The OLD TESTAMENT STUDY GUIDE

The OLD TESTAMENT STUDY GUIDE

START TO FINISH

GENERAL EDITOR
THOMAS R. VALLETTA

ASSOCIATE EDITORS

BRUCE L. ANDREASON
RANDALL C. BIRD
LEE L. DONALDSON
JOHN L. FOWLES
NORMAN W. GARDNER
RYAN C. JENKINS
ROBERT E. LUND
GEORGE R. SIMS
BRUCE G. STEWART
DIANE C. THOMAS

SALT LAKE CITY, UTAH

Visit us at deseretbook.com

Library of Congress Cataloging-in-Publication Data

(CIP data on file)
ISBN 978-1-62972-947-3

Printed in the United States of America
LSC Communications, Crawfordsville, IN

10 9 8 7 6 5 4 3 2 1

CONTENTS

INTRODUCTION TO

THE OLD TESTAMENT STUDY GUIDE

"The Old Testament is one of the standard works, or scriptures, accepted by The Church of Jesus Christ of Latter-day Saints, which values it for its prophetic, historical, doctrinal, and moral teachings. The Old Testament recounts an epochal series of ancient dispensations during which people received guidance through divine covenants and commandments, many of which remain basic and timeless" (Rasmussen, "Old Testament," 489). Elder Richard G. Scott testified: "I have found precious truths in the pages of the Old Testament that are key ingredients to the platform of truth that guides my life and acts as a resource when I try to share a gospel message with others. For that reason, I love the Old Testament" ("Power of Scripture," 6–7).

However, for a variety of reasons, "many Latter-day Saint readers find the Old Testament to be the most difficult of the Standard Works of the Church. Yet rather than paying the necessary price to discover its beautiful truths, they avoid it" (Jackson, "God's Testament to Ancient Israel," 10). Even in the apostle Paul's day, members of the Church had difficulty in understanding the Old Testament. Speaking of the children of Israel in Moses' day, Paul explained that they "were blinded: for until this day remaineth [a] veil untaken away in the reading of the old testament; which veil is done away in Christ. But even unto this day, when Moses is read, the veil is upon their heart" (2 Corinthians 3:14–15).

Though there are some challenges for modern readers in studying the Old Testament, the benefits are worth the effort. A latter-day educator wrote: "The scriptures, the words of life, are designed to point the children of God in every generation to Jesus Christ for deliverance from sin and death and all our earthly problems. The Old Testament is no exception; as with every volume of scripture, it is intended to turn our hearts and minds to our Deliverer, the Lord Jesus Christ" (Schank, "'I Am That I Am,'" 33).

The Prophet Joseph Smith declared: "We believe the Bible to be the word of God as far as it is translated correctly" (Articles of Faith 1:8). As we study the Bible, we discover that "in spite of its limitations, the Bible is an inspired work of great purity and beauty. The Lord's hand has been at work in preserving this sacred volume. He has done it in such a way that a great many of its truths have been retained" (Pearson, *Old Testament*, 22–23). In order to draw out the inspired truths found in this ancient record, "members of the Church . . . need information about the background, purposes, and difficult passages of each book of the Old

Testament to help them unlock the spiritual treasures in this magnificent volume of ancient scripture" (Ludlow, *Unlocking the Old Testament*, 1).

The Old Testament Study Guide (like its companion volumes *The Book of Mormon Study Guide* and *The New Testament Study Guide*) was developed by faithful, believing students of the scriptures to help Latter-day Saints better understand God's revealed word as recorded in the Old Testament. Readers can, through their study, strengthen their faith in the Lord Jesus Christ and better comprehend His divine mission in our Heavenly Father's plan. This study guide for use with the Old Testament will help readers reflect on Jesus Christ and His dealings as Jehovah with God's children in the ancient world. Through the innovative approach of this study guide, students of the scriptures will dig deeper into the meaning and power of the Old Testament. Students and teachers alike will find thought-provoking questions and edifying insights as well as helpful approaches to studying, pondering, and applying the doctrine and principles of the gospel.

What will I find in this book?

Typically, Bible commentaries are helpful in introducing modern readers to the ancient world of the Bible. This guide helps readers to not only see and understand the past but encourages them to apply sacred principles in the Old Testament. In order to contain this study guide to a single volume, we carefully considered the vast length of the Old Testament record. After surveying chapters emphasized in Old Testament courses taught in both the Seminaries and Institutes of Religion and in Church Sunday School materials, chapters for inclusion were recommended, reviewed, and selected. As students of the scriptures study these, they will have access to relevant prophetic statements and inspirational commentary from other General Authorities and General Officers of the Church. In addition, there are explanatory notes from many respected Latter-day Saint authors and other noted biblical scholars. Readers will also gain relevant background information that brings this ancient scripture to life, including insights into nuances of the historical and cultural context, word meanings, symbolism, and unique literary qualities of the Old Testament. In this way, this study guide unlocks ancient scripture and allows readers to reflect on its teachings in ways that will empower them to live as Latter-day Saints in the twenty-first century.

The Old Testament Study Guide has at least three unique characteristics:

- First, it is driven by thoughtful questions that prepare the mind and heart to better understand the scriptures, receive spiritual promptings, and apply gospel truths that the scriptures are teaching. These questions can be used to improve personal and family scripture study, as well as enhance classroom discussions.
- Second, questions and notes are presented in columns alongside the 2013 edition of the scriptures, with an important distinction. Because of space constraints, not every verse of the 2013 scriptures is reproduced here. For those chapters and verses that are not represented, we have included a summary of the missing material in the commentary column and a decorative element ∽ in the scripture column. The 2013 edition of

the English-language scriptures includes study aids and adjustments to chapter headings, corrections to spelling, minor typographical errors, and punctuation. Arranging the scripture text side by side with the study guide allows readers to study the Old Testament without having to turn to other books or to open multiple screens.

- Third, the eBook edition of *The Old Testament Study Guide* contains hyperlinks to hundreds of pages of additional commentary from authoritative sources to enrich your Old Testament study. An icon ⊕ in the printed book indicates where additional information may be accessed from within the eBook. Also, this unique eBook format allows you to link to other books that will deepen your understanding of the Old Testament.

How will studying the Old Testament benefit me?

President Spencer W. Kimball taught that "Jesus Christ was the God of the Old Testament, and it was He who conversed with Abraham and Moses. It was He who inspired Isaiah and Jeremiah; it was He who foretold through those chosen men the happenings of the future, even to the latest day and hour" ("Revelation," 76). "The Old Testament is like the root system of a great scriptural tree. . . . We will discover deeper meaning in all other standard works when we realize that they all receive strength from their thoroughly imbedded Old Testament roots. The scriptures are connected, and they stand together—like a mighty tree of scriptural knowledge. The Savior Jesus Christ is the great taproot, the major source of our strength in all scripture. The Old Testament is the 'book of beginnings' for our mortal sojourn. The Lord wants us to know its message, learn its lessons, and live its precepts. It could rightfully be called 'The First Testament of Jesus Christ,' and for each of us it is *an indispensable foundation*" (Horton, "Indispensable Foundation," 41).

As you use *The Old Testament Study Guide* we hope that the teachings of ancient prophets who prophesied of Jesus Christ will come to life for you. May it deepen your appreciation for how God established everlasting covenants and fulfilled promises with His children and also help you to cultivate your love for ancient Israelites who sacrificed much to give us an example of being faithful in challenging times. But above all, we hope that you will see that "the message of the Old Testament is the message of Christ and his coming and his atonement" (Romney, "Message of the Old Testament").

President Russell M. Nelson challenged the young adults of the Church "to consecrate a portion of their time each week to study *everything* Jesus said and did as recorded in the standard works" ("Drawing the Power of Jesus Christ into Our Lives," 39). We believe this challenge applies to all of us. We hope that readers will increase their faith in Jesus Christ and His role as the premortal Jehovah as they study the scriptures with this helpful Old Testament study guide.

OLD TESTAMENT GEOGRAPHY

The World of the Old Testament

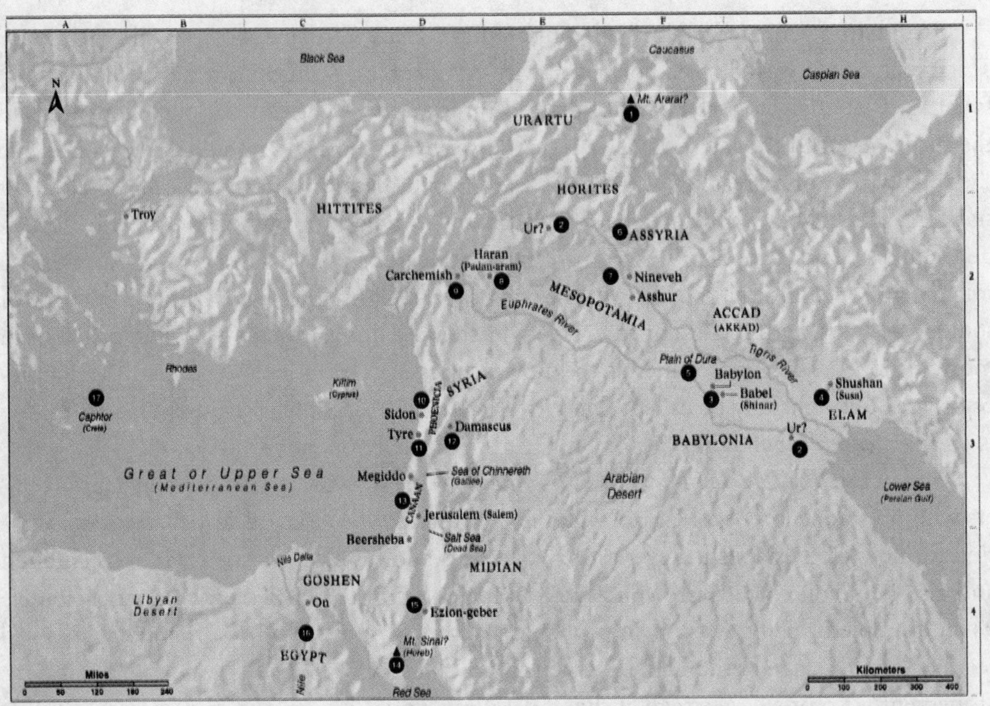

1. **Mount Ararat** The traditional site where Noah's ark landed (Gen. 8:4). The exact location is unknown.
2. **Ur** First residence of Abraham, near the mouth of the Euphrates, where he was almost a victim of human sacrifice, saw the angel of Jehovah, and received the Urim and Thummim (Gen. 11:28–12:1; Abr. 1; 3:1). (Note also a possible alternate site for Ur in northern Mesopotamia.)
3. **Babylon, Babel (Shinar)** First settled by Cush, the son of Ham, and by Nimrod. Area of origin of Jaredites at the time of the Tower of Babel in the plains of Shinar. Later provincial capital of Babylonia and residence of Babylonian kings, including Nebuchadnezzar who carried many Jews captive to this city following the destruction of Jerusalem (587 B.C.). The Jews remained in captivity in Babylon for seventy years until the time of King Cyrus, who permitted the Jews to return to Jerusalem to rebuild the temple. Daniel the prophet also resided here under Nebuchadnezzar, Belshazzar, and Darius I (Gen. 10:10; 11:1–9; 2 Kgs. 24–25; Jer. 27:1–29:10; Ezek. 1:1; Dan. 1–12; Omni 1:22; Ether 1:33–43).

4. **Shushan (Susa)** Capital city of the Persian Empire under the reigns of Darius I (Darius the Great), Xerxes (Ahasuerus), and Artaxerxes. Residence of Queen Esther, whose courage and faith saved the Jews. Daniel and later Nehemiah served here (Neh. 1:1; 2:1; Esth. 1:1; Dan. 8:2).
5. **Plain of Dura** Shadrach, Meshach, and Abed-nego were cast into a fiery furnace when they refused to worship a golden image created by Nebuchadnezzar; the Son of God preserved them, and they emerged from the furnace unharmed (Dan. 3).
6. **Assyria** Asshur was Assyria's first capital, followed by Nineveh. Assyrian rulers Shalmaneser V and Sargon II conquered the Northern Kingdom of Israel and carried away the ten tribes captive in 721 B.C. (2 Kgs. 14–15; 17–19). Assyria was a threat to Judah until 612 B.C., when Assyria was conquered by Babylon.
7. **Nineveh** The capital of Assyria. Assyria attacked the land of Judah during the reign of Hezekiah and the ministry of the prophet Isaiah. Jerusalem, the capital city of Judah, was miraculously saved when an angel smote 185,000 Assyrian soldiers (2 Kgs. 19:32–37). The Lord told the prophet Jonah to call this city to repentance (Jonah 1:2; 3:1–4).
8. **Haran** Abraham settled here for a time before going to Canaan. Abraham's father and brother remained here. Rebekah (Isaac's wife), and Rachel, Leah, Bilhah, and Zilpah (Jacob's wives) came from this area (Gen. 11:31–32; 24:10; 29:4–6; Abr. 2:4–5).
9. **Carchemish** Pharaoh Necho was defeated here by Nebuchadnezzar, which ended Egyptian power in Canaan (2 Chr. 35:20–36:6).
10. **Sidon** This city was founded by Sidon, a grandson of Ham, and is the northernmost Canaanite city (Gen. 10:15–20). It was the home of Jezebel, who introduced Baal worship into Israel (1 Kgs. 16:30–33).
11. **Tyre** This was an important commercial seaport city in Syria. Hiram of Tyre sent cedar and gold and workmen to aid Solomon in building his temple (1 Kgs. 5:1–10, 18; 9:11).
12. **Damascus** Abraham rescued Lot near here. It was the chief city of Syria. During King David's reign, the Israelites conquered the city. Elijah anointed Hazael to be king over Damascus (Gen. 14:14–15; 2 Sam. 8:5–6; 1 Kgs. 19:15).
13. **Canaan** Abraham, Isaac, Jacob, and their descendants were given this land for an everlasting possession (Gen. 17:8; 28).
14. **Mount Sinai (Horeb)** The Lord spoke to Moses from a burning bush (Ex. 3:1–2). Moses was given the Law and the Ten Commandments (Ex. 19–20). The Lord spoke to Elijah in a still, small voice (1 Kgs. 19:8–12).
15. **Ezion-geber** King Solomon built a "navy of ships" in Ezion-geber (1 Kgs. 9:26). Probably at this port the queen of Sheba, after hearing of the fame of Solomon, landed to see him (1 Kgs. 10:1–13).
16. **Egypt** Abraham traveled here because of a great famine in Ur (Abr. 2:1, 21). The Lord told Abraham to teach the Egyptians what He had revealed to him (Abr. 3:15). After Joseph's brothers sold him into slavery (Gen. 37:28), Joseph became a ruler of Potiphar's house here. He was cast into prison. He interpreted Pharaoh's dream and was given a position of authority in Egypt. Joseph and his brothers were brought together. Jacob and his family moved here (Gen. 39–46). The children of Israel dwelt in Goshen during their sojourn in Egypt (Gen. 47:6).

    The Israelites multiplied "and waxed exceeding mighty"; they were then placed in bondage by the Egyptians (Ex. 1:7–14). After a series of plagues Pharaoh allowed Israel to leave Egypt (Ex. 12:31–41). Jeremiah was taken to Egypt (Jer. 43:4–7).
17. **Caphtor (Crete)** The ancient land of the Minoans.

Canaan in Old Testament Times

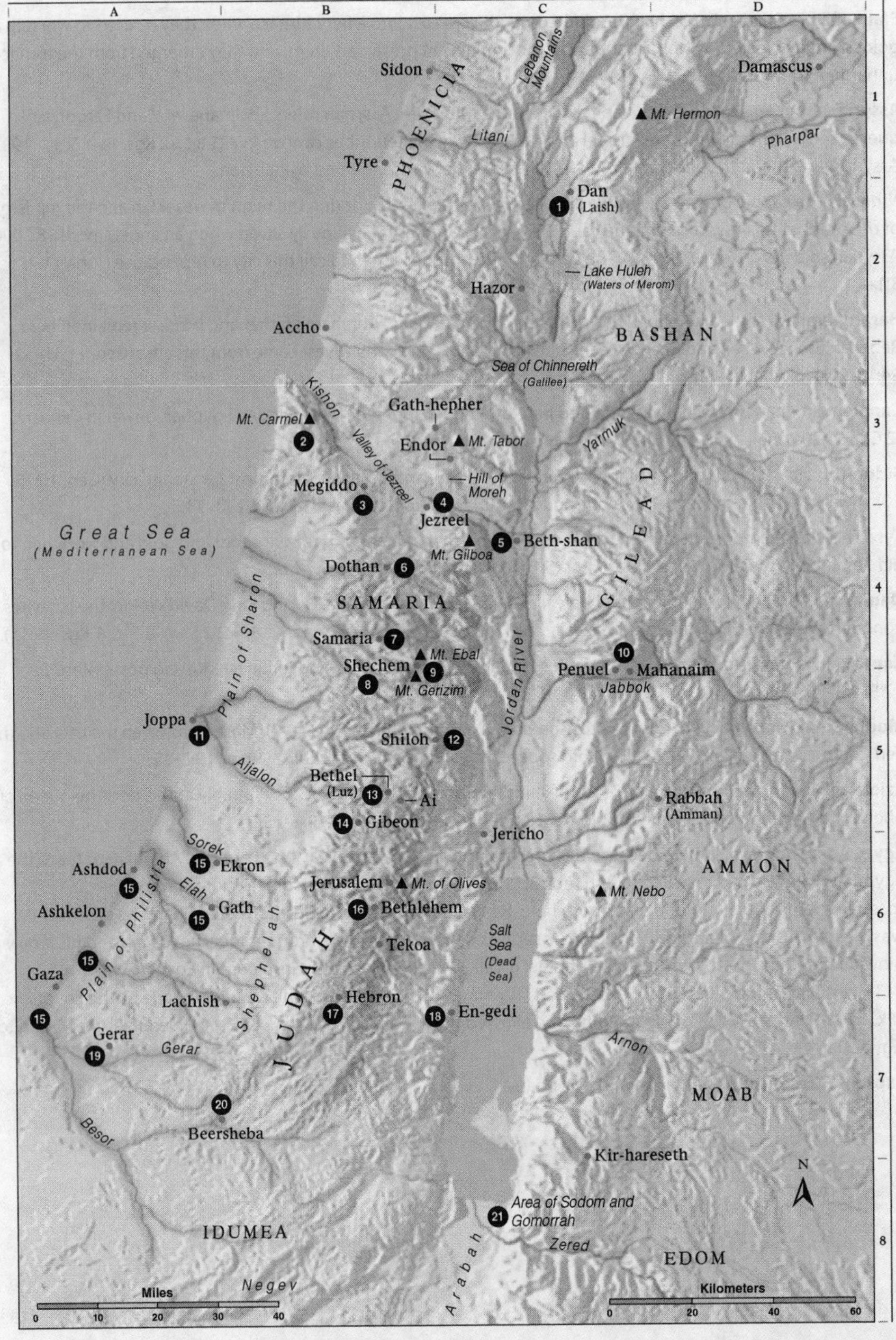

1. **Dan (Laish)** Jeroboam set up a golden calf for the Northern Kingdom to worship (1 Kgs. 12:26–33). Dan was the northern limit of ancient Israel.
2. **Mount Carmel** Elijah challenged the prophets of Baal and opened the heavens for rain (1 Kgs. 18:17–46).
3. **Megiddo** A place of many battles (Judg. 4:13–16; 5:19; 2 Kgs. 23:29; 2 Chr. 35:20–23). Solomon raised a levy to build up Megiddo (1 Kgs. 9:15). King Josiah of Judah was mortally wounded in a battle against Pharaoh Necho of Egypt (2 Kgs. 23:29–30). At the Second Coming of the Lord, a great and final conflict will take place in the Jezreel Valley as part of the battle of Armageddon (Joel 3:14; Rev. 16:16; 19:11–21). The name *Armageddon* is a Greek transliteration from the Hebrew *Har Megiddon,* or Mountain of Megiddo.
4. **Jezreel** The name of a city in the largest and most fertile valley of Israel by the same name. The kings of the Northern Kingdom built a palace here (2 Sam. 2:8–9; 1 Kgs. 21:1–2). Queen Jezebel lived and died here (1 Kgs. 21; 2 Kgs. 9:30).
5. **Beth-shan** Israel faced the Canaanites here (Josh. 17:12–16). Saul's body was fastened to the walls of this fortress (1 Sam. 31:10–13).
6. **Dothan** Joseph was sold into slavery by his brothers (Gen. 37:17, 28; 45:4). Elisha had a vision of the mountain full of horses and chariots (2 Kgs. 6:12–17).
7. **Samaria** The Northern Kingdom's capital (1 Kgs. 16:24–29). King Ahab built a temple to Baal (1 Kgs. 16:32–33). Elijah and Elisha ministered (1 Kgs. 18:2; 2 Kgs. 6:19–20). In 721 B.C. the Assyrians conquered it, completing the capture of the ten tribes (2 Kgs. 18:9–10).
8. **Shechem** Abraham built an altar (Gen. 12:6–7). Jacob lived near here. Simeon and Levi massacred all the males of this city (Gen. 34:25). Joshua's encouragement to "choose . . . this day" to serve God came in Shechem (Josh. 24:15). Here Jeroboam established the first capital of the Northern Kingdom (1 Kgs. 12).
9. **Mount Ebal and Mount Gerizim** Joshua divided Israel on these two mounts—the blessings of the law were proclaimed from Mount Gerizim, while the cursings came from Mount Ebal (Josh. 8:33). The Samaritans later built a temple on Gerizim (2 Kgs. 17:32–33).
10. **Penuel (Peniel)** Here Jacob wrestled all night with a messenger of the Lord (Gen. 32:24–32). Gideon destroyed a Midianite fortress (Judg. 8:5, 8–9).
11. **Joppa** Jonah sailed from here toward Tarshish to avoid his mission to Nineveh (Jonah 1:1–3).
12. **Shiloh** During the time of the Judges, Israel's capital and the tabernacle were located here (1 Sam. 4:3–4).
13. **Bethel (Luz)** Here Abraham separated from Lot (Gen. 13:1–11) and had a vision (Gen. 13; Abr. 2:19–20). Jacob had a vision of a ladder reaching into heaven (Gen. 28:10–22). The tabernacle was located here for a time (Judg. 20:26–28). Jeroboam set up a golden calf for the Northern Kingdom to worship (1 Kgs. 12:26–33).
14. **Gibeon** Hivite people from here tricked Joshua into a treaty (Josh. 9). The sun stood still while Joshua won a battle (Josh. 10:2–13). This was also a temporary site of the tabernacle (1 Chr. 16:39).
15. **Gaza, Ashdod, Ashkelon, Ekron, Gath** (the five cities of the Philistines) From these cities the Philistines often made war on Israel.
16. **Bethlehem** Rachel was buried nearby (Gen. 35:19). Ruth and Boaz lived here (Ruth 1:1–2; 2:1, 4). It was called the city of David (Luke 2:4).
17. **Hebron** Abraham (Gen. 13:18), Isaac, Jacob (Gen. 35:27), David (2 Sam. 2:1–4), and Absalom (2 Sam. 15:10) lived here. This was the first capital of Judah under King David (2 Sam. 2:11). It is believed that Abraham, Sarah, Isaac, Rebekah, Jacob, and Leah were buried here in the cave of Machpelah (Gen. 23:17–20; 49:31, 33).
18. **En-gedi** David hid from Saul and spared Saul's life (1 Sam. 23:29–24:22).
19. **Gerar** Abraham and Isaac lived here for a time (Gen. 20–22; 26).
20. **Beersheba** Abraham dug a well here and covenanted with Abimelech (Gen. 21:31). Isaac saw the Lord (Gen. 26:17, 23–24), and Jacob lived here (Gen. 35:10; 46:1).
21. **Sodom and Gomorrah** Lot chose to live in Sodom (Gen. 13:11–12; 14:12). God destroyed Sodom and Gomorrah because of wickedness (Gen. 19:24–26). Jesus later used these cities as symbols of wickedness (Matt. 10:15).

TO THE MOST HIGH AND MIGHTY PRINCE

JAMES

BY THE GRACE OF GOD

KING OF GREAT BRITAIN, FRANCE, AND IRELAND, DEFENDER OF THE FAITH, &C.

THE TRANSLATORS OF THE BIBLE WISH GRACE, MERCY, AND PEACE, THROUGH JESUS CHRIST OUR LORD

Great and manifold were the blessings, most dread Sovereign, which Almighty God, the Father of all mercies, bestowed upon us the people of *England,* when first he sent Your Majesty's Royal Person to rule and reign over us. For whereas it was the expectation of many, who wished not well unto our *Sion,* that upon the setting of that bright

Why did James I, king of England, become involved with the new translation of the Bible? (Title) "In 1604, James I held the Hampton Court Conference, called to settle differences between the Puritan and Anglican elements of the Church. In the course of the Conference, the President of the Corpus Christi College, Oxford (Dr. Reynolds), the leader of the moderate Puritan party, referred to the imperfections and disagreements of the existing English versions of the Bible, and suggested a new version to be prepared by the best scholars of the country. The Conference was a failure and did nothing about the suggestion of Dr. Reynolds. But King James moved forward" (Clark, *Why the King James Version*, 183).

Who Wrote "The Epistle Dedicatory" Located at the Beginning of the King James Version of the Bible?

The team that translated the 1611 Authorized Version of the King James Bible consisted of roughly fifty experts who were divided into six companies. One team member, Miles Smith, is believed to have written the introduction, or "Epistle Dedicatory," to King James. He was a "member of the First Oxford Company (Isaiah–Malachi) and general revision committee and participant in the final review, was a doctor of divinity, prebendary [clergyman] of Hereford and Exeter Cathedrals, and later bishop of Gloucester (1612), and was expert in Hebrew and other Semitic languages. . . .

"Miles Smith received the assignment to draft the translators' preface. In that eleven-page introduction, 'The Translators to the Reader,' he stated eloquently, 'So hard a thing it is to please all, even when we please God best, and do seek to approve ourselves to every one's conscience.' The preface set forth the reasoning behind the making of the new translation: the translators believed that the Bible was God's word and that it should be available in the language of the people. Even in translation, Smith wrote, the words of scripture are of great worth: 'If we be ignorant, they will instruct us; if out of the way, they will bring us home; if out of order, they will reform us; if in heaviness, comfort us; if dull, quicken us; if cold, inflame us. . . . Love the Scriptures, and wisdom will love thee.' A simple suggestion by John Rainolds at Hampton Court [to make a new translation of the Bible] initiated what would become the most popular English Bible of all time. Yet its popularity would take some time and some convincing" (Blumell and Whitchurch, "Coming Forth of the King James Bible," 53–55).

Occidental Star, Queen *Elizabeth* of most happy memory, some thick and palpable clouds of darkness would so have overshadowed this Land, that men should have been in doubt which way they were to walk; and that it should hardly be known, who was to direct the unsettled State; the appearance of Your Majesty, as of the *Sun* in his strength, instantly dispelled those supposed and surmised mists, and gave unto all that were well affected exceeding cause of comfort; especially when we beheld the Government established in Your Highness, and Your hopeful Seed, by an undoubted Title, and this also accompanied with peace and tranquillity at home and abroad.

But among all our joys, there was no one that more filled our hearts, than the blessed continuance of the preaching of God's sacred Word among us; which is that inestimable treasure, which excelleth all the riches of the earth; because the fruit thereof extendeth itself, not only to the time spent in this transitory world, but directeth and disposeth men unto that eternal happiness which is above in heaven.

Then not to suffer this to fall to the ground, but rather to take it up, and to continue it in that state, wherein the famous Predecessor of Your Highness did leave it: nay, to go forward with the confidence and resolution of a Man in maintaining the truth of Christ, and propagating it far and near, is that which hath so bound and firmly knit the hearts of all Your Majesty's loyal and religious people unto You, that Your very name is precious among them: their eye doth behold You with comfort, and they bless You

What caused such dark clouds during Queen Elizabeth's reign? (Para. 1) "Though work on what would become the King James Bible would commence the following year under the patronage of James, at the time of his coronation in July 1603 he had as of yet no intention of sponsoring a new translation of the Bible. The idea for a new translation came about as a direct result of the religious tensions that had been simmering during Elizabeth's reign. When word began to spread throughout England that James would be the next monarch, both Catholics and Protestants felt optimistic that their voices could now finally be heard" (Blumell and Whitchurch, "Coming Forth of the King James Bible," 44).

How do Latter-day Saints and other Christians feel about the Bible, which has been described as an "inestimable treasure"? (Para. 2) "Tens of millions of individuals have come to a faith in God and in Jesus Christ through seeking truth in the Holy Bible. Countless numbers of them had nothing *but* the Bible to feed and guide their faith. . . .

"How grateful we should be for the Holy Bible. In it we learn not only of the life and teachings and doctrines of Christ, we learn of His Church and of His priesthood and of the organization which He established and named the Church of Jesus Christ in those former days. We believe in that Church, and we believe that The Church of Jesus Christ of Latter-day Saints is that same Church, restored to earth, complete, with the same organization and the same priesthood" (Ballard, "Miracle of the Holy Bible," 81).

How did King James I ensure that the translation of the Bible went forth? (Para. 3) "King James, following failure of the Hampton Court Conference, took an active part in moving forward on the suggestion made at the Conference that a translation of the Bible be prepared calculated to heal differences between Anglican and Puritan elements of the Church. . . . The personnel and organization of the translation groups . . . were to be made up of scholars from the two universities. The translators, beginning their labors near the end of 1607, finished in about two years. . . . [The new Bible] was printed and issued in 1611" (Clark, *Why the King James Version*, 183).

in their hearts, as that sanctified Person, who, under God, is the immediate Author of their true happiness. And this their contentment doth not diminish or decay, but every day increaseth and taketh strength, when they observe, that the zeal of Your Majesty toward the house of God doth not slack or go backward, but is more and more kindled, manifesting itself abroad in the farthest parts of *Christendom,* by writing in defence of the Truth, (which hath given such a blow unto that man of sin, as will not be healed,) and every day at home, by religious and learned discourse, by frequenting the house of God, by hearing the Word preached, by cherishing the Teachers thereof, by caring for the Church, as a most tender and loving nursing Father.

There are infinite arguments of this right Christian and religious affection in Your Majesty; but none is more forcible to declare it to others than the vehement and perpetuated desire of accomplishing and publishing of this work, which now with all humility we present unto Your Majesty. For when Your Highness had once out of deep judgment apprehended how convenient it was, that out of the Original Sacred Tongues, together with comparing of the labours, both in our own, and other foreign Languages, of many worthy men who went before us, there should be one more exact Translation of the holy Scriptures into the *English Tongue;* Your Majesty did never desist to urge and to excite those to whom it was commended, that the work might be hastened, and that the business might be expedited in so decent a manner, as a matter of such importance might justly require.

And now at last, by the mercy of God, and the continuance of our labours, it being brought unto such a conclusion, as that we have great hopes that the Church of *England* shall reap good fruit thereby; we

How far has the influence of the King James Version of the Bible reached? (Para. 3) "The King James Version most likely can never be completely replaced *because* it is such a vital part of the heritage of English-speaking nations. Its language . . . has become 'part and parcel of our common tongue—bone of its bone and flesh of its flesh.' In one fifty-year period alone, this Bible was the source of more than eleven hundred titles of published books, a credit to its 'terse and telling imagery'" (Read, "How the Bible Came to Be," 55).

How did King James feel about the completed Bible? (Para. 4) "In 1611, King James's Bible was completed. It is said he felt more pride in seeing this work accomplished than in a recent military victory over Spain. And he had every right to feel proud. The Bible was handsome—both inside and out. Of special satisfaction to him, no doubt, was its flattering dedication" (Read, "How the Bible Came to Be," 52).

How did the King James translators provide "one more exact translation"? (Para. 4) The King James Bible translators "were divided into six committees called 'companies': two from Cambridge, two from Oxford, and two from Westminster, with each company assigned to translate a different section of the Bible. By spring or early summer of 1604, Bancroft had drafted a document providing detailed rules to be used throughout the translation process. It is presumed that the rules were written in consultation with, and under the direction of, King James. The rules were put in place so as to minimize the possibility that the Bible might be biased and lend credibility to any one group" (Blumell and Whitchurch, "Coming Forth of the King James Bible," 48).

How did these translators fulfill their "labours"? (Para. 5) "This work was to be a revision only, not a fresh translation, and the work they were to revise was the Bishops' Bible. They were granted permission, however, to refer to Tyndale's, Coverdale's, and the

Geneva versions; and where any of those agreed more closely with the Hebrew and Greek texts that were available, they could use them instead.

"There is strong evidence that the scholars worked much more independently than these instructions indicate. For example, according to their own accounts, they consulted every translation or scholarly work currently available" (Read, "How the Bible Came to Be," 50).

Why is it important to make the Bible "more known unto the people"—even today? (Para. 5) "Latter-day Saints value the Bible for many reasons. The Bible presents the revelations of God in several dispensations or eras, each headed by prophets. They also read and follow the Bible for the instructional and spiritual value of the events it describes. While some of the Old Testament describes the law of Moses that Latter-day Saints believe was fulfilled with the atonement of Christ (3 Ne. 9:17), nevertheless the Old Testament stories, commandments, ordinances, proverbs, and prophetic writings still express the basic patterns of God's will toward his children and how they should act toward him" (Hedengren, "LDS Belief in the Bible," 48).

hold it our duty to offer it to Your Majesty, not only as to our King and Sovereign, but as to the principal Mover and Author of the work: humbly craving of Your most Sacred Majesty, that since things of this quality have ever been subject to the censures of illmeaning and discontented persons, it may receive approbation and patronage from so learned and judicious a Prince as Your Highness is, whose allowance and acceptance of our labours shall more honour and encourage us, than all the calumniations and hard interpretations of other men shall dismay us. So that if, on the one side, we shall be traduced by Popish Persons at home or abroad, who therefore will malign us, because we are poor instruments to make God's holy Truth to be yet more and more known unto the people, whom they desire still to keep in ignorance and darkness; or if, on the other side, we shall be maligned by selfconceited Brethren,

First Presidency Statement on the King James Version of the Bible (1992)

"Since the days of the Prophet Joseph Smith, The Church of Jesus Christ of Latter-day Saints has used the King James Version of the Bible for English-speaking members.

"The Bible, as it has been transmitted over the centuries, has suffered the loss of many plain and precious parts. 'We believe the Bible to be the word of God as far as it is translated correctly; we also believe the Book of Mormon to be the word of God' (Articles of Faith 1:8).

"Many versions of the Bible are available today. Unfortunately, no original manuscripts of any portion of the Bible are available for comparison to determine the most accurate version. However, the Lord has revealed clearly the doctrines of the gospel in these latter-days. The most reliable way to measure the accuracy of any biblical passage is not by comparing different texts, but by comparison with the Book of Mormon and modern-day revelations.

"While other Bible versions may be easier to read than the King James Version, in doctrinal matters latter-day revelation supports the King James Version in preference to other English translations. All of the Presidents of the Church, beginning with the Prophet Joseph Smith, have supported the King James Version by encouraging its continued use in the Church. In light of all the above, it is the English language Bible used by The Church of Jesus Christ of Latter-day Saints.

"The LDS edition of the Bible (1979) contains the King James Version supplemented and clarified by footnotes, study aids, and cross-references to the Book of Mormon, the Doctrine and Covenants, and the Pearl of Great Price. These four books are the standard works of the Church. We encourage all members to have their own copies of the complete standard works and to use them prayerfully in regular personal and family study, and in Church meetings and assignments.

"Sincerely your brethren,

"Ezra Taft Benson

"Gordon B. Hinckley

"Thomas S. Monson"

(Benson, Hinckley, and Monson, "First Presidency Statement on the King James Version of the Bible," 80).

who run their own ways, and give liking unto nothing, but what is framed by themselves, and hammered on their anvil; we may rest secure, supported within by the truth and innocency of a good conscience, having walked the ways of simplicity and integrity, as before the Lord; and sustained without by the powerful protection of Your Majesty's grace and favour, which will ever give countenance to honest and Christian endeavours against bitter censures and uncharitable imputations.

The Lord of heaven and earth bless Your Majesty with many and happy days, that, as his heavenly hand hath enriched Your Highness with many singular and extraordinary graces, so You may be the wonder of the world in this latter age for happiness and true felicity, to the honour of that great GOD, and the good of his Church, through Jesus Christ our Lord and only Saviour.

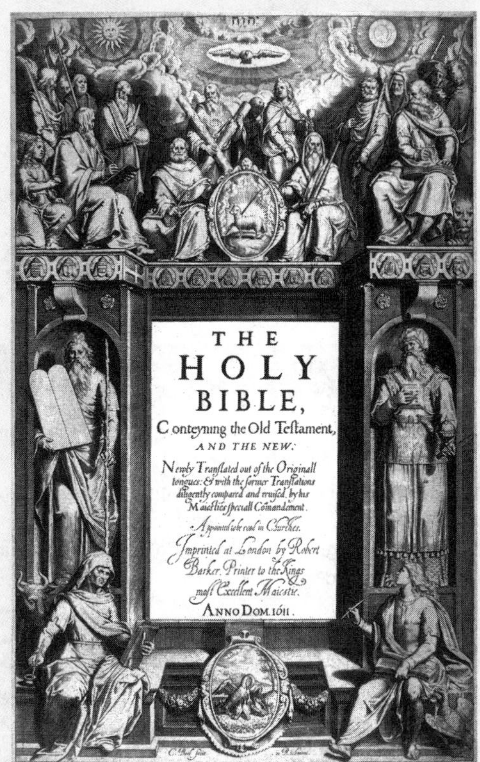

THE HOLY BIBLE,
Conteyning the Old Teſtament,
AND THE NEW:
Newly Tranſlated out of the Originall tongues: & with the former Tranſlations diligently compared and reuiſed, by his Maieſties ſpeciall Cōmandement.
Appointed to be read in Churches.
Imprinted at London by Robert Barker, Printer to the Kings moſt Excellent Maieſtie.
ANNO DOM. 1611.

Title page from the 1611 edition of the King James Version of the Bible.

THE FIRST BOOK OF MOSES

CALLED

GENESIS

Introduction

"The name *Genesis* is derived from the ancient Greek version of the Bible called the Septuagint. *Genesis* means 'origin'" (Pearson, *Old Testament*, 26). "And, indeed, Genesis is about beginnings. Genesis naturally divides into two parts: Genesis 1–11 describes the origins of the whole world—beginning with the Creation and ending with the scattering of the people at the Tower of Babel—and Genesis 12–50 describes the origins of Israel—beginning with its creation through the Abrahamic Covenant and ending with the establishment of Joseph as the birthright son with temporal and spiritual stewardship over the house of Israel" (Holzapfel, et al., *Jehovah and the World of the Old Testament*, 20).

The Bible Dictionary produced by The Church of Jesus Christ of Latter-day Saints states: "In latter-day revelation we find many sources of information that clarify and substantiate the record of Genesis. The Joseph Smith Translation especially, a portion of which is presented in the book of Moses, offers the best available account of the early chapters. Of exceptional worth is Moses 1, giving an account of some visions and experiences of Moses previous to and in preparation for writing Genesis. This chapter is an introduction to Genesis, just as Genesis is an introduction to the remainder of the Bible" (Bible Dictionary, "Genesis").

"Sometime after his call at the 'burning bush' (Moses 1:17; Ex. 3:4), Moses was given visions of the earth, its many lands and inhabitants, and its past and future (Moses 1:25–29). . . . The Lord . . . [then] commanded Moses to write and preserve the information (Moses 1:33, 35, 40; 2:1).

"Through these revelations, Moses was being prepared by the Lord to leave his refuge in Sinai and return to Egypt to lead the children of Israel out of bondage to the land promised long before. . . .

"[These visions and revelations] helped Moses know why the Israelites needed to be rescued from bondage and death in Egypt and be established in the land of promise. It also helped him (and it helps us) understand why the Lord would conduct that rescue operation in which the Egyptians and the Canaanites suffered and Israel was saved" (Rasmussen, *Latter-day Saint Commentary on the Old Testament*, 1–2).

"The book of Genesis is the true and original birthplace of all theology. It contains the ideas of God and man, of righteousness and judgment, of responsibility and moral government, of failure and hope, that are presupposed through the rest of the Old Testament and that prepare the way for the mission of Christ" (Bible Dictionary, "Genesis").

"It is interesting that this one book, which comprises no more than 5 percent of the total volume of the Bible, covers over 50 percent of its time span, nearly twenty-five hundred years. . . . The contents of Genesis are merely highlights of important events. Those events, however, carefully chosen by the great historian, give us an important understanding about God and his dealings with man" (Pearson, *Old Testament*, 26).

CHAPTER 1

God creates this earth and its heaven and all forms of life in six days—The creative acts of each day are described—God creates man, both male and female, in His own image—Man is given dominion over all things and is commanded to multiply and fill the earth.

1 In the beginning God created the heaven and the earth.

Genesis 1:1–5. On the First Day God Creates the Earth and Separates Light from Darkness

What occurred "in the beginning"? (1:1) Joseph Smith taught: "In the beginning the head of the Gods called a council of the Gods, and . . . concocted [prepared] a plan to create the world and people it" (Joseph Smith Papers, "History, 1838–1856, volume E-1 [1 July 1843–30 April 1844]," 1972). The Father directed His Son to create the earth (see Moses 1:32; JST, John 1:1–3). Speaking to some of the "noble and great ones . . . who were with him," the Lord declared: "We will go down, . . . and we will take of these materials, and will make an earth whereon these [the Father's spirit children] may dwell; and we will prove them herewith, to see if they will do all things whatsoever the Lord their God shall command them" (Abraham 3:22, 24–25). ⊕

What does modern revelation reveal about how the earth was created? (1:1) According to Abraham 4:1 we learn that "at the beginning, . . . they, that is the Gods, organized and formed the heavens and the earth." What did they organize and form it from? The Prophet Joseph Smith taught: "[The] doctors say, [God] created the earth out of nothing. *Bara'*, 'create'; it meant to organize. God had materials to organize the world" (Jackson, *Joseph Smith's Commentary on the Bible*, 3). ⊕

What Is the Purpose of the Creation Accounts? (Genesis 1:1)

Kent P. Jackson suggested: "The detailed process by which the Lord brought the universe and planet Earth into existence is not known by man. It is not unlikely that the principles of science as understood today will *never* be able to explain the divine powers and the divine actions that created these things. . . . In his own discussion of the Creation, Elder Bruce R. McConkie wrote: 'Our analysis properly begins with the frank recital that our knowledge about the Creation is limited. We do not know the how and why and when of all things. Our finite limitations are such that we could not comprehend them if they were revealed to us in all their glory, fulness, and perfection'" ("Genesis and the Early Experiences of Mankind," 26–27).

Through revelation given to the Prophet Joseph Smith, we learn that God created the earth to provide a place for His spirit children to dwell so He could "prove them herewith, to see if they will do all things whatsoever the Lord their God shall command them" (Abraham 3:25).

Susan Easton Black has written: "Latter-day Saints accept four accounts of the Creation of the earth and the Fall of Adam. These accounts are found in the Bible, the book of Moses, the book of Abraham, and in temple worship. According to Hugh Nibley, the accounts are 'like the four Gospels, but not conflicting if each is put into its proper context' (*Old Testament and Related Studies*, 64)" (*400 Questions and Answers about the Old Testament*, 27).

"Perhaps the most powerful message that is contained in the Genesis creation account (and in the other accounts as well) is that the Creation was a deliberate act of God. The scriptures leave no room for the idea that the existence of life on Earth is accidental. While we may not know the details, we can be assured that God was in control of his creative process" (Jackson, "Genesis and the Early Experiences of Mankind," 28).

How does modern revelation help us better understand the phrase "without form and void"? (1:2) The book of Abraham describes the state of the earth following its creation or "organization" by the Gods: "The earth, after it was formed, was *empty* and *desolate*, because they [the Gods] had not formed anything but the earth" (Abraham 4:2; emphasis added). Clearly there was more to do in the process of creation.

2 And the earth was without form, and void; and darkness *was* upon the face of the deep. And the Spirit of God moved upon the face of the waters.

What is the light which God commands to appear? (1:3–5) "A single short word in Hebrew, translated by the English phrase 'let there be,' expresses God's will that the divine emanation of 'light' be brought to bear directly upon the formative earth. The light bathing the incipient planet was probably not that of the sun but rather the activating power called the Light of Christ" (Rasmussen, *Latter-day Saint Commentary on the Old Testament*, 4). This light "proceedeth forth from the presence of God to fill the immensity of space" (D&C 88:12) and is the power by which the heavens and earth were made (see D&C 88:7–10).

3 And God said, Let there be light: and there was light.

4 And God saw the light, that *it was* good: and God divided the light from the darkness.

5 And God called the light Day, and the darkness he called Night. And the evening and the morning were the first day.

Genesis 1:6–8. On the Second Day God Separates the Waters on the Earth from the Clouds above the Earth

What are the waters above the firmament? (1:6–7) "The waters above the firmament is a reference to the clouds and the waters which exist in the atmosphere above the earth" (Smith, *Answers to Gospel Questions*, 4:116). The "word 'expanse' found in Abraham [4:6–8] better describes the earth's atmosphere in which moisture ('the waters above') is suspended in the form of clouds and humidity to fall as rain and dew ('the waters below')" (Draper, et al., *Pearl of Great Price*, 197). ⊕

6 ¶ And God said, Let there be a firmament in the midst of the waters, and let it divide the waters from the waters.

7 And God made the firmament, and divided the waters which *were* under the firmament from the waters which *were* above the firmament: and it was so.

8 And God called the firmament Heaven. And the evening and the morning were the second day.

Genesis 1:9–13. On the Third Day God Makes the Dry Land Appear and Causes Plants to Grow

9 ¶ And God said, Let the waters under the heaven be gathered together unto one place, and let the dry *land* appear: and it was so.

10 And God called the dry *land* Earth; and the gathering together of the waters called he Seas: and God saw that *it was* good.

Why does the text emphasize "after his kind"? (1:11–12) The Prophet Joseph Smith declared: "It is a decree of the Lord that every tree, fruit, or herb bearing seed should bring forth after its kind and cannot come forth after any other law or principle" (Jackson,

11 And God said, Let the earth bring forth grass, the herb yielding seed, *and* the fruit tree yielding fruit after his kind, whose seed *is* in itself, upon the earth: and it was so.

12 And the earth brought forth grass, *and*
herb yielding seed after his kind, and the tree
yielding fruit, whose seed *was* in itself, after
his kind: and God saw that *it was* good.

13 And the evening and the morning were
the third day.

14 ¶ And God said, Let there be lights in the
firmament of the heaven to divide the day
from the night; and let them be for signs,
and for seasons, and for days, and years:

15 And let them be for lights in the firmament of the heaven to give light upon the
earth: and it was so.

16 And God made two great lights; the
greater light to rule the day, and the lesser
light to rule the night: *he made* the stars also.

17 And God set them in the firmament of
the heaven to give light upon the earth,

18 And to rule over the day and over the
night, and to divide the light from the darkness: and God saw that *it was* good.

19 And the evening and the morning were
the fourth day.

20 And God said, Let the waters bring forth
abundantly the moving creature that hath
life, and fowl *that* may fly above the earth in
the open firmament of heaven.

21 And God created great whales, and every
living creature that moveth, which the waters
brought forth abundantly, after their kind,

Joseph Smith's Commentary on the Bible, 4). "There was no provision for . . . change from one species to another" (McConkie, "Christ and the Creation," 12).

Why does Abraham 4:13 use the word "time" instead of "day" in the creation account? (1:13) President Russell M. Nelson noted, "The physical Creation itself was staged through ordered periods of time. In Genesis and Moses, those periods are called days. But in the book of Abraham, each period is referred to as a time. Whether termed a day, a time, or an age, each phase was a period between two identifiable events—a division of eternity" ("Creation," 84).

Genesis 1:14–19. On the Fourth Day God Sets the Sun, Moon, and Stars in Their Places

What is the purpose of the "lights in the firmament"? (1:14–18) President Russell M. Nelson explained: "Lights in the expanse of the heaven were organized so there could be seasons and other means of measuring time. During this period, the sun, the moon, the stars, and the earth were placed in proper relationship to one another. The sun, with its vast stores of hydrogen, was to serve as a giant furnace to provide light and heat for the earth and life upon it" ("Creation," 85).

Genesis 1:20–23. On the Fifth Day God Creates Animals in the Sea and Birds in the Air

What happens on the fifth day of creation? (1:20–21) There is an exwplosion of life. God orders the waters to "swarm with swarms of living creatures" (Genesis 1:20*b*). "They were given the command: 'Be fruitful, and multiply, and fill the waters in the sea; and let fowl multiply in the earth.' This command—as with a similar decree given to man and applicable to all animal life—they could not then keep, but they soon would be able to do so. Appended to this command to multiply was the heaven-sent restriction that the creatures in the waters could only bring forth 'after their kind,' and that 'every winged fowl' could only bring forth 'after his kind'" (McConkie, "Christ and the Creation," 12).

Genesis 1:24–31. On the Sixth Day God Creates Land Animals and Man and Woman

Why are "cattle" distinct from the "beast[s] of the earth"? (1:24–25) "In the sixth creative period came the *cattle*, the English word used to translate a Hebrew word that is often used for herbivorous and domesticated animals in contrast to the 'beasts,' or carnivores and wild animals" (Rasmussen, *Latter-day Saint Commentary on the Old Testament*, 7). Abraham 4:24 adds that "the Gods saw they [creatures of the earth] would obey" which "seems to include what we would call 'instinct' in animals—their innate knowledge and capability to do those things which cause them to thrive and prosper" (Draper, et al., *Pearl of Great Price*, 209).

Why does God say: "Let *us* go down"? (1:26–27) Elder Bruce R. McConkie wrote that God is not only "the Father of all spirits, Christ's included," but is also "the Creator of the physical body of man. Though Jehovah and Michael and many of the noble and great ones played their assigned roles in the various creative events, yet when it came time to place man on earth, the Lord God himself performed the creative acts. 'I, God, created man in mine own image, in the image of mine Only Begotten created I him; male and female created I them' (Moses 2:27)" (*New Witness for the Articles of Faith*, 63). ⊕

and every winged fowl after his kind: and God saw that *it was* good.

22 And God blessed them, saying, Be fruitful, and multiply, and fill the waters in the seas, and let fowl multiply in the earth.

23 And the evening and the morning were the fifth day.

24 ¶ And God said, Let the earth bring forth the living creature after his kind, cattle, and creeping thing, and beast of the earth after his kind: and it was so.

25 And God made the beast of the earth after his kind, and cattle after their kind, and every thing that creepeth upon the earth after his kind: and God saw that *it was* good.

26 ¶ And God said, Let us make man in our image, after our likeness: and let them have dominion over the fish of the sea, and over the fowl of the air, and over the cattle, and over all the earth, and over every creeping thing that creepeth upon the earth.

27 So God created man in his *own* image, in the image of God created he him; male and female created he them.

What Do We Learn in Genesis about the Spiritual Creation? (Genesis 1–2)

President Joseph Fielding Smith explained: "There is no account of the creation of man or other forms of life when they were created as spirits. There is just the simple statement that they were so created before the physical creation. The statements in Moses 3:5 and Genesis 2:5 are interpolations thrown into the account of the physical creation, explaining that all things were first created in the spirit existence in heaven before they were placed upon this earth" (*Doctrines of Salvation*, 1:75–76).

"While it is true that all things were created spiritually, or as spirits, before they were naturally upon the face of the earth, this creation, we are informed, was in heaven. This applies to animals of all descriptions and also to plant life, before there was flesh upon the earth, or in the water, or in the air. The account of the creation of the earth as given in Genesis, and the Book of Moses, and as given in the temple, is the creation of the physical earth, and of physical animals and plants. I think the temple account, which was given by revelation, is the clearest of all of these. These physical creations were made out of the natural elements" (*Doctrines of Salvation*, 1:75).

Elder Bruce R. McConkie testified: "This earth, all men [and women], animals, fish, fowls, plants, all things—all lived first as spirit entities. Their home was heaven, and the earth was created to be the place where they could take upon themselves mortality" ("Christ and the Creation," 13).

28 And God blessed them, and God said
unto them, Be fruitful, and multiply, and
replenish the earth, and subdue it: and have
dominion over the fish of the sea, and over
the fowl of the air, and over every living thing
that moveth upon the earth.

29 ¶ And God said, Behold, I have given you
every herb bearing seed, which *is* upon the
face of all the earth, and every tree, in the
which *is* the fruit of a tree yielding seed; to
you it shall be for meat.

30 And to every beast of the earth, and to
every fowl of the air, and to every thing that
creepeth upon the earth, wherein *there is* life,
I have given every green herb for meat: and
it was so.

31 And God saw every thing that he had
made, and, behold, *it was* very good. And the
evening and the morning were the sixth day.

Why are Adam and Eve commanded to be "fruitful"? (1:28) The Lord brings together "Adam and Eve, his first male and first female on this earth, and perform[ed] a holy marriage ceremony to make them husband and wife. . . . Hardly had he performed the ceremony than he said to them: 'Multiply, and replenish the earth" (Kimball, *Spencer W. Kimball* [manual], 192). *Replenish* comes from a "Hebrew verb . . . meaning fill, to fill, or make full" (Smith, *Answers to Gospel Questions*, 1:208). Leaders of The Church of Jesus Christ of Latter-day Saints have written: "We declare that God's commandment for His children to multiply and replenish the earth remains in force" ("The Family: A Proclamation to the World," [2010], 129).

Why are Adam and Eve given "dominion" over all things on the earth? (1:28–30) God's charge to Adam and Eve to "multiply, and replenish the earth" included "dominion over . . . every living thing" (Abraham 4:28). Hugh Nibley explained what that meant: "There are two clearly marked departments—the earth itself as a storehouse and source of life, which Adam is to keep replenished (*filled* is the word), and the creatures that move about on and over the earth. . . . As Brigham Young explains it, while 'subduing the earth' we must be about 'multiplying those organisms of plants and animals God has designed shall dwell upon it,' namely 'all forms of life,' each to multiply in its sphere and element and have joy therein" (*Nibley on the Timely and the Timeless*, 87).

What does it mean when God declares each phase of His creation as "good"? (1:31) "In both Hebrew and English, words meaning 'good' are used to describe that which functions properly, constructively, harmoniously; in contrast, words meaning 'bad' or 'evil' connote that which functions improperly, destructively, disharmoniously, or disruptively. Good is repeated in verses 10, 12, 18, 21, and 25, evaluating each phase of the Creation; then, in verse 31, 'very good' describes the whole Creation" (Rasmussen, *Latter-day Saint Commentary on the Old Testament*, 4). ⊕

CHAPTER 2

The Creation is completed—God rests on the seventh day—The prior spirit creation is explained—Adam and Eve are placed in the Garden of Eden—They are forbidden to eat of the tree of knowledge of good and evil—Adam names every living creature—Adam and Eve are married by the Lord.

1 Thus the heavens and the earth were finished, and all the host of them.

Genesis 2:1–3. God Rests on the Seventh Day and Calls It Holy

What is earth's condition when God finishes its creation? (2:1) "The creation was accomplished; it was done. This earth, and man, and life in all its forms and varieties existed in physical form. . . . The great Creator had created a paradisiacal earth, an edenic earth, an earth of the kind and nature that will exist during the Millennium, when it will be renewed and receive again its paradisiacal glory" (McConkie, *New Witness for the Articles of Faith*, 84; see also Articles of Faith 1:10).

2 And on the seventh day God ended his work which he had made; and he rested on the seventh day from all his work which he had made.

3 And God blessed the seventh day, and sanctified it: because that in it he had rested from all his work which God created and made.

Why does God bless the seventh day? (2:2–3) "Moses came down from the quaking, smoking Mount Sinai and brought to the wandering children of Israel the Ten Commandments. This was not the origin of these specific laws, for Adam and his posterity knew the gospel and had been commanded to live them. This spectacular experience was neither the beginning nor the end. The laws of God were premortal. They were part of the test for mortals spoken of in the council in heaven.

"The law of the Sabbath, as with other laws, antedated earth life and has been reiterated through the dispensations to that of the Fulness of Times. It distinguished the early Israelites from pagans" (Kimball, "Fourth Commandment," 54). ⊕

Genesis 2:4–7. All Things Are First Created Spiritually

4 ¶ These *are* the generations of the heavens and of the earth when they were created, in the day that the LORD God made the earth and the heavens,

5 And every plant of the field before it was in the earth, and every herb of the field before it grew: for the LORD God had not caused it to rain upon the earth, and *there was* not a man to till the ground.

6 But there went up a mist from the earth, and watered the whole face of the ground.

What does "LORD God" connote? (2:4) "Thus far in Genesis, Deity is called 'God' (Heb., *Elohim* . . .). From this point on through Genesis 2 and 3, two words are used together to designate Deity: LORD God (Heb., *Jehovah Elohim*). The meaning of this combination title may be 'Jehovah of the Gods,' for *elohim* can be used as a plural common noun and Hebrew permits a genitive relationship of two nouns thus placed together without a preposition between them. Alternatively, the meaning may be 'the Lord Omnipotent,' which is a divine title for Jehovah, or Jesus, that is used several times in the Book of Mormon (e.g., Mosiah 3:5, 17, 18; 5:2, 15)" (Rasmussen, *Latter-day Saint Commentary on the Old Testament*, 9). ⊕

How do these verses help us understand the spiritual creation? (2:4–6) According to the Prophet Joseph Smith's inspired revision of these verses, the Lord declared: "For I, the Lord God, created all things of which I have spoken, spiritually, before they were naturally upon the face of the earth. . . . And I, the Lord God, had created all the children of men; . . . for in heaven created I them; and there was not yet flesh upon the earth neither in the water, neither in the air" (Moses 3:5).

7 And the LORD God formed man *of* the dust of the ground, and breathed into his nostrils the breath of life; and man became a living soul.

How does man, formed from the "dust of the ground," become a "living soul"? (2:7) "The dust of the ground means simply that the physical body of man was formed from the elements found in the earth. . . . The placing of man's preexistent spirit in this physical body produces a living being, a 'soul.' The Abrahamic account is more detailed: the Gods '*took his spirit (that is, the man's spirit), and put it into him; and breathed into his nostrils the breath of life, and man became a living soul*' [Abraham 5:7]. . . . A spirit in a physical body constitutes a 'soul,' as we read, 'The spirit and the body are the soul of man' (D&C 88:15)" (Draper, et al., *Pearl of Great Price*, 223; see also Moses 6:59). ⊕

8 ¶ And the LORD God planted a garden eastward in Eden; and there he put the man whom he had formed.

9 And out of the ground made the LORD God to grow every tree that is pleasant to the sight, and good for food; the tree of life also in the midst of the garden, and the tree of knowledge of good and evil.

Genesis 2:8–17. Adam Is Placed in the Garden of Eden

What does Eden mean and where was it located? (2:8–9) "The word *Eden* refers to a well-watered place, suggesting a luxurious park. The word translated 'garden' does not typically refer to vegetable plots but orchards or parks containing trees" (Walton, et al., *IVP Bible Background Commentary*, 31). "In accord with the revelations given to the Prophet Joseph Smith, we

What Does the Church Believe about Evolution? (Genesis 2; Moses 2–4; Abraham 5)

"The Church has no official position on the theory of evolution. Organic evolution, or changes to species' inherited traits over time, is a matter for scientific study. Nothing has been revealed concerning evolution. Though the details of what happened on earth before Adam and Eve, including how their bodies were created, have not been revealed, our teachings regarding man's origin are clear and come from revelation.

"Before we were born on earth, we were spirit children of heavenly parents, with bodies in their image. God directed the creation of Adam and Eve and placed their spirits in their bodies. We are all descendants of Adam and Eve, our first parents, who were created in God's image. There were no spirit children of Heavenly Father on the earth before Adam and Eve were created. In addition, 'for a time they lived alone in a paradisiacal setting where there was neither human death nor future family.' They fell from that state, and this Fall was an essential part of Heavenly Father's plan for us to become like Him. (See Elder Jeffrey R. Holland of the Quorum of the Twelve Apostles, 'Where Justice, Love, and Mercy Meet,' [*Ensign*, May 2015, 104–6].)

"For further reference, see 'The Origin of Man,' *Improvement Era*, Nov. 1909, 78; *Ensign*, Feb. 2002, 29. See also *Encyclopedia of Mormonism*, 5 vols. (1992), 'Evolution,' 2:478" ("What Does the Church Believe about Evolution?" 41).

teach that *the Garden of Eden was on the American continent located where the City Zion, or the New Jerusalem, will be built.* When Adam and Eve were driven out of the Garden, they eventually dwelt at a place called *Adam-ondi-Ahman*, situated in what is now Daviess County, Missouri. . . .

"We are committed to the fact that Adam dwelt on this American continent" (Smith, *Doctrines of Salvation*, 3:74).

What do rivers in the Mesopotamia have to do with the Garden of Eden? (2:10–14) Along with whatever changes occurred to the world during the Fall of Adam, "the Flood and subsequent cataclysms drastically changed the topography and geography of the earth. The descendants of Noah evidently named some rivers, and perhaps other landmarks, after places they had known before the Flood. This theory would explain why rivers in Mesopotamia now bear the names of rivers originally on the American continent. It is also possible that some present river systems are remnants of the antediluvian river systems on the one great continent that existed then" (*Old Testament Student Manual: Genesis–2 Samuel*, 33).

10 And a river went out of Eden to water the garden; and from thence it was parted, and became into four heads.

11 The name of the first *is* Pison: that *is* it which compasseth the whole land of Havilah, where *there is* gold;

12 And the gold of that land *is* good: there *is* bdellium and the onyx stone.

13 And the name of the second river *is* Gihon: the same *is* it that compasseth the whole land of Ethiopia.

14 And the name of the third river *is* Hiddekel: that *is* it which goeth toward the east of Assyria. And the fourth river *is* Euphrates.

15 And the LORD God took the man, and put him into the garden of Eden to dress it and to keep it.

Why would God plant a tree in the Garden of Eden and then command Adam not to partake of it? (2:16–17) Moses 3:17 reveals that though Adam was commanded not to partake of the tree of knowledge of good and evil, the Lord told him: "nevertheless, thou mayest choose for thyself, for it is given unto thee." "As it turns out, our Father is serious about agency—serious enough that in some respects and in many circumstances, our agency is allowed even to override His will. Imagine, He cared about us enough to provide us with a true test, a true probation—one in which we could actually make our own choices" (Dew, *God Wants a Powerful People*, 27). ⊕

16 And the LORD God commanded the man, saying, Of every tree of the garden thou mayest freely eat:

17 But of the tree of the knowledge of good and evil, thou shalt not eat of it: for in the day that thou eatest thereof thou shalt surely die.

Genesis 2:18–25. Adam and Eve Are Married by the Lord

18 ¶ And the LORD God said, *It is* not good that the man should be alone; I will make him an help meet for him.

19 And out of the ground the LORD God formed every beast of the field, and every fowl of the air; and brought *them* unto Adam to see what he would call them: and whatsoever Adam called every living creature, that *was* the name thereof.

20 And Adam gave names to all cattle, and to the fowl of the air, and to every beast of the field; but for Adam there was not found an help meet for him.

21 And the LORD God caused a deep sleep to fall upon Adam, and he slept: and he took one of his ribs, and closed up the flesh instead thereof;

22 And the rib, which the LORD God had taken from man, made he a woman, and brought her unto the man.

23 And Adam said, This *is* now bone of my bones, and flesh of my flesh: she shall be called Woman, because she was taken out of Man.

24 Therefore shall a man leave his father and his mother, and shall cleave unto his wife: and they shall be one flesh.

25 And they were both naked, the man and his wife, and were not ashamed.

What is "an help meet"? (2:18) *Help meet* literally means "a helper suited to, worthy of, or corresponding to him" (see Genesis 2:18*b*). "It seems that some of the original purpose and power of the term *helpmeet* has been lost through the ages. In today's vernacular, *helpmeet* would seem to indicate a person of lesser stature, a subject, a subordinate. Yet a careful examination of this venerable expression yields an altogether different meaning. 'Even with or equal to' is the meaning attributed to it by the *Oxford English Dictionary*" (Campbell, *Eve and the Choice Made in Eden*, 23–24). ⊕

What is significant in the account of Eve's creation? (2:21–24) "The story of the rib, of course, is figurative" (Kimball, "Blessings and Responsibilities of Womanhood," 71). "The rib, coming as it does from the side, seems to denote partnership. The rib signifies . . . a lateral relationship as partners, to work and to live, side by side" (Nelson, "Lessons from Eve," 87). ⊕

What can we learn from Adam and Eve's union in the Garden of Eden? (2:24) Elder D. Todd Christofferson testified that "the role of marriage and family rest[s] not on social science but on the truth that they are God's creation. It is He who in the beginning created Adam and Eve in His image, male and female, and joined them as husband and wife to become 'one flesh' and to multiply and replenish the earth. Each individual carries the divine image, but it is in the matrimonial union of male and female as one that we attain perhaps the most complete meaning of our having been made in the image of God—male and female" ("Why Marriage, Why Family," 52).

CHAPTER 3

The serpent (Lucifer) deceives Eve—She and then Adam partake of the forbidden fruit—Her Seed (Christ) will bruise the serpent's head—The roles of woman and of man are explained—Adam and Eve are cast out of the Garden of Eden—Adam presides—Eve becomes the mother of all living.

Genesis 3:1–6. Through Lucifer's Deception, Eve—and Then Adam—Partakes of the Forbidden Fruit

How Do Latter-day Saints View the Fall of Adam? (3:1)

"Latter-day Saints embrace the doctrine of the Fall as taught by latter-day prophets as a restoration of one of the 'plain and precious' (1 Nephi 13:28) principles that had been lost to mankind through apostasy. Latter-day prophets acknowledge that 'Adam's fall was a step downward,' but teach that 'it was also a step forward . . . in the eternal march of human progress.' Latter-day leaders have also taught that mankind 'should rejoice with [Adam and Eve], that through their fall and the atonement of Jesus Christ, the way of eternal life has been opened up to us.' Instead of disdainfully looking at the Fall as a tragedy, Latter-day Saints believe Adam and Eve's eating from 'the tree of the knowledge of good and evil' (Genesis 2:17) to be one of the most theologically significant and fortunate events in human history" (Judd, "Fortunate Fall of Adam and Eve," 298).

President Russell M. Nelson noted, "The creation of Adam and Eve was a *paradisiacal creation*, one that required a significant change before they could fulfill the commandment to have children. . . .

"The Fall of Adam (and Eve) constituted the *mortal creation* and brought about the required changes in their bodies, including the circulation of blood and other modifications as well. They were now able to have children. They and their posterity also became subject to injury, disease, and death. And a loving Creator blessed them with healing power by which the life and function of precious physical bodies could be preserved" ("Atonement," 33).

Daniel H. Ludlow explained the following concerning the Fall of Adam and Eve:

"A correct concept of the fall of Adam is necessary to an understanding of the basic claims of Christianity. The churches of the world, however, have largely lost sight of the essential differences in the status of Adam and Eve before and after the fall. The general conditions of Adam and Eve before the fall are listed on the left side of the chart which follows; the corresponding general conditions of Adam and Eve after the fall are listed on the right side of the chart.

Status of Adam and Eve before the fall	Status of Adam and Eve after the fall
1. They were in the presence of God.	1. They were cast out of the presence of God—that is, they suffered a spiritual death.
2. They were not mortal—that is, they were not subject to physical death (2 Nephi 2:22).	2. They became mortal (subject to physical death).
3. They were in a state of innocence—that is, they did not know the difference between good and evil (2 Nephi 2:23).	3. They knew good from evil.
4. They "would have had no children" (2 Nephi 2:23).	4. They had children.

"Thus, . . . two major conclusions [can be reached] from these teachings: (1) the fall was necessary in order for 'men to be'—that is, in order for Adam and Eve to have children. (2) A major purpose of man's existence is for him to have 'joy.' True joy was not possible for Adam and Eve before the fall.

"These truths are stated clearly . . . in 2 Nephi 2:22–23: 'And now, behold, if Adam had not transgressed he would not have fallen . . . and they (Adam and Eve) *would have had no children*; wherefore they would have remained in a state of innocence, *having no joy*, for they knew no misery; doing no good, for they knew no sin' ([emphasis] added)" (*Companion to Your Study of the Book of Mormon*, 126–27).

1 Now the serpent was more subtil than any beast of the field which the Lord God had made. And he said unto the woman, Yea, hath God said, Ye shall not eat of every tree of the garden?

2 And the woman said unto the serpent, We may eat of the fruit of the trees of the garden:

3 But of the fruit of the tree which *is* in the midst of the garden, God hath said, Ye shall not eat of it, neither shall ye touch it, lest ye die.

4 And the serpent said unto the woman, Ye shall not surely die:

5 For God doth know that in the day ye eat thereof, then your eyes shall be opened, and ye shall be as gods, knowing good and evil.

Why did Satan use the "serpent" to tempt Eve? (3:1) It was Satan who "put it into the heart of the serpent . . . to beguile Eve, for . . . he sought to destroy the world" (Moses 4:6). "Lucifer possesses snakelike qualities. He 'beguiles' (Moses 4:19), deceives (Rev. 12:9), poisons minds, generates fear, strikes quickly, and brings death with his venom. Further, of all the beasts of the field, he is the most subtle (Moses 4:5). For these and other reasons Satan is known as 'that old serpent, who is the devil, who is the father of all lies' (2 Ne. 2:18; D&C 76:28)" (McConkie and Parry, *A Guide to Scriptural Symbols*, 98). ⊕

How did Satan twist the truth to tempt Eve? (3:1–3) "The truth was, of course, that God had benevolently allowed [Adam and Eve] to freely eat of every tree and had warned against only one. Satan's cunning question presumes the opposite and presupposes a God not of benevolence but of restriction, causing Eve to focus on the restriction as she answered that they could eat from all the trees but one, whose fruit would bring death" (Clark, *Echoes of Eden*, 51). When might you have been tempted to consider God as being restrictive or unkind? Why is this an effective tool of the adversary?

How did Satan persuade Eve to partake of the fruit? (3:3–5) "The serpent's first assault was an invitation to Eve to reassess God's command that 'ye shall not eat of every tree of the garden' (Moses 4:7; Gen. 3:1). Eve's subsequent assessment, rationale, and perhaps outright questioning of God's directive led to the Fall. Although the serpent told Eve the truth that 'when she should eat of the tree of knowledge of good and evil they should become as Gods,' according to George Q. Cannon, 'he accompanied it with a lie as he always does. He never tells the complete truth.'

"Before speaking to Eve, the serpent waited to approach her until she was alone. Eve made a life-altering decision without consulting Adam" (Black, *400 Questions and Answers about the Old Testament*, 30). ⊕

6 And when the woman saw that the tree *was* good for food, and that it *was* pleasant to the eyes, and a tree to be desired to make *one* wise, she took of the fruit thereof, and did eat, and gave also unto her husband with her; and he did eat.

Why did Eve partake of the tree of knowledge of good and evil? (3:6) "There has been much speculation, but no revelation, about what the 'fruit' was that the woman saw and perceived to be 'good for food,' 'pleasant to the eyes,' and 'a tree to be desired to make one wise.' She partook of it partly because of those perceptions and partly because she was deceived (Gen. 3:13; 1 Tim. 2:14–15). Later, when she fully understood the potential of her choice (made available through the plan of redemption), she rejoiced about it (Moses 5:4–11). It was good that she gave the fruit also to her husband and that he did eat, so that procreation, with all its positive potential, could proceed (Moses 5:11; 2 Ne. 2:22–27)" (Rasmussen, *Latter-day Saint Commentary on the Old Testament,* 15).

What did partaking of the fruit represent? (3:6) Elder Bruce R. McConkie said, "The account is speaking figuratively. What is meant by partaking of the fruit of the tree of the knowledge of good and evil is that our first parents complied with whatever laws were involved so that their bodies would change from their state of paradisiacal immortality to a state of natural mortality" ("Christ and the Creation," 15).

Genesis 3:7–21. God Appears and Explains to Adam and Eve the Consequences of the Fall

What changed for Adam and Eve after partaking of the fruit? (3:7–8) "The fall had a twofold direction—downward, yet forward. It brought man into the world and set his feet upon progression's highway" (Whitney, *Saturday Night Thoughts*, 93). ⊕

Why did God ask questions of Adam and Eve when He already knew the answers? (3:9–13) God knows all things. He asked this question and the question in verse 13 so he could help Adam and Eve. Elder Jeffrey R. Holland said, "It is obvious that the questions [in vv. 9 and 13] are for the children's sake, giving Adam and Eve the responsibility of replying honestly" ("Rending the Veil of Unbelief," 14). ⊕

Why did Adam partake of the fruit? (3:12) "When God united Adam and Eve as husband and wife, he commanded them to 'multiply and replenish the earth' (Moses 2:28), something they could do only in a mortal state" (McConkie, *Answers*, 185). Instead of blaming Eve, Adam was obedient to this important commandment of the Lord. Brigham Young said that "we should never blame Mother Eve," for through her and then Adam's transgression, humankind could

7 And the eyes of them both were opened, and they knew that they *were* naked; and they sewed fig leaves together, and made themselves aprons.

8 And they heard the voice of the LORD God walking in the garden in the cool of the day: and Adam and his wife hid themselves from the presence of the LORD God amongst the trees of the garden.

9 And the LORD God called unto Adam, and said unto him, Where *art* thou?

10 And he said, I heard thy voice in the garden, and I was afraid, because I *was* naked; and I hid myself.

11 And he said, Who told thee that thou *wast* naked? Hast thou eaten of the tree, whereof I commanded thee that thou shouldest not eat?

12 And the man said, The woman whom thou gavest *to be* with me, she gave me of the tree, and I did eat.

13 And the LORD God said unto the woman, What *is* this *that* thou hast done? And the woman said, The serpent beguiled me, and I did eat.

come to "know good from evil, the bitter from the sweet, the things of God from the things not of God" (*Discourses of Brigham Young*, 103).

14 And the LORD God said unto the serpent, Because thou hast done this, thou *art* cursed above all cattle, and above every beast of the field; upon thy belly shalt thou go, and dust shalt thou eat all the days of thy life:

15 And I will put enmity between thee and the woman, and between thy seed and her seed; it shall bruise thy head, and thou shalt bruise his heel.

Who is the "seed of the woman" in these verses? (3:14–15) "In the promise given of God following the fall—that though the devil . . . should have the power to bruise the heel of Adam's posterity, through the seed of the woman should come the power to bruise the adversary's head. It is significant that this assurance of eventual victory . . . was to be realized through the offspring of woman; the promise was not made specifically to the man, nor to the pair. The only instance of offspring from woman dissociated from mortal fatherhood is the birth of Jesus the Christ, who was the earthly Son of a mortal mother, begotten by an immortal Father" (Talmage, *Jesus the Christ*, 40). ⊕

16 Unto the woman he said, I will greatly multiply thy sorrow and thy conception; in sorrow thou shalt bring forth children; and thy desire *shall be* to thy husband, and he shall rule over thee.

What does it mean that God will multiply Eve's sorrow? (3:16) "Appreciating the Hebrew meaning for words in God's response to Eve reinforces our understanding of His intent to bless her. He told her that He would 'greatly multiply thy sorrow' (Genesis 3:16; Moses 4:22). The Hebrew word translated 'sorrow' does not imply feeling sorry over something; it means pain or hurt. Furthermore, 'multiply' in this passage means repetition or something happening over and over again, not something being added to or increased. Therefore, God promised Eve that life in the fallen world would require her to do painful things over and over again" (Olson, *Women of the Old Testament*, 16). ⊕

How may the phrase "rule over" give the wrong impression? (3:16) President Spencer W. Kimball taught: "I have a question about the word *rule*. It gives the wrong impression. I would prefer to use the word *preside* because that's what he does. A righteous husband presides over his wife and family" ("Blessings and Responsibilities of Womanhood," 72). "By divine design, fathers are to preside over their families in love and righteousness. . . . Mothers are primarily responsible for the nurture of their children. In these sacred responsibilities, fathers and mothers are obligated to help one another as equal partners" ("The Family: A Proclamation to the World" [2010], 129).

17 And unto Adam he said, Because thou hast hearkened unto the voice of thy wife, and hast eaten of the tree, of which I commanded thee, saying, Thou shalt not eat of it: cursed *is* the ground for thy sake; in sorrow shalt thou eat *of* it all the days of thy life;

Why did God curse the ground for Adam's sake? (3:17–19) "We often hear it said that Adam was cursed because he partook of the forbidden fruit. The record says 'the ground' was cursed, not Adam. Then the Lord added 'for thy sake.' This means for his benefit" (Smith, "Opposition in Order to Strengthen Us," 62).

"Adam was told that the ground is cursed with thorns and thistles for our sakes (see Gen. 3:17–18). Likewise, mortality is 'cursed' with the thorns of worldly temptation and the slivers of sin so that we can be tested and prove ourselves. This is necessary for our eternal progression" (Faust, "Crown of Thorns, a Crown of Glory," 68).

18 Thorns also and thistles shall it bring forth to thee; and thou shalt eat the herb of the field;

19 In the sweat of thy face shalt thou eat bread, till thou return unto the ground; for out of it wast thou taken: for dust thou *art*, and unto dust shalt thou return.

20 And Adam called his wife's name Eve; because she was the mother of all living.

21 Unto Adam also and to his wife did the LORD God make coats of skins, and clothed them.

What were the "coats of skin" used to clothe Adam and Eve? (3:21) "The Hebrew word for nakedness is *erwah*, meaning 'uncleanness' or 'shame.' To cover the nakedness of Adam and Eve, the Lord made garments [coats] of skins or sacred vestments (see Gen. 3:21). According to Shon Hopkin, 'The symbolism of the coat of skins shows God's willingness to protect Adam and Eve (as the coat would do in the newly fallen world)'" (Black, *400 Questions and Answers about the Old Testament*, 31–32). Also, "this notice illustrates that death is in force in the animal kingdom, for the skins most likely came from animals" (Draper, et al., *Pearl of Great Price*, 49). ⊕

Genesis 3:22–24. Adam and Eve Are Cast Out of the Garden of Eden

22 ¶ And the LORD God said, Behold, the man is become as one of us, to know good and evil: and now, lest he put forth his hand, and take also of the tree of life, and eat, and live for ever:

23 Therefore the LORD God sent him forth from the garden of Eden, to till the ground from whence he was taken.

24 So he drove out the man; and he placed at the east of the garden of Eden Cherubims, and a flaming sword which turned every way, to keep the way of the tree of life.

Why did God place "Cherubims, and a flaming sword" at the tree of life? (3:24) "If Adam had put forth his hand immediately, and partaken of the tree of life, he would have lived forever, . . . having no space for repentance; . . . and the great plan of salvation would have been frustrated" (Alma 42:5). "The mortal learning experience, represented by the *tree of knowledge*, is so necessary that God placed cherubim and a flaming sword to guard the way of the *tree of life* until Adam and Eve completed, and we, their posterity, complete this preparatory schooling. . . . But he cannot fully receive us and give us the gift of celestial life—partaking of God's very nature—until we have *learned by our own experience* to distinguish good from evil" (Hafen, *Broken Heart*, 30).

CHAPTER 4

Eve bears Cain and Abel—They offer sacrifices—Cain slays Abel and is cursed by the Lord, who also sets a mark upon him—The children of men multiply—Adam begets Seth, and Seth begets Enos.

1 And Adam knew Eve his wife; and she conceived, and bare Cain, and said, I have gotten a man from the LORD.

Genesis 4:1–8. Cain Slays His Brother Abel

Who was the firstborn child of Adam and Eve? (4:1) It is uncertain who was the firstborn child of Adam and Eve. According to Moses 5:1–15, Adam and Eve had a variety of experiences over an extended period of time before Cain was born. For example, Adam and Eve had brought into the world many "sons and daughters" which "began to multiply and replenish the earth" (Moses 5:2). ⊕

2 And she again bare his brother Abel. And Abel was a keeper of sheep, but Cain was a tiller of the ground.

3 And in process of time it came to pass, that Cain brought of the fruit of the ground an offering unto the LORD.

4 And Abel, he also brought of the firstlings of his flock and of the fat thereof. And the LORD had respect unto Abel and to his offering:

5 But unto Cain and to his offering he had not respect. And Cain was very wroth, and his countenance fell.

Why wasn't Cain's offering acceptable unto the Lord? (4:2–5) "It was Satan who commanded Cain to make an offering to the Lord. When Cain followed Satan's instruction, his offering was rejected by the Lord. In the words of Moses, 'Satan commanded him, saying: Make an offering unto the Lord. . . . But unto Cain, and to his offering, [the Lord] had not respect. Now Satan knew this, and it pleased him' (Moses 5:18, 21).

"Earlier instructions from an angel to Adam and Eve had emphasized that animal sacrifice 'is a similitude of the sacrifice of the Only Begotten of the Father' [Moses 5:7]. . . . Thus, Cain already knew what was acceptable to God, but he refused to follow counsel (*TPJS*, pp. 58, 169)" (Harris, "Cain"). ⊕

Sacrificial Offering (Genesis 4:2–5)

How severe was Cain's apostasy? (4:6–8) "According to Moses, Cain chose to follow Satan and swore an oath to follow him in secret to 'murder to get gain' (Moses 5:29–31). Driven by anger of his rejection and his desire to take his brother's flocks, Cain went into the field and killed his brother Abel. . . . This story represents the causes and effects of following Satan" (Holzapfel, et al., *Jehovah and the World of the Old Testament*, 26). ⊕

Genesis 4:9–15. The Lord Curses Cain for Killing Abel

Why is Cain's question about being his brother's keeper important? (4:9) "Cain killed Abel. The scriptures say that he did so 'for the sake of getting gain' (Moses 5:50), the flocks of his brother (JST, Gen. 5:18; Moses 5:33). Seeing this, the Lord asked Cain, 'Where is Abel thy brother?' Cain first attempted to cover his sin with a lie: 'I know not.' Then he added a rationalization: 'Am I my brother's keeper?' (Gen. 4:9; Moses 5:34).

"Are we our brothers' keepers? In other words, are we responsible to look after the well-being of our neighbors as we seek to earn our daily bread? The Savior's Golden Rule says we are. Satan says we are not" (Oaks, "Brother's Keeper," 20). ⊕

What do we learn about judgment when God asks: "What hast thou done"? (4:10) "After looking down at the crumpled body at his feet, and especially after the torments of hell began to persecute him and the ghost of his brother began to follow him, Cain must have wished that he would give Abel's life back. The Lord did not curse Cain; it was Cain who, breaking eternal law, cursed himself" (Kimball, "Love vs. Lust," 14). ⊕

6 And the LORD said unto Cain, Why art thou wroth? and why is thy countenance fallen?

7 If thou doest well, shalt thou not be accepted? and if thou doest not well, sin lieth at the door. And unto thee *shall be* his desire, and thou shalt rule over him.

8 And Cain talked with Abel his brother: and it came to pass, when they were in the field, that Cain rose up against Abel his brother, and slew him.

9 ¶ And the LORD said unto Cain, Where *is* Abel thy brother? And he said, I know not: *Am* I my brother's keeper?

10 And he said, What hast thou done? the voice of thy brother's blood crieth unto me from the ground.

What Influenced Cain's Decision to Kill His Brother? (Genesis 4)

"While Genesis 4 opens with the birth of Cain and Abel, the passage in Moses 5 restores some important details to the story of Adam and Eve that help us to better understand the biblical narrative. According to the book of Moses, after Adam and Eve were expelled from the garden the Lord taught them the fullness of the gospel (see Moses 5:4–11).

"From Moses we learn that, having been taught the gospel, Adam and Eve 'blessed the name of God, and they made all things known unto their sons and daughters.' But the record continues: 'And Satan came among them, saying I am also a son of God' (Moses 5:12–13). Satan's unrelenting influence is manifest throughout the Old Testament as people chose between Jehovah's will or the Adversary's" (Holzapfel, et al., *Jehovah and the World of the Old Testament*, 25).

11 And now *art* thou cursed from the earth, which hath opened her mouth to receive thy brother's blood from thy hand;

12 When thou tillest the ground, it shall not henceforth yield unto thee her strength; a fugitive and a vagabond shalt thou be in the earth.

13 And Cain said unto the LORD, My punishment *is* greater than I can bear.

14 Behold, thou hast driven me out this day from the face of the earth; and from thy face shall I be hid; and I shall be a fugitive and a vagabond in the earth; and it shall come to pass, *that* every one that findeth me shall slay me.

15 And the LORD said unto him, Therefore whosoever slayeth Cain, vengeance shall be taken on him sevenfold. And the LORD set a mark upon Cain, lest any finding him should kill him.

25 ¶ And Adam knew his wife again; and she bare a son, and called his name Seth: For God, *said she,* hath appointed me another seed instead of Abel, whom Cain slew.

What does it mean that Abel's "blood crieth unto me from the ground"? (4:10) "Abel, in one sense a 'prophet' (Lk 11:50–51), 'still speaks, even though he is dead' (Heb 11:4), for his spilled blood continues to cry out to God against all those who do violence to their human brothers. But the blood of Christ 'speaks a better word' (Heb 12:24)" (*NIV Study Bible*, 12).

Why would God declare that Cain would be "a fugitive and a vagabond"? (4:10–14) "Though Cain had thought murder would give him greater prosperity, God showed him that such sin never brings what we truly want. Instead, Cain would lose the prosperity that he already had. He would become a fugitive and vagabond, or someone who wanders the earth. This does not mean that he was becoming nomadic, for nomads are not fugitives and they don't wander; they move with knowledgeable purpose. Rather, Cain would have no means of sustaining himself and would never find peace or feel at home anywhere, and would not be welcome among any group" (Muhlestein, *Scripture Study Made Simple*, 13). ⊕

What do we know about the mark put upon Cain? (4:15) "A mark was set on Cain to distinguish him from the other sons of Adam (see Gen. 4:15; Moses 5:40). The purpose of the mark was to prevent others from assuming the right to punish him. Cain and his posterity lived apart from other descendants of Adam (see Moses 7:22)" (Black, *400 Questions and Answers about the Old Testament*, 34–35). ⊕

Summary of Genesis 4:16–24

Cain becomes a wanderer in the land of Nod. He has a large family. They continue in wickedness and follow Satan instead of the Lord (see Moses 5:41–57). Cain's son Enoch (see Genesis 4:17) should not be confused with the Enoch of Seth's lineage (see Genesis 5:18–24; Moses 6:21–27).

Genesis 4:25–26. Seth Is Born to Adam and Eve

What was noble and unique about Seth? (4:25) "Modern revelation provides additional insight into the life of Adam's noble son, Seth: He 'was a perfect man and his likeness . . . seemed to be like unto his father in all things and could be distinguished from him only by his age' (D&C 107:43; Moses 6:10; Gen. 5:3). . . . He was an obedient son who 'rebelled not, but offered an acceptable sacrifice, like unto his brother Abel' (Moses 6:3). . . .

"President Joseph F. Smith saw Seth as one of the 'great and mighty ones' assembled in the 'congregations of the righteous' at the time of the Savior's visit to the spirit world following his crucifixion (D&C 138:38, 40)" (Brewster, *Doctrine and Covenants Encyclopedia*, 511).

What did Adam and Eve do to teach their family? (4:26) Following their expulsion from the Garden of Eden on, Adam and Eve "blessed the name of God" and "made all things known unto their sons and their daughters" (Moses 5:12). Unfortunately, "Satan [had come] among them," and many of their children "believed it not" (Moses 5:13). "Thus, in the beginning, the perfect pattern is set for perfecting the family. The man and the woman are together in worship; they are together in teaching their children; they are together in establishing the family unit that hopefully will endure in the eternities ahead, thus giving eternal life to all those who earn it" (McConkie, "Our Sisters from the Beginning," 62).

26 And to Seth, to him also there was born a son; and he called his name Enos: then began men to call upon the name of the LORD.

Genesis 5:1–20. A Genealogy from Adam to Enoch Is Kept

Why is this genealogy important? (5:1–2) "Genesis 5 lists the genealogies of the lineage through whom the priesthood and the covenants of the gospel continued, beginning with Adam and ending with the sons of Noah. Little is given outside of the genealogical information. One can imagine that great things were manifest in the lives of those people whom we call the Patriarchs; yet the Lord has seen fit to withhold their histories from us" (Jackson, "Genesis and the Early Experiences of Mankind," 31–32).

Why did God call Adam and Eve by the name "Adam"? (5:2) *Adam* in Hebrew can be translated as "man" (Genesis, *Hebrew-Chaldee Lexicon*, 13). This implies that God named Adam and Eve together man or mankind, as He created them "in His own image, male and female" (Genesis 1:27).

"As we read scripture designating Adam as the addressee, many assume God is speaking only of or to the man Adam. Such an assumption would lead to the belief that Eve stood by throughout the entire Garden period without a voice, without acquiring knowledge, without a significant role. . . . [But Eve had] a pivotal

CHAPTER 5

The generations of Adam are Adam, Seth, Enos, Cainan, Mahalaleel, Jared, Enoch (who walked with God), Methuselah, Lamech, and Noah (who begat Shem, Ham, and Japheth).

1 This *is* the book of the generations of Adam. In the day that God created man, in the likeness of God made he him;

2 Male and female created he them; and blessed them, and called their name Adam, in the day when they were created.

3 ¶ And Adam lived an hundred and thirty years, and begat *a son* in his own likeness, after his image; and called his name Seth:

4 And the days of Adam after he had begotten Seth were eight hundred years: and he begat sons and daughters:

5 And all the days that Adam lived were nine hundred and thirty years: and he died.

6 And Seth lived an hundred and five years, and begat Enos:

7 And Seth lived after he begat Enos eight hundred and seven years, and begat sons and daughters:

8 And all the days of Seth were nine hundred and twelve years: and he died.

9 ¶ And Enos lived ninety years, and begat Cainan:

10 And Enos lived after he begat Cainan eight hundred and fifteen years, and begat sons and daughters:

11 And all the days of Enos were nine hundred and five years: and he died.

12 ¶ And Cainan lived seventy years, and begat Mahalaleel:

13 And Cainan lived after he begat Mahalaleel eight hundred and forty years, and begat sons and daughters:

14 And all the days of Cainan were nine hundred and ten years: and he died.

15 ¶ And Mahalaleel lived sixty and five years, and begat Jared:

16 And Mahalaleel lived after he begat Jared eight hundred and thirty years, and begat sons and daughters:

17 And all the days of Mahalaleel were eight hundred ninety and five years: and he died.

18 ¶ And Jared lived an hundred sixty and two years, and he begat Enoch:

19 And Jared lived after he begat Enoch eight hundred years, and begat sons and daughters:

role in this phase of the plan. Being aware of inclusive language, we can feel confident that God's instructions, concerns for, and advancement of principles and laws were directed to Eve as they were to Adam" (Campbell, *Eve and the Choice Made in Eden*, 60–61). ⊕

What did Adam do for his posterity just prior to his death? (5:5) While describing a vision he had, the Prophet Joseph Smith taught: "I saw Adam in the valley of Adam-ondi-Ahman. He called together his children and blessed them with a patriarchal blessing. The Lord appeared in their midst. And he (Adam) blessed them all and foretold what should befall them to the latest generation" (Joseph Smith Papers, "History, 1838–1856, volume C-1," 11 [addenda]; see also D&C 107:53–56).

20 And all the days of Jared were nine hundred sixty and two years: and he died.

21 ¶ And Enoch lived sixty and five years, and begat Methuselah:

22 And Enoch walked with God after he begat Methuselah three hundred years, and begat sons and daughters:

23 And all the days of Enoch were three hundred sixty and five years:

24 And Enoch walked with God: and he *was* not; for God took him.

Genesis 5:21–24. Enoch and His City Are Taken into Heaven

What does it mean that Enoch "was not" and that "God took him"? (5:24) According to Moses 7:69, "Enoch and all his people walked with God, and dwelt in the midst of Zion; and . . . Zion was not, for God received it up into his own bosom" (Moses 7:69). *Translated beings* are "persons who are changed so that they do not experience pain or death until their resurrection to immortality" (Guide to the Scriptures, "Translated Beings"). The Prophet Joseph Smith taught: "Many may have supposed that the doctrine of translation was a doctrine whereby men were taken immediately into the presence of God and into an Eternal fulness, but this is a mistaken idea. Their place of habitation is that of the terrestrial order and a place prepared for such characters, he held in reserve to be ministering Angels unto many Planets, and who as yet have not entered into so great a fulness as those who are resurrected from the dead" (Joseph Smith Papers, "History, 1838–1856, volume C-1," 17 [addenda]).

Enoch's Ministry as Found in the Book of Moses (5:21–24)

"The prophet-patriarch Enoch remains an enigmatic figure in the religious world, an ancient character shrouded in mystery. This is certainly in part due to the fact that so little information concerning Enoch is contained in the biblical canon. . . . It is to the Prophet Joseph Smith that we turn for a detailed and authoritative account of Enoch—his call, ministry, and ultimate translation" (Millet, "Enoch and His City," 131).

From the Prophet Joseph Smith's translation of the Bible, we learn the following about Enoch's ministry as recorded in the Book of Moses:

God calls Enoch as a prophet and gives him the gift of seership (Moses 6:26–36).

Enoch testifies against the sins of the people and teaches the gospel and the importance of priesthood ordinances (Moses 6:37–68).

Enoch prophesies (Moses 7:1–12).

Enoch performs miracles and establishes the city of Zion (Moses 7:13–21).

Enoch sees all things, even to the end of the world (Moses 7:23–68).

God translates Enoch and his city and takes them into heaven (Moses 7:69).

Note: The Joseph Smith Translation changes Enoch's age to at least 430 years old because he is sixty-five years old when Methuselah is born and he establishes Zion after his birth. Also, part of Enoch's record is quoted by Jude (see Jude 1:14–16).

Genesis 5:25–32. The Generations from Methuselah to Noah Are Listed

25 And Methuselah lived an hundred eighty and seven years, and begat Lamech:

26 And Methuselah lived after he begat Lamech seven hundred eighty and two years, and begat sons and daughters:

Why did Methuselah remain on earth when Enoch and the righteous were translated? (5:25) The Joseph Smith Translation notes that Methuselah was left on the earth at the time of the translation of Enoch and his city "that the covenants of the Lord might be fulfilled, which he made to Enoch; for he truly covenanted with Enoch, that Noah should be of the fruit of his loins" (Moses 8:2). This enabled Noah to go "forth and declare [the] Gospel unto the children of men, even as it was given unto Enoch" (Moses 8:19). Noah taught faith, repentance, baptism, and the gift of the Holy Ghost (see Moses 8:24). This is the message which the people rejected.

27 And all the days of Methuselah were nine hundred sixty and nine years: and he died.

28 ¶ And Lamech lived an hundred eighty and two years, and begat a son:

Why did ancient patriarchs who lived before the Flood live so long? (5:27) "First . . . , modern revelation supports the scriptural indication that many Old Testament patriarchs lived incredibly long lives (see Moses 8:1–13; D&C 107:41–53). Second, early prophets of this dispensation understood these scriptural references to be literal. . . . And third, early historians took these statements literally. . . . The reasons . . . are not made completely clear in scripture. . . . Some have interpreted 2 Nephi 2:21 as referring to [those living before the Flood]: 'The days of the children of men were prolonged, according to the will of God, that they might repent while in the flesh.' . . . Others have suggested that it was righteousness that [increased] the longevity of their lives" (Valletta, "Length of the Lives of the Ancient Patriarchs," 61). ⊕

29 And he called his name Noah, saying, This *same* shall comfort us concerning our work and toil of our hands, because of the ground which the LORD hath cursed.

30 And Lamech lived after he begat Noah five hundred ninety and five years, and begat sons and daughters:

31 And all the days of Lamech were seven hundred seventy and seven years: and he died.

32 And Noah was five hundred years old: and Noah begat Shem, Ham, and Japheth.

What can we learn about Noah from the Prophet Joseph Smith? (5:29–32) "The Priesthood was first given to Adam; he obtained the First Presidency, and held the keys of it from generation to generation. . . . Then to Noah, who is Gabriel; he stands next in authority to Adam in the Priesthood; he was called of God to this office, and was the father of all living in his day, and to him was given the dominion. These men held keys first on earth, and then in heaven" (Smith, *Joseph Smith* [manual], 104). ⊕

CHAPTER 6

The sons of God marry the daughters of men—Men turn to wickedness, the earth is filled with violence, and all flesh is corrupted—The Flood is promised—God establishes His covenant with Noah, who builds an ark to save his family and various living things.

1 And it came to pass, when men began to
multiply on the face of the earth, and daughters were born unto them,

2 That the sons of God saw the daughters of
men that they *were* fair; and they took them
wives of all which they chose.

3 And the LORD said, My spirit shall not always strive with man, for that he also *is* flesh:
yet his days shall be an hundred and twenty
years.

4 There were giants in the earth in those
days; and also after that, when the sons of
God came in unto the daughters of men, and
they bare *children* to them, the same *became*
mighty men which *were* of old, men of renown.

5 ¶ And GOD saw that the wickedness of
man *was* great in the earth, and *that* every
imagination of the thoughts of his heart *was*
only evil continually.

Genesis 6:1–8. God Sees His Children Become Very Wicked, So He Promises to Destroy Them

Who were these "sons of God"? (6:2) Through revelation given to Joseph Smith, we learn that the *sons of God* were those who were obedient to the Lord's teachings. The record states, "And Noah and his sons hearkened unto the Lord, and gave heed, and they were called the sons of God" (Moses 8:13). However, the *sons of men* were those who did not give heed to the Lord. ⊕

Who were these giants? (6:4) "Rather than indicating that they were mythical giants and demigods, as some readers have imagined, the Hebrew name of these vaunted children of the mixed marriages, when they became 'mighty men,' merely supplied a rationale for unrighteous boasting by their parents and for rejecting Noah's warnings (Moses 8:21). Their Hebrew name, *Nephilim*, is apparently derived from the verb *naphal*, 'fall'; they are therefore thought by rabbinical commentators to have been 'fallen ones' (rather than persons of gigantic stature; the Greek Septuagint rendered the Hebrew word as *gigantes*, for reasons unknown). *Nephilim* is one of four different Hebrew words translated 'giants' in the King James Version of the Old Testament" (Rasmussen, *Latter-day Saint Commentary on the Old Testament*, 26).

What were the conditions on the earth before the flood? (6:5) "By the time of Noah, men had become so wicked, despite God's repeated calling upon them to repent, that . . . unprecedented words are recorded concerning them [see Genesis 6:5]. This generation was found to be so wicked that its people were no longer allowed to pollute the earth by their presence on it or to bring innocent spirits into its decadent environment (see Gen. 6:11–13). . . . The generation of Noah was so wicked that only an act of cleansing of immense magnitude could allow the next generations a chance to live by higher principles" (Jackson, "Genesis and the Early Experiences of Mankind," 30–31).

6 And it repented the LORD that he had made man on the earth, and it grieved him at his heart.

7 And the LORD said, I will destroy man whom I have created from the face of the earth; both man, and beast, and the creeping thing, and the fowls of the air; for it repenteth me that I have made them.

8 But Noah found grace in the eyes of the LORD.

9 ¶ These *are* the generations of Noah: Noah was a just man *and* perfect in his generations, *and* Noah walked with God.

10 And Noah begat three sons, Shem, Ham, and Japheth.

11 The earth also was corrupt before God, and the earth was filled with violence.

12 And God looked upon the earth, and, behold, it was corrupt; for all flesh had corrupted his way upon the earth.

What does it mean that God "repented"? (6:6) The Joseph Smith Translation makes it clear that Noah is the one that "repents" (see JST, Gen. 8:13): "And it repented Noah, and his heart was pained, that the Lord had made man" (see also Ex. 32:12, 14; 1 Sam. 15:11; 2 Sam. 24:16; Joel 2:13; Amos 7:3, 6; 3 Ne. 27:32; Moses 8:25).

Genesis 6:9–22. Noah Is Commanded to Build an Ark

What did Noah do as a just and perfect man? (6:9) Noah was a righteous patriarch who was a "'just man and perfect in his generations,' one who 'walked with God.' . . . Ordained to the priesthood at an early age, 'he became a preacher of righteousness and declared the gospel of Jesus Christ, . . . teaching faith, repentance, baptism, and the reception of the Holy Ghost'" (Monson, "Models to Follow," 60–61). Noah's "perfection" does not mean that he "never made mistakes. . . . Mortal perfection can be achieved as we try to perform every duty, keep every law, and strive to be as perfect in our sphere as our Heavenly Father is in his" (Nelson, "Perfection Pending," 86).

What do we know about Noah's sons? (6:10) "The sons of Noah and his wife were listed in Genesis 5:32; they were to become forefathers of the peoples who would inhabit the earth (Gen. 9:19), details of which follow in Genesis 10. Restored sources (Moses 8:12) indicate that Japheth was forty-two years older than Shem, and Shem was eight years older than Ham; thus, Ham was the youngest son (cf. Gen. 9:24)" (Rasmussen, *Latter-day Saint Commentary on the Old Testament*, 32).

In what ways does Noah's time parallel our day? (6:11) "We are told . . . that some conditions preceding the second coming of the Savior will be as in the days of Noah (see Matthew 24:37–39). . . . Noah's time was one of disobedience and wickedness. People were uncomprehending and 'knew not until the flood came' (Matt. 24:39; see also Gen. 6:5, 1 Pet. 3:20). The choking cares and pleasures of this life led to the general rejection of Noah's prophetic message. Two especially interesting words are used in the Bible to describe Noah's time: *violence* and *corruption* (Gen. 6:11). Violence and corruption, seldom strangers to the human scene, appear to be increasing today" (Maxwell, "For I Will Lead You Along," 7).

Why did God send the flood to destroy the wicked? (6:13) God does all things for the "benefit of the world" (2 Nephi 26:24). John Taylor noted that "Wickedness increased until it was decided that they should be destroyed, that they might be deprived of the privilege of perpetuating their species. Why? . . . Let us suppose that you and I were there as spirits awaiting the privilege of taking bodies, and that we could see the wickedness and corruption that was going on upon the earth. . . . Is it right and just that we who have done no wrong should have to enter into such corrupt bodies and partake of the influences with which they are surrounded? 'No,' says the Father, 'it is not just.' . . . It was an act of justice and righteousness" (*Gospel Kingdom*, 99).

What is significant about the coating of pitch? (6:14) "The ark was built of gopher wood, referring to a tree biblical scholars have not been able to identify. Noah was instructed to 'pitch it within and without' (Gen. 6:14). In other words, he was to cover the wood with a waterproofing substance. The Hebrew word (*kpr*), translated *pitch* in this verse, is used many other times in the Bible. The word as used in Genesis 6:14 denotes a protective covering. In every other instance where this Hebrew word is found, it refers to the atonement. The atonement of Jesus Christ provides us with a protective covering; it shields us from the power of the adversary, just as the pitch protected the ark from the life-threatening waters" (Parry and Parry, *Symbols and Shadows*, 88–89).

Why did God provide Noah with the design of the ark? (6:14–16) "It is significant that, apart from the Tabernacle of Moses and the Temple of Solomon, Noah's Ark is the only manmade structure mentioned in the Bible whose design was directly revealed by God. Noah's Ark seems to have been 'designed as a temple,' specifically a prefiguration of the Tabernacle. . . .

"The Ark's three decks suggest both the three divisions of the Tabernacle and the threefold layout of the Garden of Eden. Indeed, each of the decks of Noah's Ark was exactly 'the same height as the Tabernacle and three times the area of the Tabernacle court'" (Bradshaw, "Frequently Asked Questions about Science and Genesis," 224–25).

What do we know about the window in the ark? (6:16) "The Hebrew word rendered *window* is a word for something shining or bright (Gen. 6:16*a*). Light and ventilation would of course be requisite in a vessel

13 And God said unto Noah, The end of all flesh is come before me; for the earth is filled with violence through them; and, behold, I will destroy them with the earth.

14 ¶ Make thee an ark of gopher wood; rooms shalt thou make in the ark, and shalt pitch it within and without with pitch.

15 And this *is the fashion* which thou shalt make it *of:* The length of the ark *shall be* three hundred cubits, the breadth of it fifty cubits, and the height of it thirty cubits.

16 A window shalt thou make to the ark, and in a cubit shalt thou finish it above; and the door of the ark shalt thou set in the side thereof; *with* lower, second, and third *stories* shalt thou make it.

'tight like unto a dish, . . . tight like unto the ark of Noah,' as the Book of Mormon describes both the ark and the Jaredite vessels. Those vessels were lighted by miraculously luminous stones (Ether 2:22–25; 3:1–6; 6:7)" (Rasmussen, *Latter-day Saint Commentary on the Old Testament*, 28).

17 And, behold, I, even I, do bring a flood of waters upon the earth, to destroy all flesh, wherein *is* the breath of life, from under heaven; *and* every thing that *is* in the earth shall die.

18 But with thee will I establish my covenant; and thou shalt come into the ark, thou, and thy sons, and thy wife, and thy sons' wives with thee.

19 And of every living thing of all flesh, two of every *sort* shalt thou bring into the ark, to keep *them* alive with thee; they shall be male and female.

20 Of fowls after their kind, and of cattle after their kind, of every creeping thing of the earth after his kind, two of every *sort* shall come unto thee, to keep *them* alive.

21 And take thou unto thee of all food that is eaten, and thou shalt gather *it* to thee; and it shall be for food for thee, and for them.

22 Thus did Noah; according to all that God commanded him, so did he.

What can we learn from Noah's obedience and faithfulness in building and boarding the ark prior to the rain? (6:17–22) President Spencer W. Kimball explained that when Noah built the ark, "there was no evidence of rain and flood. . . . His warnings were considered irrational. . . . How foolish to build an ark on dry ground with the sun shining and life moving forward as usual! But time ran out. The ark was finished. The floods came. The disobedient and rebellious were drowned. The miracle of the ark followed the faith manifested in its building" (*Spencer W. Kimball* [manual], 140–41).

How does Noah's example help us overcome challenges in our day? (6:22) "There is no need for you or for me, in this enlightened age when the fulness of the gospel has been restored, to sail uncharted seas or to travel unmarked roads in search of truth. A loving Heavenly Father has plotted our course and provided an unfailing guide—even *obedience*. A knowledge of truth and the answers to our greatest questions come to us as we are obedient to the commandments of God. . . .

"There are rules and laws to help ensure our physical safety. Likewise, the Lord has provided guidelines and commandments to help ensure our spiritual safety so that we might successfully navigate this often-treacherous mortal existence and return eventually to our Heavenly Father" (Monson, "Obedience Brings Blessings," 89, 90).

CHAPTER 7

Noah's family and various beasts and fowl enter the ark—The Flood comes, and water covers the whole earth—All other life that breathes is destroyed.

1 And the LORD said unto Noah, Come thou
and all thy house into the ark; for thee have
I seen righteous before me in this generation.

2 Of every clean beast thou shalt take to thee
by sevens, the male and his female: and of
beasts that *are* not clean by two, the male and
his female.

3 Of fowls also of the air by sevens, the male
and the female; to keep seed alive upon the
face of all the earth.

4 For yet seven days, and I will cause it to rain
upon the earth forty days and forty nights;
and every living substance that I have made
will I destroy from off the face of the earth.

5 And Noah did according unto all that the
LORD commanded him.

6 And Noah *was* six hundred years old when
the flood of waters was upon the earth.

7 ¶ And Noah went in, and his sons, and his
wife, and his sons' wives with him, into the
ark, because of the waters of the flood.

8 Of clean beasts, and of beasts that *are* not
clean, and of fowls, and of every thing that
creepeth upon the earth,

9 There went in two and two unto Noah into
the ark, the male and the female, as God had
commanded Noah.

10 And it came to pass after seven days, that
the waters of the flood were upon the earth.

Genesis 7:1–9. Noah, His Family, and the Animals Enter the Ark

Why was Noah commanded to take seven of every clean animal and two of every unclean animal? (7:2–3) "'Clean' describes the animals suitable for food or for sacrifice ([Bible Dictionary], 'Clean and Unclean'). For the year and more they would be aboard the ark . . . , there could have been a need for more than one pair of each of the 'clean' beasts (see Gen. 8:20)" (Rasmussen, *Latter-day Saint Commentary on the Old Testament*, 29). "[Genesis] 6:19–20 refers to the minimum number needed for regeneration of the species, whereas 7:2–3 includes the additional clean animals to meet the needs of sacrifices after the Flood" (Sarna, *Genesis*, 54).

Genesis 7:10–16. The Flood Begins

What did the flood symbolically represent? (7:10–12) "Latter-day Saints look upon the earth as a living organism, one which is gloriously filling 'the measure of its creation.' They look upon the flood as a baptism of the earth, symbolizing a cleansing of the impurities of the past, and the beginning of a new life" (Widtsoe, *Evidences and Reconciliations*, 127). The question of whether the earth was entirely submerged by the Flood is considered in the commentary in this volume for Genesis 7:17–20. ⊕

11 ¶ In the six hundredth year of Noah's life, in the second month, the seventeenth day of the month, the same day were all the fountains of the great deep broken up, and the windows of heaven were opened.

What happened when the "windows of heaven" were opened? (7:11) President John Taylor stated: "The windows of heaven were opened'—that is, the waters that exist throughout the space surrounding the earth from whence come these clouds from which the rain descends. That was one cause. Another cause was 'the fountains of the great deep were broken up' . . . by the power of God" (in *Journal of Discourses*, 26:75). ⊕

12 And the rain was upon the earth forty days and forty nights.

13 In the selfsame day entered Noah, and Shem, and Ham, and Japheth, the sons of Noah, and Noah's wife, and the three wives of his sons with them, into the ark;

14 They, and every beast after his kind, and all the cattle after their kind, and every creeping thing that creepeth upon the earth after his kind, and every fowl after his kind, every bird of every sort.

15 And they went in unto Noah into the ark, two and two of all flesh, wherein *is* the breath of life.

16 And they that went in, went in male and female of all flesh, as God had commanded him: and the LORD shut him in.

What do the forty days and nights of rain represent? (7:12) "In scripture, the number represents a period of trial, testing, probation, or mourning. In the days of Noah it is said to have rained some forty days and forty nights (see Genesis 7:12). This cleansing of the earth, both literal and symbolic, gave God and Noah reason to mourn (see Moses 7:27–38; 8:22–30). One typologist added that Noah's faith was tested and found to be all that it should be" (Gaskill, *Lost Language of Symbolism*, 137).

Genesis 7:17–24. The Flood Covers the Earth

17 And the flood was forty days upon the earth; and the waters increased, and bare up the ark, and it was lift up above the earth.

18 And the waters prevailed, and were increased greatly upon the earth; and the ark went upon the face of the waters.

19 And the waters prevailed exceedingly upon the earth; and all the high hills, that *were* under the whole heaven, were covered.

20 Fifteen cubits upward did the waters prevail; and the mountains were covered.

21 And all flesh died that moved upon the earth, both of fowl, and of cattle, and of beast, and of every creeping thing that creepeth upon the earth, and every man:

How widespread was the flood? (7:17–20) The reality of the Flood is established throughout the scriptures. Ellis Rasmussen wrote: "The Genesis account of the Flood concerns a universal cataclysm, not a local one, as confirmed by many other scriptures (Gen. 7:21–24 and fn.; [Topical Guide], 'Flood, Noah's'; 'Earth, Cleansing of'; [Bible Dictionary], 'Noah'). Besides the record of the Judaeo-Christian scriptures, legends of such a deluge and renewal have been preserved by other peoples" (*Latter-day Saint Commentary on the Old Testament*, 30).

While the account in Genesis describes the Flood as covering the mountains, its exact nature and extent is unknown. "The Old Testament records a flood that was just over fifteen cubits (sometimes assumed to be about twenty-six feet) deep and covered the entire landscape. . . . Scientifically this account leaves many questions unanswered, especially how a measurable depth could cover mountains" (Petersen, "Earth," 2:432). ⊕

Why does it state that those with the breath of life died? (7:22) "By repeated use of the words . . . 'the breath of life,' . . . the Lord is perhaps informing us that there are in the world those plants and animals . . . that merit the designation of being living souls. . . . In contrast to these are plants and animals that are alive but are not living souls because their independent existence terminates with death. . . . What this means in relationship to the ark is that all life forms that now exist . . . did not need to have place on board. . . . Only animals of an eternal nature needed to accompany Noah aboard the ark" (Christianson, "Noah, the Ark, the Flood," 44, 47).

22 All in whose nostrils *was* the breath of life, of all that *was* in the dry *land,* died.

23 And every living substance was destroyed which was upon the face of the ground, both man, and cattle, and the creeping things, and the fowl of the heaven; and they were destroyed from the earth: and Noah only remained *alive,* and they that *were* with him in the ark.

24 And the waters prevailed upon the earth an hundred and fifty days.

CHAPTER 8

The Flood ceases—Noah sends forth a dove, which returns with an olive leaf—He releases all living things from the ark—He offers sacrifices—Seedtime, harvest, and seasons are ensured.

Genesis 8:1–5. The Waters Retreat and the Dry Land Appears

What does the wind from God symbolize? (8:1) "Wind often functions as a divine agent in the Bible. . . . As the waters are the symbol of chaos, the undoing of Creation, so the movement of the wind, Hebrew, *rauch*, heralds the reimposition of order" (Sarna, *Genesis*, 6, 56).

How long were Noah and his family in the ark? (8:4) "We read that it was in the seventeenth day of the second month when the great deep was broken up, and the rain was forty days. The Ark landed at Ararat on the seventeenth day of the seventh month, therefore there were five full months of travel when the Lord drove the Ark to its final destiny" (Smith, *Answers to Gospel Questions*, 2:93).

1 And God remembered Noah, and every living thing, and all the cattle that *was* with him in the ark: and God made a wind to pass over the earth, and the waters assuaged;

2 The fountains also of the deep and the windows of heaven were stopped, and the rain from heaven was restrained;

3 And the waters returned from off the earth continually: and after the end of the hundred and fifty days the waters were abated.

4 And the ark rested in the seventh month, on the seventeenth day of the month, upon the mountains of Ararat.

5 And the waters decreased continually until the tenth month: in the tenth *month,* on the first *day* of the month, were the tops of the mountains seen.

Genesis 8:6–12. Noah Sends Out a Raven and a Dove

What can the raven and the dove represent? (8:6–7) The text points out that the raven went to and fro, but the dove found no rest. The raven was a

6 ¶ And it came to pass at the end of forty days, that Noah opened the window of the ark which he had made:

7 And he sent forth a raven, which went forth to and fro, until the waters were dried up from off the earth.

8 Also he sent forth a dove from him, to see if the waters were abated from off the face of the ground;

9 But the dove found no rest for the sole of her foot, and she returned unto him into the ark, for the waters *were* on the face of the whole earth: then he put forth his hand, and took her, and pulled her in unto him into the ark.

10 And he stayed yet other seven days; and again he sent forth the dove out of the ark;

11 And the dove came in to him in the evening; and, lo, in her mouth *was* an olive leaf plucked off: so Noah knew that the waters were abated from off the earth.

12 And he stayed yet other seven days; and sent forth the dove; which returned not again unto him any more.

13 ¶ And it came to pass in the six hundredth and first year, in the first *month,* the first *day* of the month, the waters were dried up from off the earth: and Noah removed the covering of the ark, and looked, and, behold, the face of the ground was dry.

14 And in the second month, on the seven and twentieth day of the month, was the earth dried.

15 ¶ And God spake unto Noah, saying,

16 Go forth of the ark, thou, and thy wife, and thy sons, and thy sons' wives with thee.

17 Bring forth with thee every living thing that *is* with thee, of all flesh, *both* of fowl, and of cattle, and of every creeping thing that creepeth upon the earth; that they may breed abundantly in the earth, and be fruitful, and multiply upon the earth.

"scavenger bird symbolizing evil, mortification, corruption, sin, wandering, unrest, uncleanliness, carrion, impurity, destruction, deceit, and death" (Gaskill, *Lost Language of Symbolism*, 311). The dove on the other hand "was the emblem chosen from the beginning to represent truth, innocence, and the Spirit itself" (Merrill, "Behold, the Lamb of God," 135).

What does the olive leaf symbolize? (8:11) "Olive trees are special in the Holy Land. The olive branch is universally regarded as a symbol of peace. This tree provides food, light, heat, lumber, ointments, and medicine. It is now, as it was then, crucial to life in Israel" (Nelson, "Why This Holy Land?" 17).

Genesis 8:13–22. Noah's Family and the Animals Leave the Ark and Noah Offers Sacrifices to the Lord

What does it mean that the Lord smelled "a sweet savour"? (8:20–21) Significant changes have been made to verses 20–22 in the Joseph Smith Translation (see JST, Genesis 9:4–6). "The Joseph Smith Translation of verse 21 informs us that Noah was the one who smelled the sweet savour, and it also reveals that Noah prayed that the Lord would 'not again smite any more every thing living' (JST, Genesis 9:6)" (Valletta, et al., *Old Testament for Latter-day Saint Families*, 20).

Genesis 9:1–7. The Lord Blesses Noah and Gives Him Commandments

How was Noah similar to Adam? (9:1) "Following the Flood, Noah and his three sons and their wives received a calling much like that given to Adam and Eve. They were commanded to 'multiply and replenish the earth,' which would fulfill a prophecy made by Methuselah 'that from [Noah's] loins should spring all the kingdoms of the earth' (Moses 8:3). As the Prophet Joseph Smith explained, 'Noah was born to save seed of everything, when the earth was washed of its wickedness by the flood.' Noah fulfilled his specific calling just as Adam and Eve did in opening earth life and as the Savior did in redeeming earth life" (Romney, "Noah," 28).

18 And Noah went forth, and his sons, and his wife, and his sons' wives with him:

19 Every beast, every creeping thing, and every fowl, *and* whatsoever creepeth upon the earth, after their kinds, went forth out of the ark.

20 ¶ And Noah builded an altar unto the LORD; and took of every clean beast, and of every clean fowl, and offered burnt offerings on the altar.

21 And the LORD smelled a sweet savour; and the LORD said in his heart, I will not again curse the ground any more for man's sake; for the imagination of man's heart *is* evil from his youth; neither will I again smite any more every thing living, as I have done.

22 While the earth remaineth, seedtime and harvest, and cold and heat, and summer and winter, and day and night shall not cease.

CHAPTER 9

Noah and his sons are commanded to multiply and fill the earth—They are given dominion over all forms of life—The death penalty is decreed for murder—God will not again destroy the earth by a flood—Canaan is cursed; Shem and Japheth are blessed.

1 And God blessed Noah and his sons, and said unto them, Be fruitful, and multiply, and replenish the earth.

2 And the fear of you and the dread of you shall be upon every beast of the earth, and upon every fowl of the air, upon all that moveth *upon* the earth, and upon all the fishes of the sea; into your hand are they delivered.

3 Every moving thing that liveth shall be meat for you; even as the green herb have I given you all things.

4 But flesh with the life thereof, *which is* the blood thereof, shall ye not eat.

5 And surely your blood of your lives will I require; at the hand of every beast will I require it, and at the hand of man; at the hand of every man's brother will I require the life of man.

6 Whoso sheddeth man's blood, by man shall his blood be shed: for in the image of God made he man.

7 And you, be ye fruitful, and multiply; bring forth abundantly in the earth, and multiply therein.

8 ¶ And God spake unto Noah, and to his sons with him, saying,

9 And I, behold, I establish my covenant with you, and with your seed after you;

10 And with every living creature that *is* with you, of the fowl, of the cattle, and of every beast of the earth with you; from all that go out of the ark, to every beast of the earth.

11 And I will establish my covenant with you; neither shall all flesh be cut off any more by the waters of a flood; neither shall there any more be a flood to destroy the earth.

12 And God said, This *is* the token of the covenant which I make between me and you and every living creature that *is* with you, for perpetual generations:

13 I do set my bow in the cloud, and it shall be for a token of a covenant between me and the earth.

14 And it shall come to pass, when I bring a cloud over the earth, that the bow shall be seen in the cloud:

15 And I will remember my covenant, which *is* between me and you and every living creature of all flesh; and the waters shall no more become a flood to destroy all flesh.

Why was Noah's family forbidden to eat flesh with blood? (9:4) Significant changes have been made to these verses in the Joseph Smith Translation (see JST, Genesis 9:10–14). The Joseph Smith Translation for verse 4 reads, "And surely, blood shall not be shed only for meat, to save your lives" (JST, Genesis 9:11). President Joseph F. Smith wrote: "I do not believe any man should kill animals or birds unless he needs them for food, and then he should not kill innocent little birds that are not intended for food for man. I think it is wicked for men to thirst in their souls to kill almost everything which possesses animal life. It is wrong" (*Gospel Doctrine*, 266).

Genesis 9:8–19. The Lord Makes a Covenant with Noah

What do we know about rainbows prior to the covenant God made with Noah? (9:13–17) "The Lord's covenant with Noah was that the earth would never again be covered with a flood and 'neither shall all flesh be cut off any more by the waters of a flood' (Gen. 9:11). An outward token of that covenant was the rainbow (see Gen. 9:13; Ezek. 1:28; Rev. 4:3, 10:1). According to the LDS Bible Dictionary, 'The rainbow no doubt existed *before* the Flood, but with Noah the rainbow took on a new significance as the token of the covenant'" (Black, *400 Questions and Answers About the Old Testament*, 40).

Genesis 9:20–29. Canaan Is Cursed, and Shem Is Blessed

Was Noah really drunk? (9:21) "Do we have a better explanation for Noah's unexpected behavior? Yes. According to a late, secondhand remembrance of a statement by Joseph Smith, Noah 'was not drunk, but in a vision.' If we only had this statement to go by, it would be reasonable to discount it entirely. However, the Prophet's view agrees with the Genesis Apocryphon [from the Dead Sea Scrolls] which, immediately after describing a ritual where Noah and

16 And the bow shall be in the cloud; and I will look upon it, that I may remember the everlasting covenant between God and every living creature of all flesh that *is* upon the earth.

17 And God said unto Noah, This *is* the token of the covenant, which I have established between me and all flesh that *is* upon the earth.

18 ¶ And the sons of Noah, that went forth of the ark, were Shem, and Ham, and Japheth: and Ham *is* the father of Canaan.

19 These *are* the three sons of Noah: and of them was the whole earth overspread.

20 And Noah began *to be* an husbandman, and he planted a vineyard:

21 And he drank of the wine, and was drunken; and he was uncovered within his tent.

The Rainbow—A Token of the Covenant (Genesis 9)

The rainbow has at least four meanings:

1. A token that the city of Enoch will return to the earth. "And the bow shall be in the cloud; and I will look upon it, that I may remember the everlasting covenant, which I made unto thy father Enoch; that, when men should keep all my commandments, Zion should again come on the earth, the city of Enoch which I have caught up unto myself. And this is mine everlasting covenant, that when thy posterity shall embrace the truth, and look upward, then shall Zion look downward" (JST, Gen. 9:21–22).

2. A sign that God will never again destroy the earth by flood. "The Lord answered Noah's prayers. He made a covenant with him that there would be no more floods, and there would always be seed time and harvest. Then He gave him the rainbow in the sky as the sign of the covenant" (Petersen, *Noah and the Flood*, 70).

3. A symbol of God's mercy. "A rainbow radiates out from and encircles the royal seat [see Rev. 4:2–3], sign of the covenant between God and Noah, suggesting that his judgment does not eclipse his mercy (see Gen. 9:8–17)" (Draper, *Opening the Seven Seals*, 45).

4. An absence of the rainbow as a signal of the Second Coming of Jesus Christ. The Prophet Joseph Smith stated, "I have asked of the Lord concerning His coming; and while asking the Lord, He gave a sign and said, 'In the days of Noah I set a bow in the heavens as a sign and token that in any year that the bow should be seen the Lord would not come; but there should be seed time and harvest during that year: but whenever you see the bow withdrawn, it shall be a token that there shall be famine, pestilence, and great distress among the nations, and that the coming of the Messiah is not far distant" (*Joseph Smith* [manual], 252).

his family drank wine, reports in detail a divine dream vision that revealed the fate of Noah's posterity" (Bradshaw, "Was Noah Drunk or in a Vision?").

22 And Ham, the father of Canaan, saw the nakedness of his father, and told his two brethren without.

23 And Shem and Japheth took a garment, and laid *it* upon both their shoulders, and went backward, and covered the nakedness of their father; and their faces *were* backward, and they saw not their father's nakedness.

24 And Noah awoke from his wine, and knew what his younger son had done unto him.

25 And he said, Cursed *be* Canaan; a servant of servants shall he be unto his brethren.

26 And he said, Blessed *be* the LORD God of Shem; and Canaan shall be his servant.

27 God shall enlarge Japheth, and he shall dwell in the tents of Shem; and Canaan shall be his servant.

28 ¶ And Noah lived after the flood three hundred and fifty years.

29 And all the days of Noah were nine hundred and fifty years: and he died.

What may Noah's garment represent? (9:22–23) "The tradition associated with the supernatural qualities of Adam's garment weaves its way through much of the Old Testament. The garment is said to have descended from Adam to Enoch, and from him to Methuselah, who gave it to Noah, who took it with him on the ark. Ham is accused of stealing it and giving it to his firstborn son, Cush. (This is offered as the explanation for the difficult story in Genesis 9 where Ham finds Noah drunk and tells his brothers that he has seen his father's nakedness, for which Ham's son is cursed. It is suggested that the story is an allegorical expression for a priesthood garment and birth right struggle)" (McConkie, *Gospel Symbolism*, 139). ⊕

CHAPTER 10

The descendants of Noah are Japheth, whose descendants are Gentiles; Ham, whose descendants include the Canaanites; and Shem, of whom came Peleg (in whose days the earth was divided).

1 Now these *are* the generations of the sons of Noah, Shem, Ham, and Japheth: and unto them were sons born after the flood.

Genesis 10:1–5. The Descendants of Japheth

What does this genealogy depict? (10:1) "Now we are given a genealogy of the nations. The Table of Nations, as it has come to be known . . . [has] three major groupings . . . that characterize the human race . . . One may safely assume that making the offspring of Noah's sons total seventy is a literary device to convey the notion of the totality of the human race. The same device is employed in rabbinic literature, where the phrases 'seventy peoples' or 'seventy languages' express humanity in its entirety" (Sarna, *Genesis*, 67,

69). This is "a historical record of the genesis of the nations, founded upon a tradition handed down from the fathers" (Keil and Delitzsch, *Commentary* [on Genesis 10, Introduction]). ⊕

Who were the Gentiles? (10:2–5) "Peoples of the Greek islands and peninsula and broadly northward through the Caucasus are generally the 'Gentiles,' or Japhetic nations" (Bible Dictionary, "Gentiles").

"The basic meaning of the Hebrew word (*goyim*) frequently translated as 'gentile' is 'nations' or 'peoples.' However, in time, *gentile* came to mean 'stranger' or 'foreigner.' Thus, to a member of a particular group, a gentile is any person who does not belong to that group. To a Hebrew (a descendant of Abraham), a gentile is a person who is not a Hebrew. To an Israelite (a descendant of Jacob or Israel), a gentile is a person who is not an Israelite. To a Jew (a descendant of Judah; a citizen of the Kingdom of Judah or a descendant of such a citizen), a gentile is a non-Jew" (Ludlow, *Companion to Your Study of the Old Testament*, 121–22).

2 The sons of Japheth; Gomer, and Magog, and Madai, and Javan, and Tubal, and Meshech, and Tiras.

3 And the sons of Gomer; Ashkenaz, and Riphath, and Togarmah.

4 And the sons of Javan; Elishah, and Tarshish, Kittim, and Dodanim.

5 By these were the isles of the Gentiles divided in their lands; every one after his tongue, after their families, in their nations.

Genesis 10:6–20. The Descendants of Ham

What nations are described in this second major group? (10:6–20) "These comprise four primary subgroupings, listed from south to north. The first three are situated in Africa, while the last constitutes the land bridge between Africa and Asia" (Sarna, *Genesis*, 72). "Traditionally Cush has been translated as 'Ethiopia' in reference to his descendants . . . [Mizraim] is the Hebrew word for *Egypt*" (Brandt, "Early Families of the Earth," 17).

6 ¶ And the sons of Ham; Cush, and Mizraim, and Phut, and Canaan.

7 And the sons of Cush; Seba, and Havilah, and Sabtah, and Raamah, and Sabtecha: and the sons of Raamah; Sheba, and Dedan.

Who was Nimrod and what evil did he do? (10:8–12) Nimrod is highlighted in this chapter. The Bible says Nimrod was "a mighty hunter before the Lord," but the JST omits the phrase "before the Lord" [JST, Genesis 10:5]. Nimrod "boasted that no animal could escape his bow, turned that bow against men as well as animals . . . ruling all the earth with his inspired violence. He was the mortal enemy and rival of Abraham, and whereas Abraham gave Adam's blessing to the beasts, 'Nimrod ordered thousands of . . . cattle brought, . . . and sacrificed them.' This he was able to do through possession of the garment of the priesthood that had once belonged to Adam and that Ham had stolen from Noah" (Nibley, *Brother Brigham Challenges the Saints*, 17–18).

8 And Cush begat Nimrod: he began to be a mighty one in the earth.

9 He was a mighty hunter before the Lord: wherefore it is said, Even as Nimrod the mighty hunter before the Lord.

10 And the beginning of his kingdom was Babel, and Erech, and Accad, and Calneh, in the land of Shinar.

11 Out of that land went forth Asshur, and builded Nineveh, and the city Rehoboth, and Calah,

12 And Resen between Nineveh and Calah: the same *is* a great city.

13 And Mizraim begat Ludim, and Anamim, and Lehabim, and Naphtuhim,

14 And Pathrusim, and Casluhim, (out of whom came Philistim,) and Caphtorim.

15 ¶ And Canaan begat Sidon his firstborn, and Heth,

16 And the Jebusite, and the Amorite, and the Girgasite,

17 And the Hivite, and the Arkite, and the Sinite,

18 And the Arvadite, and the Zemarite, and the Hamathite: and afterward were the families of the Canaanites spread abroad.

19 And the border of the Canaanites was from Sidon, as thou comest to Gerar, unto Gaza; as thou goest, unto Sodom, and Gomorrah, and Admah, and Zeboim, even unto Lasha.

20 These *are* the sons of Ham, after their families, after their tongues, in their countries, *and* in their nations.

21 ¶ Unto Shem also, the father of all the children of Eber, the brother of Japheth the elder, even to him were *children* born.

22 The children of Shem; Elam, and Asshur, and Arphaxad, and Lud, and Aram.

23 And the children of Aram; Uz, and Hul, and Gether, and Mash.

24 And Arphaxad begat Salah; and Salah begat Eber.

Why are the borders of the Canaanites highlighted? (10:19) The Table of Nations (Genesis 10) is a record of Noah's descendants and where they went after the Flood. "The Table of Nations displays this exceptional interest in the territorial boundaries of Canaan because it is leading up to the progenitors of Abraham, whose descendants are to inherit the land" (Sarna, *Genesis*, 77).

Genesis 10:21–32. The Descendants of Shem

Why is Shem's name important? (10:21–31) In Hebrew *Shem* means "name." Literally and symbolically, Shem's descendants are the people who have received the name or the covenant. President Dallin H. Oaks taught, "Similarly, in modern revelations the Lord refers to temples as houses built 'unto my holy name' (D&C 124:39; D&C 105:33; D&C 109:2–5). In the inspired dedicatory prayer of the Kirtland Temple, the Prophet Joseph Smith asked the Lord for a blessing upon 'thy people upon whom thy name shall be put in this house' (D&C 109:26)" ("Taking upon Us the Name of Jesus Christ," 82). Also, modern revelation calls Shem "the great high priest" (D&C 138:41).

Can members of the Church today be called Hebrews? (10:21) "Yes, as scriptures define the term. You are related to Abraham, who was the great 'Eber' from which the term Hebrew was derived (see Genesis

10:21; 14:13; see also 2 Corinthians 11:22). (Nelson, "Thanks for the Covenant," 60).

How was the earth divided? (10:25) "Traditionally, this has been taken as a reference to the confusion of languages and the dispersal of mankind described in the next chapter" (Sarna, *Genesis*, 79). However, Joseph Fielding Smith wrote it was the "breaking asunder of the continents, thus dividing the land surface and creating the Eastern Hemisphere and Western Hemisphere. . . . Of course, there have been many changes on the earth's surface since the beginning. We are informed by revelation that the time will come when this condition will be changed and that the land surface of the earth will come back as it was in the beginning and all be in one place [see D&C 133:18–20]" (*Answers to Gospel Questions*, 5:73).

25 And unto Eber were born two sons: the name of one *was* Peleg; for in his days was the earth divided; and his brother's name *was* Joktan.

26 And Joktan begat Almodad, and Sheleph, and Hazarmaveth, and Jerah,

27 And Hadoram, and Uzal, and Diklah,

28 And Obal, and Abimael, and Sheba,

29 And Ophir, and Havilah, and Jobab: all these *were* the sons of Joktan.

30 And their dwelling was from Mesha, as thou goest unto Sephar a mount of the east.

31 These *are* the sons of Shem, after their families, after their tongues, in their lands, after their nations.

32 These *are* the families of the sons of Noah, after their generations, in their nations: and by these were the nations divided in the earth after the flood.

CHAPTER 11

All men speak the same language—They build the Tower of Babel—The Lord confounds their language and scatters them over all the earth—The generations of Shem include Abram, whose wife is Sarai—Abram leaves Ur and settles in Haran.

Genesis 11:1–9. The Tower of Babel Is Built

What was the "one language" until the Tower of Babel? (11:1) The language spoken by Adam was "a language which was pure and undefiled" (Moses 6:5–6). Orson Pratt indicated that this pure language continued from Adam to the Tower of Babel. When the people tried to build the tower, the Lord "caused the people to forget their own mother tongue, and . . . scattered them abroad upon the face of the whole earth" (in *Journal of Discourses*, 3:100).

1 And the whole earth was of one language, and of one speech.

Where is Shinar? (11:2) "*Shinar* is the ancient name for the land later known as Babylonia where modern-day Iraq is located (see . . . Bible Dictionary, s.v. "Shinar,

2 And it came to pass, as they journeyed from the east, that they found a plain in the land of Shinar; and they dwelt there.

Plain of," 774)" (Valletta, et al., *Old Testament for Latter-day Saint Families*, 23).

3 And they said one to another, Go to, let us make brick, and burn them throughly. And they had brick for stone, and slime had they for mortar.

Why did they burn the bricks thoroughly? (11:3) "Ordinary mud brick, baked in the sun, could only be used to build so high, and then it crumbled under the stress. But the 'brick . . . burned thoroughly' (i.e., in an oven) could be stacked quite high; the ziggurats at Babylon are three hundred feet high. In the Bible, bricks are mentioned only in connection with this tower, pharaoh's buildings, and idolatrous altars. This detail suggests the impudence in the people's feelings for the Lord in this society which had developed since the Flood" (Donaldson, et al., "Is There Additional Background Information on the Tower of Babel?" 60).

4 And they said, Go to, let us build us a city and a tower, whose top *may reach* unto heaven; and let us make us a name, lest we be scattered abroad upon the face of the whole earth.

5 And the LORD came down to see the city and the tower, which the children of men builded.

6 And the LORD said, Behold, the people *is* one, and they have all one language; and this they begin to do: and now nothing will be restrained from them, which they have imagined to do.

7 Go to, let us go down, and there confound their language, that they may not understand one another's speech.

8 So the LORD scattered them abroad from thence upon the face of all the earth: and they left off to build the city.

9 Therefore is the name of it called Babel; because the LORD did there confound the language of all the earth: and from thence did the LORD scatter them abroad upon the face of all the earth.

Why did they want to build a tower? (11:4) The tower was an apostate attempt to build a temple. "First, the impetus in building this temple was to make themselves a *name*. In other words, Nimrod was proposing that they build a temple to receive the name of God without making eternal covenants. Second, they wanted to build this tower-temple so they would not be 'scattered' (Gen. 11:4). . . . Nimrod and his people were building their own temple, their gate to heaven, without divine approval or priesthood keys. It is easy to see why an apostate people, having some understanding of temple ordinances and temple purpose, would construct an edifice symbolizing to them . . . [an] imitation of true temple worship" (Donaldson, et al., "Is There Additional Background Information on the Tower of Babel?" 61).

What does Babel represent? (11:9) *Babel* in Hebrew means confusion. "Because of her great iniquity, ancient Babel, or Babylon, has become a long-standing scriptural symbol for 'wickedness' (see D&C 133:14). Specifically, Babylon represents any people who 'have strayed from mine [the Lord's] ordinances, and have broken mine everlasting covenant" (Parry, "Flood and the Tower of Babel," 38). By way of contrast, in Akkadian, "The name of the tower, Babel, is composed of the syllables *bab*, meaning 'gate,' and *el*, meaning 'God,' suggesting that Babel is the gate of God. This definition explains that the purpose of the Tower of Babel was to create a structure or monument to human achievement that reaches heaven" (Black, *400 Questions and Answers about the Old Testament*, 41–42). ⊕

How were the languages confounded? (11:9) "The book of Ether, depicting the uprooting and scattering from the tower . . . shows them going forth not individually but in groups, and not merely family groups but groups of friends and associates [Ether 1:41]. . . . There is nothing said in our text about every man suddenly speaking a new language. We are told in the book of Ether that languages were confounded with and *by* the 'confounding' of the people: 'Cry unto the Lord,' says Jared (Ether 1:34), 'that he will not confound us that we may not understand our *words*.' . . . The Lord, we are told (Ether 1:35–37), 'did not confound the language of Jared; and Jared and his brother were not confounded'" (Nibley, *Lehi in the Desert/World of the Jaredites*, 165–66).

Genesis 11:10–26. The Genealogy of Abram's Ancestors Is Given

Why does the record shift to Shem's family? (11:10) "Immediately after the description of Babel in Genesis 11, the Old Testament record moves quickly to Abraham, a descendant of Shem, and ceases thereafter to be a record of *all* the descendants of Noah; instead, it focuses almost entirely on the Lord's covenant people, presumably a relatively small part of the earth's total population at that time. We know very little about the remainder of Noah's seed, except that in time they wandered throughout the extent of the land to become the heathen nations of the earth" (Johnson, "Who and Where Are the Lamanites?" 15).

10 ¶ These *are* the generations of Shem: Shem *was* an hundred years old, and begat Arphaxad two years after the flood:

11 And Shem lived after he begat Arphaxad five hundred years, and begat sons and daughters.

12 And Arphaxad lived five and thirty years, and begat Salah:

13 And Arphaxad lived after he begat Salah four hundred and three years, and begat sons and daughters.

14 And Salah lived thirty years, and begat Eber:

15 And Salah lived after he begat Eber four hundred and three years, and begat sons and daughters.

16 And Eber lived four and thirty years, and begat Peleg:

17 And Eber lived after he begat Peleg four hundred and thirty years, and begat sons and daughters.

18 And Peleg lived thirty years, and begat Reu:

19 And Peleg lived after he begat Reu two hundred and nine years, and begat sons and daughters.

20 And Reu lived two and thirty years, and begat Serug:

21 And Reu lived after he begat Serug two hundred and seven years, and begat sons and daughters.

22 And Serug lived thirty years, and begat Nahor:

23 And Serug lived after he begat Nahor two hundred years, and begat sons and daughters.

24 And Nahor lived nine and twenty years, and begat Terah:

25 And Nahor lived after he begat Terah an hundred and nineteen years, and begat sons and daughters.

26 And Terah lived seventy years, and begat Abram, Nahor, and Haran.

Why is Abram's birth a momentous point in the Old Testament? (11:26) "A major figure in the history and destiny of the world, Abram, who became Abraham, is introduced in Genesis 11. The eleven chapters of Genesis, to this point, are an introduction to all the scriptures that follow. They provide selected bits of information about the Creation and the purposes of the earth, survey a few epochal events from thousands of years of history, and briefly sketch ten generations of patriarchs from Adam to Noah and ten more from Noah's son Shem to Abram. The remaining thirty-nine chapters of Genesis cover only about three hundred years and provide far more detail about Abraham and three generations of his descendants than was provided about all twenty generations of his ancestors" (Rasmussen, *Latter-day Saint Commentary on the Old Testament*, 35–36). ⊕

Genesis 11:27–32. Abram Marries Sarai and Moves to Haran

27 ¶ Now these *are* the generations of Terah: Terah begat Abram, Nahor, and Haran; and Haran begat Lot.

How many generations were there from Shem to Abram and what does that represent? (11:27) Abraham "is the tenth generation from Shem, just as Noah was the tenth generation from Adam. From the scriptural point of view, the birth of Abraham constitutes a turning point in human history" (Sarna, *Genesis*, 84). The ten generations from Adam to Noah is meant to describe the origin of the world and the first divine covenants to God's servants, while the ten generations from Noah to Abraham portray the origin of His covenant nation, Israel.

Who was Sarai? (11:29) Sarai is later known as Sarah. "Sarah means 'princess.' . . . From Gen. 11:29–17:15 the form of the name used is *Sarai*" (Bible Dictionary, "Sarah or Sarai"). Sarai would play a major role in establishing the covenant people by demonstrating "marital skill, not groveling submission, that made [her] the model, obedient wife. It was that skill that earned her a full and equal partnership in the fulfillment of God's promise" (Hurd, *Our Sisters in the Bible*, 15).

Why is Sarai's barrenness highlighted? (11:30) "Barrenness was a heavy burden for any woman in Near Eastern cultures but would have been felt as a particularly searing inadequacy by a woman whose husband had received divine promises of endless posterity" (Durham, "Sarah," 3:1260). "It points up the striking contrast between the impending divine promises to Abraham of abundant posterity and the harsh reality that tries his faith" (Sarna, *Genesis*, 87).

Genesis 12:1–9. Abram Is Called by the Lord

Why did Abram have to leave Ur? (12:1) There was a famine in Ur and the Lord commanded Abram to leave Ur and go to Canaan (see Abraham 2:3–4). "Abraham's inheritance in Canaan, for himself and his seed after him, was to be an eternal inheritance, one that would endure in time and in eternity" (McConkie, *Doctrinal New Testament Commentary*, 2:71). The Prophet "Joseph Smith wrote, 'Abraham was guided in all his family affairs by the Lord; was told where to go, and when to stop; was conversed with by angels, and by the Lord; and prospered exceedingly in all that he put his hand unto; it was because he and his family obeyed the counsel of the Lord' (*Times and Seasons*, 15 July 1842, 857)" (see Valletta, et al., *Old Testament for Latter-day Saint Families*, 25).

28 And Haran died before his father Terah in the land of his nativity, in Ur of the Chaldees.

29 And Abram and Nahor took them wives: the name of Abram's wife *was* Sarai; and the name of Nahor's wife, Milcah, the daughter of Haran, the father of Milcah, and the father of Iscah.

30 But Sarai was barren; she *had* no child.

31 And Terah took Abram his son, and Lot the son of Haran his son's son, and Sarai his daughter in law, his son Abram's wife; and they went forth with them from Ur of the Chaldees, to go into the land of Canaan; and they came unto Haran, and dwelt there.

32 And the days of Terah were two hundred and five years: and Terah died in Haran.

CHAPTER 12

Abram will become a great nation—He and his seed will bless all the families of the earth—He travels from Haran to the land of Canaan—Because of famine, he goes down into Egypt—Abram and Sarai are tested in Pharaoh's court.

1 Now the LORD had said unto Abram, Get thee out of thy country, and from thy kindred, and from thy father's house, unto a land that I will shew thee:

2 And I will make of thee a great nation, and I will bless thee, and make thy name great; and thou shalt be a blessing:

3 And I will bless them that bless thee, and curse him that curseth thee: and in thee shall all families of the earth be blessed.

In what ways did the Lord promise to bless Abram? (12:2–3) In the fuller version of this covenant blessing found in Abraham 2, we find "the clearest description of the elements of the Abrahamic covenant found in the scriptures. God's promises to Abraham are: (1) a promised land for him and his posterity (Abraham 2:6), (2) the blessing of numerous posterity (Abraham 2:9), (3) a right to the priesthood for himself and his righteous posterity (Abraham 2:11), (4) the right and responsibility to preach the Gospel to all the world, thereby blessing all nations (Abraham 2:9), and (5) salvation and exaltation (Abraham 2:11). In turn, Abraham promises to be obedient to all the commandments of the Lord (Abraham 2:13). His omnipotence and omniscience ensure that [God] can fulfill all that He promises" (Draper, et al., *Pearl of Great Price*, 263–64). See commentary in this volume for Genesis 12:3 and Genesis 17:10. ⊕

How has the Lord's covenant with Abram blessed the families of the earth? (12:3) President Joseph Fielding Smith wrote: "When the Lord called Abraham out of Ur, the land of his fathers, he made certain covenants with him because of his faithfulness. One promise was that through him and his seed after him all nations of the earth should be blessed. This blessing is accomplished in several ways.

1. Through Jesus Christ . . .
2. Through the priesthood . . .
3. Through the scattering of Israel among all nations by which the blood of Israel was sprinkled among the nations, . . .
4. In the fact that the Lord covenanted with Abraham that after his time all who embraced the gospel should be called by his name" (*Doctrines of Salvation*, 3:246). See commentary in this volume for Genesis 2–3 and Genesis 17:10. ⊕

4 So Abram departed, as the LORD had spoken unto him; and Lot went with him: and Abram *was* seventy and five years old when he departed out of Haran.

What was Abram's actual age when he left Haran? (12:4) "From the Book of Abraham we learn that Abraham was sixty-two and not seventy-five years of age when he left Haran (Genesis 12:4; Abr. 2:14), showing at least that much of an error in the Old Testament account" (McConkie, *Doctrinal New Testament Commentary*, 2:71).

5 And Abram took Sarai his wife, and Lot his brother's son, and all their substance that they had gathered, and the souls that they had gotten in Haran; and they went forth to go into the land of Canaan; and into the land of Canaan they came.

What did Abraham do to bring souls to God? (12:5) "Abraham lost no time in seeking to reestablish Zion, for by the time he left Haran, he did so, as he comments in the Book of Abraham, with 'the souls that we had won in Haran' (Abr. 2:15). How had they been won? Abraham had lived in Haran for a number of years, and from the moment he arrived there, says Jewish tradition, he attracted attention by his exemplary and magnanimous manner of life. 'The people . . . saw that Abram was good and upright with God and men, and that the Lord his God was with him'" (Clark, *Blessings of Abraham*, 85).

Who were the Canaanites? (12:6) "'Canaanite' here, as often, is used generically for all the pre-Israelite inhabitants. God promised the land to Abram (v. 7), even though it was then occupied by others" (Sarna, *Genesis*, 91).

"The Canaanites were the inhabitants of Canaan, the more ancient name of Palestine. The Heb. form of Canaan apparently was taken from Hurrian, signifying 'belonging to the land of red-purple.' From the fourteenth century B.C. on this designation came to be employed of the country in which the 'Canaanite' or Phoenician traders exchanged for their commodities their most important commercial product, red-purple, which was obtained from the murex mollusks of coastal Palestine and used for dying" (*New Unger's Bible Dictionary*, 202).

Why did Abram build altars and offer sacrifice? (12:7–8) Abraham frequently built altars, offered sacrifice (see Abraham 2:18), and called upon the name of the Lord. The Prophet Joseph Smith taught:

"That the offering of sacrifice was only to point the mind forward to Christ, we infer from these remarkable words of Jesus to the Jews: 'Your Father Abraham rejoiced to see my day: and he saw it, and was glad' [John 8:56]. So, then, because the ancients offered sacrifice it did not hinder their hearing the Gospel; but served, as we said before, to open their eyes, and enable them to look forward to the time of the coming of the Savior, and rejoice in His redemption" (*Joseph Smith* [manual], 49).

Genesis 12:10–20. Abram Is Tested in Egypt

Why did Abram call Sarai his sister rather than his wife? (12:11–13) The fundamental reason Abraham told Sarai to identify herself as his sister is because the Lord commanded them to do so (Abraham 2:24). It seems that Abraham's life was in danger because of Sarai's beauty. "Abraham could validly state that Sarah was his sister. In the Bible the Hebrew words *brother*

6 ¶ And Abram passed through the land unto the place of Sichem, unto the plain of Moreh. And the Canaanite *was* then in the land.

7 And the LORD appeared unto Abram, and said, Unto thy seed will I give this land: and there builded he an altar unto the LORD, who appeared unto him.

8 And he removed from thence unto a mountain on the east of Beth-el, and pitched his tent, *having* Beth-el on the west, and Hai on the east: and there he builded an altar unto the LORD, and called upon the name of the LORD.

9 And Abram journeyed, going on still toward the south.

10 ¶ And there was a famine in the land: and Abram went down into Egypt to sojourn there; for the famine *was* grievous in the land.

11 And it came to pass, when he was come near to enter into Egypt, that he said unto Sarai his wife, Behold now, I know that thou *art* a fair woman to look upon:

12 Therefore it shall come to pass, when the Egyptians shall see thee, that they shall say,

This *is* his wife: and they will kill me, but they will save thee alive.

13 Say, I pray thee, thou *art* my sister: that it may be well with me for thy sake; and my soul shall live because of thee.

14 ¶ And it came to pass, that, when Abram was come into Egypt, the Egyptians beheld the woman that she *was* very fair.

15 The princes also of Pharaoh saw her, and commended her before Pharaoh: and the woman was taken into Pharaoh's house.

16 And he entreated Abram well for her sake: and he had sheep, and oxen, and he asses, and menservants, and maidservants, and she asses, and camels.

17 And the LORD plagued Pharaoh and his house with great plagues because of Sarai Abram's wife.

18 And Pharaoh called Abram, and said, What *is* this *that* thou hast done unto me? why didst thou not tell me that she *was* thy wife?

19 Why saidst thou, She *is* my sister? so I might have taken her to me to wife: now therefore behold thy wife, take *her,* and go thy way.

20 And Pharaoh commanded *his* men concerning him: and they sent him away, and his wife, and all that he had.

CHAPTER 13

Abram returns from Egypt—He and Lot part—The Lord will make Abram's seed as the dust of the earth in number—Abram settles in Hebron.

1 And Abram went up out of Egypt, he, and his wife, and all that he had, and Lot with him, into the south.

and *sister* are often used for other blood relatives. (See Genesis 14:14, in which Lot, Abraham's nephew, is called 'his brother.') Because Abraham and Haran, Sarah's father, were brothers, Sarah was Abraham's niece and thus could be called *sister*" (*Old Testament Student Manual: Genesis–2 Samuel*, 66). See commentary in this volume for Genesis 20:12.

Why would the Egyptians want to kill Abram? (12:15) "To kill the husband in order to possess himself of his wife seems to have been a common royal custom in those days. A papyrus tells of a Pharaoh who, acting on the advice of one of his princes, sent armed men to fetch a beautiful woman and make away with her husband. Another Pharaoh is promised by his priest on his tombstone, that even after death he will kill Palestinian sheiks and include their wives in his harem" (Kasher, *Encyclopedia of Biblical Interpretation*, 2:128).

Why would Pharaoh send Abram on his way and not punish him? (12:19–20) There is a story in the Genesis Apocryphon, found in the Dead Sea scrolls, "in which Abraham heals the ailing Pharaoh by laying his hands upon his head and blessing him . . . ; that ordinance marks both the end of the King's attempt to raise up a royal line by Sarah, and the acknowledgment of Abraham's true relationship to Sarah the Queen" (Nibley, *Abraham in Egypt*, 215). ⊕

Genesis 13:1–18. Abram and Lot Separate to Avoid Contention between Their Herdsmen

Where was the area referred to as "into the south"? (13:1) *Negev* (also *Negeb*) is the "name of the southern region of Palestine (Gen. 12:9; Num. 13:17; et al.); thus the term acquired the additional meaning 'south' (e.g., Gen. 13:14; the Heb. term is usually so rendered in the KJV). The physical characteristics of the Negeb are the rolling hills that abruptly terminate in the desert region. . . . It is a land where the water supply is scarce because of a very meager amount of rainfall in the summer months. At other seasons of the year, however, it is used by the nomads for pasturage" (*Zondervan Illustrated Bible Dictionary*, 1007).

What can we learn from Abram's wealth? (13:2) "The scriptures warn of the dangers of wealth so often that occasionally some people assume that wealth in and of itself is evil and that all wealthy people are automatically wicked. Without question, the temptation to set one's heart upon the things of the world is one to which many people succumb. But Paul taught that the '*love* of money is the root of all evil,' not the money itself (1 Timothy 6:10; emphasis added).

"Abraham provides an example of one who had great wealth (see Genesis 13:2) and yet was a man of great faith and righteousness" (*Old Testament Student Manual: Genesis–2 Samuel*, 66).

Why did Abram return to the altar in Bethel? (13:4) Bethel is the place where the Lord appeared to Abram before he went into Egypt. It may be that he returned to Bethel to give thanks after he had journeyed to his promised land. "Abram regularly built altars as he moved along, and he called upon the name of the Lord. . . . [He returned] to call again on the name of the Lord, as was his consistent practice" (Rasmussen, *Latter-day Saint Commentary on the Old Testament*, 38, 39).

What caused the strife between the herdsmen? (13:7) "It is so easy for some to become obsessed with what they possess and to lose eternal perspective. When Abraham went out of Egypt, his nephew Lot went with him to Bethel. Both Abraham and Lot had flocks and herds and tents, 'and the land was not able to bear them'" (Faust, "What's in It for Me?" 20). Abraham took action to eliminate the strife between his herdsman and Lot's herdsman before it could injure the relationship between him and his nephew.

2 And Abram *was* very rich in cattle, in silver, and in gold.

3 And he went on his journeys from the south even to Beth-el, unto the place where his tent had been at the beginning, between Beth-el and Hai;

4 Unto the place of the altar, which he had made there at the first: and there Abram called on the name of the LORD.

5 ¶ And Lot also, which went with Abram, had flocks, and herds, and tents.

6 And the land was not able to bear them, that they might dwell together: for their substance was great, so that they could not dwell together.

7 And there was a strife between the herdmen of Abram's cattle and the herdmen of Lot's cattle: and the Canaanite and the Perizzite dwelled then in the land.

8 And Abram said unto Lot, Let there be no strife, I pray thee, between me and thee, and between my herdmen and thy herdmen; for we *be* brethren.

9 *Is* not the whole land before thee? separate thyself, I pray thee, from me: if *thou wilt take* the left hand, then I will go to the right; or if *thou depart* to the right hand, then I will go to the left.

10 And Lot lifted up his eyes, and beheld all the plain of Jordan, that it *was* well watered every where, before the LORD destroyed Sodom and Gomorrah, *even* as the garden of the LORD, like the land of Egypt, as thou comest unto Zoar.

11 Then Lot chose him all the plain of Jordan; and Lot journeyed east: and they separated themselves the one from the other.

12 Abram dwelled in the land of Canaan, and Lot dwelled in the cities of the plain, and pitched *his* tent toward Sodom.

13 But the men of Sodom *were* wicked and sinners before the LORD exceedingly.

What does the phrase "pitched his tent toward Sodom" indicate? (13:12) In referring to King Benjamin's address, Randal Chase said, "Their tent doors were oriented toward the temple so that families could 'remain in their tents and hear the words which king Benjamin should speak unto them' (v. 6). The direction in which tents were pitched revealed what the people valued. For example, contrast these people with Lot, who 'pitched his tent toward Sodom' (Genesis 13:12). At first Lot only lived near the wicked city of Sodom, but he pitched his tent toward the city, and eventually he and his family lived in the city of Sodom itself (Genesis 14:12)" (*Making Precious Things Plain,* 1:225). ⊕

14 ¶ And the LORD said unto Abram, after that Lot was separated from him, Lift up now thine eyes, and look from the place where thou art northward, and southward, and eastward, and westward:

15 For all the land which thou seest, to thee will I give it, and to thy seed for ever.

16 And I will make thy seed as the dust of the earth: so that if a man can number the dust of the earth, *then* shall thy seed also be numbered.

17 Arise, walk through the land in the length of it and in the breadth of it; for I will give it unto thee.

18 Then Abram removed *his* tent, and came and dwelt in the plain of Mamre, which *is* in Hebron, and built there an altar unto the LORD.

When and how will the Lord's promises of this land be fulfilled? (13:14–15) The Joseph Smith Translation adds the following to the end of this verse: "and remember the covenant which I make with thee; for it shall be an everlasting covenant; and thou shalt remember the days of Enoch thy father" (JST, Genesis 13:12–13).

"Enoch had received the blessings of the Lord and established a great people who were ultimately caught up into heaven. . . . Enoch was also promised that a time would come when his people and their city would be reunited with the people of the earth. . . . The blessings that the posterity of Abraham would receive would be similar. The land inheritance indicated would be eternally permanent" (Hyde, *Comprehensive Commentary [Genesis]*, 176).

What land did the Lord promise to Abram and his seed? (13:14–17) "Abraham had no seed as yet. 'And I will make thy seed as the dust of the earth.' Now that is literal. The seed of Abraham shall be as the dust of the earth in number, meaning he will have eternal increase. 'So that if a man can number the dust of the earth, then shall thy seed also be numbered.' This involves celestial marriage. . . . Abraham's seed will have the land of Palestine in the resurrection" (McConkie, "Promises Made to the Fathers," 55). Ultimately, this promise of an "everlasting" inheritance of land is fulfilled when the righteous inherit the earth in its celestial glorified state (see D&C 88:25–26).

Genesis 14:1–12. Abram and the Battle of the Kings

What do we know about the kings mentioned in these verses? (14:1–2) One historian observed that "for once we are given in a story about Abraham the kind of specific detail that a historian likes to have. The first eleven verses read like a transcript from an ancient chronicle, one so ancient indeed that places and peoples in the area had to be identified by their later names so that those listening to the story would be able to follow what was going on.

"It is unfortunate that so far none of the great monarchs, who came from as far away as Elam (Persia) and Shinar (Babylonia), has been certainly equated with any known ruler" (Gibson, *Genesis*, 2:44). ⊕

What is unprecedented about this event in the Bible? (14:2–3) This is the first military battle in the Bible. "This story does not, at first glance, seem to be organically related either to the preceding or following events in the life of the patriarch. In fact, however, the literary connectives are present. Lot is still at Sodom (14:12, 13:12), and Abram still resides by the terebinths of Mamre (14:13, 13:18). There also is the irony inherent in the situation depicted in chapter 13: Lot has greedily picked the best part of the country, but now his choice turns out to have been disastrous, and his very life depends on the selflessness and loyalty of the uncle he has alienated" (Sarna, *Genesis*, 102).

CHAPTER 14

Lot is captured in the battles of the kings—He is rescued by Abram—Melchizedek administers bread and wine and blesses Abram—Abram pays tithes—He declines to accept the spoils of conquest.

1 And it came to pass in the days of Amraphel king of Shinar, Arioch king of Ellasar, Chedorlaomer king of Elam, and Tidal king of nations;

2 *That these* made war with Bera king of Sodom, and with Birsha king of Gomorrah, Shinab king of Admah, and Shemeber king of Zeboiim, and the king of Bela, which is Zoar.

3 All these were joined together in the vale of Siddim, which is the salt sea.

4 Twelve years they served Chedorlaomer, and in the thirteenth year they rebelled.

5 And in the fourteenth year came Chedorlaomer, and the kings that *were* with him, and smote the Rephaims in Ashteroth Karnaim, and the Zuzims in Ham, and the Emims in Shaveh Kiriathaim,

6 And the Horites in their mount Seir, unto El-paran, which *is* by the wilderness.

7 And they returned, and came to En-mishpat, which *is* Kadesh, and smote all the country of the Amalekites, and also the Amorites, that dwelt in Hazezon-tamar.

8 And there went out the king of Sodom, and the king of Gomorrah, and the king of Admah, and the king of Zeboiim, and the king of Bela (the same *is* Zoar;) and they joined battle with them in the vale of Siddim;

9 With Chedorlaomer the king of Elam, and with Tidal king of nations, and Amraphel king of Shinar, and Arioch king of Ellasar; four kings with five.

10 And the vale of Siddim *was full of* slime-pits; and the kings of Sodom and Gomorrah fled, and fell there; and they that remained fled to the mountain.

11 And they took all the goods of Sodom and Gomorrah, and all their victuals, and went their way.

12 And they took Lot, Abram's brother's son, who dwelt in Sodom, and his goods, and departed.

How were Lot and his family taken captive? (14:12) "Lot had taken up his abode in a district which, . . . was subdivided among a number of small kings . . . For twelve years this whole district had been tributary to *Chedorlaomer*. . . . In the fourteenth [year], the hordes of Chedorlaomer and of his three confederates swept over the intervening district, carrying desolation with them. . . . Two of the Canaanitish kings were killed, the rest fled in wild confusion; Sodom and Gomorrah were plundered, and their inhabitants—Lot among them—[were] carried away captives by the retreating host" (Edersheim, *Bible History*, 1:84).

Genesis 14:13–16. Abram and His Servants Rescue Lot and His Servants from Captivity

13 ¶ And there came one that had escaped, and told Abram the Hebrew; for he dwelt in the plain of Mamre the Amorite, brother of Eshcol, and brother of Aner: and these *were* confederate with Abram.

14 And when Abram heard that his brother was taken captive, he armed his trained *servants,* born in his own house, three hundred and eighteen, and pursued *them* unto Dan.

15 And he divided himself against them, he and his servants, by night, and smote them, and pursued them unto Hobah, which *is* on the left hand of Damascus.

16 And he brought back all the goods, and also brought again his brother Lot, and his goods, and the women also, and the people.

Where does the word *Hebrew* come from and what does it mean? (14:13) "The first person in the Bible called a Hebrew is Abram (Gen. 14:13). Thereafter, his descendants, . . . were known as 'Hebrews.' . . . The origin of the name *Hebrew* offers a difficult problem. The term may be derived from the prominent Semitic progenitor, Eber, the ancestor of Abraham (Gen. 10:21)" (*New Unger's Bible Dictionary*, 547). It is interesting to note that in the Joseph Smith Translation the words "the man of God" follow after the word *Hebrew* (see JST, Genesis 14:12).

How was Lot rescued and his goods returned? (14:16) "One who had escaped from the rout brought Abram tidings of the disaster. He immediately armed his own trained servants, three hundred and eighteen in number; and . . . followed in pursuit of Chedorlaomer and his allies. . . . Abram, having divided his force, fell upon them, in the dead of night, from several sides at the same time, inflicted a great slaughter, and pursued them to close by Damascus. All the spoil and all the captives, among them Lot also, were rescued and brought back" (Edersheim, *Bible History*, 1:85).

Genesis 14:17–24. Melchizedek Blesses Abram and Abram Pays Tithes

17 ¶ And the king of Sodom went out to
meet him after his return from the slaughter
of Chedorlaomer, and of the kings that *were*
with him, at the valley of Shaveh, which *is*
the king's dale.

18 And Melchizedek king of Salem brought
forth bread and wine: and he *was* the priest
of the most high God.

Who was Melchizedek? (14:18) "The Joseph Smith Translation provides an additional 16 verses in Genesis 14 (JST, Gen. 14:25–40) that preserve these details. As a child Melchizedek had such faith as to stop the mouths of lions. . . . He was ordained a high priest after the order of the Son of God. He was a prophet like unto Enoch who had power through his faith over the elements, over the nations of the earth, and the power to stand in the presence of God. . . . In addition to his biblical title 'King of peace' (Heb. 7:2), . . . we learn Melchizedek was called by his people 'the Prince of peace,' . . . identifying him as a type foreshadowing the ministry of Jesus Christ" (Seely, "Joseph Smith Translation," 14). ⊕

In what way does this meal prefigure the sacrament? (14:18) "Gen. 14:18 reports that Melchizedek brought forth bread and wine for himself and Abraham. However, the Joseph Smith Translation rewords this verse as follows: 'Melchizedek . . . brake bread and blest it; and he blest the wine, he being the priest of the most high God.' This wording suggests that there were two blessings, one for the bread and one for the wine. That would be unusual procedure for a regular meal. It almost suggests a prefigurement of the sacramental emblems of the atonement of Jesus Christ, which would take place many centuries later" (Matthews, *Bible! A Bible!*, 38–39). ⊕

19 And he blessed him, and said, Blessed *be*
Abram of the most high God, possessor of
heaven and earth:

What part does Melchizedek play in Abram's life? (14:19) "And he lifted up his voice, and he blessed Abram, being the high priest, and the keeper of the storehouse of God; him whom God had appointed to receive tithes for the poor. Wherefore, Abram paid unto him tithes of all that he had, of all the riches which he possessed. . . . God blessed Abram, and gave unto him riches, and honor, and lands for an everlasting possession; according to the covenant which he had made, and according to the blessing wherewith Melchizedek had blessed him" (JST, Gen. 14:37–40).

We also know from modern revelation that Abraham received the high priesthood from Melchizedek (see D&C 84:14).

20 And blessed be the most high God, which hath delivered thine enemies into thy hand. And he gave him tithes of all.

21 And the king of Sodom said unto Abram, Give me the persons, and take the goods to thyself.

How was the law of tithing practiced in the Old Testament? (14:20) "The Joseph Smith Translation explains more about the meeting between Melchizedek and Abram: 'And [Melchizedek] lifted up his voice, and he blessed Abram, being the high priest, and the keeper of the storehouse of God; him whom God had appointed to receive tithes for the poor. Wherefore, Abram paid unto him tithes of all that he had, of all the riches which he possessed, which God had given him more than that which he had need' (JST, Genesis 14:37–39)" (Valletta, et al., *Old Testament for Latter-day Saint Families*, 29). ⊕

22 And Abram said to the king of Sodom, I have lift up mine hand unto the LORD, the most high God, the possessor of heaven and earth,

Why does Abram remind the King that he is under oath? (14:22) "The king of Sodom knew nothing about Abraham's covenant with the Lord; Abraham could have made himself rich by receiving of the king's generosity. But he had made an oath which he would not violate. Oh, that all of God's children would be so true" (Kimball, "Example of Abraham," 6).

23 That I will not *take* from a thread even to a shoelatchet, and that I will not take any thing that *is* thine, lest thou shouldest say, I have made Abram rich:

Why is Abram mentioning "threads" and "shoelatchets"? (14:23) "This was certainly a proverbial mode of expression, the full meaning of which is perhaps not known. Among the rabbinical writers . . . *chut*, or . . . *chuti*, signifies a fillet [ribbon] worn by young women to tie up their hair; taken in this sense it will give a good meaning here. As Abram had rescued both the men and women . . . and the king of Sodom had offered him all the goods, claiming only the persons, he answers . . . : 'I have vowed unto the Lord, the proprietor of heaven and earth, that I will not receive the smallest portion of the property either of the women or men, from a girl's fillet to a man's shoe-tie'" (*Adam Clarke's Commentary* [on Genesis 14:23]).

24 Save only that which the young men have eaten, and the portion of the men which went with me, Aner, Eshcol, and Mamre; let them take their portion.

What do we learn about Abram's character in this chapter? (14:24) "In these episodes, Abraham demonstrated his fairness, integrity, and faith. And the Lord rewarded him with both spiritual and earthly blessings so that ultimately he prospered far more than Lot" (Faust, "We Seek after These Things," 44).

CHAPTER 15

Abram desires offspring—The Lord promises him seed in number as the stars—Abram believes the promise—His seed will be strangers in Egypt—Then, after four generations, they will inherit Canaan.

1 After these things the word of the LORD came unto Abram in a vision, saying, Fear not, Abram: I *am* thy shield, *and* thy exceeding great reward.

Genesis 15:1-6. The Lord Promises Abram That He Will Have Children

How is the Lord our "shield" from spiritual danger? (15:1) God declared that He would be a shield to Abraham. The Lord also promises to be a shield to His righteous servants in this dispensation (see D&C 35:14). Elder Robert D. Hales taught that God's "light will form a protective shield between you and the darkness of the adversary as you live worthy of it" ("Out of Darkness into His Marvelous Light," 70). Elder Neal A. Maxwell promised, "If we will keep our covenants, the covenants will keep us spiritually safe" ("Overcome . . . Even As I Also Overcame," 71).

2 And Abram said, Lord GOD, what wilt thou give me, seeing I go childless, and the steward of my house *is* this Eliezer of Damascus?

3 And Abram said, Behold, to me thou hast given no seed: and, lo, one born in my house is mine heir.

4 And, behold, the word of the LORD *came* unto him, saying, This shall not be thine heir; but he that shall come forth out of thine own bowels shall be thine heir.

Who would become Abram's heir if he had no children? (15:2–4) "According to a custom described in the Nuzi tablets from eastern Mesopotamia, one born in a man's house could become his heir. Was Abram's heir to be one born to his steward, Eliezer of Damascus?" (Rasmussen, *Latter-day Saint Commentary on the Old Testament*, 42). Abram struggled to understand how the promised blessings of the covenant might be fulfilled. Yet the Lord emphasized that the heir of the covenant would be Abram's own child.

5 And he brought him forth abroad, and said, Look now toward heaven, and tell the stars, if thou be able to number them: and he said unto him, So shall thy seed be.

6 And he believed in the LORD; and he counted it to him for righteousness.

What did the Old Testament prophets know of Jesus Christ and His gospel? (15:5–6) Adam Clarke observed, "This I conceive to be one of the most important passages in the whole Old Testament" (*Adam Clarke's Commentary* [on Genesis 15:6]).

"In the Joseph Smith Translation, four significant verses are added between verses 5 and 6 of the Genesis account: [See JST, Genesis 15:9–12].

"Once again it is clear that the early patriarchs knew far more about Christ and His mission than the present Old Testament record indicates (see Mosiah 13:33)" (*Old Testament Student Manual: Genesis–2 Samuel*, 68).

What did Abram see in this vision? (15:5–6) "The Joseph Smith Translation gives the wonderful insight that Abram was permitted to look into the future and see the days of Jesus Christ (see JST, Genesis 15:12).

During New Testament times the Savior confirmed that Abram had seen His day (see John 8:56). Also, in the Joseph Smith Translation Abraham is assured that he will be heir over this land even after he is dead (see JST, Genesis 15:11)" (Valletta, et al., *Old Testament for Latter-Day Saint Families*, 30–31).

7 And he said unto him, I *am* the LORD that brought thee out of Ur of the Chaldees, to give thee this land to inherit it.

8 And he said, Lord GOD, whereby shall I know that I shall inherit it?

9 And he said unto him, Take me an heifer of three years old, and a she goat of three years old, and a ram of three years old, and a turtledove, and a young pigeon.

Genesis 15:7–21. The Lord Covenants with Abram That His Children Will Inherit Canaan

What was the purpose in sacrificing these animals to make a covenant with the Lord? (15:9) "In answer to Abram's desire for confirmation of the promise of the land, the Lord instructed him to sacrifice three animals, each of them three years old (two females and one male), and also a turtledove and a pigeon" (Rasmussen, *Latter-day Saint Commentary on the Old Testament*, 43). The Prophet Joseph Smith noted, "The offering of sacrifice was only to point the mind forward to Christ. . . . We conclude that whenever the Lord revealed Himself to men in ancient days, and commanded them to offer sacrifice to Him, that it was done that they might look forward in faith to the time of His coming, and rely upon the power of that atonement for a remission of their sins" (*Joseph Smith* [manual], 49).

10 And he took unto him all these, and divided them in the midst, and laid each piece one against another: but the birds divided he not.

11 And when the fowls came down upon the carcases, Abram drove them away.

Why did Abram divide and cut the animals? (15:10) "Why did the Lord instruct Abram to use three different animals, each three years old, and two birds? . . . What did the divided animals symbolize? . . . Though the scriptural account does not provide answers to all these questions, an understanding of ancient covenant-making practices . . . can help us gain additional insight. . . .

"From what we know of second millennium B.C. covenant rituals, it seems clear that Jehovah

Old Testament Prophets Knew of Christ and His Ministry

According to the Joseph Smith Translation of Genesis 15:9–12, Abraham saw a vision of Jesus' mortal ministry and the Resurrection:

> *And Abram said, Lord God, how wilt thou give me this land for an everlasting inheritance?*
> *And the Lord said, Though thou wast dead, yet am I not able to give it thee?*
> *And if thou shalt die, yet thou shalt possess it, for the day cometh, that the Son of Man shall live; but how can he live if he be not dead? he must first be quickened.*
> *And it came to pass, that Abram looked forth and saw the days of the Son of Man, and was glad, and his soul found rest,* and he believed in the Lord; and *the Lord* counted it unto him for righteousness (JST, Genesis 15:9–12).

condescended to cut a covenant with Abram. Instead of a parity treaty or loyalty oath on Abram's part, God instructed Abram to slaughter three animals and divide them so he could demonstrate the absolute surety of his promises" (Parker, "Cutting Covenants," 114).

Why did Abram experience such darkness in his dream? (15:12) "The presence of God is often described using contradictory terms, typically including phrases that depict both light and darkness, both glory and fear. The darkness seems to protect the Lord from profane presences and profane presences from the Lord. The fear seems to come from realizing that one is in the presence of a being too great for our current state. This account first highlights the dark/hiding element as well as the element of fear or respect or awe" (Muhlestein, *Scripture Study Made Simple*, 26–27).

What would happen to Abram's posterity? (15:13) The "horror" noted in the previous verse "is enhanced as the Lord promises Abram that his descendants would spend a long time in bondage before the covenant would be fully realized" (Muhlestein, *Scripture Study Made Simple*, 27). According to President Joseph Fielding Smith, this prophecy was fulfilled when the posterity of Abram "went down into Egypt and there remained four hundred years and in the fourth generation under Moses a great multitude of people came out of Egypt, for the time had come for them to possess their inheritance in the land of Canaan" (*Progress of Man*, 121–22).

Who determines when a people's iniquity "is not yet full"? (15:15–16) President John Taylor taught: "There were times when the iniquity of these people was not yet full. In Abraham's day the Lord told that Patriarch that he should go to his fathers in peace, but in the fourth generation his posterity should 'come hither again: for the iniquity of the Amorites is not yet full:' by the days of Moses they appear to have filled the cup of their iniquity, for he enjoined upon the Israelites, 'thou shalt utterly destroy them,' 'as the Lord thy God hath commanded thee.' . . . Thus men and nations are adjudged by the Almighty, according to the infinite and eternal laws and principles which exist in the heavens" (in *Journal of Discourses*, 26:36).

What is a covenant? (15:18) "A covenant is a sacred agreement between God and a person or group of people. God sets specific conditions, and He promises to bless us as we obey those conditions. When we choose not to keep covenants, we cannot receive the

12 And when the sun was going down, a deep sleep fell upon Abram; and, lo, an horror of great darkness fell upon him.

13 And he said unto Abram, Know of a surety that thy seed shall be a stranger in a land *that is* not theirs, and shall serve them; and they shall afflict them four hundred years;

14 And also that nation, whom they shall serve, will I judge: and afterward shall they come out with great substance.

15 And thou shalt go to thy fathers in peace; thou shalt be buried in a good old age.

16 But in the fourth generation they shall come hither again: for the iniquity of the Amorites *is* not yet full.

17 And it came to pass, that, when the sun went down, and it was dark, behold a smoking furnace, and a burning lamp that passed between those pieces.

18 In the same day the LORD made a covenant with Abram, saying, Unto thy seed have I given this land, from the river of Egypt unto the great river, the river Euphrates:

19 The Kenites, and the Kenizzites, and the Kadmonites,

20 And the Hittites, and the Perizzites, and the Rephaims,

21 And the Amorites, and the Canaanites, and the Girgashites, and the Jebusites.

CHAPTER 16

Sarai gives Hagar to Abram as his wife—Hagar flees from Sarai—An angel commands Hagar to return and submit herself to Sarai—Hagar bears Ishmael.

1 Now Sarai Abram's wife bare him no children: and she had an handmaid, an Egyptian, whose name *was* Hagar.

2 And Sarai said unto Abram, Behold now, the LORD hath restrained me from bearing: I pray thee, go in unto my maid; it may be that I may obtain children by her. And Abram hearkened to the voice of Sarai.

3 And Sarai Abram's wife took Hagar her maid the Egyptian, after Abram had dwelt ten years in the land of Canaan, and gave her to her husband Abram to be his wife.

4 ¶ And he went in unto Hagar, and she conceived: and when she saw that she had conceived, her mistress was despised in her eyes.

blessings, and in some instances we suffer a penalty as a consequence of our disobedience" (Gospel Topics, "Covenant"). ⊕

Genesis 16:1–16. Abram's Wife Hagar Has a Son Named Ishmael

What do we know about Hagar? (16:1) Hagar was "a native of Egypt, servant of Abraham (Gen. 21:9–10) and handmaid of Sarah (16:1). Sarah, continuing childless for so long a time, determined to become a mother by proxy (not uncommon in the East) through her maid, whom she gave to Abraham as a secondary wife (Gen. 16), c. 2050 B.C." (*New Unger's Bible Dictionary,* 513). She was also the "mother of Abraham's son Ishmael (Gen. 16; 21:9–21; 25:12). After the birth of Isaac, the 'child of promise,' Hagar and her son were expelled. Paul uses the story as an allegory to show the difference between the two covenants, the one a covenant of bondage and the other one of freedom (Gal. 4:24)" (Bible Dictionary, "Hagar").

Why did Sarai give Hagar to Abraham as a wife? (16:3) The scriptures teach that "God commanded Abraham, and Sarah gave Hagar to Abraham to wife. And why did she do it? Because this was the law; and from Hagar sprang many people. This, therefore, was fulfilling, among other things, the promises. Was Abraham, therefore, under condemnation? Verily I say unto you, Nay; for I, the Lord, commanded it" (D&C 132:34–35).

What was Hagar's relationship to Abram? (16:3) "In biblical times, a concubine was a legally married wife, usually of a second class status either because of social order, economic position, race, or nationality (a foreigner). Concubines had legal status and rights as wives, although not always of the same order or magnitude as the rights of 'first wives.'

"It should be remembered that concubines in Old Testament times were part of polygynous marriages, where the husband could legally have more than one wife at the same time" (Ludlow, *Companion to Your*

Study of the Old Testament, 11). "The relationship of a concubine to a husband was 'provided for by the law of Moses and no moral stigma was attached to it' (Smith, *New Smith's Bible Dictionary,* 70)" (Black, *400 Questions and Answers About the Old Testament,* 50).

Why was Sarai despised? (16:5) "Hagar is referred to as a 'concubine' (Genesis 25:6; D&C 132:37). With none of the immoral overtones inherent in the label today, a concubine in the ancient Near East was a legal wife who was elevated from servant status by her marriage. Her increased status did not, however, equal that of the chief wife, who was always a free woman. . . . Sarai's remorse after Hagar became pregnant may have been out of fear that Hagar would supplant her as chief wife. Likewise, Hagar's 'despising' of Sarai suggests that Sarai's importance and status had diminished in Hagar's eyes" (Olson, *Women of the Old Testament,* 37, 38).

Why would the Lord send an angel to Hagar? (16:7) The "main service of angels on earth is clearly to be helpers to humankind. They are watchmen, protecting and ministering to us in hours of need. President John Taylor says, 'The angels are our watchmen.' . . . It would seem from a careful perusal of the scriptures, that the angels, while God has Saints upon the earth, stay in this lower world to ward off evil' (*Gospel Kingdom,* 31). The scriptures are replete with evidence, that these heavenly visitors are ministering angels for the righteous. Thus an angel brought courage to Hagar (Gen. 16:7)" (Widtsoe, *Evidences and Reconciliations,* 402).

How does the posterity of Ishmael help fulfill the Lord's promise to Abram? (16:10) "Hagar was given to Abraham in accordance with the will of God, and from her 'sprang many people' (D&C 132:34–35, 65). This was a partial fulfillment of the promise given Abraham that he would be the 'father of many nations' (Gen. 17:4–5).

"Hagar also received promises from angelic visitors that her descendants would be multitudinous (Gen. 16:10; 21:17–18)" (Brewster, *Doctrine and Covenants Encyclopedia,* 227–28).

What does Hagar's comment teach us about God's nature? (16:13) The Joseph Smith Translation clarifies what Hagar declared: "And she called the name of the angel of the Lord. And he spake unto her, saying, Knowest thou that God seest thee? And she said,

5 And Sarai said unto Abram, My wrong *be* upon thee: I have given my maid into thy bosom; and when she saw that she had conceived, I was despised in her eyes: the LORD judge between me and thee.

6 But Abram said unto Sarai, Behold, thy maid *is* in thy hand; do to her as it pleaseth thee. And when Sarai dealt hardly with her, she fled from her face.

7 ¶ And the angel of the LORD found her by a fountain of water in the wilderness, by the fountain in the way to Shur.

8 And he said, Hagar, Sarai's maid, whence camest thou? and whither wilt thou go? And she said, I flee from the face of my mistress Sarai.

9 And the angel of the LORD said unto her, Return to thy mistress, and submit thyself under her hands.

10 And the angel of the LORD said unto her, I will multiply thy seed exceedingly, that it shall not be numbered for multitude.

11 And the angel of the LORD said unto her, Behold, thou *art* with child, and shalt bear a son, and shalt call his name Ishmael; because the LORD hath heard thy affliction.

12 And he will be a wild man; his hand *will be* against every man, and every man's hand against him; and he shall dwell in the presence of all his brethren.

13 And she called the name of the LORD that spake unto her, Thou God seest me: for she said, Have I also here looked after him that seeth me?

14 Wherefore the well was called Beer-lahai-roi; behold, *it is* between Kadesh and Bered.

15 ¶ And Hagar bare Abram a son: and Abram called his son's name, which Hagar bare, Ishmael.

16 And Abram *was* fourscore and six years old, when Hagar bare Ishmael to Abram.

I know that God seest me, for I have also here looked after him" (JST, Gen. 16:14–16).

Why did the angel instruct Hagar to name her son Ishmael? (16:15) "Hagar, who fled the wrath of Sarai, was instructed by an angel of the Lord that she would bear a son, and was further told that she was to name him Ishmael, 'because the Lord hath heard thy affliction' (Genesis 16:11). The name *Ishmael* means 'God hears'" (McConkie, *Gospel Symbolism,* 182). "He was the child 'born after the flesh' (Gal. 4:23) and not the child 'by promise' and was sent from home after mocking Isaac (Gen. 21:8–21; see also 25:9–17; 28:9; 36:3). His descendants, the Ishmaelites, appear to have been a wandering race (16:12), living by plunder, having commercial relations and intermarrying with the heathen nations of Canaan" (Bible Dictionary, "Ishmael").

CHAPTER 17

Abram is commanded to be perfect—He will be a father of many nations—His name is changed to Abraham—The Lord covenants to be a God unto Abraham and his seed forever—Also, the Lord gives Abraham the land of Canaan for an everlasting possession—Circumcision becomes a token of the everlasting covenant between God and Abraham—Sarai's name is changed to Sarah—She will bear Isaac, with whom the Lord will establish His covenant—Abraham and the men of his house are circumcised.

1 And when Abram was ninety years old and nine, the LORD appeared to Abram, and said unto him, I *am* the Almighty God; walk before me, and be thou perfect.

2 And I will make my covenant between me and thee, and will multiply thee exceedingly.

Genesis 17:1–10. Abram's Name Is Changed to Abraham as a Part of the Covenant Made with God

What does it mean to walk before God and be perfect? (17:1) "When we walk in the Lord's presence by the way we live, surely then we are on the path toward perfection. We walk before the Lord in our actions and thoughts, and we become one with him because our desires are united with his" (Ludlow, *Principles and Practices of the Restored Gospel,* 215). President Russell M. Nelson further taught: "Mortal perfection can be achieved as we try to perform every duty, keep every law, and strive to be as perfect in our sphere as our Heavenly Father is in his. If we do the best we can, the Lord will bless us according to our deeds and the desires of our hearts" ("Perfection Pending," 86). ⊕

3 And Abram fell on his face: and God talked with him, saying,

Why did the Lord command circumcision? (17:3–4) "The restored version of Genesis explains that the old covenant of baptism made known in Adam's time (Gen. 17:3*a*; Moses 6:52–66; 7:11) had been corrupted,

The Abrahamic Covenant (Genesis 15; 17; Abraham 2)

The Land Promise. *Read Genesis 15:18; 17:8; Abraham 2:6.*

Temporal Significance

The land of Canaan was promised to Abraham and his descendants, even though he never personally possessed it (see Genesis 17:7; 13:15; 17:8).

"The Lord gave the promise to Abraham that he should have Palestine, or the land of Canaan, as an everlasting possession. Yet, as Stephen said at the time of his martyrdom, Abraham never received as much as a foot of it as a possession while he lived.

"Then what did the Lord mean in making a promise to Abraham of that kind, giving him that portion of the earth as an everlasting possession for himself and his posterity, the righteous part of it, forever? Simply this, that the time would eventually come, after the resurrection from the dead, when Abraham and his children who have been faithful in the keeping of the commandments of the Lord, should possess that land, and they shall also spread forth as far as it is necessary for them to receive an inheritance" (Smith, *Doctrines of Salvation,*1:88).

Eternal Significance

Abraham's righteous descendants will inherit the earth.

"Following the millennium plus 'a little season' (D&C 29:22–25), the earth will die, be resurrected, and becoming like a 'sea of glass' (D&C 130:7), attain unto 'its sanctified, immortal, and eternal state' (D&C 77:1–2). Then the poor and the meek—that is, the godfearing and the righteous—shall inherit the earth; it will become an abiding place for the Father and the Son, and celestial beings will possess it forever and ever (D&C 88:14–26, 111)" (McConkie, *Mormon Doctrine,* 211).

The Posterity Promise. *Read Abraham 2:9; Genesis 17:4–6; 16; Abraham 3:14.*

Temporal Significance

Abraham was one hundred years old before his covenant son, Isaac, was born. Abraham had eight sons in all; however, from Isaac the covenant people developed; through Ishmael came many of the Arab nations (see D&C 132:34). Through Keturah's sons came the Midianites and others.

"The vast population of the Arab, Moslem, and Israeli world which claim to be descendants of Abraham numbers approximately one hundred million. When one adds to that figure the deceased ancestors, and the estimates of future posterities of those groups, plus other descendants of Abraham such as the past, present, and future members of the Nephite-Lamanite cultures, the lost ten tribes, and the Latter-day Saints, he sees what the Lord meant concerning the innumerable and unmeasurable blessing of posterity" (Nyman, in *Sperry Lecture Series,* 1975, 13).

Eternal Significance

In a literal sense Abraham's posterity will have no end because his righteous descendants will go on through eternity bringing forth posterity (see D&C 132:30).

The Priesthood Promise. *Read Abraham 1:18–19; 2:9–11.*

Temporal Significance

As Noah was given the priesthood and commissioned to preach the gospel, so Abraham received the priesthood that he might preach and bless others with the gospel. The mission of the covenant people is to serve the Lord by blessing others with the gospel.

"We go to the promise made to Abraham, which was that in him and in his seed all the families of the earth should be blessed. Moses, as I have said was of his seed, and he was the deliverer of the whole of that nation. And who were the prophets that existed among ancient Israel? They were descendants of Abraham; and to them came the word of God and the light of revelation. Who was Jesus? After the flesh of the seed of Abraham. Who were his Twelve Apostles? Of the seed of Abraham. Who were the people that came to this continent—Lehi and his family, about 600 years B.C.? Of the seed of Abraham. Who were the Apostles they had among them that spread forth among the millions that then lived upon this continent? Of the seed of Abraham. Who was Joseph Smith? Of the seed of Abraham" (John Taylor, in *Journal of Discourses,* 20:224).

Eternal Significance

"As descendants of Abraham, if we remain true and faithful to our charge to bless our own family and others with the blessings of the gospel, we will continue to do so throughout all eternity. Also, we will be heirs to all that the Father has through Christ (see D&C 84:38–39)"

(*Old Testament Student Manual: Genesis–2 Samuel*, 71–72.)

4 As for me, behold, my covenant *is* with thee, and thou shalt be a father of many nations.

5 Neither shall thy name any more be called Abram, but thy name shall be Abraham; for a father of many nations have I made thee.

6 And I will make thee exceeding fruitful, and I will make nations of thee, and kings shall come out of thee.

7 And I will establish my covenant between me and thee and thy seed after thee in their generations for an everlasting covenant, to be a God unto thee, and to thy seed after thee.

8 And I will give unto thee, and to thy seed after thee, the land wherein thou art a stranger, all the land of Canaan, for an everlasting possession; and I will be their God.

9 ¶ And God said unto Abraham, Thou shalt keep my covenant therefore, thou, and thy seed after thee in their generations.

10 This *is* my covenant, which ye shall keep, between me and you and thy seed after thee; Every man child among you shall be circumcised.

11 And ye shall circumcise the flesh of your foreskin; and it shall be a token of the covenant betwixt me and you.

along with other ordinances, both in doctrine and practice. But now Abraham and his seed were commanded by the Lord, 'Keep all my covenants wherein I covenanted with thy fathers,' as well as those newly given them (JST, Gen. 17:12; Gen. 17:7*a*); then circumcision was instituted as a sign of the covenant" (Rasmussen, *Latter-day Saint Commentary on the Old Testament*, 46). See commentary in this volume for Genesis 17:11–14.

Why did the Lord change Abram's name to Abraham? (17:5) "Abram ('exalted father') was instructed by the Lord that his name was to be changed to Abraham ('father of a multitude') in the context of the Abrahamic covenant, in which the Lord promised him an endless seed (Genesis 17:5). At the same time his wife Sarai (possibly meaning 'contentions,' though probably another form of Sarah) was directed to change her name to Sarah ('princess'). The same promise given to Abraham and Sarah in their eternal union is renewed with each couple who are married for time and eternity (D&C 132:30–31). Thus, through the covenant of eternal marriage, each man becomes a 'father of multitudes' and each woman a 'princess'" (McConkie, *Gospel Symbolism*, 182). ⊕

What is the Abrahamic covenant? (17:10): The Abrahamic covenant "is of transcendent significance. It contained several promises: Abraham's posterity would be numerous, entitled to eternal increase and to bear the priesthood; he would become a father of many nations; Christ and kings would come through Abraham's lineage; certain lands would be inherited; all nations of the earth would be blessed by his seed; that covenant would be everlasting—even through 'a thousand generations'" (Nelson, "Children of the Covenant," 33). See commentary in this volume for Genesis 12:2–3. ⊕

Genesis 17:11–22. God Promises Sarah a Son Named Isaac

Why is circumcision a token of the covenant? (17:11–14) "In the Joseph Smith Translation of the Bible of this passage, we learn that circumcision was instituted as a token of the covenant; but the token was given because the people were in a state of apostasy, had lost sight of the true meaning of the ordinance of baptism, and were washing their children and sprinkling them with blood so that they would be free from sin. Circumcision reminded the people that, while children were born in the covenant, they were not to be held accountable until they reached eight years of age (see JST, Gen. 17:4–11)" (Lund, *Jesus Christ*, 57–58).

Why was Sarai's name changed to Sarah? (17:15–16) "Sarai's new name foretold a change from her way of struggle and persistence to prevail. *Sarai* is derived from the Hebrew root *srh* ('prevail'), the same root from which the Hebrew *yisrael*, or *Israel*, was later derived. Sarah, 'Princess,' is the feminine form of the word meaning 'chieftain,' 'chief,' 'ruler,' 'official,' 'captain,' or 'prince.' Thus the promise 'kings of people shall be of her' (Gen. 17:16) was a play on the meaning of her new name" (Rasmussen, *Latter-day Saint Commentary on the Old Testament*, 46–47).

Why would Abraham laugh at God's promise that he would have a son? (17:17) The Joseph Smith Translation replaces the word "laughed" with the word "rejoiced" (JST, Genesis 17:23).

Why did Isaac receive the birthright instead of Ishmael? (17:18–21) "The birthright was given to Isaac, the first son of the first wife, rather than to Ishmael, who was the first son of Abraham and Hagar and was about fourteen years older than Isaac. The Lord made it clear that in accordance with the original promise Abraham's son by Sarah would bear the covenant responsibility. Yet, Ishmael, through his twelve sons, was also to be the father of a great nation" (*Old Testament Student Manual: Genesis–2 Samuel*, 70). "Abraham's posterity has a divinely decreed potential. The Lord declared that Ishmael would become a great nation and that the seed of Abraham, Isaac, and Jacob would bless all the nations of the earth" (Nelson, "Blessed Are the Peacemakers," 40).

What does Isaac's name teach us about his birth? (17:19) The name *Isaac* means "He laugheth" [or rejoices] in Hebrew (see Genesis 17:17*b*). He was "the

12 And he that is eight days old shall be circumcised among you, every man child in your generations, he that is born in the house, or bought with money of any stranger, which *is* not of thy seed.

13 He that is born in thy house, and he that is bought with thy money, must needs be circumcised: and my covenant shall be in your flesh for an everlasting covenant.

14 And the uncircumcised man child whose flesh of his foreskin is not circumcised, that soul shall be cut off from his people; he hath broken my covenant.

15 ¶ And God said unto Abraham, As for Sarai thy wife, thou shalt not call her name Sarai, but Sarah *shall* her name *be*.

16 And I will bless her, and give thee a son also of her: yea, I will bless her, and she shall be *a mother* of nations; kings of people shall be of her.

17 Then Abraham fell upon his face, and laughed, and said in his heart, Shall *a child* be born unto him that is an hundred years old? and shall Sarah, that is ninety years old, bear?

18 And Abraham said unto God, O that Ishmael might live before thee!

19 And God said, Sarah thy wife shall bear thee a son indeed; and thou shalt call his name Isaac: and I will establish my covenant with him for an everlasting covenant, *and* with his seed after him.

20 And as for Ishmael, I have heard thee: Behold, I have blessed him, and will make him fruitful, and will multiply him exceedingly; twelve princes shall he beget, and I will make him a great nation.

21 But my covenant will I establish with Isaac, which Sarah shall bear unto thee at this set time in the next year.

22 And he left off talking with him, and God went up from Abraham.

only son of Abraham by Sarah. The name Isaac was fitly chosen by Jehovah in commemoration of the child's miraculous birth (Gen. 17:19) and of the *laughing* joy it occasioned. . . . The birth of Isaac occurred (about 2061 B.C.) when Abraham was a hundred years old and Sarah ninety (Gen. 21:5; cf. 17:17)" (*New Unger's Bible Dictionary*, 627).

23 ¶ And Abraham took Ishmael his son, and all that were born in his house, and all that were bought with his money, every male among the men of Abraham's house; and circumcised the flesh of their foreskin in the selfsame day, as God had said unto him.

24 And Abraham *was* ninety years old and nine, when he was circumcised in the flesh of his foreskin.

25 And Ishmael his son *was* thirteen years old, when he was circumcised in the flesh of his foreskin.

26 In the selfsame day was Abraham circumcised, and Ishmael his son.

27 And all the men of his house, born in the house, and bought with money of the stranger, were circumcised with him.

Genesis 17:23–27. Abraham Circumcises His Household

Who does the word "stranger" refer to in this verse? (17:27) "This word generally denotes a person from a foreign land residing in Palestine. Such persons enjoyed many privileges in common with the Jews, but still were separate from them. The relation of the Jews to strangers was regulated by special laws (Deuteronomy 23:3; 24:14–21; 25:5; 26:10–13). A special signification is also sometimes attached to this word. In Genesis 23:4 it denotes one resident in a foreign land; Exodus 23:9, one who is not a Jew; Numbers 3:10, one who is not of the family of Aaron; Psalm 69:8, an alien or an unknown person. The Jews were allowed to purchase strangers as slaves (Leviticus 25:44, 45), and to take usury [money] from them (Deuteronomy 23:20)" (Easton, *Easton's Bible Dictionary*, s.v. "stranger").

CHAPTER 18

Abraham entertains three holy men—They promise that Sarah will have a son—Abraham will command his children to be just—The Lord appears to him—They discuss the destruction of Sodom and Gomorrah.

Genesis 18:1–8. Abraham and Sarah Serve Three Heavenly Visitors

1 And the LORD appeared unto him in the plains of Mamre: and he sat in the tent door in the heat of the day;

2 And he lift up his eyes and looked, and, lo, three men stood by him: and when he saw *them*, he ran to meet them from the tent door, and bowed himself toward the ground,

3 And said, My Lord, if now I have found favour in thy sight, pass not away, I pray thee, from thy servant:

Who were these three men? (18:2) Throughout this scripture account the Joseph Smith Translation clarifies that these three men were "three angels" (JST, Gen. 19:1) who "were holy men, and were sent forth after the order of God" (JST, Gen. 18:22). "Perhaps the obviously deliberate reference to their eating (see Gen. 18:5–8) is intended to inform us that they were mortals and not angelic beings and that 'angels' is meant to be understood in its original sense (both in English and in Hebrew) as 'messengers'" (Jackson, *Restored Gospel and the Book of Genesis*, 144). ⊕

Why would Abraham offer to have their feet washed? (18:4) "In these verses we find a delightful picture of primitive hospitality. In those ancient times shoes such as ours were not in use; and the foot was protected only by *sandals* or *soles*, which fastened round the foot with straps. It was therefore a great refreshment in so hot a country to get the feet washed at the end of a day's journey; and this is the *first* thing that Abraham proposes" (*Adam Clarke's Commentary* [on Genesis 18:4]).

4 Let a little water, I pray you, be fetched, and wash your feet, and rest yourselves under the tree:

5 And I will fetch a morsel of bread, and comfort ye your hearts; after that ye shall pass on: for therefore are ye come to your servant. And they said, So do, as thou hast said.

6 And Abraham hastened into the tent unto Sarah, and said, Make ready quickly three measures of fine meal, knead *it*, and make cakes upon the hearth.

7 And Abraham ran unto the herd, and fetcht a calf tender and good, and gave *it* unto a young man; and he hasted to dress it.

8 And he took butter, and milk, and the calf which he had dressed, and set *it* before them; and he stood by them under the tree, and they did eat.

Genesis 18:9–15. The Three Messengers Promise Abraham and Sarah a Son

9 ¶ And they said unto him, Where *is* Sarah thy wife? And he said, Behold, in the tent.

10 And he said, I will certainly return unto thee according to the time of life; and, lo, Sarah thy wife shall have a son. And Sarah heard *it* in the tent door, which *was* behind him.

11 Now Abraham and Sarah *were* old *and* well stricken in age; *and* it ceased to be with Sarah after the manner of women.

12 Therefore Sarah laughed within herself, saying, After I am waxed old shall I have pleasure, my lord being old also?

13 And the LORD said unto Abraham, Wherefore did Sarah laugh, saying, Shall I of a surety bear a child, which am old?

14 Is any thing too hard for the LORD? At the time appointed I will return unto thee, according to the time of life, and Sarah shall have a son.

15 Then Sarah denied, saying, I laughed not; for she was afraid. And he said, Nay; but thou didst laugh.

What feelings did Abraham and Sarah experience at this extraordinary announcement? (18:10) "Can you imagine the joy that Abraham and Sarah must have felt—joy accompanied by deep gratitude and an undeniable realization of the power of God and the surety of his promises. They had waited for such a long time, yearning and praying and living righteously. The blessing had finally come. . . . In their old age they could quietly witness the continued fulfillment of God's promises through Isaac" (Dahl, "Abrahamic Test," 56).

How can Abraham and Sarah's trial increase our faith in the Lord? (18:13–14) "The Lord has often chosen to instruct His people in their times of trial . . . Indeed, one might say that to teach His people, the Lord employs the unlikely. . . .

"Everyone 'knows' that *old* women do not bear children. So upon whom did the Lord call to bear Abraham's birthright son? Sarah, at age ninety! When told this was to be, she asked a logical question: 'Shall I [which am old] of a surety bear a child?' (Gen. 18:13). From heaven came this reply 'Is any thing too hard for the Lord?' (Gen. 18:14).

"So decreed, she gave birth to Isaac, to carry the crucial Abrahamic covenant into the second generation" (Nelson, "With God Nothing Shall Be Impossible," 33).

16 ¶ And the men rose up from thence, and looked toward Sodom: and Abraham went with them to bring them on the way.

17 And the LORD said, Shall I hide from Abraham that thing which I do;

18 Seeing that Abraham shall surely become a great and mighty nation, and all the nations of the earth shall be blessed in him?

19 For I know him, that he will command his children and his household after him, and they shall keep the way of the LORD, to do justice and judgment; that the LORD may bring upon Abraham that which he hath spoken of him.

Genesis 18:16–21. The Messengers Tell Abraham They Are Going to Destroy Sodom

How does Abraham's faithfulness inspire his posterity? (18:19) Abraham was an example of righteousness to his family. President Spencer W. Kimball taught: "Abraham's desire to do God's will in all things led him to preside over his family in righteousness. Despite all his other responsibilities, he knew that if he failed to teach and exemplify the gospel to his children he would have failed to fulfill the most important stewardship he had received" ("Example of Abraham," 5).

In what ways do Sodom and Gomorrah's sins serve as a warning to us? (18:20) "Nothing happened in Sodom and Gomorrah which exceeds in wickedness and depravity that which surrounds us now.

"Words of profanity, vulgarity, and blasphemy are heard everywhere. Unspeakable wickedness and perversion were once hidden in dark places; now they are in the open, even accorded legal protection.

"At Sodom and Gomorrah these things were localized. Now they spread across the world, and they are among us" (Packer, "One Pure Defense," 4). See also Ezekiel 16:49–50. ⊕

20 And the LORD said, Because the cry of Sodom and Gomorrah is great, and because their sin is very grievous;

21 I will go down now, and see whether they have done altogether according to the cry of it, which is come unto me; and if not, I will know.

Genesis 18:22–33. Abraham Pleads with the Lord Not to Destroy Sodom If There Are Some Righteous Left

What does it mean that "the men turned their faces from thence"? (18:22) The Joseph Smith Translation makes it clear that the Lord sent three "angels which were holy men" ahead to Sodom while Abraham conversed with the Lord (see JST, Gen. 18:19–23).

22 And the men turned their faces from thence, and went toward Sodom: but Abraham stood yet before the LORD.

23 ¶ And Abraham drew near, and said, Wilt thou also destroy the righteous with the wicked?

24 Peradventure there be fifty righteous within the city: wilt thou also destroy and not spare the place for the fifty righteous that *are* therein?

How does the Lord reveal His merciful nature to Abraham? (18:25) "[The Lord] would grant the prayer of His servant if the necessary conditions were

25 That be far from thee to do after this manner, to slay the righteous with the

In What Ways Are the Nations of the Earth Blessed by Abraham? (Genesis 18:18)

"My name is Jehovah, and I know the end from the beginning; therefore my hand shall be over thee.

"And I will make of thee a great nation, and I will bless thee above measure, and make thy name great among all nations, and thou shalt be a blessing unto thy seed after thee, that in their hands they shall bear this ministry and Priesthood unto all nations; and I will bless them through thy name; for as many as receive this Gospel shall be called after thy name, and shall be accounted thy seed, and shall rise up and bless thee, as their father; and I will bless them that bless thee, and curse them that curse thee; and in thee (that is, in thy Priesthood) and in thy seed (that is, thy Priesthood), for I give unto thee a promise that this right shall continue in thee, and in thy seed after thee (that is to say, the literal seed, or the seed of the body) shall all the families of the earth be blessed, even with the blessings of the Gospel, which are the blessings of salvation, even of life eternal" (Abraham 2:8–11).

Elder Bruce R. McConkie wrote: "God gave Abraham a promise, and that promise has been planted in my heart because I am a descendant of Abraham. What God said to Abraham was, 'Your descendants,' meaning, as we shall see, the ones through Isaac and Jacob, 'shall have a right to the priesthood, to the gospel and to eternal life.' . . . For our purposes here, let us talk about eternal life as consisting of a continuation of the family unit in eternity. And that means celestial marriage. Celestial marriage opens the door to the continuation of the family unit in eternity. If the family unit continues in eternity, then people have eternal increase. They have, in Joseph Smith's language, spirit children in the resurrection" ("Promises Made to the Fathers," 54–55).

wicked: and that the righteous should be as the wicked, that be far from thee: Shall not the Judge of all the earth do right?

forthcoming. They were not, however, as the people of Sodom were universally depraved; but Abraham learned that God prefers mercy to judgment, and that those who have the least claim on His mercy receive it, as was the case with Lot and his family. Nor should we overlook another side of this narrative, viz. the value of a good man. Ten righteous men in Sodom will save the city. . . . While Abraham thought all along that the righteous would perish with the wicked unless the whole city was saved. God distinguished between the innocent and the guilty, and saved four persons" (*John Dummelow's Commentary* [on Genesis 18:23–32]).

26 And the LORD said, If I find in Sodom fifty righteous within the city, then I will spare all the place for their sakes.

27 And Abraham answered and said, Behold now, I have taken upon me to speak unto the Lord, which *am but* dust and ashes:

28 Peradventure there shall lack five of the fifty righteous: wilt thou destroy all the city for *lack of* five? And he said, If I find there forty and five, I will not destroy *it.*

29 And he spake unto him yet again, and said, Peradventure there shall be forty found there. And he said, I will not do *it* for forty's sake.

30 And he said *unto him,* Oh let not the Lord be angry, and I will speak: Peradventure there shall thirty be found there. And he said, I will not do *it,* if I find thirty there.

31 And he said, Behold now, I have taken upon me to speak unto the Lord: Peradventure there shall be twenty found there. And he said, I will not destroy *it* for twenty's sake.

32 And he said, Oh let not the Lord be angry, and I will speak yet but this once: Peradventure ten shall be found there. And he said, I will not destroy *it* for ten's sake.

33 And the LORD went his way, as soon as he had left communing with Abraham: and Abraham returned unto his place.

Why does Abraham want to save the righteous in Sodom? (18:26–32) "Consider why the Lord let Abraham go through the long process of pleading on behalf of those wicked places, knowing (as Gen. 19:29 implies) that it was Lot's family Abraham wished to save when he asked that the places be spared even if only as many as ten righteous could be found in them (Gen. 18:23–32). Evidently the Lord lets us exercise our intelligence and agency in order to develop, for if all things were done by the Divine initiative alone, there would be no challenges to help us grow in faith, hope, charity, intelligence, and judgment" (Rasmussen, *Latter-day Saint Commentary on the Old Testament,* 48).

CHAPTER 19

Lot entertains holy men—The men of Sodom seek to abuse Lot's guests and are smitten with blindness—Lot is sent out of Sodom—The Lord rains brimstone and fire upon Sodom and Gomorrah—Lot's daughters preserve his seed in the land.

1 And there came two angels to Sodom at even; and Lot sat in the gate of Sodom: and Lot seeing *them* rose up to meet them; and he bowed himself with his face toward the ground;

2 And he said, Behold now, my lords, turn in, I pray you, into your servant's house, and tarry all night, and wash your feet, and ye shall rise up early, and go on your ways. And they said, Nay; but we will abide in the street all night.

3 And he pressed upon them greatly; and they turned in unto him, and entered into his house; and he made them a feast, and did bake unleavened bread, and they did eat.

4 ¶ But before they lay down, the men of the city, *even* the men of Sodom, compassed the house round, both old and young, all the people from every quarter:

5 And they called unto Lot, and said unto him, Where *are* the men which came in to thee this night? bring them out unto us, that we may know them.

6 And Lot went out at the door unto them, and shut the door after him,

7 And said, I pray you, brethren, do not so wickedly.

8 Behold now, I have two daughters which have not known man; let me, I pray you, bring them out unto you, and do ye to them as *is* good in your eyes: only unto these men do nothing; for therefore came they under the shadow of my roof.

Genesis 19:1–7. Lot Serves Three Messengers from God

How many angels visited Lot in Sodom? (19:1) The Joseph Smith Translation clarifies that three, not two, angels visited Lot in Sodom (JST, Genesis 19:1).

Why is Lot concerned for his guests? (19:2) Lot is a gracious host, but does seem to warn his guests. "The strangers are urged to get out of town before the people of Sodom become aware of their presence" (Sarna, *Genesis,* 135).

What does "know" mean in this context? (19:5) "'Know' is used both in Hebrew and English in this kind of context as a euphemism in place of a sexual word. Judg. 19:22 (22–28); Isa. 3:9" (Genesis 19:5*a*).

Genesis 19:8–10. The Wicked Men of Sodom Seek to Abuse the Three Visitors and Lot's Daughters

How does the Joseph Smith Translation change our understanding of this story? (19:8–10) "The Joseph Smith Translation adds a few clarifications to the account of the rescue of Lot's family. When the wicked men of the city wanted Lot to surrender his guests, 'that we may know them' (Gen. 19:5), the Bible has Lot perversely offering instead his two daughters

9 And they said, Stand back. And they said *again,* This one *fellow* came in to sojourn, and he will needs be a judge: now will we deal worse with thee, than with them. And they pressed sore upon the man, *even* Lot, and came near to break the door.

10 But the men put forth their hand, and pulled Lot into the house to them, and shut to the door.

11 And they smote the men that *were* at the door of the house with blindness, both small and great: so that they wearied themselves to find the door.

12 ¶ And the men said unto Lot, Hast thou here any besides? son in law, and thy sons, and thy daughters, and whatsoever thou hast in the city, bring *them* out of this place:

13 For we will destroy this place, because the cry of them is waxen great before the face of the LORD; and the LORD hath sent us to destroy it.

14 And Lot went out, and spake unto his sons in law, which married his daughters, and said, Up, get you out of this place; for the LORD will destroy this city. But he seemed as one that mocked unto his sons in law.

(see Gen. 19:8). The Joseph Smith Translation explains that the citizens demanded both the visitors and the daughters, but Lot refused both. All of this evil, the Joseph Smith Translation adds, 'was after the wickedness of Sodom' (see JST, Gen. 19:12)" (Jackson, *Restored Gospel and the Book of Genesis,* 141).

Genesis 19:11–29. Sodom and Gomorrah Are Destroyed

What is inferred that the antagonists were smote with blindness? (19:11) The "blindness was not so much loss of sight as a sudden striking of the tormentors with severe disorientation that frustrated their purpose" (Guthrie, et al., *New Bible Commentary: Revised,* 98). There are other examples in the scriptures where antagonists to the Lord's purposes were temporarily blinded. For example, Elisha asked the Lord to smite an approaching Syrian army with blindness. Once the Syrian army was subdued, they received their sight again. See 2 Kings 6:18–23.

Lot Resists the Wickedness of Sodom, and Angels Protect Him (Genesis 19:8–10)

"And they said unto him, Stand back, And they were angry with him.

"And they said *among themselves,* This one *man* came in to sojourn *among us,* and he will needs *now make himself to be* a judge; now we will deal worse with *him* than with them.

"Wherefore they said unto the man, We will have the men, and thy daughters also; and we will do with them as seemeth us good.

"Now this was after the wickedness of Sodom.

"And Lot said, Behold now, I have two daughters which have not known man; I pray you, *plead with my brethren that I may not* bring them out unto you; and ye *shall not* do unto them as seemeth good in your eyes;

"For God will not justify his servant in this thing; wherefore, let me plead with my brethren, this once only, that unto these men ye do nothing, that they may have peace in my house; for therefore came they under the shadow of my roof.

"*And they were angry with Lot* and came near to break the door, but the *angels of God, which were holy men,* put forth their hand and pulled Lot into them, and shut the door" (JST, Genesis 19:9–15; changes emphasized).

How did the Lord show mercy to Lot's family? (19:15–16) Even after Lot had been warned that the Lord would destroy Sodom, he delayed his departure from the city. Nevertheless, the messengers still took the hands of Lot, his wife, and his daughters and set them outside the city. When has the Lord been merciful to you even though you delayed obedience to His counsel?

15 ¶ And when the morning arose, then the angels hastened Lot, saying, Arise, take thy wife, and thy two daughters, which are here; lest thou be consumed in the iniquity of the city.

16 And while he lingered, the men laid hold upon his hand, and upon the hand of his wife, and upon the hand of his two daughters; the LORD being merciful unto him: and they brought him forth, and set him without the city.

How might the counsel to "not look behind thee" apply to us today? (19:17) We have been counseled by the Lord to remove ourselves from Babylon, or from the wickedness of the world, prior to the destruction that will accompany the Second Coming. "Go ye out from among the nations, even from Babylon, from the midst of wickedness, which is spiritual Babylon. But verily, thus saith the Lord, let not your flight be in haste, but let all things be prepared before you; and he that goeth, let him not look back lest sudden destruction shall come upon him" (D&C 133:14–15).

17 ¶ And it came to pass, when they had brought them forth abroad, that he said, Escape for thy life; look not behind thee, neither stay thou in all the plain; escape to the mountain, lest thou be consumed.

18 And Lot said unto them, Oh, not so, my Lord:

19 Behold now, thy servant hath found grace in thy sight, and thou hast magnified thy mercy, which thou hast shewed unto me in saving my life; and I cannot escape to the mountain, lest some evil take me, and I die:

20 Behold now, this city *is* near to flee unto, and it *is* a little one: Oh, let me escape thither, (*is* it not a little one?) and my soul shall live.

21 And he said unto him, See, I have accepted thee concerning this thing also, that I will not overthrow this city, for the which thou hast spoken.

22 Haste thee, escape thither; for I cannot do any thing till thou be come thither. Therefore the name of the city was called Zoar.

23 ¶ The sun was risen upon the earth when Lot entered into Zoar.

Why is Sodom and Gomorrah's judgment a warning to us in our day? (19:24) As recorded by President Wilford Woodruff, the prophet Joseph Smith taught: "And where there is a Priest of God, a minister who has power & authority from God to administer in the ordinances of the gospel & officiate in the Priesthood

24 Then the LORD rained upon Sodom and upon Gomorrah brimstone and fire from the LORD out of heaven;

25 And he overthrew those cities, and all the plain, and all the inhabitants of the cities, and that which grew upon the ground.

of God, there is the kingdom of God & in consequence of rejecting the gospel of Jesus Christ & the Prophets whom God hath sent, the judgments of God hath rested upon people cities & nations in various ages of the world, which was the case with the cities of Sodom & Gomorrah who were destroyed for rejecting the Prophets" (Joseph Smith Papers, "Discourse, 22 Jan. 1843, as Reported by Wilford Woodruff," 4; spelling modernized).

26 ¶ But his wife looked back from behind him, and she became a pillar of salt.

27 ¶ And Abraham gat up early in the morning to the place where he stood before the LORD:

28 And he looked toward Sodom and Gomorrah, and toward all the land of the plain, and beheld, and, lo, the smoke of the country went up as the smoke of a furnace.

29 ¶ And it came to pass, when God destroyed the cities of the plain, that God remembered Abraham, and sent Lot out of the midst of the overthrow, when he overthrew the cities in the which Lot dwelt.

30 ¶ And Lot went up out of Zoar, and dwelt in the mountain, and his two daughters with him; for he feared to dwell in Zoar: and he dwelt in a cave, he and his two daughters.

31 And the firstborn said unto the younger, Our father *is* old, and *there is* not a man in the earth to come in unto us after the manner of all the earth:

32 Come, let us make our father drink wine, and we will lie with him, that we may preserve seed of our father.

33 And they made their father drink wine that night: and the firstborn went in, and lay with her father; and he perceived not when she lay down, nor when she arose.

34 And it came to pass on the morrow, that the firstborn said unto the younger, Behold, I lay yesternight with my father: let us make him drink wine this night also; and go thou

Why did Lot's wife look back to Sodom? (19:26) "Just what did Lot's wife do that was so wrong? As a student of history, I have thought about that and offer a partial answer. Apparently, what was wrong with Lot's wife was that she wasn't just looking back; in her heart she wanted to go back. It would appear that even before she was past the city limits, she was already missing what Sodom and Gomorrah offered her" (Holland, "Best Is Yet to Be," 24). ⊕

Genesis 19:30–38. Lot's Daughters Do a Wicked Thing and Have Two Sons

Why did Lot's daughters rationalize their actions? (19:31) "Lot's daughters' rationalizing their incest makes it appear that they too may have been imbued with the ways of Sodom. Their purpose could not justify such a means, for it was not a righteous way nor was it likely the only way.

"Some commentators have supposed this account of illicit acts was contrived to impugn the Moabites and Ammonites; but that is a poor argument, for equally scandalous stories are preserved later concerning even the royal line of Judah. Doubtless such accounts were kept to provide vicarious experiences that should help others avoid such rationalization. There is, of course, no implication that because prominent people of the Bible did such things their actions were approved" (Rasmussen, *Latter-day Saint Commentary on the Old Testament*, 49).

Who were the Moabites? (19:37) The Moabites were an important group in this area. Moab was the father of the Moabites. He was the "son of Lot's eldest daughter (Gen. 19:37). The land of Moab lay east of the Dead Sea. The Moabites were akin to the Israelites and spoke a language that closely resembled Hebrew, but there was constant warfare between the two nations (Num. 22–25; Judg. 3:12–30; 11:17; 2 Sam. 8:2; 2 Kgs. 3:6–27; 13:20; 24:2; 1 Chr. 18:2; 2 Chr. 20:1–25)" (Bible Dictionary, "Moab").

Who were the children of Ammon? (19:38) The Ammonites were "worshippers of Molech or Milcom (1 Kgs. 11:7, 33); they were settled east of Mount Gilead, from the Jabbok southwards, and in the time of the Judges laid claim to the Israelite settlements in Gilead (Judg. 11) but were repulsed by Jephthah and again by Saul (1 Sam. 11) and finally reduced to subjection by David (2 Sam. 10; 11:1; 12:9, 26, 31). They regained their independence after David's death and maintained it, as allies of their Aramean neighbors and bitter enemies of Israel, till they fell under the power of Assyria and Chaldea (2 Kgs. 24:2; Ezek. 25:2–10; Amos 1:13–15; Zeph. 2:8). Nor were they less hostile to the Jews after the Captivity (Neh. 4)" (Bible Dictionary, "Ammon, Ammonites").

Genesis 20:1–8. Abraham Sojourns to Gerar and Meets Abimelech

Who was Abimelech? (20:2) "A king or kings of Gerar (in the land of the Philistines) named Abimelech associated with Abraham and Isaac over the course of about one hundred years. Two or more kings of the city may have carried the same name. In fact, the name 'Abimelech' means 'my father—a king,' which easily could have been a title or hereditary name. Or,

in, *and* lie with him, that we may preserve seed of our father.

35 And they made their father drink wine that night also: and the younger arose, and lay with him; and he perceived not when she lay down, nor when she arose.

36 Thus were both the daughters of Lot with child by their father.

37 And the firstborn bare a son, and called his name Moab: the same *is* the father of the Moabites unto this day.

38 And the younger, she also bare a son, and called his name Ben-ammi: the same *is* the father of the children of Ammon unto this day.

CHAPTER 20

Abimelech desires Sarah, who is preserved by the Lord—Abraham prays for Abimelech, and the Lord blesses him and his household.

1 And Abraham journeyed from thence toward the south country, and dwelled between Kadesh and Shur, and sojourned in Gerar.

2 And Abraham said of Sarah his wife, She *is* my sister: and Abimelech king of Gerar sent, and took Sarah.

3 But God came to Abimelech in a dream by night, and said to him, Behold, thou *art but* a dead man, for the woman which thou hast taken; for she *is* a man's wife.

4 But Abimelech had not come near her: and he said, Lord, wilt thou slay also a righteous nation?

5 Said he not unto me, She *is* my sister? and she, even she herself said, He *is* my brother: in the integrity of my heart and innocency of my hands have I done this.

6 And God said unto him in a dream, Yea, I know that thou didst this in the integrity of thy heart; for I also withheld thee from sinning against me: therefore suffered I thee not to touch her.

Abimelech may have been one king who lived a long time.

"His first episode with Abraham and Sarah came at the time she carried Isaac. Abimelech desired Sarah as a wife or concubine, but the Lord spoke to him in a dream to prevent him from such action, . . . Abraham and Abimelech made a covenant of peace at Beersheba" (Ludlow, *Unlocking the Old Testament,* 15–16).

How is Sarah related to Abraham? (20:2–5) "The incident involving Abraham and Abimelech parallels in several particulars a similar incident involving Pharaoh. Sarah was Abraham's 'sister' in being of the same paternal line from Terah; but her maternal line was that of Haran's wife" (Rasmussen, *Latter-day Saint Commentary on the Old Testament*, 50). See commentary in this volume for Genesis 12:11–13.

How does Abraham's experience with Abimelech parallel his encounter with the Pharaoh? (20:6–7) This is the second of the recorded events regarding Abraham's encounters with the kings of Egypt (see Gen. 12:10–20; 20:2–6; 26:1–11). Hugh Nibley thoughtfully refers to these stories as ritualistic history: "That

Abraham and the Kings (Genesis 20:2–12)

"The book of Genesis contains a trilogy of incidents in which the wife/sister motif was used by either Abraham or Isaac. The first account describes Abraham's journey into Egypt after a famine enveloped the land of Canaan (see Genesis 12:10–13:4). Similar situations arose later when both Abraham and Isaac dwelt in the city of Gerar (see Genesis 20:1–2; 26:7–8). Although in each instance the patriarch identified his wife as his sister to avert a potentially dangerous situation, these accounts have puzzled many readers and scholars because of the apparent deception involved. Why did the patriarchs resort to such action? That is a difficult theological issue. In attempting to justify the patriarchs' actions, writers have proposed a number of different explanations that offer some significant insights into the three episodes; however, we can gain a still greater understanding, especially of the episode of Abraham's sojourn in Egypt, if we take into account the insights provided by the book of Abraham and the Genesis Apocryphon (1QapGen), one of the scrolls from the Dead Sea corpus. By doing so, we see the hand of God in Abraham's request of Sarah, for Abraham's actions initiated a confrontation between himself and Pharaoh. Because of Abraham's obedience, God was able to introduce Himself to the Egyptian Pharaoh in power and glory. Even though it was only the first of a series of such encounters, it is clear that the God of Abraham was announcing His jurisdiction over all the families of the earth and not just over Abraham and his descendants. . . .

"It appears that Abraham's major motivation for asking Sarah to say she was his sister was the beauty of Sarah, which put his life in danger. . . .

"The second biblical passage relating to Sarah's and Abraham's non-marital relationship is found in Genesis 20:12. Here Abraham justified identifying Sarah as his sister to Abimelech by saying that 'indeed *she* is my sister; she *is* the daughter of my father, but not the daughter of my mother' (Genesis 20:12). In other words, Abraham claimed that Sarah was his half-sister. . . .

"So where does that leave us? Although these hypotheses have some merit in adding to our understanding of a difficult passage of scripture, they fail to take into account the insights provided by the book of Abraham and the Genesis Apocryphon. Both of these texts demonstrate that Abraham acted not merely out of an interest in self-preservation but in obedience to a divine command" (Strathearn, "Wife/Sister Experience," 152, 154–55).

we are dealing here with ritually conditioned events rather than unique historical occurrences is apparent from the complete repetition of Sarah's Egyptian experience with *another* king many years later. Abimelech, the king of Gerar, a small state lying between Canaan and Egypt, also took Sarah to wife and would have put Abraham to death had she not again announced that he was her brother" (*Abraham in Egypt*, 351–52).

Genesis 20:9–18. Abraham Encounters Abimelech; He and Sarah Are Preserved by the Lord Because of Their Obedience to the Lord's Directions

Why did Abraham choose not to reveal Sarah's true relationship as his wife? (20:12) The Bible version suggests that it was Abraham's idea to not be forthcoming about the true identity of Sarah as his wife. However, as modern revelation clarifies, "the Lord said unto me: Behold, Sarai, thy wife, is a very fair woman to look upon; therefore it shall come to pass, when the Egyptians shall see her, they will say—She is his wife; and they will kill you, but they will save her alive; therefore see that ye do on this wise: Let her say unto the Egyptians, she is thy sister, and thy soul shall live" (Abraham 2:22–24). ⊕

What does "a covering of the eyes" mean? (20:16) The Joseph Smith Translation clarifies, "he shall give unto thee a covering of the eyes, and it shall be a token unto all that thou mayest not be taken again from Abraham thy husband" (JST, Genesis 20:17).

7 Now therefore restore the man *his* wife; for he *is* a prophet, and he shall pray for thee, and thou shalt live: and if thou restore *her* not, know thou that thou shalt surely die, thou, and all that *are* thine.

8 Therefore Abimelech rose early in the morning, and called all his servants, and told all these things in their ears: and the men were sore afraid.

9 Then Abimelech called Abraham, and said unto him, What hast thou done unto us? and what have I offended thee, that thou hast brought on me and on my kingdom a great sin? thou hast done deeds unto me that ought not to be done.

10 And Abimelech said unto Abraham, What sawest thou, that thou hast done this thing?

11 And Abraham said, Because I thought, Surely the fear of God *is* not in this place; and they will slay me for my wife's sake.

12 And yet indeed *she is* my sister; she *is* the daughter of my father, but not the daughter of my mother; and she became my wife.

13 And it came to pass, when God caused me to wander from my father's house, that I said unto her, This *is* thy kindness which thou shalt shew unto me; at every place whither we shall come, say of me, He *is* my brother.

14 And Abimelech took sheep, and oxen, and menservants, and womenservants, and gave *them* unto Abraham, and restored him Sarah his wife.

15 And Abimelech said, Behold, my land *is* before thee: dwell where it pleaseth thee.

16 And unto Sarah he said, Behold, I have given thy brother a thousand *pieces* of silver: behold, he *is* to thee a covering of the eyes, unto all that *are* with thee, and with all *other:* thus she was reproved.

17 ¶ So Abraham prayed unto God: and God healed Abimelech, and his wife, and his maidservants; and they bare *children.*

18 For the LORD had fast closed up all the wombs of the house of Abimelech, because of Sarah Abraham's wife.

Sarah was told "to procure thee a veil to conceal thy beauty (unto all that are with thee, and with all other) from all thy own kindred and acquaintance, and from all strangers, that none, seeing thou art another's wife; may covet thee on account of thy comeliness" (*Adam Clarke's Commentary* [on Genesis 20:16]).

CHAPTER 21

Sarah bears Isaac—He is circumcised—Hagar and her son are cast out of Abraham's household—The Lord saves Hagar and Ishmael—Abraham and Abimelech deal honorably with each other.

1 And the LORD visited Sarah as he had said, and the LORD did unto Sarah as he had spoken.

2 For Sarah conceived, and bare Abraham a son in his old age, at the set time of which God had spoken to him.

3 And Abraham called the name of his son that was born unto him, whom Sarah bare to him, Isaac.

4 And Abraham circumcised his son Isaac being eight days old, as God had commanded him.

5 And Abraham was an hundred years old, when his son Isaac was born unto him.

Genesis 21:1–8. The Lord Blesses Sarah with a Son in Her Old Age

Why did Abraham circumcise his son Isaac? (21:4) "Circumcision was practiced in many ancient cultures. It was usually a rite of passage performed as boys went through significant social developmental stages. Before Abraham, the performance of infant circumcision was very unusual. Some of the symbolism implied through circumcision depicted their inclusion in the covenant from birth" (Muhlestein, *Scriptural Study Made Simple*, 29). See commentary in this volume for Genesis 17:11–14.

6 ¶ And Sarah said, God hath made me to laugh, *so that* all that hear will laugh with me.

7 And she said, Who would have said unto Abraham, that Sarah should have given children suck? for I have born *him* a son in his old age.

Why did Sarah say, "God hath made me to laugh"? (21:6) "Although the King James Version (KJV) reports that Sarah laughed, reflecting a sense of disbelief, the JST states that Sarah 'rejoiced.' (It should be noted that the Hebrew word for *rejoice* in this scripture can be translated either 'rejoice' or 'laugh.' The name *Isaac* means 'laugh' and 'rejoice.')" (Black, *400 Questions and Answers about the Old Testament*, 50; see also JST, Genesis 21:5).

8 And the child grew, and was weaned: and Abraham made a great feast the *same* day that Isaac was weaned.

Why would this event cause such a celebration? (21:8) "Breast-feeding in traditional societies often continues much longer than in the West, so that a child may not be weaned until he is three (2 Macc 7:27). The importance of this occasion was marked by a great feast to celebrate it. . . . In a society where infant mortality was high, to reach the age of two or three would be regarded as a significant achievement, so this in part explains the magnitude of the celebrations. From now on Isaac looks relatively certain to be Abraham's heir" (Wenham, *Genesis 16–50*, 81).

Genesis 21:9–13. Hagar's Son, Ishmael, Makes Fun of Isaac

Why did Sarah act so harshly toward Hagar? (21:9–10) "Sarah's strong opinion that Hagar and Ishmael should leave the clan appears stark and selfish. The only background in the text to her perspective is that teenaged Ishmael 'mocked' young Isaac (Genesis 21:9–10). According to the apostle Paul, Ishmael 'persecuted' Isaac (Galatians 4:29). In his history of the Jewish people, Josephus claimed that Sarah loved Ishmael 'with an affection not inferior to that of her own son' until she feared that, due to the significant difference in the two boys' ages, Ishmael should 'do [Isaac] injuries when their father should be dead' (*Antiquities*, 1.12.3). Perhaps Sarah's servitude in Pharaoh's house years before heightened feelings of distrust for Hagar the Egyptian rather than forming a bond of sympathy" (Olson, *Women of the Old Testament*, 42). ⊕

How did God comfort Abraham? (21:12–13) "This revelation must have comforted Abraham. Ishmael was his son also. Here the Lord explains that Abraham's seed would grow through both Isaac and Ishmael, for God promised Abraham that he would become a 'father of many nations' (Genesis 17:4–5)" (Valletta, et al., *Old Testament for Latter-day Saint Families*, 43).

Genesis 21:14–21. God Saves Hagar and Her Son Ishmael

9 ¶ And Sarah saw the son of Hagar the Egyptian, which she had born unto Abraham, mocking.

10 Wherefore she said unto Abraham, Cast out this bondwoman and her son: for the son of this bondwoman shall not be heir with my son, *even* with Isaac.

11 And the thing was very grievous in Abraham's sight because of his son.

12 ¶ And God said unto Abraham, Let it not be grievous in thy sight because of the lad, and because of thy bondwoman; in all that Sarah hath said unto thee, hearken unto her voice; for in Isaac shall thy seed be called.

13 And also of the son of the bondwoman will I make a nation, because he *is* thy seed.

14 And Abraham rose up early in the morning, and took bread, and a bottle of water, and gave *it* unto Hagar, putting *it* on her shoulder, and the child, and sent her away: and she departed, and wandered in the wilderness of Beer-sheba.

15 And the water was spent in the bottle, and she cast the child under one of the shrubs.

16 And she went, and sat her down over against *him* a good way off, as it were a bowshot: for she said, Let me not see the death of the child. And she sat over against *him,* and lift up her voice, and wept.

17 And God heard the voice of the lad; and the angel of God called to Hagar out of heaven, and said unto her, What aileth thee, Hagar? fear not; for God hath heard the voice of the lad where he *is.*

18 Arise, lift up the lad, and hold him in thine hand; for I will make him a great nation.

19 And God opened her eyes, and she saw a well of water; and she went, and filled the bottle with water, and gave the lad drink.

20 And God was with the lad; and he grew, and dwelt in the wilderness, and became an archer.

21 And he dwelt in the wilderness of Paran: and his mother took him a wife out of the land of Egypt.

How did Ishmael's descendants become great? **(21:18)** "Hagar prefigures Israel. . . . A foreshadowing of Jacob's twelve sons, Hagar would become a mother of the twelve tribes of Ishmael, divinely destined to bless the earth. Centuries later, the apostle Paul drew on this symbolism to teach the restrictiveness of the law of Moses in contrast to the Lord's higher law. In the allegory, Hagar and her descendants represented the lesser law while Sarah and her descendants symbolized the law of Christ (Galatians 4:21–31). Both the higher law and the law of Moses came from God, but the higher law promises something greater. Ishmael's descendants, although great, would need to come to Isaac's descendants for the promises of the covenant and the Savior's greatest blessings" (Olson, *Women of the Old Testament,* 43–44). ⊕

22 ¶ And it came to pass at that time, that Abimelech and Phichol the chief captain of his host spake unto Abraham, saying, God *is* with thee in all that thou doest:

23 Now therefore swear unto me here by God that thou wilt not deal falsely with me, nor with my son, nor with my son's son: *but* according to the kindness that I have done unto thee, thou shalt do unto me, and to the land wherein thou hast sojourned.

24 And Abraham said, I will swear.

25 And Abraham reproved Abimelech because of a well of water, which Abimelech's servants had violently taken away.

26 And Abimelech said, I wot not who hath done this thing: neither didst thou tell me, neither yet heard I *of it,* but to day.

Genesis 21:22–34. Abraham Settles a Dispute with His Neighbor

27 And Abraham took sheep and oxen, and
gave them unto Abimelech; and both of
them made a covenant.

28 And Abraham set seven ewe lambs of the
flock by themselves.

29 And Abimelech said unto Abraham, What
mean these seven ewe lambs which thou hast
set by themselves?

30 And he said, For *these* seven ewe lambs
shalt thou take of my hand, that they may
be a witness unto me, that I have digged this
well.

31 Wherefore he called that place Beer-
sheba; because there they sware both of them.

32 Thus they made a covenant at Beer-sheba:
then Abimelech rose up, and Phichol the
chief captain of his host, and they returned
into the land of the Philistines.

33 ¶ And *Abraham* planted a grove in Beer-
sheba, and called there on the name of the
LORD, the everlasting God.

34 And Abraham sojourned in the Philistines'
land many days.

How was the covenant made binding on both Abimelech and Abraham? (21:30–32) "Abraham's Philistine neighbors, acknowledging to Abraham that 'God is with thee in all thou doest' (Gen. 21:22), proposed that a covenant of peace be made between them. People could see in Abraham's way of life and in his prudence evidences of the power of the living God in his life. So they made the covenant and named the well—which Abraham had dug and which Abimelech's servants had taken over but then restored—*Beer-sheva* (anglicized, *Beer-sheba*), 'Well of the Covenant.' Abraham gave Abimelech seven lambs in token of that agreement. The Hebrew root *sheva* bears the meaning of 'seven' and also of 'swearing' an oath in making a covenant" (Rasmussen, *Latter-day Saint Commentary on the Old Testament,* 51). ⊕

Who planted the grove in Beersheba? (21:32–33) The Prophet Joseph Smith changed this in his inspired translation of the Bible. "Abimelech, and Phicol, the chief captain of his hosts, rose up, and they planted a grove in Beer-sheba, and called there on the name of the Lord" (JST, Genesis 21:31).

CHAPTER 22

Abraham is commanded to sacrifice Isaac, his son—Both father and son yield to the will of God—Abraham's seed will be as the stars and the sand in number—In his seed, all nations will be blessed—Rebekah is born to Bethuel.

1 And it came to pass after these things, that
God did tempt Abraham, and said unto him,
Abraham: and he said, Behold, *here* I *am.*

2 And he said, Take now thy son, thine only
son Isaac, whom thou lovest, and get thee
into the land of Moriah; and offer him there
for a burnt offering upon one of the mountains which I will tell thee of.

Genesis 22:1–14. God Commands Abraham to Offer Isaac as a Sacrifice

Why would God ask Abraham to offer his only son as an offering? (22:1–2) The context for this passage is a "testing" or "proving" of Abraham, rather than God "tempting" (see Abr. 3:25). "The Lord told Abraham to take Isaac up on Mount Moriah and sacrifice him. Abraham believed God and knew that if he did offer the sacrifice that God would raise Isaac from the dead (see Heb. 11:17–19), so that in Isaac his seed would flourish according to the promises. The Book of Mormon tells us that the offering of Abraham on the

3 ¶ And Abraham rose up early in the morning, and saddled his ass, and took two of his young men with him, and Isaac his son, and clave the wood for the burnt offering, and rose up, and went unto the place of which God had told him.

4 Then on the third day Abraham lifted up his eyes, and saw the place afar off.

5 And Abraham said unto his young men, Abide ye here with the ass; and I and the lad will go yonder and worship, and come again to you.

6 And Abraham took the wood of the burnt offering, and laid *it* upon Isaac his son; and

mount, his willingness to sacrifice his only begotten son, was in similitude of the sacrifice of God our Father and his only son on the cross when our Lord worked out the infinite and eternal atoning sacrifice (Jacob 4:5)" (McConkie, "Promises Made to the Fathers," 57). ⊕

What role does Abraham's name play in this similitude of the Lord's sacrifice? (22:3) "Abraham obviously was a type or similitude of the Father. Interestingly enough, his name, *Abram*, means 'exalted father,' and *Abraham* means 'father of a great multitude' (see Genesis 17:5). Both are names appropriate of Heavenly Father" (*Old Testament Student Manual: Genesis–2 Samuel*, 77).

What do the number of days it took to travel between Beersheba and Moriah foreshadow? (22:4) "The journey from Mount Moriah back to their home in Beersheba, . . . took Abraham and Isaac three days, the same interval as that between the sacrifice of the Savior and his return to life as the resurrected Lord" (Nelson, *Power within Us*, 47).

Why did Isaac go willingly with his father? (22:5–6) "As we honor Abraham, we honor Isaac as well, for Jewish tradition holds that Isaac was no child, but a mature man who also knowingly and willing obeyed. If so, this component of the similitude further typified the willingness and obedience that characterized the atoning sacrifice of the Savior of the world" (Nelson, *Power within Us*, 47).

Sacrifice of Isaac: A Similitude of God's Sacrifice (Genesis 22:2–12)

"It was accounted unto Abraham in the wilderness to be obedient unto the commands of God in offering up his son Isaac, which is a similitude of God and his Only Begotten Son" (Jacob 4:5).

Isaac

1. Isaac was Abraham's only covenant son (see Gen. 22:2).
2. The sacrifice of Isaac took place in "the land of Moriah," or Jerusalem (Gen.22:2).
3. Isaac carried the wood for the sacrifice (see Gen. 22:6).
4. Isaac's limbs were bound upon the altar (see Gen. 22:9).
5. Isaac did not resist but was a willing sacrifice (see Gen. 22:9).
6. Isaac was to have his blood shed (see Gen. 22:10).
7. In the moment of sacrifice, an angel appeared to stop it (see Gen. 22:11–12).
8. Abraham loved God and obeyed Him and was willing to sacrifice his son (see Gen. 22:12).

Christ

1. Jesus is the Only Begotten Son of God (see John 3:16).
2. The sacrifice of Christ took place on Golgatha, at Jerusalem (see Mark 15:22).
3. Christ carried His cross (see John 19:17).
4. Christ's limbs were nailed to the cross (see Luke 23:33).
5. Christ did not resist, and willingly did the will of the Father (see Luke 22:42).
6. Jesus Christ shed His blood (see John 19:34; Luke 22:44).
7. During Christ's agony, an angel appeared to strengthen Him (see Luke 22:42).
8. God loves the world and sacrificed His Only Begotten Son (see John 3:16).

(Valletta, et al., *Old Testament for Latter-day Saint Families*, 47).

In what way does Isaac typify Christ? (22:6–7) "When they arrived at Moriah, the Genesis account says, 'Abraham took the wood of the burnt offering, and laid it upon Isaac his son' (Genesis 22:6). The Joseph Smith Translation, however, reads, 'laid it upon his back' (JST, Genesis 22:7). Some have seen in this action a similarity to Christ's carrying of the cross upon His shoulders on the way to His Crucifixion (see Clarke, *Bible Commentary*, 1:139; John 19:17)" (*Old Testament Student Manual: Genesis–2 Samuel*, 77).

How did God prove or test Abraham's faith? (22:11–12) "In spite of the mind-boggling contradictions of the situation, Abraham had faith to proceed. He had full confidence that *somehow* God could and would fulfill all his promises, even though the one through whom the promises were to come was bound on an altar and Abraham's knife was raised to slay him. It was not until the last, precarious moment that the Lord stopped Abraham. . . .

"What faith! What discipline! What a sterling example! No wonder Abraham is held up as the model" (Dahl, "Abrahamic Test," 57).

Why is Jehovah-jireh noteworthy? (22:14) "This epochal event occurred in 'the land of Moriah . . . upon one of the mountains, the place that later became the Temple Mount (Gen. 22:2*a–d*; commentary on Gen. 12:6–10). A map of Jerusalem (Bible Map [12]) reveals that the Garden Tomb and the Hill of Golgotha are on a higher part of the same mount or ridge northwest of the temple site; thus it may be that the Savior, the divine Seed of Abraham, was offered nearly two thousand years later on a higher eminence of the same mount where the birthright son of Abraham was a 'type' of Him" (Rasmussen, *Latter-day Saint Commentary on the Old Testament*, 52).

he took the fire in his hand, and a knife; and they went both of them together.

7 And Isaac spake unto Abraham his father, and said, My father: and he said, Here *am* I, my son. And he said, Behold the fire and the wood: but where *is* the lamb for a burnt offering?

8 And Abraham said, My son, God will provide himself a lamb for a burnt offering: so they went both of them together.

9 And they came to the place which God had told him of; and Abraham built an altar there, and laid the wood in order, and bound Isaac his son, and laid him on the altar upon the wood.

10 And Abraham stretched forth his hand, and took the knife to slay his son.

11 And the angel of the Lord called unto him out of heaven, and said, Abraham, Abraham: and he said, Here *am* I.

12 And he said, Lay not thine hand upon the lad, neither do thou any thing unto him: for now I know that thou fearest God, seeing thou hast not withheld thy son, thine only *son* from me.

13 And Abraham lifted up his eyes, and looked, and behold behind *him* a ram caught in a thicket by his horns: and Abraham went and took the ram, and offered him up for a burnt offering in the stead of his son.

14 And Abraham called the name of that place Jehovah-jireh: as it is said *to* this day, In the mount of the Lord it shall be seen.

Genesis 22:15–19. An Angel Reveals to Abraham His Blessings for Obeying God

15 ¶ And the angel of the LORD called unto
Abraham out of heaven the second time,

16 And said, By myself have I sworn, saith
the LORD, for because thou hast done this
thing, and hast not withheld thy son, thine
only *son:*

17 That in blessing I will bless thee, and in
multiplying I will multiply thy seed as the
stars of the heaven, and as the sand which *is*
upon the sea shore; and thy seed shall possess
the gate of his enemies;

18 And in thy seed shall all the nations of the
earth be blessed; because thou hast obeyed
my voice.

19 So Abraham returned unto his young
men, and they rose up and went together
to Beer-sheba; and Abraham dwelt at Beer-
sheba.

What did Abraham learn from this profound test? (22:15–17) "Why was Abraham commanded to go up on that mountain (traditionally Mount Moriah in Jerusalem) and offer as a sacrifice his only hope for the promised posterity? President [Hugh B.] Brown wisely replied, 'Abraham needed to learn something about Abraham.' By being tested, all of us will one day know how much our hearts are really set on the kingdom of God" (Madsen, *Joseph Smith the Prophet*, 93). ⊕

What did Abraham learn about the blessings that come from obedience? (22:18) "Abraham had been tried and tested, and for his faithfulness and obedience the Lord gave him this glorious promise: 'In thy seed shall all the nations of the earth be blessed; because thou hast obeyed my voice' (Genesis 22:18).

"Although we are not asked to prove our obedience in such a dramatic and heart-wrenching way, obedience is required of us as well.

"Declared President Joseph F. Smith in October 1873, 'Obedience is the first law of heaven.' . . .

"Obedience is the hallmark of prophets; it has provided strength and knowledge to them throughout the ages. It is essential for us to realize that we, as well, are entitled to this source of strength and knowledge" (Monson, "Obedience Brings Blessings," 90).

Genesis 22:20–24. Abraham Is Told about His Brother's Family

20 ¶ And it came to pass after these things,
that it was told Abraham, saying, Behold,
Milcah, she hath also born children unto thy
brother Nahor;

21 Huz his firstborn, and Buz his brother,
and Kemuel the father of Aram,

22 And Chesed, and Hazo, and Pildash, and
Jidlaph, and Bethuel.

23 And Bethuel begat Rebekah: these eight
Milcah did bear to Nahor, Abraham's brother.

24 And his concubine, whose name *was*
Reumah, she bare also Tebah, and Gaham,
and Thahash, and Maachah.

Who was Rebekah? (22:23) Rebekah was the "daughter of Bethuel and sister of Laban; married to Isaac (Gen. 22:23; 24); mother of Esau and Jacob (25:20–28)" (Bible Dictionary, "Rebekah"). "Rebekah is unique among the wives of the patriarchs in at least two ways. First, she alone has a consistently monogamous marriage; we know of no other woman who married Isaac.

Second, she plays a more active role in the Genesis narrative than her patriarch husband; her individuality and vitality among the covenant people is striking in stories of her qualifying as Isaac's wife, receiving revelation from God for their sons, and ensuring the bestowal of the birthright on Jacob, as God intended" (Olson, *Women of the Old Testament*, 49).

Genesis 23:1–20. Abraham Purchases a Burial Place for His Wife Sarah

Who were the sons of Heth? (23:3) "Heth [was] the forefather of the nation of the *Hittites* . . . called 'sons of Heth' (Gen. 23:3, 5, 7, 10, 16, 18, 20; 25:10; 49:32). Once we hear of the 'daughters of Heth' (27:46). . . . Heth is named as a son of Canaan. . . . The Hitties were, therefore, a Hamitic race. The NIV renders all references to the 'sons of Heth' as 'the Hittites'" (*New Unger's Bible Dictionary*, 566; see also Bible Dictionary, "Hittites").

Why does Abraham refer to himself as "a stranger and sojourner?" (23:4) Abraham referred to himself with these terms because he resided in a land that belonged to others (see Hebrews 11:8–9, 13). God promised Abraham that he would inherit the land of Canaan (see Genesis 13:15–18). However, that blessing was not fulfilled during his lifetime (see Acts 7:5). "Abraham's inheritance in Canaan, for himself and his seed after him, was to be an eternal inheritance, one that would endure in time and in eternity. This promise is the hope of Israel, the hope that the meek shall inherit the earth, first during the millennial era and finally in that same immortal state when the earth becomes a celestial sphere. . . . (see D&C 38:19–20)" (McConkie, *Doctrinal New Testament Commentary*, 2:71).

CHAPTER 23

Sarah dies and is buried in the cave of Machpelah, which Abraham buys from Ephron the Hittite.

1 And Sarah was an hundred and seven and twenty years old: *these were* the years of the life of Sarah.

2 And Sarah died in Kirjath-arba; the same *is* Hebron in the land of Canaan: and Abraham came to mourn for Sarah, and to weep for her.

3 ¶ And Abraham stood up from before his dead, and spake unto the sons of Heth, saying,

4 I *am* a stranger and a sojourner with you: give me a possession of a buryingplace with you, that I may bury my dead out of my sight.

5 And the children of Heth answered Abraham, saying unto him,

6 Hear us, my lord: thou *art* a mighty prince among us: in the choice of our sepulchres bury thy dead; none of us shall withhold from thee his sepulchre, but that thou mayest bury thy dead.

7 And Abraham stood up, and bowed himself to the people of the land, *even* to the children of Heth.

8 And he communed with them, saying, If it be your mind that I should bury my dead out of my sight; hear me, and entreat for me to Ephron the son of Zohar,

9 That he may give me the cave of Machpelah, which he hath, which *is* in the end of his field; for as much money as it is worth he shall give it me for a possession of a buryingplace amongst you.

10 And Ephron dwelt among the children of Heth: and Ephron the Hittite answered Abraham in the audience of the children of Heth, *even* of all that went in at the gate of his city, saying,

11 Nay, my lord, hear me: the field give I thee, and the cave that *is* therein, I give it thee; in the presence of the sons of my people give I it thee: bury thy dead.

12 And Abraham bowed down himself before the people of the land.

13 And he spake unto Ephron in the audience of the people of the land, saying, But if thou *wilt give it,* I pray thee, hear me: I will give thee money for the field; take *it* of me, and I will bury my dead there.

14 And Ephron answered Abraham, saying unto him,

15 My lord, hearken unto me: the land *is worth* four hundred shekels of silver; what *is* that betwixt me and thee? bury therefore thy dead.

16 And Abraham hearkened unto Ephron; and Abraham weighed to Ephron the silver, which he had named in the audience of the sons of Heth, four hundred shekels of silver, current *money* with the merchant.

17 ¶ And the field of Ephron, which *was* in Machpelah, which *was* before Mamre, the field, and the cave which *was* therein, and all the trees that *were* in the field, that *were* in all the borders round about, were made sure

Why is the cave of Machpelah important? (23:9) "Machpelah[, which means "doubling," was] the field and cave bought by Abraham (Gen. 23:9, 17), where were buried Sarah (23:19), Abraham (25:9), Isaac, Rebekah, and Leah (49:30–31), and Jacob (50:13). It was situated on the top of the hill on which Hebron was built. The traditional site is now occupied by a mosque" (Bible Dictionary, "Machpelah"). ⊕

What do we learn about Abraham as he buys this cave? (23:10–16) "The account of Abraham's purchase of a cave for [Sarah's] tomb in Machpelah gives additional insight into the character and reputation of Abraham. He was honest, considerate, persistent, and straightforward. The process of bargaining to make a purchase, or a contract, is still common in the Middle East, but usually the seller overstates the price rather than understates it. In this case the seller was trying to show favor and respect for the buyer; but the buyer, Abraham, was firm in doing what he considered to be right and just" (Rasmussen, *Latter-Day Saint Commentary on the Old Testament*, 52). ⊕

Why was a cave used to bury the dead? (23:11) "The negotiations here are not concerned with the rights to dig a hole and mark a grave. Contemporary burial practices favored rock-cut or cave tombs, which were meant to accommodate the clan through generations. Bodies would be laid out on rock shelves until nothing remained but the bones, at which point the bones would either be cleared to the back of the tomb or relocated into a container of some sort to make room for another body" (Walton, *Zondervan Illustrated Bible Backgrounds Commentary*, 1:99).

Why did Abraham weigh the shekels of silver? (23:16) "Three of the most common weights were the half-shekel (or bekah), shekel, and talent—the largest standard. . . . Since weights varied from locale to locale, . . . prophets throughout the Bible advocated using just weights and balances and warned against using deceitful ones (Deut. 25:13–15; Prov. 11:1; Micah 6:10–11). To check local weights, travelers carried their own sets and compared theirs with those of local merchants. This is what Abraham did when he bought a field from Ephron for 400 shekels of silver . . . weighing the amount against the 'current money with the merchant' (Gen. 23:16)" (Tice, "Bekahs, Shekels, and Talents," 30–31).

Genesis 24:1–9. Abraham Sends His Servant to Find a Wife for Isaac

How old was Abraham when he sent his servant to find Isaac a wife? (24:1) "The scriptures say, 'Abraham was an hundred years old, when his son Isaac was born unto him' (Genesis 21:5) and 'Isaac was forty years old when he took Rebekah to wife' (Genesis 25:20). Thus, Abraham was 140 years old at this time. But he was far from being on his deathbed. He died when he was 175 (Genesis 25:7–8), and in the meantime had another wife and six children (Genesis 25:1–2)" (Packard and Packard, *Feasting Upon the Word*, 66).

What did Abraham mean when he said, "Put, I pray thee, thy hand under my thigh"? (24:2, 9) "The most generally accepted explanation for the custom is derived by considering the proximity of the thigh to the organ of procreation, reflecting that the oath was important as it pertained to Abraham's posterity and the continuation of the covenant. But the Joseph Smith Translation changes thigh to hand, rendering the oath, 'Put, I pray thee, thy hand under my hand' in both references in Genesis 24. In this context, then, the description of making an oath by placing one's hand under another's hand may be suggesting the modern-day equivalent of shaking hands to seal an agreement" (Olson, *Women of the Old Testament*, 50).

Why was Isaac not to marry a Canaanite woman? (24:3) "The gospel teaches us to marry within our faith. Genesis emphasizes the importance of doing so by recording the efforts to obtain suitable wives for

18 Unto Abraham for a possession in the presence of the children of Heth, before all that went in at the gate of his city.

19 And after this, Abraham buried Sarah his wife in the cave of the field of Machpelah before Mamre: the same *is* Hebron in the land of Canaan.

20 And the field, and the cave that *is* therein, were made sure unto Abraham for a possession of a buryingplace by the sons of Heth.

CHAPTER 24

Abraham commands that Isaac shall not marry a Canaanite—The Lord guides Abraham's servant in choosing Rebekah as a wife for Isaac—Rebekah is blessed to be the mother of thousands of millions—She marries Isaac.

1 And Abraham was old, *and* well stricken in age: and the LORD had blessed Abraham in all things.

2 And Abraham said unto his eldest servant of his house, that ruled over all that he had, Put, I pray thee, thy hand under my thigh:

3 And I will make thee swear by the LORD, the God of heaven, and the God of the earth, that thou shalt not take a wife unto my son of the daughters of the Canaanites, among whom I dwell:

4 But thou shalt go unto my country, and to my kindred, and take a wife unto my son Isaac.

Isaac and Jacob. . . . Like modern Latter-day Saints in a similar situation, Abraham wanted his son to marry a righteous woman who worshiped the true God. A polytheist Canaanite would not be acceptable. Thus he sent his servant to Aram-naharaim, the ancestral home Haran, and instructed him to find a wife there for Isaac. . . . It is unlikely that the nationality or ethnicity of potential wives was at issue" (Jackson, *Restored Gospel and the Book of Genesis*, 147).

5 And the servant said unto him, Peradventure the woman will not be willing to follow me unto this land: must I needs bring thy son again unto the land from whence thou camest?

6 And Abraham said unto him, Beware thou that thou bring not my son thither again.

7 ¶ The LORD God of heaven, which took me from my father's house, and from the land of my kindred, and which spake unto me, and that sware unto me, saying, Unto thy seed will I give this land; he shall send his angel before thee, and thou shalt take a wife unto my son from thence.

8 And if the woman will not be willing to follow thee, then thou shalt be clear from this my oath: only bring not my son thither again.

9 And the servant put his hand under the thigh of Abraham his master, and sware to him concerning that matter.

Why was Abraham's servant worried about this charge? (24:5) Abraham gave strict conditions when he instructed his servant to find a wife for his son Isaac. "First, she must come from among Abraham's relatives back in Mesopotamia, not from among the Canaanites. Second, she must consent to marry Isaac sight unseen, for Abraham forbids his servant to take Isaac on the journey. Third, she must agree to leave home and family to make her home in Canaan (i.e., she must display a faith similar to Abraham's when he received God's call to leave Haran)" (Fee and Hubbard, *Eerdman's Companion to the Bible*, 95).

10 ¶ And the servant took ten camels of the camels of his master, and departed; for all the goods of his master *were* in his hand: and he arose, and went to Mesopotamia, unto the city of Nahor.

11 And he made his camels to kneel down without the city by a well of water at the time of the evening, *even* the time that women go out to draw *water*.

12 And he said, O LORD God of my master Abraham, I pray thee, send me good speed

Genesis 24:10–28. Abraham's Servant Prayerfully Finds Rebekah

this day, and shew kindness unto my master Abraham.

13 Behold, I stand *here* by the well of water; and the daughters of the men of the city come out to draw water:

14 And let it come to pass, that the damsel to whom I shall say, Let down thy pitcher, I pray thee, that I may drink; and she shall say, Drink, and I will give thy camels drink also: *let the same be* she *that* thou hast appointed for thy servant Isaac; and thereby shall I know that thou hast shewed kindness unto my master.

15 ¶ And it came to pass, before he had done speaking, that, behold, Rebekah came out, who was born to Bethuel, son of Milcah, the wife of Nahor, Abraham's brother, with her pitcher upon her shoulder.

16 And the damsel *was* very fair to look upon, a virgin, neither had any man known her: and she went down to the well, and filled her pitcher, and came up.

Why did the servant believe that the Lord would guide him in finding a wife for Isaac? (24:14) "The Lord cares deeply about the preparation for marriage of His sons and daughters. Although wedding customs vary in different nations, cultures, and situations, President Gordon B. Hinckley has counseled us to select our marriage companions 'carefully and wisely.' As is evident in this story, the Lord blesses those who desire to build an eternal family" (Hallen, "Rebekah," 39).

How were Rebekah and Isaac related? (24:15) "[Rebekah] was the sister of Laban and the daughter of Bethuel, son of Nahor, Abraham's brother (see Genesis 22:23)—thus she was Isaac's cousin" (Pinegar and Allen, *Old Testament Who's Who*, 156).

What did Abraham's servant immediately see in Rebekah? (24:16) Rebekah's beauty, purity, and worthiness are attested to by the Joseph Smith Translation: "And the damsel, being a virgin, very fair to look upon, such as the servant of Abraham had not seen, neither had any man known the like unto her" (JST, Genesis 24:16). "[Abraham] sends his servant on a long and dangerous journey to a place called Haran. The reason he must go there is clear—holy men need holy women to stand by their sides. . . . Rebekah was prepared and worthy to make and keep sacred covenants and to become a covenant wife of Isaac. She did not have to wait and prepare herself" (Dalton, "Be Not Moved!" 123–24).

17 And the servant ran to meet her, and said, Let me, I pray thee, drink a little water of thy pitcher.

18 And she said, Drink, my lord: and she hasted, and let down her pitcher upon her hand, and gave him drink.

19 And when she had done giving him drink, she said, I will draw *water* for thy camels also, until they have done drinking.

What can we learn about Rebekah's willingness to draw water? (24:17–19) "Culturally, if someone asked for water at a well, it would be unthinkable to not assist. However, providing water for the camels meant doing much extra. The text is clear that Rebekah drew enough for the camels to finish drinking and waited until the camels had enough in order to make sure her job was done. In all, she drew water for ten camels. On a long journey, camels can drink between twenty and fifty gallons of water. . . . Her offer to draw water for all the servant's camels was generous indeed!" (Muhlestein, *Essential Old Testament Companion*, 50–51).

20 And she hasted, and emptied her pitcher
into the trough, and ran again unto the well
to draw *water,* and drew for all his camels.

21 And the man wondering at her held his
peace, to wit whether the LORD had made his
journey prosperous or not.

Rebekah at the well.

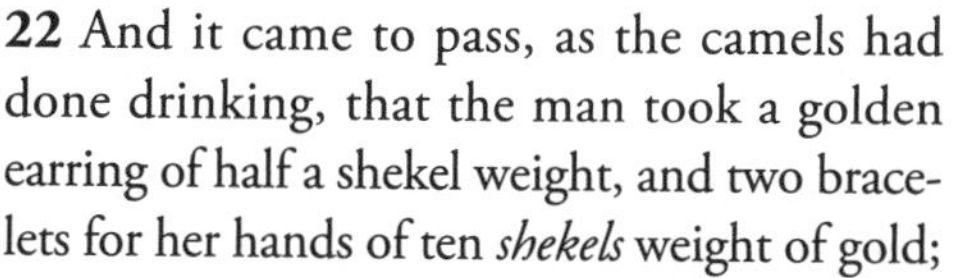

22 And it came to pass, as the camels had
done drinking, that the man took a golden
earring of half a shekel weight, and two bracelets for her hands of ten *shekels* weight of gold;

23 And said, Whose daughter *art* thou? tell
me, I pray thee: is there room *in* thy father's
house for us to lodge in?

24 And she said unto him, I *am* the daughter
of Bethuel the son of Milcah, which she bare
unto Nahor.

25 She said moreover unto him, We have
both straw and provender enough, and room
to lodge in.

26 And the man bowed down his head, and
worshipped the LORD.

27 And he said, Blessed *be* the LORD God of
my master Abraham, who hath not left destitute my master of his mercy and his truth:
I *being* in the way, the LORD led me to the
house of my master's brethren.

28 And the damsel ran, and told *them of* her
mother's house these things.

What was the earring given to Rebekah? (24:22) "The Hebrew word translated here as 'earring' should be 'ring' [see Genesis 24:22*a*]. The mention of 'shekels weight' makes it clear that these were generous gifts. That Laban notices the gifts his sister had received also shows how generous they were (see v. 30)" (Valletta, et al., *Old Testament for Latter-day Saint Families*, 50).

Why was Abraham's servant grateful to God? (24:26) Abraham's servant had received an immediate answer to his prayer for assistance (Genesis 24:12). He had witnessed the fulfillment of Abraham's promise that divine help would be given in his challenging task to find a wife for Isaac (Genesis 24:7).

Summary of Genesis 24:29–56

Abraham's servant meets Rebekah's family. He recounts Abraham's circumstances and explains why he was sent to them.

Genesis 24:57–60. Rebekah Nobly Chooses to Leave Her Family to Marry Isaac

Why did Rebekah willingly accept the opportunity to marry someone that she did not know? (24:58)

"Respect for the feelings and desires of the maiden involved was shown as Abraham had intended. . . . The gifts of silver, gold, and raiment given the bride-to-be and the precious things given her mother and brother were doubtless part of the dowry, or *mohar* (Gen. 24:51–56; [Bible Dictionary], "Marriage"). The bride was not 'purchased' thereby; she was in no sense the chattel of the husband. Her demeanor in the home, her exercise of agency and will, her initiative and effectiveness, both as an individual and as a marriage partner, illustrate that she was truly a help meet for her husband" (Rasmussen, *Latter-Day Saint Commentary on the Old Testament*, 53–54).

What does the blessing that Rebekah will be the "mother of thousands of millions" mean? (24:60)

"When Rebekah left her household, she was given a blessing. She was told: 'Be thou the mother of thousands of millions' (Gen. 24:60). That totals billions of people. This blessing came by the power of the Spirit and is speaking of the eternal increase that grows out of celestial marriage" (McConkie, "Promises Made to the Fathers," 58).

Genesis 24:61–67. Rebekah Meets and Marries Isaac

57 And they said, We will call the damsel,
and inquire at her mouth.

58 And they called Rebekah, and said unto
her, Wilt thou go with this man? And she
said, I will go.

59 And they sent away Rebekah their sister,
and her nurse, and Abraham's servant, and
his men.

60 And they blessed Rebekah, and said unto
her, Thou *art* our sister, be thou *the mother* of
thousands of millions, and let thy seed possess the gate of those which hate them.

61 ¶ And Rebekah arose, and her damsels,
and they rode upon the camels, and followed
the man: and the servant took Rebekah, and
went his way.

62 And Isaac came from the way of the well
Lahai-roi; for he dwelt in the south country.

63 And Isaac went out to meditate in the field
at the eventide: and he lifted up his eyes, and
saw, and, behold, the camels *were* coming.

64 And Rebekah lifted up her eyes, and
when she saw Isaac, she lighted off the camel.

65 For she *had* said unto the servant, What man *is* this that walketh in the field to meet us? And the servant *had* said, It *is* my master: therefore she took a veil, and covered herself.

66 And the servant told Isaac all things that he had done.

67 And Isaac brought her into his mother Sarah's tent, and took Rebekah, and she became his wife; and he loved her: and Isaac was comforted after his mother's *death*.

CHAPTER 25

Abraham marries, has descendants, dies, and is buried in the cave of Machpelah—His descendants through Ishmael are listed—Rebekah conceives, and Jacob and Esau struggle in her womb—The Lord reveals their destiny to Rebekah—Esau sells his birthright for a mess of pottage.

1 Then again Abraham took a wife, and her name *was* Keturah.

2 And she bare him Zimran, and Jokshan, and Medan, and Midian, and Ishbak, and Shuah.

3 And Jokshan begat Sheba, and Dedan. And the sons of Dedan were Asshurim, and Letushim, and Leummim.

4 And the sons of Midian; Ephah, and Epher, and Hanoch, and Abida, and Eldaah. All these *were* the children of Keturah.

5 ¶ And Abraham gave all that he had unto Isaac.

6 But unto the sons of the concubines, which Abraham had, Abraham gave gifts, and sent them away from Isaac his son, while he yet lived, eastward, unto the east country.

7 And these *are* the days of the years of Abraham's life which he lived, an hundred threescore and fifteen years.

Why did Rebekah veil her face? (24:65) "Since she had gone unveiled during the journey, Rebekah's veiling herself once Isaac is identified to her suggests that this is her way of demonstrating to him that she is his bride. Brides were veiled during the wedding but went unveiled as married women. Veil customs differed in various locations and times" (Walton, et al., *IVP Bible Background Commentary*, 56).

Genesis 25:1–11. Abraham Marries Keturah; Abraham Dies and Is Buried with His Wife Sarah in the Cave of Machpelah

Who was Keturah? (25:1) "Before Abraham died, he married a woman named Keturah, who bore six sons. Keturah is referred to in the scriptures as a concubine (see 1 Chronicles 1:32). . . . The word *concubine* is used to describe women who, in the time and culture in which they lived, were legally married to a man but had a lower social status than a wife" (*Old Testament Seminary Teacher Material* [2019], 160). In the cases of several ancient patriarchs, they were divinely authorized to marry concubines, as legal wives, in the new and everlasting covenant of marriage (see D&C 132:1, 37–39, 65).

What do we know about Abraham's children born to his concubines? (25:6) "The focus in the Old Testament is on Abraham's descendants through Sarah's son, Isaac, and Isaac's son Jacob. Through that lineage, a unique and special covenant relationship would continue. But we know also that from other marriages Abraham had additional children. . . .

"We learn through modern revelation that Abraham's marriages were not only in harmony with the Lord's will but were also eternal marriages.

. . . The Lord told Joseph Smith: 'Abraham received concubines, and they bore him children; and it was accounted unto him for righteousness, because they were given unto him, and he abode in my law" (D&C 132:29, 37)" (Jackson, *Restored Gospel and the Book of Genesis*, 145, 146).

Why did Abraham give gifts to the sons of his concubines and send them away? (25:6) Abraham provided "gifts," or an inheritance, to the sons of his concubines and sent them to live elsewhere. This was to protect Isaac who was the legitimate heir of the promised blessings of the covenant. Isaac's status as the birthright heir was emphasized in verse 11, where it shows that God blessed Isaac following Abraham's death (see Genesis 25:11; see also Bible Dictionary, "Birthright").

What does it mean that Abraham was being "gathered to his people"? (25:8) "'Gathered to his people' refers to being joined with his relatives in the afterlife" (Wenham, "Genesis," 57). "Abraham, the Friend of God, was faithful in all things. When the Lord spoke to the Prophet Joseph about him, it was revealed that Abraham is now in resurrected glory and has received his exaltation. Said the Lord: 'Abraham received all things, whatsoever he received, by revelation and commandment, by my word, saith the Lord, and hath entered into his exaltation and sitteth upon his throne' (D&C 132:29)" (Petersen, *Abraham, Friend of God*, 137).

Why was the well called Lahai-roi? (25:11) "*Beer Lahai Roi* means 'The Well of the One Who Lives and Who Sees Me.' At this well, an Angel of the Lord had appeared to Hagar (see 16:7–14)" (*NKJV Study Bible* [2018], 44).

Genesis 25:12–18. Ishmael Has Twelve Sons and He Dies at Age 137

What do we know about Ishmael's posterity? (25:12–18) Ishmael's large posterity is evidence of the fulfillment of God's promise to "multiply [Hagar's] seed exceedingly" (Genesis 16:10) and to "make [Ishmael] fruitful" (Genesis 17:20). ⊕

8 Then Abraham gave up the ghost, and died in a good old age, an old man, and full *of years;* and was gathered to his people.

9 And his sons Isaac and Ishmael buried him in the cave of Machpelah, in the field of Ephron the son of Zohar the Hittite, which *is* before Mamre;

10 The field which Abraham purchased of the sons of Heth: there was Abraham buried, and Sarah his wife.

11 ¶ And it came to pass after the death of Abraham, that God blessed his son Isaac; and Isaac dwelt by the well Lahai-roi.

12 ¶ Now these *are* the generations of Ishmael, Abraham's son, whom Hagar the Egyptian, Sarah's handmaid, bare unto Abraham:

13 And these *are* the names of the sons of Ishmael, by their names, according to their generations: the firstborn of Ishmael, Nebajoth; and Kedar, and Adbeel, and Mibsam,

14 And Mishma, and Dumah, and Massa,

15 Hadar, and Tema, Jetur, Naphish, and Kedemah:

16 These *are* the sons of Ishmael, and these *are* their names, by their towns, and by their castles; twelve princes according to their nations.

17 And these *are* the years of the life of Ishmael, an hundred and thirty and seven years: and he gave up the ghost and died; and was gathered unto his people.

18 And they dwelt from Havilah unto Shur, that *is* before Egypt, as thou goest toward Assyria: *and* he died in the presence of all his brethren.

19 ¶ And these *are* the generations of Isaac, Abraham's son: Abraham begat Isaac:

20 And Isaac was forty years old when he took Rebekah to wife, the daughter of Bethuel the Syrian of Padan-aram, the sister to Laban the Syrian.

21 And Isaac entreated the LORD for his wife, because she *was* barren: and the LORD was entreated of him, and Rebekah his wife conceived.

22 And the children struggled together within her; and she said, If *it be* so, why *am* I thus? And she went to inquire of the LORD.

23 And the LORD said unto her, Two nations *are* in thy womb, and two manner of people shall be separated from thy bowels; and *the one* people shall be stronger than *the other* people; and the elder shall serve the younger.

24 ¶ And when her days to be delivered were fulfilled, behold, *there were* twins in her womb.

Genesis 25:19–28. Rebekah Is Barren until God Blesses Her with Twins

What does it mean that Isaac "entreated the Lord" and that "the Lord was entreated by him"? (25:21) "The word 'entreat' means 'to make an earnest prayer or request, to beseech, implore.'" In the same verse, another form of the word is used in this passage to show "the prayer [was] received with favor by [Jehovah]" (*Theological Wordbook of the Old Testament*, 2:708, 709).

What did Rebekah do when she was concerned about her pregnancy? (25:22–23) "Concerned over struggles she felt in her womb, Rebekah did not go to family or friends for help but turned first to God to receive understanding and comfort. Furthermore, the biblical text is clear that Rebekah spoke directly to God and God responded directly to her, without her prophet-husband's intervention (Genesis 25:22–23). . . . She had already developed a close relationship with the Lord and the spiritual sensitivities necessary for clear communication. In response to her prayer, Rebekah learned prophetic truths: she would give birth to twin boys, each son would be a leader of a nation, and the second-born would lead the firstborn (Genesis 25:23). In time, all three prophecies were fulfilled" (Olson, *Women of the Old Testament*, 58). ⊕

Who was Esau? (25:25–27) "For nearly twenty years of their marriage, Rebekah was barren. Isaac entreated the Lord to open her womb. In answer to Isaac's prayer, Rebekah conceived. She struggled during her pregnancy. In response to her query about the struggle, the Lord told Rebekah that two nations were in her womb (see Gen. 25:22–23). Esau, whose name means 'hairy,' was the firstborn twin and favorite of Isaac. 'Esau's robust frame and 'rough' aspect were the types of a wild and daring nature. The peculiarities of his character soon began to develop; being a 'son of the desert,' he delighted to roam free and was impatient of the restraints of civilized or settled life' [Smith, *New Smith's Bible Dictionary*, 394]" (Black, *400 Questions and Answers about the Old Testament*, 53–54). ⊕

Why was Jacob considered to be "a plain man"? (25:27) "Jacob's and Esau's were the contrasting ways of hunter and husbandman. *Plain* (Gen. 25:27*b*) is used here to translate the same Hebrew word that is often translated *perfect* (Gen. 6:9; 17:1), *perfect* meaning, ideally, a 'man of integrity.' This word was used to describe Noah and to inspire Abraham. Remember also Jesus' challenge to his followers to become 'perfect' (Matt. 5:48). Jacob, like most of us, started out far from possessing that quality but achieved a degree of it later" (Rasmussen, *Latter-Day Saint Commentary on the Old Testament*, 56–57).

Genesis 25:29–34. Esau Sells His Birthright to His Younger Brother Jacob

What is pottage? (25:29) "Pottage" was a stew made of lentils (see Genesis 25:29–34). A lentil is "a small pea-like annual plant, the pods of which turn reddish-brown when boiled. It grows well even in bad soil and has provided an important source of nourishment in the Near East since ancient times" (*NIV Study Bible* [1985], 44).

Why was Esau also called Edom? (25:30) "Because Esau was red and sold his birthright for red pottage, he was called Edom, which means 'red' in Hebrew. His descendants would be the Edomites, who would fight against Israel from time to time. They inhabited the land just south of the Moabites. Thus, the land that ran parallel to the promised land on the other side of the Jordan was inhabited by, from north to south, the Ammonites (descendants of Lot through his daughter), the Moabites (descendants of Lot through his daughter), and the Edomites (descendants of Esau)" (Muhlestein, *Essential Old Testament Companion*, 52–53).

25 And the first came out red, all over like an hairy garment; and they called his name Esau.

26 And after that came his brother out, and his hand took hold on Esau's heel; and his name was called Jacob: and Isaac *was* threescore years old when she bare them.

27 And the boys grew: and Esau was a cunning hunter, a man of the field; and Jacob *was* a plain man, dwelling in tents.

28 And Isaac loved Esau, because he did eat of *his* venison: but Rebekah loved Jacob.

29 ¶ And Jacob sod pottage: and Esau came from the field, and he *was* faint:

30 And Esau said to Jacob, Feed me, I pray thee, with that same red *pottage;* for I *am* faint: therefore was his name called Edom.

31 And Jacob said, Sell me this day thy birthright.

32 And Esau said, Behold, I *am* at the point to die: and what profit shall this birthright do to me?

33 And Jacob said, Swear to me this day; and he sware unto him: and he sold his birthright unto Jacob.

What was the birthright? (25:31) "The firstborn son had the first right to receive the birthright inheritance and the birthright blessing. The birthright inheritance dealt with physical property. . . . The birthright blessing was spiritual. In the patriarchal order of the priesthood, it included the keys of the priesthood and the authority to preside as the religious leader of the family or clan. Rather than automatically belonging to the eldest son, it was given to the most righteous son. In fact, for all the patriarchal families with more than one son, the birthright blessing went to a younger son: Shem, Abraham, Isaac, Jacob, Joseph, and Ephraim each received the birthright blessing even though none of them was an eldest son" (Ludlow, *Unlocking the Old Testament*, 16–17).

34 Then Jacob gave Esau bread and pottage of lentiles; and he did eat and drink, and rose up, and went his way: thus Esau despised *his* birthright.

Why did Esau despise his birthright? (25:34) "This rationalization seems to reflect more scorn than hunger. Jacob would almost certainly have succored Esau freely if his life were in jeopardy. The point of this account seems to be primarily to show how little value Esau placed on the birthright. His immediate bodily needs were more important to him than the rights of the covenant. Additional evidence of this attitude is Esau's marriages to Canaanite women, which broke the covenant line (see Genesis 26:34–35). The birthright itself should have been a treasured thing" (*Old Testament Student Manual: Genesis–2 Samuel*, 85). ⊕

CHAPTER 26

The Lord promises Isaac posterity as the stars of heaven in number—In his seed, all nations will be blessed—The Lord prospers Isaac, temporally and spiritually, for Abraham's sake—Isaac offers sacrifices—Esau marries Hittite wives to the sorrow of his parents.

1 And there was a famine in the land, beside the first famine that was in the days of Abraham. And Isaac went unto Abimelech king of the Philistines unto Gerar.

2 And the LORD appeared unto him, and said, Go not down into Egypt; dwell in the land which I shall tell thee of:

3 Sojourn in this land, and I will be with thee, and will bless thee; for unto thee, and unto thy seed, I will give all these countries,

Genesis 26:1–5. The Lord Makes a Covenant with Isaac

What did the Lord promise Isaac? (26:3–5, 24) "Isaac was assured [by the Lord] that he could remain during the cyclical drought in the Philistine-held coastal plains near Gerar. The Lord would bless him there and confirm upon him the blessings of Abraham. The revelation declared that Abraham qualified to retain his blessings by obeying the Lord—keeping his charge, his commandments, his statutes and laws (Gen. 26:5)" (Rasmussen, *Latter-day Saint Commentary on the Old Testament*, 57). Isaac was an heir of the same covenant blessings that Jehovah promised to Abraham (Genesis 21:9–12). Latter-day revelation confirms that because Isaac was obedient to God's law, he has received exaltation and stands as an important example of righteousness (D&C 132:37; 133:55; 138:38–41).

Genesis 26:6–16. Isaac Dwells with the Philistines during a Famine

Why does Isaac tell the Philistines that Rebekah is his sister? (26:7) "The book of Genesis preserves three episodes in which a husband claims his wife is his sister: Abraham and Sarah in Egypt (Gen 12:10–20), Abraham and Sarah in the city/region of Gerar (Gen 20:1–18), and Isaac and Rebekah in Gerar (Gen 26:1–12). . . . [The first two passages] indicate Abraham's fear that because his wife Sarah was attractive she would be taken into the foreign ruler's harem and he would be killed. This suggests their perception that the ruler would be expected to negotiate with a woman's brother before taking her into his harem, but that the ruler would be more inclined to kill the husband if he desired his wife" (Holzapfel, et al., *Jehovah and the World of the Old Testament*, 52). See commentary in this volume for Genesis 12:13.

and I will perform the oath which I sware unto Abraham thy father;

4 And I will make thy seed to multiply as the stars of heaven, and will give unto thy seed all these countries; and in thy seed shall all the nations of the earth be blessed;

5 Because that Abraham obeyed my voice, and kept my charge, my commandments, my statutes, and my laws.

6 ¶ And Isaac dwelt in Gerar:

7 And the men of the place asked *him* of his wife; and he said, She *is* my sister: for he feared to say, *She is* my wife; lest, *said he,* the men of the place should kill me for Rebekah; because she *was* fair to look upon.

How Are We Made Partakers of the Abrahamic Covenant Today?

Abraham, Isaac, and Jacob all received covenant promises from the Lord (see Genesis 12:2–3; 26:3–4; 28:13–14). These same promises are made available in our day. "The Lord promised great blessings to the Prophet Joseph Smith and to other righteous Saints: 'Abraham received promises concerning his seed, and of the fruit of his loins . . . , which were to continue so long as they were in the world; . . . and out of the world should they continue as innumerable as the stars; or, if ye were to count the sand upon the seashore ye could not number them.

"'*This promise is yours also*, because ye are of Abraham, and the promise was made unto Abraham; and by this law is the continuation of the works of my Father, wherein he glorifieth himself' (D&C 132:30–31).

"Because our patriarchal blessings declare us to be of Abraham, we know the Lord is saying to each of us, 'This promise is yours also, because ye are of Abraham.'

"The Father is glorified by the exaltation of his children, and that exaltation depends on eternal marriage. This is one of the reasons marriage within the Lord's covenant is emphasized so strongly in the Old Testament. It was so critical that Abraham sent his servant on the long journey to search among his own people for a wife for his son Isaac, and Isaac sent Jacob to find a wife among the same people. By virtue of being members of the Church, part of our birthright is the privilege of going into the temple to be sealed to our companions, thus ensuring we too will have seed 'as innumerable as the stars.' This blessing will be realized in the eternities, or, as the Lord said, 'out of the world . . . they continue.' This promise is ours inasmuch as we are willing to enter 'into my law. . . . But if ye enter not into my law ye cannot receive the promise of my Father, which he made unto Abraham' (D&C 132:32–33)" (Wilcox, "Abrahamic Covenant" [*Ensign*], 44).

8 And it came to pass, when he had been there a long time, that Abimelech king of the Philistines looked out at a window, and saw, and, behold, Isaac *was* sporting with Rebekah his wife.

9 And Abimelech called Isaac, and said, Behold, of a surety she *is* thy wife: and how saidst thou, She *is* my sister? And Isaac said unto him, Because I said, Lest I die for her.

10 And Abimelech said, What *is* this thou hast done unto us? one of the people might lightly have lien with thy wife, and thou shouldest have brought guiltiness upon us.

11 And Abimelech charged all *his* people, saying, He that toucheth this man or his wife shall surely be put to death.

12 Then Isaac sowed in that land, and received in the same year an hundredfold: and the LORD blessed him.

13 And the man waxed great, and went forward, and grew until he became very great:

14 For he had possession of flocks, and possession of herds, and great store of servants: and the Philistines envied him.

15 For all the wells which his father's servants had digged in the days of Abraham his father, the Philistines had stopped them, and filled them with earth.

16 And Abimelech said unto Isaac, Go from us; for thou art much mightier than we.

Who were the Philistines? (26:8) "While the Philistines will become Israel's archenemy for a number of years, in the Genesis account the term refers to a group other than the one the Israelites will fight under Saul and David. Most likely, Abimelech and his people are Canaanites who lived in areas that would later be inhabited by Philistines. For that reason, later biblical authors refer to them as Philistines. Regardless of whether this is the reason, it is clear that the people referred to as Philistines before the time of Samuel were not the same cultural and genetic group that Israel would repeatedly fight beginning in the later period of the Judges" (Muhlestein, *Essential Old Testament Companion*, 54–55).

What did the phrase "waxed great" mean? (26:13–14) "The Hebrew words for 'waxed great' mean Isaac became very wealthy. He became so wealthy and had so many possessions that his neighbors 'envied him' or were jealous [see Genesis 26:13*a*]" (Valletta, et al., *Old Testament for Latter-day Saint Families*, 56).

Why did the Philistines vandalize the wells dug by Abraham's servants? (26:15) "In the semiarid land of southern Canaan, water is the most important commodity. Water sources are so necessary, rare, and valuable that whoever controls the water in effect controls the land. . . . Abraham had been successful in building many wells, but the local people covered them up when Abraham was gone. This allowed them to take control of the area. Isaac's flocks needed the wells, but his attempts to reopen or recreate these wells were met with great resistance. This is part of the posturing and strategy for dominance in the area. The treaty reached by Abimelech and Isaac demonstrates that they were roughly equal in power in the area" (Muhlestein, *Essential Old Testament Companion*, 55).

17 ¶ And Isaac departed thence, and pitched his tent in the valley of Gerar, and dwelt there.

Genesis 26:17–33. Isaac and His Household Move and Dig Wells

Why did Isaac give names to the wells? (26:18) "One way to designate ownership of a well or other natural resource is to give it a name. Once this has become its traditional name, title is not difficult to establish. It thus prevents later disputes or settles any that may arise" (Walton, et al., *IVP Bible Background Commentary*, 58).

What do we learn about Isaac when he decides to move? (26:20–22) To avoid the quarrels that arose over water, Isaac chose to dig new wells rather than claim his right to the wells previously dug by his father Abraham. "After patiently moving from well to well, Isaac finally went to the old well, Beer-sheba, where his father had made a covenant with the Philistines (Gen. 21:22–34). The Lord appeared at night and assured Isaac that he would continue to be blessed. . . . This is an example of the way Isaac carried out the Abrahamic mission, making known by his way of life the name, ways, and powers of the Lord (Abr. 1:18–19; 2:6–11; commentary on Gen. 26:1–5)" (Rasmussen, *Latter-Day Saint Commentary on the Old Testament*, 58).

How is Isaac an example to all followers of Jesus Christ? (26:25) "Isaac did not become an Abraham or a Jacob. He did not reach the heights of Abraham, called the 'father of the faithful' Nor was he as impressive as his son Israel, father of the twelve tribes. Yet Isaac is loved and revered. He worshiped God, cared for his home, and pursued his work. He is remembered simply as a man of peace. The eloquent simplicity of his life and his unique ability to lend importance to the commonplace made him great.

"Altar, tent, and well: his worship, his home, his work. These basic things of life signified his relationship to God, his family, and his fellowmen" (Tuttle, "Altar, Tent, Well," 66).

18 And Isaac digged again the wells of water, which they had digged in the days of Abraham his father; for the Philistines had stopped them after the death of Abraham: and he called their names after the names by which his father had called them.

19 And Isaac's servants digged in the valley, and found there a well of springing water.

20 And the herdmen of Gerar did strive with Isaac's herdmen, saying, The water *is* ours: and he called the name of the well Esek; because they strove with him.

21 And they digged another well, and strove for that also: and he called the name of it Sitnah.

22 And he removed from thence, and digged another well; and for that they strove not: and he called the name of it Rehoboth; and he said, For now the LORD hath made room for us, and we shall be fruitful in the land.

23 And he went up from thence to Beer-sheba.

24 And the LORD appeared unto him the same night, and said, I *am* the God of Abraham thy father: fear not, for I *am* with thee, and will bless thee, and multiply thy seed for my servant Abraham's sake.

25 And he builded an altar there, and called upon the name of the LORD, and pitched his tent there: and there Isaac's servants digged a well.

26 ¶ Then Abimelech went to him from Gerar, and Ahuzzath one of his friends, and Phichol the chief captain of his army.

27 And Isaac said unto them, Wherefore come ye to me, seeing ye hate me, and have sent me away from you?

28 And they said, We saw certainly that the LORD was with thee: and we said, Let there be now an oath betwixt us, *even* betwixt us and thee, and let us make a covenant with thee;

29 That thou wilt do us no hurt, as we have not touched thee, and as we have done unto thee nothing but good, and have sent thee away in peace: thou *art* now the blessed of the LORD.

30 And he made them a feast, and they did eat and drink.

31 And they rose up betimes in the morning, and sware one to another: and Isaac sent them away, and they departed from him in peace.

32 And it came to pass the same day, that Isaac's servants came, and told him concerning the well which they had digged, and said unto him, We have found water.

33 And he called it Shebah: therefore the name of the city *is* Beer-sheba unto this day.

34 ¶ And Esau was forty years old when he took to wife Judith the daughter of Beeri the Hittite, and Bashemath the daughter of Elon the Hittite:

35 Which were a grief of mind unto Isaac and to Rebekah.

Why did Abimelech want a covenant of peace with Isaac? (26:26–31) "Earlier Abimelech, acknowledging God's presence with Abraham (21:22), sought to enter into a covenant with him. Likewise, Abimelech acknowledged the Lord's presence with Isaac and sought to enter into a covenant with him. Isaac, like Abraham, was the source of blessing to those who sought him out. Isaac, like Abraham, trusted God and lived 'in peace' with his neighbors" (*Expositor's Bible Commentary [Abridged]*, 37).

Genesis 26:34–35. Isaac and Rebekah Are Saddened When Esau Marries Two Women of the Hittites

Who were the Hittites? (26:34) The Hittites were a polytheistic people who were not of the covenant nor were they followers of Jehovah. According to the Bible Dictionary: "The ancient people descended from Heth (Gen. 10:15). They were a branch of the Canaanites, and in the Bible the name denotes all the Canaanite (as distinguished from the Aramean or Syrian) nations that lived north of Palestine from the Orontes to the Euphrates (1 Kgs. 10:29; 2 Kgs. 7:6)" (Bible Dictionary, "Hittites").

Why did Isaac and Rebekah grieve over Esau's marriages? (26:35) Isaac and Rebekah waited many years to have children. They desired that their sons receive the blessings of the Abrahamic covenant. However, against the desire of his parents, Esau married two women of the Hittites. The "grief of mind" experienced by Isaac and Rebekah suggests that these women were not followers of Jehovah. In speaking of Esau's choice, Elder Bruce R. McConkie explained: "Esau married out of the Church; Esau did not marry in the everlasting covenant revealed to Abraham; Esau chose to live after the manner of the world, rather than to keep the standards of righteousness which the Lord had given them" (McConkie, "Our Sisters from the Beginning," 62).

CHAPTER 27

Rebekah guides Jacob in seeking blessings—Jacob is blessed to have dominion and rule over peoples and nations—Esau hates Jacob and plans to slay him—Rebekah fears that Jacob may marry one of the daughters of Heth.

Genesis 27:1–29. Rebekah Helps Jacob Receive the Birthright Blessings

1 And it came to pass, that when Isaac was old, and his eyes were dim, so that he could not see, he called Esau his eldest son, and said unto him, My son: and he said unto him, Behold, *here am* I.

2 And he said, Behold now, I am old, I know not the day of my death:

3 Now therefore take, I pray thee, thy weapons, thy quiver and thy bow, and go out to the field, and take me *some* venison;

4 And make me savoury meat, such as I love, and bring *it* to me, that I may eat; that my soul may bless thee before I die.

5 And Rebekah heard when Isaac spake to Esau his son. And Esau went to the field to hunt *for* venison, *and* to bring *it*.

6 ¶ And Rebekah spake unto Jacob her son, saying, Behold, I heard thy father speak unto Esau thy brother, saying,

Why did Rebekah ask Jacob to mislead Isaac? (27:6–8) "Without denigrating Isaac's authority and pure heart, Rebekah's leadership in orchestrating the birthright blessing is undeniable. As soon as she heard Isaac's instruction to Esau to 'make me savoury meat . . . that I may eat; that my soul may bless thee before I die' (Genesis 27:4), Rebekah sprang into action, advising Jacob to likewise bring fresh meat that could be prepared in the manner that his father loved. . . . Rebekah's confidence in pursuing her plan must stem in part from the revelation she received before her sons were born. She knew that God had chosen her younger son to receive the birthright" (Olson, *Women of the Old Testament*, 60).

7 Bring me venison, and make me savoury meat, that I may eat, and bless thee before the Lord before my death.

8 Now therefore, my son, obey my voice according to that which I command thee.

9 Go now to the flock, and fetch me from thence two good kids of the goats; and I will make them savoury meat for thy father, such as he loveth:

10 And thou shalt bring *it* to thy father, that he may eat, and that he may bless thee before his death.

11 And Jacob said to Rebekah his mother, Behold, Esau my brother *is* a hairy man, and I *am* a smooth man:

12 My father peradventure will feel me, and I shall seem to him as a deceiver; and I shall bring a curse upon me, and not a blessing.

13 And his mother said unto him, Upon me *be* thy curse, my son: only obey my voice, and go fetch me *them.*

14 And he went, and fetched, and brought *them* to his mother: and his mother made savoury meat, such as his father loved.

15 And Rebekah took goodly raiment of her eldest son Esau, which *were* with her in the house, and put them upon Jacob her younger son:

Why was Rebekah willing to proceed at the risk of being cursed? (27:12–13) "[It is difficult to know] why Rebekah was so strongly motivated that she risked a curse upon her son or herself (Gen. 27:6–13).... Her revelation about his destiny (Gen. 25:21–23) may have been a factor, but deceit does not get blessings (D&C 82:10*a*; 130:20–21; [Topical Guide], "Blessings"). It is not known whether she had ever shared her revelation with Isaac" (Rasmussen, *Latter-day Saint Commentary on the Old Testament*, 59).

How Did Rebekah's Plan Work? (Genesis 27:1–17)

"Rebekah's preparation of Jacob included covering him in Esau's 'goodly raiment' and putting animal skin over Jacob's skin (Genesis 27:15). Even as hairy as Esau reportedly was, it is difficult to imagine a man as [hairy] as a goat. According to a Jewish Midrash, Esau's 'wonderful garments . . . were the high-priestly raiment in which God had clothed Adam' which had been handed down to Noah, Shem, Abraham, Isaac, and finally to Esau, as Isaac's firstborn son (Ginzberg, *Legends*, 1:332). The resultant image is that the covenant son was covered with the skins of a sacrificed animal in preparation of inheriting all that his father had. Was Esau's goodly raiment symbolic of presiding priesthood authority and guardianship for the covenant that was originally given to Adam and Eve? Perhaps the covering was an outward reminder that the wearer was dedicated to the Lord to 'bear this ministry and Priesthood unto all nations' (Abraham 2:9)?

"Whatever the clothing's significance, Isaac became confused when the son before him smelled like Esau but sounded like Jacob. In the end, the feel of the goodly raiment, not the son's voice, determined the rightful recipient of the blessing. Rebekah's plan created the environment where Isaac, without his eyesight, received revelation to bestow the birthright on the foreordained son....

"A New Testament epistle confirms that Isaac acted in faith and not manipulation or deception when he blessed Jacob and Esau (Hebrews 11:20). Similarly, Jewish Midrashim assert that both Isaac and Rebekah were guided by the Spirit on this occasion (Ginzberg, *Legends*, 1:330, 334)....

"Rather than depicting Isaac as foolish and deceived, this event indicates his wisdom and commitment to follow God's commands. And rather than characterizing Rebekah as manipulative and conniving, the account shows her sagacity and efforts to enhance the power of their partnership" (Olson, *Women in the Old Testament*, 60–61).

16 And she put the skins of the kids of the goats upon his hands, and upon the smooth of his neck:

17 And she gave the savoury meat and the bread, which she had prepared, into the hand of her son Jacob.

18 ¶ And he came unto his father, and said, My father: and he said, Here *am* I; who *art* thou, my son?

19 And Jacob said unto his father, I *am* Esau thy firstborn; I have done according as thou badest me: arise, I pray thee, sit and eat of my venison, that thy soul may bless me.

20 And Isaac said unto his son, How *is it* that thou hast found *it* so quickly, my son? And he said, Because the LORD thy God brought *it* to me.

21 And Isaac said unto Jacob, Come near, I pray thee, that I may feel thee, my son, whether thou *be* my very son Esau or not.

22 And Jacob went near unto Isaac his father; and he felt him, and said, The voice *is* Jacob's voice, but the hands *are* the hands of Esau.

23 And he discerned him not, because his hands were hairy, as his brother Esau's hands: so he blessed him.

24 And he said, *Art* thou my very son Esau? And he said, I *am.*

25 And he said, Bring *it* near to me, and I will eat of my son's venison, that my soul may bless thee. And he brought *it* near to him, and he did eat: and he brought him wine, and he drank.

26 And his father Isaac said unto him, Come near now, and kiss me, my son.

27 And he came near, and kissed him: and he smelled the smell of his raiment, and blessed him, and said, See, the smell of my son *is* as the smell of a field which the LORD hath blessed:

What can we learn from Isaac's blessing? (27:27–29)
"The theme of 'blessing' points out the relationship of this narrative both to those that precede and those that follow. The promise to Abraham (12:2–3) is alluded to in the final words of the blessing. Similarly, Isaac's blessing foreshadows Jacob's later prophecy concerning

28 Therefore God give thee of the dew of heaven, and the fatness of the earth, and plenty of corn and wine:

29 Let people serve thee, and nations bow down to thee: be lord over thy brethren, and let thy mother's sons bow down to thee: cursed *be* every one that curseth thee, and blessed *be* he that blesseth thee.

30 ¶ And it came to pass, as soon as Isaac had made an end of blessing Jacob, and Jacob was yet scarce gone out from the presence of Isaac his father, that Esau his brother came in from his hunting.

31 And he also had made savoury meat, and brought it unto his father, and said unto his father, Let my father arise, and eat of his son's venison, that thy soul may bless me.

32 And Isaac his father said unto him, Who *art* thou? And he said, I *am* thy son, thy firstborn Esau.

33 And Isaac trembled very exceedingly, and said, Who? where *is* he that hath taken venison, and brought *it* me, and I have eaten of all before thou camest, and have blessed him? yea, *and* he shall be blessed.

34 And when Esau heard the words of his father, he cried with a great and exceeding bitter cry, and said unto his father, Bless me, *even* me also, O my father.

35 And he said, Thy brother came with subtilty, and hath taken away thy blessing.

36 And he said, Is not he rightly named Jacob? for he hath supplanted me these two times: he took away my birthright; and, behold, now he hath taken away my blessing. And he said, Hast thou not reserved a blessing for me?

37 And Isaac answered and said unto Esau, Behold, I have made him thy lord, and all his brethren have I given to him for servants;

the kingship of the house of Judah (cf. 49:8). Thus the words of Isaac are a crucial link in the development of the theme of the blessing of the seed of Abraham" (*Expositor's Bible Commentary [Abridged]*, 37–38).

Genesis 27:30–40. Esau Learns That Jacob Received the Birthright Blessing

Why didn't Isaac revoke the blessing given to Jacob? (27:30–35) "Whatever the explanation for the circumstances surrounding the reception of the blessing, one thing is perfectly clear. Priesthood holders are given the keys to bind *and loose* on earth and have that action validated in heaven (see Matthew 16:19). Once Isaac learned of the deception, he could have revoked the blessing and given it to Esau. Instead, he told Esau, 'Yea, and he shall be blessed' (Genesis 27:33). Later, . . . Isaac clearly gave him the blessing of Abraham (see Genesis 28:3–4), an additional proof that Jacob received the blessing meant for him and that Isaac confirmed it upon him. . . . Like anyone, he had then to live worthily in order to obtain the promised blessings" (*Old Testament Student Manual: Genesis–2 Samuel*, 85–86).

How are the "birthright" and the "blessing" different? (27:36) "The prerogative for both the birthright inheritance and the birthright blessing originally rested exclusively with the father. He could give gifts (as Abraham did to Keturah's sons in Gen. 25:6), pass out the inheritance (compare the story of the prodigal son who received his early in Luke 15:11–12) and pronounce the blessing (see Gen. 27:30–36). Jacob received his blessing initially through deceit, but eventually acquired it in full integrity. (See Gen. 27:30–36; 28:1–4.) After the time of Moses, the inheritance automatically went to the eldest son, regardless of whether or not his mother was the first or favored wife. (See Deut. 21:15–17.) The birthright blessing was still conditional" (Ludlow, *Unlocking the Old Testament*, 17). See commentary in this volume for Genesis 25:31.

and with corn and wine have I sustained
him: and what shall I do now unto thee, my
son?

38 And Esau said unto his father, Hast thou
but one blessing, my father? bless me, *even*
me also, O my father. And Esau lifted up his
voice, and wept.

39 And Isaac his father answered and said
unto him, Behold, thy dwelling shall be the
fatness of the earth, and of the dew of heaven
from above;

40 And by thy sword shalt thou live, and
shalt serve thy brother; and it shall come to
pass when thou shalt have the dominion, that
thou shalt break his yoke from off thy neck.

Genesis 27:41–46. Esau Hates Jacob and Plans to Kill Him

41 ¶ And Esau hated Jacob because of the
blessing wherewith his father blessed him:
and Esau said in his heart, The days of
mourning for my father are at hand; then
will I slay my brother Jacob.

42 And these words of Esau her elder son
were told to Rebekah: and she sent and called
Jacob her younger son, and said unto him,
Behold, thy brother Esau, as touching thee,
doth comfort himself, *purposing* to kill thee.

Why does Rebekah insist that Jacob go to her brother's house in Mesopotamia? (27:43–45)
Rebekah was worried that her sons "might either in the quarrel kill one another; or however, as one would be murdered, so the other, the murderer, must die by the hand of the civil magistrate, according to the law in Genesis 9:6; or should he escape justice being done him by men, yet the hand of God would find him; or if obliged to flee and hide himself, it would be as if he was not" (*John Gill's Exposition of the Whole Bible* [commentary on Genesis 27:45]).

How do faithful women, like Rebekah, protect and bless their families and others? (27:43–46)
"It would be impossible to measure the influence that such women have, not only on families but also on the Lord's Church, as wives, mothers, and grandmothers; as sisters and aunts; as teachers and leaders; and especially as exemplars and devout defenders of the faith. This has been true in every gospel dispensation

43 Now therefore, my son, obey my voice;
and arise, flee thou to Laban my brother to
Haran;

44 And tarry with him a few days, until thy
brother's fury turn away;

45 Until thy brother's anger turn away from
thee, and he forget *that* which thou hast done
to him: then I will send, and fetch thee from
thence: why should I be deprived also of you
both in one day?

46 And Rebekah said to Isaac, I am weary of
my life because of the daughters of Heth: if
Jacob take a wife of the daughters of Heth,
such as these *which are* of the daughters of
the land, what good shall my life do me?

CHAPTER 28

Isaac forbids Jacob to marry a Canaanite—He blesses Jacob and his seed with the blessings of Abraham—Esau marries a daughter of Ishmael—Jacob sees in vision a ladder reaching up into heaven—The Lord promises him seed as the dust of the earth in number—The Lord also promises Jacob that in him and in his seed all the families of the earth will be blessed—Jacob covenants to pay tithes.

1 And Isaac called Jacob, and blessed him, and charged him, and said unto him, Thou shalt not take a wife of the daughters of Canaan.

2 Arise, go to Padan-aram, to the house of Bethuel thy mother's father; and take thee a wife from thence of the daughters of Laban thy mother's brother.

3 And God Almighty bless thee, and make thee fruitful, and multiply thee, that thou mayest be a multitude of people;

4 And give thee the blessing of Abraham, to thee, and to thy seed with thee; that thou

since the days of Adam and Eve" (Nelson, "Plea to My Sisters," 95–96).

Why would Rebekah worry about Jacob's future wife? (27:46) "Our final glimpse of Rebekah is at the time of her plea that Jacob leave their home in Canaan to live with her brother's family in Haran. She was concerned about Jacob's physical safety in light of Esau's anger over the birthright blessing and about Jacob's spiritual safety should he, like his brother, marry outside the covenant" (Olson, *Women of the Old Testament*, 61).

Genesis 28:1–5. Isaac Commands Jacob to Find and Marry a Righteous Wife

Why did Isaac forbid Jacob to marry a Canaanite? (28:1) One generation before, Abraham told Isaac not to marry a Canaanite woman (see Genesis 24:3). The Canaanites worshipped idols and false gods. President Russell M. Nelson stated: "Celestial marriage is a pivotal part of preparation for eternal life. It requires one to be married to the right person, in the right place, by the right authority, and to obey that sacred covenant faithfully. Then one may be assured of exaltation in the celestial kingdom of God" ("Celestial Marriage," 94).

Why did Isaac instruct his servant to go to Padan-aram? (28:2) "When Abraham and Lot migrated from Haran to Canaan, the family of Nahor remained in the area at a place called Nahor. . . . The general area around Haran and Nahor was called Paddan-Aram (KJV, 'Padan'), Hebrew for 'road (or field) of Aram,' and was the home of Rebekah (Gen 25:20). It was to this same area that Jacob went to marry his wives and where most of his sons and his daughter were conceived (Gen 28:7)" (Holzapfel, et al., *Jehovah and the World of the Old Testament*, 50).

Why does Isaac confirm his previous promises to Jacob? (28:4) "Isaac both confirmed the Abrahamic covenant upon Jacob and acted to ensure that it could pass through Jacob's children. Considering his recent realization that the blessing he had intended for Esau had actually gone to Jacob, this is an important reconfirmation. As he counseled Jacob on selecting a wife, he specifically mentioned two key elements of the covenant: the promised land and innumerable posterity. He also charged Jacob to marry someone from the family, thus providing seed who could take part in the covenant" (Muhlestein, *Scripture Study Made Simple*, 49).

mayest inherit the land wherein thou art a stranger, which God gave unto Abraham.

5 And Isaac sent away Jacob: and he went to Padan-aram unto Laban, son of Bethuel the Syrian, the brother of Rebekah, Jacob's and Esau's mother.

Genesis 28:6–9. Esau Marries Contrary to His Father's Counsel

6 ¶ When Esau saw that Isaac had blessed Jacob, and sent him away to Padan-aram, to take him a wife from thence; and that as he blessed him he gave him a charge, saying, Thou shalt not take a wife of the daughters of Canaan;

7 And that Jacob obeyed his father and his mother, and was gone to Padan-aram;

8 And Esau seeing that the daughters of Canaan pleased not Isaac his father;

9 Then went Esau unto Ishmael, and took unto the wives which he had Mahalath the daughter of Ishmael Abraham's son, the sister of Nebajoth, to be his wife.

What was Esau trying to do when he married Mahalath? (28:7–9) "Esau attempted to find favor in Isaac's eyes by doing what Isaac wished. By marrying *Mahalath the daughter of Ishmael*, Esau believed he had met the standard Isaac had given Jacob (v. 1). Sadly, Esau could not regain his lost blessing. Mahalath is the same woman as Basemath, the daughter of Ishmael, in 36:2. Her name probably means 'Dance'" (*Nelson Study Bible* [NKJV], 51).

Jacob's Dream at Bethel (Genesis 28:10–15)

President Marion G. Romney described Jacob's experience and its relevance to our day: "Of all the marvelous things revealed during the restoration of the gospel, one of the most significant was a knowledge of temples and their purposes. . . .

"When Jacob traveled from Beersheba toward Haran, he had a dream in which he saw himself on the earth at the foot of a ladder that reached to heaven where the Lord stood above it. He beheld angels ascending and descending thereon, and Jacob realized that the covenants he made with the Lord there were the rungs on the ladder that he himself would have to climb in order to obtain the promised blessings—blessings that would entitle him to enter heaven and associate with the Lord.

"Because he had met the Lord and entered into covenants with him there, Jacob considered the site so sacred that he named the place Bethel, a contraction of Beth-Elohim, which means literally 'the House of the Lord.' He said of it: ' . . . this is none other but the house of God, and this is the gate of heaven' (Gen. 28:17).

"Jacob not only passed through the gate of heaven, but by living up to every covenant he also went all the way in. Of him and his forebears Abraham and Isaac, the Lord has said: ' . . . because they did none other things than that which they were commanded, they have entered into their exaltation, according to the promises, and sit upon thrones, and are not angels but are gods' (D&C 132:37).

"Temples are to us all what Bethel was to Jacob. Even more, they are also the gates to heaven for all of our unendowed kindred dead. We should all do our duty in bringing our loved ones through them" ("Temples—the Gates to Heaven," 16).

10 ¶ And Jacob went out from Beer-sheba, and went toward Haran.

11 And he lighted upon a certain place, and tarried there all night, because the sun was set; and he took of the stones of that place, and put *them for* his pillows, and lay down in that place to sleep.

12 And he dreamed, and behold a ladder set up on the earth, and the top of it reached to heaven: and behold the angels of God ascending and descending on it.

13 And, behold, the LORD stood above it, and said, I *am* the LORD God of Abraham thy father, and the God of Isaac: the land whereon thou liest, to thee will I give it, and to thy seed;

14 And thy seed shall be as the dust of the earth, and thou shalt spread abroad to the west, and to the east, and to the north, and to the south: and in thee and in thy seed shall all the families of the earth be blessed.

15 And, behold, I *am* with thee, and will keep thee in all *places* whither thou goest, and will bring thee again into this land; for I will not leave thee, until I have done *that* which I have spoken to thee of.

Genesis 28:10–15. Jacob Dreams of a Ladder Reaching to Heaven

What did Jacob see in his dream? (28:12) The Prophet Joseph Smith connected Jacob's experience with an experience of Paul's (see 2 Corinthians 12:2). "[The Apostle] Paul ascended into the third heavens, and he could understand the three principal rounds of Jacob's ladder—the telestial, the terrestrial, and the celestial glories or kingdoms, where Paul saw and heard things which were not lawful for him to utter" (Joseph Smith Papers, "History, 1838–1856, volume D-1," 1556).

What was Isaac promised at the end of his dream? (28:14–15) "Expectations of marriage and children would have intensified as he neared Haran" (Olson, *Women of the Old Testament*, 66). How might this experience have solidified the charge he received of his parents to "take thee a wife"?

How can I receive this promise from God? (28:15) "The Lord and Jacob exchanged covenants, just as we do now in our modern temples. As part of his covenant, the Lord promised Jacob: 'I am with thee, and will keep thee in all places whither thou goest. . . . I will not leave thee, until I have done that which I have spoken to thee of' (v. 15). This promised companionship and protection is a major blessing of faithful temple worship. . . . In return, 'Jacob vowed a vow, saying, If God will be with me, and will keep me in this way that I go . . . then shall the Lord be my God'" (Wilcox, *House of Glory*, 104).

16 ¶ And Jacob awaked out of his sleep, and he said, Surely the LORD is in this place; and I knew *it* not.

17 And he was afraid, and said, How dreadful *is* this place! this *is* none other but the house of God, and this *is* the gate of heaven.

18 And Jacob rose up early in the morning, and took the stone that he had put *for* his

Genesis 28:16–22. Jacob Names the Place of His Sacred Vision "Bethel"

Why would this be so "dreadful" and cause Jacob to be "afraid"? (28:17) The use of "afraid" and "dreadful" in this passage can be understood as meaning that Jacob was in awe, and said, "How awesome is this place!"

Why would Jacob declare this place as sacred and the house of God? (28:17–19) "The Latin *Templum* was the equivalent of the Hebrew *Beth Elohim*, and signified the abode of Deity; hence, as associated with Divine worship, it meant literally the HOUSE OF THE LORD" (Talmage, *House of the Lord*, 1). "What a powerful sight it must have been to see that the way to the presence of God is 'to receive all those ordinances in the house of the Lord, which are necessary for you, after you have departed this life, to enable you to walk back to the presence of the Father, passing the angels who stand as sentinels'" (Bragg, "Entering the Gate of Heaven," 66; see also *Brigham Young* [manual], 302).

How does the Joseph Smith Translation clarify the sacred context of the stone Jacob set up? (28:22) "And *the place of* this stone, which I have set for a pillar, shall be *the place of* God's house" (Wayment, *Complete Joseph Smith Translation of the Old Testament*, 105). Thus, the stone became a symbol of God's house. "Both by derivation and common usage the term 'temple,' in its literal application, is of restricted and specific meaning. The essential idea of a temple is and ever has been that of a *place* specially set apart for service regarded as sacred, and of real or assumed sanctity; in a more restricted sense, a temple is a building constructed for and exclusively devoted to sacred rites and ceremonies" (Talmage, *House of the Lord*, 1).

Why did Jacob promise God a tenth of his possessions? (28:22) "Jacob made a voluntary vow with the Lord to render a tenth of all that should come into his possession," wrote Elder James E. Talmage. "The institution of tithing [comes before] even the Mosaic dispensation, for we find both Abraham and Jacob paying tithes. Abraham, returning from a victorious battle, met Melchizedek king of Salem and 'priest of the most high God'; and, recognizing his priestly authority, 'gave him tithes of all.' . . . The Mosaic statutes were explicit in requiring tithes. . . .

"In the present dispensation the law of tithing has been given a place of great importance, and particular blessings have been promised for its faithful observance" (*Articles of Faith*, 394, 396).

pillows, and set it up *for* a pillar, and poured oil upon the top of it.

19 And he called the name of that place Beth-el: but the name of that city *was called* Luz at the first.

20 And Jacob vowed a vow, saying, If God will be with me, and will keep me in this way that I go, and will give me bread to eat, and raiment to put on,

21 So that I come again to my father's house in peace; then shall the LORD be my God:

22 And this stone, which I have set *for* a pillar, shall be God's house: and of all that thou shalt give me I will surely give the tenth unto thee.

CHAPTER 29

Jacob meets Rachel at the well—He serves Laban seven years for her—Laban gives to Jacob first Leah then Rachel in marriage—Jacob serves another seven years—Leah bears Reuben, Simeon, Levi, and Judah.

1 Then Jacob went on his journey, and came into the land of the people of the east.

2 And he looked, and behold a well in the field, and, lo, there *were* three flocks of sheep lying by it; for out of that well they watered the flocks: and a great stone *was* upon the well's mouth.

3 And thither were all the flocks gathered: and they rolled the stone from the well's mouth, and watered the sheep, and put the stone again upon the well's mouth in his place.

4 And Jacob said unto them, My brethren, whence *be* ye? And they said, Of Haran *are* we.

5 And he said unto them, Know ye Laban the son of Nahor? And they said, We know *him.*

6 And he said unto them, *Is* he well? And they said, *He is* well: and, behold, Rachel his daughter cometh with the sheep.

7 And he said, Lo, *it is* yet high day, neither *is it* time that the cattle should be gathered together: water ye the sheep, and go *and* feed *them.*

8 And they said, We cannot, until all the flocks be gathered together, and *till* they roll the stone from the well's mouth; then we water the sheep.

Genesis 29:1–14. Jacob Meets Rachel at a Well

Why would Jacob go to a well? (29:2–10) Anciently, "the 'centre' of the village was the water supply." Water, being the sustenance of life, brought many people together. "When surface water had disappeared, it was necessary to use well water for the sheep. It was customary to cover the wellhead with a large heavy stone that required several men to lift [see v. 8], thus protecting water rights." In this account Jacob seems to have removed the stone himself (v. 10). Regardless, Jacob's story is unfolding much like Abraham's servant Eliezer, who found Rebekah at the same well (Genesis 24:11). Culturally, "collecting water . . . [was] done by the older girls" (Gower, *Manners and Customs of Bible Times*, 187, 134, 44).

Who is Laban? (29:5) "Laban was the son of Bethuel, who was the youngest son of Nahor, brother of Abraham (see Genesis 22:22–23). Both Bethuel and Laban concurred with the proposal of Abraham's servant that Rebekah (Laban's sister) should become the wife of Isaac (see 24:50–51; compare 25:20). Years later, Isaac sent his son Jacob to Laban to seek a wife (28:1–5), resulting (after some subterfuge on the part of Laban) in Jacob's marrying not only Leah (Laban's older daughter), but also her sister Rachel, whom Jacob had initially chosen" (Allen and Pinegar, *Old Testament Who's Who*, 116).

What does "yet high day" mean? (29:7) "High day" has reference to "noonday, when the sun is highest; at which time in those hot countries flocks used to be made to lie down in shady places, and by still waters, to which the allusion is in Psalm 23:2; or however the sun was still up very high, and there was a great deal of the day yet to come" (*John Gill's Exposition of the Whole Bible* [commentary on Genesis 29:7]).

How is Jacob and Rachel's meeting at the well a pattern of other inspired encounters? (29:9) "In several ways Jacob's first encounter with Rachel and Laban parallels the encounter of Abraham's servant with Rebekah (24:10–33) and Moses' encounter with the daughters of Jethro (Exod. 2:15–21). (1) The hero (or his representative) goes to a distant land. (2) He stops at a well. (3) A girl (or girls) comes to the same well to draw water. (4) The hero draws water for them, or she for him. (5) The girl (or girls) returns home and reports the meeting to a brother or father. (6) The man is brought to the girl's house. (7) Subsequently a marriage takes place between the man at the well (or the man whom he represents) and the girl (or one of the girls) at the well" (Hamilton, *Book of Genesis, 18–50*, 253–54).

Why would Jacob have kissed Rachel in their first greeting? (29:11) "Kissing between relatives was part of the culture. Isaac had earlier asked his son to kiss him, thinking Jacob was Esau (27:26). Years later, Laban kissed his daughters and grandchildren goodbye (31:55). Jacob's kiss here was probably a familial kiss of a homesick young man who discovered a relative in a faraway place. But it was probably also prompted in part by the overwhelming emotion Jacob felt as he experienced God's providence in guiding him to his relatives" (*Quest Study Bible*, 43).

Genesis 29:15–20. Jacob Serves Laban for Seven Years

What does tradition tell us of Laban's daughters? (29:16–17) Ancient Jewish commentary "claims the girls were fraternal twins and that their marriages to their twin cousins Esau and Jacob were arranged by Rebekah and Laban from the time of the girls' births. . . . Another Jewish tradition explains that Leah's 'tender' or weak eyes were the result of continual weeping over a marriage contract that promised her to the wicked Esau. . . . The Bible gives no suggestion that any jealousy existed between the two sisters before their marriages. The implication is that Leah and Rachel were close confidantes who shared hopes and dreams for their future families" (Olson, *Women of the Old Testament*, 67). ⊕

9 ¶ And while he yet spake with them, Rachel came with her father's sheep: for she kept them.

10 And it came to pass, when Jacob saw Rachel the daughter of Laban his mother's brother, and the sheep of Laban his mother's brother, that Jacob went near, and rolled the stone from the well's mouth, and watered the flock of Laban his mother's brother.

11 And Jacob kissed Rachel, and lifted up his voice, and wept.

12 And Jacob told Rachel that he *was* her father's brother, and that he *was* Rebekah's son: and she ran and told her father.

13 And it came to pass, when Laban heard the tidings of Jacob his sister's son, that he ran to meet him, and embraced him, and kissed him, and brought him to his house. And he told Laban all these things.

14 And Laban said to him, Surely thou *art* my bone and my flesh. And he abode with him the space of a month.

15 ¶ And Laban said unto Jacob, Because thou *art* my brother, shouldest thou therefore serve me for nought? tell me, what *shall* thy wages *be?*

16 And Laban had two daughters: the name of the elder *was* Leah, and the name of the younger *was* Rachel.

17 Leah *was* tender eyed; but Rachel *was* beautiful and well favoured.

18 And Jacob loved Rachel; and said, I will serve thee seven years for Rachel thy younger daughter.

19 And Laban said, *It is* better that I give her to thee, than that I should give her to another man: abide with me.

What do we learn about Laban's two daughters? (29:17) "Many a reader has given Leah credit for melting, doelike eyes. The expression comes from Tyndale and was adopted by Coverdale and succeeding [Bible] versions. It is not a literal translation, for both the Hebrew and the Greek Septuagint say directly, 'The eyes of Leah were weak'" (Bridges and Weigle, *King James Bible Word Book*, 343). Others have translated "tender eyed" as gentle, sensitive, delicate, and young. On this last view, Hamilton suggests that "Leah may be older, but her eyes are the beautiful eyes of a person who looks much younger" (*Book of Genesis, 18–50*, 259).

20 And Jacob served seven years for Rachel; and they seemed unto him *but* a few days, for the love he had to her.

What are Jacob's feelings for Rachel? (29:20) "It's easy not to notice; there's much more than we're used to in those twenty-one simple words condensing seven years. But the force of that titanic tribute to the attractiveness of Rachel and the gallantry of Jacob and the power of the human soul for enduring loyalty is almost totally missed if you miss the unwritten detail between those lines, if you fail to put yourself imaginatively in Jacob's sandals herding goats and sheep in some place . . . for seven long sun-withered, wind-blasted, grit-flavored, sheep-stinking, backbreaking years of your own ardently impatient youth" (Walker, "Between Scriptural Lines," 63). ⊕

Genesis 29:21–31. Jacob Marries Leah and Rachel and Promises Seven More Years' Service

21 ¶ And Jacob said unto Laban, Give *me* my wife, for my days are fulfilled, that I may go in unto her.

22 And Laban gathered together all the men of the place, and made a feast.

23 And it came to pass in the evening, that he took Leah his daughter, and brought her to him; and he went in unto her.

24 And Laban gave unto his daughter Leah Zilpah his maid *for* an handmaid.

How much did the two sisters know of their father's plan? (29:23) "It was an early custom to give daughters in marriage according to their seniority; and it is worthy of remark that the oldest people now existing, next to the Jews, I mean the [Hindus], have this not merely as a custom, but as a positive law; and they deem it criminal to give a younger daughter in marriage while an elder daughter remains unmarried. . . . This was a custom at Mesopotamia; but Laban took care to conceal it from Jacob till after he had given him Leah" (*Adam Clarke's Commentary* [on Genesis 29:26]).

25 And it came to pass, that in the morning, behold, it *was* Leah: and he said to Laban, What *is* this thou hast done unto me? did not I serve with thee for Rachel? wherefore then hast thou beguiled me?

How did Jacob feel about being deceived? (29:25) "One can only imagine the pain that so many went through that night and the next morning. Leah knew she was marrying a man who would be disappointed to marry her and who loved someone else more. Jacob felt betrayed and upset and humiliated. Rachel seems to have loved Jacob, and had to endure knowing that her sister was marrying him instead of her. This state could only create a difficult and complicated family situation, which is what followed. While they all undoubtedly had much joy in their lives as well, there is no doubt that a great deal of heartache and difficulty would attend them" (Muhlestein, *Scripture Study Made Simple*, 51–52).

26 And Laban said, It must not be so done
in our country, to give the younger before the
firstborn.

27 Fulfil her week, and we will give thee this
also for the service which thou shalt serve
with me yet seven other years.

28 And Jacob did so, and fulfilled her week:
and he gave him Rachel his daughter to wife
also.

29 And Laban gave to Rachel his daughter
Bilhah his handmaid to be her maid.

Did Jacob actually "hate" his wife Leah? (29:30–31)

One Bible commentator observed, "[In] Hebrew a word, especially a verb, 'may be used to describe not merely its own actions, but also the omission or prevention of an opposite action'" (Hamilton, *Book of Genesis, 18–50*, 266).

Consequently, verse 30 may help clarify how the word *hate* is used in the next verse: "Jacob loved Rachel more than Leah." The phrasing "when the Lord saw that Leah was hated" could be an intentional use of hyperbole, exaggerating and contrasting the emotions felt by Jacob for his two wives, feelings that naturally would be intensified in their circumstances. This strong contrast emphasizes the Lord's subsequent actions, as He opens the womb of "hated" Leah while "loved" Rachel remains barren.

30 And he went in also unto Rachel, and he
loved also Rachel more than Leah, and served
with him yet seven other years.

31 ¶ And when the LORD saw that Leah *was*
hated, he opened her womb: but Rachel *was*
barren.

Genesis 29:32–35. Leah Bears Jacob Four Children

32 And Leah conceived, and bare a son, and
she called his name Reuben: for she said,
Surely the LORD hath looked upon my affliction; now therefore my husband will love me.

33 And she conceived again, and bare a son;
and said, Because the LORD hath heard that
I *was* hated, he hath therefore given me this
son also: and she called his name Simeon.

34 And she conceived again, and bare a son;
and said, Now this time will my husband be
joined unto me, because I have born him
three sons: therefore was his name called Levi.

35 And she conceived again, and bare a son:
and she said, Now will I praise the LORD:
therefore she called his name Judah; and left
bearing.

CHAPTER 30

Jacob marries Bilhah, and she bears Dan and Naphtali—He marries Zilpah, and she bears Gad and Asher—Leah bears Issachar and Zebulun and a daughter, Dinah—Then Rachel conceives and bears Joseph—Jacob works for Laban for wages of cattle and sheep.

1 And when Rachel saw that she bare Jacob no children, Rachel envied her sister; and said unto Jacob, Give me children, or else I die.

2 And Jacob's anger was kindled against Rachel: and he said, *Am* I in God's stead,

Genesis 30:1–8. Rachel Gives Bilhah to Jacob as a Wife, She Bears Children

What can we learn from Rachel's strong but unfulfilled desire to have children? (30:1–3) "For Rachel, not having children as Leah did had become unbearable. She decided that giving her servant as a wife to Jacob, so that she was vicariously providing him children, was the best available solution. Again we see how important family and children are. We

Jacob's Wives and Children

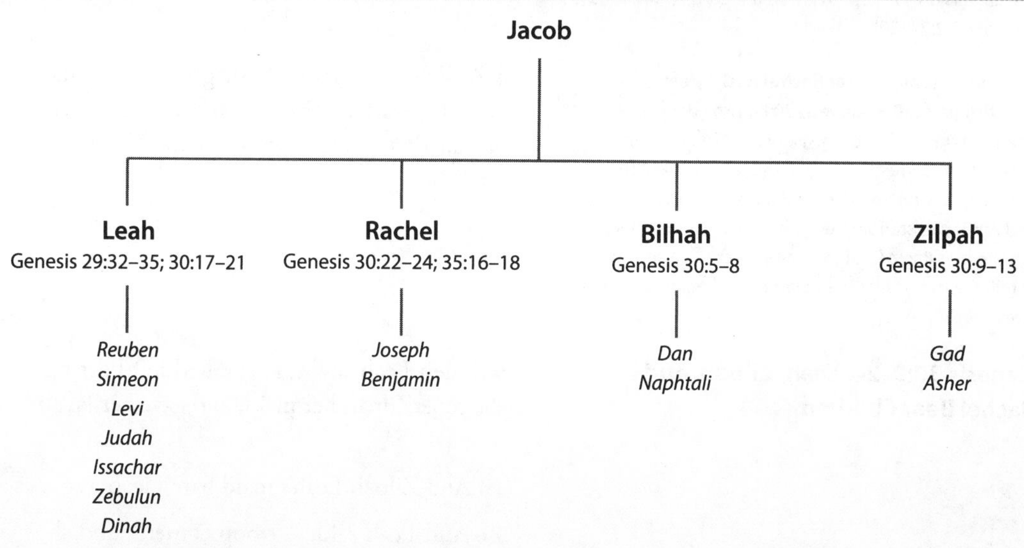

"Reuben ('see, a son') was the son of Leah.
"Simeon ('hearing' or 'that hears') was the son of Leah.
"Levi ('joined') was the son of Leah.
"Judah ('praise') was the son of Leah.
"Dan ('judging') was the son of Bilhah, Rachel's handmaid.
"Naphtali ('wrestling') was the son of Bilhah, Rachel's handmaid.
"Gad ('troop' or 'good fortune') was the son of Zilpah, Leah's handmaid.
"Asher ('my happiness') was the son of Zilpah, Leah's handmaid.
"Issachar ('God hath given me my reward') was the son of Leah.
"Zebelun ('dwelling') was the son of Leah.
"Joseph ('to add' or 'increase') was the son of Rachel.
"Benjamin ('son of my right hand' and 'son of my sorrows') was the son of Rachel"
(Black, *400 Questions and Answers about the Old Testament*, 55–56).

also see that even the greatest men and women of the scriptures went through difficult family trials. As we go through our own family difficulties, we can identify with the patriarchs and matriarchs of Genesis, all of whom had heart-wrenching family struggles" (Muhlestein, *Scripture Study Made Simple*, 53).

Why did Rachel give her handmaiden Bilhah to Jacob? (30:4) In the days of Abraham, "Sarah gave Hagar [Sarah's handmaid] to Abraham in accordance with law. . . . If a man's wife was childless, he was allowed to take a concubine and bring her into his house, though he was not to place her upon an equal footing with his first wife. This was the law in the country from which Abraham came. A concubine was a wife of inferior social rank" (Brewster, *Doctrine and Covenants Encyclopedia*, 317). Rachel exemplified great faith in accepting plural marriage (see D&C 132). She understood the work of the Father and that plural marriage is only accepted when the Lord commands it (see Jacob 2:27–30).

What does it mean that Rachel had "great wrestlings"? (30:8) Genesis 30:8*a* provides an alternate translation of the Hebrew: "The wrestlings of God have I wrestled with my sister." Rachel seems to be expressing an inner conflict of being barren and not understanding why the Lord was withholding the blessing of children, more so than a serious conflict with her sister. The name *Naphtali* means "my wrestling."

Genesis 30:9–24. Leah, Zilpah, and Rachel Bear Children

Why would Rachel want to have mandrakes? (30:14–15) "The mandrake was believed to aid a barren woman in conception; today it is known to have the effect of relaxing the womb" (Hurd, *Our Sisters in the Bible*, 29). Another author summarized: "A folk remedy

who hath withheld from thee the fruit of the womb?

3 And she said, Behold my maid Bilhah, go in unto her; and she shall bear upon my knees, that I may also have children by her.

4 And she gave him Bilhah her handmaid to wife: and Jacob went in unto her.

5 And Bilhah conceived, and bare Jacob a son.

6 And Rachel said, God hath judged me, and hath also heard my voice, and hath given me a son: therefore called she his name Dan.

7 And Bilhah Rachel's maid conceived again, and bare Jacob a second son.

8 And Rachel said, With great wrestlings have I wrestled with my sister, and I have prevailed: and she called his name Naphtali.

9 When Leah saw that she had left bearing, she took Zilpah her maid, and gave her Jacob to wife.

10 And Zilpah Leah's maid bare Jacob a son.

11 And Leah said, A troop cometh: and she called his name Gad.

12 And Zilpah Leah's maid bare Jacob a second son.

13 And Leah said, Happy am I, for the daughters will call me blessed: and she called his name Asher.

14 ¶ And Reuben went in the days of wheat harvest, and found mandrakes in the field, and brought them unto his mother Leah.

Then Rachel said to Leah, Give me, I pray thee, of thy son's mandrakes.

15 And she said unto her, *Is it* a small matter that thou hast taken my husband? and wouldest thou take away my son's mandrakes also? And Rachel said, Therefore he shall lie with thee to night for thy son's mandrakes.

16 And Jacob came out of the field in the evening, and Leah went out to meet him, and said, Thou must come in unto me; for surely I have hired thee with my son's mandrakes. And he lay with her that night.

17 And God hearkened unto Leah, and she conceived, and bare Jacob the fifth son.

18 And Leah said, God hath given me my hire, because I have given my maiden to my husband: and she called his name Issachar.

19 And Leah conceived again, and bare Jacob the sixth son.

20 And Leah said, God hath endued me *with* a good dowry; now will my husband dwell with me, because I have born him six sons: and she called his name Zebulun.

21 And afterwards she bare a daughter, and called her name Dinah.

22 ¶ And God remembered Rachel, and God hearkened to her, and opened her womb.

23 And she conceived, and bare a son; and said, God hath taken away my reproach:

24 And she called his name Joseph; and said, The LORD shall add to me another son.

for barrenness, the roots of the mandrake plant were believed to contain fertility-inducing powers. Mandrakes are an eastern plant that produces dainty purple flowers and roots that may have the appearance of a human body, or, to some analysts, the form of a newborn baby. Mandrake roots were probably boiled to prepare a tonic that was often taken as an aphrodisiac" (Olson, *Women of the Old Testament*, 71). ⊕

What does Rachel's blessing from God teach us? (30:22) "It may at times seem to us as though a loving Heavenly Father has misplaced our precious promises or He has put them on hold or filed them under the wrong name. Such were the feelings of Rachel. But with the passage of time, we encounter four of the most beautiful words in holy writ: 'And God remembered Rachel' (Genesis 30:22). . . .There are millions on earth today who are descendants of Joseph who have embraced the Abrahamic promise that through their efforts 'shall all the families of the earth be blessed, even with the blessings of the Gospel, which are the blessings of salvation, even of life eternal' (Abraham 2:11)" (Condie, "Claim the Exceeding Great and Precious Promises," 18).

What does the name Joseph mean? (30:22–24) "Finally Rachel turned to God, and he responded to her supplications. When at last a son was born to

Rachel, she named him Joseph (Heb., lit., 'He shall add'), hoping for yet more; but the name was more prophetic still, for it may be derived from a verb meaning 'He shall gather.' That concept seems implied in statements in later scriptures (e.g., Deut. 33:17; D&C 58:45)" (Rasmussen, *Latter-day Saint Commentary on the Old Testament*, 63).

Genesis 30:25–43. Jacob Settles His Wages with Laban

25 ¶ And it came to pass, when Rachel had born Joseph, that Jacob said unto Laban, Send me away, that I may go unto mine own place, and to my country.

26 Give *me* my wives and my children, for whom I have served thee, and let me go: for thou knowest my service which I have done thee.

27 And Laban said unto him, I pray thee, if I have found favour in thine eyes, *tarry: for* I have learned by experience that the LORD hath blessed me for thy sake.

28 And he said, Appoint me thy wages, and I will give *it.*

29 And he said unto him, Thou knowest how I have served thee, and how thy cattle was with me.

30 For *it was* little which thou hadst before I *came,* and it is *now* increased unto a multitude; and the LORD hath blessed thee since my coming: and now when shall I provide for mine own house also?

What are speckled, spotted, and ringstraked animals? (30:31–35) Animals of abnormal color (streaks, rings, spots, etc . . .) were described in such terms. "The Palestinian goat was commonly black. Speckled and spotted goats were a rarity, and for that reason Jacob's request for those goats . . . appeared very modest" (*Tyndale Bible Dictionary*, 55).

31 And he said, What shall I give thee? And Jacob said, Thou shalt not give me any thing: if thou wilt do this thing for me, I will again feed *and* keep thy flock:

32 I will pass through all thy flock to day, removing from thence all the speckled and spotted cattle, and all the brown cattle among the sheep, and the spotted and speckled among the goats: and *of such* shall be my hire.

33 So shall my righteousness answer for me in time to come, when it shall come for my hire before thy face: every one that *is* not speckled and spotted among the goats, and brown among the sheep, that shall be counted stolen with me.

34 And Laban said, Behold, I would it might be according to thy word.

35 And he removed that day the he goats that were ringstraked and spotted, and all the she goats that were speckled and spotted, *and* every one that had *some* white in it, and all the brown among the sheep, and gave *them* into the hand of his sons.

36 And he set three days' journey betwixt himself and Jacob: and Jacob fed the rest of Laban's flocks.

37 ¶ And Jacob took him rods of green poplar, and of the hazel and chestnut tree; and pilled white strakes in them, and made the white appear which *was* in the rods.

38 And he set the rods which he had pilled before the flocks in the gutters in the watering troughs when the flocks came to drink, that they should conceive when they came to drink.

39 And the flocks conceived before the rods, and brought forth cattle ringstraked, speckled, and spotted.

40 And Jacob did separate the lambs, and set the faces of the flocks toward the ringstraked, and all the brown in the flock of Laban; and he put his own flocks by themselves, and put them not unto Laban's cattle.

41 And it came to pass, whensoever the stronger cattle did conceive, that Jacob laid the rods before the eyes of the cattle in the gutters, that they might conceive among the rods.

42 But when the cattle were feeble, he put *them* not in: so the feebler were Laban's, and the stronger Jacob's.

43 And the man increased exceedingly, and had much cattle, and maidservants, and menservants, and camels, and asses.

What are the rods that Jacob prepared and placed in the watering troughs? (30:37–39) "Jacob's animal husbandry (Gen. 30:36–43) included the use of striped and spotted willows to engender conception of off-color animals, according to a superstition of the time. We know today that they could not have had any such effect, but similar superstitious beliefs and practices still persist in some places today. Jacob simply gave credit to the Lord for his increases in livestock" (Rasmussen, *Latter-day Saint Commentary on the Old Testament*, 63). ⊕

Genesis 31:1–16. Jacob Describes His Dream of Returning to the Land of His Inheritance to Leah and Rachel

Why did Laban seem to turn against Jacob? **(31:1–2)** "Laban had taken advantage of Jacob for 20 years. However, during his final six years with Laban, Jacob began to turn the tables on his father-in-law. As a result, Laban's sons felt that Jacob's prosperity threatened their inheritance, and Laban came to view his son-in-law as a liability" (*Quest Study Bible* [2003], 46).

How did God tell Jacob to return to his homeland? **(31:3–13)** Jacob explained to his wives that the angel of God spoke to him in a dream (see verse 11–13). "Continuous revelation from God to His Saints, through the Holy Ghost or by other means, such as visions, dreams, or visitations, makes possible daily guidance along true paths and leads the faithful soul to complete and eternal salvation in the celestial kingdom" (Bible Dictionary, "Revelation").

CHAPTER 31

The Lord commands Jacob to return to Canaan, and Jacob departs secretly—Laban pursues him; they resolve their differences and make a covenant of peace—Laban blesses his descendants, and he and Jacob part company.

1 And he heard the words of Laban's sons, saying, Jacob hath taken away all that *was* our father's; and of *that* which *was* our father's hath he gotten all this glory.

2 And Jacob beheld the countenance of Laban, and, behold, it *was* not toward him as before.

3 And the LORD said unto Jacob, Return unto the land of thy fathers, and to thy kindred; and I will be with thee.

4 And Jacob sent and called Rachel and Leah to the field unto his flock,

5 And said unto them, I see your father's countenance, that it *is* not toward me as before; but the God of my father hath been with me.

6 And ye know that with all my power I have served your father.

7 And your father hath deceived me, and changed my wages ten times; but God suffered him not to hurt me.

8 If he said thus, The speckled shall be thy wages; then all the cattle bare speckled: and if he said thus, The ringstraked shall be thy hire; then bare all the cattle ringstraked.

9 Thus God hath taken away the cattle of your father, and given *them* to me.

10 And it came to pass at the time that the cattle conceived, that I lifted up mine eyes, and saw in a dream, and, behold, the rams which leaped upon the cattle *were* ringstraked, speckled, and grisled.

11 And the angel of God spake unto me in a dream, *saying,* Jacob: And I said, Here *am* I.

12 And he said, Lift up now thine eyes, and see, all the rams which leap upon the cattle *are* ringstraked, speckled, and grisled: for I have seen all that Laban doeth unto thee.

13 I *am* the God of Beth-el, where thou anointedst the pillar, *and* where thou vowedst a vow unto me: now arise, get thee out from this land, and return unto the land of thy kindred.

14 And Rachel and Leah answered and said unto him, *Is there* yet any portion or inheritance for us in our father's house?

15 Are we not counted of him strangers? for he hath sold us, and hath quite devoured also our money.

16 For all the riches which God hath taken from our father, that *is* ours, and our children's: now then, whatsoever God hath said unto thee, do.

What does the visit of the angel of God to Jacob teach us? (31:11–13) "We read that Jacob, through his honesty of purpose, fair-dealing, and freedom from selfishness, was assisted by an holy Angel with information how to increase and multiply his flocks. . . . It is far better to build up the kingdom of God, in its temporal interests, by the Spirit of God and the wisdom of God, than by the spirit of man and the wisdom of man; on the latter principle we shall always fail, but on the former the results will always be successful" (Snow, in *Journal of Discourses*, 16:277).

How do Leah and Rachel respond to the Lord's command to leave? (31:16) "Betrayed by their earthly father, Leah and Rachel faced the temptation to distrust others close to them. . . . Here we see Rachel and Leah at their best. . . . Jacob was aware that obedience to God would anger his father-in-law and likely damage relationships between Leah and Rachel and their father. . . . Rachel and Leah were united and grounded in their reverence for God as they counseled their husband. . . . Whatever instances of rivalry had previously passed between the two sisters, they were exemplary when the moment of decision came; they were a family—bonded together in love and devotion to God and His purposes" (Olson, *Women of the Old Testament*, 75–76). ⊕

17 ¶ Then Jacob rose up, and set his sons and his wives upon camels;

18 And he carried away all his cattle, and all his goods which he had gotten, the cattle of his getting, which he had gotten in Padan-aram, for to go to Isaac his father in the land of Canaan.

19 And Laban went to shear his sheep: and Rachel had stolen the images that *were* her father's.

Genesis 31:17–42. Laban Contends with Jacob Concerning Property

Why would Rachel steal her father's images? (31:19) "One scholar theorized that these images were somehow tied in with the legal rights of inheritance (see Guthrie, *New Bible Commentary*,

104). If this theory is correct, the possessor of the teraphim had the right to inherit the father's property. This circumstance would explain why Rachel stole the images, since her father had 'stolen' her inheritance (see Genesis 31:14–16). It would also explain Laban's extreme agitation over their loss and Jacob's severe penalty offered against the guilty party (see Genesis 31:31)" (*Old Testament Student Manual: Genesis–2 Samuel*, 89). See commentary in this volume for Genesis 35:4.

20 And Jacob stole away unawares to Laban the Syrian, in that he told him not that he fled.

21 So he fled with all that he had; and he rose up, and passed over the river, and set his face *toward* the mount Gilead.

22 And it was told Laban on the third day that Jacob was fled.

23 And he took his brethren with him, and pursued after him seven days' journey; and they overtook him in the mount Gilead.

Why did the Lord warn Laban with a dream? (31:24) "Being accompanied by a number of his people, Laban might have used violence had he not been divinely warned in a dream to not impede his nephew's journey. Because of the dream, Laban allows Jacob and his daughters to escape into the borders of Canaan" (Woodger, et al., *Dreams as Revelation*, 38–39). Similarly, Abimelech was warned in a dream not to defile Sarah, Abraham's wife (see Genesis 20:3).

24 And God came to Laban the Syrian in a dream by night, and said unto him, Take heed that thou speak not to Jacob either good or bad.

Summary of Genesis 31:25–42

Laban confronts Jacob one more time before their separation. Jacob speaks of the past twenty years he has served under Laban. He testifies to Laban that Jehovah had been with him and protected him while he served in Laban's household.

Genesis 31:43–55. Jacob and Laban Separate with a Covenant

43 ¶ And Laban answered and said unto Jacob, *These* daughters *are* my daughters, and *these* children *are* my children, and *these* cattle *are* my cattle, and all that thou seest *is* mine: and what can I do this day unto these my daughters, or unto their children which they have born?

How did the arrangement of stones signify a covenant? (31:44–53) Laban proposed to make a covenant of peace with Jacob. The covenant was "properly recorded and notarized. . . . So Jacob took a stone and set it up as a pillar, while his brethren made a stone circle there and had a feast. . . . This stone witnesses in the middle between you and me today, says Laban, . . . the middle being that of the circle in which each party claimed a half (see 2 Samuel 2:13–15). 'Therefore was the name of it called Galeed' (*Gal-ed*,

44 Now therefore come thou, let us make a covenant, I and thou; and let it be for a witness between me and thee.

45 And Jacob took a stone, and set it up *for* a pillar.

46 And Jacob said unto his brethren, Gather stones; and they took stones, and made an heap: and they did eat there upon the heap.

47 And Laban called it Jegar-sahadutha: but Jacob called it Galeed.

48 And Laban said, This heap *is* a witness between me and thee this day. Therefore was the name of it called Galeed;

49 And Mizpah; for he said, The LORD watch between me and thee, when we are absent one from another.

50 If thou shalt afflict my daughters, or if thou shalt take *other* wives beside my daughters, no man *is* with us; see, God *is* witness betwixt me and thee.

51 And Laban said to Jacob, Behold this heap, and behold *this* pillar, which I have cast betwixt me and thee;

52 This heap *be* witness, and *this* pillar *be* witness, that I will not pass over this heap to thee, and that thou shalt not pass over this heap and this pillar unto me, for harm.

53 The God of Abraham, and the God of Nahor, the God of their father, judge betwixt us. And Jacob sware by the fear of his father Isaac.

54 Then Jacob offered sacrifice upon the mount, and called his brethren to eat bread: and they did eat bread, and tarried all night in the mount.

55 And early in the morning Laban rose up, and kissed his sons and his daughters, and blessed them: and Laban departed, and returned unto his place.

the circle of the sign or token)" (Parry, *Temples of the Ancient World*, 580).

Why did Jacob conclude his treaty with Laban with a sacrifice? (31:54) "The entire treaty-making process is sealed by a sacrificial meal of which all present partake" (Sarna, *Genesis*, 222). "The offering of sacrifice has ever been connected and forms a part of the duties of the Priesthood. It began with the Priesthood, and will be continued until after the coming of Christ, from generation to generation. We frequently have mention made of the offering of sacrifice by the servants of the Most High in ancient days prior to the law of Moses; which ordinances will be continued when the Priesthood is restored with all its authority, power, and blessings" (Joseph Smith Papers, "History, 1838–1856, volume C-1 [addenda]," 18 [addenda]).

Genesis 32:1–12. Jacob Prepares to Meet Esau

Why were heavenly messengers sent to help Jacob and his family? (32:1–2) "In a magnificent display of His care for him, God allowed Jacob to see that he was not traveling alone. . . . Jacob discovered that God's armies were encamped around his family's camp" (*Nelson Study Bible* [NKJV], 57). Jacob, realizing that his family camp was accompanied by God's host, referred to the place as "Mahanaim," meaning "two hosts, or camps" (see Gen. 32:2*a* and *b*).

Where is Edom? (32:3) "This country lay south of the Dead Sea, having Moab on the north and the Dead Sea on the northwest. It was not included within the limits of the land of Israel (Deut. 2:5; Josh. 24:4). From the time of the Maccabees it was known as Idumea" (Bible Dictionary, "Edom").

Why did Jacob want his messengers to show humility when meeting his brother? (32:3–5) "Hoping to ingratiate himself with Esau, who, Jacob believed, had been angry with him for twenty years, Jacob instructed the messengers to use deferential, even obsequious [flattering], language. . . . Jacob would publicly acknowledge Esau as his older brother" (Prager, *Rational Bible*, 382).

Why was Jacob so afraid? (32:6–8) Based upon the messenger's report, as well as his past relationship with Esau, Jacob was afraid and distressed. Jacob surely remembered that Esau had wanted to kill Jacob after losing the birthright blessing (see Genesis 27:41–42). Jacob was concerned that Esau's anger would extend to his family. This distress led Jacob to plead with the Lord for deliverance (Genesis 32:11). Everyone in mortality will experience fear and distress. "We live in a world of fear today. But there is no place for fear among the Latter-day Saints, among men and women who keep the commandments, who place their trust in the Almighty, who are not afraid to get down on their knees and pray to our Heavenly Father" (Benson, *Teachings of Ezra Taft Benson*, 399).

CHAPTER 32

Jacob sees angels—He asks God to preserve him from Esau, for whom he prepares presents—He wrestles all night with a messenger of God—Jacob's name is changed to Israel—He sees God face to face.

1 And Jacob went on his way, and the angels of God met him.

2 And when Jacob saw them, he said, This *is* God's host: and he called the name of that place Mahanaim.

3 And Jacob sent messengers before him to Esau his brother unto the land of Seir, the country of Edom.

4 And he commanded them, saying, Thus shall ye speak unto my lord Esau; Thy servant Jacob saith thus, I have sojourned with Laban, and stayed there until now:

5 And I have oxen, and asses, flocks, and menservants, and womenservants: and I have sent to tell my lord, that I may find grace in thy sight.

6 ¶ And the messengers returned to Jacob, saying, We came to thy brother Esau, and also he cometh to meet thee, and four hundred men with him.

7 Then Jacob was greatly afraid and distressed: and he divided the people that *was* with him, and the flocks, and herds, and the camels, into two bands;

8 And said, If Esau come to the one company, and smite it, then the other company which is left shall escape.

9 ¶ And Jacob said, O God of my father Abraham, and God of my father Isaac, the LORD which saidst unto me, Return unto thy country, and to thy kindred, and I will deal well with thee:

10 I am not worthy of the least of all the mercies, and of all the truth, which thou hast shewed unto thy servant; for with my staff I passed over this Jordan; and now I am become two bands.

11 Deliver me, I pray thee, from the hand of my brother, from the hand of Esau: for I fear him, lest he will come and smite me, *and* the mother with the children.

12 And thou saidst, I will surely do thee good, and make thy seed as the sand of the sea, which cannot be numbered for multitude.

13 ¶ And he lodged there that same night; and took of that which came to his hand a present for Esau his brother;

14 Two hundred she goats, and twenty he goats, two hundred ewes, and twenty rams,

15 Thirty milch camels with their colts, forty kine, and ten bulls, twenty she asses, and ten foals.

16 And he delivered *them* into the hand of his servants, every drove by themselves; and said unto his servants, Pass over before me, and put a space betwixt drove and drove.

17 And he commanded the foremost, saying, When Esau my brother meeteth thee, and asketh thee, saying, Whose *art* thou? and whither goest thou? and whose *are* these before thee?

18 Then thou shalt say, *They be* thy servant Jacob's; it *is* a present sent unto my lord Esau: and, behold, also he *is* behind us.

19 And so commanded he the second, and the third, and all that followed the droves, saying, On this manner shall ye speak unto Esau, when ye find him.

20 And say ye moreover, Behold, thy servant Jacob *is* behind us. For he said, I will appease

Genesis 32:13–23. Jacob Sends Gifts to His Brother Esau

Why would Jacob prepare gifts for his brother? (32:13–23) "Jacob selected a present . . . for his brother. The 520 animals Jacob selected was a sizeable gift and is a good indication of God's blessing him over the past six years. He left nothing to chance but instructed his servants what to say as they presented the gift to Esau in three installments. . . . Jacob hoped to blunt the force of Esau's past anger and deflect it with the gift" (*Zondervan KJV Commentary*, 58).

him with the present that goeth before me,
and afterward I will see his face; peradventure
he will accept of me.

21 So went the present over before him: and
himself lodged that night in the company.

22 And he rose up that night, and took his
two wives, and his two womenservants, and
his eleven sons, and passed over the ford
Jabbok.

23 And he took them, and sent them over
the brook, and sent over that he had.

24 ¶ And Jacob was left alone; and there
wrestled a man with him until the breaking
of the day.

25 And when he saw that he prevailed not
against him, he touched the hollow of his
thigh; and the hollow of Jacob's thigh was
out of joint, as he wrestled with him.

26 And he said, Let me go, for the day breaketh. And he said, I will not let thee go, except thou bless me.

27 And he said unto him, What *is* thy name?
And he said, Jacob.

28 And he said, Thy name shall be called no
more Jacob, but Israel: for as a prince hast
thou power with God and with men, and
hast prevailed.

29 And Jacob asked *him*, and said, Tell *me*, I
pray thee, thy name. And he said, Wherefore
is it *that* thou dost ask after my name? And
he blessed him there.

Genesis 32:24–32. The Lord Appears to Jacob and Changes His Name to Israel

Whom did Jacob wrestle with? (32:24) "Most scholars believe Jacob wrestled with an angel, but President Joseph Fielding Smith explained why this explanation could not be true: 'Who wrestled with Jacob on Mount Peniel? The scriptures say it was a man. The Bible interpreters say it was an angel. More than likely it was a messenger sent to Jacob to give him the blessing. To think he wrestled and held an angel who couldn't get away, is out of the question. The term *angel* as used in the scriptures, at times, refers to [human] messengers who are sent with some important instruction. Later in this chapter when Jacob said he had beheld the Lord, that did not have reference to his wrestling' (Smith, *Doctrines of Salvation*, 1:17)" (*Old Testament Student Manual: Genesis–2 Samuel*, 89). ⊕

What can we learn from Jacob's spiritual "wrestle"? (32:26) Elder Jeffrey R. Holland taught: "If you are struggling with self-control in what you look at or listen to, in what you say or what you do, I ask you to pray to your Father in Heaven for help. . . . Wrestle like Jacob did with the angel, refusing to let go until a blessing had come" ("Sanctify Yourselves," 39). ⊕

Why was Jacob's name changed? (32:28) This messenger from God had authority to change Jacob's name to Israel, meaning "one who prevails with God" or "let God prevail." Ellis Rasmussen suggested, "The new name seems to symbolize the end of his past ways and contrast them with the way he could succeed as a true patriarch, by letting God prevail in guiding his emerging mission" (*Latter-day Saint Commentary on the Old Testament*, 65). Susan Easton Black added, "While specific to Jacob, the name *Israel* equally applies to his descendants (see 2 Sam. 1:24), to a land in the Middle East, and to the Northern Kingdom. The apostle Paul claimed that *Israel* also applied to true believers in Jesus Christ (see Rom. 10:1; Gal. 6:16; Eph. 2:12)" (Black, *400 Questions and Answers about the Old Testament*, 57).

30 And Jacob called the name of the place Peniel: for I have seen God face to face, and my life is preserved.

31 And as he passed over Penuel the sun rose upon him, and he halted upon his thigh.

32 Therefore the children of Israel eat not *of* the sinew which shrank, which *is* upon the hollow of the thigh, unto this day: because he touched the hollow of Jacob's thigh in the sinew that shrank.

Why was Jacob privileged to see God face to face? (32:30) Jesus Christ has made himself known to many people in many situations. (See examples in Exodus 33:11; Abraham 2:12; Ether 3:7–16; D&C 107:53–54.) The Prophet Joseph Smith taught that when an individual strives to live the doctrine of Christ and desires righteousness, and when the Lord "thoroughly" proves that individual, he or she "will have the personage of Jesus Christ to attend him [or her] . . . and the Lord will teach him [or her] face to face" (Joseph Smith Papers, "History, 1838–1856, volume C-1 [addenda]," 9).

CHAPTER 33

Jacob and Esau meet and are reconciled—Esau receives Jacob's presents—Jacob settles in Canaan, where he builds an altar.

Genesis 33:1–7. Esau Greets His Brother, Jacob, with Kindness

1 And Jacob lifted up his eyes, and looked, and, behold, Esau came, and with him four hundred men. And he divided the children unto Leah, and unto Rachel, and unto the two handmaids.

2 And he put the handmaids and their children foremost, and Leah and her children after, and Rachel and Joseph hindermost.

Why did Jacob place Rachel and her children in the back of the group that greeted Esau? (33:2) "Some have criticized Jacob's arrangement of the clan because it appears that he is putting the handmaids and their children in the most dangerous position. It would be a natural thing, however, in the Middle East for a clan leader to show off his family and possessions in such a way that the best most highly favored is saved until last (see Clarke, Bible Commentary, 1:205)" (*Old Testament Student Manual: Genesis–2 Samuel*, 89).

3 And he passed over before them, and bowed himself to the ground seven times, until he came near to his brother.

Why would Jacob bow down seven times? (33:3) In bowing down seven times, Jacob was demonstrating respect for and seeking reconciliation with his older brother. "One way that a person showed respect for a superior in the ancient world was by bowing to the ground. To magnify the honor being given and the subservience of the person who bowed, this gesture could be repeated seven times" (Walton, et al., *IVP Bible Background Commentary*, 65–66).

What can we learn from Esau's reaction to Jacob? (33:4) "Gratefully, God, in His love and mercy for His children, has prepared a way to help us navigate these sometimes turbulent experiences of life. He has provided an escape for all who fall victim to the misdeeds of others. He has taught us that we can forgive! Even though we may be a victim once, we need not be a victim twice by carrying the burden of hate, bitterness, pain, resentment, or even revenge. We can forgive, and we can be free!" (Duncan, "Healing Ointment of Forgiveness," 33). The Doctrine and Covenants amplifies the truth that we must forgive others or we are committing the greater sin (see D&C 64:9–11). ⊕

Genesis 33:8–16. Jacob Gives Gifts to Esau

What is a "drove"? (33:8) A "drove" is "an encampment (of travellers or troops)" (see *Strong's Exhaustive Concordance*, word #h4264).

What can we learn about love and forgiveness from Jacob and Esau? (33:10–12) "The passage of time is not, by itself, an automatic cure for bad choices; but often individuals, like the prodigal son, can 'in process of time' come to their senses. The touching reunion of Jacob and Esau in the desert—so many years after their youthful rivalry, is a classic example of how generosity can replace animosity when truth is mixed with time. When we are unduly impatient, we are, in effect, trying to hasten an outcome when this kind of acceleration would be to abuse agency" (Maxwell, "Patience," 28). ⊕

What does it mean to "lead on softly"? (33:14) To "lead on softly" is to move "slowly, gently, easily, step by step" (*John Gill's Exposition of the Whole Bible* [commentary on Genesis 33:14]). Jacob's decision may also have indicated his desire to reinstill trust in his relationship with Esau. "Forgiveness and trust are not synonymous. We are required to forgive everyone

4 And Esau ran to meet him, and embraced him, and fell on his neck, and kissed him: and they wept.

5 And he lifted up his eyes, and saw the women and the children; and said, Who *are* those with thee? And he said, The children which God hath graciously given thy servant.

6 Then the handmaidens came near, they and their children, and they bowed themselves.

7 And Leah also with her children came near, and bowed themselves: and after came Joseph near and Rachel, and they bowed themselves.

8 And he said, What *meanest* thou by all this drove which I met? And he said, *These are* to find grace in the sight of my lord.

9 And Esau said, I have enough, my brother; keep that thou hast unto thyself.

10 And Jacob said, Nay, I pray thee, if now I have found grace in thy sight, then receive my present at my hand: for therefore I have seen thy face, as though I had seen the face of God, and thou wast pleased with me.

11 Take, I pray thee, my blessing that is brought to thee; because God hath dealt graciously with me, and because I have enough. And he urged him, and he took *it*.

12 And he said, Let us take our journey, and let us go, and I will go before thee.

13 And he said unto him, My lord knoweth that the children *are* tender, and the flocks and herds with young *are* with me: and if men should overdrive them one day, all the flock will die.

14 Let my lord, I pray thee, pass over before his servant: and I will lead on softly, according as the cattle that goeth before me and the children be able to endure, until I come unto my lord unto Seir.

15 And Esau said, Let me now leave with thee *some* of the folk that *are* with me. And he said, What needeth it? let me find grace in the sight of my lord.

(see D&C 64:10) but counseled to be cautious in placing our trust in others (see Matthew 7:6; Proverbs 25:19). Trust places a responsibility in people that they may not be ready to handle. Trust must be earned" (Gilliland, "Forgiveness," 48). What can you do to demonstrate trustworthy behavior? How might that bless your family members?

16 ¶ So Esau returned that day on his way unto Seir.

Genesis 33:17–20. Jacob Arrives in Canaan

17 And Jacob journeyed to Succoth, and built him an house, and made booths for his cattle: therefore the name of the place is called Succoth.

What were the booths Jacob built in Succoth? (33:17) "The little green valley of the Jabbok and the broader green valley of the Jordan must have looked good to Jacob's company, and they camped a while where the Jabbok enters the Jordan, at a place named *Succoth* ('booths'). There they built *succoth* (sheds made of posts supporting pole beams and joists and covered with willow branches), and they even built Jacob a house" (Rasmussen, *Latter-day Saint Commentary on the Old Testament*, 66).

18 ¶ And Jacob came to Shalem, a city of Shechem, which *is* in the land of Canaan, when he came from Padan-aram; and pitched his tent before the city.

19 And he bought a parcel of a field, where he had spread his tent, at the hand of the children of Hamor, Shechem's father, for an hundred pieces of money.

20 And he erected there an altar, and called it El-elohe-Israel.

Why is the name of this altar noteworthy? (33:20) El-elohe-Israel is translated as "El (God) is the God of Israel" (Genesis 33:20*a*). Altars served as a "place of worship, most frequently associated with making sacrifices and entering into or renewing covenants." They are also places "of the divine presence. Anciently, they were built on raised ground so that there was a ritual ascent as one approached the place of worship. . . . In the Bible they are clearly seen as the place from which prayers were to ascend to heaven" (McConkie, *Gospel Symbolism*, 251).

CHAPTER 34

Shechem defiles Dinah—The Hivites seek to arrange marriages with Jacob's family—Many, having been circumcised, are slain by Simeon and Levi—Jacob reproves his sons.

1 And Dinah the daughter of Leah, which she bare unto Jacob, went out to see the daughters of the land.

Genesis 34:1–5. Shechem Defiles Dinah Sexually

What happened between Shechem and Dinah? (34:2–3) Shechem sexually defiled Dinah. "The Hebrew word that is translated 'took' in the phrase 'he took her' can mean 'to take away, sometimes with violence and force; to take possession, to capture, to seize upon' (Wilson, *Old Testament Word Studies*, s.v. 'take,' 435). . . .

"'Literally, [Shechem] *spake to the heart of the damsel*—endeavoured to gain her affections, and to reconcile her to her disgrace. It appears sufficiently evident . . . that there had been no *consent* on the part of Dinah, that the whole was an act of *violence*, and that she was now detained *by force* in the house of *Shechem*' (Clarke, *Bible Commentary*, 1:207)" (*Old Testament Student Manual: Genesis–2 Samuel*, 89).

2 And when Shechem the son of Hamor the Hivite, prince of the country, saw her, he took her, and lay with her, and defiled her.

3 And his soul clave unto Dinah the daughter of Jacob, and he loved the damsel, and spake kindly unto the damsel.

4 And Shechem spake unto his father Hamor, saying, Get me this damsel to wife.

5 And Jacob heard that he had defiled Dinah his daughter: now his sons were with his cattle in the field: and Jacob held his peace until they were come.

Genesis 34:6–12. Shechem's Father Pleads with the Israelites to Intermarry with the Hivites

6 ¶ And Hamor the father of Shechem went out unto Jacob to commune with him.

7 And the sons of Jacob came out of the field when they heard *it:* and the men were grieved, and they were very wroth, because he had wrought folly in Israel in lying with Jacob's daughter; which thing ought not to be done.

8 And Hamor communed with them, saying, The soul of my son Shechem longeth for your daughter: I pray you give her him to wife.

9 And make ye marriages with us, *and* give your daughters unto us, and take our daughters unto you.

10 And ye shall dwell with us: and the land shall be before you; dwell and trade ye therein, and get you possessions therein.

Why did Shechem offer a dowry for Dinah? (34:11–12) "According to biblical law . . . a man who rapes an unattached woman must pay a fine to her father, marry her, and forfeit the right to divorce her (Deut. 22:28–29). On the other hand, biblical law elsewhere strictly forbids the marriage of an Israelite to a Hivite (one of the indigenous nations of the land of Canaan; Deut. 7:1–5), and the patriarchs have gone to great lengths to avoid intermarriage with Canaanite nations (Gen. 24; 27:46–28:9). From the perspective of these (later) laws, a happy resolution to the love-struck Shechem's dilemma is impossible" (*Jewish Study Bible*, 64–65).

11 And Shechem said unto her father and unto her brethren, Let me find grace in your eyes, and what ye shall say unto me I will give.

12 Ask me never so much dowry and gift, and I will give according as ye shall say unto me: but give me the damsel to wife.

Genesis 34:13–26. Simeon and Levi Devise an Evil Plan to Seek Revenge and Kill Shechem and the Hivites

What was wrong with Simeon and Levi's revengeful plan? (34:13–15) "Jacob's sons, Simeon and Levi, deceive the people of Shechem over the defiling of their sister Dinah, 'which thing [the defiling] ought not to be done' (Genesis 34:7). But what the brothers did, after their father's peaceful negotiation with the people of Shechem, was to roar into the city, brandishing swords. They killed every man, 'and all their little ones, and their wives took they captive' (Genesis 34:29). This in no way restored Dinah's honor. The violence was self-serving and ego-raising" (Clyde, "Old Testament Insights," 124).

Why is the "gate of their city" important? (34:20) "The city gate was a place of assembly for legal and business transactions. It could also be used for public meetings that affected all of the city's citizens. In the small towns that were the ancient cities the houses were close together and the streets were narrow. The only open areas would be the market place (if the town had one) and the area of the gate. The former would have been unsuitable for matters of public business" (Walton, et al., *IVP Bible Background Commentary*, 67).

13 And the sons of Jacob answered Shechem and Hamor his father deceitfully, and said, because he had defiled Dinah their sister:

14 And they said unto them, We cannot do this thing, to give our sister to one that is uncircumcised; for that *were* a reproach unto us:

15 But in this will we consent unto you: If ye will be as we *be,* that every male of you be circumcised;

16 Then will we give our daughters unto you, and we will take your daughters to us, and we will dwell with you, and we will become one people.

17 But if ye will not hearken unto us, to be circumcised; then will we take our daughter, and we will be gone.

18 And their words pleased Hamor, and Shechem Hamor's son.

19 And the young man deferred not to do the thing, because he had delight in Jacob's daughter: and he *was* more honourable than all the house of his father.

20 ¶ And Hamor and Shechem his son came unto the gate of their city, and communed with the men of their city, saying,

21 These men *are* peaceable with us; therefore let them dwell in the land, and trade therein; for the land, behold, *it is* large enough for them; let us take their daughters to us for wives, and let us give them our daughters.

22 Only herein will the men consent unto us for to dwell with us, to be one people, if every male among us be circumcised, as they *are* circumcised.

23 *Shall* not their cattle and their substance and every beast of theirs *be* ours? only let us

Genesis 34:27–31. Jacob Sharply Reproves His Sons for Their Deceit, Murder, and Theft

What can we learn from Jacob's response to his sons' actions? (34:27–30) Because the Lord is a perfect judge, we do not need to—nor should we—seek revenge against those who have hurt us. Simeon and Levi's actions brought serious consequences. "Israel's peace in Shalem was short-lived. An act of risk followed by an act of lust, an attempt at recompense, an agreement made in duplicity, and a violent assault by sons of Israel—all caused Israel 'to stink among the inhabitants of the land,' so Israel had to move on. Jacob's remonstrance with his guilty sons (who had reasoned they were justified in using violence to revenge the honor of their sister) may seem mild, but there were deep and lasting effects (Gen. 49:5–7)" (Rasmussen, *Latter-day Saint Commentary on the Old Testament*, 67).

consent unto them, and they will dwell with us.

24 And unto Hamor and unto Shechem his son hearkened all that went out of the gate of his city; and every male was circumcised, all that went out of the gate of his city.

25 ¶ And it came to pass on the third day, when they were sore, that two of the sons of Jacob, Simeon and Levi, Dinah's brethren, took each man his sword, and came upon the city boldly, and slew all the males.
26 And they slew Hamor and Shechem his son with the edge of the sword, and took Dinah out of Shechem's house, and went out.
27 The sons of Jacob came upon the slain, and spoiled the city, because they had defiled their sister.
28 They took their sheep, and their oxen, and their asses, and that which *was* in the city, and that which *was* in the field,
29 And all their wealth, and all their little ones, and their wives took they captive, and spoiled even all that *was* in the house.
30 And Jacob said to Simeon and Levi, Ye have troubled me to make me to stink among the inhabitants of the land, among the Canaanites and the Perizzites: and I *being* few in number, they shall gather themselves together against me, and slay me; and I shall be destroyed, I and my house.

31 And they said, Should he deal with our sister as with an harlot?

CHAPTER 35

God sends Jacob to Bethel, where he builds an altar and the Lord appears to him—God renews the promise that Jacob will be a great nation and that his name will be Israel—Jacob sets up an altar and pours a drink offering—Rachel bears Benjamin, dies in childbirth, and is buried near Bethlehem—Reuben sins with Bilhah—Isaac dies and is buried by Jacob and Esau.

1 And God said unto Jacob, Arise, go up to Beth-el, and dwell there: and make there an altar unto God, that appeared unto thee when thou fleddest from the face of Esau thy brother.

2 Then Jacob said unto his household, and to all that *were* with him, Put away the strange gods that *are* among you, and be clean, and change your garments:

3 And let us arise, and go up to Beth-el; and I will make there an altar unto God, who answered me in the day of my distress, and was with me in the way which I went.

4 And they gave unto Jacob all the strange gods which *were* in their hand, and *all their* earrings which *were* in their ears; and Jacob hid them under the oak which *was* by Shechem.

5 And they journeyed: and the terror of God was upon the cities that *were* round about them, and they did not pursue after the sons of Jacob.

6 ¶ So Jacob came to Luz, which *is* in the land of Canaan, that *is,* Beth-el, he and all the people that *were* with him.

7 And he built there an altar, and called the place El-beth-el: because there God appeared unto him, when he fled from the face of his brother.

Genesis 35:1–8. Jacob Returns to Bethel

Why did Jacob ask his family to renounce idols and earrings before going to Bethel? (35:2–4) "Before returning to Bethel, which was the equivalent of a modern temple, Jacob had his family and servants, his household, prepare themselves for the experience much as modern Saints prepare themselves. The earrings probably were more than mere jewelry, possibly amulets with inscriptions to false gods (see Keil and Delitzsch, *Commentary*, 1:1:316)" (*Old Testament Student Manual: Genesis–2 Samuel*, 89). ⊕

Where is Bethel and why is it important? (35:3) After defining Bethel as the "house of God," the Bible Dictionary explains that it was "formerly called Luz (Gen. 28:19), on the border between Benjamin and Ephraim, and one of the most sacred spots in Israel. Here Abraham built his altar on his first arrival in Canaan (Gen. 12:8; 13:3); here Jacob had his dream, set up a pillar, and gave the place its name (28:19). It was a sanctuary in the days of Samuel (1 Sam. 7:16; 10:3)" (Bible Dictionary, "Bethel"). See commentary in this volume for Genesis 28:10–15.

Why did Jacob bury the vestiges of false worship under the oak tree? (35:4) "The only previous mention of the [strange or foreign] 'gods' belonging to Jacob's household appears in the story of the 'household gods' [31:19] that Rachel stole from her father. These may be included in the term 'foreign gods' [vv. 2, 4]; but in light of the fact that the writer mentions that they bury the 'rings in their ears' (v. 4) along with these 'foreign gods,' it is likely that Jacob's household have picked up other religious objects while living in Shechem. In any case, the point of the narrative is to show that Jacob and his family are leaving such things behind and purifying themselves in preparation for their journey to Bethel" (Sailhamer, "Genesis," 1:262).

8 But Deborah Rebekah's nurse died, and she was buried beneath Beth-el under an oak: and the name of it was called Allon-bachuth.

Genesis 35:9–15. God Renews the Covenant and Jacob's Name Is Changed to Israel

9 ¶ And God appeared unto Jacob again, when he came out of Padan-aram, and blessed him.

10 And God said unto him, Thy name *is* Jacob: thy name shall not be called any more Jacob, but Israel shall be thy name: and he called his name Israel.

Why was Jacob's name changed to Israel? (35:10) Israel means "One who prevails with God or *Let God prevail.* This name was given to Jacob at Penuel (Gen. 32:28) and at Bethel (Gen. 35:10). It also applies to his descendants and to their kingdom (2 Sam. 1:24; 23:3). . . . The name Israel is . . . variously used to denote (1) the man Jacob, (2) the literal descendants of Jacob, and (3) the true believers in Christ, regardless of their lineage or geographical location" (Bible Dictionary, "Israel"). See commentary in this volume for Genesis 32:28. ⊕

11 And God said unto him, I *am* God Almighty: be fruitful and multiply; a nation and a company of nations shall be of thee, and kings shall come out of thy loins;

12 And the land which I gave Abraham and Isaac, to thee I will give it, and to thy seed after thee will I give the land.

13 And God went up from him in the place where he talked with him.

How did Israel's blessings compare to those promised to Abraham? (35:11–13) "Jacob was a grandson of Abraham. The Lord made an everlasting covenant with Abraham that was renewed with Isaac and with Jacob and his children. . . . God promised that the Israelites would be His covenant people as long as they would obey His commandments (see Deuteronomy 28:9–10). They would be a blessing to all the nations of the world by taking the gospel and the priesthood to them (see Abraham 2:9–11). Thus, they would keep their covenant with the Lord and He would keep His covenant with them" (*Gospel Principles*, 245). ⊕

14 And Jacob set up a pillar in the place where he talked with him, *even* a pillar of stone: and he poured a drink offering thereon, and he poured oil thereon.

15 And Jacob called the name of the place where God spake with him, Beth-el.

What is a drink offering? (35:14) Jacob poured wine (drink offering) and oil on the pillar as a way to dedicate the site as a sacred place. Long after Jacob, during the time of Moses, "'the *drink offering*' was often used to express thanksgiving to the Lord. It consisted of the fourth part of a hin of wine (Lev. 23:13), or about three pints. This offering was simply a libation [liquid offering] poured out before the Lord. This offering occurred every morning and every night along with the burnt offering and the meat (meal) offering (Ex. 29:39–40)" (Ludlow, *Unlocking the Old Testament*, 36).

Genesis 35:16–20. Rachel Dies While Giving Birth to Benjamin

16 ¶ And they journeyed from Beth-el; and there was but a little way to come to Ephrath: and Rachel travailed, and she had hard labour.

17 And it came to pass, when she was in hard labour, that the midwife said unto her, Fear not; thou shalt have this son also.

18 And it came to pass, as her soul was in departing, (for she died) that she called his name Ben-oni: but his father called him Benjamin.

19 And Rachel died, and was buried in the way to Ephrath, which *is* Beth-lehem.

20 And Jacob set a pillar upon her grave: that *is* the pillar of Rachel's grave unto this day.

21 ¶ And Israel journeyed, and spread his tent beyond the tower of Edar.

22 And it came to pass, when Israel dwelt in that land, that Reuben went and lay with Bilhah his father's concubine: and Israel heard *it.* Now the sons of Jacob were twelve:

23 The sons of Leah; Reuben, Jacob's firstborn, and Simeon, and Levi, and Judah, and Issachar, and Zebulun:

24 The sons of Rachel; Joseph, and Benjamin:

25 And the sons of Bilhah, Rachel's handmaid; Dan, and Naphtali:

26 And the sons of Zilpah, Leah's handmaid; Gad, and Asher: these *are* the sons of Jacob, which were born to him in Padan-aram.

27 ¶ And Jacob came unto Isaac his father unto Mamre, unto the city of Arbah, which *is* Hebron, where Abraham and Isaac sojourned.

28 And the days of Isaac were an hundred and fourscore years.

29 And Isaac gave up the ghost, and died, and was gathered unto his people, *being* old and full of days: and his sons Esau and Jacob buried him.

CHAPTER 36

The descendants of Esau, who is Edom, are listed.

What does Benjamin's name mean? (35:18) "[Rachel] named her child, *Benoni, Son of my sorrow*. But a happier fact was expressed in the name that Jacob gave him, *Benjamin, the Son of the right hand.* For the tribe of Benjamin was to play its signal part in history, since from it came Saul, the first king (1 Sam. 9:1–2), and that greater Saul of Tarsus, who was to be the apostle Paul (Phil. 3:5)" (*Interpreter's Bible*, 1:742).

Genesis 35:21–29. The Names of Israel's Sons Are Given and His Father, Isaac, Dies

How did Reuben's choice affect the birthright of Israel? (35:22) "On the surface the birthright appears to be just a temporal inheritance of land or property that is bequeathed to a firstborn son. . . . The Old Testament, however, gives many accounts of someone other than the firstborn son who inherited the birthright. . . .

"One of the underlying themes of the Old Testament is that inheritance of the birthright was based more upon the sons' worthiness than just birth order. This is evidenced later in the Old Testament when Reuben, the eldest son of Jacob (Israel), forfeits the birthright when he is immoral with his father's wife (see Genesis 35:22; see also Genesis 49:3–4)" (Top, *Peculiar Treasure*, 14). ⊕

What does it mean to be gathered unto your people? (35:29) Death is the gateway to our gathering with our family members who have passed on before us. The scriptures make it evident that Jacob is exalted and shall be in the presence of the Lord eternally (see Alma 5:24; D&C 132:37; 133:55).

Summary of Genesis 36

The descendants of Esau, Jacob's brother, are listed. Esau (sometimes called Edom) and his family live near the southeast end of the Dead Sea and are called Edomites.

Genesis 37:1–3. Jacob (Israel) Loves His Son Joseph

Why does the story of Joseph begin with "the generations of Jacob"? (37:1–2) The Prophet Joseph Smith changes this first phrase of verse two to read: "And this is the history of the generations of Jacob" (JST, Genesis 37:2). Some have suggested: "After the account of Esau and his descendants (ch. 36), we shift to *the account of Jacob*—that is, the account of his descendants. This is primarily the story of Joseph since so much of what happens to the 12 tribes of Israel is based on Joseph's enslavement and eventual rise to power in Egypt" (*Quest Study Bible* [2003], 55).

Why would Joseph report on his brothers? (37:2) "When Reuben, who was Jacob's firstborn, lost the birthright because of transgression (see Genesis 35:22; 49:4; 1 Chronicles 5:1), the blessing went to the first-born of the second wife, Rachel. And thus Joseph was given the birthright in his father's house—the house of Israel. The birthright carried with it certain prerogatives and responsibilities. It entailed an inheritance of land; but more important, it meant the right to preside in the family after the death of the father. Birthright is presidency and leadership" (Matthews, "Our Heritage from Joseph of Israel," 3). ⊕

What do we know about the coat given Joseph? (37:3) "Some scholars suggest that the coat given to Joseph was richly embroidered and had long sleeves, 'such as the better class wore.' This type of coat was called a tunic. A typical tunic was long, extending to the hands and the feet. To wear such a coat was a sign of favor. It is not clear what Joseph's tunic looked like, because the meaning of the Hebrew word that describes it is uncertain. The suggestion that the coat had many colors comes from the Greek translation of Genesis. In Joseph's case, the coat was a sign that the birthright forfeited by Reuben was given to him" (Black, *400 Questions and Answers about the Old Testament*, 57). ⊕

Genesis 37:4–11. Joseph Has a Dream Symbolizing That His Parents and Brothers Will Bow Down to Him

CHAPTER 37

Jacob loves and favors Joseph, who is hated by his brothers—Joseph dreams that his parents and brothers make obeisance to him—His brothers sell him into Egypt.

1 And Jacob dwelt in the land wherein his father was a stranger, in the land of Canaan.

2 These *are* the generations of Jacob. Joseph, *being* seventeen years old, was feeding the flock with his brethren; and the lad *was* with the sons of Bilhah, and with the sons of Zilpah, his father's wives: and Joseph brought unto his father their evil report.

3 Now Israel loved Joseph more than all his children, because he *was* the son of his old age: and he made him a coat of *many* colours.

4 And when his brethren saw that their father loved him more than all his brethren, they hated him, and could not speak peaceably unto him.

What factors seemingly led to Joseph's brothers hatred of him? (37:4–5) "It is possible that the favoritism we keep seeing in the patriarchal narratives has to do less with loving one child more than another and more to do with making it known which would be the birthright child—and perhaps even giving that child more attention and training in preparation for his responsibilities. . . .

"It seems unwise on the part of Joseph to have told his brothers about a dream that showed him as their ruler. Yet these dreams would lead to a series of actions that would result in fulfilling God's will. Perhaps Joseph was inspired to share the dreams with his brothers" (Muhlestein, *Scripture Study Made Simple*, 63).

5 ¶ And Joseph dreamed a dream, and he told *it* his brethren: and they hated him yet the more.

6 And he said unto them, Hear, I pray you, this dream which I have dreamed:

What can we learn from Joseph's experience concerning inspired dreams? (37:5–6) "In his youth, Joseph was taught through dreams, visions, and revelation about his mission in mortality. Divine dreams played a central role in his life. They were not filled with strange sequences, flights of fantasy, or haunting horrors, but with visions of meaning and eternal implications. . . . Joseph had a dream which revealed the special relationship he would have with his family and also foreshadowed the eventual mission of his posterity in the eternal salvation of the House of Israel" (Horton, "Joseph," 65).

7 For, behold, we *were* binding sheaves in the field, and, lo, my sheaf arose, and also stood upright; and, behold, your sheaves stood round about, and made obeisance to my sheaf.

8 And his brethren said to him, Shalt thou indeed reign over us? or shalt thou indeed have dominion over us? And they hated him yet the more for his dreams, and for his words.

9 ¶ And he dreamed yet another dream, and told it his brethren, and said, Behold, I have dreamed a dream more; and, behold, the sun and the moon and the eleven stars made obeisance to me.

10 And he told *it* to his father, and to his brethren: and his father rebuked him, and said unto him, What *is* this dream that thou hast dreamed? Shall I and thy mother and

What could this dream mean? (37:7–8) The "dream was indeed prophetic. It foretold the day when Joseph's brothers would bow down to him in Egypt, where he would become the prime minister (see Genesis 42:6). . . .

"Another aspect of the fulfillment of the prophecy in verse 7 . . . might well be found in Doctrine and Covenants 133:32. It foretells of the latter days when the lost ten tribes will return and receive the blessings of the gospel and the temple at the hands of 'the children of Ephraim,' who was Joseph's birthright son" (Ridges, *Old Testament Made Easier*, 277).

How could Joseph's dead mother bow to him? (37:9–11) "A possible interpretation suggests itself to Latter-day Saint readers. Since Jacob had taken his wives in accordance with the divine law of marriage wherein their covenant was eternal, . . . he knew full well that death did not dissolve the Lord's promised blessings. . . . The Lord had assured his grandfather, Abraham, that the promises given to his seed were to continue 'both in the world and out of the world' (D&C 132:30). . . . That Joseph would retain his role as a spiritual leader to his family in that sphere seems a most natural conclusion in the light of all that has been revealed on the subject in this day (D&C 138)" (McConkie, *His Name Shall Be Joseph*, 73–74). ⊕

Genesis 37:12–17. Israel Sends Joseph to Check on His Brothers

Why is Joseph's response, "Here am I," notable? (37:13) This is the same declaration that Jehovah made in the premortal life, as He accepted the responsibility to be the Savior of humankind (see Abraham 3:27). It is the declaration that many prophets, before and after Joseph, have made to show humble submission (see, for example, Genesis 22:11; 27:1; 31:11; Exodus 3:4; 1 Samuel 3:4–5; 12:3; 2 Samuel 1:7; Isaiah 6:8).

Genesis 37:18–24. Joseph's Brothers Throw Him into a Pit

Why did Reuben prevent his brothers from slaying Joseph? (37:21) "We know that Reuben has been out of favor with his father ever since the scandalous affair with Bilhah (35:22). Is Reuben's magnanimity to Joseph an attempt to rebuild some broken communication with his father? That he is Joseph's savior should pave the way for reconciliation with Jacob. It is more likely that he is here exercising the role of the oldest

thy brethren indeed come to bow down ourselves to thee to the earth?

11 And his brethren envied him; but his father observed the saying.

12 ¶ And his brethren went to feed their father's flock in Shechem.

13 And Israel said unto Joseph, Do not thy brethren feed *the flock* in Shechem? come, and I will send thee unto them. And he said to him, Here *am I*.

14 And he said to him, Go, I pray thee, see whether it be well with thy brethren, and well with the flocks; and bring me word again. So he sent him out of the vale of Hebron, and he came to Shechem.

15 ¶ And a certain man found him, and, behold, *he was* wandering in the field: and the man asked him, saying, What seekest thou?

16 And he said, I seek my brethren: tell me, I pray thee, where they feed *their flocks*.

17 And the man said, They are departed hence; for I heard them say, Let us go to Dothan. And Joseph went after his brethren, and found them in Dothan.

18 And when they saw him afar off, even before he came near unto them, they conspired against him to slay him.

19 And they said one to another, Behold, this dreamer cometh.

20 Come now therefore, and let us slay him, and cast him into some pit, and we will say, Some evil beast hath devoured him: and we shall see what will become of his dreams.

21 And Reuben heard *it*, and he delivered him out of their hands; and said, Let us not kill him.

22 And Reuben said unto them, Shed no blood, *but* cast him into this pit that *is* in the wilderness, and lay no hand upon him; that he might rid him out of their hands, to deliver him to his father again.

23 ¶ And it came to pass, when Joseph was come unto his brethren, that they stript Joseph out of his coat, *his* coat of *many* colours that *was* on him;

24 And they took him, and cast him into a pit: and the pit *was* empty, *there was* no water in it.

25 And they sat down to eat bread: and they lifted up their eyes and looked, and, behold, a company of Ishmeelites came from Gilead with their camels bearing spicery and balm and myrrh, going to carry *it* down to Egypt.

26 And Judah said unto his brethren, What profit *is it* if we slay our brother, and conceal his blood?

27 Come, and let us sell him to the Ishmeelites, and let not our hand be upon him; for he *is* our brother *and* our flesh. And his brethren were content.

28 Then there passed by Midianites merchantmen; and they drew and lifted up Joseph out of the pit, and sold Joseph to the Ishmeelites for twenty *pieces* of silver: and they brought Joseph into Egypt.

29 ¶ And Reuben returned unto the pit; and, behold, Joseph *was* not in the pit; and he rent his clothes.

30 And he returned unto his brethren, and said, The child *is* not; and I, whither shall I go?

brother, the one who is most answerable to his father for the well-being of his beloved Joseph" (Hamilton, *Book of Genesis, 18–50*, 418).

Genesis 37:25–30. Joseph's Brothers Sell Him as a Slave

Who are the Midianites and the Ishmaelites? (37:28) "In 37:25, . . . and 39:1 [the slave traders] are called Ishmaelites, but in 37:28 and 36 they are termed Midianites. Some have supposed that two groups of traders were involved, others that the variation represents the terminology of different sources. However, there is no doubt that the author of Genesis thought Ishmaelites and Midianites were alternative names for the same group of people. . . . It may be that Ishmaelite means 'nomadic trader' and Midianite refers to the tribe they belonged to, or Ishmaelites may be the larger tribal grouping of which Midianites were a smaller group" (Wenham, "Genesis," 65).

What do the twenty pieces of silver represent? (37:28) "The price received for Joseph, twenty pieces of silver, is the same price specified later in the Mosaic law for a slave between the ages of five and twenty (see Leviticus 27:5). Typically, the price for a slave was thirty pieces of silver (see Exodus 21:32)" (*Old Testament Student Manual: Genesis–2 Samuel*, 93).

Genesis 37:31–36. Joseph's Brothers Convince Their Father That Joseph Was Killed by a Wild Beast

Why did Jacob rend his clothes and put on sackcloth? (37:34) "In numerous passages the Bible reports traditional acts or signs of expressing distress or grief. Three typical practices were rending or ripping one's clothes, wearing sackcloth, and putting ashes or dust on one's head.... Mourning rites were much more visual and visceral than many Western cultures today, and these external ritual actions powerfully conveyed something about the person's inner feelings" (Holzapfel, et al., *Jehovah and the World of the Old Testament*, 245).

How did Joseph's trials turn to blessings for him and others? (37:36) "Joseph, while his father was mourning, was sold by the Midianites to Potiphar... to be first of all brought low, according to the wonderful counsel of God, and then to be exalted as ruler in Egypt, before whom his brethren would bow down, and as the savior of the house of Israel" (Keil and Delitzsch, *Commentary* [on Genesis 37:36]). How may trials you are currently experiencing become blessings as you rely on the Lord?

Genesis 38:1–11. Judah Promises His Widowed Daughter, Tamar, Marriage to His Son, Shelah

Why is Joseph's narrative interrupted with the story of Judah and Tamar? (38:1) "Upon closer examination, we can see that Genesis presents stories about Joseph and Judah that give us points of comparison to consider. First, Judah's standard of virtue is juxtaposed with that of Joseph. Joseph showed his moral fortitude in refusing the sexual advances of Potiphar's wife, even when it meant paying for his standards by going to prison. In contrast, Judah solicited a woman he believed to be a harlot but was

31 And they took Joseph's coat, and killed a kid of the goats, and dipped the coat in the blood;

32 And they sent the coat of *many* colours, and they brought *it* to their father; and said, This have we found: know now whether it *be* thy son's coat or no.

33 And he knew it, and said, *It is* my son's coat; an evil beast hath devoured him; Joseph is without doubt rent in pieces.

34 And Jacob rent his clothes, and put sackcloth upon his loins, and mourned for his son many days.

35 And all his sons and all his daughters rose up to comfort him; but he refused to be comforted; and he said, For I will go down into the grave unto my son mourning. Thus his father wept for him.

36 And the Midianites sold him into Egypt unto Potiphar, an officer of Pharaoh's, *and* captain of the guard.

CHAPTER 38

Judah has three sons by a Canaanite woman—Er and Onan are slain by the Lord—Tamar, disguised as a harlot, bears twins by Judah.

1 And it came to pass at that time, that Judah went down from his brethren, and turned in to a certain Adullamite, whose name *was* Hirah.

2 And Judah saw there a daughter of a certain Canaanite, whose name *was* Shuah; and he took her, and went in unto her.

3 And she conceived, and bare a son; and he called his name Er.

4 And she conceived again, and bare a son; and she called his name Onan.

5 And she yet again conceived, and bare a son; and called his name Shelah: and he was at Chezib, when she bare him.

6 And Judah took a wife for Er his firstborn, whose name *was* Tamar.

7 And Er, Judah's firstborn, was wicked in the sight of the LORD; and the LORD slew him.

actually his daughter-in-law, Tamar" (Olson, *Women of the New Testament*, 51).

Who is Tamar and why is her account preserved? (38:6–7) Tamar is the "wife of Er and Onan" who are the sons of Judah; Tamar becomes the "mother . . . of Pharez and Zarah" (Bible Dictionary, "Tamar"). One reason Tamar's account with Judah is documented is to preserve genealogical records important to the lineage of Judah's kings, including David, and eventually Jesus Christ (Ruth 4:18–22; Luke 3:33). Even though some of her actions were questionable, Tamar's account "can assure readers that they can excel in spite of problems in their ancestry; Jesus of Nazareth was born of that genealogical line" (Rasmussen, *Latter-day Saint Commentary on the Old Testament*, 70). ⊕

Why did the Lord slay Er? (38:7) "Like many of the other firstborn in the Bible (Cain, Ishmael, Esau, Reuben, etc.), Er is set aside by God. He was killed because he *displeased* [*Jehovah*], either by something evil he did or because he was reprehensible. The text does not give even a hint of what that sin was, and the reason for the omission is that Er's sin, and its identification, is not central to the movement of the story. But it must have been a grave sin. Not since the days of Noah and Sodom and Gomorrah has God taken the life of one who displeased him, and there it was groups who were annihilated" (Hamilton, *Book of Genesis, 18–50*, 434).

8 And Judah said unto Onan, Go in unto thy brother's wife, and marry her, and raise up seed to thy brother.

9 And Onan knew that the seed should not be his; and it came to pass, when he went in unto his brother's wife, that he spilled *it* on the ground, lest that he should give seed to his brother.

10 And the thing which he did displeased the LORD: wherefore he slew him also.

Why was Onan asked to marry his brother's widow Tamar? (38:8–11) Judah's request for Onan to marry Tamar is consistent with the traditions of their day. It is known as a levirate marriage, the "custom of a widow marrying her deceased husband's brother or sometimes a near heir. The word has nothing to do with the name Levi or the biblical Levites but is so called because of the Latin *levir*, meaning 'husband's brother,' connected with the English suffix *-ate*, thus constituting *levirate*. This system of marriage is designated in Deut. 25:5–10 (see also Gen. 38:8)" (Bible Dictionary, "Levirate marriage").

Why did the Lord slay Onan? (38:9–10) Onan's wickedness was refusing to raise up children to his deceased brother according to levirate law (see Deut. 25:5–10). "In the ancient Middle East, for a man to die without leaving a son was regarded as an incalculable loss. A person's memory was preserved in his descendants. In order to maintain the family line and the name of the deceased, a brother or another near relative would marry the man's widow and father a child that would carry on the man's family. This is called *levirate* marriage, from a Latin word meaning 'husband's brother'" (*Nelson Study Bible* [NKJV], 67). Later Biblical law gives more details of the levirate marriage custom (Deut. 25:5–10; Ruth 4:1–12).

What would be the result of Judah asking Tamar to "remain a widow" at her father's house? (38:11) "A widow without children was a woman without legal, economic or social status—a woman without a household. Judah here relegates Tamar (through his continuing authority over her) to the protection of her father's household. This is unusual in that a dowry would have been initially paid by her father precisely for the purpose of supporting her in a situation such as this. It is unlikely that her father would have had any legal obligation to support her" (*NKJV Cultural Backgrounds Study Bible*, 85).

Genesis 38:12–26. Tamar Resorts to Deception and Relies on Judah's Wickedness in Order to Have Children

Why would Tamar dress like a harlot in order to conceive with Judah? (38:12–15) "Considering the cultural and legal background of the story, one scholar proposed that 'Tamar's wearing of the veil was not to make Judah think she was a prostitute. Rather, it was intended to prevent him from recognizing her. It is not the veil but Tamar's positioning herself [alone on an open road] that made her appear to be a prostitute.' [Hamilton, *Book of Genesis, 18–50*, 442–43]. More importantly, the text does not call Tamar a harlot; Judah did (Gen. 38:15). . . . Perhaps, like Nephi in 'not knowing beforehand' what he would do (1 Ne. 4:6), Tamar was receptive to the Spirit for guidance that can only come from God" (Olson, *Women of the New Testament*, 55, 56).

11 Then said Judah to Tamar his daughter in law, Remain a widow at thy father's house, till Shelah my son be grown: for he said, Lest peradventure he die also, as his brethren *did*. And Tamar went and dwelt in her father's house.

12 ¶ And in process of time the daughter of Shuah Judah's wife died; and Judah was comforted, and went up unto his sheepshearers to Timnath, he and his friend Hirah the Adullamite.

13 And it was told Tamar, saying, Behold thy father in law goeth up to Timnath to shear his sheep.

14 And she put her widow's garments off from her, and covered her with a veil, and wrapped herself, and sat in an open place, which *is* by the way to Timnath; for she saw that Shelah was grown, and she was not given unto him to wife.

15 When Judah saw her, he thought her *to be* an harlot; because she had covered her face.

16 And he turned unto her by the way, and said, Go to, I pray thee, let me come in unto thee; (for he knew not that she *was* his daughter in law.) And she said, What wilt thou give me, that thou mayest come in unto me?

17 And he said, I will send *thee* a kid from the flock. And she said, Wilt thou give *me* a pledge, till thou send *it?*

18 And he said, What pledge shall I give thee? And she said, Thy signet, and thy bracelets, and thy staff that *is* in thine hand. And he gave *it* her, and came in unto her, and she conceived by him.

Why did Tamar insist on a pledge, signet, bracelets, and staff? (38:18) These items would ensure Judah's identity if she was later questioned about who was with her. "Judah's promise to give her a goat would ordinarily have been sufficient. However, Tamar insisted on *a pledge*. . . . The *signet* seal was an ancient means of identification. The seal was distinctively etched in stone, metal, or ivory . . . Basically, Judah gave Tamar the equivalent of a modern credit card. Presumably, Judah's *staff* was also marked in a distinctive manner" (*Nelson Study Bible* [NKJV], 67).

19 And she arose, and went away, and laid by her veil from her, and put on the garments of her widowhood.

20 And Judah sent the kid by the hand of his friend the Adullamite, to receive *his* pledge from the woman's hand: but he found her not.

21 Then he asked the men of that place, saying, Where *is* the harlot, that *was* openly by the way side? And they said, There was no harlot in this *place.*

22 And he returned to Judah, and said, I cannot find her; and also the men of the place said, *that* there was no harlot in this *place.*

23 And Judah said, Let her take *it* to her, lest we be shamed: behold, I sent this kid, and thou hast not found her.

24 ¶ And it came to pass about three months after, that it was told Judah, saying, Tamar thy daughter in law hath played the harlot; and also, behold, she *is* with child by whoredom. And Judah said, Bring her forth, and let her be burnt.

Why would Judah order Tamar burnt? (38:24) Judah's hypocritical actions led to a "twisted sense of values. He had no qualms about sending Tamar home with unfulfilled promises nor of picking up a harlot along the road. But when he heard that Tamar was pregnant he was so incensed that he ordered her put to death" (*Old Testament Student Manual: Genesis–2 Samuel*, 95).

25 When she *was* brought forth, she sent to her father in law, saying, By the man, whose these *are, am* I with child: and she said, Discern, I pray thee, whose *are* these, the signet, and bracelets, and staff.

How does Judah's confession show his spiritual growth? (38:26) "There is . . . some satisfaction to one's sense of justice in that a self-righteous man, who was willing to have his daughter-in-law punished for adultery, had to face up to his own sins" (Rasmussen, *Latter-day Saint Commentary on the Old Testament*, 70). "The evidence Tamar presents in her defense demonstrates Judah's own guilt, not only as co-adulterer but also as neglecter of his duty to her; to his credit, Judah admits her moral and legal superiority over him" (*Eerdmans Companion to the Bible*, 101).

Genesis 38:27–30. Tamar Becomes the Mother of Kings with the Birth of Her Twin Sons

What is the significance of Pharez being born first? (38:27–30) "Pharez was an ancestor of David, who was an ancestor of Christ. It is not a coincidence that Christ would be born of a Levirate marriage. There is great symbolism behind the fact that He who takes care of all that we cannot take care of ourselves was descended from a marriage that was designed to care for those who could not take care of themselves" (Muhlestein, *Scripture Study Made Simple*, 67).

Genesis 39:1–6. Potiphar Buys Joseph as a Slave and Eventually Empowers Him over All His House

Who was Potiphar? (39:1) "Potiphar was captain of Pharaoh's guard. This Pharaoh may have been one of the foreign line of Semitic rulers, called *Hyksos*, who formed the Fifteenth through the Seventeenth dynasties of Pharaohs of lower Egypt. They ruled between 1720 B.C. and 1550 B.C., the period during which, it is almost certain, Joseph lived in Egypt ([Bible Dictionary], 'Pharaoh'). This possibility is important later in the history of Joseph's family (Gen. 41:45)"

26 And Judah acknowledged *them,* and said, She hath been more righteous than I; because that I gave her not to Shelah my son. And he knew her again no more.

27 ¶ And it came to pass in the time of her travail, that, behold, twins *were* in her womb.

28 And it came to pass, when she travailed, that *the one* put out *his* hand: and the midwife took and bound upon his hand a scarlet thread, saying, This came out first.

29 And it came to pass, as he drew back his hand, that, behold, his brother came out: and she said, How hast thou broken forth? *this* breach *be* upon thee: therefore his name was called Pharez.

30 And afterward came out his brother, that had the scarlet thread upon his hand: and his name was called Zarah.

CHAPTER 39

Joseph, prospered by the Lord, becomes ruler of Potiphar's house—He resists the advances of Potiphar's wife, is falsely accused, and is cast into prison—The keeper of the prison commits the prison's affairs into Joseph's hands.

1 And Joseph was brought down to Egypt; and Potiphar, an officer of Pharaoh, captain of the guard, an Egyptian, bought him of the hands of the Ishmeelites, which had brought him down thither.

2 And the LORD was with Joseph, and he was a prosperous man; and he was in the house of his master the Egyptian.

3 And his master saw that the LORD *was* with him, and that the LORD made all that he did to prosper in his hand.

4 And Joseph found grace in his sight, and he served him: and he made him overseer over his house, and all *that* he had he put into his hand.

5 And it came to pass from the time *that* he had made him overseer in his house, and over all that he had, that the LORD blessed the Egyptian's house for Joseph's sake; and the blessing of the LORD was upon all that he had in the house, and in the field.

6 And he left all that he had in Joseph's hand; and he knew not ought he had, save the bread which he did eat. And Joseph was *a* goodly *person*, and well favoured.

7 ¶ And it came to pass after these things, that his master's wife cast her eyes upon Joseph; and she said, Lie with me.

8 But he refused, and said unto his master's wife, Behold, my master wotteth not what *is* with me in the house, and he hath committed all that he hath to my hand;

(Rasmussen, *Latter-day Saint Commentary on the Old Testament*, 70).

How long was Joseph in Potiphar's house? (39:1–4) "Altogether he served thirteen years with Potiphar and in prison. The record does not tell how long he served Potiphar before his imprisonment, but that he worked his way up to be the overseer of the prison implies some period of time before the butler and baker joined him. So it is likely that Joseph was in prison at least three years and possibly much longer" (*Old Testament Student Manual: Genesis–2 Samuel*, 95).

How was Joseph blessed to know that the Lord was with Him? (39:2–5) "Though sold to Potiphar to serve, Joseph did not become a common slave. With the Lord's gracious help, he was soon overseer of Potiphar's house and then of all he possessed" (Rasmussen, *Latter-day Saint Commentary on the Old Testament*, 70). The sixth Lecture on Faith says that it is essential to have an actual knowledge that the course of life which one is pursuing is according to the will of God. Knowing this will enable one to have that confidence in God without which no person can obtain eternal life. That confidence enabled the ancient Saints to endure all their afflictions and persecutions (see *Lectures on Faith*, 6:2–4, 11).

How does the phrase "goodly person" apply specifically to Joseph? (39:6) "The Lord was with this remarkable young man, and he seemed never to be discouraged. Though a stranger, a slave, his countenance must have radiated a special spirit. . . . Joseph had so distinguished himself to the captain that he made him ruler over his house. In authority he was the first servant; and he was made overseer over all the captain had, and the captain put his complete trust, his properties, his income, into the hands of Joseph. Joseph was a 'goodly person' and achieved a position of prominence through the help of the Lord" (Perry, "Trust in the Lord," 51–52).

Genesis 39:7–12. For Days, Potiphar's Wife Tries to Force Joseph to Break the Law of Chastity

What does "wotteth not" mean? (39:7–8) The Joseph Smith Translation explains that "wotteth not" in verse 8 means "knoweth not" (see JST, Gen. 39:8). As captain of Pharaoh's guard, Potiphar would have been a very busy and powerful man. Potiphar trusted Joseph so much that he did not even concern himself with the details of managing his household. Joseph's response to Potiphar's wife confirms the complete trust Potiphar had in Joseph and the deep betrayal it would be to give in to her seductive advances, even if they both consented. "President David O. McKay frequently said, 'It is better to be trusted than to be loved'" (Valletta, et al., *Old Testament for Latter-day Saint Families*, 77).

What do we learn about Joseph's character as he fends off Potiphar's wife? (39:9) "The primary reason for obedience to all the laws associated with chastity is to keep the commandments of God. Joseph understood that reason clearly when he resisted the entreaties of Potiphar's predatory wife (see Gen. 39:9). Joseph, who clearly noted his loyalty to his employer, Potiphar, concluded, 'How then can I do this great wickedness, and sin against God?' Joseph's obedience was an act of many-splendored loyalty—to God, to himself, to his future family, to Potiphar, and, yes, even to Potiphar's wife!" (Maxwell, "Stern but Sweet Seventh Commandment," 23–24). ⊕

What do we learn from Joseph's example? (39:10–12) "Joseph's response is as powerful now as it was then. . . . After this experience, Joseph was falsely accused and thrown into prison. However, the Lord continued to bless him because of his righteousness. He was released from prison and eventually became servant to Pharaoh himself. This put Joseph in a position to save his own family and to have a righteous posterity.

"This story has had a great influence on me throughout my life. As a teenager I faced a situation somewhat similar to Joseph's. I had treasured up Joseph's story in my mind, and, like him, I fled in the face of an imminent and dangerous moral temptation" (Rasband, "Lessons from the Old Testament," 62–64). ⊕

Why should we run from sin? (39:12) "Joseph did the very best thing he could under the circumstances. . . . In today's language—*he ran*.

"Maybe that doesn't sound like a very sophisticated thing to do, but sometimes running is the only thing to do. This was such a time. I am sure that Joseph did not know he was going to be alone with her, or he would not have gone into the house. I have great faith in Joseph.

"It is more important that we beware of compromising situations than anything else we can do. We must avoid them. If we don't, we will run the great risk of being overcome" (Rector, "Live above the Law to Be Free," 130–31). ⊕

9 *There is* none greater in this house than I;
neither hath he kept back any thing from
me but thee, because thou *art* his wife: how
then can I do this great wickedness, and sin
against God?

10 And it came to pass, as she spake to Joseph
day by day, that he hearkened not unto her,
to lie by her, *or* to be with her.

11 And it came to pass about this time, that
Joseph went into the house to do his business;
and *there was* none of the men of the house
there within.

12 And she caught him by his garment, saying, Lie with me: and he left his garment in
her hand, and fled, and got him out.

13 And it came to pass, when she saw that he had left his garment in her hand, and was fled forth,

Genesis 39:13–23. Joseph Is Falsely Imprisoned, but God Is with Joseph

Joseph as a Type of Christ (Genesis 37, 39–43)

"Joseph of Egypt was a type for Christ, Joseph Smith, and the Latter-day tribe of Joseph (i.e., Ephraim and Manasseh).

"Joseph served as a type for Christ in the following ways: . . . Both were granted a new name: Joseph was denominated Zaphnath-paaneah by Pharaoh (Gen. 41:45); Jesus' divine name was Christ" (McConkie and Parry, *Guide to Scriptural Symbols*, 71–72).

Additional types include:

- Both were good shepherds.
- Both were known as the most loved of their father.
- Both were clothed in authority and power of their father. Joseph, for instance, was given the "coat of many colours" (Gen. 37:3), a symbol of priesthood authority.
- Both were revelators, and revealed things pertaining to the future (JST, Gen. 50:24–38; Matt. 24).
- Both were fully obedient to the will and wishes of their fathers and responded to their calls to serve, saying, "Here am I" (Gen. 37:13; Abr. 3:27).
- Both were promised a future sovereignty, speaking equally of a temporal and an eternal role.
- Both were betrayed by their brothers, at which time they were stripped of their garments.
- Both were cast into a pit—Christ to the world of spirits, Joseph into an empty cistern.
- Both were betrayed with the utmost hypocrisy (Gen. 37:27; John 18:31).
- Both were sold. It was Judah that sold Joseph for twenty pieces of silver (Gen. 37:26–28), as it was Judas (Greek for Judah) who sold Jesus for thirty pieces of silver (Matt. 26:15).
- The blood-sprinkled coat of each was presented to his father. Joseph's coat of many colors was dipped in the blood of the goat (Gen. 37:31–32); the blood of Jesus Christ as the blood of the scapegoat, a sin offering, was symbolically presented to the Father.
- Both blessed those with whom they labored in prison (Gen. 39:21–23; D&C 138).
- Both were servants, and as such all that they touched were blessed.
- Both were tempted with great sin and both refused its enticements (Gen. 39; Matt. 4:1–11).
- Both were falsely accused: Joseph by Potiphar's wife, Christ by false witnesses.
- Both stood as the source of divine knowledge to their day and generation.
- Both were triumphant, overcoming all.
- Both were granted rule over all (Gen. 41:40; 1 Pet. 3:22).
- Both were thirty years old when they began their life's work (Gen. 41:46; Luke 3:23).
- Both were saviors to their people, giving them the bread of life. Joseph saved his family with a temporal salvation; Christ as the Bread of Life saves the family of humankind with a spiritual salvation.
- The rejection of both brought bondage upon the people.
- Both were unrecognized by their people (Gen. 45:3–5; D&C 45:51–53).
- Both would be recognized and accepted by their brothers only at the "second time" (Acts 7:13; D&C 45:51–53).
- As Joseph's brothers bowed to him in fulfillment of prophecy, so all will yet bow the knee to Christ (Gen. 43:26–28; D&C 76:110).
- Through both, mercy is granted to a repentant people. As Joseph's brothers sought forgiveness of him, so Christ's brothers will eventually seek forgiveness of him.
- After the reconciliation, Israel is gathered. Having manifest himself to his brothers, Joseph charged them to return and bring their father and families to Egypt. So it shall be in the last days. After Israel have returned to their God, they, like Joseph's brothers, shall be sent to bring all the family of Israel into the kingdom ruled by Christ" (adapted from McConkie and Parry, *Guide to Scriptural Symbols*, 71–72).

14 That she called unto the men of her
house, and spake unto them, saying, See, he
hath brought in an Hebrew unto us to mock
us; he came in unto me to lie with me, and I
cried with a loud voice:

15 And it came to pass, when he heard that I
lifted up my voice and cried, that he left his
garment with me, and fled, and got him out.

16 And she laid up his garment by her, until
his lord came home.

17 And she spake unto him according to
these words, saying, The Hebrew servant,
which thou hast brought unto us, came in
unto me to mock me:

18 And it came to pass, as I lifted up my
voice and cried, that he left his garment with
me, and fled out.

19 And it came to pass, when his master
heard the words of his wife, which she spake
unto him, saying, After this manner did thy
servant to me; that his wrath was kindled.

20 And Joseph's master took him, and put
him into the prison, a place where the king's
prisoners *were* bound: and he was there in
the prison.

21 ¶ But the LORD was with Joseph, and
shewed him mercy, and gave him favour in
the sight of the keeper of the prison.

22 And the keeper of the prison committed
to Joseph's hand all the prisoners that *were* in
the prison; and whatsoever they did there, he
was the doer *of it.*

23 The keeper of the prison looked not to

What do we learn of the character of Potiphar's wife? (39:16–18) "Even though this scheming woman did not succeed in defiling Joseph, her sin was most grievous. The intent was there and the desire and the lust and the coveting. She had 'already committed adultery with him in her heart and mind . . . ' as she 'cast her eyes upon Joseph day by day.' This woman's transgression did not begin when she ripped the clothes from the body of this fleeing stalwart. Her perfidy had been born and nurtured in her mind and heart in the 'day by day' of wanting him, teasing him, desiring him, lusting for him, and coveting him. Her sin was a progressive thing" (Ludlow, *Companion to Your Study of the Old Testament*, 132–33). ⊕

What can we learn from the discouraging events in Joseph's life? (39:20) "Perhaps the most significant test of Joseph's faithfulness and love of God came through his experience with Potiphar's wife, who . . . falsely accused him of trying to seduce her, and he was thrown into prison (see Gen. 39:3–20). That must have been a very discouraging turn of events to be so treated for obeying the Lord's law of chastity. Joseph's experiences with his older brothers who sold him as a slave, the false accusation by Potiphar's wife, [and imprisonment]. . . . all signify that the Lord does not make our paths easy, but he does help those who trust in him" (Matthews, *Selected Writings*, 165). ⊕

What do we learn of Joseph's character while he is in prison? (39:21–23) "Though a slave to Potiphar, Joseph refused to become the servant of sin. He had been stripped of his coat but not of his character. He had been betrayed by his brothers and imprisoned for his loyalty and purity, yet he was true to the teachings of his father, and the Lord was with him. . . . Joseph was placed in charge of all the prisoners, and given responsibility for all that happened there. Once again all that was under Joseph's charge prospered, for 'the

any thing *that was* under his hand; because the LORD was with him, and *that* which he did, the LORD made *it* to prosper.

CHAPTER 40

Joseph interprets the dreams of Pharaoh's chief butler and chief baker—The butler fails to tell Pharaoh about Joseph.

1 And it came to pass after these things, *that* the butler of the king of Egypt and *his* baker had offended their lord the king of Egypt.

2 And Pharaoh was wroth against two *of* his officers, against the chief of the butlers, and against the chief of the bakers.

3 And he put them in ward in the house of the captain of the guard, into the prison, the place where Joseph *was* bound.

4 And the captain of the guard charged Joseph with them, and he served them: and they continued a season in ward.

5 ¶ And they dreamed a dream both of them, each man his dream in one night, each man according to the interpretation of his dream, the butler and the baker of the king of Egypt, which *were* bound in the prison.

6 And Joseph came in unto them in the morning, and looked upon them, and, behold, they *were* sad.

7 And he asked Pharaoh's officers that *were* with him in the ward of his lord's house, saying, Wherefore look ye *so* sadly to day?

8 And they said unto him, We have dreamed a dream, and *there is* no interpreter of it. And Joseph said unto them, *Do* not interpretations *belong* to God? tell me *them,* I pray you.

Lord was with him'" (McConkie, *His Name Shall Be Joseph*, 75).

Genesis 40:1–4. Pharaoh's Butler and Baker Are Sent to Prison

Why was it dangerous to be Pharaoh's butler or baker? (40:2) "Though these titles may in part be ceremonial, these two men had overall responsibility for what was served to the king. The potential for assassination attempts through the king's food was real and constant, so these officials not only needed to be incorruptible themselves, but also had to be able to hire people above reproach and to identify attempts at infiltration of the staff by enemies of the king. The text is silent concerning their offense, but since both were responsible for meals, it seems logical to speculate that the king may have gotten sick from a meal" (Walton, *Zondervan Illustrated Bible Backgrounds Commentary*, 1:128). ⊕

Genesis 40:5–19. Joseph Interprets the Dreams of the Butler and the Baker

How was Joseph able to interpret dreams? (40:5–7) "Joseph exhibited the gift to interpret dreams . . . a gift the Pharaoh's chief butler came to appreciate and the Pharaoh's chief baker to loathe" (Jenkins, "Quiet Slumber," 75). "Most of the visions and dreams recorded in scripture have been given through the ministering Priesthood; but there are exceptional instances of such manifestations unto some, who, at the time, had not entered the fold. . . . Dreams with special import were given to Pharaoh, Nebuchadnezzar, and others; but it required a higher power than their own to interpret them, and Joseph and Daniel were called to officiate" (Talmage, *Articles of Faith*, 206).

Who did Joseph credit for his powerful spiritual gifts? (40:8) "Joseph of Egypt had remarkable gifts from the Lord. His gift of vision, combined with his gifts of charity and leadership, empowered him to rise up as a deliverer, as one who saves. Like the Redeemer,

Joseph also redeemed. And he did so with humility. To the butler and baker, he said, 'Do not interpretations belong to God?' (Genesis 40:8). To Pharaoh, he said, 'It is not in me: God shall give Pharaoh an answer of peace' (Genesis 41:16). Pharaoh was deeply touched by Joseph's counsel" (Allen, *Study Commentary on the Old Testament*, 66).

Why did the baker trust Joseph's prophetic gifts? (40:15–18) "'When a prophet speaketh in the name of the Lord, if the thing follow not, nor come to pass, that is the thing which the Lord hath not spoken, but the prophet hath spoken it presumptuously . . . thou shalt not be afraid of him' (Deuteronomy 18:22). It may be that Joseph's interpretation of the butler's dream gave the baker confidence to ask for an interpretation of his dream. Later in this chapter all that Joseph prophesied came to pass, in harmony with the doctrine taught in Doctrine and Covenants 1:37–38" (Valletta, et al., *Old Testament for Latter-day Saint Families*, 80).

9 And the chief butler told his dream to Joseph, and said to him, In my dream, behold, a vine *was* before me;

10 And in the vine *were* three branches: and it *was* as though it budded, *and* her blossoms shot forth; and the clusters thereof brought forth ripe grapes:

11 And Pharaoh's cup *was* in my hand: and I took the grapes, and pressed them into Pharaoh's cup, and I gave the cup into Pharaoh's hand.

12 And Joseph said unto him, This *is* the interpretation of it: The three branches *are* three days:

13 Yet within three days shall Pharaoh lift up thine head, and restore thee unto thy place: and thou shalt deliver Pharaoh's cup into his hand, after the former manner when thou wast his butler.

14 But think on me when it shall be well with thee, and shew kindness, I pray thee, unto me, and make mention of me unto Pharaoh, and bring me out of this house:

15 For indeed I was stolen away out of the land of the Hebrews: and here also have I done nothing that they should put me into the dungeon.

16 When the chief baker saw that the interpretation was good, he said unto Joseph, I also *was* in my dream, and, behold, *I had* three white baskets on my head:

17 And in the uppermost basket *there was* of all manner of bakemeats for Pharaoh; and the birds did eat them out of the basket upon my head.

18 And Joseph answered and said, This *is* the interpretation thereof: The three baskets *are* three days:

19 Yet within three days shall Pharaoh lift up thy head from off thee, and shall hang thee

on a tree; and the birds shall eat thy flesh
from off thee.

20 ¶ And it came to pass the third day, *which*
was Pharaoh's birthday, that he made a feast
unto all his servants: and he lifted up the
head of the chief butler and of the chief baker
among his servants.

21 And he restored the chief butler unto his
butlership again; and he gave the cup into
Pharaoh's hand:

22 But he hanged the chief baker: as Joseph
had interpreted to them.

23 Yet did not the chief butler remember
Joseph, but forgat him.

CHAPTER 41

Pharaoh dreams of the cattle and the ears of grain—Joseph interprets the dreams as seven years of plenty and seven of famine—He proposes a grain storage program—Pharaoh makes him ruler of all Egypt—Joseph marries Asenath—He gathers grain as the sand upon the seashore—Asenath bears Manasseh and Ephraim—Joseph sells grain to Egyptians and others during the famine.

Genesis 40:20–23. Joseph's Prophecies concerning the Butler and Baker Are Fulfilled

Why did Pharaoh display the corpse of the chief baker? (40:22) "Hanging was a way of dishonoring the corpse of the executed person (see Josh. 8:29; 2 Sam 4:12). It may involve suspensions from a rope by the neck or impalement on a stake. The actual form of execution may be stoning or beheading" (Walton, et al., *IVP Bible Background Commentary*, 72). All this was done "in the presence of *all of [Pharaoh's] servants* in order to both warn and encourage the servant household" (*Nelson Study Bible* [NKJV], 70).

What can we learn from Joseph's faithfulness despite the butler's forgetfulness? (40:23) Even though the butler forgot him, Joseph was able to stay faithful regardless of the circumstances. President Russell M. Nelson taught that "saints can be happy under every circumstance. We can feel joy even while having a bad day, a bad week, or even a bad year! . . . The joy we feel has little to do with the circumstances of our lives and everything to do with the focus of our lives.

"When the focus of our lives is on God's plan of salvation . . . and Jesus Christ and His gospel, we can feel joy regardless of what is happening—or not happening—in our lives" ("Joy and Spiritual Survival," 82).

Genesis 41:1–8. Pharaoh's Wise Men Cannot Interpret His Dreams

How long was Joseph in prison? (41:1) "Joseph was in prison for two years after he interpreted the dreams of the chief butler and baker (see Genesis 41:1). He was sold into slavery when he was about seventeen (see Genesis 37:2), and he was thirty years of age when he became vice-regent to the pharaoh (see Genesis 41:46). Altogether he served thirteen years with Potiphar and in prison . . . , but that he worked his way up to be the overseer of the prison implies some period of time before the butler and baker joined him. So it is likely that Joseph was in prison at least three years and possibly much longer" (*Old Testament Student Manual: Genesis–2 Samuel*, 95).

1 And it came to pass at the end of two full
years, that Pharaoh dreamed: and, behold, he
stood by the river.

What were the "kine" and "corn"? (41:2–5) The word "kine" means "cattle" (Bible Dictionary, "Kine"); and the word "corn" as used in the King James Bible is defined as grains "such as wheat or barley" (Bible Dictionary, "Corn").

2 And, behold, there came up out of the river
seven well favoured kine and fatfleshed; and
they fed in a meadow.
3 And, behold, seven other kine came up
after them out of the river, ill favoured and
leanfleshed; and stood by the *other* kine upon
the brink of the river.
4 And the ill favoured and leanfleshed kine
did eat up the seven well favoured and fat
kine. So Pharaoh awoke.
5 And he slept and dreamed the second time:
and, behold, seven ears of corn came up
upon one stalk, rank and good.
6 And, behold, seven thin ears and blasted
with the east wind sprung up after them.
7 And the seven thin ears devoured the seven
rank and full ears. And Pharaoh awoke, and,
behold, *it was* a dream.

Who were the magicians of Egypt? (41:8) "Many assume that the dreams of pharaoh were beyond the scope of Egypt's wise men and yet, in some ways, it is remarkable that these magicians could not have come up with some kind of logical explanation using their own well-known symbolism. . . .

"'[The magicians were] men of the priestly caste, who occupied themselves with the sacred arts and sciences of the Egyptians, the hieroglyphic writings, astrology, the interpretation of dreams, the foretelling of events, magic, and conjuring, and who were regarded as the possessors of secret arts. . . . But not one of

8 And it came to pass in the morning that
his spirit was troubled; and he sent and called
for all the magicians of Egypt, and all the
wise men thereof: and Pharaoh told them his
dream; but *there was* none that could interpret them unto Pharaoh.

9 ¶ Then spake the chief butler unto Pharaoh,
saying, I do remember my faults this day:
10 Pharaoh was wroth with his servants, and
put me in ward in the captain of the guard's
house, *both* me and the chief baker:
11 And we dreamed a dream in one night, I
and he; we dreamed each man according to
the interpretation of his dream.
12 And *there was* there with us a young man,
an Hebrew, servant to the captain of the
guard; and we told him, and he interpreted
to us our dreams; to each man according to
his dream he did interpret.
13 And it came to pass, as he interpreted to
us, so it was; me he restored unto mine office, and him he hanged.
14 ¶ Then Pharaoh sent and called Joseph,
and they brought him hastily out of the dungeon: and he shaved *himself*, and changed his
raiment, and came in unto Pharaoh.
15 And Pharaoh said unto Joseph, I have
dreamed a dream, and *there is* none that can
interpret it: and I have heard say of thee, *that*
thou canst understand a dream to interpret it.
16 And Joseph answered Pharaoh, saying, *It*
is not in me: God shall give Pharaoh an answer of peace.
17 And Pharaoh said unto Joseph, In my
dream, behold, I stood upon the bank of the
river:
18 And, behold, there came up out of the
river seven kine, fatfleshed and well favoured;
and they fed in a meadow:
19 And, behold, seven other kine came up
after them, poor and very ill favoured and

these could interpret it, although the clue to the interpretation was to be found in the religious symbols of Egypt' (Keil and Delitzsch, *Commentary*, 1:1:349)" (*Old Testament Student Manual: Genesis–2 Samuel*, 96).

Genesis 41:9–24. Pharaoh Tells Joseph His Dreams

Why does Joseph shave and put on different clothes before going to the Pharaoh? (41:14–16) "Understandably, Pharaoh takes immediate action. Joseph is to be brought before Pharaoh as quickly as possible. In preparation for his first royal audience Joseph shaves and doffs his prison garb. He does this, of course, to make himself more presentable to the head of state. We know that Semites preferred to be bearded, whereas the Egyptians were clean shaven. Joseph will look more like an Egyptian than a Hebrew, even if he is a 'Hebrew lad' (v. 12)" (Hamilton, *Book of Genesis, 18–50*, 492).

How does Joseph show his humility? (41:16) The phrase "it is not in me" likely "expresses his great modesty, that he did not arrogate such skill and wisdom to himself; declaring that he had no such power and abilities in and of himself, to interpret dreams; what he had was a gift of God, and wholly depended upon his influence . . .

"'God shall give Pharaoh an answer of peace;' such an answer to his request in the interpretation of his dream, as shall give him full content, and make his mind quiet and easy, and which shall tend to the welfare of him and his kingdom" (*John Gill's Exposition of the Whole Bible* [commentary on Genesis 41:16]).

leanfleshed, such as I never saw in all the land
of Egypt for badness:

20 And the lean and the ill favoured kine did
eat up the first seven fat kine:

21 And when they had eaten them up, it
could not be known that they had eaten
them; but they *were* still ill favoured, as at the
beginning. So I awoke.

22 And I saw in my dream, and, behold,
seven ears came up in one stalk, full and good:

23 And, behold, seven ears, withered, thin,
and blasted with the east wind, sprung up
after them:

24 And the thin ears devoured the seven good
ears: and I told *this* unto the magicians; but
there was none that could declare *it* to me.

Why did Pharaoh need someone to interpret his dreams? (41:24) "It is very unusual in Egypt for the Pharaoh to be in need of an interpreter of his dreams. Since Pharaoh was considered divine, the gods would communicate to him through dreams, and the meaning was typically presented as transparent to him" (Walton, et al., *IVP Bible Background Commentary*, 72). God had other purposes to fulfill through Pharaoh's dreams; Pharaoh's and his magicians' failed attempts allowed Joseph to reveal his divine gifts.

Genesis 41:25–36. Joseph, with the Lord's Help, Interprets Pharaoh's Dreams

25 ¶ And Joseph said unto Pharaoh, The
dream of Pharaoh *is* one: God hath shewed
Pharaoh what he *is* about to do.

26 The seven good kine *are* seven years;
and the seven good ears *are* seven years: the
dream *is* one.

27 And the seven thin and ill favoured kine
that came up after them *are* seven years; and
the seven empty ears blasted with the east
wind shall be seven years of famine.

28 This *is* the thing which I have spoken
unto Pharaoh: What God *is* about to do he
sheweth unto Pharaoh.

29 Behold, there come seven years of great
plenty throughout all the land of Egypt:

In what way were Pharaoh's two dreams related? (41:25) "Under the circumstances it would be natural that Joseph would recall his own 'doubled' dreams in which his family made obeisance to him. Dreams that have been doubled, or multiplied, should be given somber attention both in reflection and in writing, and the recipient should '[keep] all these things, and [ponder] them' (Luke 2:19)" (Jenkins, "Quiet Slumber," 75).

How did Pharaoh's dreams reveal God's purposes for Israel? (41:25–32) As we consider Pharaoh's dreams, "can we doubt that they were to prepare a people for a coming calamity? They revealed God's hand at work in the affairs of men in order that he could perform his will in their behalf. Pharaoh's dream was a small but integral part of the unfolding drama in the history of Israel as foreseen before the foundation of this world by an all-knowing Heavenly Father. Since the beginning, he has had purposes and designs for his children, a mission for Israel, and a special call for Joseph" (Horton, "Joseph," 68).

30 And there shall arise after them seven years of famine; and all the plenty shall be forgotten in the land of Egypt; and the famine shall consume the land;

31 And the plenty shall not be known in the land by reason of that famine following; for it *shall be* very grievous.

32 And for that the dream was doubled unto Pharaoh twice; *it is* because the thing *is* established by God, and God will shortly bring it to pass.

Why does Pharaoh have the same dream twice? (41:32) "When brought before the Pharaoh, Joseph was presented with two dreams of proportioned imagery. He interpreted the Pharaoh's dreams of kine and ears of corn and . . . the foreshadowing of seven years of plenty and seven years of drought. Joseph assured the Pharaoh of the interpretation . . . 'it is because the thing is established by God, and God will shortly bring it to pass' (Genesis 41:32). It was a precedent or pattern he understood from personal experience" (Jenkins, "Quiet Slumber," 75).

33 Now therefore let Pharaoh look out a man discreet and wise, and set him over the land of Egypt.

34 Let Pharaoh do *this,* and let him appoint officers over the land, and take up the fifth part of the land of Egypt in the seven plenteous years.

35 And let them gather all the food of those good years that come, and lay up corn under the hand of Pharaoh, and let them keep food in the cities.

36 And that food shall be for store to the land against the seven years of famine, which shall be in the land of Egypt; that the land perish not through the famine.

What was the significance of Joseph's proposed plan to Pharaoh? (41:33–36) "When Pharaoh himself had two dreams, one of the fat and lean kine (cows) and the other of the thin and full ears of corn (grain), Joseph was consulted and again, based on wisdom gained from the Lord, was able to prophesy the impending seven years of plenty followed by famine. For his wisdom, diligence, and integrity, Joseph was exalted to become second-in-command to the pharaoh. As foreseen through dreams, the seven years of famine struck the land, and eventually ten sons of Jacob came to Egypt seeking food" (Holzapfel, et al., *Jehovah and the World of the Old Testament*, 66). ⊕

37 ¶ And the thing was good in the eyes of Pharaoh, and in the eyes of all his servants.

38 And Pharaoh said unto his servants, Can we find *such a one* as this *is,* a man in whom the Spirit of God *is?*

Genesis 41:37–44. Joseph Becomes the Second Most Powerful Man in Egypt

How can we, like Joseph, be worthy of the Holy Ghost? (41:38) "Nothing opens the heavens quite like the combination of increased purity, exact obedience, earnest seeking, daily feasting on the words of Christ in the Book of Mormon, and regular time committed to temple and family history work" (Nelson, "Revelation for the Church, Revelation for Our Lives," 95). ⊕

How did Joseph receive the official position over the courts of Pharaoh? (41:39–40) "Pharaoh gave Joseph the Egyptian name Zaphnath-paaneah, interpreted as 'he who reveals that which is hidden,' due to his ability to interpret dreams. He further gave Joseph a signet ring, a sign of authority (see Jer. 22:24). Pharaoh appointed Joseph to be the leader of the royal granaries" (Black, *400 Questions and Answers about the Old Testament*, 58).

What power did Joseph hold in his new position? (41:41–44) "Pharaoh recognizes Joseph's wisdom and the divine presence with him, and so, at the age 30 and after 13 years of slavery and imprisonment, Joseph rises to the high position of Pharaoh's second in command (vv. 40–45). Here he assumes the task of implementing his own strategy (vv. 34–35) for saving Egypt from starvation during the seven-year famine to come" (*Eerdmans Companion to the Bible*, 102). See commentary in this volume for Genesis 42:6.

Genesis 41:45–52. Joseph Marries Asenath and Has Two Sons

Why did Joseph marry "Asenath, daughter of the priest of On"? (41:45) "In view of the emphasis placed on proper marriage in previous generations of the seed of Abraham, it is likely that Joseph's wife also was chosen for him through the Lord's influence. It may be assumed that the priests were of the same lineage as the kings of the dynasty; thus, Asenath, daughter of the priest of On, who was given to Joseph as a wife, could have been Semitic. . . . Joseph and Asenath became the parents of Manasseh and Ephraim" (Rasmussen, *Latter-day Saint Commentary on the Old Testament*, 72). See commentary in this volume for Genesis 48:1. ⊕

39 And Pharaoh said unto Joseph, Forasmuch as God hath shewed thee all this, *there is* none so discreet and wise as thou *art:*

40 Thou shalt be over my house, and according unto thy word shall all my people be ruled: only in the throne will I be greater than thou.

41 And Pharaoh said unto Joseph, See, I have set thee over all the land of Egypt.

42 And Pharaoh took off his ring from his hand, and put it upon Joseph's hand, and arrayed him in vestures of fine linen, and put a gold chain about his neck;

43 And he made him to ride in the second chariot which he had; and they cried before him, Bow the knee: and he made him *ruler* over all the land of Egypt.

44 And Pharaoh said unto Joseph, I *am* Pharaoh, and without thee shall no man lift up his hand or foot in all the land of Egypt.

45 And Pharaoh called Joseph's name Zaphnath-paaneah; and he gave him to wife Asenath the daughter of Poti-pherah priest of On. And Joseph went out over *all* the land of Egypt.

46 ¶ And Joseph *was* thirty years old when he stood before Pharaoh king of Egypt. And Joseph went out from the presence of Pharaoh, and went throughout all the land of Egypt.

47 And in the seven plenteous years the earth brought forth by handfuls.

48 And he gathered up all the food of the seven years, which were in the land of Egypt, and laid up the food in the cities: the food of the field, which *was* round about every city, laid he up in the same.

49 And Joseph gathered corn as the sand of the sea, very much, until he left numbering; for *it was* without number.

50 And unto Joseph were born two sons before the years of famine came, which Asenath the daughter of Poti-pherah priest of On bare unto him.

51 And Joseph called the name of the firstborn Manasseh: For God, *said he,* hath made me forget all my toil, and all my father's house.

What do we know about Manasseh? (41:51) Manasseh means "forgetting. [Manasseh is the] eldest son of Joseph (Gen. 41:51; 46:20; 48:1–20; 50:23; Deut. 33:13–17); also the name of the tribe descended from him; their territory west of the Jordan adjoined that of Ephraim. In addition, they had colonies east of the Jordan, in the rich pasture land of Bashan and Gilead" (Bible Dictionary, "Manasseh").

52 And the name of the second called he Ephraim: For God hath caused me to be fruitful in the land of my affliction.

What do we know about Ephraim? (41:52) Ephraim means "fruitful. [Ephraim is] the second son of Joseph (Gen. 41:52; 46:20); but at the blessing by Jacob, Ephraim was set before Manasseh, the elder son (48:19–20). Joshua belonged to this tribe, and to him was due much of its subsequent greatness. . . . Ephraim was given the birthright in Israel (1 Chr. 5:1–2; Jer. 31:9), and in the last days it has been the tribe of Ephraim's privilege first to bear the message of the Restoration of the gospel to the world and to gather scattered Israel (Deut. 33:13–17; D&C 64:36; 133:26–34)" (Bible Dictionary, "Ephraim").

53 ¶ And the seven years of plenteousness, that was in the land of Egypt, were ended.

Genesis 41:53–57. Joseph Sells Grain during the Seven Years of Famine

54 And the seven years of dearth began to come, according as Joseph had said: and the dearth was in all lands; but in all the land of Egypt there was bread.

55 And when all the land of Egypt was famished, the people cried to Pharaoh for bread: and Pharaoh said unto all the Egyptians, Go unto Joseph; what he saith to you, do.

56 And the famine was over all the face of the earth: And Joseph opened all the storehouses, and sold unto the Egyptians; and the famine waxed sore in the land of Egypt.

57 And all countries came into Egypt to Joseph for to buy *corn;* because that the famine was *so* sore in all lands.

What other countries came to Egypt during the famine to buy food? (41:57) "As there had not been a sufficiency of rains . . . to swell the Nile, to effect a proper inundation in Egypt, the same cause would produce drought, and consequently scarcity, in all the neighboring countries; and this may be all that is intended in the text" (*Adam Clarke's Commentary* [on Genesis 41:57]).

Genesis 42:1–5. Jacob's Sons Go to Egypt to Buy Food

Why do Abraham, Isaac, and Jacob each face famine in the land? (42:1) "Jacob heard from the report of others that there was plenty in Egypt. The operations of one sense, in Hebrew, are often put for those of another. Before agriculture was properly known and practiced, famines were frequent; Canaan seems to have been peculiarly vexed by them. There was one in this land in the time of Abraham [Genesis 12:10]; another in the days of Isaac [Genesis 26:1]; and now a third in the time of Jacob. To this . . . Stephen alludes [Acts 7:11]: 'there was great affliction, and our fathers found no sustenance'" (*Adam Clarke's Commentary* [on Genesis 42:1]).

What changed in Joseph's life when his brothers went down to Egypt? (42:3) "Once again, [Joseph] finds himself face to face with his brothers. On the previous, disastrous occasion, Joseph had been sent by his father to them; now it is they whom Jacob sends, unknowingly, to Joseph. Then Joseph had been at the mercy of his brothers; now he is master of the situation. . . . Underlying the phrase ["went down"] is a possible allusion to the reversal of fortunes that has taken place since Joseph was 'brought down' . . . to Egypt (Gen. 39:1)" (Sarna, *Genesis*, 291–92).

Why was Jacob concerned that "mischief" might befall Benjamin if he accompanied his brothers to buy food in Egypt? (42:4) "Jacob remembered his missing son Joseph, and he feared lest some tragedy befall Benjamin also. . . . [Perhaps] the brothers [were] not yet trustworthy in Jacob's eyes" (Petersen, *Joseph of Egypt*, 41).

Alfred Edersheim agrees: "But Benjamin, who had taken the place of Joseph in his father's heart, was not sent with them, perhaps from real fear of 'mischief' by the way, possibly because his father did not quite trust the honest intentions of his sons" (Edersheim, *Bible History*, 1:162). We see Jacob's concerns repeated in Genesis 42:38 and 44:29.

Genesis 42:6–14. Ten of Jacob's Sons Meet with Their Brother Joseph

CHAPTER 42

Jacob sends his sons to buy grain in Egypt—They bow before Joseph—He makes harsh accusations against them, imprisons Simeon, and sends them back for Benjamin.

1 Now when Jacob saw that there was corn in Egypt, Jacob said unto his sons, Why do ye look one upon another?

2 And he said, Behold, I have heard that there is corn in Egypt: get you down thither, and buy for us from thence; that we may live, and not die.

3 ¶ And Joseph's ten brethren went down to buy corn in Egypt.

4 But Benjamin, Joseph's brother, Jacob sent not with his brethren; for he said, Lest peradventure mischief befall him.

5 And the sons of Israel came to buy *corn* among those that came: for the famine was in the land of Canaan.

6 And Joseph *was* the governor over the land, *and* he *it was* that sold to all the people of the land: and Joseph's brethren came, and bowed down themselves before him *with* their faces to the earth.

What political power did Joseph have as governor? (42:6) "Joseph's appointment as second only to Pharaoh closely resembles what we know about the office of vizier in Egypt. This is evidenced by Joseph's receiving the royal seal, a signet ring. As far back as 3,000 B.C., the vizier was known in Egypt as the 'Sealbearer of the King of Lower Egypt'" (Madsen and Black, "Joseph and Joseph," 134). As governor, Joseph's brothers bowed before him, thus fulfilling one of his dreams (see Genesis 37:5–11). ⊕

How did Joseph's brothers fulfill his dreams from many years previous? (42:6, 9) "As a young man, Joseph had several dreams that foreshadowed his earthly mission and his leadership in the family. One dream was of his brothers' sheaves of grain bowing down to his sheaf. Some of his dreams are recorded in Genesis 37:5–11, and a partial fulfillment is noted in Genesis 42:6–9, when his brothers bowed before him in Egypt" (Matthews, *Selected Writings,* 165).

7 And Joseph saw his brethren, and he knew them, but made himself strange unto them, and spake roughly unto them; and he said unto them, Whence come ye? And they said, From the land of Canaan to buy food.

8 And Joseph knew his brethren, but they knew not him.

9 And Joseph remembered the dreams which he dreamed of them, and said unto them, Ye *are* spies; to see the nakedness of the land ye are come.

Why did Joseph's brothers not recognize him? (42:7–8) The passage in Genesis 42:7 of the King James Version says that Joseph "made himself strange" to his brothers. Other Bible translations suggest this could mean that Joseph "acted as a stranger" (NKJV), "pretended to be a stranger" (NIV), "treated them like strangers" (RSV), "acted as if he didn't know them" (NCV), and so on.

Joseph was seventeen years old when he was sold by his brethren (Gen. 37:2). "Joseph was thirty years of age when he was made overseer of Egypt (see Genesis 41:46); seven years later the famine began, and two years later still Joseph made himself known to his brothers, making him about thirty-nine at that time (see Genesis 45:6)" (Matthews, "Our Heritage," 3). ⊕

10 And they said unto him, Nay, my lord, but to buy food are thy servants come.

11 We *are* all one man's sons; we *are* true *men,* thy servants are no spies.

12 And he said unto them, Nay, but to see the nakedness of the land ye are come.

13 And they said, Thy servants *are* twelve brethren, the sons of one man in the land of Canaan; and, behold, the youngest *is* this day with our father, and one *is* not.

14 And Joseph said unto them, That *is it* that I spake unto you, saying, Ye *are* spies:

Why do Joseph's brothers say they are all sons of one father and "true men"? (42:10–11) "'We are all sons of one man' expresses more truth than they realized, for Joseph was also a son of Jacob. But by affirming their brotherhood, they hope to rebut the charge of spying, for spies would surely not travel together and risk the whole family by one of them being caught. 'We are honest' or 'honorable,' . . . i.e., they both tell the truth and do what is right (e.g., Num 27:7; 36:5; 2 Kgs 7:9; 17:9)" (Wenham, "Genesis 16–50," 407).

Genesis 42:15–28. Joseph Tests His Brothers by Sending Them Back to Jacob for Benjamin

Why did Joseph test his brothers? (42:15–20) In the Bible, "character is revealed primarily through speech, action, gesture" (Alter, *Art of Biblical Narrative*, 158). "Joseph wanted to test their assertion . . . because he wished to discover their feelings towards Benjamin, and see what affection they had for this son of Rachel, who had taken Joseph's place as his father's favourite. . . . Joseph had no intention whatever to administer to his brethren 'a just punishment for their wickedness towards him,' for his heart could not have stooped to such mean revenge; but he wanted to probe thoroughly the feelings of their hearts" (Keil and Delitzsch, *Commentary* [on Genesis 42:9–17]).

Why did Joseph's brothers feel anguish for forsaking their brother? (42:21–23) "Unrighteous acts that remain uncorrected leave a residue in our consciousness that at some future time will surface to our sorrow and shame. . . . [Joseph's brothers did not] know the cause of their imprisonment, but their imaginations became active. They began to argue among themselves, and Reuben said, in effect, 'I told you that you should not have mistreated our younger brother. . . . When we saw his anguish at our plan to sell him, and he pleaded for mercy, you should have listened' (see Genesis 42:21–22). That was twenty years after the selling of Joseph, but in that crisis, it all came back to trouble them" (Matthews, "Our Heritage," 5–6). ⊕

What was the money in the sacks? (42:25–27) The word translated *money* in this verse actually refers to silver. Coinage had not yet been invented. "Coined

15 Hereby ye shall be proved: By the life of Pharaoh ye shall not go forth hence, except your youngest brother come hither.

16 Send one of you, and let him fetch your brother, and ye shall be kept in prison, that your words may be proved, whether *there be any* truth in you: or else by the life of Pharaoh surely ye *are* spies.

17 And he put them all together into ward three days.

18 And Joseph said unto them the third day, This do, and live; *for* I fear God:

19 If ye *be* true *men,* let one of your brethren be bound in the house of your prison: go ye, carry corn for the famine of your houses:

20 But bring your youngest brother unto me; so shall your words be verified, and ye shall not die. And they did so.

21 ¶ And they said one to another, We *are* verily guilty concerning our brother, in that we saw the anguish of his soul, when he besought us, and we would not hear; therefore is this distress come upon us.

22 And Reuben answered them, saying, Spake I not unto you, saying, Do not sin against the child; and ye would not hear? therefore, behold, also his blood is required.

23 And they knew not that Joseph understood *them;* for he spake unto them by an interpreter.

24 And he turned himself about from them, and wept; and returned to them again, and communed with them, and took from them Simeon, and bound him before their eyes.

25 ¶ Then Joseph commanded to fill their sacks with corn, and to restore every man's money into his sack, and to give them provision for the way: and thus did he unto them.

26 And they laded their asses with the corn, and departed thence.

27 And as one of them opened his sack to give his ass provender in the inn, he espied his money; for, behold, it *was* in his sack's mouth.

28 And he said unto his brethren, My money is restored; and, lo, *it is* even in my sack: and their heart failed *them*, and they were afraid, saying one to another, What *is* this *that* God hath done unto us?

29 ¶ And they came unto Jacob their father unto the land of Canaan, and told him all that befell unto them; saying,

30 The man, *who is* the lord of the land, spake roughly to us, and took us for spies of the country.

31 And we said unto him, We *are* true *men;* we are no spies:

32 We *be* twelve brethren, sons of our father; one *is* not, and the youngest *is* this day with our father in the land of Canaan.

33 And the man, the lord of the country, said unto us, Hereby shall I know that ye *are* true *men;* leave one of your brethren *here* with me, and take *food for* the famine of your households, and be gone:

34 And bring your youngest brother unto me: then shall I know that ye *are* no spies, but *that* ye *are* true *men: so* will I deliver you your brother, and ye shall traffick in the land.

35 ¶ And it came to pass as they emptied their sacks, that, behold, every man's bundle of money *was* in his sack: and when *both* they and their father saw the bundles of money, they were afraid.

36 And Jacob their father said unto them, Me have ye bereaved *of my children:* Joseph *is* not,

money was not invented and put into common use until the sixth century B.C. Thus precious metals, gems, spices, incense and other luxury items were bartered by weight. Their relative value would also depend on scarcity. Silver was used throughout antiquity as a common item of exchange. Since Egypt lacked native silver deposits, this metal was particularly desirable as a standard for business transactions" (Walton, et al., *IVP Bible Background Commentary*, 74).

Genesis 42:29–38. Joseph's Brothers Meet with Their Father, Jacob

Why does Joseph charge them with spying, imprison Simeon, and plant money in their grain sacks? (42:29–35) "Joseph demanded they bring Benjamin to him—the last remaining son of Jacob's favored wife, Rachel. When his brothers refused out of respect for their father's love and feelings for Benjamin, Joseph ascertained that Benjamin had assumed the spot left vacant by himself, that of the favorite son. When Joseph made further food allowances contingent on his brothers bringing Benjamin to him [see Gen. 43:5], Joseph was able to see if his brothers were willing to sacrifice Benjamin in the same way that they had sacrificed Joseph" (Holzapfel, et al., *Jehovah and the World of the Old Testament*, 66–67).

and Simeon *is* not, and ye will take Benjamin
away: all these things are against me.

37 And Reuben spake unto his father, saying,
Slay my two sons, if I bring him not to thee:
deliver him into my hand, and I will bring
him to thee again.

38 And he said, My son shall not go down
with you; for his brother is dead, and he is
left alone: if mischief befall him by the way
in the which ye go, then shall ye bring down
my gray hairs with sorrow to the grave.

Why did Jacob refuse to send Benjamin? (42:37–38) "Jacob was resolute. He had lost enough sons; he didn't want to risk Benjamin, his favorite. . . . He assured his sons that risking the loss of Benjamin in addition to having lost Joseph would lead him into depression and cause his premature death" (*Nelson Study Bible* [NKJV], 75).

CHAPTER 43

Jacob is persuaded to send Benjamin to Egypt—Joseph's brothers show respect to him—They all eat and drink together.

Genesis 43:1–14. Jacob Allows Benjamin to Go to Egypt with His Brothers

1 And the famine *was* sore in the land.

2 And it came to pass, when they had eaten
up the corn which they had brought out of
Egypt, their father said unto them, Go again,
buy us a little food.

3 And Judah spake unto him, saying, The
man did solemnly protest unto us, saying, Ye
shall not see my face, except your brother *be*
with you.

4 If thou wilt send our brother with us, we
will go down and buy thee food:

5 But if thou wilt not send *him,* we will not go
down: for the man said unto us, Ye shall not
see my face, except your brother *be* with you.

6 And Israel said, Wherefore dealt ye *so* ill
with me, *as* to tell the man whether ye had
yet a brother?

7 And they said, The man asked us straitly
of our state, and of our kindred, saying, *Is*
your father yet alive? have ye *another* brother?
and we told him according to the tenor of
these words: could we certainly know that he
would say, Bring your brother down?

Why does Judah speak on behalf of the brothers? (43:3) "From this point on, Judah became the spokesman for his brothers (see vv. 8–10; 44:14–34; 46:28). His tribe would become preeminent among the 12 (see 49:8–10), and he would be an ancestor of Jesus (see Mt 1:2–3, 16–17; Lk 3:23, 33)" (*NIV Study Bible* [1985], 71).

8 And Judah said unto Israel his father, Send the lad with me, and we will arise and go; that we may live, and not die, both we, and thou, *and* also our little ones.

9 I will be surety for him; of my hand shalt thou require him: if I bring him not unto thee, and set him before thee, then let me bear the blame for ever:

10 For except we had lingered, surely now we had returned this second time.

11 And their father Israel said unto them, If *it must be* so now, do this; take of the best fruits in the land in your vessels, and carry down the man a present, a little balm, and a little honey, spices, and myrrh, nuts, and almonds:

12 And take double money in your hand; and the money that was brought again in the mouth of your sacks, carry *it* again in your hand; peradventure it *was* an oversight:

13 Take also your brother, and arise, go again unto the man:

14 And God Almighty give you mercy before the man, that he may send away your other brother, and Benjamin. If I be bereaved *of my children,* I am bereaved.

15 ¶ And the men took that present, and they took double money in their hand, and Benjamin; and rose up, and went down to Egypt, and stood before Joseph.

16 And when Joseph saw Benjamin with them, he said to the ruler of his house, Bring *these* men home, and slay, and make ready; for *these* men shall dine with me at noon.

17 And the man did as Joseph bade; and the man brought the men into Joseph's house.

18 And the men were afraid, because they were brought into Joseph's house; and they said, Because of the money that was returned in our sacks at the first time are we brought in; that he may seek occasion against us, and

What do we learn about Judah when he offers to be surety for Benjamin? (43:8–9) "It is significant that Judah, who suggested that Joseph be sold (see Genesis 37:26–27), became the one who was willing to become 'the surety' for Benjamin. There does seem to be evidence of sincere repentance on the brothers' part, and Joseph's stratagem allowed them to demonstrate this repentance. When the pressure was on, Judah's change of heart was shown to be complete (see Genesis 44:33)" (*Old Testament Student Manual: Genesis–2 Samuel*, 96).

Why are the brothers' gifts noteworthy? (43:11) "The ironic connection with the Ishmaelite traders is ingeniously reinforced by the other half of Jacob's instructions: that caravan long ago was seen (Gen. 37:25) 'carrying gum, balm, and laudanum to be taken to Egypt,' and now the brothers will constitute another such caravan, bearing exactly the same goods together with a few extra items, not bringing Joseph as a slave but headed, unawares, to the discovery of his identity as supreme master" (Alter, *Art of Biblical Narrative*, 172).

Genesis 43:15–34. Ten of Jacob's Sons Meet Again with Joseph

fall upon us, and take us for bondmen, and our asses.

19 And they came near to the steward of Joseph's house, and they communed with him at the door of the house,

20 And said, O sir, we came indeed down at the first time to buy food:

21 And it came to pass, when we came to the inn, that we opened our sacks, and, behold, *every* man's money *was* in the mouth of his sack, our money in full weight: and we have brought it again in our hand.

22 And other money have we brought down in our hands to buy food: we cannot tell who put our money in our sacks.

23 And he said, Peace *be* to you, fear not: your God, and the God of your father, hath given you treasure in your sacks: I had your money. And he brought Simeon out unto them.

24 And the man brought the men into Joseph's house, and gave *them* water, and they washed their feet; and he gave their asses provender.

25 And they made ready the present against Joseph came at noon: for they heard that they should eat bread there.

26 ¶ And when Joseph came home, they brought him the present which *was* in their hand into the house, and bowed themselves to him to the earth.

27 And he asked them of *their* welfare, and said, *Is* your father well, the old man of whom ye spake? *Is* he yet alive?

28 And they answered, Thy servant our father *is* in good health, he *is* yet alive. And they bowed down their heads, and made obeisance.

29 And he lifted up his eyes, and saw his brother Benjamin, his mother's son, and said, *Is* this your younger brother, of whom ye

What was meaningful about the brothers bowing down before Joseph? (43:26, 28) "The Hebrew words repeat those of Joseph's childhood dreams, in which his brothers' sheaves in the field gathered around and bowed down to his sheaf, and the sun, moon, and stars in the sky bowed low to him. . . .

"All eleven brothers bowed down to Joseph, just as predicted in the second of his youthful dreams (Genesis 37:9), another—perhaps the most explicit—indicator of the divine element in the Joseph story" (Prager, *Rational Bible*, 476, 490). ⊕

Why did Joseph test his older brothers' feelings about Benjamin? (43:29–34) As the meal began, Joseph favored Benjamin by providing him with "five

spake unto me? And he said, God be gracious unto thee, my son.

30 And Joseph made haste; for his bowels did yearn upon his brother: and he sought *where* to weep; and he entered into *his* chamber, and wept there.

31 And he washed his face, and went out, and refrained himself, and said, Set on bread.

32 And they set on for him by himself, and for them by themselves, and for the Egyptians, which did eat with him, by themselves: because the Egyptians might not eat bread with the Hebrews; for that *is* an abomination unto the Egyptians.

33 And they sat before him, the firstborn according to his birthright, and the youngest according to his youth: and the men marvelled one at another.

34 And he took *and sent* messes unto them from before him: but Benjamin's mess was five times so much as any of theirs. And they drank, and were merry with him.

CHAPTER 44

Joseph arranges to stop the return of his brothers to Canaan—Judah offers himself in place of Benjamin for their father's sake.

1 And he commanded the steward of his house, saying, Fill the men's sacks *with* food, as much as they can carry, and put every man's money in his sack's mouth.

2 And put my cup, the silver cup, in the sack's mouth of the youngest, and his corn money. And he did according to the word that Joseph had spoken.

3 As soon as the morning was light, the men were sent away, they and their asses.

4 *And* when they were gone out of the city, *and* not *yet* far off, Joseph said unto his steward, Up, follow after the men; and when

times so much [food] as any of [his older brothers]" (Gen. 43:34). "The Genesis text . . . [focuses] upon the problem of how one *responds* when favoritism is shown. . . . How do the brothers respond? In ch. 43, the issue is whether they can stand to have another brother favored. Would they reject him as they had Joseph? Or could they rise above hurt feelings and *rejoice with those who rejoice* (Romans 12:15)?" (*Quest Study Bible* [1994], 64).

Why would Egyptians consider eating with Hebrews offensive? (43:32) "Several Egyptian deities were represented by cattle, especially female cattle. Since the Hebrews were herdsmen who slaughtered and ate cattle, regardless of sex, this practice would have been viewed by the Egyptians as a terrible abomination. Whatever the reason, Joseph seemed to respect the custom of Egyptians and Hebrews eating separately" (*Old Testament Student Manual: Genesis–2 Samuel*, 96).

Genesis 44:1–13. Joseph Sends His Brothers Home, but Arranges for Their Capture and Return to Egypt

How did Joseph's brothers react when the cup was discovered in Benjamin's sack? (44:1–13) "Joseph continued to test the character of his brothers by commanding his servants to place his brothers' *money* in their sacks and a *silver cup* in Benjamin's sack. . . . After [Joseph's servants searched] all the brothers' sacks, the servant found the cup with Benjamin. In genuine despair for Benjamin's predicament, the brothers *tore their clothes*. They could not let Benjamin die! Ironically a few years earlier, the same brothers had been debating whether to kill Joseph. Instead of tearing their own clothes in grief, they had torn Joseph's robe in order to cover up what they had done" (*Nelson Study Bible* [NKJV], 77).

thou dost overtake them, say unto them,
Wherefore have ye rewarded evil for good?

5 *Is* not this *it* in which my lord drinketh,
and whereby indeed he divineth? ye have
done evil in so doing.

6 ¶ And he overtook them, and he spake unto
them these same words.

7 And they said unto him, Wherefore saith
my lord these words? God forbid that thy
servants should do according to this thing:

8 Behold, the money, which we found in our
sacks' mouths, we brought again unto thee
out of the land of Canaan: how then should
we steal out of thy lord's house silver or gold?

9 With whomsoever of thy servants it be
found, both let him die, and we also will be
my lord's bondmen.

10 And he said, Now also *let* it *be* according
unto your words: he with whom it is found
shall be my servant; and ye shall be blameless.

11 Then they speedily took down every man
his sack to the ground, and opened every
man his sack.

12 And he searched, *and* began at the eldest,
and left at the youngest: and the cup was
found in Benjamin's sack.

13 Then they rent their clothes, and laded
every man his ass, and returned to the city.

How are objects sometimes used in achieving God's purposes? (44:5) "Divining instruments . . . were far from unfamiliar in a biblical culture. . . . David enquired of the Urim and Thummim (seerstones) for directions concerning military strivings (see 1 Samuel 30:7–8). . . . Joseph of Egypt used a silver cup for divining (see Genesis 44:5), and the book of Revelation records the use of white stones in receiving revelation (see Revelation 2:17; D&C 130:10–11)" (Muhlestein, "Seeking Divine Interaction," 85).

Genesis 44:14–34. Joseph Arranges for Benjamin to Be His Servant

14 ¶ And Judah and his brethren came to
Joseph's house; for he *was* yet there: and they
fell before him on the ground.

15 And Joseph said unto them, What deed *is*
this that ye have done? wot ye not that such a
man as I can certainly divine?

16 And Judah said, What shall we say unto
my lord? what shall we speak? or how shall
we clear ourselves? God hath found out the
iniquity of thy servants: behold, we *are* my
lord's servants, both we, and *he* also with
whom the cup is found.

17 And he said, God forbid that I should do so: *but* the man in whose hand the cup is found, he shall be my servant; and as for you, get you up in peace unto your father.

18 ¶ Then Judah came near unto him, and said, Oh my lord, let thy servant, I pray thee, speak a word in my lord's ears, and let not thine anger burn against thy servant: for thou *art* even as Pharaoh.

19 My lord asked his servants, saying, Have ye a father, or a brother?

20 And we said unto my lord, We have a father, an old man, and a child of his old age, a little one; and his brother is dead, and he alone is left of his mother, and his father loveth him.

21 And thou saidst unto thy servants, Bring him down unto me, that I may set mine eyes upon him.

22 And we said unto my lord, The lad cannot leave his father: for *if* he should leave his father, *his father* would die.

23 And thou saidst unto thy servants, Except your youngest brother come down with you, ye shall see my face no more.

24 And it came to pass when we came up unto thy servant my father, we told him the words of my lord.

25 And our father said, Go again, *and* buy us a little food.

26 And we said, We cannot go down: if our youngest brother be with us, then will we go down: for we may not see the man's face, except our youngest brother *be* with us.

27 And thy servant my father said unto us, Ye know that my wife bare me two *sons:*

28 And the one went out from me, and I said, Surely he is torn in pieces; and I saw him not since:

What do we see in Judah when he shares his concerns about his father's well-being? (44:18–33)
"We can sense that Judah and his brothers regretted the pain they saw their father go through when they led him to believe that Joseph had died. It seems they felt so badly about Jacob's pain that they did not want to see him go through it again" (Muhlestein, *Scripture Study Made Simple*, 77). ⊕

29 And if ye take this also from me, and mischief befall him, ye shall bring down my gray
hairs with sorrow to the grave.

30 Now therefore when I come to thy servant
my father, and the lad *be* not with us; seeing
that his life is bound up in the lad's life;

31 It shall come to pass, when he seeth that
the lad *is* not *with us,* that he will die: and
thy servants shall bring down the gray hairs
of thy servant our father with sorrow to the
grave.

32 For thy servant became surety for the lad
unto my father, saying, If I bring him not
unto thee, then I shall bear the blame to my
father for ever.

33 Now therefore, I pray thee, let thy servant
abide instead of the lad a bondman to my
lord; and let the lad go up with his brethren.

34 For how shall I go up to my father, and
the lad *be* not with me? lest peradventure I
see the evil that shall come on my father.

In what ways does Judah remind us of the Savior? (44:32–34) "This is a powerful moment. The Judah we see here is not the same Judah we saw earlier. This Judah was an appropriate symbol of his great descendant, Jesus. Judah knew of the pain that his father would suffer if Benjamin did not return. He promised his father he would bring his children home to him. When one of them had been condemned, Judah in essence said that no matter what, he would bring that child home. He was willing to take the child's punishment upon himself, though he had done no wrong, so that he could return that child to his father. This is a smaller-scale version of the self-sacrifice that Christ, the Judahite, would one day take upon Himself" (Muhlestein, *Scripture Study Made Simple*, 77–78). ⊕

CHAPTER 45

Joseph makes himself known to his brothers—They rejoice together—Pharaoh invites Jacob and his family to dwell in Egypt and eat the fat of the land.

Genesis 45:1–15. Joseph Makes Himself Known to His Brothers

What powerful example of forgiveness is shown by Joseph to his brothers in these verses? (45:1–3) "Joseph 'could not refrain himself.' ... Joseph, with all tenderness of affection and delicacy of feeling, made himself known to them as the brother whom they had sold into Egypt, but whom in reality God had sent before for the purpose not only of saving their lives, but of preserving their posterity, that so His counsel of mercy with the world might be accomplished. Then let them not be grieved, for God had overruled it all. Three times must he speak it, and prove his forgiveness by the most loving marks, before they could credit his words or derive comfort from them" (Edersheim, *Bible History*, 1:171).

1 Then Joseph could not refrain himself before all them that stood by him; and he cried,
Cause every man to go out from me. And
there stood no man with him, while Joseph
made himself known unto his brethren.

2 And he wept aloud: and the Egyptians and
the house of Pharaoh heard.

3 And Joseph said unto his brethren, I *am* Joseph; doth my father yet live? And his brethren could not answer him; for they were troubled at his presence.

4 And Joseph said unto his brethren, Come near to me, I pray you. And they came near. And he said, I *am* Joseph your brother, whom ye sold into Egypt.

Why would Joseph's brothers fear when the Egyptian governor claims to be their brother? (45:3–4) "Joseph must have said ['I am Joseph'] in Hebrew and not Egyptian (42:23). Still, the brothers could not believe their ears. They had sold Joseph as a slave. He would certainly be dead. Could it be true? The Egyptian lord who held their lives in his hands was their brother! . . . Joseph realized that his physical appearance, his Egyptian manner, his high position and his total power over them all conspired to make his words unbelievable. He told them to come closer so that they could recognize his face and voice. . . . Fear overcame Joseph's brothers again. Would Joseph take revenge?" (*Nelson Study Bible* [NKJV], 78).

5 Now therefore be not grieved, nor angry with yourselves, that ye sold me hither: for God did send me before you to preserve life.

6 For these two years *hath* the famine *been* in the land: and yet *there are* five years, in the which *there shall* neither *be* earing nor harvest.

7 And God sent me before you to preserve you a posterity in the earth, and to save your lives by a great deliverance.

Why could Joseph see God's hand in his life despite his trials? (45:5–7) Joseph's faith in God enabled him to trust even when circumstances seemed hopeless. "Faith is trust—trust that God sees what we cannot and that He knows what we do not. . . . [Faith] means trusting that God loves us perfectly, that everything He does—every blessing He gives and every blessing He, for a time, withholds—is for our eternal happiness.

"With this kind of faith, though we may not understand why certain things happen or why certain prayers go unanswered, we can know that in the end everything will make sense. 'All things [will] work together for good to them that love God' (Romans 8:28)" (Uchtdorf, "Fourth Floor, Last Door," 17).

8 So now *it was* not you *that* sent me hither, but God: and he hath made me a father to Pharaoh, and lord of all his house, and a ruler throughout all the land of Egypt.

9 Haste ye, and go up to my father, and say unto him, Thus saith thy son Joseph, God hath made me lord of all Egypt: come down unto me, tarry not:

What does Joseph mean "he made me a father to the Pharaoh"? (45:8) "The use of the title 'father of Pharaoh' most likely is related to the Egyptian title *it-ntr*, 'father of the god,' used to refer to a variety of officials and priests who serve in the Pharaoh's court. 'Father' represents an advisory relationship, perhaps to be equated with the role of the priest hired by Micah in Judges 17:10 or the role of Elisha as the king of Israel's counselor in 2 Kings 6:21" (Walton, et al., *IVP Bible Background Commentary*, 74).

10 And thou shalt dwell in the land of Goshen, and thou shalt be near unto me, thou, and thy children, and thy children's children, and thy flocks, and thy herds, and all that thou hast:

11 And there will I nourish thee; for yet *there are* five years of famine; lest thou, and thy household, and all that thou hast, come to poverty.

Where is Goshen and why did Joseph settle his family there? (45:10) "In Egyptian texts the heaviest concentrations of Semites occurs in the eastern Delta region closest to Canaan. This corresponds to the biblical texts in which the region of Goshen is equated to the district of Ramesses (47:11), which is certainly in the Delta region. In the early chapters of Exodus, this is the location of the Israelite labors and towns such as Pithom and Ramesses. The region is bounded by the branches of the Nile Delta on the west and the series of lakes from the Mediterranean down to the Red Sea on the east. Crossing east to west through the center of it is the Wadi Tumilat" (Walton, *Zondervan Illustrated Bible Backgrounds Commentary,* 1:133). See commentary in this volume for Genesis 47:1.

What can families learn from Joseph forgiving his brothers? (45:14–15) "To Joseph's credit, he did not only embrace Benjamin but embraced and wept upon all his brothers. One would wish that all who read this would find it possible to reconcile with family members from whom they are estranged and whose wrongs are likely far less evil than those committed by Joseph's brothers" (Prager, *Rational Bible*, 507).

Elder Neal A. Maxwell wrote, "There is no expiation in retaliation; vengeance not only prolongs conflict, but also deepens and widens it. Thus, forgetfulness and forgiveness, by being intertwined, make strong the chords of brotherhood" (*Neal A. Maxwell Quote Book*, 130).

12 And, behold, your eyes see, and the eyes of my brother Benjamin, that *it is* my mouth that speaketh unto you.

13 And ye shall tell my father of all my glory in Egypt, and of all that ye have seen; and ye shall haste and bring down my father hither.

14 And he fell upon his brother Benjamin's neck, and wept; and Benjamin wept upon his neck.

15 Moreover he kissed all his brethren, and wept upon them: and after that his brethren talked with him.

Genesis 45:16–24. Pharaoh Shows Great Kindness to Jacob's Family

16 ¶ And the fame thereof was heard in Pharaoh's house, saying, Joseph's brethren are come: and it pleased Pharaoh well, and his servants.

17 And Pharaoh said unto Joseph, Say unto thy brethren, This do ye; lade your beasts, and go, get you unto the land of Canaan;

18 And take your father and your households, and come unto me: and I will give you the good of the land of Egypt, and ye shall eat the fat of the land.

19 Now thou art commanded, this do ye; take you wagons out of the land of Egypt for your little ones, and for your wives, and bring your father, and come.

20 Also regard not your stuff; for the good of all the land of Egypt *is* yours.

21 And the children of Israel did so: and Joseph gave them wagons, according to the commandment of Pharaoh, and gave them provision for the way.

22 To all of them he gave each man changes

of raiment; but to Benjamin he gave three hundred *pieces* of silver, and five changes of raiment.

23 And to his father he sent after this *manner;* ten asses laden with the good things of Egypt, and ten she asses laden with corn and bread and meat for his father by the way.

24 So he sent his brethren away, and they departed: and he said unto them, See that ye fall not out by the way.

What does it mean to "fall not out by the way"? (45:24) Various Bible translations have provided similar meanings for the phrase "See that ye fall not out by the way" (KJV). Many suggest that Joseph told his brothers not to quarrel while traveling home. He remembered that "the brothers had a history of quarreling. In fact, all through the narrative, beginning in 37:4, they are pictured as bitter, hateful, quarreling men. But Joseph was hoping this incident might bring harmony among them" (*Quest Study Bible* [1994], 67). One Bible commentary suggested that "the thought of their guilt could have upset the brothers and agitated their conscience, especially since they were about to confess their shameful deed to their father" (Roehrs and Franzmann, *Concordia Self-Study Commentary*, 55).

25 ¶ And they went up out of Egypt, and came into the land of Canaan unto Jacob their father,

26 And told him, saying, Joseph *is* yet alive, and he *is* governor over all the land of Egypt. And Jacob's heart fainted, for he believed them not.

27 And they told him all the words of Joseph, which he had said unto them: and when he saw the wagons which Joseph had sent to carry him, the spirit of Jacob their father revived:

28 And Israel said, *It is* enough; Joseph my son *is* yet alive: I will go and see him before I die.

Genesis 45:25–28. Jacob Realizes That His Beloved Joseph Is Still Alive

Why would Jacob not believe that Joseph was alive? (45:26) "These same sons had brought him the blood-soaked tunic twenty years before, leading Jacob to conclude Joseph was dead. . . .

"The brothers have reaped the inevitable consequence of lying—being doubted when telling the truth. Many adolescents and teens lie to their parents and when their parents respond even to the truth with skepticism, they angrily protest, 'You don't trust me!' To which the appropriate response is, 'Why should I?'" (Prager, *Rational Bible*, 509).

"When we are honest in all things, big and small," explained Sister Ann M. Dibb, "relationships are enriched because they are based on trust" ("I Believe in Being Honest and True," 116).

What persuaded Jacob that Joseph was a mighty man in Egypt? (45:26–27) "It was understandably overwhelming to Jacob to learn that Joseph was not only alive but 'governor over all the land of Egypt.' Only when he heard what Joseph had said to his brothers and saw the Egyptian wagons could the aged father believe it" (Rasmussen, *Latter-day Saint Commentary on the Old Testament*, 76).

Genesis 46:1–7. Jacob and His Family Move to Egypt

Why did Jacob offer sacrifice? (46:1–4) "'Beersheba' is some twenty-six miles (forty kilometers) south of Hebron and marks the practical southern border of the land (cf. 'from Dan to Beersheba,' 2 Sam 24:2). Beyond Beersheba, cultivation is difficult. The desert prevails until one reaches Egypt. So offering a sacrifice at this point is appropriate (cf. 31:54). Setting out on a major journey, Jacob desired God's blessing and therefore sacrificed . . . The offering of sacrifice sometimes is seen as a preliminary to prophetic inspiration (Num 23:1, 14, 29; Ps 50:5; Isa 6:6)" (Wenham, "Genesis 16–50," 440–41).

What does "visions of the night" mean? (46:2) On many occasions the Lord communicated with the Old Testament patriarchs through dreams and visions that came to them in the night. "Despite the fact that darkness and nighttime symbolically are associated with evil, spiritual giants of all ages have envisioned the things of God and of eternity during the hours of the night. Israel (Gen. 46:2), Samuel (1 Sam. 3:3ff.), Daniel (Dan. 2:19), Paul (Acts 16:9), Nephi (1 Ne. 4:23), Joseph Smith (Joseph Smith–History 1:29–30), and others have enjoyed the secrets of Deity while reposing upon their beds" (McConkie and Parry, *Guide to Scriptural Symbols,* 87).

How does moving from the promised land to live in Egypt illustrate the plan of salvation? (46:3–4) "Just as we were foreordained in the premortal life before coming to the earth, so too Jacob received a promise and a blessing from God before leaving for Egypt, 'Fear not to go down into Egypt; for I will there make of thee a great nation . . . and I will also surely bring thee up again' (Genesis 46:3–4). . . . Leaving the Promised Land is described as a descent, and returning is ascending. . . . We have the promise that we can return to [Heavenly Father's] presence again and live with Him throughout eternity if we have been faithful" (Hoskisson, "Plan of Salvation in the First Six Books," 55).

Why could Jacob courageously enter Egypt? (46:3–4) A more literal translation of the Hebrew reads: "Fear not to go down to Egypt. . . . I Myself will go down with you . . . I Myself will also bring you back; and Joseph's hand shall close your eyes." Importantly, "God's only speech in [Genesis] 37–50 reiterates the promise

CHAPTER 46

The Lord sends Jacob and his family of seventy souls to Egypt—The descendants of Jacob are named—Joseph meets Jacob.

1 And Israel took his journey with all that he had, and came to Beer-sheba, and offered sacrifices unto the God of his father Isaac.

2 And God spake unto Israel in the visions of the night, and said, Jacob, Jacob. And he said, Here *am* I.

3 And he said, I *am* God, the God of thy father: fear not to go down into Egypt; for I will there make of thee a great nation:

4 I will go down with thee into Egypt; and I will also surely bring thee up *again:* and Joseph shall put his hand upon thine eyes.

5 And Jacob rose up from Beer-sheba: and the sons of Israel carried Jacob their father, and their little ones, and their wives, in the wagons which Pharaoh had sent to carry him.

6 And they took their cattle, and their goods, which they had gotten in the land of Canaan, and came into Egypt, Jacob, and all his seed with him:

7 His sons, and his sons' sons with him, his daughters, and his sons' daughters, and all his seed brought he with him into Egypt.

28 ¶ And he sent Judah before him unto Joseph, to direct his face unto Goshen; and they came into the land of Goshen.

29 And Joseph made ready his chariot, and went up to meet Israel his father, to Goshen, and presented himself unto him; and he fell on his neck, and wept on his neck a good while.

30 And Israel said unto Joseph, Now let me die, since I have seen thy face, because thou *art* yet alive.

31 And Joseph said unto his brethren, and unto his father's house, I will go up, and shew Pharaoh, and say unto him, My brethren, and my father's house, which *were* in the land of Canaan, are come unto me;

32 And the men *are* shepherds, for their trade hath been to feed cattle; and they have

to Abraham and Isaac. . . . , assuring Jacob that his departure from the promised land will not void God's commitment to his forebears." And, that, "Joseph will lovingly attend to his father's needs at that moment of the latter's death" (*Jewish Study Bible,* 85).

What is the meaning of the promise "Joseph shall put his hand upon thine eyes"? (46:4) "An ancient Hebrew custom dictated that 'the nearest kin and the most beloved should close the eyes of the deceased person and give a parting kiss to the corpse. It was therefore a very comforting and loving thing which the Lord did when he assured Jacob that his beloved Joseph, whom he had for many years mourned as dead, should perform this filial office for him' ([Godfrey, "Making the Old Testament Live," 111])" (Black, *400 Questions and Answers about the Old Testament*, 58).

Summary of Genesis 46:8–27

Jacob's children and grandchildren who accompany him to Egypt are listed. "The fathers of the future twelve tribes of Israel were named along with their sons in a symbolic count of seventy. . . . Seventy is a tenfold multiple of seven, and seven symbolizes completeness" (Rasmussen, *Latter-day Saint Commentary on the Old Testament*, 76).

Genesis 46:28–34. Jacob and Joseph Are Reunited

How could this tender reunion between Jacob and Joseph foreshadow our reunion with the Savior? (46:29) How will the Savior greet those whom He deems worthy at the gate to eternal life? "I will tell you . . . what I think the major reason is [why he 'employeth no servant there' (2 Nephi 9:41)], as contained in another Book of Mormon scripture which says he waits for you 'with open arms' (Mormon 6:17). That's why he's there! . . . That imagery is too powerful to brush aside. . . . He does wait for us with open arms, because His love of us is perfect" (Maxwell, "But a Few Days," 7). ⊕

What was remarkable about Pharaoh allowing Joseph's large family to move to his land? (46:32–34) "Ordinarily shepherds were an 'abomination to the Egyptians' (43:32). But Pharaoh readily agreed to the settlement of these foreigners in his domain. In addition, he made provisions for adequate transport of Jacob's family to Egypt" (Roehrs and Franzmann, *Concordia Self-Study Commentary*, 55).

brought their flocks, and their herds, and all
that they have.

33 And it shall come to pass, when Pharaoh
shall call you, and shall say, What *is* your occupation?

34 That ye shall say, Thy servants' trade hath
been about cattle from our youth even until now, both we, *and* also our fathers: that
ye may dwell in the land of Goshen; for
every shepherd *is* an abomination unto the
Egyptians.

CHAPTER 47

The Israelites settle in Goshen—Jacob blesses Pharaoh—Joseph sells grain to the Egyptians—Pharaoh receives the Egyptians' cattle and lands—Jacob desires to be buried with his fathers in Canaan.

1 Then Joseph came and told Pharaoh, and
said, My father and my brethren, and their
flocks, and their herds, and all that they have,
are come out of the land of Canaan; and, behold, they *are* in the land of Goshen.

Genesis 47:1–6. Pharaoh Tells Jacob's Family to Live in the Land of Goshen

What is the significance of Jacob's family settling in the land of Goshen? (Genesis 47:1) "[Goshen was the] part of Egypt in which the Israelites dwelt. It contained pasture land (Gen. 46:33–34) and lay somewhere between Palestine and the capital of Egypt (46:28–29), probably in the eastern part of the delta of the Nile" (Bible Dictionary, "Goshen"). It was the "best of the land" (v. 6). "When Pharaoh learned that Joseph's family had come as far as Goshen and wanted permission to live there with their flocks, he assigned the land to them. . . . Thus, when the famine became more severe and fertile land was needed, no Egyptian could fault Joseph, a foreigner, for having favored his family and placing them in the best of the land, because Pharaoh had made the decision" (*Zondervan KJV Commentary*, 72).

2 And he took some of his brethren, *even* five
men, and presented them unto Pharaoh.

Why did Joseph take only five of his twelve brothers to meet Pharaoh? (47:2) It may be that Joseph selected the best, physically appealing, and strongest from among his brothers to make a good impression on Pharaoh. Another possibility is that Joseph chose the weakest of the brothers to not intimidate Pharaoh or run the risk that they might be conscripted for the Egyptian army (see *Torah: A Modern Commentary*, 294). Tradition has it that Joseph selected Reuben, Simeon, Levi, Benjamin, and Issachar (see Hamilton, *Book of Genesis, 18–50*, 2:606).

3 And Pharaoh said unto his brethren, What *is* your occupation? And they said unto Pharaoh, Thy servants *are* shepherds, both we, *and* also our fathers.

4 They said moreover unto Pharaoh, For to sojourn in the land are we come; for thy servants have no pasture for their flocks; for the famine *is* sore in the land of Canaan: now therefore, we pray thee, let thy servants dwell in the land of Goshen.

5 And Pharaoh spake unto Joseph, saying, Thy father and thy brethren are come unto thee:

6 The land of Egypt *is* before thee; in the best of the land make thy father and brethren to dwell; in the land of Goshen let them dwell: and if thou knowest *any* men of activity among them, then make them rulers over my cattle.

7 And Joseph brought in Jacob his father, and set him before Pharaoh: and Jacob blessed Pharaoh.

8 And Pharaoh said unto Jacob, How old *art* thou?

9 And Jacob said unto Pharaoh, The days of the years of my pilgrimage *are* an hundred and thirty years: few and evil have the days of the years of my life been, and have not attained unto the days of the years of the life of my fathers in the days of their pilgrimage.

10 And Jacob blessed Pharaoh, and went out from before Pharaoh.

Why would Joseph tell his family to say they were shepherds? (47:3) "Joseph wisely counseled his father and brothers to tell Pharaoh they were shepherds. The Egyptians hated shepherds (see Genesis 46:34), and Pharaoh was forced to give them land away from the main population" (Valletta, et al., *Old Testament for Latter-day Saint Families*, 94).

Genesis 47:7–11. Jacob Meets Pharaoh and Blesses Him

Why did Jacob bless Pharaoh? (47:7) "The presentation of Joseph's father *before Pharaoh* must have been a grand occasion. But surprisingly, *Jacob blessed Pharaoh* (vv. 7, 10). Pharaoh as the host might have thought of pronouncing a blessing on Jacob because of his great admiration for Joseph. But instead the visitor blessed the host in the name of the living God! Literally Jacob obeyed God's command to Abram's descendants to 'be a blessing' (see 12:2)" (*Nelson Study Bible* [NKJV], 81).

How did Jacob respond when asked about his age? (47:8–9) "When the old patriarch and shepherd was brought in for an audience with Pharaoh, Pharaoh was given a blessing by the patriarch. It was an unusual interaction between a leader with earthly power and a man with divine power.

"Note how humbly Jacob responded to Pharaoh's inquiry about his age; perhaps he counted his one hundred thirty years as 'few' because his father Isaac had lived to one hundred eighty and Abraham to one hundred seventy-five. Doubtless he counted his years as 'evil' (Gen. 47:9*b*, 'unpleasant') because of the loss of Rachel to early death, the disappearance of Joseph, and the trials incident to the famine" (Rasmussen, *Latter-day Saint Commentary on the Old Testament*, 78). ⊕

Why is the land of Goshen referred to as the "land of Rameses"? (47:11) "Following Pharaoh's orders, Joseph settles his family in Goshen, identified here as *the region of Rameses*. This phrase appears to be an editorial comment, for this terminology was not used until the thirteenth-century pharaohs of the 19th Dynasty. . . . The only way to defend the presence of this place name as early as the setting of the Joseph story, that is, as something other than an editorial insertion or an anachronism, is to suggest that the city bore this name prior to the Ramesside Dynasty, a name that simply meant 'Re has created it'" (Hamilton, *Book of Genesis, 18–50*, 2:612–13).

11 ¶ And Joseph placed his father and his brethren, and gave them a possession in the land of Egypt, in the best of the land, in the land of Rameses, as Pharaoh had commanded.

Genesis 47:12–26. Joseph Oversees Egypt during the Famine

How does ancient Joseph typify Joseph Smith? (47:12–13) Amos prophesied that God would send a famine in the last days, "not a famine of bread . . . but of hearing the words of the Lord" (Amos 8:11). "Anciently, 'when all the land of Egypt was famished, the people cried to Pharaoh for bread: and Pharaoh said unto all the Egyptians, Go unto Joseph' . . . (Gen. 41:55). In the latter days, people starving for nourishment that only the gospel can provide are again to be fed—by Joseph. The Lord declared that 'this generation shall have my word through [Joseph Smith]' (D&C 5:10). Today we 'feast upon the words of Christ' because of Joseph Smith (2 Ne. 32:3)" (Nelson, "Remnants Gathered, Covenants Fulfilled," 6).

What can we learn from the suffering of Pharaoh's people? (47:13–26) "We have a classic example of the loss of economic freedom by the misuse of free agency in the book of Genesis. The Egyptians, instead of exercising their agency to provide for themselves against a day of need, depended upon the government. As a result, when the famine came they were forced to purchase food from the government. First they used their money. When that was gone, they gave their livestock, then their lands; and finally they were compelled to sell themselves into slavery, that they might eat" (Romney, "Perfect Law of Liberty," 44–45).

12 And Joseph nourished his father, and his brethren, and all his father's household, with bread, according to *their* families.

13 ¶ And *there was* no bread in all the land; for the famine *was* very sore, so that the land of Egypt and *all* the land of Canaan fainted by reason of the famine.

14 And Joseph gathered up all the money that was found in the land of Egypt, and in the land of Canaan, for the corn which they bought: and Joseph brought the money into Pharaoh's house.

15 And when money failed in the land of Egypt, and in the land of Canaan, all the Egyptians came unto Joseph, and said, Give us bread: for why should we die in thy presence? for the money faileth.

16 And Joseph said, Give your cattle; and I will give you for your cattle, if money fail.

17 And they brought their cattle unto Joseph: and Joseph gave them bread *in exchange* for horses, and for the flocks, and for the cattle of the herds, and for the asses: and he fed them with bread for all their cattle for that year.

18 When that year was ended, they came unto him the second year, and said unto him, We will not hide *it* from my lord, how that our money is spent; my lord also hath our herds of

cattle; there is not ought left in the sight of my lord, but our bodies, and our lands:

19 Wherefore shall we die before thine eyes, both we and our land? buy us and our land for bread, and we and our land will be servants unto Pharaoh: and give *us* seed, that we may live, and not die, that the land be not desolate.

20 And Joseph bought all the land of Egypt for Pharaoh; for the Egyptians sold every man his field, because the famine prevailed over them: so the land became Pharaoh's.

21 And as for the people, he removed them to cities from *one* end of the borders of Egypt even to the *other* end thereof.

22 Only the land of the priests bought he not; for the priests had a portion *assigned them* of Pharaoh, and did eat their portion which Pharaoh gave them: wherefore they sold not their lands.

23 Then Joseph said unto the people, Behold, I have bought you this day and your land for Pharaoh: lo, *here is* seed for you, and ye shall sow the land.

24 And it shall come to pass in the increase, that ye shall give the fifth *part* unto Pharaoh, and four parts shall be your own, for seed of the field, and for your food, and for them of your households, and for food for your little ones.

25 And they said, Thou hast saved our lives: let us find grace in the sight of my lord, and we will be Pharaoh's servants.

26 And Joseph made it a law over the land of Egypt unto this day, *that* Pharaoh should have the fifth *part;* except the land of the priests only, *which* became not Pharaoh's.

Why would Joseph promise to do so much to serve the interests of the Pharaoh? (47:25–26) "[So] far as Joseph's arrangement itself was concerned, not only had he the good of the people and the interests of the king in view, but the people themselves accepted it as a favour . . . to secure the population against the danger of starvation in case the crops should fail at any future time. . . . Joseph's conduct exhibited in type how God entrusts His servants with the good things of this earth, in order that they may use them not only for the preservation of the lives of individuals and nations, but also for the promotion of the purposes of His kingdom" (Keil and Delitzsch, *Commentary* [on Genesis 47:23–27]).

Genesis 47:27–31. Jacob Desires to Be Buried in Canaan

How did Joseph make an oath with his father? (47:29) "Placing a hand under the upper leg or thigh of a seated person was a solemn means of concluding an oath or contract, similar to 'shaking hands' on an agreement in our society. Abraham requested this from his servant . . . (see Genesis 47:49). In the Abraham episode the Joseph Smith Translation changes the word 'thigh' to 'hand,' meaning 'put your hand under my hand' as a sign of the covenant" (Ludlow, *Unlocking the Old Testament*, 16). See commentary in this volume for Genesis 24:2, 9.

Why did Jacob want to be buried with his "fathers"? (47:30) "The dying [Jacob] seems to be less concerned about the unknown world he is entering than about the future of God's people. This [is] directly evident . . . [in] Jacob's sense of continuity: he must go where he belongs, and this is neither in the Egypt of Joseph nor the Mesopotamia of his ancestors, but to the land promised 'to Abraham and his seed forever'" (Kidner, *Genesis*, 1:223). Jacob knows "that there is to be no permanent residence in Egypt for his people. Egypt is to Jacob and his family what the Ark was to Noah—a temporary shelter from the disaster on the outside. Even if represented only by his decayed remains, he wants to be a part of that redemptive act of God" (Hamilton, *Book of Genesis, 18–50*, 2:625). See commentary in this volume for Genesis 49:29–32.

Genesis 48:1–11. Jacob Adopts Joseph's Sons Ephraim and Manasseh as His Own

Who were Manasseh and Ephraim? (48:1) Manasseh and Ephraim were the sons of Joseph and Asenath. "Some Latter-day Saint Church leaders have drawn

27 ¶ And Israel dwelt in the land of Egypt, in the country of Goshen; and they had possessions therein, and grew, and multiplied exceedingly.

28 And Jacob lived in the land of Egypt seventeen years: so the whole age of Jacob was an hundred forty and seven years.

29 And the time drew nigh that Israel must die: and he called his son Joseph, and said unto him, If now I have found grace in thy sight, put, I pray thee, thy hand under my thigh, and deal kindly and truly with me; bury me not, I pray thee, in Egypt:

30 But I will lie with my fathers, and thou shalt carry me out of Egypt, and bury me in their buryingplace. And he said, I will do as thou hast said.

31 And he said, Swear unto me. And he sware unto him. And Israel bowed himself upon the bed's head.

CHAPTER 48

Jacob tells of the appearance of God to him in Luz—He adopts Ephraim and Manasseh as his own children—Jacob blesses Joseph—He puts Ephraim before Manasseh—The seed of Ephraim will become a multitude of nations—The children of Israel will come again into the land of their fathers.

1 And it came to pass after these things, that *one* told Joseph, Behold, thy father *is*

sick: and he took with him his two sons, Manasseh and Ephraim.

upon the Hyksos rule of Egypt to explain not only Joseph's rise to power, but also his marriage in Egypt to 'Asenath the daughter of Poti-pherha priest of On' (Genesis 41:45), the assumption being that Asenath was then more likely to be of Hyksos, and thus Semitic, dissent, rather than the Egyptian descent" (Holzapfel, et al., *Jehovah and the World of the Old Testament*, 67).

2 And *one* told Jacob, and said, Behold, thy son Joseph cometh unto thee: and Israel strengthened himself, and sat upon the bed.

3 And Jacob said unto Joseph, God Almighty appeared unto me at Luz in the land of Canaan, and blessed me,

4 And said unto me, Behold, I will make thee fruitful, and multiply thee, and I will make of thee a multitude of people; and will give this land to thy seed after thee *for* an everlasting possession.

Why does Jacob testify again of the blessing he received at Luz (Bethel)? (48:2–4) "Joseph took his sons to Jacob for patriarchal blessings." Then, after testifying of his personal visitation from God, "the patriarch reviewed for them the promises made by the Lord concerning Canaan and the return of Israel's people to it after he had made them 'a multitude of people' (Gen. 48:4)" (Rasmussen, *Latter-day Saint Commentary on the Old Testament*, 78). ⊕

5 ¶ And now thy two sons, Ephraim and Manasseh, which were born unto thee in the land of Egypt before I came unto thee into Egypt, *are* mine; as Reuben and Simeon, they shall be mine.

6 And thy issue, which thou begettest after them, shall be thine, *and* shall be called after the name of their brethren in their inheritance.

What does it mean that Ephraim and Manasseh belong to Jacob? (48:5–6) The Joseph Smith Translation makes it clear that Jacob adopted these two grandsons as his own sons. It reads: "behold, they are mine, and the God of my fathers shall bless them; even as Reuben and Simeon they shall be blessed, for they are mine; wherefore they shall be called after my name. (Therefore they were called Israel.) And thy issue which thou begettest after them, shall be thine, and shall be called after the name of their brethren in their inheritance, in the tribes; therefore they were

The Joseph Smith Translation Additions to Genesis 48:3–11

Joseph Smith's inspired translation of the Bible added significant content concerning Joseph, his sons, and their posterity to the moment of Ephraim and Manasseh's blessings (see JST, Genesis 48:7–11). These additions read as follows:

> 7 And Jacob said unto Joseph, When the God of my fathers appeared unto me in Luz, in the land of Canaan; *he sware unto me, that he would give unto me, and unto my seed, the land for an everlasting possession.*
>
> 8 Therefore, O my son, he hath blessed me in raising thee up to be a servant unto me, in saving my house from death;
>
> 9 In delivering my people, thy brethren, from famine which was sore in the land; wherefore the God of thy fathers shall bless thee, and the fruit of thy loins, that they shall be blessed above thy brethren, and above thy father's house;
>
> 10 For thou hast prevailed, and thy father's house hath bowed down unto thee, even as it was shown unto thee, before thou wast sold into Egypt by the hands of thy brethren; wherefore *thy brethren shall bow down unto thee, from generation to generation, unto the fruit of thy loins forever;*
>
> 11 For thou shalt be a light unto my people, to deliver them in the days of their captivity, from bondage; and to bring salvation unto them, when they are altogether bowed down under sin.

called the tribes of Manasseh and of Ephraim" (JST, Genesis 48:5–6). See commentary in this volume for Genesis 47:29. ⊕

Why did Jacob highlight the death and burial of Rachel? (48:7) Rachel was Jacob's first love and she died when Benjamin was born. Jacob buried her at Bethlehem with great honor (Gen. 35:16–20). "By this adoption of his two eldest sons, Joseph was placed in the position of the first-born, so far as the inheritance was concerned (1 Chronicles 5:2). Joseph's mother [Rachel], who had died so early, was also honoured thereby. And this explains the allusion made by Jacob in [v. 7] to his beloved Rachel, the wife of his affections, and to her death—how she died by his side . . . without living to see her first-born exalted to the position of a saviour to the whole house of Israel" (Keil and Delitzsch, *Commentary* [on Genesis 48:3–7]).

Was Jacob actually blind? (48:10) The Joseph Smith translation changes this to clarify that Jacob "could not see *well*" (JST, Genesis 48:16).

Genesis 48:12–22. Jacob Gives the Birthright to Ephraim and Blesses Both Ephraim and Manasseh

Why did Jacob place Ephraim before Manasseh? (48:13–20) "Ephraim is the presiding tribe in Israel. He plays the chief role in both the scattering and the gathering of the chosen seed. It is his privilege to lay the foundation for the Second Coming, and the part he is to play has already commenced.

"All of the tribes have played and shall play their part. . . . Each has provided and shall provide prophets and seers, and the members of each stand equally before the Lord in seeking and obtaining eternal life. . . . And it is Ephraim who is to guide the destiny of the kingdom in the last days and to bring the blessings of the gospel to the other tribes in the family of Jacob" (McConkie, *Millennial Messiah*, 189). ⊕

Why was the younger Ephraim chosen to receive the birthright? (48:14) "Neither the Bible nor modern scripture explains specifically why Jacob departed from the usual practice of primogeniture, but the Joseph Smith Translation (JST, Gen. 48:5–11) and the

7 And as for me, when I came from Padan, Rachel died by me in the land of Canaan in the way, when yet *there was* but a little way to come unto Ephrath: and I buried her there in the way of Ephrath; the same *is* Beth-lehem.

8 And Israel beheld Joseph's sons, and said, Who *are* these?

9 And Joseph said unto his father, They *are* my sons, whom God hath given me in this *place*. And he said, Bring them, I pray thee, unto me, and I will bless them.

10 Now the eyes of Israel were dim for age, *so that* he could not see. And he brought them near unto him; and he kissed them, and embraced them.

11 And Israel said unto Joseph, I had not thought to see thy face: and, lo, God hath shewed me also thy seed.

12 And Joseph brought them out from between his knees, and he bowed himself with his face to the earth.

13 And Joseph took them both, Ephraim in his right hand toward Israel's left hand, and Manasseh in his left hand toward Israel's right hand, and brought *them* near unto him.

14 And Israel stretched out his right hand, and laid *it* upon Ephraim's head, who *was* the younger, and his left hand upon Manasseh's head, guiding his hands wittingly; for Manasseh *was* the firstborn.

15 ¶ And he blessed Joseph, and said, God, before whom my fathers Abraham and Isaac did walk, the God which fed me all my life long unto this day,

16 The Angel which redeemed me from all evil, bless the lads; and let my name be named on them, and the name of my fathers

Abraham and Isaac; and let them grow into a multitude in the midst of the earth.

17 And when Joseph saw that his father laid his right hand upon the head of Ephraim, it displeased him: and he held up his father's hand, to remove it from Ephraim's head unto Manasseh's head.

18 And Joseph said unto his father, Not so, my father: for this *is* the firstborn; put thy right hand upon his head.

19 And his father refused, and said, I know *it,* my son, I know *it:* he also shall become a people, and he also shall be great: but truly his younger brother shall be greater than he, and his seed shall become a multitude of nations.

20 And he blessed them that day, saying, In thee shall Israel bless, saying, God make thee as Ephraim and as Manasseh: and he set Ephraim before Manasseh.

21 And Israel said unto Joseph, Behold, I die: but God shall be with you, and bring you again unto the land of your fathers.

22 Moreover I have given to thee one portion above thy brethren, which I took out of the hand of the Amorite with my sword and with my bow.

Doctrine and Covenants (D&C 133:32–34) indicate that Jacob was directed by the Lord in giving the greater blessing to Ephraim. Thus, Ephraim received the birthright of Joseph, and Joseph received the birthright of Jacob (Israel). In a sense, then, Ephraim is the birthright son of Israel, as confirmed by the Lord through his prophet Jeremiah: 'I am a father to Israel, and Ephraim is my firstborn' (Jer. 31:9)" (Ludlow, "What Laws Governed the Inheritance of Birthright in the Old Testament?" 53). ⊕

How will Israel bless the nations through Ephraim and Manasseh? (48:20) "Joseph's sons, Ephraim and Manasseh are the 'arm' and 'strength' of the Lord [Psalm 80:1–3]. The plea is for that day when the Lord will 'make bare his arm in the eyes of all nations, in bringing about his covenants and his gospel unto those who are of the house of Israel' [1 Nephi 22:11]." In the latter-days, the descendants of Ephraim will be called to "'hold the power of the priesthood to bring again Zion . . . and to put on the authority of the priesthood, which she, Zion, has a right to by lineage . . . to return to that power which she had lost (D&C 113:8)'" (McConkie, *His Name Shall Be Joseph*, 136–37). ⊕

Why did Joseph receive a double portion of Jacob's blessings? (48:22) "The birthright now passed on to Ephraim (Jer. 31:9) through Joseph (1 Chr. 5:1). . . . From a gospel perspective the birthright included two aspects: (1) The birthright *inheritance* included a double portion of the land and possessions left by the father. With this inheritance came the responsibility to care for the needs of the mother, the sisters until they were married, to be a resource for the other brothers, and to serve as the family leader. (2) The birthright *blessing* was spiritual in nature and included the patriarchal priesthood keys and spiritual leadership. From these came the full patriarchal responsibility" (Horton, "Joseph," 79). ⊕

CHAPTER 49

Jacob blesses his sons and their seed—Reuben, Simeon, and Levi are chastened—Judah will rule until Shiloh (Christ) comes—Joseph is a fruitful bough by a well—His branches (the Nephites and Lamanites) will run over the wall—The Shepherd and Stone of Israel (Christ) will bless Joseph temporally and spiritually—Jacob chooses to be buried with his fathers in Canaan—He yields up the ghost and is gathered to his people.

1 And Jacob called unto his sons, and said, Gather yourselves together, that I may tell you *that* which shall befall you in the last days.

2 Gather yourselves together, and hear, ye sons of Jacob; and hearken unto Israel your father.

3 ¶ Reuben, thou *art* my firstborn, my might, and the beginning of my strength, the excellency of dignity, and the excellency of power:

4 Unstable as water, thou shalt not excel; because thou wentest up to thy father's bed; then defiledst thou *it:* he went up to my couch.

Genesis 49:1–7. Jacob Gathers His Twelve Sons to Bless Them before He Dies

How do Jacob's blessings promised to his sons apply to us? (49:1) Just as prophecies of Isaiah (Isa. 2:2) and Paul (1 Tim. 4:1; 2 Tim. 3:1) are set in the last days, so Jacob's blessings to the children of Israel are also latter-day prophecies. President Lorenzo Snow remarked: "Men and women can increase their spiritual knowledge; they can grow better as years multiply upon them. It was so . . . with the old prophets. When they stood on the verge of the grave, ready to give up the ghost and to pass from this life to another, they were full of the power of the Almighty, and could lay their hands on the heads of their children and tell them what would befall them down to the latest ages" (in *Journal of Discourses,* 12:148).

How should we regard patriarchal blessings? (49:2) Jacob gave his sons patriarchal—or father's—blessings. In our day, fathers who hold the priesthood may likewise give blessings to their children. We also have the opportunity to receive a blessing from an ordained Church patriarch. President Ezra Taft Benson said, "I would encourage you . . . to receive a patriarchal blessing. Study it carefully and regard it as personal scripture to you—for that is what it is" ("To the 'Youth of the Noble Birthright,'" 43).

How did Reuben show that he was "unstable as water"? (49:3–4) "His crime was, lying with Bilhah, his father's concubine (Gen. 35:22). . . . From this wickedness the injured father turns away with indignation, and passes to the third person as he repeats the words, 'my couch he has ascended.' By the withdrawal of the rank belonging to the first-born, Reuben lost the leadership in Israel; so that his tribe attained to no position of influence in the nation (compare the blessing of Moses in Deuteronomy 33:6)" (Keil and Delitzsch, *Commentary* [on Genesis 49:3–4]).

5 ¶ Simeon and Levi *are* brethren; instruments of cruelty *are in* their habitations.

6 O my soul, come not thou into their secret; unto their assembly, mine honour, be not thou united: for in their anger they slew a man, and in their selfwill they digged down a wall.

7 Cursed *be* their anger, for *it was* fierce; and their wrath, for it was cruel: I will divide them in Jacob, and scatter them in Israel.

What cruelty cost Simeon and Levi their blessings? (49:5–7) "These two brothers are strongly censured for acts of violence and cruelty. Since all the others are individually addressed, the linkage of these two most likely refers to their combined attack on the city of Shechem, which is described in chapter 34. No other instance of joint activity is recorded anywhere. Jacob's initial response to the atrocity was fear for the safety of his group (34:30). Now, with the passage of time, the patriarch renders a moral verdict on the act" (Sarna, *Genesis*, 334). Jacob denies them the birthright.

Genesis 49:8–12. Jacob Blesses Judah

8 ¶ Judah, thou *art he* whom thy brethren shall praise: thy hand *shall be* in the neck of thine enemies; thy father's children shall bow down before thee.

9 Judah *is* a lion's whelp: from the prey, my son, thou art gone up: he stooped down, he couched as a lion, and as an old lion; who shall rouse him up?

10 The sceptre shall not depart from Judah, nor a lawgiver from between his feet, until Shiloh come; and unto him *shall* the gathering of the people *be.*

11 Binding his foal unto the vine, and his ass's colt unto the choice vine; he washed his garments in wine, and his clothes in the blood of grapes:

12 His eyes *shall be* red with wine, and his teeth white with milk.

What can we learn from the blessing Jacob bestowed upon Judah? (49:8–12) Jacob gave Judah five noteworthy blessings: (1) The tribe of Judah would be a tribe of fearsome warriors. (2) The kings of Israel would come from Judah's lineage. (3) The Kingdom of Judah would retain its identity and remain intact until the coming of the Messiah (Shiloh). (4) The promised Messiah would be recognized and hailed as such by riding an ass's colt. (5) The Messiah would deliver his people by washing his "garments in wine, and his clothes in the blood of grapes" (v. 11) (adapted from Ludlow, *Unlocking the Old Testament*, 18).

Summary of Genesis 49:13–21

Jacob blesses Zebulun, Issachar, Dan, Gad, Asher, and Naphtali. Each one is given portions of the promised land as part of their blessing.

Genesis 49:22–27. Jacob Gives a Special Blessing to Rachel's Sons, Joseph and Benjamin

22 ¶ Joseph *is* a fruitful bough, *even* a fruitful bough by a well; *whose* branches run over the wall:

What promises and blessings does Jacob give to Joseph? (49:22–26) Jacob promises Joseph: (1) His posterity would expand beyond his initial inheritance to the "everlasting hills" (America). (2) Joseph's descendants would experience conflict, persecution, and hate—they will overcome them in the strength of the Lord. (3) His posterity will receive the "blessings of heaven above." (4) Joseph's genealogy would have the blessings of the earth poured out upon them. (5) They will multiply and be a fruitful people. (6) The covenant blessings of the fathers will be forever upon head of Joseph's lineage and they will administer those blessings to Israel and the world (adapted from Ludlow, *Unlocking the Old Testament*, 18). ⊕

What does the phrase "from thence is the shepherd, the stone of Israel" mean? (49:24) This does not mean that the Messiah will come from the lineage of Joseph. The footnote for this verse states: "It is from the lineage of Jacob that the Messiah comes" (49:24*a*). Another translation of the Hebrew reads: "Through the hands of the champion of Jacob, through the name of the Shepherd, and Israel's Rock, from the God of your fathers, may He aid you, Shaddai, may He bless you" (Alter, *Hebrew Bible*, 1:197). Or, alternately, "and his arms were made firm by the hands of the Mighty One of Jacob—There, the Shepherd, the Rock of Israel—the God of your father who helps you, and Shaddai who blesses you" (*Jewish Study Bible*, 98).

What are the "the everlasting hills" spoken of in this verse? (49:26) "I want to pay particular attention to the last sentence, which speaks of the 'everlasting hills' and the blessings upon him who was 'separate from his brethren.' The land of the everlasting hills we regard as the Western Hemisphere—North and South America. The matter of Joseph's being separate from his brethren was partially fulfilled by the Nephites and Lamanites dwelling for many centuries in the Western Hemisphere, separate from the other tribes of Israel. Moreover, there will be further fulfillment of this separation, for we learn from Ether 13:2–11 and 3 Nephi 20–21 that Joseph's seed shall build and inhabit the New Jerusalem on the American continent, whereas the other tribes of Israel will find inheritances in and around the old Jerusalem" (Matthews, *Selected Writings*, 168–69).

Genesis 49:28–33. Jacob Blesses His Children, Asks Them to Bury Him in Canaan, and Dies

Why does Jacob insist on being buried in the "cave that is in the field of Machpelah"? (49:29–32) "These very last words of Jacob show the same concern as in his poetic Testament, the land. Having foretold the

23 The archers have sorely grieved him, and shot *at him*, and hated him:

24 But his bow abode in strength, and the arms of his hands were made strong by the hands of the mighty *God* of Jacob; (from thence *is* the shepherd, the stone of Israel:)

25 *Even* by the God of thy father, who shall help thee; and by the Almighty, who shall bless thee with blessings of heaven above, blessings of the deep that lieth under, blessings of the breasts, and of the womb:

26 The blessings of thy father have prevailed above the blessings of my progenitors unto the utmost bound of the everlasting hills: they shall be on the head of Joseph, and on the crown of the head of him that was separate from his brethren.

27 ¶ Benjamin shall ravin *as* a wolf: in the morning he shall devour the prey, and at night he shall divide the spoil.

28 ¶ All these *are* the twelve tribes of Israel: and this *is it* that their father spake unto them, and blessed them; every one according to his blessing he blessed them.

29 And he charged them, and said unto them, I am to be gathered unto my people: bury me with my fathers in the cave that *is* in the field of Ephron the Hittite,

30 In the cave that *is* in the field of Machpelah, which *is* before Mamre, in the land of Canaan, which Abraham bought with the field of Ephron the Hittite for a possession of a buryingplace.

31 There they buried Abraham and Sarah his wife; there they buried Isaac and Rebekah his wife; and there I buried Leah.

32 The purchase of the field and of the cave that *is* therein *was* from the children of Heth.

33 And when Jacob had made an end of commanding his sons, he gathered up his feet into the bed, and yielded up the ghost, and was gathered unto his people.

tribes' glorious future in the land of Canaan, he once again insists that he should be buried there. . . .

"The phraseology here, as in other passages about the patriarchal tomb, is detailed and precise, emphasizing Israel's legal title to the burial ground (cf. 23:17–20; 25:9–10; 50:13).

"But sentiment, as well as legal title, requires that he be buried there, for that is where his mother Rebekah is buried, as well as his wife Leah, who is also the mother of six of his sons. Earlier in the narrative, the burials of Abraham, Sarah, and Isaac have been mentioned. But this is the only time that the resting place of Rebekah and Leah is recalled" (Wenham, "Genesis 16–50," 2:487–88). See commentary in this volume for Genesis 23:9.

CHAPTER 50

Jacob's body is embalmed—Joseph buries him in Canaan—Joseph comforts his brothers—The children of Israel multiply—Joseph promises that God will bring Israel out of Egypt into Canaan—Joseph dies in Egypt and is embalmed.

1 And Joseph fell upon his father's face, and wept upon him, and kissed him.

Genesis 50:1–14. Joseph Mourns the Death of Jacob

What do we learn about Joseph from his reaction to his father's death? (50:1) "These three gestures by now are strongly associated with Joseph's character. In the great recognition scene in chapter 45, he flings himself on Benjamin's neck, embraces and kisses him, and then does the same with his ten half brothers, and before this he has wept three times over the encounter with his brothers. Joseph is at once the intellectual, dispassionate interpreter of dreams and central economic planner, and the man of powerful spontaneous feeling. At his father's death bed, he only weeps, he does not speak" (Alter, *Hebrew Bible*, 1:199).

2 And Joseph commanded his servants the physicians to embalm his father: and the physicians embalmed Israel.

3 And forty days were fulfilled for him; for so are fulfilled the days of those which are embalmed: and the Egyptians mourned for him threescore and ten days.

4 And when the days of his mourning were past, Joseph spake unto the house of

Why was Jacob embalmed? (50:2–3) Joseph lived among the Egyptians most of his life. "Although it was common practice in Egypt (for any who could afford it), embalming of Israelites is found only in this chapter. The fact that the bodies of Jacob and Joseph are embalmed (Ge 50:2, 26) may suggest the desire of the Israelites to soothe the feelings of the Egyptians, but it also serves the purpose of preserving their bodies for later burial in Canaan" (*NKJV Cultural Backgrounds Study Bible*, 104). "Since this practice was customary for Egyptian monarchs, the writer depicts Jacob's receiving a royal funeral" (*New Interpreter's Bible*, 1:669).

Pharaoh, saying, If now I have found grace
in your eyes, speak, I pray you, in the ears of
Pharaoh, saying,

5 My father made me swear, saying, Lo, I
die: in my grave which I have digged for me
in the land of Canaan, there shalt thou bury
me. Now therefore let me go up, I pray thee,
and bury my father, and I will come again.

6 And Pharaoh said, Go up, and bury thy father, according as he made thee swear.

7 ¶ And Joseph went up to bury his father:
and with him went up all the servants of
Pharaoh, the elders of his house, and all the
elders of the land of Egypt,

8 And all the house of Joseph, and his brethren, and his father's house: only their little
ones, and their flocks, and their herds, they
left in the land of Goshen.

9 And there went up with him both chariots
and horsemen: and it was a very great company.

10 And they came to the threshingfloor of
Atad, which *is* beyond Jordan, and there they
mourned with a great and very sore lamentation: and he made a mourning for his father
seven days.

11 And when the inhabitants of the land, the
Canaanites, saw the mourning in the floor of
Atad, they said, This *is* a grievous mourning to
the Egyptians: wherefore the name of it was
called Abel-mizraim, which *is* beyond Jordan.

12 And his sons did unto him according as
he commanded them:

13 For his sons carried him into the land of
Canaan, and buried him in the cave of the
field of Machpelah, which Abraham bought
with the field for a possession of a buryingplace of Ephron the Hittite, before Mamre.

14 ¶ And Joseph returned into Egypt, he,
and his brethren, and all that went up with

Why does Pharaoh trust that Joseph will return to Egypt? (50:5–9) "Pharaoh is agreeable [with Joseph's leaving] and is impressed by Joseph's filial devotion. Joseph has given his word that he will return. Pharaoh believes him, and he also believes that once a promise is made, it must be fulfilled. . . . In his answer to Joseph's request, Pharaoh repeats Joseph's words with *Go and inter your father as he placed you under oath*, and he stops there. He does not end with "and then come back to me," as Joseph said he would. This is another indication of Pharaoh's implicit trust in Joseph's truthfulness" (Hamilton, *Book of Genesis, 18–50*, 2:693–94).

How was Jacob's body carried into Canaan? (50:13) "With an extensive entourage and ceremony, the mourning for Jacob and his burial at Machpelah were accomplished. Forty days of embalming and seventy days of mourning in Egypt were followed by the long journey to Hebron in Canaan, seven days of mourning at the border beyond Jordan, and finally the burial in the cave at Machpelah" (Rasmussen, *Latter-day Saint Commentary on the Old Testament*, 82). "Apparently,

him to bury his father, after he had buried
his father.

the main cortege was left at Abel-Misraim, and only Jacob's sons carried his body into Canaan to bury him at the ancestral tomb at Macpelah" (Wenham, "Genesis 16–50," 2:489).

15 ¶ And when Joseph's brethren saw that
their father was dead, they said, Joseph will
peradventure hate us, and will certainly requite us all the evil which we did unto him.

16 And they sent a messenger unto Joseph,
saying, Thy father did command before he
died, saying,

17 So shall ye say unto Joseph, Forgive, I
pray thee now, the trespass of thy brethren,
and their sin; for they did unto thee evil: and
now, we pray thee, forgive the trespass of the
servants of the God of thy father. And Joseph
wept when they spake unto him.

18 And his brethren also went and fell down
before his face; and they said, Behold, we *be*
thy servants.

19 And Joseph said unto them, Fear not: for
am I in the place of God?

20 But as for you, ye thought evil against
me; *but* God meant it unto good, to bring
to pass, as *it is* this day, to save much people
alive.

21 Now therefore fear ye not: I will nourish
you, and your little ones. And he comforted
them, and spake kindly unto them.

Genesis 50:15–21. Joseph Forgives and Loves His Brothers

What did Joseph's brothers do to cause him to weep? (50:15–17) Two actions probably disturbed Joseph. First, it appears that the brothers fabricated a story that Jacob demanded forgiveness for the brothers' previous actions (v. 16–17). Second, rather than coming to Joseph, they plead from a distance by sending a messenger (v. 16). "Whether their fear and grief grew from their present vulnerability, or as a part of the process of repentance is unclear but there was remorse as they reached their extremity during the famine." Nonetheless, "the brothers begin to fear . . . that Joseph would be vindictive and vengeful" (Horton, "Joseph," 82, 81).

What do we see in Joseph as he responds to his brothers? (50:19–21) "Each sentence of his threefold reply is a pinnacle of Old Testament (and New Testament) faith. To leave all the righting of one's wrongs to God ([v.] 19; cf. Rom. 12:19; 1 Thess. 5:15; 1 Pet. 4:19); to see his providence in man's malice ([v.] 20; [Ps. 76: 10; Acts 2:23; 4:28; 13:27; Rom. 8:28; Phil. 1:12]), and to repay evil not only with forgiveness but also with practical affection ([v.] 21; cf. Luke 6:27ff.), are attitudes which anticipate the adjective 'Christian' and even 'Christlike.' Note that in verse 21 the *I* is emphatic: Joseph was promising something more personal than philanthropy" (Kidner, *Genesis,* 1:235).

Are There Other Writings and Prophecies of Joseph? (Genesis 50:24–25)

On 3 July 1835, Joseph Smith purchased a collection of mummies and manuscripts from one Michael Chandler. Joseph noted that the manuscripts contained further writings by Abraham and Joseph (see Joseph Smith Papers, "History, 1838–1856, volume B-1," 596). Oliver Cowdery, who saw the writings, wrote : "When the translation of these valuable documents will be completed . . . judging from their size, and the comprehensiveness of the language, one might reasonable expect to see a sufficient to develop much upon the mighty acts of the ancient men of God, and of his dealing with the children of men when they saw him face to face. Be there little or much, it must be an inestimable acquisition to our present scriptures, fulfilling, in a small degree, the word of the prophet: for the earth shall be full of the knowledge of the Lord as the waters cover the sea" (*Messenger and Advocate*, vol. II, no. 3 [Dec. 1835]: 236).

Genesis 50:22–26. Joseph Dies in Egypt

What other insights do we learn about Joseph and his teachings from latter-day scripture? (50:24–25) The Joseph Smith Translation (JST, Genesis 50:24–38) and 2 Nephi 3:7–21 (assumed to be from the Brass Plates) provide us with additional teachings from Joseph of Egypt. What do you learn from these two important sources?

What happened to the house of Israel after Joseph's death? (50:25–26) "The interval between the death of Joseph and the emergence of Moses represents a dark age in two ways: (1) the Israelites in Egypt fell upon evil days; and (2) the available record is limited to a few meager references at the beginning of the book of Exodus. Nevertheless, circumstantial evidence indicates that the quest which began with the patriarchs was never completely abandoned [the quest of an inherited promised land]. It required, however, . . . the inspired leadership of Moses to reactivate the drive and give it new impetus" (Speiser, *Genesis*, 1:378).

22 ¶ And Joseph dwelt in Egypt, he, and his father's house: and Joseph lived an hundred and ten years.

23 And Joseph saw Ephraim's children of the third *generation:* the children also of Machir the son of Manasseh were brought up upon Joseph's knees.

24 And Joseph said unto his brethren, I die: and God will surely visit you, and bring you out of this land unto the land which he sware to Abraham, to Isaac, and to Jacob.

25 And Joseph took an oath of the children of Israel, saying, God will surely visit you, and ye shall carry up my bones from hence.

26 So Joseph died, *being* an hundred and ten years old: and they embalmed him, and he was put in a coffin in Egypt.

Other Insights from the Joseph Smith Translation (JST, Genesis 50:24–38)

"The Joseph Smith Translation adds twelve very significant verses to the account in the King James Version (see [JST, Gen. 50:24–38]).

"The following important concepts are discussed in these additional verses:

1. A righteous branch of Israel would be raised up out of the loins of Joseph who was sold into Egypt.
2. The Messiah (called Shiloh) would *not* be from Joseph.
3. Moses would be raised up to deliver the children of Israel from Egypt.
4. A 'choice seer . . . like unto' Moses would be raised up from the loins of Joseph in the last days—'his name shall be called Joseph, and it shall be after the name of his father' (Latter-day Saints believe this choice seer was Joseph Smith, Jr.).
5. The descendants of Judah would keep a record (the Bible) and the descendants of Joseph woud write (the Book of Mormon). In the last days these two records would 'grow together unto the confounding of false doctrines . . . and bringing . . . a knowledge of my covenants, saith the Lord.'
6. The house of Israel shall be restored 'in the last days.'

"The following commentaries substantiate the claim that Joseph Smith, Jr., was the 'choice seer' of the last days as revealed to Joseph who was sold into Egypt.

"'It was decreed in the counsels of eternity, long before the foundations of the earth were laid, that [Joseph Smith] should be the man, in the last dispensation of this world, to bring forth the word of God to the people, and receive the fulness of the keys and power of the Priesthood of the Son of God. The Lord had his eye upon him, and upon his father, and upon his father's father, and upon their progenitors clear back to Abraham, and from Abraham to the flood, from the flood to Enoch, and from Enoch to Adam. . . . He was foreordained in eternity to preside over this last dispensation' (Brigham Young, [in *Journal of Discourses*], 7:289–90).

"'God called [Joseph Smith] to occupy the position that he did . . . thousands of years ago before this world was formed. The Prophets prophesied about his coming, that a man should arise whose name should be Joseph, and that his father's name should be Joseph, and also that he should be a descendant of that Joseph who was sold into Egypt (John Taylor, [in *Journal of Discourses*], 26:106)'" (Ludlow, *Companion to Your Study of the Old Testament*, 135–36).

THE SECOND BOOK OF MOSES

CALLED

EXODUS

Introduction

"*Exodus* is the Greek word for 'going out,' the name of the book in the Greek version of the Hebrew Bible (OT). It refers to the Israelites' going out of Egypt and beginning their return to the promised land. This migration of people took place because God brought the people out of Egypt by means of miracles carried out in part by his chosen agent, Moses. The story of this event is found in Exodus 1–15 and referred to throughout the Bible. It is remembered and celebrated as the first of a series of God's actions of salvation in behalf of his people. The exodus event is foundational for the Israelites' faith and practice" (Fee, *Eerdmans Companion to the Bible*, 110).

One author sees Exodus as "a masterpiece of ancient writing" (Millet, "Call of Moses," 93). "While it is certainly a literary masterpiece in the way it maintains the expectations of the reader . . . , it is also important because it reveals in a fundamental way how God remembers his people and how he prepares a way for their deliverance" (Holzapfel, *Exodus Story*, 2).

It is also good to note "how important the Exodus is to the structure of the Bible. In *The God of Exodus*, James Plastaras writes: 'It was the . . . exodus which shaped all of Israel's understanding of history. It was only in light of the exodus that Israel was able to look back into the past and piece together her earlier history. It was also the exodus which provided the prophets with a key to the understanding of Israel's future. In this sense, the exodus stands at the center of Israel's history'" (Tate, "Typology of the Exodus Pattern in the Book of Mormon," 248).

The account Moses recorded in Exodus "is a continuation of the historical narrative found in Genesis" and is divided into "three main divisions. Part one, chapters 1–12, is an account of the oppression of the Israelites by the pharaoh of Egypt, who 'knew not Joseph' (Ex. 1:8). . . .

"Part two, chapters 13–19, describe Israel's flight from the Red Sea to Sinai. . . .

"Part three, chapters 19–40, gives a sacred narration of the solemnity of Sinai and the children of Israel being set apart as a kingdom of priests and a nation holy before God (see Ex. 19:16)" (Black, *400 Questions and Answers about the Old Testament*, 61).

"The high point of the book concentrates on the great display of divine power used to assist the Israelites in their escape from Egypt, and Jehovah's offer to renew his full covenant with them. Indeed, the book reveals the greatest direct intervention by the Lord in the affairs of men this side of the great Flood. . . .

"There will come another day, however, in the not-too-distant future when Jehovah will once again display such power. So great will that display be that men will no longer refer to the days of Moses, but to this greater day when the Lord will again make bare his arm before the nations (see Jeremiah 16:14–15)" (Pearson, *Old Testament*, 27, 28).

Finally, the "Exodus story reminds us that the Lord delivers his covenant sons and daughters from temporal captivity from time to time to not only relieve suffering but to remind them that it is his ultimate purpose to deliver them from spiritual captivity" (Holzapfel, *Exodus Story*, 2–3).

Exodus 1:1–6. Joseph and All His Brothers Die in Peace in Egypt

Who accompanied Jacob into Egypt and how many were there? (1:1–5) The Hebrew title for the book of Exodus is named "after the first two words, *we'elleh shemoth* ('these are the names of')" and refers to the list of souls Jacob took into Egypt (see Holzapfel, *Exodus Story*, 2).

The seventy souls "obviously did not include the wives of the sons, grandsons, and so on. . . .

"Most Bible scholars estimate that the number of Israelites who migrated into Egypt totaled several hundred. Jacob was 130 years old at the time (Gen. 47:9), his sons would have been at least 60 years of age, and many of his grandsons were mature men with children of their own" (Ludlow, *Companion to Your Study of the Old Testament*, 137).

Exodus 1:7–14. The Israelites Grow in Number but Are Enslaved by the Egyptians

Who was this new king over Egypt? (1:8) "Exodus 1:8 reports that there came to power 'a new king over Egypt, which knew not Joseph.' This is best understood as an indication of Egyptian king Ahmose I and his forces banishing the Hyksos from power in the Nile Delta by 1530 B.C. and establishing the New Kingdom Period of Egyptian history ([1550–1069]). The kings of this new eighteenth dynasty and the early kings of the subsequent nineteenth dynasty would have been in power during the time the Israelites served as forced laborers, as depicted in the book of Exodus" (Holzapfel, et al., *Jehovah and the World of the Old Testament*, 78).

What does the name Pharaoh mean? (1:11) The word *pharaoh* means "great house." It was a "title of the kings of ancient Egypt" and the "recorded rulers of this country, constituting twenty-six separate dynasties. . . . The term *pharaoh* can be traced back to the 22nd dynasty (945–745 [B.C.]), when it became commonly attached to the monarch's name. Thus 'Pharaoh Neco' and 'Pharaoh Hophra' are exact Hebrew translations of the Egyptian title. Pharaohs of Egypt are mentioned in various OT contexts" (*Zondervan Illustrated Bible Dictionary*, 1115–16).

CHAPTER 1

The children of Israel multiply—They are placed in bondage by the Egyptians—Pharaoh seeks to destroy the sons born to Hebrew women.

1 Now these *are* the names of the children of Israel, which came into Egypt; every man and his household came with Jacob.

2 Reuben, Simeon, Levi, and Judah,

3 Issachar, Zebulun, and Benjamin,

4 Dan, and Naphtali, Gad, and Asher.

5 And all the souls that came out of the loins of Jacob were seventy souls: for Joseph was in Egypt *already*.

6 And Joseph died, and all his brethren, and all that generation.

7 ¶ And the children of Israel were fruitful, and increased abundantly, and multiplied, and waxed exceeding mighty; and the land was filled with them.

8 Now there arose up a new king over Egypt, which knew not Joseph.

9 And he said unto his people, Behold, the people of the children of Israel *are* more and mightier than we:

10 Come on, let us deal wisely with them; lest they multiply, and it come to pass, that, when there falleth out any war, they join also unto our enemies, and fight against us, and *so* get them up out of the land.

11 Therefore they did set over them taskmasters to afflict them with their burdens. And they built for Pharaoh treasure cities, Pithom and Raamses.

12 But the more they afflicted them, the more they multiplied and grew. And they were grieved because of the children of Israel.

13 And the Egyptians made the children of Israel to serve with rigour:

What do we know about the treasure cities Pithom and Raamses? (1:11) "Pithom and Rameses are located about twenty miles apart in the eastern Nile Delta. The sites included large grain storage facilities to support palace, temple and military staff. The ruins at Tell el-Dab'a, the site of Avaris, have been identified as the Egyptian city Pi-Rameses, 'House of Rameses.' This huge city was built at the command of Rameses II (1279–1213 B.C.). This is presumably the second of two supply cities that the enslaved Israelites help build and a starting point of the Exodus (Exod 1:11; 12:37; Num 33:5)" (Holzapfel, et al., *Jehovah and the World of the Old Testament*, 81).

14 And they made their lives bitter with hard bondage, in mortar, and in brick, and in all manner of service in the field: all their service, wherein they made them serve, *was* with rigour.

Why did the Egyptians purposely make the Israelites' lives "bitter with hard bondage"? (1:14) "The Israelites had multiplied greatly in the land during the period from the death of Jacob, and the leaders of the country feared that the people of Israel—a power to be reckoned with—might choose to join themselves to the enemies of Egypt. It was determined by the Egyptians that life should be made more difficult for the Israelites, that perhaps the birth rate might decline thereby. 'Therefore they set over them taskmasters to afflict them with their burdens.' The desired result, however, was not forthcoming" (Millet, "Call of Moses," 95).

Exodus 1:15–22. Pharaoh Commands Every Male Israelite Child Be Killed at Birth

15 ¶ And the king of Egypt spake to the Hebrew midwives, of which the name of the one *was* Shiphrah, and the name of the other Puah:

16 And he said, When ye do the office of a midwife to the Hebrew women, and see *them* upon the stools; if it *be* a son, then ye shall kill him: but if it *be* a daughter, then she shall live.

17 But the midwives feared God, and did not as the king of Egypt commanded them, but saved the men children alive.

18 And the king of Egypt called for the midwives, and said unto them, Why have ye done this thing, and have saved the men children alive?

Who were these Hebrew midwives? (1:15–16) "Most likely, these two women headed a guild of midwives. One thing is certain: They knew the living God (see vv. 17, 21). Their names, *Shiprah* ('Beautiful One') and *Puah* ('Splendid One'), are preserved in this account because they were godly women with a courageous faith. At the same time, the names of the pharaohs—the 'important' people of the day—are omitted" (*Nelson Study Bible* [NKJV], 91).

Why were the midwives' actions so significant? (1:17) "Faced with an irreconcilable conflict between obedience to the sovereign's depraved law and allegiance to the moral law of God, the midwives chose morality" (Sarna, "Who Was the Pharaoh Who 'Knew Not Joseph'?" 57). Their courageous work spared the life of a future prophet (see Exodus 2:10) and merited for them God's blessing (see Exodus 1:20).

In what way did God make "houses" for these faithful midwifes? (1:21) "In acknowledgement of their reverence for life and Him who gives that life God 'made houses' for Shiprah and Puah (Exodus 1:21). The context of the story suggests a clear distinction between a physical building that the women could inhabit and a family or posterity. Because Shiprah and Puah saved others' children, the Lord blessed them with their own children" (Olson, *Women of the Old Testament*, 180).

Why did Pharaoh want to kill all Hebrew sons? (1:22) "Both the ancient Jewish historian Josephus and Jonathan ben Uzziel, another ancient Jewish writer, recorded that the pharaoh had a dream wherein he was shown that a man soon to be born would deliver Israel from bondage, and this dream motivated the royal decree to drown the male children (see Josephus, *Antiquities of the Jews*, [2.9.2]; Clarke, Bible Commentary, 1:294)" (*Old Testament Student Manual: Genesis–2 Samuel*, 104).

Exodus 2:1–4. Moses Is Born

Why was it important that Moses was from the house of Levi? (2:1) "As a new law was to be given and a new priesthood formed, God chose a religious family out of which the lawgiver and the high priest were both to spring" (*Adam Clarke's Commentary* [on Exodus 2:1]). "The work of ministering in the sanctuary was assigned to this tribe" (Bible Dictionary, "Levites").

What are the parallels between Noah's ark and Moses being found in an ark? (2:3) "In all of the Old Testament, this Hebrew word [*tebah*, or ark] is found only here and in the Flood story (Gen. 6:14–9:18). . . .

19 And the midwives said unto Pharaoh, Because the Hebrew women *are* not as the Egyptian women; for they *are* lively, and are delivered ere the midwives come in unto them.

20 Therefore God dealt well with the midwives: and the people multiplied, and waxed very mighty.

21 And it came to pass, because the midwives feared God, that he made them houses.

22 And Pharaoh charged all his people, saying, Every son that is born ye shall cast into the river, and every daughter ye shall save alive.

CHAPTER 2

Moses is born to Levite parents, is raised by Pharaoh's daughter, slays an Egyptian in defense of an Israelite, flees to Midian, and marries Zipporah—Israel in bondage cries to the Lord.

1 And there went a man of the house of Levi, and took *to wife* a daughter of Levi.

2 And the woman conceived, and bare a son: and when she saw him that he *was a* goodly *child*, she hid him three months.

3 And when she could not longer hide him, she took for him an ark of bulrushes, and daubed it with slime and with pitch, and put the child therein; and she laid *it* in the flags by the river's brink.

4 And his sister stood afar off, to wit what would be done to him.

(1) Both Noah and Moses are specifically selected to forego a tragic, watery fate; (2) both are placed on an 'ark' treated with bitumen and are carried to safety on the very body of water that brings destruction to others; and (3) both are the vehicles through whom God 'creates' a new people for his own purposes. Furthermore, Moses' safe passage through the waters of the Nile not only looks backward to the Flood story, but forward to the passage through the sea in Exodus 14 for all of God's people" (Enns, "Exodus," 62).

5 ¶ And the daughter of Pharaoh came down to wash *herself* at the river; and her maidens walked along by the river's side; and when she saw the ark among the flags, she sent her maid to fetch it.

6 And when she had opened *it,* she saw the child: and, behold, the babe wept. And she had compassion on him, and said, This *is one* of the Hebrews' children.

Exodus 2:5–10. Pharaoh's Daughter Finds and Cares for Baby Moses

Who was this "daughter of Pharaoh" and why did she help a Hebrew child? (2:5–6) "Josephus calls her Thermuthis/Thuoris, indicating his belief that she was the daughter of Rameses II. Josephus further explains that Thermuthis' desire to adopt the infant Moses grew out of the impossibility that she could produce a legitimate heir of her own because she was married to the infant heir of the throne of Lower Egypt when she was an adult woman. . . .

"Modern revelation also indicates that generations before, Joseph had prophesied that a daughter of Pharaoh would assist in Israel's future, saying that Moses 'shall be nursed by the king's daughter, and shall be called her son' (JST, Genesis 50:29)" (Olson, *Women of the Old Testament*, 91).

7 Then said his sister to Pharaoh's daughter, Shall I go and call to thee a nurse of the Hebrew women, that she may nurse the child for thee?

8 And Pharaoh's daughter said to her, Go.

Why did Moses' sister offer to find the Hebrew baby a nurse? (2:7–9) "Miriam's [Moses' sister] quick thinking and wise timing created a way for the baby to have a continued relationship with his birth family (Exodus 2:7–9). Wet-nursing agreements are common in ancient Near Eastern documents. The agreement

Who Was Moses? (Exodus 2:1–10)

"Moses is revered in biblical and later Jewish tradition as the great prophet-leader and lawgiver who, with Jehovah's power and direction, helped forge the identity of biblical Israel by leading Israelites out from Egyptian bondage and into a covenant relationship with Jehovah and by gathering them to a homeland in Canaan. From Moses' time on, no prophetic leader matched his power or accomplishments (Deut 34:10–12). This is not surprising to Latter-day Saints, given Moses' foreordination, his prophesied mission, and his role as the head of his dispensation (e.g., Gen 15:13–14; 2 Ne 3:9–10; D&C 110:11). The books of Exodus, Leviticus, Numbers, and Deuteronomy present us with an overview of significant aspects of Moses' life and his prophetic mission and teachings" (Holzapfel, et al., *Jehovah and the World of the Old Testament*, 78).

"So great was Moses that forever after the Lord and his people have used him as a standard, or model, of a prophet. Even Jesus Christ was called a prophet like unto Moses (see Acts 3:22; 7:37; Deuteronomy 18:15, 18–19; 1 Nephi 22:20–21; 3 Nephi 20:23–24). Indeed, Moses was a similitude or living symbol of Jesus Christ (see Moses 1:6)" (*Old Testament Student Manual: Genesis–2 Samuel*, 103).

Miriam suggested to Pharaoh's daughter allowed the infant Moses to live in his parents' home until he was weaned, at about the age of three years" (Olson, *Women of the Old Testament*, 91–92).

What did Moses' name foreshadow? (2:10) "*Moses*, an Egyptian name meaning 'give birth' and often part of Egyptian names joined with the name of a god (e.g., Thutmoses, Ahmoses, Rameses), is given a Hebrew etymology ('he who draws out') in anticipation of Moses' role in drawing his people through the sea ([Exodus] 14:21–29)" (*New Oxford Annotated Bible*, 85).

And the maid went and called the child's mother.

9 And Pharaoh's daughter said unto her, Take this child away, and nurse it for me, and I will give *thee* thy wages. And the woman took the child, and nursed it.

10 And the child grew, and she brought him unto Pharaoh's daughter, and he became her son. And she called his name Moses: and she said, Because I drew him out of the water.

Exodus 2:11–14. Moses Kills an Egyptian

Why did Moses slay the Egyptian taskmaster? (2:12) "The same Hebrew verb translated *smiting* in verse 11 is translated *slew* in verse 12; it is a verb used to describe what soldiers do in battle. Thus Moses did to the Egyptian what he was doing to the Hebrew. His action destroyed a life but was in defense of a life" (Rasmussen, *Latter-day Saint Commentary on the Old Testament*, 86).

11 ¶ And it came to pass in those days, when Moses was grown, that he went out unto his brethren, and looked on their burdens: and he spied an Egyptian smiting an Hebrew, one of his brethren.

12 And he looked this way and that way, and when he saw that *there was* no man, he slew the Egyptian, and hid him in the sand.

13 And when he went out the second day, behold, two men of the Hebrews strove together: and he said to him that did the wrong, Wherefore smitest thou thy fellow?

14 And he said, Who made thee a prince and a judge over us? intendest thou to kill me, as thou killedst the Egyptian? And Moses feared, and said, Surely this thing is known.

Exodus 2:15–25. Moses Flees to Midian for Safety

Where was the land of Midian and who were the Midianites? (2:15) Midian was "a region in the desert of [northwest] Arabia inhabited by the Midianites, a group of semi-nomadic tribes descended from Midian, son of Abraham and Keturah. After he fled from Egypt, Moses spent 40 years in Midian, which at that time apparently extended as far as the [south] and [east] parts of the Sinai Peninsula" (*Revell Bible Dictionary*, 1128).

Why were seven daughters watering flocks? (2:16–17) "Normally women would have been shepherdesses only when there were no sons in the family. The disadvantages of this situation are highlighted in this account, where the other shepherds bully the girls" (Walton, et al., *IVP Bible Background Commentary*, 79).

15 Now when Pharaoh heard this thing, he sought to slay Moses. But Moses fled from the face of Pharaoh, and dwelt in the land of Midian: and he sat down by a well.

16 Now the priest of Midian had seven daughters: and they came and drew *water*, and filled the troughs to water their father's flock.

17 And the shepherds came and drove them away: but Moses stood up and helped them, and watered their flock.

18 And when they came to Reuel their father, he said, How *is it that* ye are come so soon to day?

19 And they said, An Egyptian delivered us out of the hand of the shepherds, and also drew *water* enough for us, and watered the flock.

20 And he said unto his daughters, And where *is* he? why *is* it *that* ye have left the man? call him, that he may eat bread.

Why is Moses' father-in-law called Reuel here but Jethro elsewhere? (2:18) "The father-in-law of Moses is given two different names within a few verses: 'Reuel' in Exodus 2:18 and 'Jethro' as in Exodus 3:1. It is not unusual for Semites to have more than one name, as evidenced in Abraham (Abram) and Israel (Jacob)" (Ludlow, *Companion to Your Study of the Old Testament*, 139). Interestingly, the name *Reuel* means "friend of God" (Bible Dictionary, "Reuel").

21 And Moses was content to dwell with the man: and he gave Moses Zipporah his daughter.

22 And she bare *him* a son, and he called his name Gershom: for he said, I have been a stranger in a strange land.

How was Moses blessed by dwelling with Reuel and his family? (2:21–22) "Moses married Jethro's [Reuel's] daughter Zipporah, had two sons—Gershom and Eliezer, and settled in the area for the next forty years of his life (Ex. 2:16–22; 18:3; Acts 7:29–30). We suppose that it was in Midian that Moses began to be taught the true gospel and to be introduced to the teachings of the God of Abraham, Isaac, and Jacob, for we know also by modern revelation that Moses received the higher priesthood from Jethro (D&C 84:6)" (Millet, "Call of Moses," 97).

23 ¶ And it came to pass in process of time, that the king of Egypt died: and the children of Israel sighed by reason of the bondage, and they cried, and their cry came up unto God by reason of the bondage.

Who was the "king of Egypt" that died? (2:23) The "process of time" during which this Egyptian king died was about forty years (see Acts 7:30). Both Egyptian records and the Bible are silent on the name of this king. However, "a logical solution would be to see the Pharaoh who died as the predecessor of Rameses II, Seti I, who reigned between 1309 and 1291 B.C., who would thus count as the Pharaoh whose oppression of Israel begins the book of Exodus" (Lundquist, "Exodus," 122).

24 And God heard their groaning, and God remembered his covenant with Abraham, with Isaac, and with Jacob.

25 And God looked upon the children of Israel, and God had respect unto *them.*

Why did God hear the children of Israel now? (2:24–25) Abraham had learned by revelation that his descendants would be in bondage to another nation but would be delivered after 400 years (see Genesis 15:13–14). Notice the theme of deliverance found in Exodus 2: "Moses is supposed to die as a baby, but is spared. He then helps deliver others. Finally, God hears the Israelites and is ready to deliver them" (Muhlestein, *Essential Old Testament Companion*, 92). The time had finally come for God to judge Egypt and prepare the way for Israel to "come out with great substance" (Genesis 15:14).

CHAPTER 3

The Lord appears to Moses at the burning bush—Moses is called to deliver Israel from bondage—The Lord identifies Himself as the God of Abraham, Isaac, and Jacob, and as the Great I AM—He promises to smite Egypt and bring His people out with great wealth.

1 Now Moses kept the flock of Jethro his
father in law, the priest of Midian: and he
led the flock to the backside of the desert,
and came to the mountain of God, *even* to
Horeb.

2 And the angel of the LORD appeared unto
him in a flame of fire out of the midst of a
bush: and he looked, and, behold, the bush
burned with fire, and the bush *was* not consumed.

3 And Moses said, I will now turn aside,
and see this great sight, why the bush is not
burnt.

4 And when the LORD saw that he turned
aside to see, God called unto him out of the
midst of the bush, and said, Moses, Moses.
And he said, Here *am* I.

5 And he said, Draw not nigh hither: put
off thy shoes from off thy feet, for the place
whereon thou standest *is* holy ground.

6 Moreover he said, I *am* the God of thy

Exodus 3:1–6. The Lord Appears to Moses in a Burning Bush

How did Jethro receive the Holy Priesthood? (3:1) "The priesthood of Jethro descended from a prophet by the name of Esaias who was a contemporary of Abraham (D&C 84:7–13). It was from this line that Moses was ordained. That there was such an alternate line of authority is indicative of the foreknowledge of God" (Pearson, *Old Testament*, 85–86).

What was the "mountain of God" referred to as Horeb? (3:1) "The mountain where Moses encountered the burning bush was given the name 'Horeb' in Exodus 3:1. In verse 12, the Lord indicated that the children of Israel should be given the opportunity to 'serve God upon this mountain.' In Exodus 19:11 the name 'mount Sinai' is given to the place where the Lord spoke to Moses and was heard by the Israelites. Thus, many biblical scholars believe Horeb and Sinai are the same mountain. It may be that *Horeb* refers to the mountain range whereas *Sinai* is the name of a particular mountain or peak within that range" (Ludlow, *Companion to Your Study of the Old Testament*, 140).

Who appeared to Moses at the burning bush? (3:2) The Joseph Smith Translation of Exodus 3:2 states: "And *again* the *presence* of the Lord appeared unto him in a flame of fire *in* the midst of a bush" (Wayment, *Complete Joseph Smith Translation of the Old Testament*, 114). In other words, "it is the Lord God Jehovah himself who addressed the prophet, rather than an angelic minister as the King James version seems to imply" (Hyde, *Comprehensive Commentary [Exodus]*, 14).

What occurred on this mount that testifies of its sacredness? (3:5) Just as mountains were used anciently as sacred places, "some of the most holy places on earth today are the temples (houses of the Lord), where the presence of the Lord can be felt by many.

father, the God of Abraham, the God of
Isaac, and the God of Jacob. And Moses hid
his face; for he was afraid to look upon God.

7 ¶ And the LORD said, I have surely seen the
affliction of my people which *are* in Egypt,
and have heard their cry by reason of their
taskmasters; for I know their sorrows;

8 And I am come down to deliver them out
of the hand of the Egyptians, and to bring
them up out of that land unto a good land
and a large, unto a land flowing with milk
and honey; unto the place of the Canaanites,
and the Hittites, and the Amorites, and the
Perizzites, and the Hivites, and the Jebusites.

9 Now therefore, behold, the cry of the children of Israel is come unto me: and I have
also seen the oppression wherewith the
Egyptians oppress them.

10 Come now therefore, and I will send thee
unto Pharaoh, that thou mayest bring forth
my people the children of Israel out of Egypt.

11 ¶ And Moses said unto God, Who *am*
I, that I should go unto Pharaoh, and that I
should bring forth the children of Israel out
of Egypt?

Here, also, the counsel is to remove shoes worn in the world 'for the place whereon thou standest is holy ground'" (Ludlow, *Companion to Your Study of the Old Testament*, 140).

Exodus 3:7–10. The Lord Promises Moses That He Will Deliver Israel from Bondage

What is unique about this promise by the Lord? (3:8) According to Nahum M. Sarna, milk and honey was a "recurrent symbol of the land's fertility.... For the demoralized, enslaved masses of Israel, however, such an enticement would carry weight....

"Milk in the Bible is generally from the goat, 'the little man's cow.' A plentiful supply presupposes an abundance of goats, which in turn points to ample pasturage and the prospect of much meat, hide, and wool.

"Honey in the Bible (Heb. *devash*) is predominantly the thick, sweet syrup produced from dates and known to Arabas as *dibs*" (*Exodus*, 16).

Why had the time arrived for the children of Israel to be brought out of Egypt? (3:9–10) "The Lord is aware of the suffering and the prayers of people and He brings the relief that circumstances warrant. At the time Israel was in urgent need of a homeland, the occupants of Canaan were ripe in iniquity, and so the land could be made available to the Israelites if they could make themselves worthy of God's help (Gen. 15:16; Lev. 18:24–29; 1 Ne. 17:32–35)" (Rasmussen, *Latter-day Saint Commentary on the Old Testament*, 87–88).

Exodus 3:11–18. Moses Doubts His Own Abilities, but the Lord Comforts and Encourages Him

Why does Moses question the Lord about appearing before Pharaoh? (3:11) "Moses' response to the Lord's call is typical of the response of most of the humble servants of God.... Both Enoch (Moses 6:31) centuries before Moses, and Jeremiah (Jer. 1:6) centuries after, demonstrated great concern over their inadequacies when called to the work of the Lord. But the heavens compensate for those who will be taught and will allow the powers of the Spirit to work a mighty change. Indeed, marvelous miracles are wrought by those who acknowledge their own nothingness, while, at the same time, acknowledging and relying upon the Lord's omnipotence" (Millet, "Call of Moses," 98).

What was the "token" or sign the Lord offered to Moses to assure him? (3:12) "The token given Moses . . . was the Lord himself. *He* would be with Moses. Moses and the Israelites would successfully escape because of *his* presence and would therefore worship *him* as instructed. The token was their successful deliverance, and the deliverance would be possible because of *him*" (Ferrell, *Hidden Christ*, 86).

Why was Moses concerned about the name he should use to identify the God who sent him? (3:13) "Perhaps after such long exposure to the idolatry and ways of the Egyptians, and after encountering the dozens of foreign gods of the cultures Egypt traded with, the memory of the true god and his name had become dim. Whatever the reason, when Moses mentioned the name of God, the Israelites would know that Moses did not represent one of the many gods they had heard of" (Lund, *Jesus Christ, Key to the Plan of Salvation*, 76). "To the Semite, knowledge of God's name was an absolute necessity for establishing any kind of relationship" (Plastaras, *God of Exodus*, 87).

Who is the "I AM" that spoke to Moses? (3:14–15) "When the premortal Lord spoke to Moses from the

12 And he said, Certainly I will be with thee; and this *shall be* a token unto thee, that I have sent thee: When thou hast brought forth the people out of Egypt, ye shall serve God upon this mountain.

13 And Moses said unto God, Behold, *when* I come unto the children of Israel, and shall say unto them, The God of your fathers hath sent me unto you; and they shall say to me, What *is* his name? what shall I say unto them?

14 And God said unto Moses, I AM THAT I AM: and he said, Thus shalt thou say unto

I AM THAT I AM (Exodus 3:14–15)

"In English the words *I am* signify the state of being (the first person present tense of the verb *to be*). (In Latin, the verb of *being* is *esse,* which is the root source of *essence.*) Thus, when Moses asked to know the name of God, he was asking to know the essence or nature of God, and God answered in those same terms. The [*Interpreter's*] Bible dictionary . . . concludes:

"'The uses of the word "name" in the OT [Old Testament] are all related to the central conception of name as denoting essential being. This applies with regard to both man and God. . . .

"'The name in the OT is the essence of personality, the expression of innermost being' [*Interpreter's Dictionary,* 3:501].

"Similarly, the *Oxford Universal Dictionary* lists several secondary meanings of the word *name,* 'chiefly of Biblical origin,' including: (1) the name of God 'as symbolizing the divine nature of power' and (2) the name of a person 'as implying his individual characteristics' (*Oxford Universal Dictionary,* 1308). Each of these meanings came into the English language in time to influence the usage of the word *name* in the key English language translations of the Bible.

"The fact that 'God's self, his real person, is concentrated in his name' (*Interpreter's Dictionary,* 2:408) explains the sacredness of God's name in ancient thought. The [*Interpreter's*] Bible dictionary explains:

"'Because the divine name discloses God's nature, it is laden with the authority, power, and holiness of God himself. This accounts for the great reverence for the name which is one of the distinctive features of Israel's faith [ibid.].

"'In the post-exilic period (after 538 B.C.), however, the sacred name was withdrawn from popular usage for fear that it would be profaned' (*Interpreter's Dictionary,* 2:817). Such reactions seem to be attributable to the concept that a name signifies or even embodies the essence of the one named. The sacred beginning of the book of John ('IN the beginning was the Word, and the Word was with God, and the Word was God' [John 1:1]) also seems to be related to this subject.

"This brief discussion has only scratched the surface of a subject that is holy and deep and little understood" (Oaks, *His Holy Name*, 48–50).

the children of Israel, I AM hath sent me unto you.

15 And God said moreover unto Moses, Thus shalt thou say unto the children of Israel, The LORD God of your fathers, the God of Abraham, the God of Isaac, and the God of Jacob, hath sent me unto you: this *is* my name for ever, and this *is* my memorial unto all generations.

16 Go, and gather the elders of Israel together, and say unto them, The LORD God of your fathers, the God of Abraham, of Isaac, and of Jacob, appeared unto me, saying, I have surely visited you, and *seen* that which is done to you in Egypt:

17 And I have said, I will bring you up out of the affliction of Egypt unto the land of the Canaanites, and the Hittites, and the Amorites, and the Perizzites, and the Hivites, and the Jebusites, unto a land flowing with milk and honey.

18 And they shall hearken to thy voice: and thou shalt come, thou and the elders of Israel, unto the king of Egypt, and ye shall say unto him, The LORD God of the Hebrews hath met with us: and now let us go, we beseech thee, three days' journey into the wilderness, that we may sacrifice to the LORD our God.

19 ¶ And I am sure that the king of Egypt will not let you go, no, not by a mighty hand.

20 And I will stretch out my hand, and smite Egypt with all my wonders which I will do in the midst thereof: and after that he will let you go.

21 And I will give this people favour in the sight of the Egyptians: and it shall come to pass, that, when ye go, ye shall not go empty:

burning bush on Mt. Horeb, he identified himself as 'I Am.' By this name he was to be known among the children of Israel (Ex. 3:14). Many years later, during his mortal ministry, the Savior once again identified himself by this title during a confrontation with the Jews (John 8:56–58). And we find him addressing himself as 'the Great I Am' in latter-day revelation (D&C 29:1; 38:1; 39:1)" (Brewster, *Doctrine and Covenants Encyclopedia*, 223–24). "Although this is the first time this name appears in the Bible, it is obvious that if the name had not been known to the Israelites, its value for identifying the Lord would have been useless" (*Old Testament Student Manual: Genesis–2 Samuel*, 105). ⊕

Why did the Lord tell Moses to request from Pharaoh a "three day journey"? (3:18) "The request to Pharaoh is for a three-day religious pilgrimage into the wilderness. This would generally consist of one day for travel each way and one full day for the religious ceremonies. The refusal adds religious oppression to the crimes of Pharaoh" (Walton, et al., *IVP Background Commentary*, 80).

Exodus 3:19–22. The Lord Promises a Miraculous Deliverance for Israel

How would God reveal His "mighty hand" in Egypt? (3:19–20) God promised to overcome Pharaoh's power with "a mighty hand" represented by "my wonders." "*My wonders* are the ten plagues of chs. 7–12. The word refers to things only God can do, and which are designed to inspire reverence in His worshipers and fear in His enemies" (*Nelson Study Bible* [NKJV], 94–95).

What was the Lord suggesting by having the Israelites "borrow" from their neighbors? (3:21–22) "The Hebrew word translated 'borrow' means 'to ask.' Evidently the women of the Israelites were to ask the Egyptian women for their jewels, perhaps in payment for favors or work given previously. The King James word 'spoil' is the translation of a Hebrew root meaning 'empty out.' The sentence in Hebrew has no connotation of stealing or of borrowing for temporary use only" (Ludlow, *Companion to Your Study of the Old Testament*, 141).

Exodus 4:1–9. The Lord Shows Moses His Power

What do we know about the first sign given to Moses? (4:2–5) "The rod, in the Bible, is frequently emblematic of royalty, power, and authority. As a scepter, it belonged to the ceremonial insignia of Egyptian kings. Sometimes the pharaohs hold a serpent staff in their hand. The uraeus or stylized representation of the sacred cobra, patron goddess of Lower Egypt whose chief shrine was in the marshes of the Delta, was worn by all the pharaohs on the forehead as the symbol of imperial sovereignty, and as an omen of death to the enemies of the monarch. Accordingly, the feat that Moses is told to perform may well have signified his being endowed with leadership and authority, thus enabling him to handle effectively the mighty power of the Egyptian crown" (Sarna, *Exploring Exodus*, 60).

What did Moses demonstrate by picking up the serpent by the tail? (4:4) "Considering the light in which Moses had viewed this serpent, it required considerable faith to induce him thus implicitly to obey the command of God; but he obeyed, and the noxious serpent became instantly the miraculous rod in his hand! Implicit faith and obedience conquer all difficulties; and he who believes in God, and obeys him in all things, has really nothing to fear" (*Adam Clarke's Commentary* [on Exodus 4:4]).

What did the miracle of the leprous hand symbolize? (4:6–7) "The second sign inflicts a skin disease, often translated 'leprosy,' on Moses' hand. In fact,

22 But every woman shall borrow of her
neighbour, and of her that sojourneth in her
house, jewels of silver, and jewels of gold, and
raiment: and ye shall put *them* upon your
sons, and upon your daughters; and ye shall
spoil the Egyptians.

CHAPTER 4

The Lord gives signs to Moses—Aaron is chosen as a spokesman—Israel is the Lord's firstborn and must be released to serve Him—Moses' son is circumcised—Moses and Aaron lead Israel in worship.

1 And Moses answered and said, But, behold, they will not believe me, nor hearken
unto my voice: for they will say, The LORD
hath not appeared unto thee.

2 And the LORD said unto him, What *is* that
in thine hand? And he said, A rod.

3 And he said, Cast it on the ground. And
he cast it on the ground, and it became a serpent; and Moses fled from before it.

4 And the LORD said unto Moses, Put forth
thine hand, and take it by the tail. And he
put forth his hand, and caught it, and it became a rod in his hand:

5 That they may believe that the LORD God
of their fathers, the God of Abraham, the
God of Isaac, and the God of Jacob, hath appeared unto thee.

6 ¶ And the LORD said furthermore unto
him, Put now thine hand into thy bosom.
And he put his hand into his bosom: and

when he took it out, behold, his hand *was* leprous as snow.

7 And he said, Put thine hand into thy bosom again. And he put his hand into his bosom again; and plucked it out of his bosom, and, behold, it was turned again as his *other* flesh.

8 And it shall come to pass, if they will not believe thee, neither hearken to the voice of the first sign, that they will believe the voice of the latter sign.

9 And it shall come to pass, if they will not believe also these two signs, neither hearken unto thy voice, that thou shalt take of the water of the river, and pour *it* upon the dry *land:* and the water which thou takest out of the river shall become blood upon the dry *land.*

however, the Hebrew term used describes many dermatological conditions . . . Nonetheless, when inflicted in the Bible it is consistently a punishment for hubris [excessive pride]—when an individual in pride presumptuously assumes a divinely appointed role (Num 12:1–12; 2 Kings 5:22–27; 2 Chron 26:16–21), thus demonstrating God's intention to punish Pharaoh. Its result is to drive the individual from God's presence, since it rendered the afflicted unclean" (Walton et al., *IVP Background Commentary*, 80).

What did turning the Nile River water to blood symbolize? (4:9) "The Nile was considered holy by the ancient Egyptians and it was the residence of several of their gods, such as Sobek, Hep, and Heket. Because it sustained the lives of the people and the land, the Nile was seen as the means by which the gods blessed their faithful followers. Thus, to turn the water of the Nile to blood was tantamount to bringing defilement and death to the Egyptian gods and their heavens. . . . Therefore, this final of the three signs would have been quite offensive, and would have made a rather bold and dramatic statement to the Egyptians who witnessed it" (Gaskill, *Miracles of the Old Testament*, 52–53).

Exodus 4:10–17. The Lord Promises to Be with Moses as Israel Is Delivered

10 ¶ And Moses said unto the LORD, O my Lord, I *am* not eloquent, neither heretofore, nor since thou hast spoken unto thy servant: but I *am* slow of speech, and of a slow tongue.

11 And the LORD said unto him, Who hath made man's mouth? or who maketh the dumb, or deaf, or the seeing, or the blind? have not I the LORD?

Considering Moses' background, why would he think he was ineloquent in speaking? (4:10) According to the Prophet Joseph Smith, Moses was concerned with his "stammering lips, and [being] slow of speech" [Exodus 2:30*a*], possibly a speech impediment. Another thought is that "Moses had been absent from Egypt for nearly forty years. During that time he spoke the language of the Midianites. . . . Whatever he may have once mastered as a prince of Egypt, a forty-year hiatus from the Egyptian language would have made him somewhat rusty linguistically" (Hyde, *Comprehensive Commentary [Exodus]*, 43). Despite either concern, the Lord promised that "I will be with thy mouth, and teach thee what thou shalt say" (Exodus 4:12).

12 Now therefore go, and I will be with thy mouth, and teach thee what thou shalt say.

13 And he said, O my Lord, send, I pray thee, by the hand *of him whom* thou wilt send.

What can we learn from the Lord's promise to teach Moses "what thou shalt say"? (4:12) "We embrace [the prophet today] as we would have embraced Peter or Moses. . . . God told Moses, 'I will be with thy mouth, and teach thee what thou shalt say' (Exodus 4:12).

We listen to the Lord's prophet with the faith that his words are 'from [the Lord's] own mouth' (D&C 21:5).

"Is this blind faith? No, it is not. We each have a spiritual witness of the truthfulness of . . . the gospel of Jesus Christ. By our own will and choice, we . . . sustain the Lord's prophet with our 'confidence, faith, and prayer[s]' (D&C 107:22)" (Andersen, "Prophet of God," 25).

How else did Jehovah help resolve Moses' concern over his speaking abilities? (4:14–16) "Aaron was the brother of Moses. He was three years older than Moses. When the Lord called Moses as the leader of the children of Israel while they were in Egypt, Moses protested that he had a stammering tongue and that he was not capable of leadership. The Lord did not accept his excuse, but, rather, He told Moses that he should be the leader and that his brother Aaron should be his voice.

"Moses and Aaron went together to ask Pharaoh to let the children of Israel leave Egypt. . . .

"When the children of Israel eventually fled Egypt under Moses' leadership, Aaron was his assistant" (Hinckley, "Aaronic Priesthood–a Gift from God," 45). ⊕

Why was the "rod" important? (4:17) "That rod will accompany Moses for the rest of his life, serving both as a link to his first encounter with God at the burning bush, and as a reminder of his humble origins as a shepherd. Moses will remain a shepherd, though his new flock will be the Hebrew nation.

"That Moses wages the battle with the Egyptians using a simple shepherd's rod rather than sophisticated weaponry is reminiscent of the sling and the five smooth stones with which the young shepherd David confronted and prevailed over the Philistine giant Goliath ([1 Samuel] 17:40–51). With God on their side, Moses and David overcame foes far mightier than the Israelites on whose behalf they fought" (Prager, *Rational Bible*, 55).

Exodus 4:18–26. Moses Leaves Midian and Takes His Family to Egypt

14 And the anger of the LORD was kindled against Moses, and he said, *Is* not Aaron the Levite thy brother? I know that he can speak well. And also, behold, he cometh forth to meet thee: and when he seeth thee, he will be glad in his heart.

15 And thou shalt speak unto him, and put words in his mouth: and I will be with thy mouth, and with his mouth, and will teach you what ye shall do.

16 And he shall be thy spokesman unto the people: and he shall be, *even* he shall be to thee instead of a mouth, and thou shalt be to him instead of God.

17 And thou shalt take this rod in thine hand, wherewith thou shalt do signs.

18 ¶ And Moses went and returned to Jethro his father in law, and said unto him, Let me go, I pray thee, and return unto my brethren which *are* in Egypt, and see whether they be yet alive. And Jethro said to Moses, Go in peace.

19 And the LORD said unto Moses in Midian, Go, return into Egypt: for all the men are dead which sought thy life.

20 And Moses took his wife and his sons, and set them upon an ass, and he returned to the land of Egypt: and Moses took the rod of God in his hand.

21 And the LORD said unto Moses, When thou goest to return into Egypt, see that thou do all those wonders before Pharaoh, which I have put in thine hand: but I will harden his heart, that he shall not let the people go.

Why would the Lord "harden [Pharaoh's] heart"? (4:21) "The Lord does not harden the hearts of men, they harden their own hearts. In the scriptures where is says the Lord hardened Pharaoh's heart, it is a mistranslation in every case. In the corrected verses of the Inspired Version the Lord said to Moses:

"'And Pharaoh will harden his heart, as I said unto thee; and thou shalt multiply my signs, and my wonders, in the land'" (Smith, *Answers to Gospel Questions*, 3:136). ⊕

22 And thou shalt say unto Pharaoh, Thus saith the LORD, Israel *is* my son, *even* my firstborn:

23 And I say unto thee, Let my son go, that he may serve me: and if thou refuse to let him go, behold, I will slay thy son, *even* thy firstborn.

What does it mean that Israel is God's firstborn son? (4:22) "The announcement that Israel was God's . . . 'firstborn' . . . may have stunned Pharaoh; for he was accustomed to regarding himself alone as the 'son of the gods.' But for a whole people to be a 'son' of the deity was a little surprising. . . . Here, God meant 'first in rank,' firstborn by way of *preeminence*, with all the rights, privileges, and responsibilities of a 'firstborn.' . . . The penalty that Pharaoh would ultimately pay for his refusal to acknowledge Israel as the Lord's son and firstborn, however, would be aimed at his own firstborn" (*Expositor's Bible Commentary [Abridged]*, 72).

24 ¶ And it came to pass by the way in the inn, that the LORD met him, and sought to kill him.

25 Then Zipporah took a sharp stone, and cut off the foreskin of her son, and cast *it* at his feet, and said, Surely a bloody husband *art* thou to me.

26 So he let him go: then she said, A bloody husband *thou art*, because of the circumcision.

Why was the Lord angry with Moses? (4:24–26) No Bible verses "contain more problems for the interpreter than these few verses which have continued to baffle throughout the centuries" (Childs, *Book of Exodus*, 95). According to the Joseph Smith Translation, Moses incurred Jehovah's anger because he "had not circumcised his son" (JST, Exodus 4:24). After Zipporah performed the rite for him, "Moses was ashamed, and hid his face from the Lord, and said, I have sinned before the Lord" (JST, Exodus 4:26). "The phrase 'bloody husband' is . . . [an] idiom that designated the recipient of the covenant of circumcision. Doubtless Moses, as a previous recipient, should have performed the rite on his son" (Rasmussen, *Latter-day Saint Commentary on the Old Testament*, 91).

Exodus 4:27–31. Moses and Aaron Meet with the Elders of Israel and Convey Jehovah's Message of Deliverance

27 ¶ And the LORD said to Aaron, Go into the wilderness to meet Moses. And he went,

What do we know about Moses' brother, Aaron? (4:27) "Aaron was from the tribe of Levi and was

Moses's older brother. He served faithfully with Moses until he died just before Israel entered the promised land. Though he sometimes had some difficulties, he remained faithful to the Lord and Moses, served as the first high priest in the Aaronic Priesthood, and participated with Moses in many holy manifestations and miraculous events" (Muhlestein, *Essential Old Testament Companion*, 96).

What do we learn about the elders of Israel as Moses and Aaron met with them? (4:30–31) "What can be said of the people who had to be converted by signs (see Matthew 12:38–39; D&C 63:7–12)? Although their initial reaction when they saw the signs was very positive, at the first indication of challenge and adversity their commitment began to waver (see Exodus 5:20–23)" (*Old Testament Student Manual: Genesis–2 Samuel*, 107).

Exodus 5:1–9. Instead of Letting Israel Go, Pharaoh Adds to Their Burdens

What can we learn from Pharaoh's response to Moses? (5:2) "Pharaoh responded as anticipated (Ex. 3:19; 4:21–23). He asked a question, the answer to which he and many others have had to learn by hard experience. Many, like Pharaoh, who do not know the Lord, seem unwilling to learn about Him. Pharaoh even became vindictive, increasing the burdens, the beatings, and the demands made of his Israelite slaves" (Rasmussen, *Latter-day Saint Commentary on the Old Testament*, 91). "Pharaoh [was] under the common persuasion that every place and people had a tutelary [guardian] deity, and he supposed that this Jehovah might be the tutelary [guardian] deity of the Israelites, to whom he, as an Egyptian, could be under no kind of obligation" (*Adam Clarke's Commentary* [on Exodus 5:2]).

Why did Moses request a "three days' journey into the desert"? (5:3) "Was Moses lying about the

and met him in the mount of God, and
kissed him.

28 And Moses told Aaron all the words of
the LORD who had sent him, and all the signs
which he had commanded him.

29 ¶ And Moses and Aaron went and gathered together all the elders of the children of
Israel:

30 And Aaron spake all the words which the
LORD had spoken unto Moses, and did the
signs in the sight of the people.

31 And the people believed: and when they
heard that the LORD had visited the children
of Israel, and that he had looked upon their
affliction, then they bowed their heads and
worshipped.

CHAPTER 5

Moses and Aaron ask Pharaoh to free Israel—Pharaoh responds, Who is the Lord?—He places greater burdens upon the children of Israel.

1 And afterward Moses and Aaron went in,
and told Pharaoh, Thus saith the LORD God
of Israel, Let my people go, that they may
hold a feast unto me in the wilderness.

2 And Pharaoh said, Who *is* the LORD, that I
should obey his voice to let Israel go? I know
not the LORD, neither will I let Israel go.

3 And they said, The God of the Hebrews
hath met with us: let us go, we pray thee,

three days' journey into the desert, and sacrifice unto the LORD our God; lest he fall upon us with pestilence, or with the sword.

4 And the king of Egypt said unto them, Wherefore do ye, Moses and Aaron, let the people from their works? get you unto your burdens.

5 And Pharaoh said, Behold, the people of the land now *are* many, and ye make them rest from their burdens.

6 And Pharaoh commanded the same day the taskmasters of the people, and their officers, saying,

three-day trip? (5:3) No. Moses was simply countering Pharaoh's refusal of the first request to release the people. Moses posed the question differently to try to convince Pharaoh that the Israelites were under God's authority and needed to worship" (*Quest Study Bible* [2011], 85). See commentary in this volume for Exodus 3:18.

Who were the "officers" assisting the taskmasters? (5:6) "In the Egyptian corvée [unpaid, free labor] system the workers were organized into manageable gangs, each headed by a foreman ['officer'] from among their own. He, in turn, was directly responsible to his superior, the 'taskmaster.' . . . The foremen were Israelites, the taskmasters, Egyptian. The foremen kept careful logs of their wards and the activities of each. Several such logs are extant, some from the time of Ramses II. Hebrew *shoter*, 'foreman,' in fact derives from a stem meaning 'to write,' a denotation reflected in the Septuagint rendering *grammateus*, 'scribe, keeper of records'" (Sarna, *Exodus*, 28).

7 Ye shall no more give the people straw to make brick, as heretofore: let them go and gather straw for themselves.

8 And the tale of the bricks, which they did make heretofore, ye shall lay upon them; ye shall not diminish *ought* thereof: for they *be* idle; therefore they cry, saying, Let us go *and* sacrifice to our God.

9 Let there more work be laid upon the men, that they may labour therein; and let them not regard vain words.

10 ¶ And the taskmasters of the people went out, and their officers, and they spake to the people, saying, Thus saith Pharaoh, I will not give you straw.

11 Go ye, get you straw where ye can find it: yet not ought of your work shall be diminished.

Why was straw so important in making bricks? (5:7–8) "Straw serves as a bonding agent in the brick as it is heated. Without sufficient straw or with poor-quality stubble, the bricks would not form as easily and a higher proportion would fall apart, thus making the quota harder to achieve. Quotas found in Egyptian literature often do not clarify the number in the crew or the time period involved, but we do know that the quotas were often not met" (Walton, et al., *IVP Bible Background Commentary*, 81). ⊕

Exodus 5:10–19. The Children of Israel Must Gather Their Own Straw

How did Pharaoh mock the Lord? (5:10) "Introducing Pharaoh's words with *Thus says Pharaoh* sets him in opposition to the Lord, whose words are similarly announced [see Exodus 4:22]" (*New Oxford Annotated Bible*, 89). In your experience, what happens when a person chooses to mock and challenge the God of Israel?

What was the "stubble" that the Israelites gathered? (5:12) "Without straw as a binder to prevent mud bricks from splitting as they dried, the slaves were compelled to find an alternative material, such as hair, dried reeds, or slender sticks, to bind the bricks, or to make additional bricks to compensate for those that broke. Such requirements, added to an already demanding burden, create a test that builds either faith or bitter feelings toward God" (Olson, *Women of the Old Testament*, 92).

12 So the people were scattered abroad
throughout all the land of Egypt to gather
stubble instead of straw.

13 And the taskmasters hasted *them,* saying,
Fulfil your works, *your* daily tasks, as when
there was straw.

14 And the officers of the children of
Israel, which Pharaoh's taskmasters had set
over them, were beaten, *and* demanded,
Wherefore have ye not fulfilled your task in
making brick both yesterday and to day, as
heretofore?

How did Pharaoh respond to the complaints of the Israelite officers? (5:15–19) "The Hebrew leaders of the work gangs, the officers or subordinate officials, understandably complained about the new work rules. Pharaoh repeated his excuse that the people were idle (v. 8) and ordered them to continue. The Hebrew crew chiefs were in a more precarious position than ever" (*Nelson Study Bible* [NKJV], 98).

Why did Pharaoh call the Israelites "idle" in his response to Moses' request for time off? (5:17–18) "'Slackers!' Pharaoh deems them such, of course, because of the request for time off from work. The reason for the request—going into the desert to worship—Pharaoh sees merely as an excuse. But time off from work for worship was not unheard of in Egypt. A collection of texts has been preserved from the New Kingdom site of Deir el-Medina, where many Egyptian workers were stationed in order to construct and decorate royal tombs. Records list workers who were absent for a variety of reasons, including participation in religious rituals and festivities. Pharaoh does not want to give the Hebrews time off for any reason" (Walton, *Zondervan Illustrated Bible Backgrounds Commentary*, 1:180–81).

15 ¶ Then the officers of the children of
Israel came and cried unto Pharaoh, saying,
Wherefore dealest thou thus with thy servants?

16 There is no straw given unto thy servants,
and they say to us, Make brick: and, behold,
thy servants *are* beaten; but the fault *is* in
thine own people.

17 But he said, Ye *are* idle, *ye are* idle: therefore ye say, Let us go *and* do sacrifice to the
LORD.

18 Go therefore now, *and* work; for there
shall no straw be given you, yet shall ye deliver the tale of bricks.

19 And the officers of the children of Israel
did see *that* they *were* in evil *case,* after it was
said, Ye shall not minish *ought* from your
bricks of your daily task.

Exodus 5:20–23. The People Blame Moses for Their Troubles

20 ¶ And they met Moses and Aaron, who
stood in the way, as they came forth from
Pharaoh:

21 And they said unto them, The LORD
look upon you, and judge; because ye have
made our savour to be abhorred in the eyes
of Pharaoh, and in the eyes of his servants, to
put a sword in their hand to slay us.

22 And Moses returned unto the LORD, and said, Lord, wherefore hast thou *so* evil entreated this people? why *is* it *that* thou hast sent me?

23 For since I came to Pharaoh to speak in thy name, he hath done evil to this people; neither hast thou delivered thy people at all.

What was the "evil" that Moses felt had come upon his people? (5:22) "These were hard words that Moses spoke to the Lord. But God knew what he was about. There was purpose in all he did, and as he permitted Pharaoh to resist, he also was teaching the monarch that the God of Israel was mightier than the gods of Egypt. This lesson was not alone for the Egyptians, either, for the Israelites themselves had to learn that great fact, inasmuch as many of them had become worshipers of the Egyptian deities.

"The Lord was under covenant to bring his people out, and he would keep his word" (Petersen, *Moses*, 61).

What had Moses forgotten in the midst of his trials? (5:23) "It seems that Moses expected Pharaoh to cave in as soon as he heard the use of the Lord's name [Jehovah] (3:14, 15; 5:1). Yet God had warned Moses that Pharaoh would do the opposite (3:19; 4:21). Moses had forgotten this clear revelation" (*Nelson Study Bible* [NKJV], 98).

CHAPTER 6

The Lord identifies Himself as Jehovah—The genealogies of Reuben, Simeon, and Levi are listed.

1 Then the LORD said unto Moses, Now shalt thou see what I will do to Pharaoh: for with a strong hand shall he let them go, and with a strong hand shall he drive them out of his land.

2 And God spake unto Moses, and said unto him, I *am* the LORD:

3 And I appeared unto Abraham, unto Isaac, and unto Jacob, by *the name of* God Almighty, but by my name JEHOVAH was I not known to them.

4 And I have also established my covenant with them, to give them the land of Canaan, the land of their pilgrimage, wherein they were strangers.

5 And I have also heard the groaning of the children of Israel, whom the Egyptians keep in bondage; and I have remembered my covenant.

Exodus 6:1–8. God Will Deliver Israel with Great Power

By whose "strong hand" will Israel be driven from Egypt? (6:1) "The strong hand is the hand of Jehovah, not of Pharaoh" (*John Dummelow's Commentary* [on Exodus 6:1]). The New International Version of the Bible clarifies the Lord's promise to Moses with: "Because of my mighty hand [Pharaoh] will let [Israel] go; because of my mighty hand [Pharaoh] will drive them out of his country" (NIV, Exodus 6:1; see also Exodus 6:6).

When was Jehovah's name first known? (6:3) According to the Joseph Smith Translation, God here declared: "I am the Lord God Almighty; the Lord JEHOVAH. And was not my name known unto them?" (JST, Exodus 6:3). Clearly, ancient Israel was familiar with the name of God. "The Bible has hundreds of references to the name of God, a sacred word which usually refers to God the Father, or Elohim (see Genesis; John 3:16). The ancient prophets also knew and revered the name of Jehovah, the Holy One of Israel, Jesus Christ, whom the Bible usually refers to as the Lord (see JST, Ex. 6:3; Abr. 1:16, 2:8; Ether 3; Isa. 43:3)" (Oaks, "Reverent and Clean," 50). See commentary in this volume for Exodus 3:13 and 3:14–15. ⊕

What was the Lord referring to with His "stretched out arm" and "judgments"? (6:6) The Lord "had heard the 'groaning' of Israel; he was remembering his covenant and would redeem them 'with a stretched out arm' (meaning a manifestation of his identity and power). He would respond 'with great judgments,' implying there would be justifiable punishments for the oppressors" (Rasmussen, *Latter-day Saint Commentary on the Old Testament*, 92). ⊕

Why did Jehovah say He would take Israel to Him "for a people"? (6:7) "The Lord often uses a specific promise in the Abrahamic covenant to remind us that what is happening is part of that covenant. Thus, when He tells Israel 'I will take you to me for a people, and I will be to you a God' (Ex. 6:7), He is drawing on the part of the Abrahamic covenant that states He will be Abraham's God. His word choice serves as a subtle reminder" (Muhlestein, *Essential Old Testament Companion*, 98).

How has modern revelation clarified the phrase, "I am the Lord"? (6:8) The phrase "I am the Lord" should read "I the Lord *will do it*" according to the Joseph Smith Translation (see Wayment, *Complete Joseph Smith Translation of the Old Testament*, 116).

Exodus 6:9–13. The Children of Israel Will Not Listen to Moses

What do we learn about ancient Israel's spiritual state in this passage? (6:9) "The brief narrative suggests that Moses addressed gospel beginners, not seasoned believers. Even then, the enslaved people struggled to believe his message, on account of the bitter and hopeless state of their bondage (Exodus 4:27–31; 6:9)" (Olson, *Women of the Old Testament*, 89). When has your belief been challenged with sore trials?

What did Moses mean by telling the Lord he had "uncircumcised lips"? (6:12) Moses was constantly plagued by concerns about his ability to speak to either the Israelites or to Pharaoh. "The King James Version states that Moses had 'uncircumcised lips' (Exodus 6:30). The Joseph Smith Translation clarifies this statement by saying that Moses had 'stammering lips' and was 'slow of speech' (JST, Exodus 6:29). Exodus 4:10 in the New English Bible reports that Moses was 'slow and hesitant in speech.' This characteristic may explain Moses' original hesitation to be God's spokesman" (*Old Testament Student Manual: Genesis–2 Samuel*, 107).

6 Wherefore say unto the children of Israel, I *am* the LORD, and I will bring you out from under the burdens of the Egyptians, and I will rid you out of their bondage, and I will redeem you with a stretched out arm, and with great judgments:

7 And I will take you to me for a people, and I will be to you a God: and ye shall know that I *am* the LORD your God, which bringeth you out from under the burdens of the Egyptians.

8 And I will bring you in unto the land, concerning the which I did swear to give it to Abraham, to Isaac, and to Jacob; and I will give it you for an heritage: I *am* the LORD.

9 ¶ And Moses spake so unto the children of Israel: but they hearkened not unto Moses for anguish of spirit, and for cruel bondage.

10 And the LORD spake unto Moses, saying,

11 Go in, speak unto Pharaoh king of Egypt, that he let the children of Israel go out of his land.

12 And Moses spake before the LORD, saying, Behold, the children of Israel have not hearkened unto me; how then shall Pharaoh hear me, who *am* of uncircumcised lips?

13 And the LORD spake unto Moses and
unto Aaron, and gave them a charge unto the
children of Israel, and unto Pharaoh king of
Egypt, to bring the children of Israel out of
the land of Egypt.

28 ¶ And it came to pass on the day *when* the
LORD spake unto Moses in the land of Egypt,
29 That the LORD spake unto Moses, saying,
I *am* the LORD: speak thou unto Pharaoh
king of Egypt all that I say unto thee.
30 And Moses said before the LORD, Behold,
I *am* of uncircumcised lips, and how shall
Pharaoh hearken unto me?

CHAPTER 7

Moses is appointed to give the word of the Lord to Pharaoh—The Lord will multiply signs and wonders in Egypt—Aaron's rod becomes a serpent—The river is turned into blood—The magicians imitate the miracles of Moses and Aaron.

1 And the LORD said unto Moses, See, I have
made thee a god to Pharaoh: and Aaron thy
brother shall be thy prophet.
2 Thou shalt speak all that I command thee:
and Aaron thy brother shall speak unto

Why did Moses feel unprepared or doubt his call to deliver Israel from Pharaoh's bondage? (6:13) "Moses' own people did not believe him so he was afraid that Pharaoh would not believe him or obey him because of his speech problem. Still, God again gave Moses 'a charge,' or an assignment, to bring his people out of Egypt. President Thomas S. Monson counseled, 'If any brethren who hold the priesthood of God feel unprepared—even incapable—of responding to a call to serve, to sacrifice, to bless the lives of others, remember this truth: "Whom God calls, God qualifies"' (*Live the Good Life*, 17)" (Valletta, et al., *Old Testament for Latter-day Saint Families*, 112).

Summary of Exodus 6:14–27

Moses writes the names of the family heads of the children of Israel who will be delivered from four generations of bondage as promised to Abraham (see Genesis 15:16). He also focuses heavily on the family history of Levi, from whom Israel's priests would one day come.

Exodus 6:28–30. Moses Is Afraid Pharaoh Will Not Listen to Him

How do Moses' doubts affect his ability to deliver Israel? (6:28–30) Here, on the eve of one of the greatest manifestations of God's power recorded in scripture, His chosen deliverer once again humbly expressed his doubts about his ability to persuade Pharaoh to let Israel go. "But the Lord would yet turn Moses' humility and weakness into strength, and he would become a man 'mighty in words and in deeds' (Acts 7:22; Ether 12:27)" (Rasmussen, *Latter-day Saint Commentary on the Old Testament*, 92).

Exodus 7:1–7. The Lord Calls Aaron as a Spokesman for Moses

What does it mean that Moses was to be a "god to Pharaoh"? (7:1) "This passage has Moses becoming 'a god to Pharaoh: and Aaron thy brother shall be thy prophet.' It is corrected in the JST to read 'I have made thee a *prophet* to Pharaoh: and Aaron thy brother shall be thy *spokesman*'" (Horton, "Insights into Exodus, Leviticus, Numbers, and Deuteronomy," 80). "See,

I have set thee in God's stead to Pharaoh" (Jewish Publication Society translation) is more correct and, incidentally, more in harmony with the Joseph Smith Translation. . . . A prophet is basically a spokesman" (Rasmussen, *Latter-day Saint Commentary on the Old Testament*, 93).

Why would God harden Pharaoh's heart? (7:3) "There are a number of lessons for life which emerge from the narrative of Moses' encounter with Pharaoh. . . . Moses and Aaron approached Pharaoh and boldly insisted that he set the Israelites free. They represented God; surely the king of Egypt would comply, they supposed. But, as we learn repeatedly from the Prophet Joseph Smith's translation of the book of Exodus, *Pharaoh hardened his heart* and refused to either yield to the wishes of the God of gods or to be motivated by the miraculous" (Millet, "Call of Moses," 102). See commentary in this volume for Exodus 4:21.

Why did God perform these miracles? (7:5) "Not only would Israel know what was meant by the name 'LORD,' but so would the Egyptians. In addition to understanding the significance of that name (Heb. YHWH or Yahweh), these miracles would also be an invitation for the Egyptians to personally believe in Israel's Lord. Thus the invitation was pressed repeatedly in 7:5; 8:10, 22; 9:14, 16, 29; 14:4, 18—and some apparently did believe, for there was 'a mixed multitude' ([KJV, 12:38]) that left Egypt with Israel" (*Expositor's Bible Commentary [Abridged]*, 76).

Exodus 7:8–13. Aaron's Rod Becomes a Serpent

What did the serpent symbolize in these verses? (7:9–10) "The Hebrew word for 'snake' in this verse is different from the one used in 4:3. The word here can refer to a sea-monster, dragon, crocodile, or snake. . . . The sign with Moses' staff was for the Israelite elders. . . . The sign with Aaron's staff is for Pharaoh and his officials and demonstrates what appears to be an assault on Egyptian ideology. If Aaron's staff did indeed become a snake, then its devouring of the magicians' snakes, on the one hand, demonstrates an overpowering of the magicians and even a commandeering of their own abilities and expertise. . . . it could also serve as an attack on the snake as a symbol of Egyptian power" (Walton, *Zondervan Illustrated Bible Backgrounds Commentary,* 1:188). See commentary in this volume for Exodus 4:2–5.

Pharaoh, that he send the children of Israel
out of his land.

3 And I will harden Pharaoh's heart, and
multiply my signs and my wonders in the
land of Egypt.

4 But Pharaoh shall not hearken unto you,
that I may lay my hand upon Egypt, and
bring forth mine armies, *and* my people the
children of Israel, out of the land of Egypt by
great judgments.

5 And the Egyptians shall know that I *am* the
LORD, when I stretch forth mine hand upon
Egypt, and bring out the children of Israel
from among them.

6 And Moses and Aaron did as the LORD
commanded them, so did they.

7 And Moses *was* fourscore years old, and
Aaron fourscore and three years old, when
they spake unto Pharaoh.

8 ¶ And the LORD spake unto Moses and
unto Aaron, saying,

9 When Pharaoh shall speak unto you, saying, Shew a miracle for you: then thou shalt
say unto Aaron, Take thy rod, and cast *it* before Pharaoh, *and* it shall become a serpent.

10 ¶ And Moses and Aaron went in unto
Pharaoh, and they did so as the LORD had
commanded: and Aaron cast down his rod
before Pharaoh, and before his servants, and
it became a serpent.

11 Then Pharaoh also called the wise men and the sorcerers: now the magicians of Egypt, they also did in like manner with their enchantments.

12 For they cast down every man his rod, and they became serpents: but Aaron's rod swallowed up their rods.

13 And he hardened Pharaoh's heart, that he hearkened not unto them; as the LORD had said.

How did Pharaoh's magicians imitate Aaron's miracle? (7:11–12) "Another category of miracles, so-called, are the tricks that some magicians and religious practitioners stage in order to produce astonishing events in aid of their professions or ministries. You will remember that the magicians in Pharaoh's court duplicated some of the miracles Moses produced through the power of God (see Ex. 7–8). Perhaps these magicians were servants of the devil, using his power, but I think it more likely that they were simply skilled practitioners of magic tricks that they used to reinforce their position in Pharaoh's court" (Oaks, "Miracles," 6). ⊕

What did it mean when Aaron's rod devoured all the other rods? (7:12) "This rod, whether a common staff, an ensign of office, or a shepherd's crook, was now consecrated for the purpose of working miracles; . . . God gave it the miraculous power, and Moses and Aaron used it. . . . As Egypt was remarkably addicted to magic, sorcery, etc., it was necessary that God should permit Pharaoh's wise men to act to the utmost of their skill in order to imitate the work of God, that His superiority might be clearly seen, and His powerful working incontestably ascertained; and this was fully done when *Aaron's rod swallowed up their rods*" (*Adam Clarke's Commentary* [on Exodus 7:9, 12]).

14 ¶ And the LORD said unto Moses, Pharaoh's heart *is* hardened, he refuseth to let the people go.

15 Get thee unto Pharaoh in the morning; lo, he goeth out unto the water; and thou shalt stand by the river's brink against he come; and the rod which was turned to a serpent shalt thou take in thine hand.

16 And thou shalt say unto him, The LORD God of the Hebrews hath sent me unto thee, saying, Let my people go, that they may serve me in the wilderness: and, behold, hitherto thou wouldest not hear.

17 Thus saith the LORD, In this thou shalt know that I *am* the LORD: behold, I will smite with the rod that *is* in mine hand upon the waters which *are* in the river, and they shall be turned to blood.

Exodus 7:14–25. The Lord Turns the Waters in Egypt to Blood

How were the plagues presented to Pharaoh? (7:15–18) "Observe, as the account proceeds, that nine of the plagues occurred in three cycles of three, after which there was one final plague. The first in each cycle was announced to Pharaoh at the river in the morning, and when he did not yield, the plague came. The second plague in each cycle was announced with a warning, and when it came, Pharaoh supplicated for relief; [then] he hardened his heart once again. The third plague in each cycle was inflicted without warning and Pharaoh's response was only a hardened heart" (Rasmussen, *Latter-day Saint Commentary on the Old Testament*, 93–94). See commentary in this volume for Exodus 8:20. ⊕

Why did the Lord send plagues upon Pharaoh and his people? (7:17) "In the providence of God the account of Moses' confrontation with Pharaoh has been preserved as a memorial for all generations to witness the difference between the powers of heaven and the priesthoods of the prince of darkness. The majesty of

Egypt with its mighty palaces, pyramids, and temples was being challenged by a desert prophet. . . . What a spectacle it must have presented as Moses and Aaron, armed with nothing more than a shepherd's crook. . . . Mocking, Pharaoh challenged, 'Show a miracle that I may know you' ([JST, Exodus 7:9]). And a God who will not be mocked showed forth his hand and his might that all men, then and in future ages, might know that his name was the Lord" (McConkie, *Gospel Symbolism*, 45–46). ⊕

What was the result of the water turning to blood? (7:19) "With the first plague (see Exodus 7:17–25) the Lord turned to blood the precious, life-giving water of the Nile, which the Egyptians deified and worshipped as the source of fertility in their desert country. 'In this,' the Lord said, 'thou shalt know that I am the Lord' (Ex. 7:17). But it was more than just the water from the

18 And the fish that *is* in the river shall die,
and the river shall stink; and the Egyptians
shall lothe to drink of the water of the river.

19 ¶ And the LORD spake unto Moses, Say
unto Aaron, Take thy rod, and stretch out
thine hand upon the waters of Egypt, upon
their streams, upon their rivers, and upon
their ponds, and upon all their pools of
water, that they may become blood; and *that*

The Ten Plagues (Exodus 7:17)

The plagues of Egypt accomplished at least four major objectives. First, they increased the faith of the Israelites in Jehovah, and convinced them to accept Moses as their prophet leader. Second, they helped to convince the Egyptians to let Israel go. Third, they showed the supremacy of the God of Israel over the gods of Egypt because the plagues sent upon the Egyptians either represented or affected gods the Egyptians worshiped. A very similar contest of deities occurred between the God of Israel and the gods of the Canaanites in the days of Elijah. Fourth, the plagues served to give an example of the kinds of plagues that will devastate the earth prior to the second coming of Jesus Christ. Consider the following chart.

The Plague	Egyptian god	Latter-day prophecy
1. Water to blood (Ex. 7:17–25)	Hapi (or Hopi) controlled the waters of the Nile. The Nile itself was considered sacred.	Rev. 8:8; 16:3–6
2. Frogs (Ex. 8:2–6)	Heqt (or Heket) is represented as a frog goddess	Rev. 16:12–14
3. Lice, or gnats (Ex. 8:16–17)	The god of the earth, Seth, was turned into lice, or gnats.	
4. Flies (Ex. 8:21–24)	Possibly Uachit, represented by a fly	D&C 29:18–20
5. Plague on the cattle (Ex. 9:2–7)	Apis and Mnevis were bull gods; Hathor was a cow goddess; Khnum was a ram god	
6. Boils and blains (Ex. 9:8–11)	Sekhmet, goddess with power over disease; Sunu, the pestilence god; Isis, goddess of healing	
7. Hail and fire (Ex. 9:22–26)	Nut, the sky goddess; Osiris, god of crops and fertility	Rev. 8:7
8. Locusts (Ex. 10:12–15)	Osiris, god of crops and fertility	Rev. 9:3
9. Three days of darkness (Ex. 10:21–23)	Ra, or Amun-Re, the god of the sun	Rev. 8:12; D&C 112:23–24
10. Death of the firstborn (Ex. 12:21–30)	Pharaoh, who was considered a god, had no power to save his own son from death; Isis, goddess who protected children	

there may be blood throughout all the land of Egypt, both in *vessels of* wood, and in *vessels of* stone.

20 And Moses and Aaron did so, as the LORD commanded; and he lifted up the rod, and smote the waters that *were* in the river, in the sight of Pharaoh, and in the sight of his servants; and all the waters that *were* in the river were turned to blood.

21 And the fish that *was* in the river died; and the river stank, and the Egyptians could not drink of the water of the river; and there was blood throughout all the land of Egypt.

22 And the magicians of Egypt did so with their enchantments: and Pharaoh's heart was hardened, neither did he hearken unto them; as the LORD had said.

23 And Pharaoh turned and went into his house, neither did he set his heart to this also.

24 And all the Egyptians digged round about the river for water to drink; for they could not drink of the water of the river.

25 And seven days were fulfilled, after that the LORD had smitten the river.

CHAPTER 8

The Lord sends plagues of frogs, lice, and flies upon Egypt—Pharaoh hardens his heart.

1 And the LORD spake unto Moses, Go unto Pharaoh, and say unto him, Thus saith the LORD, Let my people go, that they may serve me.

2 And if thou refuse to let *them* go, behold, I will smite all thy borders with frogs:

3 And the river shall bring forth frogs abundantly, which shall go up and come into thine house, and into thy bedchamber, and upon thy bed, and into the house of thy servants, and upon thy people, and into thine ovens, and into thy kneadingtroughs:

Nile that turned to blood—all water, whether in rivers, streams, pools, ponds, or vessels of wood or stone, turned to blood. As a result, all the fish, a principal source of food, died" (Vorhaus, "I Have a Question," 64).

Exodus 8:1–7. The Lord Sends a Plague of Frogs

Why did this plague of frogs offend the Egyptians? (8:2–3) "Some scholars see a direct cause-and-effect relationship between the plague of blood and this plague of frogs. If the Nile, never in short supply of frogs, were to become uninhabitable, where else would the frogs go but up onto the land? This is speculative at best. Another idea is that this plague is one more attack on Egyptian ideology, with the frog goddess Heket as its particular target. Heket was a giver of life. [See Breakout Box in this volume for Exodus 7:17.]

"If there is symbolic meaning in the account of this plague, it may simply be to point out the inability of Pharaoh and the Egyptian gods to maintain proper order" (Wells, "Exodus," 191).

What power did Aaron's rod possess? (8:5) Aaron's power came from his faith in the priesthood of God, not a magical physical rod. Aaron's rod simply served as a means to focus his faith. "The Old Testament account of Moses and his brother Aaron recounted several instances of using rods to manifest God's will (see Exodus 7:9–12; Numbers 17:8). Many Christians in Joseph Smith and Oliver Cowdery's day similarly believed in divining rods as instruments for revelation. Oliver was among those who believed in and used a divining rod" (Cannon, "Oliver Cowdery's Gift").

Why would the magicians choose to duplicate the plague of the frogs? (8:7) "This is only the second plague, but it is the last one that Pharaoh's magicians are able to reproduce. But what purpose is there for them to do so? Would not duplicating this plague severely add to Egypt's misery?! Apart from the recurring question of how Pharaoh's magicians are able to make 'frogs come up on the land of Egypt' (8:7), it is somewhat curious why they choose to increase the number of frogs rather than rid Egypt of this menace. Furthermore, it is after the magicians have their turn that Pharaoh asks Moses to make the plague stop. Apparently, this double dose of frogs is too much for him" (Enns, "Exodus," 206).

Why did Pharaoh ask Moses and Aaron and not his magicians to take the frogs away? (8:7–8) "This miracle was also imitated by the Egyptian augurs [foretellers] with their secret arts, and frogs were brought upon the land by them. But if they were able to bring the plague, they could not take it away. The latter is not expressly stated, it is true; but it is evident from the fact that Pharaoh was obliged to send for Moses and Aaron to intercede with Jehovah to take them away. The king would never have applied to Moses and Aaron for help if his charmers could have charmed the plague away" (Keil and Delitzsch, *Commentary* [on Exodus 8:7]).

Exodus 8:9–15. Pharaoh Breaks His Promise to Let the Israelites Go

Why would Moses allow Pharaoh to set the time for the frogs to be destroyed? (8:9–10) "When Moses said, 'Pharaoh, Glory over me,' he was giving Pharaoh

4 And the frogs shall come up both on thee, and upon thy people, and upon all thy servants.

5 ¶ And the LORD spake unto Moses, Say unto Aaron, Stretch forth thine hand with thy rod over the streams, over the rivers, and over the ponds, and cause frogs to come up upon the land of Egypt.

6 And Aaron stretched out his hand over the waters of Egypt; and the frogs came up, and covered the land of Egypt.

7 And the magicians did so with their enchantments, and brought up frogs upon the land of Egypt.

8 ¶ Then Pharaoh called for Moses and Aaron, and said, Entreat the LORD, that he may take away the frogs from me, and from my people; and I will let the people go, that they may do sacrifice unto the LORD.

9 And Moses said unto Pharaoh, Glory over me: when shall I entreat for thee, and for thy servants, and for thy people, to destroy the

frogs from thee and thy houses, *that* they
may remain in the river only?

10 And he said, To morrow. And he said, *Be*
it according to thy word: that thou mayest
know that *there is* none like unto the LORD
our God.

11 And the frogs shall depart from thee, and
from thy houses, and from thy servants, and
from thy people; they shall remain in the
river only.

12 And Moses and Aaron went out from
Pharaoh: and Moses cried unto the LORD
because of the frogs which he had brought
against Pharaoh.

13 And the LORD did according to the word
of Moses; and the frogs died out of the houses,
out of the villages, and out of the fields.

14 And they gathered them together upon
heaps: and the land stank.

15 But when Pharaoh saw that there was re-
spite, he hardened his heart, and hearkened
not unto them; as the LORD had said.

the right to decide when the frogs would be taken away (see [Exodus 8:9*a*]). Moses was showing that the God of Israel could get rid of the frogs anytime He wanted to. This was an additional proof of the Lord's power" (Valletta, et al., *Old Testament for Latter-day Saint Families*,115). Keil and Delitzsch add: "To give Jehovah the glory, Moses placed himself below Pharaoh, and left him to fix the time for the frogs to be removed through his intercession" (Keil and Delitzsch, *Commentary* [on Exodus 8:9–10]).

Why would Pharaoh "harden" his heart yet again after witnessing God's miracles? (8:15) "Pharaoh's behavior exhibits a pattern. During the time of stress, Pharaoh was willing to promise anything. But as soon as the stress ended, he *hardened his heart* and became unwilling to do what he had promised" (*Nelson Study Bible* [NKJV], 102). Have you ever seen anyone become so angry that he or she stops thinking about what is right or good? Why do you think Pharaoh was willing to watch his people suffer rather than let the Hebrews go? See commentary in this volume for Exodus 4:21.

Exodus 8:16–19. The Lord Sends a Plague of Lice

16 ¶ And the LORD said unto Moses, Say
unto Aaron, Stretch out thy rod, and smite
the dust of the land, that it may become lice
throughout all the land of Egypt.

17 And they did so; for Aaron stretched out
his hand with his rod, and smote the dust
of the earth, and it became lice in man, and
in beast; all the dust of the land became lice
throughout all the land of Egypt.

Why is "dust" used to describe the lice? (8:16–17) "With this plague and that of flies, it is impossible to be precise about the insects named here. Biting gnats, stinging mosquitoes, lice, or any number of other insects could be in view" (Wells, "Exodus," 195).

Why did the Lord limit the power of the magicians to duplicate or stop plagues? (8:18) "In this confrontation with Moses the priests of Egypt had also turned rods to snakes, changed water to blood, and called forth plagues of frogs. Their ability to work miracles was impressive, yet it must not have been lost upon their people that though they could imitate the plagues they had no power to rebuke them. They had power to further curse their people, but not the power to bless them. When Moses brought forth the plague of lice, their attempts to imitate it failed, illustrating that there are limits to the powers of the kingdom of darkness" (McConkie, *Gospel Symbolism*, 47–48).

What are the magicians admitting to when they say "This is the finger of God?" (8:19) "When the magicians of Pharaoh's Court could not do what they saw Moses and Aaron do, they said, 'This is the finger of God.' That expression is used throughout the Scriptures, and means the *presence*, or *the power*, or *the purpose of God*" (Sjodahl and Reynolds, *Commentary on the Book of Mormon*, 7:6).

According to Egyptian theology, what impact would a hard heart have on Pharaoh in the afterlife? (8:19) According to the Book of the Dead, "at judgment, a person's heart was placed on a scale and weighed against an ostrich feather, representing Maat, the goddess and principle of truth, order, and rightness. If one's heart was heavier than Maat, due to sin, the devouring monster would gobble the heart up and the person had no afterlife—they ceased to be. Not only does modern revelation show that Pharaoh's heart was unresponsive to Jehovah's influence, but Egyptian imagery also seems to indicate that the Egyptian ruler's hard and heavy heart would bring him to a tragic end" (Holzapfel, et al., *Jehovah and the World of the Old Testament*, 89). See commentary in this volume for Exodus 4:21.

Exodus 8:20–24. The Lord Sends a Plague of Flies

What do the three cycles of plagues symbolize? (8:20) "The plagues were sent in three cycles of three. The first plague of each cycle was 'announced to the Pharaoh, at the river, in the morning' (see Exodus 7:15). The second plague of each cycle was announced with a warning. The third plague of each cycle was inflicted without warning. Of course, anciently, the number three was an indicator that something was of divine influence or origin. Thus, to send the plagues in cycles

18 And the magicians did so with their enchantments to bring forth lice, but they could not: so there were lice upon man, and upon beast.

19 Then the magicians said unto Pharaoh, This *is* the finger of God: and Pharaoh's heart was hardened, and he hearkened not unto them; as the LORD had said.

20 ¶ And the LORD said unto Moses, Rise up early in the morning, and stand before Pharaoh; lo, he cometh forth to the water; and say unto him, Thus saith the LORD, Let my people go, that they may serve me.

21 Else, if thou wilt not let my people go, behold, I will send swarms *of flies* upon thee, and upon thy servants, and upon thy people, and into thy houses: and the houses of the Egyptians shall be full of swarms *of flies,* and also the ground whereon they *are.*

22 And I will sever in that day the land of Goshen, in which my people dwell, that no swarms *of flies* shall be there; to the end thou mayest know that I *am* the LORD in the midst of the earth.

23 And I will put a division between my people and thy people: to morrow shall this sign be.

24 And the LORD did so; and there came a grievous swarm *of flies* into the house of Pharaoh, and *into* his servants' houses, and into all the land of Egypt: the land was corrupted by reason of the swarm *of flies.*

25 ¶ And Pharaoh called for Moses and for Aaron, and said, Go ye, sacrifice to your God in the land.

26 And Moses said, It is not meet so to do; for we shall sacrifice the abomination of the Egyptians to the LORD our God: lo, shall we sacrifice the abomination of the Egyptians before their eyes, and will they not stone us?

27 We will go three days' journey into the wilderness, and sacrifice to the LORD our God, as he shall command us.

28 And Pharaoh said, I will let you go, that ye may sacrifice to the LORD your God in the wilderness; only ye shall not go very far away: entreat for me.

29 And Moses said, Behold, I go out from thee, and I will entreat the LORD that the swarms *of flies* may depart from Pharaoh,

of three would have sent a message to all in Egypt that this was God's doing—that divine displeasure was being manifest" (Gaskill, *Miracles of the Old Testament,* 62). See commentary in this volume for Exodus 7:15.

What was unique about this plague of flies to the Egyptians? (8:21–24) "By this plague, in which a separation and deliverance was established between the people of God and the Egyptians, Pharaoh was to be taught that the God who sent this plague was not some deity of Egypt, *but 'Jehovah in the midst of the land'* (of Egypt); i.e., . . . (*a*) that Israel's God was the author of the plague; (*b*) that He had also authority over Egypt; and (*c*) that He possessed supreme authority: . . . that Israel's God was the Absolute God, who ruled both in and over Egypt with free and boundless omnipotence" (Keil and Delitzsch, *Commentary* [on Exodus 8:23]).

Exodus 8:25–32. Pharaoh Again Breaks His Promise to Let the Israelites Go

Why did Moses refer to their sacrifice of animals as "the abomination of the Egyptians"? (8:25–27) "The request of Moses that the children of Israel be allowed to go 'into the wilderness' to offer their sacrifice so they would not be stoned by the Egyptians was certainly understandable and reasonable. The sacrifices of the Israelites frequently required the killing of animals, and cattle (cows and bulls) were sacred to the Egyptians!" (Ludlow, *Companion to Your Study of the Old Testament,* 143).

Why would Pharaoh not want the Israelites to go very far to offer sacrifices? (8:28) "Pharaoh relented because the hand of God was heavy upon him; but he was not willing to give up his gain. The Israelites were very profitable to him; they were slaves of the state, and their hard labour was very productive: hence he professed a willingness, first to tolerate their religion in the land, (Ex 8:25); or to permit them to go into the wilderness, so that they went not far away, and would soon return. How ready is foolish man, when the hand of God presses him sore, to compound with his Maker! He will consent to give up some sins, provided God will permit him to keep others" (*Adam Clarke's Commentary* [on Exodus 8:28]).

from his servants, and from his people, to morrow: but let not Pharaoh deal deceitfully any more in not letting the people go to sacrifice to the LORD.

30 And Moses went out from Pharaoh, and entreated the LORD.

31 And the LORD did according to the word of Moses; and he removed the swarms *of flies* from Pharaoh, from his servants, and from his people; there remained not one.

32 And Pharaoh hardened his heart at this time also, neither would he let the people go.

CHAPTER 9

The Lord destroys the cattle of the Egyptians, but not of the Israelites—Boils and blains are sent upon the Egyptians—The Lord sends hail and fire upon the people of Pharaoh, but not upon the people of Israel.

Exodus 9:1–7. The Lord Plagues the Egyptians' Cattle

1 Then the LORD said unto Moses, Go in unto Pharaoh, and tell him, Thus saith the LORD God of the Hebrews, Let my people go, that they may serve me.

2 For if thou refuse to let *them* go, and wilt hold them still,

3 Behold, the hand of the LORD is upon thy cattle which *is* in the field, upon the horses, upon the asses, upon the camels, upon the oxen, and upon the sheep: *there shall be* a very grievous murrain.

What is "murrain" and how does it affect animals? (9:3) "The murrain is a very contagious disease among cattle, the symptoms of which are a hanging down and swelling of the head, abundance of gum in the eyes, rattling in the throat, difficulty of breathing, palpitation of the heart, staggering, a hot breath, and a shining tongue; which symptoms prove that a general inflammation has taken place. . . . Our English word murrain comes either from the French *mourir*, to die, or from the Greek μαραινω maraino, to grow lean, waste away. The term mortality would be the nearest in sense to the original, as no particular disorder is specified by the Hebrew word" (*Adam Clarke's Commentary* [on Exodus 9:3]).

4 And the LORD shall sever between the cattle of Israel and the cattle of Egypt: and there shall nothing die of all *that is* the children's of Israel.

How were the Egyptians able to save some of their cattle from the plague? (9:4–5) The Lord "made a clear distinction between the Egyptians and Hebrews. Only the Egyptian field animals were affected by the

5 And the LORD appointed a set time, saying, To morrow the LORD shall do this thing in the land.

6 And the LORD did that thing on the morrow, and all the cattle of Egypt died: but of the cattle of the children of Israel died not one.

7 And Pharaoh sent, and, behold, there was not one of the cattle of the Israelites dead. And the heart of Pharaoh was hardened, and he did not let the people go.

8 ¶ And the LORD said unto Moses and unto Aaron, Take to you handfuls of ashes of the furnace, and let Moses sprinkle it toward the heaven in the sight of Pharaoh.

9 And it shall become small dust in all the land of Egypt, and shall be a boil breaking forth *with* blains upon man, and upon beast, throughout all the land of Egypt.

10 And they took ashes of the furnace, and stood before Pharaoh; and Moses sprinkled it up toward heaven; and it became a boil breaking forth *with* blains upon man, and upon beast.

11 And the magicians could not stand before Moses because of the boils; for the boil was upon the magicians, and upon all the Egyptians.

plague. . . . Advance warning gave those Egyptians who feared God sufficient time to bring their livestock in from the fields and out of danger" (*Zondervan KJV Commentary*, 99).

How was the death of cattle in Egypt symbolic of God's power over Egyptian gods? (9:6) "The livestock that were killed by this plague are symbolically significant, so as to send a message to Pharaoh that would have been unmistakable. Scholars indicate that each of the animals killed in this plague were worshiped as a god by the Egyptians. . . . Rather plainly, Moses is informing Pharaoh that Jehovah has power over Egypt's gods. If he will not submit to the demands of the God of Israel then the sacrifice of all that is sacred in Egypt will be the penalty" (Gaskill, *Miracles of the Old Testament*, 64). ⊕

Exodus 9:8–12. The Lord Plagues the Egyptians with Boils

What is meant by "handfuls of ashes of the furnace"? (9:8–9) "The [ash-like] soot was taken from a furnace where bricks were made—a symbol of the Israelites' bondage. As such, it provided a visual aid for Pharaoh. Just as the staff was used to initiate earlier plagues, so this action—the tossing of soot [KJV *ashes*]—tied the boils to Moses and the God whom he represented. Some also think there was a symbolic link between the soot created by the sweat of God's people doing hard labor and the soot that produced boils on the Israelites' slave masters" (*Quest Study Bible* [2003], 90).

What are boils and blains and how do they affect mankind? (9:9) "'Boils' are terribly painful sores on the skin. 'Blains' are infected blisters that break out from the boils (see [Exodus 9:9*c*])" (Valletta, et al., *Old Testament for Latter-day Saint Families*, 117). Adam Clarke adds, "This word is generally [meant as], an inflammatory swelling, a burning boil; one of the most poignant afflictions, not immediately mortal, that can well affect the surface of the human body. If a single boil on any part of the body throws the whole system into a fever, what anguish must a multitude of them on the body at the same time occasion!" (*Adam Clarke's Commentary* [on Exodus 9:9]).

Why couldn't the magicians stand before Moses during this plague? (9:11) This verse has been interpreted in various ways. Some suggest that the magicians could not stand before Moses because they were aware of their own inability in not being able to either replicate or reverse this plague. Others suggest that the magicians could not stand before Moses because they were victims of the painful plague themselves and were physically unable to stand (see Enns, "Exodus," 218fn61; *John Gill's Exposition of the Whole Bible* [commentary on Exodus 9:11]). Others have written that "the 'boils of Egypt' (Dt 28:27) seriously affected the knees and legs (see Dt 28:35)" (*NIV Study Bible*, 155). All of these and other interpretations could be accurate.

Exodus 9:13–26. The Lord Sends Hail and Fire upon Egypt

How were the ten plagues of Egypt organized to show God's omnipotence? (9:13) See commentary in this volume for Exodus 7:15 and Exodus 8:20.

Why are the words "cause" and "in" italicized in this verse? (9:16) "The words '*cause*' and '*in*' are italicized, indicating that their equivalents are not found in the Hebrew. Notice the difference in meaning when these words are deleted: '. . . for this______ have I raised thee up, for to shew ______ thee my power'" (Ludlow, *Companion to Your Study of the Old Testament*, 143). Ellis T. Rasmussen explains that "leaving out those italicized words makes the meaning more like it was in Hebrew (Ex. 9:16 and fn.)" (*Latter-day Saint Commentary on the Old Testament*, 95).

How does God use Pharaoh to show His power? (9:16) "The Lord knew that Pharaoh would be so proud and stubborn that it would take great miracles to make him finally let the Israelites go. In fact, according to the Prophet Joseph Smith, the Lord raised this man up to be the Pharaoh so his stubbornness would give God the opportunity to show the entire world His great power (see [Joseph Smith Papers, "Discourse,

12 And the LORD hardened the heart of Pharaoh, and he hearkened not unto them; as the LORD had spoken unto Moses.

13 ¶ And the LORD said unto Moses, Rise up early in the morning, and stand before Pharaoh, and say unto him, Thus saith the LORD God of the Hebrews, Let my people go, that they may serve me.

14 For I will at this time send all my plagues upon thine heart, and upon thy servants, and upon thy people; that thou mayest know that *there is* none like me in all the earth.

15 For now I will stretch out my hand, that I may smite thee and thy people with pestilence; and thou shalt be cut off from the earth.

16 And in very deed for this *cause* have I raised thee up, for to shew *in* thee my power; and that my name may be declared throughout all the earth.

17 As yet exaltest thou thyself against my people, that thou wilt not let them go?

18 Behold, to morrow about this time I will cause it to rain a very grievous hail, such as hath not been in Egypt since the foundation thereof even until now.

16 May 1841, as Reported by *Times and Seasons*," 430])" (Valletta, et al., *Old Testament for Latter-day Saint Families*, 118).

19 Send therefore now, *and* gather thy cattle, and all that thou hast in the field; *for upon* every man and beast which shall be found in the field, and shall not be brought home, the hail shall come down upon them, and they shall die.

20 He that feared the word of the LORD among the servants of Pharaoh made his servants and his cattle flee into the houses:

21 And he that regarded not the word of the LORD left his servants and his cattle in the field.

How does the Lord continue to show his mercy upon the Egyptians in the midst of plagues? (9:19) "The fact that God was judging Pharaoh does not mean He was unmerciful. The Lord could have destroyed Pharaoh and his people in a moment (v. 15), but He did not. He could have brought each plague without warning, but in most cases He served notice (see 7:16). In anticipation of this plague, He warned the Egyptians to *gather* their *livestock* so they might be spared the hailstorm. Even some members of Pharaoh's court now took the *word of the Lord* seriously" (*Nelson Study Bible* [NKJV], 104). ⊕

22 ¶ And the LORD said unto Moses, Stretch forth thine hand toward heaven, that there may be hail in all the land of Egypt, upon man, and upon beast, and upon every herb of the field, throughout the land of Egypt.

23 And Moses stretched forth his rod toward heaven: and the LORD sent thunder and hail, and the fire ran along upon the ground; and the LORD rained hail upon the land of Egypt.

24 So there was hail, and fire mingled with the hail, very grievous, such as there was none like it in all the land of Egypt since it became a nation.

25 And the hail smote throughout all the land of Egypt all that *was* in the field, both man and beast; and the hail smote every herb of the field, and brake every tree of the field.

What do hail and fire in the plagues upon Egypt symbolize in the last days? (9:24) Elder Bruce R. McConkie said, in reference to the last days, "Of the nation that shall rise to fight his people in that day, the Lord says: 'And I will plead against him with pestilence and with blood; and I will rain upon him, and upon his bands, and upon the many people that are with him, an overflowing rain, and great hailstones, fire, and brimstone' (Ezek. 38:22). By these means a third of all the trees and green grass on earth are to be destroyed. The plague of hail and fire rained upon Pharaoh's Egypt, in the days of the deliverance of Israel from bondage, was perhaps symbolical of this greater deliverance of the Lord's people by the forces of nature in the latter-days (Ex. 9:22–26)" (*Doctrinal New Testament Commentary*, 3:500).

26 Only in the land of Goshen, where the children of Israel *were*, was there no hail.

Where is the land of Goshen? (9:26) "During their long sojourn in Egypt, the Israelites lived in Goshen, an area adjacent to the eastern side of the Nile Delta, north of present-day Cairo. Goshen was a pasture land in which the Israelites could thrive while living apart from the main body of the Egyptian people . . . (see D&C 84:6)" (Allen, *Study Commentary on the Old Testament*, 70). See commentary in this volume for Genesis 45:10 and 47:1.

Exodus 9:27–35. Pharaoh Again Breaks His Promise to Let the Israelites Go

27 ¶ And Pharaoh sent, and called for Moses and Aaron, and said unto them, I have sinned this time: the LORD *is* righteous, and I and my people *are* wicked.

28 Entreat the LORD (for *it is* enough) that there be no *more* mighty thunderings and hail; and I will let you go, and ye shall stay no longer.

29 And Moses said unto him, As soon as I am gone out of the city, I will spread abroad my hands unto the LORD; *and* the thunder shall cease, neither shall there be any more hail; that thou mayest know how that the earth *is* the LORD's.

30 But as for thee and thy servants, I know that ye will not yet fear the LORD God.

What is Moses doing while he prays? (9:29) "The ancient Israelite gesture of raising both hands in praise or supplication is mentioned in twenty-four scriptural passages, of which twenty-two are from the Old Testament, . . .

"Six Hebrew idioms are used in the Old Testament to describe the gesture of raising both hands in prayer. The first two idioms deal with lifting up the hands while a third idiom, pāraś kappayim, means 'spread or stretch out the hands.' This is the most common Hebrew idiom used for the raising of both hands in worship, and it is found in many biblical books, including the historical books" (Calabro, "Gestures of Praise," 105–6).

31 And the flax and the barley was smitten: for the barley *was* in the ear, and the flax *was* bolled.

32 But the wheat and the rie were not smitten: for they *were* not grown up.

33 And Moses went out of the city from Pharaoh, and spread abroad his hands unto the LORD: and the thunders and hail ceased, and the rain was not poured upon the earth.

34 And when Pharaoh saw that the rain and the hail and the thunders were ceased, he sinned yet more, and hardened his heart, he and his servants.

35 And the heart of Pharaoh was hardened, neither would he let the children of Israel go; as the LORD had spoken by Moses.

Why were flax and barley essential to the Egyptians? (9:31) "In Egypt flax was normally sown at the beginning of January and was in bloom three weeks later; barley was sown in August and harvested in February. Flax was grown primarily for its linen fiber, which was made into yarn, woven into cloth, and then bleached. The linen-making industry was of considerable importance in the economy of Egypt because linen was the preferred fabric for clothing. Barley was cultivated extensively in Egypt; it was used for bread and brewed into beer. The destruction of these crops would be a severe blow" (Sarna, *Exodus*, 47).

CHAPTER 10

The Lord sends a plague of locusts—This is followed by thick darkness in all Egypt for three days—Moses is cast out from the presence of Pharaoh.

1 And the LORD said unto Moses, Go in unto Pharaoh: for I have hardened his heart, and the heart of his servants, that I might shew these my signs before him:

2 And that thou mayest tell in the ears of thy son, and of thy son's son, what things I have wrought in Egypt, and my signs which I have done among them; that ye may know how that I *am* the LORD.

3 And Moses and Aaron came in unto Pharaoh, and said unto him, Thus saith the LORD God of the Hebrews, How long wilt thou refuse to humble thyself before me? let my people go, that they may serve me.

4 Else, if thou refuse to let my people go, behold, to morrow will I bring the locusts into thy coast:

5 And they shall cover the face of the earth, that one cannot be able to see the earth: and they shall eat the residue of that which is escaped, which remaineth unto you from the hail, and shall eat every tree which groweth for you out of the field:

6 And they shall fill thy houses, and the houses of all thy servants, and the houses of all the Egyptians; which neither thy fathers, nor thy fathers' fathers have seen, since the day that they were upon the earth unto this day. And he turned himself, and went out from Pharaoh.

7 And Pharaoh's servants said unto him, How long shall this man be a snare unto us? let the men go, that they may serve the LORD their God: knowest thou not yet that Egypt is destroyed?

Exodus 10:1–11. Pharaoh Will Let Only the Israelite Men Go

What is one reason the Lord gives for pouring out plagues upon Pharaoh and Egypt? (10:1–2) The Joseph Smith Translation states, "he hath hardened his heart, and the hearts of his servants, therefore I will show these my signs before him" (JST, Exodus 10:1). Ellis T. Rasmussen adds, "It was thus necessary, over a period of time, to show Pharaoh many facets of God's omnipotence before he would finally recognize the unseen God, Jehovah (Ex. 9:13–17; 10:3)" (*Latter-day Saint Commentary on the Old Testament*, 93).

What profound impact did the plague of locusts have upon Egypt? (10:4–5) "Locusts were all too common in the ancient Near East and were notorious for the devastation and havoc they brought. . . . A locust will consume its own weight each day. Locust swarms have been known to cover as many as four hundred square miles and even one square mile could teem with over one hundred million insects. Certainly anything that had survived the hail was now destroyed" (Walton, et al., *IVP Bible Background Commentary*, 83, 84). ⊕

What does "coast" or "coasts" mean in this chapter? (10:4) The words "coast" and "coasts" are used in Exodus 10 to refer to the boundaries of Egypt and the land enclosed within those borders. Verse 4 is translated by Robert Alter: "For if you refuse to send off My people, look, I am about to bring tomorrow locust in all your territory" (*Hebrew Bible*, 2:252).

What do Pharaoh's servants mean by saying "Egypt is destroyed"? (10:7) "It is difficult to accurately assess the extent of the damage. Some of the plagues affected the people directly (boils and biting insects, for instance). But other plagues caused economic setbacks (loss of livestock and crops). Typically even one such catastrophe was enough to cause severe hardship. Pharaoh's own officials believed that the land was ruined, suggesting that they expected economic recovery would be long in coming. But perhaps the greatest damage to Egypt was that its religious system was eroded. Each plague demonstrated the superiority of the God of Israel and undermined the authority of the false gods of Egypt" (*Quest Study Bible* [2003], 91).

Why does Pharaoh allow only the men to go? (10:11) "Pharaoh decreed that Moses must be satisfied with taking just the Hebrew *men* on the journey. It was not to be a family outing, for the Hebrew women and children would be forced to remain in Egypt as collateral to ensure the Hebrews' return. . . . Pharaoh may have believed that his decree, however minimally, had satisfied [the Lord's] requirements and settled this bothersome matter once and for all. What the king failed to realize was that in attempting to force this compromise upon Moses, the king had once again compromised his nation" (*Zondervan KJV Commentary*, 103).

Exodus 10:12–15. The Lord Sends a Plague of Locusts upon Egypt

How might the east wind prefigure the experience at the Red Sea? (10:13) "The locust plague provides connections not only to what has been but to what will come. (1) The locusts come on the land by an east wind (v. 13); an east wind also causes the Red Sea to part (14:21). We have, in other words, a preview of coming attractions. (2) The fact that the locusts meet their demise in the Red Sea clearly alludes to the drowning of the Egyptian army in 14:28. Even the language of 10:19 and 14:28 is similar," for not one of the locusts nor the Egyptians remained (Enns, "Exodus," 226). ⊕

How does the plague of locusts foreshadow what will happen in the last days? (10:15) "In its dreadful character, this Egyptian plague is a type of the plagues which will precede the last judgment, and forms the

8 And Moses and Aaron were brought again unto Pharaoh: and he said unto them, Go, serve the LORD your God: *but* who *are* they that shall go?

9 And Moses said, We will go with our young and with our old, with our sons and with our daughters, with our flocks and with our herds will we go; for we *must hold* a feast unto the LORD.

10 And he said unto them, Let the LORD be so with you, as I will let you go, and your little ones: look *to it;* for evil *is* before you.

11 Not so: go now ye *that are* men, and serve the LORD; for that ye did desire. And they were driven out from Pharaoh's presence.

12 ¶ And the LORD said unto Moses, Stretch out thine hand over the land of Egypt for the locusts, that they may come up upon the land of Egypt, and eat every herb of the land, *even* all that the hail hath left.

13 And Moses stretched forth his rod over the land of Egypt, and the LORD brought an east wind upon the land all that day, and all *that* night; *and* when it was morning, the east wind brought the locusts.

14 And the locusts went up over all the land of Egypt, and rested in all the coasts of Egypt: very grievous *were they;* before them there were no such locusts as they, neither after them shall be such.

15 For they covered the face of the whole earth, so that the land was darkened; and they did eat every herb of the land, and all the fruit of the trees which the hail had left: and there remained not any green thing in the trees, or in the herbs of the field, through all the land of Egypt.

groundwork for the description in Revelation 9:3–10; just as Joel discerned in the plagues which burst upon Judah in his own day a presage of the day of the Lord (Joel 1:15; Joel 2:1), i.e., of the great day of judgment, which is advancing step by step in all the great judgments of history or rather of the conflict between the kingdom of God and the powers of this world, and will be finally accomplished in the last general judgment" (Keil and Delitzsch, *Commentary* [on Exodus 10:13–14]).

Exodus 10:16–20. Pharaoh Continues to Break His Promise to Let the Israelites Go

16 ¶ Then Pharaoh called for Moses and Aaron in haste; and he said, I have sinned against the LORD your God, and against you.

17 Now therefore forgive, I pray thee, my sin only this once, and entreat the LORD your God, that he may take away from me this death only.

18 And he went out from Pharaoh, and entreated the LORD.

What hint do we have that Pharaoh is about to allow Israel to leave? (10:16) "This 'plague,' so much dreaded at all times, came now slowly, from far-off Arabia, upon the doomed land, more grievous than such visitation had ever been known, and to the utter destruction of every green thing still left in Egypt—Goshen alone being again excepted. Pharaoh felt it, and for the first time not only confessed his sin, but asked forgiveness, and entreated that 'this death' might be taken away (10:16, 17). . . . No sooner had his request been granted, than his rebellion returned" (Edersheim, *Bible History*, 2:182). By this plague, what dangers do you see in Pharaoh's attitude and words to Moses and Aaron? What do you feel is the spiritual cure for Pharaoh and like-minded people?

19 And the LORD turned a mighty strong west wind, which took away the locusts, and cast them into the Red sea; there remained not one locust in all the coasts of Egypt.

What do we know about the west wind that took away the locusts? (10:19) "The literal meaning is 'sea wind,' but because of the geographical situation of ancient Israel, 'sea' (that is, the Mediterranean) is often used to designate the west. Again, the wind reference reflects the geography of Canaan" (Alter, *Hebrew Bible*, 2:255).

20 But the LORD hardened Pharaoh's heart, so that he would not let the children of Israel go.

What do we learn from the contrast between Pharaoh and Moses? (10:20) "Moses was meek and allowed himself to be led by the hand of God. Consequently, great and mighty miracles were performed by him to deliver God's chosen people, Israel, from bondage.

"The pharaoh, on the other hand, was self-centered, power hungry, cruel, and hard-hearted. He was largely unimpressed with the power of the Lord. He preferred to follow the counterfeit power of Satan, which allowed him the false belief that he was a god on earth" (*Old Testament Student Manual: Genesis–2 Samuel*, 108).

Exodus 10:21–23. The Lord Sends Three Days of Darkness on Egypt

How is this darkness over Egypt a symbol of the spiritual darkness that exists in the world today? (10:21) "The Hebrew expression *thick darkness* comes from a pair of words. The first is the common word for darkness. The second is used less often and describes deep gloom. . . . This calamity would have affected the Egyptians the most. They worshipped many gods, but none so much as the sun. Even a normal solar eclipse would have had an impact, but an enshrouding darkness that lasted *for three days* was a frontal attack on their gods, on their Pharaoh and his supposed control of nature, and on all Pharaoh's counselors who were as helpless as he was. . . . The people must have been terrified" (*Nelson Study Bible* [NKJV], 106).

What does "darkness which may be felt" mean? (10:21–22) There are many interpretations of what caused a darkness that could be "felt." Some suggest that it may be the result of a desert wind or an eclipse. Others have suggested that the use of the phrase is meant to be descriptive of the intense and absolute darkness. Robert Alter writes that the text "beautifully conveys the claustrophobic palpability of absolute darkness, [which] is diminished by those who try to provide a naturalistic explanation for this plague (or indeed, for any of the others). . . . They are all emphatically presented as extraordinary interventions by God . . . that demonstrate His power over the created world" (Alter, *Hebrew Bible*, 255).

How do the three days of darkness in this plague correlate to the three days that occurred at the Savior's atoning sacrifice? (10:21–22) Elder Tad Callister has written that at the time of the Savior's Atonement, "those lands where the Savior's physical presence was absent no doubt responded with more powerful elemental reactions as a compensating witness. . . . Darkness, thick, vaporous, total darkness enveloped the land for three days. This was not a shadowy darkness, a dim-lit darkness, a darkness to which the eyes eventually adjust; no, this was impenetrable blackness, 'so that there could not be any light at all' (3 Nephi 8:21). . . . This was darkness similar to that which was cast over Egypt in Moses' day, 'even darkness which may be felt' . . . (Exodus 10:21–22)" (*Infinite Atonement*, 126). ⊕

21 ¶ And the LORD said unto Moses, Stretch out thine hand toward heaven, that there may be darkness over the land of Egypt, even darkness *which* may be felt.

22 And Moses stretched forth his hand toward heaven; and there was a thick darkness in all the land of Egypt three days:

23 They saw not one another, neither rose any from his place for three days: but all the children of Israel had light in their dwellings.

24 ¶ And Pharaoh called unto Moses, and said, Go ye, serve the LORD; only let your flocks and your herds be stayed: let your little ones also go with you.

25 And Moses said, Thou must give us also sacrifices and burnt offerings, that we may sacrifice unto the LORD our God.

26 Our cattle also shall go with us; there shall not an hoof be left behind; for thereof must we take to serve the LORD our God; and we know not with what we must serve the LORD, until we come thither.

Exodus 10:24–29. Pharaoh Will Let the People Go but Not Their Flocks and Herds

Why did Pharaoh allow Israel to leave without their herds? (10:24) "The cruelty of this demand is not more evident than its avarice. Had six hundred thousand men, besides women and children, gone three days' journey into the wilderness without their cattle, they must have inevitably perished, being without milk for their little ones, and animal food for their own sustenance, in a place where little as a substitute could possibly be found. It is evident from this that Pharaoh intended the total destruction of the whole Israelitish host" (*Adam Clarke's Commentary* [on Exodus 10:24]).

What Are We to Learn from the Plagues on Egypt? (Exodus 10)

"The entire story of the plagues is about a contest between the will of the pharaoh and the will of the God whom only the Israelites recognized. The pharaoh was a self-proclaimed god, the object of worship by his subjects. The theory of his divinity was sustained by the religious and political institutions of the Egyptian state. Consequently, the plagues, the ignoble defeat, and the ignominious end of the god-king constitute a saga that breathes contempt for Egyptian paganism" (Sarna, *Exploring Exodus*, 80).

S. Kent Brown wrote, "When Moses received the divine call to lead the Israelites out of Egyptian bondage, he likely had no idea of the lengths to which God would go in order to deliver the Hebrew slaves. There would be plagues that affected Egyptians but not Israelites, divine protection from the angel of death, a miraculous escape through the Red Sea, water and manna in the desert, and, finally, the great revelations on Mount Sinai. The Exodus showed the Israelites that the Lord was faithful and that they were his people.

"Undoubtedly, the Exodus is one of God's most memorable acts in Israel's behalf before the Atonement. Its display of sheer power and sublime affirmation of God's love showed the Lord's ability to rescue and sustain his people and also foreshadowed Christ's atonement. Prophets, leaders, and teachers both in Israel and in the Book of Mormon lands often referred to the Exodus to strengthen faith in God's ability to deliver his people—not only physically, but also spiritually—by the power of Christ's atonement. Time and again, those lessons were repeated in varying degrees when subsequent generations of the Lord's people escaped persecution through faith in their almighty God. . . .

"Following the Atonement, the Exodus diminished in its overall importance because, for the followers of Jesus, the Atonement replaced it as the primary symbol of faith and hope. Pre-Atonement authors in the Book of Mormon even drew on language and description associated with the Exodus to illuminate the effects of the Atonement more fully.

"Jacob, for example, compared the results of the yet-to-be Atonement to 'deliverance' and 'escape' in a long sermon filled with terms describing the Exodus. He quoted Isaiah, whose prophecies of the gathering of Israel in the last days form what some commentators have come to call the 'Second Exodus'—the event in which 'the Messiah will set himself again the second time to recover his people' (2 Ne. 6:14).

"In applying this Exodus terminology to the Atonement, Jacob wrote:

"'O how great the goodness of our God, who prepareth a way for our *escape* from the grasp of this awful monster . . . death and hell. . . . And because of the way of *deliverance* of our God, the Holy One of Israel, this death, of which I have spoken, which is the temporal, shall *deliver* up its dead; which death is the grave' (2 Ne. 9:10–11; emphasis added; see also Isa. 50–52)" ("Exodus," 56).

Exodus 11:1–2. The Israelites Ask for Payment for Their Years of Service as Slaves

What does the final plague on Egypt foreshadow? (11:1) "In the typology of the Passover, the children of God (Israel) are in bondage to an evil power (Egypt). Similarly, all of God's children come into a world of sin and may find themselves in bondage to Satan and the powers of sin. . . . Thus, the pharaoh could be thought of as a type or symbol of Satan. . . . It should be noted that what finally released the children of Israel from the bondage of the pharaoh . . . was the death of the firstborn of Egypt. In like manner the atoning sacrifice of the Firstborn Son of God freed the children of God from death, a bondage to Satan" (*Old Testament Student Manual: Genesis–2 Samuel,* 118).

If the Israelites are leaving Egypt, then why "borrow" items since they won't be returning? (11:2) "This is certainly not a very correct translation: the original word שׁאל *shaal* signifies simply to *ask, request, demand, require, inquire,* etc.; but it does not signify to borrow in the proper sense of that word, though in a very few places of Scripture it is thus used. In this and the parallel place, Exodus 12:35, the word signifies to *ask* or *demand,* and not *to borrow,* which is a *gross mistake*" (*Adam Clarke's Commentary* [on Exodus 3:22]). ⊕

Exodus 11:3–10. The Lord Declares That the Firstborn of Every Egyptian Family Will Die

Why were Moses and the Hebrews so highly favored by the Egyptians? (11:3) "Another remarkable

27 ¶ But the LORD hardened Pharaoh's heart, and he would not let them go.

28 And Pharaoh said unto him, Get thee from me, take heed to thyself, see my face no more; for in *that* day thou seest my face thou shalt die.

29 And Moses said, Thou hast spoken well, I will see thy face again no more.

CHAPTER 11

The departing Israelites are authorized to ask for jewels and gold from their neighbors—The Lord promises to slay the firstborn in every Egyptian home—He puts a difference between the Egyptians and the Israelites.

1 And the LORD said unto Moses, Yet will I bring one plague *more* upon Pharaoh, and upon Egypt; afterwards he will let you go hence: when he shall let *you* go, he shall surely thrust you out hence altogether.

2 Speak now in the ears of the people, and let every man borrow of his neighbour, and every woman of her neighbour, jewels of silver, and jewels of gold.

3 And the LORD gave the people favour in the sight of the Egyptians. Moreover the man

Moses *was* very great in the land of Egypt, in the sight of Pharaoh's servants, and in the sight of the people.

4 And Moses said, Thus saith the LORD, About midnight will I go out into the midst of Egypt:

5 And all the firstborn in the land of Egypt shall die, from the firstborn of Pharaoh that sitteth upon his throne, even unto the firstborn of the maidservant that *is* behind the mill; and all the firstborn of beasts.

6 And there shall be a great cry throughout all the land of Egypt, such as there was none like it, nor shall be like it any more.

7 But against any of the children of Israel shall not a dog move his tongue, against man or beast: that ye may know how that the LORD doth put a difference between the Egyptians and Israel.

8 And all these thy servants shall come down unto me, and bow down themselves unto me, saying, Get thee out, and all the people that follow thee: and after that I will go out. And he went out from Pharaoh in a great anger.

9 And the LORD said unto Moses, Pharaoh shall not hearken unto you; that my wonders may be multiplied in the land of Egypt.

10 And Moses and Aaron did all these wonders before Pharaoh: and the LORD hardened

component of the Exodus was the Egyptians' *favor* (or grace) toward the Hebrews and admiration for their leader. After all that had happened, we might expect the opposite. But the positive feelings for Moses were shared, amazingly enough, even by *Pharaoh's servants*. This, too, is a part of the wit and irony of this great victory the Lord had won over His enemy Pharaoh (who represents evil, sin, ungodliness, and even Satan)" (*Nelson Study Bible* [NKJV], 106).

Since Pharaoh promised to put Moses to death if he saw him again, when did Moses declare this final plague? (11:5) "The announcement made by Jehovah to Moses, which is recorded here, occurred before the last interview between Moses and Pharaoh (Exodus 10:24–29); but it is introduced by the historian in this place, as serving to explain the confidence with which Moses answered Pharaoh (Exodus 10:29). This is evident from Exodus 11:4–8, where Moses is said to have foretold to the king, before leaving his presence, the last plague and all its consequences" (Keil and Delitzsch, *Commentary* [on Exodus 11:1]).

What does "not a dog move his tongue" mean? (11:7) "Unlike all the other plagues, this time the Lord himself would march through the land of Egypt. The firstborn of all Egyptian families—slaves and cattle—would die at midnight (the exact day was not specified). An unprecedented outpouring of grief would follow, but among the Israelites there would be such tranquility on that evening that not a dog would have occasion to bark! Moses' final word was that the Egyptians on bent knee would beg the Israelites to leave immediately" (*Expositor's Bible Commentary [Abridged]*, 83–84).

According to the Joseph Smith Translation, who was angry in this verse? (11:8) "The statement 'And he went out from Pharaoh in a great anger' seems to indicate that Moses was angry. However, the Joseph Smith Translation puts this sentence in the context of verse 10, which changes the entire meaning: 'And Moses and Aaron did all these wonders before Pharaoh, and they went out from Pharaoh, and he was in great anger'"(Ludlow, *Companion to Your Study of the Old Testament*, 143).

How do the plagues upon Egypt signify God's love toward His children? (11:9–10) "There have been numerous attempts through the ages to explain the plagues described in these chapters of Exodus. Some have tried to show that the various plagues were the result of some natural phenomenon. . . . It is not possible at present to explain how the Lord brought about these miraculous events. . . . God often works through natural means to bring about His purposes, but that fact does not lessen the miraculous nature of His work. In the plagues and eventual deliverance of Israel from the bondage of Egypt is a record of remarkable and miraculous intervention by God in behalf of His children. *How* He actually intervened is not nearly so significant as that He *did* intervene" (*Old Testament Student Manual: Genesis–2 Samuel*, 107–8).

Pharaoh's heart, so that he would not let the
children of Israel go out of his land.

CHAPTER 12

The Lord institutes the Passover and the Feast of Unleavened Bread—Lambs without blemish are slain—Israel is saved by their blood—The firstborn of all Egyptians are slain—Israel is thrust out of Egypt after 430 years—No bones of the paschal lambs are to be broken.

Exodus 12:1–10. The Passover Lamb Must Be an Unblemished Male

Why is this chapter so important to the children of Israel? (12:1) In this chapter, there is an interlude from the unfolding drama of history to the Lord revealing a sacred ceremony to help future generations remember the importance of these events. Peter Enns wrote: "This is much more than an aside or an intrusion of legal, ritualistic mumbo jumbo. It is the institution of a powerful, everlasting observance whereby God's love for his people Israel will be remembered—indeed, reenacted—until the end of time. These verses go into considerable detail concerning the Passover meal and the Feast of Unleavened Bread. . . .

"The purpose of these celebrations is clearly for the benefit of those generations who did not participate in the Exodus itself" ("Exodus," 246, 247).

1 And the LORD spake unto Moses and Aaron
in the land of Egypt, saying,

Why was the calendar changed for the children of Israel? (12:2) The deliverance from Egypt was so significant that "the Lord indicated that Israel's calendar was to begin its cycle from this event and was to be the beginning of the year (see Ex. 12:2). Symbolically speaking, the deliverance from the bondage of sin marks a new beginning, a new time, a new life, as it were" (Lund, *Jesus Christ, Key to the Plan of Salvation*, 63). "Passover was not just a night of remembering, but it was also a night of intense expectation. It was a night of watching for the coming of the Lord" (Plastaras, *God of Exodus*, 146).

2 This month *shall be* unto you the beginning of months: it *shall be* the first month of
the year to you.

Why is the tenth day important? (12:3) The time of Egyptian bondage was complete. "In the Bible, ten appears numerous times. It usually signifies completeness

3 ¶ Speak ye unto all the congregation of
Israel, saying, In the tenth *day* of this month
they shall take to them every man a lamb,

according to the house of *their* fathers, a
lamb for an house:

4 And if the household be too little for the
lamb, let him and his neighbour next unto
his house take *it* according to the number of
the souls; every man according to his eating
shall make your count for the lamb.

5 Your lamb shall be without blemish, a male
of the first year: ye shall take *it* out from the
sheep, or from the goats:

6 And ye shall keep it up until the fourteenth
day of the same month: and the whole assembly of the congregation of Israel shall kill
it in the evening.

7 And they shall take of the blood, and strike
it on the two side posts and on the upper
door post of the houses, wherein they shall
eat it.

8 And they shall eat the flesh in that night,
roast with fire, and unleavened bread; *and*
with bitter *herbs* they shall eat it.

9 Eat not of it raw, nor sodden at all with
water, but roast *with* fire; his head with his
legs, and with the purtenance thereof.

10 And ye shall let nothing of it remain until

or wholeness: The Ten Commandments represent the essential code of human behavior. Abraham bargains with God over the fate of Sodom and Gomorrah until he reaches the number ten; fewer than this number of righteous souls would not constitute a community worth saving. God brings Ten Plagues upon Egypt to demonstrate divine power" (Frankell and Teutsch, *Encyclopedia of Jewish Symbols*, 173).

What did the lamb symbolize? (12:5) "The Passover lamb . . . anticipated Jesus' death. This lamb, like Jesus, was unblemished (Ex. 12:5; 1 Pet. 1:18–19), male (Ex. 12:5), did not experience broken bones at his death (Ex. 12:46; John 19:33), and made atonement for the people (Num. 28:22). The Passover lamb's blood saved ancient Israelites from physical death, and Christ's atoning blood saves souls from spiritual death (Ex. 12:13; Hel. 5:9). The lamb's meat was edible and clean according to Mosaic law, and the Israelites partook of it in anticipation of Jesus' broken flesh. In comparable ways, we now partake of sacramental bread in remembrance of his broken flesh" (Parry and Parry, *Symbols and Shadows*, 140).

Why were bitter herbs part of the Passover meal? (12:8) Plants "belonging to the Mustard and Daisy families, are frequently collected and used as pot-herbs and salad plants . . . possibly consumed by the people of the Exodus in their Passover meals" (Zohary, *Plants of the Bible*, 100). "It is evident that the bitter herbs were not intended to be regarded as a savory accompaniment, by which more flavor was imparted to the sweeter food, but had a more profound

How Does the Passover Serve as a Reminder of the Atonement of Jesus Christ? (Exodus 12)

"When the Israelites left Egypt, the Lord gave them the passover. They were to take a lamb without blemish; they were not to break any of its bones. They were to kill it, cook it, and eat it with bitter herbs and unleavened bread. This feast they were to remember annually thereafter until Christ should come. This was also in the similitude of the sacrifice of Jesus Christ. . . .

"All these things point to his coming and to his ministry" (Smith, *Doctrines of Salvation*, 1:22).

Passover (Symbolic)	Atonement of Jesus Christ (Fulfillment)
Male lamb without blemish (Ex. 12:5)	Jesus Christ is the male without blemish
Eating bitter herbs (Ex. 12:8) was a reminder of the bitterness of sin and bondage Leavened bread symbolized corruption and being spoiled with mold	Jesus Christ removes bondage and the bitterness of sin Jesus Christ is the unleavened bread that removes corruption and sin in order to preserve us forever
Blood of the lamb is a token to pass over and spare people from destruction (Ex. 12:13)	The blood of Jesus Christ covers sin and is a token to spare us from destruction

(Adapted from the *Old Testament Seminary Teacher Manual*, 156–57.)

Israel's Exodus from Egypt and Entry into Canaan

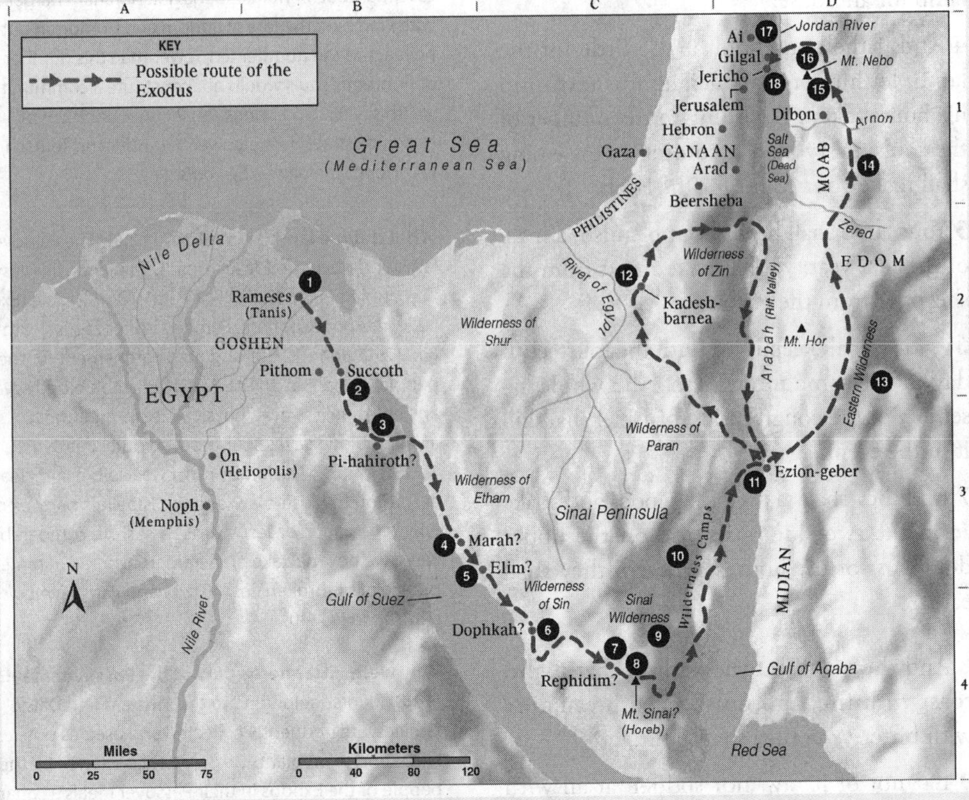

1. **Rameses** Israel was thrust out of Egypt (Ex. 12; Num. 33:5).
2. **Succoth** After the Hebrews left this first campsite, the Lord attended them in a cloud by day and in a pillar of fire by night (Ex. 13:20–22).
3. **Pi-hahiroth** Israel passed through the Red Sea (Ex. 14; Num. 33:8).
4. **Marah** The Lord healed the waters of Marah (Ex. 15:23–26).
5. **Elim** Israel camped by 12 springs (Ex. 15:27).
6. **Wilderness of Sin** The Lord sent manna and quail to feed Israel (Ex. 16).
7. **Rephidim** Israel fought with Amalek (Ex. 17:8–16).
8. **Mount Sinai** (Mount Horeb or Jebel Musa) The Lord revealed the Ten Commandments (Ex. 19–20).
9. **Sinai Wilderness** Israel constructed the tabernacle (Ex. 25–30).
10. **Wilderness Camps** Seventy elders were called to help Moses govern the people (Num. 11:16–17).
11. **Ezion-geber** Israel passed through the lands of Esau and Ammon in peace (Deut. 2).
12. **Kadesh-barnea** Moses sent spies into the promised land; Israel rebelled and failed to enter the land; Kadesh served as the main camp of Israel for many years (Num. 13:1–3, 17–33; 14; 32:8; Deut. 2:14).
13. **Eastern Wilderness** Israel avoided conflict with Edom and Moab (Num. 20:14–21; 22–24).
14. **Arnon River Israel** destroyed the Amorites who fought against them (Deut. 2:24–37).
15. **Mount Nebo** Moses viewed the promised land (Deut. 34:1–4). Moses delivered his last three sermons (Deut. 1–32).
16. **Plains of Moab** The Lord told Israel to divide the land and dispossess the inhabitants (Num. 33:50–56).
17. **Jordan River** Israel crossed the Jordan River on dry ground. Near Gilgal, stones from the bottom of the Jordan River were placed as a monument of Jordan's waters being divided (Josh. 3:1–5:1).
18. **Jericho** The children of Israel captured and destroyed the city (Josh. 6).

the morning; and that which remaineth of it
until the morning ye shall burn with fire.

11 ¶ And thus shall ye eat it; *with* your loins
girded, your shoes on your feet, and your
staff in your hand; and ye shall eat it in haste:
it *is* the LORD's passover.

12 For I will pass through the land of Egypt
this night, and will smite all the firstborn in
the land of Egypt, both man and beast; and
against all the gods of Egypt I will execute
judgment: I *am* the LORD.

13 And the blood shall be to you for a token
upon the houses where ye *are:* and when I
see the blood, I will pass over you, and the
plague shall not be upon you to destroy *you,*
when I smite the land of Egypt.

14 And this day shall be unto you for a memorial; and ye shall keep it a feast to the
LORD throughout your generations; ye shall
keep it a feast by an ordinance for ever.

15 Seven days shall ye eat unleavened bread;
even the first day ye shall put away leaven out
of your houses: for whosoever eateth leavened
bread from the first day until the seventh day,
that soul shall be cut off from Israel.

signification. The bitter herbs were to call to mind the bitterness of life experienced by Israel in Egypt (1:14), and this bitterness was to be overpowered by the sweet flesh of the lamb" (Keil and Delitzsch, *Commentary* [on Exodus 12:8, 9]).

Exodus 12: 11–20. Other Requirements for the Passover Meal Are Outlined

What did the word *Passover* mean anciently? (12:11) "The term Passover is from the Hebrew word *pesach* (Greek *paschal*), to pass by, and from the incident of the angel passing by the homes where the sign of the blood of the lamb was found, the lamb slain and eaten at the feast of the Passover is known as the Paschal lamb. This lamb had to be a male of the first year, and without spot or blemish, which was the requirement in all sacrifices, and not a bone was to be broken. The reason for this is that the sacrifice was typical of the great sacrifice which should be made by Jesus Christ" (Smith, *Church History and Modern Revelation*, 1:120).

In what way do we keep Passover in our day? (12:14) "The Passover was a law given to Israel which was to continue until Christ, and was to remind the children of Israel of the coming of Christ who would become the sacrificial Lamb. After he was crucified the law was changed by the Savior himself, and from that time forth the law of the sacrament was instituted. We now observe the law of the sacrament instead of the Passover because the Passover was consummated in full by the death of Jesus Christ" (Smith, *Answers to Gospel Questions*, 5:153). "The law of sacrifice was fulfilled with the Crucifixion. The Lord instituted the sacrament in its place. That is the ordinance we shall keep forever!" (Packer, "Word of Wisdom," 19). ⊕

What does seven days eating the unleavened bread mean? (12:14–20) "The Feast of Unleavened Bread is celebrated during the seven days after Passover. As a commemoration of the exodus from Egypt, it conveys that in their haste the Israelites were not able to bring any leaven and therefore had to bake their bread without it. Leaven was produced from the barley content of the dough that fermented and served as yeast. Small amounts would be kept from one batch, allowed to ferment, then used in another.

Passover as a Type for the Savior's Atoning Sacrifice (Exodus 12)

Elder Bruce R. McConkie noted: "At the time appointed for their deliverance from Egyptian bondage, the Lord commanded each family in Israel to sacrifice a lamb, to sprinkle its blood on their doorposts, and then to eat unleavened bread for seven more days—all to symbolize the fact that the destroying angel would pass over the Israelites as he went forth slaying the firstborn in the families of all the Egyptians; and also to show that, in haste, Israel should go forth from slavery to freedom. As a pattern for all the Mosaic instructions yet to come, the details of the performances here involved were so arranged as to bear testimony both of Israel's deliverance and of her Deliverer. Among other procedures, the Lord commanded, as found in Exodus 12:

1. 'Your lamb shall be without blemish, a male of the first year,' signifying that the Lamb of God, pure and perfect, without spot or blemish, in the prime of his life, as the Paschal Lamb, would be slain for the sins of the world.
2. They were to take of the blood of the lamb and sprinkle it upon the doorposts of their houses, having this promise as a result: 'And the blood shall be to you for a token upon the houses where ye are: and when I see the blood, I will pass over you, and the plague shall not be upon you to destroy you,' signifying that the blood of Christ, which should fall as drops in Gethsemane and flow in a stream from a pierced side as he hung on the cross, would cleanse and save the faithful; and that, as those in Israel were saved temporally because the blood of a sacrificial lamb was sprinkled on the doorposts of their houses, so the faithful of all ages would wash their garments in the blood of the Eternal Lamb and from him receive an eternal salvation. And may we say that as the angel of death passed by the families of Israel because of their faith—as Paul said of Moses, 'through faith he kept the passover, and the sprinkling of blood, lest he that destroyed the firstborn should touch them' (Hebrew 11:28)—even so shall the Angel of Life give eternal life to all those who rely on the blood of the Lamb.
3. As to the sacrifice of the lamb, the decree was, 'Neither shall ye break a bone thereof,' signifying that when the Lamb of God was sacrificed on the cross, though they broke the legs of the two thieves to induce death, yet they brake not the bones of the Crucified One 'that the scripture should be fulfilled, A bone of him shall not be broken' (John 19:31–36).
4. As to the eating the flesh of the sacrificial lamb, the divine word was, 'No uncircumcised person shall eat thereof,' signifying that the blessings of the gospel are reserved for those who come into the fold of Israel, who join the Church, who carry their part of the burden in bearing off the kingdom; signifying also that those who eat his flesh and drink his blood, as he said, shall have eternal life and he will raise them up at the last day (John 6:54).
5. As 'the Lord smote all the firstborn in the land of Egypt' because they believed not the word of the Lord delivered to them by Moses and Aaron, even so should the Firstborn of the Father, who brings life to all who believe in his holy name, destroy worldly people at the last day, destroy all those who are in the Egypt of darkness, whose hearts are hardened as were those of Pharaoh and his minions.
6. On the first and seventh days of the Feast of Unleavened Bread, the Israelites were commanded to hold holy convocations in which no work might be done except the preparation of their food. These were occasions for preaching and explaining and exhorting and testifying. We go to sacrament meetings to be built up in faith and in testimony. Ancient Israel attended holy convocations for the same purposes. Knowing that all things operate by faith, would it be amiss to draw the conclusion that it is as easy for us to look to Christ and his spilt blood for eternal salvation as it was for them of old to look to the blood of the sacrificed lamb, sprinkled on doorposts, to give temporal salvation, when the angel of death swept through the land of Egypt?

"It was, of course, while Jesus and the Twelve were keeping the Feast of the Passover that our Lord instituted the ordinance of the sacrament, to serve essentially the same purposes served by the sacrifices of the preceding four millenniums. After that final Passover day and its attendant lifting up upon the cross of the true Paschal Lamb, the day for the proper celebration of the ancient feast ceased. After that Paul was able to say: 'Christ our passover is sacrificed for us,' and to give the natural exhortation that flowed therefrom: 'Therefore let us keep the feast, not with old leaven, neither with the leaven of malice and wickedness; but with the unleavened bread of sincerity and truth' (1 Corinthians 5:7–8)" (*Promised Messiah*, 429–31).

With no 'starter' set aside to ferment, the process would have to begin again, taking seven to twelve days to reach the necessary level of fermentation" (Walton, et al., *IVP Bible Background Commentary,* 85).

16 And in the first day *there shall be* an holy convocation, and in the seventh day there shall be an holy convocation to you; no manner of work shall be done in them, save *that* which every man must eat, that only may be done of you.

What does the Passover mean for Latter-day Saints? (12:16) "Following His brief mortal ministry, this purest of all Passover sheep prepared His disciples for His death by introducing the sacrament of the Lord's Supper. . . . There would still be an offering, it would still involve a sacrifice, but it would be with symbolism much deeper, much more introspective and personal than the bloodletting of a firstborn lamb. . . . It is crucial for us to remember that we are still commanded to 'go to the house of prayer and offer up thy sacraments upon my holy day'" (Holland, "Behold the Lamb of God," 45).

17 And ye shall observe *the feast of* unleavened bread; for in this selfsame day have I brought your armies out of the land of Egypt: therefore shall ye observe this day in your generations by an ordinance for ever.

18 ¶ In the first *month,* on the fourteenth day of the month at even, ye shall eat unleavened bread, until the one and twentieth day of the month at even.

19 Seven days shall there be no leaven found in your houses: for whosoever eateth that which is leavened, even that soul shall be cut off from the congregation of Israel, whether he be a stranger, or born in the land.

20 Ye shall eat nothing leavened; in all your habitations shall ye eat unleavened bread.

Why was leaven restricted during Passover week? (12:19) "The unleavened bread, or 'the bread of affliction' that was to be eaten during Passover week to remind the Israelites of their Exodus in haste from Egypt (see Ex. 12:39; Deut. 16:3), provides an important type of the Savior. Leaven, which produces fermentation, was often used in the scriptures as a symbol of sin, false doctrine, and hypocrisy (see Matt. 16:11–12; Mark 8:14–16; Luke 12:1). Jesus was the 'unleavened bread' who was without sin or corruption and who led Israel out of the bondage of Egypt. The Apostle Paul linked the partaking of the unleavened bread under the old covenant with the symbols of the sacrament of the Lord's Supper [see 1 Cor. 5:7–8]" (Valletta, "True Bread of Life," 10).

Exodus 12:21–28. Moses Explains How Israel Must Keep the Passover

21 ¶ Then Moses called for all the elders of Israel, and said unto them, Draw out and take you a lamb according to your families, and kill the passover.

22 And ye shall take a bunch of hyssop, and dip *it* in the blood that *is* in the basin, and strike the lintel and the two side posts with the blood that *is* in the basin; and none of you shall go out at the door of his house until the morning.

What does hyssop symbolize? (12:22) "Though we are not sure exactly why, we do know that in Old Testament times the woody herb hyssop was used in purification rituals to sprinkle blood or water (see Ex. 12:22; Ps. 51:7; Heb. 9:19). It was one of most insignificant and unimposing shrubs in Palestine and was often associated with humility. Thus the use of the hyssop stressed the necessity of humility in sacrifice, as well as purification" (Lund, *Jesus Christ, Key to the Plan of Salvation*, 60). "In Christianity it signifies penitence; humility; its purgative properties depict innocence regained, hence baptism" (Cooper, *Illustrated Encyclopaedia of Traditional Symbols*, 86).

How is this promise extended to modern Israel? (12:23) "Obedience to the Word of Wisdom keeps one free. . . . 'And I, the Lord, give unto them a promise, that the destroying angel shall pass by them, as the children of Israel, and not slay them' (D&C 89:21.) This reference to the first Passover reminds us that, *in faith*, ancient Israel was obedient to the commandment to take blood and 'strike it on the two side posts and on the upper door post of the houses.' . . . So, in faith, modern Israel is commanded to obey the Word of Wisdom. It becomes our token of a covenant with the Lord—a spiritual separator of covenant Israel from the rest of the world" (Nelson, *Power within Us*, 80).

Exodus 12:29–42. The Firstborn of the Egyptians Are Killed While Israel Escapes

How did the final plague change Pharaoh? (12:30–31) This final plague, unlike the previous plagues, changed Pharaoh's heart. For the other plagues: "The [Joseph Smith Translation] reports, 'And *Pharaoh* hardened his heart, that he hearkened not unto them' (Exodus 7:13). In fact, the [JST correctly changes] systematically . . . all nine occurrences in this

23 For the LORD will pass through to smite the Egyptians; and when he seeth the blood upon the lintel, and on the two side posts, the LORD will pass over the door, and will not suffer the destroyer to come in unto your houses to smite *you*.

24 And ye shall observe this thing for an ordinance to thee and to thy sons for ever.

25 And it shall come to pass, when ye be come to the land which the LORD will give you, according as he hath promised, that ye shall keep this service.

26 And it shall come to pass, when your children shall say unto you, What mean ye by this service?

27 That ye shall say, It *is* the sacrifice of the LORD's passover, who passed over the houses of the children of Israel in Egypt, when he smote the Egyptians, and delivered our houses. And the people bowed the head and worshipped.

28 And the children of Israel went away, and did as the LORD had commanded Moses and Aaron, so did they.

29 ¶ And it came to pass, that at midnight the LORD smote all the firstborn in the land of Egypt, from the firstborn of Pharaoh that sat on his throne unto the firstborn of the captive that *was* in the dungeon; and all the firstborn of cattle.

30 And Pharaoh rose up in the night, he, and all his servants, and all the Egyptians; and there was a great cry in Egypt; for *there was* not a house where *there was* not one dead.

31 ¶ And he called for Moses and Aaron by

night, and said, Rise up, *and* get you forth
from among my people, both ye and the children of Israel; and go, serve the LORD, as ye
have said.

32 Also take your flocks and your herds, as
ye have said, and be gone; and bless me also.

33 And the Egyptians were urgent upon the
people, that they might send them out of the
land in haste; for they said, We *be* all dead
men.

34 And the people took their dough before
it was leavened, their kneadingtroughs being
bound up in their clothes upon their shoulders.

35 And the children of Israel did according
to the word of Moses; and they borrowed of
the Egyptians jewels of silver, and jewels of
gold, and raiment:

36 And the LORD gave the people favour in
the sight of the Egyptians, so that they lent
unto them *such things as they required.* And
they spoiled the Egyptians.

37 ¶ And the children of Israel journeyed
from Rameses to Succoth, about six hundred
thousand on foot *that were* men, beside children.

38 And a mixed multitude went up also with
them; and flocks, and herds, *even* very much
cattle.

39 And they baked unleavened cakes of
the dough which they brought forth out of
Egypt, for it was not leavened; because they
were thrust out of Egypt, and could not tarry,
neither had they prepared for themselves any
victual.

40 ¶ Now the sojourning of the children of
Israel, who dwelt in Egypt, *was* four hundred
and thirty years.

41 And it came to pass at the end of the four
hundred and thirty years, even the selfsame

particular context (cf. JST, Exodus 4:21; 7:13; 9:12; 10:1, 20, 27; 11:10; 14:8, 17)" (Horton, "Insights into Exodus, Leviticus, Numbers, and Deuteronomy," 79). However, it is different with this plague. ⊕

According to the Joseph Smith Translation, why were the children of Israel freed from their bondage? (12:33) "And the Egyptians were urgent upon the people, that they might send them out of the land in haste; for they said, *We have found our firstborn all dead, therefore get ye out of the land lest we die also*" (JST, Exodus 12:33).

Why did they "borrow" jewels? (12:35) "The Hebrew indicates that the Israelites *asked for* (not *borrowed*) the jewels and raiment, and the Egyptians 'let them have' (not *lent*) such things as they required. It should be remembered that the Lord earlier had commanded Moses to have the Israelites follow this procedure in order that they would not 'go empty' out of Egypt" (Ludlow, *Companion to Your Study of the Old Testament*, 145). See commentary in this volume for Exodus 11:2.

Where was Rameses? (12:37) "Ra'amses is a 'store city' for which the Israelites made construction bricks (Exodus 1:11). It is also the starting point for the Exodus (Exodus 12:37; Numbers 33:3). This is likely to be equated with the Delta capital built by and named for Ramesses II, that is, Pi-Ramesses, 'the house of Ramesses,' . . . [it was] a massive city that . . . occupied about six square miles. Egyptian records tell us that during the reign of Ramesses IX (1099–1069 B.C.), Pi-Ramesses was abandoned. . . . The fact that the city of Pi-Ramesses had a history limited to the period from c. 1275–1075 B.C. is extremely significant for the appearance of a Delta site named Ra'amses in the Exodus narrative" (Hoffmeier, "Out of Egypt," 10–12).

day it came to pass, that all the hosts of the LORD went out from the land of Egypt.

42 It *is* a night to be much observed unto the LORD for bringing them out from the land of Egypt: this *is* that night of the LORD to be observed of all the children of Israel in their generations.

43 ¶ And the LORD said unto Moses and Aaron, This *is* the ordinance of the passover: There shall no stranger eat thereof:

44 But every man's servant that is bought for money, when thou hast circumcised him, then shall he eat thereof.

45 A foreigner and an hired servant shall not eat thereof.

Exodus 12:43–51. The Law of the Passover

Why were uncircumcised strangers not allowed to partake of Passover and how can that relate to partaking of the sacrament? (12:43) God established Passover to bless His covenant people. There is a "connection between the sacrament prayers (Moroni 4–5) and Passover.... Both prayers begin by addressing God the Eternal Father in the name of the Son. The next phrase is 'to bless and sanctify.' Throughout the traditional Passover, the head of the household at the beginning blesses and sanctifies the occasion.... The next phrase is 'to the souls of all those who partake of it.' The Passover was specifically designated for those

How Many People Left Egypt with Moses?

"It seems difficult to determine with any accuracy the total number of the Twelve Tribes at the time of the exodus" (Petersen, *Moses*, 81).

There are several possibilities regarding how many people left with Moses during the Exodus.

1. *Two to three million people*. Adam Clarke estimated the population to be 3,263,000 (*Adam Clarke's Commentary* [on Exodus 12:37]).

2. *5,500 to 20,000 people*. A "total Israelite population of over two million souls, [is] a number that poses intractable problems.... In response to these problems, it has been suggested that Hebrew *'elef*, usually rendered 'thousand,' here means a 'clan' or that it signifies a small military unit—the number of fighting men levied from each tribe" (Sarna, *Exodus*, 62). If one accepts the smaller number, then this number parallels the number of Saints who left Nauvoo in 600 wagons under Brigham Young's direction (see Hartley, "Pioneer Trek," 32).

This smaller number helps the reader understand why the children of Israel felt vulnerable to Pharaoh's army of 600 chariots (Exodus 14:7). These chariots would not have been a great threat to 600,000 fighting soldiers.

Also, there are several verses in Deuteronomy that make more sense if this is a smaller group to leave Egypt. "When the Lord thy God shall bring thee into the land whither thou goest to possess it, and hath cast out many nations before thee, the Hittites, and the Girgashites, and the Amorites, and the Canaanites, and the Perizzites, and the Hivites, and the Jebusites, *seven nations greater and mightier than thou*" (Deut. 7:1; emphasis added); "The Lord did not set his love upon you, nor choose you, *because ye were more in number than any people; for ye* were the fewest of all people" (Deut. 7:7; emphasis added); "then will the Lord drive out all these nations from before you, *and ye shall possess greater nations and mightier than yourselves*" (Deut. 11:23; emphasis added).

"On the surface, those census lists of Numbers Chapters 1 and 25 can be interpreted this way. Thus instead of Reuben's '46,500 grown males,' there would be forty-six units, namely, five hundred persons; Simeon's count would be fifty-nine units corresponding to three hundred persons; and so forth for each of the tribes.... The sum total of the census would be 598 units, which corresponds to 5,550 persons" (Sarna, *Exploring Exodus*, 99).

3. *Population during David's reign*. The record likens the exodus to a later time so the reader felt as if he were in the exodus. "This population figure more or less represents the historic reality of the period of the united monarch, the period of David and Solomon.... Viewed from this perspective, ... it represents the Israelite population at the time of David and Solomon, which was seen to be the culmination of the Exodus era" (Sarna, *Exploring Exodus*, 101–2).

46 In one house shall it be eaten; thou shalt not carry forth ought of the flesh abroad out of the house; neither shall ye break a bone thereof.

47 All the congregation of Israel shall keep it.

48 And when a stranger shall sojourn with thee, and will keep the passover to the LORD, let all his males be circumcised, and then let him come near and keep it; and he shall be as one that is born in the land: for no uncircumcised person shall eat thereof.

49 One law shall be to him that is homeborn, and unto the stranger that sojourneth among you.

50 Thus did all the children of Israel; as the LORD commanded Moses and Aaron, so did they.

51 And it came to pass the selfsame day, *that* the LORD did bring the children of Israel out of the land of Egypt by their armies.

CHAPTER 13

The firstborn of man and of beasts are to be sanctified unto the Lord—The Feast of Unleavened Bread is to be kept in the land of Canaan—Moses takes Joseph's bones out of Egypt—The Lord attends Israel in a pillar of cloud by day and a pillar of fire by night.

1 And the LORD spake unto Moses, saying,

2 Sanctify unto me all the firstborn, whatsoever openeth the womb among the children of Israel, *both* of man and of beast: it *is* mine.

who were members of the covenant—those who were circumcised. . . . Since the sacrament is a formal renewal of the baptismal covenant, it is efficacious only for those who are baptized" (Seely, "Last Supper," 97).

What was foreshadowed by not breaking a bone of the sacrificial lamb? (12:46) "As to the sacrifice of the lamb, the decree was, 'Neither shall ye break a bone thereof,' signifying that when the Lamb of God was sacrificed on the cross, though they broke the legs of the two thieves to induce death, yet they brake not the bones of the Crucified One 'that the scripture should be fulfilled, A bone of him shall not be broken' (John 19:31–36)" (McConkie, *Promised Messiah*, 430).

Exodus 13:1–10. God Institutes Symbols to Remind Israel about Their Liberation

Why were the firstborn set apart to the Lord? (13:2) "All Israel was holy unto the Lord: see on Exodus 19:5, Exodus 19:6. But the firstborn of man and beast were specially consecrated to Him, as the part representing the whole. There was a special fitness in the consecration of the firstborn, seeing they had been spared in the destruction which overtook the Egyptians. The firstborn of mankind were to be consecrated to the service of Jehovah as priests; the firstborn of animals were to be offered in sacrifice, if clean animals; if not, they were to be redeemed at a price. Afterwards the whole tribe of Levi was consecrated to the priestly service in lieu of the firstborn: see Numbers 3:40–51" (*John Dummelow's Commentary* [on Exodus 13:1–16]).

What is the house of bondage? (13:3) The house of bondage is "literally, 'house of slaves.' This designation for Egypt, frequent in Deuteronomy, gives voice to the particular experience of Israel in that land. It may derive from the Egyptian practice of settling the labor gangs in workmen's villages in proximity to the site of the project for which they were conscripted. These villages were wholly enclosed by walls. One such has been uncovered at Deir el-Medinah, near Thebes. It served the laborers engaged in the construction of royal tombs in the Valley of the Kings. To the Israelite conscripts, such a village may have appeared to be a gigantic 'slave house'" (Sarna, *Exodus*, 65).

What makes this verse pivotal for the Israelites? (13:5) "This verse is important for many reasons. First Moses was formally instituting the time and manner of keeping the Passover and Feast of Unleavened Bread. Second, he was reminding the people of the bounty of the promised land. And third, he was outlining the many groups who lived in that land whom they would have to conquer. This list will be used numerous times throughout the Exodus period" (Muhlestein, *Scripture Study Made Simple*, 92).

Why did they hold a feast on the seventh day of eating unleavened bread? (13:6) "By tradition it was on the seventh day of the Exodus that the pursuing Egyptians drowned in the Sea of Reeds" (Sarna, *Exodus*, 66). Also, "seven symbolizes fulness, completion, entirety or totality" (Gaskill, *Lost Language of Symbolism*, 124). This feast also represented that their time in Egypt was complete.

How did ancient Israel remember the sign upon the hand and memorial between the eyes? (13:9) The Israelites wore "amulets fastened on the forehead or on the left arm. They were small strips of parchment inscribed with texts (see Ex. 13:1–10, 11–16; Deut. 6:4–9; 11:13–21) and enclosed in leather cases (see

3 ¶ And Moses said unto the people, Remember this day, in which ye came out from Egypt, out of the house of bondage; for by strength of hand the LORD brought you out from this *place:* there shall no leavened bread be eaten.

4 This day came ye out in the month Abib.

5 ¶ And it shall be when the LORD shall bring thee into the land of the Canaanites, and the Hittites, and the Amorites, and the Hivites, and the Jebusites, which he sware unto thy fathers to give thee, a land flowing with milk and honey, that thou shalt keep this service in this month.

6 Seven days thou shalt eat unleavened bread, and in the seventh day *shall be* a feast to the LORD.

7 Unleavened bread shall be eaten seven days; and there shall no leavened bread be seen with thee, neither shall there be leaven seen with thee in all thy quarters.

8 ¶ And thou shalt shew thy son in that day, saying, *This is done* because of that *which* the LORD did unto me when I came forth out of Egypt.

9 And it shall be for a sign unto thee upon thine hand, and for a memorial between thine eyes, that the LORD's law may be in thy mouth: for with a strong hand hath the LORD brought thee out of Egypt.

10 Thou shalt therefore keep this ordinance in his season from year to year.

11 ¶ And it shall be when the LORD shall bring thee into the land of the Canaanites, as he sware unto thee and to thy fathers, and shall give it thee,

12 That thou shalt set apart unto the LORD all that openeth the matrix, and every firstling that cometh of a beast which thou hast; the males *shall be* the LORD's.

13 And every firstling of an ass thou shalt redeem with a lamb; and if thou wilt not redeem it, then thou shalt break his neck: and all the firstborn of man among thy children shalt thou redeem.

14 ¶ And it shall be when thy son asketh thee in time to come, saying, What *is* this? that thou shalt say unto him, By strength of hand the LORD brought us out from Egypt, from the house of bondage:

15 And it came to pass, when Pharaoh would hardly let us go, that the LORD slew all the firstborn in the land of Egypt, both the firstborn of man, and the firstborn of beast: therefore I sacrifice to the LORD all that openeth the matrix, being males; but all the firstborn of my children I redeem.

16 And it shall be for a token upon thine hand, and for frontlets between thine eyes: for by strength of hand the LORD brought us forth out of Egypt.

17 ¶ And it came to pass, when Pharaoh had let the people go, that God led them not *through* the way of the land of the Philistines, although that *was* near; for God said, Lest peradventure the people repent when they see war, and they return to Egypt:

18 But God led the people about, *through*

Matt. 23:5)" (Bible Dictionary, "Phylacteries"). "The basis for using phylacteries comes from this verse [Exodus 13:9].... The phylactery might be worn on the forehead and also on the left arm near the heart" (Ludlow, *Companion to Your Study of the Old Testament*, 145).

Exodus 13:11–16. The Firstborn Are Sanctified

How does dedicating the firstborn to the Lord remind us of Jesus Christ? (13:12) "Inasmuch as the Lord saved the firstborn of the faithful ancient Israelites from death, He rightly claimed them as His (see Ex. 13:2). He commanded that their firstborn sons be dedicated to Him and that their firstborn male animals be sacrificed to Him (see Ex. 13:12). We are similarly indebted to Jesus Christ. He is justified in requesting that we serve Him, for we 'are bought with a price' (1 Cor. 6:20). The Passover instituted through Moses for the ancient Israelites is an enduring symbol that teaches us what Jesus Christ has done to bring salvation to all mankind" (Bird, "Moses and the Passover," 33). ⊕

Exodus 13:17–22. Israel Goes into the Wilderness

Why was Israel commanded to avoid the way of the land of the Philistines? (13:17) The Israelites followed God's command to take another way. "Early in the 13th century B.C., Pharaoh Seti I built the tight network of strongholds along the coast of northern Sinai referred to as the 'way of the Philistines' in Exodus 13:17. This military road remained under the strict control of the Egyptians throughout that century. It might easily have become a trap for the wandering Israelites; hence, the command . . . to avoid this route" (Malamat, "Let My People Go and Go and Go," 26).

the way of the wilderness of the Red sea: and
the children of Israel went up harnessed out
of the land of Egypt.

What evidence is there that the bones of other patriarchs were carried out of Egypt with Joseph's? (13:19) "It is supposed that the Israelites carried with them the bones or remains of *all the twelve sons of Jacob*, each tribe taking care of the bones of its own patriarch, while Moses took care of the bones of Joseph. St. Stephen expressly says, Acts 7:15,16, that not only Jacob, but the *fathers* were carried from Egypt into Sychem; and this . . . was the only opportunity that seems to have presented itself for doing this: and certainly the reason that rendered it proper to remove the bones of Joseph to the promised land, had equal weight in reference to those of the other patriarchs" (*Adam Clarke's Commentary* [on Exodus 13:19]).

19 And Moses took the bones of Joseph with
him: for he had straitly sworn the children of
Israel, saying, God will surely visit you; and
ye shall carry up my bones away hence with
you.

20 ¶ And they took their journey from
Succoth, and encamped in Etham, in the
edge of the wilderness.

Why does the Lord go before them with a pillar of fire? (13:21) "As they traveled in the wilderness, Jehovah created a pillar of smoke by day and a pillar of fire by night that rested over the Tabernacle. This was a visible—and dramatic!—token of Jehovah's guiding and guarding presence. The pillar of fire is not just a symbol. It was real enough that it kept Pharaoh and his chariots at bay all that night before the Israelites passed through the Red Sea the next day (see Exodus 14:19–20). There are numerous references to this amazing phenomenon [see Exod. 14:24; Numbers 9:15–16; 10:34; Deuteronomy 1:33]" (Lund, *Second Coming of the Lord*, 214). ⊕

21 And the Lord went before them by day
in a pillar of a cloud, to lead them the way;
and by night in a pillar of fire, to give them
light; to go by day and night:

How would future Jews remember this divine guidance of Jehovah? (13:22) "This column of smoke was intended to serve as a sign of Yahweh's special presence in the midst of the worshipping community. This ritual sign told the Israelites that Yahweh was truly present to hear their prayers . . . The pillar of cloud which rose from the incense altar of the Jerusalem temple [reminded the people] . . . that they were together with the Israelites of the exodus in experiencing the same guiding and protecting presence of Yahweh" (Plastaras, *God of Exodus*, 186–87).

22 He took not away the pillar of the cloud
by day, nor the pillar of fire by night, *from*
before the people.

CHAPTER 14

Israel goes out of Egypt—Israel passes through the Red Sea on dry ground—The Lord overthrows the Egyptians in the midst of the sea.

1 And the LORD spake unto Moses, saying,

2 Speak unto the children of Israel, that they turn and encamp before Pi-hahiroth, between Migdol and the sea, over against Baal-zephon: before it shall ye encamp by the sea.

3 For Pharaoh will say of the children of Israel, They *are* entangled in the land, the wilderness hath shut them in.

4 And I will harden Pharaoh's heart, that he shall follow after them; and I will be honoured upon Pharaoh, and upon all his host; that the Egyptians may know that I *am* the LORD. And they did so.

5 ¶ And it was told the king of Egypt that the people fled: and the heart of Pharaoh and of his servants was turned against the people, and they said, Why have we done this, that we have let Israel go from serving us?

6 And he made ready his chariot, and took his people with him:

7 And he took six hundred chosen chariots, and all the chariots of Egypt, and captains over every one of them.

8 And the LORD hardened the heart of Pharaoh king of Egypt, and he pursued after the children of Israel: and the children of Israel went out with an high hand.

9 But the Egyptians pursued after them, all the horses *and* chariots of Pharaoh, and his horsemen, and his army, and overtook them encamping by the sea, beside Pi-hahiroth, before Baal-zephon.

Exodus 14:1–12. Israel Leaves Egypt, the Exodus Begins, and the Egyptians Follow Them

Why did Israel camp by the sea? (14:2–3) "The liberated Israelites, having reached the edge of the wilderness, were suddenly ordered to change course. This new direction, fraught with great danger, was actually a stratagem to mislead the Egyptians and lure them to their doom. It was the culminating defeat of Pharaoh. Thereafter, Egypt does not again appear in Israelite history until the time of King Solomon" (Sarna, *Exodus*, 70). ⊕

According to the Joseph Smith Translation, who hardens Pharaoh's heart? (14:4) The Joseph Smith Translation points out this is a prophetic verse and Pharaoh will use his agency and hardens his own heart. "And *Pharaoh* will harden *his* heart" (JST, Exodus 14:4; emphasis added). See commentary in this volume for Exodus 4:21; 7:3.

In what way did the Lord use Pharaoh's greed to strengthen His people? (14:5) "Once they began their exodus, Pharaoh had another change of heart, as he had so many times before. He began to think of the economic loss his nation would incur by not having the slave labor of the Israelites, and so Pharaoh called together his armies and pursued the Israelites. The Lord had warned Moses that this would happen, and suggested to him that it had a divine purpose; namely, to establish for the Egyptians that the God of Israel was the true and living God (see Exodus 14:4)" (Gaskill, *Miracles of the Old Testament*, 79).

Exodus 14:13–20. Moses Commands Israel Not to Fear

What lesson did the children of Israel need to learn? (14:14) "Part of the Lord's program for the Israelites was to force them to come to trust and rely upon Him for all of their needs. This process took place over time, beginning with the first interview of Moses and Aaron with Pharaoh and ending several weeks after they had left Egypt. The point of the growing lesson was that the Lord could be trusted and, indeed, had to be trusted. In effect, He left the Israelites without any resource upon which to call except Himself. It is my own view that the Israelites had to be brought to this state of mind and heart to become fully free" (Brown, "Trust in the Lord," 93). ⊕

What lesson do we learn from Moses stretching his hand over the sea? (14:16) "Moses is not instructed to strike the sea. In verse 21 the action of Moses with his rod is the signal for the strong wind to blow back the waters. Isaiah (63:12) makes clear that it is God who splits the sea" (Sarna, *Exodus*, 72).

10 ¶ And when Pharaoh drew nigh, the children of Israel lifted up their eyes, and, behold, the Egyptians marched after them; and they were sore afraid: and the children of Israel cried out unto the LORD.

11 And they said unto Moses, Because *there were* no graves in Egypt, hast thou taken us away to die in the wilderness? wherefore hast thou dealt thus with us, to carry us forth out of Egypt?

12 *Is* not this the word that we did tell thee in Egypt, saying, Let us alone, that we may serve the Egyptians? For *it had been* better for us to serve the Egyptians, than that we should die in the wilderness.

13 ¶ And Moses said unto the people, Fear ye not, stand still, and see the salvation of the LORD, which he will shew to you to day: for the Egyptians whom ye have seen to day, ye shall see them again no more for ever.

14 The LORD shall fight for you, and ye shall hold your peace.

15 ¶ And the LORD said unto Moses, Wherefore criest thou unto me? speak unto the children of Israel, that they go forward:

16 But lift thou up thy rod, and stretch out thine hand over the sea, and divide it: and the children of Israel shall go on dry *ground* through the midst of the sea.

17 And I, behold, I will harden the hearts of the Egyptians, and they shall follow them: and I will get me honour upon Pharaoh, and upon all his host, upon his chariots, and upon his horsemen.

18 And the Egyptians shall know that I *am* the LORD, when I have gotten me honour upon Pharaoh, upon his chariots, and upon his horsemen.

19 ¶ And the angel of God, which went before the camp of Israel, removed and went behind them; and the pillar of the cloud went from before their face, and stood behind them:

20 And it came between the camp of the Egyptians and the camp of Israel; and it was a cloud and darkness *to them,* but it gave light by night *to these:* so that the one came not near the other all the night.

How is the pillar of cloud symbolic of the Lord's protection? (14:20) The "pillar of cloud moved from the front to the rear of the Israelitish camp.... This cloud had two sides, one dark and the other luminous: the luminous side gave light to . . . Israel during the night of passage; and the dark side, turned towards the pursuing Egyptians, prevented them from receiving any benefit from that light" (*Adam Clarke's Commentary* [on Exodus 14:20]). "The day of Christ's return is known as 'the great and dreadful day of the Lord' . . . because it will be great for the righteous and dreadful for the wicked. This is well depicted by the presence of God in this miracle that brought darkness to the Egyptians and light to the Israelites" (Gaskill, *Miracles of the Old Testament*, 81).

Exodus 14:21–31. Israel Crosses the Red Sea on Dry Ground

21 And Moses stretched out his hand over the sea; and the LORD caused the sea to go *back* by a strong east wind all that night, and made the sea dry *land,* and the waters were divided.

22 And the children of Israel went into the midst of the sea upon the dry *ground:* and the waters *were* a wall unto them on their right hand, and on their left.

23 ¶ And the Egyptians pursued, and went in after them to the midst of the sea, *even* all Pharaoh's horses, his chariots, and his horsemen.

24 And it came to pass, that in the morning watch the LORD looked unto the host of the Egyptians through the pillar of fire and

What power was behind the crossing of the Red Sea? (14:21–22) President Spencer W. Kimball taught: "Hopelessness, fear, despair must have gripped their hearts, and then the miracle came. It was born of the faith of their indomitable leader. A cloud hid them from the view of their enemies. A strong east wind blew all the night; the waters were parted; the bed of the sea was dry; and Israel crossed to another world and saw the returning sea envelop and destroy their pursuers. Israel was safe. Faith had been rewarded, and Moses was vindicated. The impossible had happened. An almost superhuman faith had given birth to an unaccountable and mysterious miracle that was to be the theme of the sermons and warnings of Israel and their prophets for centuries" (in Conference Report, Oct. 1952, 49).

of the cloud, and troubled the host of the Egyptians,

25 And took off their chariot wheels, that they drave them heavily: so that the Egyptians said, Let us flee from the face of Israel; for the LORD fighteth for them against the Egyptians.

26 ¶ And the LORD said unto Moses, Stretch out thine hand over the sea, that the waters may come again upon the Egyptians, upon their chariots, and upon their horsemen.

27 And Moses stretched forth his hand over the sea, and the sea returned to his strength when the morning appeared; and the Egyptians fled against it; and the LORD overthrew the Egyptians in the midst of the sea.

28 And the waters returned, and covered the chariots, and the horsemen, *and* all the host of Pharaoh that came into the sea after them; there remained not so much as one of them.

What does "took off their chariot wheels" mean? (14:25) The Lord hedged up the way of the Egyptians and in contrast helped the children of Israel walk across on dry ground (Exodus 14:29). It may be that the chariot wheels "became clogged with the soft ooze in the sea bed" (*John Dummelow's Commentary* [on Exodus 14:25]).

What is significant about the Egyptians' suffering death by drowning? (14:27) "It has been suggested that a sort of 'tit for tat' is at play here in the taking of Egyptian lives by water. Some eighty years earlier, Pharaoh had taken the lives of the male Israelite children by drowning them in the Nile. Now Israel's God would drown Pharaoh's armies in the Red Sea. Ironically, the very man God used to bring to pass the watery destruction of the Egyptians was Moses, who Himself was rescued by God from the Nile when he was but an infant" (Gaskill, *Miracles of the Old Testament*, 80).

Israel's Exodus as a Type of God's Plan (Exodus 14)

"The Exodus was not only a real event, but also 'a type and shadow of things' representing both escape from the wicked world and redemption from the bondage of sin" (Nibley, *Approach to the Book of Mormon*, 146). "The Exodus pattern is repeated and echoed throughout the scriptures. It is a type of the 'great plan of happiness.' The Exodus and the plan of salvation are both reminders that there is a way out of darkness and bondage, and that way is by the design and power of God. Our Heavenly Father loves us and has sent his Son, our Redeemer, to show us the way back home, 'beyond this vale of sorrow into a far better land of promise' (Alma 37:45)" (Valletta, "Exodus," 189).

Exodus Plan of Redemption

Israel in the Promised Land	*Premortality with Heavenly Father*
Dissension	War in Heaven
Joseph and Israel into Egypt	Sent to Earth to Be Proven
Pharaoh Who Knew Not Joseph	Satan Seeks Our Misery
Israel in Bondage in Egypt	Captive of the Devil
Moses Called to Help Deliver Us	Christ Is Our Redeemer
Israel Is Liberated through death of Firstborn	Jesus Christ, the Firstborn of the Father, Liberates Mankind through the Atonement
Crossing of the Red Sea; Burying the Pharaoh's Forces	Baptism and Other Ordinances; Begin Putting Off the World
Cloud and Pillar of Fire	Guided by the Holy Ghost
Manna from Heaven	Sustained by the Word of God
Mount Sinai and the Tabernacle	Temple Worship
Forty Years of Wilderness: Old Generation Dies	Trials and Tests of Life: Disobedience Dies
Joshua Leads Israelites into Canaan	Jesus Leads Us Home

(Adapted from Valletta, "Exodus," 187).

29 But the children of Israel walked upon dry *land* in the midst of the sea; and the waters *were* a wall unto them on their right hand, and on their left.

30 Thus the LORD saved Israel that day out of the hand of the Egyptians; and Israel saw the Egyptians dead upon the sea shore.

31 And Israel saw that great work which the LORD did upon the Egyptians: and the people feared the LORD, and believed the LORD, and his servant Moses.

CHAPTER 15

The children of Israel sing the song of Moses—They extol the Lord as a man of war and rejoice in their deliverance from Egypt—The waters of Marah are healed—The Lord promises to free Israel from the diseases of Egypt.

1 Then sang Moses and the children of Israel this song unto the LORD, and spake, saying, I will sing unto the LORD, for he hath triumphed gloriously: the horse and his rider hath he thrown into the sea.

2 The LORD *is* my strength and song, and he is become my salvation: he *is* my God, and I will prepare him an habitation; my father's God, and I will exalt him.

3 The LORD *is* a man of war: the LORD *is* his name.

4 Pharaoh's chariots and his host hath he cast into the sea: his chosen captains also are drowned in the Red sea.

Exodus 15:1–19. Moses and Israel Sing the Song of the Sea

What song did the children of Israel sing? (15:1–19) The "Israelites sang a triumphant song celebrating Pharaoh's defeat and Jehovah's deliverance of his people on dry land in the midst of the sea. Exodus 15:1–19, known as the Song of the Sea, is one of the earliest examples of Israelite poetry in the Old Testament. A sort of ballad commemorating the monumental liberation of Israel, these verses became one of the foundational documents in the collective cultural memory and spiritual awareness of the Israelites for centuries to come" (Seely and Welch, "Zenos and the Texts of the Old Testament," 323). ⊕

Why is the Lord called "a man of war"? (15:3) "The Hebrew literally says, 'The Lord is a Man of War.' This strikes those moderns for whom war is by definition immoral as a morally primitive way of describing God. Many people are much more comfortable saying 'God is Love.' But sometimes the only way to stop evil and increase love is through war. God must therefore be both Love and Warrior. In this case, when the Israelites are fleeing heavily armed professional troops, God acts as a warrior on their behalf. That was the only thing a God of Love could do" (Prager, *Rational Bible*, 172).

What role does the song of Moses play in later history? (15:4–6) This song or poem is found in Jewish prayer books. It becomes an expression of victory over

Israel's enemies. "In this spirit, John reminds us of what we have already learned [Revelation 15]. . . .

"Those who have endured to this end will sing the song of victory, just as Moses and the children of Israel sang a song of joy when the Egyptian host was destroyed in the Red Sea. . . .

"The focus of Moses' song is the execution of God's judgment over the warring forces of Pharaoh contrasted with the mercy extended to His own people . . .

"As Pharaoh was defeated, so too has Christ overcome his enemies; hence the song of the Lamb is also mentioned. Both physical and spiritual death have been conquered" (Wilcox, *Who Shall Be Able to Stand?* 217).

What does the Lord's right hand symbolize? (15:6)
"The right hand of God is associated with righteousness (Ps. 48:10; Isa. 41:10), power (Ex. 15:6; Ps. 89:13), and covenant making (Isa. 62:8). With his right hand, the Lord executes justice (3 Ne. 29:4, 9), dispenses the law (Deut. 33:2), . . . saves his people (Ps. 17:7; 20:6), [and] created the heavens and the earth (Isa. 48:13). After the divine judgment, the righteous will dwell eternally at the right hand of God (Mosiah 26:23–24; D&C 29:27)" (Parry and Parry, *Understanding the Book of Revelation*, 23).

Where is the Lord's place among the gods? (15:11)
"The Israelites never looked upon the holy war as a contest between gods because they believed that [Jehovah] had no equals, that his power was without limit. Significantly, it is never suggested in the exodus narratives that [Jehovah] is pitted against the gods of the Egyptians. It is mere man (Pharaoh) who attempts to oppose the plan of [Jehovah]. Because the Egyptians are mere men, there really is no contest at all" (Plastaras, *God of Exodus*, 180–81).

5 The depths have covered them: they sank into the bottom as a stone.

6 Thy right hand, O Lord, is become glorious in power: thy right hand, O Lord, hath dashed in pieces the enemy.

7 And in the greatness of thine excellency thou hast overthrown them that rose up against thee: thou sentest forth thy wrath, *which* consumed them as stubble.

8 And with the blast of thy nostrils the waters were gathered together, the floods stood upright as an heap, *and* the depths were congealed in the heart of the sea.

9 The enemy said, I will pursue, I will overtake, I will divide the spoil; my lust shall be satisfied upon them; I will draw my sword, my hand shall destroy them.

10 Thou didst blow with thy wind, the sea covered them: they sank as lead in the mighty waters.

11 Who *is* like unto thee, O Lord, among the gods? who *is* like thee, glorious in holiness, fearful *in* praises, doing wonders?

12 Thou stretchedst out thy right hand, the earth swallowed them.

13 Thou in thy mercy hast led forth the people *which* thou hast redeemed: thou hast guided *them* in thy strength unto thy holy habitation.

14 The people shall hear, *and* be afraid: sorrow shall take hold on the inhabitants of Palestina.

15 Then the dukes of Edom shall be amazed; the mighty men of Moab, trembling shall take hold upon them; all the inhabitants of Canaan shall melt away.

16 Fear and dread shall fall upon them; by the greatness of thine arm they shall be *as* still as a stone; till thy people pass over, O LORD, till the people pass over, *which* thou hast purchased.

17 Thou shalt bring them in, and plant them in the mountain of thine inheritance, *in* the place, O LORD, *which* thou hast made for thee to dwell in, *in* the Sanctuary, O Lord, *which* thy hands have established.

18 The LORD shall reign for ever and ever.

19 For the horse of Pharaoh went in with his chariots and with his horsemen into the sea, and the LORD brought again the waters of the sea upon them; but the children of Israel went on dry *land* in the midst of the sea.

20 ¶ And Miriam the prophetess, the sister of Aaron, took a timbrel in her hand; and all the women went out after her with timbrels and with dances.

21 And Miriam answered them, Sing ye to the LORD, for he hath triumphed gloriously; the horse and his rider hath he thrown into the sea.

22 So Moses brought Israel from the Red sea, and they went out into the wilderness of Shur; and they went three days in the wilderness, and found no water.

What does "thy holy habitation" indicate? (15:13) "With the Egyptian menace finally eliminated, the movement of the poem shifts from the events that occurred at the sea and now focus on the march to the promised land" (Sarna, *Exodus*, 80). "The deliverance from Egypt and guidance through the Red Sea were a pledge to the redeemed people of their entrance into the promised land. The holy habitation of God was Canaan (Psalm 78:54), which had been consecrated as a sacred abode for Jehovah in the midst of His people by the revelations made to the patriarchs there, and especially by the appearance of God at Bethel (Genesis 28:16, Exodus 31:13; Exodus 35:7)" (Keil and Delitzsch, *Commentary* [on Exodus 15:13]).

What is "the mountain of thine inheritance"? (15:17) "The Song at the Sea closes with an affirmation of confidence in the promise that God's redemption of Israel from Egypt will culminate in the building of a Temple" (Sarna, *Exodus*, 81). "In twenty-five lines of verse, the poem moves through the whole story of the parting of the sea and the destruction of the Egyptians and onward (in a historical telescoping) through two and a half centuries involving the conquest of the Land and the establishment of the sanctuary in Jerusalem" (Alter, *Art of Biblical Poetry*, 50).

Exodus 15:20–22. Miriam Leads the Women in Praising God

What role did the song of Miriam play anciently? (15:20–21) "A recently published Dead Sea Scroll fragment suggests that in one tradition at least Miriam did indeed have her own song, which was different from the Song of the Sea, and that this tradition survived at least until the time of the Dead Sea Scrolls. (This particular manuscript is dated to about 75–50 B.C.E.) Moreover, this new text can best be appreciated as part of a genre of women's songs that not only celebrates God's victories, but in which God accomplishes this by a kind of reversal: The victory is brought about surprisingly through the weak and downtrodden; God's victory is shame for the proud, the arrogant and the mighty, and victory belongs to the powerless" (Brooke, "Power to the Powerless," 63).

Exodus 15:23–27. The Waters of Marah Are Made Sweet

What happens when people murmur? (15:23) President Jedediah M. Grant noted: "With Saints, what is the practical result of that murmuring? It shuts down the gate between you and heaven, between you and the Almighty, and you cannot get the Spirit of God. The murmurings and rebellions of ancient Israel prevented Moses from leading them to the land of Canaan. So soon as they had to endure hardship they began to murmur against Moses, and the result was the Lord would not give them His Spirit; the same has been the result in this dispensation" (in *Journal of Discourses*, 4:71–72).

What does *Marah* mean? (15:23) *Marah* is "'bitter' in Hebrew. The site has been plausibly identified with 'Ain Hawarah, a spring just south of Wadi 'Amarah, a name that probably gave rise to Marah as word play" (Sarna, *Exodus*, 84).

What can we learn from the tree cast into the waters? (15:25) "Jehovah made Himself known to the people of Israel as their Physician, and for this purpose appointed the wood for the healing of the bitter water, which threatened Israel with disease and death" (Keil and Delitzsch, *Commentary* [on Exodus 15:25–26]). "Many suppose that this tree which healed the bitter waters was symbolical of the cross of our blessed Redeemer, that has been the means of healing infected nature, and through the virtue of which the evils and bitters of life are sweetened" (*Adam Clarke's Commentary* [on Exodus 15:25]).

23 ¶ And when they came to Marah, they could not drink of the waters of Marah, for they *were* bitter: therefore the name of it was called Marah.

24 And the people murmured against Moses, saying, What shall we drink?

25 And he cried unto the LORD; and the LORD shewed him a tree, *which* when he had cast into the waters, the waters were made sweet: there he made for them a statute and an ordinance, and there he proved them,
26 And said, If thou wilt diligently hearken to the voice of the LORD thy God, and wilt do that which is right in his sight, and wilt give ear to his commandments, and keep all his statutes, I will put none of these diseases upon thee, which I have brought upon the Egyptians: for I *am* the LORD that healeth thee.
27 ¶ And they came to Elim, where *were* twelve wells of water, and threescore and ten palm trees: and they encamped there by the waters.

CHAPTER 16

Israel murmurs for want of bread and lusts for the fleshpots of Egypt—The Lord rains bread from heaven and sends quail for meat—Israel is given manna each day, except the Sabbath, for forty years.

1 And they took their journey from Elim, and all the congregation of the children of Israel came unto the wilderness of Sin, which *is* between Elim and Sinai, on the fifteenth day of the second month after their departing out of the land of Egypt.

2 And the whole congregation of the children of Israel murmured against Moses and Aaron in the wilderness:

3 And the children of Israel said unto them, Would to God we had died by the hand of the LORD in the land of Egypt, when we sat by the flesh pots, *and* when we did eat bread to the full; for ye have brought us forth into this wilderness, to kill this whole assembly with hunger.

4 ¶ Then said the LORD unto Moses, Behold, I will rain bread from heaven for you; and the people shall go out and gather a certain rate every day, that I may prove them, whether they will walk in my law, or no.

5 And it shall come to pass, that on the sixth day they shall prepare *that* which they bring in; and it shall be twice as much as they gather daily.

6 And Moses and Aaron said unto all the children of Israel, At even, then ye shall know that the LORD hath brought you out from the land of Egypt:

Exodus 16:1–8. The Lord Gives the Children of Israel Manna from Heaven

Why was the whole congregation engaged in murmuring? (16:2–3) "The phrase 'whole congregation' indicates that this was not the [behavior] of a few trouble makers but a wholesale rebellion that was brewing. . . . They moan that they would have been better off if the Lord had 'mercifully' wiped their nation out back in Egypt. . . . The reason they would have been better off dead in Egypt is that at least they would have been corpses with full bellies. Remarkably, they have the gall to accuse Aaron and Moses of having brought their nation *into this wilderness, to kill this whole assembly*" (*Zondervan KJV Commentary*, 113).

What were the "fleshpots" in Egypt? (16:3) "In Egypt, the children of Israel were slaves to the Egyptians, who gave them their food. Flesh pots were big metal kettles used to cook over fires (see *Tyndale New Bible Dictionary,* s.v. "Fleshpots," 380)" (Valletta, et al., *Old Testament for Latter-day Saint Families*, 127).

"The Hebrew [for fleshpots] indicates something like a cauldron in which meat is cooked, but the King James Version's rendering of 'fleshpots' ('flesh' of course meaning 'meat' in seventeenth-century English) has become proverbial in the language and deserves to be retained" (Alter, *Hebrew Bible*, 1:279).

What symbolism is there in the miraculous raining of bread from heaven? (16:4–6) "One of the most remarkable miracles described in the Old Testament is the manner in which the Lord preserved and fed the Israelites as they wandered in the wilderness. . . .

"Jesus reminded the Jews of something that had been lost from their collective doctrinal memory—that all must eat of the Bread of Life in order to find eternal life. He explicitly stated that manna was merely a symbol of something far greater than mere physical food. He further reminded them that Moses did not provide the miracle of manna, but rather the Father sent this bread from heaven to save them" (Top, *Peculiar Treasure*, 175). ⊕

Why is it important to not murmur against the Lord's servants? (16:8) "Is it easier in our own age to follow a living prophet than it was in the days of Moses or Nephi? Would those who murmured against Moses and Nephi not also murmur today? The same question can be asked in reverse. Those who murmur today would also have murmured as did Laman and Lemuel or the children of Israel against the prophet of their day with the same disastrous consequences" (Workman, "Beware of Murmuring," 86). The Lord's servants are His representatives: "For he that receiveth my servants receiveth me" (D&C 84:36), and "whether by mine own voice or by the voice of my servants, it is the same" (D&C 1:38). ⊕

Exodus 16:9–12. The Children of Israel See the Glory of the Lord

Why did the Lord use a "cloud" as a sign of his presence? (16:10) "They have complained to Moses and Aaron, but Moses reminds them that their real complaint is against God (vv. 7–8). He is the one they are distrusting and even mocking by their display of thanklessness. God responds again by giving the people another glimpse of his Exodus might. There, out in the desert, they see 'the glory of the LORD appearing in the cloud' (v. 10). The last time the Lord appeared in a cloud was in [Exodus]14:24 as they were making their way through the sea. The cloud was then a sign of God's presence with and protection of his people, just as it is now" (Enns, "Exodus," 2:325–26).

Exodus 16:13–15. The Lord Sends Quail in the Evenings and Manna in the Mornings

How did the Lord provide quail for the children of Israel? (16:13) "The Sinai is on the migratory route of quail. Quail do not fly well, so when they migrate they fly until exhaustion; when they land, they are unable to fly again for some time. Most likely the Lord had quail land in their exhausted state right next to Israel, where they would be able to gather the quail that could not escape them" (Muhlestein, *Scripture Study Made Simple*, 99). ⊕

7 And in the morning, then ye shall see the
glory of the LORD; for that he heareth your
murmurings against the LORD: and what *are*
we, that ye murmur against us?

8 And Moses said, *This shall be,* when the
LORD shall give you in the evening flesh to
eat, and in the morning bread to the full;
for that the LORD heareth your murmurings
which ye murmur against him: and what *are*
we? your murmurings *are* not against us, but
against the LORD.

9 ¶ And Moses spake unto Aaron, Say unto
all the congregation of the children of Israel,
Come near before the LORD: for he hath
heard your murmurings.

10 And it came to pass, as Aaron spake unto
the whole congregation of the children of
Israel, that they looked toward the wilderness, and, behold, the glory of the LORD appeared in the cloud.

11 ¶ And the LORD spake unto Moses, saying,

12 I have heard the murmurings of the children of Israel: speak unto them, saying, At
even ye shall eat flesh, and in the morning ye
shall be filled with bread; and ye shall know
that I *am* the LORD your God.

13 And it came to pass, that at even the quails
came up, and covered the camp: and in the
morning the dew lay round about the host.

14 And when the dew that lay was gone up,
behold, upon the face of the wilderness *there*
lay a small round thing, *as* small as the hoar
frost on the ground.

15 And when the children of Israel saw *it,* they said one to another, It *is* manna: for they wist not what it *was.* And Moses said unto them, This *is* the bread which the LORD hath given you to eat.

What was manna? (16:15) "Natural agricultural products do not match the scriptural description of manna. When the Israelites first saw the small scale-like substance, they turned to one another and said, *'Man hu,'* which translates as, 'What is it?' (see Ex. 16:31–35; Num. 11:7–9). Manna came with regularity to the wandering Israelites 'every morning, except Sabbath; was small, round like hoarfrost; must be gathered early before melting; was prepared by grinding and baking, and tasted like fresh oil, and like wafers made with honey, agreeable to all palates.' Manna came with regularity from heaven until corn was made available to the Israelites in Canaan" (Black, *400 Questions about the Old Testament,* 69).

Exodus 16:16–26. The Lord Gives the Children of Israel Rules for Gathering Manna

16 ¶ This *is* the thing which the LORD hath commanded, Gather of it every man according to his eating, an omer for every man, *according to* the number of your persons; take ye every man for *them* which *are* in his tents.

17 And the children of Israel did so, and gathered, some more, some less.

18 And when they did mete *it* with an omer, he that gathered much had nothing over, and he that gathered little had no lack; they gathered every man according to his eating.

19 And Moses said, Let no man leave of it till the morning.

20 Notwithstanding they hearkened not unto Moses; but some of them left of it until the morning, and it bred worms, and stank: and Moses was wroth with them.

What is an omer? (16:16) An *omer* is "a measure of capacity, being one-tenth of an ephah, i.e., about half a gallon (Ex. 16:22)" (Bible Dictionary, "Omer").

Israel Shall Know the Lord (Exodus 16:12)

"Undoubtedly, the Exodus constituted one of God's most memorable acts in Israel's behalf before the Atonement. Its display of sheer power and sublime affirmation of God's love represented the Lord's ability to rescue and sustain his people and also foreshadowed Christ's atonement. Prophets, leaders, and teachers both in Israel and in the Book of Mormon lands often referred to the Exodus to strengthen faith in God's ability to deliver his people not only physically but also, by the power of Christ's atonement, spiritually. Time and again, those lessons were repeated in varying degrees when subsequent generations of the Lord's people escaped persecution through faith in their almighty God" (Brown, "Exodus," 54).

What "manna" should we gather every day? (16:21) Just as the children of Israel gathered "manna" every morning for physical survival, it is vital for us to read the scriptures daily for spiritual survival. President Thomas S. Monson encouraged us to "participate in daily scripture study. Crash courses are not nearly so effective as the day-to-day reading and application of the scriptures in our lives. Become acquainted with the lessons the scriptures teach. Learn the background and setting of the Master's parables and the prophets' admonitions. Study them as though they were speaking to you, for such is the truth" ("Be Your Best Self," 68).

What is the significance of the use of the word "Sabbath" in this verse? (16:23) The Hebrew word for sabbath means to "cease, desist, [or] rest" (*Strong's Exhaustive Concordance*, word #h7673). While this is the first time the word appears in the Old Testament, the sabbath was previously "instituted to commemorate God's seventh day of rest at the Creation (Ex. 20:10–11), and also the redemption from Egyptian bondage (Deut. 5:15)" (Bible Dictionary, "Sabbath").

What other miracle happened with the manna on the Sabbath? (16:23–24) "The children of Israel were miraculously sustained in the wilderness for over forty years. . . . On the sixth day, prior to the Sabbath, twice as much manna fell as on the other days (see Ex. 16:5). The children of Israel were instructed by the Lord to gather twice as much so that it would last for two days because the manna did not fall on the Sabbath day. When they did this, a third miracle happened. On the Sabbath day the manna gathered the day before did not stink, and there were no worms in it, for it was preserved for Sabbath day use (see Ex. 16:24)" (Faust, "Lord's Day," 34).

21 And they gathered it every morning, every man according to his eating: and when the sun waxed hot, it melted.

22 ¶ And it came to pass, *that* on the sixth day they gathered twice as much bread, two omers for one *man:* and all the rulers of the congregation came and told Moses.

23 And he said unto them, This *is that* which the LORD hath said, To morrow *is* the rest of the holy sabbath unto the LORD: bake *that* which ye will bake *to day*, and seethe that ye will seethe; and that which remaineth over lay up for you to be kept until the morning.

24 And they laid it up till the morning, as Moses bade: and it did not stink, neither was there any worm therein.

Lessons to Be Learned by Gathering Manna (Exodus 16:16–26)

"Jehovah . . . gave Moses several strict rules for the people on how to gather and store the manna (see Ex. 16:13, 16, 19, 23). These commandments taught them important eternal truths:

1. They were to collect only one omer (about five pints) per person per day. Some gathered more, while others gathered less, but when they came to prepare and eat the manna, everyone had the same amount to eat (see Ex. 16:17–18). Jehovah knew what they needed, and He provided it for them.

2. If an Israelite tried to hoard extra manna, 'it bred worms, and stank' (Ex. 16:20). They needed to trust that Jehovah would provide.

3. The double portion of manna to be gathered the day before the Sabbath did not spoil. Thus, the manna was preserved in a way that enabled them to keep the Sabbath day holy (see Ex. 16:22–26).

4. Jehovah commanded Moses, 'Fill an omer of [manna] to be kept for your generations; that they may see the bread wherewith I have fed you in the wilderness' (Ex. 16:32). This pot of manna became a continual symbol of what Jehovah had done for His people" (Ferrel, "Lord Is among Us!" 34–35).

25 And Moses said, Eat that to day; for to
day *is* a sabbath unto the LORD: to day ye
shall not find it in the field.

26 Six days ye shall gather it; but on the
seventh day, *which is* the sabbath, in it there
shall be none.

How did Sabbath-day observance begin? (16:25–26) "God bestowed His gift in such a manner, that the Sabbath was sanctified by it. . . . It is perfectly clear from this event, that the Israelites were not acquainted with any sabbatical observance at that time, but that, whilst the way was practically opened, it was through the decalogue that it was raised into a legal institution (see [Exodus] 10:8ff). . . .

"On the seventh day some of the people went out to gather manna, notwithstanding Moses' command, but they found nothing. Whereupon God reproved their resistance to His commands, and ordered them to remain quietly at home on the seventh day" (Keil and Delitzsch, *Commentary* [on Exodus 16:22–31]).

Exodus 16:27–36. The Lord Gives the Children of Israel the Law of the Sabbath

27 ¶ And it came to pass, *that* there went out
some of the people on the seventh day for to
gather, and they found none.

28 And the LORD said unto Moses, How
long refuse ye to keep my commandments
and my laws?

29 See, for that the LORD hath given you the
sabbath, therefore he giveth you on the sixth
day the bread of two days; abide ye every
man in his place, let no man go out of his
place on the seventh day.

30 So the people rested on the seventh day.

How were the boundaries of "every man in his place" determined? (16:29) "This verse forms the basis of the 'Sabbath day's journey' which became the custom among Jewish people. The Bible Dictionary entry indicates 'the rabbis, by means of a forced and unnatural interpretation of Ex. 16:29, fixed this at 2,000 cubits, being the distance between the Ark and the people during the march in the wilderness (Josh. 3:4), and also according to tradition, the distance between the tabernacle and the furthest part of the camp.' A Sabbath day's journey is thus about 3,000 feet, or 1,000 yards" (Ludlow, *Companion to Your Study of the Old Testament*, 146–47).

31 And the house of Israel called the name
thereof Manna: and it *was* like coriander
seed, white; and the taste of it *was* like wafers
made with honey.

What was manna supposed to represent to the children of Israel? (16:31) "Jesus corrected [the Jews], asserting that 'Moses gave you not that bread from heaven; but my Father giveth you the true bread from heaven' ([John 6:32]). He then stated His preeminent point: 'The bread of God is he which cometh down from heaven, and giveth life unto the world' (v. 33). . . . The manna of Moses' time was a type of the true bread given of the Father, and that is none other than the Son. . . . To their request for this bread, Jesus unambiguously announced, 'I am the bread of life; he that cometh to me shall never hunger; and he that believeth on me shall never thirst' (v. 35)" (Valletta, "True Bread of Life," 11). ⊕

How did future generations of Jews remember what the Lord had done? (16:32–34) "It is clear from Jesus' bread of life discourse that manna was a type for him and his atoning sacrifice, just as the sacramental emblems of bread and water are a 'remembrance' of the same. There is also a significant Old Testament link between manna and the sacrament. Not only was a jar of manna kept in the sacred ark of the covenant as a reminder, but also loaves of shewbread and a flask of wine were kept in the temple to serve as types and symbols of the flesh and blood of Christ" (Top, *Peculiar Treasure*, 176). ⊕

Exodus 17:1–7. The Children of Israel Complain Because They Have No Water

Where was "the wilderness of Sin"? (17:1) "*Sin* here is a Hebrew word, not English, and is related to the name *Sinai*; the word probably refers to the series of valleys between the mountains southeastward from the coastal oasis Elim and inland to Rephidim and Sinai [see Bible Map 2]" (Rasmussen, *Latter-day Saint Commentary on the Old Testament*, 102).

32 ¶ And Moses said, This *is* the thing which the LORD commandeth, Fill an omer of it to be kept for your generations; that they may see the bread wherewith I have fed you in the wilderness, when I brought you forth from the land of Egypt.

33 And Moses said unto Aaron, Take a pot, and put an omer full of manna therein, and lay it up before the LORD, to be kept for your generations.

34 As the LORD commanded Moses, so Aaron laid it up before the Testimony, to be kept.

35 And the children of Israel did eat manna forty years, until they came to a land inhabited; they did eat manna, until they came unto the borders of the land of Canaan.

36 Now an omer *is* the tenth *part* of an ephah.

CHAPTER 17

Israel murmurs for want of water—Moses smites a rock in Horeb, and water gushes forth—Aaron and Hur uphold Moses' hands so that Joshua prevails against Amalek.

1 And all the congregation of the children of Israel journeyed from the wilderness of Sin, after their journeys, according to the commandment of the LORD, and pitched in Rephidim: and *there was* no water for the people to drink.

2 Wherefore the people did chide with Moses, and said, Give us water that we may drink. And Moses said unto them, Why chide ye with me? wherefore do ye tempt the LORD?

3 And the people thirsted there for water; and the people murmured against Moses, and said, Wherefore *is* this *that* thou hast brought us up out of Egypt, to kill us and our children and our cattle with thirst?

4 And Moses cried unto the LORD, saying, What shall I do unto this people? they be almost ready to stone me.

5 And the LORD said unto Moses, Go on before the people, and take with thee of the elders of Israel; and thy rod, wherewith thou smotest the river, take in thine hand, and go.

What has been the general reaction toward living prophets throughout history? (17:4) President George Q. Cannon spoke about prophets in ancient days: "Was there ever a prophet of God—a man who had a message from God who was received by the generation among whom he lived? They had very few indeed. . . . From Noah down one prophet after another was rejected by the generations unto whom they were sent and unto whom they bore messages from the Almighty. . . . Jesus was persecuted; Jesus was derided; Jesus was . . . rejected because he did not come according to the ideas, the preconceived notions of the people—that is of his own kindred unto whom he was sent" (Cannon, in *Journal of Discourses,* 22:177).

6 Behold, I will stand before thee there upon the rock in Horeb; and thou shalt smite the rock, and there shall come water out of it, that the people may drink. And Moses did so in the sight of the elders of Israel.

7 And he called the name of the place Massah, and Meribah, because of the chiding of the children of Israel, and because they tempted the LORD, saying, Is the LORD among us, or not?

How does the water coming forth from the rock symbolize Jesus Christ? (17:6) "Because of its durability, exchangeability, solidity, and strength, a rock is a perfect symbol of Christ. . . .

"The fact that God answered Israel's prayers through a rock has been seen as significant, not simply because the rock was a symbol of Christ, but also because of the unlikely source it was for water. In other words, if God had caused a desert spring to suddenly be discovered, such a resolve to their problem of thirst would be expected. But to use that which does not have water to produce water is a surprise" (Gaskill, *Miracles of the Old Testament,* 118–19). See also 1 Corinthians 10:4.

8 ¶ Then came Amalek, and fought with Israel in Rephidim.

Exodus 17:8–13. When Moses' Arms Are Raised, the Children of Israel Defeat the People of Amalek

9 And Moses said unto Joshua, Choose us out men, and go out, fight with Amalek: to morrow I will stand on the top of the hill with the rod of God in mine hand.

10 So Joshua did as Moses had said to him, and fought with Amalek: and Moses, Aaron, and Hur went up to the top of the hill.

11 And it came to pass, when Moses held up his hand, that Israel prevailed: and when he let down his hand, Amalek prevailed.

Who was Joshua? (17:9) See commentary in this volume for the introduction to the Book of Joshua.

What do we know about the identity of Hur? (17:10) "Multiple traditions suggest the identity of Miriam's husband, but no reliable source gives greater support to one theory than another. Josephus claims that Miriam married Hur, a trusted companion to Moses and Aaron and the leader who resolved conficts while Moses was receiving instruction on Mount Sinai (*Antiquities,* 3.2.4; Exodus 17:10, 12; 24:24)" (Olson, *Women of the Old Testament,* 100).

12 But Moses' hands *were* heavy; and they took a stone, and put *it* under him, and he

How are the prophet's hands supported and strengthened today? (17:12) "The wicked who now oppose the work of the Lord, while different from, are no less terrible than the plundering Amalekites. The sustaining of the prophet is still an essential ongoing part of the safety of this people. Should age and infirmity cause his hands to grow heavy, they are held up by his counselors at his side. Both are prophets, seers, and revelators, as is each member of the Quorum of the Twelve" (Packer, "Shield of Faith," 8). "Only as we keep our eyes upon the presidency of the Church will we be assured of victory. . . . We note the need for strong and able assistants to our leaders when they become weary from the burdens of leadership or their arms become heavy from advancing age" (Millet, "Call of Moses," 107).

Exodus 17:14–16. The Lord Tells Moses That the Time Will Come When the People of Amalek Will No Longer Be Remembered

Why did God command Moses to destroy the people of Amalek? (17:14) "The Amalekites may have been descendants of Esau (see Genesis 36:12, 16). They attacked the Israelites in a most cowardly way, killing first the feeble, the faint, and the weary at the rear of the marching nation (see Deuteronomy 25:17–19). For this lack of respect toward God, the Amalekites were cursed by the Lord. The Israelites were subsequently commanded to 'utterly put out the remembrance of Amalek from under heaven' (Exodus 17:14)" (*Old Testament Student Manual: Genesis–2 Samuel,* 123).

What does "Jehovah-nissi" mean? (17:15) "In some stages of Israel's history the battle will be one of words, a war of opinions, but there are also occasions enough when the battle will be one of cold steel. In either case Israel must take up her arms and fight. It must always be remembered that though Israel fights, the victory is the Lord's. Their dependence is always upon him. The name of Moses' altar, *Jehovah-nissi*, interpreted is 'the Lord my banner,' for it is under such that Israel must march" (McConkie, *Gospel Symbolism*, 58).

sat thereon; and Aaron and Hur stayed up his hands, the one on the one side, and the other on the other side; and his hands were steady until the going down of the sun.

13 And Joshua discomfited Amalek and his people with the edge of the sword.

14 And the LORD said unto Moses, Write this *for* a memorial in a book, and rehearse *it* in the ears of Joshua: for I will utterly put out the remembrance of Amalek from under heaven.

15 And Moses built an altar, and called the name of it Jehovah-nissi:

16 For he said, Because the LORD hath sworn *that* the LORD *will have* war with Amalek from generation to generation.

CHAPTER 18

Jethro comes to Moses bringing Moses' wife and sons and offers sacrifices to the Lord—Moses sits in the judgment seat and hears all cases—Jethro counsels Moses to teach the law, to appoint lesser judges, and to delegate power to them.

1 When Jethro, the priest of Midian, Moses' father in law, heard of all that God had done for Moses, and for Israel his people, *and* that the LORD had brought Israel out of Egypt;

2 Then Jethro, Moses' father in law, took Zipporah, Moses' wife, after he had sent her back,

3 And her two sons; of which the name of the one *was* Gershom; for he said, I have been an alien in a strange land:

4 And the name of the other *was* Eliezer; for the God of my father, *said he, was* mine help, and delivered me from the sword of Pharaoh:

5 And Jethro, Moses' father in law, came with his sons and his wife unto Moses into the wilderness, where he encamped at the mount of God:

6 And he said unto Moses, I thy father in law Jethro am come unto thee, and thy wife, and her two sons with her.

7 ¶ And Moses went out to meet his father in law, and did obeisance, and kissed him; and they asked each other of *their* welfare; and they came into the tent.

8 And Moses told his father in law all that the LORD had done unto Pharaoh and to the Egyptians for Israel's sake, *and* all the travail that had come upon them by the way, and *how* the LORD delivered them.

9 And Jethro rejoiced for all the goodness which the LORD had done to Israel, whom he had delivered out of the hand of the Egyptians.

10 And Jethro said, Blessed *be* the LORD, who hath delivered you out of the hand of the Egyptians, and out of the hand of Pharaoh, who hath delivered the people from under the hand of the Egyptians.

Exodus 18:1–12. Jethro Comes to Moses, and They Rejoice and Worship Together

Who was Jethro? (18:1) "Jethro is called the priest of Midian, which name implies that he had priestly duties at a shrine, a temple, or a mountain altar in the land of Midian. Jethro fills prominent roles as a father, priest, and mentor in the book of Exodus. As a father, Jethro becomes Moses' father-in-law after Moses marries one of Jethro's seven daughters. As a priest, Jethro descends from a long line of Melchizedek Priesthood holders and appears to have ministered over a desert region that included the mountain of God (Sinai)" (Rivera, "Jethro, Prophet and Priest of Midian," 22). "Joseph Smith changed Exodus 18:1 to read 'the *high* priest of Midian' (emphasis added), confirming what is recorded in Doctrine and Covenants 84:6–7, that Jethro held the Melchizedek Priesthood" (*Old Testament Student Manual: Genesis–2 Samuel,* 124). ⊕

Where was Jethro prior to coming to Moses in the wilderness? (18:6) "Moses . . . 'dwelt in the land of Midian' (Exodus 2:15), where he became acquainted with Jethro (Reuel), the priest of . . . Midian. Jethro was a descendant of Abraham through Keturah (Gen. 25:1–4). Moses married Jethro's daughter Zipporah, had two sons—Gershom and Eliezer, and settled in the area for the next forty years of his life (Ex. 2:16–22; 18:3; Acts 7:29–30). We suppose that it was in Midian that Moses began to be taught the true gospel and to be introduced to the teachings of the God of Abraham, Isaac, and Jacob, for we know also by modern revelation that Moses received the higher priesthood from Jethro (D&C 84:6)" (Millet, "Call of Moses," 97).

What did Israel believe about one God? (18:11) "Similar expressions about God being greater than other gods are found throughout the Old Testament. It is not clear whether these expressions mean that the people believed there were other gods but knew that Jehovah was the most true and most powerful God, or whether they knew He was the only God, and that this is just an idiomatic way of expressing this. The latter seems most likely, though it is possible that even many worshippers of Jehovah were influenced enough by the culture around them to believe that there was more than one god" (Muhlestein, *Scripture Study Made Simple*, 102).

What qualified Jethro to be offering up sacrifices to God? (18:12) "We have already seen that sacrifices were instituted by God himself as soon as sin entered into our world; and we see that they were continued and regularly practised among all the people who had the knowledge of the only true God, from that time until they became a legal establishment. Jethro, who was a *priest* ([Exodus 2:16]), had a right to offer these sacrifices; nor can there be a doubt of his being a worshipper of the true God" (*Adam Clarke's Commentary* [on Exodus 18:12]).

Exodus 18:13–27. Jethro Counsels Moses to Give Authority and Duties to Others

11 Now I know that the LORD *is* greater than all gods: for in the thing wherein they dealt proudly *he was* above them.

12 And Jethro, Moses' father in law, took a burnt offering and sacrifices for God: and Aaron came, and all the elders of Israel, to eat bread with Moses' father in law before God.

13 ¶ And it came to pass on the morrow, that Moses sat to judge the people: and the people stood by Moses from the morning unto the evening.

14 And when Moses' father in law saw all that he did to the people, he said, What *is* this thing that thou doest to the people? why sittest thou thyself alone, and all the people stand by thee from morning unto even?

15 And Moses said unto his father in law, Because the people come unto me to inquire of God:

16 When they have a matter, they come unto me; and I judge between one and another, and I do make *them* know the statutes of God, and his laws.

17 And Moses' father in law said unto him, The thing that thou doest *is* not good.

18 Thou wilt surely wear away, both thou, and this people that *is* with thee: for this thing *is* too heavy for thee; thou art not able to perform it thyself alone.

19 Hearken now unto my voice, I will give thee counsel, and God shall be with thee: Be thou for the people to God-ward, that thou mayest bring the causes unto God:

20 And thou shalt teach them ordinances and laws, and shalt shew them the way wherein they must walk, and the work that they must do.

What did Jethro teach Moses and how can it apply to us today? (18:20) "We often note how Jethro counseled Moses to delegate by appointing judges to handle the personal conflicts. But Jethro also gave Moses counsel that illustrates the importance of the personal line: 'Thou shalt teach them ordinances and laws, and shalt shew them the way wherein they must walk, and the work that *they* must do' ([Exodus18:20]; emphasis added)'

"In other words, Israelites who followed Moses should be taught not to bring every question to that priesthood leader [v.15]. They should understand the commandments and seek inspiration to work out most problems for themselves" (Oaks, "Two Lines of Communication," 85). ⊕

21 Moreover thou shalt provide out of all the people able men, such as fear God, men of truth, hating covetousness; and place *such* over them, *to be* rulers of thousands, *and* rulers of hundreds, rulers of fifties, and rulers of tens:

22 And let them judge the people at all seasons: and it shall be, *that* every great matter they shall bring unto thee, but every small matter they shall judge: so shall it be easier for thyself, and they shall bear *the burden* with thee.

How did Jethro's counsel bless Moses? (18:21–22) "Jethro made a valuable contribution to Moses in suggesting an organization of leaders over units of ten, fifty, one hundred and one thousand to instruct and to judge the people in all but the most difficult of matters, which would be passed up through the system of inferior and superior courts if necessary, until they reached Moses at the head" (Rasmussen, *Introduction to the Old Testament*, 1:82–83).

23 If thou shalt do this thing, and God command thee *so,* then thou shalt be able to endure, and all this people shall also go to their place in peace.

24 So Moses hearkened to the voice of his father in law, and did all that he had said.

25 And Moses chose able men out of all Israel, and made them heads over the people, rulers of thousands, rulers of hundreds, rulers of fifties, and rulers of tens.

26 And they judged the people at all seasons:
the hard causes they brought unto Moses,
but every small matter they judged themselves.

27 ¶ And Moses let his father in law depart;
and he went his way into his own land.

CHAPTER 19

The Lord covenants to make Israel a peculiar treasure, a kingdom of priests, and a holy nation—The people sanctify themselves—The Lord appears on Sinai amid fire, smoke, and earthquakes.

Exodus 19:1–6. The Children of Israel Go to Mount Sinai

What do we know about this mountain? (19:2) "This mountain is constantly called Sinai so long as Israel stayed there . . . and the place of their encampment by the mountain is also called the *'desert of Sinai.'* . . . But

1 In the third month, when the children
of Israel were gone forth out of the land of
Egypt, the same day came they *into* the wilderness of Sinai.

2 For they were departed from Rephidim,
and were come *to* the desert of Sinai, and had
pitched in the wilderness; and there Israel
camped before the mount.

Mount Sinai (Horeb) and the Sinai Wilderness

There are several possible sites for Mount Sinai. One of the traditional locations is Jebel Musa (Mountain of Moses), pictured here.

3 And Moses went up unto God, and the LORD called unto him out of the mountain, saying, Thus shalt thou say to the house of Jacob, and tell the children of Israel;

4 Ye have seen what I did unto the Egyptians, and *how* I bare you on eagles' wings, and brought you unto myself.

5 Now therefore, if ye will obey my voice indeed, and keep my covenant, then ye shall be a peculiar treasure unto me above all people: for all the earth *is* mine:

6 And ye shall be unto me a kingdom of priests, and an holy nation. These *are* the words which thou shalt speak unto the children of Israel.

7 ¶ And Moses came and called for the elders of the people, and laid before their faces all these words which the LORD commanded him.

8 And all the people answered together, and said, All that the LORD hath spoken we will do. And Moses returned the words of the people unto the LORD.

9 And the LORD said unto Moses, Lo, I come unto thee in a thick cloud, that the people

in Ex. 33:6 this spot is designated as 'Mount Horeb,'. . . And whilst the general identity of Sinai and Horeb may be inferred from this; the fact, that wherever the intention of the writer is to give a precise and geographical description of the place where the law was given, the name Sinai is employed, leads to the conclusion that the term Horeb was more general and comprehensive than that of Sinai; in other words, that Horeb was the range of which Sinai was one particular mountain" (Keil and Delitzsch, *Commentary* [on Exodus 19:1–2]).

Where can we worship or commune with God? (19:3) Elder Neal A. Maxwell stated: "We need not be atop high mountains or in sacred groves for God to be there. God is also there even in the mildest expressions of His presence. . . . In a hundred ways, Deity will always be there" ("Yet Thou Art There," 32).

How does being carried by eagle wings represent the Lord's caring for Israel? (19:4) "Although no one has succeeded in squaring this grand image with ornithological behavior, the soaring eagle's supremacy among birds is meant to suggest the majestic divine power that miraculously swept up the Hebrews and bore them off from the house of bondage. The metaphorical implication is that the Hebrews themselves are helpless fledglings, unable to fly on their own (compare Deuteronomy 32:11)" (Alter, *Hebrew Bible*, 1:291).

What does it mean to be a peculiar people? (19:5) "The great emphasis on Israel is that it's a holy people, set apart. The word *peculiar,* [segullah], 'treasure, possession,' is a word they use, which strongly resembles the Latin *sigillum* 'seal'—a sealed people: peculiar, treasured, set apart, reserved to me" (Nibley, *Eloquent Witness*, 170). ⊕

Exodus 19:7–15. Moses Prepares the Children of Israel to Enter the Lord's Presence

How can we accept and sustain prophetic counsel? (19:8) Sister Carol F. McConkie taught: "To be in harmony with heaven's divine purposes, we sustain the prophet and choose to live according to his words" ("Live according to the Words of the Prophets," 77; see also D&C 21:4–6).

President Russell M. Nelson asked: "How do we really sustain a prophet? Long before he became

President of the Church, President Joseph F. Smith explained, 'It is an important duty resting upon the Saints who . . . sustain the authorities of the Church, to do so not only by the lifting of the hand, the mere form, but in *deed* and in truth' [*Joseph F. Smith* (manual), 211]" ("Sustaining the Prophets," 74).

Why did the Lord command Moses to sanctify his people by having them wash their clothes? (19:10–11) "The cleansing of one's garments was ritually important in ancient Israel as a necessary preparation for appearing before God. . . .

"This washing was to prepare the people for meeting the Lord and becoming a 'kingdom of priests' (Exodus 19:5–11). As such, it was an initiation into a new relationship with the God of their fathers, who had rescued them from bondage in Egypt" (Tvedtnes, "Priestly Clothing in Bible Times," 687, 688).

Exodus 19:16–19. The Lord Descends upon Mount Sinai in Fire and Smoke

Why is the Lord oftentimes associated with fire? (19:18) "Flames are a manifestation of the godly or celestial nature of a thing. They represent holiness, illumination, inspiration, enlightenment, and purification" (Gaskill, *Lost Language of Symbolism*, 299). The Prophet

may hear when I speak with thee, and believe thee for ever. And Moses told the words of the people unto the LORD.

10 ¶ And the LORD said unto Moses, Go unto the people, and sanctify them to day and to morrow, and let them wash their clothes,

11 And be ready against the third day: for the third day the LORD will come down in the sight of all the people upon mount Sinai.

12 And thou shalt set bounds unto the people round about, saying, Take heed to yourselves, *that ye* go *not* up into the mount, or touch the border of it: whosoever toucheth the mount shall be surely put to death:

13 There shall not an hand touch it, but he shall surely be stoned, or shot through; whether *it be* beast or man, it shall not live: when the trumpet soundeth long, they shall come up to the mount.

14 ¶ And Moses went down from the mount unto the people, and sanctified the people; and they washed their clothes.

15 And he said unto the people, Be ready against the third day: come not at *your* wives.

16 ¶ And it came to pass on the third day in the morning, that there were thunders and lightnings, and a thick cloud upon the mount, and the voice of the trumpet exceeding loud; so that all the people that *was* in the camp trembled.

17 And Moses brought forth the people out of the camp to meet with God; and they stood at the nether part of the mount.

18 And mount Sinai was altogether on a smoke, because the LORD descended upon it in fire: and the smoke thereof ascended as the smoke of a furnace, and the whole mount quaked greatly.

19 And when the voice of the trumpet sounded long, and waxed louder and louder, Moses spake, and God answered him by a voice.

Joseph Smith said, "God Almighty himself dwells in Eternal fire, flesh and blood cannot go there for all corruption is devoured by the fire—Our God is a consuming fire" (Joseph Smith Papers, "Discourse, 12 May 1844, as Reported by Thomas Bullock," [2]). When the Father and the Son appeared to Joseph Smith, he described them as being "above the brightness of the sun" (JS–H 1:16). ⊕

20 And the LORD came down upon mount Sinai, on the top of the mount: and the LORD called Moses *up* to the top of the mount; and Moses went up.

21 And the LORD said unto Moses, Go down, charge the people, lest they break through unto the LORD to gaze, and many of them perish.

22 And let the priests also, which come near to the LORD, sanctify themselves, lest the LORD break forth upon them.

Exodus 19:20–25. The Lord Commands the People to Not Come Up to His Presence

Why are priests mentioned, when there was not a Levitical Priesthood established yet? (19:22) "What compounds the difficult nature of this passage is the reference to priests in verse 22. This is the first reference to Israelite priests in the Old Testament. Officially, the priesthood is not established until chapter 28. So, where do they come from? Do the Israelites have 'priests' in a looser sense of the word before they are officially established? Some commentators reconcile this difficulty by suggesting that the elders or young men function as priests at this stage. We should not dismiss this too quickly, especially in light of 24:5 (which has young men sacrificing). Still, nowhere are these men called *priests*, the term used here" (Enns, "Exodus," 2:393–94).

23 And Moses said unto the LORD, The people cannot come up to mount Sinai: for thou chargedst us, saying, Set bounds about the mount, and sanctify it.

Why was this mountain sanctified? (19:23) "The sanctity of the mountain of God is also to be seen in its tripartite division. . . . At the top of the mountain, where Moses is summoned, God himself is immediately present, just as he is in the Most Holy Place in the soon-to-be-built tabernacle. Aaron, Nadab, Abihu, and the elders have access to the mountain, but not to its summit, corresponding to the Holy Place in the tabernacle. The rest of the people stay at the foot of the mountain, corresponding to the outer court of the tabernacle and later the temple. It presumably anticipates the same divisions that are to be given to Moses in the design and building of the tabernacle that follows" (Kaiser, "Exodus," 1:476).

Why did the people want Moses to deliver the words of God to them? (19:24–25) "The Israelites spent two days cleansing themselves physically and spiritually prior to the manifestation of God to them on Mount Sinai. As a whole community, they heard the voice of the Lord as he delivered the Ten Commandments (see Deut. 4:33; 5:4, 24). This experience so humbled and terrified them that they requested that any future words from the Lord should come through Moses (see Ex. 20:18–22; Deut. 5:5, 23–33)" (Ludlow, *Unlocking the Old Testament*, 25). ⊕

24 And the LORD said unto him, Away, get thee down, and thou shalt come up, thou, and Aaron with thee: but let not the priests and the people break through to come up unto the LORD, lest he break forth upon them.

25 So Moses went down unto the people, and spake unto them.

CHAPTER 20

The Lord reveals the Ten Commandments—Israel is to bear witness that the Lord has spoken from heaven—The children of Israel are forbidden to make gods of silver or gold—They are to make altars of unhewn stones and sacrifice to the Lord thereon.

1 And God spake all these words, saying,

2 I *am* the LORD thy God, which have brought thee out of the land of Egypt, out of the house of bondage.

Exodus 20:1–11. The Lord Gives the First Four Commandments

How important are these words that God gave to Moses? (20:1) President Gordon B. Hinckley declared: "What Moses brought down from Mount Sinai were not *The Ten Suggestions*. . . .

"Think about that for a moment. What Moses brought down were Ten Commandments, written by the finger of Jehovah on tablets of stone for the salvation and safety, for the security and happiness of the children of Israel, and for all of the generations which were to come after them" ("Our Solemn Responsibilities," 51).

How are the first two commandments linked together? (20:3–6) "The first two commandments are essentially one. The Lord declared his identity as the One who freed them and forbade worship or acknowledgment of any other force, entity, or idea as a 'god.' The phrase 'before me' is used here to translate the Hebrew *al-panai* ('against my face'); it permits no other deity whatsoever—neither in addition to, subordinate to, nor in contrast to the only true and living God. Anything else that people 'worship' is forbidden in our time as urgently as it was in theirs ([Topical Guide], 'Idolatry, Idol')" (Rasmussen, *Latter-day Saint Commentary on the Old Testament,* 104).

3 Thou shalt have no other gods before me.

4 Thou shalt not make unto thee any graven image, or any likeness *of any thing* that *is* in heaven above, or that *is* in the earth beneath, or that *is* in the water under the earth:

What does it mean that God is a "jealous God"? (20:5) "The second of the Ten Commandments elaborates the direction to have no other gods and identifies what should be the ultimate priority in our

5 Thou shalt not bow down thyself to them, nor serve them: for I the LORD thy God *am* a jealous God, visiting the iniquity of the

fathers upon the children unto the third and fourth *generation* of them that hate me;

6 And shewing mercy unto thousands of them that love me, and keep my commandments.

lives as His children. . . . More than merely forbidding physical idols, this states a fundamental priority for all time. Jehovah explains, 'For I the Lord thy God am a jealous God, . . . shewing mercy unto . . . them that love me, and keep my commandments' (Exodus 20:5–6). The meaning of *jealous* is revealing. Its Hebrew origin means 'possessing sensitive and deep feelings' ([Exodus 20:5*b*]). Thus we offend God when we 'serve' other gods—when we have other first priorities" (Oaks, "No Other Gods," 72).

7 Thou shalt not take the name of the LORD thy God in vain; for the LORD will not hold him guiltless that taketh his name in vain.

What does taking the name of the Lord in vain mean? (20:7) "The third commandment forbids swearing, profaning, or invoking the names of God for any false or vain purpose. It may also be understood to forbid using a name of the true God as a name for anything else.

"Profanity is a common violation of this commandment. The prophets and Jesus admonished against it or any other inappropriate use of the divine names. . . .

"Furthermore, to make a covenant or promise in the name of the Lord and then break it is a way of taking his name in vain by our acts" (Rasmussen, *Latter-day Saint Commentary on the Old Testament,* 105). See D&C 63:61–62.

The Ten Commandments (Exodus 20:1–17)

President Spencer W. Kimball stated: "The commandments which the Lord gave to the children of Israel set minimum standards of conduct. . . .

"But living by the letter of the Ten Commandments is only the beginning of perfection. Jesus taught the sanctity of the Ten Commandments, but emphasized repeatedly that there was more.

"It is not enough to acknowledge the Lord as supreme and refrain from worshiping idols; we should love the Lord with all our heart, might, mind, and strength, realizing the great joy he has in the righteousness of his children.

"It is not enough to refrain from profanity or blasphemy. We need to make important in our lives the name of the Lord. . . .

"It is not enough to refrain from [leisure activities and] unnecessary labor on the Sabbath. Constructive use of the Sabbath day includes studying the scriptures, attending church meetings to learn and to worship, . . . comforting the sorrowing, visiting the sick, and, in general, doing what the Lord would have us do on this, his holy day.

"If we truly honor our parents as we are commanded to do, we will seek to emulate their best characteristics and to fulfill their highest aspirations for us. Nothing we could give them materially would be more prized than our righteous living.

"It is not enough to refrain from killing. We are rather under solemn obligation to respect life and to foster it. Far from taking a life, we must be generous in helping others to enjoy the necessities of life. . . .

"It is not enough to refrain from adultery. We need to make the marriage relationship sacred, to sacrifice and work to maintain the warmth and respect which we enjoyed during courtship. God intended marriage to be eternal, sealed by the power of the priesthood, to last beyond the grave. . . .

"'Thou shalt not steal,' the Lord said on Sinai (Ex. 20:15). Thus it is for us to be honest in every way. . . .

"Bearing false witness and coveting the belongings of others are further evidences of selfishness. 'Love thy neighbour as thyself,' Jesus taught. On this and on the love of God 'hang all the law and the prophets' (Matt. 22:39–40)" ("Hold Fast to the Iron Rod," 6).

What are some reasons the Lord has given for honoring the Sabbath? (20:8–11) "Timeless truths and principles of the gospel were and are important to people of ancient and modern Israel. The Sabbath day, for example, was honored for different reasons through the generations. From the time of Adam to Moses, the Sabbath was observed as a day of rest from the labor of creation (see Ex. 20:8–11; 31:16–17). From the time of Moses to the Resurrection of the Lord, the Sabbath also commemorated the liberation of the Israelites from their bondage in Egypt (see Deut. 5:12–15; Isa. 58:13; Ezek. 20:20; 44:24; Mosiah 13:19). In latter-days, Saints keep the Sabbath day holy in memory of the Atonement of Jesus Christ (see Acts 20:7; 1 Cor. 16:2; Rev. 1:10; D&C 59:9–19)" (Nelson, "Exodus Repeated," 10–11).

8 Remember the sabbath day, to keep it holy.

9 Six days shalt thou labour, and do all thy work:

10 But the seventh day *is* the sabbath of the LORD thy God: *in it* thou shalt not do any work, thou, nor thy son, nor thy daughter, thy manservant, nor thy maidservant, nor thy cattle, nor thy stranger that *is* within thy gates:

11 For *in* six days the LORD made heaven and earth, the sea, and all that in them *is*, and rested the seventh day: wherefore the LORD blessed the sabbath day, and hallowed it.

Exodus 20:12–17. The Lord Gives Six More Commandments to Israel

What is the specific promise that comes from honoring one's parents? (20:12) President Henry B. Eyring taught, "The Lord gave you a commandment with a promise: 'Honor thy father and thy mother, that thy days may be long upon the land which the Lord thy God giveth thee' [Exodus 20:12]. It is the only one of the Ten Commandments with a promise. You may not have parents that are living. In some cases, you may not feel that your parents are worthy of the honor and respect of their children. You may not even have ever known them. But you owe them life. And in every case, even if your life is not lengthened, its quality will be improved simply by remembering your parents with honor" ("Our Perfect Example," 72).

12 ¶ Honour thy father and thy mother: that thy days may be long upon the land which the LORD thy God giveth thee.

13 Thou shalt not kill.

14 Thou shalt not commit adultery.

15 Thou shalt not steal.

How does a person bear false witness? (20:16) Brother Robert J. Matthews taught that to bear false witness is "more than a prohibition against inventing falsehoods. The language of the commandment requires that an honest and straightforward answer be given whenever we are asked to share our knowledge of the truth" ("Thou Shalt Not Bear False Witness," 54).

16 Thou shalt not bear false witness against thy neighbour.

How does not coveting directly apply to many of the other Ten Commandments? (20:17) The Hebrew word for *covet* means to desire, or take pleasure in (see Exodus 20:17*a*). When we refuse to covet we keep ourselves from falling "into the traps of adultery or theft, for we will be free of the unrighteous desires that precede those sins. Thus, the commandment 'Thou shalt not covet' is intrinsically related to all of the other commandments" (Top, "Thou Shalt Not Covet," 22).

17 Thou shalt not covet thy neighbour's house, thou shalt not covet thy neighbour's wife, nor his manservant, nor his maidservant, nor his ox, nor his ass, nor any thing that *is* thy neighbour's.

18 ¶ And all the people saw the thunderings, and the lightnings, and the noise of the trumpet, and the mountain smoking: and when the people saw *it,* they removed, and stood afar off.

19 And they said unto Moses, Speak thou with us, and we will hear: but let not God speak with us, lest we die.

20 And Moses said unto the people, Fear not: for God is come to prove you, and that his fear may be before your faces, that ye sin not.

21 And the people stood afar off, and Moses drew near unto the thick darkness where God *was.*

Exodus 20:18–21. The Children of Israel See the Power of the Lord

Why did the children of Israel receive a lesser law? (20:19) "Israel still refused to see God, and Moses alone approached the divine presence. Joseph Smith teaches that this lack of faith was the great downfall of Israel: 'when God offers a blessing or knowledge to a man and he refuses to receive it, he will be damned. [Such is] the case of the Israelites praying that God would speak to Moses and not to them, in consequence of which he cursed them with a carnal law' (*Joseph Smith's Commentary on the Bible*, Kent P. Jackson, comp. and ed., 29)" (Muhlestein, *Scripture Study Made Simple*, 107). ⊕

22 ¶ And the Lord said unto Moses, Thus thou shalt say unto the children of Israel, Ye have seen that I have talked with you from heaven.

23 Ye shall not make with me gods of silver, neither shall ye make unto you gods of gold.

24 ¶ An altar of earth thou shalt make unto me, and shalt sacrifice thereon thy burnt offerings, and thy peace offerings, thy sheep, and thine oxen: in all places where I record my name I will come unto thee, and I will bless thee.

25 And if thou wilt make me an altar of stone, thou shalt not build it of hewn stone: for if thou lift up thy tool upon it, thou hast polluted it.

26 Neither shalt thou go up by steps unto mine altar, that thy nakedness be not discovered thereon.

Exodus 20:22–26. The Lord Commands Israel to Worship Him

How are these additional laws given to Moses different from the ten commandments? (20:22) "The people were already awestruck by spiritual experiences at the beginning of the great revelation at Mount Sinai . . . , and at the end they moved 'afar off,' overwhelmed by the voice of the Lord as he spoke the commandments (Ex. 20:22; Deut. 4:33–36; 5:2–5, 22–30). It was an unusual revelation for a great assembly of people, and Moses comforted them. He explained that God's purpose was to 'prove' them and to increase their reverence and their defense against sin (Ex. 20:20 and fn.). He again warned them against making any images of Him (Ex. 20:23*a*; Deut. 4:15–16)" (Rasmussen, *Latter-day Saint Commentary on the Old Testament*, 108). ⊕

How are burnt offerings and peace offerings different? (20:24) The Book of Mormon helps explain this difference. "When Lehi 'made an offering unto the Lord, and gave thanks' (1 Ne. 2:7; also 5:9; 7:22), he was sacrificing a peace offering which served as a thanksgiving for safety in travel, whether for oneself or for others. . . .

"When he offered 'burnt offerings unto the Lord' ([1 Ne.] 5:9; also 7:22), Lehi was bringing to the altar sacrifices that would atone for sin, sin that would stain the camp and those within it. . . . Here, Lehi sought to free his extended family from the taint of unworthiness so that he and they would be able to carry out the purposes of the Lord" (Brown, *From Jerusalem to Zarahemla*, 6).

Summary of Exodus 21

This chapter contains additional detailed instructions regarding the law of Moses, including judgments of servants' behavior, family and marriage relations, stealing of property, treatment of parents, and ownership of animals. Abinadi taught, "It was expedient that there should be a law given to the children of Israel, yea, even a very strict law; for they were a stiffnecked people, quick to do iniquity, and slow to remember the Lord their God; therefore there was a law given them, yea, a law of performances and of ordinances, a law which they were to observe strictly from day to day, to keep them in remembrance of God and their duty towards him" (Mosiah 13:29–30).

The principle of an "'eye for an eye,' was given [to Israel's] judges so that their judgments might be just, and so that retribution might be taken out of the hands of individuals" (Morton, "I Have a Question," 29). Paul taught that the Law was added because of transgressions and served as a schoolmaster to bring the people to Jesus Christ (see Galatians 3:19, 24). This chapter is part of what is known as "carnal commandments," which remained with Israel until the coming of John the Baptist (see D&C 84:27).

CHAPTER 21

The Lord reveals His laws pertaining to servants, marriage, the death penalty for various offenses, the giving of an eye for an eye and a tooth for a tooth, and the damage done by oxen.

The Law of Moses (Exodus 21)

"The law of Moses encompasses hundreds of laws, rules, and regulations. The Jews have identified 613 particular laws as recorded by Moses in the books of the Torah (or the Pentateuch: Genesis, Exodus, Leviticus, Numbers, and Deuteronomy). The Ten Commandments and other familiar laws are included in this body, but most of the laws are unfamiliar, and seem outdated and strange to contemporary Bible readers.

"Rather than trying to identify every single law, it is helpful to recognize that there are two major types of commandments within the law of Moses—eternal and temporary. . . .

"The temporary laws were given for a particular dispensation. However, similar laws or 'carnal commandments' were usually given to other dispensations to fulfill similar purposes. Sometimes these peculiar laws were to test the obedience of God's children, but they usually had symbolic, physical, and social values as well. Included among them would be the following types of laws:

1. Religious festivals and holy days. . . .
2. Elaborate system of special sacrifices and offerings. . . .
3. Particular ordinances, usually symbolic of ceremonial cleanliness. . . .
4. Dietary laws. . . .
5. Laws of purification or sanitation" (Ludlow, *Unlocking the Old Testament*, 27–28).

CHAPTER 22

The Lord reveals His laws pertaining to stealing, destructions by fire, care of the property of others, borrowing, lascivious acts, sacrifices to false gods, afflicting widows, usury, reviling God, and the firstborn of men and of animals—The men of Israel are commanded to be holy.

1 If a man shall steal an ox, or a sheep, and kill it, or sell it; he shall restore five oxen for an ox, and four sheep for a sheep.

2 ¶ If a thief be found breaking up, and be smitten that he die, *there shall* no blood *be shed* for him.

3 If the sun be risen upon him, *there shall be* blood *shed* for him; *for* he should make full restitution; if he have nothing, then he shall be sold for his theft.

4 If the theft be certainly found in his hand alive, whether it be ox, or ass, or sheep; he shall restore double.

5 ¶ If a man shall cause a field or vineyard to be eaten, and shall put in his beast, and shall feed in another man's field; of the best of his own field, and of the best of his own vineyard, shall he make restitution.

6 ¶ If fire break out, and catch in thorns, so that the stacks of corn, or the standing corn, or the field, be consumed *therewith;* he that kindled the fire shall surely make restitution.

7 ¶ If a man shall deliver unto his neighbour money or stuff to keep, and it be stolen out of the man's house; if the thief be found, let him pay double.

8 If the thief be not found, then the master of the house shall be brought unto the judges, *to see* whether he have put his hand unto his neighbour's goods.

9 For all manner of trespass, *whether it be* for ox, for ass, for sheep, for raiment, *or* for any manner of lost thing, which *another*

Exodus 22:1–15. The Book of the Covenant Continues with Laws Regarding Property Rights

Why was restitution vital for satisfying a broken law? (22:4) "The idea [of restitution] is one of restoring a violated relationship by a compensatory payment. Restitution is one of the most significant concepts in [Old Testament] criminal law. The person who steals or misappropriates another's property is directly responsible to his victim. [Old Testament] law directed the criminal to repay double. His own property or labor is demanded as recompense for the harm he did to his neighbor.

"This principle is very different from that embedded in our criminal law. In our system of justice a criminal is responsible to society, not to his victim.... The [Old Testament] system is undoubtedly superior, both in its concern for the victim and in its holding the criminal responsible for his or her acts" (Richards, *Zondervan Expository Dictionary of Bible Words*, 526). ⊕

Who were the judges that were to hear these disputes? (22:8–9) In the King James Version, this passage reads *judges* where the Hebrew reads *Elohim*, or Gods. It can be inferred that these judges were to make decisions under the direction and power of God (see Rushdoony, *Institutes of Biblical Law*, 1:197).

Jethro counseled Moses to share the responsibility of judging various matters (see Ex. 18:13–16). "Rulers" or judges were to be appointed over "thousands, and rulers of hundreds, rulers of fifties, and rulers of tens" (Ex. 18:21). R. J. Rushdoony suggested that "Since the basic governmental structure of Israel was by families (and hence by tribes of families), it is safe to conclude that the tens refers to ten families. For each ten families, one judge was appointed to deal with minor matters and to refer other cases to a higher jurisdiction" (*Institutes of Biblical Law*, 1:624). See commentary in this volume for Exodus 18:21–22.

Exodus 22:16–24. Rules of Conduct Are Set Forth

How did the law help to protect young women from crimes of passion? (22:16–17) "This was an exceedingly wise and humane law, and must have operated powerfully against seduction and fornication; because the person who might feel inclined to take the advantage of a young woman knew that he must marry her, and give her a dowry, if her parents consented; and if they did not consent . . . he was obliged to give her the full dowry which could have been demanded had she been still a virgin. . . . This one consideration was a powerful curb on disorderly passions, and must tend greatly to render marriages respectable, and prevent all crimes of this nature" (*Adam Clarke's Commentary* [on Exodus 22]). ⊕

How does the Joseph Smith Translation clarify this reference to witches? (22:18) In this case, the Joseph Smith Translation changes "witch" to "murderer" so that the text should read, "Thou shalt not suffer a

challengeth to be his, the cause of both parties shall come before the judges; *and* whom the judges shall condemn, he shall pay double unto his neighbour.

10 If a man deliver unto his neighbour an
ass, or an ox, or a sheep, or any beast, to
keep; and it die, or be hurt, or driven away,
no man seeing *it:*

11 *Then* shall an oath of the LORD be between them both, that he hath not put his
hand unto his neighbour's goods; and the
owner of it shall accept *thereof,* and he shall
not make *it* good.

12 And if it be stolen from him, he shall
make restitution unto the owner thereof.

13 If it be torn in pieces, *then* let him bring it
for witness, *and* he shall not make good that
which was torn.

14 ¶ And if a man borrow *ought* of his
neighbour, and it be hurt, or die, the owner
thereof *being* not with it, he shall surely make
it good.

15 *But* if the owner thereof *be* with it, he
shall not make *it* good: if it *be* an hired *thing,*
it came for his hire.

16 ¶ And if a man entice a maid that is not
betrothed, and lie with her, he shall surely
endow her to be his wife.

17 If her father utterly refuse to give her unto
him, he shall pay money according to the
dowry of virgins.

18 ¶ Thou shalt not suffer a witch to live.

19 ¶ Whosoever lieth with a beast shall surely
be put to death.

20 ¶ He that sacrificeth unto *any* god, save unto the LORD only, he shall be utterly destroyed.

21 ¶ Thou shalt neither vex a stranger, nor oppress him: for ye were strangers in the land of Egypt.

22 ¶ Ye shall not afflict any widow, or fatherless child.

23 If thou afflict them in any wise, and they cry at all unto me, I will surely hear their cry;

24 And my wrath shall wax hot, and I will kill you with the sword; and your wives shall be widows, and your children fatherless.

25 ¶ If thou lend money to *any of* my people *that is* poor by thee, thou shalt not be to him as an usurer, neither shalt thou lay upon him usury.

26 If thou at all take thy neighbour's raiment to pledge, thou shalt deliver it unto him by that the sun goeth down:

27 For that *is* his covering only, it *is* his raiment for his skin: wherein shall he sleep? and it shall come to pass, when he crieth unto me, that I will hear; for I *am* gracious.

28 ¶ Thou shalt not revile the gods, nor curse the ruler of thy people.

29 ¶ Thou shalt not delay *to offer* the first of thy ripe fruits, and of thy liquors: the firstborn of thy sons shalt thou give unto me.

30 Likewise shalt thou do with thine oxen, *and* with thy sheep: seven days it shall be with his dam; on the eighth day thou shalt give it me.

31 ¶ And ye shall be holy men unto me: neither shall ye eat *any* flesh *that is* torn of beasts in the field; ye shall cast it to the dogs.

murderer to live" (JST, Exodus 22:18; emphasis added). In other Old Testament passages, the children of Israel were forbidden from pursuing abominable practices and evil vocations such as witches, charmers, and necromancers (see Deuteronomy 18:9–12; Leviticus 20:27).

Why is it important to care for strangers, widows, and orphans? (22:21–24) "Pure religion and undefiled before God and the Father is this, to visit the fatherless and widows in their affliction, and to keep himself unspotted from the world" (James 1:27). "The injunction to protect the 'alien' [stranger] is always based on the remembrance of the exodus and the alien status of the Israelites before they settled in Palestine (see Deut. 24:17–22). . . . Orphans, [strangers], and widows formed the three classes of powerless persons in ancient society. God took special care of these people because of their basic vulnerability, requiring that they not be oppressed and cursing those who did oppress with the threat of becoming orphans themselves" (Walton, et al., *IVP Bible Background Commentary*, 101). ⊕

Exodus 22:25–31. The Law Continues with Other Regulations

Why would it be important to promptly offer the "first" of what we have to the Lord? (22:29) Elder Carl B. Pratt said: "[The Lord] expects us to pay tithing not from our abundance nor from the 'leftovers' of the family budget but, as He commanded anciently, from the 'firstlings' of our income, be it scarce or abounding. The Lord has commanded, 'Thou shalt not delay to offer the first . . . fruits' (Exodus 22:29). It has been my personal experience that the surest way to pay tithing faithfully is to pay it as soon as I receive any income. In fact, I've found it to be the only way. . . . Let us show our faith in the Lord by paying our tithing. Pay it first; pay it honestly" ("Lord's Richest Blessings," 102).

CHAPTER 23

The Lord reveals His laws pertaining to integrity and godly conduct—The land is to rest during a sabbatical year—The children of Israel are to keep three annual feasts—An angel, bearing the Lord's name, will guide them—Sickness will be removed—The nations of Canaan will be driven out gradually.

1 Thou shalt not raise a false report: put not thine hand with the wicked to be an unrighteous witness.

2 ¶ Thou shalt not follow a multitude to *do* evil; neither shalt thou speak in a cause to decline after many to wrest *judgment:*

3 ¶ Neither shalt thou countenance a poor man in his cause.

4 ¶ If thou meet thine enemy's ox or his ass going astray, thou shalt surely bring it back to him again.

5 If thou see the ass of him that hateth thee lying under his burden, and wouldest forbear to help him, thou shalt surely help with him.

6 Thou shalt not wrest the judgment of thy poor in his cause.

7 Keep thee far from a false matter; and the innocent and righteous slay thou not: for I will not justify the wicked.

8 ¶ And thou shalt take no gift: for the gift blindeth the wise, and perverteth the words of the righteous.

9 ¶ Also thou shalt not oppress a stranger: for ye know the heart of a stranger, seeing ye were strangers in the land of Egypt.

Exodus 23:1–9. Rules of Conduct in the Book of the Covenant Are Continued

Which of the poor shouldn't receive preferential treatment? (23:3) The Joseph Smith Translation changes "poor" to "wicked" so that the text should read, "Neither shalt thou countenance a *wicked* man in his cause" (JST, Exodus 23:3; emphasis added). The footnote for this passage suggests "countenance" can also be rendered as "favor" (Exodus 23:3*a*).

Why is it essential for each of us to serve others, even those who hate us? (23:5) "Service changes people. It refines, purifies, gives a finer perspective, and brings out the best in each one of us. It gets us looking outward instead of inward. It prompts us to consider others' needs ahead of our own. Righteous service is the expression of true charity, such as the Savior showed" (Cuthbert, "Spirituality of Service," 12).

What did the law demand of judges? (23:6–9) "These verses concern legal justice. . . . A judge was not to withhold justice from the *poor* (v. 6). Perversions of justice were to be avoided. Taking a bribe was forbidden. The resident sojourner in the land was not to be deprived of justice, since the Hebrews *were strangers in . . . Egypt* (v. 9)" (*Zondervan KJV Commentary*, 123).

What is the danger of taking a gift or bribe? (23:8) "All gifts come from God and are freely given. It is a risky business when men start dealing in gifts—the careful reckoning of who gives what and how much, and who gets what and how much from whom, leads to dangerous complications and bloodshed in the gift-giving of heroic literature or the legends of the gods—the gifts always lead to trouble. . . . Whenever

10 And six years thou shalt sow thy land, and shalt gather in the fruits thereof:

11 But the seventh *year* thou shalt let it rest and lie still; that the poor of thy people may eat: and what they leave the beasts of the field shall eat. In like manner thou shalt deal with thy vineyard, *and* with thy oliveyard.

12 Six days thou shalt do thy work, and on the seventh day thou shalt rest: that thine ox and thine ass may rest, and the son of thy handmaid, and the stranger, may be refreshed.

13 And in all *things* that I have said unto you be circumspect: and make no mention of the name of other gods, neither let it be heard out of thy mouth.

14 ¶ Three times thou shalt keep a feast unto me in the year.

15 Thou shalt keep the feast of unleavened bread: (thou shalt eat unleavened bread seven days, as I commanded thee, in the time appointed of the month Abib; for in it thou camest out from Egypt: and none shall appear before me empty:)

16 And the feast of harvest, the firstfruits of thy labours, which thou hast sown in the

we accept a gift from another we are under obligation to him" (Nibley, *Approaching Zion*, 139).

Exodus 23:10–19. Laws Concerning Religious Observance

How could the people eat if they were not to harvest their crops in the seventh year? (23:10–11) "The key to resolving this seeming contradiction is to recognize the difference between harvesting and living off the land. Harvesting was for trade and profit; taking just enough to live on was more like subsistence farming—relying on crops that sprouted on their own. During the sabbath year, landowners could take no more than the poor who typically lived off the land" (*Quest Study Bible* [2003], 179). "Sabbatical years of 'rest' for the land allowed it to lie fallow to renew itself even as it provided food for the poor, who could harvest volunteer crops that grew" (Rasmussen, *Latter-day Saint Commentary on the Old Testament*, 110). ⊕

What Three Feasts Were Adult Males Required to Attend Each Year? (Exodus 23:14–17)

"*Three times . . . in the year* (v. 14), every Hebrew adult male was required to appear before God at Israel's central location of worship, originally the tabernacle and later on, the temple. The first of these three pilgrimage festivals was *the feast of unleavened bread* (which as used here is inclusive of the day of Passover; v. 15). The people were not to come empty-handed *before* the Lord but rather bearing the Passover sacrifice. The second pilgrimage feast was *the feast of harvest* (v. 16), held seven weeks after Passover. Also known as Shabuoth, this feast is called the 'feast of weeks' in 34:22 and was called Pentecost in New Testament times. On this occasion, Israel was to come before the Lord with the first-fruits of the wheat harvest, baked into special loaves. The third pilgrimage festival was the eight-day *feast of ingathering* (also called the Feast of Booths and the Feast of Tabernacles), held every autumn. Israel was to appear before the Lord with the abundance of their crops at the climax of the year's agricultural cycle" (*Zondervan KJV Commentary*, 123).

Why was leavened bread prohibited to be used with blood sacrifice? (23:18) "Yeast and leavened dough were strictly prohibited from use in animal sacrifice. This is based on the association of yeast with the process of corruption. Sacrificial blood, associated with life, might therefore be debased or corrupted if brought into contact with leaven" (Walton, et al., *IVP Bible Background Commentary*, 103).

What does it mean to "seethe a kid in his mother's milk"? (23:19) This scripture passage became the basis for the requirement in rabbinic dietary regulations to keep meat and dairy foods separate. "The commandment 'Thou shalt not seethe a kid in his mother's milk' warns the Israelites not to participate in the practice of fertility cults of boiling (seething) baby goats (kids) in the . . . milk of the mother goat. This practice had evidently been adopted by fertility cultists in the false belief such food would make them more desirous of sensual pleasures" (Ludlow, *Companion to Your Study of the Old Testament*, 153–54). ⊕

Exodus 23:20–33. Epilogue of the Book of the Covenant

Who was the angel to be sent before Israel? (23:20–22) "Assurance is given . . . of the personal presence of Jehovah in that ANGEL, in Whom is the Name of the Lord (ver. 20). This was no common angel, . . . but a manifestation of Jehovah Himself, prefigurative of, and preparatory to His manifestation in the flesh in the Person of our Lord and Saviour Jesus Christ. For all that is here said of Him is attributed to the Lord Himself in Exodus 13:21. . . . Accordingly, all obedience is to be shown to His guidance, and every contact with idolatry and idolaters avoided. In that case the Lord would fulfill every good and gracious promise to His people, and cause them to possess the land in all its extent" (Edersheim, *Bible History*, 2:211).

field: and the feast of ingathering, *which is* in the end of the year, when thou hast gathered in thy labours out of the field.

17 Three times in the year all thy males shall appear before the Lord God.

18 Thou shalt not offer the blood of my sacrifice with leavened bread; neither shall the fat of my sacrifice remain until the morning.

19 The first of the firstfruits of thy land thou shalt bring into the house of the LORD thy God. Thou shalt not seethe a kid in his mother's milk.

20 ¶ Behold, I send an Angel before thee, to keep thee in the way, and to bring thee into the place which I have prepared.

21 Beware of him, and obey his voice, provoke him not; for he will not pardon your transgressions: for my name *is* in him.

22 But if thou shalt indeed obey his voice, and do all that I speak; then I will be an enemy unto thine enemies, and an adversary unto thine adversaries.

23 For mine Angel shall go before thee, and bring thee in unto the Amorites, and the Hittites, and the Perizzites, and the Canaanites, the Hivites, and the Jebusites: and I will cut them off.

24 Thou shalt not bow down to their gods, nor serve them, nor do after their works: but thou shalt utterly overthrow them, and quite break down their images.

25 And ye shall serve the LORD your God, and he shall bless thy bread, and thy water; and I will take sickness away from the midst of thee.

26 ¶ There shall nothing cast their young, nor be barren, in thy land: the number of thy days I will fulfil.

27 I will send my fear before thee, and will destroy all the people to whom thou shalt come, and I will make all thine enemies turn their backs unto thee.

28 And I will send hornets before thee, which shall drive out the Hivite, the Canaanite, and the Hittite, from before thee.

29 I will not drive them out from before thee in one year; lest the land become desolate, and the beast of the field multiply against thee.

30 By little and little I will drive them out from before thee, until thou be increased, and inherit the land.

31 And I will set thy bounds from the Red sea even unto the sea of the Philistines, and from the desert unto the river: for I will deliver the inhabitants of the land into your hand; and thou shalt drive them out before thee.

32 Thou shalt make no covenant with them, nor with their gods.

33 They shall not dwell in thy land, lest they make thee sin against me: for if thou serve their gods, it will surely be a snare unto thee.

What did God promise to do on behalf of Israel? (23:27–31) "In a breath-taking crescendo of 'I wills,' God promised that He Himself would be responsible for the expulsion of *the Canaanites* (v. 28) from the Promised Land. He would be like a swarm of *hornets* from which *the Canaanites* would eventually flee. God would not *drive* (v. 29) the land's inhabitants *out* all at once, or even within *one year*, but in gradual stages, little by little, to prevent the land's desolation and its becoming overrun by wild animals. As the Israelites' presence in the land increased, the Canaanites would proportionately decrease until the Hebrews enjoyed their entire geographic inheritance" (*Zondervan KJV Commentary*, 124).

Exodus 24:1–11. Moses Binds the Children of Israel to the Covenant They Made with the Lord

Who accompanied Moses to Mt. Sinai? (24:1–2) Aaron was Moses' older brother. "Nadab and Abihu, Aaron's two eldest sons, would have been the next high priests in the line. They died, however, under God's judgment (Nu 3:4) because of their perverse deed (Lev 10:1–2; Nu 3:4). The official 'seventy elders' of Nu 11:16 had not been formally appointed yet. They were selected here to represent the twelve tribes, perhaps representing Jacob's seventy descendants. [In verse 2] Moses alone was to function as the mediator between God and the Israelites, just as Christ is designated the second Moses in Heb 3:1–6 and thus is the Mediator of the new covenant (Heb 12:24)" (*Expositor's Bible Commentary [Abridged]*, 108).

Why did Moses rehearse "all the words of the Lord" to the people? (24:3–11) "The ceremony described in . . . 24:3–11 is called 'the covenant which Jehovah made with Israel' [v. 8]. It was opened by Moses, who recited to the people '*all the words of Jehovah*' (i.e., not the decalogue, for the people had heard this directly from the mouth of God Himself, but the words in Exodus 20:22–26), and '*all the rights*' ([Exodus] 21–23); whereupon the people answered unanimously . . . '*All the words which Jehovah hath spoken will we do.*' This constituted the preparation for the conclusion of the covenant. . . . The covenant itself was commenced by Moses writing all the words of Jehovah . . . for the purpose of preserving them in an official record" (Keil and Delitzsch, *Commentary* [on Exodus 24:3–4]).

What did the altar and the twelve pillars represent? (24:4) "The altar represents [Jehovah], and the pillars represent the twelve tribes of Israel. The pillars, or standing stones, also serve as a witness to or a memorial of the covenant" (Hardison, "Theophany on Sinai," 225).

What was the "book of the covenant" Moses read to the audience? (24:7) The "book of the covenant" was possibly the instructions and judgments recorded by Moses in Exodus 20:22–23:33 (see also Exodus 24:3–4). "The so-called lost books of the Bible are those documents that are mentioned in the Bible in

CHAPTER 24

Israel accepts the word of the Lord by covenant—Moses sprinkles the blood of the covenant—He, Aaron, Nadab, Abihu, and seventy of the elders of Israel see God—The Lord calls Moses on to the mount to receive the tables of stone and commandments.

1 And he said unto Moses, Come up unto the LORD, thou, and Aaron, Nadab, and Abihu, and seventy of the elders of Israel; and worship ye afar off.

2 And Moses alone shall come near the LORD: but they shall not come nigh; neither shall the people go up with him.

3 ¶ And Moses came and told the people all the words of the LORD, and all the judgments: and all the people answered with one voice, and said, All the words which the LORD hath said will we do.

4 And Moses wrote all the words of the LORD, and rose up early in the morning, and builded an altar under the hill, and twelve pillars, according to the twelve tribes of Israel.

5 And he sent young men of the children of Israel, which offered burnt offerings, and sacrificed peace offerings of oxen unto the LORD.

6 And Moses took half of the blood, and put *it* in basins; and half of the blood he sprinkled on the altar.

7 And he took the book of the covenant, and read in the audience of the people: and they said, All that the LORD hath said will we do, and be obedient.

8 And Moses took the blood, and sprinkled *it* on the people, and said, Behold the blood of the covenant, which the LORD hath made with you concerning all these words.

9 ¶ Then went up Moses, and Aaron, Nadab, and Abihu, and seventy of the elders of Israel:

10 And they saw the God of Israel: and *there was* under his feet as it were a paved work of a sapphire stone, and as it were the body of heaven in *his* clearness.

such a way that it is evident they were considered authentic and valuable but that are not found in the Bible today. . . . To [the] rather clear references to inspired writings other than our current Bible may be added another list that has allusions to writings that may or may not be contained within our present text but may perhaps be known by a different title; for example, the book of the covenant (Ex. 24:7), which may or may not be included in the current book of Exodus" (Bible Dictionary, "Lost Books").

Why did Moses sprinkle the sacrificial blood on the people? (24:8) "This act symbolically bound the nation to the stipulations of the covenant, as it was now the most solemn of covenants, a covenant ratified by blood. The Mosaic covenant's successor and replacement, the new covenant, would later be ratified by the Messiah's superior blood (Matt. 26:28; Luke 22:20)" (*Zondervan KJV Commentary*, 124–25). ⊕

Why were these additional witnesses of Jehovah so important? (24:9–10) "Jehovah appeared to 'Moses, and Aaron, [and Aaron's sons] Nadab, and Abihu, and seventy of the elders of Israel [after they had gone partway up Mount Sinai]: And they saw the God of Israel' . . . (Exod 24:9–10). All Israelites had earlier heard the voice of God revealing the Ten Commandments (Exod 20). Moses had then received further revelation (Exod 21–23). The people had accepted the covenant opportunity offered by Jehovah (Exod 24). Now these seventy-four leaders became special witnesses of Jehovah's existence, his personal nature, and his holiness. Such a manifestation to so many is not recorded elsewhere in the Old Testament" (Holzapfel, et al., *Jehovah and the World of the Old Testament*, 99). ⊕

What does the phrase "the body of heaven in his clearness" indicate? (24:10) The footnote for this passage suggests that the appearance of the God of Israel was "clear as the very heavens" (Exodus 24:10*c*). The Book of Mormon describes such an appearance:

What Is the Book of the Covenant Referred to in Exodus? (Exodus 24:7)

The text in Exodus 20:22–23:33 may be the "book of the covenant" referred to in Exodus 24:7. It is also possible that this passage alludes to a lost manuscript known as the "book of the covenant" (see Bible Dictionary, "Lost Books").

"These few chapters outline how God expected Israel to act as part of the covenant. . . . God states that the blessings of the covenant are contingent on Israel keeping the statutes, judgments, and commandments He had given Israel. . . . Moses first took the Covenant Code (or Book of the Covenant) and presented it to all Israel. His job was to get all Israel to enter into this covenant" (Muhlestein, *Scripture Study Made Simple*, 108–9).

"Behold, the Lord showed himself unto [the brother of Jared], and said: . . .

"Behold, I am he who was prepared from the foundation of the world to redeem my people. Behold, I am Jesus Christ. . . .

"Behold, this body, which ye now behold, is the body of my spirit; and man have I created after the body of my spirit; and even as I appear unto thee to be in the spirit will I appear unto my people in the flesh" (Ether 3:13–14, 16).

How was eating and drinking a part of the covenant ceremony? (24:11) "The covenant meal was the one instance, in many cases, in which common people could be present and actually partake of the blessings of renewal that the temple ceremonies promised. In the context of Exodus 24, we have a people, formerly unsanctified (Exodus 19) and unqualified to enter the presence of deity, now ritually sanctified and covenanted on the basis of the revealed law and permitted to attend a sacral meal in the deity's presence" (Lundquist, "Temple, Covenant, and Law," 289).

11 And upon the nobles of the children of Israel he laid not his hand: also they saw God, and did eat and drink.

Exodus 24:12–18. Moses Receives the Tablets of Stone Containing the Law of God

12 ¶ And the LORD said unto Moses, Come up to me into the mount, and be there: and I will give thee tables of stone, and a law, and commandments which I have written; that thou mayest teach them.

13 And Moses rose up, and his minister Joshua: and Moses went up into the mount of God.

14 And he said unto the elders, Tarry ye here for us, until we come again unto you: and, behold, Aaron and Hur *are* with you: if any man have any matters to do, let him come unto them.

15 And Moses went up into the mount, and a cloud covered the mount.

16 And the glory of the LORD abode upon mount Sinai, and the cloud covered it six days: and the seventh day he called unto Moses out of the midst of the cloud.

How does "fire" represent the "glory of the Lord"? (24:17) Fire is "a symbol of the presence of the Lord. God dwells in 'everlasting burnings.' . . . Fire represents divine power, glory and holiness" (McConkie, *Gospel Symbolism*, 259).

17 And the sight of the glory of the LORD *was* like devouring fire on the top of the mount in the eyes of the children of Israel.

18 And Moses went into the midst of the cloud, and gat him up into the mount: and Moses was in the mount forty days and forty nights.

What does "forty days and forty nights" represent? (24:18) "In scripture, the number represents a period of trial, testing, probation, or mourning. . . . Moses was on Mount Sinai forty days while the children of Israel were being tested by Jehovah. They failed miserably because, lacking faith in the true God, they chose to create the golden calf as an image of their god (see Exodus 24:18). After the episode with the idol, Moses again went up upon the mount for an additional forty days (see Deuteronomy 9:18, 25)" (Gaskill, *Lost Language of Symbolism*, 137, 138).

CHAPTER 25

Israel is commanded to donate property and build a tabernacle, the ark of testimony (with the mercy seat and cherubims), a table (for the shewbread), and the candlestick, all according to patterns shown to Moses on the mount.

1 And the LORD spake unto Moses, saying,

2 Speak unto the children of Israel, that they bring me an offering: of every man that giveth it willingly with his heart ye shall take my offering.

3 And this *is* the offering which ye shall take of them; gold, and silver, and brass,

4 And blue, and purple, and scarlet, and fine linen, and goats' *hair,*

5 And rams' skins dyed red, and badgers' skins, and shittim wood,

6 Oil for the light, spices for anointing oil, and for sweet incense,

7 Onyx stones, and stones to be set in the ephod, and in the breastplate.

8 And let them make me a sanctuary; that I may dwell among them.

Exodus 25:1–9. The Lord Commands Israel to Build a Tabernacle of the Finest Material

What and why were the people asked to contribute for the construction of the tabernacle? (25:1–7) "While the children of Israel were still in the wilderness of Sinai, Jehovah directed that they should construct a sanctuary where they might worship him. Because of their migratory status, this structure was to be portable. Nevertheless, it was to be made of the finest materials and workmanship available. It was to be the house of the Lord, comparable to our modern temples. To this end, the Lord directed Moses to call on the people for an offering of such materials as gold and silver, fine linens, and precious stones (see Exodus 25:1–7). God's people must always be willing to sacrifice in order to provide these holy sanctuaries (see D&C 109:5; 124:26–27)" (Cowan, *Temples to Dot the Earth*, 3).

What is shittim wood? (25:5, 10) "Most scholars feel the shittim tree was a species of acacia. This tree grows to a diameter of three to four feet, and its wood is close-grained, very hard, and orange-brown in color, making it ideal for cabinet work" (Ludlow, *Companion to Your Study of the Old Testament*, 155).

How is the commandment to build a sanctuary in Moses' day relevant in every dispensation? (25:8) "One has only to read the scriptures carefully, particularly the modern scriptures, to discover that temples must have been built and used in antiquity, even in the days of the antediluvian patriarchs. In Doctrine and Covenants 124:39, the Lord speaks of his holy house '. . . which my people are always commanded to build unto my holy name.' . . . And why should not temples be as necessary for the giving of holy endowments to the living in the days of the ancient patriarchs as now?" (Sperry, "Ancient Temples and Their Functions," 67).

How can temple worship bring one closer to the Lord? (25:8) "The all-pervading and all-controlling thought in the erection of this portable sanctuary was that of expressing the close association between Jehovah and His people. The people were to consider themselves specifically the people of God, and amongst them should be His dwelling" (Talmage, *House of the Lord*, 23).

"Temples have always symbolized being in the presence of the Lord. . . . There is a closeness to God that comes through consistent worship in the house of the Lord. We can come to know Him and feel welcome, 'at home,' in His house" (Sorensen, "Small Temples—Large Blessings," 65).

How did Moses know how to build the tabernacle? (25:9) "We have it upon the highest authority, that, not only in its grand outlines, but in all minutest details, everything was to be made 'after the pattern' which God showed to Moses on the mount (Exod. 25:9). And so we also read in Acts 7:44, and Hebrews 8:5; 9:23, teaching us, that Moses was shown by

9 According to all that I shew thee, *after* the pattern of the tabernacle, and the pattern of all the instruments thereof, even so shall ye make *it*.

The Tabernacle Represented Mount Sinai (Exodus 25:8)

"Mount Sinai was not a temple built of marble or cedar, for it is not necessary for a sanctuary to be an edifice or structure. Rather, Sinai was a sacred place built by [Jehovah] himself (Exodus 15:17) and, as such, was the precursor and prototype of later Israelite sanctuaries, the model from which later temples were copied. . . .

"The tabernacle of Moses and the temple of Solomon were but copies of the genuine mountain temple. Each structure became, in its time, the 'architectural embodiment' of the cosmic mountain. They became small, man-made mountains designed to replace Sinai as the dwelling place of [Jehovah]. In the case of the tabernacle, it was a mobile mountain, so to speak, a moving dwelling place; and in the instance of the temple of Jerusalem, it also became a residence for [Jehovah]. Consequently, Sinai became known as the 'mountain of God'; the tabernacle was called 'the tent of God'; and the Jerusalem temple was referred to as 'the house of God' (Parry, "Sinai as Sanctuary and Mountain of God," 482, 484).

"'Mount Sinai is the archetype of the Tabernacle, and is similarly divided into three gradations of holiness. Its summit is the Holy of Holies; God's voice issues forth from there (Exodus 19:20) as from the inner shrine (Exodus 25:22; Numbers 7:89); the mountaintop is off limits to priest and layman alike (Exodus 19:24) and its very sight is punishable by death (Exodus 19:21), and so with its Tabernacle counterpart (cf. Leviticus 16:2 and Numbers 4:20); finally, Moses alone is privileged to ascend to the top (Exodus 19:20; see 34:2) just as later, the high priest is permitted to enter the inner shrine under special safeguards (Leviticus 16:2–4). The second division of Sinai is the equivalent of the outer shrine, marked off from the rest of the mountain by being enveloped in a cloud (Exodus 20:21; 24:15–18) just as the cloud overspreads the entirety of the Tabernacle (Numbers 9:15–22). . . . Below the cloud is the third division. . . . Here is where the altar and stelae are erected (Exodus 24:4). It is equivalent to the courtyard, the sacred enclosure of the Tabernacle' [Milgrom, *Studies in Levitical Terminology*, 44–45]" (quoted in Parry, "Sinai as Sanctuary and Mountain of God," 488).

God an actual pattern or model of all that he was to make in and for the sanctuary. . . . For, God showed Moses every detail to indicate that every detail had its special meaning, and hence could not be altered in any, even the minutest, particular, without destroying that meaning, and losing that significance which alone made it of importance" (Edersheim, *Bible History*, 2:213–14). ⊕

Exodus 25:10–22. The Description of the Ark of the Covenant Is Given

10 ¶ And they shall make an ark *of* shittim wood: two cubits and a half *shall be* the length thereof, and a cubit and a half the breadth thereof, and a cubit and a half the height thereof.

11 And thou shalt overlay it with pure gold, within and without shalt thou overlay it, and shalt make upon it a crown of gold round about.

12 And thou shalt cast four rings of gold for it, and put *them* in the four corners thereof; and two rings *shall be* in the one side of it, and two rings in the other side of it.

13 And thou shalt make staves *of* shittim wood, and overlay them with gold.

14 And thou shalt put the staves into the rings by the sides of the ark, that the ark may be borne with them.

15 The staves shall be in the rings of the ark: they shall not be taken from it.

16 And thou shalt put into the ark the testimony which I shall give thee.

17 And thou shalt make a mercy seat *of* pure gold: two cubits and a half *shall be* the length

What was the ark of the covenant? (25:10–22) "The ark of the covenant was a [wooden] chest, or box . . . overlaid with gold. . . . The ark was placed inside the inner room of the tabernacle known as the most holy place, or Holy of Holies. The ark was viewed with the greatest reverence by the Israelites . . . The covering [or lid] was made of solid gold and on it were formed two cherubim with wings which came up and overshadowed the lid or mercy seat. . . . Between these cherubim on the mercy seat, God told Moses, He would meet with him and commune with him" (*Old Testament Student Manual: Genesis–2 Samuel*, 148). See commentary for Exodus 26:34 in this volume.

What is the "testimony" that was to be placed into the ark? (25:16) "The chest was to contain *the Testimony* (v. 16), the two stone tablets of the Ten Commandments, which Moses had yet to receive. The ark would also contain a golden jar of manna (16:33; Heb. 9:4–5) and Aaron's rod (Num. 17:10). It was common practice in the ancient world to house important documents, such as covenants, law codes, treaties, and so on, in specially constructed containers" (*Zondervan KJV Commentary*, 126).

What were the mercy seat and the cherubim? (25:17–18) The mercy seat was "the golden covering of the Ark of the Covenant in the Holy of Holies. It was the place of the manifestation of God's glory and His meeting place with His people (Ex. 25:22; Lev. 16:2; Num. 7:89); and was regarded as the Throne of God (Num. 7:89; see also Ex. 30:6; 1 Sam. 4:4). Here the blood of the sin offering was sprinkled on the Day of Atonement (Lev. 16:14–15)" (Bible Dictionary, "Mercy Seat"). The cherubim were "figures representing heavenly creatures, the exact form being unknown. They are found in the Holy of Holies, on the Mercy Seat of the Ark (Ex. 25:18, 22; 1 Kgs. 6:23–28; Heb. 9:5), and in the visions of Ezekiel (Ezek. 10; 11:22). In the account of the Fall, cherubim are represented as keeping "the way of the tree of life" (Gen. 3:24)" (Bible Dictionary, "Cherubim"). See also the graphic of the mercy seat for Exodus 25:10–12.

How can we commune with the Lord in the temple? (25:22) Jehovah explained that He would commune with Moses in the tabernacle. President Russell M. Nelson promised that we could also experience God's power: "Our need to be in the temple on a regular basis has never been greater. . . . If you have reasonable access to a temple, I urge you to find a way to

thereof, and a cubit and a half the breadth thereof.

18 And thou shalt make two cherubims *of* gold, *of* beaten work shalt thou make them, in the two ends of the mercy seat.

19 And make one cherub on the one end, and the other cherub on the other end: *even* of the mercy seat shall ye make the cherubims on the two ends thereof.

20 And the cherubims shall stretch forth *their* wings on high, covering the mercy seat with their wings, and their faces *shall look* one to another; toward the mercy seat shall the faces of the cherubims be.

21 And thou shalt put the mercy seat above upon the ark; and in the ark thou shalt put the testimony that I shall give thee.

22 And there I will meet with thee, and I will commune with thee from above the mercy seat, from between the two cherubims which *are* upon the ark of the testimony, of all *things* which I will give thee in commandment unto the children of Israel.

Tabernacle Furnishings (Exodus 25:10–22)

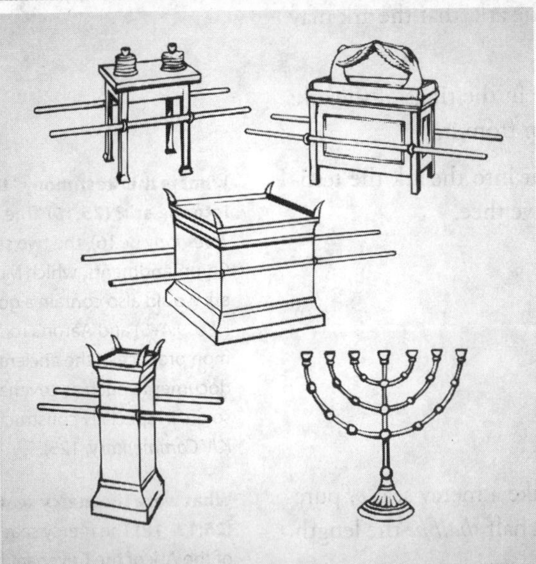

23 ¶ Thou shalt also make a table *of* shittim wood: two cubits *shall be* the length thereof, and a cubit the breadth thereof, and a cubit and a half the height thereof.

24 And thou shalt overlay it with pure gold, and make thereto a crown of gold round about.

25 And thou shalt make unto it a border of an hand breadth round about, and thou shalt make a golden crown to the border thereof round about.

26 And thou shalt make for it four rings of gold, and put the rings in the four corners that *are* on the four feet thereof.

27 Over against the border shall the rings be for places of the staves to bear the table.

28 And thou shalt make the staves *of* shittim wood, and overlay them with gold, that the table may be borne with them.

29 And thou shalt make the dishes thereof, and spoons thereof, and covers thereof, and bowls thereof, to cover withal: *of* pure gold shalt thou make them.

30 And thou shalt set upon the table shewbread before me alway.

make an appointment regularly with the Lord—to be in His holy house—then keep that appointment with exactness and joy. I promise you that the Lord will bring the miracles He knows you need as you make sacrifices to serve and worship in His temples" ("Becoming Exemplary Latter-day Saints," 114).

Exodus 25:23–40. Dimensions and Details of the Table and Shewbread and Candlestick Are Given

What was the shewbread? (25:30) "The first of the items of furniture in the holy place to be described is the table, standing on the north side (26:35).... On it was placed the bread of the Presence [KJV, "the shewbread"], so that it was probably meant to portray God as the giver of food and sustainer of His people. ... *The bread of the Presence* is so named because it was set out before the *Presence* (lit. 'face') of God. It consisted of twelve cakes baked from flour and arranged ... in two rows (or piles; cf. on Lev. 24:6) of six each. When they were replaced each sabbath they became the property of the priests (Lev. 24:5–9)" (Bruce, *International Bible Commentary*, 175). ⊕

What was the candlestick? (25:31) "The article described in this passage is the seven-branched menorah, or lamp fixture. It was not a candlestick as we understand that term; it had seven cups for oil with wicks for burning ([Bible Dictionary], "Candlestick"). Many varieties of the menorah have been crafted from ancient times to the present, and it is one of the best known symbols in Judaism. An ancient carved image of it, as it was taken from Jerusalem by the Romans, may still be seen on the arch of Titus in Rome.

"Note the emphasis that things be made according to the revealed 'pattern, which was shewed thee in the mount' (Ex. 25:40)" (Rasmussen, *Latter-day Saint Commentary on the Old Testament*, 113).

31 ¶ And thou shalt make a candlestick *of*
pure gold: *of* beaten work shall the candlestick be made: his shaft, and his branches, his
bowls, his knops, and his flowers, shall be of
the same.

32 And six branches shall come out of the
sides of it; three branches of the candlestick
out of the one side, and three branches of the
candlestick out of the other side:

33 Three bowls made like unto almonds,
with a knop and a flower in one branch; and
three bowls made like almonds in the other
branch, *with* a knop and a flower: so in the
six branches that come out of the candlestick.

What Did the Tabernacle Look Like? (Exodus 25:40)

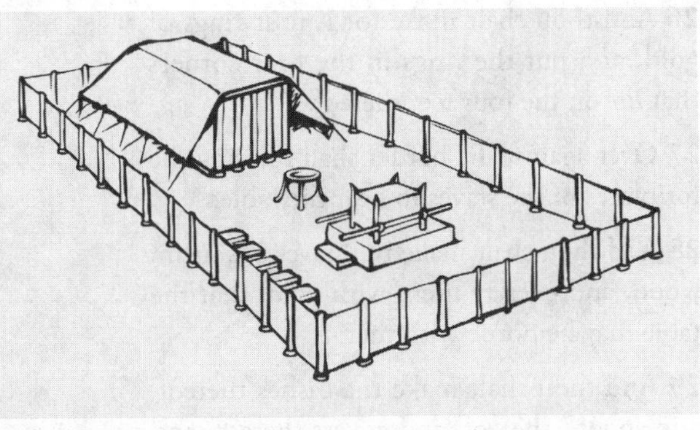

"The Lord showed Moses in vision the 'pattern' of the Tabernacle, the furnishings, and the vestments of the priests (Exod 25–31)....

"The Tabernacle was a sacred space that was divided into three zones, according to degrees of holiness: the outer courtyard, the holy place, and the Holy of Holies. The outer courtyard measured 100 x 50 cubits—a cubit is generally understood to be 18 inches, thus the courtyard measured 150 x 75 feet. A fence surrounded the Tabernacle courtyard, separating the holy space from the people....

"The Tabernacle proper measured 45 x 15 feet and was divided into two rooms: the first, called the holy place, measured 30 x 15 feet, and the second, called the most holy place or the Holy of Holies, was a perfect cube of 10 cubits, or 15 feet.... The Tabernacle was oriented to face the rising sun, with the gate in the east and the Holy of Holies in the west.

"Numerous furnishings were essential parts of Israelite worship and probably symbolic instruction. In the courtyard in front of the Tabernacle, there were two objects: the altar of sacrifice and the laver (described in Exod 30; 38)....

"Entering the Tabernacle through a veil, the priest came to the holy place, in which were found three furnishings (described in Exod 25; 30; 37): the table for the bread of the presence (KJV, the 'shewbread'), the lampstand or menorah (KJV, 'candlestick'), and the incense altar....

"An elaborately embroidered veil depicting representations of cherubim—traditional guardians of kings and thrones elsewhere in the ancient Near East—separated the holy place from the most holy place, or Holy of Holies. The Holy of Holies was a room in the shape of a perfect cube of 15 feet and contained only one object: the ark of the covenant. The ark was a gold-plated chest made of acacia wood measuring three feet, eight inches by two feet, three inches. On the top was a golden plate, called by the KJV the 'mercy seat,' bounded on two sides by golden cherubim, vthe winged angelic guardians whose wings stretched over the top of the ark to touch in the middle....

"The Tabernacle served as the religious center for the worship of the God of Israel for more than two hundred years until Solomon built his Temple in Jerusalem" (Holzapfel, et al., *Jehovah and the World of the Old Testament*, 104–7).

34 And in the candlestick *shall be* four bowls made like unto almonds, *with* their knops and their flowers.

35 And *there shall be* a knop under two branches of the same, and a knop under two branches of the same, and a knop under two branches of the same, according to the six branches that proceed out of the candlestick.

36 Their knops and their branches shall be of the same: all it *shall be* one beaten work *of* pure gold.

37 And thou shalt make the seven lamps thereof: and they shall light the lamps thereof, that they may give light over against it.

38 And the tongs thereof, and the snuffdishes thereof, *shall be of* pure gold.

39 *Of* a talent of pure gold shall he make it, with all these vessels.

40 And look that thou make *them* after their pattern, which was shewed thee in the mount.

What did the seven sources of light emphasize? (25:37) "Although a number of features in the Mosaic tabernacle had numerical significance, the seven branches of the candlestick placed between the Holy Place and the Holy of Holies seems particularly significant (see Exodus 25:31–32). It was the only light in that windowless chamber and thus served as the source of light or direction to pass from the outer (telestial) court to the Holy of Holies (or equivalent of the celestial room). As a symbol for the Holy Ghost, the seven branches serve to highlight the perfect nature of that gift" (Gaskill, *Lost Language of Symbolism*, 125).

CHAPTER 26

The tabernacle is to be built with ten curtains and with boards—A veil is to separate the holy place from the most holy place—The ark of testimony (with the mercy seat) is to be put in the most holy place.

Summary of Exodus 26:1–30

The Lord reveals to Moses the pattern for building the tabernacle that will house the furniture and provide a place for ancient Israel to worship. They are to build the ancient tabernacle so it can be taken apart and moved from place to place.

Exodus 26:31–37. Instructions Are Provided for the Veil and Placement of the Furniture within the Temple

31 ¶ And thou shalt make a veil *of* blue, and purple, and scarlet, and fine twined linen of cunning work: with cherubims shall it be made:

What was the veil of the temple? (26:31) "The innermost room of the tabernacle, the 'most holy place,' also known as the 'Holy of Holies,' . . . was separated from the 'holy place' by a beautiful veil of pure white 'fine twined linen' adorned with cherubim and other figures embroidered in blue, purple, and scarlet. A latter-day revelation (D&C 132:19) speaks of angels as guardians along the way to exaltation in the kingdom of God. Hence the veil may have symbolized the division between God and man" (Cowan, *Temples to Dot the Earth*, 6).

How can these instructions about the tabernacle help us to appreciate the sacred nature of the temple today? (26:33) "President Russell M. Nelson emphasized the vital balance between the sacred nature of temple ceremonies and the valuable information about temples published by the Church that is accurate, appropriate, and available publicly. He explained: 'I recommend that members . . . read entries in the Bible Dictionary that are related to the temple, such as 'Anoint,' 'Covenant,' 'Sacrifices,' and 'Temple.' One may also wish to read Exodus, chapters 26–29 and Leviticus, chapter 8. The Old Testament, as well as the books of Moses and Abraham in the Pearl of Great Price, underscores the antiquity of temple work and the enduring nature of its ordinances'" (Bednar, "Prepared to Obtain Every Needful Thing," 104).

Summary of Exodus 27

The Lord reveals the pattern for the altar of sacrifice. A horn is attached at each of the four corners, symbolizing help and the atoning power. Instructions are given to make items needed for handling the meat of the sacrificial animals and the ash. Pure olive oil is specified for use in the candlestick within the tabernacle.

32 And thou shalt hang it upon four pillars of shittim *wood* overlaid with gold: their hooks *shall be of* gold, upon the four sockets of silver.

33 ¶ And thou shalt hang up the veil under the taches, that thou mayest bring in thither within the veil the ark of the testimony: and the veil shall divide unto you between the holy *place* and the most holy.

34 And thou shalt put the mercy seat upon the ark of the testimony in the most holy *place*.

35 And thou shalt set the table without the veil, and the candlestick over against the table on the side of the tabernacle toward the south: and thou shalt put the table on the north side.

36 And thou shalt make an hanging for the door of the tent, *of* blue, and purple, and scarlet, and fine twined linen, wrought with needlework.

37 And thou shalt make for the hanging five pillars *of* shittim *wood*, and overlay them with gold, *and* their hooks *shall be of* gold: and thou shalt cast five sockets of brass for them.

CHAPTER 27

The tabernacle is to contain an altar for burnt offerings and a court surrounded by pillars—A light is to burn always in the tabernacle of the congregation.

CHAPTER 28

Aaron and his sons are to be consecrated and anointed to minister in the priest's office—Aaron's garments are to include a breastplate, an ephod, a robe, a coat, a miter, and a girdle—The breastplate of judgment is to contain twelve precious stones with the names of the tribes of Israel thereon—The Urim and Thummim are to be carried in the breastplate.

1 And take thou unto thee Aaron thy brother, and his sons with him, from among the children of Israel, that he may minister unto me in the priest's office, *even* Aaron, Nadab and Abihu, Eleazar and Ithamar, Aaron's sons.

2 And thou shalt make holy garments for Aaron thy brother for glory and for beauty.

3 And thou shalt speak unto all *that are* wise hearted, whom I have filled with the spirit of wisdom, that they may make Aaron's garments to consecrate him, that he may minister unto me in the priest's office.

4 And these *are* the garments which they shall make; a breastplate, and an ephod, and a robe, and a broidered coat, a mitre, and a girdle: and they shall make holy garments for Aaron thy brother, and his sons, that he may minister unto me in the priest's office.

5 And they shall take gold, and blue, and purple, and scarlet, and fine linen.

Exodus 28:1–5. Aaron and His Sons Are Called to Serve the Lord and His People in the Tabernacle

How long did Aaron and his posterity have chief responsibility ministering in the priest's office? (28:1) "'And the Lord confirmed a priesthood also upon Aaron and his seed, throughout all their generations. . . .' (D&C 84:18). This was the priesthood in general usage in ancient Israel. It was hereditary; that is, it was disseminated by virtue of who one's father and mother were. From Aaron to John the Baptist the hereditary nature of the Levitical Priesthood was in active operation (D&C 84:18, 26–27, 30). This order of priesthood was conferred only upon the worthy members of the special lineage chosen to receive it" (McConkie, *Aaronic Priesthood*, 30). See D&C 68:14–20; 84:18. ⊕

Why is the Lord specific about sacred clothing, and how does it relate to us? (28:2–4) "[Wearing the sacred garment] is symbolic of an inner commitment to strive each day to become more like the Lord. It also reminds us to remain faithful each day to covenants made and to walk on the covenant path each day in a higher and holier way" (Nelson, "Closing Remarks," 121). "To Church members, the modest temple garment worn under normal clothing and the symbolic vestments worn during temple worship represent the sacred and personal aspect of their relationship with God and their commitment to live good, honorable lives" ("Sacred Temple Clothing" [video]). ⊕

What could be the possible interpretations of "breastplate"? (28:4–5) "There have been endless latter-day efforts to reconstruct the wardrobe and to parse the technical sartorial terms that are used to represent it, but these can be no more than amalgams of guesses and approximations. Though the present translation assumes that 'breastplate' is still plausible for the Hebrew ḥoshen (etymology uncertain), others contend it is a smaller 'breastpiece' or even a 'pouch.' The ephod (the Hebrew root suggests 'binding' or 'wrapping around') evidently was a kind of apron, although opinions differ on this" (Alter, *Hebrew Bible*, 1:325). ⊕

Summary of Exodus 28:6–29

The Lord continues to provide specifics to the ceremonial clothing Aaron and his sons should wear in their priestly duties.

Exodus 28:30–43. Additional Details on the Breastplate and Clothing Are Given

Why did Aaron place the Urim and Thummim over his heart? (28:30) "The Urim and Thummim are mentioned in the Bible in connection with priestly functions. They were to be used in making the will of the Lord clear and comprehensible to the priest. Aaron was instructed to wear the Urim and Thummim 'upon his heart,' when he went to 'secure judgment' from the Lord and his successors were instructed to use the Urim and Thummim when they asked 'counsel' from the Lord. Clearly, the Urim and Thummim were used in official communication with the Lord. Beyond that, little is known of them (see Ex. 28:30; Lev. 8:8; Num. 27:21; Deut. 33:8; 1 Sam. 28:6; Ezra 2:63; Neh. 7:65)" (Widtsoe, *Evidences and Reconciliations*, 89). ⊕

30 ¶ And thou shalt put in the breastplate of judgment the Urim and the Thummim; and they shall be upon Aaron's heart, when he goeth in before the LORD: and Aaron shall bear the judgment of the children of Israel upon his heart before the LORD continually.

31 ¶ And thou shalt make the robe of the ephod all *of* blue.

32 And there shall be an hole in the top of it, in the midst thereof: it shall have a binding of woven work round about the hole of it, as it were the hole of an habergeon, that it be not rent.

33 ¶ And *beneath* upon the hem of it thou shalt make pomegranates *of* blue, and *of* purple, and *of* scarlet, round about the hem thereof; and bells of gold between them round about:

34 A golden bell and a pomegranate, a golden bell and a pomegranate, upon the hem of the robe round about.

35 And it shall be upon Aaron to minister: and his sound shall be heard when he goeth

Priestly Clothing (Exodus 28:4–43)

"Anciently, the priests, descendants of Aaron, wore special garments when serving in the tabernacle and later in the temple. Exodus 29:29 refers to 'the holy garments of Aaron' . . . the priest Ezra refers to 'the holy garment' he wore. . . . The priesthood garments used in the tabernacle and temple in Old Testament times are described in Exodus 28 and 39 and [Leviticus 8]. . . . The principal elements for the high priest's clothing were linen breeches, a coat, a robe, a bonnet with a gold mitre [cap] and a gold engraved frontlet attached, a girdle, and a garment called the ephod to which was attached a breastplate" (Tvedtnes, "Priestly Clothing in Bible Times," 663).

"To those outside a particular faith, the rituals and clothing may seem unfamiliar. But for the participants, they can stir the deepest feelings of the soul, motivate them to do good, and even shape the course of a whole life of service. . . . Not all such religious clothing is on public display. Some clothing is seen only in places of worship. For example, temple robes of The Church of Jesus Christ of Latter-day Saints, known as the robes of the holy priesthood, are worn only inside Latter-day Saint temples and are reserved for the most sacred ceremonies of their faith" ("Sacred Temple Clothing" [video]).

in unto the holy *place* before the LORD, and when he cometh out, that he die not.

36 ¶ And thou shalt make a plate *of* pure gold, and grave upon it, *like* the engravings of a signet, HOLINESS TO THE LORD.

37 And thou shalt put it on a blue lace, that it may be upon the mitre; upon the forefront of the mitre it shall be.

38 And it shall be upon Aaron's forehead, that Aaron may bear the iniquity of the holy things, which the children of Israel shall hallow in all their holy gifts; and it shall be always upon his forehead, that they may be accepted before the LORD.

39 ¶ And thou shalt embroider the coat of fine linen, and thou shalt make the mitre *of* fine linen, and thou shalt make the girdle *of* needlework.

40 ¶ And for Aaron's sons thou shalt make coats, and thou shalt make for them girdles, and bonnets shalt thou make for them, for glory and for beauty.

41 And thou shalt put them upon Aaron thy brother, and his sons with him; and shalt anoint them, and consecrate them, and sanctify them, that they may minister unto me in the priest's office.

42 And thou shalt make them linen breeches to cover their nakedness; from the loins even unto the thighs they shall reach:

How is the phrase "Holiness to the Lord" as important today as it was in the days of Aaron? (28:36) President Russell M. Nelson stated: "Inscribed on each temple are the words 'Holiness to the Lord.' That statement designates both the temple and its purposes as holy. Those who enter the temple are also to bear the attribute of holiness. It may be easier to ascribe holiness to a building than it is to a people. We can acquire holiness only by enduring and persistent personal effort. Through the ages, servants of the Lord have warned against unholiness" ("Personal Preparation for Temple Blessings," 32). ⊕

What did the anointing of Aaron and his sons symbolize? (28:41) "The oil with which the priests were anointed was understood by the ancients to represent the necessity of those on the Lord's errand being filled with his Spirit. . . . One must be consumed by the power of the Holy Ghost to stand in the presence of God. . . . This is why Moses sought to sanctify Israel that they might enjoy that presence (D&C 84:23). The symbolism is perfect. The priests entering the Holy Place, and the high priest entering the Holy of Holies, must be sanctified and filled with the Spirit, which is symbolized in the anointing" (McConkie, *Gospel Symbolism*, 115). Exodus 29 gives further details on this anointing.

What do the "linen breeches" symbolize? (28:42) "The 'coats of skins' made for Adam and Eve, the 'linen breeches' of the priests of old, and some of the temple clothing of the Latter-day Saints represent the flesh of Christ and the purity and glory that he and his Father possess through their supernal righteousness" (Gaskill, *Lost Language of Symbolism*, 71). President Boyd K. Packer stated. "The garment, covering the body, is a visual and tactile reminder of . . . covenants. For many Church members the garment has formed a barrier of protection when the wearer has been faced with temptation. Among other things it symbolizes our deep respect for the laws of God—among them the moral standard" (*Holy Temple*, 79).

Why is sacred clothing necessary when one enters the House of the Lord? (28:43) "The clothing of the tabernacle or temple dramatized the necessity for purity in every part of worship, the centrality of the atonement of Christ, the purity and justice of the Savior, and the absolute necessity of that holiness without which none can see the Lord" (McConkie, *Gospel Symbolism*, 114). How has your study of Exodus 28 broadened your understanding of sacred clothing associated with temple worship? How can honoring sacred temple clothing better prepare you for temple worship? ⊕

Summary of Exodus 29

Aaron and his sons are to be washed, anointed with oil, and then dressed in special ceremonial clothing. "Those who received the anointing were sanctified and set apart from the profane world" (Parry, "Ritual Anointing," 265).

Aaron and his sons also perform certain sacrifices to show their willingness to serve the Lord. Jehovah promises to be their God and speak to them (see Exodus 29:42). He also promises to sanctify the tabernacle with His glory and dwell among the children of Israel. See commentary in this volume for Leviticus 8.

Exodus 30:1–10. The Altar and Its Functions Are Described

What is the altar of incense? (30:1–10) "The third piece of furniture in the Holy Place . . . was the altar of incense. It stood directly in front of the veil. . . . Hot coals were placed on the altar, and each morning and evening the high priest would burn incense upon it. . . . On the altar of burnt offering we saw Christ as a sacrifice for sin; now, on the altar of incense (the symbol for sweetness and fragrance, perfectly typified in the life of Christ), we see the Savior as our intercessor. His prayers and petitions, carried upon the wings of the perfect goodness and righteousness of his

43 And they shall be upon Aaron, and upon his sons, when they come in unto the tabernacle of the congregation, or when they come near unto the altar to minister in the holy *place;* that they bear not iniquity, and die: *it shall be* a statute for ever unto him and his seed after him.

CHAPTER 29

Aaron and his sons are to be washed, anointed, and consecrated—Various sacrificial rites are to be performed—Atonement is to be made for the sins of the people—The Lord promises to dwell among them.

CHAPTER 30

An altar of incense is to be placed before the veil—Atonement is to be made with the blood of the sin offering—Atonement money is to be paid to ransom each male—Priests are to use holy anointing oil and perfume.

1 And thou shalt make an altar to burn incense upon: *of* shittim wood shalt thou make it.

2 A cubit *shall be* the length thereof, and a cubit the breadth thereof; foursquare shall it be: and two cubits *shall be* the height thereof: the horns thereof *shall be* of the same.

3 And thou shalt overlay it with pure gold, the top thereof, and the sides thereof round about, and the horns thereof; and thou shalt make unto it a crown of gold round about.

4 And two golden rings shalt thou make to it under the crown of it, by the two corners thereof, upon the two sides of it shalt thou make *it;* and they shall be for places for the staves to bear it withal.

5 And thou shalt make the staves *of* shittim wood, and overlay them with gold.

6 And thou shalt put it before the veil that *is* by the ark of the testimony, before the mercy seat that *is* over the testimony, where I will meet with thee.

7 And Aaron shall burn thereon sweet incense every morning: when he dresseth the lamps, he shall burn incense upon it.

8 And when Aaron lighteth the lamps at even, he shall burn incense upon it, a perpetual incense before the LORD throughout your generations.

9 Ye shall offer no strange incense thereon, nor burnt sacrifice, nor meat offering; neither shall ye pour drink offering thereon.

10 And Aaron shall make an atonement upon the horns of it once in a year with the blood of the sin offering of atonements: once in the year shall he make atonement upon it throughout your generations: it *is* most holy unto the LORD.

life, allow men to approach God" (McConkie, *Gospel Symbolism*, 108).

How was the perpetual burning of incense accomplished? (30:8) "The duty of offering [incense] twice daily fell upon the high priest. . . . Live coals were brought from the brazen altar of burnt offering and placed on the golden altar of incense; then the priest to whom the lot had fallen entered alone into the Holy Place, carrying in a censer the incense, which he cast on the fire. Then, bowing reverently toward the Holy of Holies, he returned to the congregation, who were praying outside, and pronounced the blessing in Num. 6:24–26. The choir of Levites at once started to sing the daily psalms" (Bible Dictionary, "Incense").

What was considered strange incense? (30:9) "There was to be no deviation from the divine recipe for the incense to be burned on the table (30:34–38). Aaron's sons, Nadab and Abihu, would later commit that error (Lev. 10:1–2). In addition, nothing besides incense was ever to be offered on the table" (*Zondervan KJV Commentary*, 131–32).

What did it mean to make an atonement on temple objects? (30:10) "This Day of Atonement was later specified in Lev. 16. The 'atoning' of objects such as this was a ritual cleansing to make these objects holy before the Lord. Since man was sinful, the things he came in contact with were associated with his sinfulness. Once a year, everything in the tabernacle that man touched had to be ceremonially cleansed" (*Nelson Study Bible* [NKJV], 140).

Exodus 30:11–16. The Lord Explains How the Service of the Tabernacle Will Be Sustained

What was the atonement money required of the children of Israel? (30:12–16) "In order to play a role in the atonements made by the Levites, adult Israelite males were required to pay 'atonement money'; this money would assure the Israelites 'that there be no plague among them,' as well as support 'the service of the tabernacle' (Ex. 30:11–16). This act of paying atonement money has particular significance for the latter days: just as the Israelites were commanded to offer atonement money to avert plagues, we are commanded to pay tithing so that we are not burned at Jesus' coming (D&C 64:23)" (Parry and Parry, *Symbols and Shadows*, 35). ⊕

11 ¶ And the LORD spake unto Moses, saying,

12 When thou takest the sum of the children
of Israel after their number, then shall they
give every man a ransom for his soul unto
the LORD, when thou numberest them; that
there be no plague among them, when *thou*
numberest them.

13 This they shall give, every one that passeth
among them that are numbered, half a shekel
after the shekel of the sanctuary: (a shekel *is*
twenty gerahs:) an half shekel *shall be* the offering of the LORD.

14 Every one that passeth among them that
are numbered, from twenty years old and
above, shall give an offering unto the LORD.

15 The rich shall not give more, and the poor
shall not give less than half a shekel, when
they give an offering unto the LORD, to make
an atonement for your souls.

16 And thou shalt take the atonement
money of the children of Israel, and shalt appoint it for the service of the tabernacle of
the congregation; that it may be a memorial
unto the children of Israel before the LORD,
to make an atonement for your souls.

Exodus 30:17–21. The Laver of Brass for Washing Is Revealed

Why would the Lord require Aaron and the other priests to wash before going into the tabernacle? (30:18–21) "In Aaron's situation, God's mandate was that anyone approaching the Lord or rendering service in his name 'shall wash their hands and their feet . . . that they die not' (KJV, Exodus 30:19–20), clearly teaching the absolute necessity of being clean before entering the service or the presence of the Lord. In addition to purification and cleansing, the washing may have also represented the symbolic bestowal of other attributes and blessings as well. In the ancient Near East, ceremonial washings, or ablutions, were believed to purify the initiate, avert evil, give life and strength,

17 ¶ And the LORD spake unto Moses, saying,

18 Thou shalt also make a laver *of* brass, and
his foot *also of* brass, to wash *withal:* and
thou shalt put it between the tabernacle of
the congregation and the altar, and thou shalt
put water therein.

19 For Aaron and his sons shall wash their
hands and their feet thereat:

20 When they go into the tabernacle of the
congregation, they shall wash with water,
that they die not; or when they come near to
the altar to minister, to burn offering made
by fire unto the LORD:

21 So they shall wash their hands and their feet, that they die not: and it shall be a statute for ever to them, *even* to him and to his seed throughout their generations.

CHAPTER 31

Artisans are inspired in building and furnishing the tabernacle—Israel is commanded to keep the Lord's Sabbaths—The death penalty is decreed for Sabbath desecration—Moses receives the stone tablets.

1 And the LORD spake unto Moses, saying,

2 See, I have called by name Bezaleel the son of Uri, the son of Hur, of the tribe of Judah:

3 And I have filled him with the spirit of God, in wisdom, and in understanding, and in knowledge, and in all manner of workmanship,

4 To devise cunning works, to work in gold, and in silver, and in brass,

5 And in cutting of stones, to set *them,* and in carving of timber, to work in all manner of workmanship.

6 And I, behold, I have given with him Aholiab, the son of Ahisamach, of the tribe of Dan: and in the hearts of all that are wise hearted I have put wisdom, that they may make all that I have commanded thee;

7 The tabernacle of the congregation, and the ark of the testimony, and the mercy seat that *is* thereupon, and all the furniture of the tabernacle,

8 And the table and his furniture, and the pure candlestick with all his furniture, and the altar of incense,

and at times, symbolize a rebirth" (Redd, "Aaron's Consecration," 122).

Summary of Exodus 30:22–38

The Lord reveals the oil to be used in the holy anointing. Moses is instructed to anoint the sacred objects and furnishings as well as Aaron in his sons.

Exodus 31:1–11. The Lord Prepares Workers to Build the Tabernacle

When you consider the Lord's work and purposes, what do these verses teach you? (31:2–6) "The two master craftsmen just mentioned by name would of course have needed large crews of men with the requisite skills to work under them. Putting wisdom in the hearts of the wise-hearted men is a kind of positive counterpart to hardening the heart of Pharaoh: the capacity for skillful artisanship is innate, one of the person's attributes, but God is the ultimate source of all such capacities and the enabling force for their realization" (Alter, *Hebrew Bible,* 1:336). Just as the Lord prepared individuals to build His tabernacle, He has prepared the "wise-hearted" to continue His work today.

How does the calling of Bezaleel emphasize the importance of workers prepared to build temples? (31:2) "Divine direction was manifest in the appointment of men who should be in charge of the labor. Bezaleel . . . [was] designated by revelation as the master [craftsman] under whose direction the other workers should labor until all had been finished in direct accord with the revealed pattern and plan" (Talmage, *House of the Lord,* 19). "The gifts of the Spirit described here are like some in other dispensations (Ex. 31:3*a–c*). With them, Bezaleel would become chief artisan; he and his assistant would supervise all the 'wise hearted' who would make all that had been commanded" (Rasmussen, *Latter-day Saint Commentary on the Old Testament,* 118). ⊕

Exodus 31:12–18. The Lord Emphasizes the Importance of the Sabbath

How does our Sabbath observance represent a sign between us and God? (31:13) "How do we *hallow* the Sabbath day? In my much younger years, I studied the work of others who had compiled lists of things to do and things *not* to do on the Sabbath. It wasn't until later that I learned from the scriptures that my conduct and my attitude on the Sabbath constituted a *sign* between me and my Heavenly Father. With that understanding, I no longer needed lists of dos and don'ts. When I had to make a decision whether or not an activity was appropriate for the Sabbath, I simply asked myself, 'What *sign* do I want to give to God?' That question made my choices about the Sabbath day crystal clear" (Nelson, "Sabbath Is a Delight," 130). ⊕

Why did the Lord impose death for those who worked on the sabbath? (31:15) "Perhaps this was the only way that these former slaves could be taught the law of obedience and be brought to an understanding of the commandments of the Lord. . . . In our own day it would seem that he recognized the intelligence of his people, and assumed that they would catch the total spirit of worship and of the Sabbath observance when he said to them: 'Thou shalt offer a sacrifice unto the Lord thy God in righteousness, even that of a broken heart and a contrite spirit' (D&C 59:8)" (Kimball, *Teachings of Spencer W. Kimball*, 217–18). ⊕

What will you do to keep this continuous covenant? (31:16) "Perhaps most important, the Sabbath was given as a perpetual covenant, a constant reminder that the Lord may sanctify His people. . . . How can you ensure that your behavior on the Sabbath will lead to joy and rejoicing? In addition to your going to church, partaking of the sacrament, and being diligent in your specific call to serve, what other activities would help to make the Sabbath a delight for you? What sign will you give to the Lord to show your love for Him?" (Nelson, "Sabbath Is a Delight," 129, 130).

9 And the altar of burnt offering with all his furniture, and the laver and his foot,

10 And the cloths of service, and the holy garments for Aaron the priest, and the garments of his sons, to minister in the priest's office,

11 And the anointing oil, and sweet incense for the holy *place:* according to all that I have commanded thee shall they do.

12 ¶ And the LORD spake unto Moses, saying,

13 Speak thou also unto the children of Israel, saying, Verily my sabbaths ye shall keep: for it *is* a sign between me and you throughout your generations; that *ye* may know that I *am* the LORD that doth sanctify you.

14 Ye shall keep the sabbath therefore; for it *is* holy unto you: every one that defileth it shall surely be put to death: for whosoever doeth *any* work therein, that soul shall be cut off from among his people.

15 Six days may work be done; but in the seventh *is* the sabbath of rest, holy to the LORD: whosoever doeth *any* work in the sabbath day, he shall surely be put to death.

16 Wherefore the children of Israel shall keep the sabbath, to observe the sabbath throughout their generations, *for* a perpetual covenant.

17 It *is* a sign between me and the children of Israel for ever: for *in* six days the LORD made heaven and earth, and on the seventh day he rested, and was refreshed.

18 ¶ And he gave unto Moses, when he had made an end of communing with him upon mount Sinai, two tables of testimony, tables of stone, written with the finger of God.

How do you feel about your personal Sabbath-day activities? (31:17) "Now I understand that my behavior on the Sabbath is my sign to the Lord of my regard [respect and love] for him and for the covenant under which I was born. If . . . my interests on the Sabbath were turned to pro football games or worldly movies, the sign from me to him would clearly be that my devotion would *not* favor the Lord. If, on the other hand, my Sabbath interests were focused on the Lord and his teachings, my family, or the sick, or the poor, and the needy, that sign would likewise be visible to God" (Nelson, *Power within Us*, 127).

CHAPTER 32

Aaron makes a golden calf, which Israel worships—Moses serves as a mediator between God and rebellious Israel—Moses breaks the tablets of stone—The Levites slay about 3,000 rebels—Moses pleads and intercedes for the people.

1 And when the people saw that Moses delayed to come down out of the mount, the people gathered themselves together unto Aaron, and said unto him, Up, make us gods, which shall go before us; for *as for* this Moses, the man that brought us up out of the land of Egypt, we wot not what is become of him.

Exodus 32:1–6. Aaron Makes a Golden Calf

Why did the children of Israel turn to an idol so quickly? (32:1) "It seems likely that Israel believed their worst fears had come true. When Moses did not return from the mount for some time, they may have assumed that he had perished in the presence of God, as they had feared they would. Instead of finding another way to turn to God, they asked Aaron to help them approach God on their own. Despite having just made a covenant that had emphasized not making any images, they asked Aaron to do so. Because many of their idolatrous neighbors, including Egypt, used the image of an animal that was associated with a god to remind them of the god himself, the calf was likely intended to help them think of God" (Muhlestein, *Scripture Study Made Simple*, 111) ⊕

2 And Aaron said unto them, Break off the golden earrings, which *are* in the ears of your wives, of your sons, and of your daughters, and bring *them* unto me.

3 And all the people brake off the golden earrings which *were* in their ears, and brought *them* unto Aaron.

Why did Aaron obey the people? (32:2) "Aaron, not knowing what else to do, foolishly complied with their demand" (Smith, "Second Commandment," 37). Elder L. Tom Perry summarized the account: "Aaron succumbed to the will of the people" ("We Believe All That God Has Revealed," 87). Elder Orson F. Whitney concluded that he was "perhaps fearful of consequences if he refused" (*Gospel Themes*, 117). Joseph Smith was told early in his ministry: "How oft you have transgressed the commandments and the laws of God, and have gone on in the persuasions of men. . . . You should not have feared man more than God. Although men set at naught the counsels of God, and despise his words" (D&C 3:6–7).

Why did Aaron choose to make their melted gold into a calf? (32:4) "Some may wonder why Aaron made an image of a calf for the people to worship, rather than an image of a man. The answer is that the Egyptians worshiped and held sacred many animals, among them the bull and the cow. Their imaginary god Apis was represented by the image of a bull, and bulls without blemish were tenderly and sacredly protected, as was also the cow. Their god Hathor was worshiped in the image of a cow, and carvings of these animals were found in their shrines and many other places" (Smith, "Second Commandment," 38).

What does the description "rose up to play" imply? (32:6) "This feast was the kind of worship that false religions practiced (see Exodus 34:12–17). The phrase 'rose up to play' refers to serious sin, as can be seen in verse 25" (Valletta, et al., *Old Testament for Latter-day Saint Families*, 143). Compare 1 Nephi 18:9–10. Paul refers to this event in a letter to Corinth: "Now these things were our examples, to the intent we should not lust after evil things, as they also lusted. Neither be ye idolaters, as were some of them; as it is written, The people sat down to eat and drink, and rose up to play. Neither let us commit fornication, as some of them committed" (1 Corinthians 10:6–8).

Exodus 32:7–14. Moses Pleads with God to Forgive Israel

What was the condition of the people when Moses returned? (32:7–8) "They corrupted (Heb., lit., 'debased') themselves through idolatrous worship, whereas worship of the true God would exalt them. . . . The Israelites did not make the golden calf in ignorance but in 'mischief' (Ex. 32:22)" (Rasmussen, *Latter-day Saint Commentary on the Old Testament*, 119). "There they were at the foot of the mountain, busily fashioning a golden calf to worship, in the very hour that Jehovah, at the summit of the mountain, had been telling Moses, 'Thou shalt have no other gods before me' and 'Thou shalt not make unto thee any graven image.' Moses was *not* happy with his flock of wandering Israelites that day!" (Holland, "Tomorrow the Lord Will Do Wonders among You," 124).

4 And he received *them* at their hand, and fashioned it with a graving tool, after he had made it a molten calf: and they said, These *be* thy gods, O Israel, which brought thee up out of the land of Egypt.

5 And when Aaron saw *it*, he built an altar before it; and Aaron made proclamation, and said, To morrow *is* a feast to the LORD.

6 And they rose up early on the morrow, and offered burnt offerings, and brought peace offerings; and the people sat down to eat and to drink, and rose up to play.

7 ¶ And the LORD said unto Moses, Go, get thee down; for thy people, which thou broughtest out of the land of Egypt, have corrupted *themselves:*

8 They have turned aside quickly out of the way which I commanded them: they have made them a molten calf, and have worshipped it, and have sacrificed thereunto, and said, These *be* thy gods, O Israel, which have brought thee up out of the land of Egypt.

9 And the LORD said unto Moses, I have seen this people, and, behold, it *is* a stiffnecked people:

10 Now therefore let me alone, that my wrath may wax hot against them, and that I may consume them: and I will make of thee a great nation.

11 And Moses besought the LORD his God,
and said, LORD, why doth thy wrath wax hot
against thy people, which thou hast brought
forth out of the land of Egypt with great
power, and with a mighty hand?

12 Wherefore should the Egyptians speak,
and say, For mischief did he bring them out,
to slay them in the mountains, and to consume them from the face of the earth? Turn
from thy fierce wrath, and repent of this evil
against thy people.

13 Remember Abraham, Isaac, and Israel, thy
servants, to whom thou swarest by thine own
self, and saidst unto them, I will multiply
your seed as the stars of heaven, and all this
land that I have spoken of will I give unto
your seed, and they shall inherit *it* for ever.

14 And the LORD repented of the evil which
he thought to do unto his people.

15 ¶ And Moses turned, and went down
from the mount, and the two tables of the
testimony *were* in his hand: the tables *were*
written on both their sides; on the one side
and on the other *were* they written.

16 And the tables *were* the work of God, and
the writing *was* the writing of God, graven
upon the tables.

17 And when Joshua heard the noise of the
people as they shouted, he said unto Moses,
There is a noise of war in the camp.

18 And he said, *It is* not the voice of *them
that* shout for mastery, neither *is it* the voice
of *them that* cry for being overcome: *but* the
noise of *them that* sing do I hear.

19 ¶ And it came to pass, as soon as he came
nigh unto the camp, that he saw the calf, and
the dancing: and Moses' anger waxed hot,
and he cast the tables out of his hands, and
brake them beneath the mount.

How did Moses try to intervene with the Lord on behalf of the people? (32:12–14) According to the Joseph Smith Translation, the last part of verse 12 should read: "Turn from thy fierce wrath. *Thy people will* repent of this evil; *therefore come thou not out against them.*" Verse 14 reads: "And the Lord *said unto Moses, If they will repent* of the evil which *they have done, I will spare them, and turn away my fierce wrath; but, behold, thou shalt execute judgment upon all that will not repent of this evil this day. Therefore, see thou do this thing that I have commanded thee, or I will execute all that which I had* thought to do unto *my* people" (compare Exodus 32:12*b*, 14 and JST, Exodus 32:12, 14).

Exodus 32:15–24. Moses Returns to Camp and Destroys the Stone Tablets and the Golden Calf

What did the people forfeit for their disobedience? (32:15–19) "There was considerably more on those tablets than the Ten Commandments. When Moses descended the mountain and found some of his people in naked, riotous activity worshiping a golden calf, he was furious. The contrast between what he had just seen, heard, and felt in the presence of the Lord compared with the debauchery and idol worship he now witnessed must have been devastating in the extreme. Furthermore, such an extreme difference between what was and what could have been helps us understand the severity of the penalty the Israelites paid in losing for well over a thousand years the [Melchizedek] priesthood, gospel, and temple blessings they could have enjoyed in abundance" (Holland, *Christ and the New Covenant*, 144). ⊕

Why did Moses force the Israelites to drink the powder of the destroyed golden calf? (32:20) In a later account we learn that Moses casts the remnants of the gold calf into the "brook that descended out of the mount" (Deut. 9:21). The brook would have been a natural water source for the people. Another view is: "He destroyed their idol and obliged the people to drink the ashes of it, strewn on water, demonstrating the idol's lack of any power" (Rasmussen, *Latter-day Saint Commentary on the Old Testament,* 120).

What can we learn from Aaron's moment of weakness? (32:22–24) "Even the very elite have sometimes succumbed to the temptation to blame others for their disobedience or their failure to receive blessings. Aaron blamed the children of Israel when Moses charged him with bringing a great sin upon them by making a molten calf.... When faced with the consequences of transgression, rather than looking to ourselves as the source of the discomfort which always accompanies sin, many of us tend to blame someone else... we fault our neighbor for our pain and try to pass it on" (Howard, "Repentance," 13). How can we better take accountability for our actions? ⊕

Exodus 32:25–29. The Sons of Levi Slay the Israelites Who Do Not Repent

Why is Moses' question to choose sides relevant today? (32:26) "We can take our choice which territory we want to live in, that of our Heavenly Father or that of Satan. I have many times repeated what my grandfather said.... 'There is a line of demarcation, well defined. On one side of the line is the Lord's territory. On the other side of the line is the devil's territory.' And... 'If you will stay on the Lord's side of the line, you are perfectly safe, because the adversary of all righteousness cannot cross that line.' [This] means to me that those who are living righteous lives, keeping all of the commandments of our Heavenly Father are perfectly safe" (Smith, in Conference Report, Oct. 1949, 5–6). ⊕

Why would the Lord command that the rebellious be slain? (32:28) "Who can say what the Almighty can and cannot do? The Prophet Joseph Smith observed, 'It is the constitutional disposition of mankind to set up stakes and set bounds to the works and ways of the Almighty.'... Yet the Lord 'willeth to take even them whom he will take, and preserveth in life them whom he will preserve' (D&C 63:3). Evidently God had judged

20 And he took the calf which they had made, and burnt *it* in the fire, and ground *it* to powder, and strawed *it* upon the water, and made the children of Israel drink *of it.*

21 And Moses said unto Aaron, What did this people unto thee, that thou hast brought so great a sin upon them?

22 And Aaron said, Let not the anger of my lord wax hot: thou knowest the people, that they *are set* on mischief.

23 For they said unto me, Make us gods, which shall go before us: for *as for* this Moses, the man that brought us up out of the land of Egypt, we wot not what is become of him.

24 And I said unto them, Whosoever hath any gold, let them break *it* off. So they gave *it* me: then I cast it into the fire, and there came out this calf.

25 ¶ And when Moses saw that the people *were* naked; (for Aaron had made them naked unto *their* shame among their enemies:)

26 Then Moses stood in the gate of the camp, and said, Who *is* on the LORD's side? *let him come* unto me. And all the sons of Levi gathered themselves together unto him.

27 And he said unto them, Thus saith the LORD God of Israel, Put every man his sword by his side, *and* go in and out from gate to gate throughout the camp, and slay every man his brother, and every man his companion, and every man his neighbour.

28 And the children of Levi did according to the word of Moses: and there fell of the people that day about three thousand men.

[some of the children of Israel] and found [them] guilty. . . . Man does not have the right to adjust the application of God's laws. But God has every right to do so; and when he does, he will reveal his decisions to his servants, the prophets" (Turner, "Why Did the Lord Command Nephi to Slay Laban?" 63).

29 For Moses had said, Consecrate yourselves to day to the LORD, even every man upon his son, and upon his brother; that he may bestow upon you a blessing this day.

What does it mean to consecrate yourself to the Lord" (32:29) Elder D. Todd Christofferson offered "five of the elements of a consecrated life. . . . As the Savior demonstrated, the consecrated life is a pure life. . . . A consecrated life is a life of labor. . . . A consecrated life respects the incomparable gift of one's physical body, a divine creation in the very image of God. . . . Those who quietly and thoughtfully go about doing good offer a model of consecration. . . . A consecrated life is a life of integrity" ("Reflections on a Consecrated Life, 16–18).

Exodus 32:30–35. Moses Offers Himself as a Sacrifice for the Sins of the Children of Israel

30 ¶ And it came to pass on the morrow, that Moses said unto the people, Ye have sinned a great sin: and now I will go up unto the LORD; peradventure I shall make an atonement for your sin.

31 And Moses returned unto the LORD, and said, Oh, this people have sinned a great sin, and have made them gods of gold.

32 Yet now, if thou wilt forgive their sin—; and if not, blot me, I pray thee, out of thy book which thou hast written.

Why did Moses offer himself as an atonement for the people? (32:30–32) "The scriptures give a number of examples of self-sacrifice because of love. . . . In his compassion, Moses pleaded before the Lord. . . . Moses was willing to forfeit his place in eternity in his heartfelt desire to help save his people's spiritual lives" (Parry and Parry, *Symbols and Shadows*, 303). "Moses' status as a mediator thus becomes—as all things in the law of Moses were—a type and shadow of a greater mediatory labor that was to be when the Messiah of whom Moses testified came to work out the infinite and eternal atonement. . . . Salvation is in Christ, not in Moses" (McConkie, *Promised Messiah*, 440–41). See also Ether 12:10–11.

33 And the LORD said unto Moses, Whosoever hath sinned against me, him will I blot out of my book.

34 Therefore now go, lead the people unto *the place* of which I have spoken unto thee: behold, mine Angel shall go before thee: nevertheless in the day when I visit I will visit their sin upon them.

What did the Lord mean that those guilty of sin would be blotted out of His book? (32:33) "The Lord's reply was based on the principle that a person shall be punished only for his own sins (Ex. 32:33*a–c*). Moses was innocent of the Israelites' sin, because he had instructed them and committed them to obedience before leaving them (Ex. 24:3–4) and had left a leader over them" (Rasmussen, *Latter-day Saint Commentary on the Old Testament*, 121). "How do we apportion the blame when all share in it? We cannot. The law of Moses insists with great strictness that every individual man, woman, and child, rich and poor, shall pay 'ransom for his soul' of exactly the same amount—one-half shekel, no more, no less (see Exodus 30:11–16)" (Nibley, *Approaching Zion*, 569).

Why did the Lord continue to plague Israel? (32:35) "According to eternal law, the consequences that follow from the justice of God are severe and permanent. When a commandment is broken, a commensurate penalty is imposed. This happens automatically. . . . 'There is a law given, and a punishment affixed,' the prophet Alma taught, and 'justice claimeth the creature and executeth the law, and the law inflicteth the punishment' [Alma 42:22]. . . . Abinadi added that the Lord 'cannot deny justice when it has its claim' (Mosiah 15:27). By itself, justice is uncompromising. The justice of God holds each of us responsible for our own transgressions and automatically imposes the penalty" (Oaks, *With Full Purpose of Heart*, 115).

35 And the LORD plagued the people, because they made the calf, which Aaron made.

CHAPTER 33

The Lord promises to be with Israel and drive out the people of the land—The tabernacle of the congregation is moved away from the camp—The Lord speaks to Moses face to face in the tabernacle—Later, Moses sees the glory of God but not His face.

Exodus 33:1–3. The Lord Commands Moses to Lead Israel to the Promised Land

1 And the LORD said unto Moses, Depart, *and* go up hence, thou and the people which thou hast brought up out of the land of Egypt, unto the land which I sware unto Abraham, to Isaac, and to Jacob, saying, Unto thy seed will I give it:

2 And I will send an angel before thee; and I will drive out the Canaanite, the Amorite, and the Hittite, and the Perizzite, the Hivite, and the Jebusite:

Why would the Lord promise to drive the designated nations from the promised land? (33:2) "The six nations or people mentioned in this verse worshipped false gods and would have been a threat to the house of Israel. Joshua and the armies of Israel will be given the assignment to drive them out of the land [see Joshua 6–12]" (Valletta, et al., *Old Testament for Latter-day Saint Families*, 145).

3 Unto a land flowing with milk and honey: for I will not go up in the midst of thee; for thou *art* a stiffnecked people: lest I consume thee in the way.

Why did the Lord refuse to be "in the midst" of the people? (33:3) "The children of Israel were still called to their mission in the land of promise and would still be blessed with divine guidance. Nevertheless, many people had demonstrated by their actions at the time the commandments were spoken on Sinai and at the time of their presentation on tablets of stone that they did not have the capacity to 'endure his presence' and to keep his commandments (Ex. 20:18–21; Ex. 32; D&C 84:22–26). They had forfeited the privilege of having the Lord 'in the midst' of them" (Rasmussen, *Latter-day Saint Commentary on the Old Testament*, 121).

What does the phrase "a stiffnecked people" symbolize? (33:3) "Since the bowing of the head is a sign of humility, to be stiff-necked is the symbol of pride" (Lund, "Understanding Scriptural Symbols," 25). A stiffnecked people are those who murmur and are disobedient: "The Lord promised the children of Israel that He would send an angel to drive out the Canaanites, that Israel might inherit a land of milk and honey (see Ex. 33:1–3). . . .

"When Israel reached the borders of Canaan, . . . then began the murmuring. They questioned the commandment given through Moses, their living prophet. They spread their questioning to others. . . . [Their] questioning turned to rationalization and excuses. . . . The murmuring became disobedience" (Workman, "Beware of Murmuring," 85).

4 ¶ And when the people heard these evil tidings, they mourned: and no man did put on him his ornaments.

5 For the LORD had said unto Moses, Say unto the children of Israel, Ye *are* a stiffnecked people: I will come up into the midst of thee in a moment, and consume thee: therefore now put off thy ornaments from thee, that I may know what to do unto thee.

6 And the children of Israel stripped themselves of their ornaments by the mount Horeb.

Exodus 33:4–8. Moses Moves the Tabernacle Outside the Camp of Israel

Why was it necessary for the people to remove their jewelry and other ornaments? (33:4–6) "Besides telling Israel that they could no longer be in His presence, God . . . wanted to see if they were willing to rid themselves of everything that had to do with the golden calf, including the ornaments from which it had been made.

"Verses 4–6 can be confusing because verse 5 and 6 seem to recount the event that led to verse 4. We could profitably reword it . . . : 'When the Lord said to Moses that Israel was stiffnecked and if He were there with them He might consume them, He told them to strip their ornaments off so that He would know what He should do with them. When the people had heard this bad news, they stripped off their ornaments'" (Muhlestein, *Scripture Study Made Simple*, 116, 115). ⊕

7 And Moses took the tabernacle, and pitched it without the camp, afar off from the camp, and called it the Tabernacle of the congregation. And it came to pass, *that* every one which sought the LORD went out unto the tabernacle of the congregation, which *was* without the camp.

8 And it came to pass, when Moses went out unto the tabernacle, *that* all the people rose

Why did the Lord ask Moses to move the tabernacle outside of the camp? (33:7) "When the children of Israel were disobedient, the privilege of enjoying the blessings of having the tabernacle in their midst was removed from them. We read: 'And Moses took the tabernacle . . . afar off from the camp . . . [and] every one which sought the Lord went out unto the tabernacle of the congregation, which was without the camp' (Ex. 33:7).

"When the children of Israel again found favor in the sight of the Lord, the tabernacle was moved with them from place to place as they went about their quest for the promised land. It led them by day and was their security by night" (Perry, "Family Traditions," 19–20). ⊕

Exodus 33:9–11. Moses Speaks with the Lord Face to Face

What do we learn about God from Moses' experience? (33:9–11) "The Prophet Joseph Smith said, 'It is the first principle of the Gospel to know for a certainty the character of God and to know that we may converse with him as one man converses with another' . . . The prophets have known of him and have borne witness to the people concerning his attributes and his laws. He created Adam 'in the image of his own body' (Moses 6:9) and then walked and talked with him, with the very man whom he had created in his own likeness. He sent his Firstborn spirit Son, Jehovah, to commune with Moses 'face to face, as a man speaketh unto his friend'" (McConkie, in Conference Report, Apr. 1952, 55–56).

Exodus 33:12–23. Moses Asks the Lord to Be with the Children of Israel as They Travel to the Land of Promise

How does Moses' pleading for Israel typify Jesus Christ? (33:12–17) "Here Moses again serves as a type, or symbol, of Christ. The Israelites being cast out of God's presence is reminiscent of our sinful actions alienating us from God. When Moses pleads and God agrees that His grace be extended to all Israel, it is parallel with how the Savior's grace will cover us and allow us to be in God's presence again. The Lord's willingness to pardon Israel should comfort us as we realize how willing He is to continually forgive and pardon us" (Muhlestein, *Essential Old Testament Companion*, 120–21).

What can we learn from the Lord's promise to send His presence among the people? (33:14) This passage "continues the issues raised in vv. 1–6 concerning God's presence among the people. Moses asked God whom he planned to send with him on the journey to the land of promise. God responded that his presence would go with them (v. 14). It is not clear if this means that God had now decided to come back into the midst of his people (34:9 may indicate that he had not) or if God was identifying himself as the angel who

up, and stood every man *at* his tent door, and looked after Moses, until he was gone into the tabernacle.

9 And it came to pass, as Moses entered into the tabernacle, the cloudy pillar descended, and stood *at* the door of the tabernacle, and *the LORD* talked with Moses.

10 And all the people saw the cloudy pillar stand *at* the tabernacle door: and all the people rose up and worshipped, every man *in* his tent door.

11 And the LORD spake unto Moses face to face, as a man speaketh unto his friend. And he turned again into the camp: but his servant Joshua, the son of Nun, a young man, departed not out of the tabernacle.

12 ¶ And Moses said unto the LORD, See, thou sayest unto me, Bring up this people: and thou hast not let me know whom thou wilt send with me. Yet thou hast said, I know thee by name, and thou hast also found grace in my sight.

13 Now therefore, I pray thee, if I have found grace in thy sight, shew me now thy way, that I may know thee, that I may find grace in thy sight: and consider that this nation *is* thy people.

14 And he said, My presence shall go *with thee,* and I will give thee rest.

15 And he said unto him, If thy presence go not *with me,* carry us not up hence.

16 For wherein shall it be known here that I and thy people have found grace in thy sight? *is it* not in that thou goest with us? so shall we be separated, I and thy people, from all the people that *are* upon the face of the earth.

17 And the LORD said unto Moses, I will do this thing also that thou hast spoken: for thou hast found grace in my sight, and I know thee by name.

18 And he said, I beseech thee, shew me thy glory.

19 And he said, I will make all my goodness pass before thee, and I will proclaim the name of the LORD before thee; and will be gracious to whom I will be gracious, and will shew mercy on whom I will shew mercy.

20 And he said, Thou canst not see my face: for there shall no man see me, and live.

21 And the LORD said, Behold, *there is* a place by me, and thou shalt stand upon a rock:

22 And it shall come to pass, while my glory passeth by, that I will put thee in a clift of the rock, and will cover thee with my hand while I pass by:

23 And I will take away mine hand, and thou shalt see my back parts: but my face shall not be seen.

CHAPTER 34

Moses hews new tables of stone—He goes up into Mount Sinai for forty days—The Lord proclaims His name and attributes and reveals His law—He makes another covenant with Israel—The skin of Moses' face shines, and he wears a veil.

1 And the LORD said unto Moses, Hew thee two tables of stone like unto the first: and I

would go before the people" (Wright, "Revelations in the Wilderness of Sinai," 138).

Why is it significant that God knows Moses by name? (33:17) Modern revelation adds clarity and context to this verse: "When Moses says that God knows his name, he may be referring to the encounter he had with God that is recorded in Moses 1. There, when God first speaks with Moses, He says, 'Moses, my son' (Moses 1:6)" (Muhlestein, *Essential Old Testament Companion*, 120).

Who cannot see God's face and live? (33:20) Without the Joseph Smith Translation, the text in verse 20 would be confusing and seem to contradict verse 11 where God spoke to Moses "face to face." However, the Joseph Smith Translation clarifies these verses this way: "Thou canst not see my face *at this time, lest mine anger be kindled against thee also, and I destroy thee, and thy people;* for there shall no man *among them* see me *at this time,* and live, *for they are exceeding sinful. And no sinful man hath at any time, neither shall there be any sinful man at any time, that shall see my face and live*" (JST, Exodus 33:20). ⊕

How might we understand the phrase "thou shalt see my back parts"? (33:23) Revelation indicates that the natural man (mortal man), must be "transfigured" in order to behold God in His glory (D&C 84:19–24). "However, a certain privilege was accorded Moses at the time here under consideration (Exodus 33:21–23), and in 'the natural man' he was allowed to see the Lord's departure" (Rasmussen, *Introduction to the Old Testament and Its Teachings*, 1:94).

Exodus 34:1–4. Moses Makes Two Additional Stone Tablets

Why did the Lord command Moses to make another set of stone tablets? (34:1–2) The Joseph

Smith Translation explains: "And the Lord said unto Moses, Hew thee two *other* tables of stone, like unto the first, and I will write upon *them also,* the words *of the law, according as they were written at the* first *on the* tables which thou brakest; *but it shall not be according to the first, for I will take away the priesthood out of their midst....*

"But I will give unto them the law as at the first, but it shall be after the law of a carnal commandment. ... Therefore do as I have commanded thee, and be ready in the morning" (JST, Exodus 34:1–2; emphasis added). ⊕

will write upon *these* tables the words that
were in the first tables, which thou brakest.

2 And be ready in the morning, and come
up in the morning unto mount Sinai, and
present thyself there to me in the top of the
mount.

3 And no man shall come up with thee, neither let any man be seen throughout all the
mount; neither let the flocks nor herds feed
before that mount.

4 ¶ And he hewed two tables of stone like
unto the first; and Moses rose up early in the
morning, and went up unto mount Sinai, as
the LORD had commanded him, and took in
his hand the two tables of stone.

Exodus 34:5–9. The Lord Appears to Moses

What does the phrase mean that God "proclaimed the name of the Lord"? (34:5) "In reconfirming the covenant, God formally stated His name and His characteristics. He begins by saying 'Jehovah is Jehovah' (a more literal translation than is in the KJV), similar to when He told Moses His name on the same mount, saying 'I am that I am,' which was just a different form of the same verb from which the name *Jehovah* stems (see Exodus 3)" (Muhlestein, *Scripture Study Made Simple*, 118).

5 And the LORD descended in the cloud, and
stood with him there, and proclaimed the
name of the LORD.

How is God longsuffering, merciful, and just? (34:6–7) "The word *longsuffering* refers to the Lord's patience with and mercy for His children, and the phrase 'by no means clear the guilty' means the Lord is perfectly just and will hold the rebellious accountable for their actions" (*Old Testament Seminary Teacher Manual*, 302). "God will not forgive the guilty—or as the Joseph Smith Translation says, 'the rebellious' (JST, Exodus 34:7). As the Lord revealed to Alma the Elder: 'as oft as my people repent will I forgive them' (Mosiah 26:30)" (Valletta, et al., *Old Testament for Latter-day Saint Families*, 147).

6 And the LORD passed by before him, and
proclaimed, The LORD, The LORD God, merciful and gracious, longsuffering, and abundant in goodness and truth,

7 Keeping mercy for thousands, forgiving
iniquity and transgression and sin, and that
will by no means clear *the guilty;* visiting the
iniquity of the fathers upon the children, and
upon the children's children, unto the third
and to the fourth *generation.*

Why will the sins of parents be visited on their children? (34:7) "It is hard for some to understand how the Lord can punish the children of wicked people 'unto the third and to the fourth generation.' But Elder Neal A. Maxwell explained: 'Small equivocations [failures in spiritual commitment] in parents can produce large deviations [changes in spiritual behavior] in their children' ['Settle This in Your Hearts,' 65]. ... In

8 And Moses made haste, and bowed his
head toward the earth, and worshipped.

9 And he said, If now I have found grace in
thy sight, O Lord, let my Lord, I pray thee,
go among us; for it *is* a stiffnecked people;
and pardon our iniquity and our sin, and
take us for thine inheritance.

other words, when children follow the bad examples of their parents, they will suffer the same punishment" (Valletta, et al., *Old Testament for Latter-day Saint Families*, 147). ⊕

10 ¶ And he said, Behold, I make a covenant:
before all thy people I will do marvels, such
as have not been done in all the earth, nor in
any nation: and all the people among which
thou *art* shall see the work of the LORD: for
it *is* a terrible thing that I will do with thee.
11 Observe thou that which I command thee
this day: behold, I drive out before thee the
Amorite, and the Canaanite, and the Hittite,
and the Perizzite, and the Hivite, and the
Jebusite.
12 Take heed to thyself, lest thou make a
covenant with the inhabitants of the land
whither thou goest, lest it be for a snare in
the midst of thee:
13 But ye shall destroy their altars, break
their images, and cut down their groves:
14 For thou shalt worship no other god: for
the LORD, whose name *is* Jealous, *is* a jealous
God:
15 Lest thou make a covenant with the inhabitants of the land, and they go a whoring
after their gods, and do sacrifice unto their
gods, and *one* call thee, and thou eat of his
sacrifice;
16 And thou take of their daughters unto thy
sons, and their daughters go a whoring after

Exodus 34:10–17. God Gives Moses Another Covenant for Israel

What was the "terrible thing" the Lord would do? (34:10) Scholars also interpret this phrase *terrible thing* to mean *awesome* or *awe-inspiring*. "Moses had pleaded that the Lord would remain with Israel on the journey and consider them still his special people (as stated in Ex. 19:5–6), forgiving their obstinacy, iniquity, and sinfulness. In response, the Lord promised to help Israel take an inheritance from the idolatrous people in Canaan (Gen. 15:13–16; 17:7–9;1 Ne. 17:23–35); however, they had to keep their covenants and take to heart the 'terrible' (awesome) things he would do with them. They were neither to marry nor worship with the idolaters, lest they be corrupted (Ex. 34:13–16 and fn.)" (Rasmussen, *Latter-day Saint Commentary on the Old Testament*, 122). ⊕

What were the groves Israel was to cut down, and why were they commanded to do so? (34:12–13) Groves in Hebrew were "called Asherah (of which the plural is Asherim or Asheroth), either a living tree or a tree-like pole, set up as an object of worship, being symbolic of the female or productive principle in nature. Every Phoenician altar had an asherah near it. The word is often translated 'green trees' or 'grove.' This 'nature worship' became associated with gross immorality, and so the practice of setting up such 'groves' or idols was forbidden by Hebrew prophets (Deut. 16:21; Isa. 17:8; see also Num. 25:3; Judg. 2:11–13; 1 Sam. 7:3–4; 1 Kgs. 11:5; Micah 5:13–14)" (Bible Dictionary, "Grove").

What do we learn about the Lord's name being "Jealous" in this verse? (34:14) The Joseph Smith Translation indicates that the first use of the word "jealous" should be translated *Jehovah* (see Exodus 34:14*c*). "The second word translated 'jealous' here is from a Hebrew word (*qanah*) with a Semitic root meaning 'to become very red' through an emotional response. As indicated in the commentary for Exodus 20:5, the word could have been translated 'zealous.' The basic idea is that God is not casual or nonchalant about us and our response to his teachings; as a loving and concerned parent, he is quickly and deeply responsive to our actions and attitudes" (Ludlow, *Companion to Your Study of the Old Testament*, 160).

Summary of Exodus 34:18–28

The Lord makes another covenant with Israel and requires that feasts and sacrifices be done in a certain way. As Moses fasts for forty days and nights, he writes the ten commandments upon his stone tables.

Exodus 34:29–35. Moses Returns to the Camp of Israel Filled with the Light of God

In addition to representing light, what else might the word "shone" have symbolized? (34:29) The light on Moses' face shining could be symbolic of heavenly power: "For the Spirit of the Lord was upon [Abinadi]; and his face shone with exceeding luster, even as Moses' . . . while speaking with the Lord. And he spake with power and authority from God" (Mosiah 13:5–6). Or perhaps, "The word *shone* is used to translate the Hebrew verb *qaran*, which is from a noun meaning 'horn.' It here depicts radial beams of light, like the 'horns' of morning—the rays seen over the horizon before sunrise. (A mistranslation in the Latin Bible of Michelangelo's time caused him to put horns on the head of his heroic statue of Moses!)" (Rasmussen, *Latter-day Saint Commentary on the Old Testament*, 123).

their gods, and make thy sons go a whoring after their gods.

17 Thou shalt make thee no molten gods.

29 ¶ And it came to pass, when Moses came
down from mount Sinai with the two tables
of testimony in Moses' hand, when he came
down from the mount, that Moses wist not
that the skin of his face shone while he talked
with him.

30 And when Aaron and all the children of
Israel saw Moses, behold, the skin of his face
shone; and they were afraid to come nigh him.
31 And Moses called unto them; and Aaron
and all the rulers of the congregation returned
unto him: and Moses talked with them.

What Was Written on the Two New Stones Hewn by Moses? (Exodus 34:28)

In addition to the Ten Commandments, Moses recorded a series of laws that included feasts, ceremonies, and rituals to remind the children of Israel of their covenants with God. The Law of Moses is "the name assigned to the whole collection of written laws given through Moses to the house of Israel, as a replacement of the higher law that they had failed to obey. The law of Moses consisted of many ceremonies, rituals, and symbols, to remind the people frequently of their duties and responsibilities. It included a law of carnal commandments and performances, added to the basic laws of the gospel. Faith, repentance, baptism in water, and remission of sins were part of the law, as were also the Ten Commandments. Although inferior to the fulness of the gospel, there were many provisions in the law of Moses of high ethical and moral value that were equal to the divine laws of any dispensation. . . . The law functioned under the Aaronic Priesthood and was a preparatory gospel to bring its adherents to Christ. . . .

"The law as given through Moses was a good law, although adapted to a lower spiritual capacity than is required for obedience to the gospel in its fulness. However, the Jewish leaders had added many unauthorized provisions, ceremonies, and prohibitions to the original law, until it became extremely burdensome. These innovations were known as the 'traditions of the elders.' By New Testament times among the Jews the law had become so altered it had lost much of its spiritual meaning. It is this form of the law that is so harshly spoken against by Jesus and by Paul (see Matt. 15:1–9; Mark 7:1–13; Gal. 2:16–21). There is no evidence that the law of Moses had become as altered among the Nephites as among the Jews, and this may partially explain why the Nephites had less trouble in giving it up when the Savior came" (Bible Dictionary, "Law of Moses").

32 And afterward all the children of Israel came nigh: and he gave them in commandment all that the Lord had spoken with him in mount Sinai.

33 And *till* Moses had done speaking with them, he put a veil on his face.

34 But when Moses went in before the Lord to speak with him, he took the veil off, until he came out. And he came out, and spake unto the children of Israel *that* which he was commanded.

35 And the children of Israel saw the face of Moses, that the skin of Moses' face shone: and Moses put the veil upon his face again, until he went in to speak with him.

What meaning might we gain from Moses' veil? (34:33) "The veil which Moses wore after his forty-day sojourn on Mount Sinai represented the veiling (or the removal) of the fullness of the gospel of Jesus Christ from the presence of the tribes of Israel. What remained unto the children of Israel were the 'lesser priesthood . . . and the preparatory gospel . . . and the law of carnal commandments' (D&C 84:26–27). However, when Christ fulfilled the law of Moses, the veil of Moses was symbolically removed (2 Cor. 3:1–18)" (McConkie and Parry, *A Guide to Scriptural Symbols,* 105).

Who was the "him" Moses spoke with after speaking to the people? (34:35) According to the Joseph Smith Translation of Exodus 34:35, the word "him" is changed to "the Lord" (see JST, Exodus 34:35). Obviously, "the skin of Moses' face shone" because he had been transfigured. When people are transfigured, they are "temporarily changed in appearance and nature—that is, lifted to a higher spiritual level—so that they can endure the presence and glory of heavenly beings" (Guide to the Scriptures, "Transfiguration").

CHAPTERS 35–39

Israel is admonished to observe the Sabbath—Free gifts are offered for the tabernacle—The calls and inspiration of certain artisans are confirmed.

Wise-hearted men are chosen to work on the tabernacle—Moses restrains the people from donating any more material.

Bezaleel makes the ark, the mercy seat, and the cherubims—He makes the table, the vessels, the candlestick, the incense altar, the holy anointing oil, and the sweet incense.

Summary of Exodus 35–39

Once the Lord has revealed all that is needed for Israel to appropriately worship him, it is time for the work to begin. Moses invites those with "a willing heart" (Exodus 35:5) to give their gold and silver freely to build the tabernacle. Israel gives more than was needed (see Exodus 36). The Lord calls Bezaleel and "filled him with the spirit of God" (Exodus 35:31) to lead the effort to build all of the furnishings for the tabernacle (see Exodus 37:1, 6, 10, 17, 25). Others weave the sacred clothing for the priests (see Exodus 39). The children of Israel complete the tabernacle just as the Lord commanded them (see Exodus 39:32).

Bezaleel and others make the altar of burnt offerings and all things pertaining to the tabernacle—Offerings are made by 603,550 men.

Holy garments are made for Aaron and the priests—The breastplate is made—The tabernacle of the congregation is finished—Moses blesses the people.

CHAPTER 40

The tabernacle is reared—Aaron and his sons are washed and anointed and given an everlasting priesthood—The glory of the Lord fills the tabernacle—A cloud covers the tabernacle by day, and fire rests on it by night.

12 And thou shalt bring Aaron and his sons unto the door of the tabernacle of the congregation, and wash them with water.

13 And thou shalt put upon Aaron the holy garments, and anoint him, and sanctify him; that he may minister unto me in the priest's office.

14 And thou shalt bring his sons, and clothe them with coats:

15 And thou shalt anoint them, as thou didst anoint their father, that they may minister unto me in the priest's office: for their anointing shall surely be an everlasting priesthood throughout their generations.

16 Thus did Moses: according to all that the LORD commanded him, so did he.

Summary of Exodus 40:1–11

The Lord instructs Moses to set up the tabernacle with sacred furnishings. Each furnishing is then to be sanctified with holy oil for sacred use.

Exodus 40:12–16. Aaron and His Sons Are Cleansed and Dressed in Priesthood Robes

How did the priests prepare for their sacred service? (40:12–15) "Consecration to the priestly office consisted of two parts: ceremonial and sacrificial. Their ceremonial functions were: (1) They were washed at the door of the tabernacle. (2) They were clothed with the priestly garments (coats, girdles, and miters or turbans). (3) They were anointed (Ex. 40:15) with holy oil. Their sacrificial function included [offerings] . . . (1) a bullock as a sin offering . . . (2) a ram as a burnt offering . . . (3) a ram as a peace or consecration offering . . . [the blood was placed] on the priest's right ear, the thumb of his right hand, and the great toe of his right foot" (Bible Dictionary, "Priests").

In what way was Aaron's priesthood "everlasting"? (40:15) The Prophet Joseph Smith explained: "There was a priesthood conferred upon the sons of Levi throughout the generations of the Jews. They were born heirs to that priesthood by lineage or descent and held the keys of the first principles of the gospel. . . .

"[It was] forever hereditary, fixed on the head of Aaron down to Zacharias, the father of John" (Jackson, *Joseph Smith's Commentary on the Bible*, 30–31).

Symbolism of the Tabernacle (Exodus 40)

"There are three major divisions or areas in the tabernacle: the outer courtyard; the first room of the tabernacle proper, or holy place; and the inner room, or Holy of Holies. In modern temples three levels of life are also depicted by rooms in the temple: the world, or telestial, room; the terrestrial room; and the celestial room. The significance of these rooms is described thus:

"[The world] room depicts the world in which we live and die. Here instruction is given regarding man's second estate and the manner in which he may overcome the obstacles of mortality.

"The terrestrial room is symbolic of the peace that may be attained by men as they overcome their fallen condition through obedience to the laws and ordinances of the gospel.

"The celestial room symbolizes the eternal joy and peace found in the presence of God. Something of the spirit of God's infinite promises to the obedient has been captured in the design of this beautiful room" (*Narrative for The House of the Lord: Filmstrip Script*, frames 43, 48, 51).

"If we compare the three divisions of the tabernacle with these three levels of spiritual life, we find some interesting parallels and insights.

"The outer courtyard (the world or telestial room). The first thing encountered as one entered the main gate was the altar of sacrifice. Here the various animals and other offerings were slain and offered to the Lord. Strict obedience and sacrifice were thus required as the first step in the symbolic progression toward perfection and entry into God's presence. This first step could be likened to having faith in Christ . . . The sacrificial fires of the great altar thus signified that 'spiritual purification would come by the Holy Ghost, whom the Father would send because of the Son' (McConkie, *Promised Messiah*, 431).

The presence of God	**Holy of Holies**	**CELESTIAL**
Angelic guardians		
Prayer	Veil	
Live by light of Spirit and flesh and blood of Christ	altar of incense; table of shew-bread; sacred lampstand	**TERRESTRIAL**
	Holy Place	
Baptism and remission of sins	laver	
Obedience and sacrifice	altar of sacrifice	**TELESTIAL**
	Outer Courtyard	

"Directly in line next in the courtyard was the laver, or basin of water, which was used for washing and cleansing (see Exodus 30:19–20). . . . Once this cleansing is done, he is prepared to leave the world, or a telestial way of living, and 'be born' (John 3:5) into a higher state of spiritual life.

"The holy place (the terrestrial room). Three articles of furniture were found in the first room of the tabernacle: the table of shewbread, the sacred candlestick, and the altar of incense. Each article had its own significance. The table of shewbread, which had the bread and wine changed each Sabbath day, was a symbol similar to the sacramental emblems of today. They typified the body and blood of the Son of God, of which the spiritual person partakes consistently so that he can have spiritual life in Christ (see John 6:53–56). The candlestick, or lampstand, with its seven branches and its olive oil symbolized the perfect light of the Spirit (see D&C 45:56–57) through which the spiritually reborn person sees all truth (see John 14:16–17; 15:26). In the sacramental covenants there is a strong tie between the emblems of the body and the blood of the Savior and the power of the Spirit, for the Lord promises that as one always remembers Him, He will always have His Spirit to be with Him (see 3 Nephi 18:7, 11).

"The third article in the holy place was the altar of incense, a symbol of prayer (see Revelation 5:8), which stood directly in front of the veil. . . . The fact that the incense was consumed on coals of fire would suggest that even our prayers should be directed and influenced by the Holy Ghost (see 3 Nephi 19:24; Romans 8:26).

"The Holy of Holies (the celestial room). Just as the celestial room in modern temples symbolizes the kingdom where God dwells, so did the holy of holies in the ancient tabernacle. The only article of furniture in this inner room was the ark of the covenant, which the Lord Himself said was the place where He would meet Moses and commune with the people (see Exodus 25:22). Both on the veil, separating the holy place from the most holy, and on the lid of the ark were cherubim, or angels. This use of angels provides a beautiful representation of the concept taught in latter-day scripture that one passes by the angels on his way to exaltation (see D&C 132:19).

"In summary, the tabernacle and its plan and the ordinances thereof illustrate the grand and glorious symbolism of mankind's progress from a state of being alienated from God to one of full communion with Him" (*Old Testament Student Manual: Genesis–2 Samuel*, 155–56).

Summary of Exodus 40:17–33

According to the Lord's design, Moses places the sacred pieces in the Tabernacle in preparation for the dedicatory services.

Exodus 40:34–38. The Glory of the Lord Fills the Tabernacle

How did the Lord show His acceptance of the Tabernacle? (40:34–38) "The Lord manifested his acceptance of the tabernacle as his 'dwelling' on earth and as a place of worship and communication. When the glorious cloud filled the tabernacle, even Moses could not enter. Compare the spiritual phenomena similarly manifested when the first temple of the latter days was dedicated [see Doctrine and Covenants 110:1–10]. . . . Thereafter, when the cloud moved from the tabernacle, the children of Israel moved; and when it stopped, they stopped and made camp. They should have felt very secure under such a divine favor (Ex. 40:36–38; but see Num. 10–11)" (Rasmussen, *Latter-day Saint Commentary on the Old Testament*, 127). ⊕

34 ¶ Then a cloud covered the tent of the congregation, and the glory of the LORD filled the tabernacle.

35 And Moses was not able to enter into the tent of the congregation, because the cloud abode thereon, and the glory of the LORD filled the tabernacle.

36 And when the cloud was taken up from over the tabernacle, the children of Israel went onward in all their journeys:

37 But if the cloud were not taken up, then they journeyed not till the day that it was taken up.

38 For the cloud of the LORD *was* upon the tabernacle by day, and fire was on it by night, in the sight of all the house of Israel, throughout all their journeys.

THE THIRD BOOK OF MOSES

CALLED

LEVITICUS

Introduction

Leviticus is the third of five books (the Pentateuch) written by Moses. It focuses on the tribe of Levi, who were called by the Lord "to have charge of the whole congregation before the tabernacle and to do the service of the tabernacle. Aaron and his sons were designated the priests that officiated in the tabernacle (see Numbers 3). Non-Levites could not be priests or even hold the Levitical Priesthood" (Renlund and Renlund, *Melchizedek Priesthood,* 16).

"Leviticus receives its name from the Septuagint (the Greek translation of the Old Testament) and means 'relating to the Levites.' Its Hebrew title, *wayyiqra'*, is the first word in the Hebrew text of the book and means 'and He [i.e., the Lord] called.' Although Leviticus does not deal only with the special duties of the Levites, it is so named because it concerns mainly the service of worship at the tabernacle, which was conducted by the priests (who were the sons of Aaron), assisted by many from the rest of the tribe of Levi" (*Zondervan KJV Commentary*, 140). "Since all of this was the special prerogative of the priests of the Aaronic Priesthood, the duties of the lesser Levites are not catalogued in this book but are given in the book of Numbers" (Pearson, *The Old Testament,* 29).

Leviticus also "emphasizes the holiness of God and the code by which His people could live to become holy" (Guide to the Scriptures, "Leviticus"). Holzapfel, Pike, and Seely explain: "In Leviticus the Lord teaches ancient Israel about holiness in three areas: space, condition, and time. First, God reveals principles of holiness as manifested in sacred space—the building of the Tabernacle, which involves the laws of sacrifice, the consecration and functioning of the priests, and the laws of clean and unclean that are mediated at the Tabernacle (Lev 1–10). Second, Leviticus emphasizes the sacred condition of people as taught through a series of moral and ritual commandments with instructions about how a person can repent of sin and be cleansed from ritual impurity. In conjunction with these laws, the Lord reveals the principles of repentance and reconciliation that lead to atonement (Lev 11–22). Finally, the Lord institutes in the law moments of sacred time: the Sabbath and the festivals, during which the people learn holiness through their worship at these sacred times (Lev 23–25)" (*Jehovah and the World of the Old Testament,* 112).

"Part of the value of the book of Leviticus for us today is its emphasis on the absolute need for an atonement to cleanse people from sin and bring them into communion with their God, who is likewise pure and holy. We are reminded that every sin is offensive to God and carries a penalty that must be paid in the manner prescribed by him. This suggests the vital importance in our daily lives of placing faith in the Savior's own 'great and last' atoning sacrifice for the sins of all mankind (Alma 34:14)" (Ricks, "Law of Sacrifice," 25).

CHAPTER 1

Animals without blemish are sacrificed as an atonement for sins—Burnt offerings are a sweet savor unto the Lord.

1 And the LORD called unto Moses, and spake unto him out of the tabernacle of the congregation, saying,

Leviticus 1:1–9. Animals Are Sacrificed to Make an Atonement for Sin

What was the tabernacle of the congregation? (1:1) The tabernacle was the "center place of Israel's worship activities during the wanderings and until the building of the temple in Solomon's day. The tabernacle was in fact a portable temple. It was an inner tent, the area available for sacred purposes (Ex. 26:7; 36:14)" (Bible Dictionary, "Tabernacle").

President Boyd K. Packer further explained, "The tabernacle served . . . as the focal point of the Israelites' communication with God while they were in the wilderness" (*Holy Temple*, 93).

Who could take offerings to the Lord? (1:2) Anyone could take an offering to the priests. The King James Version wording "any man of you" is translated in many other Bible editions as "any one of you" or "any of you." The phrase "any man of you" included women and those who were not of the tribes of Israel. If they had faith and believed in God, they could take an offering of an animal for sacrifice. The priests then did the procedure of the sacrifice and offering (see *Nelson Study Bible* [NKJV], 160).

What kind of offering did God require? (1:2–3) The animal had to be male "'without blemish' [which] means to be sound or whole. . . . All sacrificial animals had to meet two other requirements. They had to be of the category that the Lord declared clean (see Leviticus 11), and they also had to be from domesticated herds and flocks (see Leviticus 1:2). . . .

"This offering was to be 'voluntary' (Leviticus 1:3). It was not forced, but served as a free expression of gratitude on the part of the individual" (*Old Testament Student Manual: Genesis–2 Samuel*, 160–61).

What three elements were a part of an acceptable offering? (1:3–7) In his nineteenth-century biblical work, Andrew Jukes explained that "in each offering there are at least *three distinct objects* presented to us. There is the *offering*, the *priest*, the *offerer*. A definite knowledge of the precise import of each of these is absolutely requisite if we would understand the offerings.

"What, then, is *the offering?* what *the priest?* what *the offerer?* Christ is the offering, Christ is the priest, Christ is the offerer. . . . [These] distinct classes [give] us one particular view of Christ, either in His character, or in His work, or person" (*Law of the Offerings*, 42–43).

How does the burnt offering symbolize the Savior and His Atonement? (1:4) "Laying hands upon the head of the animal before it was slain exemplified the transfer of suffering for sin, later done for us by the Savior. The ascending smoke and vapors from the burnt offering, as 'a sweet savour unto the Lord' (Lev. 1:9), represented a communication of gratitude and supplication [prayer] from earth to heaven" (Rasmussen, *Latter-day Saint Commentary on the Old Testament*, 128).

2 Speak unto the children of Israel, and say
unto them, If any man of you bring an offering unto the LORD, ye shall bring your offering of the cattle, *even* of the herd, and of the
flock.

3 If his offering *be* a burnt sacrifice of the
herd, let him offer a male without blemish: he
shall offer it of his own voluntary will at the
door of the tabernacle of the congregation before the LORD.

4 And he shall put his hand upon the head
of the burnt offering; and it shall be accepted
for him to make atonement for him.

5 And he shall kill the bullock before the LORD: and the priests, Aaron's sons, shall bring the blood, and sprinkle the blood round about upon the altar that *is by* the door of the tabernacle of the congregation.

6 And he shall flay the burnt offering, and cut it into his pieces.

7 And the sons of Aaron the priest shall put fire upon the altar, and lay the wood in order upon the fire:

8 And the priests, Aaron's sons, shall lay the parts, the head, and the fat, in order upon the wood that *is* on the fire which *is* upon the altar:

9 But his inwards and his legs shall he wash in water: and the priest shall burn all on the altar, *to be* a burnt sacrifice, an offering made by fire, of a sweet savour unto the LORD.

Why were blood sacrifices necessary? (1:5) "It must be shedding the blood of the Only Begotten to atone for man, for this was the plan of redemption, and without the shedding of blood was no remission. And as the sacrifice was instituted for a type by which man was to discern the great Sacrifice which God had prepared, to offer a sacrifice contrary to that, no faith could be exercised, because redemption was not purchased in that way, nor the power of atonement instituted after that order; consequently Cain could have no faith; and whatsoever is not of faith, is sin" (*Joseph Smith* [manual], 48).

Why did they wash the bullock's inwards and legs? (1:9) The washing of the inwards and legs indicates that we need to spiritually purify ourselves in regards to both our actions and our desires by following the example of Jesus Christ. Andrew Jukes explained, "'*The legs'* and *'the inwards'* are the walk and affections. *'The water'* represents the Spirit acting through the Word [Christ]. . . . Christ, though without spot or blemish, yet as a man in His feelings and walk submitted to God's Word and Spirit. . . . Jesus, as man, fully did so: every step, every feeling, obeyed" (Jukes, *Law of the Offerings,* 74–75).

Summary of Leviticus 1:10–17

The Lord details the process for acceptable sacrifices and offerings. Sacrificial animals include cattle, sheep, goats, turtledoves, and young pigeons.

CHAPTER 2

How offerings of flour with oil and incense are made.

Summary of Leviticus 2

Leviticus 2 describes the meal offering (KJV, "meat"). The Hebrew term is *minchah.* "The English word meat in this context is used in the older sense of 'food.' The Minchah consisted chiefly of grain (or flour and cakes made from grain) and wine, seasoned with salt, and offered with incense. The Minchah could not be offered with a sin offering, but no burnt or peace offering was complete without it. Part was placed on the altar of burnt offering; the remainder was usually eaten by the priests in a holy place (Lev. 6:14–18, 23; Mal. 1:11). It was such an important part of the daily burnt offering that the term is sometimes used to denote the whole morning or evening sacrifice (2 Kgs. 3:20)" (Bible Dictionary, "Meat offering or meal offering").

Summary of Leviticus 3

"Peace offerings, as the name indicates, presupposed that the sacrificer was at peace with God; they were offered for the further realization and enjoyment of that peace. The characteristic rite was the sacrificial meal. A feast symbolized fellowship and friendship among all its partakers and providers, and also a state of joy and gladness" (Bible Dictionary, "Sacrifices").

Leviticus 4:1–26. Offerings Are Prescribed for Unintentional Sins of Priests, Congregation, and Rulers

What allowances did the Law make for those who sinned in ignorance? (4:2) "Remedies were given for sins committed in ignorance of the law, whether by a priest (Lev. 4:3), a whole congregation (Lev. 4:13), a ruler (Lev. 4:22), or one of the people (Lev. 4:27).... Penalties for breaking the law unwittingly were not as great as those for willful sinning" (Rasmussen, *Latter-day Saint Commentary on the Old Testament*, 129).

Elder Bruce C. Hafen added, "King Benjamin taught that the Atonement applies fully to ignorant transgression as well as to deliberate transgression, even though the degree of wrongful motive varies so widely between these two categories that they hardly seem sinful in the same sense [see Mosiah 3:11–12]" (*Broken Heart*, 16). See also verses 13 and 22.

Why are hands laid upon the animal's head before it is slain? (4:4) "Before making a blood sacrifice, the person making the offering, not the priest, laid hands on the victim [the animal, in this case]. The act signified the transference of guilt to, or self-identification with, the victim" (*Tyndale Bible Dictionary*, 570). "The laying on of hands ... dedicated the animal to God and made it the sacrificer's representative and substitute" (Bible Dictionary, "Sacrifices"). See also verses 15 and 24. See commentary in this volume for Leviticus 1:4.

What did the blood symbolize? (4:5–7) Blood "represents life—'the life of the flesh is in the blood' (Lev. 17:11). In scriptural language the shedding of blood is the taking of life. The atoning power of animal sacrifice came from the shedding of the animal's blood, which represented the life of the animal, as a type for the atoning sacrifice of Christ. Christ literally shed his blood both in Gethsemane and on Calvary.... Thus, the blood also symbolizes an atoning sacrifice.

CHAPTER 3

Peace offerings are made with animals without blemish, whose blood is sprinkled on the altar—Israel is forbidden to eat fat or blood.

CHAPTER 4

Sinners are forgiven through sin offerings of animals without blemish—Priests thereby make an atonement for the sins of the people.

1 And the LORD spake unto Moses, saying,

2 Speak unto the children of Israel, saying, If a soul shall sin through ignorance against any of the commandments of the LORD *concerning things* which ought not to be done, and shall do against any of them:

3 If the priest that is anointed do sin according to the sin of the people; then let him bring for his sin, which he hath sinned, a young bullock without blemish unto the LORD for a sin offering.

4 And he shall bring the bullock unto the door of the tabernacle of the congregation before the LORD; and shall lay his hand upon the bullock's head, and kill the bullock before the LORD.

5 And the priest that is anointed shall take of the bullock's blood, and bring it to the tabernacle of the congregation:

6 And the priest shall dip his finger in the blood, and sprinkle of the blood seven times before the LORD, before the veil of the sanctuary.

7 And the priest shall put *some* of the blood upon the horns of the altar of sweet incense before the LORD, which *is* in the tabernacle of the congregation; and shall pour all the blood of the bullock at the bottom of the altar of the burnt offering, which *is at* the door of the tabernacle of the congregation.

8 And he shall take off from it all the fat of the bullock for the sin offering; the fat that covereth the inwards, and all the fat that *is* upon the inwards,

9 And the two kidneys, and the fat that *is* upon them, which *is* by the flanks, and the caul above the liver, with the kidneys, it shall he take away,

10 As it was taken off from the bullock of the sacrifice of peace offerings: and the priest shall burn them upon the altar of the burnt offering.

11 And the skin of the bullock, and all his flesh, with his head, and with his legs, and his inwards, and his dung,

12 Even the whole bullock shall he carry forth without the camp unto a clean place, where the ashes are poured out, and burn him on the wood with fire: where the ashes are poured out shall he be burnt.

13 ¶ And if the whole congregation of Israel sin through ignorance, and the thing be hid from the eyes of the assembly, and they have done *somewhat against* any of the commandments of the LORD *concerning things* which should not be done, and are guilty;

14 When the sin, which they have sinned against it, is known, then the congregation shall offer a young bullock for the sin, and bring him before the tabernacle of the congregation.

15 And the elders of the congregation shall lay their hands upon the head of the bullock

Moses said, 'It is the blood that maketh an atonement for the soul' (Lev. 17:11). Through the blood of the Savior we are both redeemed and sanctified (D&C 27:2; Moses 6:60)" (McConkie, *Gospel Symbolism*, 253). See also verses 16–18, 25.

Why put blood on the horns of the altar? (4:7) "The horns of the altar' (Leviticus 4:7, 30) symbolized power. The scriptures refer to the Savior as the 'horn of salvation' (Luke 1:69), which indicates His power to save (see Psalm 18:2).... There were four horns on the altar. In the scriptures, the number four can represent the entire earth [Revelation 7:1]. Thus, placing blood on the horns could symbolize that there is power in the Savior's Atonement to save all of God's children who ever have or ever will live on the earth" (*Old Testament Seminary Teacher Material* [2018], 312). See also verses 18 and 25.

In what ways did burning the sin offering outside the camp teach of Christ's Atonement? (4:12) "The atoning sacrifice ... could be thought of as an offering for sin, for that was its purpose.... Christ stood ... as though He were guilty of all sins, even though He was guilty of none. He became a sin offering for all mankind. This sacrifice involved more than the suffering in the Garden of Gethsemane. The completion of the sacrifice took place on the cross outside the city walls. Thus, Paul saw in Christ's sacrifice a fulfilment of the typology of the sin offering being burned outside the camp [see Hebrews 13:11–13]" (*Old Testament Student Manual: Genesis–2 Samuel*, 167). See also verse 21.

before the LORD: and the bullock shall be
killed before the LORD.

16 And the priest that is anointed shall bring
of the bullock's blood to the tabernacle of the
congregation:

17 And the priest shall dip his finger *in some*
of the blood, and sprinkle *it* seven times before the LORD, *even* before the veil.

18 And he shall put *some* of the blood upon
the horns of the altar which *is* before the
LORD, that *is* in the tabernacle of the congregation, and shall pour out all the blood at
the bottom of the altar of the burnt offering,
which *is at* the door of the tabernacle of the
congregation.

19 And he shall take all his fat from him, and
burn *it* upon the altar.

20 And he shall do with the bullock as he did
with the bullock for a sin offering, so shall
he do with this: and the priest shall make an
atonement for them, and it shall be forgiven
them.

21 And he shall carry forth the bullock without the camp, and burn him as he burned
the first bullock: it *is* a sin offering for the
congregation.

22 ¶ When a ruler hath sinned, and done
somewhat through ignorance *against* any of
the commandments of the LORD his God
concerning things which should not be done,
and is guilty;

23 Or if his sin, wherein he hath sinned,
come to his knowledge; he shall bring his
offering, a kid of the goats, a male without
blemish:

24 And he shall lay his hand upon the head
of the goat, and kill it in the place where they
kill the burnt offering before the LORD: it *is*
a sin offering.

25 And the priest shall take of the blood of

Why did the priests have specific instructions regarding the sacrifices and offerings of the animals? (4:20) The apostle Paul in the New Testament taught that the law of Moses was a "schoolmaster" to lead the people to faith in Christ (see Galatians 3:23–24). What role might these sacrificial instructions have played in building faith in Christ?

Why were particular animals required for different sacrifices? (4:23) "Every sin offering required the slaughtering of a substitutionary animal. But the kind of sacrificial animal and the rites of atonement varied according to specified circumstances. Account was taken of the offender and the kind of misdeed committed" (Roehrs and Franzmann, *Concordia Self-Study Commentary*, 92). "Less valuable animals were sacrificed for those with lesser standing in the community or of lesser economic means. Thus a bull was required for the high priest (v. 3) and the whole community (v. 14), but a male goat for a civic leader (v. 23) and

the sin offering with his finger, and put *it* upon the horns of the altar of burnt offering, and shall pour out his blood at the bottom of the altar of burnt offering.

26 And he shall burn all his fat upon the altar, as the fat of the sacrifice of peace offerings: and the priest shall make an atonement for him as concerning his sin, and it shall be forgiven him.

CHAPTERS 5–6

The people are to confess and make amends for their sins—Forgiveness comes through a trespass offering—Priests thereby make an atonement for sin.

The people must first make restitution for sin, then offer a trespass offering, and thereby gain forgiveness through atonement made by the priests.

a female goat (v. 28) or lamb (v. 32) for an ordinary Israelite. If an offerer was too poor, then doves and pigeons were sufficient (5:7)" (*NIV Study Bible*, 151–52).

Summary of Leviticus 4:27–35

The Lord gives sin offering instructions regarding unintentional sins of the common people. Many of the specific commands parallel those given earlier in this chapter.

Summary of Leviticus 5–6

The Lord teaches the Israelites about sin and repentance. He emphasizes the importance of confession and restitution (see Leviticus 5:5, 16; 6:4–5). However, "The rituals of sacrifice were not automatic in their effect. The worshiper had to recognize, acknowledge, and repent of the sin. . . . A guiding principle of biblical law and ethics is that when a person has caused harm to another, whether to God or to another human being, the one offending is responsible to make good the loss. . . . The restitution and fine were paid first, as evidence of the offender's genuine repentance. Then the priest sacrificed the ram as atonement" (*Nelson Study Bible* [NKJV], 165, 166).

Sacrifice Then and Now (Leviticus 1–7)

President M. Russell Ballard taught how the law of sacrifice continued ever after Christ fulfilled the law of Moses: "The law of sacrifice with its system of offerings given to Moses was still being practiced in New Testament times. Jesus Christ of the New Testament was Jehovah of the Old Testament—He who gave the law of Moses in the first place, prescribing elements of the law that specifically pointed to His future atoning sacrifice. He was, then, the one with authority to fulfill that law, and His final words—'It is finished' (John 19:30)—indicate that this had been done. . . .

"After His mortal ministry, Christ elevated the law of sacrifice to a new level. In describing how the law would continue, Jesus told his Nephite Apostles that He would no longer accept burnt offerings but that His disciples should offer 'a broken heart and a contrite spirit' (3 Ne. 9:19–20; see also D&C 59:8, 12). Instead of the Lord requiring our animals or grain, now He wants us to give up all that is ungodly. This higher practice of the law of sacrifice reaches into the inner soul of a person. Elder Neal A. Maxwell of the Quorum of the Twelve Apostles said: 'Real, personal sacrifice never was placing an animal on the altar. Instead, it is a willingness to put the animal in us upon the altar and letting it be consumed!' ("Deny Yourselves of All Ungodliness," *Ensign*, May 1995, 68)" ("Law of Sacrifice," 10).

Summary of Leviticus 7

"More specifications were given regarding trespass offerings, peace offerings, portions to be eaten and not to be eaten, types of flesh never to be eaten, portions to be given to the priest, and pertinent regulations" (Rasmussen, *Latter-day Saint Commentary on the Old Testament*, 130).

Leviticus 8:1–13. Aaron and His Sons Are Set Apart and Prepared to Work in the Tabernacle

How does Leviticus 8 relate to Exodus 29? (8:1)

In Exodus 29, Moses receives a revelation from the Lord about how to prepare Aaron and his sons for their priesthood ministry. Leviticus 8 "shows in a very interesting way the relationship of Leviticus to Exodus.

CHAPTER 7

Laws governing various sacrifices are listed—The children of Israel are forbidden to eat fat or blood—They worship by sacrifice—Through sacrifice they gain forgiveness, make vows, consecrate their property, render thanks, and are reconciled to God.

CHAPTER 8

Aaron and his sons are washed, anointed, clothed in their priesthood robes, and consecrated before all Israel—Moses and Aaron offer sacrifices to make reconciliation and atonement with the Lord.

1 And the LORD spake unto Moses, saying,

Sacrifices and Offerings of the Mosaic Law (Leviticus 1–7)

The first seven chapters of Leviticus detail the various sacrifices and offerings commanded by the Lord within the Law of Moses. The following chart provides an overview:

Type of Sacrifice	Item	Purpose	Leviticus Reference
Burnt Offering First practiced by Adam and then the other patriarchs.	Whole animal	To give a total offering to God, "a similitude of the sacrifice of the Only Begotten, even Jesus Christ" (Moses 5:7).	1:3–17; 6:9–13
Meat or Meal Offering Usually cakes made from grain.	Flour and oil	To give a gift to God and His servants.	2:1–16; 6:14–23; 7:9–10
Peace Offering	Unblemished animal	To give thanks, renew covenants, and show voluntary obedience to God.	3:1–17; 7:11–38
Sin Offering	Bull, goat, lamb, doves, and pigeons	To prepare the people to receive forgiveness.	4:1–5; 5:1–13; 6:25–30
Trespass Offering	Ram	To atone for deliberate sin.	5:14–26; 6:1–7; 7:1–10

(Valletta, et al., *Old Testament for Latter-day Saint Families*, 153)

They are parts of a unified whole. The consecration of the priests [in Leviticus 8] is the fulfillment of the commands in Ex. 29 (cf. vv. 1–37).... Exodus ends with the setting up of the tabernacle. Leviticus proceeds with the directions for the offerings. Then Leviticus tell how the priests began their ministry, using the terms of the directions already given in Exodus" (*Expositor's Bible Commentary [Abridged]*, 135).

2 Take Aaron and his sons with him, and the garments, and the anointing oil, and a bullock for the sin offering, and two rams, and a basket of unleavened bread;

3 And gather thou all the congregation together unto the door of the tabernacle of the congregation.

4 And Moses did as the LORD commanded him; and the assembly was gathered together unto the door of the tabernacle of the congregation.

5 And Moses said unto the congregation, This *is* the thing which the LORD commanded to be done.

6 And Moses brought Aaron and his sons, and washed them with water.

7 And he put upon him the coat, and girded him with the girdle, and clothed him with the robe, and put the ephod upon him, and he girded him with the curious girdle of the ephod, and bound *it* unto him therewith.

8 And he put the breastplate upon him: also he put in the breastplate the Urim and the Thummim.

9 And he put the mitre upon his head; also upon the mitre, *even* upon his forefront, did he put the golden plate, the holy crown; as the LORD commanded Moses.

10 And Moses took the anointing oil, and anointed the tabernacle and all that *was* therein, and sanctified them.

11 And he sprinkled thereof upon the altar seven times, and anointed the altar and all his

How did Aaron and his sons' callings differ from other priesthood holders of their day? (8:2) The priesthood confirmed upon Aaron and his seed "was of lesser power and authority than the priesthood of Melchizedek and was used to administer the outward ordinances, particularly as characterized by ... the law of Moses.... The lesser priesthood was conferred only upon men of the tribe of Levi. However, within the tribe, only Aaron and his sons could hold the office of priest. And, still further, from the firstborn of Aaron's sons (after Aaron) was selected the high priest (or president of the priests). Thus Aaron and his sons after him had greater offices in the Levitical Priesthood than did the other Levites" (Bible Dictionary, "Aaronic Priesthood"; see also D&C 84:18).

Why wash the priests with water? (8:6) "Not only must the sacrifices be without blemish, but those who offer them must also be properly purified. The next section of Leviticus describes the consecration of the priests" (Ramsay, *Westminster Guide to the Books of the Bible*, 52). Gaye Strathearn explained why the priests must be purified: "Although God is the ultimate source of the power to sanctify, at times he also uses certain people or places to sanctify, and therefore the Old Testament also describes them as [holy].... The sacrificial court of the Tabernacle or Temple is described as a holy place ... because the sacrifices bring people into the realm of holiness. Those who administer the sacrifices are also described as [holy]" ("Holiness to the Lord," 223). ⊕

vessels, both the laver and his foot, to sanctify them.

12 And he poured of the anointing oil upon Aaron's head, and anointed him, to sanctify him.

13 And Moses brought Aaron's sons, and put coats upon them, and girded them with girdles, and put bonnets upon them; as the LORD commanded Moses.

What does anointing with oil symbolize? (8:12) President Dallin H. Oaks explained: "Anointings were declared to be for sanctification [see Leviticus 8:10–12] and perhaps can also be seen as symbolic of the blessings to be poured out from heaven as a result of this sacred act" ("Healing the Sick," 48). Alonzo L. Gaskill adds, "From antiquity to the present, oil has served as a standard symbol for the Holy Ghost" (*Lost Language of Symbolism*, 50). See commentary in this volume for 1 Samuel 10:1 and 2 Samuel 5:3.

Summary of Leviticus 8:14–21

A sacrifice of animals is made on behalf of Aaron and his sons.

Leviticus 8:22–36. Moses Offers Additional Sacrifices

22 ¶ And he brought the other ram, the ram of consecration: and Aaron and his sons laid their hands upon the head of the ram.

23 And he slew *it;* and Moses took of the blood of it, and put *it* upon the tip of Aaron's right ear, and upon the thumb of his right hand, and upon the great toe of his right foot.

24 And he brought Aaron's sons, and Moses put of the blood upon the tip of their right ear, and upon the thumbs of their right hands, and upon the great toes of their right feet: and Moses sprinkled the blood upon the altar round about.

25 And he took the fat, and the rump, and all the fat that *was* upon the inwards, and the caul *above* the liver, and the two kidneys, and their fat, and the right shoulder:

26 And out of the basket of unleavened bread, that *was* before the LORD, he took one unleavened cake, and a cake of oiled bread, and one wafer, and put *them* on the fat, and upon the right shoulder:

Why was blood placed on these body parts? (8:22–24) "The priest put some of [the] blood [from the offering] upon the tip of the right ear, the right thumb, and the great toe of the right foot of the person to be consecrated, in order that the organ of hearing, with which he hearkened to the word of the Lord, and those used in acting and walking according to His commandments, might thereby be sanctified through the power of the atoning blood of the sacrifice" (Keil and Delitzsch, *Commentary* [on Leviticus 14:13–14]; emphasis added). See commentary in this volume for Leviticus 14:14.

27 And he put all upon Aaron's hands, and upon his sons' hands, and waved them *for* a wave offering before the LORD.

28 And Moses took them from off their hands, and burnt *them* on the altar upon the burnt offering: they *were* consecrations for a sweet savour: it *is* an offering made by fire unto the LORD.

29 And Moses took the breast, and waved it *for* a wave offering before the LORD: *for* of the ram of consecration it was Moses' part; as the LORD commanded Moses.

30 And Moses took of the anointing oil, and of the blood which *was* upon the altar, and sprinkled *it* upon Aaron, *and* upon his garments, and upon his sons, and upon his sons' garments with him; and sanctified Aaron, *and* his garments, and his sons, and his sons' garments with him.

31 ¶ And Moses said unto Aaron and to his sons, Boil the flesh *at* the door of the tabernacle of the congregation: and there eat it with the bread that *is* in the basket of consecrations, as I commanded, saying, Aaron and his sons shall eat it.

32 And that which remaineth of the flesh and of the bread shall ye burn with fire.

33 And ye shall not go out of the door of the tabernacle of the congregation *in* seven days, until the days of your consecration be at an end: for seven days shall he consecrate you.

34 As he hath done this day, *so* the LORD hath commanded to do, to make an atonement for you.

35 Therefore shall ye abide *at* the door of the tabernacle of the congregation day and night seven days, and keep the charge of the LORD, that ye die not: for so I am commanded.

36 So Aaron and his sons did all things which the LORD commanded by the hand of Moses.

What do we learn from the wave offering? (8:27–29) "The wave offering, sometimes called the heave offering, was performed in connection with a peace offering (Lev. 8:29), the firstfruits of the harvest (Lev. 23:11–12), and of the two loaves at the Feast of Weeks (Lev. 23:20). It was also used in connection with the cleansing of a leper (Lev. 14:12, 24). The 'waving' or 'heaving' consisted of taking the breast and the right shoulder of a sacrificial animal or the firstfruits of the harvest and moving them horizontally in the direction of the sanctuary. It was to signify that these choice parts of the sacrifice were first presented to God and then returned to the officiating priests for their use" (Ludlow, *Unlocking the Old Testament*, 36–37). See commentary in this volume for Leviticus 14:24.

Why did the high priest stay at the tabernacle for seven days and nights? (8:33–35) "The high priest may not leave for any reason because this would expose him to uncleanness" (Walton, et al., *IVP Bible Background Commentary*, 153). Joseph Fielding McConkie and Donald W. Parry described the symbolic significance of seven: "The root of the Hebrew word for seven (sheva) is identical to the Hebrew verb that means 'to take an oath,' thus connecting the word seven to covenants and covenant making. Further, the word seven denotes perfection and completion" (*Guide to Scriptural Symbols*, 99). These seven days were part of a completion of their spiritual cleansing. See commentary in this volume for Leviticus 9:1.

Leviticus 9:1–7. Moses Calls on Aaron, the Priests, and the Children of Israel to Gather at the Tabernacle with Their Offerings

Why did Aaron and his sons begin their ministry on the eighth day? (9:1) "The number eight is associated with the concepts of resurrection, new beginnings, rebirth, and baptism. . . . Aaron and his sons were consecrated on the eighth day, after waiting 'at the door of the tabernacle of the congregation day and night seven days' (Leviticus 8:35; 9:1). The number eight here is likely a symbol, both of their new beginning as consecrated priests and also of their typification of Christ, whose number is eight" (Gaskill, *Lost Language of Symbolism*, 129, 130).

What does the sequence of the sin, burnt, peace, and meat offerings teach us? (9:2–4) "A young bull was the prescribed sin offering for the high priest (4:3). Before he could offer the sacrifices of others, his own sin needed atonement. The bull of the sin offering and the ram of the burnt offering (1:4, 10) accomplished this. . . . All four of the regular public offerings—burnt, sin, peace, and grain—were performed on this first day of Israel's sacrificial worship in the tabernacle. The first two were specifically to atone for sin; the second two were for a feast of fellowship with God. Only the trespass, or reparation, offering was missing because it was a private offering (5:14–6:7)" (*Nelson Study Bible* [NKJV], 172).

What does "glory of the Lord" mean? (9:6) "An expression that occurs frequently in the Old Testament. It sometimes denotes the fulness of the majesty of God, revealed in the world and made known to men (Num. 14:21–22; Isa. 6:3; 66:19); in other places it denotes some outward and visible manifestation of God's presence (Ex. 33:17–23; Ezek. 1:28; 9:3; 10:4, 18–19; 11:23; 43:2–5; Luke 2:9; 9:32; John 1:14)" (Bible Dictionary, "Glory of the Lord, or of Jehovah").

CHAPTER 9

Aaron makes an atonement by sacrifice for himself and all Israel—He and his sons offer sacrifices—The glory of the Lord appears to all—Fire from the Lord consumes the offerings on the altar.

1 And it came to pass on the eighth day, *that* Moses called Aaron and his sons, and the elders of Israel;

2 And he said unto Aaron, Take thee a young calf for a sin offering, and a ram for a burnt offering, without blemish, and offer *them* before the LORD.

3 And unto the children of Israel thou shalt speak, saying, Take ye a kid of the goats for a sin offering; and a calf and a lamb, *both* of the first year, without blemish, for a burnt offering;

4 Also a bullock and a ram for peace offerings, to sacrifice before the LORD; and a meat offering mingled with oil: for to day the LORD will appear unto you.

5 ¶ And they brought *that* which Moses commanded before the tabernacle of the congregation: and all the congregation drew near and stood before the LORD.

6 And Moses said, This *is* the thing which the LORD commanded that ye should do: and the glory of the LORD shall appear unto you.

7 And Moses said unto Aaron, Go unto the altar, and offer thy sin offering, and thy burnt offering, and make an atonement for thyself, and for the people: and offer the offering

of the people, and make an atonement for
them; as the LORD commanded.

Summary of Leviticus 9:8–22

Aaron and his sons offer sacrifices at the altar as prescribed by the Lord.

Leviticus 9:23–24. The Lord Accepts Aaron's Offering by Sending Down Fire from Heaven to Consume It

23 And Moses and Aaron went into the tabernacle of the congregation, and came out, and blessed the people: and the glory of the LORD appeared unto all the people.

How was the Lord's glory revealed to the children of Israel? (9:23) Elder Orson Pratt described the manifestation of the Lord: "In that tabernacle the Lord showed forth his power among Israel. It became visible not only on the inside, but on the outside the glory of God was made manifest and rested upon it. By this the Children of Israel knew that God was near unto them. They not only believed, but the testimony manifested before their eyes gave them a knowledge that God was in the midst of their camp" (in *Journal of Discourses*, 19:312). ⊕

24 And there came a fire out from before the LORD, and consumed upon the altar the burnt offering and the fat: *which* when all the

Why did divine fire consume the sacrifices on the altar? (9:24) "Miraculous fire came from the Lord to consume the offering and to show the divine acceptance. That this was miraculous fire could easily be

Levitical Priesthood Responsibilities (Leviticus 9:8–22)

"The high priest (Aaron and his male descendants), priests (all male descendants of Moses and Aaron), and Levites (other male descendants of Levi) had many duties in ancient Israel. Some responsibilities were restricted to particular offices, while most of them were done jointly. Among them were:

1. Use Urim and Thummim (Ex. 28:30; Num. 27:21); high priest only.
2. Administer worship in the tabernacle (or later in the temple: Lev. 24:5–9; Ex. 30:7–10, 22–38); high priest and priests.
3. Serve as religious judges in Israel (Lev. 13, 14; Num. 35:6–32); high priest and priests.
4. Care for sacred articles of tabernacle or temple (Num. 4:5–20); high priest and priests.
5. Supervise circumcisions, washings, and baptisms (Ex. 40:12; Josh. 5:8; D&C 84:26–27); priests.
6. Assist in sacrifices (Lev. 6:12, 9:13, Ex. 29:38–44); high priest (Day of Atonement), priests, and Levites.
7. Teach Israel the laws and covenants (Lev. 10:11; Deut. 33:10); all offices.
8. Collect and distribute tithes and offerings (Lev. 9:16–22); all offices.
9. Move tabernacle and maintain tabernacle and fences (later temple and courtyards: Num. 3:5–13, 23–37; 4); all offices.
10. Blow the silver trumpets to announce religious festivals and holy days or to call men to war (Num. 10:1–8); Levites.
11. Work in all types of service at the tabernacle or temple (1 Chr. 6:48); Levites.

"Although the contemporary holders of the Aaronic Priesthood do not have all these responsibilities, they continue in some of them, and much of their work and service compares to the responsibilities of the ancient Levites. One can make many comparisons between these two groups of priesthood holders" (Ludlow, *Unlocking the Old Testament*, 37–38).

distinguished by its suddenness, intensity, etc. It emphasized the fact that when the sacrifices were burned year after year, God himself accepted them and blessed the people accordingly. The fire was sacred and was not to be allowed to go out" (*Expositor's Bible Commentary [Abridged]*, 136).

Leviticus 10:1–7. Nadab and Abihu, Disobedient Sons of Aaron, Are Punished by God

What important lesson can we learn from Nadab and Abihu's actions in the tabernacle? (10:1–2) "An important story recorded in Leviticus 10 served as a warning to the priests and to all of ancient Israel to honor and respect the sanctity of holy places. On the inaugural day of the Tabernacle, Aaron's sons Nadab and Abihu were serving as priests in the sanctuary. They attempted to make an unauthorized offering, described as 'strange fire' (Lev 10:1). Their attempt was met with 'fire from the Lord' that 'devoured them, and they died before the Lord' (Lev 10:2). This story established for the congregation of Israel the critical importance of respecting the sacred space of the altar and the Tabernacle and of obedience to the Lord" (Holzapfel, et al., *Jehovah and the World of the Old Testament*, 116). See commentary in this volume for Leviticus 16:1. ⊕

Why does Aaron remain silent when his sons die? (10:3) "Aaron's silence is in contrast to the loud wailing that usually accompanied mourning" (Walton, et al., *IVP Bible Background Commentary*, 127). Aaron was grieving, but he understood his sons had rebelled against God (see *Nelson Study Bible* [NKJV], 174). Keil and Delitzsch concluded that "the Holy One . . . is not to be mocked. . . . [Aaron] was obliged to acknowledge the righteousness of the holy God" (Keil and Delitzsch, *Commentary* [on Leviticus 10:1–3]).

Why were Aaron's remaining sons forbidden to mourn their brothers' deaths? (10:6) In Biblical times

people saw, they shouted, and fell on their faces.

CHAPTER 10

Nadab and Abihu perform unauthorized sacrifices and are slain by a fire from the Lord—Aaron and his other sons are forbidden to mourn for them—Aaron and his sons are to abstain from wine and strong drink—They are to teach all that the Lord revealed to Moses.

1 And Nadab and Abihu, the sons of Aaron, took either of them his censer, and put fire therein, and put incense thereon, and offered strange fire before the Lord, which he commanded them not.

2 And there went out fire from the Lord, and devoured them, and they died before the Lord.

3 Then Moses said unto Aaron, This *is it* that the Lord spake, saying, I will be sanctified in them that come nigh me, and before all the people I will be glorified. And Aaron held his peace.

4 And Moses called Mishael and Elzaphan, the sons of Uzziel the uncle of Aaron, and said unto them, Come near, carry your brethren from before the sanctuary out of the camp.

5 So they went near, and carried them in their coats out of the camp; as Moses had said.

6 And Moses said unto Aaron, and unto Eleazar and unto Ithamar, his sons, Uncover not your heads, neither rend your clothes; lest ye die, and lest wrath come upon all the people: but let your brethren, the whole house of Israel, bewail the burning which the LORD hath kindled.

7 And ye shall not go out from the door of the tabernacle of the congregation, lest ye die: for the anointing oil of the LORD *is* upon you. And they did according to the word of Moses.

8 ¶ And the LORD spake unto Aaron, saying,

9 Do not drink wine nor strong drink, thou, nor thy sons with thee, when ye go into the tabernacle of the congregation, lest ye die: *it shall be* a statute for ever throughout your generations:

10 And that ye may put difference between holy and unholy, and between unclean and clean;

11 And that ye may teach the children of Israel all the statutes which the LORD hath spoken unto them by the hand of Moses.

when one learned of another's death, it was customary to tear one's clothes, put on sackcloth, remove a head covering and put dirt in its place, among other acts (see *Tyndale Bible Dictionary*, 918). "Aaron's other sons were forbidden to officially mourn the death of their brothers, for this action would imply that the Lord had been unjust in the punishment" (*Old Testament Student Manual: Genesis–2 Samuel*, 169).

Leviticus 10:8–11. Aaron Is Taught by the Lord to Practice and Teach Holiness

Why were the priests commanded to avoid "strong drink" while serving in the tabernacle? (10:9) "That this rule follows immediately after the record of the incident involving Aaron's sons may imply that intoxication caused them to fail in discerning 'between holy and unholy, and between unclean and clean' (Lev. 10:10) in their sacred service.

"In any case, this passage is a 'word of wisdom' restricting use of intoxicants by the priests, for alcohol can distort one's discernment and discretion. It would surely impair one's ability to teach and one's spiritual dignity as a teacher (Lev. 10:11)" (Rasmussen, *Latter-day Saint Commentary on the Old Testament*, 131). See commentary in this volume for Leviticus 16:1. ⊕

Why did Moses teach "all" the statutes? (10:11) "This emphasis makes the real burden of the book clear. God is holy; therefore, he cannot dwell in unholy temples nor among unholy people, nor, for that matter, they with him (see Moses 6:57; D&C 97:17). The charge to the priest was, then, twofold: to teach the people how to be holy, and to cleanse the people and the sanctuary when they were defiled" (Pearson, *Old Testament*, 29). In modern day revelation the Lord said, "For I the Lord cannot look upon sin with the least degree of allowance" (D&C 1:31).

Summary of Leviticus 10:12–20

Moses instructs the workers in the tabernacle to finish their sacrificial duties and partake of the flesh offerings properly. Aaron is excused from partaking of the sin offering.

Leviticus 11:1–8. The Lord Reveals Which Animals Should Be Eaten and Which Should Not

Why did the Lord distinguish between clean and unclean animals? (11:1–8) "Orthodox Jews still will not eat pork or other foods that are not kosher, 'clean.' Some of these rules may originally have been for the prevention of disease. Some may have been related to pagan practices that Israel was to avoid. . . . But probably the main reason for such food laws was to provide a daily reminder that Israel was to be different from all the other people. They were to be a 'holy nation,' a 'priestly kingdom,' separate in every aspect of life from their pagan neighbors" (Ramsay, *Westminster Guide to the Books of the Bible*, 53).

CHAPTER 11

The Lord reveals which living things may and may not be eaten, and which things are clean and unclean—He commands Israel: Be holy, for I am holy.

1 And the LORD spake unto Moses and to Aaron, saying unto them,

2 Speak unto the children of Israel, saying, These *are* the beasts which ye shall eat among all the beasts that *are* on the earth.

3 Whatsoever parteth the hoof, and is clovenfooted, *and* cheweth the cud, among the beasts, that shall ye eat.

4 Nevertheless these shall ye not eat of them that chew the cud, or of them that divide the hoof: *as* the camel, because he cheweth the cud, but divideth not the hoof; he *is* unclean unto you.

5 And the coney, because he cheweth the cud, but divideth not the hoof; he *is* unclean unto you.

6 And the hare, because he cheweth the cud, but divideth not the hoof; he *is* unclean unto you.

7 And the swine, though he divide the hoof, and be clovenfooted, yet he cheweth not the cud; he *is* unclean to you.

The Law of Moses: Spiritual Meaning of Clean and Unclean (Leviticus 11:1–8)

Joseph Fielding McConkie wrote: "The Mosaic system consisted of a host of ritualistic reminders to Israel that they were a nation set apart, a nation consecrated to God and his service—and that as such they needed to be pure. . . .

"The Hebrew word for clean used in the dietary law reached far beyond that of physical cleanliness. Synonyms include pure, unadulterated, uncontaminated, innocent, and holy. . . .

"The Mosaic dietary code can only properly be understood when viewed as a symbol of a people consecrated or dedicated to the Lord. Every meal was a reminder to Israel of who they were and what they had covenanted to be. It has been suggested that strength comes from living such a law, vision from understanding it" (*Gospel Symbolism*, 91, 92).

The Guide to the Scriptures explains that, "In a spiritual sense, to be clean is to be free from sin and sinful desires. In this sense the word is used to describe a person who is virtuous and has a pure heart (Ps. 24:4). God's covenant people have always had special instructions to be clean (3 Ne. 20:41; D&C 38:42; 133:5)" (Guide to the Scriptures, "Clean and Unclean").

8 Of their flesh shall ye not eat, and their carcase shall ye not touch; they *are* unclean to you.

9 ¶ These shall ye eat of all that *are* in the waters: whatsoever hath fins and scales in the waters, in the seas, and in the rivers, them shall ye eat.

10 And all that have not fins and scales in the seas, and in the rivers, of all that move in the waters, and of any living thing which *is* in the waters, they *shall be* an abomination unto you:

11 They shall be even an abomination unto you; ye shall not eat of their flesh, but ye shall have their carcases in abomination.

12 Whatsoever hath no fins nor scales in the waters, that *shall be* an abomination unto you.

13 ¶ And these *are they which* ye shall have in abomination among the fowls; they shall not be eaten, they *are* an abomination: the eagle, and the ossifrage, and the ospray,

14 And the vulture, and the kite after his kind;

15 Every raven after his kind;

16 And the owl, and the night hawk, and the cuckow, and the hawk after his kind,

17 And the little owl, and the cormorant, and the great owl,

18 And the swan, and the pelican, and the gier eagle,

Leviticus 11:9–12. The Lord Distinguishes between Clean and Abominable Water Creatures

How is "an abomination" different from "unclean"? (11:9–12) "A water creature had to possess both fins and scales in order to be eaten. . . . The phrasing is careful, deliberate, and repetitive to remove any possibility of finding any exception anywhere. Abomination is a stronger word than unclean. It implies not just avoidance, but active, fierce repulsion. Fins and scales are 'appropriate' for water creatures. Fish that have them are clean. Water creatures that appear to mix categories—suggesting disorder—are not merely unclean; they are an abomination. There are good health reasons for being cautious in eating some of these creatures, but this was not the main reason for classifying them as unclean" (*Nelson Study Bible* [NKJV], 176).

Leviticus 11:13–23. The Lord Distinguishes between Clean and Unclean Flying Creatures

The Law of Moses: Examples of Clean and Unclean Creatures (Leviticus 11:1–23)

Clean or Edible	Unclean or Inedible
Sheep, cows, oxen	Camels, badgers, rabbits, pigs, lizards, snakes, weasels, mice
Sea creatures with fins and scales	Sea creatures without fins and scales, such as oysters, clams, crabs, lobsters, shrimp, eels, sharks, dolphins
All birds not listed as unclean, and locusts, grasshoppers, crickets	Eagles, vultures, hawks, ostrich, raven, owls, gulls, swans, storks, herons, bats

(Adapted from Valletta, et al., *Old Testament for Latter-day Saint Families*, 156)

19 And the stork, the heron after her kind, and the lapwing, and the bat.

20 All fowls that creep, going upon *all* four, *shall be* an abomination unto you.

21 Yet these may ye eat of every flying creeping thing that goeth upon *all* four, which have legs above their feet, to leap withal upon the earth;

22 *Even* these of them ye may eat; the locust after his kind, and the bald locust after his kind, and the beetle after his kind, and the grasshopper after his kind.

23 But all *other* flying creeping things, which have four feet, *shall be* an abomination unto you.

Summary of Leviticus 11:24–43

The Lord reveals other rules to keep the Israelites clean. The Lord also shows that even touching or handling animals in certain ways can make a person unclean.

Leviticus 11:44–47. The Lord Commands Israel to Be Holy

44 For I *am* the LORD your God: ye shall therefore sanctify yourselves, and ye shall be holy; for I *am* holy: neither shall ye defile yourselves with any manner of creeping thing that creepeth upon the earth.

45 For I *am* the LORD that bringeth you up out of the land of Egypt, to be your God: ye shall therefore be holy, for I *am* holy.

46 This *is* the law of the beasts, and of the fowl, and of every living creature that moveth in the waters, and of every creature that creepeth upon the earth:

47 To make a difference between the unclean and the clean, and between the beast that may be eaten and the beast that may not be eaten.

What does holy mean? (11:44–45) One who is holy is "sacred, having a godly character, or spiritually and morally pure. The opposite of holy is common or profane" (Guide to the Scriptures, "Holy"). "Holiness indicates purity of a person's heart and intent" (Guide to the Scriptures, "Holiness"). The words holy and holiness appear over 100 times in the book of Leviticus alone.

"Individuals in Israel were expected to move others towards the divine state, like God himself did. The ordinances performed were not simply busy work given because the people were wicked, but were in fact meant to transform the people of Israel into 'partakers of the divine nature'" (Belnap, "That I May Dwell among Them," 22–23). ⊕

How can one "be holy"? (11:45) "This call to 'be holy, for I am holy' is one of the slogans of Leviticus. It is repeated twice here (vv. 44, 45) and comes again another three times (19:2; 20:7, 26)." (Wenham, *Book of Leviticus*, 180). Sister Carol F. McConkie explained that holiness is gained "in the striving and the struggle to keep the commandments and to honor the covenants we have made with God. Holiness is making the choices that will keep the Holy Ghost as our guide. Holiness is setting aside our natural tendencies and becoming 'a saint through the atonement of Christ the Lord' [Mosiah 3:19]" ("Beauty of Holiness," 9).

CHAPTERS 12–13

The Lord reveals the law of purification of women after childbirth, including a sin offering.

Laws and tokens are revealed for discerning and controlling leprosy—Leprous garments are to be burnt.

Summary of Leviticus 12–13

Leviticus chapters 11–27 contain the Lord's special instructions to the children of Israel of how they are to become a holy people and how the tabernacle/ sanctuary can once more become the dwelling place of Jehovah. Specific to chapters 12 and 13 are a variety of laws, rites, and sacrifices given to help women and men purify themselves and to control a variety of skin infections, including the dreaded disease of leprosy.

"'The term unclean in this and the following cases, is generally understood in a mere legal sense, the rendering a person unfit for sacred ordinances' [*Adam Clarke's Commentary* (on Lev. 15:11)]. This point is very important to understanding the Lord's revelations on these matters. The ordinances of the Mosaic law were all designed to symbolize spiritual truths. The more nearly one approached perfection in the performance of the law, the more closely one approached the true symbolic meaning of the ordinance. The physical body and its natural functions remind one that he is of the earth, of the physical. Therefore, to say that a man or woman was unclean (that is, not to perform sacred ordinances) at certain times was to suggest to the mind that the natural man must be put aside in order to approach God" (*Old Testament Student Manual: Genesis–2 Samuel*, 174).

CHAPTER 14

Laws, rites, and sacrifices are revealed for cleansing lepers, their garments, and leprous houses.

1 And the LORD spake unto Moses, saying,

2 This shall be the law of the leper in the day of his cleansing: He shall be brought unto the priest:

Leviticus 14:1–24. The Rules and Laws for Cleansing Lepers Are Outlined

What is a "leper" as noted in Leviticus? (14:2) "Leviticus' description of the symptoms gives an idea not of one, but of various skin diseases grouped together in various stages." Other skin disorders anciently considered leprosy include "perhaps skin cancer, which comes out in big red pimples, makes scabs and dries out; perhaps psoriasis; probably tropical ulcers and yaws; the major infectious diseases, plague, smallpox, mumps, chickenpox, measles. . . . Hansen's disease [leprosy] which the Leviticus writer does not emphasize, [includes] the gross swelling of the limbs, the local numbness, eventual loss of toes and fingers, and facial deformity" (Douglas, *Leviticus as Literature*, 183–84).

What was the purpose of the cleansing rituals? (14:3) "These rites were not for healing. They were to confirm and celebrate the healing that already had occurred, to cleanse the recovered patient, and to readmit him or her into the community and its worship" (*Nelson Study Bible* [NKJV], 181). As such, "the priest was to examine the leper *outside* the camp; and *if* he found the leprosy cured and gone," only then would he send for the necessary items to begin the purification of the individual (Keil and Delitzsch, *Commentary* [on Leviticus 14:2–4]; emphasis added). The first phase of the ritual cleansing occurred outside the camp (Lev. 14:1–8).

What did the two birds, cedar wood, scarlet, and hyssop represent? (14:4) "The birds symbolized the candidate. . . . Cedar wood is still used today because of its ability to preserve surrounding objects from decay and corruption; its meaning is obvious. . . . *Scarlet* (Lev. 14:4) really meant a piece of wool dyed bright red, a reminder of blood, which is the symbol of life and also of atonement (see Lev. 17:11). . . . In Old Testament times the herb hyssop was associated with purification (see Exod. 12:22; Ps. 51:7; Heb. 9:19)" (Lund, "Old Testament Types and Symbols," 45). The elements of the ritual point to the atoning blood of Jesus Christ, through which those who repent are cleansed from sin and preserved throughout mortality.

Why was the shaving off of all hair part of the cleansing ritual? (14:8–9) "This act [of shaving], including even the eyebrows, would make a person look very much like a newborn infant, who is typically virtually without hair. Thus, after going through the process of rebirth symbolically, the candidate graphically demonstrated on his own person that he was newborn spiritually" (Lund, "Old Testament Types and Symbols," 46).

What was the purpose of the trespass and sin offerings? (14:10–13) "*Sin and Trespass Offerings* were for the purpose of achieving reconciliation following violations of the laws of society or God. When one was

3 And the priest shall go forth out of the
camp; and the priest shall look, and, behold,
if the plague of leprosy be healed in the leper;

4 Then shall the priest command to take for
him that is to be cleansed two birds alive *and*
clean, and cedar wood, and scarlet, and hyssop:

5 And the priest shall command that one of
the birds be killed in an earthen vessel over
running water:

6 As for the living bird, he shall take it, and
the cedar wood, and the scarlet, and the hyssop, and shall dip them and the living bird in
the blood of the bird *that was* killed over the
running water:

7 And he shall sprinkle upon him that is to
be cleansed from the leprosy seven times, and
shall pronounce him clean, and shall let the
living bird loose into the open field.

8 And he that is to be cleansed shall wash his
clothes, and shave off all his hair, and wash
himself in water, that he may be clean: and
after that he shall come into the camp, and
shall tarry abroad out of his tent seven days.

9 But it shall be on the seventh day, that he
shall shave all his hair off his head and his
beard and his eyebrows, even all his hair he
shall shave off: and he shall wash his clothes,
also he shall wash his flesh in water, and he
shall be clean.

10 And on the eighth day he shall take two
he lambs without blemish, and one ewe lamb
of the first year without blemish, and three

tenth deals of fine flour *for* a meat offering, mingled with oil, and one log of oil.

11 And the priest that maketh *him* clean shall present the man that is to be made clean, and those things, before the LORD, *at* the door of the tabernacle of the congregation:

12 And the priest shall take one he lamb, and offer him for a trespass offering, and the log of oil, and wave them *for* a wave offering before the LORD:

13 And he shall slay the lamb in the place where he shall kill the sin offering and the burnt offering, in the holy place: for as the sin offering *is* the priest's, *so is* the trespass offering: it *is* most holy:

14 And the priest shall take *some* of the blood of the trespass offering, and the priest shall put *it* upon the tip of the right ear of him that is to be cleansed, and upon the thumb

guilty of violating any of the revealed laws, atonement had to be made by taking the prescribed animal to the priests at the sanctuary. . . . Sin and trespass offerings were the same, except that trespass offerings required restitution as well. The priests offered up the sacrifice in behalf of the worshiper, and through the animal's death the worshiper was reconciled with the law and thereby made ritually clean. These offerings . . . symbolized the Atonement of the Savior with its power to remove sin from our lives" (Jackson, "Law of Moses and the Atonement of Christ," 162).

Why was the lamb offered in the holy place as a burnt offering? (14:13) "In the premortal councils of heaven, God had promised Adam and Eve (and all the rest of us) that help would come from His pure, unblemished Firstborn Son, the Lamb of God 'slain from the foundation of the world,' as the Apostle John would later describe Him. By offering their own little symbolic lambs in mortality, Adam and his posterity were expressing their understanding of and their dependence upon the atoning sacrifice of Jesus the Anointed One. Later, the wilderness tabernacle would become the setting for this ordinance and, after that, the temple that Solomon would build" (Holland, "Behold the Lamb of God," 44–45).

Why did the priest place the blood of the offering on these specific body parts? (14:14) "In Hebrew the word which is usually translated *atonement* literally means 'to cover.' Thus, when the priest touched something with the blood, his action suggested the

Cleansing the Leper Foreshadows the Atonement of Jesus Christ (14:1–32)

"In Leviticus 14 we have a detailed description of the ritual that was to take place when a person's leprosy had been healed. Because of the nature of the ritual, many people have seen it as a primitive, superstitious, and abhorrent rite which makes the Israelites barely more than pagan. However, when we apply our guidelines for interpreting symbols, we find that the ritual is a beautiful representation of gospel truths. . . .

"Leprosy in its various forms was a loathsome disease that involved decay and putrefaction of the living body; it required the sufferer to be ostracized and cut off from any fellowship with the rest of the house of Israel. Because of these characteristics, leprosy was also an appropriate type or symbol of what happens to a man spiritually when he sins. Sin introduces decay and corruption into the spiritual realm as leprosy does into the physical. Also, a sinful person was cut off from fellowship with spiritual Israel and could not be part of the Lord's covenant people. So the leper himself provided a type or similitude of what King Benjamin called the 'natural man' (see Mosiah 3:19). . . .

"The priest served as the official representative of the Lord, authorized to cleanse the leper and bring him back into full fellowship. . . . The priest was also a type of Christ.

"In the ritual cleansing, 'the first bird was killed by the shedding of its blood, signifying that the leper (the natural man) had to give up his life. The second bird, after being bound together with other symbols, was released, signifying that the man had been freed from the bondage of sin'" (Lund, "Old Testament Types and Symbols," 44–45).

sanctification of, or atonement made for, that thing. In this case we find the blood of the lamb sanctifying the organ of hearing or obedience (the ear), the organ of action (the hand), and the organ of following or walking in the proper way (the foot). Thus, every aspect of the person's life was touched and affected by the atonement of Christ" (Lund, "Old Testament Types and Symbols," 46). See commentary in this volume for Leviticus 8:22–24. ⊕

What is a log of oil and what does it symbolize? (14:15–18) A "log" was a measure of capacity for liquids, only mentioned in Leviticus 14:10. Derived from items in common use, a log was equivalent to 2/3 US liquid pints (see *Harper's Bible Dictionary*, 813). "'The olive tree from the earliest times has been the emblem of peace and purity.' Modern revelation further instructs us that olive oil symbolizes the Holy Ghost (see D&C 45:55–57). To touch with oil suggests the effect of the Spirit on the same organs of living and acting that had previously been cleansed by the blood of Christ. Thus, every aspect of the candidate's life was purified and sanctified by both the Atonement and the Holy Ghost" (Lund, "Old Testament Types and Symbols," 46).

How were the poor accommodated for this cleansing ritual? (14:21–22) "In cases of poverty on the part of the person to be consecrated, the burnt-offering and sin-offering were reduced to a pair of turtle-doves or young pigeons, and the meat-offering to a tenth of an ephah of meal and oil; but no diminution was allowed in the trespass-offering as the consecration-offering [see vv. 12–13], since this was the [indispensable condition] of reinstatement in full covenant rights. On account of the importance of all the details

of his right hand, and upon the great toe of his right foot:

15 And the priest shall take *some* of the log of oil, and pour *it* into the palm of his own left hand:

16 And the priest shall dip his right finger in the oil that *is* in his left hand, and shall sprinkle of the oil with his finger seven times before the LORD:

17 And of the rest of the oil that *is* in his hand shall the priest put upon the tip of the right ear of him that is to be cleansed, and upon the thumb of his right hand, and upon the great toe of his right foot, upon the blood of the trespass offering:

18 And the remnant of the oil that *is* in the priest's hand he shall pour upon the head of him that is to be cleansed: and the priest shall make an atonement for him before the LORD.

19 And the priest shall offer the sin offering, and make an atonement for him that is to be cleansed from his uncleanness; and afterward he shall kill the burnt offering:

20 And the priest shall offer the burnt offering and the meat offering upon the altar: and the priest shall make an atonement for him, and he shall be clean.

21 And if he *be* poor, and cannot get so much; then he shall take one lamb *for* a trespass offering to be waved, to make an atonement for him, and one tenth deal of fine flour mingled with oil for a meat offering, and a log of oil;

22 And two turtledoves, or two young pigeons, such as he is able to get; and the one shall be a sin offering, and the other a burnt offering.

23 And he shall bring them on the eighth day for his cleansing unto the priest, unto the door of the tabernacle of the congregation, before the LORD.

24 And the priest shall take the lamb of the trespass offering, and the log of oil, and the priest shall wave them *for* a wave offering before the LORD:

CHAPTER 15

Laws, rites, and sacrifices are revealed for cleansing those who have a discharge and other types of uncleanness.

CHAPTER 16

How and when Aaron must enter the holy place is explained—Sacrifices are offered to reconcile Israel to God—The scapegoat carries away the sins of the people—The sins of all Israel are forgiven on the Day of Atonement.

1 And the LORD spake unto Moses after the death of the two sons of Aaron, when they offered before the LORD, and died;

of this law, every point is repeated a second time in vv. 21–32" (Keil and Delitzsch, *Commentary* [on Leviticus 14:21–32]).

What was a wave offering? (14:24) "[A wave offering] seems to mean moving the arms back and forth in a horizontal motion. . . . The wave offering, according to several translators of the English Bible and the works of Jewish commentators, was toward the sanctuary, while the so-called heave offering was a vertical motion toward heaven and thus dedicated to the Lord. However, based on an Egyptian relief from Karnac, Jacob Milgrom argues persuasively that the so-called wave offering should now be understood as an elevation offering, a ritual of elevating and lifting the offering in dedication to God" (*New Interpreter's Bible*, 1:1054). See commentary in this volume for Leviticus 8:27–29.

Summary of Leviticus 14:25–57

Other instructions are given to the priest to further explain the trespass offering and how to cleanse leprosy from individuals and their houses.

Summary of Leviticus 15

The Law details ways in which the children of Israel can cleanse, by sacrifices, those who are unclean, including those who have touched other people who are unclean.

Leviticus 16:1–22. Aaron Is to Make Sacrifices for the Children of Israel

How did Nadab and Abihu offend God? (16:1) "While it is difficult to understand the precise form of Nadab and Abihu's transgression [see Leviticus 10:1–2], the nature of their sin . . . was in doing that which [Jehovah] 'had not commanded them.' . . . Ultimately, the brothers manifested a lack of the fear of [Jehovah], which led to their negligence (whatever the form of their disobedience). Within the broader context of the structure of Leviticus . . . it appears quite plausible that Nadab and Abihu had attempted to penetrate the Presence of God within the holy of holies" (Morales, *Who Shall Ascend the Mountain of the Lord?* 146–47). See commentary in this volume for Leviticus 10:1–2 and Leviticus 10:8–11. ⊕

What was the "holy place within the veil"? (16:2) "Also called 'Most Holy Place.' The most sacred room in the tabernacle and, later, in the temple" (Bible Dictionary, "Holy of Holies"). "The Holy of Holies contained only one piece of furniture: the Ark of the Covenant, or the Ark of the Testimony (Ex. 25:22). . . . Upon the ark and forming the lid was the mercy seat. It served, with the ark beneath, as an altar on which the highest atonement known to the Jewish law was effected. On it was sprinkled the blood of the sin offering of the Day of Atonement (Lev. 16:14–15). The mercy seat was the place of the manifestation of God's glory (Ex. 25:22). It was God's throne in Israel" (Bible Dictionary, "Tabernacle").

What was the holy linen that Aaron was to put on? (16:4) "Aaron and his successors had to be properly prepared and clothed in the garments of the priesthood before entering the holy place beyond the veil of the tabernacle on the 'day of atonement,' the most holy day of the year (Lev. 16:2–34). The special clothing included linen underclothing ('breeches'), a robe ('coat'), sash ('girdle'), and cap ('mitre'); the priest was washed before being clothed in those garments of the

2 And the LORD said unto Moses, Speak unto Aaron thy brother, that he come not at all times into the holy *place* within the veil before the mercy seat, which *is* upon the ark; that he die not: for I will appear in the cloud upon the mercy seat.

3 Thus shall Aaron come into the holy *place:* with a young bullock for a sin offering, and a ram for a burnt offering.

4 He shall put on the holy linen coat, and he shall have the linen breeches upon his flesh, and shall be girded with a linen girdle, and with the linen mitre shall he be attired: these *are* holy garments; therefore shall he wash his flesh in water, and *so* put them on.

The Day of Atonement (Leviticus 16)

Atonement is the centerpiece of Leviticus 16. It also establishes what is now called the Day of Atonement, or Yom Kippur. "The day of atonement (Yom Kippur) is still observed by Jews throughout the world, although animal sacrifice has not been part of the observance since the destruction of the temple in A.D. 70.

"The Lord indicated that the day of atonement should be 'in the seventh month, on the tenth day of the month' according to the calendar then in use. Changes in the Jewish calendar have placed Yom Kippur near Rosh Hashanah (literally 'head of the year') or New Year's Day, which usually occurs in September or October" (Ludlow, *Companion to Your Study of the Old Testament*, 167).

"Without question, the day of atonement was at the heart of Israel's calendar and life. . . . Indeed, the high priest's narrated entry within the veil of God's house is, for the reader, an entrance within the inner sanctum of the Pentateuch's theology, the keystone of the cultic system of forgiveness of sins. After expulsion from the Garden of Eden, this entrance into the Tabernacle holy of holies presents the nearest human approach to God's Presence. As such, the Day of Atonement is dubbed a *šabbat šabbātôn*, a Sabbath of solemn rest or, . . . 'the Sabbath of Sabbaths'" (Morales, *Who Shall Ascend the Mountain of the Lord?* 167–68).

"The Day of Atonement, which took place each autumn, was the most sacred and solemn of all Israelite festivals. In it, the typology or symbolism of Christ's work for Israel fairly shines. A day of national fasting, it signified that the sins of Israel had been atoned for and that the nation and its people were restored to fellowship with God" (Lund, "Old Testament Types and Symbols," 48).

5 And he shall take of the congregation of the children of Israel two kids of the goats for a sin offering, and one ram for a burnt offering.

6 And Aaron shall offer his bullock of the sin offering, which *is* for himself, and make an atonement for himself, and for his house.

7 And he shall take the two goats, and present them before the LORD *at* the door of the tabernacle of the congregation.

8 And Aaron shall cast lots upon the two goats; one lot for the LORD, and the other lot for the scapegoat.

9 And Aaron shall bring the goat upon which the LORD's lot fell, and offer him *for* a sin offering.

10 But the goat, on which the lot fell to be the scapegoat, shall be presented alive before the LORD, to make an atonement with him, *and* to let him go for a scapegoat into the wilderness.

11 And Aaron shall bring the bullock of the sin offering, which *is* for himself, and shall make an atonement for himself, and for his house, and shall kill the bullock of the sin offering which *is* for himself:

12 And he shall take a censer full of burning coals of fire from off the altar before the LORD, and his hands full of sweet incense beaten small, and bring *it* within the veil:

13 And he shall put the incense upon the fire before the LORD, that the cloud of the incense may cover the mercy seat that *is* upon the testimony, that he die not:

priesthood" (Rasmussen, *Latter-day Saint Commentary on the Old Testament*, 133). ⊕

Why did Aaron first sacrifice for himself and his house? (16:5–6) "Before [Aaron] could make atonement for the people, he had to purge himself of sin" (*Torah: A Modern Commentary*, 864). Aaron was to "bring an ox (bullock) for a sin-offering . . . as a sacrifice for himself and his house. . . . Only . . . *'with this,'* i.e., with the sacrifices, dress, purifications, and means of expiation mentioned afterwards, could he go into 'the holy place'" (Keil and Delitzsch, *Commentary* [on Leviticus 16:3–5]).

What was "[casting] lots upon the two goats"? (16:7–8) "According to the Mishnah [a collection of oral Jewish commentary on the law] the goats were stationed in front of the high priest, one to his right and one to his left. Two disks inscribed respectively 'for the Lord' and 'for [the scapegoat],' had been placed in an urn. The high priest put both hands into the urn, picked one disk in each hand, and place them on the heads of the goats. It was considered a good omen if the disc for the Lord came up in his right hand" (*Torah: A Modern Commentary*, 864). Some scholars suggest that the high priest may have used the Urim and Thummim to designate the scapegoat (see Tyndale Old Testament Commentaries, 3:208).

What did the scapegoat represent? (16:10) The original Hebrew word is *Azazel*, which interpreted means "goat of departure" (*Strong's Exhaustive Concordance*, word #h5799). "The term 'scapegoat' was apparently coined by William Tyndale, the first great English Bible translator. Thereafter, it came to be used for a person, animal, or object to which the impurity or guilt of the community was formally transferred and then removed. . . . The original notion of a scapegoat included the public acknowledgment by the community of its own transgressions" (*Torah: A Modern Commentary*, 860).

14 And he shall take of the blood of the bullock, and sprinkle *it* with his finger upon the
mercy seat eastward; and before the mercy
seat shall he sprinkle of the blood with his
finger seven times.

15 ¶ Then shall he kill the goat of the sin
offering, that *is* for the people, and bring his
blood within the veil, and do with that blood
as he did with the blood of the bullock, and
sprinkle it upon the mercy seat, and before
the mercy seat:

16 And he shall make an atonement for the
holy *place,* because of the uncleanness of the
children of Israel, and because of their transgressions in all their sins: and so shall he do
for the tabernacle of the congregation, that
remaineth among them in the midst of their
uncleanness.

What can we learn from the Day of Atonement? (16:16) "The word 'atonement' can be explained best with the two following definitions: (a) the payment of a penalty or price for wrong-doing, and (b) a reconciliation, i.e., the bringing together again of two parties that had been alienated.... Because of our sins, we are unworthy to enter into the presence of God. Jesus resolved that situation by taking upon himself the

Sacrifices and Rites of the Day of Atonement (Leviticus 16:11–22)

The rites and ceremony of the Day of Atonement may be summarized in four parts. Phase one was a purification offering for Aaron and his house, usually understood to be all of the priests of Israel since the priestly functions resided in the "house" of Aaron. The bull was sacrificed, and the unused portions burned outside the camp (v. 27). Now purified, Aaron, as high priest, entered the veil and sprinkled the blood of the bull seven times on both the east side and front of the mercy seat which was the lid of the ark of the covenant (v. 14). To protect himself from the wrath of God, the high priest prepared a censer full of hot charcoal taken from the altar of burnt offering and sprinkled with incense. The smoke of the incense was to cover the mercy seat, so that the high priest would not be killed (vv. 12–13). The smoke also created a screen which prevented the high priest from directly looking upon the glory of the Lord.

In the second part of the ritual, the high priest brought the two goats to the Tabernacle before all the people. The casting of lots determined which of the goats would be sacrificed and which became the scapegoat, or "goat of departure," upon whose head the sins of all Israel were to be placed. The public nature of this choosing assured that everyone knew which goat was to be sacrificed and which goat was to be sent away.

In phase three, the high priest sacrificed the goat which was designated to the Lord as a purification offering for the people of Israel. The high priest again entered the veil of the Tabernacle and sprinkled the blood of the goat in the same manner upon the mercy seat of the ark (vv. 16–17). Exiting the holy place, the high priest sprinkled both the blood of the bull and the blood of the goat seven times upon the altar of sacrifice and the outer tent of the Tabernacle, declaring them to be clean (vv. 18–20).

In conclusion, the high priest then laid his hands upon the chosen scapegoat and confessed the sins and iniquities of the children of Israel, thus placing them upon the head of the goat. The goat was then sent into the wilderness, carrying the burden of sin away from Israel (see *New International Commentary on the Old Testament*, 3:231–34).

"The apostle Paul in the book of Hebrews drew heavily on the typology of the Day of Atonement to teach the mission of Christ. In that epistle he pointed out that Christ is the great 'High Priest' who, unlike the high priest of the Aaronic Priesthood, was holy and without spot and did not need to make atonement for his own sins before he could be worthy to officiate for Israel and enter the Holy of Holies (Heb. 3:1; 7:26–27). His perfect life was the ultimate fulfillment of the symbol of wearing white garments" (Lund, "Old Testament Types and Symbols," 49).

17 And there shall be no man in the tabernacle of the congregation when he goeth in to make an atonement in the holy *place,* until he come out, and have made an atonement for himself, and for his household, and for all the congregation of Israel.

18 And he shall go out unto the altar that *is* before the LORD, and make an atonement for it; and shall take of the blood of the bullock, and of the blood of the goat, and put *it* upon the horns of the altar round about.

19 And he shall sprinkle of the blood upon it with his finger seven times, and cleanse it, and hallow it from the uncleanness of the children of Israel.

20 ¶ And when he hath made an end of reconciling the holy *place,* and the tabernacle of the congregation, and the altar, he shall bring the live goat:

21 And Aaron shall lay both his hands upon the head of the live goat, and confess over him all the iniquities of the children of Israel, and all their transgressions in all their sins, putting them upon the head of the goat, and shall send *him* away by the hand of a fit man into the wilderness:

22 And the goat shall bear upon him all their iniquities unto a land not inhabited: and he shall let go the goat in the wilderness.

responsibility for our sins and by receiving the agonizing punishment that we deserve for them and that will fall on us if we have to pay for them ourselves. . . . Having been made clean through the blood of Christ, we then could be reconciled to God and enter his presence" (Jackson, "Law of Moses and the Atonement of Jesus Christ," 165).

How can blood cleanse? (16:19) "The verb *tihher*, 'to cleanse, purify,' describes a variety of acts. Purification in this instance was accomplished by the use of sacrificial blood . . . although blood has no real cleansing properties. . . . It is therefore preferable to translate *tihher* as 'to purify' rather than as 'to cleanse.' The root *t-h-r* has, as its primary connotation, a physical purity" (Levine, *Leviticus*, 105–6).

Summary of Leviticus 16:23–34

The Lord tells Moses how Aaron should complete the ceremony by having the scapegoat carry away the sins of Israel. These instructions include setting apart the Day of Atonement as a Sabbath (v. 30–31). Hence the reference to the Day of Atonement as the Sabbath of Sabbaths. See commentary in this volume for Leviticus 16:11–22. This is to be an everlasting statute in Israel (v. 34).

Summary of Leviticus 17

This chapter introduces a code of holiness for ancient Israel. The first nine verses specify that they should offer all sacrifices at the authorized altar. The rest of the chapter commands the children of Israel not to eat blood and that shedding their own blood would not atone for the sin of taking someone's life.

Summary of Leviticus 18

"Chapter 18 is the most systematic and complete collection of laws within the Torah dealing with the subject of incest, and other forbidden sexual unions. . . . Chapter 18 opens . . . and closes . . . with admonitions that state the consequences of transgressing God's commandments in the area of forbidden sexual activity" (Levine, *Leviticus*, 117, 118).

Leviticus 19:1–18. Israel Is Counseled on How to Become Holy

Why must the Israelites be holy? (19:1–2) Earlier the Lord said to the Israelites, "Ye shall therefore sanctify yourselves, and ye shall be holy; for I am holy" (Leviticus 11:44). Holiness is the central theme of the book of Leviticus, and all of its laws were established to achieve it. "The Israelites were [to be] a holy people because they stood in a special relationship to Jehovah. . . . Israel must be holy in character because the God of Israel was holy (Jer. 7:4–7; see also Matt. 5:48). The Law of Holiness (Lev. 17–26) shows how the attempt was made by means of ceremonial observances to secure this holiness of character" (Bible Dictionary, "Holiness").

Why would the Lord command Israel to "fear" their mothers and fathers? (19:3) "The Hebrew word *yareh* translated here as 'fear' also means 'revere.' In fact, this same Hebrew word is translated as 'reverence' in verse 30 of this chapter [see *Strong's Exhaustive Concordance*,

CHAPTER 17

Sacrifices are to be offered only to the Lord at the tabernacle of the congregation—Israel is forbidden to sacrifice to devils—All eating of blood is forbidden—Shedding of blood is required for an atonement for sins.

CHAPTER 18

Israel shall not live as the Egyptians and the Canaanites—Marriages to many close relatives and others are forbidden—Homosexual behavior and other sexual perversions are an abomination—The land expels those nations that practice sexual abominations.

CHAPTER 19

Israel is commanded: Be holy, live righteously, love your neighbor, and keep the commandments—The Lord reveals and reaffirms sundry laws and commandments—Enchantments, wizardry, prostitution, and all evil practices are forbidden.

1 And the LORD spake unto Moses, saying,

2 Speak unto all the congregation of the children of Israel, and say unto them, Ye shall be holy: for I the LORD your God *am* holy.

3 ¶ Ye shall fear every man his mother, and his father, and keep my sabbaths: I *am* the LORD your God.

4 ¶ Turn ye not unto idols, nor make to yourselves molten gods: I *am* the LORD your God.

yârê, word #h3372]. To 'fear' mother, father, and God is to revere them or to stand in awe or reverence of them; the word in this context does not mean you should dread them, nor feel great anxiety or apprehension when near them" (Ludlow, *Companion to Your Study of the Old Testament*, 168–69).

What does the phrase *the Lord your God* represent? (19:3–4) "The terms 'I am the Lord' or 'I am the Lord your God' appear at least sixteen times in this one chapter. The phrase not only indicates that the teachings come directly from God (rather than fashioned from the philosophies of man) but also places a 'seal of approval' on these admonitions" (Ludlow, *Companion to Your Study of the Old Testament*, 168).

5 ¶ And if ye offer a sacrifice of peace offerings unto the LORD, ye shall offer it at your own will.

6 It shall be eaten the same day ye offer it, and on the morrow: and if ought remain until the third day, it shall be burnt in the fire.

7 And if it be eaten at all on the third day, it *is* abominable; it shall not be accepted.

8 Therefore *every one* that eateth it shall bear his iniquity, because he hath profaned the hallowed thing of the LORD: and that soul shall be cut off from among his people.

Why were the children of Israel only given two days to eat their peace offerings? (19:5–8) "Moses repeats the warning (7:15–20) that meat used for the *peace offering* (fellowship offering; v. 5) must be consumed by the second day, or it must be *burnt in the fire* on the *third day* (v. 6). The reason for this is obvious: the meat would spoil and be contaminated. The spoiled meat *is abominable; it shall not be accepted* (v. 7). Anyone eating such meat *hath profaned the hollowed thing of the Lord* (v. 8) and would be *cut off from among his people*. . . . The laws also gave invaluable lessons about God's holy demands. Spiritual lessons accompanied practical lessons" (*Zondervan KJV Commentary*, 162).

Leviticus 19 in Context

"[Leviticus] chapters 18 and 20 are written in parallel so as to frame chapter 19, both dealing with prohibitions against various sexual offenses and idolatry. By contrast, chapter 19 offers positive rules and is unified by the Decalogue, with all ten commandments being either alluded to or quoted. This central chapter may be summarized by its own center, the admonition to 'Love your neighbor as yourself' in 19:18. . . . Chapters 18 and 20 serve to *separate* Israel from the detestable religious customs of the nations, while chapter 19 sets out the life that accords with Israel's . . . access to [Jehovah's] presence" (Morales, *Who Shall Ascend the Mountain of the Lord*, 208, 212).

"Chapter 19 may be characterized as a brief *torah* (instruction). . . . More specifically, it echoes the Ten Commandments.

"Leviticus 19	*"The Ten Commandments*
"Reverence for parents . . .	"Honoring parents (no. 5)
"The Sabbath . . .	"The Sabbath (no. 4)
"Idolatry . . .	"Idolatry; worship of other Gods (no. 2)
"Stealing and deceitful conduct . . .	"Stealing (no. 8)
"False oaths . . .	"False oaths (no. 1)
"'I am the Lord your God' . . .	"'I am the Lord . . .' (no. 1)"

(Levine, *Leviticus*, 124–25).

What are gleanings and why are they left in the field? (19:9–10) "Although the word *gleaning* may conjure up a romantic image of cloud filled skies, tall sheaves of grain and joyous peasant girls, the actual biblical custom was rooted in the practical necessity of caring for the poor. The Mosaic law stipulated that owners allow needy persons to gather the grain that remained after the reapers had made a single sweep of their fields [Deuteronomy 24:19–21]. . . . Gleaning symbolizes the misery of poverty" (*Dictionary of Biblical Imagery*, 329, 330).

How did the Law of Moses ensure righteous judgment? (19:15) "The Law of Moses is usually considered a harsh system of justice, but in many ways it was more fair and helpful to individuals and society than our current system of justice. Justice under the Law of Moses had three main criteria: (1) the rights of the victim were of greatest priority, (2) the burden of responsibility rested upon the offender, and (3) the offender was helped toward repentance. . . .

"The Mosaic law was concerned with helping the victim. Only if a guilty party could not be found to compensate the victim would society assume the burden of caring for the victim and his family" (Ludlow, *Unlocking the Old Testament*, 38, 40).

What do these passages teach us about loving others? (19:17–18) "Many persons wrongfully assume that the commandment 'love thy neighbour as thyself' comes only from the New Testament, but here it appears in the Old Testament, and it is also in the writings of many other religious groups. Verse 34 expounds the principle of loving the stranger 'as thyself.'

"The Lord also counsels not to 'hate thy brother in thine heart.' In other words, do not cherish or harbor hate, even when righteous rebuke is necessary [see

9 ¶ And when ye reap the harvest of your land, thou shalt not wholly reap the corners of thy field, neither shalt thou gather the gleanings of thy harvest.

10 And thou shalt not glean thy vineyard, neither shalt thou gather *every* grape of thy vineyard; thou shalt leave them for the poor and stranger: I *am* the LORD your God.

11 ¶ Ye shall not steal, neither deal falsely, neither lie one to another.

12 ¶ And ye shall not swear by my name falsely, neither shalt thou profane the name of thy God: I *am* the LORD.

13 ¶ Thou shalt not defraud thy neighbour, neither rob *him:* the wages of him that is hired shall not abide with thee all night until the morning.

14 ¶ Thou shalt not curse the deaf, nor put a stumblingblock before the blind, but shalt fear thy God: I *am* the LORD.

15 ¶ Ye shall do no unrighteousness in judgment: thou shalt not respect the person of the poor, nor honour the person of the mighty: *but* in righteousness shalt thou judge thy neighbour.

16 ¶ Thou shalt not go up and down *as* a talebearer among thy people: neither shalt thou stand against the blood of thy neighbour: I *am* the LORD.

17 ¶ Thou shalt not hate thy brother in thine heart: thou shalt in any wise rebuke thy neighbour, and not suffer sin upon him.

18 ¶ Thou shalt not avenge, nor bear any grudge against the children of thy people, but thou shalt love thy neighbour as thyself: I *am* the LORD.

1 John 3:13–19]" (Ludlow, *Companion to Your Study of the Old Testament*, 169). ⊕

19 ¶ Ye shall keep my statutes. Thou shalt not let thy cattle gender with a diverse kind: thou shalt not sow thy field with mingled seed: neither shall a garment mingled of linen and woollen come upon thee.

20 ¶ And whosoever lieth carnally with a woman, that *is* a bondmaid, betrothed to an husband, and not at all redeemed, nor freedom given her; she shall be scourged; they shall not be put to death, because she was not free.

21 And he shall bring his trespass offering unto the LORD, unto the door of the tabernacle of the congregation, *even* a ram for a trespass offering.

22 And the priest shall make an atonement for him with the ram of the trespass offering before the LORD for his sin which he hath done: and the sin which he hath done shall be forgiven him.

23 ¶ And when ye shall come into the land, and shall have planted all manner of trees for food, then ye shall count the fruit thereof as uncircumcised: three years shall it be as uncircumcised unto you: it shall not be eaten of.

24 But in the fourth year all the fruit thereof shall be holy to praise the LORD *withal.*

25 And in the fifth year shall ye eat of the fruit thereof, that it may yield unto you the increase thereof: I *am* the LORD your God.

26 ¶ Ye shall not eat *any thing* with the blood: neither shall ye use enchantment, nor observe times.

27 Ye shall not round the corners of your heads, neither shalt thou mar the corners of thy beard.

Leviticus 19:19–29. The Lord Warns Israel about Certain Sins and Describes How They Can Repent

What does uncircumcised fruit represent? (19:23–25) "This analogy of fruit to foreskin, a little startling to the modern ear, includes both the idea of leaving a natural growth uncut and the notion, readily understandable in a society in which all male infants were circumcised, of something prohibited. These three verses [23–25] reflect prudent arboricultural practice rather than any ethical imperative" (Alter, *Hebrew Bible*, 433).

Why were they commanded not to cut the corners of their beards? (19:27) "It seems probable that this fashion had been learned by the Israelites in Egypt, for the ancient Egyptians had their dark locks cropped short or shaved with great nicety, so that what remained on the crown appeared in the form of a circle surrounding the head, while the beard was dressed into a square form. This kind of coiffure had a highly idolatrous meaning; and it was adopted, with some slight variations, by almost all idolaters in ancient times. (Jeremiah 9:25, Jeremiah 9:26; Jeremiah 25:23, where 'in the utmost corners' means having the corners of their hair cut.)" (*Jamieson-Fausset-Brown Bible Commentary* [on Lev. 19:27])

What does it mean to print any marks on you? (19:28) It is "*tattooing*, imprinting figures of flowers, leaves, stars, and other fanciful devices on various parts of their person" (*Jamieson-Fausset-Brown Bible Commentary* [on Lev. 19:28]). "In teaching about how to care for our bodies, prophets have warned against tattooing or excessive piercing (see Leviticus 19:28; [Hinckley], "Great Shall Be the Peace of Thy Children," *Ensign*, Nov. 2000, 52)" (Gospel Topics, "Tattooing and Body Piercing").

Leviticus 19:30–37. Israel Is to Keep the Lord's Statutes and Judgments to Be Different from the World

Why does the Lord want us to keep His sabbaths and reverence His holy places? (19:30) "It is crucial for us to remember that we are still commanded to 'go to the house of prayer and offer up thy sacraments upon my holy day.'... The sacrament of the Lord's Supper [is] the sacred, acknowledged focal point of our weekly worship experience. We are to remember in as personal a way as possible that Christ died from a heart broken by shouldering entirely alone the sins and sorrows of the whole human family.... As we unite across the globe each week... we hope [there] is an increasingly sacred acknowledgment of Christ's majestic atoning gift to all humankind" (Holland, "Behold the Lamb of God," 45, 46). See commentary in this volume for Exodus 20:8–11 and Genesis 2:2–3.

Why is Israel commanded not to seek familiar spirits and wizards? (19:31) "True fear of God... awakens confidence in the Lord and His guidance, and excludes all superstitious and idolatrous ways and methods of discovering the future.... בוֹא [pronounced 'ōb] denotes a departed spirit, who was called up to make disclosures with regard to the future, hence a familiar spirit.... [Wizard], so to speak [a] 'clever man,'... denotes unquestionably a person acquainted with necromancy, or a conjurer who devoted himself to the invocation of spirits" (Keil and Delitzsch, *Commentary* [on Leviticus 19:31]). "While verse 26 prohibited

28 Ye shall not make any cuttings in your flesh for the dead, nor print any marks upon you: I *am* the LORD.

29 ¶ Do not prostitute thy daughter, to cause her to be a whore; lest the land fall to whoredom, and the land become full of wickedness.

30 ¶ Ye shall keep my sabbaths, and reverence my sanctuary: I *am* the LORD.

31 ¶ Regard not them that have familiar spirits, neither seek after wizards, to be defiled by them: I *am* the LORD your God.

32 ¶ Thou shalt rise up before the hoary head, and honour the face of the old man, and fear thy God: I *am* the LORD.

33 ¶ And if a stranger sojourn with thee in your land, ye shall not vex him.

34 *But* the stranger that dwelleth with you shall be unto you as one born among you, and thou shalt love him as thyself; for ye were strangers in the land of Egypt: I *am* the LORD your God.

35 ¶ Ye shall do no unrighteousness in judgment, in meteyard, in weight, or in measure.

36 Just balances, just weights, a just ephah, and a just hin, shall ye have: I *am* the LORD your God, which brought you out of the land of Egypt.

37 Therefore shall ye observe all my statutes, and all my judgments, and do them: I *am* the LORD.

CHAPTER 20

The death penalty is prescribed for sacrificing children to Molech, cursing father and mother, adultery, homosexual behavior, bestiality, spiritualism, and other abominations—Various laws and ordinances are listed.

individuals from performing divination, this verse prohibits them from going to others who do so and, in particular, those who claim to contact the dead" (Sklar, *Leviticus*, 251). See commentary in this volume for 1 Samuel 28:3 and Isaiah 29:4.

What is our responsibility to strangers? (19:33–34)
"We know that reaching out to others with love matters to the Lord. Consider these scriptural admonitions:

"The stranger that dwelleth with you shall be unto you as one born among you, . . . love him as thyself' [Leviticus 19:34]. . . .

"And the Savior said: 'For I was an hungered, and ye gave me meat: I was thirsty, and ye gave me drink: I was a stranger, and ye took me in: Naked, and ye clothed me: I was sick, and ye visited me' [Matt. 25:35–36]. . . .

"He also told the parable of the good Samaritan, which He concluded saying, 'Go, and do thou likewise' [Luke 10:37]" (Burton, "I Was a Stranger," 14). ⊕

Summary of Leviticus 20

In ancient Israel, the law of Moses condemned people to death for committing certain serious sins. The Lord and His prophets denounced idol worship, sexual sins, and other abominations. He wanted His children to be clean and free from the sin that surrounded them.

Physical death may not be the penalty for these types of sins today, but the Lord's desire for all His children to avoid spiritual death remains constant. Under the Lord's direction, prophets continue to proclaim His love and His laws. President Russell M. Nelson reminds us: "God's laws are motivated entirely by His infinite love for us and His desire for us to become all we can become. . . . Sometimes we are accused of being uncaring as we teach the Father's requirements for exaltation in the celestial kingdom. But wouldn't it be far more uncaring for us not to tell the truth—not to teach what God has revealed? It is precisely because we do care deeply about all of God's children that we proclaim His truth. We may not always tell people what they want to hear. Prophets are rarely popular. But we will always teach the truth!" ("Love and Laws of God").

CHAPTER 21

The priests are to be holy—The high priest is not to marry a widow, a divorced person, or a harlot—Descendants of Aaron with physical blemishes may not offer the bread of God upon the altar.

Summary of Leviticus 21:1–15

The Lord declares that priests must be holy. He gives inspired guidelines regarding marriage for priests to help ensure their worthiness and example before the children of Israel.

16 ¶ And the LORD spake unto Moses, saying,

Leviticus 21:16–24. Physical Blemishes Restrict the Performance of Certain Priesthood Services

Why would physical blemishes or disabilities prohibit a man from performing certain priesthood services? (21:17) "Just as the offering was to be without blemish, in the similitude of the Only Begotten Son of the Father, so also was the priest who offered the sacrifice to be without blemish, in similitude of the Father who offered his Son. . . . Nothing in modern revelation, however, bars one who is physically impaired from holding any priesthood office or functioning in any priesthood ordinance, in or out of the temple" (Rasmussen, *Latter-day Saint Commentary on the Old Testament*, 139). ⊕

Why was a blemished priest allowed to eat the priestly portions? (21:21–23) A portion of most sacrificial offerings was set aside for the priests as compensation for their service (see Leviticus 10:12–15). While imperfections might limit priests from performing certain ceremonies, they could still serve in a variety of other functions. "The physical deformity does not disqualify the man from his priestly perquisite [benefit] of a share in the sacrifices. Otherwise, he would have no source of sustenance. But he is not permitted (verse 23) to approach the altar ('come in') to offer the sacrifice" (Alter, *Hebrew Bible*, 440).

What does "profane not my sanctuaries" mean? (21:23) "*My sanctuaries* probably refers to the two divisions of the tabernacle: (1) the holy place, where

17 Speak unto Aaron, saying, Whosoever *he be* of thy seed in their generations that hath *any* blemish, let him not approach to offer the bread of his God.

18 For whatsoever man *he be* that hath a blemish, he shall not approach: a blind man, or a lame, or he that hath a flat nose, or any thing superfluous,

19 Or a man that is brokenfooted, or brokenhanded,

20 Or crookbackt, or a dwarf, or that hath a blemish in his eye, or be scurvy, or scabbed, or hath his stones broken;

21 No man that hath a blemish of the seed of Aaron the priest shall come nigh to offer the offerings of the LORD made by fire: he hath a blemish; he shall not come nigh to offer the bread of his God.

22 He shall eat the bread of his God, *both* of the most holy, and of the holy.

23 Only he shall not go in unto the veil, nor come nigh unto the altar, because he hath a blemish; that he profane not my sanctuaries: for I the LORD do sanctify them.

24 And Moses told *it* unto Aaron, and to his sons, and unto all the children of Israel.

the altar of incense stood; and (2) the Most Holy Place, where the ark of the covenant rested. This implies that the person with a physical defect had access to the outer court around the tabernacle as long as he did not come too close to the *altar* of burnt offering, which stood in the outer court" (*Nelson Study Bible* [NKJV], 194).

CHAPTER 22

Those of the priests and their families who may eat of the holy things are described—Sacrificial animals are to be perfect and without blemish.

Summary of Leviticus 22

The Lord reiterates the need for cleanliness among the priests and their family members who partake of the holy offerings. Worshippers should make offerings of their own free will with sacrificial animals who are perfect and without blemish.

CHAPTERS 23–24

Israel is to hold a holy convocation on each weekly Sabbath—Israel is to keep the Feasts of the Passover, of Unleavened Bread, of Pentecost or Firstfruits, of Trumpets, of the Day of Atonement, and of Tabernacles.

A perpetual fire is to burn outside the veil in the tabernacle—A blasphemer is put to death by stoning—Israel's law is one of an eye for an eye and a tooth for a tooth.

Summary of Leviticus 23–24

The Law establishes a weekly Sabbath observance (see Leviticus 23:1–3) and four special feasts (see Leviticus 23:33–44) to provide the children of Israel with opportunities to honor and show one's gratitude to the Lord God. The strictness of the law of Moses, highlighted in the phrase "eye for eye, tooth for tooth" (Leviticus 24:20), reminds the children of Israel to draw close to God. See commentary in this volume for Exodus 21:24.

CHAPTER 25

Each seventh year is to be kept as a sabbath year—Each fiftieth year is to be one of jubilee, in which liberty is proclaimed throughout the land—Laws are revealed for the sale and redemption of lands, houses, and servants—The land is the Lord's, as are the servants—Usury is forbidden.

1 And the LORD spake unto Moses in mount Sinai, saying,

2 Speak unto the children of Israel, and say unto them, When ye come into the land

Leviticus 25:1–7. The Lord Declares That Each Seventh Year Should Be a Sabbath Year

What was a sabbath year? (25:2–4) "As was the seventh day in every week and the seventh month in every year, so also was every seventh year consecrated to the Lord. The land, inasmuch as it was the Lord's, was to keep a Sabbath unto Him (Lev. 25:2–7)" (Bible Dictionary, "Sabbatical Year").

"In the sabbatical year the Israelites were neither to sow, to prune, nor to harvest—except to gather enough volunteer produce to supply the needs of the family, servants, and 'strangers' (nonresidents who might need food); they should show gratitude for their land and their freedom (Deut. 5:6, 12–15; [Bible Dictionary], 'Sabbatical Year')" (Rasmussen, *Latter-day Saint Commentary on the Old Testament*, 141).

How did honoring the sabbath year show their faith? (25:6–7) The sabbath year "illustrates the commitment of faith and trust in God that was required of one who truly followed the law. The Israelite was told that once in every seven years he was to trust wholly in God rather than in the fruits of his own labor for sustenance" (*Old Testament Student Manual: Genesis–2 Samuel*, 188). How do you show similar faith and commitment to God in your life?

Leviticus 25:8–17. A "Jubilee" Year Is to Be Celebrated Every Fiftieth Year

How did the Sabbatical year differ from the year of Jubilee? (25:8–10) "A Sabbatical year and a year of Jubilee were not one and the same. Just as the Sabbath day was every seventh day, the Sabbath year was every seventh year. Jubilee was every fiftieth year. . . . *Jubilee* is defined as 'a sabbath of sabbatical years plus one (that is 7 x 7 plus one)' [Ludlow, *Companion to Your Study of the Old Testament*, 171]. . . . To begin the Jubilee year, trumpets blew on the Day of Atonement, the law of Moses was read to the people, and much religious instruction was given" (Black, *400 Questions and Answers*, 78). ⊕

which I give you, then shall the land keep a
sabbath unto the LORD.

3 Six years thou shalt sow thy field, and six
years thou shalt prune thy vineyard, and
gather in the fruit thereof;

4 But in the seventh year shall be a sabbath
of rest unto the land, a sabbath for the LORD:
thou shalt neither sow thy field, nor prune
thy vineyard.

5 That which groweth of its own accord
of thy harvest thou shalt not reap, neither
gather the grapes of thy vine undressed: *for* it
is a year of rest unto the land.

6 And the sabbath of the land shall be meat
for you; for thee, and for thy servant, and for
thy maid, and for thy hired servant, and for
thy stranger that sojourneth with thee,

7 And for thy cattle, and for the beast that
are in thy land, shall all the increase thereof
be meat.

8 ¶ And thou shalt number seven sabbaths of
years unto thee, seven times seven years; and
the space of the seven sabbaths of years shall
be unto thee forty and nine years.

9 Then shalt thou cause the trumpet of the
jubilee to sound on the tenth *day* of the seventh month, in the day of atonement shall
ye make the trumpet sound throughout all
your land.

10 And ye shall hallow the fiftieth year, and
proclaim liberty throughout *all* the land unto
all the inhabitants thereof: it shall be a jubilee
unto you; and ye shall return every man unto
his possession, and ye shall return every man
unto his family.

11 A jubilee shall that fiftieth year be unto
you: ye shall not sow, neither reap that which

groweth of itself in it, nor gather *the grapes* in it of thy vine undressed.

12 For it *is* the jubilee; it shall be holy unto you: ye shall eat the increase thereof out of the field.

13 In the year of this jubilee ye shall return every man unto his possession.

14 And if thou sell ought unto thy neighbour, or buyest *ought* of thy neighbour's hand, ye shall not oppress one another:

15 According to the number of years after the jubilee thou shalt buy of thy neighbour, *and* according unto the number of years of the fruits he shall sell unto thee:

16 According to the multitude of years thou shalt increase the price thereof, and according to the fewness of years thou shalt diminish the price of it: for *according* to the number *of the years* of the fruits doth he sell unto thee.

17 Ye shall not therefore oppress one another; but thou shalt fear thy God: for I *am* the LORD your God.

How did the Jubilee bless Israel? (25:13–17) "*Jubile*, or *jubilee*, from the Hebrew *yovel* ('the trill of the ram's horn'; Lev. 25:9*a*), has come to mean 'rejoicing.' It was a signal to proclaim liberty for servants in bondage, and the return of a heritage to its rightful heirs. Thus land was conveyed only for the number of years remaining in each half-century after the jubilee, and no one was to take advantage of either buyer or seller in calculating those years (Lev. 25:10, 14–17)" (Rasmussen, *Latter-day Commentary on the Old Testament*, 141).

How was the selling or purchase of land linked to the year of Jubilee? (25:14–16) As indicated in Leviticus 25:13, land was returned to its original owners in the year of Jubilee. "To *buy* or *sell* [land] was never a permanent transaction. We would understand it as something similar to a lease. This law helped the people remember that God was the real landowner and they were simply his tenants, unable to permanently sell something that didn't actually belong to them" (*Quest Study Bible* [1994], 170). To ensure equity among the people, the price of land would be based on the number of harvests before the year of Jubilee. More years of harvest before the year of Jubilee would increase the price, while fewer years would decrease the price of the land (see verses 14–16).

Summary of Leviticus 25:18–55

The Lord gives laws regarding the sale and redemption of land, houses, and servants. All these things remind Israel that they should show mercy to others, as God has shown mercy to them.

CHAPTER 26

Temporal and spiritual blessings will abound in Israel if the people keep the commandments—Cursing, scourging, and desolation will be theirs if they disobey the Lord—When His people repent, the Lord will show mercy unto them.

1 Ye shall make you no idols nor graven image, neither rear you up a standing image,

Leviticus 26:1–13. The Lord Promises Great Blessings for Obedience

Why would the Lord forbid "a standing image"? (26:1) A standing image "was a stone or wooden column erected to represent a pagan god or goddess.

It was not a likeness, but a symbol. Together, the four terms used in this verse cover all the possibilities for pagan images. [The Lord] confronts the Israelites with a choice of allegiances. Would they love the living God or idols?" (*Nelson Study Bible* [NKJV], 202).

neither shall ye set up *any* image of stone in
your land, to bow down unto it: for I *am* the
LORD your God.

2 ¶ Ye shall keep my sabbaths, and reverence
my sanctuary: I *am* the LORD.

3 ¶ If ye walk in my statutes, and keep my
commandments, and do them;

4 Then I will give you rain in due season, and
the land shall yield her increase, and the trees
of the field shall yield their fruit.

What does "your threshing shall reach unto the vintage" mean? (26:5) *Threshing* refers to the harvesting of grain. "Reach unto the vintage" means that the stores of grain or food will last until the next grape harvest (see Valletta, et al., *Old Testament for Latter-day*

5 And your threshing shall reach unto the
vintage, and the vintage shall reach unto the
sowing time: and ye shall eat your bread to
the full, and dwell in your land safely.

Blessings and Curses for Israel (Leviticus 26)

"Leviticus 26 is one of the most powerful chapters in the Old Testament. The Lord put the options facing Israel so clearly that they could not be misunderstood. If Israel was obedient, they would be blessed" (*Old Testament Student Manual: Genesis–2 Samuel*, 189).

"There are four categories of blessings [for Israel's obedience]: the 'rain in due season' (Lev 26:4) that will bring bounteous harvests; 'peace in the land' (Lev 26:6) and protection from enemies; posterity, in that the Lord will 'make you fruitful, and multiply you' (Lev 26:9); and finally, Jehovah's promise that 'I will set my tabernacle among you: and my soul shall not abhor you. And I will walk among you, and will be your God, and ye shall be my people' (Lev 26:11–12).

"The curses are the horrific reversal of these blessings. Disobedience will bring famine, defeat at the hand of enemies, and destruction and scattering of posterity. The curses are couched in the language of prophecy because in the end the Lord promises his people, after they have suffered the consequences of their covenant breaking, a blessing of return and restoration" (Holzapfel, et al., *Jehovah and the World of the Old Testament*, 123).

Referring to Leviticus 26, President Spencer W. Kimball reminded the Saints of this dispensation that "the day has come when we should take stock of ourselves and see if we are worthy to ask [for the Lord's blessings] or if we have been breaking the commandments, making ourselves unworthy of receiving the blessings. . . .

"The Lord [stated]: 'These are the statutes and judgments and laws, which the Lord made between him and the children of Israel in Mount Sinai by the hand of Moses' (Lev. 26:46).

"This applies to you and me.

"Would this be a good time to deeply concern ourselves with these matters? Is this a time when we should return to our homes, our families, our children? Is this the time we should remember our tithes and our offerings, a time when we should desist from our abortions, our divorces, our Sabbath breaking, our eagerness to make the holy day a holiday?

"Is this a time to repent of our sins, our immoralities, our doctrines of devils?

"Is this a time for all of us to make holy our marriages, live in joy and happiness, rear our families in righteousness? . . .

"Is this the time to set our face firmly against unholy and profane things, and whoredoms, irregularities, and related matters? . . .

"We deal with many things which are thought to be not so spiritual; but all things are spiritual with the Lord, and he expects us to listen, and to obey, and to follow the commandments. And I beg of you—all of us—that we live the commandments of the Lord" (Kimball, "The Lord Expects His Saints to Follow the Commandments," 4, 5–6, 7).

Saint Families, 164). If the Israelites are obedient to the commandments, the Lord will provide food in abundance.

6 And I will give peace in the land, and ye shall lie down, and none shall make *you* afraid: and I will rid evil beasts out of the land, neither shall the sword go through your land.

7 And ye shall chase your enemies, and they shall fall before you by the sword.

8 And five of you shall chase an hundred, and an hundred of you shall put ten thousand to flight: and your enemies shall fall before you by the sword.

9 For I will have respect unto you, and make you fruitful, and multiply you, and establish my covenant with you.

10 And ye shall eat old store, and bring forth the old because of the new.

11 And I will set my tabernacle among you: and my soul shall not abhor you.

12 And I will walk among you, and will be your God, and ye shall be my people.

13 I *am* the LORD your God, which brought you forth out of the land of Egypt, that ye should not be their bondmen; and I have broken the bands of your yoke, and made you go upright.

How do we receive the Lord's peace in our day? (26:6) "In our homes we come unto Christ by learning to follow His commandments, by studying the scriptures and praying together, and by helping one another stay on the covenant path. . . .

"As we live with devotion born of faith in Jesus Christ, we will feel the peaceful presence of the Holy Ghost, who guides us to truth, inspires us to live worthy of the Lord's blessings, and bears witness that God lives and loves us. All this within the fortress of our own homes. But remember, our homes are only as powerful as the spiritual strength of each one of us within the walls" (Rasband, "Build a Fortress of Spirituality and Protection," 108). How will you increase peace in your home?

How did the Lord make it possible for Israel to "go upright"? (26:13) "As slaves in Egypt, the people were burdened with work like oxen bound to a yoke (see Jer. 28:10–14). God has broken this yoke of bondage, freeing them of their heavy burdens and allowing them to stand upright like free men and women. Their freedom and human dignity have thus been restored" (Walton, et al., *IVP Bible Background Commentary,* 141).

14 ¶ But if ye will not hearken unto me, and will not do all these commandments;

15 And if ye shall despise my statutes, or if your soul abhor my judgments, so that ye will not do all my commandments, *but* that ye break my covenant:

16 I also will do this unto you; I will even appoint over you terror, consumption, and the burning ague, that shall consume the eyes,

Leviticus 26:14–39. Punishments for Disobedience Are Outlined

and cause sorrow of heart: and ye shall sow your seed in vain, for your enemies shall eat it.

17 And I will set my face against you, and ye shall be slain before your enemies: they that hate you shall reign over you; and ye shall flee when none pursueth you.

18 And if ye will not yet for all this hearken unto me, then I will punish you seven times more for your sins.

Why would the Lord escalate His punishments by seven times? (26:18) The number seven symbolizes that which is whole or complete (see Gaskill, *Lost Language of Symbolism,* 124). "'Seven-fold' describes the punishment as far greater than what preceded and as a kind of full or complete punishment. God's attempt to break Israel's pride contrasts with the blessing of breaking the yoke of Egyptian slavery [see 26:13] . . . [This phrase] provides a literary means of expressing God's increasing anger and judgment as Israel continues to rebel" (Hess, "Leviticus," 1:815, 816).

19 And I will break the pride of your power; and I will make your heaven as iron, and your earth as brass:

20 And your strength shall be spent in vain: for your land shall not yield her increase, neither shall the trees of the land yield their fruits.

How would God break down Israelite pride? (26:19) "If [Israel] persisted in their disobedience even when the judgments reached to this height, God would . . . break down their strong pride by fearful drought. . . . The eminence or pride of strength includes everything upon which a nation rests its might . . . ; here it signifies the pride of a nation, puffed up by the fruitfulness and rich produce of its land. God would make their heaven (the sky of their land) like iron and their earth like brass, i.e., as hard and dry as metal, so that not a drop of rain and dew would fall from heaven to moisten the earth, and not a plant could grow out of the earth" (Keil and Delitzsch, *Commentary* [on Leviticus 26:18–20]).

21 ¶ And if ye walk contrary unto me, and will not hearken unto me; I will bring seven times more plagues upon you according to your sins.

22 I will also send wild beasts among you, which shall rob you of your children, and destroy your cattle, and make you few in number; and your *high* ways shall be desolate.

Why would the high ways be abandoned? (26:22) If the people continued to rebel, God "would smite them sevenfold for their sin by sending beasts of prey and childlessness. By beasts of prey He would destroy their cattle, and by barrenness He would make the nation so small that the ways would be deserted, that high roads would cease because there would be no traveller upon them on account of the depopulation of the land (Isaiah 33:8; Zephaniah 3:6), and the few inhabitants who still remained would be afraid to venture because of the wild beasts (Ezekiel 14:15)" (Keil and Delitzsch, *Commentary* [on Leviticus 26:21–22]).

23 And if ye will not be reformed by me by these things, but will walk contrary unto me;

24 Then will I also walk contrary unto you, and will punish you yet seven times for your sins.

25 And I will bring a sword upon you, that shall avenge the quarrel of *my* covenant: and when ye are gatherèd together within your

Why would Israel gather into cities? (26:25) "When enemies invaded a land in the ancient world, the people living in unwalled villages fled to the walled

cities, I will send the pestilence among you; and ye shall be delivered into the hand of the enemy.

26 *And* when I have broken the staff of your bread, ten women shall bake your bread in one oven, and they shall deliver *you* your bread again by weight: and ye shall eat, and not be satisfied.

27 And if ye will not for all this hearken unto me, but walk contrary unto me;

28 Then I will walk contrary unto you also in fury; and I, even I, will chastise you seven times for your sins.

29 And ye shall eat the flesh of your sons, and the flesh of your daughters shall ye eat.

30 And I will destroy your high places, and cut down your images, and cast your carcases upon the carcases of your idols, and my soul shall abhor you.

31 And I will make your cities waste, and bring your sanctuaries unto desolation, and I will not smell the savour of your sweet odours.

32 And I will bring the land into desolation: and your enemies which dwell therein shall be astonished at it.

33 And I will scatter you among the heathen, and will draw out a sword after you: and your land shall be desolate, and your cities waste.

34 Then shall the land enjoy her sabbaths, as long as it lieth desolate, and ye *be* in your enemies' land; *even* then shall the land rest, and enjoy her sabbaths.

35 As long as it lieth desolate it shall rest; because it did not rest in your sabbaths, when ye dwelt upon it.

36 And upon them that are left *alive* of you I will send a faintness into their hearts in the

cities for refuge, causing great overcrowding. If a city then was besieged for a long time unsanitary conditions led to *pestilence*, epidemics of deadly communicable diseases. Another result of a long siege was famine. The flour ration allotted to *ten women* would be so small that they would bake it all together in *one oven*. The bread itself would be weighed to ensure equal distribution" (*Nelson Study Bible* [NKJV], 204).

When was this prophecy fulfilled? (26:29–33) "This prophecy was literally fulfilled during the Babylonian siege of Jerusalem (see 2 Kings 25:1–7, 21) and later during the Roman siege in A.D. 70" (Valletta, et al., *Old Testament for Latter-day Saint Families,* 165).

Why would the Lord destroy Israel's "high places"? (26:30) High places were "places of worship, usually on an eminence. The name is sometimes applied to places used for the worship of Jehovah, but in later times the 'high places' were condemned as idolatrous" (*John Dummelow's Commentary* [on Leviticus 26:30]). For the Lord "to defile them [high places] with human *carcasses* would make them permanently unfit for worship" (*Nelson Study Bible* [NKJV], 204).

How can the land "enjoy her sabbaths"? (26:34–36) "Here we see the significance of the command in [Leviticus 26] verse 2: 'Observe my sabbaths.' The Lord's sabbaths include weekly Sabbaths, ceremonial sabbaths, and sabbatical fallow years, which acknowledge his lordship over the people and the land. If the people deplete the land by failing to grant its sabbatical respites, they will be deleted from it. It is as if the exhausted land heaves a mighty sigh of relief and settles down to a long nap to recover from its sleep deficit" (Gane, *Leviticus, Numbers*, 454).

lands of their enemies; and the sound of a
shaken leaf shall chase them; and they shall
flee, as fleeing from a sword; and they shall
fall when none pursueth.

37 And they shall fall one upon another, as
it were before a sword, when none pursueth:
and ye shall have no power to stand before
your enemies.

38 And ye shall perish among the heathen,
and the land of your enemies shall eat you
up.

39 And they that are left of you shall pine
away in their iniquity in your enemies' lands;
and also in the iniquities of their fathers shall
they pine away with them.

40 If they shall confess their iniquity, and the
iniquity of their fathers, with their trespass
which they trespassed against me, and that
also they have walked contrary unto me;

41 And *that* I also have walked contrary unto
them, and have brought them into the land
of their enemies; if then their uncircumcised
hearts be humbled, and they then accept of
the punishment of their iniquity:

42 Then will I remember my covenant with
Jacob, and also my covenant with Isaac, and
also my covenant with Abraham will I remember; and I will remember the land.

43 The land also shall be left of them, and
shall enjoy her sabbaths, while she lieth desolate without them: and they shall accept of
the punishment of their iniquity: because,
even because they despised my judgments,
and because their soul abhorred my statutes.

44 And yet for all that, when they be in the
land of their enemies, I will not cast them
away, neither will I abhor them, to destroy
them utterly, and to break my covenant with
them: for I *am* the LORD their God.

Leviticus 26:40–46. The Lord Shows Mercy to Those Who Repent

How does Israel receive the Lord's mercy? (26:40–42) "Israel must qualify for the blessings of living in a promised land or be driven out as were others before them (recall Lev. 18:24–28). But they or their descendants could be gathered again upon remembering and fulfilling God's covenants, for he will certainly remember and perform his part (Lev. 26:40–46)" (Rasmussen, *Latter-day Saint Commentary on the Old Testament,* 142–43).

"And thus mercy can satisfy the demands of justice, and encircles them in the arms of safety, while he that exercises no faith unto repentance is exposed to the whole law of the demands of justice; therefore only unto him that has faith unto repentance is brought about the great and eternal plan of redemption" (Alma 34:16). ⊕

How do the Lord's actions with the children of Israel show His love? (26:44) "Our Heavenly Father's goal in parenting is not to have His children *do* what is right; it is to have His children *choose* to do what is right and ultimately become like Him. If He simply wanted us to be obedient, He would use immediate rewards and punishments to influence our behaviors.

45 But I will for their sakes remember the covenant of their ancestors, whom I brought forth out of the land of Egypt in the sight of the heathen, that I might be their God: I *am* the LORD.

46 These *are* the statutes and judgments and laws, which the LORD made between him and the children of Israel in mount Sinai by the hand of Moses.

CHAPTER 27

How properties are consecrated unto the Lord is explained—Israel is commanded to pay tithes of their crops, flocks, and herds.

"But God is not interested in His children just becoming trained and obedient 'pets' who will not chew on His slippers in the celestial living room. No, God wants His children to grow up spiritually and join Him in the family business" (Renlund, "Choose You This Day," 104). How have you learned about Heavenly Father's love by choosing Him and keeping His commandments? ⊕

Summary of Leviticus 27

All things belong to God, and His people should recognize His hand in their lives by paying a tithe on all that they have. One LDS scholar wrote: "Leviticus shows us the laws governing Saints in former days [see Leviticus 27:34]. Many of them embrace principles that still apply to us" (Rasmussen, *Latter-day Saint Commentary on the Old Testament*, 143).

THE FOURTH BOOK OF MOSES

CALLED

NUMBERS

Introduction

Numbers is the fourth book of "the five books of Moses . . . known collectively as 'the Pentateuch,' i.e., 'the fivefold book'" (Millet, "Lessons in the Wilderness," 173). The name comes from the Septuagint or Greek version of the Old Testament whose translators "chose to label it 'Arithmoi,' 'Numbers,' because of the repeated use of census figures and counting of the Israelites. In reality, . . . [only] chapters 1–4 and 26 contain many numbers; the majority of the story in this phase of Israel's dramatic exodus involves the people's encounter with their God and his prophet, and with lessons painfully learned 'in the desert'" (Millet, "Lessons in the Wilderness," 173).

"In Hebrew [Numbers] is called the 'in the wilderness' book. It picks up the Exodus historical narrative of Israel after their eleven-month sojourn at Sinai. After explaining why Israel was not ready to enter the promised land of Canaan at the time, it skips to the end of their thirty-eight years of wandering and highlights their travels around Edom and Moab" (Ludlow, *Unlocking the Old Testament*, 41).

"Numbers emphasizes . . . [that] before God established his covenant with the Israelites at Sinai their lack of faith was not punished; after Sinai, it was. Israel's repeated failures and chastisements by God, though depressing in and of themselves, do leave at least one message of consolation: Jehovah is shown to be a God of grace and mercy who repeatedly offers to Israel another chance to live the covenant" (Pearson, *Old Testament*, 30).

"The book has four main parts. Part one, chapters 1–10:10, tells of preparations made to leave Sinai. . . . Part two, [chapter 10, verse 11 through chapter 14], is a record of the Israelite journey from Sinai to Mt. Pisgah, located near the borders of Canaan. . . . Part three, chapters 15–19, tells of the Mosaic laws that governed the Israelites and of the problems that arose in keeping those laws. Part four, chapters 20–36, is an account of their continued travels and encampments. . . .

"Although doctrinal discourses in Numbers are rare, the biblical text is significant because it presents a history of the wandering Israelites not found elsewhere" (Black, *400 Questions and Answers about the Old Testament*, 79).

CHAPTER 1

Moses and the princes in Israel count from each tribe (except Levi) those males twenty years of age and older—They total 603,550—The Levites are appointed to attend the tabernacle.

1 And the LORD spake unto Moses in the
wilderness of Sinai, in the tabernacle of the
congregation, on the first *day* of the second
month, in the second year after they were
come out of the land of Egypt, saying,

Numbers 1:1–4. A Census Is Taken and Leaders Are Appointed over Every Tribe

How long had the children of Israel been in the "wilderness [or desert] of Sinai"? (1:1) As Numbers chapter one opens on "the first day of the second month, in the second year," the Israelites have been camping at the base of Mount Sinai for almost a year. "In ancient times, the first day of each month was a holiday and provided a convenient opportunity to bring the people together for important announcements. . . . The sanctuary, called the 'Tent of Meeting,' had been completed one month earlier (Exod. 40:17)" (Milgrom, *Numbers*, 4).

2 Take ye the sum of all the congregation of the children of Israel, after their families, by the house of their fathers, with the number of *their* names, every male by their polls;
3 From twenty years old and upward, all that are able to go forth to war in Israel: thou and Aaron shall number them by their armies.
4 And with you there shall be a man of every tribe; every one head of the house of his fathers.

Why did the Lord command Moses to number the children of Israel? (1:2–3) "Chapter one of the book of Numbers begins with the Lord's command to Moses to number the males in all the tribes of Israel over twenty years of age; this would represent the potential army of Israel, the fighting force needed to face the enemies of the people of God. If the figures are to be taken literally, the average number of fighting males per tribe was a little over 50,000, with the tribe of Judah furnishing the greater number (74,600) and the tribe of Manasseh the least (32,200)" (Millet, "Lessons in the Wilderness," 176). "The 'numbering' of the Israelite males for military duty was conducted by tribe, clan, and extended family (Num 1:1–46)" (Holzapfel, et al., *Jehovah and the World of the Old Testament*, 124). See commentary in this volume for Exodus 12:37.

Summary of Numbers 1:5–46

A census of the tribes of Israel counts the adult males able to fight in war except for the Levites due to their responsibilities for the tabernacle. The total number of males age twenty and older reaches 603,550. However, the word translated in this account as "thousand" may actually mean "clan" or "military company." If this is the case, the total number of fighting men would be much smaller (see Holzapfel, et al., *Jehovah and the World of the Old Testament*, 126).

47 ¶ But the Levites after the tribe of their fathers were not numbered among them.
48 For the Lord had spoken unto Moses, saying,
49 Only thou shalt not number the tribe of Levi, neither take the sum of them among the children of Israel:

Numbers 1:47–54. The Levites Are Not Included in the Military Census

Why was the tribe of Levi numbered separately? (1:49–50) In addition to the "numbering" of males for military duty, a "separate census of Israelite firstborn males is also recorded (Num 3:40–43). The Levites, however, were not included in either census because they were consecrated to the Lord (Num 1:47–51; see also 3:11–39). They were, however, numbered separately for the purpose of organizing their services at the Tabernacle (Num 3:39; 4:46–48)" (Holzapfel, et al., *Jehovah and the World of the Old Testament*, 124).

50 But thou shalt appoint the Levites over the tabernacle of testimony, and over all the vessels thereof, and over all things that *belong*

What was the Levites' role in moving the tabernacle from place to place? (1:50) "The Levites were numbered later (Num. 3) and appointed to assemble

to it: they shall bear the tabernacle, and all the vessels thereof; and they shall minister unto it, and shall encamp round about the tabernacle.

51 And when the tabernacle setteth forward, the Levites shall take it down: and when the tabernacle is to be pitched, the Levites shall set it up: and the stranger that cometh nigh shall be put to death.

52 And the children of Israel shall pitch their tents, every man by his own camp, and every man by his own standard, throughout their hosts.

53 But the Levites shall pitch round about the tabernacle of testimony, that there be no wrath upon the congregation of the children of Israel: and the Levites shall keep the charge of the tabernacle of testimony.

54 And the children of Israel did according to all that the LORD commanded Moses, so did they.

the tabernacle at all the long-term camping places, conduct services, and disassemble and carry the parts of the tabernacle and its furnishings" (Rasmussen, *Latter-day Saint Commentary on the Old Testament*, 145–46).

Why were strangers punished so harshly for approaching the tabernacle? (1:51) A better translation for "stranger" is "anyone unauthorized" (Numbers 1:51*a*). Only Levites were called, set apart, and sanctified to "keep the charge of the tabernacle of testimony" (Numbers 1:53). "The sense of *comes near* [cometh nigh] is [to] encroach; the encroacher is executed on the spot by Levitical guards (see [Numbers 18:7])" (*New Oxford Annotated Bible*, 190). ⊕

Why were the Levites commanded to camp surrounding the tabernacle? (1:53) "The Levites . . . are charged to encamp around [the tabernacle], protect it from casual contact, maintain it, carry it during the journey, and pitch it at each stop. . . . This action is in the interests of the community, so that it not experience the wrath of God, which may cause death, often through a plague ([Numbers 16:46–50; 31:16]). These strict measures are instituted to preserve a proper relationship between God and the people" (*New Oxford Annotated Bible* [2010], 190).

Why Did the Children of Israel Set Up Their Camp around the Tabernacle? (Numbers 1:50–53)

"Reviewing man's history reveals examples of obedience yielding blessings and disobedience yielding sorrow and destruction. The course we are to follow is revealed through His holy prophets, who direct us to be obedient to the Lord's instructions.

"One example is the Lord's directions to the children of Israel as they journeyed in the wilderness. In order that they would have a centerpiece for their worship and activity, the Lord instructed Moses to build a tabernacle. The tabernacle was a forerunner of the temple, made portable so they could easily carry it with them. . . .

"This tabernacle became the center of their camp as they journeyed to the promised land. Here sacred services could be performed. . . .

"Because of the disobedience of the children of Israel, 'Moses took the tabernacle [out of their midst], and pitched it without the camp' [Exodus 33:7].

"Now their centerpiece, the tabernacle, was away from them. They could no longer be guided and protected by its presence. Now only the faithful were allowed to come to the tabernacle" (Perry, "We Believe All That God Has Revealed," 87).

CHAPTER 2

The order and leaders of the tribes and armies of Israel in their tents are given.

Summary of Numbers 2

God establishes the pattern of Israel's camp and the order for their march when moving. They organize the camp into four groups of three tribes each. The tribes of Judah, Issachar, and Zebulun camp on the east side of the tabernacle. Reuben, Simeon, and Gad camp on the south side. The west side of the tabernacle is where Ephraim, Manasseh, and Benjamin camp. Finally, Dan, Asher, and Naphtali are on the north side of the tabernacle. The Levites camp immediately around the tabernacle. When marching, the tribes on the east of the tabernacle make up the first rank. The tribes on the south follow them, then the tribes on the west, and the tribes on the north march in the last rank. The Levites carry the tabernacle and its furnishings in the middle of the company.

The Camp of Israel in the Wilderness (Numbers 2)

"The arrangement of the camp of Israel as outlined in Numbers 2 is highly symbolic as well as functional. The Tabernacle was to be set up in the center of camp, emphasizing the significance of God's presence among the Israelites and the restriction on outsiders' access. The Israelites pitched their tents by tribe, three on each side of the Tabernacle and at some distance away. The placement of Judah in front of the Tabernacle (on the east) and the Joseph tribes—Ephraim and Manasseh—behind the Tabernacle foreshadow the significance these tribes would have after the Israelites settled in Canaan" (Holzapfel, et al., *Jehovah and the World of the Old Testament*, 124).

CAMP OF ISRAEL

North

Naphtali
Dan
Asher

Manasseh
Levites
Zebulun

West
Ephraim
Levites
TABERNACLE
Levites
Judah
East

Benjamin
Levites
Issachar

Simeon
Reuben
Gad

South

Summary of Numbers 3–4

The two sons of Aaron die after they offer "strange fire before the Lord" (Numbers 3:4). (See commentary in this volume for Leviticus 10:1–2.) Jehovah redeems the firstborn of all the tribes He had previously claimed (Exodus 13:1–16) by "claiming" the Levites as replacements. Since the number of the "firstborn" in the other tribes exceed that of the Levites, the tribes are to "redeem" them with money paid to the priests. It outlines the order of encampment for the Levitical families. The Levites are instructed regarding their priesthood duties and instructed how to move the tabernacle and its furnishings. Although we do not know exactly why the Lord chose the tribe of Levi to officiate in the priesthood, on one occasion the tribe of Levi showed greater faith than the other tribes. When Moses asked Israel who was on the Lord's side, only the Levites responded affirmatively (see Exodus 32:26).

CHAPTERS 3–4

Aaron and his sons minister in the priest's office—The Levites are chosen to do the service of the tabernacle—They are the Lord's, replacing the firstborn of all families of Israel—Their number, charge, and service are given.

When the camps of Israel move, Aaron and his sons cover the holy things in the tabernacle—The Levites of the families of Kohath, Gershon, and Merari carry the burden of the tabernacle.

Summary of Numbers 5

Because the tabernacle is within the camp, and represents the Lord's presence, those who become ritually unclean must leave the camp for a time until they are considered purified. The Lord reveals to Moses specific laws to both prevent or remove wickedness from the camp of Israel and other laws on how offenders could return. These laws include removing people considered impure, such as lepers, and also detail how to provide restitution to those who have been wronged. They present women suspected of marital infidelity before the priest. God will punish the guilty.

CHAPTER 5

Lepers are put out of the camp—Sinners must confess and make restitution to gain forgiveness—Women believed to be immoral undergo a trial of jealousy before the priests.

CHAPTER 6

The law of the Nazarite is explained, whereby the children of Israel may consecrate themselves to the Lord by a vow—They drink no wine nor strong drink and if defiled must shave their heads—The Lord reveals the blessing to be used by Aaron and his sons in blessing Israel.

Numbers 6:1–8. The Lord Reveals the Special Vow of a Nazarite

1 And the LORD spake unto Moses, saying,

What was a Nazarite? (6:2) "Within the law of Moses, the Lord made a special provision for men and women who wanted 'to separate themselves unto the LORD' and devote themselves to his service (Num 6:2). This is called the Nazirite vow, from the Hebrew word nazir, 'to separate, consecrate, or abstain.' One who

2 Speak unto the children of Israel, and say unto them, When either man or woman shall separate *themselves* to vow a vow of a Nazarite, to separate *themselves* unto the LORD:

3 He shall separate *himself* from wine and strong drink, and shall drink no vinegar of wine, or vinegar of strong drink, neither shall he drink any liquor of grapes, nor eat moist grapes, or dried.

4 All the days of his separation shall he eat nothing that is made of the vine tree, from the kernels even to the husk.

5 All the days of the vow of his separation there shall no razor come upon his head: until the days be fulfilled, in the which he separateth *himself* unto the LORD, he shall be holy, *and* shall let the locks of the hair of his head grow.

6 All the days that he separateth *himself* unto the LORD he shall come at no dead body.

7 He shall not make himself unclean for his father, or for his mother, for his brother, or for his sister, when they die: because the consecration of his God *is* upon his head.

8 All the days of his separation he *is* holy unto the LORD.

takes such a vow is called a Nazirite. The KJV 'Nazarite' is more correctly spelled Nazirite" (Holzapfel, et al., *Jehovah and the World of the Old Testament*, 128). "The inclusion of [women] indicates that the Nazirite vow was widely practiced. . . . At the end of the Second Temple period, many women took the vow, which accounts for the technical term for the female Nazirite, *nezirah*, and for the many laws pertaining to her status" (Milgrom, *Numbers*, 44).

Summary of Numbers 6:9–27

The Lord explains how Nazarites who become defiled can reclaim their vows and also how to be released from their vows. The Lord reveals a blessing Aaron and his sons would impart upon the children of Israel.

The Nazarite Vow (Numbers 6:2–8)

"The term *Nazarite* comes from a Hebrew word whose root meaning is 'to separate, cut off, or keep oneself from.' There were two main ways that a Nazarite would 'separate' himself.

"First, a Nazarite would 'separate from' certain products or actions. Specifically, he was not to eat any fruit of the vine (grapes, raisins, grape juice, wine, etc.). He was not to cut his hair while under the vow. And he was not to touch a dead person (even a member of his own family).

"Secondly, the Nazarite would 'separate toward' certain vows or obligations of his own choice. These could include personal goals, community service, religious duties, or whatever he desired. The vows were to be voluntary and from the heart.

"The vow of a Nazarite lasted anywhere from a month to a lifetime. Either men or women could enter the vow (for example, Samson and his mother). Parents could even raise their child as a Nazarite and as the child matured he could decide if he wanted to honor his parents' desire and continue the vow on his own.

"Noted examples of Nazarites are Samson (Judg. 13:5), Samuel (1 Sam. 1:11), and John the Baptist (Luke 1:15)" (Ludlow, *Unlocking the Old Testament*, 47).

Summary of Numbers 7–8

Now that the Camp of Israel is organized, the leaders of each of the twelve tribes present gifts for the dedication of the tabernacle. Moses then gives Israel final instructions for the tabernacle, such as the lighting of the menorah and preparing Aaron, his sons, and the Levites for service in the tabernacle.

CHAPTERS 7–8

The princes of Israel make offerings for the tabernacle at its dedication—The Lord speaks to Moses from the mercy seat, between the cherubim, upon the ark.

The Levites are washed, consecrated, and set apart by the laying on of hands—They are the Lord's in place of the firstborn of every family—They are a gift to Aaron and his sons to do the service of the tabernacle.

CHAPTER 9

Israel is again commanded to keep the Passover—A cloud rests upon the tabernacle by day and by night, plus a fire by night—When the cloud rests, Israel camps; when it lifts, they journey.

Numbers 9:1–14. The Children of Israel Celebrate Their Second Passover

1 And the LORD spake unto Moses in the wilderness of Sinai, in the first month of the second year after they were come out of the land of Egypt, saying,

2 Let the children of Israel also keep the passover at his appointed season.

3 In the fourteenth day of this month, at even, ye shall keep it in his appointed season: according to all the rites of it, and according to all the ceremonies thereof, shall ye keep it.

4 And Moses spake unto the children of Israel, that they should keep the passover.

5 And they kept the passover on the fourteenth day of the first month at even in the wilderness of Sinai: according to all that the LORD commanded Moses, so did the children of Israel.

6 ¶ And there were certain men, who were defiled by the dead body of a man, that they could not keep the passover on that day: and

What was the purpose of observing the Passover again? (9:2–3) "The Israelites were again commanded to observe the Passover ritual and to commemorate the night in Egypt when the angel of death spared the chosen of the Lord, those upon whose door posts was found the blood of the lamb (Ex. 12; Num. 9:1–14). The spiritually sensitive among the children of Israel would surely recognize the remarkable typology in the celebration of this event and the accompanying week of feasting: the blood of the 'lamb slain from the foundation of the world' (Rev. 13:8) would deliver all the obedient and observant from the universal commonality—death" (Millet, "Lessons in the Wilderness," 182). ⊕

How did God provide for those who were impure and couldn't celebrate the Passover? (9:6–12) "Because of their defilement from touching the body of a dead person ([Numbers] 5:2), there were some [which

they came before Moses and before Aaron on
that day:

7 And those men said unto him, We *are* defiled by the dead body of a man: wherefore
are we kept back, that we may not offer an
offering of the LORD in his appointed season
among the children of Israel?

8 And Moses said unto them, Stand still,
and I will hear what the LORD will command
concerning you.

9 ¶ And the LORD spake unto Moses, saying,

10 Speak unto the children of Israel, saying,
If any man of you or of your posterity shall
be unclean by reason of a dead body, or *be* in
a journey afar off, yet he shall keep the passover unto the LORD.

11 The fourteenth day of the second month
at even they shall keep it, *and* eat it with unleavened bread and bitter *herbs*.

12 They shall leave none of it unto the morning, nor break any bone of it: according to
all the ordinances of the passover they shall
keep it.

13 But the man that *is* clean, and is not in
a journey, and forbeareth to keep the passover, even the same soul shall be cut off from
among his people: because he brought not
the offering of the LORD in his appointed
season, that man shall bear his sin.

14 And if a stranger shall sojourn among you,
and will keep the passover unto the LORD;
according to the ordinance of the passover,
and according to the manner thereof, so shall
he do: ye shall have one ordinance, both for
the stranger, and for him that was born in
the land.

15 ¶ And on the day that the tabernacle was
reared up the cloud covered the tabernacle,
namely, the tent of the testimony: and at even

had been removed from the camp] who *could not keep the Passover* at its appointed time. These people came willingly to ask Moses what they might do. God's intent was that the Passover would be celebrated by all of His people. Reasons of ritual impurity should not prevent a person from enjoying the night. Neither should one think that the celebration was unnecessary. Thus the ritually impure would celebrate the Passover a month later" (*Nelson Study Bible* [NKJV], 225).

Why did Moses seek even more revelation from the Lord? (9:8–9) President James E. Faust discussed the necessity for constant revelation: "Much revelation received, in this time as well as anciently, has been doctrinal. Some of it has been operational and tactical. Much of it is not spectacular. President John Taylor reminds us: 'Adam's revelation did not instruct Noah to build his ark; nor did Noah's revelation tell Lot to forsake Sodom; nor did either of these speak of the departure of the children of Israel from Egypt. These all had revelations for themselves' (*Millennial Star*, 1 Nov. 1847, 323)" ("Continuing Revelation," 5).

What were the symbolic elements of the Passover? (9:12) "Special considerations included:

- The selection of a firstling of the flock, without blemish [see Lev. 5:18; 27:26],
- The sacrifice of the animal's life by the shedding of its blood [see Lev. 9:18],
- Death of the animal without breaking a bone [see Ex. 12:46; Num. 9:12], and
- One animal could be sacrificed as a vicarious act for another [see Lev. 16:10].

"The Atonement of Christ fulfilled these prototypes of the Old Testament. He was the firstborn Lamb of God, without blemish. His sacrifice occurred by the shedding of blood. No bones of His body were broken—noteworthy in that both malefactors crucified with the Lord had their legs broken [see John 19:31–33]. And His was a vicarious sacrifice for others" (Nelson, "Atonement," 34–35).

Numbers 9:15–23. The Fire and Cloud Lead the Israelites through the Wilderness

What did the cloud by day and fire at night symbolize? (9:15–17) "This statement is the most comprehensive on the law of the Lord concerning the movement of the camp of Israel. Since the cloud of smoke and fire was a visible sign of God's presence, Israel learned to literally follow the Lord. They made camp, broke camp, traveled, and performed their services at the command of the Lord—the Hebrew reads, 'at the mouth of Jehovah' (see v. 18). In very deed they were schooled to follow Jehovah, who has ever directed His church and kingdom, and yet many of them did not transfer the meaning from this miraculous physical demonstration to its more important spiritual corollary" (*Old Testament Student Manual: Genesis–2 Samuel*, 200). ⊕

there was upon the tabernacle as it were the appearance of fire, until the morning.

16 So it was alway: the cloud covered it *by day*, and the appearance of fire by night.

17 And when the cloud was taken up from the tabernacle, then after that the children of Israel journeyed: and in the place where the cloud abode, there the children of Israel pitched their tents.

18 At the commandment of the LORD the children of Israel journeyed, and at the commandment of the LORD they pitched: as long as the cloud abode upon the tabernacle they rested in their tents.

19 And when the cloud tarried long upon the tabernacle many days, then the children of Israel kept the charge of the LORD, and journeyed not.

20 And *so* it was, when the cloud was a few days upon the tabernacle; according to the commandment of the LORD they abode in their tents, and according to the commandment of the LORD they journeyed.

21 And *so* it was, when the cloud abode from even unto the morning, and *that* the cloud was taken up in the morning, then they journeyed: whether *it was* by day or by night that the cloud was taken up, they journeyed.

22 Or *whether it were* two days, or a month, or a year, that the cloud tarried upon the tabernacle, remaining thereon, the children of Israel abode in their tents, and journeyed not: but when it was taken up, they journeyed.

23 At the commandment of the LORD they rested in the tents, and at the commandment of the LORD they journeyed: they kept the charge of the LORD, at the commandment of the LORD by the hand of Moses.

CHAPTER 10

Silver trumpets are used to call assemblies and to blow alarms—The cloud is taken from the tabernacle, and the children of Israel march forth in their prescribed order—The ark of the covenant goes before them in their journeyings.

CHAPTER 11

Fire from the Lord consumes the rebels in Israel—Israel murmurs and lusts for meat instead of manna—Moses complains that he cannot bear the burden alone—He is commanded to choose seventy elders to assist him—The Lord promises meat until it becomes loathsome to the Israelites—The seventy elders are chosen, they prophesy, the Lord comes down, and Eldad and Medad prophesy in the camp—Israel is provided with quail—The people lust, a great plague follows, and many die.

1 And *when* the people complained, it displeased the LORD: and the LORD heard *it;* and his anger was kindled; and the fire of the LORD burnt among them, and consumed *them that were* in the uttermost parts of the camp.

2 And the people cried unto Moses; and when Moses prayed unto the LORD, the fire was quenched.

3 And he called the name of the place Taberah: because the fire of the LORD burnt among them.

4 ¶ And the mixed multitude that *was* among them fell a lusting: and the children of Israel also wept again, and said, Who shall give us flesh to eat?

Summary of Numbers 10

The children of Israel finally leave Sinai and begin traveling toward the promised land. At the Lord's command, trumpets direct the people to take their places to march through the wilderness. The camp of Israel, with the ark of the covenant in front, follows the fire and the cloud for a three-day journey to the wilderness of Paran.

Numbers 11:1–9. The Israelites' Complaining Displeases Moses and the Lord

Why was the Lord so displeased with this episode of complaining? (11:1) "The grammatical construction of the Hebrew is unusual—literally, 'And the people became [or were] as complainers of evil.' Some understand this as an indication of persistence in the activity of complaint, though it is at least as plausible to construe it as conveying the initiation of the activity. The likelihood of the latter construction is reinforced by the fact that this episode is the first of the numerous episodes of 'murmuring' that punctuate Numbers" (Alter, *Hebrew Bible*, 1:513).

What do we learn from the Lord's severe punishment of His people? (11:1–3) "Only three days into their march, the people reverted to the disloyal complaining they had expressed a year earlier. . . . The response of the Lord to this outbreak of murmuring was one of wrath" (*Expositor's Bible Commentary [Abridged]*, 196). ⊕

Who were the mixed multitude which stirred up unrest among Israelites? (11:4) "Evidence suggests that those who made up the Israelite host were not all direct descendants of Jacob's twelve sons. The narrative reads, 'A *mixed multitude* went up also with them; and flocks, and herds, even very much cattle' (Exodus 12:38; emphasis added; see also Numbers 11:4). In addition to Israelites, the slaves conscripted by the Egyptians likely included other Semitic people from Canaan who came to Egypt at various times for numerous reasons such as famine and greater opportunities available under the Hyksos' regime. Egyptian texts and art portray a variety of Semitic peoples and Nubians (from south of Egypt) among their enslaved groups" (Olson, *Women of the Old Testament*, 95–96).

Why would the Israelites want to return to Egyptian bondage? (11:5–6) "So quickly after being taught the dangers of murmuring, Israel fell right back into the practice, remembering the good aspects of Egypt while forgetting the bad—forgetting all that God had done for them and forgetting how grateful they once were for manna. The repeated exposure to the blessing of manna had not only made it commonplace, but tiresome. We are all in danger of repeating their actions in our own lives" (Muhlestein, *Scripture Study Made Simple*, 122). How can you better develop a consistent attitude of humility and gratitude for what God has done for you?

What do we know about manna? (11:7–9) See commentary in this volume for Exodus 16:14–36.

Numbers 11:10–15. Moses Complains to the Lord about His Burdens

Why did Moses complain to the Lord? (11:10–13) "Clearly the murmuring of Israel had worn Moses down so much that even he was complaining and questioning what God could do for them. The Old Testament is powerful in its consistent presentation of both the high and low points of the great men and women of God, allowing us to realize that even the best among us have our human moments" (Muhlestein, *Scripture Study Made Simple*, 123).

5 We remember the fish, which we did eat in Egypt freely; the cucumbers, and the melons, and the leeks, and the onions, and the garlick:

6 But now our soul *is* dried away: *there is* nothing at all, beside this manna, *before* our eyes.

7 And the manna *was* as coriander seed, and the colour thereof as the colour of bdellium.

8 *And* the people went about, and gathered *it*, and ground *it* in mills, or beat *it* in a mortar, and baked *it* in pans, and made cakes of it: and the taste of it was as the taste of fresh oil.

9 And when the dew fell upon the camp in the night, the manna fell upon it.

10 ¶ Then Moses heard the people weep throughout their families, every man in the door of his tent: and the anger of the LORD was kindled greatly; Moses also was displeased.

11 And Moses said unto the LORD, Wherefore hast thou afflicted thy servant? and wherefore have I not found favour in thy sight, that thou layest the burden of all this people upon me?

12 Have I conceived all this people? have I begotten them, that thou shouldest say unto me, Carry them in thy bosom, as a nursing father beareth the sucking child, unto the land which thou swarest unto their fathers?

13 Whence should I have flesh to give unto all this people? for they weep unto me, saying, Give us flesh, that we may eat.

14 I am not able to bear all this people alone, because *it is* too heavy for me.

15 And if thou deal thus with me, kill me, I pray thee, out of hand, if I have found favour in thy sight; and let me not see my wretchedness.

What can we do when we feel overwhelmed like Moses? (11:14–15) "Even the great prophet Moses felt so overwhelmed and discouraged at one point that he wanted to give up and die [see Numbers 11:14–15]. But God did not give up on Moses.

"My dear brothers and sisters, if we look at ourselves only through our mortal eyes, we may not see ourselves as good enough. But our Heavenly Father sees us as who we truly are and who we can become. He sees us as His sons and daughters, as beings of eternal light with everlasting potential and with a divine destiny [see 1 John 3:1–3]. . . .

"God will help you become something greater than you ever thought possible" (Uchtdorf, "It Works Wonderfully," 23).

Numbers 11:16–30. The Lord Assigns Seventy Men to Assist Moses

16 ¶ And the LORD said unto Moses, Gather unto me seventy men of the elders of Israel, whom thou knowest to be the elders of the people, and officers over them; and bring them unto the tabernacle of the congregation, that they may stand there with thee.

17 And I will come down and talk with thee there: and I will take of the spirit which *is* upon thee, and will put *it* upon them; and they shall bear the burden of the people with thee, that thou bear *it* not thyself alone.

18 And say thou unto the people, Sanctify yourselves against to morrow, and ye shall eat flesh: for ye have wept in the ears of the LORD, saying, Who shall give us flesh to eat? for *it was* well with us in Egypt: therefore the LORD will give you flesh, and ye shall eat.

19 Ye shall not eat one day, nor two days, nor five days, neither ten days, nor twenty days;

How did the Lord respond to Moses' anguished request? (11:16–18) "In answer to Moses' request for help, seventy men were chosen and endowed with the 'spirit that was upon him' (i.e., upon Moses; it means they were endowed with some of the same authority and spiritual gifts) so that they were able also to 'prophesy'" (Rasmussen, *Introduction to the Old Testament*, 1:115). The Lord then promised that they would "eat flesh" the next day. Though Moses expressed his surprise that the Lord could provide enough meat for so many, with the Lord's encouragement, Moses immediately told the people the words of the Lord (see Numbers 11:21–24).

20 *But* even a whole month, until it come out
at your nostrils, and it be loathsome unto you:
because that ye have despised the LORD which
is among you, and have wept before him, saying, Why came we forth out of Egypt?
21 And Moses said, The people, among
whom I *am, are* six hundred thousand footmen; and thou hast said, I will give them
flesh, that they may eat a whole month.
22 Shall the flocks and the herds be slain for
them, to suffice them? or shall all the fish of
the sea be gathered together for them, to suffice them?

23 And the LORD said unto Moses, Is the
LORD's hand waxed short? thou shalt see now
whether my word shall come to pass unto
thee or not.

What "spirit" was put upon the seventy elders selected by Moses? (11:24–25) "Recall the previous seventy who were privileged to go up the mount and become divine witnesses, seeing the Lord, eating and drinking together there (Ex. 24:1–11). When this new group of seventy elders met at the tabernacle by appointment and the Lord endowed them with the Spirit Moses possessed, they were blessed with the gift of prophecy. It came even upon two of them who did not meet at the appointed time and place. Some, including Joshua, objected when those two also were endowed with the Spirit; but Moses accepted them" (Rasmussen, *Latter-day Saint Commentary on the Old Testament*, 152).

24 ¶ And Moses went out, and told the
people the words of the LORD, and gathered
the seventy men of the elders of the people,
and set them round about the tabernacle.

25 And the LORD came down in a cloud, and
spake unto him, and took of the spirit that
was upon him, and gave *it* unto the seventy
elders: and it came to pass, *that,* when the
spirit rested upon them, they prophesied,
and did not cease.

What do we learn about Moses' character from the account of Eldad and Medad? (11:26–29) "In this material is another evidence of Moses' greatness. Some leaders would be threatened if subordinates evidenced gifts and abilities similar to their own because then their own status and position would be jeopardized. Not so with Moses. . . . Not only was he not threatened by this remarkable sharing of his spiritual power, but he expressed the desire to have every single Israelite share the same power with him" (*Old Testament Student Manual: Genesis–2 Samuel*, 201).

26 But there remained two *of the* men in the
camp, the name of the one *was* Eldad, and
the name of the other Medad: and the spirit
rested upon them; and they *were* of them
that were written, but went not out unto the
tabernacle: and they prophesied in the camp.
27 And there ran a young man, and told
Moses, and said, Eldad and Medad do prophesy in the camp.

28 And Joshua the son of Nun, the servant of
Moses, *one* of his young men, answered and
said, My lord Moses, forbid them.

29 And Moses said unto him, Enviest thou for my sake? would God that all the LORD's people were prophets, *and* that the LORD would put his spirit upon them!

30 And Moses gat him into the camp, he and the elders of Israel.

Why did Moses wish that all Israelites would be prophets? (11:29) "The primary responsibility of a prophet is to stand as a witness of the Lord Jesus. . . . And what is true of prophets is equally true of members of the Church who have received the gift of the Holy Ghost. Prophets are our pattern; they receive and deliver the witness and thus set the example for us to follow. As Moses concluded, 'Would God that all the Lord's people were prophets, and that the Lord would put his spirit upon them' (Numbers 11:29)" (Millet, *Life in Christ*, 14).

Numbers 11:31–35. The Lord Sends Wind to Carry Quails into the Israelites' Camp

31 ¶ And there went forth a wind from the LORD, and brought quails from the sea, and let *them* fall by the camp, as it were a day's journey on this side, and as it were a day's journey on the other side, round about the camp, and as it were two cubits *high* upon the face of the earth.

32 And the people stood up all that day, and all *that* night, and all the next day, and they gathered the quails: he that gathered least gathered ten homers: and they spread *them* all abroad for themselves round about the camp.

33 And while the flesh *was* yet between their teeth, ere it was chewed, the wrath of the LORD was kindled against the people, and the LORD smote the people with a very great plague.

34 And he called the name of that place Kibroth-hattaavah: because there they buried the people that lusted.

35 *And* the people journeyed from Kibroth-hattaavah unto Hazeroth; and abode at Hazeroth.

What was "the wind from the Lord"? (11:31) "God answers both Moses and the people through His *ruaḥ*, a term that means either spirit or wind. God's spirit on Moses has been shared by the elders. Now it is God's wind that brings meat to the people. Wind and spirit are two aspects of the same divine agency (cf. 1 Kings 22:19–23). God employs a wind to drive back the waters of Creation (Gen. 1:2; Ps. 104:4), the Flood (Gen. 8:1), and the Red Sea (Exod. 14:21), to endanger Jonah's ship (Jon. 1:4), and to remove the plague of the locusts (Exod. 10:13,19)" (Milgrom, *Numbers*, 91).

Why did the miracle of the quail become a curse? (11:31–34) "Migratory quail often come through the Sinai on their way north from the Sudan to Europe. . . . They generally fly with the wind and are driven to ground . . . if caught in a crosswind. In their exhaustion it is not unusual for them to fly so low that they can be easily caught" (Walton, et al., *IVP Bible Background Commentary*, 149). "When God sent the quail . . . , the people turned gluttonous. . . . The greedy lust for more than they could use brought a just punishment upon the people. How many died in the plague is not recorded, but the place was called 'Graves of the Craving' . . . (see v. 34)" (*Old Testament Student Manual: Genesis–2 Samuel*, 201).

What lesson was taught with the miracle of the quail? (11:34–35) "The Lord is trying to make Israel into the kind of people who are so full of faith that they will rely on Him enough to inherit the promised land. In order to do that, He will have to punish them in such a way that it forces them to rely on Him and nothing else. Many of the judgments Israel receives are specifically designed to shape them into a group of people who have faith in God and who fully rely on His ability to deliver them" (Muhlestein, *Essential Old Testament Companion*, 131).

Numbers 12:1–16. Aaron and Miriam Criticize Moses

Who was the "Ethiopian woman" that Moses married? (12:1) "Aaron and Miriam in their declining years seem to have objected to the idea that Moses was the sole spokesman for the Lord, and they justified their fault-finding by berating him for his marriage in Egypt to an Ethiopian. Josephus (*Antiquities of the Jews* 2:10:2) indeed recorded an account of such a marriage, proposed by the princess and the king of Ethiopia for military and political reasons, but the Bible mentions it nowhere else. That marriage is not to be confused with his marriage in Midian to Zipporah, daughter of the high priest Jethro (Ex. 2:15–22)" (Rasmussen, *Latter-day Saint Commentary on the Old Testament*, 153).

What was the sin of Miriam and Aaron? (12:2) "Herein lies the true reason for Miriam and Aaron's complaint; the previous one was only a pretext. What they were really after was a share in Moses' leadership" (Milgrom, *Numbers*, 94).

"It appears that both drank too deeply of the sweet wine of pride, the dregs of which leave the bitter aftertaste of jealousy. Intoxicated by such foolish spirits, they brought accusation against Moses and claimed themselves his equal. . . .

"That Miriam was the instigator of this rebellion needs no other proof than the punishment God inflicted upon her" (McConkie, *Gospel Symbolism*, 69–70).

What can we learn from Moses' example of meekness? (12:3) "'Moses was learned in all the wisdom of the Egyptians, and was mighty in words and in deeds' [Acts 7:22]. Yet he 'was very meek, above all the men which were upon the face of the earth' [Numbers 12:3]. His knowledge and competence could have caused him to be prideful. Instead, the attribute and spiritual gift of meekness with which he was blessed attenuated arrogance in his life and magnified Moses as an instrument to accomplish God's purposes" (Bednar, "Meek and Lowly of Heart," 32).

CHAPTER 12

Aaron and Miriam complain against Moses, the most meek of all men—The Lord promises to speak to Moses mouth to mouth and to reveal to him the similitude of the Lord—Miriam becomes leprous for a week.

1 And Miriam and Aaron spake against Moses because of the Ethiopian woman whom he had married: for he had married an Ethiopian woman.

2 And they said, Hath the LORD indeed spoken only by Moses? hath he not spoken also by us? And the LORD heard *it*.

3 (Now the man Moses *was* very meek, above all the men which *were* upon the face of the earth.)

4 And the LORD spake suddenly unto Moses, and unto Aaron, and unto Miriam, Come out ye three unto the tabernacle of the congregation. And they three came out.

5 And the LORD came down in the pillar of the cloud, and stood *in* the door of the tabernacle, and called Aaron and Miriam: and they both came forth.

6 And he said, Hear now my words: If there be a prophet among you, *I* the LORD will make myself known unto him in a vision, *and* will speak unto him in a dream.

7 My servant Moses *is* not so, who *is* faithful in all mine house.

8 With him will I speak mouth to mouth, even apparently, and not in dark speeches; and the similitude of the LORD shall he behold: wherefore then were ye not afraid to speak against my servant Moses?

9 And the anger of the LORD was kindled against them; and he departed.

What distinguished Moses from others who had the gift of prophecy? (12:6–8) Moses stood at the head of one of the principal dispensations in earth's history (see Bible Dictionary, "Dispensations"). Elder Bruce R. McConkie taught: "Dispensations are those periods of time when the plan of salvation . . . is dispensed to men on earth. . . . I am speaking of those great eras or periods, of those designated portions of the earth's history, when the Lord, through one man, gives his word to the whole world and makes all the prophets, and all the seers, and all the administrators, and all the apostles of that period subject to, and exponents of, what came through that individual" (McConkie, "This Generation," 54). ⊕

What did it mean that God spoke to Moses "mouth to mouth"? (12:8) "God is not an 'it,' as many Christians assert. He is not a thing. He is not some neuter force, not some ethereal nonsubstance. The scriptures not only refer to God as our Father in Heaven, but as 'him' or 'he' in verse after verse. Why? Because God is a male personage.

"Consistent with being a male personage, God has a corporeal body. Jacob declared: 'I have seen God *face* to *face*' (Genesis 32:30). Paul spoke of a '*face* to *face*' encounter with the Lord (1 Corinthians 13:12), and John saw the day when the worthy would approach the throne of God and 'see his *face*' (Revelation 22:4)" (Callister, *Inevitable Apostasy*, 118). ⊕

10 And the cloud departed from off the tabernacle; and, behold, Miriam *became* leprous, *white* as snow: and Aaron looked upon Miriam, and, behold, *she was* leprous.

What type of leprosy afflicted Miriam? (12:10) "As further evidence that Miriam was the instigator and chief complainant against Moses, the Lord chastened her alone with a week-long bout of 'leprosy,' a condition that, under the law of Moses, required a seven-day purification process (Leviticus 13:32–37). Various impurities affecting the skin caused *tzara'at*, or 'leprosy,' as it is translated in the King James Bible. *Tzara'at* was a condition that differs substantially from Hansen's disease, the infection we call leprosy today. Symptoms of *tzara'at* included skin erosion that produced swelling, rash, or snow-white scales similar to those of psoriasis and eczema, or like vitiligo, which develops white spots without scales (Leviticus 13:6, 25–27, 42)" (Olson, *Women of the Old Testament*, 102–3). See commentary in this volume for Leviticus 14:2. ⊕

11 And Aaron said unto Moses, Alas, my lord, I beseech thee, lay not the sin upon us, wherein we have done foolishly, and wherein we have sinned.

What are the spiritual consequences of murmuring against the Lord's prophet? (12:11) "Cursed are all those that shall lift up the heel against mine anointed, saith the Lord, and cry [the prophets] have sinned when they have not sinned before me, saith the Lord, but have done that which was meet in mine eyes, and which I commanded them" (D&C 121:16).

Sister Carol F. McConkie explained, "We have a choice. We may choose to ignore, trifle with, trample upon, or rebel against the words of Christ spoken by His ordained servants. But the Savior taught that those who do so will be cut off from His covenant people [see 3 Nephi 20:23]" ("Live according to the Words of the Prophets," 79).

What special concession did the camp of Israel make for Miriam? (12:15–16) "Miriam's deep humiliation for her outburst may have been exacerbated by the fact that the entire community waited the seven days for her cleansing before moving on to the next camp (Numbers 12:15–16). . . . On the other hand, the week-long hiatus from travel may have been an outpouring of the company's love and support for Miriam. Waiting for her to be reinstated could have offered a similar repentance period for all the Israelites. Acknowledging their own sins of slander and criticism against their leaders, perhaps all the children of Israel willingly stopped in order to receive the Lord's cleansing and healing" (Olson, *Women of the Old Testament*, 104). ⊕

Numbers 13:1–20. Twelve Spies Are Sent to the Land of Canaan

Who were the twelve spies? (13:2–17) "Moses formed the group by choosing one of the chief rulers from each of the tribes. Oshea of the tribe of Ephraim was apparently designated to be their leader. Not satisfied with Oshea's name, however, Moses changed it to Joshua (Numbers 13:16). . . . As earlier noted, Joshua is the Hebrew form of the name Jesus. The story is an obvious type, saying to Israel of all future generations that the only way they can escape the wilderness of life and obtain the eternal inheritance promised them is to follow Jesus and the Twelve" (McConkie, *Gospel Symbolism*, 71).

12 Let her not be as one dead, of whom the flesh is half consumed when he cometh out of his mother's womb.

13 And Moses cried unto the LORD, saying, Heal her now, O God, I beseech thee.

14 ¶ And the LORD said unto Moses, If her father had but spit in her face, should she not be ashamed seven days? let her be shut out from the camp seven days, and after that let her be received in *again*.

15 And Miriam was shut out from the camp seven days: and the people journeyed not till Miriam was brought in *again*.

16 And afterward the people removed from Hazeroth, and pitched in the wilderness of Paran.

CHAPTER 13

Moses sends twelve spies to search the land of Canaan—Ten of them bring an evil report, telling only of the strength of the inhabitants.

1 And the LORD spake unto Moses, saying,

2 Send thou men, that they may search the land of Canaan, which I give unto the children of Israel: of every tribe of their fathers shall ye send a man, every one a ruler among them.

3 And Moses by the commandment of the LORD sent them from the wilderness of Paran: all those men *were* heads of the children of Israel.

4 And these *were* their names: of the tribe of Reuben, Shammua the son of Zaccur.

5 Of the tribe of Simeon, Shaphat the son of Hori.

6 Of the tribe of Judah, Caleb the son of Jephunneh.

7 Of the tribe of Issachar, Igal the son of Joseph.

8 Of the tribe of Ephraim, Oshea the son of Nun.

9 Of the tribe of Benjamin, Palti the son of Raphu.

10 Of the tribe of Zebulun, Gaddiel the son of Sodi.

11 Of the tribe of Joseph, *namely,* of the tribe of Manasseh, Gaddi the son of Susi.

12 Of the tribe of Dan, Ammiel the son of Gemalli.

13 Of the tribe of Asher, Sethur the son of Michael.

14 Of the tribe of Naphtali, Nahbi the son of Vophsi.

15 Of the tribe of Gad, Geuel the son of Machi.

16 These *are* the names of the men which Moses sent to spy out the land. And Moses called Oshea the son of Nun Jehoshua.

17 ¶ And Moses sent them to spy out the land of Canaan, and said unto them, Get you up this *way* southward, and go up into the mountain:

18 And see the land, what it *is;* and the people that dwelleth therein, whether they *be* strong or weak, few or many;

19 And what the land *is* that they dwell in, whether it *be* good or bad; and what cities *they be* that they dwell in, whether in tents, or in strong holds;

20 And what the land *is,* whether it *be* fat or lean, whether there be wood therein, or not.

What was the mission of the twelve spies? (13:17–20) "The reconnaissance mission was two-fold. The first was to observe the enemy that had to be conquered. Moses asked the spies to learn how many people they would be dealing with, how strong they were, how big their cities were, and how strong the fortifications of those cities were. . . .

"The second mission for the spies was to learn about the agricultural possibility of the land. . . . Having come from Egypt, no one had seen the promised land before and none of them had experience with land that had trees and forests. They wanted to know what it would be like to live in this land once they had successfully conquered it" (Muhlestein, *Scripture Study Made Simple,* 126).

Numbers 13:21–33. After Forty Days the Spies Return

What areas did the twelve spies investigate? (13:21–22) "The Wilderness of Zin is the area going south from an imaginary line drawn between the southern tip of the Dead Sea and the Mediterranean, an area also referred to as the Negev. It constitutes the southern border of Canaan. Rehob has often been identified with Tell el-Balat Beth-rehob, almost halfway from the Mediterranean to Hazor. Lebo Hamath is most likely modern Lebweh on one of the sources of the Orontes. This was the southern border of the land of Hamath and therefore the northern border of Canaan. These reference points suggest the scouts explored the land between the Jordan River and the Mediterranean up and down its full 350-mile length" (Walton, et al., *IVP Bible Background Commentary*, 150).

Why did the spies' reports differ? (13:25–31) "Caleb and the other spies possessed the same facts about Canaan and its inhabitants. But their perspective was different. An old chorus sums up the difference. 'Others saw the giants. Caleb saw the Lord.' We should face difficulties realistically. But most of all we need to remain aware of God, and share Caleb's confidence that 'we can certainly do it' with His help" (Richards, *Bible Reader's Companion*, 100).

And be ye of good courage, and bring of the
fruit of the land. Now the time *was* the time
of the firstripe grapes.

21 ¶ So they went up, and searched the land
from the wilderness of Zin unto Rehob, as
men come to Hamath.

22 And they ascended by the south, and
came unto Hebron; where Ahiman, Sheshai,
and Talmai, the children of Anak, *were.*
(Now Hebron was built seven years before
Zoan in Egypt.)

23 And they came unto the brook of Eshcol,
and cut down from thence a branch with one
cluster of grapes, and they bare it between
two upon a staff; and *they brought* of the
pomegranates, and of the figs.

24 The place was called the brook Eshcol, because of the cluster of grapes which the children of Israel cut down from thence.

25 And they returned from searching of the
land after forty days.

26 ¶ And they went and came to Moses,
and to Aaron, and to all the congregation of
the children of Israel, unto the wilderness of
Paran, to Kadesh; and brought back word
unto them, and unto all the congregation,
and shewed them the fruit of the land.

27 And they told him, and said, We came
unto the land whither thou sentest us, and
surely it floweth with milk and honey; and
this *is* the fruit of it.

28 Nevertheless the people *be* strong that
dwell in the land, and the cities *are* walled,
and very great: and moreover we saw the
children of Anak there.

29 The Amalekites dwell in the land of the
south: and the Hittites, and the Jebusites,
and the Amorites, dwell in the mountains:
and the Canaanites dwell by the sea, and by
the coast of Jordan.

30 And Caleb stilled the people before Moses, and said, Let us go up at once, and possess it; for we are well able to overcome it.

31 But the men that went up with him said, We be not able to go up against the people; for they *are* stronger than we.

What were the consequences of fearing to enter the promised land? (13:31) "According to the Torah, the wilderness period was marked by two egregious sins: the apostasy of the golden calf (Exod. 32–34) and the faithlessness of the scouts (Num. 13–14). Only these two sins are singled out for special mention in the survey of the wilderness trek given by Deuteronomy (1:22–45; 9:12–25).... The scouts' factual but negative report (13:28–29) sets off a wave of murmuring (13:30a): The exaggerated description of the dangers (13:32–33) leads to organized vocal opposition (14:1–3) and a threat to return to Egypt under new leadership (14:4–10)" (Milgrom, *Numbers*, 99).

32 And they brought up an evil report of the land which they had searched unto the children of Israel, saying, The land, through which we have gone to search it, *is* a land that eateth up the inhabitants thereof; and all the people that we saw in it *are* men of a great stature.

33 And there we saw the giants, the sons of Anak, *which come* of the giants: and we were in our own sight as grasshoppers, and so we were in their sight.

What is the "evil report" that was brought by the spies? (13:32–33) "The majority of the search party gave a very discouraging report on the promised land and its inhabitants. Although they found a land that was beautiful and desirable and flowing with milk and honey, they also found that the cities were walled and formidable and that the people, the 'sons of Anak,' looked like giants. The Israelite scouts said that they felt like grasshoppers in comparison" (Kimball, "Give Me This Mountain," 79). "Their words became exaggerations and distortions. The Anakites were now said to be Nephilim [people of great size and strength]. The reference to the Nephilim seems deliberately intended to evoke fear. The exaggeration of the faithless led to their final folly" (*NIV Study Bible* [1985], 210).

CHAPTER 14

Israel murmurs and speaks of returning to Egypt—Joshua and Caleb give a good report of Canaan—Moses mediates between Israel and the Lord—The adults of Israel will not enter the promised land—The Lord slays the false spies by a plague—Some rebels try to go alone and are slain by the Amalekites and Canaanites.

1 And all the congregation lifted up their voice, and cried; and the people wept that night.

Numbers 14:1–10. The Israelites Complain and Rebel against the Lord

2 And all the children of Israel murmured against Moses and against Aaron: and the whole congregation said unto them, Would

Why did the Israelites murmur against Moses? (14:2) "The people repudiated Moses, and even the Lord, when the majority began to protest and declared that they would be better off in Egypt. The camp of God's own people turned into a place of hopelessness, with constant murmuring against what was happening to them. Against this unbelief and lack of trust and its dire results are directed all the 'warnings of the book of Hebrews (2:1–4; 3:7–19; 5:11–6:12; 10:19–39; 12:25–29)' (Unger, *Commentary*, 202)" (*Zondervan KJV Commentary*, 192).

Why did the Israelites demand a captain? (14:4) "Here was a formal renunciation of the authority of Moses, and flat rebellion against God. And it seems from Nehemiah 9:17; that they had actually appointed another leader, under whose direction they were about to return to Egypt. How astonishing is this! Their lives were made bitter, because of the rigor with which they were made to serve in the land of Egypt; and yet they are willing, yea eager, to get back into the same circumstances again! . . . They had partly forgot their Egyptian bondage, and now smart under a little discouragement, having totally lost sight of their high calling, and of the power and goodness of God" (*Adam Clarke's Commentary* [on Numbers 14:4]).

Why did Joshua and Caleb rend their clothes? (14:6–10) "Rending the garment is a sign of mourning. . . . Joshua and Caleb are not only frustrated by the negative report of the other scouts but they fear God's harsh punishment, as evidenced by their plea to the people not to rebel against God. The imminence of Israel's rebellion is apparent by the people's intent to stone Moses and Aaron, and probably also Joshua and Caleb (cf. Exod. 17:4)" (*Jewish Study Bible* [2014], 296).

Why did the Israelites feel justified in stoning their leaders? (14:10) "Stoning was public execution for blasphemy or a profound offense against the community (such as giving children to Molech, Lev. 20:2). The people felt that Moses, Aaron, Caleb and Joshua had committed such an offense by urging them to enter an apparently dangerous land. The people still stubbornly refused to believe God was for them even after all his demonstrations of power and provision on their behalf" (*Quest Study Bible* [2003], 209).

God that we had died in the land of Egypt!
or would God we had died in this wilderness!

3 And wherefore hath the LORD brought
us unto this land, to fall by the sword, that
our wives and our children should be a prey?
were it not better for us to return into Egypt?

4 And they said one to another, Let us make
a captain, and let us return into Egypt.

5 Then Moses and Aaron fell on their faces
before all the assembly of the congregation of
the children of Israel.

6 ¶ And Joshua the son of Nun, and Caleb
the son of Jephunneh, *which were* of them
that searched the land, rent their clothes:

7 And they spake unto all the company of
the children of Israel, saying, The land, which
we passed through to search it, *is* an exceeding good land.

8 If the LORD delight in us, then he will bring
us into this land, and give it us; a land which
floweth with milk and honey.

9 Only rebel not ye against the LORD, neither
fear ye the people of the land; for they *are*
bread for us: their defence is departed from
them, and the LORD *is* with us: fear them not.

10 But all the congregation bade stone them
with stones. And the glory of the LORD appeared in the tabernacle of the congregation
before all the children of Israel.

11 ¶ And the LORD said unto Moses, How long will this people provoke me? and how long will it be ere they believe me, for all the signs which I have shewed among them?

12 I will smite them with the pestilence, and disinherit them, and will make of thee a greater nation and mightier than they.

Numbers 14:11–25. Moses Pleads with the Lord to Forgive Faithless Israel

Why was the Lord prepared to smite the Israelites? (14:11–12) "Refusing to tolerate his people's faithlessness, which amounts to outright rejection of the covenant he has established with them, God again determines to dispossess Abraham's descendants and create an even greater nation through Moses. . . . Moses intercedes on the Israelites' behalf, and God pardons them" (*Eerdmans Companion to the Bible*, 146). "This moment in Old Testament history is what some prophets have called 'the provocation, in the day of temptation in the wilderness' (Heb. 3:8). These prophets have used the story of what happened to the children of Israel at this point in their history to teach their people the importance of repenting before it is too late (see Jacob 1:7–8; Alma 12:36–37)" (Wilcox, "12 Spies," 36).

13 ¶ And Moses said unto the LORD, Then the Egyptians shall hear *it,* (for thou broughtest up this people in thy might from among them;)

14 And they will tell *it* to the inhabitants of this land: *for* they have heard that thou LORD *art* among this people, that thou LORD art seen face to face, and *that* thy cloud standeth over them, and *that* thou goest before them, by day time in a pillar of a cloud, and in a pillar of fire by night.

15 ¶ Now *if* thou shalt kill *all* this people as one man, then the nations which have heard the fame of thee will speak, saying,

16 Because the LORD was not able to bring this people into the land which he sware unto them, therefore he hath slain them in the wilderness.

17 And now, I beseech thee, let the power of my Lord be great, according as thou hast spoken, saying,

18 The LORD *is* longsuffering, and of great mercy, forgiving iniquity and transgression, and by no means clearing *the guilty,* visiting the iniquity of the fathers upon the children unto the third and fourth *generation.*

What was Moses' reason to pardon Israel? (14:13–19) "As Gen. 22 records the divine testing of Abraham, this chapter records the divine testing of Moses. Moses might have accepted the Lord's offer and stood aside while the Lord swept the desert clean of this rebellious people. Instead, Moses protested that this drastic act of judgment would taint the reputation of God among the nations. Moses argued that *the Egyptians* would *hear it,* and that the great victory of God over their gods would be dismissed by their reinterpretation of events, if God were not able to bring His people into their new home. Then Moses quoted the Lord concerning His great mercy (v. 18 cites Ex. 34:6, 7) and begged Him to pardon the iniquity of the people" (*Nelson Study Bible* [NKJV], 234).

How were the children of Israel punished for their rebellion? (14:23–24) "The Israelites will spend one year wandering in the wilderness for each day the spies spent in Canaan (14:25, 34). In this way, God will grant the faithless generation's careless wish to die in the desert (14:2). Not only will Joshua and Caleb escape punishment, but Caleb will also realize God's blessing for his obedient spirit (14:24)" (Fee and Hubbard, *Eerdman's Companion to the Bible*, 146). "From Caleb's example we learn very important lessons. Just as Caleb had to struggle and remain true and faithful to gain his inheritance, so we must remember that, while the Lord has promised us a place in his kingdom, we must ever strive constantly and faithfully so as to be worthy to receive the reward" (Kimball, "Give Me This Mountain," 79).

Where is "the wilderness by the way of the Red sea?" (14:25) "These instructions require the Israelites, who fear moving directly north into Canaan, to proceed south from Kadesh in the Wilderness of Paran to the area of Elath on the Gulf of Aqaba. *Yam Suph* in this verse is therefore not the Red Sea but, as in Numbers 21:4 and Deuteronomy 1:40; 2:1, refers to the Gulf of Aqaba on the eastern coast of the Sinai peninsula" (Walton, et al., *IVP Bible Background Commentary*, 151–52).

Summary of Numbers 14:26–45

The Lord lists the consequences of Israel's disobedience. None of the children of Israel over the age of twenty will inherit the promised land, except for Caleb and Joshua. Their children will have to wander for forty years in the wilderness. The ten spies that caused

19 Pardon, I beseech thee, the iniquity of this people according unto the greatness of thy mercy, and as thou hast forgiven this people, from Egypt even until now.

20 And the LORD said, I have pardoned according to thy word:

21 But *as* truly *as* I live, all the earth shall be filled with the glory of the LORD.

22 Because all those men which have seen my glory, and my miracles, which I did in Egypt and in the wilderness, and have tempted me now these ten times, and have not hearkened to my voice;

23 Surely they shall not see the land which I sware unto their fathers, neither shall any of them that provoked me see it:

24 But my servant Caleb, because he had another spirit with him, and hath followed me fully, him will I bring into the land whereinto he went; and his seed shall possess it.

25 (Now the Amalekites and the Canaanites dwelt in the valley.) To morrow turn you, and get you into the wilderness by the way of the Red sea.

Ten Times When Israel Tested Jehovah

The children of Israel rarely comprehended the great blessings they received from Jehovah. Rather, they continually murmured and complained against Moses and the Lord. For example: "(1) at the Red Sea, where it seemed that Pharaoh's army would destroy them (Ex 14:10–12); (2) at Marah, where they found bitter water (Ex 15:22–24); (3) in the Desert of Sin, as they hungered (Ex 16:1–3); (4) in the Desert of Sin, as they paid no attention to Moses concerning the storing of the manna until the morning (Ex 16:19–20); (5) in the Desert of Sin, as they disregarded Moses concerning the gathering of the manna on the seventh day (Ex 16:27–30); (6) at Rephidim, as they complained for water (Ex 17:1–4); (7) at Mount Sinai, as Aaron led the people in making the golden calf (Ex 32:1–35); (8) at Taberah, where the people raged against the Lord (Nu 11:1–3); (9) at Kibroth Hattaavah, in the grumbling provoked by the rabble for quail (Nu 11:4–34); (10) at Kadesh in the Desert of Paran, when the people refused to receive the good report of Joshua and Caleb but rather wished themselves dead (Nu 14:1–3)" (*Expositor's Bible Commentary [Abridged]*, 202).

so many to murmur and rebel because of their evil report die by a plague. Israel defies the Lord's warning and attempts to enter the promised land. They attack the Canaanites but Israel is defeated.

CHAPTER 15

Various sacrificial ordinances bring forgiveness to repentant Israel—Those who sin willfully are cut off from among the people—A man is stoned for gathering sticks on the Sabbath day—The Israelites are to look on the fringes of their garments and remember the commandments.

Summary of Numbers 15

The Lord teaches Israel to offer sacrifices for forgiveness of sin and provides a way to remember the commandments. The Israelites are to make fringes on the hems of their garments to remind them to keep the commandments.

CHAPTER 16

Korah, Dathan, Abiram, and 250 leaders rebel and seek priestly offices—The earth swallows the three rebels and their families—Fire from the Lord consumes the 250 rebels—Israel murmurs against Moses and Aaron for slaying the people—The Lord sends a plague, from which 14,700 die.

1 Now Korah, the son of Izhar, the son of Kohath, the son of Levi, and Dathan and Abiram, the sons of Eliab, and On, the son of Peleth, sons of Reuben, took *men:*

Numbers 16:1–11. Korah and His Allies Rebel against Moses

Who led the rebellion against Moses? (16:1) "The leaders of the revolt are listed in verse 1, Korah, a Levite of the Kohathite clan, and Dathan, Abiram and On of the tribe of Reuben (On is not mentioned again). According to 2:10ff. and 3:29, both Reubenites and the Kohathites were to encamp on the south side of the tabernacle. The proximity of their tents explains their mutual involvement and their common fate. However, it is clear from 27:3 that members of other tribes were also involved in the revolt, referred to in verse 2 as *leaders of the congregation*. And though the Kohathites and Reubenites camped near each other and made common cause against Moses and Aaron, it seems that their objectives were rather different" (Wenham, *Numbers*, 149).

2 And they rose up before Moses, with certain of the children of Israel, two hundred and fifty princes of the assembly, famous in the congregation, men of renown:

3 And they gathered themselves together against Moses and against Aaron, and said

What did the rebels demand of Moses? (16:2–3) "These Levites . . . desired the right to officiate in the tabernacle. As Korathite priests they resented their assignment to the lesser tasks and sought the position of high priests. . . . The Reubenites . . . demanded authority suited to the descendants of the firstborn of Jacob. . . . Acting as spokesman for the rebellion, Korah demanded that Moses recognize the 'holiness' of all Israel and allow increased participation in the government of Israel" (Wright, "Prophet's Voice of Authority," 39–40).

What was the function of "censers"? (16:6–7) "The censers are most likely long-handled pans that could also shovel up the hot coals [from the altar of the tabernacle]. They served as portable altars, because the incense was actually burned in them. . . . Burning incense purifies the area of the altar and signifies God's presence. . . . Moses proposes a test, ordering the followers of the rebellious Korah to offer incense in a censer before God. This was the exclusive prerogative of priests and could be very dangerous for anyone, priest or nonpriests, who might do it incorrectly (Lev 10:1–2)" (Walton, et al., *IVP Bible Background Commentary*, 153).

What "priesthood" office would Korah, who was already a Levite, be seeking? (16:10) The Joseph Smith Translation changes the last phrase of this verse to read: "seek ye the *high* priesthood also?" "It is difficult to tell whether the JST clarification ('seek ye the *high* priesthood also?') is making reference to the Melchizedek Priesthood, the keys of which were held by Moses . . . or the high priesthood or position of Aaron, the keys of which were held by Aaron (note the chapter heading to chapter 16 in the LDS edition of the KJV, prepared by Elder Bruce R. McConkie: 'Korah, Dathan, and Abiram and 250 leaders rebel and *seek priestly offices*')" (Millet, "Lessons in the Wilderness," 193fn23).

unto them, *Ye take* too much upon you, seeing all the congregation *are* holy, every one of them, and the LORD *is* among them: wherefore then lift ye up yourselves above the congregation of the LORD?

4 And when Moses heard *it*, he fell upon his face:

5 And he spake unto Korah and unto all his company, saying, Even to morrow the LORD will shew who *are* his, and *who is* holy; and will cause *him* to come near unto him: even *him* whom he hath chosen will he cause to come near unto him.

6 This do; Take you censers, Korah, and all his company;

7 And put fire therein, and put incense in them before the LORD to morrow: and it shall be *that* the man whom the LORD doth choose, he *shall be* holy: *ye take* too much upon you, ye sons of Levi.

8 And Moses said unto Korah, Hear, I pray you, ye sons of Levi:

9 *Seemeth it but* a small thing unto you, that the God of Israel hath separated you from the congregation of Israel, to bring you near to himself to do the service of the tabernacle of the LORD, and to stand before the congregation to minister unto them?

10 And he hath brought thee near *to him*, and all thy brethren the sons of Levi with thee: and seek ye the priesthood also?

11 For which cause *both* thou and all thy company *are* gathered together against the LORD: and what *is* Aaron, that ye murmur against him?

12 ¶ And Moses sent to call Dathan and Abiram, the sons of Eliab: which said, We will not come up:

13 *Is it* a small thing that thou hast brought us up out of a land that floweth with milk and honey, to kill us in the wilderness, except thou make thyself altogether a prince over us?

14 Moreover thou hast not brought us into a land that floweth with milk and honey, or given us inheritance of fields and vineyards: wilt thou put out the eyes of these men? we will not come up.

15 And Moses was very wroth, and said unto the LORD, Respect not thou their offering: I have not taken one ass from them, neither have I hurt one of them.

16 And Moses said unto Korah, Be thou and all thy company before the LORD, thou, and they, and Aaron, to morrow:

17 And take every man his censer, and put incense in them, and bring ye before the LORD every man his censer, two hundred and fifty censers; thou also, and Aaron, each *of you* his censer.

18 And they took every man his censer, and put fire in them, and laid incense thereon, and stood in the door of the tabernacle of the congregation with Moses and Aaron.

19 And Korah gathered all the congregation against them unto the door of the tabernacle of the congregation: and the glory of the LORD appeared unto all the congregation.

20 And the LORD spake unto Moses and unto Aaron, saying,

21 Separate yourselves from among this congregation, that I may consume them in a moment.

22 And they fell upon their faces, and said, O God, the God of the spirits of all flesh,

Numbers 16:12–22. Confrontation between the Rebellious Israelites and Moses and Aaron

What outrageous lie ignites Moses' anger? (16:14–15) Dathan and Abiram accuse Moses of planning to gouge out his critics' eyes. "Where do Dathan and Abiram get the idea that Moses himself might be planning to take such vindictive action?—from his announcement of the Lord's decision that they would not see the land of Canaan (cf. 14:23)?

"Moses has put up with a lot in the past, but the outrageous defamations hurled at him by Dathan and Abiram turn him into an anti-intercessor (16:15). This is the only place where the Pentateuch says that Moses was 'very angry'" (Gane, *Leviticus, Numbers*, 635).

What does burning incense symbolize? (16:17–18) "During the tabernacle service, the officiating priest was required to sprinkle incense on the burning coals on the altar of incense, which stood directly in front of the veil of the tabernacle. Other scriptures indicate that the burning of incense was a symbol of prayer. . . . Here, Korah and his supporters were asked to bring fire before the Lord as a symbol of their prayers and supplication for His support of their cause. Instead, the earth opened up and swallowed the leaders of the rebellion (see Numbers 16:31–33), and fire came down and consumed the other two hundred and fifty who presumed to take priesthood power unto themselves (see v. 35)" (*Old Testament Student Manual: Genesis–2 Samuel*, 207).

What did the phrase "the God of the spirits of all flesh" mean to early Israel? (16:22) "Latter-day Saint commentators have used this verse as evidence of a doctrinal understanding on the part of ancient Israel of the role of God as the Father of spirits; as such it may provide an insight to us that many particulars of the Plan of Salvation were had millennia before the coming of Christ. This is consistent with what we find in the Book of Moses in the Pearl of Great Price: marvelous theology among the ancients" (Millet, "Lessons in the Wilderness," 193).

Numbers 16:23–40. Judgment Is Carried Out on the Enemies of Jehovah

Why did Moses personally prescribe the rebels' punishment? (16:28–35) "Moses called for a sign from God because he did not want anyone to think that what was about to happen was merely coincidence. . . . In answer to Moses' prayer, God's judgment was sudden, dramatic, and memorable. He caused the earth to swallow the rebels alive[,] . . . a sudden action, like that of a sinkhole that opens with great speed. The families of Dathan and Abiram died with those two men. But the family of Korah was spared ([Numbers] 26:11). In fact, Korah's descendants contributed a considerable number of psalms for temple worship (see Ps. 42)—yet another example of God displaying His mercy even as He justly punished rebels" (*Nelson Study Bible* [NKJV], 238).

shall one man sin, and wilt thou be wroth with all the congregation?

23 ¶ And the LORD spake unto Moses, saying,

24 Speak unto the congregation, saying, Get you up from about the tabernacle of Korah, Dathan, and Abiram.

25 And Moses rose up and went unto Dathan and Abiram; and the elders of Israel followed him.

26 And he spake unto the congregation, saying, Depart, I pray you, from the tents of these wicked men, and touch nothing of theirs, lest ye be consumed in all their sins.

27 So they gat up from the tabernacle of Korah, Dathan, and Abiram, on every side: and Dathan and Abiram came out, and stood in the door of their tents, and their wives, and their sons, and their little children.

28 And Moses said, Hereby ye shall know that the LORD hath sent me to do all these works; for *I have* not *done them* of mine own mind.

29 If these men die the common death of all men, or if they be visited after the visitation of all men; *then* the LORD hath not sent me.

30 But if the LORD make a new thing, and the earth open her mouth, and swallow them up, with all that *appertain* unto them, and they go down quick into the pit; then ye shall understand that these men have provoked the LORD.

31 ¶ And it came to pass, as he had made an end of speaking all these words, that the ground clave asunder that *was* under them:

32 And the earth opened her mouth, and

swallowed them up, and their houses, and all the men that *appertained* unto Korah, and all *their* goods.

33 They, and all that *appertained* to them, went down alive into the pit, and the earth closed upon them: and they perished from among the congregation.

34 And all Israel that *were* round about them fled at the cry of them: for they said, Lest the earth swallow us up *also.*

35 And there came out a fire from the LORD, and consumed the two hundred and fifty men that offered incense.

36 ¶ And the LORD spake unto Moses, saying,

37 Speak unto Eleazar the son of Aaron the priest, that he take up the censers out of the burning, and scatter thou the fire yonder; for they are hallowed.

38 The censers of these sinners against their own souls, let them make them broad plates *for* a covering of the altar: for they offered them before the LORD, therefore they are hallowed: and they shall be a sign unto the children of Israel.

39 And Eleazar the priest took the brasen censers, wherewith they that were burnt had offered; and they were made broad *plates for* a covering of the altar:

40 *To be* a memorial unto the children of Israel, that no stranger, which *is* not of the seed of Aaron, come near to offer incense before the LORD; that he be not as Korah, and as his company: as the LORD said to him by the hand of Moses.

41 ¶ But on the morrow all the congregation of the children of Israel murmured against Moses and against Aaron, saying, Ye have killed the people of the LORD.

42 And it came to pass, when the congregation was gathered against Moses and against

Why did the censers become a covering for the altar? (16:37–40) "The censers used by Korah and his company are collected and made into a covering for the altar, as a memorial of their sin and punishment, and a warning to others against profaning holy things: cp. Judges 1:11" (*John Dummelow's Commentary* [on Numbers 16:36–39]).

Numbers 16:41–50. A Plague Kills Thousands of Israelites

What reason did the people give for turning against Moses and Aaron? (16:41–42) "With all the results of murmuring against Moses, Aaron, and the Lord, one would think that the people would have had their bellies' worth of grumbling. Nevertheless, they were at it again. On the next day following the terrible judgment of God against the apostate nobles, the would-be priests of God, we read that the entire Israelite community grumbled against Moses—again! . . .

"The attack on Moses and Aaron was audacious in its language. The pronoun 'you' is emphatic; they said to them, 'You are responsible! You have killed the men of [Jehovah]!' Oblivious to the vindication of Moses and Aaron by the Lord, the frenzied crowd, mad as rabid wolves, pressed in on them" (Allen, "Numbers," 2:255).

What was the purpose in using Aaron's censer to make "atonement for the people"? (16:46–48) "Aaron is told to take *the* (i.e., a particular) *censer* and to *make atonement* on behalf of the Israelites. . . . Aaron was to prepare this censer in the normal way with coals from the altar (they would be holy) and incense (cf. 16:6–7, 17), and to avert the disaster by this means. It is unclear why this means was chosen, since it is unusual to *make atonement* without a blood sacrifice (but cf. Exod. 30:15). One explanation is that [Jehovah] gave these instructions to Moses and Aaron during prayer. Since the original offense had been given by an illegitimate incense offering (16:17), the remedy would be a legitimate offering of the same kind. Since no rationale is mentioned in the text itself, this remains a conjecture" (Ashley, *Book of Numbers,* 327–28).

Numbers 17:1–13. The Budding of Aaron's Staff

What did Aaron's budding rod typify? (17:2–8) "The symbolism associated with this test was most deliberate: A rod, or branch, had been chosen to represent each of the twelve tribes or families of Israel, each had

Aaron, that they looked toward the tabernacle of the congregation: and, behold, the cloud covered it, and the glory of the LORD appeared.

43 And Moses and Aaron came before the tabernacle of the congregation.

44 ¶ And the LORD spake unto Moses, saying,

45 Get you up from among this congregation, that I may consume them as in a moment. And they fell upon their faces.

46 ¶ And Moses said unto Aaron, Take a censer, and put fire therein from off the altar, and put on incense, and go quickly unto the congregation, and make an atonement for them: for there is wrath gone out from the LORD; the plague is begun.

47 And Aaron took as Moses commanded, and ran into the midst of the congregation; and, behold, the plague was begun among the people: and he put on incense, and made an atonement for the people.

48 And he stood between the dead and the living; and the plague was stayed.

49 Now they that died in the plague were fourteen thousand and seven hundred, beside them that died about the matter of Korah.

50 And Aaron returned unto Moses unto the door of the tabernacle of the congregation: and the plague was stayed.

CHAPTER 17

As a test, a rod for each tribe is placed in the tabernacle of witness—Aaron's rod buds and blossoms and brings forth almonds—It is kept as a token against rebels.

1 And the LORD spake unto Moses, saying,

2 Speak unto the children of Israel, and take of every one of them a rod according to the house of *their* fathers, of all their princes according to the house of their fathers twelve rods: write thou every man's name upon his rod.

3 And thou shalt write Aaron's name upon the rod of Levi: for one rod *shall be* for the head of the house of their fathers.

4 And thou shalt lay them up in the tabernacle of the congregation before the testimony, where I will meet with you.

5 And it shall come to pass, *that* the man's rod, whom I shall choose, shall blossom: and I will make to cease from me the murmurings of the children of Israel, whereby they murmur against you.

6 ¶ And Moses spake unto the children of Israel, and every one of their princes gave him a rod apiece, for each prince one, according to their fathers' houses, *even* twelve rods: and the rod of Aaron *was* among their rods.

7 And Moses laid up the rods before the LORD in the tabernacle of witness.

8 And it came to pass, that on the morrow Moses went into the tabernacle of witness; and, behold, the rod of Aaron for the house of Levi was budded, and brought forth buds, and bloomed blossoms, and yielded almonds.

9 And Moses brought out all the rods from before the LORD unto all the children of Israel: and they looked, and took every man his rod.

10 ¶ And the LORD said unto Moses, Bring Aaron's rod again before the testimony, to be kept for a token against the rebels; and thou shalt quite take away their murmurings from me, that they die not.

11 And Moses did *so:* as the LORD commanded him, so did he.

12 And the children of Israel spake unto Moses, saying, Behold, we die, we perish, we all perish.

13 Whosoever cometh any thing near unto

its name carefully placed upon it. By tradition the rod, as a staff or sceptre, represented one's position and authority. Together all were presented before the Lord. By making Aaron's rod bud, blossom, and put forth fruit, the Lord demonstrated once again that it was for him to choose those who will stand in his stead, be filled with his power, and bring forth his fruits" (McConkie, *Gospel Symbolism*, 73). ⊕

What did the almonds symbolize? (17:8) "The Hebrew word for almond and almond tree is *shaked*, which denotes to wake up early, and the almond tree is 'so called from its early waking out of winter's sleep.' In Israel, the almond tree buds and blossoms early in the season. As an almond tree, Aaron's rod symbolizes that Jesus Christ was the first to awaken at the resurrection; just as Aaron's rod budded and blossomed, and as the almond tree 'wakes up early' in the spring, even so Jesus, as the firstfruits, woke up early in the resurrection. The rod was stored in the ark of the covenant with the tablets and jar of manna" (Parry and Parry, *Symbols and Shadows*, 127)

the tabernacle of the Lord shall die: shall we be consumed with dying?

Summary of Numbers 18

The Lord outlines some of the priests' duties. The tithes and offerings given by the people could support the priests and their families. The Levites will not receive an inheritance of land in Canaan but would live among all the tribes of Israel.

CHAPTER 18

Aaron and his sons are called to minister in the priest's office—Levites are called to minister in the service of the tabernacle—Levites receive no land inheritance but are supported by the tithes of the people.

CHAPTER 19

Directions are given for the sacrifice of a red heifer—The water of separation is used for purification from sin—Ceremonially unclean persons are sprinkled with the water of separation.

1 And the Lord spake unto Moses and unto Aaron, saying,

2 This *is* the ordinance of the law which the Lord hath commanded, saying, Speak unto the children of Israel, that they bring thee a red heifer without spot, wherein *is* no blemish, *and* upon which never came yoke:

3 And ye shall give her unto Eleazar the priest, that he may bring her forth without the camp, and *one* shall slay her before his face:

4 And Eleazar the priest shall take of her blood with his finger, and sprinkle of her blood directly before the tabernacle of the congregation seven times:

5 And *one* shall burn the heifer in his sight; her skin, and her flesh, and her blood, with her dung, shall he burn:

6 And the priest shall take cedar wood, and hyssop, and scarlet, and cast *it* into the midst of the burning of the heifer.

7 Then the priest shall wash his clothes, and he shall bathe his flesh in water, and

Numbers 19:1–10. The Sacrifice of a Red Heifer

What did the sacrifice of a red heifer represent? (19:2–10) "The sacrifice of the heifer is symbolic of Jesus Christ's divine sacrifice; its blood points to Jesus' blood, and the fact that the heifer was a female and potential life-giver anticipates the life-giving force of Jesus' atonement" (Parry and Parry, *Symbols and Shadows*, 142–43). ⊕

What is the purpose of the sacrifice of a red heifer? (19:2) "Purification ceremonies differed [in the law of Moses], depending on the deed and reason for needing to be purified. Regardless of the ritualistic ceremony, according to William Smith, upon being pronounced pure the recipient was 'absolved from the taint of uncleanness.'

"The most interesting purification ceremony was performed for those who had been in the presence of a corpse. They were pronounced clean after a red heifer was slain, burned, and the ashes laid aside. Then the ashes were placed in pure water and the mixture sprinkled upon those who had been defiled. This was known as 'the water of separation,' since by it one was separated, or purified, from sin. Failure to avail oneself of the cleansing power in this way resulted in being 'cut off from among the congregation'" (Black, *400 Questions about the Old Testament*, 83–84).

afterward he shall come into the camp, and the priest shall be unclean until the even.

8 And he that burneth her shall wash his clothes in water, and bathe his flesh in water, and shall be unclean until the even.

9 And a man *that is* clean shall gather up the ashes of the heifer, and lay *them* up without the camp in a clean place, and it shall be kept for the congregation of the children of Israel for a water of separation: it *is* a purification for sin.

10 And he that gathereth the ashes of the heifer shall wash his clothes, and be unclean until the even: and it shall be unto the children of Israel, and unto the stranger that sojourneth among them, for a statute for ever.

Summary of Numbers 19:11–22

Those who had touched a dead body were considered unclean for seven days. The unclean could purify themselves on the third and seventh day by the "water of separation" made from the ashes of a red heifer.

CHAPTER 20

Miriam dies—Moses smites a rock at Meribah and brings forth water—The king of Edom refuses to let Israel pass peacefully through his land—Aaron dies, and Eleazar becomes the high priest.

1 Then came the children of Israel, *even* the whole congregation, into the desert of Zin in the first month: and the people abode in Kadesh; and Miriam died there, and was buried there.

2 And there was no water for the congregation: and they gathered themselves together against Moses and against Aaron.

3 And the people chode with Moses, and spake, saying, Would God that we had died when our brethren died before the Lord!

4 And why have ye brought up the congre-

Numbers 20:1–6. The Children of Israel Murmur against Moses

What can we assume about Miriam at the time of her death? (20:1) "Jewish tradition relates that Miriam, Moses, and Aaron all died sinless (Ginzberg, *Legends*, 3:444). . . .

"Although no further chapters of her life are recorded between her chastisement with leprosy and her death some thirty-eight years later, the silence testifies to her meekness, likely inspired by that of her 'little brother.' Rather than becoming distraught and withdrawn after her public humiliation, Miriam appears to have trusted in God's forgiveness. . . . She discovered expanded ways to exercise her spiritual gift while sincerely sustaining the prophet. Returning to leadership and influence, she added deep humility to her strengths while giving all the glory to the Lord" (Olson, *Women of the Old Testament*, 104–5).

gation of the LORD into this wilderness, that
we and our cattle should die there?

5 And wherefore have ye made us to come
up out of Egypt, to bring us in unto this evil
place? it *is* no place of seed, or of figs, or of
vines, or of pomegranates; neither *is* there
any water to drink.

6 And Moses and Aaron went from the presence of the assembly unto the door of the
tabernacle of the congregation, and they fell
upon their faces: and the glory of the LORD
appeared unto them.

Numbers 20:7–13. Moses Strikes a Rock, and the Lord Provides Water

7 ¶ And the LORD spake unto Moses, saying,

8 Take the rod, and gather thou the assembly
together, thou, and Aaron thy brother, and
speak ye unto the rock before their eyes; and
it shall give forth his water, and thou shalt
bring forth to them water out of the rock:
so thou shalt give the congregation and their
beasts drink.

9 And Moses took the rod from before the
LORD, as he commanded him.

What can we learn from Moses' mistake at Meribah? (20:10–12) Elder Neal A. Maxwell explained, "At a place called Meribah, one of the greatest ever, Moses, was fatigued by people clamoring for water. Momentarily, Moses 'spake unadvisedly,' saying, 'Must we fetch you water?' (Ps. 106:33; Num. 20:10; see also Deut. 4:21). The Lord mentored remarkable Moses through the pronoun problem and further magnified him. We would do well to be as meek as Moses (see Num. 12:3)" ("Consecrate Thy Performance," 37). ⊕

10 And Moses and Aaron gathered the congregation together before the rock, and he
said unto them, Hear now, ye rebels; must we
fetch you water out of this rock?

11 And Moses lifted up his hand, and with
his rod he smote the rock twice: and the
water came out abundantly, and the congregation drank, and their beasts *also*.

12 ¶ And the LORD spake unto Moses and
Aaron, Because ye believed me not, to sanctify me in the eyes of the children of Israel,
therefore ye shall not bring this congregation
into the land which I have given them.

13 This *is* the water of Meribah; because the
children of Israel strove with the LORD, and
he was sanctified in them.

Summary of Numbers 20:14–29

Aaron is not allowed to enter the promised land. He dies, and his son Eleazar is ordained the high priest.

CHAPTER 21

The children of Israel destroy those Canaanites who fight against them—The Israelites are plagued with fiery serpents—Moses lifts up a serpent of brass to save those who look thereon—Israel defeats the Amorites, destroys the people of Bashan, and occupies their lands.

1 And *when* king Arad the Canaanite, which
dwelt in the south, heard tell that Israel came
by the way of the spies; then he fought against
Israel, and took *some* of them prisoners.

2 And Israel vowed a vow unto the LORD,
and said, If thou wilt indeed deliver this
people into my hand, then I will utterly destroy their cities.

3 And the LORD hearkened to the voice of
Israel, and delivered up the Canaanites; and
they utterly destroyed them and their cities:
and he called the name of the place Hormah.

Numbers 21:1–3. Canaanite King Attacks the Israelites

Why is the battle of Hormah meaningful? (21:3) "After Israel's defection from God's leadership following the report of the spies (14:1–10a), [Jehovah] condemned the old generation to wander forty years and to die in the wilderness without claiming the land

Why Was Moses Not Allowed into the Holy Land? (20:7–13)

"Rebellion among the children of Israel was not at all uncommon in their desert wanderings. The rebellion described in these verses, however, was especially serious because it apparently led Moses, the prophet of God, to momentarily forget what the Lord had commanded him to do. The Lord had told Moses to provide water for murmuring Israel in a special way. Pointing out a certain rock, the Lord told Moses, 'Speak ye unto the rock before their [Israel's] eyes; and it shall give forth his water' (v. 8). But Moses was weary and angry with Israel. 'Hear now, ye rebels,' he said. 'Must *we* fetch you water out of this rock?' (v. 10; emphasis added). Then, instead of speaking to the rock as God commanded, Moses 'smote the rock twice' and water gushed forth (v. 11). The Lord then chided Moses and Aaron for their failure to sanctify Him in the eyes of the people and told both men that neither of them would be allowed to bring Israel into the promised land (see v. 12). Not only did they not follow the Lord's instructions carefully but they also suggested by the use of *we* that they were the ones who provided the water.

"This incident, taken together with other scripture, creates a number of questions. Did Moses really sin against the Lord? Was that the reason Moses was not permitted to enter the promised land? Did Moses really assume glory to himself, or was he simply angry with the lack of faith exhibited by the children of Israel? Was this one error enough to cancel out years of great faith, obedience, and devotion?

"At least two other Old Testament passages indicate that Moses did sin in striking the rock at Meribah (see Numbers 27:12–14; Deuteronomy 32:51–52). Other passages, however, help to clarify the matter. Deuteronomy 3:26 and 4:21 indicate that the Lord told Moses that the reason he could not enter the promised land was that the Lord was angry with him *'for your sakes'* (emphasis added). This statement could imply that there were reasons other than the error of Moses for the prohibition. Two other facts strengthen this supposition. First, both Moses and the higher priesthood were taken from Israel because of the people's unworthiness, not Moses' (see D&C 84:23–25). Second, Moses was translated when his mortal ministry was finished (see Alma 45:19). In other words, Moses was privileged to enter a land of promise far greater than the land of Canaan. He had finished his calling in mortality, and a new leader was to take Israel into the promised land. And, Moses was translated—hardly a punishment for sinning against God" (*Old Testament Student Manual: Genesis–2 Samuel*, 208).

of promise (14:10b–38). In a misguided attempt to put things right, the people then tried to go into Canaan from the south, only to be humiliated and pursued as far as a place called Hormah. . . . If one assumes that 21:1–3 took place around the time of Aaron's death, as the placement of texts seems to indicate, then the time is 38 years later (33:38). The Hebrews have returned to the same area, but this time it is not their own destruction that is related, but that of the Canaanites" (Ashley, *Book of Numbers*, 398).

Numbers 21:4–9. Poisonous Snakes Are Sent to Humble the Israelites

What does the fiery serpent "set . . . upon a pole" teach us? (21:4–9) "This miracle tells us what Israel needed to do to be saved; namely, 'look to God and live' (Alma 37:47). But it also tells us a bit about what Christ needed to do to save us; namely, give His life. 'The fashioning of the brazen serpent alone was not enough! It had to be lifted up! The coming of Jesus into the world alone was not enough. His deeds must have been lifted up!' [Trent, *Types of Christ in the Old Testament*, 108]. Christ lived the perfect life, but He also needed to die the perfect death. This miracle highlights that fact, as well as the power resident in Christ's death to heal and to save!" (Gaskill, *Miracles of the Old Testament*, 158–59).

Moses and the brass serpent.

4 ¶ And they journeyed from mount Hor
by the way of the Red sea, to compass the
land of Edom: and the soul of the people was
much discouraged because of the way.

5 And the people spake against God, and
against Moses, Wherefore have ye brought us
up out of Egypt to die in the wilderness? for
there is no bread, neither *is there any* water;
and our soul loatheth this light bread.

6 And the LORD sent fiery serpents among
the people, and they bit the people; and
much people of Israel died.

7 ¶ Therefore the people came to Moses, and
said, We have sinned, for we have spoken
against the LORD, and against thee; pray unto
the LORD, that he take away the serpents
from us. And Moses prayed for the people.

8 And the LORD said unto Moses, Make thee
a fiery serpent, and set it upon a pole: and it
shall come to pass, that every one that is bitten, when he looketh upon it, shall live.

9 And Moses made a serpent of brass, and
put it upon a pole, and it came to pass, that
if a serpent had bitten any man, when he beheld the serpent of brass, he lived.

What can we do today to receive healing from the Savior? (21:9) "The principle of activating blessings that flow from God is eternal. Like those ancient Israelites, we too must act on our faith in Jesus Christ to be blessed. God has revealed that 'there is a law, irrevocably decreed in heaven before the foundations of this world, upon which all blessings are predicated—and when we obtain any blessing from God, it is by obedience to that law upon which it is predicated' [D&C 130:20–21]. That being said, you do not earn a blessing—that notion is false—but you do have to qualify for it. Our salvation comes only through the merits and grace of Jesus Christ" (Renlund, "Abound with Blessings," 71).

Summary of Numbers 21:10–35

Israel defeats the Amorites and the people of Bashan and takes over their land.

CHAPTER 22

Balak offers money, cattle, and great honors to Balaam to curse Israel—The Lord forbids Balaam to do so—An angel opposes Balaam on the way.

1 And the children of Israel set forward, and pitched in the plains of Moab on this side Jordan *by* Jericho.

2 ¶ And Balak the son of Zippor saw all that Israel had done to the Amorites.

3 And Moab was sore afraid of the people, because they *were* many: and Moab was distressed because of the children of Israel.

4 And Moab said unto the elders of Midian, Now shall this company lick up all *that are* round about us, as the ox licketh up the grass of the field. And Balak the son of Zippor *was* king of the Moabites at that time.

Numbers 22:1–21. Balak Offers to Pay Balaam to Curse Israel

Who was Balaam? (22:2–5) "Balak, king of Moab, sent [messengers] to Balaam, a non-Israelite who was an inspired prophet. We do not know from which people Balaam was descended. Perhaps he was a Midianite, which could explain both how he was a prophet of God (remember that Moses's father-in-law who ordained him was a Midianite) and why the story of Balaam begins with Balak seeking an alliance with Midian. On the other hand, he [may have come] from Aram, or the area of Syria. There were some Midianites in that area in other stories, so they could have been there in Moses's day as well. In any case, Balak . . . was willing to pay Balaam if he would cast a curse upon Israel" (Muhlestein, *Scripture Study Made Simple*, 131). ⊕

Who were the Moabites? (22:4) "The Moabites . . . are descendants of Lot, Abraham's nephew. When Sodom and Gomorrah were destroyed, Lot's two daughters, believing that the world had come to an end, intoxicated their father and deceived him into fathering children by them. . . . The Moabites, lived along the eastern bank of the Jordan River and east of the Dead Sea. They warred constantly with Israel" (Tvedtnes, "Who Is an Arab?" 28).

5 He sent messengers therefore unto Balaam the son of Beor to Pethor, which *is* by the river of the land of the children of his people, to call him, saying, Behold, there is a people come out from Egypt: behold, they cover the face of the earth, and they abide over against me:

6 Come now therefore, I pray thee, curse me this people; for they *are* too mighty for me: peradventure I shall prevail, *that* we may smite them, and *that* I may drive them out of the land: for I wot that he whom thou blessest *is* blessed, and he whom thou cursest is cursed.

7 And the elders of Moab and the elders of Midian departed with the rewards of divination in their hand; and they came unto Balaam, and spake unto him the words of Balak.

8 And he said unto them, Lodge here this night, and I will bring you word again, as the LORD shall speak unto me: and the princes of Moab abode with Balaam.

9 And God came unto Balaam, and said, What men *are* these with thee?

10 And Balaam said unto God, Balak the son of Zippor, king of Moab, hath sent unto me, *saying,*

11 Behold, *there is* a people come out of Egypt, which covereth the face of the earth: come now, curse me them; peradventure I shall be able to overcome them, and drive them out.

12 And God said unto Balaam, Thou shalt not go with them; thou shalt not curse the people: for they *are* blessed.

13 And Balaam rose up in the morning, and said unto the princes of Balak, Get you into your land: for the LORD refuseth to give me leave to go with you.

14 And the princes of Moab rose up, and they went unto Balak, and said, Balaam refuseth to come with us.

15 ¶ And Balak sent yet again princes, more, and more honourable than they.

16 And they came to Balaam, and said to him, Thus saith Balak the son of Zippor, Let nothing, I pray thee, hinder thee from coming unto me:

17 For I will promote thee unto very great honour, and I will do whatsoever thou sayest unto me: come therefore, I pray thee, curse me this people.

How did Balak tempt Balaam to curse Israel? (22:16–17) "The honors we sometimes receive from our peers are potentially a strength, but we need to remember that Satan can turn these to our detriment also. We must be careful that we do not become like the prophet Balaam. The Apostle Peter said that Balaam 'loved the wages of unrighteousness' (2 Peter 2:15), which Elder Bruce R. McConkie of the Quorum of the Twelve interpreted as 'the honors of men and the wealth of the world' [*Doctrinal New Testament Commentary*, 3:361]. Honors may come, but we should beware that they not deflect our priorities and commitments away from the things of God" (Oaks, "Our Strengths Can Become Our Downfall," 14).

18 And Balaam answered and said unto the servants of Balak, If Balak would give me his house full of silver and gold, I cannot go beyond the word of the LORD my God, to do less or more.

19 Now therefore, I pray you, tarry ye also here this night, that I may know what the LORD will say unto me more.

20 And God came unto Balaam at night, and said unto him, If the men come to call thee, rise up, *and* go with them; but yet the word which I shall say unto thee, that shalt thou do.

21 And Balaam rose up in the morning, and saddled his ass, and went with the princes of Moab.

22 ¶ And God's anger was kindled because he went: and the angel of the LORD stood in the way for an adversary against him. Now he was riding upon his ass, and his two servants *were* with him.

23 And the ass saw the angel of the LORD standing in the way, and his sword drawn in his hand: and the ass turned aside out of the way, and went into the field: and Balaam smote the ass, to turn her into the way.

What did Balaam understand about God? (22:18) "Balaam knew God too well to suppose he could reverse any of his purposes; and he respected him too much to attempt to do anything without his permission. Though he was covetous, yet he dared not, even when strongly tempted both by riches and honors, to go contrary to the command of his God" (*Adam Clarke's Commentary* [on Numbers 22:18]).

Numbers 22:22–35. The Angel of the Lord Stops Balaam on the Road

Why did God open the mouth of the donkey? (22:22–31) "On the trip to Moab, the angel of the Lord appears to Balaam's donkey three times, but the false prophet apparently cannot see him until the third appearance. . . .

"After . . . three beatings, God gave the donkey utterance, and she chastisingly queried why Balaam kept beating her. Balaam rebukes the ass. . . . The animal reminds Balaam of the years of service that she has provided him; at which point, Balaam's eyes were opened, and, for the first time, he too saw the angel with the drawn sword standing before them. Balaam, likely in fear, falls to the ground before the angel (Numbers 22:22–31)" (Gaskill, *Miracles of the Old Testament*, 163, 164).

The angel appearing to Balaam.

How did Balaam respond to the donkey speaking? (22:28) "If the ass had opened her own mouth, and reproved the rash prophet, we might well be astonished; but when God opens the mouth, an ass can speak as well as a man. It is worthy of remark here, that Balaam testifies no surprise at this miracle, because he saw it was the Lord's doing" (*Adam Clarke's Commentary* [on Numbers 22:28]).

What does the drawn sword represent? (22:31) "The 'drawn sword' in the angel's hand was a manifestation of the wrath of God" (Keil and Delitzsch, *Commentary* [on Numbers 22:31]).

24 But the angel of the LORD stood in a path of the vineyards, a wall *being* on this side, and a wall on that side.

25 And when the ass saw the angel of the LORD, she thrust herself unto the wall, and crushed Balaam's foot against the wall: and he smote her again.

26 And the angel of the LORD went further, and stood in a narrow place, where *was* no way to turn either to the right hand or to the left.

27 And when the ass saw the angel of the LORD, she fell down under Balaam: and Balaam's anger was kindled, and he smote the ass with a staff.

28 And the LORD opened the mouth of the ass, and she said unto Balaam, What have I done unto thee, that thou hast smitten me these three times?

29 And Balaam said unto the ass, Because thou hast mocked me: I would there were a sword in mine hand, for now would I kill thee.

30 And the ass said unto Balaam, *Am* not I thine ass, upon which thou hast ridden ever since *I was* thine unto this day? was I ever wont to do so unto thee? And he said, Nay.

31 Then the LORD opened the eyes of Balaam, and he saw the angel of the LORD standing in the way, and his sword drawn in his hand: and he bowed down his head, and fell flat on his face.

32 And the angel of the LORD said unto him, Wherefore hast thou smitten thine ass these three times? behold, I went out to withstand thee, because *thy* way is perverse before me:

33 And the ass saw me, and turned from me these three times: unless she had turned from me, surely now also I had slain thee, and saved her alive.

34 And Balaam said unto the angel of the LORD, I have sinned; for I knew not that thou stoodest in the way against me: now therefore, if it displease thee, I will get me back again.

35 And the angel of the LORD said unto Balaam, Go with the men: but only the word that I shall speak unto thee, that thou shalt speak. So Balaam went with the princes of Balak.

Summary of Numbers 22:36–41

Balak is anxious to have Balaam begin the work of cursing Israel.

CHAPTER 23

The Lord commands Balaam to bless Israel—He does so, saying, Who can count the dust of Jacob? and, What hath God wrought!

1 And Balaam said unto Balak, Build me here seven altars, and prepare me here seven oxen and seven rams.

2 And Balak did as Balaam had spoken; and Balak and Balaam offered on *every* altar a bullock and a ram.

Numbers 23:1–10. Balaam Makes His First Prophecy about Israel

Why were seven altars and fourteen animals used in this sacrifice? (23:1–2) "At Balaam's command Balak built seven altars, and then selected seven bullocks and seven rams, which they immediately sacrificed, namely, one bullock and one ram upon each altar. . . . The erection of *seven* altars, and the sacrifice of *seven* animals of each kind, are to be explained from the sacredness acquired by this number, through the creation of the world in seven days, as being the stamp of work that was well-pleasing to God. The sacrifices were burnt-offerings, and were offered by themselves to Jehovah, whom Balaam acknowledged as his God" (Keil and Delitzsch, *Commentary* [on Numbers 23:1–2]). ⊕

3 And Balaam said unto Balak, Stand by thy burnt offering, and I will go: peradventure the LORD will come to meet me: and whatsoever he sheweth me I will tell thee. And he went to an high place.

4 And God met Balaam: and he said unto him, I have prepared seven altars, and I have offered upon *every* altar a bullock and a ram.

5 And the LORD put a word in Balaam's mouth, and said, Return unto Balak, and thus thou shalt speak.

Why does Balaam continually petition the Lord to curse Israel? (23:3–12) "When Balaam did ask the Lord, he learned that Israel was a blessed people, so he refused to do as Balak asked. Balak asked again, promising great riches if Balaam will curse Israel. Balaam said that there was no way he could curse Israel against God's will. Balaam asked again, and God told Balaam that he could go with Balak to prophesy, but that he could only prophesy what God told him to. Balaam went with Balak, king of Moab. It appears that Balaam was struggling to keep the charge to prophesy only what God would have him say" (Muhlestein, *Scripture Study Made Simple*, 131).

6 And he returned unto him, and, lo, he stood by his burnt sacrifice, he, and all the princes of Moab.

What does "he took up his parable" mean? (23:7) The word "parable" is translated from a Hebrew word (*mashal*) that is sometimes translated as a "proverb," "oracle" or "poem." In this context, it might be appropriately translated as "prophecy." Many translations refer to this phrase as a person who spoke under the influence of the spirit. "In Balaam's first oracle [prophecy], which has been described as exquisite poetry (vv. 7–10), he stated that he could not curse whom *God hath not cursed* (v. 8). From lofty heights, he saw God's work with Israel. They shall *dwell alone, and shall not be reckoned among the nations* (v. 9). . . . Balaam wanted to die as one who is *righteous* (v. 10), not as one who defied God. Balak was furious at Balaam's refusal to curse Israel (vv. 11–12)" (*Zondervan KJV Commentary*, 203).

7 And he took up his parable, and said, Balak the king of Moab hath brought me from Aram, out of the mountains of the east, *saying*, Come, curse me Jacob, and come, defy Israel.

8 How shall I curse, whom God hath not cursed? or how shall I defy, *whom* the LORD hath not defied?

9 For from the top of the rocks I see him, and from the hills I behold him: lo, the people shall dwell alone, and shall not be reckoned among the nations.

What does "who can count the dust of Jacob" mean? (23:10) "The blessings of Abraham, Isaac, and Jacob had continued with the covenant people, notwithstanding their frequent rebellions and their general recalcitrant attitude toward complete compliance with the word of the Lord. Their posterity would continue as the stars of heaven, as the sands of the sea, and as the dust of the earth. In them all of the blessings of eternity were embodied. Balaam could have asked for nothing greater for himself" (Hyde, *Comprehensive Commentary [Numbers and Deuteronomy]*, 233).

10 Who can count the dust of Jacob, and the number of the fourth *part* of Israel? Let me die the death of the righteous, and let my last end be like his!

Numbers 23:11–17. Balak Tries Again to Get Balaam to Curse Israel

11 And Balak said unto Balaam, What hast thou done unto me? I took thee to curse mine enemies, and, behold, thou hast blessed *them* altogether.

12 And he answered and said, Must I not take heed to speak that which the LORD hath put in my mouth?

Why would Balak propose a second place to offer sacrifices? (23:13–17) "Trying to cover all the angles, Balak attempted to reduce the power of the people by selecting a point where their immense numbers would be obscured. Alas for Balak, the oracle that followed exceeded the first in its blessing on Israel. Again we sense the idea of numbers in this text. There was a power in numbers in the ancient world. If one were confronted only with a small percentage of the whole,

13 And Balak said unto him, Come, I pray thee, with me unto another place, from whence thou mayest see them: thou shalt see but the utmost part of them, and shalt not see them all: and curse me them from thence.

Balak reasoned, the enormity of the nation would not cause the gods to bless when they were requested to curse Israel" (Allen, "Numbers," 2:319).

14 ¶ And he brought him into the field of Zophim, to the top of Pisgah, and built seven altars, and offered a bullock and a ram on *every* altar.

15 And he said unto Balak, Stand here by thy burnt offering, while I meet *the LORD* yonder.

16 And the LORD met Balaam, and put a word in his mouth, and said, Go again unto Balak, and say thus.

17 And when he came to him, behold, he stood by his burnt offering, and the princes of Moab with him. And Balak said unto him, What hath the LORD spoken?

18 And he took up his parable, and said, Rise up, Balak, and hear; hearken unto me, thou son of Zippor:

19 God *is* not a man, that he should lie; neither the son of man, that he should repent: hath he said, and shall he not do *it?* or hath he spoken, and shall he not make it good?

20 Behold, I have received *commandment* to bless: and he hath blessed; and I cannot reverse it.

21 He hath not beheld iniquity in Jacob, neither hath he seen perverseness in Israel: the LORD his God *is* with him, and the shout of a king *is* among them.

22 God brought them out of Egypt; he hath as it were the strength of an unicorn.

23 Surely *there is* no enchantment against Jacob, neither *is there* any divination against Israel: according to this time it shall be said of Jacob and of Israel, What hath God wrought!

24 Behold, the people shall rise up as a great lion, and lift up himself as a young lion: he shall not lie down until he eat *of* the prey, and drink the blood of the slain.

Why did Balak take Balaam to Zophim and Mount Pisgah? (23:14) "The 'field of the watchers,' or 'spies (*zophim*), upon the top of *Pisgah*,' corresponds, no doubt, to 'the field of Moab, upon the top of *Pisgah*,' on the west of Heshbon (see at Numbers 21:20)" (Keil and Delitzsch, *Commentary* [on Numbers 23:11–17]). "Balak thought that the sight of such an immense camp had intimidated Balaam, and this he might gather from what he said in the tenth verse: Who can count the dust of Jacob, etc.; he thought therefore that he might get Balaam to curse them in detached parties, till the whole camp should be devoted to destruction by successive execrations" (*Adam Clarke's Commentary* [on Numbers 23:13]).

Numbers 23:18–30. Balaam Makes a Second Prophecy about Israel

What does it mean that "God is not a man that he should lie"? (23:19) Contrasting Jehovah to the multiple gods of Canaan and their whimsy, this verse highlights God's truthful nature as one who cannot lie. "The constancy of God's intention and action contrasts with the gods' caprice, which can be appealed to by man" (Milgrom, *Numbers*, 199).

In what way does "unicorn" describe God's strength? (23:22) "In scripture horns are used as symbols of power and strength, whether good or evil. . . .

"'In Hebrew literature the word "horn" is equivalent to power. "To break the horns" of a people signifies defeat, "to raise the horns" means pride, victory. Balaam described God as having horns like a wild ox' (Numbers 23:22)" (Gaskill, *Lost Language of Symbolism*, 49).

The word that is translated *unicorn* in the King James Version is from a Hebrew word meaning *wild ox* (see Numbers 23:22*a*).

What is Balak asking Balaam to do? (23:25–28) "Every time Balak thought the prophet would curse Israel, Balaam instead blesses Israel. Now it is almost as if Balak is saying he would pay Balaam to say nothing! He thinks that they just need to find a better location from which to offer sacrifice and make the curse" (Valletta, et al., *Old Testament for Latter-day Saint Families,* 186).

25 ¶ And Balak said unto Balaam, Neither curse them at all, nor bless them at all.

26 But Balaam answered and said unto Balak, Told not I thee, saying, All that the LORD speaketh, that I must do?

27 ¶ And Balak said unto Balaam, Come, I pray thee, I will bring thee unto another place; peradventure it will please God that thou mayest curse me them from thence.

28 And Balak brought Balaam unto the top of Peor, that looketh toward Jeshimon.

29 And Balaam said unto Balak, Build me here seven altars, and prepare me here seven bullocks and seven rams.

30 And Balak did as Balaam had said, and offered a bullock and a ram on *every* altar.

CHAPTER 24

Balaam sees in vision and prophesies of the destiny of Israel—He prophesies of the Messiah: There will come a Star out of Jacob, and a Sceptre will rise out of Israel.

Summary of Numbers 24:1–9

Balaam again prophesies blessings instead of cursings for Israel. Balaam prophesies that those who bless Israel will be blessed and those who curse Israel will be cursed.

Numbers 24:10–19. Balaam Sees the Coming of Jesus Christ

How did Balaam respond to Balak's anger? (24:10–14) "Balak was beside himself with anger. . . . He raged and struck his hands while ranting. He observed that at this point Balaam had given three distinct blessings on Israel (v.10). At least Balak got that much right. In his disgust with the failure of Balaam to curse Israel, Balak now dismissed him without pay—the ultimate insult in answer to his greed (2Pe 2:15).

"Balaam was ready to leave; the whole situation must have been uncomfortable for him as well! But before he left, he was constrained by the Lord to speak again—this time his greatest oracle. In the phrase 'in days to come,' we recognize the signal in biblical

10 ¶ And Balak's anger was kindled against Balaam, and he smote his hands together: and Balak said unto Balaam, I called thee to curse mine enemies, and, behold, thou hast altogether blessed *them* these three times.

11 Therefore now flee thou to thy place: I thought to promote thee unto great honour; but, lo, the LORD hath kept thee back from honour.

12 And Balaam said unto Balak, Spake I not

also to thy messengers which thou sentest unto me, saying,

13 If Balak would give me his house full of silver and gold, I cannot go beyond the commandment of the LORD, to do *either* good or bad of mine own mind; *but* what the LORD saith, that will I speak?

14 And now, behold, I go unto my people: come *therefore, and* I will advertise thee what this people shall do to thy people in the latter days.

15 ¶ And he took up his parable, and said, Balaam the son of Beor hath said, and the man whose eyes are open hath said:

16 He hath said, which heard the words of God, and knew the knowledge of the most High, *which* saw the vision of the Almighty, falling *into a trance,* but having his eyes open:

literature for the distant future" (Allen, "Numbers," 2:328–29).

How are spiritual trances a source of revelation? (24:16) "From what we can deduce from scriptural writ, it appears that a trance is a state in which the body and its functions become quiescent [calm] in order that the full powers of the Spirit may be centered on the revelations of heaven. Freed from the

Balaam's Seven Prophecies (Numbers 23–24)

All seven prophecies which Balaam makes take the form of Hebrew poetry. "All these oracular speeches of Balaam are in hemistich metre in the original. They are highly dignified, and may be considered as immediate poetic productions of the Spirit of God" (*Adam Clarke's Commentary* [on Numbers 23:7]).

Balaam's First Prophecy (Numbers 23:7–10) "Balak imagined, like all the heathen, that Balaam, as a . . . magician, could distribute blessings and curses according to his own will, and put such constraint upon his God as to make Him subservient to his own will (see at Numbers 22:6)" (Keil and Delitzsch, *Commentary* [on Numbers 23:8–10]). Of course, Balaam could not curse Israel as it was against the will of God.

Balaam's Second Prophecy (Numbers 23:18–24) The second prophecy is addressed to Balak. "This seems to be spoken to correct the foregoing supposition of Balak that God could change his mind. Even the heathen would not allow that their supreme god could be caught in a falsity" (*Adam Clarke's Commentary* [on Numbers 23:19]).

Balaam's Third Prophecy (Numbers 24:3–9) These prophecies were delivered by Balaam and are "evident prophecies of the victories which the Israelites should gain over their enemies, and of their firm possession of the promised land. They may also refer to the great victories to be obtained by the Lord Jesus Christ, that Lion of the tribe of Judah, over sin, death, and Satan, the grand enemies of the human race" (*Adam Clarke's Commentary* [on Numbers 24:9]).

Balaam's Fourth Prophecy (Numbers 24:14–19) The high point of this fourth prophecy is that a Star would come out of Jacob. Many commentators believe this prophecy refers to the Messiah, Jesus Christ.

Balaam's Fifth Prophecy (Numbers 24:20) The fifth prophecy is a curse upon Amalek, which was "the most ancient and most powerful of all the nations or states then within the view of Balaam; but his latter end shall be that he perish for ever, or his posterity ואחריתו acharitho, shall be destroyed, or shall utterly fail" (*Adam Clarke's Commentary* m[on Numbers 24:20]).

Balaam's Sixth Prophecy (Numbers 24:21–22) "This oracle [prophecy] makes a wordplay between the word *Kenite* and the similar Hebrew word for *nest. Asshur* is Assyria" (*Nelson Study Bible* [NKJV], 251).

Balaam's Seventh Prophecy (Numbers 24:23–24) In this last prophecy it is difficult to identify which nation is which. However, the message is that one nation would rise against another only to see its own destruction.

fetters of a mortal body, man's spirit can be ushered into the divine presence; it can hear what otherwise could not be heard and see what otherwise could not be seen—even the visions of eternity and even the Almighty himself. Yet the trance, . . . is subject to counterfeiting. Such counterfeits were common, for instance, to the frontier camp meetings of the United States" (McConkie and Millet, *Doctrinal Commentary on the Book of Mormon*, 3:140). ⊕

When was Balaam's prophecy fulfilled? (24:17) "It is claimed by some Jewish interpreters that David fulfilled, at least in part, this prophecy, since he did smite Moab and Edom [2 Samuel 8:2, 14]. From early times, however, Jewish commentators have held the passage to be Messianic. The 'Star' that should arise out of Israel being held to have reference to 'David's greater Son,' the Messiah, rather than to David. So held Rabbi Sohar Cadash (14th cent.), commenting on [Numbers 24:17]. This 'Star' to arise in Israel 'is the Messiah' (Sohar on [Num. 24:17], vol. 85., c. 340)" (Roberts, *Rasha—the Jew*, 39). Robert Millet adds, "This prophecy was certainly fulfilled in David and will be fulfilled ultimately in the second coming of Jesus Christ" ("Lessons in the Wilderness," 202). ⊕

17 I shall see him, but not now: I shall behold him, but not nigh: there shall come a Star out of Jacob, and a Sceptre shall rise out of Israel, and shall smite the corners of Moab, and destroy all the children of Sheth.

18 And Edom shall be a possession, Seir also shall be a possession for his enemies; and Israel shall do valiantly.

19 Out of Jacob shall come he that shall have dominion, and shall destroy him that remaineth of the city.

Numbers 24:20–25. Prophecies against Israel's Enemies

In what way was Amalek "the first"? (24:20) Amalek, or the Amalekites, "were the first enemies to attack Israelites under Moses at the battle of Rephidim (Ex. 17:8–14). Because they attacked without provocation, God promised to have them completely destroyed some day in the future (later fulfilled by King Saul, 1 Sam. 15:2–9)" (*Revell Bible Dictionary*, 53).

What is the purpose of these final three prophecies? (24:21–24) "The remaining three oracles [prophecies] seem to spring almost involuntarily from the fourth oracle. They overlap the promise of the victory of Israel over all enemies; hence these oracles are 'curse oracles.' It may be that these were very similar to the types of oracles that Balaam intended to present against Israel; instead these harsh words lash out against the foes of the covenant community. Here is the final irony: Balak and Balaam had plotted to bring Israel under a curse, but in their machinations they only ensured their own doom" (Allen, "Numbers," 2:911–12).

20 ¶ And when he looked on Amalek, he took up his parable, and said, Amalek *was* the first of the nations; but his latter end *shall be* that he perish for ever.

21 And he looked on the Kenites, and took up his parable, and said, Strong is thy dwellingplace, and thou puttest thy nest in a rock.

22 Nevertheless the Kenite shall be wasted, until Asshur shall carry thee away captive.

23 And he took up his parable, and said, Alas, who shall live when God doeth this!

24 And ships *shall come* from the coast of Chittim, and shall afflict Asshur, and shall afflict Eber, and he also shall perish for ever.

25 And Balaam rose up, and went and returned to his place: and Balak also went his way.

CHAPTER 25

The Israelites who worship false gods are slain—Phinehas slays the adulterers and stays the plague—Israel is commanded to vex the Midianites who beguiled them.

Summary of Numbers 25

Despite all that the Lord promised Israel, the Moabite and Midianite women tempt the Israelites to join them in the immoral worship of their idols. The Lord sends a plague which stops only when Phinehas, Aaron's grandson, kills a rebel and a wicked Midianite woman whom he brought into the Israelite camp.

CHAPTER 26

Moses and Eleazar count the Israelites on the plains of Moab near Jericho—The males twenty years and older, excluding Levites, total 601,730—Only Caleb and Joshua remain from those numbered at Sinai.

Summary of Numbers 26

Prior to entering the promised land, Moses and Eleazar count the male members of each tribe twenty years and older with the Levites exempted. As the Lord promised, Joshua and Caleb are the only ones Moses counted in the first numbering of Israel who are still alive for the second census thirty-eight years later (see Numbers 26:65; and 14:26–30). The reason for the second census is to prepare for dividing the land among the various tribes (see Numbers 26:53–56 and 33:54).

CHAPTER 27

The law of inheritances to sons, daughters, and kinsmen is explained—Moses will see but not enter the promised land—Joshua is called and set apart to lead Israel.

1 Then came the daughters of Zelophehad, the son of Hepher, the son of Gilead, the son of Machir, the son of Manasseh, of the families of Manasseh the son of Joseph: and these *are* the names of his daughters; Mahlah, Noah, and Hoglah, and Milcah, and Tirzah.

2 And they stood before Moses, and before Eleazar the priest, and before the princes and all the congregation, *by* the door of the tabernacle of the congregation, saying,

3 Our father died in the wilderness, and he was not in the company of them that gathered themselves together against the LORD in the company of Korah; but died in his own sin, and had no sons.

4 Why should the name of our father be done away from among his family, because he hath no son? Give unto us *therefore* a possession among the brethren of our father.

Numbers 27:1–11. The Law of Succession and Inheritance

What important legal case did the daughters of Zelophedad bring before Moses? (27:1–4) "When he [Zelophedad] died in the wilderness, the five daughters petitioned the Lord God through Moses that they might receive their inheritances despite the fact they were women. The Lord awarded their petition and set the pattern by which daughters could represent their father's line in the absence of their being sons. . . .

"Although we cannot with certainty provide all of the ages of the daughters of Zelophehad, we can say that the eldest, Mahlah, could have been no more than 59 years old at the time the request was made of Moses and the princes of Israel" (Hyde, *Comprehensive Commentary [Numbers and Deuteronomy]*, 296–97).

How does revelation help solve the serious issue of land inheritance? (27:5–11) "Again a problem was solved through revelation. Land inheritances usually passed to sons because daughters would go away to live with their husbands; but in this case, a father without male heirs had died and his daughters brought the question of inheritance to Moses, Eleazar, and the princes of Israel. Moses 'brought their cause before the Lord,' and a law was established to give women rights of inheritance. Israel was very early among the nations of the world in establishing such rights" (Rasmussen, *Latter-day Saint Commentary on the Old Testament*, 161–62).

5 And Moses brought their cause before the LORD.

6 ¶ And the LORD spake unto Moses, saying,

7 The daughters of Zelophehad speak right: thou shalt surely give them a possession of an inheritance among their father's brethren; and thou shalt cause the inheritance of their father to pass unto them.

8 And thou shalt speak unto the children of Israel, saying, If a man die, and have no son, then ye shall cause his inheritance to pass unto his daughter.

9 And if he have no daughter, then ye shall give his inheritance unto his brethren.

10 And if he have no brethren, then ye shall give his inheritance unto his father's brethren.

11 And if his father have no brethren, then ye shall give his inheritance unto his kinsman that is next to him of his family, and he shall possess it: and it shall be unto the children of Israel a statute of judgment, as the LORD commanded Moses.

Numbers 27:12–23. Joshua Replaces Moses as the Prophet of Israel

Where is Mount Abarim and why did Moses go there? (27:12) The Lord wanted Moses to view the Promised Land before he was to depart from his mortal life. Abarim is a "mountainous area located east of the Jordan River and the Dead Sea, and extending northward from the plains of Moab. From the highest point on Mt. Nebo, [which may have been] called Pisgah, located on Abarim (2,642 feet; 805 meters), Moses looked into the Promised Land" (*Tyndale Bible Dictionary*, 2).

12 ¶ And the LORD said unto Moses, Get thee up into this mount Abarim, and see the land which I have given unto the children of Israel.

What do we know about the deaths of Aaron and Moses? (27:13) "It is recorded that Aaron died on Mount Hor (Numbers 33:39) and maybe that is what happened. However, while it was recorded of Moses that he died and was buried by the hand of the Lord (Deuteronomy 34:5–7), Alma said that he 'was taken up by the Spirit,' or, more specifically, 'the scriptures saith the Lord took Moses unto himself'(Alma 45:18–19). Moses was translated, as were many, like strangers and pilgrims on earth before him (D&C 45:11–14; Hebrews 11:5, 11–16)" (McConkie, *Aaronic Priesthood*,

13 And when thou hast seen it, thou also shalt be gathered unto thy people, as Aaron thy brother was gathered.

14 For ye rebelled against my commandment in the desert of Zin, in the strife of the congregation, to sanctify me at the water before their eyes: that *is* the water of Meribah in Kadesh in the wilderness of Zin.

15 ¶ And Moses spake unto the LORD, saying,

16 Let the LORD, the God of the spirits of all flesh, set a man over the congregation,

17 Which may go out before them, and which may go in before them, and which may lead them out, and which may bring them in; that the congregation of the LORD be not as sheep which have no shepherd.

18 ¶ And the LORD said unto Moses, Take thee Joshua the son of Nun, a man in whom *is* the spirit, and lay thine hand upon him;

19 And set him before Eleazar the priest, and before all the congregation; and give him a charge in their sight.

20 And thou shalt put *some* of thine honour upon him, that all the congregation of the children of Israel may be obedient.

21 And he shall stand before Eleazar the priest, who shall ask *counsel* for him after the judgment of Urim before the LORD: at his word shall they go out, and at his word they shall come in, *both* he, and all the children of Israel with him, even all the congregation.

22 And Moses did as the LORD commanded him: and he took Joshua, and set him before Eleazar the priest, and before all the congregation:

23 And he laid his hands upon him, and gave him a charge, as the LORD commanded by the hand of Moses.

CHAPTERS 28–29

Sacrifices are to be offered each morning and evening, on the Sabbath, on the first day of each month, at Passover, on each day of the Feast of Unleavened Bread, and at the Feast of Firstfruits.

21). See commentary in this volume for Deuteronomy 32:48–52; 34:5–7; and Joshua 1:1. ⊕

How did the Israelites know who would succeed Moses? (27:15–18) See commentary in this volume for introduction to the book of Joshua.

Why was laying hands upon him important? (27:18–19) "One of our Articles of Faith declares that 'a man must be called of God, by prophecy, and by the laying on of hands by those who are in authority' [Articles of Faith 1:5]. Why do you think it was important that Joshua was set apart and given 'a charge,' or his calling to be the new leader, in front of the children of Israel? How does it increase your confidence to know that Church leaders today are also called of God, by prophecy, and by the laying on of hands by those who are in authority?" (Valletta, et al., *Old Testament for Latter-day Saint Families*, 189). See commentary in this volume for Deuteronomy 34:9. ⊕

Who possessed the Urim and Thummim and what was its purpose? (27:21) "Moses' prayer in Deuteronomy 33:8 indicates a desire that the tribe of Levi would continue to be a possessor of the Urim and Thummim in the future, demonstrating a connection between the Urim and Thummim and the authority and power of the office of the Israelite high priest. The Urim and Thummim held by the high priest are closely connected with receiving revelation in other Old Testament passages. Numbers 27:21 indicates that Eleazar the priest should ask 'after the judgment of Urim before the Lord' in order to determine the will of the Lord concerning Joshua and all of Israel. In this case 'judgment' appears more closely connected to the decisions of the Lord regarding his people" (Hopkin, "Peter, Stones, and Seers," 115–16). ⊕

Summary of Numbers 28–29

The Lord reveals to Moses the rituals Israelites should perform as they worship God. These rituals include daily sacrifices, Sabbath sacrifices, and offerings at the beginning of each month, on Passover and Pentecost, and for the New Year, Day of Atonement, and on special feast days.

Sacrifices are to be offered during the seventh month, including at the Feast of Trumpets and at the Feast of Tabernacles.

Summary of Numbers 30

The Lord commands His people to faithfully keep their vows (oaths). God gives special directions concerning oaths made by wives and daughters to release them honorably from certain vows.

CHAPTER 30

Vows and oaths must be kept—Fathers may disallow vows of daughters, and husbands may disallow vows of wives.

Summary of Numbers 31

Jehovah commands Moses to send Israel to war against the Midianites because they tried to destroy Israel through immorality and idolatry. Moses' army destroys the Midianites with no losses to their army. Among those who died in the battle was Balaam, who disobeyed God and turned against Israel. In gratitude for their victory, the Israelites give much of what they captured to the Lord.

CHAPTER 31

Moses sends forth 12,000 warriors who destroy the Midianites—The prey is divided in Israel—None in the armies of Israel are lost.

Summary of Numbers 32

A new season of life begins for the Israelites as they settle in the promised land. Although the tribes of Reuben, Gad, and half of the tribe of Manasseh are appointed to settle on the east side of the Jordan River, they covenant to help the other tribes in conquering the territory on the west side of the Jordan River.

CHAPTER 32

Reuben, Gad, and half the tribe of Manasseh receive their inheritances east of the Jordan—They covenant to join other tribes in conquering Canaan.

Summary of Numbers 33

A summary of Israel's travels from Egypt to the promised land. A list of locations where they camped during their journey reminds the reader of the great miracles the Lord provided for His people in bringing them out of Egyptian slavery. The Lord commands Israel to drive out all the inhabitants of Canaan.

CHAPTER 33

Israel's journeys from Egypt to Canaan are reviewed—The people are commanded to drive out the inhabitants of the land—Any remaining inhabitants will vex Israel.

Summary of Numbers 34

The Lord defines the boundaries of the promised land and identifies the leaders who will assign inheritances in the land. The boundaries extend from the mountains of Lebanon in the north to Kadesh on the south.

CHAPTER 34

Moses specifies the borders of Israel's inheritance in Canaan and names the princes of the tribes who will divide the land.

CHAPTER 35

The Levites are to possess their own cities—Cities of refuge are established for those guilty of manslaughter—Murderers are to be executed by the revenger of blood.

CHAPTER 36

Some daughters in Israel are directed to marry within their own tribe—Inheritances are not to move from tribe to tribe.

Summary of Numbers 35

Jehovah gives the Levites an inheritance of forty-eight towns after the other tribes have received their inheritances. Israel establishes cities of refuge for those who have taken another's life. The Lord gives very detailed rules for these cities, making clear the difference between those who kill on purpose and those who kill by accident. The Lord details conditions for different cases.

Summary of Numbers 36

The book of Numbers concludes with the end of Israel's wandering in the wilderness. Moses counsels the daughters of each tribe to marry within their own tribe. The land given to each tribe is to remain with that tribe.

THE FIFTH BOOK OF MOSES
CALLED
DEUTERONOMY

Introduction

The book of Deuteronomy is part of a series of books called the Pentateuch attributed to Moses. "Deuteronomy is the Greek name of the fifth book of the Bible. It means 'Second Law,' or 'A Copy of the Law.' The Hebrew name of the Book, *elleh haddebarim* ('These Are the Words'), is taken from the first words of Deuteronomy: 'These are the words which Moses spake unto all Israel on this side Jordan in the wilderness, in the plain. . . . according unto all that the Lord had given him in commandment unto them' ([Deut. 1:1, 3]). It is also familiarly known to the Jews as *mishneh hattora*, 'copy of the law' (17:18)" (Meservy, "Good News of Moses," 206).

"Much of the book is a series of addresses delivered by Moses to Israel as they prepared to enter the promised land. There is an urgency in Deuteronomy as Moses pleads with the people to remember God and live his law" (Pearson, *Old Testament*, 32). This preparation required a sacred covenant before entering into the Promised Land. "The whole book of Deuteronomy seems to have the structure of a covenant ceremony. Throughout history, especially among ancient peoples, such covenant-making and covenant renewal were regular and consistent" (Ricks, "Deuteronomy," 57).

"Anciently, these covenants that man made with God were entered into with a specific formula which bound both parties. The biblical scholar George Mendenhall identified six common steps in ancient covenants and treaties (*Interpreter's Dictionary,* 1:714). These elements are as follows: (1) the preamble, (2) historical prologue, (3) stipulations, (4) blessings and curses, (5) witnesses, and (6) deposit and public reading of the covenant.

"Each element of the covenant making process is vital. For instance, the preamble demonstrates the authority of the people making the covenant. The historical prologue to the covenant forms the foundation for the history of a covenant people. The stipulations lay out the requirements of the covenant for both parties. The blessings and curses graphically illustrate the consequences of keeping or breaking the pact. The witnesses serve to show God's people that all his actions were done without secret covenants. Finally, the deposit and public reading remind God's people of their promises and illustrate that his covenants stretch beyond an isolated time and people" (Donaldson, "Plates of Ether," 70).

Deuteronomy is organized around this ancient covenant pattern:

1. Preamble (1:1–5); 2. Historical prologue (1:6–4:49); 3a. General stipulations (chapters 5–11); 3b. Specific stipulations (chapters 12–26); 4. Blessings and curses (Chapters 27–28); 5. Witnesses (see 30:19; 31:19; 32:1–43); 6. Deposit and public reading of the covenant (Deut. 27:1–8; Deut. 31:1, 9, 24–26) (see Craigie, *Book of Deuteronomy*, 24).

"Thus, the book of Deuteronomy is more than Moses' review of his earlier teachings. It goes beyond a 'last lecture' and becomes a capstone for the covenant relationship between the Lord and Israel. This covenant formula in Deuteronomy was not only for the generation of Israelites listening to Moses but it should also be accepted by each following generation" (Ludlow, *Unlocking the Old Testament*, 52).

This reading of the covenant "consists of a series of three sermons which Moses delivered to the Israelites in Moab near the end of his life: *First Speech:* Chapters 1–4. This speech is a recitation of the events that took place between the departure from Sinai and the arrival east of the Jordan River. *Second Speech:* Chapters 5–26. This discourse contains Moses' account of the events that took place at Sinai, and the instructions that Israel received there, often called the Deuteronomic Law (chapters 12–26). *Third Speech:* Chapters 27–30. These chapters contain Moses' final instructions to his people, including blessings and curses that he promised to them, based on their behavior" (Meservy, "Good News of Moses," 206).

CHAPTER 1

Moses begins the recitation of all that befell Israel during forty years in the wilderness—The children of Israel are commanded to go into and possess Canaan—Judges and rulers are chosen to assist Moses—Israel's spies bring an evil report—The adults of Israel will perish—The Amorites defeat the armies of Israel.

1 These *be* the words which Moses spake unto all Israel on this side Jordan in the wilderness, in the plain over against the Red *sea,* between Paran, and Tophel, and Laban, and Hazeroth, and Dizahab.

2 (*There are* eleven days' *journey* from Horeb by the way of mount Seir unto Kadesh-barnea.)

Deuteronomy 1:1–5. Moses Addresses the Children of Israel

Who wrote the introduction to the book of Deuteronomy? (1:1–5) "A general introduction to the book of Deuteronomy, the first five verses may have been supplied by an editor after Moses' time, but the verses confirm that the book contains Moses' words in Moab and at various times and places from the Red Sea to the Jordan" (Rasmussen, *Latter-day Saint Commentary on the Old Testament*, 168).

Why would the Lord allow Israel to wander for forty years in the wilderness when it is only an eleven days' journey? (1:2) It took the children of Israel about three months to travel from Egypt to Mount Sinai (see Exodus 19:1). They spent nearly an entire year at Sinai (see Numbers 10:11–12). Then it was another eleven days from Sinai (also called Horeb) to Kadesh-barnea (see Deuteronomy 1:2). It was from Kadesh-barnea that Moses sent the twelve spies into the land of Canaan. After forty days they brought back the report that frightened the children of Israel and caused them to rebel against Moses (see Deuteronomy 1:22–46). Israel's lack of faith in

Introduction (continued)

Deuteronomy 1–4	Deuteronomy 5–26	Deuteronomy 27–34
Moses' First Sermon	***Moses' Second Sermon***	***Moses' Third Sermon***
History: Review of Wandering in the Wilderness	*Legal:* Review of the Law: What God Expects of Israel	*Prophecy:* Future of Israel Foretold: What God Will Do for Israel
Theme: Remember	*Theme:* Obey	*Theme:* Trust
Deut. 1–3 Israelite history since leaving Egypt	Deut. 5–11 Decalogue	Deut. 27–28 Ratifying the Covenant: Tablets of Stone and Blessings and Curses
Deut. 4:1–40 Call to obey	Deut. 12–16:17 Ceremonial Laws	Deut. 29–30 Israel's Future
Deut. 4:41–49 Three cities of refuge	Deut. 16:18–20 Civil Laws	Deut. 31–34 Moses' Last Days: Song of Moses; Blessing of Moses; End of Moses
	Deut. 21–26 Social Laws	

"Historical evidence gives indication that Lehi was especially familiar with the book of Deuteronomy. . . .

"Lehi's last address to his people appears to invoke at least fourteen important themes and verbal formulations from the final addresses of Moses as recorded in Deuteronomy" (Reynolds, "Israelite Background of Moses Typology in the Book of Mormon," 10, 20).

the Lord's power to help them defeat their enemies resulted in the Lord condemning that generation to wander in the wilderness until all who rebelled had died (see Deuteronomy 2:14–15). This forty-year period also served as a time when their children, who would inherit the promised land, were humbled, tried, and proven (see Deuteronomy 8:2–3).

What happened in the fortieth year? (1:3) "Moses begins addressing the Israelites slightly less than forty years (thirty-nine years, nine months, sixteen days) after they departed from Egypt (first year, first month, and fifteenth day—the day after their first Passover celebration; Ex 12:18), ca. 1406 B.C. . . . Since the Israelite crossing of the Jordan River (Jos 4:19—forty-first year, first month, tenth day) represented the beginning of the conquest of Canaan, the transition from Moses to Joshua (with Moses preaching the content of Deuteronomy, his death, burial, and the transferral of leadership to Joshua) occurred within about one and one-third months of Moses' addressing the Israelites with this material" (Grisanti, "Deuteronomy," 2:476).

3 And it came to pass in the fortieth year, in
the eleventh month, on the first *day* of the
month, *that* Moses spake unto the children
of Israel, according unto all that the LORD
had given him in commandment unto them;
4 After he had slain Sihon the king of the
Amorites, which dwelt in Heshbon, and Og
the king of Bashan, which dwelt at Astaroth
in Edrei:

5 On this side Jordan, in the land of Moab,
began Moses to declare this law, saying,

Deuteronomy 1:6–18. Moses Recalls God's Direction at Mt. Sinai

Why was it time for the children of Israel to take possession of the promised land? (1:6–8) The Lord had given His Law. "The events of Horeb [Sinai] were completed and it was time to move. The formation of the covenant at Horeb [Sinai] has made the Israelites potentially a nation; there could be no rest until that potential was a reality. Hence at Horeb [Sinai], and again at Mount Seir, and now in the plains of Moab, where Moses addressed the people, the call comes constantly to move on, until the promised land is the possessed land" (Craigie, *Book of Deuteronomy*, 80–81).

6 The LORD our God spake unto us in Horeb,
saying, Ye have dwelt long enough in this
mount:

7 Turn you, and take your journey, and go
to the mount of the Amorites, and unto all
the places nigh thereunto, in the plain, in the
hills, and in the vale, and in the south, and
by the sea side, to the land of the Canaanites,
and unto Lebanon, unto the great river, the
river Euphrates.

8 Behold, I have set the land before you:
go in and possess the land which the LORD
sware unto your fathers, Abraham, Isaac, and
Jacob, to give unto them and to their seed
after them.

9 ¶ And I spake unto you at that time, saying, I am not able to bear you myself alone:

10 The LORD your God hath multiplied you,
and, behold, ye *are* this day as the stars of
heaven for multitude.

11 (The LORD God of your fathers make you
a thousand times so many more as ye *are*,
and bless you, as he hath promised you!)

12 How can I myself alone bear your cum-
brance, and your burden, and your strife?

How do we claim the blessing of being made "a thousand times so many more as ye are"? (1:11) "It is my testimony and apostolic blessing to each one of you that you will feel in your heart and mind this sublime truth for yourselves. Live in faith, dear friends . . . and 'the Lord [our] God [will] increase you a thousand times and bless you as he has promised!' [NIV, Deut. 1:11 (2011)]" (Uchtdorf, "Fourth Floor, Last Door," 18).

13 Take you wise men, and understanding,
and known among your tribes, and I will
make them rulers over you.

14 And ye answered me, and said, The thing
which thou hast spoken *is* good *for us* to do.

15 So I took the chief of your tribes, wise
men, and known, and made them heads over
you, captains over thousands, and captains
over hundreds, and captains over fifties, and
captains over tens, and officers among your
tribes.

What is one way that wise men are known or recognized? (1:13) The Prophet Joseph Smith said: "The way to get along in any important matter is to gather unto yourselves wise men, experienced and aged men, to assist in council in all times of trouble. . . . You will always discover in the first glance of a man, in the outlines of his features, something of his mind" (Joseph Smith Papers, "History, 1838–1856, volume D-1 [1 Aug. 1842–1 Jul. 1843]," 1550).

16 And I charged your judges at that time,
saying, Hear *the causes* between your brethren,
and judge righteously between *every* man and
his brother, and the stranger *that is* with him.

How does one cultivate the ability to judge righteously? (1:16) "The only safe way for us to [judge righteously], as individuals, is to live so humbly, so righteously and so faithfully before God, that we may possess His Spirit to that extent that we will be able to judge righteously" (Smith, in *Journal of Discourses*, 24:193). "For behold, the Spirit of Christ is given to every man, that he may know good from evil; wherefore, I show unto you the way to judge" (Moroni 7:16).

17 Ye shall not respect persons in judgment;
but ye shall hear the small as well as the great;
ye shall not be afraid of the face of man; for
the judgment *is* God's: and the cause that is
too hard for you, bring *it* unto me, and I will
hear it.

18 And I commanded you at that time all
the things which ye should do.

What is part of the Lord's criteria for righteous judgment? (1:17) "In the administration of justice, no distinction was to be made between *the small and the great*, that is, the poor and the rich, the unimportant and the important. Nor were the judges to be afraid of man, if untoward pressure was brought to bear on them, for the measure by which they adjudicated was that of God. The principle *that judgment belongs to God* was enormously important, for it removed the basis and the authority of the law from the human realm and placed it firmly on an absolute principle of divine authority. But . . . cases *too hard* for the judges . . . were to be referred to Moses" (Craigie, *Book of Deuteronomy*, 84).

19 ¶ And when we departed from Horeb,
we went through all that great and terrible
wilderness, which ye saw by the way of the

Deuteronomy 1:19–46. Moses Recalls Events at Kadesh-Barnea

mountain of the Amorites, as the LORD our God commanded us; and we came to Kadesh-barnea.

20 And I said unto you, Ye are come unto the mountain of the Amorites, which the LORD our God doth give unto us.

21 Behold, the LORD thy God hath set the land before thee: go up *and* possess *it*, as the LORD God of thy fathers hath said unto thee; fear not, neither be discouraged.

22 ¶ And ye came near unto me every one of you, and said, We will send men before us, and they shall search us out the land, and bring us word again by what way we must go up, and into what cities we shall come.

23 And the saying pleased me well: and I took twelve men of you, one of a tribe:

24 And they turned and went up into the mountain, and came unto the valley of Eshcol, and searched it out.

25 And they took of the fruit of the land in their hands, and brought *it* down unto us, and brought us word again, and said, *It is* a good land which the LORD our God doth give us.

26 Notwithstanding ye would not go up, but rebelled against the commandment of the LORD your God:

27 And ye murmured in your tents, and said, Because the LORD hated us, he hath brought us forth out of the land of Egypt, to deliver us into the hand of the Amorites, to destroy us.

28 Whither shall we go up? our brethren have discouraged our heart, saying, The people *is* greater and taller than we; the cities *are* great and walled up to heaven; and moreover we have seen the sons of the Anakims there.

How do we counter discouragement? (1:21) The Prophet Joseph Smith said that we should "not be discouraged on account of the greatness of the work; only be humble and faithful. . . . He who scattered Israel has promised to gather them; therefore inasmuch as you are to be instrumental in this great work, He will endow you with power, wisdom, might and intelligence, and every qualification necessary; while your minds will expand wider and wider, until you can circumscribe the earth and the heavens, reach forth into eternity, and contemplate the mighty acts of Jehovah in all their variety and glory" (Joseph Smith Papers, "History, 1838–1856, volume C-1 [2 November 1838–31 July 1842]," 1058).

What rumors fueled the children of Israel's fear of entering the promised land? (1:26–28) The "people's vision had not been on the goodness of the land, but on the difficulty they would experience in possessing it. . . . The 'facts' were the same for both, but Moses, the man of vision and faith, could minimize the difficulties because of his strong conviction in the Lord's promise; the people, with little vision, could not lift their sight above the formidableness of their opponents" (Craigie, *Book of Deuteronomy*, 87). "Though Israel had seen one of the mightiest armies on earth, that of Egypt, defeated and destroyed by the hand of the Lord, they were afraid that He could not bring them into His rest in the promised land" (Muhlestein, "Israel's Exodus and Deliverance," 49).

29 Then I said unto you, Dread not, neither be afraid of them.

30 The Lord your God which goeth before you, he shall fight for you, according to all that he did for you in Egypt before your eyes;

31 And in the wilderness, where thou hast seen how that the Lord thy God bare thee, as a man doth bear his son, in all the way that ye went, until ye came into this place.

What does it take for the Lord to fight our battles? (1:30) "God will fight our battles if we honor him and serve him with all our hearts, might, mind, and strength" (Kimball, *Teachings of Spencer W. Kimball*, 416). How do you demonstrate that you honor God? What does it take to give all of your heart, might, mind, and strength to God? What does this request teach you about God and the relationship He seeks with you?

32 Yet in this thing ye did not believe the Lord your God,

33 Who went in the way before you, to search you out a place to pitch your tents *in,* in fire by night, to shew you by what way ye should go, and in a cloud by day.

34 And the Lord heard the voice of your words, and was wroth, and sware, saying,

35 Surely there shall not one of these men of this evil generation see that good land, which I sware to give unto your fathers,

36 Save Caleb the son of Jephunneh; he shall see it, and to him will I give the land that he hath trodden upon, and to his children, because he hath wholly followed the Lord.

How do we avoid becoming like those who couldn't enter the promised land? (1:35) "Brethren and sisters, let us be faithful, keep our covenants, and press onward until that time [of testing] shall come. . . . If we do not do this, the Lord can raise up a people that will. . . . He will give [the blessings] to somebody else. Ancient Israel transgressed, and would not keep the covenants and obey the Lord; consequently, they could not enter into the promised land. But was it much trouble to raise up a people that would? No" (Wells, in *Journal of Discourses*, 5:44).

37 Also the Lord was angry with me for your sakes, saying, Thou also shalt not go in thither.

38 *But* Joshua the son of Nun, which standeth before thee, he shall go in thither: encourage him: for he shall cause Israel to inherit it.

Why did the Lord display His anger with Moses? (1:37) "In this verse Moses places at least part of the blame for his not being able to enter the promised land upon the wickedness of the people" (Ludlow, *Companion to Your Study of the Old Testament*, 184).

39 Moreover your little ones, which ye said should be a prey, and your children, which in that day had no knowledge between good and evil, they shall go in thither, and unto them will I give it, and they shall possess it.

40 But *as for* you, turn you, and take your journey into the wilderness by the way of the Red sea.

What does it mean that the people went up "presumptuously"? (1:43) The Lord reminded the Israelites of their disobedience when battling the Amorites. "The verb (*zūd*) suggests an action undertaken with insolence, which was just the attitude taken by the Israelites toward their God. . . . The result of their insolent and presumptuous action was inevitable. When the Israelites met the Amorites, they were defeated and put to flight, because the Lord was not in their midst. . . . The Amorites pursued them *as bees do*, a suggestive simile describing the headlong flight of the Israelites from battle" (Craigie, *Book of Deuteronomy*, 90).

Why would the Lord not listen to the Israelites? (1:45) The children of Israel's return was not a "true conversion to repentance, but simply the giving up of their rash enterprise, which they had undertaken in opposition to the commandment of God—the return from a defiant attitude to unbelieving complaining on account of the misfortune that had come upon them. Such complaining God never hears" (Keil and Delitzsch, *Commentary* [on Deuteronomy 1:45–46]). This is reminiscent of the Nephites who "did struggle for their lives without calling upon that Being who created them" (Mormon 5:2).

Summary of Deuteronomy 2

Moses recounts Israel's wandering in the wilderness. Though it was challenging and demanding, he recalls the Lord's kindness and mercy to them. They passed through many lands in peace, and when the Amorites attacked them, they were given divine strength to win the battle.

41 Then ye answered and said unto me, We have sinned against the LORD, we will go up and fight, according to all that the LORD our God commanded us. And when ye had girded on every man his weapons of war, ye were ready to go up into the hill.

42 And the LORD said unto me, Say unto them, Go not up, neither fight; for I *am* not among you; lest ye be smitten before your enemies.

43 So I spake unto you; and ye would not hear, but rebelled against the commandment of the LORD, and went presumptuously up into the hill.

44 And the Amorites, which dwelt in that mountain, came out against you, and chased you, as bees do, and destroyed you in Seir, *even* unto Hormah.

45 And ye returned and wept before the LORD; but the LORD would not hearken to your voice, nor give ear unto you.

46 So ye abode in Kadesh many days, according unto the days that ye abode *there*.

CHAPTER 2

The children of Israel press forward to their promised land—They pass through the lands of Esau and of Ammon in peace but destroy the Amorites.

CHAPTER 3

The children of Israel destroy the people of Bashan—Their lands, on the east of the Jordan, are given to Reuben and Gad—Moses sees Canaan from Pisgah but is denied entrance thereto—He counsels and strengthens Joshua.

Summary of Deuteronomy 3

Moses reminds the children of Israel of their military victories in the wilderness. Moses sees the promised land (Canaan) but is not allowed to enter. He charges Joshua to lead the people of Israel into Canaan. Another form of the name Joshua is Jesus. Therefore, Joshua leading Israel into the promised land symbolizes Jesus leading us back to a promised land of celestial glory.

CHAPTER 4

Moses exhorts the children of Israel to keep the commandments, to teach them to their children, and to be exemplary before all nations—They are forbidden to make graven images or worship other gods—They are to witness that they have heard the voice of God—They will be scattered among all nations when they worship other gods—They will be gathered again in the latter days when they seek the Lord their God—Moses extols the mercy and goodness of God to Israel.

1 Now therefore hearken, O Israel, unto the statutes and unto the judgments, which I teach you, for to do *them,* that ye may live, and go in and possess the land which the LORD God of your fathers giveth you.

2 Ye shall not add unto the word which I command you, neither shall ye diminish *ought* from it, that ye may keep the commandments of the LORD your God which I command you.

3 Your eyes have seen what the LORD did because of Baal-peor: for all the men that followed Baal-peor, the LORD thy God hath destroyed them from among you.

Deuteronomy 4:1–13. Moses Pleads with Israel to Keep the Commandments

Why does God give His commandments and ordinances? (4:1) Obedience to God's commandments and ordinances is vital. President Packer taught: "Ordinances and covenants become our credentials for admission into [God's] presence. To worthily receive them is the quest of a lifetime; to keep them thereafter is the challenge of mortality" ("Covenants," 24). President Russell M. Nelson added: "The greatest compliment that can be earned here in this life is to be known as a covenant keeper. The rewards for a covenant keeper will be realized both here and hereafter" ("Covenants," 88).

What qualifies one prophet adding to the words of another? (4:2) "Virtually every prophet of the Old *and* New Testament has added scripture to that received by his predecessors. If the Old Testament words of Moses were sufficient, as some could have mistakenly thought them to be, then why, for example, the subsequent prophecies of Isaiah or of Jeremiah, who follows him? To say nothing of Ezekiel and Daniel, of Joel, Amos, and all the rest. If one revelation to one prophet in one moment of time is sufficient for *all* time, what justifies these many others? What justifies them was made clear by Jehovah Himself when He said to Moses, 'My works are without end, and . . . my words . . . never cease' [Moses 1:4]" (Holland, "My Words . . . Never Cease," 92).

What does it mean to cleave unto the Lord? (4:4) The Hebrew word in this verse which is translated as "cleave" is *chakam* which means "intelligent . . . endowed with reason and using it" (*Gesenius' Hebrew-Chaldee Lexicon to the Old Testament*, 277). These Israelites were wise to attach themselves to God. "Surely this great nation [is] a wise and understanding people" (Deut. 4:6).

In what way does God accomplish His purposes by blessing Israel? (4:5–8) "Here is an excellent statement of the mission of Israel and of every true believer in the Lord and his gospel. It is related to Jesus' basic charge to believers: 'Let your light so shine before men, that they may see your good works, and glorify your Father which is in heaven' (Matthew 5:16; Deut. 4:5–6)" (Rasmussen, *Latter-day Saint Commentary on the Old Testament*, 170).

How does the command to teach our children apply to us? (4:10) "On one particular occasion, while Moses and his people were in the plains of Moab before entering the promised land, the Lord inspired him to admonish his people concerning their responsibility to learn the statutes and covenants they had received from the Lord and to teach them to their posterity, many of whom had not personally experienced the crossing of the Red Sea or the revelation given on Mount Sinai. . . . God's prophets have consistently instructed that we need to raise our families 'in the nurture and admonition of the Lord' [Ephesians 6:4; Enos 1:1]" (Soares, "How Can I Understand?" 6–7). ⊕

4 But ye that did cleave unto the LORD your God *are* alive every one of you this day.

5 Behold, I have taught you statutes and judgments, even as the LORD my God commanded me, that ye should do so in the land whither ye go to possess it.

6 Keep therefore and do *them;* for this *is* your wisdom and your understanding in the sight of the nations, which shall hear all these statutes, and say, Surely this great nation *is* a wise and understanding people.

7 For what nation *is there so* great, who *hath* God *so* nigh unto them, as the LORD our God *is* in all *things that* we call upon him *for?*

8 And what nation *is there so* great, that hath statutes and judgments *so* righteous as all this law, which I set before you this day?

9 Only take heed to thyself, and keep thy soul diligently, lest thou forget the things which thine eyes have seen, and lest they depart from thy heart all the days of thy life: but teach them thy sons, and thy sons' sons;

10 *Specially* the day that thou stoodest before the LORD thy God in Horeb, when the LORD said unto me, Gather me the people together, and I will make them hear my words, that they may learn to fear me all the days that they shall live upon the earth, and *that* they may teach their children.

11 And ye came near and stood under the mountain; and the mountain burned with fire unto the midst of heaven, with darkness, clouds, and thick darkness.

12 And the LORD spake unto you out of the midst of the fire: ye heard the voice of the words, but saw no similitude; only *ye heard* a voice.

13 And he declared unto you his covenant, which he commanded you to perform, *even* ten commandments; and he wrote them upon two tables of stone.

14 ¶ And the LORD commanded me at that time to teach you statutes and judgments, that ye might do them in the land whither ye go over to possess it.

15 Take ye therefore good heed unto yourselves; for ye saw no manner of similitude on the day *that* the LORD spake unto you in Horeb out of the midst of the fire:

16 Lest ye corrupt *yourselves,* and make you a graven image, the similitude of any figure, the likeness of male or female,

17 The likeness of any beast that *is* on the earth, the likeness of any winged fowl that flieth in the air,

18 The likeness of any thing that creepeth on the ground, the likeness of any fish that *is* in the waters beneath the earth:

19 And lest thou lift up thine eyes unto heaven, and when thou seest the sun, and the moon, and the stars, *even* all the host of heaven, shouldest be driven to worship them, and serve them, which the LORD thy God hath divided unto all nations under the whole heaven.

20 But the LORD hath taken you, and brought you forth out of the iron furnace, *even* out of Egypt, to be unto him a people of inheritance, as *ye are* this day.

21 Furthermore the LORD was angry with me for your sakes, and sware that I should not go over Jordan, and that I should not go in unto that good land, which the LORD thy God giveth thee *for* an inheritance:

Deuteronomy 4:14–24. Israel Is Forbidden to Worship Other Gods

How can we take "good heed" of ourselves? (4:15) This life is a time to prepare to meet God (Alma 34:32). This preparation requires that we "take good heed" of our lives. "The Spirit speaketh the truth and lieth not. Wherefore, it speaketh of things as they really are, and of things as they really will be; wherefore, these things are manifested unto us plainly, for the salvation of our souls" (Jacob 4:13). In what ways can you assess your spiritual progress and see things as "they really are"?

How do we make graven images unto the Lord today? (4:16) "Few men have ever knowingly and deliberately chosen to reject God and his blessings. Rather, we learn from the scriptures that because the exercise of faith has always appeared to be more difficult than relying on things more immediately at hand, carnal man has tended to transfer his trust in God to material things. Therefore, in all ages when men have fallen under the power of Satan and lost the faith, they have put in its place a hope in the 'arm of flesh' and in 'gods of silver, and gold, of brass, iron, wood, and stone, which see not, nor hear, nor know' (Dan. 5:23)—that is, in idols" (Kimball, *Teachings of Spencer W. Kimball*, 76).

What did the iron furnace represent? (4:20) The "iron furnace" referred to Israel's time in Egypt. "Through the 'furnace of affliction,' the Lord's people are refined, purified, and sanctified before the Lord (Isa. 48:10; 1 Pet. 1:7; Deut. 4:20)" (McConkie and Parry, *Guide to Scriptural Symbolism*, 57).

What happened to Moses at the end of his life? (4:22) Though this verse says that Moses "must die in this land," it should be noted that he was actually translated. President Joseph Fielding Smith said, "It is a very reasonable thought to believe that both Moses and Alma, like Elijah and John, were translated to accomplish some work which the Lord had in store for them at some future day" (*Answers to Gospel Questions*, 5:38). See commentary in this volume for Deuteronomy 34:5–7.

Why would Moses say that God is a consuming fire? (4:24) The Prophet Joseph Smith taught, "God Almighty Himself dwells in eternal fire; flesh and blood cannot go there, for all corruption is devoured by the fire" (Joseph Smith Papers, "History, 1838–1856, volume F-1 [1 May 1844–8 August 1844]," 20).

Deuteronomy 4:25–40. The Scattering and Gathering of Israel Are Explained

Why would Moses prophesy that Israel would be scattered? (4:25–31) "Moses had no illusions about how long Israel would remain obedient. Here he prophetically foresaw one of the most common themes in the Old Testament: the scattering of Israel because of their wickedness, but also the great gathering that is to take place 'in the latter days' (v. 30). The Lord pointed out two reasons why Israel shall be regathered. First, many of latter-day Israel will turn to the Lord (see v. 29); second, the covenants Jehovah made with Israel's fathers (the patriarchs) will be kept (see v. 31, 37). This gathering involves a return to the lands of Israel's inheritance, but, more important, it involves a spiritual gathering, that is, a return to the covenants and laws of God" (*Old Testament Student Manual: Genesis–2 Samuel*, 217). ⊕

How was Moses' prophesy fulfilled? (4:26–29) "When the Prophet Joseph saw his vision [of the Father and the Son], the whole Christian world believed in a God without body, parts, or passions. That means he had no eyes; he couldn't see. He had no ears; he couldn't hear. He had no mouth; he couldn't speak. Moses knew that this condition would prevail, for when he went to lead the children of Israel into the Promised Land, he told them that they would not remain there long, but that they would be scattered among the nations, and that they would worship gods made by the hands of man (that's man's doing) that could neither see, nor hear, nor taste, nor smell (see Deut. 4:26–28)" (Richards, "Things of God and Man," 21–22).

22 But I must die in this land, I must not go
over Jordan: but ye shall go over, and possess
that good land.

23 Take heed unto yourselves, lest ye forget
the covenant of the LORD your God, which
he made with you, and make you a graven
image, *or* the likeness of any *thing,* which the
LORD thy God hath forbidden thee.

24 For the LORD thy God *is* a consuming
fire, *even* a jealous God.

25 ¶ When thou shalt beget children, and
children's children, and ye shall have remained
long in the land, and shall corrupt *yourselves,*
and make a graven image, *or* the likeness of
any *thing,* and shall do evil in the sight of the
LORD thy God, to provoke him to anger:

26 I call heaven and earth to witness against
you this day, that ye shall soon utterly perish from off the land whereunto ye go over
Jordan to possess it; ye shall not prolong *your*
days upon it, but shall utterly be destroyed.

27 And the LORD shall scatter you among the
nations, and ye shall be left few in number
among the heathen, whither the LORD shall
lead you.

28 And there ye shall serve gods, the work of
men's hands, wood and stone, which neither
see, nor hear, nor eat, nor smell.

29 But if from thence thou shalt seek the
LORD thy God, thou shalt find *him,* if thou
seek him with all thy heart and with all thy
soul.

30 When thou art in tribulation, and all
these things are come upon thee, *even* in

the latter days, if thou turn to the LORD thy
God, and shalt be obedient unto his voice;

31 (For the LORD thy God *is* a merciful
God;) he will not forsake thee, neither destroy thee, nor forget the covenant of thy fathers which he sware unto them.

32 For ask now of the days that are past,
which were before thee, since the day that
God created man upon the earth, and *ask*
from the one side of heaven unto the other,
whether there hath been *any such thing* as this
great thing *is,* or hath been heard like it?

33 Did *ever* people hear the voice of God
speaking out of the midst of the fire, as thou
hast heard, and live?

34 Or hath God assayed to go *and* take him
a nation from the midst of *another* nation,
by temptations, by signs, and by wonders,
and by war, and by a mighty hand, and by
a stretched out arm, and by great terrors, according to all that the LORD your God did
for you in Egypt before your eyes?

35 Unto thee it was shewed, that thou
mightest know that the LORD he *is* God;
there is none else beside him.

36 Out of heaven he made thee to hear his
voice, that he might instruct thee: and upon
earth he shewed thee his great fire; and thou
heardest his words out of the midst of the fire.

37 And because he loved thy fathers, therefore he chose their seed after them, and

Covenant of the Fathers (Deuteronomy 4)

- If Israel seek the Lord and are obedient, they will find Him (vv. 29–30)
- The Lord has and will show Israel by mighty works, like no other nation, that "there is none else beside him" (vv. 33–35)
- The Lord will instruct Israel out of the heavens (v. 36)
- The Lord chose Israel and chooses her seed after them (v. 37)
- The Lord will give Israel the promised land of their inheritance (v. 38)
- If obedient, "all will go well" with Israel and her children (v. 40)
- If obedient, Israel's days will be prolonged upon the earth (v. 40)
- All of Israel's promises apply in the latter days (v. 30)

brought thee out in his sight with his mighty power out of Egypt;

38 To drive out nations from before thee greater and mightier than thou *art,* to bring thee in, to give thee their land *for* an inheritance, as *it is* this day.

39 Know therefore this day, and consider *it* in thine heart, that the LORD he *is* God in heaven above, and upon the earth beneath: *there is* none else.

40 Thou shalt keep therefore his statutes, and his commandments, which I command thee this day, that it may go well with thee, and with thy children after thee, and that thou mayest prolong *thy* days upon the earth, which the LORD thy God giveth thee, for ever.

Summary of Deuteronomy 4:41–49

Moses finishes his first sermon to the children of Israel by outlining God's judgments.

Summary of Deuteronomy 5

Moses reviews the covenant which God made with the children of Israel on Mount Sinai (Horeb). He declares that the Ten Commandments are still in force. He implores them to be obedient and promises mercy for those who obey the commandments.

CHAPTER 5

Moses tells of the covenant God made with Israel in Horeb—He reviews the Ten Commandments—Sabbath observance also commemorates the deliverance from Egypt—God talks with man—Blessings flow from obedience.

CHAPTER 6

Moses proclaims, The Lord our God is one Lord, and, Thou shalt love the Lord thy God—The children of Israel are commanded to teach their children—Moses exhorts them to keep the commandments, testimonies, and statutes of the Lord that they may prosper.

Deuteronomy 6:1–15. Israel Is Commanded to Always Remember the Lord

1 Now these *are* the commandments, the statutes, and the judgments, which the LORD your God commanded to teach you, that ye might do *them* in the land whither ye go to possess it:

2 That thou mightest fear the LORD thy God, to keep all his statutes and his commandments, which I command thee, thou, and thy son, and thy son's son, all the days of thy life; and that thy days may be prolonged.

3 ¶ Hear therefore, O Israel, and observe to do *it;* that it may be well with thee, and that ye may increase mightily, as the LORD God of thy fathers hath promised thee, in the land that floweth with milk and honey.

4 Hear, O Israel: The LORD our God *is* one LORD:

What does it mean that God is one? (6:4–9) "We find the first of many common misunderstandings of Deuteronomy 6:4–5 within the King James translation of the phrase 'The Lord our God is one Lord.' Many people regard the phrase as an obvious argument for monotheism—that there is only one God, no more. . . . However, the *Jewish Study Bible* . . . warns readers against interpreting Deuteronomy 6:4 'as an assertion of monotheism, a view that is anachronistic. In the context of ancient Israelite religion, it served as a public proclamation of exclusive loyalty to YHVH [i.e., Jehovah] as the sole Lord of Israel.' Thus their better English rendering of the phrase as: 'The Lord is our God, the Lord alone'" (Bradshaw, "What Are the Most Cited, Recited, and Misunderstood Verses in Deuteronomy?").

5 And thou shalt love the LORD thy God with all thine heart, and with all thy soul, and with all thy might.

6 And these words, which I command thee this day, shall be in thine heart:

What does the Lord require of each of us? (6:5) "The scriptures invite us to place all we are and are becoming on the altar of love and service. In the Old Testament, Deuteronomy enjoins us to 'love the Lord thy God' with all our heart, soul, and might [Deuteronomy 6:5]. . . . We rejoice in the invitation to devote our whole souls to seeking higher and holier ways to love God and those around us and to strengthen our faith in Heavenly Father and Jesus Christ in our hearts and in our homes and at church" (Gong, "Our Campfire of Faith," 42).

Hear, O Israel: A Jewish Confession of Faith (Deuteronomy 6: 4–9)

"Deuteronomy 6:4–9 is part of what is known as the Shema (from the Hebrew word meaning 'hear'). The entire Shema, which consists of Deuteronomy 6:4–9; 11:13–21; and Numbers 15:37–41 (in that order), is recited twice daily by all devout Jews as an evening and a morning prayer. When Jesus was asked which was the greatest commandment, he quoted the Shema (see Matthew 22:36–37). President Ezra Taft Benson said, 'When we put God first, all other things fall into their proper place or drop out of our lives' (*Ensign*, May 1988, 4)" (Valletta, et al, *Old Testament for Latter-day Saint Families*, 196).

"Moses opened his overview of divine laws with a proclamation: 'Hear, O Israel: JEHOVAH is our God; JEHOVAH is one' (Deut. 6:4, translation mine). The first word, *hear*, is *shema* in Hebrew, so the whole verse is called the Shema by Jews; they recite it on special occasions, and the deeply religious desire to repeat the verse at the moment of death" (Rasmussen, *Latter-day Saint Commentary on the Old Testament*, 173).

What does God expect of parents? (6:7) "Parents have a divine duty to teach their children to love the Lord" (Nelson, "Listen to Learn," 23). "Parents are commanded to 'bring up' their children 'in light and truth' (D&C 93:40). They are to teach them the plan of salvation (Moses 6:57–60), and the whole law of the whole gospel (Deut. 6:4–9). Theirs is the specific obligation to 'teach their children to pray, and to walk uprightly before the Lord,' as also 'to understand the doctrine of repentance, faith in Christ the Son of the living God, and of baptism and the gift of the Holy Ghost by the laying on of the hands, when eight years old' (D&C 68:25–28)" (McConkie, *Doctrinal New Testament Commentary*, 2:521). ⊕

Deuteronomy 6:16–25. Israel Is Promised They Will Prosper as They Keep the Commandments

What does it mean to tempt the Lord? (6:16–19) "Moses warns Israel against questioning [Jehovah's] ability to keep his promise to them. Rather than concerning themselves with his capacity to do what he said, the Israelites need to commit themselves to unreserved submission to his requirements.... 'Testing' of this kind involves a question about the capacity of the one being tested....

"Jesus quoted from this passage when Satan suggested that he cast himself from the pinnacle of the temple (Mt 4:7; Lk 4:12). Jesus did not question

7 And thou shalt teach them diligently unto thy children, and shalt talk of them when thou sittest in thine house, and when thou walkest by the way, and when thou liest down, and when thou risest up.

8 And thou shalt bind them for a sign upon thine hand, and they shall be as frontlets between thine eyes.

9 And thou shalt write them upon the posts of thy house, and on thy gates.

10 And it shall be, when the LORD thy God shall have brought thee into the land which he sware unto thy fathers, to Abraham, to Isaac, and to Jacob, to give thee great and goodly cities, which thou buildedst not,

11 And houses full of all good *things*, which thou filledst not, and wells digged, which thou diggedst not, vineyards and olive trees, which thou plantedst not; when thou shalt have eaten and be full;

12 *Then* beware lest thou forget the LORD, which brought thee forth out of the land of Egypt, from the house of bondage.

13 Thou shalt fear the LORD thy God, and serve him, and shalt swear by his name.

14 Ye shall not go after other gods, of the gods of the people which *are* round about you;

15 (For the LORD thy God *is* a jealous God among you) lest the anger of the LORD thy God be kindled against thee, and destroy thee from off the face of the earth.

16 ¶ Ye shall not tempt the LORD your God, as ye tempted *him* in Massah.

17 Ye shall diligently keep the commandments of the LORD your God, and his testimonies, and his statutes, which he hath commanded thee.

18 And thou shalt do *that which is* right and good in the sight of the LORD: that it may be well with thee, and that thou mayest go in and possess the good land which the LORD sware unto thy fathers,

19 To cast out all thine enemies from before thee, as the LORD hath spoken.

20 *And* when thy son asketh thee in time to come, saying, What *mean* the testimonies, and the statutes, and the judgments, which the LORD our God hath commanded you?

21 Then thou shalt say unto thy son, We were Pharaoh's bondmen in Egypt; and the LORD brought us out of Egypt with a mighty hand:

22 And the LORD shewed signs and wonders, great and sore, upon Egypt, upon Pharaoh, and upon all his household, before our eyes:

23 And he brought us out from thence, that he might bring us in, to give us the land which he sware unto our fathers.

24 And the LORD commanded us to do all these statutes, to fear the LORD our God, for our good always, that he might preserve us alive, as *it is* at this day.

25 And it shall be our righteousness, if we observe to do all these commandments before the LORD our God, as he hath commanded us.

God's ability to rescue him, but he knew that 'such an act would trivialize the power of God and his care for those he loves'" (Grisanti, "Deuteronomy," 2:561–62).

Why were the Israelites told to remember their bondage in Egypt? (6:21) "The proclamation of the covenant law always began . . . 'I am the LORD, your God, who freed you from the land of Egypt, the house of bondage.' . . . It was essential that later generations should realize that 'we were once slaves in Egypt.' Israel insisted on this point, not just for setting the stage for a rag-to-riches story, but because it revealed something essential in God's plan of salvation. . . . God who by his grace calls slaves to freedom. . . . The exodus narratives stress the fact that God came to save because he had heard the 'outcry' of an oppressed people" (Plastaras, *God of Exodus*, 27, 28).

What was the purpose of sending signs and wonders upon Egypt? (6:22) "Egypt . . . represents the stage upon which God's power and justice were first demonstrated to the world. 'With signs and wonders, with a strong hand and an outstretched arm' [Exodus 13:14], God brought the Children of Israel forth from bondage into freedom" (Frankel and Teutsch, *Encyclopedia of Jewish Symbols*, 46).

How does God work with His children? (6:24) "In His selfless plan, the Lord doeth nothing save it be for the benefit of the children of men (see 2 Nephi 26:24). He labors, lovingly and constantly, as Moses and Jeremiah declared, 'for our good always' (Deuteronomy 6:24; see also Jeremiah 32: 38–40). In His grand design, His 'work' and 'glory' are 'to bring to pass the immortality and eternal life of man' (Moses 1:39). Thus, even when we truly learn to love God, we must humbly acknowledge that He loved us first (see 1 John 4:19)" (Maxwell, "Great Plan of the Eternal God," 21).

Summary of Deuteronomy 7

Because of the extreme wickedness of the people living in Canaan, God commands the Israelites to drive them out or destroy them. The children of Israel are commanded not to marry the wicked inhabitants of the land because they would lead Israel into apostasy. However, if Israel obeys God's command, He will prosper them, show mercy to them, and heal them of their sicknesses.

CHAPTER 7

Israel is to destroy the seven nations of Canaan—Marriages with them are forbidden lest apostasy result—Israel has a mission as a holy and chosen people—The Lord shows mercy unto those who love Him and keep His commandments—He promises to remove sickness from the children of Israel if they obey.

CHAPTER 8

The Lord tested the children of Israel in the wilderness for forty years—Eating manna taught them that man lives by the word of God—Their clothing did not wear out—The Lord chastened them—If they serve other gods, they will perish.

Deuteronomy 8:1–10. Moses Reviews the Children of Israel's Desert Wandering

1 All the commandments which I command thee this day shall ye observe to do, that ye may live, and multiply, and go in and possess the land which the LORD sware unto your fathers.

2 And thou shalt remember all the way which the LORD thy God led thee these forty years in the wilderness, to humble thee, *and* to prove thee, to know what *was* in thine heart, whether thou wouldest keep his commandments, or no.

3 And he humbled thee, and suffered thee to hunger, and fed thee with manna, which thou knewest not, neither did thy fathers know; that he might make thee know that man doth not live by bread only, but by every *word* that proceedeth out of the mouth of the LORD doth man live.

What lesson did the Lord teach the children of Israel by giving them manna? (8:3) "Feeding with manna is called a humiliation, inasmuch as God intended to show to the people . . . that man does not live by bread alone, that the power to sustain life does not rest upon bread only . . . , or belong simply to it, but to all that goeth forth out of the mouth of Jehovah. . . . Hence all means [are] designed and appointed by the Lord for the sustenance of life. In this sense Christ quotes these words in reply to the tempter (Matthew 4:4). . . . The Messiah lives not by (material) bread only, but by the fulfilment of the will of God, or by trusting in the sustaining word of God" (Keil and Delitzsch, *Commentary* [on Deuteronomy 8:3]).

4 Thy raiment waxed not old upon thee, neither did thy foot swell, these forty years.

5 Thou shalt also consider in thine heart, that, as a man chasteneth his son, *so* the LORD thy God chasteneth thee.

6 Therefore thou shalt keep the commandments of the LORD thy God, to walk in his ways, and to fear him.

7 For the LORD thy God bringeth thee into a good land, a land of brooks of water, of fountains and depths that spring out of valleys and hills;

8 A land of wheat, and barley, and vines, and fig trees, and pomegranates; a land of oil olive, and honey;

9 A land wherein thou shalt eat bread without scarceness, thou shalt not lack any *thing* in it; a land whose stones *are* iron, and out of whose hills thou mayest dig brass.

10 When thou hast eaten and art full, then thou shalt bless the LORD thy God for the good land which he hath given thee.

11 Beware that thou forget not the LORD thy God, in not keeping his commandments, and his judgments, and his statutes, which I command thee this day:

12 Lest *when* thou hast eaten and art full, and hast built goodly houses, and dwelt *therein;*

What is meant by "thy raiment waxed not old upon thee"? (8:4) "The words used by Moses affirm the idea that the clothes of the Israelites did not wear out because God gave them a miraculous durability. Some early rabbis and Christian theologians interpreted this passage to mean that the clothes of the younger generation grew upon their backs like the shells of snails. Israel did, however, have limited means for producing some items of clothing" (*Old Testament Student Manual: Genesis–2 Samuel*, 220).

Why was water one of the first things mentioned about the promised land? (8:7) "The description of the land contained in these verses is expressed in glowing terms; it has been suggested, quite plausibly, that the description may be modelled on, or even quoted from, a hymn-like poem extolling the beauties of the land. There is first a description of the bountiful water supply of the land (*brooks of water, springs and deep waters*), which stands in contrast to the dryness of the desert mentioned in the previous verses" (Craigie, *Book of Deuteronomy*, 158). ⊕

Why might this list of produce in the promised land have been encouraging to the Israelites? (8:8) "The gifts of God in the rich and beautiful land of Canaan are a motive to thankfulness and obedience" (*John Dummelow's Commentary* [on Deuteronomy 8:7–9]). "These products—grapes, olives, and wheat—were the staple produce of the eastern Mediterranean lands, and in fact it has been said that the Israelites did not colonize any area where these three products would not grow together. Other main types of produce grown in Israel anciently are mentioned . . . barley, figs, pomegranates, and honey. Wheat was grown successfully in the fairly well watered highland areas of Samaria and, east of the Jordan River, in Gilead. In areas of less rainfall south of Jerusalem, barley was grown" (Lundquist, "Life in Ancient Biblical Lands," 40).

Deuteronomy 8:11–20. If Israel Serves Other Gods, Israel Will Perish

Why is prosperity spiritually dangerous in any generation? (8:11–14) "Affluence, prosperity, and ease can be tests in our day equal to or greater in intensity than the persecution and physical hardships endured by the Saints who volunteered to march in Zion's Camp. . . . Now is the time to show that we are watching and preparing to withstand the latter-day trials of prosperity and pride, of affluence and ease, and of hard hearts and forgetting the Lord our God.

Now is the time to show that we will be true at all times in whatsoever things we are entrusted by our Heavenly Father and His Beloved Son" (Bednar, "Who's on the Lord's Side?"). ⊕

What were fiery serpents? (8:15) "Much has been written on the question of the 'fiery serpents' of [Num. 21:6, 8; see also Deuteronomy 8:15], with which, it is usual to erroneously identify, the 'fiery flying serpent' of [Isa. 14:29 and 30:6]. The word 'fiery' probably signifies 'burning,' in allusion to the sensation produced by the bite" (*Smith's Bible Dictionary*, "Serpent").

How can we avoid pride in our accomplishments and possessions? (8:17) "Before enjoying the harvests of righteous efforts, let us therefore first acknowledge God's hand. Otherwise, the rationalizations appear, and they include, 'My power and the might of mine hand hath gotten me this wealth' (Deuteronomy 8:17). Or, we 'vaunt' ourselves, as ancient Israel would have done (except for Gideon's deliberately small army), by boasting that 'mine own hand hath saved me' (Judges 7:2). Touting our own 'hand' makes it doubly hard to confess God's hand in all things (see Alma 14:11; D&C 59:21)" (Maxwell, "Consecrate Thy Performance," 37).

How are idolatry and prosperity interwoven? (8:18–20) Prosperity "is a curse in disguise. Prosperity *per se* is not an enemy to religion, but prosperity may often lead to idolatry. The danger of all progress is idolatry, because the temptation all of the time is to set up something in the place of God. And the more tempting the progress is—and material prosperity is tempting—the more dangerous it is. Think of the idols of prosperity: the car, the camper, the boat (bane of bishops), the color TV, the football game, two weeks of hunting. These become idols when more enthusiasm and time are given to them than to the worship of God" (King, *Abundance of the Heart*, 48).

13 And *when* thy herds and thy flocks multiply, and thy silver and thy gold is multiplied, and all that thou hast is multiplied;

14 Then thine heart be lifted up, and thou forget the LORD thy God, which brought thee forth out of the land of Egypt, from the house of bondage;

15 Who led thee through that great and terrible wilderness, *wherein were* fiery serpents, and scorpions, and drought, where *there was* no water; who brought thee forth water out of the rock of flint;

16 Who fed thee in the wilderness with manna, which thy fathers knew not, that he might humble thee, and that he might prove thee, to do thee good at thy latter end;

17 And thou say in thine heart, My power and the might of *mine* hand hath gotten me this wealth.

18 But thou shalt remember the LORD thy God: for *it is* he that giveth thee power to get wealth, that he may establish his covenant which he sware unto thy fathers, as *it is* this day.

19 And it shall be, if thou do at all forget the LORD thy God, and walk after other gods, and serve them, and worship them, I testify against you this day that ye shall surely perish.

20 As the nations which the LORD destroyeth before your face, so shall ye perish; because ye would not be obedient unto the voice of the LORD your God.

CHAPTER 9

Other nations are driven out of Canaan because of their wickedness—Moses rehearses the rebellions of Israel and tells how he mediated between the people and the Lord—On two occasions he went without food and water for forty days.

1 Hear, O Israel: Thou *art* to pass over Jordan this day, to go in to possess nations greater and mightier than thyself, cities great and fenced up to heaven,

2 A people great and tall, the children of the Anakims, whom thou knowest, and *of whom* thou hast heard *say,* Who can stand before the children of Anak!

3 Understand therefore this day, that the LORD thy God *is* he which goeth over before thee; *as* a consuming fire he shall destroy them, and he shall bring them down before thy face: so shalt thou drive them out, and destroy them quickly, as the LORD hath said unto thee.

4 Speak not thou in thine heart, after that the LORD thy God hath cast them out from before thee, saying, For my righteousness the LORD hath brought me in to possess this land: but for the wickedness of these nations the LORD doth drive them out from before thee.

5 Not for thy righteousness, or for the uprightness of thine heart, dost thou go to possess their land: but for the wickedness of these nations the LORD thy God doth drive them out from before thee, and that he may perform the word which the LORD sware unto thy fathers, Abraham, Isaac, and Jacob.

6 Understand therefore, that the LORD thy God giveth thee not this good land to possess it for thy righteousness; for thou *art* a stiffnecked people.

Deuteronomy 9:1–6. The Wicked Canaanites Are Driven from the Promised Land

Why did the surrounding nations fear the children of Anak? (9:2) The name Anakim means "long necked" and refers to an ancient people who were considered a giant race. Goliath of Gath whom young David slew with a sling may have descended from this race (see Bible Dictionary, "Giants").

Why did the Lord not allow these nations to inherit the land? (9:4) "Moses and the Lord wanted Israel to know that it is not because of favoritism that one nation is displaced by another by the hand of the Lord. It was earlier revealed to Abraham that his seed could not inherit the land promised as long as 'the iniquity of the Amorites is not yet full' (Gen. 15:16; 1 Ne. 17:33–35). Even in Moses' time, Israelites were only relatively righteous compared to Canaanites; thus, they were warned not to pride themselves on their own supposed worthiness (Deut. 9:4–5)" (Rasmussen, *Latter-day Saint Commentary on the Old Testament*, 175).

Why is Moses so harsh with the Israelites? (9:6) "Moses' castigation of Israel for disobedience was proportionate to the great amount of light they had received. If no law had been given, then no disobedience would have been possible. But, as modern Israel learned: 'Unto whom much is given much is required; and he who sins against the greater light shall receive the greater condemnation' (D&C 82:3–4). One must read Moses' comments regarding Israel's persistent disobedience in the light of their high calling and their great revelations. Similarly, the Lord in the Doctrine and Covenants often scolded his modern Saints" (Meservy, "Good News of Moses," 211–12).

Summary of Deuteronomy 9:7–29

Moses reminds Israel that many of their fathers succumbed to temptation, created a golden calf, and worshipped it. Still, not only does Moses plead with the Lord not to destroy Israel (see Exodus 32), but to redeem them "through thy greatness, which thou hast brought forth out of Egypt with a mighty hand" (Deuteronomy 9:26).

Summary of Deuteronomy 10

After reviewing with the children of Israel why a second set of stone tablets was given, Moses explains that this second set of tablets was placed in the ark of the covenant as a reminder to Israel of all that God had done for them. The Joseph Smith Translation notes that the second set of tablets were the same "save the words of the everlasting covenant of the holy priesthood" (JST, Deuteronomy 10:1–2).

Deuteronomy 11:1–9. Israel Is to Love the Lord and Keep His Commandments

Why does Moses recount several episodes from Israel's exodus from Egypt? (11:2–8) "Forgetting God has been such a persistent problem among His children since the world began. Think of the times of Moses, when God provided manna and in miraculous and visible ways led and protected His children. Still, the prophet warned the people who had been so blessed . . . 'Take heed to thyself, and keep thy soul diligently, lest thou forget the things which thine eyes have seen, and lest they depart from thy heart all the days of thy life' (Deuteronomy 4:9)" (Eyring, "O Remember, Remember," 67). "Throughout the scriptures the Lord asks us to *remember*. Remembering our shared legacy of faith, devotion, and perseverance gives us perspective and strength as we face the challenges of our day" ("Message from the First Presidency," in *Saints*, 1:xv).

CHAPTER 10

The tables of stone containing the Ten Commandments are placed in the ark—All that God requires is that Israel love and serve Him—How great and mighty is the Lord!

CHAPTER 11

Thou shalt love and obey the Lord thy God—If the children of Israel obey, they will be blessed with rain and harvests and will drive out mighty nations—Israel must learn God's laws and teach them—Blessings flow from obedience; cursings attend disobedience.

1 Therefore thou shalt love the LORD thy God, and keep his charge, and his statutes, and his judgments, and his commandments, alway.

2 And know ye this day: for *I speak* not with your children which have not known, and which have not seen the chastisement of the LORD your God, his greatness, his mighty hand, and his stretched out arm,

3 And his miracles, and his acts, which he did in the midst of Egypt unto Pharaoh the king of Egypt, and unto all his land;

4 And what he did unto the army of Egypt, unto their horses, and to their chariots; how he made the water of the Red sea to overflow them as they pursued after you, and *how* the LORD hath destroyed them unto this day;

5 And what he did unto you in the wilderness, until ye came into this place;

6 And what he did unto Dathan and Abiram, the sons of Eliab, the son of Reuben: how the earth opened her mouth, and swallowed them up, and their households, and their tents, and all the substance that *was* in their possession, in the midst of all Israel:

7 But your eyes have seen all the great acts of the LORD which he did.

8 Therefore shall ye keep all the commandments which I command you this day, that ye may be strong, and go in and possess the land, whither ye go to possess it;

9 And that ye may prolong *your* days in the land, which the LORD sware unto your fathers to give unto them and to their seed, a land that floweth with milk and honey.

What is the purpose of remembering sacred history? (11:8) "Within this section of Deuteronomy, a few principles are mightily emphasized. . . . While reminding them of the danger of a pride or wickedness cycle, God also showed Israel a righteousness cycle and pled with them to be part of that. If Israel would just remember God, it would keep them on a cycle that would spiral them to unimaginable blessings. The elements of this cycle as outlined in Deuteronomy are strikingly similar to the sacrament prayers, which promise that if we remember and obey we will receive the greatest of blessings that will help us continue to remember and obey" (Muhlestein, *Scripture Study Made Simple*, 140).

10 ¶ For the land, whither thou goest in to possess it, *is* not as the land of Egypt, from whence ye came out, where thou sowedst thy seed, and wateredst *it* with thy foot, as a garden of herbs:

11 But the land, whither ye go to possess it, *is* a land of hills and valleys, *and* drinketh water of the rain of heaven:

12 A land which the LORD thy God careth for: the eyes of the LORD thy God *are* always upon it, from the beginning of the year even unto the end of the year.

13 ¶ And it shall come to pass, if ye shall hearken diligently unto my commandments which I command you this day, to love the LORD your God, and to serve him with all your heart and with all your soul,

Deuteronomy 11:10–21. The Lord Promises Blessings for Obedience

What does it mean to drink "water of the rain of heaven"? (11:11) "In Egypt, the land could be made to produce a crop from the planted seed only when it was irrigated by artificial means. *You used to sow your seed and water it with your foot, like a vegetable garden*—the reference to watering the land by foot probably reflects the practice of marking the ground with footdug channels, through which irrigating water would flow. In the promised land, a vegetable garden might be watered artificially (11:10b), but in contrast, virtually the whole Egyptian agricultural system depended on irrigation. The land the Israelites were about to possess was watered directly by *the rain of heaven* (v. 11). In the promised land, therefore, they would be dependent not on human techniques, but on the provision of God" (Craigie, *Book of Deuteronomy*, 178).

Why is the promise of rain for their land important to Israel? (11:14) "Deity intervenes in temporal things, even controlling and moderating the elements for the faithful. True, he makes the sun to shine and sends his rains upon the just and the unjust (Matthew 5:45), . . . but he maintains special watch care over those who by obedience and righteousness become his especial friends. For them storms are stilled, barren soil becomes productive (Isaiah 35), special needed rains fall and bounteous harvests mature (Lev. 26:3–5; Deut. 11:13–15; 28:11–12), vines do not cast off their ripened fruits untimely (Mal. 3:11), climatic conditions of whole regions are changed, mountains are moved, and rivers are turned out of their courses. (Moses 6:34; 7:13–14)" (McConkie, *Doctrinal New Testament Commentary*, 1:307).

What is the first rain and the latter rain? (11:14) "By the *first* or *former* rain we are to understand that which fell in Judea about November, when they sowed their seed, and this served to moisten and prepare the ground for the vegetation of the seed. The *latter rain* fell about April, when the corn was well grown up, and served to fill the ears, and render them plump and perfect. Rain rarely fell in Judea at any other seasons than these. If the *former* rain were withheld, or not sent in due season, there could be no vegetation: if the *latter rain* were withheld, or not sent in its *due season*, there could be no full corn in the ear, and consequently no harvest" (*Adam Clarke's Commentary* [on Deuteronomy 11:14]).

Where does God want His children to bind His words? (11:18) "God had commanded Israel to show their love for God by binding His law 'upon thine hand,' and 'between thine eyes,' and 'upon the posts of thy house' (Deuteronomy 6:8–9). Some Jews still do this literally by wearing phylacteries and placing mezuzahs on their doorposts. In a similar way, children can place their parents' teachings in their heart and express those teachings in their day-to-day actions" (Valletta, et al., *Old Testament for Latter-day Saint Families*, 452).

14 That I will give *you* the rain of your land in his due season, the first rain and the latter rain, that thou mayest gather in thy corn, and thy wine, and thine oil.

15 And I will send grass in thy fields for thy cattle, that thou mayest eat and be full.

16 Take heed to yourselves, that your heart be not deceived, and ye turn aside, and serve other gods, and worship them;

17 And *then* the LORD's wrath be kindled against you, and he shut up the heaven, that there be no rain, and that the land yield not her fruit; and *lest* ye perish quickly from off the good land which the LORD giveth you.

18 ¶ Therefore shall ye lay up these my words in your heart and in your soul, and bind them for a sign upon your hand, that they may be as frontlets between your eyes.

19 And ye shall teach them your children, speaking of them when thou sittest in thine house, and when thou walkest by the way, when thou liest down, and when thou risest up.

20 And thou shalt write them upon the door posts of thine house, and upon thy gates:

21 That your days may be multiplied, and the days of your children, in the land which the LORD sware unto your fathers to give them, as the days of heaven upon the earth.

22 ¶ For if ye shall diligently keep all these
commandments which I command you, to
do them, to love the LORD your God, to walk
in all his ways, and to cleave unto him;

23 Then will the LORD drive out all these nations from before you, and ye shall possess
greater nations and mightier than yourselves.

24 Every place whereon the soles of your feet
shall tread shall be yours: from the wilderness and Lebanon, from the river, the river
Euphrates, even unto the uttermost sea shall
your coast be.

25 There shall no man be able to stand before you: *for* the LORD your God shall lay the
fear of you and the dread of you upon all the
land that ye shall tread upon, as he hath said
unto you.

26 ¶ Behold, I set before you this day a blessing and a curse;

27 A blessing, if ye obey the commandments
of the LORD your God, which I command
you this day:

28 And a curse, if ye will not obey the commandments of the LORD your God, but turn
aside out of the way which I command you
this day, to go after other gods, which ye have
not known.

29 And it shall come to pass, when the LORD
thy God hath brought thee in unto the land
whither thou goest to possess it, that thou
shalt put the blessing upon mount Gerizim,
and the curse upon mount Ebal.

30 *Are* they not on the other side Jordan, by
the way where the sun goeth down, in the land
of the Canaanites, which dwell in the cham-
paign over against Gilgal, beside the plains of
Moreh?

31 For ye shall pass over Jordan to go in to
possess the land which the LORD your God

Deuteronomy 11:22–32. Blessings Follow Obedience; Curses Follow Disobedience

Why did the Lord set before Israel both a blessing and a curse? (11:26) "Let us remember that with every commandment, God has promised a blessing. If we expect to claim the blessing, we must keep the commandment. Otherwise, if we ignore or break the commandment, we are cursed by losing the blessing. . . . It is a very simple but serious arrangement" (Asay, "Oath and Covenant of the Priesthood," 44). "There is a law, irrevocably decreed in heaven before the foundations of this world, upon which all blessings are predicated—and when we obtain any blessing from God, it is by obedience to that law upon which it is predicated" (D&C 130:20–21).

How did the Lord illustrate the blessings and curses? (11:29) "The children of Israel were to gather in the center of the land of promise, in a valley at Shechem between Mount Ebal on the north and Mount Gerizim on the south; half were to be on the slope of each mountain to hear from Ebal lists of evils that would lead to curses and from Gerizim lists of good deeds that would bring blessings. This place for launching the commonwealth of Israel was also the place of Abraham's first altar in the land of promise, and it was the place of Jacob's first camp upon arriving back from Haran, where he also built an altar (Deut. 11:29*a–b*; Gen. 12:6–7; 33:18–20)" (Rasmussen, *Latter-day Saint Commentary on the Old Testament*, 177). See commentary in this volume for Deuteronomy 27:11–14.

giveth you, and ye shall possess it, and dwell therein.

32 And ye shall observe to do all the statutes and judgments which I set before you this day.

CHAPTER 12

Israel is to destroy the Canaanite gods and places of worship—The Lord will designate where His people will worship—The eating of blood is forbidden—Israel's worship must conform to the divine standard.

1 These *are* the statutes and judgments, which ye shall observe to do in the land, which the LORD God of thy fathers giveth thee to possess it, all the days that ye live upon the earth.

2 Ye shall utterly destroy all the places, wherein the nations which ye shall possess served their gods, upon the high mountains, and upon the hills, and under every green tree:

3 And ye shall overthrow their altars, and break their pillars, and burn their groves with fire; and ye shall hew down the graven images of their gods, and destroy the names of them out of that place.

4 Ye shall not do so unto the LORD your God.

5 But unto the place which the LORD your God shall choose out of all your tribes to put his name there, *even* unto his habitation shall ye seek, and thither thou shalt come:

6 And thither ye shall bring your burnt offerings, and your sacrifices, and your tithes, and heave offerings of your hand, and your vows, and your freewill offerings, and the firstlings of your herds and of your flocks:

7 And there ye shall eat before the LORD your God, and ye shall rejoice in all that ye put

Deuteronomy 12:1–16. Israel Is Commanded to Destroy the Canaanite Gods and Establish the Worship of Jehovah

Why was it necessary to destroy everything connected with idol worship? (12:2–3) "The conduct of the Canaanites in almost every respect was abhorrent to the God of Heaven. Their depravity exceeded that of Egypt and the other great nations of the world. . . . The worship of Baal, Ashteroth, and similar deities was unbridled among the inhabitants of the land of Canaan. Whole regions of the country were dedicated to the licentious practices in which the devotees reveled. The children of Israel were to eradicate any evidence that such rituals had ever taken place. Groves, shrines, objects of sacrifice, and even the nomenclature were to be completely erased from the land, lest any of the covenant people be enticed to sin" (Hyde, *Comprehensive Commentary [Deuteronomy]*, 81–82). ⊕

Why is it important for the Lord to choose the place of His worship? (12:5) "Whereas the heathen seeks and worships his nature-gods, . . . the place of [the true God's] worship depended upon the choice which God Himself should make, and which would be made known by the fact that He 'put His name,' i.e., actually manifested His own immediate presence, in one definite spot. . . . The unity of the worship, therefore, which Moses here enjoined, was not to consist in the fact that the people of Israel brought all their sacrificial offerings to the tabernacle, but in their offering them only in the spot where the Lord made His name (that is to say, His presence) known" (Keil and Delitzsch, *Commentary* [on Deuteronomy 12:4–5]). ⊕

your hand unto, ye and your households, wherein the LORD thy God hath blessed thee.

8 Ye shall not do after all *the things* that we do here this day, every man whatsoever *is* right in his own eyes.

9 For ye are not as yet come to the rest and to the inheritance, which the LORD your God giveth you.

10 But *when* ye go over Jordan, and dwell in the land which the LORD your God giveth you to inherit, and *when* he giveth you rest from all your enemies round about, so that ye dwell in safety;

11 Then there shall be a place which the LORD your God shall choose to cause his name to dwell there; thither shall ye bring all that I command you; your burnt offerings, and your sacrifices, your tithes, and the heave offering of your hand, and all your choice vows which ye vow unto the LORD:

12 And ye shall rejoice before the LORD your God, ye, and your sons, and your daughters, and your menservants, and your maidservants, and the Levite that *is* within your gates; forasmuch as he hath no part nor inheritance with you.

13 Take heed to thyself that thou offer not thy burnt offerings in every place that thou seest:

14 But in the place which the LORD shall choose in one of thy tribes, there thou shalt offer thy burnt offerings, and there thou shalt do all that I command thee.

15 Notwithstanding thou mayest kill and eat flesh in all thy gates, whatsoever thy soul lusteth after, according to the blessing of the LORD thy God which he hath given thee: the unclean and the clean may eat thereof, as of the roebuck, and as of the hart.

16 Only ye shall not eat the blood; ye shall pour it upon the earth as water.

Instead of land, what did the Lord reserve for the Levites? (12:12) "The Levites were dedicated to the service of the Lord to execute the ordinances for the children of Israel. The Levites were themselves offered on behalf of the children of Israel (Num. 8:11–22); they thus became God's peculiar property, given to Him in place of the firstborn (Num. 8:16).... They had no land inheritance in Canaan (Num. 18:23–24), but they received the tithe (Num. 18:21), forty-eight cities [with the surrounding areas for their fields and pastures; see Numbers 35:2–7], and a right to receive the alms of the people at feast times (Deut. 12:18–19; 14:27–29)" (Guide to the Scriptures, "Levi").

Summary of Deuteronomy 12:17–28

The Lord establishes guidelines for the consumption of sacrificial offerings.

Deuteronomy 12:29–32. The Lord Warns the Israelites to Do as He Has Commanded

29 ¶ When the LORD thy God shall cut off
the nations from before thee, whither thou
goest to possess them, and thou succeedest
them, and dwellest in their land;

30 Take heed to thyself that thou be not
snared by following them, after that they be
destroyed from before thee; and that thou inquire not after their gods, saying, How did
these nations serve their gods? even so will I
do likewise.

What dangers come with inquiring after false worship practices? (12:30) "Nothing was to remain of the wicked practices that had been perpetrated by the former inhabitants of Canaan in their desires to serve the spirit of the natural man. Curiosity was not to be an excuse for delving into the rituals of the heathen. No doubt there were those who wished to seem sophisticated and objectively learned in their acquisition of knowledge. The Lord, however, made it clear that their inquisitiveness would ultimately destroy them if they succumbed to that kind of thinking" (Hyde, *Comprehensive Commentary [Deuteronomy]*, 87).

31 Thou shalt not do so unto the LORD thy
God: for every abomination to the LORD,
which he hateth, have they done unto their
gods; for even their sons and their daughters
they have burnt in the fire to their gods.

Which false Canaanite god required the burning of children as an act of worship? (12:31) Molech was a "Semitic deity honored by the sacrifice of children, in which they were caused to pass through or into the fire. Palestinian excavations have uncovered evidences of infant skeletons in burial places around heathen shrines. . . . Worship of Molech was stringently prohibited by Hebrew law (Lev. 18:21; 20:1–5). . . . No form of ancient Semitic idolatry was more abhorrent than Molech worship" (*New Unger's Bible Dictionary,* 488).

32 What thing soever I command you, observe to do it: thou shalt not add thereto, nor
diminish from it.

What did Moses mean that nothing could be added or diminished from what he commanded? (12:32) "A careful reading . . . of these [scriptural] admonitions makes it clear that *man* is not to make changes in the revelations of the Lord: *man* is not to add to or take from the words of God. There is no indication or intimation that God could not, or would not, add to or take from; nor would any reasonable person with a belief in the divine powers of God consciously believe that God would be so restricted. Without question he would have the right and power to give additional revelation for the guidance of his children in any age and to add additional scripture" (Hunter, "No Man Shall Add to or Take Away," 65). See commentary in this volume for Deuteronomy 4:2.

CHAPTER 13

The Lord tests His people to see if they will worship false gods—Prophets, dreamers, relatives, or friends who advocate worship of false gods will be put to death—Idolatrous cities will be destroyed.

1 If there arise among you a prophet, or a
dreamer of dreams, and giveth thee a sign or
a wonder,

2 And the sign or the wonder come to pass,
whereof he spake unto thee, saying, Let us go
after other gods, which thou hast not known,
and let us serve them;

3 Thou shalt not hearken unto the words of
that prophet, or that dreamer of dreams: for
the LORD your God proveth you, to know
whether ye love the LORD your God with all
your heart and with all your soul.

4 Ye shall walk after the LORD your God, and
fear him, and keep his commandments, and
obey his voice, and ye shall serve him, and
cleave unto him.

5 And that prophet, or that dreamer of
dreams, shall be put to death; because he hath
spoken to turn *you* away from the LORD your
God, which brought you out of the land of
Egypt, and redeemed you out of the house of
bondage, to thrust thee out of the way which
the LORD thy God commanded thee to walk
in. So shalt thou put the evil away from the
midst of thee.

6 ¶ If thy brother, the son of thy mother, or
thy son, or thy daughter, or the wife of thy
bosom, or thy friend, which *is* as thine own
soul, entice thee secretly, saying, Let us go
and serve other gods, which thou hast not
known, thou, nor thy fathers;

7 *Namely,* of the gods of the people which *are*
round about you, nigh unto thee, or far off
from thee, from the *one* end of the earth even
unto the *other* end of the earth;

Deuteronomy 13:1–5. Israel Is Warned against Heeding False Prophets

What are some ways we can discern false prophets? (13:1–3) "Let us beware of false prophets and false teachers, both men and women, who are self-appointed declarers of the doctrines of the Church and who seek to spread their false gospel and attract followers. . . . Beware of those who speak and publish in opposition to God's true prophets and who actively proselyte others with reckless disregard for the eternal well-being of those whom they seduce. . . . They 'set themselves up for a light unto the world, that they may get gain and praise of the world; but they seek not the welfare of Zion' (2 Ne. 26:29)" (Ballard, "Beware of False Prophets and False Teachers," 63). See commentary in this volume for Deuteronomy 18:22. ⊕

Deuteronomy 13:6–11. Individuals Who Entice Others to Serve False Gods Are Subject to the Death Penalty

Why was a serious penalty and required report needed for those who turned others away from the Lord? (13:6–10) "The teacher of idolatry was to be put to death; . . . because this was the highest offense that could be committed against God, and the most destructive to society; hence the severest laws were enacted against it" (*Adam Clarke's Commentary* [on Deuteronomy 13:6]). In the light of Israel's social structure based on the extended family, one relative had significant potential to influence other relatives for evil or for good. "By exterminating the guilty party, they . . . remove the evil (and evil influence) from the midst of the covenantal nation as a sobering deterrent for others" (Grisanti, "Deuteronomy," 2:622). ⊕

8 Thou shalt not consent unto him, nor hearken unto him; neither shall thine eye pity him, neither shalt thou spare, neither shalt thou conceal him:

9 But thou shalt surely kill him; thine hand shall be first upon him to put him to death, and afterwards the hand of all the people.

10 And thou shalt stone him with stones, that he die; because he hath sought to thrust thee away from the LORD thy God, which brought thee out of the land of Egypt, from the house of bondage.

11 And all Israel shall hear, and fear, and shall do no more any such wickedness as this is among you.

Deuteronomy 13:12–18. Penalties for Cities or Communities Guilty of Idol Worship Are Set Forth

12 ¶ If thou shalt hear *say* in one of thy cities, which the LORD thy God hath given thee to dwell there, saying,

13 *Certain* men, the children of Belial, are gone out from among you, and have withdrawn the inhabitants of their city, saying, Let us go and serve other gods, which ye have not known;

14 Then shalt thou inquire, and make search, and ask diligently; and, behold, *if it be* truth, *and* the thing certain, *that* such abomination is wrought among you;

15 Thou shalt surely smite the inhabitants of that city with the edge of the sword, destroying it utterly, and all that *is* therein, and the cattle thereof, with the edge of the sword.

16 And thou shalt gather all the spoil of it into the midst of the street thereof, and shalt burn with fire the city, and all the spoil thereof every whit, for the LORD thy God: and it shall be an heap for ever; it shall not be built again.

17 And there shall cleave nought of the cursed thing to thine hand: that the LORD may turn from the fierceness of his anger, and shew

Why would an Israelite community that worshipped false gods have to be completely destroyed? (13:15–16) "The Lord had designated the promised land as holy, but it had been occupied for hundreds of years by people who refused to obey His commandments. To prevent the Israelites from being contaminated by the wickedness of those people, the Lord gave the Israelites specific instructions as they prepared to enter the promised land" (*Old Testament Seminary Teacher Material* [2018], 370). If a community became "unholy" and fell into apostasy by worshipping false gods, the community would be under the same condemnation as the Canaanites and be destroyed.

What is the "cursed thing"? (13:17) The term *cursed* in this context "refers to anything sacrificed to idols or made to represent an idol or made to be used in the

thee mercy, and have compassion upon thee, and multiply thee, as he hath sworn unto thy fathers;

18 When thou shalt hearken to the voice of the LORD thy God, to keep all his commandments which I command thee this day, to do *that which is* right in the eyes of the LORD thy God.

CHAPTER 14

The Israelites are children of the Lord Jehovah—Unclean beasts, fish, and fowl are not to be eaten—The Israelites are to tithe all the increase of their seed annually.

1 Ye *are* the children of the LORD your God: ye shall not cut yourselves, nor make any baldness between your eyes for the dead.

2 For thou *art* an holy people unto the LORD thy God, and the LORD hath chosen thee to be a peculiar people unto himself, above all the nations that *are* upon the earth.

22 Thou shalt truly tithe all the increase of thy seed, that the field bringeth forth year by year.

23 And thou shalt eat before the LORD thy God, in the place which he shall choose to place his name there, the tithe of thy corn, of thy wine, and of thine oil, and the firstlings of thy herds and of thy flocks; that thou mayest learn to fear the LORD thy God always.

worship of idols. Cursed things were to be avoided by the Israelites altogether" (*Old Testament Student Manual: Genesis–2 Samuel*, 221). The serious nature of retaining those things the Lord called "cursed" is well documented in Joshua 7.

Deuteronomy 14:1–2. The Israelites Are a Holy People unto the Lord

Why were the pagan practices of cutting oneself and ritualistic shaving condemned? (14:1) "Because of their identity, God's chosen people need to manifest their distinctiveness by avoiding all pagan mourning practices. They are prohibited from self-mutilation . . . and shaving the front part of their heads [as a sign of mourning for the dead]. The prophets of Baal repeatedly cut themselves as a means of inciting Baal to action (1 Kings 18:28). . . . God demanded that Israel not cloud their identity as his special possession by accepting practices that had clear pagan connotations" (Grisanti, "Deuteronomy," 2:624–25).

Summary of Deuteronomy 14:3–21

Regulations given concerning clean and unclean beasts are reviewed. See commentary in this volume for Leviticus 11.

Deuteronomy 14:22–29. The Payment of Tithes and the Care of the Poor Are Outlined

Why has the Lord often commanded that we pay tithing? (14:22–23) "Tithing is a test of faith with eternal blessings. . . . Tithing has been established in these latter days as an essential law for members of the Lord's restored Church. It is one of the basic ways we witness our faith in Him and our obedience to His laws and commandments. . . . By sacrificing to the Lord what we may think we need or want for ourselves, we learn to rely on Him. . . . We learn to trust that what we have been given, through the blessings of the Lord and our own diligent efforts, is sufficient for our needs" (Hales, "Tithing," 26, 27). In what ways can your attitude about tithing influence your family? See commentary in this volume for Deuteronomy 26:12–15.

What tithing modifications were made for Israelites that lived far from the center of worship? (14:24–26) "The tithe, or tenth, of all increase, was ordinarily contributed 'in kind' [such as the firstlings of their flocks and herds, grain, wine, or oil]; but if the contributor lived too far from the place specified to take it, he could instead sell the tithing goods [and] carry the proceeds to the place of worship. . . . Therewith he could make his contributions and prepare the thank-feast associated with tithe-paying. Some of the food items contributed were to be used by the priests and Levites, and some were given to the poor" (Rasmussen, *Latter-day Saint Commentary on the Old Testament*, 179).

How could tithing funds be appropriately used to purchase items "lusted after"? (14:26) "In the [KJV], the phrase 'lusteth after' is used to translate a word meaning simply 'desires' or 'yearns for'" (Rasmussen, *Latter-day Saint Commentary on the Old Testament*, 179). Tithing funds could be used to purchase whatever items the giver needed in order to participate in the thanksgiving feast that accompanied tithe paying. In this context, the term does not have inappropriate connotations.

What provisions were made to care for the poor with tithing funds? (14:28–29) "Every third year . . . they were to separate the whole of the tithe from the year's produce ('bring forth,' sc., from the granary), and leaven it in their gates (i.e., their towns), and feed the Levites, the strangers, and the widows and orphans with it. They were not to take it to the sanctuary, therefore; but . . . , after bringing it out, were to make confession to the Lord of what they had done, and pray for His blessing" (Keil and Delitzsch, *Commentary* [on Deuteronomy 14:28–29]).

Deuteronomy 15:1–6. All Debts Are to Be Forgiven in a Sabbatical Year

What was the purpose of discharging the debts of their fellow Israelites? (15:1–6) "Israelites were not to exact repayment of loans from fellow Israelites beyond any sabbatical year; however, they were not expected to release strangers from their responsibility

24 And if the way be too long for thee, so that thou art not able to carry it; *or* if the place be too far from thee, which the LORD thy God shall choose to set his name there, when the LORD thy God hath blessed thee:

25 Then shalt thou turn *it* into money, and bind up the money in thine hand, and shalt go unto the place which the LORD thy God shall choose:

26 And thou shalt bestow that money for whatsoever thy soul lusteth after, for oxen, or for sheep, or for wine, or for strong drink, or for whatsoever thy soul desireth: and thou shalt eat there before the LORD thy God, and thou shalt rejoice, thou, and thine household,

27 And the Levite that *is* within thy gates; thou shalt not forsake him; for he hath no part nor inheritance with thee.

28 ¶ At the end of three years thou shalt bring forth all the tithe of thine increase the same year, and shalt lay *it* up within thy gates:

29 And the Levite, (because he hath no part nor inheritance with thee,) and the stranger, and the fatherless, and the widow, which *are* within thy gates, shall come, and shall eat and be satisfied; that the LORD thy God may bless thee in all the work of thine hand which thou doest.

CHAPTER 15

Every seven years, all debts are to be released—The people are admonished to care for the poor—Hebrew servants are to be released and given gifts during the seventh year—The firstling males of herds and flocks are the Lord's.

1 At the end of *every* seven years thou shalt make a release.

to repay. If Israelites would obey God's commandments, they would be blessed with prosperity and be able to lend to others and have no need of borrowing from them (Deut. 15:1*a–b*; 15:4*a*; Ex. 21:1–6; [Topical Guide], "Sabbatical Year")" (Rasmussen, *Latter-day Saint Commentary on the Old Testament*, 179).

2 And this *is* the manner of the release: Every creditor that lendeth *ought* unto his neighbour shall release *it;* he shall not exact *it* of his neighbour, or of his brother; because it is called the LORD's release.

3 Of a foreigner thou mayest exact *it again:* but *that* which is thine with thy brother thine hand shall release;

4 Save when there shall be no poor among you; for the LORD shall greatly bless thee in the land which the LORD thy God giveth thee *for* an inheritance to possess it:

5 Only if thou carefully hearken unto the voice of the LORD thy God, to observe to do all these commandments which I command thee this day.

6 For the LORD thy God blesseth thee, as he promised thee: and thou shalt lend unto many nations, but thou shalt not borrow; and thou shalt reign over many nations, but they shall not reign over thee.

7 ¶ If there be among you a poor man of one of thy brethren within any of thy gates in thy land which the LORD thy God giveth thee, thou shalt not harden thine heart, nor shut thine hand from thy poor brother:

8 But thou shalt open thine hand wide unto him, and shalt surely lend him sufficient for his need, *in that* which he wanteth.

9 Beware that there be not a thought in thy wicked heart, saying, The seventh year, the year of release, is at hand; and thine eye be

What can we learn from this symbolic pattern of debt forgiveness? (15:2) "As used in the scriptures, money or property owed to another causes the borrower to be in a form of bondage. In another sense, Jesus taught that we should ask the Father to forgive us our debts, or release us from paying the price for our sins—through the Atonement of Jesus Christ—after we have forgiven others for their offences against us (Matt. 6:12; 3 Ne. 13:11)" (Guide to the Scriptures, "Debt"). Are you willing to extend forgiveness to others, no matter the debt incurred? How might the Lord be inviting you to develop this Christlike characteristic?

Deuteronomy 15:7–11. The Poor Are to Be Treated with Compassion

How does the Lord expect us to treat the poor? (15:7–8) "To help others is the path of discipleship. Faith, hope, love, compassion, and service refine us as disciples. Through your efforts to help the poor and the needy, to reach out to those in distress, your own character is purified and forged, your spirit is enlarged, and you walk a little taller. But this love cannot come with expectations of repayment. It cannot be the kind of service that expects recognition, adulation, or favor. True disciples of Jesus Christ love God and His children without expectation of something in return" (Uchtdorf, "Your Great Adventure," 88). How might the Lord's invitations in Deuteronomy 12:7–8 and Mosiah 4:16–19 change how you treat the poor?

Why did Moses warn about having a "wicked heart" during a sabbatical year? (15:9–10) "If a man were to request aid at the beginning of a seven year cycle, the lender might be more than happy to serve as a creditor. The closer the year of release came, the more hesitant a natural man would find himself calculating his losses, pondering whether making the loan was worth his time and means. The lender was to avoid this sort of thinking at all hazards, because those sentiments would be the antithesis of the whole spirit of the Gospel of Jesus Christ. . . . If a man makes an earnest petition for help, the more fortunate man is under covenant to respond positively, without condemnation or recrimination" (Hyde, *Comprehensive Commentary [Deuteronomy]*, 96).

Deuteronomy 15:12–18. Servants Are to Be Released during the Sabbatical Year

Why might some of the slaves or servants be Hebrews? (15:12) "Being unable to provide for oneself (or experiencing some other financial distress) could lead a person voluntarily to become a slave (an 'indentured' servant) to obtain basic needs or to pay off a debt" (Grisanti, "Deuteronomy," 2:632). "Other slaves may have been the victims of war or extreme poverty" (Hyde, *Comprehensive Commentary [Deuteronomy]*, 96).

What was the responsibility of those who released servants? (15:14) "[The released servant] is not to be sent away empty, as the probable result would be a return to slavery. He is to be liberally furnished, so as to be in a position to earn a livelihood and make a fresh start in life. This is a very wise as well as humane prescription" (*John Dummelow's Commentary* [on Deuteronomy 15:12–18]). Honoring the service of the servant was also an opportunity to honor God (see Mosiah 4:17–21).

Why was a servant's ear pierced when they chose to stay in service? (15:17) "If a slave elect to remain in the master's service instead of accepting release, a formal compact must be made to that effect. In Exodus 21:6 the ceremony is performed in public before the magistrates; here it seems to be private. The boring of the ear and the fastening it to the doorpost with the awl [a sharp, pointed tool used to puncture holes in leather or wood] signified that the person was permanently attached to the house and was bound to obey the words of his master" (*John Dummelow's Commentary* [on Deuteronomy 15:16]).

evil against thy poor brother, and thou givest him nought; and he cry unto the LORD against thee, and it be sin unto thee.

10 Thou shalt surely give him, and thine heart shall not be grieved when thou givest unto him: because that for this thing the LORD thy God shall bless thee in all thy works, and in all that thou puttest thine hand unto.

11 For the poor shall never cease out of the land: therefore I command thee, saying, Thou shalt open thine hand wide unto thy brother, to thy poor, and to thy needy, in thy land.

12 ¶ *And* if thy brother, an Hebrew man, or an Hebrew woman, be sold unto thee, and serve thee six years; then in the seventh year thou shalt let him go free from thee.

13 And when thou sendest him out free from thee, thou shalt not let him go away empty:

14 Thou shalt furnish him liberally out of thy flock, and out of thy floor, and out of thy winepress: *of that* wherewith the LORD thy God hath blessed thee thou shalt give unto him.

15 And thou shalt remember that thou wast a bondman in the land of Egypt, and the LORD thy God redeemed thee: therefore I command thee this thing to day.

16 And it shall be, if he say unto thee, I will not go away from thee; because he loveth thee and thine house, because he is well with thee;

17 Then thou shalt take an awl, and thrust *it* through his ear unto the door, and he shall be thy servant for ever. And also unto thy maidservant thou shalt do likewise.

18 It shall not seem hard unto thee, when thou sendest him away free from thee; for he hath been worth a double hired servant *to thee,* in serving thee six years: and the LORD thy God shall bless thee in all that thou doest.

19 ¶ All the firstling males that come of thy herd and of thy flock thou shalt sanctify unto the LORD thy God: thou shalt do no work with the firstling of thy bullock, nor shear the firstling of thy sheep.

20 Thou shalt eat *it* before the LORD thy God year by year in the place which the LORD shall choose, thou and thy household.

21 And if there be *any* blemish therein, *as if it be* lame, or blind, *or have* any ill blemish, thou shalt not sacrifice it unto the LORD thy God.

22 Thou shalt eat it within thy gates: the unclean and the clean *person shall eat it* alike, as the roebuck, and as the hart.

23 Only thou shalt not eat the blood thereof; thou shalt pour it upon the ground as water.

Deuteronomy 15:19–23. All Firstling Males of Herds and Flocks Are to Be Dedicated to the Lord

Why were the firstborn bulls not allowed to work? (15:19–23) "The command, which the Lord had given when first they came out of Egypt (Exodus 13:2, 12), that all the first-born of the herd and flock should be sanctified to Him, is repeated here by Moses, with the express injunction that they were not to work with the first-born of cattle (by yoking them to the plough or wagon), and not to shear the first-born of sheep; that is to say, they were not to use the first-born animals which were sanctified to the Lord for their own earthly purposes, but to offer them year by year as sacrifices to the Lord, and consume them in sacrificial meals " (Keil and Delitzsch, *Commentary* [on Deuteronomy 15:19–23]).

CHAPTER 16

Israel is to keep the Passover, the Feast of Unleavened Bread, the Feast of Weeks, and the Feast of Tabernacles—All males are to appear annually before the Lord at these three feasts—Judges are not to make dishonest judgments nor take gifts.

Summary of Deuteronomy 16

Israel is commanded to observe three feasts to remind them of the Lord and their identity as God's chosen people. All Israelite men should travel to the central place of worship during these feasts "to appear before the Lord" (Deuteronomy 16:16). The king must study the laws of God daily.

CHAPTER 17

Those who worship false gods will be put to death—Priests and judges are to determine the hard cases—Kings are not to acquire horses, wives, or gold for themselves—The king must study the laws of God daily.

Summary of Deuteronomy 17:1–7

The death penalty is declared for those who worship idols.

Deuteronomy 17:8–13. Priests and Levites Are to Judge in Difficult Cases

How were the Levites and priests involved in judgment? (17:8–12) "Matters of judgment were part of the responsibility of the priests and Levites, along with teaching and officiating at the altars of the Lord. Theirs was a vital part of the Israelite government" (Rasmussen, *Latter-day Saint Commentary on the Old Testament*, 181). "The local judges and officials must relegate to the central tribunal, made up of priests and a chief judge, cases that are too difficult for them to adjudicate. This body will issue a binding decision, and all who fail to abide by it will face the death penalty. . . . The fundamental point is that whatever verdict is rendered by this central tribunal, its decision is totally nonnegotiable" (Grisanti, "Deuteronomy," 2:645).

How is the instruction to "come unto the priests" continued in our day? (17:9) "Modern bishops in the Church are judges in Israel (see D&C 58:14–17; 64:40). Upon their shoulders rests the heavy responsibility of hearing and judging cases involving Church membership or worthiness. Anciently, priests of the Aaronic Priesthood performed similar functions (see Deuteronomy 17:9)" (*Old Testament Student Manual: Genesis–2 Samuel*, 225).

Why was execution the punishment for not abiding by the imposed sentence? (17:12) "The man who refused to abide by this final determination forfeited his life, as being then in a state of rebellion against the highest authority, and consequently the public could have no pledge for his conduct" (*Adam Clarke's Commentary* [on Deuteronomy 17:12]). "These instructions may seem harsh and perhaps excessive to the modern mind, yet at the heart of that which was being commanded was the preservation of the meek and the innocent. Those who sought to usurp the authority of the Lord's anointed would receive swift judgment" (Hyde, *Comprehensive Commentary [Deuteronomy]*, 106).

8 ¶ If there arise a matter too hard for thee
in judgment, between blood and blood, between plea and plea, and between stroke and
stroke, *being* matters of controversy within
thy gates: then shalt thou arise, and get thee
up into the place which the LORD thy God
shall choose;

9 And thou shalt come unto the priests the
Levites, and unto the judge that shall be in
those days, and inquire; and they shall shew
thee the sentence of judgment:

10 And thou shalt do according to the sentence, which they of that place which the
LORD shall choose shall shew thee; and thou
shalt observe to do according to all that they
inform thee:

11 According to the sentence of the law
which they shall teach thee, and according to
the judgment which they shall tell thee, thou
shalt do: thou shalt not decline from the sentence which they shall shew thee, *to* the right
hand, nor *to* the left.

12 And the man that will do presumptuously, and will not hearken unto the priest
that standeth to minister there before the
LORD thy God, or unto the judge, even that
man shall die: and thou shalt put away the
evil from Israel.

13 And all the people shall hear, and fear,
and do no more presumptuously.

Deuteronomy 17:14–20. The Lord Instructs the Future Kings of Israel

How was an Israelite king to be selected? (17:15) "As a theocratic state, Israel's only true king was the

14 ¶ When thou art come unto the land
which the LORD thy God giveth thee, and
shalt possess it, and shalt dwell therein, and
shalt say, I will set a king over me, like as all
the nations that *are* about me;

15 Thou shalt in any wise set *him* king over
thee, whom the LORD thy God shall choose:

one from among thy brethren shalt thou set king over thee: thou mayest not set a stranger over thee, which *is* not thy brother.

16 But he shall not multiply horses to himself, nor cause the people to return to Egypt, to the end that he should multiply horses: forasmuch as the LORD hath said unto you, Ye shall henceforth return no more that way.

17 Neither shall he multiply wives to himself, that his heart turn not away: neither shall he greatly multiply to himself silver and gold.

18 And it shall be, when he sitteth upon the throne of his kingdom, that he shall write him a copy of this law in a book out of *that which is* before the priests the Levites:

19 And it shall be with him, and he shall read therein all the days of his life: that he may learn to fear the LORD his God, to keep all the words of this law and these statutes, to do them:

20 That his heart be not lifted up above his brethren, and that he turn not aside from the commandment, *to* the right hand, or *to* the left: to the end that he may prolong *his* days in his kingdom, he, and his children, in the midst of Israel.

Lord, and there was a sense in which it would seem presumptuous for a man to assume the title; the legislation given here makes certain that the king would remain aware both of his human status as a man among his brethren, and also of his status in relation to the kingship of God. . . . Just as the sanctuary's location would be chosen by God [see Deut. 12], so too would his royal representative be chosen. . . . Therefore, the office of the king would not be dependent on either popularity or military strength; it would be filled by a man approved by God" (Craigie, *Book of Deuteronomy,* 214, 215).

What influence could multiple wives have on a king? (17:17) Marriages between a king and foreign princesses "would necessarily lead to foreign alliances, and be the means of introducing the manners and customs of other nations, and their idolatry also. Solomon sinned against this precept, and brought ruin on himself and on the land by it; see 1 Kings 11:4" (*Adam Clarke's Commentary* [on Deuteronomy 17:17]). "A richly furnished harem, and the accumulation of silver and gold, were inseparably connected with the luxury of Oriental monarchs generally; so that the fear was a very natural one, that the future king of Israel might follow the general customs of the heathen in these respects" (Keil and Delitzsch, *Commentary* [on Deuteronomy 17:14–17]).

How would the anticipated king be guided? (17:18–20) "Moses mandates that as soon as a new king takes the throne of Israel, he must commission the making of a fresh copy of this covenantal text. Once the copy is made, the king must not live as though it does not exist. Rather, it must be with him and he must read it 'all the days of his life' [Deuteronomy 17:19]. . . . If he genuinely fears [God], he will consistently live in accordance with God's covenantal demands. He will realize that he, just like his fellow Israelites, is not above God's law" (Grisanti, "Deuteronomy," 2:647). King Benjamin epitomizes the example of a holy king guided by God and His laws (see Mosiah 2:10–19).

CHAPTER 18

How priests are supported—Divination, spiritualism, and the like are abominations—A Prophet (Christ) will arise like unto Moses.

Summary of Deuteronomy 18:1–8

The Levite priests are to be provided for by the other tribes of Israel so they can fulfill their call to be completely dedicated to God's service.

9 ¶ When thou art come into the land which the LORD thy God giveth thee, thou shalt not learn to do after the abominations of those nations.

10 There shall not be found among you *any one* that maketh his son or his daughter to pass through the fire, *or* that useth divination, *or* an observer of times, or an enchanter, or a witch,

11 Or a charmer, or a consulter with familiar spirits, or a wizard, or a necromancer.

12 For all that do these things *are* an abomination unto the LORD: and because of these abominations the LORD thy God doth drive them out from before thee.

13 Thou shalt be perfect with the LORD thy God.

14 For these nations, which thou shalt possess, hearkened unto observers of times, and unto diviners: but as for thee, the LORD thy God hath not suffered thee so *to do.*

Deuteronomy 18:9–14. Israel Is to Shun the Evil Beliefs and Practices of Canaan

What are the Canaanite abominations Israel is forbidden to practice? (18:9–12) "The Canaanites were a superstitious people who believed in and practiced divination and black magic. An enchanter inspects the entrails of dead animals, watches the flight of birds, or uses other means to predict the future. A charmer employs spells and incantations in predicting future events. Consulters with familiar spirits try to contact the spirit of a departed person to learn things not known to human beings. A wizard is a male witch. A necromancer, like one who consults with familiar spirits, seeks the secrets of the spirit world by inquiring of the dead. All of these activities were forbidden to ancient Israel. They were admonished to heed the words of their living prophet" (*Old Testament Student Manual: Genesis–2 Samuel*, 226).

15 ¶ The LORD thy God will raise up unto thee a Prophet from the midst of thee, of thy brethren, like unto me; unto him ye shall hearken;

16 According to all that thou desiredst of the LORD thy God in Horeb in the day of the assembly, saying, Let me not hear again

Deuteronomy 18:15–22. Moses Prophesies of Another Prophet Who Will Save Israel

What event is the Lord referring to in this verse? (18:16) "The Lord is referring to the time when the children of Israel feared to enter God's presence in an unworthy state at Mount Horeb [Sinai]. As in this case, a prophet becomes the spokesman for God to deliver

the voice of the LORD my God, neither let me see this great fire any more, that I die not.

17 And the LORD said unto me, They have well *spoken that* which they have spoken.

18 I will raise them up a Prophet from among their brethren, like unto thee, and will put my words in his mouth; and he shall speak unto them all that I shall command him.

19 And it shall come to pass, *that* whosoever will not hearken unto my words which he shall speak in my name, I will require *it* of him.

20 But the prophet, which shall presume to speak a word in my name, which I have not commanded him to speak, or that shall speak in the name of other gods, even that prophet shall die.

21 And if thou say in thine heart, How shall we know the word which the LORD hath not spoken?

22 When a prophet speaketh in the name of the LORD, if the thing follow not, nor come to pass, that *is* the thing which the LORD hath not spoken, *but* the prophet hath spoken it presumptuously: thou shalt not be afraid of him.

CHAPTER 19

Cities of refuge are appointed for cases of manslaughter—Murderers will be put to death—Two or three witnesses are required in court cases—False witnesses will be punished.

His words to the people (see Exodus 20:19)" (Valletta, et al., *Old Testament for Latter-day Saint Families*, 205).

Who is the prophet like unto Moses? (18:18–19) "At least four other scriptures refer to the prophet like unto Moses (see Acts 3:22–23; 1 Nephi 22:21; 3 Nephi 20:23; JS–H 1:40). In each instance these scriptures make it clear that the prophet like unto Moses was the Savior, Jesus Christ. When Jesus visited the Nephites, . . . he identified himself in this way: 'Behold, I am he of whom Moses spake, saying: A prophet shall the Lord your God raise up unto you of your brethren, like unto me; him shall ye hear in all things whatsoever he shall say unto you. And it shall come to pass that every soul who will not hear that prophet shall be cut off from among the people' (3 Nephi 20:23)" (*Old Testament Student Manual: Genesis–2 Samuel*, 226).

How can we discern a true prophet? (18:22) "*When is a prophet a prophet? Whenever he speaks under the inspiration and influence of the Holy Ghost. . . .* When prophets write and speak on the principles of the gospel, they should have the guidance of the Spirit. If they do, then all that they say will be in harmony with the revealed word. If they are in harmony then we know that they have not spoken presumptuously. *Should a man speak or write, and what he says is in conflict with the standards which are accepted, with the revelations the Lord has given, then we may reject what he has said, no matter who he is*" (Smith, *Doctrines of Salvation*, 1:187).

Summary of Deuteronomy 19:1–14

Individuals who kill someone can escape to cities of refuge to await trial. If a killing is accidental, the person is allowed to live. If the individual is found guilty of murder, a death sentence is carried out.

Deuteronomy 19:15–21. The Law of Witnesses Is Established

How does the law of witnesses function? (19:15) "Two or three witnesses are required to determine the truth of any matter. The intent of this commandment is to assure that no one is ever convicted on insufficient evidence, and particularly when a human life hangs in the balance" (Hyde, *Comprehensive Commentary [Deuteronomy]*, 114–15). "This was a just and necessary provision. One may be mistaken, or so violently prejudiced as to impose even on his own judgment, or so wicked as to endeavor through malice to compass the life of his neighbor: but it is not likely that two or more should be of this kind; and even were they, their separate examination would lead to a discovery of the truth, and to their conviction" (*Adam Clarke's Commentary* [on Numbers 35:30]).

What was the purpose of the punishments stipulated in the law of Moses? (19:19–21) "In each case when a punishment was pronounced or administered for failure to abide by the law of Moses, it was to rid evil from Israel. Punishment was meted out or 'apportioned on the principle of righteous retribution,' such as 'life for life, wound for wound, beast for beast,' which suggests retributive justice (see Ex. 21:23–25; Lev. 24:17–23). For murder, the punishment was stoning (see Deut. 17:5), and for idolatry, it was being slain by the sword (see Deut. 13:15). For lesser crimes, it was equal retributive justice but not excessive punishment. . . . There was also a distinction between criminal and societal law. Criminal law was based on justice, whereas societal law was based on love" (Black, *400 Questions and Answers about the Old Testament*, 88).

Why would the Lord demand such strict punishment for false witnesses? (19:21) "Deuteronomy prescribed that if one was found to be a lying witness, that person was to suffer the punishment of the crime which he or she was leveling against the other (Deut. 19:16–21)" (Wright, "Laws and the Sanctuary," 149). "The judges would make a diligent investigation of the case [Deut. 19:18] and pass judgment on the basis of their findings. If it turned out that the witness bringing the charge was giving false testimony, then his punishment would be determined on the basis of the intention of the crime; the lex talionis ['law of retaliation'] would become operative [19:19]" (Craigie, *Book of Deuteronomy*, 228).

15 ¶ One witness shall not rise up against a man for any iniquity, or for any sin, in any sin that he sinneth: at the mouth of two witnesses, or at the mouth of three witnesses, shall the matter be established.

16 ¶ If a false witness rise up against any man to testify against him *that which is* wrong;

17 Then both the men, between whom the controversy *is,* shall stand before the LORD, before the priests and the judges, which shall be in those days;

18 And the judges shall make diligent inquisition: and, behold, *if* the witness *be* a false witness, *and* hath testified falsely against his brother;

19 Then shall ye do unto him, as he had thought to have done unto his brother: so shalt thou put the evil away from among you.

20 And those which remain shall hear, and fear, and shall henceforth commit no more any such evil among you.

21 And thine eye shall not pity; *but* life *shall go* for life, eye for eye, tooth for tooth, hand for hand, foot for foot.

CHAPTER 20

Laws are revealed for selecting soldiers and making war—Hittites, Amorites, Canaanites, Perizzites, Hivites, and Jebusites will be utterly destroyed.

1 When thou goest out to battle against thine enemies, and seest horses, and chariots, *and* a people more than thou, be not afraid of them: for the LORD thy God *is* with thee, which brought thee up out of the land of Egypt.

2 And it shall be, when ye are come nigh unto the battle, that the priest shall approach and speak unto the people,

3 And shall say unto them, Hear, O Israel, ye approach this day unto battle against your enemies: let not your hearts faint, fear not, and do not tremble, neither be ye terrified because of them;

4 For the LORD your God *is* he that goeth with you, to fight for you against your enemies, to save you.

10 ¶ When thou comest nigh unto a city to fight against it, then proclaim peace unto it.

11 And it shall be, if it make thee answer of peace, and open unto thee, then it shall be, *that* all the people *that is* found therein shall be tributaries unto thee, and they shall serve thee.

12 And if it will make no peace with thee, but will make war against thee, then thou shalt besiege it:

Deuteronomy 20:1–4. The Lord Will Be with Israel When They Go to War

How does the Lord help us overcome our fear? (20:1–4) "We are . . . not ignorant of the challenges of the world, nor are we unaware of the difficulties of our times. But this does not mean that we should burden ourselves or others with constant fear. Rather than dwelling on the immensity of our challenges, would it not be better to focus on the infinite greatness, goodness, and absolute power of our God, trusting Him and preparing with a joyful heart for the return of Jesus the Christ?

"As His covenant people, we need not be paralyzed by fear because bad things might happen. Instead, we can move forward with faith, courage, determination, and trust in God as we approach the challenges and opportunities ahead" (Uchtdorf, "Perfect Love Casteth Out Fear," 106).

Summary of Deuteronomy 20:5–9

Circumstances when men may be excused from going to battle are outlined, such as the building of a new house (verse 5), planting a new vineyard (verse 6), or having been newly married (verse 7).

Deuteronomy 20:10–18. Directives on How to Conduct Warfare among the Tribes in the Promised Land

Why did the Israelites first proclaim peace to the city before fighting? (20:10–11) "On advancing against a town to attack it, they were *'to call to it for peace,'* i.e., to summon it to make a peaceable surrender and submission (cf. Judges 21:13). *'If it answered peace,'* i.e., returned an answer conducing to peace, and *'opened'* (sc., its gates), the whole of its inhabitants were to become tributary to Israel, and serve it; consequently even those who were armed were not to be put to death, for Israel was not to shed blood unnecessarily" (Keil and Delitzsch, *Commentary* [on Deuteronomy 20:10–11]).

How could annihilating these nations show mercy? (20:16–18) "The Canaanites against whom Israel waged war were under judicial sentence of death by God. They were spiritually and morally degenerate. Virtually every kind of perversion was a religious act. . . . Thus, God ordered all the Canaanites to be killed (Deut. 2:34; 3:6; 20:16–18; Josh. 11:14), both because they were under God's death sentence, and to avoid the contamination of Israel" (Rushdoony, *Institutes of Biblical Law*, 279).

Summary of Deuteronomy 20:19–20

The land is to be preserved in time of war.

Summary of Deuteronomy 21–24

Moses delivers detailed instructions concerning family relationships, lost property, wearing appropriate clothing, fidelity in marriage, and punishment for sexual sins. Justice, mercy, and the love of God are illustrated in each case of judgment. The Lord reminds the people of their captivity in Egypt and their redemption through His mighty power. The Israelites are to treat others mercifully.

13 And when the LORD thy God hath delivered it into thine hands, thou shalt smite
every male thereof with the edge of the sword:
14 But the women, and the little ones, and
the cattle, and all that is in the city, *even* all
the spoil thereof, shalt thou take unto thyself;
and thou shalt eat the spoil of thine enemies,
which the LORD thy God hath given thee.
15 Thus shalt thou do unto all the cities
which are very far off from thee, which *are*
not of the cities of these nations.

16 But of the cities of these people, which
the LORD thy God doth give thee *for* an inheritance, thou shalt save alive nothing that
breatheth:
17 But thou shalt utterly destroy them;
namely, the Hittites, and the Amorites, the
Canaanites, and the Perizzites, the Hivites,
and the Jebusites; as the LORD thy God hath
commanded thee:
18 That they teach you not to do after all
their abominations, which they have done
unto their gods; so should ye sin against the
LORD your God.

CHAPTERS 21–24

How amends are made for murders by unknown persons—Equity is required in dealing with wives and children—Stubborn and rebellious sons will be put to death.

Moses sets forth laws pertaining to lost property, wearing of proper clothes, caring for interests of others, marrying virgins, and sexual immorality.

Moses specifies those who may and may not enter the congregation—He sets forth laws concerning sanitation, servants, usury, and vows.

Laws are given concerning divorce, newly married persons, making merchandise of men, taking pledges, leprosy, oppression of servants, and leaving gleanings of crops.

CHAPTER 25

Judges prescribe punishment for the wicked—The marriage law provides for a brother's widow—Just weights and measures are required—Israel is commanded to blot out the Amalekites from under heaven.

Summary of Deuteronomy 25

Chapter 25 continues Moses' instructions from chapter 12 to Israel pertaining to the command to live by that "which is altogether just" ("righteous"; see *Strong's Exhaustive Concordance*, word #h6664) (Deut. 16:20). These somewhat disparate laws are linked under the obligation to live righteous lives, and only righteous lives. Moses' instructions in this chapter may be characterized by the following:

Verses 1–3. Laws that preserve righteousness in the administration of justice.

Verse 4. Laws that preserve righteousness in the treatment of animals.

Verses 5–12. Laws that preserve righteousness in male/female sexuality and the family.

Verses 13–16. Laws that preserve righteousness in business affairs (see Clements, "Book of Deuteronomy," 2:471–75).

CHAPTER 26

The children of Israel are to offer to the Lord a basket of the firstfruits of Canaan—They are commanded to keep the law of tithing—They covenant to keep the commandments, and the Lord promises to make them a holy people and a great nation.

1 And it shall be, when thou *art* come in unto the land which the LORD thy God giveth thee *for* an inheritance, and possessest it, and dwellest therein;

2 That thou shalt take of the first of all the fruit of the earth, which thou shalt bring of thy land that the LORD thy God giveth thee,

Deuteronomy 26:1–11. After They Conquer the Land of Promise, the Children of Israel Are to Offer Their First Crops to the Lord

Why did the Lord command Israel to bring the first fruits of the land to His servants? (26:1–4) "The natural man has a tendency to think only of himself—not only to place himself first, but rarely, if ever, to place anyone else second, including God. For the natural man, sacrifice does not come naturally. He has an insatiable appetite for more. . . .

"Because the natural man tends to hoard or consume everything, the Lord wisely commanded ancient

Israel to sacrifice not the last and poorest of the flock, but the firstlings—not the leftovers of the field, but the firstfruits (see Deut. 26:2; Mosiah 2:3; Moses 5:5). Genuine sacrifice has been a hallmark of the faithful from the beginning" (Robbins, "Tithing," 34).

Why did God require them to confess their faith? (26:5–10) As Israel gave of their first fruits, the Lord required them to verbally remember "the purposes of Jehovah in choosing the seed of Abraham especially and separating them from other peoples and nations, and taking them under His especial care and guidance, and leading them as he did out of Egyptian bondage with a mighty hand and an outstretched arm" (Snow, *Journal of Discourses*, 23:181). This remembrance came in three parts: The wanderings of Jacob and his family (v. 5); the mistreatment of Israel at the hands of the Egyptians (vv. 6–7); and, the redemption of Israel by His mighty hand and outstretched arm (vv. 8–10).

Deuteronomy 26:12–15. The Children of Israel Are Commanded to Pay Tithes and Offerings to the Lord and They Promise to Keep God's Commandments

What are the "tithes of thine increase"? (26:12) "The word denotes a tenth part, given for the service of

and shalt put *it* in a basket, and shalt go unto the place which the LORD thy God shall choose to place his name there.

3 And thou shalt go unto the priest that shall be in those days, and say unto him, I profess this day unto the LORD thy God, that I am come unto the country which the LORD sware unto our fathers for to give us.

4 And the priest shall take the basket out of thine hand, and set it down before the altar of the LORD thy God.

5 And thou shalt speak and say before the LORD thy God, A Syrian ready to perish *was* my father, and he went down into Egypt, and sojourned there with a few, and became there a nation, great, mighty, and populous:
6 And the Egyptians evil entreated us, and afflicted us, and laid upon us hard bondage:

7 And when we cried unto the LORD God of our fathers, the LORD heard our voice, and looked on our affliction, and our labour, and our oppression:

8 And the LORD brought us forth out of Egypt with a mighty hand, and with an outstretched arm, and with great terribleness, and with signs, and with wonders:

9 And he hath brought us into this place, and hath given us this land, *even* a land that floweth with milk and honey.

10 And now, behold, I have brought the firstfruits of the land, which thou, O LORD, hast given me. And thou shalt set it before the LORD thy God, and worship before the LORD thy God:

11 And thou shalt rejoice in every good *thing* which the LORD thy God hath given unto thee, and unto thine house, thou, and the Levite, and the stranger that *is* among you.

12 ¶ When thou hast made an end of tithing all the tithes of thine increase the third year, *which is* the year of tithing, and hast given *it* unto the Levite, the stranger, the fatherless, and the widow, that they may eat within thy gates, and be filled;

13 Then thou shalt say before the LORD thy God, I have brought away the hallowed things out of *mine* house, and also have given them unto the Levite, and unto the stranger, to the fatherless, and to the widow, according to all thy commandments which thou hast commanded me: I have not transgressed thy commandments, neither have I forgotten *them:*

14 I have not eaten thereof in my mourning, neither have I taken away *ought* thereof for *any* unclean *use,* nor given *ought* thereof for the dead: *but* I have hearkened to the voice of the LORD my God, *and* have done according to all that thou hast commanded me.

15 Look down from thy holy habitation, from heaven, and bless thy people Israel, and the land which thou hast given us, as thou swarest unto our fathers, a land that floweth with milk and honey.

God. . . . The law enforced the payment and provided rules with regard to the use to which the tithe should be put. . . .

"Blessings from the payment of tithing are both temporal and spiritual, and failure to pay an honest tithe is a form of robbery. . . .

"Latter-day revelation emphasizes the law of the tithe as a duty and a test of faithfulness (D&C 64:23–25; 85:3; 97:11; 119). The honest payment of tithing sanctifies both the individual and the land on which he lives" (Bible Dictionary, "Tithe"). See commentary in this volume for Genesis 14:20.

The Payment of Tithing and the Remembrance of Blessings (Deuteronomy 26:12–15)

Upon the payment of tithes on their increase (separate and differentiated from the offering of their first fruits), the Lord required Israel to verbally acknowledge the extent of their offering. Elder Franklin D. Richards remarked: "Here is a curious saying: When thou hast made an end of this tithing, and eaten within thy gates [Deut. 26:12], then thou shalt say before the Lord: 'I have brought away the hallowed things out of mine house, and also have I given them unto the Levite, and unto the stranger, to the fatherless, and to the widow, according to all thy commandments which thou hast commanded me: I have not transgressed thy commandments, neither have I forgotten them' [Deut. 26:13]. Now, supposing there was an ordinance of that kind instituted among us that at the close of each annual settlement, it was required of each man to say, I have paid my tithing, the tenth of all the Lord has given unto me; I have delivered it to my Bishop or to the storehouse of the Lord, as the Lord has required. And then to say, I have done all things according to the commandments of the Lord my God, and have not failed in any of these things. How many of us could lift up our hands and say that we have done all that God has required? There was the point—God brought it home to the people, and when a man could say this his neighbors knew he was living the law of God. This was something that created confidence and fellowship between man and man. When they could thus testify that they had done all that was required of them, they could also, with good grace and faith, ask the blessings of God upon them and their land as written in the 15th verse of the chapter just quoted: 'Look down from thy holy habitation, from heaven, and bless thy people Israel, and the land which thou hast given us, as thou swarest unto our fathers, a land that floweth with milk and honey' [Deut. 26:15]. As the Lord has in like manner said unto us" (In *Journal of Discourses*, 23:318).

Deuteronomy 26:16–19. Israel Promises to Keep God's Commandments, and He Promises to Bless Them More Than All Other People

What does "avouched" mean? (26:17) Avouch ('âmar) is a primitive word with a wide range of uses. In this particular context it is to be understood as to certify, to avow, to plainly promise, "to answer, to say in one's heart" (*Strong's Exhaustive Concordance*, word #h0559).

What does "peculiar" mean? (26:18) "The term *peculiar* as used in the scriptures is quite different. In the Old Testament, the Hebrew term from which *peculiar* was translated is *segullah*, which means 'valued property,' or 'treasure.' In the New Testament, the Greek term from which *peculiar* was translated is *peripoiesis*, which means 'possession,' or 'an obtaining.'

"Thus, we see that the scriptural term *peculiar* signifies 'valued treasure,' 'made' or 'selected by God.' For us to be identified by servants of the Lord as his *peculiar* people is a compliment of the highest order" (Nelson, "Children of the Covenant," 34). See commentary in this volume for Exodus 19:5.

Deuteronomy 27:1–10. The Children of Israel Build a Monument in the Land of Promise to Remind Them of the Lord's Help

What does Moses ask of the elders of Israel? (27:1–5) "Moses instructed the nation to observe a unique ceremony immediately upon their entrance into the Promised Land. They were to 'coat three great stones . . . with plaister' (v. 2; perhaps lime is meant) and, while the plaister still pliable, clearly inscribe 'all the words of this law' (v. 3). Most likely, the covenant's general and specific stipulations (Deut. 12–26) are meant here. The practice of inscribing plaster—or lime—covered stones was a common Egyptian practice, a skill with which the eldest members of the conquest generation would still be familiar. The stones were to remain uncut and unadorned and were to be erected into an altar (v. 5)" (*Zondervan KJV Commentary*, 262).

What was the purpose of setting up monuments of stones in ancient Israel? (27:2) Following ancient tradition the Hebrew people erected monuments of stone to evoke sacred memories of Jehovah's

16 ¶ This day the LORD thy God hath commanded thee to do these statutes and judgments: thou shalt therefore keep and do them with all thine heart, and with all thy soul.

17 Thou hast avouched the LORD this day to be thy God, and to walk in his ways, and to keep his statutes, and his commandments, and his judgments, and to hearken unto his voice:

18 And the LORD hath avouched thee this day to be his peculiar people, as he hath promised thee, and that *thou* shouldest keep all his commandments;

19 And to make thee high above all nations which he hath made, in praise, and in name, and in honour; and that thou mayest be an holy people unto the LORD thy God, as he hath spoken.

CHAPTER 27

The children of Israel are to cross the Jordan, build an altar, and worship the Lord—They are the Lord's people but will be cursed if they do not obey Him.

1 And Moses with the elders of Israel commanded the people, saying, Keep all the commandments which I command you this day.

2 And it shall be on the day when ye shall pass over Jordan unto the land which the LORD thy God giveth thee, that thou shalt set thee up great stones, and plaster them with plaster:

3 And thou shalt write upon them all the words of this law, when thou art passed over, that thou mayest go in unto the land which the LORD thy God giveth thee, a land that floweth with milk and honey; as the LORD God of thy fathers hath promised thee.

4 Therefore it shall be when ye be gone over Jordan, *that* ye shall set up these stones, which I command you this day, in mount Ebal, and thou shalt plaster them with plaster.

5 And there shalt thou build an altar unto the LORD thy God, an altar of stones: thou shalt not lift up *any* iron *tool* upon them.

6 Thou shalt build the altar of the LORD thy God of whole stones: and thou shalt offer burnt offerings thereon unto the LORD thy God:

7 And thou shalt offer peace offerings, and shalt eat there, and rejoice before the LORD thy God.

8 And thou shalt write upon the stones all the words of this law very plainly.

9 ¶ And Moses and the priests the Levites spake unto all Israel, saying, Take heed, and hearken, O Israel; this day thou art become the people of the LORD thy God.

interactions and covenants with His people. Jacob set up stone pillars at Bethel to remember his heavenly dream, in which God reaffirmed his covenant with him (Genesis 28). Moses built twelve standing stones at the foot of Mount Sinai after receiving the Ten Commandments and other laws (Exodus 24). The Israelites erected standing stones to remember their miraculous crossing of the Jordan River (Joshua 4). Joshua built a standing stone when the covenant was renewed at Shechem (Joshua 24). Samuel erected the Ebenezer stone celebrating Israel's victory over the Philistines (1 Samuel 7).

Why were the Israelites instructed to not use iron tools in building God's altar? (27:5) "The Lord gave the Israelites specific instructions on how they could approach Him. Forging *iron* was not a skill as characteristic of Israel as of some other Middle Eastern peoples. The Lord rejected an impressive altar for a humble altar of whole *stones*, that is, uncut stones. Perhaps an impressive altar would have diverted the worshipers' attention from God (Ex. 20:25)" (*Nelson Study Bible* [NKJV], 309).

Mount Ebal and Mount Gerizim (Deuteronomy 27:1–10)

The ancient site of Shechem. In the foreground is Mount Gerizim, and beyond it, Mount Ebal. Shechem is situated between these two mountains.

10 Thou shalt therefore obey the voice of the
LORD thy God, and do his commandments
and his statutes, which I command thee this
day.

11 ¶ And Moses charged the people the same
day, saying,

12 These shall stand upon mount Gerizim
to bless the people, when ye are come over
Jordan; Simeon, and Levi, and Judah, and
Issachar, and Joseph, and Benjamin:

13 And these shall stand upon mount Ebal
to curse; Reuben, Gad, and Asher, and
Zebulun, Dan, and Naphtali.

14 ¶ And the Levites shall speak, and say
unto all the men of Israel with a loud voice,

15 Cursed *be* the man that maketh *any* graven
or molten image, an abomination unto the
LORD, the work of the hands of the craftsman, and putteth *it* in *a* secret *place*. And all
the people shall answer and say, Amen.

16 Cursed *be* he that setteth light by his father or his mother. And all the people shall
say, Amen.

17 Cursed *be* he that removeth his neighbour's landmark. And all the people shall say,
Amen.

Deuteronomy 27:11–26. Moses and Priesthood Leaders Are to Remind Israel to Obey the Lord

Why were Mount Ebal and Mount Gerizim selected as the place for Israel to establish a covenant with God? (27:11–14) "During the covenant renewal ceremony with the second generation of Israel, the Lord used the topography of the land for dramatic, visual effect. *Mount Ebal*, because of topographical and climatic conditions, is normally a barren peak while *Mount Gerizim* is usually covered with vegetation. Consequently, Mount Ebal was an ideal place for the curses to be recited, and Mount Gerizim was suitable for the blessings. The association of the place and the word would have been unforgettable. Furthermore, the two mountains are quite close, so they would serve as a natural amphitheater for the recitation of the curses and blessings by the *Levites*" (*Nelson Study Bible* [NKJV], 310).

Why are only the curses listed? (27:15–26) "There now follow in vv. 15–26 the twelve curses, the so-called Dodecalog [the twelve words or commandments]. To each curse *all the people* respond 'Amen.' This word, which refers back to what has immediately preceded, indicates assent and agreement to what has been proclaimed. Thus, by saying 'Amen,' the people indicate understanding and agreement and thereby remove any possible excuse for their conduct, if at some subsequent time they were to disobey the law of the covenant. It is difficult to determine a single unifying theme underlying the various acts that are placed under the curse" (Craigie, *Book of Deuteronomy*, 277).

The Raising of Stones and the Formalizing of Israel's Covenant (27:1–10)

Moses' mandate to erect stones on Mount Ebal as a token of Israel's covenant brought together the three essential covenant elements: Jehovah, Israel, and the Land. The ceremonial erecting of the stones on Mount Ebal may be seen as an essential four-part process:

1. They were to wait to build the memorial until the promises of the Lord would be fulfilled and they received the promised land of inheritance (v. 2).

2. Not only was the erecting of "stones" and the writing of the law upon the stones patterned after the original archetype of Sinai, but the writing on stone declared and established the permanence of the Law in Israel (vv. 2–4).

3. The Law was to be presented with clarity—no misunderstanding possible—as Moses directed that "thou shalt write upon the stones all the words of this law *very plainly*" (v. 8; emphasis added).

4. The erecting and the writing upon the stones was ritualized by the sacred and the holy as Moses was commanded to build a separate and distinct "altar of the Lord God of whole stones" where burnt offerings and peace offerings were to be offered. At this altar Israel would ritually feast and rejoice (vv. 5–7) (see Keil and Delitzsch, *Commentary* [on Deuteronomy 27:1–10]; see also Rasmussen, *Latter-day Saint Commentary on the Old Testament*, 186).

18 Cursed *be* he that maketh the blind to wander out of the way. And all the people shall say, Amen.

19 Cursed *be* he that perverteth the judgment of the stranger, fatherless, and widow. And all the people shall say, Amen.

20 Cursed *be* he that lieth with his father's wife; because he uncovereth his father's skirt. And all the people shall say, Amen.

21 Cursed *be* he that lieth with any manner of beast. And all the people shall say, Amen.

22 Cursed *be* he that lieth with his sister, the daughter of his father, or the daughter of his mother. And all the people shall say, Amen.

23 Cursed *be* he that lieth with his mother in law. And all the people shall say, Amen.

24 Cursed *be* he that smiteth his neighbour secretly. And all the people shall say, Amen.

25 Cursed *be* he that taketh reward to slay an innocent person. And all the people shall say, Amen.

26 Cursed *be* he that confirmeth not *all* the words of this law to do them. And all the people shall say, Amen.

CHAPTER 28

If the children of Israel are obedient, they will be blessed temporally and spiritually—If they are disobedient, they will be cursed, smitten, and destroyed; diseases, plagues, and oppression will come upon them; they will serve false gods and become a byword among all nations; fierce nations will enslave them; and they will eat their own children and be scattered among all nations.

Summary of Deuteronomy 28

"This chapter of Deuteronomy is very similar to Leviticus 26, in which the Lord specifically outlined the blessings that would accrue to Israel if they were obedient (see vv. 1–14) and also the punishments they would suffer if they turned from the Lord (see vv. 15–68). One particularly gruesome prediction added in this chapter concerned a siege so terrible that cannibalism would result (see vv. 49–57). When Jerusalem fell to Babylonian forces under Nebuchadnezzar, conditions were so terrible that the people did turn to cannibalism to survive (see Lamentations 4:1–10). But in the siege of Jerusalem by the Romans in A.D. 70, the prophecy seems to have been fulfilled with particular preciseness" (*Old Testament Student Manual: Genesis–2 Samuel*, 230–31).

Summary of Deuteronomy 29

The Lord continues to ask Israel to promise to obey Him. If they obey, they will be blessed. If they don't, they will be destroyed and scattered to other lands. Other nations will see what will happen to Israel when they disobey the Lord and will be amazed at His anger.

CHAPTER 29

The children of Israel make a covenant with the Lord under which they will be blessed if they are obedient, and cursed if they are disobedient—If they are disobedient, their land will be as brimstone and salt.

CHAPTER 30

The scattered Israelites will be gathered from all nations when they remember the covenant—Moses places life or death, blessing or cursing, before the people.

1 And it shall come to pass, when all these things are come upon thee, the blessing and the curse, which I have set before thee, and thou shalt call *them* to mind among all the nations, whither the LORD thy God hath driven thee,

2 And shalt return unto the LORD thy God, and shalt obey his voice according to all that I command thee this day, thou and thy children, with all thine heart, and with all thy soul;

3 That then the LORD thy God will turn thy captivity, and have compassion upon thee, and will return and gather thee from all the nations, whither the LORD thy God hath scattered thee.

4 If *any* of thine be driven out unto the outmost *parts* of heaven, from thence will the LORD thy God gather thee, and from thence will he fetch thee:

Deuteronomy 30:1–9. When Israel Remembers the Lord, He Will Gather Them

Why did Moses command Israel to recall their history? (30:1) "The Lord commanded Israel to remember what He had done for them in times past. Their journey from Egypt began with, 'Remember this day' . . . (Exod 13:3). This command is repeated in the book of Deuteronomy: 'Remember that thou wast a servant in the land of Egypt' . . . (Deut 5:15). The Hebrew verb *zakar*, 'to remember,' is used no fewer than 169 times in the Old Testament in one form or another. In Deuteronomy the divine call to remember is repeated on numerous occasions (see Deut 4:9–10; 5:15; 7:18; 8:2, 18; 9:7; 15:15; 16:3, 12; 24:18, 22; 32:7). Often called the Deuteronomic imperative, the call to remember could be appropriately identified as the 'Eleventh Commandment' (Holzapfel, et al., *Jehovah and the World of the Old Testament*, 138). ⊕

How is scattered Israel to be gathered from the nations? (30:3–4) Six hundred years before the mortal ministry of Jesus Christ, Nephi prophesied of the role latter-day scripture plays in this gathering: "And the Lord will set his hand again the second time to restore his people from their lost and fallen state. Wherefore, he will proceed to do a marvelous work and a wonder among the children of men.

"Wherefore, he shall bring forth his words unto them, which words shall judge them at the last day, for they shall be given them for the purpose of convincing them of the true Messiah, who was rejected by them; and unto the convincing of them that they need not look forward any more for a Messiah to come" (2 Nephi 25:17–18). ⊕

5 And the LORD thy God will bring thee into the land which thy fathers possessed, and thou shalt possess it; and he will do thee good, and multiply thee above thy fathers.

6 And the LORD thy God will circumcise thine heart, and the heart of thy seed, to love the LORD thy God with all thine heart, and with all thy soul, that thou mayest live.

7 And the LORD thy God will put all these curses upon thine enemies, and on them that hate thee, which persecuted thee.

8 And thou shalt return and obey the voice of the LORD, and do all his commandments which I command thee this day.

9 And the LORD thy God will make thee plenteous in every work of thine hand, in the fruit of thy body, and in the fruit of thy cattle, and in the fruit of thy land, for good: for the LORD will again rejoice over thee for good, as he rejoiced over thy fathers:

10 If thou shalt hearken unto the voice of the LORD thy God, to keep his commandments and his statutes which are written in this book of the law, *and* if thou turn unto the LORD thy God with all thine heart, and with all thy soul.

11 ¶ For this commandment which I command thee this day, it *is* not hidden from thee, neither *is* it far off.

12 It *is* not in heaven, that thou shouldest say, Who shall go up for us to heaven, and bring it unto us, that we may hear it, and do it?

13 Neither *is* it beyond the sea, that thou shouldest say, Who shall go over the sea for us, and bring it unto us, that we may hear it, and do it?

14 But the word *is* very nigh unto thee, in thy mouth, and in thy heart, that thou mayest do it.

How does inheriting land fulfill God's covenant with Israel? (30:5–9) "Regardless of their location of exile, the Lord will regather them (v. 4) to the land of his promise and will bless them even more abundantly than their ancestors (v. 5). Once the Lord reinstates them in the land, he will reconstitute Israel and give them the ability to obey him and to enjoy his continued blessings. By an act of God alone, these returned Israelites and their descendants will be given the ability to love the Lord ('circumcise your hearts') and consequently experience the abundant blessings of the covenant (v. 6). In addition to this great blessing, he will transfer the curses endured by the children of Israel to the nations that brought about Israel's exile (v. 7)" (Grisanti, "Deuteronomy," 2:763). ⊕

Deuteronomy 30:10–14. The Children of Israel Have the Word of the Lord

Who wrote these commandments? (30:10) "Internal evidence indicates that Moses wrote these scriptures during his life, provided for their preservation, and ordered their public review every seven years [see Deut. 31:10–13]" (Rasmussen, *Latter-day Saint Commentary on the Old Testament*, 188). Moses' writings were presented to the priests of Levi and preserved in the Ark of the Covenant (see Deut. 31:9).

In what way were the commandments and statutes written by Moses to be available and "not hidden"? (30:11–14) See commentary in this volume for Deuteronomy 31:11–13.

Deuteronomy 30:15–20. The Children of Israel Can Choose to Do Right or Wrong

How does the Lord present the doctrine of agency in these verses? (30:15–17) "Moses prophesied the scattering and the gathering of Israel, and for every person then or now the principle is clear: 'See, I have set before thee this day life and good, and death and evil' (Deut. 30:15). It is the eternal principle of agency: Choose what you will, and do what you must to get it; or do what you will, and content yourself with what you must get. The Lord plainly set before Israel the alternatives, and he pleaded with the people to love him enough to obey his voice; for only thereby would any people be free from captivity" (Rasmussen, *Latter-day Saint Commentary on the Old Testament*, 187–88; see also 2 Nephi 2:27–30). ⊕

What does Moses mean by "denounce"? (30:18) The Hebrew meaning for *denounce* in this verse is "declare" (see Deuteronomy 30:18*a*).

According to Moses, what must be a part of our love for the Lord? (30:20) How does the following statement sustain Moses' teaching? President Dallin H. Oaks taught we must not forget the first commandment "to love God with all our heart, soul, and mind. We show that love by 'keep[ing] [His] commandments' [John 14:15]. God requires us to obey His commandments because only through that obedience, including repentance, can we return to live in His presence and become perfect as He is" ("Two Great Commandments," 73–74).

Deuteronomy 31:1–6. Moses Tells Israel That Joshua Will Lead Them into the Promised Land

How is Moses' life arranged in the scriptures? (31:2) The books of Exodus through Deuteronomy divide Moses' life of 129 years into three distinct periods of forty years—his life as a prince in Egypt (see Exodus 2:1–15), his life in the Midian desert (see Exodus

15 ¶ See, I have set before thee this day life
and good, and death and evil;

16 In that I command thee this day to love
the LORD thy God, to walk in his ways, and to
keep his commandments and his statutes and
his judgments, that thou mayest live and multiply: and the LORD thy God shall bless thee
in the land whither thou goest to possess it.

17 But if thine heart turn away, so that thou
wilt not hear, but shalt be drawn away, and
worship other gods, and serve them;

18 I denounce unto you this day, that ye
shall surely perish, *and that* ye shall not prolong *your* days upon the land, whither thou
passest over Jordan to go to possess it.

19 I call heaven and earth to record this day
against you, *that* I have set before you life and
death, blessing and cursing: therefore choose
life, that both thou and thy seed may live:

20 That thou mayest love the LORD thy God,
and that thou mayest obey his voice, and that
thou mayest cleave unto him: for he *is* thy life,
and the length of thy days: that thou mayest dwell in the land which the LORD sware
unto thy fathers, to Abraham, to Isaac, and to
Jacob, to give them.

CHAPTER 31

Moses counsels Joshua and all Israel to be strong and of good courage—The law is to be read to all Israel every seven years—The children of Israel will follow false gods and corrupt themselves.

1 And Moses went and spake these words
unto all Israel.

2 And he said unto them, I *am* an hundred
and twenty years old this day; I can no more
go out and come in: also the LORD hath said
unto me, Thou shalt not go over this Jordan.

3 The LORD thy God, he will go over before thee, *and* he will destroy these nations from before thee, and thou shalt possess them: *and* Joshua, he shall go over before thee, as the LORD hath said.

4 And the LORD shall do unto them as he did to Sihon and to Og, kings of the Amorites, and unto the land of them, whom he destroyed.

5 And the LORD shall give them up before your face, that ye may do unto them according unto all the commandments which I have commanded you.

6 Be strong and of a good courage, fear not, nor be afraid of them: for the LORD thy God, he *it is* that doth go with thee; he will not fail thee, nor forsake thee.

7 ¶ And Moses called unto Joshua, and said unto him in the sight of all Israel, Be strong and of a good courage: for thou must go with this people unto the land which the LORD hath sworn unto their fathers to give them; and thou shalt cause them to inherit it.

8 And the LORD, he *it is* that doth go before thee; he will be with thee, he will not fail thee, neither forsake thee: fear not, neither be dismayed.

9 ¶ And Moses wrote this law, and delivered it unto the priests the sons of Levi, which bare the ark of the covenant of the LORD, and unto all the elders of Israel.

10 And Moses commanded them, saying, At the end of *every* seven years, in the solemnity of the year of release, in the feast of tabernacles,

2:16–4:17), and his life in the Sinai wilderness (see Exodus 4:18–Deuteronomy 34:12).

How does the counsel to be strong and of good courage apply today? (31:3–6) See commentary in this volume for Deuteronomy 20:1–4.

Deuteronomy 31:7–13. Moses Teaches and Blesses Joshua

Who was Joshua? (31:7) His name means "*God is help.* The name also occurs in the Old Testament under the various forms Jehoshua, Hoshea, Jeshua, and Jesus; son of Nun, and successor of Moses; born in Egypt before the Exodus (Num. 14:26–31); fought with Amalek (Ex. 17:13–14); was Moses' minister (24:13; 32:17; 33:11); one of the 12 spies (Num. 13:8); appointed Moses' successor (27:18–19; 34:17; see also Deut. 1:38; 3:28; 31:3, 23; 34:9). The book of Joshua . . . contains the history of his conquest of Palestine. He died at the age of 110 and was buried in his own city, Timnath-Serah. He is the highest type of the devout warrior" (Bible Dictionary, "Joshua").

What is the Feast of Tabernacles? (31:10) "The Feast of Tabernacles (Lev. 23:34) or of Ingathering (Ex. 23:16), called by later Jews the Feast (John 7:37) and reckoned by them to be the greatest and most joyful of all, was celebrated on the 15th to 21st days of the seventh month. To the seven days was added an eighth, 'the last day, that great day of the feast' (John 7:37), a day of holy convocation, which marked the ending not only of this particular feast, but of the whole festival season. The events celebrated were the sojourning of the children of Israel in the wilderness (Lev. 23:43) and the gathering-in of all the fruits of the year (Ex. 23:16)" (Bible Dictionary, "Feasts").

What was the purpose of the public reading of the law every seven years? (31:11–13) "In the sabbatical year the fields are allowed to lie fallow, and the festival of huts (Succoth), the fall harvest festival, would conclude all harvesting from the previous year, thus leaving the entire people, with its agriculturally based economy, free to come to the central sanctuary and listen to the public reading of the book of teaching" (Alter, *Hebrew Bible*, 1:724). "The purpose of the deposit and public reading of the covenant is to remind the people of their obligations" (Holzapfel, et al., *Jehovah and the World of the Old Testament*, 141). ⊕

11 When all Israel is come to appear before the LORD thy God in the place which he shall choose, thou shalt read this law before all Israel in their hearing.

12 Gather the people together, men, and women, and children, and thy stranger that *is* within thy gates, that they may hear, and that they may learn, and fear the LORD your God, and observe to do all the words of this law:

13 And *that* their children, which have not known *any thing*, may hear, and learn to fear the LORD your God, as long as ye live in the land whither ye go over Jordan to possess it.

Summary of Deuteronomy 31:14–30

God instructs Moses to bring Joshua to the tabernacle of the congregation where He will charge him with the power to lead Israel. The Lord appears to Moses and Joshua in a pillar of cloud which overshadows the tabernacle door. The Lord commands Moses to write a song as a witness against the future wickedness of Israel. They preserve the song of Moses in the ark of the covenant. Moses gathers all the elders and officers of the tribes. He speaks the words of his song to all the congregation.

CHAPTER 32

Israel will sing the song of Moses and acclaim: God speaks to heaven and earth; the children of Israel were known in the premortal life; God chose them in this life; they forgot the Rock of their salvation; He sent terror, a sword, and vengeance upon them; there is no God beside Him—Moses will be gathered to his people.

1 Give ear, O ye heavens, and I will speak; and hear, O earth, the words of my mouth.

2 My doctrine shall drop as the rain, my speech shall distil as the dew, as the small rain upon the tender herb, and as the showers upon the grass:

Deuteronomy 32:1–6. Israel Will Forget the Rock (Christ) of Their Salvation

What is a modern-day parallel to Moses' song? (32:1–6) A careful reading of Doctrine and Covenants 1, given by the Lord to the Church in November 1831 as His preface to the Doctrine and Covenants, reveals some interesting parallels to Moses' Song to Israel (see Deuteronomy 32:1–43). For example: "Hearken, O ye people . . . listen together;" "iniquities shall be

3 Because I will publish the name of the LORD: ascribe ye greatness unto our God.

4 *He is* the Rock, his work *is* perfect: for all his ways *are* judgment: a God of truth and without iniquity, just and right *is* he.

5 They have corrupted themselves, their spot *is* not *the spot* of his children: *they are* a perverse and crooked generation.

6 Do ye thus requite the LORD, O foolish people and unwise? *is* not he thy father *that* hath bought thee? hath he not made thee, and established thee?

7 ¶ Remember the days of old, consider the years of many generations: ask thy father, and he will shew thee; thy elders, and they will tell thee.

8 When the most High divided to the nations their inheritance, when he separated the sons of Adam, he set the bounds of the people according to the number of the children of Israel.

spoken from the housetops, their secret acts shall be revealed;" "the voice of warning;" "commandments . . . [published to the] inhabitants of the earth" (D&C 1:1–6). In addition, latter-day peoples will break God's everlasting covenant as will Israel (see D&C 1:15–16; Deuteronomy 32:5–6). And the Lord will re-establish His covenant with His people (see D&C 1:17–30; Deuteronomy 32:43).

Deuteronomy 32:7–14. The Lord Has Watched Over and Blessed Israel since Premortal Life

Why is this special appointment of the children of Israel noteworthy? (32:7–8) Elder Bruce R. McConkie noted the unique identity of Israel: "Israel is an eternal people. She came into being as a chosen and separate congregation before the foundations of the earth were laid; she was a distinct and a peculiar people in preexistence, even as she is in this sphere. Her numbers were known before their mortal birth, and the very land surface of the earth was 'divided to the nations [for] their inheritance . . . according to the number of the children of Israel' (Deuteronomy 32:8)" (*New Witness for the Articles of Faith*, 510). See also Acts 17:24–26 and Romans 8:28–30. ⊕

What Is the "Rock" in Moses' Song to Israel? (Deuteronomy 32:4, 15, 18, 30–31)

Robert J. Matthews explained: "An examination of the Doctrine and Covenants shows that in this dispensation the Lord frequently has referred to his gospel and also to himself as a rock [Deut. 32:4] or the rock upon which the Church would be established. For example:

"Christ, the rock. . . . D&C 50:44.

"The gospel is the rock. . . . D&C 6:34; 10:69; 11:16; 11:24; 18:4, 5, 17; 33:1, 12–13.

"It was a common Hebrew metaphor to refer to God, or the Messiah, as the Rock, as is shown in the following biblical references:

"Deut. 32:4, 31. . . . He is our Rock.

"1 Sam. 2:2. . . . There is no rock like our God.

"2 Sam. 22:2–3. . . . The Lord is my rock.

"Ps. 42:9. . . . God is my rock.

"1 Cor. 10:1–4. . . . Christ is the spiritual Rock.

"Eph. 2:20. . . . Jesus Christ is the chief cornerstone.

"Ps. 118:22; Matt. 21:42. . . . The stone which the builders rejected is become the head of the corner.

"Whatever one concludes as to the Lord's meaning of the term *rock*, it is readily seen that there is a common element in all of the usages listed above, and that common element is Jesus Christ. In each instance it is either the gospel of Christ, the testimony of Christ, the revelation of Christ, or Christ himself that is the rock" (*Behold the Messiah*, 240).

What does "the Lord's portion is his people" mean? (32:9) "It would seem very clear, then, that those born to the lineage of Jacob, who was later to be called Israel, and his posterity, who were known as the children of Israel, were born into the most illustrious lineage of any of those who came upon the earth as mortal beings.

"All these rewards were seemingly promised, or foreordained, before the world was. Surely these matters must have been determined by the kind of lives we had lived in that premortal spirit world" (Lee, "Understanding Who We Are Brings Self-Respect," 5).

How is the Lord's sincere concern for Israel described here? (32:10–12) "Having determined that Israel's inheritance was in Canaan, [Jehovah] sets about bringing his people there. These verses explore [Jehovah's] care of Israel during the wilderness period after leaving Egypt. The picture begins (v. 10) with the *barren* . . . and *howling waste* of the desert. . . . [Jehovah's] care during this period is depicted using three metaphors: as an encircling . . . protector who guarded Israel as *the apple of his eye* . . . ; as an eagle that stirs up her young and *hovers* . . . over them, spreading its wings to catch and carry them . . . ; and as a kindly shepherd or leader who guides his people . . . , without any *foreign god* to help him. . . . Emphasis is placed on the fact that *the LORD alone* led Israel" (Tyndale Old Testament Commentaries, 5:312).

Deuteronomy 32:15–18. Israel Will Forget Their Rock and Worship False Gods

Why did Israel (Jeshurun) forsake God? (32:15–18) George A. Smith stated: "I know this people will bear poverty and affliction, they will bear persecution, they will suffer their houses to be burned, their property to be destroyed, and sacrifice what the Lord has given them of earthly goods, expose themselves to suffering and hardship for the sake of the principles they have received, joyfully; but how many of these, when the smiles of Providence have beamed upon them, when prosperity has surrounded them, and they have been blessed and are in affluent circumstances, have forgotten the Lord, like the Prophet said of Jeshurun, 'They waxed fat, and kicked, and forgot the Lord'" (in *Journal of Discourses*, 10:68). How do you avoid complacency and indifference toward God amidst your multitude of blessings?

9 For the LORD's portion *is* his people; Jacob *is* the lot of his inheritance.

10 He found him in a desert land, and in the waste howling wilderness; he led him about, he instructed him, he kept him as the apple of his eye.

11 As an eagle stirreth up her nest, fluttereth over her young, spreadeth abroad her wings, taketh them, beareth them on her wings:

12 *So* the LORD alone did lead him, and *there was* no strange god with him.

13 He made him ride on the high places of the earth, that he might eat the increase of the fields; and he made him to suck honey out of the rock, and oil out of the flinty rock;

14 Butter of kine, and milk of sheep, with fat of lambs, and rams of the breed of Bashan, and goats, with the fat of kidneys of wheat; and thou didst drink the pure blood of the grape.

15 ¶ But Jeshurun waxed fat, and kicked: thou art waxen fat, thou art grown thick, thou art covered *with fatness;* then he forsook God *which* made him, and lightly esteemed the Rock of his salvation.

16 They provoked him to jealousy with strange *gods,* with abominations provoked they him to anger.

17 They sacrificed unto devils, not to God; to gods whom they knew not, to new *gods that* came newly up, whom your fathers feared not.

18 Of the Rock *that* begat thee thou art unmindful, and hast forgotten God that formed thee.

Summary of Deuteronomy 32:19–47

Moses' song warns Israel of the Lord's anger against the future wickedness of Israel. He will scatter them, for they are a nation that will not hearken to counsel. The Lord affirms that there are no gods other than Himself and He will render judgment against His enemies.

Deuteronomy 32:48–52. God Tells Moses to Go to a Mountain Where He Can See the Promised Land

48 And the Lord spake unto Moses that selfsame day, saying,

49 Get thee up into this mountain Abarim, *unto* mount Nebo, which *is* in the land of Moab, that *is* over against Jericho; and behold the land of Canaan, which I give unto the children of Israel for a possession:

50 And die in the mount whither thou goest up, and be gathered unto thy people; as Aaron thy brother died in mount Hor, and was gathered unto his people:

51 Because ye trespassed against me among the children of Israel at the waters of Meribah-Kadesh, in the wilderness of Zin; because ye sanctified me not in the midst of the children of Israel.

52 Yet thou shalt see the land before *thee;* but thou shalt not go thither unto the land which I give the children of Israel.

Why wasn't Moses allowed into the promised land? (32:48–52) Moses incurred the Lord's displeasure when he took credit for getting water from a rock and for not properly following the Lord's directions (see Numbers 20).

"However . . . I gather from reading D&C 84:20–[25] that the Lord was angry not with Moses, but with the children of Israel. They did not deserve Moses any longer, so Moses was translated and taken to heaven. . . . If the Lord was too angry with Moses to let him go into the promised land, it seems strange that he would yet be pleased enough with him to take him into heaven. Moses was given the greater blessing of being translated" (Matthews, *Bible! A Bible!* 67). See commentary in this volume for Numbers 27:13; Deuteronomy 34:5–7; and Joshua 1:1.

CHAPTER 33

Moses blesses the tribes of Israel—Levi is blessed to teach the Lord's judgments and His law—Joseph is blessed above all; the Lord will gather Israel in the latter days—Israel will triumph.

Summary of Deuteronomy 33:1–12

Moses, at the end of his life, blesses the tribes of Israel. The people remember that he was a man of God. He was their teacher, and he loved them. The tribes of Reuben, Judah, Levi, and Benjamin are blessed. The tribe of Levi is responsible for keeping the Urim and Thummim and teaching judgment and the law to Israel. In addition, the tribe of Levi will administer the sacrifices and offerings of the temple in Israel.

Deuteronomy 33:13–17. Moses Gives a Special Blessing to Joseph and His Sons

13 ¶ And of Joseph he said, Blessed of the
Lord *be* his land, for the precious things of
heaven, for the dew, and for the deep that
coucheth beneath,
14 And for the precious fruits *brought forth*
by the sun, and for the precious things put
forth by the moon,
15 And for the chief things of the ancient
mountains, and for the precious things of the
lasting hills,
16 And for the precious things of the earth
and fulness thereof, and *for* the good will of
him that dwelt in the bush: let *the blessing*
come upon the head of Joseph, and upon
the top of the head of him *that was* separated
from his brethren.

What was the principal blessing given to Joseph? (33:15–16) "Moses gave . . . Joseph a blessing of a new land in the utmost bounds of the everlasting hills. [In] describing that land, Moses used the word 'precious' five times in just a few verses in the Bible, telling what a marvelous land the Lord had for Joseph and he would be separated from his brethren" (Richards, in Conference Report, April 1963, 117). "Joseph was given a multifaceted blessing; it alluded to lands and precious things 'of the ancient mountains' and the 'lasting hills.' It included promises of leadership, glory, and the power ('horns') to gather the other tribes at last from all ends of the earth. . . . It is apparent that the mission of Joseph's seed through Manasseh and Ephraim was to be far-reaching in time and in eternity" (Rasmussen, *Latter-day Saint Commentary on the Old Testament*, 191). See commentary in this volume for Genesis 49:22–26. ⊕

17 His glory *is like* the firstling of his bullock, and his horns *are like* the horns of unicorns: with them he shall push the people
together to the ends of the earth: and they
are the ten thousands of Ephraim, and they
are the thousands of Manasseh.

Who will push the gathering of Israel? (33:17) "How shall Israel be gathered? . . . It will not be an easy work. Every lost sheep must be taught the gospel; every new convert must believe the Book of Mormon; all must repent and forsake the world and come voluntarily, often in the face of great opposition, into the latter-day kingdom of the God of their fathers. Missionaries must labor with zeal and in the face of great odds. They must 'push the people together.' And who shall do this work? Moses says: 'They are the ten thousands of Ephraim, and they are the thousands of Manasseh' (Deuteronomy 33:17). And such is an apt and accurate definition of the missionary force of the great latter-day kingdom" (McConkie, *New Witness for the Articles of Faith*, 528–29).

Summary of Deuteronomy 33:18–29

Moses blesses the tribes of Zebulun, Issachar, Gad, Dan, Naphtali, and Asher.

CHAPTER 34

Moses sees the promised land and is taken by the Lord—Joshua leads Israel—Moses was Israel's greatest prophet.

1 And Moses went up from the plains of Moab unto the mountain of Nebo, to the top of Pisgah, that *is* over against Jericho. And the LORD shewed him all the land of Gilead, unto Dan,

2 And all Naphtali, and the land of Ephraim, and Manasseh, and all the land of Judah, unto the utmost sea,

3 And the south, and the plain of the valley of Jericho, the city of palm trees, unto Zoar.

4 And the LORD said unto him, This *is* the land which I sware unto Abraham, unto Isaac, and unto Jacob, saying, I will give it unto thy seed: I have caused thee to see *it* with thine eyes, but thou shalt not go over thither.

5 ¶ So Moses the servant of the LORD died there in the land of Moab, according to the word of the LORD.

6 And he buried him in a valley in the land of Moab, over against Beth-peor: but no man knoweth of his sepulchre unto this day.

7 ¶ And Moses *was* an hundred and twenty years old when he died: his eye was not dim, nor his natural force abated.

Deuteronomy 34:1–4. Moses Sees the Land of Promise from a High Mountain

Why did the Lord have Moses ascend Mount Nebo? (34:1–4) "After blessing the people, Moses ascended Mount Nebo, according to the command of God (Deut. 32:48–51), and there the Lord showed him, in all its length and breadth, that promised land into which he was not to enter . . . in all its different districts. . . . This sight of every part of the land . . . was not an ecstatic vision, but a sight with the bodily eyes, whose natural power of vision was miraculously increased by God, to give Moses a glimpse at least of the glorious land which he was not to tread, and delight his eye with a view of the inheritance intended for his people" (Keil and Delitzsch, *Commentary* [on Deuteronomy 34:1–4]).

Deuteronomy 34:5–12. Moses Is Translated, or Taken into Heaven

What was the ultimate fate of Moses? (34:5–7) "The statements in the Bible concerning the 'death' of Moses are confusing, both here and in Jude, verse 9. The Book of Mormon makes it clear that Moses was translated (see Alma 45:19). . . .

"This is also made clear in [JST] Deuteronomy 34:6: 'For the Lord took him unto his fathers, in a valley in the land of Moab, over against Beth-peor; therefore no man knoweth of his sepulcher unto this day.'

"Josephus claims that when Moses left the children of Israel he was accompanied by 'the senate, and Eleazar . . . , and Joshua.' After the senate left,

Moses 'was going to embrace Eleazar and Joshua. and was still talking with them when a cloud stood over him and he disappeared' (*Antiquities of the Jews*, 103)" (Ludlow, *Companion to Your Study of the Old Testament*, 200–201). See commentary in this volume for Numbers 27:13; Deuteronomy 32:48–52; and Joshua 1:1). ⊕

Why did Moses lay his hands upon Joshua? (34:9) "When Moses was about to depart, God required of him that he should lay his hands upon another man to take his place to act as the leader of the people of Israel. He laid his hands upon Joshua, and a portion of that spirit and power that had attended the ministrations of Moses in the midst of Israel was immediately manifested through Joshua and God confirmed the selection and impressed upon the people by the signs and the mighty works which Joshua accomplished that he was indeed God's chosen servant. . . . And the people, if they had had any doubts whatever, had those doubts removed by those manifestations of power" (Cannon, in *Journal of Discourses*, 26:58).

Why was no other prophet in ancient Israel like unto Moses? (34:10) "This remark concerning Moses does not presuppose that a long series of prophets had already risen up since the time of Moses. . . . The conviction might already have become established in Israel, that no other prophet would arise like Moses, to whom the Lord had manifested Himself with such signs and wonders before the Egyptians and the eyes of Israel. . . . Moses was the founder and mediator of the old covenant. As long as this covenant was to last, no prophet could arise in Israel like unto Moses. There is but One who is worthy of greater honour than Moses, namely, . . Jesus Christ, the founder and mediator of the new and everlasting covenant" (Keil and Delitzsch, *Commentary* [on Deuteronomy 34:9–12]).

8 ¶ And the children of Israel wept for Moses in the plains of Moab thirty days: so the days of weeping *and* mourning for Moses were ended.

9 ¶ And Joshua the son of Nun was full of the spirit of wisdom; for Moses had laid his hands upon him: and the children of Israel hearkened unto him, and did as the LORD commanded Moses.

10 ¶ And there arose not a prophet since in Israel like unto Moses, whom the LORD knew face to face,

11 In all the signs and the wonders, which the LORD sent him to do in the land of Egypt to Pharaoh, and to all his servants, and to all his land,

12 And in all that mighty hand, and in all the great terror which Moses shewed in the sight of all Israel.

THE BOOK OF JOSHUA

Introduction

"The Book of Joshua is one of the most important writings in the [Old Testament], and should never be separated from the Pentateuch [five books of Moses], of which it is at once both the continuation and completion. Between this Book and the five Books of Moses, there is the same analogy as between the four Gospels and the Acts of the Apostles" (*Adam Clarke's Commentary* [on Joshua, Book Overview]). Joshua was the "name given by Moses to Hoshea, son of Nun (Nu 13:16). 'Hoshea' means 'salvation,' while 'Joshua' means 'The LORD saves.' . . . Joshua was from the tribe of Ephraim (Nu 13:8), one of the most powerful of the 12 tribes. . . . Joshua's military prowess uniquely suited him to be the conqueror of Canaan 40 years later, while his faith in God and loyalty to Moses suited him to be Moses' 'aide' (24:13; 33:11) and successor (see Dt 1:38; 3:28; 31:14; 34:9; Jos 1:5)" (*NIV Study Bible* [2020], 128).

Joshua's succession as the leader of Israel was publicly announced by Moses in Numbers 27:18–23. Moses took Joshua before the priests and all the people and "laid his hands upon him, and gave him a charge" (Numbers 27:23). "The book [of Joshua] was regarded by the Jews as the first of the 'former prophets,' but it is more properly a continuation of the first Five Books" (Bible Dictionary, "Joshua, book of").

"We do not know for certain who wrote the book of Joshua. . . . Near the end of Joshua's ministry, . . . the book's narrator reports that 'Joshua wrote these words in the book of the law of God' (Joshua 24:26). This passage may indicate that Joshua wrote at least a portion of the book that is named for him" (*Old Testament Seminary Teacher Material*, 378). "It is apparent that the book came to its final form after the death of Joshua but before the time of the kings of Israel. But the writer recorded those kinds of particulars which only an eyewitness would know. Therefore, it would seem that the original composition was Joshua's. Probably he recorded the events of his administration, following the example of Moses, and later this material was edited by one of the prophets (who many feel was Samuel) and placed with other holy works" (Pearson, *Old Testament*, 34).

The book of Joshua "describes (1) the conquest of Canaan (Josh. 1–12); (2) the allotment of the land among the tribes and Joshua's final exhortations (Josh. 13–24)" (Bible Dictionary, "Joshua, book of"). "The account of the conquest shows that as the Israelites strictly obeyed the Lord's commandments, the Lord made them victorious over their enemies. The book's final two chapters (Joshua 23–24) emphasize the importance of serving the Lord rather than the false gods in the land of Canaan, foreshadowing an important problem the Israelites would struggle with in the future, as recorded in the book of Judges and many other books of the Old Testament" (*Old Testament Seminary Teacher Material*, 378–79).

"The book presents Joshua as a second Moses of sorts, while still appreciating the differences between the two men. Obvious parallels between these two leaders and their experiences include the Red Sea parting for Moses (Exod 14) and the Jordan River parting for Joshua (Josh 3); Jehovah's promise to be with Joshua as he was with Moses (Josh 1:5; 3:7); the sending of spies to scout out the land (Num 13–14; Josh 2); the removal of sandals when a location became holy through divine manifestation (Exod 3:1–6; Josh 5:13–15); and the Israelites' response to Joshua after crossing into Canaan: 'On that day the Lord magnified Joshua in the sight of all Israel; and they feared him, as they feared Moses, all the days of his life' (Josh 4:14)" (Holzapfel, et al., *Jehovah and the World of the Old Testament*, 149).

CHAPTER 1

The Lord speaks to Joshua—He is commanded to be of good courage, to meditate upon the law, and to keep the commandments—He prepares Israel to enter Canaan.

1 Now after the death of Moses the servant of the LORD it came to pass, that the LORD spake unto Joshua the son of Nun, Moses' minister, saying,

2 Moses my servant is dead; now therefore arise, go over this Jordan, thou, and all this people, unto the land which I do give to them, *even* to the children of Israel.

3 Every place that the sole of your foot shall tread upon, that have I given unto you, as I said unto Moses.

4 From the wilderness and this Lebanon even unto the great river, the river Euphrates, all the land of the Hittites, and unto the great

Joshua 1:1–9. The Lord Commands Joshua to Meditate on the Scriptures and Gives Him Courage

What do we know about the death of Moses? (1:1) Moses was translated and did not die. "As was the case with many of the ancient prophets, Moses' ministry extended beyond the limits of his own mortal lifetime. In company with Elijah, he came to the Mount of Transfiguration and bestowed keys of the priesthood upon Peter, James, and John [see Matt. 17:3–4]. From this event . . . we understand that Moses was a translated being and had not died as reported in Deut. 34 (Alma 45:19). It was necessary that he be translated, in order to have a body of flesh and bones at the time of the Transfiguration, since the Resurrection had not yet taken place" (Bible Dictionary, "Moses"). See commentary in this volume for Numbers 27:13; Deuteronomy 32:48–52 and 34:5–7.

What was the first recorded revelation given to Joshua? (1:2) "In the first recorded revelation to Joshua as Israel's leader, the Lord gave him his life's mission: to lead Israel into the land of their inheritance. The Lord promised help and encouraged him.

"The boundaries of the promised land were reviewed (Josh. 1:1–9 and fn). Israelite control did not reach all those boundaries until the time of David and Solomon" (Rasmussen, *Latter-day Saint Commentary on the Old Testament*, 195).

How large was the land which the Lord promised Israel? (1:3–4) "When the Lord tells Joshua that every place his foot treads upon will be given to him, the Lord is drawing upon a cultural symbol. Throughout the ancient Near East, one demonstrates control over something by measuring it out, or by placing it under one's foot. These images are combined by speaking of Joshua's foot treading throughout the land. It is as

The Prophet Joshua Is a Type of Jesus Christ

Jesus is "the Greek form of the Hebrew name *Joshua*. The name means 'Jehovah saves'" (McConkie, *Gospel Symbolism*, 263).

"The book of Joshua . . . [continues] the typology, or symbolism, of Christ, just as did the law of Moses. Indeed, Latter-day Saints are taught that Moses was 'in the similitude of [the] Only Begotten' [Moses 1:6; see also McConkie, *Promised Messiah*, 442–48]. Just as Moses, in his role as prophet, lawgiver, mediator, and deliverer, was a type of Jesus Christ, so Joshua, who led Israel into the promised land, was also a type of Jesus, who leads all the faithful into the ultimate land of promise, the celestial kingdom (see Alma's comparison of the promised land to eternal life in Alma 37:45)" (*Old Testament Student Manual: Genesis–2 Samuel*, 236).

sea toward the going down of the sun, shall be your coast.

if he comes to control the land by placing it under his feet and by pacing off the measurements of their inheritance" (Muhlestein, *Essential Old Testament Companion,* 165).

5 There shall not any man be able to stand before thee all the days of thy life: as I was with Moses, *so* I will be with thee: I will not fail thee, nor forsake thee.

6 Be strong and of a good courage: for unto this people shalt thou divide for an inheritance the land, which I sware unto their fathers to give them.

How might the Lord's promise to be with Joshua have affected him? (1:5) Jehovah's promise to Moses "I will be with thee" (Ex. 3:12) is extended to Joshua (1:9; 3:7). "Of special comfort to Joshua would have been the fact that God would be with him in the same way He had been with Moses. Joshua had been present during the many demonstrations of God's presence in Moses' life and would have known how significant this promise was" (*Nelson Study Bible* [NKJV], 328).

7 Only be thou strong and very courageous, that thou mayest observe to do according to all the law, which Moses my servant commanded thee: turn not from it *to* the right hand or *to* the left, that thou mayest prosper whithersoever thou goest.

8 This book of the law shall not depart out of thy mouth; but thou shalt meditate therein day and night, that thou mayest observe to do according to all that is written therein: for then thou shalt make thy way prosperous, and then thou shalt have good success.

What blessings come from daily meditating on the scriptures? (1:8) As with Joshua, scripture study can help us have a successful life. "I would encourage all of us to continue to read and study the scriptures, that we might understand them and apply in our lives the lessons we find there. . . .

"Spending time each day in scripture study will, without doubt, strengthen our foundations of faith and our testimonies of truth" (Monson, "How Firm a Foundation," 68).

"As you ponder and pray about doctrinal principles, the Holy Ghost will speak to your mind and your heart. From events portrayed in the scriptures, new insights will come and principles relevant to your situation will distill upon your heart" (Nelson, "Living by Scriptural Guidance," 18). ⊕

9 Have not I commanded thee? Be strong and of a good courage; be not afraid, neither be thou dismayed: for the LORD thy God *is* with thee whithersoever thou goest.

How does exercising courage bless our lives? (1:9) "The Lord knew the prophet Joshua and the children of Israel would need great courage during this time. In the first chapter of the book of Joshua, the Lord tells him several times to 'be strong and of a good courage.' The word *courage* is defined as 'mental or moral strength to . . . persevere, and withstand danger, fear, or difficulty.' . . . Through their courage and obedience, Joshua and the children of Israel were able to enter the land of promise. . . .

"In our day we too are striving to enter a 'land of promise.' Our greatest goal is to obtain eternal life with our Heavenly Father" (Dibb, "Be of a Good Courage," 114). ⊕

Joshua 1:10–18. Joshua Prepares the People for Battle in the Promised Land

Why did Joshua command Israel to prepare "victuals"? (1:10–11) The word "victuals" (*tsedah*) referred to "prey or provisions as [the Israelites] had taken from the conquered countries, such as corn, oxen, sheep, etc.; for the word signifies prey, or what is taken by hunting, etc. This was necessary, as they were about to undergo considerable fatigue in marching, and in making preparations for the passage of the Jordan" (*Adam Clarke's Commentary* [on Joshua 1:11]).

Why did the Lord demand a pledge from the tribes of Rueben, Gad, and Manasseh? (1:12–14) "The tribes of Reuben, Gad, and Manasseh, who were to inherit lands already conquered on the east side of the Jordan, were charged to join the other tribes in conquering the rest of the land. These tribes showed their loyalty by accepting that charge and covenanting to put to death any who refused to do so" (*Old Testament Student Manual: Genesis–2 Samuel*, 236).

In what ways can we respond to the Lord's commands as ancient Israel did? (1:16–18) "The scriptures are full of accounts of men and women who showed great courage to do whatever the Lord commanded, even when the tasks seemed impossible, even when they may have wanted to give up. What does the Lord want you to do? He wants you to be . . . valiant and virtuous . . . , dedicated to living each day so that you can be worthy to receive the blessings of the temple and return to Him. In today's world that will take courage" (Cook, "Never, Never, Never Give Up," 117).

10 ¶ Then Joshua commanded the officers of the people, saying,

11 Pass through the host, and command the people, saying, Prepare you victuals; for within three days ye shall pass over this Jordan, to go in to possess the land, which the LORD your God giveth you to possess it.

12 ¶ And to the Reubenites, and to the Gadites, and to half the tribe of Manasseh, spake Joshua, saying,

13 Remember the word which Moses the servant of the LORD commanded you, saying, The LORD your God hath given you rest, and hath given you this land.

14 Your wives, your little ones, and your cattle, shall remain in the land which Moses gave you on this side Jordan; but ye shall pass before your brethren armed, all the mighty men of valour, and help them;

15 Until the LORD have given your brethren rest, as *he hath given* you, and they also have possessed the land which the LORD your God giveth them: then ye shall return unto the land of your possession, and enjoy it, which Moses the LORD's servant gave you on this side Jordan toward the sunrising.

16 ¶ And they answered Joshua, saying, All that thou commandest us we will do, and whithersoever thou sendest us, we will go.

17 According as we hearkened unto Moses in all things, so will we hearken unto thee: only the LORD thy God be with thee, as he was with Moses.

18 Whosoever *he be* that doth rebel against thy commandment, and will not hearken unto thy words in all that thou commandest him, he shall be put to death: only be strong and of a good courage.

CHAPTER 2

Joshua sends spies to Jericho—They are received and concealed by Rahab—They promise to preserve Rahab and her household.

1 And Joshua the son of Nun sent out of Shittim two men to spy secretly, saying, Go view the land, even Jericho. And they went, and came into an harlot's house, named Rahab, and lodged there.

2 And it was told the king of Jericho, saying, Behold, there came men in hither to night of the children of Israel to search out the country.

3 And the king of Jericho sent unto Rahab, saying, Bring forth the men that are come to thee, which are entered into thine house: for they be come to search out all the country.

4 And the woman took the two men, and hid them, and said thus, There came men unto me, but I wist not whence they *were:*
5 And it came to pass *about the time* of shutting of the gate, when it was dark, that the men went out: whither the men went I wot not: pursue after them quickly; for ye shall overtake them.

6 But she had brought them up to the roof of the house, and hid them with the stalks of flax, which she had laid in order upon the roof.

7 And the men pursued after them the way to Jordan unto the fords: and as soon as they

Joshua 2:1–7. Rahab Saves the Lives of the Israelite Spies

Who was Rahab? (2:1) "Whether Rahab had been a harlot, as it says in the King James Version of the Bible, or an innkeeper, as many early Jews and some Christians have traditionally argued, we do not know (see Fallows, *Bible Encyclopedia*, s.v. 'Rahab,' 3:1424). Here we learn that she did many good things for Israel and sought to follow the Lord. For example, she was spared for her courage and loyalty to Israel, while the rest of Jericho was destroyed (see Joshua 6:17). She married Salmon, an Israelite (see Matthew 1:5). She was cited as an example of faith (see Hebrews 11:31; James 2:24–25) and was an ancestor of Jesus Christ (see Matthew 1:5)" (Valletta, et al., *Old Testament for Latter-day Saint Families*, 222).

How were Israel's spies discovered so quickly? (2:3) "The Israelite spies had been recognized as soon as they entered the city gates, and though they were not taken at that moment, word was sent to the king. . . .

"It may be wondered how the spies could have been so readily recognized as they entered Jericho. Archaeologists say that the city occupied only from six to ten acres of land. Strangers therefore were quickly noticed, since all the inhabitants of the city evidently knew each other well. The fact that the circumference of the city was so small also makes more understandable how the Israelite army could march around it so easily each day for a week" (Petersen, *Joshua*, 36, 38).

How was Rahab able to hide the two men? (2:4–6) "Probably she secreted them for the time being in some private corner, till she had the opportunity of concealing them on the house-top in the manner mentioned [Joshua 2:6]. . . .

"All the houses in the east were made flat-roofed; for which a law is given [Deuteronomy 22:8]. On these flat roofs the Asiatics to this day walk, converse, and oftentimes even sleep and pass the night. It is probable that this hiding was after that referred to in the fourth verse" (*Adam Clarke's Commentary* [on Joshua 2:4 and 2:6]).

Joshua 2:8–24. The Israelite Spies Promise to Save Rahab and Her Family

What does Rahab's belief that God had given Israel the land reveal about her faith? (2:9) "Rahab's statement 'I know that the Lord hath given you the land' (v. 9) reveals her prior knowledge and faith in the Lord as well as her understanding of the futility of opposing his will" (Ludlow, *Companion to Your Study of the Old Testament*, 202).

Rahab then quotes "the Song of the Sea (Exodus 15:15–16), merely reversing the order of terms in the poem. . . . Her words are a verbatim confirmation of the assertion in the Song that the great news of the crossing of the sea had reached the Canaanites and dismayed them" (Alter, *Hebrew Bible*, 2:12).

How did Rahab's kindness bring her blessings? (2:12) "Kindness is the essence of greatness and the fundamental characteristic of the noblest men and women I have known. Kindness is a passport that opens doors and fashions friends. It softens hearts and molds relationships that can last lifetimes. . . .

"Kindness is the essence of a celestial life. Kindness is how a Christlike person treats others. Kindness should permeate all of our words and actions at work, at school, at church, and especially in our homes" (Wirthlin, "Virtue of Kindness," 26).

Was it common to have one's house built upon the wall? (2:15) "Houses built into the side of the city wall were common to this period. This benefited the city by adding extra width and support for the wall and benefited the resident by providing a firm wall to support the house. Excavations at Jericho have discovered houses built on the plaster rampart between the two walls with their backs up against the inside of the outer wall" (Walton, et al., *IVP Bible Background Commentary*, 214).

which pursued after them were gone out,
they shut the gate.

8 ¶ And before they were laid down, she
came up unto them upon the roof;

9 And she said unto the men, I know that
the LORD hath given you the land, and that
your terror is fallen upon us, and that all the
inhabitants of the land faint because of you.

10 For we have heard how the LORD dried
up the water of the Red sea for you, when ye
came out of Egypt; and what ye did unto the
two kings of the Amorites, that *were* on the
other side Jordan, Sihon and Og, whom ye
utterly destroyed.

11 And as soon as we had heard *these things*,
our hearts did melt, neither did there remain
any more courage in any man, because of
you: for the LORD your God, he *is* God in
heaven above, and in earth beneath.

12 Now therefore, I pray you, swear unto me
by the LORD, since I have shewed you kindness, that ye will also shew kindness unto my
father's house, and give me a true token:

13 And *that* ye will save alive my father, and
my mother, and my brethren, and my sisters,
and all that they have, and deliver our lives
from death.

14 And the men answered her, Our life for
yours, if ye utter not this our business. And
it shall be, when the LORD hath given us the
land, that we will deal kindly and truly with
thee.

15 Then she let them down by a cord through
the window: for her house *was* upon the town
wall, and she dwelt upon the wall.

16 And she said unto them, Get you to the
mountain, lest the pursuers meet you; and
hide yourselves there three days, until the
pursuers be returned: and afterward may ye
go your way.

17 And the men said unto her, We *will be* blameless of this thine oath which thou hast made us swear.

Why were the Israelite spies concerned about being blameless of their oath with Rahab? (2:17) Their concern illustrates "the value placed upon an oath or promise by men of ancient times. Unfortunately, men of that day were more faithful to their covenants with other men than they were to those made with God. A token was agreed upon as proof of their intention to protect Rahab and her family from destruction in return for her assistance. Rahab was to place a 'line of scarlet thread' in the window of her house (v. 18). This thread would serve as a reminder to attacking Israel that Rahab and all within her house were to be spared from destruction" (*Old Testament Student Manual: Genesis–2 Samuel*, 237).

18 Behold, *when* we come into the land, thou shalt bind this line of scarlet thread in the window which thou didst let us down by: and thou shalt bring thy father, and thy mother, and thy brethren, and all thy father's household, home unto thee.

What symbolism might the "line of scarlet thread" have conveyed? (2:18) The *"line of scarlet thread"* was likely a "piece of scarlet cloth, or, this cloth (made) of scarlet thread" (*Adam Clarke's Commentary* [on Joshua 2:18]). "The *line of scarlet thread in the window* (v. 18) was the 'cord' by which Rahab had assisted the spies' escape over the wall (2:15). . . . Now, however, the function of the red marker as prescribed by the spies was to be similar to that of the blood of the Passover lamb when the Lord struck down the firstborn of Egypt (Exod. 12:13, 22–23), to mark and identify for preservation her house and its inhabitants. The early church viewed the blood-colored cord as a type (symbol) of Christ's atonement" (*Zondervan KJV Commentary*, 280). ⊕

19 And it shall be, *that* whosoever shall go out of the doors of thy house into the street, his blood *shall be* upon his head, and we *will be* guiltless: and whosoever shall be with thee in the house, his blood *shall be* on our head, if *any* hand be upon him.

20 And if thou utter this our business, then we will be quit of thine oath which thou hast made us to swear.

How was the promise of Rahab's scarlet cord similar to another promise given to Israel? (2:19–21) "The Israelite spies promise Rahab that all her family that are found in her house will be spared if she marks the window with the red cord. This is similar to the promise given to the Israelites who marked their doors with lamb's blood on the night of Passover (see Exodus 12:7, 13)" (Valletta, et al., *The Old Testament for Latter-day Saint Families*, 223).

21 And she said, According unto your words, so *be* it. And she sent them away, and they departed: and she bound the scarlet line in the window.

22 And they went, and came unto the mountain, and abode there three days, until the pursuers were returned: and the pursuers sought *them* throughout all the way, but found *them* not.

Why did Rahab send the spies to the nearby mountains? (2:21–22) "At Rahab's [suggestion], the spies hid themselves for three days. The hills around Jericho are full of caves, and so would have given them ample cover. They then returned to Joshua, probably by swimming the Jordan, with their report of the utter despondency and alarm of the Canaanites" (*New Bible Commentary: Revised*, 236–37).

Joshua 3:1–6. Joshua Prepares the People to Cross over Jordan

Why were the Israelites commanded to follow the ark of the covenant? (3:3) "The ark was the symbol of the presence of the Lord. . . . As Israel is always to be led by the Lord and by the word of his mouth, so the ark of the covenant was to go before them as they journeyed to their land of promise. This taught the necessity of Israel in all ages following the path marked by the Lord and giving heed to his voice" (McConkie, *Gospel Symbolism*, 110).

About how far is two thousand cubits? (3:4) "A 'cubit' is about eighteen inches ([see] Bible Dictionary, s.v. "Weights and Measures," . . .). Two thousand cubits would be about one thousand yards or nine hundred meters" (Valletta, et al., *The Old Testament for Latter-day Saint Families*, 224). What lessons might the Lord want to teach with this distance between the sacred and the common? In what ways can we better reverence sacred places like temples and sacred time like the Sabbath?

Why do you think prophets, both ancient and modern, instruct their people to sanctify themselves? (3:5) "If gospel standards seem high and the personal improvement needed in the days ahead seems out of reach, remember Joshua's encouragement to his people when they faced a daunting future. 'Sanctify yourselves,' he said, 'for to morrow the Lord will do

23 ¶ So the two men returned, and descended from the mountain, and passed over, and came to Joshua the son of Nun, and told him all *things* that befell them:

24 And they said unto Joshua, Truly the LORD hath delivered into our hands all the land; for even all the inhabitants of the country do faint because of us.

CHAPTER 3

Joshua leads Israel to the Jordan—The Lord cuts off the water of the Jordan; it stands up as a heap, and Israel passes over on dry ground.

1 And Joshua rose early in the morning; and they removed from Shittim, and came to Jordan, he and all the children of Israel, and lodged there before they passed over.

2 And it came to pass after three days, that the officers went through the host;

3 And they commanded the people, saying, When ye see the ark of the covenant of the LORD your God, and the priests the Levites bearing it, then ye shall remove from your place, and go after it.

4 Yet there shall be a space between you and it, about two thousand cubits by measure: come not near unto it, that ye may know the way by which ye must go: for ye have not passed *this* way heretofore.

5 And Joshua said unto the people, Sanctify yourselves: for to morrow the LORD will do wonders among you.

6 And Joshua spake unto the priests, saying, Take up the ark of the covenant, and pass over before the people. And they took up the ark of the covenant, and went before the people.

7 ¶ And the LORD said unto Joshua, This day will I begin to magnify thee in the sight of all Israel, that they may know that, as I was with Moses, *so* I will be with thee.

8 And thou shalt command the priests that bear the ark of the covenant, saying, When ye are come to the brink of the water of Jordan, ye shall stand still in Jordan.

9 ¶ And Joshua said unto the children of Israel, Come hither, and hear the words of the LORD your God.

10 And Joshua said, Hereby ye shall know that the living God *is* among you, and *that* he will without fail drive out from before you the Canaanites, and the Hittites, and the Hivites, and the Perizzites, and the Girgashites, and the Amorites, and the Jebusites.

11 Behold, the ark of the covenant of the Lord of all the earth passeth over before you into Jordan.

12 Now therefore take you twelve men out of the tribes of Israel, out of every tribe a man.

13 And it shall come to pass, as soon as the soles of the feet of the priests that bear the

wonders among you.' I declare that same promise.... It is the promise of this Church. It is the promise of Him who performs those wonders" (Holland, "Tomorrow the Lord Will Do Wonders among You," 127). ⊕

Joshua 3:7–17. The Lord Stops the River Jordan to Show the People That He Is Still Leading Them

How does the Lord magnify His prophets? (3:7) "A portion of that spirit and power that had attended the ministrations of Moses in the midst of Israel was immediately manifested through Joshua, and God confirmed the selection and impressed upon the people by the signs and the mighty works which Joshua accomplished that he was indeed God's chosen servant. He magnified him in the midst of the people; he was enabled to perform mighty works, and the people, if they had had any doubts whatever, had those doubts removed by those manifestations of power" (Cannon, in *Journal of Discourses*, 26:56). In our day, the Lord has commanded us to receive the words of our modern prophet "as if from [His] own mouth, in all patience and faith" (D&C 21:5).

Why might the Lord have provided for a miracle at the River Jordan? (3:8–13) Israel is about to begin the dangerous task of invading the promised land and certainly they had mixed feelings regarding the venture. "The manner by which God is about to bring Israel across the Jordan River, the watery boundary of the promised land, will bring assurance that the one true God is with them and that he will surely dislodge the present inhabitants of Canaan" (*NIV Study Bible* [1997], 295).

What is the symbolism of passing through the River Jordan? (3:8) "As Moses was magnified by the Lord in the eyes of Israel when God parted the Red Sea, so Joshua was magnified in the same way through the parting of the Jordan River. In both instances Israel passed through the water into a newness of life.... In each instance the passage represented a new covenant agreement. Israel passed over the River Jordan on the first day of the Passover (see Joshua 3:17; 4:19; compare Exodus 12:3)" (*Old Testament Student Manual: Genesis–2 Samuel*, 237).

ark of the LORD, the Lord of all the earth,
shall rest in the waters of Jordan, *that* the waters of Jordan shall be cut off *from* the waters
that come down from above; and they shall
stand upon an heap.

14 ¶ And it came to pass, when the people
removed from their tents, to pass over
Jordan, and the priests bearing the ark of the
covenant before the people;

15 And as they that bare the ark were come
unto Jordan, and the feet of the priests that
bare the ark were dipped in the brim of the
water, (for Jordan overfloweth all his banks
all the time of harvest,)

What did the priests demonstrate by stepping into the flowing water? (3:15) "Interestingly, the waters did not part as the children of Israel stood on the banks of the river waiting for something to happen; rather, the soles of their feet were wet before the water parted. The faith of the Israelites was manifested in the fact that they walked into the water *before* it parted. They walked into the river Jordan with a future-facing assurance of things hoped for" (Bednar, "Seek Learning by Faith," 63). ⊕

16 That the waters which came down from
above stood *and* rose up upon an heap
very far from the city Adam, that *is* beside
Zaretan: and those that came down toward
the sea of the plain, *even* the salt sea, failed,
and were cut off: and the people passed over
right against Jericho.

How was this miracle similar to parting the Red Sea? (3:16–17) "These events naturally call to mind the Red Sea crossing in Exodus 14–15. There too God miraculously separated the waters that allowed the Israelites to cross on dry ground. There too the waters stood in a 'heap' (Exod 15:8). There too the miracle was for the immediate purpose of crossing a great watery barrier, but it was for the larger purpose of glorifying God and confirming his chosen leader (Moses) in the eyes of the people (Exod 14:31), just as the later miracle glorified God (3:10; 4:24) and confirmed his chosen leader, Joshua (3:7; 4:14)" (Howard, *Joshua*, 131).

17 And the priests that bare the ark of the
covenant of the LORD stood firm on dry
ground in the midst of Jordan, and all the
Israelites passed over on dry ground, until all
the people were passed clean over Jordan.

How can miracles like this apply to you? (3:17) "As we demonstrate our faith in Christ's delivering power, even to the point of getting our feet wet, the Lord will part the waters and bring about our redemption. We see in Israel's journey the pattern which we must follow in order to inherit our promised land. Whether it be 11 days or 40 years that lie ahead of us, we must follow the instructions of the Lord and have faith in His delivering power. As we do this, there is no doubt that He will bring us into the celestial kingdom" (Muhlestein, "Israel's Exodus and Deliverance," 51).

CHAPTER 4

Joshua places twelve stones to commemorate the crossing of the Jordan—Joshua is magnified before the children of Israel as they cross the Jordan—After the priests bearing the ark pass over, the river returns to its course.

Summary of Joshua 4

While the priests "[stand] firm" (Joshua 4:3) in the Jordan and the waters of the river are still raised up "upon an heap" (Joshua 3:16), Joshua commands a man from each of the tribes of Israel to carry out a stone from the riverbed. With these stones they build a monument to help the people always remember the great miracle the Lord did for Israel. After the children of Israel cross the river and the stones are collected, Joshua commands the priests carrying the ark of the covenant to come up out of the river. The river then begins to flow again.

"The account of the Israelites miraculously crossing the Jordan River on dry ground demonstrated Jehovah's power and that he was still with the Israelites (Josh 3; reminiscent of the parting of the Red Sea). This power was manifest when the flow of the Jordan River stopped as the priests carried the ark of the covenant, the most visible and sacred symbol of Jehovah's presence, into the water (Josh 3:15–17; 4:17–18)" (Holzapfel, et al., *Jehovah and the World of the Old Testament*, 149).

CHAPTER 5

The inhabitants of Canaan fear Israel—The males of Israel are circumcised—Israel keeps the Passover, eats the fruit of the land, and manna ceases—The captain of the Lord's host appears to Joshua.

Summary of Joshua 5:1–9

The Canaanite fear of Israel provides time for Joshua to follow the Lord's command to circumcise all of Israel's males.

Joshua 5:10–15. After Israel Arrives in the Promised Land, Manna Ceases and Joshua Sees the Captain of the Lord's Host

10 ¶ And the children of Israel encamped in Gilgal, and kept the passover on the fourteenth day of the month at even in the plains of Jericho.

11 And they did eat of the old corn of the land on the morrow after the passover, unleavened cakes, and parched *corn* in the selfsame day.

Why was Israel's first Passover in the promised land so important? (5:10–12) "The first Passover kept by the Israelites in Canaan took place forty years after the Passover was inaugurated in Egypt on the eve of Israel's march to freedom (Josh. 5:10a; Ex. 12:11; Num. 28:16; 32:13; Deut. 29:5). The children of Israel crossed the Jordan 'on the tenth day of the first month, and encamped in Gilgal' on the day each family was to select a lamb in preparation for the Passover [Josh. 4:19;

5:10]. On the next day, after the Passover, they ate unleavened cakes made with grain from the previous year's harvest in Canaan, and the manna ceased to fall" (Rasmussen, *Latter-day Saint Commentary on the Old Testament*, 198).

Who was the captain of the Lord's host? (5:13–14) "The divinity of the messenger is indicated by his instructions to Joshua, which, like those that Moses had been given at the burning bush, were to show reverence because the place had become holy (Josh. 5:13–15*a–b*). His message was encouraging, and Joshua was reverent and grateful" (Rasmussen, *Latter-day Saint Commentary on the Old Testament*, 198).

Why is this place holy? (5:15) "The statement 'the place whereon thou standest' (v. 15) may have referred to (1) an event in the past that occurred there, or (2) the incident occurring to Joshua, or (3) a sacred event to occur in the future. The Savior visited in the area of Jericho several times, healing the blind and performing other miracles (Matt. 20:29–34; Mark 10:46–52; Luke 18:35–43; 19:1–27). It was also in the river Jordan which flows near Jericho, where he was baptized (Matt. 3:13–16)" (Ludlow, *Companion to Your Study of the Old Testament*, 203–4).

Joshua 6:1–16. The Lord Tells Joshua How to Bring Down the Walls of Jericho

What does it mean that "Jericho was straitly shut up" because of Israel? (6:1) The indication that Jericho is *straitly [tightly] shut up* "is understandable since the fearful inhabitants of the city have anticipated the arrival of the Israelites. With the recent visit of the spies, the people of Jericho suspect an imminent attack and set in place special measures of security in order to protect the city and its inhabitants. In reality, Jericho is now under siege. As a rule, walled cities opened their gates every day to allow the inhabitants to plow the surrounding fields, to permit foreign merchants to come in for business purposes, and to enable travelers to enter the city" (Dallaire, "Joshua," 2:895).

12 ¶ And the manna ceased on the morrow after they had eaten of the old corn of the land; neither had the children of Israel manna any more; but they did eat of the fruit of the land of Canaan that year.

13 ¶ And it came to pass, when Joshua was by Jericho, that he lifted up his eyes and looked, and, behold, there stood a man over against him with his sword drawn in his hand: and Joshua went unto him, and said unto him, *Art* thou for us, or for our adversaries?

14 And he said, Nay; but *as* captain of the host of the LORD am I now come. And Joshua fell on his face to the earth, and did worship, and said unto him, What saith my lord unto his servant?

15 And the captain of the LORD's host said unto Joshua, Loose thy shoe from off thy foot; for the place whereon thou standest *is* holy. And Joshua did so.

CHAPTER 6

Jericho is taken and destroyed—Only Rahab and her household are saved.

1 Now Jericho was straitly shut up because of the children of Israel: none went out, and none came in.

2 And the LORD said unto Joshua, See, I have given into thine hand Jericho, and the king thereof, *and* the mighty men of valour.

3 And ye shall compass the city, all *ye* men of war, *and* go round about the city once. Thus shalt thou do six days.

4 And seven priests shall bear before the ark seven trumpets of rams' horns: and the seventh day ye shall compass the city seven times, and the priests shall blow with the trumpets.

5 And it shall come to pass, that when they make a long *blast* with the ram's horn, *and* when ye hear the sound of the trumpet, all the people shall shout with a great shout; and the wall of the city shall fall down flat, and the people shall ascend up every man straight before him.

6 ¶ And Joshua the son of Nun called the priests, and said unto them, Take up the ark of the covenant, and let seven priests bear seven trumpets of rams' horns before the ark of the LORD.

7 And he said unto the people, Pass on, and compass the city, and let him that is armed pass on before the ark of the LORD.

8 ¶ And it came to pass, when Joshua had spoken unto the people, that the seven priests bearing the seven trumpets of rams' horns passed on before the LORD, and blew with the trumpets: and the ark of the covenant of the LORD followed them.

9 ¶ And the armed men went before the priests that blew with the trumpets, and the rearward came after the ark, *the priests* going on, and blowing with the trumpets.

10 And Joshua had commanded the people, saying, Ye shall not shout, nor make any noise with your voice, neither shall *any* word proceed out of your mouth, until the day I bid you shout; then shall ye shout.

11 So the ark of the LORD compassed the city, going about *it* once: and they came into the camp, and lodged in the camp.

12 ¶ And Joshua rose early in the morning, and the priests took up the ark of the LORD.

13 And seven priests bearing seven trumpets of rams' horns before the ark of the LORD

What does the number seven represent or symbolize? (6:4) "The number seven figures prominently in this passage: seven priests, seven trumpets, seven days, and seven trips around the city. Seven is a significant number in the Scriptures, beginning with the seven days for creation. It is a number that signifies completion. Its use here helps to demonstrate that the conquest of Jericho was part of a larger spiritual exercise that sanctified the people and the land for God" (*NKJV Study Bible* [2018], 316).

How did this unconventional battle plan show Israel's trust in the Lord? (6:8–16) "By striving to live by every word of God we open ourselves to . . . new perspectives on life here and hereafter. Consider for a moment the rather fascinating manner in which Joshua and the children of Israel were instructed to conquer the city of Jericho . . . It would certainly have been easier for Jehovah to sweep the land of Jericho with fire and destroy all the inhabitants and then have the Israelites move into their new digs. But God didn't do it that way. Rather, he announced a plan that required the descendants of Abraham to give perfect heed to his word, to follow his instructions with exactness—to do things just as their Lord instructed them, down to the minutest detail" (Millet, *Men of Covenant*, 87). ⊕

Joshua 6:17–27. The Walls of Jericho Fall but Rahab and Her Family Are Saved

What were the "accursed" things Joshua spoke of? (6:18) Joshua 6:18*a* states that the "accursed thing[s]" are "those things under a ban for the people to take, or dedicated for a sacrifice to the Lord. Josh. 7:1; 1 Chr. 2:7." There was a general rule that no one should loot and selfishly keep spoils for themselves or "from laying hold on, secreting, and enjoying as their own, what was devoted to another use: . . . *when ye take of the accursed thing* [it would bring a curse on the entire camp of Israel, *and trouble it*, since it was] . . . done secretly, and not known who did it, the whole body of the people would be chargeable with it, and suffer" (*John Gill's Exposition of the Whole Bible* [commentary on Joshua 6:18]).

What lessons can be drawn from the walls of Jericho falling down? (6:20) Elder Neil L. Andersen uses the example of Jericho's fallen walls to emphasize the need to follow modern prophets even if what is asked is not completely understood or scoffed at by the world: "[When] Joshua spoke, . . . [we] can almost hear the whining of the skeptics as Joshua announced his battle plans for taking the city of Jericho. . . . They would quietly . . . circle the city one time for each of six

went on continually, and blew with the
trumpets: and the armed men went before
them; but the rearward came after the ark of
the LORD, *the priests* going on, and blowing
with the trumpets.

14 And the second day they compassed the
city once, and returned into the camp: so
they did six days.

15 And it came to pass on the seventh day,
that they rose early about the dawning of the
day, and compassed the city after the same
manner seven times: only on that day they
compassed the city seven times.

16 And it came to pass at the seventh time,
when the priests blew with the trumpets,
Joshua said unto the people, Shout; for the
LORD hath given you the city.

17 ¶ And the city shall be accursed, *even* it,
and all that *are* therein, to the LORD: only
Rahab the harlot shall live, she and all that
are with her in the house, because she hid the
messengers that we sent.

18 And ye, in any wise keep *yourselves* from
the accursed thing, lest ye make *yourselves* accursed, when ye take of the accursed thing,
and make the camp of Israel a curse, and
trouble it.

19 But all the silver, and gold, and vessels
of brass and iron, *are* consecrated unto the
LORD: they shall come into the treasury of
the LORD.

20 So the people shouted when *the priests*
blew with the trumpets: and it came to pass,
when the people heard the sound of the
trumpet, and the people shouted with a great
shout, that the wall fell down flat, so that
the people went up into the city, every man
straight before him, and they took the city.

days. Then on the seventh day they would compass the city seven times. Following, the priests would blow the trumpets, and at that time all the people would shout with a great shout. Then, Joshua assured them, the walls would come down. . . . When the walls came down, the skeptics were quiet" ("Prophets and Spiritual Mole Crickets," 16).

21 And they utterly destroyed all that *was* in the city, both man and woman, young and old, and ox, and sheep, and ass, with the edge of the sword.

22 But Joshua had said unto the two men that had spied out the country, Go into the harlot's house, and bring out thence the woman, and all that she hath, as ye sware unto her.

23 And the young men that were spies went in, and brought out Rahab, and her father, and her mother, and her brethren, and all that she had; and they brought out all her kindred, and left them without the camp of Israel.

24 And they burnt the city with fire, and all that *was* therein: only the silver, and the gold, and the vessels of brass and of iron, they put into the treasury of the house of the LORD.

Why did they have to destroy everything except Rahab and her family? (6:21–23) "God requires punishment for the wicked and unrepentant as this miracle suggests. However, this miracle also highlights God's desire to send mercy, even to those whose wickedness is nearing the point of no return, if they will repent and turn to Him (see 2 Chronicles 7:14; Jeremiah 18:8). God did not will the destruction of Jericho, nor the destruction of Rahab—one of its residents. But Jericho was unrepentant, whereas Rahab changed her life and conformed to God's will (see Hebrews 11:31). Consequently, the former was destroyed and the latter was saved" (Gaskill, *Miracles of the Old Testament*, 199).

25 And Joshua saved Rahab the harlot alive, and her father's household, and all that she had; and she dwelleth in Israel *even* unto this day; because she hid the messengers, which Joshua sent to spy out Jericho.

How could Rahab have been spared when the walls fell down? (6:25) "German excavations from the early 1900s uncovered a portion of the wall that did not fall. It had houses built against it that were still intact. These houses were between the lower wall and another wall built just above them, making them 'in' the city's wall. Rahab's house could have been in this portion of the wall that did not fall. One way or the other, she was miraculously spared" (Muhlestein, *Scripture Study Made Simple*, 151).

26 ¶ And Joshua adjured *them* at that time, saying, Cursed *be* the man before the LORD, that riseth up and buildeth this city Jericho: he shall lay the foundation thereof in his firstborn, and in his youngest *son* shall he set up the gates of it.

27 So the LORD was with Joshua; and his fame was *noised* throughout all the country.

How has this curse on Jericho been fulfilled? (6:26) "Joshua cursed any attempts at rebuilding Jericho. The city was occupied sporadically after that ([Joshua] 18:21; Judg. 3:13; 2 Sam. 10:5), but never to the previous extent. Joshua's curse found a dramatic fulfillment many centuries later when Hiel of Bethel laid its foundation and rebuilt its gates at great personal cost (1 Kin. 16:34). The language of the 1 Kings account consciously echoes that of this passage" (*Nelson Study Bible* [NKJV], 337).

Joshua 7:1–15. The Israelites Are Defeated at Ai

Who was Achan? (7:1) Achan was "a man of the tribe of Judah who seized and attempted to hide the spoils from the battle of Jericho, against the counsel of Joshua. His disobedience resulted in Israel's defeat at Ai. His transgression was detected through revelation to Joshua, and he was stoned to death. Josh. 7; 22:20" (Bible Dictionary, "Achan").

What did Achan's family do to bring God's fury upon all Israel? (7:1–5) "The principle of collective responsibility is powerfully taught in Joshua 7. All Israelites were supposed to abide by the 'ban' on taking booty from Jericho. Everything belonged to the Lord. Achan disobeyed and took booty and hid it in his tent. Despite his individual action, the text states, 'The children of Israel committed a trespass in the accursed thing' (Josh 7:1), and 'Israel hath sinned, and they have also transgressed my covenant . . . for they have even taken of the accursed thing [*herem*]' (Josh 7:11). This resulted in the defeat of Israelite forces in their initial attack on the city of Ai (Josh 7:2–9)" (Holzapfel, et al., *Jehovah and the World of the Old Testament*, 153–54).

Why were the Israelites defeated by Ai's men? (7:5–12) Elder James E. Talmage observed: "Consider the defeat of Israel by the men of Ai; a law of righteousness had been violated, and things that were accursed had been introduced into the camp of the covenant people; this transgression interposed resistance to the current of divine help, and until the people had sanctified themselves the power was not renewed unto them" (*Articles of Faith*, 95). ⊕

Why was Joshua so upset that he tore his clothes, fell on his face, and put dust on his head? (7:6–9) "The ancient Israelites openly expressed their grief in customs—tearing clothes, wearing scratchy material called sackcloth, going without sandals or headgear, putting dirt on their heads and rolling in dust or ashes—that have almost no modern counterparts. Joshua was alarmed and grieved to discover that God had abandoned them in their battle against Ai [v. 7–9]. In anguish he prostrated himself before the ark in the presence of the Lord" (*Quest Study Bible* [1994], 292).

CHAPTER 7

Israel is defeated by the people of Ai—Joshua complains to the Lord—Achan and his household are destroyed because he disobeyed the Lord by taking the spoils of Jericho.

1 But the children of Israel committed a trespass in the accursed thing: for Achan, the son of Carmi, the son of Zabdi, the son of Zerah, of the tribe of Judah, took of the accursed thing: and the anger of the LORD was kindled against the children of Israel.

2 And Joshua sent men from Jericho to Ai, which *is* beside Beth-aven, on the east side of Beth-el, and spake unto them, saying, Go up and view the country. And the men went up and viewed Ai.

3 And they returned to Joshua, and said unto him, Let not all the people go up; but let about two or three thousand men go up and smite Ai; *and* make not all the people to labour thither; for they *are but* few.

4 So there went up thither of the people about three thousand men: and they fled before the men of Ai.

5 And the men of Ai smote of them about thirty and six men: for they chased them *from* before the gate *even* unto Shebarim, and smote them in the going down: wherefore the hearts of the people melted, and became as water.

6 ¶ And Joshua rent his clothes, and fell to the earth upon his face before the ark of the LORD until the eventide, he and the elders of Israel, and put dust upon their heads.

7 And Joshua said, Alas, O Lord GOD, wherefore hast thou at all brought this people over Jordan, to deliver us into the hand of the Amorites, to destroy us? would to God we had been content, and dwelt on the other side Jordan!

8 O Lord, what shall I say, when Israel turneth their backs before their enemies!

9 For the Canaanites and all the inhabitants of the land shall hear *of it,* and shall environ us round, and cut off our name from the earth: and what wilt thou do unto thy great name?

10 ¶ And the LORD said unto Joshua, Get thee up; wherefore liest thou thus upon thy face?

11 Israel hath sinned, and they have also transgressed my covenant which I commanded them: for they have even taken of the accursed thing, and have also stolen, and dissembled also, and they have put *it* even among their own stuff.

12 Therefore the children of Israel could not stand before their enemies, *but* turned *their* backs before their enemies, because they were accursed: neither will I be with you any more, except ye destroy the accursed from among you.

Why did the Lord give Joshua instructions on finding who had transgressed His commandment? (7:10–15) "God's response to Joshua and the elders' mourning reinforced the importance of holiness. Israel—not just Achan—had sinned, and God would not tolerate it. This passage also shows that God had consistent standards for both Israel and the Canaanites. He had ordered Israel to exterminate the Canaanites because of their sin; He could not allow Israel to accommodate corruption, even that of one man, especially when the instructions concerning the infraction were so clear (v. 11; Deut. 7:26)" (*Nelson Study Bible* [NKJV], 338).

13 Up, sanctify the people, and say, Sanctify yourselves against to morrow: for thus saith the LORD God of Israel, *There is* an accursed thing in the midst of thee, O Israel: thou canst not stand before thine enemies, until ye take away the accursed thing from among you.

14 In the morning therefore ye shall be brought according to your tribes: and it shall be, *that* the tribe which the LORD taketh shall come according to the families *thereof;* and the family which the LORD shall take shall come by households; and the household which the LORD shall take shall come man by man.

15 And it shall be, *that* he that is taken with the accursed thing shall be burnt with fire, he and all that he hath: because he hath transgressed the covenant of the LORD, and because he hath wrought folly in Israel.

How was the offender to be discovered? (7:13–15) The Prophet Joseph Smith taught that "a man must have the discerning of spirits, . . . to understand these things, and how is he to obtain this gift if there are no gifts of the Spirit? And how can these gifts be obtained without revelation? . . . [This same power] existed through the medium of the Priesthood in different ages. Moses could detect the magician's power, and show that he [himself] was God's servant. . . . [It was by this same power that] Joshua knew how to detect the man who had stolen the wedge of gold and the Babylonish garment" (Joseph Smith Papers, "History, 1838–1856, volume C-1 [2 November 1838–31 July 1842]," 1307).

Joshua 7:16–26. The Lord Reveals That Achan Is the Man Who Caused the Israelite Defeat

What lessons can be learned from Achan's tragic mistake? (7:16–21) "We cannot hide sins from the Lord. In an attempt to encourage Achan to confess, the Lord told Joshua to have each tribe present themselves before Him and He would point out to which tribe the offender belonged. . . . Achan was certainly present as the number of possible offenders was being narrowed. Then each man in the guilty family was brought one at a time before the Lord until it was Achan's turn. When confronted, Achan finally confessed (see Josh. 7:20). At each step in the identification process, the Lord had given Achan an opportunity to come forward and admit his sin, but he had refused until he was directly exposed" (Morgan, "Sin of Achan," 44).

Why was Achan's coveting such a serious matter? (7:21) "To understand the meaning of the word *covet* as it is used in the tenth commandment, we must focus on *what* and *why* we covet. The word itself is used in both negative and positive senses in the Bible, and its application depends on the root word from which the English is translated. The Hebrew word translated as *covet* in Ex. 20:17 is *lo takhmodh*, which denotes an inordinate, consuming, selfish desire, arising from improper or evil motives" (Top, "Thou Shalt Not Covet," 22).

16 ¶ So Joshua rose up early in the morning, and brought Israel by their tribes; and the tribe of Judah was taken:

17 And he brought the family of Judah; and he took the family of the Zarhites: and he brought the family of the Zarhites man by man; and Zabdi was taken:

18 And he brought his household man by man; and Achan, the son of Carmi, the son of Zabdi, the son of Zerah, of the tribe of Judah, was taken.

19 And Joshua said unto Achan, My son, give, I pray thee, glory to the LORD God of Israel, and make confession unto him; and tell me now what thou hast done; hide *it* not from me.

20 And Achan answered Joshua, and said, Indeed I have sinned against the LORD God of Israel, and thus and thus have I done:

21 When I saw among the spoils a goodly Babylonish garment, and two hundred shekels of silver, and a wedge of gold of fifty shekels weight, then I coveted them, and took them; and, behold, they *are* hid in the earth in the midst of my tent, and the silver under it.

22 ¶ So Joshua sent messengers, and they ran unto the tent; and, behold, *it was* hid in his tent, and the silver under it.

23 And they took them out of the midst of the tent, and brought them unto Joshua, and unto all the children of Israel, and laid them out before the LORD.

24 And Joshua, and all Israel with him, took Achan the son of Zerah, and the silver, and the garment, and the wedge of gold, and his sons, and his daughters, and his oxen, and his asses, and his sheep, and his tent, and all that he had: and they brought them unto the valley of Achor.

25 And Joshua said, Why hast thou troubled us? the LORD shall trouble thee this day. And all Israel stoned him with stones, and burned them with fire, after they had stoned them with stones.

26 And they raised over him a great heap of stones unto this day. So the LORD turned from the fierceness of his anger. Wherefore the name of that place was called, The valley of Achor, unto this day.

CHAPTER 8

Joshua uses an ambush, takes Ai, and slays its inhabitants—He builds an altar in Mount Ebal—The words of the law, both blessings and cursings, are read to the people.

CHAPTER 9

The Gibeonites by craft obtain a league with Israel—Joshua makes them servants to the congregation of Israel.

Why was Achan's family also destroyed? (7:25) "It is unclear whether only Achan was killed for his sin or all the members of his family were executed: 'And all Israel stoned *him* with stones, and burned *them* with fire, after they had stoned *them* with stones. And they raised over *him* a great heap of stones.' (Italics added.) Obviously Achan perished, but the next pronoun *them* could refer to the possessions, rather than the family, of Achan.

"Deuteronomy 24:16 specifically states 'neither shall the children be put to death for the [sins of the] fathers'" (Ludlow, *Companion to Your Study of the Old Testament*, 204).

Summary of Joshua 8

The Lord again blesses Israel, after the wickedness of Achan is removed (see Joshua 7). Joshua destroys the city of Ai. Then, as Moses had commanded (see Deuteronomy 27:1–8), Joshua builds an altar of stones whereon he writes all the words of the Law. Joshua teaches the people and reminds them of all the blessings the Lord promised if they are faithful and all the punishments promised if they are wicked.

Summary of Joshua 9

"Most of the leaders of the city-states in Canaan prepared to fight against the Israelites (Josh 9:1–2). However, the people of Gibeon intentionally set out to deceive the Israelites. Their envoys pretended to have traveled for a great distance (Josh 9:3–13), when actually the city of Gibeon is only about six miles northwest of Jerusalem and about thirty miles south of Shechem. Their stratagem proved successful. The biblical narrative notes that the Israelites 'asked not counsel at the mouth of the Lord. And Joshua made peace with them, and made a league [covenant/treaty] with them, to let them live: and the princes of the congregation sware unto them' (Josh 9:14–15). The power of this covenant, sworn with an oath, kept the Israelites from destroying the Gibeonites even after discovering their deception. Alternatively, they imposed work on the Gibeonites, to provide wood and water for the Tabernacle service (Josh 9:16–27)" (Holzapfel, et al., *Jehovah and the World of the Old Testament*, 155).

Joshua 10:1–14. Five Amorite Kings Attack the Gibeonites for Making Peace with Israel and the Israelites Come to Their Aid

Why were Canaanite kings concerned about Gibeon's alliance with Israel? (10:2–4) "One of the major passes from the hill country to the plains, from the Beth Horon pass into the Valley of Aijalon, was in the area controlled by Gibeon. With Jericho, Ai and Bethel already defeated, that gave Israel control of the primary lateral route across Palestine (from the Jordan rift to the coast). . . .

"Royal cities would be the administrative centers of larger districts. The Egyptians had a number of cities during the Amarna period where their governors were housed, such as Gaza and Beth Shan. Cities like Shechem and Hazor could also have been considered royal cities because of the large areas they controlled. Gibeon's strategic location and fortifications give it the potential to be such a city" (Walton, et al., *IVP Bible Background Commentary*, 223).

Why did the men of Gibeon ask for Joshua's help? (10:6–7) "The Gibeonites' words to Joshua were an urgent appeal for protection. . . . Because of the treaty they had just concluded with the Israelites, they were able to make such an appeal [and this became] a test of Israel's commitment and faithfulness to its word. The number of verbs found in their appeal—all imperatives—add to this sense of urgency: *'Do not let* your hands *drop* from your servants; *get up* to us quickly and *deliver* us and *help* us!' The appeal to *'deliver'* is an emphatic imperative—perhaps best rendered as *'you* must *deliver us!'*—adding even more

CHAPTER 10

Israel defeats the Amorites and their allies, and the Lord casts stones from heaven upon them—The sun and moon stand still—Many kings and cities are destroyed—The Lord fought for Israel.

1 Now it came to pass, when Adoni-zedek king of Jerusalem had heard how Joshua had taken Ai, and had utterly destroyed it; as he had done to Jericho and her king, so he had done to Ai and her king; and how the inhabitants of Gibeon had made peace with Israel, and were among them;

2 That they feared greatly, because Gibeon *was* a great city, as one of the royal cities, and because it *was* greater than Ai, and all the men thereof *were* mighty.

3 Wherefore Adoni-zedek king of Jerusalem sent unto Hoham king of Hebron, and unto Piram king of Jarmuth, and unto Japhia king of Lachish, and unto Debir king of Eglon, saying,

4 Come up unto me, and help me, that we may smite Gibeon: for it hath made peace with Joshua and with the children of Israel.

5 Therefore the five kings of the Amorites, the king of Jerusalem, the king of Hebron, the king of Jarmuth, the king of Lachish, the king of Eglon, gathered themselves together, and went up, they and all their hosts, and encamped before Gibeon, and made war against it.

6 ¶ And the men of Gibeon sent unto Joshua to the camp to Gilgal, saying, Slack not thy hand from thy servants; come up to us quickly, and save us, and help us: for all the kings of the Amorites that dwell in the mountains are gathered together against us.

7 So Joshua ascended from Gilgal, he, and all the people of war with him, and all the mighty men of valour.

to this impression. Joshua did just as the Gibeonites requested (v. 7), coming up from Gilgal with a force of his own against the Amorite coalition (see on v. 2)" (Howard, *Joshua*, 136).

8 ¶ And the LORD said unto Joshua, Fear them not: for I have delivered them into thine hand; there shall not a man of them stand before thee.

9 Joshua therefore came unto them suddenly, *and* went up from Gilgal all night.

10 And the LORD discomfited them before Israel, and slew them with a great slaughter at Gibeon, and chased them along the way that goeth up to Beth-horon, and smote them to Azekah, and unto Makkedah.

11 And it came to pass, as they fled from before Israel, *and* were in the going down to Beth-horon, that the LORD cast down great stones from heaven upon them unto Azekah, and they died: *they were* more which died with hailstones than *they* whom the children of Israel slew with the sword.

How did the Lord assist Joshua in defeating the powerful Amorites? (10:8–11) "The Amorites who dwelt in the mountains were the strongest of all the Canaanites. . . . [The Lord] renewed the assurance of His help in this particular war, in which Joshua was about to fight for the first time with several allied kings of Canaan. . . . The large stones [see verse 11] which the Lord threw . . . were hail-stones . . . , not stone-hail, or a shower of stones . . . which hail fell upon the foe in pieces as large as stones . . . , and slew a greater number of them than the swords of the Israelites" (Keil and Delitzsch, *Commentary* [on Joshua 10:6–11]).

12 ¶ Then spake Joshua to the LORD in the day when the LORD delivered up the Amorites before the children of Israel, and he said in the sight of Israel, Sun, stand thou still upon Gibeon; and thou, Moon, in the valley of Ajalon.

13 And the sun stood still, and the moon stayed, until the people had avenged themselves upon their enemies. *Is* not this written in the book of Jasher? So the sun stood still in the midst of heaven, and hasted not to go down about a whole day.

Why does the sun stand still? (10:12–14) "Surely the Lord who created the heavens and the earth 'and all things that in them are' (3 Ne. 9:15) could cause the sun and the moon to stand still (or the earth to stand still so the heavenly bodies would appear to be stationary) as indicated here (see Hel. 12:13–15).

"Another biblical account even has the sun reversing its direction (see 2 Kgs. 20:8–11 and Isa. 38:7–8).

"There should be no question concerning the reality of this miracle, although we may not understand the exact manner in which it was accomplished.

"The lengthening out of the day prevented the Amorites from regrouping and greatly assisted Joshua and the Israelites in their victory" (Ludlow, *Companion to Your Study of the Old Testament*, 204–5). ⊕

What is the book of Jasher? (10:13) "Like numerous other books mentioned in the Old and New Testament but not contained within their pages, the book of Jasher appears to have been a source that contained accounts of heroic deeds in ancient Israel. It is thought by many to have been written in verse, but it likely contained some prose as well. A book with this title is currently available, but it is of doubtful origin, according to most scholars, and probably is not the one mentioned in the Old Testament" (*Old Testament Student Manual: Genesis–2 Samuel*, 241).

14 And there was no day like that before it or after it, that the LORD hearkened unto the voice of a man: for the LORD fought for Israel.

What do we learn about faith-filled prayer? (10:14) Joshua's prayer was in tune with the will of God: "He that asketh in the Spirit asketh according to the will of God; wherefore it is done even as he asketh" (D&C 46:30). We learn from the Book of Mormon that because of Nephi's righteousness, the Lord declared, "I will bless thee forever . . . yea, even that all things shall be done unto thee according to thy word, for thou shalt not ask that which is contrary to my will" (Helaman 10:5). In addition, Enoch asked the Lord "that the earth might never more be covered by the floods. And the Lord . . . covenanted with Enoch . . . that he would stay the floods" (Moses 7:50–51).

Summary of Joshua 10:15–43

Joshua leads the Israelite armies in a resounding victory over all the nations in the southern portion of the promised land "because the Lord God of Israel fought for Israel" (Joshua 10:42). However, there were battles yet to be fought that are recorded in the final chapters of Joshua's record.

CHAPTER 11

Joshua and Israel conquer the whole land, destroying many cities and nations.

Summary of Joshua 11

After "a long time" (Joshua 11:18), Joshua and the armies of Israel conquer the remaining nations in the land of Canaan, putting some to tribute (see Joshua 11:19). The Joseph Smith Translation adds this insight concerning the command to retake the promised land: "For it was of the Lord *to destroy them utterly, because they hardened their hearts*" (JST, Joshua 11:20; emphasis added). "The note in verse 22 is of interest because the Anakim were a race of giants (see Numbers 13:32–33) and because Goliath came from Gath (see 1 Samuel 17:4)" (*Old Testament Student Manual: Genesis–2 Samuel*, 241). Joshua completes everything the Lord has asked him to do (see Joshua 11:23).

CHAPTERS 12–22

Two kings on the east of the Jordan and thirty-one on the west are conquered by Israel.

Summary of Joshua 12–22

These chapters describe how "Joshua divides the land of promise among the twelve tribes of Israel. The Lord gives the children of Israel all the land that He had promised to their fathers Abraham, Isaac, and Jacob (see Genesis 13:14–15; 26:1–3; 28:3–4; Joshua 21:43–45)" (Valletta, et al., *Old Testament for Latter-day Saint Families*, 232). Also, the children of Israel place

There remain some lands yet to be possessed—Some inhabitants are not expelled—The inheritances of Reuben, Gad, and one half of Manasseh are confirmed.

The land is divided by lot among 9½ tribes—Caleb inherits Hebron as a special reward for his faithfulness.

Judah is given an inheritance in Canaan—The Jebusites dwell with Judah at Jerusalem.

The children of Joseph (Ephraim and Manasseh) receive their inheritances—Some Canaanites continue to dwell among the Ephraimites.

Manasseh and Ephraim both receive an additional inheritance—Ephraim is to drive out the Canaanites from the hill country.

The tabernacle of the congregation is set up at Shiloh—Benjamin receives an inheritance by lot.

the tabernacle in the city of Shiloh. "The tabernacle accompanied the children of Israel during their wanderings in the desert and in the different stages of the conquest of the land of Canaan. The conquest complete, it was fixed in Shiloh as the place that the Lord had chosen (Josh. 18:1)" (Bible Dictionary, "Tabernacle").

Shiloh (Joshua 18)

In this western view, the ruins of the ancient city of Shiloh are just left of center. The tabernacle was established here soon after the children of Israel settled in Canaan.

"Give Me This Mountain" (Joshua 14:12)

Caleb was one of the spies sent to scout out the promised land. Full of faith, he provided a good report of the land to the children of Israel (Numbers 13:30). The Lord promised Caleb that he would eventually receive an inheritance in the land (Deuteronomy 1:36). Forty-five years later, he expressed his faith once again by requesting an inheritance in the hill country of Hebron where the Anakims dwelt. Knowing this would be a challenge, he declared: "If it so be the Lord will be with me, then I shall be able to drive them out" (Joshua 14:12). President Spencer W. Kimball drew upon this account to teach: "From Caleb's example we learn very important lessons. Just as Caleb had to struggle and remain true and faithful to gain his inheritance, so we must remember that, while the Lord has promised us a place in his kingdom, we must ever strive constantly and faithfully so as to be worthy to receive the reward.

"Caleb concluded his moving declaration with a request and a challenge with which my heart finds full sympathy. The Anakims, the giants, were still inhabiting the promised land, and they had to be overcome. Said Caleb, now at 85 years, 'Give me this mountain' (Josh. 14:12).

"This is my feeling for the work at this moment. There are great challenges ahead of us, giant opportunities to be met. I welcome that exciting prospect and feel to say to the Lord, humbly, 'Give me this mountain,' give me these challenges" ("Give Me This Mountain," 79).

Simeon, Zebulun, Issachar, Asher, Naphtali, and Dan receive their inheritances by lot.

Six cities of refuge are appointed for those guilty of manslaughter.

The Levites receive forty-eight cities with their suburbs—The Lord fulfills all His promises and gives Israel rest.

The 2½ tribes are dismissed with a blessing—They build an altar of testimony by the Jordan to show they are the Lord's people—It is not an altar for sacrifices or burnt offerings.

CHAPTER 23

Joshua exhorts Israel to be courageous, keep the commandments, love the Lord, and neither marry among nor cleave unto the remnants of the Canaanites who remain in the land—When the children of Israel serve other gods, they will be cursed and dispossessed.

1 And it came to pass a long time after that the LORD had given rest unto Israel from all their enemies round about, that Joshua waxed old *and* stricken in age.

2 And Joshua called for all Israel, *and* for their elders, and for their heads, and for their judges, and for their officers, and said unto them, I am old *and* stricken in age:

Joshua 23:1–11. God Will Continue to Bless Israel if They Are Faithful

Why did Joshua gather Israel and his leaders? **(23:1–2)** "In his old age (he died at age one hundred ten; Josh. 24:29), Joshua called the first of two assemblies to give his farewell instructions and a charge. He repeated the promises and urged Israel not to backslide and affiliate with Canaanite remnants, lest they suffer as they had been warned" (Rasmussen, *Latter-day Saint Commentary on the Old Testament*, 207). What other accounts in scripture do we have of fathers/prophets—just before their deaths—giving instructions and counsel to their children and people? What are common themes and doctrines in these messages?

3 And ye have seen all that the LORD your God hath done unto all these nations because of you; for the LORD your God *is* he that hath fought for you.

Why did God fight for them? (23:3) "Joshua reminds the leaders that *You yourselves have seen* what God did. . . . In the past, the God of Israel fought on behalf of Israel. God will continue to fight to drive out the remaining nations. The expression *it was the Lord your God who fought for you* is repeated word for word in the Hebrew text of verse 10. This is a key theme of Joshua's address. Israel did not win the battles through its own skill. God won Israel's battles. He would go on doing so only if Israel remained faithful" (Hess, *Joshua*, 325).

4 Behold, I have divided unto you by lot these nations that remain, to be an inheritance for your tribes, from Jordan, with all the nations that I have cut off, even unto the great sea westward.

Why did the Lord have them divide the promised land by casting lots? (23:4) "Even before the land was completely taken, Joshua was instructed to *divide this land* [Joshua 13:7] by lot *for an inheritance*. By casting lots, the assignment of land to the individual tribes fell to the choice of God (Prov. 16:33). It was His to give to the tribes as He chose, and no one could charge Joshua and the assisting elders with tribal favoritism" (*Zondervan KJV Commentary*, 298).

Where Is the Land Which the Children of Israel Inherited? (23:4)

"Biblical Israel is generally thought of as that region south and southwest of the Lebanon mountains, north and east of Egypt, east of the Mediterranean coastal plain, and west of the Arabian desert. In dimension, Israel was roughly 150 miles from Dan to Beersheba, and at its greatest width it was about 75 miles across. The Lord promised Joshua that the original extent of the land promised to Abraham was to be given to Israel (see Genesis 15:18; Joshua 1:4)" (*Old Testament Student Manual: Genesis–2 Samuel*, 236). See Bible Map 3, "The Division of the 12 Tribes."

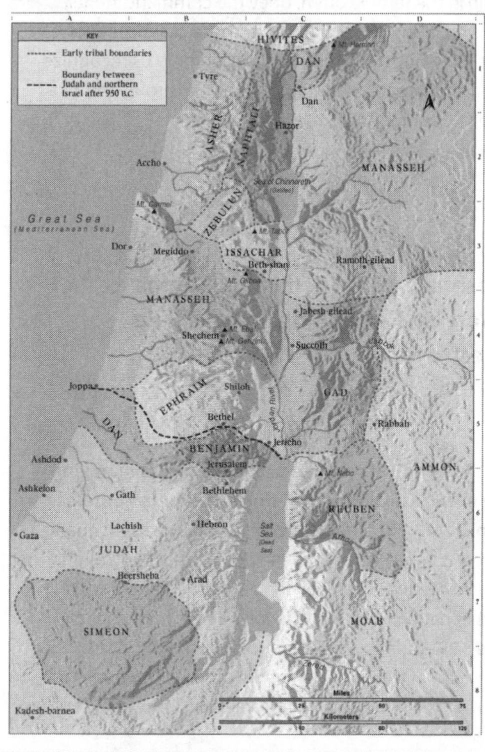

Why would the Lord "expel" some people from their lands and cities? (23:5) "By the time of Moses and Joshua, the Canaanites (or Amorites) had become grossly wicked, for the Lord warned Israel repeatedly not to allow any of the Canaanite ways of life to infiltrate her own. . . . Rather than allowing [the wicked] to continue to pollute the earth by their wickedness and to contaminate the unborn generations by their perversions, the Lord's righteous judgments took them from the earth" (Meservy, "Why Did the Lord Permit Israel to War Against People in the Land of Promise?" 59). ⊕

When were the people of Canaan finally expelled from the land? (23:7) "In this chapter Joshua continually mentions the people who are still left in the land, clearly demonstrating that his successful battles had not wiped out all of Canaan and had not ended Israel's work. It would not be until the days of David, hundreds of years later, that the job would be finished" (Muhlestein, *Essential Old Testament Companion*, 177).

What can we do to "cleave unto the Lord"? (23:8) "We cleave unto the Lord as we hold personal and family scripture study, personal and family prayer, and family [councils]. We also cleave unto Him as we partake of the sacrament, magnify our callings, worship in the temple often, obey the commandments, and repent when we fall short. These practices allow the Holy Ghost to abide with us and help us recognize and avoid snares and traps" (Choi, "Be Strong and of a Good Courage," 21).

Joshua 23:12–16. If Israel Begins to Worship False Gods, They Will Be Destroyed

Why were God's people prohibited from marrying or even associating with those of non-Israelite nations? (23:13) "The danger of apostasy was Joshua's great concern here. Thus the people must not 'ally' . . . themselves to any pagan nations. Alliances with other nations frequently involved intermarriage (cf. Ge 34:9–10) and respect for their gods (cf. 1 Ki 11:1–6). Because of the great danger involved in intermarriage, it was strictly prohibited for Israel (Ex 34:12–16;

5 And the LORD your God, he shall expel them from before you, and drive them from out of your sight; and ye shall possess their land, as the LORD your God hath promised unto you.

6 Be ye therefore very courageous to keep and to do all that is written in the book of the law of Moses, that ye turn not aside therefrom *to* the right hand or *to* the left;

7 That ye come not among these nations, these that remain among you; neither make mention of the name of their gods, nor cause to swear *by them,* neither serve them, nor bow yourselves unto them:

8 But cleave unto the LORD your God, as ye have done unto this day.

9 For the LORD hath driven out from before you great nations and strong: but *as for* you, no man hath been able to stand before you unto this day.

10 One man of you shall chase a thousand: for the LORD your God, he *it is* that fighteth for you, as he hath promised you.

11 Take good heed therefore unto yourselves, that ye love the LORD your God.

12 Else if ye do in any wise go back, and cleave unto the remnant of these nations, *even* these that remain among you, and shall make marriages with them, and go in unto them, and they to you:

13 Know for a certainty that the LORD your God will no more drive out *any of* these nations from before you; but they shall be snares and traps unto you, and scourges in your sides, and thorns in your eyes, until ye perish from off this good land which the LORD your God hath given you.

Dt 7:1–6). . . . Just as faithfulness had been essential for Israel to acquire the land, so now it was indispensable if they were to continue to live in the land" (*Expositor's Bible Commentary [Abridged]*, 324).

14 And, behold, this day I *am* going the way of all the earth: and ye know in all your hearts and in all your souls, that not one thing hath failed of all the good things which the LORD your God spake concerning you; all are come to pass unto you, *and* not one thing hath failed thereof.

Why is it sometimes difficult to trust in God's promises? (23:14) "The Lord makes generous promises, and He certifies that He will not vary from these promises, for, said He, 'I, the Lord, am bound when ye do what I say; but when ye do not what I say, ye have no promise' (D&C 82:10). . . . Sometimes, in our earthly impatience, we may lose sight of the Lord's precious promises and disconnect our obedience from the fulfillment of these promises. . . . The Apostle Peter testified that 'the Lord is not slack concerning his promise, as some men count slackness; but is longsuffering' toward us (2 Peter 3:9)" (Condie, "Claim the Exceeding Great and Precious Promises," 16, 17, 18).

15 Therefore it shall come to pass, *that* as all good things are come upon you, which the LORD your God promised you; so shall the LORD bring upon you all evil things, until he have destroyed you from off this good land which the LORD your God hath given you.

16 When ye have transgressed the covenant of the LORD your God, which he commanded you, and have gone and served other gods, and bowed yourselves to them; then shall the anger of the LORD be kindled against you, and ye shall perish quickly from off the good land which he hath given unto you.

Why did Joshua remind Israel about possible punishments and curses? (23:15–16) "Joshua's logic as he concluded his speech was that, just as surely as the Lord's promises had come true for Israel's good, so also his swift and devastating punishment would come upon the Israelites if they violated the covenant. God's anger would burn . . . against his people, and, indeed, this did happen many times in Israel's history. Whenever the Lord's anger burned against his people, they suffered, usually at the hands of a foreign enemy" (Howard, *Joshua*, 425).

CHAPTER 24

Joshua recites how the Lord has blessed and led Israel—Joshua and all the people covenant to choose the Lord and serve Him only—Joshua and Eleazar die—The bones of Joseph, taken from Egypt, are buried in Shechem.

1 And Joshua gathered all the tribes of Israel to Shechem, and called for the elders of Israel, and for their heads, and for their judges, and for their officers; and they presented themselves before God.

Joshua 24:1–13. Joshua Tells How the Lord Has Blessed the Children of Israel

Why did the children of Israel present themselves before God in Shechem? (24:1) "When the period of desert wandering was over and when Israel had conquered (at least partially) the Promised Land, we will see the tribes gathered at the Shechem sanctuary to renew the covenant made long ago at Sinai. Many of the details of the two covenant ceremonies are different, but all the essential features are the same. They stood at the foot of Mt. Gerizim and Mt. Ebal, rather than at the foot of Sinai. Moses was gone, so Joshua now played the role of covenant mediator. The rite, however is the same" (Plastaras, *God of Exodus*, 204–5).

What flood was Joshua referring to? (24:2–3) "The word translated as 'flood' here is the word we usually translate as 'river.' Joshua is situating Israel geographically, but thus also culturally and religiously, as being between two areas that survive off of their rivers. Abraham grew up either in Mesopotamia or somewhere around southern Turkey, both of which survive agriculturally because of rivers. As Moses had instructed Israel, they would not survive in Canaan because of rivers, but because of rain that came when they were obedient. Thus their geography also separated them religiously, for they would truly only survive when they relied solely and wholly on Jehovah. In many ways this reference is to the journey Abraham made from an idolatrous background to having only God as his God in the promised land" (Muhlestein, *Scripture Study Made Simple*, 153).

Why did Joshua recount this portion of Israel's history? (24:2–13) "In accordance with the common ancient Near Eastern practice of making treaties (covenants), a brief recital of the past history of the relationship precedes the making of covenant commitments. Joshua here focuses on the separation of Abraham from his polytheistic family, the deliverance of Israel from Egypt and the Lord's establishment of his people in Canaan" (*NIV Study Bible* [1995], 319).

2 And Joshua said unto all the people, Thus saith the LORD God of Israel, Your fathers dwelt on the other side of the flood in old time, *even* Terah, the father of Abraham, and the father of Nachor: and they served other gods.

3 And I took your father Abraham from the other side of the flood, and led him throughout all the land of Canaan, and multiplied his seed, and gave him Isaac.

4 And I gave unto Isaac Jacob and Esau: and I gave unto Esau mount Seir, to possess it; but Jacob and his children went down into Egypt.

5 I sent Moses also and Aaron, and I plagued Egypt, according to that which I did among them: and afterward I brought you out.

6 And I brought your fathers out of Egypt: and ye came unto the sea; and the Egyptians pursued after your fathers with chariots and horsemen unto the Red sea.

7 And when they cried unto the LORD, he put darkness between you and the Egyptians, and brought the sea upon them, and covered them; and your eyes have seen what I have done in Egypt: and ye dwelt in the wilderness a long season.

8 And I brought you into the land of the Amorites, which dwelt on the other side Jordan; and they fought with you: and I gave them into your hand, that ye might possess their land; and I destroyed them from before you.

9 Then Balak the son of Zippor, king of Moab, arose and warred against Israel, and sent and called Balaam the son of Beor to curse you:

10 But I would not hearken unto Balaam; therefore he blessed you still: so I delivered you out of his hand.

11 And ye went over Jordan, and came unto Jericho: and the men of Jericho fought against you, the Amorites, and the Perizzites, and the Canaanites, and the Hittites, and the Girgashites, the Hivites, and the Jebusites; and I delivered them into your hand.

12 And I sent the hornet before you, which drave them out from before you, *even* the two kings of the Amorites; *but* not with thy sword, nor with thy bow.

13 And I have given you a land for which ye did not labour, and cities which ye built not, and ye dwell in them; of the vineyards and oliveyards which ye planted not do ye eat.

14 ¶ Now therefore fear the Lord, and serve him in sincerity and in truth: and put away the gods which your fathers served on the other side of the flood, and in Egypt; and serve ye the Lord.

15 And if it seem evil unto you to serve the Lord, choose you this day whom ye will serve; whether the gods which your fathers served that *were* on the other side of the flood, or the gods of the Amorites, in whose land ye dwell: but as for me and my house, we will serve the Lord.

What does the hornet represent? (24:12) "The biblical passages which contain [tsir'âh; hornet] all refer to a divine intervention on Israel's behalf in driving out the inhabitants of Canaan.... Interpreted as a metaphor, [Jehovah's] preparatory onslaught would so numb the Canaanites that they would be unable to defend themselves against the Hebrew tribes. It indicates that [Jehovah] played as much the decisive role in the conquest of Canaan as he had in the exodus from Egypt" (Frerichs, "Hornet," 2:645).

Joshua 24:14–25. The Children of Israel Covenant to Obey the Lord

How are we to "put away the gods" of this world? (24:14) "We show that we serve the Lord by the way in which we live the commandments received from Him, by the work we do to help establish the kingdom of God on earth, and by the way we act towards our neighbor. Putting away worldly gods means keeping impure thoughts out of our minds, shedding all hateful feelings from our hearts, and ridding our lives of everything which may prevent the Holy Ghost from being always with us.... Whatever the situation, in each one of us there is the power to change our life.... The Lord Jesus Christ will give us this power and will help us" (Damiani, "Serving the Lord," 28). ⊕

Why is our choice to serve the Lord so vital? (24:15) "Our Heavenly Father's goal in parenting is not to have His children *do* what is right; it is to have His children *choose* to do what is right and ultimately become like Him. If He simply wanted us to be obedient, He would use immediate rewards and punishments to influence our behaviors.... The magnitude of our eternal happiness depends on choosing the living God.... So, choose faith in Christ; choose repentance; choose to be baptized and receive the Holy Ghost; choose to conscientiously prepare for and worthily partake of the sacrament; choose to make covenants in the temple; and choose to serve the living God and His children" (Renlund, "Choose You This Day," 104, 106). ⊕

How did Joshua's generation of Israelites do at keeping their word? (24:16–18) "An earlier generation had covenanted to serve the Lord, and then failed to keep their promise (Ex. 32:15–35); later generations also failed to serve the Lord. However, the generation that made this promise of faithfulness evidently kept their word as indicated in Judges 2:6–10. Unfortunately the following generation (and many generations thereafter) 'knew not the Lord, nor yet the works which he had done for Israel' (Judg. 2:10)" (Ludlow, *Companion to Your Study of the Old Testament*, 208).

16 And the people answered and said, God forbid that we should forsake the LORD, to serve other gods;

17 For the LORD our God, he *it is* that brought us up and our fathers out of the land of Egypt, from the house of bondage, and which did those great signs in our sight, and preserved us in all the way wherein we went, and among all the people through whom we passed:

18 And the LORD drave out from before us all the people, even the Amorites which dwelt in the land: *therefore* will we also serve the LORD; for he *is* our God.

What warning does Joshua give the children of Israel? (24:19–20) "Before accepting the covenant renewal the people were offering [see verses 16–18], Joshua warned them of the dangers of breaking the covenant. . . . God knows we are not yet beings who are capable of perfectly keeping our covenants. When we break them, there will be consequences or punishments. But, . . . one of the main themes of [the Old Testament] is that God punishes His covenant people in a way that is designed to help them return to the covenant; then He accepts them back. He knows we will stray, and He has accounted for that in the plan; He will never give up on us and never stop working with us" (Muhlestein, *Scripture Study Made Simple*, 154). ⊕

19 And Joshua said unto the people, Ye cannot serve the LORD: for he *is* an holy God; he *is* a jealous God; he will not forgive your transgressions nor your sins.

20 If ye forsake the LORD, and serve strange gods, then he will turn and do you hurt, and consume you, after that he hath done you good.

21 And the people said unto Joshua, Nay; but we will serve the LORD.

Why were witnesses needed here? (24:22) Joshua ensured that the children of Israel understood that they "were made witnesses of the covenant and of the events taking place. Witnesses were necessary to make the mutual promises legally binding" (Ostler, "Covenant Tradition in the Book of Mormon," 233). Now that the covenant was made sure or legal, the children of Israel were accountable to it.

22 And Joshua said unto the people, Ye *are* witnesses against yourselves that ye have chosen you the LORD, to serve him. And they said, *We are* witnesses.

How can we incline our heart unto the Lord? (24:23) "Choose to incline your heart to God. Strive each day to find Him. Learn to love Him. And then let that love inspire you to learn, understand, and follow His teachings and learn to keep God's commandments. . . . If you hesitate in this adventure because you doubt your ability, remember that discipleship is not about doing things perfectly; it's about doing things intentionally. . . . Even when you fail, you can choose not to give up, but rather discover your courage, press forward, and

23 Now therefore put away, *said he,* the strange gods which *are* among you, and incline your heart unto the LORD God of Israel.

24 And the people said unto Joshua, The LORD our God will we serve, and his voice will we obey.

rise up. That is the great test of the journey" (Uchtdorf, "Your Great Adventure," 87).

25 So Joshua made a covenant with the people that day, and set them a statute and an ordinance in Shechem.

What does it mean that Joshua "set them a statute and an ordinance in Shechem"? (24:25) "God placed his people in the center of the ancient world, for there they could, if they remained righteous, holy, and peculiar, exert their beneficial influence on, and be an example to, all the nations of the earth. . . . There is, however, a chance that a peculiar, covenant, and elect people may allow the world's cultures, laws, values, and standards to infiltrate their own. They become like the world rather than serving as an example to the world. . . . For that reason the prophets constantly reminded them of their responsibility to choose between being distinguished from the world or being part of the world" (Wilcox, "Abrahamic Covenant," in *Witness of Jesus Christ*, 277).

Joshua 24:26–33. Joshua Dies and Is Buried

26 ¶ And Joshua wrote these words in the book of the law of God, and took a great stone, and set it up there under an oak, that *was* by the sanctuary of the LORD.

27 And Joshua said unto all the people, Behold, this stone shall be a witness unto us; for it hath heard all the words of the LORD which he spake unto us: it shall be therefore a witness unto you, lest ye deny your God.

28 So Joshua let the people depart, every man unto his inheritance.

In what way can a stone be a witness? (24:26–27) "Two possible explanations might answer this question. First, the stone was a part of this earth. This earth has an intelligence and it will become a Urim and Thummim in the eternities (D&C 130:9). Perhaps the earth was in some way able to record the history of that event upon the rock. Second, the stone could serve as a witness or reminder to the Israelites. As they would see the stone in later years, they would remember the earlier event. Plymouth Rock, Massachusetts, serves a similar role for many Americans today" (Ludlow, *Unlocking the Old Testament*, 61).

29 ¶ And it came to pass after these things, that Joshua the son of Nun, the servant of the LORD, died, *being* an hundred and ten years old.

30 And they buried him in the border of his inheritance in Timnath-serah, which *is* in mount Ephraim, on the north side of the hill of Gaash.

Why was it notable that Joshua died at 110 years old? (24:29) "This event probably took place shortly after this public assembly; for he was old and stricken in years when he held the assembly mentioned Joshua 23:2; and as his work was now all done, and his soul ripened for a state of blessedness, God took him to himself, being one hundred and ten years of age; exactly the same age as that of the patriarch Joseph. See Genesis 50:26" (*Adam Clarke's Commentary* [on Joshua 24:29]).

31 And Israel served the LORD all the days of Joshua, and all the days of the elders that overlived Joshua, and which had known all the works of the LORD, that he had done for Israel.

Why was Israel so committed to the covenant they made with the Lord? (24:31) Seeing that the children of Israel not only served the Lord "all the days of Joshua" but also "all the days of the elders that overlived [him]" we see that Joshua's inspiring "example and influence [was] one cause of the fidelity of that generation" (Rasmussen, *Latter-day Saint Commentary on the Old Testament*, 208). Who has had a similar inspiring influence on your life?

Why is the burial of Joseph's bones significant? (24:32) "Joseph asked his sons to take his bones to Canaan upon their return (Ex. 13:19). . . . He reminded them of God's promise to bring them out of Egypt into the land he gave to their fathers. Then he 'took an oath' of them. . . .

"During forty years of wandering, Moses saw to it that the bones of Joseph were carried with the Israelites (Ex. 13:19). It fell to the lot of Joshua (an Ephraimite) to take the bones into Canaan, where he placed them in Shechem on a parcel of ground purchased earlier by Jacob (Josh. 24:32)" (Horton, "Joseph," 83, 87).

32 ¶ And the bones of Joseph, which the children of Israel brought up out of Egypt, buried they in Shechem, in a parcel of ground which Jacob bought of the sons of Hamor the father of Shechem for an hundred pieces of silver: and it became the inheritance of the children of Joseph.

33 And Eleazar the son of Aaron died; and they buried him in a hill *that pertained to* Phinehas his son, which was given him in mount Ephraim.

THE BOOK OF JUDGES

Introduction

The books of Judges and Ruth contain "all the Jewish history that has been preserved to us of the times between the death of Joshua and the birth of Samuel. . . .

"The book of Judges helps us to understand the development of the house of Israel after the settlement in Canaan. During the period that the book covers, the Israelites formed a confederation of tribes rather than a compact nation. The tribes were united by their recognition of a common descent and still more by their common worship of Jehovah; but, except when the approach of a formidable enemy compelled them to act together, their unity seldom found practical expression and was often overborne by local jealousies. It was only in time of war that a single leader became indispensable and was invested by general consent with something of kingly authority. . . . The lack of unity is vividly called to the reader's attention in the closing sentence of the book (Judg. 21:25): 'In those days there was no king in Israel: every man did that which was right in his own eyes'" (Bible Dictionary, "Judges, book of").

"A set chronology for the book of Judges is difficult, if not impossible, to construct. . . . Even the editor or editors are not known, though the prophet Samuel appears as a most likely candidate, since he was the last of the judges and would have had access to the material. One must remember, however, that the book of Judges is a fragmentary and short account at best. It cannot be viewed as a complete history of the era or of the rule of the judges" (Pearson, *Old Testament*, 36).

Judges records the interventions of 12 single leaders referred to as judges. "In Jewish literature, these judges were called *shophetim*—leaders who pronounced judgment and were chosen at various times to deliver different Israelite tribes from enemies intent on attacking and suppressing them. These judges labored during eras of spiritual turmoil, tribal divisions, and Baal worship, facing a great deal of temptation and opposition in their attempts to lead" (Litchman, "Deborah and the Book of Judges," 32).

"[The book of] Judges consists of three parts: (1) an introduction (Judg. 1:1–3:6); (2) the history of the Twelve Judges, which falls into a succession of periods of rebellion against God, and the oppressions and deliverances by which they were followed (3:7–16:31); (3) two narratives, which specially show the tendency to idolatry and lawlessness (Judg. 17–21)" (Bible Dictionary, "Judges, book of").

Similar to the Book of Mormon, the book of Judges repeatedly describes Israel's cycle of apostasy and repentance. "Initially the people willingly followed the Lord's prophet Joshua. Then their wickedness required external, forced humility before they followed inspired judges" (Ludlow, *Unlocking the Old Testament*, 65). During these cycles of wickedness and judges, we can see repeated examples of the Lord's love, patience, and rescue.

Judges 1:1–8. The Tribes of Judah and Simeon Slay Canaanites and Perizzites

Why did the Lord choose the tribe of Judah to begin a war against the Canaanites? (1:1–2) "Presumably, Israel *asked the* L*ORD* through the high priest, who used the Urim and Thummim . . . to obtain divine direction. . . .

"The book begins and ends (see 20:18) with Judah going up first to battle. The selection of Judah was appropriate. It was the largest of the tribes (Num. 26:22) and was also the first to be assigned territory west of the Jordan (Joshua 15). The leadership role of the tribe of Judah had been anticipated in the blessing of Jacob (Gen. 49:8–12)" (*Zondervan KJV Commentary,* 318).

Who were the "Perizzites"? (1:4) "The term 'Perizzites' occurs regularly in various lists of the pre-Israelite inhabitants of the Promised Land (e.g., Ge 15:20; 34:20; Ex 3:8; 33:2; Jos 3:10; 7:1; 12:8; Jdg 3:5; 1Ki 9:20; Ezr 9:1; Ne 9:8). On two other occasions in the [Old Testament] outside of Judges 1:4–5 (Ge 13:7; 34:30), 'Canaanites' and 'Perizzites' appear in a two-name list of the inhabitants of the land. It is possible that 'Perizzite' is derived from the term *perizzî* ('rural country'), so that the term 'Canaanites' indicates those in fortified urban space, while 'Perizzites,' those in the rural areas (unwalled villages, farms). But it may be that the distinction is along ethnic lines and that, in the light of Genesis 15:19–21; Joshua 11:3; 17:15, they were located in the territory between Judah and Ephraim" (Boda, "Judges," 2:1071).

Why were the king's thumbs and big toes cut off? (1:5–7) "Judah's soldiers wanted to humiliate and cripple the conquered king. Without thumbs, he would no longer be able to wield a weapon. Without big toes, he would no longer be able to run in battle. This sort of treatment of war prisoners was common among many nations at that time. The defeated king accepted his fate philosophically (1:7). He knew his punishment was no worse than what he had done to those he had conquered" (*Quest Study Bible* [1994], 320).

How complete was the Israelite victory over the Jebusites in Jerusalem? (1:8) Though the Israelites captured Jerusalem and portions were burned, they

CHAPTER 1

Judah, Simeon, and Joseph continue to conquer the Canaanites—Remnants of the Canaanites remain in the lands of Judah, Manasseh, Ephraim, Zebulun, Asher, Naphtali, and Dan.

1 Now after the death of Joshua it came to pass, that the children of Israel asked the LORD, saying, Who shall go up for us against the Canaanites first, to fight against them?

2 And the LORD said, Judah shall go up: behold, I have delivered the land into his hand.

3 And Judah said unto Simeon his brother, Come up with me into my lot, that we may fight against the Canaanites; and I likewise will go with thee into thy lot. So Simeon went with him.

4 And Judah went up; and the LORD delivered the Canaanites and the Perizzites into their hand: and they slew of them in Bezek ten thousand men.

5 And they found Adoni-bezek in Bezek: and they fought against him, and they slew the Canaanites and the Perizzites.

6 But Adoni-bezek fled; and they pursued after him, and caught him, and cut off his thumbs and his great toes.

7 And Adoni-bezek said, Threescore and ten kings, having their thumbs and their great toes cut off, gathered *their meat* under my table: as I have done, so God hath requited me. And they brought him to Jerusalem, and there he died.

8 Now the children of Judah had fought against Jerusalem, and had taken it, and smitten it with the edge of the sword, and set the city on fire.

did not settle there at this time. According to Joshua 15:63, the Jebusites "stubbornly held on to Jerusalem because the tribe of Judah did not destroy them completely. . . . [However, Judges 1:21] states that Benjamin (not Judah) failed to drive out the Jebusites. This is because Jerusalem sat astride the boundary between Benjamin and Judah. In the early period, Jerusalem did not strictly belong to either tribe. The tribe of Judah did capture Jerusalem . . . , but Benjamin did not drive out the Jebusites in their portion (Judges 1:21). Apparently Judah took the unfortified southwestern hill, while the tribe of Benjamin failed to take the walled city on the eastern hill" (*NKJV Study Bible* [2007], 353).

Summary of Judges 1:9–26

Soldiers from Judah, Benjamin, and Joseph continue to defeat various Canaanite cities. Some enemies, however, such as the Philistines in the coastal plains and Jebusites in Jerusalem, are not driven out.

Judges 1:27–36. The Tribes of Israel Fail to Drive Out or Destroy All the Canaanite Inhabitants as Commanded by God

27 ¶ Neither did Manasseh drive out *the inhabitants of* Beth-shean and her towns, nor Taanach and her towns, nor the inhabitants of Dor and her towns, nor the inhabitants of Ibleam and her towns, nor the inhabitants of Megiddo and her towns: but the Canaanites would dwell in that land.

What did their failure to drive out the Canaanites indicate for the Israelites? (1:27–36) As they prepared to enter the promised land, the Lord commanded Israel to "drive out all the inhabitants of the land" and not "cleave unto the remnant of these nations" (see Numbers 33:52–53; Joshua 23:12). After the death of Joshua, "they failed to expel the remaining nations. That failure was a sign of their failure to keep the commandment that had been given them. It was also a sign of Israel's failure to serve the Lord to the degree necessary to have him drive those nations from before them [see Joshua 23:5, 12–13]. . . . Having failed to remove the ungodly elements around them, the Israelites condemned themselves to certain sin" (Ferrell, *Hidden Christ*, 140, 141).

28 And it came to pass, when Israel was strong, that they put the Canaanites to tribute, and did not utterly drive them out.

29 ¶ Neither did Ephraim drive out the Canaanites that dwelt in Gezer; but the Canaanites dwelt in Gezer among them.

30 ¶ Neither did Zebulun drive out the inhabitants of Kitron, nor the inhabitants of

Why didn't the Israelites destroy their enemies as the Lord commanded? (1:28) Instead of destroying their enemies, the Israelites often compelled their captives to live and provide forced labor. This labor was a "tribute to be paid in service (1 Kings 9:21), a condition of serfdom (Josh. 16:10; 17:13; Judg. 1:28)" (*New Unger's Bible Dictionary*, 438). Interestingly, this is just how "Israel had been treated in Egypt" (*John Dummelow's* Commentary [on Judges 1:28]).

Nahalol; but the Canaanites dwelt among
them, and became tributaries.

31 ¶ Neither did Asher drive out the inhabitants of Accho, nor the inhabitants of Zidon,
nor of Ahlab, nor of Achzib, nor of Helbah,
nor of Aphik, nor of Rehob:

32 But the Asherites dwelt among the
Canaanites, the inhabitants of the land: for
they did not drive them out.

33 ¶ Neither did Naphtali drive out the inhabitants of Beth-shemesh, nor the inhabitants of Beth-anath; but he dwelt among the
Canaanites, the inhabitants of the land: nevertheless the inhabitants of Beth-shemesh and
of Beth-anath became tributaries unto them.

34 And the Amorites forced the children of
Dan into the mountain: for they would not
suffer them to come down to the valley:

35 But the Amorites would dwell in mount
Heres in Aijalon, and in Shaalbim: yet the
hand of the house of Joseph prevailed, so that
they became tributaries.

36 And the coast of the Amorites *was* from
the going up to Akrabbim, from the rock,
and upward.

CHAPTER 2

An angel rebukes Israel for not serving the Lord—As a pattern of future events, a new generation arises that forsakes the Lord and serves Baal and Ashtaroth—The Lord is angry with the children of Israel and ceases to preserve them—He raises up judges to guide and lead them—The Canaanites are left in the land to test Israel.

1 And an angel of the LORD came up from
Gilgal to Bochim, and said, I made you to go
up out of Egypt, and have brought you unto
the land which I sware unto your fathers; and
I said, I will never break my covenant with
you.

Judges 2:1–5. An Angel of the Lord Tells Israel That God Will No Longer Help Them Drive Out the Canaanites

What do we know about the angel sent to the Israelites? (2:1) "The Hebrew noun *mal'ak* used here designates both divine and human 'messengers' in the Bible" (Holzapfel, et al., *Jehovah and the World of the Old Testament*, 174). The Lord may speak Himself or through various messengers. Regardless how He chooses to communicate, He has taught, "Whether by mine own voice or by the voice of my servants, it is the same" (D&C 1:38).

2 And ye shall make no league with the inhabitants of this land; ye shall throw down their altars: but ye have not obeyed my voice: why have ye done this?

3 Wherefore I also said, I will not drive them out from before you; but they shall be *as thorns* in your sides, and their gods shall be a snare unto you.

Why did the Lord withdraw His promise to help drive out the Canaanites? (2:2–3) "The Lord reminds Israel that they had made a covenant or sacred promise with Him. But they had not kept their promise to destroy the altars of the Canaanites. In latter days, the Lord explained, 'I, the Lord, am bound when ye do what I say; but when ye do not what I say, ye have no promise' (D&C 82:10). Because Israel didn't keep their covenant, they would no longer have the Lord's help in driving the Canaanites out of the land" (Valletta, et al., *Old Testament for Latter-day Saint Families,* 236).

4 And it came to pass, when the angel of the LORD spake these words unto all the children of Israel, that the people lifted up their voice, and wept.

5 And they called the name of that place Bochim: and they sacrificed there unto the LORD.

Where is Bochim? (2:4–5) Bochim (meaning *weepers*) was a place near Gilgal, "the site of the first Hebrew camp after the crossing of the Jordan (Joshua 4:19)" (*John Dummelow's Commentary* [on Judges 2:1]). Bochim was "a place where the angel of the Lord reproved the Israelites for entering into a league with the people of the land. This caused them bitterly to weep, and hence the name of the place (Judges 2:1, 5)" (*Easton's Bible Dictionary*, "Bochim").

Judges 2:6–23. The Younger Generation Grows Up Not Knowing Jehovah and They Follow Other Gods

6 ¶ And when Joshua had let the people go, the children of Israel went every man unto his inheritance to possess the land.

Why does this section of scripture seem to be a break in the story? (2:6–19) "Between verses 6 and 19, the story is interrupted as the author explicitly conveys the theme of the book of Judges. In these few verses, the author tells how Israel continually forsakes God and how God brings them back to Him, only for the cycle to start over again. After he has helped us see this theme, the author returns to the story he is presenting, knowing we will be able to make more sense of the story because of his explanation" (Muhlestein, *Scripture Study Made Simple*, 157).

7 And the people served the LORD all the days of Joshua, and all the days of the elders that outlived Joshua, who had seen all the great works of the LORD, that he did for Israel.

8 And Joshua the son of Nun, the servant of the LORD, died, *being* an hundred and ten years old.

Why is Joshua's death mentioned both in Joshua 24 and Judges 2? (2:7–9) "In a history written in terms of great men, Joshua deserves mention as representing a watershed between two eras of Israel's national life. The report of his death not only closes the book that bears his name but also marks the end of the period when 'the people served the Lord' (Josh. 24:29, 31). The account of his passing appears . . . in the Book of Judges in order to introduce the reader to the radical change that was about to take place after his influence waned" (Roehrs and Franzmann, *Concordia Self-Study Commentary*, 160).

9 And they buried him in the border of his inheritance in Timnath-heres, in the mount of Ephraim, on the north side of the hill Gaash.

10 And also all that generation were gathered unto their fathers: and there arose another generation after them, which knew not the LORD, nor yet the works which he had done for Israel.

How are the children of the rising generation affected when they are not taught to know the Lord? (2:10) "All that the future holds in store for each sacred child of God will be shaped by his or her parents, family, friends, and teachers. Thus, our faith *now* becomes part of our posterity's faith *later*" (Nelson, "Face the Future with Faith," 34). Elder Neal A. Maxwell cautioned: "The human family is seldom more than one generation away from deep doubt and even disbelief. Laman and Lemuel doubted and murmured because, wrote Nephi, 'they knew not the dealings of that God who had created them' (1 Ne. 2:12); they were provincial, just like forgetful Israel" ("God Will Yet Reveal," 52). ⊕

11 ¶ And the children of Israel did evil in the sight of the LORD, and served Baalim:

12 And they forsook the LORD God of their fathers, which brought them out of the land of Egypt, and followed other gods, of the gods of the people that *were* round about them, and bowed themselves unto them, and provoked the LORD to anger.

13 And they forsook the LORD, and served Baal and Ashtaroth.

Why would Israel worship Baal and Ashtaroth? (2:11–13) "Baal [plural *Baalim*] was the great male weather god, while Ashtart [plural *Ashtaroth*] was the fertility goddess. Together they were responsible for the proper combination of moisture and earth and of germination and growth to ensure a successful harvest.... The cycles of spring and summer, fertility and drought, life and death, were all combined by the Canaanites into the story of Baal. Their religion gave them the false hope that they could control these cycles and have power to guarantee fertility of the soil. To release this power, they reenacted the life of Baal in his temple or shrine through pageantry, ritual, female idols, naked images, phallic sculptures, and religious prostitution" (Ludlow, *Unlocking the Old Testament*, 66, 67).

14 ¶ And the anger of the LORD was hot against Israel, and he delivered them into the hands of spoilers that spoiled them, and he sold them into the hands of their enemies round about, so that they could not any longer stand before their enemies.

15 Whithersoever they went out, the hand of the LORD was against them for evil, as the LORD had said, and as the LORD had sworn unto them: and they were greatly distressed.

How was the anger of the Lord displayed against Israel? (2:14–15) "The Lord became angry at Israel's apostasy and turned the Israelites over to their enemies.... God 'sold them' as one sells a slave (3:8; Dt 32:30). Israel's crops, supposedly guaranteed by the worship of Baal, were carried off year after year. The strong hand of the Lord now acted to secure Israel's defeat (cf. Dt 28:25)" (*Expositor's Bible Commentary [Abridged]*, 333). See commentary in this volume for Judges 3:8.

16 ¶ Nevertheless the LORD raised up judges, which delivered them out of the hand of those that spoiled them.

Who were the judges that served Israel at this time? (2:16) "During this era, Israel is a loose conglomeration of tribes that sometimes band together

17 And yet they would not hearken unto their judges, but they went a whoring after other gods, and bowed themselves unto them: they turned quickly out of the way which their fathers walked in, obeying the commandments of the LORD; *but* they did not so.

18 And when the LORD raised them up judges, then the LORD was with the judge, and delivered them out of the hand of their enemies all the days of the judge: for it repented the LORD because of their groanings by reason of them that oppressed them and vexed them.

19 And it came to pass, when the judge was dead, *that* they returned, and corrupted *themselves* more than their fathers, in following other gods to serve them, and to bow down unto them; they ceased not from their own doings, nor from their stubborn way.

20 ¶ And the anger of the LORD was hot against Israel; and he said, Because that this people hath transgressed my covenant which I commanded their fathers, and have not hearkened unto my voice;

against common enemies and sometimes fight among themselves. Though there is no particular governing system outside of the tribe and clan patriarchal system, leaders rise from time to time, at various times guiding the affairs of one tribe, many tribes, or even all the tribes. These leaders are called judges. . . . The term *judge*, or *shophat*, is used differently in Hebrew than it is in English. *Shophat* means leader and can refer to a military, religious, political, or judiciary leader—often meaning all of them at once" (Muhlestein, *Essential Old Testament Companion*, 180, 181).

What does "repented the Lord" mean? (2:18)
"The Joseph Smith Translation changes the words 'it repented the Lord' to 'the Lord hearkened' (JST, Judges 2:18). It is the people who must repent, not the Lord. It seems that through the judges' leadership the Lord answered the people's prayer-like 'groanings,' or expressions of deep pain and sorrow, which came because of the afflictions caused by their enemies" (Valletta, et al., *Old Testament for Latter-day Saint Families*, 238).

Cycle of Sin and Deliverance in the Book of Judges (Judges 2:20–23)

"The book of Judges describes a recurring cycle of apostasy, oppression, repentance, and deliverance, with Jehovah playing a pivotal role in that cycle. When the Israelites abandoned the worship of Jehovah for the rites of the Canaanite deities, Jehovah allowed the neighboring nations to afflict them. Following a period of oppression, the Israelites became humble and prayerful and begged the Lord for deliverance from their enemies. In response to their cries, Jehovah sent a war hero ('judge') to deliver the people.

"This cycle of apostasy, oppression, repentance, and deliverance occurs several times in Judges. . . . Each instance of apostasy and oppression is a confirmation of the prophetic promises of Moses and serves as a warning to future generations" (Parry and Ricks, "Judges of Israel," 241).

1. The Israelites sin against the Lord.

2. The Israelites are afflicted by their enemies.

3. The Israelites cry unto the Lord for deliverance.

4. The Lord raises up judges, who deliver the Israelites from their enemies.

Judges 3:1–4. The Nations Israel Spared Become Their Enemies

Why might the Lord desire to "prove" Israel? (3:1–4)
"The nations were left to 'prove' (test, try) Israel because the Israelites had failed to pass the first test—they had not observed several of the important commandments of the Lord, obedience to which would have enabled him to help them defeat their enemies" (Ludlow, *Companion to Your Study of the Old Testament,* 209).

The scriptures teach that among the reasons for Heavenly Father sending His children into mortality is to "prove them herewith, to see if they will do all things whatsoever the Lord their God shall command them" (Abraham 3:25).

How will it benefit Israel "to teach them war"? (3:2)
For the Israelites, living among hostile nations may have fulfilled an additional role. "It was not only a punishment, or an opportunity to test the nation's fidelity; it was also to provide them with experience in the art of warfare. . . . Israel was to be in a hostile environment for the major part of her history, due either to the pressures of the petty kingdoms which surrounded her or, at a later stage, due to her strategic position between the successive world-powers of Assyria, Babylonia, Persia and Greece on the one hand and Egypt on the other hand. Military prowess was a necessary accomplishment, humanly speaking, if she was to survive" (Cundall and Morris, *Judges and Ruth,* 73).

21 I also will not henceforth drive out any from before them of the nations which Joshua left when he died:

22 That through them I may prove Israel, whether they will keep the way of the LORD to walk therein, as their fathers did keep *it,* or not.

23 Therefore the LORD left those nations, without driving them out hastily; neither delivered he them into the hand of Joshua.

CHAPTER 3

The children of Israel intermarry with the Canaanites, worship false gods, and are cursed—Othniel judges the Israelites—They serve Moab and are delivered by Ehud, who slays Eglon.

1 Now these *are* the nations which the LORD left, to prove Israel by them, *even* as many *of Israel* as had not known all the wars of Canaan;

2 Only that the generations of the children of Israel might know, to teach them war, at the least such as before knew nothing thereof;

3 *Namely,* five lords of the Philistines, and all the Canaanites, and the Sidonians, and the Hivites that dwelt in mount Lebanon, from mount Baal-hermon unto the entering in of Hamath.

4 And they were to prove Israel by them, to know whether they would hearken unto the commandments of the LORD, which he commanded their fathers by the hand of Moses.

5 ¶ And the children of Israel dwelt among the Canaanites, Hittites, and Amorites, and Perizzites, and Hivites, and Jebusites:

6 And they took their daughters to be their wives, and gave their daughters to their sons, and served their gods.

7 And the children of Israel did evil in the sight of the LORD, and forgat the LORD their God, and served Baalim and the groves.

8 ¶ Therefore the anger of the LORD was hot against Israel, and he sold them into the hand of Chushan-rishathaim king of Mesopotamia: and the children of Israel served Chushan-rishathaim eight years.

9 And when the children of Israel cried unto the LORD, the LORD raised up a deliverer to the children of Israel, who delivered them, *even* Othniel the son of Kenaz, Caleb's younger brother.

10 And the Spirit of the LORD came upon him, and he judged Israel, and went out to war: and the LORD delivered Chushan-rishathaim king of Mesopotamia into his hand; and his hand prevailed against Chushan-rishathaim.

11 And the land had rest forty years. And Othniel the son of Kenaz died.

Judges 3:5–7. Intermarriage with the Canaanite People Leads to Serving Their False Gods

Why did the Lord warn the Israelites against intermarriage with the Canaanites? (3:5–7)
Intermarriage with the Canaanites led to forgetting the "Lord their God and serving 'Balaam and the groves' [v. 7]. The groves were local worship centers for heathen gods and included a tree or pole and altars, often among groves of trees. The practice of idolatry which broke the covenant and which was sustained from generation to generation corrupted the house of Israel. One of the most important reminders to Israel that the Lord gave through Moses before they entered the promised land went unheeded (see Deuteronomy 7:3–5)" (*Old Testament Student Manual: Genesis–2 Samuel*, 253).

Judges 3:8–14. Israel Repents and Receives Righteous Othniel as a Judge, after Which They Return to Wickedness and Captivity

What are we to understand by the phrase "the anger of the Lord was hot against Israel"? (3:8)
"Righteous anger is an attribute of Deity. His anger is everlastingly kindled against the wicked (D&C 1:13; 5:8; 60:2; 63:11, 32; 84:24). Similarly, an inspired man might speak or act in righteous anger, as when Moses broke the tablets upon which the Ten Commandments were written, or as when our Lord drove the money changers from the temple" (McConkie, *Doctrinal New Testament Commentary*, 2:515–16).

How did these judges receive their positions and authority? (3:9–10) "It is evident that the Judges were not merely individuals who became leaders through their charismatic qualities. Many scriptures demonstrate that the Judges were appointed and chosen by Jehovah to deliver Israel from its frequent bondage. The New Testament says that the Lord 'gave unto them judges' (Acts 13:20); similar language in Judges says that 'the Lord raised up judges' (2:16) and 'the Lord raised up a deliverer' (3:9, 15). . . . The epistle to the Hebrews states that many of the Judges 'subdued kingdoms' through their faith (Heb. 11:33).

"Many Judges, such as Othniel (3:10), Gideon (6:34), and Jephthah (11:29), were blessed with the 'Spirit of the Lord'" (Parry and Ricks, "Judges of Israel," 245).

Where did Eglon and the Moabites live? (3:12–13) "The land of Moab lay east of the Dead Sea [see Bible Map 3]. The Moabites were akin to the Israelites and spoke a language that closely resembled Hebrew, but there was constant warfare between the two nations" (Bible Dictionary, "Moab").

"Moabite forces crossed the Jordan and occupied Jericho. . . . Jericho had been cursed by Joshua (Jos 6:26) and was probably unoccupied when King Eglon moved in. From this strategic base Eglon dominated the Israelites for eighteen years" (*Expositor's Bible Commentary [Abridged]*, 334).

Judges 3:15–31. The Lord Raises Up Another Judge to Free Israel from the Moabites

How was Ehud able to successfully take the king's life? (3:16–22) Bible commentator John Dummelow suggests that the dagger with two edges (v. 16) was actually a sword "about 14 [inches] in the blade. Being, on his right thigh (convenient for his left hand) the guards would not notice it" (*John Dummelow's Commentary* [on Judges 3:7–11]). Regarding how he would have been able to get close enough to do the deed, Robert Alter suggests that King Eglon would have been "inclined to trust [Ehud] as a vassal bringing tribute and that the 'secret' he promises to confide to the king [v. 19] will thus be understood as a piece of intelligence volunteered by an Israelite collaborator" (*Art of Biblical Narrative*, 39).

Why was Ehud delivering a "present" to Eglon? (3:17–18) "In the [Old Testament] this term [translated 'present' in the KJV] is used most often of gift offerings made to God as an expression of gratitude and reverence, but it is also used for a voluntary gift of homage (Gen. 32:14, 19, 21) or political friendship (2 Kin. 20:12). Here it applies to the tribute required of a vassal by a superior. This was an ancient and widespread practice in the ancient Near East. The present text does not describe the nature of the tribute. The most valued items would have been precious metals, silver and gold, but other items were often included" (Keener, *NKJV Cultural Backgrounds Study Bible*, 430–31).

How might we view Ehud's assassination of Eglon? (3:21–22) "When the children of Israel cried unto the Lord, the Lord raised them up a deliverer, Ehud the son

12 ¶ And the children of Israel did evil again in the sight of the LORD: and the LORD strengthened Eglon the king of Moab against Israel, because they had done evil in the sight of the LORD.

13 And he gathered unto him the children of Ammon and Amalek, and went and smote Israel, and possessed the city of palm trees.

14 So the children of Israel served Eglon the king of Moab eighteen years.

15 But when the children of Israel cried unto the LORD, the LORD raised them up a deliverer, Ehud the son of Gera, a Benjamite, a man lefthanded: and by him the children of Israel sent a present unto Eglon the king of Moab.

16 But Ehud made him a dagger which had two edges, of a cubit length; and he did gird it under his raiment upon his right thigh.

17 And he brought the present unto Eglon king of Moab: and Eglon *was* a very fat man.

18 And when he had made an end to offer the present, he sent away the people that bare the present.

19 But he himself turned again from the quarries that *were* by Gilgal, and said, I have a secret errand unto thee, O king: who said, Keep silence. And all that stood by him went out from him.

20 And Ehud came unto him; and he was sitting in a summer parlour, which he had for himself alone. And Ehud said, I have a message from God unto thee. And he arose out of *his* seat.

21 And Ehud put forth his left hand, and took the dagger from his right thigh, and thrust it into his belly:

22 And the haft also went in after the blade; and the fat closed upon the blade, so that he could not draw the dagger out of his belly; and the dirt came out.

23 Then Ehud went forth through the porch, and shut the doors of the parlour upon him, and locked them.

24 When he was gone out, his servants came; and when they saw that, behold, the doors of the parlour *were* locked, they said, Surely he covereth his feet in his summer chamber.

25 And they tarried till they were ashamed: and, behold, he opened not the doors of the parlour; therefore they took a key, and opened *them:* and, behold, their lord *was* fallen down dead on the earth.

26 And Ehud escaped while they tarried, and passed beyond the quarries, and escaped unto Seirath.

27 And it came to pass, when he was come, that he blew a trumpet in the mountain of Ephraim, and the children of Israel went down with him from the mount, and he before them.

28 And he said unto them, Follow after me: for the LORD hath delivered your enemies the Moabites into your hand. And they went down after him, and took the fords of Jordan toward Moab, and suffered not a man to pass over.

29 And they slew of Moab at that time about ten thousand men, all lusty, and all men of valour; and there escaped not a man.

30 So Moab was subdued that day under the hand of Israel. And the land had rest fourscore years.

31 ¶ And after him was Shamgar the son of Anath, which slew of the Philistines six hundred men with an ox goad: and he also delivered Israel.

of Gera, a Benjamite" (Judges 3:15). "The left-handed Benjamite was an authentic hero. All alone, and purely by his wits, he cut down the king of Moab, who had established himself in Canaan near Jericho" (*NIV Study Bible* [1985], 333). The scriptures do not indicate if Ehud's actions were sanctioned by the Lord, but it is clear he was raised up to deliver Israel. It might be helpful to note that Ehud's actions led to eighty years of peace.

What do we know about Shamgar, the next deliverer of Israel? (3:31) "Shamgar is the first of six minor judges and a contemporary of Deborah (see 5:6–7). His name is foreign, so he may not have been an Israelite. . . . [The phrase] *Son of Anath* indicates either that Shamgar came from the town of Beth-anath (see 1:33) or that his family worshiped the goddess Anath. Since Anath, Baal's sister, was a goddess of war who fought for Baal, the expression 'son of Anath' may have been a military title, meaning 'a warrior.' His weapon was an *ox goad*, which was a long, wooden rod, sometime with a metal tip, used for driving draft animals (see 1 Sam. 13:21)" (*Zondervan KJV Commentary*, 323).

Judges 4:1–16. The Prophetess Deborah Leads Israel in a Successful Battle against the Canaanites

Who was King Jabin? (4:2–3) "The person bearing the name Jabin here is not to be confused with the Jabin who ruled Hazor at least 30 or 40 years earlier, and who headed an alliance of Canaanite forces against Joshua in Josh. 11:1–15. In the ancient Near East, royal names were commonly repeated and even took on the form of dynastic names (e.g., Rameses I–XI).... The present text identifies Jabin as 'king of Canaan,' suggesting he had recaptured for Hazor the dominant position among Canaanite cities that had not fallen into Israelite control" (Keener, *NKJV Cultural Backgrounds Study Bible*, 433).

Why was the area of Hazor so important? (4:2–3) Hazor "stood at a strategic point in northern Galilee (ten miles north of the Sea of Galilee) on the road between Damascus to Megiddo. The Joshua account describes it as 'the head of all those kingdoms' (Josh 11:10), and in both Joshua and in Judges, its king Jabin is defeated (Josh 11:13; Judg 4:24; see also 1 Sam 12:9).... Subsequently the city was refortified by Solomon (1 Kings 9:15) and remained a major center of commerce and a key to Israel's northern border until the Assyrian conquest (2 Kings 15:29)" (Walton, et al., *IVP Bible Background Commentary*, 249).

What is a prophetess? (4:4) A prophetess is "a woman who has received a testimony of Jesus and enjoys the spirit of revelation. A prophetess does not hold the priesthood or its keys. Though only a few women in the scriptures are called prophetesses, many prophesied" (Guide to the Scriptures, "Prophetess"). "Six women are presented in scripture as prophetesses. In addition to Miriam, the sister of Moses,... Huldah, Anna, Isaiah's wife, Ezekiel's wife, and Deborah are all called by that title" (Hurd, *Our Sisters in the Bible*, 44).

Why did the children of Israel come to Deborah for judgment? (4:5) "Known for her wisdom and respected as a leader, Deborah is introduced in the biblical record with no indication that the fact of a woman's holding such influence was inappropriate or surprising.... Although other individuals showed

CHAPTER 4

Deborah, a prophetess, judges Israel—She and Barak deliver Israel from the Canaanites—Jael, a woman, slays Sisera, the Canaanite.

1 And the children of Israel again did evil in
the sight of the LORD, when Ehud was dead.
2 And the LORD sold them into the hand of
Jabin king of Canaan, that reigned in Hazor;
the captain of whose host *was* Sisera, which
dwelt in Harosheth of the Gentiles.
3 And the children of Israel cried unto the
LORD: for he had nine hundred chariots of
iron; and twenty years he mightily oppressed
the children of Israel.

4 ¶ And Deborah, a prophetess, the wife of
Lapidoth, she judged Israel at that time.

5 And she dwelt under the palm tree of
Deborah between Ramah and Beth-el in
mount Ephraim: and the children of Israel
came up to her for judgment.

6 And she sent and called Barak the son of
Abinoam out of Kedesh-naphtali, and said
unto him, Hath not the LORD God of Israel
commanded, *saying,* Go and draw toward
mount Tabor, and take with thee ten thousand men of the children of Naphtali and of
the children of Zebulun?

7 And I will draw unto thee to the river
Kishon Sisera, the captain of Jabin's army,
with his chariots and his multitude; and I will
deliver him into thine hand.

8 And Barak said unto her, If thou wilt go
with me, then I will go: but if thou wilt not
go with me, *then* I will not go.

9 And she said, I will surely go with thee:
notwithstanding the journey that thou takest
shall not be for thine honour; for the LORD
shall sell Sisera into the hand of a woman.
And Deborah arose, and went with Barak to
Kedesh.

10 ¶ And Barak called Zebulun and Naphtali
to Kedesh; and he went up with ten thousand men at his feet: and Deborah went up
with him.

11 Now Heber the Kenite, *which was* of the
children of Hobab the father in law of Moses,
had severed himself from the Kenites, and
pitched his tent unto the plain of Zaanaim,
which *is* by Kedesh.

inspiring courage and faith in God to assist in Israel's victory, Deborah was the catalyst that ignited the Israelite surge. Her conviction that God would deliver His people from twenty years of Canaanite oppression inspired an army to rise up and win freedom for Israel" (Olson, *Women of the Old Testament,* 107). ⊕

What gave Deborah power to lead and inspire others to go to battle? (4:8–9) "One Bible scholar explains that the term *wife of Lapidoth* [see v. 4] could also have been translated in Hebrew to read 'a woman of a torch-like spirit' (in [Edersheim, *Bible History,* 3:121]). . . .

"Deborah's torch-like spirit had the power to instill courage in others and to inspire them to follow the command of the Lord. Where did this power come from? Remember, Deborah was a prophetess. The scriptures teach that '*the testimony of Jesus* is the spirit of prophecy' (Revelation 19:10; emphasis added). Perhaps Deborah's strength of spirit came from her testimony of Christ" (Freeman, *Written on Our Hearts,* 42). ⊕

Why did Deborah tell Barak that he would not be honored for his part in the battle? (4:9) "Deborah was more than willing to go with Barak but she also wanted him and all Israel to know that it was God who would deliver them, not their own power. Because the point of God's punishments and deliverances was to get Israel to return to Him, God wanted to make sure He delivered them in a way that they would not come to rely more heavily on themselves but rather would realize how much they needed God. Thus, He promises He would deliver them in such a way that Israel would not be able to claim the ability to defeat the Canaanites on their own. Having the mightiest Canaanite warrior fall prey to someone who clearly could not defeat him on his or her own would thus serve God's purposes" (Muhlestein, *Scripture Study Made Simple,* 159).

Who was Heber the Kenite? (4:11–12) "Since the name Kenite is closely related to the word for (copper) smith in both Arabic and Aramaic, it may be that this tribe was something of a trade guild of wandering smiths who offered their skills where needed" (Elwell and Comfort, *Tyndale Bible Dictionary,* 769). "Heber appears to have lived separate from the rest of the Kenites, leading a patriarchal life. He must have been a person of some consequence from its being stated that there was peace between the house of Heber and the powerful King Jabin" (*New Unger's Bible Dictionary,* 546).

How did the Lord bring victory to the less powerful army of Israel? (4:13–16) "The River Kishon flows in a northwest direction through the Jezreel Valley. . . . Because the land is quite flat, the river is usually not much more than a sluggish stream. In times of unusually hard rains, however, it may overflow its banks and flood the surrounding land, making it marshy and nearly impassable.

"The Song of Deborah [Judges 5] seems to suggest that just such an unexpected downpour, accompanied by thunder and lightning, suddenly struck the area. The chariots of Sisera bogged down in the resulting overflow of the Kishon River, making it possible for the smaller forces of Deborah and Barak to achieve victory" (*Old Testament Student Manual: Genesis–2 Samuel,* 254). ⊕

How important was the conquering of Sisera? (4:15) "Deborah's war against the Canaanites, which took place around 1125 B.C. according to most biblical scholars, was so important to her people's history that its events are recounted twice in the book of Judges—in chapter 4 and in chapter 5. . . . Deborah's War broke the main Canaanite power in the north, opening the way for territorial expansion that united the Galilee tribes with the territory of Ephraim to the south. Under Deborah's rallying call, a joint cooperative effort among the Israelite tribes produced victory against a common enemy. After the battle, Barak, according to Josephus, 'was the commander of the Israelites for forty years' [Whiston, trans., *Work of Flavius Josephus,* 115]" (Litchman, "Deborah and the Book of Judges," 34–35).

Judges 4:17–24. The Canaanite Captain Sisera Flees the Battle but Does Not Find Safety

What was unique about Jael's role in Sisera's death? (4:18–22) "In the 'world-turned-upside-down' theme employed in Judges, many customs or everyday actions are reversed (see the correct sequence of events in a hospitality situation in Gen. 18:2–8). Thus a woman instead of her husband offers Sisera hospitality. As a guest Sisera is not supposed to ask for

12 And they shewed Sisera that Barak the son of Abinoam was gone up to mount Tabor.

13 And Sisera gathered together all his chariots, *even* nine hundred chariots of iron, and all the people that *were* with him, from Harosheth of the Gentiles unto the river of Kishon.

14 And Deborah said unto Barak, Up; for this *is* the day in which the LORD hath delivered Sisera into thine hand: is not the LORD gone out before thee? So Barak went down from mount Tabor, and ten thousand men after him.

15 And the LORD discomfited Sisera, and all *his* chariots, and all *his* host, with the edge of the sword before Barak; so that Sisera lighted down off *his* chariot, and fled away on his feet.

16 But Barak pursued after the chariots, and after the host, unto Harosheth of the Gentiles: and all the host of Sisera fell upon the edge of the sword; *and* there was not a man left.

17 Howbeit Sisera fled away on his feet to the tent of Jael the wife of Heber the Kenite: for *there was* peace between Jabin the king of Hazor and the house of Heber the Kenite.

18 ¶ And Jael went out to meet Sisera, and said unto him, Turn in, my lord, turn in to me; fear not. And when he had turned in unto her into the tent, she covered him with a mantle.

19 And he said unto her, Give me, I pray thee, a little water to drink; for I am thirsty. And she opened a bottle of milk, and gave him drink, and covered him.

20 Again he said unto her, Stand in the door of the tent, and it shall be, when any man doth come and inquire of thee, and say, Is there any man here? that thou shalt say, No.

21 Then Jael Heber's wife took a nail of the tent, and took an hammer in her hand, and went softly unto him, and smote the nail into his temples, and fastened it into the ground: for he was fast asleep and weary. So he died.

22 And, behold, as Barak pursued Sisera, Jael came out to meet him, and said unto him, Come, and I will shew thee the man whom thou seekest. And when he came into her *tent,* behold, Sisera lay dead, and the nail *was* in his temples.

23 So God subdued on that day Jabin the king of Canaan before the children of Israel.

24 And the hand of the children of Israel prospered, and prevailed against Jabin the king of Canaan, until they had destroyed Jabin king of Canaan.

anything, but he asks for both a drink as well as sentry duty on Jael's part. Finally, murdering a guest is never a part of the protocol of hospitality. However, Jael may have been justified in killing Sisera" (Walton, et al., *IVP Bible Background Commentary*, 251). ⊕

What is memorable about Israel's victory? (4:23–24) "Deborah's story shows that many Israelites played a part in overcoming the Canaanites. Barak as the military captain, Jael as Sisera's slayer, Deborah as the prophetess, and the ten thousand obedient soldiers were all vital to the outcome. No one of them, however, could have accomplished the victory alone. No one of them was the essential hero. The victory was the Lord's. Only with Him did they become conquerors" (Olson, *Women of the Old Testament*, 124).

CHAPTER 5

Deborah and Barak sing a song of praise because Israel is delivered from Canaanite bondage.

Summary of Judges 5

"Two accounts of Deborah's story are contained in the Bible, one in prose (Judges 4) and the other in verse, presumably written by Deborah and performed with the Israelite captain Barak after their military victory (Judges 5). The song of Deborah exhibits linguistic traits that mark it as very early Hebrew writing. Because words of song and poetry endured without revisions over time, it is likely that this song is one of the oldest pieces of text in the biblical canon. . . . Deborah's composition is a hymn of thanksgiving in which she praises God for His gracious acts in their behalf" (Olson, *Women of the Old Testament*, 107–8).

Judges 6:1–6. The Children of Israel Are in Bondage to the Midianites

Who were the people of Midian? (6:1–2) "The Midianites were descendants of Abraham through his second wife Keturah [see Gen. 25:1–6]" (*Lion Encyclopedia of the Bible*, 309). They were "Nomadic traders who occupied the land of Midian. A band of Midianites probably bought Joseph and sold him as a slave in Egypt (Gen. 37:28)" (Knight and Ray, *Illustrated Everyday Bible Companion*, 222). Moses married the daughter of Jethro, a member of a tribe of Midianites (see Exod. 2:16; 3:1).

What was noteworthy about the destruction levied against Israel by her enemies? (6:3–6) "The destruction wrought by the Midianites, the Amalekites, and the children of the east in their separate regions effectively destroyed the vast majority of the harvest for that following year. The flocks and herds of the Israelites also fell into the hands of their enemies. The whole House of Israel would be suffering famine in a short period of time" (Hyde, *Comprehensive Commentary [Judges]*, 85).

Judges 6:7–18. An Angel Calls Gideon to Deliver Israel from the Midianites

Why did the Lord send a prophet at this time? (6:7–10) "The children of Israel appear to have turned to the Lord in their extremity as a last resort, which hardly indicates a vital religious faith. The reason for their misfortune was brought home to them by an unnamed prophet whose words were similar to those of the angel of the Lord at Bochim [Judges 2:1]. The fundamental failure of the Israelites was their forgetfulness of the implications of the covenant-relationship, the God who had done great things for them required loyal obedience, which they failed conspicuously to give" (Cundall and Morris, *Judges and Ruth*, 103).

CHAPTER 6

Israel is in bondage to the Midianites—An angel appears to Gideon and calls him to deliver Israel—He overthrows the altar of Baal, the Spirit of the Lord rests upon him, and the Lord gives him a sign to show he is called to deliver Israel.

1 And the children of Israel did evil in the sight of the LORD: and the LORD delivered them into the hand of Midian seven years.

2 And the hand of Midian prevailed against Israel: *and* because of the Midianites the children of Israel made them the dens which *are* in the mountains, and caves, and strong holds.

3 And *so* it was, when Israel had sown, that the Midianites came up, and the Amalekites, and the children of the east, even they came up against them;

4 And they encamped against them, and destroyed the increase of the earth, till thou come unto Gaza, and left no sustenance for Israel, neither sheep, nor ox, nor ass.

5 For they came up with their cattle and their tents, and they came as grasshoppers for multitude; *for* both they and their camels were without number: and they entered into the land to destroy it.

6 And Israel was greatly impoverished because of the Midianites; and the children of Israel cried unto the LORD.

7 ¶ And it came to pass, when the children of Israel cried unto the LORD because of the Midianites,

8 That the LORD sent a prophet unto the children of Israel, which said unto them, Thus saith the LORD God of Israel, I brought you up from Egypt, and brought you forth out of the house of bondage;

9 And I delivered you out of the hand of the Egyptians, and out of the hand of all that oppressed you, and drave them out from before you, and gave you their land;

10 And I said unto you, I *am* the LORD your God; fear not the gods of the Amorites, in whose land ye dwell: but ye have not obeyed my voice.

11 ¶ And there came an angel of the LORD, and sat under an oak which *was* in Ophrah, that *pertained* unto Joash the Abi-ezrite: and his son Gideon threshed wheat by the winepress, to hide *it* from the Midianites.

12 And the angel of the LORD appeared unto him, and said unto him, The LORD *is* with thee, thou mighty man of valour.

13 And Gideon said unto him, Oh my Lord, if the LORD be with us, why then is all this befallen us? and where *be* all his miracles which our fathers told us of, saying, Did not the LORD bring us up from Egypt? but now the LORD hath forsaken us, and delivered us into the hands of the Midianites.

14 And the LORD looked upon him, and said, Go in this thy might, and thou shalt save Israel from the hand of the Midianites: have not I sent thee?

15 And he said unto him, Oh my Lord, wherewith shall I save Israel? behold, my family *is* poor in Manasseh, and I *am* the least in my father's house.

16 And the LORD said unto him, Surely I will be with thee, and thou shalt smite the Midianites as one man.

17 And he said unto him, If now I have found grace in thy sight, then shew me a sign that thou talkest with me.

What kind of servants does the Lord often call to help in His work? (6:12) "Once again [the Lord] sought to deliver the Israelites out of the prevailing darkness of the day into his marvelous light. Jehovah then did what he so often does to awaken and retrieve his wandering sons and daughters: he called upon a man—a common man, a good man—and then empowered and qualified and prepared that good man for greatness. An angel appeared to one Gideon 'and said unto him, *The Lord is with thee, thou mighty man of valour*' (Judges 6:7–12; emphasis added). Gideon was then taught and shaped and readied to save his people and return them to the worship of Jehovah" (Millet, *Men of Valor*, 1).

How can we overcome feelings of inadequacy? (6:14–16) "Start where you are. Sometimes we feel discouraged because we are not 'more' of something. . . . But remember, our weaknesses can help us to be humble and turn us to Christ, who will 'make weak things become strong' [Ether 12:27]. Satan, on the other hand, uses our weaknesses to the point that we are discouraged from even trying. . . .

"God will take you as you are at this very moment and begin to work with you. All you need is a willing heart, a desire to believe, and trust in the Lord.

"Gideon saw himself as a poor farmer. . . . But God saw him as a mighty man of valor [see Judges 6:12–16]" (Uchtdorf, "It Works Wonderfully!" 22, 23).

Why was it appropriate for Gideon to ask God for a sign? (6:17) "Viewed as a whole, the scriptures contain apparently conflicting teachings and examples on whether signs should be used as proof. But the instructions to modern Israel are clear. Signs are not acceptable to produce conversions, but they are acceptable—even promised—to confirm them.

"The Old Testament contains memorable examples of miracles that amounted to signs. . . . Gideon asked for and received a sign that he was chosen to deliver Israel (Judg. 6:17)" (Oaks, *Lord's Way*, 77–78).

18 Depart not hence, I pray thee, until I come unto thee, and bring forth my present, and set *it* before thee. And he said, I will tarry until thou come again.

Judges 6:19–32. Gideon Receives a Sign That the Lord Is with Israel and Is Told to Throw Down False Gods' Altars and Replace Them with an Altar to the Lord

What sign does Gideon seek? (6:19–21) "When Gideon asked for a 'sign' he seemed only to want a sign that the messenger was a bona fide emissary of the LORD (v. 17). On this latter point, note that messengers may sometimes be from the wrong source and discernment is important (see, e.g., D&C 129; see another consideration of the problem in 2 Corinthians 11:13–15; 1 Corinthians 12:10; and 1 John 4:1–2). (Signs *may be* given, based upon man's faith and the will of God; D&C 63:10.)

"When Gideon made a meal of meat, cakes and broth, and the angel turned it into a miraculous burnt offering, this 'sign' was sufficient to overwhelm Gideon. But the LORD kindly gave him comfort and peace, and Gideon gratefully named the monument he built there 'LORD of Peace'" (Rasmussen, *Introduction to the Old Testament and Its Teachings*, 150).

19 ¶ And Gideon went in, and made ready a kid, and unleavened cakes of an ephah of flour: the flesh he put in a basket, and he put the broth in a pot, and brought *it* out unto him under the oak, and presented *it*.

20 And the angel of God said unto him, Take the flesh and the unleavened cakes, and lay *them* upon this rock, and pour out the broth. And he did so.

21 ¶ Then the angel of the LORD put forth the end of the staff that *was* in his hand, and touched the flesh and the unleavened cakes; and there rose up fire out of the rock, and consumed the flesh and the unleavened cakes. Then the angel of the LORD departed out of his sight.

22 And when Gideon perceived that he *was* an angel of the LORD, Gideon said, Alas, O Lord GOD! for because I have seen an angel of the LORD face to face.

23 And the LORD said unto him, Peace *be* unto thee; fear not: thou shalt not die.

24 Then Gideon built an altar there unto the LORD, and called it Jehovah-shalom: unto this day it *is* yet in Ophrah of the Abi-ezrites.

What might Gideon tearing down one altar and replacing it with another symbolize? (6:25–27) "The first step the Lord asks Gideon to take as He begins to deliver Israel is to cast down the altar of Baal and then build up an altar to Jehovah. This has a parallel to what we must do in our lives as we try to draw closer to God. We must first get rid of that which leads us away

25 ¶ And it came to pass the same night, that the LORD said unto him, Take thy father's young bullock, even the second bullock of seven years old, and throw down the altar of Baal that thy father hath, and cut down the grove that *is* by it:

26 And build an altar unto the Lord thy God upon the top of this rock, in the ordered place, and take the second bullock, and offer a burnt sacrifice with the wood of the grove which thou shalt cut down.

27 Then Gideon took ten men of his servants, and did as the Lord had said unto him: and *so* it was, because he feared his father's household, and the men of the city, that he could not do *it* by day, that he did *it* by night.

28 ¶ And when the men of the city arose early in the morning, behold, the altar of Baal was cast down, and the grove was cut down that *was* by it, and the second bullock was offered upon the altar *that was* built.

29 And they said one to another, Who hath done this thing? And when they inquired and asked, they said, Gideon the son of Joash hath done this thing.

30 Then the men of the city said unto Joash, Bring out thy son, that he may die: because he hath cast down the altar of Baal, and because he hath cut down the grove that *was* by it.

31 And Joash said unto all that stood against him, Will ye plead for Baal? will ye save him? he that will plead for him, let him be put to death whilst *it is yet* morning: if he *be* a god, let him plead for himself, because *one* hath cast down his altar.

32 Therefore on that day he called him Jerubbaal, saying, Let Baal plead against him, because he hath thrown down his altar.

33 ¶ Then all the Midianites and the Amalekites and the children of the east were gathered together, and went over, and pitched in the valley of Jezreel.

from Him and then replace it with things that draw us closer to Him" (Muhlestein, *Essential Old Testament Companion*, 186–87).

How did Joash defend his son Gideon? (6:31–32)
When Gideon obeyed the command to destroy the altar of Baal and replace it with an altar to the Lord, the men of the city demanded that Gideon be killed. His father Joash saved his son by questioning the idol-worshiping men of the city. "Joash's questions are rhetorical. He refused to put his son to death, arguing that Baal should be able to take care of himself if he were indeed a god.... Gideon's father *called him Jerubbaal* to deride those who would put their trust in Baal. The name means 'Let Baal Plead,' and it echoes the question of v. 31. Thus Gideon became a living reminder of Baal's impotence" (*NKJV Study Bible* [2007], 380).

Judges 6:33–40. The Lord Sends Another Sign to Gideon

What is significant about the Midianites and the Amalekites camping in the Jezreel Valley? (6:33)
"The Jezreel Valley is a huge valley that is not only incredibly fertile but also is a junction between several trade routes. As a valley that spans from the Jordan

Valley nearly to the Mediterranean Sea, it is the only east-west route by which travelers can easily cut through the many hills and mountains of Israel. By camping in the Jezreel Valley, the Midianites were able to control both Israel's agriculture and their ability to gather against them" (Muhlestein, *Scripture Study Made Simple*, 162).

What does it mean that the Spirit of the Lord "came upon" Gideon? (6:34) "Having established himself in the eyes of the people as a servant of God, Gideon became more confident in doing what the Lord commanded. As harvesttime neared, the Midianites again gathered, this time in the valley of Jezreel (see Bible Dictionary, "Jezreel," 713). 'The Spirit of the Lord came upon Gideon, and he blew a trumpet,' mustering an army of 32,000 men from throughout Israel (see Judg. 6:34). Gideon then asked for and received a spiritual confirmation that the Lord would save Israel (see Judg. 6:36–40). So off to battle they went" (Schütze, "Sword of the Lord and of Gideon," 48). ⊕

What did the miracles of the fleece teach Gideon? (6:36–40) "Gideon simply wishes to know whether this is the time and place that the deliverance was going to take place. The seal of approval would be in two parts so that no doubt would remain that he was to move forward at that time. . . . The sign provided an anchor to his soul as he moved further and further into the miracle of the destruction of the Midianite armies. . . . We should not criticize Gideon any more than we do Moses when the latter sought for assurances that he would be able to accomplish the enormous task of the exodus in the face of the whole Egyptian empire" (Hyde, *Comprehensive Commentary [Judges]*, 96, 97). ⊕

34 But the Spirit of the LORD came upon Gideon, and he blew a trumpet; and Abi-ezer was gathered after him.

35 And he sent messengers throughout all Manasseh; who also was gathered after him: and he sent messengers unto Asher, and unto Zebulun, and unto Naphtali; and they came up to meet them.

36 ¶ And Gideon said unto God, If thou wilt save Israel by mine hand, as thou hast said,

37 Behold, I will put a fleece of wool in the floor; *and* if the dew be on the fleece only, and *it be* dry upon all the earth *beside,* then shall I know that thou wilt save Israel by mine hand, as thou hast said.

38 And it was so: for he rose up early on the morrow, and thrust the fleece together, and wringed the dew out of the fleece, a bowl full of water.

39 And Gideon said unto God, Let not thine anger be hot against me, and I will speak but this once: let me prove, I pray thee, but this once with the fleece; let it now be dry only upon the fleece, and upon all the ground let there be dew.

40 And God did so that night: for it was dry upon the fleece only, and there was dew on all the ground.

CHAPTER 7

Gideon's army is reduced to 300—They frighten the Midianite armies with trumpets and lights—The Midianites fight among themselves, flee, and are defeated by Israel.

1 Then Jerubbaal, who *is* Gideon, and all the people that *were* with him, rose up early, and pitched beside the well of Harod: so that the host of the Midianites were on the north side of them, by the hill of Moreh, in the valley.

2 And the LORD said unto Gideon, The people that *are* with thee *are* too many for me to give the Midianites into their hands, lest Israel vaunt themselves against me, saying, Mine own hand hath saved me.

3 Now therefore go to, proclaim in the ears of the people, saying, Whosoever *is* fearful and afraid, let him return and depart early from mount Gilead. And there returned of the people twenty and two thousand; and there remained ten thousand.

4 And the LORD said unto Gideon, The people *are* yet *too* many; bring them down unto the water, and I will try them for thee there: and it shall be, *that* of whom I say unto thee, This shall go with thee, the same shall go with thee; and of whomsoever I say unto thee, This shall not go with thee, the same shall not go.

5 So he brought down the people unto the water: and the LORD said unto Gideon, Every one that lappeth of the water with his tongue, as a dog lappeth, him shalt thou set by himself; likewise every one that boweth down upon his knees to drink.

6 And the number of them that lapped, *putting* their hand to their mouth, were three hundred men: but all the rest of the people bowed down upon their knees to drink water.

Judges 7:1–8. The Lord Reduces the Size of Israel's Army So They Will Trust Him

Why is Gideon referred to as Jerubbaal? (7:1) Jerubbaal means "contender with Baal" and is the name given to Gideon "because he destroyed the altar of Baal" (*Easton's Bible Dictionary*, "Jerubbaal"). See Judges 6:31–32; Bible Dictionary, "Jerubbaal."

Why would the Lord instruct Gideon to reduce the size of his army? (7:2–3) "Had [Gideon] led up a numerous host against his enemies, the excellence of the power by which they were discomfited might have appeared to be of man and not of God. By the manner in which this whole transaction was conducted, both the Israelites and Midianites must see that the thing was of God. This would inspire the Israelites with confidence, and the Midianites with fear" (*Adam Clarke's Commentary* [on Judges 7:2]).

"The Lord can do remarkable miracles with a person of ordinary ability who is humble, faithful, and diligent in serving the Lord and seeks to improve himself. This is because God is the ultimate source of power" (Faust, "Acting for Ourselves and Not Being Acted Upon," 47).

What was the significance of lapping water as opposed to kneeling while drinking? (7:4–6) "If we ask about the rationale of this means of distinction, we conclude, of course, that it indicated the bravest and most ardent warriors, who would not stoop to kneel, but hastily quenched their thirst out of the hollow of their hands, in order to hasten to battle. But Jewish tradition assigns another and deeper meaning to it. It declares that the practice of kneeling was characteristic of the service of Baal. . . . Thus the three hundred would represent those in the host of Israel—'all the knees which have not bowed unto Baal' [1 Kings 19:18]" (Edersheim, *Bible History*, 3:138).

What does the Lord teach ancient and modern covenant Israel by reducing the size of Israel's army? (7:7) "The Lord has never chosen to display the majesty of the gospel in worldly trappings. . . . Rather, he said, 'I call upon the weak things of the world, those who are unlearned and despised, to [thresh] the nations by the power of my Spirit' (D&C 35:13). . . .

"Again and again in the scriptures we see the simplicity of faith arrayed against the physical or intellectual powers of the world. We find Gideon and his army of three hundred routing the thousands of Midian. . . . The power of the gospel is to be kept clearly independent from the 'arm of flesh' (D&C 1:19)" (McConkie, *Gospel Symbolism*, 21).

7 And the LORD said unto Gideon, By the three hundred men that lapped will I save you, and deliver the Midianites into thine hand: and let all the *other* people go every man unto his place.

8 So the people took victuals in their hand, and their trumpets: and he sent all *the rest of* Israel every man unto his tent, and retained those three hundred men: and the host of Midian was beneath him in the valley.

Judges 7:9–14. The Lord Sends Gideon at Night into the Midianite Camp, Where He Hears the Prophetic Dream of an Enemy Soldier

How does the Lord reassure Gideon of victory? (7:9–14) "The summons to attack the Midianites, although accompanied by an absolute assurance of victory, provided for a further strengthening of Gideon's faith. . . . Gideon and his servant Phurah went down into the valley and crossed to the encampment of the enemy. . . . The two men overheard a couple of the Midianite sentries conversing about a *dream* which one had had. . . . The meaning of the dream . . . provided Gideon with the final assurance which he sought. With gratitude in his heart for such an encouraging sign he first worshipped the One who had dealt so graciously with him and then returned to his own small company" (Cundall and Morris, *Judges and Ruth*, 109, 110).

How may we liken Gideon's army to modern missionaries? (7:12) "The Lord was with Gideon and his army even though the Midianites outnumbered them as 'grasshoppers upon the land.' Similar counsel is given to missionaries who are battling for the souls of men. The Lord said to the early missionaries of our time 'for I will go before your face. I will be on your right hand and on your left, and my Spirit shall be in your hearts, and mine angels round about you, to bear you up' (D&C 84:88)" (Valletta, et al., *Old Testament for Latter-day Saint Families*, 245).

9 ¶ And it came to pass the same night, that the LORD said unto him, Arise, get thee down unto the host; for I have delivered it into thine hand.

10 But if thou fear to go down, go thou with Phurah thy servant down to the host:

11 And thou shalt hear what they say; and afterward shall thine hands be strengthened to go down unto the host. Then went he down with Phurah his servant unto the outside of the armed men that *were* in the host.

12 And the Midianites and the Amalekites and all the children of the east lay along in the valley like grasshoppers for multitude; and their camels *were* without number, as the sand by the sea side for multitude.

13 And when Gideon was come, behold, *there was* a man that told a dream unto his fellow, and said, Behold, I dreamed a dream, and, lo, a cake of barley bread tumbled into the host of Midian, and came unto a tent, and smote it that it fell, and overturned it, that the tent lay along.

14 And his fellow answered and said, This *is* nothing else save the sword of Gideon the son of Joash, a man of Israel: *for* into his hand hath God delivered Midian, and all the host.

15 ¶ And it was *so,* when Gideon heard the telling of the dream, and the interpretation thereof, that he worshipped, and returned into the host of Israel, and said, Arise; for the LORD hath delivered into your hand the host of Midian.

16 And he divided the three hundred men *into* three companies, and he put a trumpet in every man's hand, with empty pitchers, and lamps within the pitchers.

17 And he said unto them, Look on me, and do likewise: and, behold, when I come to the outside of the camp, it shall be *that,* as I do, so shall ye do.

18 When I blow with a trumpet, I and all that *are* with me, then blow ye the trumpets also on every side of all the camp, and say, *The sword* of the LORD, and of Gideon.

19 ¶ So Gideon, and the hundred men that *were* with him, came unto the outside of the camp in the beginning of the middle watch; and they had but newly set the watch: and they blew the trumpets, and brake the pitchers that *were* in their hands.

20 And the three companies blew the trumpets, and brake the pitchers, and held the lamps in their left hands, and the trumpets in their right hands to blow *withal:* and they cried, The sword of the LORD, and of Gideon.

21 And they stood every man in his place round about the camp: and all the host ran, and cried, and fled.

22 And the three hundred blew the trumpets, and the LORD set every man's sword against his fellow, even throughout all the host: and the host fled to Beth-shittah in

Judges 7:15–25. Gideon Prepares His Troops and Leads Them into Victory under the Lord's Power

What can we learn from Gideon's small band of men? (7:17–21) "Their weaponry consisted of a trumpet, a pitcher, and a lamp. His counsel to them was clear, 'Look on me, and do likewise . . . as I do, so shall ye do' (Judges 7:17). . . . They focused on Gideon, . . . a man who had come to trust the Lord—implicitly. 'And they stood every man in his place' (Judges 7:21).

"'May we always remember this profound lesson: that we are banner bearers of the Lord Jesus Christ, upheld by the Holy Spirit of God, faithful and true to the end, each one devoted to give our all to the cause of Zion and bound by covenant to stand close together' ([Uchtdorf, "Lift Where You Stand," 56])" (Freeman, *Written on Our Hearts*, 45). ⊕

Zererath, *and* to the border of Abel-meholah, unto Tabbath.

23 And the men of Israel gathered themselves together out of Naphtali, and out of Asher, and out of all Manasseh, and pursued after the Midianites.

24 ¶ And Gideon sent messengers throughout all mount Ephraim, saying, Come down against the Midianites, and take before them the waters unto Beth-barah and Jordan. Then all the men of Ephraim gathered themselves together, and took the waters unto Beth-barah and Jordan.

25 And they took two princes of the Midianites, Oreb and Zeeb; and they slew Oreb upon the rock Oreb, and Zeeb they slew at the winepress of Zeeb, and pursued Midian, and brought the heads of Oreb and Zeeb to Gideon on the other side Jordan.

CHAPTER 8

Gideon pursues and destroys the Midianites—He frees the children of Israel but refuses their invitation to reign as king over them—Gideon dies, and Israel returns to idolatry.

1 And the men of Ephraim said unto him, Why hast thou served us thus, that thou calledst us not, when thou wentest to fight with the Midianites? And they did chide with him sharply.

2 And he said unto them, What have I done now in comparison of you? *Is* not the gleaning of the grapes of Ephraim better than the vintage of Abi-ezer?

3 God hath delivered into your hands the princes of Midian, Oreb and Zeeb: and what was I able to do in comparison of you? Then their anger was abated toward him, when he had said that.

Judges 8:1–3. The Men of Ephraim Are Upset Because They Have Not Been Called to Assist in the Attack

Why were the Ephraimites angry with Gideon? (8:1–3) "The tribe of Ephraim had a proud heritage (see 1:22) and felt insulted by Gideon's failure to call on them earlier. They had cooperated honorably with Ehud (3:26–29) and Barak (5:13–14a) and wondered why they were left out this time. Gideon decided to adopt a course of appeasement. He praised them for their great victory over Oreb and Zeeb, assuring them that in comparison his accomplishments were small. . . . Gideon's flattery calmed their anger and avoided the civil war that later flared up between Ephraim and Manasseh (12:4–6)" (*Expositor's Bible Commentary [Abridged]*, 344).

4 ¶ And Gideon came to Jordan, *and* passed over, he, and the three hundred men that *were* with him, faint, yet pursuing *them.*

5 And he said unto the men of Succoth, Give, I pray you, loaves of bread unto the people that follow me; for they *be* faint, and I am pursuing after Zebah and Zalmunna, kings of Midian.

6 ¶ And the princes of Succoth said, *Are* the hands of Zebah and Zalmunna now in thine hand, that we should give bread unto thine army?

7 And Gideon said, Therefore when the LORD hath delivered Zebah and Zalmunna into mine hand, then I will tear your flesh with the thorns of the wilderness and with briers.

8 ¶ And he went up thence to Penuel, and spake unto them likewise: and the men of Penuel answered him as the men of Succoth had answered *him.*

9 And he spake also unto the men of Penuel, saying, When I come again in peace, I will break down this tower.

10 ¶ Now Zebah and Zalmunna *were* in Karkor, and their hosts with them, about fifteen thousand *men,* all that were left of all the hosts of the children of the east: for there fell an hundred and twenty thousand men that drew sword.

11 ¶ And Gideon went up by the way of them that dwelt in tents on the east of Nobah and Jogbehah, and smote the host: for the host was secure.

12 And when Zebah and Zalmunna fled, he pursued after them, and took the two kings of Midian, Zebah and Zalmunna, and discomfited all the host.

Judges 8:4–21. Gideon and His Men Follow and Defeat the Remaining Midianites

Why did the people of Succoth and Penuel refuse to provide bread for Gideon's army? (8:4–9)

"Gideon's tiny attack force did not inspire people's confidence that it was a long-lasting protective army. The people of Succoth and [Penuel] felt that their security in the long run depended on maintaining good relations with the Midianites. . . . Therefore, rather than risk revenge from the Midianites later, they treated Gideon's request coolly and refused to give him supplies" (*Quest Study Bible* [2003], 345).

Why were Succoth and Penuel punished by Gideon? (8:16–17) Succoth and Penuel were towns of Gad. "Since the Midianites lived in the deserts of Arabia, Gad and the other tribes east of the Jordan were most vulnerable to their marauding raids. Yet instead of joining Gideon in his attempt to eliminate the threat once and for all, these Gadites flatly refused to get involved.

"Gideon was furious and promised that once he finished with the Midianites he would return to deal with these traitors....

"Such harsh punishment was justified because in their refusal to help Gideon's army, Succoth and Penuel threatened the whole nation of Israel. Their act was thus equivalent to high treason" (*Old Testament Student Manual: Genesis–2 Samuel*, 255).

Why did Gideon put these men to death? (8:18–21) Zebah and Zalmunna were two kings of Midian (see Judges 8:5). "Gideon repaid the two kings of Midian, who had been taken prisoners.... We learn that these kings had put the brothers of Gideon to death, and apparently not in open fight; but they had murdered them in an unrighteous and cruel manner. And Gideon made them atone for this with their own lives" (Keil and Delitzsch, *Commentary* [on Judges 8:18–21]).

13 ¶ And Gideon the son of Joash returned
from battle before the sun *was up,*

14 And caught a young man of the men of
Succoth, and inquired of him: and he described unto him the princes of Succoth, and
the elders thereof, *even* threescore and seventeen men.

15 And he came unto the men of Succoth,
and said, Behold Zebah and Zalmunna,
with whom ye did upbraid me, saying, *Are*
the hands of Zebah and Zalmunna now in
thine hand, that we should give bread unto
thy men *that are* weary?

16 And he took the elders of the city, and
thorns of the wilderness and briers, and with
them he taught the men of Succoth.

17 And he beat down the tower of Penuel,
and slew the men of the city.

18 ¶ Then said he unto Zebah and Zalmunna,
What manner of men *were they* whom ye slew
at Tabor? And they answered, As thou *art,* so
were they; each one resembled the children of
a king.

19 And he said, They *were* my brethren, *even*
the sons of my mother: *as* the LORD liveth,
if ye had saved them alive, I would not slay
you.

20 And he said unto Jether his firstborn, Up,
and slay them. But the youth drew not his
sword: for he feared, because he *was* yet a
youth.

21 Then Zebah and Zalmunna said, Rise
thou, and fall upon us: for as the man *is, so*

is his strength. And Gideon arose, and slew Zebah and Zalmunna, and took away the ornaments that *were* on their camels' necks.

22 ¶ Then the men of Israel said unto Gideon, Rule thou over us, both thou, and thy son, and thy son's son also: for thou hast delivered us from the hand of Midian.

23 And Gideon said unto them, I will not rule over you, neither shall my son rule over you: the LORD shall rule over you.

24 ¶ And Gideon said unto them, I would desire a request of you, that ye would give me every man the earrings of his prey. (For they had golden earrings, because they *were* Ishmaelites.)

25 And they answered, We will willingly give *them*. And they spread a garment, and did cast therein every man the earrings of his prey.

26 And the weight of the golden earrings that he requested was a thousand and seven hundred *shekels* of gold; beside ornaments, and collars, and purple raiment that *was* on the kings of Midian, and beside the chains that *were* about their camels' necks.

27 And Gideon made an ephod thereof, and put it in his city, *even* in Ophrah: and all Israel went thither a whoring after it: which thing became a snare unto Gideon, and to his house.

28 ¶ Thus was Midian subdued before the children of Israel, so that they lifted up their heads no more. And the country was in quietness forty years in the days of Gideon.

Judges 8:22–27. Gideon Rejects Israel's Invitation to Be Their King

What does Gideon's refusal to become Israel's king reveal about his character? (8:22–23) "The deliverance of Israel was now complete. It had been wrought most unexpectedly, and by apparently quite inadequate means. In the circumstances, it was natural that, in measure as the people failed to recognize the direct agency of Jehovah, they should exalt Gideon as the great national hero. Accordingly, they now offered him the hereditary rule over, at least, the northern tribes. Gideon had spiritual discernment and strength sufficient to resist this temptation. He knew that he had only been called to a temporary work, and that the 'rule' which they wished could not be made hereditary. Each 'judge' must be specially called, and qualified by the influence of the Holy Spirit" (Edersheim, *Bible History*, 3:144).

What does it mean that Israel went "a whoring after" Gideon's ephod? (8:24–27) "The idiom 'Israel went thither a whoring after it' (the ephod or, more probably, an ornament to adorn the priest's ephod) means the Israelites started to look upon it as an idol. . . . Anyone guilty of [idolatry] was unfaithful to the Lord just as a husband would be unfaithful to his wife by following after a woman of ill repute" (Ludlow, *Companion to Your Study of the Old Testament*, 210).

Judges 8:28–35. Gideon Dies and Israel Returns to the Worship of Baalim

Why did the children of Israel so quickly return to rebel against the Lord? (8:33–35) "They were both unthankful and unholy. Though they had the clearest proofs of God's power and goodness before their eyes, yet they forgot him. And although they were under the greatest obligations to Gideon, and were once so sensible of them that they offered to settle the kingdom on him and his family, yet they forgot him also; for, becoming foes to God, they could not be friends to [Gideon]" (*Adam Clarke's Commentary* [on Judges 8:35]).

Summary of Judges 9

"Gideon [also known as Jerubbaal] reportedly fathered seventy sons (Judg 9:2, 5, 18; perhaps an idealized number), plus one named Abimelech with his concubine from Shechem (Judg 8:31). Having aspirations to be a king, Abimelech, with aid from some Shechemites, killed his half-brothers (except Jotham, who escaped), and established himself as a local king. Later, Abimelech turned and fought against Shechem, killing many of its inhabitants. Abimelech himself died attacking another city (Judg 9). This episode highlights the dangers of royal pretensions not sanctioned by Jehovah. It also emphasizes the principle of divine restitution (Judg 9:23–24, 56–57)" (Holzapfel, et al., *Jehovah and the World of the Old Testament*, 178).

29 ¶ And Jerubbaal the son of Joash went and dwelt in his own house.

30 And Gideon had threescore and ten sons of his body begotten: for he had many wives.

31 And his concubine that *was* in Shechem, she also bare him a son, whose name he called Abimelech.

32 ¶ And Gideon the son of Joash died in a good old age, and was buried in the sepulchre of Joash his father, in Ophrah of the Abi-ezrites.

33 And it came to pass, as soon as Gideon was dead, that the children of Israel turned again, and went a whoring after Baalim, and made Baal-berith their god.

34 And the children of Israel remembered not the LORD their God, who had delivered them out of the hands of all their enemies on every side:

35 Neither shewed they kindness to the house of Jerubbaal, *namely,* Gideon, according to all the goodness which he had shewed unto Israel.

CHAPTER 9

Gideon's son Abimelech is made king—He slays his seventy brothers—Jotham tells a fable of trees choosing a king—The Shechemites conspire against Abimelech—He is slain at Thebez.

CHAPTER 10

Tola and then Jair judge Israel—The children of Israel worship false gods, are forsaken by the Lord, and are distressed by their enemies—They repent and ask the Lord for deliverance.

Summary of Judges 10

Tola, the son of Puah, judges Israel for twenty-three years, followed by Jair, who judges for twenty-two years. Surrounding nations again influence Israel to serve false gods. For eighteen years the Lord allows Israel to fall under bondage to the Philistines and the children of Ammon. The Lord reminds them, "Ye have forsaken me, and served other gods" (Judges 10:13). He suggests that they "go and cry unto the gods which ye have chosen; let them deliver you in the time of your tribulation" (Judges 10:14). The children of Israel admit they have sinned and then "put away the strange gods from among them, and [serve] the Lord" (Judges 10:16).

CHAPTER 11

Jephthah is chosen as the captain of the armies of Israel—The Ammonites assail Israel in war—Jephthah is guided by the Spirit and defeats Ammon with a great slaughter—He makes a rash vow, which leads to the sacrifice of his only daughter.

Summary of Judges 11

"The circumstances of Jephthah's birth brought him great persecution. He was 'the son of an harlot' [Judges 11:1], for which he was persecuted and finally cast out from among his people [Judges 11:2–3]. But he 'was a mighty man of valour' [Judges 11:1], and when the children of Ammon came against Israel, the elders of the people went to fetch Jephthah and to beg him to come and deliver them" (Ferrell, *Hidden Christ*, 145).

"Jephthah was acquainted with the Lord's powers and had faith in his help, but he mistakenly believed he could secure that help by promising to offer as a burnt sacrifice whatever might come out from the doors of his house to meet him.

"He did indeed succeed in the campaign, and when his beloved daughter came to meet him, he tragically felt he must fulfill his vow. Because the Lord does not require human sacrifice, it may only be hoped that she was dedicated to the service of the Lord rather than sacrificed as a burnt offering (Judg. 11:34–37; Jer. 32:35)" (Rasmussen, *Latter-day Saint Commentary on the Old Testament*, 219).

CHAPTER 12

The Gileadites slay 42,000 Ephraimites—Jephthah, Ibzan, Elon, and Abdon each in turn judge Israel.

Summary of Judges 12

Jephthah gathers the men of Gilead in a civil war against the tribe of Ephraim. He serves as judge for six years before dying. Jephthah is succeeded by Ibzan, Elon, and Abdon.

Judges 13:1–5. Manoah's Wife Is Promised a Son Who Will Be Dedicated to the Lord

Who were the Philistines? (13:1) The Philistines were "a tribe that originally came from Caphtor (Crete, or perhaps part of Egypt) (Amos 9:7) and occupied before the days of Abraham (Gen. 21:32) the rich lowland on the Mediterranean coast from Joppa to the Egyptian desert. . . . For many years there was a struggle for supremacy between them and the Israelites, Philistine power being at its height at the time of Saul's death but rapidly declining during the reign of David" (Bible Dictionary, "Philistines"). "The Bible is understandably hostile to the Philistines, describing them as a pleasure loving, warlike society of pagans ruled by 'tyrants' who threatened ancient Israel's existence" (Dothan, "What We Know about the Philistines," 20). See commentary in this volume for Genesis 26:8. ⊕

What is the location and significance of the city of Zorah? (13:2) "Zorah, the home of Samson, had been assigned originally to the tribe of Judah (see Joshua 15:33), but was later inhabited by the tribe of Dan, which had been unable to take over the land assigned to it as its inheritance" (*Old Testament Student Manual: Genesis–2 Samuel*, 259).

How is Samson's birth similar to others in the Bible? (13:3) "Six barren women in the Bible receive an annunciation from God promising an end to their barrenness. . . . These six stories share a basic tripartite structure: (1) Each begins with an indication of the woman's barrenness, (2) followed by a promise that the woman's barrenness will end—a promise made to Sarah by three divine visitors, to Manoah's wife by an angel of the Lord, to Rebecca by an oracle, to Rachel by God remembering her, to Hannah by Eli the priest and to the Shunammite woman by the prophet Elisha, a man of God; and (3) concluding with the conception and birth of the promised son" (Ackerman, "Child Sacrifice," 20).

What was a Nazarite? (13:4–5) "'The primary meaning of the Heb. verb *nazar* is to separate. Hence the *nazir* [Nazarite] is "the separated," "consecrated," "devoted"' (Hastings, *Bible Dictionary,* s.v. 'Nazarite,'

CHAPTER 13

Israel is in Philistine bondage for forty years—An angel comes to Manoah's wife and promises a son who will begin to deliver Israel—The angel comes again; he ascends in a flame from the altar—Samson is born, and the Spirit of the Lord moves upon him.

1 And the children of Israel did evil again in the sight of the LORD; and the LORD delivered them into the hand of the Philistines forty years.

2 ¶ And there was a certain man of Zorah, of the family of the Danites, whose name *was* Manoah; and his wife *was* barren, and bare not.

3 And the angel of the LORD appeared unto the woman, and said unto her, Behold now, thou *art* barren, and bearest not: but thou shalt conceive, and bear a son.

4 Now therefore beware, I pray thee, and drink not wine nor strong drink, and eat not any unclean *thing:*

5 For, lo, thou shalt conceive, and bear a son; and no razor shall come on his head: for the child shall be a Nazarite unto God from the womb: and he shall begin to deliver Israel out of the hand of the Philistines.

pp. 647–48). A Nazarite therefore, was one who was separated from others by a special vow of self-dedication to Jehovah. The term 'set apart' is used to mean that one has been given a special calling or position and is thus separated from others" (*Old Testament Student Manual: Genesis–2 Samuel*, 259). In this case, the angel commanded Samson's mother to live as a Nazarite until the birth of her son (see Judg. 13:4). See commentary in this volume for Numbers 6:1–8.

Summary of Judges 13:6–14

An angel of the Lord continues to teach Manoah and his wife regarding Samson's foreordained birth and the responsibilities of a Nazarite. In this special case, Samson is consecrated from birth for a mission to deliver Israel.

15 ¶ And Manoah said unto the angel of the LORD, I pray thee, let us detain thee, until we shall have made ready a kid for thee.

Judges 13:15–25. Samson Is Born

16 And the angel of the LORD said unto Manoah, Though thou detain me, I will not eat of thy bread: and if thou wilt offer a burnt offering, thou must offer it unto the LORD. For Manoah knew not that he *was* an angel of the LORD.

17 And Manoah said unto the angel of the LORD, What *is* thy name, that when thy sayings come to pass we may do thee honour?

18 And the angel of the LORD said unto him, Why askest thou thus after my name, seeing it *is* secret?

What did the angel mean by saying his name was "secret"? (13:17–18) "Interestingly, the 'man of God' [13:6] appeared both times to the woman, who in turn informed her husband. . . . The name was *secret* (v. 18), that is, 'incomprehensible, wonderful.' In Isaiah 9:6, the Hebrew for this phrase (translated 'Wonderful') applies to One who would come as 'The mighty God.' . . . The angel . . . *ascended in the flame of the altar* (v. 20). This finally made Manoah aware that he had been in the presence of the angel of the Lord" (*Zondervan KJV Commentary*, 338, 339).

19 So Manoah took a kid with a meat offering, and offered *it* upon a rock unto the LORD: and *the angel* did wondrously; and Manoah and his wife looked on.

20 For it came to pass, when the flame went up toward heaven from off the altar, that the angel of the LORD ascended in the flame of the altar. And Manoah and his wife looked on *it*, and fell on their faces to the ground.

Why was Manoah worried that they would die? (13:19–22) "The idea of sacredness was so strong that we continually see characters in the Old Testament fearing they will not survive because they have come into contact with something sacred. As an example, Manoah and his wife fear their death when they see an angel ascend to heaven" (Muhlestein, *Essential Old Testament Companion*, 191).

21 But the angel of the LORD did no more
appear to Manoah and to his wife. Then
Manoah knew that he *was* an angel of the
LORD.

22 And Manoah said unto his wife, We shall
surely die, because we have seen God.

23 But his wife said unto him, If the LORD
were pleased to kill us, he would not have received a burnt offering and a meat offering at
our hands, neither would he have shewed us
all these *things*, nor would as at this time have
told us *such things* as these.

24 ¶ And the woman bare a son, and called
his name Samson: and the child grew, and
the LORD blessed him.

What do we know about Samson's name? (13:24) "Samson seems clearly to have been a Canaanite personal name. Whether or not Samson is to be regarded as originally the hero of a sun myth . . . the connection of his name with the sun is indubitable. His birthplace was across the Valley of Sorek . . . a short distance from the city Beth-shemesh, 'house of the sun,' the site of a shrine of the sun-god" (*Interpreter's Dictionary of the Bible*, 4:198).

25 And the Spirit of the LORD began to move
him at times in the camp of Dan between
Zorah and Eshtaol.

In what land does Samson grow up? (13:25) "Zorah, where Samson was born, was about halfway between Jerusalem and the Mediterranean, along the coast of which the Philistines lived. . . . At the time of his birth the Israelites had been in bondage to the Philistines for forty years because they had done evil in the sight of the Lord" (*Zondervan Illustrated Bible Dictionary*, 1278–79). The Philistines, "whose major settlements lay along the seacoast, established outposts and villages as far east as the Jordan Valley, threatening the very existence of Israel as a separate people! In view of this threat, Samson's preoccupation with personal affronts and vengeance is a grim commentary on his character" (Richards, *Bible Reader's Companion*, 168).

CHAPTER 14

Samson slays a young lion with his bare hands—He marries a Philistine wife, propounds a riddle, is deceived by his wife, and slays thirty Philistines.

Judges 14:1–11. Samson Desires a Wife of the Philistines

1 And Samson went down to Timnath, and
saw a woman in Timnath of the daughters of
the Philistines.

2 And he came up, and told his father and
his mother, and said, I have seen a woman in
Timnath of the daughters of the Philistines:
now therefore get her for me to wife.

3 Then his father and his mother said unto
him, *Is there* never a woman among the
daughters of thy brethren, or among all my
people, that thou goest to take a wife of the
uncircumcised Philistines? And Samson said
unto his father, Get her for me; for she pleaseth me well.

4 But his father and his mother knew not
that it *was* of the LORD, that he sought an occasion against the Philistines: for at that time
the Philistines had dominion over Israel.

5 ¶ Then went Samson down, and his father
and his mother, to Timnath, and came to the
vineyards of Timnath: and, behold, a young
lion roared against him.

6 And the Spirit of the LORD came mightily
upon him, and he rent him as he would have
rent a kid, and *he had* nothing in his hand:
but he told not his father or his mother what
he had done.

7 And he went down, and talked with the
woman; and she pleased Samson well.

How could Samson's request to marry a Philistine woman be considered "of the Lord"? (14:2–4) "To marry with any that did not belong to the Israelitish stock, was contrary to the law, Exodus 34:16; Deuteronomy 7:3. But this marriage of Samson was said to be of the Lord, Judges 14:4; that is, God permitted it (for in no other sense can we understand the phrase), that it might be a means of bringing about the deliverance of Israel" (*Adam Clarke's Commentary* [on Judges 14:3]).

What did the author mean by using the phrase, "the Spirit of the Lord"? (14:6) "Samson's remarkable strength was a gift of God derived from and sustained by the Nazarite vow he was under. Perhaps when the author of Judges used the phrase 'the Spirit of God' he . . . used it more in the way that one would now use the phrase 'spiritual gifts.' One may say of another, 'The way he taught the lesson demonstrated that he has a spiritual gift.' Samson's gift was strength, and each time he used that gift in a remarkable manner, the writer of the scripture gave credit to the Lord, the true source of the gift, by saying 'the Spirit of the Lord' came mightily upon him" (*Old Testament Student Manual: Genesis–2 Samuel*, 260). ⊕

What was Samson's weakness that caused his downfall? (14:7) "In the book of Judges . . . we learn about Samson. Samson was born with great potential. His mother was promised, 'He shall begin to deliver Israel out of the hand of the Philistines' [Judges 13:5]. But as Samson grew, he looked more to the world's temptations than to God's direction. He made choices because they 'pleased [him] well' [Judges 14:3] rather than because those choices were right. . . . Instead of arising and shining forth to fulfill his great potential, Samson was overcome by the world, lost his God-given power, and died a tragic, early death" (Dibb, "Arise and Shine Forth," 118).

What was notable about Samson eating honey found in the carcass of the lion? (14:8–9) "Samson returned to the [*carcass*] *of the lion* (v. 8), a probable violation of the Nazarite vow. His silence concerning his whereabouts (v. 6) and activity (v. 9) strongly hints of his awareness of a broken Nazarite vow. The *honey* taken from the dead lion was considered unclean" (*Zondervan KJV Commentary*, 340).

Judges 14:12–20. Samson Gives a Riddle to Thirty Philistines

What was the purpose of riddles in the ancient world? (14:12) To *put forth a riddle* literally meant, "'riddle a riddle.' The word *chidah* is derived from a root 'to tie in a knot' and so 'to be intricate.' As a source of entertainment the riddle was much loved in all ages. The queen of Sheba came to test Solomon's wisdom with riddles [1 Kings 10:1], and God told Ezekiel to pose a riddle to the house of Israel [Ezek. 27:2])" (Cohen, *Joshua and Judges*, 271).

What was the result of Samson's riddle at his wedding party? (14:14–20) "At Samson's seven-day wedding celebration he proposed a riddle. When his wife revealed the answer to the thirty Philistine guests to save her own life (see vs. 15) and Samson lost the wager, he was furious and wreaked havoc on the Philistines at Ashkelon to get the spoils necessary to pay his debt. Probably for spite, his father-in-law gave Samson's wife to the man 'used as his friend' (vs. 20), that is his best man at the wedding" (*Old Testament Student Manual: Genesis–2 Samuel*, 260).

8 ¶ And after a time he returned to take her, and he turned aside to see the carcase of the lion: and, behold, *there was* a swarm of bees and honey in the carcase of the lion.

9 And he took thereof in his hands, and went on eating, and came to his father and mother, and he gave them, and they did eat: but he told not them that he had taken the honey out of the carcase of the lion.

10 ¶ So his father went down unto the woman: and Samson made there a feast; for so used the young men to do.

11 And it came to pass, when they saw him, that they brought thirty companions to be with him.

12 ¶ And Samson said unto them, I will now put forth a riddle unto you: if ye can certainly declare it me within the seven days of the feast, and find *it* out, then I will give you thirty sheets and thirty change of garments:

13 But if ye cannot declare *it* me, then shall ye give me thirty sheets and thirty change of garments. And they said unto him, Put forth thy riddle, that we may hear it.

14 And he said unto them, Out of the eater came forth meat, and out of the strong came forth sweetness. And they could not in three days expound the riddle.

15 And it came to pass on the seventh day, that they said unto Samson's wife, Entice thy husband, that he may declare unto us the riddle, lest we burn thee and thy father's house with fire: have ye called us to take that we have? *is it* not *so?*

16 And Samson's wife wept before him, and said, Thou dost but hate me, and lovest me not: thou hast put forth a riddle unto the children of my people, and hast not told *it* me. And he said unto her, Behold, I have not told *it* my father nor my mother, and shall I tell *it* thee?

17 And she wept before him the seven days, while their feast lasted: and it came to pass on the seventh day, that he told her, because she lay sore upon him: and she told the riddle to the children of her people.

18 And the men of the city said unto him on the seventh day before the sun went down, What *is* sweeter than honey? and what *is* stronger than a lion? And he said unto them, If ye had not plowed with my heifer, ye had not found out my riddle.

19 ¶ And the Spirit of the LORD came upon him, and he went down to Ashkelon, and slew thirty men of them, and took their spoil, and gave change of garments unto them which expounded the riddle. And his anger was kindled, and he went up to his father's house.

20 But Samson's wife was *given* to his companion, whom he had used as his friend.

CHAPTER 15

Samson burns the grain of the Philistines—They burn his wife and father-in-law—Samson slays a thousand Philistines at Lehi with the jawbone of an ass.

1 But it came to pass within a while after, in the time of wheat harvest, that Samson visited his wife with a kid; and he said, I will go in to my wife into the chamber. But her father would not suffer him to go in.

2 And her father said, I verily thought that thou hadst utterly hated her; therefore I gave her to thy companion: *is* not her younger sister fairer than she? take her, I pray thee, instead of her.

3 ¶ And Samson said concerning them, Now shall I be more blameless than the Philistines, though I do them a displeasure.

Judges 15:1–8. Samson Burns the Crops of the Philistines

How did Samson's desire for revenge harm both the Philistines and his own family? (15:4–6) In anger over his father-in-law's actions, Samson chooses to retaliate against the Philistines, capturing foxes to carry out his plan. "The *three hundred foxes* were probably jackals. The two animals are similar, and the same Hebrew word is used for both. Foxes are solitary animals, but jackals travel in packs and large numbers of them could be caught more easily. . . .

"Shocks are bundles of wheat stacked together in the fields. Samson's jackals burned whole crops of grain, grapes, and olives. The damage naturally outraged the Philistines. According to the law, anyone who burned someone else's fields had to pay restitution (Ex. 22:6)" (*Nelson Study Bible* [NKJV], 396).

What kind of a man had Samson become? (15:7) "Judges 15 continues to portray Samson as more reactionary and vengeful than inspired. Other judges had raised armies and delivered their people from oppression. Samson continued to kill Philistines (Judg 15:14–16), but he always worked alone and for selfish reasons and never completely delivered his people" (Holzapfel, et al., *Jehovah and the World of the Old Testament*, 179–80).

What is the meaning of the phrase "hip and thigh"? (15:8) Hip and thigh was "a formulaic expression describing complete devastation" (*New Oxford Annotated Bible* [1991], 322).

Judges 15:9–13. Men of Judah Bind Samson and Give Him to the Philistines

What does the name *Lehi* mean? (15:9) "Lehi is an unknown location situated somewhere along the Philistine frontier [Meir Lubetshi, "Lehi," in Freedman, *Anchor Bible Dictionary*]. The name 'Lehi' means 'jaw' (or 'cheek'); and, thus, it appears that the city was named 'Lehi' after Samson slew a thousand Philistine men in that location, using the 'jawbone' of an ass as his weapon [see Wolf, "Judges," in Gaebelein, ed., *Expositor's Bible Commentary*]" (Gaskill, *Miracles of the Old Testament*, 228). ⊕

Why would the men of Judah try to capture Samson? (15:11–13) "The men of Judah were well aware of Samson's capabilities, and even with their large force, they did not attempt to tie him up without

4 And Samson went and caught three hundred foxes, and took firebrands, and turned
tail to tail, and put a firebrand in the midst
between two tails.

5 And when he had set the brands on fire,
he let *them* go into the standing corn of the
Philistines, and burnt up both the shocks,
and also the standing corn, with the vineyards *and* olives.

6 ¶ Then the Philistines said, Who hath done
this? And they answered, Samson, the son in
law of the Timnite, because he had taken his
wife, and given her to his companion. And
the Philistines came up, and burnt her and
her father with fire.

7 ¶ And Samson said unto them, Though ye
have done this, yet will I be avenged of you,
and after that I will cease.

8 And he smote them hip and thigh with a
great slaughter: and he went down and dwelt
in the top of the rock Etam.

9 ¶ Then the Philistines went up, and pitched
in Judah, and spread themselves in Lehi.

10 And the men of Judah said, Why are ye
come up against us? And they answered, To
bind Samson are we come up, to do to him
as he hath done to us.

11 Then three thousand men of Judah
went to the top of the rock Etam, and said
to Samson, Knowest thou not that the
Philistines *are* rulers over us? what *is* this *that*

thou hast done unto us? And he said unto them, As they did unto me, so have I done unto them.

12 And they said unto him, We are come down to bind thee, that we may deliver thee into the hand of the Philistines. And Samson said unto them, Swear unto me, that ye will not fall upon me yourselves.

13 And they spake unto him, saying, No; but we will bind thee fast, and deliver thee into their hand: but surely we will not kill thee. And they bound him with two new cords, and brought him up from the rock.

14 ¶ *And* when he came unto Lehi, the Philistines shouted against him: and the Spirit of the LORD came mightily upon him, and the cords that *were* upon his arms became as flax that was burnt with fire, and his bands loosed from off his hands.

15 And he found a new jawbone of an ass, and put forth his hand, and took it, and slew a thousand men therewith.

16 And Samson said, With the jawbone of an ass, heaps upon heaps, with the jaw of an ass have I slain a thousand men.

17 And it came to pass, when he had made an end of speaking, that he cast away the jawbone out of his hand, and called that place Ramath-lehi.

18 ¶ And he was sore athirst, and called on the LORD, and said, Thou hast given this great deliverance into the hand of thy servant: and now shall I die for thirst, and fall into the hand of the uncircumcised?

19 But God clave an hollow place that *was* in the jaw, and there came water thereout; and when he had drunk, his spirit came again, and he revived: wherefore he called the name thereof En-hakkore, which *is* in Lehi unto this day.

his consent (vv. 12–13). . . . Much of Judah was under Philistine rule, and the tribe apparently was content to accept it. So they mustered a force, not to support Samson, but to capture him for the Philistines" (*Zondervan KJV Commentary*, 341).

Judges 15:14–20. Samson Kills a Thousand Philistines with a Jawbone

What does it mean that Samson killed a thousand Philistines? (15:14–16) "The supernatural strength with which Samson rent asunder the fetters bound upon him, when the Philistines thought they had him safely in their power, filled them with fear and awe as before a superior being, so that they fled, and he pursued them, smiting one heap after another, as he overtook them, with an ass's jaw-bone which he found in the way. The number given, viz., a thousand, is of course a round number signifying a very great multitude" (Keil and Delitzsch, *Commentary* [on Judges 15:15]).

What do these verses teach us about receiving blessings from God? (15:18–19) "Samson's thirst is interpreted as a result of the battle, but it also has educational meaning. He realizes that his might and life are dependent upon God's will. This time . . . Samson represents himself as a servant before his master and admits that the victory came from God" (*Jewish Study Bible* [2004], 544).

"God's responsiveness did not automatically mean Samson's deeds were approved. Samson, despite his arrogance and violence, cried out to God, as the Israelites had in the desert (Ex 17:1–7; Nu 20:2–13). God, in his mercy, graciously supplied Samson's need" (*Quest Study Bible* [2003], 358).

What did Samson accomplish during his reign? (15:20) "And Samson became the judge over Israel and ruled for twenty years and the Philistines did not plunder the land any more because they were afraid of the strength of Samson.

"But Samson did nothing to free his people from the Philistines. He was content to think that fear of him might keep them away always. So in pride and vainglory Samson annoyed the enemies of his people rather than using his strength in wisdom to subdue them" (Jacob, *Message of the Old Testament,* 124).

20 And he judged Israel in the days of the Philistines twenty years.

CHAPTER 16

Samson carries away the doors of the gate of Gaza—He loves Delilah, who delivers him to the Philistines—He destroys a building, killing himself and 3,000 others.

Judges 16:1–14. Delilah Tries to Find the Source of Samson's Strength

1 Then went Samson to Gaza, and saw there an harlot, and went in unto her.

2 *And it was told* the Gazites, saying, Samson is come hither. And they compassed *him* in, and laid wait for him all night in the gate of the city, and were quiet all the night, saying, In the morning, when it is day, we shall kill him.

3 And Samson lay till midnight, and arose at midnight, and took the doors of the gate of the city, and the two posts, and went away with them, bar and all, and put *them* upon his shoulders, and carried them up to the top of an hill that *is* before Hebron.

Who was Delilah? (16:4) "The name *Delilah* may be related to an Arabic root that means 'flirt'" (*New Oxford Annotated Bible* [1991], 323). Alternately, the Bible Dictionary suggests her name could mean "weak, delicate." Regardless of the meaning of her name, Delilah was "a Philistine woman from the valley of Sorek who had such influence over Samson that she obtained from him the secret of his strength and betrayed him, which was the cause of his being blinded and imprisoned at Gaza (Judg. 16)" (Bible Dictionary, "Delilah").

4 ¶ And it came to pass afterward, that he loved a woman in the valley of Sorek, whose name *was* Delilah.

What was the bribe really worth? (16:5) "One correlation as to the relative value of these 'pieces of silver' in the economy of that Israelite time period is found in the next chapter. A Levite from Bethlehem

5 And the lords of the Philistines came up unto her, and said unto her, Entice him, and see wherein his great strength *lieth,* and by what *means* we may prevail against him, that we may bind him to afflict him: and we will give thee every one of us eleven hundred *pieces* of silver.

moved north to the tribal area of Ephraim and was enticed to become a personal family priest to a man named Micah ([Judges] 17:7–9). His yearly wages were to be an allotment of food and clothing along with 'ten pieces of silver a year' (17:10). The Levite accepted these wages. Thus, if a man could receive food, clothes, and only ten pieces of silver annually for a salary, one can imagine what value and use Delilah would have made of her 5,500 pieces of silver (the wages of one man for 550 years)" (Ludlow, *Unlocking the Old Testament*, 73).

6 ¶ And Delilah said to Samson, Tell me, I pray thee, wherein thy great strength *lieth,* and wherewith thou mightest be bound to afflict thee.

How does Samson's life reflect Israel at that time? (16:6) "If the secret of Samson's strength lay in the faithful observance of his Nazarite vow, his weakness sprung from his natural character. The parallel, so far as Israel is concerned cannot fail to be seen. And as Samson's sin finally assumed the form of adulterous love for Delilah, so that of his people was spiritual unfaithfulness. Thus, if the period of the Judges reached its highest point in Samson, the Nazarite, it also sunk to its lowest in Samson the man of carnal lusts, who yielded his secret to Delilah" (Edersheim, *Bible History*, 3:165).

7 And Samson said unto her, If they bind me with seven green withs that were never dried, then shall I be weak, and be as another man.

8 Then the lords of the Philistines brought up to her seven green withs which had not been dried, and she bound him with them.

9 Now *there were* men lying in wait, abiding with her in the chamber. And she said unto him, The Philistines *be* upon thee, Samson. And he brake the withs, as a thread of tow is broken when it toucheth the fire. So his strength was not known.

10 And Delilah said unto Samson, Behold, thou hast mocked me, and told me lies: now tell me, I pray thee, wherewith thou mightest be bound.

What are "green withs"? (16:7) Green withs, or "fresh [uncured] thongs or bow strings were sometimes made of the intestines of cattle. Sumerian literature refers to deriving bow strings from a sheep's leg (presumably the tendons) or from ram's gut, while Ugaritic literature refers to tendons from a bull's leg. They were usually laid out to dry before being put to use. Others have preferred to think of vines being used. The fact that seven are used also suggests a magical element to the procedure" (Walton, et al., *IVP Bible Background Commentary*, 269).

11 And he said unto her, If they bind me fast with new ropes that never were occupied, then shall I be weak, and be as another man.

12 Delilah therefore took new ropes, and bound him therewith, and said unto him, The Philistines *be* upon thee, Samson. And

Why would Samson specify that "new" ropes should be used? (16:11) "Ropes have been found preserved in Egyptian tombs made of green papyrus or of date-palm fiber. In Israel the stem of the sparrow-wort, a desert shrub, was one of the most suitable and convenient materials. New ropes would have been less brittle and therefore more resilient" (Walton, et al., *IVP Bible Background Commentary*, 268).

there were liers in wait abiding in the chamber. And he brake them from off his arms
like a thread.

What was "the web" and "the pin" that Delilah used to bind Samson's hair? (16:13–14) "*The web* and *the pin* were parts of a loom" (*New Oxford Annotated Bible,* [1991], 323). "Delilah, we may understand, having the sleeping Samson's head in her lap (as in v. 19), weaves his hair into the warp and beats it up into the web *with the pin*, a flat piece of wood, so that his hair actually becomes part of the woven material. The loom would be the primitive type with two upright posts fixed into the ground, one holding the yarn-beam and the other the cloth-beam. When Samson wakes up, he goes off, loom and all fixed to his hair, dragging the upright posts out of the ground" (Guthrie, et al., *New Bible Commentary: Revised*, 272).

13 And Delilah said unto Samson, Hitherto
thou hast mocked me, and told me lies: tell
me wherewith thou mightest be bound. And
he said unto her, If thou weavest the seven
locks of my head with the web.

14 And she fastened *it* with the pin, and
said unto him, The Philistines *be* upon thee,
Samson. And he awaked out of his sleep, and
went away with the pin of the beam, and
with the web.

Judges 16:15–25. Samson Tells the Secret of His Strength, and He Is Captured and Blinded

What led to Samson's ruin? (16:15–17) "Samson's entanglement with Delilah, whose sympathies were with the Philistines, brought about his downfall. Three times he successfully repulsed the Philistines when the woman betrayed him into their hands. However, when he revealed the secret of his power to her and his hair was cut, Samson lost his strength" (Shultz, *Old Testament Speaks*, 112). ⊕

15 ¶ And she said unto him, How canst
thou say, I love thee, when thine heart *is* not
with me? thou hast mocked me these three
times, and hast not told me wherein thy great
strength *lieth.*

16 And it came to pass, when she pressed
him daily with her words, and urged him, *so*
that his soul was vexed unto death;

17 That he told her all his heart, and said
unto her, There hath not come a razor upon
mine head; for I *have been* a Nazarite unto
God from my mother's womb: if I be shaven,
then my strength will go from me, and I shall
become weak, and be like any *other* man.

18 And when Delilah saw that he had told
her all his heart, she sent and called for the
lords of the Philistines, saying, Come up this
once, for he hath shewed me all his heart.
Then the lords of the Philistines came up
unto her, and brought money in their hand.

What was the true source of Samson's strength? (16:19–20) "These last words are very important to observe in order to form a correct idea of the affair.

19 And she made him sleep upon her knees;
and she called for a man, and she caused him
to shave off the seven locks of his head; and

she began to afflict him, and his strength went from him.

20 And she said, The Philistines *be* upon thee, Samson. And he awoke out of his sleep, and said, I will go out as at other times before, and shake myself. And he wist not that the LORD was departed from him.

21 ¶ But the Philistines took him, and put out his eyes, and brought him down to Gaza, and bound him with fetters of brass; and he did grind in the prison house.

22 Howbeit the hair of his head began to grow again after he was shaven.

23 Then the lords of the Philistines gathered them together for to offer a great sacrifice unto Dagon their god, and to rejoice: for they said, Our god hath delivered Samson our enemy into our hand.

24 And when the people saw him, they praised their god: for they said, Our god hath delivered into our hands our enemy, and the destroyer of our country, which slew many of us.

25 And it came to pass, when their hearts were merry, that they said, Call for Samson, that he may make us sport. And they called for Samson out of the prison house; and he made them sport: and they set him between the pillars.

26 And Samson said unto the lad that held him by the hand, Suffer me that I may feel the pillars whereupon the house standeth, that I may lean upon them.

27 Now the house was full of men and women; and all the lords of the Philistines *were* there; and *there were* upon the roof about three thousand men and women, that beheld while Samson made sport.

Samson had said to Delilah, 'If my hair were cut off, *my strength* would depart from me' (v. 17). The historian observes, on the other hand, that '*Jehovah* had departed from him.' The superhuman strength of Samson did not reside in his hair as hair, but in the fact that Jehovah was with or near him. But Jehovah was with him so long as he maintained his condition as a Nazarite. As soon as he broke away from this by sacrificing the hair which he wore in honour of the Lord, Jehovah departed from him, and with Jehovah went his strength" (Keil and Delitzsch, *Commentary* [on Judges 16:20]).

Why did they punish Samson so severely? (16:21) To "put out" literally means "'bored,' a form of mutilation common in ancient times (cf. [1 Sam. 11:2]; [2 Kings 25:7]). . . . The Rabbis remarked that the eyes are the agents of sin. Samson's eyes had lusted after Philistine women, and that part of his body suffered punishment" (Cohen, *Joshua and Judges,* 283).

Who was the deity named "Dagon"? (16:23) "The head of the Philistine pantheon appears to have been the Canaanite god, Dagon" (Dothan, "What We Know about the Philistines," 30). "*Dagon* [was] a deity of the Philistines with a temple to his worship in Ashdod ([1 Sam. 5:2ff]). The name has been associated with *dag*, 'a fish,' or *dagan*, 'corn,' and thought of as half man and half fish or a god of agriculture. The data point to his being a Semite god worshipped even in Babylonia" (Cohen, *Joshua and Judges*, 284).

Judges 16:26–31. Samson Dies Taking Revenge on the Philistines One Last Time

What can we learn from Samson's final act? (16:30)
"It is not until the very last chapter of Samson's short life that he breaks out of the narrow confines of his narcissism and becomes a true biblical hero. In a single harrowing moment, he gives, in Lincoln's words, 'the full measure of devotion,' redeeming himself as God's choice to liberate his people from the Philistine yoke. . . . By deciding to sacrifice his life for the greater good, Samson gives meaning to his life and death and leaves a legacy of freedom and heroism to the Israelite tribes" (Rosenblatt, "Esther and Samson," 23, 47).

Summary of Judges 17–21

After the days of Samson, the children of Israel become more and more wicked. The record states that during these days, "there was no king in Israel, but every man did that which was right in his own eyes" (Judges 17:6; see also Judges 21:25). These final chapters of Judges contain accounts that illustrate the spiritual decline of the Israelites. "The stories of Micah the Levite and the Danite migration, in chapters 17 and 18, and the account of the rape of the concubine at Gibeah and the subsequent punishment of the Benjamites, in chapters 19–21, are samples of Israel's worst days. Nothing in the stories show the Israelites doing what was right" (*Old Testament Student Manual: Genesis–2 Samuel*, 261). "Probably no historical book of the Old Testament has so transparent a 'philosophy of history' as does the book of Judges. . . . The writer of Judges has driven home the inescapable lesson of the period of the Judges: apostasy and disobedience will inevitably result in sorrow and affliction" (Parry and Ricks, "The Judges of Israel," 246–47).

28 And Samson called unto the LORD, and said, O Lord GOD, remember me, I pray thee, and strengthen me, I pray thee, only this once, O God, that I may be at once avenged of the Philistines for my two eyes.

29 And Samson took hold of the two middle pillars upon which the house stood, and on which it was borne up, of the one with his right hand, and of the other with his left.

30 And Samson said, Let me die with the Philistines. And he bowed himself with *all his* might; and the house fell upon the lords, and upon all the people that *were* therein. So the dead which he slew at his death were more than *they* which he slew in his life.

31 Then his brethren and all the house of his father came down, and took him, and brought *him* up, and buried him between Zorah and Eshtaol in the buryingplace of Manoah his father. And he judged Israel twenty years.

CHAPTERS 17–21

Micah has a house of gods (images) and consecrates his own priests.

The Danites send men to seek an inheritance—They take Micah's images and priest, burn the city of Laish, and set up idolatry.

A Levite's concubine returns to her father—Her husband takes her back, and they lodge overnight in Gibeah—The men of Gibeah abuse the concubine and she dies—The Levite husband cuts her into twelve pieces and sends them to the tribes of Israel.

All Israel arises against the Benjamites, who refuse to deliver up the men of Gibeah—The Benjamites are smitten and destroyed.

The people lament the desolation of Benjamin—The inhabitants of Jabesh-gilead are destroyed for not engaging in the war with Benjamin—Wives are provided for the remnant of Benjamin.

THE BOOK OF RUTH

Introduction

"The book of Ruth is one of the most loved stories in the Old Testament. . . . We love the story because it is so well told, because it has characters we can identify with, because it weaves a plot we can relate to that has a wonderful resolution. Yet, we often do not recognize a deeper symbolism in the text. The book of Ruth carries within its pages some of the most fundamental and powerful doctrines of the kingdom. It speaks of and symbolically demonstrates God's redeeming power; it teaches us of how we can access that power and exemplifies how we should emulate our Redeemer. Numerous elements of the story serve as types of Christ" (Muhlestein, "Ruth, Redemption, Covenant, and Christ," 187).

Ruth is a narrative that begins with "a Judean man named Elimelech, who lived in the town of Bethlehem, fled the land with his wife, Naomi, and their two sons, Mahlon and Chilion. The family traveled to Moab, a kingdom on the eastern borders of the Dead Sea" (*Old Testament Student Manual: Genesis–2 Samuel*, 262). "The book of Ruth serves as an appendix to the book of Judges. It tells of some nobler events that 'came to pass in the days when the judges ruled' (Ruth 1:1). It is reassuring to read about Israelites of that time who were good, even exemplary—showing faith, love, loyalty, generosity, and devotion to duty. Perhaps they represent many other Israelites of the time whose family history we do not have" (Rasmussen, *Latter-day Saint Commentary on the Old Testament*, 224).

"The story of Ruth beautifully illustrates the conversion of a non-Israelite into the fold of Israel, giving up her former god and former life to unite with the household of faith in the service of the God of Israel (see Ruth 1:16)" (Bible Dictionary, "Ruth"). Finally, "As long as ordinary people who demonstrate the simple virtues of loyalty, love, and generosity are valued, the book of Ruth will remain a cherished part of our biblical heritage" (Ricks, "Ruth," 257).

The book of Ruth also typifies the return of scattered Israel. "The narrative from Exodus to Deuteronomy relates the return of this people from Egypt to the land they have been promised. . . . The Book of Ruth, too, is about exile and return, land and people. Like Abraham, and like the family of Jacob (see the story of Joseph), the family of Elimelech was forced by famine to leave its home in the land of Israel and to preserve itself in a foreign land. When the famine abates, Naomi returns to Bethlehem. Far from being a casual move, the importance of returning is emphasized in chapter 1 by the repetition of the root *shuv*, 'return,' twelve times as Naomi bids her daughters-in-law return to their families in Moab" (Berlin, "Ruth," 43, 47).

CHAPTER 1

Elimelech and his family go to Moab because of famine—His sons marry—The father and sons die—Ruth, the Moabitess, her husband having died, remains constant to Naomi—They come to Bethlehem.

1 Now it came to pass in the days when the
judges ruled, that there was a famine in the

Ruth 1:1–5. Naomi's Sons Marry and Eventually Die in Moab

Who were the Moabites? (1:1) "The Moabites were Semitic people related to Abraham, the father of the Hebrews; they were descendants of Lot and one of his

land. And a certain man of Beth-lehem-judah went to sojourn in the country of Moab, he, and his wife, and his two sons.

2 And the name of the man *was* Elimelech, and the name of his wife Naomi, and the name of his two sons Mahlon and Chilion, Ephrathites of Beth-lehem-judah. And they came into the country of Moab, and continued there.

3 And Elimelech Naomi's husband died; and she was left, and her two sons.

4 And they took them wives of the women of Moab; the name of the one *was* Orpah, and the name of the other Ruth: and they dwelled there about ten years.

5 And Mahlon and Chilion died also both of them; and the woman was left of her two sons and her husband.

6 ¶ Then she arose with her daughters in law, that she might return from the country of Moab: for she had heard in the country of Moab how that the Lord had visited his people in giving them bread.

7 Wherefore she went forth out of the place where she was, and her two daughters in law with her; and they went on the way to return unto the land of Judah.

8 And Naomi said unto her two daughters in law, Go, return each to her mother's house: the Lord deal kindly with you, as ye have dealt with the dead, and with me.

9 The Lord grant you that ye may find rest, each *of you* in the house of her husband. Then she kissed them; and they lifted up their voice, and wept.

daughters (see Gen. 19:30–38)" (Ludlow, *Companion to Your Study of the Old Testament*, 212).

What do the names in Naomi's family mean? (1:2) "The name *Elimelech* means 'my God is king' and characterizes the religious loyalty of the man and his family.

"*Naomi* means 'pleasantness, sweetness,' and though this good woman later became so depressed that she thought *Mara* ('bitter sorrow') would be a more appropriate name, she recovered her pleasantness and showed wisdom and faith as well.

"*Mahlon* is possibly derived from *mahlah*, implying 'illness,' and seems to have anticipated his short life.

"*Chilion* is possibly derived from *kalah*, which has one root meaning 'to be ended, spent, consumed,' also anticipating a short life and early death" (Rasmussen, *Latter-day Saint Commentary on the Old Testament*, 225). ⊕

What are the meanings of the names Orpah and Ruth? (1:4) "*Orpah* was taken by some of the Jewish commentators as signifying 'the back of the neck,' and explained by her having turned her back on Naomi. *Ruth* may be 'friend' or 'refreshment': the Talmud takes the latter view, 'because David sprang from her, who refreshed the Holy One with songs and praises'" (*John Dummelow's Commentary* [on Ruth 1:2]).

Ruth 1:6–15. Naomi Tells Her Daughters-in-Law to Stay with Their Families in Moab

What was Naomi's concern for Ruth? (1:8–13) "Both Ruth and Orpah insisted that they should stay with Naomi. But Naomi convinced them that it was not worth it. She reminded them that she had no way of providing them with a brother in law whom they could marry under the Levirate law of marriage ([see Genesis 38]). If they were to stay with her, they would be husbandless and childless their entire lives" (Muhlestein, *Scripture Study Made Simple*, 172). ⊕

What happened to Orpah? (1:14–15) "Because Orpah's name means 'back of neck' or 'neck' [Brown, et al., *Hebrew and English Lexicon,* 298–99, 791c, 1093], she has been characterized as one who turned her back. In Jewish Midrash, Orpah is described as the mother of Goliath, the giant warrior who faced Ruth's great-grandson David and lost his life, suggesting that she relocated to Philistia [Ginzberg, *Legends of the Jews*, 4:85]. But the scriptural text does not describe Orpah as the opposite of Ruth. On the contrary, her fine character serves to highlight the unusually remarkable character of Ruth [Campbell, *Ruth*, 78, 82]" (Olson, *Women of the New Testament*, 80).

Who was the god of the Moabites? (1:15) Chemosh was "the national deity of the Moabites ([Numbers 21:29; Jeremiah 48:7, 13, 46]) In [Judges 11:24, he] also appears as the god of the Ammonites. Solomon introduced, and Josiah abolished, the worship of *Chemosh* at Jerusalem (1 Kings 11:7; 2 Kings 23:13). Also identified with *Baal-peor, Baalzebub, Mars* and *Saturn*" (*Smith's Bible Dictionary*, 53).

Ruth 1:16–22. Ruth Testifies That She Will Always Follow Naomi and Her God

What blessings did Ruth receive for her loyalty to Naomi? (1:16) "When Naomi sensed the true depth of Ruth's love and loyalty, she consented and the two made their way back to Bethlehem. There, through the mediating role of Naomi, Ruth met Boaz, 'a mighty man of wealth' (Ruth 2:1), and they married. From this

10 And they said unto her, Surely we will return with thee unto thy people.

11 And Naomi said, Turn again, my daughters: why will ye go with me? *are* there yet *any more* sons in my womb, that they may be your husbands?

12 Turn again, my daughters, go *your way;* for I am too old to have an husband. If I should say, I have hope, *if* I should have an husband also to night, and should also bear sons;

13 Would ye tarry for them till they were grown? would ye stay for them from having husbands? nay, my daughters; for it grieveth me much for your sakes that the hand of the LORD is gone out against me.

14 And they lifted up their voice, and wept again: and Orpah kissed her mother in law; but Ruth clave unto her.

15 And she said, Behold, thy sister in law is gone back unto her people, and unto her gods: return thou after thy sister in law.

16 And Ruth said, Entreat me not to leave thee, *or* to return from following after thee: for whither thou goest, I will go; and where thou lodgest, I will lodge: thy people *shall be* my people, and thy God my God:

17 Where thou diest, will I die, and there will I be buried: the LORD do so to me, and more also, *if ought* but death part thee and me.

18 When she saw that she was steadfastly minded to go with her, then she left speaking unto her.

19 ¶ So they two went until they came to Beth-lehem. And it came to pass, when they were come to Beth-lehem, that all the city was moved about them, and they said, *Is* this Naomi?

20 And she said unto them, Call me not Naomi, call me Mara: for the Almighty hath dealt very bitterly with me.

21 I went out full, and the LORD hath brought me home again empty: why *then* call ye me Naomi, seeing the LORD hath testified against me, and the Almighty hath afflicted me?

22 So Naomi returned, and Ruth the Moabitess, her daughter in law, with her, which returned out of the country of Moab: and they came to Beth-lehem in the beginning of barley harvest.

CHAPTER 2

Ruth gleans in the fields of Boaz, a near relative of Naomi—He treats Ruth kindly.

1 And Naomi had a kinsman of her husband's, a mighty man of wealth, of the family of Elimelech; and his name *was* Boaz.

2 And Ruth the Moabitess said unto Naomi, Let me now go to the field, and glean ears of corn after *him* in whose sight I shall find grace. And she said unto her, Go, my daughter.

union came a son named Obed, who fathered a son named Jesse, who fathered a son named David, the greatest king in Israel's history. Thus Ruth's love for and loyalty to Naomi not only brought gospel blessings to Ruth, but ultimately blessed the entire Israelite nation" (Holland, "Real Friendship," 64–65). ⊕

How was Ruth's life changed by choosing to follow Naomi and to worship Jehovah? (1:16–19) This "is a radical thought because it signals that Ruth is changing her identity in a world where that was almost inconceivable. The ancient world had no mechanism for religious conversion or change of citizenship; the very notion was unthinkable. Religion and peoplehood defined one's ethnic identity, and this could no more be changed than the color of one's skin. A Moabite was always a Moabite, wherever he or she lived. And indeed, Ruth is referred to throughout the story as 'the Moabitess.' But from Ruth's point of view, she is becoming an Israelite" (Berlin, "Ruth," 48).

How did God demonstrate He had not abandoned Naomi? (1:20–21) "It seemed to Naomi that 'the Almighty [had] dealt very bitterly' with her. Nevertheless God, in his never-flagging love, directed the subsequent events which led to the marriage of Ruth and Boaz and the birth of Obed, whom Naomi lovingly held in her bosom and for whom she acted as a nurse at the end of the story" (Ricks, "Ruth," 256).

When did the barley harvest begin? (1:22) "The poor people's bread, barley was limited to areas with sparse rainfall. . . . Since it ripens a month or more before wheat, it was taken for the *omer* offerings at the Passover feast while the first grains of wheat were offered at the Feast of Pentecost" (Zohary, *Plants of the Bible*, 76). "The occasion would be the commencement of the general harvesting season. . . . This is about April" (*Five Megilloth*, 48).

Ruth 2:1–7. Ruth Gathers Grain in Boaz's Fields

In what way was Boaz a "mighty man"? (2:1) "At the first mention of Boaz in the LXX [Septuagint, or Greek translation of the Bible], he is called 'a mighty man of the kindred of Elimelech' (Ruth 2:1). The Hebrew word translated 'mighty' here is otherwise translated a person 'of substance' or 'a worthy' individual. In the King James translation of the verse, he is called 'a mighty man of wealth.' Later, Boaz used the same Hebrew word to describe Ruth when he told her that 'all the city of my people doth know that thou art a virtuous woman' (Ruth 3:11)" (Olson, *Women of the New Testament*, 83).

Why was Ruth gleaning in the fields? (2:3) "Amid the rejoicing of harvest-time a kindly Israelitish law upheld the custom whereby the poor, orphans and strangers, were allowed to glean grain, grapes and olives (Lv. 19:9–10; 23:22; Dt. 24:19). Ruth took full advantage of the practice (Ru. 2:2ff)" (Cundall and Morris, *Judges and Ruth*, 423). ⊕

Ruth 2:8–17. Boaz Is Kind to Ruth and Naomi

What do Boaz's actions toward Ruth reveal about him? (2:8–12) "The good qualities of Boaz may be seen in the way he greeted the workmen, in his enquiry about [Ruth], and in his generous treatment of [her] after learning she was the Moabite daughter-in-law to Naomi. Ruth's humility and appreciation are also noteworthy. It is evident here, as it was earlier, that she had become a converted follower of the true God" (Rasmussen, *Latter-day Saint Commentary on the Old Testament*, 226). "Boaz blesses Ruth [v. 12], in a statement which may be taken as a prayer. . . . Boaz believes that Ruth deserves the best for her piety and choice of Israel's God, and is convinced that a just God will see that she is well rewarded. Boaz, who utters this prayer, is the means by which it is answered. God often uses one who prays as His agent to answer that prayer" (Richards, *Bible Reader's Companion*, 176).

What can we learn from Ruth's difficult choices? (2:11–12) "The choice to forsake family, friends, or other familiar circumstances is a difficult choice that new converts and others sometimes make because they have gained a testimony of the truths of the

3 And she went, and came, and gleaned in
the field after the reapers: and her hap was
to light on a part of the field *belonging* unto
Boaz, who *was* of the kindred of Elimelech.

4 ¶ And, behold, Boaz came from Bethlehem, and said unto the reapers, The LORD
be with you. And they answered him, The
LORD bless thee.

5 Then said Boaz unto his servant that was
set over the reapers, Whose damsel *is* this?

6 And the servant that was set over the reapers answered and said, It *is* the Moabitish
damsel that came back with Naomi out of
the country of Moab:

7 And she said, I pray you, let me glean and
gather after the reapers among the sheaves: so
she came, and hath continued even from the
morning until now, that she tarried a little in
the house.

8 Then said Boaz unto Ruth, Hearest thou
not, my daughter? Go not to glean in another field, neither go from hence, but abide
here fast by my maidens:

9 *Let* thine eyes *be* on the field that they do
reap, and go thou after them: have I not
charged the young men that they shall not
touch thee? and when thou art athirst, go
unto the vessels, and drink of *that* which the
young men have drawn.

10 Then she fell on her face, and bowed herself to the ground, and said unto him, Why
have I found grace in thine eyes, that thou
shouldest take knowledge of me, seeing I *am*
a stranger?

11 And Boaz answered and said unto her, It
hath fully been shewed me, all that thou hast
done unto thy mother in law since the death
of thine husband: and *how* thou hast left thy

father and thy mother, and the land of thy nativity, and art come unto a people which thou knewest not heretofore.

12 The LORD recompense thy work, and a full reward be given thee of the LORD God of Israel, under whose wings thou art come to trust.

13 Then she said, Let me find favour in thy sight, my lord; for that thou hast comforted me, and for that thou hast spoken friendly unto thine handmaid, though I be not like unto one of thine handmaidens.

14 And Boaz said unto her, At mealtime come thou hither, and eat of the bread, and dip thy morsel in the vinegar. And she sat beside the reapers: and he reached her parched *corn,* and she did eat, and was sufficed, and left.

15 And when she was risen up to glean, Boaz commanded his young men, saying, Let her glean even among the sheaves, and reproach her not:

16 And let fall also *some* of the handfuls of purpose for her, and leave *them,* that she may glean *them,* and rebuke her not.

17 So she gleaned in the field until even, and beat out that she had gleaned: and it was about an ephah of barley.

18 ¶ And she took *it* up, and went into the city: and her mother in law saw what she had gleaned: and she brought forth, and gave to her that she had reserved after she was sufficed.

19 And her mother in law said unto her, Where hast thou gleaned to day? and where wroughtest thou? blessed be he that did take knowledge of thee. And she shewed her

restored gospel and have put their trust in the Lord. Like Ruth, they exercise great faith as they make changes to align their lives to the new truths they have been taught" (Dalton, "Lessons from Ruth and Hannah," 36). "There are many young women today who have given up everything to join the Church. The Lord is mindful of their sacrifices, and he will bless and reward them as he did Ruth of old, who was converted and followed the Lord's way without faltering" (Hale, "Lessons in Womanhood," 71). ⊕

How much is an ephah? (2:17) "The weight of an ephah has been variously estimated at from twenty-nine to fifty pounds, which represents sufficient to last Ruth and Naomi for several days, if not some weeks (cf. 1 Sam. 17:17, where an ephah is mentioned as satisfying several fighting men)....

"That Ruth gathered an ephah (i.e. 29–50 pounds) of barley in one day [is evidence of] her success in gleaming" (Ricks, "Ruth," 251fn4, 252).

Ruth 2:18–23. Naomi and Ruth Know the Lord Has Blessed Them Greatly

Why did Naomi rejoice when she learned that Ruth had gleaned in the fields of Boaz? (2:19–20) "The *goël*, 'kinsman,' had both rights and duties. He had the right of buying the property of his dead relative before it was offered for public sale; he was the avenger of the blood in the event of murder; it was his duty to redeem his relative who sold himself as a slave. Naomi recognized in Boaz the *goël* who would close the painful wound which death had torn open in the lives of two women" (*Five Megilloth*, 54). ⊕

mother in law with whom she had wrought, and said, The man's name with whom I wrought to day *is* Boaz.

20 And Naomi said unto her daughter in law, Blessed *be* he of the LORD, who hath not left off his kindness to the living and to the dead. And Naomi said unto her, The man *is* near of kin unto us, one of our next kinsmen.

21 And Ruth the Moabitess said, He said unto me also, Thou shalt keep fast by my young men, until they have ended all my harvest.

22 And Naomi said unto Ruth her daughter in law, *It is* good, my daughter, that thou go out with his maidens, that they meet thee not in any other field.

23 So she kept fast by the maidens of Boaz to glean unto the end of barley harvest and of wheat harvest; and dwelt with her mother in law.

CHAPTER 3

By Naomi's instruction, Ruth lies at the feet of Boaz—He promises as a relative to take her as his wife.

1 Then Naomi her mother in law said unto her, My daughter, shall I not seek rest for thee, that it may be well with thee?

Ruth 3:1–5. Naomi Tells Ruth How to Get a Husband in the Lord's Way

What does it mean that Naomi wanted "rest" for Ruth? (3:1) In proposing to "seek rest" for Ruth, "Naomi suggested that Ruth consider a levirate marriage (Ruth 3:1*a*). It was proper for Naomi to propose this option because she was the responsible parent. She knew the threshing would be done during the time of evening breezes. For Ruth to return thereafter and lie at his feet as a humble servant would bring her status to Boaz's attention, and Naomi was confident that he would tell Ruth what to do. There would have been moral danger in such proceedings except for the known character of Ruth and Boaz—in which Naomi implicitly trusted" (Rasmussen, *Latter-day Saint Commentary on the Old Testament*, 227). See commentary in this volume for Genesis 38:8–11.

2 And now *is* not Boaz of our kindred, with whose maidens thou wast? Behold, he winnoweth barley to night in the threshingfloor.

What was the threshing floor? (3:2) "The threshing floor was a circular parcel of ground anywhere from 50 to 320 feet in diameter. Generally, one threshing floor was prepared for an entire village, and farmers took turns using it. As in the time when Deborah judged in

Israel, the threshing floor was also used for determining legal outcomes (Judg. 4:5). This custom may have influenced Naomi's idea to send Ruth to the threshing floor to petition Boaz for marriage [see Matthews, *Manners and Customs,* 54]. The farmer or his servants typically spent nights on the threshing floor to guard against thieves" (Olson, *Women of the New Testament,* 81).

3 Wash thyself therefore, and anoint thee, and put thy raiment upon thee, and get thee down to the floor: *but* make not thyself known unto the man, until he shall have done eating and drinking.

4 And it shall be, when he lieth down, that thou shalt mark the place where he shall lie, and thou shalt go in, and uncover his feet, and lay thee down; and he will tell thee what thou shalt do.

Why did Naomi tell Ruth to lay at Boaz's feet? (3:3–4) "Ruth would remove the edge of Boaz's outer garment from his feet and lie down by his uncovered feet. Touching and holding his feet was an act of submission. This was a daring and dramatic action that would call for a decision on his part to be her protector—and, likely, her husband" (*Nelson Study Bible* [NKJV], 412).

5 And she said unto her, All that thou sayest unto me I will do.

6 ¶ And she went down unto the floor, and did according to all that her mother in law bade her.

Ruth 3:6–13. Boaz Accepts Ruth's Offer and Promises That He or Another Relative Will Marry Her

7 And when Boaz had eaten and drunk, and his heart was merry, he went to lie down at the end of the heap of corn: and she came softly, and uncovered his feet, and laid her down.

8 ¶ And it came to pass at midnight, that the man was afraid, and turned himself: and, behold, a woman lay at his feet.

9 And he said, Who *art* thou? And she answered, I *am* Ruth thine handmaid: spread therefore thy skirt over thine handmaid; for thou *art* a near kinsman.

What was the "skirt" that Ruth requested to have spread over her? (3:9) *Skirt* literally means "'wing,' a metaphor . . . used as a symbol of marriage" (*Five Megilloth,* 57). "When Boaz first met Ruth, he spoke of how she had come to trust in being under the Lord's wing (see Ruth 2:12). When Ruth approaches Boaz at the threshing floor, she asks him to spread his wing, or skirt, over her (see Ruth 3:9). The word for 'wing' and 'skirt' (*canaph*) is the same in Hebrew and seems to be an intentional way of asking Boaz to be the answer to her prayers—in other words, to be the Lord's wing and take care of her" (Muhlestein, *Essential Old Testament Companion,* 202–3). ⊕

Why was Ruth known as a virtuous woman? (3:10–11) "Ruth became a widow at a relatively young age. She was a committed convert and made great sacrifices as she left home and relatives for Bethlehem. . . . She showed complete loyalty and faithfulness to her widowed mother-in-law as she supported her in many ways, including providing food she gleaned from the fields of Boaz. . . .

"Ruth was known to all the people of the city as a virtuous woman (see Ruth 3:11). Other women, seeing how good Ruth was to her mother-in-law and how she loved and cared for her, paid the extraordinary compliment that she was 'better to [Naomi] than seven sons' (Ruth 4:15)" (Palmer, "Enduring Influence of Righteous Women," 50).

Why couldn't Boaz immediately agree to marry Ruth? (3:12–13) "When a husband died in ancient Israel, his nearest kin was to marry the husband's widow and raise up a son to the name of the deceased (see Deut. 25:5–10). Boaz was not the nearest of kin to Ruth, but he agreed to take Ruth in marriage if the closest relative would not. Failure on the part of an unnamed relative to accept Ruth opened the way for Boaz to marry the Moabite" (Black, *400 Questions and Answers about the Old Testament*, 101).

Summary of Ruth 3:14–18

Ruth returns to Naomi in the morning and tells what happened.

Ruth 4:1–12. The Nearest Relative Refuses to Marry Ruth

What did people do at the gate of the city? (4:1) The gate "was a fairly large edifice, where men might sit in the comfort of the shade during the heat of the day. In front of it was a broad open space. This was the market-place where the court normally held its sessions and people met for the interchange of news and the settlement of disputes" (*Five Megilloth*, 60).

10 And he said, Blessed *be* thou of the Lord,
my daughter: *for* thou hast shewed more
kindness in the latter end than at the beginning, inasmuch as thou followedst not young
men, whether poor or rich.

11 And now, my daughter, fear not; I will
do to thee all that thou requirest: for all the
city of my people doth know that thou *art* a
virtuous woman.

12 And now it is true that I *am thy* near kinsman: howbeit there is a kinsman nearer than I.
13 Tarry this night, and it shall be in the
morning, *that* if he will perform unto thee the
part of a kinsman, well; let him do the kinsman's part: but if he will not do the part of
a kinsman to thee, then will I do the part of a
kinsman to thee, *as* the Lord liveth: lie down
until the morning.

CHAPTER 4

The nearest relative declines, and Boaz takes Ruth to wife—Ruth bears Obed, through whom came David the king.

1 Then went Boaz up to the gate, and sat
him down there: and, behold, the kinsman
of whom Boaz spake came by; unto whom
he said, Ho, such a one! turn aside, sit down
here. And he turned aside, and sat down.

2 And he took ten men of the elders of the
city, and said, Sit ye down here. And they sat
down.

3 And he said unto the kinsman, Naomi, that
is come again out of the country of Moab,
selleth a parcel of land, which *was* our brother
Elimelech's:

4 And I thought to advertise thee, saying, Buy *it* before the inhabitants, and before the elders of my people. If thou wilt redeem *it,* redeem *it:* but if thou wilt not redeem *it, then* tell me, that I may know: for *there is* none to redeem *it* beside thee; and I *am* after thee. And he said, I will redeem *it.*

5 Then said Boaz, What day thou buyest the field of the hand of Naomi, thou must buy *it* also of Ruth the Moabitess, the wife of the dead, to raise up the name of the dead upon his inheritance.

6 ¶ And the kinsman said, I cannot redeem *it* for myself, lest I mar mine own inheritance: redeem thou my right to thyself; for I cannot redeem *it.*

Why did the nearest kinsman decline to marry Ruth? (4:6) "True to his word and to Naomi's prediction (3:18), Boaz does not delay in assembling a quorum of elders at the city gate . . . to settle the issue of Ruth's redemption. Elimelech's closest relative changes his mind about taking the opportunity to buy Elimelech's land when he discovers that Ruth comes with the package, for at this point he realizes that the inheritance will not simply be added to his own territorial claim but will instead revert to Ruth's sons (through him!) in order to maintain Elimelech's inheritance separately. In addition, Ruth and her children will add to the relative's expenses by becoming his dependents" (Fee and Hubbard, *Eerdmans Companion to the Bible*, 200).

7 Now this *was the manner* in former time in Israel concerning redeeming and concerning changing, for to confirm all things; a man plucked off his shoe, and gave *it* to his neighbour: and this *was* a testimony in Israel.

8 Therefore the kinsman said unto Boaz, Buy *it* for thee. So he drew off his shoe.

Why did the man take off his shoe? (4:7–8) "Boaz implies that the acquisition of Ruth as wife is necessarily tied to the redemption of land. . . . The [shoe] represents the conveying of goods or rights from one party to another. . . . In their view, the act symbolizes that [the nearest kinsman] relinquishes the obligation and the privilege of redeeming the land and marrying Ruth" (*Jewish Study Bible* [2004], 1585).

9 ¶ And Boaz said unto the elders, and *unto* all the people, Ye *are* witnesses this day, that I have bought all that *was* Elimelech's, and all that *was* Chilion's and Mahlon's, of the hand of Naomi.

10 Moreover Ruth the Moabitess, the wife of Mahlon, have I purchased to be my wife, to raise up the name of the dead upon his inheritance, that the name of the dead be not

In what way had Boaz purchased Ruth's hand in marriage? (4:9–10) "By purchasing all of Naomi's property and goods, Boaz has undertaken the total care of Naomi and the obligation to support her in life and provide for her in death. By acquiring Ruth, he has obligated himself to give her the opportunity to bear children, the first of whom would them become the heir of Elimelech and his sons" (Walton, et al., *IVP Bible Background Commentary*, 280). ⊕

cut off from among his brethren, and from the gate of his place: ye *are* witnesses this day.

11 And all the people that *were* in the gate, and the elders, said, *We are* witnesses. The LORD make the woman that is come into thine house like Rachel and like Leah, which two did build the house of Israel: and do thou worthily in Ephratah, and be famous in Beth-lehem:

How was the Lord involved in Ruth's life? (4:11) "As with other stories in the Bible, the narrative of Ruth seems to emphasize the way God works behind the scenes to accomplish his will. On the surface everything seems to move through human agents without divine interference. The events, which appear as a chain of natural occurrences, evolve from one to another to reveal themselves in the end as the outcome of God's plan. In so doing they serve as a testimony of the quiet, yet wonderful way in which God leads men toward their destinies" (Pearson, *Old Testament*, 38).

12 And let thy house be like the house of Pharez, whom Tamar bare unto Judah, of the seed which the LORD shall give thee of this young woman.

What does the union of Ruth and Boaz teach us? (4:12) "Boaz and Ruth became the parents of Obed, who was the father of Jesse, who was the father of King David. This means that Boaz and Ruth were the great-grandparents of King David. The direct ancestral line of Boaz and Ruth also includes the kings of Judah and the King of Kings, Jesus Christ (see Ruth 4:22; 1 Chr. 2:12; Matt. 1:5–6)" (Black, *400 Questions and Answers about the Old Testament*, 101). In addition, according to the Babylonian Talmud and the Midrash Aggadah, Orpah was the great-grandmother of Goliath, which sets up the future confrontation between David and Goliath.

Summary of Ruth 4:13–22

Naomi rejoices in the blessings Ruth receives from the Lord. Boaz marries Ruth, and they have a son named Obed. Their posterity includes David, the king of Israel, and Jesus Christ, the Savior of the world (see Matthew 1:1).

THE FIRST BOOK OF
SAMUEL
OTHERWISE CALLED
THE FIRST BOOK OF THE KINGS

Introduction

"This and the three following books were formerly termed the first, second, third, and fourth books of Kings" (*Adam Clarke's Commentary* [on 1 Samuel, Book Overview]). The books of 1 Samuel and 2 Samuel "were originally one. The division between the two was first introduced in the Septuagint [Greek Bible], which called them First and Second kingdoms followed by Third and Fourth kingdoms (1 and 2 Kings). Later, the term *kingdoms* became *kings*" (Pearson, *Old Testament*, 38–39). "The books begin with the birth of Samuel (hence the title) and carry us down nearly to the death of David, a period of about 130 years" (Bible Dictionary, "Samuel, books of").

"The book of 1 Samuel recounts the ministry of the prophet Samuel, who 'restored law and order and regular religious worship in the land' (Bible Dictionary, "Samuel") after the Israelites had forgotten the Lord and worshipped idols many times throughout the reign of the judges. One of the major themes of 1 Samuel is the importance of honoring the Lord" (*Old Testament Seminary Teacher Material*, 422). "The first book of Samuel contains a historic announcement: 'all Israel from Dan even to Beer-sheba knew that Samuel was established to be a prophet of the Lord' (1 Sam. 3:20). For the first time since the days of Moses and Joshua, the tribes became somewhat united, first under the prophet Samuel and then under the first two kings, Saul and David. Samuel was an inspired judge and a prophet, able to motivate the people to defense or to repentance. He influenced Israel to begin again to become the holy people they were called to be (Ex. 19:5–6)" (Rasmussen, *Latter-day Saint Commentary on the Old Testament*, 230).

"It is uncertain who the author was or when he wrote. In order to compile his narrative he no doubt used various writings that he found already in existence, including the state chronicles (among which were writings by Samuel, Nathan, and Gad, 1 Sam. 10:25; 1 Chr. 29:29)" (Bible Dictionary, "Samuel, books of").

"The main theme of Samuel is the rise of kingship in Israel. Samuel, as the prophet and priest, was responsible for calling and anointing the first two kings of Israel. . . . The institution of kingship dramatically changed the political, social, and economic world of ancient Israel. Before there was a king, Jehovah led his people through prophets, priests, and judges. After the establishment of kingship, there continued to be priests and prophets; in cases where the kings were wicked, the Lord sent his prophets to call them to repentance" (Holzapfel, et al., *Jehovah and the World of the Old Testament*, 190).

CHAPTER 1

Hannah prays for a son and vows to give him to the Lord—Eli the priest blesses her—Samuel is born—Hannah loans him to the Lord.

1 Now there was a certain man of Ramathaim-zophim, of mount Ephraim, and his name *was* Elkanah, the son of Jeroham, the son of Elihu, the son of Tohu, the son of Zuph, an Ephrathite:

1 Samuel 1:1–18. Hannah Prays with Great Faith to Have a Son

Who is Hannah and what lessons can we learn from her? (1:2–5) "Hannah is a powerful example of faithfulness. Her petition to be blessed with a child was granted after the trial of her faith. She covenanted with the Lord that she would give her son to His service when her son was old enough, and she remained committed to her covenant. . . .

"It is interesting to note that Hannah's story begins with a cry of distress and sorrow to the Lord and ends with a song of praise and thanksgiving to the Lord. We do not always have the option of choosing our situations in life, but we can respond with faith and trust in the Savior. We can know that He knows and loves us and will be with us" (Dalton, "Lessons from Ruth and Hannah," 36).

Why did Elkanah have two wives? (1:2) "In biblical times, the Lord commanded some of His people to practice plural marriage—the marriage of one man and more than one woman [see Doctrine and Covenants 132:34–39; Jacob 2:30; see also Genesis 16]" (Gospel Topics, "Plural Marriage in Kirtland and Nauvoo").

Why did Elkanah offer sacrifices in Shiloh? (1:3) "As Elkanah went each year 'to sacrifice unto the Lord of hosts in Shiloh,' he might well have been of the tribe of Levi. Thus Samuel, if worthy, may have had a right later to perform some of the priestly functions by right of his birth, even without the special vows of his mother and his training with Eli.

"Shiloh is the name of a place as well as a title referring to Jesus Christ [see Gen. 49:10]. . . . The *place* Shiloh is first mentioned in Joshua 18:1; it was founded when the tabernacle and the ark of the covenant were placed there" (Ludlow, *Companion to Your Study of the Old Testament*, 214).

What was the "portion" Hannah received? (1:4–5) "When Elkanah took his wives and their families to Shiloh (where the tabernacle had been located after the tribes conquered Canaan) to offer sacrifices, a peace offering was made. After the fat, kidneys, and other parts were burned, the priest customarily received the breast and right shoulder. The rest of the sacrificial animal was given back to the offerer to be eaten in a special feast. From his part, Elkanah gave portions of the meat to his family. Hannah received either more than the others or else a more choice portion because of Elkanah's love for her" (*Old Testament Student Manual: Genesis–2 Samuel*, 267).

2 And he had two wives; the name of the one *was* Hannah, and the name of the other Peninnah: and Peninnah had children, but Hannah had no children.

3 And this man went up out of his city yearly to worship and to sacrifice unto the LORD of hosts in Shiloh. And the two sons of Eli, Hophni and Phinehas, the priests of the LORD, *were* there.

4 ¶ And when the time was that Elkanah offered, he gave to Peninnah his wife, and to all her sons and her daughters, portions:

5 But unto Hannah he gave a worthy portion; for he loved Hannah: but the LORD had shut up her womb.

6 And her adversary also provoked her sore, for to make her fret, because the LORD had shut up her womb.

7 And *as* he did so year by year, when she went up to the house of the LORD, so she provoked her; therefore she wept, and did not eat.

8 Then said Elkanah her husband to her, Hannah, why weepest thou? and why eatest thou not? and why is thy heart grieved? *am* not I better to thee than ten sons?

9 ¶ So Hannah rose up after they had eaten in Shiloh, and after they had drunk. Now Eli the priest sat upon a seat by a post of the temple of the LORD.

10 And she *was* in bitterness of soul, and prayed unto the LORD, and wept sore.

11 And she vowed a vow, and said, O LORD of hosts, if thou wilt indeed look on the affliction of thine handmaid, and remember me, and not forget thine handmaid, but wilt give unto thine handmaid a man child, then I will give him unto the LORD all the days of his life, and there shall no razor come upon his head.

12 And it came to pass, as she continued praying before the LORD, that Eli marked her mouth.

13 Now Hannah, she spake in her heart; only her lips moved, but her voice was not heard: therefore Eli thought she had been drunken.

14 And Eli said unto her, How long wilt thou be drunken? put away thy wine from thee.

15 And Hannah answered and said, No, my lord, I *am* a woman of a sorrowful spirit: I have drunk neither wine nor strong drink, but have poured out my soul before the LORD.

How did Hannah respond to Peninnah's taunts for having no children? (1:6–7) "Hannah's sorrows were further magnified by the reproaches of Elkanah's other wife, Peninnah, who had borne him many children (see 1 Sam. 1:4). Certainly each child Peninnah bore would have deepened Hannah's anguish over her own apparent barrenness. To make matters worse, Peninnah 'provoked her sore' for being barren (see 1 Sam. 1:6)....

"Throughout these circumstances Hannah's character and strength of testimony were revealed....

"As painful as the insults must have been, Hannah chose neither retaliation nor use of Elkanah's love as a shield. Instead, she appealed to the Lord" (Campbell, "Hannah," 46). ⊕

Why was Hannah's barrenness attributed to God? (1:6) "Like several wives of the patriarchs, Hannah was barren 'because the Lord had shut up her womb' (1 Samuel 1:6). Judgments against infertile women had not improved among the people of the covenant since the days of Sarah and Rebekah. Their society continued to see barren women as a disgrace to their husbands and without purpose in their communities. The Lord had an important mission and lesson for Hannah that became apparent to her only through her struggles with barrenness" (Olson, *Women of the Old Testament*, 127). ⊕

What do we learn about Hannah with her vow? (1:11) "This was no idle appeal nor selfish bargain, since it meant Hannah would have only a short time to enjoy her child. Her pledge that 'there shall no razor come upon his head' (1 Sam. 1:11) apparently was a reference to the Nazarite vow, a promise to consecrate a man for either a temporary period of time or, as in Hannah's prayer, his entire life. He would then be set apart in a special way to prepare to serve the Lord and fulfill his purposes (see Bible Dictionary, s.v. "Nazarite").... Hannah's vow would have required that she yield back to the Lord the one blessing she had earnestly sought—surely one of her greatest tests of commitment." (Campbell, "Hannah," 46).

What was "a daughter of Belial"? (1:16) A daughter of Belial means "'a daughter of worthlessness' i.e. a worthless woman. 'Belial' came to be used as a name for Satan (2 Corinthians 6:15)" (*John Dummelow's Commentary* [on 1 Samuel 1:16]).

1 Samuel 1:19–28. Samuel Is Named and Hannah Gives Him to the Lord

Why does the Lord sometimes delay or withhold blessings from His children? (1:19–20) "Some blessings come soon, some come late, and some don't come until heaven; but for those who embrace the gospel of Jesus Christ, *they come*. Of that I personally attest" (Holland, "High Priest of Good Things to Come," 38).

Why was the name "Samuel" chosen? (1:20) "The name [Samuel] means 'heard of God' and is a testimony that the Lord heard the prayers of his mother Hannah, who had been barren" (McConkie, *Gospel Symbolism*,186). "The miraculous circumstances surrounding the birth and the call of Samuel make it clear that he had a divine calling before he entered mortality, and that he was chosen to play an important role in the history of Israel" (Seely, "Samuel," 271).

How old was Samuel when he was weaned and taken to the tabernacle? (1:22) "Weaning took place very late among the Israelites. . . . the Hebrew mothers were in the habit of suckling their children for three years. When the weaning had taken place, Hannah would bring her son up to the sanctuary, to appear before the face of the Lord, and remain there for ever. . . . [Some claim] that a child of three years old could only have been a burden to Eli. . . . [However,] his earliest training might have been superintended by one of the women who worshipped at the door of the tabernacle (1 Samuel 2:22)" (Keil and Delitzsch, *Commentary* [on 1 Samuel 1:22]).

Why did Hannah bring a young bull, wine, and flour to the temple? (1:24–25) "According to Numbers 15:8–12 the flour and the wine were to accompany a bull [burnt] offering ['or for a sacrifice in performing a vow']. The text is more easily understood as referring to three bulls rather than to a three-year-old bull. This would be supported by the fact that they also bring three times the required amount of

16 Count not thine handmaid for a daughter of Belial: for out of the abundance of my complaint and grief have I spoken hitherto.

17 Then Eli answered and said, Go in peace: and the God of Israel grant *thee* thy petition that thou hast asked of him.

18 And she said, Let thine handmaid find grace in thy sight. So the woman went her way, and did eat, and her countenance was no more *sad*.

19 ¶ And they rose up in the morning early, and worshipped before the LORD, and returned, and came to their house to Ramah: and Elkanah knew Hannah his wife; and the LORD remembered her.

20 Wherefore it came to pass, when the time was come about after Hannah had conceived, that she bare a son, and called his name Samuel, *saying*, Because I have asked him of the LORD.

21 And the man Elkanah, and all his house, went up to offer unto the LORD the yearly sacrifice, and his vow.

22 But Hannah went not up; for she said unto her husband, *I will not go up* until the child be weaned, and *then* I will bring him, that he may appear before the LORD, and there abide for ever.

23 And Elkanah her husband said unto her, Do what seemeth thee good; tarry until thou have weaned him; only the LORD establish his word. So the woman abode, and gave her son suck until she weaned him.

24 ¶ And when she had weaned him, she took him up with her, with three bullocks, and one ephah of flour, and a bottle of wine, and brought him unto the house of the LORD in Shiloh: and the child *was* young.

25 And they slew a bullock, and brought the child to Eli.

26 And she said, Oh my lord, *as* thy soul liveth, my lord, I *am* the woman that stood by thee here, praying unto the LORD.

27 For this child I prayed; and the LORD hath given me my petition which I asked of him:

28 Therefore also I have lent him to the LORD; as long as he liveth he shall be lent to the LORD. And he worshipped the LORD there.

flour and wine. If there are three bull offerings to be made, this may indicate the generosity of Elkanah and Hannah" (Walton, et al., *IVP Bible Background Commentary*, 283).

How can Hannah's example help us when it seems our prayers are not answered? (1:27) "Many of the so-called difficulties about prayer arise from forgetting [that God is our Father, and we are His children]. Prayer is the act by which the will of the Father and the will of the child are brought into correspondence with each other. The object of prayer is not to change the will of God but to secure for ourselves and for others blessings that God is already willing to grant but that are made conditional on our asking for them. Blessings require some work or effort on our part before we can obtain them. Prayer is a form of work and is an appointed means for obtaining the highest of all blessings" (Bible Dictionary, "Prayer").

CHAPTER 2

Hannah sings praises to the Lord—Samuel ministers before the Lord—Eli blesses Elkanah and Hannah, and they have sons and daughters—The sons of Eli reject the Lord and live in wickedness—The Lord rejects the house of Eli.

1 And Hannah prayed, and said, My heart rejoiceth in the LORD, mine horn is exalted in the LORD: my mouth is enlarged over mine enemies; because I rejoice in thy salvation.

2 *There is* none holy as the LORD: for *there is* none beside thee: neither *is there* any rock like our God.

3 Talk no more so exceeding proudly; let *not* arrogancy come out of your mouth: for the LORD *is* a God of knowledge, and by him actions are weighed.

4 The bows of the mighty men *are* broken, and they that stumbled are girded with strength.

5 *They that were* full have hired out themselves for bread; and *they that were* hungry ceased:

1 Samuel 2:1–11. Hannah Offers a Prayer (Psalm) to Praise the Lord

In what way is Hannah's psalm prophetic? (2:1–10) "Hannah's poetic song of thanksgiving, with its prophetic insight and appreciation, is in some ways like Mary's (Luke 1:46–55). In poetic parallels and figurative phrases she praises God, his powers, and goodness. Her language is sometimes terse but always clear; for instance, she knows that birth, life, death, and resurrection are all prerogatives of the Lord (1 Sam. 2:5–6). She prophesies of the ultimate kingdom, when the Lord will be acclaimed as ruler, judge, and kingmaker. The 'horn' symbolizes the power of the 'anointed' one. Hannah was a prophetess" (Rasmussen, *Latter-day Saint Commentary on the Old Testament*, 232). "In a general sense a prophet is anyone who has a testimony of Jesus Christ by the Holy Ghost" (Bible Dictionary, "Prophet").

What does it mean that Hannah's horn is exalted or lifted? (2:1) The Hebrew "for 'horn,' used figuratively, means 'power,'[or] 'capacity'" (1 Samuel 2:1*c*). Another commentator suggests that the phrase "horn is exalted," originated from "an animal carrying its head high and proudly conscious of its strength" (Goldman, *Samuel*, 8).

"This poem echoes themes of the omnipotence of God, his love for his children, and the justice that he metes out to them. It ends with the phrase 'he shall give strength unto his king, and exalt the horn of his anointed' (1 Sam. 2:10), which is a clear allusion to the establishment of kingship in Israel in which Samuel was to play a part" (Seely, "Samuel," 272).

so that the barren hath born seven; and she that hath many children is waxed feeble.

6 The LORD killeth, and maketh alive: he bringeth down to the grave, and bringeth up.

7 The LORD maketh poor, and maketh rich: he bringeth low, and lifteth up.

8 He raiseth up the poor out of the dust, *and* lifteth up the beggar from the dunghill, to set *them* among princes, and to make them inherit the throne of glory: for the pillars of the earth *are* the LORD's, and he hath set the world upon them.

9 He will keep the feet of his saints, and the wicked shall be silent in darkness; for by strength shall no man prevail.

10 The adversaries of the LORD shall be broken to pieces; out of heaven shall he thunder

"Hannah's Psalm" (1 Samuel 2:1–10)

"Considered verse by verse, Hannah's psalm as recorded in 1 Samuel is a remarkable example of joy, wisdom, and inspired perspective amid life's trials. After she gave her all to the Lord, she could only see what great things He had done for her. . . ."

"**2:1** Hannah described her joy as though her 'horn' were exalted or lifted up. . . . By knowing that salvation comes only from the Lord, Hannah's 'mouth is enlarged over her enemies,' or, she no longer fears her enemies. The Lord is her salvation.

"**2:2** Aware of people all around her who believed in other gods, Hannah definitively declared that 'there is none beside [God]: neither is there any rock like our God.' He is the Rock, as 'broad as eternity' (Moses 7:53), upon which, if we build, we 'cannot fall' (Helaman 5:12).

"**2:3–4** With new perspective gained through willing sacrifice and the knowledge that Christ is the only One to fill our void, Hannah learned true humility. . . .

"**2:4–9** Hannah could now sing with conviction that God gives us weakness and trials to help us gain strength in Him. In these six verses, Hannah described the cyclical patterns of life. With little or no warning, the sick are brought to good health and the healthy become sick; the poor find wealth while the rich fall into poverty; the fruitful become barren and the barren are filled.

"Hannah's new perspective did not emerge because she bore a child but because she learned that only the Savior's perfect love fills our emptiness. She could then recognize that if we have been at the bottom of the wheel, we are less likely to forget the poor when we are on top. . . .

"**2:10** Finally, Hannah prophesied of the Lord's strength and victory in the future. She announced that Israel would have a monarchy and that the kings would be 'anointed.' Interestingly, it would be Hannah's son Samuel who would anoint Saul and David as the first two kings of Israel. . . .

"Hannah bore witness of the Judge of us all, the King of kings, the Anointed One. The definition of a prophet or prophetess is someone who possesses a 'testimony of Jesus' (Revelation 19:10). Naturally, as a prophetess Hannah would testify of the Messiah, which in Hebrew means 'the anointed one.' If indeed Hannah's psalm prophesied of the Savior's coming, Hannah is also the first person in recorded scripture to speak of Him as 'the Anointed One'" (Olson, *Women of the Old Testament*, 139–40, 141).

upon them: the LORD shall judge the ends of the earth; and he shall give strength unto his king, and exalt the horn of his anointed.

11 And Elkanah went to Ramah to his house. And the child did minister unto the LORD before Eli the priest.

12 ¶ Now the sons of Eli *were* sons of Belial; they knew not the LORD.

13 And the priests' custom with the people *was, that,* when any man offered sacrifice, the priest's servant came, while the flesh was in seething, with a fleshhook of three teeth in his hand;

14 And he struck *it* into the pan, or kettle, or caldron, or pot; all that the fleshhook brought up the priest took for himself. So they did in Shiloh unto all the Israelites that came thither.

15 Also before they burnt the fat, the priest's servant came, and said to the man that sacrificed, Give flesh to roast for the priest; for he will not have sodden flesh of thee, but raw.

16 And *if* any man said unto him, Let them not fail to burn the fat presently, and *then* take *as much* as thy soul desireth; then he would answer him, *Nay;* but thou shalt give *it me* now: and if not, I will take *it* by force.

17 Wherefore the sin of the young men was very great before the LORD: for men abhorred the offering of the LORD.

18 ¶ But Samuel ministered before the LORD, *being* a child, girded with a linen ephod.

19 Moreover his mother made him a little coat, and brought *it* to him from year to year, when she came up with her husband to offer the yearly sacrifice.

1 Samuel 2:12–26. The Sons of Eli Do Evil in the House of the Lord and Eli Reproves Them

What evil things were the sons of Eli doing? (2:12) "The term *Belial* means 'worthless' or 'wicked' [see Bible Dictionary, 'Belial']. They were men of greed and lust. They used their authority as priests to extort from the people the best of the meat brought before them for sacrifice (see 1 Sam. 2:13–16). In essence they were taking their portion before giving a portion to God! They were also committing immoral acts with the women who gathered at the tabernacle (see 1 Sam. 2:22). Eli knew what they were doing, and when the people saw that the priesthood at Shiloh was corrupt, they 'abhorred the offering of the Lord' (1 Sam. 2:17)" (Grahl, "Eli and His Sons," 18).

Why were the actions of the sons of Eli so detestable? (2:15–17) "To take the flesh of the sacrificial animal and roast it . . . was a crime which was equivalent [equal] to a robbery of God. . . . Moreover, the priests could not claim any of the flesh which the [offerer] of the sacrifice boiled for the sacrificial meal, . . . to say nothing of their taking it forcibly out of the pots while it was being boiled. . . . This . . . was a great sin in the sight of the Lord, as they thereby brought the sacrifice of the Lord into contempt [disgrace]" (Keil and Delitzsch, *Commentary* [on 1 Samuel 2:15–17]). ⊕

What was the linen ephod that Samuel wore? (2:18) An ephod was "a priestly garment worn by those who served before the Lord at his sanctuary (see 22:18; 2Sa 6:14). It was a close-fitting, sleeveless pullover, usually of hip length, and is to be distinguished from the special ephod worn by the high priest" (*NIV Study Bible* [1995], 375; see also Bible Dictionary, "Ephod").

How did Hannah stay close to young Samuel who lived with Eli? (2:19) "In the years that followed, even though Samuel was not with her, Hannah remembered her precious gift from the Lord. She spent countless hours sewing for her son. Once every year she visited the beloved child that she had pled for and brought him what must surely have been a token of her love—a handmade little coat. . . . We know how important each of those little coats must have been to Samuel. If they hadn't been, he wouldn't have remembered to write them into the history of his life. I am confident that Samuel wore each of those coats and thought of his mother" (Freeman, *Written on Our Hearts*, 51–52). ⊕

How did the Lord continue to bless Hannah? (2:20–21) "As the Lord promises all his children, once a test is fully met, the blessings are then bestowed, whether in this life or the next (see D&C 58:3–4). Hannah was likewise blessed once the commitment to her vow had been fully tested. . . . Hannah was eventually granted three more sons and two daughters (see 1 Sam. 2:20–21). At last her cup truly overflowed with blessings of great joy.

"Hannah's testimony reaches across dispensations to our time, and her story is an invitation to apply the same principles of righteousness. Through doing so we, too, might rejoice in the Lord as we experience his innumerable blessings in our lives" (Campbell, "Hannah," 48–49).

In what ways did both Eli and his sons sin against the Lord? (2:22–25) "Eli knew of his sons' grave violations not only of their priestly privileges (they had the right to certain portions of flesh and other food items offered in sacrifice, but they took more than allowed and demanded choice parts) but also of the commandments (their abuse of women worshippers emulated the behavior of the priests of fertility cults in Canaan). The priest reproved his sons, but he did not effectively restrain them. The tragic results of his failings and their faults became evident later (1 Sam. 2:27–36; 3:11–14; 4:12–22)" (Rasmussen, *Latter-day Saint Commentary on the Old Testament*, 232–33).

20 ¶ And Eli blessed Elkanah and his wife, and said, The LORD give thee seed of this woman for the loan which is lent to the LORD. And they went unto their own home.

21 And the LORD visited Hannah, so that she conceived, and bare three sons and two daughters. And the child Samuel grew before the LORD.

22 ¶ Now Eli was very old, and heard all that his sons did unto all Israel; and how they lay with the women that assembled *at* the door of the tabernacle of the congregation.

23 And he said unto them, Why do ye such things? for I hear of your evil dealings by all this people.

24 Nay, my sons; for *it is* no good report that I hear: ye make the LORD's people to transgress.

25 If one man sin against another, the judge shall judge him: but if a man sin against the LORD, who shall entreat for him? Notwithstanding they hearkened not unto the voice of their father, because the LORD would slay them.

26 And the child Samuel grew on, and was in favour both with the LORD, and also with men.

Summary of 1 Samuel 2:27–36

With their sins revealed, a man of God prophesies that the wicked sons of Eli will die and the Lord will raise up a righteous prophet [Samuel] to take their place. The Lord honors those who honor Him.

CHAPTER 3

The Lord calls Samuel—The house of Eli will not be purged by sacrifices and offerings—Samuel is recognized as a prophet by all Israel—The Lord appears to him.

1 And the child Samuel ministered unto the LORD before Eli. And the word of the LORD was precious in those days; *there was* no open vision.

2 And it came to pass at that time, when Eli *was* laid down in his place, and his eyes began to wax dim, *that* he could not see;

3 And ere the lamp of God went out in the temple of the LORD, where the ark of God *was,* and Samuel was laid down *to sleep;*

4 That the LORD called Samuel: and he answered, Here *am* I.

5 And he ran unto Eli, and said, Here *am* I; for thou calledst me. And he said, I called not; lie down again. And he went and lay down.

6 And the LORD called yet again, Samuel. And Samuel arose and went to Eli, and said, Here *am* I; for thou didst call me. And he answered, I called not, my son; lie down again.

7 Now Samuel did not yet know the LORD,

1 Samuel 3:1–14. The Lord Speaks to Samuel in the Night

Why was the "word of the Lord" so precious in the days of Samuel? (3:1) The expression the "word of the Lord was precious" indicates the scarcity of revelation. "'The story commences with a significant statement. "And the child Samuel ministered unto the Lord before Eli. And the word of the Lord was precious in those days; there was no open vision" (1 Samuel 3:1). . . . That means that there was no prophet upon the earth through whom the Lord could reveal his will, either by personal experience, or by revelation' ([Lee, 'But Arise and Stand upon Thy Feet,' 2])" (*Old Testament Student Manual: Genesis–2 Samuel*, 269). ⊕

Why did the Lord want the lamp continually burning in the temple? (3:3) The light from the lamp was a reminder of the Lord's presence and it was commanded that the temple lamp "burn always" (Exodus 27:20). "The lamps on the seven-branched lampstand (Ex 25:31–37) were filled with olive oil, lit at twilight (30:8), and kept burning 'before the LORD from evening till morning' (27:20–21; cf. Lev 24:2–4; 2 Ch 13:11). Thus Samuel's encounter with the Lord on his bed in the tabernacle compound . . . took place during the night, since the 'lamp of God had not yet gone out'" (Youngblood, "1, 2 Samuel," 3:67).

What can we learn about responding to the Spirit from Samuel's example? (3:4–10) President Boyd K. Packer taught: "The Spirit does not get our attention by shouting or shaking us with a heavy hand. Rather it whispers. It caresses so gently that if we are preoccupied we may not feel it at all. . . .

"Occasionally it will press just firmly enough for us to pay heed. But most of the time, if we do not heed the gentle feeling, the Spirit will withdraw and wait until we come seeking and listening and say in our manner and expression, like Samuel of ancient times, 'Speak [Lord], for thy servant heareth' [1 Sam. 3:10]" ("Candle of the Lord," 53). ⊕

1 Samuel 3:15–21. Eli and All of Israel Know That the Lord Is with Samuel

Why did Samuel fear Eli's reaction to his vision? (3:15–18) Samuel "reverenced [Eli] as a father, and he feared to distress him by showing what the Lord had purposed to do. . . .

"[Eli] suspected that God had threatened severe judgments, for he knew that his house was very criminal; and he wished to know what God had spoken. The words imply thus much: 'If thou do not tell me fully what God has threatened, may the same and greater curses fall on thyself.'

"[Thus,] Samuel told him every whit . . . [for Eli] there is much of a godly submission, as well as a deep sense of his own unworthiness" (*Adam Clarke's Commentary* [on 1 Samuel 3:15, 17, and 18]).

neither was the word of the LORD yet revealed unto him.

8 And the LORD called Samuel again the third
time. And he arose and went to Eli, and said,
Here *am* I; for thou didst call me. And Eli
perceived that the LORD had called the child.

9 Therefore Eli said unto Samuel, Go, lie
down: and it shall be, if he call thee, that thou
shalt say, Speak, LORD; for thy servant heareth.
So Samuel went and lay down in his place.

10 And the LORD came, and stood, and called
as at other times, Samuel, Samuel. Then
Samuel answered, Speak; for thy servant
heareth.

11 ¶ And the LORD said to Samuel, Behold,
I will do a thing in Israel, at which both the
ears of every one that heareth it shall tingle.

12 In that day I will perform against Eli all
things which I have spoken concerning his
house: when I begin, I will also make an end.

13 For I have told him that I will judge his
house for ever for the iniquity which he
knoweth; because his sons made themselves
vile, and he restrained them not.

14 And therefore I have sworn unto the
house of Eli, that the iniquity of Eli's house
shall not be purged with sacrifice nor offering
for ever.

15 ¶ And Samuel lay until the morning, and
opened the doors of the house of the LORD.
And Samuel feared to shew Eli the vision.

16 Then Eli called Samuel, and said, Samuel,
my son. And he answered, Here *am* I.

17 And he said, What *is* the thing that *the*
LORD hath said unto thee? I pray thee hide
it not from me: God do so to thee, and more
also, if thou hide *any* thing from me of all the
things that he said unto thee.

18 And Samuel told him every whit, and hid nothing from him. And he said, It *is* the LORD: let him do what seemeth him good.

19 ¶ And Samuel grew, and the LORD was with him, and did let none of his words fall to the ground.

Why should we follow the living prophets? (3:19) In modern revelation the Lord stated: "For his [the prophet's] word ye shall receive, as if from mine own mouth, in patience and faith. For by doing these things the gates of hell shall not prevail against you" (D&C 2:5–6). President Wilford Woodruff declared: "The Lord will never permit me or any other man who stands as President of this Church to lead you astray. It is not in the programme. It is not in the mind of God. If I were to attempt that, the Lord would remove me out of my place, and so He will any other man who attempts to lead the children of men astray from the oracles of God and from their duty" (Official Declaration 1).

20 And all Israel from Dan even to Beersheba knew that Samuel *was* established *to be* a prophet of the LORD.

In what way was Samuel "established to be a prophet of the Lord"? (3:20) "Although the Hebrew word *nabi'* (prophet) is used previous to Samuel in reference to Abraham, Moses, Miriam, and Deborah, Jewish tradition, in a certain sense of the word, regards Samuel as the 'first of the prophets.' This tradition is expressed in New Testament times by Peter in his speech in the temple where he said that, '*all* the prophets from Samuel and those that follow after, as many as have spoken, have likewise foretold of these days' (Acts 3:24).... Paul also alluded to Samuel as the first of the prophets, as well as the last of the judges, when he said that God gave the people of Israel judges 'until Samuel the prophet' (Acts 13:20)" (Seely, "Samuel," 272). ⊕

21 And the LORD appeared again in Shiloh: for the LORD revealed himself to Samuel in Shiloh by the word of the LORD.

What pattern has the Lord established with both His ancient and modern prophets? (3:21) Consider the following declaration: "I declare with all solemnity that continuous revelation has been received and is being received through channels the Lord has established.... I personally testify that... guidance for the Church, as a whole, comes to the President and prophet of the Church." (Cook, "Blessing of Continuing Revelation," 98, 99). How has the Lord's consistent pattern of revealing His will to prophets blessed your life?

CHAPTER 4

The Israelites are smitten and defeated by the Philistines, who also capture the ark of God—Eli's sons are slain, Eli dies in an accident, and his daughter-in-law dies in childbirth.

Summary of 1 Samuel 4

The Philistines defeat the armies of Israel, kill the sons of Eli, and capture the ark of the covenant. Eli falls backward and dies when he learns that the ark of God has been taken.

Summary of 1 Samuel 5

The Philistines place the captured ark of the covenant in the temple of the false god Dagon. The following day, the image of Dagon has fallen on its face in front of the ark. The Philistines "were filled with consternation when they found the object of their stupid veneration prostrate before the symbol of the divine presence. Though set up, it fell again, and lay in a state of complete mutilation; its head and arms, severed from the trunk, were lying in distant and separate places, as if violently cast off, and only the fishy part remained. . . . It lay in the attitude of a vanquished enemy and a suppliant, and this picture of humiliation significantly declared the superiority of the God of Israel" (*Jamieson-Fausset-Brown Bible Commentary* [on 1 Samuel 5:3–4]).

CHAPTER 5

The Philistines place the ark in the house of Dagon, their god—The Philistines in Ashdod, then Gath, and then Ekron are plagued and slain because the ark is lodged with them.

Summary of 1 Samuel 6

For seven months, God smote the Philistines with plagues wherever they took the ark throughout Ashdod, Gath, and Ekron. The Philistines finally provide gifts and return the ark to the Israelites.

"The point of this narrative is simple and significant. The capture of the ark of the covenant did not signify that Jehovah the God of Israel was powerless. Just as he had defeated Egypt with his 'mighty hand,' so he defeated Dagon and the Philistines 'with his hand.' . . . The message for Israel was that if they suffered defeat at the hands of their enemies, it was due to their own unrighteousness, not the powerlessness of their God" (Holzapfel, et al., *Jehovah and the World of the Old Testament*, 195).

CHAPTER 6

The Philistines send back the ark with an offering—The Lord smites and slays the Israelites in Beth-shemesh who look into the ark.

Summary of 1 Samuel 7

In mighty faith, the prophet Samuel helps the Israelites repent and return to the Lord. Israel restores fasting and praying to seek the Lord's divine help. As Israel repents, they regain power over the Philistines and again are blessed.

CHAPTER 7

Samuel exhorts Israel to forsake Ashtaroth and Baalim and serve the Lord—Israel fasts and seeks the Lord—The Philistines are subdued—Samuel judges Israel.

CHAPTER 8

Samuel's sons take bribes and pervert judgment—The Israelites seek for a king to rule over them—Samuel rehearses the nature and evils of kingly rule—The Lord consents to give them a king.

1 And it came to pass, when Samuel was old, that he made his sons judges over Israel.

2 Now the name of his firstborn was Joel; and the name of his second, Abiah: *they were* judges in Beer-sheba.

3 And his sons walked not in his ways, but turned aside after lucre, and took bribes, and perverted judgment.

4 Then all the elders of Israel gathered themselves together, and came to Samuel unto Ramah,

5 And said unto him, Behold, thou art old, and thy sons walk not in thy ways: now make us a king to judge us like all the nations.

6 ¶ But the thing displeased Samuel, when they said, Give us a king to judge us. And Samuel prayed unto the LORD.

1 Samuel 8:1–22. Israel Refuses to Follow Samuel's Counsel and Desires a King

What was faulty about Israel's reasoning for a king? (8:3–6) "Joel and Abijah, [Samuel's] designated successors, are unrighteous and unjust, being easily bribed in their judgments. Dynastic succession had not been effective among the judges or the priests (Judg. 9:1–57; 1 Sam. 2:12–17). Israel had been down this path before. . . . Perhaps there would be a better way. . . .

"The problem arises in the nature of their suggestion. This request for a king (really, it is a demand) is the fundamental problem that finds resolution in chapters 8–12 and actually overshadows the rest of 1 Samuel. . . . The Israelite demand for a king in 8:5 is sinful in its motives, selfish in its timing, and cowardly in its spirit" (Arnold, *1 and 2 Samuel*, 149).

Why was Samuel so displeased with Israel's request for a king? (8:6) "Samuel struggled to anoint a king due to the perplexity and harm he perceived would come to Israel after the Lord showed him the dark side or consequences that would befall Israel under monarchial rule. Although he expressed woeful prophecies about monarchs (see 1 Sam. 8:9–18), Samuel bowed to the will of the people and ordained Saul king of Israel at God's direction (see Sam. 9:16–17).

Context for Israel Demanding a King (1 Samuel 8:1–22)

"Great changes throughout the ancient Near East in the twelfth to tenth centuries B.C. contributed to the inception of the monarchy in Israel. In archaeological terms this was the shift from the Late Bronze Age to the Iron Age. A population shift also occurred, involving the incursion of the Sea Peoples, including the Philistines, who spread along the southeastern Mediterranean coast. In this same period the Israelites established themselves in Canaan; their 'judges' helped them fight their enemies. Many of the prominent cities on the coast were violently destroyed at the beginning of this period. The Philistines settled on the coast of Canaan on the borders with the Israelites and attempted to conquer and displace the tribes from their homes in the hill country. This threat led the people to demand of Samuel and of the Lord a king, largely in order to defeat the Philistines; Saul and David spent years fighting the Philistines" (Holzapfel, et al., *Jehovah and the World of the Old Testament*, 192).

"The woeful prophecies of Samuel were all too soon fulfilled. George Washington used these prophecies to reject the 'proposal that he become a king in the American colonies freed from England by the American Revolutionary War'" (Black, *400 Questions and Answers about the Old Testament*, 105).

Who did the people reject? (8:7) "Whenever people fail to hearken to the true prophet of God, they fail to hearken to God himself. As the Lord has said in this dispensation, 'whether by mine own voice or by the voice of my servants, it is the same' (D&C 1:38.) Thus the Lord said to Samuel: 'They [the rebellious people] have not rejected thee, but they have rejected me'" (Ludlow, *Companion to Your Study of the Old Testament*, 215).

In what ways do God's children often unwittingly serve other Gods? (8:8) President Dallin H. Oaks noted: "We offend God when we 'serve' other gods—when we have other first priorities. What other priorities are being 'served' ahead of God by persons—even religious persons—in our day? Consider these possibilities, all common in our world:

- Cultural and family traditions
- Political correctness
- Career aspirations
- Material possessions
- Recreational pursuits
- Power, prominence, and prestige. . . .

"The principle is not whether we have other priorities. The question posed by the second commandment is 'What is our *ultimate* priority?' Are we serving priorities or gods ahead of the God we profess to worship?" ("No Other Gods," 72).

Why did the Lord want Samuel to "protest solemnly" before granting the people their desire for a king? (8:9) "The Lord accepted the desires of the people of the covenant to raise up unto themselves a king, but this with an inspired caution from the servant of the Lord regarding what they should expect from those whom they would have rule over them. . . .

"Samuel presented the problems . . . associated with the rule of kings in a manner that they could understand. He illustrated the physical impositions that a king would make of his people, the social disparity between the noble classes and the common people, and the financial distresses that would come as the wealth of the nation was focused upon a privileged few" (Hyde, *Comprehensive Commentary [1 Samuel]*, 67).

7 And the LORD said unto Samuel, Hearken unto the voice of the people in all that they say unto thee: for they have not rejected thee, but they have rejected me, that I should not reign over them.

8 According to all the works which they have done since the day that I brought them up out of Egypt even unto this day, wherewith they have forsaken me, and served other gods, so do they also unto thee.

9 Now therefore hearken unto their voice: howbeit yet protest solemnly unto them, and shew them the manner of the king that shall reign over them.

10 ¶ And Samuel told all the words of the LORD unto the people that asked of him a king.

11 And he said, This will be the manner of the king that shall reign over you: He will take your sons, and appoint *them* for himself, for his chariots, and *to be* his horsemen; and *some* shall run before his chariots.

12 And he will appoint him captains over thousands, and captains over fifties; and *will set them* to ear his ground, and to reap his harvest, and to make his instruments of war, and instruments of his chariots.

13 And he will take your daughters *to be* confectionaries, and *to be* cooks, and *to be* bakers.

14 And he will take your fields, and your vineyards, and your oliveyards, *even* the best *of them,* and give *them* to his servants.

15 And he will take the tenth of your seed, and of your vineyards, and give to his officers, and to his servants.

16 And he will take your menservants, and your maidservants, and your goodliest young men, and your asses, and put *them* to his work.

17 He will take the tenth of your sheep: and ye shall be his servants.

18 And ye shall cry out in that day because of your king which ye shall have chosen you; and the LORD will not hear you in that day.

What were some of the consequences for rejecting the Lord's counsel? (8:11–18) "There is a great lesson on this point, as it affected a whole nation, in Israel's rejecting judges, which were recommended by the Lord, and choosing to be ruled by kings. . . . [The Lord] refused to interfere with Israel's right of choice, even though their choice was to reject Him. Israel, having been warned by both their God and his prophet Samuel, exercised their agency, contrary to the advice of both. They got their king, and they suffered the consequences. In due time their kingdom was divided, they were taken captive, and ultimately they became slaves" (Romney, in Conference Report, Oct. 1968, 66).

Why did the Lord warn the Israelites that He would refuse to hear their cries? (8:18) "Instead of crying out because of their enemies (Judg. 3:9, 15; 6:6–7; 10:10) they will cry out because of their king, and God who answered their cry in the past will then refrain from answering them" (*Jewish Study Bible* [2004], 575).

19 ¶ Nevertheless the people refused to obey the voice of Samuel; and they said, Nay; but we will have a king over us;

20 That we also may be like all the nations; and that our king may judge us, and go out before us, and fight our battles.

21 And Samuel heard all the words of the people, and he rehearsed them in the ears of the LORD.

Why did the Israelites reject their Heavenly King? (8:19–20) "They had set their hearts on an earthly king to lead them in battle and give them a sense of national identity, security, and unity. Their request reflected a lack of faith and trust in their covenant relationship with the Lord. Did they think the Lord was not king enough? He had never broken His promise to be their protector, if they would but believe in Him, and had repeatedly demonstrated His power for their sakes . . .

"They wanted a king the world could admire rather than the unseen King who could only be known by faith" (Lee, "King for Israel," 22). ⊕

Why doesn't God prevent being governed by kings? (8:22) "Sometimes [God] temporarily grants to men their unwise requests in order that they might learn from their own sad experiences. Some refer to this as the 'Samuel principle.' The children of Israel wanted a king like all the other nations. The prophet Samuel was displeased and prayed to the Lord about it. The Lord responded by saying, Samuel, 'they have not rejected thee, but they have rejected me, that I should not reign over them.' The Lord told Samuel to warn the people of the consequences if they had a king. Samuel gave them the warning. But they still insisted on their king. So God gave them a king and let them suffer" (Benson, "Jesus Christ—Gifts and Expectations," 17).

22 And the Lord said to Samuel, Hearken
unto their voice, and make them a king. And
Samuel said unto the men of Israel, Go ye
every man unto his city.

1 Samuel 9:1–14. Saul, Kish's Son, Travels and Sees the Prophet Samuel

What do we know about Saul? (9:1–2) Saul's name means *asked*. "Saul was the first king of Israel, his reign lasting from around 1095 [B.C.] to the middle of that century. . . . As part of Saul's transition to leadership, the Lord gave him 'another heart' (1 Samuel 10:9), and the Spirit of the Lord came upon him such that he was able to prophesy. . . . However, soon after assuming the role of king in Israel, Saul began to forget the Lord and arrogate to himself the abilities of righteous judgment and priesthood authority" (Pinegar and Allen, *Old Testament Who's Who*, 168–69).

Why was Saul described as a choice and goodly young man? (9:2) "Saul's life began with great promise. . . . Saul was personally chosen by God to be king [see 1 Samuel 9:17]. He had every advantage—he was physically imposing [see 1 Samuel 10:23], and he came from an influential family [see 1 Samuel 9:1]" (Uchtdorf, "Matter of a Few Degrees," 58).

Goodly also refers to Saul's personal characteristics. "All that the Bible reveals indicates that Saul was honest, reliable, considerate of his parents, and altogether a very promising person for the great task ahead. . . . Saul was potentially the hero and man of valour all Israel sought. [Even physically,] he was about a foot taller than those of his generation" (*Old Testament Student Manual: Genesis–2 Samuel*, 271).

CHAPTER 9

Saul, the son of Kish, a Benjamite, is a choice and goodly person—He is sent to seek his father's asses—The Lord reveals to Samuel the seer that Saul is to be king—Saul goes to Samuel and is entertained by him.

1 Now there was a man of Benjamin, whose
name *was* Kish, the son of Abiel, the son
of Zeror, the son of Bechorath, the son of
Aphiah, a Benjamite, a mighty man of power.

2 And he had a son, whose name *was* Saul,
a choice young man, and a goodly: and *there*
was not among the children of Israel a good-
lier person than he: from his shoulders and
upward *he was* higher than any of the people.

3 And the asses of Kish Saul's father were
lost. And Kish said to Saul his son, Take now
one of the servants with thee, and arise, go
seek the asses.

4 And he passed through mount Ephraim,
and passed through the land of Shalisha,
but they found *them* not: then they passed
through the land of Shalim, and *there they
were* not: and he passed through the land of
the Benjamites, but they found *them* not.

5 *And* when they were come to the land of
Zuph, Saul said to his servant that *was* with
him, Come, and let us return; lest my father
leave *caring* for the asses, and take thought
for us.

6 And he said unto him, Behold now, *there is*
in this city a man of God, and *he is* an honourable man; all that he saith cometh surely
to pass: now let us go thither; peradventure
he can shew us our way that we should go.

7 Then said Saul to his servant, But, behold,
if we go, what shall we bring the man? for the
bread is spent in our vessels, and *there is* not
a present to bring to the man of God: what
have we?

8 And the servant answered Saul again, and
said, Behold, I have here at hand the fourth
part of a shekel of silver: *that* will I give to the
man of God, to tell us our way.

9 (Beforetime in Israel, when a man went to
inquire of God, thus he spake, Come, and let
us go to the seer: for *he that is* now *called* a
Prophet was beforetime called a Seer.)

10 Then said Saul to his servant, Well said;
come, let us go. So they went unto the city
where the man of God *was*.

11 ¶ *And* as they went up the hill to the city,
they found young maidens going out to draw
water, and said unto them, Is the seer here?

What is remarkable about Saul's journey to find lost animals? (9:3–8) "Saul's story, or history, commences in 1 Samuel 9 when the unknown young man . . . is instantly elevated to a position of national prominence and importance. When the Bible introduces us to Saul, he is searching unsuccessfully for his father's stray asses. He returns with a very different kind of find—he has been made king over all of Israel, the first person ever to hold this position. He searched for asses and found a kingship. . . . On the providential plane, which is concealed from Saul, he is, instead of the seeker, the sought. On one level, he is looking for something; on another, he is himself the object of a quest" (Fokkelman, "Saul and David," 20).

What is a seer? (9:9) "A seer is one who sees with spiritual eyes. He perceives the meaning of that which seems obscure [unclear or hidden] to others; therefore he is an interpreter and clarifier of eternal truth. He foresees the future from the past and the present. This he does by the power of the Lord operating through him directly, or indirectly with the aid of divine instruments such as the Urim and Thummim. In short, he is one who sees, who walks in the Lord's light with open eyes [see Mosiah 8:15–17]" (Widtsoe, *Evidences and Reconciliations*, 258). ⊕

Why was Israel offering sacrifice in the high places? (9:12–14) "*A high place* was an elevated site of worship located on a hill or on an artificial platform in a temple. The Canaanites were known for building their places of worship on hills (see Num. 33:52; Deut. 12:2–5). Nevertheless, pious Israelites appear to have used such facilities legitimately after the destruction of Shiloh and before the construction of Solomon's temple (see 1 Kin. 3:2). Sadly, the misuse of such high places to worship false gods eventually undermined the worship of God and contributed to the rise of idolatry in Israel (see 1 Kin. 11:7; 12:26–33)" (*Nelson Study Bible* [NKJV], 431).

Summary of 1 Samuel 9:15–27

The Lord reveals to Samuel that Saul is to be king. Samuel privately visits with Saul. Through their visit together, Samuel receives confirmation that Saul is to become the king.

1 Samuel 10:1–8. Samuel Anoints Saul

Why did Samuel anoint Saul with oil? (10:1) "While priests had been anointed since the days of Moses, anointing kings in the kingdom of Israel began when Samuel anointed Saul. From that time forward a few kings of Israel were anointed—it is presumed others were as well. . . . The ancient act of anointing, whether to priesthood or kingship, was a 'symbol of endowment with the Spirit of God; as the oil itself, by virtue of the strength which it gives to the vital spirits, was a symbol of the Spirit of God' (see Lev. 8:12)" (Black, *400 Questions and Answers about the Old Testament*, 105–6). See commentary in this volume for Leviticus 8:12 and 2 Samuel 5:3.

Why were these three men going to Bethel and why did they give Saul bread? (10:3–4) "The fact that the three men were going up to God at Bethel,

12 And they answered them, and said, He is; behold, *he is* before you: make haste now, for he came to day to the city; for *there is* a sacrifice of the people to day in the high place:

13 As soon as ye be come into the city, ye shall straightway find him, before he go up to the high place to eat: for the people will not eat until he come, because he doth bless the sacrifice; *and* afterwards they eat that be bidden. Now therefore get you up; for about this time ye shall find him.

14 And they went up into the city: *and* when they were come into the city, behold, Samuel came out against them, for to go up to the high place.

CHAPTER 10

Samuel anoints Saul to be captain over the Lord's inheritance—Samuel manifests the gift of seership—Saul prophesies among the prophets, and the Lord gives him a new heart—He is chosen king at Mizpeh.

1 Then Samuel took a vial of oil, and poured *it* upon his head, and kissed him, and said, *Is it* not because the LORD hath anointed thee *to be* captain over his inheritance?

2 When thou art departed from me to day, then thou shalt find two men by Rachel's sepulchre in the border of Benjamin at Zelzah; and they will say unto thee, The asses which thou wentest to seek are found: and, lo, thy father hath left the care of the asses, and sorroweth for you, saying, What shall I do for my son?

3 Then shalt thou go on forward from thence, and thou shalt come to the plain of Tabor, and there shall meet thee three men going up to God to Beth-el, one carrying three kids, and another carrying three loaves of bread, and another carrying a bottle of wine:

4 And they will salute thee, and give thee two *loaves* of bread; which thou shalt receive of their hands.

shows that there was still a place of sacrifice consecrated to the Lord at Bethel, where Abraham and Jacob had erected altars to the Lord . . . ; for the kids and loaves and wine were sacrificial gifts which they were about to offer. . . . The meaning of this double sign consisted in the fact that these men gave Saul two loaves from their sacrificial offerings. In this he was to discern a homage paid to the anointed of the Lord; and he was therefore to accept the gift in this sense at their hand" (Keil and Delitzsch, *Commentary* [on 1 Samuel 10:3–4]). See commentary in this volume for Genesis 28:17–19.

5 After that thou shalt come to the hill of God, where *is* the garrison of the Philistines: and it shall come to pass, when thou art come thither to the city, that thou shalt meet a company of prophets coming down from the high place with a psaltery, and a tabret, and a pipe, and a harp, before them; and they shall prophesy:

6 And the Spirit of the LORD will come upon thee, and thou shalt prophesy with them, and shalt be turned into another man.

7 And let it be, when these signs are come unto thee, *that* thou do as occasion serve thee; for God *is* with thee.

8 And thou shalt go down before me to Gilgal; and, behold, I will come down unto thee, to offer burnt offerings, *and* to sacrifice sacrifices of peace offerings: seven days shalt thou tarry, till I come to thee, and shew thee what thou shalt do.

9 ¶ And it was *so,* that when he had turned his back to go from Samuel, God gave him another heart: and all those signs came to pass that day.

Why would these holy men accompany themselves with music? (10:5) "Music was a [recognized] means of promoting the exaltation of spirit necessary for inspiration (2 Kings 3:15)" (*John Dummelow's Commentary* [on 1 Samuel 10:5]). President J. Reuben Clark Jr. said, "We get nearer to the Lord through music than perhaps through any other thing except prayer" (In Conference Report, Oct. 1936, 111). Sister Cheryl A. Esplin remarked, "Inspiring music is just one of the many ways we can feel the Spirit whisper to us, filling us with light and truth" ("Filling Our Homes with Light and Truth," 8).

1 Samuel 10:9–16. God Gives Saul a Change of Heart and Saul Speaks by the Power of the Spirit

How can we invite the Lord to change our hearts? (10:9) "As you exercise a little faith and begin your walk as a peaceable follower of our Lord Jesus Christ, your heart will change. Your whole being will be filled with light.

"God will help you become something greater than you ever thought possible. And you will discover that the gospel of Jesus Christ is indeed working in your life. . . .

"I pray that we will focus on 'the simplicity that is in Christ' [2 Corinthians 11:3] and allow His grace to lift and carry us during our journey from where we are now to our glorious destiny in our Father's presence" (Uchtdorf, "It Works Wonderfully!" 23).

Who were the company of prophets? (10:10) "In ancient times, there was a school of the prophets. The members of this school were termed the 'sons of the prophets,' which is a Hebrew idiom meaning 'of the class or group of the prophets.' . . . Samuel was perhaps the first head of this school. While his father had not been a prophet (nor had the father of Amos; see Amos 7:14), we find that many of these 'sons of the prophets' were actually sons of members of the school" (Tvedtnes, *Church of the Old Testament*, 20). See commentary in this volume for 1 Samuel 19:29.

10 And when they came thither to the hill,
behold, a company of prophets met him; and
the Spirit of God came upon him, and he
prophesied among them.

Why were those who observed Saul prophesying among the prophets surprised? (10:11–12) "[This] episode demonstrates that Saul has become another man (v. 6). . . . Kish is a well-known and prosperous citizen, and his son's conduct arouses astonishment. . . . The other prophets do not come from distinguished families like Saul, which makes his affiliation with them even more astonishing. [The question] 'Is Saul [also] among the prophets?' . . . expresses surprise at a person who engages in something foreign to him or associates with people unlike himself" (*Jewish Study Bible* [2014], 565).

11 And it came to pass, when all that knew
him beforetime saw that, behold, he prophesied among the prophets, then the people
said one to another, What *is* this *that* is come
unto the son of Kish? *Is* Saul also among the
prophets?

12 And one of the same place answered
and said, But who *is* their father? Therefore
it became a proverb, *Is* Saul also among the
prophets?

13 And when he had made an end of prophesying, he came to the high place.

14 ¶ And Saul's uncle said unto him and to
his servant, Whither went ye? And he said,
To seek the asses: and when we saw that *they*
were no where, we came to Samuel.

15 And Saul's uncle said, Tell me, I pray thee,
what Samuel said unto you.

16 And Saul said unto his uncle, He told
us plainly that the asses were found. But of
the matter of the kingdom, whereof Samuel
spake, he told him not.

1 Samuel 10:17–27. Samuel Announces That Saul Is King

17 ¶ And Samuel called the people together
unto the LORD to Mizpeh;

18 And said unto the children of Israel, Thus
saith the LORD God of Israel, I brought up
Israel out of Egypt, and delivered you out
of the hand of the Egyptians, and out of the
hand of all kingdoms, *and* of them that oppressed you:

19 And ye have this day rejected your God, who himself saved you out of all your adversities and your tribulations; and ye have said unto him, *Nay,* but set a king over us. Now therefore present yourselves before the LORD by your tribes, and by your thousands.

20 And when Samuel had caused all the tribes of Israel to come near, the tribe of Benjamin was taken.

21 When he had caused the tribe of Benjamin to come near by their families, the family of Matri was taken, and Saul the son of Kish was taken: and when they sought him, he could not be found.

22 Therefore they inquired of the LORD further, if the man should yet come thither. And the LORD answered, Behold, he hath hid himself among the stuff.

23 And they ran and fetched him thence: and when he stood among the people, he was higher than any of the people from his shoulders and upward.

24 And Samuel said to all the people, See ye him whom the LORD hath chosen, that *there is* none like him among all the people? And all the people shouted, and said, God save the king.

25 Then Samuel told the people the manner of the kingdom, and wrote *it* in a book, and laid *it* up before the LORD. And Samuel sent all the people away, every man to his house.

26 ¶ And Saul also went home to Gibeah; and there went with him a band of men, whose hearts God had touched.

Why might Saul have hidden among the *stuff*? (10:22) The *stuff* likely was "the travelling baggage of the people who had assembled at Mizpeh. Saul could neither have wished to avoid accepting the monarchy, nor have imagined that the lot would not fall upon him if he hid himself. For he knew that God had chosen him; and Samuel had anointed him already. He did it therefore simply from humility and modesty" (Keil and Delitzsch, *Commentary* [on 1 Samuel 10:22]).

Why did the Lord give the people a king when He knew that was not what was best for them? (10:24) "The people had been looking for a king because they had been looking to the world for guidance. Thus, God gave them a king who had the worldly appearance of being all they asked for. Alma teaches that God will grant us our desires, even if it leads to our destruction (see Alma 29:4). . . . Israel had asked for a king, even though it was not what God wanted for them, and He gave them a king that was big enough to inspire them in battle. They would have to wait to find a leader who was the kind of man God was looking for. They were too influenced by the world at this point" (Muhlestein, *Scripture Study Made Simple*, 186).

What does it mean that Samuel described the "manner of the kingdom"? (10:25) "Samuel not only announced the Lord's choice of king but also made the occasion a kind of constitutional convention, for he 'told the people the manner of the kingdom, and wrote it in a book, and laid it up before the Lord' (1 Sam. 10:25). Recall the prophetic instructions for Israelite kings given by Moses (Deut. 17:14–20). The consenting, sustaining voice of the people was also a factor, as seen

27 But the children of Belial said, How shall this man save us? And they despised him, and brought him no presents. But he held his peace.

in the installation of kings Saul, David, Solomon, and Rehoboam (1 Sam. 10:24)" (Rasmussen, *Latter-day Saint Commentary on the Old Testament*, 239).

CHAPTER 11

The Ammonites encamp against the Israelites of Jabesh-gilead—Saul rescues them and defeats the Ammonites—His kingship is renewed in Gilgal.

Summary of 1 Samuel 11:1–5

The first challenge of Israel's new king comes from Nahash, the Ammonite king. He threatens to enslave and blind the right eye of all Israelites living east of the Jordan River. Messengers are sent to King Saul to tell him of the crisis.

1 Samuel 11:6–11. The Spirit of the Lord Guides Saul in Uniting Israel to Defeat the Ammonites

6 And the Spirit of God came upon Saul when he heard those tidings, and his anger was kindled greatly.

How could the Spirit kindling Saul's anger become a blessing for Israel? (11:6) "At that time, when danger threatened Israel, . . . the Spirit and power of Almighty God, and the anointing that he had received under the hands of the Prophet of God, descended upon that young man, Saul, and his anger was kindled at the insult that had been offered to his nation, . . .

"He had gone about his business; but when the crisis arose, when there was a necessity for someone to step forward and take the leading position, then the spirit of that position to which he had been anointed, . . . rested upon him, and he emerged from his obscurity and arose in their midst a king, a leader in very deed and in truth" (Cannon, in *Journal of Discourses*, 26:57–58).

7 And he took a yoke of oxen, and hewed them in pieces, and sent *them* throughout all the coasts of Israel by the hands of messengers, saying, Whosoever cometh not forth after Saul and after Samuel, so shall it be done unto his oxen. And the fear of the LORD fell on the people, and they came out with one consent.

How would sending pieces of oxen to the various Israelite communities provoke the people? (11:7) "The intent is to evoke a strong reaction, reinforced by the threat that those who do not respond may suffer similar treatment. As Gordon observes, the dismemberment of the oxen 'evokes the world of execration and treaty curse where the threat was directed not so much at the individual's property as at the individual himself' (Gordon, *1 & 2 Samuel*, 124). The ancient Near East was accustomed to gruesome actions intended to prompt a certain response" (Long, "1 and 2 Samuel," 2:323).

8 And when he numbered them in Bezek, the
children of Israel were three hundred thousand, and the men of Judah thirty thousand.

9 And they said unto the messengers that
came, Thus shall ye say unto the men of
Jabesh-gilead, To morrow, by *that time* the
sun be hot, ye shall have help. And the messengers came and shewed *it* to the men of
Jabesh; and they were glad.

10 Therefore the men of Jabesh said, To morrow we will come out unto you, and ye shall
do with us all that seemeth good unto you.

11 And it was *so* on the morrow, that Saul
put the people in three companies; and they
came into the midst of the host in the morning watch, and slew the Ammonites until the
heat of the day: and it came to pass, that they
which remained were scattered, so that two
of them were not left together.

12 ¶ And the people said unto Samuel, Who
is he that said, Shall Saul reign over us? bring
the men, that we may put them to death.

13 And Saul said, There shall not a man be
put to death this day: for to day the LORD
hath wrought salvation in Israel.

14 Then said Samuel to the people, Come,
and let us go to Gilgal, and renew the kingdom there.

15 And all the people went to Gilgal; and
there they made Saul king before the LORD
in Gilgal; and there they sacrificed sacrifices
of peace offerings before the LORD; and there
Saul and all the men of Israel rejoiced greatly.

CHAPTER 12

Samuel testifies of his own just dealings in Israel—He reproves the people for their ingratitude—He exhorts them to keep the commandments lest the Lord consume them and their king.

1 Samuel 11:12–15. Saul Credits God for Protecting Israel; Samuel Gathers Israel in Gilgal to Formalize Saul's Call as King

What can we learn from Saul's willingness to forgive those who opposed him? (11:12–13) President Gordon B. Hinckley's following counsel relates to Saul's action toward the Israelites who opposed him: "I submit that it takes neither strength nor intelligence to brood in anger over wrongs suffered, to go through life with a spirit of vindictiveness, to dissipate one's abilities in planning retribution. There is no peace in the nursing of a grudge. There is no happiness in living for the day when you can 'get even'" ("Of You It Is Required to Forgive," 4). How has the spirit of the Lord been different when you willingly forgive?

Summary of 1 Samuel 12

The aging Samuel defends his actions as the Lord's prophet. He rebukes the people for repeatedly forgetting the Lord and calls upon them to repent. He admonishes them to fear the Lord and serve Him with all their hearts.

1 Samuel 13:1–7. The Philistines Greatly Outnumber the Israelites in Battle

How much time passed since Saul was anointed King? (13:1) "Problems of chronology arise here. How much time passed from Saul's anointing as a young man, . . . until the Ammonite war and the public sustaining of King Saul at Gilgal? (1 Sam 11:14–15). The problems arise because the translation of 1 Samuel 13:1 states 'Saul reigned one year; and when he had reigned two years,' the events related in chapter 13 occurred; but Saul was by then a mature man with a mature son, Jonathan, in the army with him (1 Sam. 13:3, 16). Perhaps these events happened two years after the confirmation of Saul's kingship at Gilgal" (Rasmussen, *Latter-day Saint Commentary on the Old Testament,* 240, 241).

How many soldiers defended this "garrison of the Philistines"? (13:3) "Given Jonathan's contingent of 1,000 men (v. 2) and the heralding of his victory, it seems likely that he would have defeated a Philistine garrison of at least comparable size, if not greater. Saul regarded the victory as an outstanding military triumph. The Hebrews fielded men in organized units of 1,000, 100, 50 and 10 (Ex 18:25). Archaeology suggests that the Philistines may have organized their military similarly" (*Quest Study Bible* [1994], 373).

How accurate are the numbers cited in this verse? (13:5) Saul's 3,000 soldiers (see v. 2) were most certainly outnumbered by the Philistines who appeared to have as many "people as the sand which is on the sea shore." Adam Clarke suggested that the number of Philistine chariots could not be 30,000. "There is no proportion here between the chariots and the cavalry. The largest armies ever brought into the field, even by mighty emperors, never were furnished with thirty thousand chariots" (*Adam Clarke's Commentary* [on 1 Samuel 13:5]). Another commentator pointed out that "this inflated figure is reduced to three thousand in the Septuagint" (Alter, *Hebrew Bible,* 2:223). ⊕

How can we overcome fear when frightening circumstances surround us? (13:6–7) President Henry B. Eyring taught that the Lord "tells us, that when we stand with faith upon His rock, doubt and fear are diminished; the desire to do good increases. . . . Faith always defeats fear" ("Fear Not to Do Good,"

CHAPTER 13

Saul offers a burnt offering—The Lord rejects him and chooses another captain over His people.

1 Saul reigned one year; and when he had reigned two years over Israel,

2 Saul chose him three thousand *men* of Israel; *whereof* two thousand were with Saul in Michmash and in mount Beth-el, and a thousand were with Jonathan in Gibeah of Benjamin: and the rest of the people he sent every man to his tent.

3 And Jonathan smote the garrison of the Philistines that *was* in Geba, and the Philistines heard *of it.* And Saul blew the trumpet throughout all the land, saying, Let the Hebrews hear.

4 And all Israel heard say *that* Saul had smitten a garrison of the Philistines, and *that* Israel also was had in abomination with the Philistines. And the people were called together after Saul to Gilgal.

5 ¶ And the Philistines gathered themselves together to fight with Israel, thirty thousand chariots, and six thousand horsemen, and people as the sand which *is* on the sea shore in multitude: and they came up, and pitched in Michmash, eastward from Beth-aven.

6 When the men of Israel saw that they were in a strait, (for the people were distressed,) then the people did hide themselves in caves, and in thickets, and in rocks, and in high places, and in pits.

7 And *some of* the Hebrews went over Jordan to the land of Gad and Gilead. As for Saul, he *was* yet in Gilgal, and all the people followed him trembling.

101, 103). Can faith and fear exist at the same time? When was a time when faith allowed you to overcome your fears?

1 Samuel 13:8–16. Without God's Authority, Saul Makes a Burnt Offering to the Lord and Samuel Chastens Him for His Foolish Action

8 ¶ And he tarried seven days, according to the set time that Samuel *had appointed:* but Samuel came not to Gilgal; and the people were scattered from him.

9 And Saul said, Bring hither a burnt offering to me, and peace offerings. And he offered the burnt offering.

10 And it came to pass, that as soon as he had made an end of offering the burnt offering, behold, Samuel came; and Saul went out to meet him, that he might salute him.

What was wrong with Saul's actions? (13:8–9) Saul "gathered the people together and did something he had no priesthood authority to do—he offered the sacrifice himself" (Uchtdorf, "Matter of a Few Degrees," 58). Elder James E. Talmage explained that "unauthorized ministrations in priestly functions are not alone invalid, but also grievously sinful. In His dealings with mankind God recognizes and honors the Priesthood established by His direction, and countenances [approves] no unauthorized assumption of authority. . . . [Saul forgot] that though he occupied the throne, wore the crown, and bore the scepter, these insignia of kingly power gave him no right to officiate even as a deacon in the Priesthood of God" (*Articles of Faith*, 183–85).

11 ¶ And Samuel said, What hast thou done? And Saul said, Because I saw that the people were scattered from me, and *that* thou camest not within the days appointed, and *that* the Philistines gathered themselves together at Michmash;

12 Therefore said I, The Philistines will come down now upon me to Gilgal, and I have not made supplication unto the LORD: I forced myself therefore, and offered a burnt offering.

13 And Samuel said to Saul, Thou hast done foolishly: thou hast not kept the commandment of the LORD thy God, which he commanded thee: for now would the LORD have established thy kingdom upon Israel for ever.

What did Saul reveal about his character by not waiting for the prophet Samuel? (13:11–13) President Dieter F. Uchtdorf observed, "The prophet Samuel recognized a critical weakness in Saul's character. When pressured by outside influences, Saul did not have the self-discipline to stay on course, trust the Lord and His prophet, and follow the pattern God had established. . . .

"Saul's failure to hold fast to the counsel of the prophet just a little longer, may seem minor. But even small errors over time can make a dramatic difference in our lives" ("Matter of a Few Degrees," 58).

14 But now thy kingdom shall not continue: the LORD hath sought him a man after his own heart, and the LORD hath commanded him *to be* captain over his people, because thou hast not kept *that* which the LORD commanded thee.

How do you develop a heart "after [the Lord's] own heart"? (13:14) Perhaps Samuel was teaching Saul to live as the people described in Helaman 3:35 whose hearts were sanctified, "which sanctification cometh because of their yielding their hearts unto God.

"The phrase 'yield our hearts' means to surrender or give our hearts to God. When one yields his or her heart to God, he is surrendering his personal desires in exchange for the Lord's desires" (*Book of Mormon Student Manual: Genesis–2 Samuel*, 266). Consider how different the circumstances would have been for Saul had he surrendered his personal desires and kept the Lord's commandments.

15 And Samuel arose, and gat him up from
Gilgal unto Gibeah of Benjamin. And Saul
numbered the people *that were* present with
him, about six hundred men.

16 And Saul, and Jonathan his son, and the
people *that were* present with them, abode in
Gibeah of Benjamin: but the Philistines encamped in Michmash.

1 Samuel 13:17–23. Samuel Left Saul, and the Philistines Attacked the Israelites

17 ¶ And the spoilers came out of the camp
of the Philistines in three companies: one
company turned unto the way *that leadeth to*
Ophrah, unto the land of Shual:

18 And another company turned the way *to*
Beth-horon: and another company turned *to*
the way of the border that looketh to the valley of Zeboim toward the wilderness.

What disadvantage did Israel's armies have? (13:19–22) "Scholars believe that at this time the Israelites did not know how to work with iron. The Philistines guarded the secret carefully to maintain superiority in weapons over the softer brass weapons of the Israelites. As a result, the Israelites did not have the superior chariots of iron, nor could they manufacture swords and spears of iron. The other instruments mentioned, 'share,' 'coulter,' 'axe,' 'mattock,' and 'goad,' had to be taken to the Philistines for sharpening. A *share* was a metal instrument used to plough the ground, and a *coulter* was a small garden hoe. . . . A *mattock* was an Egyptian hoe or grubbing axe, and a *goad* was a sharp rod about eight feet long" (*Old Testament Student Manual: Genesis–2 Samuel*, 274).

19 ¶ Now there was no smith found throughout all the land of Israel: for the Philistines
said, Lest the Hebrews make *them* swords or
spears:

20 But all the Israelites went down to the
Philistines, to sharpen every man his share,
and his coulter, and his axe, and his mattock.

21 Yet they had a file for the mattocks, and
for the coulters, and for the forks, and for the
axes, and to sharpen the goads.

22 So it came to pass in the day of battle,
that there was neither sword nor spear found
in the hand of any of the people that *were*
with Saul and Jonathan: but with Saul and
with Jonathan his son was there found.

23 And the garrison of the Philistines went
out to the passage of Michmash.

CHAPTER 14

Jonathan smites the garrison of the Philistines—Saul instructs the people to eat no food until evening—Unaware of the oath, Jonathan eats, and Saul decrees his death—He is rescued by the people—Saul vexes his enemies on every hand.

CHAPTER 15

Saul is commanded to smite and destroy the Amalekites and all that they have—He saves some animals to sacrifice—Saul is rejected as king and told that to obey is better than sacrifice—Samuel destroys Agag.

1 Samuel also said unto Saul, The LORD sent me to anoint thee *to be* king over his people, over Israel: now therefore hearken thou unto the voice of the words of the LORD.

2 Thus saith the LORD of hosts, I remember *that* which Amalek did to Israel, how he laid *wait* for him in the way, when he came up from Egypt.

3 Now go and smite Amalek, and utterly destroy all that they have, and spare them not; but slay both man and woman, infant and suckling, ox and sheep, camel and ass.

4 And Saul gathered the people together, and numbered them in Telaim, two hundred thousand footmen, and ten thousand men of Judah.

Summary of 1 Samuel 14

Saul seeks the Lord's help in battle by unwisely commanding the Israelites to fast on the day of their battle with the Philistines. He declares that anyone who does not fast will be put to death. His oath is not made under the direction of the Lord's Spirit. Saul's son Jonathan is not present and does not know about his father's command. Jonathan eats some honey while pursuing the Philistines. Saul decrees that Jonathan must be killed for his actions. The Israelites defend Jonathan and plead with Saul not to carry out his foolish oath. Saul listens to their plea, and Jonathan is spared.

1 Samuel 15:1–9. The Lord Commands Saul to Destroy the Amalekites and All They Have

What evil had the Amalekites previously done to Israel? (15:2) For generations, the Amalekites "were constant enemies of Israel" (*Wycliffe Bible Commentary*, 285). For example, prior to the Israelites entering the promised land, the Amalekites "came at the rear of the camp [of Israel], smote the hindmost of the people, even all that were feeble behind, when they were faint and weary. . . . The baggage, no doubt, was the object of their avarice [greed]; but finding the women, children, aged and infirm persons, behind with the baggage, they smote them and took away their spoils [see Deuteronomy 25:17–18]. . . . God then purposed that Amalek, as a nation, should be blotted out from under heaven; which purpose was now fulfilled" (*Adam Clarke's Commentary* [on Exodus 17:8; 1 Samuel 15:2]).

Why would God command everyone to be killed? (15:3) "Some people think it is not like God to take *vengeance* upon people, because he is a merciful God. The fact is *he takes vengeance upon the ungodly because he is merciful*. He is merciful to them in removing them and shows consideration for all *others* who keep his commandments. It was for this very reason that he destroyed Sodom and Gomorrah, . . . and destroyed so many Nephite cities at the time of his crucifixion. It was the meek and lowly Nazarene who did all of these things, because in his mercy and justice he had to cleanse the earth for the benefit of the sinful as well as for the righteous who remained" (Smith, *Doctrines of Salvation*, 3:44–45; see also 1 Nephi 17:35). ⊕

Why were the Kenites treated kindly by Saul? (15:6) "This kindness seems to reflect the aid given by Hobab, son of Reuel, who was their guide in the wilderness (Nm. 10:29–31)" (*Tyndale Bible Dictionary*, 769). See commentary in this volume for Judges 4:11–12.

Why did Saul spare the life of the Amalekite king and the best of their animals? (15:8–9) "Agag should have been slain as well, but Saul thought to modify the Lord's commands in order to satisfy his own desire for outward display of power and authority" (Hyde, *Comprehensive Commentary [1 Samuel]*, 128).

1 Samuel 15:10–23. The Lord Rejects Saul as King of Israel

How should verse 11 be correctly understood? (15:11) The Joseph Smith Translation (JST) reads, "I have set up Saul to be a king, *and he repenteth not that he hath sinned*" (see 1 Samuel 15:11*a*). Thereby noting that it was Saul who was in need of repentance, not the Lord.

Why would Saul declare he had obeyed the Lord's command when he had not? (15:13–15) "In [Saul's] arrogant and haughty state he took things in his own hands wholly disregarding the commandments of the Lord. . . . Saul rationalized. . . . Why not keep the fat sheep and cattle? Was not his royal judgment superior to that of lowly Samuel? Who was Samuel that his

5 And Saul came to a city of Amalek, and laid wait in the valley.

6 ¶ And Saul said unto the Kenites, Go, depart, get you down from among the Amalekites, lest I destroy you with them: for ye shewed kindness to all the children of Israel, when they came up out of Egypt. So the Kenites departed from among the Amalekites.

7 And Saul smote the Amalekites from Havilah *until* thou comest to Shur, that *is* over against Egypt.

8 And he took Agag the king of the Amalekites alive, and utterly destroyed all the people with the edge of the sword.

9 But Saul and the people spared Agag, and the best of the sheep, and of the oxen, and of the fatlings, and the lambs, and all *that was* good, and would not utterly destroy them: but every thing *that was* vile and refuse, that they destroyed utterly.

10 ¶ Then came the word of the LORD unto Samuel, saying,

11 It repenteth me that I have set up Saul *to be* king: for he is turned back from following me, and hath not performed my commandments. And it grieved Samuel; and he cried unto the LORD all night.

12 And when Samuel rose early to meet Saul in the morning, it was told Samuel, saying, Saul came to Carmel, and, behold, he set him up a place, and is gone about, and passed on, and gone down to Gilgal.

13 And Samuel came to Saul: and Saul said unto him, Blessed *be* thou of the LORD: I have performed the commandment of the LORD.

14 And Samuel said, What *meaneth* then this bleating of the sheep in mine ears, and the lowing of the oxen which I hear?

15 And Saul said, They have brought them from the Amalekites: for the people spared the best of the sheep and of the oxen, to sacrifice unto the LORD thy God; and the rest we have utterly destroyed.

16 Then Samuel said unto Saul, Stay, and I will tell thee what the LORD hath said to me this night. And he said unto him, Say on.

17 And Samuel said, When thou *wast* little in thine own sight, *wast* thou not *made* the head of the tribes of Israel, and the LORD anointed thee king over Israel?

18 And the LORD sent thee on a journey, and said, Go and utterly destroy the sinners the Amalekites, and fight against them until they be consumed.

19 Wherefore then didst thou not obey the voice of the LORD, but didst fly upon the spoil, and didst evil in the sight of the LORD?

20 And Saul said unto Samuel, Yea, I have obeyed the voice of the LORD, and have gone the way which the LORD sent me, and have brought Agag the king of Amalek, and have utterly destroyed the Amalekites.

21 But the people took of the spoil, sheep and oxen, the chief of the things which should have been utterly destroyed, to sacrifice unto the LORD thy God in Gilgal.

22 And Samuel said, Hath the LORD *as great* delight in burnt offerings and sacrifices, as in obeying the voice of the LORD? Behold, to obey *is* better than sacrifice, *and* to hearken than the fat of rams.

words should be obeyed implicitly, and who would know anyway? . . . [Saul] could do the expedient things but could find alibis as to the things which countered his own desires" (Kimball, in Conference Report, Oct. 1954, 51).

Why might it be important to view ourselves as "little in [our] own sight"? (15:16–17) Samuel reminded Saul of a time "when [he was] little in [his] own sight" (verse 17). What important attribute did Samuel observe that Saul had lost? President Howard W. Hunter taught: "Humility is an attribute of godliness possessed by true Saints. It is easy to understand why a proud man fails. He is content to rely upon himself only. . . . The proud man shuts himself off from God, and when he does he no longer lives in the light" (*Teachings of Howard W. Hunter*, 266). What do you think caused Saul to lose humility and shut himself off from God? ⊕

Why would Saul try to blame others for his sins? (15:20–21) Elder Marion D. Hanks taught that the "tendency in man to excuse himself has ever been with us. Saul was sent on a great mission. Saul failed and then blamed it on his people when he was confronted by the Prophet Samuel. Saul told a falsehood, and Samuel said, 'Then what is this bleating I hear in my ear' . . . and then Saul blamed his defection [disobedience] on his people" ("Thou Art You," 1091).

Why is obedience better than sacrifice? (15:22) "Obedience is the first law of heaven. . . . These laws affect not only our happiness and well-being here upon the earth, but are essential to our eternal life" (Tanner, "Obedience," 93).

"The ordinance of sacrifice, which looked forward to the atonement of the Savior, was later replaced by the sacrament ordinance. It is important to . . . partake of the sacrament, but without obedience to the gospel, the ordinance is meaningless and can even be detrimental [see 3 Nephi 18:29].

"The blessings of every ordinance are based on obedience to the gospel of Jesus Christ. How foolish Saul was to think that he and the people could receive the Spirit of God through ordinances only!" (Burgess, *New Insights into the Old Testament*, 145–46).

How is rebellion and stubbornness like witchcraft and idolatry? (15:23) "Rebellion makes a statement about our loyalty and our understanding of what God is really like and what he really wants. Saul, who understood the method but not the meaning of his sacrifice, and the Latter-day Saint who faithfully goes to sacrament meeting but is no more merciful or patient or forgiving as a result, [is] much the same as the witch and the idolator. They go through the motions of the ordinances without loyalty to or understanding of the reasons for which these ordinances were established—obedience, gentleness, and loving kindness in the search for forgiveness of their sins" (Holland, "I Stand All Amazed," 70).

23 For rebellion *is as* the sin of witchcraft, and stubbornness *is as* iniquity and idolatry. Because thou hast rejected the word of the LORD, he hath also rejected thee from *being* king.

1 Samuel 15:24–35. Saul Confesses His Sin

How can we overcome popular opinion and better obey God? (15:24) President Russell M. Nelson taught: "The temptation to be popular may prioritize public opinion above the word of God. Political campaigns and marketing strategies widely employ public opinion polls to shape their plans. Results of those polls are informative. But they could hardly be used as grounds to justify disobedience to God's commandments! Even if 'everyone is doing it,' wrong is never right. Evil, error, and darkness will never be truth, even if popular. A scriptural warning so declares: 'Woe unto them that call evil good, and good evil; that put darkness for light, and light for darkness' (Isaiah 5:20)" ("Let Your Faith Show," 30–31).

24 ¶ And Saul said unto Samuel, I have sinned: for I have transgressed the commandment of the LORD, and thy words: because I feared the people, and obeyed their voice.

25 Now therefore, I pray thee, pardon my sin, and turn again with me, that I may worship the LORD.

What did Saul lose when the Lord rejected him? (15:26–28) "While it was not too late for Saul to repent personally, it was too late for his full kingship to be maintained. Having forsaken God twice in order to follow the ideas of men, Saul would not be given more chances. . . .

"[In verse 27, Saul] seemed to think that if he could physically restrain Samuel, somehow the Lord would change His mind. . . .

"Samuel continued with the symbolism of Saul's action, telling him that as his cloak had been torn, so would the kingdom be torn from Saul. Symbolic action was the most powerful way to convey what Samuel was teaching" (Muhlestein, *Scripture Study Made Simple*, 192–93).

26 And Samuel said unto Saul, I will not return with thee: for thou hast rejected the word of the LORD, and the LORD hath rejected thee from being king over Israel.

27 And as Samuel turned about to go away, he laid hold upon the skirt of his mantle, and it rent.

28 And Samuel said unto him, The LORD hath rent the kingdom of Israel from thee this day, and hath given it to a neighbour of thine, *that is* better than thou.

29 And also the Strength of Israel will not lie nor repent: for he *is* not a man, that he should repent.

30 Then he said, I have sinned: *yet* honour me now, I pray thee, before the elders of my people, and before Israel, and turn again with me, that I may worship the LORD thy God.

31 So Samuel turned again after Saul; and Saul worshipped the LORD.

32 ¶ Then said Samuel, Bring ye hither to me Agag the king of the Amalekites. And Agag came unto him delicately. And Agag said, Surely the bitterness of death is past.

What does it mean that Agag came to Samuel "delicately"? (15:32) "The Hebrew word translated 'delicately' does not make much sense in this context, even with such possible alternate translations as 'daintily' and 'cheerfully.' The original writer may have meant to convey the idea that Agag was putting on a fake front of optimism and bravado. Agag's statement 'Surely the bitterness of death is past' seems to mean 'Let's let bygones be bygones.' Saul indicates by his subsequent savage handling of the king of the Amalekites that he is not about to be flattered by Agag" (Ludlow, *Companion to Your Study of the Old Testament*, 218).

33 And Samuel said, As thy sword hath made women childless, so shall thy mother be childless among women. And Samuel hewed Agag in pieces before the LORD in Gilgal.

Why would a prophet of God put another man to death? (15:33) "The Lord often used his people as instruments of righteous judgment (Gen. 9:6; Lev. 24:17–23). There was nothing inconsistent about a 'man of God,' in response to the clear command of the Lord, putting to death sinners who deserved to die. In this case, Samuel executed Agag (since Saul had refused) to fulfill the Lord's command (15:3)" (*Quest Study Bible* [1994], 378).

34 ¶ Then Samuel went to Ramah; and Saul went up to his house to Gibeah of Saul.

35 And Samuel came no more to see Saul until the day of his death: nevertheless Samuel mourned for Saul: and the LORD repented that he had made Saul king over Israel.

How does the Joseph Smith Translation help us better understand this verse? (15:35) The Joseph Smith Translation (JST) changes verse 35 to read, "the Lord *rent the kingdom from Saul whom* he had made king over Israel" (see 1 Samuel 15:35*a*).

CHAPTER 16

The Lord chooses David of Bethlehem as king—He is anointed by Samuel—Saul chooses David as his companion and armor bearer.

1 And the LORD said unto Samuel, How long wilt thou mourn for Saul, seeing I have rejected him from reigning over Israel? fill thine horn with oil, and go, I will send thee to Jesse the Beth-lehemite: for I have provided me a king among his sons.

1 Samuel 16:1–13. Samuel Finds and Anoints David as King of Israel

Why was Samuel afraid that Saul would kill him? (16:2) "This fear on the part of the prophet, who did not generally show himself either hesitating or timid, can only be explained, as we may see from 1 Samuel 16:14, on the supposition that Saul was already given up to the power of the evil spirit, so that the very worst might be dreaded from his madness, if he discovered that Samuel had anointed another king" (Keil and Delitzsch, *Commentary* [on 1 Samuel 16:2–3]).

Why did the elders of the town tremble at Samuel's arrival? (16:4) "Because it was strange and unexpected to them, this being but an obscure town, and remote from Samuel, and therefore they justly thought there was some extraordinary reason for it. . . . The Hebrew phrase, comest thou in peace, is as much as to say (in our phrase) is all well?" (*Wesley's Explanatory Notes* [on 1 Samuel 16:4]).

Who is Eliab and why did the Lord refuse him? (16:6–7) Eliab was the "eldest son of Jesse of Bethlehem and the elder brother of David. . . . Eliab served as a soldier in Saul's wars against the Philistines." His physical stature impressed Samuel. "Samuel's line of thinking was not far afield; it was completely consistent with the criteria that [they] apparently had used to select Saul. Saul had been physically head and shoulders taller than anyone else in Israel. Should not the next king have the same sort of appearance? The Lord suggested that there was to be another set of requirements used to determine the next ruler of Israel" (Hyde, *Comprehensive Commentary [1 Samuel]*, 140).

Why is it so important to remember that "the Lord looketh on the heart"? (16:7) President Dieter F. Uchtdorf said: "Heavenly Father's interest in you does not depend on how rich or beautiful or healthy or smart you are. He sees you not as the world sees you; He sees who you really are. He looks on your heart" ("Your Wonderful Journey Home," 128). President Uchtdorf also taught, "God does not look on the outward appearance. I believe that He doesn't care one bit if we live in a castle or a cottage, if we are handsome or homely, if we are famous or forgotten. Though we are incomplete, God loves us completely. Though we are imperfect, He loves us perfectly" ("Love of God," 22). ⊕

2 And Samuel said, How can I go? if Saul hear *it,* he will kill me. And the LORD said, Take an heifer with thee, and say, I am come to sacrifice to the LORD.

3 And call Jesse to the sacrifice, and I will shew thee what thou shalt do: and thou shalt anoint unto me *him* whom I name unto thee.

4 And Samuel did that which the LORD spake, and came to Beth-lehem. And the elders of the town trembled at his coming, and said, Comest thou peaceably?

5 And he said, Peaceably: I am come to sacrifice unto the LORD: sanctify yourselves, and come with me to the sacrifice. And he sanctified Jesse and his sons, and called them to the sacrifice.

6 ¶ And it came to pass, when they were come, that he looked on Eliab, and said, Surely the LORD's anointed *is* before him.

7 But the LORD said unto Samuel, Look not on his countenance, or on the height of his stature; because I have refused him: for *the LORD seeth* not as man seeth; for man looketh on the outward appearance, but the LORD looketh on the heart.

8 Then Jesse called Abinadab, and made him pass before Samuel. And he said, Neither hath the LORD chosen this.

9 Then Jesse made Shammah to pass by. And he said, Neither hath the LORD chosen this.

10 Again, Jesse made seven of his sons to pass before Samuel. And Samuel said unto Jesse, The LORD hath not chosen these.

11 And Samuel said unto Jesse, Are here all *thy* children? And he said, There remaineth yet the youngest, and, behold, he keepeth the sheep. And Samuel said unto Jesse, Send and fetch him: for we will not sit down till he come hither.

12 And he sent, and brought him in. Now he *was* ruddy, *and* withal of a beautiful countenance, and goodly to look to. And the LORD said, Arise, anoint him: for this *is* he.

What does "ruddy" mean? (16:12) "Usually this designates the red hair and fair skin regarded as beautiful in southern countries, where the hair and the complexion are generally dark. However, . . . 'ruddy,' may refer to the youth's physical prowess. David and Esau are the only two in the OT referred to by this term. Perhaps the word 'warrior' would be a better translation than *ruddy*" (*Wycliffe Bible Commentary* [1962], 286).

13 Then Samuel took the horn of oil, and anointed him in the midst of his brethren: and the Spirit of the LORD came upon David from that day forward. So Samuel rose up, and went to Ramah.

What did anointing signify? (16:13) "In Israel individuals called to three specific offices were anointed: prophets (1 Kgs 19:16), priests (Exod 29:7–9; Lev 8:10–12), and kings (1 Sam 10:1). . . . Anointing was done with olive oil. . . . Olive oil was associated with prosperity, wealth, cleansing, healing, and purity and symbolized the Spirit. One who was anointed was called *meshiah*, 'anointed one,' which derives from the Hebrew verb *mashah*, 'to anoint.' Thus the prophets, priests, and kings could all be properly referred to as messiahs. King David as the 'anointed one' was a type of the future Davidic king who is referred to as the Messiah" (Holzapfel, et al., *Jehovah and the World of the Old Testament,* 197). See commentary in this volume for Leviticus 8:12. ⊕

14 ¶ But the Spirit of the LORD departed from Saul, and an evil spirit from the LORD troubled him.

15 And Saul's servants said unto him, Behold now, an evil spirit from God troubleth thee.

16 Let our lord now command thy servants, *which are* before thee, to seek out a man, *who is* a cunning player on an harp: and it shall come to pass, when the evil spirit from God is upon thee, that he shall play with his hand, and thou shalt be well.

What important changes did the Joseph Smith Translation make to these verses? (16:14–16) "There are four verses changed in chapter 16 of 1 Samuel, but all four changes are the same. This is the account of King Saul being bothered by an evil spirit. The KJV calls it 'an evil spirit from the Lord.' The JST corrects the text to read 'an evil spirit *which was not of* the Lord' or '*not of God*' (vv. 14, 15–16, 23). God does not send evil spirits. Chapter 18 (v. 10) and chapter 19 (v. 9) each have the same correction. The Prophet apparently observed the error and followed the account until all of the corrections were made" (Nyman, "Contribution of the JST," 92).

17 And Saul said unto his servants, Provide me now a man that can play well, and bring *him* to me.

Why did Saul ask for a musician to play for him? (16:17) When "the Spirit of the Lord departed from Saul . . . an evil spirit" filled the vacancy and "troubled him" (v. 14). Saul sought music to clear his troubled soul. Elder Richard G. Scott taught of a better way, "You can regain peace of conscience by repenting of personal transgressions that cause you internal turmoil. . . . Try as you might, you will not find enduring happiness until, through repentance, you satisfy personally broken law to restore peace to a troubled conscience" ("Peace of Conscience and Peace of Mind," 16).

18 Then answered one of the servants, and said, Behold, I have seen a son of Jesse the Beth-lehemite, *that is* cunning in playing, and a mighty valiant man, and a man of war, and prudent in matters, and a comely person, and the LORD *is* with him.

19 ¶ Wherefore Saul sent messengers unto Jesse, and said, Send me David thy son, which *is* with the sheep.

20 And Jesse took an ass *laden* with bread, and a bottle of wine, and a kid, and sent *them* by David his son unto Saul.

21 And David came to Saul, and stood before him: and he loved him greatly; and he became his armourbearer.

22 And Saul sent to Jesse, saying, Let David, I pray thee, stand before me; for he hath found favour in my sight.

23 And it came to pass, when the *evil* spirit from God was upon Saul, that David took an harp, and played with his hand: so Saul was refreshed, and was well, and the evil spirit departed from him.

How did the Joseph Smith Translation correct this verse? (16:23) See commentary in this chapter for 1 Samuel 16:14–16.

David: "The Lord Is with Him" (1 Samuel 16:18)

"Excluding Moses, there is no character more prominent to the story of the Old Testament than David, the son of Jesse. Virtually every recorded event to the time of his great sin seems fraught with symbolic meaning pointing to Christ" (McConkie, *Gospel Symbolism*, 158).

Consider the following likenesses between Jesus Christ and David:

- David, like the Son of God, was born under humble circumstances in the village of Bethlehem (1 Sam. 16:1).
- During David's early years, he was despised by his brothers (1 Sam. 17:28).
- David was a good shepherd.
- Christ's ancestry came through the lineage of David (Matt. 9:27; 12:23).
- The name of David is a prophetic name for Christ (Ezek. 34:23–24).
- With only the armor of faith, David slew Goliath, Israel's great enemy, and Jesus slew the last enemy of Israel, which is death.
- Without justification, David was opposed by Saul, similar to Christ and His servants who are opposed by those who follow another king.
- David was anointed with holy oil (1 Sam. 16:12–13) and became king (2 Sam. 5:4–5), uniting the kingdom of Israel under one head. David's reign thus symbolizes the glorious reign of the Lord during the millennial period.
- David's name means "beloved," and Jesus is called the "beloved Son" (Matt. 3:17).

(Adapted from McConkie, *Gospel Symbolism*, 158; and McConkie and Parry, *Guide to Scriptural Symbols*, 38).

CHAPTER 17

Israel and the Philistines engage in war—Goliath of Gath, a giant, defies Israel and challenges any Israelite to personal combat—David goes against him in the name of the Lord—David slays Goliath with a sling and a stone—Israel defeats the Philistines.

1 Now the Philistines gathered together their armies to battle, and were gathered together at Shochoh, which *belongeth* to Judah, and pitched between Shochoh and Azekah, in Ephes-dammim.

2 And Saul and the men of Israel were gathered together, and pitched by the valley of Elah, and set the battle in array against the Philistines.

3 And the Philistines stood on a mountain on the one side, and Israel stood on a mountain on the other side: and *there was* a valley between them.

4 ¶ And there went out a champion out of the camp of the Philistines, named Goliath, of Gath, whose height *was* six cubits and a span.

5 And *he had* an helmet of brass upon his head, and he *was* armed with a coat of mail; and the weight of the coat *was* five thousand shekels of brass.

6 And *he had* greaves of brass upon his legs, and a target of brass between his shoulders.

7 And the staff of his spear *was* like a weaver's beam; and his spear's head *weighed* six hundred shekels of iron: and one bearing a shield went before him.

8 And he stood and cried unto the armies of Israel, and said unto them, Why are ye come out to set *your* battle in array? *am* not I a Philistine, and ye servants to Saul? choose you a man for you, and let him come down to me.

9 If he be able to fight with me, and to kill me, then will we be your servants: but if I

1 Samuel 17:1–11. Goliath Challenges Israel to a Battle

What is significant about the detailed descriptions of Goliath? (17:4–7) "According to the weights and measurements assigned by most biblical scholars, Goliath would have been over nine feet tall, with a 'coat of mail' (armor) weighing about 125 pounds and a spear with a head weighing about 15 pounds!" (Ludlow, *Companion to Your Study of the Old Testament,* 218). ⊕

What is meant by "and there went out a champion"? (17:4) "The obvious answer is that a champion is a man who has proven himself on the battlefield. However, the Hebrew text suggests that the word *champion* describes a middleman, a man who tries to settle disputes between two opposing forces, whether armies or nations. In the days of King Saul, it was 'not unusual for opposing armies, which were generally quite small, to select one representative [champion] from each side to fight a personal contest. The outcome of that contest determined the winner of the battle'" (Black, *400 Questions and Answers about the Old Testament,* 107).

How tall was Goliath? (17:4) "Goliath's height was six cubits and a span. The most widely accepted opinion of the length of a cubit is about eighteen inches or, roughly, the distance from the elbow to the tip of the extended middle finger. A span is said to be one-half the distance from the thumb to the end of the little finger when the fingers are spread as wide as possible. These measurements would make the height of Goliath approximately nine feet, nine inches! It is not too surprising that the Philistines would have picked such a champion or that no man in Israel wanted to be Saul's champion" (*Old Testament Student Manual: Genesis–2 Samuel,* 278). ⊕

1 Samuel 17:12–31. David Offers to Fight Goliath in the Name of the Lord and on Behalf of Israel

Why did Goliath present himself for forty days? (17:16) The number forty "suggests a period of trial, testing, probation" (Gaskill, *Lost Language of Symbolism,* 320). Goliath's presentation "may have been forty literal days, or 'forty' may serve as a way of saying 'a long time.' In either case, the standoff between the armies became lengthy as Goliath continued to hurl his challenge to the cowering Israelites. To their credit, while they cowered about the personal combat, they did not go home, but rather stayed and protected their homeland. As long as the Philistines did not advance, they were accomplishing their purpose" (Muhlestein, *Scripture Study Made Simple,* 197).

What can we learn from David's response to Goliath's challenge? (17:20–26) David's faith in God and mortal courage was vital to Israel's success. Have you ever been around someone who speaks against or rebels against God? President Thomas S. Monson presents a question to ponder: "The battle for our immortal souls is no less important than the battle

prevail against him, and kill him, then shall ye be our servants, and serve us.

10 And the Philistine said, I defy the armies of Israel this day; give me a man, that we may fight together.

11 When Saul and all Israel heard those words of the Philistine, they were dismayed, and greatly afraid.

12 ¶ Now David *was* the son of that Ephrathite of Beth-lehem-judah, whose name *was* Jesse; and he had eight sons: and the man went among men *for* an old man in the days of Saul.

13 And the three eldest sons of Jesse went *and* followed Saul to the battle: and the names of his three sons that went to the battle *were* Eliab the firstborn, and next unto him Abinadab, and the third Shammah.

14 And David *was* the youngest: and the three eldest followed Saul.

15 But David went and returned from Saul to feed his father's sheep at Beth-lehem.

16 And the Philistine drew near morning and evening, and presented himself forty days.

17 And Jesse said unto David his son, Take now for thy brethren an ephah of this parched *corn,* and these ten loaves, and run to the camp to thy brethren;

18 And carry these ten cheeses unto the captain of *their* thousand, and look how thy brethren fare, and take their pledge.

19 Now Saul, and they, and all the men of Israel, *were* in the valley of Elah, fighting with the Philistines.

20 ¶ And David rose up early in the morning, and left the sheep with a keeper, and took, and went, as Jesse had commanded him; and he came to the trench, as the host was going forth to the fight, and shouted for the battle.

21 For Israel and the Philistines had put the battle in array, army against army.

22 And David left his carriage in the hand of the keeper of the carriage, and ran into the army, and came and saluted his brethren.

23 And as he talked with them, behold, there came up the champion, the Philistine of Gath, Goliath by name, out of the armies of the Philistines, and spake according to the same words: and David heard *them*.

24 And all the men of Israel, when they saw the man, fled from him, and were sore afraid.

25 And the men of Israel said, Have ye seen this man that is come up? surely to defy Israel is he come up: and it shall be, *that* the man who killeth him, the king will enrich him with great riches, and will give him his daughter, and make his father's house free in Israel.

26 And David spake to the men that stood by him, saying, What shall be done to the man that killeth this Philistine, and taketh away the reproach from Israel? for who *is* this uncircumcised Philistine, that he should defy the armies of the living God?

27 And the people answered him after this manner, saying, So shall it be done to the man that killeth him.

28 ¶ And Eliab his eldest brother heard when he spake unto the men; and Eliab's anger was kindled against David, and he said, Why camest thou down hither? and with whom hast thou left those few sheep in the wilderness? I know thy pride, and the naughtiness of thine heart; for thou art come down that thou mightest see the battle.

29 And David said, What have I now done? *Is there* not a cause?

30 ¶ And he turned from him toward another, and spake after the same manner: and

fought by David. The enemy is no less formidable, the help of Almighty God no farther away. What will our action be?" (*Teachings of Thomas S. Monson*, 72).

Why did David ask, "Is there not a cause?" (17:29)

"David's comment, 'Is there not a cause?' suggests that there are times when all of us should stand up and be counted on the side of truth and righteousness. . . . Sometimes God expects us to stand up . . . for the cause of truth and righteousness and fight such things as pornography, immorality, bigotry, and injustice in our neighborhoods and communities. In David's case, the Philistines were mocking God and his covenants and were striving to take away his people's agency and freedom" (Burgess, *New Insights into the Old Testament*, 151). What does God expect you to stand up for?

1 Samuel 17:32–58. David Defeats Goliath

Why did David refuse to wear Saul's armor? (17:39)
David had not proven the armor. "The Hebrew word translated 'proved' here could have been translated as 'test' or 'try.' It is even translated as 'tempted' in Exodus 17:7 wherein the children of Israel 'tempted [tried, tested, proved] the Lord'" (Ludlow, *Companion to Your Study of the Old Testament*, 218).

"In ancient times it required considerable exercise and training to make a man expert in the use of such heavy armor; armor which in the present day scarcely a man is to be found who is able to carry; and so it

the people answered him again after the former manner.

31 And when the words were heard which David spake, they rehearsed *them* before Saul: and he sent for him.

32 ¶ And David said to Saul, Let no man's heart fail because of him; thy servant will go and fight with this Philistine.

33 And Saul said to David, Thou art not able to go against this Philistine to fight with him: for thou *art but* a youth, and he a man of war from his youth.

34 And David said unto Saul, Thy servant kept his father's sheep, and there came a lion, and a bear, and took a lamb out of the flock:

35 And I went out after him, and smote him, and delivered *it* out of his mouth: and when he arose against me, I caught *him* by his beard, and smote him, and slew him.

36 Thy servant slew both the lion and the bear: and this uncircumcised Philistine shall be as one of them, seeing he hath defied the armies of the living God.

37 David said moreover, The LORD that delivered me out of the paw of the lion, and out of the paw of the bear, he will deliver me out of the hand of this Philistine. And Saul said unto David, Go, and the LORD be with thee.

38 ¶ And Saul armed David with his armour, and he put an helmet of brass upon his head; also he armed him with a coat of mail.

39 And David girded his sword upon his armour, and he assayed to go; for he had not proved *it*. And David said unto Saul, I cannot go with these; for I have not proved *them*. And David put them off him.

40 And he took his staff in his hand, and chose
him five smooth stones out of the brook, and
put them in a shepherd's bag which he had,
even in a scrip; and his sling *was* in his hand:
and he drew near to the Philistine.

41 And the Philistine came on and drew near
unto David; and the man that bare the shield
went before him.

42 And when the Philistine looked about,
and saw David, he disdained him: for he was
but a youth, and ruddy, and of a fair countenance.

43 And the Philistine said unto David, *Am*
I a dog, that thou comest to me with staves?
And the Philistine cursed David by his gods.

44 And the Philistine said to David, Come
to me, and I will give thy flesh unto the fowls
of the air, and to the beasts of the field.

45 Then said David to the Philistine, Thou
comest to me with a sword, and with a spear,
and with a shield: but I come to thee in the
name of the LORD of hosts, the God of the
armies of Israel, whom thou hast defied.

46 This day will the LORD deliver thee into
mine hand; and I will smite thee, and take
thine head from thee; and I will give the carcases of the host of the Philistines this day
unto the fowls of the air, and to the wild
beasts of the earth; that all the earth may
know that there is a God in Israel.

47 And all this assembly shall know that the
LORD saveth not with sword and spear: for
the battle *is* the LORD's, and he will give you
into our hands.

must have been then, until that practice which arises from frequent use had made the proprietor perfect" (*Adam Clarke's Commentary* [on 1 Samuel 17:39]).

What smooth stones should we choose for our personal battles? (17:40) President Thomas S. Monson urged us to make personal application of this account: "Just as David went to the brook, well might we go to our source of supply—the Lord. What polished stones will you select to defeat the Goliath that is robbing you of your happiness by smothering your opportunities? May I offer suggestions. . . .

"The stone of COURAGE will melt the Goliath of fear. The stone of EFFORT will bring down the Goliath of indecision and procrastination. And the Goliaths of pride, of envy, of lack of self-respect will not stand before the power of the stones of HUMILITY, PRAYER, and DUTY" ("Meeting Your Goliath," 4–5).

Why did Goliath refer to a dog? (17:43–44) "The Hebrews, . . . viewed [dogs] with utter disgust. In the Bible the dog . . . is usually described as a scavenger. . . . When applied to a person 'dog' becomes a term of disregard and humiliation and in Ps. 22:16 enemies are called 'dogs.' In 1 Sam. 17:43 Goliath ridicules David's weapons by saying 'Am I a dog, that you come to me with sticks?'" (*Harper's Bible Dictionary*, 224). Jewish historian Josephus records that David replied, "No, not for a dog, but for a creature worse than a dog" (*Antiquities of the Jews*, 6.9.4).

How did David use imagery to testify of his faith in the Lord? (17:45–47) "*Hosts* refers to the armies of heaven and of Israel over whom God is Commander in Chief. . . .

"David intended his victory to demonstrate to *all the earth* that (1) the God of Israel exists and (2) He delivers His own against overwhelming odds. David's words *the battle is the Lord's* put the contest into proper perspective" (*NKJV Study Bible* [2007], 446).

48 And it came to pass, when the Philistine arose, and came and drew nigh to meet David, that David hasted, and ran toward the army to meet the Philistine.

49 And David put his hand in his bag, and took thence a stone, and slang *it,* and smote the Philistine in his forehead, that the stone sunk into his forehead; and he fell upon his face to the earth.

50 So David prevailed over the Philistine with a sling and with a stone, and smote the Philistine, and slew him; but *there was* no sword in the hand of David.

51 Therefore David ran, and stood upon the Philistine, and took his sword, and drew it out of the sheath thereof, and slew him, and cut off his head therewith. And when the Philistines saw their champion was dead, they fled.

52 And the men of Israel and of Judah arose, and shouted, and pursued the Philistines, until thou come to the valley, and to the gates of Ekron. And the wounded of the Philistines fell down by the way to Shaaraim, even unto Gath, and unto Ekron.

53 And the children of Israel returned from chasing after the Philistines, and they spoiled their tents.

54 And David took the head of the Philistine, and brought it to Jerusalem; but he put his armour in his tent.

55 ¶ And when Saul saw David go forth against the Philistine, he said unto Abner, the captain of the host, Abner, whose son *is* this youth? And Abner said, *As* thy soul liveth, O king, I cannot tell.

56 And the king said, Inquire thou whose son the stripling *is.*

57 And as David returned from the slaughter of the Philistine, Abner took him, and

How common was the sling and how did it work? (17:49–50) Slings were "among the most ancient instruments of warfare (see Job 41:28). This weapon was common among the Egyptians, Assyrians, and Hebrews" (*New Unger's Bible Dictionary*, 105). They were "devised originally by shepherds to drive off animals molesting their flocks.... In the hands of a trained slinger a missile could be hurled as far as 600 feet.... The slinger held his arms above his head.... After swinging the sling several times around his head with great force ... he suddenly released the end of one of the thongs to discharge the missile" (*Tyndale Bible Dictionary*, 111–12).

brought him before Saul with the head of the Philistine in his hand.

58 And Saul said to him, Whose son *art* thou, *thou* young man? And David answered, *I am* the son of thy servant Jesse the Beth-lehemite.

CHAPTER 18

Jonathan loves David—Saul sets David over his armies—David is honored by the people, and Saul becomes jealous—David marries Michal, a daughter of Saul.

1 And it came to pass, when he had made an end of speaking unto Saul, that the soul of Jonathan was knit with the soul of David, and Jonathan loved him as his own soul.

2 And Saul took him that day, and would let him go no more home to his father's house.

1 Samuel 18:1–4. Jonathan and David Promise to Be Friends

How did Jonathan demonstrate to David they were true friends? (18:1) "Aristotle said once that friendship is a single soul dwelling in two bodies. No definition of friendship could better describe the relationship of David and Jonathan in the Old Testament. Jonathan, the son of King Saul, was a valiant soldier in his own right and a worthy young prince in Israel. But when David came onto the scene fresh from his mighty victory over Goliath, having already been anointed by the prophet Samuel, it was he, not Jonathan, who would be successor to the increasingly disobedient Saul.

"To a lesser man—or a lesser friend—than Jonathan, David would have been a terrible threat, a natural rival. But he wasn't" (Holland, "Real Friendship," 62). ⊕

3 Then Jonathan and David made a covenant, because he loved him as his own soul.

4 And Jonathan stripped himself of the robe that *was* upon him, and gave it to David, and his garments, even to his sword, and to his bow, and to his girdle.

What do we learn about covenants from Jonathan and David? (18:3–4) "In the Hebrew Bible, 'the covenant' usually describes the entire relationship between God and the children of Israel. Terms such as 'contract,' 'agreement,' 'treaty,' 'obligation,' 'brotherhood,' 'law,' and 'cutting' or 'binding' express facets of the covenant. But none of these alone is sufficient to capture the full meaning of this distinctive, self-contained Israelite religious concept. It has been said that according to the Israelite concept of covenant, one enters into a fellowship of the strongest order with another party, virtually becoming like that person himself, as in the covenant between Jonathan and David in 1 Samuel 18:1, 3–4" (Welch, "Word Studies from the New Testament," 29).

1 Samuel 18:5–16. Saul Becomes Jealous and Angry as David Is Praised after a Battle

5 ¶ And David went out whithersoever Saul
sent him, *and* behaved himself wisely: and
Saul set him over the men of war, and he was
accepted in the sight of all the people, and
also in the sight of Saul's servants.

Why was Saul "very wroth"? (18:6–8) President Ezra Taft Benson explained: "Saul became an enemy to David through pride. He was jealous because the crowds of Israelite women were singing that 'Saul hath slain his thousands, and David his ten thousands' (1 Sam. 18:6–8).

"The proud stand more in fear of men's judgment than of God's judgment (see D&C 3:6–7; D&C 30:1–2; D&C 60:2). 'What will men think of me?' weighs heavier than 'What will God think of me?' . . . Fear of men's judgment manifests itself in competition for men's approval. The proud love 'the praise of men more than the praise of God' (John 12:42–43)" ("Beware of Pride," 5). ⊕

6 And it came to pass as they came, when
David was returned from the slaughter of the
Philistine, that the women came out of all
cities of Israel, singing and dancing, to meet
king Saul, with tabrets, with joy, and with instruments of musick.
7 And the women answered *one another* as
they played, and said, Saul hath slain his
thousands, and David his ten thousands.
8 And Saul was very wroth, and the saying
displeased him; and he said, They have ascribed unto David ten thousands, and to me
they have ascribed *but* thousands: and *what*
can he have more but the kingdom?
9 And Saul eyed David from that day and
forward.

What role did dancing play in ancient celebrations? (18:6) "Among the Jews, dancing was always a favorite social pastime among girls and women (Jer. 31:4), imitated by children playing on the street (Job 21:11; Matt. 11:17; Luke 7:32), and was engaged in by female companies in honor of national joys, especially victories (1 Sam. 18:6) and religious festivities (Ex. 15:20; Judg. 21:21). . . . The dances . . . were accompanied by women beating tambourines (Judg. 11:34). At national festivities other instruments were played" (*New Unger's Bible Dictionary*, 274).

How does the Joseph Smith Translation change this verse? (18:10) The Joseph Smith Translation (JST) makes an important change to this verse: "The evil spirit *which was not of* God . . ." (see 1 Samuel 18:10*a*).

10 ¶ And it came to pass on the morrow, that
the evil spirit from God came upon Saul,
and he prophesied in the midst of the house:
and David played with his hand, as at other
times: and *there was* a javelin in Saul's hand.
11 And Saul cast the javelin; for he said, I
will smite David even to the wall *with it.* And
David avoided out of his presence twice.
12 ¶ And Saul was afraid of David, because
the LORD was with him, and was departed
from Saul.

What did Saul hope to accomplish by making David a captain in the military? (18:13–16) "Saul promotes David because he is afraid to have David nearby and hopes that David will be killed in battle. . . . [But] *all Israel and Judah loved David* . . . and anticipates

13 Therefore Saul removed him from him,
and made him his captain over a thousand;
and he went out and came in before the
people.

14 And David behaved himself wisely in all his ways; and the LORD *was* with him.

15 Wherefore when Saul saw that he behaved himself very wisely, he was afraid of him.

16 But all Israel and Judah loved David, because he went out and came in before them.

David's rule over both north and south. The army was devoted to David because of his military success" (*New Oxford Annotated Bible* [2010], 428).

Summary of 1 Samuel 18:17–30

Saul plans to use his daughter Michal to place David where he will be killed on the battlefield. Instead, David is successful beyond Saul's expectations and becomes even more popular.

CHAPTER 19

Saul seeks to kill David—Michal saves David by artifice—David joins Samuel and the company of prophets.

Summary of 1 Samuel 19:1–17

After being influenced by an evil spirit (see 1 Samuel 19:9*a*), Saul solicits his son Jonathan to kill David. Instead, Jonathan warns David to find a secret place to avoid Saul's wrath. Michal, Saul's daughter and David's wife, helps him escape her father's plan.

18 ¶ So David fled, and escaped, and came to Samuel to Ramah, and told him all that Saul had done to him. And he and Samuel went and dwelt in Naioth.

19 And it was told Saul, saying, Behold, David *is* at Naioth in Ramah.

1 Samuel 19:18–24. David Finds Refuge with the Prophet Samuel

Why would David turn to the prophet Samuel for help? (19:18) "There has always been a desperate need for the steady and reassuring voice of a living prophet of God: one who will speak the mind and will of God in showing the way to spiritual safety and personal peace and happiness. . . . The greatest security of members of The Church of Jesus Christ of Latter-day Saints comes from learning to listen to and obey the words and commandments that the Lord has given through living prophets" (Hales, "Hear the Prophet's Voice and Obey," 15). How have the teachings of modern prophets and apostles strengthened your faith in Jesus Christ and helped you in times of worry, temptation, or sorrow?

20 And Saul sent messengers to take David: and when they saw the company of the prophets prophesying, and Samuel standing *as* appointed over them, the Spirit of God was upon the messengers of Saul, and they also prophesied.

How did David escape Saul's messengers? (19:20) "David had sought refuge with Samuel in what scholars called 'Schools of the Prophets' (Keil and Delitzsch, *Commentary*, 2:2:199). These scholars showed that such prophets as Samuel, Elijah, and Elisha conducted special schools that were called here 'the company of the prophets' (v. 20). Elsewhere, the men who attended these schools were called 'sons of the prophets' (1 Kings 20:35). This fact is of interest to Latter-day Saints because Joseph Smith set up a similar school in Kirtland, Ohio, to help teach priesthood holders their special duties" (*Old Testament Student Manual: Genesis–2 Samuel*, 279; see also Bible Dictionary, "School of the Prophets"). See commentary in this volume for 1 Samuel 10:10. ⊕

Why did Saul strip off his clothes? (19:23–24) "The spirit of prophecy is, as it were, infectious; Saul's messengers and the king himself are forced to succumb to the power of the Spirit of God in this abode of the prophets, and they 'prophesy' despite themselves" (Guthrie, et al., *New Bible Commentary: Revised*, 298). "After Saul was touched by the Spirit, he seemed to realize how wicked he was, and he wanted to humble himself, Thus he became naked (most likely stripped to a girdle-like undergarment), an expression of humility or humiliation" (Muhlestein, *Scripture Study Made Simple*, 204). ⊕

21 And when it was told Saul, he sent other
messengers, and they prophesied likewise.
And Saul sent messengers again the third
time, and they prophesied also.

22 Then went he also to Ramah, and came
to a great well that *is* in Sechu: and he asked
and said, Where *are* Samuel and David? And
one said, Behold, *they be* at Naioth in Ramah.

23 And he went thither to Naioth in Ramah:
and the Spirit of God was upon him also,
and he went on, and prophesied, until he
came to Naioth in Ramah.

24 And he stripped off his clothes also, and
prophesied before Samuel in like manner,
and lay down naked all that day and all that
night. Wherefore they say, *Is* Saul also among
the prophets?

CHAPTER 20

David and Jonathan make a covenant of friendship and peace—They take leave of each other.

1 Samuel 20:1–23. David and Jonathan Invite the Lord into Their Everlasting Friendship

1 And David fled from Naioth in Ramah,
and came and said before Jonathan, What
have I done? what *is* mine iniquity? and what
is my sin before thy father, that he seeketh
my life?

2 And he said unto him, God forbid; thou
shalt not die: behold, my father will do nothing either great or small, but that he will
shew it me: and why should my father hide
this thing from me? it *is* not *so*.

3 And David sware moreover, and said,
Thy father certainly knoweth that I have
found grace in thine eyes; and he saith, Let
not Jonathan know this, lest he be grieved:
but truly *as* the LORD liveth, and *as* thy soul
liveth, *there is* but a step between me and
death.

4 Then said Jonathan unto David, Whatsoever thy soul desireth, I will even do *it* for thee.

Why did Jonathan pledge his loyalty to David?
(20:4) "The friendship of David and Jonathan was one of the closest friendships of all times. We are told that when David was brought into the court of Saul, 'the soul of Jonathan was knit with the soul of David, and Jonathan loved him as his own soul' (1 Sam. 18:1). The interesting thing about his relationship is that Jonathan was the heir-designate and was meant to occupy the throne upon the death of his father, Saul. Still, he recognized early in their relationship that David was the one chosen of the Lord, and he desired only to be able to serve at David's side" (Bassett, "King Called David," 66–67).

5 And David said unto Jonathan, Behold, to morrow *is* the new moon, and I should not fail to sit with the king at meat: but let me go, that I may hide myself in the field unto the third *day* at even.

6 If thy father at all miss me, then say, David earnestly asked *leave* of me that he might run to Beth-lehem his city: for *there is* a yearly sacrifice there for all the family.

7 If he say thus, *It is* well; thy servant shall have peace: but if he be very wroth, *then* be sure that evil is determined by him.

What is the new moon and why is it important?
(20:5) "The Hebrew religious calendar was based on lunar months. Religious festivals were held on days calculated from the new moon. The Jewish people also celebrated the beginning of a lunar month with a New Moon festival, including sacrifices and feasts (1 Sam. 20:5–24; 2 Ki. 4:23; Neh. 10:33; Isa. 1:13, 14; Hos. 5:7; Amos 8:5)" (*Revell Bible Dictionary*, 706–7).

8 Therefore thou shalt deal kindly with thy servant; for thou hast brought thy servant into a covenant of the LORD with thee: notwithstanding, if there be in me iniquity, slay me thyself; for why shouldest thou bring me to thy father?

9 And Jonathan said, Far be it from thee: for if I knew certainly that evil were determined by my father to come upon thee, then would not I tell it thee?

10 Then said David to Jonathan, Who shall tell me? or what *if* thy father answer thee roughly?

11 ¶ And Jonathan said unto David, Come, and let us go out into the field. And they went out both of them into the field.

12 And Jonathan said unto David, O LORD God of Israel, when I have sounded my

How do David and Jonathan demonstrate Christlike characteristics in their friendship?
(20:8–23) "We can learn a great lesson from the friendship of David and Jonathan, which was based on a covenant to be faithful to the Lord. . . . What kinds of friends do we select, adopt, confide in, and visit with? Are we strong enough to refuse to be a friend of the world and its representatives? Is to be a friend to be complacent and surrender to lower standards, or is it to maintain Christlike standards and defend them? Do we consider mutual friendship as a way to maintain and develop the foundation of our testimony of Christ? . . . Be committed to be his friend!" (Didier, "Friend or Foe," 24).

father about to morrow any time, *or* the third
day, and, behold, *if there be* good toward
David, and I then send not unto thee, and
shew it thee;

13 The LORD do so and much more to
Jonathan: but if it please my father *to do* thee
evil, then I will shew it thee, and send thee
away, that thou mayest go in peace: and the
LORD be with thee, as he hath been with my
father.

14 And thou shalt not only while yet I live
shew me the kindness of the LORD, that I die
not:

15 But *also* thou shalt not cut off thy kindness from my house for ever: no, not when
the LORD hath cut off the enemies of David
every one from the face of the earth.

16 So Jonathan made *a covenant* with the
house of David, *saying*, Let the LORD even require *it* at the hand of David's enemies.

17 And Jonathan caused David to swear
again, because he loved him: for he loved him
as he loved his own soul.

18 Then Jonathan said to David, To morrow
is the new moon: and thou shalt be missed,
because thy seat will be empty.

19 And *when* thou hast stayed three days,
then thou shalt go down quickly, and come
to the place where thou didst hide thyself
when the business was *in hand*, and shalt remain by the stone Ezel.

Why did Jonathan ask David to covenant not to "cut off" his house? (20:15) "Whatever the outcome of the rift between Saul and David, Jonathan appealed to David to protect his own life and the lives of his descendants. Jonathan knew that David might someday take the throne—and he was well aware of the ancient custom of a new king killing the offspring of his predecessor (see 1 Kin. 15:29; 16:11; 2 Kin. 10:7)" (*Nelson Study Bible* [NKJV], 451). Jonathan was so concerned about this that he "caused David to swear again" (1 Samuel 20:17).

What can we learn from David and Jonathan about keeping covenants and promises? (20:16) "How important is it to you to keep your word? to be trusted? to do what you say you will do? to strive to honor your sacred covenants? to have integrity? By living true to our promises to the Lord and to others, we walk the covenant path back to our Father in Heaven and we feel His love in our lives. Our Savior, Jesus Christ, is our great Exemplar when it comes to making and keeping promises and covenants. . . . Keeping promises is not a habit; it is a characteristic of being a disciple of Jesus Christ" (Rasband, "Standing by Our Promises and Covenants," 53).

What do Jonathan's words to David convey? (20:18–23) "The elaborate speeches of Jonathan (1 Sam. 20:12–15, 16, 18–23) contain more than a simple plan to determine Saul's intentions toward David. Acknowledging that David will certainly one day be king, Jonathan confirms his covenant commitment to David and desires to protect his own children when David in fact becomes king. He also speaks frankly and prophetically about David's

20 And I will shoot three arrows on the side *thereof,* as though I shot at a mark.

21 And, behold, I will send a lad, *saying,* Go, find out the arrows. If I expressly say unto the lad, Behold, the arrows *are* on this side of thee, take them; then come thou: for *there is* peace to thee, and no hurt; *as* the LORD liveth.

22 But if I say thus unto the young man, Behold, the arrows *are* beyond thee; go thy way: for the LORD hath sent thee away.

23 And *as touching* the matter which thou and I have spoken of, behold, the LORD *be* between thee and me for ever.

CHAPTERS 21–23

David gets help from Ahimelech the priest—He eats the shewbread—He goes to Gath, where he pretends madness.

David gains followers—He goes from one place to another, fleeing from Saul—Saul slays the priests who showed kindness to David.

David smites the Philistines and saves Keilah—He continues to flee from Saul—Jonathan comforts him in Ziph.

future international rule, which is a new theme in the books of Samuel. These speeches of Jonathan have been called 'the thematic centerpiece of the story of Jonathan,' for they legitimize David's rule as the rightful successor to the throne of Israel and underscore the future relationship between the house of Saul and the house of David" (Arnold, *1 and 2 Samuel*, 297).

Summary of 1 Samuel 20:24–42

Jonathan returns home and Saul is angered that David does not accompany him. His anger extends to Jonathan for favoring and protecting David, and he threatens Jonathan's life. Jonathan and David meet again, and take comfort in each other's presence.

Summary of 1 Samuel 21–23

David flees as a fugitive to Nob to escape Saul's attempts to have him killed. He and his companions receive help and food from the priest Ahimelech. While traveling among the Philistines, David feigns insanity to relieve the concerns of those who feared his reputation. He moves his parents to safety so they are beyond Saul's reach. Saul learns of the help David received at Nob and orders the slaughter of the priests there. Abiathar is the only one to survive, and he joins with David for refuge. David and his men deliver the people of Keilah from the Philistines. Saul continues to fail in his efforts to capture David.

CHAPTER 24

David finds Saul in a cave and spares his life—Saul confesses that David is more righteous than he—David swears that he will not cut off the seed of Saul.

1 Samuel 24:1–15. David Refuses to Slay Saul and Pleads for Reconciliation

Where is En-gedi? (24:1) The name denotes "*Fountain of the kid.* [It is] a place on the western shore of the Dead Sea" (Bible Dictionary, "En-gedi"). "En-Gedi has been an oasis in the desert for thousands of years, with immense fountains of water emerging from underground springs. . . . Here is Israel's only waterfall that runs year-round. The water drops nearly 300 feet" (Berrett, *Discovering the World of the Bible*, 431).

"The wilderness of En-gedi was one of two places where David refused to lift up his hand to remove 'the anointed of the Lord'" (Rasmussen, *Latter-day Saint Commentary on the Old Testament*, 249).

1 And it came to pass, when Saul was returned from following the Philistines, that it was told him, saying, Behold, David *is* in the wilderness of En-gedi.

2 Then Saul took three thousand chosen men out of all Israel, and went to seek David and his men upon the rocks of the wild goats.

What are "sheepcotes"? (24:3) They are "sheepfolds; shelters, probably caves with stone walls about the entrance" (see 1 Samuel 24:3*a*).

3 And he came to the sheepcotes by the way, where *was* a cave; and Saul went in to cover his feet: and David and his men remained in the sides of the cave.

Why did David cut off "the skirt of Saul's robe"? (24:4) "Like the elaborately decorated hem on the high priest's garments (Ex 28:33–34), Saul's robe would also have had a distinctive fringe or design marking him as the king. It may have been specially dyed or contained a special stitching reserved only for the king's use, and it symbolized his power and authority" (Walton, et al., *IVP Bible Background Commentary*, 315).

4 And the men of David said unto him, Behold the day of which the LORD said unto thee, Behold, I will deliver thine enemy into thine hand, that thou mayest do to him as it shall seem good unto thee. Then David arose, and cut off the skirt of Saul's robe privily.

5 And it came to pass afterward, that David's heart smote him, because he had cut off Saul's skirt.

6 And he said unto his men, The LORD forbid that I should do this thing unto my master, the LORD's anointed, to stretch forth mine hand against him, seeing he *is* the anointed of the LORD.

What did it mean that David "stayed" his servants? (24:7) "The word is a very strong one and shows that David had to exert [make use of] all his authority" (*John Dummelow's Commentary* [on 1 Samuel 24:7]). David's servants fully believed that the Lord had delivered David's enemy into his hands and would have taken Saul's life for him if needed.

7 So David stayed his servants with these words, and suffered them not to rise against Saul. But Saul rose up out of the cave, and went on *his* way.

8 David also arose afterward, and went out of the cave, and cried after Saul, saying, My lord the king. And when Saul looked behind him,

David stooped with his face to the earth, and
bowed himself.

9 ¶ And David said to Saul, Wherefore hearest thou men's words, saying, Behold, David
seeketh thy hurt?

10 Behold, this day thine eyes have seen how
that the LORD had delivered thee to day into
mine hand in the cave: and *some* bade *me* kill
thee: but *mine eye* spared thee; and I said,
I will not put forth mine hand against my
lord; for he *is* the LORD's anointed.

11 Moreover, my father, see, yea, see the skirt
of thy robe in my hand: for in that I cut off
the skirt of thy robe, and killed thee not,
know thou and see that *there is* neither evil
nor transgression in mine hand, and I have
not sinned against thee; yet thou huntest my
soul to take it.

Why did David refer to Saul as his father? (24:11) "The king himself knows that David has just now had a unique opportunity to kill him, but David refused to seize it. . . . When [David] addresses Saul as 'my father,' he is probably not simply using a term of respect but is reminding the king that he is, after all, Saul's son-in-law (cf. 18:17–27; 22:14) and thus holds him in high regard (Saul will later respond to David as 'my son,' v. 16)" (*Expositor's Bible Commentary [Abridged]*, 529).

12 The LORD judge between me and thee,
and the LORD avenge me of thee: but mine
hand shall not be upon thee.

13 As saith the proverb of the ancients,
Wickedness proceedeth from the wicked: but
mine hand shall not be upon thee.

14 After whom is the king of Israel come
out? after whom dost thou pursue? after a
dead dog, after a flea.

What does this proverb mean? (24:12–15) David used scriptures to try to explain how he saw his relationship with the king. "The meaning of the proverb ['Wickedness proceedeth from the wicked'] is that only a wicked man would seek to do evil against another. Since David did not take advantage of the opportunity to kill Saul, he was most certainly a good man. . . . David likened himself to a *dead dog* and a *flea* in contrast with *the king of Israel*. How could something as worthless as a dead dog or as insignificant as a flea be of any danger to Saul?" (*Nelson Study Bible* [NKJV], 458). David's words and behavior demonstrated that he "places himself in God's hands rather than in Saul's [see v. 15]" (*New Bible Commentary: Revised*, 300).

15 The LORD therefore be judge, and judge
between me and thee, and see, and plead my
cause, and deliver me out of thine hand.

What does this account tell us about David's early character? (24:15) "When I consider this story and the admirable perspective and actions of David, I am awed. I cannot think of another account that compares to this one as an example of honoring an anointed servant of the Lord, even when that servant, by any accounting, did not appear worthy of it" (Crookston, "Natural Blessings of the Law," 4). President Romney added: "It seems to me that David's conduct under these trying circumstances teaches a great lesson on reverence for the priesthood, that is, for bearers of the priesthood who represent the Lord" (Romney, "Reverence," 5).

1 Samuel 24:16–22. Saul Acknowledges That the Lord Is with David

How did Saul know that David would be king? (24:20) "David's behaviour towards [Saul] had conquered for the moment the evil demon of his heart, and completely altered his feelings. In this better state of mind he felt impelled even to give utterance to these words, 'I know that thou wilt be king. . . .' Saul could not prevent this conviction from forcing itself upon him, . . . now that better feelings had arisen in his mind, he uttered it without envy, and merely asked David to promise on oath that he would not cut off his descendants after his death, and seek to exterminate his name from his father's house" (Keil and Delitzsch, *Commentary* [on 1 Samuel 24:20–21]).

16 ¶ And it came to pass, when David had made an end of speaking these words unto Saul, that Saul said, *Is* this thy voice, my son David? And Saul lifted up his voice, and wept.

17 And he said to David, Thou *art* more righteous than I: for thou hast rewarded me good, whereas I have rewarded thee evil.

18 And thou hast shewed this day how that thou hast dealt well with me: forasmuch as when the LORD had delivered me into thine hand, thou killedst me not.

19 For if a man find his enemy, will he let him go well away? wherefore the LORD reward thee good for that thou hast done unto me this day.

20 And now, behold, I know well that thou shalt surely be king, and that the kingdom of Israel shall be established in thine hand.

21 Swear now therefore unto me by the LORD, that thou wilt not cut off my seed after me, and that thou wilt not destroy my name out of my father's house.

22 And David sware unto Saul. And Saul went home; but David and his men gat them up unto the hold.

CHAPTER 25

Samuel dies—Nabal rebuffs David and refuses to give him food—Abigail intercedes, saves Nabal, and gives David a present—David is pacified, Nabal dies, and David marries Abigail.

1 And Samuel died; and all the Israelites were gathered together, and lamented him, and buried him in his house at Ramah. And David arose, and went down to the wilderness of Paran.

1 Samuel 25:1–13. Nabal Chooses to Be Selfish and Indifferent with His Wealth

Why did all Israel lament the death of Samuel? (25:1) "The books of 1 and 2 Samuel cover the time period from the birth of Samuel (shortly before 1125 B.C.) to a period just prior to the death of David (around 1015 B.C.). . . . Against the backdrop of intrigue and pride reflected in the vacillating character of Saul, we perceive the principled ministry of the prophet Samuel as a mirror of divine purpose and truth. . . . The Psalmist remembered Samuel in this inspiring exhortation: 'Exalt ye the Lord our God, and worship at his

2 And *there was* a man in Maon, whose possessions *were* in Carmel; and the man *was* very great, and he had three thousand sheep, and a thousand goats: and he was shearing his sheep in Carmel.

3 Now the name of the man *was* Nabal; and the name of his wife Abigail: and *she was* a woman of good understanding, and of a beautiful countenance: but the man *was* churlish and evil in his doings; and he *was* of the house of Caleb.

4 ¶ And David heard in the wilderness that Nabal did shear his sheep.

5 And David sent out ten young men, and David said unto the young men, Get you up to Carmel, and go to Nabal, and greet him in my name:

6 And thus shall ye say to him that liveth *in prosperity,* Peace *be* both to thee, and peace *be* to thine house, and peace *be* unto all that thou hast.

7 And now I have heard that thou hast shearers: now thy shepherds which were with us, we hurt them not, neither was there ought missing unto them, all the while they were in Carmel.

8 Ask thy young men, and they will shew thee. Wherefore let the young men find favour in thine eyes: for we come in a good day: give, I pray thee, whatsoever cometh to thine hand unto thy servants, and to thy son David.

9 And when David's young men came, they spake to Nabal according to all those words in the name of David, and ceased.

footstool; for he is holy. Moses and Aaron among his priests, and Samuel . . . ; they called upon the Lord, and he answered them' (Psalm 99:5–6)" (Allen and Pinegar, *Old Testament Who's Who*, "Samuel").

What does Nabal mean? (25:2–3) "Names describing personality or temperament might include Nabal ('fool')" (Gaskill, *Lost Language of Symbolism*, 386). "Readers have wondered why parents would name their child 'Fool.' . . . Perhaps it was a later nickname or epithet. It is possible, too, that the name of Abigail's husband was not given in the narrator's sources, so that his true name was not known to the writer (Nabal is first introduced in the text as an anonymous 'man in Maon'; v. 2). . . . Perhaps he took his cue from a line of dialogue traditionally attributed to Abigail ('Fool is his name . . .'; v. 25) and adopted it as an apt designation" (Owen, "Habakkuk Principle," 158–59).

Why was David justified in asking Nabal for assistance? (25:5–9) "Forming an army of six hundred supporters, David . . . strengthened Israel's occupation of the land by protecting the southern boundaries from enemy invasion. For a time David and his men camped in the Judean wilderness near Carmel, the area where Nabal's flocks grazed. Protecting Israel's borders also meant shielding the property of Israelite families from predators and thieves. According to one of Nabal's servants, David's army was 'a wall' of protection for them and was regarded as an exceptional blessing (1 Samuel 25:16). . . . David sent ten of his men to greet Nabal and request a gift for him and his men, . . . in return for their service to his shepherds" (Olson, *Women of the Old Testament*, 202).

Why was David going to take vengeance on Nabal? (25:10–13) "Nabal's rude reply [verse 10] expresses contempt. By implying that they are runaway slaves he insults both David, who escaped from Saul, and his men, who fled from society. . . . David is determined to use force: girding the swords is mentioned three times [verse 13]" (*Jewish Study Bible* [2014], 593).

1 Samuel 25:14–35. Abigail Seeks Out David to Make Restitution for Her Husband's Decisions

How did Abigail react after being told that Nabal insulted David's servants? (25:14–18) "No sooner had David's men gone than one of the servants told Abigail what had happened. He reminded her that David's request was just and went on to speak rather frankly about the master. Obviously, the household had come to rely on Abigail's better judgment. She lost no time making amends. With the safety of her household at stake, she didn't pause to debate the matter or even to inform her husband" (Hurd, *Our Sisters in the Bible*, 74).

Who is Abigail? (25:14) "It will surprise no one familiar with the ironic transformations of biblical scripture if the textbook case of a just man living by his faith turns out to be a just woman, namely Abigail, first the wife of Nabal and then of David. . . . We meet her in 1 Sam. 25, in an episode that is ostensibly the story of a random confrontation and its timely resolution but which then becomes something more consequential, both for Abigail and for the united kingdom of Israel" (Owen, "Habakkuk Principle," 183). ⊕

10 ¶ And Nabal answered David's servants, and said, Who *is* David? and who *is* the son of Jesse? there be many servants now a days that break away every man from his master.

11 Shall I then take my bread, and my water, and my flesh that I have killed for my shearers, and give *it* unto men, whom I know not whence they *be?*

12 So David's young men turned their way, and went again, and came and told him all those sayings.

13 And David said unto his men, Gird ye on every man his sword. And they girded on every man his sword; and David also girded on his sword: and there went up after David about four hundred men; and two hundred abode by the stuff.

14 ¶ But one of the young men told Abigail, Nabal's wife, saying, Behold, David sent messengers out of the wilderness to salute our master; and he railed on them.

15 But the men *were* very good unto us, and we were not hurt, neither missed we any thing, as long as we were conversant with them, when we were in the fields:

16 They were a wall unto us both by night and day, all the while we were with them keeping the sheep.

17 Now therefore know and consider what thou wilt do; for evil is determined against our master, and against all his household: for he *is such* a son of Belial, that *a man* cannot speak to him.

18 ¶ Then Abigail made haste, and took two hundred loaves, and two bottles of wine, and five sheep ready dressed, and five measures of parched *corn,* and an hundred clusters of raisins, and two hundred cakes of figs, and laid *them* on asses.

19 And she said unto her servants, Go on before me; behold, I come after you. But she
told not her husband Nabal.

20 And it was *so, as* she rode on the ass, that
she came down by the covert of the hill,
and, behold, David and his men came down
against her; and she met them.

21 Now David had said, Surely in vain have
I kept all that this *fellow* hath in the wilderness, so that nothing was missed of all that
pertained unto him: and he hath requited me
evil for good.

22 So and more also do God unto the enemies
of David, if I leave of all that *pertain* to him
by the morning light any that pisseth against
the wall.

23 And when Abigail saw David, she hasted,
and lighted off the ass, and fell before David
on her face, and bowed herself to the ground,

24 And fell at his feet, and said, Upon me, my
lord, *upon* me *let this* iniquity *be:* and let thine
handmaid, I pray thee, speak in thine audience, and hear the words of thine handmaid.

25 Let not my lord, I pray thee, regard this
man of Belial, *even* Nabal: for as his name *is,*
so *is* he; Nabal *is* his name, and folly *is* with
him: but I thine handmaid saw not the young
men of my lord, whom thou didst send.

26 Now therefore, my lord, *as* the LORD
liveth, and *as* thy soul liveth, seeing the LORD
hath withholden thee from coming to *shed*
blood, and from avenging thyself with thine
own hand, now let thine enemies, and they
that seek evil to my lord, be as Nabal.

27 And now this blessing which thine handmaid hath brought unto my lord, let it even
be given unto the young men that follow my
lord.

28 I pray thee, forgive the trespass of thine
handmaid: for the LORD will certainly make

What does Abigail's attitude toward David convey? (25:23–28) "When Abigail found David in the wilderness, she bowed before him and humbly asked him to spare her household despite her husband's iniquities. In this account, Abigail is a powerful type, or symbol, of Jesus Christ. Not only does she ask for her household to be spared, but she is also willing to take Nabal's iniquity upon herself and asks for David's forgiveness" (*Old Testament Seminary Student Material* [2019], 449–50). ⊕

How is your life "bound in the bundle of life with the Lord"? (25:29) "The metaphor is taken from the custom of binding up valuable things in a bundle, to prevent their being injured. The words do not refer primarily to eternal life with God in heaven, but only to the safe preservation of the righteous on this earth in the grace and fellowship of the Lord. But whoever is so hidden in the gracious fellowship of the Lord in this life, . . . the Lord will not allow to perish, even though temporal death should come, but will then receive him into eternal life" (Keil and Delitzsch, *Commentary* [on 1 Samuel 25:29]). What does this phrase convey to you? When have you felt the Lord's protection and blessings?

my lord a sure house; because my lord fighteth the battles of the LORD, and evil hath not been found in thee *all* thy days.

29 Yet a man is risen to pursue thee, and to seek thy soul: but the soul of my lord shall be bound in the bundle of life with the LORD thy God; and the souls of thine enemies, them shall he sling out, *as out* of the middle of a sling.

30 And it shall come to pass, when the LORD shall have done to my lord according to all the good that he hath spoken concerning thee, and shall have appointed thee ruler over Israel;

31 That this shall be no grief unto thee, nor offence of heart unto my lord, either that thou hast shed blood causeless, or that my lord hath avenged himself: but when the LORD shall have dealt well with my lord, then remember thine handmaid.

Abigail as a Type of Jesus Christ (1 Samuel 25:18–44)

"What amazing grace! Upon hearing of the wrong committed by another, Abigail raced to gather what the aggrieved—David and his men—had been denied by Nabal's mistreatment. She then sought out David with her gift—to save him from avenging himself, wherewith he would begin to fight his own battles rather than the Lord's, and commit an 'offence of heart' that would keep him from receiving 'all the good that [the Lord had] spoken concerning [him].'

"Upon delivering to David all that he needed and more, thereby atoning for Nabal's sin, she then took Nabal's sin on her own head when she pleaded, 'upon me let this iniquity be.' And then, incredibly to me, in an utterance that teaches us just what it means to take upon oneself the sins of another, she pleaded, 'forgive the trespass of thine handmaid.' Think of it: The one who had done no wrong asked for the mistreated person to forgive her—not Nabal, the actual perpetrator of the wrong, but her! In her mind, as she knelt before David, Nabal's sin was now hers. She had taken it upon her, claiming it as her own.

"'Forgive the trespass of thine handmaid.' No purer words have ever been spoken—except, that is, by Him in whose similitude she uttered them. Consider how closely Abigail's story parallels the Savior's:

- She atoned for the wrong committed by another.
- She provided all that was needed to him who was harmed.
- She took the sinner's iniquity on her own head, even though she herself had done no wrong.
- She pled for the avenger to give up vengeance.
- And . . . she was the means of delivering peace.

"When we think of the Atonement, we most often think about how the Savior filled in the gaps for our own sins, which he surely did. That is, we are all sinners, and someone had to bridge for each of us the otherwise impassable chasm between us and eternal life that we have created through sin. So normally we think of the Atonement as something that Christ has done for us—for ourselves. But Abigail invites us to look at the Atonement from a different angle—not from the perspective of how Christ has atoned for our own sins, but rather from the equally true perspective that he has atoned for the sins of others" (Ferrell, *Hidden Christ*, 167–68).

32 ¶ And David said to Abigail, Blessed *be*
the LORD God of Israel, which sent thee this
day to meet me:

33 And blessed *be* thy advice, and blessed *be*
thou, which hast kept me this day from coming to *shed* blood, and from avenging myself
with mine own hand.

34 For in very deed, *as* the LORD God of
Israel liveth, which hath kept me back from
hurting thee, except thou hadst hasted and
come to meet me, surely there had not been
left unto Nabal by the morning light any that
pisseth against the wall.

35 So David received of her hand *that* which
she had brought him, and said unto her, Go
up in peace to thine house; see, I have hearkened to thy voice, and have accepted thy
person.

36 ¶ And Abigail came to Nabal; and, behold, he held a feast in his house, like the
feast of a king; and Nabal's heart *was* merry
within him, for he *was* very drunken: wherefore she told him nothing, less or more, until
the morning light.

37 But it came to pass in the morning, when
the wine was gone out of Nabal, and his wife
had told him these things, that his heart died
within him, and he became *as* a stone.

38 And it came to pass about ten days *after*,
that the LORD smote Nabal, that he died.

39 ¶ And when David heard that Nabal was
dead, he said, Blessed *be* the LORD, that hath
pleaded the cause of my reproach from the
hand of Nabal, and hath kept his servant
from evil: for the LORD hath returned the
wickedness of Nabal upon his own head. And
David sent and communed with Abigail, to
take her to him to wife.

40 And when the servants of David were
come to Abigail to Carmel, they spake unto

Why did David feel that Abigail had been sent by the Lord? (25:32) "[Abigail] was sinless in the dispute between David and her husband. Yet she took upon herself the sin of her husband to save his life. At the same time, she helped turn David from committing mortal sin. Though both Nabal and David were undeserving, she made intercession for them both. . . . In our lives, we also are sometimes unwise, unjust, and sinful, as Nabal was. We are hasty and quick to judge others—and to exact justice, as David was. The atonement [of Jesus Christ] is for those who are sinful. It is also for those who are sinned against—and who then respond in a sinful way" (Parry and Parry, *Symbols and Shadows*, 95).

1 Samuel: 25:36–44. The Lord's Judgment Falls upon Nabal and Abigail Marries David

What was the fate of Nabal? (25:37) "The scriptural text reports that upon hearing Abigail's report of her generous offering and agreement with David, Nabal 'became as a stone' (1 Samuel 25:37). Did his shock reflect the terror he felt when he realized what might have happened had Abigail not intervened? Was it a reaction to his estimate of assets he had lost to feed David's army a feast? Or was it due to his wife disregarding his law and humiliating him in the face of his enemy? Whatever the cause, Nabal had what was likely a stroke. Ten days later, Nabal died from a second stroke or complications related to his weakened condition (1 Samuel 25:38)" (Olson, *Women of the Old Testament*, 208).

Why is it significant that Abigail was willing to wash the feet of the servants? (25:41) The Lord gave David many wives and concubines. "Abigail, as one of these 'given' wives, consents to it willingly. But here, as all along, her submissiveness seems not primarily to David but to the Lord. 'Behold,' she says, ostensibly to David's men, 'your handmaid will be a menial to wash the feet of my lord's servants.' With the removal of the comma (which does not exist in biblical Hebrew) we have, conceivably, the familiar *Behold your handmaid*. This phrasing might represent the proper feminine reply to the Lord's call" (Owen, "Habakkuk Principle," 154–55).

How were David and Abigail lawfully wedded according to God's law? (25:42) "Although there was no general 'temple marriage' in David's Israel (and as yet no temple), prophets of the Lord held the Melchizedek Priesthood and had the power to seal such ordinances. David, as the Lord's anointed, was married in this way, as the Lord explained to Joseph Smith: 'David's wives and concubines were given unto him of me, by the hand of Nathan, my servant, and others of the prophets who had the keys of this power' (D&C 132:39)" (Owen, "Habakkuk Principle," 155).

What is known of Ahinoam? (25:43) "About the same time as his betrothal to Abigail, David married a woman named Ahinoam and lost his first wife, Michal, to another man (1 Samuel 25:43–44). No account of Ahinoam appears in the Bible, except that she was from Jezreel, a community not far from Nabal's Carmel" (Olson, *Women of the Old Testament*, 209, 213).

Summary of 1 Samuel 26–27

David continues to avoid being captured and killed by Saul. He once again finds himself in a position to take Saul's life, and his servants encourage him to do so. Abishai, one of David's men, tells him that "God hath delivered thine enemy into thine hand this day: now therefore let me smite him, I pray thee" (1 Samuel 26:8). David, still unwilling to shed Saul's blood, commands Abishai, "Destroy him not: for who can stretch forth his hand against the Lord's anointed, and be guiltless?" (1 Samuel 26:9).

To distance himself from Saul, David and his men go live among the Philistines for sixteen months. To retain the Philistine king's favor, David pretends that he has become a traitor while attacking and destroying towns that threaten the people of Israel.

her, saying, David sent us unto thee, to take
thee to him to wife.

41 And she arose, and bowed herself on *her*
face to the earth, and said, Behold, *let* thine
handmaid *be* a servant to wash the feet of the
servants of my lord.

42 And Abigail hasted, and arose, and rode
upon an ass, with five damsels of hers that
went after her; and she went after the messengers of David, and became his wife.

43 David also took Ahinoam of Jezreel; and
they were also both of them his wives.

44 ¶ But Saul had given Michal his daughter, David's wife, to Phalti the son of Laish,
which *was* of Gallim.

CHAPTERS 26–27

David again spares Saul's life—He again refuses to stretch forth his hand against the Lord's anointed—Saul and David separate.

David flees to Achish at Gath—He dwells among the Philistines for sixteen months.

CHAPTER 28

Saul inquires of the witch of Endor for revelation—She foretells his death, the death of his sons, and the defeat of Israel by the Philistines.

1 And it came to pass in those days, that the Philistines gathered their armies together for warfare, to fight with Israel. And Achish said unto David, Know thou assuredly, that thou shalt go out with me to battle, thou and thy men.

2 And David said to Achish, Surely thou shalt know what thy servant can do. And Achish said to David, Therefore will I make thee keeper of mine head for ever.

3 ¶ Now Samuel was dead, and all Israel had lamented him, and buried him in Ramah, even in his own city. And Saul had put away those that had familiar spirits, and the wizards, out of the land.

4 And the Philistines gathered themselves together, and came and pitched in Shunem: and Saul gathered all Israel together, and they pitched in Gilboa.

5 And when Saul saw the host of the Philistines, he was afraid, and his heart greatly trembled.

6 And when Saul inquired of the Lord, the Lord answered him not, neither by dreams, nor by Urim, nor by prophets.

1 Samuel 28:1–20. Saul Lives in a State of Fear and Turns to a False Source for Revelation

Why did Achish place David in a position of trust? (28:1–2) Since David could not trust Saul's conciliatory words (see 1 Samuel 26:21–25), "he fled with six hundred men to the Philistine city of Gath and for sixteen months served Achish, its king. During that time [David] led a series of bloody raids to the south against various Canaanitish peoples" (Turner, "Two Davids," 242). "Because Achish trusted David, he was willing to set him in battle against the Israelites and make him his personal bodyguard," or "captain of the bodyguard" (Rasmussen, *Latter-day Saint Commentary on the Old Testament*, 251; see also 1 Samuel 28:2*a*).

Who were those with familiar spirits that Saul banished from the land? (28:3) "'Familiar spirits' (Leviticus 19:31) connoted those who today would be called spiritualists, or spirit mediums. They supposedly had the power to communicate through a séance with departed spirits. The Hebrew word for *familiar spirit* means 'ventriloquist,' suggesting in the very name itself the fraudulent [fake] character of such people" (*Old Testament Student Manual: Genesis–2 Samuel*, 187). See commentary in this volume for Leviticus 19:31 and Isaiah 29:4.

Why was Saul unable to receive an answer from the Lord? (28:6) Saul had turned from the truth and was disobedient and full of iniquity. "Men and women should become settled in the truth, and founded in the knowledge of the gospel, depending upon no person for borrowed or reflected light, but trusting only upon the Holy Spirit. . . . They will then have light everlasting which cannot be obscured. The only safe way for us to do, as individuals, is to live so humbly, so righteously and so faithfully before God that we may possess his Spirit to that extent that we shall be able to judge righteously, and discern between truth and error, between right and wrong" (*Joseph F. Smith* [manual], 270).

Why did Saul seek guidance from familiar spirits after banning them from Israel? (28:7–8) "It is clear that the woman whom Saul visited was one of the class placed under ban, by the commandment of God, because they practiced divination with familiar spirits [for example, see 1 Samuel 28:3, 6]. . . . Saul had tried every legitimate means to obtain supernatural guidance, but, as he had departed from the Lord, the Lord had departed from him. There was no answer from heaven to his inquiries. . . . In his desperation, Saul turned to the opposite power. In that he sinned. He knew that he was violating the law of the Lord. . . . When he fell into darkness he sought the ways of darkness and sealed his own doom" (Smith, *Answers to Gospel Questions*, 4:105). ⊕

What was happening as this woman appeared to speak to the deceased prophet Samuel? (28:11–15) "After Saul had assured the woman that he would not disclose her, she agreed to bring up Samuel. Upon doing so she recognized Saul and was again assured of her safety by him. Samuel then spoke to Saul. However, from the Joseph Smith Translation account it appears to be a false spirit representing Samuel, although the message is not false. . . . The Lord does not give messages through false mediums, but the devil might give true messages in order to deceive. Because the JST says it is the 'words of Samuel' instead of Samuel himself, it suggests that there was probably deception" (Nyman, "Joseph Smith Translation's Doctrinal Contributions," 65–66). ⊕

Why is this account of Samuel appearing to Saul doctrinally incorrect? (28:15) "When God has anything to reveal, it will come in the way, by the means and through the persons whom he has appointed. . . . By permission of the Lord, persons on either side of the veil may be manifest to those on the other,

7 ¶ Then said Saul unto his servants, Seek
me a woman that hath a familiar spirit, that
I may go to her, and inquire of her. And
his servants said to him, Behold, *there is* a
woman that hath a familiar spirit at En-dor.
8 And Saul disguised himself, and put on
other raiment, and he went, and two men
with him, and they came to the woman by
night: and he said, I pray thee, divine unto
me by the familiar spirit, and bring me *him*
up, whom I shall name unto thee.
9 And the woman said unto him, Behold,
thou knowest what Saul hath done, how he
hath cut off those that have familiar spirits,
and the wizards, out of the land: wherefore
then layest thou a snare for my life, to cause
me to die?
10 And Saul sware to her by the LORD, saying, *As* the LORD liveth, there shall no punishment happen to thee for this thing.
11 Then said the woman, Whom shall I
bring up unto thee? And he said, Bring me
up Samuel.
12 And when the woman saw Samuel, she
cried with a loud voice: and the woman spake
to Saul, saying, Why hast thou deceived me?
for thou *art* Saul.
13 And the king said unto her, Be not afraid:
for what sawest thou? And the woman said
unto Saul, I saw gods ascending out of the
earth.
14 And he said unto her, What form *is* he of?
And she said, An old man cometh up; and he
is covered with a mantle. And Saul perceived
that it *was* Samuel, and he stooped with *his*
face to the ground, and bowed himself.
15 ¶ And Samuel said to Saul, Why hast
thou disquieted me, to bring me up? And
Saul answered, I am sore distressed; for the
Philistines make war against me, and God
is departed from me, and answereth me no

more, neither by prophets, nor by dreams:
therefore I have called thee, that thou mayest
make known unto me what I shall do.

16 Then said Samuel, Wherefore then dost
thou ask of me, seeing the LORD is departed
from thee, and is become thine enemy?

17 And the LORD hath done to him, as he
spake by me: for the LORD hath rent the
kingdom out of thine hand, and given it to
thy neighbour, *even* to David:

18 Because thou obeyedst not the voice of
the LORD, nor executedst his fierce wrath
upon Amalek, therefore hath the LORD done
this thing unto thee this day.

19 Moreover the LORD will also deliver Israel
with thee into the hand of the Philistines:
and to morrow *shalt* thou and thy sons *be*
with me: the LORD also shall deliver the host
of Israel into the hand of the Philistines.

20 Then Saul fell straightway all along on
the earth, and was sore afraid, because of the
words of Samuel: and there was no strength
in him; for he had eaten no bread all the day,
nor all the night.

but this will certainly be by law and according to the order which God has established. By observing that law and refraining from association with persons and influences that know not God and obey not his gospel, the Latter-day Saints will save themselves from subtle deception and much sorrow, and will be more susceptible to the light and inspiration and revelations that proceed from the Eternal Father!" (Smith, *Answers to Gospel Questions*, 4:110).

How can we avoid living in a state of fear like Saul? (28:20) "Perhaps our Heavenly Father's greatest hope is that through our fears we may choose to turn to him. The uncertainties of earth life can help to remind each of us that we are dependent on him. But that reminder is not automatic. It involves our agency. We must choose to take our fears to him, choose to trust him, and choose to allow him to direct us. . . . As we try to live his commandments and pray to him, there are things he will direct us to do that will help calm our fears. These actions often require great courage and direction from the Holy Ghost" (Pearce, "Fear," 90).

Summary of 1 Samuel 28:21–25

The witch of Endor takes note of Saul's weak physical state and prepares a meal for him and his servants. After rest and a meal, they leave her home later that night.

Summary of 1 Samuel 29–31

As Israel prepares for battle with the Philistines, David and his army successfully defeat the Amalekites. In David's absence, the long-awaited battle with the Philistines takes place and they defeat Israel. Three of Saul's sons, including Jonathan, are killed in the battle. Saul hears of his sons' deaths and falls on his own sword. In a show of strength, the Philistines nail the bodies of Saul and his sons to a city wall. Courageous Gileadites retrieve their bodies and Israel mourns.

CHAPTERS 29–31

Israel and the Philistines gather for war—The Philistine princes send David away.

The Amalekites spoil Ziklag and the borders of Judah—David smites Amalek and regains and divides the spoil.

The Philistines defeat Israel—Saul and his three sons are slain—Their bodies are retrieved by the Gileadites and burned.

THE SECOND BOOK OF
SAMUEL
OTHERWISE CALLED THE SECOND BOOK OF THE KINGS

Introduction

The unnamed author of the second book of Samuel lists the following sources from which the book was written: "'The acts of David the king, first and last, behold, they *are* written in the book of Samuel the seer, and in the book of Nathan the prophet, and in the book of Gad the seer' [1 Chronicles 29:29]. Using these memoirs, the unknown author was able to record an accurate and insightful history of the establishment of the Israelite monarchy" (Pearson, *Old Testament*, 39). "Samuel was originally one book that was divided into two when the Hebrew text was translated into Greek, to accommodate the work to the length of scrolls typically used in classical antiquity" (*Dictionary for Theological Interpretation of the Bible*, 717). "Second Samuel recounts the triumphs and defeats of King David. From [David's] rise to the throne to his famous last words, this biography describes a remarkable, divinely inspired leader. As king, David took a divided and defeated Israel from his predecessor King Saul and built a prominent nation. . . . Like most political biographies, 2 Samuel highlights the character traits that enabled David to succeed—his reliance on God for guidance (2:1), his sincerity (5:1–5), and his courage (5:6, 7). But the book also describes the tragic consequences of David's lust (12:1–23) and pride (24:1–17)" (*Nelson Study Bible* [NKJV], 505). "Though there is a great deal of historical material, the overriding concern of [this book] is to establish the national and religious significance of Israel's decision to be governed by mortal kings. . . . The story of the kings points out the tragic fact that even excellent kings can fall, thus leaving people in extreme jeopardy" (Pearson, *Old Testament*, 40).

CHAPTER 1

David learns of the death of Saul and Jonathan—He slays the Amalekite who claims to have killed Saul—David laments the passing of Saul and Jonathan with a song.

1 Now it came to pass after the death of Saul, when David was returned from the slaughter of the Amalekites, and David had abode two days in Ziklag;

2 It came even to pass on the third day, that, behold, a man came out of the camp from Saul with his clothes rent, and earth upon his head: and *so* it was, when he came to David, that he fell to the earth, and did obeisance.

2 Samuel 1:1–12. David Mourns the Death of Saul and Jonathan

Where do we learn of David's battle with the Amalekites? (1:1) "There is no break between the two books of Samuel; they really form one continuous narrative. This [verse] is a continuation of 1 Samuel 30, which describes David's successful attack upon [the Amalekites who had conquered] Ziklag." (*John Dummelow's Commentary* [on 2 Samuel 1:1]).

Why was this Amalekite stranger present at the battle between Israel and the Philistines? (1:2–10) "It is not necessary to conclude from v. 3 that this Amalekite was a member of Saul's army. His statement that he 'happened to be on Mount Gilboa' (v. 6) is probably not as innocent as it appears. He may have been there as a scavenger to rob the fallen soldiers of their valuables and weapons. It is ironic that Saul's death is reported by an Amalekite (see 1 Sa 15)" (*NIV Study Bible* [1995], 419).

3 And David said unto him, From whence comest thou? And he said unto him, Out of the camp of Israel am I escaped.

4 And David said unto him, How went the matter? I pray thee, tell me. And he answered, That the people are fled from the battle, and many of the people also are fallen and dead; and Saul and Jonathan his son are dead also.

5 And David said unto the young man that told him, How knowest thou that Saul and Jonathan his son be dead?

6 And the young man that told him said, As I happened by chance upon mount Gilboa, behold, Saul leaned upon his spear; and, lo, the chariots and horsemen followed hard after him.

7 And when he looked behind him, he saw me, and called unto me. And I answered, Here *am* I.

8 And he said unto me, Who *art* thou? And I answered him, I *am* an Amalekite.

9 He said unto me again, Stand, I pray thee, upon me, and slay me: for anguish is come upon me, because my life *is* yet whole in me.

10 So I stood upon him, and slew him, because I was sure that he could not live after that he was fallen: and I took the crown that *was* upon his head, and the bracelet that *was* on his arm, and have brought them hither unto my lord.

11 Then David took hold on his clothes, and rent them; and likewise all the men that *were* with him:

12 And they mourned, and wept, and fasted until even, for Saul, and for Jonathan his son, and for the people of the LORD, and for the house of Israel; because they were fallen by the sword.

13 ¶ And David said unto the young man that told him, Whence *art* thou? And he answered, I *am* the son of a stranger, an Amalekite.

14 And David said unto him, How wast thou not afraid to stretch forth thine hand to destroy the LORD's anointed?

15 And David called one of the young men, and said, Go near, *and* fall upon him. And he smote him that he died.

16 And David said unto him, Thy blood *be* upon thy head; for thy mouth hath testified against thee, saying, I have slain the LORD's anointed.

2 Samuel 1:13–16. David Condemns the Young Amalekite to Death because He Claims to Have Killed the Lord's Anointed

Why would David punish this Amalekite for killing Saul, David's enemy? (1:15–16) "[The] messenger is offering [David] a self-serving fiction, or at best an embroidered version of the truth. . . . David asks the messenger about his origins. . . . As soon as he admits his race and his action, he loses the protection that belonged to a resident alien. His death is a further example of David propagating the doctrine that [Jehovah's] anointed must remain inviolate. . . . The Amalekite may or may not have done what he claimed, and all he claimed was to have administered the coup de grâce. But, for David's purposes, he had done what David had twice refrained from doing" (Auld, "2 Samuel," 230).

17 ¶ And David lamented with this lamentation over Saul and over Jonathan his son:

18 (Also he bade them teach the children of Judah *the use of* the bow: behold, *it is* written in the book of Jasher.)

2 Samuel 1:17–27. David Writes a Poetic Song, or "Psalm," about the Deaths of Saul and Jonathan

What was the instruction regarding the "bow"? (1:18) "The Hebrew wording of this statement in parenthesis is incomplete. A possible translation to convey the idea is: 'And he said to teach the sons of Judah (the Song of) the Bow. Behold, it is written in the book of Jasher'" (Ludlow, *Companion to Your Study of the Old Testament*, 221). "The use of the bow (v. 18) could be rendered 'the song of the bow.' Perhaps David taught his men to sing this lament while they practiced the bow (Israel's most common weapon; see, e.g., 22:35) as a motivation to master the weapon thoroughly so they would not experience a similar defeat" (*Zondervan KJV Commentary*, 414).

What was the book of Jasher? (1:18) "The Israelites apparently kept the *Book of Jashar* to record the exploits of their national heroes. The account of Joshua's defeat of the Amorites on the day the sun stood still (Joshua 10:13), for example quotes this book. . . . Although the *Book of Jashar* was familiar to David's contemporaries, it has not survived to modern times" (*Quest Study Bible* [1994], 401). "Various other collections of the book of Jasher are available today and may be of some worth but do not appear to be the one spoken of in the Bible" (Bible Dictionary, "Jasher, book of").

Who were the "mighty" that were fallen? (1:19) "'How are the mighty fallen!' (2 Sam. 1:19). These were the words David used as a refrain in his exquisite lament over the father and son whom he had reverenced as the 'Lord's anointed.' It is ironic that the same words could characterize his own later life. . . . The lament over the death of Saul and Jonathan, the beautiful historical poem in the midst of this prose history, may be compared to some of the loveliest psalms" (Madsen, "David, the King of Israel," 293). ⊕

Given that Saul and Jonathan had divided loyalties, how did they remain so close? (1:23) "Notwithstanding their difference of character, and the very opposite attitude which they assumed towards David, the noble Jonathan did not forsake his father, although his fierce hatred towards the friend whom Jonathan loved as his own soul might have undermined his attachment to his father. The two predicates, בהאנ, loved and amiable, and םיענ, affectionate or kind, apply chiefly to Jonathan; but they were also suitable to Saul in the earliest years of his reign, when he manifested the virtues of an able ruler, which secured for him the lasting affection and attachment of the people" (Keil and Delitzsch, *Commentary* [on 2 Samuel 1:23–24]). ⊕

What type of love did David have for Jonathan? (1:26) "When men receive the everlasting Gospel and the Priesthood, there is a love begotten in their hearts for their fellowmen such as they never have felt before. Like the love of Jonathan for David. . . . It is a love that comes from God. It is the love of the Holy Ghost, the love of purity, the love of truth, the love that we would have for holy beings—a part of the love that we have for God Himself and for our Lord and Savior Jesus. This love unites them together with a bond and strength of affection that was never known before" (Cannon, *Gospel Truth*, 298–99).

19 The beauty of Israel is slain upon thy high places: how are the mighty fallen!

20 Tell *it* not in Gath, publish *it* not in the streets of Askelon; lest the daughters of the Philistines rejoice, lest the daughters of the uncircumcised triumph.

21 Ye mountains of Gilboa, *let there be* no dew, neither *let there be* rain, upon you, nor fields of offerings: for there the shield of the mighty is vilely cast away, the shield of Saul, *as though he had* not *been* anointed with oil.

22 From the blood of the slain, from the fat of the mighty, the bow of Jonathan turned not back, and the sword of Saul returned not empty.

23 Saul and Jonathan *were* lovely and pleasant in their lives, and in their death they were not divided: they were swifter than eagles, they were stronger than lions.

24 Ye daughters of Israel, weep over Saul, who clothed you in scarlet, with *other* delights, who put on ornaments of gold upon your apparel.

25 How are the mighty fallen in the midst of the battle! O Jonathan, *thou wast* slain in thine high places.

26 I am distressed for thee, my brother Jonathan: very pleasant hast thou been unto me: thy love to me was wonderful, passing the love of women.

27 How are the mighty fallen, and the weapons of war perished!

CHAPTER 2

David is anointed king over the house of Judah—Ishbosheth becomes the king of Israel—David's followers defeat Abner and the men of Israel.

1 And it came to pass after this, that David inquired of the LORD, saying, Shall I go up into any of the cities of Judah? And the LORD said unto him, Go up. And David said, Whither shall I go up? And he said, Unto Hebron.

2 So David went up thither, and his two wives also, Ahinoam the Jezreelitess, and Abigail Nabal's wife the Carmelite.

3 And his men that *were* with him did David bring up, every man with his household: and they dwelt in the cities of Hebron.

4 And the men of Judah came, and there they anointed David king over the house of Judah. And they told David, saying, *That* the men of Jabesh-gilead *were they* that buried Saul.

2 Samuel 2:1–4. The People of Judah Make David Their King

Why did the Lord choose Hebron for the site of David's anointing as king? (2:1–4) "David asked divine guidance when accession to his great responsibility was imminent. Apparently he desired to know where first to proclaim his kingship and was told to go to Hebron. It was sacred as the home of father Abraham and was central to the territory of Judah. When the ten northern tribes were won over, a more central capital was chosen.

"No information is recorded about how the people of Judah were assembled or how the anointing was administered. Only a single verse tells of the inauguration, and it also tells of David's learning that Gileadites from Jabesh-gilead had buried the bodies of Saul and his sons (2 Sam. 2:4*a-c*)" (Rasmussen, *Latter-day Saint Commentary on the Old Testament*, 256).

Why was David anointed twice to become king? (2:4) "Almost immediately after the death of Saul, David became king over his own tribe of Judah. Whereas, Samuel had anointed David to become king, the men of Judah anointed David in Hebron to be their king (2 Sam 2:4). However, he would have to fight a long and bitter war against Saul's surviving son Ishbaal/Ish-bosheth and his followers to reunify the kingdom. David assembled an army and successfully fought and defeated Ishbaal/Ish-bosheth, who was killed. Seven years after the death of Saul, David was proclaimed and anointed king over all of Israel, again in Hebron (2 Sam 5:3)" (Holzapfel, et al., *Jehovah and the World of the Old Testament*, 206). See commentary in this volume for 1 Samuel 10:1 and Leviticus 8:12.

5 ¶ And David sent messengers unto the men of Jabesh-gilead, and said unto them, Blessed *be* ye of the LORD, that ye have shewed this kindness unto your lord, *even* unto Saul, and have buried him.

6 And now the LORD shew kindness and truth unto you: and I also will requite you this kindness, because ye have done this thing.

2 Samuel 2:5–13. Abner Makes Saul's Son Ish-bosheth the King over the Rest of Israel

Who was "Ish-bosheth"? (2:8) "Ish-bó-sheth [means] 'man of shame.' . . . The youngest of Saul's four sons[,] . . . Ishbosheth was the only son who survived his father, his three brothers being slain with Saul in the battle of Gilboa" (*New Unger's Bible Dictionary* [2005], 631). "In I Chron. [8:33; 9:39] the name is *Eshbaal,* i.e. 'man of the lord,' and there is little doubt that this was his original name. In later years, because of the association of the name Baal with the Canaanite deities and their worship, *bosheth* 'shame' was substituted for Baal. Cf. the substitution of Mephibosheth for Merib-baal ([4:4]; I Chron. [8:34]) and Jerubbesheth for Jerubbaal ([11:21]; Judg. [8:35])" (Goldman, *Samuel*, 194). ⊕

How can we reconcile the lengths of David's and Ish-Bosheth's reigns? (2:10–11) "David reigned in Hebron *seven years and six months* (v. 11). Compare Ish-bosheth's two-year reign in Mahanaim (v. 10). Because it appears that David was made king over all Israel shortly after Ish-bosheth's death (5:1–5) and moved his capital to Jerusalem not long afterward (5:6–12), reconciling the lengths of David's and Ish-bosheth's reigns is difficult. The difficulty is best resolved by assuming that it took Ish-bosheth a number of years to be recognized as his father's successor and that the two years of his reign roughly correspond to the last two or three years of David's reign in Hebron" (*Zondervan KJV Commentary*, 415–16).

Who was Joab? (2:13) Joab was the "eldest son of Zeruiah, David's sister, and captain of David's army. He was closely associated with all the chief events of David's reign, and was generally faithful to his master" (Bible Dictionary, "Joab") He was "the dominant figure in David's regime, to whom more than any other David owed the success of his reign. . . . Though loyal to David's throne, [Joab] appears to have been politically shrewder and more forceful than David, and he turned his position as commander-in-chief into an independent power base within the kingdom. . . . [Joab] takes responsibility for killing David's rebellious son [Absalom] himself—against direct royal orders (2 Sam. 18:9–15)" (*Eerdmans Dictionary of the Bible*, 714–15). Joab is ultimately executed for conspiracy against Solomon. ⊕

7 Therefore now let your hands be strengthened, and be ye valiant: for your master Saul is dead, and also the house of Judah have anointed me king over them.

8 ¶ But Abner the son of Ner, captain of Saul's host, took Ish-bosheth the son of Saul, and brought him over to Mahanaim;

9 And made him king over Gilead, and over the Ashurites, and over Jezreel, and over Ephraim, and over Benjamin, and over all Israel.

10 Ish-bosheth Saul's son *was* forty years old when he began to reign over Israel, and reigned two years. But the house of Judah followed David.

11 And the time that David was king in Hebron over the house of Judah was seven years and six months.

12 ¶ And Abner the son of Ner, and the servants of Ish-bosheth the son of Saul, went out from Mahanaim to Gibeon.

13 And Joab the son of Zeruiah, and the servants of David, went out, and met together by the pool of Gibeon: and they sat down, the one on the one side of the pool, and the other on the other side of the pool.

CHAPTERS 3–4

The houses of David and Saul engage in a long war—David grows stronger—Abner joins David but is slain by Joab—David mourns for Abner.

Two of Saul's captains slay Ishbosheth—They take his head to David, who has them slain for killing a righteous person.

CHAPTER 5

All Israel anoints David king—He takes Jerusalem and is blessed of the Lord—He conquers the Philistines.

1 Then came all the tribes of Israel to David unto Hebron, and spake, saying, Behold, we *are* thy bone and thy flesh.

2 Also in time past, when Saul was king over us, thou wast he that leddest out and broughtest in Israel: and the LORD said to thee, Thou shalt feed my people Israel, and thou shalt be a captain over Israel.

3 So all the elders of Israel came to the king to Hebron; and king David made a league with them in Hebron before the LORD: and they anointed David king over Israel.

Summary of 2 Samuel 2:14–32

The struggle for control of the country begins in Gibeon when twelve of Abner's soldiers face twelve of Joab's soldiers in a contest of hand-to-hand combat. All twenty-four soldiers kill one another. Following this contest, hostility increases between the two armies.

Summary of 2 Samuel 3–4

David leads Judah in a long war against Israel. Abner senses the waning of his power against Judah and vows to deliver the northern tribes to David if he can regain Michal as his wife. Joab considers Abner to be a spy and has him killed. David curses the house of Joab and honors Abner as a great man in Israel. Two of Israel's army commanders assassinate Ishbosheth thinking to gain a reward from King David. However, David honors the fallen Ishbosheth by having the two men executed.

"David showed great wisdom and judgment by executing the two men who killed Ishbosheth. Although he was at war with Ishbosheth, David did not condone the treachery of the assassins and put them to death. His wisdom and goodness finally united the tribes into one kingdom loyal to David" (*Old Testament Student Manual: Genesis–2 Samuel*, 288).

2 Samuel 5:1–3. All Israel Gathers in Hebron before the Lord to Anoint David King

What did the tribes of Israel mean by claiming they were David's "bone" and "flesh"? (5:1) "The word *bone* is used to denote a familial relationship between two parties, both in a physical and spiritual sense. After the rib was taken from Adam, he said, referring to Eve, 'This is now bone of my bones, and flesh of my flesh' (Gen. 2:23). . . . It was the twelve tribes of Israel who made the claim to King David, 'Behold, we are thy bone and thy flesh' (2 Sam. 5:1)" (McConkie and Parry, *Guide to Scriptural Symbols*, 23). ⊕

What did David's anointing represent? (5:3) "Anointing signified several things. First, it indicated a change of status or setting apart to a divinely inspired calling. Second, anointing was a symbol of purification. . . . Third, anointing was a symbol of consecration—or the making of something or someone 'holy.' . . . Fourth, anointing was often connected with the Spirit" (Holzapfel, et al., *Jehovah and the World of the Old Testament*, 197). "As David had earlier been anointed king over Judah (2:4), so now he is anointed king over Israel, 'as the Lord had promised through Samuel' (1 Ch. 11:3). The news of the anointing would soon become well enough known to cause concern in the hearts of the Philistines (v. 17)" (*Expositor's Bible Commentary [Abridged]*, 443). See commentary in this volume for 1 Samuel 10:1 and Leviticus 8:12.

2 Samuel 5:4–12. David Conquers the City of Jerusalem, and It Becomes the Capital City of His Nation

4 ¶ David *was* thirty years old when he began to reign, *and* he reigned forty years.

5 In Hebron he reigned over Judah seven years and six months: and in Jerusalem he reigned thirty and three years over all Israel and Judah.

6 ¶ And the king and his men went to Jerusalem unto the Jebusites, the inhabitants of the land: which spake unto David, saying, Except thou take away the blind and the lame, thou shalt not come in hither: thinking, David cannot come in hither.

7 Nevertheless David took the strong hold of Zion: the same *is* the city of David.

8 And David said on that day, Whosoever getteth up to the gutter, and smiteth the Jebusites, and the lame and the blind, *that are* hated of David's soul, *he shall be chief and captain.* Wherefore they said, The blind and the lame shall not come into the house.

9 So David dwelt in the fort, and called it the city of David. And David built round about from Millo and inward.

10 And David went on, and grew great, and the LORD God of hosts *was* with him.

11 ¶ And Hiram king of Tyre sent messengers to David, and cedar trees, and carpenters, and masons: and they built David an house.

12 And David perceived that the LORD had established him king over Israel, and that he had exalted his kingdom for his people Israel's sake.

Why did David select Jerusalem as the new capital of the kingdom? (5:6) "[Jerusalem] had very large walls, a spring that was protected by a massive gate with even more massive towers, and it sat on a hill with steep, essentially unassailable, valleys on three sides. . . . David determined to conquer the city and make it his capital. The history of the world was changed with this decision, for Jerusalem became arguably the most important city in the world from that time" (Muhlestein, *Scripture Study Made Simple*, 212). ⊕

What was "the gutter" referred to in this passage? (5:8) "The Bible quotes David as saying, 'Whoever would smite the Jebusites, let him touch the *tsinnor* [usually translated "watershaft"]' (2 Samuel 5:8). That Warren's Shaft—named for the British explorer and engineer who discovered it in 1867—is the much-disputed *tsinnor* was a viable suggestion until [studies] in the 1980s proved . . . that the Warren's Shaft system was not created until . . . long after David's conquest of the city" (Faust, "Warren's Shaft," 70). "Canaanites were constructing water-shafts several centuries before David's assault on the Jebusite fortress at Jerusalem. It is certainly reasonable therefore that there may well have been such a water-shaft in existence in Jebusite Jerusalem" (Kleven, "Up the Waterspout," 34–35). It may be that Joab used a Canaanite water-shaft.

Who was Hiram, the king of Tyre? (5:11–12) "About midway between present-day Beirut and Haifa in Israel was the port city of Tyre, one of the ancient and most important cities of the Phoenicians. The name *Hiram* appears to have been the family name for a king or series of kings of Tyre who were contemporaries of David and Solomon. Best known of these Hirams is he who sent masons, carpenters, and cedars from Lebanon to build David's palace in Jerusalem (see

13 ¶ And David took *him* more concubines
and wives out of Jerusalem, after he was
come from Hebron: and there were yet sons
and daughters born to David.

14 And these *be* the names of those that were
born unto him in Jerusalem; Shammua, and
Shobab, and Nathan, and Solomon,

15 Ibhar also, and Elishua, and Nepheg, and
Japhia,

16 And Elishama, and Eliada, and Eliphalet.

17 ¶ But when the Philistines heard that they
had anointed David king over Israel, all the
Philistines came up to seek David; and David
heard *of it,* and went down to the hold.

18 The Philistines also came and spread
themselves in the valley of Rephaim.

19 And David inquired of the LORD, saying,
Shall I go up to the Philistines? wilt thou deliver them into mine hand? And the LORD
said unto David, Go up: for I will doubtless
deliver the Philistines into thine hand.

20 And David came to Baal-perazim, and
David smote them there, and said, The LORD
hath broken forth upon mine enemies before
me, as the breach of waters. Therefore he
called the name of that place Baal-perazim.

2 Samuel 5:11; 1 Chronicles 14:1). Later, Solomon was greatly assisted in the building of the temple in Jerusalem by this same Hiram, or another of the same name (see 1 Kings 9; 2 Chronicles 2)" (*Old Testament Student Manual: Genesis–2 Samuel*, 289).

2 Samuel 5:13–16. David Takes More Concubines and Wives

Who authorized David to take additional wives and concubines? (5:13–16) "The polygamy of patriarchal times was still practiced, especially by rulers, and David exercised that prerogative (a comment on which is made in modern scripture, D&C 132:38–39)" (Rasmussen, *Latter-day Saint Commentary on the Old Testament*, 259). The Lord revealed: "David also received many wives and concubines . . . as also many others of my servants . . . and in nothing did they sin save in those things which they received not of me. David's wives and concubines were given unto him of me, by the hand of Nathan, my servant" (D&C 132:38–39).

2 Samuel 5:17–20. The Philistines Learn That David Has Been Anointed King of Israel

Why did the Philistines view David as a threat? (5:17–18) "There is no indication that the Philistines interfered with David's ascendancy as king in Hebron. It is possible that they simply regarded him as a vassal as long as the rest of Israel, being torn by civil warfare, offered no unified resistance.

"But they became alarmed when David gained the acceptance of the whole nation. A Philistine attack ([2 Sam.] 5:17–25 and [1 Chron.] 14:8–17) very likely took place before the conquest and occupation of Zion. Twice David defeated them, thus preventing their interference in the unification of Israel under the new king" (Schultz, *Old Testament Speaks*, 131).

Summary of 2 Samuel 5:21–25

Through the Lord's direction and help, David and his armies defeat the Philistines. David's men capture the Philistine idols and burn them.

2 Samuel 6:1–9. The Israelites Do Not Follow the Lord's Instructions While Moving the Ark of the Covenant

What was the "ark of God"? (6:2) The Ark of the Covenant, "also known as the Ark of Jehovah and the Ark of the Testimony [was] an oblong chest of acacia or shittim wood overlaid with gold, [2.5] cubits long, [1.5] broad and high, made by Moses at God's command (Ex. 25). It was the oldest and most sacred of the religious symbols of the Israelites, and the Mercy Seat which formed its covering was regarded as the earthly dwelling place of Jehovah (Ex. 25:22)" (Bible Dictionary, "Ark of the Covenant").

What does it mean to try to "steady the ark"? (6:3–7) "The ark of the covenant was a sacred vessel that housed some of the holiest objects in Israel's history. To touch the ark or its contents was strictly forbidden by the Lord. Only authorized Levites, and they only under certain specified conditions, could handle the sacred instruments (see Numbers 4:15). Uzzah may have exhibited some bold presumption when he sought to touch that which God had forbidden to be touched. Even if Uzzah's intention was simply to keep the ark from falling, it should be remembered that God was fully capable of steadying His own ark had He wished to do so" (*Old Testament Student Manual: Genesis–2 Samuel*, 289). ⊕

CHAPTER 6

David takes the ark to the city of David—Uzzah is smitten for steadying the ark and dies—David dances before the Lord, causing a breach between him and Michal.

1 Again, David gathered together all *the* chosen *men* of Israel, thirty thousand.

2 And David arose, and went with all the people that *were* with him from Baale of Judah, to bring up from thence the ark of God, whose name is called by the name of the LORD of hosts that dwelleth *between* the cherubims.

3 And they set the ark of God upon a new cart, and brought it out of the house of Abinadab that *was* in Gibeah: and Uzzah and Ahio, the sons of Abinadab, drave the new cart.

4 And they brought it out of the house of Abinadab which *was* at Gibeah, accompanying the ark of God: and Ahio went before the ark.

5 And David and all the house of Israel played before the LORD on all manner of *instruments made of* fir wood, even on harps,

How Can the Story of Uzzah Serve as a Warning Today? (2 Samuel 6:3–7)

"The story of Uzzah, who aided the men of Israel in the transport of the ark to Jerusalem, illustrates an important lesson for Latter-day Saints. The Lord had specified that the ark was always to be carried by the poles and only by duly authorized persons. . . . The disregard for the Lord's established order brought judgment upon Israel and Uzzah" (Brandt, "What Was the Ark of the Covenant, and Does It Exist in Any Form Today?" 50).

President David O. McKay taught: "It is a little dangerous for us to go out of our own sphere and try unauthoritatively to direct the efforts of a brother. You remember the case of Uzzah who stretched forth his hand to steady the ark [see 1 Chronicles 13:7–10]. He seemed justified when the oxen stumbled in putting forth his hand to steady that symbol of the covenant. We today think his punishment was very severe. Be that as it may, the incident conveys a lesson of life. Let us look around us and see how quickly men who attempt unauthoritatively to steady the ark die spiritually. Their souls become embittered, their minds distorted, their judgment faulty, and their spirit depressed. Such is the pitiable condition of men who, neglecting their own responsibilities, spend their time in finding fault with others" (in Conference Report, Apr. 1936, 60).

and on psalteries, and on timbrels, and on cornets, and on cymbals.

6 ¶ And when they came to Nachon's threshingfloor, Uzzah put forth *his hand* to the ark of God, and took hold of it; for the oxen shook *it.*

7 And the anger of the LORD was kindled against Uzzah; and God smote him there for *his* error; and there he died by the ark of God.

8 And David was displeased, because the LORD had made a breach upon Uzzah: and he called the name of the place Perez-uzzah to this day.

9 And David was afraid of the LORD that day, and said, How shall the ark of the LORD come to me?

10 So David would not remove the ark of the LORD unto him into the city of David: but David carried it aside into the house of Obed-edom the Gittite.

11 And the ark of the LORD continued in the house of Obed-edom the Gittite three months: and the LORD blessed Obed-edom, and all his household.

12 ¶ And it was told king David, saying, The LORD hath blessed the house of Obed-edom, and all that *pertaineth* unto him, because of the ark of God. So David went and brought up the ark of God from the house of Obed-edom into the city of David with gladness.

13 And it was *so,* that when they that bare the ark of the LORD had gone six paces, he sacrificed oxen and fatlings.

14 And David danced before the LORD with all *his* might; and David *was* girded with a linen ephod.

15 So David and all the house of Israel brought up the ark of the LORD with shouting, and with the sound of the trumpet.

2 Samuel 6:10–23. The Ark of the Covenant Is Moved to Jerusalem, David's City

Where are some of the places the Ark of the Covenant has resided? (6:10–12) The Lord blessed Obed-edom during the time that the ark remained in his house. Then "[the ark] was brought by David to Jerusalem, the journey being interrupted at Perezuzzah (2 Sam. 6; 1 Chr. 13:11). In Jerusalem it was placed in a separate tent, which David pitched for it (2 Sam. 7:2; 1 Chr. 16:1). It accompanied the army in the war against Ammon (2 Sam. 11:11)... .On the completion of Solomon's temple it was placed in the Holy of Holies (1 Kgs. 8:1–8).... It had certainly disappeared before the building of the second temple. It was seen by John in his vision of heaven (Rev. 11:19)" (Bible Dictionary, "Ark of the Covenant").

Why did David want to move the ark to Jerusalem? (6:12) David saw the house of Obed-edom being blessed while the ark resided there. He therefore transferred it to Jerusalem. "In the transfer of the ark to Jerusalem [the prophet Nathan; 2 Sam. 2:1–17] saw a climax of a long sequence of events that began in the wilderness of Transjordan when Moses first promised the children of Israel 'rest from their enemies all around' (Deut.12:10).... The ark's arrival in Jerusalem, therefore, is a critical moment in this larger design: [Jehovah's] name is in its place and Israel is soon to have the promised 'rest from all [her] enemies' (7:11)" (McCarter, *II Samuel*, 174, 175). ⊕

Why was Michal offended by David's celebration of the return of the ark of the covenant? (6:16) "When the ark came (*i.e.* was carried) into the city of David, Michal the daughter of Saul looked out of the window, and there she saw king David leaping and dancing before Jehovah, and despised him in her heart. . . . Michal is intentionally designated the daughter of Saul here, instead of the wife of David, because on this occasion she manifested her father's disposition rather than her husband's. In Saul's time people did not trouble themselves about the ark of the covenant [1 Chronicles13:3]; public worship was neglected, and the soul for vital religion had died out in the family of the king" (Keil and Delitzsch, *Commentary* [on 2 Samuel 6:16]). ⊕

16 And as the ark of the LORD came into the city of David, Michal Saul's daughter looked through a window, and saw king David leaping and dancing before the LORD; and she despised him in her heart.

17 ¶ And they brought in the ark of the LORD, and set it in his place, in the midst of the tabernacle that David had pitched for it: and David offered burnt offerings and peace offerings before the LORD.

18 And as soon as David had made an end of offering burnt offerings and peace offerings, he blessed the people in the name of the LORD of hosts.

19 And he dealt among all the people, *even* among the whole multitude of Israel, as well to the women as men, to every one a cake of bread, and a good piece *of flesh,* and a flagon *of wine.* So all the people departed every one to his house.

20 ¶ Then David returned to bless his household. And Michal the daughter of Saul came out to meet David, and said, How glorious was the king of Israel to day, who uncovered himself to day in the eyes of the handmaids of his servants, as one of the vain fellows shamelessly uncovereth himself!

21 And David said unto Michal, *It was* before the LORD, which chose me before thy father, and before all his house, to appoint me ruler over the people of the LORD, over Israel: therefore will I play before the LORD.

22 And I will yet be more vile than thus, and will be base in mine own sight: and of the maidservants which thou hast spoken of, of them shall I be had in honour.

23 Therefore Michal the daughter of Saul had no child unto the day of her death.

CHAPTER 7

David offers to build a house for the Lord—The Lord, through Nathan, says He has not asked David to do so—The Lord will establish David's house and kingdom forever—David offers a prayer of thanksgiving.

1 And it came to pass, when the king sat in his house, and the LORD had given him rest round about from all his enemies;

2 That the king said unto Nathan the prophet, See now, I dwell in an house of cedar, but the ark of God dwelleth within curtains.

3 And Nathan said to the king, Go, do all that *is* in thine heart; for the LORD *is* with thee.

4 ¶ And it came to pass that night, that the word of the LORD came unto Nathan, saying,

5 Go and tell my servant David, Thus saith the LORD, Shalt thou build me an house for me to dwell in?

6 Whereas I have not dwelt in *any* house since the time that I brought up the children of Israel out of Egypt, even to this day, but have walked in a tent and in a tabernacle.

7 In all *the places* wherein I have walked with all the children of Israel spake I a word with any of the tribes of Israel, whom I commanded to feed my people Israel, saying, Why build ye not me an house of cedar?

8 Now therefore so shalt thou say unto my servant David, Thus saith the LORD of hosts, I took thee from the sheepcote, from following the sheep, to be ruler over my people, over Israel:

9 And I was with thee whithersoever thou wentest, and have cut off all thine enemies out of thy sight, and have made thee a great name, like unto the name of the great *men* that *are* in the earth.

2 Samuel 7:1–11. David Desires to Build a Temple unto the Lord

Why did Nathan change his position regarding David's request to build the Lord's temple? (7:1–3)

"The scriptures do not teach a doctrine of prophetic infallibility. When David told Nathan that he had decided to build a temple, Nathan said, 'Go, do all that is in thine heart; for the Lord is with thee.' That night Nathan learned that the Lord did not want David to build the temple, for that privilege was to be reserved for David's son. Nathan then reversed himself on the matter (2 Samuel 7:3–16)" (McConkie, *Prophets and Prophecy*, 78).

What was the "house" the Lord promised David? (7:11) The phrase *He will make thee an house* "is a pun on the two meanings of the word *house*—'dwelling place' and 'dynasty.' . . . The [verse] promises David an eternal seed without mentioning a house, but the [writer] chooses this word deliberately to show that if God requires a house, it will not be one made with human hands but one consisting of human lives and of his own fashioning. Whether this prophecy was intended to be read messianically we cannot say; but it was clearly susceptible of such an interpretation" (*Interpreter's Bible*, 2:1084).

2 Samuel 7:12–17. David's Son Will Build the House of the Lord

Why was David denied the opportunity to build the Lord's house? (7:12–13) "David's motivation for wanting to build a permanent house for the Lord (the tabernacle built by Moses in the wilderness was then about three hundred years old) was proper and good, but the Lord, through Nathan, denied him permission to do so. No specific reason was given here, only a blessing on David's house. In the account in Chronicles, however, David told Solomon that it was revealed to him that he had seen too much war and bloodshed to build the house of the Lord (see 1 Chronicles 22:8)" (*Old Testament Student Manual: Genesis–2 Samuel*, 289–90). ⊕

How was David's throne to be "established for-ever"? (7:16) "This verse is an example of a dualistic prophecy, that is, a prophecy with a double meaning. . . . It promised that David's lineage would continue on the throne, and unlike Saul's lineage, would not be overthrown after his death. But it is clearly a Messianic prophecy as well. Jesus, the Messiah, was called David, He would hold the key of David, and He would sit upon the throne of David. Clearly, only one person can sit upon the throne of David (that is, rule over the house

10 Moreover I will appoint a place for my people Israel, and will plant them, that they may dwell in a place of their own, and move no more; neither shall the children of wickedness afflict them any more, as beforetime,

11 And as since the time that I commanded judges *to be* over my people Israel, and have caused thee to rest from all thine enemies. Also the LORD telleth thee that he will make thee an house.

12 ¶ And when thy days be fulfilled, and thou shalt sleep with thy fathers, I will set up thy seed after thee, which shall proceed out of thy bowels, and I will establish his kingdom.

13 He shall build an house for my name, and I will stablish the throne of his kingdom for ever.

14 I will be his father, and he shall be my son. If he commit iniquity, I will chasten him with the rod of men, and with the stripes of the children of men:

15 But my mercy shall not depart away from him, as I took *it* from Saul, whom I put away before thee.

16 And thine house and thy kingdom shall be established for ever before thee: thy throne shall be established for ever.

17 According to all these words, and according to all this vision, so did Nathan speak unto David.

CHAPTER 8

David defeats and subjects many nations—The Lord is with him—He executes judgment and justice unto all his people.

CHAPTER 9

David seeks to honor the house of Saul—He finds Mephibosheth, the son of Jonathan, to whom he restores all the land of Saul.

of Israel) forever and ever, and that one is Christ. He came into mortality as a descendant of David and as an heir to his throne both physically and spiritually" (*Old Testament Student Manual: Genesis–2 Samuel*, 290). ⊕

Summary of 2 Samuel 7:18–29

David meditates before the Lord thanking Him for His goodness and blessings. He states there is "none like thee, neither is there any God beside thee" (v. 22). David further testifies that "the Lord of hosts is the God over Israel: and thy servant David will be established forever" (v. 26).

Summary of 2 Samuel 8

David's victories that extended the boundaries of the kingdom are listed. He dedicates the riches obtained through war to the Lord. The record states, "And David reigned over all Israel; and [he] executed judgment and justice unto all his people" (v. 15).

Summary of 2 Samuel 9

David desires to find Saul's family members so he can bless them and keep the covenant he made with Jonathan. The covenant stated: "Thou shalt not cut off thy kindness from my house for ever: no, not when the Lord had cut off the enemies of David every one from the face of the earth. So Jonathan made a covenant with the house of David, saying, Let the Lord even require it at the hand of David's enemies. And Jonathan caused David to swear again, because he loved him: for he loved him as he loved his own soul" (1 Samuel 20:14–17). David restores the property of Saul to Mephibosheth, the son of Jonathan, who was the only surviving male descendant of Saul. In addition, David

The Davidic Covenant and the House of David (2 Samuel 7:16)

"When David asked Nathan the prophet to inquire of the Lord if he could build a permanent house for the Ark of the Lord, he received an answer which stunned him. To the related question about building a temple he was told that his descendant would build it (2 Sam. 7:12–13). But the Lord went on to promise David: 'Thine house and *thy kingdom shall be established for ever* before thee: *thy throne shall be established for ever'* (2 Sam. 7:16). This has come to be known as the Davidic Covenant and is reiterated in many other places (see 2 Sam. 23:5; Isa. 9:7; 55:3–4)" (Madsen, "David, the King of Israel," 303).

"The biblical description of the covenant made with David seems markedly different from the one Jehovah made with Moses and the Israelites. The Mosaic covenant was based on revealed law, with blessings for obedience and curses for disobedience. Scholars, however, describe the Davidic covenant as a royal grant, modeled on an ancient Near Eastern practice in which a king gifted land or some other favor to a loyal subject. The biblical text gives little evidence that David, having already proved his loyalty to Jehovah, had to do more than accept God's seemingly unconditional gift of kingship" (Holzapfel, et al., *Jehovah and the World of the Old Testament,* 207).

makes provisions for him to eat at the kings' table "as one of the kings' sons" (v. 11). Mephibosheth's servants would take care of the land, but Jonathan's son would always be cared for in a special manner. This story illustrates David's generosity and efforts to honor his friend Jonathan.

Summary of 2 Samuel 10

After Nahash, king of Ammon, dies, David chooses to be kind to his son Hanun because Nahash had showed kindness to him. Therefore, David sends servants to Hanun to honor him, but Hanun's princes think David's servants are spies. In turn, Hanun ridicules and embarrasses David's servants by shaving off half of their beards and cutting off a portion of their garments. When David learns of Hanun's offenses, he sends Joab, the commander of his military forces, to go to battle against the Ammonites and the Syrians. After a great battle the Ammonites and Syrians retreat and their kings make peace with David.

2 Samuel 11:1–13. David Commits Adultery with Bathsheba

How did David defile himself when he chose to tarry at Jerusalem? (11:1) "There are so many ways to keep the shielding seventh commandment firmly in place. Instructively, for instance, David's fall, at least in part, was facilitated because he was not where duty lay. . . . Then, as you know, came the lustful view from the roof and all the sadness that followed. Implicit, therefore, in the instruction 'Stand ye in holy places' [D&C 87:8] is to avoid indulgent tarrying" (Maxwell, "Seventh Commandment," 79). ⊕

Why should we be quick to recognize and avoid temptation? (11:2–3) "[David] was on a rooftop courtyard of his palace, and looking below in a neighboring yard, he saw something he never should have seen. That was the adversary's bait. Modesty, chastity, and good judgment required that David turn away immediately and not watch, but he didn't do either thing. Instead, he allowed his mind to turn to forbidden fantasies, those thoughts led to actions, and things quickly spiraled downward from bad to worse to fatal. David was trapped, and for him the consequences were eternal" (Clayton, "Blessed Are the Pure in Heart," 52). When has controlling your thoughts helped you avoid temptation? ⊕

CHAPTER 10

David's messengers are abused by the Ammonites —Israel defeats the Ammonites and Syrians.

CHAPTER 11

David lies with Bathsheba, and she conceives— He then arranges for the death in battle of her husband, Uriah.

1 And it came to pass, after the year was expired, at the time when kings go forth *to battle,* that David sent Joab, and his servants with him, and all Israel; and they destroyed the children of Ammon, and besieged Rabbah. But David tarried still at Jerusalem.

2 ¶ And it came to pass in an eveningtide, that David arose from off his bed, and walked upon the roof of the king's house: and from the roof he saw a woman washing herself; and the woman *was* very beautiful to look upon.

3 And David sent and inquired after the woman. And *one* said, *Is* not this Bath-sheba, the daughter of Eliam, the wife of Uriah the Hittite?

4 And David sent messengers, and took her; and she came in unto him, and he lay with her; for she was purified from her uncleanness: and she returned unto her house.

5 And the woman conceived, and sent and told David, and said, I *am* with child.

What was Bathsheba's role in her adultery with David? (11:4) "Did Bathsheba want to come? Was she forced or seduced? Did she raise no objection on moral grounds? Perhaps she was not a faithful wife. The commentaries variously speculate that she might have been afraid to say nay to the king, or she might have been flattered to be asked. . . . The story has nothing to say on the subject. It does not raise Bathsheba's feelings or opinions as an issue" (Segal, "II Samuel," 120). ⊕

6 ¶ And David sent to Joab, *saying,* Send me Uriah the Hittite. And Joab sent Uriah to David.

Who was Uriah? (11:6) "Uriah the Hittite was one of David's mighty men ([2 Samuel] 23:39). The name Uriah means 'Flame of the Lord' or 'The Lord is Light.' The fact that he is called a Hittite suggests that he may have been a foreign mercenary who had become a worshiper of Israel's God. Immediately, a contrast is set before the reader. On the one hand there was David, the Lord's anointed, the regent of God on earth. On the other hand there was Uriah, a convert—a man who was not born in the faith of Israel, but who willingly chose it for his own" (*NKJV Study Bible* [2007], 487).

7 And when Uriah was come unto him, David demanded *of him* how Joab did, and how the people did, and how the war prospered.

8 And David said to Uriah, Go down to thy house, and wash thy feet. And Uriah departed out of the king's house, and there followed him a mess *of meat* from the king.

9 But Uriah slept at the door of the king's house with all the servants of his lord, and went not down to his house.

10 And when they had told David, saying, Uriah went not down unto his house, David said unto Uriah, Camest thou not from *thy* journey? why *then* didst thou not go down unto thine house?

11 And Uriah said unto David, The ark, and Israel, and Judah, abide in tents; and my lord Joab, and the servants of my lord, are encamped in the open fields; shall I then go into mine house, to eat and to drink, and to lie with my wife? *as* thou livest, and *as* thy soul liveth, I will not do this thing.

Why did David send for Uriah? (11:7–13) "Uriah, Bathsheba's husband, was brought home from the battle field. He is mentioned earlier as one of David's hand-picked thirty mighty men (1 Chron. 11:41). The tragic irony of the situation is obvious. While Uriah, David's loyal soldier, was fighting for his master in enemy territory, David was taking Uriah's wife. This irony was heightened by Uriah's refusal to sleep with his wife when he returned home. When Israel went to war the warriors consecrated themselves to continence. While the war lasted they remained consecrated in this way. Even after David tried to overcome his resistance by drink, Uriah would not go in to Bathsheba. Uriah's loyalty foiled David's strategy" (Madsen, "David, the King of Israel," 306).

12 And David said to Uriah, Tarry here to day also, and to morrow I will let thee depart. So Uriah abode in Jerusalem that day, and the morrow.

13 And when David had called him, he did eat and drink before him; and he made him drunk: and at even he went out to lie on his bed with the servants of his lord, but went not down to his house.

2 Samuel 11:14–27. David Causes the Death of Uriah

Who was Joab? (11:14) See commentary in this volume for 2 Samuel 2:13.

What was David's plan for Uriah? (11:15) "It is chilling how easily cover-up plan shifts to murder plot. As before, it begins with a message from David to Joab, but this time Uriah must carry the cruel order for his own death (v. 14). The letter orders Joab to place Uriah in the midst of heavy fighting and withdraw support (v. 15). Thus Uriah is to be given a hero's death in battle. He is to be honored in death for the sake of preserving David's honor in life. . . . God's anointed king has become an agent of death. Self-interested use of power has led David into a deadly chain of events from seizure to deception to death" (Birch, "First and Second Books of Samuel," 2:1287). ⊕

14 ¶ And it came to pass in the morning, that David wrote a letter to Joab, and sent *it* by the hand of Uriah.

15 And he wrote in the letter, saying, Set ye Uriah in the forefront of the hottest battle, and retire ye from him, that he may be smitten, and die.

16 And it came to pass, when Joab observed the city, that he assigned Uriah unto a place where he knew that valiant men *were*.

17 And the men of the city went out, and fought with Joab: and there fell *some* of the people of the servants of David; and Uriah the Hittite died also.

18 ¶ Then Joab sent and told David all the things concerning the war;

19 And charged the messenger, saying, When thou hast made an end of telling the matters of the war unto the king,

20 And if so be that the king's wrath arise, and he say unto thee, Wherefore approached ye so nigh unto the city when ye did fight? knew ye not that they would shoot from the wall?

Why did Joab give this instruction to the messenger? (11:21) Joab didn't follow David's orders exactly, and many other valiant soldiers were killed along with Uriah. "The reference is to Judges 9:50–57, where in the siege of Thebez Abimelech went so close to the wall that a woman was able to kill him by hurling an upper millstone on top of him. Joab, the military commander, knew better than to go close to the wall, but he had had to do so in response to the king's command; now the king must take the blame.

21 Who smote Abimelech the son of Jerubbesheth? did not a woman cast a piece of a millstone upon him from the wall, that he died in Thebez? why went ye nigh the wall? then say thou, Thy servant Uriah the Hittite is dead also.

22 ¶ So the messenger went, and came and shewed David all that Joab had sent him for.

23 And the messenger said unto David, Surely the men prevailed against us, and came out unto us into the field, and we were upon them even unto the entering of the gate.

24 And the shooters shot from off the wall upon thy servants; and *some* of the king's servants be dead, and thy servant Uriah the Hittite is dead also.

25 Then David said unto the messenger, Thus shalt thou say unto Joab, Let not this thing displease thee, for the sword devoureth one as well as another: make thy battle more strong against the city, and overthrow it: and encourage thou him.

26 ¶ And when the wife of Uriah heard that Uriah her husband was dead, she mourned for her husband.

27 And when the mourning was past, David sent and fetched her to his house, and she became his wife, and bare him a son. But the thing that David had done displeased the LORD.

The fact that a woman was involved is subtly hinted at by Joab, who has formed his own interpretation of David's activities in Jerusalem. He is not mistaken" (Baldwin, *1 and 2 Samuel*, 250).

What was David's response to the news that Uriah had been killed? (11:25) "In his reply David fails to register any of the anger expected of him by Joab. Instead he takes the losses in his stride as part of the cost of the war, refusing to take notice of the inference that he had initiated the situation by his orders concerning Uriah. 'David poses as Joab's mild and understanding superior. However, in [14, 15] we have already been informed about the man behind this mask, and therefore v. 25 sounds all the more cynical and merciless' [Fokkelman, *Narrative Art and Poetry in the Books of Samuel*, 63]. By saying to Joab, *Do not let this matter trouble you* ('displease thee'. . .), David is at the same time speaking to himself and placating his own conscience" (Baldwin, *1 and 2 Samuel*, 251).

What do we know about the eternal consequences of David's sins? (11:27) "Suppose a man violates his covenants by committing a heinous sin and afterwards humbly . . . forsakes it and seeks forgiveness with all his heart; . . . what will be required of him? . . . David committed a dreadful crime, and all his life afterwards sought for forgiveness. . . . [Yet] David is still paying for his sin. He did not receive the resurrection at the time of the resurrection of Jesus Christ. . . . The Prophet Joseph Smith has said, 'David sought repentance at the hand of God carefully with tears, for the murder of Uriah; but he could only get . . . a promise that his soul should not be left in hell' (*Teachings of the Prophet Joseph Smith*, 229)" (Smith, *Answers to Gospel Questions*, 1:73).

2 Samuel 12:1–14. The Prophet Nathan Confronts David with His Sins

Who was Nathan? (12:1) Nathan was the "Hebrew prophet who lived in the reigns of David and Solomon. The first mention of him is in a consultation with David, in which he advises him to build the Temple (2 Sam. 7:2–3); but after a vision he informed David that he was not to carry out his intention (vv. 4–17) . . .

"About a year after David's sin with Bathsheba and the death of Uriah, Nathan comes forth to reprove him. The reason for this delay seems to be set forth by David in Ps. 32, where he describes the state of his heart during this period and the sufferings he endured while trying to conceal his crime" (*New Unger's Bible Dictionary*, 905). See commentary for 2 Samuel 7:1–3 in this volume.

Why did Nathan use a parable of the ewe lamb to confront David? (12:1–4) "The parable Nathan used was well chosen, for it appealed to David's upbringing as a shepherd boy. Since we know David risked his life for his sheep, we can imagine him caring for little lambs the way the poor shepherd was described in Nathan's parable. This imagery would surely catch David's attention and passion, making it all the more powerful as a device designed to force David to look at the reality of his serious sin" (Muhlestein, *Scripture Study Made Simple*, 216).

What did David learn from Nathan's parable of the lamb? (12:7–9) "King David learned in a most powerful way the injury that adultery inflicts upon others, both the transgressors and the innocent victims. . . .With the parable of the lamb, Nathan rebuked David's abominable sins and showed him that as terrible as it would be to steal a poor man's prized ewe, it was far, far worse to steal another man's wife" (Top, *Peculiar Treasure*, 48, 49).

"While in [2 Samuel] 7 the Lord out of grace promised him an enduring house, here he announces

CHAPTER 12

Nathan tells David the parable of the ewe lamb—The Lord gave many wives to David, who is now cursed for taking Bathsheba—David fasts and prays for his son, but the Lord takes him—Solomon is born—David conquers the royal city of the Ammonites.

1 And the LORD sent Nathan unto David. And he came unto him, and said unto him, There were two men in one city; the one rich, and the other poor.

2 The rich *man* had exceeding many flocks and herds:

3 But the poor *man* had nothing, save one little ewe lamb, which he had bought and nourished up: and it grew up together with him, and with his children; it did eat of his own meat, and drank of his own cup, and lay in his bosom, and was unto him as a daughter.

4 And there came a traveller unto the rich man, and he spared to take of his own flock and of his own herd, to dress for the wayfaring man that was come unto him; but took the poor man's lamb, and dressed it for the man that was come to him.

5 And David's anger was greatly kindled against the man; and he said to Nathan, *As* the LORD liveth, the man that hath done this *thing* shall surely die:

6 And he shall restore the lamb fourfold, because he did this thing, and because he had no pity.

7 ¶ And Nathan said to David, Thou *art* the man. Thus saith the LORD God of Israel, I anointed thee king over Israel, and I delivered thee out of the hand of Saul;

8 And I gave thee thy master's house, and thy master's wives into thy bosom, and gave thee the house of Israel and of Judah; and if *that had been* too little, I would moreover have given unto thee such and such things.

9 Wherefore hast thou despised the commandment of the Lord, to do evil in his sight? thou hast killed Uriah the Hittite with the sword, and hast taken his wife *to be* thy wife, and hast slain him with the sword of the children of Ammon.

10 Now therefore the sword shall never depart from thine house; because thou hast despised me, and hast taken the wife of Uriah the Hittite to be thy wife.

11 Thus saith the Lord, Behold, I will raise up evil against thee out of thine own house, and I will take thy wives before thine eyes, and give *them* unto thy neighbour, and he shall lie with thy wives in the sight of this sun.

12 For thou didst *it* secretly: but I will do this thing before all Israel, and before the sun.

13 And David said unto Nathan, I have sinned against the Lord. And Nathan said unto David, The Lord also hath put away thy sin; thou shalt not die.

14 Howbeit, because by this deed thou hast given great occasion to the enemies of the Lord to blaspheme, the child also *that is* born unto thee shall surely die.

15 ¶ And Nathan departed unto his house. And the Lord struck the child that Uriah's wife bare unto David, and it was very sick.

16 David therefore besought God for the child; and David fasted, and went in, and lay all night upon the earth.

17 And the elders of his house arose, *and went* to him, to raise him up from the earth:

that David for his own deeds will experience misery in his house, for David has *despised* the Lord [2 Samuel 13:10] and the word of the Lord [13:9]" (Tsumura, *Second Book of Samuel*, 189).

What was the curse Nathan pronounced upon David? (12:10–11) "David's rather callous message to Joab, 'the sword sometimes consumes one way and sometimes another' [2 Sam. 11:25], is now thrown back in his face. The story of David's sons, not to speak of his descendants and later generations, will in fact turn out to be a long tale of conspiracy, internecine struggle, and murder. One of the most extraordinary features of the whole David narrative is that the story of the founding of the great dynasty of Judah is, paradoxically, already a tale of the fall of the house of David" (Alter, *Hebrew Bible*, 2:353).

In what way had the Lord "put away" David's sin? (12:13) The footnote for this verse points out that David was not immediately punished with death, as the law dictated, but neither did he escape punishment. In the Joseph Smith Translation, the Prophet changed this verse to read: "The Lord also hath *not* put away thy sin *that* thou shalt not die" (2 Sam. 12:13*b*). "David prayed that his soul would not be left forever in 'hell.' . . . That hope is provided by our divine Redeemer, who raises every soul from the disembodied state by resurrection. But the eternal state of resurrected souls differs according to worthiness" (Rasmussen, *Latter-day Saint Commentary on the Old Testament*, 264). See commentary for 2 Samuel 11:27 in this volume.

2 Samuel 12:15–23. David and Bathsheba's Newborn Son Dies

What does the writer of this incident want readers to understand? (12:15–19) "It should be noted . . . that the writer has contrived to repeat 'dead' five times, together with one use of the verb 'died,' in these two verses: the [inescapable] bleak fact of death is hammered home to us just before David's grim acceptance of it" (Alter, *Hebrew Bible*, 2:354). "The opening of this bitter story leaves no room for doubt: 'The Lord struck the child that Uriah's wife bore to David and it became very ill. . . . The death that David brought to another family now enters his own. In the view of this narrator, there was a cost to be paid, and the Lord is the agent exacting the moral cost of David's deathly crimes" (Birch, "First and Second Books of Samuel," 1297). ⊕

Why did David lay upon the earth as he fasted? (12:16) "Although Nathan said the child would die ([2 Samuel] 12:14), David agonized in prayer and fasting for his son's life. When the Lord took his son, David was bereft but not bitter. He accepted God's will in contentment and came into the house of the Lord, and worshipped (v. 20). In this way, David clearly demonstrated his humble acceptance of the disciplinary results of his sin. . . .

"David's fasting and weeping were not signs of grief but expressions of his repentance and supplication to God that He would spare the child's life. When the child died, David accepted the will of the Lord" (*Zondervan KJV Commentary*, 432).

Why didn't David appear to mourn the death of his son? (12:20–23) "Custom dictates that mourning should begin, with its attendant lamentation and ceremonies of grief. Instead of these practices, David begins a series of purposeful actions not usually associated with the time of mourning (v. 20). The verbs dominate the story: David rose, washed, anointed himself, changed clothes, entered the house of the Lord, worshiped, went to his own house, requested food, and ate. In short, David resumed his life and the practices of his customary routines. . . . David accepted the reality of death and rejected fasting and weeping in favor of relinquishment and resumption of life" (Birch, "First and Second Books of Samuel," 1297). ⊕

What do we learn of David in this verse? (12:23) "If the episode of Bathsheba and Uriah is the great turning point of the David story, these haunting words are the pivotal moment in the turning point. . . . Every instance of David's speech in the preceding narrative has been crafted to serve political ends. . . . Now, after the dire curse pronounced by Nathan . . . is fulfilled . . . , David speaks for the first time not out of political need but of existential nakedness. . . . The words he utters have a stark simplicity . . . and his recognition of the irreversibility of his son's death also makes him think of his own mortality" (Alter, *Hebrew Bible*, 2:355). ⊕

but he would not, neither did he eat bread with them.

18 And it came to pass on the seventh day, that the child died. And the servants of David feared to tell him that the child was dead: for they said, Behold, while the child was yet alive, we spake unto him, and he would not hearken unto our voice: how will he then vex himself, if we tell him that the child is dead?

19 But when David saw that his servants whispered, David perceived that the child was dead: therefore David said unto his servants, Is the child dead? And they said, He is dead.

20 Then David arose from the earth, and washed, and anointed *himself,* and changed his apparel, and came into the house of the LORD, and worshipped: then he came to his own house; and when he required, they set bread before him, and he did eat.

21 Then said his servants unto him, What thing *is* this that thou hast done? thou didst fast and weep for the child, *while it was* alive; but when the child was dead, thou didst rise and eat bread.

22 And he said, While the child was yet alive, I fasted and wept: for I said, Who can tell *whether* GOD will be gracious to me, that the child may live?

23 But now he is dead, wherefore should I fast? can I bring him back again? I shall go to him, but he shall not return to me.

2 Samuel 12:24–25. David and Bathsheba Have Another Son and Name Him Solomon

24 ¶ And David comforted Bath-sheba his wife, and went in unto her, and lay with her: and she bare a son, and he called his name Solomon: and the LORD loved him.

25 And he sent by the hand of Nathan the prophet; and he called his name Jedidiah, because of the LORD.

Why did David name his son Solomon? (12:24–25) "David named his son Solomon, which could mean 'peaceful.' But the Lord sent Nathan the prophet to give the newborn son the name Jedediah, meaning 'beloved of the Lord' (*Tyndale New Bible Dictionary*, s.v. "Solomon," 1127)" (Valletta, et al., *Old Testament for Latter-day Saint Families*, 306).

2 Samuel 12:26–31. David Conquers the Capital City of the Ammonites

26 ¶ And Joab fought against Rabbah of the children of Ammon, and took the royal city.

Where was Rabbah? (12:26) "A strong place on the [east] of the Jordan, which, when its name is first introduced in the sacred records, was the chief city of the Ammonites. In five passages (Deut. 3:11; 2 Sam. 12:26; 17:27; Jer. 49:2; Ezek. 21:20) it is called Rabbah of the sons of Ammon; elsewhere (Josh. 13:25; 2 Sam. 11:1; 12:27, 29; 1 Chron. 20:1; Jer. 49:3; Ezek. 25:5; Amos 1:14) simply Rabbah. . . . Rabbah was made the main point of attack, Joab in command (2 Sam. 11:1); and after a siege, probably of two years, it was taken (12:26–29; 1 Chron. 20:1). We are not told whether the city was demolished or whether David was satisfied with the slaughter of its inhabitants" (*New Unger's Bible Dictionary*, 1058).

27 And Joab sent messengers to David, and said, I have fought against Rabbah, and have taken the city of waters.

28 Now therefore gather the rest of the people together, and encamp against the city, and take it: lest I take the city, and it be called after my name.

29 And David gathered all the people together, and went to Rabbah, and fought against it, and took it.

What is the "city of waters"? (12:27–29) The phrase "city of waters" alludes to "the lower town of Rabbah, on the Jabbok. It received this name because of a perennial stream which rises within it and which still flows through it" (*John Dummelow's Commentary* [on 2 Samuel 12:27]). ⊕

30 And he took their king's crown from off his head, the weight whereof *was* a talent of gold with the precious stones: and it was *set* on David's head. And he brought forth the spoil of the city in great abundance.

Why was the crown of the Ammonite king placed on David's head? (12:30) "The transfer of the crown from the head of the Ammonite king (whose name is not mentioned now, despite its repetition in 2 Sam. 10:1–5) to the head of David symbolized the transfer of power over Ammon to the Israelite king. The weight of the gold (the *talent* was about 30 kg, or 66 lb) and the crown jewel were indicative of the splendour of

Ammon's throne" (Baldwin, *1 and 2 Samuel*, 262). "A crown of such weight . . . would have been worn only briefly and on very special occasions. Perhaps it was worn only once in a symbolic act of transferring to David sovereignty over Ammon" (*NIV Study Bible*, 480).

What does it mean that the Ammonites were placed "under saws, and under harrows of iron"? (12:31) "The population was subjected to forced labour, not to torture, as used to be thought. . . . A century ago the traditional interpretation was questioned. It has now become the generally accepted view that forced labour, not torture, is implied by the text; the various tools and occupations suggest that David set up building projects throughout Ammonite territory. These would be needed in order to repair the fortifications damaged in the recent fighting, and probably also to house his own garrisons, whose task it would be to keep the conquered people subservient" (Baldwin, *1 and 2 Samuel*, 262–63).

31 And he brought forth the people that *were* therein, and put *them* under saws, and under harrows of iron, and under axes of iron, and made them pass through the brickkiln: and thus did he unto all the cities of the children of Ammon. So David and all the people returned unto Jerusalem.

CHAPTER 13

Amnon desires Tamar, his sister, and forces her—He is slain by Absalom's command—Absalom flees to Geshur.

Summary of 2 Samuel 13:1–18

Amnon desires his half-sister Tamar. Through Jonadab's subtle and wicked strategy, Amnon deceives his father, David, and commits a grievous sin by violently forcing himself on Tamar, against her will.

2 Samuel 13:19–29. Absalom Slays Amnon for His Wickedness

Why did Tamar put ashes on her head? (13:19) "Tamar's sense of desolation was every bit as great as if she were in mourning, hence the expressions of grief that everyone she met could see and hear. At least there was for her no unhealthy repression of wounded feelings, though her future was bleak. Her face daubed with [ashes] (cf. 1 Sam. 4:12), her torn robe (cf. 2 Sam. 1:2) and her loud crying eloquently depicted grievous loss; *she laid her hand on her head* is a gesture mentioned in Jeremiah 2:37 [symbolizing shame], but in reliefs and tomb paintings it appears to symbolize captivity" (Baldwin, *1 and 2 Samuel*, 266).

19 ¶ And Tamar put ashes on her head, and rent her garment of divers colours that *was* on her, and laid her hand on her head, and went on crying.

20 And Absalom her brother said unto her, Hath Amnon thy brother been with thee? but hold now thy peace, my sister: he *is* thy brother; regard not this thing. So Tamar remained desolate in her brother Absalom's house.

21 ¶ But when king David heard of all these things, he was very wroth.

22 And Absalom spake unto his brother Amnon neither good nor bad: for Absalom hated Amnon, because he had forced his sister Tamar.

23 ¶ And it came to pass after two full years, that Absalom had sheepshearers in Baalhazor, which *is* beside Ephraim: and Absalom invited all the king's sons.

24 And Absalom came to the king, and said, Behold now, thy servant hath sheepshearers; let the king, I beseech thee, and his servants go with thy servant.

25 And the king said to Absalom, Nay, my son, let us not all now go, lest we be chargeable unto thee. And he pressed him: howbeit he would not go, but blessed him.

26 Then said Absalom, If not, I pray thee, let my brother Amnon go with us. And the king said unto him, Why should he go with thee?

27 But Absalom pressed him, that he let Amnon and all the king's sons go with him.

28 ¶ Now Absalom had commanded his servants, saying, Mark ye now when Amnon's heart is merry with wine, and when I say unto you, Smite Amnon; then kill him, fear not: have not I commanded you? be courageous, and be valiant.

29 And the servants of Absalom did unto Amnon as Absalom had commanded. Then all the king's sons arose, and every man gat him up upon his mule, and fled.

30 ¶ And it came to pass, while they were in the way, that tidings came to David, saying, Absalom hath slain all the king's sons, and there is not one of them left.

31 Then the king arose, and tare his garments, and lay on the earth; and all his servants stood by with their clothes rent.

What were Absalom's motives for killing Amnon? (13:28–29) "Tamar's full brother, Absalom, determined to avenge her. His motives may not have been fully revenge, for while he was David's third son, the second [son] Kileab [Chileab], son of Abigail [2 Samuel 3:3], presumably died in infancy (we never hear anything of him after his birth). Thus, eliminating Amnon would put Absalom in line for the throne" (Muhlestein, *Scripture Study Made Simple*, 220). ⊕

2 Samuel 13:30–39. Absalom Flees for His Life

32 And Jonadab, the son of Shimeah David's
brother, answered and said, Let not my lord
suppose *that* they have slain all the young
men the king's sons; for Amnon only is dead:
for by the appointment of Absalom this hath
been determined from the day that he forced
his sister Tamar.

33 Now therefore let not my lord the king
take the thing to his heart, to think that all the
king's sons are dead: for Amnon only is dead.

34 But Absalom fled. And the young man
that kept the watch lifted up his eyes, and
looked, and, behold, there came much people
by the way of the hill side behind him.

35 And Jonadab said unto the king, Behold,
the king's sons come: as thy servant said, so
it is.

36 And it came to pass, as soon as he had
made an end of speaking, that, behold, the
king's sons came, and lifted up their voice
and wept: and the king also and all his servants wept very sore.

37 ¶ But Absalom fled, and went to Talmai,
the son of Ammihud, king of Geshur. And
David mourned for his son every day.

38 So Absalom fled, and went to Geshur, and
was there three years.

39 And *the soul of* king David longed to go
forth unto Absalom: for he was comforted
concerning Amnon, seeing he was dead.

How does Jonadab's subtlety continue in this verse when he speaks to David? (13:32) "Jonadab, exercising his 'wisdom,' is careful not to condemn Absalom immediately, but instead uses a plural verb [they] with an unspecified agent. Then he introduces Absalom as the source of the determination to kill Amnon, choosing a verb, 'abused' [KJV: forced], that concedes the crime of rape. Whether or not this was a possibility he had in mind when he offered counsel to Amnon, he now implicitly distances himself from Amnon's act" (Alter, *Hebrew Bible*, 2:362–63).

Who was Talmai and why did Absalom flee to him? (13:37) Talmai was Absalom's "grand-father on his mother's side, who was *king of Geshur*, a buffer-state between Israel and Syria, to the north of Gilead (2 Sam. 3:3). There he escaped being brought to justice, but at the same time he forfeited any likelihood of inheriting the throne of Israel. His father, meanwhile, continued in mourning *for his son*: for Amnon, presumably, though there is ambiguity here" (Baldwin, *1 and 2 Samuel*, 269).

What does it mean that David "longed to go forth unto" Absalom? (13:39) "We find that he had a very strong paternal affection for this young man, who appears to have had little to commend him but the beauty of his person. David wished either to go to him, or to bring him back; for the hand of time had now wiped off his tears for the death of his son Amnon. Joab had marked this disposition, and took care to work on it, in order to procure the return of Absalom. It would have been well for all parties had Absalom ended his days at Geshur. His return brought increasing wretchedness to his unfortunate father. And it may be generally observed that those undue, unreasonable paternal attachments are thus rewarded" (*Adam Clarke's Commentary* [on 2 Samuel 13:39]).

CHAPTER 14

Joab arranges by artifice to bring Absalom home after three years—After two more years, Absalom sees the king, and they are reconciled.

1 Now Joab the son of Zeruiah perceived that the king's heart *was* toward Absalom.

2 And Joab sent to Tekoah, and fetched thence a wise woman, and said unto her, I pray thee, feign thyself to be a mourner, and put on now mourning apparel, and anoint not thyself with oil, but be as a woman that had a long time mourned for the dead:

3 And come to the king, and speak on this manner unto him. So Joab put the words in her mouth.

21 ¶ And the king said unto Joab, Behold now, I have done this thing: go therefore, bring the young man Absalom again.

22 And Joab fell to the ground on his face, and bowed himself, and thanked the king:

2 Samuel 14:1–3. Joab Hires a "Wise Woman" from Tekoah to Convince David to Allow Absalom's Return to Jerusalem

What was Joab attempting to accomplish through this deception? (14:2–3) "There has been some debate about the character and role of the woman from Tekoa. The use of the adjective 'wise' . . . probably does not indicate a formal office (sage or teacher). It may indicate that she was 'clever' or 'shrewd.' Joab may have given her the words that define the hypothetical case she brings to David, but her interaction with David and the skill with which she manipulates his response draw the reader's attention" (Birch, "First and Second Books of Samuel," 2:1313).

Where is Tekoah? (14:2) "Some scholars have assumed Tekoa must have been a village particularly noted for its wisdom, based on this passage and the fact that Amos, the eighth-century prophet, was from Tekoa. But more likely, Joab simply needs to be sure that the king will not recognize the woman, as might happen in the case of a local woman. Tekoa is in the hills of Judah, approximately ten miles south of Jerusalem" (Arnold, *1 and 2 Samuel*, 566). ⊕

Summary of 2 Samuel 14:4–20

The wise woman from Tekoah tells the king that one of her two sons accidentally killed the other during a fight. And now many people seek to kill her son that he might pay for his sin. She tells the king that her son is all the family she has left and his death would leave her alone. David sympathizes with her and offers to spare her son's life. As planned, she then reminds the king that he has not forgiven Absalom for the death of Amnon. David realizes that she has come at the request of Joab.

2 Samuel 14:21–33. David Finally Agrees to See Absalom after Five Years

What are the consequences of David allowing Absalom to return? (14:21–24) "Joab's persuasion got Absalom back from his foreign refuge, but David refused to reconcile with him, and Absalom remained ostracized for two more crucial years. The bitterness engendered in Absalom during that time spawned ideas of revolt by the handsome and popular prince (2 Sam. 14:25; 15:1–12). Only by violent means and harsh words did he finally get audience with his father the king; but it was too late, and ultimate tragedy was inevitable" (Rasmussen, *Latter-day Saint Commentary on the Old Testament*, 266).

and Joab said, To day thy servant knoweth
that I have found grace in thy sight, my lord,
O king, in that the king hath fulfilled the request of his servant.

23 So Joab arose and went to Geshur, and
brought Absalom to Jerusalem.

24 And the king said, Let him turn to his
own house, and let him not see my face. So
Absalom returned to his own house, and saw
not the king's face.

25 ¶ But in all Israel there was none to be
so much praised as Absalom for his beauty:
from the sole of his foot even to the crown of
his head there was no blemish in him.

26 And when he polled his head, (for it was
at every year's end that he polled *it:* because
the hair was heavy on him, therefore he
polled it:) he weighed the hair of his head at
two hundred shekels after the king's weight.

27 And unto Absalom there were born three
sons, and one daughter, whose name *was*
Tamar: she was a woman of a fair countenance.

28 ¶ So Absalom dwelt two full years in
Jerusalem, and saw not the king's face.

Why is the reference to Absalom's beauty inserted into the story? (14:25–27) "Nothing is said of Absalom's wisdom and piety. . . . All that is here said of him is, . . . that he was a very handsome man" (*Matthew Henry's Commentary* [on 2 Samuel 14:21–27]). "The extravagant description conveys the impression that [Absalom] was totally taken up with his appearance, especially with his hair. . . . Ironically, it was his hair that would . . . cause his death. Mention of his sons and lovely daughter suggests the popularity of this proud and good-looking family, but the name *Tamar* acts as a warning reminder of Absalom's raped sister, after whom his daughter has been named" (Baldwin, *1 and 2 Samuel*, 273).

What does it mean that Absalom polled his head? (14:26) "*To poll* means 'to thin' by means of combing or cutting. Thus, when Absalom's hair became either too thick or too long, he had it polled. Evidently, Absalom's hair was extremely thick, and this information was probably introduced into the narrative here because Absalom's hair seems to have played a part in his death (see 2 Samuel 18:9–17). Exactly how much weight is meant by two hundred shekels is not completely clear; this number may either be incorrect or an exaggeration of the total weight for literary purposes" (*Old Testament Student Manual: Genesis–2 Samuel*, 296).

29 Therefore Absalom sent for Joab, to have
sent him to the king; but he would not come
to him: and when he sent again the second
time, he would not come.

30 Therefore he said unto his servants, See,
Joab's field is near mine, and he hath barley
there; go and set it on fire. And Absalom's
servants set the field on fire.

Why did Absalom set Joab's field on fire? (14:29–32) "After Absalom had sat for two whole years in his house at Jerusalem without seeing the king's face, he sent to Joab that he might obtain for him the king's full forgiveness. But as Joab would not come to him, even after he had sent for him twice, Absalom commanded his servants to set fire to one of Joab's fields which adjoined his own and was then full of barley, for the purpose of compelling him to come, as he foresaw that Joab would not take this destruction of his property

31 Then Joab arose, and came to Absalom unto *his* house, and said unto him, Wherefore have thy servants set my field on fire?

32 And Absalom answered Joab, Behold, I sent unto thee, saying, Come hither, that I may send thee to the king, to say, Wherefore am I come from Geshur? *it had been* good for me *to have been* there still: now therefore let me see the king's face; and if there be *any* iniquity in me, let him kill me.

33 So Joab came to the king, and told him: and when he had called for Absalom, he came to the king, and bowed himself on his face to the ground before the king: and the king kissed Absalom.

quietly, but would come to him to complain" (Keil and Delitzsch, *Commentary* [on 2 Samuel 14:28–30]).

What happened at the meeting between Absalom and David? (14:33) "Perhaps David's kiss could have signaled a restored relationship, but we have the impression that the kiss came at least two years late. . . . When the kiss finally comes, it is because Absalom forces the moment. . . . Even when official forgiveness allows Absalom's return to Jerusalem [2 Samuel 14:21, 24], David makes it clear that personal forgiveness is not offered. David's mind was on Absalom (14:1), but he seems unable to allow the father in him to take precedence over the king. The text is clear: it is the king who kisses Absalom, not the father" (Birch, *First and Second Books of Samuel*, 2:1316).

CHAPTERS 15–16

Absalom conspires against David and gains the support of the people—David flees, and Absalom enters Jerusalem.

Mephibosheth is alleged to be seeking to be king—Shimei, of the house of Saul, curses David—Ahithophel counsels Absalom, and Absalom takes his father's concubines.

Summary of 2 Samuel 15–16

Absalom uses his popularity to undermine David by suggesting that he would be a wiser and more just king. Absalom flatters the people by agreeing with their complaints against the king. David is forced to flee his beloved Jerusalem because of Absalom's influence over the people. David takes the ark and the high priests with him but sends them back to Jerusalem and trusts the Lord to oversee events. David strategizes to have Hushai, a trusted counselor, return to Jerusalem and become his informant as Absalom's advisor.

Ziba, Mephibosheth's servant, supplies David with sustenance and transportation but lies to him concerning his master's plans. David gives all that belonged to Mephibosheth to Ziba. David is confronted by Shimei, of Saul's family, who curses and assaults him for taking Saul's kingdom. David's guards want to put Shimei to death for his actions, but David does not allow it. When Absalom arrives in Jerusalem he is greeted by Hushai, who offers his services. Absalom is counseled by Ahithophel to take David's concubines as a sign that he has taken the kingdom.

Summary of 2 Samuel 17–18

Ahithophel counsels Absalom to take action against David and kill him, but Absalom is dissuaded by Hushai. Absalom and his men decide that the Lord was behind Hushai's counsel. Hushai secretly warns David that civil war may be imminent should Absalom change his mind. When Ahithophel determines that his counsel will not be followed, he hangs himself. David and his men prepare for war.

Absalom's and David's armies clash in the woods of Ephraim. David's army kills twenty thousand of the army of Israel. During the battle Absalom catches his hair in the branches of an oak tree and is slain by Joab. Word is sent to David of Absalom's death. David mourns his son and wishes he had died instead of Absalom.

Summary of 2 Samuel 19–21

Joab rebukes David for loving his enemies more than his friends. David replaces Joab as his commander with Amasa. Shimei, who assaulted David, is acquitted, though he may not be forgiven. Mephibosheth remains loyal to David. David rethinks his earlier decision and divides Saul's estate between Mephibosheth and Ziba. Tensions continue between Judah and Israel.

David returns to Jerusalem and his household. Opposition to the king continues and Sheba takes command of the rebels. David orders his armies against Sheba. Joab kills Amasa and once again takes command of David's men. A wise woman intervenes on behalf of the people in the besieged city of Sheba. The people in the city execute Sheba, and Joab spares them. With the death of Sheba, David's army returns to Jerusalem.

During the reign of king Saul, he violates a treaty by attacking and killing some of the Gibeonites. The Lord sends three years of famine in consequence of this bloody deed. David counsels with the Gibeonites and determines to send seven of Saul's sons to be punished for the crime. The seven sons of Saul are hanged in retribution at Gibeah. David reclaims the bones of Saul and Jonathan and they are returned to the land of Benjamin for burial.

The Philistines continue to seek revenge for the death of Goliath.

CHAPTERS 17–18

Ahithophel's counsel is overthrown by Hushai's—David is warned and flees over the Jordan—Ahithophel hangs himself—The people prepare for war.

The Israelites are smitten in the woods of Ephraim—Joab slays Absalom—Tidings of his death are taken to David, who mourns for his son.

CHAPTERS 19–21

Joab rebukes David for favoring his enemies instead of his friends—David replaces Joab with Amasa—Shimei, who cursed David, is pardoned—Mephibosheth pledges allegiance to David—The men of Judah take David back to Jerusalem.

Sheba leads the tribes of Israel away from David—Joab slays Amasa and pursues Sheba—A wise woman intercedes—The death of Sheba ends the insurrection.

The Lord sends a famine—David understands that the famine came because Saul smote the Gibeonites, contrary to the oath of Israel—David delivers up seven sons of Saul to be hanged by the Gibeonites—Israel and the Philistines continue their wars.

CHAPTERS 22–24

David praises the Lord in a psalm of thanksgiving—The Lord is his fortress and savior, He is mighty and powerful in deliverance, He rewards men according to their righteousness, He shows mercy to the merciful, His way is perfect, He lives, and blessed is He.

David speaks by the power of the Holy Ghost—Rulers must be just, ruling in the fear of God—David's mighty men are named and their deeds extolled.

David sins in numbering Israel and Judah—The men of war total 1,300,000—The Lord destroys 70,000 men by pestilence—David sees an angel, offers sacrifice, and the plague is stayed.

Summary of 2 Samuel 22–24

2 Samuel concludes with David's songs of thanksgiving for God's role in their deliverance from their enemies. God is the source of David's safety and security. When David calls, God hears and answers. As God delivered his people in times past, He delivers David from his enemies. The Lord is good to those who serve Him. The Lord strengthens and preserves David. David proclaims the Lord as the rock of his salvation.

The Lord speaks through David by the power of His Spirit. The Spirit rests upon David and brings peace and prosperity to his people. Through an everlasting covenant God orders all things. David names the mighty warriors that helped him establish his kingdom. He remembers his deliverance from the Philistines by the bravery of three of his chief warriors. He honors Abishai and Benaiah for their bravery and victories. David continues to name those followers of great note, including Uriah the Hittite, husband of Bathsheba.

David is guilty of pride as he glories in the size of his armies and their victories, instead of recognizing the hand of the Lord in their successes. The Lord sends a plague and pestilence against David's people and many die. David sees an angel and repents. David purchases the threshing floor of Araunah and builds an altar and offers burnt offerings to the Lord. The Lord stays the plague.

David loves music, and as he nears the end of his life, he praises the Lord in song for His power to deliver. He also praises his mighty warriors who have stood by him for many years.

THE FIRST BOOK OF THE
KINGS
COMMONLY CALLED
THE THIRD BOOK OF THE KINGS

Introduction

The books of 1 and 2 Kings are a continuation of the historical narrative of the house of Israel recorded in 1 and 2 Samuel. Originally, they were "regarded by the Jews as forming one book. The Greek version [Septuagint] divided the book of Samuel and the book of Kings each into two parts, calling the four portions the four books of the Kings" (Bible Dictionary, "Kings, books of").

"Although we may only speculate about the many editors that have influenced the current text of the books of the Kings, we may rest assured that the prophets who lived in the days of Solomon and the kings of Judah and Israel who followed him, diligently recorded the events through which they passed" (Hyde, *Comprehensive Commentary [1 Kings]*, 14).

Since no author is mentioned in the text of 1 Kings, it is assumed that "an unknown editor or compiler used a number of records to complete this work. He probably lived during the reign of Jehoiachin, one of the last kings of Judah, and finished this book by 590 B.C. . . .

"The compiler followed the pattern of other ancient historians. He used available records, selected the desired material, and added his own commentary and those additional items which he felt were essential. . . .

"Like Mormon extracting, compiling, and commenting on the large plates of Nephi (which contained a secular history), the compiler of the book of Kings used secular historical records to demonstrate how the kings' and people's religious behavior had affected their military and political conditions" (Ludlow, *Unlocking the Old Testament*, 83–86).

"The first half of the first book of the Kings (1 Kgs. 1–11) relates the transmission of the kingdom from David to his son Solomon. It recounts Solomon's consolidation and further expansion of the kingdom and the establishment of Jerusalem as the religious capital with a glorious new temple. . . . But then Solomon declined and fell, as did the previous two kings.

"The second half (1 Kgs. 12–22) illustrates what Jesus once said: 'Every kingdom divided against itself is brought to desolation; and every city or house divided against itself shall not stand' (Matt. 12:25). Ancient Israel deteriorated, lost the concept of the divine Abrahamic mission of Israel, and lost the blessings promised those who faithfully perform it" (Rasmussen, *Latter-day Saint Commentary on the Old Testament*, 274).

1 Kings illustrates "the fulfillment of the word of God in the history of the Israelites. Moses had clearly and unequivocally foretold what would happen as the people obeyed or rebelled (Deuteronomy 28). Therefore fate, chance, luck—good or ill—are not part of the narrative. God was intimately associated with all that transpired with this vacillating and weak-willed people. . . . The message is clear: all Israel fell when they turned from God and broke the covenant" (Pearson, *Old Testament*, 41–42).

CHAPTER 1

Abishag cherishes David in his extreme age—Adonijah aspires to be king—Bathsheba and Nathan advise David of Adonijah's plotting—David names Solomon as king, and he is anointed by Zadok—Adonijah's cause fails.

CHAPTER 2

David charges Solomon to keep the commandments and walk in the ways of the Lord—King David dies and Solomon reigns—Adonijah, Joab, and Shimei are put to death, and Abiathar is rejected as high priest—The kingdom is established with Solomon.

1 Now the days of David drew nigh that he should die; and he charged Solomon his son, saying,

2 I go the way of all the earth: be thou strong therefore, and shew thyself a man;

3 And keep the charge of the LORD thy God, to walk in his ways, to keep his statutes, and his commandments, and his judgments, and his testimonies, as it is written in the law of Moses, that thou mayest prosper in all that

Summary of 1 Kings 1

Exploiting his father's advancing age, Adonijah, one of David's sons, aspires to be king. He organizes an unauthorized feast for his supporters, proclaiming himself Israel's ruler. Bathsheba and the prophet Nathan inform David of Adonijah's unlawful actions. David instructs Nathan and the priest Zadok to anoint Solomon king, causing much joy and rejoicing among all the people. Adonijah fears retribution, but Solomon promises no harm will come to him if "he will shew himself a worthy man" (1 Kings 1:52).

1 Kings 2:1–12. David Gives Final Words of Counsel to Solomon

How can we heed David's counsel to Solomon to be strong? (2:2–4) "We will all face fear, experience ridicule, and meet opposition. Let us—all of us—have the courage to defy the consensus, the courage to stand for principle. Courage, not compromise, brings the smile of God's approval. Courage becomes a living and an attractive virtue when it is regarded not only as a willingness to die manfully but also as the

An Overview of the Book of 1 Kings

The book of 1 Kings can be divided into three main sections:

"**1 Kings 1–11** Before his death, King David has his son Solomon anointed king. Solomon rules his kingdom with great wisdom. Solomon builds a temple and his palace at Jerusalem, beginning the period known as the 'golden age of Israel.' The Queen of Sheba visits Solomon. Solomon's wives lure him away from worshipping the Lord and encourage him to worship false gods. Solomon's kingdom is threatened by Jeroboam.

"**1 Kings 12–16** All the tribes of Israel except Judah and Benjamin rebel against Solomon's son Rehoboam. The kingdom is divided, and Jeroboam becomes the ruler of the Northern Kingdom (also known as Israel), leaving Rehoboam to rule the Southern Kingdom (also known as Judah). Jeroboam and Rehoboam both establish idol worship in their kingdoms, and many rulers of both kingdoms follow this pattern of idol worship.

"**1 Kings 17–22** The prophet Elijah causes a drought in the land. He raises a widow's son from the dead. With great power from God, Elijah competes with the priests of Baal and shows that Jehovah is God. After this miracle, Jezebel, the wife of King Ahab and a supporter of Baal, tries to kill Elijah. Elijah travels to Mount Horeb, where the Lord speaks to him in a still, small voice. Elijah meets Elisha, who will succeed him as prophet. Elijah prophesies the deaths of Ahab and Jezebel. Following Ahab's death, Ahaziah, the son of Ahab, reigns in wickedness" (*Old Testament Seminary Teacher Material*, 491).

determination to live decently. As we move forward, striving to live as we should, we will surely receive help from the Lord and can find comfort in His words" (Monson, "Be Strong and of a Good Courage," 69).

Why did David counsel Solomon to slay certain leaders in Israel? (2:5–9) "David had Solomon kill those people who had been political threats to him. As an ensconced and powerful king, David could survive such threats and show mercy. As a new king trying to consolidate power in the face of rivals, Solomon did not have such luxury. By disposing of those who had been threats to David, Solomon not only got rid of those who could cause him problems but showed himself loyal to David and a legitimate part of his legacy, setting a tradition that opposition to the king would not be tolerated" (Muhlestein, *Essential Old Testament Companion*, 247).

Who was Barzillai the Gileadite? (2:7) "*Barzillai of Gilead* appears in 2 Samuel 17:27–29 as one of those who provided for David while he was in Mahanaim. Later ([2 Samuel] 19:31–39), the king tried to return the compliment, but Barzillai declined his offer on the grounds of old age. His family is now commended to Solomon's care: he is to provide for them as they had provided for David" (Provan, *1 & 2 Kings*, 32).

Who was Shimei the son of Gera? (2:8) "Shimei, son of Gera, was a Benjamite of the house of Saul who actively and aggressively opposed David during the uprising of Absalom (see 2 Samuel 16:5–8). Following

thou doest, and whithersoever thou turnest thyself:

4 That the LORD may continue his word which he spake concerning me, saying, If thy children take heed to their way, to walk before me in truth with all their heart and with all their soul, there shall not fail thee (said he) a man on the throne of Israel.

5 Moreover thou knowest also what Joab the son of Zeruiah did to me, *and* what he did to the two captains of the hosts of Israel, unto Abner the son of Ner, and unto Amasa the son of Jether, whom he slew, and shed the blood of war in peace, and put the blood of war upon his girdle that *was* about his loins, and in his shoes that *were* on his feet.

6 Do therefore according to thy wisdom, and let not his hoar head go down to the grave in peace.

7 But shew kindness unto the sons of Barzillai the Gileadite, and let them be of those that eat at thy table: for so they came to me when I fled because of Absalom thy brother.

8 And, behold, *thou hast* with thee Shimei the son of Gera, a Benjamite of Bahurim, which cursed me with a grievous curse in the day when I went to Mahanaim: but he came down to meet me at Jordan, and I sware to him by the LORD, saying, I will not put thee to death with the sword.

The Rise and Fall of King Solomon (1 Kings 1–11)

"Many kings ascended the throne of Israel from the time of Saul to the dissolution of both the Northern Kingdom and the Southern Kingdom. None of these kings, however, obtained the power and prestige that Solomon did. Nearly a thousand years before Solomon, Abraham had been promised that his seed would receive the land of Canaan for their inheritance, including territory as far north as the Euphrates River (see Genesis 12:7; 13:15; 15:18). But not until Solomon's time was this promise fully realized. . . .

"At the beginning of his reign, Solomon loved the God of Israel and covenanted with God that he would walk in obedience throughout his administration as king of Israel. Solomon was promised wisdom, riches, honor, and long life if he would continue in righteousness before the Lord. The promise was fulfilled. . . .

"Nevertheless, at the end of Solomon's reign, Israel became temporally and spiritually bankrupt. Deterioration and strife were everywhere. Within a year of Solomon's death, the land was divided into two kingdoms, and the course of Israel's history was permanently altered" (*Old Testament Student Manual: 1 Kings–Malachi*, 1).

9 Now therefore hold him not guiltless: for thou *art* a wise man, and knowest what thou oughtest to do unto him; but his hoar head bring thou down to the grave with blood.

10 So David slept with his fathers, and was buried in the city of David.

11 And the days that David reigned over Israel *were* forty years: seven years reigned he in Hebron, and thirty and three years reigned he in Jerusalem.

12 ¶ Then sat Solomon upon the throne of David his father; and his kingdom was established greatly.

the defeat and death of Absalom (18:15), Shimei came back with a host of his colleagues to demonstrate his subservient contrition before David (see 19:19–20), who magnanimously pardoned him (see 19:21–23) but warned Solomon of the man's duplicity (see 1 Kings 2:9). When Shimei violated an oath not to journey away from Jerusalem, King Solomon ordered his execution (see 1 Kings 2:36–46)" (Pinegar and Allen, *Old Testament Who's Who*, 173).

Where was David buried? (2:10) "[King David's] burial 'in the city of David' (1 Kgs. 2:10) was unusual; burials were typically outside Israelite cities. The traditional site of his burial is venerated to this day on 'Mount Zion' southwest of the Old City of Jerusalem" (Rasmussen, *Latter-day Saint Commentary on the Old Testament*, 276). The city of David "was the name afterwards given to the castle and royal palace on Mount Zion, as distinguished from Jerusalem generally (1 Kings 3:1 ; 8:1). It was on the south-west side of Jerusalem, opposite the temple mount, with which it was connected by a bridge over the Tyropoeon valley" (*Easton's Bible Dictionary*, "David, City of").

How was Solomon able to establish his kingdom "greatly"? (2:12) "Solomon's forty-year reign was characterized by economic prosperity and political stability (968–928 B.C.). While David created Israel as an empire through his military success, Solomon ruled in peace and extended Israel's international sphere through diplomacy, trade, and marriages. Solomon distinguished himself as a man of wisdom, as a merchant, and as a builder" (Holzapfel, et al., *Jehovah and the World of the Old Testament*, 213).

Summary of 1 Kings 2:13–46

Adonijah again attempts to become king by trying to arrange a marriage with Abishag, one of David's wives. Knowing the implications of this request, Solomon orders Adonijah's execution. Joab is also slain, both for his support of Adonijah and his unsanctioned actions while David's captain (see 1 Kings 2:5–6). Shimei violates the orders of the king's pardon and is put to death.

1 Kings 3:1–15. Solomon Asks the Lord for Wisdom

What does it mean that Solomon "made affinity" with Pharaoh? (3:1) "The Hebrew words translated 'made affinity with' might have been translated 'made a marriage alliance with'" (Ludlow, *Companion to Your Study of the Old Testament*, 226).

This verse is corrected in the Joseph Smith Translation: "And *the Lord was not pleased with Solomon,* for he made affinity with Pharaoh, king of Egypt, and took Pharaoh's daughter *to wife . . . ; and the Lord blessed Solomon for the people's sake only*" (Wayment, *Complete Joseph Smith Translation of the Old Testament*, 136).

Why were the Israelites sacrificing in "high places" like Gibeon? (3:2–4) "As Solomon commenced his reign, 'he began to love the Lord' and 'called on the name of the Lord' (JST, 1 Kgs. 3:3). His worship included frequent offerings, which were made at the high places (outdoor places of worship), because the temple had not yet been built" (Szink, "Reign of Solomon," 14). "The tabernacle built by Moses was at this time located in Gibeon along with the great altar upon which sacrifices had been offered since the days of Moses. That is why Solomon went to Gibeon to offer sacrifices (see 1 Chronicles 21:29; 2 Chronicles 1:2–3)" (*Old Testament Student Manual: 1 Kings–Malachi*, 4).

How often did the Lord appear to Solomon? (3:5) "The Lord appeared to Solomon at Gibeon (see [also] 2 Chr. 1:7) and in the temple at Jerusalem (see 1 Kgs. 9:2). The first appearance was in answer to Solomon's prayer for wisdom to rule and to discern between good and evil. His prayer was granted on condition of faithfulness. In the second appearance, which occurred in the temple, the Lord promised Solomon that he would keep the throne as long as Israel remained obedient" (Black, *400 Questions and Answers about the Old Testament*, 112).

What can we learn from Solomon's gratitude for God's goodness and greatness? (3:6) "The consistency of pleas from prophets to reflect on the goodness of God is striking. Our Heavenly Father wants us to recall His and His Beloved Son's goodness, not for Their

CHAPTER 3

Solomon loves the Lord and keeps His commandments—The Lord appears to Solomon and promises him a wise and an understanding heart—He judges between two harlots and determines who is the mother of a child.

1 And Solomon made affinity with Pharaoh
king of Egypt, and took Pharaoh's daughter,
and brought her into the city of David, until he had made an end of building his own
house, and the house of the LORD, and the
wall of Jerusalem round about.

2 Only the people sacrificed in high places,
because there was no house built unto the
name of the LORD, until those days.

3 And Solomon loved the LORD, walking in
the statutes of David his father: only he sacrificed and burnt incense in high places.

4 And the king went to Gibeon to sacrifice
there; for that *was* the great high place: a
thousand burnt offerings did Solomon offer
upon that altar.

5 ¶ In Gibeon the LORD appeared to Solomon
in a dream by night: and God said, Ask what
I shall give thee.

6 And Solomon said, Thou hast shewed unto
thy servant David my father great mercy, according as he walked before thee in truth,
and in righteousness, and in uprightness of

heart with thee; and thou hast kept for him this great kindness, that thou hast given him a son to sit on his throne, as *it is* this day.

7 And now, O Lord my God, thou hast made thy servant king instead of David my father: and I *am but* a little child: I know not *how* to go out or come in.

8 And thy servant *is* in the midst of thy people which thou hast chosen, a great people, that cannot be numbered nor counted for multitude.

9 Give therefore thy servant an understanding heart to judge thy people, that I may discern between good and bad: for who is able to judge this thy so great a people?

10 And the speech pleased the Lord, that Solomon had asked this thing.

11 And God said unto him, Because thou hast asked this thing, and hast not asked for thyself long life; neither hast asked riches for thyself, nor hast asked the life of thine enemies; but hast asked for thyself understanding to discern judgment;

12 Behold, I have done according to thy words: lo, I have given thee a wise and an understanding heart; so that there was none like thee before thee, neither after thee shall any arise like unto thee.

13 And I have also given thee that which thou hast not asked, both riches, and honour: so that there shall not be any among the kings like unto thee all thy days.

own gratification but for the influence such remembrance has on us. By considering Their kindness, our perspective and understanding are enlarged. By reflecting on Their compassion, we become more humble, prayerful, and steadfast" (Renlund, "Consider the Goodness and Greatness of God," 41). When have you been grateful for the Lord's goodness and greatness?

Why did Solomon ask God for an understanding heart? (3:7–9) "Solomon, probably in his early twenties, was distraught with the responsibility thrust upon him. He felt inadequate. . . .

"The overwhelming weight of the crown pressed heavily upon him. No doubt there were many in this favored nation who were older and wiser than he. How could he govern so great a people as this? And so he pled with the Lord for an understanding heart. . . . Because he righteously desired and asked for this gift, he was rewarded. The Lord gave him a wise and understanding heart. . . . With the gift of wisdom, Solomon's mind began, in part, to partake of the mind of God" (Callister, *Infinite Atonement*, 275–76).

How can we develop an understanding heart? (3:9) "If the Lord was pleased because of that which Solomon had asked of him [an understanding heart; see 1 Kings 3:6–13] surely he would be pleased with each of us if we had the desire to acquire an understanding heart. This must come from conscious effort coupled with faith and firm determination. An understanding heart results from the experiences we have in life if we keep the commandments of God" (*Teachings of Howard W. Hunter*, 255). When has an understanding heart been a blessing in your life?

What does God's response to Solomon's request teach us about Him? (3:11–13) The Prophet Joseph Smith taught: "If we seek first the kingdom of God, all good things will be added. So [it was] with Solomon. First he asked wisdom, and God gave it him—and with it every desire of his heart" (Jackson, *Joseph Smith's Commentary on the Bible*, 36). What are some other examples from the scriptures of unselfish requests made to the Lord?

What does the Joseph Smith Translation help us understand about this verse? (3:14) "Rather than *commendation* of David, the Joseph Smith Translation refers to *condemnation* of David, with a promise to Solomon if he proves worthy:

"'And if thou wilt walk in my ways to keep my statutes, and my commandments, then I will lengthen thy days, *and thou shalt not walk in unrighteousness, as did thy father David*' (italics added)" (Ludlow, *Companion to Your Study of the Old Testament*, 226–27).

"There are numerous places in the historical books where David is held up as an example of one who was pleasing in God's sight. The Prophet Joseph Smith corrected each of those references to show that David was being used by the Lord as an example of what David's successors should not do" (*Old Testament Student Manual: 1 Kings–Malachi*, 4). ⊕

1 Kings 3:16–28. Solomon Wisely Settles a Dispute between Two Mothers

Why would the king hear the case of two harlots? (3:16) "Despite being prohibited by law (Lev 19:29; Deut 23:18), prostitution was apparently tolerated among the Israelites. . . . Solomon's willingness to hear the case of the two prostitutes . . . fits in well with his image as a 'just king'" (Walton, et al., *IVP Bible Background Commentary*, 359).

How does the suggested resolution of the conflict between the two women demonstrate Solomon's wisdom? (3:17–27) "In this famous illustration of Solomon's wisdom, it is surprising that his solution to the question worked out at all. Normally two women who both desired the same baby would *both* have objected to the crude suggestion that it be cut in two. His wisdom must have been in his insight to see that one would be brazen enough to consent. Naturally the true mother gave in rather than consent to the death of the child" (Rasmussen, *Latter-day Saint Commentary on the Old Testament*, 278).

14 And if thou wilt walk in my ways, to keep my statutes and my commandments, as thy father David did walk, then I will lengthen thy days.

15 And Solomon awoke; and, behold, *it was* a dream. And he came to Jerusalem, and stood before the ark of the covenant of the LORD, and offered up burnt offerings, and offered peace offerings, and made a feast to all his servants.

16 ¶ Then came there two women, *that were* harlots, unto the king, and stood before him.

17 And the one woman said, O my lord, I and this woman dwell in one house; and I was delivered of a child with her in the house.

18 And it came to pass the third day after that I was delivered, that this woman was delivered also: and we *were* together; *there was* no stranger with us in the house, save we two in the house.

19 And this woman's child died in the night; because she overlaid it.

20 And she arose at midnight, and took my son from beside me, while thine handmaid slept, and laid it in her bosom, and laid her dead child in my bosom.

21 And when I rose in the morning to give my child suck, behold, it was dead: but when

I had considered it in the morning, behold, it was not my son, which I did bear.

22 And the other woman said, Nay; but the living *is* my son, and the dead *is* thy son. And this said, No; but the dead *is* thy son, and the living *is* my son. Thus they spake before the king.

23 Then said the king, The one saith, This *is* my son that liveth, and thy son *is* the dead: and the other saith, Nay; but thy son *is* the dead, and my son *is* the living.

24 And the king said, Bring me a sword. And they brought a sword before the king.

25 And the king said, Divide the living child in two, and give half to the one, and half to the other.

26 Then spake the woman whose the living child *was* unto the king, for her bowels yearned upon her son, and she said, O my lord, give her the living child, and in no wise slay it. But the other said, Let it be neither mine nor thine, *but* divide *it*.

27 Then the king answered and said, Give her the living child, and in no wise slay it: she *is* the mother thereof.

28 And all Israel heard of the judgment which the king had judged; and they feared the king: for they saw that the wisdom of God *was* in him, to do judgment.

How did the people of Israel react when they heard of Solomon's wisdom? (3:28) "The fame of Solomon's wisdom spread throughout Israel, and even beyond: people from other nations came to visit him and hear his wisdom" (Szink, "Reign of Solomon," 15). "Solomon himself was famous for his intellectual achievements. He was renowned as a botanist, who catalogued plant life, and a zoologist, who gathered birds, animals, and insects (1 Ki. 4:29–34). In addition he is said to have spoken 'three thousand proverbs and his songs [psalms] numbered a thousand and five'" (*Revell Bible Dictionary*, 933).

Summary of 1 Kings 4

Solomon's kingdom spreads beyond the borders established by his father, David. The kingdom of Israel is bordered by the land of the Philistines on the west, the great Euphrates River on the northeast, and Egypt on the south. Because of the increase in territory, Solomon organizes his government into twelve districts. His obedience to the Lord increases his wealth, prosperity, and wisdom. Leaders of other nations seek his counsel.

Summary of 1 Kings 5

The Lord promised David that his son Solomon would be privileged to build a temple (see 1 Chronicles 22:8–10). Solomon makes an agreement with Hiram, king of Tyre, to trade wheat and oil in exchange for cedar wood from Lebanon. Solomon and Hiram commission men to prepare the wood and cut the stones to be used in the temple construction. In time, "they brought great stones, . . . hewed stones, to lay the foundation of the [Lord's] house" (1 Kings 5:17).

1 Kings 6:1–14. The Lord Promises Solomon That He Will Dwell in the Temple as Israel Obeys His Words

How did Solomon know how to build a temple? (6:1) Though the tabernacle existed as a pattern, and David had provided his revealed pattern concerning the building of the temple (see 1 Chronicles 28:11–13), Solomon was still young and inexperienced (see 1 Chronicles 22:5). "The pattern of this temple, the length and breadth, and height of the inner and outer courts, with all the fixtures thereunto appertaining, were given to Solomon by revelation, through the proper source. And why was this revelation-pattern necessary? Because Solomon had never built a temple, and did not know what was necessary in the arrangement of the different apartments, any better than Moses did what was needed in the tabernacle" (*Discourses of Brigham Young*, 414).

Why did Solomon construct such a glorious temple? (6:2–9) "In Hebrew the Temple is referred to as *beth yhwh*, 'house of Jehovah,' or *hekal*, 'palace,' which indicates that the Temple was understood first and foremost as the dwelling place of Jehovah among his covenant people. . . .

CHAPTER 4

The officers in Solomon's court are listed—Solomon reigns in peace and prosperity over a large kingdom—His wisdom and understanding exceed that of all men.

CHAPTER 5

Solomon solicits and gains Hiram's help in getting timber to build the temple—The Israelites hew stones and cut timber for the temple.

CHAPTER 6

Solomon builds the temple—The Lord promises to dwell among the Israelites if they are obedient—The ornaments of the temple are described.

1 And it came to pass in the four hundred and eightieth year after the children of Israel were come out of the land of Egypt, in the fourth year of Solomon's reign over Israel, in the month Zif, which *is* the second month, that he began to build the house of the Lord.

2 And the house which king Solomon built for the Lord, the length thereof *was* threescore cubits, and the breadth thereof twenty *cubits*, and the height thereof thirty cubits.

3 And the porch before the temple of the house, twenty cubits *was* the length thereof, according to the breadth of the house; *and* ten cubits *was* the breadth thereof before the house.

4 And for the house he made windows of narrow lights.

5 ¶ And against the wall of the house he built chambers round about, *against* the walls of the house round about, *both* of the temple and of the oracle: and he made chambers round about:

6 The nethermost chamber *was* five cubits broad, and the middle *was* six cubits broad, and the third *was* seven cubits broad: for without *in the wall* of the house he made narrowed rests round about, that *the beams* should not be fastened in the walls of the house.

7 And the house, when it was in building, was built of stone made ready before it was brought thither: so that there was neither hammer nor axe *nor* any tool of iron heard in the house, while it was in building.

"The space around the Temple was demarcated in various levels of holiness, symbolizing the need for greater holiness in approaching the presence of God. . . . The Temple is described as being located on the 'mountain of his holiness' (Ps 48:1–4), suggesting that as worshippers ascended toward the Temple they were approaching Jehovah. . . . As the earthly dwelling place of God, the Temple served as the link between heaven and earth" (Holzapfel, et al., *Jehovah and the World of the Old Testament*, 223–24). ⊕

What was the "oracle"? (6:5) "The word *oracle* literally means 'to speak' and connotes the means whereby divine messages are conveyed to man. In the scriptures, the term is used in three different ways: (1) any sacred place where God speaks his will to his children, such as Mount Sinai, the Sacred Grove, temples, and other holy sites (D&C 124:39); (2) the inspired messages or revelations from God to man (Romans 3:2; D&C 124:126); and (3) the Lord's authorized servants who receive these revelations (2 Samuel 16:23; 1 Peter 4:11; D&C 90:4)" (Top, "Oracles," 464). In Solomon's temple, the Holy of Holies was sometimes "translated as 'oracle' in the KJV" (Muhlestein, *Scripture Study Made Simple*, 228). ⊕

Why were certain tools not used near the temple site? (6:7) "As an iron tool was thought to violate a holy structure, the dressing of the stone would have to be done at the *quarry* (cf. Exod. 20:25)" (Wiseman, *1 and 2 Kings*, 115). "Masons used large picks (weighing thirty to thirty-five pounds) for quarrying and smaller

The Construction of Solomon's Temple (1 Kings 6)

"Soon after Solomon's accession to the throne he set about the labor [of building the temple], which, as heritage and honor, had come to him with his crown. He laid the foundation in the fourth year of his reign, and the building was completed within seven years and a half. With the great wealth accumulated by his kingly father and specifically reserved for the building of the Temple, Solomon was able to put the [surrounding lands] under tribute, and to enlist the co-operation of nations in his great undertaking. The temple workmen numbered scores of thousands, and every department was in [the] charge of master craftsmen. To serve on the great structure in any capacity was an honor; and labor acquired a dignity never before recognized. Masonry became a profession, and the graded orders therein established have endured until this day. The erection of the Temple of Solomon was an epoch-making event, not alone in the history of Israel, but in that of the world. . . .

"In architecture and construction, in design and costliness, it is known as one of the most remarkable buildings in history" (Talmage, *House of the Lord,* 5–6).

Sidney B. Sperry explained: "The materials for the permanent house of the Lord, known as Solomon's Temple, were accumulated mostly by David (2 Sam. 7; 1 Chr. 28:11; 1 Chr. 29:9). It is estimated that he gathered a total of 108,000 talents of gold, 10,000 darics [Persian coins] of gold, and 1,017,000 talents of silver for the prospective structure and its furnishings. With these metals and other materials for which Solomon made arrangements, the king built a most lavish temple to the Lord. It was completed in seven and one-half years" (Sperry, "Ancient Temples and Their Functions," 69).

picks (weighing twelve or fifteen pounds) for shaping of the stone" (Walton, et al., *IVP Bible Background Commentary*, 362). "The rock was precut at the quarry for its proper fit in the temple building, so *no . . . tool was heard* at the temple itself. This required a high degree of skill in measuring, cutting, and fitting the immense stones in place" (*Nelson Study Bible* [NKJV], 569).

How have modern prophets continued to speak of the promised temple blessings? (6:11–13) "For me, the greatest motivation to be worthy of temple experiences is what the Lord has said of His holy houses:

"' . . . My presence shall be there, for I will come into it, and all the pure in heart that shall come into it shall see God' [D&C 97:16].

"President Russell M. Nelson made clear for us that we can 'see' the Savior in the temple in the sense that He becomes no longer unknown to us. President Nelson said this: 'We understand Him. We comprehend His work and His glory. And we begin to feel the infinite impact of His matchless life'" (Eyring, "I Love to See the Temple," 29–30).

Summary of 1 Kings 6:15–38

The temple is extensively decorated with beautiful embellishments of gold, carvings, and furnishings. It takes seven years to complete the temple construction.

Summary of 1 Kings 7

While the temple is being constructed, Solomon begins to build himself a house. The furnishings of the temple are carefully crafted, including the "molten sea" or baptismal font, which rested on the backs of twelve oxen (see 1 Kings 7:23–26). That pattern is reflected in the baptismal fonts located in our modern-day temples.

8 The door for the middle chamber *was* in the right side of the house: and they went up with winding stairs into the middle *chamber*, and out of the middle into the third.

9 So he built the house, and finished it; and covered the house with beams and boards of cedar.

10 And *then* he built chambers against all the house, five cubits high: and they rested on the house with timber of cedar.

11 ¶ And the word of the LORD came to Solomon, saying,

12 *Concerning* this house which thou art in building, if thou wilt walk in my statutes, and execute my judgments, and keep all my commandments to walk in them; then will I perform my word with thee, which I spake unto David thy father:

13 And I will dwell among the children of Israel, and will not forsake my people Israel.

14 So Solomon built the house, and finished it.

CHAPTER 7

Solomon builds himself a house—Hiram of Tyre makes the two pillars, the molten sea, the ten bases, the ten lavers, and all the vessels for the temple—The molten sea (baptismal font) rests on the backs of twelve oxen.

CHAPTER 8

The ark, containing the two tablets of stone, is placed in the holy of holies—The glory of the Lord fills the temple—Solomon offers the dedicatory prayer—He asks for temporal and spiritual blessings upon repentant and prayerful Israel—The people sacrifice and worship for fourteen days.

1 Then Solomon assembled the elders of Israel, and all the heads of the tribes, the chief of the fathers of the children of Israel, unto king Solomon in Jerusalem, that they might bring up the ark of the covenant of the LORD out of the city of David, which *is* Zion.

2 And all the men of Israel assembled themselves unto king Solomon at the feast in the month Ethanim, which *is* the seventh month.

3 And all the elders of Israel came, and the priests took up the ark.

4 And they brought up the ark of the LORD, and the tabernacle of the congregation, and all the holy vessels that *were* in the tabernacle, even those did the priests and the Levites bring up.

5 And king Solomon, and all the congregation of Israel, that were assembled unto him, *were* with him before the ark, sacrificing sheep and oxen, that could not be told nor numbered for multitude.

6 And the priests brought in the ark of the covenant of the LORD unto his place, into the oracle of the house, to the most holy *place, even* under the wings of the cherubims.

7 For the cherubims spread forth *their* two wings over the place of the ark, and the cherubims covered the ark and the staves thereof above.

8 And they drew out the staves, that the ends of the staves were seen out in the holy *place* before the oracle, and they were not seen without: and there they are unto this day.

1 Kings 8:1–11. The Ark Is Placed in the Holy of Holies

What was the significance of moving the ark of the covenant into the new temple? (8:1–11) "Also called the 'ark of the testimony' (Ex. 25:22), . . . this divine vessel was connected with the divine presence of God" (McConkie and Parry, *Guide to Scriptural Symbols*, 15). "After seven years of labor, the temple was finished (see 1 Kings 6:38). On the day of its dedication, priests took the ark of the covenant and placed it beneath the wings of the cherubim in the holy of holies. When they emerged, a cloud of glory, symbolizing God's presence, filled the building (1 Kgs. 8:1–11 . . .)" (Szink, "Reign of Solomon," 16).

Why were there winged cherubim or angels in the Holy of Holies? (8:6–7) The lid of the ark of the covenant had two winged cherubim fashioned thereon. For decorative purposes Solomon had placed in the Holy of Holies larger replicas of the cherubim. "The . . . two large cherubim (each fifteen feet high, with wing spans of fifteen feet) was not in violation of the commandment against engraven idols (or 'images,' as translated in the King James Version). The cherubim were not to be worshipped, but were for beautification and for representation of heavenly powers" (Ludlow, *Companion to Your Study of the Old Testament*, 228).

What was missing from inside the ark of the covenant? (8:9) "It is curious that the only thing inside the ark were the two tables of stone. At one point, it also had a bowl or pot of manna and Aaron's rod that blossomed [see Ex. 16:32–34; Num. 17:10]" (Muhlestein, *Scripture Study Made Simple*, 229–30). Although some speculate possible reasons, it is not known what happened to the manna or the rod.

What was the meaning of a cloud filling Solomon's temple? (8:10–11) "When the sanctuary [in the wilderness] was completed, the cloud which had evidenced the protection and presence of the Lord from the beginning of their wilderness march filled the dwelling" (McConkie, *Gospel Symbolism*, 68). Similarly, at Solomon's Temple dedication, when the temple singers "praised the Lord, saying, For he is good; for his mercy endureth for ever: that then the house was filled with a cloud, even the house of the Lord" (2 Chron. 5:13).

Describing the cloud's presence in the holy edifice, Joseph Fielding McConkie wrote that "such was the symbol of the divine presence. . . . Further, the cloud was a symbol of his presence and their right to appear before him and seek his blessings" (*Gospel Symbolism*, 68–69). See also commentary in this volume for 1 Kings 8:1–11. ⊕

9 *There was* nothing in the ark save the two tables of stone, which Moses put there at Horeb, when the LORD made *a covenant* with the children of Israel, when they came out of the land of Egypt.

10 And it came to pass, when the priests were come out of the holy *place,* that the cloud filled the house of the LORD,

11 So that the priests could not stand to minister because of the cloud: for the glory of the LORD had filled the house of the LORD.

1 Kings 8:12–22. Solomon Praises the Lord

12 ¶ Then spake Solomon, The LORD said that he would dwell in the thick darkness.

13 I have surely built thee an house to dwell in, a settled place for thee to abide in for ever.

14 And the king turned his face about, and blessed all the congregation of Israel: (and all the congregation of Israel stood;)

15 And he said, Blessed *be* the LORD God of Israel, which spake with his mouth unto David my father, and hath with his hand fulfilled *it,* saying,

16 Since the day that I brought forth my people Israel out of Egypt, I chose no city out of all the tribes of Israel to build an house, that my name might be therein; but I chose David to be over my people Israel.

17 And it was in the heart of David my father to build an house for the name of the LORD God of Israel.

18 And the LORD said unto David my father, Whereas it was in thine heart to build an house unto my name, thou didst well that it was in thine heart.

19 Nevertheless thou shalt not build the house; but thy son that shall come forth out of thy loins, he shall build the house unto my name.

20 And the LORD hath performed his word that he spake, and I am risen up in the room of David my father, and sit on the throne of Israel, as the LORD promised, and have built an house for the name of the LORD God of Israel.

21 And I have set there a place for the ark, wherein *is* the covenant of the LORD, which he made with our fathers, when he brought them out of the land of Egypt.

22 ¶ And Solomon stood before the altar of the LORD in the presence of all the congregation of Israel, and spread forth his hands toward heaven:

Why didn't David build the temple? (8:17–19) David desired "to build unto the Lord of hosts a house, a temple. [However, the] Lord, in one place, alludes to his life, saying that he had been a man of war and blood; that he had gone forth and fought his enemies, and because of this the Lord was not disposed to accept his offer [see 1 Chr. 22:8], but . . . according to the prediction of the Lord God, through Nathan the Prophet, Solomon was raised up and did accomplish the work which his father David had desired to do" (Cannon, in *Journal of Discourses*, 14:123).

What was unique about the way Solomon dedicated the temple to the Lord? (8:22) As Solomon offered the dedicatory prayer for the temple, not only did he "spread forth his hands toward heaven" (1 Kings 8:22), he also "[knelt] on his knees" (1 Kings 8:54). "The account of Solomon praying on his knees is the first recorded instance of a kneeling prayer in the Old Testament. Usually the Israelites prostrated themselves when praying" (Black, *400 Questions and Answers about the Old Testament*, 114). ⊕

Summary of 1 Kings 8:23–53

Solomon's dedicatory prayer sets a pattern for future temple dedications. He praises the Lord and invites Him to bless the temple. He pleads for the Lord's blessings and urges the people to be faithful. Finally, Solomon seeks compassion and forgiveness for the people's sins. "Solomon's dedicatory prayer gives a good insight into the state of Solomon's heart at the time. His closeness to the Lord is very evident" (*Old Testament Student Manual: 1 Kings–Malachi*, 7).

1 Kings 8:54–66. After the Dedication of the Temple, Solomon Blesses His People

What can happen when we "incline" our hearts to God? (8:57–58) "The more we incline our hearts and minds toward God, the more heavenly light distills upon our souls. And each time we willingly and earnestly seek that light, we indicate to God our readiness to receive more light. Gradually, things that before seemed hazy, dark, and remote become clear, bright, and familiar to us" (Uchtdorf, "Receiving a Testimony of Light and Truth," 22). How has the temple helped you "incline" your heart to God? What light and understanding have you received in your life because of temple service?

How can we know when our hearts are "perfect with the Lord"? (8:61) "The scriptures say that when we desire righteousness our 'heart is right' with God. The Psalmist condemned the people of ancient Israel because 'their heart was not right with [God]' (Psalm 78:37). When King Solomon blessed the people at the dedication of the temple, he concluded with these words: 'Let your heart therefore be perfect with the Lord our God, to walk in his statutes, and to keep his commandments, as at this day' (1 Kings 8:61). . . .

"Our heart is right or perfect with God when we desire what God desires" (Oaks, *Pure in Heart*, 4–5). When have God's desires become your desires? How has that made a difference in your relationship with Him?

54 And it was *so,* that when Solomon had made an end of praying all this prayer and supplication unto the LORD, he arose from before the altar of the LORD, from kneeling on his knees with his hands spread up to heaven.

55 And he stood, and blessed all the congregation of Israel with a loud voice, saying,

56 Blessed *be* the LORD, that hath given rest unto his people Israel, according to all that he promised: there hath not failed one word of all his good promise, which he promised by the hand of Moses his servant.

57 The LORD our God be with us, as he was with our fathers: let him not leave us, nor forsake us:

58 That he may incline our hearts unto him, to walk in all his ways, and to keep his commandments, and his statutes, and his judgments, which he commanded our fathers.

59 And let these my words, wherewith I have made supplication before the LORD, be nigh unto the LORD our God day and night, that he maintain the cause of his servant, and the cause of his people Israel at all times, as the matter shall require:

60 That all the people of the earth may know that the LORD *is* God, *and that there is* none else.

61 Let your heart therefore be perfect with the LORD our God, to walk in his statutes, and to keep his commandments, as at this day.

62 ¶ And the king, and all Israel with him, offered sacrifice before the LORD.

63 And Solomon offered a sacrifice of peace offerings, which he offered unto the LORD, two and twenty thousand oxen, and an hundred and twenty thousand sheep. So the king and all the children of Israel dedicated the house of the LORD.

64 The same day did the king hallow the middle of the court that *was* before the house of the LORD: for there he offered burnt offerings, and meat offerings, and the fat of the peace offerings: because the brasen altar that *was* before the LORD *was* too little to receive the burnt offerings, and meat offerings, and the fat of the peace offerings.

Why did Solomon offer so many sacrifices? (8:63–64) "Solomon offered a sacrifice of peace offerings (v. 63), sacrifices that involved a communion meal. Although the numbers of two and twenty thousand oxen and an hundred and twenty thousand sheep may seem large, vast numbers of people participated in the dedication ceremony, which lasted fourteen days (see 8:1–2; see also v. 65). The number was so large, however, that the bronze altar was inadequate, so Solomon consecrated the center of the temple court and utilized it as a huge altar for the sacrifices. The congregation (v. 65) of Israelites represented . . . nearly the entire area of Solomon's dominion" (*Zondervan KJV Commentary*, 475). ⊕

65 And at that time Solomon held a feast, and all Israel with him, a great congregation, from the entering in of Hamath unto the river of Egypt, before the LORD our God, seven days and seven days, *even* fourteen days.

66 On the eighth day he sent the people away: and they blessed the king, and went unto their tents joyful and glad of heart for all the goodness that the LORD had done for David his servant, and for Israel his people.

Why did Solomon's dedicatory feast last so long? (8:65–66) Apparently the seven-day celebration for the temple dedication was immediately followed by the Feast of Tabernacles which took place from the 15th to the 21st days of the seventh month (see *NIV Study Bible* [1995], 484). "The festival for the first seven days of the seventh month would have included the solemn Day of Atonement. The second seven days would have been the joyful Feast of Tabernacles, or Sukkoth, ending on the eighth day with Simchas Torah, 'Joy in the Torah' ([see Bible Dictionary], 'Fasts'; 'Feasts')" (Rasmussen, *Latter-day Saint Commentary on the Old Testament*, 283).

CHAPTER 9

The Lord again appears to Solomon—The Lord promises great blessings if the Israelites are obedient and great cursings if they forsake Him—Solomon reigns in splendor, levies tribute upon the non-Israelites, and builds a navy of ships.

1 And it came to pass, when Solomon had finished the building of the house of the LORD, and the king's house, and all Solomon's desire which he was pleased to do,

2 That the LORD appeared to Solomon the second time, as he had appeared unto him at Gibeon.

1 Kings 9:1–9. The Lord Appears to Solomon a Second Time

How did the appearance of the Lord help remind Solomon of the need to remain faithful? (9:2–9) "God had already signally honored Solomon by appearing to him at Gibeon. Now once again God appeared to him to encourage him to remain faithful and to walk in God's ways" (*Expositor's Bible Commentary [Abridged]*, 512). "The effects of keeping or breaking one's covenants were reiterated in a revelation confirming the covenant promises made at the temple dedication. David was again cited as an exemplar of integrity of faith in the Lord, having never turned to other gods (recall, however, that by his sins he fell from his exaltation; D&C 132:39; [Bible Dictionary], 'David')" (Rasmussen, *Latter-day Saint Commentary on the Old Testament*, 283).

What was meant by the Lord saying He would "put [His] name there for ever"? (9:3) "The Old Testament contains scores of references to the name of the Lord in a context where it clearly means the authority of the Lord. . . .

"The Lord told [the children of Israel] that when they entered the promised land there should be a place where the Lord their God would 'cause his name to dwell' [Deut. 12:11]. . . . The Lord and his servants referred to the future temple as a house for 'the name' of the Lord God of Israel [1 Kings 3:2]. . . . After the temple was dedicated, the Lord appeared to Solomon and told him that He had hallowed the temple 'to put my name there for ever' [1 Kgs. 9:3]" (Oaks, "Taking upon Us the Name of Jesus Christ," 81).

What was included in the Lord's promise to David? (9:4–5) God's promise to David about the building of the temple, given in 2 Samuel 7:12–13, 16, links the words "house" and "throne." "[It] was much more than a promise of a physical house for the Lord, built by a son of David. Solomon's construction of the physical temple was but a type and shadow of the covenant's deeper promise, which is revealed as one ponders the dual meaning of the word *house*.

"When the Lord said that he would make David a house, he did not mean that he would construct a physical structure for David to dwell in. . . . Rather, the Lord was making a promise regarding the 'house of David'—that is, the *family* of David" (Ferrell, *Hidden Christ*, 174). ⊕

Why did the Lord warn that the temple would be "cast out of [his] sight"? (9:6–9) "The glorious pre-eminence of this splendid structure was of brief duration. Thirty-four years after its dedication, and but five years subsequent to the death of Solomon, its decline began; and this decline was soon to develop into general spoliation [destruction], and finally to become an actual desecration. Solomon the king, the man of wisdom, the master-builder, had been led astray by the wiles of idolatrous women, and his wayward ways had fostered iniquity in Israel. . . . The Temple soon lost its sanctity. The gift became depreciated by the perfidy [betrayal] of the giver, and Jehovah withdrew His protecting presence from the place no longer holy" (Talmage, *House of the Lord*, 6–7).

3 And the LORD said unto him, I have heard
thy prayer and thy supplication, that thou
hast made before me: I have hallowed this
house, which thou hast built, to put my
name there for ever; and mine eyes and mine
heart shall be there perpetually.

4 And if thou wilt walk before me, as David
thy father walked, in integrity of heart, and
in uprightness, to do according to all that
I have commanded thee, *and* wilt keep my
statutes and my judgments:

5 Then I will establish the throne of thy
kingdom upon Israel for ever, as I promised
to David thy father, saying, There shall not
fail thee a man upon the throne of Israel.

6 *But* if ye shall at all turn from following
me, ye or your children, and will not keep
my commandments *and* my statutes which
I have set before you, but go and serve other
gods, and worship them:

7 Then will I cut off Israel out of the land
which I have given them; and this house,
which I have hallowed for my name, will
I cast out of my sight; and Israel shall be a
proverb and a byword among all people:

8 And at this house, *which* is high, every one
that passeth by it shall be astonished, and

shall hiss; and they shall say, Why hath the LORD done thus unto this land, and to this house?

9 And they shall answer, Because they forsook the LORD their God, who brought forth their fathers out of the land of Egypt, and have taken hold upon other gods, and have worshipped them, and served them: therefore hath the LORD brought upon them all this evil.

CHAPTER 10

The queen of Sheba visits Solomon—His wealth and wisdom exceed that of all the kings of the earth.

1 And when the queen of Sheba heard of the fame of Solomon concerning the name of the LORD, she came to prove him with hard questions.

2 And she came to Jerusalem with a very great train, with camels that bare spices, and very much gold, and precious stones: and when she was come to Solomon, she communed with him of all that was in her heart.

3 And Solomon told her all her questions: there was not *any* thing hid from the king, which he told her not.

Summary of 1 Kings 9:10–28

Twenty cities are gifted to King Hiram as repayment for wood, gold, and other services he had provided, but the king is dissatisfied. Solomon continues to employ the levy of working men (see 1 Kings 5:13–15) to build a navy of ships for the kingdom.

1 Kings 10:1–13. The Queen of Sheba Hears of Solomon's Greatness and Visits Him

Why did the Queen of Sheba come to ask "hard questions" of Solomon? (10:1) "The *queen of Sheba* came to ask Solomon *hard questions* to satisfy her own mind and to examine his wisdom. She serves as an example of what must have happened on a lesser scale throughout the reign of Solomon. His wisdom, which became proverbial ([1 Kings] 4:29–34), was an attractive force. Wise men and sages from other cultures came to Jerusalem and learned of the wisdom that is rooted in the fear of God (Prov. 1:7). This suggests a lively intellectual climate in Jerusalem during the reign of Solomon the Wise" (*Nelson Study Bible* [NKJV], 578). ⊕

Why did the Queen of Sheba bring such wealth to Jerusalem? (10:2) The gold, precious stones, and spices Sheba brought with her may indicate intentions of establishing trade with Solomon (see *Quest Study Bible* [2011], 483). "[Sheba] profited from the sea trade of India and east Africa by transporting luxury commodities north to Damascus and Gaza on caravan routes through the Arabian Desert. It is possible that Solomon's fleet of ships [1 Kings 9:26–28; 10:11–12] threatened Sheba's continued dominance of the trading business" (*NIV Study Bible* [1995], 485–86).

4 And when the queen of Sheba had seen all Solomon's wisdom, and the house that he had built,

5 And the meat of his table, and the sitting of his servants, and the attendance of his ministers, and their apparel, and his cupbearers, and his ascent by which he went up unto the house of the LORD; there was no more spirit in her.

What do the observations of Solomon's house and table signify? (10:5) "One expression of extreme wealth would be the display of quantities and varieties of food on the royal table. It was a singular honor to eat at the king's table and the number of persons who could be accommodated there was a sign of the power of the ruler.... Royal banquets in the ancient Near East featured an extensive and sophisticated *haute cuisine*....

"The size of Solomon's bureaucracy and power as a monarch might be estimated by the number who would regularly be seated at his table. It was also a further expression of wealth of his kingdom that he could continuously provide for these men" (Walton, et al., *IVP Bible Background Commentary*, 430).

What does it mean that there was "no more spirit in her"? (10:5) "The queen of Sheba [was] overwhelmed by Solomon's wealth and wisdom" (*New Oxford Annotated Bible*, 506). "She had no courage left wherewith to continue to compete with him in the interchange of wise and hidden sayings" (*Interpreter's Bible*, 3:97).

Why was the Queen of Sheba so impressed with her visit with Solomon? (10:6–9) "Solomon's brilliant replies to the queen of Sheba's difficult *questions* (v. 3), as well as the skillful use of his wisdom for the needs and interests of his kingdom convinced her that such wisdom must be divinely bestowed. Her acknowledgement of Solomon's God and the Lord's covenant faithfulness toward Israel does not necessarily mean

6 And she said to the king, It was a true report that I heard in mine own land of thy acts and of thy wisdom.

7 Howbeit I believed not the words, until I came, and mine eyes had seen *it:* and, behold, the half was not told me: thy wisdom and prosperity exceedeth the fame which I heard.

Who Was the Queen of Sheba? (1 Kings 10:1–13)

"Ancient Sheba is most likely located in the southwest corner of the Arabian peninsula, known as Saba. In the Bible, Sheba is known as the home of merchants that trade in gold (Isa 60:6; Ezek 27:22), precious stones (Ezek 27:22), and incense (Isa 60:6; Jer 6:20)—all of which are found in the area....

"The Queen of Sheba is mentioned in the Old and New Testaments (1 Kgs 10:1–13; cf. 2 Chr 9:1–12; Matt 12:42) as well as the Quran (27:15–45). The Queen of Sheba 'heard of the fame of Solomon'; and came to test his wisdom—'to prove him with hard questions'—and to see the great Temple that he had built and the wealth of his court.... After Solomon answered all of her questions and she had marveled at his wealth, she exclaimed: 'Blessed be the LORD thy God, which delighted in thee, to set thee on the throne of Israel' (1 Kgs 10:9)" (Holzapfel, et al., *Jehovah and the World of the Old Testament*, 217).

"The scriptural account of the Queen of Sheba and Solomon does not suggest a romantic relationship. However, 'a long dynasty of kings of Ethiopia, which ended with Haile Selassie (1891–1975), claimed descent from the queen of Sheba and Solomon' [Rasmussen, *Latter-day Saint Commentary on the Old Testament*, 285]" (Black, *400 Questions and Answers about the Old Testament*, 115).

8 Happy *are* thy men, happy *are* these thy servants, which stand continually before thee, *and* that hear thy wisdom.

9 Blessed be the LORD thy God, which delighted in thee, to set thee on the throne of Israel: because the LORD loved Israel for ever, therefore made he thee king, to do judgment and justice.

10 And she gave the king an hundred and twenty talents of gold, and of spices very great store, and precious stones: there came no more such abundance of spices as these which the queen of Sheba gave to king Solomon.

11 And the navy also of Hiram, that brought gold from Ophir, brought in from Ophir great plenty of almug trees, and precious stones.

12 And the king made of the almug trees pillars for the house of the LORD, and for the king's house, harps also and psalteries for singers: there came no such almug trees, nor were seen unto this day.

13 And king Solomon gave unto the queen of Sheba all her desire, whatsoever she asked, beside *that* which Solomon gave her of his royal bounty. So she turned and went to her own country, she and her servants.

that she made a commitment of personal faith in the Lord. Such recognition of foreign deities was common in the literature of the ancient world. However, the possibility exists that she experienced a spiritual awakening as a result of her time with Solomon (see [1 Kings] 5:7)" (*Nelson Study Bible* [NKJV], 578).

What were "almug trees"? (10:11–12) *"Almug wood* [was] a precious wood of uncertain species (traditionally sandalwood)" (*New Oxford Annotated Bible*, 507).

Summary of 1 Kings 10:14–29

Solomon's vast wealth of gold, silver, chariots, horses, and ships is described. His wealth exceeds "all the kings of the earth for riches" (1 Kings 10:23) and his wisdom is so famous that "all the earth sought to [him], to hear his wisdom, which God had put into his heart" (1 Kings 10:24).

CHAPTER 11

Solomon marries non-Israelite women, and his wives turn his heart to the worship of false gods—The Lord stirs up adversaries against him, including Jeroboam, the son of Nebat—Ahijah promises Jeroboam that he will be the king of the ten tribes—Solomon dies and Rehoboam reigns in his stead.

1 But king Solomon loved many strange women, together with the daughter of Pharaoh, women of the Moabites, Ammonites, Edomites, Zidonians, *and* Hittites;

2 Of the nations *concerning* which the LORD said unto the children of Israel, Ye shall not go in to them, neither shall they come in unto you: *for* surely they will turn away your heart after their gods: Solomon clave unto these in love.

3 And he had seven hundred wives, princesses, and three hundred concubines: and his wives turned away his heart.

4 For it came to pass, when Solomon was old, *that* his wives turned away his heart after other gods: and his heart was not perfect with the LORD his God, as *was* the heart of David his father.

5 For Solomon went after Ashtoreth the goddess of the Zidonians, and after Milcom the abomination of the Ammonites.

1 Kings 11:1–8. Solomon Marries outside of the Covenant

Who were the "strange women" Solomon married and why did he marry them? (11:1–2) "Solomon married 'strange women,' that is, foreign women, or those not of the covenant. Solomon's marriages were for political expediency . . . and perhaps for personal reasons as well. But these women brought to Israel their idols and heathen worship, which corrupted not only Solomon but the people also" (*Old Testament Student Manual: 1 Kings–Malachi*, 9). ⊕

What can we learn from Solomon's marriages? (11:3) "Solomon— . . . who had been blessed by the Lord with 'wisdom and understanding exceeding much, and largeness of heart . . .' (1 Kings 4:29) and who had built the Lord's house and received personal visitations from the Lord Jehovah (see 1 Kings 3:5; 9:2)—disobeyed the Lord's command and married many wives not of the covenant. . . .

"Just as Solomon and his Israelite seed ultimately lost their kingdom due to their marrying out of the Abrahamic covenant, so too will we lose our 'thrones, kingdoms, principalities, and powers' (D&C 132:19) if we . . . set at naught the only covenant of marriage that can produce kings and queens, priests and priestesses" (Top, *Peculiar Treasure*, 17, 18).

Was David's heart "perfect with the Lord"? (11:4) As the writer of Kings points out the tragic fall of Solomon whose heart had been turned away by his wives, he extolls the perfect heart of David. The Joseph Smith Translation clarifies this idea by saying that Solomon's "heart was not perfect with the Lord his God, *and it became* as the heart of David his father [JST, 1 Kings 11:4]" (Wayment, *Complete Joseph Smith Translation of the Old Testament*, 138).

The Joseph Smith Translation of verse 6 confirms this truth: "And Solomon did evil in the sight of the

6 And Solomon did evil in the sight of the LORD, and went not fully after the LORD, as *did* David his father.

7 Then did Solomon build an high place for Chemosh, the abomination of Moab, in the hill that *is* before Jerusalem, and for Molech, the abomination of the children of Ammon.

8 And likewise did he for all his strange wives, which burnt incense and sacrificed unto their gods.

9 ¶ And the LORD was angry with Solomon, because his heart was turned from the LORD God of Israel, which had appeared unto him twice,

10 And had commanded him concerning this thing, that he should not go after other gods: but he kept not that which the LORD commanded.

11 Wherefore the LORD said unto Solomon, Forasmuch as this is done of thee, and thou hast not kept my covenant and my statutes, which I have commanded thee, I will surely rend the kingdom from thee, and will give it to thy servant.

12 Notwithstanding in thy days I will not do it for David thy father's sake: *but* I will rend it out of the hand of thy son.

13 Howbeit I will not rend away all the kingdom; *but* will give one tribe to thy son for David my servant's sake, and for Jerusalem's sake which I have chosen.

Lord, *as David his father*, and went not fully after the Lord" (Wayment, *Complete Joseph Smith Translation of the Old Testament*, 138).

1 Kings 11:9–13. Most of Solomon's Kingdom Is Given to Jeroboam

What was the source of the Lord's anger with Solomon? (11:9–10) "David and Solomon were . . . given direction through the legal administrators of their day to take additional wives, and they enjoyed the approbation of heaven while they stayed within the bounds the Lord had set. When they moved outside those bounds, however, and began to acquire wives and concubines for selfish or lustful reasons (for example, David in the case of Bathsheba, 2 Samuel 11; Solomon in taking 'strange women' as wives 'who turned away his heart from the things of righteousness,' 1 Kings 11), they offended God and forfeited their eternal rewards that might have been theirs" (Millet, *Precept upon Precept*, 330).

Why did the Lord eventually "rend the kingdom" from Solomon? (11:11–12) "[King Solomon's] heart . . . was turned aside from the Lord our God, because he took to himself strange wives, women of the nations with whom God had commanded Israel not to marry, and because of this he was led as he grew in years into idolatry. He built in the groves where the strange nations performed their idolatrous rites, places of worship, and to gratify these wives he went and worshipped with them; and God in His anger, . . . said that the nation should be rent asunder; and . . . the greater portion of the kingdom was taken from the house of David, and given to another" (Cannon, in *Journal of Discourses*, 25:364).

How was the Lord's prophecy fulfilled? (11:13) "At the end of Solomon's forty-year reign, Israel was temporally and spiritually marred with strife. Within a year of [Solomon's] death (about 922 B.C.), the kingdom of Israel was divided in two [see *Old Testament Student Manual: 1 Kings–Malachi*, 1]. Judah united with Rehoboam, the son of Solomon, whose dynasty lasted nineteen generations before Jerusalem succumbed to Babylonian captivity in 587 B.C. The Northern

Kingdom united with Jeroboam, formerly an official in Solomon's kingdom" (Black, *400 Questions and Answers about the Old Testament*, 118).

Summary for 1 Kings 11:14–25

The Lord allows enemies, such as Hadad of Edom (in league with Pharaoh) and Rezon, to come against Solomon in battle because of his continued wickedness.

1 Kings 11:26–40. The Prophet Ahijah Promises Jeroboam He Will Reign in Solomon's Stead over a Divided Israel

What do we know about Jeroboam? (11:26–28) Jeroboam was an Ephraimite. The land inheritance of the tribe of Ephraim lay north of Jerusalem and included the sites of Bethel, Shechem, and Shiloh. "As a member of Solomon's bureaucracy, Jeroboam was a local leader of the regional corvee, a corps of men drafted into temporary service (porterage, construction), within the district of 'the House of Joseph' (Ephraim/Manasseh)" (Walton, et al., *IVP Bible Background Commentary*, 366). ⊕

What was Ahijah's purpose in giving Jeroboam ten pieces of cloth torn from a "new garment"? (11:29–32) "Ahijah's tearing the robe . . . symbolizes the removal of the kingship from the current king and its bestowal upon a new king. . . . The robe is torn into twelve pieces, for the twelve tribes" (*Jewish Study Bible* [2014], 683).

Jeroboam "was told by the prophet Ahijah that he would rule over ten of the tribes of Israel. The tribe of Judah, however, was to continue under the reign of David's line so that the promise that the Messiah would come through the lineage of David and from the tribe of Judah would be fulfilled (see Genesis 49:10). The kingdom of Judah would include half the small tribe of Benjamin, the Levites, and the strangers that were in Judah's territory" (*Old Testament Student Manual: 1 Kings–Malachi*, 9).

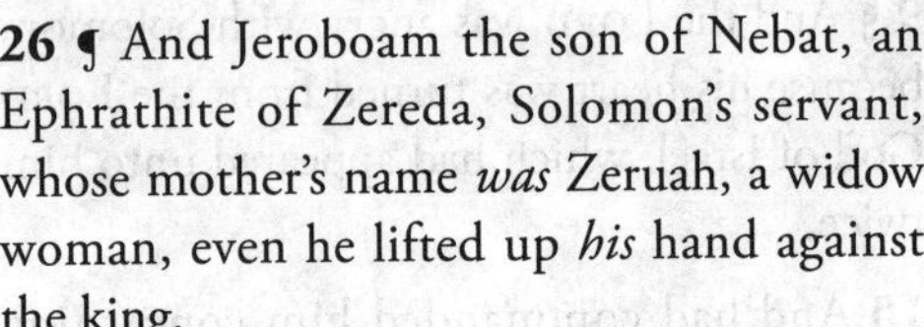

26 ¶ And Jeroboam the son of Nebat, an Ephrathite of Zereda, Solomon's servant, whose mother's name *was* Zeruah, a widow woman, even he lifted up *his* hand against the king.

27 And this *was* the cause that he lifted up *his* hand against the king: Solomon built Millo, *and* repaired the breaches of the city of David his father.

28 And the man Jeroboam *was* a mighty man of valour: and Solomon seeing the young man that he was industrious, he made him ruler over all the charge of the house of Joseph.

29 And it came to pass at that time when Jeroboam went out of Jerusalem, that the prophet Ahijah the Shilonite found him in the way; and he had clad himself with a new garment; and they two *were* alone in the field:

30 And Ahijah caught the new garment that *was* on him, and rent it *in* twelve pieces:

31 And he said to Jeroboam, Take thee ten pieces: for thus saith the LORD, the God of Israel, Behold, I will rend the kingdom out of the hand of Solomon, and will give ten tribes to thee:

32 (But he shall have one tribe for my servant David's sake, and for Jerusalem's sake, the city which I have chosen out of all the tribes of Israel:)

33 Because that they have forsaken me, and have worshipped Ashtoreth the goddess of the Zidonians, Chemosh the god of the Moabites, and Milcom the god of the children of Ammon, and have not walked in my ways, to do *that which is* right in mine eyes, and *to keep* my statutes and my judgments, as *did* David his father.

34 Howbeit I will not take the whole kingdom out of his hand: but I will make him prince all the days of his life for David my servant's sake, whom I chose, because he kept my commandments and my statutes:

35 But I will take the kingdom out of his son's hand, and will give it unto thee, *even* ten tribes.

36 And unto his son will I give one tribe, that David my servant may have a light alway before me in Jerusalem, the city which I have chosen me to put my name there.

37 And I will take thee, and thou shalt reign according to all that thy soul desireth, and shalt be king over Israel.

38 And it shall be, if thou wilt hearken unto all that I command thee, and wilt walk in my ways, and do *that is* right in my sight, to keep my statutes and my commandments, as David my servant did; that I will be with thee, and build thee a sure house, as I built for David, and will give Israel unto thee.

39 And I will for this afflict the seed of David, but not for ever.

What was the "light" that Ahijah promised would remain in Jerusalem? (11:36) "The *lamp* [KJV "light"] was symbolic of God's living presence. God had promised David that he would always have a living representative on the throne in Jerusalem. This was considered a Messianic promise, and it was ultimately fulfilled by Jesus Christ. Several passages use this metaphor in connection with David and his house ([1 Kings] 15:4; [2 Samuel] 21:17; [2 Kings] 8:19)" (*Quest Study Bible* [2011], 486). How might knowing how God fulfilled promises anciently help us trust that He will keep His promises in our day?

Why was Jeroboam told that the Lord would afflict the seed of David? (11:38–39) "The Joseph Smith Translation of these verses [see 1 Kings 11:39*a*] indicates:

1. Solomon sinned greatly as did David, but Solomon was not repentant and so the Lord could not forgive him.
2. David was blessed by the Lord when he was obedient to the Lord's commandments.
3. Because of the sins of Solomon, the right of reigning over ten of the twelve tribes was taken from him (and his descendants).
4. Because of the sins of David, the descendants of David would be afflicted, 'but not for ever'" (Ludlow, *Companion to Your Study of the Old Testament*, 230).

Why did Solomon seek to kill Jeroboam? (11:40) The ten pieces of torn cloth given to Jeroboam by the prophet Ahijah "symbolized the Lord's taking ten tribes away from Solomon because of his apostasy. Out of respect for David, however, they would be taken only after Solomon's death. If Jeroboam would stay close to the Lord, the Lord would preserve him.

"When Solomon heard of this prophecy, he tried to have Jeroboam killed, but the future ruler of the Northern Kingdom of Israel escaped to Egypt, where he stayed until Solomon died (1 Kgs. 11:26–40)" (Szink, "Reign of Solomon," 19). ⊕

40 Solomon sought therefore to kill Jeroboam.
And Jeroboam arose, and fled into Egypt,
unto Shishak king of Egypt, and was in Egypt
until the death of Solomon.

1 Kings 11:41–43. Solomon Dies and Is Buried in the City of David

Where can we read the "book of the acts of Solomon"? (11:41) The "book of the acts of Solomon" is considered lost scripture. "The Bible is of inestimable worth; nevertheless, it testifies to its own incompleteness. It mentions sacred works that are no longer available [1 Kings 11:41]. . . .

"Latter-day Saints recognize that many ancient scriptures have been lost. Some contents of these sacred records are known, but much remains obscure. Latter-day Saints look forward to a time when all things revealed from God will be restored and made known again" (Cloward, "Lost Scripture," 422).

What do we know about Solomon's burial? (11:43) "By stating that Solomon 'slept with his father,' the biblical writers were describing how Solomon was buried near where David was buried. No one has ever been able to figure out exactly where the kings of Judah were buried" (Muhlestein, *Scripture Study Made Simple*, 241).

41 ¶ And the rest of the acts of Solomon, and
all that he did, and his wisdom, *are* they not
written in the book of the acts of Solomon?

42 And the time that Solomon reigned in
Jerusalem over all Israel *was* forty years.

43 And Solomon slept with his fathers, and
was buried in the city of David his father:
and Rehoboam his son reigned in his stead.

1 Kings 12:1–11. Rehoboam Seeks Counsel from Advisors but Rejects Their Advice

Who was Rehoboam? (12:1) Rehoboam was the "Son of Solomon by the Ammonite princess Naamah (1 Kgs. 14:21, 31), and his successor in the kingdom (1 Kgs. 11:43). During his reign the division took place between north and south (1 Kgs. 12), being mainly the result of an old rivalry between Judah and Ephraim, which Rehoboam tried to pacify by going to Shechem to be crowned. Much discontent had also been

CHAPTER 12

Rehoboam seeks to impose greater burdens upon the people—The ten tribes revolt and turn to Jeroboam—Jeroboam turns to idolatry and worships false gods.

1 And Rehoboam went to Shechem: for all
Israel were come to Shechem to make him
king.

caused by the rigor of Solomon's government, and by Rehoboam's refusal to relieve the burdens placed upon the people (1 Kgs. 12:1–11)" (Bible Dictionary, "Rehoboam").

Why did they go to Shechem to make Rehoboam king? (12:1) "In the distribution of the land, Shechem fell to Ephraim (Josh. 20:7) but was assigned to the Levites and became a city of refuge ([Joshua] 21:20–21). It was the scene of the promulgation of the law, when its blessings were heard from Gerizim and its curses from Ebal (Deut. 27:11; Josh. 8:33–35). . . . All Israel assembled at Shechem, and Rehoboam, Solomon's successor, went there to be inaugurated as king. Here, at this same place, the ten tribes [would renounce] the house of David and [transfer] their allegiance to Jeroboam ([1 Kings]12:16), under whom Shechem became for a time the capital of his kingdom" (*New Unger's Bible Dictionary* [2005], 1173–74).

2 And it came to pass, when Jeroboam the son of Nebat, who was yet in Egypt, heard *of it,* (for he was fled from the presence of king Solomon, and Jeroboam dwelt in Egypt;)

Why was Jeroboam dwelling in Egypt? (12:2–3) When Solomon heard Ahijah's prophecy about the division of the kingdom, he sought to kill Jeroboam. Jeroboam fled to Egypt for safety (see 1 Kings 11:40; see also Carlson, "When the Lord Commands," 38).

3 That they sent and called him. And Jeroboam and all the congregation of Israel came, and spake unto Rehoboam, saying,

4 Thy father made our yoke grievous: now therefore make thou the grievous service of thy father, and his heavy yoke which he put upon us, lighter, and we will serve thee.

What was the grievous yoke that Solomon put on his people? (12:4) "A system of forced labor had been imposed by Solomon to accomplish and maintain his building projects (see [1 Kings] 5:13–18). Because this burdensome service was especially hateful to the northern tribes, relief from it was a crucial issue" (*NKJV Study Bible* [2018], 513).

5 And he said unto them, Depart yet *for* three days, then come again to me. And the people departed.

6 ¶ And king Rehoboam consulted with the old men, that stood before Solomon his father while he yet lived, and said, How do ye advise that I may answer this people?

Who were the old men that gave counsel to Rehoboam? (12:6–8) "These were the officials of Solomon's government, such as Adoniram ([1 Kings] 4:6) and the district governors (4:7–19), who had had ample opportunity to witness the schism that was developing among the tribes and that would ultimately divide the nation if critical grievances were not addressed. These men reminded Rehoboam, *'If thou wilt be a servant . . .'* (v. 7). Authority in the kingdom of God is for service, not for personal aggrandizement" (*Zondervan KJV Commentary*, 482).

7 And they spake unto him, saying, If thou wilt be a servant unto this people this day, and wilt serve them, and answer them, and speak good words to them, then they will be thy servants for ever.

8 But he forsook the counsel of the old men, which they had given him, and consulted

What was the meaning of the imagery used by Rehoboam's peers? (12:11) "The advice of Rehoboam's own advisors was that the system of forced labor should be intensified until its sting became like that of a scorpion. *Scourges* [KJV "scorpions"] were leather whips that could have more than one tail to which barbed points or metal spikes were attached" (*NKJV Study Bible* [2018], 513).

1 Kings 12:12–20. Rehoboam Rejects the Counsel of His Elders and Follows His Peers

Why would Rehoboam reject the counsel of the older men? (12:13–14) "The *elders*—who had, no doubt, had the benefit of Solomon's own wisdom (cf. 1 Kgs. 10:8) and had little hope of or desire for further advancement from his son—give Rehoboam wise advice. . . .

"But he chooses instead to accept the foolish advice of his younger contemporaries (v. 8). They, of course, owe their position in life to him, and they give him advice that he evidently wishes to hear. He should take a hard line (vv. 8–11), substituting *scorpions* (perhaps a particularly vicious form of whip) for mere *whips*" (Provan, *1 & 2 Kings*, 104).

How did Rehoboam's decision to follow the counsel of his peers fulfill the Lord's "cause"? (12:15) "At this point the author of Kings interrupts the narrative (v.15) to point out that the decision of Rehoboam and his counselors was in accordance with a turn of affairs arranged by God's sovereign disposition, as prophesied previously by Ahijah (cf. 1 Ki 11:29–39;

with the young men that were grown up with him, *and* which stood before him:

9 And he said unto them, What counsel give ye that we may answer this people, who have spoken to me, saying, Make the yoke which thy father did put upon us lighter?

10 And the young men that were grown up with him spake unto him, saying, Thus shalt thou speak unto this people that spake unto thee, saying, Thy father made our yoke heavy, but make thou *it* lighter unto us; thus shalt thou say unto them, My little *finger* shall be thicker than my father's loins.

11 And now whereas my father did lade you with a heavy yoke, I will add to your yoke: my father hath chastised you with whips, but I will chastise you with scorpions.

12 ¶ So Jeroboam and all the people came to Rehoboam the third day, as the king had appointed, saying, Come to me again the third day.

13 And the king answered the people roughly, and forsook the old men's counsel that they gave him;

14 And spake to them after the counsel of the young men, saying, My father made your yoke heavy, and I will add to your yoke: my father *also* chastised you with whips, but I will chastise you with scorpions.

15 Wherefore the king hearkened not unto the people; for the cause was from the LORD, that he might perform his saying, which the LORD spake by Ahijah the Shilonite unto Jeroboam the son of Nebat.

16 ¶ So when all Israel saw that the king hearkened not unto them, the people answered the king, saying, What portion have we in David? neither *have we* inheritance in the son of Jesse: to your tents, O Israel: now see to thine own house, David. So Israel departed unto their tents.

17 But *as for* the children of Israel which dwelt in the cities of Judah, Rehoboam reigned over them.

18 Then king Rehoboam sent Adoram, who *was* over the tribute; and all Israel stoned him with stones, that he died. Therefore king Rehoboam made speed to get him up to his chariot, to flee to Jerusalem.

19 So Israel rebelled against the house of David unto this day.

20 And it came to pass, when all Israel heard that Jeroboam was come again, that they sent and called him unto the congregation, and made him king over all Israel: there was none that followed the house of David, but the tribe of Judah only.

21 ¶ And when Rehoboam was come to Jerusalem, he assembled all the house of Judah, with the tribe of Benjamin, an hundred and fourscore thousand chosen men, which were warriors, to fight against the house of Israel, to bring the kingdom again to Rehoboam the son of Solomon.

2 Ch 10:15). While the decision and responsibility for all that took place rested with the human participants, none of it took God by surprise. Indeed, God utilized everything to accomplish his will in judgment against Solomon and the people (cf. 1 Ki 11:33)" (Patterson and Austel, "1, 2 Kings," 740).

How did Israel rebel against the house of David? (12:16–20) "Under the direction of Solomon's son, Rehoboam, the tribe of Judah together with the assimilated Simeonites of that region and half of the tribe of Benjamin joined together to form the southern monarchy called the kingdom of Judah.

"The ten and one-half tribes in the north united under the leadership of a strong military officer, Jeroboam, to establish the northern kingdom called Israel or sometimes Ephraim, after the preeminent tribe" (Brandt, "Time of the Divided Kingdoms," 30).

"The northern tribes viewed the house of David as pertaining only to the tribe of Judah, hearkening back to the days before David's united kingship when division, and not unity, characterized the relationship between the two groups of tribes" (Lundquist, "Life in Ancient Biblical Lands," 36).

Why did the people of Israel kill Rehoboam's representative Adoram? (12:18) *Adoram* is elsewhere called *Adoniram* (see 1 Kings 4:6; 5:14). He was the "receiver-general of the imposts [levies or taxes] in the reigns of David, Solomon, and Rehoboam (1 Kings 4:6). During his extended term of office he rendered both himself and the tribute so odious to the people, in sustaining the immense public works of Solomon, that when Rehoboam rashly sent him to enforce the collection of the taxes the exasperated populace rose upon him and stoned him to death" (*New Unger's Bible Dictionary* [2005], 27).

Was the tribe of Judah alone in supporting the house of David? (12:20) According the Septuagint, the house of David, also called the kingdom of Judah after the division of the kingdoms, was supported by the tribes of Judah and Benjamin (see 1 Kings 12:20*b*). See commentary in this volume for 1 Kings 12:16–20.

1 Kings 12:21–24. Rehoboam Is Counseled Not to Go to War against the Kingdom of Israel

Why didn't Rehoboam go to war with the northern tribes? (12:21–24) "Only Judahites had shown loyalty to Rehoboam at the assembly in Shechem, but some Benjamites joined them, perhaps because Jerusalem was virtually on the border between the tribes of Judah and Benjamin.

"Thanks to the inspired advice of a 'man of God,' a prophet, who warned Rehoboam against making war on the northern tribes to force them back under his subjection, Rehoboam's military forces turned back. His action is surprising—and commendable—but it also confirmed the divided state of Israel.

"The southern Israelite nation of Judah thereafter included the tribes of Judah and Simeon, some of the tribe of Benjamin, and all the faithful of the tribe of Levi" (Rasmussen, *Latter-Day Saint Commentary on the Old Testament*, 288).

1 Kings 12:25–33. Jeroboam Establishes His Kingdom and Makes Two Golden Calves

Why did Jeroboam make two golden calves?

(12:26–30) "[Jeroboam] determined that having his subjects go to Jerusalem for religious reasons would be bad for him politically. . . . He dealt with this dilemma by building two national shrines for his new kingdom, one in Dan, near the northern border of his kingdom, and one in Bethel, near the southern border. . . .

"The redactors of 1 Kings clearly thought Jeroboam's substitution of these two shrines for worship at the Jerusalem Temple was apostate and sinful" (Holzapfel, et al., *Jehovah and the World of the Old Testament*, 251).

What was the feast that Jeroboam organized?

(12:31–33) "[Jeroboam] inaugurates a feast day (probably to rival the Feast of Tabernacles; vv. 32–33; Lev. 23:34–43), and appoints non-Levitical priests. In trying to tighten his grip on political power, however, Jeroboam seals his own doom, for he forgets the conditions of his appointment to kingship, namely, covenantal fidelity (cf. [1 Kings] 11:38). Israelite history would ultimately point to Jeroboam as the model of

22 But the word of God came unto Shemaiah the man of God, saying,

23 Speak unto Rehoboam, the son of Solomon, king of Judah, and unto all the house of Judah and Benjamin, and to the remnant of the people, saying,

24 Thus saith the LORD, Ye shall not go up, nor fight against your brethren the children of Israel: return every man to his house; for this thing is from me. They hearkened therefore to the word of the LORD, and returned to depart, according to the word of the LORD.

25 ¶ Then Jeroboam built Shechem in mount Ephraim, and dwelt therein; and went out from thence, and built Penuel.

26 And Jeroboam said in his heart, Now shall the kingdom return to the house of David:

27 If this people go up to do sacrifice in the house of the LORD at Jerusalem, then shall the heart of this people turn again unto their lord, *even* unto Rehoboam king of Judah, and they shall kill me, and go again to Rehoboam king of Judah.

28 Whereupon the king took counsel, and made two calves *of* gold, and said unto them, It is too much for you to go up to Jerusalem: behold thy gods, O Israel, which brought thee up out of the land of Egypt.

29 And he set the one in Beth-el, and the other put he in Dan.

30 And this thing became a sin: for the people went *to worship* before the one, *even* unto Dan.

31 And he made an house of high places, and made priests of the lowest of the people, which were not of the sons of Levi.

32 And Jeroboam ordained a feast in the eighth month, on the fifteenth day of the month, like unto the feast that *is* in Judah, and he offered upon the altar. So did he

in Beth-el, sacrificing unto the calves that
he had made: and he placed in Beth-el the
priests of the high places which he had made.

33 So he offered upon the altar which he
had made in Beth-el the fifteenth day of the
eighth month, *even* in the month which he
had devised of his own heart; and ordained
a feast unto the children of Israel: and he
offered upon the altar, and burnt incense.

the unfaithful king by measuring later rulers against the standard of 'the sins of Jeroboam' (14:9–10)" (Fee and Hubbard, *Eerdmans Companion to the Bible*, 237).

CHAPTERS 13–14

Jeroboam is smitten and then healed by a prophet from Judah—The prophet delivers his message, is led astray by a prophet from Bethel, and is slain by a lion for his disobedience—Jeroboam continues false worship in Israel.

Ahijah foretells the ruin of Jeroboam's house, the death of his child, and the scattering of the Israelites because of their idolatry—Jeroboam dies and Nadab reigns—Judah, under Rehoboam, turns to wickedness—Shishak of Egypt takes treasures from the temple—Rehoboam dies and Abijam reigns.

Summary of 1 Kings 13–14

A man of God confronts Jeroboam with a prophecy that a king named Josiah will be raised up and bring religious reform. When Jeroboam challenges his words, two signs are given: his hand is withered and the altar at Beth-el is split. After he appeals to the prophet, his hand is restored to normal. Still, Jeroboam returns to his wickedness. Finally, Ahijah the prophet warns Jeroboam that his family will be destroyed and he will lose his kingdom if he does not change. Destruction comes upon Jeroboam as promised. In the southern kingdom, Rehoboam permits idol worship to continue. Rehoboam's kingdom becomes as wayward in apostasy as Jeroboam's. Shishak, the king of Egypt, enters Jerusalem and takes precious treasures from the temple and the king's house.

CHAPTERS 15–16

Abijam reigns in wickedness and then Asa reigns in righteousness in Judah—Nadab and then Baasha reign in wickedness in Israel—Baasha destroys the house of Jeroboam.

Jehu prophesies evil upon Baasha and his house—Elah, Zimri, Omri, and Ahab reign in wickedness—Zimri destroys the house of Baasha—Ahab marries Jezebel, worships Baal, and provokes the Lord to anger.

Summary of 1 Kings 15–16

After the deaths of Jeroboam and Rehoboam, new kings rule in Israel and Judah. Asa, king of Judah, pleases the Lord when he does away with the idolatrous worship in the southern kingdom. Ahab, king of Israel, enters into a politically advantageous marriage to the Phoenician princess Jezebel, and makes Baal worship official in the northern kingdom. Ahab does "more to provoke the Lord God of Israel to anger than all the kings of Israel that were before him" (1 Kings 16:33).

1 Kings 17:1–7. Elijah Seals the Heavens, and a Drought Occurs in Israel

Who was Elijah? (17:1) "Elijah was a fierce defender of Jehovah, as reflected by the meaning of his name '(my) God is Jehovah.' He is called 'the Tishbite who was of the inhabitants of Gilead,' meaning he came from east of the Jordan River, and he prophesied in northern Israel during the reign of the wicked king Ahab (873–852 B.C.) and his Phoenician wife Jezebel (1 Kgs 17–19; 21; 2 Kgs 1–2), who promoted the worship of Baal.

"There is no account of Elijah's call. Elijah first appears standing before King Ahab declaring that the Lord would send a drought on account of apostasy" (Holzapfel, et al., *Jehovah and the World of the Old Testament*, 258).

Why did Elijah declare that there would be no dew nor rain? (17:1) "Could such a dearth of life-giving moisture be justified as an act of God or of his servant? As terrible as such a curse may be, there are worse things. The physical suffering and calamity occasioned by drought are not nearly so dreadful as moral delinquency and spiritual apostasy. One makes mortality miserable; the other threatens eternity" (Merrill, *Elijah*, 11). ⊕

Why was Elijah commanded to hide himself? (17:3) "While Ahab and Elijah do not appear to be enemies at the beginning of the drought, it appears that God—in His foreknowledge—sent Elijah away (once the drought started) because He knew that Ahab and

CHAPTER 17

Elijah seals the heavens and is fed by the ravens—At his command the barrel of flour and the jar of oil of the widow of Zarephath never become empty—He raises her son from death.

1 And Elijah the Tishbite, *who was* of the inhabitants of Gilead, said unto Ahab, *As* the LORD God of Israel liveth, before whom I stand, there shall not be dew nor rain these years, but according to my word.

2 And the word of the LORD came unto him, saying,

3 Get thee hence, and turn thee eastward, and hide thyself by the brook Cherith, that *is* before Jordan.

Elijah Held the Sealing Keys of the Melchizedek Priesthood (1 Kings 17:1)

"The authority given to Elijah was that authority which pertains to the sealing ordinances of the gospel, such as we obtain in the temples of the Lord. . . . The keys of the Melchizedek Priesthood were held by ancient prophets and by Israel's prophets until the time of Moses. When the Lord took these keys away from Israel and left them the Aaronic Priesthood, there was still the necessity for the Lord to maintain prophets who held the Melchizedek Priesthood, but they were especially called and ordained in each instance by the direct edict from the Lord. . . .

"We read in [1 Kings 17] that power had been given to Elijah to close the heavens that there would be no rain except by his word. He had power given him to bless the widow's oil and meal and to bring down fire from heaven to consume his offering and destroy the false doctrines of the priests of Baal. The fact that Elijah had this great power and authority did not prevent other prophets from also holding some divine authority in the Melchizedek Priesthood which was essential to the faithful in the House of Israel. We should also remember the fact that in the days of the Savior's ministry this authority held by Elijah was bestowed by Elijah, and the authority held by Moses was restored by Moses to Peter, James, and John" (Smith, *Answers to Gospel Questions*, 4:6–8).

4 And it shall be, *that* thou shalt drink of the brook; and I have commanded the ravens to feed thee there.

5 So he went and did according unto the word of the LORD: for he went and dwelt by the brook Cherith, that *is* before Jordan.

6 And the ravens brought him bread and flesh in the morning, and bread and flesh in the evening; and he drank of the brook.

7 And it came to pass after a while, that the brook dried up, because there had been no rain in the land.

8 ¶ And the word of the LORD came unto him, saying,

9 Arise, get thee to Zarephath, which *belongeth* to Zidon, and dwell there: behold, I have commanded a widow woman there to sustain thee.

10 So he arose and went to Zarephath. And when he came to the gate of the city, behold, the widow woman *was* there gathering of sticks: and he called to her, and said, Fetch me, I pray thee, a little water in a vessel, that I may drink.

11 And as she was going to fetch *it,* he called to her, and said, Bring me, I pray thee, a morsel of bread in thine hand.

12 And she said, *As* the LORD thy God liveth, I have not a cake, but an handful of meal in a barrel, and a little oil in a cruse: and, behold, I *am* gathering two sticks, that I may go in and dress it for me and my son, that we may eat it, and die.

13 And Elijah said unto her, Fear not; go *and* do as thou hast said: but make me thereof a little cake first, and bring *it* unto me, and after make for thee and for thy son.

his wife would be angered by it and would eventually seek out the prophet in order to slay him, as a means of ending the drought and Israel's woes" (Gaskill, *Miracles of the Old Testament*, 255).

Why did the Lord have ravens provide Elijah with food? (17:4) "The ravens brought 'bread and flesh' morning and evening (1 Kings 17:6), reminiscent of the bread (manna) and flesh (quail) miraculously provided to the children of Israel as they wandered in the desert under Moses' leadership centuries earlier (see Numbers 11). Some commentators feel that the word ravens should be read 'merchants' or 'Arabs,' depending on the way they view the Hebrew text. Most, though, concur that the word really is ravens. It does not seem likely that the Lord would send Elijah to a desolate area to hide and then send people twice a day to feed him" (Merrill, *Elijah*, 14).

1 Kings 17:8–16. A Miracle Is Performed for a Widow in Zarephath

Who was the widow of Zarephath? (17:9) "*Zarephath* [was] a coastal town located between Tyre and Sidon, in the territory ruled by Jezebel's father. . . . Elijah was commanded to go and reside in the heart of the very land from which the Baal worship being promoted in Israel had come. . . . Elijah, as the bearer of God's word, was now to be sustained by human hands, but they were the hands of a poor widow facing starvation (v. 12). She was, moreover, from outside the circle of God's own people (see Luke 4:25–26); in fact, she was from the pagan nation that at that time (much like Egypt earlier and Babylon later) represented the forces arrayed against God's kingdom" (*Zondervan KJV Commentary*, 495).

Why would Elijah insist that the widow feed him first? (17:13) "We would expect Elijah to be the provider and the poor woman to be the one provided for. . . . But in this case, the Lord turned the tables. He

14 For thus saith the LORD God of Israel, The barrel of meal shall not waste, neither shall the cruse of oil fail, until the day *that* the LORD sendeth rain upon the earth.

commanded the one who had nothing to give as if she had everything. In like manner, God required the one who had been so blessed and richly endowed to ask for help from the lowest in the social, religious, and economic order. . . . With only an Israelite's word that her supply of oil and grain would inexplicably continue throughout the duration of the drought, . . . the widow put her trust in Elijah's God" (Olson, *Women of the Old Testament*, 228, 229–30). ⊕

15 And she went and did according to the saying of Elijah: and she, and he, and her house, did eat *many* days.

What do we know about the faith of this widow? (17:15) "Elijah was on the Lord's errand. Israel's future—including the future of this very widow and her son—was at stake. His prophetic duty made him more bold than he might normally have wanted to be. . . .

"Then this understated expression of faith—as great, under these circumstances, as any I know in the scriptures. The record says simply, 'And she went and did according to the saying of Elijah.' Perhaps uncertain what the cost of her faith would be not only to herself but to her son as well, she first took her small loaf to Elijah, obviously trusting that if there were not enough bread left over, at least she and her son would have died in an act of pure charity" (Holland, "Handful of Meal and a Little Oil," 29). ⊕

16 *And* the barrel of meal wasted not, neither did the cruse of oil fail, according to the word of the LORD, which he spake by Elijah.

How can we obtain faith like the widow of Zarephath? (17:16) "Sometimes we think our circumstances so extreme as to be impossible of resolution. Would the Lord do any less for us than he did for the widow long ago? Does he have any less love for us? No, he promises and he fulfills, for he is 'the same yesterday, today, and forever' (Mormon 9:9). There is, however, one warning regarding our expectation of blessings. It is that 'God will give liberally to him that asketh . . . if [he] ask not amiss' (2 Nephi 4:35)" (Merrill, *Elijah*, 20). When have you been sustained by the Lord's merciful power?

1 Kings 17:17–24. Elijah Raises the Woman's Son from the Dead

17 ¶ And it came to pass after these things, *that* the son of the woman, the mistress of the house, fell sick; and his sickness was so sore, that there was no breath left in him.

18 And she said unto Elijah, What have I to do with thee, O thou man of God? art thou come unto me to call my sin to remembrance, and to slay my son?

Did the widow's son die because of a sin? (17:17–18) "It seems evident from the narrative that the widow believed that some forgotten sin in her past was the reason that her son had died. However, we know that such is not doctrinally accurate. This episode brings to mind Jesus's conversation with the disciples in John 9, where they ask if a man born blind was so afflicted because his parents had sinned. Jesus responded, 'Neither hath this man sinned, nor his parents: but [he was born blind] that the works of God

19 And he said unto her, Give me thy son. And he took him out of her bosom, and carried him up into a loft, where he abode, and laid him upon his own bed.

20 And he cried unto the LORD, and said, O LORD my God, hast thou also brought evil upon the widow with whom I sojourn, by slaying her son?

21 And he stretched himself upon the child three times, and cried unto the LORD, and said, O LORD my God, I pray thee, let this child's soul come into him again.

22 And the LORD heard the voice of Elijah; and the soul of the child came into him again, and he revived.

23 And Elijah took the child, and brought him down out of the chamber into the house, and delivered him unto his mother: and Elijah said, See, thy son liveth.

24 ¶ And the woman said to Elijah, Now by this I know that thou *art* a man of God, *and* that the word of the LORD in thy mouth *is* truth.

CHAPTER 18

Elijah is sent to meet Ahab—Obadiah saves a hundred prophets and meets Elijah—Elijah challenges the prophets of Baal to call down fire from heaven—They fail—He calls down fire, slays the prophets of Baal, and opens the heavens for rain.

1 And it came to pass *after* many days, that the word of the LORD came to Elijah in the third year, saying, Go, shew thyself unto Ahab; and I will send rain upon the earth.

2 And Elijah went to shew himself unto Ahab. And *there was* a sore famine in Samaria.

3 And Ahab called Obadiah, which *was* the governor of *his* house. (Now Obadiah feared the LORD greatly:

should be made manifest in him' (John 9:3)" (Gaskill, *Miracles of the Old Testament*, 272).

How did Elijah stretch himself upon the child? (17:21) "In the King James Version of the Bible, Elijah *stretched* himself on the boy three times as he petitioned God to return him to life (1 Kings 17:21). The Hebrew reads literally, 'he *measured* or *extended* himself three times upon or over the boy' as he prayed. This reading appears nowhere else in the Hebrew Bible. A likely meaning of the passage is that three times Elijah extended himself to God in a prayer, perhaps with his hand stretched heavenward, on behalf of the boy" (Olson, *Women of the Old Testament*, 231–32).

1 Kings 18:1–6. A Sore Famine Continues throughout King Ahab's Kingdom

Who was Obadiah who cared for the prophets? (18:3–4) "[Obadiah] is a highly sympathetic figure, whose great faith in God and heroic actions help us gain a more balanced picture of the situation of people of faith in Israel at the time. . . . Obadiah was Ahab's palace official and minister of state, in both cases serving as the king's personal representative. . . . That there could be one hundred prophets for Obadiah to hide may be seen from the fact that associations of prophets who met and may even have lived together are known from this period onward (see 1 Sam. 10:5; 2 Kin. 2:3–7; 6:1, 2). . . . Caves have been found in the vicinity of Mt. Carmel, many of them capable of holding 50 men" (*NKJV Study Bible* [2018], 522). ⊕

Why was Ahab concerned about his "horses and mules"? (18:5) "Keeping horses alive was important to maintain military preparedness in a world where there was nearly always the threat of new hostilities" (*Nelson Study Bible* [NKJV], 522).

"If ever there was a time when Ahab and his people should have been brought to the depths of humility, it should have been at [this] moment. . . . We can only imagine the suffering, the complaints to the king, and the demands for relief. . . . We cannot help but wonder if he was as concerned about his subjects as he apparently was about maintaining the royal animals" (Merrill, *Elijah*, 25).

Summary of 1 Kings 18:7–16

Ahab tries in vain to locate Elijah. Occasionally, someone reports seeing Elijah, but Elijah is gone when Ahab arrives. Then Ahab has those individuals killed. Obadiah fears Elijah will not keep his word to meet with Ahab and that he will be killed (see vv. 12–16). Elijah promises Obadiah that he will surely show himself to Ahab (see v. 15).

1 Kings 18:17–40. Elijah Challenges the Prophets of Baal

Why did Ahab accuse Elijah of creating problems for Israel? (18:17–18) "Ahab, hoping to deal with Elijah from a position of strength, greeted him with the charge of being a troublemaker in Israel. Possibly the king was implying that the famine was all Elijah's fault; because of Elijah's hostile attitude, Baal had become angered and so had withheld rain for the past three years. Elijah's reply is particularly instructive. Not he, but Ahab and his family were the real troublers, because they had made Baal worship the state religion" (*Expositor's Bible Commentary [Abridged]*, 529).

What is meant by Baalim? (18:18) "The word most often associated with idolatry in the Old Testament is *Baal*. The gods of a people—in the plural—may be

4 For it was *so,* when Jezebel cut off the prophets of the Lord, that Obadiah took an hundred prophets, and hid them by fifty in a cave, and fed them with bread and water.)

5 And Ahab said unto Obadiah, Go into the land, unto all fountains of water, and unto all brooks: peradventure we may find grass to save the horses and mules alive, that we lose not all the beasts.

6 So they divided the land between them to pass throughout it: Ahab went one way by himself, and Obadiah went another way by himself.

17 ¶ And it came to pass, when Ahab saw Elijah, that Ahab said unto him, *Art* thou he that troubleth Israel?

18 And he answered, I have not troubled Israel; but thou, and thy father's house, in that ye have forsaken the commandments of the Lord, and thou hast followed Baalim.

19 Now therefore send, *and* gather to me all
Israel unto mount Carmel, and the prophets of Baal four hundred and fifty, and the
prophets of the groves four hundred, which
eat at Jezebel's table.
20 So Ahab sent unto all the children of
Israel, and gathered the prophets together
unto mount Carmel.

21 And Elijah came unto all the people, and
said, How long halt ye between two opinions? if the LORD *be* God, follow him: but
if Baal, *then* follow him. And the people answered him not a word.
22 Then said Elijah unto the people, I, *even* I
only, remain a prophet of the LORD; but Baal's
prophets *are* four hundred and fifty men.
23 Let them therefore give us two bullocks;
and let them choose one bullock for themselves, and cut it in pieces, and lay *it* on
wood, and put no fire *under:* and I will dress
the other bullock, and lay *it* on wood, and
put no fire *under:*
24 And call ye on the name of your gods,
and I will call on the name of the LORD: and
the God that answereth by fire, let him be
God. And all the people answered and said,
It is well spoken.

referred to as Baalim, as in 1 Kings 18:18. Thus, Baalism refers to the worship of anything or anyone other than the true and living God" (Madsen, "No Other Gods Before Me," 48).

Why did Elijah designate Mount Carmel for this confrontation? (18:19) "The name *Carmel* [means] 'vineyard of El,' and was probably considered by the Canaanites to be sacred to the old Canaanite God, as well as to Baal and to the Canaanites' two chief goddesses. . . . As the most prominent piece of land in the area, it was considered part of the body of Anath, the earth goddess. Furthermore, because it is the highest mountain in the region, during thunderstorms it receives more lightning strikes than other points; probably this was thought to indicate Baal's presence. The mountain also receives more rainfall than any other spot in Israel, making it an even more suitable representation of Anath, on whom Baal sends his rain" (Tvedtnes, "Elijah," 54).

What does the phrase "halt ye between two opinions" mean? (18:21) "The literal translation of the phrase 'How long halt ye between two opinions?' in the past has been interpreted as 'How long hop ye about upon two boughs?' The phrase is a metaphor that uses birds that hop from bough to bough, not knowing where to stay" (Black, *400 Questions and Answers about the Old Testament*, 124).

"The question for Israelites . . . implied a dangerous double-mindedness (1 Kgs. 18:21*a*). It was Elijah's dramatic way of trying to turn the hearts of the children of Israel back to the covenants of the Lord with their forefathers" (Rasmussen, *Latter-Day Saint Commentary on the Old Testament*, 293). ⊕

What might the use of fire symbolize in this contest? (18:24) "The contest Elijah proposed should have appealed to the prophets of Baal, since they believed their god rode on the thunderstorm and used lightning as his weapon. Surely he could send down fire from heaven. Elijah's comparison between the number of prophets of Baal and the number of prophets of the Lord (see v. 22) was intended to show the great power of the only true God" (Valletta, et al., *Old Testament for Latter-day Saint Families*, 327).

Why did Elijah allow the priests of Baal to make the first attempt? (18:25) "By letting the priests of Baal go first, Elijah again gave them a favorable position. Throughout the contest, he did everything he could to demonstrate how much God has power and how the Phoenician gods were not gods at all and thus had no power at all. He did this by giving the Phoenician priests every possible advantage in the contest, such as holding it in a place sacred for El, letting Baal's priests go first, and giving them a very long time to attempt their sacrifice" (Muhlestein, *Scripture Study Made Simple*, 255).

Why did Elijah mock the priests? (18:27) "[Elijah's] insults were even stronger than they seem at first glance. Can one worship a god who likes to take trips and leave the world to run itself without supervision? Or a god who is so busy talking that he would not interrupt his chat to respond to the pleas of his ardent followers? The phrase 'he is pursuing' actually should read 'he has gone aside,' which some commentators interpret as a euphemism to mean 'he has gone to the bathroom.' . . . There are moments when [sarcasm] is used in a divine manner to expose or ridicule evil designs and hearts" (Merrill, *Elijah*, 39–40).

Why did Elijah repair the broken altar? (18:30–32) "It is possible that the altar had been built by people of the northern ten tribes after the division of the kingdom . . . and that it had been destroyed by the agents of Jezebel (vv. 4, 13; 19:10, 14). . . .

"[By using twelve stones to rebuild the altar] Elijah called attention to the covenant unity of Israel as the people of God in spite of her political division. What was about to happen concerned the entire nation, not just the northern ten tribes" (*NIV Study Bible* [1995], 512).

Why did Elijah have water poured upon the sacrifice and the wood three times? (18:33–35) "Elijah undoubtedly drenched the altar and sacrifice with water as much for the heathen priests as for the people. He wanted to convince them that there was no trickery and to show them that the power of the Lord was manifest. It was a bold and dramatic move

25 And Elijah said unto the prophets of Baal, Choose you one bullock for yourselves, and dress *it* first; for ye *are* many; and call on the name of your gods, but put no fire *under.*

26 And they took the bullock which was given them, and they dressed *it,* and called on the name of Baal from morning even until noon, saying, O Baal, hear us. But *there was* no voice, nor any that answered. And they leaped upon the altar which was made.

27 And it came to pass at noon, that Elijah mocked them, and said, Cry aloud: for he *is* a god; either he is talking, or he is pursuing, or he is in a journey, *or* peradventure he sleepeth, and must be awaked.

28 And they cried aloud, and cut themselves after their manner with knives and lancets, till the blood gushed out upon them.

29 And it came to pass, when midday was past, and they prophesied until the *time* of the offering of the *evening* sacrifice, that *there was* neither voice, nor any to answer, nor any that regarded.

30 And Elijah said unto all the people, Come near unto me. And all the people came near unto him. And he repaired the altar of the LORD *that was* broken down.

31 And Elijah took twelve stones, according to the number of the tribes of the sons of Jacob, unto whom the word of the LORD came, saying, Israel shall be thy name:

32 And with the stones he built an altar in the name of the LORD: and he made a trench about the altar, as great as would contain two measures of seed.

33 And he put the wood in order, and cut the bullock in pieces, and laid *him* on the wood, and said, Fill four barrels with water, and pour *it* on the burnt sacrifice, and on the wood.

34 And he said, Do *it* the second time. And they did *it* the second time. And he said, Do *it* the third time. And they did *it* the third time.

35 And the water ran round about the altar; and he filled the trench also with water.

36 And it came to pass at *the time of* the offering of the *evening* sacrifice, that Elijah the prophet came near, and said, LORD God of Abraham, Isaac, and of Israel, let it be known this day that thou *art* God in Israel, and *that* I *am* thy servant, and *that* I have done all these things at thy word.

37 Hear me, O LORD, hear me, that this people may know that thou *art* the LORD God, and *that* thou hast turned their heart back again.

38 Then the fire of the LORD fell, and consumed the burnt sacrifice, and the wood, and the stones, and the dust, and licked up the water that *was* in the trench.

39 And when all the people saw *it,* they fell on their faces: and they said, The LORD, he *is* the God; the LORD, he *is* the God.

40 And Elijah said unto them, Take the prophets of Baal; let not one of them escape. And they took them: and Elijah brought them down to the brook Kishon, and slew them there.

that demonstrated his absolute confidence in the power of the true God" (*Old Testament Student Manual: 1 Kings–Malachi*, 61).

Had the Lord already turned the hearts of Israel back to Him? (18:37) The Joseph Smith Translation for 1 Kings 18:37 changes "that thou hast turned their heart back again" to "thou *mayest turn* their heart back again" (see Wayment, *Complete Joseph Smith Translation of the Old Testament*, 140). The Israelites would still need to exercise their agency to choose the Lord and fully turn their hearts to Him.

How did this miracle reveal the futility of worshipping false gods? (18:38) "Elijah's challenge specifically targets the Canaanite religion. Baal is celebrated as being able to cast lightning or fire down from the sky. . . . The contest takes place at a sacred place for the chief Canaanite god, El, who is also symbolized by the bullock they offer. Asherah is represented by the many trees in the area and the wood that is burned. Anat is symbolized by the dirt and dust that is burned, and Mot is represented by the water. In this way the Lord either consumes symbols of all these gods or shows that He is the one who can really do godly things" (Muhlestein, *Essential Old Testament Companion*, 269).

Why were the priests of Baal executed? (18:40) "Elijah availed himself of this enthusiasm of the people for the Lord, to deal a fatal blow at the prophets of Baal, who turned away the people from the living God. He commanded the people to seize them, and had them slain at the brook Kishon, and that not so much from revenge, i.e., because it was at their instigation that queen Jezebel had murdered the prophets of the true God (1 Kings 18:13), as to carry out the fundamental law of the Old Testament kingdom of God, which prohibited idolatry on pain of death, and commanded that false prophets should be destroyed (Deuteronomy 17:2–3; Deuteronomy 13:13.)" (Keil and Delitzsch, *Commentary* [on 1 Kings 18:40–46]).

1 Kings 18:41–46. The Drought Ends with Much Rain Sent by the Lord

Why did Elijah put his face between his knees? (18:42–44) "This was a posture of prayer [Elijah] put himself into, and continued in; . . . expressive of his humility, and of his earnestness, and vehement desire, and continued importunity, that rain might fall" (*John Gill's Exposition of the Whole Bible* [commentary on 1 Kings 18:42]; paragraphing altered).

"'*Seven times*' [1 Kings 18:43], . . . the servant of Elijah was sent to scan the sea for a sign of a cloud. On the seventh time, he saw a small cloud arising *out of the sea* (v. 44), that is, appearing on the western horizon. The Lord's last proof of his supremacy over Baal was to do what the storm god could not do—send the rain God had shut off three and a half years earlier" (*Zondervan KJV Commentary*, 499).

How was Elijah able to run to Jezreel and arrive before Ahab? (18:46) "Ahab headed speedily for Jezreel, which lay about seventeen miles away, easterly across the plains of Esdraelon. . . . A person running on foot can cover a given distance in a relatively straight line more quickly than can an entourage in chariots following roads. But even so, the Lord must have given Elijah mighty strength to reach the city before the king. . . . At the close of one of the most memorable days in history, it seems most appropriate that the prophet of God should have reached Jezreel first, being placed geographically, as well as spiritually, 'before' the king" (Merrill, *Elijah*, 48–49).

1 Kings 19:1–8. Elijah's Discouragement Is Lifted by an Angel from God

41 ¶ And Elijah said unto Ahab, Get thee up,
eat and drink; for *there is* a sound of abundance of rain.
42 So Ahab went up to eat and to drink. And
Elijah went up to the top of Carmel; and he cast himself down upon the earth, and put his face between his knees,
43 And said to his servant, Go up now, look
toward the sea. And he went up, and looked, and said, *There is* nothing. And he said, Go again seven times.
44 And it came to pass at the seventh time,
that he said, Behold, there ariseth a little cloud out of the sea, like a man's hand. And he said, Go up, say unto Ahab, Prepare *thy chariot,* and get thee down, that the rain stop thee not.
45 And it came to pass in the mean while,
that the heaven was black with clouds and wind, and there was a great rain. And Ahab rode, and went to Jezreel.
46 And the hand of the LORD was on Elijah;
and he girded up his loins, and ran before Ahab to the entrance of Jezreel.

CHAPTER 19

Jezebel seeks the life of Elijah—An angel sends him to Horeb—The Lord speaks to Elijah, not in the wind nor the earthquake nor the fire, but in a still, small voice—Elisha joins Elijah.

1 And Ahab told Jezebel all that Elijah had
done, and withal how he had slain all the prophets with the sword.

2 Then Jezebel sent a messenger unto Elijah, saying, So let the gods do *to me,* and more also, if I make not thy life as the life of one of them by to morrow about this time.

3 And when he saw *that,* he arose, and went for his life, and came to Beer-sheba, which *belongeth* to Judah, and left his servant there.

How does Jezebel respond to Ahab's report of Elijah's miracle? (19:2) "These verses show how powerful and corrupt Jezebel was. Even after the miraculous fire from heaven, this woman was moved only to anger and swore she would take Elijah's life in revenge. Elijah fled, first into the territory of Judah (at Beersheba) and then to Mount Horeb (or Sinai) 150 miles further south. . . .

"It must have been very lonely for Elijah during this period. Men were seeking his life, he felt himself to be the only faithful prophet left in Israel, and he was hiding in a cave" (*Old Testament Student Manual: 1 Kings–Malachi*, 61).

4 ¶ But he himself went a day's journey into the wilderness, and came and sat down under a juniper tree: and he requested for himself that he might die; and said, It is enough; now, O LORD, take away my life; for I *am* not better than my fathers.

5 And as he lay and slept under a juniper tree, behold, then an angel touched him, and said unto him, Arise *and* eat.

6 And he looked, and, behold, *there was* a cake baken on the coals, and a cruse of water at his head. And he did eat and drink, and laid him down again.

7 And the angel of the LORD came again the second time, and touched him, and said, Arise *and* eat; because the journey *is* too great for thee.

Why did Elijah pray that the Lord would end his life? (19:4) "The deep despondency of Elijah's soul found utterance in the entreaty to be released from work and suffering. He was not better than his fathers; like them he had vainly toiled; like them he had failed; why should his painful mission be prolonged? . . . Like Moses of old, he must at least gain distant view of the sweet land of beauty and rest. As so often, God in His tender mercy gave His beloved the precious relief of sleep. And more than that—he was to have evidence that even there he was not forsaken" (Edersheim, *Bible History Old Testament*, 696).

Why did the Lord send an angel to help Elijah? (19:5–7) "Elijah should have recognized God's concern for his prophet in the angel's supplying his need for nourishment for the journey that lay ahead. The narrator expects the reader to make the connection between the Kerith Ravine [the brook Cherith] incident ([1 Kings] 17:2–6) and the miraculous supply at the widow of Zarephath's home (17:13–16). In the latter case the correlation is unmistakable, for the Hebrew words used for 'the cake of bread' and 'jar' [cruse] are those used previously in 17:13–14" (Patterson and Austel, "1, 2 Kings," 782).

8 And he arose, and did eat and drink, and went in the strength of that meat forty days and forty nights unto Horeb the mount of God.

Why did it take forty days for Elijah to travel to Horeb? (19:8) Horeb is another name for Mt. Sinai. "The forty days and forty nights are not to be taken as a measure of the distance of Horeb from the prophet's starting-point (1 Kings 19:3–4), for this (about 180 [miles]) could be traversed in a much shorter time, but are meant to associate Elijah with Moses (see Exodus 24:18; [Deuteronomy 9:11, 18]). In solitary communion with God, such as Moses had enjoyed, the prophet would recover his fortitude" (*John Dummelow's Commentary* [on 1 Kings 19:1–21]).

1 Kings 19:9–18. The Lord Teaches Elijah about the Still Small Voice

9 ¶ And he came thither unto a cave, and lodged there; and, behold, the word of the LORD *came* to him, and he said unto him, What doest thou here, Elijah?

10 And he said, I have been very jealous for the LORD God of hosts: for the children of Israel have forsaken thy covenant, thrown down thine altars, and slain thy prophets with the sword; and I, *even* I only, am left; and they seek my life, to take it away.

11 And he said, Go forth, and stand upon the mount before the LORD. And, behold, the LORD passed by, and a great and strong wind rent the mountains, and brake in pieces the rocks before the LORD; *but* the LORD *was* not in the wind: and after the wind an earthquake; *but* the LORD *was* not in the earthquake:

12 And after the earthquake a fire; *but* the LORD *was* not in the fire: and after the fire a still small voice.

13 And it was *so,* when Elijah heard *it,* that he wrapped his face in his mantle, and went out, and stood in the entering in of the cave. And, behold, *there came* a voice unto him, and said, What doest thou here, Elijah?

14 And he said, I have been very jealous for the LORD God of hosts: because the children of Israel have forsaken thy covenant, thrown down thine altars, and slain thy prophets with the sword; and I, *even* I only, am left; and they seek my life, to take it away.

15 And the LORD said unto him, Go, return on thy way to the wilderness of Damascus: and when thou comest, anoint Hazael *to be* king over Syria:

16 And Jehu the son of Nimshi shalt thou anoint *to be* king over Israel: and Elisha the

What can we learn from Elijah about how God communicates with His servants? (19:11–12) President Gordon B. Hinckley explained: "The best way I could describe the process is to liken it to the experience of Elijah. . . . Elijah spoke to the Lord, and there was a wind, a great wind, and the Lord was not in the wind. And there was an earthquake, and the Lord was not in the earthquake. And there was a fire, and the Lord was not in the fire. And after the fire a still, small voice, which I describe as the whisperings of the Spirit. . . . The things of God are understood by the Spirit of God, and one must have and seek and cultivate that Spirit" (Hinckley, "This Thing Was Not Done in a Corner," 51).

son of Shaphat of Abel-meholah shalt thou anoint *to be* prophet in thy room.

17 And it shall come to pass, *that* him that escapeth the sword of Hazael shall Jehu slay: and him that escapeth from the sword of Jehu shall Elisha slay.

Did Elisha slay anyone? (19:17) "There is no record of Elisha slaying anyone. This passage may mean that Elisha would prophesy the death of certain people. Of course, the Bible record as it is now is fragmentary at best, and the details of the incident referred to here may be lost" (*Old Testament Student Manual: 1 Kings–Malachi*, 62).

18 Yet I have left *me* seven thousand in Israel, all the knees which have not bowed unto Baal, and every mouth which hath not kissed him.

What does it mean that 7,000 in Israel had not kissed Baal? (19:18) "The Lord reassured Elijah that he was not the only true worshipper of Jehovah remaining in Israel: 'Yet I have left me seven thousand in Israel . . .' (1 Kgs 19:18). Their mouths having not kissed Baal reiterates the sense of the previous phrase: they had not bowed down or worshipped Baal. Egyptian and Mesopotamian texts refer to kissing the feet of or the ground in front of deities as an act of devoted submission" (Holzapfel, et al., *Jehovah and the World of the Old Testament*, 260).

1 Kings 19:19–21. Elijah Calls Elisha to the Ministry

19 ¶ So he departed thence, and found Elisha the son of Shaphat, who *was* plowing *with* twelve yoke *of oxen* before him, and he with the twelfth: and Elijah passed by him, and cast his mantle upon him.

20 And he left the oxen, and ran after Elijah, and said, Let me, I pray thee, kiss my father and my mother, and *then* I will follow thee. And he said unto him, Go back again: for what have I done to thee?

21 And he returned back from him, and took a yoke of oxen, and slew them, and boiled their flesh with the instruments of the oxen, and gave unto the people, and they did eat. Then he arose, and went after Elijah, and ministered unto him.

Why was Elisha plowing with so many oxen? (19:19) "Elijah used symbolic action to call Elisha. There is symbolism in the fact that he was plowing with twelve yoke of oxen. Plowing is how a field is prepared for planting. Plowing rips the ground apart and beats it up so it can receive seeds. This would be Elisha's role among the twelve tribes. It is also worth noting that having twelve yoke of oxen (twenty-four oxen in all) meant that Elisha was somewhat well-to-do" (Muhlestein, *Scripture Study Made Simple*, 259).

Why did Elijah throw his mantle upon Elisha? (19:19) "The temporary passing of Elijah's mantle to Elisha symbolized his calling; later it was permanently bestowed (2 Kgs. 2:8, 13–14). Note that Elisha was required to leave all that he had to perform his new calling (cf. Matt. 4:18–22)" (Rasmussen, *Latter-day Saint Commentary on the Old Testament*, 295).

Summary of 1 Kings 20–21

Ben-hadad leads Syria to battle twice against Israel and is defeated both times. Ahab disobeys the Lord's counsel and allows Syria's king to go free (see 1 Kings 20:34). This disobedience brings the judgments of God upon Ahab and his household. Ahab's wife Jezebel forms a murderous scheme to acquire the property and vineyard of Naboth for her husband. False witnesses accuse Naboth of blasphemy and he is stoned to death. The prophet Elijah arrives and pronounces divine judgment upon Ahab and Jezebel for their wickedness.

Summary of 1 Kings 22

The prophet Micaiah declares that wicked king Ahab will not survive the battle with the Syrians. Though Ahab is disguised, an arrow finds its mark between pieces of his armor and kills Ahab. The words of Elijah are fulfilled as Ahab's blood runs into his chariot and is later licked up by dogs in Samaria. His son Ahaziah reigns in his stead and continues to worship Baal. In contrast, Jehoshaphat, the new king of Judah, reigns in righteousness.

CHAPTERS 20–21

Benhadad of Syria makes war with Israel—The Syrians are defeated twice—Ahab lets Benhadad go free, contrary to the will of the Lord.

Ahab desires the vineyard of Naboth—Jezebel arranges for false witnesses, and Naboth is stoned for blasphemy—Elijah prophesies that Ahab and Jezebel and their house will be destroyed.

CHAPTER 22

Jehoshaphat of Judah and Ahab of Israel join forces against Syria—Ahab's prophets foretell success—Micaiah foretells the defeat and death of Ahab—Ahab is slain and dogs lick up his blood—Jehoshaphat reigns in righteousness in Judah—Ahaziah reigns in Israel and serves Baal.

THE SECOND BOOK OF THE
KINGS
COMMONLY CALLED
THE FOURTH BOOK OF THE KINGS

Introduction

1 and 2 Kings were originally one book. "Second Kings continues the story of the Hebrew monarchies. Chapters 1–17 describe the period from the reigns of Ahaziah of Israel and Jehoshaphat of Judah until the fall of Samaria and the end of the kingdom of Israel in 721 B.C. Chapters 18–25 relate the story of the kingdom of Judah from the fall of the kingdom of Israel to the fall of Judah with the capture and destruction of Jerusalem by Nebuchadnezzar in 586 B.C., ending with a brief account of the governorship of Gedaliah and the elevation of King Jehoiachin in exile. . . . The fall of both Israel and Judah is interpreted in terms of the judgment of the Lord" (*New Oxford Annotated Bible* [1991], 463). See commentary in this volume for introduction to the first book of the Kings.

"The Second Book of the Kings is a book of tragedy. Once the nation of Israel stood unified under the leadership of Saul, David, and Solomon. The sad story of the divided kingdoms of Judah and Israel continues until both are taken captive by their enemies. In spite of the powerful ministries of Elijah, Elisha, and other prophets, the northern kingdom of Israel is conquered in 722 B.C. by Assyria (see 2 Kings 17) and the southern kingdom of Judah is conquered by the Babylonians in 587 B.C. (see 2 Kings 25). History loses sight of the northern tribes of Israel taken captive to Assyria (known as the ten lost tribes) but faithfully records the tribe of Judah's return to Jerusalem seventy years after they were conquered (see Ezra 1–6)" (Valletta, et al, *Old Testament for Latter-day Saint Families*, 333).

"It should be further noted that the narratives in Kings concerning Elijah and Elisha are among the best scriptural accounts of the function of prophets in Israel. The writer(s) or editor(s) of Kings attempted to preserve a complete account of each king in both the Northern and the Southern Kingdoms and devised an ingenious system that allowed the telling of both histories simultaneously. The system consists of a series of simple formulas that provide the relevant information for each king in both kingdoms and allow both histories to be told in sequence, alternating between the Southern and the Northern Kingdom. The formulas differed slightly for the North and the South, generally including more information from the South. Important historical events are narrated in the reign of the king in which they occurred, and a relative chronology is maintained throughout the book" (Seely, "Kings and Chronicles," 7–8).

"In the original Hebrew, the book of Kings was the longest book in the Bible. . . . This history was compiled from documents and state chronicles written toward the end of the Babylonian exile" (Black, *400 Questions and Answers*, 110–11). "The [book describes] a people without direction, leaders who failed to lead, and a God who was forced to discipline His rebellious people" (*Nelson Study Bible* [NJKV], 607).

CHAPTER 1

Ahaziah turns to Baalzebub to learn if he will live—Elijah prophesies Ahaziah's death—Elijah calls down fire from heaven to consume the soldiers sent to apprehend him.

1 Then Moab rebelled against Israel after the death of Ahab.

2 Kings 1:1–2. The King of Israel, Ahaziah, Seeks Help from False Gods

Who were the Moabites? (1:1) "The Moabites occupied the territory east of the Dead Sea. They were the descendants of Lot (see Genesis 19:37). Years earlier David had conquered them. . . . The Moabites now saw an opportunity to break connection with the Israelites, and they were determined to make the most of it. Their king, a man named Mesha, was so proud of the Moabites' rebellion that he wrote about it on a large black stone that has been discovered by archeologists. . . . Mesha recorded on the stone the account of hundreds of cities being added to his kingdom and how he built reservoirs, aqueducts, and fortifications" (*Old Testament Student Manual:1 Kings–Malachi*, 63).

Why did the king of Israel seek revelation from a false god? (1:2) "This dramatic episode shows how deeply apostate this Israelite king had become and how vigorously the Lord, through his prophet Elijah, tried to correct the presumption of such a king, even though it involved removing some servants of the king from this life.

"Because of his attitudes and actions, Ahaziah died after only two years of rule, as the true prophet had predicted.

"The name of the idol god Baal-zebub appears as 'Beelzebub' in the New Testament (Matt. 12:24), where he is referred to as 'the prince of the devils.' The name means 'Lord of flies,' and he was the Philistine god of both disease and healing" (Rasmussen, *Latter-day Saint Commentary on the Old Testament*, 300).

2 Kings 1:3–18. Elijah Calls Down Fire from Heaven

Why is Elijah referred to as the Tishbite? (1:3) "Elijah is here called 'the Tishbite, who was of the inhabitants of Gilead.' Some scholars say that Elijah came from Tishbeh, in upper Galilee (see [Keil and Delitzsch], *Commentary on the Old Testament*, 3:1:234). Adam Clarke suggested a different place. Elijah came, he said, from Gilead beyond the Jordan in the land given to the tribe of Gad (see [*Holy Bible with Commentary*], 2:452). Whichever is correct, it is clear that the title *Tishbite* refers to the place from which Elijah came" (*Old Testament Student Manual:1 Kings–Malachi*, 59).

Why did the king's messengers not finish their assignment? (1:5–6) At the Lord's behest Elijah intercepts the king's messengers on their way to enquire of false gods on the king's behalf. The Lord apparently did not want Ahaziah to be encouraged by a false message since he had already received the word of God (see *Nelson Study Bible* [NKJV], 609).

2 And Ahaziah fell down through a lattice in
his upper chamber that *was* in Samaria, and
was sick: and he sent messengers, and said
unto them, Go, inquire of Baal-zebub the
god of Ekron whether I shall recover of this
disease.

3 But the angel of the LORD said to Elijah the
Tishbite, Arise, go up to meet the messengers
of the king of Samaria, and say unto them,
Is it not because *there is* not a God in Israel,
that ye go to inquire of Baal-zebub the god
of Ekron?

4 Now therefore thus saith the LORD, Thou
shalt not come down from that bed on which
thou art gone up, but shalt surely die. And
Elijah departed.

5 ¶ And when the messengers turned back
unto him, he said unto them, Why are ye
now turned back?

6 And they said unto him, There came a man
up to meet us, and said unto us, Go, turn
again unto the king that sent you, and say
unto him, Thus saith the LORD, *Is it* not because *there is* not a God in Israel, *that* thou

sendest to inquire of Baal-zebub the god of Ekron? therefore thou shalt not come down from that bed on which thou art gone up, but shalt surely die.

7 And he said unto them, What manner of man *was he* which came up to meet you, and told you these words?

8 And they answered him, *He was* an hairy man, and girt with a girdle of leather about his loins. And he said, It *is* Elijah the Tishbite.

Why was Elijah called a "hairy" man? (1:8) "The reference to 'hairy' could mean that Elijah wore long hair and a full beard or, more likely, refers to his wearing a garment of animal skins covered with hair or wool on the outside. Most individuals in society would have worn clothing made from woven materials instead. It appears that the mantle of the prophet was easily recognizable as something relatively unique because of the way the messengers mentioned it. Their description parallels that given of John the Baptist, who 'was clothed with camel's hair, and a with a girdle of a skin about his loins' (Mark 1:6). The description, though seemingly brief and vague, was sufficient to be immediately recognized by King Ahaziah" (Merrill, *Elijah*, 72).

9 Then the king sent unto him a captain of fifty with his fifty. And he went up to him: and, behold, he sat on the top of an hill. And he spake unto him, Thou man of God, the king hath said, Come down.

10 And Elijah answered and said to the captain of fifty, If I *be* a man of God, then let fire come down from heaven, and consume thee and thy fifty. And there came down fire from heaven, and consumed him and his fifty.

11 Again also he sent unto him another captain of fifty with his fifty. And he answered and said unto him, O man of God, thus hath the king said, Come down quickly.

12 And Elijah answered and said unto them, If I *be* a man of God, let fire come down from heaven, and consume thee and thy fifty. And the fire of God came down from heaven, and consumed him and his fifty.

13 ¶ And he sent again a captain of the third fifty with his fifty. And the third captain of fifty went up, and came and fell on his knees

Why would God destroy these men with fire? (1:9–14) "Some have blamed the prophet for destroying these men, by bringing down fire from heaven upon them. But they do not consider that it was no more possible for Elijah to bring down fire from heaven, than for them to do it. God alone could send the fire; and as he is just and good, he would not have destroyed these men had there not been a sufficient cause to justify the act.... Elijah, personally, had no concern in the business. God led him simply to announce on these occasions what he himself had determined to do" (*Adam Clarke's Commentary* [on 2 Kings 1:10]). ⊕

Why was there a different outcome for this group of soldiers sent to slay Elijah? (1:13) "Whether or not the third captain of fifty had received instructions to immediately slay the prophet Elijah..., this captain of fifty was far more circumspect in his treatment of the man of God. It may have been that this man, together with his company, were men who in reality had remained somewhat in touch with the faith of their fathers. They could not afford to be disobedient to the king, but they nonetheless knew that their lives would be forfeit if they tried to bully the prophet as had their predecessors" (Hyde, *Comprehensive Commentary [1 and 2 Kings]*, 23).

How many different individuals named Jehoram are mentioned in this verse? (1:17) "The Vulgate, Septuagint, and Syriac say, Jehoram His Brother reigned in his stead, in the second year of Jehoram. There were two Jehorams who were contemporary: the first, the son of Ahab, brother to Ahaziah, and his successor in the kingdom of Israel; the second, the son of Jehoshaphat, king of Judah, who succeeded his father in Judah" (*Adam Clarke's Commentary* [on 2 Kings 1:17]). Thus, both the king of Israel and the king of Judah at this time had been given the name Jehoram.

What is the book of the chronicles mentioned here referring to? (1:18) "*The book of the chronicles of the kings of Israel* is mentioned often in 1 Kings as an early source book for the history of the northern kingdom. These chronicles should not be confused with the biblical books of 1 and 2 Chronicles" (*NKJV Study Bible* [2007], 546). A footnote in the Latter-day Saint edition of the Bible states: "It is significant that the kings of Israel and Judah kept official records; these records are no longer extant; they were used as source books by the author(s) of our books of Kings; they are not our books of Chronicles" (1 Kings 14:19*a*).

before Elijah, and besought him, and said unto him, O man of God, I pray thee, let my life, and the life of these fifty thy servants, be precious in thy sight.

14 Behold, there came fire down from heaven, and burnt up the two captains of the former fifties with their fifties: therefore let my life now be precious in thy sight.

15 And the angel of the LORD said unto Elijah, Go down with him: be not afraid of him. And he arose, and went down with him unto the king.

16 And he said unto him, Thus saith the LORD, Forasmuch as thou hast sent messengers to inquire of Baal-zebub the god of Ekron, *is it* not because *there is* no God in Israel to inquire of his word? therefore thou shalt not come down off that bed on which thou art gone up, but shalt surely die.

17 ¶ So he died according to the word of the LORD which Elijah had spoken. And Jehoram reigned in his stead in the second year of Jehoram the son of Jehoshaphat king of Judah; because he had no son.

18 Now the rest of the acts of Ahaziah which he did, *are* they not written in the book of the chronicles of the kings of Israel?

CHAPTER 2

Elisha and the prophets know that Elijah is to be translated—Elijah divides the waters of the Jordan and is taken up into heaven in a whirlwind—The mantle of Elijah falls on Elisha, who also divides the waters of the Jordan—Elisha heals the waters of Jericho—Youths are torn by bears for mocking Elisha.

1 And it came to pass, when the LORD would take up Elijah into heaven by a whirlwind, that Elijah went with Elisha from Gilgal.

2 And Elijah said unto Elisha, Tarry here, I pray thee; for the LORD hath sent me to Beth-el. And Elisha said *unto him, As* the LORD liveth, and *as* thy soul liveth, I will not leave thee. So they went down to Beth-el.

3 And the sons of the prophets that *were* at Beth-el came forth to Elisha, and said unto him, Knowest thou that the LORD will take away thy master from thy head to day? And he said, Yea, I know *it;* hold ye your peace.

4 And Elijah said unto him, Elisha, tarry here, I pray thee; for the LORD hath sent me to Jericho. And he said, *As* the LORD liveth, and *as* thy soul liveth, I will not leave thee. So they came to Jericho.

5 And the sons of the prophets that *were* at Jericho came to Elisha, and said unto him, Knowest thou that the LORD will take away thy master from thy head to day? And he answered, Yea, I know *it;* hold ye your peace.

6 And Elijah said unto him, Tarry, I pray thee, here; for the LORD hath sent me to Jordan. And he said, *As* the LORD liveth, and

2 Kings 2:1–8. Elisha Learns That Elijah Will Be Translated

What does it mean that "the Lord would take up Elijah into heaven"? (2:1) "Elijah was taken to heaven in 'a chariot of fire,' without tasting death (2 Kgs. 2:1–11). In other words, he became a translated being with temporary power over death. This was necessary in order that he might return to the Mount of Transfiguration and bestow keys of authority on Peter, James, and John, for he had to possess a tangible earthly body for that mission" (Brewster, *Doctrine & Covenants Encyclopedia*, 151). Translated "refers to the condition whereby God alters the physical condition of selected mortals, thus making them temporarily impervious to the frailties of the flesh, including death. . . . At the appropriate future time, each of these translated beings will pass through an instantaneous death and be resurrected" (Brewster, *Doctrine & Covenants Encyclopedia*, 600). ⊕

Who were the "sons of the prophets"? (2:3–7) The school of the prophets was "the name given to bands of prophets or 'sons of prophets' living together for instruction and worship under Samuel, Elijah, and Elisha. Little is known about these schools, but they seem to have been important religious institutions in Israel and references to them are frequent (1 Sam. 10:11; 19:19–20; 2 Kgs. 2:3, 5; 4:38; 6:1). Not all the 'sons of the prophets' claimed to have a supernatural gift; they were simply trained religious teachers, while some inspired prophets had received no training in the schools (Amos 7:14; see also D&C 88:127, 136–38; 90:7; 95:10, 17)" (Bible Dictionary, "Schools of the Prophets"). ⊕

as thy soul liveth, I will not leave thee. And
they two went on.

7 And fifty men of the sons of the prophets
went, and stood to view afar off: and they
two stood by Jordan.

8 And Elijah took his mantle, and wrapped
it together, and smote the waters, and they
were divided hither and thither, so that they
two went over on dry ground.

What can be understood by Elijah's smiting the waters with his mantle? (2:8) "Elijah's use of his rolled-up cloak to perform this miracle has caused many commentators to link this imagery to Moses's use of his staff to smite and part the waters of the Red Sea (see Exodus 14:21–31). The staff and cloak each appear to be utilized as 'the symbol of [their] office' [Wiseman, *1 and 2 Kings*, 195]" (Gaskill, *Miracles of the Old Testament*, 303).

2 Kings 2:9–11. Elijah Is Taken Away in a Chariot of Fire

9 ¶ And it came to pass, when they were
gone over, that Elijah said unto Elisha, Ask
what I shall do for thee, before I be taken
away from thee. And Elisha said, I pray thee,
let a double portion of thy spirit be upon me.

10 And he said, Thou hast asked a hard
thing: *nevertheless,* if thou see me *when I am*
taken from thee, it shall be so unto thee; but
if not, it shall not be *so.*

11 And it came to pass, as they still went
on, and talked, that, behold, *there appeared* a
chariot of fire, and horses of fire, and parted
them both asunder; and Elijah went up by a
whirlwind into heaven.

What is a double portion of the spirit? (2:9) "Elijah asked his student-prophet what he would desire of him before his departure. 'I pray thee, let a double portion of thy spirit be upon me,' Elisha replied (2 Kgs. 2:9). The term *double portion* refers to Elisha's desire for the special inheritance that belongs to the worthy firstborn male in a family (see Bible Dictionary, "Firstborn," 675). Elijah deferred the granting of this request to the will of the Lord, saying, 'If thou see me when I am taken from thee, it shall be so unto thee' (2 Kgs. 2:10)" (Andreason, "Mantle of Elijah," 26). ⊕

What is the symbolism behind the imagery of a "chariot of fire" and "horses of fire"? (2:11) "A chariot and horses of fire made an instant appearance and a dramatic departure. Since there is no indication of anything actually being burned, the use of the word *fire* here is probably a reference to the appearance of heavenly glory. The scriptures often refer to the manifestation of glory as fire" (Merrill, *Elijah*, 85). ⊕

2 Kings 2:12–18. Elisha Takes Up Elijah's Mantle

12 ¶ And Elisha saw *it,* and he cried, My father, my father, the chariot of Israel, and the
horsemen thereof. And he saw him no more:
and he took hold of his own clothes, and rent
them in two pieces.

13 He took up also the mantle of Elijah that
fell from him, and went back, and stood by
the bank of Jordan;

What does Elisha receiving Elijah's mantle symbolize? (2:12–13) The mantle "was an emblem of authority. Elijah's placing of his mantle upon Elisha symbolized both a call and the conferring of spiritual power (1 Kgs. 19:19; 2 Kgs. 2:14)" (McConkie, *Gospel Symbolism*, 265). ⊕

14 And he took the mantle of Elijah that fell from him, and smote the waters, and said, Where *is* the LORD God of Elijah? and when he also had smitten the waters, they parted hither and thither: and Elisha went over.

Parallels between Elijah's Ministry and Our Ministry (2:11)

"In describing Elijah's work and some of the events during his ministry, we have also described the work of The Church of Jesus Christ of Latter-day Saints and some of the events that will precede the second coming of Jesus Christ. Not only is the work in which we are engaged done with the keys which Elijah restored, it is also much the *same work* done by Elijah. . . .

"These parallels between Elijah's work and the work to be done in these latter days may help explain why it was Elijah who came to restore the keys of the work of sealing on earth and in the heavens. His work is our work."

Elijah's Ministry	Our Ministry
"1. Elijah helped reawaken Israel by drawing the people away from the false gods they had worshipped; in doing so, he built a new altar to worship the true God. Specific reference is made to turning the hearts of the people (see 1 Kgs. 18:17–39)."	"1. We are to reawaken Israel by drawing them away from false teachings and helping them to make true covenants at newly built altars in modern-day temples. (In our case, such work is being done for both the living and the dead.)"
"2. While the earth was suffering from a general physical and spiritual drought in Elijah's time, he was sustained by nourishment from heaven brought by ravens. He also received angelic ministrations (see 1 Kgs. 17:1–6; 19:5–8)."	"2. We will receive spiritual nourishment from heaven in the midst of worldwide spiritual drought."
"3. As shown by his blessing a widow's meal and the oil, Elijah had the power to multiply nourishment so that it would not cease until the Lord himself sent rain from heaven. He used this power to bring nourishment to a widow and her fatherless child (see 1 Kgs. 17:8–16)."	"3. We are to lead men to the spiritual nourishment of Christ—nourishment that is *never-ceasing* and therefore eternal, as Christ taught when he said, 'I am the bread of life: he that cometh to me shall never hunger; and he that believeth on me shall never thirst' (see John 6:35)."
"4. Elijah used his priesthood power to restore the dead to life (see 1 Kgs. 17:17–24)."	"4. We are to perform ordinances that will help redeem the dead—help them gain eternal life—through temple work."
"5. He used his powers to seal and unseal the heavens (see 1 Kgs. 17:1)."	"5. Elijah restored priesthood keys in our day that can seal and unseal the heavens—or, in other words, ratify ordinations on earth and in heaven. This work occurs as revelation is dispensed from heaven and the children of God are sealed up to eternal life. Not only can living families be sealed together, but living families can be sealed to deceased family members. These sealings are recognized by God and will endure in the heavens."
"6. Elijah called down fire from heaven to destroy the wicked (see 2 Kgs. 1:10–12)."	"6. The end of the ministry of this day will end as Elijah's mortal ministry did just before his ascent into heaven—with fire coming down from heaven to destroy the wicked [see Luke 17:29–30]."
"7. Elijah was taken into heaven without tasting death (see 2 Kgs. 2:11)."	"7. In that day, the scriptures teach, the faithful, like Elijah, will be taken into heaven without tasting death (see 1 Thes. 4:17)."

(Read, "Elijah and Elisha," 26–27; paragraphing altered).

How have we witnessed the transfer of authority [taking up the mantle] in the latter days? (2:15–18) "Six weeks after the Prophet Joseph Smith's martyrdom, a meeting of the Saints was held in Nauvoo, Illinois. . . . The purpose of the meeting was to determine . . . who had the right . . . to lead the Church—Sidney Rigdon, . . . or the Quorum of the Twelve with Brigham Young at their head. . . . Many in attendance received a divine witness that Brigham Young was to be the next leader: some Saints specifically state that as Brigham Young addressed the congregation he sounded and appeared remarkably like Joseph Smith, others simply say that the 'mantle of Joseph' . . . rested on Brigham Young" (Jorgensen, "Mantle of the Prophet Joseph Passes to Brother Brigham," 125–26). See commentary in this volume for 1 Kings 19:19.

15 And when the sons of the prophets which *were* to view at Jericho saw him, they said, The spirit of Elijah doth rest on Elisha. And they came to meet him, and bowed themselves to the ground before him.

16 ¶ And they said unto him, Behold now, there be with thy servants fifty strong men; let them go, we pray thee, and seek thy master: lest peradventure the Spirit of the LORD hath taken him up, and cast him upon some mountain, or into some valley. And he said, Ye shall not send.

17 And when they urged him till he was ashamed, he said, Send. They sent therefore fifty men; and they sought three days, but found him not.

18 And when they came again to him, (for he tarried at Jericho,) he said unto them, Did I not say unto you, Go not?

2 Kings 2:19–22. Elisha Heals the Water in Jericho

Why did Elisha use salt to heal the waters? (2:21) "Anciently salt was a vital part of everyday life as well as religious practice. It was a condiment or seasoning agent, a preservative, a purgative, a medicine, and a crucial element in the sacrificial system of Mosaic law. . . . The reputation of the life-giving and curative powers of salt prompted Elisha to use it to purify the spring at Jericho" (Millet, et al., in *LDS Beliefs*, 554).

19 ¶ And the men of the city said unto Elisha, Behold, I pray thee, the situation of this city *is* pleasant, as my lord seeth: but the water *is* naught, and the ground barren.

20 And he said, Bring me a new cruse, and put salt therein. And they brought *it* to him.

21 And he went forth unto the spring of the waters, and cast the salt in there, and said, Thus saith the LORD, I have healed these waters; there shall not be from thence any more death or barren *land*.

22 So the waters were healed unto this day, according to the saying of Elisha which he spake.

2 Kings 2:23–25. Several Youth Mock Elisha the Prophet

Why would Elisha send bears to attack the youth? (2:23–25) "Evidence suggests that the mocking youths in the Elisha story were not simply calling him a baldheaded man when they called him *qērēaḥ*. Rather, they were speaking to Elisha figuratively. . . . Certainly they were not simply teasing Elisha by calling him 'baldy,' as some interpreters have suggested.

23 ¶ And he went up from thence unto Beth-el: and as he was going up by the way, there came forth little children out of the city, and mocked him, and said unto him, Go up, thou bald head; go up, thou bald head.

24 And he turned back, and looked on them, and cursed them in the name of the LORD. And there came forth two she bears out of the wood, and tare forty and two children of them.

25 And he went from thence to mount Carmel, and from thence he returned to Samaria.

Instead, they were accusing him of being a usurper of authority, an act that warranted serious consequences for speaking evil against the Lord's prophet. As a result, they incurred the vengeance of God who had previously warned, 'And if you walk contrary to me, . . . I will send wild beasts among you, which shall rob you of your children' (Lev. 26:21–22)" (Woods, "Elisha and the Children," 55).

How old were these "little children"? (2:23) These "little children" were "youths" (see 2 Kings 2:23*a*). According to Craig Keener: "The age of the mockers is uncertain. The Hebrew can refer to prepubescent children, but can also refer to 'the younger generation'; the same Hebrew word describes Rehoboam's peers in 1 Kin. 12:8 ('young men'), and they are over 40. This is probably a group of young teens" (Keener, *NKJV Cultural Backgrounds Study Bible*, 648).

CHAPTER 3

Jehoram of Israel and Jehoshaphat of Judah join forces against Moab—Elisha promises them water for their animals and victory in the war—The Moabites are defeated.

1 Now Jehoram the son of Ahab began to reign over Israel in Samaria the eighteenth year of Jehoshaphat king of Judah, and reigned twelve years.

2 And he wrought evil in the sight of the LORD; but not like his father, and like his mother: for he put away the image of Baal that his father had made.

3 Nevertheless he cleaved unto the sins of Jeroboam the son of Nebat, which made Israel to sin; he departed not therefrom.

4 ¶ And Mesha king of Moab was a sheepmaster, and rendered unto the king of Israel an hundred thousand lambs, and an hundred thousand rams, with the wool.

5 But it came to pass, when Ahab was dead, that the king of Moab rebelled against the king of Israel.

6 ¶ And king Jehoram went out of Samaria the same time, and numbered all Israel.

2 Kings 3:1–10. Israel and Judah Unite to Fight the Moabites

How did Jehoram's sins differ from that of his parents? (3:1–3) "Jehoram, the new king of Israel, was nearly as wicked as all the kings before him. He replaced the worship of the false Canaanite gods with the worship of golden calves. Aaron made the first golden calf when Israel was in the wilderness (see Exodus 32:1–6) and Jeroboam, the first king of the northern kingdom, set up two golden calves in Israel and made the children of Israel worship them (see 1 Kings 12:25–30)" (Valletta, et al., *Old Testament for Latter-day Saint Families*, 339).

What do we know about Mesha, the king of Moab? (3:4) "The king of Moab who was tributary to Ahab, (2 Kings 3:4) but when Ahab fell at Ramoth-gilead, Mesha refused to pay tribute to his successor, Jehoram. . . . The Moabites were defeated, and [Mesha] took refuge in his last stronghold, and defended himself with the energy of despair. With 700 fighting men he made a vigorous attempt to cut his way through the beleaguering army, and when beaten back, he withdrew to the wall of his city, and there, in sight of the allied host, offered his first-born son, his successor in the kingdom, as a burnt offering to Chemosh, the ruthless fire-god of Moab" (*Smith's Bible Dictionary*, 444).

2 Kings 3:11–20. Elisha Promises Victory to the Kings of Judah and Israel

Why would Elisha respond with disgust to the king seeking his advice? (3:11–14) "Jehoshaphat, king of Judah, desired the advice of a true prophet of God before he went into battle because he was a follower of Jehovah. The kings went to the prophet Elisha, who was irritated by the presence of Jehoram, king of Israel. Elisha sarcastically advised him to seek the counsel of the false prophets of his father (see v. 13).

"A minstrel, or harpist, was then called to soothe Elisha before he complied with King Jehoshaphat's request to seek the Lord's direction. It seems ironic that even though they were not willing to follow Elisha's counsel, they were anxious to have his blessing on their endeavor" (*Old Testament Student Manual: 1 Kings–Malachi*, 74). ⊕

7 And he went and sent to Jehoshaphat the king of Judah, saying, The king of Moab hath rebelled against me: wilt thou go with me against Moab to battle? And he said, I will go up: I *am* as thou *art*, my people as thy people, *and* my horses as thy horses.

8 And he said, Which way shall we go up? And he answered, The way through the wilderness of Edom.

9 So the king of Israel went, and the king of Judah, and the king of Edom: and they fetched a compass of seven days' journey: and there was no water for the host, and for the cattle that followed them.

10 And the king of Israel said, Alas! that the LORD hath called these three kings together, to deliver them into the hand of Moab!

11 But Jehoshaphat said, *Is there* not here a prophet of the LORD, that we may inquire of the LORD by him? And one of the king of Israel's servants answered and said, Here *is* Elisha the son of Shaphat, which poured water on the hands of Elijah.

12 And Jehoshaphat said, The word of the LORD is with him. So the king of Israel and Jehoshaphat and the king of Edom went down to him.

13 And Elisha said unto the king of Israel, What have I to do with thee? get thee to the prophets of thy father, and to the prophets of thy mother. And the king of Israel said unto him, Nay: for the LORD hath called these three kings together, to deliver them into the hand of Moab.

14 And Elisha said, *As* the LORD of hosts liveth, before whom I stand, surely, were it not that I regard the presence of Jehoshaphat the king of Judah, I would not look toward thee, nor see thee.

15 But now bring me a minstrel. And it came to pass, when the minstrel played, that the hand of the LORD came upon him.

16 And he said, Thus saith the LORD, Make this valley full of ditches.

17 For thus saith the LORD, Ye shall not see wind, neither shall ye see rain; yet that valley shall be filled with water, that ye may drink, both ye, and your cattle, and your beasts.

18 And this is *but* a light thing in the sight of the LORD: he will deliver the Moabites also into your hand.

Why would Elisha invite a "minstrel" [musician] to visit him prior to making a decision for the king? (3:15) "Appropriate music can invite the Spirit. 'Good music—especially sacred music—makes spiritual things more understandable.'... [Said Elder Richard G. Scott:] 'It prepares emotions for response to promptings of the Holy Spirit' (*Church News,* 30 Aug. 1997). In the 1985 hymnal, the First Presidency said, 'Inspirational music is an essential part of our church meetings. The hymns invite the Spirit of the Lord, create a feeling of reverence, unify us as members, and provide a way for us to offer praises to the Lord. ... Hymns move us to repentance and good works, build testimony and faith, comfort the weary, console the mourning, and inspire us to endure to the end' (*Hymns,* ix)" (Valletta, et al., *Old Testament for Latter-day Saint Families,* 340).

19 And ye shall smite every fenced city, and every choice city, and shall fell every good tree, and stop all wells of water, and mar every good piece of land with stones.

20 And it came to pass in the morning, when the meat offering was offered, that, behold, there came water by the way of Edom, and the country was filled with water.

What were the three actions Elisha commanded Israel to take against their enemies? (3:19) "The prophet Elisha commanded Israel to do three things as they went through the land of Moab: (1) cut down all trees that could be used to build fortifications (see Deuteronomy 20:19–20 for the justification of this practice); (2) destroy the wells that provided the life-giving waters of the land; and (3) throw rocks on the fields. A large army passing through an area could quickly cover the land with rocks. It would then take months of hard work to uncover the land so crops could again be grown. The reasoning was that the defeated enemy would have to spend its labor in recovering from war rather than in preparing to wage it again" (*Old Testament Student Manual: 1 Kings–Malachi,* 74).

2 Kings 3:21–27. The Moabites Are Defeated

21 ¶ And when all the Moabites heard that the kings were come up to fight against them, they gathered all that were able to put on armour, and upward, and stood in the border.

22 And they rose up early in the morning, and the sun shone upon the water, and the Moabites saw the water on the other side *as* red as blood:

23 And they said, This *is* blood: the kings are surely slain, and they have smitten one another: now therefore, Moab, to the spoil.

How were the Moabites deceived to flee without fighting? (3:21–24) The king of Edom also joined the alliance of Israel and Judah to defeat the Moabites. "On hearing the report of the march of the allied kings, Moab had raised all the men that were capable of bearing arms, and stationed them on the frontier. In the morning, when the sun had risen above the water, the Moabites saw the water opposite to them like blood, and said: 'That is blood: the (allied) kings have destroyed themselves and smitten one another; and now to the spoil, Moab!' Coming with this expectation to the Israelitish camp, they were received by the allies, who were ready for battle, and put to flight" (Keil and Delitzsch, *Commentary* [on 2 Kings 3:20–23]). ⊕

Why would the Moabite king offer his son as a sacrifice? (3:27) "The king of Moab made a desperate attempt to flee the city because of its imminent destruction. But his flight was stopped by the Edomites, and he was forced back into the city. When his attempted flight failed, the king offered his firstborn son, who would have succeeded him, as a burnt offering. Chemosh, god of the Moabites, was frequently offered human sacrifice to appease his anger. This custom may have prompted the Moabite king in this case.

"With the death of the heir, Israel lifted their siege and departed, perhaps feeling that Moab's power as a nation had ended. This feeling, however, was a mistake (see 2 Kings 13:20)" (*Old Testament Student Manual: 1 Kings–Malachi*, 74).

2 Kings 4:1–7. Elisha Increases a Widow's Oil

Why could children be taken away from parents to satisfy debts? (4:1) "In drastic circumstances, where there was no collateral, a debtor could pledge a son, daughter, or slave. The value of the child's or slave's labor could then be credited against both interest and principal. An account in the Bible of a widow's two sons about to go into slavery shows how cruel

24 And when they came to the camp of Israel, the Israelites rose up and smote the Moabites, so that they fled before them: but they went forward smiting the Moabites, even in *their* country.

25 And they beat down the cities, and on every good piece of land cast every man his stone, and filled it; and they stopped all the wells of water, and felled all the good trees: only in Kir-haraseth left they the stones thereof; howbeit the slingers went about *it*, and smote it.

26 ¶ And when the king of Moab saw that the battle was too sore for him, he took with him seven hundred men that drew swords, to break through *even* unto the king of Edom: but they could not.

27 Then he took his eldest son that should have reigned in his stead, and offered him *for* a burnt offering upon the wall. And there was great indignation against Israel: and they departed from him, and returned to *their own* land.

CHAPTER 4

Elisha multiplies the widow's oil—He promises a son to a Shunammite woman—The child dies and is raised to life by Elisha—He makes the poisonous food harmless—Bread and grain are multiplied for the people to eat.

1 Now there cried a certain woman of the wives of the sons of the prophets unto Elisha, saying, Thy servant my husband is dead; and thou knowest that thy servant did fear the LORD: and the creditor is come to take unto him my two sons to be bondmen.

2 And Elisha said unto her, What shall I do for thee? tell me, what hast thou in the house? And she said, Thine handmaid hath not any thing in the house, save a pot of oil.

3 Then he said, Go, borrow thee vessels abroad of all thy neighbours, *even* empty vessels; borrow not a few.

4 And when thou art come in, thou shalt shut the door upon thee and upon thy sons, and shalt pour out into all those vessels, and thou shalt set aside that which is full.

5 So she went from him, and shut the door upon her and upon her sons, who brought *the vessels* to her; and she poured out.

6 And it came to pass, when the vessels were full, that she said unto her son, Bring me yet a vessel. And he said unto her, *There is* not a vessel more. And the oil stayed.

7 Then she came and told the man of God. And he said, Go, sell the oil, and pay thy debt, and live thou and thy children of the rest.

8 ¶ And it fell on a day, that Elisha passed to Shunem, where *was* a great woman; and she constrained him to eat bread. And *so* it was, *that* as oft as he passed by, he turned in thither to eat bread.

9 And she said unto her husband, Behold now, I perceive that this *is* an holy man of God, which passeth by us continually.

10 Let us make a little chamber, I pray thee, on the wall; and let us set for him there a bed, and a table, and a stool, and a candlestick: and it shall be, when he cometh to us, that he shall turn in thither.

11 And it fell on a day, that he came thither, and he turned into the chamber, and lay there.

12 And he said to Gehazi his servant, Call this Shunammite. And when he had called her, she stood before him.

the custom could be (2 Kgs. 4:1–7)" (*Tyndale Bible Dictionary*, 369). "Debt slavery was a fact of life for people who could not meet their financial and tax obligations. Sometimes such people were redeemed from bondage; often they were not" (Holzapfel, et al., *Jehovah and the World of the Old Testament*, 265).

After gathering the pots to her home, why was the woman instructed to close the door? (4:4) "The impending miracle was not intended to be a public sensation but to demonstrate privately God's mercy and grace to this widow. . . . She did not hesitate to respond to the instructions of the Lord's prophet in faith and obedience" (*NIV Study Bible* [1995], 529).

What might the word "stayed" symbolize in this verse? (4:6–7) "While there was a vessel to fill, there was oil sufficient; and it only ceased to flow when there was no vessel to receive it. This is a good emblem of the grace of God. While there is an empty, longing heart, there is a continual overflowing fountain of salvation. If we find in any place or at any time that the oil ceases to flow, it is because there are no empty vessels there, no souls hungering and thirsting for righteousness" (*Adam Clarke's Commentary* [on 2 Kings 4:6]). ⊕

2 Kings 4:8–17. Elisha Promises a Barren Woman That She Will Bear a Son

What was a "little chamber"? (4:10) "The *aliyah*, 'chamber,' is an upper room of an Eastern house, being sometimes built on the roof, and sometimes making a second story to the porch, to which it has access by stairs. . . . It is usually well furnished, and kept as a room for the entertainment of honored guests" (Freeman, *Handbook of Bible Manners and Customs*, 171). ⊕

Why does the woman answer Elisha's question by saying, "I dwell among mine own people"? (4:13) "The Shunammite woman felt secure and content in the community of her own family and tribe, and she had no need or desire for favors from high government officials" (*NIV Study Bible* [1995], 529).

13 And he said unto him, Say now unto her,
Behold, thou hast been careful for us with all
this care; what *is* to be done for thee? wouldest thou be spoken for to the king, or to
the captain of the host? And she answered, I
dwell among mine own people.

14 And he said, What then *is* to be done for
her? And Gehazi answered, Verily she hath
no child, and her husband is old.

15 And he said, Call her. And when he had
called her, she stood in the door.

16 And he said, About this season, according to the time of life, thou shalt embrace a
son. And she said, Nay, my lord, *thou* man of
God, do not lie unto thine handmaid.

17 And the woman conceived, and bare a
son at that season that Elisha had said unto
her, according to the time of life.

Why would the Shunammite woman accuse the prophet of lying? (4:16) "The promise of a son within a year's time seemed to be the greatest possible blessing for the woman. But she responded, 'Nay, my lord' (2 Kings 4:16). Rather than a lack of faith in the prophet's power, the woman revealed a fear of disappointment when she declined Elisha's proffered gift. For how long had she learned to accept the probability that she would never bear or rear a child? Now, even the mention of the possibility seemed to reopen wounds and portend greater pain" (Olson, *Women of the Old Testament*, 243–44).

2 Kings 4:18–37. The Woman's Son Dies and Is Raised from the Dead by Elisha

Why would the promised child be taken from his mother? (4:18–21) "The child, given as an evidence of God's grace and the reliability of his word, was suddenly taken from the woman in a severe test of her faith. Her subsequent actions demonstrate the strength of her faith in the face of great calamity" (*NIV Study Bible,* [1995], 529).

18 ¶ And when the child was grown, it fell
on a day, that he went out to his father to the
reapers.

19 And he said unto his father, My head, my
head. And he said to a lad, Carry him to his
mother.

20 And when he had taken him, and brought
him to his mother, he sat on her knees till
noon, and *then* died.

21 And she went up, and laid him on the bed
of the man of God, and shut *the door* upon
him, and went out.

22 And she called unto her husband, and
said, Send me, I pray thee, one of the young
men, and one of the asses, that I may run to
the man of God, and come again.

How does the Shunammite woman demonstrate her powerful faith? (4:21–25) This heart-stricken mother needed Elisha's help and prepared to find him. "The distance from Shunem to the area of Carmel is about twenty miles" (Walton, et al., *IVP Bible Background*, 389). "The Shunammite's action speaks strongly of her faith. Despite her overwhelming sorrow, she placed the fate of her child close to Elisha, through whose word, and by means of God's mercy, she had gained her son in the first place. Placing the body on the bed of the man of God also kept his death a secret until she could reach Elisha, from whom she had once seen the impossible accomplished" (*Nelson Study Bible* [NKJV], 614).

23 And he said, Wherefore wilt thou go to him to day? *it is* neither new moon, nor sabbath. And she said, *It shall be* well.

Why was the husband of the Shunammite woman questioning his wife concerning the day on which she went to find Elisha? (4:23) "The Shunammite's husband did not connect his wife's proposed visit to the prophet with the death of his child, but with some religious duty. The new moon (i.e. the first day of the month) and the sabbath were feasts at which the prophets might be asked to preside, as Samuel did at the feast held at the high place of Ramah (1 Samuel 9:12–13)" (*John Dummelow's Commentary* [on 2 Kings 4:23]).

24 Then she saddled an ass, and said to her servant, Drive, and go forward; slack not *thy* riding for me, except I bid thee.

25 So she went and came unto the man of God to mount Carmel. And it came to pass, when the man of God saw her afar off, that he said to Gehazi his servant, Behold, *yonder is* that Shunammite:

26 Run now, I pray thee, to meet her, and say unto her, *Is it* well with thee? *is it* well with thy husband? *is it* well with the child? And she answered, *It is* well.

27 And when she came to the man of God to the hill, she caught him by the feet: but Gehazi came near to thrust her away. And the man of God said, Let her alone; for her soul *is* vexed within her: and the LORD hath hid *it* from me, and hath not told me.

28 Then she said, Did I desire a son of my lord? did I not say, Do not deceive me?

29 Then he said to Gehazi, Gird up thy loins, and take my staff in thine hand, and go thy way: if thou meet any man, salute him not; and if any salute thee, answer him not again: and lay my staff upon the face of the child.

30 And the mother of the child said, *As* the LORD liveth, and *as* thy soul liveth, I will not leave thee. And he arose, and followed her.

31 And Gehazi passed on before them, and laid the staff upon the face of the child; but *there was* neither voice, nor hearing. Wherefore he went again to meet him, and told him, saying, The child is not awaked.

Why would Elisha lay upon the child in order to raise him from the dead? (4:34) "He [Elisha] uses every natural means in his power to restore life, while praying to the Author of it to exert a miraculous influence. Natural means are in our power; those that are supernatural belong to God. We should always do our own work, and beg of God to do his" (*Adam Clarke's Commentary* [on 2 Kings 4:34]). Elisha was probably familiar with a similar miracle performed by Elijah (see 1 Kings 17:21) (see Ludlow, *Companion to Your Study of the Old Testament*, 238).

What is so significant about the child sneezing seven times? (4:35) Because seven symbolizes perfection, completion, and wholeness in Hebrew, the unusual detail of the boy's sneezes may signify that the child was made completely whole. Some scholars have linked Elisha's method of healing to a Mesopotamian procedure to ward off evil spirits. The Mesopotamian healer touched his head to the head of the patient, hand to hand, and foot to foot (see *Jewish Study Bible* [2004], 713). "Elisha's mode of resuscitating the boy may point to the ultimate victory of the Savior. . . . Furthermore, when both Elisha and the boy rose again, the miracle testified that not only would Jesus Christ be resurrected but also that all the children of God will live again" (Olson, *Women of the Old Testament*, 246).

2 Kings 4:38–41. Elisha Heals Poisonous Stew at Gilgal

How was the "seethe pottage" or stew poisoned? (4:38–40) "When Elisha stopped to visit a group of sons of the prophets in a time of dearth [famine] and they tried to prepare food, they unknowingly put a noxious gourd into their stew. Such a gourd, still known in the Jordan valley, can be used in small amounts as a laxative, but in large quantity it can cause death. Elisha knew how to remedy its effects" (Rasmussen, *Latter-day Saint Commentary on the Old Testament*, 303).

32 And when Elisha was come into the house, behold, the child was dead, *and* laid upon his bed.

33 He went in therefore, and shut the door upon them twain, and prayed unto the LORD.

34 And he went up, and lay upon the child, and put his mouth upon his mouth, and his eyes upon his eyes, and his hands upon his hands: and he stretched himself upon the child; and the flesh of the child waxed warm.

35 Then he returned, and walked in the house to and fro; and went up, and stretched himself upon him: and the child sneezed seven times, and the child opened his eyes.

36 And he called Gehazi, and said, Call this Shunammite. So he called her. And when she was come in unto him, he said, Take up thy son.

37 Then she went in, and fell at his feet, and bowed herself to the ground, and took up her son, and went out.

38 ¶ And Elisha came again to Gilgal: and *there was* a dearth in the land; and the sons of the prophets *were* sitting before him: and he said unto his servant, Set on the great pot, and seethe pottage for the sons of the prophets.

39 And one went out into the field to gather herbs, and found a wild vine, and gathered thereof wild gourds his lap full, and came and shred *them* into the pot of pottage: for they knew *them* not.

40 So they poured out for the men to eat. And it came to pass, as they were eating of the pottage, that they cried out, and said, O *thou* man of God, *there is* death in the pot. And they could not eat *thereof.*

41 But he said, Then bring meal. And he cast *it* into the pot; and he said, Pour out for the people, that they may eat. And there was no harm in the pot.

42 ¶ And there came a man from Baal-shalisha, and brought the man of God bread of the firstfruits, twenty loaves of barley, and full ears of corn in the husk thereof. And he said, Give unto the people, that they may eat.

43 And his servitor said, What, should I set this before an hundred men? He said again, Give the people, that they may eat: for thus saith the LORD, They shall eat, and shall leave *thereof.*

44 So he set *it* before them, and they did eat, and left *thereof,* according to the word of the LORD.

CHAPTER 5

Naaman, the Syrian, comes to Elisha to be healed of leprosy—He rejects the prophet's instruction at first but relents and dips himself in the Jordan seven times; he is healed—Elisha refuses to accept a reward—Gehazi accepts a gift from Naaman and is cursed with leprosy.

1 Now Naaman, captain of the host of the king of Syria, was a great man with his master, and honourable, because by him the LORD had given deliverance unto Syria: he was also a mighty man in valour, *but he was* a leper.

2 Kings 4:42–44. Elisha Blesses Bread and Grain and Feeds a Hundred Men

How do Elisha's actions foreshadow the Savior? (4:42–44) "That twenty barley loaves and a portion of roasted grains of corn were not a sufficient quantity to satisfy a hundred men, is evident from the fact that one man was able to carry the whole of this gift in a sack, and still more so from the remark of the servant, which shows that there was no proportion between the whole of this quantity and the food required by a hundred persons. In this respect the food, which was so blessed by the word of the Lord that a hundred men were satisfied by so small a quantity and left some over, forms a type of the miraculous feeding of the people by Christ" (Keil and Delitzsch, *Commentary* [on 2 Kings 4:42–44]).

2 Kings 5:1–7. Naaman, a Syrian Captain, Has Leprosy

What do we know about Naaman? (5:1) "Naaman was a remarkable figure in biblical history. This verse is filled with phrases describing his character, his honor, and his ability. Surprisingly, we read that his military victories were granted by the Lord. The Hebrew word translated *leper* refers to any of several serious skin diseases (Lev. 13:1–46; Num. 5:1–4), including certain fungi (Lev. 13:47–56; 14:33–57)" (*NKJV Study Bible* [2007], 572). "It is ironic that despite Naaman's strength and success, in the eyes of Israel and most of the ancient world his disease of leprosy was associated with uncleanliness. Thus, Naaman was dying as an unclean man, and that fact completely eclipsed his greatness!" (Anderson, "Naaman, Baptism, and Cleansing," 28).

What is known about the little maid who waited on Naaman's wife? (5:2) "Only part of the Little Maid's background can be deduced from the few details given in the scriptural text. She could have become a slave in a foreign country for a number of reasons. She might have been born to Israelites who were already enslaved in that country, or she might have been sold by her parents to pay a debt, as was almost the case with the Israelite widow's children (2 Kings 4:1–7). . . . She was captured and carried back to Damascus by a Syrian 'company' after an attack or a marauding expedition in Israel (2 Kings 5:2)" (Olson, *Women of the Old Testament*, 255).

How might this little maid's account be considered a story of faith? (5:3) "There is no scriptural evidence that Elisha or another prophet at that time had ever healed a 'leper,' yet the Little Maid believed a true prophet of God could. One wonders what circumstances she had observed, heard about, or experienced to lead her to this unshakeable faith in priesthood power. Had she or someone she knew been sick, discouraged, or lost, only to be found or healed by a power not of this world? . . . This little girl bore witness to Naaman's wife that a prophet . . . could cure him, if he would just inquire (2 Kings 5:3)" (Olson, *Women of the Old Testament*, 256).

What is the approximate value of the gift accompanying Naaman? (5:5) "The gift accompanying Naaman is exorbitant—a king's ransom. Ten talents equal thirty thousand shekels, about seven hundred fifty pounds of silver. The six thousand shekels of gold equal about one hundred fifty pounds (one gold shekel equaled fifteen silver shekels). Converted to today's buying power, it would be in the vicinity of three-quarters of a billion dollars. One can get an idea of the proportions by understanding that a typical wage would have been ten silver shekels per year, and one gold shekel would purchase one ton of grain" (Walton, et al., *IVP Bible Background Commentary*, 390–91).

2 And the Syrians had gone out by companies, and had brought away captive out of the land of Israel a little maid; and she waited on Naaman's wife.

3 And she said unto her mistress, Would God my lord *were* with the prophet that *is* in Samaria! for he would recover him of his leprosy.

4 And *one* went in, and told his lord, saying, Thus and thus said the maid that *is* of the land of Israel.

5 And the king of Syria said, Go to, go, and I will send a letter unto the king of Israel. And he departed, and took with him ten talents of silver, and six thousand *pieces* of gold, and ten changes of raiment.

6 And he brought the letter to the king of Israel, saying, Now when this letter is come unto thee, behold, I have *therewith* sent Naaman my servant to thee, that thou mayest recover him of his leprosy.

7 And it came to pass, when the king of Israel had read the letter, that he rent his clothes, and said, *Am* I God, to kill and to make alive, that this man doth send unto me to recover a man of his leprosy? wherefore consider, I pray you, and see how he seeketh a quarrel against me.

8 ¶ And it was *so,* when Elisha the man of
God had heard that the king of Israel had
rent his clothes, that he sent to the king, saying, Wherefore hast thou rent thy clothes? let
him come now to me, and he shall know that
there is a prophet in Israel.

9 So Naaman came with his horses and with
his chariot, and stood at the door of the
house of Elisha.

10 And Elisha sent a messenger unto him,
saying, Go and wash in Jordan seven times,
and thy flesh shall come again to thee, and
thou shalt be clean.

11 But Naaman was wroth, and went away,
and said, Behold, I thought, He will surely
come out to me, and stand, and call on the
name of the LORD his God, and strike his
hand over the place, and recover the leper.

12 *Are* not Abana and Pharpar, rivers of
Damascus, better than all the waters of Israel?
may I not wash in them, and be clean? So he
turned and went away in a rage.

13 And his servants came near, and spake
unto him, and said, My father, *if* the prophet
had bid thee *do some* great thing, wouldest
thou not have done *it?* how much rather then,
when he saith to thee, Wash, and be clean?

14 Then went he down, and dipped himself
seven times in Jordan, according to the saying of the man of God: and his flesh came
again like unto the flesh of a little child, and
he was clean.

2 Kings 5:8–14. Naaman Washes in the Jordan River Seven Times

Why was Naaman angry upon hearing what was necessary to be cleansed? (5:11–12) Elisha told Naaman to wash seven times in the River Jordan to become clean (see 2 Kings 5:10). "Although it seemed like an unusual command, it was a clear instruction from the prophet of God. The mighty Naaman was taken aback and confused. He had anticipated that the Israelite prophet would work a miracle on the spot—calling on the name of the Lord and, in a sweeping demonstration of great power, 'strike his hand over the place' to cure his leprosy (2 Kgs. 5:11). He became upset and in a fit of anger stormed away from Elisha's house" (Hardy, "Namaan and Gehazi," 28). ⊕

How should we react to seemingly small things we are asked to do in the Lord's gospel? (5:13–14) "Some of us suppose that if we were called to a high office in the Church immediately we would be loyal, and would show the dedication necessary. We would step forward and valiantly commit ourselves to this service. . . .

"If you will not be loyal in the small things you will not be loyal in the large things. If you will not respond to the so-called insignificant or menial tasks which need to be performed in the Church and kingdom, there will be no opportunity for service in the so-called greater challenges" (Packer, "Follow the Brethren," 4). ⊕

What might Naaman have felt like on being made whole again? (5:14) "What a humbling thing it must have been for Naaman to realize how close he came to allowing his own pride and his unwillingness to listen to the counsel of the prophet to prevent him from receiving such a great, cleansing blessing. And what a humbling thing it is to contemplate how many of us might miss out on great and promised blessings because we do not listen *and then do* the relatively simple things our prophet is telling us to do today" (Ballard, "His Word Ye Shall Receive," 66).

2 Kings 5:15–19. Elisha Refuses Naaman's Attempt to Pay for the Miracle

Why would Naaman carry soil back to his homeland? (5:17–19) "Generally speaking, deities in the ancient world were conceived to be limited to the territories of the people who worshiped them. When one crossed an international frontier, one also passed from the territory of one god to the territory of another. The story of Naaman illustrates this. Naaman came to Elisha seeking a cure for his leprosy. After he was freed from the disease he asked Elisha's permission to take two donkey loads of earth back to Syria so that he could worship the Lord Jehovah on Jehovah's own ground (see 2 Kgs. 5:17–18)" (Brown, "Biblical Egypt," 49).

2 Kings 5:20–27. Elisha's Servant Lies and Is Given Gifts

What sin did Gehazi suffer from that was greater than the disease of leprosy? (5:20–24) Elder Marvin J. Ashton taught: "It is a sin to lie. It is a tragedy to be the victim of lies. Being trapped in the snares of dishonesty and misrepresentation does not happen instantaneously. One little lie or dishonest act leads to another until the perpetrator is caught in the web of deceit" ("This Is No Harm," 9).

15 ¶ And he returned to the man of God,
he and all his company, and came, and stood
before him: and he said, Behold, now I know
that *there is* no God in all the earth, but in
Israel: now therefore, I pray thee, take a
blessing of thy servant.

16 But he said, *As* the LORD liveth, before
whom I stand, I will receive none. And he
urged him to take *it;* but he refused.

17 And Naaman said, Shall there not then, I
pray thee, be given to thy servant two mules'
burden of earth? for thy servant will henceforth offer neither burnt offering nor sacrifice
unto other gods, but unto the LORD.

18 In this thing the LORD pardon thy servant, *that* when my master goeth into the
house of Rimmon to worship there, and he
leaneth on my hand, and I bow myself in the
house of Rimmon: when I bow down myself
in the house of Rimmon, the LORD pardon
thy servant in this thing.

19 And he said unto him, Go in peace. So he
departed from him a little way.

20 ¶ But Gehazi, the servant of Elisha the
man of God, said, Behold, my master hath
spared Naaman this Syrian, in not receiving
at his hands that which he brought: but, *as*
the LORD liveth, I will run after him, and take
somewhat of him.

21 So Gehazi followed after Naaman. And
when Naaman saw *him* running after him, he
lighted down from the chariot to meet him,
and said, *Is* all well?

22 And he said, All *is* well. My master hath
sent me, saying, Behold, even now there be
come to me from mount Ephraim two young

men of the sons of the prophets: give them, I pray thee, a talent of silver, and two changes of garments.

23 And Naaman said, Be content, take two talents. And he urged him, and bound two talents of silver in two bags, with two changes of garments, and laid *them* upon two of his servants; and they bare *them* before him.

24 And when he came to the tower, he took *them* from their hand, and bestowed *them* in the house: and he let the men go, and they departed.

25 But he went in, and stood before his master. And Elisha said unto him, Whence *comest thou,* Gehazi? And he said, Thy servant went no whither.

26 And he said unto him, Went not mine heart *with thee,* when the man turned again from his chariot to meet thee? *Is it* a time to receive money, and to receive garments, and oliveyards, and vineyards, and sheep, and oxen, and menservants, and maidservants?

27 The leprosy therefore of Naaman shall cleave unto thee, and unto thy seed for ever. And he went out from his presence a leper *as white* as snow.

Why did Gehazi deserve this divine punishment? (5:27) "We need not overly mourn for the servant of Gehazi. This was a man who had chosen poorly. He had not effectively put off the natural man, but had partaken of the temptations of the flesh, and succumbed to the passions of his mind and his heart" (Hyde, *Comprehensive Commentary [1 and 2 Kings]*, 56).

CHAPTER 6

Elisha causes an ax to float—He reveals to the king how to conduct a war with Syria—Horses and chariots of fire protect Elisha—The Syrians are smitten with blindness—Benhadad besieges Samaria, and foodstuff sells for a great price.

1 And the sons of the prophets said unto Elisha, Behold now, the place where we dwell with thee is too strait for us.

2 Let us go, we pray thee, unto Jordan, and take thence every man a beam, and let us make us a place there, where we may dwell. And he answered, Go ye.

2 Kings 6:1–7. Elisha Causes an Axe Head to Float

3 And one said, Be content, I pray thee, and
go with thy servants. And he answered, I will
go.

4 So he went with them. And when they
came to Jordan, they cut down wood.

How does this event demonstrate God's involvement in our lives? (6:5–7) "In another helpful miracle, Elisha relieved the distress of one who lost the iron head of a borrowed axe in the water. Miraculously, the iron axe head floated and was retrieved" (Rasmussen, *Latter-day Saint Commentary on the Old Testament*, 304). "We see a faithful man in Israel felling a beam with a borrowed axe; the head comes off and falls into the water. Then at the word of the prophet Elisha—mark it well—'the iron did swim,' and the axe head is recovered (2 Kgs. 6:1–7). Solid iron swims in water as though it were a cork because Jehovah and his prophets, by faith, have power over the waters" (McConkie, *Mortal Messiah*, 2:357).

5 But as one was felling a beam, the axe head
fell into the water: and he cried, and said,
Alas, master! for it was borrowed.

6 And the man of God said, Where fell it?
And he shewed him the place. And he cut
down a stick, and cast *it* in thither; and the
iron did swim.

7 Therefore said he, Take *it* up to thee. And
he put out his hand, and took it.

2 Kings 6:8–12. Elisha Helps Jehoram in the War against Syria

8 ¶ Then the king of Syria warred against
Israel, and took counsel with his servants,
saying, In such and such a place *shall be* my
camp.

How did Elisha show loyalty to Israel? (6:9–10) After unsolicited counsel from Elisha, "The king sent spies to see if what Elisha had told him was true. By so doing he avoided great loss to his armies. This transpired on several occasions; the king of Syria's ambush attempts all failed. . . . The king of Damascus was so frustrated at not being able to make a surprise attack on the forces of the king of Israel that he began to accuse the members of his own cabinet of [treachery]" (Hyde, *Comprehensive Commentary [1 and 2 Kings]*, 57, 58).

9 And the man of God sent unto the king
of Israel, saying, Beware that thou pass not
such a place; for thither the Syrians are come
down.

10 And the king of Israel sent to the place
which the man of God told him and warned
him of, and saved himself there, not once nor
twice.

Why should we put our faith and trust in the prophets of God? (6:11–12) "[The prophets] represent the Lord Jesus Christ and have the right to declare His mind and will as it is revealed to them. I testify that there is safety in following their counsel. The Lord is inspiring them to emphasize strengthening our faith in Heavenly Father and in His Son, Jesus Christ, and in His Atonement so that we will not waver as we face the challenges of our day" (Soares, "Confide in God Unwaveringly," 33). How can you better follow the counsel of prophets in times of uncertainty?

11 Therefore the heart of the king of Syria
was sore troubled for this thing; and he called
his servants, and said unto them, Will ye not
shew me which of us *is* for the king of Israel?

12 And one of his servants said, None, my
lord, O king: but Elisha, the prophet that *is*
in Israel, telleth the king of Israel the words
that thou speakest in thy bedchamber.

13 ¶ And he said, Go and spy where he *is*, that I may send and fetch him. And it was told him, saying, Behold, *he is* in Dothan.

14 Therefore sent he thither horses, and chariots, and a great host: and they came by night, and compassed the city about.

15 And when the servant of the man of God was risen early, and gone forth, behold, an host compassed the city both with horses and chariots. And his servant said unto him, Alas, my master! how shall we do?

16 And he answered, Fear not: for they that *be* with us *are* more than they that *be* with them.

17 And Elisha prayed, and said, LORD, I pray thee, open his eyes, that he may see. And the LORD opened the eyes of the young man; and he saw: and, behold, the mountain *was* full of horses and chariots of fire round about Elisha.

18 And when they came down to him, Elisha prayed unto the LORD, and said, Smite this people, I pray thee, with blindness. And he smote them with blindness according to the word of Elisha.

19 ¶ And Elisha said unto them, This *is* not the way, neither *is* this the city: follow me, and I will bring you to the man whom ye seek. But he led them to Samaria.

20 And it came to pass, when they were come into Samaria, that Elisha said, LORD, open the eyes of these *men*, that they may see. And the LORD opened their eyes, and they saw; and, behold, *they were* in the midst of Samaria.

21 And the king of Israel said unto Elisha, when he saw them, My father, shall I smite *them?* shall I smite *them?*

22 And he answered, Thou shalt not smite *them:* wouldest thou smite those whom thou

2 Kings 6:13–23. God Protects Elisha with Horses and Chariots of Fire

How does God surround His children with help? (6:16–17) "In the gospel of Jesus Christ you have help from both sides of the veil and you must never forget that. When disappointment and discouragement strike—and they will—you remember and never forget that if our eyes could be opened we would see horses and chariots of fire as far as the eye can see riding at reckless speed to come to our protection. They will always be there, these armies of heaven, in defense of Abraham's [children]" (Holland, "For Times of Trouble," 15). ⊕

How was Elisha able to move a great host of people from Dothan to Samaria? (6:18–20) "The ten-mile trip would have taken some time when trying to lead a debilitated army of confused men who cannot see" (Walton, et al., *IVP Bible Background Commentary*, 393). "With the help of the Lord, Elisha and his servant were able to make it safely to Samaria, leading the entire Syrian army captive behind them. Safely protected by the Lord, they accomplished an unbelievable feat without weapons, without even the help of an army—simply with the assistance of the Lord" (Freeman, *Written on Our Hearts*, 67–68).

Why did the king of Israel call Elisha "my father"? (6:21) "*Father* was a term of honor and respect. The king recognized the prophet's spiritual authority (see 13:14). In the same way, Elisha had also called his mentor Elijah *my father* (2:12), and the servants of Naaman referred to their master in a similar way (5:13)" (*Quest Study Bible* [1994], 495).

Why did Elisha insist that the Syrian soldiers be treated kindly? (6:21–23) "The Aramean soldiers had been taken captive by the power of the Lord, not by Joram's military prowess. The Lord's purpose was to demonstrate to them and their king and to the Israelites and their king that Israel's national security ultimately was grounded in the Lord, not in military forces or strategies" (*NIV Study Bible* [2002], 537). ⊕

hast taken captive with thy sword and with thy bow? set bread and water before them, that they may eat and drink, and go to their master.

23 And he prepared great provision for them: and when they had eaten and drunk, he sent them away, and they went to their master. So the bands of Syria came no more into the land of Israel.

Summary of 2 Kings 6:24–33

Because of wickedness in Israel, the Syrians besiege Samaria and a terrible famine inflicts all the land. Some eat their own children.

Summary of 2 Kings 7

In the midst of terrible famine caused by the Syrian siege, the Lord shows mercy upon Israel. God sends "the noise of a great host" upon the Syrian army (2 Kings 7:6) and they abandon their camp in fear for their lives. Four lepers from the gates of Samaria discover the deserted camp and deliver the news to the king's house. The people of Samaria are saved by the spoils of the Syrian army.

Summary of 2 Kings 8

Elisha's warning to the Shunammite woman of a seven-year famine in Israel saves her family. Elisha travels to Damascus and prophesies of the great evil that Hazael, the future king of Syria, will practice upon Israel. In the kingdom of Judah, Jehoram, the son of Jehoshaphat, follows the example of the Israelite kings and does evil in the sight of God. His son, Ahaziah, then continues to reign in wickedness.

Summary of 2 Kings 9

Elisha sends one of his disciples to anoint Jehu as king of Israel. Jehu is told to cut off the whole house of Ahab and does so by killing both Joram and Ahaziah, king of Judah. He also has Jezebel thrown out of her window where she is trodden to death by horses and eaten by dogs, thus fulfilling the Lord's prophecy concerning her (see 1 Kings 21:23).

CHAPTER 7

Elisha prophesies incredible plenty in Samaria—The Syrian hosts flee at a noise of battle and leave their possessions—Israel takes spoil from the Syrians.

CHAPTER 8

Elisha prophesies a seven-year famine—The Shunammite woman is preserved through the famine—Jehoram and then Ahaziah reign in wickedness in Judah.

CHAPTER 9

A prophet anoints Jehu king over Israel and prophesies the destruction of the house of Ahab and the death of Jezebel—Jehu kills Joram in the field of Naboth—Jezebel is killed by Jehu and is eaten by dogs.

CHAPTERS 10–12

Ahab's seventy sons are slain—Jehu destroys the house of Ahab and all the worshippers of Baal, but he continues to worship the golden calves in Bethel and Dan.

Athaliah destroys the royal family in Judah and reigns herself in Judah—Joash is preserved and crowned king when seven years old—Jehoiada the priest destroys the house of Baal.

Jehoash (Joash) reigns in righteousness—The breaches in the temple are repaired—The safety of Jerusalem is purchased with the hallowed things in the temple—Joash is slain and Amaziah reigns.

Summary of 2 Kings 10–12

Jehu sends a letter to the elders of Samaria and arranges for the killing of Ahab's sons and Ahaziah's brothers. He also gathers together all Baal worshippers in Israel and puts them to death. Following the death of Jehu, Athaliah, daughter of Ahab, puts to death all of the royal family of Jehu except Joash, who is hidden for six years. Later, the high priest Jehoiada secretly calls the nobles into the temple and anoints Joash as king. Upon hearing this news, Athaliah comes to the temple, where she is seized and put to death. Joash rules in Jerusalem for forty years and is obedient to God, rebuilds the temple, and attempts to appease Hazael, king of Syria, who is laying siege to Jerusalem, by giving him sacred items from the temple. The servants of Joash plot against and kill him.

CHAPTER 13

Jehoahaz and his successors reign in wickedness in Israel—Elisha prophesies that Joash will defeat Syria—Elisha dies—A dead Israelite is restored to life after touching Elisha's bones.

Summary of 2 Kings 13

Jehoahaz, son of Jehu, rules in wickedness over the Northern Kingdom of Israel. Though Jehoahaz eventually seeks the Lord (vv. 4–9), his son Jehoash rules for sixteen years in wickedness (vv. 9–13). Jehoash has respect for Elisha but he lacks faith in God, who guides the prophet. The dying Elisha warns Jehoash that he will only have limited success over Syria (vv. 14–19). Later, a dead man is placed in Elisha's sepulcher. When his dead body makes contact with Elisha's, the dead man miraculously returns to life (vv. 20–21). Some view this miracle as the Lord showing His power to heal the spiritually dead in Israel.

Who Were the Kings of Israel and Judah? (2 Kings 13)

"After the death of Solomon, a power struggle for the leadership of Israel ensued. Under the direction of Solomon's son, Rehoboam, the tribe of Judah together with the assimilated Simeonites of that region and half of the tribe of Benjamin joined together to form the southern monarchy called the kingdom of Judah.

"The ten and one-half tribes in the north united under the leadership of a strong military officer, Jeroboam, to establish the northern kingdom called Israel or sometimes Ephraim, after the preeminent tribe.

"The record of the era of the divided kingdoms is a difficult seesaw account. Time lapses in the narrative and only selected mention of events is characteristic of the interwoven chronicle of these kingdoms" (Brandt, "Time of the Divided Kingdoms," 30).

Summary of 2 Kings 14–15

Amaziah, king of Judah, avenges his father Joash's murder. After successfully overcoming Edom, he initiates war with Israel. The army of Judah suffers a decisive defeat. Later Amaziah is killed by a conspiracy and succeeded by his son Azariah. Both Azariah and his son Jotham gain favor in the Lord's sight, but fail to remove the "high places" of idolatry in Judah (see 2 Kings 15:4, 35).

In the kingdom of Israel, wickedness and conspiracy abound, and the prophet Jonah is rejected. The rising Assyrian empire invades Israel. During the reign of Pekah, the northern areas including Gilead and Galilee are conquered and the people are carried captive to Assyria, commencing the scattering of Israel.

CHAPTERS 14–15

Amaziah reigns well in Judah—Israel defeats Judah in battle—Jeroboam reigns in wickedness in Israel.

Many kings reign in Israel and in Judah—Their wickedness, wars, conspiracies, and evils are described—Much of Israel is carried captive to Assyria by Tiglath-pileser.

2 Kings 16:1–4. Ahaz Reestablishes Idolatry in Judah

Who was Ahaz? (16:1–2) "Ahaz was the worst of the Davidic kings. He had the great prophet Isaiah to advise him and would have done better by accepting his advice" (Rasmussen, *Latter-day Saint Commentary on the Old Testament*, 314). "[Ahaz] comes to power as a twenty-year-old, then rules officially for sixteen

CHAPTER 16

Ahaz reigns in wickedness in Judah—He offers his son in heathen sacrifice—He makes a new altar, destroys the brazen sea, and changes the method for sacrificing in the temple.

1 In the seventeenth year of Pekah the son of Remaliah Ahaz the son of Jotham king of Judah began to reign.

2 Twenty years old *was* Ahaz when he began to reign, and reigned sixteen years in

The Rise of Assyria (2 Kings 15)

"Assyria, named for the god Ashur (highest in the pantheon of Assyrian gods), was located in the Mesopotamian plain. It was bordered on the west by the Syrian desert, on the south by Babylonia, and on the north and east by the Persian and Urarthian hills (see [Douglas, ed., *Illustrated Bible Dictionary*], s.v. "Assyria," 1:137). This area today is primarily the nation of Iraq. . . .

"Assyria's ascent as a formidable power in the Near East was due in large measure to strong kings who increased her borders and subjected other nations as tributaries. . . . Under these kings Assyria reached its greatest apex of power, controlling the area that included not only Assyria but also Babylonia, Armenia, Media, Judea, Syria, Phoenicia, Sumeria, Elam, and Egypt. . . .

"The most vital part of the Assyrian government was its army. Warfare was a science to the leaders of Assyria. Infantry, chariots, cavalry (introduced by Ashurnasirpal to aid the infantry and chariots), sappers, armor made from iron, siege machines, and battering rams were all developed or perfected by the Assyrians. Strategy and tactics were also well understood by the Assyrian officers. . . .

"Assyria was at the height of its power, and its reputation for terror and brutality should have been sufficient to turn Israel back to their God, but they would not heed. Under the reign of Tiglath-pileser II, Assyria began consolidating its power in the western part of the empire. Around 738 B.C. he demanded and received tribute from Damascus, the capital of Syria, and Samaria, the capital of Israel (see 2 Kings 15:19–20). But four years later, the two Syrian states rebelled, and once again Tiglath-pileser moved in. Damascus was conquered, as was part of the territory of the Northern Kingdom, and the people were carried off into captivity (see 2 Kings 15:29)" (*Old Testament Student Manual: 1 Kings–Malachi*, 113, 114).

Jerusalem, and did not *that which was* right in the sight of the LORD his God, like David his father.

3 But he walked in the way of the kings of Israel, yea, and made his son to pass through the fire, according to the abominations of the heathen, whom the LORD cast out from before the children of Israel.

4 And he sacrificed and burnt incense in the high places, and on the hills, and under every green tree.

years. The text notes that he becomes king in Pekah's [the king of Israel] seventeenth year, which is 735 B.C., and rules sixteen years, though dates for later kings indicate his era ends in 715 B.C." (House, *1, 2 Kings*, 335).

In what ways did Ahaz follow the wicked kings of Israel? (16:3–4) Ahaz came to power in Judah following several moderately righteous kings. However, like the monarchs of the northern kingdom, Ahaz rejected the true God of Israel. He led his people in blatant worship of false Canaanite gods, including the performance of human sacrifices.

"We have here the first instance of an actual Moloch-sacrifice among the Israelites, i.e., of one performed by slaying and burning. . . . The offering of his son for Moloch took place, in all probability, during the severe oppression of Ahaz by the Syrians, and was intended to appease the wrath of the gods, as was done by the king of the Moabites in similar circumstances (2 Kings 3:27)" (Keil and Delitzsch, *Commentary* [on 2 Kings 16:3–4]). ⊕

5 ¶ Then Rezin king of Syria and Pekah son of Remaliah king of Israel came up to Jerusalem to war: and they besieged Ahaz, but could not overcome *him.*

6 At that time Rezin king of Syria recovered Elath to Syria, and drave the Jews from Elath: and the Syrians came to Elath, and dwelt there unto this day.

7 So Ahaz sent messengers to Tiglath-pileser king of Assyria, saying, I *am* thy servant and thy son: come up, and save me out of the hand of the king of Syria, and out of the hand of the king of Israel, which rise up against me.

8 And Ahaz took the silver and gold that was found in the house of the LORD, and in the treasures of the king's house, and sent *it for* a present to the king of Assyria.

9 And the king of Assyria hearkened unto him: for the king of Assyria went up against Damascus, and took it, and carried *the people of* it captive to Kir, and slew Rezin.

2 Kings 16:5–9. Syria and Israel Unite against Judah, and Ahaz Seeks Favor from Assyria

Why did Ahaz submit to Assyria? (16:7) "Ignoring both Isaiah's assurance about an attack by Syria and Israel and his warning about the growing dangers form Assyria (Isa. 7), Ahaz tried a pressure-play against the Syrians and northern Israelites by giving tribute to Assyria's king, even adopting his religion, to curry favor with him" (Rasmussen, *Latter-day Saint Commentary on the Old Testament*, 314).

2 Kings 16:10–20. Ahaz Replaces the Altar and Desecrates the Temple

Why does Ahaz have a new temple altar built? (16:10) "Tiglath-pileser is subjugating Damascus and Ahaz goes there, probably to pay tribute. An altar catches his fancy, and he decides to have one like it built in Jerusalem. The altar was Assyrian and Ahaz was doing honour to the gods of Assyria" (*New Bible Commentary: Revised*, 361).

What does the phrase "made it against King Ahaz came from Damascus" mean? (16:11) "This phrase means that Urijah had the altar made by the time King Ahaz got back. Evidently, while in Damascus, Ahaz saw an altar, probably to a false god, that caught his admiration. He had a duplicate made in Jerusalem and set aside the great altar in the temple to use the new one in its place (compare with 2 Chronicles 28:23–5)" (*Old Testament Student Manual: 1 Kings–Malachi*, 126).

10 ¶ And king Ahaz went to Damascus to meet Tiglath-pileser king of Assyria, and saw an altar that *was* at Damascus: and king Ahaz sent to Urijah the priest the fashion of the altar, and the pattern of it, according to all the workmanship thereof.

11 And Urijah the priest built an altar according to all that king Ahaz had sent from Damascus: so Urijah the priest made *it* against king Ahaz came from Damascus.

12 And when the king was come from Damascus, the king saw the altar: and the king approached to the altar, and offered thereon.

13 And he burnt his burnt offering and his meat offering, and poured his drink offering, and sprinkled the blood of his peace offerings, upon the altar.

14 And he brought also the brasen altar, which *was* before the LORD, from the forefront of the house, from between the altar and the house of the LORD, and put it on the north side of the altar.

15 And king Ahaz commanded Urijah the priest, saying, Upon the great altar burn the morning burnt offering, and the evening meat offering, and the king's burnt sacrifice, and his meat offering, with the burnt offering of all the people of the land, and their meat offering, and their drink offerings; and sprinkle upon it all the blood of the burnt offering, and all the blood of the sacrifice: and the brasen altar shall be for me to inquire *by*.

16 Thus did Urijah the priest, according to all that king Ahaz commanded.

17 ¶ And king Ahaz cut off the borders of the bases, and removed the laver from off them; and took down the sea from off the brasen oxen that *were* under it, and put it upon a pavement of stones.

18 And the covert for the sabbath that they had built in the house, and the king's entry without, turned he from the house of the LORD for the king of Assyria.

What is a "covert for the sabbath"? (16:18) "It is very likely that this means either a sort of canopy which was erected on the Sabbath days for the accommodation of the people who came to worship, and which Ahaz took away to discourage them from that worship; or a canopy under which the king and his family reposed themselves, and which he transported to some other place to accommodate the king of Assyria when he visited him" (*Adam Clarke's Commentary* [on 2 Kings 16:18]).

19 ¶ Now the rest of the acts of Ahaz which he did, *are* they not written in the book of the chronicles of the kings of Judah?

20 And Ahaz slept with his fathers, and was buried with his fathers in the city of David: and Hezekiah his son reigned in his stead.

What were "the rest of the acts of Ahaz"? (16:19–20) "Ahaz went yet further in his apostasy. According to the Chronicler (2Ch 28:24–25; cf. 29:7), he went so far as to desecrate the temple furniture and close the temple itself so that the services within the Holy Place were discontinued. 'Worship services' would henceforth be held only in connection with the new altar or at one of the several altars erected throughout Jerusalem or at the high places dedicated to the various gods established throughout Judah by royal edict ([2Ch] 28:24–25). All his innovations speak volumes as to Ahaz's depraved spiritual condition. It is small wonder, then, that the Chronicler reports that Ahaz provoked the Lord's anger ([2 Chr.] 28:25)" (Patterson and Austel, "1, 2 Kings," 3:893).

CHAPTER 17

Hoshea reigns in Israel and is subject to the Assyrians—The Israelites forsake the Lord, worship idols, serve Baal, and reject all that the Lord has given them—The ten tribes are carried away captive by the kings of Assyria—The land of Israel (Samaria) is repopulated by other people—Many forms of false worship are found among the Samaritans.

1 In the twelfth year of Ahaz king of Judah began Hoshea the son of Elah to reign in Samaria over Israel nine years.

2 And he did *that which was* evil in the sight of the LORD, but not as the kings of Israel that were before him.

3 ¶ Against him came up Shalmaneser king of Assyria; and Hoshea became his servant, and gave him presents.

4 And the king of Assyria found conspiracy in Hoshea: for he had sent messengers to So

2 Kings 17:1–6. After Conspiring against Assyria, Israel Is Carried into Captivity

Who was Hoshea, king of Israel? (17:1–4) "Hoshea, the last king of the northern ten tribes of Israel, conspired against [his predecessor] King Pekah and slew him. . . . The account concedes that the evil [Hoshea] did was not as bad as the evil done by the kings before him. He paid Assyria tribute as three kings before him had done, but like Pekah before him, he could not keep Assyria appeased. When he tried to get Egypt's help against Assyria, Shalmaneser of Assyria imprisoned him and besieged the capital city, Samaria, for three years. Finally, Shalmaneser took the city and sent thousands of Israelites into slavery" (Rasmussen, *Latter-day Saint Commentary on the Old Testament,* 315).

Which Assyrian king conquered Israel in 722–721 B.C.? (17:3–4) "Hoshea reigned only a few years in Israel before a failure to render tribute to Assyria brought down on him the wrath of Tiglath-pileser's successor Shalmaneser V (727–722 B.C.), who imprisoned Hoshea and laid siege to Samaria. It is Shalmaneser who is identified in biblical tradition as the eventual conqueror of Samaria around 722 B.C. after a three-year siege ([2 Kings] 17:5–6; 18:9–10). Extrabiblical tradition possibly speaks with two voices on the subject, however. The Babylonian Chronicle does indeed identify Shalmaneser V as Samaria's besieger and conqueror, but Shalmaneser's successor, Sargon II (722–705 B.C.), also takes this honor for himself in his inscriptions" (Provan, "2 Kings," 3:177).

king of Egypt, and brought no present to the
king of Assyria, as *he had done* year by year:
therefore the king of Assyria shut him up,
and bound him in prison.

5 ¶ Then the king of Assyria came up
throughout all the land, and went up to
Samaria, and besieged it three years.

Why are these cities named when the Israelites are relocated? (17:6) "It was ancient practice to deport large numbers of influential citizens of a conquered country or city to decrease the possibility of rebellion. . . . Such a mixing of populations would break down ethnic distinctions and weaken the loyalties that the people had. It would also help create a sense of empire. The cities recorded here may indicate the order for a caravan or relocated people" (*Nelson Study Bible* [NKJV], 640, 641). ⊕

6 ¶ In the ninth year of Hoshea the king of
Assyria took Samaria, and carried Israel away
into Assyria, and placed them in Halah and
in Habor *by* the river of Gozan, and in the
cities of the Medes.

2 Kings 17:7–23. Reasons for the Fall of the Kingdom of Israel

7 For *so* it was, that the children of Israel had
sinned against the LORD their God, which
had brought them up out of the land of
Egypt, from under the hand of Pharaoh king
of Egypt, and had feared other gods,

8 And walked in the statutes of the heathen,
whom the LORD cast out from before the
children of Israel, and of the kings of Israel,
which they had made.

What are the towers and the fenced city? (17:9) "Towers were built by owners of vineyards (see 2 Chronicles 26:10) so they could observe the countryside and protect their possessions. The expression 'from the tower of the watchmen to the fenced city' simply means from thinly populated areas to heavily populated areas. It is another way of saying that all Israel, the Northern Kingdom, had turned to the worship of idols" (*Old Testament Student Manual: 1 Kings–Malachi*, 126).

9 And the children of Israel did secretly *those*
things that *were* not right against the LORD
their God, and they built them high places in
all their cities, from the tower of the watchmen to the fenced city.

10 And they set them up images and groves
in every high hill, and under every green tree:

11 And there they burnt incense in all the
high places, as *did* the heathen whom the
LORD carried away before them; and wrought
wicked things to provoke the LORD to anger:

12 For they served idols, whereof the LORD had said unto them, Ye shall not do this thing.

13 Yet the LORD testified against Israel, and against Judah, by all the prophets, *and by* all the seers, saying, Turn ye from your evil ways, and keep my commandments *and* my statutes, according to all the law which I commanded your fathers, and which I sent to you by my servants the prophets.

14 Notwithstanding they would not hear, but hardened their necks, like to the neck of their fathers, that did not believe in the LORD their God.

15 And they rejected his statutes, and his covenant that he made with their fathers, and his testimonies which he testified against them; and they followed vanity, and became vain, and went after the heathen that *were* round about them, *concerning* whom the LORD had charged them, that they should not do like them.

16 And they left all the commandments of the LORD their God, and made them molten images, *even* two calves, and made a grove, and worshipped all the host of heaven, and served Baal.

17 And they caused their sons and their daughters to pass through the fire, and used divination and enchantments, and sold themselves to do evil in the sight of the LORD, to provoke him to anger.

18 Therefore the LORD was very angry with Israel, and removed them out of his sight: there was none left but the tribe of Judah only.

19 Also Judah kept not the commandments of the LORD their God, but walked in the statutes of Israel which they made.

20 And the LORD rejected all the seed of Israel, and afflicted them, and delivered them into the hand of spoilers, until he had cast them out of his sight.

Why is it important to understand the role of prophets? (17:13) "Prophets speak by the power of the Holy Spirit. They testify of Christ and His divine mission on earth. They represent the mind and heart of the Lord and are called to represent Him and teach us what we must do to return to live in the presence of God and His Son, Jesus Christ. We are blessed as we exercise our faith and follow their teachings. By following them, our lives are happier and less complicated, our difficulties and problems are easier to bear, and we create a spiritual armor around us that will protect us from the attacks of the enemy in our day" (Soares, "Prophets Speak by the Power of the Holy Spirit," 99).

How did Israel follow vanity? (17:15) "Rejecting the Lord's guidance, the children of Israel 'followed vanity,' or things that are empty and of no lasting value. As a result, they 'became vain,' or were led astray as they worshipped false gods who could not answer their prayers or give them guidance (see [*Strong's Exhaustive Concordance*, #h1892, #h1891])" (Valletta, et al., *Old Testament for Latter-day Saint Families*, 349).

What does it mean that the Israelites worshipped "all the host of heaven"? (17:16) "This is the first time this form of idolatry is mentioned in the Northern Kingdom. To worship the host of heaven was to worship the sun, moon, and stars—something that Moses had forbidden the people to do (see Deuteronomy 4:19; 17:3)" (*Old Testament Student Manual: 1 Kings–Malachi*, 126).

Which tribes were carried away into captivity? (17:18) "The statement that 'there was none left but the tribe of Judah only' can be understood correctly only if one realizes that at this time Benjamin, Levi, and all other Israelites who had left the nation of Israel and joined Judah were included under the title of Judah. The ten tribes carried into captivity at this time were Reuben, Simeon, Issachar, Zebulon, Gad, Dan, Asher, Naphtali, Ephraim, and Manasseh. The three remaining tribes were Judah, Benjamin, and Levi. Some of the tribe of Levi were still with Israel (the ten tribes), however, and some of Ephraim, Manasseh, and other tribes were with Judah. So, the division is not as clear as a superficial reading might indicate" (*Old Testament Student Manual: 1 Kings–Malachi*, 127).

21 For he rent Israel from the house of David; and they made Jeroboam the son of Nebat king: and Jeroboam drave Israel from following the LORD, and made them sin a great sin.

22 For the children of Israel walked in all the sins of Jeroboam which he did; they departed not from them;

23 Until the LORD removed Israel out of his sight, as he had said by all his servants the prophets. So was Israel carried away out of their own land to Assyria unto this day.

2 Kings 17:24–29. The Land of the Kingdom of Israel Is Occupied

What became of those Israelites left behind by the Assyrians? (17:24) "The foreigners mentioned in verse 24, and their descendants, eventually intermarried with many of the Israelites who remained in Samaria after the ten tribes were taken into captivity. The offspring of these mixed marriages were the 'Samaritans,' who were not acceptable to the orthodox of Judah because of their mixed blood.

"The scorn of most Jews for the Samaritans was still evident in New Testament times and provided the background for the visit of Jesus with the woman

24 ¶ And the king of Assyria brought *men* from Babylon, and from Cuthah, and from Ava, and from Hamath, and from Sepharvaim, and placed *them* in the cities of Samaria instead of the children of Israel: and they possessed Samaria, and dwelt in the cities thereof.

25 And *so* it was at the beginning of their dwelling there, *that* they feared not the

Lessons from the Scattering of Israel (2 Kings 17:1–23)

"As descendants of Abraham, the tribes of ancient Israel had access to priesthood authority and blessings of the gospel, but eventually the people rebelled. They killed the prophets and were punished by the Lord. Ten tribes were carried captive into Assyria. From there they became lost to the records of mankind. (Obviously, the ten tribes are not lost to the Lord.) Two remaining tribes continued a short time and then, because of their rebellion, were taken captive into Babylon" (Nelson, "Gathering of Scattered Israel," 79).

Reflecting on the Israelites' exercise of their agency in these circumstances, Elder Quentin L. Cook reminded us: "God intended that men and women would be free to make choices between good and evil. When evil choices become the dominant characteristic of a culture or nation, there are serious consequences both in this life and the life to come. People can become enslaved or put themselves in bondage not only to harmful, addictive substances but also to harmful, addictive philosophies that detract from righteous living.

"Turning from the worship of the true and living God and worshipping false gods like wealth and fame and engaging in immoral and unrighteous conduct result in bondage in all its insidious manifestations. These include spiritual, physical, and intellectual bondage and sometimes bring destruction. . . .

"These messages have echoed and been reinforced across the centuries in all dispensations. They are at the heart of the Restoration of the gospel of Jesus Christ in this, the final dispensation. . . .

"We learn valuable lessons from this tragic period. We should do everything within our power to avoid the sin and rebellion that lead to bondage" ("Lamentations of Jeremiah," 88–89).

What can we learn from the scattering of Israel? How can we avoid becoming spiritually "scattered" in a time of rampant wickedness and individual justification for unrighteous actions? President Dieter F. Uchtdorf counseled, "There is too much at stake for us as individuals, as families, and as Christ's Church to give only a halfhearted effort. . . .

"Being a disciple of Jesus Christ is not an effort of once a week or once a day. It is an effort of once and for all" ("Are You Sleeping through the Restoration?" 61).

LORD: therefore the LORD sent lions among them, which slew *some* of them.

26 Wherefore they spake to the king of Assyria, saying, The nations which thou hast removed, and placed in the cities of Samaria, know not the manner of the God of the land: therefore he hath sent lions among them, and, behold, they slay them, because they know not the manner of the God of the land.

27 Then the king of Assyria commanded, saying, Carry thither one of the priests whom ye brought from thence; and let them go and dwell there, and let him teach them the manner of the God of the land.

28 Then one of the priests whom they had carried away from Samaria came and dwelt in Beth-el, and taught them how they should fear the LORD.

29 Howbeit every nation made gods of their own, and put *them* in the houses of the high places which the Samaritans had made, every nation in their cities wherein they dwelt.

CHAPTER 18

Hezekiah reigns in righteousness in Judah—He destroys idolatry and breaks the brazen serpent made by Moses because the children of Israel burn incense to it—Sennacherib, king of Assyria, invades Judah—In a blasphemous speech, Rabshakeh asks Jerusalem to surrender to the Assyrians.

1 Now it came to pass in the third year of Hoshea son of Elah king of Israel, *that* Hezekiah the son of Ahaz king of Judah began to reign.

2 Twenty and five years old was he when he began to reign; and he reigned twenty and

of Samaria at Jacob's well (John 4:3–42) as well as the story of the good Samaritan who proved to be a neighbor to the man who fell among thieves (Luke 10:25–37)" (Ludlow, *Companion to Your Study of the Old Testament*, 240).

Why was an Israelite priest returned to Samaria? (17:27) "When the new settlers faced the menace of lions roaming freely through the area, they immediately suspected that 'the god of the land' was punishing them because of their failure to worship him. . . . The Israelite priest sent back to the northern kingdom would teach the false worship instituted by Jeroboam. The result was a mixture of truth combined with the corrupted experience of Israel (now deepened by two centuries of growing apostasy) and the pagan rites brought by the new settlers" (Patterson and Austel, "1, 2 Kings," 3:900).

Summary for 2 Kings 17:30–41

The inhabitants of Samaria practice a mixed religion, making sacrifices to the true God, Jehovah, and to the numerous false gods of the people.

2 Kings 18:1–8. King Hezekiah Begins His Reign in Judah and Destroys the Idols Found in His Kingdom

Who was King Hezekiah? (18:1–2) Hezekiah was the King of Judah and "son of King Ahaz. . . . [He] reconquered many of the cities that his father had lost" (Isbouts, *National Geographic Who's Who in the Bible*, 138). Hezekiah was "a great religious and political reformer (2 Kgs. 18:1–21:3; 2 Chr. 29:1–33:3; Isa. 36–39). He suppressed idolatry and reconstituted the temple services. In his reforms both in church and state he had the assistance of the great prophet Isaiah. . . . [Judah experienced two Assyrian invasions.] After a time of great anxiety the city was at length delivered, probably by a pestilence that broke out in the Assyrian camp. A year later Hezekiah died, after a reign of 29 years" (Bible Dictionary, "Hezekiah").

How did Hezekiah differ from the kings who preceded him? (18:3–4) "To be compared with King David was one of the best compliments Hebrew writers could give a king. Only two [prior] kings carried this honor: Asa (1 Kings 15:11) and Jehoshaphat (1 King 22:43). King Hezekiah was greater however, because these other two did not tear down the 'high places' or altars that had been used for idol worship" (Valletta, et al., *Old Testament for Latter-day Saint Families,* 351).

Why did Hezekiah call the brass serpent *Nehushtan*? (18:4) "The brass serpent was preserved in Israel and, in time, became an object of adoration and was worshiped by the Israelites much as they worshiped idols. In his zeal to eradicate all forms of idolatry in Judah, King Hezekiah had the brazen serpent destroyed along with the idols. The word *nehushtan* comes from the Hebrew and means an object made of brass. The implication may be that Hezekiah was speaking contemptuously of the object being worshiped, saying it was merely a 'thing of brass' and nothing more" (*Old Testament Student Manual: 1 Kings–Malachi,* 127).

What can we learn from the description of Hezekiah in these verses? (18:5–6) "The divine evaluation is a favorable one: (1) There was none who equaled Hezekiah in his trust of the Lord (v.5); (2) he followed the Lord faithfully (v.6a); and (3) he obeyed implicitly the law of God (v.6b). Hence God was with him and blessed him with success (v.7). Hezekiah's character stands as a reminder that living for God's glory is for the believer's good also (cf. v.7 with 2Ch 31:20–21)" (Patterson and Austel, "1, 2 Kings," 3:903). How might you better develop these faithful characteristics in yourself?

How did Hezekiah rebel against Assyria? (18:7) "Judah had become a vassal to Assyria under Ahaz . . . which required at least formal recognition of Assyrian deities. Hezekiah reversed the policy of his father Ahaz and sought independence from Assyrian dominance. . . . Hezekiah refused to pay the annual tribute due the Assyrians" (*NIV Study Bible* [1995], 553). "In addition to refusing to serve any longer as a vassal of *Assyria,*

nine years in Jerusalem. His mother's name also *was* Abi, the daughter of Zachariah.

3 And he did *that which was* right in the sight of the LORD, according to all that David his father did.

4 ¶ He removed the high places, and brake the images, and cut down the groves, and brake in pieces the brasen serpent that Moses had made: for unto those days the children of Israel did burn incense to it: and he called it Nehushtan.

5 He trusted in the LORD God of Israel; so that after him was none like him among all the kings of Judah, nor *any* that were before him.

6 For he clave to the LORD, *and* departed not from following him, but kept his commandments, which the LORD commanded Moses.

7 And the LORD was with him; *and* he prospered whithersoever he went forth: and he rebelled against the king of Assyria, and served him not.

8 He smote the Philistines, *even* unto Gaza, and the borders thereof, from the tower of the watchmen to the fenced city.

9 ¶ And it came to pass in the fourth year of king Hezekiah, which *was* the seventh year of Hoshea son of Elah king of Israel, *that* Shalmaneser king of Assyria came up against Samaria, and besieged it.

10 And at the end of three years they took it: *even* in the sixth year of Hezekiah, that *is* the ninth year of Hoshea king of Israel, Samaria was taken.

11 And the king of Assyria did carry away Israel unto Assyria, and put them in Halah and in Habor *by* the river of Gozan, and in the cities of the Medes:

12 Because they obeyed not the voice of the LORD their God, but transgressed his covenant, *and* all that Moses the servant of the LORD commanded, and would not hear *them,* nor do *them.*

13 ¶ Now in the fourteenth year of king Hezekiah did Sennacherib king of Assyria come up against all the fenced cities of Judah, and took them.

14 And Hezekiah king of Judah sent to the king of Assyria to Lachish, saying, I have offended; return from me: that which thou puttest on me will I bear. And the king of Assyria appointed unto Hezekiah king of Judah three hundred talents of silver and thirty talents of gold.

15 And Hezekiah gave *him* all the silver that was found in the house of the LORD, and in the treasures of the king's house.

Hezekiah also conquered the *Philistines*. This helped establish Judah as an independent nation and new power in the region. No longer was Judah under the threat of military incursions from neighboring states simply because of its weakness" (*Nelson Study Bible* [NKJV], 643).

2 Kings 18:9–16. The Northern Kingdom of Israel Is Carried Captive into Assyria and Judah Is Invaded

Why does this passage retell the event found in 2 Kings 17:1–6? (18:9–12) "This text repeats information already covered in 2 Kgs 17:1–6, with the intention of demonstrating Hezekiah's awareness of the dangers inherent in opposing Assyria. The passage also reminds readers that the fundamental reason [Israel] fell was its spiritual rebellion, not merely its refusal to obey Assyria any longer. Therefore, Hezekiah may not disobey the Lord and survive. The issue that awaits an appropriate answer is whether or not Hezekiah can serve the Lord, disobey Assyria, and survive. Since he cannot serve the Lord and maintain ties with an oppressive, murderous country, Hezekiah will be forced to discover the answer to this question" (House, *1, 2 Kings*, 8:360).

How did Hezekiah attempt to appease King Sennacherib? (18:13–16) "The beginning of the Assyrian assault is reported in verses 13–16, as a new king (*Sennacherib*) attacks *all the fortified cities* and captures them. This is not a very promising beginning. It seems that Hezekiah may indeed be about to suffer the same fate as Hoshea, regardless of his trust in God (v. 5). For all that Hezekiah has been lauded as a king quite unlike anyone who preceded him, his first reaction to foreign attack is a familiar one; he raids the royal *treasuries* and *the temple*, even stripping the *gold* from its *doors and doorposts* (cf. 1 Kgs. 15:18ff.; 2 Kgs. 12:17–18; 16:7ff.)" (Provan, *1 and 2 Kings*, 7:255).

2 Kings 18:17–27. Assyrian Emissaries Mock and Threaten Judah from Outside the Walls of Jerusalem

Why did the king of Assyria send emissaries to Jerusalem? (18:17) "The three Assyrian titles mean roughly 'field marshal' [Tartan], 'chief officer' [Rabsaris], . . . and 'chief administrator' [Rab-shakeh]. . . . The *Rabshakeh* was a highly placed Assyrian official. He was obviously well informed about Hezekiah's political alliances (v. 21), religious activities (v. 22), able to speak the local language, 'Judean' (v. 26), and knowledgeable about Israelite religion (v. 25). His speech, although formally directed to the leaders, was intended for the ears of the common folk so that they would pressure their king to give in to Assyria" (*Jewish Study Bible* [2014], 745). The emissaries were accompanied by a great army (see verse 17), which would have added an element of physical intimidation.

What was the purpose of the Assyrian message? (18:19–22) "The Assyrian Rabshakeh's propaganda was diabolical. He taunted the people of Judah with offers of horses if they could find riders for them. He used vulgarity to frighten them with the horrors of famine. He promised to take them to a land better and more productive. He asserted that the Lord would not help them because Hezekiah had ordered altars on the high places destroyed—wrongly assuming that those altars were for worship of the Lord. . . . [Rabshakeh] boasted that the Lord could not defend Jerusalem against Assyria even if he wanted to do so, citing the failure of gods of other lands to defend them" (Rasmussen, *Latter-day Saint Commentary on the Old Testament*, 317).

Why is Egypt referred to as a "bruised reed"? (18:21) Egypt, while a some-time political ally of Judah, had diminished in power under Assyrian expansion. "The figure of Egypt as a splintered [bruised or broken] reed is appropriate. The Nile River was rich in the reeds that were so important to Egyptian life. . . . Sennacherib's evaluation of Egypt harmonized with the prophecies of Isaiah (Isa. 20; 30:3–5; 31:1–3). . . . What kind of trust can they hope to place in such a splintered reed?" (Patterson and Austel, "1, 2 Kings," 3:908; paragraphing altered).

16 At that time did Hezekiah cut off *the gold*
from the doors of the temple of the LORD,
and *from* the pillars which Hezekiah king of
Judah had overlaid, and gave it to the king
of Assyria.

17 ¶ And the king of Assyria sent Tartan
and Rabsaris and Rab-shakeh from Lachish
to king Hezekiah with a great host against
Jerusalem. And they went up and came to
Jerusalem. And when they were come up,
they came and stood by the conduit of the
upper pool, which *is* in the highway of the
fuller's field.

18 And when they had called to the king,
there came out to them Eliakim the son of
Hilkiah, which *was* over the household, and
Shebna the scribe, and Joah the son of Asaph
the recorder.

19 And Rab-shakeh said unto them, Speak
ye now to Hezekiah, Thus saith the great
king, the king of Assyria, What confidence *is*
this wherein thou trustest?

20 Thou sayest, (but *they are but* vain words,)
I have counsel and strength for the war. Now
on whom dost thou trust, that thou rebellest
against me?

21 Now, behold, thou trustest upon the staff
of this bruised reed, *even* upon Egypt, on
which if a man lean, it will go into his hand,
and pierce it: so *is* Pharaoh king of Egypt
unto all that trust on him.

22 But if ye say unto me, We trust in the
LORD our God: *is* not that he, whose high
places and whose altars Hezekiah hath
taken away, and hath said to Judah and
Jerusalem, Ye shall worship before this altar
in Jerusalem?

23 Now therefore, I pray thee, give pledges
to my lord the king of Assyria, and I will
deliver thee two thousand horses, if thou be
able on thy part to set riders upon them.

24 How then wilt thou turn away the face of one captain of the least of my master's servants, and put thy trust on Egypt for chariots and for horsemen?

25 Am I now come up without the LORD against this place to destroy it? The LORD said to me, Go up against this land, and destroy it.

26 Then said Eliakim the son of Hilkiah, and Shebna, and Joah, unto Rab-shakeh, Speak, I pray thee, to thy servants in the Syrian language; for we understand *it:* and talk not with us in the Jews' language in the ears of the people that *are* on the wall.

27 But Rab-shakeh said unto them, Hath my master sent me to thy master, and to thee, to speak these words? *hath he* not *sent me* to the men which sit on the wall, that they may eat their own dung, and drink their own piss with you?

Why were the Assyrians asked to speak the Syrian language of Aramaic? (18:26–27) "The Assyrian envoy's use of [Hebrew] was early 'psychological warfare.' He wanted all to understand his ridicule and promises, to weaken the will to resist" (Richards, *Bible Reader's Companion*, 256).

Summary of 2 Kings 18:28–37

Rab-shakeh mocks the Lord and proclaims that no god could rescue the people or stand against the might of Assyria. Obedient to Hezekiah's command, the people do not respond to Rab-shakeh's taunts.

CHAPTER 19

Hezekiah seeks counsel from Isaiah to save Jerusalem—Isaiah prophesies the defeat of the Assyrians and the death of Sennacherib—Hezekiah prays for deliverance—Sennacherib sends a blasphemous letter—Isaiah prophesies that the Assyrians will be destroyed and that a remnant of Judah will flourish—An angel slays 185,000 Assyrians—Sennacherib is slain by his sons.

1 And it came to pass, when king Hezekiah heard *it,* that he rent his clothes, and covered himself with sackcloth, and went into the house of the LORD.

2 Kings 19:1–7. King Hezekiah Goes to the Temple and Isaiah Prophesies of Jerusalem's Deliverance

Why did Hezekiah rend (or tear) his clothes? (19:1) "When Hezekiah had heard from his counsellors the report of Rabshakeh's words, he rent his clothes with horror at his daring mockery of the living God" (Keil and Delitzsch, *Commentary* [on 2 Kings 19:1–2]). "Hezekiah knew that a battle at Jerusalem was inevitable. He immediately began to mourn. He then went to the temple. He also sent his officers to Isaiah, seeking the word of the Lord and hoping that God would be offended by the blasphemous words of the Assyrians and would come out in anger against them" (Muhlestein, *Scripture Study Made Simple*, 283).

Why did Hezekiah send two of his trusted leaders to Isaiah the prophet? (19:2) "Many scholars believe that Isaiah's ministry took place between the years 740 and 700 (or perhaps 699) B.C.—approximately forty years. According to Isaiah 1:1, Isaiah served as a prophet during the reign of several kings in Judah, including Uzziah [Azariah], Jotham, Ahaz, and Hezekiah. He had personal dealings with at least two of those kings. According to one ancient Jewish source, Isaiah's wife was a daughter of one of the kings of Judah, making Isaiah a member of the royal family by marriage" (Parry, et al., *Understanding Isaiah*, 2).

What is meant by the imagery of childbirth? (19:3) "[This is] a figure denoting extreme danger, the most desperate circumstances. If the woman in travail has not strength to bring forth the child which has come to the mouth of the womb, both the life of the child and that of the mother are exposed to the greatest danger; and this was the condition of the people here" (Keil and Delitzsch, *Commentary* [on 2 Kings 19:3]).

What was the "blast" that Sennacherib would "hear a rumor" about? (19:5–7) "Isaiah replied with this comforting promise: Hezekiah was not to be afraid of the blasphemous words of the Assyrian king; the Lord would frighten him with a report, so that he would return to his own land, and there would He cause him to fall by the sword" (Keil and Delitzsch, *Commentary* [on 2 Kings 19:5–7]). Another scholar has expressed, "The blast was that which slew one hundred and eighty-five thousand of them in one night, see 2 Kings 19:35" (*Adam Clarke's Commentary* [on 2 Kings 19:7]).

Summary of 2 Kings 19:8–31

Sennacherib sends a letter to Hezekiah, declaring that no gods have withstood Assyria. Hezekiah goes to the temple and spreads the letter out before the Lord and prays for their deliverance. Isaiah prophesies that Judah will be preserved and Assyria's army defeated.

2 And he sent Eliakim, which *was* over the
household, and Shebna the scribe, and the elders of the priests, covered with sackcloth, to
Isaiah the prophet the son of Amoz.

3 And they said unto him, Thus saith
Hezekiah, This day *is* a day of trouble, and of
rebuke, and blasphemy: for the children are
come to the birth, and *there is* not strength to
bring forth.

4 It may be the LORD thy God will hear all
the words of Rab-shakeh, whom the king of
Assyria his master hath sent to reproach the
living God; and will reprove the words which
the LORD thy God hath heard: wherefore lift
up *thy* prayer for the remnant that are left.

5 So the servants of king Hezekiah came to
Isaiah.

6 ¶ And Isaiah said unto them, Thus shall
ye say to your master, Thus saith the LORD,
Be not afraid of the words which thou hast
heard, with which the servants of the king of
Assyria have blasphemed me.

7 Behold, I will send a blast upon him, and
he shall hear a rumour, and shall return to his
own land; and I will cause him to fall by the
sword in his own land.

2 Kings 19:32–37. The Lord's Promise to Deliver Judah Is Fulfilled

32 Therefore thus saith the LORD concerning the king of Assyria, He shall not come into this city, nor shoot an arrow there, nor come before it with shield, nor cast a bank against it.

33 By the way that he came, by the same shall he return, and shall not come into this city, saith the LORD.

34 For I will defend this city, to save it, for mine own sake, and for my servant David's sake.

How would Judah's victory be won? (19:32–34) "The final portion of God's response quite specifically promises that the Assyrians will not conquer Jerusalem. In fact, their armies will not surround the city, lay a siege ramp, or shoot an arrow against it. Hezekiah's prayers are answered. [Jehovah] proves greater than the gods of defeated lands, and therefore is worthy of honor, praise, and worship. Jerusalem is spared. The king's faithfulness is rewarded. In fact, this faithfulness was 'all' that was required for the victory" (House, *1, 2 Kings*, 370–71).

What does "cast a bank against it" mean? (19:32) The phrase "cast a bank against it" means to "build a ramp of dirt to allow soldiers to climb over the city walls" (Valletta, et al., *Old Testament for Latter-day Saint Families*, 352).

35 ¶ And it came to pass that night, that the angel of the LORD went out, and smote in the camp of the Assyrians an hundred fourscore and five thousand: and when they arose early in the morning, behold, they *were* all dead corpses.

36 So Sennacherib king of Assyria departed, and went and returned, and dwelt at Nineveh.

How does the Joseph Smith Translation clarify this verse? (19:35) A Joseph Smith Translation change is found in "an amusing story, as worded in the KJV, concerning an angel of the Lord smiting one hundred eighty-five thousand Assyrians. The story is also recorded in chapter 37 of Isaiah. The account ends with the statement, 'And when they arose early in the morning, behold, they were all dead corpses' (2 Kings 19:35; Isaiah 37:36). This KJV reading sounds as if it is those who were killed that arose. However, the JST in both the 2 Kings and Isaiah account adds 'when they *who were left* arose,' showing that it was not those who were killed that arose" (Nyman, "Contribution of the JST to the Old Testament Historical Books," 98).

37 And it came to pass, as he was worshipping in the house of Nisroch his god, that Adrammelech and Sharezer his sons smote him with the sword: and they escaped into the land of Armenia. And Esarhaddon his son reigned in his stead.

How was Isaiah's prophecy about Senacherib's fall fulfilled? (19:37) "The Babylonian Chronicle reports the death of Sennacherib as taking place in 681 B.C., during an insurrection led by his son, but not Esarhaddon, the son who ascended to the throne in the aftermath. Esarhaddon describes the events surrounding his accession to the throne at greater length. He identifies himself as the youngest son of Sennacherib, yet chosen as successor by his father. He claims that he drove the assassins out of the country. A letter to Esarhaddon, found in the royal archives of the Sargonid Dynasty at Nineveh, identifies one of the assassins as Arad-Mullissu—probably the Adrammelech of the Biblical text (2 Kin. 19:37)" (Keener, *NKJV Cultural Backgrounds Study Bible*, 690).

2 Kings 20:1–11. Hezekiah Pleads with the Lord to Lengthen His Life

What did Hezekiah understand about the power of prayer? (20:1–3) "King Hezekiah had an abscess and illness which, if allowed to run its course, would have caused his death; but just as any of us might do, the king prayed humbly and sincerely to be healed" (Rasmussen, *Latter-day Saint Commentary on the Old Testament*, 319). "The object of prayer is not to change the will of God but to secure for ourselves and for others blessings that God is already willing to grant but that are made conditional on our asking for them. Blessings require some work or effort on our part before we can obtain them" (Bible Dictionary, "Prayer"). ⊕

How might Hezekiah's prayer have influenced the Lord's response? (20:2–3) "Hezekiah was able to plead with the Lord by pointing out how wholeheartedly he had served God. He was able to lay claim on the covenant, having kept it. Presumably Hezekiah would have gone to the temple to pray, but his sore made him ritually unclean so that he could not enter. Instead he prayed toward a wall, presumably toward the temple wall" (Muhlestein, *Scripture Study Made Simple*, 286).

Why did Hezekiah wait to enter the temple? (20:5) Hezekiah's illness likely included skin lesions or boils and would need to be "cleansed" or cleared up; showing evidence that he had been healed. "After an illness that had kept one from entering the temple was cured, it was customary to wash and go before the priests to be pronounced clean" (Parry, et al., *Understanding Isaiah*, 335). Being declared clean by the priests allowed a previously unclean person to again enter the temple.

Why were figs used to treat Hezekiah's illness? (20:7) Applying "a poultice of figs was well known in the ancient world as a means of softening and opening hard boils" (*Interpreter's Bible*, 3:306). "Some scholars have suggested that the illness could not have been very serious if a poultice of *figs* . . . was sufficient

CHAPTER 20

Hezekiah is told he will die and pleads with the Lord; his life is lengthened fifteen years—The shadow goes back ten degrees on the sundial of Ahaz—Isaiah prophesies the Babylonian captivity of Judah.

1 In those days was Hezekiah sick unto death. And the prophet Isaiah the son of Amoz came to him, and said unto him, Thus saith the LORD, Set thine house in order; for thou shalt die, and not live.

2 Then he turned his face to the wall, and prayed unto the LORD, saying,

3 I beseech thee, O LORD, remember now how I have walked before thee in truth and with a perfect heart, and have done *that which is* good in thy sight. And Hezekiah wept sore.

4 And it came to pass, afore Isaiah was gone out into the middle court, that the word of the LORD came to him, saying,

5 Turn again, and tell Hezekiah the captain of my people, Thus saith the LORD, the God of David thy father, I have heard thy prayer, I have seen thy tears: behold, I will heal thee: on the third day thou shalt go up unto the house of the LORD.

6 And I will add unto thy days fifteen years; and I will deliver thee and this city out of the hand of the king of Assyria; and I will defend this city for mine own sake, and for my servant David's sake.

7 And Isaiah said, Take a lump of figs. And they took and laid *it* on the boil, and he recovered.

8 ¶ And Hezekiah said unto Isaiah, What
shall be the sign that the LORD will heal me,
and that I shall go up into the house of the
LORD the third day?

9 And Isaiah said, This sign shalt thou have
of the LORD, that the LORD will do the thing
that he hath spoken: shall the shadow go forward ten degrees, or go back ten degrees?

10 And Hezekiah answered, It is a light thing
for the shadow to go down ten degrees: nay,
but let the shadow return backward ten degrees.

11 And Isaiah the prophet cried unto the
LORD: and he brought the shadow ten degrees backward, by which it had gone down
in the dial of Ahaz.

12 ¶ At that time Berodach-baladan, the son
of Baladan, king of Babylon, sent letters and
a present unto Hezekiah: for he had heard
that Hezekiah had been sick.

13 And Hezekiah hearkened unto them,
and shewed them all the house of his precious things, the silver, and the gold, and the
spices, and the precious ointment, and *all* the
house of his armour, and all that was found
in his treasures: there was nothing in his
house, nor in all his dominion, that Hezekiah
shewed them not.

14 ¶ Then came Isaiah the prophet unto king
Hezekiah, and said unto him, What said
these men? and from whence came they unto
thee? And Hezekiah said, They are come
from a far country, *even* from Babylon.

15 And he said, What have they seen in thine
house? And Hezekiah answered, All *the things*

to heal him. This ignores, however, the divine element which lies behind the story" (*New Bible Commentary: Revised*, 364). Other Christian sources cite imagery in the figs representing the miracle of healing brought about by the Holy Ghost (see Gaskill, *Miracles of the Old Testament*, 409–10).

What did the Lord's sign of healing have to do with the sundial of Ahaz? (20:8–11) Ahaz's sundial "appears to have consisted of a series of graduated lines, or steps, over which a column towered. As the earth moved, the sun would cast a shadow at a certain angle and thus measure the passing of the hours" (*Old Testament Student Manual: 1 Kings–Malachi*, 129). "This miraculous sign ([see also] 2 Chr. 32:24) is also an integral part of Isaiah 38:1–8 and cannot be dismissed as later prophetic 'legend.' A sign to authenticate a prophet's word that it is God who is acting is not uncommon. It was natural . . . for the shadow to move forward, so this reversal of the natural order by regression would be more significant and less unmistakable than a rapid advance" (Wiseman, *1 and 2 Kings*, 306).

2 Kings 20:12–21. Hezekiah Allows Babylonian Envoys to See the Kingdom of Judah's Treasures

Why would Hezekiah show Judah's wealth to the Babylonian envoys? (20:13) One scholar proposed: "Whether from the euphoria that accompanied the destruction of the Assyrians or the sense of wellbeing that accompanied his recovery from his near-fatal disease, Hezekiah welcomed the messengers from Merodachbaladan effusively and took them on an exhaustive tour of the city of Jerusalem. He unwisely showed the men the residual wealth that remained in store" (Hyde, *Comprehensive Commentary [2 Kings]*, 200).

What was the meaning of Isaiah's warning to Hezekiah? (20:14–18) "Isaiah confronted the king concerning his all-too-ready reception and disclosures to the Babylonian embassy (cf. Isa 39:5). Hezekiah had been foolish. Not only would the extent of Jerusalem's wealth now be known and desired by all, but also one day this same Babylon would invade the land and carry off its populace and all its treasures (v.17). Even

Hezekiah's own descendants would be taken captive and employed in the service of a Babylonian king (v.18; cf. 24:12–16; 2Ch 33:11; [Dan.] 1:3–5). Quite out of keeping with his righteous character, Hezekiah's folly would prove to be a contributing factor in the fulfillment of the ancient prophecies (Lev 26:33; Dt 28:64–67; 30:3)" (Patterson and Austel, "1, 2 Kings," 3:925).

What was the "good" in this prophecy? (20:19)
"Hezekiah's humility before the Lord is clear here, as is his gratitude that he would not have to personally see any more destruction" (Muhlestein, *Scripture Study Made Simple*, 287).

What was the conduit Hezekiah made? (20:20)
Earlier, when "the Assyrians moved toward Jerusalem, Hezekiah had prepared for a long siege. Second Kings notes, 'how he made a pool and a conduit, and brought water into the city' (2 Kgs 20:20), . . . resulting in the remarkable technological feat known as Hezekiah's tunnel. This tunnel brought water from the Gihon spring to the Pool of Siloam, providing safer and increased access to water within the city walls" (Holzapfel, et al., *Jehovah and the World of the Old Testament*, 304).

Summary of 2 Kings 21

Unlike his righteous father, Hezekiah, Manasseh "seduced [the people of Judah] to do more evil than did the nations whom the Lord destroyed before the children of Israel" (2 Kings 21:9). Manasseh rebuilds the false altars his father destroyed and restores idol worship among the people. He ignores prophetic counsel and warnings and leads the kingdom in continual wickedness. His son Amon follows his evil example.

that *are* in mine house have they seen: there is nothing among my treasures that I have not shewed them.

16 And Isaiah said unto Hezekiah, Hear the word of the Lord.

17 Behold, the days come, that all that *is* in thine house, and that which thy fathers have laid up in store unto this day, shall be carried into Babylon: nothing shall be left, saith the Lord.

18 And of thy sons that shall issue from thee, which thou shalt beget, shall they take away; and they shall be eunuchs in the palace of the king of Babylon.

19 Then said Hezekiah unto Isaiah, Good *is* the word of the Lord which thou hast spoken. And he said, *Is it* not *good*, if peace and truth be in my days?

20 ¶ And the rest of the acts of Hezekiah, and all his might, and how he made a pool, and a conduit, and brought water into the city, *are* they not written in the book of the chronicles of the kings of Judah?

21 And Hezekiah slept with his fathers: and Manasseh his son reigned in his stead.

CHAPTER 21

Manasseh turns Judah to idolatry, even sacrificing a son to a heathen god—Prophets foretell the destruction of Judah and Jerusalem—Wickedness continues under Amon.

CHAPTER 22

Josiah reigns in righteousness in Judah—Hilkiah repairs the temple and finds the book of the law—Josiah sorrows because of the wickedness of his fathers—Huldah prophesies wrath upon the people but blessings upon Josiah.

1 Josiah *was* eight years old when he began to reign, and he reigned thirty and one years in Jerusalem. And his mother's name *was* Jedidah, the daughter of Adaiah of Boscath.

2 And he did *that which was* right in the sight of the LORD, and walked in all the way of David his father, and turned not aside to the right hand or to the left.

3 ¶ And it came to pass in the eighteenth year of king Josiah, *that* the king sent Shaphan the son of Azaliah, the son of Meshullam, the scribe, to the house of the LORD, saying,

4 Go up to Hilkiah the high priest, that he may sum the silver which is brought into the house of the LORD, which the keepers of the door have gathered of the people:

5 And let them deliver it into the hand of the doers of the work, that have the oversight of the house of the LORD: and let them give it to the doers of the work which *is* in the house of the LORD, to repair the breaches of the house,

6 Unto carpenters, and builders, and masons, and to buy timber and hewn stone to repair the house.

7 Howbeit there was no reckoning made with them of the money that was delivered into their hand, because they dealt faithfully.

2 Kings 22:1–7. Josiah Reigns in Righteousness and Repairs the Temple

How did Josiah develop as a righteous man? (22:2) "King Josiah was a king of Judah who reigned in righteousness. When he was only eight years old, he succeeded his father as king. Scripture tells us that although he was just a boy, Josiah 'did that which was right in the sight of the Lord, . . . and turned not aside to the right hand or to the left' (2 Kgs. 22:2)" (Wirthlin, "Straight and Narrow Way," 64). "Saying that Josiah departed neither to the 'right hand or to the left' is a way of saying that he never varied from trying to follow God and encouraged the kingdom to do so also" (Muhlestein, *Scripture Study Made Simple*, 289).

What were the duties of a scribe? (22:3) Shaphan the scribe was likely the secretary to the king, the same position held by Seraiah under King David (see 2 Samuel 8:17). "Their education made them indispensable in many civilizations, as they were needed to keep all military, government, legal, and financial records" (*Eerdmans Dictionary of the Bible*, 1173). In the time of Joash, the royal scribe was also given responsibility for the monetary affairs of the temple (see 2 Kings 12:10). This responsibility appears to have been continued with Shaphan (see 2 Kings 22:3–7).

Why didn't they reckon or calculate the money used by the craftsmen who were repairing the temple? (22:7) "Apparently the workmen were just as desirous as the king to see the improvements made and were not of a mind to squander or misuse the funds in any way" (Hyde, *Comprehensive Commentary [2 Kings]*, 212).

2 Kings 22:8–20. The Book of the Law Is Found in the Temple

What book of the law did the high priest find? (22:8) Dummelow suggested: "As the book found in the Temple was brief enough to be read at a single assembly (2 Kings 23:2), whereas the reading of the Law by Ezra occupied several days (Nehemiah 8:18), it can scarcely have included the whole of the Pentateuch; and the religious reforms that Josiah carried out after its discovery and perusal [2 Kings 23:4 and following] point to its being Deuteronomy only" (*John Dummelow's Commentary* [on 2 Kings 22:8]).

Why did Josiah rend his clothes? (22:11) "When the king heard words from the book, telling what people should do and what would befall them if they did evil instead, he rent his clothes in repentance and asked his scribes and Hilkiah the priest to inquire of the Lord whether His wrath would fall upon all for their many violations. They may have read warnings in the books of Moses (Lev. 18:26–28; 26:21–46; Deut. 4:23–30; 28:58–68) and feared they were applicable to Israel in their time" (Rasmussen, *Latter-day Saint Commentary on the Old Testament*, 322).

Who was Huldah the prophetess? (22:14) "It is important to remember that in the Old Testament the word *prophet* (or *prophetess*) is used differently than how we use it. We use the phrase to refer to our presiding high priest, but in the Old Testament it is used to refer to any who are inspired to speak on behalf of the Lord. Huldah was the person so known for receiving God's inspiration, so it was she to whom the king's counselors turned when they sought to learn more about the newly rediscovered book" (Muhlestein, *Scripture Study Made Simple*, 290). ⊕

8 ¶ And Hilkiah the high priest said unto Shaphan the scribe, I have found the book of the law in the house of the LORD. And Hilkiah gave the book to Shaphan, and he read it.

9 And Shaphan the scribe came to the king, and brought the king word again, and said, Thy servants have gathered the money that was found in the house, and have delivered it into the hand of them that do the work, that have the oversight of the house of the LORD.

10 And Shaphan the scribe shewed the king, saying, Hilkiah the priest hath delivered me a book. And Shaphan read it before the king.

11 And it came to pass, when the king had heard the words of the book of the law, that he rent his clothes.

12 And the king commanded Hilkiah the priest, and Ahikam the son of Shaphan, and Achbor the son of Michaiah, and Shaphan the scribe, and Asahiah a servant of the king's, saying,

13 Go ye, inquire of the LORD for me, and for the people, and for all Judah, concerning the words of this book that is found: for great *is* the wrath of the LORD that is kindled against us, because our fathers have not hearkened unto the words of this book, to do according unto all that which is written concerning us.

14 So Hilkiah the priest, and Ahikam, and Achbor, and Shaphan, and Asahiah, went unto Huldah the prophetess, the wife of Shallum the son of Tikvah, the son of Harhas, keeper of the wardrobe; (now she dwelt in Jerusalem in the college;) and they communed with her.

15 ¶ And she said unto them, Thus saith the LORD God of Israel, Tell the man that sent you to me,

16 Thus saith the LORD, Behold, I will bring evil upon this place, and upon the inhabitants thereof, *even* all the words of the book which the king of Judah hath read:

17 Because they have forsaken me, and have burned incense unto other gods, that they might provoke me to anger with all the works of their hands; therefore my wrath shall be kindled against this place, and shall not be quenched.

18 But to the king of Judah which sent you to inquire of the LORD, thus shall ye say to him, Thus saith the LORD God of Israel, *As touching* the words which thou hast heard;

19 Because thine heart was tender, and thou hast humbled thyself before the LORD, when thou heardest what I spake against this place, and against the inhabitants thereof, that they should become a desolation and a curse, and hast rent thy clothes, and wept before me; I also have heard *thee,* saith the LORD.

20 Behold therefore, I will gather thee unto thy fathers, and thou shalt be gathered into thy grave in peace; and thine eyes shall not see all the evil which I will bring upon this place. And they brought the king word again.

CHAPTER 23

Josiah reads the book of the covenant to the people—They covenant to keep the commandments—Josiah overturns the worship of false gods, removes the sodomites, and puts down idolatry—Idolatrous priests are slain—Judah holds a solemn Passover—Egypt subjects the land of Judah.

1 And the king sent, and they gathered unto him all the elders of Judah and of Jerusalem.

2 And the king went up into the house of the LORD, and all the men of Judah and all the inhabitants of Jerusalem with him, and the priests, and the prophets, and all the

What did it mean to dwell "in the college"? (22:14) "The Hebrew words translated 'in the college' have also been translated 'in the second part' or 'in the second quarter'" (Ludlow, *Companion to Your Study of the Old Testament*, 243). This area may have been located "between the first and second walls in the northwest part of Jerusalem" (*NIV Study Bible* [1995], 561).

How was Huldah's promise to Josiah fulfilled? (22:19–20) "The manner in which Josiah died has . . . been a cause for speculation, because Huldah prophesied that he would die in peace. Being fatally shot by the pharaoh's archers does not sound like a peaceful way to die (2 Kings 23:29–30; 2 Chronicles 35:22–24). One explanation is that Huldah's prophecy was not about the manner of death but about the peaceful conditions Judah enjoyed throughout Josiah's mortal life" (Olson, *Women of the Old Testament*, 159).

2 Kings 23:1–3. King Josiah Reads the Scriptures to His People

Which prophets may have accompanied Josiah on this occasion? (23:2) "The record does not make clear exactly what prophets were present on this occasion. [However,] Jeremiah, Habakkuk, and Zephaniah all lived about this time" (Ludlow, *Companion to Your Study of the Old Testament*, 243).

people, both small and great: and he read in their ears all the words of the book of the covenant which was found in the house of the LORD.

3 ¶ And the king stood by a pillar, and made
a covenant before the LORD, to walk after the
LORD, and to keep his commandments and his
testimonies and his statutes with all *their* heart
and all *their* soul, to perform the words of this
covenant that were written in this book. And
all the people stood to the covenant.

What does it mean to "stand" to a covenant? (23:3) "King Josiah personally entered into the covenant as outlined in the book of the law. He also directed his people as they entered into this covenant. Presumably they entered into the same covenant and performed the same covenant ceremony that Moses and the children of Israel had performed when they entered into the covenant with God just prior to their entering the promised land, as recorded in Deuteronomy 27–30" (Muhlestein, *Scripture Study Made Simple*, 291). "'Stood to' represents the Hebrew, and probably describes the actual ritual of standing within the covenant symbols" (*New Bible Commentary: Revised*, 365).

Summary of 2 Kings 23:4–24

King Josiah removes the groves, idols, and high places of the false gods and completely destroys them. Those who seek familiar spirits, wizardry, or any other abominations are abolished from the land. He directs the people to celebrate the Passover.

2 Kings 23:25–28. Josiah Turns to the Lord with All His Heart, but God's Wrath Is Not Turned Away

25 And like unto him was there no king before him, that turned to the LORD with all
his heart, and with all his soul, and with all
his might, according to all the law of Moses;
neither after him arose there *any* like him.

How did Josiah compare to other righteous rulers of Judah? (23:25) "In summary, it could be said of Josiah that none of the kings of Israel and Judah was his equal in zeal for the law (v.25). As Moses was unequaled among the early prophets (Dt 34:10–12), as David was noted for his heart devotion to God (1Ki 9:4), and as Hezekiah was noted for his faith (18:5), so Josiah knew no rival in uncompromising adherence to the law of Moses. The statement in v.25 forms an inclusion with 22:2, thus framing the entire picture of Josiah's righteous life" (Patterson and Austel, "1, 2 Kings," 3:940).

26 ¶ Notwithstanding the LORD turned not
from the fierceness of his great wrath, wherewith his anger was kindled against Judah, because of all the provocations that Manasseh
had provoked him withal.

27 And the LORD said, I will remove Judah
also out of my sight, as I have removed Israel,
and will cast off this city Jerusalem which I

What effect did Josiah's reforms have on the people of Judah? (23:26) "It is true that Josiah had exterminated outward and gross idolatry throughout the land by his sincere conversion to the Lord, and by his zeal for the restoration of the lawful worship of Jehovah, and had persuaded the people to enter into covenant with its God once more; but a thorough conversion of the people to the Lord he had not been able to effect. . . . [Jeremiah bears] witness to the deep inward apostasy of the people from the Lord, not only

have chosen, and the house of which I said, My name shall be there.

28 Now the rest of the acts of Josiah, and all that he did, *are* they not written in the book of the chronicles of the kings of Judah?

before and during Josiah's reform of worship, but also afterwards" (Keil and Delitzsch, *Commentary* [on 2 Kings 23:26]). The destruction foretold by prophets was now assured.

Summary of 2 Kings 23:29–37

Josiah is killed in battle at Megiddo. His son Jehoahaz reigns in wickedness and is taken captive by the Egyptian pharaoh. Jehoiakim continues in his own sinful reign.

CHAPTER 24

Jerusalem is besieged and taken by Nebuchadnezzar—Many of the people of Judah are carried captive into Babylon—Zedekiah becomes king in Jerusalem—He rebels against Babylon.

Summary of 2 Kings 24:1–9

After defeating Assyria and Egypt, Babylon comes to power and King Nebuchadnezzar compels Judah to become a vassal state.

10 ¶ At that time the servants of Nebuchadnezzar king of Babylon came up against Jerusalem, and the city was besieged.

11 And Nebuchadnezzar king of Babylon came against the city, and his servants did besiege it.

12 And Jehoiachin the king of Judah went out to the king of Babylon, he, and his mother, and his servants, and his princes, and his officers: and the king of Babylon took him in the eighth year of his reign.

13 And he carried out thence all the treasures of the house of the LORD, and the treasures of the king's house, and cut in pieces all the vessels of gold which Solomon king of Israel had made in the temple of the LORD, as the LORD had said.

14 And he carried away all Jerusalem, and all the princes, and all the mighty men of valour, *even* ten thousand captives, and all the

2 Kings 24:10–16. Nebuchadnezzar Lays Siege to Jerusalem and Carries Many People and Much Treasure into Babylon

Why did Jehoiachin surrender himself to the Babylonians? (24:12) "Young Jehoiachin, because he surrendered, was spared with his family and taken to Babylon, where he would live the rest of his life. The Babylonians looted the city and the Temple. They carried away with them the treasures of the palace, and they 'cut in pieces all the vessels of gold which Solomon king of Israel had made in the temple of the LORD' (2 Kgs. 24:13)" (Holzapfel, et al., *Jehovah and the World of the Old Testament*, 324). See commentary in this volume for 2 Kings 25:27.

Who were the people exiled to Babylon? (24:14–16) "The objective of the exile was to demilitarize, not punish, Judah by removing the court, high officials, administrators, military officials, and professional soldiers, as well as craftsmen who could manufacture new arms" (*Jewish Study Bible* [2014], 757). The Babylonians "took into exile . . . the Judahite elite, . . . all to serve in Babylon (2 Kgs 24:11–16). Ezekiel was among these exiles (Ezek 33:21); he went to Babylonia and settled with his family on the banks of the Chebar River" (Holzapfel, et al., *Jehovah and the World of the Old Testament*, 328).

Summary of 2 Kings 24:17–20

Zedekiah is appointed king by Nebuchadnezzar and imprudently rebels against Babylon.

2 Kings 25:1–7. Nebuchadnezzar Overwhelms Jerusalem and Captures Zedekiah

What happened during the siege of Jerusalem? (25:2) "The besieged city of Jerusalem held out for eighteen months. As foretold by Jeremiah, famine and pestilence decimated the city" (Holzapfel, et al., *Jehovah and the World of the Old Testament*, 330). "When Nebuchadnezzar's troops were forced to withdraw momentarily to deal with an Egyptian relief column . . . , the misguided Jerusalemites prematurely assumed that they had been delivered from the siege (Jer. 37:6–10). . . . Finally, when strength and provisions were completely exhausted . . . , the Neo-Babylonian troops breached the walls and poured into the city" (Patterson and Austel, "1, 2 Kings," 3:949).

craftsmen and smiths: none remained, save the poorest sort of the people of the land.

15 And he carried away Jehoiachin to Babylon, and the king's mother, and the king's wives, and his officers, and the mighty of the land, *those* carried he into captivity from Jerusalem to Babylon.

16 And all the men of might, *even* seven thousand, and craftsmen and smiths a thousand, all *that were* strong *and* apt for war, even them the king of Babylon brought captive to Babylon.

CHAPTER 25

Nebuchadnezzar again besieges Jerusalem—Zedekiah is captured, Jerusalem and the temple are destroyed, and most of the people of Judah are carried into Babylon—Gedaliah, left to govern the remnant, is slain—The remnant flee to Egypt—Jehoiachin is shown favor in Babylon.

1 And it came to pass in the ninth year of his reign, in the tenth month, in the tenth *day* of the month, *that* Nebuchadnezzar king of Babylon came, he, and all his host, against Jerusalem, and pitched against it; and they built forts against it round about.

2 And the city was besieged unto the eleventh year of king Zedekiah.

3 And on the ninth *day* of the *fourth* month the famine prevailed in the city, and there was no bread for the people of the land.

4 ¶ And the city was broken up, and all the men of war *fled* by night by the way of the gate between two walls, which *is* by the king's garden: (now the Chaldees *were* against the city round about:) and *the king* went the way toward the plain.

5 And the army of the Chaldees pursued after the king, and overtook him in the plains of Jericho: and all his army were scattered from him.

6 So they took the king, and brought him up to the king of Babylon to Riblah; and they gave judgment upon him.

7 And they slew the sons of Zedekiah before his eyes, and put out the eyes of Zedekiah, and bound him with fetters of brass, and carried him to Babylon.

How did Zedekiah escape? (25:4) The walls through which "Zedekiah and his army slipped out of Jerusalem probably lay at the extreme southeastern corner of the city, which gave direct access to the Kidron Valley (cf. Ne. 3:15)" (Patterson and Austel, "1, 2 Kings," 3:949). "Zedekiah and his army . . . were overtaken by the army of the Chaldeans and brought before Nebuchadnezzar (2 Kgs. 25:4–6). . . . No mercy was shown to the rebellious Zedekiah: he first was forced to witness the execution of his sons, then his eyes were put out, and finally he was bound in chains and transported to Babylon . . . (2 Kgs. 25:7)" (Walker, "Fall of the Kingdom of Judah," 175).

What clues do we have about the survival of Zedekiah's son Mulek? (25:7) "The first clue of the existence and escape of Mulek, son of Zedekiah, can be found in 2 Kings 25:1–10, which reports that Nebuchadnezzar and '*all* his host' scattered '*all* the men' and '*all* [the king's] army' and burnt '*all* the

The Book of Mormon and the Scattering and Gathering of Israel (2 Kings 24–25)

"Around 600 B.C., during the time Jeremiah was still prophesying, the prophet Lehi—a descendant of Joseph—began his ministry in Jerusalem. As prophets before him had done, he warned that if the people did not repent, Jerusalem would be destroyed and those who survived would be taken captive by the Babylonians (see 1 Ne. 1:13, 18). Lehi's warnings fell on deaf ears, and he fled with his family into southern desert lands. In about 587 B.C. the inhabitants of Jerusalem were conquered by Babylon and later became subject to other nations. . . .

"The Book of Mormon account of the Lehites and the Mulekites, two groups of Israelites who were dispersed from Jerusalem just before the main Babylonian invasion, is also important in the story of the scattering of Israel. For Lehi, the commandment to leave Jerusalem resulted in the preservation of a branch of the house of Israel, a branch that Joseph of old foresaw would be 'carried into a far country' and would eventually be visited by the Messiah (see JST, Gen. 50:25, Bible appendix). The Book of Mormon tells of their journey, their voyage across the ocean, and their arrival in the Western Hemisphere. We also learn of the Mulekites' arrival on the American continent sometime after Lehi. The book of Omni informs us that the two peoples became one several hundred years later and were identified as Nephites" (Browning, "Gathering Scattered Israel," 57–58, 59).

"The story of Lehi and his family in the Book of Mormon is a record of a scattered remnant of the house of Israel. Yet the Book of Mormon introduces all of scattered Israel to the Restoration and latter-day prophets who preach the same gospel of Christ taught by ancient prophets. When the resurrected Christ spoke of the doctrine of the gathering of a covenant people to the Saints in the land of Bountiful (see 3 Ne. 20:25–31), He reminded them of the ancient covenant He, as Jehovah, had made with Abraham some 2,000 years before (see [Gen. 12:1–3; 17:19–21; 22:18]), to gather scattered Israel. In plainness and simplicity, the Book of Mormon testifies that the intent of all scripture is to invite Israel home" (Coleman, "Book of Mormon," 47).

"The coming forth of the Book of Mormon is a sign to the entire world that the Lord has commenced to gather Israel and fulfill covenants He made to Abraham, Isaac, and Jacob [see Genesis 12:2–3; 26:3–4; 35:11–12; and chapter headings for 3 Nephi 21; 29]. We not only teach this doctrine, but we participate in it. . . .

"The Book of Mormon is central to this work. It declares the doctrine of the gathering [see 1 Nephi 10:14]. It causes people to learn about Jesus Christ, to believe His gospel, and to join His Church. In fact, if there were no Book of Mormon, the promised gathering of Israel would not occur (Nelson, "Gathering of Scattered Israel," 80).

houses of Jerusalem,' and with '*all* the army' they destroyed the walls. In the midst of all this, however, 2 Kings 25:7 omits the word *all* when it reports only that 'the sons' of Zedekiah were killed, leaving open the question whether all of his sons were slain" (Smith and Urrutia, "New Information about Mulek, Son of the King," 143). ⊕

Summary of 2 Kings 25:8–26

The city of Jerusalem is sacked and destroyed, and the temple is burned. Gedaliah is appointed governor, but conspirators kill him.

2 Kings 25:27–30. Jehoiachin Is Released from Prison and Ends His Days in Babylon

What do we know about Jehoiachin's life in captivity? (25:27) "The favor granted to the former king of Judah is unexplained, unless the new Babylonian king found it politic to make with him a sort of government-in-exile to help control the Jews in Babylon. A grandson of Jehoiachin named Zerubbabel (1 Chr. 3:17–19; Ezra 2:1–2; [Bible Dictionary], "Zerubbabel") was later made governor of the Jews who were permitted by the Persians to return to Judah; and his lineage continued on down to Joseph and Mary (his name is spelled *Zorobabel* in Matt. 1:12).... [Jehoiachin] may have been divinely preserved to perpetuate the Davidic line into which the Messiah would be born" (Rasmussen, *Latter-day Saint Commentary on the Old Testament*, 326–27).

27 ¶ And it came to pass in the seven and thirtieth year of the captivity of Jehoiachin king of Judah, in the twelfth month, on the seven and twentieth *day* of the month, *that* Evil-merodach king of Babylon in the year that he began to reign did lift up the head of Jehoiachin king of Judah out of prison;

28 And he spake kindly to him, and set his throne above the throne of the kings that *were* with him in Babylon;

29 And changed his prison garments: and he did eat bread continually before him all the days of his life.

30 And his allowance *was* a continual allowance given him of the king, a daily rate for every day, all the days of his life.

THE FIRST BOOK OF THE CHRONICLES

Introduction

"The two books of Chronicles counted as one in the Hebrew canon. They give a short history of events from the Creation down to the proclamation of Cyrus allowing the Jews to return to their homeland" (Bible Dictionary, "Chronicles"). The first time that this account is divided into 1 Chronicles and 2 Chronicles is in the Septuagint, the Greek translation of the Hebrew Bible. The Greek title for Chronicles is *Paraleipomena*, a word meaning "things left out." Just as combining the three synoptic gospels (Matthew, Mark, and Luke) gives a richer view of the Savior's life in the New Testament, so combining 1 and 2 Chronicles helps us understand things which were "left out" of 1 and 2 Samuel and 1 and 2 Kings.

"First and 2 Chronicles is a history similar to 1 Samuel through 2 Kings. At an unknown point in time, but probably in the third or fourth century B.C., an inspired person or group of people gathered the records they had and created an abridged history. The chronicler(s) relates the history, but is more didactic than the author(s) of Samuel and Kings, meaning that morals and lessons are pointed out more frequently and directly in Chronicles" (Muhlestein, *Essential Old Testament Companion*, 272).

"The central theme in Chronicles is the restoration of the life and practice [of Israel] . . . centered on the Temple. . . . Chronicles intertwines history and theology into an appeal for the people to return both to the Land and the God of [Israel] through a Davidic type of king. The chronicler . . . interprets [Israel's] history, emphasizing the continuity of the past through the Davidic dynasty, the sovereignty of God, common worship through the Temple, obedience to the *Torah* and the warnings of the prophets, and a Messianic hope" (Stern, *Complete Jewish Bible*, 1111).

"According to Jewish tradition, which was universally received down to the middle of the seventeenth century, Ezra was regarded as the author of the Chronicles. There are many points of resemblance and of contact between the Chronicles and the Book of Ezra which seem to confirm this opinion. The conclusion of the one and the beginning of the other are almost identical in expression. In their spirit and characteristics they are the same, showing thus also an identity of authorship" (*Easton's Bible Dictionary*, "Chronicles, Books of")

The Chronicler paints a very favorable picture of the monarchs. For example, he "deviates from the mostly parallel account in Samuel–Kings: he omits all references to David's rebellious war against Saul and to his alliance with the Philistines, whereas in Samuel both events are recounted in great detail (1 Sam. 19:18–26:25, 27:1–29:11). Similarly, there is no mention in Chronicles of David's dispute with Nabal the Carmelite or of Nabal's rather mystifying death, after which David married his widow, Abigail (1 Sam. 25:1–42). Likewise omitted is the tale of David's illicit affair with Bathsheba, the wife of Uriah the Hittite (2 Sam. 11:2–12:25). . . . Nothing is said of Solomon's taking in marriage foreign women from neighboring nations" (Talmon, "1 and 2 Chronicles," 366).

According to Glenn L. Pearson, the Chronicles speak of "matters of religion such as the worship of God, the temple, the function of priests and Levites, and state-allowed or state-encouraged idolatry. . . . At the same time, the troubles within the royal house of David and Solomon are passed over as though their personal lives were tranquil and flawless. . . . The emphasis on the duties of priests and Levites would help push the work of the rebuilding and rededication of the temple; the undisputed right of the Davidic line would narrow the field of would-be rulers; while the stress on the devastating effects of idolatry would serve as a warning to the infant nation" (*Old Testament*, 44).

Summary of 1 Chronicles 1–9

These chapters give a detailed genealogy of covenant Israel from Adam to Esau. Listed are the families of the twelve tribes from Jacob (Israel) to the days of Saul, which enable Israel to resettle and become established after their foreign exile. The Chronicler highlights David's descendants and the priestly lines. There is a special emphasis on the Levites (who are appointed to oversee the vessels and instruments of the tabernacle), political leaders, gatekeepers, and others who returned to Jerusalem after the Babylonian captivity.

CHAPTERS 1–9

The genealogies and family ties from Adam to Abraham are given—The posterity of Abraham is listed.

The descendants of Israel, Judah, Jesse, Caleb, and others are listed.

David's sons are named—The successors of Solomon to Jeconiah and beyond are listed.

The families and descendants of Judah, Simeon, and others are chronicled—Various princes in their families are named.

The sons of Joseph received Reuben's birthright—Judah and his descendants became rulers in Israel—The line of Reuben down to the captivity is given—The Assyrians carry the Reubenites, Gadites, and half of Manasseh into captivity.

The sons of Levi, including David's singers, are listed—The responsibilities of Aaron and his descendants are given—Levite cities are designated in the areas of the various tribes.

The sons and families are named for Issachar, Benjamin, Naphtali, Manasseh, Ephraim, and Asher.

The sons and chief men of Benjamin are named.

The inhabitants of Jerusalem are listed—The responsibilities of the Levites and the areas where they are to serve are listed—The family of Saul is named.

CHAPTER 10

The Philistines defeat Israel—Saul dies for his transgressions.

1 Now the Philistines fought against Israel; and the men of Israel fled from before the Philistines, and fell down slain in mount Gilboa.

2 And the Philistines followed hard after Saul, and after his sons; and the Philistines slew Jonathan, and Abinadab, and Malchi-shua, the sons of Saul.

3 And the battle went sore against Saul, and the archers hit him, and he was wounded of the archers.

4 Then said Saul to his armourbearer, Draw thy sword, and thrust me through therewith; lest these uncircumcised come and abuse me. But his armourbearer would not; for he was sore afraid. So Saul took a sword, and fell upon it.

5 And when his armourbearer saw that Saul was dead, he fell likewise on the sword, and died.

6 So Saul died, and his three sons, and all his house died together.

1 Chronicles 10:1–6. Saul Dies and His Descendants Lose the Throne (see also 1 Samuel 31:1–6)

Why did Saul choose such a drastic course of action to kill himself? (10:3–4) "The Philistines could not only harm Saul personally, but bring shame on the nation that had him as their leader. Saul was driven to an extreme course of action. Suicide was a very rare occurrence among the Hebrews of Old Testament times (see v. 5; 2 Sam. 17:23; 1 Kin. 16:18)" (*Nelson Study Bible* [NKJV], 677).

Why does the text say that "all his house died together"? (10:6) These verses specifically state that three of Saul's sons were killed, including Saul's armor-bearer. "This [house] cannot mean 'all his family,' since Ish-bosheth and others of his children survived him (2 Samuel 2:8; 2 Samuel 21:8), but must refer to those of his household who attended him at Gilboa" (*John Dummelow's Commentary* [on 1 Chronicles 10:6]). This marks the end of the 40 years of Saul's house ruling over Israel and gives way to the 425 years of David's dynasty. The purpose of these verses is "to narrate the death of Saul and of his sons, in order to point out how the supreme power came to David" (Keil and Delitzsch, *Commentary* [on 1 Chronicles 10:1–7]).

1 Chronicles 10:7–14. Saul's Enemies Disgrace and Mock His Body (see also 1 Samuel 31:7–13)

7 And when all the men of Israel that *were*
in the valley saw that they fled, and that Saul
and his sons were dead, then they forsook
their cities, and fled: and the Philistines came
and dwelt in them.

8 ¶ And it came to pass on the morrow,
when the Philistines came to strip the slain,
that they found Saul and his sons fallen in
mount Gilboa.

9 And when they had stripped him, they
took his head, and his armour, and sent
into the land of the Philistines round about,
to carry tidings unto their idols, and to the
people.

10 And they put his armour in the house
of their gods, and fastened his head in the
temple of Dagon.

11 ¶ And when all Jabesh-gilead heard all
that the Philistines had done to Saul,

12 They arose, all the valiant men, and took
away the body of Saul, and the bodies of his
sons, and brought them to Jabesh, and buried their bones under the oak in Jabesh, and
fasted seven days.

13 ¶ So Saul died for his transgression which
he committed against the LORD, *even* against
the word of the LORD, which he kept not,
and also for asking *counsel* of *one that had* a
familiar spirit, to inquire *of it;*

14 And inquired not of the LORD: therefore
he slew him, and turned the kingdom unto
David the son of Jesse.

Why did the Philistines strip Saul and take his armor? (10:9) Unlike the account in Samuel where Saul is stripped of his armor, Chronicles points out that the Philistines first stripped Saul, then beheaded him, and took his armor. "Nakedness is used to denote shame" (McConkie and Parry, *Guide to Scriptural Symbols*, 85). In his death, Saul was shamed and humiliated.

What were some of Saul's transgressions? (10:13–14) Saul transgressed "in having spared the king of the Amalekites and taken the flocks of the people as spoils (1 Samuel 15:9), as well as in having consulted a pythoness [woman who practices divination] (1 Samuel 28:7). Both of these acts were great sins. . . . *And inquired not of the Lord*—he had done so in form (1 Samuel 28:6), but not in the spirit of a humble penitent, nor with the believing confidence of a sincere worshipper. His enquiry was, in fact, a mere mockery, and his total want of all right religious impressions was manifested by his rushing from God to a wretched impostor in the service of the devil (1 Samuel 28:7)" (*Jamieson-Fausset-Brown Bible Commentary* [on 1 Chronicles 10:13–14]).

CHAPTERS 11–14

David is anointed king in Hebron—He takes Zion, the City of David—His valiant warriors are named and their deeds recounted.

David's mighty men are cataloged—The armies of the tribes of Israel join David at Hebron—Israel rejoices because of King David.

David fetches the ark from Kirjath-jearim—Uzza is slain by the Lord when he steadies the ark—The house of Obed-edom prospers because they care for the ark.

David marries wives, begets children, and defeats the Philistines; his fame spreads to all nations.

Summary of 1 Chronicles 11–14

The people tell David they want him as their king. David leaves Hebron and conquers Jerusalem. The chronicler lists his faithful soldiers and their heroic deeds. David honors three of them by not drinking water from a Bethlehem well, which they obtained by risking their lives. There is a list of those who were faithful to David during his stay in Ziklag, those who helped him when he was in the mountains, and those who joined him before Saul's last battle with the Philistines. David brings the ark from Kirjath-jearim and Uzza dies as he tries to steady the ark. Hiram, the king of Tyre, sends craftsmen and cedar to Jerusalem to build David a house. David marries additional wives and has more children. The Philistines come to battle against David. By following the directions of the Lord, David gains the promise of victory and successfully leads Israel to triumph. David's fame increases (see also 2 Samuel 5:11–25).

CHAPTER 15

David prepares a place for the ark—The Levites bring the ark to Jerusalem—They sing and minister before the Lord.

Summary of 1 Chronicles 15:1–11

David builds more palaces for his family and a tabernacle to house the ark of the covenant. David ensures that only the Levites will carry the ark, as the Lord commanded Moses.

1 Chronicles 15:12–16. David Calls on the Levites to Sanctify and Prepare Themselves to Bring the Ark into Jerusalem

12 And said unto them, Ye *are* the chief of the fathers of the Levites: sanctify yourselves, *both* ye and your brethren, that ye may bring up the ark of the LORD God of Israel unto *the place that* I have prepared for it.

What does it mean to sanctify yourself? (15:12) We lose a desire to sin when we sanctify ourselves. President Spencer W. Kimball noted that there is "an attitude which is basic to the sanctification we should all be seeking, and thus to the repentance which merits forgiveness. It is that the former transgressor must have reached a 'point of no return' to sin wherein there is not merely a renunciation but also a deep abhorrence of the sin—where the sin becomes most distasteful to him and where the desire or urge to sin is cleared out of his life" (*Miracle of Forgiveness*, 354–55).

What was the "due order" of carrying the ark? (15:13) The "breach" the Lord had made on Israel was the death of Uzza for steadying the ark. The "due order" the Lord had given included specific instructions that the sons of Kohath were to carry the ark on poles (see Numbers 7:9) and "required that the ark, upon which Jehovah sits enthroned, should be carried by Levites, and touched by no unholy person, or one who is not a priest (Numbers 4:15)" (Keil and Delitzsch, *Commentary* [on 1 Chronicles 15:13]).

13 For because ye *did it* not at the first, the LORD our God made a breach upon us, for that we sought him not after the due order.

14 So the priests and the Levites sanctified themselves to bring up the ark of the LORD God of Israel.

15 And the children of the Levites bare the ark of God upon their shoulders with the staves thereon, as Moses commanded according to the word of the LORD.

16 And David spake to the chief of the Levites to appoint their brethren *to be* the singers with instruments of musick, psalteries and harps and cymbals, sounding, by lifting up the voice with joy.

Summary of 1 Chronicles 15:17–24

Musicians and doorkeepers are appointed to celebrate the arrival of the ark into Jerusalem.

1 Chronicles 15:25–29. David Leads the Procession to Bring the Ark into Jerusalem (see also 2 Samuel 6:12–23)

Why did they sacrifice seven bullocks and seven rams? (15:26) "The Levites seem to have entered on this duty with fear and trembling; and finding that they might advance without any such indications of divine wrath as Uzza had experienced (1 Chronicles 13:10), they offered an ox and a fatted sheep immediately after starting (2 Samuel 6:13), and seven bullocks and seven rams—a perfect sacrifice, at the close of the procession (1 Chronicles 16:1)" (*Jamieson-Fausset-Brown Bible Commentary* [on 1 Chronicles 15:26]).

25 ¶ So David, and the elders of Israel, and the captains over thousands, went to bring up the ark of the covenant of the LORD out of the house of Obed-edom with joy.

26 And it came to pass, when God helped the Levites that bare the ark of the covenant of the LORD, that they offered seven bullocks and seven rams.

27 And David *was* clothed with a robe of fine linen, and all the Levites that bare the ark, and the singers, and Chenaniah the master of the song with the singers: David also *had* upon him an ephod of linen.

28 Thus all Israel brought up the ark of the covenant of the LORD with shouting, and with sound of the cornet, and with trumpets, and with cymbals, making a noise with psalteries and harps.

29 ¶ And it came to pass, *as* the ark of the covenant of the LORD came to the city of David, that Michal the daughter of Saul looking out at a window saw king David dancing and playing: and she despised him in her heart.

CHAPTER 16

People offer sacrifices and praise the Lord—David delivers a psalm of thanksgiving—He praises the Lord—Asaph, Obed-edom, Zadok, and others minister before the Lord.

Summary of 1 Chronicles 16:1–6

The ark is brought into the Jerusalem tabernacle. David, as king, gives burnt and peace offerings and blesses the people. David appoints certain Levites to minister before the ark and gives praise to God (see also 2 Samuel 6:12–19).

1 Chronicles 16:7–36. David Gives a Psalm of Thanksgiving

7 ¶ Then on that day David delivered first *this psalm* to thank the LORD into the hand of Asaph and his brethren.

What is unique about this psalm? (16:7) This was the first psalm David did "ordain to give thanks unto the Lord, by the hand of . . . Asaph" (*John Dummelow's Commentary* [on 1 Chronicles 16:7]). "Among the other preparations for this solemn inauguration, the royal bard had composed a special hymn for the occasion. Doubtless it had been previously in the hands of Asaph and his assistants, but it was now publicly committed to them as they entered for the first time on the performance of their sacred duties. It occupies the greater part of this chapter (1 Chronicles 16:8–36), and seems to have been compiled from other psalms of David, previously known to the Israelites" (*Jamieson-Fausset-Brown Bible Commentary* [on 1 Chronicles 16:7]).

8 Give thanks unto the LORD, call upon his name, make known his deeds among the people.

9 Sing unto him, sing psalms unto him, talk ye of all his wondrous works.

10 Glory ye in his holy name: let the heart of them rejoice that seek the LORD.

What is the purpose of psalms? (16:8–9) "The Psalms collectively are called in Hebrew *Tehillim* or 'Praises'" (Bible Dictionary, "Psalms"). They are praises to God which are "presented as liturgical songs to be intoned to the accompaniment of the lyre, the ten-stringed instrument, cymbals, drums, and whatever else was once used to fill the temple courts with melody" (Alter, *Art of Biblical Poetry*, 111). Latter-day scripture also praises God through hymns (see D&C 25:12; 109:79; 128:22; 136:28). ⊕

Why should we continually seek the face of the Lord? (16:11) "Does it seem unseemly to seek such a spiritual reward as seeing the face of the Lord? . . . Hear this divine counsel to the saints: 'Care for the soul, and for the life of the soul. And seek the face of the Lord always, that in patience ye may possess your souls, and ye shall have eternal life' (D&C 101:37–38). We seek eternal life. . . . To receive this greatest of all the gifts of God, we must be worthy to dwell in that Celestial Presence. Ought we not . . . then become worthy, here and now, and thus qualify for the divine association that we hope to enjoy forever in the realms ahead?" (McConkie, *New Witness for the Articles of Faith*, 493). ⊕

What does it mean to be mindful of our covenants? (16:15–17) Being mindful means remembering. It "does not mean simply inner reflections, or merely awareness of or curiosity about the past, or even detailed information to be recalled. . . . Remembrance refers to action. This action springs from realizing the meaning of past events" (Midgely, "Ways of Remembrance," 169).

Who do you offend when you mistreat the Lord's anointed? (16:22) "Grievous the sin and heavy the penalty incurred by those who mistreat the servants of the Master. . . .

"Again that ancient admonition, sounding down the centuries, 'Touch not mine anointed, and do my prophets no harm!' blending with the Savior's solemn warning to the world: 'Inasmuch as ye have done it unto one of the least of these, my brethren, ye have done it unto Me'" (Whitney, *Saturday Night Thoughts*, 221).

What does it mean that "the gods of the people are idols"? (16:26) The Hebrew word for idol is *éliyl*, which means "of nothing, of nought, empty, vain" (*Gesenius' Hebrew-Chaldee Lexicon to the Old*

11 Seek the LORD and his strength, seek his face continually.

12 Remember his marvellous works that he hath done, his wonders, and the judgments of his mouth;

13 O ye seed of Israel his servant, ye children of Jacob, his chosen ones.

14 He *is* the LORD our God; his judgments *are* in all the earth.

15 Be ye mindful always of his covenant; the word *which* he commanded to a thousand generations;

16 *Even of the covenant* which he made with Abraham, and of his oath unto Isaac;

17 And hath confirmed the same to Jacob for a law, *and* to Israel *for* an everlasting covenant,

18 Saying, Unto thee will I give the land of Canaan, the lot of your inheritance;

19 When ye were but few, even a few, and strangers in it.

20 And *when* they went from nation to nation, and from *one* kingdom to another people;

21 He suffered no man to do them wrong: yea, he reproved kings for their sakes,

22 *Saying,* Touch not mine anointed, and do my prophets no harm.

23 Sing unto the LORD, all the earth; shew forth from day to day his salvation.

24 Declare his glory among the heathen; his marvellous works among all nations.

25 For great *is* the LORD, and greatly to be praised: he also *is* to be feared above all gods.

26 For all the gods of the people *are* idols: but the LORD made the heavens.

27 Glory and honour *are* in his presence; strength and gladness *are* in his place.

28 Give unto the LORD, ye kindreds of the people, give unto the LORD glory and strength.

29 Give unto the LORD the glory *due* unto his name: bring an offering, and come before him: worship the LORD in the beauty of holiness.

Testament, 116). That is, the idol is powerless. "Once an idol was created, it was nailed or anchored to keep it from tipping over. Ironically, the anchoring of the idol emphasizes its powerlessness (Judg. 6:25–31). The Lord, however, could never be restrained" (Parry, et al., *Understanding Isaiah*, 346).

What is the "beauty of holiness" we can offer the Lord? (16:29) Carol F. McConkie shared: "I see the beauty of holiness in [Latter-day Saints] whose hearts are centered on all that is good, who want to become more like the Savior. They offer their whole soul, heart, might, mind, and strength to the Lord in the way that they live every day. Holiness is in the striving and the struggle to keep the commandments and to honor the covenants we have made with God. Holiness is making the choices that will keep the Holy Ghost as our guide. Holiness is setting aside our natural tendencies and becoming 'a saint through the atonement of Christ the Lord.' 'Every moment of [our lives] must be holiness to the Lord'" ("Beauty of Holiness," 9).

30 Fear before him, all the earth: the world also shall be stable, that it be not moved.

31 Let the heavens be glad, and let the earth rejoice: and let *men* say among the nations, The LORD reigneth.

32 Let the sea roar, and the fulness thereof: let the fields rejoice, and all that *is* therein.

33 Then shall the trees of the wood sing out at the presence of the LORD, because he cometh to judge the earth.

In what way does worshipping God bring stability to our lives? (16:30) "Without Christ, we are driven like a vessel tossed about upon the waves. We have no power because we have no sail. We have no stability, especially in times of storm, because we have no anchor. We have no direction or purpose because we don't have anything with which to steer. . . . In order to face, overcome, and be prepared for the crosswinds and crosscurrents of life, we must obey God's commandments; become humble, willing, and determined lifelong learners; serve others; and establish Jesus Christ as the foundation of our lives. As we do so we dramatically increase our spiritual stability" (Renlund, "Constructing Spiritual Stability," 5–6).

34 O give thanks unto the LORD; for *he is* good; for his mercy *endureth* for ever.

35 And say ye, Save us, O God of our salvation, and gather us together, and deliver us from the heathen, that we may give thanks to thy holy name, *and* glory in thy praise.

36 Blessed *be* the LORD God of Israel for ever and ever. And all the people said, Amen, and praised the LORD.

Why is mercy highlighted so often as a godly attribute? (16:34) The Hebrew word for mercy is *hesed*. "The concept of *hesed* . . . is unfamiliar to most Bible readers. . . . The term is difficult to translate, the KJV providing no less than fifteen different terms to signify the presence of *hesed* in the text, the most common being mercy, kindness, and loving-kindness. Yet the principle of *hesed* may be one of the most important doctrinal concepts in the Old Testament, as it appears 245 times in the Hebrew Bible and embodies both the manner in which Israel was expected to act and the true nature of God. . . . *Hesed* is clearly associated with the divine and may even be used to define godly experience" (Belnap, "How Excellent Is Thy Lovingkindness," 170–71).

Summary of 1 Chronicles 16:37–43

David appoints priests to minister before the ark of the covenant. "Zadok and the priests subordinate to him were stationed at Gibeon to perform the sacred service before the ancient tabernacle which still remained there" (*Jamieson-Fausset-Brown Bible Commentary* [on 1 Chronicles 16:39–40]).

Summary of 1 Chronicles 17

David wants to build a temple for the Lord, and Nathan agrees. However, the Lord comes to Nathan and directs that it will be David's son who constructs the temple (see 1 Chronicles 17; see also 2 Samuel 7). God reminds David of the blessings he received in establishing the Lord's kingdom. David praises and thanks the Lord and accepts His direction.

Summary of 1 Chronicles 18–21

David turns his energy to strengthening his kingdom by defeating the Philistines, Moabites, and Syrians (see 1 Chronicles 18; see also 2 Samuel 8). David sends messengers to the Ammonites who mock and mistreat them. When the Ammonites learn of David's indignation, they prepare to battle Israel by enlisting the Syrians. David sends Joab to battle, who defeats the Syrians, and the Ammonites retreat to Rabbah (see 1 Chronicles 19; see also 2 Samuel 10). Joab returns to battle the Ammonites, and Israel defeats the Philistines in three different battles (see 1 Chronicles 20; see also 2 Samuel 11:1; 12:26–31; 21:15–22). David orders an unauthorized census, either to determine the number of warriors he could use to conquer other lands, or to establish a royal tax. This action angers the Lord and He sends Gad the seer to offer David three options as his punishment: Three years of famine, three months to be destroyed by his enemies, or three days of pestilence in the land. David chooses pestilence and thousands die. The Lord in His mercy tells the angel to stay his hand as it was enough (JST, 1 Chronicles 21:15). God stops the plague when David repents, builds an altar, and offers sacrifices (see also 2 Samuel 24:1–25). Afterward, David chooses the temple site.

CHAPTER 17

Nathan first approves David's building of a house of the Lord, then restrains him—David's son will build the temple—The triumph of Israel is foretold—David thanks the Lord for His goodness to Israel.

CHAPTERS 18–21

David subdues all the adversaries of Israel and reigns in justice over the people.

The Ammonites insult David's messengers and plan war against Israel—David defeats the Ammonites and the Syrians.

The Ammonites are overcome—Israel defeats the Philistines.

David sins by numbering Israel—The Lord sends pestilence upon the people—David offers sacrifices and the plague is stayed.

CHAPTER 22

David prepares gold, silver, brass, iron, stone, and cedar wood for the temple—He charges Solomon to do the work of building it.

1 Then David said, This *is* the house of the LORD God, and this *is* the altar of the burnt offering for Israel.

2 And David commanded to gather together the strangers that *were* in the land of Israel; and he set masons to hew wrought stones to build the house of God.

3 And David prepared iron in abundance for the nails for the doors of the gates, and for the joinings; and brass in abundance without weight;

4 Also cedar trees in abundance: for the Zidonians and they of Tyre brought much cedar wood to David.

5 And David said, Solomon my son *is* young and tender, and the house *that is* to be builded for the LORD *must be* exceeding magnifical, of fame and of glory throughout all countries: I will *therefore* now make preparation for it. So David prepared abundantly before his death.

1 Chronicles 22:1–5. David Prepares the Materials Needed to Build "the House of the Lord"

Why is it so important that the Houses of the Lord be so "exceeding magnifical, of fame and of glory"? (22:5) "Others may dispute the reality of the First Vision of the Prophet Joseph Smith in the grove in Palmyra, New York. They may doubt the divine origin of the Book of Mormon. They may question the return of Peter, James, and John and the appearance in Kirtland, Ohio, of the prophet Elijah to restore priesthood keys to the world, but every temple we build stands as a witness of our faith, that those glorious events occurred" (Eyring, "Temples Are a Witness of Our Faith").

6 ¶ Then he called for Solomon his son, and charged him to build an house for the LORD God of Israel.

7 And David said to Solomon, My son, as for me, it was in my mind to build an house unto the name of the LORD my God:

1 Chronicles 22:6–19. David Entrusts Solomon to Build the Temple

Why was Solomon, not David, able to build the temple? (22:6) "David, the king, sought to build a temple to the Lord but the prophet Nathan told him that he was wanting in some spiritual dimensions and that instead his son Solomon would build the temple. The temple of Solomon, finished about 1005 B.C., would be a symbol for temples for thousands of years" (Packer, *Holy Temple*, 94). "David was a man of war—literally, it was said, 'a man of blood.' The Lord would not allow him to build the temple for that reason" (Petersen, *Three Kings of Israel*, 111).

8 But the word of the LORD came to me, saying, Thou hast shed blood abundantly, and hast made great wars: thou shalt not build an house unto my name, because thou hast shed much blood upon the earth in my sight.

What does the name Solomon symbolize? (22:9) "Biblical names especially are symbolic" (Bible Dictionary, "Symbolism"). Solomon comes "from שלם shalam, he was peaceable; and therefore, says the Lord, alluding to the name, I will give Peace, שלום Shalom, in his days" (*Adam Clarke's Commentary* [on 1 Chronicles 22:9]).

9 Behold, a son shall be born to thee, who shall be a man of rest; and I will give him rest from all his enemies round about: for his name shall be Solomon, and I will give peace and quietness unto Israel in his days.

10 He shall build an house for my name; and he shall be my son, and I *will be* his father; and I will establish the throne of his kingdom over Israel for ever.

11 Now, my son, the LORD be with thee; and prosper thou, and build the house of the LORD thy God, as he hath said of thee.

12 Only the LORD give thee wisdom and understanding, and give thee charge concerning Israel, that thou mayest keep the law of the LORD thy God.

What are the conditions that allow one to prosper? (22:13) "For the Lord God hath said: Inasmuch as ye shall keep my commandments ye shall prosper in the land; but inasmuch as ye will not keep my commandments ye shall be cut off from my presence" (2 Nephi 4:4). President Gordon B. Hinckley observed, "The happiness of the Latter-day Saints, the peace of the Latter-day Saints, the progress of the Latter-day Saints, the prosperity of the Latter-day Saints, and the eternal salvation and exaltation of this people lie in walking in obedience" ("If Ye Be Willing and Obedient," 126).

13 Then shalt thou prosper, if thou takest heed to fulfil the statutes and judgments which the LORD charged Moses with concerning Israel: be strong, and of good courage; dread not, nor be dismayed.

14 Now, behold, in my trouble I have prepared for the house of the LORD an hundred thousand talents of gold, and a thousand thousand talents of silver; and of brass and iron without weight; for it is in abundance: timber also and stone have I prepared; and thou mayest add thereto.

15 Moreover *there are* workmen with thee in abundance, hewers and workers of stone and timber, and all manner of cunning men for every manner of work.

16 Of the gold, the silver, and the brass, and the iron, *there is* no number. Arise *therefore,* and be doing, and the LORD be with thee.

17 ¶ David also commanded all the princes of Israel to help Solomon his son, *saying,*

18 *Is* not the LORD your God with you? and hath he *not* given you rest on every side? for he hath given the inhabitants of the land into mine hand; and the land is subdued before the LORD, and before his people.

19 Now set your heart and your soul to seek the LORD your God; arise therefore, and build ye the sanctuary of the LORD God, to bring the ark of the covenant of the LORD, and the holy vessels of God, into the house that is to be built to the name of the LORD.

Why is it important to seek the Lord before building a temple? (22:19) Brigham Young observed that "we never began to build a temple without the bells of hell beginning to ring" (*Brigham Young* [manual], 300). Temple building requires both the heart and soul. President Boyd K. Packer, in referring to temple work, noted: "No work is more spiritually refining. No work we do gives us more power. No work requires a higher standard of righteousness" ("Holy Temple," 35).

CHAPTERS 23–27

Solomon is made king—The Levites are numbered and assigned their various religious duties.

The sons of Aaron and the rest of the sons of Levi are divided into groups and assigned their duties by lot.

The Levite singers and musicians are assigned their duties by lot.

The Levites are assigned as porters—They have charge of the treasures, serve as officers and judges, and conduct the outward business pertaining to the Israelites.

The officers who serve the king are named—The princes of the tribes of Israel are set forth.

Summary of 1 Chronicles 23–27

David relinquishes the kingdom to his son Solomon. David organizes the Levites and assigns their duties before he steps down. These duties include purifying the temple instruments, providing the shewbread, and offering prayers and sacrifices for Israel. The Levites are counted and ordered by family and placed into twenty-four divisions or courses. The temple singers and musicians are also placed into twenty-four courses. This may explain why the number twenty-four has a priesthood association with the temple and the throne of God in John's vision (see Revelation 4:4; 19:4). Temple porters, or sentries, are organized into four classes, which are assigned to the four gates of the temple. David organizes the army into twelve divisions with a captain placed over each division. He appoints leaders over each of the twelve tribes and selects caretakers over the royal treasury, vineyards, and flocks.

CHAPTER 28

David assembles the leaders of Israel—Solomon is appointed to build the temple—David exhorts Solomon and the people to keep the commandments—David gives Solomon the pattern and materials for the temple.

1 And David assembled all the princes of Israel, the princes of the tribes, and the captains of the companies that ministered to the king by course, and the captains over the thousands, and captains over the hundreds, and the stewards over all the substance and possession of the king, and of his sons, with the officers, and with the mighty men, and with all the valiant men, unto Jerusalem.

2 Then David the king stood up upon his feet, and said, Hear me, my brethren, and my people: *As for me,* I *had* in mine heart to build an house of rest for the ark of the covenant of the LORD, and for the footstool of our God, and had made ready for the building:

3 But God said unto me, Thou shalt not build an house for my name, because thou *hast been* a man of war, and hast shed blood.

4 Howbeit the LORD God of Israel chose me before all the house of my father to be king over Israel for ever: for he hath chosen Judah *to be* the ruler; and of the house of Judah, the house of my father; and among the sons of my father he liked me to make *me* king over all Israel:

5 And of all my sons, (for the LORD hath given me many sons,) he hath chosen Solomon my son to sit upon the throne of the kingdom of the LORD over Israel.

6 And he said unto me, Solomon thy son, he shall build my house and my courts: for I have chosen him *to be* my son, and I will be his father.

1 Chronicles 28:1–10. David Gives a Charge to Israel and Reaffirms Solomon as the New King

What was "the footstool of our God"? (28:2) "God seated between the cherubim, at the two extremities of the ark, might be said to be enthroned in His glory, and the coverlet of the ark to be His footstool" (*Jamieson-Fausset-Brown Bible Commentary* [on 1 Chronicles 28:2]) "The ark served as God's footstool (Ps. 99:5; 132:7) as it was situated under his throne. The ark, being associated with Deity, brought blessings to believers of the Israelite faith (Josh. 3–4; 1 Sam. 7:1; 2 Sam. 6:2–17) and cursings to the unbelievers (Josh. 6; 1 Sam. 5:1–7; 6:19)" (Parry and McConkie, *Guide to Scriptural Symbols*, 15). "It is symbolic of subjection, something beneath one and over which power is exercised" (Brewster, *Doctrine and Covenants Encyclopedia*, 191).

In what way does the house of David rule over Israel forever? (28:4) "Kingship belongs to Jesus the Messiah both by lineage and by divine decree. He alone possesses 'the key of the house of David' (Isa. 22:22; see also Rev. 3:7), the key to the governance of Israel. The house of David reigns forever because the Son of David reigns forever. He will be the God-King of this celestialized earth" (Turner, "Two Davids," 255).

7 Moreover I will establish his kingdom for ever, if he be constant to do my commandments and my judgments, as at this day.

8 Now therefore in the sight of all Israel the congregation of the LORD, and in the audience of our God, keep and seek for all the commandments of the LORD your God: that ye may possess this good land, and leave *it* for an inheritance for your children after you for ever.

9 ¶ And thou, Solomon my son, know thou the God of thy father, and serve him with a perfect heart and with a willing mind: for the LORD searcheth all hearts, and understandeth all the imaginations of the thoughts: if thou seek him, he will be found of thee; but if thou forsake him, he will cast thee off for ever.

10 Take heed now; for the LORD hath chosen thee to build an house for the sanctuary: be strong, and do *it*.

11 ¶ Then David gave to Solomon his son the pattern of the porch, and of the houses thereof, and of the treasuries thereof, and of the upper chambers thereof, and of the inner parlours thereof, and of the place of the mercy seat,

12 And the pattern of all that he had by the spirit, of the courts of the house of the LORD, and of all the chambers round about, of the treasuries of the house of God, and of the treasuries of the dedicated things:

What is a willing mind? (28:9) "Having 'a willing mind' connotes giving our best effort and finest thinking and seeking God's wisdom. It suggests that our most devoted lifetime study should be of things that are eternal in nature. It means that there must be an inextricable relationship between hearing the word of God and obeying it" (Hallstrom, "Heart and a Willing Mind," 32).

1 Chronicles 28:11–12. David Gives the Pattern for the Temple

How is David's role in building the temple portrayed in 1 Chronicles? (28:11) "Although Chronicles agrees with Samuel that David was not suited to build the temple (2 Sam. 22:1–17; 1 Kgs. 5:3; 1 Chron. 22:8), David is closely associated in Chronicles with the foundation of the temple ritual. In fact, Chronicles records that the pattern of the temple was revealed to David by the Spirit (1 Chron. 28:11–12), which allowed him to make preparations for its building and which he then passed on to his son Solomon" (Seely, "Kings and Chronicles," 10).

How did David receive the pattern for the building the temple? (28:12) "Although David was forbidden of the Lord to build the temple (1 Chr. 17:1–15; 22:1–10), the Lord revealed the pattern of the temple 'by the spirit' (v. 12). Here David reveals the pattern to Solomon 'in writing by his hand' (v. 19)" (Ludlow, *Companion to Your Study of the Old Testament*, 247). "Brigham Young drew a parallel with Moses and Solomon and emphasized that without this direct vision, Joseph Smith 'could not know what was wanting, having never seen one [a temple], and not having experienced its use'" (Anderson, *Joseph Smith's Kirtland*, 157). ⊕

Summary of 1 Chronicles 28:13–21

David gives the details of the furnishings, instruments, and vessels for temple worship. He also charges Solomon to be strong and of good courage by trusting in God. The priesthood and government are organized to support Solomon as he builds the temple and institutes temple worship.

CHAPTER 29

All Israel makes a liberal offering for the temple—David blesses and praises the Lord and instructs the people—David dies—Solomon reigns as king—The books of Nathan and Gad are mentioned.

1 Furthermore David the king said unto all the congregation, Solomon my son, whom alone God hath chosen, *is yet* young and tender, and the work *is* great: for the palace *is* not for man, but for the LORD God.

1 Chronicles 29:1–9. David Details the Offerings and Sacrifices as Israel Prepares to Build the Temple

Why remind Israel that they were building a house for God and not man? (29:1) Building the "palace" or House of the Lord required their best efforts. Joseph Smith faced a smiliar situation. "At a meeting in Kirtland, Joseph Smith asked the brethren for their views about how the temple was to be constructed. Lucy Mack Smith described their responses: 'Some were in favor of building a frame house, but others were of a mind to put up a log house. Joseph reminded them that they were not building a house for a man, but for God; "and shall we, brethren," said he, "build a house for our God, of logs? No, I have a better plan than that. I have a plan of the house of the Lord"'" (Anderson, *Joseph Smith's Kirtland*, 157–58).

2 Now I have prepared with all my might for the house of my God the gold for *things to be made* of gold, and the silver for *things* of silver, and the brass for *things* of brass, the iron for *things* of iron, and wood for *things* of wood; onyx stones, and *stones* to be set, glistering stones, and of divers colours, and all manner of precious stones, and marble stones in abundance.

In what ways did David set an example in providing for temple building and worship? (29:2–4) 1 Chronicles highlights that David's "affection to the house of . . . God" drove his careful financial preparations for the building of the temple, but these efforts are not found in 2 Samuel. David described the "precious things he had gathered in preparation for building the temple. He challenged tribal leaders and other people to contribute; they responded with good hearts and offered willingly to the Lord—for which the king rejoiced" (Rasmussen, *Latter-day Saint Commentary on the Old Testament*, 339).

3 Moreover, because I have set my affection to the house of my God, I have of mine own proper good, of gold and silver, *which* I have given to the house of my God, over and above all that I have prepared for the holy house,

4 *Even* three thousand talents of gold, of the gold of Ophir, and seven thousand talents of refined silver, to overlay the walls of the houses *withal:*

5 The gold for *things* of gold, and the silver for *things* of silver, and for all manner of work *to be made* by the hands of artificers. And who *then* is willing to consecrate his service this day unto the LORD?

6 ¶ Then the chief of the fathers and princes of the tribes of Israel, and the captains of thousands and of hundreds, with the rulers of the king's work, offered willingly,

7 And gave for the service of the house of God of gold five thousand talents and ten thousand drams, and of silver ten thousand talents, and of brass eighteen thousand talents, and one hundred thousand talents of iron.

8 And they with whom *precious* stones were found gave *them* to the treasure of the house of the LORD, by the hand of Jehiel the Gershonite.

9 Then the people rejoiced, for that they offered willingly, because with perfect heart they offered willingly to the LORD: and David the king also rejoiced with great joy.

10 ¶ Wherefore David blessed the LORD before all the congregation: and David said, Blessed *be* thou, LORD God of Israel our father, for ever and ever.

11 Thine, O LORD, *is* the greatness, and the power, and the glory, and the victory, and the majesty: for all *that is* in the heaven and in the earth *is thine;* thine *is* the kingdom, O LORD, and thou art exalted as head above all.

12 Both riches and honour *come* of thee, and thou reignest over all; and in thine hand *is* power and might; and in thine hand *it is* to make great, and to give strength unto all.

What does it mean to "consecrate his service"? (29:5) The Hebrew phrase is "*lemalloth yado*, to fill his hand; to bring an offering to the Lord" (*Adam Clarke's Commentary* [on 1 Chronicles 29:5]). "In the most ancient practice [of consecration] the offerings were placed in the hands of the priest" (Beck, "Consecrate," 677). David was asking them to bring their offerings to the Lord.

Why was it important that the people willingly give their offering? (29:6) "In all this, the Chronicler insists, the people of Israel in David's time met the Mosaic Law's 'willingness' requirements in their sacrifices and offerings. In Exodus 25:2, the Lord had commanded Moses: 'Speak unto the children of Israel, that they bring me an offering: of every man that giveth it *willingly* [*yiddĕbenû*] with his heart ye shall take my offering.' . . . [There is] a close connection—perhaps an ideal connection—between the identity of [Jehovah's] 'people' and their 'willingness,' all this in the context of temple. In the end, what else would (or should) distinguish a 'people of the Lord' from other people other than their 'willingness'?" (Bowen, "My People Are Willing," 87).

1 Chronicles 29:10–19. David Prays and Gives Thanks for the Temple

Why would David describe Jehovah as Israel's father? (29:10) The Book of Mormon clarifies this doctrine that we become the children of Jehovah by making and keeping our covenants: "And now, because of the covenant which ye have made ye shall be called the *children* of Christ, his sons, and his daughters; for behold, this day he hath spiritually begotten you; for ye say that your hearts are *changed* through faith on his name; therefore, ye are born of him and have *become his sons and his daughters*" (Mosiah 5:7; emphasis added). ⊕

Why would David say they were strangers and sojourners? (29:15) "It seems somewhat ironic that both the Lord and his servants would refer to God's people as *gērîm* or 'sojourners' even after they have reached the land that God has prepared for them. However, these references to the Israelites as *gērîm* in the land of Canaan forcefully remind us that even in the promised land the Lord's people will not feel entirely at home, for they will understand that their inheritance lies beyond and surpasses any earthly blessing, including their geographical 'promised land'" (Boehm, "Wanderers in the Promised Land," 196; see also Hebrews 11:13–16).

Why does God try the heart? (29:17) "By being tested, all of us will one day know how much our hearts are really set on the kingdom of God" (Madsen, *Joseph Smith the Prophet*, 92). "Why, then, are some things so hard? Though the record in Brigham Young's office journal of 1857 is not complete, he apparently was asked, 'Why are [we] left alone and often sad?' His response was that man has to learn to 'act as an independent being . . . to see what he will do . . . to practice him . . . to be righteous in the dark—to be the friend of God'" (Maxwell, *That Ye May Believe*, 194–95).

What is a perfect heart? (29:19) It is "a whole (undivided) heart" (Keil and Delitzsch, *Commentary* [on 1 Chronicles 29:19]). The "concept of having a 'perfect' heart is directly connected to faithfully worshipping Jehovah" (Judd, "Be Ye Therefore Perfect," 124). The "heart" was in David's thinking. In verse 17 he points out that God "tries" our hearts. In verse 18 he asks the Lord to "prepare [Israel's] heart unto thee." And then he asks God to "give unto Solomon my son a perfect heart." It's as if, after a long life of tribulation and struggling with weakness, David had learned the crucial significance of the heart. No wonder "the Lord requireth the heart and a willing mind" (D&C 64:34). ⊕

13 Now therefore, our God, we thank thee, and praise thy glorious name.

14 But who *am* I, and what *is* my people, that we should be able to offer so willingly after this sort? for all things *come* of thee, and of thine own have we given thee.

15 For we *are* strangers before thee, and sojourners, as *were* all our fathers: our days on the earth *are* as a shadow, and *there is* none abiding.

16 O LORD our God, all this store that we have prepared to build thee an house for thine holy name *cometh* of thine hand, and *is* all thine own.

17 I know also, my God, that thou triest the heart, and hast pleasure in uprightness. As for me, in the uprightness of mine heart I have willingly offered all these things: and now have I seen with joy thy people, which are present here, to offer willingly unto thee.

18 O LORD God of Abraham, Isaac, and of Israel, our fathers, keep this for ever in the imagination of the thoughts of the heart of thy people, and prepare their heart unto thee:

19 And give unto Solomon my son a perfect heart, to keep thy commandments, thy testimonies, and thy statutes, and to do all *these things*, and to build the palace, *for* the which I have made provision.

Summary of 1 Chronicles 29:20–30

Solomon becomes king. A feast is held and sacrifices are offered up to the Lord. David, who had reigned for forty years, passes away (see also 1 Kings 1:28–2:11).

THE SECOND BOOK OF THE CHRONICLES

Introduction

"When it was first written, Second Chronicles brought a ray of hope to a people desperately in need of encouragement. The Israelite community, reduced to a tiny minority in exile among the Babylonians, was struggling to understand its place. Had God's promises to Abraham and David been revoked because of the nation's sins? Was there any hope of reviving David's dynasty? Could Judaism survive without the temple? Second Chronicles addressed questions like these. Its answers came in a historical review of God's faithfulness to the Israelites" (*Nelson Study Bible* [NKJV], 710).

The author of 2 Chronicles "wants to demonstrate the hand of God in human affairs, especially in the house of Israel. He portrays the moral order and covenant relationship of God with his children. He also stresses the observance of rightful forms of worship for the Israelite community and teaches that God's revelations were given not only in the past but are given in the present as a living word of truth" (Ludlow, *Unlocking the Old Testament*, 110–11).

"The first nine chapters of 2 Chronicles deal with achievements of Solomon in his reign over the united kingdom of Israel, with emphasis on the building of the temple, the work of the priests and Levites, and the reinstating of the Mosaic sacrifices and rituals. The remaining chapters cover the reigns of Solomon's descendants from Rehoboam to Zedekiah, ending with the commencement of the Babylonian captivity. The closing verses anticipate the return of many Judahites to their homeland from Babylon by the grace of God through the sympathy of King Cyrus of Persia. Thus the book anticipates its sequels, the books of Ezra, Nehemiah, and Esther" (Rasmussen, *Latter-day Saint Commentary on the Old Testament*, 342).

2 Chronicles focuses on Judah and the history of the southern kingdom. Unlike Kings, historical events not related to the kingdom of Judah are not included. For example, Elijah and Elisha are not mentioned in 2 Chronicles because they are prophets of the northern kingdom of Israel. The only exception is Elijah's letter to Jehoram, the king of Judah (2 Chronicles 21).

CHAPTER 1

The Lord honors Solomon before all Israel—The Lord appears to him—Solomon chooses and is given wisdom—His kingdom is blessed with splendor and riches.

1 And Solomon the son of David was
strengthened in his kingdom, and the LORD
his God *was* with him, and magnified him
exceedingly.

2 Then Solomon spake unto all Israel, to the
captains of thousands and of hundreds, and

2 Chronicles 1:1–6. Solomon and His Leaders Assemble at Gibeon (see also 1 Kings 3:4)

Who gathered to Gibeon with Solomon? (1:2–3)
"Solomon's speech to all levels of the Israelite leadership emphasizes the breadth of unity and oneness

to the judges, and to every governor in all
Israel, the chief of the fathers.

3 So Solomon, and all the congregation
with him, went to the high place that *was* at
Gibeon; for there was the tabernacle of the
congregation of God, which Moses the servant of the LORD had made in the wilderness.

4 But the ark of God had David brought up
from Kirjath-jearim to *the place which* David
had prepared for it: for he had pitched a tent
for it at Jerusalem.

5 Moreover the brasen altar, that Bezaleel
the son of Uri, the son of Hur, had made, he
put before the tabernacle of the LORD: and
Solomon and the congregation sought unto it.

6 And Solomon went up thither to the
brasen altar before the LORD, which *was*
at the tabernacle of the congregation, and
offered a thousand burnt offerings upon it.

CHAPTERS 2–7

Solomon engages Huram of Tyre to supply timber for the temple—Laborers are organized to do the work.

Solomon begins to build the temple—He makes the veil and the pillars, and uses much gold and many precious stones.

that shapes this pilgrimage to Gibeon by the Israelite community. A gathering of a similar group of individuals was organized by David to announce that Solomon would build the temple for the Lord (1Ch 28:1–8) as well as the procession that accompanied David in moving the ark of the covenant from Kiriath Jearim to Jerusalem (1Ch 13 and 15)" (Mabie, "1 and 2 Chronicles," 158).

Why did the leaders of Israel choose Gibeon as the gathering place? (1:5) The "high place at Gibeon was chosen for the performance of the sacred rites, because the tabernacle and all the ancient furniture connected with the national worship were deposited there. . . . The brazen altar, 'before the tabernacle of the Lord,' on which the burnt offerings were appointed by the law to be made, was at Gibeon. . . . Solomon considered it his duty to present his offerings on the legally appointed spot 'before the tabernacle,' and on the time-honored altar prepared by the skill of Bezaleel in the wilderness (Exodus 38:1)" (*Jamieson-Fausset-Brown Bible Commentary* [on 2 Chronicles1:2–5]).

Summary of 2 Chronicles 1:7–17

God appears to Solomon and asks him what blessing he desires. Solomon asks for wisdom and God grants his request and also promises him riches, possessions, and honor (see also 1 Kings 3:5–14). Solomon returns from his journey to worship the Lord at Gibeon (see also 1 Kings 3:15). Solomon brings horses from Egypt, contrary to the Mosaic command to not multiply horses (see Deuteronomy 17:16).

Summary of 2 Chronicles 2–7

As Solomon determines to build the House of the Lord, he prepares both the workers and the needed materials. He directs the construction of the temple including the cherubim, the veil, and two pillars. He also makes the altar and the brazen sea which is supported by twelve oxen. The ten lavers, ten lampstands, ten tables, and the courts for the temple are finished. Huram (Hiram), the king of Tyre, provided skilled artisans to complete the furnishings. The Levite priests bring the ark of the covenant into the temple and place it in the Holy of Holies. As a sign of acceptance, the Lord fills the temple with His glory. Solomon then offers the dedicatory prayer in which he reminds the people that God has kept His promise to the children of Israel (see also 1 Kings 5–8). The Lord shows that He accepts the temple by having heavenly fire consume the burnt offerings. The people are promised prosperity if they are obedient.

Summary of 2 Chronicles 8–9

Solomon fortifies his kingdom and conquers other cities. As he defeats his enemies, he enslaves them. The children of Israel keep their religious feasts and the Levites fulfill their assigned duties. Solomon launches his first fleet of ships which Huram (or Hiram, king of Tyre; see 1 Kings 5:1) gave him. The queen of Sheba visits Solomon and is impressed with his wisdom and also his wealth. Solomon rules for forty years and passes away. Rehoboam, his son, becomes the new king.

Solomon makes a basin and places it on twelve oxen—The altar, basins, pots, and various items are made.

The temple is finished, and the ark of the covenant is placed in the holy of holies—The glory of the Lord fills the temple.

Solomon blesses the congregation of Israel—He offers the dedicatory prayer for the temple—He prays for mercy and blessings for penitent Israel.

Fire comes down from heaven and consumes the sacrifices and burnt offerings—The Lord appears to Solomon and promises to bless the people—The Israelites will prosper if they keep the commandments.

CHAPTERS 8–9

Solomon builds cities—He offers sacrifices according to the law of Moses—Priests and Levites are appointed to serve the Lord.

The queen of Sheba visits Solomon—He excels in wisdom, wealth, and magnificence—After reigning forty years, Solomon dies, and Rehoboam becomes king.

CHAPTERS 10–12

The people request relief, but Rehoboam promises to increase the burdens upon the people—Israel rebels and the kingdom is divided.

Rehoboam strengthens the kingdom of Judah but is forbidden to subdue Israel—Jeroboam leads the kingdom of Israel into idolatry—Rehoboam takes many wives and concubines.

Rehoboam forsakes the law of the Lord—The Egyptians plunder Jerusalem and take the treasures of the house of the Lord—The people repent and receive partial deliverance—Rehoboam dies.

Summary of 2 Chronicles 10–12

Jeroboam, the son of Nebat, asks Rehoboam to reduce his father's labor demands, but Rehoboam increases them. All of Israel except Judah rebel against David's family. Rehoboam mobilizes the army to reclaim Israel, but the Lord sends a prophet to stop Rehoboam's plan. Jeroboam becomes the first king of the northern kingdom of Israel. The Levites return to Judah because Jeroboam sets up idols. Rehoboam, in his pride, turns away from the Lord, so Shishak, king of Egypt, attacks Jerusalem. Shemaiah, the prophet, calls Rehoboam to repent or suffer the consequences. He humbles himself and the anger of the Lord is turned away. Rehoboam dies and Abijah becomes king (see also 1 Kings 9–14).

The Kingdoms of Israel and Judah at a Glance (2 Chronicles 10–12)

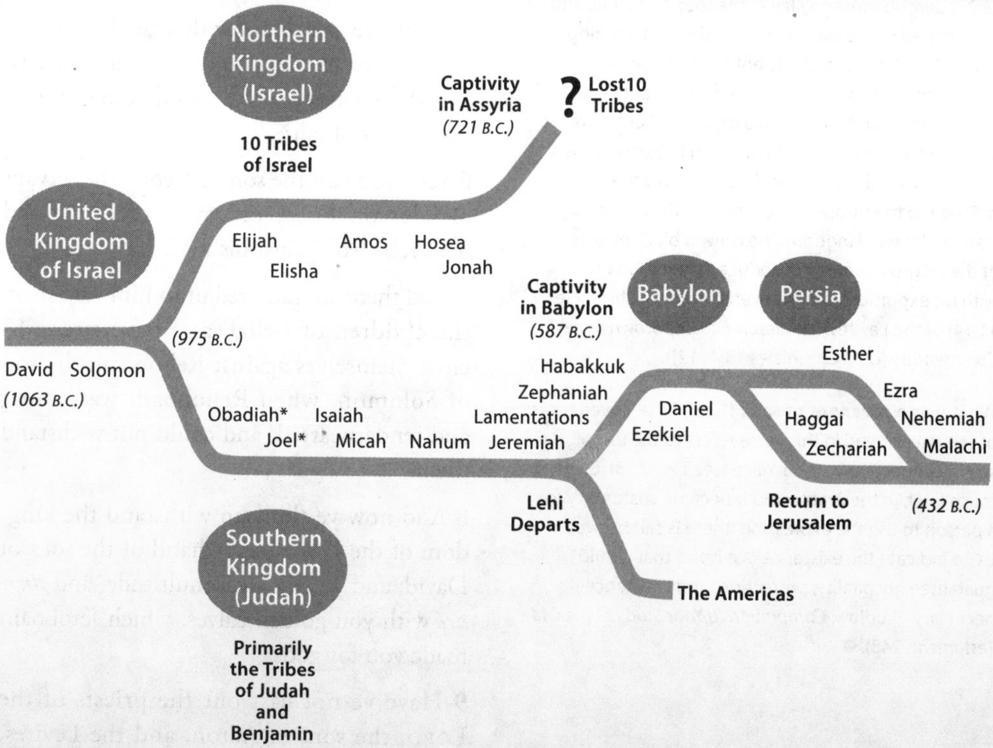

United Kingdom of Israel

David Solomon

(1063 B.C.)

(975 B.C.)

Northern Kingdom (Israel)

10 Tribes of Israel

Elijah Elisha Amos Hosea Jonah

Captivity in Assyria

(721 B.C.)

? Lost10 Tribes

Southern Kingdom (Judah)

Primarily the Tribes of Judah and Benjamin

Obadiah* Joel* Isaiah Micah Nahum Lamentations Jeremiah Zephaniah Habakkuk

Captivity in Babylon

(587 B.C.)

Babylon

Daniel Ezekiel

Persia

Esther Haggai Zechariah Ezra Nehemiah Malachi

Return to Jerusalem

(432 B.C.)

Lehi Departs

The Americas

**Time of ministry uncertain*

2 Chronicles 13:1–22. The Army of Judah Defeats a Large Army of Israel

What do we learn from the differing accounts regarding Abijah? (13:1–8) The name *Abijah* means my "father is Jehovah." In 1 Kings 15 he is referred to as Abijam (which name seems to have Canaanite roots). Rasmussen observes that the "picture [in 2 Chronicles 13] of King Abijah is very different from the one in Kings (cf. 1 Kgs. 15:1-8), in which he was shown to be sinful like his father and engaged in war all his years as king. Here he is depicted as a valiant champion of the Lord, calling on Jeroboam and northern Israel to repent and return to the true priesthood and worship of the living God" (*Latter-day Saint Commentary on the Old Testament*, 349).

How did Abijah appeal to Jeroboam's army? (13:4–12) Abijah "entered the enemy's territory and was encamped on an eminence near Beth-el (Joshua 18:22). Jeroboam's army lay at the foot of the hill, and as a pitched battle was expected, Abijah, according to the singular usage of ancient times, harangued the enemy. The speakers in such circumstances, while always extolling their own merits, poured out torrents of invective and virulent abuse upon the adversary. So did Abijah. He dwelt on the divine right of the house of David to the throne . . . contrasting the religious state of the two kingdoms, he drew a black picture of the . . . gross idolatry introduced by Jeroboam, with his expulsion and impoverishment (2 Chronicles 11:14) of the Levites" (*Jamieson-Fausset-Brown Bible Commentary* [on 2 Chronicles 13:4–12]).

What was a covenant of salt? (13:5) "The 'covenant of salt' mentioned in this verse refers to the use of salt in connection with sacrifice (see Lev. 2:13). Even much later, in the Arab world it became customary for a person to use the expression 'there is salt between us' to indicate the existence of a bond that would guarantee hospitality, protection, and assistance if necessary" (Ludlow, *Companion to Your Study of the Old Testament*, 248).

CHAPTER 13

Abijah reigns in Judah—He defeats Jeroboam and the armies of Israel—The Lord strikes Jeroboam, and he dies.

1 Now in the eighteenth year of king Jeroboam began Abijah to reign over Judah.

2 He reigned three years in Jerusalem. His mother's name also *was* Michaiah the daughter of Uriel of Gibeah. And there was war between Abijah and Jeroboam.

3 And Abijah set the battle in array with an army of valiant men of war, *even* four hundred thousand chosen men: Jeroboam also set the battle in array against him with eight hundred thousand chosen men, *being* mighty men of valour.

4 ¶ And Abijah stood up upon mount Zemaraim, which *is* in mount Ephraim, and said, Hear me, thou Jeroboam, and all Israel;

5 Ought ye not to know that the LORD God of Israel gave the kingdom over Israel to David for ever, *even* to him and to his sons by a covenant of salt?

6 Yet Jeroboam the son of Nebat, the servant of Solomon the son of David, is risen up, and hath rebelled against his lord.

7 And there are gathered unto him vain men, the children of Belial, and have strengthened themselves against Rehoboam the son of Solomon, when Rehoboam was young and tenderhearted, and could not withstand them.

8 And now ye think to withstand the kingdom of the LORD in the hand of the sons of David; and ye *be* a great multitude, and *there are* with you golden calves, which Jeroboam made you for gods.

9 Have ye not cast out the priests of the LORD, the sons of Aaron, and the Levites, and have made you priests after the manner of the nations of *other* lands? so that whosoever cometh to consecrate himself with a young bullock and seven rams, *the same* may be a priest of *them that are* no gods.

10 But as for us, the LORD *is* our God, and we have not forsaken him; and the priests, which minister unto the LORD, *are* the sons of Aaron, and the Levites *wait* upon *their* business:

11 And they burn unto the LORD every morning and every evening burnt sacrifices and sweet incense: the shewbread also *set they in order* upon the pure table; and the candlestick of gold with the lamps thereof, to burn every evening: for we keep the charge of the LORD our God; but ye have forsaken him.

12 And, behold, God himself *is* with us for *our* captain, and his priests with sounding trumpets to cry alarm against you. O children of Israel, fight ye not against the LORD God of your fathers; for ye shall not prosper.

13 ¶ But Jeroboam caused an ambushment to come about behind them: so they were before Judah, and the ambushment *was* behind them.

14 And when Judah looked back, behold, the battle *was* before and behind: and they cried unto the LORD, and the priests sounded with the trumpets.

15 Then the men of Judah gave a shout: and as the men of Judah shouted, it came to pass, that God smote Jeroboam and all Israel before Abijah and Judah.

16 And the children of Israel fled before Judah: and God delivered them into their hand.

17 And Abijah and his people slew them with a great slaughter: so there fell down slain of Israel five hundred thousand chosen men.

Why did the army of Judah prevail, and what we can learn from it? (13:18) Judah was caught in the middle with the battle "before and behind" (2 Chronicles 13:14). However, they trusted in God and were delivered. "Even as we are 'troubled on every side,' we are 'not in despair' (2 Corinthians 4:8).... The scriptures also teach that He will deliver those who put their trust in Him (see 1 Samuel 17:37, 45–46; Psalm 34:22; Proverbs 3:5–6; Alma 36:27; 38:5)" (Oaks, "Stand as Witnesses of God," 33). In what way can we demonstrate this same faith in our lives?

Who was Iddo? (13:22) Iddo was a prophet whose vision or story we do not have. The Bible mentions other lost books containing prophetic records such as Nathan's record, the prophecy of Abijah, and the book of Shemaiah (see 2 Chronicles 9:29; 12:15).

2 Chronicles 14:1–8. Asa Becomes King and Guides Judah to Worship Jehovah (see also 1 Kings 15:9–12)

How does the 2 Chronicles record of Asa differ from the account in 1 Kings? (14:3–5) "Three whole chapters here give far more credit to Asa and his worthy actions than the mere sixteen verses in Kings, which tell only briefly of his religious reforms and deal mostly with his war with northern Israel's king Baasha (1 Kgs. 15:9–24).

"Chronicles reports Asa's removing idolatrous facilities and practices, strengthening Judah's northern borders, and fighting a defensive war against 'Zera the Ethiopian' (Heb., Cushi; probably an Arabian tribe rather than the distant Ethiopians of the Nile), which he won after a humble prayer" (Rasmussen, *Latter-day Saint Commentary on the Old Testament*, 346).

18 Thus the children of Israel were brought under at that time, and the children of Judah prevailed, because they relied upon the LORD God of their fathers.

19 And Abijah pursued after Jeroboam, and took cities from him, Beth-el with the towns thereof, and Jeshanah with the towns thereof, and Ephrain with the towns thereof.

20 Neither did Jeroboam recover strength again in the days of Abijah: and the LORD struck him, and he died.

21 ¶ But Abijah waxed mighty, and married fourteen wives, and begat twenty and two sons, and sixteen daughters.

22 And the rest of the acts of Abijah, and his ways, and his sayings, *are* written in the story of the prophet Iddo.

CHAPTER 14

Asa reigns in Judah, rebuilds the cities, and defeats and plunders the Ethiopians, who attack Judah.

1 So Abijah slept with his fathers, and they buried him in the city of David: and Asa his son reigned in his stead. In his days the land was quiet ten years.

2 And Asa did *that which was* good and right in the eyes of the LORD his God:

3 For he took away the altars of the strange *gods,* and the high places, and brake down the images, and cut down the groves:

4 And commanded Judah to seek the LORD God of their fathers, and to do the law and the commandment.

5 Also he took away out of all the cities of Judah the high places and the images: and the kingdom was quiet before him.

6 ¶ And he built fenced cities in Judah: for the land had rest, and he had no war in those years; because the LORD had given him rest.

7 Therefore he said unto Judah, Let us build these cities, and make about *them* walls, and towers, gates, and bars, *while* the land *is* yet before us; because we have sought the LORD our God, we have sought *him,* and he hath given us rest on every side. So they built and prospered.

8 And Asa had an army *of men* that bare targets and spears, out of Judah three hundred thousand; and out of Benjamin, that bare shields and drew bows, two hundred and fourscore thousand: all these *were* mighty men of valour.

CHAPTER 15

Azariah prophesies that Judah will prosper if the people keep the commandments—Asa does away with false worship in Judah—Many from Ephraim, Manasseh, and Simeon migrate to Judah—The people covenant to serve the Lord and are blessed.

Why did the people of Judah prosper? (14:6–7) Asa and his people sought the Lord and He blessed them with prosperity. President Russell M. Nelson noted: "As Saints learn and obey the commandments of God, they will prosper. This promise has been recorded by prophets throughout time and in diverse places (see [Josh. 1:7; 1 Kgs. 2:3; 2 Chr. 24:20, 31:21; Ezra 6:14; 1 Ne. 2:20, 4:14; 2 Ne. 1:9, 20, 4:4; Jarom 1:9; Omni 1:6; Mosiah 1:7, 2:22, 31; Alma 9:13, 36:1, 30, 37:13, 38:1, 48:15, 25])" ("In the Lord's Own Way," 26).

Summary of 2 Chronicles 14:9–15

Asa defeats Zerah the Ethiopian, who mounted a large army against Judah. Zerah's entire army is destroyed and Asa credits the Lord with the victory.

Summary of 2 Chronicles 15:1–8

The prophet Azariah calls on God's people to repent. He testifies that Israel's prosperity and happiness depend on their faithfulness to Jehovah. Asa gains courage from Azariah's words and he removes all apostate idols out of the land. He also restores the altar in front of the temple.

2 Chronicles 15:9–15. Asa Leads Judah into a Covenant with the Lord (see also 1 Kings 15:13–15)

Why is it important to recognize that there were people from the tribes of Ephraim and Manasseh living in Jerusalem? (15:9) "Azariah led a reform movement. . . . [He] also 'gathered all Judah and Benjamin, and *the strangers with them out of Ephraim and Manasseh* . . . (v. 9; italics added). . . . This scripture is of particular interest to Latter-day Saints, for the Book of Mormon claims that hundreds of years later—even after the ten tribes comprising the northern kingdom had been taken captive and dispersed—descendants of Ephraim and Manasseh were living in Jerusalem" (Ludlow, *Companion to your Study of the Old Testament*, 249; see also 1 Nephi 5:14; Alma 10:3).

Why would Judah covenant to put nonbelievers to death? (15:13) "Those who 'would not seek the Lord' are those who turn to other gods. This putting the unbeliever to death was a commandment given by the Lord to Moses (see Deuteronomy 13:6–9). President John Taylor explained why such extreme action was commanded by the Lord: 'In forsaking God, they lose sight of their eternal existence, corrupt themselves, and entail misery on their posterity. Hence it was better to destroy a few individuals, than to entail misery on many. And hence the inhabitants of the old world and of the cities of Sodom and Gomorrah were destroyed, because it was better for them to die, and thus be deprived of their agency . . . and bring ruin upon millions of unborn persons' (as quoted in Smith, *Answers to Gospel Questions*, 3:55)" (Valletta, et al., *Old Testament for Latter-day Saint Families*, 359).

Summary of 2 Chronicles 15:16–19

Asa's mother, Maachah, is dethroned for making an idol. Asa worships the Lord with all his heart and brings back the sacred vessels to the temple.

9 And he gathered all Judah and Benjamin,
and the strangers with them out of Ephraim
and Manasseh, and out of Simeon: for they
fell to him out of Israel in abundance, when
they saw that the LORD his God *was* with him.

10 So they gathered themselves together at
Jerusalem in the third month, in the fifteenth
year of the reign of Asa.

11 And they offered unto the LORD the same
time, of the spoil *which* they had brought,
seven hundred oxen and seven thousand
sheep.

12 And they entered into a covenant to seek
the LORD God of their fathers with all their
heart and with all their soul;

13 That whosoever would not seek the LORD
God of Israel should be put to death, whether
small or great, whether man or woman.

14 And they sware unto the LORD with a
loud voice, and with shouting, and with
trumpets, and with cornets.

15 And all Judah rejoiced at the oath: for
they had sworn with all their heart, and
sought him with their whole desire; and he
was found of them: and the LORD gave them
rest round about.

CHAPTER 16

Asa employs Syria to defeat Israel—Hanani the seer reproves Asa for lack of faith—Asa suffers from disease and dies.

CHAPTERS 17–21

Jehoshaphat reigns well and prospers in Judah—Priests travel and teach out of the book of the law of the Lord.

Jehoshaphat of Judah joins Ahab of Israel to fight Syria—Ahab's false prophets foretell victory—Micaiah prophesies the fall and death of Ahab—The Syrians slay Ahab.

Jehoshaphat is rebuked for helping ungodly Ahab—He helps the people return to the Lord, sets up judges, and administers justice.

The Ammonites and others attack Judah—Jehoshaphat and all the people fast and pray—Jahaziel prophesies the deliverance of Judah—Judah's attackers war among and destroy themselves.

Jehoram slays his brothers, marries Ahab's daughter, and reigns in wickedness—Elijah prophesies a plague upon the people and the death of Jehoram—The Philistines and others war against Judah—Jehoram dies of sore diseases.

Summary of 2 Chronicles 16

Asa takes gold and silver from the temple to secure an alliance with Ben-hadad, the king of Syria, against Israel. The seer Hanani condemns Asa for trusting in the arm of flesh rather than in God. Asa is angry with Hanani and throws him into prison. Asa becomes ill and dies (see also 1 Kings 15:16–24).

Summary of 2 Chronicles 17–21

Jehoshaphat becomes king and serves the Lord. He builds a storehouse and strengthens Judah. However, he creates an unholy alliance with Ahab, king of Israel. The Lord reproves Jehoshaphat, and he repents. The Moabites march against Jehoshaphat and his armies. Jehoshaphat goes to the temple and seeks the Lord's blessing against their enemies. God hears their prayers and delivers Judah (see also 1 Kings 22). Jehoshaphat dies and Jehoram becomes king by killing his brothers. Elijah warns Jehoram to repent or suffer from a plague. Jehoram refuses; the Lord sends a plague that slays Jehoram.

Summary of 2 Chronicles 22–25

Ahaziah becomes king and follows his wicked father's example. He allies with Israel against Syria, but is later slain by Jehu. Ahaziah's mother Athaliah seizes power in Judah and destroys all the royal family except Joash, who is safely hidden during Athaliah's rule. Jehoiada the priest leads a rebellion against Athaliah and calls on Judah to repent. The people overthrow Athaliah, and Joash becomes king. The people then destroy Baal worship in Judah and restore the temple. Jehoiada dies of old age. Judah's leaders induce Joash to turn from the temple and to worship idols. Zechariah, a prophet, calls Joash to repent, but they execute Zechariah in the temple. The Syrian army conquers Judah and Joash is assassinated by his own servants (see also 2 Kings 8–12). When Amaziah becomes king, he executes the men who killed his father. He organizes an army and hires mercenaries from the kingdom of Israel. A prophet warns him he will lose the battle if he uses mercenaries, so he sends them home to Ephraim. Amaziah leads Judah to victory against the Edomites. After taking their idols, he bows down to the idols and worships them. God sends a prophet to confront him, but Amaziah dismisses the prophet. Amaziah declares war on King Joash (or Jehoash; see 2 Kings 14) of Israel. Joash warns him to back down, but Amaziah refuses to listen. Israelites capture him and receive a ransom from the temple treasury for his return. Amaziah unsuccessfully flees a conspiracy and is slain at Lachish (see also 2 Kings 14).

Summary of 2 Chronicles 26:1–15

Uzziah becomes king at sixteen years of age. At first he keeps the commandments and prospers. He builds up the country and places forts [towers] throughout the land (see also 2 Kings 14:21–15:5).

2 Chronicles 26:16–23. Uzziah Becomes Arrogant and Attempts to Burn Incense in the Temple and Is Smitten

What flaw overtook Uzziah? (26:16–19) "His transgression was like that of King Saul; he assumed priestly prerogatives and burned incense upon the altar.

CHAPTERS 22–25

Ahaziah reigns in wickedness and is slain by Jehu; his mother, Athaliah, reigns in his stead.

Jehoiada the priest makes Joash king—Athaliah is slain—Worship of the Lord is restored, and the priest of Baal is slain.

Joash and Jehoiada receive contributions and repair the house of the Lord—Jehoiada dies—Joash falls into idolatry, slays a prophet named Zechariah, and is himself slain in a conspiracy.

Amaziah reigns, smites the Edomites, and worships false gods—A prophet foretells Amaziah's destruction—Judah is defeated by Israel, and Amaziah is slain in a conspiracy.

CHAPTER 26

Uzziah reigns and prospers as long as he keeps the commandments—He transgresses, attempts to burn incense upon the altar, and is cursed with leprosy.

16 ¶ But when he was strong, his heart was
lifted up to *his* destruction: for he transgressed against the LORD his God, and went

into the temple of the LORD to burn incense upon the altar of incense.

17 And Azariah the priest went in after him, and with him fourscore priests of the LORD, *that were* valiant men:

18 And they withstood Uzziah the king, and said unto him, *It appertaineth* not unto thee, Uzziah, to burn incense unto the LORD, but to the priests the sons of Aaron, that are consecrated to burn incense: go out of the sanctuary; for thou hast trespassed; neither *shall it be* for thine honour from the LORD God.

19 Then Uzziah was wroth, and *had* a censer in his hand to burn incense: and while he was wroth with the priests, the leprosy even rose up in his forehead before the priests in the house of the LORD, from beside the incense altar.

20 And Azariah the chief priest, and all the priests, looked upon him, and, behold, he *was* leprous in his forehead, and they thrust him out from thence; yea, himself hasted also to go out, because the LORD had smitten him.

21 And Uzziah the king was a leper unto the day of his death, and dwelt in a several house, *being* a leper; for he was cut off from the house of the LORD: and Jotham his son *was* over the king's house, judging the people of the land.

22 ¶ Now the rest of the acts of Uzziah, first and last, did Isaiah the prophet, the son of Amoz, write.

23 So Uzziah slept with his fathers, and they buried him with his fathers in the field of the burial which *belonged* to the kings; for they said, He *is* a leper: and Jotham his son reigned in his stead.

When he was corrected, he flew into a rage and was punished with leprosy. For the rest of his life the government was in the hands of his son Jotham, who later succeeded him as king (2 Chr. 26:15–23)" (Rasmussen, *Latter-day Saint Commentary on the Old Testament*, 357). President Ezra Taft Benson warned: "The proud cannot accept the authority of God giving direction to their lives (see Hel. 12:6). They pit their perceptions of truth against God's great knowledge, their abilities versus God's priesthood power, their accomplishments against His mighty works" ("Beware of Pride," 5).

What does leprosy represent? (26:19) "Leprosy was 'the disease [that] was regarded as a living death.' . . . Throughout the scriptures, leprosy is symbolically linked to sins and transgressions—those things that lead us to spiritual death" (Parry and Parry, *Symbols and Shadows*, 42). See commentary in this volume for Leviticus 13.

Summary of 2 Chronicles 27–28

Jotham rules over Judah. He is righteous but the people become wicked. He builds the Upper Gate of the temple and fortifies Judah. His son Ahaz follows him as king. Ahaz turns from his father's example and worships the idols of Baal. God allows the king of Syria to defeat him and deport many of his people. The army of Israel also defeats his army. The prophet Oded warns Israel to not keep the Judean captives. They set them free. Ahaz aligns with the king of Assyria against Edom. The Lord afflicts Judah for Ahaz's sins, but he will not repent. He closes the temple and makes idolatrous altars (see also 2 Kings 15:32–16).

Summary of 2 Chronicles 29–32

Hezekiah becomes king and rules over Judah for 29 years. He repairs the temple doors and opens them for worship. He gathers the Levites and invites them to sanctify themselves and the temple. Hezekiah directs the burnt and sin offerings for his nation. The temple workers are consecrated so the house of the Lord is set in order. Hezekiah invites all of Israel and Judah to come to the temple to celebrate Passover. Though most of the people reject his invitation, the faithful gather to worship at the temple. Those who attend Passover return home and tear down the idolatrous altars and centers of worship. Hezekiah and the priests are overwhelmed by the generous tithes and offerings of the faithful and are enabled to care for the needy. When Sennacherib, king of Assyria, invades Judah, Hezekiah blocks the water sources outside the city so they are unusable by the Assyrians. He builds a tunnel to the source to provide water for Jerusalem. Hezekiah also reinforces the city walls. Sennacherib mocks Hezekiah's efforts and religious practices and boasts that he will destroy Judah. Hezekiah and Isaiah plead with the Lord for help. The Lord sends an angel to destroy the Assyrian army. In his later years, Hezekiah reigns in righteousness, is healed of a life-threatening illness, and prospers (see also 2 Kings 18–20).

CHAPTERS 27–28

Jotham reigns, builds up the kingdom, and subdues the Ammonites.

Ahaz reigns in wickedness and practices idolatry; his people are defeated by Israel—The captives are freed by the command of a prophet—The Edomites and Philistines attack Judah—Ahaz continues his idolatrous ways.

CHAPTERS 29–32

Hezekiah reigns in righteousness and restores the worship of Jehovah—The Levites cleanse and sanctify the house of the Lord—The priests offer sacrifices and make reconciliation and atonement for the people—Hezekiah and all the people worship the Lord and praise His name.

Hezekiah invites all Israel to a solemn Passover in Jerusalem—Some accept the call; others laugh him to scorn—The faithful Israelites worship the Lord in Jerusalem.

The faithful Israelites overthrow false worship among them—The people pay tithes and offerings—The Levites administer in temporal matters—Hezekiah serves faithfully.

Sennacherib invades Judah and besieges the cities—He rails against the Lord—Isaiah and Hezekiah pray, and an angel destroys the leaders of the Assyrian armies—Hezekiah reigns in righteousness despite some pride in his heart.

CHAPTER 33

Manasseh reigns in wickedness and worships false gods—He is taken captive into Assyria—He repents and serves the Lord—Amon reigns in unrighteousness and is slain.

Summary of 2 Chronicles 33

Manasseh becomes king when he is twelve years old. He proves unfaithful and reintroduces idol worship. He places an idol in the temple. He ignores prophetic warnings, and the Assyrians capture him and send him in chains to Babylon. Once he repents, God restores him to his throne. He removes the foreign idols and rebuilds the temple altar. He dies, and Amon succeeds him. Unfortunately, Amon sacrifices to carved images. Finally, Amon's servants slay him.

CHAPTERS 34–35

Josiah destroys idolatry in Judah—The people of Judah repair the house of the Lord—Hilkiah finds a book of the law—Huldah the prophetess reveals the desolations to come upon the people—Josiah and the people covenant to serve the Lord.

Josiah and all Judah keep a most solemn Passover—Josiah is mortally wounded by the Egyptians at Megiddo.

Summary of 2 Chronicles 34–35

Amon's son Josiah becomes king when he is eight years old and faithfully serves like his ancestor David. He removes idol worship from the land and establishes a way to pay for repairing the temple. While the temple is being repaired, Hilkiah finds a book of the law. "The law book is easily recognizable as Deuteronomy, and so King Josiah's purge is usually known as the Deuternomic reform of the temple" (Barker, "What Did King Josiah Reform?" 523). Huldah, the prophetess, foretells the curses that will come upon those who turn from the Lord. Josiah and his people make a covenant to follow God and prepare and keep an incomparable Passover. Eventually, Josiah dies in a battle at Megiddo while fighting the Egyptians.

CHAPTER 36

Various kings rule in Judah—Nebuchadnezzar overruns Judah and makes Zedekiah king—Zedekiah rebels, the people reject the prophets, and the Chaldeans burn the temple and destroy Jerusalem—Cyrus of Persia decrees the building of the temple.

Summary of 2 Chronicles 36

Josiah's son, Jehoahaz, becomes king. In time, other kings rule in wickedness. King Nebuchadnezzar overruns Judah and takes temple treasures to Babylon. Zedekiah is appointed king by the Babylonians. Unfortunately, Zedekiah rejects Jeremiah's counsel and warnings. As the people reject the prophets, the temple is destroyed and the people are taken captive into Babylon. They remain there for seventy years until Cyrus, king of Persia, allows them to return to their homeland and rebuild the temple (see also 2 Kings 21–25).

EZRA

Introduction

Ezra was "a famous priest and scribe who brought back part of the exiles from captivity [in Babylon] (Ezra 7–10; Neh. 8; 12). The object of his mission was 'to teach in Israel statutes and judgments.' . . .

"The book of Ezra contains also an introductory section (Ezra 1–6) describing events that happened from 60 to 80 years before the arrival of Ezra in Jerusalem, that is, the decree of Cyrus, 537 B.C., and the return of Jews under Zerubbabel; the attempt to build the temple and the hindrances due to the Samaritans; the preaching of Haggai and Zechariah and the completion of the temple, 516 B.C. There is no record in the book of any events between this date and the mission of Ezra" (Bible Dictionary, "Ezra").

The book "is a witness of the fulfillment of prophecies by Isaiah and Jeremiah about the return of the Jews to Jerusalem after seventy years of captivity (see Isaiah 44:28; Jeremiah 25:12–14). Ezra tells about the rebuilding of Solomon's temple and the problems that arise between the Jews and the Samaritans (see Ezra 1–6). Prophets, such as Haggai and Zechariah, encourage the people to rebuild the temple (see Ezra 5:1). The final chapters contain the story of Ezra's efforts to increase the spirituality of the people (see Ezra 7–10)" (Valletta, et al., *Old Testament for Latter-day Saint Families*, 373).

"The books of the Bible do not fall into chronological order. Their position is determined usually by whether they are historical or prophetic books. . . .

"The books of Ezra and Nehemiah are actually the last two historical books of the Old Testament.

"Zechariah and Haggai were prophets during this same period. Malachi is the only prophet known to have served in Israel between the time of Ezra and Nehemiah and the beginning of the New Testament.

"The books of Ezra and Nehemiah tell the story of Israel's history from the first return to Jerusalem until the end of Nehemiah's second term as governor of Judah (538 B.C. to shortly before 400 B.C.)" (*Old Testament Student Manual: 1 Kings–Malachi*, 319).

CHAPTER 1

King Cyrus of Persia lets the Jews go back to Jerusalem to build the temple—Cyrus returns the vessels of the house of the Lord taken by Nebuchadnezzar.

1 Now in the first year of Cyrus king of Persia,
that the word of the LORD by the mouth of
Jeremiah might be fulfilled, the LORD stirred
up the spirit of Cyrus king of Persia, that he
made a proclamation throughout all his kingdom, and *put it* also in writing, saying,

Ezra 1:1–11. Cyrus Issues a Decree to Return the Jews to Their Homeland

Who was Cyrus, king of Persia? (1:1–2) Cyrus was the "king of Persia who fulfilled Isaiah's prophecy (2 Chr. 36:22–23; Isa. 44:28; 45:1) by allowing the Jews to return to Jerusalem to rebuild the temple, thus partially ending the Babylonian captivity" (Guide to the Scriptures, "Cyrus"). "The Persians were a tribe who in the 8th century B.C. inhabited a district east of Elam. Cyrus united the Medes and Persians, conquered Babylon (538 B.C.), and founded the Persian

2 Thus saith Cyrus king of Persia, The LORD God of heaven hath given me all the kingdoms of the earth; and he hath charged me to build him an house at Jerusalem, which *is* in Judah.

3 Who *is there* among you of all his people? his God be with him, and let him go up to Jerusalem, which *is* in Judah, and build the house of the LORD God of Israel, (he *is* the God,) which *is* in Jerusalem.

Empire, which extended from Afghanistan to the Mediterranean, including Asia Minor. . . . Judea was a subject province to the Persian Empire from 530 until 334 B.C." (Bible Dictionary, "Persia").

How might God use Gentile kings to fulfill His word? (1:1–3) "God, the Father of us all, uses the men of the earth, especially good men, to accomplish his purposes. It has been true in the past, it is true today, it will be true in the future" (Benson, "Civic Standards for the Faithful Saints," 59). "God does not rule in nations, but He is mindful of them. He can and does place people in positions of influence who want what is best for the people" (Eyring, "Trust in God, Then Go and Do," 73). ⊕

Why did only some of the Jews return to Jerusalem? (1:3–4) "Every one was at liberty to go, but none was obliged to go" (*Adam Clarke's Commentary* [on Ezra 1:4]). "Ezra 2:64–65 indicates that approximately fifty thousand people made the first trip back to Jerusalem. Ezra 1:4 tells of the responsibilities of the Jews who remained in Babylonia. By far, most of the expatriated Jews chose not to return to Jerusalem at this time, a decision that indicates how well they had been absorbed into the Babylonian way of life" (*Old Testament Student Manual: 1 Kings–Malachi*, 319).

4 And whosoever remaineth in any place where he sojourneth, let the men of his place help him with silver, and with gold, and with goods, and with beasts, beside the freewill offering for the house of God that *is* in Jerusalem.

5 ¶ Then rose up the chief of the fathers of Judah and Benjamin, and the priests, and the Levites, with all *them* whose spirit God had raised, to go up to build the house of the LORD which *is* in Jerusalem.

6 And all they that *were* about them strengthened their hands with vessels of silver, with gold, with goods, and with beasts, and with precious things, beside all *that* was willingly offered.

7 ¶ Also Cyrus the king brought forth the vessels of the house of the LORD, which Nebuchadnezzar had brought forth out of Jerusalem, and had put them in the house of his gods;

What were the remaining Jews in Persia inspired to do? (1:4–6) "The returning Jews were . . . inspired by the Lord: 'Then rose up the chief of the fathers of Judah and Benjamin, and the priests, and the Levites, with all them whose spirit God had raised, to go up to build the house of the Lord which is in Jerusalem' (Ezra 1:5). And those who were staying in Babylonia willingly contributed resources to help make possible the return of some (Ezra 1:4–6)" (Holzapfel, et al., *Jehovah and the World of the Old Testament*, 362).

What are the "vessels of the house of the Lord"? (1:7) "The Lord repeatedly says in the scriptures, 'Be ye clean, that bear the vessels of the Lord.' . . . Let me tell you what that phrase 'bear the vessels of the Lord' means. Anciently [it] . . . refers to the recovery and return to Jerusalem of various temple implements that had been carried into Babylon by King Nebuchadnezzar. In physically handling the return of these items, the Lord reminded those early brethren of the sanctity of anything related to the temple" (Holland, "Sanctify Yourselves," 39).

Who was Sheshbazzar? (1:8) "The name *Shesh-bazzar* (possibly Persian 'fire-worshipper') occurs only four times in the Bible—all in the book of Ezra (1:8, 11; 5:14, 16). Some scholars believe *Shesh-bazzar* is simply another name for *Zerub-babel* ('born in Babylon'), since both of them were of royal blood ('princes of Judah'), had Babylonian names, and were prominent in the return of the exiles. The Septuagint version of the Bible, however, distinguishes between them, showing that they were probably two different people (1 Esdras 6:18)" (Ludlow, *Companion to Your Study of the Old Testament*, 253).

What were these gold and silver items? (1:9–11) "After more than 60 years in Babylonian captivity, the Jews as a people began to return to their beloved Jerusalem. Cyrus, the conqueror of Babylon and founder of the Persian Empire, issued a decree giving them permission to reclaim their homeland and rebuild their temple (see 2 Chron. 36:22–23; Ezra 1:2–3). Cyrus even gave back to them 5,400 gold and silver 'vessels of the house of the Lord' that Nebuchadnezzar had taken out of Jerusalem (see Ezra 1:7–11).... Led by Zerubbabel, a prince of Judah, and the prophets Haggai and Zechariah, the people joyously dedicated the temple in 516 B.C. (see Ezra 3:1–6:16)" (Garner, "Ezra Unfolds the Scriptures," 47).

8 Even those did Cyrus king of Persia bring
forth by the hand of Mithredath the treasurer, and numbered them unto Sheshbazzar, the prince of Judah.

9 And this *is* the number of them: thirty
chargers of gold, a thousand chargers of silver, nine and twenty knives,

10 Thirty basins of gold, silver basins of a
second *sort* four hundred and ten, *and* other vessels a thousand.

11 All the vessels of gold and of silver *were*
five thousand and four hundred. All *these* did Sheshbazzar bring up with *them of* the captivity that were brought up from Babylon unto Jerusalem.

CHAPTER 2

The descendants of the Jews taken captive who return to Jerusalem and to Judah are listed—The children of priests whose genealogy is lost are denied the priesthood—Faithful people contribute to the building of the temple.

Summary of Ezra 2:1–60

"[Ezra 2:1–2] announces that the list which follows it (vv. 3–67) contains the number of the men of the people of Israel who returned to Jerusalem and Judah from the captivity in Babylon, under the conduct of Zerubbabel, Joshua, and other leaders. It is composed of separate lists: of the families of the people, vv. 3–35; of the priests and Levites, Ezra 2:36–42; of the Nethinims and servants of Solomon, vv. 43–58; of

61 ¶ And of the children of the priests: the
children of Habaiah, the children of Koz,
the children of Barzillai; which took a wife
of the daughters of Barzillai the Gileadite,
and was called after their name:

62 These sought their register *among* those
that were reckoned by genealogy, but they
were not found: therefore were they, as polluted, put from the priesthood.

63 And the Tirshatha said unto them, that
they should not eat of the most holy things,
till there stood up a priest with Urim and
with Thummim.

64 ¶ The whole congregation together *was*
forty and two thousand three hundred *and*
threescore,

65 Beside their servants and their maids, of
whom *there were* seven thousand three hundred thirty and seven: and *there were* among
them two hundred singing men and singing
women.

66 Their horses *were* seven hundred thirty
and six; their mules, two hundred forty and
five;

67 Their camels, four hundred thirty and
five; *their* asses, six thousand seven hundred
and twenty.

families who could not prove their Israelite descent, and of certain priests whose genealogy could not be found, Ezra 2:59–63; and it closes with the sum-total of the persons, and of their beasts of burden, Ezra 2:64–67. This is followed by an enumeration of the gifts which they brought with them for the temple ([Ezra 2:68–69]), and by a final statement with regard to the entire list (Ezra 2:70)" (Keil and Delitzsch, *Commentary* [on Introduction to Ezra 2]).

Ezra 2:61–70. Unworthy Priests Are Excluded from Priesthood Service; the Urim and Thummim Is Identified and the Faithful Contribute to the Building of the Temple

Why did the Lord refer to this passage in the Doctrine and Covenants? (2:61–62) "On November 27, 1832, the Lord specifically mentioned [Ezra 2:61–62] to Joseph Smith in regard to the apostasy of priesthood members in the latter days. Such 'shall not find an inheritance among the saints of the Most High; Therefore, it shall be done unto them as unto the children of the priest, as will be found recorded in the second chapter and sixty-first and second verses of Ezra' (D&C 85:11–12)" (Ludlow, *Companion to Your Study of the Old Testament*, 253).

What was the Urim and Thummim? (2:63) "Moses delivered to the Aaronic high priest two objects to be 'worn' in a pouch behind the breastplate: the Urim and Thummim—the transliterated forms of two Hebrew words that mean 'lights' and 'perfections.' In the Old Testament these objects are mysterious. Their form is not described, their function is never fully explained, and they are not mentioned in the text after the time of David (1 Sam 23:6) except in reference to their future restoration (Ezra 2:63). Yet it is clear that they represented the power and authority of the high priest to inquire and receive the will of the Lord on behalf of the people" (Holzapfel, et al., *Jehovah and the World of the Old Testament*, 109). See commentary in this volume for Exodus 28:30.

68 ¶ And *some* of the chief of the fathers,
when they came to the house of the LORD
which *is* at Jerusalem, offered freely for the
house of God to set it up in his place:

69 They gave after their ability unto the treasure of the work threescore and one thousand drams of gold, and five thousand pound of silver, and one hundred priests' garments.

70 So the priests, and the Levites, and *some*
of the people, and the singers, and the porters, and the Nethinims, dwelt in their cities, and all Israel in their cities.

CHAPTER 3

The altar is rebuilt—Regular sacrifices are reinstituted—The foundations of the temple are laid amid great rejoicing.

Summary of Ezra 3

"The returned Jews, under the direction of Zerubbabel and Jeshua (the leader of the priests), began rebuilding the temple. They began with the altar so they could perform the sacrifices commanded in the law of Moses. Then they began the foundation. When the foundation was complete, they had a celebration. Those who could remember the temple of Solomon wept when they saw this temple because they knew it would not be nearly as beautiful as the one they remembered" (*Old Testament Student Study Guide* [1998], 122).

In addition, Zerubbabel reinstituted the regular daily and monthly worship services, including the holy days and the Feast of Unleavened Bread, the Feast of Weeks, and the Feast of Tabernacles as described in Exodus 23:14–17 and Deut. 16:16.

CHAPTER 4

The Samaritans offer help, then hinder the work—The building of the temple and of the walls of Jerusalem ceases.

1 Now when the adversaries of Judah and
Benjamin heard that the children of the captivity builded the temple unto the LORD God of Israel;

Ezra 4:1–10. Jewish Rulers Reject the Samaritans' Offer to Help Rebuild the Temple

Who were the "adversaries" who wanted to help build the temple? (4:1) "The 'adversaries of Judah and Benjamin' [were] part-Israelitish people living in the lands of Samaria (hence, *Samaritans*), where the peoples of the ten northern tribes had previously lived. The Israelites who had remained in the area at the time of the Assyrian captivity (about 722 B.C.) intermarried with the foreigners who moved in. These mixed-blooded peoples were not considered to be pure Israelites by the returning exiles and were not allowed to assist in the rebuilding of the temple" (Ludlow, *Companion to Your Study of the Old Testament*, 254). ⊕

2 Then they came to Zerubbabel, and to the chief of the fathers, and said unto them, Let us build with you: for we seek your God, as ye *do;* and we do sacrifice unto him since the days of Esar-haddon king of Assur, which brought us up hither.

What motivated the Samaritan offer to help build the temple? (4:2) The Samaritans "proposed to join with them . . . which proposal at first sight might seem very agreeable and welcome, and would have been so had they been sincere, but they were not; they hoped, by getting among them, to have . . . disunited them; and so by these or other means to have retarded the building; or if it went forward, that they might have a claim to it as theirs, at least as to set up their own idols in a part of it; the reasons they gave [*for we seek your God as ye do*] which was false, for they did not worship him alone, but with idols, nor in the same manner as the Jews did" (*John Gill's Exposition of the Whole Bible* [commentary on Ezra 4:2]). ⊕

3 But Zerubbabel, and Jeshua, and the rest of the chief of the fathers of Israel, said unto them, Ye have nothing to do with us to build an house unto our God; but we ourselves together will build unto the LORD God of Israel, as king Cyrus the king of Persia hath commanded us.

4 Then the people of the land weakened the hands of the people of Judah, and troubled them in building,

5 And hired counsellors against them, to frustrate their purpose, all the days of Cyrus king of Persia, even until the reign of Darius king of Persia.

6 And in the reign of Ahasuerus, in the beginning of his reign, wrote they *unto him* an accusation against the inhabitants of Judah and Jerusalem.

Why did the leaders of Judah use the king's order as a reason to reject help? (4:3) "The fact that they were not authorised to extend to others the privileges conferred upon them by Cyrus was probably not the only motive that actuated the Jews. They no doubt felt that to admit to closer association such a hybrid community as the Samaritans, with their mixture of Hebrew and heathen rites of worship, would neutralise the impulse in the direction of purity of religion which they had derived from their experiences as exiles" (*John Dummelow's Commentary* [on Ezra 4:3]).

How did the Samaritans slow down the building of the temple? (4:5) "Exasperated by this repulse, the Samaritans endeavored by every means to molest the workmen as well as obstruct the progress of the building; and, though they could not alter the decree which Cyrus had issued regarding it, yet by bribes and clandestine arts indefatigably plied at court, they labored to frustrate the effects of the edict. Their success in those underhand dealings was great; for Cyrus, being frequently absent and much absorbed in his warlike expeditions, left the government in the hands of his son Cambyses, a wicked prince, and extremely hostile to the Jews and their religion. The same arts were assiduously practiced during the reign of his successor" (*Jamieson-Fausset-Brown Bible Commentary* [on Ezra 4:4–5]).

7 ¶ And in the days of Artaxerxes wrote Bishlam, Mithredath, Tabeel, and the rest of their companions, unto Artaxerxes king of Persia; and the writing of the letter *was* written in the Syrian tongue, and interpreted in the Syrian tongue.

What was the Syrian tongue? (4:7) "The language shifts from Hebrew to Aramaic (Ezra 4:8–6:18) in reporting these letters and their results; Hebrew is then resumed for the rest of the book of Ezra except for one other Aramaic passage (Ezra 7:12–26). . . . Aramaic, the official language of the Persian empire, was the language of international communication and trade for centuries. Later the scriptures were orally translated and explained to the people in that language (Neh. 8)" (Rasmussen, *Latter-day Saint Commentary on the Old Testament*, 370).

Ezra 4:11–24. Feeling Spiteful after Being Rejected, the Samaritans Make False Legal Claims against the Jews to the King of Persia

Why would the Samaritans falsely accuse the Jews of rebelling against the Persian king? (4:12) "After all these years of trying [to frustrate Jewish purposes], the enemies of the Jews tried again by making charges against the loyalty of the Jews who were trying to rebuild Jerusalem. They laid out a case that the people in Jerusalem had habitually and continually rebelled against outside rulers, as could be attested by a simple search of historical records. They told the king that if he continued to let the Jews rebuild Jerusalem they would surely rebel again and make it so that he received no taxes or other support from that portion of his empire" (Muhlestein, *Scripture Study Made Simple*, 303). ⊕

8 Rehum the chancellor and Shimshai the scribe wrote a letter against Jerusalem to Artaxerxes the king in this sort:

9 Then *wrote* Rehum the chancellor, and Shimshai the scribe, and the rest of their companions; the Dinaites, the Apharsathchites, the Tarpelites, the Apharsites, the Archevites, the Babylonians, the Susanchites, the Dehavites, *and* the Elamites,

10 And the rest of the nations whom the great and noble Asnappar brought over, and set in the cities of Samaria, and the rest *that are* on this side the river, and at such a time.

11 ¶ This *is* the copy of the letter that they sent unto him, *even* unto Artaxerxes the king; Thy servants the men on this side the river, and at such a time.

12 Be it known unto the king, that the Jews which came up from thee to us are come unto Jerusalem, building the rebellious and the bad city, and have set up the walls *thereof*, and joined the foundations.

13 Be it known now unto the king, that, if this city be builded, and the walls set up *again, then* will they not pay toll, tribute, and custom, and *so* thou shalt endamage the revenue of the kings.

14 Now because we have maintenance from *the king's* palace, and it was not meet for us to see the king's dishonour, therefore have we sent and certified the king;

15 That search may be made in the book of the records of thy fathers: so shalt thou find in the book of the records, and know that this city *is* a rebellious city, and hurtful unto kings and provinces, and that they have moved sedition within the same of old time: for which cause was this city destroyed.

16 We certify the king that, if this city be builded *again,* and the walls thereof set up,

by this means thou shalt have no portion on
this side the river.

17 ¶ *Then* sent the king an answer unto
Rehum the chancellor, and *to* Shimshai the
scribe, and *to* the rest of their companions
that dwell in Samaria, and *unto* the rest beyond the river, Peace, and at such a time.

18 The letter which ye sent unto us hath
been plainly read before me.

19 And I commanded, and search hath been
made, and it is found that this city of old
time hath made insurrection against kings,
and *that* rebellion and sedition have been
made therein.

20 There have been mighty kings also over
Jerusalem, which have ruled over all *countries*
beyond the river; and toll, tribute, and custom, was paid unto them.

21 Give ye now commandment to cause
these men to cease, and that this city be not
builded, until *another* commandment shall
be given from me.

22 Take heed now that ye fail not to do this:
why should damage grow to the hurt of the
kings?

23 ¶ Now when the copy of king Artaxerxes'
letter *was* read before Rehum, and Shimshai
the scribe, and their companions, they went
up in haste to Jerusalem unto the Jews, and
made them to cease by force and power.

24 Then ceased the work of the house of God
which *is* at Jerusalem. So it ceased unto the
second year of the reign of Darius king of
Persia.

Why is there opposition when building temples? (4:23–24) The false reports of the Samaritans delayed the construction of the temple for many years. President Gordon B. Hinckley spoke of the opposition the Saints experience as they seek to build latter-day temples: "We might expect that the adversary of righteousness would seek to thwart [temple] construction and the work to be done therein. He had done so in the days of Kirtland. . . . He did so in the days of Far West. . . . It was so in the days of Nauvoo. . . . It was so here in this Temple Square when, during the forty years of the temple construction, there was one threat after another" ("War We Are Winning," 43–44). ⊕

How do you respond to adversity? (4:24) "The [ancient] Jews faced bitter disappointment in rebuilding the temple. Elder Richard G. Scott counseled: 'When you face adversity, you can be led to ask many questions. Some serve a useful purpose; others do not. To ask, Why does this have to happen to me? Why do I have to suffer this, now? What have I done to cause this? will lead you into blind alleys. It really does no good to ask questions that reflect opposition to the will of God. Rather ask, What am I to do? What am I to learn from this experience?' (["Trust in the Lord," 17]). How can this counsel help you when you face disappointment?" (Valletta, et al., *Old Testament for Latter-day Saint Families*, 378). ⊕

Summary of Ezra 5

"In 520 B.C. the people of Judah, encouraged by the prophets Haggai and Zechariah, resumed work on rebuilding the temple. Tatnai, the local governor under Persia, challenged the builders on account of Artaxerxes' edict (Ezra 4:21–23) and demanded the names of the leaders who were directing the building (in Ezra 5:4, *we* should be *he*, according to the Septuagint, which makes better sense). When the governor's complaint went to Darius, however, it also contained the Jews' assertion that Cyrus had earlier authorized the work and aided them in building the house of God in Jerusalem, and they requested that a search be made for Cyrus' decree (Ezra 5:6–17)" (Rasmussen, *Latter-day Saint Commentary on the Old Testament*, 370).

"The Jews had spent a number of years on a costly detour, both politically and spiritually. The nation had yet to recover, but the community of faith had wound its way back through the Judean hills, arriving at Jerusalem. Critical to their faith was the reconstruction of the temple. But in the process of resettlement, they had veered off course. The temple wreckage lay in the dust like a forgotten idea. It was at this point that God spoke through two prophets, Haggai and Zechariah. They called the people back to their original purpose; they unfolded the map of God's design and pointed them in the right direction—the completion of the temple" (Larson and Dahlen, *Ezra, Nehemiah, Esther*, 55).

CHAPTER 5

Haggai and Zechariah prophesy—Zerubbabel renews the building of the temple—The Samaritans challenge the Jews' right to continue their building work.

Why Is It Important to Trust the Lord's Prophets? (Ezra 5:1–2)

The Lord directed two prophets, Haggai and Zechariah, to encourage the people of Judah to rebuild the temple. (For details of their prophecies see Haggai 2:3–4; Zechariah 1:12–17.) Under the direction of Zerubbabel, the people were able to complete the reconstruction of the temple. Their righteous efforts to follow the prophets and commence again building the temple were rewarded when king Darius confirmed the prior king's decree. Why is it important to trust prophets?

"Prophets see ahead. They see the harrowing dangers the adversary has placed or will yet place in our path. Prophets also foresee the grand possibilities and privileges awaiting those who listen *with the intent to obey*. I know this is true! I have experienced it for myself over and over again . . .

"You may not always understand every declaration of a living prophet. But when you know a prophet is a prophet, you can approach the Lord in humility and faith and ask for your own witness about whatever His prophet has proclaimed" (Nelson, "Stand as True Millennials," 31).

"Trusting in and following the prophets is more than a blessing and a privilege. President Ezra Taft Benson declared that 'our [very] salvation hangs on' following the prophet. He described what he called 'Fourteen Fundamentals in Following the Prophet.' . . .

"'First: The prophet is the only man who speaks for the Lord in everything.

"'Second: The living prophet is more vital to us than the standard works.

CHAPTER 6

Darius renews the decree of Cyrus to build the temple—It is finished and dedicated, and sacrifices and feasts commence again.

1 Then Darius the king made a decree, and
search was made in the house of the rolls,
where the treasures were laid up in Babylon.

Ezra 6:1–12. Darius Searches for and Honors Cyrus's Decree to Allow the Jews to Build the Temple

Who was king Darius? (6:1) "Darius I, the third king of the Persian Empire, was a great organizer. . . . Darius's building projects included a canal from the Red Sea to the Nile River, and Persepolis, a new capital. . . .

"Darius expanded and improved his empire's network of roads, including the Royal Road, which ran 1,700 miles from Susa (southwestern Persia) to Sardis (western Anatolia). This transportation network had great commercial, political, and military value. . . .

"Darius reaffirmed Persian support for Jewish efforts to rebuild their Temple in Jerusalem, originally approved by Cyrus (Ezra 4:24). Zerubbabel, Jeshua, the prophets Haggai and Zechariah, and the rest of the population of Jerusalem completed and dedicated their new Temple in the sixth year of Darius's reign (Ezra 6:1–15)" (Holzapfel, et al., *Jehovah and the World of the Old Testament*, 355, 357).

"'Third: The living prophet is more important to us than a dead prophet.

"'Fourth: The prophet will never lead the Church astray.

"'Fifth: The prophet is not required to have any particular earthly training or credentials to speak on any subject or act on any matter at any time.

"'Sixth: The prophet does not have to say "Thus saith the Lord" to give us scripture.

"'Seventh: The prophet tells us what we need to know, not always what we want to know.

"'Eighth: The prophet is not limited by men's reasoning.

"'Ninth: The prophet can receive revelation on any matter, temporal or spiritual.

"'Tenth: The prophet may be involved in civic matters.

"'Eleventh: The two groups who have the greatest difficulty in following the prophet are the proud who are learned and the proud who are rich.

"'Twelfth: The prophet will not necessarily be popular with the world or the worldly.

"'Thirteenth: The prophet and his counselors make up the First Presidency—the highest quorum in the Church.

"'Fourteenth: [Follow] . . . the living prophet and the First Presidency . . . and be blessed; reject them and suffer.'

"Brothers and sisters . . . we can choose to follow the prophet, or we can look to the arm of flesh. May we have the wisdom to trust in and follow the counsel of the living prophets and apostles" (Duncan, "Our Very Survival," 35–36).

Why would king Darius allow the Jews to renew their work on the temple? (6:1–3) "The Persian King Darius seems, like Cyrus, to have felt some motivation to please 'the God of heaven.' . . . With the king's political and economic help and with the spiritual guidance of the prophets Haggai and Zechariah complementing the work of the priests and Levites, the work prospered" (Rasmussen, *Latter-day Saint Commentary on the Old Testament*, 371). "Darius recognized the role of God in human affairs. During his reign, Darius adopted the religion of Zoroastrianism for the Persian Empire. Darius probably thought that the god he worshiped also wanted the temple of Judah rebuilt. And, the decrees of one king were often honored by his successors" (*Old Testament Student Manual: 1 Kings–Malachi*, 321).

What were Achmetha and Medes? (6:2) "*Achmetha* (i.e., Ecbatana; v.2) was one of the four capitals (along with Babylon, Persepolis, and Susa) of the Persian Empire. Located in what is today the Iranian city of Hamadan. . . . The *Medes* were a people whose homeland was Media, in northwestern Iran. They were an Indo-European tribe related to the Persians. After the rise of Cyrus in 550 B.C., they became subordinate to the Persians" (*Zondervan KJV Commentary*, 645).

What did king Darius do to endorse the rebuilding of the temple? (6:3–5) "Darius searched the records and found the decree made by Cyrus. He issued his own directives to the Satrap ('the governor on this side of the river') that not only should the Jews be allowed to build, but that they should be aided in doing so. He also threatened punishment for any who tried to hinder them" (Muhlestein, *Scripture Study Made Simple*, 304).

Who was Tatnai? (6:6–8) "King Darius made two decrees: that the decree of Cyrus be sought, and when found, that it be vigorously implemented. Tatnai, the governor 'beyond the river,' may well have regretted having ever brought up the matter, for he was commanded to cease his obstruction and even contribute to the building project" (Rasmussen, *Latter-day Saint Commentary on the Old Testament*, 371).

2 And there was found at Achmetha, in the palace that *is* in the province of the Medes, a roll, and therein *was* a record thus written:

3 In the first year of Cyrus the king *the same* Cyrus the king made a decree *concerning* the house of God at Jerusalem, Let the house be builded, the place where they offered sacrifices, and let the foundations thereof be strongly laid; the height thereof threescore cubits, *and* the breadth thereof threescore cubits;

4 *With* three rows of great stones, and a row of new timber: and let the expenses be given out of the king's house:

5 And also let the golden and silver vessels of the house of God, which Nebuchadnezzar took forth out of the temple which *is* at Jerusalem, and brought unto Babylon, be restored, and brought again unto the temple which *is* at Jerusalem, *every one* to his place, and place *them* in the house of God.

6 Now *therefore,* Tatnai, governor beyond the river, Shethar-boznai, and your companions the Apharsachites, which *are* beyond the river, be ye far from thence:

7 Let the work of this house of God alone; let the governor of the Jews and the elders of the Jews build this house of God in his place.

8 Moreover I make a decree what ye shall do to the elders of these Jews for the building of this house of God: that of the king's goods, *even* of the tribute beyond the river, forthwith expenses be given unto these men, that they be not hindered.

9 And that which they have need of, both young bullocks, and rams, and lambs, for the burnt offerings of the God of heaven, wheat, salt, wine, and oil, according to the appointment of the priests which *are* at Jerusalem, let it be given them day by day without fail:

10 That they may offer sacrifices of sweet savours unto the God of heaven, and pray for the life of the king, and of his sons.

11 Also I have made a decree, that whosoever shall alter this word, let timber be pulled down from his house, and being set up, let him be hanged thereon; and let his house be made a dunghill for this.

12 And the God that hath caused his name to dwell there destroy all kings and people, that shall put to their hand to alter *and* to destroy this house of God which *is* at Jerusalem. I Darius have made a decree; let it be done with speed.

13 ¶ Then Tatnai, governor on this side the river, Shethar-boznai, and their companions, according to that which Darius the king had sent, so they did speedily.

14 And the elders of the Jews builded, and they prospered through the prophesying of Haggai the prophet and Zechariah the son of Iddo. And they builded, and finished *it,* according to the commandment of the God of Israel, and according to the commandment of Cyrus, and Darius, and Artaxerxes king of Persia.

15 And this house was finished on the third day of the month Adar, which was in the sixth year of the reign of Darius the king.

Ezra 6:13–15. With the King's Support and the Encouragement of the Prophets Haggai and Zechariah, the Temple Is Completed and Dedicated

How did the reconstructed temple differ from the original temple of Solomon? (6:15) "In many respects the Temple of Zerubbabel appeared poor in comparison with its splendid predecessor. . . . Critical scholars specify the following features characteristic of the Temple of Solomon and lacking in the Temple of Zerubbabel: (1) the Ark of the Covenant; (2) the sacred fire; (3) the Shekinah, or glory of the Lord, manifested of old as the Divine Presence; (4) the Urim and Thummim . . . ; (5) the genius or spirit of prophecy. . . . Notwithstanding these differences the Temple of Zerubbabel was recognized of God and was undoubtedly the site or seat of Divine revelation to duly constituted prophets" (Talmage, *House of the Lord*, 42–43). ⊕

Summary of Ezra 6:16–22

The dedication of the temple brings great joy and happiness to the children of Israel. Priests offer sacred offerings and sacrifices. The year following the dedication, the Jews restore the feasts of the Passover and unleavened bread with their festivals in the new temple.

Ezra 7:1–11. The Families That Travel to Jerusalem from Babylon Are Listed; Ezra Prepares His Heart to Seek the Law of the Lord

Who was Ezra? (7:1) "The Lord raised up a Levite, a direct descendant of Aaron, named Ezra (see Ezra 7:1–5). Born in captivity, Ezra was inspired to ask Artaxerxes, king of Persia, for permission to lead another group of Jews back to Jerusalem in 459 B.C. (see Ezra 7:6–7). The king granted him everything he asked, providing him with an impressive letter of introduction and credentials that entitled Ezra to whatever he and his group needed during their journey (see Ezra 7:11–27).

"Now, Ezra was no ordinary priest of Aaron, for he was a 'ready scribe in the law of Moses . . . even a scribe of the words of the commandments of the Lord, and of his statutes to Israel' (Ezra 7:6, 11)" (Garner, "Ezra Unfolds the Scriptures," 48).

What was Ezra's role among the people? (7:6) "Although the entire book was named after Ezra, the first time he is mentioned in the book is 7:1. A listing of his genealogy ([7:1–5]) proves he is a descendant of Aaron and thus entitled to the priesthood. Throughout the rest of the book, Ezra is referred to by such titles as 'the priest, the scribe, even a scribe of the words of the commandments of the Lord' (v. 11); the title *prophet* is not used for Ezra.

"The letter from King Artaxerxes gives permission to Ezra 'to set magistrates and judges, which may judge all the people that are beyond the river'; Ezra thus held some civil power over the people to go with his priestly authority" (Ludlow, *Companion to Your Study of the Old Testament*, 255).

CHAPTER 7

Ezra goes up to Jerusalem—Artaxerxes provides for beautifying the temple and sustains the Jews in their worship.

1 Now after these things, in the reign of Artaxerxes king of Persia, Ezra the son of Seraiah, the son of Azariah, the son of Hilkiah,

2 The son of Shallum, the son of Zadok, the son of Ahitub,

3 The son of Amariah, the son of Azariah, the son of Meraioth,

4 The son of Zerahiah, the son of Uzzi, the son of Bukki,

5 The son of Abishua, the son of Phinehas, the son of Eleazar, the son of Aaron the chief priest:

6 This Ezra went up from Babylon; and he *was* a ready scribe in the law of Moses, which the LORD God of Israel had given: and the king granted him all his request, according to the hand of the LORD his God upon him.

7 And there went up *some* of the children of Israel, and of the priests, and the Levites, and the singers, and the porters, and the Nethinims, unto Jerusalem, in the seventh year of Artaxerxes the king.

8 And he came to Jerusalem in the fifth month, which *was* in the seventh year of the king.

9 For upon the first *day* of the first month began he to go up from Babylon, and on the first *day* of the fifth month came he to Jerusalem, according to the good hand of his God upon him.

10 For Ezra had prepared his heart to seek the law of the LORD, and to do *it,* and to teach in Israel statutes and judgments.

How can I prepare my heart to be obedient to God's law? (7:10) "The idea that scripture reading can lead to inspiration and revelation opens the door to the truth that a scripture is not limited to what it meant when it was written but may also include what that scripture means to a reader today. Even more, scripture reading may also lead to current revelation on whatever else the Lord wishes to communicate to the reader at that time. We do not overstate the point when we say that the scriptures can be a Urim and Thummim to assist each of us to receive personal revelation" (Oaks, "Scripture Reading and Revelation," 8). ⊕

11 ¶ Now this *is* the copy of the letter that the king Artaxerxes gave unto Ezra the priest, the scribe, *even* a scribe of the words of the commandments of the LORD, and of his statutes to Israel.

What was Ezra's role as a scribe? (7:11) "The word *scribe* 'does not merely signify a *speedy writer* or an *excellent penman*, but one who was eminently skillful in expounding the law.' Ezra was a teacher, well versed in the scriptures, who had devoted himself to the study and observance of their commands and decrees. Furthermore, he 'had prepared his heart to seek the law of the Lord, and to do it' (Ezra 7:10).

"Ezra and his group made the difficult journey of about 1,100 miles in just four months, so that Ezra could 'teach in Israel statutes and judgments' (Ezra 7:10). Thus the Lord had made ready a man of God to end the long famine 'of hearing the words of the Lord' (see Amos 8:11–12)" (Garner, "Ezra Unfolds the Scriptures," 48).

Summary of Ezra 7:12–28

In a letter to Ezra, Artaxerxes gives him authority to organize Jewish leaders in Jerusalem and provide for beautifying the temple. He also gives him the resources he needs to complete this task.

CHAPTER 8

Those who go up from Babylon to Jerusalem are listed—The Levites are called to accompany them—Ezra and the people fast and pray for and gain guidance and protection in going to Jerusalem.

Summary of Ezra 8

A genealogy of the major families who traveled with Ezra to Jerusalem is given. Ezra finds that there are no Levites among them, and sends to the city for priests to minister to the people. They offer sacrifices of burnt offerings, and the gold, silver, and sacred vessels are carried to Jerusalem and presented to the high priest.

Summary of Ezra 9

"When Ezra, some time after his arrival, was in the temple at Jerusalem, the princes of the people informed him that the Israelites had mingled themselves by marriage with the people of the lands (Ezra 9:1–2). Deeply moved by this communication, he sat astonished till the time of the evening sacrifice, while all who feared God's word assembled about him [Ezra 9:3–4]. At the evening sacrifice he fell upon his knees and prayed, making a touching confession of sin before God, in the name of the congregation [Ezra 9:5–15]" (Keil and Delitzsch, *Commentary* [on Introduction to Ezra 9]). "In his prayer, Ezra confessed his shame and concern for his people and recognized the grace and patience of God. He contrasted the Lord's grace with the infidelity, carelessness, and rebelliousness of Israel (Ezra 9:4–15; compare the prayer of Nephi, son of Helaman, in Hel. 7:6–29)" (Rasmussen, *Latter-day Saint Commentary on the Old Testament*, 373–74).

Summary of Ezra 10

Ezra was particularly troubled by the non-covenant marriages of the people, and saw that they "were 'doing according to [the] abominations . . . of the Canaanites, the Hittites, the Perizzites, the Jebusites, the Ammonites, the Moabites, the Egyptians, and the Amorites.' Marriage with these exact groups had been specifically forbidden by the Lord (see Ex. 23:20–33; Deut. 7:1–6). . . . 'All the congregation' agreed to separate themselves 'from the people of the land, and from [their foreign] wives,' and the list of the offenders included 'sons of priests' (vs. 18–22), 'Levites' (v. 23), 'the singers' (v. 24), and '[others] of Israel' (vs. 25–43)" (Ludlow, *Companion to Your Study of the Old Testament*, 255).

CHAPTER 9

Many Jews intermarry with the Canaanites and others and follow their abominations—Ezra prays and confesses the sins of all the people.

CHAPTER 10

The Jews covenant to put away their wives taken from the Canaanites and others—Ezra assembles the people at Jerusalem—The Levites who married non-Israelite women are listed.

THE BOOK OF NEHEMIAH

Introduction

The books of Ezra and Nehemiah are important historical texts that can help us understand the Jewish people's return from Babylon. The books of Nehemiah and Ezra "were originally considered one book, which constituted a continuation of the history of Israel given in 1 and 2 Chronicles. The last two verses of 2 Chronicles (2 Chron. 36:22–23) are repeated in Ezra 1:1–3. . . . Chronicles was written sometime after the return of the Jews from Babylon, and the records of Ezra and Nehemiah were added to it later, perhaps around 400 B.C. Ezra 7–10 and Nehemiah constitute the last chapter in this history of Israel. Although the Jews seemed determined to neglect the law and the prophets were taken from them, the work of these two pious men demonstrated that the Lord was still willing to grant his wayward people some degree of help and prosperity" (Lamoreaux, "Work of Ezra and Nehemiah," 374–75).

"Nehemiah stands out as one of the noble men in the Old Testament. As he fulfilled a necessary mission in his day, he demonstrated the highest level of dedication and courage, both in the practical matter of rebuilding the walls of Jerusalem and also in the spirit matter of rebuilding the religious life of his people" (*Old Testament Student Manual: 1 Kings–Malachi*, 335).

John Dummelow explained: "The book of Nehemiah carries the history of the Jewish people down to a later date than any other of the avowedly historical works in the canon of the [Old Testament]. Its interest is manifold, since it describes not only the rebuilding of the walls of Jerusalem, but the reconstruction of the Jewish ecclesiastical organisation" (*John Dummelow's Commentary* [on Introduction to Nehemiah]).

Raymond Brown thoughtfully observed: "Nehemiah is a visible reminder to the Israelite people of the unchanging mercy of God. Life has changed for them, and some of their treasured institutions were no more, but the Lord was with them, raising up new people to refine and invigorate the vulnerable community. A trusted wine steward in a pagan palace becomes God's instrument for Israel's renewal" (*Message of Nehemiah*, 17).

CHAPTER 1

Nehemiah mourns, fasts, and prays for the Jews in Jerusalem.

1 The words of Nehemiah the son of Hachaliah. And it came to pass in the month Chisleu, in the twentieth year, as I was in Shushan the palace,

2 That Hanani, one of my brethren, came, he and *certain* men of Judah; and I asked them concerning the Jews that had escaped, which were left of the captivity, and concerning Jerusalem.

Nehemiah 1:1–3. Hanani Reports to Nehemiah about Jerusalem

Who was Nehemiah? (1:1) Nehemiah was a Jew living in exile. Though not much is known about his background, he likely "was born after Cyrus decreed that the Jews were allowed to return to their homeland" (*Old Testament Student Manual: 1 Kings–Malachi*, 335). The record does state that "Nehemiah was a cup-bearer for the king of Persia. This role, which resembles that of a kind of personal butler, was very important, since it was up to the cup-bearer to ensure that the king was not poisoned and that he was taken care of. Thus, the cup-bearer was usually a person very trusted by and close to the king. Nehemiah would make two different trips to rebuild Jerusalem, each one sanctioned by the king" (Muhlestein, *Scripture Study Made Simple*, 308).

Nehemiah 1:4–11. Nehemiah Prays and Fasts for the Jews in Jerusalem

What can we learn from Nehemiah's spiritual devotion? (1:4–6) Nehemiah's prayers throughout his book are instructive about his faith in God. "It begins with prayer in Persia (1:4) and closes with prayer in Jerusalem (13:31). . . . Here is a believer who hurries to the place of prayer to share his present griefs (1:4), confess his past failures (1:6–7) and discover his future work (1:11). . . .

"Nehemiah's immediate reaction to the news of his people's trouble was to go into the presence of God. Throughout the book this gifted leader is vividly portrayed as a man of earnest prayer [including] this, the first of his nine recorded prayers" (Brown, *Message of Nehemiah*, 22, 33).

Why was Nehemiah distressed over Hanani's report on the condition in Jerusalem? (1:4) "The lack of a city wall meant that the people were defenseless against their enemies. . . . When Nebuchadnezzar assaulted Jerusalem, he battered and broke down the walls around it (2Ki 25:10). Most, however, do not believe that Nehemiah's distress was caused by Nebuchadnezzar's destruction in 586 [B.C.] but by the episode of Ezr 4:7–23. The Jews had attempted to rebuild the walls earlier in the reign of Artaxerxes I; but after the protest of Rehum and Shimshai, the king ordered the Jews to desist" (*NIV Study Bible* [1985], 694).

What qualifies a person for God's mercy rather than His "terrible" justice? (1:5) The meaning of "the great and terrible God" in Hebrew is "the God, the great, the revered" (see Nehemiah 1:5*a*). Stephen Robinson, writing about this, said: "The choice before us is mercy or justice. Either choice can be accommodated, and either choice is compatible with the nature and plan of God, but, as in the choice between the Lord and Satan, there are no third alternatives. Again, life has default settings, and they are set for justice. We can choose the mercy that is offered through the gospel covenant, but if we refuse that mercy, we will receive justice" (*Believing Christ*, 60).

3 And they said unto me, The remnant that are left of the captivity there in the province *are* in great affliction and reproach: the wall of Jerusalem also *is* broken down, and the gates thereof are burned with fire.

4 ¶ And it came to pass, when I heard these words, that I sat down and wept, and mourned *certain* days, and fasted, and prayed before the God of heaven,

5 And said, I beseech thee, O LORD God of heaven, the great and terrible God, that keepeth covenant and mercy for them that love him and observe his commandments:

6 Let thine ear now be attentive, and thine eyes open, that thou mayest hear the prayer of thy servant, which I pray before thee now, day and night, for the children of Israel thy servants, and confess the sins of the children of Israel, which we have sinned against thee: both I and my father's house have sinned.

7 We have dealt very corruptly against thee, and have not kept the commandments, nor the statutes, nor the judgments, which thou commandedst thy servant Moses.

8 Remember, I beseech thee, the word that thou commandedst thy servant Moses, saying, *If* ye transgress, I will scatter you abroad among the nations:

9 But *if* ye turn unto me, and keep my commandments, and do them; though there were of you cast out unto the uttermost part of the heaven, *yet* will I gather them from thence, and will bring them unto the place that I have chosen to set my name there.

10 Now these *are* thy servants and thy people, whom thou hast redeemed by thy great power, and by thy strong hand.

11 O Lord, I beseech thee, let now thine ear be attentive to the prayer of thy servant, and to the prayer of thy servants, who desire to fear thy name: and prosper, I pray thee, thy servant this day, and grant him mercy in the sight of this man. For I was the king's cupbearer.

CHAPTER 2

Artaxerxes sends Nehemiah to Jerusalem—Sanballat and others oppose Nehemiah in rebuilding the walls and gates of Jerusalem.

1 And it came to pass in the month Nisan, in the twentieth year of Artaxerxes the king, *that* wine *was* before him: and I took up the wine, and gave *it* unto the king. Now I had not been *beforetime* sad in his presence.

2 Wherefore the king said unto me, Why *is* thy countenance sad, seeing thou *art* not sick? this *is* nothing *else* but sorrow of heart. Then I was very sore afraid,

3 And said unto the king, Let the king live for ever: why should not my countenance be sad, when the city, the place of my fathers' sepulchres, *lieth* waste, and the gates thereof are consumed with fire?

What does the Lord promise scattered Israel? (1:8–9) Anciently the tribes of Israel rebelled, "killed the prophets[,] and were punished by the Lord. Ten tribes were carried captive into Assyria. . . . Two remaining tribes continued a short time and then . . . were taken captive into Babylon. . . .

"God's promise for the gathering of scattered Israel was equally emphatic. Isaiah, for example, foresaw that in the latter days the Lord would send 'swift messengers' to these people who were so 'scattered and peeled' [Isaiah 18:2, 7].

"This promise of the gathering, woven all through the fabric of the scriptures, will be fulfilled just as surely as were the prophecies of the scattering of Israel" (Nelson, "Gathering of Scattered Israel," 79).

What did Nehemiah understand about the extent of God's love? (1:10–11) In his pleading with the Lord, saying that Jews were "thy servant and thy people," Nehemiah demonstrated his doctrinal understanding of the teachings of the law of Moses regarding God's grace and love given to Israel because of His covenant with them. The Lord told Moses that even if the people were scattered "unto the uttermost part of the heaven" (Deuteronomy 30:1–5), He would still gather them. Obviously, even those who have died and are in the spirit world are not beyond the reach of the Lord who is gathering His people.

Nehemiah 2:1–11. King Artaxerxes Allows Nehemiah to Go to Jerusalem

Who was Artaxerxes? (2:1) Artaxerxes was the king of Persia during this time period. Known also as "Longimanus, [he was a] son of Xerxes . . . , 465–425 B.C.; [he hindered] Jews from building (Ezra 4:7–23); [and gave] commission to Ezra (6:14; 7:1–21; 8:1) and to Nehemiah (Neh. 2:1; 5:14; 13:6)" (Bible Dictionary, "Artaxerxes").

4 Then the king said unto me, For what dost thou make request? So I prayed to the God of heaven.

5 And I said unto the king, If it please the king, and if thy servant have found favour in thy sight, that thou wouldest send me unto Judah, unto the city of my fathers' sepulchres, that I may build it.

6 And the king said unto me, (the queen also sitting by him,) For how long shall thy journey be? and when wilt thou return? So it pleased the king to send me; and I set him a time.

7 Moreover I said unto the king, If it please the king, let letters be given me to the governors beyond the river, that they may convey me over till I come into Judah;

Why did Nehemiah request letters from the king and where is "beyond the river"? (2:7) "Nehemiah . . . requested from the king letters to the governors beyond (west of) the river (Euphrates), to allow him to travel unmolested through their provinces to Judah . . . ; and a letter to Asaph, the keeper (inspector) of the royal forests, to give him timber to make beams for the gates of the citadel by the temple, and for the walls of the city, and for the governor's own house. These requests were also granted" (Keil and Delitzsch, *Commentary* [on Nehemiah 2:7–8]). The phrase "beyond the river" refers to the west side of the Euphrates River, which was then occupied by the Persian Empire (see Nehemiah 2:7*a*).

8 And a letter unto Asaph the keeper of the king's forest, that he may give me timber to make beams for the gates of the palace which *appertained* to the house, and for the wall of the city, and for the house that I shall enter into. And the king granted me, according to the good hand of my God upon me.

9 ¶ Then I came to the governors beyond the river, and gave them the king's letters. Now the king had sent captains of the army and horsemen with me.

10 When Sanballat the Horonite, and Tobiah the servant, the Ammonite, heard *of it,* it grieved them exceedingly that there was come a man to seek the welfare of the children of Israel.

Why would Nehemiah need wood from the king's forest? (2:8) "The gates of the city were typically made of wood. Babylon had burned the gates of Jerusalem so that nothing was left. The areas around Jerusalem do not grow the kinds of trees that could be used to build large gates, which was why David and Solomon sought cedars from the city-states of Lebanon. Thus it is important that Artaxerxes ordered the keeper of his forests to provide Nehemiah with the wood needed to rebuild the gates and certain houses. Without wood from elsewhere in the empire, Nehemiah could not have been successful" (Muhlestein, *Essential Old Testament Companion,* 311).

Who was Sanballat? (2:10) Sanballat was the governor of Samaria who opposed Nehemiah. He and "the governors of other nearby areas opposed the plans of the Jews for Jerusalem and resented the protection given them by the Persian king. A deep bitterness had developed between the Samaritans and the Jews

11 So I came to Jerusalem, and was there
three days.

17 ¶ Then said I unto them, Ye see the distress that we *are* in, how Jerusalem *lieth*
waste, and the gates thereof are burned with
fire: come, and let us build up the wall of
Jerusalem, that we be no more a reproach.

18 Then I told them of the hand of my God
which was good upon me; as also the king's
words that he had spoken unto me. And
they said, Let us rise up and build. So they
strengthened their hands for *this* good *work.*
19 But when Sanballat the Horonite, and
Tobiah the servant, the Ammonite, and
Geshem the Arabian, heard *it,* they laughed
us to scorn, and despised us, and said, What
is this thing that ye do? will ye rebel against
the king?
20 Then answered I them, and said unto
them, The God of heaven, he will prosper us;
therefore we his servants will arise and build:
but ye have no portion, nor right, nor memorial, in Jerusalem.

who had returned with Zerubbabel [see Ezra 4]. For Nehemiah to return with full power from the emperor to refortify Jerusalem was a great setback for the Samaritans, and they openly opposed it. Sanballat of Samaria led this group (see v. 19) and made it necessary for Nehemiah to arm those who worked on the walls of Jerusalem [see Nehemiah 4, 6]" (*Old Testament Student Manual: 1 Kings–Malachi,* 335).

Summary of Nehemiah 2:12–16

Nehemiah secretly views the destroyed walls and gates of Jerusalem and desires to rebuild them.

Nehemiah 2:17–20. Nehemiah Announces They Will Rebuild Jerusalem's Walls

Why was Nehemiah adamant that they rebuild the walls of Jerusalem? (2:17–20) "Nehemiah's call to rebuild the walls of Jerusalem was much more than a simple renovation project. It was a call for the Jews to take control of their lives, land, and destiny as the people of God.

"But when Sanballat, Tobiah, and others heard Nehemiah's plan, they laughed and ridiculed him and the people. They did not want the Jews to rise again to political prominence in the region. But Nehemiah answered them, 'The God of heaven, he will prosper us; therefore we his servants will arise and build' (Neh. 2:20)" (Amistad, "Wanted: Modern Nehemiahs," 45).

How are we blessed by following righteous leaders? (2:18) "There are many today who find themselves spiritually similar to that of the Jews in Nehemiah's time—in danger of long-term captivity because of unrighteousness. In God's great mercy, He gives His children opportunities to return to Him.

"What helped the Jews succeed in the face of tremendous opposition? They had a great leader—Nehemiah. He was humble, self-motivated, confident in the will of God, willing to take the lead, full of faith, fearless, an organizer, obedient, and just. He was able to gain the love, trust, and confidence of his people.

"Today we are blessed with a living prophet, apostles, and many faithful men and women who lead the Church" (Amistad, "Wanted: Modern Nehemiahs," 46).

Why were Sanballat, Tobiah, and Gehshem opposed to the building of the walls? (2:19) "From their perspective, Nehemiah's appointment had disrupted the political balance of that region and put Sanballat and Tobiah out of a job as far as Jerusalem and Judah were concerned. . . .

"From a political perspective, biblical and other evidence suggests that Sanballat's administrative responsibilities for Samaria may have included jurisdiction over the greater Jerusalem area. Now, Nehemiah had arrived in the city with the king's specific authority, and the Samaritan leader was angry that he had been robbed of his former authority over the Israelite people" (Brown, *Message of Nehemiah*, 60). ⊕

Summary of Nehemiah 3

Under Nehemiah's direction, families and other groups rebuild the portions of Jerusalem's walls and gates nearest to their homes. The work proceeds in a counterclockwise manner, beginning with the Sheep Gate on the city's northeast side.

Eliashib, the high priest, joins with other priests to help in this project beginning at the sheep gate. "From the fact of its restoration by the priests the inference has been drawn that the gate was near the Temple. Probably it was so named because the small cattle brought into the city for sacrifice passed through this gate, situated in the north-east of the capital" (Slotki, *Daniel, Ezra, Nehemiah*, 193).

Nehemiah 4:1–12. Nehemiah Seeks God's Help in Trying to Rebuild the Walls of Jerusalem

Why did Nehemiah face opposition to the work of rebuilding the walls at Jerusalem? (4:1–3) Those who seek to do God's work will always face opposition from those who do not believe. "We may remark here, in general, that the enemies of God's work [rebuilding Jerusalem's walls and gates] endeavor by all means to discredit and destroy it, and those who are employed in it" (*Adam Clarke's Commentary* [on Nehemiah 4:2]).

CHAPTER 3

The names and order of those who help to build the walls and gates of Jerusalem are listed.

CHAPTER 4

The Jews' enemies seek to prevent them from rebuilding the walls of Jerusalem—Nehemiah arms the laborers and keeps the work progressing.

1 But it came to pass, that when Sanballat heard that we builded the wall, he was wroth, and took great indignation, and mocked the Jews.

2 And he spake before his brethren and the army of Samaria, and said, What do these feeble Jews? will they fortify themselves? will they sacrifice? will they make an end in a day? will they revive the stones out of the heaps of the rubbish which are burned?

3 Now Tobiah the Ammonite *was* by him, and he said, Even that which they build, if a fox go up, he shall even break down their stone wall.

4 Hear, O our God; for we are despised: and turn their reproach upon their own head, and give them for a prey in the land of captivity:

5 And cover not their iniquity, and let not their sin be blotted out from before thee: for they have provoked *thee* to anger before the builders.

6 So built we the wall; and all the wall was joined together unto the half thereof: for the people had a mind to work.

7 ¶ But it came to pass, *that* when Sanballat, and Tobiah, and the Arabians, and the Ammonites, and the Ashdodites, heard that the walls of Jerusalem were made up, *and* that the breaches began to be stopped, then they were very wroth,

8 And conspired all of them together to come *and* to fight against Jerusalem, and to hinder it.

9 Nevertheless we made our prayer unto our God, and set a watch against them day and night, because of them.

10 And Judah said, The strength of the bearers of burdens is decayed, and *there is* much rubbish; so that we are not able to build the wall.

11 And our adversaries said, They shall not know, neither see, till we come in the midst among them, and slay them, and cause the work to cease.

12 And it came to pass, that when the Jews which dwelt by them came, they said unto us ten times, From all places whence ye shall return unto us *they will be upon you.*

13 ¶ Therefore set I in the lower places behind the wall, *and* on the higher places, I even set the people after their families with their swords, their spears, and their bows.

14 And I looked, and rose up, and said unto the nobles, and to the rulers, and to the rest of the people, Be not ye afraid of them:

How did Nehemiah and the people respond to the opposition from Sanballat and others? (4:4–6) "Nehemiah took action to meet that opposition: he prayed, set out guards and defenders, kept the workmen armed and encouraged their faith, and kept a trumpeter at hand to summon help if needed. Thus with vigilance, day and night, he moved the work forward despite problems external or internal" (Rasmussen, *Latter-day Saint Commentary on the Old Testament,* 378). Equally, when the Church faces opposition on different issues, instead of engaging in the fight, we should simply go about our work (see Packer, "Come, All Ye Sons of God," 69). ⊕

How were the workers affected by the tactics of their enemies ? (4:10–12) The Jews worked under duress as they labored on the wall, not only because of the hard work that taxed them physically, but also because of the persecution inflicted by outsiders that taxed them mentally. "The neighboring people under Sanballat of Samaria . . . [used] taunts and threats. . . . The builders temporarily [succumbed] to the difficulties of the work and their opponents' intimidation" (*New Oxford Annotated Bible* [2010], 690–91).

Nehemiah 4:13–23. Nehemiah Arms His People with Weapons and Continues to Build in Faith

How did Nehemiah inspire his people to resume work on the walls? (4:14) "Nehemiah's faith-filled and stirring leadership is proclaimed throughout the book that bears his name. When Sanballat, Tobiah, and other regional adversaries attempted to interrupt the work of rebuilding the walls and gates of Jerusalem, 'we made our prayer unto our God, and set a watch against them day and night' (Neh 4:9). Sounding somewhat like Captain Moroni (Alma 46:10–13), Nehemiah encouraged his people, 'Be not ye afraid of them: remember the Lord, which is great and terrible, and fight for your brethren, your sons, and your daughters, your wives, and your houses' (Neh 4:14)" (Holzapfel, et al., *Jehovah and the World of the Old Testament*, 370–71).

remember the Lord, *which is* great and terrible, and fight for your brethren, your sons, and your daughters, your wives, and your houses.

15 And it came to pass, when our enemies heard that it was known unto us, and God had brought their counsel to nought, that we returned all of us to the wall, every one unto his work.

16 And it came to pass from that time forth, *that* the half of my servants wrought in the work, and the other half of them held both the spears, the shields, and the bows, and the habergeons; and the rulers *were* behind all the house of Judah.

17 They which builded on the wall, and they that bare burdens, with those that laded, *every one* with one of his hands wrought in the work, and with the other *hand* held a weapon.

18 For the builders, every one had his sword girded by his side, and *so* builded. And he that sounded the trumpet *was* by me.

The Saints in Kirtland and Nauvoo Were Also Persecuted While Building Their Temples (Nehemiah 4:16–18)

"In every age when the people of God set out to build up Zion, the enemies of God do their best to stop it. The circumstances in Jerusalem of Nehemiah's time were almost duplicated when the Saints at Kirtland were trying to build the temple there. The mob was so determined to stop the building that the Saints had to arm themselves even while carrying on the work" (England, "Let Us Rise Up and Build").

Brigham Young recounted "the great Prophet Joseph, in the stone quarry, quarrying rock with his own hands; and the few then in the Church, following his example of obedience and diligence wherever most needed; with laborers on the walls, holding the sword in one hand to protect themselves from the mob, while they placed the stone and moved the trowel with the other, the Kirtland temple—the second house of the Lord, that we have any published record of on the earth, was so far completed as to be dedicated" (*Discourses of Brigham Young*, 415).

President George Q. Cannon remarked about the circumstances in which the Nauvoo Temple was built: "The workmen who labored upon [the Nauvoo Temple], were like the Jews in the days of Nehemiah, when they undertook to rebuild the walls of Jerusalem, and had to labor a portion of the time at least, and a great portion of it too, with their instruments of labor in one hand, and weapons to defend themselves in the other. We were surrounded by mobs, and living in a constant state, it may be said of fear, because of the threats which were made and the combinations which were formed, and the attacks upon our outlying settlements in the burning of houses, in the destruction of grain, in the shooting down of cattle, and in the driving out of the people from their homes" (in *Journal of Discourses*, 25:167).

19 ¶ And I said unto the nobles, and to the rulers, and to the rest of the people, The work *is* great and large, and we are separated upon the wall, one far from another.

20 In what place *therefore* ye hear the sound of the trumpet, resort ye thither unto us: our God shall fight for us.

21 So we laboured in the work: and half of them held the spears from the rising of the morning till the stars appeared.

22 Likewise at the same time said I unto the people, Let every one with his servant lodge within Jerusalem, that in the night they may be a guard to us, and labour on the day.

23 So neither I, nor my brethren, nor my servants, nor the men of the guard which followed me, none of us put off our clothes, *saving that* every one put them off for washing.

CHAPTER 5

Many Jews are in bondage to their fellow Jews—At Nehemiah's direction they are freed, their lands are restored, and the taking of usury is discontinued.

How did the Jews organize the work to finish building the wall? (4:21–23) "Interestingly, the dual assignments of guard duty and working on the construction did more than provide protection. It also gave some variety to the workers, resting them and improving their morale. Militarily, of course, the alliance of leaders mentioned in verse 7 could completely surround and overwhelm the Jews. But the plotters knew Nehemiah had the support of the powerful Persian government, which they feared. Of course, the greatest protection the Jews had was their faith in God" (*Quest Study Bible* [1994], 649).

How did they sacrifice in rebuilding the walls and gates of the city? (4:23) "Nehemiah was so fervent in the work that he got his people to work from sunup to sundown. Because they had to be ready to defend themselves, no one went back to their own farms or homes, but rather slept in Jerusalem, fully clothed and weapons by their side, so they could have a full militia ready to defend the city at any given moment. Surely this long and stressful work situation wore upon the people, and we will see that they paid the price. But their dedication also paid off" (Muhlestein, *Scripture Study Made Simple*, 311). ⊕

Summary of Nehemiah 5

"The effectiveness of Nehemiah's leadership is seen again in his response to the complaints of the poor and of the recently returned exiles who were impoverished by drought, taxes, debts, and many other demands upon their means and labor to help build the wall. Evidently the Jews who had returned earlier had greater wealth, and the poorer ones had borrowed from them. Unable to repay, they had indentured sons and daughters into service or bondage. Nehemiah's anger, rebuke, persuasion, and good example brought about relief" (Rasmussen, *Latter-day Saint Commentary on the Old Testament*, 378). The people are released from their debts upon Nehemiah's becoming governor.

Nehemiah 6:1–14. Sanballat and Tobiah Secretly Combine against Nehemiah

How did Nehemiah know that this invitation was a plot against him? (6:1–2) "The invitation appeared innocent, but was a thinly disguised death sentence. . . . The governor was discerning, resolute and inflexible. . . .

"He was a man of prayer and unlikely to receive an invitation of this sort without taking it unto God's presence. . . . Now he was being warned by the Lord that this consultation idea was nothing but artful and highly dangerous bluff. The time Nehemiah spent with God made him sensitive to divine guidance and warning. He was prompted by God to refuse the invitation, knowing that his enemies were set on his destruction" (Brown, *Message of Nehemiah*, 101).

How can "doing a great work" bless our lives? (6:3–4) "Nehemiah's enemies became more desperate. Four times they entreated him to leave the safety of the city and meet with them under the pretense of resolving the conflict, but Nehemiah knew that their intent was to do him harm. Each time they approached him, he responded with the same answer: 'I am doing a great work, so that I cannot come down' [Nehemiah 6:3].

"What a remarkable response! With that clear and unchanging purpose of heart and mind, with that great resolve, the walls of Jerusalem rose until they were rebuilt in an astonishing 52 days [see Nehemiah 6:15]" (Uchtdorf, "We Are Doing a Great Work and Cannot Come Down," 61).

Why did Sanballat send "an open letter"? (6:5) Sanballat "refers to rumors among the neighboring nations that the real purpose of the wall was to rebel and to proclaim Nehemiah as king. . . .

"The scheming of Sanballat became clear to Nehemiah. Another proof of Sanballat's dishonest intentions is that he sent *an open letter*, i.e., not sealed, as was the custom in those days. With the open letter, which could be read by anyone on the way, he was responsible for the further spreading of the rumor" (Fensham, *Books of Ezra and Nehemiah*, 201, 202).

CHAPTER 6

Sanballat engages in intrigue against Nehemiah and the building of the wall—The Jews finish the construction of the wall.

1 Now it came to pass, when Sanballat, and Tobiah, and Geshem the Arabian, and the rest of our enemies, heard that I had builded the wall, and *that* there was no breach left therein; (though at that time I had not set up the doors upon the gates;)

2 That Sanballat and Geshem sent unto me, saying, Come, let us meet together in *some one of* the villages in the plain of Ono. But they thought to do me mischief.

3 And I sent messengers unto them, saying, I *am* doing a great work, so that I cannot come down: why should the work cease, whilst I leave it, and come down to you?

4 Yet they sent unto me four times after this sort; and I answered them after the same manner.

5 Then sent Sanballat his servant unto me in like manner the fifth time with an open letter in his hand;

6 Wherein *was* written, It is reported among the heathen, and Gashmu saith *it, that* thou and the Jews think to rebel: for which cause thou buildest the wall, that thou mayest be their king, according to these words.

7 And thou hast also appointed prophets to preach of thee at Jerusalem, saying, *There is* a king in Judah: and now shall it be reported to the king according to these words. Come now therefore, and let us take counsel together.

8 Then I sent unto him, saying, There are no such things done as thou sayest, but thou feignest them out of thine own heart.

9 For they all made us afraid, saying, Their hands shall be weakened from the work, that it be not done. Now therefore, *O God,* strengthen my hands.

10 Afterward I came unto the house of Shemaiah the son of Delaiah the son of Mehetabeel, who *was* shut up; and he said, Let us meet together in the house of God, within the temple, and let us shut the doors of the temple: for they will come to slay thee; yea, in the night will they come to slay thee.

11 And I said, Should such a man as I flee? and who *is there,* that, *being* as I *am,* would go into the temple to save his life? I will not go in.

12 And, lo, I perceived that God had not sent him; but that he pronounced this prophecy against me: for Tobiah and Sanballat had hired him.

13 Therefore *was* he hired, that I should be afraid, and do so, and sin, and *that* they might have *matter* for an evil report, that they might reproach me.

14 My God, think thou upon Tobiah and Sanballat according to these their works, and on the prophetess Noadiah, and the rest of the prophets, that would have put me in fear.

15 ¶ So the wall was finished in the twenty and fifth *day* of *the month* Elul, in fifty and two days.

16 And it came to pass, that when all our enemies heard *thereof,* and all the heathen that *were* about us saw *these things,* they were much cast down in their own eyes: for they perceived that this work was wrought of our God.

Why did Shemaiah attempt to draw Nehemiah into the holy place of the temple? (6:10–13) After being hired by Sanballat (v. 12), "Shemaiah proposed that they [he and Nehemiah] enter the holy place to be safe from assassins. Shemaiah's suggestion was for Nehemiah to flee into the sanctuary. It was lawful for an Israelite to seek refuge at the altar outside the temple (see Ex. 21:13, 14), but only a priest could enter the holy place. Nehemiah's enemies were tempting him. If they could trap him in sin, this would discredit him and the work. Then people would cease to follow him, and the work on the wall would stop" (*Nelson Study Bible* [NKJV], 794).

Nehemiah 6:15–19. The Wall of Jerusalem Is Finished

How were Nehemiah and his people able to finish the work in such a short period of time? (6:15) "To the dismay of Sanballat and his allies, the work succeeded. People labored day and night for fifty-two days, apparently stopping only for Sabbaths" (Brown and Holzapfel, *Between the Testaments*, 25–26). ⊕

Why were Nehemiah's enemies "much cast down"? (6:16) The enemies who opposed the rebuilding of Jerusalem's walls were despondent because of the miraculous completion of the project. They had to acknowledge that it was God's work. A later Jewish sage, Gamaliel, counseled those opposed to the work of

Peter and John, "And now I say unto you, Refrain from these men, and let them alone: for if this counsel or this work be of men, it will come to nought: But if it be of God, ye cannot overthrow it; lest haply ye be found even to fight against God" (Acts 5:38–39).

17 ¶ Moreover in those days the nobles of Judah sent many letters unto Tobiah, and *the letters* of Tobiah came unto them.

18 For *there were* many in Judah sworn unto him, because he *was* the son in law of Shechaniah the son of Arah; and his son Johanan had taken the daughter of Meshullam the son of Berechiah.

19 Also they reported his good deeds before me, and uttered my words to him. *And* Tobiah sent letters to put me in fear.

Summary of Nehemiah 7

"The building of the wall being now concluded, Nehemiah first made arrangements for securing the city against hostile attacks (Nehemiah 7:1–3); then took measures to increase the inhabitants of Jerusalem (7:4–73)" (Keil and Delitzsch, *Commentary* [on Introduction to Nehemiah 7]). After Nehemiah placed people to oversee the protection of Jerusalem, he searched the genealogical records of those who had returned from Babylon, and found records which showed by lineage which men should hold the priesthood. Nehemiah "found this genealogical record [v. 5] from Israel's past and used it to inspire her present and future needs. In his hands, this century-old archive testifies afresh to the governor's priorities in the exercise of his stewardship. . . . There is more to this archive than a list of forgotten names; it is a declaration of a godly community's spiritual commitment" (Brown, *Message of Nehemiah*, 126).

CHAPTER 7

Provision is made to protect Jerusalem—The genealogy is given of the Jews who returned from Babylon—Priests without genealogical records are denied the priesthood.

Nehemiah 8:1–12. Ezra Reads the Law of Moses to the People

How did Ezra reward the faithful Jews? (8:1–2)

"Ezra the scribe, after bringing the people of Judah back to the land of Judea from their seventy-year captivity in Babylon, gathered them together so he could read the Old Testament to them. He translated as he read because the scriptures were written in Hebrew and the younger Jews spoke only Aramaic, the language of Babylon. Probably for the first time in their lives these Jews heard and understood the scriptures in their own tongue, and they wept and rejoiced (see Nehemiah 8)" (Matthews, *Bible! A Bible!* 4).

CHAPTER 8

Ezra reads and interprets the law of Moses to the people—They keep the Feast of Tabernacles.

1 And all the people gathered themselves together as one man into the street that *was* before the water gate; and they spake unto Ezra the scribe to bring the book of the law of Moses, which the LORD had commanded to Israel.

2 And Ezra the priest brought the law before the congregation both of men and women, and all that could hear with understanding, upon the first day of the seventh month.

3 And he read therein before the street that *was* before the water gate from the morning until midday, before the men and the women, and those that could understand; and the ears of all the people *were attentive* unto the book of the law.

Why was this reading of the Law so extraordinary? (8:3) "The reading of the law to the people by Ezra the scribe is of particular importance because it appears to have been the first time a synagogue, or a place to read and expound the scriptures, was established in Jerusalem after the return from Babylon" (*Old Testament Student Manual: 1 Kings–Malachi*, 336).

4 And Ezra the scribe stood upon a pulpit of wood, which they had made for the purpose; and beside him stood Mattithiah, and Shema, and Anaiah, and Urijah, and Hilkiah, and Maaseiah, on his right hand; and on his left hand, Pedaiah, and Mishael, and Malchiah, and Hashum, and Hashbadana, Zechariah, *and* Meshullam.

Why did they erect a wooden platform to read the Law? (8:4) "Surrounded by the elders, Ezra stood 'upon a pulpit of wood, which they had made for the purpose,' and read from the Law 'from morning until midday.' The makeshift platform was probably positioned just below the southern wall of the temple so that Ezra could see the people in an open area that sloped down toward the 'water gate,' located at the extreme south end of the city ('all the people gathered themselves together as one man into the street that was before the water gate' [Neh. 8:1])" (England, "Let Us Rise Up and Build"). This is similar to King Benjamin erecting his tower for his people to hear his address (see Mosiah 2–5).

5 And Ezra opened the book in the sight of all the people; (for he was above all the people;) and when he opened it, all the people stood up:

6 And Ezra blessed the LORD, the great God. And all the people answered, Amen, Amen, with lifting up their hands: and they bowed their heads, and worshipped the LORD with *their* faces to the ground.

7 Also Jeshua, and Bani, and Sherebiah, Jamin, Akkub, Shabbethai, Hodijah, Maaseiah, Kelita, Azariah, Jozabad, Hanan, Pelaiah, and the Levites, caused the people to understand the law: and the people *stood* in their place.

8 So they read in the book in the law of God distinctly, and gave the sense, and caused *them* to understand the reading.

What does it mean to give "sense" to the Law? (8:8) "The Israelites, having been lately brought out of the Babylonish captivity, in which they had continued seventy years, . . . were not only extremely corrupt, but it appears that they had in general lost the knowledge of the ancient Hebrew to such a degree, that when the book of the law was read, they did not understand it: but certain Levites stood by, and gave the sense, i.e., translated into [Aramaic]" (*Adam Clarke's Commentary* [on Nehemiah 8:17]).

9 ¶ And Nehemiah, which *is* the Tirshatha, and Ezra the priest the scribe, and the Levites that taught the people, said unto all the people, This day *is* holy unto the LORD your God; mourn not, nor weep. For all the people wept, when they heard the words of the law.

Why is the reading of the law (scriptures) so important today? (8:9) The Book of Mormon prophet Alma taught, "And now, as the preaching of the word had a great tendency to lead the people to do that which was just—yea, it had had more powerful effect upon the minds of the people than the sword, or anything else, which had happened unto them—therefore Alma thought it was expedient that they should try the virtue of the word of God" (Alma 31:5).

What does "joy of the Lord" mean in Hebrew? (8:10) Truman G. Madsen tells the story: "'I'm writing a book on joy,' said a rabbi to a colleague of mine in New York. That book found that one root of the word *joy* in the Old Testament is *chemdah*. When it is conjoined with the phrase 'of the Lord,' it means three things. It means gladness; it means togetherness or being joined one with another; and it means something about the temple. Nehemiah was the rebuilder of the temple. The phrase 'joy of the Lord' attends his invitation to the newly rebuilt temple" ("Joy of the Lord Is Your Strength (Nehemiah 8:10)," 1).

Nehemiah 8:13–18. The Feast of Tabernacles Is Observed according to the Law of Moses

How did the Jewish leaders and families respond after meeting with Ezra? (8:13–15) "Many priests and Levites help teach the law to the people.... Ezra and Nehemiah proclaim it a holy day.... Nehemiah tells the people to rejoice and to feast.... The heads of families gather the next day with Ezra in order to learn the law even better. They learn that they should be keeping the Feast of Tabernacles, so they go forward to keep the celebration. They all build booths and keep the festival for its full seven days, studying the law every day. When it finishes they hold a solemn assembly" (Muhlestein, *Essential Old Testament Companion*, 316). ⊕

10 Then he said unto them, Go your way, eat the fat, and drink the sweet, and send portions unto them for whom nothing is prepared: for *this* day *is* holy unto our Lord: neither be ye sorry; for the joy of the LORD is your strength.

11 So the Levites stilled all the people, saying, Hold your peace, for the day *is* holy; neither be ye grieved.

12 And all the people went their way to eat, and to drink, and to send portions, and to make great mirth, because they had understood the words that were declared unto them.

13 ¶ And on the second day were gathered together the chief of the fathers of all the people, the priests, and the Levites, unto Ezra the scribe, even to understand the words of the law.

14 And they found written in the law which the LORD had commanded by Moses, that the children of Israel should dwell in booths in the feast of the seventh month:

15 And that they should publish and proclaim in all their cities, and in Jerusalem,

Ezra and the Reading of the Law (Nehemiah 8:8)

"If Nehemiah chapter 8 follows chronologically the arrival of Ezra, he did not wait long. After all, Ezra carried the solemn charge to 'teach' to his people 'the laws of ... God' (Ezra 7:25).... It was October and the Feast of Tabernacles. Standing with friends and officials 'upon a pulpit of wood, which they had made for the purpose,' Ezra read until time for the midday meal. These friends and officials translated the Hebrew of Ezra's copy of the law into Aramaic so the audience could understand clearly the meaning, an indicator that people had begun to lose their abilities with Hebrew, the language of the country before the destruction of Jerusalem by Nebuchadnezzar (8:4–8). This is the first occasion we know of when an interpretation of scripture was made in another language. This practice would eventually grow into a written tradition that became known as the targums.... The response to Ezra's reading was touching: 'All the people wept, when they heard the words of the law' (8:9).

"Matters did not stop there. During each day of the feast, Ezra continued to read out of the Law (Nehemiah 8:13, 18), with an immediate impact. For example, when people learned they were to celebrate the Feast of Tabernacles by dwelling 'in booths' and by carrying 'olive branches and pine branches' and the like, they gladly conformed (8:14–17). Clearly, doing so was a learning experience for them. Moreover, at the end of the month, separating themselves from others in their midst, the Jews 'assembled with fasting' and entered 'into an oath, to walk in God's law, which was given by Moses' (9:1; 10:29). Significantly, they pledged to live in accord with the stipulations of the Law, including keeping the Sabbath properly, making the required donations to the temple, and not intermarrying with outsiders (10:30–39)" (Brown and Holzapfel, *Lost 500 Years*, 25).

saying, Go forth unto the mount, and fetch olive branches, and pine branches, and myrtle branches, and palm branches, and branches of thick trees, to make booths, as *it is* written.

16 ¶ So the people went forth, and brought *them,* and made themselves booths, every one upon the roof of his house, and in their courts, and in the courts of the house of God, and in the street of the water gate, and in the street of the gate of Ephraim.

17 And all the congregation of them that were come again out of the captivity made booths, and sat under the booths: for since the days of Jeshua the son of Nun unto that day had not the children of Israel done so. And there was very great gladness.

18 Also day by day, from the first day unto the last day, he read in the book of the law of God. And they kept the feast seven days; and on the eighth day *was* a solemn assembly, according unto the manner.

CHAPTER 9

The Jews fast and confess their sins—The Levites bless and praise the Lord and recite His goodness toward Israel.

1 Now in the twenty and fourth day of this month the children of Israel were assembled with fasting, and with sackclothes, and earth upon them.

2 And the seed of Israel separated themselves from all strangers, and stood and confessed their sins, and the iniquities of their fathers.

3 And they stood up in their place, and read in the book of the law of the LORD their God *one* fourth part of the day; and *another* fourth part they confessed, and worshipped the LORD their God.

4 ¶ Then stood up upon the stairs, of the Levites, Jeshua, and Bani, Kadmiel,

Nehemiah 9:1–6. The Children of Israel Fast and Pray in Gratitude to the Lord

What does Israel appear to be doing in these verses? (9:2–4) "After disassociating themselves from all non-Jews, hearing the law for a fourth of the day, and confessing their sins and worshiping the Lord for another fourth of the day, they made a covenant to obey the Law of Moses (Neh. 9:2–3, 38; 10:29). The covenant was made after the leaders of the Jews rehearsed the history of God's dealings with Israel (Neh. 9:4–35), which they rightly understood to be a history of disobedience on the part of their forefathers. The priests, Levites, and other family heads signed their names to this covenant, in addition to Nehemiah" (Lamoreaux, "Work of Ezra and Nehemiah," 379). ⊕

Why were the people crying out to the Lord? (9:4) "The whole reading of the Torah becomes a week of rededication and rejoicing, as at a new birth. [Nehemiah] 9 renews the public confession of sins, perhaps on the model of the Day of Atonement" (Carmody, et al., *Exploring the Hebrew Bible*, 385). "The Rabbis understand the people's cry as a confession for idolatrous practices that are said to have caused the destruction of the sanctuary, the burning of the temple, the murder of the righteous, and the Babylonian exile" (*Jewish Study Bible* [2004], 1701).

Shebaniah, Bunni, Sherebiah, Bani, *and* Chenani, and cried with a loud voice unto the LORD their God.

5 Then the Levites, Jeshua, and Kadmiel, Bani, Hashabniah, Sherebiah, Hodijah, Shebaniah, *and* Pethahiah, said, Stand up *and* bless the LORD your God for ever and ever: and blessed be thy glorious name, which is exalted above all blessing and praise.

6 Thou, *even* thou, *art* LORD alone; thou hast made heaven, the heaven of heavens, with all their host, the earth, and all *things* that *are* therein, the seas, and all that *is* therein, and thou preservest them all; and the host of heaven worshippeth thee.

Nehemiah 9:7–31. The Levites Recount Israel's Long History

7 Thou *art* the LORD the God, who didst choose Abram, and broughtest him forth out of Ur of the Chaldees, and gavest him the name of Abraham;

8 And foundest his heart faithful before thee, and madest a covenant with him to give the land of the Canaanites, the Hittites, the Amorites, and the Perizzites, and the Jebusites, and the Girgashites, to give *it, I say,* to his seed, and hast performed thy words; for thou *art* righteous:

9 And didst see the affliction of our fathers in Egypt, and heardest their cry by the Red sea;

10 And shewedst signs and wonders upon Pharaoh, and on all his servants, and on all the people of his land: for thou knewest that they dealt proudly against them. So didst thou get thee a name, as *it is* this day.

11 And thou didst divide the sea before them, so that they went through the midst of the sea on the dry land; and their persecutors thou threwest into the deeps, as a stone into the mighty waters.

12 Moreover thou leddest them in the day by a cloudy pillar; and in the night by a pillar of fire, to give them light in the way wherein they should go.

13 Thou camest down also upon mount Sinai, and spakest with them from heaven, and gavest them right judgments, and true laws, good statutes and commandments:

14 And madest known unto them thy holy sabbath, and commandedst them precepts, statutes, and laws, by the hand of Moses thy servant:

15 And gavest them bread from heaven for their hunger, and broughtest forth water for them out of the rock for their thirst, and promisedst them that they should go in to possess the land which thou hadst sworn to give them.

16 But they and our fathers dealt proudly, and hardened their necks, and hearkened not to thy commandments,

17 And refused to obey, neither were mindful of thy wonders that thou didst among them; but hardened their necks, and in their rebellion appointed a captain to return to their bondage: but thou *art* a God ready to pardon, gracious and merciful, slow to anger, and of great kindness, and forsookest them not.

18 Yea, when they had made them a molten calf, and said, This *is* thy God that brought thee up out of Egypt, and had wrought great provocations;

19 Yet thou in thy manifold mercies forsookest them not in the wilderness: the pillar of the cloud departed not from them by day, to lead them in the way; neither the pillar of fire by night, to shew them light, and the way wherein they should go.

20 Thou gavest also thy good spirit to instruct them, and withheldest not thy manna from their mouth, and gavest them water for their thirst.

Why is it so critical to not forget what God has done for us? (9:15–17) "Forgetting God has been such a persistent problem among His children since the world began. Think of the times of Moses, when God provided manna and in miraculous and visible ways led and protected His children. Still, the prophet warned the people who had been so blessed, as prophets always have warned and always will: 'Take heed to thyself, and keep thy soul diligently, lest thou forget the things which thine eyes have seen, and lest they depart from thy heart all the days of thy life (Deut. 4:9)" (Eyring, "O Remember, Remember," 67).

How did the Lord uniquely bless the children of Israel in the wilderness? (9:21) "This miracle is seldom mentioned but is nevertheless extraordinary. For forty years in the wilderness the clothes of the children of Israel 'waxed not old, and their feet swelled not.' The Lord had reminded the children of Israel of this miracle just before they entered the promised land (see Deut. 29:5; see also 8:4)" (Ludlow, *Companion to Your Study of the Old Testament*, 259).

What happened to Israel because of their disobedience? (9:26–27) "Moses prophesied that if wickedness and disobedience came among the people of Israel, they would be scattered among the nations (Deut. 28:25). Beginning with the conciliatory treaty of King Ahab of Israel with Syria (1 Kings 20:34) until the final captivity of Judah by Babylonia, the scattering or dispersion of the Lord's people followed as a consequence of their broken covenants. Most of the people who were scattered never returned to the land of promise, and their posterity continued to be spread throughout the earth" (Brandt, "Exile and First Return of Judah," 12). ⊕

21 Yea, forty years didst thou sustain them in the wilderness, *so that* they lacked nothing; their clothes waxed not old, and their feet swelled not.

22 Moreover thou gavest them kingdoms and nations, and didst divide them into corners: so they possessed the land of Sihon, and the land of the king of Heshbon, and the land of Og king of Bashan.

23 Their children also multipliedst thou as the stars of heaven, and broughtest them into the land, concerning which thou hadst promised to their fathers, that they should go in to possess *it*.

24 So the children went in and possessed the land, and thou subduedst before them the inhabitants of the land, the Canaanites, and gavest them into their hands, with their kings, and the people of the land, that they might do with them as they would.

25 And they took strong cities, and a fat land, and possessed houses full of all goods, wells digged, vineyards, and oliveyards, and fruit trees in abundance: so they did eat, and were filled, and became fat, and delighted themselves in thy great goodness.

26 Nevertheless they were disobedient, and rebelled against thee, and cast thy law behind their backs, and slew thy prophets which testified against them to turn them to thee, and they wrought great provocations.

27 Therefore thou deliveredst them into the hand of their enemies, who vexed them: and in the time of their trouble, when they cried unto thee, thou heardest *them* from heaven; and according to thy manifold mercies thou gavest them saviours, who saved them out of the hand of their enemies.

28 But after they had rest, they did evil again before thee: therefore leftest thou them in the hand of their enemies, so that they had the dominion over them: yet when they returned, and cried unto thee, thou heardest *them* from heaven; and many times didst thou deliver them according to thy mercies;

29 And testifiedst against them, that thou mightest bring them again unto thy law: yet they dealt proudly, and hearkened not unto thy commandments, but sinned against thy judgments, (which if a man do, he shall live in them;) and withdrew the shoulder, and hardened their neck, and would not hear.

30 Yet many years didst thou forbear them, and testifiedst against them by thy spirit in thy prophets: yet would they not give ear: therefore gavest thou them into the hand of the people of the lands.

31 Nevertheless for thy great mercies' sake thou didst not utterly consume them, nor forsake them; for thou *art* a gracious and merciful God.

What do latter-day prophets and apostles teach about God's mercies? (9:31) Elder Jeffrey R. Holland added his witness regarding the teachings of the Prophet Joseph: "In the words of that prophet I, too, declare: 'Our Heavenly Father is more liberal in His views, and boundless in His mercies and blessings, than we are ready to believe or receive. . . . God does not look on sin with [the least degree of] allowance, but . . . the nearer we get to our heavenly Father, the more we are disposed to look with compassion on perishing souls; we feel that we want to take them upon our shoulders, and cast their sins behind our backs'" ("Grandeur of God," 73).

32 Now therefore, our God, the great, the mighty, and the terrible God, who keepest covenant and mercy, let not all the trouble seem little before thee, that hath come upon us, on our kings, on our princes, and on our priests, and on our prophets, and on our fathers, and on all thy people, since the time of the kings of Assyria unto this day.

33 Howbeit thou *art* just in all that is brought upon us; for thou hast done right, but we have done wickedly:

34 Neither have our kings, our princes, our priests, nor our fathers, kept thy law, nor hearkened unto thy commandments and

Nehemiah 9:32–38. The Jews Renew Their Covenant with the Lord

thy testimonies, wherewith thou didst testify against them.

35 For they have not served thee in their kingdom, and in thy great goodness that thou gavest them, and in the large and fat land which thou gavest before them, neither turned they from their wicked works.

36 Behold, we *are* servants this day, and *for* the land that thou gavest unto our fathers to eat the fruit thereof and the good thereof, behold, we *are* servants in it:

37 And it yieldeth much increase unto the kings whom thou hast set over us because of our sins: also they have dominion over our bodies, and over our cattle, at their pleasure, and we *are* in great distress.

38 And because of all this we make a sure *covenant,* and write *it;* and our princes, Levites, *and* priests, seal *unto it.*

What was the "sure covenant" the Jews made? **(9:38)** "It was an important oath that the Jews had taken. All in the community who were clean and thus separated from the foreigners took on themselves to keep *and* practice the law of God, the Pentateuch. With the renewal of the covenant they came into a renewed relationship with God, a relationship of obedience to the precepts of his law" (Fensham, *Books of Ezra and Nehemiah*, 238). ⊕

CHAPTERS 10–12

The people covenant not to marry outside of Israel—They also covenant to honor the Sabbath, to pay tithes, and to keep the commandments.

The people and their overseers are elected by lot to dwell in Jerusalem and the other cities.

The priests and Levites who came up from Babylon are named—The walls of Jerusalem are dedicated—The offices of priests and Levites are appointed in the temple.

Summary of Nehemiah 10–12

These chapters include a series of lists. One list was of those who promised to marry in the covenant and to walk in God's paths. Another contains a list of the people and overseers who were appointed to dwell in Jerusalem. One out of every ten persons was to live in Jerusalem while the others were to settle outside the holy city. They list temple workers, singers, and Levites.

"Chapter 11 and most of 12 (vv. 1–26) list the people who had returned to Judah from areas of Babylon after it became part of the Persian empire. The remainder of chapter 12 (vv. 27–47) tells of their completion of the wall around Jerusalem and of its dedication" (Rasmussen, *Latter-day Saint Commentary on the Old Testament*, 375–76).

"When all was said and done, Nehemiah and Ezra had assisted their people immensely in and around Jerusalem. Perhaps significantly, they were both outsiders from Babylon. Through the forceful and charismatic efforts of Nehemiah, the wall of Jerusalem was erected, bringing security and strength to a crestfallen people" (Brown and Holzapfel, *Lost 500 Years*, 26–27).

CHAPTER 13

The Ammonites and Moabites are denied a place in the congregation of God—Tobiah is ejected from his dwelling place in the temple—Nehemiah corrects abuses and reinstitutes Sabbath observance—Some Jews are rebuked for marrying non-Israelite women and defiling the priesthood.

Summary of Nehemiah 13

"Chapter 13 brings the narrative to conclusion on the theme of separation and purification. The text in mind at the outset may be Deuteronomy 23:3–5" (Carmody, et al., *Exploring the Hebrew Bible*, 387). Although "Nehemiah was the political reformer" and commissioned "to rebuild the walls of the city of Jerusalem," he is also "credited with 'cleans[ing] the temple of a resident apostate' (Neh. 13:4–8). In addition, he is credited with prohibiting the buying and selling of merchandise on the Sabbath (see Neh. 13:15–21) and advising Israelite men to marry Israelite women" (Black, *400 Questions and Answers about the Old Testament*, 140–41).

THE BOOK OF
ESTHER

Introduction

"Esther is a story of courage and sacrifice. Esther lived in Susa [Shushan], the capital city of Persia, probably between 482 and 478 B.C. This was a time when Persia had conquered Babylon, and the Jews had been in captivity for over 100 years. Some Jews had returned to Jerusalem with Zerubbabel to rebuild Solomon's temple, but many chose to stay and live in their new lands. Though the Jews had dangerous enemies in Persia, the Lord prepared Esther to save them in their hour of need (see Esther 4:14)" (Valletta, et al., *Old Testament for Latter-day Saint Families,* 394).

Esther is a Persian name meaning "star." This name was given to "a Jewish girl named Hadassah ('myrtle') who became the wife of King Ahasuerus and queen of Persia. Esther is a heroine in that she interceded on behalf of her people with the king and preserved them from a massacre. . . .

"This story became widely read [among the scattered] Jews who faced persecution and sometimes destruction. Mordecai and Esther, like Daniel, became important examples of the power of individuals to deliver their people by attaining high positions or influence in the government" (Holzapfel, et al., *Jehovah and the World of the Old Testament,* 356).

"Although we do not know who wrote the book of Esther, . . . it is clear that the author was a Jew, both from his emphasis on the origin of a Jewish festival and from the Jewish nationalism that permeates the story. The author's knowledge of Persian customs, the setting of the story in the city of Susa and the absence of any reference to the land of Judah or to Jerusalem suggest that he was a resident of a Persian city. . . .

"An outstanding feature of this book—one that has given rise to considerable discussion—is the complete absence of any explicit reference to God, worship, prayer, or sacrifice. . . . It appears that the author has deliberately refrained from mentioning God or any religious activity as a literary device to heighten the fact that it is God who controls and directs all the seemingly insignificant coincidences . . . that make up the plot and issue in deliverance for the Jews. God's sovereign rule is assumed at every point . . . , an assumption made all the more effective by the total absence of reference to him" (*NIV Study Bible* [1995], 709, 710).

"The events recorded in this book took place about the same time as those recorded in Nehemiah. Thus, Esther is a companion to the books of Ezra and Nehemiah" (Pearson, *Old Testament,* 47).

CHAPTER 1

Ahasuerus of Persia and Media makes royal feasts—Vashti disobeys the king and is deposed as queen.

1 Now it came to pass in the days of
Ahasuerus, (this *is* Ahasuerus which reigned,
from India even unto Ethiopia, *over* an hundred and seven and twenty provinces:)

Esther 1:1–12. Queen Vashti Disobeys King Ahasuerus during a Celebration

Who was Ahasuerus? (1:1) Ahasuerus is the Hebrew name for Xerxes. Xerxes was the son of Darius I the Great of Persia. His kingdom extended from India to Ethiopia (see *New Unger's Bible Dictionary* [2005], 37).

2 *That* in those days, when the king Ahasuerus sat on the throne of his kingdom, which *was* in Shushan the palace,

Where was Shushan located? (1:2) Shushan, also known as Susa, was the capital "of the Elamite Empire until King Ashurbanipal of Assyria destroyed the city in 645 B.C. and exiled its inhabitants to Samaria. Under the Medes and Persians it once again became an important city. Darius 1 built a splendid palace here. The ruins, in modern Iran, can still be seen.

"The story of Esther, the Jewish girl who became queen of Persia, took place at the royal court in Susa [Shushan]. It was here, too, that Nehemiah acted as royal cup-bearer. The city was later captured by Alexander the Great" (*Lion Encyclopedia of the Bible*, 277).

3 In the third year of his reign, he made a feast unto all his princes and his servants; the power of Persia and Media, the nobles and princes of the provinces, *being* before him:

4 When he shewed the riches of his glorious kingdom and the honour of his excellent majesty many days, *even* an hundred and fourscore days.

5 And when these days were expired, the king made a feast unto all the people that were present in Shushan the palace, both unto great and small, seven days, in the court of the garden of the king's palace;

6 *Where were* white, green, and blue, *hangings,* fastened with cords of fine linen and purple to silver rings and pillars of marble: the beds *were of* gold and silver, upon a pavement of red, and blue, and white, and black, marble.

7 And they gave *them* drink in vessels of gold, (the vessels being diverse one from another,) and royal wine in abundance, according to the state of the king.

Why are both Persia and Media named here? (1:3) "In about 550 B.C., the Medes were conquered by Cyrus the Great, who then became king of the Medes as well as the Persians. . . . Many Medes were brought into the Persian administration and with them many Median customs and laws" (*Revell Bible Dictionary*, 684).

An Overview of the Book of Esther (Esther 1–10)

"The first chapter of Esther sets the stage for Esther's dilemma. The second tells how she became a queen in Persia and how her cousin and guardian, Mordecai, attained honorable status. The adversary, Haman, is introduced in the third chapter, and the development moves quickly toward a crisis. The fourth chapter tells how Queen Esther was faced with a challenge and rose to meet it. The fifth and sixth chapters become tense as Esther's plan and Haman's plot progressed simultaneously and Esther barely managed to execute her plan in time to save her people from Haman's plot. The last chapters show how he who planned to destroy others was himself destroyed, and the Jews gained a victory over those who had sought to destroy them. The festival of Purim, still celebrated by Jews to this day, was thereby originated, according to this account" (Rasmussen, *Latter-day Saint Commentary on the Old Testament*, 385–86).

What was the law for drinking in the king's presence? (1:8) "By *law* or special decree the king set aside a rule of etiquette governing royal banquets. Ordinarily guests were required to drink only as the king raised his goblet or as the master of ceremonies gave the appropriate signal. At these drinking bouts such restrictions did not apply. *As every man desired*, he could imbibe to his heart's content" (Roehrs and Franzmann, *Concordia Self-Study Commentary*, 300).

8 And the drinking *was* according to the law;
none did compel: for so the king had appointed to all the officers of his house, that
they should do according to every man's pleasure.

9 Also Vashti the queen made a feast for the
women *in* the royal house which *belonged* to
king Ahasuerus.

What were the duties of a chamberlain? (1:10) A chamberlain was a confidential servant of the king (see Bible Dictionary, "Chamberlain"). Other definitions include, "the (one) over the bedchamber . . . an officer who had various duties in the houses of the kings and nobles. . . . 'A person who manages the domestic affairs of a family, in general, a manager, a steward,' is translated 'chamberlain' in the KJV" (*Vine's Complete Expository Dictionary*, 95).

10 ¶ On the seventh day, when the heart
of the king was merry with wine, he commanded Mehuman, Biztha, Harbona, Bigtha,
and Abagtha, Zethar, and Carcas, the seven
chamberlains that served in the presence of
Ahasuerus the king,

11 To bring Vashti the queen before the king
with the crown royal, to shew the people and
the princes her beauty: for she *was* fair to
look on.

Why might Queen Vashti have refused to appear before the king's guests? (1:12) The guests had been allowed to drink the king's wine in any quantity they wished. "After seven days of heavy drinking, the guests were probably quite inebriated, and she may have considered it beneath the dignity of the queen to parade before such a lot simply to display her beauty" (*Old Testament Student Manual: 1 Kings–Malachi*, 329). "Queen Vashti was not merely a trophy wife; she showed moxie. When the king summoned her to parade her beauty in front of his inebriated guests, she flatly refused" (Olson, *Women of the Old Testament*, 163). "With character equal to her beauty, Vashti made a stand for modesty. She refused to be viewed as a sex object, and was denounced, dethroned, and divorced" (Hurd, *Our Sisters in the Bible*, 82). ⊕

12 But the queen Vashti refused to come at
the king's commandment by *his* chamberlains: therefore was the king very wroth, and
his anger burned in him.

Esther 1:13–22. Queen Vashti Loses Her Royal Title

What did it mean to know "the times"? (1:13–14) Kings often relied on soothsayers and others for advice. "These 'wise men' [who knew the times] were court magicians or astrologers who tried to foretell the future by reading stars and planets. Isaiah warned that such men have 'no light in them' (Isaiah 8:19–20)" (Valletta, et al., *Old Testament for Latter-day Saint Families*, 395). This phrase also implies that these seven

13 ¶ Then the king said to the wise men,
which knew the times, (for so *was* the king's
manner toward all that knew law and judgment:

14 And the next unto him *was* Carshena,
Shethar, Admatha, Tarshish, Meres, Marsena,
and Memucan, the seven princes of Persia

and Media, which saw the king's face, *and* which sat the first in the kingdom;)

15 What shall we do unto the queen Vashti according to law, because she hath not performed the commandment of the king Ahasuerus by the chamberlains?

16 And Memucan answered before the king and the princes, Vashti the queen hath not done wrong to the king only, but also to all the princes, and to all the people that *are* in all the provinces of the king Ahasuerus.

17 For *this* deed of the queen shall come abroad unto all women, so that they shall despise their husbands in their eyes, when it shall be reported, The king Ahasuerus commanded Vashti the queen to be brought in before him, but she came not.

18 *Likewise* shall the ladies of Persia and Media say this day unto all the king's princes, which have heard of the deed of the queen. Thus *shall there arise* too much contempt and wrath.

19 If it please the king, let there go a royal commandment from him, and let it be written among the laws of the Persians and the Medes, that it be not altered, That Vashti come no more before king Ahasuerus; and let the king give her royal estate unto another that is better than she.

20 And when the king's decree which he shall make shall be published throughout all his empire, (for it is great,) all the wives shall give to their husbands honour, both to great and small.

21 And the saying pleased the king and the princes; and the king did according to the word of Memucan:

22 For he sent letters into all the king's provinces, into every province according to the writing thereof, and to every people after their language, that every man should bear

men knew the civic laws and customs "of the times." As these seven princes were the closest counselors to the king, their views would greatly influence the king's judgments.

Why was Vashti accused of offending the entire kingdom? (1:16) "[Prince] Memucan voiced the opinion of the council of seven. Not only the king's honour but male supremacy generally was at stake, therefore strong sanctions must be applied" (*New Bible Commentary: Revised*, 415). "Fearing Vashti's influence would spread to their wives and all the other women in the court, the king's princely advisers counseled the king to regard her disobedience as a personal affront and to depose her (Esther 1:10–22)" (Olson, *Women of the Old Testament*, 163).

Why was the decree against Vashti written so it could not be altered? (1:19) "An edict issued by the king, entered among the laws of the Persians and Medes, and sealed with the royal signet (Esther 8:8), does not pass away, i.e., remains in force, is irrevocable (comp. Daniel 6:9). The counsellors press for the issue of such an edict, for the purpose of making it impossible to the king to take Vashti again into favour, lest they should experience her vengeance on the restoration of her influence" (Keil and Delitzsch, *Commentary* [on Esther 1:19–20]).

How should we read this ancient injunction that men "should bear rule" in their homes? (1:22) Men in ancient Persia considered themselves rulers over women. However, the scriptures make it clear that men should never exercise "unrighteous dominion" over women (see D&C 121:39–42). Speaking of the relationship between husbands and wives, President Spencer W. Kimball said: "I have a question about the word *rule.* It gives the wrong impression. I would prefer to use the word *preside* because that's what he does. A righteous husband presides over his wife and family" ("Blessings and Responsibilities of Womanhood," 72).

Summary of Esther 2:1–4

The fair young women of the kingdom are gathered to Shushan so king Ahasuerus can select a new queen to replace Vashti.

Esther 2:5–11. Esther Is Brought to the King's Palace and Mordecai Forbids Revealing Her Jewish Heritage

Who was Mordecai? (2:5) Mordecai was "the son of Jair of the tribe of Benjamin who raised his cousin Hadassah from childhood in the days of Ahasuerus the king of Persia. . . . Mordecai is referred to as a Jew even though he hailed from the tribe of Benjamin. Clearly at this point in the history of the covenant people, the term Jew had come to be more of a political term than a genealogical one" (Hyde, *Comprehensive Commentary [Esther]*, 18).

By what other names was king Jeconiah known? (2:6) Jeconiah was also known as Jehoiachin and Coniah (see Bible Dictionary, "Jehoiachin"). See 2 Kings 24:8–17; see commentary in this volume for 2 Kings 24:12 and 25:27.

What is the meaning of Esther's name? (2:7) "Esther's name is interesting. Her Hebrew name was Hadassah, which is also the name of a hardy, perennial ground cover plant called myrtle. It bears five-petal flowers that are like little blue or white stars. *Esther* is an English rendition of a Persian word meaning 'star.' That name also appears sometimes as *Ishtar*, the name of the goddess-companion to *Marduk*, which name has the same root as *Mordecai*. Some symbolism therein may be significant.

"An eminent Jewish women's organization for social and civic service is called by the name 'Hadassah'" (Rasmussen, *Latter-day Saint Commentary on the Old Testament*, 387).

rule in his own house, and that *it* should be published according to the language of every people.

CHAPTER 2

Ahasuerus seeks a new queen—Mordecai presents Esther—Esther pleases the king and is chosen as queen—Mordecai exposes a plot against the king.

5 ¶ *Now* in Shushan the palace there was a certain Jew, whose name *was* Mordecai, the son of Jair, the son of Shimei, the son of Kish, a Benjamite;

6 Who had been carried away from Jerusalem with the captivity which had been carried away with Jeconiah king of Judah, whom Nebuchadnezzar the king of Babylon had carried away.

7 And he brought up Hadassah, that *is,* Esther, his uncle's daughter: for she had neither father nor mother, and the maid *was* fair and beautiful; whom Mordecai, when her father and mother were dead, took for his own daughter.

8 ¶ So it came to pass, when the king's commandment and his decree was heard, and when many maidens were gathered together unto Shushan the palace, to the custody of Hegai, that Esther was brought also unto the king's house, to the custody of Hegai, keeper of the women.

9 And the maiden pleased him, and she obtained kindness of him; and he speedily gave her her things for purification, with such things as belonged to her, and seven maidens, *which were* meet to be given her, out of the king's house: and he preferred her and her maids unto the best *place* of the house of the women.

10 Esther had not shewed her people nor her kindred: for Mordecai had charged her that she should not shew *it.*

11 And Mordecai walked every day before the court of the women's house, to know how Esther did, and what should become of her.

12 ¶ Now when every maid's turn was come to go in to king Ahasuerus, after that she had been twelve months, according to the manner of the women, (for so were the days of their purifications accomplished, *to wit,* six months with oil of myrrh, and six months with sweet odours, and with *other* things for the purifying of the women;)

13 Then thus came *every* maiden unto the king; whatsoever she desired was given her to go with her out of the house of the women unto the king's house.

14 In the evening she went, and on the morrow she returned into the second house of the women, to the custody of Shaashgaz, the king's chamberlain, which kept the concubines: she came in unto the king no more, except the king delighted in her, and that she were called by name.

Why had Mordecai forbidden Esther from revealing her nationality? (2:10) "Mordecai was aware that Esther's ethnic background could put her at a disadvantage, even in danger, because of potential anti-Jewish sentiment in the palace. The existence of this hostility throughout the empire is demonstrated by the large numbers of *enemies of the Jews* in chapter 9" (*Quest Study Bible* [2003], 696).

Esther 2:12–20. Esther Is Chosen to Become Queen

Why was such an extended preparation needed for the young women? (2:12) The most beautiful of all the young virgins of the provinces "were prepared in the house of the women to be presented to the king for his liking; . . . the [oil of myrrh] was used to make the skin smooth and soft, and [the 'sweet odours'] to remove all ill scents through sweat, or any other cause. . . . Such a space of time was observed not only for the thorough purification of them, but partly was of state and grandeur, and partly that it might be a clear case they were not with child by another, before they came to the king" (*John Gill's Exposition of the Whole Bible* [commentary on Esther 2:12]).

What were the circumstances of a concubine in the Persian court? (2:14) "Concubines were girls who came to a marriage without a dowry. They had not been taken into the harem in connection with political alliances with other countries nor for associations to be made between the crown and a wealthy family. As concubines they would continue to be supported as a member of the royal household but would be unlikely to enjoy any of the king's attention in the future. . . . While the women enjoyed every sort of material comfort and were indulged and pampered in many ways, . . . the special relationship found with a husband

[or] raising children within a family setting—these pleasures were denied them" (Walton, et al., *IVP Bible Background Commentary*, 486, 485).

What may have set Esther apart from the other virgins? (2:15–17) "[Esther] distances herself from the tawdry flamboyance of the court, and her success is due to her restraint in taking with her only what Hegai, who knows the king's tastes, advises. Chances are that Hegai also knows women quite well and knows precisely what will enhance Esther's already distinctive beauty. . . . While Esther won favor in connection with Hegai, who oversaw her and was her superior . . . , more publicly she wins grace, . . . —a probable testimony both to her stunning beauty and to her demeanor" (Phillips, "Esther," 4:618).

Why was Mordecai sitting in the king's gate? (2:19) "The biblical text frequently portrays Mordecai as 'sitting at the king's gate' (Esther 2:19, 21; 5:13; 6:10). This has given some the impression that Mordecai was a kind of unemployed hanger-on who frequented the palace entrance. In fact, the king's gate was not simply an architectural unit at the entrance to the royal compound. It was the center of auxiliary buildings belonging to the palace and included all the offices of management, both of palace administration and supplies. 'To sit' here means . . . to be stationed, to have an office at a particular place. The plot of the two bodyguards to kill the king became known to Mordecai in his official capacity at the king's gate" (Heltzer, "Book of Esther," 29).

15 ¶ Now when the turn of Esther, the daughter of Abihail the uncle of Mordecai, who had
taken her for his daughter, was come to go in
unto the king, she required nothing but what
Hegai the king's chamberlain, the keeper of
the women, appointed. And Esther obtained
favour in the sight of all them that looked
upon her.

16 So Esther was taken unto king Ahasuerus
into his house royal in the tenth month,
which *is* the month Tebeth, in the seventh
year of his reign.

17 And the king loved Esther above all the
women, and she obtained grace and favour in
his sight more than all the virgins; so that he
set the royal crown upon her head, and made
her queen instead of Vashti.

18 Then the king made a great feast unto
all his princes and his servants, *even* Esther's
feast; and he made a release to the provinces,
and gave gifts, according to the state of the
king.

19 And when the virgins were gathered together the second time, then Mordecai sat in
the king's gate.

20 Esther had not *yet* shewed her kindred nor
her people; as Mordecai had charged her: for
Esther did the commandment of Mordecai,
like as when she was brought up with him.

21 ¶ In those days, while Mordecai sat in the king's gate, two of the king's chamberlains, Bigthan and Teresh, of those which kept the door, were wroth, and sought to lay hand on the king Ahasuerus.

22 And the thing was known to Mordecai, who told *it* unto Esther the queen; and Esther certified the king *thereof* in Mordecai's name.

23 And when inquisition was made of the matter, it was found out; therefore they were both hanged on a tree: and it was written in the book of the chronicles before the king.

CHAPTER 3

Mordecai, the Jew, refuses to bow to Haman—Haman arranges a decree to kill all the Jews in the kingdom.

1 After these things did king Ahasuerus promote Haman the son of Hammedatha the Agagite, and advanced him, and set his seat above all the princes that *were* with him.

2 And all the king's servants, that *were* in the king's gate, bowed, and reverenced Haman: for the king had so commanded concerning him. But Mordecai bowed not, nor did *him* reverence.

3 Then the king's servants, which *were* in the king's gate, said unto Mordecai, Why transgressest thou the king's commandment?

Esther 2:21–23. Mordecai Foils a Plot to Assassinate the King

What was the duty of those who "kept the door" for the king? (2:21–22) "Kings in ancient times were keenly aware of the risk of assassination and were well guarded. But Bigthan and Teresh 'kept the door' (v. 21), or, in other words, were part of the king's personal bodyguard and watched over his personal quarters. Their conspiracy to kill the king was especially dangerous because they had access to him. Mordecai somehow learned of this plot and reported it to the king through Esther. The account of Mordecai's loyalty was inserted here because of the central part it plays later in the narrative" (*Old Testament Student Manual: 1 Kings–Malachi*, 330).

Esther 3:1–6. Mordecai Refuses to Reverence and Honor Haman

Who was Haman? (3:1) Haman was the "Chief minister of Ahasuerus (Esth. 3–9); his unsuccessful attempt to destroy the Jews gave rise to the Jewish Feast of Purim" (Bible Dictionary, "Haman"). Haman's position in the Persian court was similar to that of a prime minister. "Haman is called an Agagite. Jewish tradition identifies him as a descendant of the Amalekite king [Agag], whose people Saul failed to destroy (cf. Ex. 17:8–14; 1 Sam. 15:7–33). Mordecai was of Saul's tribe (cf. Es. 2:5). So rabbinical commentators see this conflict as the historic struggle of the Jewish people with Gentile enemies whose unreasoning hatred persists for thousands of years" (Richards, *Bible Reader's Companion*, 325).

Why didn't Mordecai bow to Haman? (3:2–3) "Obedience to the second commandment (Ex 20:4) is not the issue in Mordecai's refusal to bow down to Haman, for the Jews were willing to bow down to kings (see 1Sa 24:8; 2Sa 14:4; 1Ki 1:16) and to other persons (see Ge 23:7; 33:3; 44:14). Only the long-standing enmity between the Jews and the Amalekites accounts both for Mordecai's refusal and for Haman's intent to destroy all the Jews (vv. 5–6)" (*NIV Study Bible* [1995], 714).

4 Now it came to pass, when they spake
daily unto him, and he hearkened not unto
them, that they told Haman, to see whether
Mordecai's matters would stand: for he had
told them that he *was* a Jew.
5 And when Haman saw that Mordecai
bowed not, nor did him reverence, then was
Haman full of wrath.
6 And he thought scorn to lay hands on
Mordecai alone; for they had shewed
him the people of Mordecai: wherefore
Haman sought to destroy all the Jews that
were throughout the whole kingdom of
Ahasuerus, *even* the people of Mordecai.

Esther 3:7–15. Haman Plots to Have the Jews Killed

What was the significance of casting lots? (3:7) "Apparently Haman was so angered by Mordecai's refusal to bow down to him (see v. 5) that he cast Pur or lots to determine the day and the month that he would seek to bring about the death of the Jews in Persia. Anciently lots were cast 'for the purpose of making a choice' [Bible Dictionary, 'Lots, casting of']" (Valletta, et al., *Old Testament for Latter-day Saint Families*, 396).

7 ¶ In the first month, that *is,* the month
Nisan, in the twelfth year of king Ahasuerus,
they cast Pur, that *is,* the lot, before Haman
from day to day, and from month to month,
to the twelfth *month,* that *is,* the month Adar.

Why did Haman lie to the king about "certain people" in the kingdom? (3:8–9) "Haman carefully avoided naming the Jews when he accused them to the king of having their own law, which was true, and of disregarding the law of the land, which was not true, except in the one detail that concerned his status [see Esther 3:2]. They had been taught to seek the peace of the city of their exile (cf. Jer. 29:7) and had done so. This subtle blend of truth and error provided a plausible case for ridding the land of such a stubborn and potentially dangerous element in the population" (*New Bible Commentary: Revised*, 417).

8 ¶ And Haman said unto king Ahasuerus,
There is a certain people scattered abroad and
dispersed among the people in all the provinces of thy kingdom; and their laws *are* diverse from all people; neither keep they the
king's laws: therefore it *is* not for the king's
profit to suffer them.
9 If it please the king, let it be written that
they may be destroyed: and I will pay ten
thousand talents of silver to the hands of
those that have the charge of the business, to
bring *it* into the king's treasuries.

What was notable about the king giving Haman his ring? (3:10) "Signet rings were used by people in authority in the ancient world as official seals. They were engraved with the wearer's personal insignia, which would be used to make an impression on soft wax or clay in order to authorize important documents (3:12). By giving Haman his signet ring, [Ahasuerus] gave him authority to do whatever he wished in the king's name" (*Quest Study Bible* [2003], 697).

10 And the king took his ring from his
hand, and gave it unto Haman the son of
Hammedatha the Agagite, the Jews' enemy.
11 And the king said unto Haman, The silver
is given to thee, the people also, to do with
them as it seemeth good to thee.

12 Then were the king's scribes called on the thirteenth day of the first month, and there was written according to all that Haman had commanded unto the king's lieutenants, and to the governors that *were* over every province, and to the rulers of every people of every province according to the writing thereof, and *to* every people after their language; in the name of king Ahasuerus was it written, and sealed with the king's ring.

13 And the letters were sent by posts into all the king's provinces, to destroy, to kill, and to cause to perish, all Jews, both young and old, little children and women, in one day, *even* upon the thirteenth *day* of the twelfth month, which *is* the month Adar, and *to take* the spoil of them for a prey.

14 The copy of the writing for a commandment to be given in every province was published unto all people, that they should be ready against that day.

15 The posts went out, being hastened by the king's commandment, and the decree was given in Shushan the palace. And the king and Haman sat down to drink; but the city Shushan was perplexed.

What was the Persian communication system like? (3:13) "Darius I, the third king of the Persian Empire, was a great organizer. . . . [He] expanded and improved his empire's network of roads, including the Royal Road, which ran 1,700 miles from Susa (southwestern Persia) to Sardis (western Anatolia [Turkey]). This transportation network had great commercial, political, and military value. Darius also established a 'pony express' mail system along the Royal Road. So effective was the Persian communication network that Herodotus, a fifth-century Greek historian, claimed, 'There is nothing in the world which travels faster than these Persian couriers. . . . Nothing stops these couriers from covering their allotted stage in the quickest possible time—neither snow, rain, heat, nor darkness' ([*Histories*], 8:98)" (Holzapfel, et al., *Jehovah and the World of the Old Testament*, 357).

Why was nearly a year of notice given for the Jews' destruction? (3:13) "The motive seems to have been . . . to cause many Jews to leave their property and escape to other lands, for the sake of preserving their lives. Thus Haman would attain his object. He would be relieved of the presence of the Jews, and be able to enrich himself by the appropriation of their possessions. On the other hand, the providence of God [overruled] the event in the interest of the Jews. . . . It was only because there was so long an interval . . . that it was possible for the Jews to take means for averting the destruction with which they were threatened" (Keil and Delitzsch, *Commentary* [on Esther 3:15]).

Esther 4:1–9. Mordecai Mourns and Requests That Esther Petition the King

Why did Mordecai and many Jews dress in sackcloth with ashes? (4:1–3) Mordecai and the Jews demonstrated their deep feelings about Haman's decree by enacting Jewish mourning rituals in anticipation of their destruction. Sackcloth was a "coarse, rough cloth usually made of goat's hair, . . . worn anciently by those who wished to display an attitude of mourning (Gen. 37:34; 2 Sam. 3:31), extreme humility (Ps. 35:13), or repentance (Hel. 11:9; Matt. 11:21). The custom of donning sackcloth was often accompanied by the rending of garments, sitting in ashes, weeping, fasting, and prayer (Mosiah 11:25; Jonah 3:6–8; Dan. 9:3)" (McConkie and Parry, *Guide to Scriptural Symbols*, 95–96).

Why did Esther send clothing to Mordecai? (4:4) While their previous communications during Esther's tenure in the court have been discreet, "at this point, however, Mordecai's actions are dangerously unsuitable given her position. . . . By dispatching clothing to Mordecai Esther attempts to quell his outburst as effectively and quickly as possible, lest it have bad ramifications for her. His traditional reaction appears extreme, and the ritual sackcloth appears acutely distasteful and unseemly. Esther has spent five years functioning according to court protocol and is undoubtedly concerned for what the *king* will think and how he will respond. . . . That Mordecai refuses to remove his sackcloth is indicative of his complete identity with the national crisis" (Phillips, "Esther," 4:631).

Why did Mordecai charge Esther to go directly to the king? (4:8–9) "It was a common necessity of proper court function that there must be limited access to the king. . . . Many commentators have wondered why Esther could not have simply gone through proper channels to secure an audience with the king

CHAPTER 4

Mordecai and the Jews mourn and fast because of the king's decree—Esther, at the peril of her life, prepares to go in unto the king.

1 When Mordecai perceived all that was done, Mordecai rent his clothes, and put on sackcloth with ashes, and went out into the midst of the city, and cried with a loud and a bitter cry;

2 And came even before the king's gate: for none *might* enter into the king's gate clothed with sackcloth.

3 And in every province, whithersoever the king's commandment and his decree came, *there was* great mourning among the Jews, and fasting, and weeping, and wailing; and many lay in sackcloth and ashes.

4 ¶ So Esther's maids and her chamberlains came and told *it* her. Then was the queen exceedingly grieved; and she sent raiment to clothe Mordecai, and to take away his sackcloth from him: but he received *it* not.

5 Then called Esther for Hatach, *one* of the king's chamberlains, whom he had appointed to attend upon her, and gave him a commandment to Mordecai, to know what it *was*, and why it *was*.

6 So Hatach went forth to Mordecai unto the street of the city, which *was* before the king's gate.

7 And Mordecai told him of all that had happened unto him, and of the sum of the money that Haman had promised to pay to the king's treasuries for the Jews, to destroy them.

8 Also he gave him the copy of the writing of the decree that was given at Shushan to destroy them, to shew *it* unto Esther, and to declare *it* unto her, and to charge her that she should go in unto the king, to make supplication unto him, and to make request before him for her people.

9 And Hatach came and told Esther the words of Mordecai.

10 ¶ Again Esther spake unto Hatach, and gave him commandment unto Mordecai;

11 All the king's servants, and the people of the king's provinces, do know, that whosoever, whether man or woman, shall come unto the king into the inner court, who is not called, *there is* one law of his to put *him* to death, except such to whom the king shall hold out the golden sceptre, that he may live: but I have not been called to come in unto the king these thirty days.

12 And they told to Mordecai Esther's words.

13 Then Mordecai commanded to answer Esther, Think not with thyself that thou shalt escape in the king's house, more than all the Jews.

14 For if thou altogether holdest thy peace at this time, *then* shall there enlargement and deliverance arise to the Jews from another place; but thou and thy father's house shall be destroyed: and who knoweth whether thou art come to the kingdom for *such* a time as this?

15 ¶ Then Esther bade *them* return Mordecai *this answer,*

or perhaps even waited longer to see if she would be summoned (the set time [for the Jews' destruction] was many months away). If, however Haman holds the office [of directing the king's guards], she would have to make arrangements through him and thereby jeopardize the whole plan" (Walton, et al., *IVP Bible Background Commentary*, 488).

Esther 4:10–17. Esther Courageously Plans to Make an Uninvited Visit to the King

What was the golden scepter? (4:11) A scepter is "a staff borne by a ruler as the badge of his authority. . . . Sometimes scepters were short like a mace, sometimes long and garnished with royal insignia" (*New Unger's Bible Dictionary*, 1138). By extending the scepter toward a supplicant, the king showed clemency and willingness to hear a petition.

Why did Esther tell Mordecai that she had not been called to the king for thirty days? (4:11) "Esther understood that Mordecai was asking her to risk her life. She was understandably fearful. Her fear was compounded by the fact that the king had not summoned her for *thirty days*, implying that she had not been enjoying the king's favor recently. Who knew if he would still have regard for her at all?" (*Nelson Study Bible* [NKJV], 817).

What was Mordecai's warning to Esther? (4:13–14) "Mordecai's answer was stern and to the point. He warned Esther that she must not think she was safe from destruction. In a purge, secrets such as hers had a way of leaking out and being used. Still, his most persuasive argument was not based on fear, but on his understanding of the way God worked—an understanding he expected Esther to share. He reminded her that the Jews would be saved—if not by her hand, by some other means. The privileges she had enjoyed . . . were not hers because she had won them, but by the grace of God. If she held her peace now, she would lose her opportunity to serve and be swept aside" (Hurd, *Our Sisters in the Bible*, 87).

Why was Esther told that she had come "for such a time as this"? (4:14) Mordecai correctly indicated that Esther had been prepared and probably foreordained to help save her nation. During a BYU Women's Conference, Wendy Watson Nelson taught: "Queen Esther . . . at great peril to herself, stepped forward in a most crucial way to save her people. She was the right person, at the right place, at the right time, with the right preparation to do what the Lord needed her to do" ("For Such a Time as This," 1). ⊕

What do we learn about Esther when she asks the Jews to fast for her? (4:16) "At the moment of truth, Esther not only makes a choice that will benefit her people but also demonstrates, through her actions and her request, that she knows who she is and what she can do when hard things come. . . . She knows God, she knows the power of fasting and prayer, and she uses that understanding when she needs courage and strength" (Hughes, "Lessons from the Old Testament," 38).

Esther 5:1–8. Esther Invites the King and Haman to a Special Banquet

What enabled Esther to stand before the king? (5:2) Esther prepared herself spiritually by asking "all of the Jews of the kingdom to fast and pray with her. It was then she made personal preparation by looking her most beautiful, as she went in to see the king.

"With every step she must have wondered, 'Will he hold out the royal sceptre?' 'Will he condemn me to death?' 'Will he drop me into poverty and oblivion?' She stood before him, young, beautiful, calm—knowing that she was totally vulnerable. She also knew that she had appealed to God for help and that there was a great moral wrong about to be committed. She had to be responsible to God who made her, no matter what the mortal consequences" (Smith, "Women for the Latter Day," 107).

What was the king really saying to Esther? (5:3) "The king rightly surmised that Esther dared to act 'against the law' [of entering the king's presence without being summoned] because she needed his help in a matter of grave concern to her. Anticipating a costly request, he used the stereotyped formula *even to the half of my kingdom* to indicate that he was willing to grant even such a favor" (Roehrs and Franzmann, *Concordia Self-Study Commentary*, 303).

16 Go, gather together all the Jews that are present in Shushan, and fast ye for me, and neither eat nor drink three days, night or day: I also and my maidens will fast likewise; and so will I go in unto the king, which *is* not according to the law: and if I perish, I perish.

17 So Mordecai went his way, and did according to all that Esther had commanded him.

CHAPTER 5

The king receives Esther—She invites him and Haman to a banquet—Haman plans to have Mordecai hanged.

1 Now it came to pass on the third day, that Esther put on *her* royal *apparel,* and stood in the inner court of the king's house, over against the king's house: and the king sat upon his royal throne in the royal house, over against the gate of the house.

2 And it was so, when the king saw Esther the queen standing in the court, *that* she obtained favour in his sight: and the king held out to Esther the golden sceptre that *was* in his hand. So Esther drew near, and touched the top of the sceptre.

3 Then said the king unto her, What wilt thou, queen Esther? and what *is* thy request? it shall be even given thee to the half of the kingdom.

4 And Esther answered, If *it seem* good unto the king, let the king and Haman come this day unto the banquet that I have prepared for him.

5 Then the king said, Cause Haman to make haste, that he may do as Esther hath said. So the king and Haman came to the banquet that Esther had prepared.

6 ¶ And the king said unto Esther at the banquet of wine, What *is* thy petition? and it shall be granted thee: and what *is* thy request? even to the half of the kingdom it shall be performed.

7 Then answered Esther, and said, My petition and my request *is;*

8 If I have found favour in the sight of the king, and if it please the king to grant my petition, and to perform my request, let the king and Haman come to the banquet that I shall prepare for them, and I will do to morrow as the king hath said.

Why did Esther invite the king and Haman to a second banquet? (5:8) Esther's words "the banquet I shall prepare for them" (v. 8) convey that "the party is as much for Haman as for the king—a clever rhetorical move to make Haman think he is the center of attention. And so he will be" (*Jewish Study Bible* [2014], 1628).

Esther 5:9–14. Haman Secretly Plans to Hang Mordecai

9 ¶ Then went Haman forth that day joyful and with a glad heart: but when Haman saw Mordecai in the king's gate, that he stood not up, nor moved for him, he was full of indignation against Mordecai.

10 Nevertheless Haman refrained himself: and when he came home, he sent and called for his friends, and Zeresh his wife.

11 And Haman told them of the glory of his riches, and the multitude of his children, and all *the things* wherein the king had promoted him, and how he had advanced him above the princes and servants of the king.

12 Haman said moreover, Yea, Esther the queen did let no man come in with the king unto the banquet that she had prepared but myself; and to morrow am I invited unto her also with the king.

Why did Haman grow more angry with Mordecai? (5:9) "Haman was elated as he came away from the queen's party, until he saw Mordecai. . . . Despite the king's edict consigning Mordecai and all his people to destruction, Mordecai gave no outward sign of recognition to the author of all his troubles, not by even a flicker of recognition acknowledging his presence. . . . Mordecai simply remained seated at his accustomed place at the King's Gate . . . , in his regular clothes . . . , as if nothing had happened" (Moore, *Esther*, 60).

13 Yet all this availeth me nothing, so long
as I see Mordecai the Jew sitting at the king's
gate.

14 ¶ Then said Zeresh his wife and all his
friends unto him, Let a gallows be made
of fifty cubits high, and to morrow speak
thou unto the king that Mordecai may be
hanged thereon: then go thou in merrily with
the king unto the banquet. And the thing
pleased Haman; and he caused the gallows to
be made.

Why was the gallows of such excessive height? (5:14) "The gallows was probably not an elaborate gallows, but rather a high pole or stake. . . . The higher the stake, the farther it could be seen" (*Old Testament Student Manual: 1 Kings–Malachi*, 331). "The extreme height of the gallows (fifty cubits, or seventy-five feet) is probably a reflection of the extreme hatred of Haman and his family for Mordecai" (Ludlow, *Companion to Your Study of the Old Testament*, 262).

Summary of Esther 6

During a sleepless night, the king reads past court records. He learns how Mordecai saved his life by exposing the assassination plot of his personal bodyguards (see Esther 2:21–23). The king determines to honor Mordecai for his loyalty and asks Haman how best to honor one who has pleased the king. Haman, certain the king intends to honor Haman himself, petitions that the man should wear the king's apparel and ride a royal horse while his good deeds are proclaimed before the city. The king charges Haman to bestow this public demonstration upon Mordecai, the very man Haman is plotting to kill.

CHAPTER 6

Mordecai receives great honors—Haman mourns and is counseled by his wife.

CHAPTER 7

Esther reveals Haman's plot to destroy the Jews—He is hanged on his own gallows.

Esther 7:1–6. Esther Reveals Haman's Plot to Kill the Jews

1 So the king and Haman came to banquet
with Esther the queen.

2 And the king said again unto Esther on the
second day at the banquet of wine, What *is*
thy petition, queen Esther? and it shall be
granted thee: and what *is* thy request? and
it shall be performed, *even* to the half of the
kingdom.

3 Then Esther the queen answered and said,
If I have found favour in thy sight, O king,
and if it please the king, let my life be given
me at my petition, and my people at my request:

Why did Esther say that she and her people had been "sold to be destroyed"? (7:3–4) "[Esther] builds her case on her personal relationship to the king. . . . Esther equates her life (self) with her people, but does not name them as the Jews. [She says] *we have been sold,* perhaps a hint of Haman's attempted bribe, which Esther learned about from Mordecai in

4 For we are sold, I and my people, to be destroyed, to be slain, and to perish. But if we had been sold for bondmen and bondwomen, I had held my tongue, although the enemy could not countervail the king's damage.

5 ¶ Then the king Ahasuerus answered and said unto Esther the queen, Who is he, and where is he, that durst presume in his heart to do so?

6 And Esther said, The adversary and enemy *is* this wicked Haman. Then Haman was afraid before the king and the queen.

7 ¶ And the king arising from the banquet of wine in his wrath *went* into the palace garden: and Haman stood up to make request for his life to Esther the queen; for he saw that there was evil determined against him by the king.

8 Then the king returned out of the palace garden into the place of the banquet of wine; and Haman was fallen upon the bed whereon Esther *was*. Then said the king, Will he force the queen also before me in the house? As the word went out of the king's mouth, they covered Haman's face.

9 And Harbonah, one of the chamberlains, said before the king, Behold also, the gallows fifty cubits high, which Haman had made for Mordecai, who had spoken good for the king, standeth in the house of Haman. Then the king said, Hang him thereon.

10 So they hanged Haman on the gallows that he had prepared for Mordecai. Then was the king's wrath pacified.

4:7; or, perhaps the sense is 'handed over, betrayed.' . . . But Esther may be subtly recasting Haman's offer of money as a treasonous act against the king. An entire people could become enslaved only if another political entity conquered them. The implication is that Haman wanted to take ownership of some of the king's subjects—an act of treason" (*Jewish Study Bible* [2014], 1629).

Esther 7:7–10. Haman Is Hanged on the Gallows Built for Mordecai

Why did Haman fall on Esther's bed? (7:8) "The king left the banquet *in his wrath* (v. 7), setting the stage for the final twist that would seal Haman's fate. Meals were customarily eaten while reclining on a couch (Amos 6:4–7; John 13:23), so the king returned to find Haman *fallen upon the bed whereon Esther was* (v. 8), to beg for his life. It is ironic that Haman, who had been angry when the Jew Mordecai would not bow down (which set the whole story in motion), now fell before the Jewess Esther (see 6:13)" (*Zondervan KJV Commentary*, 684).

What was implied when the soldiers covered Haman's face? (7:8) "The covering of Haman's face (v. 8) presages his execution, which follows swiftly on the gallows now identified to [the king] as Haman's intended instrument for death for the faithful Mordecai" (Fee and Hubbard, *Eerdmans Companion to the Bible*, 299).

CHAPTER 8

Mordecai is honored and placed over the house of Haman—Ahasuerus issues a decree to preserve the Jews.

1 On that day did the king Ahasuerus give the house of Haman the Jews' enemy unto Esther the queen. And Mordecai came before the king; for Esther had told what he *was* unto her.

2 And the king took off his ring, which he had taken from Haman, and gave it unto Mordecai. And Esther set Mordecai over the house of Haman.

3 ¶ And Esther spake yet again before the king, and fell down at his feet, and besought him with tears to put away the mischief of Haman the Agagite, and his device that he had devised against the Jews.

4 Then the king held out the golden sceptre toward Esther. So Esther arose, and stood before the king,

5 And said, If it please the king, and if I have found favour in his sight, and the thing *seem* right before the king, and I *be* pleasing in his eyes, let it be written to reverse the letters devised by Haman the son of Hammedatha the Agagite, which he wrote to destroy the Jews which *are* in all the king's provinces:

6 For how can I endure to see the evil that shall come unto my people? or how can I endure to see the destruction of my kindred?

Esther 8:1–6. Esther Pleads for Her People

Why did the king give Mordecai his ring? (8:2) "The bestowal of the ring implied that Mordecai was appointed to be a minister of State, since the ring was used for giving authority to royal decrees (see Esther 8:8)" (*John Dummelow's Commentary* [on Esther 8:1–17]). See commentary in this volume for Esther 3:10.

Why was Esther still pleading for the Jews after Haman's death? (8:5–6) "The earlier order to kill the Jews could not be rescinded because it had been 'written in the king's name, and sealed with the king's ring' (v. 8). Now a new letter is sent out, written in the name of the king and 'sealed . . . with the king's ring' authorizing the Jews to defend themselves" (Ludlow, *Companion to Your Study of the Old Testament*, 262).

Summary of Esther 8:7–14

The king cannot abolish Haman's sanctioned decree to slay the Jews. However, Mordecai is permitted to write a new edict giving the Jews power to defend themselves and legally fight their enemies.

15 ¶ And Mordecai went out from the presence of the king in royal apparel of blue and
white, and with a great crown of gold, and
with a garment of fine linen and purple:
and the city of Shushan rejoiced and was
glad.

16 The Jews had light, and gladness, and joy,
and honour.

17 And in every province, and in every city,
whithersoever the king's commandment and
his decree came, the Jews had joy and gladness, a feast and a good day. And many of the
people of the land became Jews; for the fear
of the Jews fell upon them.

CHAPTERS 9–10

The Jews slay their enemies, including Haman's ten sons—The Feast of Purim is instituted to commemorate their deliverance and victory.

Mordecai, the Jew, stands next to Ahasuerus in power and might.

Esther 8:15–17. Mordecai Is Honored and the Jews Rejoice

What does it mean that "many of the people became Jews"? (8:17) "The word translated with the phrase 'became Jews' occurs here only, and since it is not the word usually used to describe religious conversion, it may simply mean that some [people] 'judaized' themselves by sympathetic actions" (Rasmussen, *Latter-day Saint Commentary on the Old Testament*, 390).

Summary of Esther 9–10

The Jews defend themselves and defeat their enemies in battle. They establish the feast of Purim to remember the day Esther helped save them from destruction. Mordecai is placed next to the king in power.

What Is the Feast of Purim? (Esther 9)

"This feast was instituted by Mordecai, at the suggestion of Esther, in memory of the extraordinary deliverance of the Jews of Persia from the murderous plot of Haman. . . .

"The name *Purim,* 'lots,' was given to this festival because of the casting of lots by Haman to decide when he should carry into effect the decree issued by the king for the extermination of the Jews (Esther 9:24). The name was probably given to the festival in irony. . . .

"Mordecai ordered the 14th and 15th of Adar to be kept annually by the Jews; that these two days should be days of feasting and joy, of the interchange of presents, and of sending gifts to the poor. . . . The day preceding (13th Adar) is kept as a fast day (called 'the Fast of Esther'), in accordance with the command of the queen ([Esther] 4:15–16)" (*New Unger's Bible Dictionary*, 421–22).

"Held usually in mid-winter, Purim includes a reading of Esther in the synagogue. The children are dressed in costumes and parade through their Jewish neighborhoods. Then the story is read and acted out. Each girl hopes to be selected to portray Esther. Everyone has noisemakers and they are loudly used whenever the name of Haman is mentioned in the story, in order to drown out any sound of his name. The pageant has the effect of a melodrama. Candy, treats, gifts, and games (usually involving dice or 'lots') are an important part of the festival" (Ludlow, *Unlocking the Old Testament*, 117).

"One of the most common treats associated with the holiday is a triangle-shaped pastry known as 'Haman's ears,' which people eat in celebration of the destruction of Haman, enemy of the Jews" (Muhlestein, *Essential Old Testament Companion*, 325).

THE BOOK OF
JOB

Introduction

Not much is known about Job as a person outside of the sparse information in the first few verses of the Book of Job. The book does not reference his genealogy, "nor to the time when Job lived, as is the pattern with prophetic literature in the Old Testament" (Tanner, "Book of Job," 392). "There is no scholarly consensus on the date, author, structure, stages of composition (if any), nature (history, narrative, story, or dramatic fiction), or meaning of the book" (Stirling, "Job," 99).

Commentators categorize the book of Job as "wisdom literature," along with Proverbs and Ecclesiastes. "Unlike prophetic and historical biblical texts, wisdom texts are less concerned with the unfolding history of a covenant people through time than they are with the timeless truths of the individual's relationship to moral and religious principles" (Tanner, "Book of Job," 392).

"Scriptures confirm the fact that Job was an actual man by listing him among the prophets. For example, the three great men the Lord mentions to Ezekiel are Noah, Daniel, and Job (see Ezek. 14:14, 20). James also refers to Job (see James 5:11). Latter-day scriptural confirmation of Job's existence is Doctrine and Covenants 121:10, where the Lord refers to Job in answer to a plea of the Prophet Joseph Smith" (Adams, "Job," 73).

The book of Job "narrates the afflictions that befell a righteous man and discusses the moral problem such sufferings present. Job's 'three friends' discuss with him the meaning of his sufferings; they give their interpretation, that they are a sign of God's anger and a punishment for sin; but this Job will not admit. . . .

"The book of Job does not entirely answer the question as to why Job (or any human) might suffer pain and the loss of his goods. It does make it clear that affliction is not necessarily evidence that one has sinned. The book suggests that affliction, if not for punishment, may be for experience, discipline, and instruction (see also D&C 122)" (Bible Dictionary, "Job, book of").

"The book of Job comprises the following major sections: opening prologue and framework, teaching that God permits Satan to try to test Job, who encounters daunting adversity and decries his situation (chapters 1–3); Job's three friends (Eliphaz, Bildad, and Zophar) discuss with him the implications of his suffering, . . . (chapters 4–18); Job declares his faith in God's design and confirms his enduring testimony (chapter 19); Job continues his dialogue with his friends, . . . (chapters 20–28); Job reviews his condition (chapters 29–31); Elihu intervenes with a sermon on man's weakness and God's majesty (chapters 31–37); God speaks with Job and teaches him truths from the divine perspective (chapters 38–41); Job repents and is blessed (chapter 42)" (Pinegar and Allen, *Old Testament Who's Who*, 103–4).

CHAPTER 1

Job, a just and perfect man, is blessed with great riches—Satan obtains permission from the Lord to tempt and try Job—Job's property and children are destroyed, and yet he praises and blesses the Lord.

1 There was a man in the land of Uz, whose name *was* Job; and that man was perfect and upright, and one that feared God, and eschewed evil.

2 And there were born unto him seven sons and three daughters.

3 His substance also was seven thousand sheep, and three thousand camels, and five hundred yoke of oxen, and five hundred she asses, and a very great household; so that this man was the greatest of all the men of the east.

4 And his sons went and feasted *in their* houses, every one his day; and sent and called for their three sisters to eat and to drink with them.

5 And it was so, when the days of *their* feasting were gone about, that Job sent and sanctified them, and rose up early in the morning, and offered burnt offerings *according* to the number of them all: for Job said, It may be

Job 1:1–5. The Lord Greatly Blesses Job and His Family

Was Job a real person? (1:1) An important evidence that Job was a real person can be found in the Lord's comparison between the Prophet Joseph Smith's suffering at Liberty Jail and Job (see D&C 121:7–10). "If Job were not real and his suffering, therefore, were merely the figment of some author's imagination, and Joseph Smith on the other hand was very real, and his suffering and that of his people were not imaginary, then for the Lord to chide him because his circumstances were not as bad as Job's were, would provide an intolerable comparison, since one cannot compare real with unreal things. On the other hand, since the Lord did make the comparison, . . . Job was a very real person" (Meservy, "Job," 155).

How could Job be considered "perfect"? (1:1) "Jesus is the only person to have lived without committing any sin. Job was not 'sinless,' as was Christ, but is described as becoming perfect. Job's righteousness is similar to that of others in scripture who are also described as 'perfect' (1 Kings 15:14; D&C 107:43). For example, Noah is described as 'perfect in his generations' (Genesis 6:9), but the Hebrew word translated here as *perfect* means 'complete, whole, having integrity' ([Genesis 6:9*c*])" (Valletta, et al., *Old Testament for Latter-day Saint Families*, 404).

What does it mean that Job was "the greatest of all the men of the east"? (1:3) "Job's situation is described as being blessed in the greatest ways a person could be. He was righteous. He had a large family that also seemed to be righteous and who afforded him great joy. They had great unity and looked after one another. Job was a good spiritual shepherd for his family. He also had a tremendous amount of all that the land could offer in terms of goods" (Muhlestein, *Scripture Study Made Simple*, 321).

Job 1:6–12. The Lord Permits Satan to Test and Tempt Job

Who were the "sons of God"? (1:6) The Joseph Smith Translation makes a change to Job 1:6 and also to Job 2:1 where "sons of God" is rendered "*children* of God" (see Job 1:6*a* and also Job 2:1*a*). "The scriptures indeed tell of a time when all the children of God gathered in the Council in Heaven, and Lucifer was there until he became 'Satan'" (Rasmussen, *Latter-Day Saint Commentary on the Old Testament*, 394).

Why was Satan permitted to go "to and fro in the earth"? (1:7) "Satan is shown here in his role of testing Job, as he may test every earthbound soul. Because the narrative of Job is a particular example of the general predicament of man, any of us may relate Job's experiences to the tests and trials we have in life" (Rasmussen, *Latter-Day Saint Commentary on the Old Testament*, 394).

"Satan, also called the adversary or the devil, is the enemy of righteousness and those who seek to follow God. . . .

"Heavenly Father allows Satan and Satan's followers to tempt us as part of our experience in mortality (see 2 Nephi 2:11–14; D&C 29:39). . . . [Satan] and his followers try to lead us away from righteousness. He directs his most strenuous opposition at the most important aspects of Heavenly Father's plan of happiness" (*True to the Faith*, "Satan").

What was being suggested about Job's character? (1:9–11) "Satan comes among the 'sons of God' and makes his presence known in the council of [Jehovah]. . . . [Jehovah] and Satan then begin a theological discussion that centers on the figure of Job, specifically

that my sons have sinned, and cursed God in their hearts. Thus did Job continually.

6 ¶ Now there was a day when the sons of God came to present themselves before the LORD, and Satan came also among them.

7 And the LORD said unto Satan, Whence comest thou? Then Satan answered the LORD, and said, From going to and fro in the earth, and from walking up and down in it.

8 And the LORD said unto Satan, Hast thou considered my servant Job, that *there is* none like him in the earth, a perfect and an upright man, one that feareth God, and escheweth evil?

9 Then Satan answered the LORD, and said, Doth Job fear God for nought?

10 Hast not thou made an hedge about him, and about his house, and about all that he

Viewing Job as a Similitude of Jesus Christ

"Surely [Job] serves as an example, and reference to his life gives one hope in building patience, endurance, and faith. But, as we shall see, Job's example is extremely distinctive, for in his life we find a type of some of the most distinctive and divine traits of the Savior" (Farley, "Job," 26).

Some ways that Job's life was a similitude of Jesus Christ include:

- He was perfect and upright (Job 1:8).
- There was none like him in all the earth (Job 1:8).
- Satan desired to destroy him (Job 1:9–19; 2:4–7).
- He suffered immeasurably for no wrong or fault of his own (Job 1:12–2:8).
- He was mocked and scorned by his 'friends' (see, for example, Job 16:20; 17:2).
- He remained absolutely steadfast (see, for example, Job 13:15).
- He endured all the sufferings without murmuring (see, for example, Job 1:21–22; 2:10).
- As a result of his faithfulness, sinners can be accepted before the Lord through him and do not have to suffer for their own sins (Job 42:7–10).
- He gained everything after he endured the sufferings (Job 42:10–13)" (Ferrell, *Hidden Christ*, 220).

hath on every side? thou hast blessed the
work of his hands, and his substance is increased in the land.

11 But put forth thine hand now, and touch
all that he hath, and he will curse thee to thy
face.

12 And the LORD said unto Satan, Behold,
all that he hath *is* in thy power; only upon
himself put not forth thine hand. So Satan
went forth from the presence of the LORD.

whether Job is loyal to [Jehovah] in spite of his suffering or because Job hasn't yet been subjected to true suffering. In other words, is Job prosperous because he is pious [devoted to God], or is he pious because he is prosperous? If he loses his prosperity, will his piety fall away as well? In order to determine Job's true nature, Satan seeks and receives [Jehovah's] divine authorization to afflict Job in any fashion short of killing him" (Frederick, "Old Wine in New Bottles," 247).

Would God participate in an arrangement with Satan? (1:12) "The premise of the whole book is established with two scenes in which God and Satan meet in a council with the 'sons of God' and cordially discuss the righteousness of Job (see Job 1–2). Satan contends that Job is righteous only because he is prosperous, but God wagers that Job will maintain his integrity even in the face of trials. It is likely that these scenes are a figurative depiction of how God allows Satan to test his children" (Holzapfel, et al., *Jehovah and the World of the Old Testament*, 242). ⊕

Job 1:13–22. Job's Family and Possessions Are Destroyed, but He Remains Faithful to God

13 ¶ And there was a day when his sons and
his daughters *were* eating and drinking wine
in their eldest brother's house:

14 And there came a messenger unto Job,
and said, The oxen were plowing, and the
asses feeding beside them:

15 And the Sabeans fell *upon them*, and took
them away; yea, they have slain the servants
with the edge of the sword; and I only am
escaped alone to tell thee.

16 While he *was* yet speaking, there came
also another, and said, The fire of God is
fallen from heaven, and hath burned up the
sheep, and the servants, and consumed them;
and I only am escaped alone to tell thee.

17 While he *was* yet speaking, there came
also another, and said, The Chaldeans made
out three bands, and fell upon the camels,
and have carried them away, yea, and slain
the servants with the edge of the sword; and I
only am escaped alone to tell thee.

What do we know about those who brought about Job's extreme losses? (1:13–19) "Job's custom was to make offerings for his family. The very day he made these offerings, this devastation took place. The coming of the messengers of misfortune, each on the heels of the other, all on that one fateful day, has its dramatic effect heightened by the narrator's style. We are informed, however, that it is really the work of the Accuser, this master of evil, who can and does use both the elements of nature and humankind to accomplish his purpose. Satan is a great juggler and has manifested himself as such in Paradise (Eden) and in the temptation of Jesus Christ" (*Expositor's Bible Commentary [Abridged]*, 746–47).

18 While he *was* yet speaking, there came
also another, and said, Thy sons and thy
daughters *were* eating and drinking wine in
their eldest brother's house:

19 And, behold, there came a great wind
from the wilderness, and smote the four corners of the house, and it fell upon the young
men, and they are dead; and I only am escaped alone to tell thee.

20 Then Job arose, and rent his mantle, and
shaved his head, and fell down upon the
ground, and worshipped,

How can a knowledge of God's plan help during times of trial? (1:20) "From the account of Job's personal tragedies and his ultimate triumph we gain insight into the role that suffering and sorrow play in the testing process of the plan of salvation. Job's unfailing faith in the Lord and his purposes is a relevant example for us today as we struggle with our own trials and utter heartfelt pleadings such as 'Why me?' 'Why this?' and 'Why now?' Job teaches us that essential adversity-enduring strength and power come with a personal knowledge of God" (Top, *Peculiar Treasure*, 126).

21 And said, Naked came I out of my mother's
womb, and naked shall I return thither: the
LORD gave, and the LORD hath taken away;
blessed be the name of the LORD.

Why did God permit Job to be afflicted with so many trials? (1:21) "Into the brief, fleeting time allotted to each of us must be crowded challenges that will help us, in our weaknesses, to develop the qualities we now lack. The presence of stress may be needed for their development. Otherwise, the adversary could taunt us as he did Job by saying that an insulated Job was an untested Job (see Job 1:8–12). The same availability to experience adversity will be ours, for 'the Lord seeth fit to chasten his people; yea, he trieth their patience and their faith' (Mosiah 23:21). To expect immunity is naiveté!" (Maxwell, *Notwithstanding My Weakness*, 20–21). ⊕

22 In all this Job sinned not, nor charged
God foolishly.

Why wasn't Job angry with God? (1:22) "In the Bible Job offers the classic portrait of patience. In the face of losing his vast empire, including his children, Job was able, because of his unfailing faith, to proclaim, 'The Lord gave, and the Lord hath taken away; blessed be the name of the Lord.' Through all of his tribulation and pain, 'Job sinned not, nor charged God foolishly' (Job 1:21–22).

"How often do we hear oppressed souls ask foolishly, 'How could God do this to me?' when really they should be praying for strength to 'beareth' and 'endureth all things'" (Oaks, "Power of Patience," 15).

CHAPTER 2

Satan obtains permission from the Lord to afflict Job physically—Job is smitten with boils—Eliphaz, Bildad, and Zophar come to comfort him.

1 Again there was a day when the sons of God came to present themselves before the LORD, and Satan came also among them to present himself before the LORD.

2 And the LORD said unto Satan, From whence comest thou? And Satan answered the LORD, and said, From going to and fro in the earth, and from walking up and down in it.

3 And the LORD said unto Satan, Hast thou considered my servant Job, that *there is* none like him in the earth, a perfect and an upright man, one that feareth God, and escheweth evil? and still he holdeth fast his integrity, although thou movedst me against him, to destroy him without cause.

4 And Satan answered the LORD, and said, Skin for skin, yea, all that a man hath will he give for his life.

5 But put forth thine hand now, and touch his bone and his flesh, and he will curse thee to thy face.

6 And the LORD said unto Satan, Behold, he *is* in thine hand; but save his life.

7 ¶ So went Satan forth from the presence of the LORD, and smote Job with sore boils from the sole of his foot unto his crown.

Job 2:1–10. God Allows Satan to Test Job Physically, but Job Will Not Curse God

How might the "sons of God" continue to present themselves before Him? (2:1) "We know of no second Council in Heaven, but it may be that the ongoing interaction between God, mankind, and the Devil is here particularized to Job's case, for it is true that any of God's children on earth are tested and tried again and again. Satan can challenge, use, and abuse the God-given agency of man to work for his own gain" (Rasmussen, *Latter-Day Saint Commentary on the Old Testament*, 394).

What can we learn about the importance of integrity from Job's example? (2:3) "Integrity is the value we set on ourselves. It is a fulfillment of the duty we owe ourselves. An honorable man or woman will personally commit to live up to certain self-imposed expectations. They need no outside check or control. They are honorable in their inner core. . . .

"Integrity is the light that shines from a disciplined conscience. . . .

"God help us to be honest and true. May we always be thoroughly dependable, standing firm and upright though others may fail, and be fearless, constant, and just. May we say with the much-tested Job: 'Till I die I will not remove mine integrity from me' (Job 27:5)" (Faust, "Integrity, the Mother of Many Virtues," 47, 49).

What did Satan mean by "skin for skin"? (2:4) "The origin of the proverb *skin for skin* utilized by Satan is disputed. Some think it may have originated from the practice of bartering animal skins. Others believe that the phrase is similar to the proverb 'life for life, eye for eye, tooth for tooth' (Ex. 21:23–25). In the last half of the verse Satan charges that Job would be willing to lose his possessions or even his family, as long as his life was spared" (*NKJV Study Bible* [2018], 731). ⊕

What are boils? (2:7) "A boil is a painful sore filled with infection. Sometimes boils ooze or bleed" (Valletta, et al., *Old Testament for Latter-day Saint Families*, 407). "Sore boils. . . . What this diabolical disorder was, interpreters are not agreed. Some think it was the leprosy, and this is the reason why he dwelt by himself, and had his habitation in an unclean place, without the city . . . and the reason why his friends beheld him afar off, Job 2:12, was because they knew that the disorder was infectious" (*Adam Clarke's Commentary* [on Job 2:7]).

What is a potsherd? (2:8) "Job and his wife were now destitute, having lost everything, including their children. . . . To sit on the ash heap was a sign of utter poverty and despair. Job scraped his skin with a broken piece of pottery (a *potsherd*) to remove the sores and the loose flesh" (*Zondervan KJV Commentary*, 693).

Why did Job's wife encourage him to curse God? (2:9–10) "Certainly Job's wife was experiencing tragedies of her own. It is hard to imagine, however, that she was unsympathetic toward the man with whom she had ten children. Job's wife, for all of her difficulties, was not suffering excruciating disease. But she could not bear to see him in his fallen state. These words should probably be understood as an expression of abject sorrow and despair, rather than as censure. . . . Job does not judge his companion; he does not say that she is a foolish woman, but that she is talking like one" (Hyde, *Comprehensive Commentary [Job]*, 14, 15).

Job 2:11–13. Job's Three Friends Come to Visit and Comfort Him

Why didn't Job's friends recognize him? (2:11–13) "When three of Job's friends hear about the personal disasters that have befallen their comrade, they travel to Job's home from areas in Arabia and Edom. The calamities have so transformed Job that they barely recognize him. They first mourn for him and then grieve with him for a full week. Their silence recognizes that words are inadequate to comfort their friend" (Fee and Hubbard, *Eerdmans Companion to the Bible*, 310).

8 And he took him a potsherd to scrape himself withal; and he sat down among the ashes.

9 ¶ Then said his wife unto him, Dost thou
still retain thine integrity? curse God, and die.
10 But he said unto her, Thou speakest as
one of the foolish women speaketh. What?
shall we receive good at the hand of God,
and shall we not receive evil? In all this did
not Job sin with his lips.

11 ¶ Now when Job's three friends heard of
all this evil that was come upon him, they
came every one from his own place; Eliphaz
the Temanite, and Bildad the Shuhite, and
Zophar the Naamathite: for they had made
an appointment together to come to mourn
with him and to comfort him.

12 And when they lifted up their eyes afar
off, and knew him not, they lifted up their
voice, and wept; and they rent every one his
mantle, and sprinkled dust upon their heads
toward heaven.

13 So they sat down with him upon the
ground seven days and seven nights, and
none spake a word unto him: for they saw
that *his* grief was very great.

CHAPTERS 3–13

Job curses the circumstances of his birth—He asks, Why died I not from the womb?

Eliphaz reproves Job, asking such questions as, Are the righteous cut off? Shall a man be more pure than his maker?

Eliphaz counsels Job: Man is born unto trouble, seek unto God, and happy is the man whom God corrects.

Job bemoans his grief—He prays that God will grant his petitions—Those who are afflicted should be pitied—How forcible are right words!

Job asks, Is there an appointed time for man on earth? What is man that Thou shouldst magnify him? Why dost Thou not pardon my transgression?

Bildad asks, Doth God pervert judgment?—Bildad says, Our days upon earth are a shadow, and God will not cast away a perfect man.

Summary of Job 3–13

Job's misery leads him to curse the day of his birth, but he retains his trust in God (see Job 3:1–3). Job's friends suggest that disobedience is the source of suffering (see Job 4:7–9; 8:3–6). Job complains that his friends offer no help, like a dry riverbed unable to provide water to weary travelers in the desert. Because of the shallow advice from his three friends, Job describes them as "forgers of lies" and "physicians of no value" (Job 13:4). Job is convinced that his sins do not justify the perceived punishment. While Job does not understand why he has been afflicted so severely, he chooses not to lose his faith in God.

Finding Purpose in Suffering (Job 3–13)

"In the pain, the agony, and the heroic endeavors of life, we pass through a refiner's fire, and the insignificant and the unimportant in our lives can melt away like dross and make our faith bright, intact, and strong. In this way the divine image can be mirrored from the soul. It is part of the purging toll exacted of some to become acquainted with God. In the agonies of life, we seem to listen better to the faint, godly whisperings of the Divine Shepherd. . . .

"For some, the refiner's fire causes a loss of belief and faith in God, but those with eternal perspective understand that such refining is part of the perfection process" (Faust, "Refined in Our Trials," 4).

"Sometimes suffering and sorrow can actually be our greatest benefactors. They can turn our attention toward God, intensify our devotion to him, and strengthen our faith. God's use of adversity to turn the hearts and minds of his children to him not only is found in the account of Job but is also a recurring theme throughout all of the Old Testament (see Leviticus 26; 1 Kings 8:35–36; 2 Chronicles 20:9; Isaiah 30:20; 48:10; Hosea 5:15)" (Top, *Peculiar Treasure*, 129).

Job acknowledges the justice and greatness of God and concludes that man cannot contend against Him.

Job is weary of life—He reasons with God about his afflictions—He asks, Why hast Thou brought me forth out of the womb?

Zophar asks, Canst thou by searching find out God?—Zophar says that the hope of the wicked will fade away as though it had died.

Job says, The souls of all things are in the hands of the Lord, with the ancient is wisdom, and the Lord governs in all things.

Job testifies of his confidence in the Lord and says, Though He slay me, yet will I trust in Him, and He also will be my salvation.

Summary of Job 14–18

Job declares that death may be the only way to find relief from his suffering. He wishes he could be hidden in a grave until God's wrath is completed (Job 14:13). Job ceases his efforts to declare his innocence to his "miserable comforters" (see Job 16:2–7).

CHAPTERS 14–18

Job testifies of the shortness of life, the certainty of death, and the guarantee of a resurrection—He asks, If a man die, will he live again?—Job answers that he will await the Lord's call to come forth from the grave.

Eliphaz sets forth the disquietude of wicked men—They do not believe they will return out of darkness and be resurrected.

Job speaks against the wicked who oppose him—Though even his friends scorn him, he testifies that his witness is in heaven and his record is on high.

Job speaks of the sorrow of death and of the grave in that day when the body returns to the dust.

Bildad tells of the damned state of the wicked who know not God.

CHAPTER 19

Job tells of the ills that have befallen him and then testifies, I know that my Redeemer lives—Job prophesies that he will be resurrected and that in his flesh he will see God.

Summary of Job 19:1–22

Job strongly objects to the accusations given by his friends. Job reviews the challenges with which God has afflicted him. Job expresses the feelings of being abandoned by God, his family, and friends.

Job 19:23–29. Job Testifies of Jesus Christ and of the Resurrection

23 Oh that my words were now written! oh that they were printed in a book!

24 That they were graven with an iron pen and lead in the rock for ever!

What was the "iron pen and lead" that Job wished to use to record his words? (19:23–24) "Against [the] uncharitable and groundless accusations [of his friends] he wishes (Job 19:23) that the testimony of his innocence, to which [his friends] will not listen, might be recorded in a book for posterity, or because a book may easily perish, graven in a rock (therefore not on leaden plates) with an iron style, and the addition of lead, with which to fill up the engraved letters, and render them still more imperishable" (Keil and Delitzsch, *Commentary* [on Job 19:21–25]). "[Job's] wish was granted, for peace has come into many souls as they have read his strong testimony" (Kimball, in Conference Report, April 1969, 31).

How can we, as Job, declare such a strong testimony? (19:25) "At some time every one of us must face the question which Job faced, and because of the Atonement wrought by Jesus Christ we may answer it as Job answered it. . . .

"The Spirit has borne witness in our hearts so that we too can testify that Jesus Christ is the resurrection and the life, and that he that believeth in Him, though he were dead, yet shall he live; and he that liveth and believeth in Him shall never die (see John 11:25–26)" (Hinckley, "Empty Tomb Bore Testimony," 66).

How does our knowledge of the resurrection prepare us to understand death? (19:26) "When Christ rose from the grave, becoming the firstfruits of the Resurrection, He made that gift available to all. And with that sublime act, He softened the devastating, consuming sorrow that gnaws at the souls of those who have lost precious loved ones. . . .

"[Death] is not the end of existence. 'If in this life only we have hope in Christ, we are of all men most miserable' [1 Cor. 15:19]. Because of the risen Christ, 'death is swallowed up in victory' [1 Cor. 15:54].

"Because of our beloved Redeemer, we can lift up our voices, even in the midst of our darkest Fridays, and proclaim, 'O death, where is thy sting? O grave, where is thy victory?' (1 Corinthians 15:55)" (Wirthlin, "Sunday Will Come," 29, 30).

What are "reins"? (19:27) "Reins" is a term used to refer to "heart," "kidneys," "loins," "waist," or other "inward parts" (see *New Unger's Bible Dictionary*, 1072).

25 For I know *that* my redeemer liveth, and *that* he shall stand at the latter *day* upon the earth:

26 And *though* after my skin *worms* destroy this *body*, yet in my flesh shall I see God:

27 Whom I shall see for myself, and mine eyes shall behold, and not another; *though* my reins be consumed within me.

28 But ye should say, Why persecute we him, seeing the root of the matter is found in me?

29 Be ye afraid of the sword: for wrath *bringeth* the punishments of the sword, that ye may know *there is* a judgment.

CHAPTERS 20–21

Zophar shows the condition of the wicked—He says, The triumphing of the wicked is short, and the joy of the hypocrite is but for a moment.

Job admits that the wicked sometimes prosper in this life—Then he testifies that their judgment will be hereafter in the day of wrath and destruction.

Summary of Job 20–21

Zophar takes offense at Job's rebuke and describes his view of how heaven punishes the wicked. Job confronts his friends with his perspective that sometimes the Lord allows the wicked to prosper. "Job expresses himself as puzzled by the dispensations of Divine Providence, because of the unequal distribution of temporal goods; he shows that wicked men often live long, prosper in their families, in their flocks, and in all their substance, and yet live in defiance of God and sacred things [Job 21:1–16]. At other times their prosperity is suddenly blasted, and they and their families come to ruin, Job 21:17–21. God, however, is too wise to err; and he deals out various lots to all according to his wisdom: some come sooner, others later, to the grave: the strong and the weak, the prince and the peasant, come to a similar end in this life; but the wicked are reserved for a day of wrath, Job 21:22–33" (*Adam Clarke's Commentary* [on Introduction to Job 21]).

CHAPTERS 22–26

Eliphaz accuses Job of various sins and exhorts him to repent.

Job seeks the Lord and asserts his own righteousness—He says, When the Lord has tried me, I will come forth as gold.

Summary of Job 22–26

Eliphaz attributes all of Job's sufferings and losses to disobedience and disfavor before God, a common belief anciently. Job even wonders why so many of the wicked seem to go unpunished while they take advantage of the innocent. Malachi asks a similar question: "Ye have said, It is vain to serve God: and what profit is it that we have kept his ordinance, and that we have walked mournfully before the LORD of hosts? And now we call the proud happy; yea, they that work wickedness are set up; yea, they that tempt God are even delivered" (Malachi 3:14–15).

Eliphaz then suggests that Job repent, saying: "Is not thy wickedness great? And thine iniquities infinite?" He insists that Job would have all of his

Joseph Smith's Teachings on Being Tried through Affliction (Job 23)

"There is no safety, only in the arm of Jehovah. None else can deliver, and he will not deliver unless we do prove ourselves faithful to him in the severest trouble. For he that will have his robes washed in the blood of the Lamb must come up through great tribulation [see Revelation 7:13–14], even the greatest of all affliction. . . .

"Men have to suffer that they may come upon Mount Zion and be exalted above the heavens. . . .

"God hath said that He would have a tried people, that He would purge them as gold [see Malachi 3:3]. . . .

"Trials will only give us the knowledge necessary to understand the minds of the ancients. For my part, I think I never could have felt as I now do, if I had not suffered the wrongs that I have suffered. All things shall work together for good to them that love God [see Romans 8:28]. . . .

"You will have all kinds of trials to pass through. And it is quite as necessary for you to be tried as it was for Abraham and other men of God, and . . . God will feel after you, and He will take hold of you and wrench your very heart strings, and if you cannot stand it you will not be fit for an inheritance in the Celestial Kingdom of God" (*Joseph Smith* [manual], 230–31).

fortunes restored if he would only repent (see Job 22:5, 21–28). Job responds to Eliphaz by declaring the Lord "knoweth the way that I take: when he hath tried me, I shall come forth as gold" (Job 23:10). Job knew that "in the pain, the agony, and the heroic endeavors of life, we pass through a refiner's fire, and the insignificant and the unimportant in our lives can melt away like dross and make our faith bright, intact, and strong. In this way the divine image can be mirrored from the soul. It is part of the purging toll exacted of some to become acquainted with God. In the agonies of life, we seem to listen better to the faint, godly whisperings of the Divine Shepherd" (Faust, "Refiner's Fire," 54).

Murderers, adulterers, those who oppress the poor, and wicked people in general often go unpunished for a little while.

Bildad bemoans the lowly state of man and classifies him as a worm.

Job reproves Bildad's lack of empathy—He extols the power, greatness, and strength of the Lord.

CHAPTER 27

Job asserts his righteousness—When the wicked are buried in death, terrors will take hold of them.

Job 27:1–6. Job Says He Will Always Be Righteous

1 Moreover Job continued his parable, and said,

2 *As* God liveth, *who* hath taken away my judgment; and the Almighty, *who* hath vexed my soul;

3 All the while my breath *is* in me, and the spirit of God *is* in my nostrils;

4 My lips shall not speak wickedness, nor my tongue utter deceit.

What does Job mean that he will not speak wickedly or with deceit? (27:4) "In this long eternal quest to be more like our Savior, may we try to be 'perfect' men and women in at least this one way now—by offending not in word, or more positively put, by speaking with a new tongue, the tongue of angels. Our words, like our deeds, should be filled with faith and hope and charity, the three great Christian imperatives so desperately needed in the world today" (Holland, "Tongue of Angels," 18). ⊕

5 God forbid that I should justify you: till I die I will not remove mine integrity from me.

What is integrity? (27:5) "Integrity is defined as moral soundness, genuineness, wholeness, and incorruptibility. It includes our beliefs, the way we think and speak, and the way we act, especially when no one is watching. It is being honest with ourselves, others, and God. When we have integrity, we 'live by our beliefs and standards.' President Gordon B. Hinckley . . . instructed us that keeping our covenants with honor is a part of integrity. It is thinking and doing what is right, no matter where we are or what the consequences might be" (Lewis, "Integrity," 50).

6 My righteousness I hold fast, and will not let it go: my heart shall not reproach *me* so long as I live.

Like Job, how can you hold firmly to righteousness? (27:6) "Regardless of gender, marital status, or age, individuals can choose to link themselves directly to the Savior, hold fast to the rod of His truth, and lead by the light of that truth. By so doing, they become examples of righteousness to whom others will want to cling" (Nelson, "Set in Order Thy House," 69). "If we exercise faith and diligently obey the commandments of the Lord, we can more easily choose the right" (Soares, "Hold On to the Rod," 60).

7 Let mine enemy be as the wicked, and he that riseth up against me as the unrighteous.

Job 27:7–23. Job Explains That the Wicked Will Be Punished according to the Judgment of God

8 For what *is* the hope of the hypocrite, though he hath gained, when God taketh away his soul?

9 Will God hear his cry when trouble cometh upon him?

10 Will he delight himself in the Almighty? will he always call upon God?

What does Job say is the fate of the hypocrite? (27:8–10) Job's point here seems to be that the hypocrite has no hope—he has lost his soul and God will not answer his petition when trouble comes upon him. A latter-day apostle has also warned about the dangers of hypocrisy: "The Lord's prophets have ever raised a warning voice against those who 'draw near [to the Lord] with their mouth, and with their lips do honour [Him], but have removed their heart far from [Him]' [Isaiah 29:13]. . . .

"Such artificial discipleship not only keeps us from seeing ourselves as who we really are, but it also prevents us from truly changing through the miracle of the Savior's Atonement" (Uchtdorf, "On Being Genuine," 81, 83).

11 I will teach you by the hand of God: *that* which *is* with the Almighty will I not conceal.

12 Behold, all ye yourselves have seen *it;* why then are ye thus altogether vain?

What did Job mean that he would teach "by the hand of God"? (27:11) "Most people don't come to church looking merely for a few new gospel facts or to see old friends, though all of that is important. They come seeking a spiritual experience. They want peace. They want their faith fortified and their hope renewed. . . . Those of us who are called upon to speak or teach or lead have an obligation to help provide that, as best we possibly can. We can only do that if we ourselves are striving to know God, if we ourselves are continually seeking the light of His Only Begotten Son" (Holland, "Teacher Come from God," 26).

13 This *is* the portion of a wicked man with God, and the heritage of oppressors, *which* they shall receive of the Almighty.

What is the fate of the wicked? (27:13–23) "The fate of the wicked is . . . expounded in verses 13–23. . . . Job is instructing the friends by turning their argument against them, warning that this could happen to them.

This . . . fits well with the emphasis in verse 11 that Job is going to instruct them, and it makes sense if the friends are seen as the enemy (v. 7) who will receive the portion of the wicked (v. 13). The friends have misrepresented God and have wronged Job with their counsel so that their . . . identification with the wicked is an appropriate warning to them" (Belcher, *Finding Favour in the Sight of God*, 111).

What is the imagery of the moth's house? (27:18) "While most of the calamities that befall the wicked that Job outlines in this segment are easily understandable, a few are less so. In this verse Job compares the homes of the wicked to temporary things. They will last as long as the cocoon of a moth, which is used for a very short period, never to be returned to, and which blows away in the wind. Their homes are also like a temporary hut that is set up by those who need to stay in the field to watch animals for a time" (Muhlestein, *Scripture Study Made Simple*, 328).

Why does the "rich man" experience terror when facing death? (27:19–22) "This wicked person's loss of all his wealth is but the beginning of his end. He himself will have to pass through a tunnel of horror that leads to his own death. *Terrors . . . overtake him.* He is panic-stricken, as when a person walking in a wadi suddenly faces a rushing torrent. Or *in the night the tempest snatches . . . him from his place.* His *place* is the center of his rule, his wealth, and his security.

"The evildoer feels as though the hot *east wind lifts him up* and *sweeps him* away *from his place*. On nights when the sirocco [hot wind] blows, the dry heat makes it difficult to sleep; a person's restless mind is troubled by nightmares. As God's instrument of punishment, this wind torments the wicked person. It pursues him relentlessly as he tries desperately to escape its force" (Hartley, *Book of Job*, 360).

What is meant by men "clap[ping] their hands at [God]"? (27:23) This verse is similar to Lamentations 2:15, "All that pass by clap their hands at thee; they hiss and wag their head." When men "clap their hands . . . and shall hiss," they do so "in derisive mockery and contempt" (Reichert, *Job*, 139).

14 If his children be multiplied, *it is* for the sword: and his offspring shall not be satisfied with bread.

15 Those that remain of him shall be buried in death: and his widows shall not weep.

16 Though he heap up silver as the dust, and prepare raiment as the clay;

17 He may prepare *it,* but the just shall put *it* on, and the innocent shall divide the silver.

18 He buildeth his house as a moth, and as a booth *that* the keeper maketh.

19 The rich man shall lie down, but he shall not be gathered: he openeth his eyes, and he *is* not.

20 Terrors take hold on him as waters, a tempest stealeth him away in the night.

21 The east wind carrieth him away, and he departeth: and as a storm hurleth him out of his place.

22 For *God* shall cast upon him, and not spare: he would fain flee out of his hand.

23 *Men* shall clap their hands at him, and shall hiss him out of his place.

CHAPTER 28

Wealth comes out of the earth—Wisdom cannot be purchased—The fear of the Lord is wisdom, and to depart from evil is understanding.

CHAPTERS 29–31

Job recalls his former prosperity and greatness—He was blessed because of his righteousness, his charity, and his good deeds.

Job is derided by the children of vile and base men—In his afflicted state, he cries to the Lord—Job says that he wept for those in trouble.

Job invites judgment so that God may know his integrity—If he has done ill, Job welcomes the penalties for so doing.

CHAPTERS 32–37

Elihu, in anger, answers Job and his three friends—Elihu says, There is a spirit in man, and the inspiration of the Almighty gives understanding—He also says, Great men are not always wise.

Elihu says, God is greater than man, He speaks to man in dreams and visions, He ransoms those cast into the pit, and He delivers their souls and gives them life.

Summary of Job 28

"Chapter 28 of Job is a stand-alone poem often called the Hymn to Wisdom, which argues that human beings can never find wisdom themselves because only God is truly wise" (Austin, *Re-reading Job*, 59). Amid his infirmities, Job expresses that wisdom leads a person to feel reverence for the Lord (see Job 28:28).

Summary of Job 29–31

Job assures his friends and others that in his days of prosperity he was justified before the Lord for his treatment toward others. While his friends deride him, Job confidently conveys that God knows the goodness of his heart and, if there were something amiss in his life, he accepts the judgments. Job demonstrates great faith throughout his whole trial. The *Lectures on Faith* teach that for anyone to have true faith, he or she needs to have "first, the idea that [God] actually exists. Secondly, a correct idea of [His] character, perfections and attributes. Thirdly, an actual knowledge that the course of life which he [or she] is pursuing is according to [His] will" (*Lectures on Faith* [1985], 38). Job believes that his life is in harmony with the will of God.

Job exclaims, "Let me be weighed in an even balance, that God may know mine integrity" (Job 31:6). Similarly, Joseph Smith taught that the Saints' trials would be "a trial of our faith equal to that of Abraham, and that the [Ancients] will not have, whereof, to boast over us in the day of Judgment, as being called to pass through heavier afflictions, that we may hold an even weight in the balances with them" (Joseph Smith Papers, "History, 1838–1856, volume C-1 [2 November 1838–31 July 1842][a]," 904[a]).

Summary of Job 32–37

These chapters introduce a fourth young man into the dialogue named Elihu. "Elihu's comments do not have the poetic majesty of the earlier dialogue, but they contain sound theological messages that shift attention from Job's question of justice to the divine perspective of the creation. While many scholars feel the Elihu discourse is a later addition to Job, it fits the story well by elevating Job and his friends' attention from his own problems to becoming more receptive to communication from the Lord. Elihu provides the link between the earlier questions and speeches and the divine response" (Ludlow, *Unlocking the Old Testament*, 122).

Elihu teaches, God cannot be unjust, commit iniquity, pervert judgment, or respect persons—Man should bear chastisement and do iniquity no more.

Elihu contrasts the weakness of man and the power of God—Our wickedness hurts other men, and our righteousness helps them—Man should trust in the Lord.

Elihu says, Those who are righteous are prospered—The wicked perish and die without knowledge—Elihu praises the greatness of God.

Elihu concludes, saying, The Lord controls the laws of nature—God reigns in terrible majesty.

CHAPTER 38

God asks Job where he was when the foundations of the earth were laid, when the morning stars sang together, and when all the sons of God shouted for joy—The phenomena of nature show the greatness of God and the weakness of man.

1 Then the LORD answered Job out of the whirlwind, and said,

Job 38:1–7. Job Learns Why He Should Not Question God

Why did God speak out of a whirlwind? (38:1) "Job is taught first by the winds of adversity. A great wind collapses the roof of the eldest son's house (Job 1:19), crushing all Job's children. This disaster culminates a series of external calamities that lead Job to question why humans endure seemingly senseless suffering. Hence a literal desert storm hurls Job into a spiritual maelstrom. By corollary, Job's inquiry is ended by a whirlwind.... Thus Job learns wisdom from the winds of affliction and of revelation" (Tanner, "Book of Job," 391).

2 Who *is* this that darkeneth counsel by words without knowledge?

3 Gird up now thy loins like a man; for I will demand of thee, and answer thou me.

Who is being accused as one who darkeneth counsel? (38:2) "We sense Job's powerful integrity and genuine depth of feelings for God, qualities seemingly absent from his coldly correct friends. Yet we also sense a measure of pride and even arrogance, that he, Job, a mere man, should think himself sufficient to prosecute a case against God. No wonder Job stands condemned by the Lord in the final chapters as one 'that darkeneth counsel by words without knowledge.' . . . Humbled by the voice from the whirlwind, Job repents: 'Behold, I am vile . . . therefore have I uttered that I understood not; things too wonderful for me, which I knew not' (Job 40:4; 42:3)" (Tanner, "Book of Job," 400).

4 Where wast thou when I laid the foundations of the earth? declare, if thou hast understanding.

5 Who hath laid the measures thereof, if thou knowest? or who hath stretched the line upon it?

6 Whereupon are the foundations thereof fastened? or who laid the corner stone thereof;

7 When the morning stars sang together, and all the sons of God shouted for joy?

Where was Job when Jehovah laid the foundation of the earth? (38:4–7) "Would the Lord have asked these questions of Job had Job not had a preexistence, had there not been a plan of life and of salvation developed before the foundations of the earth were laid? And then we read that at that very time of which these questions relate, that 'the morning stars sang together and all of the sons of God shouted for joy.' Job participated in that singing and so did we. Joseph Smith, the Prophet, leaves us no doubt on that subject. He says: 'At the first organization in heaven we were all present and saw the Savior chosen and appointed and the plan of salvation made, and we sanctioned it'" (Moyle, in Conference Report, Apr. 1955, 71).

Why did we shout for joy in the premortal world? (38:7) "Why were we then happy? I think it was because good had triumphed over evil and the whole human family was on the Lord's side. We turned our backs on the adversary and aligned ourselves with the forces of God, and those forces were victorious. But having made that decision, why should we have to make it again and again after our birth into mortality? I cannot understand why so many have betrayed in life the decision they once made when the great war occurred in heaven" (Hinckley, "Dawning of a Brighter Day," 81).

Summary of Job 38:8–41

God explains the wonders of nature to Job so he will better understand how great God is and how weak men are in comparison to God.

Summary of Job 39–41

The Lord poses rhetorical questions to contrast the infinite power of God and the mortal limitations of Job. Job's responses to the Lord's questions and statements reveal the development of his understanding and wisdom. The Lord rebukes Job by saying, "Shall he that contendeth with the Almighty instruct him?" (Job 40:2). After which Job replies, "Behold I am vile; what shall I answer thee? I will lay mine hand upon my mouth" (Job 40:4).

The Lord tells Job to "gird up his loins now like a man" (Job 40:7). "Webster defines gird as 'to encircle or fasten . . . , surround . . . , clothe or invest with power . . . , prepare for a struggle.' Thus, if one has girded up his loins, he has clothed himself with power in preparation for the ongoing struggle with Satan, that father of lies who would rob [Job] of virtue and spiritual strength" (Brewster, *Doctrine and Covenants Encyclopedia*, 212). The Lord assures Job He is all powerful and can help him.

"The Lord's power over the behemoth (hippopotamus) and the leviathan (crocodile) provide simple illustrations of mortal weaknesses when compared to God ([Job] 40–41). Job finally confesses the rightness of the Lord and his need to repent of any thoughts questioning the justice of God" (Ludlow, *Unlocking the Old Testament*, 123).

Job 42:1–6. Job Is Remorseful for Having Questioned God's Ways

Why does Job have total trust and faith in God? (42:2) Job had a spiritual witness that God had all knowledge and that He was the creator of all things. Other prophets have also testified: "He knoweth all things, and there is not anything save he knows it" (2 Nephi 9:20). "He knows all the thoughts and intents of the heart" (Alma 18:32). He knows the "things that come into your mind" (Ezekiel 11:5). King Benjamin pleaded, "Believe in God; believe that he is, and that he created all things, both in heaven and in earth; believe that he has all wisdom, and all power, both in heaven and in earth; believe that man doth not comprehend all the things which the Lord can comprehend" (Mosiah 4:9).

CHAPTERS 39–41

Man's weakness and ignorance are compared with God's mighty works—Does man even know how the laws of nature operate?

The Lord challenges Job, and Job replies humbly—The Lord speaks of His power to Job—He asks, Hast thou an arm like God?—He points to His power in the behemoth.

The Lord points to His power in the leviathan—All things under the whole heaven are the Lord's.

CHAPTER 42

Job repents in dust and ashes—He sees the Lord with his eyes—The Lord chastises Job's friends, accepts Job, blesses him, and makes his latter days greater than his beginning.

1 Then Job answered the LORD, and said,

2 I know that thou canst do every *thing*, and *that* no thought can be withholden from thee.

3 Who *is* he that hideth counsel without knowledge? therefore have I uttered that I understood not; things too wonderful for me, which I knew not.

4 Hear, I beseech thee, and I will speak: I will demand of thee, and declare thou unto me.

What were the wonderful things that Job did not understand or know? (42:3) "Job quickly and fully acknowledges that he has been speaking of things that were beyond his ability to comprehend. In some ways this is the point of the entire play [see introduction to Book of Job]. It explores many avenues of thought regarding the nature of suffering, and then it states clearly that man is not capable of understanding God's thoughts or ways—and thus, in some ways, suffering must be endured without full understanding. This is really the main and most salient point of the book. We may not understand why we suffer, but God knows and understands more than we do, and He is in charge" (Muhlestein, *Scripture Study Made Simple*, 329).

5 I have heard of thee by the hearing of the ear: but now mine eye seeth thee.

6 Wherefore I abhor *myself,* and repent in dust and ashes.

In what ways did Job "see" God? (42:5) "It is true that some have actually seen the Savior, but when one consults the dictionary, he learns that there are many other meanings of the word *see*, such as coming to know Him, discerning Him, recognizing Him and His work, perceiving His importance, or coming to understand Him" (Haight, "Temples and Work Therein," 61). It appears from the text that Job had most likely "seen" God in all aspects of knowing Him.

7 ¶ And it was *so,* that after the LORD had spoken these words unto Job, the LORD said to Eliphaz the Temanite, My wrath is kindled against thee, and against thy two friends: for ye have not spoken of me *the thing that is* right, as my servant Job *hath.*

8 Therefore take unto you now seven bullocks and seven rams, and go to my servant Job, and offer up for yourselves a burnt offering; and my servant Job shall pray for you: for him will I accept: lest I deal with you *after your* folly, in that ye have not spoken of me *the thing which is* right, like my servant Job.

9 So Eliphaz the Temanite and Bildad the Shuhite *and* Zophar the Naamathite went, and did according as the LORD commanded them: the LORD also accepted Job.

Job 42:7–9. God Tells Job's Friends to Offer Sacrifice

Why did God command Job's friends to offer "a burnt offering"? (42:8–9) Anciently, the burnt offering was offered for those who needed repentance. "The 'burnt offering' was not an offering for a specific sin, but rather for the sinful heart or sin-nature which required an atonement if the worshiper was to have access to God" (*Revell Bible Dictionary*, 180).

10 And the LORD turned the captivity of Job, when he prayed for his friends: also the LORD gave Job twice as much as he had before.

11 Then came there unto him all his brethren, and all his sisters, and all they that had

Job 42:10–17. The Lord Blesses Job with More Than He Had before His Trials Began

How might Job's experience inspire us with hope in our trials? (42:10) "And so great was the goodness of God extended to Job, that we are told he was more blessed in his latter days than in his former days. And it was as the devil had said, God put a hedge around about [Job] (Job 1:10) and so he does about us, and we do not know it" (Taylor, in *Journal of Discourses*, 22:320). "The book of Job provides what may be taken as an allegorical lesson of hope for all of us, in the afterlife" (Rasmussen, *Latter-day Saint Commentary on the Old Testament*, 412). In what ways has God provided you with strength in your trials?

been of his acquaintance before, and did eat bread with him in his house: and they bemoaned him, and comforted him over all the evil that the LORD had brought upon him: every man also gave him a piece of money, and every one an earring of gold.

12 So the LORD blessed the latter end of Job more than his beginning: for he had fourteen thousand sheep, and six thousand camels, and a thousand yoke of oxen, and a thousand she asses.

Why are the names of the daughters mentioned but not the sons? (42:13–14) "The narrator lingers on the daughters, giving their names. . . . The image of a joyful and harmonious society is underscored by the note that Job gave his daughters an inheritance along with the brothers. That this detail should receive special mention apparently indicates that it was not the normal state of affairs (cf. Num 27:3–4)" (Newsom, "Book of Job," 635).

13 He had also seven sons and three daughters.

14 And he called the name of the first, Jemima; and the name of the second, Kezia; and the name of the third, Keren-happuch.

In what ways were the daughters of Job considered to be "fair"? (42:15) The Hebrew word for "fair" [*yâpeh*] means beautiful, beauty, comely, fair, goodly, pleasant, or well (see *Strong's Exhaustive Concordance*, word #h3303). "Women of God can never be like women of the world. The world has enough women who are tough; we need women who are tender. There are enough women who are coarse; we need women who are kind. There are enough women who are rude; we need women who are refined. We have enough women of fame and fortune; we need more women of faith. We have enough greed; we need more goodness. We have enough vanity; we need more virtue. We have enough popularity; we need more purity" (Nadauld, "Joy of Womanhood," 15). See commentary in this volume for Proverbs 31.

15 And in all the land were no women found *so* fair as the daughters of Job: and their father gave them inheritance among their brethren.

16 After this lived Job an hundred and forty years, and saw his sons, and his sons' sons, *even* four generations.

17 So Job died, *being* old and full of days.

THE BOOK OF
PSALMS

Introduction

The book of Psalms is "Israel's ancient collection of hymns of praise and worship, widely used in Temple and synagogue worship and particularly cherished by God's people in every age" (*New Unger's Bible Dictionary*, 1048). "The word *psalms* comes from the Hebrew word *tehillim*, meaning 'praises.' The book of Psalms is part of the poetic corpus [writings] of the Old Testament. Psalms contains sacred hymns sung to music and/or shouted with rejoicing. The name *Psalms* originated from the Greek *psalmoi*, meaning 'songs of praise'" (Black, *400 Questions and Answers about the Old Testament*, 148).

"The Psalms became a very important part of scripture and were used in temple performances, solemn feasts and festivals, coronations, pilgrimages, covenant renewals, regular Sabbath worship, times of mourning, and in all kinds of prayers" (Muhlestein, *Essential Old Testament Companion*, 334).

Of the 150 psalms, "seventy-three of [them] are ascribed to David, and so it was natural that the whole collection should be referred to as his, and that this convenient way of speaking should give rise in time to the popular belief that 'the sweet psalmist of Israel' himself wrote all the so-called Psalms of David" (Bible Dictionary, "Psalms"). "In the King James Version of the Bible we find the following breakdown according to author and number written: David, seventy-three; Solomon, two; the sons of Korah, ten; Asaph, twelve; Heman, one; Ethan, one; psalms bearing no name, fifty-nine. Ezra is credited with having gathered, edited, and arranged the order of the psalms, thus providing Judah with a standard hymnal as part of their sacred literature" (Pearson, *Old Testament*, 52).

"Martin Luther called it a work through which we are shown the heart of all the saints. It is perhaps best understood as a celebration of, and guide to, [an] intimate relationship with God. As such, the Psalms is one of the most significant, most personal, and most rewarding of the books of the Bible" (*Revell Bible Dictionary*, 833). "No book of the Old Testament is more Christian in its inner sense or more fully attested as such by the use made of it than the Psalms" (Bible Dictionary, "Psalms"). "Of the 283 direct quotes from the Old Testament cited in the New Testament, 116 were taken from Psalms. Such love of the psalms by the early Christians came because of the insights into the nature, goodness, mercy, and mission of the Lord which are revealed in many of these inspired poems" (Pearson, *Old Testament*, 52).

"The greatest value of the psalms for the modern Church . . . is what draws most people to them. They provide doctrinal insights and exhortations to do good. Because many of the biblical psalms are hymns of praise to God, they tell us much about God and our relationship to him. From the psalms, we learn that God is a loving, trustworthy, and wise Father to whom we can turn in all circumstances. We learn that even in times of tribulation we can turn to him and receive comfort, support, healing, and forgiveness" (Tvedtnes, "Ancient Israelite Psalters," 247–48).

Psalm 1:1–6. The Righteous Will Be Blessed and the Wicked Punished

What does "standeth in the way of sinners" mean? (1:1) In this case, the phrase "standeth in the way of sinners" should not be confused with "getting in the way to oppose sinners." Rather, this phrase commends those who do not participate in or support sinful behavior. For example, one modern translation of this verse reads: "Happy are those who do not follow the advice of the wicked, or take the path that sinners tread, or sit in the seat of scoffers" (NRSV, Psalm 1:1).

What is the "law of the Lord"? (1:2) "The law of the Lord can be found in scripture. Joshua 1:8 commands us to meditate or think about the scriptures 'day and night,' and not just to ponder them, but to 'observe to do' or live by their teachings" (Valletta, et al., *Old Testament for Latter-day Saint Families*, 415). "As members of The Church of Jesus Christ of Latter-day Saints, we are blessed to know how and where true happiness is found. It is found in carefully living the gospel established by our Lord and Savior, Jesus Christ, and in striving to become more like Him" (Craven, "Careful versus Casual," 9; see also Mosiah 2:41).

PSALM 1

Blessed are the righteous—The ungodly will perish.

1 Blessed *is* the man that walketh not in the counsel of the ungodly, nor standeth in the way of sinners, nor sitteth in the seat of the scornful.

2 But his delight *is* in the law of the LORD; and in his law doth he meditate day and night.

3 And he shall be like a tree planted by the rivers of water, that bringeth forth his fruit in his season; his leaf also shall not wither; and whatsoever he doeth shall prosper.

How Was the Book of Psalms Organized? (Psalms 1–150)

"In the traditional Hebrew Bible, the book of Psalms consists of 150 psalms (chapters), divided into five sections: 1–41; 42–72; 73–89; 90–106; 107–150. The Jewish Talmud suggests this correlates with the five books of Moses, and certain psalms . . . emphasize obedience to the law. . . .

"Although psalms express different emotions, they often overlap, making strict categorization difficult. There are, however, a few dominant categories. The most common type of biblical psalm is the lament. There are both individual and community lamentations in the book of Psalms. . . . Another general category of psalms is praise. . . . Psalms 146–150 particularly focus on praising Jehovah, especially for his 'mighty acts.' . . . A particular type of praise is rendered in thanksgiving psalms, which express gratitude for blessings received, including healing, deliverance, and forgiveness. . . . There are a number of royal psalms associated with Israel's kings. Many Christians believe certain of these royal psalms contain messianic imagery that points to various aspects of Jesus' redeeming mission" (Holzapfel, et al., *Jehovah and the World of the Old Testament*, 233, 234, 235).

"The traditional Hebrew titles ascribed to most of the poems in Psalms associate many of them with various individuals, who presumably authored or grouped the songs or to whom they were dedicated. The musically gifted shepherd-king David—by far the most frequently mentioned—appears in 73 of these headings. . . . Some psalm titles relate the songs to specific historical circumstances or specify musical directions, such as prescriptions for instrumental accompaniment" (*Eerdmans Companion to the Bible*, 319).

Susan Easton Black added: "Some superscriptions refer to the way each psalm was to be sung or accompanied. For example, *Negin* means that the psalm could be accompanied by a stringed instrument, whereas *Nehiloth* implies a wind instrument accompaniment. Other titles suggest the character of the psalm. For example, *Maschil* means 'to give instruction,' whereas *Gittith* refers to the 'melody or instrument' to be used [see Bible Dictionary, 'Psalms']" (*400 Questions and Answers about the Old Testament*, 151).

4 The ungodly *are* not so: but *are* like the chaff which the wind driveth away.

Why are the ungodly compared to chaff? (1:4) Unlike the righteous who are compared to a well-watered, fruitful tree, the ungodly are compared to *chaff.* "Anciently, threshers of grain understood well the art of separating the seed from the husks, or chaff. This simple matter was accomplished by tossing the grain into the air. By so doing, the valuable seed immediately returned to the threshing floor, and the slightest breeze would carry the worthless chaff away. So it is with the wicked" (McConkie and Parry, *Guide to Scriptural Symbols*, 28).

5 Therefore the ungodly shall not stand in the judgment, nor sinners in the congregation of the righteous.

6 For the Lord knoweth the way of the righteous: but the way of the ungodly shall perish.

What qualifies a person to be called ungodly? (1:5) "You will find in the Scriptures of the Old and New Testaments, and in the other revelations of God, that there is a clear distinction made between the sinner and the ungodly [see Psalm 1:5; 1 Peter 4:18]. A person to be ungodly must have known godliness, and must have a knowledge of what the Lord requires concerning him. There are many in the midst of this people who believe the Gospel with all their hearts, but yet do wickedly; this makes them ungodly" (Young, in *Journal of Discourses*, 2:258).

PSALMS 2–7

A messianic psalm—The heathen will rage against the Lord's anointed—The Lord speaks of His Son, whom He has begotten.

David cries unto the Lord and is heard—Salvation is of the Lord.

A Psalm of David, when he fled from Absalom his son.

Summary of Psalms 2–7

These psalms were written by David. They include some of David's petitions to the Lord for protection and deliverance from enemies and his pleadings for vindication. David testifies that salvation comes from the Lord and that we can trust in God's power. David is convinced of his innocence against the charges of those who oppose him and he pleads to the Lord for vindication and judgment.

Some of the headings of these psalms include superscriptions, indicating information about the psalm or how it was to be performed. The superscriptions of these psalms begin to provide musical

What Purpose Does Psalm 1 Serve? (Psalm 1:1–6)

"Psalm 1 serves to introduce the book as a whole. In a tone reminiscent of the Wisdom literature, it begins: 'Blessed [or, happy] is the man that walketh not in the counsel of the ungodly, nor standeth in the way of sinners. . . . But his delight is in the law of the Lord; and in his law doth he meditate day and night.' . . . Such a person is compared to a sturdy, productive, well-watered tree. The psalmist knew . . . 'meditation' and 'delight' did not take place in isolation from the events of a challenging world but also realized they are essential to finding peace and knowing the Lord. The psalms were to help in this process" (Holzapfel, et al., *Jehovah and the World of the Old Testament*, 234).

Elder Jeffrey R. Holland added: "[Psalm 1] is intended to be something of a backdrop against which all the psalms that follow are considered. It is the reminder that in the quest for a peaceful and productive life, we shouldn't be so foolish as to *choose* trouble. Life is difficult enough without our adding stupidity to our list of mistakes. How frustrating it must be to God when, wanting to help us and knowing full well the dangers along the way, He sees us willingly, willfully choose to walk in the counsel of the ungodly, stand in the way of sinners, and sit in the seat of the scornful" (*For Times of Trouble*, 16–17).

instructions. For example, some refer to the use of instruments such as Nehiloth, a flute or wind instrument, Neginoth and Sheminith, stringed instruments, or a style of music, Shiggaion, which is a psalm of lament (see Walton, et al., *IVP Bible Background Commentary*, 517, 518). Also, the word *Selah* begins to appear in some of the psalms. It is likely "a pause in singing for narration, instructions on dynamics to the choir or to instrumental accompaniment" (*Harper's Bible Dictionary* [1985], 922).

What is "Gittith"? (Psalm 8 superscription) *Gittith* "may relate either to the melody or to the instrument" used while performing the psalm (see Bible Dictionary, "Psalms").

Psalm 8:1–9. God Created Man and Is Mindful of Him

What is the significance of the phrase "O LORD our Lord"? (8:1) This phrase literally means "Jehovah, our Lord" (see *John Dummelow's Commentary* [on Psalm 8:1]). The name or title *LORD* "is one of the most frequently used titles for Jesus in the scriptures, especially when referencing Jehovah in the Old Testament. Its most common synonym is *Master*, suggesting governance and authority over possessions, property, and people, such as a medieval 'lord of the manor' or 'master of the house'" (Holland, *Witness for His Names*, 101).

David pleads for mercy—He counsels, Put your trust in the Lord.

To the chief Musician on Neginoth, A Psalm of David.

David asks the Lord to hear his voice—The Lord hates workers of iniquity—He blesses and shields the righteous.

To the chief Musician upon Nehiloth, A Psalm of David.

David cries unto the Lord for mercy—He asks to be healed and saved.

To the chief Musician on Neginoth upon Sheminith, A Psalm of David.

David trusts in the Lord, who will judge the people—God is angry with the wicked.

Shiggaion of David, which he sang unto the LORD, concerning the words of Cush the Benjamite.

PSALM 8

A messianic psalm of David—He says that babes and children praise the Lord—He asks, What is man, that Thou art mindful of him?

To the chief Musician upon Gittith, A Psalm of David.

1 O LORD our Lord, how excellent *is* thy name in all the earth! who hast set thy glory above the heavens.

2 Out of the mouth of babes and sucklings hast thou ordained strength because of thine enemies, that thou mightest still the enemy and the avenger.

What strength can be gained from children? (8:2) Referring to 3 Nephi 26:14, Elder Jeffrey R. Holland wrote: "Given the power and majesty of the teachings the Savior had given these Nephites . . . it is amazing to think that what these children knew and said was even greater than the things Jesus taught their parents. . . .

"All of us can respect our children and listen to them. In so many ways we need to be more like them, because 'of such is the kingdom of heaven' [Matthew 19:14]. Children come 'trailing clouds of glory . . . from God, who is [their] home' [Wordsworth, in *New Oxford Book of English Verse*, 509], and thereby they will frequently be the source of God's inspiration and utterance to us" (*For Times of Trouble*, 35–36). ⊕

3 When I consider thy heavens, the work of thy fingers, the moon and the stars, which thou hast ordained;

4 What is man, that thou art mindful of him? and the son of man, that thou visitest him?

5 For thou hast made him a little lower than the angels, and hast crowned him with glory and honour.

What is the place of God's children among all of His creations? (8:3–5) "Just think of it: You are known and remembered by the most majestic, powerful, and glorious Being in the universe! You are loved by the King of infinite space and everlasting time!

"He who created and knows the stars knows you and your name. . . .

"God loves you because you are His child. He loves you even though at times you may feel lonely or make mistakes.

"The love of God and the power of the restored gospel are redemptive and saving. . . . You are closer to heaven than you suppose. You are destined for more than you can possibly imagine" (Uchtdorf, "Forget Me Not," 123).

What does it mean that man was made "a little lower than the angels"? (8:5) "[Man] is unique among the creations of God—with a unique creation, a unique relationship to the Creator, and a unique stewardship over all other creations (Genesis 1:26–28; Moses 1:26–31; 6:8–10, 22). Man—all men and women—are thus unique in that they are the offspring of God. . . . Within this context, we can see that man, as the Psalmist declared, is only 'a little lower than the angels [in Hebrew the word is *Elohim*, the Gods], and [God] has crowned him with glory and honour' (Psalm 8:5). As the offspring of God, all men and women have the potential to become . . . exalted and like God" (Top, "Man," 402). ⊕

6 Thou madest him to have dominion over the works of thy hands; thou hast put all *things* under his feet:

7 All sheep and oxen, yea, and the beasts of the field;

Why did God give His children dominion over His creations? (8:6–9) "A human, made in the image of God, is certainly 'less than the gods' (Ps. 8:5*a*) but is given opportunity to earn 'glory and honor.'

"'Dominion' over others of God's creatures gives God's children opportunities to learn the ways of godliness (Ps. 8:6–8). They violate their dominion if they exploit animals or resources selfishly" (Rasmussen, *Latter-day Saint Commentary on the Old Testament*, 416). What have you learned about becoming like God as you have had "dominion" over some earthly things? ⊕

Summary of Psalms 9–15

This group of psalms includes Hebrew notations such as Muth-labben, Higgaion, and Sheminith, which may refer to musical instruments, tunes, or other directions for performing the psalms. David rejoices in thanksgiving to the Lord for bringing punishment to his enemies and is confident that the Lord will bring judgment to the wicked. He laments that God sometimes keeps His distance from those who experience trouble, but expresses confidence that the Lord will yet bless the humble. Finally, David contrasts the deceitful flattery of men with God's pure words. Those who seek to dwell with the Lord in the "holy hill of Zion" (JST, Psalm 15:1), must be truthful, be neighborly, fear the Lord, and have integrity. These psalms show the importance of turning to the Lord in every circumstance.

8 The fowl of the air, and the fish of the sea, *and whatsoever* passeth through the paths of the seas.

9 O Lord our Lord, how excellent *is* thy name in all the earth!

PSALMS 9–15

A messianic psalm of David—He praises the Lord for rebuking the nations—The Lord will judge the world in righteousness—He will dwell in Zion—The wicked will be sent to hell.

To the chief Musician upon Muth-labben,
A Psalm of David.

David speaks of various acts of the wicked—God is not in their thoughts—But the Lord is King forever and ever—He will judge the fatherless and oppressed.

David rejoices that the Lord is in His holy temple—The Lord tests the righteous and hates the wicked.

To the chief Musician, *A Psalm* of David.

David decries flattering lips and proud tongues—He says, The words of the Lord are pure words.

To the chief Musician upon Sheminith,
A Psalm of David.

David trusts in the Lord's mercy and rejoices in His salvation.

To the chief Musician, A Psalm of David.

David says, The fool has said in his heart, there is no God—Israel will rejoice in the day of restoration.

To the chief Musician, *A Psalm* of David.

David asks, Who will dwell in the Lord's holy hill?—He answers, The righteous, the upright, and those with integrity.

A Psalm of David.

PSALM 16

A messianic psalm of David—He rejoices in the Saints who are on the earth, in his own future redemption from hell, in the fact that God will not suffer His Holy One (the Messiah) to see corruption, and in the fulness of joy that is found in the Lord's presence.

Michtam of David.

1 Preserve me, O God: for in thee do I put my trust.

2 *O my soul,* thou hast said unto the LORD, Thou *art* my Lord: my goodness *extendeth* not to thee;

3 *But* to the saints that *are* in the earth, and *to* the excellent, in whom *is* all my delight.

4 Their sorrows shall be multiplied *that* hasten *after* another *god:* their drink offerings of blood will I not offer, nor take up their names into my lips.

5 The LORD *is* the portion of mine inheritance and of my cup: thou maintainest my lot.

6 The lines are fallen unto me in pleasant *places;* yea, I have a goodly heritage.

What was a "Michtam"? (Psalm 16 superscription) "This word occurs in the titles of six psalms ([Psalm] 16, 56–60), all of which are ascribed to David. . . . In the Geneva version [of the Bible] it is described as 'a certain tune.' From the position which it occupies in the title we may infer that *michtam* is a term applied to these psalms to denote their musical character, but beyond this everything is obscure" (*Smith's Bible Dictionary*, "Michtam"). Another source notes, "Some translate the word 'golden', i.e., precious. . . . The root of the word means to stamp or [en]grave, and hence it is regarded as denoting a composition so precious as to be worthy to be engraven on a durable tablet for preservation" (*Easton's Bible Dictionary*, "Michtam").

Psalm 16:1–11. David Praises the Lord for Promising to Redeem Him from Hell

What are the "lines" that provided David with a pleasant inheritance? (16:5–6) "Here is an allusion to the ancient division of the land by lot among the Israelites, the breadth and length being ascertained by lines which were used in measuring" (*Adam Clarke's Commentary* [on Psalm 16:6]). But David was not referring only to an earthly inheritance. "The lines have fallen to him in a charming district, [namely], in the pleasurable fellowship of God, this most blessed domain of love has become his paradisaic possession" (Keil and Delitzsch, *Commentary* [on Psalm 16:6–8]).

What do "reins" symbolize in this verse? (16:7) "The *reins*, an archaic word for 'kidneys,' represent the seat of emotions and the core of one's inner self (Ps. 7:9; 73:21; Prov. 23:16)" (McConkie and Parry, *Guide to Scriptural Symbols*, 93). David points out that it was often during "*the night*" that "God *instructs* him [through David's feelings], involving both correction and direction" (*New Bible Commentary: Revised*, 460).

To what hope was David referring? (16:9–10) "Speaking of his own resurrection and that of his Lord, David wrote: 'My flesh also shall rest in hope,' meaning, 'My body shall come forth from the grave,' 'For thou wilt not leave my soul in hell,' meaning, 'My spirit shall not remain in hell forever, but shall be joined with my body when I am resurrected.' Death and hell shall thus deliver up dead David who is in them. Then David came forth with the great Messianic pronouncement, 'Neither wilt thou suffer thine Holy One to see corruption' (Ps. 16:7–11). That is, 'The Holy One of Israel shall come forth in his resurrection before his dead body is permitted to decay and become dust'" (McConkie, *Promised Messiah*, 272–73). ⊕

Why did David refer to his soul being left in hell? (16:10) In speaking of David's condition, the Prophet Joseph Smith said: "A murderer, . . . one that sheds innocent blood, cannot have forgiveness. David sought repentance at the hand of God, carefully with tears, but he could only get it through Hell. He got a promise that his soul should not be left in Hell" (Jackson, *Joseph Smith's Commentary on the Bible*, 35). Psalm 51 records David's repentant pleading that resulted in this promise. President Boyd K. Packer explained: "Forgiveness will come eventually to all repentant souls who have not committed the unpardonable sin (see Matt. 12:31). Forgiveness does not, however, necessarily assure exaltation, as is the case with David (see D&C 132:38–39; see also Ps. 16:10; Acts 2:25–27)" ("Brilliant Morning of Forgiveness," 21fn15).

How can we obtain a fulness of joy in this life? (16:11) "Joy is a gift for the faithful [see 2 Nephi 9:18]. It is the gift that comes from intentionally trying to live a righteous life, as taught by Jesus Christ [see 2 Nephi 27:30; Alma 27:16–18]. . . .

"Heed these words of the Psalmist: 'I have set the Lord always before me: because he is at my right hand, I shall not be moved. . . . In [His] presence is fulness of joy' [Psalm 16:8, 11]. As this principle is embedded in our hearts, each and every day can be a day of joy and gladness [see Isaiah 35:10; 2 Nephi 8:3]" (Nelson, "Joy and Spiritual Survival," 84). What can you do this week to prepare to receive a fulness of joy?

7 I will bless the LORD, who hath given me counsel: my reins also instruct me in the night seasons.

8 I have set the LORD always before me: because *he is* at my right hand, I shall not be moved.

9 Therefore my heart is glad, and my glory
rejoiceth: my flesh also shall rest in hope.
10 For thou wilt not leave my soul in hell; neither wilt thou suffer thine Holy One to see corruption.

11 Thou wilt shew me the path of life: in thy presence *is* fulness of joy; at thy right hand *there are* pleasures for evermore.

PSALMS 17–21

David pleads with the Lord to hear his voice and to preserve him from men of the world—David hopes to behold the Lord's face in righteousness.

A Prayer of David.

David praises the Lord for His greatness and preserving care—The Lord's way is perfect—The Lord has given marvelous blessings—David testifies, The Lord lives, and blessed be my Rock.

To the chief Musician, *A Psalm* of David, the servant of the LORD, who spake unto the LORD the words of this song in the day *that* the LORD delivered him from the hand of all his enemies, and from the hand of Saul: And he said,

David testifies, The heavens declare the glory of God, the law of the Lord is perfect, and the judgments of the Lord are true and righteous altogether.

To the chief Musician, A Psalm of David.

David prays that the Lord will hear in time of trouble—The Lord saves His anointed.

To the chief Musician, A Psalm of David.

A messianic psalm of David—He tells of the glory of the great King—The King will triumph over all His enemies—Their evil designs will fail.

To the chief Musician, A Psalm of David.

Summary of Psalms 17–21

These psalms reveal David's love for the Lord, who continually preserves him. Because of this love, David proclaims, "The Lord is my rock, and my fortress, and my deliverer; my God, my strength, in whom I will trust; my buckler [defensive shield]; and the horn of my salvation, and my high tower" (Psalm 18:2).

In another messianic psalm, David praises the eternal reign of Jesus Christ (see Psalm 21). David also teaches about the cleansing of the earth in preparation for the return of the Messiah.

What is "Aijeleth Shahar"? (Psalm 22 superscription) This phrase is "found once only in the Bible, in the title of Ps. 22. It probably describes to the musician the melody to which the psalm was to be played" (*Smith's Bible Dictionary*, "Aijeleth Shahar"). Another Bible commentator added: "It is probably the name of some song or tune to the measure of which the psalm was to be chanted. Some, however, understand by the name some instrument of music, or an allegorical allusion to the subject of the psalm" (*Easton's Bible Dictionary*, "Aijeleth Shahar").

Psalm 22:1–21. David's Psalm Foretells Moments of the Savior's Life

What do we learn about the Savior in this verse? (22:1) "The Holy Ghost, through David, said: 'My God, my God, why hast thou forsaken me?' (Ps. 22:1)—thus revealing aforetime the very words Jesus would speak on the cross in that moment when, left alone that he might drink the dregs of the bitter cup to the full, the Father would entirely withdraw his sustaining power [see Matthew 27:46]" (McConkie, *Promised Messiah*, 530). ⊕

When did people "shoot out the lip" or "shake [their] head" at the Lord? (22:7–8) To "shoot out the lip" and "shake the head" were "gestures of contempt and hatred" (*John Dummelow's Commentary* [on Psalm 22:7]). This passage leads us to consider the accounts of Jesus hanging on the cross when "they that passed by railed on him, wagging their heads, and saying, Ah, thou that destroyest the temple, and buildest it in three days, Save thyself, and come down from the cross. Likewise also the chief priests mocking said among themselves with the scribes, He saved others; himself he cannot save" (Mark 15:29–31; see also Matthew 27:39–43; Luke 23:35–37).

PSALM 22

A messianic psalm of David—He foretells events in the Messiah's life—The Messiah will say, My God, my God, why hast Thou forsaken me?—They will pierce His hands and feet—He will yet govern among all nations.

To the chief Musician upon Aijeleth Shahar, A Psalm of David.

1 My God, my God, why hast thou forsaken me? *why art thou so* far from helping me, *and from* the words of my roaring?

2 O my God, I cry in the daytime, but thou hearest not; and in the night season, and am not silent.

3 But thou *art* holy, *O thou* that inhabitest the praises of Israel.

4 Our fathers trusted in thee: they trusted, and thou didst deliver them.

5 They cried unto thee, and were delivered: they trusted in thee, and were not confounded.

6 But I *am* a worm, and no man; a reproach of men, and despised of the people.

7 All they that see me laugh me to scorn: they shoot out the lip, they shake the head, *saying,*

8 He trusted on the Lord *that* he would deliver him: let him deliver him, seeing he delighted in him.

9 But thou *art* he that took me out of the womb: thou didst make me hope *when I was* upon my mother's breasts.

10 I was cast upon thee from the womb: thou *art* my God from my mother's belly.

11 Be not far from me; for trouble *is* near; for *there is* none to help.

12 Many bulls have compassed me: strong *bulls* of Bashan have beset me round.

13 They gaped upon me *with* their mouths, *as* a ravening and a roaring lion.

What were the "bulls of Bashan"? (22:12) "Bashan was a very fertile region east of the Jordan River, well known for its sheep and plump cattle. In this prime cattle-grazing area, one could find pampered cattle being raised for the market, as well as a breed of ferocious undomesticated cattle that roamed free" (Walton, et al., *IVP Bible Background Commentary*, 523).

Theologian John Gill suggested that "the chief priests, elders, Scribes, and Pharisees, . . . and Herod and Pontius Pilate . . . [were] comparable to bulls for their fierceness, rage, and fury against Christ, Psalm 2:1; and for their pushing at him with their horns of power and authority, and for their trampling him under their feet" (*John Gill's Exposition of the Whole Bible* [commentary on Psalm 22:12]).

14 I am poured out like water, and all my bones are out of joint: my heart is like wax; it is melted in the midst of my bowels.

15 My strength is dried up like a potsherd; and my tongue cleaveth to my jaws; and thou hast brought me into the dust of death.

What might it mean to be "poured out like water"? (22:14) "David uses striking imagery to describe his distress. He is surrounded by animals—*bulls* and *lions*. Moreover, David's distress is so profound that he feels as if his life has been drained from him, as one might empty a jug of water. These words become even more poignant when they are applied to the sufferings of Jesus on the Cross (see John 19:34)" (*Nelson Study Bible* [NKJV], 897). ⊕

Messianic Prophecies in the Psalms (Psalm 22)

Reflecting on the two disciples who walked with the risen Lord along the road to Emmaus, Elder Gerald N. Lund wrote: "Wouldn't you love to have been able to walk along behind the three of them and hear that conversation? I have often wondered to which scriptures he referred. To what things did he point their minds? . . .

"Perhaps Psalm 22 was [a] scripture he cited. The opening lines are, 'My God, my God, why hast thou forsaken me?' (v. 1). Had they been at the cross? Had they heard that last agonized cry? (see Matt. 27:46). A few verses later in that same psalm we read, 'All they that see me laugh me to scorn: they shoot out the lip [a Hebrew idiom meaning to mock and ridicule], they shake the head, saying, He trusted on the Lord that he would deliver him: let him deliver him, seeing he delighted in him' (Ps. 22:7–8). Did the disguised Savior gently remind them how some at the cross had mocked him and challenged him to come down if he were truly the Son of God? (see Matt. 27:39–43). And then in verse sixteen, we read: 'For dogs have compassed me: the assembly of the wicked have enclosed me: they pierced my hands and my feet.' And verse eighteen, 'They part my garments among them, and cast lots upon my vesture' (see Matt. 27:35). To anyone who had witnessed the Crucifixion, those prophecies would have been electrifying.

"Perhaps he pointed their minds to Psalm 41:9: 'Yea, mine own familiar friend, in whom I trusted, which did eat of my bread, hath lifted up his heel against me.' Certainly these two men knew by now about Judas's betrayal of the Master.

"Or perhaps Psalm 69 may have been another scripture he quoted. Verses twenty and twenty-one read, 'Reproach hath broken my heart; and I am full of heaviness: and I looked for some to take pity, but there was none; and for comforters, but I found none. They gave me also gall for my meat; and in my thirst they gave me vinegar to drink.' Would these men have seen or heard from other witnesses that a soldier gave Jesus vinegar to drink just before he died? (see John 19:29–30). Did the disciples realize, as John apparently did, that the Savior died of a broken heart? [see Talmage, 620–21; see also John 19:34–35]. What remorse they must have felt as they thought how no one, not even themselves, had stayed through the ordeal to comfort the Master" (*Jesus Christ, Key to the Plan of Salvation*, 41–42).

Why is David talking about being surrounded by dogs who then part his garments? (22:16–18) Elder Bruce R. McConkie explained: "[This] is exactly what transpired on the gloomy day of [Christ's] crucifixion. . . . Matthew says, 'And they [the Roman soldiers] crucified him, and parted his garments, casting lots; that it might be fulfilled which was spoken by the prophet, They parted my garments among them, and upon my vesture did they cast lots' (Matt. 27:35)" (*Promised Messiah*, 531). "People whose lives are unworthy and reprobate are often referred to as dogs. . . . [like] those who crucified Jesus (Ps. 22:16)" (McConkie and Parry, *Guide to Scriptural Symbols*, 40).

16 For dogs have compassed me: the assembly of the wicked have inclosed me: they pierced my hands and my feet.

17 I may tell all my bones: they look *and* stare upon me.

18 They part my garments among them, and cast lots upon my vesture.

Why is David pleading with the Lord for help? (22:19–21) "The psalmist implores God to listen to his prayer because of the utter despair and meaninglessness of his situation. There is no way out. In view of the absence of any other alternative, he prays that the Lord may spare his 'life' [KJV, 'my darling']. Life alone was left in him, because he was to his enemies nothing but skin and bones (v. 17) and his inner self was sick from anxiety. . . . But he is not ready to die. Only the Lord can deliver him and restore life to him" (VanGemeren, "Psalms," 245–46).

19 But be not thou far from me, O LORD: O my strength, haste thee to help me.

20 Deliver my soul from the sword; my darling from the power of the dog.

21 Save me from the lion's mouth: for thou hast heard me from the horns of the unicorns.

Summary of Psalm 22:22–31

David praises the Lord and speaks of the growing number of those who will praise Jehovah. He foretells the day when "the ends of the world" will "turn unto the Lord" and worship Him (see Psalm 22:27).

Psalm 23:1–6. The Lord Is My Shepherd

Why shall we "not want" if the Lord is our Shepherd? (23:1–3) "The Savior's mortal ministry was indeed characterized by love, compassion, and empathy. He did not disdainfully walk the dusty roads of Galilee and Judea, flinching at the sight of sinners. He did not dodge them in abject horror. No, He ate with them [see Luke 15:1–2]. He helped and blessed, lifted and edified, and replaced fear and despair with hope and joy. Like the true shepherd He is, He seeks us and finds us to offer relief and hope [see Matthew 18:11]. Understanding His compassion and love helps us exercise faith in Him—to repent and be healed" (Renlund, "Our Good Shepherd," 30).

PSALM 23

David declares, The Lord is my shepherd.

A Psalm of David.

1 The LORD *is* my shepherd; I shall not want.

2 He maketh me to lie down in green pastures: he leadeth me beside the still waters.

3 He restoreth my soul: he leadeth me in the paths of righteousness for his name's sake.

4 Yea, though I walk through the valley of the shadow of death, I will fear no evil: for thou *art* with me; thy rod and thy staff they comfort me.

5 Thou preparest a table before me in the presence of mine enemies: thou anointest my head with oil; my cup runneth over.

6 Surely goodness and mercy shall follow me all the days of my life: and I will dwell in the house of the LORD for ever.

PSALM 24

David testifies, The earth is the Lord's and the fulness thereof, he who has clean hands and a pure heart will ascend unto the hill of the Lord, and the Lord of Hosts is the King of Glory.

A Psalm of David.

1 The earth *is* the LORD's, and the fulness thereof; the world, and they that dwell therein.

2 For he hath founded it upon the seas, and established it upon the floods.

What is the difference between a rod and a staff? (23:4) "The rod was a weapon, an aid in times of conflict; the staff, a walking stick useful in all times and ways of life" (Rasmussen, *Latter-day Saint Commentary on the Old Testament*, 421). "Ancient shepherds used the rod and staff to rescue, protect, and guide the sheep. . . . The sheep are not alone; their Shepherd is standing over them, guiding them into safety—just as the Lord stands over us and protects us" (*Nelson Study Bible* [NKJV], 898). ⊕

What did David mean by proclaiming he would dwell in the house of the Lord? (23:6) The Hebrew "for ever" literally means *for length of days*. In other words, David was implying: "During the rest of my life, I shall not be separated from God's house, nor from God's ordinances; and shall at last dwell with him in glory" (*Adam Clarke's Commentary* [on Psalm 23:6]).

Psalm 24:1–10. All Who Have Clean Hands and a Pure Heart Will Be Able to Live with the Lord

Why is it important to remember that the earth and its fulness belong to the Lord? (24:1) "Think for a moment how that simple concept would alter people's thinking if they would really accept it. We clutch things to our bosom and say, 'These are mine.' Individuals rob,

How Is the Lord Our Shepherd? (Psalm 23)

"Not only is Psalm 23 the world's favorite psalm, but is arguably the most familiar and most quoted scripture in all of canonized writ. Its opening line—for all intents and purposes its title—must surely rank among the most readily identified phrases in the English language. Furthermore, quite apart from the theology expressed, it is acknowledged to be one of the most beautiful song-poems ever written. It is beloved of Christians and Jews, young and old, believers and non-believers, the sure and the uncertain. If someone is going to memorize a full, albeit short, chapter of scripture, it will likely be this one.

"What is there in this passage that is so compelling and so comforting to such a wide variety of readers? As one gifted Jewish rabbi has said (after decades of studying the psalms):

"'In a mere fifty-seven words of Hebrew and just about twice that number in English translation, the author of the Twenty-third Psalm gives us . . . a more practical theology than we can find in many books. . . . If we are anxious, the psalm gives us courage and we overcome our fears. If we are grieving, it offers comfort and we find our way through the valley of the shadow [of death]. If our lives are embittered by unpleasant people, it teaches us how to deal with them. If the world threatens to wear us down, the psalm guides us to replenish our souls. If we are obsessed with what we lack, it teaches gratitude for what we have. And most of all, if we feel alone and adrift in a friendless world, it offers us the priceless reassurance that "Thou art with me"' [Kushner, *The Lord Is My Shepherd*, 9]" (Holland, *For Times of Trouble*, 202–3).

cheat, and steal, or they manipulate and maneuver so they may be able to claim things as their own. . . .

"If we truly believed that God was the owner of all things, that man was only a user and a borrower, our approach to life would alter drastically" (Lund, *Jesus Christ, Key to the Plan of Salvation*, 117).

What is required to "ascend into the hill of the Lord"? (24:3–4) "Please notice that both clean hands and a pure heart are required to ascend into the hill of the Lord and to stand in His holy place.

"Let me suggest that hands are made clean through the process of putting off the natural man and by overcoming sin and the evil influences in our lives through the Savior's Atonement. Hearts are purified as we receive His strengthening power to do good and become better. . . . It is the Atonement of Jesus Christ that provides both a *cleansing and redeeming power* that helps us to overcome sin and a *sanctifying and strengthening power* that helps us to become better than we ever could by relying only upon our own strength" (Bednar, "Clean Hands and a Pure Heart," 82). ⊕

What was the meaning of the word *Selah*? (24:6, 10) "Selah is used more than seventy times in the Psalms. We are not sure of its exact meaning or use. It was likely a musical term, perhaps combining liturgy with music—in other words, giving directions for the musicians as to how to interact with a ritual or event. Many think it means something like 'pause and ponder'" (Muhlestein, *Essential Old Testament Companion*, 335). Holzapfel, Pike, and Seely add that in the Greek Septuagint, *selah* "is rendered as *diapsalma*, signifying an interlude" (Holzapfel, et al., *Jehovah and the World of the Old Testament*, 236).

Why is Christ called the "King of glory"? (24:7–10) "This title refers to Christ's role as 'King of kings' (1 Timothy 6:15) in the theocratic governance of the kingdom of God both in heaven and on earth. . . . To [those] on both sides of the veil who have taken upon themselves His name, Christ is . . . King, but to the rest of the human family He is King-in-Waiting until the time of His triumphant Second Coming. Then, as is appropriate in the presence of royalty, every knee shall bow and every tongue confess that He is the Messiah; the King of Zion; the True, Living, and Everlasting King of Nations; King over All the Earth" (Holland, *Witness for His Names*, 92). ⊕

What are the gates that the King of glory approaches? (24:9) "David establishes that the Lord will come to His temple, but He does so in a way that

3 Who shall ascend into the hill of the LORD? or who shall stand in his holy place?

4 He that hath clean hands, and a pure heart; who hath not lifted up his soul unto vanity, nor sworn deceitfully.

5 He shall receive the blessing from the LORD, and righteousness from the God of his salvation.

6 This *is* the generation of them that seek him, that seek thy face, O Jacob. Selah.

7 Lift up your heads, O ye gates; and be ye lift up, ye everlasting doors; and the King of glory shall come in.

8 Who *is* this King of glory? The LORD strong and mighty, the LORD mighty in battle.

9 Lift up your heads, O ye gates; even lift *them* up, ye everlasting doors; and the King of glory shall come in.

10 Who is this King of glory? The LORD of hosts, he *is* the King of glory. Selah.

makes it seem as if there are gatekeepers who will not allow just anyone to come to the temple (a detail already established by the fact that only those with pure intents and actions can enter). These gatekeepers question who it is that wants to enter. The emphatic answer is that it is Jehovah Himself who has come. For the Lord of Hosts, the King of Glory, the gates must open as He comes to claim the home that has always belonged to Him" (Muhlestein, *Essential Old Testament Companion*, 338–39).

PSALM 25

David pleads for truth and asks for pardon—Mercy and truth are for those who keep the commandments.

A Psalm of David.

Summary of Psalm 25

Psalm 25 is the first of the acrostic poems in Psalms. David expresses his trust and hope in the Lord. David pleads with the Lord to show him His ways and to remember His great mercy and love as He guides him in all truth. David waits upon the Lord and prays that the Lord God will redeem Israel.

PSALM 26

David says that he has walked in integrity and obedience—He loves the Lord's house.

A Psalm of David.

Summary of Psalm 26

David appeals to the Lord for vindication because of the goodness and willingness of David's heart to walk in His ways. David loves the house of the Lord and blesses Jehovah as he worships there.

What Is an Acrostic Psalm? (Psalm 25)

An acrostic poem is a "composition in verse, in which the first letters of the lines, taken in order, form the name of a person, kingdom, city, etc., which is the subject of the composition" (*Webster's American Dictionary of the English Language* [1828] "Acrostic").

"Psalm 25 is an acrostic: each verse begins with a word whose initial letter is in the Hebrew alphabetical order, which, unfortunately, is lost in translation. That pattern makes this psalm a song of praise and supplication, covering the qualities and blessings the worshipper desires, as it were, from A to Z (in Hebrew, from *aleph* to *tau*). Several psalms have this alphabetic pattern: 34, 37, 111, 112, 119, and 145" (Rasmussen, *Latter-day Saint Commentary on the Old Testament*, 422).

PSALM 27

David says, The Lord is my light and my salvation—He desires to dwell in the house of the Lord forever—He counsels, Wait on the Lord and be of good courage.

A Psalm of David.

When in David's life was this psalm written? (Psalm 27 superscription) "In the Vulgate, Septuagint, Arabic, and Ethiopic [bibles], it has this title: 'A Psalm of David, before he was anointed.' . . . For this title there is no authority in fact. However, it may be just necessary to state that David appears to have received the royal unction [anointing] three times:

"• In Bethlehem from the hand of Samuel, in the house of his father Jesse; 1 Samuel 16:13.

"• At Hebron after the death of Saul, by the men of Judah; 2 Samuel 2:4.

"• By the elders of Israel, at Hebron, after the death of Ishbosheth, when he was acknowledged king over all the tribes; 2 Samuel 5:3" (*Adam Clarke's Commentary* [on Introduction to Psalm 27]). ⊕

Psalm 27:1–5. David Looks to the Lord for Light and Desires to Dwell in the House of the Lord

1 The LORD *is* my light and my salvation;
whom shall I fear? the LORD *is* the strength of
my life; of whom shall I be afraid?

2 When the wicked, *even* mine enemies and
my foes, came upon me to eat up my flesh,
they stumbled and fell.

What blessings can we receive when the Lord is our light? (27:1) "It is often difficult to be different and to stand alone in a crowd. It is natural to fear what others might think or say. Comforting are the words of the psalm: 'The Lord is my light and my salvation; whom shall I fear? . . .' As we make Christ the center of our lives, our fears will be replaced by the courage of our convictions.

"Life is perfect for none of us, and at times the challenges and difficulties we face may become overwhelming, causing our light to dim. However, with help from our Heavenly Father, coupled with support from others, we can regain that light which will illuminate our own path once again and provide the light others may need" (Monson, "Be an Example and a Light," 88). ⊕

3 Though an host should encamp against me,
my heart shall not fear: though war should
rise against me, in this *will* I *be* confident.

How has the Lord helped you to overcome fear? (27:3) "Christ's perfect love allows us to walk with humility, dignity, and a bold confidence as followers of our beloved Savior. Christ's perfect love gives us the confidence to press through our fears and place our complete trust in the power and goodness of our Heavenly Father and of His Son, Jesus Christ.

"In our homes, in our places of business, in our Church callings, in our hearts, let us replace fear with Christ's perfect love. Christ's love will replace fear with faith!" (Uchtdorf, "Perfect Love Casteth Out Fear," 107). What principles are taught in this psalm that can help you overcome fear and despair? How does your faith and hope in Jesus Christ help you set your fears aside?

4 One *thing* have I desired of the LORD, that will I seek after; that I may dwell in the house of the LORD all the days of my life, to behold the beauty of the LORD, and to inquire in his temple.

5 For in the time of trouble he shall hide me in his pavilion: in the secret of his tabernacle shall he hide me; he shall set me up upon a rock.

How can the temple constantly influence our lives? (27:4–5) "As a practical matter we cannot be in the temple always, and we don't really go there to 'hide.' After our allotted time in its sacred precincts, we willingly leave and reenter life to face the issues of mortality. But in our hearts we can cherish this experience and cling to the wish that, if we could, we would 'dwell in the house of the Lord all the days of my life, to behold the beauty of the Lord.' That experience will add to the beauty and joy we can find in every other setting and circumstance" (Holland, *For Times of Trouble*, 63).

Psalm 27:6–10. David Pleads That the Lord Not Forsake Him in Times of Trouble

6 And now shall mine head be lifted up above mine enemies round about me: therefore will I offer in his tabernacle sacrifices of joy; I will sing, yea, I will sing praises unto the LORD.

7 Hear, O LORD, *when* I cry with my voice: have mercy also upon me, and answer me.

8 *When thou saidst,* Seek ye my face; my heart said unto thee, Thy face, LORD, will I seek.

9 Hide not thy face *far* from me; put not thy servant away in anger: thou hast been my help; leave me not, neither forsake me, O God of my salvation.

Why did David feel to sing praises to the Lord? (27:6) The righteous express their love for the Lord in song. "When ancient Israel was delivered from Egypt, 'then sang Moses and the children of Israel [a] song unto the Lord' (Exodus 15:1). As the Jaredites crossed the ocean, 'they did sing praises unto the Lord' (Ether 6:9). And when the early Latter-day Saints dedicated the Kirtland Temple, they sang William W. Phelps's new hymn 'The Spirit of God Like a Fire Is Burning.' In every dispensation of the gospel, the children of God have lifted their voices to praise Him with music. . . . Our songs—whether of praise, gratitude, knowledge, remembrance, or commitment—are pleasing to the Lord" ("Worship through the Hymns," 64, 67).

The Righteous Seek the Lord's Face (Psalm 27:7–8)

The Saints in all dispensations enjoy the privilege of seeking the face of the Lord. The accompanying promise is that He will "unveil his face unto you" (D&C 88:68). President Spencer W. Kimball stated this promise as follows: "Joseph Smith saw the Lord's face in reality, as have numerous of the prophets of God. But this is [for everyone]. If [they] will do those several things without limitation or question, [everyone] 'shall see my face and know that I am'" ("To See the Face of the Lord"). Joseph Smith restored the ancient mandate and requirements to see the face of the Lord:

D&C 67:10	Strip yourself of jealousies and fears. Humble yourself.
D&C 76:116–18	Love the Lord. Purify yourself. Cultivate the Spirit.
D&C 84:20–22	Participate in the ordinances of the gospel.
D&C 88:67–69	Sanctify yourself. Cast away idle thoughts. Cast away excess laughter.
D&C 93:1	Forsake your sins. Come unto the Lord through prayer. Obey His voice and keep the commandments.
D&C 110:7–8	Do not pollute the temple of the Lord.

These are they, in the Lord's own due time, "to whom he grants this privilege of seeing and knowing for themselves; that through the power and manifestation of the Spirit, while in the flesh, they may be able to bear his presence in the world of glory" (D&C 76:117–18).

How will the Lord "take [David] up"? (27:10)

"Unfortunately there is that rare father or mother who abdicates his or her responsibility, who flees home and hearth either literally or figuratively, forsaking the child who looks to that parent for love. . . . To any child who experiences such a loss . . . the Psalmist offers an assurance that will never fail, a love that never grows cold, a parenthood that never walks out the door or out of our life. He offers the love of a heavenly parent.

"The love of God toward His children is secure. His parenthood is His most treasured role; of all His titles He most prefers that of 'Father.' He will 'take [us] up' [Psalm 27:10] in His strong arms when no earthly parent is there to do so. He will *never* forsake us" (Holland, *For Times of Trouble*, 64–65).

Psalm 27:11–14. David Knows That if He Waits on the Lord, the Lord Will Teach Him, Lead Him, and Deliver Him

What does it mean to "wait on the Lord"? (27:14)

"To wait upon the Lord means planting the seed of faith and nourishing it (see Alma 32:41).

"It means praying as the Savior did—to God, our Heavenly Father—saying: 'Thy kingdom come. Thy will be done' (Matthew 6:10; Luke 11:2). It is a prayer we offer with our whole souls in the name of our Savior, Jesus Christ.

"Waiting upon the Lord means pondering in our hearts and 'receiv[ing] the Holy Ghost' so that we can know 'all things what [we] should do' (2 Nephi 32:5).

"As we follow the promptings of the Spirit, we discover that 'tribulation worketh patience' (Romans 5:3) and we learn to 'continue in patience until [we] are perfected' (D&C 67:13)" (Hales, "How to Wait on the Lord," 48).

Summary of Psalms 28–30

David pleads for mercy for himself and for his people. He asks for judgment and retribution upon their enemies for their evil deeds. David praises the Lord as his strength and his shield. He proclaims the majesty of the Lord and counsels Israel to worship the Lord God in beauty and holiness. Citing his own deliverance, David then instructs all to praise and give thanks to the Lord God.

10 When my father and my mother forsake me, then the Lord will take me up.

11 Teach me thy way, O Lord, and lead me in a plain path, because of mine enemies.

12 Deliver me not over unto the will of mine enemies: for false witnesses are risen up against me, and such as breathe out cruelty.

13 *I had fainted,* unless I had believed to see the goodness of the Lord in the land of the living.

14 Wait on the Lord: be of good courage, and he shall strengthen thine heart: wait, I say, on the Lord.

PSALMS 28–30

David pleads with the Lord to hear his voice and grant his petitions—David prays, Save Thy people and bless Thine inheritance.

A Psalm of David.

David counsels, Worship the Lord in the beauty of holiness—David sets forth the wonder and power of the voice of the Lord.

A Psalm of David.

David sings praises and gives thanks to the Lord—David pleads for mercy.

A Psalm *and* Song *at* the dedication of the house of David.

PSALM 31

David trusts in the Lord and rejoices in His mercy—Speaking as the Messiah he says, Into Thine hand I commit my spirit—He counsels, O love the Lord, all ye His Saints, for the Lord preserves the faithful.

To the chief Musician, A Psalm of David.

1 In thee, O LORD, do I put my trust; let me never be ashamed: deliver me in thy righteousness.

2 Bow down thine ear to me; deliver me speedily: be thou my strong rock, for an house of defence to save me.

3 For thou *art* my rock and my fortress; therefore for thy name's sake lead me, and guide me.

4 Pull me out of the net that they have laid privily for me: for thou *art* my strength.

Psalm 31:1–8. David Trusts in the Lord

What does it mean to put your trust in the Lord? (31:1) "This life is an experience in profound trust—trust in Jesus Christ, trust in His teachings, trust in our capacity as led by the Holy Spirit to obey those teachings for happiness now and for a purposeful, supremely happy eternal existence. To trust means to obey willingly without knowing the end from the beginning (see Prov. 3:5–7). To produce fruit, your trust in the Lord must be more powerful and enduring than your confidence in your own personal feelings and experience.

"To exercise faith is to trust that the Lord knows what He is doing with you and that He can accomplish it for your eternal good even though you cannot understand how He can possibly do it" (Scott, "Trust in the Lord," 17).

How is the Lord our rock and fortress? (31:3) Helaman instructed his sons to "remember that it is upon the rock of our Redeemer, who is Christ, the Son of God, that ye must build your foundation; that when the devil shall send forth his mighty winds, yea, his shafts in the whirlwind, yea, when all his hail and his mighty storm shall beat upon you, it shall have no power over you . . . because of the rock upon which ye are built" (Helaman 5:12). The prophet Jacob identified the Lord as "the stone upon which [we] might build and have safe foundation." This stone shall be "the great, and the last, and the only sure foundation" (Jacob 4:15–16).

What was important about David committing his spirit into the Lord's hand? (31:5) "These words . . . were in the highest credit among our ancestors; by whom they were used in all dangers, difficulties, and in the article of death. . . . [These] words are particularly sanctified, or set apart for this purpose, by the use made of them by our blessed Lord just before he expired on the cross" (*Adam Clarke's Commentary* [on Psalm 31:5]).

How has the Lord "considered [your] trouble" and "known [your] soul in adversity"? (31:7) Though David spoke these words in the context of his own adversities and transgressions, the prophet Alma clarified that these words are eternal and beautiful in their application. Alma noted that Jesus Christ would "go forth, suffering pains and afflictions and temptations of every kind. . . . And he will take upon him . . . their infirmities, that his bowels may be filled with mercy, according to the flesh, that he may know according to the flesh how to succor his people according to their infirmities" (Alma 7:11–12). How has your appreciation for Jesus Christ grown as you have relied on Him in your troubles and adversities?

Psalm 31:9–19. David Speaks of the Misery because of His Sins

Why do times of trouble often lead us to seek for the Lord's mercy? (31:9) "Much that happens to us in this life we cannot control; we only respond. Knowing what God has promised can provide the courage and faith we need. We are assured in the scriptures that we may know of a surety that the Lord does visit his people in their afflictions (see Mosiah 24:13–14). And that 'whosoever shall put their trust in God shall be supported in their trials, and their troubles, and their afflictions, and shall be lifted up at the last day' (Alma 36:3)" (Hanks, "Loving, Communicating God," 64). ⊕

Why did David feel like a broken vessel? (31:10–14) Because of his sins, David felt abandoned by his friends like a piece of broken pottery. "Whatever your struggle, my brothers and sisters—mental or emotional or physical or otherwise . . . [trust] in God. Hold on in His love. Know that one day the dawn will break brightly and all shadows of mortality will flee. Though we may feel we are 'like a broken vessel,' as

5 Into thine hand I commit my spirit: thou hast redeemed me, O LORD God of truth.

6 I have hated them that regard lying vanities: but I trust in the LORD.

7 I will be glad and rejoice in thy mercy: for thou hast considered my trouble; thou hast known my soul in adversities;

8 And hast not shut me up into the hand of the enemy: thou hast set my feet in a large room.

9 Have mercy upon me, O LORD, for I am in trouble: mine eye is consumed with grief, *yea*, my soul and my belly.

10 For my life is spent with grief, and my years with sighing: my strength faileth because of mine iniquity, and my bones are consumed.

11 I was a reproach among all mine enemies, but especially among my neighbours, and a fear to mine acquaintance: they that did see me without fled from me.

12 I am forgotten as a dead man out of mind: I am like a broken vessel.

13 For I have heard the slander of many: fear *was* on every side: while they took counsel together against me, they devised to take away my life.

14 But I trusted in thee, O LORD: I said, Thou *art* my God.

15 My times *are* in thy hand: deliver me from the hand of mine enemies, and from them that persecute me.

16 Make thy face to shine upon thy servant: save me for thy mercies' sake.

17 Let me not be ashamed, O LORD; for I have called upon thee: let the wicked be ashamed, *and* let them be silent in the grave.

18 Let the lying lips be put to silence; which speak grievous things proudly and contemptuously against the righteous.

19 *Oh* how great *is* thy goodness, which thou hast laid up for them that fear thee; *which* thou hast wrought for them that trust in thee before the sons of men!

PSALM 32

David says, Blessed is the man unto whom the Lord imputes not iniquity—David acknowledges his sin—He recommends that the righteous be glad in the Lord and rejoice.

A Psalm of David, Maschil.

the Psalmist says (Psalm 31:12), we must remember, that vessel is in the hands of the divine potter.... While God is at work making those repairs, the rest of us can help by being merciful, nonjudgmental, and kind" (Holland, "Like a Broken Vessel," 42).

What did David mean that his "times" were in the Lord's hand? (31:15) "In all the important decisions in our lives, what is most important is to do the right thing. Second, and only slightly behind the first, is to do the right thing at the right time" (Oaks, "Timing," 10). "The issue for us is trusting God enough to trust also His timing. If we can truly believe He has our welfare at heart, may we not let His plans unfold as He thinks best? The same is true with the second coming and with all those matters wherein our faith needs to include faith in the Lord's timing for us personally, not just in His overall plans and purposes" (Maxwell, *Even as I Am*, 93).

Summary of Psalm 31:20–24

The Lord hears and answers David's prayer. David invites the faithful to love the Lord and have faith that He will help them.

Summary of Psalm 32

David recognizes the great blessing of forgiveness. He promises mercy for those who trust the Lord. David invites all the upright in heart to be glad in the Lord and shout for joy.

What does "Maschil" mean? (Psalm 32 superscription) "The Psalm heading marks the first appearance in the Psalter of the Hebrew term *maśkil* in a heading (a noun based on the verb *śkl*, 'make someone keen/clever; instruct'). The term is well known in the wisdom literature, where it is frequently used to mean 'instruct, make perceptive'" (Wilson, *Psalms, Vol. 1*, 544–45).

Psalm 33:1–9. David Sings Praises to the Lord for His Righteousness and Judgment

What is a psaltery? (33:2) The Hebrew word for "psaltery" is *nebel* and is "sometimes translated 'viol' or 'lute.' A large harp, much used for accompanying religious music" (Bible Dictionary, "Psaltery"). "None of [the ancient Hebrew] instruments survive. . . . Because of [the Jewish] laws forbidding graphic depictions, the appearance of their musical instruments is not known. . . . Yet a picture scratched on a floor at Megiddo by some non-Hebrew centuries before David's time shows a woman playing a harp" (*Harper's Bible Dictionary*, "Music"). ⊕

Why was Israel singing a "new song"? (33:3) "This psalm is a hymn of praise to [Jehovah], celebrating his righteous character, creative power, and sovereignty—qualities that make him the only reliable foundation for trust and hope. As a communal hymn of praise and rejoicing, Psalm 33 roots out of the command in 32:11 that the 'righteous' (cf. 32:11 and 33:1) and the 'upright in heart' (cf. 32:11; 33:1) 'rejoice' and 'sing.' In its present position, and especially without its own psalm heading, Psalm 33 is bound closely to the preceding psalm and provides the song of rejoicing requested there" (Wilson, *Psalms, Vol. 1*, 555).

Who is the creator of the heavens and the earth? (33:6–7) "Christ is the Creator and Redeemer of worlds so numerous that they cannot be numbered by man. As to his infinite and eternal creative and redemptive enterprises the divine word attests: 'And worlds without number have I created,' saith the Father, 'and I also created them for mine own purpose; and by the Son I created them, which is mine Only Begotten" [Moses 1:33]" (McConkie, "Christ and the Creation," 10). ⊕

Psalm 33:10–14. The Lord Looks upon All the Inhabitants of the Earth

PSALM 33

Rejoice in the Lord—Sing unto Him a new song—He loves righteousness and judgment—Blessed is the nation whose God is the Lord.

1 Rejoice in the LORD, O ye righteous: *for* praise is comely for the upright.

2 Praise the LORD with harp: sing unto him with the psaltery *and* an instrument of ten strings.

3 Sing unto him a new song; play skilfully with a loud noise.

4 For the word of the LORD *is* right; and all his works *are done* in truth.

5 He loveth righteousness and judgment: the earth is full of the goodness of the LORD.

6 By the word of the LORD were the heavens made; and all the host of them by the breath of his mouth.

7 He gathereth the waters of the sea together as an heap: he layeth up the depth in storehouses.

8 Let all the earth fear the LORD: let all the inhabitants of the world stand in awe of him.

9 For he spake, and it was *done;* he commanded, and it stood fast.

10 The LORD bringeth the counsel of the heathen to nought: he maketh the devices of the people of none effect.

11 The counsel of the LORD standeth for ever, the thoughts of his heart to all generations.

12 Blessed *is* the nation whose God *is* the LORD; *and* the people *whom* he hath chosen for his own inheritance.

13 The LORD looketh from heaven; he beholdeth all the sons of men.

14 From the place of his habitation he looketh upon all the inhabitants of the earth.

How does a nation choose the Lord as their God? (33:12) President Gordon B. Hinckley noted: "Now, brothers and sisters, we must do our duty, whatever that duty might be. Peace may be denied for a season. Some of our liberties may be curtailed. We may be inconvenienced. We may even be called on to suffer in one way or another. But God our Eternal Father will watch over this nation and all of the civilized world who look to Him. He has declared, 'Blessed is the nation whose God is the Lord' (Ps. 33:12). Our safety lies in repentance. Our strength comes of obedience to the commandments of God" (Hinckley, "Times in Which We Live," 74). ⊕

15 He fashioneth their hearts alike; he considereth all their works.

16 There is no king saved by the multitude of an host: a mighty man is not delivered by much strength.

17 An horse *is* a vain thing for safety: neither shall he deliver *any* by his great strength.

Psalm 33:15–22. The Lord Is Our Shield and Will Deliver in Mercy Those Who Hope

Why was it vain to trust in a horse for safety? (33:17) "The Israelites had no cavalry, and the chariots and horsemen of their enemies appeared specially formidable to them" (*John Dummelow's Commentary* [on Psalm 33:17]). "Even the horse, with all his fleetness, is no sure means of escape from danger: the lion or the tiger can overtake him or he may stumble, fall, and destroy his rider" (*Adam Clarke's Commentary* [on Psalm 33:17]).

18 Behold, the eye of the LORD *is* upon them that fear him, upon them that hope in his mercy;

19 To deliver their soul from death, and to keep them alive in famine.

20 Our soul waiteth for the LORD: he *is* our help and our shield.

21 For our heart shall rejoice in him, because we have trusted in his holy name.

How do our lives change when we recognize that the Lord's eyes are on us? (33:18) "It would . . . be a great blessing for a people to really understand that the eye of the Lord is upon all his works—that nothing escapes his notice, and that all is composed, organized, and brought forth for the glory, benefit, and use of intelligent beings. . . . If we could at all times strictly realize this, do you not think that God would be continually in all our thoughts? Could we but behold and realize . . . that he has created and ordained everything for the benefit of his creatures, would not that bring us to sense, realize, and understand the hand of the Lord in all things?" (Young, in *Journal of Discourses*, 6:143).

22 Let thy mercy, O LORD, be upon us, according as we hope in thee.

Why did David prize having hope in the Lord? (33:22) "Hope is a gift of the Spirit. It is a hope that through the Atonement of Jesus Christ and the power of His Resurrection, we shall be raised unto life eternal and this because of our faith in the Savior. This kind of hope is both a principle of promise as well as a commandment, and, as with all commandments, we have the responsibility to make it an active part of our lives and overcome the temptation to lose hope. Hope in our Heavenly Father's merciful plan of happiness leads to peace, mercy, rejoicing, and gladness. The hope of salvation is like a protective helmet; it is the foundation of our faith and an anchor to our souls" (Uchtdorf, "Infinite Power of Hope," 21–22).

PSALM 34

David blesses the Lord at all times—He counsels, Keep your tongue from evil; do good and seek peace—He says that not one of the Messiah's bones will be broken.

A Psalm of David, when he changed his behaviour before Abimelech; who drove him away, and he departed.

What happened that caused David to change his behavior before Abimelech? (Psalm 34 superscription) "The phrase . . . apparently refers to the account in 1 Sam. 21:10–15 of how David acted insane when in the presence of Achish, the king of Gath. . . . 'Abimelech' (literally, 'my father is king') was an official title for Philistine kings, just as *Pharaoh* was an official title for Egyptian kings. The main point . . . is for modern readers to take the incident in David's life as an interpretive key as to how to read and use this psalm. It is a psalm of thanks to God and instruction for God's people, which is appropriately used in times when God's deliverance has been experienced" (deClaissé-Walford, et al., *Book of Psalms*, 321).

Psalm 34:1–3. David Remembers and Honors the Lord at All Times

1 I will bless the LORD at all times: his praise *shall* continually *be* in my mouth.

2 My soul shall make her boast in the LORD: the humble shall hear *thereof*, and be glad.

3 O magnify the LORD with me, and let us exalt his name together.

Why does David bless the Lord? (34:1–3): "The Old Testament . . . contains many passages in which individuals such as Abraham, Moses, David, Solomon, and Daniel, in a seeming reversal of roles, invoked a blessing on God or encouraged other people to bless God. . . .

"When ancient Israelites 'blessed' Jehovah, either in spontaneous expression or through more formal means, they were in effect praising and worshiping their God. . . . They pronounced and invoked blessings or praise upon God. Praise is any worshipful expression in which the greatness and goodness of God are affirmed" (Pike, "I Will Bless the Lord at All Times," 137, 143).

In what ways were women allowed to take part in the feasts of Israel? (34:2) "Here we may have one of the few psalms that can be identified as having been sung during the feast of Tabernacles temple drama by the Israelite women. . . . The evidence that the song was sung by women is: 'My soul shall make her boast in the Lord'" (Baker and Ricks, *Who Shall Ascend into the Hill of the Lord?* 426–27).

Psalm 34:4–7. David Testifies of the Ways of the Lord in His Own Deliverance

4 I sought the LORD, and he heard me, and delivered me from all my fears.

In what way do we seek the Lord? (34:4) "The term translated 'sought' (*drš*) is never used of seeking someone or something whose location is unknown. When one seeks God in this fashion, one does so knowing full well where he is, but is seeking either a restored relationship with him or, most commonly, information, guidance, or direction from him. This seeking may be accomplished through prayer or . . . receiving the word of a prophet. Such seeking is serious, purposeful searching, not confused wondering or wandering" (Wilson, *Psalms, Vol. 1*, 568). ⊕

5 They looked unto him, and were lightened: and their faces were not ashamed.

6 This poor man cried, and the LORD heard *him*, and saved him out of all his troubles.

What does it mean that as we look to the Lord we will be "lightened"? (34:5) The Hebrew word translated "lightened" (נָהַר *nâhar*) means "to *sparkle*, i.e. [figuratively] *be cheerful*, [to shine, be radiant like] a running stream." But it also means to "flow" or to "flow (together)" (*Strong's Exhaustive Concordance*, word #h5102). Isaiah 60:2–5 uses this Hebrew word (נָהַר *nâhar*) multiple times, and in both senses. In this passage the earth is covered in darkness. In the last days, the Lord's glory is seen upon His people, who radiate and shine with His light. When seen, the Gentiles "flow" and "gather" to them that they might be "nursed at [their] side." Then the hearts of the radiant will be "enlarged" as the "Gentiles come unto [them]" (Isaiah 60:4–5).

7 The angel of the LORD encampeth round about them that fear him, and delivereth them.

What does it mean to fear the Lord? (34:7) "This phrase is often misunderstood. It can be viewed as the paradoxical awareness that one is fragile, mortal, and [sinful], on the one hand, and that the Lord is rock-solid, immortal, and gracious, on the other. To fear the Lord is therefore simultaneously both to tremble in dread anticipation and to tremble in joyous anticipation" (deClaissé-Walford, et al., *Book of Psalms*, 325). Study the results of King Benjamin's sermon in Mosiah 4:1–3. Note how the "fear of the Lord" is seen from both of these perspectives. Why should you fear the Lord? From David's and Benjamin's perspectives, what are the blessings that come from fearing the Lord? Identify how David uses fearing the Lord in the verses that follow (see verses 8–22).

Psalm 34:8–22. The Lord Distinguishes Goodness and Righteousness from Evil

How are we blessed when we trust in the Lord? (34:8–22) Elder Marion D. Hanks spoke of what trust in the Lord can mean in our lives: "Our religion is 'not weight, it is wings.' It can carry us through the dark times, the bitter cup. It will be with us in the fiery furnace and the deep pit. It will accompany us to the hospital room and to the place of bereavement. It can guarantee us the presence of a Captain on the rough voyage. It is, in short, not the path to easy disposition of problems, but the comforting assurance of the eternal light, by which we may see, and the eternal warmth, which we may feel. 'The Lord is good: Blessed is the man that trusteth in him' (Ps. 34:8)" ("Trust in the Lord," 14).

What does it mean to "taste and see" the goodness of the Lord? (34:8) "God's people have spiritual feasts and pure delicacies. . . . Whoever have touched with the taste of their hearts the sweetness of the justice and mercy of God, by which all his ordinances are carried out, and have drunk from the experiences of supernal joys . . . , they will despise the corruptible and temporal good in their admiration of the eternal, and they will glow in that fire that the love of God kindles. As when cold is changed to warmth and night is changed to daylight, the Holy Spirit by one stroke in the hearts of the faithful takes away darkness and destroys sin" (Leo the Great, "Feast beyond Compare," Sermon 50.2). See 1 Nephi 8:10–12 and Alma 36:24–26. ⊕

What is required that the Lord's eyes may be upon us? (34:12–16) Peter quoted these verses in his first apostolic letter (1 Peter 3). To David's teachings that encourage the eyes of the Lord to be upon us, Peter added: (1) be of one mind; (2) have compassion on one another; (3) instead of rendering evil for evil, render blessings for evil; and (4) loving life and seeing good days requires that our lips speak no evil or guile (see 1 Peter 3:8–12). Peter also asked: "Who is he that will harm you, if ye be followers of that which is good?" and declared: "If ye suffer for righteousness' sake, happy are ye" (1 Peter 3:13–14).

8 O taste and see that the Lord *is* good: blessed *is* the man *that* trusteth in him.

9 O fear the Lord, ye his saints: for *there is* no want to them that fear him.

10 The young lions do lack, and suffer hunger: but they that seek the Lord shall not want any good *thing*.

11 Come, ye children, hearken unto me: I will teach you the fear of the Lord.

12 What man *is he that* desireth life, *and* loveth *many* days, that he may see good?

13 Keep thy tongue from evil, and thy lips from speaking guile.

14 Depart from evil, and do good; seek peace, and pursue it.

15 The eyes of the Lord *are* upon the righteous, and his ears *are open* unto their cry.

16 The face of the Lord *is* against them that do evil, to cut off the remembrance of them from the earth.

17 *The righteous* cry, and the Lord heareth, and delivereth them out of all their troubles.

18 The LORD *is* nigh unto them that are of a broken heart; and saveth such as be of a contrite spirit.

19 Many *are* the afflictions of the righteous: but the LORD delivereth him out of them all.

20 He keepeth all his bones: not one of them is broken.

21 Evil shall slay the wicked: and they that hate the righteous shall be desolate.

22 The LORD redeemeth the soul of his servants: and none of them that trust in him shall be desolate.

PSALMS 35–37

David complains of his enemies and their wrong dealings—He asks the Lord to judge him according to his righteousness.

A Psalm of David.

David praises the Lord for His mercy, His righteousness, and His loving kindness—The fountain of life is with the Lord.

To the chief Musician, *A Psalm* of
David the servant of the LORD.

How did Roman soldiers fulfill this prophecy about broken bones? (34:20) "It is a wrenching thing indeed to realize that the only supportive thing that can be said of those soldiers who witnessed the greatest act of love ever offered in the history of all mankind is that they did not break the Savior's bones. That was because, as noted by John, Jesus was already dead and therefore did not need to have the process of His death hastened by the accelerated asphyxiation that would have come by the standard practice of breaking the leg bone, an act which took away the victim's ability to relieve the constriction on his lungs by 'standing up' on the nails driven into his feet" (Holland, *For Times of Trouble*, 196).

Summary of Psalms 35–37

David entreats the Lord to contend with his enemies and promises to rejoice and praise Him. David asks, "Who is like the Lord?" and promises to testify of the Lord's righteousness that vindicated him against his enemies. David expresses his confidence to withstand the proud and the wicked and praises the Lord's "lovingkindness" as a priceless gift.

David counsels his people to not trouble themselves because of their enemies, but to find delight and rest through trusting the Lord and committing to walk in His ways. The Lord will uphold the righteous, but the wicked shall perish.

Psalm 34 and the Crucifixion of Jesus Christ (Psalm 34:20)

"John, the apostle and beloved friend of Jesus, was near the cross when the Savior died. In recounting the experience, he reminded his readers of [Psalm 34]. . . . The scene, if it represented a prophecy about the Savior's atoning sacrifice, would have been this one:

"'Now there stood by the cross of Jesus his mother, and his mother's sister, Mary the wife of Cleophas, and Mary Magdalene. When Jesus therefore saw his mother, and the disciple standing by, whom he loved, he saith unto his mother, Woman, behold thy son! Then saith he to the disciple, Behold thy mother! And from that hour that disciple took her unto his own home. . . .

"Then came the soldiers, and brake the legs of the first, and of the other which was crucified with him. But when they came to Jesus, and saw that he was dead already, they brake not his legs: But one of the soldiers with a spear pierced his side, and forthwith came there out blood and water. And he that saw it bare record, and his record is true: and he knoweth that he saith true, that ye might believe. For these things were done, that the scripture should be fulfilled, A bone of him shall not be broken (John 19:25–27, 32–36)" (Baker and Ricks, *Who Shall Ascend into the Hill of the Lord?* 309; paragraphing altered).

David counsels, Trust in the Lord and do good—Rest in the Lord and wait patiently for Him—Cease from anger and forsake wrath—The meek will inherit the earth—The Lord loves justice and does not forsake His Saints.

A *Psalm* of David.

Summary of Psalm 38

Sorrowful for his sins, David teaches of hope in Christ. He pleads with the Lord for compassion.

PSALM 38

David sorrows for his sins—They rest as a disease upon him—He asks the Lord to be compassionate.

A Psalm of David, to bring to remembrance.

Summary of Psalms 39–40

David continues to ask the Lord to forgive him for his sins. He thanks the Lord for all He has done. David prays that he will be able to continue to do God's will.

PSALMS 39–40

David seeks to control his tongue—Man is altogether vanity—He is a stranger and a sojourner on the earth.

To the chief Musician, *even* to Jeduthun,
A Psalm of David.

A messianic psalm of David—The Messiah will come and preach righteousness—He will declare salvation—The righteous will say, The Lord be magnified.

To the chief Musician, A Psalm of David.

PSALM 41

A messianic psalm of David—Blessed is he who considers the poor—The treachery of Judas is foretold.

To the chief Musician, A Psalm of David.

1 Blessed *is* he that considereth the poor: the Lord will deliver him in time of trouble.
2 The Lord will preserve him, and keep him alive; *and* he shall be blessed upon the earth:

Psalm 41:1–3. David Pleads for Blessings on Those Who Regard the Weak and the Poor

How does the Lord bless those who are compassionate toward the poor? (41:1) The Apostle Peter declared: "And above all things have fervent charity among yourselves: for charity shall cover the multitude of sins" (1 Pet. 4:8). Joseph Smith slightly

and thou wilt not deliver him unto the will of his enemies.

3 The LORD will strengthen him upon the bed of languishing: thou wilt make all his bed in his sickness.

4 I said, LORD, be merciful unto me: heal my soul; for I have sinned against thee.

5 Mine enemies speak evil of me, When shall he die, and his name perish?

6 And if he come to see *me,* he speaketh vanity: his heart gathereth iniquity to itself; *when* he goeth abroad, he telleth *it.*

7 All that hate me whisper together against me: against me do they devise my hurt.

8 An evil disease, *say they,* cleaveth fast unto him: and *now* that he lieth he shall rise up no more.

9 Yea, mine own familiar friend, in whom I trusted, which did eat of my bread, hath lifted up *his* heel against me.

10 But thou, O LORD, be merciful unto me, and raise me up, that I may requite them.

11 By this I know that thou favourest me, because mine enemy doth not triumph over me.

12 And as for me, thou upholdest me in mine integrity, and settest me before thy face for ever.

changed the wording to read: "Charity *preventeth* a multitude of sins" (JST, 1 Pet. 4:8). Notably, Joseph continued to use both Peter's original sentiment as well as his slight modification as he spoke to the Saints (see Joseph Smith Papers, "History, 1838–1856, volume E-1 [1 Jul. 1843–30 Apr. 1844]," 1992). In both renderings—whether charity compensates for many of our sins, or whether the tenderness of charity tempers our sinful nature—the Lord blesses those who show compassion and love for the downtrodden. ⊕

How does the Lord preserve His charitable children? (41:1–3) Elder Gene R. Cook stated: "Magnifying that gift from God [charity] will bring a new heart, a pure heart, and ever-increasing love and peace. As we increasingly think and act like Him, the attributes of the natural man will slip away to be replaced by the heart and the mind of Christ. We will become like Him and then truly receive Him" ("Charity," 83).

Psalm 41:4–13. David Praises God for His Mercy

Why does David plead with the Lord for mercy? (41:4–8) "[David] is treated in his distress of soul in a manner totally different from the way just described [vv. 1–3] which is so rich in promises of blessing. He is himself just such a [poor soul], towards whom one ought to manifest [sympathy]. But, whilst he is addressing God . . . for mercy and help, his enemies speak evil to him . . . wishing that he might die and that his name might perish" (Keil and Delitzsch, *Commentary* [on Psalm 41:4–6]).

What event in scripture fulfilled the phrase "familiar friend . . . lifted up his heel against me"? (41:9) "*Familiar friend* describes a close, intimate relationship. The outrage of betrayal by one so close is nearly unbearable (Matt. 26:14–16). The fulfillment of this verse in the experience of Jesus and Judas is remarkable. Not only did the two eat a meal together . . . but Jesus also called Judas a 'friend' at the moment of betrayal (Matt. 26:50). Moreover Jesus quoted this verse, noting its fulfillment in Judas (John 13:18)" (*Nelson Study Bible* [NJKV], 920).

Why is the benediction of "Amen, and Amen" important? (41:13) The book of Psalms has been divided into five books or sections. "[Verse] 13 is a doxology [expression of praise] that does not end Psalm 41, but rather marks the close of the entirety of Book I of the [Psalms]" (Longman, *Psalms*, 191). "This verse is not an integral part of the Psalm but an editorial flourish to mark the end of the first of the five books (on the model of the Torah) into which the redactors retroactively divided the book of Psalms" (Alter, *Hebrew Bible*, 3:112).

Summary of Psalms 42–44

Psalms 42, 43, and 44 were written for the sons of Korah, who were apparently the singers who assisted in sacred worship at the temple or other places of worship. It appears that Psalms 42 and 43 were originally one psalm, as they both quote an identical thought (see Psalms 42:5, 11; 43:5). They use the imagery of thirsting for water to teach about the heartfelt desire of the righteous for their God. Psalm 44 describes how true Saints praise the Lord even when suffering persecution.

What is "Shoshannim"? (Psalm 45 superscription) "'To the chief musician upon Shoshannim' is a musical direction to the leader of the temple choir which occurs in [Psalm 45] and most probably indicates the melody 'after' or 'in the manner of' . . . which the psalms were to be sung. [It has] no meaning in the present text, and must therefore be regarded as probably a fragment of the beginning of an older psalm with which the choir were familiar" (*Smith's Bible Dictionary*, "Shoshannim").

Psalm 45:1–7. The Messiah Shall Be Fairer Than Mortal Men

What does it mean to "indite"? (45:1) "Indite meant originally to dictate a form of words to be repeated or written down by someone else; it came soon to be

13 Blessed *be* the LORD God of Israel from everlasting, and to everlasting. Amen, and Amen.

PSALMS 42–44

The souls of the righteous thirst for God—The wicked say, Where is your God?

To the chief Musician, Maschil, for the sons of Korah.

The righteous praise God and cry, Send out Thy light and Thy truth.

The Saints praise the Lord and boast in His name forever—They are persecuted, maligned, and considered as sheep for the slaughter.

To the chief Musician for the sons of Korah, Maschil.

PSALM 45

A messianic psalm—The Messiah is fairer than the children of men—He is anointed with the oil of gladness above His fellows—His name will be remembered in all generations.

To the chief Musician upon Shoshannim, for the sons of Korah, Maschil, A Song of loves.

1 My heart is inditing a good matter: I speak of the things which I have made touching the king: my tongue *is* the pen of a ready writer.

used for the act of expressing one's thoughts in words, in any form of literary composition, without implication as to who wrote them down. . . .

"The Hebrew verb, however, is more vivid. It means to bubble up, seethe, boil over. . . . [The Revised Standard Version] reads: 'My heart overflows with a goodly theme; / I address my verses to the king; / my tongue is like the pen of a ready scribe'" (Bridges and Weigle, *King James Bible Word Book*, 186).

2 Thou art fairer than the children of men: grace is poured into thy lips: therefore God hath blessed thee for ever.

3 Gird thy sword upon *thy* thigh, O *most* mighty, with thy glory and thy majesty.

How was grace "poured into" the Messiah's lips? (45:2) At the beginning of Jesus' ministry He declared that the words of Isaiah were fulfilled: "The Spirit of the Lord is upon me, because he hath anointed me to preach the gospel to the poor; he hath sent me to heal the brokenhearted, to preach deliverance to the captives, and recovering of sight to the blind, to set at liberty them that are bruised" (Luke 4:18). At that time "all bare him witness, and wondered at the gracious words which proceeded out of his mouth" (Luke 4:22). All through His ministry, Jesus' words were those He learned of His Father (see John 8:25–30). As we follow His words, we will be led back to Heavenly Father.

4 And in thy majesty ride prosperously because of truth and meekness *and* righteousness; and thy right hand shall teach thee terrible things.

What is the meaning of God's "right hand" teaching terrible things? (45:4) Adam Clarke explained how other Bibles have translated this phrase: "The Arabic: 'And with admiration shall thy right hand direct thee.' The Septuagint: 'And thy right hand shall

Many Were Healed through Christ's Grace (Psalm 45:2)

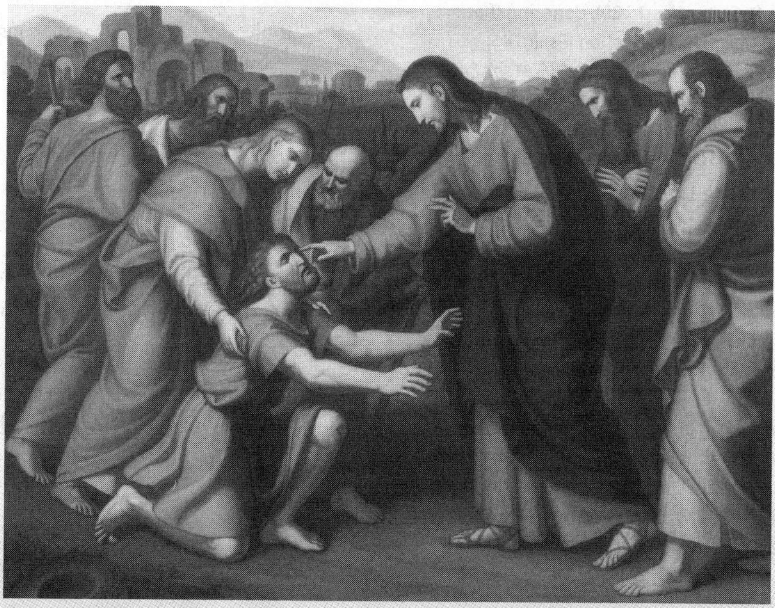

lead thee wonderfully.' To the same purpose are the Vulgate, Anglo-Saxon, and the old Psalter. The meaning is, nothing shall be able to resist thee, and the judgments which thou shalt inflict on thine enemies shall be terrible" (*Adam Clarke's Commentary* [on Psalm 45:4]). Another commentator wrote, "The victories of the king's hand would be awesome [terrible], a symbol pointing . . . forward to the works of the Savior Jesus" (*NKJV Study Bible* [2007], 863).

5 Thine arrows *are* sharp in the heart of the king's enemies; *whereby* the people fall under thee.

What does it mean to be anointed with "the oil of gladness"? (45:6–7) "Oil was symbolically associated with joy, festivity, ceremony, honor, light, and health (both spiritual and physical), while its absence spelled sorrow [Joel 1:10] and the withdrawal of all that is good in life" (*Tyndale Bible Dictionary*, 974).

"What a wonderful thought that in the end we might, with Christ, be anointed 'with the oil of gladness,' to be truly happy forever, almost as it were with a priesthood ordinance to that effect" (Holland, *For Times of Trouble*, 172). ⊕

6 Thy throne, O God, *is* for ever and ever: the sceptre of thy kingdom *is* a right sceptre.

7 Thou lovest righteousness, and hatest wickedness: therefore God, thy God, hath anointed thee with the oil of gladness above thy fellows.

Summary of Psalm 45:8–17

The Messiah's name shall be remembered in all generations and praised forever.

PSALM 46

God is our refuge and strength—He dwells in His city, does marvelous things, and says, Be still and know that I am God.

To the chief Musician for the sons of Korah, A Song upon Alamoth.

What is "Alamoth"? (Psalm 46 superscription) "Some interpret it to mean a musical instrument, and others a melody" (*Smith's Bible Dictionary*, "al'Amoth"). "A musical term (1 Chronicles 15:20), denoting that the psalm which bears this inscription (Psalm 46) was to be sung by soprano or female voices" (*Easton's Bible Dictionary*, "Alamoth").

Psalm 46:1–11. God—Our Refuge, Strength, and the Lord of Hosts—Shall Be with Us on Earth

1 God *is* our refuge and strength, a very present help in trouble.

How can we be sustained during commotions and calamities? (46:2–3) "The first stanza of the psalm is a triumphant confession of fearless trust in God and portrays the Lord as a *refuge and strength* (v. 1) in the midst of natural disaster (vv. 1–3). God's people have no need to *fear*, even if an earthquake breaks up the continents and causes them to sink beneath the resurging waters of the seas. God provides security even if the creation itself seems to become uncreated and all appears to be going down into the primeval deep" (*Zondervan KJV Commentary*, 767).

2 Therefore will not we fear, though the earth be removed, and though the mountains be carried into the midst of the sea;

3 *Though* the waters thereof roar *and* be troubled, *though* the mountains shake with the swelling thereof. Selah.

4 *There is* a river, the streams whereof shall
make glad the city of God, the holy *place* of
the tabernacles of the most High.

5 God *is* in the midst of her; she shall not
be moved: God shall help her, *and that* right
early.

Where is the "city of God"? (46:4) Historically "Jerusalem is the holy city. It was made sacred in bygone days by the presence of God's sanctuary, sanctified by righteous prophets and Apostles who walked her streets, and hallowed by the life, ministry, and infinite atonement of Jesus Christ. The city's many names and titles describe her sacred calling and divine mission" (McConkie and Parry, *Guide to Scriptural Symbols*, 70). A similar title, "city of the living God," is found in D&C 76:66. It refers to a future city of Zion. "This city is the New Jerusalem, which is to occupy the site now known as Independence, Jackson County, Missouri [D&C 57:1–4; Ether 13:2–10]" (Brewster, *Doctrine and Covenants Encyclopedia*, rev. ed., 87).

The Joseph Smith Translation Emphasizes the Prophetic Nature of Psalm 46

"Around two hundred verses in some fifty different psalms saw revision at the hands of Joseph Smith. Because he worked from the King James Version without reference to Hebrew or Greek texts, many of the changes have to do with KJV difficulties rather than difficulties arising from the original texts, though such difficulties certainly do exist. . . .

"We should mention a change that is somewhat representative of changes made in several other places (Ps. 11, 12, and 24 contain such examples). The present tense of the verb found in Psalm 46:3–11 of the KJV is altered to the future tense in the JST. When one reads Psalm 46 in the KJV, the feeling is that the Psalmist is magnifying God because of a recent or even concurrent trial at the hands of 'heathens.' While reading the JST, on the other hand, one gets the feeling that it is a prophetic insight on the part of the Psalmist concerning some far-distant occurrence. This impression is confirmed upon arriving at the end of verse 8: 'in the latter days' is added in the JST. What this means is that the Prophet read some psalms as prophetic oracles concerning the latter days which the KJV read as historical occurrences within ancient Israel.

"One of the results of reading many psalms in this prophetic, latter-day-looking manner is that Joseph Smith found additional material concerning the founding of a latter-day Zion. It is clear, even from a cursory reading of the Doctrine and Covenants, that the formation of Zion was one of the main objects of Joseph Smith's ministry. Indeed, one could easily be justified in adding a subtitle to this latter-day collection of revelations: 'A Guide for the Establishment and Maintenance of Zion.' In Psalm 46:5 we read from the KJV of a very concrete, very present, city: 'God is in the midst of her [the city of God]; she shall not be moved: God shall help her, and that right early.' In the JST we read of a city not yet a reality: 'For Zion shall come, and God shall be in the midst of her; she shall not be moved; God shall help her right early'" (Burton, "Hymnal of Ancient Israel," 408, 409)

The following are samples of the JST changes in Psalm 46. Crossed-out are words removed, and bold italics are words added or restored in the JST. The Prophet Joseph Smith did not make any changes to verse 10:

"5 ***For Zion shall come, and*** God ~~is~~ ***shall be*** in the midst of her; she shall not be moved***;*** : God shall help her~~, and that~~ right early.

"6 The heathen ***shall be enraged*** ~~raged~~, ***and*** ~~the~~ ***their*** kingdoms ~~were~~ ***shall be*** moved~~,: he uttered~~ ***and the Lord shall utter*** his voice, ***and*** the earth ***shall be*** melted.

"7 The Lord of hosts ~~is~~ ***who shall be*** with us***,*** ; the God of Jacob is our refuge. Selah.

"8 Come, behold the works of the Lord, what desolations he ~~hath made~~ ***shall make*** in the earth ***in the latter days***.

"9 He maketh wars to cease unto the end of the earth; he breaketh the bow, and cutteth the spear in sunder; he burneth the chariot in the fire***,*** : ***and saith unto the nations,***

[10 Be still, and know that I am God: I will be exalted among the heathen, I will be exalted in the earth.]

"11 The LORD of hosts ~~is~~ ***shall be*** with us***,*** the God of Jacob ~~is~~ our refuge. Selah" (Hite, et al., *Old Testament with the Joseph Smith Translation*, 277).

Why will the Lord's voice melt the earth? (46:6) The Book of Mormon explains: "And now, I speak also concerning those who do not believe in Christ. Behold, will ye believe in the day of your visitation—behold, when the Lord shall come, yea, even that great day when the earth shall be rolled together as a scroll, and the elements shall melt with fervent heat, yea, in that great day when ye shall be brought to stand before the Lamb of God—then will ye say that there is no God?" (Mormon 9:1–2; see also 3 Nephi 26:3; D&C 101:24–25). See commentary in this volume for Isaiah 64:1–3.

When will the Lord cause wars to cease? (46:9) "The millennial day is one in which the Lord himself will dwell with men. . . . We can scarcely conceive of the glory and wonder of it all. The Lord Jesus Christ, the King of heaven, our Savior and Redeemer, the Lord God Omnipotent dwelling among men! . . .

"In that day there will be peace on earth; wars will be unknown and unheard of; crime and evil and carnality will vanish away; and the Son of Righteousness shall replace evil with good. . . . Where there is peace, there is neither crime nor war. . . . 'He maketh wars to cease unto the end of the earth' (Ps. 46:9)" (McConkie, *Millennial Messiah*, 652, 654). ⊕

How can we "be still" and why is it necessary? (46:10) President Boyd K. Packer taught the need for being still: "Inspiration comes more easily in peaceful settings. Such words as *quiet*, *still*, *peaceable*, *Comforter* abound in the scriptures: 'Be *still*, and know that I am God' (Ps. 46:10, italics added). And the promise, 'You shall receive my Spirit, the Holy Ghost, even the Comforter, which shall teach you the *peaceable* things of the kingdom' (D&C 36:2, italics added)" ("Reverence Invites Revelation," 21). ⊕

Summary of Psalms 47–49

These psalms conclude a series of psalms written for the sons of Korah to sing. They sing of God as their King (see Psalm 47:2, 6–9), God's future glorious city of Zion (see Psalm 48:1–3, 8, 11–12), and how God, not wealth, can redeem us from death (see Psalm 49:6–8, 13–15). The holiness of God and the city of Zion are emphasized in these psalms.

6 The heathen raged, the kingdoms were moved: he uttered his voice, the earth melted.

7 The LORD of hosts *is* with us; the God of Jacob *is* our refuge. Selah.

8 Come, behold the works of the LORD, what desolations he hath made in the earth.

9 He maketh wars to cease unto the end of the earth; he breaketh the bow, and cutteth the spear in sunder; he burneth the chariot in the fire.

10 Be still, and know that I *am* God: I will be exalted among the heathen, I will be exalted in the earth.

11 The LORD of hosts *is* with us; the God of Jacob *is* our refuge. Selah.

PSALMS 47–49

The Lord is King over all the earth—Sing praises to His name, for He reigns over all.

To the chief Musician, A Psalm for the sons of Korah.

Zion, the city of God, the joy of the whole earth, will be established forever.

A Song *and* Psalm for the sons of Korah.

Men cannot be ransomed or redeemed by wealth—God alone can redeem a soul from the grave—The glory of a rich man ceases with his death.

To the chief Musician, A Psalm for the sons of Korah.

PSALM 50

Asaph speaks of the Second Coming—The Lord accepts the sacrifices of the righteous and will deliver them—Those whose conduct is right will see the salvation of God.

A Psalm of Asaph.

1 The mighty God, *even* the LORD, hath spoken, and called the earth from the rising of the sun unto the going down thereof.

2 Out of Zion, the perfection of beauty, God hath shined.

3 Our God shall come, and shall not keep silence: a fire shall devour before him, and it shall be very tempestuous round about him.

4 He shall call to the heavens from above, and to the earth, that he may judge his people.

Who is "Asaph"? (Psalm 50 superscription) Asaph is "a cymbal-playing Levite appointed leader of David's choir. Founded a family of singers called the 'sons of Asaph' or 'children of Asaph'; mentioned in the titles of various Psalms [see Psalms 50; 73–83]" (Bible Dictionary, "Asaph").

Psalm 50:1–6. The Lord Shall Appear and Judge His People

What is "the perfection of beauty" that will come out of Zion? (50:2) "The two words most commonly used to describe Zion are *beauty* and *joy*, and the same two words most often relate to heaven and paradise. Beauty comes first, for beauty is whatever gives joy. . . . These are more than figures of speech. As President Joseph F. Smith put it, 'Things upon the earth, so far as they have not been perverted by wickedness, are typical of things in heaven. Heaven was the prototype of this beautiful creation when it came from the hand of the Creator, and was pronounced "good" [in *Journal of Discourses*, 23:175].' There you have the environment of Zion; and for a foretaste of it, all we have to do is go to the canyons and look around us" (Nibley, *Approaching Zion*, 7). ⊕

How will the Lord's Second Coming differ from His First Coming? (50:3–4) Elder Orson Pratt taught: "[Jesus Christ] came in a very meek and humble manner; his birth and advent into this world were in the most humble position. . . . This last coming, or the coming here spoken of by the Psalmist, represents him as coming with power" (in *Journal of Discourses*, 15:54).

"When the Savior comes again, He will come in power and glory to claim the earth as His kingdom. His Second Coming will mark the beginning of the Millennium.

"The Second Coming will be a fearful, mournful time for the wicked, but it will be a day of peace for the righteous" (*True to the Faith* [2004], 159–60). See also D&C 88:88–92. ⊕

Who are the Lord's saints? (50:5) Psalm 50:5 describes the saints who are gathered as "those that have made a covenant with me by sacrifice." Following His resurrection, the Lord explained the sacrifice He requires: "And ye shall offer for a sacrifice unto me a broken heart and a contrite spirit" (3 Nephi 9:20).

Elsewhere, "the scriptures use the word *Saint* to refer to those who have come out of the darkness of the world into the 'marvellous light' of Christ (1 Peter 2:9), have accepted Jesus Christ as their Lord and Savior, and have come into his Church. Saints are striving to put off the natural man and put on Christ (Mosiah 3:19)" (Millet, "Saint," 551).

Who is the God who will "judge his people"? (50:6) "'The Father judgeth no man, but hath committed all judgment unto the Son: that all men should honour the Son, even as they honour the Father' (John 5:22–23). And this Son of Man, in a not far-distant day, shall come again, in all the glory of his Father's kingdom, to take vengeance upon the ungodly and to give glory and honor to the righteous" (McConkie, *New Witness for the Articles of Faith*, 69).

Summary of Psalm 50:7–23

The Lord asks His people for offerings of thanksgiving and their prayers to Him. The wicked who forget God will be reproved.

Psalm 51:1–9. David Pleads for Forgiveness

Why is David seeking to be made clean from sin? (51:2) When confronted by the prophet Nathan, David acknowledged his need to repent and be made clean by the Lord (see 2 Samuel 12). "If we wish to return to our Father, we absolutely must learn how to feel the power of our Savior's Atonement through the remission of our sins. Lovingly, the resurrected Christ told His disciples on the American continent:

"'No unclean thing can enter into his kingdom' [3 Nephi 27:19]. . . .

5 Gather my saints together unto me; those that have made a covenant with me by sacrifice.

6 And the heavens shall declare his righteousness: for God *is* judge himself. Selah.

PSALM 51

David pleads for forgiveness after he went in to Bathsheba—He pleads, Create in me a clean heart, and renew a right spirit within me.

To the chief Musician, A Psalm of David, when Nathan the prophet came unto him, after he had gone in to Bath-sheba.

1 Have mercy upon me, O God, according to thy lovingkindness: according unto the multitude of thy tender mercies blot out my transgressions.

2 Wash me throughly from mine iniquity, and cleanse me from my sin.

3 For I acknowledge my transgressions: and my sin *is* ever before me.

4 Against thee, thee only, have I sinned, and done *this* evil in thy sight: that thou mightest be justified when thou speakest, *and* be clear when thou judgest.

"Oh, to be clean! This is the great challenge of our mortal probation. It is also the only way to the indescribable joy of truly knowing our Savior. He has promised us, 'Blessed are the pure in heart: for they shall see God' [Matthew 5:8]" (Andersen, *Divine Gift of Forgiveness*, 13, 14).

5 Behold, I was shapen in iniquity; and in sin did my mother conceive me.

Why did David say he was born in sin? (51:5) "The line has been used as a proof text for original sin. . . . But the point of the line is to make another personal statement about the suppliant's [David's] particular life" (Goldingay, *Psalms, Vol. 2*, 129). "In the midst of his sorrow because he violated the moral law, he may have felt his sin keenly and in this manner expressed himself, but this did not make the statement true that his parents were guilty of sin and that he partook of it in his birth. Let it be remembered also that David was speaking only for and of himself, and that his words cannot . . . be universally applied" (Smith, *Answers to Gospel Questions*, 3:15). ⊕

6 Behold, thou desirest truth in the inward parts: and in the hidden *part* thou shalt make me to know wisdom.

How do we receive truth "in the inward parts"? (51:6) The phrase "inward parts" refers to our hearts. When we receive truth in our hearts, we desire to live the gospel with all our hearts and are truly converted to it (see Jeremiah 31:33). Elder Ronald A. Rasband taught: "One by one we gain a witness from the Holy Spirit as He speaks to our own spirit, teaching 'truth in the inward parts' [Psalm 51:6]. When we live the gospel of Jesus Christ, when we draw upon the Savior's Atonement and press forward with faith, not fear, we are fortified against the wiles of the adversary. Our testimonies connect us to the heavens, and we are blessed with 'the truth of all things' [Moroni 10:5]" ("Build a Fortress of Spirituality and Protection," 110).

7 Purge me with hyssop, and I shall be clean: wash me, and I shall be whiter than snow.

How can the consequences of sin be made "whiter than snow"? (51:7) "There is no such thing as a spotted, cream-colored repenter. There is no black mark that emerges from the waters of baptism, no stain that survives the rigors of repentance. The repentant soul becomes as white as the driven snow. For such a saint, it is as though the act were never even committed. That is the miracle of repentance. As Elder Matthew Cowley said, 'I believe when we repent there is some erasing going on up there so that when we get there we will be judged as we are for what we are and maybe not for what we have been.' He also commented, 'That's what I like about it—the erasing' [Smith, *Matthew Cowley, Man of Faith*, 295]" (Callister, *Infinite Atonement*, 193–94).

8 Make me to hear joy and gladness; *that* the bones *which* thou hast broken may rejoice.

9 Hide thy face from my sins, and blot out all mine iniquities.

What brings joy and gladness to one who has sinned? (51:8–9) "We have all made incorrect choices. If we have not already corrected such choices, I assure you that there is a way to do so. The process is called repentance. . . . Our Savior died to provide you and me that blessed gift. Although the path is not easy, the promise is real. . . . The sooner you begin to make your way back, the sooner you will find the sweet peace and joy that come with the miracle of forgiveness" (Monson, *Teachings of Thomas S. Monson*, 253–54). When did you last feel the joy and gladness of repentance?

Psalm 51:10–19. David Asks the Lord to Make Him Clean Again

10 Create in me a clean heart, O God; and renew a right spirit within me.

11 Cast me not away from thy presence; and take not thy holy spirit from me.

12 Restore unto me the joy of thy salvation; and uphold me *with thy* free spirit.

13 *Then* will I teach transgressors thy ways; and sinners shall be converted unto thee.

What did David desire to regain through his repentance? (51:10–12) "David, a great man of such tremendous ability and potential, recognized that through his wrongdoing as a mature man he had lost the relationship he had with his Father in Heaven. That relationship allowed him to have sufficient faith to personally challenge Goliath, sufficient faith to lead great armies, and sufficient faith and the Spirit of the Lord to compose beautiful psalms and to do all the things which he had done in an otherwise seemingly great life. Now, by his sin, he had cast away his ability to call upon the Spirit" (West, "Are You on the Lord's Side?" 14). In what ways can you regain the companionship of the Spirit, once lost?

14 Deliver me from bloodguiltiness, O God, thou God of my salvation: *and* my tongue shall sing aloud of thy righteousness.

15 O Lord, open thou my lips; and my mouth shall shew forth thy praise.

16 For thou desirest not sacrifice; else would I give *it:* thou delightest not in burnt offering.

What is "bloodguiltiness"? (51:14) This "probably meant that the death penalty should have been imposed for David's sins. Most likely this was David's plea for mercy so that he would be spared from vengeance and death" (*Quest Study Bible* [1994], 773). "The translation 'bloodguiltiness' occurs only in Psalm 51:14. The plural form almost invariably means the shedding of blood, but the singular can mean blood itself, bloodshed, or the guilt incurred by bloodshed (i.e., by killing). The idea that killing was punishable by death pervades the Bible; killing was generally done by literally shedding another's blood" (*Tyndale Bible Dictionary*, 228).

17 The sacrifices of God *are* a broken spirit: a broken and a contrite heart, O God, thou wilt not despise.

18 Do good in thy good pleasure unto Zion: build thou the walls of Jerusalem.

What does it mean for us to offer as a sacrifice a broken heart and contrite spirit? (51:17) Marie K. Hafen shared how observing well-trained horses helped her understand the scriptural term *broken*: "A horse that is well broken is a horse that is well trained. When the Lord asks us for our broken hearts, He is asking in part, for us to take His word into us, to put His bit in our mouths, to wear His bridle so our ears can

19 Then shalt thou be pleased with the sacrifices of righteousness, with burnt offering and whole burnt offering: then shall they offer bullocks upon thine altar.

PSALMS 52–55

David says that wicked tongues devise mischief and the wicked trust in riches—The Saints trust in the mercy of God forever.

To the chief Musician, Maschil, *A Psalm* of David, when Doeg the Edomite came and told Saul, and said unto him, David is come to the house of Ahimelech.

David says, The fool says there is no God—There is none who does good—Gathered Israel will rejoice.

To the chief Musician upon Mahalath, Maschil, *A Psalm* of David.

David pleads for salvation and promises to serve God.

To the chief Musician on Neginoth, Maschil, *A Psalm* of David, when the Ziphims came and said to Saul, Doth not David hide himself with us?

David prays morning, noon, and night—He seeks protection and help against his enemies.

To the chief Musician on Neginoth, Maschil, *A Psalm* of David.

become attuned to His voice. . . . Contrition of spirit when added to a state of brokenheartedness moves us toward Christ because we want His help. . . . A contrite spirit is eager to repent" (*Contrite Spirit*, xiv, xv).

Summary of Psalms 52–55

These hymns, attributed to David's authorship, express his confidence in God in contrast to the foolishness of evil disbelievers. He prays for deliverance from those who would kill him. He pleads, "Hear my prayer, O God; give ear to the words of my mouth. For strangers are risen up against me . . . they have not set God before them" (Psalm 54:2–3).

PSALM 56

David seeks mercy, trusts in and praises the Lord, and thanks Him for deliverance.

To the chief Musician upon Jonath-elem-rechokim, Michtam of David, when the Philistines took him in Gath.

What do the words *Jonath–elem–rechokim* mean? (Psalm 56 superscription) "Dove of the dumbness of the distance; i.e., 'the silent dove in distant places'" (*Easton's Bible Dictionary*, "Jonath-Elem-Rechokim"). Some translators believe these words are "the beginning of a song; and others think they are the name of a musical instrument: but they seem rather to design the subject matter of the psalm . . . ; and refer to David, who, when he wrote this psalm, was among the Philistines, who were aliens from the commonwealth of Israel, afar off from God and his law, and from righteousness . . . and, what gave him most concern, from the house and worship of God; and here he was as a mute dove" (*John Gill's Exposition of the Whole Bible* [commentary on Introduction to Psalm 56]).

What was a "Michtam"? (Psalm 56 superscription) See commentary in this volume for Psalm 16 superscription.

Psalm 56:1–9. David's Enemies Oppress Him Daily, but He Trusts in the Lord

What can we do when people and circumstances try to "swallow" us up? (56:2–4) As the Psalmist put his trust in God (see vv. 3–4), so Elder Richard G. Scott reminded us: "This life is an experience in profound trust—trust in Jesus Christ, trust in His teachings, trust in our capacity as led by the Holy Spirit to obey those teachings for happiness now and for a purposeful, supremely happy eternal existence. To trust means to obey willingly without knowing the end from the beginning (see Prov. 3:5–7)" ("Trust in the Lord," 17). The Book of Mormon adds, "The Lord in his great infinite goodness doth bless and prosper those who put their trust in him" (Helaman 12:1). When has trusting in the Lord helped you through difficult relationships or experiences? ⊕

1 Be merciful unto me, O God: for man would swallow me up; he fighting daily oppresseth me.

2 Mine enemies would daily swallow *me* up: for *they be* many that fight against me, O thou most High.

3 What time I am afraid, I will trust in thee.

4 In God I will praise his word, in God I have put my trust; I will not fear what flesh can do unto me.

5 Every day they wrest my words: all their thoughts *are* against me for evil.

6 They gather themselves together, they hide themselves, they mark my steps, when they wait for my soul.

7 Shall they escape by iniquity? in *thine* anger cast down the people, O God.

8 Thou tellest my wanderings: put thou my tears into thy bottle: *are they* not in thy book?

9 When I cry *unto thee,* then shall mine enemies turn back: this I know; for God *is* for me.

How can you be assured God is "for you"? (56:9) Elder Jeffrey R. Holland testified: "That truth has to be seared into our hearts, written in bold letters across the tissue of our brains, and never forgotten. . . . We ought to have some such figurative reminder constantly before our eyes and always in our hearts that God is for us. . . . No matter what the trouble and trial of the day may be, we start and finish with the eternal truth that God is for us. He loves us. He is our Heavenly Father. He never sleeps nor slumbers in His watchcare over us. His work and His glory are to save us, to exalt us, to see us safely home with Him" (*For Times of Trouble*, 12).

Summary of Psalm 56:10–13

Because the Psalmist trusts the Lord, he has no fear of any man. He ends his psalm with praise and a promise to walk before God.

PSALMS 57–60

David pleads for mercy and acclaims the glory and exaltation of God.

To the chief Musician, Al-taschith, Michtam of David, when he fled from Saul in the cave.

David reproves wicked judges—They go astray and speak lies.

To the chief Musician, Al-taschith, Michtam of David.

David prays to be delivered from his enemies—God rules in Jacob unto the ends of the earth.

To the chief Musician, Al-taschith, Michtam of David; when Saul sent, and they watched the house to kill him.

David says that the Lord has scattered His people—The Lord places Ephraim at the head and makes Judah His lawgiver.

To the chief Musician upon Shushaneduth, Michtam of David, to teach; when he strove with Aram-naharaim and with Aram-zobah, when Joab returned, and smote of Edom in the valley of salt twelve thousand.

Summary of Psalms 57–60

All of these psalms are prayers: prayers for deliverance from enemies (Psalms 57, 59); a prayer asking God to correct wicked judges (Psalm 58); and a prayer on behalf of the nation of Israel who has suffered a military defeat (Psalm 60).

Summary of Psalms 61–66

David declares Jehovah to be his protector, rock, salvation, and defense. He praises and worships the Lord and prays for safety. The Psalmist declares "He is my defence; I shall not be moved. In God is my salvation and my glory . . . ye people, pour out your heart before him" (Psalm 62:6–8). The Lord will send tests, trials, and blessings. "For thou, O God, hast proved us: thou hast tried us, as silver is tried. . . . We went through fire and through water: but thou broughtest us out into a wealthy place" (Psalm 66:10, 12).

PSALMS 61–66

David finds shelter in the Lord, abides in the Lord's presence, and keeps his own vows.

To the chief Musician upon Neginah, *A Psalm* of David.

David praises God as his defense, his rock, and his salvation—The Lord judges men according to their works.

To the chief Musician, to Jeduthun, A Psalm of David.

David thirsts for God, whom he praises with joyful lips.

A Psalm of David, when he was in the wilderness of Judah.

David prays for safety—The righteous will be glad in heart.

To the chief Musician, A Psalm of David.

David speaks of the blessedness of God's chosen—The Lord sends rain and good things upon the earth.

To the chief Musician, A Psalm *and* Song of David.

Praise and worship the Lord—He tests and tries men—Sacrifices are to be offered in His house.

To the chief Musician, A Song *or* Psalm.

PSALM 67

A messianic psalm—The Lord will cause His face to shine upon men—He will judge and govern in righteousness.

To the chief Musician on Neginoth, A Psalm *or* Song.

1 God be merciful unto us, and bless us; *and*
cause his face to shine upon us; Selah.

2 That thy way may be known upon earth,
thy saving health among all nations.

3 Let the people praise thee, O God; let all
the people praise thee.

4 O let the nations be glad and sing for joy:
for thou shalt judge the people righteously,
and govern the nations upon earth. Selah.

5 Let the people praise thee, O God; let all
the people praise thee.

6 *Then* shall the earth yield her increase; *and*
God, *even* our own God, shall bless us.

7 God shall bless us; and all the ends of the
earth shall fear him.

What are "Neginoth"? (Psalm 67 superscription) Neginoth are "songs with instrumental accompaniment, found in the titles of Psalm 4; 6; 54; 55; 67; 76; rendered 'stringed instruments' [Habakkuk 3:19]. It denotes all kinds of stringed instruments, [such] as the 'harp,' 'psaltery,' 'viol,' etc. The 'chief musician on Neginoth' is the leader of that part of the temple choir which played on stringed instruments" (*Easton's Bible Dictionary,* "Neginoth").

Psalm 67:1–7. May All the Earth Know and Praise God

What is the "saving health among all nations"? (67:2–7) "The theme of this excellent psalm, stated in the second verse, is missionary work; it is the essence of the original call of Abraham. He and his seed are to minister unto all families of all nations; they are to bring knowledge of the name, blessings, and power of the only true and living God ([Topical Guide], 'Abrahamic Covenant'). Thereby all nations shall be blessed. This psalm is a prayer for God's blessing to help the faithful fulfill that mission. Then all nations may sing for joy, when God shall govern the nations and all shall worship him" (Rasmussen, *Latter-day Saint Commentary on the Old Testament*, 435; see also Abraham 2:9–11).

How are we helping all nations come to know the gladness and joy of the Lord? (67:4–5) "Church leaders have emphasized the clarion call 'Every member a missionary!' for decades.

"Members of the Church of Jesus Christ—both in past times as well as in ours—have enthusiastically and joyfully shared the gospel with friends and acquaintances. Their hearts are aflame with the testimony of Jesus Christ, and they sincerely want others to experience the same joy they have found in the Savior's gospel" (Uchtdorf, "Missionary Work," 16). ⊕

PSALM 68

A messianic psalm of David—He extols JAH—The Lord gave the word—He takes captivity captive—He delivers us from death—Sing praises unto the Lord.

To the chief Musician, A Psalm *or* Song of David.

Psalm 68:1–6. Jehovah Leads Israel out of Egypt

1 Let God arise, let his enemies be scattered:
let them also that hate him flee before him.

2 As smoke is driven away, *so* drive *them*
away: as wax melteth before the fire, *so* let the
wicked perish at the presence of God.

3 But let the righteous be glad; let them rejoice before God: yea, let them exceedingly
rejoice.

4 Sing unto God, sing praises to his name:
extol him that rideth upon the heavens by his
name JAH, and rejoice before him.

Why is Jehovah's name referenced as "JAH" in this psalm? (68:4) "*Yahweh* is the name of the God of the Hebrews. The Anglicized or English rendition of this name is *Jehovah*. The shortened form of *Yahweh* is *Yah*, and the contracted form of *Jehovah* (*Jahveh* or *Yahweh*) is *Jah*. Thus David writes: 'Sing unto God, sing praises to his name: extol him that rideth upon the heavens by his name JAH, and rejoice before him' (Ps. 68:4)" (McConkie, *Promised Messiah*, 111). "The original pronunciation of [Jehovah's] name has possibly been lost, as the Jews, in reading, never mentioned it but substituted one of the other names of God, usually Adonai. . . . In the KJV, the Jewish custom has been followed, and the name is generally denoted by LORD or GOD, printed in small capitals" (Bible Dictionary, "Jehovah").

5 A father of the fatherless, and a judge of the
widows, *is* God in his holy habitation.

6 God setteth the solitary in families: he
bringeth out those which are bound with
chains: but the rebellious dwell in a dry *land*.

How can Jehovah be the "father of the fatherless" while dwelling "in his holy habitation"? (68:5–6) Jehovah "is enthroned in heaven, *his holy habitation*, yet He is intimately aware of human needs: He is a father to orphans and the protector of the weak and lonely (cf. Ex. 22:22, 23; Jn. 14:18); He cares for the solitary and He delivers the oppressed. . . . He has especially blessed Israel in having brought them out of Egyptian bondage into comparative prosperity; on the other hand, the bodies of rebellious folk who could not enter in because of disbelief were left in *a parched land*" (Guthrie, et al., *New Bible Commentary: Revised*, 492).

18 Thou hast ascended on high, thou hast led captivity captive: thou hast received gifts for men; yea, *for* the rebellious also, that the Lord God might dwell *among them.*

19 Blessed *be* the Lord, *who* daily loadeth us *with benefits, even* the God of our salvation. Selah.

20 *He that is* our God *is* the God of salvation; and unto God the Lord *belong* the issues from death.

21 But God shall wound the head of his enemies, *and* the hairy scalp of such an one as goeth on still in his trespasses.

Summary of Psalm 68:7–17

David recounts how Jehovah had led Israel and provided for them as they sojourned through the wilderness and into the promised land. The Lord also led them to victory over their enemies.

Psalm 68:18–21. Jehovah Is Victor over All, Including Death

In what way can these verses describe the Savior and His mission? (68:18–21) The apostle Paul applied Psalm 68:18 to the Savior when he taught the Ephesians, "Wherefore he saith, When he ascended up on high, he led captivity captive, and gave gifts unto men" (Ephesians 4:8). "Metaphors express the prophecy of the Lord's subduing the earth by ascending 'on high' via the cross and the Resurrection, whereby he 'received gifts for men' in the Atonement so that all may come unto him. . . . He is 'the God of salvation,' for unto him belong 'the issues from death,' meaning all who arise from death. He is the Savior, Eve's 'Seed,' who did 'bruise' or 'wound' the head of the adversary (Gen. 3:15; Ps. 68:19–20, 21*a*)" (Rasmussen, *Latter-day Saint Commentary on the Old Testament*, 436).

After Ascending on High, Christ Appeared to His Disciples (Psalm 68:18–21)

Summary of Psalm 68:22–35

Psalm 68 appears to be a processional hymn, perhaps celebrating David's returning the ark to Jerusalem (see 2 Sam. 6; 1 Chron. 13). Also a prayer to the Lord asking Him for a demonstration of strength against those nations who will not submit to Him. Finally, a triumphal hymn calling for all kingdoms to praise the God of Israel.

What is "Shoshannim"? (Psalm 69 superscription)

Shoshannim is direction to the musical leader. See commentary in this volume for Psalm 45.

Psalm 69:1–12. David Pleads to the Lord for Help

What do "deep waters" symbolize? (69:1–2)

President Russell M. Nelson noted: "The expression *deep water* means danger!" ("With God Nothing Shall Be Impossible," 33). "In the biblical text, water carries both the connotation of cleansing and also of chaos" (Gaskill, *Lost Language of Symbolism*, 265). Even though deep waters might be dangerous or chaotic, the Prophet Joseph Smith declared: "Deep water is what I am wont to swim in" (D&C 127:2).

Why is it futile to hide sins from God? (69:5)

Brigham Young taught: "It has been the doctrine of some . . . that all the sin you can hide from your brethren and sisters, no matter what its nature and magnitude, will not be brought against you in the day of judgment. Such persons are greatly mistaken. For the sins you commit against yourselves and your God, unless repented of and forgiven, the Lord will hold his private council and judge. . . . You need not think that you can hide your sins. . . . The doctrine of hiding sin is a false doctrine" (in *Journal of Discourses*, 8:362; see also Alma 38:8; 2 Nephi 9:20; D&C 1:1–2).

PSALM 69

A messianic psalm of David—The zeal of the Lord's house has eaten Him up—Reproach has broken His heart—He is given gall and vinegar to drink—He is persecuted—He will save Zion.

To the chief Musician upon Shoshannim, *A Psalm* of David.

1 Save me, O God; for the waters are come in unto *my* soul.

2 I sink in deep mire, where *there is* no standing: I am come into deep waters, where the floods overflow me.

3 I am weary of my crying: my throat is dried: mine eyes fail while I wait for my God.

4 They that hate me without a cause are more than the hairs of mine head: they that would destroy me, *being* mine enemies wrongfully, are mighty: then I restored *that* which I took not away.

5 O God, thou knowest my foolishness; and my sins are not hid from thee.

6 Let not them that wait on thee, O Lord
God of hosts, be ashamed for my sake: let
not those that seek thee be confounded for
my sake, O God of Israel.

7 Because for thy sake I have borne reproach;
shame hath covered my face.

8 I am become a stranger unto my brethren,
and an alien unto my mother's children.

9 For the zeal of thine house hath eaten
me up; and the reproaches of them that re-
proached thee are fallen upon me.

10 When I wept, *and chastened* my soul with
fasting, that was to my reproach.

11 I made sackcloth also my garment; and I
became a proverb to them.

In what way might those who "seek" Israel be confounded? (69:6) "I have noted recently, as I have many times in the past, that whenever or wherever a Latter-day Saint is mentioned in a news story—whether it be for appointment to high government office or for law-breaking—the 'Mormon' connection is usually mentioned. Other denominations rarely receive that distinction. I consider this a compliment because it is evidence that the world is becoming more and more aware of what we stand for and expects more of us. The example we set before the world will determine, in large measure, whether we gain friends or enemies" (Tanner, "Power of Example," 2).

What does it mean to become a "proverb"? (69:11) According to Dummelow, the word "proverb" is translated as "byword" (see *John Dummelow's Commentary* [on Psalm 69:11]). Another biblical scholar suggested that when one becomes a "byword," they are the "subject of derision" (Cohen, *Psalms*, 218). For example, the New International Version of this verse says: "When I put on sackcloth, people make sport of me" (NIV, Psalm 69:11).

Messianic Prophecies in Psalm 69 (Psalm 69:4)

"Much of Psalm 69 will sound familiar to you from the New Testament. This psalm is the second most quoted psalm in the New Testament. It is second only to Psalm 22" (Longman, *How to Read the Psalms*, 133). The New Testament shows how the prophecies in Psalm 69 were fulfilled.

Prophecy of Jesus	New Testament Fulfillment
Psalm 69:4—Jesus would be hated "without a cause"	John 15:23–25—"That the word might be fulfilled that is written in their law, They hated me without a cause"
Psalm 69:9—Jesus would be moved to "zeal" to cleanse the temple	John 2:13–17—"His disciples remembered that it was written, The zeal of thine house hath eaten me up"
Psalm 69:9—Jesus would suffer by taking upon Himself the "reproaches of them"	Romans 15:3—"As it is written, The reproaches of them that reproached thee fell on me"
Psalm 69:21—Jesus would thirst on the cross and be given "gall" and "vinegar"	Matthew 27:34; see also John 19:28–30—"Gave him vinegar to drink mingled with gall: and when he had tasted thereof, he would not drink"
Psalm 69:22–23—Jesus' persecutors' actions would be a "snare" and a "trap" for them	Romans 11:5–10—"David saith, Let their table be made a snare, and a trap, and a stumblingblock, and a recompence unto them"
Psalm 69:25—Judas' betrayal of Jesus would lead to his losing his "habitation" and his "tent" (family), becoming "desolate"	Acts 1:15–20—"For it is written in the book of Psalms, Let his habitation be desolate, and let no man dwell therein"

What was said by those who sat "in the gate"? (69:12) "At the gates were the courts for public justice; there were complaints lodged, and causes heard. No doubt many vexatious complaints were made against the poor captives; and false accusations, through which they grievously suffered; so that, literally, they were often 'obliged to restore that which they had not taken away.' See Psalm 69:4" (*Adam Clarke's Commentary* [on Psalm 69:12]).

12 They that sit in the gate speak against me; and I *was* the song of the drunkards.

Psalm 69:13–21. David Prays That God Will Rescue Him

13 But as for me, my prayer *is* unto thee, O LORD, *in* an acceptable time: O God, in the multitude of thy mercy hear me, in the truth of thy salvation.

14 Deliver me out of the mire, and let me not sink: let me be delivered from them that hate me, and out of the deep waters.

15 Let not the waterflood overflow me, neither let the deep swallow me up, and let not the pit shut her mouth upon me.

What is the pit that will shut her mouth? (69:15) "Known as the 'horrible pit' (Ps. 40:2), the 'pit of destruction' (Ps. 55:23), the 'deeps' (Ps. 88:6), and 'prison' (Isa. 24:22), the pit is hell, the realm where the spirits of the unrighteous dwell while awaiting the judgment (2 Ne. 24:15; Ezek. 32:21–23)" (McConkie and Parry, *Guide to Scriptural Symbols*, 90).

16 Hear me, O LORD; for thy lovingkindness *is* good: turn unto me according to the multitude of thy tender mercies.

17 And hide not thy face from thy servant; for I am in trouble: hear me speedily.

18 Draw nigh unto my soul, *and* redeem it: deliver me because of mine enemies.

Why do some experience the Lord's lovingkindness and tender mercies? (69:16) Nephi explained: "I, Nephi, will show unto you that the tender mercies of the Lord are over all those whom he hath chosen, because of their faith, to make them mighty even unto the power of deliverance" (1 Nephi 1:20). Later, in one of his many dreams, note how Lehi experienced the Lord's lovingkindness: "And after I had traveled for the space of many hours in darkness, I began to pray unto the Lord that he would have mercy on me, according to the multitude of his tender mercies" (1 Nephi 8:8). In what ways have you experienced the Lord's lovingkindness and tender mercies? ⊕

19 Thou hast known my reproach, and my shame, and my dishonour: mine adversaries *are* all before thee.

20 Reproach hath broken my heart; and I am full of heaviness: and I looked *for some* to take pity, but *there was* none; and for comforters, but I found none.

What is "reproach"? (69:19–20) *Reproach* means "disgrace . . . [or] shame" (*Strong's Exhaustive Concordance*, word #h2781).

21 They gave me also gall for my meat; and in my thirst they gave me vinegar to drink.

What does this verse teach us about the Savior's life and death? (69:21) "Irony may involve not only unexpected suffering but also undeserved suffering. . . . Christ, long, long ago, as Creator, provided habitable conditions for us on this earth, generously providing all the essential atmospheric conditions for life, including essential water (see Moses 1:33; D&C 76:24). When he was aflame with thirst on the cross, 'they gave him vinegar to drink mingled with gall: and when he had tasted thereof, he would not drink' (Matt. 27:34; see also Ps. 69:21). Even so, there was no railing but a forgiving Christ (see Luke 23:34)" (Maxwell, "Irony," 63).

Summary of Psalm 69:22–28

David prays that God's divine justice might come upon his enemies who so persecute him. New Testament writers saw Messianic themes in these verses. For example, the Apostle Paul suggests that verses 22 and 23 also apply to the Jews who reject Christ (see Romans 11:9–10). In Luke's record, he saw that the promised end mentioned in verse 25 is directly tied to Judas Iscariot (see Acts 1:16, 20).

29 But I *am* poor and sorrowful: let thy salvation, O God, set me up on high.

30 I will praise the name of God with a song, and will magnify him with thanksgiving.

31 *This* also shall please the LORD better than an ox *or* bullock that hath horns and hoofs.

32 The humble shall see *this, and* be glad: and your heart shall live that seek God.

33 For the LORD heareth the poor, and despiseth not his prisoners.

34 Let the heaven and earth praise him, the seas, and every thing that moveth therein.

35 For God will save Zion, and will build the cities of Judah: that they may dwell there, and have it in possession.

Psalm 69:29–36. David Expresses Hope and Confidence in God to Save His People

How is singing praises to God "better than an ox or bullock"? (69:30–31) "Devout worship and praise of [Jehovah] please God much more than rituals and sacrifices" (Walton, et al., *IVP Bible Background Commentary*, 539). The Lord notes: "For my soul delighteth in the song of the heart; yea, the song of the righteous is a prayer unto me, and it shall be answered with a blessing upon their heads" (D&C 25:12). See commentary in this volume for 1 Samuel 15:22.

Who are the poor who have the Lord's attention? (69:33) "The term *poor* is used basically in two senses. . . . In most cases it refers to those who are needy or destitute. . . .

"There is another group of 'poor' spoken of in scripture, usually in association with the 'meek' (D&C 35:15; 88:17). These are 'the poor in spirit who come unto me,' declared the Savior. They are 'the meek [who] shall inherit the earth' (3 Ne. 12:3, 5; D&C 56:18; 88:17, 26)" (Brewster, *Doctrine and Covenants Encyclopedia*, 428).

What blessing comes to those who love the Lord's name? (69:36) "David humbly prayed for salvation 'on high' along with the humble and poor, and he looked to the time when Zion shall be redeemed and the cities of Judah be built, so that the seed of the Lord's servants may inherit it and 'they that love his name shall dwell therein' [Ps. 69:29–36]" (Rasmussen, *Latter-day Saint Commentary on the Old Testament*, 436–37).

Summary of Psalms 70–71

These two psalms, of both thanksgiving and expressions of sadness, are related to each other. The first (Psalm 70) pleads to God for help with overcoming his enemies. The second (Psalm 71) praises God for His willingness to always help and support His children.

Psalm 72:1–14. The Greatness of Israel's King

What does this Psalm teach us about Jesus Christ, the rightful king of Israel? (72:1) "Although it was David's prayer . . . that this psalm of the ideal king speak of Solomon (who did reign in righteousness and power for a time), in actuality the words typify the glorious millennial reign of Jesus Christ, when the Perfect King will fulfill all parts of the psalm, bringing peace, righteousness, and judgment to earth's inhabitants" (Parry and Parry, *Understanding the Signs of the Times*, 454).

How does God judge His people "with righteousness"? (72:2) "The ancient Jews, like ourselves, think of God's judgment in terms of an earthly court of justice. The difference is that the Christian pictures the case to be tried as a criminal case with himself in the dock; the Jew pictures it as a civil case with himself as the plaintiff [or accuser]. The one hopes for acquittal or rather for pardon; the other hopes for a resounding triumph with heavy damages. . . . The good king

36 The seed also of his servants shall inherit it: and they that love his name shall dwell therein.

PSALMS 70–71

David proclaims, Let God be magnified.

To the chief Musician, *A Psalm* of David, to bring to remembrance.

David praises God with thanksgiving—Who is like unto the Lord!

PSALM 72

David speaks of Solomon, who is made a type of the Messiah—He will have dominion—His name will endure forever—All nations will call him blessed—The whole earth will be filled with the glory of the Lord.

A Psalm for Solomon.

1 Give the king thy judgments, O God, and thy righteousness unto the king's son.

2 He shall judge thy people with righteousness, and thy poor with judgment.

in Psalm 72:2 will 'judge' the people rightly; that is, he will 'defend the poor.' When God 'arises to judgement' he will 'help all the meek upon earth' (76:9), all the timid, helpless people whose wrongs have never been righted yet" (Lewis, *Reflections on the Psalms*, 9–10). ⊕

3 The mountains shall bring peace to the people, and the little hills, by righteousness.

4 He shall judge the poor of the people, he shall save the children of the needy, and shall break in pieces the oppressor.

5 They shall fear thee as long as the sun and moon endure, throughout all generations.

6 He shall come down like rain upon the mown grass: as showers *that* water the earth.

7 In his days shall the righteous flourish; and abundance of peace so long as the moon endureth.

What are the mountains which bring us peace? (72:3) Mountains are "an image of the temple or house of the Lord; also representative of revelation, inspiration, separation from the world" (Gaskill, *Lost Language of Symbolism*, 322). "The temple provides purpose for our lives. It brings peace to our souls—not the peace provided by men but the peace promised by the Son of God when He said, 'Peace I leave with you, my peace I give unto you'" (Monson, "Blessings of the Temple," 15).

8 He shall have dominion also from sea to sea, and from the river unto the ends of the earth.

9 They that dwell in the wilderness shall bow before him; and his enemies shall lick the dust.

What does the phrase "from the river to the end of the earth" mean? (72:8) "The *River* is the Euphrates, the eastern geographical boundary familiar to the Hebrews. The phrase really covers the whole of the then known world" (Cohen, *Psalms*, 228).

10 The kings of Tarshish and of the isles shall bring presents: the kings of Sheba and Seba shall offer gifts.

How was this prophecy about Tarshish and Sheba bringing Solomon gifts fulfilled? (72:10) "Though Solomon did not reign over Cilicia, of which Tarsus was the capital, yet he might receive gifts, not in the sense of tribute; for מנחה *minchah*, the word here used, signifies a gratitude or friendly offering. [As to the] *kings of Sheba and Seba*—Both countries of Arabia[,] from the former came the queen of Sheba, to hear the wisdom of Solomon. And she brought exceeding great presents or gifts" (*Adam Clarke's Commentary* [on Psalm 72:10]).

11 Yea, all kings shall fall down before him: all nations shall serve him.

12 For he shall deliver the needy when he crieth; the poor also, and *him* that hath no helper.

13 He shall spare the poor and needy, and shall save the souls of the needy.

Who will rule over the kings and redeem the poor? (72:11–14) "From a prayer of David we extract these words which are clearly Messianic, though some of them, as originally given, applied to contemporary events. It was the prophetic practice among the Hebrews to use local circumstances as similitudes to teach the glories and wonders of the gospel and of the Messiah who would come to save his people. . . . In substance and in thought content they all shall surely come to pass" (McConkie, *Millennial Messiah*,

593). By "taking advantage of the ambiguity of Hebrew verb tenses, the poem manages at once to be prayer, prophecy, portrait, and benediction" (Alter, *Art of Biblical Poetry*, 131).

Psalm 72:15–20. David's Prayer for the King

What does "a handful of corn on the top of the mountain" represent? (72:16) "The main crop of biblical times was wheat [sometimes translated as 'corn']. The fields were not irrigated and were fully dependent upon the highly unstable rainfall" (Zohary, *Plants of the Bible*, 74). This represents a prayer to have an abundant crop. As one Bible translation has it: "May there be abundance of grain in the land; on the tops of the mountains may it wave" (RSV, Psalm 72:16).

Why do these verses twice bless the Lord and end with double amens? (72:18–19) The "last three verses of Psalm 72, . . . clearly belong to the editorial formula of conclusion to Book Two of Psalms, and not to the poem itself" (Alter, *Art of Biblical Poetry*, 130). The Psalms are a "collection of five parts (alluding to the Pentateuch), each of which concludes with a doxology [prayer]" (*Zondervan Illustrated Bible Dictionary*, 1190). These five parts or books are Book 1 (Psalms 1–41), Book 2 (Psalms 42–72), Book 3 (Psalms 73–89), Book 4 (Psalms 90–106), and Book 5 (Psalms 107–50). "Verses 18–19 is the doxology that ends Book 2; it is not part of the psalm" (Clifford, *Psalms 1–72*, 331). See commentary in this volume for Psalm 41:13.

Why does it say that the "prayers of David" are ended? (72:20) This is the only postscript in the book of Psalms. "This was most probably the last Psalm he ever wrote. There may be several in the after part of this book which were written by him; but they were probably composed in a former period of his life, for this was the end of the poetic prayers of David the son of Jesse" (*Adam Clarke's Commentary* [on Psalm 72:20]).

14 He shall redeem their soul from deceit and violence: and precious shall their blood be in his sight.

15 And he shall live, and to him shall be given of the gold of Sheba: prayer also shall be made for him continually; *and* daily shall he be praised.

16 There shall be an handful of corn in the earth upon the top of the mountains; the fruit thereof shall shake like Lebanon: and *they* of the city shall flourish like grass of the earth.

17 His name shall endure for ever: his name shall be continued as long as the sun: and *men* shall be blessed in him: all nations shall call him blessed.

18 Blessed *be* the LORD God, the God of Israel, who only doeth wondrous things.

19 And blessed *be* his glorious name for ever: and let the whole earth be filled *with* his glory; Amen, and Amen.

20 The prayers of David the son of Jesse are ended.

PSALMS 73–77

God is good to Israel—The wicked and ungodly prosper in this world—They will be consumed with terrors hereafter—Those who trust in the Lord will be received up unto glory.

A Psalm of Asaph.

O God, remember Thy chosen congregation—The wicked destroy the sanctuary and burn the synagogues—O God, remember them for their deeds, and save Thy people.

Maschil of Asaph.

The righteous praise and thank the God of Jacob—They will be exalted—God is the judge, and the wicked will be condemned.

To the chief Musician, Al-taschith,
A Psalm *or* Song of Asaph.

God is known in Judah and dwells in Zion—He will save the meek of the earth.

To the chief Musician on Neginoth,
A Psalm *or* Song of Asaph.

The righteous cry unto the Lord—They remember the wonders of old, how He redeemed the sons of Jacob and led Israel like a flock.

To the chief Musician, to Jeduthun,
A Psalm of Asaph.

Summary of Psalms 73–77

Sometimes it seems as if those who ignore God prosper more than those who are faithful. These psalms declare that God's followers have what really matters, that God's fairness will properly judge all men and deliver the righteous from their enemies. Psalm 77 concludes with a prayer of the righteous pleading with God to deliver them from their trials as He had previously done for His righteous children.

PSALM 78

The Israelites are to teach the Lord's law to their children—Disobedient Israel provoked the Lord in the wilderness—The Egyptian plagues are recounted—The Lord chooses and blesses Judah and David.

Maschil of Asaph.

To what does "Maschil" refer? (Psalm 78 superscription) *Maschil* is instruction for the music leader. See the introduction to the Book of Psalms in this volume.

Summary of Psalm 78:1–8

Parents must make known unto their children the things of the Lord. The children should then teach lessons learned from their parents to help each new generation be faithful to the Lord.

Psalm 78:9–16. Israel Is Delivered from Egypt

Why does the psalmist recite part of Israel's history? (78:9–12) "Psalm 78 is the voice of a teacher. It is largely composed of narrative, a telling of the story of the LORD's way with Israel. In this respect it is similar to Psalms 105; 106; and 136. Because of this common dominant feature, this group of psalms is often classified as 'historical psalms'" (Mays, *Psalms*, 254). "The purpose of the psalm, at the time it was written, may have been to teach and warn the people of Judah in later years to be true to the covenant and the law, so that they might return from Babylon and be saved for their destiny" (Rasmussen, *Latter-day Saint Commentary on the Old Testament*, 440). ⊕

What happened in the field of Zoan? (78:12–16) Zoan was a "city on the Tanitic branch of the Nile, called by the Greeks Tanis. . . . This great and important city was the capital of the Hyksos, or Shepherd kings, who ruled Egypt for more than 500 years. It was the frontier town of Goshen. Here Pharaoh was holding his court at the time of his various interviews with Moses and Aaron. . . . This city was also called 'the Field of Zoan' (Psalm 78:12, 43) and 'the Town of Rameses,' (q.v.) because the oppressor rebuilt and embellished it, probably by the forced labour of the Hebrews, and made it his northern capital" (*Easton's Bible Dictionary*, "Zoan").

9 The children of Ephraim, *being* armed, *and* carrying bows, turned back in the day of battle.

10 They kept not the covenant of God, and refused to walk in his law;

11 And forgat his works, and his wonders that he had shewed them.

12 Marvellous things did he in the sight of their fathers, in the land of Egypt, *in* the field of Zoan.

13 He divided the sea, and caused them to pass through; and he made the waters to stand as an heap.

14 In the daytime also he led them with a cloud, and all the night with a light of fire.

15 He clave the rocks in the wilderness, and gave *them* drink as *out of* the great depths.

16 He brought streams also out of the rock, and caused waters to run down like rivers.

17 And they sinned yet more against him by provoking the most High in the wilderness.

18 And they tempted God in their heart by asking meat for their lust.

19 Yea, they spake against God; they said, Can God furnish a table in the wilderness?

20 Behold, he smote the rock, that the waters gushed out, and the streams overflowed; can he give bread also? can he provide flesh for his people?

21 Therefore the LORD heard *this,* and was wroth: so a fire was kindled against Jacob, and anger also came up against Israel;

22 Because they believed not in God, and trusted not in his salvation:

23 Though he had commanded the clouds from above, and opened the doors of heaven,

24 And had rained down manna upon them to eat, and had given them of the corn of heaven.

25 Man did eat angels' food: he sent them meat to the full.

26 He caused an east wind to blow in the heaven: and by his power he brought in the south wind.

27 He rained flesh also upon them as dust, and feathered fowls like as the sand of the sea:

28 And he let *it* fall in the midst of their camp, round about their habitations.

29 So they did eat, and were well filled: for he gave them their own desire;

30 They were not estranged from their lust. But while their meat *was* yet in their mouths,

31 The wrath of God came upon them, and slew the fattest of them, and smote down the chosen *men* of Israel.

32 For all this they sinned still, and believed not for his wondrous works.

Psalm 78:17–39. Israel Is Quick to Forget God's Miracles

In what way had the children of Israel "sinned yet more" in the wilderness? (78:17–18) "Evidently the more God gives, the less we appreciate it. This grudging response to a string of miracles is not unlike the sequel to the feeding of the five thousand: a demand for a further and better sign (John 6:26, 30f.). The whole history of unbelief in the wilderness supports our Lord's refusal; it is also an answer to the perennial demands for better proofs. In appealing to this very psalm (24; cf. John 6:31), the arguers were handling too sharp a weapon" (Kidner, *Psalms 73–150*, 312–13). "Therefore the LORD . . . was wroth: so a fire was kindled against . . . Israel" (Psalm 78:21).

Why did the children of Israel struggle with faith in the wilderness? (78:22) "We have seen that deliverance always requires humility before God. It takes submission to His will. It takes prayer and the willingness to obey" (Eyring, "Power of Deliverance," 5). Similarly, the Book of Mormon prophet Jacob concluded that his people's unbelief in Christ was their core challenge in the wilderness: "Wherefore we labored diligently among our people, that we might persuade them to come unto Christ, and partake of the goodness of God, that they might enter into his rest" (Jacob 1:7).

What do the east and south winds represent? (78:26) The east wind "was perceived as the instrument of God's wrath. . . . Not only did Israel attribute the parting of the Red Sea to this divinely sent zephyr (see Exodus 14:21), but it was also the stated source of the plague of locusts that annoyed Pharaoh's kingdom during the ministry of Moses (see Exodus 10:13)" (Gaskill, *Lost Language of Symbolism*, 153–54). The south wind "applies to the winds which brought the quails, as stated in the Book of Numbers" (Burgess, *Journal of Sacred Literature and Biblical Record*, 405).

In what way was Israel's desire for the quails a curse rather than a blessing for Israel? (78:30–31) "The manna was a typological symbol of Christ. Thus, Israel's rejection of the manna in preference for flesh [vv. 17–18] was a strong metaphor of the dangers of loving the things of this world (symbolized by the meat) more than the things of God (represented by the manna)" (Gaskill, *Miracles of the Old Testament*, 108).

Why is one's heart a more reliable measure of the soul than one's words? (78:36–37) The "laws of God are concerned with spiritual things. Spiritual consequences are affected by actions, but they are also affected by desires or thoughts, independent of actions. Gospel consequences flow from the desires of our hearts" (Oaks, "Desires of Our Hearts," 64).

33 Therefore their days did he consume in vanity, and their years in trouble.

34 When he slew them, then they sought him: and they returned and inquired early after God.

35 And they remembered that God *was* their rock, and the high God their redeemer.

36 Nevertheless they did flatter him with their mouth, and they lied unto him with their tongues.

37 For their heart was not right with him, neither were they steadfast in his covenant.

38 But he, *being* full of compassion, forgave *their* iniquity, and destroyed *them* not: yea, many a time turned he his anger away, and did not stir up all his wrath.

39 For he remembered that they *were but* flesh; a wind that passeth away, and cometh not again.

Summary of Psalm 78:40–53

Even after the Lord uses a variety of displays of power to free Israel from Egypt's bondage, the children of Israel continue to rebel against God.

Psalm 78:54–64. Israel Persists in Her Rebellious Ways

What does the right hand symbolize? (78:54) "There are numerous passages in the scriptures referring to the right hand, indicating that it is a symbol of righteousness and was used in the making of covenants" (Smith, *Answers to Gospel Questions*, 1:157).

What is a "deceitful bow"? (78:56–57) "The eastern bow, which when at rest is in the form of a [curved figure], must be recurved, or turned the contrary way, in order to be what is called bent and strung. If a person who is unskillful or weak [attempts] to recurve and string one of these bows, if he take not great heed it will spring back and regain its quiescent position, and perhaps break his arm. . . . These Israelites, when

54 And he brought them to the border of his sanctuary, *even to* this mountain, *which* his right hand had purchased.

55 He cast out the heathen also before them, and divided them an inheritance by line, and made the tribes of Israel to dwell in their tents.

56 Yet they tempted and provoked the most high God, and kept not his testimonies:

57 But turned back, and dealt unfaithfully like their fathers: they were turned aside like a deceitful bow.

brought out of their natural bent, soon recoiled, and relapsed into their former state" (*Adam Clarke's Commentary* [on Psalm 78:57]).

58 For they provoked him to anger with their high places, and moved him to jealousy with their graven images.

59 When God heard *this,* he was wroth, and greatly abhorred Israel:

In what way do we have "graven images"? (78:58) President Spencer W. Kimball taught: "Few men have ever knowingly and deliberately chosen to reject God and his blessings. Rather . . . when men have fallen under the power of Satan and lost the faith, they have put in its place a hope in the 'arm of flesh' . . . —that is, in idols. This I find to be a dominant theme in the Old Testament. Whatever thing a man sets his heart and his trust in most is his god; and if his god doesn't also happen to be the true and living God of Israel, that man is laboring in idolatry" (*Spencer W. Kimball* [manual], 146).

60 So that he forsook the tabernacle of Shiloh, the tent *which* he placed among men;

61 And delivered his strength into captivity, and his glory into the enemy's hand.

62 He gave his people over also unto the sword; and was wroth with his inheritance.

63 The fire consumed their young men; and their maidens were not given to marriage.

64 Their priests fell by the sword; and their widows made no lamentation.

What was the "tabernacle of Shiloh" and how was it forsaken? (78:60) Shiloh is a "sacred city of the Holy Land, [9.25] miles north from Bethel and [11.5] miles south from Shechem, in the tribe of Ephraim (Josh. 18:1; Judg. 18:31). The tabernacle was here during the greater part of the period of the Judges, and the place continued to be the religious center of the nation (1 Sam. 1:3) until after the loss of the Ark in the disastrous battle of Ebenezer" (Bible Dictionary, "Shiloh"). See commentary in this volume for 1 Samuel 1:3.

Who were the priests that fell by the sword? (78:64) This verse refers to "Hophni and Phinehas, who were slain in that unfortunate battle against the Philistines in which the ark of the Lord was taken, 1 Samuel 4:11. A Chaldee Targum [interpretation of] this passage says, 'In the time in which the ark of the Lord was taken by the Philistines, Hophni and Phinehas, the two priests, fell by the sword at Shiloh; and when the news was brought, their wives made no lamentation, for they both died the same day'" (*Adam Clarke's Commentary* [on Psalm 78:64]).

Summary of Psalm 78:65–72

As the recital of Israel's history continues, the Lord eventually refuses to help the tribe of Joseph any longer but blesses Judah and the house of David as they turn to Him.

Summary of Psalms 79–81

Psalms 79 and 80 express sadness for what Israel lost because of wickedness. Psalm 79 appears to be written after the fall of Jerusalem and the ruin of the temple by the Babylonians. The prayer is a plea for forgiveness and rescue. Similarly, Psalm 80 speaks of the earlier destruction of the northern kingdom by the Assyrians and their cry for the Lord to restore the children of Israel to their lands of inheritance. In Psalm 81, Israel is commanded to sing praises unto the God of Israel and to remember the Lord God Almighty, who delivered them out of Egyptian bondage. The Lord will answer His people when they call upon Him. Psalm 81 was probably composed for the Feast of Trumpets (Rosh Hashanah) which occurred on the first day of the seventh month (see Lev. 23:24).

Psalm 82:1–8. We Are the Children of God

What is the "congregation of the mighty"? (82:1)

"The word 'mighty' in this verse is a translation of the Hebrew word *ale* which very properly could have been translated 'gods' or 'heavenly beings.' More perfect renderings of this verse are found in modern translations. For instance: 'God takes his stand in the courts of heaven to deliver judgment among the gods themselves' (New English Bible). . . . 'God presides in the divine council, in the midst of the gods adjudicates' (Anchor Bible Series). Latter-day Saints . . . immediately recognize it as a companion passage to Abraham 3 [vv. 3:22–28] where the Lord shows Abraham a vision of the assembly of spirits destined to come to this earth" (McConkie, "Joseph Smith and the Poetic Writings," 115–16).

PSALMS 79–81

The heathen nations destroy Jerusalem and defile the temple—Israel pleads for forgiveness and deliverance.

A Psalm of Asaph.

Israel pleads with the Shepherd of Israel for deliverance, for salvation, and for His face to shine upon them.

To the chief Musician upon Shoshannim-Eduth, A Psalm of Asaph.

Israel is commanded to sing praises to God—If the Israelites had walked in the Lord's ways, they would have triumphed over their enemies.

To the chief Musician upon Gittith, *A Psalm* of Asaph.

PSALM 82

Thus says the Lord, Ye are gods and children of the Most High.

A Psalm of Asaph.

1 God standeth in the congregation of the mighty; he judgeth among the gods.

2 How long will ye judge unjustly, and accept the persons of the wicked? Selah.

3 Defend the poor and fatherless: do justice to the afflicted and needy.

4 Deliver the poor and needy: rid *them* out of the hand of the wicked.

5 They know not, neither will they understand; they walk on in darkness: all the foundations of the earth are out of course.

6 I have said, Ye *are* gods; and all of you *are* children of the most High.

7 But ye shall die like men, and fall like one of the princes.

8 Arise, O God, judge the earth: for thou shalt inherit all nations.

What correction is made in the Joseph Smith Translation? (82:2) The Joseph Smith Translation corrects this verse to read, "How long will ye *suffer them to* judge unjustly?" (JST, Psalm 82:2; emphasis added).

What does it mean to be "children of the most High"? (82:6) "However many generations in your mortal ancestry, no matter what race or people you represent, the pedigree of your spirit can be written on a single line. You are a child of God!" (Packer, "To Young Women and Men," 54). "That doctrine is not hidden away in an obscure verse. It is taught over and over again in scripture. These clear examples are from the Bible: 'All of you are children of the most High' (Psalm 82:6), and 'We are the offspring of God' (Acts 17:29). . . . What could inspire one to purity and worthiness more than to possess a spiritual confirmation that we are the children of God?" (Packer, *Let Not Your Heart Be Troubled*, 288, 292).

PSALM 83

God is asked to confound the enemies of His people—Jehovah is the Most High over all the earth.

A Song *or* Psalm of Asaph.

Summary of Psalm 83

This psalm is the last one attributed to Asaph. Here he calls upon God to use His power to save Judah from their enemies. It praises the Lord Jehovah because He is the Most High over all the earth.

PSALM 84

The righteous cry unto the living God—It is better to be a doorkeeper in the house of the Lord than to dwell in the tents of wickedness—No good thing is withheld from those who walk uprightly.

To the chief Musician upon Gittith,
A Psalm for the sons of Korah.

What is the "Gittith" and who are the sons of Korah? (superscription) See introduction to the Book of Psalms in this volume.

Psalm 84:1–4. Blessed Are They Who Dwell in Temples

Why did this psalmist long for the temple? (84:1–3) "The temple, the dwelling place of deity, was a place where one enjoyed favor and blessing. The verb used here is similar to the English idiom of 'missing' someone or something. It carries a bit of nostalgia; one longs for the return of a fondly remembered circumstance or situation. Here the pilgrim misses being around the temple" (Walton, et al., *IVP Bible Background Commentary*, 543).

How is a person blessed by going to the house of the Lord? (84:4) "As we attend the temple, there can come to us a dimension of spirituality and a feeling of peace which will transcend any other feeling which could come into the human heart. We will grasp the true meaning of the words of the Savior when He said: 'Peace I leave with you, my peace I give unto you. . . . Let not your heart be troubled, neither let it be afraid'" (Monson, "Blessings of the Temple," 91–92).

1 How amiable *are* thy tabernacles, O Lord of hosts!

2 My soul longeth, yea, even fainteth for the courts of the Lord: my heart and my flesh crieth out for the living God.

3 Yea, the sparrow hath found an house, and the swallow a nest for herself, where she may lay her young, *even* thine altars, O Lord of hosts, my King, and my God.

4 Blessed *are* they that dwell in thy house: they will be still praising thee. Selah.

Psalm 84:5–12. Blessed Is the Man Whose Strength Is in the Lord

What is the valley of Baca? (84:6) "Baca, evidently the singular of the word translated 'balsam trees' or . . . 'aspens' (2 Sam. 5:23), is thought to indicate a tree or shrub which grows in arid places; hence . . . 'the thirsty valley'" (Kidner, *Psalms 73–150*, 336).

What does it mean to go from "strength to strength"? (84:7) The word *strength* (Hebrew, *chayil*) can mean "*strength, power, might* (especially warlike), *valour*" (*Gesenius' Hebrew-Chaldee Lexicon to the Old Testament*, 275). The faithful move from power to power or virtue to virtue which culminates in appearing before the Lord and asking Him to give ear to their

5 Blessed *is* the man whose strength *is* in thee; in whose heart *are* the ways *of them.*

6 *Who* passing through the valley of Baca make it a well; the rain also filleth the pools.

7 They go from strength to strength, *every one of them* in Zion appeareth before God.

8 O Lord God of hosts, hear my prayer: give ear, O God of Jacob. Selah.

9 Behold, O God our shield, and look upon the face of thine anointed.

10 For a day in thy courts *is* better than a thousand. I had rather be a doorkeeper in the house of my God, than to dwell in the tents of wickedness.

11 For the LORD God *is* a sun and shield: the LORD will give grace and glory: no good *thing* will he withhold from them that walk uprightly.

12 O LORD of hosts, blessed *is* the man that trusteth in thee.

prayer (see verse 8). *Chayil* comes from the root word *chuwl "to dance* in a circle" (*Gesenius' Hebrew-Chaldee Lexicon to the Old Testament*, s.v. "*chuwl*").

Why would one want to be a doorkeeper in the Lord's house? (84:10) "The higher you get in heaven, the lower you get in this world. The Psalmist says, 'I would rather be a doorkeeper in the house of God, than dwell in the pavilions of the princes of the wicked' (Psalm 84:10). Better the lowest position in the best of worlds than the highest position in the lowest of worlds, which is what Satan wanted, remember? . . . 'Better to reign in hell, than serve in heaven.' If Satan could only be top man, he would accept that position in the worst possible world. Whereas the Psalmist says, Even if it means I must be the lowest man, give me the best possible world" (Nibley, *Approaching Zion*, 549).

PSALM 85

The Lord speaks peace to His people—Truth will spring out of the earth (the Book of Mormon), and righteousness will look down from heaven.

To the chief Musician, A Psalm for the sons of Korah.

1 LORD, thou hast been favourable unto thy land: thou hast brought back the captivity of Jacob.

2 Thou hast forgiven the iniquity of thy people, thou hast covered all their sin. Selah.

3 Thou hast taken away all thy wrath: thou hast turned *thyself* from the fierceness of thine anger.

4 Turn us, O God of our salvation, and cause thine anger toward us to cease.

Psalm 85:1–5. The Lord Is Kind to Jacob

How does the Lord cover sin? (85:2) The "Hebrew term for atonement, *kippur*, can be thought of as roughly approximating the English word 'cover.' In the Mosaic temple, the idea of *kippur* related to the *kapporet* that formed the lid of the ark of the temple where Jehovah stood to forgive—or cover—the sins of the people" (Bradshaw, "Meaning of the Atonement").

What is the wrath of God? (85:3) "The 'wrath of God' is a term usually indicating his disapproval of the deeds of the wicked and justifying the inevitable punishments that will befall them if they do not repent. Latter-day Saints believe that his response is a natural application of the law of justice (Mosiah 3:26), which requires that punishments be exacted when God's laws have been violated. . . . The scriptures state that God sends cursings, judgments, and destruction upon the unbelieving and the rebellious, including all who reject the Savior or his prophets and are not willing to confess his hand in all things (D&C 1:6–13; 59:21; 63:6; 88:85; 104:8; 124:48, 52; Moses 7:1)" (Gilchrist, "Wrath of God," 4:1598).

Psalm 85:5–13. Truth Shall Spring Out of the Earth

In what ways will the Lord "revive" Israel? (85:6) "We are part of a great movement—the gathering of scattered Israel. . . . This promise of the gathering, woven all through the fabric of the scriptures, will be fulfilled. . . . As prophesied by Peter and Paul, *all* things were to be restored in this dispensation. Therefore, there must come, as part of that restoration, the long-awaited gathering of scattered Israel. It is a necessary prelude to the Second Coming of the Lord" (Nelson, "Gathering of Scattered Israel," 79, 80). ⊕

How has the Lord provided to "speak" to Israel in the day of the gathering? (85:8) The Book of Mormon prophesies: "And he [Joseph Smith] shall be like unto me [Joseph of Egypt]; for the thing [the Book of Mormon], which the Lord shall bring forth by his hand, by the power of the Lord shall bring my people unto salvation" (2 Nephi 3:15). The Prophet Joseph Smith noted: "The great benefits to the world which result from the Book of Mormon and the Revelations, . . . the Lord has seen fit in His infinite wisdom to grant unto us for our salvation, and for the salvation of all that will believe" (Joseph Smith Papers, "History, 1838–1856, volume A-1 [23 Dec. 1805–30 Aug. 1834]," 173).

How will truth "spring out of the earth"? (85:11) "What think ye of the Book of Mormon? Who can tell its wonder and worth? . . . It is a book, a holy book, a book of sacred, saving scripture. It is a voice from the dust, a voice that whispers low out of the earth, telling of a fallen people who sank into an endless oblivion because they forsook their God. It is truth springing out of the earth as righteousness looks down from heaven" (McConkie, "What Think Ye of the Book of Mormon?" 74; see also Moses 7:62). ⊕

Summary of Psalm 86

This psalm is entitled "A Prayer of David." He petitions the Lord for mercy and protection. He also prays for godliness: "Teach me thy way" (Psalm 86:11). He praises God for delivering his soul "from the lowest hell" (Psalm 86:13). He also seeks for deliverance from enemies who seek his life .

5 Wilt thou be angry with us for ever? wilt thou draw out thine anger to all generations?

6 Wilt thou not revive us again: that thy people may rejoice in thee?

7 Shew us thy mercy, O LORD, and grant us thy salvation.

8 I will hear what God the LORD will speak: for he will speak peace unto his people, and to his saints: but let them not turn again to folly.

9 Surely his salvation *is* nigh them that fear him; that glory may dwell in our land.

10 Mercy and truth are met together; righteousness and peace have kissed *each other.*

11 Truth shall spring out of the earth; and righteousness shall look down from heaven.

12 Yea, the LORD shall give *that which is* good; and our land shall yield her increase.

13 Righteousness shall go before him; and shall set *us* in the way of his steps.

PSALM 86

David implores God for mercy and is saved from the lowest hell—The Lord is good and generous in mercy—All nations will worship before Him.

A Prayer of David.

PSALM 87

The Lord loves the gates of Zion, and He Himself will establish Zion.

A Psalm *or* Song for the sons of Korah.

1 His foundation *is* in the holy mountains.

2 The LORD loveth the gates of Zion more than all the dwellings of Jacob.

3 Glorious things are spoken of thee, O city of God. Selah.

4 I will make mention of Rahab and Babylon to them that know me: behold Philistia, and Tyre, with Ethiopia; this *man* was born there.

Who are the sons of Korah? (Psalm 87 superscription) See commentary in this volume for Psalm 42 superscription.

Psalm 87:1–7. The Lord Loves Jerusalem

What mountains or hills was Jerusalem built upon? (87:1–3) "Jerusalem was founded on the mountains or hills of Zion and Moriah. The after increase of the population obliged the inhabitants to [enclose] all the contiguous hills; but [Mount] Zion and Moriah were the principal. We know that ancient Rome was built on seven hills" (*Adam Clarke's Commentary* [on Psalm 87:1]).

What does it mean that God's "foundation is in the holy mountains"? (87:1–3) "What is clear is that this [psalm] is a song that celebrates and praises Zion as the city where God resides and as the primeval birthplace of the world. . . . [The] term *mountain* here . . . reflects 'the cosmic primal mountain that as both world-mountain and mountain of paradise[,] gives the earth stability and life.' Verse 2 declares Zion the place of God's heart. Verse 3 reminds that Zion will always be remembered. The section as a whole gives praise to Zion because God chose this city as the place of residence" (deClassé-Wolford, et al., *Book of Psalms*, 664, 665). The psalm as a whole may serve as an introduction for the celebration of Zion.

What might the "gates of Zion" symbolize in this psalm? (87:2) "The builder, we are told, had special fondness for *the gates of Zion*, at once a synonym for the whole city, and a reference to the massive and proudly wrought portals that were its protection" (*Interpreter's Bible*, 4:469). "God has a special love for the place where His name is worshipped. The *gates of Zion* are the conspicuous entrance to the city. The verb *loves* includes the idea of choice (see Deut. 6:5) as well as emotion. God chose Jerusalem, and He also has an enduring affection for the city" (*Nelson Study Bible* [NKJV], 968).

Why are these geographical names important to the Jews? (87:4) "*Rahab* is a symbolic name for Egypt (Is. 30:7) that has negative connotations. It alludes to the arrogance of the Egyptians. . . . *Babylon* was the proverbial seat of apostasy and idolatry (Gen. 10:10). *To those who know Me* may be rephrased 'as those who know Me.' Thus the verse anticipates a time when foreigners would know and worship the living God.

Among those who came to Zion to worship the Lord were people from Egypt, Babylon, *Philistia, Tyre, and Ethiopia*. At the time of the writing of this psalm, perhaps in the later period of Hezekiah's reign, foreigners were worshiping God in the temple along with Jews" (*Nelson Study Bible* [NKJV], 968).

Who could be counted as an inhabitant of Zion? (87:5–7) "Zion is the pure in heart, a people of one heart and one mind, dwelling in righteousness with no poor among them [Moses 7:18]. The Prophet Joseph Smith stated, 'We ought to have the building up of Zion as our greatest object' [*Joseph Smith* (manual), 186]. We build up Zion in our homes, wards, branches, and stakes through unity, godliness, and charity" (Christofferson, "Preparing for the Lord's Return," 82).

5 And of Zion it shall be said, This and that man was born in her: and the highest himself shall establish her.

6 The Lord shall count, when he writeth up the people, *that* this *man* was born there. Selah.

7 As well the singers as the players on instruments *shall be there:* all my springs *are* in thee.

Summary of Psalm 88

In desperation, the author of this psalm cries out to God for relief from trouble. The dread of death has eroded any sense of hope or comfort. He feels as though he is drowning from affliction (see Psalm 88:17). He prays to God because all others have abandoned him.

What does "Mahalath Leannoth, Maschil" mean in this superscription? (Psalm 88 superscription) "*Maḥalath leannoth*, probably [refers to] a melody. The term 'maḥalath' may be related to the word 'maḥalah,' 'illness,' making this a sad melody or a melody for the sick" (*Jewish Study Bible* [2004], 1380). For "Maschil," see commentary in this volume for Psalm 32 superscription.

Who was Heman the Ezrahite? (Psalm 88 superscription) Heman was the "grandson of Samuel (1 Chronicles 6:33; 15:17), to whom the 88th Psalm probably was inscribed. He was one of the 'seers' named in 2 Chronicles 29:14, 30, and took a leading part in the administration of the sacred services" (*Easton's Bible Dictionary*, "Heman"). "Along with Ethan (in Ps 89), Heman is listed as one of the famous wise men of Solomon's time (1 Kings 4:31) and was appointed one of the Levitical musicians during the time of David (1 Chron 15; 17, 19)" (Walton, et al., *IVP Bible Background Commentary*, 544).

PSALM 88

A prayer of one who feels forsaken and who asks whether the Lord's loving kindness will be declared in the grave.

A Song *or* Psalm for the sons of Korah, to the chief Musician upon Mahalath Leannoth, Maschil of Heman the Ezrahite.

PSALM 89

A messianic psalm—A song setting forth the mercy, greatness, justice, and righteousness of the Holy One of Israel—The Lord will establish David's seed and throne forever—God's Firstborn will be made higher than the kings of the earth.

Maschil of Ethan the Ezrahite.

What is "Maschil"? (Psalm 89 superscription) "The word *Maschil* in the superscription may mean 'making wise'; but the contents do not seem to be especially so directed, except that anyone who has repented and has been forgiven is wiser than he was" (Rasmussen, *Latter-day Saint Commentary on the Old Testament*, 424). Susan Easton Black suggests that "other titles [superscriptions] suggest the character of the psalm. For example, Maschil means 'to give instruction'" (*400 Questions and Answers about the Old Testament*, 151). See commentary in this volume for Psalm 32 superscription.

Psalm 89:1–4. God's Promises to David Are Acclaimed

1 I will sing of the mercies of the LORD for ever: with my mouth will I make known thy faithfulness to all generations.

2 For I have said, Mercy shall be built up for ever: thy faithfulness shalt thou establish in the very heavens.

How did David experience God's mercy and faithfulness? (89:1) "The mercies of the Lord in this psalm center on the covenant He made with David, promising him an eternal dynasty (see 2 Sam. 7)" (*Nelson Study Bible* [NKJV], 970). Mercy is "the spirit of compassion, tenderness, and forgiveness. Mercy is one of the attributes of God. Jesus Christ offers mercy to us through His atoning sacrifice" (Guide to the Scriptures, "Merciful, Mercy").

"The Lord had promised that His mercy would always rest on David's son" (*Nelson Study Bible* [NKJV], 970).

3 I have made a covenant with my chosen, I have sworn unto David my servant,

4 Thy seed will I establish for ever, and build up thy throne to all generations. Selah.

What is the covenant that God made with David? (89:3–4) "Special covenant promises were given to David. These promises revealed the fact that God intends to keep His promises to Abraham through the agency of a Ruler who will be one of David's physical descendants. Until the birth of that King, commonly called the Messiah, or Anointed One, David would always have a descendant on the throne of Israel, or qualified to sit on that throne. These promises . . . are celebrated in this psalm" (Richards, *Bible Reader's Companion*, 370).

The Two Parts of Psalm 89

"The Psalm divides itself into two grand parts; the first extends, verses 1–37, in which the psalmist shows God's mercy to the house of David, and the promises which he has given to it of support and perpetuity. The second part begins with Psalm 89:38, and ends with the Psalm; and in it the author complains that notwithstanding these promises, the kingdom of Judah is overthrown and the royal family ruined; and he entreats the Lord to remember his covenant made with that family, and restore them from their captivity" (*Adam Clarke's Commentary* [on Psalm 89 Introduction]).

Psalm 89:5–18. A Celebration of God's Covenant Established with David

How has God calmed the storms in your life? (89:9) "Sometimes we don't understand death, illness, mental and physical disabilities, personal tragedies, war, and other conflict. Some of these are a necessary part of our mortal probation. Others, as Enoch foresaw, are part of the preparation for the Savior's Second Coming. . . .

5 And the heavens shall praise thy wonders, O LORD: thy faithfulness also in the congregation of the saints.

6 For who in the heaven can be compared unto the LORD? *who* among the sons of the mighty can be likened unto the LORD?

7 God is greatly to be feared in the assembly of the saints, and to be had in reverence of all *them that are* about him.

8 O LORD God of hosts, who *is* a strong LORD like unto thee? or to thy faithfulness round about thee?

9 Thou rulest the raging of the sea: when the waves thereof arise, thou stillest them.

10 Thou hast broken Rahab in pieces, as one that is slain; thou hast scattered thine enemies with thy strong arm.

"Joseph Smith and the Poetic Writings"

"From what Joseph Smith learned by revelation about the poetic writings and from the changes he made in them in his inspired translation, we can draw the following conclusions:

"1. All scripture is not of equal worth. Indeed not everything claiming sanctuary in the holy writ is deserving of such protection. Joseph Smith paid relatively little attention to those books that do not contain the testimony of Christ, the doctrines of the kingdom, or prophetic utterances. . . .

"2. If not directly from the Prophet Joseph Smith, then certainly from the abuse of the poetic writings which he sought to correct, we learn that you do not establish doctrine from poetry, from allegory, or might we add parables. They may be used to sustain good doctrine, but only after that doctrine has been plainly established in the form of unambiguous revelation. As [President] Boyd K. Packer so wisely taught us in . . . general conference, doctrines basic to the salvation of men are not relegated to obscure passages of scripture.

"3. As we learn from the messianic psalms and from the psalmic prophecies of the last days, there is no meaningful understanding of revelation without revelation. Many passages given contemporary explanations contain prophecy of future events. Much in the book of Psalms, like the rest of the Bible, is sealed to those who read without the light of revelation, be it the personal promptings of the Holy Ghost, commentary in the form of modern revelation, or the statements of living prophets.

"4. David, along with many Old Testament prophets, described the apostasy and scattering of Israel and their latter-day gathering. He and others of the Psalmists knew the story of the Restoration in marvelous detail, even as they knew of events in the life of Christ in minute detail.

"It was the apostle Paul who taught us that while the things of man can be understood by the spirit of man, the things of God are understood only by the Spirit of God (see 1 Corinthians 2:11). Thus we learn that it takes prophets to understand prophets, scripture to understand scripture, and the Spirit to understand the things of the Spirit. This was the principle that enabled Joseph Smith to read books sealed to the understanding of the supposedly learned (Isaiah 29:11–12). Describing what it meant for him and Oliver Cowdery to receive the Holy Ghost, Joseph Smith said: 'Our minds being now enlightened, we began to have the scriptures laid open to our understandings, and the true meaning and intention of their more mysterious passages revealed unto us in a manner which we never could attain to previously, nor ever before had thought of' (JS–H 1:74)" (McConkie, "Joseph Smith and the Poetic Writings," 117–18).

"Our faith in Him and obedience to His commandments will bring 'a perfect brightness of hope' [2 Ne. 31:20] and dispel the darkness and gloom of despair in these troubled times. The One who had power to calm the elements of earth has power to calm our souls, to give us refuge from the storm: 'Peace, be still' [Mark 4:39]" (Hales, "Faith through Tribulation Brings Peace and Joy," 18).

11 The heavens *are* thine, the earth also *is* thine: *as for* the world and the fulness thereof, thou hast founded them.

12 The north and the south thou hast created them: Tabor and Hermon shall rejoice in thy name.

What doctrine do these verses emphasize about one of Jesus Christ's significant roles? (89:11–12) "Christ was 'in the world, and the world was made by him, and the world knew him not' (John 1:10). The religious leaders during the time of the Savior's ministry did not recognize Him as the Creator of the world, as John so boldly testified.

"How blessed we are—and how confirming to absolute truth it is—to have messianic prophecies that testify that Christ is the Creator" (Tingey, *Old Testament Prophecies of Jesus Christ*, 33).

13 Thou hast a mighty arm: strong is thy hand, *and* high is thy right hand.

14 Justice and judgment *are* the habitation of thy throne: mercy and truth shall go before thy face.

What view was held by some Jews that caused them to expect that Christ would come as a great military leader? (89:13–14) "For those who first read these Psalms [45, 89, 110] as poems about the birth of Christ, that birth primarily meant something very militant; the hero, the 'judge' or champion or giant-killer, who was to fight and beat death, hell, and the devils, had at last arrived" (Lewis, *Reflections on the Psalms*, 108).

15 Blessed *is* the people that know the joyful sound: they shall walk, O LORD, in the light of thy countenance.

16 In thy name shall they rejoice all the day: and in thy righteousness shall they be exalted.

17 For thou *art* the glory of their strength: and in thy favour our horn shall be exalted.

What is the "joyful sound" mentioned in this verse and how does it correlate with the joy we have in the gospel today? (89:15) "*The [joyful] shout* could well be the cry at the Feast of Tabernacles acknowledging the Lord as King" (*New Bible Commentary: Revised*, 507). Elder David A. Bednar, talking about joy, said: "A common dictionary definition of joy is 'a *feeling* of great pleasure [or] happiness.' In comparison, the Guide to the Scriptures describes joy as 'a *condition* of great happiness [that results] from righteous living.' Interestingly, our gospel perspective helps us to understand that joy is more than a fleeting feeling or emotion; rather, it is a spiritual gift and a state of being and becoming" ("Jesus Christ," 18).

18 For the LORD *is* our defence; and the Holy One of Israel *is* our king.

Why is Jesus Christ referred to as the King of the Jews? (89:18) "At the time of the Savior's birth, Israel was ruled by [outside] monarchs. The rights of the royal Davidic family were unrecognized; and the ruler of the Jews was an appointee of Rome. Had Judah been a free and independent nation, ruled by her rightful sovereign, Joseph the carpenter would have been her crowned king; and his lawful successor to the throne would have been Jesus of Nazareth, the King of the Jews" (Talmage, *Jesus the Christ*, 82).

Summary of Psalm 89:19–52

The Psalmist reaffirms that God has called Israel to be his covenant nation and that David's descendants are to rule. Knowing all this, the Psalmist becomes frustrated that the nation has been pillaged and the kingly rule has come to an end.

Summary of Psalm 90

This psalm has been called "a prayer of Moses: the man of God" (see superscription for Psalm 90). In this psalm attributed to Moses, he emphasizes the eternal nature of God. Moses recognizes man's fallen nature and hopes that God's grace will bring man back to His presence.

Psalm 91:1–8. Those That Trust in the Lord Need Not Fear

What is the "secret place of the Most High"? (91:1) The description of a "secret place" could be translated as a shelter. "This word . . . sometimes designates the temple . . . , the immediate reference may be to the worshippers in the sanctuary and possibly also to the inhabitants of Jerusalem. It is clear, from the usage of the same word in 32:7 . . . ; that it is capable of a metaphorical meaning. *Shadow* (or 'shade') is another figure for the Lord's protection" (*Interpreter's Bible*, 4:494).

What are the dangers from which the Lord offers protection? (91:3–6) A "fowler" is one who hunts wild birds. The term evokes "the images of a bird trap and various types of disease [as] a general description of dangers that might come to helpless people" (*Nelson Study Bible* [NKJV], 974). "Most of these dangers are of a kind which strike unseen, against which the strong are as helpless as the weak. Some, like *the snare of the fowler* [v. 3], are obviously metaphors for the plots which would entangle our affairs (140:1–5) or compromise our loyalty (119:110). Others are ills that attack the mind [v. 5] or the body, by human or non-human agency [vv. 5, 6]. The pictures of *pestilence that stalks* . . . and *destruction that wastes* (i.e. devastates) are poetic personifications" (Kidner, *Psalms 73–150*, 364).

PSALM 90

A prayer of Moses, the man of God—God is from everlasting to everlasting—Man's days last but seventy years—Moses implores the Lord to give mercy and blessings to His people.

A Prayer of Moses the man of God.

PSALM 91

A messianic psalm—The Lord will deliver the Messiah from terror, pestilence, and war—The Lord will give His angels charge over the Messiah and deliver Him and honor Him.

1 He that dwelleth in the secret place of the most High shall abide under the shadow of the Almighty.

2 I will say of the Lord, *He is* my refuge and my fortress: my God; in him will I trust.

3 Surely he shall deliver thee from the snare of the fowler, *and* from the noisome pestilence.

4 He shall cover thee with his feathers, and under his wings shalt thou trust: his truth *shall be thy* shield and buckler.

5 Thou shalt not be afraid for the terror by night; *nor* for the arrow *that* flieth by day;

6 *Nor* for the pestilence *that* walketh in darkness; *nor* for the destruction *that* wasteth at noonday.

7 A thousand shall fall at thy side, and ten thousand at thy right hand; *but* it shall not come nigh thee.

8 Only with thine eyes shalt thou behold and see the reward of the wicked.

9 Because thou hast made the LORD, *which is* my refuge, *even* the most High, thy habitation;

10 There shall no evil befall thee, neither shall any plague come nigh thy dwelling.

11 For he shall give his angels charge over thee, to keep thee in all thy ways.

12 They shall bear thee up in *their* hands, lest thou dash thy foot against a stone.

13 Thou shalt tread upon the lion and adder: the young lion and the dragon shalt thou trample under feet.

14 Because he hath set his love upon me, therefore will I deliver him: I will set him on high, because he hath known my name.

Psalm 91:9–16. The Lord Protects Those Who Call upon Him

How did Satan use this psalm in tempting Jesus Christ? (91:11–12) "The wonderful Old Testament messianic prophecy referred to by Satan as he enticed Christ to derive fame by successfully casting Himself from the pinnacle of the temple is found in Psalms:

"'For he shall give his angels charge over thee, to keep thee in all thy ways. They shall bear thee up in their hands, lest thou dash thy foot against a stone' (Psalm 91:11–12).

"How prophetic and accurate are these messianic prophecies, which foretold events that would occur many centuries later. How marvelous that Christ was able to confound Satan and not only foil the temptation but further affirm the divinity of our Lord and Savior, Jesus Christ" (Tingey, *Old Testament Prophecies of Jesus Christ*, 32). ⊕

Moroni, Joseph Smith, and the Book of Psalms

"Joseph Smith was still in his teens when he learned of the prophetic significance of the book of Psalms. We can virtually identify the very moment—it was during the night and early morning hours of [21 and 22 September] 1823, when Moroni first visited him. It was Oliver Cowdery who, after a lengthy conversation with the Prophet, preserved this knowledge for us. . . . In his account of what the Prophet told him, Oliver lists more than two dozen such passages, among which are five of the Psalms. . . . Though Moroni's explanation of these passages has not been preserved for us, their interpretation in the context of Moroni's instruction to Joseph Smith will be obvious" (McConkie, "Joseph Smith and the Poetic Writings," 109).

Joseph Fielding McConkie gave us additional insight into Psalm 91:6. He said: "This is a messianic psalm, the introductory verses of which are refrains of praise and rejoicing in the protection afforded Israel through faith in God. The sixth verse speaks of pestilence and of a 'destruction that wasteth at noonday.'

"Moroni placed the passage in the same context as Joel's prophecy that the moon would turn to blood and the stars fall from heaven (see Joel 2:31), and Isaiah's prophecy of the earth reeling to and fro as a drunken man (see Isaiah 24:20). Oliver's account records, 'The Lord will bring to the knowledge of his people his commandments and statutes, that they may be prepared to stand when the . . . nations tremble, and the destroying angel goes forth to waste the inhabitants at noon-day: for so great are to be the calamities which are to come upon the inhabitants of the earth, before the coming of the Son of Man the second time, that whoso is not prepared cannot abide; but such as are found faithful, and remain, shall be gathered with his people and caught up to meet the Lord in the cloud, and so shall they inherit eternal life' [*Messenger and Advocate*, 1:108–12]. Moroni would obviously have emphasized to Joseph Smith his role in restoring the 'commandments and statutes' of the Lord that a people might be prepared to stand when the Lord comes" ("Joseph Smith and the Poetic Writings," 109).

How might angels have charge over us in our lives? (91:11–12) Elder Jeffrey R. Holland, knowing the need for angelic help as we wrestle with trials, testified: "But God knew the challenges [His children] would face, and He certainly knew how lonely and troubled they would sometimes feel. So He watched over His mortal family constantly, heard their prayers always, and sent prophets (and later apostles) to teach, counsel, and guide them. But in times of special need, He sent angels, divine messengers, to bless His children, reassure them that heaven was always very close and that His help was always very near" ("Ministry of Angels," 29). ⊕

Summary of Psalm 92

"The first third of this Sabbath worship psalm and song expresses praise and appreciation for the help and good given by the Lord to the righteous. The second part contrasts with it the way the 'brutish' and the wicked respond to the Lord and the way he affects their lives. The third segment tells of ways the Lord helps the righteous overcome their enemies and increases their power so that they may flourish and grow in the courts of the Lord and bear fruit even in old age—all of which demonstrate the firmness and uprightness of the Lord" (Rasmussen, *Latter-day Saint Commentary on the Old Testament*, 445–46).

Summary of Psalm 93

This psalm has no name or title. Its subject is that God is all powerful and reigns supreme in the heavens above. The Babylonian Talmud teaches that the Jews sing this song on the sixth day of the week in celebration of the world's creation (see Legge, "Sovereign's Psalm").

Summary of Psalm 94

This psalm was given when the church of God was being persecuted, and it is an appeal to God for help against Israel's enemies. Elder Jeffrey R. Holland added, "These passages are a gentle rebuke to those who may be tempted to consider themselves so bright they are smarter than God. Perhaps the only serious risk I have seen in the world of academic accomplishment is the pride and vanity that can come with it, the arrogance of a few who say not to the hand or to the foot but to God Himself, 'I have no need of thee [1 Corinthians 12:21].' . . .

"Everyone needs to guard against vanity and arrogance, but especially bright, talented people need to be careful because, truth be told, they have the most to be vain and arrogant about" (*For Times of Trouble*, 115–16).

15 He shall call upon me, and I will answer him: I *will be* with him in trouble; I will deliver him, and honour him.

16 With long life will I satisfy him, and shew him my salvation.

PSALM 92

A psalm or song for the Sabbath day—Give thanks unto the Lord—His enemies will perish—The righteous will flourish—There is no unrighteousness in the Lord.

A Psalm *or* Song for the sabbath day.

PSALM 93

The Lord reigns—He is from everlasting—Holiness adorns the house of the Lord forever.

PSALM 94

The Lord will judge the earth and all men—Blessed is he whom the Lord teaches and chastens—The Lord will not forsake His people, but He will cut off the wicked.

PSALM 95

Let us sing unto the Lord—Let us worship and bow down before Him—Israel provoked the Lord and failed to enter into His rest.

1 O come, let us sing unto the LORD: let us make a joyful noise to the rock of our salvation.

2 Let us come before his presence with thanksgiving, and make a joyful noise unto him with psalms.

3 For the LORD *is* a great God, and a great King above all gods.

4 In his hand *are* the deep places of the earth: the strength of the hills *is* his also.

5 The sea *is* his, and he made it: and his hands formed the dry *land.*

6 O come, let us worship and bow down: let us kneel before the LORD our maker.

7 For he *is* our God; and we *are* the people of his pasture, and the sheep of his hand. To day if ye will hear his voice,

8 Harden not your heart, as in the provocation, *and* as *in* the day of temptation in the wilderness:

9 When your fathers tempted me, proved me, and saw my work.

10 Forty years long was I grieved with *this* generation, and said, It *is* a people that do err in their heart, and they have not known my ways:

11 Unto whom I sware in my wrath that they should not enter into my rest.

Psalm 95:1–6. Acknowledge the Lord as the Great God and King and Worship Him

What truth is underscored for the true disciple? (95:6) "Jesus confirmed this most basic of all commands when he said: 'Thou shalt worship the Lord thy God, and him only shalt thou serve' (Luke 4:8); and the constant cry of all the prophets of all the ages is: 'O come, let us worship and bow down: let us kneel before the Lord our maker. For he is our God; and we are the people of his pasture, and the sheep of his hand' (Ps. 95:6–7)" (McConkie, "How to Worship," 129).

Psalm 95:7–11. Worship Him by Hearing and Obeying His Voice, Which Israel in the Wilderness Failed to Do

What lesson from Israel's history is illustrated in this psalm? (95:8–11) The "language and imagery of Psalm 95 recall the exodus event and the subsequent response of the people. The mention of 'sea' in verse 5 is reminiscent of Exodus 15:1, and 'dry land' in verse 5 recalls the path the people took through the sea (Exod. 14:16, 22, 29; 15:19). In this context, 'my work' in verse 9 is certainly an allusion to the exodus. . . . In the book of Exodus, the sequence of deliverance and proclamation of God's reign should have led to immediate obedience, but instead it led to immediate complaining. Psalm 95 says, in effect, 'Do not repeat that mistake'" (McCann, *Theological Introduction to the Book of Psalms*, 47). ⊕

Summary of Psalms 96–99

"Many modern biblical scholars characterize Psalms 47, 93, and 96–99 as 'royal enthronement psalms,' which take the human phenomenon of the coronation of a king and project it onto God. Thus, this group of psalms is sung when we, as it were, enthrone God as our sovereign" (Polish, *Keeping Faith with the Psalms*, 8).

What might the superscription *a psalm of praise* indicate about this psalm? (Psalm 100 superscription) This superscription has been interpreted in several other Bible editions to indicate that it is a psalm for giving thanks. "Perhaps it indicates that the psalm was to accompany a thank offering (see Lev. 7:12)" (*NIV Study Bible*, 891).

Psalm 100:1–5. A Call to Praise the Lord

What might it mean to come into the presence of the Lord? (100:1–5) "This Psalm begins with the announcement that all the earth must declare the Lord and serve him joyfully. It is an invitation for the worthy of all nations to 'come before his presence,' which is an Old Testament phrase meaning 'to come to the temple.' The witness of the Psalmist is that the truths taught therein endure from generation to generation, unchanged. This, we learn from Moroni, was the day for which David longed and often prayed. Further, we are told that David knew that such a day could not come 'until the knowledge of the glory of God covered all lands, or all the earth' [*Messenger and Advocate*, 1:108]" (McConkie, "Joseph Smith and the Poetic Writings," 109).

PSALMS 96–99

Sing praises unto the Lord—Declare His name among the nations—Worship the Lord in the beauty of holiness—He comes to judge His people and the world.

The Lord reigns in millennial glory—The hills melt at His presence—Those who love the Lord hate evil.

Sing unto the Lord—All the ends of the earth will see His salvation—He comes to judge all men with equity and righteousness.

A Psalm.

The Lord is great in Zion—Exalt the Lord and worship at His footstool, for He is holy.

PSALM 100

Serve the Lord with gladness, all who are His people—Be thankful unto Him and bless His name.

A Psalm of praise.

1 Make a joyful noise unto the Lord, all ye lands.

2 Serve the Lord with gladness: come before his presence with singing.

3 Know ye that the Lord he *is* God: *it is* he *that* hath made us, and not we ourselves; *we are* his people, and the sheep of his pasture.

4 Enter into his gates with thanksgiving, *and* into his courts with praise: be thankful unto him, *and* bless his name.

5 For the Lord *is* good; his mercy *is* everlasting; and his truth *endureth* to all generations.

PSALM 101

David sings of mercy and justice—He will forsake the company of evildoers.

A Psalm of David.

Summary of Psalm 101

God will give mercy to all people who come unto Him and live by His teachings. Those who choose not to repent and keep His commandments will receive His judgments. David chooses to not associate with those who choose evil.

PSALM 102

The psalmist offers a prayer of the afflicted—Zion will be built up when the Lord appears in His glory—Though the heaven and earth perish, the Lord who created them will endure forever.

A Prayer of the afflicted, when he is overwhelmed, and poureth out his complaint before the LORD.

Summary of Psalm 102

"This psalm has direct overtones of a latter-day/millennial time in which Zion's favored day arrives and 'all the kings of the earth' shall acknowledge the One True King, Jesus Christ, who will 'appear in his glory.' As always, this will be a King particularly mindful of the poor and the 'destitute.' In a very conspicuous way, a line like verse 20—that this Deliverer will 'hear the groaning of the prisoner' and 'loose those that are appointed to death'—echoes Isaiah's great Messianic passage (one of the greatest of all Messianic passages in the Old Testament) that begins: 'The Spirit of the Lord God is upon me; because the Lord hath anointed me to preach good tidings unto the meek; he hath sent me to bind up the brokenhearted, to proclaim liberty to the captives, and the opening of the prison to them that are bound' [Isaiah 61:1]" (Holland, *For Times of Trouble*, 182).

The Thanksgiving Psalm (Psalm 100)

"Elder B. H. Roberts of the Seventy was a chaplain in the United States Armed Forces during World War I. The war finally ended, and the peace treaty was signed on November 11, 1918. Two weeks later, on Thanksgiving Day, a group of American soldiers were gathered together in France 'in one grand Thanksgiving service.

"'The large attendance included high-ranking military officers and the services were conducted by the chaplains, who were seated on the grandstand.

"'Elder Roberts was relegated to one of the rear seats. He had not been asked in advance to participate on the program, therefore, it was with great surprise that he heard the chaplain in charge announce: "Elder Roberts, the Mormon chaplain from Utah, will now step up and read the Thanksgiving Psalm."

"'Elder Roberts had never heard of the Thanksgiving Psalm but, hiding his personal embarrassment and possible impending embarrassment to the Church, he arose and walked to the podium, not knowing what he should say.

"'Years later he testified that, during the long walk to the front, he distinctly heard an audible voice announce: "The 100th Psalm."

"'It was as clear as though another person had spoken at his side.

"'Elder Roberts faced the crowd, paused, then opened his Bible and read Psalm 100. . . .

"'After Brother Roberts had closed his Bible and was returning to his seat, he noticed that his fellow chaplains refused to look at him; their eyes were immovably fixed on the floor. . . . It was then he realized that his part on the program had been a deliberate attempt to embarrass him, the Church and the priesthood. He acknowledged the help which he had received from the Lord in his moment of need and, when he returned to his tent that night, he checked the Book of Psalms, discovering that the 100th Psalm contained the most pertinent and appropriate sentiments on Thanksgiving'" (*Old Testament Study Guide for Home-Study Seminary Students*, Unit 23: Day 2, Psalms, Part 3).

Psalm 103:1–12. Praise God for His Love and Mercy

How can being forgiven of our sins also heal us? (103:3) "I am amazed at the Savior's encircling arms of mercy and love for the repentant, no matter how selfish the forsaken sin. I testify that the Savior is able and eager to forgive our sins. . . . What a marvelous privilege for each of us to turn away from our sins and to come unto Christ. Divine forgiveness is one of the sweetest fruits of the gospel, removing guilt and pain from our hearts and replacing them with joy and peace of conscience. Jesus declares, 'Will ye not now return unto me, and repent of your sins, and be converted, that I may heal you?' [3 Nephi 9:13]" (Andersen, "Repent . . . That I May Heal You," 40–41).

What is the relationship between renewed eagles and youth? (103:5) Each year the eagle sheds its old feathers and receives new ones. The phrase "thy youth is renewed like the eagle's" may symbolically teach us the need to cast off our sins and become new again through the Atonement of Christ (see *Adam Clarke's Commentary* [on Psalm 103:5]).

How can being "slow to anger" help you extend mercy and grace like the Savior? (103:8–9) "The Lord has warned that from the beginning and throughout history, Satan would stir up people's hearts to anger. . . . Wherever we live in the world, we have been molded as a people to be the instruments of the Lord's peace. . . . We cannot afford to be caught up in a world prone to give and to take offense. Rather, as the Lord revealed to both Paul and Mormon, we must neither envy nor be puffed up in pride. We are not easily provoked, nor do we behave unseemly. We rejoice not in iniquity but in the truth. Surely this is the pure love of Christ which we represent" (Wood, "Instruments of the Lord's Peace," 93, 95).

PSALM 103

David exhorts the Saints to bless the Lord for His mercy—The Lord is merciful unto those who keep His commandments.

A Psalm of David.

1 Bless the LORD, O my soul: and all that is within me, *bless* his holy name.

2 Bless the LORD, O my soul, and forget not all his benefits:

3 Who forgiveth all thine iniquities; who healeth all thy diseases;

4 Who redeemeth thy life from destruction; who crowneth thee with lovingkindness and tender mercies;

5 Who satisfieth thy mouth with good *things; so that* thy youth is renewed like the eagle's.

6 The LORD executeth righteousness and judgment for all that are oppressed.

7 He made known his ways unto Moses, his acts unto the children of Israel.

8 The LORD *is* merciful and gracious, slow to anger, and plenteous in mercy.

9 He will not always chide: neither will he keep *his anger* for ever.

10 He hath not dealt with us after our sins; nor rewarded us according to our iniquities.

11 For as the heaven is high above the earth, *so*
great is his mercy toward them that fear him.

12 As far as the east is from the west, *so* far
hath he removed our transgressions from us.

How does God show His mercy toward us? (103:11–12) "Mercy is compassion, kindness, empathy, forgiveness. While grace might be described as blessings and favor from God that we do not necessarily deserve, mercy represents not receiving what we do deserve because of the patience and love of the Master. It is an attribute of Deity. Christ's mercy to man comes by reason of his infinite atoning sacrifice and perfect love" (Top, "Mercy," 422–23).

13 Like as a father pitieth *his* children, *so* the
LORD pitieth them that fear him.

14 For he knoweth our frame; he remembereth that we *are* dust.

15 *As for* man, his days *are* as grass: as a flower
of the field, so he flourisheth.

16 For the wind passeth over it, and it is gone;
and the place thereof shall know it no more.

17 But the mercy of the LORD *is* from everlasting to everlasting upon them that fear him,
and his righteousness unto children's children;

18 To such as keep his covenant, and to
those that remember his commandments to
do them.

19 The LORD hath prepared his throne in the
heavens; and his kingdom ruleth over all.

20 Bless the LORD, ye his angels, that excel in
strength, that do his commandments, hearkening unto the voice of his word.

21 Bless ye the LORD, all *ye* his hosts; *ye* ministers of his, that do his pleasure.

22 Bless the LORD, all his works in all places
of his dominion: bless the LORD, O my soul.

Psalm 103:13–22. Nothing Compares to God's Goodness

Why are men's days like grass? (103:15) "Grass and wild flowers, so brief in their glory, are a favourite theme, sometimes for comparison, sometimes for contrast. . . . Our Lord gave a new turn to this analogy from nature, arguing from God's care for things as fragile as flowers to his far greater care for us" (Kidner, *Psalms 73–150*, 399–400).

How do the scriptures teach that we should fear the Lord? (103:17) "We know that the Lord is merciful and kind and that he does not rejoice in causing fear in the hearts of the righteous; nor does he command them to approach him in the spirit of fear in the sense in which this term is usually interpreted. It is true that the wicked will fear and tremble before him in that great day of judgment and that he is angry with the wicked, and dreadful fear and trembling will fill their hearts at his coming. The fear spoken of in these passages is in connection with the spirit of obedience, and the seeking of knowledge is quite a different thing" (Smith, *Answers to Gospel Questions*, 2:2).

Who are the angels of God mentioned in this verse? (103:20) "Who are the angels of God if not those who work his will and keep his commandments? Once they are standing on higher ground, the servants of God can reach out to those that stand in need of comfort, those who need to be strengthened, those who desire to receive the blessings of Heaven. Angels in many forms bless and benefit the children of men. They are men [and women] who have partaken of the divine nature and desire others do the same" (Hyde, *Comprehensive Commentary [Psalms]*, 231).

Summary of Psalms 104–106

God's assurance that He will protect Israel from their enemies is found in these psalms. Israel's protection comes from obedience to God's laws, but Israel often fails to obey and thus suffers oppression by its enemies and eventually deliverance from God, who displays His mercy toward them.

Psalm 107:1–8. Israel Praises the Lord for His Goodness and Wonderful Works

Who are the "redeemed of the Lord"? (107:2) "The redeemed of the Lord [are] people who have heard the message of redemption, obeyed the ordinances of redemption, received the Gospel of redemption, and [are] the people of God, the people of Christ" (Pratt, in *Journal of Discourses*, 21:274). The word *redeem* means "to deliver, to purchase, or to ransom, such as to free a person from bondage by payment. *Redemption* refers to the Atonement of Jesus Christ and to deliverance from sin. Jesus' Atonement redeems all mankind from physical death. Through His Atonement, those who have faith in Him and who repent are also redeemed from spiritual death" (Guide to the Scriptures, "Redeem, Redeemed, Redemption"). In the context of this psalm, the "redeemed of the Lord" also refers to being redeemed physically to a place of safety.

PSALMS 104–106

The Lord is clothed with honor and majesty—He makes His angels spirits and His ministers a flaming fire—Through His providence He sustains all forms of life—His glory endures forever.

Make the Lord's doings known among all men—Show His covenant with Abraham and His dealings with Israel—Touch not His anointed, and do His prophets no harm—Israel is to observe His statutes and keep His laws.

Praise the Lord for His mercy and mighty works—Israel rebelled and did wickedly—Moses mediated between Israel and the Lord—Israel was scattered and slain for worshipping false gods.

PSALM 107

The people of Israel are to praise and thank the Lord when they are gathered and redeemed—Oh, that men would praise the Lord!—The Lord's providences prevail in the lives of men.

1 O give thanks unto the Lord, for *he is* good: for his mercy *endureth* for ever.

2 Let the redeemed of the Lord say *so*, whom he hath redeemed from the hand of the enemy;

3 And gathered them out of the lands, from the east, and from the west, from the north, and from the south.

4 They wandered in the wilderness in a solitary way; they found no city to dwell in.

5 Hungry and thirsty, their soul fainted in them.

6 Then they cried unto the LORD in their trouble, *and* he delivered them out of their distresses.

7 And he led them forth by the right way, that they might go to a city of habitation.

8 Oh that *men* would praise the LORD *for* his goodness, and *for* his wonderful works to the children of men!

What made their wanderings "solitary"? (107:4–6) Elder Orson Pratt recounted a latter-day pioneer illustration of this psalm: "Are there not many sitting on these seats who can reflect back to the time when they wandered over the solitary plains, the arid deserts, and rugged mountains? . . . Oh, how solitary it was except for the [Native Americans], buffalo, a few antelope, some elk, deer, and howling wolves! It was indeed solitary; no road broken for us, no bridges across the streams. . . . And thus we continued, month after month, to wander in this solitary way, in this wilderness, as it were, and when we entered these valleys we found no city already built for us" (in *Journal of Discourses*, 12:89).

Summary of Psalm 107:9–43

The Lord is extolled for His continued mercy toward Israel and their deliverance from all distress.

PSALM 108

David praises and exalts God—Judah is the Lord's lawgiver.

A Song *or* Psalm of David.

Summary of Psalm 108

David's heart is "fixed" and steadfast in praising God (Psalm 108:1). He honors the Lord for delivering His people from their enemies such as Moab, Edom, and Philistia (see Psalm 108:9).

PSALM 109

David speaks of the cursings due to the wicked and deceitful—He prays that his enemies will be confounded.

To the chief Musician, A Psalm of David.

Summary of Psalm 109

This psalm is a prayer of protection against all manner of adversaries. David condemns the evil words and actions of his enemies and prays to the Lord for retribution upon them.

The Final "Book" of Psalms (Psalms 107–150)

"The book of Psalms is subdivided into five 'Books': [1–41, 42–72, 73–89, 90–106, 107–150]. The division into books is marked by the insertion of doxologies, short hymnic praises of God, at the end of each book. . . . The last psalm, Ps 150, serves as the concluding doxology for Book [5] and for the book of Psalms as a whole" (*Jewish Study Bible* [2014], 1265).

Book 5 (Psalms 107–150) "contains forty-four [psalms], the vast majority of which are of late date. The contents of these [psalms] are a surer guide to the period to which they belong than is the case in the other books, as many of them give either direct references or unmistakable hints regarding experiences of the exile or the return. Thus Psalm 107:10–16 refers to the years of captivity, as does also Psalm 137. Other [psalms], such as 126, refer to the joy of the return, and others still, e.g. 132, are prompted by the rebuilding of the Temple" (*John Dummelow's Commentary* [on Book 5]).

Psalm 110:1–7. Jesus Christ Will Be a Priest Forever after the Order of Melchizedek

Who was the second "Lord" addressed in this psalm? (110:1) "With the fairly common reference in the psalms of one Lord—the Father—speaking to another Lord—the Son—this passage places Christ on the traditional 'right hand' of the Father, a relationship that allows for the unity of the Father and the Son in every possible spiritual way but underscores the separateness of their physical being" (Holland, *For Times of Trouble*, 184). This verse was cited by Jesus Christ Himself as He taught the Pharisees and others (see Matthew 22:43–45; Mark 12:36–37; Luke 20:42–44), testifying of His relationship to the Father and His role as the Messiah. This verse was also taught by the Apostle Peter in Acts 2:34–35.

What is the dew of youth? (110:3) "The phrase . . . 'thou hast the dew of thy youth' suggests that the king [in the psalm] was ordained rather early on in the drama, when he was represented as being the prince, heir-apparent, rather than as a mature king" (Baker and Ricks, *Who Shall Ascend into the Hill of the Lord?* 241).

What was notable about being called a "priest after the order of Melchizedek"? (110:4) "This psalm is . . . one of only two places in the Old Testament where the great High Priest Melchizedek is mentioned by name—in this passage and in Genesis 14:18–20, wherein it is recorded that Abraham paid 'tithes of all' to Melchizedek. The Apostle Paul quoted these verses from Psalm 110 not once but twice in his epistle to the Hebrews in his effort to stress Christ's divine authority [see Hebrews 5:6; 7:17, 21]. . . . Melchizedek is clearly a very specific Old Testament type for the Christ that was to come in New Testament times" (Holland, *For Times of Trouble*, 184–85). ⊕

Why are there warlike images in these verses? (110:5–7) While these verses may borrow from battlefield images related to King David's war victories (see *NIV Study Bible* [1995], 900), another writer proposed a different setting. "At the time of the second coming of the Lord Jesus Christ, the rebellious nations of the earth will suffer greatly as a consequence of their individual and collective sins. . . . For one who is modestly familiar with the prophecies concerning the events of the latter days, it requires no imagination at all to perceive the manner in which this prophecy will be fulfilled. Hundreds of millions of the wicked will perish before the final wind-up scene takes place" (Hyde, *Comprehensive Commentary [Psalms]*, 277).

PSALM 110

A messianic psalm of David—Christ will sit on the Lord's right hand—He will be a priest forever after the order of Melchizedek.

A Psalm of David.

1 The LORD said unto my Lord, Sit thou at my right hand, until I make thine enemies thy footstool.

2 The LORD shall send the rod of thy strength out of Zion: rule thou in the midst of thine enemies.

3 Thy people *shall be* willing in the day of thy power, in the beauties of holiness from the womb of the morning: thou hast the dew of thy youth.

4 The LORD hath sworn, and will not repent, Thou *art* a priest for ever after the order of Melchizedek.

5 The Lord at thy right hand shall strike through kings in the day of his wrath.

6 He shall judge among the heathen, he shall fill *the places* with the dead bodies; he shall wound the heads over many countries.

7 He shall drink of the brook in the way: therefore shall he lift up the head.

PSALM 111

The Lord is gracious and full of compassion—Holy and reverend is His name—The fear of the Lord is the beginning of wisdom.

1 Praise ye the LORD. I will praise the LORD with *my* whole heart, in the assembly of the upright, and *in* the congregation.

2 The works of the LORD *are* great, sought out of all them that have pleasure therein.

3 His work *is* honourable and glorious: and his righteousness endureth for ever.

4 He hath made his wonderful works to be remembered: the LORD *is* gracious and full of compassion.

5 He hath given meat unto them that fear him: he will ever be mindful of his covenant.

6 He hath shewed his people the power of his works, that he may give them the heritage of the heathen.

7 The works of his hands *are* verity and judgment; all his commandments *are* sure.

8 They stand fast for ever and ever, *and are* done in truth and uprightness.

9 He sent redemption unto his people: he hath commanded his covenant for ever: holy and reverend *is* his name.

10 The fear of the LORD *is* the beginning of wisdom: a good understanding have all they that do *his commandments:* his praise endureth for ever.

Psalm 111:1–10. Praise the Lord for His Love toward Us

Why are we exhorted to praise the Lord? (111:1–10) "Psalm 111 is the first of the Hallelujah Psalms, which comprise Psalms 111 through 113 in one set and Psalms 146 through 150 in another. Each begins with the Hebrew word *hallelujah*, meaning 'praise ye Jehovah.'

"Three varieties of the Lord's 'works' described in Psalm 111 are more specific in Hebrew: his 'deeds,' his 'work,' and his 'wonders,' each of which is exemplified" (Rasmussen, *Latter-day Saint Commentary on the Old Testament*, 452). What are some of the Lord's deeds, works, or wonders for which you can praise Him? How are your relationships with Heavenly Father and Jesus Christ strengthened as you recognize and praise Them for these blessings? ⊕

What is the "assembly of the upright"? (111:1) To be *upright* means to be righteous, honorable, and true. The "assembly of the upright" refers to a group of righteous people who have come together to worship. In Doctrine and Covenants 101:22, the Lord commanded: "Behold, it is my will, that all they who call on my name, and worship me according to mine everlasting gospel, should gather together, and stand in holy places."

What are these "works of the Lord"? (111:2–9) This hymn focuses on "what God has done for His people. These powerful and benevolent acts are a reflection of God's righteous character. The provision of food [v. 5] is illustrative of His bountiful provisions for the daily needs of His people (see Matt. 6:11). He is faithful to His *covenant* (v. 5) promises, and His word is absolutely trustworthy (*sure*; v. 7), based in *truth and uprightness* (v. 8). The Lord redeemed Israel from death and bondage because of His *covenant* (v. 9) promises. The Lord's works on behalf of Israel demonstrate His holiness" (*Zondervan KJV Commentary*, 802).

What does "heritage of the heathen" mean? (111:6) The "heritage of the heathen" refers to the land formerly possessed by non-believers (see Valletta, et al., *Old Testament for Latter-day Saint Families*, 437). The Lord had shown the children of Israel "the power of his works" in delivering them from Egypt and from the influence of the wicked Canaanites, and by leading them to the promised land.

How might fear of the Lord lead a person to wisdom? (111:10) "Men of understanding have left on record . . . that 'the fear of the Lord is the beginning of wisdom' (Psalm 111:10). It is the sure foundation upon which all true knowledge is based. Men may acquire extensive information and learning; but unless accompanied by faith in and fear of God such acquirements are not so profitable unto them as they might be. A knowledge of the truth as revealed by the Lord furnishes men who obtain it a sure foundation on which to stand. . . . He who fears God and receives the truths He reveals can safely trust them" (Cannon, *Gospel Truth*, 281). See also John 7:17. ⊙

Psalm 112:1–10. Blessed Is the Man Who Loves and Serves the Lord

What does it mean to delight "greatly" in the commandments? (112:1) "To delight in Him is to acknowledge His hand in our lives. Our gospel duty is to do what is right and to love and delight in what is right. When we delight to serve Him, our Father in Heaven delights to bless us" (Tanner, "My Soul Delighteth in the Things of the Lord," 83).

"It is not enough to fear God, we must also love him: fear will deter us from evil; love will lead us to obedience. And the more a man fears and loves God, the more obedient will he be; till at last he will delight greatly in the commandments of his Maker" (*Adam Clarke's Commentary* [on Psalm 112:1]).

Who is "he" in this verse? (112:4) "It is important for us to know that the 'he' in verse 4 can be understood in two very different ways. It might refer to God shining as a light. In that case, it speaks about how God deals kindly with the good person. But because the subject of all the other verses is the good person himself, it is more likely that this verse is part of the description of the God-revering person. . . . So this verse, and the situation it describes, is a perfect example of the good person embodying in himself (and herself) the qualities that we understand as God's attributes" (Polish, *Keeping Faith with the Psalms*, 260).

How does the Joseph Smith Translation change this verse? (112:8) "The words 'his desire' should read 'judgment executed,' according to the Joseph Smith Translation" (Ludlow, *Companion to Your Study of the Old Testament*, 273).

What is the significance of the horn in this verse? (112:9) "Horns are representative of power and strength (1 Sam. 2:10; Jer. 48:25; Ps. 75:10)" (McConkie and Parry, *Guide to Scriptural Symbols*, 66). In the Book of Mormon, "Christ promises the Nephites that through their faithfulness he will 'make their horn iron' (3 Nephi 20:19), implying that they will be invincible. . . . Anciently kings were usually anointed with oil that

PSALM 112

Blessed is the man who fears the Lord—The righteous will be remembered always.

1 Praise ye the LORD. Blessed *is* the man *that* feareth the LORD, *that* delighteth greatly in his commandments.

2 His seed shall be mighty upon earth: the generation of the upright shall be blessed.

3 Wealth and riches *shall be* in his house: and his righteousness endureth for ever.

4 Unto the upright there ariseth light in the darkness: *he is* gracious, and full of compassion, and righteous.

5 A good man sheweth favour, and lendeth: he will guide his affairs with discretion.

6 Surely he shall not be moved for ever: the righteous shall be in everlasting remembrance.

7 He shall not be afraid of evil tidings: his heart is fixed, trusting in the LORD.

8 His heart *is* established, he shall not be afraid, until he see *his desire* upon his enemies.

9 He hath dispersed, he hath given to the poor; his righteousness endureth for ever; his horn shall be exalted with honour.

was carried in a horn (see 1 Samuel 16:13; 1 Kings 1:39; Psalm 92:10), implying that they should be directed by God's Spirit and would be empowered by it if they lived and served faithfully" (Gaskill, *Lost Language of Symbolism*, 50). In this psalm, the Lord promises that the righteous people will have power to be "exalted with honor."

10 The wicked shall see *it*, and be grieved; he shall gnash with his teeth, and melt away: the desire of the wicked shall perish.

What does it mean to gnash one's teeth? (112:10) To gnash one's teeth means "to grind the teeth. In the [Old Testament], gnashing of teeth expresses hostility and anger. . . . In the Gospels, grinding the teeth expresses the frustration and pain of those condemned to eternal torment" (*Revell Bible Dictionary*, 437).

PSALM 113

Blessed be the name of the Lord—Who is like unto the Lord our God?

1 Praise ye the LORD. Praise, O ye servants of the LORD, praise the name of the LORD.

Psalm 113:1–9. Israel Praises the Lord for His Goodness and Wonderful Works

What is the main message of this psalm? (113:1–9) "Praise for God, who is exalted above all in the cosmos, should extend throughout the world because God is everywhere in the world. The psalm is pure praise; there is no hint of petition. . . . [In verse 1] *servants* [are] either a specific group in the Temple, or general worshippers. The idea of worshipping is serving God, as a servant serves a master. [Verses 2 and 3 instruct worshippers to] praise . . . God at all times and in all places" (*Jewish Study Bible* [2014], 1397).

2 Blessed be the name of the LORD from this time forth and for evermore.

3 From the rising of the sun unto the going down of the same the LORD's name *is* to be praised.

4 The LORD *is* high above all nations, *and* his glory above the heavens.

5 Who *is* like unto the LORD our God, who dwelleth on high,

6 Who humbleth *himself* to behold *the things that are* in heaven, and in the earth!

What reasons do you have to bless the name of the Lord? (113:2) "Our Heavenly Father wants us to recall His and His Beloved Son's goodness, not for Their own gratification but for the influence such remembrance has on us. By considering Their kindness, our perspective and understanding are enlarged. By reflecting on Their compassion, we become more humble, prayerful, and steadfast. . . . Every time we use, benefit from, or even think of these gifts, we ought to consider the sacrifice, generosity, and compassion of the givers. Reverence for the givers does more than just make us grateful. Reflecting on Their gifts can and should transform us" (Renlund, "Consider the Goodness and Greatness of God," 41, 42). How are you being transformed by remembering to bless the name of the Lord?

7 He raiseth up the poor out of the dust, *and* lifteth the needy out of the dunghill;

8 That he may set *him* with princes, *even* with the princes of his people.

What do these verses teach us about God's compassion? (113:7–9) "The true uniqueness of the Lord is not His meriting of universal, endless praise, nor the sheer fact of His transcendence, but [v. 7] that He draws near to the needy to deliver them, [v. 8] to transform their state and [v. 9] to satisfy their longings"

(*New Bible Commentary: Revised*, 523). "In Psalm 113, we encounter God taking care of the poor and needy in a way that completely overcomes their marginality and reverses their position in the social order" (Polish, *Keeping Faith with the Psalms*, 273).

How might this promise to women be fulfilled today? (113:9) "The promise to every worthy woman is that she will have a chance to marry in time or in eternity, and an equal promise to every worthy woman is that she will have an opportunity to 'keep house, and to be a joyful mother of children' somewhere, sometime, someday.

"We do not know all the particulars of how that is done or under what circumstances the miracle of that promise will unfold, but it will unfold. This promise is meant to be a great assurance to those who have worthy desires of marriage and children and family life with their eternal bonds of love.

"Those desires will be realized. God has promised it. And it will be a joyful experience" (Holland, *For Times of Trouble*, 119–20).

Summary of Psalm 114

This psalm may be read as an illustration of God's characteristics outlined in Psalm 113. His sovereignty over all things and His abiding power with Israel are praised.

9 He maketh the barren woman to keep house, *and to be* a joyful mother of children. Praise ye the LORD.

PSALM 114

The Lord governs the sea and the land for the blessing of His people.

Were Psalms 113 and 114 Sung by Jesus and His Disciples at the Last Supper?

Elder Merrill J. Bateman of the Seventy taught:

"It is likely that many hymns were sung that evening. Matthew indicates that the Lord and His Apostles concluded the Last Supper with a hymn before leaving for the Mount of Olives (see Matt. 26:30). What did they sing? Although we have no way of knowing the concluding hymn, we do know one song. It is called the *Hallel*, which consists of Psalms 113–18. From before the time of Christ down to the present day, it is traditional for Jewish families to sing Psalms 113–14 before the Passover meal and Psalms 115–18 after. Why are these hymns important to the celebration? What is their message?

"Psalms 113–14 praise God for delivering Israel from the Egyptians. They indicate that He rules both water and land in that He parted the Red Sea for Israel to pass through and brought forth water when Moses struck the rock at Meribah (see Ex. 14:21–22; Ex. 17:6–7). At the Passover meal, one would expect Israel to be singing about deliverance from the angel of death, preservation in the desert, the parting of the Red Sea, and the greatness of the God of Jacob.

"In fact, the angel of death's Passover in Egypt was a messianic type. After the meal, the hymns turn to the ultimate deliverance of the soul (Ps. 116:4), the breaking of the bonds of death, both physical (Ps. 116:8, 16) and spiritual (Ps. 118:22, 29). The Atonement, represented by the cup of salvation, is the centerpiece of the festivities following the meal. All who celebrated the Passover that evening in A.D. 33 would have sung about 'the stone which the builders refused,' which became 'the head stone of the corner' (Ps. 118:22). The stone or rock, which is Christ, was refused or crucified by the builders, the Jewish leaders. As a result, Christ became the chief cornerstone or name by which salvation comes.

"Imagine, if you will, the Savior of the world singing these hymns with His disciples, which foreshadowed the events that followed later that evening and the next day" ("Power of Hymns," 17, 19).

PSALM 115

Our God is in the heavens—Idols are false gods—Trust in the Lord.

PSALM 116

Gracious is the Lord, and righteous—Precious in the sight of the Lord is the death of His Saints.

1 I love the LORD, because he hath heard my voice *and* my supplications.

2 Because he hath inclined his ear unto me, therefore will I call upon *him* as long as I live.

3 The sorrows of death compassed me, and the pains of hell gat hold upon me: I found trouble and sorrow.

4 Then called I upon the name of the LORD; O LORD, I beseech thee, deliver my soul.

5 Gracious *is* the LORD, and righteous; yea, our God *is* merciful.

6 The LORD preserveth the simple: I was brought low, and he helped me.

7 Return unto thy rest, O my soul; for the LORD hath dealt bountifully with thee.

8 For thou hast delivered my soul from death, mine eyes from tears, *and* my feet from falling.

9 I will walk before the LORD in the land of the living.

10 I believed, therefore have I spoken: I was greatly afflicted:

11 I said in my haste, All men *are* liars.

Summary of Psalm 115

Our God is superior to all idols of silver and gold that are made by man. He is mindful of his people and worthy of their praise forever. Because of His goodness and gracious promises, all should praise the Lord.

Psalm 116:1–8. The Lord Hears and Answers Prayers

How can we invite the Lord to "incline His ear" to our prayers? (116:2) "When God has commanded us to pray, He has used words like 'pray unceasingly' and 'pray always' and 'mighty prayer.'

"Those commands do not require using many words. In fact, the Savior has told us that we need not multiply words when we pray. The diligence in prayer which God requires does not take flowery speech nor long hours of solitude. . . .

"We can and must go often and carefully to the word of God. If we become casual in our study of the scriptures, we will become casual in our prayers" (Eyring, "Prayer," 16, 17).

Why does the Lord treat us with such grace and mercy? (116:5–8) "I marvel to think that the Son of God would condescend to save us, as imperfect, impure, mistake-prone, and ungrateful as we often are. I have tried to understand the Savior's Atonement with my finite mind, and the only explanation I can come up with is this: God loves us deeply, perfectly, and everlastingly. I cannot even begin to estimate 'the breadth, and length, and depth, and height . . . [of] the love of Christ' [Ephesians 3:18–19]" (Uchtdorf, "Gift of Grace," 107). What are some ways the Lord has treated you with grace and mercy?

Psalm 116:9–19. We Bless the Lord by Keeping His Covenants and Serving Him

What can we give to the Lord when He has given us so much? (116:12) "Our beloved Father simply asks that we live by the truth we have received and that we follow the path He has provided. Therefore, let us take courage and trust in the guidance of the Spirit. Let us in word and in deed share with our fellowmen the amazing and awe-inspiring message of God's plan of happiness. May our motive be our love for God and for His children, for they are our brothers and sisters. This is the beginning of what we can do in return for so much" (Uchtdorf, "O How Great the Plan of Our God!" 22). What will you do this week to live the truths of the gospel? How will you share the message of God's plan?

What is the "cup of salvation"? (116:13) The word translated "salvation" is a Hebrew word meaning "deliverance . . . aid, victory, prosperity" (see *Strong's Exhaustive Concordance*, word #h3444). In this verse, "the psalmist vows a public thanksgiving offering. . . . [The] *cup of deliverance* [refers to] a libation [drink] celebrating the psalmist's deliverance. This may be taken literally, as referring to the libation accompanying the thanksgiving offering, or metaphorically, as a kind of 'toast' to God invoking His name to publicize His great deeds" (*Jewish Study Bible* [2014], 1399).

Why is the death of a saint precious to the Lord? (116:15) "Tears at the passing of good people are the price we pay for love in this world. We realize how precious these people are to us and how precious their lives have been, so it is very easy to see why they are indeed 'precious in the sight of the Lord.' In that sense, even as we feel such loss in our lives, how joyful it must be for that person, other loved ones, and the Lord Himself to have such a joyful reunion beyond the veil. Nothing is more 'precious' than a humble, worthy, loving life" (Holland, *For Times of Trouble*, 121–22). ⊕

How do we offer a "sacrifice of thanksgiving" in our day? (116:17) "Expressing gratitude is pleasing to God, and true worship includes thanking Him. We should give thanks to the Lord for all things" (Guide to the Scriptures, "Thankful, Thanks, Thanksgiving"). The Lord has asked that we offer "unto [Him] a broken heart and a contrite spirit. And whoso cometh unto me with a broken heart and a contrite spirit, him will I baptize with fire and with the Holy Ghost" (3 Nephi 9:20). In what ways could offering a broken heart and contrite spirit be a sacrifice of thanksgiving?

12 What shall I render unto the LORD *for* all his benefits toward me?

13 I will take the cup of salvation, and call upon the name of the LORD.

14 I will pay my vows unto the LORD now in the presence of all his people.

15 Precious in the sight of the LORD *is* the death of his saints.

16 O LORD, truly I *am* thy servant; I *am* thy servant, *and* the son of thine handmaid: thou hast loosed my bonds.

17 I will offer to thee the sacrifice of thanksgiving, and will call upon the name of the LORD.

18 I will pay my vows unto the LORD now in the presence of all his people,

19 In the courts of the LORD's house, in the midst of thee, O Jerusalem. Praise ye the LORD.

PSALM 117

Praise the Lord for His mercy and truth.

Summary of Psalm 117

The Lord's merciful kindness is great, and His truth endures forever.

PSALM 118

A messianic psalm—Let all Israel say of the Lord, His mercy endures forever—The Stone that the builders refused is become the headstone of the corner—Blessed is he who comes in the name of the Lord.

1 O give thanks unto the LORD; for *he is* good: because his mercy *endureth* for ever.

2 Let Israel now say, that his mercy *endureth* for ever.

3 Let the house of Aaron now say, that his mercy *endureth* for ever.

4 Let them now that fear the LORD say, that his mercy *endureth* for ever.

5 I called upon the LORD in distress: the LORD answered me, *and set me* in a large place.

6 The LORD *is* on my side; I will not fear: what can man do unto me?

7 The LORD taketh my part with them that help me: therefore shall I see *my desire* upon them that hate me.

Psalm 118:1–7. The Lord Will Strengthen Those on His Side

What benefits may come as we give thanks to the Lord? (118:1–2) "Let such who have had an experience of [the Lord's mercy] acknowledge and declare it to others; not only believe in it with their hearts, and privately give thanks for it, but with the mouth make confession of it. . . . [The house of] Israel whom God has chosen, Christ has redeemed, and the Spirit effectually calls and sanctifies; such who are Israelites indeed, who have been encouraged to hope in the Lord, and in his mercy, and are made partakers of it; these should speak of the grace and mercy of God, and the continuance of it, for the encouragement of others" (*John Gill's Exposition of the Whole Bible* [commentary on Psalm 118:2]). How can you be an example to your family of giving thanks to the Lord?

What is the significance of being "set in a large place"? (118:5) When one is distressed or afflicted, it is like being confined in a narrow, constricted space. Contrast that with being set in a large place "where [one] is free to roam unconfined by the threats and dangers that had hemmed [that one] in" (*NIV Study Bible* [1995], 795).

Why is it important to have the Lord on our side? (118:6) "The enemy of our souls is alert and awake. He is trying by new methods to corrupt men and women. There is not a man or woman who lives that shall not be tried, whose position shall not be assailed, and if Satan can make an entrance he will endeavor to capture that soul. . . .

"But those who are on the Lord's side will close the ranks, fortify themselves, adhere to the standards, live in harmony with those blessed principles of the gospel which Christ has given, depending absolutely upon his leadership. And as sure as we live, victory shall come for Christ and his own" (Ballard, "Struggle for the Soul," 38, 39).

Summary of Psalm 118:8–20

Trust in the Lord, for He is mightier than all the nations of the earth. "The Lord is my strength and song, and is become my salvation" (Psalm 118:14). All Israel should rejoice, for the Lord will not give His people over to death.

Psalm 118:21–29. Rejoice in the Lord and Praise His Name

How does Jesus Christ fulfill this prophecy? (118:22) "Nothing in all of human history equals the wonder, the splendor, the magnitude, or the fruits of the matchless life of the Son of God. . . .

"He is the chief cornerstone of the church which bears His name, The Church of Jesus Christ of Latter-day Saints. There is no other name given among men whereby we can be saved (see Acts 4:12). He is the author of our salvation, the giver of eternal life (see Hebrews 5:9). . . . Thanks be to God for the gift of His Beloved Son, who gave His life that we might live and who is the chief, immovable cornerstone of our faith and His Church" (Hinckley, "Four Cornerstones of Faith," 4–5).

How can we be glad and rejoice in the days we are given? (118:24) "So often we get caught up in the illusion that there is something just beyond our reach that would bring us happiness: a better family situation, a better financial situation, or the end of a challenging trial. . . .

"We shouldn't wait to be happy until we reach some future point, only to discover that happiness was already available—all the time! Life is not meant to be appreciated only in retrospect. . . .

"No matter our circumstances, no matter our challenges or trials, there is something in each day to embrace and cherish. There is something in each day that can bring gratitude and joy if only we will see and appreciate it" (Uchtdorf, "Of Regrets and Resolutions," 23–24).

How were these words fulfilled? (118:26) "These words were used to greet travelers coming to Jerusalem for the Feast of Unleavened Bread (Passover). The crowd shouted these words with additional vigor when Jesus triumphantly entered Jerusalem before Passover" (*Quest Study Bible* [2005], 869). "At the Lord's triumphal entry into Jerusalem, the multitudes cried 'Hosanna' ['save now'; see Psalm 118:25] and spread palm branches for Jesus to ride upon, thus demonstrating their understanding that Jesus was the same Lord who had delivered Israel anciently" (Guide to the Scriptures, "Hosanna").

21 I will praise thee: for thou hast heard me, and art become my salvation.

22 The stone *which* the builders refused is become the head *stone* of the corner.

23 This is the LORD's doing; it *is* marvellous in our eyes.

24 This *is* the day *which* the LORD hath made; we will rejoice and be glad in it.

25 Save now, I beseech thee, O LORD: O LORD, I beseech thee, send now prosperity.

26 Blessed *be* he that cometh in the name of the LORD: we have blessed you out of the house of the LORD.

27 God *is* the LORD, which hath shewed us light: bind the sacrifice with cords, *even* unto the horns of the altar.

28 Thou *art* my God, and I will praise thee: *thou art* my God, I will exalt thee.

29 O give thanks unto the LORD; for *he is* good: for his mercy *endureth* for ever.

PSALM 119

א ALEPH

Blessed are they who keep the commandments.

ב BETH

Ponder the precepts and ways of the Lord.

ג GIMEL

O Lord, open our eyes, that we may behold wondrous things out of Thy law.

ד DALETH

O Lord, grant us Thy law, and make us to understand Thy precepts.

ה HE

O Lord, teach us Thy statutes, Thy law, and Thy commandments.

ו VAU

O Lord, give us mercy, truth, and salvation.

41 Let thy mercies come also unto me, O LORD, *even* thy salvation, according to thy word.

42 So shall I have wherewith to answer him that reproacheth me: for I trust in thy word.

43 And take not the word of truth utterly out of my mouth; for I have hoped in thy judgments.

Summary of Psalm 119:1–40

The psalmist pleads that our eyes may be open to behold and understand the wondrous law of the Lord.

Psalm 119:41–48. We Can Trust in the Lord's Mercy and Truth

How Is Psalm 119 Different from Other Psalms?

Psalm 119 is divided into twenty-two segments of eight verses apiece. Each segment begins with one of the twenty-two letters of the Hebrew alphabet, beginning with the first letter, *Aleph*, and ending with the letter *Tau*. See commentary in this volume for Psalm 25 regarding acrostic poetry.

44 So shall I keep thy law continually for ever and ever.

45 And I will walk at liberty: for I seek thy precepts.

46 I will speak of thy testimonies also before kings, and will not be ashamed.

How can being tied to the Lord's teachings result in freedom? (119:45) "There are many among us, and throughout the world, young and old (though perhaps we too often confine the lesson to the young) who have the idea that freedom, the freedom of which we speak, can be found in unlicensed liberty. But this freedom which Jesus taught is not the freedom of irresponsibility or unrighteousness, but the freedom which accompanies obedience. . . .

"My humble testimony is that real freedom is not irresponsibility or license, but that real freedom accompanies faith in God, the understanding of his word, and obedience to it. (And each of us, I believe, knows personally the difference between the freedom of faith and obedience, and the bondage of sin.)" (Hanks, in Conference Report, Oct. 1954, 101, 102). ⊕

47 And I will delight myself in thy commandments, which I have loved.

48 My hands also will I lift up unto thy commandments, which I have loved; and I will meditate in thy statutes.

How have you learned to love the Lord's commandments? (119:47) "We may feel at times that God's laws restrict our personal freedom, take from us our agency, and limit our growth. But as we seek for greater understanding, as we allow our Father to teach us, we will begin to see that His laws are a manifestation of His love for us and obedience to His laws is an expression of our love for Him" (Stephens, "If Ye Love Me, Keep My Commandments," 119). What is the relationship between our obedience to the Lord's commandments and our love for Him?

Summary of Psalm 119:49–64

Remember the Lord, do not delay to keep His commandments, and He will comfort you. Though the wicked afflict you, seek faithful companions who fear the Lord.

ז ZAIN

The Lord's statutes and judgments comfort us during our pilgrimage.

ח CHETH

Make faithful people our companions.

Psalm 119:65–72. The Lord's Statutes Protect Us during Affliction

ט TETH

O Lord, teach us Thy statutes.

65 Thou hast dealt well with thy servant, O Lord, according unto thy word.

66 Teach me good judgment and knowledge: for I have believed thy commandments.

67 Before I was afflicted I went astray: but now have I kept thy word.

68 Thou *art* good, and doest good; teach me thy statutes.

69 The proud have forged a lie against me: *but* I will keep thy precepts with *my* whole heart.

70 Their heart is as fat as grease; *but* I delight in thy law.

What does it mean that the heart of the proud "is as fat as grease"? (119:70) Other Bible versions of this verse offer help with this description. The New International Version uses the phrase "Their hearts are callous and unfeeling" (NIV, Psalm 119:70). The same phrase is recorded in a Hebrew translation as "Their minds are thick like fat" (see *Jewish Study Bible* [2014], 1406). Another writer observed that this phrase describes individuals who "have gradually become less sensitive to the truth and have forgotten much that they once knew and understood" (Hyde, *Comprehensive Commentary [Psalms]*, 299).

71 *It is* good for me that I have been afflicted; that I might learn thy statutes.

72 The law of thy mouth *is* better unto me than thousands of gold and silver.

How can we be blessed by experiencing afflictions? (119:71) Elder Jeffrey R. Holland declared: "The point is that faith means trusting God in good times and bad, even if that includes some suffering until we see His arm revealed in our behalf. That can be difficult in our modern world when many have come to believe that the highest good in life is to avoid all suffering, that no one should ever anguish over anything. But that belief will never lead us to the 'measure of the stature of the fulness of Christ'" ("Waiting on the Lord," 116).

י JOD

O Lord, let Thy tender mercies come upon us.

כ CAPH

All the Lord's commandments are faithful.

ל LAMED

O Lord, save us, for we have sought Thy precepts.

Summary of Psalm 119:73–96

A kind and merciful God gives commandments to His children so they might know how to live righteously. The commandments of God are faithful and will save all who seek after them.

Psalm 119:97–112. The Scriptures Guide Our Lives

Why are the Lord's words compared to honey? (119:103) "The honeycomb . . . was the sweetest substance known in the ancient world. No refined sugar was available, but bees were plentiful in the agricultural highlands of Palestine, and their produce was highly valued by the Israelites. To say that Scripture is sweeter than honey is to say the psalmist values it more than any pleasure" (Richards, *Bible Reader's Companion*, 377).

How can the scriptures help you receive spiritual light? (119:105) "We have scriptures that reveal the word of God to mankind through the ages. When we feast upon the word of God, we open our minds to eternal truths and our hearts to the gentle whisperings of the Holy Ghost. Truly God's word, through scriptures and modern-day prophets, is a 'lamp unto [our] feet, and a light unto [our] path' [Psalm 119:105]" (Wirthlin, "One Step after Another," 26). What scripture study skill could you apply this week that will help you strengthen the spiritual light you receive?

What is a freewill offering of the mouth? (119:108) "Sometimes we are forced to say the right things, as if righteousness could be coerced. . . . Required expressions have their place, but how much more wonderful when, of our own volition, we offer to the Lord and others 'the freewill offerings of [our] mouth.'

מ MEM

The Lord's law and His testimonies should be our meditation all the day.

97 O how love I thy law! it *is* my meditation all the day.

98 Thou through thy commandments hast made me wiser than mine enemies: for they *are* ever with me.

99 I have more understanding than all my teachers: for thy testimonies *are* my meditation.

100 I understand more than the ancients, because I keep thy precepts.

101 I have refrained my feet from every evil way, that I might keep thy word.

102 I have not departed from thy judgments: for thou hast taught me.

103 How sweet are thy words unto my taste! *yea, sweeter* than honey to my mouth!

104 Through thy precepts I get understanding: therefore I hate every false way.

נ NUN

The Lord's word is a lamp unto our feet.

105 Thy word *is* a lamp unto my feet, and a light unto my path.

106 I have sworn, and I will perform *it*, that I will keep thy righteous judgments.

107 I am afflicted very much: quicken me, O Lord, according unto thy word.

108 Accept, I beseech thee, the freewill offerings of my mouth, O Lord, and teach me thy judgments.

109 My soul *is* continually in my hand: yet do I not forget thy law.

110 The wicked have laid a snare for me: yet I erred not from thy precepts.

111 Thy testimonies have I taken as an heritage for ever: for they *are* the rejoicing of my heart.

112 I have inclined mine heart to perform thy statutes alway, *even unto* the end.

These might include—but are not limited to—words of love, words of kindness, words of patience, words of compassion.

"We make a freewill offering of our mouth every time we offer a prayer that is honest and from the heart. We make a freewill offering of our mouth every time we bear a testimony or teach a truth. Furthermore, we can give such expressions even more freely and generously than we do" (Holland, *For Times of Trouble*, 137).

The Scriptures Increase Our Spiritual Power and Understanding (Psalm 119:97–112)

Psalm 119:97–112 confirms the blessings that come from scripture study. Elder Jay E. Jensen of the Seventy taught: "The Lord has promised us specific blessings for reading and studying the scriptures.... Most promises that come to us for reading and studying the scriptures pertain to mortality....

"Consider the following five promises of power:

"Power to overcome *evil*—Nephi taught: 'Whoso would hearken unto the word of God, and would hold fast unto it, ... the fiery darts of the adversary [could not] overpower them unto blindness' (1 Ne. 15:24; see also Ps. 17:4; Ps. 119:98–101, 104; Hel. 3:29–30).

"Power to live *righteously*—Alma 'did ... preach the word of God unto them, to stir them up in remembrance of their duty' (Alma 4:19). The Psalmist said, 'Thy word is a lamp unto my feet, and a light unto my path' (Ps. 119:105; see also 2 Tim. 3:15–17; Hel. 15:7–8).

"Power to teach convincingly—Alma and the sons of Mosiah 'had searched the scriptures diligently ... and when they taught, they taught with power and authority of God' (Alma 17:2–3; see also 2 Tim. 3:16). To Hyrum Smith the Lord said: 'First seek to obtain my word ...; then, if you desire, you shall have my Spirit and my word, yea, the power of God unto the convincing of men' (D&C 11:21; see also 2 Tim. 3:15–17; Alma 4:19; Alma 31:5; D&C 84:85).

"Power to call down the powers of heaven—Jacob said that 'we search the prophets ... and our faith becometh unshaken, insomuch that we truly can command in the name of Jesus and the very trees obey us, or the mountains, or the waves of the sea' (Jacob 4:6; Hel. 10:4–5).

"Power to change the heart and disposition—Samuel taught the Nephites that the Lamanites were 'led to believe the holy scriptures, ... which are written, which leadeth them to faith on the Lord, and unto repentance, which faith and repentance bringeth a change of heart unto them' (Hel. 15:7; see also 1 Ne. 15:20)....

"Consider now the following promises of increase:

"Increase in hope and joy—The Apostle Paul taught that 'we through patience and comfort of the scriptures might have hope' (Rom. 15:4; see also 1 Ne. 11:25; Jacob 2:8; Jacob 4:6; Alma 44:5; D&C 19:23).

"Increase in spirituality—'The preaching of the word had a great tendency to lead the people to do that which was just' (Alma 31:5; see also 2 Ne. 4:15–16; Moro. 6:4).

"Increase in knowledge and understanding—Nephi taught that 'the words of Christ will tell you all things what ye should do' (2 Ne. 32:3). To Joseph Smith the Lord said: 'The holy scriptures are given of me for your instruction' (D&C 33:16; see also Ps. 19:7; Ps. 119:98–101; 2 Tim. 3:15–17; Alma 12:10; Alma 17:2–3; D&C 18:34–36).

"Increase in the power of discernment—'The word of God ... is quick and powerful, which shall divide asunder all the cunning and the snares and the wiles of the devil' (Hel. 3:29). 'And whoso treasureth up my word, shall not be deceived' (JS–M 1:37; see also Heb. 4:12).

"Increase in testimony—From the Doctrine and Covenants: 'You can testify that you have heard my voice, and know my words' (D&C 18:36; see also Ps. 19:7)" ("Remember Also the Promises," 81). How are you seeking after these promises of scripture study?

Summary of Psalm 119:113–176

As we are righteous, the Lord will guide us and give us His love and peace. All the ways of the Lord are righteous.

ס SAMECH

Depart from evildoers and keep the commandments of God.

ע AIN

O Lord, we are Thy servants; give us understanding.

פ PE

The Lord's testimonies are wonderful.

צ TZADDI

The Lord's law is the truth.

ק KOPH

O Lord, hear the voice of Thy servants according to Thy loving kindness.

ר RESH

Great are Thy tender mercies, O Lord.

ש SCHIN

Those who love the Lord's law have peace.

ת TAU

All the Lord's commandments are righteousness.

PSALM 120

Call upon the Lord when in distress.

A Song of degrees.

PSALM 121

Help comes from the Lord—He is the guardian of Israel.

A Song of degrees.

1 I will lift up mine eyes unto the hills, from whence cometh my help.

2 My help *cometh* from the LORD, which made heaven and earth.

3 He will not suffer thy foot to be moved: he that keepeth thee will not slumber.

Summary of Psalm 120

The Lord will help us in our times of need.

Psalm 121:1–8. The Lord, Who Protects Israel, Does Not Sleep

Why would the Psalmist look to the hills for help?

(121:1) "The 'hills, from whence cometh my help' are the mountains of the Lord's house; thus it is made clear that 'my help cometh from the Lord' (Ps. 121:1–2)" (Rasmussen, *Latter-day Saint Commentary on the Old Testament,* 460). "As we attend the temple, there can come to us a dimension of spirituality and a feeling of peace which will transcend any other feeling which could come into the human heart. We will grasp the true meaning of the words of the Savior when He said: 'Peace I leave with you, my peace I give unto you. . . . Let not your heart be troubled, neither let it be afraid' [John 14:27]" (Monson, "Blessings of the Temple," 91–92).

What does this psalm teach us about God?

(121:2–8) "Psalm 121 speaks explicitly of God as a helper. In an image that is echoed in virtually every verse of this psalm, God is spoken of as a *shomer*—a guard. The word is used to describe someone who stands watch. Not only does God watch over us, but, unlike human counterparts, we are assured that God will 'neither slumber nor sleep.' By employing a series of paired opposites, the psalmist conveys a sense that God's help and protection is constant and consistent. Thus, we are reminded that God made 'heaven and

What Are the Songs of Degrees? (Psalms 120–135)

Psalm 120 begins a series of fifteen psalms, ending with Psalm 135, each with a variation of the title "A song of degrees."

"These psalms are also called 'songs of ascents,' meaning songs of 'rising' or 'going up.' These fifteen psalms may have been sung by Israelite pilgrims as they traveled up to Jerusalem for religious festivals. (See [Bible Dictionary], 'Feasts.') In some translations they are called the 'pilgrim songs' or the 'pilgrim book of devotions.' Another possibility is that priests and Levites may have sung these psalms during the festivals as they ascended the steps and courtyards approaching the temple, especially the fifteen steps leading from the women's court to the men's court. In either case, these psalms were part of the liturgy [rituals of worship] of the Jerusalem temple and ancient Israelite religious holidays. As such, they could be compared with the Easter, Christmas, or Thanksgiving hymns of our age" (Ludlow, *Unlocking the Old Testament*, 137).

earth,' that God protects us by day and night, and that God guards us as we 'go out and . . . come in,' now and always" (Polish, *Keeping Faith with the Psalms*, 187).

Why would the God of Israel "neither slumber nor sleep"? (121:4) Elder Jeffrey R. Holland stated: "Please understand that He who never sleeps nor slumbers cares for the happiness and ultimate exaltation of His children above all else that a divine being has to do. He is pure love, gloriously personified, and Merciful Father is His name" ("Waiting on the Lord," 116).

How can we know that the Lord is paying attention to our circumstances? (121:5) To the heavily burdened, Elder Jeffrey R. Holland affirmed: "At least one of the purposes of . . . the teachings of the prophets down through the ages is to declare to these very people that the Lord is equally fervent in trying to reach them, that when there is trouble His hopes and His striving and His efforts greatly exceed our own and it never ceases. . . .

"Christ and His angels and His prophets forever labor to buoy up our spirits, steady our nerves, calm our hearts, send us forth with renewed strength and resolute hope. They wish all to know that 'if God be for us, who can be against us?' [Romans 8:31]" ("Peaceable Things of the Kingdom," 83).

Summary of Psalms 122–125

The Lord blesses, protects, and gives mercy to those who trust in Him.

4 Behold, he that keepeth Israel shall neither slumber nor sleep.

5 The LORD *is* thy keeper: the LORD *is* thy shade upon thy right hand.

6 The sun shall not smite thee by day, nor the moon by night.

7 The LORD shall preserve thee from all evil: he shall preserve thy soul.

8 The LORD shall preserve thy going out and thy coming in from this time forth, and even for evermore.

PSALMS 122–125

David says, Go into the house of the Lord—Give thanks unto Him.

A Song of degrees of David.

Lift up your eyes unto the Lord, and plead with Him for mercy.

A Song of degrees.

David says, Israel's help is in the name of the Lord.

A Song of degrees of David.

Blessed are they who trust in the Lord—Peace will be upon Israel.

A Song of degrees.

PSALM 126

The Lord has done great things for His people, Israel.

A Song of degrees.

1 When the LORD turned again the captivity of Zion, we were like them that dream.

2 Then was our mouth filled with laughter, and our tongue with singing: then said they among the heathen, The LORD hath done great things for them.

3 The LORD hath done great things for us; *whereof* we are glad.

4 Turn again our captivity, O LORD, as the streams in the south.

5 They that sow in tears shall reap in joy.

6 He that goeth forth and weepeth, bearing precious seed, shall doubtless come again with rejoicing, bringing his sheaves *with him.*

Psalm 126:1–6. The Lord Did Great Things in Delivering His People

Why did Israel consider their deliverance like a dream? (126:1–6) "The return of Judah from Babylon after it was conquered by Persia (ca. 538–537 B.C.) was like a dream come true; but though 'the Lord [had] done great things' for them, there was yet 'captivity' in mortality itself, from which they desired redemption. If they who sow in tears go forth in life to sow 'precious seed,' then the Lord will lift them up with joy as they come 'bringing . . . sheaves' to the Judgment Day. Redemption from Babylon was like a dream; but redemption from the wicked world of 'Babylon' (D&C 1:16) will be a dream come true. Thus this psalm too sings of the ultimate elevation of man by the Lord" (Rasmussen, *Latter-day Saint Commentary on the Old Testament*, 461–62).

PSALM 127

Children are a heritage from the Lord.

A Song of degrees for Solomon.

1 Except the LORD build the house, they labour in vain that build it: except the LORD keep the city, the watchman waketh *but* in vain.

2 *It is* vain for you to rise up early, to sit up late, to eat the bread of sorrows: *for* so he giveth his beloved sleep.

Psalm 127:1–2. Nothing We Do Will Succeed without God

What is the "bread of sorrows"? (127:2) "The phrase 'to eat the bread of sorrows' refers to the food we earn by our hard work (see Genesis 3:17)" (Valletta, et al., *Old Testament for Latter-day Saint Families*, 441).

3 Lo, children *are* an heritage of the LORD: *and* the fruit of the womb *is his* reward.

4 As arrows *are* in the hand of a mighty man; so *are* children of the youth.

5 Happy *is* the man that hath his quiver full of them: they shall not be ashamed, but they shall speak with the enemies in the gate.

Psalm 127:3–5. Children Are a Blessing from God

How can we safeguard the God-given heritage of children? (127:3) The First Presidency and Quorum of the Twelve Apostles have taught: "Husband and wife have a solemn responsibility to love and care for each other and for their children. 'Children are an heritage of the Lord' (Psalm 127:3). Parents have a sacred duty to rear their children in love and righteousness, to provide for their physical and spiritual needs, and to teach them to love and serve one another, observe the commandments of God, and be law-abiding citizens wherever they live. Husbands and wives—mothers and fathers—will be held accountable before God for the discharge of these obligations" ("Family: A Proclamation to the World" [2017], 145).

Summary of Psalms 128–132

The Lord blesses those who love and obey Him, but those who hate Him will wither as grass. The Messiah will come from the family line of King David and save Israel in fulfillment of the promises made to Abraham.

Summary of Psalms 133–134

Psalms 133 and 134 continues the last of the "songs of degrees" or "also called 'songs of ascents,' meaning songs of 'rising' or 'going up.' These fifteen psalms may have been sung by Israelite pilgrims as they traveled up to Jerusalem for religious festivals" (Ludlow, *Unlocking the Old Testament*, 137; see commentary in this volume for Psalms 120–135). These songs of ascent were also "thought to have been sung by the Levites standing atop a special choir stairway in the temple" (Tvedtnes, "Ancient Israelite Psalters," 242). In Psalm 133:1, David suggests "how pleasant it is . . . to dwell together in unity." In Psalm 134:2, he also points out that God blesses those who "lift up [their] hands in the sanctuary [temple], and bless the Lord."

PSALMS 128–132

Blessed are those who fear the Lord and walk in His ways.

A Song of degrees.

The Lord is righteous—Let those be confounded who hate Zion.

A Song of degrees.

O Lord, hear our prayers, forgive iniquity, and redeem Israel.

A Song of degrees.

David says, Let Israel hope in the Lord forever.

A Song of degrees of David.

A messianic psalm—Of the fruit of David's loins will the Lord set One upon His throne—The Lord will bless Zion, and her Saints will shout for joy.

A Song of degrees.

PSALMS 133–134

David says, It is pleasant for brethren to dwell together in unity!

A Song of degrees of David.

Bless the Lord, and He will bless you.

A Song of degrees.

PSALMS 135–138

Praise and bless the Lord—Our Lord is above all gods; idols cannot see, hear, or speak.

Give thanks unto God for all things, for His mercy endures forever.

While in captivity, the Jews wept by the rivers of Babylon—Because of sorrow, they could not bear to sing the songs of Zion.

David praises the Lord for His loving kindness and truth—He worships toward the holy temple.

A Psalm of David.

PSALM 139

David says that the Lord knows all man's thoughts and doings—He asks, Where can man go to escape from the spirit and presence of the Lord?—Man is fearfully and wonderfully made.

To the chief Musician, A Psalm of David.

1 O Lord, thou hast searched me, and known *me*.

2 Thou knowest my downsitting and mine uprising, thou understandest my thought afar off.

3 Thou compassest my path and my lying down, and art acquainted *with* all my ways.

4 For *there is* not a word in my tongue, *but*, lo, O Lord, thou knowest it altogether.

5 Thou hast beset me behind and before, and laid thine hand upon me.

6 *Such* knowledge *is* too wonderful for me; it is high, I cannot *attain* unto it.

Summary of Psalms 135–138

These psalms praise the Lord for His power and mercy, though Psalm 137 includes a song of sorrow over the captivity of the Jews in Babylon. David also declares that he will worship "towards [the Lord's] holy temple" (Psalm 138:2) and that one day the kings of the earth will also praise the Lord (see Psalm 138:4).

Psalm 139:1–12. David Acknowledges That He Cannot Hide Anything from the Lord

How does the Lord's omniscience allow us to exercise faith in Him? (139:1–3) "The omniscience of the Lord is dramatically declared in this famous psalm, and the gratitude of those who are comfortable in the presence of the Lord is beautifully stated. It is marvelous and comforting that there is no hiding place God does not know. The psalmist expresses trust in God and desire for his help in the process of repentance" (Rasmussen, *Latter-day Saint Commentary on the Old Testament*, 466).

Why is it not possible to hide from the Lord? (139:7–10) "There is not a single thought of our hearts which he does not comprehend; there is nothing connected with us he does not know. We may hide ourselves in the bowels of the earth, but we cannot conceal ourselves from his all-piercing sight. We may climb the highest mountains or descend into the deepest valleys or we may go to the uttermost parts of the earth, but wherever we may go he is there [see Psalm 139:7–10], his power is there, his vision is there to hear and to comprehend the desires and the wishes of our hearts [see D&C 67:1; 137:9]" (Cannon, in *Journal of Discourses*, 21:73–74). ⊕

Psalm 139:13–24. David Praises the Lord for His Omniscience

What does "fearfully and wonderfully made" mean? (139:13–15) As David reflected on his miraculous body, he explained how God "possessed my reins" or, in other words, "created my inward parts" (Psalm 139:13*a*). "The . . . human body is the most complicated and curious that can be conceived. It is, indeed, wonderfully made; and it is withal so exquisitely nice and delicate, that the slightest accident may impair or destroy in a moment some of those parts essentially necessary to the continuance of life; therefore, we are fearfully made. And God has done so to show us our frailty, that we should walk with death, keeping life in view; and feel the necessity of depending on the all-wise . . . care and providence of God" (*Adam Clarke's Commentary* [on Psalm 139:14]). ⊕

What was David's substance that was seen by the Lord? (139:16) "A most obscure verse. 'Thine eyes beheld my' (yet) 'unformed substance, and in thy book were they all written,' (even) 'the days which were preordained when as yet there was none of them.' The Psalmist himself, all his days, and all their happenings, were in the mind of God before he was born" (*John Dummelow's Commentary* [on Psalm 139:16]). Similarly, Jehovah said to Jeremiah: "Before I formed thee in the belly I knew thee; and before thou camest forth out of the womb I sanctified thee" (Jeremiah 1:5).

What did David mean by hating those that hate the Lord? (139:19–22) David's impassioned expression to God was a "declaration of loyalty that echoes the

7 Whither shall I go from thy spirit? or whither shall I flee from thy presence?

8 If I ascend up into heaven, thou *art* there: if I make my bed in hell, behold, thou *art there.*

9 *If* I take the wings of the morning, *and* dwell in the uttermost parts of the sea;

10 Even there shall thy hand lead me, and thy right hand shall hold me.

11 If I say, Surely the darkness shall cover me; even the night shall be light about me.

12 Yea, the darkness hideth not from thee; but the night shineth as the day: the darkness and the light *are* both alike *to thee.*

13 For thou hast possessed my reins: thou hast covered me in my mother's womb.

14 I will praise thee; for I am fearfully *and* wonderfully made: marvellous *are* thy works; and *that* my soul knoweth right well.

15 My substance was not hid from thee, when I was made in secret, *and* curiously wrought in the lowest parts of the earth.

16 Thine eyes did see my substance, yet being unperfect; and in thy book all *my members* were written, *which* in continuance were fashioned, when *as yet there was* none of them.

17 How precious also are thy thoughts unto me, O God! how great is the sum of them!

18 *If* I should count them, they are more in number than the sand: when I awake, I am still with thee.

19 Surely thou wilt slay the wicked, O God: depart from me therefore, ye bloody men.

20 For they speak against thee wickedly, *and* thine enemies take *thy name* in vain.

21 Do not I hate them, O Lord, that hate thee? and am not I grieved with those that rise up against thee?

22 I hate them with perfect hatred: I count them mine enemies.

23 Search me, O God, and know my heart: try me, and know my thoughts:

24 And see if *there be any* wicked way in me, and lead me in the way everlasting.

pledge required by ancient Near Eastern kings of their vassals (e.g., 'With my friend you shall be friend, and with my enemy you shall be enemy,' from a treaty between Mursilis II, a Hittite king, and Tette of Nuhassi, 14th century B.C.)" (*NIV Study Bible* [1995], 926).

Why would David invite the Lord to "search [him]" and to "know" his heart and thoughts? (139:23–24) The Lord knows all things, so it is crucial that "in every waking hour of our lives and every moment of our discipleship we say with honesty, 'Search me, O God, and know my heart; try me, and know my thoughts.' That is an interview the Lord is constantly giving us (whether we agree to it or not). He is searching our hearts, and He surely knows our thoughts. We would do well to be worthy of such examinations 'at all times and in all things, and in all places' [Mosiah 18:9]" (Holland, *For Times of Trouble*, 146).

PSALMS 140–143

David prays for deliverance from his enemies—The Lord maintains the cause of the poor and afflicted.

To the chief Musician, A Psalm of David.

David pleads with the Lord to hear his prayers—The reproof of the righteous is a kindness.

A Psalm of David.

David prays for preservation from his persecutors.

Maschil of David; A Prayer when he was in the cave.

David prays for favor in judgment—He meditates on the Lord's works and trusts in Him.

A Psalm of David.

Summary of Psalms 140–143

In this set of psalms, David pleads with the Lord to hear his prayers and to deliver him from his enemies. David's pleas rely on temple imagery, such as incense, lifting up hands, and sacrifice (see Psalm 141:2; see also Rev. 8:3–5). David also declares: "Keep me from the snares which they have laid for me" (Psalm 141:9). For example, as David hid from Saul in a cave, he prayed for deliverance from his persecutor (see Psalm 142). Despite his challenges, David expresses his trust in the Lord (see Psalm 143:8). The word *maschil* in the superscription of Psalm 142 identifies it as a song of lament or of instruction. For additional information on this superscription, see commentary in this volume for Psalm 32 superscription.

Psalm 144:1–8. David Praises the Lord for His Goodness and for Subduing His Enemies

Why did David suggest that Jehovah taught him to fight? (144:1–2) "Many of [Israel's] Judges were called *moshi'a* (the Hebrew word meaning 'deliverer' or 'savior'). As such they acted as temporal saviors for Israel. Jehovah is the ultimate *moshi'a* (Isa. 43:3; 45:15; Ps. 40:17; 144:2) in both a spiritual and a temporal sense. He is the power that made the Judges successful in bringing deliverance to Israel. As a 'man of war' (Ex. 15:3), the Lord went out before the Israelite army (4:14). Israel's battles were 'the Lord's battles' (1 Sam. 18:17; 25:28), and the enemies of Israel were the foes of Jehovah" (Parry and Ricks, "Judges of Israel," 245–46).

Why was David in awe of the Lord's interest in His mortal children? (144:3–4) "And while we may look at the vast expanse of the universe and say, 'What is man in comparison to the glory of creation?' God Himself said we are the reason He created the universe! His work and glory—the purpose for this magnificent universe—is to save and exalt mankind [see Moses 1:38–39]. In other words, the vast expanse of eternity, the glories and mysteries of infinite space and time are all built for the benefit of ordinary mortals like you and me. Our Heavenly Father created the universe that we might reach our potential as His sons and daughters" (Uchtdorf, "You Matter to Him," 20). ⊕

What was the significance of the Lord touching the mountains? (144:5–6) "The figure of Omnipotence, 'He toucheth the mountains and they smoke,' is . . . taken from the mountains that smoked at the giving of the Law [see Exodus 19:18; 20:15]. The mountains . . . point to the worldly powers. God only needs to touch these as with the tip of His finger, and the inward fire, which will consume them, at once makes itself known by the smoke, which ascends from them" (Keil and Delitzsch, *Commentary* [on Psalm 144:5–8]).

PSALM 144

David blesses the Lord for deliverance and temporal prosperity—Happy is that people whose God is the Lord.

A Psalm of David.

1 Blessed *be* the LORD my strength, which teacheth my hands to war, *and* my fingers to fight:

2 My goodness, and my fortress; my high tower, and my deliverer; my shield, and *he* in whom I trust; who subdueth my people under me.

3 LORD, what *is* man, that thou takest knowledge of him! *or* the son of man, that thou makest account of him!

4 Man is like to vanity: his days *are* as a shadow that passeth away.

5 Bow thy heavens, O LORD, and come down: touch the mountains, and they shall smoke.

6 Cast forth lightning, and scatter them: shoot out thine arrows, and destroy them.

7 Send thine hand from above; rid me, and deliver me out of great waters, from the hand of strange children;

8 Whose mouth speaketh vanity, and their right hand *is* a right hand of falsehood.

Psalm 144:9–15. David Extols the Blessings That Come to a People Who Love the Lord

9 I will sing a new song unto thee, O God: upon a psaltery *and* an instrument of ten strings will I sing praises unto thee.

10 *It is he* that giveth salvation unto kings: who delivereth David his servant from the hurtful sword.

11 Rid me, and deliver me from the hand of strange children, whose mouth speaketh vanity, and their right hand *is* a right hand of falsehood:

12 That our sons *may be* as plants grown up in their youth; *that* our daughters *may be* as corner stones, polished *after* the similitude of a palace:

13 *That* our garners *may be* full, affording all manner of store: *that* our sheep may bring forth thousands and ten thousands in our streets:

14 *That* our oxen *may be* strong to labour; *that there be* no breaking in, nor going out; that *there be* no complaining in our streets.

15 Happy *is that* people, that is in such a case: *yea,* happy *is that* people, whose God *is* the Lord.

What was a psaltery and a ten-stringed instrument? (144:9) The psaltery "was a stringed instrument of music to accompany the voice" and in many instances in the Bible "is translated *viol*. The ancient viol was a six-stringed guitar" (*Smith's Bible Dictionary*, "Psaltery"). "[The] *ten-stringed lyre* [was a] musical instrument made of wood, probably of Syrian origin. It may have looked something like a modern guitar and was played like a harp" (*Quest Study Bible* [2011], 900).

Why did David compare the daughters of Zion to cornerstones? (144:12) "Much in the Hebraic tradition of the scriptures deals with sons and priesthood principles. Yet so often we fail to recognize how many stunningly beautiful things are said about women—our mothers and daughters and sisters. What could be more inspiring than to think of our daughters as the corner stones of a palace, even corner stones of the temple—like unto Christ, who is 'the chief corner stone' of the Church and of our lives [see Ephesians 2:20]" (Holland, *For Times of Trouble*, 150).

What is one way we can achieve happiness as a people? (144:15) "Who are the happy people today? Not those who forsake the Lord and devote themselves entirely to the pleasures of life and the physical things of the world. The truly happy people are those who have faith in the Lord and keep the laws of the gospel, those who forget self in their desire and effort to bless others. . . . One has true joy when he knows that he pleases God, and again, when he is assured that God is pleased with him" (Anderson, "Road to Happiness," 29, 31; see also Mosiah 2:41; 4 Nephi 1:15–18).

Why is this psalm of David unique? (Psalm 145 superscription) "The whole book of Psalms is called, in Hebrew, *Tehillim*, 'Praises'; but only this one is called 'David's Psalm of praise' in a superscription. The last of this series of eight psalms of David, Psalm 145 is also a prelude to the remaining group of Hallelujah Psalms, each of which begins with *hallelujah*, 'praise ye Jehovah'" (Rasmussen, *Latter-day Saint Commentary on the Old Testament*, 467).

Psalm 145:1–7. The Lord Deserves Great Praise

Why does David use so many names for the Lord? (145:1–7) "In the Psalms, eleven of which were sung on festive days in honor of royalty, there are many composite names—sentence names or titles—such as the 'God of Gods,' 'the Most High God,' '[Jehovah] the Exalted,' and 'the Most High [Jehovah].' Some Psalms are 'a litany of sacred names' as is Psalm 145, which introduces new titles in verses 1, 3, 5, 6, and 7. Praise here becomes synonymous with prayer and vice versa. In the Psalms, the most frequent order of praising is first of [Jehovah], then of his works, and finally his name" (Madsen, "Putting on the Names," 461).

How can we share the Lord's "mighty acts" through our generations? (145:4–6) Elder Jeffrey R. Holland testified: "We ought to bear testimony often. We certainly ought to bear testimony to those who have not heard what we have heard and seen what we have seen. Among those several audiences, no group deserves to hear the testimony, receive stories, and hear of our convictions more than our own children" (*For Times of Trouble*, 105). When have you heard of mighty acts from your parents or grandparents? What opportunities do you have to share such mighty acts from your generation to another? ⊕

Psalm 145:8–21. The Lord Is Merciful and Holy

How does the Lord show compassion for His children? (145:8–9) "[The Lord] extends the hand of blessing, the hand of fellowship, to His children all the day long. The Father thus outlined the plan of salvation in the premortal councils. The central feature of that plan is the atonement of Jesus Christ. . . . Truly, 'grace and truth came by Jesus Christ' (John 1:17). Thus, we sing with humble fervor: 'Come, thou Fount of every blessing'" (Millet, *Grace Works*, 20–21).

PSALM 145

David proclaims the greatness and majesty of God—The Lord is good to all—His kingdom is an everlasting kingdom—He is near to all who call upon Him, and He preserves those who love Him.

David's *Psalm* of praise.

1 I will extol thee, my God, O king; and I will bless thy name for ever and ever.

2 Every day will I bless thee; and I will praise thy name for ever and ever.

3 Great *is* the LORD, and greatly to be praised; and his greatness *is* unsearchable.

4 One generation shall praise thy works to another, and shall declare thy mighty acts.

5 I will speak of the glorious honour of thy majesty, and of thy wondrous works.

6 And *men* shall speak of the might of thy terrible acts: and I will declare thy greatness.

7 They shall abundantly utter the memory of thy great goodness, and shall sing of thy righteousness.

8 The LORD *is* gracious, and full of compassion; slow to anger, and of great mercy.

9 The LORD *is* good to all: and his tender mercies *are* over all his works.

10 All thy works shall praise thee, O LORD; and thy saints shall bless thee.

11 They shall speak of the glory of thy kingdom, and talk of thy power;

12 To make known to the sons of men his mighty acts, and the glorious majesty of his kingdom.

13 Thy kingdom *is* an everlasting kingdom, and thy dominion *endureth* throughout all generations.

When will the saints speak of the glory to the Lord's kingdom? (145:10–13) "When will the Lord's kingdom come? When will it be set up again on earth as it once was . . . with power and magnificence? . . . It was reserved for our day, and the promised consummation is not far distant. What is more appropriate, then, than to have David himself prophesy of his even greater Son who will one day sit on his father's throne and reign over the house of Israel forever? . . .

"Those with spiritual insight find in the Psalms priceless pearls of wisdom and revelation. Truly, their pleasant words and sweet similitudes open the eyes of our understanding with reference to the coming reign of the Son of David" (McConkie, *Millennial Messiah*, 592, 594).

14 The LORD upholdeth all that fall, and raiseth up all *those that be* bowed down.

15 The eyes of all wait upon thee; and thou givest them their meat in due season.

16 Thou openest thine hand, and satisfiest the desire of every living thing.

In what way does the Lord "[uphold] all that fall"? (145:14–16) Elder Jeffrey R. Holland said: "Nothing is more certain in the scriptures (and in the psalms) than that God will not falter or fail us, that He sleeps not neither does He slumber, that when we are weary and can run no longer He will lift us on the wings of eagles. The intent of this book is to show that divine love for us, to show God's light shining in the dark places of our lives. But such an outreach to those in darkness or difficulty would not be complete (or even responsible) if it did not conclude with the understanding that we should never *choose* darkness, we should never wallow in despair, we should never make a habit of courting trouble or looking for it if we haven't had any recently" (*For Times of Trouble*, 152–53).

17 The LORD *is* righteous in all his ways, and holy in all his works.

18 The LORD *is* nigh unto all them that call upon him, to all that call upon him in truth.

19 He will fulfil the desire of them that fear him: he also will hear their cry, and will save them.

20 The LORD preserveth all them that love him: but all the wicked will he destroy.

21 My mouth shall speak the praise of the LORD: and let all flesh bless his holy name for ever and ever.

Why do we see the word "all" so many times in this psalm? (145:17–18) David used the word *all* at least twelve times in this psalm. "The word *all* appears twice in each of these verses, and another three times before the psalm concludes, . . . emphasizing God's incomparability" (*New Oxford Annotated Bible*, 891). In these two verses we learn that because of *all* that the Lord is, He will be near *all* those "that call upon him." No one left out; no exceptions.

What do we learn from David's request to bless God's name? (145:21) David begins this psalm with "I will bless thy name for ever and ever," and ends it with "let all flesh bless his holy name for ever and ever." This is known as an *inclusio*, "a literary device where the writer states a theme or idea at both the beginning and end of a story. It's intended to introduce and conclude a main point. Everything in-between is to be read with the inclusio theme in mind. When you think of inclusio, think bookends" (Weis, "Inclusio and the Gospels").

PSALM 146

Happy are they whose hope is in the Lord—The Lord frees the prisoners, loves the righteous, and reigns forever.

1 Praise ye the LORD. Praise the LORD, O my soul.

2 While I live will I praise the LORD: I will sing praises unto my God while I have any being.

3 Put not your trust in princes, *nor* in the son of man, in whom *there is* no help.

4 His breath goeth forth, he returneth to his earth; in that very day his thoughts perish.

5 Happy *is he* that *hath* the God of Jacob for his help, whose hope *is* in the LORD his God:

6 Which made heaven, and earth, the sea, and all that therein *is:* which keepeth truth for ever:

Psalm 146:1–10. Happy Is the Person Who Goes to the Lord for Help

Why shouldn't we put our trust in princes or men? (146:3) "Trusting in man—either common or extraordinary (rulers)—is a gross error, and [Psalm] 60:11–12, which states that the 'help of man is *worthless*,' could have been part of the influence which persuaded Nephi to say: 'I will not put my trust in the arm of flesh; for I know that cursed is he that putteth his trust in the arm of flesh' (2 Ne. 4:34). It is clear from the Old Testament that trusting in men is not only foolish and disappointing but also a most serious breach of the covenant relationship between God and Israel" (Burton, "Nature of God in the Psalms," 427fn5).

Why does hope in the Lord engender happiness? (146:5) "The scriptures are clear and certain about the importance of hope. The Apostle Paul taught that the scriptures were written to the end that we 'might have hope' [Romans 15:4]. Hope has the power to fill our lives with happiness [see Psalm 146:5]. Its absence—when this desire of our heart is delayed—can make 'the heart sick' [Proverbs 13:12]. Hope is a gift of the Spirit [see Moroni 8:26]. It is a hope that through the Atonement of Jesus Christ and the power of His

The Hallelujah Psalms (Psalms 146–150)

The last five psalms of the Book of Psalms are known as the Hallelujah Psalms. One reason for this grouping is that each psalm begins and ends with the word *hallelujah*. Bruce R. McConkie explained:

"One of the most interesting of all the prophetic pronouncements revealing that Jehovah and Christ are one and the same in person and identity is the great liturgical call of praise given to each of them by inspired authors. Let us note with particularity the words used and their meaning both in the original Hebrew and in the tongues into which they have been transliterated.

"*Yahweh* is the name of the God of the Hebrews. The Anglicized or English rendition of this name is *Jehovah*. The shortened form of *Yahweh* is *Yah*, and the contracted form of *Jehovah (Jahveh* or *Yahweh)* is *Jah*. Thus David writes: 'Sing unto God, sing praises to his name: extol him that rideth upon the heavens by his name JAH, and rejoice before him' (Ps. 68:4). Most Old Testament passages containing the name *Jah* (for *Jehovah*) have been translated *Lord*.

"*Halleluyah* is the Hebrew term meaning 'Praise ye Yah,' or as we would say, 'praise ye the Lord.' The transliterated form of *Halleluyah* is *Hallelujah (Hallelu-Jah)*. It is thus clear how ancient Israel sang praises to her God who was the Lord Jehovah" (McConkie, *Promised Messiah*, 111).

Resurrection, we shall be raised unto life eternal and this because of our faith in the Savior [see Moroni 7:41]" (Uchtdorf, "Infinite Power of Hope," 21). ⊕

7 Which executeth judgment for the oppressed: which giveth food to the hungry. The LORD looseth the prisoners:

8 The LORD openeth *the eyes of* the blind: the LORD raiseth them that are bowed down: the LORD loveth the righteous:

Why does the Lord help the disadvantaged? (146:7–9) "All those who are marginal and helpless are depicted as the object of God's concern, care, and active assistance. Thus, we read of the oppressed . . . and those who are characterized as 'humble' or humbled by the circumstances of their lives. . . . God is represented as especially concerned with the humble, the stranger, the widow and the fatherless. They were the most defenseless members of biblical society, virtually helpless. They had no given place in the communal structure and no one to defend them, if not God. Perhaps this is why they are mentioned repeatedly as special recipients of God's concern in so many psalms" (Polish, *Keeping Faith with the Psalms,* 275–76).

9 The LORD preserveth the strangers; he relieveth the fatherless and widow: but the way of the wicked he turneth upside down.

10 The LORD shall reign for ever, *even* thy God, O Zion, unto all generations. Praise ye the LORD.

What does it mean that the Lord will turn the wicked upside down? (146:9) A literal translation from Hebrew is "'causeth to turn aside' (into the trackless desert, where it disappears)" (*John Dummelow's Commentary* [on Psalm 146:9]). In other words, the Lord will "turn aside" the wicked from the paths of the righteous. "God's justice is complete; *the way of the wicked he brings to ruin,* before their plans reach fruition" (*New Oxford Annotated Bible,* 891).

PSALMS 147–148

Praise the Lord for His power—His understanding is infinite—He sends His commandments, His word, His statutes, and His judgments unto Israel.

Let all things praise the Lord: men and angels, the heavenly bodies, the elements and the earth, and all things thereon.

Summary of Psalms 147–148

Both of these hymns, as part of the Hallelujah Psalms, ask all of God's creations to praise Him for His power and mercy, for His laws, commandments, and revelations. One specific way the Lord shall extend His power and mercy is when He "gathereth together the outcasts of Israel" (Psalm 147:2). "The physical gathering of Israel means that the covenant people will be 'gathered home to the lands of their inheritance, and shall be established in all their lands of promise' (2 Nephi 9:2)" (*Gospel Principles*, 248). And also in many other ways the Lord provides for His people, "even of the children of Israel, a people near unto him. Praise ye the LORD" (Psalm 148:14).

Psalm 149:1–9. Let Israel Rejoice in the Lord

Why are we asked to praise the Lord in song? (149:1–2) "In our Latter-day Saint hymns, we sing praises to the Lord, pray unto the Lord, recite great religious truths—in effect sermons—and our minds and spirits are elevated and spiritually stimulated. . . .

"As we sing our hymns, let us be conscious of the beauty and import of each hymn, and as we do, our singing will deeply move our souls, bring us in closer harmony with the Holy Spirit, and strengthen our testimonies" (Richards, "LDS Hymns—Worshiping with Song," 22, 24). How have the hymns and other sacred music helped you to praise the Lord?

Why does the Lord take pleasure in those who are meek? (149:4) "Meekness is a defining attribute of the Redeemer and is distinguished by righteous responsiveness, willing submissiveness, and strong self-restraint.

"The Christlike quality of meekness often is misunderstood in our contemporary world. Meekness is strong, not weak; active, not passive; courageous, not timid; restrained, not excessive; modest, not self-aggrandizing; and gracious, not brash. A meek person is not easily provoked, pretentious, or overbearing and readily acknowledges the accomplishments of others" (Bednar, "Meek and Lowly of Heart," 32).

How does a "two-edged sword" relate to a person's mouth? (149:6) "A sword whose blade is sharpened on both sides is able to penetrate and cut at every contact point and with every movement. This means that it can be thrust more quickly and deeply and can cut more easily. . . .

"In his analogy of the armor of God, the Apostle Paul compared the sword of the Spirit to the word of God (see Ephesians 6:17).

"In the Bible, both the Greek and Hebrew words for *two-edged* mean 'two-mouthed,' referring to how the blade consumes what it touches. But because the mouth is also where speech is produced, the original Bible languages inherently contain an association between a two-edged sword and the word" ("Two-Edged Sword," 72, 73).

PSALM 149

Praise the Lord in the congregation of the Saints—He will beautify the meek with salvation.

1 Praise ye the LORD. Sing unto the LORD a new song, *and* his praise in the congregation of saints.

2 Let Israel rejoice in him that made him: let the children of Zion be joyful in their King.

3 Let them praise his name in the dance: let them sing praises unto him with the timbrel and harp.

4 For the LORD taketh pleasure in his people: he will beautify the meek with salvation.

5 Let the saints be joyful in glory: let them sing aloud upon their beds.

6 *Let* the high *praises* of God *be* in their mouth, and a twoedged sword in their hand;

7 To execute vengeance upon the heathen, *and* punishments upon the people;

Why does this psalm change from worship to exacting vengeance? (149:7–9) "Israel's unique honor has two sides: She has been granted salvation (in fact and in promise), and she has been armed to execute God's sentence of judgment on the world powers that have launched their attacks against the kingdom of God—she is the earthly contingent of the armies of the King of heaven" (*NIV Study Bible* [1995], 933). "The contrasts both reveal the nations to be powerless and emphasize the praiseworthiness of the Lord. While the Lord is to be praised as king and creator (v. 2), the kings of the nations are to be bound with iron fetters (v. 8)" (Prinsloo, "Psalms," 435).

8 To bind their kings with chains, and their nobles with fetters of iron;

9 To execute upon them the judgment written: this honour have all his saints. Praise ye the LORD.

What were the fetters and chains used to bind enemy kings and nobles? (149:8) "Fetters [are] shackles or chains used for binding prisoners either by the wrists or ankles. . . . Chains are used as a symbol of oppression or punishment (Ps. 149:8). . . . Iron is used in scripture as the symbol of *strength*, . . . of severe *affliction*, . . . [and a] harsh exercise of *power*" (*New Unger's Bible Dictionary*, 424, 217, 626). Binding nobles and kings in such a way was considered an act of humiliation.

PSALM 150

Praise God in His sanctuary—Let everything that has breath praise the Lord.

1 Praise ye the LORD. Praise God in his sanctuary: praise him in the firmament of his power.

2 Praise him for his mighty acts: praise him according to his excellent greatness.

Psalm 150:1–6. Let Everything That Breathes Praise the Lord

Why does this psalm repeat the invitation to praise God so many times? (150:1–6) "This is 'the grand Finale of the spiritual concert,' and worthily closes not only this little Hallelujah group [Psalms 146–150], but the whole Psalter [or Book of Psalms]" (*John Dummelow's Commentary* [on Psalm 150]). "This Psalm is without title and author in the Hebrew, and in all the ancient versions. It is properly the full chorus of all voices and instruments in the temple, at the conclusion of the grand Hallelujah" (*Adam Clarke's Commentary* [on Psalm 150]). ⊕

3 Praise him with the sound of the trumpet: praise him with the psaltery and harp.

4 Praise him with the timbrel and dance: praise him with stringed instruments and organs.

5 Praise him upon the loud cymbals: praise him upon the high sounding cymbals.

How did ancient Israel use music in worshiping the Lord? (150:3–5) "In its present form, Psalms preserves no understandable musical notation that might indicate what tunes accompanied the lyrics, what metrical measurements were used, where verses began and ended, etc. Although many of the unknown terms in the superscriptions . . . may very well provide such information, scholars have arrived at no general consensus about their meaning. The ancient traditions, where not entirely lacking, are of little help.

"The book of Psalms itself speaks much of its own musical nature and of music and musical instruments. Consider the following [example: Psalm 150:3–5]" (Burton, "Hymnal of Ancient Israel," 414).

How can the book of Psalms inspire us to "praise the Lord"? (150:6) "This final, grand hallelujah psalm begins each clause with *hallelu*, 'Praise ye.' . . . This is the book of Psalms, the book of praises, testimonies, supplications, outcries of despair, hope, confidence, and gratitude, and even more praises. They are voiced by ordinary people, priests, a king, other leaders, exiles. Their language is sometimes strange to us but often strangely familiar. Their times were different, long ago; but in the present many things are like their times. Thus the psalms are valuable for history, for heritage, and for worship" (Rasmussen, *Latter-day Saint Commentary on the Old Testament*, 470).

6 Let every thing that hath breath praise the
Lord. Praise ye the Lord.

Were There Other Ancient Psalms? (Psalm 150)

"Whereas the traditional Hebrew book of Psalms contains 150 psalms, the Septuagint (LXX) has 151. This has led scholars to wonder if in antiquity there were other ancient psalms that were not preserved because they did not make it into the canon. In 1956 a large psalm scroll, part of the Dead Sea Scrolls, was discovered in Cave 11 at Qumran. . . . Interspersed among the 41 canonical psalms on the scroll were eight other psalms: four non-canonical psalms known from other apocryphal works and four psalms that were previously unknown. From this remarkable scroll we learn that in antiquity there were different collections of psalms, some better attested than others. . . . Among the non-canonical psalms in 11 QPsa was a Hebrew copy of Psalm 151, which is also preserved in the Septuagint, in which David recounts his boyhood as a shepherd, how he was called and anointed by God, and how he went forth to fight Goliath.

"Psalm 151 (translated from the LXX):
"I was small among my brothers.
"and the youngest in my father's house;
"I tended my father's sheep.
"My hands made a harp;
"my fingers fashioned a lyre.
"And who would tell my Lord?
"The Lord himself; it is he who hears.
"It was he who sent his messenger
"and took me from my father's sheep,
"and anointed me with his anointing oil.
"My brothers were handsome and tall,
"but the Lord was not pleased with them.
"I went out to meet the Philistine,
"and he cursed me by his idols.
"But I drew his own sword;
"I beheaded him, and took away disgrace from the
"people of Israel." (NRSV)
(Holzapfel, et al., *Jehovah and the World of the Old Testament*, 237).

THE PROVERBS

Introduction

"The book of Proverbs contains many brief but wise statements about how to live a godly life. Although the book was written in ancient Israel, its messages remain applicable in the modern world. . . . [The reader] can learn wisdom that will help them draw closer to the Lord" (*Old Testament Seminary Teacher Material*, 605).

"A proverb is usually defined as 'a maxim, an adage, a pithy saying.' As such it represents an attempt to render concisely in words a lesson learned through experience. . . . The Hebrew word *māšāl* is usually rendered 'proverb' in the KJV, as it is in the title, 'The Proverbs.' . . . Additionally, the word *māšāl* is rendered as 'parable' more than a dozen times in the KJV, in passages such as Numbers 23:7; Psalm 49:4; Ezekiel 20:49; and Micah 2:4" (Pike, "Proverbs," 450).

A proverb is also a "distillation of a wise idea into a succinct, well-expressed form [which] made it easy to remember; if it were easier to remember it would be easier to pass from one generation to another. And this was the intent—to pass wisdom from the parent to the child" (Meservy, "How Did Proverbs Come to Be—and How Were They Used in Olden Times?" 60).

"The authorship of [Proverbs] is commonly ascribed to Solomon [see Prov. 1:1; 10:1; 25:1]. . . . According to the Book of 1 Kings, Solomon was a very wise man who was the author of a large number of proverbs [see 1 Kings 4:29–32]. . . . We can see no real reason to doubt that a good proportion of the proverbs ascribed to Solomon are really his, though at the same time admitting that they were collected, or 'copied out,' edited, and put into various collections at a later time" (Sperry, *Spirit of the Old Testament*, 77, 78–79).

The following is a helpful organization of Proverbs: "The first part (chapters 1–8) represents the admonitions, directions, and cautions of a teacher or parent to a student or child. The second part (chapters 9–22:16) contains the proverbs of Solomon proper [in the strictest sense]. The third part (chapters 22:17–25:28) again contains instructions of a teacher to a student. The fourth part (chapters 26–29) is stated to be a collection of Solomon's proverbs made by men (probably Isaiah, Hosea, and Micah) under the direction of King Hezekiah. The final portion (chapters 30–31) forms a kind of appendix in which the teacher, Agur, instructs his pupils, Ithiel and Ucal, and an unnamed mother instructs her son Lemuel" (Pearson, *Old Testament*, 52–53).

The commentary provided for Proverbs 10–30 in this volume will change from a sequential review to a topical study of the proverbs. This approach may assist the reader to better appreciate the breadth of the practical counsel found in Proverbs.

CHAPTER 1

The fear of the Lord is the beginning of knowledge—If sinners entice you, do not consent—Those who hearken to wisdom will dwell safely.

1 The proverbs of Solomon the son of David, king of Israel;

2 To know wisdom and instruction; to perceive the words of understanding;

3 To receive the instruction of wisdom, justice, and judgment, and equity;

4 To give subtilty to the simple, to the young man knowledge and discretion.

5 A wise *man* will hear, and will increase learning; and a man of understanding shall attain unto wise counsels:

6 To understand a proverb, and the interpretation; the words of the wise, and their dark sayings.

Proverbs 1:1–7. Proverbs Help Us Gain Knowledge and Wisdom

Why is wisdom so valuable? (1:1–7) "Wisdom is a gift of God obtained only by diligent searching, and God will watch over and protect those who receive it and remain faithful to it. This promise can be understood only when one remembers that to Israel, wisdom meant obedience to God's laws" (*Old Testament Student Manual: 1 Kings–Malachi*, 14).

"As it is used in Proverbs, wisdom encompasses many things. Primarily it is the right way to act—and included in that idea is righteousness. If one is wise, one will automatically choose to act the way God would have him or her act, which is righteousness. Wisdom is also the desire and ability to learn righteousness" (Muhlestein, *Essential Old Testament Companion*, 346).

Why was Solomon exceptionally wise? (1:1–2) The Lord blessed Solomon with "a wise and an understanding heart" which he exercised in helpful and edifying ways (see 1 Kings 3–4, 10). In modern revelation the Lord states: "Verily I say unto you, to some is given, by the Spirit of God, the word of wisdom" (D&C 46:17). Why should we seek to obtain the gift of wisdom? How should it help us bless others?

Why will the Lord help those who are wise to hear? (1:5) "The question is never whether God is speaking to us, but rather, can we hear? Are we hearkening to the voice of the Spirit? Just as there are many mechanical sounds that drown out the human voice, so the adversary will use every conceivable method to create road noise along the highway of life in an effort to drown out the voice of the Spirit" (Kapp, *Rejoice! His Promises Are Sure*, 74–75). How does exercising wisdom help a person to recognize the voice of the Spirit?

What are "dark sayings"? (1:6) "The first verses of Proverbs state that one purpose of this collection of wisdom is to help men understand the 'dark sayings' of the wise. The Hebrew idiom *dark sayings* connotes riddles or puzzles. The idea here is that the sayings of the wise are hidden or puzzling to those who are not wise" (*Old Testament Student Manual: 1 Kings–Malachi*, 13–14).

Bible commentator Adam Clarke adds that *dark sayings* are "enigmas [some known thing concealed under obscure language] or riddles. . . . I believe parables, such as those delivered by our Lord, nearly express the meaning" (*Adam Clarke's Commentary* [on Proverbs 1:6]).

7 ¶ The fear of the LORD *is* the beginning of knowledge: *but* fools despise wisdom and instruction.

How can a "fear of the Lord" increase our knowledge? (1:7) *Fear* in this verse "is not dread, but 'reverence of God expressed in submission to His will.' This is in fact the basic sense of 'fear of the Lord' throughout the [Old Testament], where it might often be rendered 'reverential awe' or even 'faith.' . . . But why is fear of God the 'beginning' or the starting point? Because the conviction that God is—and is to be honored—the only door that opens to true wisdom. Only when all is oriented to the Lord can true moral knowledge or wisdom be gained" (Richards, *Bible Reader's Companion*, 387).

Godly fear "is the beginning of knowledge" (Proverbs 1:7), a "strong confidence" (14:26), and "a fountain of life" (14:27). ⊕

Why does Proverbs teach that it is foolish to "despise wisdom and instruction"? (1:7) "A single bad choice may cause one an entire lifetime of suffering. We can learn to make better judgments by studying models of excellence and making firm, long term decisions based on God's standards of right and wrong. We can also increase the quality of our judgment by learning to understand what causes weakness and foolishness. . . . With a well-trained conscience and a set of good habits, we can learn to increase our judgment. Too many faults and too many weaknesses can make fools out of even wise men, whereas the integrity and strength of high personal codes of honor will put inferior procedures out of bounds where they are not eligible for consideration" (Sill, *Wealth of Wisdom*, 87–88).

Proverbs 1:8–33. Counsel and Appeals to Youth

8 My son, hear the instruction of thy father, and forsake not the law of thy mother:

9 For they *shall be* an ornament of grace unto thy head, and chains about thy neck.

10 ¶ My son, if sinners entice thee, consent thou not.

Who is "my son" referencing in verse 8? (1:8–10) Israelite wisdom literature includes "the addressing of wise instructions to children, especially sons. . . . While in some cases the son may have been the child of the parents giving instructions, this is mainly a literary device to represent admonition from a superior to a subordinate. One of several examples in Proverbs is: 'My son, hear the instruction of thy father, and forsake not the law of thy mother' (Prov 1:8)" (Holzapfel, et al., *Jehovah and the World of the Old Testament*, 239). ⊕

Summary of Proverbs 1:11–19

Wisdom's enemies include peers who entice one to seek gain from other people through dishonest means. They are like birds who will be caught in a net.

Proverbs 1:20–33. Wisdom Is Personified, Warning Those Who Would Ignore Her

Why is wisdom personified as a woman? (1:20) "Personification, especially in poetic texts, is commonly employed in scripture as a literary device for helping render abstract qualities or ideas more concretely. . . . One of the most striking features of Israelite wisdom literature is the personification of wisdom as a woman. . . . Although scholars have suggested that Lady Wisdom represents a pagan goddess in sanitized form, it is clear that in the biblical context 'she' is both an attribute of and a gift from God . . . 'Her' voice is the Lord's voice; 'her' teachings are the Lord's teachings" (Pike, "Proverbs," 456). See additional examples in Proverbs 1:21; 4:5–9; Mosiah 8:20. ⊕

Why is wisdom described as crying out in public? (1:20–21) "Wisdom is represented as calling out its message in the streets and public thoroughfares. . . . The prophets also proclaimed their message in the streets and public places" (Guthrie and Motyer, *New Bible Commentary: Revised*, 551). The call of wisdom in public places also suggests that wisdom is important in daily living for all people (see *Expositor's Bible Commentary [Abridged]*, 943).

What does it mean to "turn" at reproof? (1:23) This passage is about the principle of repentance. "In the scriptures the word *repentance* is translated from the Hebrew word *shuv* (Old Testament) and the Greek word *metanoia* (New Testament) and generally means 'to turn' or to 'turn around' by turning *from* sin and turning *to* God. Repentance is a comprehensive turning or changing of one's heart (desires), mind (attitudes), and behavior (deeds)" (Top, "Repentance," 523).

What does it mean that God has stretched out his hand? (1:24) The Lord's stretched-out hand may sometimes be viewed as an act of mercy. However, John Gee uses similar passages in ancient scripture to demonstrate that "a stretched forth hand . . . is a hand administering punishment ['his anger is not turned away' see Isa. 5:25, 9:12, 10:4]. The Hebrew is also clear on the subject. The idiom is *yadô neṭûyâ*, which means that the hand is hanging over, threatening or bent. It is thus a threatening gesture" ("Different Way," 114).

20 ¶ Wisdom crieth without; she uttereth her voice in the streets:

21 She crieth in the chief place of concourse, in the openings of the gates: in the city she uttereth her words, *saying,*

22 How long, ye simple ones, will ye love simplicity? and the scorners delight in their scorning, and fools hate knowledge?

23 Turn you at my reproof: behold, I will pour out my spirit unto you, I will make known my words unto you.

24 ¶ Because I have called, and ye refused; I have stretched out my hand, and no man regarded;

25 But ye have set at nought all my counsel, and would none of my reproof:

26 I also will laugh at your calamity; I will mock when your fear cometh;

27 When your fear cometh as desolation, and your destruction cometh as a whirlwind; when distress and anguish cometh upon you.

28 Then shall they call upon me, but I will not answer; they shall seek me early, but they shall not find me:

29 For that they hated knowledge, and did not choose the fear of the LORD:

30 They would none of my counsel: they despised all my reproof.

31 Therefore shall they eat of the fruit of their own way, and be filled with their own devices.

32 For the turning away of the simple shall slay them, and the prosperity of fools shall destroy them.

33 But whoso hearkeneth unto me shall dwell safely, and shall be quiet from fear of evil.

CHAPTER 2

The Lord gives wisdom, knowledge, and understanding—Walk in the way of good men.

1 My son, if thou wilt receive my words, and hide my commandments with thee;

2 So that thou incline thine ear unto wisdom, *and* apply thine heart to understanding;

3 Yea, if thou criest after knowledge, *and* liftest up thy voice for understanding;

4 If thou seekest her as silver, and searchest for her as *for* hid treasures;

5 Then shalt thou understand the fear of the LORD, and find the knowledge of God.

6 For the LORD giveth wisdom: out of his mouth *cometh* knowledge and understanding.

7 He layeth up sound wisdom for the righteous: *he is* a buckler to them that walk uprightly.

8 He keepeth the paths of judgment, and preserveth the way of his saints.

Proverbs 2:1–9. Seeking for the Lord's Wisdom, Knowledge, and Understanding

Why is seeking wisdom, knowledge, and understanding from God vital? (2:1–6) "The Book of Mormon specifically relates God's wisdom to his knowledge [see 2 Nephi 2:24]. . . . It is possible . . . for [one] to be knowledgeable about many things and still be short on wisdom. . . .

"The inspiration of the Lord can and often does compensate for unknown facts—that is, for lack of knowledge. For example, if a stranger at the crossroads, not knowing which way to turn, can receive inspiration from God, his decision will be as wise as if he had known all the facts. Why? Because God 'knoweth all things.' Inspiration from him is an expression of total wisdom" (Romney, "Converting Knowledge into Wisdom," 5).

What is a "buckler"? (2:7) "A buckler is a small shield generally held with the left hand to stop or parry the blows of an enemy. Speaking in a symbolic sense, the Lord is a buckler 'to all them that trust in him' (2 Sam. 22:31; Ps. 18:2) and 'to them that walk uprightly' (Prov. 2:7), meaning that he will shield and protect the righteous from the fiery darts and evil weaponry of the devil and his host" (McConkie and Parry, *Guide to Scriptural Symbols*, 27).

9 Then shalt thou understand righteousness, and judgment, and equity; *yea,* every good path.

Summary of Proverbs 2:10–22

The benefits of receiving wisdom from the Lord include discretion, understanding, and protection from evil men and women.

CHAPTER 3

Write mercy and truth upon the tablet of your heart—Trust in the Lord—Honor Him with your substance—Whom the Lord loves He corrects—Happy is the man who finds wisdom.

1 My son, forget not my law; but let thine heart keep my commandments:

2 For length of days, and long life, and peace, shall they add to thee.

3 Let not mercy and truth forsake thee: bind them about thy neck; write them upon the table of thine heart:

4 So shalt thou find favour and good understanding in the sight of God and man.

5 ¶ Trust in the LORD with all thine heart; and lean not unto thine own understanding.

Proverbs 3:1–8. Keeping the Lord's Commandments and Trusting in Him Will Bring His Guidance and Blessings

What blessings come from keeping the Lord's commandments? (3:1–2) "Obedience and righteousness lead to blessings, which lead to joy. Conversely, disobedience and wickedness lead to punishment, which leads to sorrow. . . . The pathway to happiness begins with righteousness through obedience to the commandments. The commandments have been given to us as a divine playbook to direct us away from many of the calamities of mortality. . . . Some people find it counterintuitive that the commandments are at the trailhead of the path to happiness rather than something to be carried along the way. . . . When we begin with righteousness and obedience, we will end with blessings and joy" (Stevenson, "Safety and Peace of Keeping the Commandments," 64, 65).

What does it mean to trust with all our heart? (3:5) "This life is an experience in profound trust—trust in Jesus Christ, trust in His teachings, trust in our capacity as led by the Holy Spirit to obey those teachings for happiness now and for a purposeful, supremely happy

When Wisdom Enters the Heart, We Are Delivered from Evil (Proverbs 2:10–12)

"Paul's warnings describe apostasy and other dangers of our day. Some of these perils are contrary to God's purposes and are championed by persuasive people possessing more ability than morality, more knowledge than wisdom. Their rationalization breeds justification. The Bible affirms that the 'way of a fool is right in his own eyes' (Prov. 12:15). Indeed, individuals with malignity of purpose often wear the mask of honesty. So we must constantly be on guard.

"To build a house straight and strong, you do not choose crooked boards. So to build your eternal destiny, you cannot—you must not—limit lessons only to those warped to exclude revelation from God. The Book of Mormon offers this note of caution and hope:

"'Seek not to counsel the Lord, but to take counsel from his hand. For behold, ye yourselves know that he counseleth in wisdom, and in justice, and in great mercy, over all his works' (Jacob 4:10). . . .

"The light of the gospel of Jesus Christ beams as the hope of the world. . . . The Lord hides His wisdom from no one: 'If any of you lack wisdom, let him ask of God' (James 1:5)" (Nelson, "Where Is Wisdom?" 8).

eternal existence. To trust means to obey willingly without knowing the end from the beginning (see Prov. 3:5–7). To produce fruit, your trust in the Lord must be more powerful and enduring than your confidence in your own personal feelings and experience" (Scott, "Trust in the Lord," 17).

6 In all thy ways acknowledge him, and he shall direct thy paths.

How can I acknowledge the Lord in all my ways? (3:6) "Our meek and perfect Lord is not asking for mere ritual acknowledgment or for superficial praise of the tongue. . . . In addition to *acknowledging* Him by obeying Him, *confessing* His hand means to *avow* [declare openly and without shame, with a view to defend]. . . .

"There is a tendency to acknowledge only 'big blessings' without acknowledging the multiplicity of 'small blessings'" (Maxwell, *That Ye May Believe*, 25, 30).

"One's realization about Jesus' role may commence with only an *acknowledgment* of Him and ripen into real *appreciation*, then into deep *admiration*, and then proceed into genuine *adoration* and, finally, into reverent *emulation*. Our ultimate praise, therefore, is to pattern our lives after His" (Maxwell, *One More Strain of Praise*, 52).

7 ¶ Be not wise in thine own eyes: fear the LORD, and depart from evil.

8 It shall be health to thy navel, and marrow to thy bones.

What happens when we are "wise in [our] own eyes"? (3:7) "This description refers to those who believe they know more than God or their fellow beings" (Parry, et al., *Understanding Isaiah*, 58). The Book of Mormon cautions against "the vainness, and the frailities, and the foolishness of men! When they are learned they think they are wise, and they hearken not unto the counsel of God, for they set it aside, supposing they know of themselves, wherefore, their wisdom is foolishness and it profiteth them not. And they shall perish" (2 Nephi 9:28; see also Isaiah 5:21). "The wise among us know the source of all that is good and we trust in him. Those doing otherwise come short of the glory of God and will never obtain a fulness of truth" (McConkie and Millet, *Doctrinal Commentary on the Book of Mormon*, 1:254).

Proverbs 3:9–12. Honor the Lord with Your Substance and Be Humble with His Chastisement

9 Honour the LORD with thy substance, and with the firstfruits of all thine increase:

10 So shall thy barns be filled with plenty, and thy presses shall burst out with new wine.

How do we "honour the Lord with [our] substance"? (3:9–10) "The sacrifices and offerings that were required under the Law of Moses are referenced here, as are the statutes revealed in these latter days. Tithing fulfills in part the requirements for these commandments. Greater commandments invite us to contribute even more for the building up of the Kingdom of God and the establishment of Zion. . . .

"As counterintuitive as it may seem, the presenting of tithes and offerings bring temporal blessings beyond measure to the obedient. The Lord promises an abundance that cannot be adequately held in barns and barrels" (Hyde, *Comprehensive Commentary [Proverbs]*, 13).

Why should we not despise the Lord's chastening? (3:11–12) Our loving God may chasten us for various reasons. He does so when we need to forgive others (D&C 64:8), if we murmur against Him or His servants (1 Nephi 16:25; D&C 75:7–8), when we neglect family members (D&C 93:50), when we haven't been praying as He has commanded (Ether 2:14), when we attempt to hide our sins (D&C 58:60), if it is the only way we can learn obedience (D&C 105:6), to strengthen and purify us (D&C 90:36; Mosiah 23:21), and because He loves us (Proverbs 3:11–12; Revelation 3:19; Helaman 15:3; D&C 95:1; see also Heb. 12:6–7, 9–10). (See Olson, "Chasten," 103–4.)

11 ¶ My son, despise not the chastening of the Lord; neither be weary of his correction:

12 For whom the Lord loveth he correcteth; even as a father the son *in whom* he delighteth.

Summary of Proverbs 3:13–35

Wisdom is a most valuable possession, more so than the riches of the earth. The Lord used wisdom in the creation. We are urged to keep and value the Lord's wisdom to bless and protect our lives. Instructions are offered on relationships with others.

CHAPTER 4

Keep the commandments and live—With all your getting, get understanding—Go not in the way of evil men.

Summary of Proverbs 4:1–4

An appeal addressed to children by a loving father. Perhaps Solomon speaks the words of his father, David, who urged his son to keep the commandments.

Proverbs 4:5–13. Get Wisdom and Understanding

5 Get wisdom, get understanding: forget *it* not; neither decline from the words of my mouth.

6 Forsake her not, and she shall preserve thee: love her, and she shall keep thee.

7 Wisdom *is* the principal thing; *therefore* get wisdom: and with all thy getting get understanding.

How does one seek understanding? (4:7) "Understanding in this context follows intelligence, knowledge, experience, wisdom, and promptings from the Holy Ghost—all of which lead us to knowing and doing what is right. . . . To manage [the] very important things that we 'get,' we must also obtain 'understanding,' as the scripture teaches. This understanding comes through an interdependence of study and prayer. Said another way, we must trust in and rely on the Lord Jesus Christ. Alma described this when he likened the word unto a seed. As he stated, 'It beginneth to enlighten my *understanding*, yea, it beginneth to be delicious to me' (Alma 32:28; emphasis added)" (Stevenson, "With All Thy Getting, Get Understanding," 30).

8 Exalt her, and she shall promote thee: she shall bring thee to honour, when thou dost embrace her.

How does one "exalt" wisdom? (4:8) "To exalt something is to elevate it or, in the case of wisdom, to make it a priority. Doctrine and Covenants 136:32 teaches us we can gain more wisdom by 'humbling [ourselves] and calling upon the Lord'" (Valletta, et al., *Old Testament for Latter-day Saint Families*, 447).

9 She shall give to thine head an ornament of grace: a crown of glory shall she deliver to thee.

10 Hear, O my son, and receive my sayings; and the years of thy life shall be many.

How does wisdom give an "ornament of grace" and a "crown of glory"? (4:9) Ornaments and crowns were part of the apparel at weddings and feasts (see *Zondervan King James Version Commentary*, 833). "The image of a marriage feast is given substance with the bestowing of the traditional symbols of union by the bride (wisdom) and her protégé (groom).... In the metaphorical sense it could also be paralleled with Isaiah 28:5, where God becomes a 'glorious crown, a beautiful wreath' for the Israelites" (Walton, et al., *IVP Bible Background Commentary*, 562).

11 I have taught thee in the way of wisdom; I have led thee in right paths.

12 When thou goest, thy steps shall not be straitened; and when thou runnest, thou shalt not stumble.

13 Take fast hold of instruction; let *her* not go: keep her; for she *is* thy life.

Where does the path of wisdom lead? (4:11–13) The wise father taught that to follow the "way of wisdom" and the "right paths" is possible if one takes "fast hold of instruction" and "let her not go" (vv. 11, 13). This might remind us of Lehi's vision in the Book of Mormon, where one "group of people witnessed by Lehi obtained the path, pressed forward in righteousness, caught hold of the rod of iron, and held fast to that rod.... It would appear that this was the one group of persons who remained steadfast to the gospel cause, proved faithful to their covenants with the Lord, and qualified for those transcendent privileges associated with exaltation in the highest heaven" (McConkie and Millet, *Doctrinal Commentary on the Book of Mormon*, 1:60).

Summary of Proverbs 4:14–27

A faithful father admonishes his children to stay off the dark and wicked path of evil men and, instead, concentrate on the path of righteous living.

Summary of Proverbs 5

This chapter exhorts a son against associating with immoral women (vv. 1–6). He is taught that the consequences of infidelity are mourning and regret (vv. 7–14). He is encouraged to find blessings in fidelity to one's wife (vv. 15–23).

Proverbs 6:1–5. Avoid Surety, Especially with Strangers

What is "surety" and is why it denounced? (6:1–5)
"These verses warn against putting up *surety* (see 11:15), or cosigning a loan. This does not mean we should never be generous or helpful if we have the means, only that we should not promise what we cannot deliver. In Solomon's day, a cosigner who could not pay could lose all he had and be reduced to slavery besides. Even though laws differ today, inability to pay a debt is still a form of bondage and can be a serious problem. Modern conditions are different than in [Old Testament] times, but the warning still applies" (*NKJV Study Bible* [2007], 971). Notice in verse 1 there is a special warning against being surety for strangers, perhaps foreign traders (see Guthrie and Motyer, *New Bible Commentary: Revised*, 556).

Proverbs 6:6–15. Counsel to Avoid Laziness and Divisiveness

What can the sluggard learn from the ant? (6:6–8)
A *sluggard* is a habitually lazy person (see *Merriam-Webster.com Dictionary*, "sluggard"). "Since the ant is a lowly creature, this comparison is somewhat degrading. But the sluggard can learn diligence from its ways. . . . The description of the ant's activities shows that although it appears to have no leader (even though it actually does have organization and cooperation), it provides for the future with great industry. The classic example of such foresight and industry is Joseph in [Genesis] 41" (*Expositor's Bible Commentary [Abridged]*, 950–51).

What does this proverb imply about the importance of work and the consequences of laziness? (6:9–11)
"Sleep in proper measure and at the right time is a good thing, but too much sleep and sleeping at the wrong times will lead to poverty and actual endangerment. . . .

CHAPTER 5

Those who associate with immoral women will go down to hell—Rejoice with the wife of your youth.

CHAPTER 6

Six things that the Lord hates are named—Those who commit adultery destroy their own souls.

1 My son, if thou be surety for thy friend, *if* thou hast stricken thy hand with a stranger,

2 Thou art snared with the words of thy mouth, thou art taken with the words of thy mouth.

3 Do this now, my son, and deliver thyself, when thou art come into the hand of thy friend; go, humble thyself, and make sure thy friend.

4 Give not sleep to thine eyes, nor slumber to thine eyelids.

5 Deliver thyself as a roe from the hand *of the hunter,* and as a bird from the hand of the fowler.

6 ¶ Go to the ant, thou sluggard; consider her ways, and be wise:

7 Which having no guide, overseer, or ruler,

8 Provideth her meat in the summer, *and* gathereth her food in the harvest.

9 How long wilt thou sleep, O sluggard? when wilt thou arise out of thy sleep?

10 *Yet* a little sleep, a little slumber, a little folding of the hands to sleep:

11 So shall thy poverty come as one that travelleth, and thy want as an armed man.

Hard work is an antidote to poverty (see 12:11; 14:23; 28:19)" (*Zondervan KJV Commentary*, 836).

"We, likewise, speak of 'working out our salvation,' of the 'law of the harvest,' and of the 'sweat of the brow' [see Moses 5:1; see also JST, Gen. 4:1]. These are not idle phrases. Instead, they underscore the importance of work. In fact . . . work is always a spiritual necessity even if, for some, work is not an economic necessity" (Maxwell, "Put Your Shoulder to the Wheel," 37–38).

12 ¶ A naughty person, a wicked man, walketh with a froward mouth.

13 He winketh with his eyes, he speaketh with his feet, he teacheth with his fingers;

14 Frowardness *is* in his heart, he deviseth mischief continually; he soweth discord.

15 Therefore shall his calamity come suddenly; suddenly shall he be broken without remedy.

What is the "naughty person" guilty of? (6:12–15)
"There is wry humor in the characterization of the 'naughty person'; he is 'a good-for-nothing,' according to the Hebrew term used; his perverseness (Prov. 6:12*a*) is implemented by expressions, gestures, and motions calculated to disarm, deceive, drive wedges of doubt, and sow discord. For all this he is to be punished" (Rasmussen, *Latter-day Saint Commentary on the Old Testament*, 474).

"Such a person deliberately divides people from one another, using subtle, manipulative gestures and words. God hates division and strife and those who deliberately cause it in friendships, family or churches can expect God's judgment" (*Quest Study Bible* [1994], 872).

16 ¶ These six *things* doth the LORD hate: yea, seven *are* an abomination unto him:

17 A proud look, a lying tongue, and hands that shed innocent blood,

18 An heart that deviseth wicked imaginations, feet that be swift in running to mischief,

19 A false witness *that* speaketh lies, and he that soweth discord among brethren.

20 ¶ My son, keep thy father's commandment, and forsake not the law of thy mother:

Proverbs 6:16–23. Seven Sins and Keeping Parental Commandments

What are "thy father's commandments"? (6:20)
These are most likely "the words of Solomon to his son; and not to his son only, in a strict natural relation, but to everyone that came to him for and put himself under his instruction; and to everyone that stood in such a relation to a religious father; for not the divine Being, the Father of all, is here meant, according to some Jewish writers; though the commandment no doubt is the commandment of God taught by godly parents; or such a system of precepts that is founded upon and agrees unto the revealed will of God, and which being so should be laid up and kept in the heart, and not forgotten" (*John Gill's Exposition of the Whole Bible* [commentary on Proverbs 6:20]).

How might one bind commandments and laws upon their heart and about their neck? (6:21–22) "*Bind* the teachings (figuratively) like a pendant on a cord about your neck, so that they will rest over your heart. These are metaphors for keeping a valuable object close to oneself always, and they stress the beauty and worth of the teachings [see also Exod. 28:29 and Prov. 3:3]" (*Jewish Study Bible* [2014], 1447).

21 Bind them continually upon thine heart, *and* tie them about thy neck.

22 When thou goest, it shall lead thee; when thou sleepest, it shall keep thee; and *when* thou awakest, it shall talk with thee.

How do commandments light the way of life? (6:23) "A commandment *is* a lamp to show us the right course, and indeed the law defines that course that we are to follow. . . . The commandments of the Lord are principles upon which *our* lives must be built if we are to find happiness, success, and peace. . . .

"We need simply to remember that which is expected of us if we wish a blessing. The Lord will remember that which is expected of him" (Christiansen, "The Laws of God Are Blessings," 23, 24). See commentary in this volume for Psalm 119:105.

23 For the commandment *is* a lamp; and the law *is* light; and reproofs of instruction *are* the way of life:

Summary of Proverbs 6:24–35

Strong warnings are given to avoid lust, jealousy, and immoral behavior. Adultery destroys one's soul.

"Six Things Doth the Lord Hate; Yea, Seven Are an Abomination unto Him" (Proverbs 6:16–19)

The seven things the Lord "hates" are

- a proud look
- a lying tongue
- hands that shed innocent blood
- an heart that deviseth wicked imaginations
- feet that be swift in running to mischief
- a false witness that speaketh lies
- he that soweth discord among brethren

"All of these sins address the treatment of one's fellow men. There is no salvation possible for one who abuses the children of God. These sinners partake of the spirit of the natural man, feeling that they can, because of their superior strength or intellect, take advantage of the weak, naïve, and innocent" (Hyde, *Comprehensive Commentary [Proverbs]*, 20).

"There is something of a contrasting parallel arrangement with the Beatitudes in [Matt.] 5, which has seven blessed things to answer these seven hated things; moreover, the first beatitude ('Blessed are the poor in spirit,' [Matt.] 5:5) contrasts the first hated thing ['haughty eyes,' v. 17; i.e., 'a proud look'] and the seventh ('peacemakers,' [Matt.] 5:7) with the seventh abomination ['soweth discord,' v. 19]" (*Expositor's Bible Commentary [Abridged]*, 951).

Two of these seven sins relate to dishonesty. "The Savior constantly rebuked those who *professed* one thing publicly but lived differently in their hearts. He praised those who lived without deception. . . . Light, spiritual answers, and heavenly direction are unalterably linked to your own honesty and truth. Many of your lasting satisfactions at school and work will come as you continually elevate your commitment to personal honesty. . . . Honesty, integrity, and truth are eternal principles that significantly shape our experience in mortality and help determine our eternal destiny. For a disciple of Christ, honesty is at the very heart of spirituality" (Andersen, "Spiritual Power of Honesty," 4).

CHAPTER 7

An immoral woman leads a man to destruction as an ox to the slaughter—The house of an adulterous woman is the way to hell.

Summary of Proverbs 7

The writer warns of the hazards of adultery. Proverbs 7 warns that a young man who falls prey to an evil woman is like an ox being taken to slaughter (v. 22). Elder Jeffrey R. Holland explained that immorality is such a serious sin because "one who uses the God-given body of another without divine sanction abuses the very soul of that individual, abuses the central purpose and processes of life, 'the very key' to life, as President Boyd K. Packer once called it. In exploiting the body of another—which means exploiting his or her soul—one desecrates the Atonement of Christ, which saved that soul and which makes possible the gift of eternal life. And when one mocks the Son of Righteousness, one steps into a realm of heat hotter and holier than the noonday sun. You cannot do so and not be burned" ("Personal Purity," 76).

CHAPTER 8

Wisdom is greatly to be desired—The Lord and the sons of men possessed wisdom in the premortal life.

Summary of Proverbs 8

In Proverbs 8 wisdom speaks in stark contrast to the subject of the previous chapter. Wisdom speaks truth and righteousness, and offers instruction and knowledge more valuable than riches (vv. 10–11, 18). Wisdom existed before God created the earth (vv. 22–30). We are invited to listen and be blessed by wisdom's teachings (vv. 32–34).

CHAPTER 9

Rebuke a wise man and he will love you—The fear of the Lord is the beginning of wisdom—The guests of an immoral woman are in the depths of hell.

Summary of Proverbs 9

Proverbs 9 summarizes themes addressed in Proverbs 1–8. Wisdom offers a house with a banquet for all to come and feast. "The fear of the Lord is the beginning of wisdom: and the knowledge of the holy is understanding" (v. 10). In contrast to wisdom is the "foolish woman" who is "simple, and knoweth nothing" (v. 13). The banquet offered to her guests is "the depths of hell" (v. 18).

Summary of Proverbs 10–31

"Beginning with [chapter] 10 there is a notable change to the form of the material. No longer do we find the forceful admonitions to seek wisdom, the lengthy poems, or the developed pictures and personifications. Instead we find what more closely corresponds to the title 'Proverbs'—a collection of independent, miscellaneous aphorisms, dealing mostly with the consequences of right or wrong actions on various topics" (*Expositor's Bible Commentary [Abridged]*, 957). The following section highlights a selection of useful topics to study from Proverbs 10–31.

Suggested Topics to Study in Proverbs 10–31

Care for the Poor and Needy

"He that oppresseth the poor reproacheth his Maker: but he that honoureth him hath mercy on the poor" (Proverbs 14:31).

Related passages: Proverbs 14:20–21; 17:5; 19:17; 21:13; 22:9, 22–23; 28:27; 29:7

President Russell M. Nelson taught: "Lessons from the Old Testament remind us that when the Lord sent prophets to call Israel back from apostasy, in almost every instance, one of the first charges made was that the poor had been neglected.

"Scriptures teach us that the poor—especially widows, orphans, and strangers—have long been the concern of God and the godly. . . .

"To those who cared for the poor, blessings were promised. The Lord would deliver them in time of trouble (see Ps. 41:1). Truths were taught by these proverbs: 'He that hath mercy on the poor, happy is he' (Prov. 14:21). 'The righteous considereth the cause of the poor: but the wicked regardeth not to know it' (Prov. 29:7)" ("In the Lord's Own Way," 25–26).

Elder Jeffrey R. Holland said: "From the beginning of His ministry, Jesus loved the impoverished and the disadvantaged in an extraordinary way. He was born into the home of two of them and grew up among many more of them. We don't know all the details of His temporal life, but He once said, 'Foxes have holes, and . . . birds . . . have nests; but the Son of man hath not where to lay his head' [Matthew 8:20]. Apparently the Creator of heaven and earth 'and all things that in them are' [2 Nephi 2:14; 3 Nephi 9:15] was, at least in His adult life, homeless.

"Down through history, poverty has been one of humankind's greatest and most widespread challenges. Its obvious toll is usually physical, but the spiritual and emotional damage it can bring may be even more debilitating. In any case, the great Redeemer has issued no more persistent call than for us to join Him in lifting this burden from the people" ("Are We Not All Beggars?" 40).

Avoid Anger

"A soft answer turneth away wrath: but grievous words stir up anger" (Proverbs 15:1).

Related passages: Proverbs 14:17, 29; 15:18; 16:32; 17:28; 25:28; 30:32–33

President Gordon B. Hinckley taught: "It was said of old that 'a soft answer turneth away wrath' [Prov. 15:1]. It is interesting to me that in this revelation the Lord spoke of consoling words in the spirit of meekness.

"There is so much of argument in the homes of the people. It is so destructive. It is so corrosive. It leads only to bitterness, heartbreak, and tears. How well advised we would be, each of us, when there is tension, when there is friction, when there is affliction, to speak with consoling words in the spirit of meekness" ("If Thou Art Faithful," 91).

Elder Lynn G. Robbins explained: "Anger is a yielding to Satan's influence by surrendering our self-control. . . .

"Anger is an uncivil attempt to make another feel guilty or a cruel way of trying to correct them. It is often mislabeled as discipline but is almost always counterproductive. . . .

"Choice and accountability are inseparable principles. Because anger is a choice, there is a strong warning in the proclamation 'that individuals . . . who abuse spouse or offspring, . . . will one day stand accountable before God.'

"Understanding the connection between agency and anger is the first step in eliminating it from our lives. We can choose not to become angry. And we can make that choice today, right now: 'I will never become angry again'" ("Agency and Anger," 80–81).

Prayer

"The Lord is far from the wicked: but he heareth the prayer of the righteous" (Proverbs 15:29).

Related passages: Proverbs 15:8; 28:9

Elder David A. Bednar explained: "Morning and evening prayers—and all of the prayers in between—are not unrelated, discrete events; rather, they are linked together each day and across days, weeks, months, and even years. This is in part how we fulfill the scriptural admonition to 'pray always' (Luke 21:36; 3 Nephi 18:15, 18; D&C 31:12). Such meaningful prayers are instrumental in obtaining the highest blessings God holds in store for His faithful children" ("Morning and Evening Prayers," 4).

Elder Bruce R. McConkie said: "It is written: 'The Lord . . . heareth the prayer of the righteous' (Proverbs 15:29). It is also written: 'And whatsoever we ask, we receive of him, because we keep his commandments, and do those things that are pleasing in his sight' (1 John 3:22; see also 5:14–15). And it was Jesus himself who said: 'If ye abide in me, and my words abide in you, ye shall ask what ye will, and it shall be done unto you' (John 15:7). Thus, prayers are heard and prayers are answered when those who seek their God do so in righteousness. Only the true and living God hears prayers. He alone grants the petitions of the penitent, and as with all else that he does, he is bound by the laws of obedience and faith and personal righteousness that he himself has ordained" (*New Witness for the Articles of Faith*, 385).

Humility and Pride

"Pride goeth before destruction, and an haughty spirit before a fall" (Proverbs 16:18).

Related passages: Proverbs 13:10; 15:31–32; 16:5, 19–20; 22:4; 27:1–2; 29:23

Elder Dieter F. Uchtdorf explained: "Some suppose that humility is about beating ourselves up. Humility does not mean convincing ourselves that we are worthless, meaningless, or of little value. Nor does it mean denying or withholding the talents God has given us. We don't discover humility by thinking less of ourselves; we discover humility by thinking less *about* ourselves. It comes as we go about our work with an attitude of serving God and our fellowman.

"Humility directs our attention and love toward others and to Heavenly Father's purposes. Pride does the opposite. Pride draws its energy and strength from the deep wells of selfishness. The moment we stop obsessing with ourselves and lose ourselves in service, our pride diminishes and begins to die" ("Pride and the Priesthood," 58).

President Ezra Taft Benson: "The central feature of pride is enmity—enmity toward God and enmity toward our fellowmen. *Enmity* means 'hatred toward, hostility to, or a state of opposition.' It is the power by which Satan wishes to reign over us.

"Pride is essentially competitive in nature. We pit our will against God's. When we direct our pride toward God, it is in the spirit of 'my will and not thine be done.' . . .

"Another major portion of this very prevalent sin of pride is enmity toward our fellowmen. We are tempted daily to elevate ourselves above others and diminish them (see Hel. 6:17; D&C 58:41).

"The proud make every man their adversary by pitting their intellects, opinions, works, wealth, talents, or any other worldly measuring device against others" *(Ezra Taft Benson* [manual], 232–33).

Wise Use of Language

"Whoso keepeth his mouth and his tongue keepeth
his soul from troubles" (Proverbs 21:23).

Related passages: Proverbs 10:18–19; 11:13; 12:22; 15:2, 4; 17:27–28; 27:2

Elder Jeffrey R. Holland taught: "Like all gifts 'which cometh from above,' words are 'sacred, and must be spoken with care, and by constraint of the Spirit' [D&C 63:64].

"It is with this realization of the power and sanctity of words that I wish to caution us, if caution is needed, regarding how we speak to each other and how we speak of ourselves. . . .

"The voice that bears profound testimony, utters fervent prayer, and sings the hymns of Zion can be the same voice that berates and criticizes, embarrasses and demeans, inflicts pain and destroys the spirit of oneself and of others in the process. . . .

"So, brothers and sisters, in this long eternal quest to be more like our Savior, may we try to be 'perfect' men and women in at least this one way now—by offending not in word, or more positively put, by speaking with a new tongue, the tongue of angels. Our words, like our deeds, should be filled with faith and hope and charity, the three great Christian imperatives so desperately needed in the world today. With such words, spoken under the influence of the Spirit, tears can be dried, hearts can be healed, lives can be elevated, hope can return, confidence can prevail" ("Tongue of Angels," 16, 18).

Responsibility of Parents

"Train up a child in the way he should go: and when he is old,
he will not depart from it" (Proverbs 22:6).

Related passages: Proverbs 19:18; 20:7; 29:17

"Husband and wife have a solemn responsibility to love and care for each other and for their children. 'Children are an heritage of the Lord' (Psalm 127:3). Parents have a sacred duty to rear their children in love and righteousness, to provide for their physical and spiritual needs, and to teach them to love and serve one another, observe the commandments of God, and be law-abiding citizens wherever they live" ("Family: A Proclamation to the World" [2010], 129).

Elder L. Tom Perry added, "Lessons taught in the home by goodly parents are becoming increasingly important in today's world, where the influence of the adversary is so widespread. As we know, he is attempting to erode and destroy the very foundation of our society—the family. In clever and carefully camouflaged ways, he is attacking commitment to family life throughout the world and undermining the culture and covenants of faithful Latter-day Saints. Parents must resolve that teaching in the home is a most sacred and important responsibility. While other institutions such as church and school can assist parents to 'train up a child in the way he [or she] should go' [Proverbs 22:6] this responsibility ultimately rests on the parents. According to the great plan of happiness, it is goodly parents who are entrusted with the care and development of Heavenly Father's children" ("Becoming Goodly Parents," 27).

Learn from Those Who Are Wise

"Bow down thine ear, and hear the words of the wise, and apply thine heart unto my knowledge. . . . Have not I written to thee excellent things in counsels and knowledge, that I might make thee know the certainty of the words of truth; that thou mightest answer the words of truth to them that send unto thee?" (Proverbs 22:17, 20–21).

Related passages: Proverbs 8:32–33; 13:14; 15:31–33; 16:16; 18:15; 19:20; 23:12

President Russell M. Nelson said: "Members, learn to listen, and listen to learn from Church leaders. Faithful members love the Savior and honor His servants, having faith in the Lord's declaration that 'whether by mine own voice or by the voice of my servants, it is the same' [D&C 1:38]. . . .

"Gratefully we thank God for a prophet to guide us in these latter days. But many turn a deaf ear to his teachings, oblivious to his prophetic position. They do so at great risk. . . .

"Wise members listen to learn from Church leaders" ("Listen to Learn," 23, 24).

Elder David A. Bednar stated: "Each member of The Church of Jesus Christ of Latter-day Saints has an individual responsibility to learn and live the Lord's teachings and to receive by proper authority the ordinances of salvation and exaltation. We should not expect the Church as an organization to teach or tell us everything we need to know and do to become devoted disciples and endure valiantly to the end. Rather, our personal responsibility is to learn what we should learn, to live as we know we should live, and to become who the Master would have us become. And our homes are the ultimate setting for learning, living, and becoming" ("Prepared to Obtain Every Needful Thing," 102).

Righteous Thoughts and Feelings of the Heart

"For as he thinketh in his heart, so is he" (Proverbs 23:7).

Related passages: Proverbs 12:5; 15:13, 26, 28; 16:3; 17:22; 23:17; 24:1–2, 9; 30:32

President Gordon B. Hinckley said: "You have heard [Proverbs 23:7] many times. I submit that it is profound in its implications. A man or woman largely becomes the product of his or her beliefs. Our behavior is governed by our thoughts, our beliefs. And these become our standards of conduct" (*Teachings of Gordon B. Hinckley*, 651).

Elder Gerald N. Lund shared: "We feel things in our hearts. In the scriptures, the prophets teach that personal revelation is closely linked to the heart. For example:

"Mormon taught, 'Because of meekness and lowliness of heart cometh the visitation of the Holy Ghost.' . . .

"Isn't that something we all seek, brothers and sisters—to be visited by the Holy Ghost, to have the Lord draw closer to us, to find joy and consolation in our lives? If so, then carefully assessing the condition of our hearts is one of the most essential things we can do in this life" ("Opening Our Hearts," 32–33).

Responsibility of Children to Honor Parents

"Hearken unto thy father that begat thee, and despise not thy mother when she is old. . . . The father of the righteous shall greatly rejoice: and he that begetteth a wise child shall have joy of him. Thy father and thy mother shall be glad, and she that bare thee shall rejoice" (Proverbs 23:22, 24–25).

Related passages: Proverbs 10:1, 5; 13:1; 17:6; 20:20

President Dallin H. Oaks taught: "The commandment to honor our parents echoes the sacred spirit of family relationships in which—at their best—we have sublime expressions of heavenly love and care for one another. We sense the importance of these relationships when we realize that our greatest expressions of joy or pain in mortality come from the members of our families. . . .

"[The Savior] reminded the scribes and Pharisees that we are commanded to honor our father and our mother and that God had directed that whoever cursed father or mother should be put to death (see Lev. 20:9; Deut. 21:18–21; Matt. 15:4; Mark 7:10). In this day, failing to honor our parents is not a capital crime in any country of which I am aware. However, the divine direction to honor our father and our mother has never been revoked (see Mosiah 13:20; Matt. 19:19; Luke 18:20).

"Like many scriptures, this commandment has multiple meanings.

"To young people, honoring parents is appropriately understood to focus on obedience, respect, and emulation of righteous parents. . . .

"If you honor your parents, you will love them, respect them, confide in them, be considerate of them, express appreciation for them, and demonstrate all of these things by following their counsel in righteousness and by obeying the commandments of God.

"To persons whose parents are dead, honoring parents is likely to involve thoughts of family reunions, family histories, temple work, and commitment to the great causes in which departed parents spent their lives.

"Middle-aged persons are likely to think of the commandment to honor our fathers and our mothers in terms of caring for aged parents. . . .

"In time to come, each of us will be judged by the Lord God of Israel, who commanded us to honor our fathers and our mothers" ("Honour Thy Father and Thy Mother," 15, 17).

Repentance

"He that covereth his sins shall not prosper: but whoso confesseth and forsaketh them shall have mercy" (Proverbs 28:13).

Related passages: Proverbs 16:6; 20:9; 28:9; 30:12

President Russell M. Nelson explained: "Repentance is a resplendent gift. It is a process never to be feared. It is a gift for us to receive with joy and to use—even embrace—day after day as we seek to become more like our Savior. . . .

"True repentance is not an event. It is a never-ending privilege. It is *fundamental* to progression and having peace of mind, comfort, and joy" ("Savior's Four Gifts of Joy," 4).

Elder Richard G. Scott taught: "The joyful news for anyone who desires to be rid of the consequences of past poor choices is that the Lord sees weaknesses differently than He does rebellion. Whereas the Lord warns that unrepented rebellion will bring punishment, when the Lord speaks of weaknesses, it is always with mercy. . . .

"Each of us has had times in our lives when we have made poor choices. We are all in desperate need of the redemptive power of the Atonement of Jesus Christ. Each of us must repent of any rebellion. 'For I the Lord cannot look upon sin with the least degree of allowance' [D&C 1:31]. He cannot because He knows what it takes to become like Him" ("Personal Strength through the Atonement of Jesus Christ," 83, 84).

Obedience to God's Commandments

"Whoso walketh uprightly shall be saved: but he that is perverse in his ways shall fall at once" (Proverbs 28:18).

Related passages: Proverbs 13:13; 15:29; 16:7; 21:3; 28:1, 4–7, 10; 29:2, 6, 18; 30:5

Elder Quentin L. Cook taught: "With respect to righteousness, this life is the time for all of us to prepare to meet God. The Book of Mormon provides multiple examples of the tragic consequences when individuals or groups fail to keep the commandments of God.

"During my lifetime, worldly issues and concerns have moved from one extreme to another—from frivolous and trivial pursuits to serious immorality. . . .

"As we look around, we see the devastation of wickedness and addiction at every turn. If, as individuals, we are really concerned about the Savior's ultimate judgment of us, we should seek repentance. I am afraid many people no longer feel accountable to God and do not turn to the scriptures or the prophets for guidance" ("Prepare to Meet God," 115–16).

Elder Dale G. Renlund stated: "The principle of activating blessings that flow from God is eternal. Like [the] ancient Israelites, we . . . must act on our faith in Jesus Christ to be blessed. God has revealed that 'there is a law, irrevocably decreed in heaven before the foundations of this world, upon which all blessings are predicated—and when we obtain any blessing from God, it is by obedience to that law upon which it is predicated' [D&C 130:20–21]. That being said, you do not earn a blessing—that notion is false—but you do have to qualify for it. Our salvation comes only through the merits and grace of Jesus Christ" ("Abound with Blessings," 71).

A Virtuous Woman

"Who can find a virtuous woman? for her price is far above rubies" (Proverbs 31:10).

Related passages: Proverbs 31:11–12, 20, 25–26, 28–30

Sister Barbara W. Winder, former Relief Society General President, taught: "The virtuous woman described in Proverbs was a woman who was prepared. She worked willingly, stretched out her hand to the poor, saw to the physical needs of her household, sought after knowledge. She had profound reverence for the Lord. While many of her tasks may appear to be temporal in nature, her blessings were eternal ones" ("Becoming a Prepared People," 88).

President Spencer W. Kimball declared: "To be a righteous woman is a glorious thing in any age. To be a righteous woman during the winding up scenes on this earth, before the second coming of our Savior, is an especially noble calling. The righteous woman's strength and influence today can be tenfold what it might be in more tranquil times. . . .

"Much of the major growth that is coming to the Church in the last days will come because many of the good women of the world (in whom there is often such an inner sense of spirituality) will be drawn to the Church in large numbers. This will happen to the degree that the women of the Church reflect righteousness and articulateness in their lives and to the degree that the women of the Church are seen as distinct and different—in happy ways—from the women of the world. . . . Thus it will be that female exemplars of the Church will be a significant force in both the numerical and the spiritual growth of the Church in the last days" (*Spencer W. Kimball* [manual], 217, 222–23).

ECCLESIASTES

OR, THE PREACHER

Introduction

The name Ecclesiastes is a translation of the Hebrew word *koheleth*, which means "one who convenes an assembly" or simply a preacher (see Bible Dictionary, "Ecclesiastes"). "Throughout this book, the writer presents a series of questions in search of the purpose of life. His questions and subsequent conclusions illustrate his own journey of seeking to understand why we are here on the earth. As [individuals] study this book, they can likewise consider the purpose of mortality and discover with the writer that everyone will one day have to stand before God and be judged" (*Old Testament Seminary Teacher Material*, 618).

"As literature, Ecclesiastes belongs, along with Proverbs, Job, [and other biblical writings], . . . in the category of wisdom. Wisdom texts reflect on the nature of the world and the God who created and controls it, and on the place of humans in this divine creation" (*Jewish Study Bible*, 1603). "The structure of Ecclesiastes is important for understanding the book and the several different interpretations of the book. . . . Ecclesiastes is similar to . . . [a] first-person style of autobiography. . . . The first eleven verses of the book introduce the author, state the [theme] of the book, ask a key question and then present the words of [the Preacher] that preview the argument of the book. The end of the book ([Ecclesiastes] 12:8–14) restates the [theme] of the book, gives an evaluation of the words of [the Preacher] and points to the solution of the problems [the Preacher] addressed. The structure of the book can be called an autobiography cast in a frame, or a framed autobiography" (Belcher, *Finding Favor in the Sight of God*, 135).

"The book of Ecclesiastes seems permeated with a pessimistic flavor but must be read in the light of one of its key phrases: 'under the sun' (1:9), meaning 'from a worldly point of view.' The term *vanity* also needs clarification, since as used in Ecclesiastes it means 'transitory' or 'fleeting.' Thus the Preacher laments that as things appear from the point of view of the world, everything is temporary and soon gone—nothing is permanent. . . . The most spiritual part of the book appears in chapters 11 and 12, where it is concluded that the only activity of lasting and permanent value comes from obedience to God's commandments, since all things will be examined in the judgment that God will render on man" (Bible Dictionary, "Ecclesiastes").

CHAPTER 1

Everything under the sun is vanity and vexation of spirit—He who increases in knowledge increases in sorrow.

1 The words of the Preacher, the son of David, king in Jerusalem.

1:1–11. All Earthly Things Are Insignificant

Who is the Preacher spoken of in Ecclesiastes? (1:1)
"Preacher is used to translate *koheleth*, whose root *kahal* means 'to gather, convoke, or call together.' *Ecclesiastes* is a Greek word meaning 'assemblyman.' Why the author of these lifetime experiments so identified himself is not known. Neither is it known whether the author really was Solomon, or whether he merely chose and discussed experiences and

2 Vanity of vanities, saith the Preacher, vanity of vanities; all *is* vanity.

3 What profit hath a man of all his labour which he taketh under the sun?

4 *One* generation passeth away, and *another* generation cometh: but the earth abideth for ever.

5 The sun also ariseth, and the sun goeth down, and hasteth to his place where he arose.

6 The wind goeth toward the south, and turneth about unto the north; it whirleth about continually, and the wind returneth again according to his circuits.

7 All the rivers run into the sea; yet the sea *is* not full; unto the place from whence the rivers come, thither they return again.

8 All things *are* full of labour; man cannot utter *it:* the eye is not satisfied with seeing, nor the ear filled with hearing.

9 The thing that hath been, it *is that* which shall be; and that which is done *is* that which shall be done: and *there is* no new *thing* under the sun.

10 Is there *any* thing whereof it may be said, See, this *is* new? it hath been already of old time, which was before us.

11 *There is* no remembrance of former *things;* neither shall there be *any* remembrance of *things* that are to come with *those* that shall come after.

12 ¶ I the Preacher was king over Israel in Jerusalem.

13 And I gave my heart to seek and search out by wisdom concerning all *things* that

values typical in a life like that of Solomon. Perhaps who he was does not matter, for he can represent a person of any era; he lived in our world, and for the worldly, much is still the same today as it was then" (Rasmussen, *Latter-day Saint Commentary on the Old Testament*, 487).

What is the Preacher referring to when he says that "all is vanity"? (1:2–11) The Preacher states that earthly things, such as worldly learning, are empty and hollow. He is sorrowful as he ponders the different things men seek after. "While the earth lasts, mankind and his works come and go. The sun's work is never done, neither is the wind's or a river's. Likewise, men work but their labors do not amount to anything lasting. No one does anything new; everything has been done before. Just as we do not remember the great works of the past, so will our works not be remembered by those in the future" (Muhlestein, *Essential Old Testament Companion*, 359).

1:12–18. The Preacher Sought Knowledge and Wisdom

What is the meaning of the word *vanity* in Ecclesiastes? (1:14) The word *vanity* is from the Hebrew [word *heḇel*]. This means "emptiness, something transitory and unsatisfactory" (*Strong's Exhaustive Concordance*, word #h1892). Referring to the idea of a transitory, empty life, Elder Dieter F. Uchtdorf noted: "The ancient King Solomon was one of the most outwardly successful human beings in history. He seemed to have everything—money, power, adoration, honor. But after decades of self-indulgence and luxury, how did King Solomon sum up his life? 'All is vanity' [Eccl. 1:1–2], he said" ("Believe, Love, Do," 46).

Why did the Preacher find pain and sorrow in obtaining knowledge and wisdom? (1:17–18) As he grapples with the afflictions of the human condition, "the Preacher explains the anguish of the secular philosopher, even though he be a Solomon-back-from-the-dead.... The attempt to solve the problem of life by wisdom in fact only enlarged the problem (v. 18). So long as wisdom is restricted to the realm 'under the sun', it sees the throbbing tumult of creation, life scurrying round its ever-repetitive circuits, and nothing more. 'The more you understand, the more you ache' (Moffatt)" (Eaton, *Ecclesiastes*, 75–76).

Ecclesiastes 2:1–17. Pleasure and Wealth Are Empty and All Will Die

How did the Preacher view his attempts to find happiness? (2:1–11) President Harold B. Lee noted, "In King Solomon's 'personal diary,' as someone has called the Book of Ecclesiastes, this wise king gives us an enumeration [record] of the things he had acquired, but which did not make him rich toward God" ("Communion with Deity," 1144). From verses 1–11, make a list of the ways the Preacher sought to find happiness and meaning in his life. Note how this list encompasses the whole of life for the pleasure-seeker. How have you fallen into the trap of thinking these temporalities will bring you happiness and closer to

are done under heaven: this sore travail hath
God given to the sons of man to be exercised
therewith.

14 I have seen all the works that are done
under the sun; and, behold, all *is* vanity and
vexation of spirit.

15 *That which is* crooked cannot be made
straight: and that which is wanting cannot be
numbered.

16 I communed with mine own heart, saying, Lo, I am come to great estate, and have
gotten more wisdom than all *they* that have
been before me in Jerusalem: yea, my heart
had great experience of wisdom and knowledge.

17 And I gave my heart to know wisdom,
and to know madness and folly: I perceived
that this also is vexation of spirit.

18 For in much wisdom *is* much grief: and he
that increaseth knowledge increaseth sorrow.

CHAPTER 2

All the riches and wealth of the king are vanity and vexation of spirit—Wisdom is better than folly—God gives wisdom, knowledge, and joy to man.

1 I said in mine heart, Go to now, I will prove
thee with mirth, therefore enjoy pleasure:
and, behold, this also *is* vanity.

2 I said of laughter, *It is* mad: and of mirth, What doeth it?

3 I sought in mine heart to give myself unto wine, yet acquainting mine heart with wisdom; and to lay hold on folly, till I might see what *was* that good for the sons of men, which they should do under the heaven all the days of their life.

4 I made me great works; I builded me houses; I planted me vineyards:

5 I made me gardens and orchards, and I planted trees in them of all *kind of* fruits:

6 I made me pools of water, to water therewith the wood that bringeth forth trees:

7 I got *me* servants and maidens, and had servants born in my house; also I had great possessions of great and small cattle above all that were in Jerusalem before me:

8 I gathered me also silver and gold, and the peculiar treasure of kings and of the provinces: I gat me men singers and women singers, and the delights of the sons of men, *as* musical instruments, and that of all sorts.

9 So I was great, and increased more than all that were before me in Jerusalem: also my wisdom remained with me.

10 And whatsoever mine eyes desired I kept not from them, I withheld not my heart from any joy; for my heart rejoiced in all my labour: and this was my portion of all my labour.

11 Then I looked on all the works that my hands had wrought, and on the labour that I had laboured to do: and, behold, all *was* vanity and vexation of spirit, and *there was* no profit under the sun.

God? How does the gospel of Jesus Christ prepare a person to find joy and purpose in this life? ⊕

Why does the writer compare laughter to madness? (2:2) Ecclesiastes "does not speak here of a sober enjoyment of the things of this world, but of intemperate pleasure, whose two attendants, laughter and mirth, are introduced by a beautiful [figure of speech] as two persons; and the contemptuous manner wherewith he treats them has something remarkably striking. He tells the former to her face that she is mad; but as to the latter, he thinks her so much beneath his notice, that he only points at her, and instantly turns his back" (*Adam Clarke's Commentary* [on Ecclesiastes 2:2]). Elder Richard G. Scott noted: "Loud, inappropriate laughter will offend the Spirit. A good sense of humor helps revelation; loud laughter does not" ("How to Obtain Revelation and Inspiration for Your Personal Life," 46).

Why does the "Preacher" believe even the wise man dies a fool? (2:12–17) "This section is pivotal toward understanding how [the Preacher's] thinking is affected by his fear of death. . . . [It] leads him to contemplate the benefits of wisdom in the light of his impending death. . . . Death renders all things, including wisdom, meaningless" (Longman, *Book of Ecclesiastes*, 94). This depressing thought was, itself, rendered null and void by the Prophet Joseph Smith, who taught that our knowledge will remain with us after death: "Whatever principle of intelligence we attain unto in this life, it will rise with us in the resurrection" (D&C 130:18–19).

12 ¶ And I turned myself to behold wisdom, and madness, and folly: for what *can* the man *do* that cometh after the king? *even* that which hath been already done.

13 Then I saw that wisdom excelleth folly, as far as light excelleth darkness.

14 The wise man's eyes *are* in his head; but the fool walketh in darkness: and I myself perceived also that one event happeneth to them all.

15 Then said I in my heart, As it happeneth to the fool, so it happeneth even to me; and why was I then more wise? Then I said in my heart, that this also *is* vanity.

16 For *there is* no remembrance of the wise more than of the fool for ever; seeing that which now *is* in the days to come shall all be forgotten. And how dieth the wise *man?* as the fool.

17 Therefore I hated life; because the work that is wrought under the sun *is* grievous unto me: for all *is* vanity and vexation of spirit.

Ecclesiastes 2:18–26. The Emptiness of Earthly Work

18 ¶ Yea, I hated all my labour which I had taken under the sun: because I should leave it unto the man that shall be after me.

19 And who knoweth whether he shall be a wise *man* or a fool? yet shall he have rule over all my labour wherein I have laboured, and wherein I have shewed myself wise under the sun. This *is* also vanity.

20 Therefore I went about to cause my heart to despair of all the labour which I took under the sun.

21 For there is a man whose labour *is* in wisdom, and in knowledge, and in equity; yet to a man that hath not laboured therein shall he leave it *for* his portion. This also *is* vanity and a great evil.

22 For what hath man of all his labour, and of the vexation of his heart, wherein he hath laboured under the sun?

23 For all his days *are* sorrows, and his travail grief; yea, his heart taketh not rest in the night. This is also vanity.

24 ¶ *There is* nothing better for a man, *than* that he should eat and drink, and *that* he should make his soul enjoy good in his labour. This also I saw, that it *was* from the hand of God.

25 For who can eat, or who else can hasten *hereunto,* more than I?

How can a focus on the simple things of life increase our appreciation for God? (2:24) "With this verse [the Preacher] begins the first major summary of his thinking in 1:13–2:23. He gives his practical advice in the light of his conclusion that meaning may not be found in either wisdom or hard work. . . .

"The lifestyle he advocates is the pursuit of the basic necessities of life: food, drink, and enjoyment in work. One wonders how [he] ever expected anyone to enjoy their work after reading the previous section, but perhaps that was not his real intention. Certainly, he understands, as we can see from the second half of the verse, that no one is able to enjoy even these simple pleasures unless God allows it" (Longman, *Book of Ecclesiastes*, 107).

26 For *God* giveth to a man that *is* good in his sight wisdom, and knowledge, and joy: but to the sinner he giveth travail, to gather and to heap up, that he may give to *him that is* good before God. This also *is* vanity and vexation of spirit.

How does God give that which is good in a world that seems meaningless? (2:26) "In this chapter, the Preacher continues his theme and takes it one step farther. He begins where the last chapter left off—he listed many things that we often think bring us joy or satisfaction and demonstrates that they do not. After doing this, he finally introduces God. Once God is part of the equation, we learn that we can actually achieve joy. In this way the Preacher shows that none of the things of the world can give joy, but God can" (Muhlestein, *Essential Old Testament Companion*, 360–61). ⊕

CHAPTER 3

To every thing there is a season—Whatever God does, it will be forever—God will judge the righteous and the wicked.

1 To every *thing there is* a season, and a time to every purpose under the heaven:

Ecclesiastes 3:1–15. A Time for Everything

What does it mean to do things in their time and season? (3:1) "*Sequentially* is a big word meaning to do things one at a time at different times. The book of Ecclesiastes says: 'To every thing there is a season, and a time to every purpose under . . . heaven'" (Faust, "How Near the Angels," 96). "In many respects this chapter is a continuation of the previous one. There are many aspects of this mortal experience over which we have little or no control. This our Father in Heaven administers to us according to His divine wisdom and love" (Hyde, *Comprehensive Commentary [Ecclesiastes]*, 13). ⊕

How do we experience the realities of life? (3:2–8) "The Preacher identifies two basic kinds of seasons or times in which we tend our lots—disquiets and delights" (Eswing, *Recovering Eden*, 119). Read verses 2–8 and make two lists: one that addresses the worries and anxieties of life and another that addresses enjoyments and pleasures of life. How do these adverse conditions work together to define our lives? How are we to cope with the anxieties that sometimes seem to overwhelm us? In what ways do the delightful things of life give us hope and keep the trials we experience in perspective?

What does it mean that God set the world in our hearts? (3:11) A more accurate translation of the Hebrew (עָלוֹם *'ôlâm* [world]) is "continuance, eternal, (for, everlasting)" (*Strong's Exhaustive Concordance*, word #h5769). Therefore, a better translation for this phrase is God "hath set the eternal in their heart without which man cannot find out the work that God hath done" (Ecclesiastes 3:11*b*). "The Preacher, in the course of his observations and meditations, had realized that there is much beauty in life that humankind can appreciate only by the spark of the eternal within, which inspires the heart of mortals" (Rasmussen, *Latter-day Saint Commentary on the Old Testament*, 489).

2 A time to be born, and a time to die; a time to plant, and a time to pluck up *that which is* planted;

3 A time to kill, and a time to heal; a time to break down, and a time to build up;

4 A time to weep, and a time to laugh; a time to mourn, and a time to dance;

5 A time to cast away stones, and a time to gather stones together; a time to embrace, and a time to refrain from embracing;

6 A time to get, and a time to lose; a time to keep, and a time to cast away;

7 A time to rend, and a time to sew; a time to keep silence, and a time to speak;

8 A time to love, and a time to hate; a time of war, and a time of peace.

9 What profit hath he that worketh in that wherein he laboureth?

10 I have seen the travail, which God hath given to the sons of men to be exercised in it.

11 He hath made every *thing* beautiful in his time: also he hath set the world in their heart, so that no man can find out the work that God maketh from the beginning to the end.

12 I know that *there is* no good in them, but for *a man* to rejoice, and to do good in his life.

13 And also that every man should eat and drink, and enjoy the good of all his labour, it *is* the gift of God.

This Is Your Time (Ecclesiastes 3:1)

"As I have pondered . . . , I have thought of the scripture from Ecclesiastes, or the Preacher: 'To every thing there is a season, and a time to every purpose under the heaven.' This is your time. What will you do with it? Are you where you want to be with your life? If not, what are you going to do about it? . . . To help us focus our answers, we may wish to consider this formula for success: Be where we ought to be. Be what we ought to be. Say what we ought to say. Do what we ought to do" (Monson, "Three Gates to Open").

14 I know that, whatsoever God doeth, it
shall be for ever: nothing can be put to it, nor
any thing taken from it: and God doeth *it,*
that *men* should fear before him.

15 That which hath been is now; and that
which is to be hath already been; and God
requireth that which is past.

16 ¶ And moreover I saw under the sun the
place of judgment, *that* wickedness *was* there;
and the place of righteousness, *that* iniquity
was there.

17 I said in mine heart, God shall judge the
righteous and the wicked: for *there is* a time
there for every purpose and for every work.

18 I said in mine heart concerning the estate
of the sons of men, that God might manifest them, and that they might see that they
themselves are beasts.

19 For that which befalleth the sons of men
befalleth beasts; even one thing befalleth
them: as the one dieth, so dieth the other; yea,
they have all one breath; so that a man hath
no preeminence above a beast: for all *is* vanity.

20 All go unto one place; all are of the dust,
and all turn to dust again.

21 Who knoweth the spirit of man that
goeth upward, and the spirit of the beast that
goeth downward to the earth?

22 Wherefore I perceive that *there is* nothing
better, than that a man should rejoice in his
own works; for that *is* his portion: for who
shall bring him to see what shall be after him?

What does the Preacher understand about the character of God? (3:14) In this verse, the Preacher addresses a doctrine only slightly alluded to in the Old and New Testaments, but clearly enunciated in modern revelation—that God is an eternal, unchangeable Being. Moroni declared: "If there were miracles wrought then, why has God ceased to be a God of miracles and yet be an unchangeable Being? And behold, I say unto you he changeth not; if so he would cease to be God; and he ceaseth not to be God" (Mormon 9:19; see also commentary in *Book of Mormon Study Guide: Start to Finish, Revised Edition*, on Mormon 9:19).

Ecclesiastes 3:16–22. All Must Die and Give an Accounting

What constitutes God's judgment? (3:17) "Judgment . . . will occur after the Resurrection. God, through Jesus Christ, will judge each person to determine the eternal glory [he or she] will receive. This judgment will be based on each person's obedience to God's commands, including [his or her] acceptance of the atoning sacrifice of Jesus Christ" (Guide to the Scriptures, "Judgment, The Last"). There will be "unfailing consequence of blessings for righteous thoughts and acts, and punishment for unrepented sin. Justice is an eternal law that requires a penalty each time a law of God is broken (Alma 42:13–24). The sinner must pay the penalty if he does not repent (Mosiah 2:38–39; D&C 19:17). If he does repent, the Savior pays the penalty through the Atonement, invoking mercy (Alma 34:16)" (Guide to the Scriptures, "Justice").

Ecclesiastes 4:1–3. There Are Sorrows on the Earth

What is the cause of earthly sorrows? (4:1–3) "The author intends to convey the sense that he saw the pervasiveness of oppression. Perhaps he means that he has seen all kinds of oppressions. . . . The text does not say who the oppressors are, nor what their outrages entail, however. It states only that in the face of this pervasive oppression, 'there is none to comfort the oppressed.'" Unlike Job and Lamentations, who find God culpable for earthly sorrow and oppression (Job 10:7, Lam. 1:21), Ecclesiastes suggests that "injustice is simply laid out as a fact of life, something that everyone who is alive sees" (Seow, *Ecclesiastes*, 186–87).

Ecclesiastes 4:4–12. Both the Wise and Foolish Labor

What does the Preacher observe about work? (4:4) "The Preacher sees that the main motivation for work is human rivalry. Effort put forth (*toil*) and success in techniques acquired (*skill*) often hide the scramble for wealth, leadership, power or status. The ancient world too had its international tensions, labour disputes and class conflict. Beneath the surface of human energies the Preacher sees the restless desire to outclass others. . . . If his toil originates in ambition (4:4), if its progress is liable to be inhibited by folly (2:19, 21), if its results may be nil (1:3; 5:15), any hope of gain can come only from God (3:13; 5:18f.). Admittedly the Preacher is generalizing, and a different perspective will come later (9:10)" (Eaton, *Ecclesiastes*, 106–7).

What responsibilities do these verses place upon us? (4:9–10) "You are under covenant . . . that . . . you accepted a responsibility for whatever you might do or fail to do for the salvation of others however difficult and dangerous that might appear to be for you.

"[Your covenant] . . . brings with it an obligation to 'lift up the hands which hang down, and strengthen

CHAPTER 4

Oppression and evil deeds are vanity—The strength of two is better than one—Better is a poor and wise child than an old and foolish king.

1 So I returned, and considered all the oppressions that are done under the sun: and behold the tears of *such as were* oppressed, and they had no comforter; and on the side of their oppressors *there was* power; but they had no comforter.

2 Wherefore I praised the dead which are already dead more than the living which are yet alive.

3 Yea, better *is he* than both they, which hath not yet been, who hath not seen the evil work that is done under the sun.

4 ¶ Again, I considered all travail, and every right work, that for this a man is envied of his neighbour. This *is* also vanity and vexation of spirit.

5 The fool foldeth his hands together, and eateth his own flesh.

6 Better *is* an handful *with* quietness, than both the hands full *with* travail and vexation of spirit.

7 ¶ Then I returned, and I saw vanity under the sun.

8 There is one *alone,* and *there is* not a second; yea, he hath neither child nor brother: yet *is there* no end of all his labour; neither is his eye satisfied with riches; neither *saith he,* For whom do I labour, and bereave my soul of good? This *is* also vanity, yea, it *is* a sore travail.

9 ¶ Two *are* better than one; because they have a good reward for their labour.

10 For if they fall, the one will lift up his fellow: but woe to him *that is* alone when he falleth; for *he hath* not another to help him up.

11 Again, if two lie together, then they have heat: but how can one be warm *alone?*

12 And if one prevail against him, two shall withstand him; and a threefold cord is not quickly broken.

the feeble knees' [D&C 81:5] of those around you. You are the Lord's servant covenanted to do for others, as best you can, what He would do.

"Your great opportunity and your responsibility are described in Ecclesiastes:

"'Two are better than one; . . . for if they fall, the one will lift up his fellow' [Ecclesiastes 4:9–10]" (Eyring, "Man Down!" 64).

Ecclesiastes 4:13–16. Following Kings or Political Leaders, Hoping They Will Save Us, Is Also Vain and Useless

13 ¶ Better *is* a poor and a wise child than an old and foolish king, who will no more be admonished.

14 For out of prison he cometh to reign; whereas also *he that is* born in his kingdom becometh poor.

15 I considered all the living which walk under the sun, with the second child that shall stand up in his stead.

16 *There is* no end of all the people, *even* of all that have been before them: they also that come after shall not rejoice in him. Surely this also *is* vanity and vexation of spirit.

How can age and status bring foolishness? (4:13–16) Brigham Young saw his own experience in this passage: "When I was baptized into this Church, it was in its infancy, although a considerable number had been baptized before me, and many of them were older when they were baptized than I was. They improved, their minds expanded, they received truth and intelligence, increased in the knowledge of the things of God, and bid fair to become full-grown men in Christ Jesus. But some of them, when they had gained a little spiritual strength and knowledge, apparently stopped in their growth. . . . Like the fruit-trees, they have ceased to grow and increase and bear the fruits of the Spirit" (in *Journal of Discourses*, 7:335–36).

CHAPTER 5

God is in heaven—A fool's voice is known by a multitude of words—Keep your vows—Riches and wealth are the gift of God.

1 Keep thy foot when thou goest to the house of God, and be more ready to hear, than to give the sacrifice of fools: for they consider not that they do evil.

Ecclesiastes 5:1–7. The Foolishness of Empty Promises

2 Be not rash with thy mouth, and let not thine heart be hasty to utter *any* thing before God: for God *is* in heaven, and thou upon earth: therefore let thy words be few.

3 For a dream cometh through the multitude of business; and a fool's voice *is known* by multitude of words.

What is the danger of rash, harsh words "before God"? (5:2) "Like all gifts 'which cometh from above,' words are 'sacred, and must be spoken with care, and by constraint of the Spirit' [D&C 63:64]. . . . Some things we say can be destructive, even venomous—and that is a chilling indictment for a Latter-day Saint! The voice that bears profound testimony, utters fervent prayer, and sings the hymns of Zion *can be* the same voice that berates and criticizes, embarrasses and demeans, inflicts pain and destroys the spirit of oneself and of others in the process. 'Out of the same mouth proceedeth blessing and cursing,' James grieves. 'My brethren [and sisters], these things ought not so to be' [James 3:2–10]" (Holland, "Tongue of Angels," 16).

What vows do we make with God today? (5:4–5)
"We meet as disciples of the Lord Jesus Christ. We love him, and we want to help him in doing that which has to be done.... We can be part of that process through our commitment....

"Every member of this Church takes upon himself a sacred vow as he submits himself to the waters of baptism [Mosiah 18:8–30; D&C 20:37]. One day in seven, each Sabbath day, we assemble to renew that sacred vow and commitment as we partake of the sacrament [3 Ne. 18:1–16; D&C 20:75–79]" (Simpson, "These Four Things," 57). ⊕

Ecclesiastes 5:8–20. The Foolishness of Riches

What is the insidious nature of greed? (5:10–11)
"Too many ... have been screaming ever louder for more and more of the things we cannot take with us and paying less and less attention to the real sources of the very happiness we seek. We have been measuring our fellowmen more by balance sheets and less by moral standards. We have developed frightening physical power and fallen into pathetic spiritual weakness. We have become so concerned over the growth of our earning capacity that we have neglected the growth of our character" (Monson, in Conference Report, Oct. 1964, 141). ⊕

How should we look upon our daily work? (5:12)
"When [one] finds no joy in his daily work, goes to it in the morning with regret, has no feeling of thankfulness that he has work to do, and dislikes the hours in which he does it, there is something wrong.... Someone has said, 'Happy is the man who has work he loves to do,' but somebody else has added the basic fundamental thought, 'Happy is the man who

4 When thou vowest a vow unto God, defer not to pay it; for *he hath* no pleasure in fools: pay that which thou hast vowed.

5 Better *is it* that thou shouldest not vow, than that thou shouldest vow and not pay.

6 Suffer not thy mouth to cause thy flesh to sin; neither say thou before the angel, that it *was* an error: wherefore should God be angry at thy voice, and destroy the work of thine hands?

7 For in the multitude of dreams and many words *there are* also *divers* vanities: but fear thou God.

8 ¶ If thou seest the oppression of the poor, and violent perverting of judgment and justice in a province, marvel not at the matter: for *he that is* higher than the highest regardeth; and *there be* higher than they.

9 ¶ Moreover the profit of the earth is for all: the king *himself* is served by the field.

10 He that loveth silver shall not be satisfied with silver; nor he that loveth abundance with increase: this *is* also vanity.

11 When goods increase, they are increased that eat them: and what good *is there* to the owners thereof, saving the beholding *of them* with their eyes?

12 The sleep of a labouring man *is* sweet, whether he eat little or much: but the abundance of the rich will not suffer him to sleep.

13 There is a sore evil *which* I have seen under the sun, *namely,* riches kept for the owners thereof to their hurt.

14 But those riches perish by evil travail: and he begetteth a son, and *there is* nothing in his hand.

15 As he came forth of his mother's womb, naked shall he return to go as he came, and shall take nothing of his labour, which he may carry away in his hand.

16 And this also *is* a sore evil, *that* in all points as he came, so shall he go: and what profit hath he that hath laboured for the wind?

17 All his days also he eateth in darkness, and *he hath* much sorrow and wrath with his sickness.

18 ¶ Behold *that* which I have seen: *it is* good and comely *for one* to eat and to drink, and to enjoy the good of all his labour that he taketh under the sun all the days of his life, which God giveth him: for it *is* his portion.

19 Every man also to whom God hath given riches and wealth, and hath given him power to eat thereof, and to take his portion, and to rejoice in his labour; this *is* the gift of God.

20 For he shall not much remember the days of his life; because God answereth *him* in the joy of his heart.

loves the work he has to do'" (Bennion, in Conference Report, Apr. 1955, 110–11).

CHAPTERS 6–10

Unless a man's soul is filled with good, his riches, wealth, honor, and posterity are vanity.

Wisdom gives life to them that have it—All men are sinners—God has made man upright.

None have power to avoid death—It will not be well with the wicked; he turns to pleasure and cannot find wisdom.

Summary of Ecclesiastes 6–10

"This . . . section marks the middle of the book [and] a transition in [the Preacher's] focus. There is overlap between the two halves of the book, but [the Preacher] here leaves his explicit search for meaning and in the second half of the book focuses on advice and commentary about the future" (Longman, *Book of Ecclesiastes*, 176). These chapters contain sensible advice, including: life's purpose is not found in the pursuit of worldly wealth and honor; a good name and reputation should be protected; the race of life is won by those who endure in righteousness; and wisdom exceeds strength and brings success.

God's providence rules over all—All men are subject to time and chance—Wisdom is better than strength—One sinner destroys much good.

A little folly destroys the reputation of the wise and honorable—The words of a wise man's mouth are gracious—A fool is full of words.

CHAPTER 11

Do good and give to them who need—God will bring all men to judgment.

1 Cast thy bread upon the waters: for thou shalt find it after many days.

2 Give a portion to seven, and also to eight; for thou knowest not what evil shall be upon the earth.

3 If the clouds be full of rain, they empty *themselves* upon the earth: and if the tree fall toward the south, or toward the north, in the place where the tree falleth, there it shall be.

4 He that observeth the wind shall not sow; and he that regardeth the clouds shall not reap.

5 As thou knowest not what *is* the way of the spirit, *nor* how the bones *do grow* in the womb of her that is with child: even so thou knowest not the works of God who maketh all.

Ecclesiastes 11:1–10. Life's True Rewards

What does it mean to "cast [our] bread upon the waters"? (11:1) President Thomas S. Monson, speaking to the priesthood but applicable to all, noted: "I am confident we at times wonder if we are affecting the lives of others in a favorable manner. The instructor in the quorum who prepares so diligently . . . the quorum officers who reach out to rescue perhaps will never fully know the far-reaching influence of their service. This is particularly true of the faithful missionaries who day after day carry on in the service of the Master. Never complaining, ever serving, always sacrificing for the benefit of others. . . . The simple words from Ecclesiastes, or the Preacher, carry an assurance that brings comfort and inspires effort: 'Cast thy bread upon the waters: for thou shalt find it after many days'" ("Search and Rescue," 50).

What are we to understand by the phrase "give a portion to seven, and also to eight"? (11:2) "Even though the recipient of your charity be unknown to you, be generous in giving—'to seven, and also to eight' (Eccl. 11:2) means going beyond the norm—and be hopeful that someone will be charitable to you in future, unforeseen times of need. Perhaps his observation that when clouds form it rains and where a tree falls it lies is a kind of persuasion to live in charitable ways, suggesting that certain laws of cause and effect are constant" (Rasmussen, *Latter-day Saint Commentary on the Old Testament*, 494).

How does the child grow in the womb of its mother? (11:5) President J. Reuben Clark observed: "I am not going to assume that any argument is necessary to the point that this creation of man's body

6 In the morning sow thy seed, and in the evening withhold not thine hand: for thou knowest not whether shall prosper, either this or that, or whether they both *shall be* alike good.

7 ¶ Truly the light *is* sweet, and a pleasant *thing it is* for the eyes to behold the sun:

8 But if a man live many years, *and* rejoice in them all; yet let him remember the days of darkness; for they shall be many. All that cometh *is* vanity.

9 ¶ Rejoice, O young man, in thy youth; and let thy heart cheer thee in the days of thy youth, and walk in the ways of thine heart, and in the sight of thine eyes: but know thou, that for all these *things* God will bring thee into judgment.

10 Therefore remove sorrow from thy heart, and put away evil from thy flesh: for childhood and youth *are* vanity.

billions of times in the same way since the beginning, is the offspring of chance. . . . I am going to assume that the facts are a demonstration that the whole body-building process is the offspring of intelligence, infinite in its quality, so much so that the conscious mind of man cannot ever even comprehend it all. . . . That it repeats itself over the ages shows to me that it is directed by intelligence of which it is the offspring" (*Man: God's Greatest Miracle*, 19, 21). ⊕

What is the accountability of our youth? (11:9) The Preacher uses the imperative four times to encourage youth to enjoy the fleeting years, for life is short-lived and it is God's will that we enjoy living (see Towner, "Book of Ecclesiastes," 5:353). However, "joy is to be controlled by the knowledge of God's *judgment*. [It is] right to argue that the definite article ('*the* judgment') points to a single specific event, not merely to God's general judicial activity. . . . [God] is one whose activity is fittingly described in terms of law and justice . . . for in the face of sin the LORD must take action" (Eaton, *Ecclesiastes*, 165–66). ⊕

The Meaning of the Phrase "In the Place Where the Tree Falleth, There Shall It Be" (Ecclesiastes 11:3)

On occasion, the early Brethren used these verses to speak of death, the spirit, and the resurrection. For example, President Joseph F. Smith, commenting on 1 Peter 3:18–19, when Jesus went to preach to the dead while His body lay in the tomb, noted: "This may seem strange to some, that Jesus should go to preach the Gospel unto the wicked, rebellious antediluvians; whose bodies had been destroyed in the flood because they rejected the testimony of Noah. . . . The people in Europe, where we have been preaching, were struck with wonder and astonishment when we mentioned this doctrine, and say they, 'We had supposed that, "as the tree fell so it should lie" [Eccl. 11:3].'"

President Smith then commented that this verse pertained only "to the flesh. Does the spirit lie with the body? Is the spirit confined in the grave? No. As the body falls, so it will lie until the resurrection; there is no salvation in the grave, but in Christ, who is the 'light of life' [John 8:12], and the spirit soars beyond the grave; it does not slumber in the dust, but is wafted to the place prepared for it in the spirit world, to receive its reward or punishment, having passed the first judgment of God, there to await his mercy, and the resurrection from the dead and the final judgment of the great last day" (in *Journal of Discourses*, 18:92).

CHAPTER 12

At death the spirit will return to God who gave it—The words of the wise are as goads—The whole duty of man is to fear God and keep His commandments.

1 Remember now thy Creator in the days of
thy youth, while the evil days come not, nor
the years draw nigh, when thou shalt say, I
have no pleasure in them;

2 While the sun, or the light, or the moon,
or the stars, be not darkened, nor the clouds
return after the rain:

3 In the day when the keepers of the house
shall tremble, and the strong men shall bow
themselves, and the grinders cease because
they are few, and those that look out of the
windows be darkened,

4 And the doors shall be shut in the streets,
when the sound of the grinding is low, and
he shall rise up at the voice of the bird, and all
the daughters of musick shall be brought low;

5 Also *when* they shall be afraid of *that which*
is high, and fears *shall be* in the way, and the
almond tree shall flourish, and the grasshopper shall be a burden, and desire shall fail:
because man goeth to his long home, and the
mourners go about the streets:

6 Or ever the silver cord be loosed, or the
golden bowl be broken, or the pitcher be
broken at the fountain, or the wheel broken
at the cistern.

7 Then shall the dust return to the earth as
it was: and the spirit shall return unto God
who gave it.

8 ¶ Vanity of vanities, saith the preacher; all
is vanity.

Ecclesiastes 12:1–8. Remember God All of Your Life

Why is the Preacher's viewpoint so pessimistic? (12:3–8) "This passage sounds negative, cynical, and without hope, but one must remember that the Preacher is speaking from the viewpoint of a man without God. From the standpoint of the natural man, it is difficult to argue against Ecclesiastes. When a person puts his trust in things under the sun (the things of the world), he finds no lasting spiritual benefits. Energy and labor expended, wisdom and knowledge acquired, fortune and prestige gained, goodness and virtue dispensed are empty without God and pointless in the eternal scheme of things without accompanying spiritual life. The purpose of Ecclesiastes is . . . to help us remember that there is meaning only through God and keeping His commandments" (*Old Testament Student Manual*: *1 Kings–Malachi*, 20).

Why does the spirit return to God at death? (12:7) "If the body's capacity for normal function, defense, repair, regulation, and regeneration were to prevail without limit, life here would continue in perpetuity. Yes, we would be stranded here on earth! Mercifully for us, our Creator provided for aging and other processes that would ultimately result in our physical death. Death, like birth, is part of life. Scripture teaches that 'it was not expedient that man should be reclaimed from this temporal death, for that would destroy the great plan of happiness' [Alma 42:8]. To return to God

9 And moreover, because the preacher was wise, he still taught the people knowledge; yea, he gave good heed, and sought out, *and* set in order many proverbs.

10 The preacher sought to find out acceptable words: and *that which was* written *was* upright, *even* words of truth.

11 The words of the wise *are* as goads, and as nails fastened *by* the masters of assemblies, *which* are given from one shepherd.

12 And further, by these, my son, be admonished: of making many books *there is* no end; and much study *is* a weariness of the flesh.

13 ¶ Let us hear the conclusion of the whole matter: Fear God, and keep his commandments: for this *is* the whole *duty* of man.

14 For God shall bring every work into judgment, with every secret thing, whether *it be* good, or whether *it be* evil.

through the gateway we call death is a joy for those who love Him and are prepared to meet Him [Psalm 116:15]" (Nelson, "Thanks Be to God," 79). ⊕

Ecclesiastes 12:9–14. Man's Duty

Why are we told to "fear God"? (12:13–14) "Please note that godly fear is linked inextricably to an understanding of the Final Judgment and our individual accountability for our desires, thoughts, words, and acts (see Mosiah 4:30). The fear of the Lord is not a reluctant apprehension about coming into His presence to be judged. I do not believe we will be afraid of Him at all. Rather, it is the prospect in His presence of facing things as they really are about ourselves and having 'a perfect knowledge' (2 Nephi 9:14; see also Alma 11:43) of all our rationalizations, pretenses, and self-deceptions. Ultimately, we will be left without excuse" (Bednar, "Therefore They Hushed Their Fears," 49). ⊕

Fearing God by Keeping His Commandments Is a Divine Mandate (Ecclesiastes 12:13)

President Thomas S. Monson remembered a moment with President J. Reuben Clark, Jr. that both encouraged a thoughtful study of the Book of Ecclesiastes and also identified the key message of the Preacher: "It was my great privilege to know President Clark rather well. I was his printer. On occasion, he would share with me some of his most intimate thoughts, even those scriptures around which he tailored his teachings and lived his life. Late one evening I delivered some press proofs to his office situated in his home . . . here in Salt Lake City. President Clark was reading from Ecclesiastes. He was in a quiet and reflective mood. He sat back from his large desk, which was stacked with books and papers. He held the scriptures in his hand, lifted his eyes from the printed page, and read aloud to me: 'Let us hear the conclusion of the whole matter: Fear God, and keep his commandments: for this is the whole duty of man' (Eccl. 12:13). He exclaimed, 'A treasured truth! A profound philosophy!' Through the years that conversation has remained bright in my memory. I love, I cherish the noble word *duty*" ("Call of Duty," 37).

THE SONG OF SOLOMON

Introduction

"The Song of Solomon is a song of love. And a love poem in the Old Testament demands a response. Hence it has been the most praised, and most maligned, or the most ignored book in the Old Testament. It was preserved from antiquity in the Jewish canon, where it is found in the Writings—one of the five *Megilloth*, 'little scrolls,' which, in the Jewish tradition, are read in the synagogue on the annual festivals. The Song of Solomon is read at Passover, celebrating the Lord's love for his bride, the covenant people" (Seely, "Song of Solomon," 467).

The first verse of the Song attributes the writing to Solomon. However, "whether Solomon is actually the author is doubtful. The composition has many beautiful phrases and lyrical prose, often quoted in nonreligious literature. The [Joseph Smith Translation] states that 'the Songs of Solomon are not inspired writings.' Both Jews and Christians have at times been reluctant to accept it into the canon of scripture because of its romantic content but have permitted it on the basis of its being an allegory of God's love for Israel and of the Church" (Bible Dictionary, "Song of Solomon").

Summary of Song of Solomon 1–8

"The best-known fact among Latter-day Saints about the Song of Solomon, is that Joseph Smith wrote in the manuscript of the Joseph Smith Translation, 'The Songs of Solomon are not inspired writings.' Nevertheless, we have a very significant allusion to a passage from it in modern revelation. The bride is referred to in the Song of Solomon as one 'that looketh forth as the morning, fair as the moon, clear as the sun, and terrible as an army with banners' (Song 6:10). In the book of Revelation we find the symbol of a woman who 'fled into the wilderness' (Rev. 12:5), who represents 'the church of God,' and who 'brought forth the kingdom of our God and his Christ' (JST Rev. 12:7). [See Ludlow, *Unlocking the Old Testament*, 142–44, who discusses the allusion to this imagery known in the Song of Solomon in the New Testament and the Doctrine and Covenants.] In the Doctrine and Covenants, Joseph Smith's inspired dedicatory prayer for the Kirtland Temple refers to the coming forth of the Church in the latter days with the same imagery, building on the language found in the Song of Solomon: 'That thy church may come forth out of the wilderness of darkness, and shine forth fair as the

CHAPTERS 1–8

The poet sings of love and devotion.

Beloved ones are praised and described.

A love song concerning Solomon is presented.

A song describes the beauty of the poet's beloved.

The song of love and affection continues.

The song of love continues.

The song of love continues.

Many waters cannot quench love.

moon, clear as the sun, and terrible as an army with banners; And be adorned as a bride for that day when thou shalt unveil the heavens, and cause the mountains to flow down at thy presence, and the valleys to be exalted, the rough places made smooth; that thy glory may fill the earth' (D&C 109:73–74; see also 105: 31–32)" (Seely, "Song of Solomon," 470).

THE BOOK OF THE PROPHET ISAIAH

Introduction

"Isaiah is by every standard *the* messianic prophet of the Old Testament and as such is the most penetrating prophetic voice in that record. He, more than any other witness in the Old World, saw and wrote and prophesied of the Savior's coming both in the meridian of time and again in the latter days" (Holland, *Christ and the New Covenant*, 75).

"Most of us as members of the Church know that we have been commanded to diligently search the words of Isaiah. And most of us agree that that is a hard thing to do. Isaiah is indisputably one of the most challenging books in the Bible. We probably wouldn't feel as intimidated if we had been given the special commandment to search Third Nephi or the book of Luke or most of the sections of the Doctrine and Covenants. But Isaiah seems to have been written for another time and place, in a form and language that sometimes seem to defy understanding" (Parry, et al., *Understanding Isaiah*, 1).

Yet Nephi said, "my soul delighteth in the words of Isaiah" (2 Ne. 25:5). "Isaiah's warnings and prophecies . . . foretell the first and second coming of the Messiah, the restoration of the gospel, the gathering of the house of Israel, the events and leaders before the Millennium, and some characteristics of the Millennium. As Christ said about Isaiah, 'surely he spake as touching all things concerning my people which are of the house of Israel' (3 Ne. 23:2)" (Ludlow, *Isaiah*, 2–3).

Isaiah "served as a prophet in Jerusalem during the forty-year period from 740 to 701 B.C. While his ministry was essentially to the tribe of Judah, or the southern kingdom of Israel, his prophecies extended to the northern kingdom and to gentile nations of his time, as well as to the last days. . . . While the book of Psalms is the book most frequently quoted in the New Testament, Isaiah is the Old Testament *prophet* who is most quoted by Jesus and His apostles. Furthermore, Isaiah is quoted more frequently in the Book of Mormon and the Doctrine and Covenants than any other prophet" (Brewster, *Isaiah Plain and Simple*, 2–3).

Isaiah's ministry spanned four kings of Judah: Uzziah, Jotham, Ahaz, and Hezekiah. "Tradition holds that he was martyred by being placed in a hollow log and sawn asunder by Hezekiah's wicked son and successor, Manasseh" (Winn and Ball, *Making Sense of Isaiah*, 3).

"The writings of Isaiah carry messages of warning to apostate Israel and prophecies of the scattering and gathering of Israel. But even more impressive are his prophecies about the Savior. It is Jesus that gives meaning to all of Isaiah. Therefore, the more one reads Isaiah the better he understands the nature and mission of the Savior and the relationship of that mission to the covenant with Israel which allows those of us living in the latter days to have the gospel of Jesus Christ, partake of priesthood power, gather Israel, and be prepared to meet the Lord" (Pearson, *Old Testament*, 57–58).

Ten Keys to Understanding Isaiah

"If our eternal salvation depends upon our ability to understand the writings of Isaiah as fully and truly as Nephi understood them—and who shall say such is not the case!—how shall we fare in that great day when with Nephi we shall stand before the pleasing bar of Him who said: 'Great are the words of Isaiah'? (3 Ne. 23:1). . . .

"[Isaiah's] prophetic words can and should shine brightly in the heart of every member of the Church. If there are those who truly desire to enlarge and perfect their knowledge of the plan of salvation and of the Lord's dealings with latter-day Israel—all in harmony with his command to search diligently the words of Isaiah (3 Ne. 23:1)—I can give them the key which opens the door to that flood of light and knowledge that flowed from the pen of that witness of Christ and his laws who in many respects was Israel's greatest prophet. Here, in fact, are my ten keys to understanding Isaiah:

"1. *Gain an Over-All Knowledge of the Plan of Salvation and of God's Dealings with His Earthly Children.* The book of Isaiah is not a definitive work that outlines and explains the doctrines of salvation, as do 2 Nephi and Moroni in the Book of Mormon, for instance. Rather, it is written to people who already know—among other things—that Jesus is the Lord through whose atoning blood salvation comes, and that faith, repentance, baptism, the gift of the Holy Ghost, and righteous works are essential to an inheritance in his Father's kingdom. . . .

"2. *Learn the Position and Destiny of the House of Israel in the Lord's Eternal Scheme of Things.* Isaiah's love and interests center in the chosen race. His most detailed and extensive prophecies portray the latter-day triumph and glory of Jacob's seed. . . . .

"3. *Know the Chief Doctrines about Which Isaiah Chose to Write.* His chief doctrinal contributions fall into seven categories: (a) restoration of the gospel in latter days through Joseph Smith, (b) latter-day gathering of Israel and her final triumph and glory, (c) coming forth of the Book of Mormon as a new witness for Christ and the total revolution it will eventually bring in the doctrinal understanding of men, (d) apostate conditions of the nations of the world in the latter days, (e) messianic prophecies relative to our Lord's first coming, (f) second coming of Christ and the millennial reign, and (g) historical data and prophetic utterances relative to his own day. . . .

"4. *Use the Book of Mormon.* . . . Isaiah's writings, in an even more perfect form than found in our Bible, were preserved on the brass plates, and from this source the Nephite prophets quoted 414 verses and paraphrased at least another 34. . . . And the Book of Mormon prophets—note this carefully and let its significance dawn upon you—the Book of Mormon prophets interpreted the passages they used, with the result that this volume of latter-day scripture becomes the witness for and the revealer of the truths of this chief book of Old Testament prophecies. The Book of Mormon is the world's greatest commentary on the book of Isaiah. . . .

"5. *Use Latter-Day Revelation.* The Lord by direct revelation has also taken occasion in our day to interpret, approve, clarify, and enlarge upon the writings of Isaiah. . . .

"6. *Learn How the New Testament Interprets Isaiah.* . . .

"7. *Study Isaiah in Its Old Testament Context.* . . .

"8. *Learn the Manner of Prophesying Used among the Jews in Isaiah's Day.* One of the reasons many of the Nephites did not understand the words of Isaiah was that they did not know 'concerning the manner of prophesying among the Jews' (2 Ne. 25:1). . . . Because of the wickedness of the people, Isaiah and others often spoke in figures, using types and shadows to illustrate their points. Their messages were, in effect, hidden in parables (2 Ne. 25:1–8). . . .

"9. *Have the Spirit of Prophecy.* . . . Scripture comes from God by the power of the Holy Ghost. It does not originate with man. . . . To interpret it, we must be enlightened by the power of the Holy Spirit (2 Pet. 1:20–21). It takes a prophet to understand a prophet, and every faithful member of the Church should have 'the testimony of Jesus' which 'is the spirit of prophecy' (Rev. 19:10). . . .

"10. *Devote Yourself to Hard, Conscientious Study.* Read, ponder, and pray—verse by verse, thought by thought, passage by passage, chapter by chapter!" (McConkie, "Ten Keys to Understanding Isaiah," 78–81).

CHAPTER 1

The people of Israel are apostate, rebellious, and corrupt; only a few remain faithful—The people's sacrifices and feasts are rejected—They are called upon to repent and work righteousness—Zion will be redeemed in the day of restoration.

1 The vision of Isaiah the son of Amoz, which
he saw concerning Judah and Jerusalem
in the days of Uzziah, Jotham, Ahaz, *and*
Hezekiah, kings of Judah.

2 Hear, O heavens, and give ear, O earth: for
the Lord hath spoken, I have nourished and
brought up children, and they have rebelled
against me.

3 The ox knoweth his owner, and the ass his
master's crib: *but* Israel doth not know, my
people doth not consider.

4 Ah sinful nation, a people laden with iniquity, a seed of evildoers, children that are cor-
rupters: they have forsaken the Lord, they
have provoked the Holy One of Israel unto
anger, they are gone away backward.

5 ¶ Why should ye be stricken any more? ye
will revolt more and more: the whole head is
sick, and the whole heart faint.

Isaiah 1:1–9. The Lord Charges Israel with Apostasy and Sin

What is the vision or prophecy of Isaiah? (1:1) "The first chapter is an introduction to the entire book, containing the basic themes of Isaiah's ministry, namely, the sinfulness of Judah and Jerusalem (vv. 3–8), the tender appeals of the Lord (vv. 16–19), the certainty of the coming judgment (vv. 24, 25, 29–31), and the blessedness of salvation to come (vv. 26, 27). . . . [Verse 1] is not a heading to the first chapter only, but to the entire collection of Isaiah's prophecies. . . . This verse is found in all the ancient manuscripts and versions" (Young, *Book of Isaiah*, 1:27, 28).

What does it mean when the Lord calls for us to "hear"? (1:2) This verse starts with the word "hear." President Russell M. Nelson taught: "Our Father knows that when we are surrounded by uncertainty and fear, what will help us the very most is to hear His Son.

"Because when we seek to hear—truly hear—His Son, we will be guided to know what to do in any circumstance. . . . We are to *hear* the words of the Lord, *hearken* to them, and *heed* what He has told us!

"As we seek to be disciples of Jesus Christ, our efforts to *hear Him* need to be ever more intentional. It takes conscious and consistent effort to fill our daily lives with His words, His teachings, His truths" ("Hear Him," 89).

How is Israel like an ox and an ass? (1:2–3) "These two verses appear to introduce a trial scene. Here nature serves the purposes of prophecy. The heavens and earth witness God's complaint against his people, and the ox and the donkey dumbly rebuke Israel's ingratitude. Unreasoning beasts exhibit more sense and appreciation than unthinking Israel (cf. Jer. 8:7). The words 'children' and 'they' are both emphatic in the Hebrew, underlining the unthinkable character of such filial rebellion" (*Expositor's Bible Commentary [Abridged]*, 1045).

How does Isaiah portray Israel's rebellion? (1:5–8) "In 1:5–8 Isaiah uses two graphic figures to depict the nation's spiritual condition. The first (vv. 5–6) is that of a bruised and wounded body that is left untended; the second (v. 8), that of an abandoned hut in a harvested

6 From the sole of the foot even unto the head *there is* no soundness in it; *but* wounds, and bruises, and putrifying sores: they have not been closed, neither bound up, neither mollified with ointment.

7 Your country *is* desolate, your cities *are* burned with fire: your land, strangers devour it in your presence, and *it is* desolate, as overthrown by strangers.

8 And the daughter of Zion is left as a cottage in a vineyard, as a lodge in a garden of cucumbers, as a besieged city.

9 Except the LORD of hosts had left unto us a very small remnant, we should have been as Sodom, *and* we should have been like unto Gomorrah.

10 ¶ Hear the word of the LORD, ye rulers of Sodom; give ear unto the law of our God, ye people of Gomorrah.

11 To what purpose *is* the multitude of your sacrifices unto me? saith the LORD: I am full of the burnt offerings of rams, and the fat of fed beasts; and I delight not in the blood of bullocks, or of lambs, or of he goats.

12 When ye come to appear before me, who hath required this at your hand, to tread my courts?

13 Bring no more vain oblations; incense is an abomination unto me; the new moons and sabbaths, the calling of assemblies, I cannot away with; *it is* iniquity, even the solemn meeting.

14 Your new moons and your appointed feasts my soul hateth: they are a trouble unto me; I am weary to bear *them.*

15 And when ye spread forth your hands, I will hide mine eyes from you: yea, when ye make many prayers, I will not hear: your hands are full of blood.

field. The harvesters are gone, and the winter winds have blown away most of the odds and ends used to build the hut. That is what Israel is like. Yet for all of this, it seems Israel cannot put two and two together and come up with four. If only they would turn back to the Lord, he would gladly restore the blessings he had formerly showered on them" (Oswalt, *Isaiah*, 73).

Why is Israel compared to a "lodge in a garden" or "cottage in a vineyard"? (1:8) "The verse illustrates Isaiah's powerful use of imagery. The 'daughter of Zion' is a personification of the city, Jerusalem . . . The 'shelter [cottage] in a vineyard' is an image of desolation: a rude hut used in late summer by watchmen who kept the birds away from the crops, but abandoned in every other season. And the 'city under siege [besieged city]' is an image of desperation and hunger" (Richards, *Bible Reader's Companion*, 412).

Isaiah 1:10–15. The Physical and Spiritual Consequences of Disobedience

Why would the Lord denounce Israel's animal sacrifices? (1:11–14) "Many writers have supposed these verses to mean that Jehovah had no use for sacrifices and that the ritual of Israel was distasteful to Him. Far more probable is the view that He was not denouncing sacrifices and worship as such, but only refuting their efficacy and value when performed by a wicked and hypocritical people" (Sperry, *Voice of Israel's Prophets*, 21–22).

What are "vain oblations"? (1:13) *Oblations* are offerings or sacrifices to God. "What Isaiah is saying, as you know, is that it doesn't matter what our prayer life is like or our temple work or the ordinances we've participated in or what sacred days and ceremonies we celebrate. . . . If we do not relieve the oppressed and the widow and the orphan or the minority groups or anyone else in need, then our formal religious life is vain" (Bennion, *Best of Lowell L. Bennion*, 24). How can you ensure that your religious activities are sincere and genuine, and thus worthy of the Lord's blessings? ⊕

What does it mean to "spread forth your hands"? (1:15) "In both the Old and New Testaments, the temple is referred to as 'the house of prayer.' . . . Throughout the Bible there are descriptions of individuals raising their hands during prayer. . . . This gesture was also employed when calling down the blessings of heaven" (Brown, *Gate of Heaven*, 124, 125). However, in this case, the Lord rejects their prayers because their hands are "full of bloodshed" (see Isaiah 1:15*b*).

Isaiah 1:16–20. Israel May Be Forgiven if They Repent

Why are the fatherless and widows mentioned? (1:17) "As Isaiah begins his writings, he addresses Israelites as if they were in Sodom and Gomorrah and as if those in the city of Jerusalem were harlots (see Isa. 1:10, 21). Such a beginning suggests that the society in which he lived neglected the rights of the defenseless" (Black, *400 Questions and Answers about the Old Testament*, 167). "The widow and orphan are mentioned together because of their helplessness, and they thus become a symbol of those that are weak and without help. They have no one to plead their cause or to defend them" (Young, *Book of Isaiah*, 1:74).

Why does Isaiah compare our sins to scarlet which can become white? (1:18) "The scarlet dye of the Old Testament was not only colorful but also colorfast, meaning that its vivid color stuck to the wool and would not fade no matter how many times it was washed [see 'Scarlet, Crimson, Snow, and Wool,' *Ensign*, Dec. 2016, 64–65]. Satan wields this reasoning like a club: white wool stained scarlet can never go back to being white. But Jesus Christ declares, 'My ways [are] higher than your ways' [Isaiah 55:9], and the miracle of His grace is that when we repent of our sins, His scarlet blood returns us to purity. It isn't logical, but it is nevertheless true" (Eubank, "Christ: The Light that Shines in Darkness," 75). ⊕

Isaiah 1:21–31. The Lord Pronounces His Judgment, Purges the Wicked, and Redeems the Righteous

How does Isaiah prepare Jerusalem for the judgment? (1:21–31) "Structurally, the last section of chapter 1 can stand alone as an independent pronouncement. The Lord first addresses a very wicked Jerusalem, threatening vengeance upon those who become his enemies. He then foretells a purging and a restoration of Zion, and concludes by prophesying the destruction of the wicked. This pronouncement is divided into three segments in the King James Version . . . which follow a chiastic

16 ¶ Wash you, make you clean; put away
the evil of your doings from before mine
eyes; cease to do evil;

17 Learn to do well; seek judgment, relieve
the oppressed, judge the fatherless, plead for
the widow.

18 Come now, and let us reason together,
saith the LORD: though your sins be as scarlet,
they shall be as white as snow; though they be
red like crimson, they shall be as wool.

19 If ye be willing and obedient, ye shall eat
the good of the land:

20 But if ye refuse and rebel, ye shall be devoured with the sword: for the mouth of the
LORD hath spoken *it*.

21 ¶ How is the faithful city become an harlot! it was full of judgment; righteousness
lodged in it; but now murderers.

pattern of negative-positive-negative, that is: warning first of wickedness and vengeance (vs. 21–24), then promising cleansing and redemption (vs. 25–27), and finally burning the wicked and the worldly (vs. 28–31). The primary themes of these three segments also follow the common and easily remembered pattern of apostasy-restoration-judgment" (Ludlow, *Isaiah*, 78).

22 Thy silver is become dross, thy wine mixed with water:

23 Thy princes *are* rebellious, and companions of thieves: every one loveth gifts, and followeth after rewards: they judge not the fatherless, neither doth the cause of the widow come unto them.

What does silver becoming dross and wine mixed with water symbolize? (1:22–23) "Illustration ([v.] 22) leads into reality ([v.] 23). *Silver* which has *become dross* is totally degenerate; once *wine* is touched by *water*, no particle remains undiluted. Thus sin degrades the nature it enters and leaves no part untainted. The *rulers* provide a window into society: Godward they are *rebels* (cf. 2) and break his law by consorting with *thieves*, they abuse their position for self-advantage in *bribes* and *gifts*, and have no concern for other people" (Motyer, *Isaiah*, 55).

24 Therefore saith the Lord, the LORD of hosts, the mighty One of Israel, Ah, I will ease me of mine adversaries, and avenge me of mine enemies:

25 ¶ And I will turn my hand upon thee, and purely purge away thy dross, and take away all thy tin:

26 And I will restore thy judges as at the first, and thy counsellors as at the beginning: afterward thou shalt be called, The city of righteousness, the faithful city.

27 Zion shall be redeemed with judgment, and her converts with righteousness.

When will judges be restored and Zion redeemed? (1:24–27) "This prophecy speaks of our day. Isaiah prophesies of two separate groups who will live in the last days . . . those who belong to Zion, and those who belong to the community of wickedness. In the latter days, Zion will be restored, redeemed, and cleansed; her dross and tin will be removed, her righteous judges and counselors will be restored, and once again Zion will be the faithful city. . . . The text makes clear that it is the Lord's atoning sacrifice that will cleanse members of Zion: 'I will turn my hand upon thee, and purely purge away thy dross' (1:25). Those who belong to the wicked community will be destroyed, 'consumed,' 'ashamed,' 'confounded,' and burned" (Parry, et al., *Understanding Isaiah*, 20–21).

28 ¶ And the destruction of the transgressors and of the sinners *shall be* together, and they that forsake the LORD shall be consumed.

29 For they shall be ashamed of the oaks which ye have desired, and ye shall be confounded for the gardens that ye have chosen.

30 For ye shall be as an oak whose leaf fadeth, and as a garden that hath no water.

31 And the strong shall be as tow, and the maker of it as a spark, and they shall both burn together, and none shall quench *them*.

Why would the people be "ashamed of the oaks"? (1:29) "The 'oaks' . . . are usually identified as 'terebinth' trees in modern translations. . . . Groves of terebinths were used in pagan idol worship because, among other reasons, the pagans considered these evergreen trees to represent perpetual renewal and fertility. Thus, in Isaiah, groves of trees were often synonymous with idolatry. . . . He is referring to either their coveting and yearning to have their yards and estates landscaped with groves of terebinths, or their desiring to use terebinths for places of idol worship" (Ludlow, *Isaiah*, 83–84).

CHAPTER 2

Isaiah sees the latter-day temple, gathering of Israel, and millennial judgment and peace—The proud and wicked will be brought low at the Second Coming—Compare 2 Nephi 12.

1 The word that Isaiah the son of Amoz saw concerning Judah and Jerusalem.

2 And it shall come to pass in the last days, *that* the mountain of the LORD's house shall be established in the top of the mountains, and shall be exalted above the hills; and all nations shall flow unto it.

3 And many people shall go and say, Come ye, and let us go up to the mountain of the LORD, to the house of the God of Jacob; and he will teach us of his ways, and we will walk in his paths: for out of Zion shall go forth the law, and the word of the LORD from Jerusalem.

4 And he shall judge among the nations, and shall rebuke many people: and they shall beat their swords into plowshares, and their spears into pruninghooks: nation shall not lift up sword against nation, neither shall they learn war any more.

5 O house of Jacob, come ye, and let us walk in the light of the LORD.

Isaiah 2:1–5. In the Last Days the Lord's Temple Will Be Built in the Mountains and There Will Be Peace in the World

How has establishing the Lord's house in the tops of the mountains been fulfilled? (2:2) "Ever since the Salt Lake Temple was dedicated, we have interpreted that scripture from Isaiah, repeated again in Micah (see Micah 4:1–2), as applying to this sacred house of the Lord. And of this place, since the day of its dedication, an ever-increasing number from across the world have said in effect, 'Come ye, and let us go up to the mountain of the Lord, to the house of the God of Jacob, that He might teach us of His ways, that we might walk in His paths'" (Hinckley, "An Ensign to the Nations, a Light to the World," 82). See commentary in *Book of Mormon Study Guide: Start to Finish, Revised Edition* for 2 Nephi 12:2. ⊕

What does it mean to walk in the Lord's paths? (2:3) "When we're baptized, we receive the gift of the Holy Ghost. That gift provides us guidance and direction, helps us repent and be clean, and changes our lives. These blessings are a result of living on the covenant path—or living faithfully according to the covenants we've made and will make, and doing the things that help us stay faithful. . . . As we faithfully follow the covenant path, we'll end up doing a lot of things that can help us grow, enjoy life, and be happy" ("Your Covenant Path," 13). These paths are also called the "path of the just" (Proverbs 4:18) or the "strait and narrow path" (2 Nephi 31:18).

Why does Isaiah invite the "house of Jacob" to walk in the Lord's light? (2:5) Both the Book of Mormon and the Joseph Smith Translation make it clear that all of the house of Jacob—that is, the house of Israel—have wandered off the path. "O house of Jacob, come ye, and let us walk in the light of the Lord; *yea, come, for ye have all gone astray, everyone to his wicked ways*" (2 Nephi 12:5; emphasis added). Isaiah invites God's people to walk in the light.

6 ¶ Therefore thou hast forsaken thy people the house of Jacob, because they be replenished from the east, and *are* soothsayers like the Philistines, and they please themselves in the children of strangers.

7 Their land also is full of silver and gold, neither *is there any* end of their treasures; their land is also full of horses, neither *is there any* end of their chariots:

8 Their land also is full of idols; they worship the work of their own hands, that which their own fingers have made:

9 And the mean man boweth down, and the great man humbleth himself: therefore forgive them not.

10 ¶ Enter into the rock, and hide thee in the dust, for fear of the LORD, and for the glory of his majesty.

11 The lofty looks of man shall be humbled, and the haughtiness of men shall be bowed down, and the LORD alone shall be exalted in that day.

12 For the day of the LORD of hosts *shall be* upon every *one that is* proud and lofty, and upon every *one that is* lifted up; and he shall be brought low:

13 And upon all the cedars of Lebanon, *that are* high and lifted up, and upon all the oaks of Bashan,

14 And upon all the high mountains, and upon all the hills *that are* lifted up,

15 And upon every high tower, and upon every fenced wall,

16 And upon all the ships of Tarshish, and upon all pleasant pictures.

Isaiah 2:6–18. Before Peace Comes in the Last Days, There Will Be a Time of Judgment

What Israelite sins does Isaiah denounce in his prayer? (2:6–9) "In Isaiah's day, God had abandoned His people because they had chosen not to walk in His light. Like the Philistines and other non-Israelite people around them, they had instead chosen to turn to divination and folk-magic practices" (Muhlestein, *Scripture Study Made Simple*, 334). "[This is a] criticism of the nation's sins: magic, amassing extraordinary amounts of wealth, pursuing military power, and idolatry. All of these vices embody inappropriate confidence in humanity's own powers. This confidence is not only mistaken, but offensive to God" (*Jewish Study Bible* [2014], 771). To better understand about the mean man bowing down, etc., see commentary in *Book of Mormon Study Guide: Start to Finish, Revised Edition* for 2 Nephi 12:9.

Who is to hide in the rocks for fear of the Lord? (2:10) The Book of Mormon version of this verse clarifies that it is the "wicked ones" who are to hide from God because His majesty will smite them (see 2 Nephi 12:10). The fact that they seek to "take refuge under ground or in the rocks, [is] an advice peculiarly significant in Palestine, a country full of caves, often used . . . for this very purpose [1 Samuel 13:6, 14:11; Judges 6:2]" (Alexander, *Commentary on Isaiah*, 102).

How does Isaiah symbolically portray the proud in these verses? (2:12–16) The cedars of Lebanon and the oaks of Bashan "were valued for their size, beauty, strength and durability. They would be used in the building projects (such as gates and palaces) that were the sources of pride for nations and in which they would put their trust. . . . Towers and walls were features of fortified cities [and] there were also many garrison fortresses built along trade routes and borders. . . . Trading ships [of Tarshish] . . . could feature either one or two banks of oars. A typical length would be about fifty feet, though larger ones are known" (Walton, et al., *IVP Bible Background Commentary*, 588). See commentary in *Book of Mormon Study Guide: Start to Finish, Revised Edition* for 2 Nephi 12:12–16.

Isaiah 2:19–22. Wicked People Will Try to Hide Themselves and Their Sins from the Lord

Why won't the wicked be able to hide from the Lord in the last days? (2:19) "Among the predicted commotions of nature to take place in the last days is the upheaval and shaking of the earth. As Jesus taught his disciples on the Mount of Olives . . . 'There shall be famines, and pestilences, and earthquakes, in divers places' (Matthew 24:7; see also Mark 13:8; Luke 21:11; JS–M 1:29). This declaration is repeated in a revelation given in 1831 (see D&C 45:33) and was mentioned by the ancient prophet Moroni as one of the signs of the last days (see Mormon 8:30). . . . Latter-day revelation indicates that God chastises and calls people to repentance by the voice and testimony of earthquakes (see D&C 43:25; 87:6; 88:89)" (Brewster, *Behold, I Come Quickly*, 26–27).

Why would idols of silver and gold be thrown to moles and bats? (2:20) "This verse demonstrates again the prophet's skill in irony. . . . Thus the effect is to juxtapose the supposed preciousness of the idols with the squeamishness felt toward the small, unclean rodents. Mighty gods? Hardly. The same people who made the idols *for themselves to worship* (a telling phrase) now fling them away to their true domain. The God who alone is worthy of worship has appeared" (Oswalt, *Book of Isaiah, Chapters 1–39*, 128). See commentary in *Book of Mormon Study Guide: Start to Finish, Revised Edition* for 2 Nephi 12:20.

What does "whose breath is in his nostrils" mean? (2:22) "Here is the reason why it is folly to trust in man; in his nostrils there is a breath. Man's life is transitory. God had breathed into man the breath that brings life (Gen. 2:7; 7:22). Man therefore does not exist through his own strength. As that breath was breathed into him, so also it may be taken away and depart from him (Ps. 116:4)" (Young, *Book of Isaiah*, 1:133).

17 And the loftiness of man shall be bowed down, and the haughtiness of men shall be made low: and the LORD alone shall be exalted in that day.

18 And the idols he shall utterly abolish.

19 And they shall go into the holes of the rocks, and into the caves of the earth, for fear of the LORD, and for the glory of his majesty, when he ariseth to shake terribly the earth.

20 In that day a man shall cast his idols of silver, and his idols of gold, which they made *each one* for himself to worship, to the moles and to the bats;

21 To go into the clefts of the rocks, and into the tops of the ragged rocks, for fear of the LORD, and for the glory of his majesty, when he ariseth to shake terribly the earth.

22 Cease ye from man, whose breath *is* in his nostrils: for wherein is he to be accounted of?

CHAPTER 3

Judah and Jerusalem will be punished for their disobedience—The Lord pleads for and judges His people—The daughters of Zion are cursed and tormented for their worldliness—Compare 2 Nephi 13.

1 For, behold, the Lord, the LORD of hosts, doth take away from Jerusalem and from Judah the stay and the staff, the whole stay of bread, and the whole stay of water,

2 The mighty man, and the man of war, the judge, and the prophet, and the prudent, and the ancient,

3 The captain of fifty, and the honourable man, and the counsellor, and the cunning artificer, and the eloquent orator.

4 And I will give children *to be* their princes, and babes shall rule over them.

5 And the people shall be oppressed, every one by another, and every one by his neighbour: the child shall behave himself proudly against the ancient, and the base against the honourable.

6 When a man shall take hold of his brother of the house of his father, *saying,* Thou hast clothing, be thou our ruler, and *let* this ruin *be* under thy hand:

7 In that day shall he swear, saying, I will not be an healer; for in my house *is* neither bread nor clothing: make me not a ruler of the people.

8 For Jerusalem is ruined, and Judah is fallen: because their tongue and their doings *are* against the LORD, to provoke the eyes of his glory.

Isaiah 3:1–15. The Wicked in Judah Suffer from Famine and Conquest

Why would the Lord remove these leaders from Judah? (3:2–3) The people listed in this passage indicate "that God would remove everything that supports life and social order. Specifically, this included food and water, and a host of key military (hero, warrior, captain of fifty), political (judge, elder, man of rank, and counselor), religious (prophet, soothsayer, enchanter), and economic (skilled craftsman or possibly conjurer) leaders. These people had a role and status in society that gave order and security to the common people" (Smith, *Isaiah 1–39*, 145–46). See commentary in *Book of Mormon Study Guide: Start to Finish, Revised Edition* for 2 Nephi 13:2–3.

Why would "children" and "babes" rule over Jerusalem and Judah? (3:4–5) "Only the young or inexperienced will be left in Judah to rule. Seven of the kings who ruled over Judah during the time of Isaiah up to the Babylonian captivity were between the age of eight and twenty-five when they begin their reigns, and all but one are characterized as 'evil' in the Old Testament account (see Nyman, *Great Are the Words of Isaiah*, 35). Under these circumstances, neighbors will oppress one another, and the young will lose respect for their elders" (Bytheway, *Isaiah for Airheads*, 80).

In what way is our spiritual condition reflected in our countenance? (3:9) "May your efforts to develop Christlike attributes be successful so that His image may be engraven in your countenance and His attributes manifest in your behavior. Then, when your children or others feel of your love and see your behavior, it will remind them of the Savior and draw them to Him" (Robbins, "What Manner of Men and Women Ought Ye to Be?" 105). See commentary in *Book of Mormon Study Guide: Start to Finish, Revised Edition* for 2 Nephi 13:9.

9 ¶ The shew of their countenance doth witness against them; and they declare their sin as Sodom, they hide *it* not. Woe unto their soul! for they have rewarded evil unto themselves.

10 Say ye to the righteous, that *it shall be* well *with him:* for they shall eat the fruit of their doings.

11 Woe unto the wicked! *it shall be* ill *with him:* for the reward of his hands shall be given him.

12 ¶ *As for* my people, children *are* their oppressors, and women rule over them. O my people, they which lead thee cause *thee* to err, and destroy the way of thy paths.

13 The LORD standeth up to plead, and standeth to judge the people.

14 The LORD will enter into judgment with the ancients of his people, and the princes thereof: for ye have eaten up the vineyard; the spoil of the poor *is* in your houses.

15 What mean ye *that* ye beat my people to pieces, and grind the faces of the poor? saith the Lord GOD of hosts.

Why will the Lord judge us for the way we treat the poor and needy? (3:14–15) "Down through history, poverty has been one of humankind's greatest and most widespread challenges. Its obvious toll is usually physical, but the spiritual and emotional damage it can bring may be even more debilitating. In any case, the great Redeemer has issued no more persistent call than for us to join Him in lifting this burden from the people. . . . The Lord commanded the members to 'look to the poor and . . . needy, and administer to their relief that they shall not suffer' [D&C 38:35]. Note the imperative tone of that passage—'they *shall* not suffer.' That is language God uses when He means business" (Holland, "Are We Not All Beggars?" 40).

Isaiah 3:16–26. Zion's Daughters Are Proud and Will Be Punished, and Many Men Shall Die in War

What does Isaiah's portrayal of the daughters of Zion tell us about the conditions in ancient Israel? (3:16–23) "The poet [Isaiah] offers us an image of [a] public occasion when the most self-indulgent in Jerusalem show off themselves and their extravagance. . . . So here, the poet in great detail mocks the strutting, self-announcing arrogance of those who parade themselves and their finery; he comments on necks extended, eyes cutting at an angle, feet walking in tiny steps—all gestures calculated to call attention to those who are attired in finery of the most exotic sort. All this transpires while widows and orphans are denied life!" (Brueggemann, *Isaiah 1–39*, 37).

16 ¶ Moreover the LORD saith, Because the daughters of Zion are haughty, and walk with stretched forth necks and wanton eyes, walking and mincing *as* they go, and making a tinkling with their feet:

17 Therefore the Lord will smite with a scab the crown of the head of the daughters of Zion, and the LORD will discover their secret parts.

18 In that day the Lord will take away the bravery of *their* tinkling ornaments *about their feet,* and *their* cauls, and *their* round tires like the moon,

19 The chains, and the bracelets, and the mufflers,

20 The bonnets, and the ornaments of the legs, and the headbands, and the tablets, and the earrings,

21 The rings, and nose jewels,

22 The changeable suits of apparel, and the mantles, and the wimples, and the crisping pins,

23 The glasses, and the fine linen, and the hoods, and the veils.

24 And it shall come to pass, *that* instead of sweet smell there shall be stink; and instead of a girdle a rent; and instead of well set hair baldness; and instead of a stomacher a girding of sackcloth; *and* burning instead of beauty.

Why will conditions for the worldly daughters of Zion change so drastically? (3:24) "The prophet contrasts their former beauty with the results of judgment. Because of their wickedness, the beauty, the pride, and the fashion shall become tragedy, disaster, and slavery. The girdle in verse 24 was the sash used to fasten the outer clothing. Keil and Delitzsch showed that the 'rent' which was to replace it was the rope used to bind slaves. Sackcloth was black goat's hair worn at times of great mourning. The 'burning' refers to the branding that often accompanied one's being made a slave [see Keil and Delitzsch, *Commentary* [on Isaiah 3:24]" (*Old Testament Student Manual: 1 Kings–Malachi*, 141).

25 Thy men shall fall by the sword, and thy mighty in the war.

In what way does this warning of war apply to us? (3:25) "'Thy men shall fall by the sword, and thy mighty in the war,' Isaiah says of a latter-day Zion in which there are some wicked and wanton people. . . . Let all men know of the coming wars and desolations; let them know that Armageddon is at the door; let them know that the sword of the Lord's justice hangs heavily over all men. Let not these things be hidden from them. They are entitled to be warned, and God, by the mouth of Isaiah, raises the warning voice" (McConkie, *Millennial Messiah*, 450). See commentary in *Book of Mormon Study Guide: Start to Finish, Revised Edition* for 2 Nephi 13:26.

26 And her gates shall lament and mourn; and she *being* desolate shall sit upon the ground.

What might the woman sitting on the ground symbolize? (3:26) "Sitting on the ground was a posture that denoted mourning and deep distress. The prophet Jeremiah (Lamentations 2:8) has given it the first place among many indications of sorrow, in the following elegant description of the same state of distress of his country: 'The elders of the daughter of Sion sit on the ground, they are silent: They have cast up dust on their heads; they have girded themselves with sackcloth; The virgins of Jerusalem have bowed down their heads to the ground'" (*Adam Clarke's Commentary* [on Isaiah 3:26]).

Isaiah 4:1–6. During the Millennium, the Lord Will Bless Zion, Jerusalem, and His Worthy Children

In what day were these conditions to exist? (4:1) "The [Joseph Smith Translation] and the Hebrew Bible place this verse in the previous chapter, where it fits the context much better. This condition will result from the war described in 3:25–26. While this verse has been interpreted by some as a prophecy of plural marriage in the Church, a close examination will show that it refers to the world, not the Church" (Nyman, *Great Are the Words of Isaiah*, 36). See commentary in *Book of Mormon Study Guide: Start to Finish, Revised Edition* for 2 Nephi 14:1.

What is the branch that will "be beautiful and glorious"? (4:2) "The metaphorical title indicates a person to 'spring up' or 'sprout from' David's line. Six [Old Testament] passages use this term of the coming Messiah (Isa. 4:2; 11:1; Jer. 23:5; 33:15; Zech. 3:8; 6:12). In them the Messiah is associated with washing away the sins of God's people 'in a single day' (Zech. 3:9) and with the kingdom of glory to follow. The Branch, empowered by the Spirit, is to bring justice and righteousness to earth and fulfill the covenant promises given to David (Jer. 33:15–22)" (Richards, *Bible Reader's Companion*, 413).

What blessings come to those who escape God's judgments? (4:2–5) "This section . . . deals with those who have survived the judgments of God, as listed in Isa. 3:14–26, perhaps in the dawning of the millennial day. The survivors are those who are the 'escaped of Israel and Judah' and have been 'left in Zion' (JST, Isa. 4:2) to be 'written among the living in Jerusalem' (Isa. 4:3). The survivors will love to participate in the ordinances of the Lord's temple, for they will be 'called holy' (Isa. 4:3 . . .), their filth and iniquity will be removed, and the same elements (cloud, smoke, fire, glory) that attended and protected the ancient Israelite temples will exist among them in Zion" (Parry and Parry, *Understanding the Signs of the Times*, 357). See commentary in *Book of Mormon Study Guide: Start to Finish, Revised Edition* for 2 Nephi 14:2–5.

What will the Lord create in every home in Zion? (4:5) "I rejoice in the prophecy of Isaiah that the time will come when 'upon every dwelling place of mount Zion' there shall be 'a cloud . . . by day, and . . . a flaming fire by night' (Isa. 4:5), when the Spirit of God will abide in the homes of His people continually" (Porter, "Building the Kingdom," 81). ⊕

CHAPTER 4

Zion and her daughters will be redeemed and cleansed in the millennial day—Compare 2 Nephi 14.

1 And in that day seven women shall take hold of one man, saying, We will eat our own bread, and wear our own apparel: only let us be called by thy name, to take away our reproach.

2 In that day shall the branch of the LORD be beautiful and glorious, and the fruit of the earth *shall be* excellent and comely for them that are escaped of Israel.

3 And it shall come to pass, *that he that is* left in Zion, and *he that* remaineth in Jerusalem, shall be called holy, *even* every one that is written among the living in Jerusalem:

4 When the Lord shall have washed away the filth of the daughters of Zion, and shall have purged the blood of Jerusalem from the midst thereof by the spirit of judgment, and by the spirit of burning.

5 And the LORD will create upon every dwelling place of mount Zion, and upon her assemblies, a cloud and smoke by day, and the shining of a flaming fire by night: for upon all the glory *shall be* a defence.

6 And there shall be a tabernacle for a shadow in the daytime from the heat, and for a place of refuge, and for a covert from storm and from rain.

CHAPTER 5

The Lord's vineyard (Israel) will become desolate, and His people will be scattered—Woes will come upon them in their apostate and scattered state—The Lord will lift an ensign and gather Israel—Compare 2 Nephi 15.

1 Now will I sing to my wellbeloved a song of my beloved touching his vineyard. My wellbeloved hath a vineyard in a very fruitful hill:

2 And he fenced it, and gathered out the stones thereof, and planted it with the choicest vine, and built a tower in the midst of it, and also made a winepress therein: and he looked that it should bring forth grapes, and it brought forth wild grapes.

3 And now, O inhabitants of Jerusalem, and men of Judah, judge, I pray you, betwixt me and my vineyard.

4 What could have been done more to my vineyard, that I have not done in it? wherefore, when I looked that it should bring forth grapes, brought it forth wild grapes?

5 And now go to; I will tell you what I will do to my vineyard: I will take away the hedge thereof, and it shall be eaten up; *and* break down the wall thereof, and it shall be trodden down:

6 And I will lay it waste: it shall not be pruned, nor digged; but there shall come up briers and thorns: I will also command the clouds that they rain no rain upon it.

7 For the vineyard of the Lord of hosts *is* the house of Israel, and the men of Judah his pleasant plant: and he looked for judgment, but behold oppression; for righteousness, but behold a cry.

Isaiah 5:1–7. The Lord Compares Israel to a Carefully Tended Vineyard That Brings Forth Wild Fruit

What is the nature of Isaiah's song? (5:1–7) Isaiah begins this chapter with a poetic song. "The prophet returns to words of judgment against Jerusalem and Judah, but this judgment is veiled in an allegory about his 'friend's' vineyard. . . . The prophet's friend invested time and energy into his vineyard with the expectation of a return on this investment. For crops like grapes, full production did not begin for several years after the vines were planted. The owner of the vineyard had to have confidence and patience that a harvest would come one day. But the song is about disappointment. The anticipated results of the efforts do not materialize: the vineyard produces only bitter grapes" (Hoppe, *Isaiah*, 21). ⊕

What more could the Lord have done to save His people? (5:4) "People are not plants; they have agency. So there is no adequate answer for God's question about why his vineyard brought forth wild grapes. When he laments, 'What could have been done more to my vineyard, that I have not done in it?' (Isa. 5:4), we see him revealed as a very concerned Father who strives with all the powers at his command to bring good into the lives of his children" (Meservy, "God Is with Us," 94). ⊕

What do the briers and thorns symbolize? (5:6) The "characteristics of the lowly briars and thorns render them an appropriate metaphor for pride and worldliness. More than seventy species of thorned and spiny plants are indigenous to Israel. . . . All thistles have some characteristics in common. They are invasive, noxious, and unruly, doing harm to any that would touch them—traits commonly found in the proud and worldly as well. Isaiah coupled the lowly briars and thorns with the lofty trees of the forest to illustrate and foretell the fate of the ungrateful, rebellious, and worldly, be they rich or poor, great or small" (Ball, "Isaiah's Imagery of Plants and Planting," 24).

Isaiah 5:8–25. Isaiah Pronounces Six Woes on Israel

Why would Isaiah condemn "join[ing] house to house"? (5:8) "This woe is pronounced on the wealthy landowners who covet and buy up property, thus depriving the poor of their heritage (see Micah 2:1–2). The law of ancient Israel prescribed that land could not 'be sold for ever' (Leviticus 25:23; see also 1 Kings 21). It was to remain within families as a heritage for posterity. When economical circumstances necessitated the sale of land, it was to be returned to the original owners in the year of jubilee, which occurred every fifty years" (Brewster, *Isaiah Plain and Simple*, 46). See commentary in *Book of Mormon Study Guide: Start to Finish, Revised Edition* for 2 Nephi 15:8.

What does the size of the harvest indicate? (5:10) "The seriousness of the desolation in the fields is demonstrated by the terms used in verse 10. Ordinarily, a farmer would hope to get a thirty, sixty, or even a hundred-fold increase from the seed he planted. But instead he would only get one tenth back because one homer of seed (equal to ten ephahs) would only yield one ephah of harvest. This is a type of 'reverse tithing' that results from unfaithfulness" (Ludlow, *Companion to Your Study of the Old Testament*, 286).

What role does alcohol play in the Bible? (5:11–13) "Wine in Scripture is often associated with joyful occasions. . . . Yet the [Old Testament] bluntly condemns both drunkenness and love of drink (Prov. 20:1; 21:17; 23:20–21), and the [New Testament] views alcohol abuse as characteristic of a pagan rather than a Christian lifestyle (Eph. 5:18; 1 Peter 4:3)" (Richards, *Bible Reader's Companion*, 414). "Isaiah includes several warnings in his writings concerning the evils of 'strong drink,' including the contents of [verses 11 and 22]" (Ludlow, *Companion to Your Study of the Old Testament*, 286).

8 ¶ Woe unto them that join house to house, *that* lay field to field, till *there be* no place, that they may be placed alone in the midst of the earth!

9 In mine ears *said* the LORD of hosts, Of a truth many houses shall be desolate, *even* great and fair, without inhabitant.

10 Yea, ten acres of vineyard shall yield one bath, and the seed of an homer shall yield an ephah.

11 ¶ Woe unto them that rise up early in the morning, *that* they may follow strong drink; that continue until night, *till* wine inflame them!

12 And the harp, and the viol, the tabret, and pipe, and wine, are in their feasts: but they regard not the work of the LORD, neither consider the operation of his hands.

13 ¶ Therefore my people are gone into captivity, because *they have* no knowledge: and their honourable men *are* famished, and their multitude dried up with thirst.

14 Therefore hell hath enlarged herself, and opened her mouth without measure: and their glory, and their multitude, and their pomp, and he that rejoiceth, shall descend into it.

15 And the mean man shall be brought down, and the mighty man shall be humbled, and the eyes of the lofty shall be humbled:

16 But the LORD of hosts shall be exalted in judgment, and God that is holy shall be sanctified in righteousness.

17 Then shall the lambs feed after their manner, and the waste places of the fat ones shall strangers eat.

18 Woe unto them that draw iniquity with cords of vanity, and sin as it were with a cart rope:

19 That say, Let him make speed, *and* hasten his work, that we may see *it:* and let the counsel of the Holy One of Israel draw nigh and come, that we may know *it!*

20 ¶ Woe unto them that call evil good, and good evil; that put darkness for light, and light for darkness; that put bitter for sweet, and sweet for bitter!

21 Woe unto *them that are* wise in their own eyes, and prudent in their own sight!

22 Woe unto *them that are* mighty to drink wine, and men of strength to mingle strong drink:

23 Which justify the wicked for reward, and take away the righteousness of the righteous from him!

24 Therefore as the fire devoureth the stubble, and the flame consumeth the chaff, *so* their root shall be as rottenness, and their blossom shall go up as dust: because they have cast away the law of the LORD of hosts, and despised the word of the Holy One of Israel.

25 Therefore is the anger of the LORD kindled against his people, and he hath stretched forth his hand against them, and hath smitten them: and the hills did tremble, and their carcases *were* torn in the midst of the streets. For all this his anger is not turned away, but his hand *is* stretched out still.

What does sin have to do with cords and cart ropes? (5:18) "Isaiah condemned those who think they can give up one sin and yet cling tenaciously to others. 'Woe unto them that draw iniquity with cords of vanity, and sin as it were with a cart rope' (Isaiah 5:18). Occasionally we cut the 'cords of vanity' and let go of a favorite sin, but all too often we only periodically cast off from our cart a sin here and there rather than just letting go of the cart rope" (Top, *Peculiar Treasure*, 160).

What is the danger in confusing good and evil? (5:20) "Spiritually dangerous ideas and actions frequently can appear to be attractive, desirable, or pleasurable. Thus, in our contemporary world, each of us needs to be aware of beguiling bad that pretends to be good. . . . How blessed we are to live in this latter-day dispensation when restored gospel light can shine brightly in our lives and help us to discern the adversary's dark deceptions and distractions" (Bednar, "Watchful unto Prayer Continually," 33). How do you avoid the worldly tendency to confuse good and evil?

What does it mean to "justify the wicked for [a] reward"? (5:23) "The issue is the distortion of public order, the collapse of an equitable judicial system whereby for a price courts will rule for those who exploit others; conversely, the innocent—here the vulnerable, weak, exposed innocent—have no chance for the favor of the court. The poet [Isaiah] understands that the disappearance of a reliable judiciary assures the complete collapse of a viable human community" (Brueggemann, *Isaiah 1–39*, 54–55).

Why is the Lord's hand "stretched out still"? (5:25) "When it says that God has stretched forth his hand, it is a way of saying that He is doing something. Stretching forth the hand can be to do good or bad things; it just means an action is happening. In this case, God is bringing about terrible judgments. . . . But even with all God has done, He is not yet done smiting His people. His hand is still stretched out in action, and that action is still that of punishment" (Muhlestein, *Scripture Study Made Simple*, 342).

Isaiah 5:26–30. In the Last Days, the Lord Will Signal for Israel to Return to Him and to Their Lands

What can we do to help gather Israel? (5:26) President Russell M. Nelson taught the youth: "Anytime you do *anything* that helps *anyone*—on either side of the veil—take a step toward making covenants with God and receiving their essential baptismal and temple ordinances, you are helping to gather Israel" ("Hope of Israel," 15). See commentary in *Book of Mormon Study Guide: Start to Finish, Revised Edition* for 2 Nephi 15:26.

What did Isaiah see as Israel was being gathered? (5:27–29) "Through the Lord's missionary servants the word of God will be spread as predicted by Isaiah. . . . The swiftness of travel referred to will aid in both the gathering of Israel and the missionary travels of modern-day [missionaries]" (Farley, "Nephi, Isaiah, and the Latter-Day Restoration," 233). See commentary in *Book of Mormon Study Guide: Start to Finish, Revised Edition* for 2 Nephi 15:27. ⊕

Isaiah 6:1–9. Isaiah Sees God on His Throne and Offers to Serve Him

How is Isaiah's vision similar to that of other prophets? (6:1) "Isaiah's grand vision of the Lord likely took place in 740 B.C. (the year that King Uzziah died). It is told in the first person (Isaiah uses the pronouns 'I' and 'me') and is similar to other prophetic visions such as those of Moses (Moses 1), Amos (Amos 7:1–9), Ezekiel (Ezek. 1), John (Rev. 1:10–19), and Joseph Smith (D&C 76; 110). Elsewhere we are informed that it was Jesus Christ whom Isaiah envisioned on this great occasion (2 Ne. 11:2–3; John 12:41). The temple identified in this

26 ¶ And he will lift up an ensign to the nations from far, and will hiss unto them from the end of the earth: and, behold, they shall come with speed swiftly:

27 None shall be weary nor stumble among them; none shall slumber nor sleep; neither shall the girdle of their loins be loosed, nor the latchet of their shoes be broken:

28 Whose arrows *are* sharp, and all their bows bent, their horses' hoofs shall be counted like flint, and their wheels like a whirlwind:

29 Their roaring *shall be* like a lion, they shall roar like young lions: yea, they shall roar, and lay hold of the prey, and shall carry *it* away safe, and none shall deliver *it*.

30 And in that day they shall roar against them like the roaring of the sea: and if *one* look unto the land, behold darkness *and* sorrow, and the light is darkened in the heavens thereof.

CHAPTER 6

Isaiah sees the Lord—His sins are forgiven—He is called to prophesy—He prophesies of the Jews' rejection of Christ's teachings—A remnant will return—Compare 2 Nephi 16.

1 In the year that king Uzziah died I saw also the Lord sitting upon a throne, high and lifted up, and his train filled the temple.

2 Above it stood the seraphims: each one had six wings; with twain he covered his face, and with twain he covered his feet, and with twain he did fly.

3 And one cried unto another, and said, Holy, holy, holy, *is* the LORD of hosts: the whole earth *is* full of his glory.

4 And the posts of the door moved at the voice of him that cried, and the house was filled with smoke.

5 ¶ Then said I, Woe *is* me! for I am undone; because I *am* a man of unclean lips, and I dwell in the midst of a people of unclean lips: for mine eyes have seen the King, the LORD of hosts.

6 Then flew one of the seraphims unto me, having a live coal in his hand, *which* he had taken with the tongs from off the altar:

7 And he laid *it* upon my mouth, and said, Lo, this hath touched thy lips; and thine iniquity is taken away, and thy sin purged.

section was the heavenly or celestial temple, or more specifically the throne room or holy of holies" (Parry, et al., *Understanding Isaiah*, 62). See commentary in *Book of Mormon Study Guide: Start to Finish, Revised Edition* for 2 Nephi 16:1.

What are the seraphim? (6:2) "Hebrew dictionaries define a seraph in the Old Testament as a mythological being with six wings. The fact, however, that the word 'seraphim' is not attested elsewhere in the Old Testament may suggest that Isaiah employed the word here in a unique meaning. As Isaiah and his schooled contemporaries knew, the meaning of the root from which this noun is formed denotes in its verbal aspect to burn or be fiery. Knowing this, Latter-day Saints should have no trouble recognizing that seraphim represent celestial beings who attend God at His throne (see the explanation of Revelation 4:6 in D&C 77:2)" (Hoskisson, "Latter-day Saint Reading of Isaiah," 211). See commentary in *Book of Mormon Study Guide: Start to Finish, Revised Edition* for 2 Nephi 16:2.

What might the smoke in the house of the Lord symbolize? (6:4) The scriptural phrase, "The house was filled with smoke" represents the presence of God. "Symbolically, God's presence was seen and felt when He covered Mount Sinai with smoke (Exodus 19:18). The sacred slopes of Sinai thus became a temple to Moses. Perhaps experiencing something similar to Isaiah, John saw 'the temple filled with smoke from the glory of God' (Revelation 15:8)" (Brewster, *Isaiah Plain and Simple*, 57).

How can we feel more confident before the Lord? (6:5) "When we dwell on our own weaknesses, it is easy to dwell on the feelings that we are unworthy. Somehow we need to bridge the gap between continually striving to improve and yet not feeling defeated when our actions aren't perfect all the time. We need to remove *unworthy* from our vocabulary and replace it with *hope* and *work*. This we can do if we turn to quieter, deeper, surer guidelines—the words of our prophets and leaders, past and present" (Ashton, "On Being Worthy," 23).

How is Isaiah cleansed? (6:6–7) "The live coal (v. 6) that touches Isaiah's lips symbolizes the purging of his sins, just as our ordinances of baptism and the sacrament physically represent acts of spiritual power (see [Isa. 6:6*a*]). . . . Regardless of whether the coal (or stone) came from an altar outside or inside the temple, or whether the temple was in Jerusalem or in God's presence, the important fact is that the coal represents divine fire and the cleansing power of the Atonement [of Jesus Christ]. By touching Isaiah's lips, the cleansing object not only purges him from being 'a man of unclean lips,' but it also consecrates him to speak in righteousness as a mouthpiece of the Lord (see Jer. 1:9)" (Ludlow, *Isaiah*, 131).

Isaiah 6:10–13. God Tells Isaiah That Many Will Reject His Message

Why does Isaiah prophesy that the people will not hear the message? (6:10) In this verse, the "result of the prophet's preaching [is] described as though it were the purpose [of his preaching]. Most of his hearers will stubbornly reject his message, with the result that they will become dead to all impressions" (*John Dummelow's Commentary* [on Isaiah 6:10]). See commentary in *Book of Mormon Study Guide: Start to Finish, Revised Edition* for 2 Nephi 16:10.

How many will return to Jerusalem after they are scattered? (6:13) "The Book of Mormon retains two words which give a more complete understanding of this verse: ['But yet *there* shall be a tenth, and *they* shall return' (2 Nephi 16:13; emphasis added)]. . . . Although the cities of Judah will be destroyed and the inhabitants scattered, a remnant of that 'holy seed' will return to inhabit the land. Further light is shed upon the phrase 'shall be eaten' by a marginal reading in the KJV: 'when it is returned, and hath been broused.' This has reference to a purging of those who are to be scattered. Isaiah's analogy of a tree's being pruned by animals eating the leaves, and by the natural casting off of the dead leaves, indicates that the tenth to return will be of a new generation" (Nyman, *Great Are the Words of Isaiah*, 52).

8 Also I heard the voice of the Lord, saying,
Whom shall I send, and who will go for us?
Then said I, Here *am* I; send me.

9 ¶ And he said, Go, and tell this people,
Hear ye indeed, but understand not; and see
ye indeed, but perceive not.

10 Make the heart of this people fat, and
make their ears heavy, and shut their eyes;
lest they see with their eyes, and hear with
their ears, and understand with their heart,
and convert, and be healed.

11 Then said I, Lord, how long? And he answered, Until the cities be wasted without
inhabitant, and the houses without man, and
the land be utterly desolate,

12 And the LORD have removed men far
away, and *there be* a great forsaking in the
midst of the land.

13 ¶ But yet in it *shall be* a tenth, and *it* shall
return, and shall be eaten: as a teil tree, and
as an oak, whose substance *is* in them, when
they cast *their leaves: so* the holy seed *shall be*
the substance thereof.

CHAPTER 7

Ephraim and Syria wage war against Judah—Christ will be born of a virgin—Compare 2 Nephi 17.

1 And it came to pass in the days of Ahaz the son of Jotham, the son of Uzziah, king of Judah, *that* Rezin the king of Syria, and Pekah the son of Remaliah, king of Israel, went up toward Jerusalem to war against it, but could not prevail against it.

2 And it was told the house of David, saying, Syria is confederate with Ephraim. And his heart was moved, and the heart of his people, as the trees of the wood are moved with the wind.

3 Then said the LORD unto Isaiah, Go forth now to meet Ahaz, thou, and Shear-jashub thy son, at the end of the conduit of the upper pool in the highway of the fuller's field;

4 And say unto him, Take heed, and be quiet; fear not, neither be fainthearted for the two tails of these smoking firebrands, for the fierce anger of Rezin with Syria, and of the son of Remaliah.

5 Because Syria, Ephraim, and the son of Remaliah, have taken evil counsel against thee, saying,

6 Let us go up against Judah, and vex it, and let us make a breach therein for us, and set a king in the midst of it, *even* the son of Tabeal:

7 Thus saith the Lord GOD, It shall not stand, neither shall it come to pass.

8 For the head of Syria *is* Damascus, and the head of Damascus *is* Rezin; and within threescore and five years shall Ephraim be broken, that it be not a people.

9 And the head of Ephraim *is* Samaria, and the head of Samaria *is* Remaliah's son. If ye will not believe, surely ye shall not be established.

Isaiah 7:1–9. Isaiah Warns Judah of Israel's Conspiracy with Syria and Eventual Attack

Why did the kings of Israel and Syria war against Judah? (7:1) "Rezin, king of Syria, and Pekah, king of Israel, had united to resist the westward expansion of Assyria (7:1–2). They tried to coerce Ahaz into joining the alliance, but when he resisted, they prepared to attack Jerusalem and set up another king, 'the son of Tabeel,' in his place (v. 6)" (Barker, "Isaiah," 505).

Why would Isaiah take Shearjashub to meet with Ahaz? (7:3) "The Lord's commandment for Isaiah to take his son Shearjashub with him to meet Ahaz is apparently purposeful. . . . The meaning of his son's name [was] 'The remnant shall return.' This meaning comes from the prophecy given by the Lord to Isaiah at the time of his call ([Isaiah] 6:13). The son's presence may have served either of two purposes. It may have been to remind Ahaz of the prophecy that Judah would not be utterly destroyed, or it may have been a reminder that the Lord had prophesied concerning Judah in order to prepare Ahaz for the prophecy which Isaiah was to deliver" (Nyman, *Great Are the Words of Isaiah*, 54).

In what way does Isaiah encourage Ahaz to exercise faith? (7:7–9) A "wordplay [a *paronomasia*] occurs as the prophet concludes his words of assurance to Ahaz in verses 7b–9. One way to preserve that wordplay in English translation is to render verse 9b: 'If you do not make yourself *firm* (in the Lord), you will not be *affirmed* (by the Lord).' Note the words for firm/affirmed are forms of the Hebrew root *'mn*, which we know from the word 'Amen.' The prophet asserts that Ahaz need do nothing to save Judah but have confidence in God's words of assurance. . . . [However,] he was unwilling to accept the prophet's assurances that the Lord was going to protect Judah" (Hoppe, *Isaiah*, 31).

Isaiah 7:10–16. Christ Shall Be Born of a Virgin

Who was the virgin that would give birth? (7:14) This prophecy points to Mary, the mother of Jesus. "Most scholars believe that the expected woman was Isaiah's own wife . . . because the Hebrew term translated 'virgin' (*'almah*) can be rendered 'a young woman' who is married. . . . But the reference to the 'virgin' and to the name Immanuel appears to envision an era far from that of Isaiah. . . . The Jewish translator of this passage into Greek in the third century B.C. rendered the Hebrew term *'almah* with the Greek word for virgin, *parthenos*, which almost always means a woman who is unmarried and has known no man" (Brown, "Zacharias and Elisabeth, Joseph and Mary," 108). See commentary in *Book of Mormon Study Guide: Start to Finish, Revised Edition* for 2 Nephi 17:14–15. ⊕

10 ¶ Moreover the LORD spake again unto Ahaz, saying,

11 Ask thee a sign of the LORD thy God; ask it either in the depth, or in the height above.

12 But Ahaz said, I will not ask, neither will I tempt the LORD.

13 And he said, Hear ye now, O house of David; *Is it* a small thing for you to weary men, but will ye weary my God also?

14 Therefore the Lord himself shall give you a sign; Behold, a virgin shall conceive, and bear a son, and shall call his name Immanuel.

The Nativity (Isaiah 7:14)

15 Butter and honey shall he eat, that he may know to refuse the evil, and choose the good.

16 For before the child shall know to refuse the evil, and choose the good, the land that thou abhorrest shall be forsaken of both her kings.

CHAPTER 8

Christ will be as a stone of stumbling and a rock of offense—Seek the Lord, not muttering wizards—Turn to the law and to the testimony for guidance—Compare 2 Nephi 18.

1 Moreover the LORD said unto me, Take thee a great roll, and write in it with a man's pen concerning Maher-shalal-hash-baz.

2 And I took unto me faithful witnesses to record, Uriah the priest, and Zechariah the son of Jeberechiah.

3 And I went unto the prophetess; and she conceived, and bare a son. Then said the LORD to me, Call his name Maher-shalal-hash-baz.

4 For before the child shall have knowledge to cry, My father, and my mother, the riches of Damascus and the spoil of Samaria shall be taken away before the king of Assyria.

Why is it important for us to "refuse the evil, and choose the good"? (7:15) "During the ministry of President Thomas S. Monson, he . . . often taught that decisions determine destiny. In that spirit my counsel tonight is to rise above any rationalizations that prevent us from making righteous decisions, especially with respect to serving Jesus Christ. In Isaiah we are taught we must 'refuse the evil, and choose the good' [Isaiah 7:15].

"I believe it is of particular importance in our day, when Satan is raging in the hearts of men in so many new and subtle ways, that our choices and decisions be made carefully, consistent with the goals and objectives by which we profess to live. We need unequivocal commitment to the commandments and strict adherence to sacred covenants" (Cook, "Choose Wisely," 46).

Summary of Isaiah 7:17–25

Isaiah's instruction to King Ahaz to trust the Lord is ignored, and an enemy is allowed to defeat Ahaz and his people. The conquering army leaves the kingdom of Judah desolate and its people in bondage. Ahaz ignores the Lord's counsel and brings captivity instead of freedom to his people.

Isaiah 8:1–8. Isaiah Prophetically Names His Son, and Judah Rejects Christ's Living Water

What does Isaiah's son's name foreshadow? (8:3–4) "Isaiah had told King Ahaz that the threat from Syria and Ephraim (Israel) would pass and the child Immanuel would be born in Judah as part of the country's future destiny (Isa. 7:14–16). Then the promise of relief from attack was made more immediate by the Lord's assurance that before a son yet to be born to Isaiah and his wife could learn to say *avi* (daddy) and *immi* (mommy), both Damascus of Syria and Samaria of Israel would be conquered by Assyria. The name of this baby was a token of Assyria's attack on northern Israel (Isa. 8:1*d*)" (Rasmussen, *Latter-day Saint Commentary on the Old Testament*, 509). See commentary in *Book of Mormon Study Guide: Start to Finish, Revised Edition* for 2 Nephi 18:1.

Why did Isaiah contrast the waters of Shiloah with the Euphrates? (8:6–8) The waters of Shiloah is "a meager supply of water for Jerusalem [that] arose from the spring at Gehon. . . . The prophet uses the figure of this trickle of water to depict the seeming weakness of the divine promise in contrast with the awesome strength of Assyria, whose aid Ahaz had sought. But for the prophet, Assyria is just a tool of God's power ([Isaiah] 10:5), and because of Judah's despising the divine aid in favor of Assyria's, God turns the aid into terrifying judgment" (Childs, *Isaiah*, 73). See commentary in *Book of Mormon Study Guide: Start to Finish, Revised Edition* for 2 Nephi 18:6–7.

Isaiah 8:9–18. Christ Is Compared to a Stone of Stumbling for Judah

What role did the Lord call Isaiah to fulfill? (8:11–18) "These are . . . difficult verses. The Book of Mormon helps, however. Apparently Isaiah was forbidden to preach unto Judah, as Mormon was forbidden to

5 ¶ The LORD spake also unto me again, saying,

6 Forasmuch as this people refuseth the waters of Shiloah that go softly, and rejoice in Rezin and Remaliah's son;

7 Now therefore, behold, the Lord bringeth up upon them the waters of the river, strong and many, *even* the king of Assyria, and all his glory: and he shall come up over all his channels, and go over all his banks:

8 And he shall pass through Judah; he shall overflow and go over, he shall reach *even* to the neck; and the stretching out of his wings shall fill the breadth of thy land, O Immanuel.

9 ¶ Associate yourselves, O ye people, and ye shall be broken in pieces; and give ear, all ye of far countries: gird yourselves, and ye shall be broken in pieces; gird yourselves, and ye shall be broken in pieces.

10 Take counsel together, and it shall come to nought; speak the word, and it shall not stand: for God *is* with us.

11 ¶ For the LORD spake thus to me with a strong hand, and instructed me that I should not walk in the way of this people, saying,

Isaiah's Wife, the Prophetess (Isaiah 8:3–4)

"All Israelite women were not given the title of prophetess, nor was the title assigned because a woman was married to a prophet or other important man in society. Only one of the seven biblical women called 'prophetess' in the Bible was married to a prophet, as we use the term today. That woman was Isaiah's wife, as he indicated in the following verse: 'And I went unto the prophetess; and she conceived, and bare a son. Then said the Lord to me, Call his name Maher-shalal-hash-baz' (Isaiah 8:3). Nothing in the verse explains why Isaiah referred to his wife as a prophetess. . . .

"Considering the other women who were given the title 'prophetess' and the way the term has been used by both ancient and modern prophets, Isaiah's wife also must have received a personal witness of the Savior and may have been given a confirming witness to that of her husband's concerning the prophetic name for their son. In the other examples of Old Testament prophetesses, either no husband is mentioned or little is known of the woman's husband. Thus the title of prophetess speaks more about the woman herself. Women were qualified as true prophetesses by their faith in the Savior's Atonement rather than by marriage to a righteous man" (Olson, *Women of the Old Testament*, 83–84).

12 Say ye not, A confederacy, to all *them to* whom this people shall say, A confederacy; neither fear ye their fear, nor be afraid.

13 Sanctify the LORD of hosts himself; and *let* him *be* your fear, and *let* him *be* your dread.

14 And he shall be for a sanctuary; but for a stone of stumbling and for a rock of offence to both the houses of Israel, for a gin and for a snare to the inhabitants of Jerusalem.

15 And many among them shall stumble, and fall, and be broken, and be snared, and be taken.

16 Bind up the testimony, seal the law among my disciples.

17 And I will wait upon the LORD, that hideth his face from the house of Jacob, and I will look for him.

18 Behold, I and the children whom the LORD hath given me *are* for signs and for wonders in Israel from the LORD of hosts, which dwelleth in mount Zion.

19 ¶ And when they shall say unto you, Seek unto them that have familiar spirits, and unto wizards that peep, and that mutter: should not a people seek unto their God? for the living to the dead?

20 To the law and to the testimony: if they speak not according to this word, *it is* because *there is* no light in them.

21 And they shall pass through it, hardly bestead and hungry: and it shall come to pass, that when they shall be hungry, they

preach to the Nephites and was to stand as an idle witness against her (see Morm. 1:16; 3:16). The Lord had left Judah without excuse by giving her two or three witnesses: the previous testimony of Ahaz, the great roll attested to by two witnesses, and the name of the son of Isaiah. Isaiah was to sanctify the Lord of Hosts and to fear him; the Lord would then be his sanctuary" (Nyman, *Great Are the Words of Isaiah*, 65).

Who would be "a stone of stumbling and . . . a rock of offense"? (8:14) "Israel's God shall be—the tense is future—a blessing or a cursing to the whole house of Israel, to both the kingdom of Ephraim and the kingdom of Judah, and for that matter to the whole of mankind. Those who believe and obey shall find peace and rest and security in his arms; he is their sanctuary. Those who stumble at his doctrine, who are offended by his claims of divinity, shall be cast out and rejected for their disbelief" (McConkie, *Promised Messiah*, 173). See commentary in *Book of Mormon Study Guide: Start to Finish, Revised Edition* for 2 Nephi 18:14–15. ⊕

Isaiah 8:19–22. Israel Is Told to Only Seek Revelation from the Lord

What does "familiar spirits" mean? (8:19) "The expression 'familiar spirits' is not an accurate term to convey the significance of the Hebrew term used anciently. The Hebrew word '*ob* means 'a leather bottle or bag' (see [Gesenius, *Hebrew and English Lexicon of the Old Testament*, 15]). This object was used by the practitioners of necromancy, a deceptive craft of pretended communication with the dead. The art involved a kind of ventriloquism wherein the voice or message of the 'departed spirits' was called forth from the bag or sometimes a pit (see [Botterweck and Ringgren, *Theological Dictionary of the Old Testament*, 1:131, 133–34])" (*Old Testament Student Manual:1 Kings–Malachi*, 146).

What is the law and the testimony to which we should turn for truth? (8:20) A Biblical scholar understood this phrase to mean "'let us stick to the authentic instrument, laid up by the command of the Lord'" (see *Adam Clarke's Commentary* [on Isaiah 8:20]; citing Deschamps). The "authentic instrument" here consists of the standard works. The "standard works are the books accepted by Latter-day Saints as scripture: the Bible, Book of Mormon, Doctrine and Covenants, and Pearl of Great Price. In early Latter-day Saint usage, the term apparently included more writings than the scriptures. In 1874 George A. Smith described 'standard works' as the scriptures and other works published by the Church that illustrate 'the principles of life and salvation made known in the gospel of Jesus Christ.' By 1900, however, the phrase 'standard works' came to refer only to the scriptures'" (Williams, "Standard Works," 3:1415).

Isaiah 9:1–7. Isaiah Prophesies of a Messiah

Who are these people and when will they see a "great light"? (9:1–2) "The 'dimness of anguish' and the 'darkness' of exile and oppression (Isa. 8:22) are again mentioned, merging prophecies of affliction in exile with prophecies of later oppressions to come to northern Israelite lands, including Galilee. There the afflicted people would begin to see the 'great light' of the life and teachings of the Messiah" (Rasmussen, *Latter-day Saint Commentary on the Old Testament*, 511). See commentary in *Book of Mormon Study Guide: Start to Finish, Revised Edition* for 2 Nephi 19:1–2.

What are the yoke and the rod which the Messiah will break? (9:4) "Isaiah also sees again a future day when the Messiah will reign and war will be no more (vv. 4, 5; cf. Isaiah 2:4). The 'yoke of his burden,' the oppressive rule of the conqueror, will be lifted; and the bars and rods representing unjust and cruel exercise of power and authority will be broken" (Sperry, *Book of Mormon Compendium*, 207). *"The day of Midian"* likely is "referring to when Gideon defeated the hordes of Midian (see Judg. 7:22–25). While the Messiah will provide Israel's final deliverance from all oppressors, the promise of the breaking of *the yoke . . . and the staff* also looked to the more immediate deliverance from Assyria" (*Zondervan KJV Commentary*, 922).

shall fret themselves, and curse their king and their God, and look upward.

22 And they shall look unto the earth; and behold trouble and darkness, dimness of anguish; and *they shall be* driven to darkness.

CHAPTER 9

Isaiah speaks about the Messiah—The people in darkness will see a great Light—Unto us a Child is born—He will be the Prince of Peace and reign on David's throne—Compare 2 Nephi 19.

1 Nevertheless the dimness *shall* not *be* such as *was* in her vexation, when at the first he lightly afflicted the land of Zebulun and the land of Naphtali, and afterward did more grievously afflict *her by* the way of the sea, beyond Jordan, in Galilee of the nations.

2 The people that walked in darkness have seen a great light: they that dwell in the land of the shadow of death, upon them hath the light shined.

3 Thou hast multiplied the nation, *and* not increased the joy: they joy before thee according to the joy in harvest, *and* as *men* rejoice when they divide the spoil.

4 For thou hast broken the yoke of his burden, and the staff of his shoulder, the rod of his oppressor, as in the day of Midian.

5 For every battle of the warrior *is* with confused noise, and garments rolled in blood; but *this* shall be with burning *and* fuel of fire.

6 For unto us a child is born, unto us a son is given: and the government shall be upon his shoulder: and his name shall be called Wonderful, Counsellor, The mighty God, The everlasting Father, The Prince of Peace.

7 Of the increase of *his* government and peace *there shall be* no end, upon the throne of David, and upon his kingdom, to order it, and to establish it with judgment and with justice from henceforth even for ever. The zeal of the LORD of hosts will perform this.

8 ¶ The Lord sent a word into Jacob, and it hath lighted upon Israel.

9 And all the people shall know, *even* Ephraim and the inhabitant of Samaria, that say in the pride and stoutness of heart,

10 The bricks are fallen down, but we will build with hewn stones: the sycomores are cut down, but we will change *them into* cedars.

11 Therefore the LORD shall set up the adversaries of Rezin against him, and join his enemies together;

12 The Syrians before, and the Philistines behind; and they shall devour Israel with open mouth. For all this his anger is not turned away, but his hand *is* stretched out still.

13 ¶ For the people turneth not unto him that smiteth them, neither do they seek the LORD of hosts.

14 Therefore the LORD will cut off from Israel head and tail, branch and rush, in one day.

15 The ancient and honourable, he *is* the head; and the prophet that teacheth lies, he *is* the tail.

16 For the leaders of this people cause *them* to err; and *they that are* led of them *are* destroyed.

Why did Isaiah identify the Messiah by titles such as Wonderful? (9:6) "That title originated by the prophet Isaiah (with the help of the scholars who translated the King James Bible) to celebrate in prophecy the birth of the baby Jesus means literally that which astonishes, fills with surprise, or at which one marvels. We experience all of that and more when we feel the wonder of Christ's role in our salvation" (Holland, *Witness for His Names*, 157). Ponder the titles of Jesus Christ in this verse. Which means the most to you? How has the Lord fulfilled that title for you? ⊕

Isaiah 9:8–16. Isaiah Warns of Three Evils That Will Come upon Israel

What is the difference between building with brick or with stones? (9:9–10) Bricks represent things which are secular. "Buildings in ancient Egypt were constructed from either stone or mudbrick. Temples were generally built with stone that was meant to last throughout the ages. Palaces, on the other hand, were built for comfort out of mudbrick, which was cool in the day and warm at night. Each type of construction was considered specialized labor; in other words, people who did one did not do the other" (Falk, "Brick by Brick," 54). These hewn stones outlasted the mudbricks.

What does the phrase "his hand is stretched out still" teach you about the Lord? (9:12) "To all of you who think you are lost or without hope, or who think you have done too much that was too wrong for too long, to every one of you who worry that you are stranded somewhere on the wintry plains of life and have wrecked your handcart in the process, this conference calls out Jehovah's unrelenting refrain, '[My] hand is stretched out still' [Isaiah 5:25; 9:17, 21].... His mercy endureth forever, and His hand is stretched out still. His is the pure love of Christ, the charity that never faileth, that compassion which endures even when all other strength disappears' [see Moroni 7:46–47]" (Holland, "Prophets in the Land Again," 107).

Who are the head and the tail that the Lord will cut off from Israel? (9:14–16) The "ancient" or elders (see Isaiah 9:15*a*) "are the 'head[s]' or leaders of the community.... The tails are the false prophets who pretend to speak in the Lord's name and utter flattering statements that the people desire to hear. Such prophets, along with the elder and the honorable, lead the people of Israel astray and 'cause them to err' (9:16).... Since the leaders cause the people to stray from truth and justice, and since the people choose to follow, both will be destroyed (9:14)" (Parry, et al., *Understanding Isaiah*, 100). See commentary in *Book of Mormon Study Guide: Start to Finish, Revised Edition* for 2 Nephi 19:14–15.

Summary of Isaiah 9:17–21

Since Israel has accepted the counsel of false prophets and leaders, the Lord has no joy in His people (v. 17). Because of their rejection of His servants and reckless wickedness, the Lord inspires Isaiah to warn them of their coming destruction. In His wrath the Lord declares that "the people shall be as fuel of the fire" (v. 19).

Summary of Isaiah 10

Isaiah denounces unjust leaders who rob the poor, for they are the ones who need to bow down to the Lord. For this sin the Lord will punish their injustice. Jehovah raises up Assyria as the rod of His anger against unrepentant Israel. But because of Assyria's offensive idols, God will also punish the king of Assyria for his arrogance. In the end, a remnant of Israel shall return to the Lord. In the last days, the Lord will also free Judah from Assyria's yoke and humble them by cutting down their pride and haughtiness. See commentary in *Book of Mormon Study Guide: Start to Finish, Revised Edition* for 2 Nephi 20.

CHAPTER 10

The destruction of Assyria is a type of the destruction of the wicked at the Second Coming—Few people will be left after the Lord comes again—The remnant of Jacob will return in that day—Compare 2 Nephi 20.

Major Nations in the Book of Isaiah

"**Assyria (Nineveh)**—Powerful and expanding empire in Isaiah's day. Conquered and ruled by terror. Destroyed the northern kingdom of Israel and scattered the ten tribes. Under leadership of **Sennacherib**, they also besieged Jerusalem during Hezekiah's rule in Judah.

"**Israel (Ephraim)**—Northern kingdom of ten tribes, wicked and idolatrous in Isaiah's day. Led by **Pekah**. Together with Syria, attacked Judah but were turned back. United with Syria in an unsuccessful revolt against Assyria. Then carried away captive by the Assyrians and scattered, becoming the 'lost ten tribes.'

"**Syria (Damascus)**—Collection of kingdoms northeast of Israel. Grew weaker as Assyria grew stronger. Combined with northern kingdom of Israel and attacked Judah during the reign of Ahaz. Later, after a failed revolt against Assyria, Damascus was destroyed.

"**Egypt**—Powerful force in the region. Rival of Assyria. For many years the policy of the kings of Judah was to be allied with Egypt against Assyria. However, Isaiah opposed this alliance, warning against relying on Egypt and saying the Lord would deliver Judah against the Assyrians, which He did (see Isaiah 30–31; 36–37).

"**Babylon**—[Capital] of Babylonia, a rival and subject of Assyria during Isaiah's day. Isaiah prophesied of its future—that it would rise to power, conquer Judah, destroy Jerusalem and the temple, take captives from Judah back to Babylon, and eventually fall. In Isaiah, it is often a metaphor for the world and its wickedness.

"**Judah (Jerusalem)**—Southern kingdom, where Isaiah lived. During reign of King **Ahaz**, attacked by Syria and Israel. In Isaiah's day, subject to Assyria, which threatened to destroy it. Miraculously spared. Enjoyed relative prosperity under King **Hezekiah**, who was righteous and took advice from Isaiah.

"**Persia**—A great empire that conquered Babylon. Almost 200 years beforehand, Isaiah prophesied that King **Cyrus** of Persia would let the captive Jews in Babylon return to Jerusalem and rebuild the temple (see Isaiah 44:28; 45:1, 13; Ezra 1)" (Gardner and Edwards, "How Can I Understand Isaiah?" 21; paragraphing altered).

CHAPTER 11

The stem of Jesse (Christ) will judge in righteousness—The knowledge about God will cover the earth in the Millennium—The Lord will raise an ensign and gather Israel—Compare 2 Nephi 21.

1 And there shall come forth a rod out of the stem of Jesse, and a Branch shall grow out of his roots:

2 And the spirit of the LORD shall rest upon him, the spirit of wisdom and understanding, the spirit of counsel and might, the spirit of knowledge and of the fear of the LORD;

3 And shall make him of quick understanding in the fear of the LORD: and he shall not judge after the sight of his eyes, neither reprove after the hearing of his ears:

4 But with righteousness shall he judge the poor, and reprove with equity for the meek of the earth: and he shall smite the earth with the rod of his mouth, and with the breath of his lips shall he slay the wicked.

5 And righteousness shall be the girdle of his loins, and faithfulness the girdle of his reins.

Isaiah 11:1–5. The Stem of Jesse, Who Is Christ, Will Bless the Righteous

Who is the "stem of Jesse"? (11:1–5) The Prophet Joseph Smith explained that "the Stem of Jesse spoken of in the 1st, 2d, 3d, 4th, and 5th verses of the 11th chapter of Isaiah . . . is Christ" (D&C 113:1–2). "Jesse was the father of David, he who became Israel's greatest king. Christ was variously both a *branch* and a *stem* in this royal lineage" (Holland, *Witness for His Names*, 145). In verses 2–5, Isaiah describes the Savior's attributes and influence that lead to His millennial reign (see Isaiah 11:6–9). See commentary for 2 Nephi 21:1–5 in *Book of Mormon Study Guide: Start to Finish, Revised Edition*. ⊕

Who is the "rod"? (11:1–5) The rod is a "servant in the hands of Christ, who is partly a descendant of Jesse as well as of Ephraim, or of the house of Joseph, on whom there is laid much power" (D&C 113:4). Sidney B. Sperry wrote: "'Joseph [Smith] was destined to become a great "servant in the hands of Christ." Moreover, if we assume that he was the "rod" or "servant," observe how very well such an identification fits in with Moroni's mission of explaining to the latter-day Prophet his part in Isaiah's great vision of the future. . . . Joseph Smith fits naturally into Isaiah's prophecy, and it is easy to understand why Moroni quoted and explained Isaiah 11 to him'" (*Doctrine and Covenants Student Manual* [2002], 283).

6 The wolf also shall dwell with the lamb, and the leopard shall lie down with the kid; and the calf and the young lion and the fatling together; and a little child shall lead them.

Isaiah 11:6–9. The Millennium Will Be a Time of Peace

Jesus Christ Is the Main Character in Isaiah 11 (Isaiah 11:1–5)

"The Book of Mormon (2 Ne. 30:9 especially) and the Doctrine and Covenants (113) reinforce the fact that Jesus Christ is the main character in Isaiah 11. He is the Messiah who will have the 'spirit of the Lord,' the 'spirit of wisdom and understanding,' 'counsel and might,' 'knowledge,' and 'fear of the Lord' (11:2); he is the Messiah who will serve as the righteous judge (11:3); and he will be the advocate of the poor and the meek and will settle their case (11:4). In the end, the Messiah will smite the wicked of the earth with his great power at the Second Coming, resulting in the glorious conditions of the Millennium (11:6–10)" (Parry, et al., *Understanding Isaiah*, 116).

7 And the cow and the bear shall feed; their
young ones shall lie down together: and the
lion shall eat straw like the ox.

8 And the sucking child shall play on the
hole of the asp, and the weaned child shall
put his hand on the cockatrice' den.

9 They shall not hurt nor destroy in all my
holy mountain: for the earth shall be full of
the knowledge of the LORD, as the waters
cover the sea.

When will the earth be "full of the knowledge of the LORD"? (11:9) It is the millennium, a 1,000 year period, when "he (Christ) shall reveal all things—things which have passed, and hidden things which no man knew, things of the earth, by which it was made, and the purpose and the end thereof" (D&C 101:32–33). "During the Millennium, 'Christ will reign personally upon the earth' (Articles of Faith 1:10). [It] will be a time of righteousness and peace on the earth. The Lord has revealed that 'in that day the enmity of man, and the enmity of beasts, yea, the enmity of all flesh, shall cease' (Doctrine and Covenants 101:26; see also Isaiah 11:6–9)" (Gospel Topics, "Millennium").

Isaiah 11:10–16. An Ensign Is Lifted to Gather Scattered Israel Home

10 ¶ And in that day there shall be a root of
Jesse, which shall stand for an ensign of the
people; to it shall the Gentiles seek: and his
rest shall be glorious.

Who is the "root of Jesse"? (11:10) "'It is a descendant of Jesse, as well as of Joseph, unto whom rightly belongs the priesthood, and the keys of the kingdom, for an ensign, and for the gathering of my people in the last days' (D&C 113:6). There can be no question that this is describing the Prophet Joseph Smith. By way of revelation he was told that he held the right to the priesthood (see D&C 86:8–9). That the keys of the kingdom had been given to him is a matter of record; that his labors were to stand as an 'ensign' to which the nations of the earth will gather is also a matter

Moroni Quotes Isaiah 11 (Isaiah 11:10)

During Moroni's first visit to the Prophet Joseph Smith on the night of September 21, 1823, "he quoted the eleventh chapter of Isaiah, saying that it was about to be fulfilled" (JS–H 1:40). Given this fact, Joseph Smith appears to be the fulfillment of Isaiah's prophecy regarding a root of Jesse whom the Gentiles in the latter days would seek for a knowledge of the covenants of the Lord. Similar to Isaiah, Lehi explained to his son Joseph that Joseph of Egypt had foretold a latter-day seer who would be raised up out of his lineage: "For Joseph truly testified, saying: A seer shall the Lord my God raise up, who shall be a choice seer unto the fruit of my loins. Yea, Joseph truly said: Thus saith the Lord unto me: A choice seer will I raise up out of the fruit of thy loins; and he shall be esteemed highly among the fruit of thy loins. And unto him will I give commandment that he shall do a work for the fruit of thy loins, his brethren, which shall be of great worth unto them, even to the bringing of them to the knowledge of the covenants which I have made with thy fathers" (2 Nephi 3:6–7).

"The evidence seems clear that both the 'rod out of the stem of Jesse' (Isa. 11:1) and the 'root of Jesse' (Isa. 11:10) refer to the same individual—the Prophet Joseph Smith" (Jackson, *Lost Tribes and Last Days*, 92).

of scriptural promise (D&C 29:4, 7–8; 35:25; 38:33; 39:11; 45:9, 28)" (McConkie, "Joseph Smith as Found in Ancient Manuscripts," 18).

11 And it shall come to pass in that day, *that*
the Lord shall set his hand again the second
time to recover the remnant of his people,
which shall be left, from Assyria, and from
Egypt, and from Pathros, and from Cush,
and from Elam, and from Shinar, and from
Hamath, and from the islands of the sea.

12 And he shall set up an ensign for the
nations, and shall assemble the outcasts of
Israel, and gather together the dispersed of
Judah from the four corners of the earth.

When did the Lord begin to recover Israel a second time? (11:11) The restoration of the gospel through the Prophet Joseph Smith began the gathering of Israel in the latter days. Joseph Smith declared: "The time has at last [arrived] when the God of Abraham, of Isaac, and of Jacob has set his hand again the second time to recover the remnants of his people, . . . and with them to bring in the fulness of the Gentiles and establish that covenant with them which was promised when their sins should be taken away (see Romans 11, 25, 16, and 27, and also Jeremiah 31, 32, and 33)" (Joseph Smith Papers, "Letter to Noah C. Saxton, 4 January 1833," 14–15; spelling and punctuation modernized).

What is the ensign to which Israel will be gathered? (11:11–12) "[Isaiah 11, verses 11 and 12] elaborate on the gathering of Israel and the role of an ensign. The first gathering of Israel took place after the Babylonian captivity; the second gathering will see remnants return from all directions (as symbolized by different countries: Assyria = Modern Iraq; Egypt, Pathros = Egypt; Cush = Ethiopia; Elam = Iran; Shinar = Iraq; Hamath = Syria) and from various continents (islands of the sea). The Lord will also set up a church (or ensign) for the nations and the scattered outcasts of Israel" (Ludlow, *Unlocking the Old Testament*, 158–59). See commentary for 2 Nephi 21:12 in *Book of Mormon Study Guide: Start to Finish, Revised Edition.*

13 The envy also of Ephraim shall depart,
and the adversaries of Judah shall be cut off:
Ephraim shall not envy Judah, and Judah
shall not vex Ephraim.

What must take place for this prophecy to be fulfilled? (11:13) Elder LeGrand Richards taught: "I do not know how the enmity and the envy between Ephraim and Judah can disappear except that we of the house of Ephraim, who have the custody of the gospel, should lead out in trying to bring to this branch of the house of Israel the blessings of the restored gospel. . . .

"And it seems to me that the only way that the tribe of Judah can be sanctified to dwell in his presence forever and ever will be when we bring to them the gospel of the Lord Jesus Christ as the Savior promised them it would be brought in the latter days" (in Conference Report, Oct. 1956, 23, 24).

When will Israel and Judah "fly upon" their enemies? (11:14–15) This will be fulfilled in the last days as the house of Israel is gathered. "Isaiah 11 (vv. 14–15) shows the Lord's power over Israel's traditional enemies in that coming day" (Meservy, "God Is with Us," 103).

14 But they shall fly upon the shoulders of the Philistines toward the west; they shall spoil them of the east together: they shall lay their hand upon Edom and Moab; and the children of Ammon shall obey them.

15 And the LORD shall utterly destroy the tongue of the Egyptian sea; and with his mighty wind shall he shake his hand over the river, and shall smite it in the seven streams, and make *men* go over dryshod.

16 And there shall be an highway for the remnant of his people, which shall be left, from Assyria; like as it was to Israel in the day that he came up out of the land of Egypt.

What type of highway will the Lord create? (11:16) "Isaiah gives a somewhat more expansive view in these words: 'And an highway shall be there, and a way, and it shall be called The way of holiness; the unclean shall not pass over it; but it shall be for those [who are worthy, and] . . . the redeemed shall walk there.' It appears that a way will be provided to assemble the outcasts of Israel again in their promised land. The safe and secure physical arrangements, whatever they may be, will, in fact, be but symbolical of the way of holiness whereon only the righteous can find footing. The way of holiness cannot be other than the strait and narrow path" (McConkie, *Millennial Messiah*, 327). ⊕

Isaiah 12:1–6. Israel Sings Songs of Salvation

CHAPTER 12

In the millennial day, all men will praise the Lord—He will dwell among them—Compare 2 Nephi 22.

1 And in that day thou shalt say, O LORD, I will praise thee: though thou wast angry with me, thine anger is turned away, and thou comfortedst me.

2 Behold, God *is* my salvation; I will trust, and not be afraid: for the LORD JEHOVAH *is* my strength and *my* song; he also is become my salvation.

Why is "LORD JEHOVAH" capitalized? (12:2) "In the King James Version there are words set in italics and others set in all caps. The italics represent words that do not occur in the original biblical languages, but which the King James translators added to make the text read sensibly in English. Words set in all caps represent the translation of the sacred Hebrew name for God (*JHWH*)" (Skousen, "Textual Variants in the Isaiah Quotations in the Book of Mormon," 372–73). "This is one of the four times only that the name Jehovah is written out in full in the King James English Bible. See Ex. 6:3; Ps. 83:18; Isa. 26:4. In all other places LORD is used instead" (Isaiah 12:2*a*).

3 Therefore with joy shall ye draw water out of the wells of salvation.

What does the "water out of the wells of salvation" represent? (12:3) "Living water is the words of eternal life, the message of salvation, the truths about God and his kingdom; it is the doctrines of the gospel. Those who thirst are invited to come unto Christ and drink (John 7:37–38). Where there are prophets of God, there will be found rivers of living water, wells filled with eternal truths, springs bubbling forth their life-giving draughts that save from spiritual death" (McConkie, *Doctrinal New Testament Commentary*, 1:151–52). See commentary in this volume for Jeremiah 2:13. ⊕

4 And in that day shall ye say, Praise the LORD, call upon his name, declare his doings among the people, make mention that his name is exalted.

5 Sing unto the LORD; for he hath done excellent things: this *is* known in all the earth.

6 Cry out and shout, thou inhabitant of Zion: for great *is* the Holy One of Israel in the midst of thee.

Who is the "Holy One of Israel"? (12:4–6) "The prophets and peoples of olden times paid homage to Jehovah under his names Holy (Isa. 57:15), Holy One (Hab. 1:12), Holy One of Jacob (Isa. 29:23), and Holy One of Israel (Isa. 45:11), thereby being constantly aware that he being holy, so should they be (Lev. 11:45). . . .

"With the knowledge thus before us that the Holy One of Israel is Christ, the door is open to us to gain a new insight into the deeper and hidden meanings of many passages.

"Isaiah expounds about the glory and praise to be heaped upon the Holy One of Israel in the day of restoration and of millennial peace" (McConkie, *Promised Messiah*, 167, 168). ⊕

CHAPTER 13

The destruction of Babylon is a type of the destruction at the Second Coming—It will be a day of wrath and vengeance—Babylon (the world) will fall forever—Compare 2 Nephi 23.

1 The burden of Babylon, which Isaiah the son of Amoz did see.

Isaiah 13:1–13. The Righteous Are Called to Flee the Destruction of Babylon

What does the word *burden* mean in this scripture? (13:1) *Burden* "is the literal meaning of the Hebrew word *massa*. It signifies 'a lifting up' (of the spirit, or voice), hence 'a prophecy, oracle, or vision'" (Slotki, *Isaiah*, 61–62).

"Burden" is used throughout Isaiah: burden of Moab (15:1); burden of Damascus (17:1); burden of Egypt (19:1); burden of the desert, of the sea, or Babylon (21:1); burden of the valley of vision or Jerusalem (22:1); and burden of Tyre (23:1). ⊕

2 Lift ye up a banner upon the high mountain, exalt the voice unto them, shake the hand, that they may go into the gates of the nobles.

Why will the Lord's servants raise a banner? (13:2) "Isaiah 13:2–5 . . . comprises the Lord's command to us to gather Israel by hoisting a banner or ensign on a mountain; calling with a voice; and beckoning with the hand (13:2). When these three signals are given, the earth cannot doubt the veracity of the invitation to join the Saints in Zion.

"Those who gather will come from all parts of the earth (13:5), will be sanctified in the temple (13:3), and will become part of the Lord's army to serve in the holy war against evil (13:4–5), all of which will occur in preparation for the Lord's coming when he will destroy modern Babylon as he destroyed ancient Babylon" (Parry, et al., *Understanding Isaiah*, 129). See commentary for 2 Nephi 23:2 in *Book of Mormon Study Guide: Start to Finish, Revised Edition*.

Who are the Lord's "sanctified ones"? (13:3) "On the Lord's side will be the 'sanctified ones,' God's all-powerful force before whom no enemy can stand. The sanctified ones are those who 'rejoice in [God's] highness' (Isa. 13:3) and who are set apart to his service (Isa. 13:2–5)" (Meservy, "God Is with Us," 106). The Book of Mormon clarifies the meaning of this passage: "I have commanded my sanctified ones, I have also called my mighty ones, *for mine anger is not upon them that rejoice in my highness*" (2 Nephi 23:3; emphasis added).

What is "the day of the Lord"? (13:6) The day of the Lord is the coming of Jesus Christ to judge and cleanse the earth. This "imagery also appears in Deut. 32:43, which describes how the LORD appears to take vengeance on his enemies and 'to atone the land,' and in Deut. 33:2–3, which describes his coming with a host of ten thousand holy ones on the day he becomes King. *These suggest that the day of the LORD was a tradition of the first [Solomon's] temple, enacted annually on the day of Atonement when the king was reaffirmed as the LORD's son and ruler in Jerusalem*" (Barker, "Isaiah," 511).

What will happen to the wicked in the "day of the Lord"? (13:6–9) "Great destruction will come upon the wicked in the days preceding the second coming of the Lord, as well as when He actually arrives. Fear shall grip the hearts of the wicked as, in the midst of sorrow, they face the reality that 'wickedness never was happiness' (Alma 41:10). Truly, for them this will be the 'dreadful day of the Lord' (Malachi 4:5)" (Brewster, *Isaiah Plain and Simple*, 126).

3 I have commanded my sanctified ones, I have also called my mighty ones for mine anger, *even* them that rejoice in my highness.

4 The noise of a multitude in the mountains, like as of a great people; a tumultuous noise of the kingdoms of nations gathered together: the LORD of hosts mustereth the host of the battle.

5 They come from a far country, from the end of heaven, *even* the LORD, and the weapons of his indignation, to destroy the whole land.

6 ¶ Howl ye; for the day of the LORD *is* at hand; it shall come as a destruction from the Almighty.

7 Therefore shall all hands be faint, and every man's heart shall melt:

8 And they shall be afraid: pangs and sorrows shall take hold of them; they shall be in pain as a woman that travaileth: they shall be amazed one at another; their faces *shall be as* flames.

9 Behold, the day of the LORD cometh, cruel both with wrath and fierce anger, to lay the land desolate: and he shall destroy the sinners thereof out of it.

10 For the stars of heaven and the constellations thereof shall not give their light: the sun shall be darkened in his going forth, and the moon shall not cause her light to shine.

When will the sun, moon, and stars be darkened? (13:10) Modern-day revelation confirms this prophecy of the last days. "But, behold, I say unto you that before this great day shall come the sun shall be darkened, and the moon shall be turned into blood, and the stars shall fall from heaven, and there shall be greater signs in heaven above and in the earth beneath" (D&C 29:14; see also D&C 88:87).

11 And I will punish the world for *their* evil, and the wicked for their iniquity; and I will cause the arrogancy of the proud to cease, and will lay low the haughtiness of the terrible.

12 I will make a man more precious than fine gold; even a man than the golden wedge of Ophir.

13 Therefore I will shake the heavens, and the earth shall remove out of her place, in the wrath of the LORD of hosts, and in the day of his fierce anger.

When will pride cease? (13:11) President Ezra Taft Benson stated: "In the premortal council, it was pride that felled Lucifer, 'a son of the morning' (2 Ne. 24:12–15; see also D&C 76:25–27; Moses 4:3). At the end of this world, when God cleanses the earth by fire, the proud will be burned as stubble and the meek shall inherit the earth (see 3 Ne. 12:5; 25:1; D&C 29:9, JS–H 1:37; Mal. 4:1)" ("Beware of Pride," 4).

Summary of Isaiah 13:14–18

Isaiah describes the destruction of Babylon by the Medes.

Isaiah 13:19–22. Babylon Will Be Destroyed as Sodom and Gomorrah

19 ¶ And Babylon, the glory of kingdoms, the beauty of the Chaldees' excellency, shall be as when God overthrew Sodom and Gomorrah.

20 It shall never be inhabited, neither shall it be dwelt in from generation to generation: neither shall the Arabian pitch tent there; neither shall the shepherds make their fold there.

21 But wild beasts of the desert shall lie there; and their houses shall be full of doleful creatures; and owls shall dwell there, and satyrs shall dance there.

22 And the wild beasts of the islands shall cry in their desolate houses, and dragons in *their* pleasant palaces: and her time *is* near to come, and her days shall not be prolonged.

What does the Book of Mormon add to this verse? (13:22) "The Book of Mormon retains a complete sentence at the end of verse 22 regarding the destruction of the wicked and the Lord's mercy to his people—those who will accept him as their God. . . . 'And the wild beasts of the islands shall cry in their desolate houses, and dragons in their pleasant palaces; and her time is near to come, and her day shall not be prolonged. *For I will destroy her speedily; yea, for I will be merciful unto my people, but the wicked shall perish*' (2 Nephi 23:22). . . . In commenting on Isaiah's words, Nephi declared that ancient Babylon would be destroyed and that the Jews would therefore be 'scattered by other nations' (2 Nephi 25:15)" (Nyman, *Great Are the Words of Isaiah*, 83).

CHAPTER 14

Israel will be gathered and enjoy millennial rest—Lucifer was cast out of heaven for rebellion—Israel will triumph over Babylon (the world)—Compare 2 Nephi 24.

1 For the LORD will have mercy on Jacob, and will yet choose Israel, and set them in their own land: and the strangers shall be joined with them, and they shall cleave to the house of Jacob.

Isaiah 14:1–3. Israel Will Be Gathered to Their Lands of Promise

How will the Lord yet have mercy on Israel? (14:1–3) "The gathering process that restores Israel to her promised lands will be facilitated by other nations (people) who will actually assist in Israel's return from the ends of the earth. Then these other nations will espouse Israel's cause, and the captive (Israel) will become a ruler over her captors. This favored condition will be fully realized in the glorious millennial peace enjoyed by the faithful who have truly conquered Babylon (the world). (See Isaiah 14:3.) In other words, as [Keil and Delitzsch] put it, 'Babylon falls that Israel may rise' ([*Commentary*], 7:1:306)" (*Old Testament Student Manual: 1 Kings–Malachi*, 154).

2 And the people shall take them, and bring them to their place: and the house of Israel shall possess them in the land of the LORD for servants and handmaids: and they shall take them captives, whose captives they were; and they shall rule over their oppressors.

3 And it shall come to pass in the day that the LORD shall give thee rest from thy sorrow, and from thy fear, and from the hard bondage wherein thou wast made to serve,

What does the Joseph Smith Translation add to this verse? (14:2) "And the people shall take them, and bring them to their place: *yea, from far, unto the end of the earth, and they shall return to their land of promise,* and the house of Israel shall possess them in the land of the Lord for servants and handmaids: and they shall take them captives, whose captives they were; and they shall rule over their oppressors" (Wayment, *Complete Joseph Smith Translation of the Old Testament*, 187). See commentary of 2 Nephi 24:1–3 in *Book of Mormon Study Guide: Start to Finish, Revised Edition*.

4 ¶ That thou shalt take up this proverb against the king of Babylon, and say, How hath the oppressor ceased! the golden city ceased!

5 The LORD hath broken the staff of the wicked, *and* the sceptre of the rulers.

6 He who smote the people in wrath with a continual stroke, he that ruled the nations in anger, is persecuted, *and* none hindereth.

Isaiah 14:4–11. Isaiah Prophesies the Destruction of the King of Babylon

How did Isaiah depict the king of Babylon? (14:4–11) "These verses [Isa. 14:4–8] begin the *taunt-song* aimed at the once-powerful king of Babylon. Even the trees rejoice in the demise of this once-powerful king. Although the historical context of these verses is couched in ancient Babylon, the application extends to the latter days as well. It could apply to the ultimate removal of any wicked leader, particularly Satan. He will be bound at the commencement of the Millennium, reducing him to the role of a powerless prisoner for one thousand years (see D&C 88:110)" (Brewster, *Isaiah Plain and Simple*, 136–37).

7 The whole earth is at rest, *and* is quiet: they break forth into singing.

What will bring about the "rest" prophesied by Isaiah? (14:7–8) "When the law of God is observed, there is peace and tranquility in every quarter. When

8 Yea, the fir trees rejoice at thee, *and* the cedars of Lebanon, *saying,* Since thou art laid
down, no feller is come up against us.

9 Hell from beneath is moved for thee to
meet *thee* at thy coming: it stirreth up the
dead for thee, *even* all the chief ones of the
earth; it hath raised up from their thrones all
the kings of the nations.

10 All they shall speak and say unto thee, Art
thou also become weak as we? art thou become like unto us?

11 Thy pomp is brought down to the grave,
and the noise of thy viols: the worm is spread
under thee, and the worms cover thee.

12 How art thou fallen from heaven, O
Lucifer, son of the morning! *how* art thou cut
down to the ground, which didst weaken the
nations!

13 For thou hast said in thine heart, I will
ascend into heaven, I will exalt my throne
above the stars of God: I will sit also upon
the mount of the congregation, in the sides
of the north:

14 I will ascend above the heights of the
clouds; I will be like the most High.

15 Yet thou shalt be brought down to hell, to
the sides of the pit.

the love of Christ abounds, there is unity and harmony in the hearts of men and women who can then live together without strife. The quintessential time for this state of affairs is during the Millennial reign of the Lord Jesus Christ. There have been various societies in lengthy periods of human history when these principles of Zion have been embraced. The saints in Jerusalem enjoyed a brief time of unity during which the disciples of Christ were of one mind and one heart. The Nephites, after the ministry of the resurrected Christ to them in the land of Bountiful, experienced more than three generations of abundant truth and love" (Hyde, *Comprehensive Commentary [Isaiah]*, 99).

Isaiah 14:12–20. Satan, like the King of Babylon, Will Be Cast Down to Hell

Who was Lucifer? (14:12) Lucifer means "literally *the Shining One*; also *Lightbringer* or *Son of the Morning*. Lucifer is also known as Satan or the devil. The name Lucifer appears only once in the Bible (Isa. 14:12; compare Luke 10:18). Apparently Lucifer is the name of the devil before his rebellion and fall. Latter-day revelation clarifies the fall of Lucifer and equates him with Satan (D&C 76:25–38; see also Rev. 12; 2 Ne. 9:8; D&C 29:36–38; Moses 4:1–4)" (Bible Dictionary, "Lucifer"). Here, the Hebrew word for "Lucifer" means "morning star, son of dawn" (Isaiah 14:12*c*). "*Stars* and *heavens* are frequently used to represent the members of the Council in Heaven" (Baker and Ricks, *Who Shall Ascend into the Hill of the Lord?* 214fn289; see also D&C 76:26–27).

Why did Isaiah liken the Babylonian king to Lucifer? (14:12–15) "The pivotal point and most important scene lies in verses 12–15, in which Isaiah identifies the king of Babylon as Lucifer (KJV, 'bright morning star' in the Hebrew . . .). Most scholars identify the 'morning star' or Lucifer, as a mythical figure or as a figurative representation of a Babylonian king. Latter-day Saints are fortunate to have modern scripture that explains who Lucifer is. Additional modern scripture explains his actions and attitude in greater detail (compare Isa. 14:12–14 with D&C 76:25–27; 29:36–37; Moses 4:1–4)" (Ludlow, *Isaiah*, 188). See commentary for 2 Nephi 24:12–15 in *Book of Mormon Study Guide: Start to Finish, Revised Edition.* ⊕

Whose position in heaven does Lucifer ultimately desire? (14:14) Joseph Smith saw in vision that an angel of God, after his rebellion, "was thrust down from the presence of God and the Son, and was called

Perdition, for the heavens wept over him—he was Lucifer, a son of the morning" (D&C 76:25–26). Isaiah reveals that Satan continued to desire the position he once held. He specifically desired to take the position of the Son or even the Father, who is the Most High in heaven. The book of Moses recorded Satan crying out in frustration and demanding that Moses worship him: "And now, when Moses had said these words, Satan cried with a loud voice, and ranted upon the earth, and commanded, saying: I am the Only Begotten, worship me" (Moses 1:19).

What was Lucifer's goal from the beginning? (14:16–17) "Satan, or Lucifer, or the father of lies—call him what you will—is real, the very personification of evil. His motives are in every case malicious. . . . He is eternally opposed to the love of God, the Atonement of Jesus Christ, and the work of peace and salvation. He will fight against these whenever and wherever he can. He knows he will be defeated and cast out in the end, but he is determined to take down with him as many others as he possibly can" (Holland, "We Are All Enlisted," 44). ⊕

Why does Isaiah portray Lucifer as an "abominable branch"? (14:19) "The grave of Nebuchadnezzar, Babylon's king, has never been discovered, and Lucifer will never have a grave or a monument because he never received a body. The imagery of *cast out of the grave* stands opposite Jesus and his tomb ([Isaiah] 53:9), where Jesus arose from the dead and possessed 'life in himself' (John 5:26); he used his own power to arise and exit the tomb. Lucifer, the *abominable branch*, can be contrasted to the useful 'Branch' that will 'grow out of' the roots of Jesse ([Isaiah] 11:1; D&C 113:1–2)" (Parry, et al., *Understanding Isaiah*, 150). ⊕

Summary of Isaiah 14:21–32

Isaiah concludes his prophecy of the destruction of Babylon and also prophesies the destruction of Assyria and the Philistines. In the end, all the nations of the wicked will be destroyed. This will enable the Lord to establish Zion, and His people shall trust in it.

16 They that see thee shall narrowly look upon thee, *and* consider thee, *saying, Is* this the man that made the earth to tremble, that did shake kingdoms;

17 *That* made the world as a wilderness, and destroyed the cities thereof; *that* opened not the house of his prisoners?

18 All the kings of the nations, *even* all of them, lie in glory, every one in his own house.

19 But thou art cast out of thy grave like an abominable branch, *and as* the raiment of those that are slain, thrust through with a sword, that go down to the stones of the pit; as a carcase trodden under feet.

20 Thou shalt not be joined with them in burial, because thou hast destroyed thy land, *and* slain thy people: the seed of evildoers shall never be renowned.

CHAPTERS 15–21

Moab will be laid waste, and her people will howl and weep.

Moab is condemned, and her people will sorrow—The Messiah will sit on David's throne, seeking justice and hastening righteousness.

Israel was scattered because she forgot God—Yet the nations that plunder her will be destroyed.

The Lord will raise the gospel ensign, send messengers to His scattered people, and gather them to Mount Zion.

The Lord will smite and destroy Egypt—Finally He will heal her, and Egypt and Assyria will be blessed with Israel.

Assyria will overrun Egypt and make her ashamed.

Babylon is fallen, is fallen!—Other nations also are destroyed.

Summary of Isaiah 15–21

Isaiah directs chapters 15 and 16 to Moab, who serves as a type and shadow of the wickedness that fights against Zion. Chapters 17 and 18 are a warning to Syria and Ephraim regarding trusting in idols, riches, and power. Though Israel is scattered because of her sins, the nations that plunder her will be destroyed, and in the last days the Lord will send His messengers to gather His scattered people. In chapters 19 and 20 Isaiah testifies how the Lord will destroy and then heal Egypt. Though Egypt and Assyria will be blessed with Israel, eventually Assyria will destroy Egypt. Chapter 21 is a prophecy of the destruction of Babylon, Dumah (Edom), and Arabia. Babylon symbolizes the world in our day. As modern revelation declares: "Every man walketh in his own way, and after the image of his own god, whose image is in the likeness of the world, and whose substance is that of an idol, which waxeth old and shall perish in Babylon, even Babylon the great, which shall fall" (D&C 1:16).

CHAPTER 22

Jerusalem will be attacked and scourged—The people will be carried captive—The Messiah will hold the key of the house of David, inherit glory, and be fastened as a nail in a sure place.

1 The burden of the valley of vision. What aileth thee now, that thou art wholly gone up to the housetops?

2 Thou that art full of stirs, a tumultuous city, a joyous city: thy slain *men are* not slain with the sword, nor dead in battle.

3 All thy rulers are fled together, they are bound by the archers: all that are found in thee are bound together, *which* have fled from far.

4 Therefore said I, Look away from me; I will weep bitterly, labour not to comfort me, because of the spoiling of the daughter of my people.

5 For *it is* a day of trouble, and of treading down, and of perplexity by the Lord God of hosts in the valley of vision, breaking down the walls, and of crying to the mountains.

6 And Elam bare the quiver with chariots of men *and* horsemen, and Kir uncovered the shield.

Isaiah 22:1–7. Jerusalem Is in a Panic Because of the Approaching Enemy

What was the "valley of vision," and why was it so called? (22:1) "The contents of this oracle [revelation] indicate that *the valley of vision* refers to Jerusalem. No such name is known. The term is meant as a pun on the name of the Kidron Valley that defines the eastern boundary of biblical Jerusalem. Kidron means 'darkness' or 'gloom,' and Isaiah's use of the term *valley of vision* to refer to the site is a play that reverses the meaning of the valley's name to designate it as a site of vision or revelation concerning the Lord's intentions for the city of Jerusalem" (*New Oxford Annotated Bible* [2010], 996).

In what way will the Lord's "daughter" be spoiled? (22:2–5) "These events occur during the 701 B.C. campaign of Sennacherib. . . . During the course of the invasion of Palestine, they will according to Sennacherib's annals, 'lay siege to forty-six fortified cities, walled forts, and countless villages.' King Hezekiah was bottled up in Jerusalem 'like a bird in a cage.' Any of his officials who attempted to escape were captured, and many were executed. . . . The invaders eventually withdrew after Hezekiah paid a huge sum as tribute and ransom for the city of Jerusalem (2 Kings 18:13–16)" (Walton, et al., *IVP Bible Background Commentary*, 613).

Why were Elam and Kir mentioned with the Assyrian army? (22:6–7) "Sennacherib regularly conscripted levees of soldiers from subject and allied peoples. Although Elam has previously supported

The Setting of Isaiah 22

"One difficulty in understanding Isaiah is that his prophecies are not necessarily chronological. One chapter may address one time period, the next chapter an earlier time period, and the next addresses several time periods at once. Chapter 22 seems to be set in Hezekiah's day, just before the Assyrian invasion (thus around 705 B.C.). Yet there is no doubt that aspects of the prophecy also apply to the Babylonian invasion that would occur more than a hundred years later. Additionally, the principles taught are timeless and apply to every situation and era. This chapter should be read in conjunction with 2 Kings 18–19 and Isaiah 36–37" (Muhlestein, *Scripture Study Made Simple*, 347).

7 And it shall come to pass, *that* thy choicest
valleys shall be full of chariots, and the horsemen shall set themselves in array at the gate.

8 ¶ And he discovered the covering of Judah,
and thou didst look in that day to the armour of the house of the forest.

9 Ye have seen also the breaches of the city of
David, that they are many: and ye gathered
together the waters of the lower pool.

10 And ye have numbered the houses of
Jerusalem, and the houses have ye broken
down to fortify the wall.

11 Ye made also a ditch between the two
walls for the water of the old pool: but ye
have not looked unto the maker thereof, neither had respect unto him that fashioned it
long ago.

12 And in that day did the Lord GOD of
hosts call to weeping, and to mourning, and
to baldness, and to girding with sackcloth:

13 And behold joy and gladness, slaying
oxen, and killing sheep, eating flesh, and
drinking wine: let us eat and drink; for to
morrow we shall die.

14 And it was revealed in mine ears by the
LORD of hosts, Surely this iniquity shall not
be purged from you till ye die, saith the Lord
GOD of hosts.

15 ¶ Thus saith the Lord GOD of hosts, Go,
get thee unto this treasurer, *even* unto Shebna,
which *is* over the house, *and say,*

16 What hast thou here? and whom hast
thou here, that thou hast hewed thee out a
sepulchre here, *as* he that heweth him out a
sepulchre on high, *and* that graveth an habitation for himself in a rock?

17 Behold, the LORD will carry thee away with
a mighty captivity, and will surely cover thee.

the Babylonians and opposed Assyria, in this 701 [B.C.] campaign it seems clear that they have supplied a contingent of bowmen for Sennacherib's host" (Walton, et al., *IVP Bible Background Commentary*, 613).

Isaiah 22:8–14. Trust in Your Creator, Not in Your Own Strength

Despite all their preparations, wherein lies Israel's only safety? (22:9–11) "Isaiah warns of calamities coming to Jerusalem. Jerusalem will be attacked and its leaders will be taken captive, but it will be able to rejoice that it is not completely destroyed. Isaiah weeps because of the calamities coming to Jerusalem as it is besieged by a great army. Though Israel has fortified Jerusalem's wall, built new walls, and protected its water sources, she has not done the most important thing for her protection: look to God. The Lord has brought tribulation upon Israel hoping to humble her, but she refuses to be humble. Because she refused to turn to the Lord even in great need, many in Israel will be destroyed" (Muhlestein, *Essential Old Testament Companion*, 378).

What was the iniquity that would lead to a purging by death? (22:12–14) "God intervened, as he promised he would, and defended Jerusalem himself (Isa. 36:37; 2 Kgs. 18:13–19:37). The miraculous deliverance was to be seen as another opportunity to repent, but instead of repenting, the people celebrated: [see Isa. 22:12–13] . . . For that response, Isaiah wrote, they would eventually be held accountable" (Seely, "Lord Is Our Judge and Our King," 117).

Isaiah 22:15–19. Isaiah Prophesies Punishments upon Shebna for His Pride

Who was Shebna? (22:15–19) "Isaiah singles out a leading citizen and describes his selfish, vain actions. The individual selected is Shebna, the leader of the king's court, a position similar to a present-day secretary of state. Isaiah apparently confronts Shebna in the Kidron Valley near the tombs of the kings. . . . Like the dashed expectations of those in Jerusalem, Shebna's hope for a magnificent tomb in Jerusalem is destined to come to naught. Indeed, Shebna was eventually disgraced in office and demoted to the office of secretary or scribe of the king's court (Isa. 36:3). . . .

"According to some scholars, Shebna was actually a foreigner who rose to power in Jerusalem" (Ludlow, *Isaiah*, 233, 234).

Isaiah 22:20–25. Eliakim Is a Type for the Messiah

Why was Eliakim called to rule in Shebna's place? (22:20–25) "Isaiah 22:20–25 pertains to the righteousness and blessing of Eliakim, who was a priest and official in Hezekiah's house (36:3; 37:2). . . . Eliakim serves as a type of Christ in several ways: as Eliakim replaces an evil ruler of Judah (Shebna), so Christ will replace all of the temporal rulers of Judah and Israel when he takes his rightful place as King of kings; Eliakim's name is prophetic ('may God raise') and points to Christ's power to lift us from both sin and death as a priest. Eliakim points to Jesus' role as the priest (Heb. 7:17); and similar to Eliakim's ministry 'over the house' of Hezekiah, king of Judah, Christ possesses eternal power over the house of Judah or Israel" (Parry, et al., *Understanding Isaiah*, 199–200). ⊕

What did it mean to receive the "key of the house of David"? (22:22) "The key of the house of David, the right to rule, was a symbol for the real right to rule, which is only enjoyed through the holy priesthood of God. This power was focused upon and centered in the Lord Jesus Christ, to whom was given power to 'shut' and to 'open' with no one who could override that power. John and Isaiah both clearly show that the key of David, or the government, was to be upon the shoulders of the Savior of the world (see Isaiah 9:6; Revelation 3:7)" (*Old Testament Student Manual: 1 Kings–Malachi*, 159).

Who will be fastened with "a nail in a sure place"? (22:23) "The 'nail in a sure place' (Isaiah 22:23) is clearly messianic and symbolizes the terrible reality of the cross, though only a part of the total suffering of the Lord, that caused him to 'tremble because of pain, and to bleed at every pore, and to suffer both body and spirit' (D&C 19:18.) Just as the nail of the cross that was driven in the sure place secured the body of the one being crucified, so the Savior himself is, to all who will, a nail in the sure place, for he has given them power so that none need be lost (see John 17:12)" (*Old Testament Student Manual: 1 Kings–Malachi*, 159). ⊕

18 He will surely violently turn and toss thee *like* a ball into a large country: there shalt thou die, and there the chariots of thy glory *shall be* the shame of thy lord's house.

19 And I will drive thee from thy station, and from thy state shall he pull thee down.

20 ¶ And it shall come to pass in that day, that I will call my servant Eliakim the son of Hilkiah:

21 And I will clothe him with thy robe, and strengthen him with thy girdle, and I will commit thy government into his hand: and he shall be a father to the inhabitants of Jerusalem, and to the house of Judah.

22 And the key of the house of David will I lay upon his shoulder; so he shall open, and none shall shut; and he shall shut, and none shall open.

23 And I will fasten him *as* a nail in a sure place; and he shall be for a glorious throne to his father's house.

24 And they shall hang upon him all the glory of his father's house, the offspring and the issue, all vessels of small quantity, from the vessels of cups, even to all the vessels of flagons.

25 In that day, saith the LORD of hosts, shall the nail that is fastened in the sure place be removed, and be cut down, and fall; and the burden that *was* upon it shall be cut off: for the LORD hath spoken *it*.

CHAPTER 23

Tyre will be overthrown.

Summary of Isaiah 23

"For centuries, extensive trade launched from the port cities of Tyre and Sidon, on the coast of today's Lebanon, established the Phoenicians as the dominant seafaring merchants in the eastern Mediterranean. Isaiah foresees the news of Tyre's destruction passing from the city's nearest colony on Cyprus to the far reaches of its sea-trade in Egypt and Tarshish (probably Tartessus in Spain, v. 6). . . . The prophecy envisions the 'land of the Chaldeans' (Babylonia) as carrying out the destruction of Tyre (v. 13), after which the city goes unremembered for the span of a lifetime (70 years; v. 15). When Tyre does resume international trade, the material gains will benefit God's faithful (v. 18)" (Fee and Hubbard, *Eerdmans Companion to the Bible*, 391).

CHAPTER 24

Men will transgress the law and break the everlasting covenant—At the Second Coming, they will be burned, the earth will reel, and the sun will be ashamed—Then the Lord will reign in Zion and in Jerusalem.

1 Behold, the LORD maketh the earth empty, and maketh it waste, and turneth it upside down, and scattereth abroad the inhabitants thereof.

Isaiah 24:1–12. The Earth Is Cursed Because of Breaking the Covenant of the Lord

When might these judgments be carried out? (24:1) "Sometimes the prophecy seems to apply to all the world. But there are times when it seems to apply only to those who have made a covenant with God. . . . There is almost certainly a fulfillment in Isaiah's and/or Jeremiah's day (the countryside would be destroyed and emptied in both eras), but seems to also refer to the great apostasy and the spiritual emptiness that accompanies it. It may also have reference to the destruction that precedes the Second Coming. Isaiah declares that the Lord will cause chaos to reign, almost undoing His own creation" (Muhlestein, *Scripture Study Made Simple*, 348). ⊕

2 And it shall be, as with the people, so with the priest; as with the servant, so with his master; as with the maid, so with her mistress; as with the buyer, so with the seller; as with the lender, so with the borrower; as with the taker of usury, so with the giver of usury to him.

3 The land shall be utterly emptied, and utterly spoiled: for the LORD hath spoken this word.

Why are priests included in this list of people who receive the Lord's judgment? (24:2) At the time of the prophesied destruction, it won't matter what position a person held if they have been guilty of breaking the "everlasting covenant" (Isaiah 23:5). "Such voices may have to answer for their perpetuating falsehood and their failure to give true leadership in combating evil. 'As with the people, so with the priest' (Isa. 24:2). The term *priest* is here used to denote all religious leaders of any faith" (Kimball, "Voices of the Past, of the Present, of the Future," 18). See Ezekiel 22:26 as a reminder that God will hold all the guilty accountable, including those who hold priesthood authority.

4 The earth mourneth *and* fadeth away, the world languisheth *and* fadeth away, the haughty people of the earth do languish.

5 The earth also is defiled under the inhabitants thereof; because they have transgressed the laws, changed the ordinance, broken the everlasting covenant.

What did Isaiah notice about the moral condition of mankind? (24:5) "Men have forsaken the whole gospel system—its laws, ordinances, and saving truths. A covenant that is everlasting no longer continues; it has been broken by men! They have forsaken their God. For such a course they must pay the penalty. 'Therefore hath the curse devoured the earth, and they that dwell therein are desolate'—or, better, 'they that dwell therein are found guilty'—'therefore the inhabitants of the earth are burned, and few men left' (Isa. 24:4–6). The burning occurs at the Second Coming" (McConkie, *Millennial Messiah*, 38). ⊕

6 Therefore hath the curse devoured the earth, and they that dwell therein are desolate: therefore the inhabitants of the earth are burned, and few men left.

7 The new wine mourneth, the vine languisheth, all the merryhearted do sigh.

8 The mirth of tabrets ceaseth, the noise of them that rejoice endeth, the joy of the harp ceaseth.

9 They shall not drink wine with a song; strong drink shall be bitter to them that drink it.

How will the righteous be preserved by fire? (24:6) Nephi explained this coming event to his brothers. "For the day soon cometh that all the proud and they who do wickedly shall be as stubble; and the day cometh that they must be burned. . . . Wherefore, he will preserve the righteous by his power, even if it so be that the fulness of his wrath must come, and the righteous be preserved, even unto the destruction of their enemies by fire. Wherefore, the righteous need not fear; for thus saith the prophet, they shall be saved, even if it so be as by fire" (1 Nephi 22:15, 17). ⊕

10 The city of confusion is broken down: every house is shut up, that no man may come in.

11 *There is* a crying for wine in the streets; all joy is darkened, the mirth of the land is gone.

12 In the city is left desolation, and the gate is smitten with destruction.

How does one retain joy in a day of wickedness? (24:11) "You cannot do wrong and feel right. It pays to live the good, wholesome, joy-filled life. Live so you will have no serious regrets—no heartaches. Live so you can reach out and tap that unseen Power, without which no man or woman can do their best" (Benson, "Satan's Thrust—Youth," 54). Elder Richard G. Scott said: "[The Lord's] intent is that each of us finds joy. . . . Obey the commandments, have faith in the Master, and do the things that are necessary to have joy here on earth. Your joy in life depends upon your trust in Heavenly Father and His holy Son, your conviction that their plan of happiness truly can bring you joy" ("Finding Joy in Life," 24).

Isaiah 24:13–23. Signs in the Earth and Heavens at the Second Coming

13 ¶ When thus it shall be in the midst of the land among the people, *there shall be* as the shaking of an olive tree, *and* as the gleaning grapes when the vintage is done.

14 They shall lift up their voice, they shall sing for the majesty of the LORD, they shall cry aloud from the sea.

What does the "shaking of an olive tree" symbolize? (24:13) "In verse 13, Isaiah and the Lord make it clear that while they speak of lands, nations, and trees, they are really talking about people. This is a clue that we should read this chapter not only to know what God does with Israel and the world, but also to see how He deals with us. Specifically, the Lord will shake from us that which is not good. He will purge us in a painful manner, but He will not give up on us. He will do whatever He has to in order to force us to rely on Him and Him only. Then He will take us back" (Muhlestein, *Essential Old Testament Companion*, 380–81).

15 Wherefore glorify ye the LORD in the fires, *even* the name of the LORD God of Israel in the isles of the sea.

16 ¶ From the uttermost part of the earth have we heard songs, *even* glory to the righteous. But I said, My leanness, my leanness, woe unto me! the treacherous dealers have dealt treacherously; yea, the treacherous dealers have dealt very treacherously.

Where are the fires Isaiah is referring to? (24:15) "Having described the judgments which were to come upon the wicked world, Isaiah turns to the message of hope. There is to be a group in the midst of the land (the earth) who shall sing unto the Lord and glorify him. He further identifies the place as 'in the fires . . . in the isles of the sea.' A marginal note in the KJV suggests the word 'valleys' instead of 'fires.' Isaiah consistently uses the term 'isles of the sea,' undoubtedly with reference to America. Similarly, the Book of Mormon prophet Jacob spoke of the Nephites' being on 'an isle of the sea' (2 Nephi 10:20). Thus Isaiah seems to be describing the Latter-day Saints, who will be singing and glorifying God in the day of the earth's turmoils and devastation" (Nyman, *Great Are the Words of Isaiah*, 95).

17 Fear, and the pit, and the snare, *are* upon thee, O inhabitant of the earth.

What could "the pit" refer to? (24:17) The term "pit" is "known as the 'horrible pit' (Ps. 40:2), the 'pit of destruction' (Ps. 55:23), the 'deeps' (Ps. 88:6), and 'prison' (Isa. 24:22), the pit is hell [spirit prison], the realm where the spirits of the unrighteous dwell while awaiting the judgment (2 Ne. 24:15; Ezek. 32:21–23)" (McConkie, *Guide to Scriptural Symbols*, 90).

18 And it shall come to pass, *that* he who fleeth from the noise of the fear shall fall into the pit; and he that cometh up out of the midst of the pit shall be taken in the snare: for the windows from on high are open, and the foundations of the earth do shake.

Why are the wicked fleeing and what will be the end result? (24:18) "The wicked will futilely attempt to avoid God's many judgments. Although they may escape from one, they will fall into another, and if they escape from the second judgment, they will be ensnared in a third" (Ludlow, *Isaiah*, 244). Samuel the Lamanite warned the wicked Nephites of his day, "Ye shall attempt to flee and there shall be no place for refuge" (Helaman 15:2). Many of the fleeing wicked "would fain be glad if [they] could command the rocks and the mountains to fall upon [them] to hide [them] from his presence" (Alma 12:14).

In what sense will the earth be "broken down" and "clean dissolved"? (24:19) The earth "must needs be sanctified from all unrighteousness, that it may be prepared for the celestial glory; for after it hath filled the measure of its creation, it shall be crowned with glory, even with the presence of God the Father; that bodies who are of the celestial kingdom may possess it forever and ever; for, for this intent was it made and created, and for this intent are they sanctified" (D&C 88:18–20).

Who are the "prisoners" gathered in the pit? (24:22) The prisoners gathered in the pit are those in spirit prison waiting to be taught the knowledge of the truth (see D&C 138:30–34). "The knowledge that the gospel was to be taught to all, either in this life or the next, and that vicarious ordinances were to be performed for those unable to receive them in earth life, was known to the ancient Saints. There are scriptural, apocryphal, and historical references that evidence that these principles were understood anciently. Yet it is only with the knowledge we have as a result of the restoration of the gospel that these ancient sources take on significant meaning for us; otherwise they would seem as strange to Latter-day Saints as they presently do to the rest of the Christian world [see D&C 138:12–17]" (Millet and McConkie, *Life Beyond*, 156–57).

Isaiah 25:1–8. The Lord Prepares a Feast for the Righteous

What might the phrase "thy counsels of old" refer to? (25:1) "God's 'counsels of old' may refer to His 'plan of redemption, which had been prepared from the foundation of the earth' (Alma 12:30)" (Valletta, et al., *Old Testament for Latter-day Saint Families*, 494).

19 The earth is utterly broken down, the earth is clean dissolved, the earth is moved exceedingly.

20 The earth shall reel to and fro like a drunkard, and shall be removed like a cottage; and the transgression thereof shall be heavy upon it; and it shall fall, and not rise again.

21 And it shall come to pass in that day, *that* the LORD shall punish the host of the high ones *that are* on high, and the kings of the earth upon the earth.

22 And they shall be gathered together, *as* prisoners are gathered in the pit, and shall be shut up in the prison, and after many days shall they be visited.

23 Then the moon shall be confounded, and the sun ashamed, when the LORD of hosts shall reign in mount Zion, and in Jerusalem, and before his ancients gloriously.

CHAPTER 25

In Mount Zion the Lord will prepare a gospel feast of rich food—He will swallow up death in victory—It will be said, Lo, this is our God.

1 O LORD, thou *art* my God; I will exalt thee, I will praise thy name; for thou hast done wonderful *things; thy* counsels of old *are* faithfulness *and* truth.

2 For thou hast made of a city an heap; *of* a defenced city a ruin: a palace of strangers to be no city; it shall never be built.

3 Therefore shall the strong people glorify thee, the city of the terrible nations shall fear thee.

4 For thou hast been a strength to the poor, a strength to the needy in his distress, a refuge from the storm, a shadow from the heat, when the blast of the terrible ones *is* as a storm *against* the wall.

5 Thou shalt bring down the noise of strangers, as the heat in a dry place; *even* the heat with the shadow of a cloud: the branch of the terrible ones shall be brought low.

6 ¶ And in this mountain shall the LORD of hosts make unto all people a feast of fat things, a feast of wines on the lees, of fat things full of marrow, of wines on the lees well refined.

7 And he will destroy in this mountain the face of the covering cast over all people, and the veil that is spread over all nations.

8 He will swallow up death in victory; and the Lord GOD will wipe away tears from off all faces; and the rebuke of his people shall he take away from off all the earth: for the LORD hath spoken *it*.

How has the Lord provided "strength to the poor" and "strength to the needy" in our day? (25:4) "To implement his instructions to care for the poor and the needy, the Lord has in all dispensations given specific programs. . . . He has told us how to contribute to the care of his people, and he has given us our agency. We can do with it as we please, but he warns: 'Therefore, if any man shall take of the abundance which I have made, and impart not his portion, according to the law of my gospel, unto the poor and the needy, he shall, with the wicked, lift up his eyes in hell, being in torment' (D&C 104:18)" (Romney, "Caring for the Poor and Needy," 99). What can you do to assist the Lord in helping others?

When will the Lord prepare His "feast of fat things"? (25:6) Isaiah's words allude to a time where all nations will be invited to partake of the blessings of the gospel. This time is in preparation for the Second Coming of Jesus Christ. In "Mount Zion, which shall be the city of New Jerusalem" (D&C 84:2), the Lord "promised to prepare a feast of fat things. . . . This invitation is to be given first to the rich and learned, the wise and noble—classes who do not readily embrace the Gospel and then in the day of his power, the poor, the lame, and the blind, and the deaf, should come in unto the marriage of the lamb. In this manner the parable of the great supper (Luke 14) will be fulfilled" (Smith, *Church History and Modern Revelation*, 1:195). See also D&C 58:6–13.

What could the "veil that is spread over all nations" be? (25:7) "The '[veil] that is spread over all nations' is undoubtedly the veil of darkness and ignorance. It will be destroyed by the Lord's pouring out knowledge upon the heads of the Latter-day Saints, and all others who will hearken in the dispensation of the fulness of times, as spoken of in D&C 121:26–33 (see also Isaiah 11:9)" (Nyman, *Great are the Words of Isaiah*, 97).

How are Isaiah's words in this verse relevant today? (25:8) "It is my promise to you that increasing your faith in the Lord Jesus Christ will bring you added strength and greater hope. For you, the righteous, the Healer of our souls, in His time and His way, will heal all your wounds. No injustice, no persecution, no trial, no sadness, no heartache, no suffering, no wound—however deep, however wide, however painful—will be excluded from the comfort, peace, and lasting hope of Him whose open arms and whose wounded hands will welcome us back into His presence. At that day . . . 'God shall wipe away all tears from [your] eyes' [see Rev. 7:13, 15, 17]. This day will come" (Andersen, "Wounded," 86).

Isaiah 25:9–12. The Lord Will Save Those Who Wait for Him

What does it mean to "wait upon the Lord"? (25:9) "In the scriptures, the word *wait* means to hope, to anticipate, and to trust. To hope and trust in the Lord requires faith, patience, humility, meekness, long-suffering, keeping the commandments, and enduring to the end.... Waiting upon the Lord means pondering in our hearts and 'receiv[ing] the Holy Ghost' so that we can know 'all things what [we] should do'. ... As we wait upon the Lord, we are 'immovable in keeping the commandments,' knowing that we will 'one day rest from all [our] afflictions'" (Hales, "Waiting upon the Lord," 72).

What does Isaiah mean about the Lord spreading forth his hands like a swimmer? (25:11) "In divine judgment the Lord will *spread forth his hands* and destroy Moab, or the wicked, [with] the same ease of a swimmer who puts forth his arms to pass through water" (Parry, et al., *Understanding Isaiah*, 228). "As the Lord sweeps his hand through the land (like a swimmer spreads his hands through the water), he will humble the proud and haughty ones.... Reviewing Isaiah 24 and 25, one sees a pattern ... of serious warnings mingled with a note of optimism (as in chapter 24) and then follows it with a prophecy of joyful promises, concluding with a somber tone of caution (as in chapter 25)" (Ludlow, *Isaiah*, 248).

9 ¶ And it shall be said in that day, Lo, this *is* our God; we have waited for him, and he will save us: this *is* the LORD; we have waited for him, we will be glad and rejoice in his salvation.

10 For in this mountain shall the hand of the LORD rest, and Moab shall be trodden down under him, even as straw is trodden down for the dunghill.

11 And he shall spread forth his hands in the midst of them, as he that swimmeth spreadeth forth *his hands* to swim: and he shall bring down their pride together with the spoils of their hands.

12 And the fortress of the high fort of thy walls shall he bring down, lay low, *and* bring to the ground, *even* to the dust.

Isaiah 26:1–11. Jehovah Is Our Everlasting Strength

What is unique about the thoughts conveyed in this song? (26:1) "This grand song of thanks and praise for redemption credits the Lord not only with bringing about resurrection but with initiating it in raising His dead body (Isa. 26:19 and fn.; Isa. 25:8–9). These are some of the best Old Testament statements on the resurrection of the dead. Enjoy the beauty and truth in many of the poetic couplets in this prophecy (e.g., Isa. 26:3–4, 7, 12, 19–20)" (Rasmussen, *Latter-day Saint Commentary on the Old Testament*, 519).

Who is the "righteous nation" in this passage? (26:2) "Some modern students of the scriptures have suggested that 'the righteous nation which keepeth the truth' is the United States of America, which provided the basis of religious freedom necessary

CHAPTER 26

Trust in the Lord forever—Jehovah will die and be resurrected—All men will rise in the Resurrection.

1 In that day shall this song be sung in the land of Judah; We have a strong city; salvation will *God* appoint *for* walls and bulwarks.

2 Open ye the gates, that the righteous nation which keepeth the truth may enter in.

for the restoration of the true Church in the last days" (Ludlow, *Companion to Your Study of the Old Testament*, 295). Adam Clarke suggests a broader meaning: "The converted Gentiles shall have the gates opened—a full entrance into all the glories and privileges of the Gospel" (*Adam Clarke's Commentary* [on Isaiah 26:2]). Regardless, the Savior told the ruling Jews that "the kingdom of God shall be taken from [them] and given to a nation bringing forth fruits thereof" (Matthew 21:43). This was understood to be a Gentile nation.

3 Thou wilt keep *him* in perfect peace, *whose* mind *is* stayed *on thee:* because he trusteth in thee.

What blessing can come to someone who centers his or her mind on Jesus Christ? (26:3) "Let your minds be filled with the goal of being like the Lord, and you will crowd out depressing thoughts as you anxiously seek to know him and do his will. 'Let this mind be in you,' said Paul (Philip. 2:5). 'Look unto me in every thought,' said Jesus (D&C 6:36). And what will follow if we do? 'Thou wilt keep him in perfect peace, whose mind is stayed on thee' (Isa. 26:3). . . . We can rise above the enemies of despair, depression, discouragement, and despondency by remembering that God provides righteous alternatives" (Benson, "Do Not Despair," 67).

4 Trust ye in the LORD for ever: for in the LORD JEHOVAH *is* everlasting strength:

Why is JEHOVAH in capital letters? (26:4) See commentary in this volume for Isaiah 12:2.

5 ¶ For he bringeth down them that dwell on high; the lofty city, he layeth it low; he layeth it low, *even* to the ground; he bringeth it *even* to the dust.

6 The foot shall tread it down, *even* the feet of the poor, *and* the steps of the needy.

7 The way of the just *is* uprightness: thou, most upright, dost weigh the path of the just.

8 Yea, in the way of thy judgments, O LORD, have we waited for thee; the desire of *our* soul *is* to thy name, and to the remembrance of thee.

9 With my soul have I desired thee in the night; yea, with my spirit within me will I seek thee early: for when thy judgments *are* in the earth, the inhabitants of the world will learn righteousness.

When will the Lord's judgments (or precepts) lead to righteousness? (26:9) "In His mortal life, Jesus Christ was a loving judge, uncommonly wise and patient. He is known in the scriptures as 'the righteous judge' (2 Timothy 4:8; Moses 6:57). . . . The proceedings of a righteous judge are merciful, loving, and redemptive, not condemning" (Robbins, "Righteous Judge," 96, 97).

10 Let favour be shewed to the wicked, *yet* will he not learn righteousness: in the land of

Isaiah 26:12–21. All Shall Live Again and the Lord Shall Send Forth Righteous Indignation

What is Isaiah conveying by the imagery of Israel "with child"? (26:17–18) "Isaiah again uses the simile of Israel's chastisement being similar to labor pains. What God has done to Israel has been painful, but if it successfully forces her to turn to Him and thus to be born again, then the pain is turned to joy just as it is for a woman who gives birth. This simile is designed to help us understand the purposes for the Lord's punishments and to help us know how to act when those punishments happen" (Muhlestein, *Essential Old Testament Companion*, 385). ⊕

What profound truth did Isaiah emphasize in this passage? (26:19) "Christ has declared himself to be the resurrection and the life. He obtained that power through his atoning sacrifice. The keys of the resurrection are in his hands. The first resurrection is past. It took place immediately following his resurrection when he obtained power to open the graves. We are told that he is 'the Faithful Witness, and the first begotten of the dead' (Revelation 1:5). There could be no resurrection for any other, until he had come forth from the dead" (Smith, *Restoration of All Things*, 274).

uprightness will he deal unjustly, and will not behold the majesty of the LORD.

11 LORD, *when* thy hand is lifted up, they will not see: *but* they shall see, and be ashamed for *their* envy at the people; yea, the fire of thine enemies shall devour them.

12 ¶ LORD, thou wilt ordain peace for us: for thou also hast wrought all our works in us.

13 O LORD our God, *other* lords beside thee have had dominion over us: *but* by thee only will we make mention of thy name.

14 *They are* dead, they shall not live; *they are* deceased, they shall not rise: therefore hast thou visited and destroyed them, and made all their memory to perish.

15 Thou hast increased the nation, O LORD, thou hast increased the nation: thou art glorified: thou hadst removed *it* far *unto* all the ends of the earth.

16 LORD, in trouble have they visited thee, they poured out a prayer *when* thy chastening *was* upon them.

17 Like as a woman with child, *that* draweth near the time of her delivery, is in pain, *and* crieth out in her pangs; so have we been in thy sight, O LORD.

18 We have been with child, we have been in pain, we have as it were brought forth wind; we have not wrought any deliverance in the earth; neither have the inhabitants of the world fallen.

19 Thy dead *men* shall live, *together with* my dead body shall they arise. Awake and sing, ye that dwell in dust: for thy dew *is as* the dew of herbs, and the earth shall cast out the dead.

20 ¶ Come, my people, enter thou into thy
chambers, and shut thy doors about thee:
hide thyself as it were for a little moment,
until the indignation be overpast.

21 For, behold, the LORD cometh out of his
place to punish the inhabitants of the earth
for their iniquity: the earth also shall disclose
her blood, and shall no more cover her slain.

How can the Lord's people hide themselves from the punishment of the wicked? (26:20–21) The Lord will provide safety in Zion for the Saints. "It has been designed for many generations to hide up the Saints in the last days until the indignation of the Almighty be over. His wrath will be poured out upon the nations of the earth. We see the nations steadily driving along to the precipice. The Lord has spoken from the heavens, and he is about to fulfill the prophecies of his ancient and modern Prophets. . . . Let our anxiety be centered upon this one thing, the sanctification of our own hearts, the purifying of our own affections, the preparing of ourselves for the approach of the events that are hastening upon us" (Young, in *Journal of Discourses*, 9:3).

CHAPTER 27

The people of Israel will blossom and bud and fill the earth with fruit—They will be gathered one by one and will worship the Lord.

Summary of Isaiah 27

God has victory over the forces of evil. Israel shall grow and blossom and the blessings of salvation will spread over the earth. Jacob, who was exiled because of unfaithfulness, will be blessed for destroying false religious trappings. A trumpet blast will signal the start of Israel's gathering.

CHAPTER 28

Woe to the drunkards of Ephraim!—Revelation comes line upon line and precept upon precept—Christ, the sure foundation, is promised.

1 Woe to the crown of pride, to the drunkards of Ephraim, whose glorious beauty *is* a
fading flower, which *are* on the head of the fat
valleys of them that are overcome with wine!

2 Behold, the Lord hath a mighty and strong
one, *which* as a tempest of hail *and* a destroying storm, as a flood of mighty waters overflowing, shall cast down to the earth with the
hand.

3 The crown of pride, the drunkards of
Ephraim, shall be trodden under feet:

4 And the glorious beauty, which *is* on the
head of the fat valley, shall be a fading flower,
and as the hasty fruit before the summer;
which *when* he that looketh upon it seeth,
while it is yet in his hand he eateth it up.

Isaiah 28:1–17. The Lord Warns the Kingdom of Israel of Pride and Apostasy

Who and what is being identified here? (28:1–4) "The prophecy of the destruction of Ephraim—the Northern Kingdom, Israel, or Samaria—was undoubtedly given in the first half of Isaiah's ministry, because the promised destruction occurred at the hands of the Assyrians in 721 B.C. . . . Samaria was wealthy, prosperous, arrogant, and overindulgent, as reflected by the indictments pronounced by the prophets to the North (Hosea and Amos) and the archaeological evidence. . . . And the crown (a garland of fading flowers) is sitting upon the drunkard Ephraim at the head of 'fat valleys,' representing the rich agricultural resources in the North" (Seely, "Lord Is Our Judge and King," 121–22).

How is the "crown of glory" and the "crown of pride" compared and contrasted in this verse? (28:5) Note the reference to the "LORD of hosts" representing a "crown of glory" opposed to the Kingdom of Israel being referred to as the "crown of pride" (in verses 1–4). How do you see the glory and beauty of the Lord above the pride of the world? What are you doing to seek the crown of glory?

How does the comparison of wine and strong drink to Israel show us her future? (28:7–8) "When doctrines, truths, principles, and ordinances are changed from their pure form, spiritual drunkenness results. The wine in the whore's cup consists of all the apostate doctrines, creeds, and teachings, which have been spoiled and fermented. Man manipulates them for sundry reasons, often from the desire to be one with the world rather than one with the Lord. . . . When one is filled with the wine of apostasy, it becomes impossible to walk the straight and narrow path. The vision of leaders is blurred as opposed to the clear insight of seers. Judgment is impaired, and tables are filled with private interpretations brought forth from individual prejudices" (Wilcox, *Who Shall Be Able to Stand?* 244).

When should a person begin to be taught correct knowledge? (28:9) "Instructions in righteousness must begin with the young" (Isaiah 28:9*b*). The Lord stated in our dispensation: "Inasmuch as parents have children in Zion . . . that teach them not to understand the doctrine of repentance, faith in Christ the Son of the living God, and of baptism and the gift of the Holy Ghost by the laying on of the hands, when eight years old, the sin be upon the heads of the parents" (D&C 68:25).

How does Nephi use Isaiah's teachings concerning "precept upon precept"? (28:10–13) Nephi could have conveyed his sentiments from what he had read from Isaiah: "For behold, thus saith the Lord God: I will give unto the children of men line upon line, precept upon precept, here a little and there a little; and blessed are those who hearken unto my precepts, and lend an ear unto my counsel, for they shall learn wisdom; for unto him that receiveth I will give more; and from them that shall say, We have enough, from them shall be taken away even that which they have" (2 Nephi 28:30).

5 ¶ In that day shall the LORD of hosts be for a crown of glory, and for a diadem of beauty, unto the residue of his people,

6 And for a spirit of judgment to him that sitteth in judgment, and for strength to them that turn the battle to the gate.

7 ¶ But they also have erred through wine, and through strong drink are out of the way; the priest and the prophet have erred through strong drink, they are swallowed up of wine, they are out of the way through strong drink; they err in vision, they stumble *in* judgment.

8 For all tables are full of vomit *and* filthiness, *so that there is* no place *clean.*

9 ¶ Whom shall he teach knowledge? and whom shall he make to understand doctrine? *them that are* weaned from the milk, *and* drawn from the breasts.

10 For precept *must be* upon precept, precept upon precept; line upon line, line upon line; here a little, *and* there a little:

11 For with stammering lips and another tongue will he speak to this people.

12 To whom he said, This *is* the rest *wherewith* ye may cause the weary to rest; and this *is* the refreshing: yet they would not hear.

13 But the word of the LORD was unto them precept upon precept, precept upon precept; line upon line, line upon line; here a little, *and* there a little; that they might go, and fall backward, and be broken, and snared, and taken.

14 ¶ Wherefore hear the word of the LORD, ye scornful men, that rule this people which *is* in Jerusalem.

15 Because ye have said, We have made a covenant with death, and with hell are we at agreement; when the overflowing scourge shall pass through, it shall not come unto us: for we have made lies our refuge, and under falsehood have we hid ourselves:

16 ¶ Therefore thus saith the Lord GOD, Behold, I lay in Zion for a foundation a stone, a tried stone, a precious corner *stone,* a sure foundation: he that believeth shall not make haste.

Who is the tried cornerstone? (28:16) "Jesus Christ is that precious cornerstone in the foundation of Zion" (Bangerter, "Laying the Foundation of a Great Work," 15). ⊕

What do you think the Savior means when He says to the believers to "not make haste"? (28:16) Isaiah writes, "He that believeth shall not make haste." Peter's quotation of Isaiah here reads, "He that believeth on him shall not be confounded" (1 Pet. 2:6), and Paul's quotation reads, "shall not be ashamed" (Rom. 9:33; 10:11). The meaning of this phrase, then, is: "Whosoever believes in him [Christ, the stone] shall not be [confounded or] ashamed" (Parry, et al., *Understanding Isaiah*, 254).

17 Judgment also will I lay to the line, and righteousness to the plummet: and the hail shall sweep away the refuge of lies, and the waters shall overflow the hiding place.

What is the "plummet" or plumb line? (28:17) A plumb line is "a cord with a stone or metal weight, the plummet, tied to one end; used by builders to keep a wall perpendicular. Plumb line and plummet are used figuratively of God's actions in testing the uprightness of his people" (2 Ki. 21:13; Isa. 28:17; Amos 7:7–9)" (*Zondervan Illustrated Bible Dictionary*, 1154). "The Lord will measure or judge men by their works of justice and righteousness, just as stonemasons use a plumb bob and a measuring line to ensure that their work is straight. Those who are found lacking will be swept away by the wrath of God and they will not be able to hide" (Minert, *Simplified Isaiah for the Latter-day Saints*, 103–4). ⊕

Summary of Isaiah 28:18–29

Isaiah tells Israel that at a future day the Lord will rise up and perform a "strange act" (v. 21). The Lord has said in latter-day revelation that this "strange act" is "to prune my vineyard for the last time, . . . that I may pour out my Spirit upon all flesh" (D&C 95:4) and that all people "may discern between the righteous and the wicked" (D&C 101:95).

Isaiah 29:1–8. Isaiah Prophesies the Downfall of Jerusalem and Her Scattered Descendants

What correction did Joseph Smith insert in verse 2, and what city is referred to as Ariel? (29:1–2) "These verses are not quoted by Nephi. However, as the Prophet Joseph Smith worked on his inspired translation of the Bible, he made a slight alteration in verse 2, adding the phrase 'for thus hath the Lord said unto me' after the word 'sorrow,' and deleting the words 'me as' between 'unto' and 'Ariel' ['shall be heaviness and sorrow; *for thus hath the Lord said unto me*, It shall be unto ~~me as~~ Ariel'] (JST, Isaiah 29:2). Ariel (the city where David dwelt) was Jerusalem. It meant 'altar of God' or 'hearth of God.' The hearth was the highest tier of the altar of Solomon's temple and was the place where sacrifices were consumed by fire" (Brewster, *Isaiah Plain and Simple*, 152). See commentary in *Book of Mormon Study Guide: Start to Finish, Revised Edition* for 2 Nephi 27:3.

According to the Joseph Smith Translation, who is the subject of these verses? (29:3–6) "As corrected by the Prophet, the interpretation would be limited to Jerusalem. In the following verses, the pronouns in the JST are all changed to *her*, implying Jerusalem" (Nyman, "Contribution of the JST to Understanding the Old Testament Prophets," 125) ⊕

How does this passage relate to the people in the Book of Mormon? (29:4–6) "Where else in all history are there two better examples of peoples who were brought down and utterly destroyed than the Jaredites and Nephites? And whose voices, being stilled in death, yet speak from their graves for all to hear? Does not their united voice have a familiar spirit? Is it not whispering out of the ground the same prophetic message that is now and always has been the burden of the living prophets? Does not the Book of Mormon proclaim a familiar message, one already written in the Bible?" (McConkie, *New Witness for the Articles of Faith*, 432). ⊕

What is inferred by Isaiah's use of "a familiar spirit"? (29:4) "Throughout the Old Testament, . . . a familiar spirit was typically understood as the ghost of someone who had passed away. And those who consulted such spirits, usually to divine the future, were called necromancers. . . . Isaiah's use of 'familiar

CHAPTER 29

A people (the Nephites) will speak as a voice from the dust—The Apostasy, restoration of the gospel, and coming forth of a sealed book (the Book of Mormon) are foretold—Compare 2 Nephi 27.

1 Woe to Ariel, to Ariel, the city *where* David dwelt! add ye year to year; let them kill sacrifices.

2 Yet I will distress Ariel, and there shall be heaviness and sorrow: and it shall be unto me as Ariel.

3 And I will camp against thee round about, and will lay siege against thee with a mount, and I will raise forts against thee.

4 And thou shalt be brought down, *and* shalt speak out of the ground, and thy speech shall be low out of the dust, and thy voice shall be, as of one that hath a familiar spirit, out of the ground, and thy speech shall whisper out of the dust.

5 Moreover the multitude of thy strangers shall be like small dust, and the multitude of the terrible ones *shall be* as chaff that passeth away: yea, it shall be at an instant suddenly.

6 Thou shalt be visited of the LORD of hosts with thunder, and with earthquake, and great noise, with storm and tempest, and the flame of devouring fire.

spirit' in Isaiah 29, however, is quite unusual. Isaiah prophesied that after being besieged and presumably destroyed, Ariel (Jerusalem) would 'speak out of the ground, and [her] speech shall be low out of the dust, and [her] voice shall be, as of one that hath a familiar spirit' (Isaiah 29:4).... Isaiah was using necromancy as a metaphor for the sake of comparison.... Obviously, Isaiah's prophecy did not approve of illicit necromancy" ("How Are the Words of the Book of Mormon Like 'One That Hath a Familiar Spirit'?"). See commentary in this volume for Leviticus 19:31 and 1 Samuel 28:3. ⊕

7 ¶ And the multitude of all the nations that fight against Ariel, even all that fight against her and her munition, and that distress her, shall be as a dream of a night vision.

8 It shall even be as when an hungry *man* dreameth, and, behold, he eateth; but he awaketh, and his soul is empty: or as when a thirsty man dreameth, and, behold, he drinketh; but he awaketh, and, behold, *he is* faint, and his soul hath appetite: so shall the multitude of all the nations be, that fight against mount Zion.

Why do nations who fight against truth always fail? (29:7–8) "Every group that has fought, or will fight, against God's people will eventually be dispersed by God. Though these groups may seem forceful and terrible at the time, those who keep covenant with God will eventually find that the groups disappear as quickly as a terrible and frightening nightmare does when we awake. When Israel awakes to God, God will disperse her enemies, even if those enemies had been God's tool for humbling Israel" (Muhlestein, *Scripture Study Made Simple*, 361). ⊕

Isaiah 29:9–12. A Deep Sleep Covers the Nations

9 ¶ Stay yourselves, and wonder; cry ye out, and cry: they are drunken, but not with wine; they stagger, but not with strong drink.

10 For the Lord hath poured out upon you the spirit of deep sleep, and hath closed your eyes: the prophets and your rulers, the seers hath he covered.

How does a person become drunk but not with wine? (29:9–10) "They stagger and struggle like drunken men, drunk not with strong drink but with the wickedness of their actions. Elder Bruce R. McConkie suggests that 'in a spiritual sense drunkenness means apostasy.' Thus, Isaiah's imagery of the starving, intoxicated man represents the unrighteous, who because of their stubborn wickedness starve for want of spiritual food and drink. They stumble through life, unsure of their spiritual desires or heavenly origin and destiny. Isaiah further elaborates on the unrighteous nightmare, describing the wicked as asleep to the truths of the gospel" (Ludlow, *Unlocking Isaiah in the Book of Mormon*, 208). ⊕

11 And the vision of all is become unto you as the words of a book that is sealed, which *men* deliver to one that is learned, saying, Read this, I pray thee: and he saith, I cannot; for it *is* sealed:

What book does Isaiah foresee? (29:11) "Can you find a fulfillment of [this detailed prophecy] anywhere in this world like when Martin Harris took copies of the hieroglyphics from the plates from which the Book of Mormon was translated to Professor Anthon in New York? When Professor Anthon had given a certificate to say that the translation was correct, he wanted Martin Harris to bring the plates and let him translate them. Martin Harris said, 'They are sealed.' The professor repeated the very words that Isaiah spoke thousands of years ago: 'I cannot read a sealed book'" (Richards,

"Value of Holy Scriptures," 83). Note the changes in 2 Nephi 27 are also in the Joseph Smith Translation. See commentary in *Book of Mormon Study Guide: Start to Finish, Revised Edition* for 2 Nephi 27:7–8; 15–22.

How did one who "is not learned" accomplish the task given to him by the Lord? (29:12) "The Lord chose Joseph Smith, most likely considered to be one of 'the weak things of the world' (D&C 1:17–19), a man with virtually no formal learning to be the translator of this ancient record. How did the unlearned young man accomplish this great task? Here is his own testimony: 'Through the medium of the Urim and Thummim I translated the record by the gift and power of God' [*Joseph Smith* (manual), 60]. While a special instrument had been prepared to assist Joseph in the process of translation, it should be remembered that the Urim and Thummim could be used only by chosen seers who possessed the gift and power of God" (Brewster, *Isaiah Plain and Simple*, 166).

12 And the book is delivered to him that is not learned, saying, Read this, I pray thee: and he saith, I am not learned.

Isaiah 29:13–24. A Marvelous Work and a Wonder

13 ¶ Wherefore the Lord said, Forasmuch as this people draw near *me* with their mouth, and with their lips do honour me, but have removed their heart far from me, and their fear toward me is taught by the precept of men:

What constitutes "a marvelous work and wonder"? (29:14) "According to 2 Nephi 25:18, this marvelous work would be accomplished through the bringing forth of the Lord's words, specified as the words of Nephi's seed (the Book of Mormon) in 2 Nephi 29:2. This is also confirmed by the Savior's words to the Nephites after his resurrection (see 3 Nephi 21:1–9)" (Nyman, *Great Are the Words of Isaiah*, 112). Elder Jeffrey R. Holland testified: "It *is* a wonder! The Restoration of the gospel of Jesus Christ is filled with miracles, revelations, manifestations of every kind. Many of those have come in our lifetime" ("Like a Watered Garden," 33). ⊕

14 Therefore, behold, I will proceed to do a marvellous work among this people, *even* a marvellous work and a wonder: for the wisdom of their wise *men* shall perish, and the understanding of their prudent *men* shall be hid.

Why is it useless for the wicked to "seek to hide their counsel from the Lord"? (29:15–16) The Joseph Smith Translation adds a meaningful change that impacts these verses. An added phrase in verse 16, "I will show unto them, saith the Lord of Hosts, that I know all their works" (Wayment, *Complete Joseph Smith Translation of the Old Testament*, 193) clarifies that nothing can be hidden from God. Those who "seek to hide their counsel from the Lord" will fail (see verse 15; see also Nephi 9:20). See commentary in *Book of Mormon Study Guide: Start to Finish, Revised Edition* for 2 Nephi 27:27.

15 Woe unto them that seek deep to hide their counsel from the LORD, and their works are in the dark, and they say, Who seeth us? and who knoweth us?

16 Surely your turning of things upside down shall be esteemed as the potter's clay: for shall the work say of him that made it, He made me not? or shall the thing framed say of him that framed it, He had no understanding?

17 *Is* it not yet a very little while, and Lebanon shall be turned into a fruitful field, and the fruitful field shall be esteemed as a forest?

Who is turning things upside down? (29:16) "Of note is the clarification as to who is accusing whom of turning the world upside down; it is the promoters of secret combinations that point their fingers at the faithful who are attempting to establish the Kingdom of God upon the earth and in the hearts of the children of men. The conspirators will be shown that all of their dark plans have been anticipated and compensated for. The plots against the life and mission of the Prophet Joseph Smith, for example, were fruitless exercises until his work on the earth was complete. The futile attempts against the growth of the Kingdom of God" (Hyde, *Comprehensive Commentary [Isaiah]*, 157).

18 ¶ And in that day shall the deaf hear the words of the book, and the eyes of the blind shall see out of obscurity, and out of darkness.

19 The meek also shall increase *their* joy in the LORD, and the poor among men shall rejoice in the Holy One of Israel.

20 For the terrible one is brought to nought, and the scorner is consumed, and all that watch for iniquity are cut off:

How has the Book of Mormon helped you hear and see spiritual truths? (29:18–19) "Bring forth those who are blind to the light of the gospel, who cannot see that which is shown before them in the Bible; bring forth those who are deaf to the voice of the Spirit, who do not hear the voice of the Lord as it speaks from the ancient scriptures. Let them see and hear the words of the Book of Mormon where the precious truths are set forth with such plainness that none need err. Then will their eyes be opened and their ears unstopped, and the deaf shall hear and the blind see" (McConkie, *Millennial Messiah*, 173–74). See commentary in *Book of Mormon Study Guide: Start to Finish, Revised Edition* for 2 Nephi 27:29–30.

21 That make a man an offender for a word, and lay a snare for him that reproveth in the gate, and turn aside the just for a thing of nought.

How do some people today "make a man an offender for a word"? (29:21) "The translation of this phrase in the New International Version is instructive: 'Those who with a word make a man out to be guilty, who ensnare the defender in court and with false testimony deprive the innocent of justice'" (Parry, et al., *Understanding Isaiah*, 273). President Boyd K. Packer added: "Some few within the Church openly, or perhaps far worse in the darkness of anonymity, reproach their leaders in the wards and stakes and in the Church, seeking to make them 'an offender for a word,' as Isaiah said. To them the Lord said: . . . 'But those who cry transgression do it because they are the servants of sin, and are the children of disobedience themselves'" ("Twelve Apostles," 7).

22 Therefore thus saith the LORD, who redeemed Abraham, concerning the house of Jacob, Jacob shall not now be ashamed, neither shall his face now wax pale.

23 But when he seeth his children, the work of mine hands, in the midst of him, they shall

Why will Jacob's descendants sanctify the name of Jesus Christ? (29:22–23) "Let it be known that the things 'which our forefathers have awaited with anxious expectation to be revealed in the last times' are now being poured out upon the Saints. . . . The gleams of celestial light which now pierce the darkness of our souls will soon blaze forth in full celestial splendor.

The foundation has been laid; the Lord's house is now being built up on earth. God, our gracious Father, has restored in these last days the fulness of his everlasting gospel for the benefit and blessing of all his children and for the salvation and exaltation of those who believe and obey" (McConkie, "This Final Glorious Gospel Dispensation," 21).

Why do some people err in the things of God? (29:24) "There are many who unintentionally err in spirit because they believe in and are following the philosophies of men disguised as the word of the Lord [see D&C 123:12 and John 14:6].... There is only *one* way that leads to God, not multiple paths. As the apostle Paul preached, there is but 'one Lord, one faith, one baptism' (Ephesians 4:5).... To come unto Christ means that one must disavow and turn away from all error, from anything that will prevent him or her from coming to a correct understanding of His doctrines, covenants, and saving ordinances" (Brewster, *Isaiah Plain and Simple*, 175, 176).

Isaiah 30:1–13. Isaiah Identifies Israel's Shame and Rebuffing of Prophets

What does "cover with a covering" represent? (30:1) Judah "sought for a cover, a shelter, a protection from the enemy, but not from the Spirit of the Lord" (*John Gill's Exposition of the Whole Bible* [commentary on Isaiah 30:1]).

The Lord warns Judah they are errantly seeking protection by trusting in the arm of flesh, His words "directed against those who 'walk to go down into Egypt, and have not asked at my mouth; to strengthen themselves in the strength of Pharaoh, and to trust in the shadow of Egypt!' (Isa. 30:2), [referencing] Judah's constant attempts to make political alliances with Egypt (Isa. 18, 31).... Not only has Judah demonstrated lack of faith in the Lord but has not even sought his counsel in time of need" (Seely, "Lord Is Our Judge," 124).

What danger is symbolized when the children of Israel "go down into Egypt"? (30:2–3) Israel had proposed to enter into an alliance with Egypt to protect against the threat of Assyria's aggression. "The people of Israel were listening all right, but to the voices of pagan, materialistic Egypt. They had forsaken God for

sanctify my name, and sanctify the Holy One of Jacob, and shall fear the God of Israel.

24 They also that erred in spirit shall come to understanding, and they that murmured shall learn doctrine.

CHAPTER 30

Israel is scattered for rejecting the seers and prophets—Israel's people will be gathered and blessed temporally and spiritually—The Lord will come in a day of apostasy to judge and destroy the wicked.

1 Woe to the rebellious children, saith the LORD, that take counsel, but not of me; and that cover with a covering, but not of my spirit, that they may add sin to sin:

2 That walk to go down into Egypt, and have not asked at my mouth; to strengthen themselves in the strength of Pharaoh, and to trust in the shadow of Egypt!

3 Therefore shall the strength of Pharaoh be your shame, and the trust in the shadow of Egypt *your* confusion.

4 For his princes were at Zoan, and his ambassadors came to Hanes.

5 They were all ashamed of a people *that* could not profit them, nor be an help nor profit, but a shame, and also a reproach.

6 The burden of the beasts of the south: into the land of trouble and anguish, from whence *come* the young and old lion, the viper and fiery flying serpent, they will carry their riches upon the shoulders of young asses, and their treasures upon the bunches of camels, to a people *that* shall not profit *them.*

7 For the Egyptians shall help in vain, and to no purpose: therefore have I cried concerning this, Their strength *is* to sit still.

8 ¶ Now go, write it before them in a table, and note it in a book, that it may be for the time to come for ever and ever:

9 That this *is* a rebellious people, lying children, children *that* will not hear the law of the LORD:

10 Which say to the seers, See not; and to the prophets, Prophesy not unto us right things, speak unto us smooth things, prophesy deceits:

11 Get you out of the way, turn aside out of the path, cause the Holy One of Israel to cease from before us.

12 Wherefore thus saith the Holy One of Israel, Because ye despise this word, and trust in oppression and perverseness, and stay thereon:

the siren sound of the great secular strength which Egypt could offer. They thought to defend themselves with the strength of Pharaoh. They trusted in chariots because there were many, and in horsemen because they were strong. . . . Their confidence was in temporal power, and in their idols of gold and silver. . . . The Egyptians were men and not God" (Hanks, "Freedom and Responsibility," 5).

Why was Isaiah commanded to record his prophecies? (30:8) "The holy scriptures are the word of God given to us for our salvation. The scriptures are essential in receiving a testimony of Jesus Christ and His gospel. . . . These sacred records bear testimony of the Savior and lead us to Him. That is why great prophets like Enos cried unto the Lord in faith to preserve the scriptures. . . . Over two millennia ago, Isaiah wrote of the word of God, 'Now go, write it before them in a table, and note it in a book, that it may be for the time to come for ever and ever.' This world needs the scriptures today" (Hales, "Holy Scriptures," 24, 27).

What is the difference between smooth things and right things? (30:10–11) "In keeping with the Savior's own experience, there has been a long history of rejection and a painfully high price paid by prophets and apostles, missionaries and members in every generation—all those who have tried to honor God's call to lift the human family to 'a more excellent way.' . . . We have the burden of those called to bear the messianic message. . . . Unfortunately, messengers of divinely mandated commandments are often no more popular today than they were anciently" (Holland, "Cost—and Blessings—of Discipleship," 6, 7).

Using the imagery of a high wall about to break, what does the Lord teach? (30:13) "Isaiah compares Judah's iniquity to a large crack in the outside wall that protects Jerusalem. The crack expands, weakening the wall until it suddenly crumbles. Similarly, Judah's inhabitants have been weakened through sin; their iniquity increases like the crack in the wall until the nation is destroyed because its enemies are able to enter through the breach. This excellent description illustrates the effect of sin on all of us. Even a little sin, not repented of, can be like a crack in a wall, which can grow larger and larger until it leads to our spiritual destruction" (Parry, et al., *Understanding Isaiah*, 279–80).

Summary of Isaiah 30:14–33

Isaiah continues to prophesy that the Lord "will cause his glorious voice to be heard" (v. 30). It will be a voice of judgment upon the wicked. Modern revelation confirms this voice will be "the voice of thunderings, and by the voice of lightnings, and by the voice of tempests, and by the voice of earthquakes, and great hailstorms, and . . . pestilences of every kind" (D&C 43:25).

Summary of Isaiah 31–33

The strength of Egypt will not be sufficient to protect the rebellious children of Israel. If they will repent, God will protect them against Assyria. The Messiah will protect His people from oppression, and righteousness will prevail among the people. The pouring out of the Spirit will reverse the effects of Jehovah's judgments. The land will be transformed into a fruitful field. While the Assyrian invasion would flatten everything like a hailstorm, the Lord's covenant blessings would return. Isaiah prays that the Lord would destroy their enemies. Several of the attributes of God are extolled. Isaiah prophesies of the destruction of the wicked and the preservation of the righteous at the Second Coming. The people dwelling in Zion will enjoy the protection and healing of the Lord.

13 Therefore this iniquity shall be to you as a breach ready to fall, swelling out in a high wall, whose breaking cometh suddenly at an instant.

CHAPTERS 31–33

Israel is reproved for turning to Egypt for help—When the Lord comes, He will defend and preserve His people.

A king (the Messiah) will reign in righteousness—The land of Israel will be a wilderness until the day of restoration and gathering.

Apostasy and wickedness will precede the Second Coming—The Lord will come with devouring fire—Zion and its stakes will be perfected—The Lord is our Judge, Lawgiver, and King.

CHAPTER 34

The Second Coming will be a day of vengeance and judgment—The indignation of the Lord will be upon all nations—His sword will fall upon the world.

CHAPTER 35

In the day of restoration, the desert will blossom, the Lord will come, Israel will be gathered, and Zion will be built up.

1 The wilderness and the solitary place shall be glad for them; and the desert shall rejoice, and blossom as the rose.

2 It shall blossom abundantly, and rejoice even with joy and singing: the glory of Lebanon shall be given unto it, the excellency of Carmel and Sharon, they shall see the glory of the LORD, *and* the excellency of our God.

3 ¶ Strengthen ye the weak hands, and confirm the feeble knees.

4 Say to them *that are* of a fearful heart, Be strong, fear not: behold, your God will come *with* vengeance, *even* God *with* a recompence; he will come and save you.

5 Then the eyes of the blind shall be opened, and the ears of the deaf shall be unstopped.

6 Then shall the lame *man* leap as an hart, and the tongue of the dumb sing: for in the wilderness shall waters break out, and streams in the desert.

7 And the parched ground shall become a pool, and the thirsty land springs of water: in the habitation of dragons, where each lay, *shall be* grass with reeds and rushes.

Summary of Isaiah 34

Isaiah foretells of a coming day of destruction, vengeance, and of God's judgment. The Lord will pour His anger upon nations and their armies and they will be destroyed. Their destruction is compared to sacrificed animals. Future generations will read about the destruction of God's enemies in the book of the Lord.

Isaiah 35:1–7. The Desert Shall Blossom as a Rose

In what ways has "the desert" blossomed "as the rose"? (35:1–2) "These two verses are often mentioned by Latter-day Saints in relationship to the settlement of the Saints in the valleys of the Rockies. . . . However, the Doctrine and Covenants gives a broader interpretation: it refers to Jacob's flourishing in the wilderness and the Lamanites' blossoming as a rose, noting also that Zion will flourish upon the hills and be assembled to the place which the Lord has appointed (see D&C 49:24–25). Isaiah 35:1–2 is frequently said to refer to a blossoming taking place in the land of Judah; obviously, the Lord can and will make more than one place blossom as he gathers his people (see D&C 117:6–8)" (Nyman, *Great Are the Words of Isaiah,* 125–26). ⊕

What will spiritually open the eyes of the blind and the ears of the deaf? (35:5) Anciently, eyes were thought of as a symbol for a source of light, knowledge, and revelation (see Gaskill, *Lost Language of Symbolism*, 36). Ears were associated with spiritual understanding (see McConkie, *Gospel Symbolism*, 258). Isaiah prophesied that the words of the Book of Mormon would open the ears and eyes of the spiritually deaf and blind (see Isaiah 29:18; 2 Nephi 27:29). See commentary in this volume for Isaiah 29:18–19.

Isaiah 35:8–10. A Highway Shall Be Provided to Come to Zion

What is the highway that leads the ransomed back to Zion? (35:8–10) "It appears that a way will be provided to assemble the outcasts of Israel again in their promised land. The safe and secure physical arrangements, whatever they may be, will, in fact, be but symbolical of the way of holiness whereon only the righteous can find footing. The way of holiness cannot be other than the strait and narrow path. The wayward tribes, having forsaken the ancient holy way, having been scattered for their wickedness, shall now be gathered because they forsake the world and seek again that whereon the footprints of their fathers are found" (McConkie, *Millennial Messiah*, 327). ⊕

Who are the "ransomed of the Lord"? (35:10) "Those who accept the restored gospel and its covenants are the ransomed of the Lord. These people will return (*return* in Hebrew also means 'repent') from centuries of scattering and exile in various lands and will 'come to Zion' (D&C 45:71)" (Parry, et al., *Understanding Isaiah*, 319). "[Zion is] the pure in heart (D&C 97:21). Zion also means a place where the pure in heart live. . . . The Saints are counseled to build up Zion wherever they are living in the world" (Guide to the Scriptures, "Zion"). ⊕

Summary of Isaiah 36–37

Assyria was the most powerful nation on the earth. It had already destroyed and taken captive the northern kingdom of Israel and now was attacking Jerusalem. The Assyrian commander warned the people not to rely on the armies of Egypt or to listen to King Hezekiah and trust in their God, for neither could deliver them from Assyria's mighty army. Instead, they should pay tribute money to the king of Assyria and they would be spared (see Isaiah 36:1–22; also 2 Kings 18:17–37; 2 Chronicles 32:1–19). Upon hearing these things, Hezekiah wisely sought counsel from the prophet Isaiah, who prophesied that the Assyrian army would be defeated, and the king of Assyria would be killed. Hezekiah obeyed Isaiah's counsel and prayed for Jerusalem's deliverance. Just as predicted, an angel destroyed 185,000 Assyrian soldiers, and Assyria's king was later killed by his sons (see Isaiah 37:36–38; see also 2 Kings 19:1–37). See commentary in this volume for 2 Kings 18–19.

8 And an highway shall be there, and a way, and it shall be called The way of holiness; the unclean shall not pass over it; but it *shall be* for those: the wayfaring men, though fools, shall not err *therein*.

9 No lion shall be there, nor *any* ravenous beast shall go up thereon, it shall not be found there; but the redeemed shall walk *there:*

10 And the ransomed of the LORD shall return, and come to Zion with songs and everlasting joy upon their heads: they shall obtain joy and gladness, and sorrow and sighing shall flee away.

CHAPTERS 36–37

The Assyrians war against Judah and blaspheme the Lord.

Hezekiah seeks counsel from Isaiah to save Jerusalem—Isaiah prophesies the defeat of the Assyrians and the death of Sennacherib—Hezekiah prays for deliverance—Sennacherib sends a blasphemous letter—Isaiah prophesies that the Assyrians will be destroyed and that a remnant of Judah will flourish—An angel slays 185,000 Assyrians—Sennacherib is slain by his sons.

CHAPTERS 38–39

Hezekiah's life is lengthened fifteen years—The sun goes back ten degrees as a sign—Hezekiah praises and thanks the Lord.

Hezekiah reveals his wealth to Babylon—Isaiah prophesies the Babylonian captivity.

Summary of Isaiah 38–39

Chapters 38 and 39 continue in a narrative style similar to chapters 36 and 37. These chapters create a historical transition moving beyond the problems with Assyria to establish a warning that Babylon will become the future threat to God's children in Judah. In these chapters, Hezekiah became "sick unto death" (Isaiah 38:1), however, Isaiah promised the king that he would live another fifteen years. As word spread of Hezekiah's miraculous healing, the king of Babylon sent ministers to commemorate Hezekiah's recovery. Isaiah prophesied that one day Babylon would conquer Judah and Jerusalem and carry them away captive. See commentary in this volume for 2 Kings 20.

CHAPTER 40

Isaiah speaks about the Messiah—Prepare ye the way of the Lord—He will feed His flock like a shepherd—Israel's God is incomparably great.

1 Comfort ye, comfort ye my people, saith your God.

2 Speak ye comfortably to Jerusalem, and cry unto her, that her warfare is accomplished, that her iniquity is pardoned: for she hath received of the LORD's hand double for all her sins.

Isaiah 40:1–11. The Lord Will Come Again and Feed His Flock

Parallel Passages in Isaiah, 2 Kings, and 2 Chronicles (Isaiah 36–39)

"Isaiah's historical chapters repeat, with a few differences, reports in the historical books of the Old Testament: 2 Kings 18:13–37 corresponds with Isaiah 36; 2 Kings 19, with Isaiah 37; 2 Kings 20:1–11, with Isaiah 38; and 2 Kings 20:12–19, with Isaiah 39. . . .

"Two verses in 2 Kings 18 (vv. 15–16) about Hezekiah's delivering precious metals from the palace and temple to Assyria are not repeated in Isaiah. Four verses in 2 Kings 20 (vv. 8–11) about King Hezekiah asking Isaiah (and Isaiah asking the Lord) what sign would assure Hezekiah that he would recover from his illness are not repeated in Isaiah; however, a voluntary sign is reported in Isaiah.

"On the other hand, something is added in the Isaiah account: King Hezekiah's psalm of thanks and praise to the Lord for saving him after he had considered in deep sorrow the prospect of coming to the end of his life. He was grateful for his added fifteen years (Isa. 38:9–20; that item is not recorded in 2 Kgs. 20)" (Rasmussen, *Latter-day Saint Commentary on the Old Testament*, 523).

Parallel Passages in Isaiah, 2 Kings, and 2 Chronicles

Isaiah 36:2–22	*is similar to*	2 Kings 18:17–37	*and*	2 Chronicles 32:9–19
Isaiah 37:1–38	*is similar to*	2 Kings 19:1–37	*and*	2 Chronicles 32:20–23
Isaiah 38:1–22	*is similar to*	2 Kings 20:1–11	*and*	2 Chronicles 32:24–29
Isaiah 39:1–8	*is similar to*	2 Kings 20:12–19	*and*	2 Chronicles 32:31

(Adapted from Valletta, et al., *Old Testament for Latter-Day Saint Families*, 504.)

Who is crying in the wilderness to prepare for the Lord's coming? (40:3) The Lord promises that one day Judah's punishment would come to an end and they would be comforted (see Isaiah 40:1–2). It will come when a "voice . . . crieth in the wilderness" (Isaiah 40:3). "The idea that one will come who cries in the wilderness for us to prepare for the coming of the Lord has a general fulfillment in anyone who teaches of God and His plan. A very specific fulfillment of this prophecy is John the Baptist, who literally prepared Israel for the imminent coming of Jesus Christ" (Muhlestein, *Essential Old Testament Companion*, 392).

When will these changes to the earth take place? (40:4) "The millennial earth will be restored to conditions that existed before the Fall. Therefore, both desert and fertile field will enjoy changes in the new earth that will come to be during the Millennium.

"Another change to the face of the earth will be that 'every valley shall be exalted, and every mountain and hill shall be made low' (Isa. 40:4) 'for the mountains shall depart, and the hills be removed' (Isa. 54:10). In the Doctrine and Covenants the Lord included these words of Isaiah in connection with a time when the earth will tremble and 'reel to and fro like a drunkard' or 'as a drunken man' (Isa. 24:20; D&C 49:23)" (Ostler, "Isaiah's Voice on the Promised Millennium," 73–74). ⊕

How might Zion be brought into a "high mountain"? (40:9) Charles W. Penrose, a former member of the First Presidency, said that Isaiah's prophecy about Zion gathering to a "high mountain" with a good message "has been fulfilled in the coming here [Salt Lake City] of the people who are now gathered in these mountain valleys, and the word of the Lord is going forth and it is to be carried to every nation and kindred and tongue and people" (in Conference Report, Oct. 1919, 47).

How does the Savior care for us like a shepherd cares for his sheep? (40:11) "By comparing the Lord to a shepherd—and by speaking of Him carrying lambs in His bosom and gently leading the mother sheep—Isaiah paints a picture of amazing care and compassion. This verse successfully evokes images of a God who gently takes care of His people, especially those most in need. The Savior drew on this kind of imagery when He spoke of being the Good Shepherd" (Muhlestein, *Essential Old Testament Companion*, 392). ⊕

3 ¶ The voice of him that crieth in the wilderness, Prepare ye the way of the LORD, make straight in the desert a highway for our God.

4 Every valley shall be exalted, and every mountain and hill shall be made low: and the crooked shall be made straight, and the rough places plain:

5 And the glory of the LORD shall be revealed, and all flesh shall see *it* together: for the mouth of the LORD hath spoken *it*.

6 The voice said, Cry. And he said, What shall I cry? All flesh *is* grass, and all the goodliness thereof *is* as the flower of the field:

7 The grass withereth, the flower fadeth: because the spirit of the LORD bloweth upon it: surely the people *is* grass.

8 The grass withereth, the flower fadeth: but the word of our God shall stand for ever.

9 ¶ O Zion, that bringest good tidings, get thee up into the high mountain; O Jerusalem, that bringest good tidings, lift up thy voice with strength; lift *it* up, be not afraid; say unto the cities of Judah, Behold your God!

10 Behold, the Lord GOD will come with strong *hand,* and his arm shall rule for him: behold, his reward *is* with him, and his work before him.

11 He shall feed his flock like a shepherd: he shall gather the lambs with his arm, and carry *them* in his bosom, *and* shall gently lead those that are with young.

28 ¶ Hast thou not known? hast thou not heard, *that* the everlasting God, the LORD, the Creator of the ends of the earth, fainteth not, neither is weary? *there is* no searching of his understanding.

29 He giveth power to the faint; and to *them that have* no might he increaseth strength.

30 Even the youths shall faint and be weary, and the young men shall utterly fall:

31 But they that wait upon the LORD shall renew *their* strength; they shall mount up with wings as eagles; they shall run, and not be weary; *and* they shall walk, and not faint.

Summary of Isaiah 40:12–27

Isaiah reminds the Jews that no nation, regardless of its seeming power and royalty, compares to the God of Israel. The things mankind has built are like dust compared to the works of God (see v. 15). Isaiah invites his people to look throughout the earth and high into the heavens to see "the greatness of [God's] might" (v. 26).

Isaiah 40:28–31. Jehovah Strengthens and Saves Israel

What do we learn about God in these verses? (40:28–31) When Isaiah characterized the Lord Jehovah as "the everlasting God," he likely meant that He was "from the eternity past to the eternity future as far as man's understanding is concerned, from pre-existence through the temporal (mortal) life unto the eternity following the resurrection" (Smith, *Answers to Gospel Questions*, 2:127).

Erin Kramer Holmes added: "Because the Lord 'fainteth not, neither is weary,' He will be the source of our strength. . . . [Isaiah also promised] that as you wait upon the Lord, you will have the capacity to endure life's uncertainties" ("Waiting upon the Lord").

Why can't we search or comprehend God's understanding? (40:28) The Book of Mormon teaches that "it is impossible that man should find out all [God's] ways" (Jacob 4:8). Elsewhere, the Lord has revealed: "For my thoughts are not your thoughts, neither are your ways my ways, saith the Lord. For as the heavens are higher than the earth, so are my ways higher than your ways, and my thoughts than your thoughts" (Isaiah 55:8–9).

What does the Lord teach us through the imagery of eagles' wings? (40:31) "Eagles' wings represent the power of God" (Valletta, et al., *The Old Testament for Latter-day Saint Families*, 505). "When we rely on worldly strength, even the strongest will eventually fail. But when we rely on God, even the weakest cannot fail. Beautiful imagery is employed here to demonstrate how all those who trust in God will find themselves able to do more than even the mightiest can do on their own. This is true of every aspect of life" (Muhlestein, *Scripture Study Made Simple*, 371). ⊕

Summary of Isaiah 41

The children of Israel are reminded to trust in the Lord's promises. The Lord has given us that same reminder today (see D&C 1:37–38). The Lord tells His people three times to "fear not" for "I will help thee." He promises to help Israel stand against all of their enemies because they, like Abraham, are His chosen people. Israel is nothing without God. The Lord will give to Jerusalem one that brings good tidings.

Isaiah 42:1–4. Isaiah Prophesies of the Messiah

Who is this servant of God? (42:1) "Isaiah frequently speaks of a servant of the Lord. While the primary fulfillment of this servant is Jesus Christ, Isaiah describes the servant in ways that allow for many people and groups to typify this servant and thus to symbolize the Savior. In this chapter the Savior is certainly spoken of as God's servant, but the most explicit fulfillment of this role is Israel. In verse 6, Isaiah specifically identifies this servant as the covenant people and explains that God has made a covenant with them so that they can bring His light to every nation of the earth, providing spiritual sight and life for all mankind" (Muhlestein, *Essential Old Testament Companion*, 396). ⊕

What do the reed and flax symbolize? (42:3) "A reed is a marsh plant with tall, hollow stems. A bruised reed is one that is cracked, and therefore is weak. Symbolically, a *bruised reed* may be a mortal with physical weaknesses or bodily afflictions. A *smoking flax* is a wick made from flax for an oil lamp, whose flame wavers, about to go out. This may signify someone who is spiritually weak, whose light flickers and does not burn brightly. . . . A reed requires much water for it to grow properly; a flax or wick burns brightly when it has sufficient oil. Symbolically, Jesus Christ (as the waters of life) provides water to the reed, and (as the Anointed One) provides oil to the wick" (Parry, et al., *Understanding Isaiah*, 360). ⊕

CHAPTER 41

To Israel the Lord says, Ye are my servants; I will preserve you—Idols are nothing—One will bring good tidings to Jerusalem.

CHAPTER 42

Isaiah speaks about the Messiah—The Lord will bring His law and His justice, be a light to the Gentiles, and free the prisoners—Praise the Lord.

1 Behold my servant, whom I uphold; mine elect, *in whom* my soul delighteth; I have put my spirit upon him: he shall bring forth judgment to the Gentiles.

2 He shall not cry, nor lift up, nor cause his voice to be heard in the street.

3 A bruised reed shall he not break, and the smoking flax shall he not quench: he shall bring forth judgment unto truth.

4 He shall not fail nor be discouraged, till he have set judgment in the earth: and the isles shall wait for his law.

The Right Hand of God's Righteousness (Isaiah 41:10)

"The right hand or side is called the dexter and the left the sinister. *Dexter* connotes something favorable; *sinister,* on the other hand, suggests something unfavorable or unfortunate. The Lord has frequently utilized this distinction to contrast the blessed state of those who are loyal to him and keep the commandments (those on his right hand) and the pitiable condition of those who come to know his wrath and displeasure (those on his left hand)" (McConkie and Millet, *Doctrinal Commentary on the Book of Mormon*, 2:178).

5 ¶ Thus saith God the LORD, he that created the heavens, and stretched them out; he that spread forth the earth, and that which cometh out of it; he that giveth breath unto the people upon it, and spirit to them that walk therein:

6 I the LORD have called thee in righteousness, and will hold thine hand, and will keep thee, and give thee for a covenant of the people, for a light of the Gentiles;

7 To open the blind eyes, to bring out the prisoners from the prison, *and* them that sit in darkness out of the prison house.

8 I *am* the LORD: that *is* my name: and my glory will I not give to another, neither my praise to graven images.

9 Behold, the former things are come to pass, and new things do I declare: before they spring forth I tell you of them.

Isaiah 42:5–16. The Lord Brings Light to His People and Destroys Their Enemies

Who are the prisoners that God's servant will bring out from prison? (42:7) "The prophecy of Isaiah that Christ shall, in the process of the Resurrection, visit the prisoners in prison foretells the revelation to Peter following the death of Jesus Christ. We are informed that during the three-day period between the death and resurrection of our Lord, He visited and preached to the spirits in prison [spirit world] waiting since the days of Noah for the Resurrection [see 1 Peter 3:18–19]" (Tingey, *Old Testament Prophecies of Jesus Christ,* 130–31). In Joseph F. Smith's vision of the spirit world he learned that the "joy and gladness" experienced by the righteous spirits came "because the day of their deliverance was at hand" (D&C 138:15). See commentary in this volume for Isaiah 49:9–12. ⊕

Why does Isaiah sometimes speak as though the future has already occurred? (42:9) "Often when ancient prophets would speak of future events, they would use a verb form sometimes called the 'prophetic past tense.' That is, they would talk about the future as though the event had already happened. For example, one could talk about the still-future Millennium by saying: 'And at the beginning of the Millennium the Church of Jesus Christ had already

The Servant Songs of Isaiah (Isaiah 42:1–4)

"The first four verses of Isaiah 42 comprise one of the four 'major songs' or major poetic passages in which Isaiah describes a servant of the Lord. (The other three are Isa. 49:1–6; 50:4–9; 52:13–53:12.) This servant is not named, so readers and scholars often disagree about the servant's identity. Generally, the Jewish scholars believe the servant is either the prophet Isaiah or a representation of the people of Israel in their chosen role as the Lord's servants to the world. Christian scholars usually believe Jesus Christ is the servant prophesied by Isaiah. Latter-day Saint readers often recognize that the covenant members of the restored gospel serve as the Lord's servants. They as a people, and the prophet of the restoration, Joseph Smith, may be identified as Isaiah's promised servant....

"Rather than categorically stating that Isaiah's servant songs apply only to one servant, we might be wise in recognizing that the characteristics of God's servant are best exemplified in Christ and are also demonstrated through the lives of all of God's righteous children. In short, the precise identity of the servant is not as important as studying his characteristics and seeking to develop them in our own lives" (Ludlow, *Isaiah*, 358, 360).

organized over 10,000 stakes and this number increased ten-fold in ten years. The Latter-day Saints were zealous in sharing the gospel with all people.' Study Isaiah 42:9 with D&C 93:24 and see why a prophet would be so confident of the future that he would talk of it in a prophetic past tense" (Ludlow, *Unlocking the Old Testament*, 167).

What is the "new song" and when will it be sung? (42:10) "When the day comes that 'all shall know [the Lord]' (the Millennium), they shall sing a 'new song,' the words of which are found in modern revelation (D&C 84:98–102)" (Brewster, *Isaiah Plain and Simple*, 239). "A new song is to be sung in the isles when and where Israel is to be restored. Israel will be gathered from the ends of the earth, where she was previously scattered, and will give glory and praise from the tops of the mountains" (Nyman, *Great Are the Words of Isaiah*, 157). ⊕

Who was "Kedar"? (42:11) Kedar was "a desert nomadic people descended from Ishmael. They were not initially believers in [Jehovah] but are included in Isaiah's prophecy of the future kingdom of God" (*Tyndale Bible Dictionary*, 768).

Why will people of the earth "give glory unto the Lord" when He comes again? (42:11–15) Elder Neal A. Maxwell testified: "One day . . . all flesh shall see him together. All knees shall bow in his presence, and all tongues confess his name (see D&C 76:110–11; Philip. 2:10–11). Knees which never before have assumed that posture for that purpose will do so then—promptly. Tongues which have never before spoken his name, except in gross profanity, will do so then—worshipfully. . . .

"All will then acknowledge the completeness of his justice and his mercy (see Alma 12:15). Then mortals will see how human indifference to God—not God's indifference to humanity—accounts for so much misery and suffering" ("Our Acceptance of Christ," 74).

In what way will the Lord lead His people in the latter days? (42:16) "In the scriptures we read that some individuals 'grope in the dark without light' and 'stagger like a drunken man' [Job 12:25]. Stumbling along, we may become accustomed to the dimness of our surroundings and forget how glorious it is to walk in the light.

"There is a way out of the 'mists of darkness' [1 Nephi 12:17] and onto the path that leads to happiness in this life and eternal life. . . . The covenant we make at baptism and renew as we partake of the

10 Sing unto the LORD a new song, *and* his praise from the end of the earth, ye that go down to the sea, and all that is therein; the isles, and the inhabitants thereof.

11 Let the wilderness and the cities thereof lift up *their voice,* the villages *that* Kedar doth inhabit: let the inhabitants of the rock sing, let them shout from the top of the mountains.

12 Let them give glory unto the LORD, and declare his praise in the islands.

13 The LORD shall go forth as a mighty man, he shall stir up jealousy like a man of war: he shall cry, yea, roar; he shall prevail against his enemies.

14 I have long time holden my peace; I have been still, *and* refrained myself: *now* will I cry like a travailing woman; I will destroy and devour at once.

15 I will make waste mountains and hills, and dry up all their herbs; and I will make the rivers islands, and I will dry up the pools.

16 And I will bring the blind by a way *that* they knew not; I will lead them in paths *that* they have not known: I will make darkness light before them, and crooked things straight. These things will I do unto them, and not forsake them.

CHAPTER 43

To Israel the Lord says, I am your God; I will gather your descendants; beside me there is no Savior; you are my witnesses.

1 But now thus saith the LORD that created thee, O Jacob, and he that formed thee, O Israel, Fear not: for I have redeemed thee, I have called *thee* by thy name; thou *art* mine.

2 When thou passest through the waters, I *will be* with thee; and through the rivers, they shall not overflow thee: when thou walkest through the fire, thou shalt not be burned; neither shall the flame kindle upon thee.

3 For I *am* the LORD thy God, the Holy One of Israel, thy Saviour: I gave Egypt *for* thy ransom, Ethiopia and Seba for thee.

4 Since thou wast precious in my sight, thou hast been honourable, and I have loved thee: therefore will I give men for thee, and people for thy life.

5 Fear not: for I *am* with thee: I will bring thy seed from the east, and gather thee from the west;

6 I will say to the north, Give up; and to the south, Keep not back: bring my sons from far, and my daughters from the ends of the earth;

sacrament . . . includes the promise that we will always have His Spirit, that we will always have that light to be with us" (Hales, "Out of Darkness into His Marvelous Light," 71).

Summary of Isaiah 42:17–25

When Israel rebels against God, they become blind to the truth and worship false gods. The Lord promises Israel that if they will "hearken unto the messenger, the Lord's servant," they will "be made perfect notwithstanding their blindness" (JST, Isaiah 42:20).

Isaiah 43:1–13. The Lord Gathers Scattered Israel

What is the significance of the Lord's use of the names "Jacob" and "Israel" in the same message? (43:1–3) "Two names designate the people who will inherit God's blessings, *Jacob* and *Israel*. . . . It is the order of the two names that makes the repetition significant, for 'Jacob' nearly always precedes 'Israel,' hinting, perhaps, that a change in Jacob's character prompted the Lord to change his name also. Jacob, the 'supplanter,' who worried about his relationship with his twin brother, Esau, became Israel, the 'prevailer,' who worked together with God to overcome wickedness. . . . Thus, Isaiah places *Jacob* before Israel in the chapter as a way of saying that the descendants of Jacob need to rise to the character of Israel" (Ludlow, *Isaiah*, 363).

What qualifies one nation to be called "precious" by the Lord? (43:4) "Some may wonder why the children of Israel were considered 'precious' in God's sight while other nations were destroyed. Nephi taught that 'the Lord esteemeth all flesh in one; he that is righteous is favored of God. . . . And he raiseth up a righteous nation, and destroyeth the nations of the wicked' (1 Nephi 17:35, 37)" (Valletta, et al., *Old Testament for Latter-day Saint Families*, 509).

What can we learn from the Lord's promise that He will be with us? (43:5) "Believe in the Savior. He loves you, and I testify that He will not leave you alone. He has promised:

"'Fear not, I am with thee; oh, be not dismayed,
"'For I am thy God and will still give thee aid.
"'I'll strengthen thee, help thee, and cause thee to stand, . . .
"'Upheld by my righteous, omnipotent hand'

("How Firm a Foundation," *Hymns*, no. 85; see also Isa. 41:10; 43:2–5).

"I believe that each one of you has the power to change the world. Believe in yourselves. Believe that you are never alone. Believe that you will be guided" (Dalton, "Believe!" 112).

What is Isaiah describing about our day? (43:5–7) "Truly this is what has been and is transpiring in this day. The scattered remnants of Israel, hearing again the voice of their Shepherd, are believing his gospel, accepting baptism at the hands of his servants, coming into his sheepfold, taking upon themselves his name, and once again becoming his sons and his daughters" (McConkie, *Promised Messiah*, 359).

What does it mean that there was no God before or after the Lord? (43:10–13) "There is only one God of this earth, who, under the Father's direction, performs all of the mighty works that have been done in every dispensation. We are called to be His witnesses. . . . We need not be confused about the variety of 'gods' that the world has imagined and/or created. There is only one God, and He is the Lord and Savior Jesus Christ, who in Old Testament times was the God of Israel, Jehovah. This set of verses makes that fact very clear. 'Yea, before the day was [before creation] I am he [Jehovah was]'" (Chase, *Making Precious Things Plain*, 9:134).

How can we be witnesses of God? (43:12) "Be open about your faith in Christ. When the occasion presents itself, speak of His life, His teachings, and His incomparable gift to all mankind. Share His powerful truths from the Book of Mormon. . . . I promise you that as you pray often and sincerely for opportunities to 'stand as a witness of God' [Mosiah 18:9], those opportunities will come, and those who seek more light and knowledge will be put before you. . . . The Holy Ghost will carry your words to the heart of another" (Andersen, "Witness of God," 37).

Summary of Isaiah 43:14–28

Though the Lord is the God of Israel, He delivers His people to their enemies when they turn their backs on Him and do not keep their covenants.

7 *Even* every one that is called by my name: for I have created him for my glory, I have formed him; yea, I have made him.

8 ¶ Bring forth the blind people that have eyes, and the deaf that have ears.

9 Let all the nations be gathered together, and let the people be assembled: who among them can declare this, and shew us former things? let them bring forth their witnesses, that they may be justified: or let them hear, and say, *It is* truth.

10 Ye *are* my witnesses, saith the LORD, and my servant whom I have chosen: that ye may know and believe me, and understand that I *am* he: before me there was no God formed, neither shall there be after me.

11 I, *even* I, *am* the LORD; and beside me *there is* no saviour.

12 I have declared, and have saved, and I have shewed, when *there was* no strange *god* among you: therefore ye *are* my witnesses, saith the LORD, that I *am* God.

13 Yea, before the day *was* I *am* he; and *there is* none that can deliver out of my hand: I will work, and who shall let it?

CHAPTER 44

The Lord's Spirit will be poured out on the descendants of Israel—Idols of wood are as fuel for a fire—The Lord will gather, bless, and redeem Israel and rebuild Jerusalem.

CHAPTER 45

Cyrus will free the captives of Israel from Babylon—Come unto Jehovah (Christ) and be saved—To Him every knee will bow and every tongue will take an oath.

1 Thus saith the LORD to his anointed, to Cyrus, whose right hand I have holden, to subdue nations before him; and I will loose the loins of kings, to open before him the two leaved gates; and the gates shall not be shut;

2 I will go before thee, and make the crooked places straight: I will break in pieces the gates of brass, and cut in sunder the bars of iron:

3 And I will give thee the treasures of darkness, and hidden riches of secret places, that thou mayest know that I, the LORD, which call *thee* by thy name, *am* the God of Israel.

4 For Jacob my servant's sake, and Israel mine elect, I have even called thee by thy name: I have surnamed thee, though thou hast not known me.

Summary of Isaiah 44

The Lord will pour out His Spirit and blessings upon Israel's children. God scatters Israel when they serve false gods. When Israel turns her back on false gods and returns to the God of Israel, He redeems His people and opens the way for them to rebuild Jerusalem.

Isaiah 45:1–4. Isaiah Prophesies That God Will, for Israel's Sake, Give Cyrus Power to Conquer Nations

What do we know about Cyrus, the Gentile king? (45:1–4) "King Cyrus lived more than five hundred years before Christ and figured in prophecies of the Old Testament mentioned in 2 Chronicles and the book of Ezra, and by the prophets Ezekiel, Isaiah, and Daniel. The Bible states how 'the Lord stirred up the spirit of Cyrus, King of Persia' (2 Chr. 36:22). Cyrus restored certain political and social rights to the captive Hebrews, gave them permission to return to Jerusalem, and directed that Jehovah's temple should be rebuilt. . . .

"God, the Father of us all, uses the men of the earth, especially good men, to accomplish his purposes. It has been true in the past, it is true today, it will be true in the future" (Benson, "Civic Standards for the Faithful Saints," 59). ⊕

What can we learn from Cyrus' call to serve the Lord? (45:4) Sydney B. Sperry explained why the Lord blessed Cyrus: "The mission of Cyrus to restore the Lord's people from the Babylonian exile [in Isaiah 44:24–45:13] shows that the Lord who creates the heavens, orders events, and tells the future, can restore His people from exile and raise up a deliverer for Israel. Cyrus the Persian is named as the person who is the Lord's shepherd and the performer of His pleasure respecting Jerusalem. . . .

Isaiah's Prophecy of Cyrus' Deeds (Isaiah 45:1–4)

"Isaiah's prediction of the coming of Cyrus is one of the most striking prophecies in all scripture. Numerous commentators deny that Isaiah could foresee Cyrus so clearly as to be able to call him by name. They commonly claim, therefore, that this part of Isaiah was written by someone during the Exile and after Cyrus had given Israel help" (Sperry, *Voice of Israel's Prophets*, 107).

"Cyrus will be called for Israel's sake; the Lord will gird him, though the king will not have known Him. The world will realize through Cyrus that there is no god beside Him" (*Voice of Israel's Prophets*, 105–6).

Summary of Isaiah 45:5–19

The Lord announces that it is useless for anyone (Cyrus or the children of Israel) to fight against His will. The Lord invites Israel to repent and to seek out Jehovah and be saved.

Isaiah 45:20–25. God Saves the Humble from Destruction

Why does Isaiah repeatedly teach that Jehovah is the only God who can save us? (45:20–22) The Lord, through Isaiah, reminds Israel that idols and false "gods have no power to save them. The only power is in the God of Israel; 'a just God and a Saviour'" (Valletta, et al., *Old Testament for Latter-day Saint Families*, 511). "*I am the Lord, and there is none else, there is no God beside me.* In this theological revelation, Isaiah declared a number of the Lord's creative and redemptive works. Like the Father, the Son is uniquely God, and there is no other in his role. . . .

"God invites the gathered of Israel and 'all the ends of the earth' (Isa. 45:22) to look unto him and be saved" (Rasmussen, *Latter-day Saint Commentary on The Old Testament*, 527). ⊕

What does it mean to "look unto God"? (45:22) "When the Lord calls . . . to 'look unto me in every thought' [D&C 6:36] . . . , it is a call to turn away from sin and the world and to turn to Him and love and obey Him . . . , a call to trust Him completely, surrender our will and yield our hearts to Him. . . . President Russell M. Nelson has called us to look unto Jesus Christ in just this way: 'There is nothing easy or automatic about becoming such powerful disciples. Our focus must be riveted on the Savior and His gospel. It is mentally rigorous to strive to look unto Him in *every* thought. But when we do, our doubts and fears flee'" (Clark, "Look unto Jesus Christ," 55).

Why will both the wicked and righteous bow their knee and confess that Jesus is the Christ? (45:23) "Every soul eventually must become acquainted with the plan of salvation, at least as far as it is possible for him to do. We read that every knee must bow and every tongue confess Jesus Christ as the Son of God. This being true, then every soul must know something about him. . . .

20 ¶ Assemble yourselves and come; draw near together, ye *that are* escaped of the nations: they have no knowledge that set up the wood of their graven image, and pray unto a god *that* cannot save.

21 Tell ye, and bring *them* near; yea, let them take counsel together: who hath declared this from ancient time? *who* hath told it from that time? *have* not I the LORD? and *there is* no God else beside me; a just God and a Saviour; *there is* none beside me.

22 Look unto me, and be ye saved, all the ends of the earth: for I *am* God, and *there is* none else.

23 I have sworn by myself, the word is gone out of my mouth *in* righteousness, and shall not return, That unto me every knee shall bow, every tongue shall swear.

24 Surely, shall *one* say, in the LORD have I righteousness and strength: *even* to him shall *men* come; and all that are incensed against him shall be ashamed.

25 In the LORD shall all the seed of Israel be justified, and shall glory.

"All of these, however, will be called upon to repent. They will have to suffer the torments of the damned until they do, and through that suffering they will be brought to repentance and to acknowledge Jesus Christ as their Redeemer and the Son of God. Every knee must bow and every tongue confess, no matter which kingdom the inhabitants of the earth enter" (Smith, *Doctrines of Salvation*, 2:23, 184).

CHAPTER 46

Idols are not to be compared with the Lord—He alone is God and will save Israel.

Summary of Isaiah 46

Idols and false gods created by men have no power to deliver their believers from harm, nor can they compare with the God of Israel. Isaiah records that Israel must not trust in false gods, for only the Lord can save Israel from spiritual or physical bondage.

CHAPTER 47

Babylon and Chaldea will be destroyed for their iniquities—No one will save them.

Summary of Isaiah 47:1–9

The Lord warns Babylon and future wicked nations that one day He will destroy them because of their wickedness. Even though Babylon will achieve greatness for a season, the day will come when they will suffer a great destruction.

10 ¶ For thou hast trusted in thy wickedness: thou hast said, None seeth me. Thy wisdom and thy knowledge, it hath perverted thee; and thou hast said in thine heart, I *am*, and none else beside me.

Isaiah 47:10–15. The Lord Will Destroy Those Who Trust in Wickedness

What might it mean to "trust in wickedness" and be "perverted" by wisdom? (47:10) Isaiah warned that the Babylonians trusted in "wealth and power wickedly obtained; in political schemes wickedly contrived; in [their] ambition and pride, tyranny and cruelty; and especially in [their] wicked arts of astrology, divination, and magic . . . and other . . . wicked

The Fall of Babylon Expressed in Poetry (Isaiah 47)

"[Isaiah] Chapter 47 is a lyric outburst, or dirge, corresponding to the ode on the king of Babylon in 14:4–21. The song is in four strophes or stanzas as follows: (1) Vss. 1–4; (2) vss. 5–7; (3) vss. 8–11; (4) vss. 12–15. . . .

"Babylon is addressed as a 'tender and delicate' queen, who must do the work and wear the garments of a slave; the Lord will bring retribution upon her because of her crimes (47:1–4). She was chosen as the Lord's agent in the chastisement of Israel, but she showed no mercy upon her subjects; for this reason her crimes will be requited (47:5–7). She now sits securely and confident, but ruin will come upon her suddenly and completely. Her sorceries and enchantments will be of no avail (47:8–11). Babylon's counselors, astrologers, stargazers, and prognosticators will alike be unable to see the coming disaster, and will perish. There will be 'none to save thee' (47:12–15)" (Sperry, *Voice of Israel's Prophets*, 109).

actions done in the dark; but nothing can be hid from the omniscient God. . . .

"[Babylon's] high opinion of her own wisdom and knowledge in political affairs, or in magic arts, deceived her, and turned her from right to wrong ways, which issued in her ruin" (*John Gill's Exposition of the Whole Bible* [commentary on Isaiah 47:10]). How can we better discern between truth and error and reject the world's supposed wisdom?

How does Isaiah describe the fate of those who believe in diviners and soothsayers? (47:12–14)
"With vivid imagery the prophet foretells in Isaiah 47 how proud and pampered Babylon will become like a humiliated slave and be left forsaken and barren (47:1–5, 7–9). Her punishment will be just recompense for her mercilessness, haughtiness, and conceit (47:6, 7–10). All this will befall her despite her acclaimed astrologers, sorcerers, and prognosticators (47:11–13). These diviners will not be able to save Babylon—or themselves (47:14–15)" (Ball and Winn, *Making Sense of Isaiah*, 132).

What can we learn from the fall of Babylon? (47:15)
"This prophecy of the destruction of Babylon drips with irony. Babylon was a center of worldly wealth, pride, prestige, arrogance, and corruption. . . .

"Babylon was also a center of science and sorcery. The people prided themselves on their ability to foresee the future and ward off evil. . . . Yet Babylon fell quickly and unexpectedly . . . when Cyrus, king of the Persians, diverted the Euphrates River that coursed under the city walls and sent his soldiers into the heart of the city along the empty riverbed, surprising the Babylonians as they reveled at a festival.

"The prophecy and its fulfillment anciently remind us today that those who glory in their own worldly wealth, wisdom, prestige, or power are placing their future and happiness on fragile and fleeting footing" (Ball and Winn, *Making Sense of Isaiah*, 132–33).

11 ¶ Therefore shall evil come upon thee; thou shalt not know from whence it riseth: and mischief shall fall upon thee; thou shalt not be able to put it off: and desolation shall come upon thee suddenly, *which* thou shalt not know.

12 Stand now with thine enchantments, and with the multitude of thy sorceries, wherein thou hast laboured from thy youth; if so be thou shalt be able to profit, if so be thou mayest prevail.

13 Thou art wearied in the multitude of thy counsels. Let now the astrologers, the stargazers, the monthly prognosticators, stand up, and save thee from *these things* that shall come upon thee.

14 Behold, they shall be as stubble; the fire shall burn them; they shall not deliver themselves from the power of the flame: *there shall* not *be* a coal to warm at, *nor* fire to sit before it.

15 Thus shall they be unto thee with whom thou hast laboured, *even* thy merchants, from thy youth: they shall wander every one to his quarter; none shall save thee.

CHAPTER 48

The Lord reveals His purposes to Israel—Israel has been chosen in the furnace of affliction and is to depart from Babylon—Compare 1 Nephi 20.

1 Hear ye this, O house of Jacob, which are called by the name of Israel, and are come forth out of the waters of Judah, which swear by the name of the LORD, and make mention of the God of Israel, *but* not in truth, nor in righteousness.

2 For they call themselves of the holy city, and stay themselves upon the God of Israel; The LORD of hosts *is* his name.

3 I have declared the former things from the beginning; and they went forth out of my mouth, and I shewed them; I did *them* suddenly, and they came to pass.

4 Because I knew that thou *art* obstinate, and thy neck *is* an iron sinew, and thy brow brass;

5 I have even from the beginning declared *it* to thee; before it came to pass I shewed *it* thee: lest thou shouldest say, Mine idol hath done them, and my graven image, and my molten image, hath commanded them.

6 Thou hast heard, see all this; and will not ye declare *it?* I have shewed thee new things from this time, even hidden things, and thou didst not know them.

7 They are created now, and not from the beginning; even before the day when thou heardest them not; lest thou shouldest say, Behold, I knew them.

8 Yea, thou heardest not; yea, thou knewest not; yea, from that time *that* thine ear was not opened: for I knew that thou wouldest deal very treacherously, and wast called a transgressor from the womb.

Isaiah 48:1–8. The Israelites Break Their Covenants and Their Apostasy Is Described

What is the meaning of the phrase "the waters of Judah"? (48:1) A "significant addition is the phrase identifying the 'waters of Judah' as the 'waters of baptism' (v. 1). This addition fits quite well within the verse, since the people are called first by their natural name as descendants of Jacob and then by their covenant title as followers of Israel. A parallelism naturally develops if the verse is also interpreted to mean that people come first out of the 'waters of Judah' (the amniotic fluids of the womb, or the 'loins'; RSV, NIV, and other translations) and then out of the 'waters of baptism,' representing a covenant or spiritual birth. The covenant then continues through the first verses as the people also make oaths in God's name and are then called after the name of his holy city" (Ludlow, *Isaiah*, 401). See commentary in *Book of Mormon Study Guide: Start to Finish, Revised Edition* for 1 Nephi 20:1.

What are some dangers when one merely appears to be righteous? (48:1) "The Savior was understanding and compassionate with sinners whose hearts were humble and sincere. But He rose up in righteous anger against hypocrites like the scribes, Pharisees, and Sadducees—those who tried to appear righteous in order to win the praise, influence, and wealth of the world, all the while oppressing the people they should have been blessing" (Uchtdorf, "On Being Genuine," 81). What can you do to be genuine in your faith and reliance upon Jesus Christ? See commentary in *Book of Mormon Study Guide: Start to Finish, Revised Edition* for 1 Nephi 20:1–8.

How do these verses depict Israel's apostasy and rejection of Jehovah? (48:1–7) "While [the] chosen people of the Lord have 'come forth out of the waters of . . . baptism' [see 1 Nephi 20:1] 'they do not stay themselves upon the . . . Lord' (1 Nephi 20:2). In other words, they have apostatized. For this reason, the Lord elected to demonstrate His powers of omniscience. . . . [He] 'declared . . . things from the beginning,' that is, He spoke of them before their occurrence, and then 'shewed them . . . suddenly' by bringing them to pass (Isaiah 48:3). This He had done, He said, lest the apostates should say, 'Mine idol hath done them' (v. 5), or 'Behold, I knew them' (v. 7), that is to say, 'I already knew that'" (*Old Testament Student Manual: 1 Kings–Malachi*, 191).

Why was their rebelliousness described as an "iron sinew" and "brow [of] brass"? (48:4) "In more modern terminology the obstinate or stubborn of Israel could be described as having necks that would not turn—they were *stiffnecked*; and their minds were not pliant to the promptings of the Spirit—they were *hardheaded*. A stiff neck does not turn in the direction of divine guidance. By contrast, the Lord promises to 'feel after' those who 'stiffen not their necks' (D&C 112:13)" (Brewster, *Isaiah Plain and Simple*, 179). See commentary in *Book of Mormon Study Guide: Start to Finish, Revised Edition* for 1 Nephi 20:4. ⊕

What are the people being urged to "declare"? (48:6) "The meaning of the question in *Isaiah 48:6* is very obvious: they [Israel] must acknowledge and attest, even [though] against their will . . . that Jehovah has foretold all that is now confirmed by the evident fulfilment. Consequently the 'former things' are the events experienced by the people from the very earliest times . . . down to the present. . . . And as the object of the prediction was to guard Israel against ascribing to its idols that which had taken place (which can only be understood of events that had occurred in favour of Israel), the 'former things' must include the preparation for the redemption of Israel from the Babylonian captivity through the revolution brought to pass by Cyrus" (Keil and Delitzsch, *Commentary* [on Isaiah 48:6–8]).

Isaiah 48:9–11. Through Afflictions the Lord Makes Us His Chosen People

9 ¶ For my name's sake will I defer mine anger, and for my praise will I refrain for thee, that I cut thee not off.

10 Behold, I have refined thee, but not with silver; I have chosen thee in the furnace of affliction.

11 For mine own sake, *even* for mine own sake, will I do *it:* for how should *my name* be polluted? and I will not give my glory unto another.

How can our afflictions be refining with the Lord's help? (48:10) "It is challenging but vital to remain firm and steadfast when we find ourselves being refined 'in the furnace of affliction' [Isaiah 48:10], something that comes soon or late to all of us in mortality. Without God, these dark experiences tend to despondency, despair, and even bitterness. With God, comfort replaces pain, peace replaces turmoil, and hope replaces sorrow. Remaining firm in the faith of Christ will bring His sustaining grace and support. He will convert trial into blessing and, in Isaiah's words, 'give . . . beauty for ashes' [Isaiah 61:3]" (Christofferson, "Firm and Steadfast in the Faith of Christ," 32). See commentary in *Book of Mormon Study Guide: Start to Finish, Revised Edition* for 1 Nephi 20:10.

12 ¶ Hearken unto me, O Jacob and Israel, my called; I *am* he; I *am* the first, I also *am* the last.

13 Mine hand also hath laid the foundation of the earth, and my right hand hath spanned the heavens: *when* I call unto them, they stand up together.

14 All ye, assemble yourselves, and hear; which among them hath declared these *things?* The LORD hath loved him: he will do his pleasure on Babylon, and his arm *shall be on* the Chaldeans.

15 I, *even* I, have spoken; yea, I have called him: I have brought him, and he shall make his way prosperous.

16 ¶ Come ye near unto me, hear ye this; I have not spoken in secret from the beginning; from the time that it was, there *am* I: and now the Lord GOD, and his Spirit, hath sent me.

17 Thus saith the LORD, thy Redeemer, the Holy One of Israel; I *am* the LORD thy God which teacheth thee to profit, which leadeth thee by the way *that* thou shouldest go.

18 O that thou hadst hearkened to my commandments! then had thy peace been as a river, and thy righteousness as the waves of the sea:

19 Thy seed also had been as the sand, and the offspring of thy bowels like the gravel thereof; his name should not have been cut off nor destroyed from before me.

Isaiah 48:12–17. The Children of Israel Should Hearken unto the Lord and His Prophets

How do these phrases in these verses describe the power and supreme position of Jehovah? (48:12–13) "*First/last.* These words express the eternal nature of the Lord Jesus Christ. . . . Jesus was the first to be born in the spirit. He is the first in position and dominion. He is the last in that he will continue as God, preeminent over all, through all eternity. . . .

"*Right hand.* The *right hand* is the hand of authority. It is also the 'covenant hand,' or the hand we use to covenant with the Lord.

"*Laid the foundation of the earth/spanned the heavens.* God is the Creator, who has all power both in our sphere (earth) and in all other spheres (heavens).

"*I call/they stand up.* Both earth and heaven obey God's command" (Parry, et al., *Understanding Isaiah*, 418).

Why does the Lord declare that He has "not spoken in secret"? (48:16) "The Lord has not spoken in secret. From the beginning He has clearly declared His works and His will, which was in full accord with that of His Father. Verse 16 is a foreshadowing of the Savior's later declaration during His mortal ministry: 'My meat is to do the will of him that sent me, and to finish his work' (John 4:34)" (Brewster, *Isaiah Plain and Simple*, 182–83). See commentary in *Book of Mormon Study Guide: Start to Finish, Revised Edition* for 1 Nephi 21:1–7.

Isaiah 48:18–22. Living Righteously Brings Peace

How is "peace" inextricably linked to keeping God's commandments? (48:18) President Marion G. Romney taught that "since Lucifer 'is the father of contention' (3 Ne. 11:29), the antithesis of peace, the price of peace is victory over Satan" ("Price of Peace," 5).

Elder Marvin J. Ashton added, "Inner peace is the prized possession of God's valiant. A testimony of the truthfulness of the teachings of our Savior gives personal peace in times of adversity. . . . Wickedness, no matter how it is labeled or camouflaged, will eventually bring grief and heartache and wipe out inner peace.

"Peace will never be the possession of those who participate in vulgar conversations and behavior" ("Peace—A Triumph of Principles," 69–70). ⊕

How can we rejoice as we "go forth" from Babylon today? (48:20) "We do not need to adopt the standards, the mores, and the morals of Babylon. We can create Zion in the midst of Babylon. We can have our own standards for music and literature and dance and film and language. We can have our own standards for dress and deportment, for politeness and respect. We can live in accordance with the Lord's moral laws. We can limit how much of Babylon we allow into our homes by the media of communication. . . .

"We can be courageous and can walk in the Lord's paths and follow His footsteps" (Stone, "Zion in the Midst of Babylon," 92, 93). See commentary in *Book of Mormon Study Guide: Start to Finish, Revised Edition* for 1 Nephi 20:20. ⊕

20 ¶ Go ye forth of Babylon, flee ye from the Chaldeans, with a voice of singing declare ye, tell this, utter it *even* to the end of the earth; say ye, The LORD hath redeemed his servant Jacob.

21 And they thirsted not *when* he led them through the deserts: he caused the waters to flow out of the rock for them: he clave the rock also, and the waters gushed out.

22 *There is* no peace, saith the LORD, unto the wicked.

Isaiah 49:1–7. Jesus Christ and His Prophet Will Gather Israel and Provide Light for the Gentiles

How does the Book of Mormon restore meaning to this verse? (49:1) "The entire chapter of Isaiah 49 is quoted in 1 Nephi 21. Half of verse one is missing from the King James text. What was lost from the Bible is the statement that the scattering of Israel was a direct result of the wickedness of the religious leaders" (*Old Testament Student Manual: 1 Kings–Malachi*, 191). See commentary in *Book of Mormon Study Guide: Start to Finish, Revised Edition* for 1 Nephi 21:1–7. ⊕

CHAPTER 49

The Messiah will be a light to the Gentiles and will free the prisoners—Israel will be gathered with power in the last days—Kings will be the nursing fathers of Israel—Compare 1 Nephi 21.

1 Listen, O isles, unto me; and hearken, ye people, from far; The LORD hath called me from the womb; from the bowels of my mother hath he made mention of my name.

Who Is the Servant Referred to in Isaiah 49:1–6?

"In answer to the question 'Who is the servant referred to in Isaiah 49:1–6?' it seems that the limited evidence suggests that the term 'servant' generally applies to the house of Israel's major representatives throughout the ages:

"1. Isaiah, Israel's major prophet at the end of the eighth century B.C., was the last great prophet before the scattering of Israel.

"2. Jesus Christ personally fulfilled the Father's promises to Jacob.

"3. Ephraim, recipient of Jacob's birthright, is responsible for Israel's spiritual welfare and especially for her restoration in the last days.

"4. Joseph Smith was the head of the dispensation of the fulness of times and the first prophet with the keys of the gathering of Israel in the last days.

"It appears that the servant song in chapter 49 is talking more about Ephraim than the other possibilities; however, more important than identifying the exact servant described here is understanding the servant's characteristics and desiring to incorporate his traits into our own lives so that we can become true servants of the Lord (see Jacob 5:61–63)" (Ludlow, *Isaiah*, 410). See commentary in *Book of Mormon Study Guide: Start to Finish, Revised Edition* for 1 Nephi 21; see also commentary in this volume for Isaiah 42:1–4.

2 And he hath made my mouth like a sharp sword; in the shadow of his hand hath he hid me, and made me a polished shaft; in his quiver hath he hid me;

3 And said unto me, Thou *art* my servant, O Israel, in whom I will be glorified.

4 Then I said, I have laboured in vain, I have spent my strength for nought, and in vain: *yet* surely my judgment *is* with the LORD, and my work with my God.

5 ¶ And now, saith the LORD that formed me from the womb *to be* his servant, to bring Jacob again to him, Though Israel be not gathered, yet shall I be glorious in the eyes of the LORD, and my God shall be my strength.

6 And he said, It is a light thing that thou shouldest be my servant to raise up the tribes of Jacob, and to restore the preserved of Israel: I will also give thee for a light to the Gentiles, that thou mayest be my salvation unto the end of the earth.

7 Thus saith the LORD, the Redeemer of Israel, *and* his Holy One, to him whom man despiseth, to him whom the nation abhorreth, to a servant of rulers, Kings shall see and arise, princes also shall worship, because of the LORD that is faithful, *and* the Holy One of Israel, and he shall choose thee.

8 Thus saith the LORD, In an acceptable time have I heard thee, and in a day of salvation have I helped thee: and I will preserve thee, and give thee for a covenant of the people, to establish the earth, to cause to inherit the desolate heritages;

9 That thou mayest say to the prisoners, Go forth; to them that *are* in darkness, Shew yourselves. They shall feed in the ways, and their pastures *shall be* in all high places.

10 They shall not hunger nor thirst; neither shall the heat nor sun smite them: for he that

Who is this verse referring to as a "polished shaft" in God's hand? (49:2) Commentators have suggested that the servant, here identified as a "polished shaft," represents Isaiah, Israel, and/or Jesus Christ. Some Latter-day Saint writers have suggested that in addition this verse may also have reference to Joseph Smith. "The 'polished shaft' hidden in the Lord's quiver may be a direct reference to Joseph Smith. As the 'choice seer' of the latter day, he was to be the Lord's servant in a special sense (see 2 Ne. 3:6; 3 Ne. 21:10). . . . The arrow shaft is polished that it might fly truer and faster, and the shaft that is polished is generally reserved for one's most important shot. The last dispensation, when all things are gathered in one, is the Lord's most important 'shot,' so he saved his 'polished shaft' for this latter-day work" (Nyman, *Great are the Words of Isaiah*, 177). ⊕

What is the meaning of the "light to the gentiles"? (49:6) The Lord called us "to 'arise and shine forth, that thy light may be a standard for the nations' (D&C 115:4–5). Anciently He charged the Saints on two continents to be a light . . . (Matt. 5:14–16; 3 Ne. 12:14–16). Thus, the true followers of Christ, the faithful members of His Church, have always been identified as children of light; charged with the responsibility of letting that light shine. They are to be a 'light unto the Gentiles' (D&C 86:11). Ultimately, through their righteousness, these faithful followers of Christ, these children of light, will be celestial Saints and 'shine forth as the sun in the kingdom of their Father' (Matt. 13:43)" (Brewster, *Doctrine and Covenants Encyclopedia*, 81). See commentary in *Book of Mormon Study Guide: Start to Finish, Revised Edition* for 1 Nephi 21:6.

Isaiah 49:8–12. Israel Will Be Gathered in the Last Days from Her Long Dispersion

hath mercy on them shall lead them, even by the springs of water shall he guide them.

11 And I will make all my mountains a way, and my highways shall be exalted.

12 Behold, these shall come from far: and, lo, these from the north and from the west; and these from the land of Sinim.

Isaiah 49:13–17. The Lord Will Not Forget His Children

13 ¶ Sing, O heavens; and be joyful, O earth; and break forth into singing, O mountains: for the LORD hath comforted his people, and will have mercy upon his afflicted.

14 But Zion said, The LORD hath forsaken me, and my Lord hath forgotten me.

15 Can a woman forget her sucking child, that she should not have compassion on the son of her womb? yea, they may forget, yet will I not forget thee.

16 Behold, I have graven thee upon the palms of *my* hands; thy walls *are* continually before me.

17 Thy children shall make haste; thy destroyers and they that made thee waste shall go forth of thee.

How does this verse symbolize or represent Jesus Christ? (49:16) Elder Gerrit W. Gong testified: "With you, at this Easter season, I testify of God, our Eternal Father, and His Beloved Son, the living Jesus Christ. Mortal men were cruelly crucified and later resurrected. But only the living Jesus Christ in His perfect resurrected form still bears the marks of crucifixion in His hands, feet, and side. Only He can say, 'I have graven thee upon the palms of my hands' [Isaiah 49:16; 1 Nephi 21:16]. Only He can say: 'I am he who was lifted up. I am Jesus that was crucified. I am the Son of God' [D&C 45:52]" ("Hosanna and Hallelujah—The Living Jesus Christ," 55). ⊕

Isaiah 49:18–26. The Gentile Nations Shall Help Gather the House of Israel

18 ¶ Lift up thine eyes round about, and behold: all these gather themselves together, *and* come to thee. *As* I live, saith the LORD, thou shalt surely clothe thee with them all, as with an ornament, and bind them *on thee*, as a bride *doeth*.

19 For thy waste and thy desolate places, and the land of thy destruction, shall even now be too narrow by reason of the inhabitants, and they that swallowed thee up shall be far away.

20 The children which thou shalt have, after thou hast lost the other, shall say again in thine ears, The place *is* too strait for me: give place to me that I may dwell.

21 Then shalt thou say in thine heart, Who hath begotten me these, seeing I have lost my children, and am desolate, a captive, and removing to and fro? and who hath brought up these? Behold, I was left alone; these, where *had* they *been?*

22 Thus saith the Lord God, Behold, I will lift up mine hand to the Gentiles, and set up my standard to the people: and they shall bring thy sons in *their* arms, and thy daughters shall be carried upon *their* shoulders.

23 And kings shall be thy nursing fathers, and their queens thy nursing mothers: they shall bow down to thee with *their* face toward the earth, and lick up the dust of thy feet; and thou shalt know that I *am* the Lord: for they shall not be ashamed that wait for me.

24 ¶ Shall the prey be taken from the mighty, or the lawful captive delivered?

25 But thus saith the Lord, Even the captives of the mighty shall be taken away, and the prey of the terrible shall be delivered: for I will contend with him that contendeth with thee, and I will save thy children.

26 And I will feed them that oppress thee with their own flesh; and they shall be drunken with their own blood, as with sweet wine: and all flesh shall know that I the Lord *am* thy Saviour and thy Redeemer, the mighty One of Jacob.

When will nations be involved in helping to fulfill part of this prophecy? (49:22) "Though Israel has frequently been humiliated by the powerful of the world and has served them, the tables will be turned. The powerful will fulfill the servant functions for Israel as those who have chosen to follow God are justified. Many feel that at least a partial fulfillment of this occurred when Gentile nations helped establish the modern state of Israel" (Muhlestein, *Scripture Study Made Simple*, 395). See commentary in *Book of Mormon Study Guide: Start to Finish, Revised Edition* for 1 Nephi 21:22–26.

What might the phrase "kings shall be thy nursing fathers, and their queens thy nursing mothers" mean? (49:22–23) "The mighty of the earth—royalty [kings and queens], presidents, government ministers—shall assist in the process of gathering the house of Israel. This could be through financial assistance to enable them to return to their homelands, such as the Jews to the Holy Land, or it could be in removing legal barriers that heretofore have prevented the preaching and establishment of the restored gospel in their lands" (Brewster, *Isaiah Plain and Simple*, 203). See commentary in *Book of Mormon Study Guide: Start to Finish, Revised Edition* for 1 Nephi 21:23.

What is meant by the submissive gestures made by the mighty in this verse? (49:23) "The Gentile nations would come to Jerusalem, not to attack the city but to acknowledge the Lord. The oppressors who would take Israel away in exile would become *nursing fathers, and . . . mothers . . .* who would bring the people home" (*Zondervan KJV Commentary*, 955).

How and when might the Lord contend with our enemies? (49:25) The Joseph Smith Translation adds the words italicized here: "For *the mighty God shall deliver his covenant people. For thus saith the Lord,* I will contend with them" (JST, Isaiah 49:25; emphasis added). What does this teach us about how God honors those who keep His covenants? "You faithful Saints do not have to fight life's battles alone. Think of that! The Lord declared, 'I will contend with him that contendeth with thee, and I will save thy children' [Isaiah 49:25]. Later came this promise to His faithful people: 'I, the Lord, would fight their battles, and their children's battles, and their children's children's, . . . to the third and fourth generation' [D&C 98:37]" (Nelson, "Face the Future with Faith," 36).

Isaiah 50:1–3. The Lord Does Not Give Up on His People

What is a bill of divorcement? (50:1) "To understand these verses we need to keep in mind that a Jew according to the Mosaic Law was permitted to give his wife a letter of divorce to send her away or to sell her away to creditors. . . . [God] cast Israel away as His lawful wife for she has been unfaithful to Him. He is not sending Israel into exile without just cause; Israel's conduct demanded it for there was something very lewd and immoral about Israel for she had committed spiritual adultery" (Johnson, *Isaiah the Prophet*, 98). See commentary in *Book of Mormon Study Guide: Start to Finish, Revised Edition* for 2 Nephi 7:1.

Who does the Lord address in this verse? (50:2) The Joseph Smith Translation makes it clear this message is addressed to "O house of Israel." "Wherefore, when I came *there was* no man; when I called *there was* none to answer. *O house of Israel*, is my hand shortened at all, that it cannot redeem; or have I no power to deliver?" (JST, Isaiah 50:2; emphasis added).

Isaiah 50:4–9. Isaiah Prophesies of the Mortal Ministry of Jesus Christ

Who is the servant in these verses? (50:4–9) "These verses, comprising the third servant song, portray the 'servant' as the epitome of righteousness. As with the other servant songs, controversy surrounds the interpretation of these verses. The servant could be any number of people or peoples. . . . The most acceptable identification is Christ, because these verses describe events in the life of Jesus" (Ludlow, *Isaiah*, 422). See commentary in *Book of Mormon Study Guide: Start to Finish, Revised Edition* for 2 Nephi 7:4–9. ⊕

How should we react to the Lord's chastening? (50:5) "Isaiah the prophet tells us that the people of Israel had lost all hope during their long years of Babylonian captivity. In their misery they thought that God had completely forsaken and deserted them, that He had 'divorced their mother' and 'sold them to creditors' (Isaiah 50:1–3). [They] lost their nationhood and their freedom to worship. . . . But Isaiah reminded them that what was most important was how they saw and understood their captivity. His words still ring true for

CHAPTER 50

Isaiah speaks as the Messiah—He will have the tongue of the learned—He will give His back to the smiters—He will not be confounded—Compare 2 Nephi 7.

1 Thus saith the Lord, Where *is* the bill of your mother's divorcement, whom I have put away? or which of my creditors *is it* to whom I have sold you? Behold, for your iniquities have ye sold yourselves, and for your transgressions is your mother put away.

2 Wherefore, when I came, *was there* no man? when I called, *was there* none to answer? Is my hand shortened at all, that it cannot redeem? or have I no power to deliver? behold, at my rebuke I dry up the sea, I make the rivers a wilderness: their fish stinketh, because *there is* no water, and dieth for thirst.

3 I clothe the heavens with blackness, and I make sackcloth their covering.

4 The Lord God hath given me the tongue of the learned, that I should know how to speak a word in season to *him that is* weary: he wakeneth morning by morning, he wakeneth mine ear to hear as the learned.

5 ¶ The Lord God hath opened mine ear, and I was not rebellious, neither turned away back.

6 I gave my back to the smiters, and my cheeks to them that plucked off the hair: I hid not my face from shame and spitting.

7 ¶ For the Lord GOD will help me; therefore shall I not be confounded: therefore have I set my face like a flint, and I know that I shall not be ashamed.

8 *He is* near that justifieth me; who will contend with me? let us stand together: who *is* mine adversary? let him come near to me.

9 Behold, the Lord GOD will help me; who *is* he *that* shall condemn me? lo, they all shall wax old as a garment; the moth shall eat them up.

10 ¶ Who *is* among you that feareth the LORD, that obeyeth the voice of his servant, that walketh *in* darkness, and hath no light? let him trust in the name of the LORD, and stay upon his God.

11 Behold, all ye that kindle a fire, that compass *yourselves* about with sparks: walk in the light of your fire, and in the sparks *that* ye have kindled. This shall ye have of mine hand; ye shall lie down in sorrow.

those of us who suffer today. . . . We must trust God even during the 'dark night of the soul,' even when we cannot meet Him or hear Him speak" (Ross, *Table before Me*, 125, 126).

What are the implications of the phrase "I gave my back to the smiters, and my cheeks to them that plucked off the hair"? (50:6) "The servant now presents details to show how he was not rebellious. The striking language calls to mind immediately the physical sufferings of our Lord (cf. Matt. 26:67ff.; 27:26ff; John 19:1ff.). . . . There is majesty in the description as though the servant was in complete control of the situation. He sets himself forth as one who acts. Instead of saying that men beat him, he declares that he himself gave his back to those who struck him. He either voluntarily yielded himself to flogging, or he offered himself thereto. The strikers or smiters would be those who would have the public duty of beating a criminal. Beating on the back would seem also to be the custom in the punishment of evil men (cf. Prov. 10:13; 19:29; 26:3 and cf. Ps. 129:3)" (Young, *Book of Isaiah*, 3:300).

Isaiah 50:10–11. Those Who Trust in the Lord Shall Walk in His Light

Who are contrasted in these verses? (50:10–11) "Two classes of people are contrasted in these two verses. One class consists of those who fear the Lord and obey his servant (50:10). They will not walk in spiritual darkness but will have spiritual light [v. 10]. The other class consists of those who seek to be spiritually self-sufficient, relying on themselves instead of on God. They attempt to create their own light [v. 11], but their efforts produce no more than sparks [v. 11] when compared to the bright light that comes from God. Those in this group will eventually receive judgments from the Lord, resulting in sorrow [v. 11]" (Parry, et al., *Understanding Isaiah*, 444).

Isaiah 51:1–8. The Lord Calls Israel to Salvation

Who is the rock whom Israel should remember while in distress? (51:1–2) "The chapter begins with an appeal to the children of Israel to remember their heritage and to follow the righteous example of their progenitors, Abraham and Sarah. The promises God made to these grand heads of Israel's people are still in force. While the heavens and the earth may pass away, the Lord's promises and covenants will abide forever. But the people must qualify for the promised blessings through their obedience and righteousness" (Brewster, *Isaiah Plain and Simple*, 214). See commentary in *Book of Mormon Study Guide: Start to Finish, Revised Edition* for 2 Nephi 8:1–2.

When will the desert be made like the garden of the Lord? (51:3) "All these things have been spoken of and will be fulfilled; and by and by, when we are sanctified and made perfect, when we are chastised and humbled before the Lord, when we have got our eyes opened, and our hearts set upon building up the kingdom of God, then will we return and rebuild the waste places of Zion" (Woodruff, *Journal of Discourses*, 16:271). See commentary in *Book of Mormon Study Guide: Start to Finish, Revised Edition* for 2 Nephi 8:1–2, 3–6.

How can we protect ourselves from the reproach of men? (51:7) "Trying to please others before pleasing God is inverting the *first and second great commandments* (see Matthew 22:37–39). It is forgetting which way we face. And yet, we have all made that mistake because of the fear of men. In Isaiah the Lord warns us,

CHAPTER 51

In the last days, the Lord will comfort Zion and gather Israel—The redeemed will come to Zion amid great joy—Compare 2 Nephi 8.

1 Hearken to me, ye that follow after righteousness, ye that seek the LORD: look unto the rock *whence* ye are hewn, and to the hole of the pit *whence* ye are digged.

2 Look unto Abraham your father, and unto Sarah *that* bare you: for I called him alone, and blessed him, and increased him.

3 For the LORD shall comfort Zion: he will comfort all her waste places; and he will make her wilderness like Eden, and her desert like the garden of the LORD; joy and gladness shall be found therein, thanksgiving, and the voice of melody.

4 ¶ Hearken unto me, my people; and give ear unto me, O my nation: for a law shall proceed from me, and I will make my judgment to rest for a light of the people.

5 My righteousness *is* near; my salvation is gone forth, and mine arms shall judge the people; the isles shall wait upon me, and on mine arm shall they trust.

6 Lift up your eyes to the heavens, and look upon the earth beneath: for the heavens shall vanish away like smoke, and the earth shall wax old like a garment, and they that dwell therein shall die in like manner: but my salvation shall be for ever, and my righteousness shall not be abolished.

7 ¶ Hearken unto me, ye that know righteousness, the people in whose heart *is* my law; fear ye not the reproach of men, neither be ye afraid of their revilings.

8 For the moth shall eat them up like a garment, and the worm shall eat them like wool: but my righteousness shall be for ever, and my salvation from generation to generation.

'Fear ye not the reproach of men' (Isaiah 51:7; see also 2 Nephi 8:7). In Lehi's dream, this fear was triggered by the *finger of scorn* pointed from the great and spacious building, causing many to forget which way they faced and to leave the tree 'ashamed' (see 1 Nephi 8:25–28). . . . Decisions of character are made by remembering the right order of the first and second great commandments (see Matthew 22:37–39)" (Robbins, "Which Way Do You Face?" 9). See commentary in *Book of Mormon Study Guide: Start to Finish, Revised Edition* for 2 Nephi 8:7–8.

Isaiah 51:9–16. If Israel Will Turn to the Lord, He Will Give Them Great Blessings

9 ¶ Awake, awake, put on strength, O arm of the LORD; awake, as in the ancient days, in the generations of old. *Art* thou not it that hath cut Rahab, *and* wounded the dragon?

10 *Art* thou not it which hath dried the sea, the waters of the great deep; that hath made the depths of the sea a way for the ransomed to pass over?

Who is Rahab? (51:9) "*Rahab* has several possible interpretations: Egypt, primordial chaos, or Satan. More important than the specific identification of Rahab, however, is the understanding that God has power over all, even his mightiest enemies ([Isa.] 27:1; Job 26:12; Ps. 74:13–17)" (Parry, et al., *Understanding Isaiah*, 453–54). See commentary in *Book of Mormon Study Guide: Start to Finish, Revised Edition* for 2 Nephi 8:9–10.

11 Therefore the redeemed of the LORD shall return, and come with singing unto Zion; and everlasting joy *shall be* upon their head: they shall obtain gladness and joy; *and* sorrow and mourning shall flee away.

How do we become the "redeemed of the Lord"? (51:11) "In 2 Nephi 9:10, Jacob discusses the two deaths, 'that monster, death and hell, which I call the death of the body, and also the death of the spirit.' This commentary gives added meaning to several passages in Isaiah 51 that Jacob has just quoted in 2 Nephi 8. Isaiah writes, 'Art thou not he that hath cut Rahab [i.e.,the same as Jacob's "death"], and wounded the dragon [i.e., the same as Jacob's "hell"]?' (2 Ne. 8:9). Isaiah's use of the words 'ransomed' (Isa. 51:10) and 'redeemed' (Isa. 51:11) takes on broader meaning as 'sorrow and mourning shall flee away' (Isa. 51:11) because of the infinite Atonement that overcomes death and hell" (Davis, "Book of Mormon Commentary on Isaiah," 57–58). See commentary in *Book of Mormon Study Guide: Start to Finish, Revised Edition* for 2 Nephi 8:11.

12 I, *even* I, *am* he that comforteth you: who *art* thou, that thou shouldest be afraid of a man *that* shall die, and of the son of man *which* shall be made *as* grass;

13 And forgettest the LORD thy maker, that hath stretched forth the heavens, and laid the foundations of the earth; and hast feared continually every day because of the fury of the oppressor, as if he were ready to destroy? and where *is* the fury of the oppressor?

14 The captive exile hasteneth that he may be loosed, and that he should not die in the pit, nor that his bread should fail.

15 But I *am* the LORD thy God, that divided the sea, whose waves roared: The LORD of hosts *is* his name.

Isaiah 51:17–23. Two Prophets in the Last Days Will Teach and Comfort the Jews

What is the "cup of trembling"? (51:17) This is "'the cup of mortal poison.' . . . This may also allude to the ancient custom of [executing] criminals by a cup of poison" (*Adam Clarke's Commentary* [on Isaiah 51:17]).

Who are the two sons that "lie at the head of . . . the streets"? (51:18–20) Revelation 11:3 also speaks of these two witnesses who will prophesy and die in Jerusalem in the last days (see also D&C 77:15). "These are not just there to bear their testimony. They are prophets and will testify against Gog and his armies. And since the only place where we find prophets of God on earth today is within The Church of Jesus Christ of Latter-day Saints, then we can assume they will be leaders in the Church. . . .

"Sometimes we hear members of the Church speak of these two men being 'Jewish prophets.' It does not say *two Jewish prophets* will be raised up, but that these two prophets will be *raised up to the Jewish nation*" (Lund, *Second Coming of the Lord*, 305). See commentary in *Book of Mormon Study Guide: Start to Finish, Revised Edition* for 2 Nephi 8:9–10. ⊕

16 And I have put my words in thy mouth, and I have covered thee in the shadow of mine hand, that I may plant the heavens, and lay the foundations of the earth, and say unto Zion, Thou *art* my people.

17 ¶ Awake, awake, stand up, O Jerusalem, which hast drunk at the hand of the LORD the cup of his fury; thou hast drunken the dregs of the cup of trembling, *and* wrung *them* out.

18 *There is* none to guide her among all the sons *whom* she hath brought forth; neither *is there any* that taketh her by the hand of all the sons *that* she hath brought up.

19 These two *things* are come unto thee; who shall be sorry for thee? desolation, and destruction, and the famine, and the sword: by whom shall I comfort thee?

20 Thy sons have fainted, they lie at the head of all the streets, as a wild bull in a net: they are full of the fury of the LORD, the rebuke of thy God.

21 ¶ Therefore hear now this, thou afflicted, and drunken, but not with wine:

22 Thus saith thy Lord the LORD, and thy God *that* pleadeth the cause of his people, Behold, I have taken out of thine hand the cup of trembling, *even* the dregs of the cup of my fury; thou shalt no more drink it again:

23 But I will put it into the hand of them that afflict thee; which have said to thy soul, Bow down, that we may go over: and thou hast laid thy body as the ground, and as the street, to them that went over.

CHAPTER 52

In the last days, Zion will return, and Israel will be redeemed—The Messiah will deal prudently and be exalted.

1 Awake, awake; put on thy strength, O Zion; put on thy beautiful garments, O Jerusalem, the holy city: for henceforth there shall no more come into thee the uncircumcised and the unclean.

2 Shake thyself from the dust; arise, *and* sit down, O Jerusalem: loose thyself from the bands of thy neck, O captive daughter of Zion.

3 For thus saith the LORD, Ye have sold yourselves for nought; and ye shall be redeemed without money.

4 For thus saith the Lord GOD, My people went down aforetime into Egypt to sojourn there; and the Assyrian oppressed them without cause.

Isaiah 52:1–6. At the Point of Destruction, the Lord Will Personally Save the Jews

What does it mean for Israel to rise up and put on beautiful garments? (52:1) "When Elias Higbee asked the Prophet Joseph Smith for an interpretation of verse 1 of this scripture, he responded: '[Isaiah] had reference to those whom God should call in the last days, who should hold the power of priesthood to bring again Zion, and the redemption of Israel; and to put on her strength is to put on the authority of the priesthood, which she, Zion, has a right to by lineage; also to return to that power which she had lost" (D&C 113:7–8). 'Put on thy beautiful garments' is a metaphor meaning the same thing as 'put on thy strength'" (Chase, *Making Precious Things Plain*, 9:155). ⊕

What does it mean to arise from the dust and sit down? (52:2) "The Lord's people are to take action to rid themselves of the dust, which term represents sin, humiliation, and servitude. . . . The Lord's people are instructed to get up from the dust, where slaves must sit, and sit instead in a place of honor, as on a throne. In contrast, Babylon has been cast from a throne into the dust (47:1)" (Parry, et al., *Understanding Isaiah*, 460).

What does it mean that they sold themselves for nought? (52:3) "The Jews became the servants of their foreign conquerors, who paid nothing for Israel, so the Lord will redeem Israel gratuitously from sin (45:13; 55:1)" (*MacArthur Bible Commentary*, 823).

What Place Does This Chapter Take in Scripture? (Isaiah 52)

"Isaiah's writings in chapter 52 are referenced by the apostles John and Paul in the New Testament (Revelation 18:4; 2 Corinthians 6:17); quoted by such Book of Mormon prophets as Nephi (1 Nephi 22:10–11), Jacob (2 Nephi 8:24–25), Abinadi (Mosiah 12:21–24; 15:29–31), and Moroni (Moroni 10:31); taught by the resurrected Lord in the ancient Americas (3 Nephi 16, 20, 21); and found sprinkled throughout the Doctrine and Covenants (e.g., D&C 38:42; 82:14; 84:98–99).

"This is a chapter of hope, focusing on the house of Israel in the last days. Verses 8–10 of the Isaiah text are obviously significant, for they are quoted four times in the Book of Mormon, twice by Jesus Himself. He first recited these verses at the conclusion of His teachings as recorded in 3 Nephi 16, which included prophecies about the last days. He introduced the Old Testament seer's words by saying, 'And then the words of the prophet Isaiah shall be fulfilled' (3 Nephi 16:17). The people were then told to go to their homes to ponder and pray about His teachings and to prepare their minds for subsequent teachings the following day (3 Nephi 17:3)" (Brewster, *Isaiah Plain and Simple*, 230–31).

5 Now therefore, what have I here, saith
the LORD, that my people is taken away for
nought? they that rule over them make them
to howl, saith the LORD; and my name continually every day *is* blasphemed.

6 Therefore my people shall know my name:
therefore *they shall know* in that day that I *am*
he that doth speak: behold, *it is* I.

Isaiah 52:7–12. The Lord Will Bring About Zion, and the Earth Will See the Lord's Salvation

Whose beautiful feet are upon the mountains? (52:7) "Ultimately it is Christ who is beautiful upon the mountain. And it is His merciful promise of 'peace in this world,' His good tidings of 'eternal life in the world to come' [see D&C 59:23] that make us fall at His feet and call His name blessed and give thanks for the restoration of His true and living Church" (Holland, "Peaceable Things of the Kingdom," 82). ⊕

7 ¶ How beautiful upon the mountains are
the feet of him that bringeth good tidings,
that publisheth peace; that bringeth good
tidings of good, that publisheth salvation;
that saith unto Zion, Thy God reigneth!

When will Isaiah's prophecy be fulfilled? (52:8–10) "These words of Isaiah were quoted to the Lehites by the resurrected Jesus Christ, with the explanation that these words would be fulfilled *after* 'this land [the Americas]' should be given 'unto this people [the descendants of the Lehites] . . . for their inheritance' (3 Ne. 16:16–20, italics added).

"In a subsequent meeting with the righteous Lehites, the Savior provided an inspired (and inspiring) commentary on the words of Isaiah. Every serious student of the scriptures should study carefully these teachings of Jesus Christ (see 3 Ne. 20:11–46 and chapters 21–23)" (Ludlow, *Companion to Your Study of the Old Testament*, 305). See commentary in *Book of Mormon Study Guide: Start to Finish, Revised Edition* for 3 Nephi 16:18–19.

8 Thy watchmen shall lift up the voice; with
the voice together shall they sing: for they
shall see eye to eye, when the LORD shall
bring again Zion.

9 ¶ Break forth into joy, sing together, ye
waste places of Jerusalem: for the LORD hath
comforted his people, he hath redeemed
Jerusalem.

10 The LORD hath made bare his holy arm in
the eyes of all the nations; and all the ends of
the earth shall see the salvation of our God.

11 ¶ Depart ye, depart ye, go ye out from
thence, touch no unclean *thing;* go ye out of
the midst of her; be ye clean, that bear the
vessels of the LORD.

12 For ye shall not go out with haste, nor go
by flight: for the LORD will go before you;
and the God of Israel *will be* your rearward.

Isaiah 52:13–15. The Lord Will Suffer

When will the Savior be "exalted and extolled"? (52:13) "Verse 13 is almost universally accepted by Christians as a description of the Savior's being exalted on high following his persecution and crucifixion. The following two verses seem to describe his mortal life, and could well be left at that were it not for latter-day revelation which shows that these verses also apply to Joseph Smith. . . . After the Savior quoted these verses to the Nephites, he gave a sign to them to show when these things were to take place. Since he had

13 ¶ Behold, my servant shall deal prudently,
he shall be exalted and extolled, and be very
high.

already been persecuted, crucified and resurrected, his quoting these verses shows that they had not yet been completely fulfilled. He said the prophecy would begin to be fulfilled when the works of the Nephites (the Book of Mormon) would come forth among the Gentiles (see 3 Ne. 21:2–9)" (Nyman, *Great Are the Words of Isaiah*, 204).

14 As many were astonied at thee; his visage was so marred more than any man, and his form more than the sons of men:

15 So shall he sprinkle many nations; the kings shall shut their mouths at him: for *that* which had not been told them shall they see; and *that* which they had not heard shall they consider.

What does it mean to have His visage "marred"? (52:14) "The servant will be greatly disfigured by his sufferings, both in face and in body (Job 19:13–22). Certainly the pain that Jesus suffered in the Garden of Gethsemane was so great that it could be said that 'his visage' would be 'marred more than any man, and his form more than the sons of men'" (Parry, et al., *Understanding Isaiah*, 469). ⊕

CHAPTER 53

Isaiah speaks about the Messiah—His humiliation and sufferings are described—He makes His soul an offering for sin and makes intercession for the transgressors—Compare Mosiah 14.

1 Who hath believed our report? and to whom is the arm of the Lord revealed?

2 For he shall grow up before him as a tender plant, and as a root out of a dry ground: he hath no form nor comeliness; and when we shall see him, *there is* no beauty that we should desire him.

Isaiah 53:1–3. Jesus, the Son of God, Experiences Mortal Life

What is the meaning of growing up like a "tender plant"? (53:2) "When Isaiah spoke of the Savior as being a 'tender plant' without form and comeliness, he meant that Jesus was born as a small, helpless infant just as all people are. Jesus grew as other people do.

"President Joseph Fielding Smith wrote: 'Did not Christ grow up as a tender plant? There was nothing about him to cause people to single him out. In appearance he was like men; and so it is expressed here by the prophet that he had no form or comeliness, that is, he was not so distinctive, so different from others that people would recognize him as the Son of God. He appeared as a mortal man' (*Doctrines of Salvation*, 1:23)" (*Old Testament Student Manual: 1 Kings–Malachi*, 197).

3 He is despised and rejected of men; a man of sorrows, and acquainted with grief: and we hid as it were *our* faces from him; he was despised, and we esteemed him not.

In what ways was Jesus Christ "despised and rejected of men"? (53:3) "To the layman in the streets of Judea, Christ's career must have seemed a failure, a tragedy, a good man totally overwhelmed by the evils surrounding Him and the misdeeds of others. He was misunderstood or misrepresented, even hated from the beginning. No matter what He said or did, His statements were twisted, His actions suspected, His motives impugned. In the entire history of the world no one has ever loved so purely or served so selflessly—and been treated so diabolically for His effort. Yet nothing could break His faith in His Father's plan or His Father's promises. Even in those darkest hours at Gethsemane and Calvary, He pressed on, continuing to trust in the very God whom He momentarily feared had forsaken Him" (Holland, "High Priest of Good Things to Come," 37). See commentary in *Book of Mormon Study Guide: Start to Finish, Revised Edition* for Mosiah 14:3, 4. ⊕

Isaiah 53:4–12. Through Suffering the Pains, Sins, and Sorrows of the World, Jesus Christ Works Out the Atonement

How can the way we feel about the Lord influence our acceptance of His Atonement? (53:4–5) "Being converted unto the Lord starts with an unwavering commitment to God, followed by making that commitment part of who we are. Internalizing such a commitment is a lifelong process that requires patience and ongoing repentance. Eventually, this commitment becomes part of who we are, embedded in our sense of self, and ever present in our lives. Just as we never forget our own name no matter what else we are thinking about, we never forget a commitment that is etched in our hearts" (Renlund, "Unwavering Commitment to Jesus Christ," 22). How might you increase your appreciation for and commitment to the Lord? See commentary in *Book of Mormon Study Guide: Start to Finish, Revised Edition* for Mosiah 14:4–6.

How do these verses describe the Atonement of Jesus Christ? (53:4–10) "Isaiah 53 presents the 'most complete prophecy found in our Old Testament about the atoning sacrifice of the Lord Jesus Christ.' In this chapter, Isaiah prophesies that Jesus will be 'wounded for our transgressions, he was bruised for our iniquities . . . and with his stripes we are healed' (Isa. 53:5). He foretells that 'the Lord hath laid on him the iniquity of us all . . . for the transgression of my people was he stricken' (Isa. 53:6, 8). Isaiah knew that Christ would be an 'offering for sin' (Isa. 53:10)" (Black, *400 Questions and Answers about the Old Testament*, 174).

How was this prophecy fulfilled in the life of Jesus Christ? (53:7) "Herod began to question the Prisoner; but Jesus remained silent. The chief priests and scribes vehemently voiced their accusations; but not a word was uttered by the Lord. . . . As far as we know, Herod is . . . the only being who saw Christ face to face and

4 ¶ Surely he hath borne our griefs, and carried our sorrows: yet we did esteem him stricken, smitten of God, and afflicted.

5 But he *was* wounded for our transgressions, *he was* bruised for our iniquities: the chastisement of our peace *was* upon him; and with his stripes we are healed.

6 All we like sheep have gone astray; we have turned every one to his own way; and the LORD hath laid on him the iniquity of us all.

7 He was oppressed, and he was afflicted, yet he opened not his mouth: he is brought as a lamb to the slaughter, and as a sheep before her shearers is dumb, so he openeth not his mouth.

8 He was taken from prison and from judgment: and who shall declare his generation? for he was cut off out of the land of the living: for the transgression of my people was he stricken.

9 And he made his grave with the wicked, and with the rich in his death; because he had done no violence, neither *was any* deceit in his mouth.

10 ¶ Yet it pleased the LORD to bruise him; he hath put *him* to grief: when thou shalt make his soul an offering for sin, he shall see *his* seed, he shall prolong *his* days, and the pleasure of the LORD shall prosper in his hand.

11 He shall see of the travail of his soul, *and* shall be satisfied: by his knowledge shall my righteous servant justify many; for he shall bear their iniquities.

12 Therefore will I divide him *a portion* with the great, and he shall divide the spoil with the strong; because he hath poured out his soul unto death: and he was numbered with the transgressors; and he bare the sin of many, and made intercession for the transgressors.

CHAPTER 54

In the last days, Zion and her stakes will be established, and Israel will be gathered in mercy and tenderness—Israel will triumph—Compare 3 Nephi 22.

1 Sing, O barren, thou *that* didst not bear; break forth into singing, and cry aloud, thou *that* didst not travail with child: for more *are* the children of the desolate than the children of the married wife, saith the LORD.

spoke to Him, yet never heard His voice. . . . For Herod the fox He had but disdainful and kingly silence. Thoroughly piqued, Herod turned from insulting questions to acts of malignant derision. He and his men-at-arms made sport of the suffering Christ. . . . Herod had found nothing in Jesus to warrant condemnation" (Talmage, *Jesus the Christ*, 636). See commentary in *Book of Mormon Study Guide: Start to Finish, Revised Edition* for Mosiah 14:7.

In what way did Jesus "see his seed"? (53:10) "Christ tasted 'death for *every* man' (Hebrews 2:9; emphasis added), perhaps meaning for each individual person. One reading of Isaiah suggests that Christ may have envisioned each of us as the atoning sacrifice took its toll—'when thou shalt make his soul an offering for sin, he shall *see* his seed' (Isaiah 53:10; emphasis added; see also Mosiah 15:10–11). Just as the Savior blessed the 'little children, one by one' (3 Nephi 17:21); just as the Nephites felt his wounds 'one by one' (3 Nephi 11:15); just as he listens to our prayers one by one; so, perhaps, he suffered for us, one by one" (Callister, *Infinite Atonement*, 141).

Isaiah 54:1–10. The Lord's Church Shall Grow, and Nothing Will Stop It

Why would the barren woman rejoice? (54:1) "The barren woman of verse 1 is undoubtedly Israel, who has not yet brought forth the full fruits of her covenants with the Lord. Isaiah calls Israel barren because of her inability or unwillingness to produce spiritually strong offspring for the Lord.

"The woman has been separated from her husband, the Lord, because of her wickedness (compare Hosea 1–2). Thus, she has not had children. However, Isaiah tells her to break forth into song, because many children have been born to the 'desolate' or forsaken woman" (Ludlow, *Isaiah*, 459). See commentary in *Book of Mormon Study Guide: Start to Finish, Revised Edition* for 3 Nephi 22:1.

What is the meaning of Isaiah's phrase, "Enlarge the place of thy tent"? (54:2) "Isaiah, fifty-fourth chapter, verses one and two, talks about the tent which represents the gospel of Christ. He states that in the last days the cords of the tent would be stretched across the earth and stakes would be planted in every land (see Isa. 54:1–2). We literally are seeing that fulfilled today. As I have thought about these passages, I have thought of the awesome task of supporting the Brethren in carrying the gospel to every nation, kindred, tongue, and people" (Bateman, "Stretching the Cords of the Tent," 65). See commentary in *Book of Mormon Study Guide: Start to Finish, Revised Edition* for 3 Nephi 22:2.

How is separation from God only for a "small moment"? (54:6–9) "The Lord would divorce Israel when He sent her away into exile, but this abandonment would be only for a moment (vv. 5–7). The Lord would have mercy on Israel because His covenant kindness (v. 8) and commitment to Israel is everlasting. The Lord's promises to Israel are as lasting as His promise to Noah (v. 9) that He would never again destroy the earth by flood" (*Zondervan KJV Commentary*, 958). See commentary for 3 Nephi 22:6 and 3 Nephi 22:7 in *Book of Mormon Study Guide: Start to Finish, Revised Edition.*

How does the Joseph Smith Translation help personalize this verse? (54:10) "The Joseph Smith Translation replaces the word *peace* in this verse with *people*" (Valletta, et al., *Old Testament for Latter-day Saint Families*, 528). How do the Lord's covenants with His people demonstrate mercy and peace?

2 Enlarge the place of thy tent, and let them stretch forth the curtains of thine habitations: spare not, lengthen thy cords, and strengthen thy stakes;

3 For thou shalt break forth on the right hand and on the left; and thy seed shall inherit the Gentiles, and make the desolate cities to be inhabited.

4 Fear not; for thou shalt not be ashamed: neither be thou confounded; for thou shalt not be put to shame: for thou shalt forget the shame of thy youth, and shalt not remember the reproach of thy widowhood any more.

5 For thy Maker *is* thine husband; the Lord of hosts *is* his name; and thy Redeemer the Holy One of Israel; The God of the whole earth shall he be called.

6 For the Lord hath called thee as a woman forsaken and grieved in spirit, and a wife of youth, when thou wast refused, saith thy God.

7 For a small moment have I forsaken thee; but with great mercies will I gather thee.

8 In a little wrath I hid my face from thee for a moment; but with everlasting kindness will I have mercy on thee, saith the Lord thy Redeemer.

9 For this *is as* the waters of Noah unto me: for *as* I have sworn that the waters of Noah should no more go over the earth; so have I sworn that I would not be wroth with thee, nor rebuke thee.

10 For the mountains shall depart, and the hills be removed; but my kindness shall not depart from thee, neither shall the covenant of my peace be removed, saith the Lord that hath mercy on thee.

11 ¶ O thou afflicted, tossed with tempest, *and* not comforted, behold, I will lay thy stones with fair colours, and lay thy foundations with sapphires.

12 And I will make thy windows of agates, and thy gates of carbuncles, and all thy borders of pleasant stones.

13 And all thy children *shall be* taught of the LORD; and great *shall be* the peace of thy children.

14 In righteousness shalt thou be established: thou shalt be far from oppression; for thou shalt not fear: and from terror; for it shall not come near thee.

15 Behold, they shall surely gather together, *but* not by me: whosoever shall gather together against thee shall fall for thy sake.

16 Behold, I have created the smith that bloweth the coals in the fire, and that bringeth forth an instrument for his work; and I have created the waster to destroy.

17 ¶ No weapon that is formed against thee shall prosper; and every tongue *that* shall rise against thee in judgment thou shalt condemn. This *is* the heritage of the servants of the LORD, and their righteousness *is* of me, saith the LORD.

Isaiah 54:11–17. The Lord Will Again Gather and Protect His Children in the Last Days

What do these foundations laid with beautiful and precious stones symbolize? (54:11–12) "God uses a building metaphor to help us understand what He is trying to do for us. We have chosen to be unmoored; our sins and straying have made it so that we have no foundation and can be tossed about by worldly whims and Satanic huffs. But God wants to make of us a palace built on a sure foundation. Because He loves us so much, He wants to make us something grander than we have ever imagined, built on characteristics and principles that will make our footing and strength so sure we cannot fall. He will make our being so beautiful, or jewel-like, it cannot even be imagined" (Muhlestein, *Scripture Study Made Simple*, 406). See commentary in *Book of Mormon Study Guide: Start to Finish, Revised Edition* for 3 Nephi 22:12.

How does Isaiah's writing emphasize the promised blessings of righteousness? (54:14–15) "In verses 14–15, Isaiah promises the blessings of righteousness: continual protection and peace, and freedom from oppression and fear. He uses composite parallelism in verse 14 to stress the safety of the righteous: 'thou [shalt] be established,' 'thou shalt be far from oppression,' and 'thou shalt not fear'" (Ludlow, *Unlocking Isaiah in the Book of Mormon*, 250–51). In verse 15, the Joseph Smith Translation adds: "They shall surely gather together against thee."

What is the promise of the Lord pertaining to His work? (54:17) "Yes, 'the enemy is combined,' but when we are combined with the Lord's 'chariots of fire,' then 'they that be with us are more than they that be with them'! (2 Kgs. 6:16–17). Furthermore, the divine promise is that no weapon formed against the Lord's work shall finally prosper; this 'is the heritage of the servants of the Lord' (Isa. 54:17; D&C 71:9). I so assure; I so testify!" (Maxwell, "'Behold, the Enemy Is Combined' (D&C 38:12)," 79). See commentary in *Book of Mormon Study Guide: Start to Finish, Revised Edition* for 3 Nephi 22:17.

Summary of Isaiah 55

Isaiah testifies of Jesus and invites us to seek the Lord, turn from our sins, and obtain salvation, which is free. We are to constantly seek the Lord and continually call upon Him. We need to always realize that His thoughts and ways are higher than those of man.

Isaiah 56:1–8. God Invites All His Children to Be Part of His Covenant People

How can we keep the Sabbath day holy and unpolluted? (56:2) President Russell M. Nelson taught the following about one's conduct and attitude on the Sabbath: "I learned from the scriptures that my conduct and my attitude on the Sabbath constituted a *sign* between me and my Heavenly Father. With that understanding, I no longer needed lists of dos and dont's. When I had to make a decision whether or not an activity was appropriate for the Sabbath, I simply asked myself, 'What *sign* do I want to give to God?' That question made my choices about the Sabbath day crystal clear" ("Sabbath Is a Delight," 130).

CHAPTER 55

Come and drink; salvation is free—The Lord will make an everlasting covenant with Israel—Seek the Lord while He is near.

CHAPTER 56

All who keep the commandments will be exalted—Other people will join Israel—The Lord will gather others to the house of Israel.

1 Thus saith the Lord, Keep ye judgment, and do justice: for my salvation *is* near to come, and my righteousness to be revealed.

2 Blessed *is* the man *that* doeth this, and the son of man *that* layeth hold on it; that keepeth the sabbath from polluting it, and keepeth his hand from doing any evil.

The Lord's Thoughts and Ways Are Higher Than Man's (Isaiah 55:8–9)

Throughout the ages, prophets and apostles have taught that men must accept that God's ways are higher than man's ways. Consider some of the following:

1. President Howard W. Hunter said: "At various times in our lives, probably at repeated times in our lives, we do have to acknowledge that God knows what we do not know and sees what we do not see" ("Opening and Closing of Doors," 60).

2. The Prophet Joseph Smith taught: "The past, the present, and the future were and are, with Him, one eternal 'now'" (*Joseph Smith* [manual], 406). "We are looked upon by God as though we were in eternity; God dwells in eternity, and does not view things as we do" (*Joseph Smith* [manual], 475).

3. Elder Neil L. Andersen said: "Seeing through the lens of mortality does not always give a complete understanding of the workings of God. But His gentle reminder, 'My thoughts are not your thoughts, neither are your ways my ways' [Isaiah 55:8] reassures us that with time and eternal perspective we will see things 'as they really are' [Jacob 4:13] and more completely understand His perfect love" ("Power in the Priesthood," 93).

4. Elder Dieter F. Uchtdorf taught: "The purpose of faith is not to *change* God's will but to empower us to *act on* God's will. Faith is trust—trust that God sees what we cannot and that He knows what we do not [see Isaiah 55:8–9]. Sometimes, trusting our own vision and judgment is not enough" ("Fourth Floor, Last Door," 17).

5. Elder S. Dilworth Young said: "As with me, it will thrill you that the Lord takes a pure boy and teaches him the truth before he can be taught what uninspired men conceive to be truth. Perhaps you will remember that the Lord puts into the minds and hearts of his prophets what he wants them to think and say rather than the thoughts of philosophical men. Remember what he said to Isaiah: 'For my thoughts are not your thoughts, neither are your ways my ways, saith the Lord' [Isaiah 55:8]" ("For Thy Servant Heareth," 90–91).

3 ¶ Neither let the son of the stranger, that hath joined himself to the LORD, speak, saying, The LORD hath utterly separated me from his people: neither let the eunuch say, Behold, I *am* a dry tree.

4 For thus saith the LORD unto the eunuchs that keep my sabbaths, and choose *the things* that please me, and take hold of my covenant;

5 Even unto them will I give in mine house and within my walls a place and a name better than of sons and of daughters: I will give them an everlasting name, that shall not be cut off.

6 Also the sons of the stranger, that join themselves to the LORD, to serve him, and to love the name of the LORD, to be his servants, every one that keepeth the sabbath from polluting it, and taketh hold of my covenant;

7 Even them will I bring to my holy mountain, and make them joyful in my house of prayer: their burnt offerings and their sacrifices *shall be* accepted upon mine altar; for mine house shall be called an house of prayer for all people.

8 The Lord GOD which gathereth the outcasts of Israel saith, Yet will I gather *others* to him, beside those that are gathered unto him.

How does this invitation to "strangers" and "eunuchs" alter prior practices by the Israelites? (56:3–8) "The strangers in Israel's midst were usually non-Israelites who accepted Israelite rule (2 Sam. 1:13; Ezek. 14:7; see [Bible Dictionary], 'Stranger'). Strangers were usually not full citizens, though they shared certain legal rights and responsibilities. Some were barred from entering the tabernacle and even the temple courtyards (Deut. 23:3)....

"The eunuchs were particularly restricted in their social acceptance by the Israelites. Under Mosaic law, eunuchs were not allowed into full Israelite fellowship, especially in the sacrificial, tabernacle, and priesthood ordinances (Lev. 21:17–23; Deut. 23:1–2). This law was probably given to Israel because wholeness of body typified spiritual wholeness: those who had been emasculated were considered religiously unfit in Israel" (Ludlow, *Isaiah*, 472–73).

Who can receive His "everlasting name" and a place in the Lord's house? (56:4–5) Because these blessings are available to all, Elder David A. Bednar encouraged the Saints to consider "[your] willingness to take upon us the name of Jesus Christ and the blessing of protection promised to those who honorably hold a name and standing in the holy temple" ("Honorably Hold a Name and Standing," 99).

Who does the Lord want to place His everlasting name on and include in His house? (56:5–8) Isaiah testifies that God seeks to gather and bless "the Gentiles and the childless. These foreigners (strangers, KJV) and eunuchs were earlier restricted in their religious participation with the Israelites....

"The Lord's beautiful promise in verses 4 and 5 is that the Gentiles and eunuchs ... will share God's full blessings if they keep his laws.... The major blessing is given in verse 5 with the invitation to receive an everlasting name in the Lord's house, the temple. Particularly, the 'outcasts' are promised a 'name' and a 'place' (KJV)" (Ludlow, *Isaiah*, 472, 473).

Isaiah 56:9–12. Isaiah Condemns the Watchmen Who Are Blind, Ignorant, and Dumb and Greedy Dogs

Who are these watchmen identified by Isaiah? (56:9–12) "*Watchmen* are those, particularly leaders, who have the gospel and are charged to protect it from apostasy. In this passage, the watchmen themselves have become apostates. In 56:11, they are referred to as shepherds who have turned from their care of the flock. Like watchdogs who have become lazy, blind, and incapacitated, or like shepherds who have lost sight of their calling and are no longer able to recognize the enemy, these watchmen have left off caring for their flock and have turned instead to caring for their own needs and desires (Jer. 6:17; Ezek. 3:17; 34:1).

"Besides describing Israel's religious leaders in ancient times, this prophecy may also refer to leaders of apostate religions in our day (2 Ne. 28:3–9; Morm. 8:31–33, 37–39)" (Parry, et al., *Understanding Isaiah*, 500–501).

Summary of Isaiah 57

Isaiah continues his rebuke of Israel and her "watchmen," detailing her transgressions. So wicked is Israel that the righteous shall disappear from among them, and no one will notice. Nor will they be aware of the approaching evil (57:1–2). Addressing Israel directly (57:3, "ye"), Isaiah condemns the "covenant" the people have made with their pagan neighbors (57:8, "them"). Through this association, Israel has become immoral, unjust, and cruel, given to ritual sacrifice, including that of "slaying [their] children" (NIV, 57:5) in the groves and upon the mountains, and displaying pagan symbols on their doorposts (57:3–8). In summary, they became "wearied in the greatness of [God's] way" (57:10) and have discovered "[themselves] to another than [the Lord]" (57:8).

In this state of affairs, the Lord questions Israel: "Of whom hast thou been afraid or feared, that thou hast lied, and hast not remembered me, nor laid it to thy heart? have not I held my peace even of old, and thou fearest me not?" (57:11).

The Lord then reveals how He will heal and redeem Israel. He will judge the wicked, for them there will be "no peace" (57:21). But for the righteous, "I will not contend for ever, neither will I be always wroth. . . . I have seen his ways, and will heal him: I will lead him also, and restore comforts unto him and to his mourners. . . . Peace, peace to him . . . saith the Lord; and I will heal him" (57:16–20).

9 ¶ All ye beasts of the field, come to devour, *yea,* all ye beasts in the forest.

10 His watchmen *are* blind: they are all ignorant, they *are* all dumb dogs, they cannot bark; sleeping, lying down, loving to slumber.

11 Yea, *they are* greedy dogs *which* can never have enough, and they *are* shepherds *that* cannot understand: they all look to their own way, every one for his gain, from his quarter.

12 Come ye, *say they,* I will fetch wine, and we will fill ourselves with strong drink; and to morrow shall be as this day, *and* much more abundant.

CHAPTER 57

When the righteous die, they enter into peace—Mercy is promised to the penitent—There is no peace for the wicked.

CHAPTER 58

The true law of the fast, with its purposes and attendant blessings, is set forth—The commandment to keep the Sabbath is given.

1 Cry aloud, spare not, lift up thy voice like a trumpet, and shew my people their transgression, and the house of Jacob their sins.

2 Yet they seek me daily, and delight to know my ways, as a nation that did righteousness, and forsook not the ordinance of their God: they ask of me the ordinances of justice; they take delight in approaching to God.

3 ¶ Wherefore have we fasted, *say they,* and thou seest not? *wherefore* have we afflicted our soul, and thou takest no knowledge? Behold, in the day of your fast ye find pleasure, and exact all your labours.

4 Behold, ye fast for strife and debate, and to smite with the fist of wickedness: ye shall not fast as *ye do this* day, to make your voice to be heard on high.

5 Is it such a fast that I have chosen? a day for a man to afflict his soul? *is it* to bow down his head as a bulrush, and to spread sackcloth and ashes *under him?* wilt thou call this a fast, and an acceptable day to the LORD?

Isaiah 58:1–5. Fasting for the Right and Wrong Reasons Compared

Why did the Lord suggest that Isaiah's voice should be lifted up like a trumpet? (58:1) A trumpet "symbolizes the declaration of an important thing or event (Alma 29:1; Rev. 1:10; D&C 88:105–6).... The sounding of a trump figuratively calls the outcasts of Israel to gather unto the Lord (Isa. 27:13; Matt. 24:31). ... Trumpets are blown in times of impending danger (both spiritual and physical danger) as a warning to the people (D&C 88:92; 77:12; Ezek. 33:3–6; Joel 2:1)" (McConkie and Parry, *Guide to Scriptural Symbols*, 104). "Through the centuries, prophets have fulfilled their duty when they have warned people of the dangers before them. The Lord's Apostles are duty bound to watch, warn, and reach out to help those seeking answers to life's questions" (Ballard, "God Is at the Helm," 25).

Why did those who took delight in performing religious rituals need to repent? (58:1–2) "Isaiah issued a call for repentance emphasizing the need for a lifestyle of justice rather than the mere performance of religious rituals. Israel would experience . . . renewal only when they were rightly related to the Lord. . . . The people persisted in their sinful ways while pretending to seek (v.2) the Lord and to practice righteousness" (*Zondervan KJV Commentary*, 961). ⊕

Why didn't the Lord acknowledge the fasts of the Israelites? (58:3–5) "To questions about performing such ordinances as fasting and then failing to feel any spiritual results, the prophet's answer from the Lord explained that the fasting was perfunctory, for they had not lived as their ordinances had pledged them to. Fasting should increase charity in the heart and charitable deeds in the community. Real blessings, both spiritual and material, will flow from sincerely fasting and giving fast offerings (Isa. 58:9–12)" (Rasmussen, *Latter-day Saint Commentary on the Old Testament*, 534–35). ⊕

What does it mean to "fast for strife and debate"? (58:4) "In other words, 'You did it to outdo your neighbor or to show you are more righteous than he is. That's not the right reason for fasting. If you do fast that way,' he said, 'you won't get the proper benefit from fasting'" (Matthews, "How to Read Isaiah and Enjoy It!" 207). "They may also have been fasting for the wrong reasons, seeking strength for arguments or sinful endeavors" (Nyman, *Great Are the Words of Isaiah*, 222). "Fasting without spiritual motivation only engenders discomfort and irritability" (Isaiah 58:4*b*). What difference have you noticed when you fast with a true purpose rather than simply going without food?

Isaiah 58:6–14. Blessings of Fasting and the Sabbath

How can fasting "loose the bands of wickedness"? (58:6) "Our Father will free us from the bands of wickedness, He will lift our heavy burdens, and He will let the oppressed go free. In fact He promises to empower us to break every yoke. What an enabling promise, to have the power to break every yoke!

"Proper and consistent fasting can help us overcome sins, bad habits, and addictions. Is there any of us who would not want to be freed from the personal

6 *Is* not this the fast that I have chosen? to loose the bands of wickedness, to undo the heavy burdens, and to let the oppressed go free, and that ye break every yoke?

7 *Is it* not to deal thy bread to the hungry, and that thou bring the poor that are cast out to thy house? when thou seest the naked, that

Yom Kippur and the Israelite Fast in Isaiah 58

"*Yom Kippur* is held on the tenth day of the seventh month of the Jewish liturgical calendar (either in September or October). During the fast, each person evaluates his life and repents of his sins in order to be at peace with God and with others. No labor is performed—the day is observed as if it were a Sabbath (whether it falls on the Sabbath or not) (Lev. 23:27–32). *Yom Kippur* is still observed by the Jews as the most holy of all religious celebrations. . . .

"Although every *Yom Kippur* was a special holy day, another religious commemoration was celebrated along with it twice each century—the Jubilee year (see [Bible Dictionary], 'Jubilee, Year of'). Every fiftieth year, the blowing of trumpets on *Yom Kippur* proclaimed liberty throughout the land—all debts, slaves, and indentured servants were freed (Lev. 25:8–17, 25–34). When *Yom Kippur* was celebrated during the Jubilee year, Israelites had a unique opportunity to clear all their spiritual debts with the Lord and material debts with their fellow man. The celebration also provided the people an opportunity to hear a reading of the whole Mosaic law, to review their history, and to commemorate another half-century of existence and (hopefully) growth for Israel (see [Bible Dictionary], 'Sabbatical Year').

"Note the similarities between the ritual of Yom Kippur (as celebrated during a Sabbatical Year, especially the Jubilee year) and the structure of Isaiah 58:

"1. *Trumpet (58:1)*: Isaiah's voice is raised like a trumpet; the trumpet is blown each Yom Kippur and proclaims the Jubilee Year (Lev. 25:8–9).

"2. *Sins of Israel (58:1)*: Isaiah is charged to remind the people of their sins; on Yom Kippur the High Priest sacrifices a sin offering before assembled Israel for all the sins committed during the past year (Lev. 16:15–19).

"3. *Sabbath (58:3–4, 13)*: Isaiah condemns the people for pursuing their daily business on this Sabbath fast day; the Day of Atonement and Jubilee are both special Sabbaths during which no work is to be done (Lev. 16:31; 25:1–22).

"4. *Wickedness removed (58:6, 11)*: Israel is told to remove every yoke from the people, particularly wickedness and injustice; on Yom Kippur the High Priest places the sins of Israel upon the scapegoat and sends it into the wilderness (Lev. 16:20–22).

"5. *Freedom (58:6–7)*: The fast that the Lord desires includes releasing burdens (debts) and freeing the oppressed; every seven years debts and slaves were to be freed, and every fifty years land was to be returned to its original tribal owners (Lev. 25).

"6. *Mercy of the Lord (58:8)*: As Israel observes a proper fast, she is promised the glory of the Lord; as the high priest sprinkles blood before the mercy seat of the Lord each Yom Kippur, he fulfills a ritual atonement for the people that cleanses them of their sins and enables them to be worthy of the Lord's glory (Lev. 16:15, 30).

"Although the precise occasion of Isaiah's discourse on fasting is not recorded, it seems likely that it was on *Yom Kippur* during a Sabbatical year, and perhaps even during the Jubilee year" (Ludlow, *Isaiah*, 482–84).

thou cover him; and that thou hide not thyself from thine own flesh?

8 ¶ Then shall thy light break forth as the morning, and thine health shall spring forth speedily: and thy righteousness shall go before thee; the glory of the LORD shall be thy rearward.

9 Then shalt thou call, and the LORD shall answer; thou shalt cry, and he shall say, Here I *am*. If thou take away from the midst of thee the yoke, the putting forth of the finger, and speaking vanity;

10 And *if* thou draw out thy soul to the hungry, and satisfy the afflicted soul; then shall thy light rise in obscurity, and thy darkness *be* as the noonday:

11 And the LORD shall guide thee continually, and satisfy thy soul in drought, and make fat thy bones: and thou shalt be like a watered garden, and like a spring of water, whose waters fail not.

12 And *they that shall be* of thee shall build the old waste places: thou shalt raise up the foundations of many generations; and thou shalt be called, The repairer of the breach, The restorer of paths to dwell in.

burdens we carry? Fasting allows us to avail ourselves of this cleansing and purifying power.

"The key is to develop the faith and spiritual strength necessary to receive the blessings of fasting" (Bowen, "Fasting with Power," 64).

Why has the Lord commanded us to fast? (58:6–7) Elder L. Tom Perry noted: "The law of the fast has three great purposes. First, it provides assistance to the needy through the contribution of fast offerings, consisting of the value of meals from which we abstain. Second, a fast is beneficial to us physically. Third, it is to increase humility and spirituality on the part of each individual" ("Law of the Fast," 31). What can you do to better align your fasting with the true spirit of fasting? ⊕

What is the meaning of the word *rereward*? (58:8) "*Rereward* is an older word meaning 'rear guard.' The Hebrew word *asaph* has the root meaning of 'to gather' and, as used in Isaiah 58:8, 'it is applied to the gathering up of the scattered rear of an army, or the keeping it from straggling, and defending it from the attacks of an enemy' ([Wilson, *Old Testament Word Studies*, "rereward"]). A better translation would be 'the glory of Jehovah will gather thee, or keep thee together, *i.e.* be thy rear-guard' ([Keil and Delitzsch, *Commentary*], 7:2:390)" (*Old Testament Student Manual: 1 Kings–Malachi*, 205).

Who will be known as the "repairer of the breach"? (58:12) "Isaiah spoke of those who faithfully live the law of the fast and thus become for their own posterity a repairer of the breach. They are the ones who, Isaiah promises, will 'build the old waste places' [Isaiah 58:12]. In a similar way, the Savior repaired the breach, or distance, between us and Heavenly Father. He, through His great atoning sacrifice, opens the way for us to partake of God's loving power, and then we are enabled to repair the 'waste places' in our personal lives. Healing emotional distance between each other will require our acceptance of God's love, coupled with a sacrifice of our natural selfish and fearful tendencies" (Marriott, "Abiding in God and Repairing the Breach," 11–12).

In what ways is the Sabbath to be a delight? (58:13–14) President Russell M. Nelson taught, "I believe [the Lord] wanted us to understand that the Sabbath was His gift to us" ("Sabbath Is a Delight," 129). President Nelson elaborated on how keeping the Sabbath is a delight in the following six ways: (1) It is a day for personal healing and resting; (2) it is a day for the renewing of our covenants; (3) it is a day for teaching our children the gospel of Jesus Christ; (4) it is a time for family remembrance—honoring our faithful ancestors—and doing family history; (5) it is a day to render service to those afflicted and suffering; and (6) it is a day to set our pleasures aside and honor the Lord (see "Sabbath Is a Delight," 129–32).

13 ¶ If thou turn away thy foot from the sabbath, *from* doing thy pleasure on my holy day; and call the sabbath a delight, the holy of the LORD, honourable; and shalt honour him, not doing thine own ways, nor finding thine own pleasure, nor speaking *thine own* words:

14 Then shalt thou delight thyself in the LORD; and I will cause thee to ride upon the high places of the earth, and feed thee with the heritage of Jacob thy father: for the mouth of the LORD hath spoken *it*.

Isaiah 59:1–2. Israel Is Separated from God by Iniquity

What has happened between God and His people? (59:1–2) "Sin had driven a wedge between God and his people (59:2). Falsehood, unjust gain, pursuing worthless things, violence, shedding innocent blood, wicked thoughts, oppression, injustice and no concern for peace characterized the community in Isaiah 59. Though some may be wondering whether God's hand is too short to save (59:1), Isaiah is making it increasingly clear that any supposed delay in God's intervention is because his very own people are unjust and he is tarrying due to his own mercy (59:2–8)" (Abernathy, *Book of Isaiah and God's Kingdom*, 89).

CHAPTER 59

The people of Israel are separated from their God by iniquity—Their sins testify against them—The Messiah will intercede, come to Zion, and redeem the repentant.

1 Behold, the LORD's hand is not shortened, that it cannot save; neither his ear heavy, that it cannot hear:

2 But your iniquities have separated between you and your God, and your sins have hid *his* face from you, that he will not hear.

Summary of Isaiah 59:3–15

Israel is sinful. The people are full of lies, dishonesty, unfairness, hatred, and fighting. They reject truth and anyone who tries to live it. The poison of Israel's sins is bringing about their spiritual death. Israel's efforts to provide for their needs are compared to trying to weave a garment out of spider webs (59:5–6). They blindly walk in crooked paths. Even the faithful are so circumscribed by the larger evil that they lose hope (59:9–12). Truth has failed and "fallen in the street." The Lord sees all of this and is angered (59:14–15).

16 ¶ And he saw that *there was* no man, and
wondered that *there was* no intercessor: therefore his arm brought salvation unto him; and
his righteousness, it sustained him.

17 For he put on righteousness as a breastplate, and an helmet of salvation upon his
head; and he put on the garments of vengeance *for* clothing, and was clad with zeal
as a cloak.

18 According to *their* deeds, accordingly he
will repay, fury to his adversaries, recompence to his enemies; to the islands he will
repay recompence.

19 So shall they fear the name of the LORD
from the west, and his glory from the rising
of the sun. When the enemy shall come in
like a flood, the Spirit of the LORD shall lift
up a standard against him.

20 ¶ And the Redeemer shall come to Zion,
and unto them that turn from transgression
in Jacob, saith the LORD.

Isaiah 59:16–21. The Lord Promises His Spirit and Salvation to the Righteous

Who is the intercessor in these verses? (59:16–21) These prophetic verses refer "to Jesus Christ, our intercessor with the Father. He came to earth because 'there was no man' and 'there was no intercessor' (v. 16) for the people. If the Savior had not been sent, our state, because of iniquity, would have been grim indeed (see v. 1–15; compare 2 Nephi 9:8–9). Therefore, Jesus was sent to earth. 'His arm brought [man's] salvation unto him,' which was possible because 'his righteousness, it sustained him,' much as a breastplate protects a soldier in battle" (*Old Testament Student Manual: 1 Kings–Malachi*, 206). ⊕

What is the meaning of "his arm"? (59:16) "God's arm is a common metaphor for conveying his powerful action in human history (cf. Psalm 98:1), particularly in the exodus event. . . . Earlier in Isaiah there was anticipation that God's arm would devastate the Assyrians (30:30), and there was a yearning that God's arm would act to bring an even greater salvation when he took up his reign in Zion (33:2; 51:5, 9; 52:10; 53:1). . . . God's arm will establish salvation through his coming as a warrior, according to 59:16. God will take matters into his own 'arm,' bringing salvation from oppression and being sustained by his desire to set things right" (Abernathy, *Book of Isaiah and God's Kingdom*, 90).

What does it mean that the Lord put on righteousness as armor? (59:17) The Lord "will return as the Divine Warrior dressed with a breastplate of righteousness, the helmet of salvation, the garments of vengeance, and a cloak of zeal (Isa. 59:17)—an image that applies to the Redeemer both as he conquered sin and death and also as he returns to judge the world at the end of time. Vengeance will come upon the wicked, and the Spirit of the Lord will rise up against the enemy" (Seely, "Lord Will Bring Salvation," 158).

What does it mean that the "Redeemer shall come to Zion"? (59:20–21) "There is no one thing more fully revealed in the Scriptures of eternal truth, than the rise of the Zion of our God in the latter days, clothed upon with the glory of God from the heavens" (Pratt, in *Journal of Discourses*, 16:78). "Not only will Christ come to Zion but he will then go forth from Zion. Paul wrote: 'Blindness in part is happened to Israel, until the fulness of the Gentiles be come in. And so all Israel shall be saved: as it is written, There shall come out of Sion the Deliverer, and shall turn away ungodliness from Jacob: for this is my covenant unto them, when I shall take away their sins' (Rom. 11:25–27)" (Parry, et al., *Understanding Isaiah*, 527).

Summary of Isaiah 60–62

In the last days, Israel will become a mighty nation, attracting many people. Further, the New Jerusalem, the city of God, will be built and it will be known for its peace and righteousness.

Isaiah 61 includes words the Savior would later read in a synagogue in Nazareth when He announced His mortal ministry. Isaiah writes that the Messiah should come to "preach good tidings[,] . . . bind up the brokenhearted, to proclaim liberty to the captives" (Isaiah 61:1). When Jesus finished reading from these passages in Isaiah, He declared that He was this Messiah (see Luke 4:18–21). The Jews in Nazareth could not believe that Jesus the son of Joseph could be the Anointed One, so they rejected Him (see Luke 4:28–29). Isaiah explains that in the latter days this Messiah will come again and bring hope to the righteous.

He prophesies that in the last days the Lord will gather His children by lifting up "a standard for the people," which is the restored gospel of Jesus Christ. As the children of Israel live the gospel, the Lord shall call them by "a new name," and Zion will be redeemed.

Isaiah 63:1–9. All the Wicked Are Destroyed at the Second Coming

Who is coming with dyed garments? (63:1) "The meaning of this passage is that the Savior will come again, having overcome such enemies as sin and death. The metaphor is of sin and death as people whose blood stained the Redeemer's garments. In fact, when he ransomed us from sin and death, his garments were stained with his own blood" (Rasmussen, *Latter-day Saint Commentary on the Old Testament*, 536–37). See also D&C 133:46–53.

21 As for me, this *is* my covenant with them, saith the LORD; My spirit that *is* upon thee, and my words which I have put in thy mouth, shall not depart out of thy mouth, nor out of the mouth of thy seed, nor out of the mouth of thy seed's seed, saith the LORD, from henceforth and for ever.

CHAPTERS 60–62

In the last days, Israel will rise again as a mighty nation—The gentile peoples will join with and serve Israel—Zion will be established—Finally, Israel will dwell in celestial splendor.

Isaiah speaks about the Messiah—The Messiah will have the Spirit, preach the gospel, and proclaim liberty—In the last days, the Lord will call His ministers and make an everlasting covenant with the people.

In the last days, Israel will be gathered—Zion will be established—Her watchmen will teach about the Lord—The gospel standard will be lifted up—The people will be called holy, the redeemed of the Lord.

CHAPTER 63

The Second Coming will be a day of vengeance and also the year of the redeemed of the Lord—Then the Saints will praise the Lord and acknowledge Him as their father.

1 Who *is* this that cometh from Edom, with dyed garments from Bozrah? this *that is* glorious in his apparel, travelling in the greatness of his strength? I that speak in righteousness, mighty to save.

2 Wherefore *art thou* red in thine apparel, and thy garments like him that treadeth in the winefat?

3 I have trodden the winepress alone; and of the people *there was* none with me: for I will tread them in mine anger, and trample them in my fury; and their blood shall be sprinkled upon my garments, and I will stain all my raiment.

4 For the day of vengeance *is* in mine heart, and the year of my redeemed is come.

5 And I looked, and *there was* none to help; and I wondered that *there was* none to uphold: therefore mine own arm brought salvation unto me; and my fury, it upheld me.

6 And I will tread down the people in mine anger, and make them drunk in my fury, and I will bring down their strength to the earth.

7 ¶ I will mention the lovingkindnesses of the LORD, *and* the praises of the LORD, according to all that the LORD hath bestowed on us, and the great goodness toward the

Why does the Lord say He has "trodden the winepress alone"? (63:1–6) "The winepress serves as a symbol of God trampling down the enemies of Israel. Just as one who treads on the grapes will find himself stained in red, so will the Lord be covered in the blood of Israel's enemies as he destroys them in defense of the covenant people" (Muhlestein, *Essential Old Testament Companion*, 420). ⊕

What is the "day of vengeance"? (63:4) "When [the Savior] comes again he comes to take vengeance on the ungodly and to bring deliverance unto his Saints. . . . It behooves us to be made well aware which class we belong to, that if we are not already among the redeemed we may immediately join that society, that when the Son of God shall come the second time . . . arrayed in power and great glory to take vengeance on them that know not God and obey not the Gospel, or when he shall come in flaming fire, we shall be among that number who shall be ready to meet him with gladness in our hearts and hail him as our great deliverer and friend" (Taylor, in *Journal of Discourses*, 10:116).

How does the Lord display His lovingkindness? (63:7) "In the Hebrew this verse begins and ends with *kindnesses*. The word *ḥesed* [kindness] is the Lord's pledged love for his people; here plural, to intensify and amplify, a love that never changes

He Comes Again to Rule and Reign (Isaiah 63:1–6)

and that contains to the full every ingredient of true love. About this love he recalls three things. First, it has been displayed in action: *deeds... done* [KJV, 'bestowed']; the verb *gāmal* means 'to do completely' and underlines the rich sufficiency of the Lord's love in action. Secondly, it is bountiful and beneficent: *many good things*, literally 'abundant goodness' (cf. 'abundant' in 63:1). Thirdly, it is a heart-love: *compassion* (49:15; 54:7; 55:7; 63:15), emotional, passionate, personal (1 Kgs 3:26)" (Motyer, *Isaiah*, 437).

What is the hallmark of the Lord's relationship with His people? (63:8–9) "Isaiah recounts God's kind acts toward Israel, first mentioning Israel's election as the chosen people (v. 8). Isaiah calls Israel the sons of God and adds that, as such, they should never deal falsely with God. He concludes verse 8 with the remark that God's loving kindness is best manifest in his becoming their savior.

"Isaiah highlights in verse 9 the kindness and mercy of Jehovah; he reminds Israel that in all their affliction Jehovah was willing to aid them. The phrase 'the angel of his presence saved them' (v. 9, KJV) echoes Moses' words. Moses indicates that this angel is the Lord himself (Ex. 33:12–15; see D&C 133:52–53)" (Ludlow, *Isaiah*, 515).

Summary of Isaiah 63:10–19

Isaiah teaches that the relationship between Israel and the Lord is more than a legal agreement—it is personal and intimate, so Israel's rebellion grieves His heart (vv. 9–10). Isaiah recalls the sad lessons of disobedience in Israel's exodus from Egypt. Moses asks the Lord why He has suffered His people to err from His ways (JST, v. 17) and pleads with the Lord for mercy in spite of their hardness of heart.

Isaiah 64:1–12. We Should Pray for the Lord to Come Again

What does it mean that the mountains of the earth shall flow and the earth's waters shall boil? (64:1–3) Reflecting on the prophecies that speak of the earth's future transfiguration, Bruce R. McConkie observed: "When the Lord comes in his glory, in flaming fire, that fire will both cleanse the vineyard and burn the earth. In that day, so intense shall be the heat and so universal the burning, the very elements of which this earth is composed shall melt. The mountains, high and glorious and made of solid rock, shall melt like wax. They shall become molten and flow down into the valleys

house of Israel, which he hath bestowed on them according to his mercies, and according to the multitude of his lovingkindnesses.

8 For he said, Surely they *are* my people, children *that* will not lie: so he was their Saviour.

9 In all their affliction he was afflicted, and the angel of his presence saved them: in his love and in his pity he redeemed them; and he bare them, and carried them all the days of old.

CHAPTER 64

The people of the Lord pray for the Second Coming and for the salvation that will then be theirs.

1 Oh that thou wouldest rend the heavens, that thou wouldest come down, that the mountains might flow down at thy presence,

2 As *when* the melting fire burneth, the fire causeth the waters to boil, to make thy name known to thine adversaries, *that* the nations may tremble at thy presence!

3 When thou didst terrible things *which* we looked not for, thou camest down, the mountains flowed down at thy presence.

4 For since the beginning of the world *men* have not heard, nor perceived by the ear, neither hath the eye seen, O God, beside thee, *what* he hath prepared for him that waiteth for him.

5 Thou meetest him that rejoiceth and worketh righteousness, *those that* remember thee in thy ways: behold, thou art wroth; for we have sinned: in those is continuance, and we shall be saved.

6 But we are all as an unclean *thing*, and all our righteousnesses *are* as filthy rags; and we all do fade as a leaf; and our iniquities, like the wind, have taken us away.

7 And *there is* none that calleth upon thy name, that stirreth up himself to take hold of thee: for thou hast hid thy face from us, and hast consumed us, because of our iniquities.

below. The very earth itself, as now constituted, shall be dissolved. All things shall burn with fervent heat. And out of it all shall come new heavens and a new earth whereon dwelleth righteousness" (*Millennial Messiah*, 526–27). ⊕

When will the "mountains [flow] down"? (64:2–3) President Charles W. Penrose declared: "He comes! The earth shakes, and the tall mountains tremble; the mighty deep rolls back to the north as in fear, and the rent skies glow like molten brass. He comes! The dead Saints burst forth from their tombs, and 'those who are alive and remain' are 'caught up' with them to meet him. The ungodly rush to hide themselves from his presence.... His glory is a consuming fire.... He sweeps the earth 'as with the besom of destruction' [Isaiah 14:23]. He deluges the earth with the fiery floods of his wrath, and the filthiness and abominations of the world are consumed" ("Second Advent," 583).

What has the ear not heard or the eye not seen? (64:4) The Apostle Paul expressed this same sentiment in his letter to the Corinthians (see 1 Cor. 2:9). The Nephites also expressed this view when they heard Jesus pray during His ministry among them (3 Ne. 17:14–17). The expression is used twice in the Doctrine and Covenants (D&C 76:10; 133:45). The context of these statements seems to be the revelation and understanding of the mysteries and wonders of eternity and the secrets of Christ's Kingdom (D&C 76:2–10), sometimes referred to as "the deep things of God" (1 Cor. 2:9–10)—in other words, all things pertaining to the salvation of God's children, to be revealed at the time of His Second Coming (D&C 133:42–47; see also D&C 101:32–42; 121:26–32).

What does it mean that the righteousness of Israel had become as "filthy rags"? (64:5–6) "As Keil and Delitzsch translated the passage: '*All our virtues [are] like a garment soiled with blood*' (*Commentary*, 7:2:470). That is not to say that God despises virtue and views it as filthiness, but rather to say that Israel's former righteousness has now become evil. Joseph Smith changed Isaiah 64:5–6 to reflect this teaching more clearly: 'Thou meetest him that worketh righteousness, and rejoiceth him that remembereth thee in thy ways; in righteousness there is continuance, and such shall be saved. But we have sinned; we are all as an unclean thing, and all our righteousnesses are as filthy rags; and we all do fade as a leaf; and our iniquities, like the wind, have taken us away' (JST, Isaiah 64:5–6)" (*Old Testament Student Manual: 1 Kings–Malachi*, 208).

How are we clay in God's hands? (64:8) "Personal identity is much more than a passport photograph. We also have roots and branches. Divinity is rooted in each of us. 'We all are the work of [our Creator's] hand' [Isa. 64:8]. We are eternal beings. In premortal realms, we brethren were foreordained for our priesthood responsibilities [Alma 31:5]. Before the foundation of the world, women were prepared that they may bear children and glorify God [D&C 132:63].

"We came to this mortal experience to acquire a body, to be tried and tested [see D&C 101:4]. We are to form families and be sealed in holy temples, with joy and loving relationships that endure eternally. To these everlasting truths, we are personally rooted" (Nelson, "Roots and Branches," 29). See commentary in this volume for Jeremiah 18:3–4. ⊕

When are the Lord's holy places to become desolate? (64:10–12) In verses 6–9, Isaiah laments the wickedness of Israel in his day. "Then the vision shifted from the times of Israel's decadence to the last days when the 'holy cities are a wilderness, Zion is a wilderness, Jerusalem a desolation' awaiting the restoration and establishment of the Lord's kingdom on earth (Isa. 64:9–12). Note the reference to two 'holy cities'—Zion and Jerusalem (Isa. 64:10; [Topical Guide], 'Jerusalem, New'; 'Zion'; [Bible Dictionary], 'Zion')" (Rasmussen, *Latter-day Saint Commentary on the Old Testament*, 537–38). ⊕

Isaiah 65:1–10. The Lord Punishes Ancient Israel for Their Disobedience

When does the Lord reveal Himself? (65:1–2) The Joseph Smith Translation for verse 1 reads: "I am found of them who seek after me. I give unto all them that ask of me; I am not found of them that sought me not, or that inquireth not after me" (JST, Isa. 65:1). It is evident that the Lord continually reveals Himself to His people—"I have spread out my hands all the day" (64:2). If there is no revelation among the people, it is a people problem, not the Lord's intention. In these verses "[the Lord] ironically [chastises] the Israelites because he continues speaking to them though they ignore him" (Ludlow, *Isaiah*, 526). ⊕

8 But now, O LORD, thou *art* our father; we *are* the clay, and thou our potter; and we all *are* the work of thy hand.

9 ¶ Be not wroth very sore, O LORD, neither remember iniquity for ever: behold, see, we beseech thee, we *are* all thy people.

10 Thy holy cities are a wilderness, Zion is a wilderness, Jerusalem a desolation.

11 Our holy and our beautiful house, where our fathers praised thee, is burned up with fire: and all our pleasant things are laid waste.

12 Wilt thou refrain thyself for these *things*, O LORD? wilt thou hold thy peace, and afflict us very sore?

CHAPTER 65

Ancient Israel was rejected for rejecting the Lord—The Lord's people will rejoice and triumph during the Millennium.

1 I am sought of *them that* asked not *for me;* I am found of *them that* sought me not: I said, Behold me, behold me, unto a nation *that* was not called by my name.

2 I have spread out my hands all the day unto a rebellious people, which walketh in a way *that was* not good, after their own thoughts;

3 A people that provoketh me to anger continually to my face; that sacrificeth in gardens, and burneth incense upon altars of brick;

4 Which remain among the graves, and lodge in the monuments, which eat swine's flesh, and broth of abominable *things is in* their vessels;

5 Which say, Stand by thyself, come not near to me; for I am holier than thou. These *are* a smoke in my nose, a fire that burneth all the day.

6 Behold, *it is* written before me: I will not keep silence, but will recompense, even recompense into their bosom,

7 Your iniquities, and the iniquities of your fathers together, saith the LORD, which have burned incense upon the mountains, and blasphemed me upon the hills: therefore will I measure their former work into their bosom.

8 ¶ Thus saith the LORD, As the new wine is found in the cluster, and *one* saith, Destroy it not; for a blessing *is* in it: so will I do for my servants' sakes, that I may not destroy them all.

9 And I will bring forth a seed out of Jacob, and out of Judah an inheritor of my mountains: and mine elect shall inherit it, and my servants shall dwell there.

10 And Sharon shall be a fold of flocks, and the valley of Achor a place for the herds to lie down in, for my people that have sought me.

What role will the seed of Jacob and Judah play in the latter days? (65:9) "Even though the land of Israel had been promised to the descendants of Abraham, Isaac, and Jacob, they possessed it only a short time (63:18). But they are assured that the promise will indeed come to pass and that a seed of Jacob will inherit the mountains of Palestine (14:25; 57:13; 60:21). Because mountains often symbolize temples, this passage seems to indicate that the covenant people will receive the blessings of the temple" (Parry, et al., *Understanding Isaiah*, 573–74).

What Were Israel's Transgressions?

Isaiah identifies several important wrongdoings of ancient Israel that became a smoke and a stink in the Lord's nose:

1. They were a rebellious people (65:2)
2. They walked after their own ways (65:2)
3. They walked after their own thoughts (65:2)
4. They sacrificed to idols on altars in pagan groves (65:3–4)
5. They forsook the dietary laws of the Law of Moses (65:4)
6. They had become a proud and haughty people (65:5)

Of ancient Israel's behavior, it is noted: "So what was their problem? They have been 'obstinate' (*sorer*, see also Isa. 1:23; 30:1), walking in 'not good' ways that they have devised for themselves. These three ideas—obstinacy, devising one's own ways, and ways that are not good—describe in a brief compass precisely what the human problem is. Rather than obediently submitting to the ways of living that the Creator has designed for us, we have rebelled and tried to devise other ways of living for ourselves. By definition, 'good' is that which corresponds to the Creator's plan (cf. Gen. 1:3; etc.). Therefore, anything we try to replace those ways with is, by definition, 'not good'" (Oswalt, *Isaiah*, 680).

Summary of Isaiah 65:11–16

Isaiah prophesies that the children of Israel who "forsake the Lord," forget His "holy mountain" (temple), and worship false gods will be slain by the sword. In their distress they will seek after the Lord and He will not answer. They will be ashamed for not choosing the way of the Lord. Those who survive will feel sadness for refusing God's help.

Isaiah 65:17–25. In the Millennium, Israel Will Finally Praise the Lord

What does "new heavens and a new earth" mean? (65:17–18) On 27 December 1832, the Lord declared: "The earth abideth the law of a celestial kingdom, for it filleth the measure of its creation, and transgresseth not the law—wherefore, it shall be sanctified; yea, notwithstanding it shall die, it shall be quickened again, and shall abide the power by which it is quickened, and the righteous shall inherit it" (D&C 88:25–26). According to Elder Bruce R. McConkie: "It is the day 'when the earth shall be transfigured' (D&C 63:21).... It is the day when 'the earth will be renewed and receive its paradisiacal glory' [Articles of Faith 1:10]. It is the day of the 'new earth,' ... the earth which will prevail when wickedness ceases, when the millennial era is ushered in, when 'every corruptible thing ... shall be consumed' (D&C 101:24). It is the day ... of universal peace and justice, a millennial era when Christ shall reign personally upon the earth" (in Conference Report, Oct. 1967, 43).

What does it mean that a child "shall die an hundred years old"? (65:20) The Joseph Smith Translation for verse 20 reads: "In those days there shall be no more thence an infant of days, nor an old man that hath not filled his days: for the child shall not die, but shall live to be an hundred years old" (JST, Isaiah 65:20). The Doctrine and Covenants explains: "In that day an infant shall not die until he is old; and his life shall be as the age of a tree; and when he dies he shall not sleep, that is to say in the earth, but shall be changed in the twinkling of an eye, and shall be caught up, and his rest shall be glorious" (D&C 101:30–31).

17 ¶ For, behold, I create new heavens and a new earth: and the former shall not be remembered, nor come into mind.

18 But be ye glad and rejoice for ever *in that* which I create: for, behold, I create Jerusalem a rejoicing, and her people a joy.

19 And I will rejoice in Jerusalem, and joy in my people: and the voice of weeping shall be no more heard in her, nor the voice of crying.

20 There shall be no more thence an infant of days, nor an old man that hath not filled his days: for the child shall die an hundred years old; but the sinner *being* an hundred years old shall be accursed.

21 And they shall build houses, and inhabit *them;* and they shall plant vineyards, and eat the fruit of them.

22 They shall not build, and another inhabit; they shall not plant, and another eat: for as the days of a tree *are* the days of my people, and mine elect shall long enjoy the work of their hands.

23 They shall not labour in vain, nor bring forth for trouble; for they *are* the seed of the blessed of the LORD, and their offspring with them.

24 And it shall come to pass, that before they call, I will answer; and while they are yet speaking, I will hear.

25 The wolf and the lamb shall feed together, and the lion shall eat straw like the bullock: and dust *shall be* the serpent's meat. They shall not hurt nor destroy in all my holy mountain, saith the LORD.

What does the peaceful harmony of the lamb and the wolf represent? (65:25) "This new creation will be a reversal of the normal course of mortality. The Lord describes in Isaiah 65:19–25 the conditions during the Millennium: joy; end to infant mortality; building, planting, and eating; enjoyment of the labor of one's hands; and peace on earth—symbolized by the coexistence of the wolf and the lamb (see Isa. 11:7–8; 2:4)" (Seely, "Lord Will Bring Salvation," 164). "God shows that in the animal Kingdom all violence and strife will cease. Similarly, in the lives of those who have truly turned to God, peace will flow in superabundance and the rest of God will be extended" (Muhlestein, *Scripture Study Made Simple*, 416). ⊕

CHAPTER 66

At the Second Coming, Israel, as a nation, will be born in a day; the wicked will be destroyed; and the Gentiles will hear the gospel.

Summary of Isaiah 66

In his final chapter, Isaiah touches on common themes of his writings—looking forward to the day when the Messiah will finally come in His fury and triumph over the wicked. Destruction will give way to abundance (66:7–14). The great city of Zion will be established (66:8), a new Jerusalem, signaling a new heaven and a new earth (66:22). In that day both the children of Israel and many Gentiles will hear the gospel message and then "shall all flesh come to worship before [the Lord]" (66:23).

THE BOOK OF THE PROPHET JEREMIAH

Introduction

"There is more knowledge about the life of Jeremiah than any other prophet in the Old Testament. He was born, of priestly descent . . . about 645 B.C. He was called to the ministry when he was in his late teens, and he continued his ministry for over forty years" (Pearson, *Old Testament*, 58). "His preaching overlapped with the ministries of other prophets, including Lehi (see 1 Nephi 1:4, 18–20), Zephaniah (see Zephaniah 1:1), and Urijah (see Jeremiah 26:20–24). Some of Jeremiah's words were recorded before the destruction of Jerusalem (see Jeremiah 36:32)" (*Old Testament Seminary Teacher Material*, 709).

"He witnessed the events from the dissolution of the Assyrian Empire to the fall of the kingdom of Judah at the hands of the Babylonians in 587 B.C. In all of this he was not a dispassionate observer but rather an ardent patriot. Throughout his long ministry he worked to persuade Judah to turn from her evil, which would destroy their country, and follow the Lord. For this he suffered rejection, plots against his life, mobbings, imprisonment, and, if certain traditions are correct, martyrdom in Egypt" (Pearson, *Old Testament*, 58).

"The book of Jeremiah contains the prophecies, warnings, and teachings that were part of the prophet Jeremiah's ministry to the Southern Kingdom of Judah. Because many of Jerusalem's leaders and people rejected Jeremiah and other prophets and continued to sin, Jerusalem was destroyed and many Jews were taken captive to Babylon. This book illustrates that the covenant between God and Israel does not make God's people invincible. If they do not fulfill their part of the covenant and heed the Lord's word, they withdraw themselves from God's care and protection" (*Old Testament Seminary Teacher Material*, 709).

"The Lord's pronouncement of Jeremiah's mission captures the twin themes of the book of Jeremiah—destruction and restoration: 'See, I have this day set thee over the nations and over the kingdoms, to root out, and to pull down, and to destroy, and to throw down, to build, and to plant' (Jer 1:10)" (Holzapfel, et al., *Jehovah and the World of the Old Testament*, 326).

"One thing that makes the book at times difficult to understand is that whoever collected [the prophet's inspired messages] did not put them in chronological order. Jeremiah does begin with the prophet's call and end with the fall of Jerusalem. But Jeremiah 7, for example, gives us the prophet's report of his famous 'Temple sermon,' while Jeremiah 26 tells that story again. Chapter 21 is a denunciation of Zedekiah, but chapter 22 contains warnings to two of his predecessors. Clearly, the book is not organized chronologically, and it is not entirely clear just why chapters come in the order in which we have them" (Ramsay, *Westminster Guide to the Books of the Bible*, 202).

Jeremiah 1:1–10. Jeremiah Is Called to Be a Prophet before He Is Born

What do we know about Jeremiah and his family background? (1:1) The Hebrew name *Jeremiah* may mean "raised up or appointed by Jehovah" (*Easton's*

CHAPTER 1

Jeremiah was foreordained to be a prophet unto the nations—He is called as a mortal to declare the word of the Lord.

1 The words of Jeremiah the son of Hilkiah, of the priests that *were* in Anathoth in the land of Benjamin:

2 To whom the word of the LORD came in the days of Josiah the son of Amon king of Judah, in the thirteenth year of his reign.

3 It came also in the days of Jehoiakim the son of Josiah king of Judah, unto the end of the eleventh year of Zedekiah the son of Josiah king of Judah, unto the carrying away of Jerusalem captive in the fifth month.

Bible Dictionary, "Jeremiah"). Jeremiah "belonged to a priestly family living at a small town named Anathoth . . . some two miles to the [northeast] of Jerusalem. The high priest Abiathar, of the line of Ithamar, had settled there in the days of David (1 Kings 2:26). The prophet's family had apparently been owners of land in that region ever since Abiathar's time" (*John Dummelow's Commentary* [on Introduction to Jeremiah]). ⊕

4 Then the word of the LORD came unto me, saying,

5 Before I formed thee in the belly I knew thee; and before thou camest forth out of the womb I sanctified thee, *and* I ordained thee a prophet unto the nations.

What do we learn about the calling of a prophet from this passage? (1:4–5) "The account of Jeremiah's call is especially interesting because it involves a doctrinal principle not mentioned in the call of any other prophet [thus far in the Old Testament]. . . . This passage points to the fact that Jeremiah was foreordained before his birth to perform the work of a prophet" (Sperry, *Spirit of the Old Testament*, 207). The Prophet Joseph Smith testified: "Every man who has a calling to minister to the inhabitants of the world was ordained to that very purpose in the Grand Council of heaven before this world was" (*Joseph Smith* [manual], 511). ⊕

6 Then said I, Ah, Lord GOD! behold, I cannot speak: for I *am* a child.

7 ¶ But the LORD said unto me, Say not, I *am* a child: for thou shalt go to all that I shall send thee, and whatsoever I command thee thou shalt speak.

How does this phrase show Jeremiah's humility to serve as a prophet? (1:6–7) "Those who are really called of God to the sacred ministry are such as have been brought to a deep acquaintance with themselves, feel their own ignorance, and know their own weakness. They know also the awful responsibility that attaches to the work; and nothing but the authority of God can induce such to undertake it. They whom God never called run, because of worldly honor and [profit]: the others hear the call with fear and trembling, and can go only in the strength of Jehovah" (*Adam Clarke's Commentary* [on Jeremiah 1:6]).

8 Be not afraid of their faces: for I *am* with thee to deliver thee, saith the LORD.

9 Then the LORD put forth his hand, and touched my mouth. And the LORD said unto me, Behold, I have put my words in thy mouth.

Why did the Lord touch Jeremiah's mouth? (1:8–9) "The hand is the instrument of making and doing; the touching of Jeremiah's mouth by the hand of God is consequently an emblematical token that God frames in his mouth what he is to speak" (Keil and Delitzsch, *Commentary* [on Jeremiah 1:9–10]).

"When Jeremiah received his call, the Lord delivered to him his word, both symbolically when he touched his young mouth, and also literally when he spoke with Jeremiah and revealed to him his will. From then on Jeremiah could deliver with authority the phrase 'Thus saith the Lord' with the attendant message" (Seely, "I Am with Thee, to Deliver Thee," 214).

10 See, I have this day set thee over the nations and over the kingdoms, to root out,
and to pull down, and to destroy, and to
throw down, to build, and to plant.

How did these instructions from the Lord apply to Jeremiah? (1:10) "God describes Jeremiah's task by using a mixed metaphor, comparing Jeremiah's work to both farm work and construction work. Jeremiah's mission was two-fold. He would first humble Israel, like a farmer would clear land by rooting out and tearing down the plants already there. Like a builder, he would prepare for a new building by first destroying and throwing down the old one. Once Israel . . . had been prepared by being torn down, then Jeremiah would start to build and to plant" (Muhlestein, *Scripture Study Made Simple*, 417).

Jeremiah 1:11–19. The Lord Promises Destruction of the Wicked in Judah and Protection of Jeremiah

11 ¶ Moreover the word of the LORD came
unto me, saying, Jeremiah, what seest thou?
And I said, I see a rod of an almond tree.

12 Then said the LORD unto me, Thou hast
well seen: for I will hasten my word to perform it.

13 And the word of the LORD came unto me
the second time, saying, What seest thou?
And I said, I see a seething pot; and the face
thereof *is* toward the north.

14 Then the LORD said unto me, Out of the
north an evil shall break forth upon all the
inhabitants of the land.

15 For, lo, I will call all the families of the
kingdoms of the north, saith the LORD; and
they shall come, and they shall set every
one his throne at the entering of the gates
of Jerusalem, and against all the walls thereof
round about, and against all the cities of
Judah.

What did a north-facing seething (or boiling) pot and the burning of incense to other gods represent? (1:13–16) "The vision of a 'seething pot' was shown to Jeremiah, symbolizing the disaster and pain which, like the contents of a [tilted] boiling cauldron, would spill over and run down the kingdoms of the north to overwhelm Judah (see [Keil and Delitzsch, *Commentary*], 8:1:43–44).

"The burning of incense (see Jeremiah 1:16) is a symbol of prayer (see Revelation 5:8; 8:3). Far more is implied in the Lord's accusation than just a ritual of burning incense to false gods. The people were seeking help and guidance from the false gods rather than from the Lord" (*Old Testament Student Manual: 1 Kings–Malachi*, 236).

Jeremiah's Prophetic Call (Jeremiah 1:5–11)

"In 627 B.C. the word of the Lord came to Jeremiah as a youth and called him to be a prophet to the nations, delivering messages of destruction—'to destroy, and to throw down'— and of restoration—'to build, and to plant' (Jeremiah 1:10). The Lord revealed to him, 'Before I formed thee in the belly I knew thee; and before thou camest forth out of the womb I sanctified thee, and I ordained thee a prophet unto the nations' (Jeremiah 1:5). Jeremiah was overwhelmed and replied in language rather like that of Enoch and Moses, 'Ah, Lord God! behold, I cannot speak: for I am a child' (Jeremiah 1:6). The Lord commanded him to 'be not afraid' (Jeremiah 1:7) to go where he was sent and to deliver the message, which was given symbolically to Jeremiah by the touch of the Lord's hand to his mouth (see Jeremiah 1:7–10). The Lord reassured him that 'I have made thee this day a defenced city, and an iron pillar' against the kings, princes, priests, and people, and 'they shall not prevail against thee; for I am with thee' (Jeremiah 1:19; see also 1:11–19). His entire life's mission consisted of delivering the word of the Lord and witnessing the calamities that befell those who would not respond" (Seely and Seely, "Lehi and Jeremiah," 30).

16 And I will utter my judgments against them touching all their wickedness, who have forsaken me, and have burned incense unto other gods, and worshipped the works of their own hands.

17 ¶ Thou therefore gird up thy loins, and arise, and speak unto them all that I command thee: be not dismayed at their faces, lest I confound thee before them.

18 For, behold, I have made thee this day a defenced city, and an iron pillar, and brasen walls against the whole land, against the kings of Judah, against the princes thereof, against the priests thereof, and against the people of the land.

19 And they shall fight against thee; but they shall not prevail against thee; for I *am* with thee, saith the LORD, to deliver thee.

Why did the Lord tell Jeremiah to "gird up thy loins"? (1:17–19) "Returning to the commissioning of vv. 11–12 and repeating the words of v. 8, this final component encourages the prophet to stand firm against his internal opponents, the kings of Judah, its officials, priests, and the entire people (see Ezek. 2:6; 3:8). [Verse 17:] *Gird up [thy] loins*, partakes in the image of a warrior preparing for battle" (*Jewish Study Bible* [2014], 908).

CHAPTER 2

The people of Judah forsook the Lord, the fountain of living waters—They worshipped idols and rejected the prophets.

1 Moreover the word of the LORD came to me, saying,

2 Go and cry in the ears of Jerusalem, saying, Thus saith the LORD; I remember thee, the kindness of thy youth, the love of thine espousals, when thou wentest after me in the wilderness, in a land *that was* not sown.

3 Israel *was* holiness unto the LORD, *and* the firstfruits of his increase: all that devour him shall offend; evil shall come upon them, saith the LORD.

4 Hear ye the word of the LORD, O house of Jacob, and all the families of the house of Israel:

Jeremiah 2:1–4. The Lord Remembers When Israel Was Faithful

How does the Lord describe His relationship with Israel? (2:2–4) The Lord loves His covenant people and they had previously shown faithfulness to Him. Figuratively the Lord is often described as Israel's husband (see Isa. 54:5; Jer. 3:14). "To show the nation how far it had departed from the Lord, Jeremiah recalls their deliverance from Egypt. Like a devoted bridegroom, the Lord says that he still remembers their love as his true bride (cf. Hos 1–3). Proof that Jeremiah is speaking of Israel's love for God is shown by her following him in the desert at the time of their marriage, the period of her faithfulness and devotion to the Lord" (*Expositor's Bible Commentary [Abridged]*, 1158).

Why does Jeremiah address "all the families of the house of Israel"? (2:4) "In the context of the Bible, whenever the Lord had a people that he acknowledged as his own, that acknowledgment came in the form of a covenant relationship. Simply stated, the Lord's people were a covenant people. . . . The covenant and its promised blessings centered in and around the family, for salvation is a family affair. The promise given to Abraham and repeated to Isaac and Jacob was that of posterity as numberless as the stars of heaven or the sands upon the seashore (see D&C 132:30). . . . Among the Lord's ancient covenant people, salvation was a family affair, not an individual matter" (Millet and McConkie, *Our Destiny*, 8, 9). ⊕

Jeremiah 2:5–13. Israel Seeks After Worthless Idols Instead of the God Who Delivered Them from Egypt

Why would the Lord ask such an unusual question? (2:5) "The strange question in v. 5 is intended to awaken the people's consciences. The change in their relationship to God was not his fault but theirs. They had broken the marriage covenant by their infidelity in going after impure lovers. A play on words reveals how worshipers become like the objects they worship" (*Expositor's Bible Commentary [Abridged]*, 1159).

In what ways does remembering the Lord and His blessings help us remain close to Him? (2:6–7) Jehovah challenged Israel to remember that He brought their ancestors out of Egypt, through the dreaded wilderness, and into the promised land, where they spiritually turned away from Him. President Spencer W. Kimball suggested one way to help us remember the Lord's influence in our lives: "Those who keep a book of remembrance are more likely to keep the Lord in remembrance in their daily lives. Journals are a way of counting our blessings and of leaving an inventory of these blessings for our posterity" (*Teachings of Spencer W. Kimball*, 349). How have you found ways to recognize and remember the Lord's hand in your life and the life of your family? ⊕

In what context does the Lord plead with His children? (2:8–9) The word *plead* in this verse has also been translated as "bring charges against" (NKJV and NIV). These are "*charges* of apostasy and idolatry" (*NKJV Study Bible* [2007], 1150).

"In chapters 2 and 3 the Lord revealed to Jeremiah the covenantal lawsuit he was bringing against his people on account of their disobedience. The legal imagery of the Lord charging his people—a covenantal lawsuit—is a common feature in biblical prophecy. . . .

"The stipulations of the Mosaic covenant—the Law—were from the beginning inseparably connected with specific promises of blessings and curses, depending on obedience to the commandments [see, for example, 2 Ne. 1:20]" (Seely, "I Am with Thee, to Deliver Thee," 216).

5 ¶ Thus saith the LORD, What iniquity have your fathers found in me, that they are gone far from me, and have walked after vanity, and are become vain?

6 Neither said they, Where *is* the LORD that brought us up out of the land of Egypt, that led us through the wilderness, through a land of deserts and of pits, through a land of drought, and of the shadow of death, through a land that no man passed through, and where no man dwelt?

7 And I brought you into a plentiful country, to eat the fruit thereof and the goodness thereof; but when ye entered, ye defiled my land, and made mine heritage an abomination.

8 The priests said not, Where *is* the LORD? and they that handle the law knew me not: the pastors also transgressed against me, and the prophets prophesied by Baal, and walked after *things that* do not profit.

9 ¶ Wherefore I will yet plead with you, saith the LORD, and with your children's children will I plead.

10 For pass over the isles of Chittim, and see; and send unto Kedar, and consider diligently, and see if there be such a thing.

11 Hath a nation changed *their* gods, which *are* yet no gods? but my people have changed their glory for *that which* doth not profit.

12 Be astonished, O ye heavens, at this, and be horribly afraid, be ye very desolate, saith the LORD.

13 For my people have committed two evils; they have forsaken me the fountain of living waters, *and* hewed them out cisterns, broken cisterns, that can hold no water.

14 ¶ *Is* Israel a servant? *is* he a homeborn *slave?* why is he spoiled?

15 The young lions roared upon him, *and* yelled, and they made his land waste: his cities are burned without inhabitant.

16 Also the children of Noph and Tahapanes have broken the crown of thy head.

17 Hast thou not procured this unto thyself, in that thou hast forsaken the LORD thy God, when he led thee by the way?

18 And now what hast thou to do in the way of Egypt, to drink the waters of Sihor? or what hast thou to do in the way of Assyria, to drink the waters of the river?

Jeremiah 2:14–22. Israel's Consequences for Rejecting Their God

Why did Jeremiah compare Israel to slaves who were preyed upon by young lions? (2:14–15) "Now that God had established what Judah had done wrong, He moved on to describing the consequences. He started by asking why Israel would be treated like the spoils of war when they are not servants or slaves of any kind. Yet they were destroyed completely, as if they were prey to be taken by young lions. The lions may represent Assyria and Babylon" (Muhlestein, *Scripture Study Made Simple*, 421).

Why did Judah turn to foreign countries for assistance? (2:18–22) Jeremiah "ridiculed Judah's turning to decadent Egypt or to Assyria for help. Had the Israelites forgotten the Lord's defense of them during all the centuries past? Had they forgotten his planting them in the promised land, expecting them to bear fruit? Could they ever wash sin away with harsh cleansers, turn from idolatry and from indulging

Broken Cisterns, That Can Hold No Water (Jeremiah 2:13)

What was a cistern? "The rendering of a Hebrew word *Bor*, which means a receptacle for water conveyed to it; distinguished from *Beer*, which denotes a place where water rises on the spot (Jeremiah 2:13; Proverbs 5:15; Isaiah 36:16), a fountain. Cisterns are frequently mentioned in Scripture. The scarcity of springs in Palestine made it necessary to collect rain-water in reservoirs and cisterns (Numbers 21:22)" (*Easton's Bible Dictionary*, "Cistern").

What was the Lord saying to Israel? "It was bad enough for the Israelites to forsake Jehovah ('the fountain of living waters'), but they have compounded the sin by worshipping idols ('hewed them out cisterns, broken cisterns, that can hold no water')" (Ludlow, *Companion to Your Study of the Old Testament,* 315).

What "broken cisterns" today prevent one from enjoying the Lord's living water? Elder Joseph B. Wirthlin explained: "The Lord Jesus Christ is the only source of living water. It will quench the thirst of those suffering from the drought of divine truth that so afflicts the world. The words of the Lord to ancient Israel spoken by the prophet Jeremiah describe the condition of many of God's children in our own day: 'My people . . . have forsaken me the fountain of living waters, and hewed them out . . . broken cisterns, that can hold no water' (Jer. 2:13). Too many of our Heavenly Father's children spend their precious lives carving out broken cisterns of worldly gain that cannot hold the living water that satisfies fully their natural thirst for everlasting truth" ("Living Water to Quench Spiritual Thirst," 19).

their sensual urges, cease from enjoying carnal things? Evidently not" (Rasmussen, *Latter-day Saint Commentary on the Old Testament*, 543).

What is Israel's "backsliding"? (2:19) "*Backsliding* is used 13 times in Jeremiah and 3 times in Hosea as a term for Israel's turning away from God. [The Revised Standard Version] uses 'faithless' or 'faithlessness' in 10 of these passages, and 'apostasy' in 2" (Bridges and Weigle, *King James Bible Word Book*, 34). Verse 19 teaches the truth that "often, very often, we are punished as much by our sins as we are for them" (Packer, "Why Stay Morally Clean," 112).

"The phrase 'my fear is not in thee' (v. 19) refers to the fear of God. *Fear* in the Hebrew denotes a sense of reverent awe and profound respect" (*Old Testament Student Manual: 1 Kings–Malachi*, 236).

19 Thine own wickedness shall correct thee, and thy backslidings shall reprove thee: know therefore and see that *it is* an evil *thing* and bitter, that thou hast forsaken the LORD thy God, and that my fear *is* not in thee, saith the Lord GOD of hosts.

20 ¶ For of old time I have broken thy yoke, *and* burst thy bands; and thou saidst, I will not transgress; when upon every high hill and under every green tree thou wanderest, playing the harlot.

21 Yet I had planted thee a noble vine, wholly a right seed: how then art thou turned into the degenerate plant of a strange vine unto me?

22 For though thou wash thee with nitre, and take thee much soap, *yet* thine iniquity is marked before me, saith the Lord GOD.

Summary of Jeremiah 2:23–37

Along with idolatry, Israel threw off self-control and was guilty of immorality. They had become spiritually polluted. Israel killed her own prophets. They had forgotten the Lord and the serious sin of oppression of the innocent poor added to their decline.

CHAPTER 3

Israel and Judah defiled and polluted the land through wickedness—In the last days, the Lord will gather the people of Israel, one from a city and two from a family, and bring them to Zion.

1 They say, If a man put away his wife, and she go from him, and become another man's, shall he return unto her again? shall not that land be greatly polluted? but thou hast played the harlot with many lovers; yet return again to me, saith the LORD.

Jeremiah 3:1–11. The Kingdom of Judah Is as a Faithless Wife, More Treacherous Than Was the Kingdom of Israel

Why is the nation of Israel compared to a divorced woman returning to her original husband? (3:1) "Deuteronomy 24:1–4 forbids a man to remarry his divorced wife if she has remarried and been divorced in the meantime. The implication is that the woman has been defiled by the second marriage. After forsaking God, Israel had taken many other *lovers*—that is, the nation worshiped many other gods. Yet the Lord in His mercy still extended His loving hand to His unfaithful bride. The word *return* implies repentance" (*NKJV Study Bible* [2007], 1152).

2 Lift up thine eyes unto the high places, and see where thou hast not been lien with. In the ways hast thou sat for them, as the Arabian in the wilderness; and thou hast polluted the land with thy whoredoms and with thy wickedness.

3 Therefore the showers have been withholden, and there hath been no latter rain; and thou hadst a whore's forehead, thou refusedst to be ashamed.

4 Wilt thou not from this time cry unto me, My father, thou *art* the guide of my youth?

5 Will he reserve *his anger* for ever? will he keep *it* to the end? Behold, thou hast spoken and done evil things as thou couldest.

6 ¶ The LORD said also unto me in the days of Josiah the king, Hast thou seen *that* which backsliding Israel hath done? she is gone up upon every high mountain and under every green tree, and there hath played the harlot.

7 And I said after she had done all these *things,* Turn thou unto me. But she returned not. And her treacherous sister Judah saw *it.*

8 And I saw, when for all the causes whereby backsliding Israel committed adultery I had put her away, and given her a bill of divorce; yet her treacherous sister Judah feared not, but went and played the harlot also.

9 And it came to pass through the lightness of her whoredom, that she defiled the land, and committed adultery with stones and with stocks.

10 And yet for all this her treacherous sister Judah hath not turned unto me with her whole heart, but feignedly, saith the LORD.

11 And the LORD said unto me, The backsliding Israel hath justified herself more than treacherous Judah.

What is the claim against Israel of this verse? (3:2) "Upon these barren heights Israel committed physical and spiritual adultery. The word *lain* [KJV, *lien*] has strong sexual connotations. Like Arabs who were known for ambushing caravans, Israel lustily sought other gods" (*Nelson Study Bible* [1997], 1227).

Why did the Lord consider Judah to be more treacherous than Israel? (3:6–11) "Jeremiah compared Israel and Judah to two sisters who had been unfaithful to the Lord as their husband.... In a sense, Judah was more guilty than the apostate northern kingdom. Judah had seen how the Lord had given Israel *a bill of divorce* (v. 8) by sending her into exile (722 B.C.), yet Judah persisted in her sinful ways. She refused to learn the obvious lesson from Israel's tragic experience.... Judah had not turned to the Lord *with her whole heart* (v. 10) (*Zondervan KJV Commentary*, 976).

What are stones and stocks? (3:9) "Committing adultery with stone and wood [tree (NKJV) or stock (KJV)] refers to the 'spiritual adultery' of following after the Asherim (the sacred trees, i.e., wood) and the Baals (stone)" (Walton, et al., *IVP Bible Background Commentary*, 645).

"When 'backsliding Israel committed adultery I had put her away, and given her a bill of divorce; yet her treacherous sister Judah feared not, but went and played the harlot also.'

"Judah's grievous sin is that she not only committed whoredoms (by marrying with unworthy people) but she 'committed adultery with stones and with stocks' (by worshipping idols of stone and wood)" (Ludlow, *Companion to Your Study of the Old Testament*, 316).

Jeremiah 3:12–19. In the Latter Days the Lord Will Gather Israel to Zion

What is the Lord teaching regarding how and why we must repent? (3:12–13) Repentance "is not a harsh principle. . . . It is kind and merciful. The Hebrew root of the word means, simply, 'to turn' [Healey, "Repentance," in *Anchor Bible Dictionary*, 5:671] or to *re*turn, to God. Jehovah pled with the children of Israel: 'Return . . . and I will not cause mine anger to fall upon you: for I am merciful . . . and I will not keep anger for ever. Only acknowledge thine iniquity, that thou hast transgressed against the Lord thy God' [Jer. 3:12–13].

"When we acknowledge our sins, confess them and forsake them, and turn to God, He will forgive us" (Hinckley, "Repentance, a Blessing of Membership," 49).

How can this prophecy apply to the latter days? (3:14–15) President Gordon B. Hinckley suggested missionary labors: "Long ago Jeremiah said that the Lord would gather His people one of a city and two of a family and bring them to Zion and feed them with pastors after His own heart (see Jer. 3:14–15). In terms of the individual missionary, the harvest is not great in most instances, but in the aggregate it becomes tremendous. The work demands courage, it demands effort, it demands dedication, it demands the humility to get on one's knees and ask the Lord for help and direction" ("Of Missions, Temples, and Stewardship," 51).

12 ¶ Go and proclaim these words toward the north, and say, Return, thou backsliding Israel, saith the LORD; *and* I will not cause mine anger to fall upon you: for I *am* merciful, saith the LORD, *and* I will not keep *anger* for ever.

13 Only acknowledge thine iniquity, that thou hast transgressed against the LORD thy God, and hast scattered thy ways to the strangers under every green tree, and ye have not obeyed my voice, saith the LORD.

14 Turn, O backsliding children, saith the LORD; for I am married unto you: and I will take you one of a city, and two of a family, and I will bring you to Zion:

15 And I will give you pastors according to mine heart, which shall feed you with knowledge and understanding.

16 And it shall come to pass, when ye be multiplied and increased in the land, in those days, saith the LORD, they shall say no more, The ark of the covenant of the LORD: neither shall it come to mind: neither shall they remember it; neither shall they visit *it;* neither shall *that* be done any more.

17 At that time they shall call Jerusalem the throne of the LORD; and all the nations shall be gathered unto it, to the name of the

How Did Jeremiah Describe Israel and Judah's Future? (Jeremiah 3:14–19)

"In the midst of condemning Judah for their apostasy, Jeremiah turned to the future when Israel will again become a faithful wife and be reclaimed. The Lord reminded Israel that He is merciful and that all they need do to be reclaimed is to turn back to Him. The Lord's promises include the following:

- Missionary work and gathering to Zion (see v. 14).
- Knowledge and understanding taught by faithful pastors (church leaders) (see v. 15).
- The fulfillment of the old covenant and the establishment of a new covenant (see v. 16).
- The restoration of Jerusalem to righteousness (see v. 17).
- The gathering of Israel, including the return of the lost tribes from the north and the reuniting of the children of Judah in the lands of their inheritance (see vv. 18–19 ; see also Isaiah 11:16; 35:8–10; 51:9–11; D&C 133:26–35)" (*Old Testament Student Manual: 1 Kings–Malachi*, 237).

Lord, to Jerusalem: neither shall they walk any more after the imagination of their evil heart.

18 In those days the house of Judah shall walk with the house of Israel, and they shall come together out of the land of the north to the land that I have given for an inheritance unto your fathers.

19 But I said, How shall I put thee among the children, and give thee a pleasant land, a goodly heritage of the hosts of nations? and I said, Thou shalt call me, My father; and shalt not turn away from me.

CHAPTERS 4–6

Israel and Judah are called to repentance—Jeremiah laments for the miseries of Judah.

Judgments will be poured out upon the people of Judah because of their sins—Their iniquities cause blessings to be withheld from them.

Jerusalem will be destroyed because of her iniquity—She will be overrun by a great and cruel nation.

Summary of Jeremiah 3:20–25

The Lord once again urges the house of Israel to repent and return to Him that He might heal them. A repentant Israel recognizes their sin and its consequences. They declare that only "in the Lord God is the salvation of Israel" (Jeremiah 3:23).

Summary of Jeremiah 4–6

Israel and Judah are once more called to repent. Jeremiah uses figurative language to describe the calamity that Judah will suffer if they refuse to change their ways. In chapter 5 we learn that Jerusalem, much like Sodom and Gomorrah, is past the point where righteous citizens can be found (Jeremiah 5:1). Jeremiah lists their gross sins, illustrating how they are, as Nephi said, "wicked, yea, nearly unto ripeness" (1 Nephi 17:43). There are so-called prophets and priests, but they are corrupt, teaching people what they want to hear. Jerusalem rejects Jeremiah; her people "cannot hearken" and "have no delight" in his words (Jeremiah 6:10). Jeremiah prophesies that a wicked nation will come from the north and destroy them (see Jeremiah 6:22–23).

CHAPTER 7

If the people of Judah repent, they will be preserved—The temple has become a den of robbers—The Lord rejects that generation of the people of Judah for their idolatries—They offer their children as sacrifices.

Jeremiah 7:1–15. Jeremiah Warns Judah That if They Do Not Repent, the Temple Will Not Save Them

Why did Jehovah have Jeremiah deliver a message of repentance while standing at the temple gate? (7:2–4) As Jeremiah 7 transitions from King Josiah to King Jehoiakim, "there were nationalist groups in Judah who believed that the Temple in Jerusalem rendered them invincible to the Babylonians. In response to these people, Jeremiah delivered a sermon at the Temple in which he warned the people that because of their hypocrisy Jehovah would not deliver them and they would be destroyed (Jer 7; 26). Jehoiakim put Jeremiah on trial because of this message. Many in the royal court attempted to have Jeremiah put to death for speaking these words, but others defended him" (Holzapfel, et al., *Jehovah and the World of the Old Testament*, 323). Jeremiah counters the false security placed in the temple with his warning: "Trust ye not in lying words" (Jeremiah 7:4). ⊕

1 The word that came to Jeremiah from the LORD, saying,

2 Stand in the gate of the LORD's house, and proclaim there this word, and say, Hear the word of the LORD, all *ye of* Judah, that enter in at these gates to worship the LORD.

3 Thus saith the LORD of hosts, the God of Israel, Amend your ways and your doings, and I will cause you to dwell in this place.

4 Trust ye not in lying words, saying, The temple of the LORD, The temple of the LORD, The temple of the LORD, *are* these.

What must Judah change if they wish to stay in the promised land? (7:5–7) Jeremiah tells the people to "[thoroughly] amend your ways and your doings" (v. 5). He cites commandments related to what they had previously received (see Exodus 22:21–24). One writer explained that "Judah must abandon idolatry, but also (1) abandon oppression, (2) stop taking advantage of the poor ['the fatherless, and the widow'], and (3) maintain an honest justice system. Worship of God and morality are the twin pillars on which society must rest" (Richards, *Bible Reader's Companion*, 453). See commentary in this volume for Exodus 22:21–24. ⊕

5 For if ye throughly amend your ways and your doings; if ye throughly execute judgment between a man and his neighbour;

6 *If* ye oppress not the stranger, the fatherless, and the widow, and shed not innocent blood in this place, neither walk after other gods to your hurt:

7 Then will I cause you to dwell in this place, in the land that I gave to your fathers, for ever and ever.

8 ¶ Behold, ye trust in lying words, that cannot profit.

9 Will ye steal, murder, and commit adultery, and swear falsely, and burn incense unto Baal, and walk after other gods whom ye know not;

Why did the Lord declare that His house had become "a den of robbers"? (7:9–11) Jehovah accused Judah: "Ye appear in my temple to sacrifice and worship, thinking thus to appease my wrath and turn aside all punishment, that so ye may go on doing all these (in Jeremiah 7:9 enumerated) abominations. By

10 And come and stand before me in this house, which is called by my name, and say, We are delivered to do all these abominations?

11 Is this house, which is called by my name, become a den of robbers in your eyes? Behold, even I have seen *it,* saith the LORD.

12 But go ye now unto my place which *was* in Shiloh, where I set my name at the first, and see what I did to it for the wickedness of my people Israel.

13 And now, because ye have done all these works, saith the LORD, and I spake unto you, rising up early and speaking, but ye heard not; and I called you, but ye answered not;

14 Therefore will I do unto *this* house, which is called by my name, wherein ye trust, and unto the place which I gave to you and to your fathers, as I have done to Shiloh.

15 And I will cast you out of my sight, as I have cast out all your brethren, *even* the whole seed of Ephraim.

frequenting the temple, they thought to procure an indulgence for their wicked ongoings. . . .

"To expose the senselessness of such an idea, God asks if they take the temple for a den of robbers?" (Keil and Delitzsch, *Commentary* [on Jeremiah 7:10, 11]).

What happened in Shiloh, and what lesson should Judah have learned? (7:12–15) "The people did not think that God would destroy Jerusalem . . . , but they should have called to mind the fate of *Shiloh* (v. 12). The tabernacle had been set up in Shiloh after the conquest of Canaan (see Josh. 18:1). . . . The tabernacle itself was not destroyed, since it was still at Gibeon during David's reign (see 1 Chron. 21:29). The city was likely destroyed sometime after the events described in 1 Samuel 4. The fate of Shiloh should have caused the inhabitants of Jerusalem to realize that the Lord was serious when He threatened, *I will cast you out of my sight* (v. 15)" (*Zondervan KJV Commentary*, 981).

Who is the "whole seed of Ephraim"? (7:15) This phrase refers to Ephraim, "the tribe whose ancestor was the son of Joseph and the most important within the northern tribal group, here as well as elsewhere symbolizing the entirety of the Northern Kingdom, which had been defeated and deported by the Assyrians more than a century earlier" (*New Oxford Annotated Bible*, 1072).

Jeremiah 7:16–34. Judah Is Condemned for Idolatry, Including Offering Their Children as Sacrifices

16 Therefore pray not thou for this people, neither lift up cry nor prayer for them, neither make intercession to me: for I will not hear thee.

17 ¶ Seest thou not what they do in the cities of Judah and in the streets of Jerusalem?

18 The children gather wood, and the fathers kindle the fire, and the women knead *their* dough, to make cakes to the queen of heaven, and to pour out drink offerings unto other gods, that they may provoke me to anger.

Why would God command Jeremiah not to pray for Judah? (7:16–18) "The Lord's commandment that Jeremiah not pray for his people should be taken in its context. As long as they continued in their sinful state and would not repent, the Lord would not hearken to his requests (compare D&C 101:6–7). Their worship of the 'queen of heaven' (a pagan fertility goddess), was undoubtedly borrowed from the surrounding nations. . . . Jeremiah's people later returned to this practice while in Egypt (see Jeremiah 44:17)" (Nyman, *Words of Jeremiah*, 37).

Jeremiah's description of his people is similar to Mormon's description of the people in his day (see Mormon 3:11–12, 14–16). Like Mormon, Jeremiah was unable to pray in faith for such a wicked people.

What was the Lord's intended commandment behind burnt offerings and sacrifices? (7:22–23) "An inner-oriented type of worship seems to have been God's original intention, before its spirit became entangled in the letter of ritual complexity. . . . In other words, inner obedience was the original end, with outer ordinances the superadded means. The shell meant nothing without the core. Without inner righteousness and real intent, Jeremiah suggests, they might as well eat their sacrificial offerings themselves. . . . This sense is clearer in translations other than the King James Version. The New International Version, for example, translates Jeremiah 7:21 as follows: 'Go ahead, add your burnt offerings to your other sacrifices and eat the meat yourselves!'" (Halverson, "Rejection and Rehabilitation of Worship in the Old Testament," 196, 197, 201fn16).

What does the ear and a hardened neck represent? (7:26) The ear is "a figure for spiritual understanding (Moses 6:27)" (McConkie, *Gospel Symbolism*, 258). When one is worthy and receptive to the Lord, this understanding may come in the form of personal revelation (see D&C 113:10).

"In scripture the neck is most often associated with attitude or subjection. . . . When someone is described as being 'stiff-necked,' the implication is that the person is prideful, obstinate, or disobedient. On a number of occasions this term is applied to the covenant people when they resist God's commands" (Gaskill, *Lost Language of Symbolism*, 52). See commentary in this volume for Jeremiah 17:23.

19 Do they provoke me to anger? saith the LORD: *do they* not *provoke* themselves to the confusion of their own faces?

20 Therefore thus saith the Lord GOD; Behold, mine anger and my fury shall be poured out upon this place, upon man, and upon beast, and upon the trees of the field, and upon the fruit of the ground; and it shall burn, and shall not be quenched.

21 ¶ Thus saith the LORD of hosts, the God of Israel; Put your burnt offerings unto your sacrifices, and eat flesh.

22 For I spake not unto your fathers, nor commanded them in the day that I brought them out of the land of Egypt, concerning burnt offerings or sacrifices:

23 But this thing commanded I them, saying, Obey my voice, and I will be your God, and ye shall be my people: and walk ye in all the ways that I have commanded you, that it may be well unto you.

24 But they hearkened not, nor inclined their ear, but walked in the counsels *and* in the imagination of their evil heart, and went backward, and not forward.

25 Since the day that your fathers came forth out of the land of Egypt unto this day I have even sent unto you all my servants the prophets, daily rising up early and sending *them:*

26 Yet they hearkened not unto me, nor inclined their ear, but hardened their neck: they did worse than their fathers.

27 Therefore thou shalt speak all these words unto them; but they will not hearken to thee: thou shalt also call unto them; but they will not answer thee.

28 But thou shalt say unto them, This *is* a nation that obeyeth not the voice of the LORD their God, nor receiveth correction: truth is perished, and is cut off from their mouth.

29 ¶ Cut off thine hair, *O Jerusalem,* and cast *it* away, and take up a lamentation on high places; for the LORD hath rejected and forsaken the generation of his wrath.

Why did Jeremiah instruct Jerusalem to "cut off [their] hair" and "take up a lamentation"? (7:29) "The call to the people to lament is because [Jehovah] has rejected that generation. . . . No person is named, but the verbs are feminine in Hebrew and this points to Jerusalem or the nation personified. The symbol of deep mourning was the cutting off of the hair. . . . Some have seen in this a reference to the Nazarite vow (Nu. 6:7). Jerusalem has broken her vows, and so, like a faithless Nazarite, might as well cut off the hair, which was his symbol and badge" (Guthrie and Motyer, *New Bible Commentary: Revised*, 633–34).

30 For the children of Judah have done evil
in my sight, saith the LORD: they have set
their abominations in the house which is
called by my name, to pollute it.
31 And they have built the high places of
Tophet, which *is* in the valley of the son of
Hinnom, to burn their sons and their daughters in the fire; which I commanded *them*
not, neither came it into my heart.
32 ¶ Therefore, behold, the days come, saith
the LORD, that it shall no more be called
Tophet, nor the valley of the son of Hinnom,
but the valley of slaughter: for they shall bury
in Tophet, till there be no place.

What was the evil that Judah committed? (7:30–32) "The people had brazenly introduced their idols in the temple, as though to defy God to his face. Furthermore, they had set up high places (altars) in Topheth. . . . Here the idolatrous nation burned their children to appease the fire god, Molech. This passage reveals that the children were not merely made to pass through an ordeal by fire; they were actually burned up. . . . Since they so flagrantly disobeyed God, they themselves would be slaughtered where their children were slaughtered. The slaughter of the coming doom of the city would be so great that Topheth would have to be used for burial, thus changing the name of the place to The Valley of the Slaughter" (*Expositor's Bible Commentary [Abridged]*, 1175). ⊕

33 And the carcases of this people shall be
meat for the fowls of the heaven, and for the
beasts of the earth; and none shall fray *them*
away.
34 Then will I cause to cease from the cities
of Judah, and from the streets of Jerusalem,
the voice of mirth, and the voice of gladness,
the voice of the bridegroom, and the voice of
the bride: for the land shall be desolate.

How serious will be the consequences for Judah's wicked people? (7:33–34) "Apparently human beings couldn't commit much worse sins than those indicated by [Jeremiah]. . . .

"Jeremiah, of course, preached in the hopes that his people would repent. But when they didn't, it became necessary to pronounce a penalty. So Jeremiah spoke of a nation that the Lord would bring from far. It would eat up Judah's harvest, her sons and daughters, flocks and herds, vines and fig-trees, and would batter her fortified cities. Taken captive, her people should serve strangers in a land not hers. They should run the gamut of nearly every form of human suffering for their sins" (Sperry, *Spirit of the Old Testament*, 210–11).

Jeremiah 8:1–5. Jeremiah Prophesies in Detail about the Ruthless Destruction of Jerusalem

Why were the bones of Jerusalem's inhabitants dishonored by scattering them on the ground? (8:1) "In order to pour the utmost contempt upon the land, the victorious enemies dragged out of their graves, caves, and sepulchers, the bones of kings, princes, prophets, priests, and the principal inhabitants, and exposed them in the open air; so that they became, in the order of God's judgments, a reproach to them in the vain confidence they had in the sun, moon, and the host of heaven—all the planets and stars, whose worship they had set up in opposition to that of Jehovah. This custom of raising the bodies of the dead, and scattering their bones about, seems to have been general. It was the highest expression of hatred and contempt" (*Adam Clarke's Commentary* [on Jeremiah 8:1]).

What can we do to overcome "perpetual backsliding" in our lives? (8:4–5) Brother William H. Baker stated: "The Lord expects each step upward in knowledge to be followed by a step upward in performance. . . .

"Improvement in the doing arena takes great dedication. New habits can be hard to establish, and old habits can be hard to break. As my son Steve concluded his mission in England, my wife and a daughter and I joined him to travel and to visit some of the people he had baptized or helped to activate. One faithful sister talked of her growth in the Church since her baptism. She spoke of the dedicated effort required to stay on the path and then said, 'It is so easy to backslide.'

"It is indeed easy to backslide, but we can avoid it or overcome it with enough determination" ("Knowing, Doing, and Being").

CHAPTER 8

Calamities will befall the inhabitants of Jerusalem—For them the harvest is past, the summer is ended, and they are not saved.

1 At that time, saith the LORD, they shall bring out the bones of the kings of Judah, and the bones of his princes, and the bones of the priests, and the bones of the prophets, and the bones of the inhabitants of Jerusalem, out of their graves:

2 And they shall spread them before the sun, and the moon, and all the host of heaven, whom they have loved, and whom they have served, and after whom they have walked, and whom they have sought, and whom they have worshipped: they shall not be gathered, nor be buried; they shall be for dung upon the face of the earth.

3 And death shall be chosen rather than life by all the residue of them that remain of this evil family, which remain in all the places whither I have driven them, saith the LORD of hosts.

4 ¶ Moreover thou shalt say unto them, Thus saith the LORD; Shall they fall, and not arise? shall he turn away, and not return?

5 Why *then* is this people of Jerusalem slidden back by a perpetual backsliding? they hold fast deceit, they refuse to return.

Summary of Jeremiah 8:6–17

Israel continues to reject God. The people believe in the false teachings, vain priests, and false prophets. Jeremiah censures the people for their pride and interpreting the scriptures falsely. Jeremiah sorrows that due to their wickedness, God will destroy them with "serpents" (v. 17; a metaphor for an enemy army).

18 ¶ *When* I would comfort myself against sorrow, my heart *is* faint in me.

19 Behold the voice of the cry of the daughter of my people because of them that dwell in a far country: *Is* not the LORD in Zion? *is* not her king in her? Why have they provoked me to anger with their graven images, *and* with strange vanities?

20 The harvest is past, the summer is ended, and we are not saved.

Jeremiah 8:18–22. Jeremiah Laments with Judah That the Time to Repent Has Passed and There Is No Balm in Gilead

What are the consequences of delaying or refusing to repent? (8:20) Referring to Jeremiah's lament that "the harvest is past, . . . and we are not saved" [Jer. 8:20], Elder Quentin L. Cook pointed out: "When evil choices become the dominant characteristic of a culture or nation, there are serious consequences both in this life and the life to come. People can become enslaved or put themselves in bondage not only to harmful, addictive substances but also to harmful, addictive philosophies that detract from righteous living" ("Lamentations of Jeremiah," 88).

The Pen of the Scribes Is in Vain (Jeremiah 8:8)

Understanding that the word *pen* refers to the work of the scribes in recording God's law can help us understand Jeremiah's lament that "the pen of the scribes is in vain" (Jeremiah 8:8). "In enumerating the causes which will bring his judgments upon the people of Judah, the Lord says men will use their own wisdom to alter and interpret the law of the Lord. For the phrase 'the pen of the scribes is in vain,' a KJV marginal note gives an alternate reading: 'the false pen of the scribes worketh for falsehood.' The [Revised Standard Version] reads, 'But, behold, the false pen of the scribes has made it into a lie.' The new Catholic edition (1957) translates the phrase as follows: 'Indeed the lying pen of the scribes hath wrought falsehood.' These last two versions both support the KJV marginal reading, and they support the same concept taught in the JST of Luke 11:53: 'Woe unto you lawyers! For ye have taken away the key of knowledge, the *fullness of the scriptures*' (italics added). The Savior's declaration here strongly implies that by the time of his ministry there had been tampering with the text of the scriptures—of which Jeremiah 8:8 is a good example. These passages also support the eighth Article of Faith of The Church of Jesus Christ of Latter-day Saints: 'We believe the Bible to be the word of God as far as it is translated correctly.' In a similar vein, the Prophet Joseph Smith declared: 'I believe the Bible as it read when it came from the pen of the original writers. Ignorant translators, careless transcribers, or designing and *corrupt priests have committed many errors*' ([*Joseph Smith* (manual), 207; emphasis added]). This was apparently under way in Jeremiah's day or before" (Nyman, *Words of Jeremiah*, 38; see also 1 Nephi 13:24–29).

What did Jeremiah mean by the expressions "am I hurt" and "I am black"? (8:21) When Jeremiah says "am I hurt; I am black" he is likely "expressing his sympathy with the people in their affliction. . . . [These phrases are similar to saying] *I am broken*; in heart and spirit: *I am black*; with grief and sorrow. . . .

"*Astonishment hath taken hold on me*; at the miseries that were come upon his people; and there was no remedy for them" (*John Gill's Exposition of the Whole Bible* [commentary on Introduction to Jeremiah 8:21]; emphasis added).

What is the symbolism regarding the "balm in Gilead"? (8:22) "The Bible records that in ancient times there came from Gilead, beyond the Jordan, a substance used to heal and soothe. It came, perhaps, from a tree or shrub, and was a major commodity of trade in the ancient world. It was known as the Balm of Gilead. That name became symbolic for the power to soothe and heal" (Packer, "Balm of Gilead," 59). "Gilead was famous for its healing ointment (see Genesis 37:25). Nevertheless, no healing ointment, or medication, was available for rebellious Israel. The balm of salvation could be administered only through Israel's Savior, Jehovah, whom they had rejected" (*Old Testament Student Manual: 1 Kings–Malachi*, 238). ⊕

Jeremiah 9:1–8. Jeremiah Recounts the Sins of the People

How can a person become valiant? (9:3) "To be valiant, we need to focus on the power of Jesus Christ and His atoning sacrifice to overcome death and, through our repentance, to cleanse us from sin, and we need to follow the doctrine of Christ [see 2 Nephi 31:17–21]. We also need the light and knowledge of the Savior's life and teachings to guide us on the covenant pathway, including the sacred ordinances of the temple. We must be steadfast in Christ, feast upon His word, and endure to the end [see 2 Nephi 31:20–21]" (Cook, "Valiant in the Testimony of Jesus," 43).

21 For the hurt of the daughter of my people am I hurt; I am black; astonishment hath taken hold on me.

22 *Is there* no balm in Gilead; *is there* no physician there? why then is not the health of the daughter of my people recovered?

CHAPTER 9

Jeremiah sorrows greatly because of the sins of the people—They will be scattered among the nations and punished.

1 Oh that my head were waters, and mine eyes a fountain of tears, that I might weep day and night for the slain of the daughter of my people!

2 Oh that I had in the wilderness a lodging place of wayfaring men; that I might leave my people, and go from them! for they *be* all adulterers, an assembly of treacherous men.

3 And they bend their tongues *like* their bow *for* lies: but they are not valiant for the truth upon the earth; for they proceed from evil to evil, and they know not me, saith the LORD.

4 Take ye heed every one of his neighbour, and trust ye not in any brother: for every brother will utterly supplant, and every neighbour will walk with slanders.

5 And they will deceive every one his neighbour, and will not speak the truth: they have
taught their tongue to speak lies, *and* weary
themselves to commit iniquity.

6 Thine habitation *is* in the midst of deceit;
through deceit they refuse to know me, saith
the Lord.

7 Therefore thus saith the Lord of hosts,
Behold, I will melt them, and try them; for
how shall I do for the daughter of my people?

8 Their tongue *is as* an arrow shot out; it
speaketh deceit: *one* speaketh peaceably to his
neighbour with his mouth, but in heart he
layeth his wait.

Summary of Jeremiah 9:9–22

God's covenant people refuse to know Him. Instead, they turn to idols and oppress the weak. Jeremiah painfully describes how the judgments of God will overtake the cities of Judah. They will become desolate and mourn.

Jeremiah Condemns the Sins of Judah and Declares: "They Be All Adulterers!" (Jeremiah 9:2)

"What, exactly, led to the fiery destruction of Jerusalem? Jeremiah tells us that its inhabitants had become so sensual and materialistic that they had lost all sense of divine values: 'They are wise to do evil, but to do good they have no knowledge' (Jer. 4:22).

"'They be all adulterers,' Jeremiah said about the mores of that generation (Jer. 9:2). They 'assembled themselves by troops in the harlots' houses.' Like well-fed stallions, 'every one neighed after his neighbour's wife' (Jer. 5:7–8). . . .

"The people's preoccupation with sensuality was matched by their covetousness and dishonesty. Jeremiah lamented, 'From the least of them even unto the greatest of them every one is given to covetousness; and from the prophet even unto the priest every one dealeth falsely' (Jer. 6:13; Jeremiah referred to false prophets simply as prophets, as the context makes clear). He challenged anyone who doubted his words to search the streets and plazas of Jerusalem to see 'if there be any that executeth judgment, that seeketh the truth' (Jer. 5:1).

"In Jerusalem, possessing things became all-important, and any means to possessing them seemed justified. Dishonesty replaced integrity, trust disappeared, and neighbors became treacherous. Jeremiah observed:

"'They bend their tongues like their bow for lies: but they are not valiant for the truth. . . .'

"Therefore he counseled, 'Take ye heed every one of his neighbour, and trust ye not in any brother: for every brother will utterly supplant, and every neighbour will walk with slanders' (Jer. 9:2–4).

"'One speaketh peaceably to his neighbour with his mouth, but in heart he layeth his wait' (Jer. 9:8).

"As covetous, dishonest, and adulterous as that generation was, it carefully maintained its self-respect by rationalizing good into evil, and evil into good" (Meservy, "Jerusalem at the Time of Lehi and Jeremiah," 23–24).

Jeremiah 9:23–26. The Wise Will Understand and Know the Lord

How do Jeremiah's words condemn the prideful traditions in Judah? (9:23–26) "The section closes with two 'sayings' of the LORD . . . The first (vv. 23–24) points to a common misunderstanding of the Law. That misunderstanding places the Law above the Lawgiver (the LORD). . . . It is as if they do not need the LORD any more. . . . The second saying (vv. 25–26) provides a concrete example of what he means. The people of Judah naturally think of their circumcision as a sign of how they are different from those around them. . . . The LORD dismisses their distinctiveness on the grounds it is superficial only. On the inside—in their hearts—they are no different than those *uncircumcised*. . . . They 'fear the LORD' no more than their idolatrous neighbors" (Willis, *Jeremiah–Lamentations*, 117–18).

23 ¶ Thus saith the LORD, Let not the wise *man* glory in his wisdom, neither let the mighty *man* glory in his might, let not the rich *man* glory in his riches:

Why should we glory in our understanding of God more than anything else? (9:24) The Prophet Joseph Smith revealed this truth about the character of God: "Our Heavenly Father is more liberal in his views, and boundless in his mercies and blessings, than we are ready to believe or receive, and, at the same time, is more terrible to the workers of iniquity, more awful in the executions of his punishments, and more ready to detect every false way than we are apt to suppose him to be . . . ; he says, . . . 'But no good thing will I withhold from them who walk uprightly before me, and do my will in all things; who will listen to my voice, and to the voice of my servant whom I have sent'" (Joseph Smith Papers, "History, 1838–1856, volume D-1 [1 August 1842–1 July 1843] [addenda]," 4 [addenda]; spelling modernized). ⊕

24 But let him that glorieth glory in this, that he understandeth and knoweth me, that I *am* the LORD which exercise lovingkindness, judgment, and righteousness, in the earth: for in these *things* I delight, saith the LORD.

Why did the Lord describe His people as being "uncircumcised in the heart"? (9:25–26) "The time was coming when God would punish both the *circumcised* (v. 25) and the *uncircumcised* (vv. 25–26). Judah believed that they were exempt from the judgment that would fall on the uncircumcised nations that did not have a special covenant with the Lord, but the people failed to realize that they were just as deserving of judgment because they were uncircumcised in heart" (*Zondervan KJV Commentary*, 982–83).

25 ¶ Behold, the days come, saith the LORD, that I will punish all *them which are* circumcised with the uncircumcised;
26 Egypt, and Judah, and Edom, and the children of Ammon, and Moab, and all *that are* in the utmost corners, that dwell in the wilderness: for all *these* nations *are* uncircumcised, and all the house of Israel *are* uncircumcised in the heart.

CHAPTER 10

Learn not the way of other nations—Their gods are idols and molten images—The Lord is the true and living God.

CHAPTER 11

The people of Judah are cursed for breaking the covenant of obedience—The Lord will not hear their prayers.

1 The word that came to Jeremiah from the LORD, saying,

2 Hear ye the words of this covenant, and speak unto the men of Judah, and to the inhabitants of Jerusalem;

3 And say thou unto them, Thus saith the LORD God of Israel; Cursed *be* the man that obeyeth not the words of this covenant,

Summary of Jeremiah 10

"This chapter shows that there is no comparison to be made between God and the idols of the Gentiles; . . . [Jeremiah exposes] their idols, and sets forth the greatness and glory of God. Their idols are described by the matter and makers of them . . . and from their impotence to speak, to stand, to move, or do either good or evil, . . . but, on the other hand, God is described by the greatness of his name and power, and by the reverence that belongs unto him; . . . [and by] his power and wisdom, in making the heavens and the earth" (*John Gill's Exposition of the Whole Bible*, [commentary on Introduction to Jeremiah 10]).

Jeremiah 11:1–17. Jeremiah Reproves the People for Their Disobedience

What did Jeremiah mean by specifying "this covenant"? (11:1–2) "Without any introduction, the word of the Lord comes to Jeremiah. It is obvious that the prophet is the messenger of God. What follows is a serious reminder of the words of *this covenant*, the covenant given at Sinai. Like Moses, the prophet par excellence in the Old Testament, Jeremiah plays an important role in reminding the people of the covenant" (Lalleman, *Jeremiah and Lamentations*, 132).

What does it mean to be cursed by God? (11:3) "Cursings are the opposite of blessings and may be expressed as . . . words or actions by God or his representatives expressing divine displeasure with or warning against wickedness; or . . . God's chastisement of mankind. . . .

"Cursing may be the expression of divine displeasure, warning, or exclusion from God's blessing. Just as blessings are obtained by righteousness, cursings result from breaking God's law and failing to keep his commandments (Deut. 11:26–28; D&C 104:1–8; 124:48). . . . Sinning against light and knowledge has more serious consequences than sinning in ignorance (see Mosiah 2:36–37; Alma 32:19–20; 39:6). Alma$_2$ gives an example wherein the same land was simultaneously blessed for those who acted righteously and cursed for those who did not (Alma 45:16)" (Howard, "Cursings," 1:352).

How can we be God's people? (11:4) Why did ancient Israel struggle to keep their covenants with the Lord? Why do some people today struggle with being obedient? What do you need to continue to do or change for the Lord to say to you: *You are mine, you belong to me, and I am your God*?

What is the plot or conspiracy noted in this verse? (11:7–9) The Lord revealed to Jeremiah that there was a plot or conspiracy to murder him. See commentary in this volume for Jeremiah 11:18.

How deep and widespread was the apostasy of Judah in the days of Jeremiah? (11:10–12) The Jews "had turned back to the iniquities of their forefathers. . . . Their gods were as numerous as their cities, and the number of altars set up to Baal was according to the number of streets in Jerusalem. But, warned the Lord, their gods would not save them in the time of their trouble. In view of their spiritual condition the prophet was commanded not to pray for the people. Nor would the Lord hear their cries unto Him [11:9–14]" (Sperry, *Voice of Israel's Prophets*, 165–66).

4 Which I commanded your fathers in the day *that* I brought them forth out of the land of Egypt, from the iron furnace, saying, Obey my voice, and do them, according to all which I command you: so shall ye be my people, and I will be your God:

5 That I may perform the oath which I have sworn unto your fathers, to give them a land flowing with milk and honey, as *it is* this day. Then answered I, and said, So be it, O LORD.

6 Then the LORD said unto me, Proclaim all these words in the cities of Judah, and in the streets of Jerusalem, saying, Hear ye the words of this covenant, and do them.

7 For I earnestly protested unto your fathers in the day *that* I brought them up out of the land of Egypt, *even* unto this day, rising early and protesting, saying, Obey my voice.

8 Yet they obeyed not, nor inclined their ear, but walked every one in the imagination of their evil heart: therefore I will bring upon them all the words of this covenant, which I commanded *them* to do; but they did *them* not.

9 And the LORD said unto me, A conspiracy is found among the men of Judah, and among the inhabitants of Jerusalem.

10 They are turned back to the iniquities of their forefathers, which refused to hear my words; and they went after other gods to serve them: the house of Israel and the house of Judah have broken my covenant which I made with their fathers.

11 ¶ Therefore thus saith the LORD, Behold, I will bring evil upon them, which they shall not be able to escape; and though they shall cry unto me, I will not hearken unto them.

12 Then shall the cities of Judah and inhabitants of Jerusalem go, and cry unto the gods unto whom they offer incense: but they shall not save them at all in the time of their trouble.

13 For *according to* the number of thy cities were thy gods, O Judah; and *according to* the number of the streets of Jerusalem have ye set up altars to *that* shameful thing, *even* altars to burn incense unto Baal.

14 Therefore pray not thou for this people, neither lift up a cry or prayer for them: for I will not hear *them* in the time that they cry unto me for their trouble.

15 What hath my beloved to do in mine house, *seeing* she hath wrought lewdness with many, and the holy flesh is passed from thee? when thou doest evil, then thou rejoicest.

16 The LORD called thy name, A green olive tree, fair, *and* of goodly fruit: with the noise of a great tumult he hath kindled fire upon it, and the branches of it are broken.

17 For the LORD of hosts, that planted thee, hath pronounced evil against thee, for the evil of the house of Israel and of the house of Judah, which they have done against themselves to provoke me to anger in offering incense unto Baal.

18 ¶ And the LORD hath given me knowledge *of it,* and I know *it:* then thou shewedst me their doings.

19 But I *was* like a lamb *or* an ox *that* is brought to the slaughter; and I knew not that they had devised devices against me, *saying,* Let us destroy the tree with the fruit thereof, and let us cut him off from the land of the living, that his name may be no more remembered.

20 But, O LORD of hosts, that judgest righteously, that triest the reins and the heart, let me see thy vengeance on them: for unto thee have I revealed my cause.

Jeremiah 11:18–23. The Wicked Threaten to Kill Jeremiah in Order to Silence Him

How did the Lord protect Jeremiah's life against the plot to kill him? (11:18) "The men of Anathoth had conspired against his life, because he reproved them for their sins, and denounced the judgments of God against them. Of this God had given him a secret warning, that he might be on his guard" (*Adam Clarke's Commentary* [on Jeremiah 11:18]).

Why does Jeremiah make his appeal directly to God? (11:20) Jeremiah saw there was no justice to be had by men in his day and thus seeks "recourse to a righteous God. . . . This is [Jeremiah's] appeal to God, as the Judge of the whole earth, [God] will do right . . . [and try] *the reins and the heart*; of all men; as of his own, so of his enemies. . . . *Let me see thy vengeance* *on them*; which imprecation arose from [Jeremiah's] pure zeal for God, for his glory, and the honour of his justice; and not from private revenge; and so no ways inconsistent with the character of [Jeremiah]" (*John Gill's Exposition of the Whole Bible*, [commentary on Jeremiah 11:20]; paragraphing altered).

21 Therefore thus saith the LORD of the
men of Anathoth, that seek thy life, saying,
Prophesy not in the name of the LORD, that
thou die not by our hand:
22 Therefore thus saith the LORD of hosts,
Behold, I will punish them: the young men
shall die by the sword; their sons and their
daughters shall die by famine:
23 And there shall be no remnant of
them: for I will bring evil upon the men of
Anathoth, *even* the year of their visitation.

Summary of Jeremiah 12

"The enmity experienced by Jeremiah at the hands of his countrymen at Anathoth excites his displeasure at the prosperity of the wicked, who thrive and live with immunity. He therefore begins to expostulate with God, and demands from God's righteousness that they be cut off out of the land (Jeremiah 12:1–4); whereupon the Lord reproves him for this outburst of ill-nature and impatience by telling him that he must patiently endure still worse. This section . . . sets before us the greatness of God's long-suffering towards a people ripe for destruction" (Keil and Delitzsch, *Commentary* [on Jeremiah 12:1–6]).

CHAPTER 12

Jeremiah complains of the prosperity of the wicked—If other nations learn the ways of Israel, they will be numbered with Israel.

Summary of Jeremiah 13

Jeremiah utilizes symbols to depict the long captivity of Israel and Judah and to plead for their humility and repentance. But sadly, chastisement is imminent.

CHAPTER 13

Israel and Judah will be as a rotted and decayed belt—The people are commanded to repent—Judah will be taken captive and scattered as stubble.

Summary of Jeremiah 14–15

The animals and all classes of people would be affected by death, drought, and war. In Jeremiah 14–15, there is a discussion between Jeremiah and the Lord concerning the suffering caused by the extended drought and the reasons for it. In the face of critical drought, Jeremiah's plea for reprieve is rejected by the Lord because of the people's wickedness. Their coming destruction will not be averted. The Lord challenges Jeremiah to remain faithful to his call and promises that he will be delivered "out of the hand of the wicked" (Jeremiah 15:21).

CHAPTERS 14–15

Jeremiah prays because of dearth and famine—The Lord will not hear because of the wickedness of His people.

The people of Judah will suffer death, the sword, famine, and captivity—They will be scattered into all the kingdoms of the earth—Jerusalem will be destroyed.

CHAPTER 16

The utter ruin of Judah is foreseen—Israel is rejected and scattered for serving false gods—Fishers and hunters will gather Israel again, and the people will serve the Lord—The gospel is to be restored.

Summary of Jeremiah 16:1–13

Jeremiah continues to prophesy of war, famine, death, and the utter destruction of Judah.

14 ¶ Therefore, behold, the days come, saith the LORD, that it shall no more be said, The LORD liveth, that brought up the children of Israel out of the land of Egypt;

15 But, The LORD liveth, that brought up the children of Israel from the land of the north, and from all the lands whither he had driven them: and I will bring them again into their land that I gave unto their fathers.

16 ¶ Behold, I will send for many fishers, saith the LORD, and they shall fish them; and after will I send for many hunters, and they shall hunt them from every mountain, and from every hill, and out of the holes of the rocks.

Jeremiah 16:14–21. The Lord Will Send Many "Fishers" and "Hunters" to Gather Israel

Why is the gathering of Israel in the last days more important and greater than Israel's deliverance from Egypt? (16:14–15) "No image of God's delivering power and love is so oft employed in the Old Testament as the Exodus. Thus, the Lord highlights the exceptional power He will display in gathering Israel yet again when He says that such an event will replace the Exodus as the symbol of His deliverance" (Muhlestein, *Essential Old Testament Companion*, 437). See commentary in this volume for Jeremiah 31:1–14.

Who are the fishers and hunters? (16:16) "In chapter sixteen of Jeremiah [the Lord] says that he will send fishers and hunters among the Israelites [Jer. 16:16]. Latter-day Saints would recognize these individuals as being missionaries of the restored gospel. The results of these missionary activities were mentioned in chapter three of Jeremiah as the Lord told Israel:

Jeremiah's Life Is Symbolically Portrayed in Judah's Circumstances (Jeremiah 16:1–13)

"Jeremiah's day was a sad one for Judah. To symbolize that truth, the Lord told His prophet three things that he was not to do:

"1. He was not to marry or father children (see Jeremiah 16:2). So universal was the calamity bearing down upon the people that God did not want children to suffer its outrage. This commandment, like the one to Hosea to take a wife of whoredoms (see Hosea 10), may not have been a literal one. Perhaps the meaning is that Jeremiah was not to expect that his people would marry themselves to the covenant again, nor was he to expect to get spiritual children (converts) from his ministry.

"2. He was not to lament those in Judah who died by the sword or famine (see Jeremiah 16:5), since they brought these judgments upon themselves.

"3. He was not to feast or eat with friends in Jerusalem (see v. 8), since feasting was a sign of celebration and eating together a symbol of fellowship.

"In addition, Jeremiah was commanded to explain clearly to the people the reasons for his actions as well as the reasons for their coming punishment" (*Old Testament Student Manual: 1 Kings–Malachi*, 241).

'. . . I will take you one of a city, and two of a family, and I will bring you to Zion' [Jer. 3:14]" (Ludlow, *Unlocking the Old Testament*, 181–82). ⊕

Why is comparing the gathering of Israel to hunting and fishing an accurate description? (16:16) "Here on earth, missionary work is crucial to the gathering of Israel. The gospel was to be taken first to the 'lost sheep of the house of Israel' [Matt. 10:6; 15:24]. Consequently, servants of the Lord have gone forth proclaiming the Restoration. In many nations our missionaries have searched for those of scattered Israel; they have hunted for them 'out of the holes of the rocks'; and they have fished for them as in ancient days [see Jer. 16:16]" (Nelson, "Gathering of Scattered Israel," 81). ⊕

How have you come to know the Lord's hand and power in your life? (16:21) Elder Dale G. Renlund reminds us that "we need to reflect every day on the gifts we have received and on what they entailed. . . . I invite you to remember each day the greatness of Heavenly Father and Jesus Christ and what They have done for you. Let your consideration of Their goodness more firmly bind your wandering heart to Them. Ponder Their compassion, and you will be blessed with added spiritual sensitivity and become more Christlike. Contemplating Their empathy will help you 'hold out faithful to the end,' until you 'are received into heaven' to 'dwell with God in a state of never-ending happiness' [Mos. 2:41]" ("Consider the Goodness and Greatness of God," 43, 44).

Summary of Jeremiah 17:1–18

For continuing to worship idols and failing to trust in the Lord, Jeremiah prophesies that the people of Judah would lose the blessings of the righteous and be destroyed. They would lose their inheritance and serve their enemies in foreign lands.

17 For mine eyes *are* upon all their ways: they are not hid from my face, neither is their iniquity hid from mine eyes.

18 And first I will recompense their iniquity and their sin double; because they have defiled my land, they have filled mine inheritance with the carcases of their detestable and abominable things.

19 O LORD, my strength, and my fortress, and my refuge in the day of affliction, the Gentiles shall come unto thee from the ends of the earth, and shall say, Surely our fathers have inherited lies, vanity, and *things* wherein *there is* no profit.

20 Shall a man make gods unto himself, and they *are* no gods?

21 Therefore, behold, I will this once cause them to know, I will cause them to know mine hand and my might; and they shall know that my name *is* The LORD.

CHAPTER 17

The captivity of Judah comes because of sin and forsaking the Lord—Hallow the Sabbath day; doing so will save the people; otherwise they will be destroyed.

19 ¶ Thus said the LORD unto me; Go
and stand in the gate of the children of the
people, whereby the kings of Judah come in,
and by the which they go out, and in all the
gates of Jerusalem;

20 And say unto them, Hear ye the word of
the LORD, ye kings of Judah, and all Judah,
and all the inhabitants of Jerusalem, that enter in by these gates:

21 Thus saith the LORD; Take heed to yourselves, and bear no burden on the sabbath
day, nor bring *it* in by the gates of Jerusalem;

22 Neither carry forth a burden out of your
houses on the sabbath day, neither do ye any
work, but hallow ye the sabbath day, as I
commanded your fathers.

23 But they obeyed not, neither inclined
their ear, but made their neck stiff, that they
might not hear, nor receive instruction.

24 And it shall come to pass, if ye diligently
hearken unto me, saith the LORD, to bring in
no burden through the gates of this city on
the sabbath day, but hallow the sabbath day,
to do no work therein;

25 Then shall there enter into the gates of
this city kings and princes sitting upon the
throne of David, riding in chariots and on
horses, they, and their princes, the men of
Judah, and the inhabitants of Jerusalem: and
this city shall remain for ever.

Jeremiah 17:19–27. Jeremiah Stands at Jerusalem's Gates and Reproves the People for Not Hallowing the Sabbath Day

What blessings come from "hallowing" the Sabbath day? (17:19–22) Keeping the Sabbath day holy protects us from the sins and stains of the world: "Honoring the Sabbath is a form of righteousness that will bless and strengthen families, connect us with our Creator, and increase happiness. The Sabbath can help separate us from that which is frivolous, inappropriate, or immoral. It allows us to be in the world but not of the world. . . .

"Many members understand that truly keeping the Sabbath day holy is a refuge from the storms of this life. It is also a sign of our devotion to our Father in Heaven. . . . I challenge all of us to . . . improve our Sabbath worship" (Cook, "Shipshape and Bristol Fashion," 41–42). ⊕

What does it mean to make one's neck stiff? (17:23) "When Jeremiah notes the people 'made their neck stiff that they may not hear, nor receive instruction' (Jer. 17:23) the image is that of stubborn pride. The reason for this is linked to another function of the neck. It holds the head and turns it. Since the bowing of the head is a sign of humility, to be stiff-necked is the symbol of pride. . . .

"Since things are hung around the neck, it is often associated with slavery or bondage. The 'yoke' upon the neck (see Isa. 10:27; Jer. 27:2) and the 'bands of thy neck' (Isa. 52:2) provide clear and powerful imagery of spiritual, and sometimes literal, bondage" (Lund, "Understanding Scriptural Symbols," 25).

What was the Lord promising Judah in this passage? (17:24–25) "The Lord promised: 'if ye diligently hearken unto me' including '[hallowing] the sabbath day' (v. 24), 'Then shall there enter into the gates of this city [true] kings and princes upon the throne of David' (v. 25). If the Sabbath was kept holy, signifying the covenant faithfulness of Israel, the nation would retain its sovereign kings and princes. In other words, the promise of unending Davidic succession in kingship would be fulfilled (see 2 Sam 7:16)" (*Nelson Study Bible* [1997], 1257).

Summary of Jeremiah 18

Using the imagery of a potter, the Lord declares that individuals and nations (like Israel) who repent can be reshaped and molded with His help. "The potter is the Lord, and the clay is the house of Israel or Judah. Because it had become marred, it was to be returned to the mill (scattered among the nations) until it was ready to be molded by the hands of the Lord another time.

"There is a lesson which should not be overlooked regarding the clay. The quality of the vessel is determined by the quality of the clay in the potter's hand. The Lord is the master potter and will mold Israel into a beautiful earthly vessel (nation or kingdom) if the clay (Judah) is properly prepared" (Nyman, *Words of Jeremiah*, 61).

Summary of Jeremiah 19

The Lord commands Jeremiah to perform a symbolic act with a pottery jar. Jeremiah is to go to the valley of Hinnom, proclaim the evils of the people of Judah, and then break the jar as a sign of the irrevocable judgment of God upon them. "Thus saith the LORD of hosts; Even so will I break this people and this city, as one breaketh a potter's vessel, that cannot be made whole again. . . . Behold, I will bring upon this city and upon all her towns all the evil that I have pronounced against it, because they have hardened their necks, that they might not hear my words" (Jeremiah 19:11, 15).

26 And they shall come from the cities of Judah, and from the places about Jerusalem, and from the land of Benjamin, and from the plain, and from the mountains, and from the south, bringing burnt offerings, and sacrifices, and meat offerings, and incense, and bringing sacrifices of praise, unto the house of the LORD.

27 But if ye will not hearken unto me to hallow the sabbath day, and not to bear a burden, even entering in at the gates of Jerusalem on the sabbath day; then will I kindle a fire in the gates thereof, and it shall devour the palaces of Jerusalem, and it shall not be quenched.

CHAPTER 18

Israel is as potter's clay in the hands of the Lord—If nations repent, the Lord withholds the evil decreed against them—The people of Judah will be scattered.

CHAPTER 19

The Lord will bring evil upon Judah—They sacrifice their children to Baal—In the siege they will eat the flesh of their sons and daughters.

CHAPTER 20

Jeremiah is smitten and put in the stocks—He prophesies that all Judah will be taken captive by Babylon.

1 Now Pashur the son of Immer the priest, who *was* also chief governor in the house of the LORD, heard that Jeremiah prophesied these things.

2 Then Pashur smote Jeremiah the prophet, and put him in the stocks that *were* in the high gate of Benjamin, which *was* by the house of the LORD.

3 And it came to pass on the morrow, that Pashur brought forth Jeremiah out of the stocks. Then said Jeremiah unto him, The LORD hath not called thy name Pashur, but Magor-missabib.

4 For thus saith the LORD, Behold, I will make thee a terror to thyself, and to all thy friends: and they shall fall by the sword of their enemies, and thine eyes shall behold *it:* and I will give all Judah into the hand of the king of Babylon, and he shall carry them captive into Babylon, and shall slay them with the sword.

Jeremiah 20:1–6. Jeremiah Is Beaten and Humiliated for Prophesying Things People Do Not Want to Hear

What do we know about this man named Pashur? (20:1) "A senior officer at the temple was brazen enough to 'smite' the prophet, confine him in a device that holds the body in a distorted position, and keep him there overnight in a public place—all because of his prophecies. . . . [Jeremiah] prophesied Pashur would suffer terror with the exiles and die in Babylon; the royal house would fare no better" (Rasmussen, *Latter-day Saint Commentary on the Old Testament*, 556). It should be noted that the Pashur mentioned in chapter 21 is not the same individual described in chapter 20 (see Jer. 21:1).

How might Pashur's treatment of Jeremiah apply to us today? (20:2) "I think it is a very serious thing when anybody raises his hand against the prophets of God. Have you read carefully the story, of Jeremiah in the Old Testament and seen there how men and women [opposed] the prophet? I want you to know that it is just as serious for us who live today to raise our hands against these modern prophets as it was for ancient Israel to raise their hands against Jeremiah whom they put in a dungeon and whom they would have been glad to see die" (Peterson, in Conference Report, April 1949, 145). How might we raise our hands against the prophets of the Lord today? In what ways does criticism constitute raising a hand against the prophets?

Why does the Lord change Pashur's name? (20:3) "When Pashhur released Jeremiah the next morning, Jeremiah gave him the symbolic name Magor-missabib, 'terror all around.' . . . [The] significance of a new name to mark a new status is clear. Pashhur will not be a temple overseer who metes out punishment to others, but one who will himself suffer the divine judgment when terror surrounds him and the nation" (Thompson, *Book of Jeremiah*, 455). "The name Pashur appears to have meant something like 'prosperity all around'—quite the opposite of his new name (Jer. 20:3*a*)" (Rasmussen, *Latter-day Saint Commentary on the Old Testament*, 556).

Jeremiah 20:7–18. Jeremiah Testifies That the Word of the Lord Is Like a Fire in His Bones

Why did Jeremiah feel that the Lord had deceived him? (20:7–9) "The word deceived (v. 7) literally means 'seduced' (see Exod. 22:16) or 'enticed' (see 1 Kings 22:20–22). The Lord had not fully revealed to Jeremiah all the sufferings that he would experience in fulfilling his prophetic calling" (*Zondervan KJV Commentary*, 991). "In [Jeremiah's] lament . . . we learn of the unwilling human nature of the prophet in submitting himself to the will of the Lord in delivering an unpopular message. . . . Jeremiah, perhaps comforted by his own admission of weakness, went on to reaffirm his faith and to praise the Lord" (Seely, "I Am with Thee, to Deliver Thee," 232).

How did having the Lord's word "in [his] heart" enable Jeremiah to fulfill his prophetic role? (20:9) "[The Lord] knows our bearing capacities. Though we

5 Moreover I will deliver all the strength of this city, and all the labours thereof, and all the precious things thereof, and all the treasures of the kings of Judah will I give into the hand of their enemies, which shall spoil them, and take them, and carry them to Babylon.

6 And thou, Pashur, and all that dwell in thine house shall go into captivity: and thou shalt come to Babylon, and there thou shalt die, and shalt be buried there, thou, and all thy friends, to whom thou hast prophesied lies.

7 ¶ O LORD, thou hast deceived me, and I was deceived: thou art stronger than I, and hast prevailed: I am in derision daily, every one mocketh me.

8 For since I spake, I cried out, I cried violence and spoil; because the word of the LORD was made a reproach unto me, and a derision, daily.

9 Then I said, I will not make mention of him, nor speak any more in his name. But *his word* was in mine heart as a burning fire shut

A Burning Fire Shut Up in My Bones (Jeremiah 20:9)

Elder Jeffrey R. Holland taught: "A memorable account . . . comes from the life of the prophet Jeremiah. This great man felt the way most teachers or speakers or Church officers feel when called—inexperienced, inadequate, frightened. 'Ah, Lord,' he cried, 'behold, I cannot speak: for I am [but] a child.'

But the Lord reassured him: 'Be not afraid of their faces: for I am with thee. . . . Therefore gird up thy loins, and arise, and speak unto them' [Jer. 1:6, 8, 17].

"So speak unto them he did, but initially not with much success. Things went from bad to worse until finally he was imprisoned and made a laughingstock among the people. Angry that he had been so mistreated and maligned, Jeremiah vowed, in effect, never to teach another lesson, whether that be to an investigator, Primary child, new convert, or—heaven forbid—the 15-year-olds. 'I will not make mention of [the Lord], nor speak any more in his name,' the discouraged prophet said. But then came the turning point of Jeremiah's life. Something had been happening with every testimony he had borne, every scripture he had read, every truth he had taught. Something had been happening that he hadn't counted on. Even as he vowed to close his mouth and walk away from the Lord's work, he found that he could not. Why? Because 'his word was in mine heart as a burning fire shut up in my bones, and I was weary with forbearing, and I could not stay' [Jer. 20:7–9].

"That is what happens in the gospel to both the teacher and the taught. It is what happened to Nephi and Lehi when . . . 'the Holy Spirit of God did come down from heaven, and did enter into their hearts, and they were filled as if with fire, and they could speak forth marvelous words' [Hel. 5:45]" ("Teacher Come from God," 27).

up in my bones, and I was weary with forbearing, and I could not *stay*.

10 ¶ For I heard the defaming of many, fear on every side. Report, *say they*, and we will report it. All my familiars watched for my halting, *saying*, Peradventure he will be enticed, and we shall prevail against him, and we shall take our revenge on him.

11 But the LORD *is* with me as a mighty terrible one: therefore my persecutors shall stumble, and they shall not prevail: they shall be greatly ashamed; for they shall not prosper: *their* everlasting confusion shall never be forgotten.

12 But, O LORD of hosts, that triest the righteous, *and* seest the reins and the heart, let me see thy vengeance on them: for unto thee have I opened my cause.

13 Sing unto the LORD, praise ye the LORD: for he hath delivered the soul of the poor from the hand of evildoers.

14 ¶ Cursed *be* the day wherein I was born: let not the day wherein my mother bare me be blessed.

15 Cursed *be* the man who brought tidings to my father, saying, A man child is born unto thee; making him very glad.

16 And let that man be as the cities which the LORD overthrew, and repented not: and let him hear the cry in the morning, and the shouting at noontide;

ourselves may feel pushed to the breaking point, ere long, thanks to Him, these once-daunting challenges become receding milestones. Even outstanding and courageous Jeremiah was once discouraged. Being mocked and persecuted, he briefly considered refraining from speaking out anymore. But then he said God's word was 'as a burning fire shut up in my bones, . . . and I could not stay' (Jeremiah 20:9). Jeremiah reached a breaking point, but he did not break!" (Maxwell, "Precious Promise," 45–46).

How does Jeremiah's confidence in the Lord despite persecution inspire you? (20:11) Jeremiah prayed for the Lord's protection against those who plotted against him. In a similar way, the Prophet Joseph Smith trusted in God's power to preserve him against his enemies: "I understand my mission and business. God Almighty is my shield, and what can man do if God is my friend, I shall not be sacrificed until my time comes, then I shall be offered freely. . . . I thank God for preserving me from my enemies; I have no enemies but for the Truth's sake. I have no desire but to do all men good; I feel to pray for all men" (Joseph Smith Papers, "History, 1838–1856, volume D-1 [1 August 1842–1 July 1843] [addenda]," 6 [addenda]).

Why would the Lord try the righteous? (20:12) "Modern revelation indicates at least three times that each of us who seeks eternal life must one day be tried, even as Abraham. I put the question once to President Hugh B. Brown, when we were in Israel: Why was Abraham commanded to go up on that mountain (traditionally Mount Moriah in Jerusalem) and offer as a sacrifice his only hope for the promised posterity? President Brown wisely replied, 'Abraham needed to learn something about Abraham.' By being tested, all of us will one day know how much our hearts are really set on the kingdom of God" (Madsen, *Joseph Smith the Prophet*, 92–93).

Why did Jeremiah curse the circumstances of his birth? (20:14–18) "We cannot assume . . . that Jeremiah truly wished ill upon whoever bore the news of his birth. It is a rhetorical device designed to convey how difficult Jeremiah's life was. The device continues as Jeremiah says he wishes he had been a stillborn child, for then he would not have gone through his hardships. . . . Jeremiah knows God will eventually deliver him, but even when he would like to shrink from the task, he cannot stop himself from doing God's will—even though it has taken over his life and brought him great misery and suffering" (Muhlestein, *Scripture Study Made Simple*, 429).

17 Because he slew me not from the womb; or that my mother might have been my grave, and her womb *to be* always great *with me.*

18 Wherefore came I forth out of the womb to see labour and sorrow, that my days should be consumed with shame?

Summary of Jeremiah 21–22

King Zedekiah was the last king of Judah and was deceived because of his wickedness. What he wanted to hear from the prophets was that the Lord would "deal with [them] according to all his wondrous works" (Jer. 21:2) and deliver them from the Babylonians. However, he did not get the message he wanted to hear. Instead, Jeremiah detailed the eventual siege, captivity, and destruction of Jerusalem at the hands of Babylon. Zedekiah and his servants also learned what their fate would be (see Jer. 21:7). The Lord reminded Zedekiah and other leaders, "I set before you the way of life, and the way death" (Jer. 21:8). In other words, the Lord had extended His mercy and plan of happiness.

In chapter 22, Jeremiah declared that the Lord would soon bring desolation upon the Kingdom of Judah. He also described what observers would say of its desolation: "And many nations shall pass by this city, and they shall say every man to his neighbour, Wherefore hath the Lord done thus unto this great city? Then they shall answer, Because they have forsaken the covenant of the Lord their God, and worshipped other gods, and served them" (Jer. 22:8–9).

CHAPTERS 21–22

Jeremiah foretells the siege, captivity, and destruction of Jerusalem—Zedekiah is to be taken captive by Nebuchadrezzar.

David's throne stands or falls according to the obedience of the kings—The judgments of the Lord rest upon the kings of Judah.

Jeremiah 23:1–8. The Lord Will Gather and Save Israel in the Latter Days

Who were the "pastors" denounced by Jeremiah? (23:1) President Joseph Fielding Smith, commenting on who the "pastors" were that Jeremiah taught, said, "From these passages you will see that it is clear that the Lord has reference to the priests and rulers over the children of Israel and not to an order, or office, in the priesthood" (*Answers to Gospel Questions*, 1:128).

CHAPTER 23

The remnants of Israel will be gathered in the last days—The Branch, who is the King (the Messiah), will reign in righteousness—False prophets who teach lies will be cursed.

1 Woe be unto the pastors that destroy and scatter the sheep of my pasture! saith the LORD.

2 Therefore thus saith the LORD God of Israel against the pastors that feed my people; Ye have scattered my flock, and driven them away, and have not visited them: behold, I will visit upon you the evil of your doings, saith the LORD.

3 And I will gather the remnant of my flock out of all countries whither I have driven them, and will bring them again to their folds; and they shall be fruitful and increase.

How will the Lord gather the remnant of His flock? (23:3) Shortly after His resurrection the Lord emphasized to His followers: "Go ye therefore, and teach all nations" (Matt. 28:19). In our dispensation, Jesus Christ told His willing disciples: "Ye are called to bring to pass the gathering of my elect" (D&C 29:7). Elder D. Todd Christofferson wisely stated: "We should pause to remember that it is the Lord's work and He is doing it. He is the Lord of the vineyard, and we are His servants. He bids us labor in the vineyard with our might this 'last time,' and He labors with us. It would probably be more accurate to say He permits us to labor with Him" ("Preparing for the Lord's Return," 83–84). ⊕

4 And I will set up shepherds over them which shall feed them: and they shall fear no more, nor be dismayed, neither shall they be lacking, saith the LORD.

Who are the shepherds the Lord uses today to feed His flock? (23:4) "Who is a shepherd? Every man, woman, and child in the kingdom of God is a shepherd. No calling is required. From the moment we emerge from the waters of baptism, we are commissioned to this work. . . . Whenever our neighbors are in distress temporally or spiritually, we run to their aid. . . . The Lord lovingly expects this of us. And the day will come when we will be held accountable for the care we take in ministering to His flock" (Stevenson, "Shepherding Souls," 111).

5 ¶ Behold, the days come, saith the LORD, that I will raise unto David a righteous Branch, and a King shall reign and prosper, and shall execute judgment and justice in the earth.

6 In his days Judah shall be saved, and Israel shall dwell safely: and this *is* his name whereby he shall be called, THE LORD OUR RIGHTEOUSNESS.

7 Therefore, behold, the days come, saith the LORD, that they shall no more say, The LORD liveth, which brought up the children of Israel out of the land of Egypt;

8 But, The LORD liveth, which brought up and which led the seed of the house of Israel out of the north country, and from all countries whither I had driven them; and they shall dwell in their own land.

Who is the "righteous Branch" raised up unto David? (23:5–6) "The King who shall reign personally upon the earth during the Millennium . . . is the Lord Jehovah, even him whom we call Christ. . . .

"That the Branch of David is Christ is perfectly clear. We shall now see that he is also called David, that he is a new David, an Eternal David, who shall reign forever on the throne of his ancient ancestor. 'It shall come to pass in that day, saith the Lord of hosts,' that is, in the great millennial day of gathering, that 'they shall serve the Lord their God, and David their king, whom I will raise up unto them' (Jer. 30:8–9)" (McConkie, *Promised Messiah*, 192, 193).

Jeremiah 23:9–15. Jeremiah Is Brokenhearted over the False Prophets in Israel

Will we ever see a day similar to Jeremiah's, when wicked prophets and priests are found in the Church? (23:11) Though there will be no latter-day apostasy of Church leaders as in Jeremiah's day, the Lord did reveal to the Prophet Joseph Smith that "all flesh has become corrupt before my face. Behold, vengeance cometh speedily upon the inhabitants of the earth. . . . And upon my house shall it begin, and from my house shall it go forth, saith the Lord; first among those . . . who have professed to know my name and have not known me, and have blasphemed against me in the midst of my house, said the Lord" (D&C 112:23–26).

9 ¶ Mine heart within me is broken because of the prophets; all my bones shake; I am like a drunken man, and like a man whom wine hath overcome, because of the Lord, and because of the words of his holiness.

10 For the land is full of adulterers; for because of swearing the land mourneth; the pleasant places of the wilderness are dried up, and their course is evil, and their force *is* not right.

11 For both prophet and priest are profane; yea, in my house have I found their wickedness, saith the Lord.

12 Wherefore their way shall be unto them as slippery *ways* in the darkness: they shall be driven on, and fall therein: for I will bring evil upon them, *even* the year of their visitation, saith the Lord.

13 And I have seen folly in the prophets of Samaria; they prophesied in Baal, and caused my people Israel to err.

14 I have seen also in the prophets of Jerusalem an horrible thing: they commit adultery, and walk in lies: they strengthen also the hands of evildoers, that none doth return from his wickedness: they are all of them unto me as Sodom, and the inhabitants thereof as Gomorrah.

Who Is the "Seed of the House of Israel" from the "North Country"? (Jeremiah 23:8)

"A large portion of the house of Israel had been taken by Assyria from the land of their inheritance and thus were lost from the common knowledge of the tribe of Judah. . . .

"Doubtless the total number carried away was significant. . . . It may be that those taken captive by the Assyrians numbered in the hundreds of thousands. In any case, these members of the Lord's Other Tribes were taken away as colonists to the area of northwestern Mesopotamia, toward the upper reaches of the Tigris and Euphrates rivers, there to await the time of their escape. Today those areas are associated with eastern Syria, northern Iraq, northwestern Iran, and the Armenian region of eastern Turkey. . . .

"Perhaps the fall of Assyria afforded the captives the opportunity to escape. . . . Subsequently, some of the peoples held captive by Assyria migrated. This migration seems to have been under way by the early part of the sixth century B.C., for at that time Nephi wrote: 'Behold, there are many who are already lost from the knowledge of those who are at Jerusalem. Yea, the more part of *all* the tribes have been led away' (1 Ne. 22:4; italics added). . . .

"Precisely where the tribes journeyed after the fall of Assyria is another unknown, even as it is unknown to Judah where Lehi and Mulek went. . . . But seeking an actual locale is perhaps an irrelevant question, since the scriptures clearly indicate that the Other Tribes were to be scattered among many nations, even though a distinct remnant of them clearly would remain in the 'land of the north'" (Swanson, "Israel's 'Other Tribes,'" 29).

15 Therefore thus saith the LORD of hosts concerning the prophets; Behold, I will feed them with wormwood, and make them drink the water of gall: for from the prophets of Jerusalem is profaneness gone forth into all the land.

16 Thus saith the LORD of hosts, Hearken not unto the words of the prophets that prophesy unto you: they make you vain: they speak a vision of their own heart, *and* not out of the mouth of the LORD.

17 They say still unto them that despise me, The LORD hath said, Ye shall have peace; and they say unto every one that walketh after the imagination of his own heart, No evil shall come upon you.

18 For who hath stood in the counsel of the LORD, and hath perceived and heard his word? who hath marked his word, and heard *it?*

19 Behold, a whirlwind of the LORD is gone forth in fury, even a grievous whirlwind: it shall fall grievously upon the head of the wicked.

20 The anger of the LORD shall not return, until he have executed, and till he have performed the thoughts of his heart: in the latter days ye shall consider it perfectly.

21 I have not sent these prophets, yet they ran: I have not spoken to them, yet they prophesied.

22 But if they had stood in my counsel, and had caused my people to hear my words, then they should have turned them from their evil way, and from the evil of their doings.

23 *Am* I a God at hand, saith the LORD, and not a God afar off?

Jeremiah 23:16–24. True Prophets Speak the Words of the Lord, False Prophets Speak Lies from Their Own Hearts

How can we discern prophets not sent by the Lord today? (23:16–21) "We can accept nothing as authoritative but that which comes directly through the appointed channel, the constituted organizations of the Priesthood, which is the channel that God has appointed through which to make known His mind and will to the world.... And the moment that individuals look to any other source, that moment they throw themselves open to the seductive influences of Satan, and render themselves liable to become servants of the devil; they lose sight of the true order through which the blessings of the Priesthood are to be enjoyed; they step outside of the pale of the kingdom of God, and are on dangerous ground" (Smith, *Gospel Doctrine*, 41–42). ⊕

What "counsel" is being referred to in this passage? (23:18) "The root from which *counsel* or *secret* comes is the Hebrew *sod* (also rendered *sodh*, or *sode*), which should have been translated 'council.'... Hebrew dictionaries indicate to us that what we are dealing with is a circle of people assembled in a sacred or secret council. After pursuing the etymology of *sod*, Raymond Brown concludes that its basic meaning is 'council or assembly.' He further concludes that in our Jeremiah text we are clearly dealing with a heavenly assembly. What Jeremiah is telling us, then, is that all true prophets will profess to have stood in a heavenly council or assembly where they received their message and the commission to declare it" (McConkie, "Premortal Existence, Foreordinations, and Heavenly Councils," 185–86).

How do true prophets stand in the Lord's "counsel"? (23:18–22) "'The true prophet is here identified as the one who has stood in that heavenly council [spelled "counsel" in the King James Version]... and heard the words of God, which the prophet was then sent to declare to the people. The false prophets had not stood in that council' (Palmer, *Deity and Death*, 82). Jeremiah's proof that the false prophets had not stood in God's counsel was that they had not turned the people from wickedness" (Valletta, et al., *Old Testament for Latter-day Saint Families*, 555).

Why is it impossible to hide from God? (23:24)

"[God] has all wisdom, all knowledge, and all understanding; he is the All-Wise One, the All-Knowing One. There is no truth he does not know, no wisdom hidden from his view, no laws or powers or facts for him to discover. . . .

"By the power of his Spirit, God is everywhere present at one and the same time. There is no place on earth or in heaven or through all the broad expanse of boundless space where his presence is not felt. . . . His senses are infinite and there is no limit to the power of his mind. He can hear and see and know all things at one and the same time" (McConkie, *New Witness for the Articles of Faith*, 52–53).

Summary of Jeremiah 23:25–40

The Lord condemns the people for listening to false prophets. Because they prefer their own words to the word of the Lord, they will be left on their own and end up ashamed.

Summary of Jeremiah 24

Jeremiah receives further teachings from the Lord on the scattering of Judah. The Lord shows Jeremiah two baskets of figs. One basket contains good figs and the other basket evil and corrupted figs. Zedekiah, his princes, and the residue of Jerusalem are the evil figs (see Jeremiah 24:8) and would be "consumed from off the land" (Jeremiah 24:10). The good figs represent those who would be scattered to other nations. The Lord promises, "I will set my eyes upon them for good, and I will bring them again to this land. . . . I will give them an heart to know me, that I am the Lord: and they shall be my people, and I will be their God" (Jeremiah 24:6–7).

Jeremiah 25:1–7. Jeremiah and Other Prophets Tell the Jews to Repent

24 Can any hide himself in secret places that I shall not see him? saith the LORD. Do not I fill heaven and earth? saith the LORD.

CHAPTER 24

Zedekiah and the people of Judah will be cursed and scattered—Some will be gathered back from Chaldea to serve the Lord.

CHAPTER 25

Captive Judah will serve Babylon for seventy years—Various nations will be overthrown—In the last days, all the inhabitants of the earth will be at war.

1 The word that came to Jeremiah concerning all the people of Judah in the fourth year of Jehoiakim the son of Josiah king of Judah, that *was* the first year of Nebuchadrezzar king of Babylon;

2 The which Jeremiah the prophet spake unto all the people of Judah, and to all the inhabitants of Jerusalem, saying,

3 From the thirteenth year of Josiah the son of Amon king of Judah, even unto this day, that *is* the three and twentieth year, the word of the LORD hath come unto me, and I have spoken unto you, rising early and speaking; but ye have not hearkened.

4 And the LORD hath sent unto you all his servants the prophets, rising early and sending *them;* but ye have not hearkened, nor inclined your ear to hear.

5 They said, Turn ye again now every one from his evil way, and from the evil of your doings, and dwell in the land that the LORD hath given unto you and to your fathers for ever and ever:

6 And go not after other gods to serve them, and to worship them, and provoke me not to anger with the works of your hands; and I will do you no hurt.

7 Yet ye have not hearkened unto me, saith the LORD; that ye might provoke me to anger with the works of your hands to your own hurt.

8 ¶ Therefore thus saith the LORD of hosts; Because ye have not heard my words,

9 Behold, I will send and take all the families of the north, saith the LORD, and Nebuchadrezzar the king of Babylon, my servant, and will bring them against this land, and against the inhabitants thereof, and

What was significant about Jeremiah's twenty-third year of prophesying to the Jews? (25:2–3) Jeremiah was in his twenty-third year teaching and preaching unto the people (see Bible Dictionary, "Chronology"). "Jeremiah lived at a critical time in the history of the kingdom of Judah. He first prophesied of the impending Babylonian captivity and then was an eyewitness of many of the major events associated with it" (Ludlow, *Selected Writings of Daniel H. Ludlow*, 56).

What do we know of the ministry of other prophets during Jeremiah's ministry? (25:4) "Lehi was not the only prophet of that time whose name the Old Testament has forgotten. Nephi says that just prior to his father's call 'there came many prophets, prophesying unto the people that they must repent, or the great city Jerusalem must be destroyed' (1 Ne. 1:4). These were among the messengers of God that the Bible tells us were 'mocked,' their messages 'despised,' and themselves 'misused' (2 Chr. 36:15–16). No prophet who sees beyond the immediate situation to the fall of a nation is ever popular with the people of that nation; and most of the time, unfortunately, he is ignored" (Craig, "Father Lehi," 60).

Who was Jeremiah quoting in these verses? (25:5–7) There seems to be a clear connection between "They" in verse 5 and "his servants the prophets" in verse 4. Jeremiah could be quoting his contemporaries or other prophets who had previously preached to Judah. Regardless, the prophets were trying to get the people to repent so they would not forfeit the land of their inheritance. Shortly after leaving Jerusalem, Nephi described Laman and Lemuel as being part of the group who did not "believe that Jerusalem, that great city, could be destroyed according to the words of the prophets. And they were like unto the Jews who were at Jerusalem, who sought to take away the life of my father" (1 Nephi 2:13).

Jeremiah 25:8–14. Jeremiah Prophesies That Babylon Will Take the Jews to Babylon for Seventy Years

Why did the Lord refer to the Babylonian king as "my servant"? (25:9) "This expression does not imply that the Babylonian monarch worshiped Israel's God, but simply that he was used by God to fulfill His purposes (as in the case of Cyrus, who is called the Lord's 'anointed' in Is. 45:1)" (*NKJV Study Bible* [2018], 1112).

against all these nations round about, and will utterly destroy them, and make them an astonishment, and an hissing, and perpetual desolations.

10 Moreover I will take from them the voice of mirth, and the voice of gladness, the voice of the bridegroom, and the voice of the bride, the sound of the millstones, and the light of the candle.

11 And this whole land shall be a desolation, *and* an astonishment; and these nations shall serve the king of Babylon seventy years.

12 ¶ And it shall come to pass, when seventy years are accomplished, *that* I will punish the king of Babylon, and that nation, saith the LORD, for their iniquity, and the land of the Chaldeans, and will make it perpetual desolations.

13 And I will bring upon that land all my words which I have pronounced against it, *even* all that is written in this book, which Jeremiah hath prophesied against all the nations.

14 For many nations and great kings shall serve themselves of them also: and I will recompense them according to their deeds, and according to the works of their own hands.

How was this prophecy against the king of Babylon fulfilled? (25:12) "The same divine principles that worked against Judah's sin would also be effective against Babylon. Its rule was terminated by the Medes and Persians under Cyrus (c. 536–536 B.C.). . . . Babylon was not to be punished for carrying out God's will but for her own sins (cf. 50:11–13). God used Babylon, not because of her merit, but because of Israel's sin. Verse 14 indicates that Babylon would receive retribution in kind (cf. 50:29). The 'many nations' and the 'great kings' refer to the Medes and Persians with their many allies or tributary kings under Cyrus the Great. They would impose forced labor upon the once-invincible Babylonians" (Alexander, "Ezekiel," 1210).

Summary of Jeremiah 25:15–38

In the last days, all the people in the world will be at war and the wicked will be destroyed.

CHAPTER 26

Jeremiah prophesies the destruction of the people—For this he is arraigned, tried, and then acquitted.

Summary of Jeremiah 26:1–7

During the accession of Jehoiakim to the throne of Judah, Jeremiah goes to the temple and prophesies to the people. He warns them that destruction will come, leaving their house empty, because of their rejection of prophets and refusal to repent.

8 ¶ Now it came to pass, when Jeremiah had made an end of speaking all that the LORD had commanded *him* to speak unto all the people, that the priests and the prophets and all the people took him, saying, Thou shalt surely die.

9 Why hast thou prophesied in the name of the LORD, saying, This house shall be like Shiloh, and this city shall be desolate without an inhabitant? And all the people were gathered against Jeremiah in the house of the LORD.

10 ¶ When the princes of Judah heard these things, then they came up from the king's house unto the house of the LORD, and sat down in the entry of the new gate of the LORD's *house*.

11 Then spake the priests and the prophets unto the princes and to all the people, saying, This man *is* worthy to die; for he hath prophesied against this city, as ye have heard with your ears.

12 ¶ Then spake Jeremiah unto all the princes and to all the people, saying, The LORD sent me to prophesy against this house and against this city all the words that ye have heard.

Jeremiah 26:8–24. Jeremiah Warns Those Who Want to Kill Him That They Will Be Killing an Innocent Man

What was the reaction to Jeremiah's prophecy? (26:8–9) "When Jeremiah finishes speaking the word he has received from God, the priests, the prophets, and all the people seize him and threaten his life. One senses the power of the spoken word here. Jeremiah's opponents take his words seriously. This is because in the ancient Near East not only is the prophet the channel for divine messages, but in the act of speaking the message the prophet unleashes the divine action. Therefore, if the prophet has said something that the authorities or the ones in power dislike, they will want to silence him" (Voth, "Jeremiah," 4:293).

Why does Jeremiah declare that God sent him? (26:12) In Jeremiah 26–29, "Jeremiah is presented as a prophet sent by the Lord to announce Judah's judgment, captivity in Babylon that will last seventy years. The reason given is that Judah has failed to listen to the prophets whom God has sent. Jeremiah's message of doom is countered in these chapters by optimistic prophets who assure both those in Judah and those already taken captive in 597 B.C. that the Babylonian problem will last only two years. While these prophets are predictably well received, Jeremiah charges that God has not sent them. By Judah's rejection of Jeremiah and embrace of his more optimistic contemporaries, we are taken another step toward understanding the captivity of Judah" (Bracke, *Jeremiah 1–29*, 203).

How does the Joseph Smith Translation help us understand this verse? (26:13) The Joseph Smith Translation reads "And the Lord will *turn away* the evil that he hath pronounced against you" (Jeremiah 26:13*a*). "Thus, a more idiomatic translation of God repenting of the evil He intends to bring against Israel would be something like this: 'God will turn from His plans to bring terrible punishments upon you'" (Muhlestein, *Essential Old Testament Companion*, 431).

13 Therefore now amend your ways and your doings, and obey the voice of the LORD your God; and the LORD will repent him of the evil that he hath pronounced against you.

14 As for me, behold, I *am* in your hand: do with me as seemeth good and meet unto you.

15 But know ye for certain, that if ye put me to death, ye shall surely bring innocent blood upon yourselves, and upon this city, and upon the inhabitants thereof: for of a truth the LORD hath sent me unto you to speak all these words in your ears.

16 ¶ Then said the princes and all the people unto the priests and to the prophets; This man *is* not worthy to die: for he hath spoken to us in the name of the LORD our God.

17 Then rose up certain of the elders of the land, and spake to all the assembly of the people, saying,

18 Micah the Morasthite prophesied in the days of Hezekiah king of Judah, and spake to all the people of Judah, saying, Thus saith the LORD of hosts; Zion shall be plowed *like* a field, and Jerusalem shall become heaps, and the mountain of the house as the high places of a forest.

19 Did Hezekiah king of Judah and all Judah put him at all to death? did he not fear the LORD, and besought the LORD, and the LORD repented him of the evil which he had pronounced against them? Thus might we procure great evil against our souls.

20 And there was also a man that prophesied in the name of the LORD, Urijah the son of Shemaiah of Kirjath-jearim, who prophesied against this city and against this land according to all the words of Jeremiah:

21 And when Jehoiakim the king, with all his mighty men, and all the princes, heard his words, the king sought to put him to death: but when Urijah heard it, he was afraid, and fled, and went into Egypt;

22 And Jehoiakim the king sent men into Egypt, *namely*, Elnathan the son of Achbor, and *certain* men with him into Egypt.

23 And they fetched forth Urijah out of Egypt, and brought him unto Jehoiakim the king; who slew him with the sword, and cast his dead body into the graves of the common people.

24 Nevertheless the hand of Ahikam the son of Shaphan was with Jeremiah, that they should not give him into the hand of the people to put him to death.

CHAPTER 27

The Lord sends word to many nations that they are to serve Babylon—The vessels of the Lord's house will go into Babylon.

Who was the prophet Urijah? (26:20–24) "Although 1 Nephi makes no explicit statement relating Lehi's message to that of his contemporaries, the point is evident: The people in Jerusalem in Lehi's day had been warned expressly and repeatedly. Nephi also leaves the ill fate of these other prophets unstated. Only a few years earlier, for example, the prophet Urijah had been persecuted, had fled to Egypt, was extradited, convicted, and ignominiously executed for preaching the same message that the prophets were again preaching in the first year of the reign of Zedekiah" (Welch, "Calling of a Prophet," 37–38). Perhaps for these reasons Lehi's departure from Jerusalem was taken with such care and caution to avoid detection.

What is significant about Urijah's execution? (26:23) "Throughout her whole history, Israel's prophets were tortured, mocked, scourged, imprisoned, stoned, sawn asunder, and slain (Heb. 11:35–38). For instance: Jeremiah was beaten and imprisoned (Jer. 37:15–21; 38:6); Zechariah the son of Jehoiada was stoned (2 Chron. 24:18–22); Urijah the son of Shemaiah was slain (Jer. 26:20–24), as were other prophets (Neh. 9:26); and according to tradition, Isaiah was sawn asunder. . . . Prophet after prophet came, all raising the same warning voice (2 Kings 17:13; 2 Chron. 36:15–16)" (McConkie, *Doctrinal New Testament Commentary*, 1:594.

Summary of Jeremiah 27

Jeremiah delivers a revelation warning King Jehoiakim that he and the coming kings of Judah would serve under the king of Babylon. Many sacred items pertaining to the temple would be carried into Babylon. God commands Jeremiah to wear shackles and a yoke around his neck to dramatize the message to Zedekiah that Judah should submit rather than defy the rule of the Babylonian king. In the revelation the Lord warns those who thought Jerusalem could not fall and that her inhabitants would not be dispersed: "Hearken not to your [false] prophets, nor to your diviners, nor to your dreamers, nor to your enchanters, nor to your sorcerers, which speak unto you saying, Ye shall not serve the king of Babylon. For they prophesy a lie unto to you" (Jeremiah 27:9–10).

Jeremiah 28:1–11. The False Prophet Hananiah Contradicts Jeremiah

Who was Hananiah? (28:1) The contrast between true and false prophets is illustrated in this chapter. "Hananiah turns out to be a false prophet, but the difference is not immediately obvious, as he is also referred to as a prophet, just like Jeremiah. Hananiah comes from Gibeon, north of Jerusalem and not far from Jeremiah's home town of Anathoth" (Lalleman, *Jeremiah and Lamentations*, 214–15). The Prophet Joseph Smith explained: "When a man goes about prophesying, and commands men to obey his teachings, he must either be a true or false prophet. False prophets always arise to oppose the true prophets and they will prophesy so very near the truth that they will deceive almost the very chosen ones" (*Joseph Smith* [manual], 203).

What was the "yoke" that Hananiah falsely prophesied would be broken? (28:2–4) The Lord had previously instructed Jeremiah to wear a yoke around his neck (see Jer. 27:2). That symbolic act likely suggested that the people of Judah were to submit to the bondage imposed by Babylon prophesied to last seventy years (see Jer. 25:11–12). "Flatly contradicting Jeremiah's God-given counsel of submission, Hananiah predicted a return of the captives and the temple vessels within two years. . . . One can well imagine the confusion created in the minds of the populace by the spectacle of the false prophet's denying the central elements in the message of the true prophet of God" (*Expositor's Bible Commentary [Abridged]*, 1215, 1216).

Why did Jeremiah acknowledge Hananiah's false claim with "Amen: the Lord do so"? (28:6) "Hananiah claimed to know from God that King Zedekiah and his people would 'not go into captivity but that Babylonia's power (yoke) had been broken and the temple treasures and the captives would be returned within two years' (see Jer. 28:1–4). Of these claims, Jeremiah said, 'Amen: the Lord do so' (Jer. 28:6). His remark was sarcastic—a direct challenge to Hananiah's claim to commune with Jehovah" (Black, *400 Questions and Answers about the Old Testament*, 181).

CHAPTER 28

Hananiah prophesies falsely that the Babylonian yoke will be broken.

1 And it came to pass the same year, in the beginning of the reign of Zedekiah king of Judah, in the fourth year, *and* in the fifth month, *that* Hananiah the son of Azur the prophet, which *was* of Gibeon, spake unto me in the house of the LORD, in the presence of the priests and of all the people, saying,

2 Thus speaketh the LORD of hosts, the God of Israel, saying, I have broken the yoke of the king of Babylon.

3 Within two full years will I bring again into this place all the vessels of the LORD's house, that Nebuchadnezzar king of Babylon took away from this place, and carried them to Babylon:

4 And I will bring again to this place Jeconiah the son of Jehoiakim king of Judah, with all the captives of Judah, that went into Babylon, saith the LORD: for I will break the yoke of the king of Babylon.

5 ¶ Then the prophet Jeremiah said unto the prophet Hananiah in the presence of the priests, and in the presence of all the people that stood in the house of the LORD,

6 Even the prophet Jeremiah said, Amen: the LORD do so: the LORD perform thy words which thou hast prophesied, to bring again the vessels of the LORD's house, and all that is carried away captive, from Babylon into this place.

7 Nevertheless hear thou now this word that I speak in thine ears, and in the ears of all the people;

8 The prophets that have been before me and before thee of old prophesied both against many countries, and against great kingdoms, of war, and of evil, and of pestilence.

9 The prophet which prophesieth of peace, when the word of the prophet shall come to pass; *then* shall the prophet be known, that the LORD hath truly sent him.

What was Jeremiah teaching about Hananiah's prophecy of peace? (28:8–9) "To an unrepentant people, divine prophets must have appeared to be harbingers of doom, while false prophets must have seemed to be angels of peace and mercy. Jeremiah, for example, wrote to the captives in Babylonia telling them to build homes, plant gardens, and marry off their children . . . during the long years of captivity. The false prophet Hananiah, on the other hand, promised in the name of the Lord that within two years God would bring them all back to their homes in Palestine (see Jer. 28:1–4; Jer. 29:1, 4–7). When Jeremiah cried war—sword, spear, and fire—false prophets pacified the sinful people with 'Peace, peace!' (see Jer. 6:13–14, 22–29)" (Meservy, "Jerusalem at the Time of Lehi and Jeremiah," 24).

10 ¶ Then Hananiah the prophet took the yoke from off the prophet Jeremiah's neck, and brake it.

11 And Hananiah spake in the presence of all the people, saying, Thus saith the LORD; Even so will I break the yoke of Nebuchadnezzar king of Babylon from the neck of all nations within the space of two full years. And the prophet Jeremiah went his way.

Why did Hananiah take the yoke from Jeremiah and break it? (28:10–11) "Had Hananiah been sent by the Lord, he might have been satisfied with Jeremiah's opinion, and have contentedly awaited the issue. But instead of this, he seeks by means of violence to secure credence for his prophesying. He takes the yoke from off the neck of the prophet, and breaks it in pieces, as he repeats before the people his former prediction. . . . Thereupon Jeremiah went his way without answering a word, calmly entrusting to the Lord the vindication of the truth of His own word" (Keil and Delitzsch, *Commentary* [on Jeremiah 28:10–11]).

12 ¶ Then the word of the LORD came unto Jeremiah *the prophet,* after that Hananiah the prophet had broken the yoke from off the neck of the prophet Jeremiah, saying,

13 Go and tell Hananiah, saying, Thus saith the LORD; Thou hast broken the yokes of wood; but thou shalt make for them yokes of iron.

14 For thus saith the LORD of hosts, the God of Israel; I have put a yoke of iron upon the neck of all these nations, that they may serve Nebuchadnezzar king of Babylon; and they shall serve him: and I have given him the beasts of the field also.

Jeremiah 28:12–17. Jeremiah Emphasizes the Servitude That Judah Will Spend in Babylon and Predicts the Death of Hananiah

What were the "yokes of iron"? (28:13–14) "In his final response to Hananiah, Jeremiah reflected on the consequences of the false prophet's attempt to oppose the true word of the Lord. The national consequence was that Jeremiah's wooden yoke would instead become *yokes of iron* (v. 13). The wooden yoke of submission would instead be exchanged for the iron yoke of servitude (v. 14; see 38:17–33)" (*Zondervan KJV Commentary*, 999).

Why did the Lord end Hananiah's life? (28:15–17) "Jeremiah received a word from the Lord against Hananiah. First, the Lord said that he had not sent Hananiah. Second, Hananiah had misled Judah into believing lies. . . . [The Lord] decreed that Hananiah was to die that very year, and he died in two months after his wicked prophecy. He had to die because in opposing Jeremiah he instigated rebellion against the Lord. The Jews knew the penalty for apostasy (cf. Dt 13:1–5; cf. Eze 11:13; Ac 5:1–11). Jeremiah's prophecy was authenticated in the death of Hananiah, which discredited him as a fraud. Thus the authority of the true prophet was vindicated" (*Expositor's Bible Commentary [Abridged]*, 1216–17). ⊕

Jeremiah 29:1–9. Jeremiah Tells the Jews to Do Good Things during Their Time in Babylon

Why did Jeremiah send a letter to the captives in Babylon? (29:1) "As will be noted in other prophetic books of the time, the Lord did not neglect those in captivity in Babylon: Daniel and Ezekiel were there, and Jeremiah also communicated with the captives. This conciliatory letter was addressed to the exiles, including King Jeconiah [Jehoiachin] and many leading citizens, who were taken to Babylon in 598 B.C. It was sent along with the messengers of Zedekiah to the king of Babylon. It recommended that the captive peoples maintain positive attitudes and actions. It warned against false prophets and predictions, and it promised a return after seventy years" (Rasmussen, *Latter-day Saint Commentary on the Old Testament*, 561–62).

Why did the Lord permit Judah to be carried away into captivity? (29:4) "Of all peoples who ought to have understood that wickedness will be punished, it should have been the people living in the Southern Kingdom of Judah. They had seen the Northern Kingdom fall to Assyria. . . .

"Like her northern sister, Judah was soon deeply entrenched in idolatry and wickedness. . . . In that state, Judah lost the promise of divine protection. . . . The Lord sent His prophets to warn the people of their impending destruction. Jeremiah, Lehi, and many others were called (see 1 Nephi 1:4), but their warnings fell on deaf ears" (*Old Testament Student Manual: 1 Kings–Malachi*, 232).

15 ¶ Then said the prophet Jeremiah unto Hananiah the prophet, Hear now, Hananiah; The LORD hath not sent thee; but thou makest this people to trust in a lie.

16 Therefore thus saith the LORD; Behold, I will cast thee from off the face of the earth: this year thou shalt die, because thou hast taught rebellion against the LORD.

17 So Hananiah the prophet died the same year in the seventh month.

CHAPTER 29

Jeremiah tells the Jews in Babylon to prepare for seventy years of captivity—Those remaining in Jerusalem will yet be scattered—Shemaiah prophesies falsely and is cursed.

1 Now these *are* the words of the letter that Jeremiah the prophet sent from Jerusalem unto the residue of the elders which were carried away captives, and to the priests, and to the prophets, and to all the people whom Nebuchadnezzar had carried away captive from Jerusalem to Babylon;

2 (After that Jeconiah the king, and the queen, and the eunuchs, the princes of Judah and Jerusalem, and the carpenters, and the smiths, were departed from Jerusalem;)

3 By the hand of Elasah the son of Shaphan, and Gemariah the son of Hilkiah, (whom Zedekiah king of Judah sent unto Babylon to Nebuchadnezzar king of Babylon) saying,

4 Thus saith the LORD of hosts, the God of Israel, unto all that are carried away captives, whom I have caused to be carried away from Jerusalem unto Babylon;

5 Build ye houses, and dwell *in them;* and plant gardens, and eat the fruit of them;

6 Take ye wives, and beget sons and daughters; and take wives for your sons, and give your daughters to husbands, that they may bear sons and daughters; that ye may be increased there, and not diminished.

7 And seek the peace of the city whither I have caused you to be carried away captives, and pray unto the LORD for it: for in the peace thereof shall ye have peace.

8 ¶ For thus saith the LORD of hosts, the God of Israel; Let not your prophets and your diviners, that *be* in the midst of you, deceive you, neither hearken to your dreams which ye cause to be dreamed.

9 For they prophesy falsely unto you in my name: I have not sent them, saith the LORD.

10 ¶ For thus saith the LORD, That after seventy years be accomplished at Babylon I will visit you, and perform my good word toward you, in causing you to return to this place.

11 For I know the thoughts that I think toward you, saith the LORD, thoughts of peace, and not of evil, to give you an expected end.

12 Then shall ye call upon me, and ye shall go and pray unto me, and I will hearken unto you.

13 And ye shall seek me, and find *me,* when ye shall search for me with all your heart.

14 And I will be found of you, saith the LORD: and I will turn away your captivity, and I will gather you from all the nations, and from all the places whither I have driven you, saith the LORD; and I will bring you again into the place whence I caused you to be carried away captive.

How was Jeremiah's counsel meant to help the captives? (29:5–6) "As in Jerusalem, so too in Babylon the predictions of the false prophets fostered a lively hope that the domination of Nebuchadnezzar would not last long, and that the return of the exiles to their fatherland would soon come about. . . . Jeremiah makes use of . . . a letter to the exiles, exhorting them to yield with submission to the lot God had assigned to them. He counsels them to prepare, by establishing their households there, for a long sojourn in [Babylon], and to seek the welfare of that country as the necessary condition of their own" (Keil and Delitzsch, *Commentary* [on Jeremiah 29:1–3]).

Who were these prophets and diviners? (29:8–9) Even in exile there were false prophets and diviners making wild promises to the Jews. "In part [Jeremiah's] letter was a response to those false prophets in Babylon who apparently were raising the hopes of the people for a quick return (Jer. 29:7–9). The Lord even noted that two of those false prophets of the Exile would be turned over to Nebuchadnezzar and killed (Jer. 29:21)" (Seely, "Ministry of Jeremiah," 205).

Jeremiah 29:10–15. After Seventy Years, the Lord Will Gather the Jews Back to the Promised Land

What was the Lord's "expected end" for His children in Babylon? (29:11) "This verse is profound. It helps us see that though the Lord had to punish Judah, His intent was to get them to a state in which He could work with them. He did not want [captivity] to be the end. He was only doing this for a time, and then He planned on forgiving and redeeming His people. This is ever His way" (Muhlestein, *Scripture Study Made Simple*, 436).

What does it mean to search for the Lord with all our heart? (29:13) "Because a veil separates this mortality from our heavenly home, we must seek in the Spirit that which is imperceptible to mortal eyes.

"Heaven may seem distant at times. . . .

"However, seeking God with all our hearts implies much more than simply offering a prayer or pronouncing a few words inviting God into our lives. 'For this is the love of God, that we keep his commandments' [1 Jn. 5:3]. . . .

"We increase our love for our Heavenly Father and demonstrate that love by aligning our thoughts and actions with God's word" (Uchtdorf, "Love of God," 23). ⊕

Who were the prophets in Babylon? (29:15) "It should be remembered that there were true prophets raised up among the captives of Babylon. . . . Daniel and Ezekiel were called among their prospective groups after they had been taken captive (see Daniel 1:1–6; Ezekiel 1:1–3). The prophets referred to in this verse [15] are the false prophets among them. They further verify the Prophet Joseph Smith's teaching that false prophets always arise to oppose the true prophets [see *Teachings of the Prophet Joseph Smith*, 365]. There are two separate prophecies in these verses: one directed against those who follow the false prophets and one directed against two specific false prophets" (Nyman, *Words of Jeremiah*, 78–79).

Summary of Jeremiah 29:16–32

Shemaiah, a false prophet residing among the exiles, wrote a letter to the high priest in Jerusalem seeking to silence Jeremiah. The Lord declares that Shemaiah and all of his household will be punished with death.

Jeremiah 30:1–9. Israel and Judah Will Be Gathered Back to Their Promised Lands

What was the "book" Jeremiah was commanded to write? (30:2) "The book of Jeremiah is one of the few prophetic works in the Bible that makes explicit mention of writing down the words of [Jehovah] to the prophet. Jeremiah was aided in this task by Baruch, a professional scribe (see [Jer.] 36:2–4). In this passage the word translated as 'book' is a general term for a written document, and in that time period it meant a scroll" (Walton, et al., *IVP Bible Background Commentary*, 662).

What does "bring again the captivity" mean? (30:3) "Jeremiah 30:3 has several meanings. It refers to the return of the Jews after seventy years of captivity in Babylon. It also refers to the restoration of the Jews to their homeland in the last days after they have been scattered for the second time. And it refers to the return of the lost tribes from the lands of the north. Note that the Lord will bring them" (*Old Testament Student Manual: 1 Kings–Malachi*, 254).

15 ¶ Because ye have said, The LORD hath raised us up prophets in Babylon;

CHAPTER 30

In the last days, Judah and Israel will be gathered to their own lands—David, their king (the Messiah), will reign over them.

1 The word that came to Jeremiah from the LORD, saying,

2 Thus speaketh the LORD God of Israel, saying, Write thee all the words that I have spoken unto thee in a book.

3 For, lo, the days come, saith the LORD, that I will bring again the captivity of my people Israel and Judah, saith the LORD: and I will cause them to return to the land that I gave to their fathers, and they shall possess it.

4 ¶ And these *are* the words that the LORD spake concerning Israel and concerning Judah.

5 For thus saith the LORD; We have heard a voice of trembling, of fear, and not of peace.

6 Ask ye now, and see whether a man doth travail with child? wherefore do I see every man with his hands on his loins, as a woman in travail, and all faces are turned into paleness?

7 Alas! for that day *is* great, so that none *is* like it: it *is* even the time of Jacob's trouble; but he shall be saved out of it.

8 For it shall come to pass in that day, saith the LORD of hosts, *that* I will break his yoke from off thy neck, and will burst thy bonds, and strangers shall no more serve themselves of him:

9 But they shall serve the LORD their God, and David their king, whom I will raise up unto them.

CHAPTER 31

In the last days, Israel will be gathered—The Lord declares that Ephraim has the birthright as the firstborn—The Lord will make a new covenant with Israel, to be inscribed in the heart—Then all Israel will know the Lord.

1 At the same time, saith the LORD, will I be the God of all the families of Israel, and they shall be my people.

2 Thus saith the LORD, The people *which were* left of the sword found grace in the wilderness; *even* Israel, when I went to cause him to rest.

3 The LORD hath appeared of old unto me, *saying*, Yea, I have loved thee with an everlasting love: therefore with lovingkindness have I drawn thee.

Why must Israel suffer before the Lord saves them? (30:6–7) Jeremiah "mentions a period of such fear and anguish that the gestures displayed by men would be comparable to those of a woman in childbirth. This period of time, ushering in the final deliverance, would be great in suffering and distress, but would free the Israelites from their yokes as they would serve the Lord their God and David, their king whom he would raise up unto them (30:5–9). The Lord promises that he will save Israel" (Ludlow, *Unlocking the Old Testament*, 184).

Who will be the king known as "David" that Israel will serve? (30:8–9) This future king is the Lord Jesus Christ. See commentary in this volume for Jeremiah 23:5–6.

Summary of Jeremiah 30:10–24

God has inflicted judgment on His people because of their iniquity. However, the Lord will gather Israel and Judah and restore them to their lands of promise. Jesus Christ will be their king and they will dwell in peace and security.

Jeremiah 31:1–6. The Lord Promises Deliverance to All the Families of Israel

What is "lovingkindness"? (31:3) One of the many words the King James translators used for the Hebrew word *ḥesed* is "lovingkindness." "The principle of *ḥesed* may be one of the most important doctrinal concepts in the Old Testament, as it appears 245 times in the Hebrew Bible and embodies both the manner in which Israel was expected to act and the true nature of God. Thus, by studying the *ḥesed* references within their contexts and discerning the pattern in which this gospel principle is revealed, we can recognize the importance, particularly through its emphasis on acts of deliverance in the Old Testament narratives and its insight on what it means to be like God" (Belnap, "How Excellent Is Thy Lovingkindness," 170). ⊕

How might these promises have given hope to captive Israel? (31:4–5) "Here the promises of destruction were being overturned. In the day of gathering, Israel would build what had been destroyed. In that same time, the lamentations and loss of mirth would be turned into great rejoicing. . . .

"Continuing with imagery that reverses covenantal cursings and establishes covenantal blessings, God tells Israel that they will one day plant and reap in the promised land again, ending a prophecy about the destruction of their crops that had been uttered by Joel and others" (Muhlestein, *Scripture Study Made Simple*, 438).

Who are the watchmen on mount Ephraim? (31:6) "Watchmen [were] posted on heights to announce seasons of prayer and, according to Jewish tradition, the appearance of the new moon as determining the dates of festivals" (*John Dummelow's Commentary* [on Jeremiah 31:6]).

"The watchmen mentioned in verse 6 are the righteous prophets of the latter days (see also Ezekiel 3:16–21). In the last dispensation they will cry to all people to join together in proper worship of the Lord (see D&C 1:1–2)" (*Old Testament Student Manual: 1 Kings–Malachi*, 254). ⊕

4 Again I will build thee, and thou shalt be built, O virgin of Israel: thou shalt again be adorned with thy tabrets, and shalt go forth in the dances of them that make merry.

5 Thou shalt yet plant vines upon the mountains of Samaria: the planters shall plant, and shall eat *them* as common things.

6 For there shall be a day, *that* the watchmen upon the mount Ephraim shall cry, Arise ye, and let us go up to Zion unto the LORD our God.

The Angel Moroni Quoted from Prophecies of Jeremiah to Joseph Smith

"The angel Moroni quoted to Joseph Smith three verses from the book of Jeremiah. He first quoted Jeremiah 31:6: 'For there shall be a day, that the watchmen upon the mount Ephraim shall cry, Arise ye, and let us go up to Zion unto the LORD our God.' He next quoted Jeremiah 31:8: 'Behold, I will bring them from the north country, and gather them from the coasts of the earth.' The concluding quotation was Jeremiah 31:10: 'Hear the word of the LORD, O ye nations, and declare it in the isles afar off, and say, He that scattered Israel will gather him, and keep him, as a shepherd doth his flock'" (Black, *400 Questions and Answers about the Old Testament*, 181–82).

The latter-day gathering foretold by Jeremiah and other ancient prophets has commenced. The Prophet Joseph Smith declared:

"The work of the gathering spoken of in the Scriptures will be necessary to bring about the glories of the last dispensation. . . .

"The building up of Zion is a cause that has interested the people of God in every age; it is a theme upon which prophets, priests and kings have dwelt with peculiar delight; . . . but they died without the sight; we are the favored people that God has made choice of to bring about the Latter-day glory; . . . when the Saints of God will be gathered in one from every nation, and kindred, and people, and tongue" (*Joseph Smith* [manual], 513).

7 For thus saith the Lord; Sing with gladness for Jacob, and shout among the chief of the nations: publish ye, praise ye, and say, O Lord, save thy people, the remnant of Israel.

8 Behold, I will bring them from the north country, and gather them from the coasts of the earth, *and* with them the blind and the lame, the woman with child and her that travaileth with child together: a great company shall return thither.

9 They shall come with weeping, and with supplications will I lead them: I will cause them to walk by the rivers of waters in a straight way, wherein they shall not stumble: for I am a father to Israel, and Ephraim *is* my firstborn.

10 ¶ Hear the word of the Lord, O ye nations, and declare *it* in the isles afar off, and say, He that scattered Israel will gather him, and keep him, as a shepherd *doth* his flock.

11 For the Lord hath redeemed Jacob, and ransomed him from the hand of *him that was* stronger than he.

12 Therefore they shall come and sing in the height of Zion, and shall flow together to the goodness of the Lord, for wheat, and for wine, and for oil, and for the young of the flock and of the herd: and their soul shall be as a watered garden; and they shall not sorrow any more at all.

13 Then shall the virgin rejoice in the dance, both young men and old together: for I will turn their mourning into joy, and will comfort them, and make them rejoice from their sorrow.

14 And I will satiate the soul of the priests with fatness, and my people shall be satisfied with my goodness, saith the Lord.

Jeremiah 31:7–14. The Lord Will Gather Israel

Who will the Lord gather in from the "north country"? (31:8) "The Doctrine and Covenants explains that the ten tribes will return from the north with prophets and power. They will gather to 'the boundaries of the everlasting hills' to receive eternal blessings from the 'hands of the servants of the Lord, even the children of Ephraim' (D&C 133:25–34)" (Valletta, et al., *Old Testament for Latter-day Saint Families*, 563). ⊕

Why was the tribe of Ephraim emphasized in this prophecy? (31:9) "Ephraim was blessed with the birthright in Israel, and in this dispensation he has been called to stand at the head to bless the other tribes of Israel. This is the interpretation as discovered in the discourses of the leading brethren and in the blessings of the patriarchs of the Church. . . .

"There is the fact revealed through the Prophet Joseph Smith . . . that the majority of the people who have been first to receive the gospel and priesthood of the latter-day dispensation, are descendants of some of the house of Ephraim scattered among the nations, and therefore, the stick of Joseph—the Book of Mormon—is in their hands' [Franklin D. Richards, in *Contributor*, vol. 17, 428]" (Smith, *Doctrines of Salvation*, 3:247). See commentary in this volume for Genesis 48:13–20.

Jeremiah 31:15–30. Israel and Judah Are Invited to Repent

Who is "Rahel" and why is she weeping? (31:15) "*Rahel* (Rachel) *weeping for her children* (v. 15) refers to Israel's national grief over the exile. Rachel was the wife of Jacob and the grandmother of Ephraim and Manasseh (see Gen. 30:22–24; 48:1–2), the two most prominent and powerful tribes in the northern kingdom. Rachel thus represented all the women of Israel who watched their sons being carried away into exile. Matthew 2:15 refers to this passage being 'fulfilled' in connection with Herod's orders to kill all the male infants in the vicinity of Bethlehem, in the sense that the mothers who lost their infant sons in Bethlehem shared the sorrow of the women in *Ramah* who lost their sons in the exile" (*Zondervan KJV Commentary,* 1001).

How can Ephraim's willingness to turn to the Lord prepare them to be blessed by the Lord? (31:18–20) "Following Ephraim's 'bemoaning himself,' the prophet indicated that the Lord is aware of both their sorrow and their repentance and will speed the return of Ephraim and the others. The righteousness of those latter-day generations of Israel shall exceed that of the former who departed" (Rasmussen, *Latter-day Saint Commentary on the Old Testament*, 564). How does our humility and willingness to be "turned" by the Lord make it possible for Him to bless us?

What is meant by "a woman shall compass a man"? (31:22) "Many times in Hebrew writing Israel is described as a woman and sometimes as a bride. The marriage relationship between the woman (Israel) and her husband (the Lord Jesus Christ) is used to depict a very tender, intimate association. . . .

"'In the verse now before us, [the Hebrew word translated as 'compass'] signifies to encompass with

15 ¶ Thus saith the LORD; A voice was heard in Ramah, lamentation, *and* bitter weeping; Rahel weeping for her children refused to be comforted for her children, because they *were* not.

16 Thus saith the LORD; Refrain thy voice from weeping, and thine eyes from tears: for thy work shall be rewarded, saith the LORD; and they shall come again from the land of the enemy.

17 And there is hope in thine end, saith the LORD, that thy children shall come again to their own border.

18 ¶ I have surely heard Ephraim bemoaning himself *thus;* Thou hast chastised me, and I was chastised, as a bullock unaccustomed *to the yoke:* turn thou me, and I shall be turned; for thou *art* the LORD my God.

19 Surely after that I was turned, I repented; and after that I was instructed, I smote upon *my* thigh: I was ashamed, yea, even confounded, because I did bear the reproach of my youth.

20 *Is* Ephraim my dear son? *is he* a pleasant child? for since I spake against him, I do earnestly remember him still: therefore my bowels are troubled for him; I will surely have mercy upon him, saith the LORD.

21 Set thee up waymarks, make thee high heaps: set thine heart toward the highway, *even* the way *which* thou wentest: turn again, O virgin of Israel, turn again to these thy cities.

22 ¶ How long wilt thou go about, O thou backsliding daughter? for the LORD hath created a new thing in the earth, A woman shall compass a man.

23 Thus saith the LORD of hosts, the God of Israel; As yet they shall use this speech in

the land of Judah and in the cities thereof,
when I shall bring again their captivity; The
LORD bless thee, O habitation of justice, *and*
mountain of holiness.

24 And there shall dwell in Judah itself, and
in all the cities thereof together, husbandmen, and they *that* go forth with flocks.

25 For I have satiated the weary soul, and I
have replenished every sorrowful soul.

26 Upon this I awaked, and beheld; and my
sleep was sweet unto me.

27 ¶ Behold, the days come, saith the LORD,
that I will sow the house of Israel and the
house of Judah with the seed of man, and
with the seed of beast.

28 And it shall come to pass, *that* like as I
have watched over them, to pluck up, and
to break down, and to throw down, and to
destroy, and to afflict; so will I watch over
them, to build, and to plant, saith the LORD.

29 In those days they shall say no more, The
fathers have eaten a sour grape, and the children's teeth are set on edge.

30 But every one shall die for his own iniquity: every man that eateth the sour grape,
his teeth shall be set on edge.

31 ¶ Behold, the days come, saith the LORD,
that I will make a new covenant with the
house of Israel, and with the house of Judah:

love and care, to surround lovingly and carefully.... Herein is expressed a new relation of Israel to the Lord, a reference to a new covenant which the Lord, ver. 31ff., will conclude with His people, and in which He deals so condescendingly towards them that they can lovingly embrace Him ...' (Keil and Delitzsch, *Commentary*, 8:2:30)'" (*Old Testament Student Manual: 1 Kings–Malachi*, 255).

What is meant by a parent eating a sour grape? (31:29–30) "Apparently a proverb had arisen in Judah that discussed how the mistakes made by a parent could affect their children....

"The wickedness of Judah sent them into exile, causing their children to be born outside of the promised land, not having the opportunity for many of the blessings available had their parents kept the covenant. Similar things happen throughout time as the wickedness of parents deprive their children of the opportunity to be raised in an environment with full covenantal blessings. The beautiful promise God is making here is that He can undo this—He can give people a chance to overcome the consequences of their parents and experience the full covenant" (Muhlestein, *Scripture Study Made Simple*, 441).

Jeremiah 31:31–34. The Lord Will Make a New Covenant with the Children of Israel and with Judah

What is the "new covenant?" (31:31) "Jeremiah foretold the establishment of God's new and everlasting covenant with Israel and Judah.... The new and everlasting covenant is the fulness of the gospel (see D&C 39:11; 66:2). It is 'new' and 'everlasting' in contrast to the 'old' and 'temporary' covenant of the law of Moses, to which Jeremiah compared it. It was established in the Church in Jesus' day, as it had been in the times of earlier righteous Saints prior to the days of Moses. We live now in the day when it has been reestablished with Israel; thus Jeremiah's prophecy has found partial fulfillment already" (Jackson, *Lost Tribes and Last Days*, 47).

How can God's law and covenant be written on our "inward parts" and "hearts?" (31:33) "Jeremiah described the nature of this new covenant in the language of the Exodus known throughout Jeremiah [see Jer. 31:33]. . . . The 'heart' and 'inward parts' represent an internalization of the covenant in the souls of those who accept it. Paul discussed the nature of this covenant, written 'not in tables of stone, but in fleshy tables of the heart' (2 Cor. 3:3) and explained that this process of internalization can only occur through the power of the Spirit. The fulfillment of this prophecy is in process with the establishment of the new and everlasting covenant. It is 'new' because, as the Lord said, 'all old covenants have I caused to be done away in this thing'; and it is 'everlasting' because it is 'that which was from the beginning' (D&C 22:1)" (Seely, "Prophet over the Nations," 245).

Summary of Jeremiah 31:35–40

Jerusalem will be rebuilt in the last days and dedicated to the Lord.

32 Not according to the covenant that I made with their fathers in the day *that* I took them by the hand to bring them out of the land of Egypt; which my covenant they brake, although I was an husband unto them, saith the LORD:

33 But this *shall be* the covenant that I will make with the house of Israel; After those days, saith the LORD, I will put my law in their inward parts, and write it in their hearts; and will be their God, and they shall be my people.

34 And they shall teach no more every man his neighbour, and every man his brother, saying, Know the LORD: for they shall all know me, from the least of them unto the greatest of them, saith the LORD: for I will forgive their iniquity, and I will remember their sin no more.

The Day Will Come When All Will Know Jesus Christ (Jeremiah 31:34)

"Joseph Smith tells us that Jeremiah's prophecy will be fulfilled during the Millennium. The Prophet speaks of making one's calling and election sure and of the sealing power whereby 'we may be sealed up unto the day of redemption.' Then he says: 'This principle ought (in its proper place) to be taught, for God hath not revealed anything to Joseph, but what He will make known unto the Twelve, and even the least Saint may know all things as fast as he is able to bear them, for the day must come when no man need say to his neighbor, Know ye the Lord; for all shall know Him (who remain) from the least to the greatest.' These are the very words of Jeremiah's prophecy; and they will find their complete fulfillment among those 'who remain,' those who abide the day, those who gain an inheritance on the new earth when it receives its paradisiacal glory again. 'How is this to be done?' the Prophet asks. How shall men come to know the Lord and understand all the hidden mysteries of his kingdom without a teacher? His answer: 'It is to be done by this sealing power, and the other Comforter spoken of, which will be manifest by revelation' [Joseph Smith Papers, "History, 1838–1856, volume C-1 (2 November 1838–31 July 1842) (addenda)," 8 (addenda)].

"Men will know God in the millennial day because they see him. He will teach them face to face. They will know the mysteries of his kingdom because they are caught up to the third heaven, as was Paul. They will receive the Second Comforter. The millennial day is the day of the Second Comforter, and whereas but few have been blessed with this divine association in times past, great hosts will be so blessed in times to come" (McConkie, *Millennial Messiah*, 681–82).

CHAPTER 32

Jeremiah is imprisoned by Zedekiah—The prophet purchases land to symbolize the return of Israel to their land—The Lord will gather Israel and make an everlasting covenant with them.

6 ¶ And Jeremiah said, The word of the LORD came unto me, saying,

7 Behold, Hanameel the son of Shallum thine uncle shall come unto thee, saying, Buy thee my field that *is* in Anathoth: for the right of redemption *is* thine to buy *it.*

8 So Hanameel mine uncle's son came to me in the court of the prison according to the word of the LORD, and said unto me, Buy my field, I pray thee, that *is* in Anathoth, which *is* in the country of Benjamin: for the right of inheritance *is* thine, and the redemption *is* thine; buy *it* for thyself. Then I knew that this *was* the word of the LORD.

9 And I bought the field of Hanameel my uncle's son, that *was* in Anathoth, and weighed him the money, *even* seventeen shekels of silver.

10 And I subscribed the evidence, and sealed *it,* and took witnesses, and weighed *him* the money in the balances.

11 So I took the evidence of the purchase, *both* that which was sealed *according* to the law and custom, and that which was open:

12 And I gave the evidence of the purchase unto Baruch the son of Neriah, the son of Maaseiah, in the sight of Hanameel mine uncle's *son,* and in the presence of the witnesses that subscribed the book of the purchase, before all the Jews that sat in the court of the prison.

Summary of Jeremiah 32:1–5

The prophet Jeremiah is imprisoned for prophesying that Jerusalem would fall and that King Zedekiah would be taken into exile.

Jeremiah 32:6–15. Jeremiah Is Commanded to Purchase Property in the Land of Promise

Why did the Lord command Jeremiah to put the documents showing the land purchase in a clay jar? (32:12–14) "The deed (in duplicate) was given to Baruch, the trusted confidant and secretary of Jeremiah, for preservation from loss or mutilation. . . . The documents were stored in clay jars to ensure their permanence (the Dead Sea Scrolls, written on leather, have survived in earthenware jars for over two thousand years)" (*Expositor's Bible Commentary [Abridged]*, 1229). "This purchase, by the prophet who had for years prophesied the destruction of Jerusalem and the exile of her people, became a symbolic act of the Lord's intention to one day restore the people to their land" (Seely, "Ministry of Jeremiah," 206).

Summary of Jeremiah 32:16–25

Jeremiah prays and recounts the grace shown by God to Israel throughout her history. He prays for help to know why the Lord had commanded him to publicly buy the field when it was sure to be lost to the Babylonians.

Jeremiah 32:26–35. Because Israel and Judah Turned Their Backs on the Lord, He Will Not Protect Them from Their Enemies

13 ¶ And I charged Baruch before them, saying,

14 Thus saith the LORD of hosts, the God of Israel; Take these evidences, this evidence of the purchase, both which is sealed, and this evidence which is open; and put them in an earthen vessel, that they may continue many days.

15 For thus saith the LORD of hosts, the God of Israel; Houses and fields and vineyards shall be possessed again in this land.

26 ¶ Then came the word of the LORD unto Jeremiah, saying,

27 Behold, I *am* the LORD, the God of all flesh: is there any thing too hard for me?

28 Therefore thus saith the LORD; Behold, I will give this city into the hand of the Chaldeans, and into the hand of Nebuhadrezzar king of Babylon, and he shall take it:

29 And the Chaldeans, that fight against this city, shall come and set fire on this city, and burn it with the houses, upon whose roofs they have offered incense unto Baal, and poured out drink offerings unto other gods, to provoke me to anger.

30 For the children of Israel and the children of Judah have only done evil before me from their youth: for the children of Israel have only provoked me to anger with the work of their hands, saith the LORD.

31 For this city hath been to me *as* a provocation of mine anger and of my fury from the day that they built it even unto this day; that I should remove it from before my face,

32 Because of all the evil of the children of Israel and of the children of Judah, which they have done to provoke me to anger, they, their kings, their princes, their priests, and their prophets, and the men of Judah, and the inhabitants of Jerusalem.

33 And they have turned unto me the back, and not the face: though I taught them, rising up early and teaching *them,* yet they have not hearkened to receive instruction.

34 But they set their abominations in the house, which is called by my name, to defile it.

35 And they built the high places of Baal, which *are* in the valley of the son of Hinnom, to cause their sons and their daughters to pass through *the fire* unto Molech; which I commanded them not, neither came it into my mind, that they should do this abomination, to cause Judah to sin.

What abominations had occurred in the Lord's house? (32:34–35) "The height of the nation's impiety was reached when the people set up their idols in the temple of God himself. Their obscene symbols had been removed during Josiah's reforms, but they were reintroduced in the years of apostasy after Josiah's reign (cf. 7:30; 2 Ki 23:4, 6). Molech worship included human sacrifice; so along with gross idolatry went child sacrifice (cf. 19:1–13). So abhorrent was this practice that the Lord . . . says that it had never entered his mind that his favored people would stoop so low" (*Expositor's Bible Commentary [Abridged]*, 1230).

36 ¶ And now therefore thus saith the Lord, the God of Israel, concerning this city, whereof ye say, It shall be delivered into the hand of the king of Babylon by the sword, and by the famine, and by the pestilence;

37 Behold, I will gather them out of all countries, whither I have driven them in mine anger, and in my fury, and in great wrath; and I will bring them again unto this place, and I will cause them to dwell safely:

38 And they shall be my people, and I will be their God:

39 And I will give them one heart, and one way, that they may fear me for ever, for the good of them, and of their children after them:

40 And I will make an everlasting covenant with them, that I will not turn away from them, to do them good; but I will put my fear in their hearts, that they shall not depart from me.

Jeremiah 32:36–44. The Lord Will Once Again Gather Israel and Make an Everlasting Covenant with Them

What will the Lord do for Israel? (32:37–44) "The Lord promises Israel and Judah that He will not only gather them, but make a New or Everlasting Covenant with them. This we believe to be a promise of the restoration of the Gospel in the latter days, a promise which John the Revelator foresaw when he predicted the coming of an angel with the everlasting gospel (Rev. 14:6, 7). Though the world doesn't realize it, that angel has already come, and the Gospel has been restored to earth. Ephraim has been given the task of organizing the Church and is sending forth its 'fishers' and 'hunters' to gather the lost Israel. A remnant has been gathered, and the remaining tribes will in due time of the Lord come into the fold" (Sperry, *Voice of Israel's Prophets*, 181–82). ⊕

41 Yea, I will rejoice over them to do them good, and I will plant them in this land assuredly with my whole heart and with my whole soul.

42 For thus saith the LORD; Like as I have brought all this great evil upon this people, so will I bring upon them all the good that I have promised them.

43 And fields shall be bought in this land, whereof ye say, *It is* desolate without man or beast; it is given into the hand of the Chaldeans.

44 Men shall buy fields for money, and subscribe evidences, and seal *them,* and take witnesses in the land of Benjamin, and in the places about Jerusalem, and in the cities of Judah, and in the cities of the mountains, and in the cities of the valley, and in the cities of the south: for I will cause their captivity to return, saith the LORD.

Summary of Jeremiah 33

Jeremiah was in prison when the Lord invited him to "call unto me" and promised that "I will answer thee, and shew thee great and mighty things" (v. 3; see also Jer. 32:18–19). Jeremiah prophesies of Jesus Christ's mortal mission declaring that "the Branch of righteousness . . . shall execute judgment and righteousness in the land" (v. 15).

CHAPTER 33

Judah and Israel will be gathered—The Branch of Righteousness (the Messiah) is promised—The Seed of David (the Messiah) will reign forever.

What Can We Do to Assist in the Gathering of Israel? (Jeremiah 32:37–44)

President Russell M. Nelson declared: "Now, participating in the gathering of Israel will require some sacrifice on your part. It may even require some changes in your life. It will definitely take some of your time and energy and your God-given talents. . . .

"The gathering of Israel ultimately means offering the gospel of Jesus Christ to God's children on both sides of the veil. . . .

"You were sent to earth at this precise time, the most crucial time in the history of the world, to help gather Israel. There is *nothing* happening on this earth right now that is more important than that. There is *nothing* of greater consequence. Absolutely *nothing*" ("Hope of Israel," 8, 11, 12).

In a general conference message, President Nelson emphasized: "For the more than 36 years I've been an Apostle, the doctrine of the gathering of Israel has captured my attention. *Everything* about it has intrigued me. . . . When we speak of gathering Israel on both sides of the veil, we are referring, of course, to missionary, temple, and family history work. We are also referring to building faith and testimony in the hearts of those with whom we live, work, and serve. Anytime we do *anything* that helps anyone—on either side of the veil—to make and keep their covenants with God, we are helping to gather Israel" ("Let God Prevail," 92–93).

CHAPTER 34

Jeremiah prophesies the captivity of Zedekiah—The people of Judah will be removed into all the kingdoms of the earth.

Summary of Jeremiah 34

Jeremiah prophesied the fall of Jerusalem and recommended that Zedekiah should surrender to the Babylonians. As the siege continued, Zedekiah hastily made a covenant and proclaimed that all slaves should be liberated, perhaps in an effort to appease God. The failure of the people to honor that covenant and free the slaves ignited the Lord's promised judgment. Note that chapters 34 and 35 provide a contrast between Judah's disobedience and the obedience of the Rechabites. See commentary in this volume for Jeremiah 35.

CHAPTER 35

The Rechabites are commended and blessed for their obedience.

Summary of Jeremiah 35

This chapter is a flashback of several years to the time of King Jehoiakim. The Rechabite people were "descendants of Abraham through his wife Keturah and were also descendants from Jethro, Moses' father-in-law. . . . The covenant the Rechabites took was similar to the Nazarite vow" (Nyman, *Words of Jeremiah*, 79). They sought protection in Jerusalem from the invading Babylonian army. "Their faithfulness was in marked contrast with Judah's refusal to obey the commands of God. God promised through Jeremiah to bless this family for its faithfulness (Jer. 35)" (*Revell Bible Dictionary*, 849).

Who Were the Rechabites? (Jeremiah 35)

"In the time of Jeremiah, or shortly before, a certain Jonadab ben Rekhab had led a colony of permanent settlers from Jerusalem into the wilderness, where his descendants survived through all the succeeding centuries as the strange and baffling nation of the Rekhabites. What makes them baffling is their Messianic religion, which is so much like primitive Christianity in many ways that it has led some scholars to argue that those people must have been of Christian origin, though the historical evidence for their great antiquity is unquestionable. When one considers that Jonadab's project was almost contemporary (perhaps slightly prior) to Lehi's, that his name, ending in *-adab*, is of a type peculiar to the period and to the Book of Mormon, and that the Book of Mormon specifically states that the Lord had led other people out of Jerusalem beside Lehi, and that the Rekhabite teachings are strangely like those in the Book of Mormon, one is forced to admit at very least the possibility that Lehi's exodus *could* have taken place in the manner described, and the certainty that other such migrations actually did take place" (Nibley, *Approach to the Book of Mormon*, 68–69).

Jeremiah 36:1–10. Jeremiah Receives a Prophecy from the Lord, and His Servant Baruch Writes

Who was Jehoiakim? (36:1) Jehoiakim was the king of Judah from 609 to 598 B.C. He was an unfaithful ruler, rejecting the prophecies of Jeremiah. Jehoiakim was succeeded by his son Jehoiachin, who was succeeded by Zedekiah (see Bible Dictionary, "Jehoiakim"). "In 603 BC the Babylonian King Nebuchadnezzar wrested Palestine from the Egyptians, and suddenly Jehoiakim found himself a Babylonian vassal (2 Kgs 24:1). Perhaps because of Egyptian promises of aid, Jehoiakim revolted three years later bringing the might of the Babylonian army on his people" (Matthews, *Manners and Customs in the Bible*, 101).

What message was Jeremiah to record in "a roll of a book"? (36:2–4) Jeremiah was commanded to write all of the messages he had received from the Lord in a "roll of a book" or scroll of papyrus. The messages included a warning to Judah to repent in order to save the city of Jerusalem. The prophet Lehi, a contemporary of Jeremiah, was also shown a vision during which he read a similar message from a book. "Wo, wo, unto Jerusalem, for I have seen thine abominations! Yea, and many things did my father read concerning Jerusalem—that it should be destroyed, and the inhabitants thereof; many should perish by the sword, and many should be carried away captive into Babylon" (1 Nephi 1:11–13).

Who was Baruch? (36:4) "Baruch, son of Neriah, was a friend and scribe to the prophet, Jeremiah. His brother Seraiah was an official in the court of Zedekiah. . . . Baruch figures in several of the important incidents in Jeremiah's life. . . .

"Some scholars believe that because Baruch was Jeremiah's confidant and scribe he may have had a hand in writing or editing the biblical book of Jeremiah" (Holzapfel, et al., *Jehovah and the World of the Old Testament*, 325).

CHAPTER 36

Baruch writes the prophecies of Jeremiah and reads them in the house of the Lord—Jehoiakim, the king, burns the book, and judgment comes upon him—Jeremiah dictates the prophecies again and adds many more.

1 And it came to pass in the fourth year of Jehoiakim the son of Josiah king of Judah, *that* this word came unto Jeremiah from the LORD, saying,

2 Take thee a roll of a book, and write therein all the words that I have spoken unto thee against Israel, and against Judah, and against all the nations, from the day I spake unto thee, from the days of Josiah, even unto this day.

3 It may be that the house of Judah will hear all the evil which I purpose to do unto them; that they may return every man from his evil way; that I may forgive their iniquity and their sin.

4 Then Jeremiah called Baruch the son of Neriah: and Baruch wrote from the mouth of Jeremiah all the words of the LORD, which he had spoken unto him, upon a roll of a book.

5 And Jeremiah commanded Baruch, saying, I *am* shut up; I cannot go into the house of the LORD:

6 Therefore go thou, and read in the roll, which thou hast written from my mouth, the words of the LORD in the ears of the people in the LORD's house upon the fasting day: and also thou shalt read them in the ears of all Judah that come out of their cities.

7 It may be they will present their supplication before the LORD, and will return every one from his evil way: for great *is* the anger and the fury that the LORD hath pronounced against this people.

8 And Baruch the son of Neriah did according to all that Jeremiah the prophet commanded him, reading in the book the words of the LORD in the LORD's house.

9 And it came to pass in the fifth year of Jehoiakim the son of Josiah king of Judah, in the ninth month, *that* they proclaimed a fast before the LORD to all the people in Jerusalem, and to all the people that came from the cities of Judah unto Jerusalem.

10 Then read Baruch in the book the words of Jeremiah in the house of the LORD, in the chamber of Gemariah the son of Shaphan the scribe, in the higher court, at the entry of the new gate of the LORD's house, in the ears of all the people.

20 ¶ And they went in to the king into the court, but they laid up the roll in the chamber of Elishama the scribe, and told all the words in the ears of the king.

21 So the king sent Jehudi to fetch the roll: and he took it out of Elishama the scribe's chamber. And Jehudi read it in the ears of the king, and in the ears of all the princes which stood beside the king.

22 Now the king sat in the winterhouse in the ninth month: and *there was a fire* on the hearth burning before him.

Why would the Lord speak to Judah in such fury and anger? (36:7) The Lord explained to Jeremiah that the purpose of His declaration against Judah was to cause the people to repent and "return every man from his evil way" (Jer. 36:3). "Divine chastening has at least three purposes: (1) to persuade us to repent, (2) to refine and sanctify us, and (3) at times to redirect our course in life to what God knows is a better path.

"Consider first of all repentance, the necessary condition for forgiveness and cleansing. The Lord declared . . . 'And my people must needs be chastened until they learn obedience, if it must needs be, by the things which they suffer' (D&C 105:6; see also D&C 1:27)" (Christofferson, "As Many as I Love, I Rebuke and Chasten," 98).

Summary of Jeremiah 36:11–19

Since Jeremiah is restricted from going to the temple (see 36:5), Baruch reads the prophecies of Jeremiah to the princes or leaders of the people. They respond with fear and advise Baruch and Jeremiah to hide from king Jehoiakim.

Jeremiah 36:20–26. The King Cuts Up the Prophecy and Burns It

How do Jehoiakim's actions foreshadow Jerusalem's destruction? (36:20–26) "Because Jeremiah is banned from the area of the Temple, he dictates his message and has his secretary Baruch read it at a Temple gate. The scroll is seized and eventually read to King Jehoiakim. As Jehoiakim listens to the scroll in his winter house, he cuts away sections of Jeremiah's scroll as it is read and burns it in the fire. The connection to the themes of the surrounding chapters is obvious. Judah has refused to listen to and obey God's word, and that refusal is dramatically portrayed when Jehoiakim burns the scroll containing the words of Jeremiah. Because Jehoiakim has burned God's word, God will burn Jerusalem" (Bracke, *Jeremiah 30–52 and Lamentations*, 44).

Jeremiah 36:27–32. Jeremiah Is Commanded to Write His Prophecies Again on Another Scroll and Include Additional Words

What additional message does the Lord want Jeremiah to dictate? (36:27–31) "At God's command the prophet once more dictates his message to his scribe. This time a special judgment is pronounced upon Jehoiakim for burning the scroll (36:27–31). Conditions will be such at the time of his death that he will not have a royal burial but his body will be exposed to the heat by day and the frost by night" (Schultz, *Old Testament Speaks*, 337).

23 And it came to pass, *that* when Jehudi had read three or four leaves, he cut it with the penknife, and cast *it* into the fire that *was* on the hearth, until all the roll was consumed in the fire that *was* on the hearth.

24 Yet they were not afraid, nor rent their garments, *neither* the king, nor any of his servants that heard all these words.

25 Nevertheless Elnathan and Delaiah and Gemariah had made intercession to the king that he would not burn the roll: but he would not hear them.

26 But the king commanded Jerahmeel the son of Hammelech, and Seraiah the son of Azriel, and Shelemiah the son of Abdeel, to take Baruch the scribe and Jeremiah the prophet: but the LORD hid them.

27 ¶ Then the word of the LORD came to Jeremiah, after that the king had burned the roll, and the words which Baruch wrote at the mouth of Jeremiah, saying,

28 Take thee again another roll, and write in it all the former words that were in the first roll, which Jehoiakim the king of Judah hath burned.

29 And thou shalt say to Jehoiakim king of Judah, Thus saith the LORD; Thou hast burned this roll, saying, Why hast thou written therein, saying, The king of Babylon shall certainly come and destroy this land, and shall cause to cease from thence man and beast?

30 Therefore thus saith the LORD of Jehoiakim king of Judah; He shall have none to sit upon the throne of David: and his dead body shall be cast out in the day to the heat, and in the night to the frost.

31 And I will punish him and his seed and his servants for their iniquity; and I will bring upon them, and upon the inhabitants of Jerusalem, and upon the men of Judah, all the evil that I have pronounced against them; but they hearkened not.

32 ¶ Then took Jeremiah another roll, and gave it to Baruch the scribe, the son of Neriah; who wrote therein from the mouth of Jeremiah all the words of the book which Jehoiakim king of Judah had burned in the fire: and there were added besides unto them many like words.

CHAPTER 37

Jeremiah prophesies that Egypt will not save Judah from Babylon—He is cast into a dungeon—Zedekiah transfers him to the court of the prison.

1 And king Zedekiah the son of Josiah reigned instead of Coniah the son of Jehoiakim, whom Nebuchadrezzar king of Babylon made king in the land of Judah.

2 But neither he, nor his servants, nor the people of the land, did hearken unto the words of the LORD, which he spake by the prophet Jeremiah.

3 And Zedekiah the king sent Jehucal the son of Shelemiah and Zephaniah the son of Maaseiah the priest to the prophet Jeremiah, saying, Pray now unto the LORD our God for us.

4 Now Jeremiah came in and went out among the people: for they had not put him into prison.

5 Then Pharaoh's army was come forth out of Egypt: and when the Chaldeans that besieged Jerusalem heard tidings of them, they departed from Jerusalem.

6 ¶ Then came the word of the LORD unto the prophet Jeremiah, saying,

Jeremiah 37:1–10. Jeremiah Warns King Zedekiah to Not Rely on the Egyptians and Foretells Judah's Fall to Babylon

Who was Coniah, the son of Jehoiakim? (37:1)
"[Jehoiakim] was replaced by his son Jehoiachin (in Jeremiah called Jeconiah or Coniah), who reigned in Judah only three months. Nebuchadnezzar subdued Judah with restraint and exiled their king along with many others, including Ezekiel and possibly Daniel. Nebuchadnezzar then put Zedekiah—Jehoiachin's uncle and Josiah's son—on the throne (2 Kgs. 24:17)" (Seely, "Ministry of Jeremiah," 200). ⊕

How does the Book of Mormon confirm Jeremiah's warning regarding Jerusalem? (37:7–8) "This threatened invasion by the Egyptians, possibly at the request of Zedekiah (see verse 7), caused a temporary departure of the Chaldean army, but Jeremiah prophesied that they would return and destroy the city. The time frame fits into the time frame in which the Book of Mormon was begun. It was then Lehi was shown that Jerusalem would be destroyed and that many of the inhabitants would be carried into Babylon. Lehi was then called to prophesy and warn the Jews, but they were angry and sought to take away his life (see 1 Nephi 1:4–13, 18–20). Thus, the Book of Mormon serves as a second witness to the record of Jeremiah" (Nyman, *Words of Jeremiah*, 98).

Jeremiah 37:11–15. Some People Think Jeremiah Is Going to Join the Babylonians

Why did Jeremiah go to the land of Benjamin? (37:12–15) "It is very possible that Jeremiah went to the land of Benjamin to buy his uncle's field, as it had been revealed to him to do (see 32:6–15). He was, nonetheless, accused of falling away to the Chaldeans and placed in prison. This incident is also attested to in the Book of Mormon[, after] Lehi's sons had returned to Jerusalem for the second time . . . [see 1 Nephi 7:12–15]. Apparently Jeremiah had not been in prison when Lehi and his family left Jerusalem, but by the time Lehi had sent his sons back . . . , undoubtedly several weeks later, he had been cast there" (Nyman, *Words of Jeremiah*, 98–99).

Jeremiah 37:16–21. The King Speaks Secretly to Jeremiah and Lets Him Move to a Better Place in the Prison

What was it like to be held in these cabins? (37:16) "These cells were likely cramped spaces equipped with stocks. Abarbanel [a bible commentator] says it was the worst kind of prison. And we can figure as much,

7 Thus saith the LORD, the God of Israel; Thus shall ye say to the king of Judah, that sent you unto me to inquire of me; Behold, Pharaoh's army, which is come forth to help you, shall return to Egypt into their own land.

8 And the Chaldeans shall come again, and fight against this city, and take it, and burn it with fire.

9 Thus saith the LORD; Deceive not yourselves, saying, The Chaldeans shall surely depart from us: for they shall not depart.

10 For though ye had smitten the whole army of the Chaldeans that fight against you, and there remained *but* wounded men among them, *yet* should they rise up every man in his tent, and burn this city with fire.

11 ¶ And it came to pass, that when the army of the Chaldeans was broken up from Jerusalem for fear of Pharaoh's army,

12 Then Jeremiah went forth out of Jerusalem to go into the land of Benjamin, to separate himself thence in the midst of the people.

13 And when he was in the gate of Benjamin, a captain of the ward *was* there, whose name *was* Irijah, the son of Shelemiah, the son of Hananiah; and he took Jeremiah the prophet, saying, Thou fallest away to the Chaldeans.

14 Then said Jeremiah, *It is* false; I fall not away to the Chaldeans. But he hearkened not to him: so Irijah took Jeremiah, and brought him to the princes.

15 Wherefore the princes were wroth with Jeremiah, and smote him, and put him in prison in the house of Jonathan the scribe: for they had made that the prison.

16 ¶ When Jeremiah was entered into the dungeon, and into the cabins, and Jeremiah had remained there many days;

17 Then Zedekiah the king sent, and took him out: and the king asked him secretly in his house, and said, Is there *any* word from the LORD? And Jeremiah said, There is: for, said he, thou shalt be delivered into the hand of the king of Babylon.

18 Moreover Jeremiah said unto king Zedekiah, What have I offended against thee, or against thy servants, or against this people, that ye have put me in prison?

19 Where *are* now your prophets which prophesied unto you, saying, The king of Babylon shall not come against you, nor against this land?

20 Therefore hear now, I pray thee, O my lord the king: let my supplication, I pray thee, be accepted before thee; that thou cause me not to return to the house of Jonathan the scribe, lest I die there.

21 Then Zedekiah the king commanded that they should commit Jeremiah into the court of the prison, and that they should give him daily a piece of bread out of the bakers' street, until all the bread in the city were spent. Thus Jeremiah remained in the court of the prison.

CHAPTER 38

The rulers cast Jeremiah into a muddy dungeon—He is freed by Ebed-melech, an Ethiopian, and put in the court of the prison—Jeremiah counsels Zedekiah concerning the war.

1 Then Shephatiah the son of Mattan, and Gedaliah the son of Pashur, and Jucal the son of Shelemiah, and Pashur the son of Malchiah, heard the words that Jeremiah had spoken unto all the people, saying,

since Jeremiah after his release petitioned the king not to send him back there, lest he die (v 20). . . . Here real suffering of the prophet was experienced" (Lundbom, *Jeremiah 37–52*, 60).

Why did Zedekiah visit Jeremiah in secret? (37:17)
"The king questioned [Jeremiah] 'in secret,' namely, through fear of his ministers and court-officers, who were prejudiced against the prophet, perhaps also in the hope of receiving in a private interview a message from God of more favourable import. To the question of the king, 'Is there any word from [the Lord]?' Jeremiah replies in the affirmative; but the word of God is this, 'Thou shalt be given into the hand of the king of Babylon,' just as Jeremiah had previously announced to him" (Keil and Delitzsch, *Commentary* [on Jeremiah 37:16–21]).

Jeremiah 38:1–6. Leaders of the Jews Try to Kill Jeremiah by Lowering Him into a Muddy Pit

Who were these princes that counseled the king? (38:4–5) "We know very little about the city government of the Jews, save that the 'elders' played a principal role. By 'elders' has been understood 'the heads of the most influential families of the city.' This would make them identical with those princes, notables, and officials who are designated as *sarim* in the Lachish letters; the word *sarim* applies . . . to 'members of the official class, i.e., "officers" acting under the king as his counsellors and rulers.' In the Lachish letters we find the *sarim* denouncing Jeremiah to the king and demanding that he be executed because of his bad influence on the morale of the people (Jeremiah 38:4–5)" (Nibley, *Lehi in the Desert*, 7–8).

What do we know about the next dungeon Jeremiah was cast into? (38:6) "A staging area for troops would have had a cistern to store rainwater during the dry months. . . . The fact that a narrow-necked limestone cistern was available as a prison and was empty of water attests to the larger population and the desperate situation they faced. The quagmire at the bottom of the cistern . . . would have prevented Jeremiah from resting and would have been extremely unhealthy. Since the king was afraid to execute Jeremiah, he may have been relying on disease or malnutrition to rid him of the prophet" (Walton, et al., *IVP Bible Background Commentary*, 671).

Jeremiah 38:7–13. King Zedekiah Allows an Ethiopian Man to Pull Jeremiah Out of the Pit

Who was Ebed-melech? (38:7) "Ebed-melech was probably not the real name of this man, for that name means 'servant of the king.' He was a foreigner who had gained a great deal of personal trust from the king. Apparently a fervent believer in Jehovah and His true prophet, when he learned of Jeremiah's fate he went quickly to the king who sat in judgment at the northern gate of the city" (Muhlestein, *Scripture Study Made Simple: The Old Testament*, 448). ⊕

2 Thus saith the LORD, He that remaineth in this city shall die by the sword, by the famine, and by the pestilence: but he that goeth forth to the Chaldeans shall live; for he shall have his life for a prey, and shall live.

3 Thus saith the LORD, This city shall surely be given into the hand of the king of Babylon's army, which shall take it.

4 Therefore the princes said unto the king, We beseech thee, let this man be put to death: for thus he weakeneth the hands of the men of war that remain in this city, and the hands of all the people, in speaking such words unto them: for this man seeketh not the welfare of this people, but the hurt.

5 Then Zedekiah the king said, Behold, he *is* in your hand: for the king *is* not *he that* can do *any* thing against you.

6 Then took they Jeremiah, and cast him into the dungeon of Malchiah the son of Hammelech, that *was* in the court of the prison: and they let down Jeremiah with cords. And in the dungeon *there was* no water, but mire: so Jeremiah sunk in the mire.

7 ¶ Now when Ebed-melech the Ethiopian, one of the eunuchs which was in the king's house, heard that they had put Jeremiah in the dungeon; the king then sitting in the gate of Benjamin;

8 Ebed-melech went forth out of the king's house, and spake to the king, saying,

9 My lord the king, these men have done evil in all that they have done to Jeremiah the prophet, whom they have cast into the dungeon; and he is like to die for hunger in the place where he is: for *there is* no more bread in the city.

10 Then the king commanded Ebed-melech the Ethiopian, saying, Take from hence thirty men with thee, and take up Jeremiah the prophet out of the dungeon, before he die.

11 So Ebed-melech took the men with him, and went into the house of the king under the treasury, and took thence old cast clouts and old rotten rags, and let them down by cords into the dungeon to Jeremiah.

12 And Ebed-melech the Ethiopian said unto Jeremiah, Put now *these* old cast clouts and rotten rags under thine armholes under the cords. And Jeremiah did so.

13 So they drew up Jeremiah with cords, and took him up out of the dungeon: and Jeremiah remained in the court of the prison.

14 ¶ Then Zedekiah the king sent, and took Jeremiah the prophet unto him into the third entry that *is* in the house of the LORD: and the king said unto Jeremiah, I will ask thee a thing; hide nothing from me.

15 Then Jeremiah said unto Zedekiah, If I declare *it* unto thee, wilt thou not surely put me to death? and if I give thee counsel, wilt thou not hearken unto me?

16 So Zedekiah the king sware secretly unto Jeremiah, saying, *As* the LORD liveth, that made us this soul, I will not put thee to death, neither will I give thee into the hand of these men that seek thy life.

17 Then said Jeremiah unto Zedekiah, Thus saith the LORD, the God of hosts, the God of Israel; If thou wilt assuredly go forth unto the king of Babylon's princes, then thy soul shall

How did Ebed-melech use old rags to save Jeremiah? (38:11–12) "Ebed-Melech took special care to obtain *rags* for Jeremiah to cushion his armpits, preventing the *ropes* from cutting his skin. A foreigner, a once-despised Cushite, cared more for the prophet of God than did the king and the princes of Jeremiah's own people" (*Nelson Study Bible* [NKJV], 1294).

Jeremiah 38:14–20. Jeremiah Warns the King to Surrender to the Babylonians to Protect the People of Jerusalem

What divine counsel did Zedekiah reject? (38:17–20) "When the Babylonians finally came and surrounded the city, Jeremiah again counseled individuals that they could survive by surrendering to the Babylonians. Such advice weakened the hands of the defenders and made Jeremiah look as if he were a traitor (Jer. 38:2–4). Yet only God knew what was coming and could tell them how to survive.

"In the final days of the siege, Zedekiah desperately asked Jeremiah for advice. Jeremiah promised him his life and the city's salvation if he would give himself up to the Babylonians. Otherwise, the city would be destroyed. Yet Zedekiah kept the advice secret for fear of his own people, and Jeremiah's prophecy was fulfilled (38:17–27)" (Meservy, "Jerusalem at the Time of Lehi and Jeremiah," 24–25).

Summary of Jeremiah 38:21–28

Jeremiah tells the king that if he doesn't surrender to the Babylonians, the Jews, including wives and children, will be taken captive and the city burned.

Jeremiah 39:1–7. King Nebuchadrezzar Renews His Siege of Jerusalem

Why is the Babylonian king called both Nebuchadrezzar and Nebuchadnezzar? (39:1) In the King James version of the Bible, Nebuchadnezzar is the more well-known name for the Babylonian king at the time of Judah's destruction. In the book of Ezekiel, and at times in Jeremiah, the name *Nebuchadrezzar* is used, which is closer to the original Hebrew form of the name. Note that in Jeremiah 39, Nebuchadrezzar is used in verse one, whereas Nebuchadnezzar is used in verse five. This demonstrates that the translators considered the names interchangeable.

What were the consequences of this long siege? (39:1–3) "The siege, carried out with the full force of Nebuchadnezzar's troops, lasted for eighteen months. . . . As the city was gradually starved and its resistance progressively weakened, it was only a matter of time before troops could break through the walls and gain access to the city; the populace was already broken and dispirited. . . . The rest of Jeremiah's prophetic warning is now fulfilled . . . as Jerusalem, the city of God, is set ablaze" (Brown, "Jeremiah," 458, 459).

live, and this city shall not be burned with fire; and thou shalt live, and thine house:

18 But if thou wilt not go forth to the king of Babylon's princes, then shall this city be given into the hand of the Chaldeans, and they shall burn it with fire, and thou shalt not escape out of their hand.

19 And Zedekiah the king said unto Jeremiah, I am afraid of the Jews that are fallen to the Chaldeans, lest they deliver me into their hand, and they mock me.

20 But Jeremiah said, They shall not deliver *thee.* Obey, I beseech thee, the voice of the LORD, which I speak unto thee: so it shall be well unto thee, and thy soul shall live.

CHAPTER 39

Jerusalem is taken, and the people are taken captive—Jeremiah and Ebed-melech, the Ethiopian, are preserved.

1 In the ninth year of Zedekiah king of Judah, in the tenth month, came Nebuchadrezzar king of Babylon and all his army against Jerusalem, and they besieged it.

2 *And* in the eleventh year of Zedekiah, in the fourth month, the ninth *day* of the month, the city was broken up.

3 And all the princes of the king of Babylon came in, and sat in the middle gate, *even* Nergal-sharezer, Samgar-nebo, Sarsechim, Rab-saris, Nergal-sharezer, Rab-mag, with all the residue of the princes of the king of Babylon.

4 ¶ And it came to pass, *that* when Zedekiah
the king of Judah saw them, and all the men
of war, then they fled, and went forth out of
the city by night, by the way of the king's
garden, by the gate betwixt the two walls:
and he went out the way of the plain.

5 But the Chaldeans' army pursued after
them, and overtook Zedekiah in the plains of
Jericho: and when they had taken him, they
brought him up to Nebuchadnezzar king of
Babylon to Riblah in the land of Hamath,
where he gave judgment upon him.

6 Then the king of Babylon slew the sons of
Zedekiah in Riblah before his eyes: also the
king of Babylon slew all the nobles of Judah.

7 Moreover he put out Zedekiah's eyes, and
bound him with chains, to carry him to
Babylon.

How were Jeremiah's prophecies regarding Zedekiah fulfilled? (39:4–7) These verses describe "the flight, capture, torture, and imprisonment of Zedekiah. . . . Zedekiah, realizing the end of Jerusalem had come, still hoped to save his life. He and his company tried to escape [but] was captured and taken to Riblah. . . . At Riblah, Nebuchadnezzar began slaying all the resisters. . . . Only Zedekiah was spared for captivity after he saw with his own eyes the slaughter and then was blinded. . . . Thus two prophecies were fulfilled: Zedekiah would see the king of Babylon and be taken there (cf. 32:3–4), and he would die in Babylon without ever seeing it (cf. Eze. 12:13)" (*Expositor's Bible Commentary [Abridged]*, 1242).

What do we know about Zedekiah's sons? (39:6–7) "In the book of Omni, readers are introduced to the 'people of Zarahemla' who 'came out from Jerusalem at the time that Zedekiah, king of Judah, was carried away captive into Babylon' (Omni 1:15). Mosiah 25:2 explains that Zarahemla was a 'descendant of Mulek, and those who came with him into the wilderness.' Yet not until the book of Helaman do readers learn that Mulek was a 'son of Zedekiah' (Helaman 6:10), and that he was Zedekiah's only son who wasn't slain when Jerusalem was destroyed by the Babylonians (Helaman 8:21)" ("Why Should Readers Pay Close Attention to the Mulekites?").

Jeremiah 39:8–18. The Remnant of the Jews Are Carried Captive into Babylon and Jeremiah Is Released from Prison

8 ¶ And the Chaldeans burned the king's
house, and the houses of the people, with
fire, and brake down the walls of Jerusalem.

9 Then Nebuzar-adan the captain of the guard
carried away captive into Babylon the remnant of the people that remained in the city,
and those that fell away, that fell to him, with
the rest of the people that remained.

10 But Nebuzar-adan the captain of the
guard left of the poor of the people, which
had nothing, in the land of Judah, and gave
them vineyards and fields at the same time.

11 ¶ Now Nebuchadrezzar king of Babylon
gave charge concerning Jeremiah to Nebuzar-
adan the captain of the guard, saying,

How was Jeremiah treated after the collapse of Jerusalem? (39:12–14) Nebuchadnezzar placed Jeremiah under the charge of the "captain of the guard" (Jer. 39:11), who was told to "look well to him" or to "keep your eyes on him" (Jer. 39:12*a*). Interestingly, to accomplish this, Jeremiah was "placed in the custody of Gedaliah, the newly-appointed governor of Judah with whose family Jeremiah had long been friendly [Jer. 26:24; 36:10]" (*New Oxford Annotated Bible* [1991], 1023).

Why is it important to trust the Lord as did Ebed-melech? (39:16–18) Jeremiah was God's servant and did what he was instructed to do. President Henry B. Eyring taught: "You show your trust in [God] when you listen with the intent to learn and repent and then you go and do whatever He asks. If you trust God enough to listen for His message in every sermon, song, and prayer . . . , you will find it. And if you then go and do what He would have you do, your power to trust Him will grow, and in time you will be overwhelmed with gratitude to find that He has come to trust you" ("Trust in God, Then Go and Do," 73).

Summary of Jeremiah 40–41

Jeremiah is released from prison and dwells with Gedaliah, who was made governor of Judah by Nebuchadnezzar. Gedaliah submits to Babylon while many of the surviving Jews return to Judah. Ishmael is sent by the king of the Ammonites to kill Gedaliah. Johanan warns Gedaliah of this plot, but Gedaliah refuses to believe him. Ishmael kills Gedaliah by the sword and the Jews who were with him. Men from Shechem come to see Gedaliah, and are captured by Ishmael and slain. Johanan gathers men to meet Ismael in battle at the waters of Gibeon. Many desert Ishmael and join Johanan. Johanan rescues the captives taken by Ishmael, but Ishmael escapes to the Ammonites.

12 Take him, and look well to him, and do
him no harm; but do unto him even as he
shall say unto thee.

13 So Nebuzar-adan the captain of the
guard sent, and Nebushasban, Rab-saris, and
Nergal-sharezer, Rab-mag, and all the king of
Babylon's princes;

14 Even they sent, and took Jeremiah out of
the court of the prison, and committed him
unto Gedaliah the son of Ahikam the son of
Shaphan, that he should carry him home: so
he dwelt among the people.

15 ¶ Now the word of the LORD came unto
Jeremiah, while he was shut up in the court
of the prison, saying,

16 Go and speak to Ebed-melech the
Ethiopian, saying, Thus saith the LORD of
hosts, the God of Israel; Behold, I will bring
my words upon this city for evil, and not for
good; and they shall be *accomplished* in that
day before thee.

17 But I will deliver thee in that day, saith
the LORD: and thou shalt not be given into
the hand of the men of whom thou *art* afraid.

18 For I will surely deliver thee, and thou
shalt not fall by the sword, but thy life shall
be for a prey unto thee: because thou hast
put thy trust in me, saith the LORD.

CHAPTERS 40–41

The king of Babylon makes Gedaliah governor over the remnant left in Judah—Jeremiah is freed and dwells among them.

Ishmael kills Gedaliah and carries the people of Mizpah captive—They are rescued by Johanan.

CHAPTERS 42–43

Jeremiah promises Johanan and the remnant of Judah peace and safety if they remain in Judah, but the sword, famine, and pestilence if they go to Egypt.

Johanan carries Jeremiah and the remnant of Judah into Egypt—Jeremiah prophesies that Babylon will conquer Egypt.

Summary of Jeremiah 42–43

All of the captains and their forces promise Jeremiah that they will abide by the Lord's counsel. "Whether it be good, or whether it be evil we will obey the voice of the Lord our God" (Jer. 42:6). Jeremiah counsels them not to be afraid of Babylon. If the people set their faces to enter into Egypt they will receive the sword, which they feared from Babylon. The Lord's fury will be poured out as they enter Egypt and they will become "an execration and an astonishment, and a curse, and a reproach" (Jer. 42:18).

Jeremiah warns those who desired to flee to Egypt that they would not find safety there. He is accused of lying to them. Jeremiah is taken with the group to Egypt, perhaps by force. Yet Jeremiah's prophecy that the Lord would "kindle a fire in the houses of the gods of Egypt . . . and carry them away captives" would be fulfilled through the conquest by the Babylonians (Jer. 43:12).

CHAPTER 44

Jeremiah prophesies that the Jews in Egypt, save a small remnant, will be destroyed because they worship false gods.

Summary of Jeremiah 44

Jeremiah declares the word of the Lord to the Jews living in the land of Egypt. They had provoked the Lord "to anger, in that they went to burn incense, and to serve other gods" (Jer. 44:3). The children of Israel had forgotten the wickedness of their fathers. They reject Jeremiah's message and blame their situation in exile to the fact that they had been prevented to "burn incense unto the queen of heaven, and to pour out drink offerings unto her" (Jer. 44:17).

CHAPTER 45

Jeremiah promises Baruch that his life will be preserved.

Summary of Jeremiah 45

Baruch is despondent as he realizes all of the prophecies of Jeremiah will be fulfilled. He is then "admonished not to seek great things but to realize that life itself is God's gift. God assures him that his life will be spared as a prize of war. Now after the destruction of Jerusalem Baruch is still with Jeremiah, indicating that God has fulfilled his promise" (Schultz, *Old Testament Speaks*, 339).

CHAPTER 46

Jeremiah prophesies the conquest of Egypt by Babylon—Jacob will be saved and will return to his own land.

Summary of Jeremiah 46

Jeremiah 46 is separated into two parts: verses 2 through 12 and 13 through 26. The first section describes a battle "between Pharaoh-necho, king of Egypt, and Nebuchadnezzar, king of Babylon; in which the Egyptians were routed in Carchemish with great slaughter" (*Adam Clarke's Commentary* [on Jeremiah 46 Introduction]). The second section relates "how Nebuchadrezzar king of Babylon should come and smite the land of Egypt" (Jeremiah 46:13). Even with all of this, God is with and will finally save Israel.

Summary of Jeremiah 47

"Like Judah, the Philistines were caught up between the larger powers of Egypt and Mesopotamia. [In spite of] uncertainties, the intent of the prophecy is clear: the Philistine cities are to experience fearful destruction in which the northern enemy is understood to be acting as God's agent. . . . All is seen as part of the same comprehensive divine purpose to bring about the submission of all nations to the king of Babylon" (Clements, *Jeremiah*, 250–51). "The Babylonian destruction of Philistia for allying itself with Egypt took place in 604/3 B.C., when, according to the Babylonian Chronicle, Ashkelon fell after a long siege" (Seely, "Prophet over the Nations," 248).

CHAPTER 47

Jeremiah foretells desolation and destruction upon the Philistines.

Summary of Jeremiah 48

Because of idolatry and Moab magnifying itself against the Lord, it is doomed to destruction.

CHAPTER 48

Judgment and destruction will come upon the Moabites for their contempt of God.

Summary of Jeremiah 49

Revelations of judgment and destruction against Ammon (49:1–6), Edom (49:7–22), Damascus (49:23–27), Kedar and Hazor (49:28–33), and Elam (49:34–39).

CHAPTER 49

Judgment and destruction will come upon the people of Ammon, Edom, Kedar, Hazor, and Elam.

Summary of Jeremiah 50–51

Jeremiah prophesies against Babylon and her sins. Israel is reminded that "their Redeemer is strong; the Lord of hosts is his name: he shall thoroughly plead their cause" (50:34). Israel will not be forsaken but is commanded to flee Babylon. Babylon will be utterly destroyed and "shall be desolate for ever" (51:26, 62).

CHAPTERS 50–51

Babylon will be destroyed and never rise again—The scattered people of Israel will be brought again into the lands of their inheritance.

Jeremiah Prophesies against Nine Nations (Jeremiah 46–51)

"The book of Jeremiah contains prophecies against nine foreign nations in chapters 46 through 51. These oracles [prophecies], as in the other major prophets, are grouped together. They appear in no obvious chronological or geographical order: Egypt (chap. 46), Philistia (chap. 47), Moab (chap. 48), Ammon (49:1–6), Edom (49:7–22), Damascus (49:23–27), Kedar (49:28–33), Elam (49:34–39), and Babylon (chaps. 50–51). The oracles follow closely, though not exactly, the order of cities and nations listed in the passage about the cup of wrath in Jeremiah 25:15–38. They are also connected thematically with the imagery of the prophecy in that passage" (Seely, "Prophet over the Nations," 245–46).

"Since the prophets' principal mission was to their own people, . . . the messages served as warning that God punishes evil wherever he finds it. . . . The message for Judah was clear: God is in control of history, not just Judah's history but the history of all the nations. In essence the Lord is larger than they ever imagined, and he is righteous" (Huey, *Jeremiah, Lamentations*, 374).

Judgment, destruction, and desolation will come upon Babylon for her sins—Israel is commanded, Flee from Babylon—Israel is the Lord's rod to destroy all kingdoms.

CHAPTER 52

Jerusalem is besieged and taken by the Chaldeans—Many people and the vessels of the house of the Lord are carried into Babylon.

1 Zedekiah *was* one and twenty years old when he began to reign, and he reigned eleven years in Jerusalem. And his mother's name *was* Hamutal the daughter of Jeremiah of Libnah.

2 And he did *that which was* evil in the eyes of the LORD, according to all that Jehoiakim had done.

3 For through the anger of the LORD it came to pass in Jerusalem and Judah, till he had cast them out from his presence, that Zedekiah rebelled against the king of Babylon.

4 ¶ And it came to pass in the ninth year of his reign, in the tenth month, in the tenth *day* of the month, *that* Nebuchadrezzar king of Babylon came, he and all his army, against Jerusalem, and pitched against it, and built forts against it round about.

5 So the city was besieged unto the eleventh year of king Zedekiah.

Jeremiah 52:1–11. The Babylonians Capture Jerusalem and Punish Zedekiah

What happens in Jerusalem when Zedekiah begins to reign? (52:1) "The beginning of the reign of Zedekiah also marked the year that Lehi, the great patriarch and prophet of the Book of Mormon, left the city of Jerusalem. Nephi recorded: 'For it came to pass in the commencement of the first year of the reign of Zedekiah, king of Judah, (my father, Lehi, having dwelt at Jerusalem in all his days) . . . my father, Lehi . . . went forth' (1 Ne. 1:4–5)" (Ludlow, *Companion to Your Study of the Old Testament*, 329–30). Zedekiah "was the last king of Judah and Jerusalem. . . . His original name was Mattaniah, which was changed to Zedekiah by Nebuchadnezzar when he carried off his nephew Jehoiachin to Babylon, and left him on the throne of Jerusalem" (*Smith's Bible Dictionary*, "Zedekiah"). See commentary in this volume for 2 Kings 24–25; 25:4; and 25:7.

How was the Lord's anger with Judah's wickedness demonstrated in Jerusalem? (52:3) Jerusalem's wickedness led to their destruction. "The initial focus of Jeremiah 52 is on King Zedekiah, but these verses expand that focus in three ways, incorporating an account of the destruction of Jerusalem (vv. 12–16), an account of the pillage of the Temple (vv. 17–23), and an account of what the Babylonians did to some of the leading citizens of Jerusalem (vv. 24–27). For those in ancient Judah, the city of Jerusalem, the Temple, and the key religious and political leaders (remember that the monarch, King Zedekiah, was already considered in earlier verses) were all understood to have been established by the Lord and secure forever as signs of God's commitment to Judah" (Bracke, *Jeremiah 30–52 and Lamentations*, 172).

How long was Jerusalem under siege? (52:5) "A grinding year-and-a-half siege preceded Jerusalem's fiery end. As Jeremiah had predicted, thousands of citizens died by famine, fire, and sword. Jerusalem and Solomon's magnificent temple became rubble and ashes. Zedekiah, the proud monarch, saw his sons slain, before having his eyes put out. Contrary to promises made by false prophets, tens of thousands more of Jerusalem's citizens became Babylonian captives. The few survivors eventually fled to Egypt for safety" (Meservy, "Jerusalem at the Time of Lehi and Jeremiah," 22).

How did Zedekiah and his aides escape the siege? (52:7–9) "The king and his army officials may have made preparations for their escape when they saw the end approaching. Apparently they were able to make their initial getaway under the cover of darkness. In similar circumstances, others have escaped using bribes or disguises—perhaps as women, since women and children were sometimes permitted to go free" (*Quest Study Bible* [2011], 1191). "In the evening of the day Babylonian soldiers poured into the city, Zedekiah and some of his men fled, making for the Jordan and hoping to escape to safety in the desert. They got as far as Jericho before they were captured" (*Old Testament Student Manual: 1 Kings–Malachi*, 233).

6 And in the fourth month, in the ninth *day* of the month, the famine was sore in the city, so that there was no bread for the people of the land.

7 Then the city was broken up, and all the men of war fled, and went forth out of the city by night by the way of the gate between the two walls, which *was* by the king's garden; (now the Chaldeans *were* by the city round about:) and they went by the way of the plain.

8 ¶ But the army of the Chaldeans pursued after the king, and overtook Zedekiah in the plains of Jericho; and all his army was scattered from him.

9 Then they took the king, and carried him up unto the king of Babylon to Riblah in the land of Hamath; where he gave judgment upon him.

10 And the king of Babylon slew the sons of Zedekiah before his eyes: he slew also all the princes of Judah in Riblah.

11 Then he put out the eyes of Zedekiah; and the king of Babylon bound him in chains, and carried him to Babylon, and put him in prison till the day of his death.

Where Can We Learn about One of Zedekiah's Sons Who Escaped from Jerusalem and the Army of the Chaldeans? (Jeremiah 52:10)

"One important fact that the Bible does not contain is that not all of Zedekiah's sons were slain. He had at least one young son, an infant, that was secreted away during the chaos and whose life was spared. This child, Mulek, eventually found his way to the American continent along with those who sought to protect him (see Omni 1:14–17; Hel. 6:10; 8:21). These people were called 'Mulekites,' and were discovered in the city of Zarahemla by Mosiah and his people of Nephi. The name *Mulek* is an interesting one, since the Hebrew word *melek* means 'king,' and the vowel *u* implies 'last in line,' neither of which would have been known to Joseph Smith at the time he translated the Book of Mormon" (Chase, *Making Jeremiah Plain*, 86).

12 ¶ Now in the fifth month, in the tenth *day* of the month, which *was* the nineteenth year of Nebuchadrezzar king of Babylon, came Nebuzar-adan, captain of the guard, *which* served the king of Babylon, into Jerusalem,

13 And burned the house of the LORD, and the king's house; and all the houses of Jerusalem, and all the houses of the great *men*, burned he with fire:

14 And all the army of the Chaldeans, that *were* with the captain of the guard, brake down all the walls of Jerusalem round about.

15 Then Nebuzar-adan the captain of the guard carried away captive *certain* of the poor of the people, and the residue of the people that remained in the city, and those that fell away, that fell to the king of Babylon, and the rest of the multitude.

16 But Nebuzar-adan the captain of the guard left *certain* of the poor of the land for vinedressers and for husbandmen.

17 Also the pillars of brass that *were* in the house of the LORD, and the bases, and the brasen sea that *was* in the house of the LORD, the Chaldeans brake, and carried all the brass of them to Babylon.

18 The caldrons also, and the shovels, and the snuffers, and the bowls, and the spoons, and all the vessels of brass wherewith they ministered, took they away.

19 And the basins, and the firepans, and the bowls, and the caldrons, and the candlesticks, and the spoons, and the cups; *that* which *was* of gold *in* gold, and *that* which *was* of silver *in* silver, took the captain of the guard away.

20 The two pillars, one sea, and twelve brasen bulls that *were* under the bases, which king Solomon had made in the house of the LORD: the brass of all these vessels was without weight.

Jeremiah 52:12–30. The Babylonians Burn Jerusalem and Take Most of the Jews to Babylon

Why does Jeremiah specifically note that walls of Jerusalem were broken down? (52:14) Not only did Nebuchadnezzar order the burning of the temple, palaces, and dwellings of Jerusalem, but he "also undertook the dismantling of the walls of the city. Just how complete this dismantling was has been revealed by excavations on the eastern side of the city overlooking the Kidron Valley. The verb 'pull down' (*nātas*) occurs several times in the book of Jeremiah. [Jehovah] had appointed the prophet to pull down kingdoms (1:10). [Jehovah] himself might pull down a kingdom (18:7). He had pulled Israel down (31:28). Thus the use of the verb 'pull down' in reference to the walls carries with it some significant overtones" (Thompson, *Book of Jeremiah*, 776).

What does it mean that the vessels looted from the temple were "without weight"? (52:20) Clearly, the accumulation of an abundance of brass, gold, and silver that adorned the temple had physical weight. The King James Version phrase "without weight" is better rendered "was more than could be weighed"

(NIV, Jeremiah 52:20). "The Babylonians broke up the bronze pillars in front of the LORD's Temple, the bronze water carts, and the great bronze basin called the Sea, and they carried all the bronze away to Babylon. . . . The weight of the bronze from the two pillars, the Sea with the twelve bronze oxen beneath it, and the water carts was too great to be measured" (Martens and Walker, *Isaiah, Jeremiah & Lamentations*, 542).

Why were pomegranates on the pillars of the temple? (52:22–23) When the tabernacle was constructed in the wilderness, the Lord directed that colored trims in the shape of pomegranates were to decorate the priests' robes. Later when Solomon's temple was built, golden pomegranates adorned the tops of the pillars. "Its many seeds symbolize fertility. . . . The pomegranate gave its perfect shape to the golden bells that ornamented the Temple, to its furniture, embroidery, and carved column-capitals, and to the priestly garments" (Zohary, *Plants of the Bible*, 62).

21 And *concerning* the pillars, the height of
one pillar *was* eighteen cubits; and a fillet of
twelve cubits did compass it; and the thick-
ness thereof *was* four fingers: *it was* hollow.

22 And a chapiter of brass *was* upon it; and
the height of one chapiter *was* five cubits,
with network and pomegranates upon the
chapiters round about, all *of* brass. The second pillar also and the pomegranates *were*
like unto these.

23 And there were ninety and six pomegranates on a side; *and* all the pomegranates upon
the network *were* an hundred round about.

24 ¶ And the captain of the guard took
Seraiah the chief priest, and Zephaniah the
second priest, and the three keepers of the
door:

25 He took also out of the city an eunuch,
which had the charge of the men of war; and
seven men of them that were near the king's
person, which were found in the city; and
the principal scribe of the host, who mustered the people of the land; and threescore
men of the people of the land, that were
found in the midst of the city.

26 So Nebuzar-adan the captain of the guard
took them, and brought them to the king of
Babylon to Riblah.

27 And the king of Babylon smote them, and
put them to death in Riblah in the land of
Hamath. Thus Judah was carried away captive out of his own land.

28 This *is* the people whom Nebuchadrezzar
carried away captive: in the seventh year
three thousand Jews and three and twenty:

29 In the eighteenth year of Nebuchadrezzar
he carried away captive from Jerusalem eight
hundred thirty and two persons:

30 In the three and twentieth year of Nebuchadrezzar Nebuzar-adan the captain of the
guard carried away captive of the Jews seven
hundred forty and five persons: all the persons *were* four thousand and six hundred.

31 ¶ And it came to pass in the seven and
thirtieth year of the captivity of Jehoiachin
king of Judah, in the twelfth month, in
the five and twentieth *day* of the month,
that Evil-merodach king of Babylon in the
first year of his reign lifted up the head of
Jehoiachin king of Judah, and brought him
forth out of prison,

32 And spake kindly unto him, and set his
throne above the throne of the kings that
were with him in Babylon,

33 And changed his prison garments: and he
did continually eat bread before him all the
days of his life.

34 And *for* his diet, there was a continual
diet given him of the king of Babylon, every
day a portion until the day of his death, all
the days of his life.

Jeremiah 52:31–34. Jehoiachin, King of Judah, Lives Out His Life as a Captive in Babylon

Why did the king of Babylon release Jehoiachin from prison? (52:31–34) Although Jeremiah "told those in Babylon to prepare for a long stay, he promised that in seventy years there would be a return. . . . It is recorded that Nebuchadnezzar's successor Evil-merodach, in the first year of his reign, released Jehoiachin, the exiled king of Judah, out of prison and restored him to a respectable lifestyle. This foreshadowing of the restoration of Judah in 539 would serve as a type of the establishment of the 'new covenant' (Matt. 26:28) and finally the new and everlasting covenant (D&C 1:22)" (Seely, "Ministry of Jeremiah," 211–12).

THE
LAMENTATIONS
OF JEREMIAH

Introduction

The word *lamentation* means weeping or crying with great sorrow. "The book of Lamentations, traditionally attributed to Jeremiah, presents five short poems lamenting the tragedy of the fall of Jerusalem. The Hebrew text of Lamentations gives no evidence of authorship. The vividness and immediacy of the descriptions has led many to believe that it was written by an eyewitness to the destruction of Jerusalem. In the Septuagint, the tradition that Jeremiah was the author was placed in the Greek heading to the book: 'And it came to pass, after Israel was taken captive, and Jerusalem made desolate, that Jeremias sat weeping and lamented with his lamentation over Jerusalem' (LXX Lamentations, heading)" (Holzapfel, et al., *Jehovah and the World of the Old Testament*, 335).

"[Lamentations] was written shortly after the destruction of Jerusalem and the fall of the Southern Kingdom. It fully exposed the pathos felt by Jeremiah. . . . With every word one can almost hear the drop of a tear and feel the breaking of a heart" (Pearson, *Old Testament*, 59).

"Each chapter is a separate poem. The first four are acrostic poems: Each succeeding verse begins with the next letter of the 22-consonant Hebrew alphabet. Chapter 3 gives three verses to each of the 22 letters. This is a feature common in Hebrew poetry, and may have been used to aid memorization" (*Revell Bible Dictionary*, 620). Even today the poems in Lamentations "continue as a part of Jewish liturgy and are recited late each summer in remembrance of the destruction of the temples of Solomon and Herod, which occurred on the same day . . . six hundred fifty-seven years apart" (Ludlow, *Unlocking the Old Testament*, 187).

Jeremiah "stresses that Judah brought the suffering on herself. Whereas the suffering of an individual or a . . . nation cannot necessarily be attributed to sin, the suffering of a covenant nation can be. The Jews had reached a level of desperate wickedness which God could not ignore. . . . But in all this darkness there was a spark of light. . . . If Israel would repent and call upon the Lord, Jeremiah promised that the Lord would hear and a restoration would be possible" (Pearson, *Old Testament*, 59–60).

CHAPTER 1

Jeremiah laments the miserable condition of Jerusalem—Jerusalem herself complains of her deep sorrow.

1 How doth the city sit solitary, *that was* full of people! *how* is she become as a widow! she *that was* great among the nations, *and* princess among the provinces, *how* is she become tributary!

2 She weepeth sore in the night, and her tears *are* on her cheeks: among all her lovers she

Lamentations 1:1–11. Jeremiah Sorrows over the Destruction of Jerusalem

Why does Jeremiah begin his book with the word "How"? (1:1) "In the Hebrew Bible the book of Lamentations is called *eka*—'How?'. . . The initial word 'how' of three of the poems in Lamentations [chapters 1, 2, and 4] poses unanswerable questions and expresses the utter inability of the poet to articulate the agonies that had befallen Jerusalem: 'How doth the city sit solitary . . . how is she become as a widow! . . . how is she become tributary!' (Lam. 1:1). It expresses

hath none to comfort *her:* all her friends have dealt treacherously with her, they are become her enemies.

3 Judah is gone into captivity because of affliction, and because of great servitude: she dwelleth among the heathen, she findeth no rest: all her persecutors overtook her between the straits.

4 The ways of Zion do mourn, because none come to the solemn feasts: all her gates are desolate: her priests sigh, her virgins are afflicted, and she *is* in bitterness.

5 Her adversaries are the chief, her enemies prosper; for the LORD hath afflicted her for the multitude of her transgressions: her children are gone into captivity before the enemy.

6 And from the daughter of Zion all her beauty is departed: her princes are become like harts *that* find no pasture, and they are gone without strength before the pursuer.

7 Jerusalem remembered in the days of her affliction and of her miseries all her pleasant things that she had in the days of old, when her people fell into the hand of the enemy, and none did help her: the adversaries saw her, *and* did mock at her sabbaths.

8 Jerusalem hath grievously sinned; therefore she is removed: all that honoured her despise her, because they have seen her nakedness: yea, she sigheth, and turneth backward.

9 Her filthiness *is* in her skirts; she remembereth not her last end; therefore she came down wonderfully: she had no comforter. O LORD, behold my affliction: for the enemy hath magnified *himself.*

10 The adversary hath spread out his hand upon all her pleasant things: for she hath seen *that* the heathen entered into her sanctuary, whom thou didst command *that* they should not enter into thy congregation.

the afflicted's disbelief: 'How hath the Lord covered the daughter of Zion with a cloud in his anger' (Lam. 2:1)" (Seely, "Lamentations," 254).

In what ways was Jerusalem a "widow"? (1:1–5) Jeremiah "personifies the city of Zion as a widow, a pitiful woman in pain. As frequently noted in the Bible, widows are the symbol of the distressed and disenfranchised element of society who are bereft of protectors. Israel the bride of the Lord has now become a widow, as the Lord has withdrawn and even become her afflicter (Lam. 1:5). Once great among the nations, Zion now sits alone weeping. . . . This theme is repeated throughout the lament (Lam. 1:2, 9, 16, 17, 21). . . . Zion the weeping woman is a tragic figure; even death would bring her solace" (Seely, "Lamentations," 254–55).

In what ways was Jerusalem left to herself when Babylon invaded? (1:5–8) "The writer of Lamentations wrote to reveal Judah's pathetic condition as a despoiled people at the hands of the Babylonians. He likened abandoned Jerusalem to a woman whose husband was dead (see v. 1). All her 'lovers' (the false gods she worshiped) abandoned her to her enemies (see vv. 2–3). All of this came about because of Judah's wickedness (see vv. 5–8). Even the Lord forsook her in the hour of her affliction. Her enemies 'mock[ed] at her sabbaths' (v. 7)" (*Old Testament Student Manual: 1 Kings–Malachi*, 250). ⊕

In what way had Jerusalem "grievously sinned"? (1:8–9) "Jerusalem is compared to a debased prostitute, shamelessly exposing her nakedness. . . . Since prostitution is repeatedly used for Israel's idolatry and Baal worship, it is obviously implied here. The completeness of Israel's collapse has finally brought her to her senses. She knows she has no grounds for begging for a reversal of fortune . . . (cf. Isa. 10:12)" (*Expositor's Bible Commentary [Abridged]*, 1264).

What were the "pleasant things" "the adversary" laid their hands on? (1:10–11) "This is specially mentioned in [v.] 10. The enemy has spread out his hand over all her jewels (. . . the costly treasures of Jerusalem which were plundered), and even forced into the sanctuary of the Lord to spoil it of its treasures and vessels. . . . [Nor] are 'all her pleasant vessels' merely the sacred vessels of the temple. '[All] her precious vessels' [must], include . . . favourite spots, beautiful buildings, pleasure gardens. . . . Besides this disgrace, famine also comes on her. All her people . . . sigh after bread, and part with their jewels for food, merely to prolong their life" (Keil and Delitzsch, *Commentary* [on Lamentations 1:10–11]).

Lamentations 1:12–17. Jerusalem Herself Bemoans Her Deep Sorrow

Why does the text change to first person in this verse? (1:12) "The prophet [Jeremiah] became a voice for the personified city, lamenting what had come upon her, describing her, confessing her faults, but praying that the oppressors would also be punished for their wickedness" (Rasmussen, *Latter-day Saint Commentary on the Old Testament*, 578).

How does the writer's use of common metaphors intensify the tragedy of Judah's fate? (1:13–15) The book of Lamentations "employed vivid images to depict Judah's great distress, likening it to fire in the bones, a net for the feet, a yoke around the neck, the crushing of grapes in a winepress. Each allusion is an apt one. The image of the yoke or bands around the neck is also used in Isaiah 52:2. According to the interpretation given in Doctrine and Covenants 113:10, the bands on Israel's neck 'are the curses of God upon her, or the remnants of Israel in their scattered condition among the Gentiles.' Judah's seventy-year captivity in Babylon was like that described in these scriptures" (*Old Testament Student Manual: 1 Kings–Malachi*, 250).

What was the cause of Israel's "yoke" or bondage? (1:14) "We learn valuable lessons from this tragic period. We should do everything within our power to avoid the sin and rebellion that lead to bondage. We also recognize that righteous living is a prerequisite for assisting the Lord in gathering His elect and in the literal gathering of Israel.

"Bondage, subjugation, addictions, and servitude come in many forms. They can be literal physical enslavement but can also be loss or impairment of moral agency that can impede our progress. Jeremiah is clear that unrighteousness and rebellion were the main reasons for the destruction of Jerusalem and captivity in Babylon" (Cook, "Lamentations of Jeremiah," 89).

11 All her people sigh, they seek bread; they have given their pleasant things for meat to relieve the soul: see, O LORD, and consider; for I am become vile.

12 ¶ *Is it* nothing to you, all ye that pass by? behold, and see if there be any sorrow like unto my sorrow, which is done unto me, wherewith the LORD hath afflicted *me* in the day of his fierce anger.

13 From above hath he sent fire into my bones, and it prevaileth against them: he hath spread a net for my feet, he hath turned me back: he hath made me desolate *and* faint all the day.

14 The yoke of my transgressions is bound by his hand: they are wreathed, *and* come up upon my neck: he hath made my strength to fall, the Lord hath delivered me into *their* hands, *from whom* I am not able to rise up.

15 The Lord hath trodden under foot all my mighty *men* in the midst of me: he hath called an assembly against me to crush my young men: the Lord hath trodden the virgin, the daughter of Judah, *as* in a winepress.

16 For these *things* I weep; mine eye, mine eye runneth down with water, because the comforter that should relieve my soul is far from me: my children are desolate, because the enemy prevailed.

17 Zion spreadeth forth her hands, *and there is* none to comfort her: the LORD hath commanded concerning Jacob, *that* his adversaries *should be* round about him: Jerusalem is as a menstruous woman among them.

Why was Jerusalem compared to a menstruous woman? (1:17) Even as those in Jerusalem reached to the heavens for help against her enemies, no help would come. Jerusalem had become like "a menstruant, who is ritually impure, not fit to come into contact with holy things. . . . Jerusalem's 'lovers' (vv. 2, 19) distance themselves from her" (*New Oxford Annotated Bible* [2010], 1149–50). In other words, in the eyes of those who followed the law of Moses, Jerusalem had become like someone "to whom none dared to approach, either to help or comfort, because of the law [Lev. 15:19–27]" (*Adam Clarke's Commentary* [on Lamentations 1:17]).

Lamentations 1:18–22. The Lord Is Righteous

18 ¶ The LORD is righteous; for I have rebelled against his commandment: hear, I pray you, all people, and behold my sorrow: my virgins and my young men are gone into captivity.

What is a starting point for meaningful repentance? (1:18) "Jerusalem confesses 'the Lord is righteous' and 'I [have] rebelled.' This is the place to which every person or people experiencing divine discipline must come if there is to be any hope of restoration. But don't expect that confession to result in an immediate change of circumstances. Acknowledging God's righteousness and admitting our fault is a turning point, a first step that must be followed by a long hike back along the path of righteousness" (Richards, *Bible Reader's Companion*, 481).

19 I called for my lovers, *but* they deceived me: my priests and mine elders gave up the ghost in the city, while they sought their meat to relieve their souls.

What does it mean that Jerusalem's priests and elders "gave up the ghost"? (1:19) Conditions were so serious in Jerusalem that her own priests and elders were of little help to the people. In fact, they "gave up the ghost . . . while they sought their meat to relieve their souls" (Lam. 1:19) "or died in the city of Jerusalem; not by the sword of the enemy, but through famine" (*John Gill's Exposition of the Whole Bible*, [commentary on Lamentations 1:19]).

20 Behold, O LORD; for I *am* in distress: my bowels are troubled; mine heart is turned within me; for I have grievously rebelled: abroad the sword bereaveth, at home *there is* as death.

21 They have heard that I sigh: *there is* none to comfort me: all mine enemies have heard of my trouble; they are glad that thou hast done *it:* thou wilt bring the day *that* thou hast called, and they shall be like unto me.

What might the Jews have avoided if they had responded to their concerns and feelings much earlier? (1:20–22) "The bowels, or intestines, carry several symbolic meanings in scripture. In the Bible the Hebrew and Greek words translated as 'bowels' imply compassion, sympathy, love, or pity [see *Thayer's Greek-English Lexicon*, 585]. Thus the bowels are most often associated with one's feelings or emotions [see McConkie and Parry, *Guide to Scriptural Symbols*, 24]" (Gaskill, *Lost Language of Symbolism*, 32).

Summary of Lamentations 2–4

In these chapters, Jeremiah mourns over what happened to the people living in Jerusalem and Judea. He points out in Jeremiah 2:1–9 that it was the Lord who punished His people because of their iniquities. Conditions became so extreme during Babylon's siege on Jerusalem that some parents may have turned to cannibalism (Lam. 2:20; 4:10). The Lord now hoped that this would lead them to humbly return to Him. "Though he cause grief, yet will he have compassion according to the multitude of his mercies" (Lam. 3:32). Still, the people feel God has forsaken them and hope He will not leave them forever. Jeremiah laments the way Israel used to be as he compares them to what they have now become. "The precious sons of Zion, comparable to fine gold, how are they esteemed as earthen pitchers, the work of the hands of the potter!" (Lam. 4:2).

Lamentations 5:1–5. Jeremiah Prays for the Restoration of Judah

What was the "inheritance" of the Jews? (5:1–3) This inheritance refers to their promised land, which the Lord had intended to remain in the family, but had now been lost. It "had been a gift from God to Abraham. This *inheritance* was a kind of 'down payment' on the future reign of God that would include the restoration of His people to that land. God demonstrated that He owned all nations and that Israel was to be His instrument for blessing all the nations on the earth. Yet in their present condition, the people of Israel seemed to be the most helpless of all peoples" (*Nelson Study Bible* [NKJV], 1330).

Why were the people compelled to purchase wood and water? (5:4) "Water and wood are mentioned in ver. 4 as the greatest necessities of life, without which it is impossible to exist. Both of these they must buy for themselves, because the country, with its waters and forests, is in the possession of the enemy. The emphasis lies on '*our* water . . . *our* wood.' What they formerly had, as their own property, for nothing, they must now purchase" (Keil and Delitzsch, *Commentary* [on Lamentations 5:4]).

22 Let all their wickedness come before thee; and do unto them, as thou hast done unto me for all my transgressions: for my sighs *are* many, and my heart *is* faint.

CHAPTERS 2–4

Misery, sorrow, and desolation prevail in Jerusalem.

Jeremiah, speaking for Judah, laments the calamity but trusts in the Lord and prays for deliverance.

The condition of Zion is pitiful because of sin and iniquity.

CHAPTER 5

Jeremiah recites in prayer the sorrowful condition of Zion.

1 Remember, O LORD, what is come upon us: consider, and behold our reproach.

2 Our inheritance is turned to strangers, our houses to aliens.

3 We are orphans and fatherless, our mothers *are* as widows.

4 We have drunken our water for money; our wood is sold unto us.

5 Our necks *are* under persecution: we labour, *and* have no rest.

Summary of Lamentations 5:6–15

The miserable condition of the people of Judah during and after Babylon conquers them is a tragic tale. They are violently enslaved, must labor with no rest, often risk their lives to obtain food, suffer sickness, see their leaders treated brutally, and feel forsaken by the God of Israel.

Lamentations 5:16–22. Jeremiah Asks the Lord to Turn Judah unto Him

16 The crown is fallen *from* our head: woe unto us, that we have sinned!

17 For this our heart is faint; for these *things* our eyes are dim.

What was the crown that had fallen from Judah's head? (5:16) "Jeremiah wrote the book of Lamentations when Judah fell captive to Babylon.... The imagery of the crown is clear. The crown is a symbol of the power to rule; therefore, Jeremiah's imagery tells us that Judah lost the governing power she once held" (Lund, "Understanding Scriptural Symbols," 24). "Crowns are worn by royalty as a symbol of their status and authority. As a result the word was extended to refer to the abstract concept of the dignity and honor that are the natural accompaniment of status and authority. In this passage the reference is not to an actual crown that Israel wore but to the dignity and honor" (Walton, et al., *IVP Bible Background Commentary*, 689).

18 Because of the mountain of Zion, which is desolate, the foxes walk upon it.

19 Thou, O LORD, remainest for ever; thy throne from generation to generation.

20 Wherefore dost thou forget us for ever, *and* forsake us so long time?

What was the significance of foxes roaming "the mountain of Zion"? (5:18) "The temple and the city were so utterly destroyed that buildings were ruined and abandoned. The land reverted to wilderness, where rodents and small animals took up lodging. These small animals attracted jackals [foxes], a hated nuisance in Israel. Their growing presence indicated that most people had left the land" (*Quest Study Bible* [2011], 1206).

21 Turn thou us unto thee, O LORD, and we shall be turned; renew our days as of old.

22 But thou hast utterly rejected us; thou art very wroth against us.

What might Lamentations' plea demonstrate about Judah's changing heart? (5:21–22) "This woeful lament and plea could have been translated: 'Return us to you, O Jehovah, and we shall return; renew our days as of old'" (Ludlow, *Companion to Your Study of the Old Testament*, 331). "Judah has brought tribulation upon herself; she has lost the blessings of the Lord's elect people.... The poet recognized that Judah was dependent upon the Lord's mercy to repent and regain her status" (Seely, "Lamentations," 257). What do you find compelling about Jeremiah's prayer in these verses? How can you more fully turn to the Lord and be renewed?

THE BOOK OF THE PROPHET
EZEKIEL

Introduction

Ezekiel's name means *God will strengthen* (see Bible Dictionary, "Ezekiel"). All we know about him is what he recorded in his own book. "The prophet Ezekiel was born about two decades before Lehi and his family left Jerusalem. In 597 B.C., at age 25, Ezekiel was one of the many carried captive to Babylon by Nebuchadnezzar, and as best we can tell, he spent the rest of his life there. He was of the Aaronic priestly lineage, and when he was 30, he became a prophet [see Ezek. 1–3; see also Holzapfel, et al., *Jehovah and the World of the Old Testament*, 344]" (Christofferson, "Voice of Warning," 108).

With a careful reading of his work, it becomes clear that "Ezekiel, like other Old Testament prophets, was an extraordinary poet, which accounts for much of the inter-weaving of symbolism and imagery in his message. The use of this method probably gave force to his words. Unfortunately, his style sometimes hampers the modern reader. The major portion of his prophecy, however, is intelligible and edifying to today's reader" (Pearson, *Old Testament*, 60).

Ezekiel's book "can be divided into three parts. Part one, chapters 1–24, includes his judgment prophecies against the Holy City and the nation of Judah. These prophecies are a reminder that a person cannot be saved by his former righteousness (see Ezek. 18:24). Part two, chapters 25–32, consists of his prophecies against Judah's near neighbors for their mistreatment of the Lord's covenant people and promises of a hopeful future for Israel (see Ezek. 28:24–26). Part three, chapters 33–48, contains Ezekiel's prophecies about the restoration of Judah—the people and the land—and a vision of a reconstructed temple and a river flowing to the Dead Sea" (Black, *400 Questions and Answers about the Old Testament*, 184).

"The book of Ezekiel is rich with accounts of visions and prophecies. For example, the Lord showed Ezekiel a vision of the resurrection of the house of Israel, affirming that the Lord's covenant people would eventually be gathered to the lands of their inheritance (see Ezekiel 37:1–14). The Lord also described the latter-day gathering of Israel by comparing it to the uniting of the stick of Joseph (the Book of Mormon) with the stick of Judah (the Bible) (see Ezekiel 37:15–28). The book of Ezekiel includes a prophecy of a great battle that will precede the Second Coming of Jesus Christ (see Ezekiel 38–39). Additionally, Ezekiel 40–48 contains a description of a temple that will be built in Jerusalem in the latter days" (*Old Testament Seminary Teacher Material*, 736).

"Undergirding [Ezekiel's prophetic messages], as with other prophets, is the testimony that the work of the kingdom is God's. God's purposes are not frustrated but will all be fulfilled. The best course of action for the individual, therefore, is to follow the Lord" (Pearson, *Old Testament*, 61).

CHAPTER 1

Ezekiel sees in vision four living creatures, four wheels, and the glory of God on His throne.

1 Now it came to pass in the thirtieth year,
in the fourth *month*, in the fifth *day* of the
month, as I *was* among the captives by

Ezekiel 1:1–3. Ezekiel Receives the Word of the Lord

Why was Ezekiel in Babylon? (1:1) About eleven years before the final destruction of Jerusalem, Babylon attacked rebellious Judah and carried away King Jehoiachin and many of their foremost citizens: military and religious leaders and craftsmen, forcibly settled in Babylon. "Ezekiel was one of those people.

the river of Chebar, *that* the heavens were
opened, and I saw visions of God.

2 In the fifth *day* of the month, which *was*
the fifth year of king Jehoiachin's captivity,
3 The word of the LORD came expressly unto
Ezekiel the priest, the son of Buzi, in the land
of the Chaldeans by the river Chebar; and
the hand of the LORD was there upon him.

4 ¶ And I looked, and, behold, a whirlwind
came out of the north, a great cloud, and
a fire infolding itself, and a brightness *was*
about it, and out of the midst thereof as the
colour of amber, out of the midst of the fire.
5 Also out of the midst thereof *came* the likeness of four living creatures. And this *was* their
appearance; they had the likeness of a man.
6 And every one had four faces, and every
one had four wings.

. . . As Jeremiah was in Jerusalem prophesying to the Jews, Ezekiel was in Babylon, near the Chebar river, doing the same. He was a prophet in exile, teaching all the Jews, but mostly those Jews in exile. He did this at the same time that Jeremiah and Lehi were prophesying in Jerusalem" (Muhlestein, *Essential Old Testament Companion*, 452).

How did Ezekiel try to explain his vision of God? (1:1) "It is very difficult, if not impossible, for a mortal to convey in writing the message and spirit of a vision or other revelation from God so that the reader will have a complete understanding of what took place and what was communicated. Such was the challenge of Ezekiel in describing his transcendent visions of heaven. Others, too, have faced the same challenge (see 2 Corinthians 12:4; 3 Nephi 28:12–14; D&C 76:114–17). Joseph Smith said that 'could you gaze into heaven five minutes, you would know more than you would by reading all that ever was written on the subject' [*Joseph Smith* (manual), 419]. One must experience revelation to understand it fully" (*Old Testament Student Manual: 1 Kings–Malachi*, 265). ⊕

What do we learn from the phrase "the hand of the Lord was there upon him"? (1:2–3) The first three verses of Ezekiel 1 are considered a superscription or historical setting for Ezekiel's book. It emphasizes "the hand of the Lord," which is a "phrase repeated six times in the book (3:14, 22; 8:1; 33:22; 37:1; 40:1), indicating an overpowering experience of divine revelation" (*NIV Study Bible* [1995], 1224). "This expression describes God's commission of Ezekiel as a prophet (one who speaks for God). It may also have indicated the presence of God's Spirit on Ezekiel" (*Quest Study Bible* [2011], 1208).

Ezekiel 1:4–14. Ezekiel's Vision of Living Creatures

How did Ezekiel describe the first part of this vision? (1:4–5) "Ezekiel saw a number of visions that were highly symbolic. . . . His book begins with his *sôd*, or the vision in which he was called to prophesy. . . . In fact, his vision holds many similarities to the vision of John the Revelator. He saw a cloud, fire, light, four-faced beasts . . . , a fiery wheel, and a firmament. All of this seems to be the glory that surrounds the throne of God" (Muhlestein, *Scripture Study Made Simple*, 451). John's vision included "figurative expressions . . . describing heaven, the paradise of God, the happiness of man, and of beasts . . . that which is spiritual being in the likeness of that which is temporal" (D&C 77:2).

What did the "four living creatures" represent? (1:5–8, 10) "In his vision, Ezekiel saw four creatures, each of which had four faces. 'They four had the face of a man, . . . lion, . . . an ox . . . [and] the face of an eagle' (Ezekiel 1:10). The Apostle John had a similar vision. In his vision, the creatures were described as being 'like a lion, . . . like a calf, . . . [having] a face as a man, and . . . like a flying eagle (Revelation 4:7). The Prophet Joseph Smith, under inspiration from God, explained that the four beasts in John's vision were representative of classes of beings (see D&C 77:3). The faces of the creatures in Ezekiel's vision seem to represent the same thing" (*Old Testament Student Manual: 1 Kings–Malachi*, 266).

What might the wings of the four living creatures represent? (1:9–12) Ezekiel describes the four living creatures he saw as each having a set of wings, very similar to the four beasts that John saw. According to the Prophet Joseph Smith, "their wings are a representation of power, to move, to act, etc." (D&C 77:4).

7 And their feet *were* straight feet; and the sole of their feet *was* like the sole of a calf's foot: and they sparkled like the colour of burnished brass.

8 And *they had* the hands of a man under their wings on their four sides; and they four had their faces and their wings.

9 Their wings *were* joined one to another; they turned not when they went; they went every one straight forward.

10 As for the likeness of their faces, they four had the face of a man, and the face of a lion, on the right side: and they four had the face of an ox on the left side; they four also had the face of an eagle.

11 Thus *were* their faces: and their wings *were* stretched upward; two *wings* of every one *were* joined one to another, and two covered their bodies.

12 And they went every one straight forward: whither the spirit was to go, they went; *and* they turned not when they went.

13 As for the likeness of the living creatures, their appearance *was* like burning coals of fire, *and* like the appearance of lamps: it went up and down among the living creatures; and

What Did Ezekiel See When the Heavens Were Opened? (Ezekiel 1:3–4)

Once the Lord had placed His hand upon him, Ezekiel simply said: "and I looked" (see Ezekiel 1:3–4). "Thus begins Ezekiel's attempt to describe, in the inadequate words of this earth, the glories of a heavenly vision. The details of the heavenly chariot-throne are marvelous, but it must have been nearly impossible to describe. The account of Ezekiel's vision and divine visitation is much more complicated than Isaiah's general description, but they both saw the Lord. With words of reverence, Ezekiel testified, 'upon the likeness of the throne was the likeness of the appearance of a man above upon it.' He struggled with words to tell of the glory of that Being, surrounded, as it were, by 'the appearance of fire.' Using the spectrum of the rainbow as a simile for light and color, he testified, 'This was the appearance of the likeness of the glory of the Lord. And when I saw it, I fell upon my face, and I heard a voice of one that spake' (Ezek. 1:26–28)" (Rasmussen, *Latter-day Saint Commentary on the Old Testament*, 583).

the fire was bright, and out of the fire went forth lightning.

14 And the living creatures ran and returned as the appearance of a flash of lightning.

15 ¶ Now as I beheld the living creatures, behold one wheel upon the earth by the living creatures, with his four faces.

16 The appearance of the wheels and their work *was* like unto the colour of a beryl: and they four had one likeness: and their appearance and their work *was* as it were a wheel in the middle of a wheel.

17 When they went, they went upon their four sides: *and* they turned not when they went.

18 As for their rings, they were so high that they were dreadful; and their rings *were* full of eyes round about them four.

19 And when the living creatures went, the wheels went by them: and when the living creatures were lifted up from the earth, the wheels were lifted up.

20 Whithersoever the spirit was to go, they went, thither *was their* spirit to go; and the wheels were lifted up over against them: for the spirit of the living creature *was* in the wheels.

21 When those went, *these* went; and when those stood, *these* stood; and when those were lifted up from the earth, the wheels were lifted up over against them: for the spirit of the living creature *was* in the wheels.

Ezekiel 1:15–25. Ezekiel's Vision of the Wheels

What were the wheels that Ezekiel described in his vision? (1:16–21) "There are occasional uses of figurative imagery, such as Ezekiel's 'wheels' (see Ezek. 1:15–21), for which the Lord has yet given us the interpretation" (Lund, "Understanding Scriptural Symbols," 23–27). Ezekiel sees God sitting on a chariot-like throne (see Eze. 1:14–28) and his "description of this vehicle symbolically represents God's power and ability to move and to do. . . . [God's] chariot throne pulled by composite creatures draws on the imagery of 2 Samuel 6:2 (Jehovah sitting over the ark of the covenant between the cherubim). The creatures in the vision exhibit parallels with the large composite statues placed at doorways in Mesopotamian palaces displaying features of bulls, lions, humans, and other creatures, often with wings" (Holzapfel, et al., *Jehovah and the World of the Old Testament*, 344).

What might the eyes surrounding the wheels represent? (1:18) Both John and Ezekiel describe their four living creatures as being "full of eyes." According to the Doctrine and Covenants, the eyes of the beasts in John's vision "are a representation of light and knowledge, that is, they are full of knowledge" (D&C 77:4) as we would assume all creatures in heaven to be. ⊕

What additional knowledge does Ezekiel give us regarding the creatures and the wheels? (1:20–21) "In [chapter] 10, these *living creatures* are related to the cherubim [angels]—celestial beings associated with God's holiness and glory. . . . The prophet stresses the association of the wheels with the living creatures, as well as the creatures' ability to travel wherever they wished. . . . It appears that the wheels represented the flexibility and mobility of the living creatures. This is a pictorial representation of God's omnipresence" (*Nelson Study Bible* [NKJV], 1335).

What was the firmament upon the heads of the living creatures? (1:22–24) The firmament was actually some kind of an "expanse over" their heads (Ezek. 1:22*a*). One Bible commentator described it this way, "Above the heads of the four creatures is a platform sparkling like crystal or ice. Ancient Near Eastern glyptic art and sculpture contain images of winged creatures holding up a pillar, a throne or platform" (Walton, et al., *IVP Bible Background Commentary*, 691).

Ezekiel 1:26–28. Ezekiel's Vision of the Throne of God

Who was the man sitting upon the throne above the firmament? (1:26–28) "Ezekiel saw a firmament, or expanse, above or over the creatures. Above the firmament Ezekiel saw God sitting on his throne in his glory. Ezekiel used several terms to describe the brilliance, beauty, and glory of God" (*Old Testament Student Manual: 1 Kings–Malachi*, 267). ⊕

What was Ezekiel's reaction to this vision? (1:26–28) Like Isaiah (see Isa. 6), who is humbled and inspired when he sees God's throne, Ezekiel's "vision of God on his flying chariot throne, gave assurances to the exiles that the Lord had not abandoned them, but had accompanied them to Babylon. Ezekiel, like Jeremiah, spent his life preaching repentance to his people. He prophesied the destruction of the Temple and warned the people in exile not to worship the foreign gods that had led to the destruction of Jerusalem" (Holzapfel, et al., *Jehovah and the World of the Old Testament*, 342). In what ways might Ezekiel's vision have encouraged the Jews in exile? When have you been encouraged by inspired messages of the prophets of God?

22 And the likeness of the firmament upon the heads of the living creature *was* as the colour of the terrible crystal, stretched forth over their heads above.

23 And under the firmament *were* their wings straight, the one toward the other: every one had two, which covered on this side, and every one had two, which covered on that side, their bodies.

24 And when they went, I heard the noise of their wings, like the noise of great waters, as the voice of the Almighty, the voice of speech, as the noise of an host: when they stood, they let down their wings.

25 And there was a voice from the firmament that *was* over their heads, when they stood, *and* had let down their wings.

26 ¶ And above the firmament that *was* over their heads *was* the likeness of a throne, as the appearance of a sapphire stone: and upon the likeness of the throne *was* the likeness as the appearance of a man above upon it.

27 And I saw as the colour of amber, as the appearance of fire round about within it, from the appearance of his loins even upward, and from the appearance of his loins even downward, I saw as it were the appearance of fire, and it had brightness round about.

28 As the appearance of the bow that is in the cloud in the day of rain, so *was* the appearance of the brightness round about. This *was* the appearance of the likeness of the glory of the Lord. And when I saw *it*, I fell upon my face, and I heard a voice of one that spake.

CHAPTER 2

Ezekiel is called to take the word of the Lord to Israel—He sees a book in which lamentations and mourning are written.

1 And he said unto me, Son of man, stand upon thy feet, and I will speak unto thee.

2 And the spirit entered into me when he spake unto me, and set me upon my feet, that I heard him that spake unto me.

3 And he said unto me, Son of man, I send thee to the children of Israel, to a rebellious nation that hath rebelled against me: they and their fathers have transgressed against me, *even* unto this very day.

4 For *they are* impudent children and stiff-hearted. I do send thee unto them; and thou shalt say unto them, Thus saith the Lord GOD.

5 And they, whether they will hear, or whether they will forbear, (for they *are* a rebellious house,) yet shall know that there hath been a prophet among them.

6 ¶ And thou, son of man, be not afraid of them, neither be afraid of their words, though briers and thorns *be* with thee, and thou dost dwell among scorpions: be not afraid of their words, nor be dismayed at their looks, though they *be* a rebellious house.

Ezekiel 2:1–5. The Lord Calls Ezekiel

How is the phrase "Son of man" used in Ezekiel?
(2:1) "[Ezekiel] was consistently called 'son of man' (Heb., *ben-adam*, 'human') by the Lord, as if to emphasize that he was the human agent to transmit the divine messages. The phrase 'son of man' occurs many times throughout this book and is nowhere else as prominent; however, in the New Testament, Jesus chose to call himself 'Son of Man'" (Rasmussen, *Latter-day Saint Commentary on the Old Testament*, 583–84).

Ezekiel 2:6–10. The Lord Tells Ezekiel Not to Fear Warning Rebellious Israel

How does the Lord warn Ezekiel about his mission?
(2:6–7) "God immediately forestalls any hesitations by giving [Ezekiel] an exhortation to take courage (2:6–8), followed by a foretaste of his message (2:9–3:3). This in turn is followed by the promise of the power to persevere in the face of opposition (3:4–9). To judge from his subsequent ministry, Ezekiel does not give the impression of being anything but fearless. . . . It is therefore all the more illuminating to see the repeated way in

What Was Ezekiel's Mission to the House of Israel? (Ezekiel 2)

"[Ezekiel] received five specific charges from the Lord:

1. He was to warn Israel, who would be hostile and stubborn (2:1–8).
2. He was to speak only to Israel; even though they would ignore him, he would be fortified with a 'stone forehead' (like a 'tough skin' today; 3:7–9).
3. He was to receive, understand, and proclaim to the exiles all that the Lord told him (3:10–15).
4. He was to be a watchman to Israel (3:16–21; compare 33:1–20).
5. He was to return home and be dumb (not speak) until he received word of Jerusalem's destruction (which occurred seven and one half years later; 3:22–27; compare 24:27; 33:22).

"The fifth charge or commission is particularly puzzling. It is unclear whether his silence was to be only outside the house, or if he was only to speak the oracles [revelations] and prophecies given him by the Lord and nothing else, or if he was to be completely silent for the whole time" (Ludlow, *Unlocking the Old Testament*, 190).

which God has to tell him to be free of his natural fears and not to be *dismayed at their looks*. . . . And the Israelite exiles are described as *though briers and thorns are with you and you sit upon scorpions*. The prophet's feelings will be painfully hurt by the cruel and rancorous treatment he must expect to receive from the exiles in response to his oracles" (Taylor, *Ezekiel*, 65).

What kind of book did Jehovah give Ezekiel? (2:8–9) A book was "a roll of leather or papyrus used for writing. Rolls were made by sewing sheets together to make a long strip. Some rolls became very long, exceeding 100 feet. They were usually from 9 to 11 inches high. Rolls were generally wound around a stick and, as used, would be unwound from one stick onto another. Much of the Old Testament and the New Testament was probably written on rolls. Scrolls (rolls) are mentioned in Ezra 6:1; Isa. 8:1; 34:4; Jer. 36; Ezek. 2:9; 3:1; Zech. 5:1–2; Rev. 6:14" (Bible Dictionary, "Scroll").

Why is it notable that Ezekiel received a book? (2:9–10) "At the beginning of most dispensations, a book is given to the newly called prophet. Moses received tablets (see Ex. 31:18). Lehi was given a book to read concerning the destruction of Jerusalem (see 1 Ne. 1:11–14). Ezekiel was given 'a roll of a book' (Ezek. 2:9–10) containing the Lord's message for the house of Judah in his day. John the Revelator on the Isle of Patmos was shown a book with seven seals (see Revelation 5; D&C 77:6). Is it any wonder, then, that the Lord would provide a book containing the fulness of the gospel as part of the 'restitution of all things'? The Book of Mormon has the power to draw all men and women to Christ" (Bateman, "Pattern for All," 75).

Ezekiel 3:1–14. Ezekiel's Mission to the House of Israel

Why was Ezekiel asked to eat a roll? (3:1–3) Similar to John the Revelator (see Rev. 10:1–10), Ezekiel was given a roll or book to eat which represented a mission to the house of Israel "containing 'lamentations, and mourning, and woe' (Ezek. 2:10). . . . Amazingly, despite the book's content, it was like honey to the taste, perhaps symbolizing that God's gifts, of whatever sort they may be, are sweet" (Ricks, "Watchman to the House of Israel," 270). As the Lord told an enthusiastic Hyrum Smith, "Seek not to declare my word, but first seek to obtain it, and then shall your tongue be loosed" (D&C 11:21).

7 And thou shalt speak my words unto them, whether they will hear, or whether they will forbear: for they *are* most rebellious.

8 But thou, son of man, hear what I say unto thee; Be not thou rebellious like that rebellious house: open thy mouth, and eat that I give thee.

9 ¶ And when I looked, behold, an hand *was* sent unto me; and, lo, a roll of a book *was* therein;

10 And he spread it before me; and it *was* written within and without: and *there was* written therein lamentations, and mourning, and woe.

CHAPTER 3

Ezekiel is made a watchman unto the house of Israel—The blood of Israel is required at his hand unless he raises the warning voice.

1 Moreover he said unto me, Son of man, eat that thou findest; eat this roll, and go speak unto the house of Israel.

2 So I opened my mouth, and he caused me to eat that roll.

3 And he said unto me, Son of man, cause thy belly to eat, and fill thy bowels with this roll that I give thee. Then did I eat *it;* and it was in my mouth as honey for sweetness.

4 ¶ And he said unto me, Son of man, go, get thee unto the house of Israel, and speak with my words unto them.

What can we learn from the Lord asking Ezekiel to "speak with my words"? (3:4) "An essential truth we learn from the First Vision and the Prophet Joseph Smith is that God calls prophets [see Amos 3:7], seers, and revelators to instruct, guide, warn, and lead us. These men are God's mouthpieces on earth [see 2 Ne. 3:18], with the authority to speak and act in the name of the Lord [see Ezek. 3:4; Luke 1:70; Acts 3:21; D&C 1:38]. By strictly following their counsel, we will be protected and receive choice blessings in our journey on this earth" (Parrella, "Essential Truths—Our Need to Act," 115). How might ancient Israel have been similarly blessed if they had chosen to follow Ezekiel's counsel? How have you come to know that prophets speak God's words?

5 For thou *art* not sent to a people of a strange speech and of an hard language, *but* to the house of Israel;

6 Not to many people of a strange speech and of an hard language, whose words thou canst not understand. Surely, had I sent thee to them, they would have hearkened unto thee.

7 But the house of Israel will not hearken unto thee; for they will not hearken unto me: for all the house of Israel *are* impudent and hardhearted.

In what important way did Israel differ from other countries? (3:5–7) "The prophet is not sent to a foreign nation; nor to the heathen world in general. If it had been so they would have listened. But Israel will listen neither to a prophet nor to God Himself. The traditional obduracy [stubbornness] of Israel is referred to by our Lord in Mt. 11:21–24; Lk. 4:24–27" (Guthrie and Motyer, *New Bible Commentary: Revised*, 668).

8 Behold, I have made thy face strong against their faces, and thy forehead strong against their foreheads.

9 As an adamant harder than flint have I made thy forehead: fear them not, neither be dismayed at their looks, though they *be* a rebellious house.

10 Moreover he said unto me, Son of man, all my words that I shall speak unto thee receive in thine heart, and hear with thine ears.

11 And go, get thee to them of the captivity, unto the children of thy people, and speak unto them, and tell them, Thus saith the Lord GOD; whether they will hear, or whether they will forbear.

What is meant by having a strong forehead? (3:8–9) Ezekiel clearly had a daunting task before him when faced with a people the Lord described as "impudent and hardhearted" (Ezek. 3:7). However, God promised to make Ezekiel equal to the challenge. The New International Version of these verses reads: "But I will make you as unyielding and hardened as they are. I will make your forehead like the hardest stone, harder than flint. Do not be afraid of them or terrified by them, though they are a rebellious house" (*NIV Study Bible* [1995], 1226).

What feelings did Ezekiel have as his vision concluded? (3:12–14) "*Bitterness* means 'distress' and 'anguish.' Ezekiel's human perspective caused him to focus on the distasteful calling of delivering a message no one would listen to. The prophet was angry—*heat of my spirit*—and appalled. But the *hand of the LORD* was present to help him deal with these feelings and then move him on to live and work among the captives (see v. 15)" (*Nelson Study Bible* [NKJV], 1338). "When we are on the Lord's errand, we are entitled to the Lord's help. Remember that whom the Lord calls, the Lord qualifies" (Monson, "Duty Calls," 44).

Ezekiel 3:15–21. Ezekiel Is to Be a Watchman on the Tower

What did it mean for Ezekiel to be called as a "watchman unto the house of Israel"? (3:17) "Ezekiel was called to be a watchman in the service of God, whose chief task it was to warn his people in accordance with the words God had given him (Ezek. 3:16–21; cf. 33:1–9)....

"Just as the watchman of a city is liable when he fails to warn its inhabitants, so Ezekiel would be responsible if he failed to warn Israel. If he warned the wicked of the house of Israel that they would die, or the righteous who turned from their righteousness that they would die, and they did not turn from their ways and died, Ezekiel had fulfilled his duty and was innocent of their death" (Ricks, "Watchman to the House of Israel," 271–72). See commentary in this volume for Ezekiel 33:2–6. ⊕

Ancient watchtower.

12 Then the spirit took me up, and I heard
behind me a voice of a great rushing, *saying*,
Blessed *be* the glory of the LORD from his
place.

13 *I heard* also the noise of the wings of the
living creatures that touched one another,
and the noise of the wheels over against
them, and a noise of a great rushing.

14 So the spirit lifted me up, and took me
away, and I went in bitterness, in the heat
of my spirit; but the hand of the LORD was
strong upon me.

15 ¶ Then I came to them of the captivity at
Tel-abib, that dwelt by the river of Chebar,
and I sat where they sat, and remained there
astonished among them seven days.

16 And it came to pass at the end of seven
days, that the word of the LORD came unto
me, saying,

17 Son of man, I have made thee a watchman unto the house of Israel: therefore hear
the word at my mouth, and give them warning from me.

18 When I say unto the wicked, Thou shalt surely die; and thou givest him not warning, nor speakest to warn the wicked from his wicked way, to save his life; the same wicked *man* shall die in his iniquity; but his blood will I require at thine hand.

19 Yet if thou warn the wicked, and he turn not from his wickedness, nor from his wicked way, he shall die in his iniquity; but thou hast delivered thy soul.

20 Again, When a righteous *man* doth turn from his righteousness, and commit iniquity, and I lay a stumblingblock before him, he shall die: because thou hast not given him warning, he shall die in his sin, and his righteousness which he hath done shall not be remembered; but his blood will I require at thine hand.

21 Nevertheless if thou warn the righteous *man,* that the righteous sin not, and he doth not sin, he shall surely live, because he is warned; also thou hast delivered thy soul.

Why would God place the blood of the wicked on Ezekiel? (3:18–19) "Even if a prophet knows the people will not repent as a result of his preaching, he must still warn in order that his garments might be clean from the blood of that generation (see Jacob 1:18–19). The prophet Mormon cautions that even though the people reject the message of missionaries, prophets, or other representatives of God because of their own 'hardness, let us labor diligently; for if we should cease to labor, we should be brought under condemnation' [Moro. 9:6]" (Ludlow, *Companion to Your Study of the Old Testament*, 333).

Like Ezekiel, how can we deliver our souls? (3:20–21) In these verses, the Lord assures Ezekiel "that his personal responsibility is limited to delivering . . . warnings; members of his audience are accountable for their responses (18:1–32; see also 33:1–9)" (*New Oxford Annotated Bible* [2010], 1165). Similarly, we have been told that "it becometh every man who hath been warned to warn his neighbor. Therefore, they are left without excuse, and their sins are upon their own heads" (D&C 88:81–82; see also James 5:19–20). When have you felt like you have warned a neighbor? How can you continue to fulfill this divine call this week?

Summary of Ezekiel 3:22–27

After Ezekiel's vision comes to an end, he returns to dwell among the people, but in an astonished condition (see Ezek. 3:15). Soon the Lord reveals to Ezekiel that He will make him dumb and unable to speak until it is time for his mouth to be opened (see Ezek. 3:26–27). At the time, Israel was not worthy to bear prophetic messages because they were rebellious.

CHAPTERS 4–5

Ezekiel symbolically illustrates the siege and famine that will befall Jerusalem.

The judgment of Jerusalem will include famine, pestilence, war, and the scattering of her inhabitants.

Summary of Ezekiel 4–5

"Ezekiel himself went through several typological or symbolic actions to dramatize the coming disaster. For example, in chapter 4 he took a tile and drew a picture of Jerusalem on it. Then he put an iron pan against it [representing how the city would be cut off from assistance]. In that same chapter, by command of the Lord, he had to lie upon his side for many days, symbolizing the captivity, and then he was told to cook his bread with cow dung to symbolize that the people in Judah would eat defiled bread in coming times. In chapter 5 Ezekiel cut his hair and divided it unto thirds, burning some and scattering some, again symbolizing what the people would suffer" (Lund, "Ezekiel," 82–83).

Ezekiel 6:1–7. Judgments and Promises Given to Israel

Why would Ezekiel be asked to prophesy against the mountains of Israel? (6:2–3) "Ezekiel addresses the country under the figure *the mountains of Israel*, since they formed its chief feature; it is, indeed, 'a central mountain range sloping down to the narrow plains by the Mediterranean and the Jordan.' . . . Moreover, the *mountains* and *hills* are usually associated by the prophets with idolatry (*e.g.* Is. 65:7; Je. 2:6; Ho. 4:13). *Ravines* [JST 'rivers']. These and the *valleys* were used for impure rites and the worship of Molech (Je. 7:31, 32)" (Guthrie and Motyer, *New Bible Commentary: Revised*, 669). ⊕

What do we know about the idols the people of Judah were worshipping? (6:4–5) "*Idols* translates Ezekiel's characteristic term 'gillulim,' found in Lev 26.30 and thirty-nine times in Ezekiel, compared with eight times elsewhere in the Bible. The term is contemptuous, probably equating idols with sheep droppings. The people are devoted to vile futility" (*New Oxford Annotated Bible* [2010], 1168). In other words, "[Judah's] death is on the heads of these idols and altars that did nothing to save them" (Walton, et al., *IVP Bible Background Commentary*, 694).

When was this prophecy fulfilled? (6:5–6) "This was literally fulfilled by the Chaldeans. According to Baruch, 2:24, 25, they opened the sepulchres of the principal people, and threw the bones about on every side" (*Adam Clarke's Commentary* [on Ezekiel 6:5]). Keil and Delitzsch add, "The ignominy of the destruction is heightened by the bones of the slain idolaters being scattered round about the idol altars. In order that the idolatry may be entirely rooted out, the cities throughout the whole land, and all the high places, are to be devastated" (*Commentary* [on Ezekiel 6:1–7]). ⊕

CHAPTER 6

The people of Israel will be destroyed for their idolatry—A remnant only will be saved and scattered.

1 And the word of the LORD came unto me, saying,

2 Son of man, set thy face toward the mountains of Israel, and prophesy against them,

3 And say, Ye mountains of Israel, hear the word of the Lord GOD; Thus saith the Lord GOD to the mountains, and to the hills, to the rivers, and to the valleys; Behold, I, *even* I, will bring a sword upon you, and I will destroy your high places.

4 And your altars shall be desolate, and your images shall be broken: and I will cast down your slain *men* before your idols.

5 And I will lay the dead carcases of the children of Israel before their idols; and I will scatter your bones round about your altars.

6 In all your dwellingplaces the cities shall be laid waste, and the high places shall be desolate; that your altars may be laid waste and made desolate, and your idols may be broken and cease, and your images may be cut down, and your works may be abolished.

7 And the slain shall fall in the midst of you, and ye shall know that I *am* the LORD.

8 ¶ Yet will I leave a remnant, that ye may
have *some* that shall escape the sword among
the nations, when ye shall be scattered
through the countries.

9 And they that escape of you shall remember me among the nations whither they shall
be carried captives, because I am broken
with their whorish heart, which hath departed from me, and with their eyes, which
go a whoring after their idols: and they shall
lothe themselves for the evils which they have
committed in all their abominations.

10 And they shall know that I *am* the LORD,
and that I have not said in vain that I would
do this evil unto them.

11 ¶ Thus saith the Lord GOD; Smite with
thine hand, and stamp with thy foot, and
say, Alas for all the evil abominations of
the house of Israel! for they shall fall by the
sword, by the famine, and by the pestilence.

12 He that is far off shall die of the pestilence; and he that is near shall fall by the
sword; and he that remaineth and is besieged
shall die by the famine: thus will I accomplish my fury upon them.

13 Then shall ye know that I *am* the LORD,
when their slain *men* shall be among their
idols round about their altars, upon every
high hill, in all the tops of the mountains,
and under every green tree, and under every
thick oak, the place where they did offer
sweet savour to all their idols.

Ezekiel 6:8–14. A Remnant Will Survive and Be Scattered among the Nations

Why will the Lord leave a remnant? (6:8) "A careful study of [Ezekiel's] writings shows that even the most harsh and caustic predictions and judgments were counterbalanced by an immediate addendum of hope. For example, after making dire and specific predictions of Jerusalem's destruction through famine, pestilence, war, and cannibalism (see Ezekiel 5:5–17), after predicting that Israel will be smitten with such devastation that the bones of the people will lie unburied at the altars of their false gods (see Ezekiel 6:4–5), the Lord tells Ezekiel:'Yet will I leave a remnant. . . . And they that escape of you shall remember me among the nations. . . . And they shall know that I am the Lord' (Ezekiel 6:8–10)" (Lund, "Ezekiel," 85). ⊕

How did Israel demonstrate a "whorish heart"? (6:9) Jehovah's "feelings about Israel's covenantal infidelity are compared to the emotions of a husband who has been abandoned by his harlotrous wife. He grieves over their condition, here described as whorish of heart and eyes: *their promiscuous heart . . . their eyes that whored*. The word *zônâ* refers fundamentally to any immoral sexual behavior, but it is used most often in the context of marital infidelity. Here it is employed theologically, being defined more closely by the following phrase, turned away from me (*sār mēʿālay*). As Israel's redeemer and her spiritual husband, [Jehovah] was passionately protective of his relationship, and would tolerate no interference from would-be competitors" (Block, *Book of Ezekiel, Chapters 1–24*, 231).

Where and what is represented by the "wilderness toward Diblath"? (6:14) "The geographic range here, like the more familiar 'from Dan to Beersheba,' expresses God's ability to punish the Israelites from one end to the other of their territory. The desert refers to the wilderness around Beersheba. . . . [The mention of Diblah] here may refer to the city's use by Nebuchadnezzar. It was the headquarters for his army's campaign during his siege of Jerusalem in 588–586 B.C." (Walton, et al., *IVP Bible Background Commentary*, 694).

Summary of Ezekiel 7

"In chapter 7, it is no longer the single community but the whole of the people who are addressed. 'Over and over the prophet repeats his devastating message until his words pound the reader like a hammer. Disaster approaches. An end has come upon the land. Doom is near. God will not spare any of the people and will not pity them. The people are helpless against the approaching enemy. Prophets, priests, elders, and king are terrified and can do nothing. God will be known to Israel only in the irreversible judgment that will repay the people for their sins' [Wilson, "Ezekiel," 665]. This section is redolent [reminiscent] of the terror of the 'Day of the Lord' prophecies found in other prophets, perhaps most notably Amos (5:18–20; 8:1–14) and Isaiah (chap. 13), in which God would approach Israel, for good or ill, in judgment" (Ricks, "Watchman to the House of Israel," 274).

Ezekiel 8:1–6. The Image of Jealousy Is Seen

Who were the "elders of Judah"? (8:1) "The leadership in the Judahite communities appears to have been officials known as the elders. Jeremiah refers to the 'elders which were carried away captives' (Jer. 29:1) and Ezekiel to the 'elders of Judah' and 'elders of Israel' living in Babylonia (Ezek 8:1; 14:1; 20:1, 3), suggesting that the Judahites enjoyed some kind of political and religious autonomy. The Babylonians allowed exiles to practice their own religions and presumably many in the Judahite community continued the practice of worshipping the Lord God of Israel" (Holzapfel, et al., *Jehovah and the World of the Old Testament*, 347). See commentary in this volume for Jeremiah 38:4–5.

14 So will I stretch out my hand upon them, and make the land desolate, yea, more desolate than the wilderness toward Diblath, in all their habitations: and they shall know that I *am* the LORD.

CHAPTER 7

Desolation, war, pestilence, and destruction will sweep the land of Israel—The desolation of the people is foreseen.

CHAPTER 8

Ezekiel sees in vision the wickedness and abominations of the people of Judah in Jerusalem—He sees idolatry practiced in the temple itself.

1 And it came to pass in the sixth year, in the sixth *month*, in the fifth *day* of the month, *as* I sat in mine house, and the elders of Judah sat before me, that the hand of the Lord GOD fell there upon me.

2 Then I beheld, and lo a likeness as the appearance of fire: from the appearance of his loins even downward, fire; and from his loins even upward, as the appearance of brightness, as the colour of amber.

3 And he put forth the form of an hand, and took me by a lock of mine head; and the spirit lifted me up between the earth and the heaven, and brought me in the visions of God to Jerusalem, to the door of the inner gate that looketh toward the north; where *was* the seat of the image of jealousy, which provoketh to jealousy.

4 And, behold, the glory of the God of Israel *was* there, according to the vision that I saw in the plain.

5 ¶ Then said he unto me, Son of man, lift up thine eyes now the way toward the north. So I lifted up mine eyes the way toward the north, and behold northward at the gate of the altar this image of jealousy in the entry.

6 He said furthermore unto me, Son of man, seest thou what they do? *even* the great abominations that the house of Israel committeth here, that I should go far off from my sanctuary? but turn thee yet again, *and* thou shalt see greater abominations.

What was the "image of jealousy"? (8:3) "Ezekiel found himself standing at the entrance of the inner court's north gate, known also as the altar gate, because the altar of sacrifice was located just inside the gate.... As he looked northward into the outer court, he saw the 'idol [KJV, image] of jealousy.' This idol provoked the Lord to jealousy, for he had declared in the Mosaic covenant that he alone was God (Ex 20:1–3) and that all idolatry was forbidden. The idol's description is vague; thus it cannot be identified with certainty.... Jeremiah's denunciation of the worship of the Queen of Heaven may also relate to this image (Jer 7:18; 44:17–30)" (*Expositor's Bible Commentary [Abridged]*, 1285–86). ⊕

A Prophet's Temple Vision (Ezekiel 8)

"This chapter introduces a single vision which Ezekiel was given in Aug./Sept. of 592 B.C. It ... fully explains to the leaders of the exiled Jerusalem community why there is no hope for their homeland. Chapter 8 is background for the phenomenon described in chapters 9–11: the withdrawal of the presence of the Lord from the Jerusalem temple.

"Ezekiel is taken in his vision to Jerusalem, where he witnesses the idolatry practiced in the Holy City. He sees an idol ... erected within the temple compound (Ezek. 8:1–6). Going further Ezekiel is shown the leading men of Judah secretly worshiping images in private rooms inside the temple's inner court (vv. 7–13).

"Ezekiel is then shown women outside the temple compound's north gate worshiping Tammuz, a primeval fertility goddess ... (vv. 14–15). Finally Ezekiel was shown 25 men at the very entrance to the temple, turning away from it to worship the sun (vv. 16–18). Each of these pagan rites were being practiced in the very shadow of God's temple, fully illustrating abandonment of the Lord and the loss of holiness" (Richards, *Bible Reader's Companion*, 490).

"Ezekiel clearly preached against the idea that the temple alone would save the people. He recounted a vision in which he [also] saw the Lord's Spirit lift from the sanctuary, hover over the temple for a moment, and then depart to the east (see Ezek. 9:8; 10:18; 11:23). His message was both clear and simple: It was not the temple but righteousness that would be Judah's only shield. Where there was no righteousness, there was no hope" (Draper, "Prophets of the Exile," 101).

Ezekiel 8:7–12. Ezekiel's Vision of Idolatrous Abominations in Jerusalem

What were the abominations Ezekiel saw upon the wall? (8:7–11) Ezekiel, while living in Babylon, was "brought . . . in the visions of God" (Ezekiel 8:3) to the temple in Jerusalem. . . . "There he saw a hole in the wall, and on breaking through the wall, by the command of God, he saw a door, and having entered it, he saw all kinds of figures of animals engraved on the wall round about, in front of which seventy of the elders of Israel were standing and paying reverence to the images of beasts with burning incense" (Keil and Delitzsch, *Commentary* [on Ezekiel 8:7–12]). ⊕

What does it mean that the doings of Israel's ancients were "in the dark"? (8:12) "It is significant that such worship took place in the dark (see v. 12). This fact, in addition to the necessity Ezekiel was under to dig through the wall to see in, indicates that ancient Israelites knew of the Lord but sought to hide their abominable practices from Him. They said, 'The Lord seeth us not' (v. 12). Such is often the case among those who perform unrighteous acts. How foolish it is for any to assume that they can hide their acts from God's all-seeing eye!" (*Old Testament Student Manual: 1 Kings–Malachi*, 270).

7 ¶ And he brought me to the door of the court; and when I looked, behold a hole in the wall.

8 Then said he unto me, Son of man, dig now in the wall: and when I had digged in the wall, behold a door.

9 And he said unto me, Go in, and behold the wicked abominations that they do here.

10 So I went in and saw; and behold every form of creeping things, and abominable beasts, and all the idols of the house of Israel, portrayed upon the wall round about.

11 And there stood before them seventy men of the ancients of the house of Israel, and in the midst of them stood Jaazaniah the son of Shaphan, with every man his censer in his hand; and a thick cloud of incense went up.

12 Then said he unto me, Son of man, hast thou seen what the ancients of the house of Israel do in the dark, every man in the chambers of his imagery? for they say, The LORD seeth us not; the LORD hath forsaken the earth.

Ezekiel 8:13–18. Abominations Occur in the House of the Lord

Who was Tammuz? (8:14) Tammuz was "a deity worshipped both in Babylonia and in Phœnicia—the same as the Greek Adonis. He appears to have been a god of the spring, and the myth regarding him told of his early death and of the descent of Istar his bride into the underworld in search of him. The death of Tammuz [symbolized] the destruction of the spring vegetation by the heat of summer, and it was celebrated annually by seven days of women's mourning in the 4th month (June–July), which was called Tammuz.

13 ¶ He said also unto me, Turn thee yet again, *and* thou shalt see greater abominations that they do.

14 Then he brought me to the door of the gate of the LORD's house which *was* toward the north; and, behold, there sat women weeping for Tammuz.

15 ¶ Then said he unto me, Hast thou seen *this,* O son of man? turn thee yet again, *and* thou shalt see greater abominations than these.

16 And he brought me into the inner court of the LORD's house, and, behold, at the door of the temple of the LORD, between the porch and the altar, *were* about five and twenty men, with their backs toward the temple of the LORD, and their faces toward the east; and they worshipped the sun toward the east.

17 ¶ Then he said unto me, Hast thou seen *this,* O son of man? Is it a light thing to the house of Judah that they commit the abominations which they commit here? for they have filled the land with violence, and have returned to provoke me to anger: and, lo, they put the branch to their nose.

18 Therefore will I also deal in fury: mine eye shall not spare, neither will I have pity: and though they cry in mine ears with a loud voice, *yet* will I not hear them.

CHAPTER 9

Ezekiel sees the marking of the righteous and the slaughter of all others, beginning at the Lord's sanctuary.

This superstition had been introduced into Jerusalem" (*John Dummelow's Commentary* [on Ezekiel 8:14]). The women's mourning was supposed to play a role in bringing the god back to life.

What is the significance of priests worshipping the sun and having their backs toward the temple? (8:16) "As the whole nation was seen in the seventy elders, so is the entire priesthood represented here in the twenty-five leaders as deeply sunk in disgraceful idolatry. Their apostasy from the Lord is shown in the fact that they turn their back upon the temple, and therefore upon Jehovah, who was enthroned in the temple, and worship the sun, with their faces turned towards the east. The worship of the sun does not refer to the worship of Adonis, . . . but generally to the worship of the heavenly bodies, against which Moses had warned the people [Deut. 4:19; 17:3]" (Keil and Delitzsch, *Commentary* [on Ezekiel 8:14–16]).

What does the phrase "put the branch to their nose" mean? (8:17) This phrase "represents a practice which cannot with certainty be identified. Some argue from the use of the term *branch* . . . that it was associated with Tammuz–worship; some see in it an obscenity, interpreting the Hebrew word as 'stench'; others have noted that a similar action portrayed in a Assyrian relief seems to be a mark of reverence and worship" (Guthrie and Motyer, *New Bible Commentary: Revised*, 670).

Summary of Ezekiel 9

"The coming death of the remnant in Jerusalem, except the few marked to be spared, was symbolized as if accomplished by angels of death; in fact it was brought about within five years by the army of Nebuchadnezzar. The few righteous 'marked' for divine protection included, at that time, such men as Jeremiah, Ebed-melech, and the faithful scribe, Baruch (Jer. 39:11–18; 45)" (Rasmussen, *Latter-day Saint Commentary on the Old Testament*, 589).

"This mark was to be put on these faithful ones for their protection when the faithless were to be destroyed. It showed that they belonged to God. The allusion is to a very ancient custom. In Egypt a runaway slave was freed from his master if he went to the temple and gave himself up to the god, receiving certain marks upon his person to denote his consecration to the deity there worshiped. Cain had a mark put on him for his protection, as an evidence of God's promise to spare his life notwithstanding his wickedness [Gen. 4:15]. To this day all [Hindus] have some sort of mark upon their forehead signifying their consecration to their gods. Several passages in the book of Revelation represent the saints as having a mark on their foreheads [see Rev. 7:3; 9:4; 14:1; 22:4]. The followers of the 'beast' are also said to be marked in the forehead or in the hands [see Rev. 13:16–17; 14:9; 20:4]. The Romans marked their soldiers in the hand and their slaves in the forehead. The woman in scarlet, whom John saw, had a name written on her forehead [see Rev. 17:5]' (Freeman, *Manners and Customs of the Bible,* 301–2).

"In this case the mark represented the allegiance of the faithful to God. As those who belonged to God, they would be preserved" (*Old Testament Student Manual: 1 Kings–Malachi*, 270).`

Summary of Ezekiel 10

"In a vision of the temple, Ezekiel saw the beginning of the withdrawal of the glory of the Lord from the now desecrated place (cf. Ezek. 10)" (Rasmussen, *Latter-day Saint Commentary on the Old Testament*, 589). Ezekiel's vision from chapters 1–3 is repeated. Ezekiel sees again in vision the winged cherubim or angels, the four wheels, and the throne and glory of God. See commentary in this volume for Ezekiel 1–3.

Ezekiel 11:1–11. Judgment Proclaimed upon Jerusalem's Leaders

Why is Jerusalem compared to a cauldron? (11:3) Jerusalem's leaders claimed that the city would not fall to Babylon and that the people would be safe. They ridiculed the prophets, saying, "Jerusalem is the pot, and we, its inhabitants, are the flesh. The point

CHAPTER 10

He sees in vision, as before, the wheels, the cherubims, and the throne and the glory of God.

CHAPTER 11

He sees in vision the destruction of Jerusalem and the captivity of the Jews—He prophesies the latter-day gathering of Israel.

1 Moreover the spirit lifted me up, and brought me unto the east gate of the LORD's house, which looketh eastward: and behold at the door of the gate five and twenty men; among whom I saw Jaazaniah the son of Azur, and Pelatiah the son of Benaiah, princes of the people.

2 Then said he unto me, Son of man, these *are* the men that devise mischief, and give wicked counsel in this city:

3 Which say, *It is* not near; let us build houses: this *city is* the caldron, and we *be* the flesh.

4 ¶ Therefore prophesy against them, prophesy, O son of man.

of comparison is this: as the pot protects the flesh from burning, so does the city of Jerusalem protect us from destruction. . . . This saying expresses not only false confidence in the strength of Jerusalem, but also contempt and scorn of the predictions of the prophets sent by God. Ezekiel is therefore to prophesy, as he does in Ezekiel 11:5–12, against this pernicious counsel, which is confirming the people in their sins" (Keil and Delitzsch, *Commentary* [on Ezekiel 11:1–4]).

5 And the Spirit of the LORD fell upon me,
and said unto me, Speak; Thus saith the
LORD; Thus have ye said, O house of Israel:
for I know the things that come into your
mind, *every one of* them.

How does God know Ezekiel's thoughts? (11:5) The Lord declared, "I tell thee, that thou mayest know that there is none else save God that knowest thy thoughts and the intents of thy heart" (D&C 6:16). The Book of Mormon prophet Alma explained to Zeezrom that God "knows all thy thoughts, and thou seest that thy thoughts are made known unto us by his Spirit" (Alma 12:3). "In the ultimate sense, only God knows the thoughts and intents of the children of men [see Alma 18:32; D&C 6:16]. On occasion, however, he does grant to his chosen servants the discerning and revelatory powers needed to know the motives and dispositions of those they teach or confront [see Jacob 7:14; Alma 11:24; 30:42]" (McConkie and Millet, *Doctrinal Commentary on the Book of Mormon*, 3:133).

6 Ye have multiplied your slain in this city,
and ye have filled the streets thereof with the
slain.

7 Therefore thus saith the Lord GOD; Your
slain whom ye have laid in the midst of it,
they *are* the flesh, and this *city is* the caldron:
but I will bring you forth out of the midst
of it.

8 Ye have feared the sword; and I will bring a
sword upon you, saith the Lord GOD.

9 And I will bring you out of the midst
thereof, and deliver you into the hands of
strangers, and will execute judgments among
you.

10 Ye shall fall by the sword; I will judge you
in the border of Israel; and ye shall know that
I *am* the LORD.

11 This *city* shall not be your caldron, neither
shall ye be the flesh in the midst thereof; *but*
I will judge you in the border of Israel:

What punishment did the Lord pronounce upon Jerusalem's leaders? (11:6–11) "In spite of repeated warnings, they insist that the walls of Jerusalem are like a *caldron* in which *flesh* or meat is safely stored [see v. 3]. So they urge that business-as-usual be the order of the day. Ezekiel is ordered by *the Spirit* to set matters straight. Jerusalem, he declares, is not inviolate because the Lord chose it as His habitation. The city is indeed a caldron filled with *the slain* victims of the wicked policies and crimes of the leaders. But it does not offer protection from the Lord. For He will bring them *forth out of the midst of it* [judging] them by *the hands of [Babylon]*" (Roehrs and Franzmann, *Concordia Self-Study Commentary*, 543).

Summary of Ezekiel 11:12–25

"Ezekiel sees in vision the destruction of Jerusalem. The Lord reminds the people that this destruction comes because they 'have not walked in my statutes [laws], neither executed my judgments, but have done after the manners of the heathen that are round about you' (Ezekiel 11:12). Yet in the Lord's mercy, Israel will eventually be gathered so that the children of Israel 'may walk in my statutes, and keep mine ordinances, and do them: and they shall be my people, and I will be their God' (Ezekiel 11:20)" (Valletta, et al., *Old Testament for Latter-day Saint Families*, 583).

Ezekiel 12:1–16. Ezekiel Is a Type for Scattered Israel

Why did the Lord command Ezekiel to gather his things and publicly leave Jerusalem? (12:1–12)

"The prophet was instructed . . . to act out what was going to happen to those still holed up in Jerusalem. . . . Ezekiel packed a light bag. . . . [The wall he was to dig through was] not the city wall, which was made of stone and was many feet thick, but the sun-dried brick wall of his house. . . . Ezekiel was to explain that this was their *sign* (that is a sign to the people; v.11). [Ezekiel was depicting King Zedekiah and the people trying] to escape from the city [2 Kings 25:1–11]" (*Zondervan KJV Commentary*, 1040–41).

CHAPTER 12

Ezekiel makes himself a symbol of the scattering of the people of Judah from Jerusalem—He then prophesies their scattering among all nations.

1 The word of the Lord also came unto me, saying,

2 Son of man, thou dwellest in the midst of a rebellious house, which have eyes to see, and see not; they have ears to hear, and hear not: for they *are* a rebellious house.

3 Therefore, thou son of man, prepare thee stuff for removing, and remove by day in their sight; and thou shalt remove from thy place to another place in their sight: it may be they will consider, though they *be* a rebellious house.

4 Then shalt thou bring forth thy stuff by day in their sight, as stuff for removing: and thou shalt go forth at even in their sight, as they that go forth into captivity.

5 Dig thou through the wall in their sight, and carry out thereby.

6 In their sight shalt thou bear *it* upon *thy* shoulders, *and* carry *it* forth in the twilight: thou shalt cover thy face, that thou see not the ground: for I have set thee *for* a sign unto the house of Israel.

7 And I did so as I was commanded: I brought forth my stuff by day, as stuff for captivity, and in the even I digged through the wall with mine hand; I brought *it* forth in the twilight, *and* I bare *it* upon *my* shoulder in their sight.

8 ¶ And in the morning came the word of the LORD unto me, saying,

9 Son of man, hath not the house of Israel, the rebellious house, said unto thee, What doest thou?

10 Say thou unto them, Thus saith the Lord GOD; This burden *concerneth* the prince in Jerusalem, and all the house of Israel that *are* among them.

11 Say, I *am* your sign: like as I have done, so shall it be done unto them: they shall remove *and* go into captivity.

12 And the prince that *is* among them shall bear upon *his* shoulder in the twilight, and shall go forth: they shall dig through the wall to carry out thereby: he shall cover his face, that he see not the ground with *his* eyes.

13 My net also will I spread upon him, and he shall be taken in my snare: and I will bring him to Babylon *to* the land of the Chaldeans; yet shall he not see it, though he shall die there.

14 And I will scatter toward every wind all that *are* about him to help him, and all his bands; and I will draw out the sword after them.

15 And they shall know that I *am* the LORD, when I shall scatter them among the nations, and disperse them in the countries.

16 But I will leave a few men of them from the sword, from the famine, and from the pestilence; that they may declare all their abominations among the heathen whither they come; and they shall know that I *am* the LORD.

Who was "the prince in Jerusalem" who would be taken to Babylon but "not see it"? (12:10–13) "The 'burden [message of doom]' to 'the prince in Jerusalem [Zedekiah]' includes the baffling information that he should die in the land of Babylon yet should not see that land (v. 13).

"The striking way in which this apparent riddle is solved is explained in Jeremiah's account of the capture of Zedekiah (king of Judah) by Nebuchadnezzar (king of Babylon):

"Then he [Nebuchadnezzar] put out the eyes of Zedekiah; and the king of Babylon bound him in chains, and carried him to Babylon, and put him in prison till the day of his death' (Jer. 52:11)" (Ludlow, *Companion to Your Study of the Old Testament*, 334). ⊕

What was the Lord teaching Israel by sparing a few men from the sword? (12:15–16) "Ezekiel instructed the exiles that their difficult situation did have a purpose. God would use it to demonstrate that He was a personal, caring Lord. Its aim was corrective and instructive. . . . The defeat of God's people would not indicate the Lord's lack of strength, but the serious consequences of sin against Him. Yet He would demonstrate that His purpose had always been to restore His people to Himself. . . . Through the difficult experience, His people would learn that their God was both holy and loving. Sin offended Him, but He still would reach out to restore the sinner" (*Nelson Study Bible* [NKJV], 1349).

Ezekiel 12:17–28. God Declares That His Prophecies and Visions against Jerusalem Shall Be Fulfilled

17 ¶ Moreover the word of the LORD came
to me, saying,

18 Son of man, eat thy bread with quaking,
and drink thy water with trembling and with
carefulness;

19 And say unto the people of the land,
Thus saith the Lord GOD of the inhabitants
of Jerusalem, *and* of the land of Israel; They
shall eat their bread with carefulness, and
drink their water with astonishment, that her
land may be desolate from all that is therein,
because of the violence of all them that dwell
therein.

20 And the cities that are inhabited shall be
laid waste, and the land shall be desolate; and
ye shall know that I *am* the LORD.

21 ¶ And the word of the LORD came unto
me, saying,

22 Son of man, what *is* that proverb *that* ye
have in the land of Israel, saying, The days
are prolonged, and every vision faileth?

23 Tell them therefore, Thus saith the Lord
GOD; I will make this proverb to cease,
and they shall no more use it as a proverb
in Israel; but say unto them, The days are at
hand, and the effect of every vision.

24 For there shall be no more any vain vision
nor flattering divination within the house of
Israel.

25 For I *am* the LORD: I will speak, and the
word that I shall speak shall come to pass; it
shall be no more prolonged: for in your days,
O rebellious house, will I say the word, and
will perform it, saith the Lord GOD.

26 ¶ Again the word of the LORD came to
me, saying,

27 Son of man, behold, *they of* the house of
Israel say, The vision that he seeth *is* for many
days *to come,* and he prophesieth of the times
that are far off.

Why were the people directed to stop using this well-known proverb? (12:22–24) A popular saying among the people mocked prophetic visions and prophecies, saying that they were overdue or incomplete. "Ezekiel affirmed that God's words would be fulfilled and that there would not be a long delay in their fulfillment. Ezekiel also attacked the false prophets and diviners—men and women—who, through their lying oracles (which one commentator referred to as 'whistling in the dark'), had given Judah hope that had ultimately failed" (Ricks, "Watchman to the House of Israel," 277–78).

What promise does Jehovah make about His prophesies and visions? (12:23–25) One of the greatest mistakes we make is to second-guess the Lord when the timing of His pronouncements seem to have passed. The Lord's timing is not our timing. Here the Lord declares to Ezekiel that "the days are at hand" for Jerusalem's destruction and "the effect [or fulfillment] of every vision" (see Ezek. 12:23*a*). As the Lord declared in our day: "What I the Lord have spoken, I have spoken, and I excuse not myself; and though the heavens and the earth pass away, my word shall not pass away, but shall all be fulfilled" (D&C 1:38). ⊕

Why do people oftentimes ignore prophetic warnings? (12:27) Too often people ignore prophetic warnings and teachings because they feel they have

28 Therefore say unto them, Thus saith the Lord GOD; There shall none of my words be prolonged any more, but the word which I have spoken shall be done, saith the Lord GOD.

CHAPTER 13

Ezekiel reproves false prophets, both male and female, who speak lies, to whom God has not spoken.

1 And the word of the LORD came unto me, saying,

2 Son of man, prophesy against the prophets of Israel that prophesy, and say thou unto them that prophesy out of their own hearts, Hear ye the word of the LORD;

3 Thus saith the Lord GOD; Woe unto the foolish prophets, that follow their own spirit, and have seen nothing!

4 O Israel, thy prophets are like the foxes in the deserts.

5 Ye have not gone up into the gaps, neither made up the hedge for the house of Israel to stand in the battle in the day of the LORD.

6 They have seen vanity and lying divination, saying, The LORD saith: and the LORD hath not sent them: and they have made *others* to hope that they would confirm the word.

7 Have ye not seen a vain vision, and have ye not spoken a lying divination, whereas ye say, The LORD saith *it;* albeit I have not spoken?

8 Therefore thus saith the Lord GOD; Because ye have spoken vanity, and seen lies, therefore, behold, I *am* against you, saith the Lord GOD.

9 And mine hand shall be upon the prophets that see vanity, and that divine lies: they shall not be in the assembly of my people, neither shall they be written in the writing of the house of Israel, neither shall they enter into the land of Israel; and ye shall know that I *am* the Lord GOD.

more time and they can make changes later. Amulek warned, "I beseech of you that ye do not procrastinate the day of your repentance" (Alma 34:33). "Ezekiel and every prophet before and since . . . have warned all who will to turn away from Satan, the enemy of their souls, and 'choose liberty and eternal life, through the great Mediator of all men' [2 Nephi 2:27]" (Christofferson, "Voice of Warning," 108). ⊕

Ezekiel 13:1–16. Ezekiel Condemns False Prophets

In what ways were Israel's prophets considered false? (13:1–3) "False prophets do not receive visions from God; therefore their purported visions (they 'have seen nothing') come from their own minds (they 'follow their own spirit')" (Ludlow, *Companion to Your Study of the Old Testament*, 334).

Why would Ezekiel compare Israel's false prophets to foxes? (13:4–6) "The cunning of the fox in obtaining his prey has been long proverbial. These false prophets are represented as the foxes who, having got their prey by great subtlety, run to the desert to hide both themselves and it. So the false prophets, when the event did not answer to their prediction, got out of the way, that they might not be overwhelmed with the reproaches and indignation of the people" (*Adam Clarke's Commentary* [on Ezekiel 13:4]). ⊕

How were Israel's false prophets similar to untempered mortar? (13:10) "Ezekiel compared the work of false prophets to daubing a wall 'with untempered morter' (v.10). Freeman explained: . . . 'Reference is here made to "cob-walls;" that is, walls which are made of beaten earth rammed into molds or boxes, to give shape and consistency, and then emptied from the molds, layer by layer, on the wall, where it dries as the work goes on. Such walls cannot stand the effects of the weather, and houses built on this principle soon crumble and decay. . . . To protect them from the weather a very fine mortar is sometimes made, which is laid thickly on the outside of the walls. When this mortar is properly mixed with lime, it answers the purpose designed; but where the lime is left out, as is often the case, the "untempered mortar" is no protection [*Manners and Customs of the Bible*, 302]'" (*Old Testament Student Manual: 1 Kings–Malachi*, 271–72).

What is meant by "an overflowing shower"? (13:11–13) "The violent thunderstorm of God's judgment (imagery frequently used in the [Old Testament]) was about to sweep [the people of Judah] away" (*NIV Study Bible* [1985], 1242). The Lord declares that the false prophets who have done nothing to warn and prepare their people for the onslaught will no longer "be in the assembly of my people" (Ezek. 13:9). In other words, their wickedness results "in total exclusion from the community" (*NIV Study Bible* [1985], 1242).

10 ¶ Because, even because they have seduced my people, saying, Peace; and *there was* no peace; and one built up a wall, and, lo, others daubed it with untempered *mortar:*

11 Say unto them which daub *it* with untempered *mortar,* that it shall fall: there shall be an overflowing shower; and ye, O great hailstones, shall fall; and a stormy wind shall rend *it.*

12 Lo, when the wall is fallen, shall it not be said unto you, Where *is* the daubing wherewith ye have daubed *it?*

13 Therefore thus saith the Lord GOD; I will even rend *it* with a stormy wind in my fury; and there shall be an overflowing shower in mine anger, and great hailstones in *my* fury to consume *it.*

14 So will I break down the wall that ye have daubed with untempered *mortar,* and bring it down to the ground, so that the foundation thereof shall be discovered, and it shall fall, and ye shall be consumed in the midst thereof: and ye shall know that I *am* the LORD.

15 Thus will I accomplish my wrath upon the wall, and upon them that have daubed it with untempered *mortar,* and will say unto you, The wall *is* no *more,* neither they that daubed it;

16 *To wit,* the prophets of Israel which
prophesy concerning Jerusalem, and which
see visions of peace for her, and *there is* no
peace, saith the Lord GOD.

17 ¶ Likewise, thou son of man, set thy face
against the daughters of thy people, which
prophesy out of their own heart; and prophesy thou against them,

18 And say, Thus saith the Lord GOD; Woe
to the *women* that sew pillows to all armholes, and make kerchiefs upon the head of
every stature to hunt souls! Will ye hunt the
souls of my people, and will ye save the souls
alive *that come* unto you?

19 And will ye pollute me among my people
for handfuls of barley and for pieces of bread,
to slay the souls that should not die, and to
save the souls alive that should not live, by
your lying to my people that hear *your* lies?

20 Wherefore thus saith the Lord GOD;
Behold, I *am* against your pillows, wherewith
ye there hunt the souls to make *them* fly, and
I will tear them from your arms, and will let
the souls go, *even* the souls that ye hunt to
make *them* fly.

21 Your kerchiefs also will I tear, and deliver
my people out of your hand, and they shall
be no more in your hand to be hunted; and
ye shall know that I *am* the LORD.

22 Because with lies ye have made the heart
of the righteous sad, whom I have not made
sad; and strengthened the hands of the
wicked, that he should not return from his
wicked way, by promising him life:

23 Therefore ye shall see no more vanity,
nor divine divinations: for I will deliver my
people out of your hand: and ye shall know
that I *am* the LORD.

Ezekiel 13:17–23. Sorcery, Divination, and Witchcraft Denounced by the Lord

Why would the Lord tell Ezekiel to prophesy against women who prophesy "out of their own heart"? (13:17–22) "Some women purposely misused their positions of trust to teach false prophecies and doctrines with the intent to thwart God's work. . . . The prophet Ezekiel warned of women who used divination to 'prophesy out of their own heart' rather than by the Spirit [Ezek. 13:17, 22]" (Olson, *Women of the Old Testament*, 84). "The women condemned here are false prophets who prophesied out of their own imagination. . . . Ezekiel points to the divinatory side of their activities in which they employed wristbands and veils, and he indicates that they are paid for their services. The exact identity and function of these devices are unclear" (*Jewish Study Bible* [2014], 1054). ⊕

Summary of Ezekiel 14–15

Ezekiel continues to warn Israel about idol worship. The elders of Israel lust for idols yet seek the prophet's counsel on how to worship God. This two-faced allegiance causes a stumbling block for Israel. The Lord declares that even if Noah, Daniel, and Job were there, the people would still not repent. Comparing Jerusalem to a useless tree, the Lord states that it will be fuel for burning and that the land around it will become desolate.

CHAPTERS 14–15

The Lord will not answer those who worship false gods and work iniquity—Ezekiel preaches repentance—The people would not be saved though Noah, Daniel, and Job ministered among them.

Jerusalem, as a useless vine, will be burned.

CHAPTER 16

Jerusalem has become as a harlot, reveling in her idols and worshipping false gods—She has partaken of all the sins of Egypt and the nations round about, and she is rejected—Yet in the last days, the Lord will again establish His covenant with her.

1 Again the word of the Lord came unto me, saying,

2 Son of man, cause Jerusalem to know her abominations,

3 And say, Thus saith the Lord God unto Jerusalem; Thy birth and thy nativity *is* of the land of Canaan; thy father *was* an Amorite, and thy mother an Hittite.

4 And *as for* thy nativity, in the day thou wast born thy navel was not cut, neither wast thou washed in water to supple *thee;* thou wast not salted at all, nor swaddled at all.

5 None eye pitied thee, to do any of these unto thee, to have compassion upon thee; but thou wast cast out in the open field, to the lothing of thy person, in the day that thou wast born.

Ezekiel 16:1–5. Ezekiel Reveals Jerusalem's Abominations

What do we learn about Jerusalem's origin from these verses? (16:3–5) "Geographically, Jerusalem is a Canaanite city, and ethnically or politically it was a Jebusite one. Israel's own version of its history told how originally they failed to conquer it; its inhabitants were incorporated within Israel rather than annihilated. It is the pagan ways of its own people which are thus reflected in the way it has since behaved. Jerusalem's sin goes back to its foreign parenthood" (Goldingay, "Ezekiel," 635–36).

Why is Jerusalem compared to a newborn child? (16:4) "Jerusalem had been treated in a manner similar to a child left to exposure on birth. It was the custom in the ancient Near East to wash a newborn child, rub it with salt for hygienic reasons, and wrap it in cloths. . . . Such common treatment was not given to Jerusalem, by analogy, in her beginning. She was a foundering city, uncared for by the people of Canaan or by Israel in the conquest of the land, for the Hebrews failed to conquer the city of Jebus (Jos. 15:63). In fact, they allowed this city to lie as an unwanted child throughout the period of the judges (vv. 4–5)" (*Expositor's Bible Commentary [Abridged]*, 1296).

6 ¶ And when I passed by thee, and saw thee
polluted in thine own blood, I said unto thee
when thou wast in thy blood, Live; yea, I said
unto thee *when thou wast* in thy blood, Live.

7 I have caused thee to multiply as the bud of
the field, and thou hast increased and waxen
great, and thou art come to excellent ornaments: *thy* breasts are fashioned, and thine
hair is grown, whereas thou *wast* naked and
bare.

8 Now when I passed by thee, and looked
upon thee, behold, thy time *was* the time
of love; and I spread my skirt over thee, and
covered thy nakedness: yea, I sware unto thee,
and entered into a covenant with thee, saith
the Lord GOD, and thou becamest mine.

9 Then washed I thee with water; yea, I
throughly washed away thy blood from thee,
and I anointed thee with oil.

10 I clothed thee also with broidered work,
and shod thee with badgers' skin, and I
girded thee about with fine linen, and I covered thee with silk.

11 I decked thee also with ornaments, and I
put bracelets upon thy hands, and a chain on
thy neck.

12 And I put a jewel on thy forehead, and
earrings in thine ears, and a beautiful crown
upon thine head.

13 Thus wast thou decked with gold and silver; and thy raiment *was of* fine linen, and
silk, and broidered work; thou didst eat fine
flour, and honey, and oil: and thou wast exceeding beautiful, and thou didst prosper
into a kingdom.

Ezekiel 16:6–14. The Lord's Courtship and Marriage to Jerusalem

Why does Ezekiel describe Jerusalem as a maturing young woman? (16:6–7) Ezekiel uses story-form to relate Jerusalem's history. After discovering the abandoned girl-child (verses 3–5), the hero (Jehovah) "commands her to 'Live' (verse 6), a word which brings with it the provision and power of living. And so the unloved and unwanted child . . . begins to grow and comes to full maturity" (Craigie, *Ezekiel*, 108). "Although Israel in Egypt was physically developed, [she] was still spiritually and morally immature. The foundling, now grown to beautiful womanhood, is espoused by her Rescuer. The relationship between God and Israel is frequently depicted by the prophets under the metaphor of marriage" (Fisch, *Ezekiel*, 85–86).

How is the Lord's relationship with Jerusalem like a marriage? (16:8–14) "With striking, graphic, sometimes shocking language, Ezekiel described Jerusalem and Judah as a harlot (chap. 16). Although carelessly treated at her birth in Canaan, she was treated kindly by God, who 'spread his skirt' over her—a symbol of intention to marry (Ezek. 16:8). . . . Despite the marriage of the Lord and Judah, Judah proved herself constant only in her profligacy [decadence] and unfaithfulness. For her adulteries, she would be punished" (Ricks, "Watchman to the House of Israel," 279–80). Regarding the spreading of a skirt, see commentary in this volume for Ruth 3:9.

14 And thy renown went forth among the heathen for thy beauty: for it *was* perfect through my comeliness, which I had put upon thee, saith the Lord GOD.

Summary of Ezekiel 16:15–34

"Instead of being faithful to her marriage to Jehovah, Israel played the part of the harlot . . . whoring after false gods. Indeed, the Lord said, she was worse than a harlot, for such a woman is unfaithful because her lovers give her money and gifts. In her spiritual adultery, Israel actually gave gifts to her lovers—the false gods" (Lund, "Ezekiel," 84).

Summary of Ezekiel 16:35–43

Because of her serious and unrepentant sins, Judah and Jerusalem will be given over to other idol-worshipping nations. Her punishment for idol worship will be death, accomplished at the hand of Babylon.

Ezekiel 16:44–48. Judah's Sins Exceeded Those of Her Neighbors

44 ¶ Behold, every one that useth proverbs shall use *this* proverb against thee, saying, As *is* the mother, *so is* her daughter.

45 Thou *art* thy mother's daughter, that lotheth her husband and her children; and thou *art* the sister of thy sisters, which lothed their husbands and their children: your mother *was* an Hittite, and your father an Amorite.

46 And thine elder sister *is* Samaria, she and her daughters that dwell at thy left hand: and thy younger sister, that dwelleth at thy right hand, *is* Sodom and her daughters.

What do these family terms mean in this proverb? (16:44–48) "The words *mother* and *father* refer to the Hittites and Amorites who were leaders in Canaanite idolatry. *Daughter* indicates Jerusalem, a representative of Judah or Israel. The *husband* represents the Lord (see Ezekiel 16:8, 32, 38). The antecedents of both *that* and *her* are 'daughter,' not "mother.' *Children* were offered in sacrifice to Molech as part of heathen worship. The *sisters* were Samaria and Sodom (see v. 46). They and Jerusalem were all motivated by the same spirit of idolatry" (*Old Testament Student Manual: 1 Kings–Malachi,* 273).

How are the words "daughters" and "hands" related to Jerusalem? (16:46) "The words *elder* and *younger* could more clearly be rendered *greater* and *lesser.* Perhaps they are a reference to the degree of iniquity, that is, Samaria's was greater, Sodom's lesser. *Left hand* equals the direction north; *right hand* means south. The word *daughters* is used here and throughout the rest of the chapter with a different meaning than the word *daughters* in verse 45; *daughters* are cities under the domination of Samaria and Sodom, lesser cities in the surrounding areas (see Keil and Delitzsch, *Commentary,* 9:1:221–23; *Interpreter's Bible,* 6:148–49)" (*Old Testament Student Manual: 1 Kings–Malachi,* 273).

47 Yet hast thou not walked after their ways, nor done after their abominations: but, as *if that were* a very little *thing*, thou wast corrupted more than they in all thy ways.

48 *As* I live, saith the Lord GOD, Sodom thy sister hath not done, she nor her daughters, as thou hast done, thou and thy daughters.

CHAPTER 17

Ezekiel shows in a parable how Israel, while subject to Babylon, wrongfully sought help from Egypt—Yet the Lord will bring forth in the last days a goodly tree from the cedars of Lebanon.

CHAPTER 18

Men will be punished for their own sins—Sinners will die, and the righteous will surely live—A righteous man who sins will be damned, and a sinner who repents will be saved.

1 The word of the LORD came unto me again, saying,

2 What mean ye, that ye use this proverb concerning the land of Israel, saying, The fathers have eaten sour grapes, and the children's teeth are set on edge?

3 *As* I live, saith the Lord GOD, ye shall not have *occasion* any more to use this proverb in Israel.

How had Jerusalem and Judah's wickedness exceeded Sodom and "her daughters"? (16:47–48) The actions of the people in Jerusalem and the communities in the surrounding area most likely mirrored the wicked practices of nearby heathen cities. So why does the Lord declare Israelites to be more corrupt? Because, as the Lord has said, "For of him unto whom much is given much is required; and he who sins against the greater light shall receive the greater condemnation" (D&C 82:3).

Summary of Ezekiel 16:49–63

Ezekiel lists the sins for which Sodom and Samaria were famous for committing including ignoring "the poor and needy." "The condemnation in every age has been when they have neglected and have failed to set out to take care of the needy and the unfortunate" (Lee, *Teachings of Harold B. Lee*, 321). Jerusalem is named more guilty than those two—for they have committed less than half of Jerusalem's sins.

Summary of Ezekiel 17

Using a parable, Ezekiel explains how three groups from Judah are sent into exile. The first two groups are carried captive into Babylon, but the third group is taken by the Lord and planted "upon an high mountain and eminent; . . . and it shall bring forth boughs, and bear fruit" (Ezek. 17:22–23). Zedekiah's son Mulek and his company, who came to the western hemisphere (see Ezek. 17:22a–b), may have been this group saved by the Lord" (see Rasmussen, *Latter-day Saint Commentary on the Old Testament*, 594).

Ezekiel 18:1–9. The Righteous and the Wicked Shall Receive a Just Reward

Why did the Lord instruct Ezekiel to denounce this proverb? (18:1–4) "This revelation corrected a misunderstanding of a phrase in the Decalog [the Ten Commandments] about 'visiting the iniquity of the fathers upon the children unto the third and fourth generation of them that hate me' (Ex. 20:5–6). It also confirmed another teaching of the Lord through Moses that 'the fathers shall not be put to death for the children, neither shall the children be put to death for the fathers: every man shall be put to death for his own sin' (Deut. 24:16). While it is true that the sins of parents may affect children . . . the Lord will not impose punishment on children on behalf of fathers or forefathers" (Rasmussen, *Latter-day Saint Commentary on the Old Testament*, 594–95). ⊕

How did the Israelites misuse this proverb? (18:2–3) "The point of the proverb is that Israel claims that the children are unfairly enduring the consequences of their fathers' deeds. Their thinking was wrong, for they had followed in the footsteps of their fathers and were receiving the just punishment for their own sins" (*Quest Study Bible* [2003], 1207). See commentary in this volume for Jeremiah 31:29.

What did it mean to eat "upon the mountains"? (18:6) This phrase is only found in Ezekiel's writings (see Ezek. 18:6, 11, 15; 22:9). While the meaning is not entirely clear, it may refer to "eating meat sacrificed to idols on the high places" (*NIV Study Bible* [1995], 1242). One commentator noted: "Presumably this is a charge of idolatry at local high places. . . . It might be compared to the giving of Jerusalem's children as food to the gods in [Ezek.] 16:20 and to charge that the people of Judah are willing to 'worship on every high hill' throughout the land. A similar condemnation of the use of hilltop shrines can be found in Hosea 4:13" (Walton, et al., *IVP Bible Background Commentary*, 705).

What was the debtor's pledge and why was it to be restored? (18:7) Property that a debtor offered as collateral for a loan was called his *pledge*. This instruction could be associated with Exodus 22:25–27, in which "a person's only cloak could be taken in pledge for a loan, but it had to be returned if the debtor needed it" (*Jewish Study Bible* [2014], 1062).

Why was it considered wrong to collect usury on a loan? (18:8) "Usury sometimes has more than one meaning. In biblical English it often means simply charging interest on a loan. At other times it implies an unduly high rate of interest. Under the law of Moses, Israel was forbidden to charge usury . . . when lending to a fellow church member" (Bible Dictionary, "Usury"). The two Hebrew words associated with usury "refer to the two aspects of usury—it bites . . . out of the property of one party and increases that of the other. . . . The lender takes a bite . . . out of the amount stipulated when he makes the loan, whereas he demands the full measure or weight in repayment" (Greenberg, *Ezekiel 1–20*, 330).

4 Behold, all souls are mine; as the soul of the father, so also the soul of the son is mine: the soul that sinneth, it shall die.

5 ¶ But if a man be just, and do that which is lawful and right,

6 *And* hath not eaten upon the mountains, neither hath lifted up his eyes to the idols of the house of Israel, neither hath defiled his neighbour's wife, neither hath come near to a menstruous woman,

7 And hath not oppressed any, *but* hath restored to the debtor his pledge, hath spoiled none by violence, hath given his bread to the hungry, and hath covered the naked with a garment;

8 He *that* hath not given forth upon usury, neither hath taken any increase, *that* hath withdrawn his hand from iniquity, hath executed true judgment between man and man,

9 Hath walked in my statutes, and hath kept my judgments, to deal truly; he *is* just, he shall surely live, saith the Lord GOD.

19 ¶ Yet say ye, Why? doth not the son bear
the iniquity of the father? When the son hath
done that which is lawful and right, *and* hath
kept all my statutes, and hath done them, he
shall surely live.

20 The soul that sinneth, it shall die. The
son shall not bear the iniquity of the father,
neither shall the father bear the iniquity of
the son: the righteousness of the righteous
shall be upon him, and the wickedness of the
wicked shall be upon him.

21 But if the wicked will turn from all his
sins that he hath committed, and keep all
my statutes, and do that which is lawful and
right, he shall surely live, he shall not die.

22 All his transgressions that he hath committed, they shall not be mentioned unto
him: in his righteousness that he hath done
he shall live.

Summary of Ezekiel 18:10–18

Ezekiel continues the parable of a just man whose son chooses wickedness, but whose grandson then follows righteousness.

Ezekiel 18:19–32. Men Will Be Punished for Their Own Sins, but the Lord Blesses Those Who Keep His Commandments

How does latter-day scripture confirm that children don't bear their parents' sins? (18:20) These verses teach the same doctrine the Prophet Joseph Smith proclaimed: "We believe that men will be punished for their own sins and not for Adam's transgression" (Articles of Faith 1:2). ⊕

How do we receive the Lord's promise to live and not die spiritually? (18:21–22) Speaking of these verses, Elder Gary B. Sabin remarked: "What a fabulous promise, but it requires two *alls* to receive the promise of the third. Turn from all [your sins]; keep all [my statutes]; then all is forgiven. This requires being 'all in'! . . .

"The Lord requires the heart and a willing mind. Our whole heart! When we are baptized, we are fully immersed as a symbol of our promise to fully follow the Savior, not half-heartedly. When we are fully committed and 'all in,' heaven shakes for our good. When we are lukewarm or only partially committed, we lose out on some of heaven's choicest blessings" ("Stand Up Inside and Be All In," 52).

Why will the Lord not "mention" your sins when you repent? (18:22) "Our spirits are damaged when we make mistakes and commit sins. But unlike the case of our mortal bodies, when the repentance process is complete, no scars remain because of the Atonement of Jesus Christ. . . . That means that no matter what we have done or where we have been or how something happened, if we truly repent, He has promised that He would atone. And when He atoned, that settled that. There are so many of us who are thrashing around, as it were, with feelings of guilt, not knowing quite how to escape. You escape by accepting the Atonement of Christ, and all that was heartache can turn to beauty and love and eternity" (Packer, "Plan of Happiness," 28). See Doctrine and Covenants 58:42.

23 Have I any pleasure at all that the wicked should die? saith the Lord GOD: *and* not that he should return from his ways, and live?

24 ¶ But when the righteous turneth away from his righteousness, and committeth iniquity, *and* doeth according to all the abominations that the wicked *man* doeth, shall he live? All his righteousness that he hath done shall not be mentioned: in his trespass that he hath trespassed, and in his sin that he hath sinned, in them shall he die.

25 ¶ Yet ye say, The way of the Lord is not equal. Hear now, O house of Israel; Is not my way equal? are not your ways unequal?

26 When a righteous *man* turneth away from his righteousness, and committeth iniquity, and dieth in them; for his iniquity that he hath done shall he die.

27 Again, when the wicked *man* turneth away from his wickedness that he hath committed, and doeth that which is lawful and right, he shall save his soul alive.

28 Because he considereth, and turneth away from all his transgressions that he hath committed, he shall surely live, he shall not die.

29 Yet saith the house of Israel, The way of the Lord is not equal. O house of Israel, are not my ways equal? are not your ways unequal?

30 Therefore I will judge you, O house of Israel, every one according to his ways, saith the Lord GOD. Repent, and turn *yourselves* from all your transgressions; so iniquity shall not be your ruin.

What does this verse teach us about God's loving kindness? (18:23) "The Lord is emphatic: He takes no pleasure in the just punishments He must give us. Instead, it is clear that He loves us so abundantly that He will offer us every chance to return to Him, and He pleads with us to do exactly that" (Muhlestein, *Essential Old Testament Companion*, 455). "The Lord came to save sinners. He taught that it is the sick who need the physician. Therefore, he invites the sick—as well as all others—to come unto him, repent, and be cleansed, sanctified, and saved in his kingdom" (Petersen, "Salvation Comes through the Church," 111). See also 2 Nephi 26:23–33.

How does sin offset the good we have done? (18:24) "The scriptures teach that there is an opposition in all things. Thus, if the sinner who repents can have all his sins removed, then the person who commits a sin should expect all his former sins to return. One possibility cannot exist without the possibility of the other [see D&C 82:7]" (Ludlow, *Companion to Your Study of the Old Testament*, 337). President Spencer W. Kimball warned: "Having received the necessary saving ordinances—baptism, the gift of the Holy Ghost, temple ordinances and sealings—one must live the covenants made. He must endure in faith. No matter how brilliant was the service rendered . . . , if he falters later in his life and fails to live righteously 'to the end' the good works he did all stand in jeopardy" (*Miracle of Forgiveness*, 121). ⊕

31 ¶ Cast away from you all your transgressions, whereby ye have transgressed; and
make you a new heart and a new spirit: for
why will ye die, O house of Israel?

32 For I have no pleasure in the death of him
that dieth, saith the Lord GOD: wherefore
turn *yourselves,* and live ye.

How can a new heart be made within us? (18:31–32) "Our determination to cast off all that is contrary to God's will and to sacrifice all we are asked to give and to strive to follow His teachings will help us to endure in the path of Jesus Christ's gospel—even in the face of tribulation, the weakness of our souls, or the social pressure and worldly philosophies that oppose His teachings. . . .

"The scriptures teach that there is a way out of these situations—by inviting our Savior to help us to replace our stony hearts with new hearts" (Soares, "Take Up Our Cross," 114, 115).

CHAPTER 19

Ezekiel laments for Israel because she has been taken captive by other nations and has become like a vine planted in dry and thirsty ground.

Summary of Ezekiel 19

Ezekiel 19 is a lamentation, or poetic song expressing grief for the coming destruction of Judah. Ezekiel describes Judah's kings as lion cubs that are captured and carried into captivity first by Egypt and then by Babylon (see 2 Kings 23:30–34; 24:8–15; 25:27–30). Judah is then depicted as a vine with branches that have been dried up by the east wind (likely representing spiritual apostasy) and planted in the wilderness.

CHAPTER 20

From the time of their deliverance from Egypt to the day of Ezekiel, the people of Israel have rebelled and failed to keep the commandments—In the last days, the Lord will gather Israel and restore His gospel covenant.

1 And it came to pass in the seventh year, in
the fifth *month,* the tenth *day* of the month,
that certain of the elders of Israel came to inquire of the LORD, and sat before me.

2 Then came the word of the LORD unto me,
saying,

Ezekiel 20:1–4. The Wicked Cannot Receive the Lord's Guidance

What previous event did Ezekiel use to measure the passage of time? (20:1) King Jehoiachin was taken into exile in approximately 598 B.C. "Ezekiel had been taken to Babylon that same year. The precise dating gives the message a formal quality and suggests it had special significance" (*Quest Study Bible* [2003], 1211). "The political context of this prophecy was Zedekiah's foolish and sinful alignment with Egypt against Babylon in hopes of deliverance from Nebuchadnezzar's attacks. . . . [The] exiled elders [came] to Ezekiel to obtain a divine explanation of current events. They wanted to know if Egypt would save Judah from the Babylonians" (*Nelson Study Bible* [NKJV], 1362).

3 Son of man, speak unto the elders of Israel,
and say unto them, Thus saith the Lord
GOD; Are ye come to inquire of me? *As* I live,
saith the Lord GOD, I will not be inquired of
by you.

4 Wilt thou judge them, son of man, wilt
thou judge *them?* cause them to know the
abominations of their fathers:

Why does the Lord refuse to answer the elders of Israel? (20:3) "The Lord told Ezekiel to remind [the elders] of the covenant He had made with Israel and the great blessings He had given them and also of how the people had rebelled against Him. . . . If the elders really wanted God's word, they would have obeyed that which they already had from His prophets. God will not be mocked. He will not give more to those who reject that which He has already given (see Alma 12:9–11)" (*Old Testament Student Manual: 1 Kings–Malachi,* 274).

Ezekiel 20:5–9. The Lord Works in Israel's Behalf

What does the Lord lifting up His hand signify? (20:5) "There are many references in the Bible to taking an oath by raising up a hand to heaven (see Deut. 32:40; Dan. 12:7). Ezekiel uses the phrase ten times, with God being the one to take an oath by raising the hand" (Walton, et al., *IVP Bible Background Commentary*, 706). Ezekiel speaks Jehovah's commitment: "I bound myself in a covenant to them to continue to be their God, if they should be faithful, and continue to be my people" (*Adam Clarke's Commentary* [on Ezekiel 20:5]).

How can you better avoid and reject the wickedness that surrounds you? (20:7) "Spiritually dangerous ideas and actions frequently can appear to be attractive, desirable, or pleasurable. Thus, in our contemporary world, each of us needs to be aware of beguiling bad that pretends to be good. . . . Spiritual complacency and casualness make us vulnerable to the advances of the adversary. Spiritual thoughtlessness invites great danger into our lives. . . .

"Constant vigilance is required to counteract complacency and casualness. To be vigilant is the state or action of *keeping careful watch* for possible danger or difficulties. And keeping watch denotes the act of *staying awake* to guard and protect" (Bednar, "Watchful unto Prayer Continually," 33).

Why is the Lord upset about His "name's sake"? (20:9) "The *name* of [God] expresses his nature, his total personality as he has revealed himself. It is parallel to his 'glory', i.e. his glorious majesty, and it can refer to his reputation in the eyes of men. If men think right thoughts about him and recognize his attributes for what they are and so worship him, they may be said to 'sanctify' him; and conversely, to misunderstand his nature and to regard him less highly than he ought to be regarded is to *profane* his name" (Taylor, *Ezekiel*, 156).

Summary of Ezekiel 20:10–32

Ezekiel relates the physical and spiritual wanderings of the house of Israel from the time they left Egypt.

5 ¶ And say unto them, Thus saith the Lord
God; In the day when I chose Israel, and
lifted up mine hand unto the seed of the
house of Jacob, and made myself known
unto them in the land of Egypt, when I lifted
up mine hand unto them, saying, I *am* the
Lord your God;

6 In the day *that* I lifted up mine hand unto
them, to bring them forth of the land of
Egypt into a land that I had espied for them,
flowing with milk and honey, which *is* the
glory of all lands:

7 Then said I unto them, Cast ye away every
man the abominations of his eyes, and defile
not yourselves with the idols of Egypt: I *am*
the Lord your God.

8 But they rebelled against me, and would
not hearken unto me: they did not every man
cast away the abominations of their eyes, neither did they forsake the idols of Egypt: then
I said, I will pour out my fury upon them,
to accomplish my anger against them in the
midst of the land of Egypt.

9 But I wrought for my name's sake, that it
should not be polluted before the heathen,
among whom they *were*, in whose sight I
made myself known unto them, in bringing
them forth out of the land of Egypt.

33 ¶ *As* I live, saith the Lord God, surely with a mighty hand, and with a stretched out arm, and with fury poured out, will I rule over you:

34 And I will bring you out from the people, and will gather you out of the countries wherein ye are scattered, with a mighty hand, and with a stretched out arm, and with fury poured out.

35 And I will bring you into the wilderness of the people, and there will I plead with you face to face.

36 Like as I pleaded with your fathers in the wilderness of the land of Egypt, so will I plead with you, saith the Lord God.

37 And I will cause you to pass under the rod, and I will bring you into the bond of the covenant:

38 And I will purge out from among you the rebels, and them that transgress against me: I will bring them forth out of the country where they sojourn, and they shall not enter into the land of Israel: and ye shall know that I *am* the Lord.

39 As for you, O house of Israel, thus saith the Lord God; Go ye, serve ye every one his idols, and hereafter *also,* if ye will not hearken unto me: but pollute ye my holy name no more with your gifts, and with your idols.

40 For in mine holy mountain, in the mountain of the height of Israel, saith the Lord

Ezekiel 20:33–44. The Lord Desires to Save Judah

What does it mean to "pass under the rod"? (20:37) *Passing under the rod* is a phrase that "alludes to the custom of tithing the sheep. . . . The shepherd stood at the door of the fold, where only one sheep could come out at once. He had in his hand a rod dipped in vermillion; and as they came out, he counted . . . and as the tenth came out, he marked it with the rod, and [it] was set apart for the Lord" (*Adam Clarke's Commentary* [on Ezekiel 20:37]). Other writers have observed, "God's grace follows judgment, so he would ultimately bring Israel into the bond of the covenant as his special possession. When a sheep passes under his shepherd's rod, it indicates that that sheep belongs to the shepherd" (*Expositor's Bible Commentary [Abridged]*, 1305).

How were the wicked of Judah like the rebels of Moses' time? (20:38–39) "As He had in the Sinai wilderness . . . , God would *purge . . . the rebels* (v. 38) from among them. As in the first wilderness experience, many were not allowed to enter the land (see Num. 14:26–35). God probably used irony as He concluded His rebuke, *Go ye, serve ye every one his idols* (v. 39). The opposite is meant (see 1 Kings 22:15; Amos 4:4). More than this is indicated, however. He would have them choose whether to serve Him or their idols, but He did not want them to pretend to worship Him with their words while in their hearts they still worshiped idols" (*Zondervan KJV Commentary*, 1051). ⊕

GOD, there shall all the house of Israel, all of them in the land, serve me: there will I accept them, and there will I require your offerings, and the firstfruits of your oblations, with all your holy things.

41 I will accept you with your sweet savour, when I bring you out from the people, and gather you out of the countries wherein ye have been scattered; and I will be sanctified in you before the heathen.

42 And ye shall know that I *am* the LORD, when I shall bring you into the land of Israel, into the country *for* the which I lifted up mine hand to give it to your fathers.

43 And there shall ye remember your ways, and all your doings, wherein ye have been defiled; and ye shall lothe yourselves in your own sight for all your evils that ye have committed.

44 And ye shall know that I *am* the LORD, when I have wrought with you for my name's sake, not according to your wicked ways, nor according to your corrupt doings, O ye house of Israel, saith the Lord GOD.

45 ¶ Moreover the word of the LORD came unto me, saying,

46 Son of man, set thy face toward the south, and drop *thy word* toward the south, and prophesy against the forest of the south field;

47 And say to the forest of the south, Hear the word of the LORD; Thus saith the Lord GOD; Behold, I will kindle a fire in thee, and it shall devour every green tree in thee, and every dry tree: the flaming flame shall not be quenched, and all faces from the south to the north shall be burned therein.

48 And all flesh shall see that I the LORD have kindled it: it shall not be quenched.

49 Then said I, Ah Lord GOD! they say of me, Doth he not speak parables?

Ezekiel 20:45–49. Ezekiel Prophesies against Judah

Why was Ezekiel told to turn and prophesy to the south? (20:46–47) "This is a prophecy against Judah and Jerusalem. Ezekiel speaks rhetorically here, as if he were standing on the northern border of Judah. God's fire of judgment, in the form of the Babylonian army, would sweep through Judah from north to south" (*Quest Study Bible* [2003], 1213). "The forest is a figure signifying the population, or the mass of people. Individual men are trees. The green tree is a figurative representation of the righteous man, and the dry tree of the ungodly. . . . The fire which Jehovah kindles is the fire of war. . . . From the terrible fierceness of the fire, which cannot be extinguished, every one will know that God has kindled it, that it has been sent in judgment" (Keil and Delitzsch, *Commentary* [on Ezekiel 20:45–49]).

CHAPTER 21

Both the righteous and the wicked in Jerusalem will be slain—Babylon will draw a sharp and bright sword against Israel and will prevail.

1 And the word of the LORD came unto me, saying,

2 Son of man, set thy face toward Jerusalem, and drop *thy word* toward the holy places, and prophesy against the land of Israel,

3 And say to the land of Israel, Thus saith the LORD; Behold, I *am* against thee, and will draw forth my sword out of his sheath, and will cut off from thee the righteous and the wicked.

4 Seeing then that I will cut off from thee the righteous and the wicked, therefore shall my sword go forth out of his sheath against all flesh from the south to the north:

5 That all flesh may know that I the LORD have drawn forth my sword out of his sheath: it shall not return any more.

6 Sigh therefore, thou son of man, with the breaking of *thy* loins; and with bitterness sigh before their eyes.

7 And it shall be, when they say unto thee, Wherefore sighest thou? that thou shalt answer, For the tidings; because it cometh: and every heart shall melt, and all hands shall be feeble, and every spirit shall faint, and all knees shall be weak *as* water: behold, it cometh, and shall be brought to pass, saith the Lord GOD.

8 ¶ Again the word of the LORD came unto me, saying,

9 Son of man, prophesy, and say, Thus saith the LORD; Say, A sword, a sword is sharpened, and also furbished:

Ezekiel 21:1–17. Ezekiel Testifies of Judah's Coming Destruction

Why would the Lord "cut off the righteous and the wicked" together? (21:3–4) "If God had permitted none to be carried off captive but the wicked, the case of these would be utterly hopeless, as there would be none to set a good example, to preach repentance, to reprove sin, or to show God's willingness to forgive sinners. But God, in his mercy, permitted many of the righteous to be carried off also, that the wicked might not be totally abandoned, or put beyond the reach of being saved. . . . And how much was God's glory and the good of men promoted by this! What a seed of salvation was sown, even in the heathen countries, by thus cutting off the righteous with the wicked!" (*Adam Clarke's Commentary* [on Ezekiel 21:3]).

Why was Ezekiel told to sigh "with the breaking of thy loins"? (21:6) To portray the terror and pain of the judgments that would come upon Judah, Ezekiel was told to heave and groan like a woman in the pains of childbirth (see *John Gill's Exposition of the Whole Bible*, [commentary on Ezekiel 21:6]). "Ezekiel's display of intense grief is to serve as another prophetic sign and as an occasion for a new message of impending judgment" (*NIV Study Bible* [1995], 1247).

What does the sharpened and polished sword represent? (21:9–12) Ezekiel warns of Judah's imminent destruction by speaking of a sword. "It is not only drawn out of its sheath, as before, but is made sharp and bright, and ready for use. [The word *sword*] is repeated, either to show the certainty of it, or to express the terror and anguish of mind on account of it" (*John Gill's Exposition of the Whole Bible*, [commentary on Ezekiel 21:9]).

What does the word *contemn* mean? (21:10) The word *contemn* means to regard a person or object with contempt or scorn (see Webster, *American Dictionary of the English Language,* "contemn"). "The sword of Nebuchadnezzar, meaning his destructive force, had contempt for any strength or power promised to Judah (compare Genesis 49:9–10). His sword destroyed the regal government of Judah just as it had brought down other nations over which it had been wielded in power" (*Old Testament Student Manual: 1 Kings–Malachi,* 275).

What is the significance of hitting the thighs or slapping the hands together? (21:12, 14) These gestures generally express heightened emotion. In these verses, the actions demonstrate "great alarm and horror" at Jerusalem's coming destruction (see Ezek. 6:11; Jer. 31:9). They can also express "contempt (see Job 27:23), anger (see Ezekiel 22:13), . . . triumph (see Ezekiel 25:6), or [could indicate] a pledge [or promise] (see Ezekiel 21:17)" (*Old Testament Student Manual: 1 Kings–Malachi,* 275).

What is suggested by "doubling" a sword? (21:14) By clapping his hands together, "Ezekiel demonstrates the Lord's attitude of justice toward Judah's sin and encourages the sword's greater effectiveness. The judgment's intensity is emphasized by the doubling and tripling of the sword. The sword becomes three times more effective than it normally would be. Two and three swords are not present; rather, the sword's swiftness and intensity manifested in God's wrath produces two to three times the normal slaughter" (Alexander, "Ezekiel," 756).

Summary of Ezekiel 21:18–24

Ezekiel describes the false divination practices used by the king of Babylon.

10 It is sharpened to make a sore slaughter;
it is furbished that it may glitter: should we
then make mirth? it contemneth the rod of
my son, *as* every tree.

11 And he hath given it to be furbished, that
it may be handled: this sword is sharpened,
and it is furbished, to give it into the hand
of the slayer.

12 Cry and howl, son of man: for it shall
be upon my people, it *shall be* upon all the
princes of Israel: terrors by reason of the
sword shall be upon my people: smite therefore upon *thy* thigh.

13 Because *it is* a trial, and what if *the sword*
contemn even the rod? it shall be no *more,*
saith the Lord GOD.

14 Thou therefore, son of man, prophesy,
and smite *thine* hands together, and let the
sword be doubled the third time, the sword
of the slain: it *is* the sword of the great *men*
that are slain, which entereth into their privy
chambers.

15 I have set the point of the sword against
all their gates, that *their* heart may faint,
and *their* ruins be multiplied: ah! *it is* made
bright, *it is* wrapped up for the slaughter.

16 Go thee one way or other, *either* on the
right hand, *or* on the left, whithersoever thy
face *is* set.

17 I will also smite mine hands together, and
I will cause my fury to rest: I the LORD have
said *it.*

25 ¶ And thou, profane wicked prince of
Israel, whose day is come, when iniquity *shall
have* an end,

26 Thus saith the Lord GOD; Remove the
diadem, and take off the crown: this *shall* not
be the same: exalt *him that is* low, and abase
him that is high.

27 I will overturn, overturn, overturn, it: and
it shall be no *more,* until he come whose right
it is; and I will give it *him.*

28 ¶ And thou, son of man, prophesy and
say, Thus saith the Lord GOD concerning
the Ammonites, and concerning their reproach; even say thou, The sword, the sword
is drawn: for the slaughter *it is* furbished, to
consume because of the glittering:

29 Whiles they see vanity unto thee, whiles
they divine a lie unto thee, to bring thee
upon the necks of *them that are* slain, of the
wicked, whose day is come, when their iniquity *shall have* an end.

30 Shall I cause *it* to return into his sheath? I
will judge thee in the place where thou wast
created, in the land of thy nativity.

31 And I will pour out mine indignation
upon thee, I will blow against thee in the fire
of my wrath, and deliver thee into the hand
of brutish men, *and* skilful to destroy.

Ezekiel 21:25–27. The Wicked Will Be Removed from Power

Who is the "wicked prince of Israel"? (21:25) The wicked prince is Zedekiah, the last king of Judah. Zedekiah rebelled against Nebuchadnezzar, who had placed him on the throne (see 2 Kings 24:17). Zedekiah refused counsel from the prophet Jeremiah (see Jeremiah 37) and sought assistance from sources other than the Lord. He withheld tribute from Babylon and turned to the forces of Egypt as Jehoiakim had unsuccessfully done before him (see Muhlestein, *Essential Old Testament Companion*, 294, 444–45).

Why is the word *overturn* repeated three times in this verse? (21:26–27) The word "means 'wrecked' or 'ruined' and is used three times consecutively in the Hebrew text to underscore the comprehensive and intensive nature of the destruction" (*Nelson Study Bible* [NKJV], 1367). In these verses, it is the diadem or miter of the high priest and the crown of the king of Judah that would be overturned (see Ezek. 21:26). The priesthood and kingly rule would not be restored until the coming of the Messiah.

"The Hebrew word *shiloh* may be a short form of *asher-lo,* which can be rendered 'whose right it is'" (Ezek. 21:27*b*). The name or title *Shiloh* "has been regarded by many biblical scholars as a prophecy of the coming of Messiah" (Bible Dictionary, "Shiloh").

Ezekiel 21:28–32. The Lord Will Pour Out Destruction on Both Judah and Judah's Enemies

32 Thou shalt be for fuel to the fire; thy blood shall be in the midst of the land; thou shalt be no *more* remembered: for I the LORD have spoken *it*.

CHAPTER 22

Ezekiel catalogs the sins of the people of Judah in Jerusalem—They will be scattered and destroyed for their iniquities.

Summary of Ezekiel 22:1–22

Ezekiel reviews the numerous sins of Judah in Jerusalem. Although the people once boasted of being God's chosen people, their sinful downfall has now made them a source for mockery among the nations.

Ezekiel 22:23–31. The Influence of Unrighteous Leaders

23 ¶ And the word of the LORD came unto me, saying,

24 Son of man, say unto her, Thou *art* the land that is not cleansed, nor rained upon in the day of indignation.

25 *There is* a conspiracy of her prophets in the midst thereof, like a roaring lion ravening the prey; they have devoured souls; they have taken the treasure and precious things; they have made her many widows in the midst thereof.

26 Her priests have violated my law, and have profaned mine holy things: they have put no difference between the holy and profane, neither have they shewed *difference* between the unclean and the clean, and have hid their eyes from my sabbaths, and I am profaned among them.

What is this "conspiracy of prophets"? (22:25–27) "The word of the Lord through Ezekiel specifically condemned the land not cleansed, for the popular prophets were false, priests failed their duty, princes shed blood for gain and power, and the 'prophets' confirmed them in their acts. The people, too, turned to oppression and robbery, taking advantage of the poor, the needy, and the foreigner. No wonder there was not a righteous man found for whose sake the nation could be spared (Ezekiel 22:23–31)" (Rasmussen, *Latter-day Saint Commentary on the Old Testament*, 598). The Prophet Joseph Smith explained that "false prophets always arise to oppose the true prophets and they will prophesy so very near the truth that they will deceive almost the very chosen ones" (*Joseph Smith* [manual], 203).

How can we resist seeing "no difference between the holy and profane"? (22:26) "We live in a world where more and more persons of influence are teaching and acting out a belief that there is no absolute right and wrong. . . .The philosophy of moral relativism, which holds that each person is free to choose for him or herself what is right and wrong, is becoming the unofficial creed for many. . . .

"In this troubled circumstance, we who believe in God and the corollary truth of absolute right and wrong have the challenge of living in a godless and increasingly amoral world. In this circumstance, all of us—especially the rising generation—have a duty to stand up and speak out to affirm that God exists and that there are absolute truths that His commandments establish" (Oaks, "Balancing Truth and Tolerance," 25, 26).

27 Her princes in the midst thereof *are* like wolves ravening the prey, to shed blood, *and* to destroy souls, to get dishonest gain.

How do righteous leaders differ from the leaders Ezekiel describes in Jerusalem? (22:27) "The world teaches that leaders must be mighty; the Lord teaches that they must be meek. Worldly leaders gain power and influence through their talent, skill, and wealth. Christlike leaders gain power and influence 'by persuasion, by long-suffering, by gentleness and meekness, and by love unfeigned' [D&C 121:41].

"In God's eyes, the greatest leaders have always been the greatest followers. . . .

"Leadership is an expression of discipleship—it is simply a matter of helping others come unto Christ, which is what true disciples do. If you are striving to be a follower of Christ, then you can help others follow Him and you can be a leader" (Owen, "Greatest Leaders are the Greatest Followers," 75).

28 And her prophets have daubed them with untempered *mortar*, seeing vanity, and divining lies unto them, saying, Thus saith the Lord GOD, when the LORD hath not spoken.

29 The people of the land have used oppression, and exercised robbery, and have vexed the poor and needy: yea, they have oppressed the stranger wrongfully.

What is "untempered mortar" and why did the false prophets use it? (22:28) *Mortar* is "a very firm cement compounded of sand, ashes and lime . . . well pounded, sometimes mixed and sometimes coated with oil, so as to form a surface almost impenetrable to wet or the weather" (*Smith's Bible Dictionary,* "Mortar"). If the mortar was untempered, or not mixed to the proper consistency, the resulting compound was weak and simply whitened the surface it was intended to protect. "The 'prophets,' through false visions and lying divinations, have whitewashed their own impure motives and led the people astray by falsely claiming to have God's authority" (Alexander, "Ezekiel," 764).

30 And I sought for a man among them, that should make up the hedge, and stand in the gap before me for the land, that I should not destroy it: but I found none.

31 Therefore have I poured out mine indignation upon them; I have consumed them with the fire of my wrath: their own way have I recompensed upon their heads, saith the Lord GOD.

What did it mean to "stand in the gap"? (22:30) Through Ezekiel, Jehovah sought even one person to be true and faithful to Him in the midst of social and spiritual uproar. One biblical commentator observed: "In times of crisis, when governments and church leadership fail, it is no reason for despair. God always seeks one person to 'stand in the breach.' And though we may not be able to see the influence and impact of one such person, we are required to stand, not despair and conform to the tenor of our times. Ezekiel, though addressing a nation, has much to say on individual responsibility. . . . If we truly grasp his message, we will learn the responsibility of faithfulness, even in a time of faithlessness" (Craigie, *Ezekiel,* 171).

Summary of Ezekiel 23

Ezekiel describes the idolatries and foreign alliances of Samaria and Jerusalem. These actions ultimately lead to the spiritual and physical downfall of the kingdoms of Israel and Judah. Their wickedness is likened to entering immoral liaisons.

The Joseph Smith Translation makes small but significant changes in verses 17, 22, and 28. Rather than being alienated from or turned against their false lovers, their minds were turned away from God by their lovers.

Ezekiel 24:1–5. A Warning to the Rebellious House

Why did Ezekiel record this specific date? (24:1–2) "The date is January [Tevet, the 10th month of the Hebrew calendar] 588 B.C., the *very day* that Nebuchadnezzar—*king of Babylon*—began his attack on Jerusalem (see 2 Kings 25:1–3; Jer. 39:1, 2; 52:1–6). Ezekiel was commanded to *write down the name of the day*. This would be a bitter reminder of God's trustworthiness to do what He promised through the prophets. Nebuchadnezzar's siege was God's judgment on Jerusalem" (*Nelson Study Bible* [NKJV], 1372).

How does this parable serve as a warning? (24:3–5) "Ezekiel was told to symbolically announce, by a 'parable' (a symbol) of a pot with meat in it, the Babylonian conquest of Jerusalem. Tevet is the tenth month [see verse 1]; . . . the tenth day of Tevet is remembered by a fast. In the pot, choice meat with the bones was first to be boiled and then burned to powder and the pot melted. The pot represented Jerusalem and its once choice inhabitants who were destroyed in and with their city by the Babylonian siege; it was 'purified' by fire. It must have been a terrifying message for the exiles that day" (Rasmussen, *Latter-day Saint Commentary on the Old Testament*, 599–600).

Ezekiel 24:6–14. The Sins of Judah Are Condemned, and the Lord Proclaims Judgment

What does the uncovered blood on the rock represent? (24:7–8) "The city has shed blood, which is not covered with earth, but has been left uncovered, like blood poured out upon a hard rock, which the stone

CHAPTER 23

Two sisters, Samaria and Jerusalem, committed whoredoms by worshipping idols—Both are destroyed for their lewdness.

CHAPTER 24

The irrevocable judgment of Jerusalem is foretold—As a sign to the Jews, Ezekiel does not weep at his wife's death.

1 Again in the ninth year, in the tenth month, in the tenth *day* of the month, the word of the LORD came unto me, saying,

2 Son of man, write thee the name of the day, *even* of this same day: the king of Babylon set himself against Jerusalem this same day.

3 And utter a parable unto the rebellious house, and say unto them, Thus saith the Lord GOD; Set on a pot, set *it* on, and also pour water into it:

4 Gather the pieces thereof into it, *even* every good piece, the thigh, and the shoulder; fill *it* with the choice bones.

5 Take the choice of the flock, and burn also the bones under it, *and* make it boil well, and let them seethe the bones of it therein.

6 ¶ Wherefore thus saith the Lord GOD; Woe to the bloody city, to the pot whose scum *is* therein, and whose scum is not gone out of it! bring it out piece by piece; let no lot fall upon it.

7 For her blood is in the midst of her; she set it upon the top of a rock; she poured it not upon the ground, to cover it with dust;

8 That it might cause fury to come up to take
vengeance; I have set her blood upon the top
of a rock, that it should not be covered.

9 Therefore thus saith the Lord GOD; Woe to
the bloody city! I will even make the pile for
fire great.

10 Heap on wood, kindle the fire, consume
the flesh, and spice it well, and let the bones
be burned.

11 Then set it empty upon the coals thereof,
that the brass of it may be hot, and may burn,
and *that* the filthiness of it may be molten in
it, *that* the scum of it may be consumed.

12 She hath wearied *herself* with lies, and her
great scum went not forth out of her: her
scum *shall be* in the fire.

13 In thy filthiness *is* lewdness: because I
have purged thee, and thou wast not purged,
thou shalt not be purged from thy filthiness
any more, till I have caused my fury to rest
upon thee.

14 I the LORD have spoken *it:* it shall come
to pass, and I will do *it;* I will not go back,
neither will I spare, neither will I repent; according to thy ways, and according to thy
doings, shall they judge thee, saith the Lord
GOD.

cannot absorb, and which cries to God for vengeance, because it is uncovered (cf. Genesis 4:10; Job 16:18; and Isaiah 26:21). The thought is this: [Judah] has sinned in an insolent and shameless manner, and has done nothing to cover her sin, has shown no sign of repentance or atonement, by which she might have got rid of her sin. This has all been ordered by God. . . . [so that] He might be able to execute vengeance for the crime" (Keil and Delitzsch, *Commentary* [on Ezekiel 24:3–14]).

What is the filthiness Ezekiel refers to in this verse? (24:13) "In the Bible, filthiness is a term associated with sexual sin and with lewd language. . . .

"Indecent and vulgar expressions pollute the air around us. Relations that are sacred between husband and wife are branded with coarse expressions that degrade what is intimate in marriage and make commonplace what is forbidden outside it. Moral sins that should be unspeakable are in the common vernacular. Human conduct plunging downward from the merely immodest to the utterly revolting is written on the walls and shouted in the streets. . . .

"How soberly we must regard the Book of Mormon teachings that 'there cannot any unclean thing enter into the kingdom of God; wherefore there must needs be a place of filthiness prepared for that which is filthy' (1 Ne. 15:34; see also Alma 7:21)" (Oaks, "Reverent and Clean," 51).

15 ¶ Also the word of the LORD came unto
me, saying,

16 Son of man, behold, I take away from
thee the desire of thine eyes with a stroke: yet
neither shalt thou mourn nor weep, neither
shall thy tears run down.

17 Forbear to cry, make no mourning for the
dead, bind the tire of thine head upon thee,
and put on thy shoes upon thy feet, and cover
not *thy* lips, and eat not the bread of men.

Ezekiel 24:15–27. The Death of Ezekiel's Wife Foreshadows the Destruction of the Temple

Why was Ezekiel instructed not to mourn for his wife? (24:16–18) "Ezekiel was told that his wife would die suddenly but that he was not to mourn her. When asked concerning this peculiar—and, in the light of the importance of mourning rites, highly inappropriate (cf. Jer. 16:1–7)—behavior, Ezekiel was to explain that it was a symbol for Jerusalem, whose inhabitants and temple would be so suddenly destroyed that there would be no time for mourning. The sudden death of his wife and his inability to mourn for her according to custom became a symbol of the sudden destruction of God's sanctuary in Jerusalem" (Ricks, "Watchman to the House of Israel," 285). But through His prophets, the Lord promised Israel that He "would deliver them in about seventy years" (see Ludlow, *Companion to Your Study of the Old Testament*, 338).

Why was Ezekiel commanded to tell the exiled Jews about Jerusalem's destruction? (24:19–27) "When they heard of the sudden loss of all their *sons and* their *daughters* (v. 21) in Jerusalem, and the destruction of . . . God's *sanctuary* [temple], they were to recognize this as God's doing and to mourn, not for their loved ones, but for their sins. Then, the Lord declared, they would certainly know that Ezekiel was *a sign unto them*. . . . The prophet would be *no more dumb* [silent] (v. 27). Ezekiel's wife died the same day the temple was burned [2 Kings 25:8–9]. Ironically, the desire of their eyes was the sanctuary, the place of God's dwelling, not God Himself" (*Zondervan KJV Commentary*, 1058).

18 So I spake unto the people in the morning: and at even my wife died; and I did in the morning as I was commanded.

19 ¶ And the people said unto me, Wilt thou not tell us what these *things are* to us, that thou doest *so?*

20 Then I answered them, The word of the LORD came unto me, saying,

21 Speak unto the house of Israel, Thus saith the Lord GOD; Behold, I will profane my sanctuary, the excellency of your strength, the desire of your eyes, and that which your soul pitieth; and your sons and your daughters whom ye have left shall fall by the sword.

22 And ye shall do as I have done: ye shall not cover *your* lips, nor eat the bread of men.

23 And your tires *shall be* upon your heads, and your shoes upon your feet: ye shall not mourn nor weep; but ye shall pine away for your iniquities, and mourn one toward another.

24 Thus Ezekiel is unto you a sign: according to all that he hath done shall ye do: and when this cometh, ye shall know that I *am* the Lord GOD.

25 Also, thou son of man, *shall it* not *be* in the day when I take from them their strength, the joy of their glory, the desire of their eyes, and that whereupon they set their minds, their sons and their daughters,

26 *That* he that escapeth in that day shall come unto thee, to cause *thee* to hear *it* with *thine* ears?

27 In that day shall thy mouth be opened to him which is escaped, and thou shalt speak, and be no more dumb: and thou shalt be a sign unto them; and they shall know that I *am* the LORD.

CHAPTERS 25–32

The Lord's vengeance will fall on the Ammonites, on the Moabites and Edomites, and on the Philistines.

Because she rejoiced in the sorrows and fall of Jerusalem, Tyre will be destroyed.

Ezekiel laments the fall of Tyre and the loss of her riches and commerce.

Tyre and Sidon will fall and be destroyed—The Lord will gather the people of Israel to their own land—They will then dwell safely.

Egypt will be overthrown by Babylon—When Egypt rises again, it will be the basest of kingdoms.

Egypt and its helpers will be made desolate by Babylon.

Pharaoh's glory and fall are compared to that of the Assyrians.

Ezekiel laments for the fearful fall of Pharaoh and of Egypt.

Summary of Ezekiel 25–32

In these chapters, Ezekiel prophesies against the nations that surrounded Israel.

"The fall of Jerusalem seemed to be a victory of heathendom over the people of the true God, and it was needful to show that it was not so. The God of Israel who had visited His people with this punishment would send His judgments on the heathen nations also, and would convince them that He was the living God. The humiliation of these nations would clear the stage for the restoration of Israel, which would no longer be troubled by its formerly hostile neighbors" (*John Dummelow's Commentary* [on Ezekiel 25:1–32]).

Ezekiel 33:1–11. A Watchman's Responsibility Is to Warn the People

What was the role of the watchman? (33:2–6) "Watchmen were sentries stationed on a wall or in a tower in order to look out for and warn of dangers approaching from afar. They were employed to protect cities as well as vineyards, fields, or pastures. . . .

"As God's called and authorized servants, prophets are separated from the world, draw closer to Him, and are allowed to see things from a more heavenly perspective. . . .

"Prophets have a solemn responsibility to warn us of coming dangers, and they will continue to do so regardless of public opinion or trends in society. . . . By heeding prophets' warnings, we can find safety and avoid the calamities that may befall us" ("Watchmen on the Tower," 28, 29). See commentary in this volume for Ezekiel 3:17. ⊕

What does the trumpet denote in scripture? (33:3) A trumpet "symbolizes the declaration of an important thing or event (Alma 29:1; Rev. 1:10; D&C 88:105–6). For example, the Lord's missionaries blow the trumpet by preaching the gospel [D&C 24:12]. The sounding of a trump figuratively calls the outcasts of Israel to gather unto the Lord (Isa. 27:13; Matt. 24:31). It also calls forth the dead from the grave unto the bar of judgment (Morm. 9:13; 1 Cor. 15:52; 1 Thes. 4:16; Mosiah 26:24–25). . . . Trumpets are blown in times of impending danger (both spiritual and physical danger) as a warning to the people (D&C 88:92; 77:12; Ezek. 33:3–6; Joel 2:1)" (McConkie and Parry, *Guide to Scriptural Symbols*, 104–5).

How can heeding prophetic warnings deliver our souls from danger? (33:5) "Spiritually speaking, we need to stay awake and be alert to the promptings of the Holy Ghost and the signals that come from the Lord's watchmen on the towers [Ezek. 33:7]. . . . Focusing our lives in and on the Savior and His gospel enables us to overcome the tendency of the natural man to be spiritually snoozy and lazy. As we are blessed with eyes to see and ears to hear [see Matthew 13:16], the Holy Ghost can increase our

CHAPTER 33

Watchmen who raise the warning voice save their own souls—Repentant sinners are saved—The righteous who turn to sin are damned—The people of Judah in Jerusalem are destroyed because of their sins.

1 Again the word of the LORD came unto me, saying,

2 Son of man, speak to the children of thy people, and say unto them, When I bring the sword upon a land, if the people of the land take a man of their coasts, and set him for their watchman:

3 If when he seeth the sword come upon the land, he blow the trumpet, and warn the people;

4 Then whosoever heareth the sound of the trumpet, and taketh not warning; if the sword come, and take him away, his blood shall be upon his own head.

5 He heard the sound of the trumpet, and took not warning; his blood shall be upon him. But he that taketh warning shall deliver his soul.

6 But if the watchman see the sword come, and blow not the trumpet, and the people be not warned; if the sword come, and take *any* person from among them, he is taken away in his iniquity; but his blood will I require at the watchman's hand.

7 ¶ So thou, O son of man, I have set thee a watchman unto the house of Israel; therefore thou shalt hear the word at my mouth, and warn them from me.

8 When I say unto the wicked, O wicked *man,* thou shalt surely die; if thou dost not speak to warn the wicked from his way, that wicked *man* shall die in his iniquity; but his blood will I require at thine hand.

9 Nevertheless, if thou warn the wicked of his way to turn from it; if he do not turn from his way, he shall die in his iniquity; but thou hast delivered thy soul.

10 Therefore, O thou son of man, speak unto the house of Israel; Thus ye speak, saying, If our transgressions and our sins *be* upon us, and we pine away in them, how should we then live?

11 Say unto them, *As* I live, saith the Lord GOD, I have no pleasure in the death of the wicked; but that the wicked turn from his way and live: turn ye, turn ye from your evil ways; for why will ye die, O house of Israel?

capacity to look and listen when we may not typically think we need to look or listen or when we may not think anything can be seen or heard" (Bednar, "Watchful unto Prayer Continually," 33).

What is our responsibility when we have been warned by prophets? (33:7–9) "While the duty to warn is felt especially keenly by prophets, it is a duty shared by others as well. In fact, 'it becometh every man who hath been warned to warn his neighbor' [D&C 88:81]. We who have received a knowledge of the great plan of happiness—and its implementing commandments—should feel a desire to share that knowledge since it makes all the difference here and in eternity" (Christofferson, "Voice of Warning," 108). Consider the prophetic messages that have affected you personally. Who in your life might need to hear this message and how will you share it? ⊕

Who does the Lord consider to be "wicked"? (33:8) Martin Harris was called a "wicked man" because he "set at naught the counsels of God and has broken the most sacred promises which were made before God" (D&C 3:12–13; see also D&C 84:50–51). However, the "label of 'wickedness' need not be confined to those who either openly or surreptitiously *seek* sin, but also to those procrastinators who passively pursue its siren call. . . . An all-encompassing definition of the 'wicked' was given by President Joseph Fielding Smith, who said that this meant 'all who had not repented and received the Gospel' [see *Church History and Modern Revelation*, 1:258]" (Brewster, *Doctrine and Covenants Encyclopedia*, 635).

What do we learn about God's character in this verse? (33:11) "Far from being anxious to condemn, our Heavenly Father and our Savior seek our happiness and plead with us to repent, knowing full well that 'wickedness never was [and never will be] happiness' [Alma 41:10]. So Ezekiel and every prophet before and since, speaking the word of God out of a full heart, have warned all who will to turn away from Satan, the enemy of their souls, and 'choose liberty and eternal life, through the great Mediator of all men' [2 Ne. 2:27]" (Christofferson, "Voice of Warning," 108). Nephi's words deepen our appreciation, saying, "[Jesus Christ] layeth down his own life that he may draw all men unto him. Wherefore, he commandeth none that they shall not partake of his salvation" (2 Ne. 26:24).

Ezekiel 33:12–16. The Lord Teaches How to Repent

How do we turn from our sins? (33:14–15) "The word *repent* connotes 'to perceive afterwards' and implies 'change.' In Swedish, the word is *omvänd*, which simply means 'to turn around.' . . . Real repentance also includes a turning of our heart and will to God and a renunciation of sin. . . . Real repentance must involve faith in the Lord Jesus Christ. . . .

"When we 'perceive afterwards' and 'turn around' with the Savior's help, we can feel hope in His promises and the joy of forgiveness. Without the Redeemer, the inherent hope and joy evaporate, and repentance becomes simply miserable behavior modification. But by exercising faith in Him, we become converted to His ability and willingness to forgive sin" (Renlund, "Repentance," 122).

How does restitution help turn us to God? (33:15–16) "Ezekiel teaches that spiritual life after sin is possible only for those who repent of their foolishness. God's promises, based on knowing the truth—in other words, knowing things as they *really* are—are the basis of rebuilding shattered lives. Those who repent demonstrate that they are greater than their sins. Their actions show their convictions, along with their hope, that they can return to the Lord, from whom they have become estranged" (Meservy, "Ezekiel, Prophet of Hope," 59).

Summary of Ezekiel 33:17–33

The Lord will judge each person on their own merit. Ezekiel prophesies that the Lord will desolate Israel for their wickedness and abominations.

12 Therefore, thou son of man, say unto the children of thy people, The righteousness of the righteous shall not deliver him in the day of his transgression: as for the wickedness of the wicked, he shall not fall thereby in the day that he turneth from his wickedness; neither shall the righteous be able to live for his *righteousness* in the day that he sinneth.

13 When I shall say to the righteous, *that* he shall surely live; if he trust to his own righteousness, and commit iniquity, all his righteousnesses shall not be remembered; but for his iniquity that he hath committed, he shall die for it.

14 Again, when I say unto the wicked, Thou shalt surely die; if he turn from his sin, and do that which is lawful and right;

15 *If* the wicked restore the pledge, give again that he had robbed, walk in the statutes of life, without committing iniquity; he shall surely live, he shall not die.

16 None of his sins that he hath committed shall be mentioned unto him: he hath done that which is lawful and right; he shall surely live.

CHAPTER 34

The Lord reproves those shepherds who do not feed the flock—In the last days, the Lord will gather the lost sheep of Israel—The Messiah will be their Shepherd—The Lord will make His gospel covenant with them.

1 And the word of the LORD came unto me, saying,

2 Son of man, prophesy against the shepherds of Israel, prophesy, and say unto them, Thus saith the Lord GOD unto the shepherds; Woe *be* to the shepherds of Israel that do feed themselves! should not the shepherds feed the flocks?

3 Ye eat the fat, and ye clothe you with the wool, ye kill them that are fed: *but* ye feed not the flock.

4 The diseased have ye not strengthened, neither have ye healed that which was sick, neither have ye bound up *that which was* broken, neither have ye brought again that which was driven away, neither have ye sought that which was lost; but with force and with cruelty have ye ruled them.

Ezekiel 34:1–10. The Lord Holds Israel's Leaders Responsible for Not Caring for Their People

What was the Lord's complaint against Israel's leaders? (34:2) "Through Ezekiel, the Lord warns the leaders of Israel by comparing them to shepherds who do not care for their flocks. He accuses them of feeding themselves on the flock while not taking care of the sheep. In addition, they have not taken care of the sick sheep, they fail to gather in those that have strayed, and they are cruel masters. As a result, the sheep become scattered and fall prey to predators. The Lord makes it clear it is His flock that they have lost and failed to search for. As a result, the Lord will hold them accountable and remove them from being shepherds" (Muhlestein, *Essential Old Testament Companion*, 456).

What does "ye eat the fat" mean? (34:3) "The shepherds include, first, the priests and Levites; secondly, the kings, princes, and magistrates. The flock means the whole of the people. The fat and the wool [are] the tithes and offerings, the taxes and imposts. The reprehensible feeding and clothing with these, as to the priests and Levites, the using these tithes and offerings, [is] not to enable them the better to fulfill the work of the ministry, but to pamper their own bodies, and support them in an idle voluptuous life; and in reference to the state, the employing the taxes and imposts, [is] not for the support and administration of justice and good government, but to subsidize heathen powers, and maintain their own luxury and idolatrous prodigality [wastefulness]" (*Adam Clarke's Commentary* [on Ezekiel 34:2]).

What Christlike characteristics should true shepherds demonstrate? (34:4–6) Can you identify scriptural accounts, doctrine, or principles that illustrate Jesus Christ is the "chief Shepherd"? (1 Pet. 5:2–4). Unlike the shepherds Ezekiel dealt with, what Christlike characteristics do true shepherds always demonstrate? "Our Good Shepherd cautions that shepherds in Israel must not slumber, nor scatter or cause the sheep to go astray, nor look our own way for our own gain. God's shepherds are to strengthen, heal, bind up that which is broken, bring again that which was driven away, seek that which was lost" (Gong, "Good Shepherd, Lamb of God," 98). ⊕

Ezekiel 34:11–31. The Lord Is a Shepherd Who Gathers, Protects, and Nourishes His People

Why does the Lord take the responsibility upon Himself to seek after us, the sheep? (34:11–12) "Ezekiel likened the exiled Israelites' situation to that of scattered sheep. The scattering had taken place because their shepherds had been careless and had exploited the sheep (see Ezek. 34:1–10). But God himself would replace those careless shepherds with his constant care. He, as any good shepherd, would seek out the sheep, bind up their bruises, and bring them home again. . . . Christ is the shepherd both to the wandering individual and to His scattered people, and the message of hope in Ezekiel's words applies both to the one lost sheep and to the straying flock" (Meservy, "Ezekiel, Prophet of Hope," 59).

What has the Lord promised regarding the gathering of His scattered sheep? (34:12) "The message of the gathering of Israel is clear in this passage. The lost sheep of Israel will be brought back to the fold, gathered 'out from the people' and 'from the countries.' They will be restored to the covenants

5 And they were scattered, because *there is* no shepherd: and they became meat to all the beasts of the field, when they were scattered.

6 My sheep wandered through all the mountains, and upon every high hill: yea, my flock was scattered upon all the face of the earth, and none did search or seek *after them.*

7 ¶ Therefore, ye shepherds, hear the word of the LORD;

8 *As* I live, saith the Lord GOD, surely because my flock became a prey, and my flock became meat to every beast of the field, because *there was* no shepherd, neither did my shepherds search for my flock, but the shepherds fed themselves, and fed not my flock;

9 Therefore, O ye shepherds, hear the word of the LORD;

10 Thus saith the Lord GOD; Behold, I *am* against the shepherds; and I will require my flock at their hand, and cause them to cease from feeding the flock; neither shall the shepherds feed themselves any more; for I will deliver my flock from their mouth, that they may not be meat for them.

11 ¶ For thus saith the Lord GOD; Behold, I, *even* I, will both search my sheep, and seek them out.

12 As a shepherd seeketh out his flock in the day that he is among his sheep *that are* scattered; so will I seek out my sheep, and will deliver them out of all places where they have been scattered in the cloudy and dark day.

13 And I will bring them out from the people, and gather them from the countries, and will bring them to their own land, and feed them upon the mountains of Israel by the rivers, and in all the inhabited places of the country.

14 I will feed them in a good pasture, and upon the high mountains of Israel shall their fold be: there shall they lie in a good fold, and *in* a fat pasture shall they feed upon the mountains of Israel.

15 I will feed my flock, and I will cause them to lie down, saith the Lord GOD.

16 I will seek that which was lost, and bring again that which was driven away, and will bind up *that which was* broken, and will strengthen that which was sick: but I will destroy the fat and the strong; I will feed them with judgment.

17 And *as for* you, O my flock, thus saith the Lord GOD; Behold, I judge between cattle and cattle, between the rams and the he goats.

18 *Seemeth it* a small thing unto you to have eaten up the good pasture, but ye must tread down with your feet the residue of your pastures? and to have drunk of the deep waters, but ye must foul the residue with your feet?

of the gospel with Jehovah as their shepherd. He is their *true* prophet, priest, and king" (Jackson, "I Will Be Your God," 295). Joseph Smith taught that "the Good Shepherd will put forth his own sheep, and lead them out from all nations where they have been scattered in a cloudy and dark day, to Zion and to Jerusalem" (Joseph Smith Papers, "History, 1838–1856, volume A-1 [23 December 1805–30 August 1834]," 262; orthography standardized).

How was this prophecy fulfilled in our dispensation? (34:13–14) President Wilford Woodruff explained one way that this prophecy has been fulfilled: "If we had not come [to the mountains] there certainly would have been a flood of prophecy fallen unfulfilled, prophecy in regard to the mountains of Israel, and the great company gathering up thereto, with regard to the lifting up of a standard therein, and the building of cities and the Temple of God in their midst. All these things would have fallen unfulfilled if we had not come to these mountains and fulfilled them. And so with many other prophecies. We have been called together to perform the work of the Lord, and now the Lord looks to us to fulfill our covenants and keep his commandments" (in *Journal of Discourses*, 18:113).

What do these verses teach you about the Savior's nature? (34:15–16) "The language of this passage tells us of the commitment and loving care the Lord has for his sheep. He will *search* for them and *seek them out*; he will *seek* them and *deliver them*; he will *bring them out from the people* and will *gather them* and will *bring them to their own land* and will *feed them*. . . . Through Nephi we have this wonderful promise: 'He gathereth his children from the four quarters of the earth; and he numbereth his sheep, and they know him; and there shall be one fold and one shepherd; and he shall feed his sheep, and in him they shall find pasture' (1 Ne. 22:25)" (Parry and Parry, *Understanding the Signs of the Times*, 79).

What did the Lord mean when He said He would "judge between cattle and cattle"? (34:17–22) "God has a further message for the leaders of His people, but this time He reminds them that while they were asked to be shepherds, they were still His sheep. He will gather all His sheep, but He will also keep in mind which were the sheep and which were the goats, which were sheep rams and which were goat rams. The goats walked through the water, fouling it with their feet so that the sheep had to drink of filthy water. This was what the failed, wicked, and proud leadership of Judah had done, and God had noticed it. Though they were His sheep, and He would care for them, still He would have to judge them" (Muhlestein, *Scripture Study Made Simple*, 457).

19 And *as for* my flock, they eat that which
ye have trodden with your feet; and they
drink that which ye have fouled with your
feet.

20 ¶ Therefore thus saith the Lord GOD unto
them; Behold, I, *even* I, will judge between
the fat cattle and between the lean cattle.

21 Because ye have thrust with side and
with shoulder, and pushed all the diseased
with your horns, till ye have scattered them
abroad;

22 Therefore will I save my flock, and they
shall no more be a prey; and I will judge between cattle and cattle.

Who is "my servant David" in these passages? (34:23–24) "These passages refer to Jesus Christ, who was a descendant of David in the flesh and who is and ever will be the true Shepherd and King of Israel. To the ancient Israelites, David embodied the very essence of kingship . . . [This] came to mind whenever David's name was mentioned, and they provided for later Israelites not only the reminiscence of a past golden age but also the longing for a future age that would be even more glorious. Thus the name David took on symbolic significance and was applied to Israel's millennial King. He would be, as it were, a second King David, who would restore the glories of the past" (Jackson, "I Will Be Your God," 296). ⊕

23 And I will set up one shepherd over them,
and he shall feed them, *even* my servant
David; he shall feed them, and he shall be
their shepherd.

24 And I the LORD will be their God, and
my servant David a prince among them; I
the LORD have spoken *it*.

What is the "covenant of peace" mentioned in this verse? (34:25) The "Lord will make 'a covenant of peace' with his flock ([Ezek.] 34:25). In place of the curses of the Sinai covenant, which they have experienced while being under the judgment of God—wild animals, drought, famine, and the sword (Lev. 26:14–35)—they will now experience the blessings of the covenant: safety, rain in its season, fruitfulness, and peace (26:4–13). . . . This covenant is thus not so much a 'new' covenant as it is the . . . blessings promised in the original covenant" (Duguid, *Ezekiel*, 396).

25 And I will make with them a covenant of
peace, and will cause the evil beasts to cease
out of the land: and they shall dwell safely in
the wilderness, and sleep in the woods.

26 And I will make them and the places
round about my hill a blessing; and I will
cause the shower to come down in his season;
there shall be showers of blessing.

27 And the tree of the field shall yield her
fruit, and the earth shall yield her increase,
and they shall be safe in their land, and shall
know that I *am* the LORD, when I have broken the bands of their yoke, and delivered
them out of the hand of those that served
themselves of them.

28 And they shall no more be a prey to the heathen, neither shall the beast of the land devour them; but they shall dwell safely, and none shall make *them* afraid.

29 And I will raise up for them a plant of renown, and they shall be no more consumed with hunger in the land, neither bear the shame of the heathen any more.

30 Thus shall they know that I the LORD their God *am* with them, and *that* they, *even* the house of Israel, *are* my people, saith the Lord GOD.

31 And ye my flock, the flock of my pasture, *are* men, *and* I *am* your God, saith the Lord GOD.

What is the "plant of renown" that will be raised up? (34:29) "The Lord is known as the 'seed of David' (2 Tim. 2:8), the 'rod out of the stem of Jesse' (Isa. 11:1), the 'BRANCH' (Zech. 3:8), the 'vine' (John 15:1), and the 'stem' (D&C 113:1–2), all designations that describe him as the 'plant of renown' (Ezek. 34:29). . . . A plant is a perfect figure of Christ. It is set firmly in the ground. . . . Many plants produce fruit which . . . provides nutrition, and which gives vitality and physical strength to its partakers. Jehovah, as the 'plant of renown,' gives fruit to Israel, so that 'they shall be no more consumed with hunger in the land' (Ezek. 34:29)" (McConkie and Parry, *Guide to Scriptural Symbols*, 154).

CHAPTER 35

Judgment will fall upon Mount Seir and all Idumea for their hatred of Israel.

Summary of Ezekiel 35

A prophecy of judgment against the nation of Edom, also known as Idumea. In spite of their blood ties through mutual ancestry, Edom refused to come to the aid of vulnerable and beleaguered Judah. The Lord "will make [Edom] desolate" (Ezek. 35:14) because of their inaction and rejoicing at Israel's fall.

CHAPTER 36

In the last days, all the house of Israel will be gathered to their own lands—The Lord will give them a new heart and a new spirit—They will have His gospel law.

Summary of Ezekiel 36:1–24

Ezekiel prophesies that Israel will be gathered and restored to their ancestral lands in the latter days.

Ezekiel 36:25–38. Israel Is Promised a New Heart and New Spirit

25 ¶ Then will I sprinkle clean water upon you, and ye shall be clean: from all your filthiness, and from all your idols, will I cleanse you.

What does the phrase "sprinkle with clean water upon you" mean? (36:25) This phrase symbolizes "cleansing through divine forgiveness by blood (cf. Ex. 12:22; Lev. 14:4–7; 49:53; Ps 51:7; 1 Co. 6:11). For ceremonial cleansing to be more than a ritual, it was essential that the people repent and acknowledge their past iniquity about which God would remind them. As they would loathe their former transgressions with their shame and disgrace, they would understand how gracious is their cleansing. Likewise, for ceremonial cleansing to be meaningful, actual cleansing and forgiveness of sin must be made. This will be through the new covenant (Jer. 31:31–34)" (Alexander, "Ezekiel," 845).

How does one receive a "new" heart and spirit from the Lord? (36:26–27) "'Repent, and turn yourselves from all your transgressions,' the Lord admonished through Ezekiel (Ezekiel 18:30). True repentance involves a change of heart and spirit and a comprehensive abandonment of evil desires and deeds. This kind of total 'turning around' brings with it a newness of attitude, character, and being" (Top, *Peculiar Treasure*, 161). In addition, Elder Gene R. Cook testified that when we remember God's overwhelming love for us, "God will bring a new heart, a pure heart, and ever-increasing love and peace. As we increasingly think and act like Him, the attributes of the natural man will slip away to be replaced by the heart and the mind of Christ" ("Charity: Perfect and Everlasting Love," 83). ⊕

How can you retain the Lord's change to your heart? (36:26–27) "This mighty change of our spiritual hearts is just the beginning. Repentance, baptism, and confirmation are necessary but not sufficient. Indeed, equal, if not greater, care must be taken with a spiritually changed heart than with a physically transplanted heart if we are to endure to the end. . . .

"Enduring to the end can be challenging because the tendency of the natural man is to reject the spiritually changed heart and allow it to harden. No wonder the Lord cautioned to 'even let those who are sanctified take heed [D&C 20:34]'" (Renlund, "Preserving the Heart's Mighty Change," 98).

What was Ezekiel referring to when he explained that the Lord would "call for the corn"? (36:29) The people will answer to God like "a servant to his master; and shall spring up out of the earth in great abundance; and which shall grow, and increase, and bring forth much fruit; and yield bread to the eater, and seed to the sower: and which is to be understood, not of corn in a literal sense only, but of corn in a spiritual sense; of all spiritual provisions, the word and ordinances, and especially the corn of wheat, Christ Jesus; who is the sum and substance of the Gospel. . . . [There will be no famine] of bread, or of water; nor of hearing the word of the Lord; but shall have plenty of provisions, both for soul and body" (*John Gill's Exposition of the Whole Bible*, [commentary on Ezekiel 36:29]).

26 A new heart also will I give you, and a new spirit will I put within you: and I will take away the stony heart out of your flesh, and I will give you an heart of flesh.

27 And I will put my spirit within you, and cause you to walk in my statutes, and ye shall keep my judgments, and do *them.*

28 And ye shall dwell in the land that I gave to your fathers; and ye shall be my people, and I will be your God.

29 I will also save you from all your uncleannesses: and I will call for the corn, and will increase it, and lay no famine upon you.

30 And I will multiply the fruit of the tree, and the increase of the field, that ye shall receive no more reproach of famine among the heathen.

31 Then shall ye remember your own evil ways, and your doings that *were* not good, and shall lothe yourselves in your own sight for your iniquities and for your abominations.

32 Not for your sakes do I *this,* saith the Lord GOD, be it known unto you: be ashamed and confounded for your own ways, O house of Israel.

33 Thus saith the Lord GOD; In the day that I shall have cleansed you from all your iniquities I will also cause *you* to dwell in the cities, and the wastes shall be builded.

34 And the desolate land shall be tilled, whereas it lay desolate in the sight of all that passed by.

35 And they shall say, This land that was desolate is become like the garden of Eden; and the waste and desolate and ruined cities *are become* fenced, *and* are inhabited.

36 Then the heathen that are left round about you shall know that I the LORD build the ruined *places, and* plant that that was desolate: I the LORD have spoken *it,* and I will do *it.*

37 Thus saith the Lord GOD; I will yet *for* this be inquired of by the house of Israel, to do *it* for them; I will increase them with men like a flock.

38 As the holy flock, as the flock of Jerusalem in her solemn feasts; so shall the waste cities be filled with flocks of men: and they shall know that I *am* the LORD.

Why would God restore Israel to its lands even though they had committed grievous sins? (36:31–36) "A cleansed Israel will return permanently to a productive and plentiful land. . . . Israel will be God's people and the Lord will be her God. . . . Nations will observe this marvelous transformation in Israel and see the Lord as gracious and loving, for Israel did not deserve restoration (v. 32). This restoration is done for the sake of the reputation of the Lord's name. . . .

"The most important consequence of Israel's restoration will be the spread of the knowledge of the Lord throughout the nations. The nations will unequivocally know that Israel's God has accomplished this great restoration" (Alexander, "Ezekiel," 845, 846).

Why is the latter-day land of Israel compared to the Garden of Eden? (36:35) "For later biblical prophets, the Garden of Eden became a byword for prosperity and fruitfulness (see Isaiah 51:3; Ezekiel 36:35; Joel 2:3). Each of these elements—God's hand in the planting of the garden, his divine presence there, the fruit and herbs designed as food for both man and beast, and the river of water that provided a source of life for the plants—denote a place of abundance and prosperity" (Parry, "Garden of Eden," 147).

What was the "holy flock" referred to in these verses? (36:37–38) The holy flock is the true "Church of Christ, without spot, or wrinkle, or any such thing. *The flock of Jerusalem* [refers to] the Jerusalem that is from above, the city of the living God, the place where his Majesty dwells. As they came in ancient times to the solemn national feasts so shall they come when they have fully returned unto the Lord, and received his salvation by Christ Jesus" (*Adam Clarke's Commentary* [on Ezekiel 36:38]).

CHAPTER 37

Ezekiel is shown the valley of dry bones—Israel will inherit the land in the Resurrection—The stick of Judah (the Bible) and the stick of Joseph (the Book of Mormon) will become one in the Lord's hand—The children of Israel will be gathered and cleansed—David (the Messiah) will reign over them—They will receive the everlasting gospel covenant.

1 The hand of the LORD was upon me, and carried me out in the spirit of the LORD, and set me down in the midst of the valley which *was* full of bones,

2 And caused me to pass by them round about: and, behold, *there were* very many in the open valley; and, lo, *they were* very dry.

Ezekiel 37:1–14. Ezekiel's Vision of Dead Bones Brought to Life

How did Ezekiel experience this vision from the Lord? (37:1) "Sometimes prophets and worthy men and women are 'caught away' in the Spirit in the sense that they are taken into [a] vision in order to see and hear unspeakable things. On other occasions . . . they are transported bodily to another place wherein they might experience those things which God desires that they experience. Such was the case with Moses (Moses 1:1), Jesus himself (JST, Matthew 4:1–11), and [Philip] (Acts 8:39)" (McConkie and Millet, *Doctrinal Commentary on the Book of Mormon*, 1:75). Whether Ezekiel sees the valley in vision or whether he is compelled by the Spirit to go to this place is unclear. Nevertheless, the Lord communicates powerful truths through this vision to His prophet.

What are the possible meanings to this vision? (37:2–5) "Often prophetic utterances have dual meanings. Such is the case for the well-known allegory of the scattered dry bones. . . . Sidney B. Sperry wrote the

Ezekiel and the Valley of Dry Bones (Ezekiel 37:1–14)

3 And he said unto me, Son of man, can these bones live? And I answered, O Lord GOD, thou knowest.

following commentary on the [possible] dual nature of this prophecy: 'It will be seen from this passage that the doctrine of the resurrection from the dead . . . is invoked to symbolize the restoration of Israel's exiles to their own land. The exiles are represented—so it seems to me—as having lost hope (their bones are dried up) of ever living again as a nation. But the Lord shows them that they can be restored through His mighty power even as the dead will be raised in the resurrection' [*Voice of Israel's Prophets*, 225–26]" (*Old Testament Student Manual: 1 Kings–Malachi*, 282).

4 Again he said unto me, Prophesy upon these bones, and say unto them, O ye dry bones, hear the word of the LORD.

5 Thus saith the Lord GOD unto these bones; Behold, I will cause breath to enter into you, and ye shall live:

6 And I will lay sinews upon you, and will bring up flesh upon you, and cover you with skin, and put breath in you, and ye shall live; and ye shall know that I *am* the LORD.

What do these verses teach us about the Lord's sequence of the Resurrection? (37:4–6) "When the Lord brings up the children of Israel out of their graves, he will do it just as Ezekiel saw it in vision. The materials that form the bones will come together: first, the anatomy or framework, the most part of the system; then the flesh, afterwards the skin, and then the Spirit of the living God will enter into them, and they will live as immortal beings, no more to be subject to death" (Pratt, in *Journal of Discourses*, 19:290).

7 So I prophesied as I was commanded: and as I prophesied, there was a noise, and behold a shaking, and the bones came together, bone to his bone.

8 And when I beheld, lo, the sinews and the flesh came up upon them, and the skin covered them above: but *there was* no breath in them.

9 Then said he unto me, Prophesy unto the wind, prophesy, son of man, and say to the wind, Thus saith the Lord GOD; Come from the four winds, O breath, and breathe upon these slain, that they may live.

10 So I prophesied as he commanded me, and the breath came into them, and they lived, and stood up upon their feet, an exceeding great army.

How did Ezekiel describe the process of resurrection? (37:7–10) "Ezekiel witnessed the resurrection, here described as a noise, a shaking, and bones coming together, 'bone to his bone.' President [Joseph F.] Smith also used the expression 'bone to his bone' in his Vision of the Redemption of the Dead. President Smith's words, like Ezekiel's, provide a vivid description of the resurrection: 'Their sleeping dust was to be restored unto its perfect frame, bone to his bone, and the sinews and the flesh upon them, the spirit and the body to be united never again to be divided, that they might receive a fulness of joy' (D&C 138:17)" (Parry and Parry, *Understanding Death and the Resurrection*, 331).

Why might Ezekiel's vision include the resurrection in this context? (37:11–14) Kerry Muhlestein reflected, "While we often cite the first part of this chapter as evidence of resurrection, that evidence is a secondary purpose of the scripture. While it is very valid to use as a scriptural verification of resurrection, we must realize that the prophecy is really about the restoration of Israel. Thus the primary interpretation is that God will restore Israel—and resurrection is an accepted fact that is used to illustrate the principle of restoration" (*Essential Old Testament Companion,* 458). ⊕

Ezekiel 37:15–28. Ezekiel Prophesies of Two Books of Scripture in the Last Days

What can we learn from the imagery of "sticks" in these verses? (37:16–17) This prophecy is an excellent example of a dual prophecy. "The Lord has Ezekiel use sticks as a symbolic prophecy about the restoration of Israel and as symbolic of the two tribes being joined into a unified whole again. While we usually speak of the sticks as representing the scriptures from Judah and Joseph [Bible and Book of Mormon], that is . . . a secondary interpretation [which] fulfills the first, meaning that using the Book of Mormon and Bible gathers the tribes of Israel together" (Muhlestein, *Essential Old Testament Companion,* 458–59). ⊕

How have the sticks of Joseph and Judah been made "one" in the latter days? (37:19) "The stick or record of Judah—the Old Testament and the New Testament—and the stick or record of Ephraim—the Book of Mormon, which is another testament of Jesus Christ—are now woven together in such a way that as you pore over one you are drawn to the other; as you learn from one you are enlightened by the other. They are indeed one in our hands. Ezekiel's prophecy now stands fulfilled" (Packer, "Scriptures," 53). ⊕

11 ¶ Then he said unto me, Son of man, these bones are the whole house of Israel: behold, they say, Our bones are dried, and our hope is lost: we are cut off for our parts.

12 Therefore prophesy and say unto them, Thus saith the Lord GOD; Behold, O my people, I will open your graves, and cause you to come up out of your graves, and bring you into the land of Israel.

13 And ye shall know that I *am* the LORD, when I have opened your graves, O my people, and brought you up out of your graves,

14 And shall put my spirit in you, and ye shall live, and I shall place you in your own land: then shall ye know that I the LORD have spoken *it,* and performed *it,* saith the LORD.

15 ¶ The word of the LORD came again unto me, saying,

16 Moreover, thou son of man, take thee one stick, and write upon it, For Judah, and for the children of Israel his companions: then take another stick, and write upon it, For Joseph, the stick of Ephraim, and *for* all the house of Israel his companions:

17 And join them one to another into one stick; and they shall become one in thine hand.

18 ¶ And when the children of thy people shall speak unto thee, saying, Wilt thou not shew us what thou *meanest* by these?

19 Say unto them, Thus saith the Lord GOD; Behold, I will take the stick of Joseph, which *is* in the hand of Ephraim, and the tribes of Israel his fellows, and will put them with him, *even* with the stick of Judah, and make them one stick, and they shall be one in mine hand.

20 ¶ And the sticks whereon thou writest shall be in thine hand before their eyes.

21 And say unto them, Thus saith the Lord GOD; Behold, I will take the children of Israel from among the heathen, whither they be gone, and will gather them on every side, and bring them into their own land:

22 And I will make them one nation in the land upon the mountains of Israel; and one king shall be king to them all: and they shall be no more two nations, neither shall they be divided into two kingdoms any more at all:

23 Neither shall they defile themselves any more with their idols, nor with their detestable things, nor with any of their transgressions: but I will save them out of all their dwellingplaces, wherein they have sinned, and will cleanse them: so shall they be my people, and I will be their God.

24 And David my servant *shall be* king over them; and they all shall have one shepherd: they shall also walk in my judgments, and observe my statutes, and do them.

25 And they shall dwell in the land that I have given unto Jacob my servant, wherein your fathers have dwelt; and they shall dwell therein, *even* they, and their children, and their children's children for ever: and my servant David *shall be* their prince for ever.

26 Moreover I will make a covenant of peace with them; it shall be an everlasting covenant with them: and I will place them, and multiply them, and will set my sanctuary in the midst of them for evermore.

27 My tabernacle also shall be with them: yea, I will be their God, and they shall be my people.

28 And the heathen shall know that I the LORD do sanctify Israel, when my sanctuary shall be in the midst of them for evermore.

In what way is the word "stick" used in these verses? (37:20–22) "Commonly translated *stick*, the Hebrew word used is *etz*, a generic word meaning 'wood'. . . . This was wood upon which it was possible to write. Babylonian writing tablets of wood have been found hinged together and faced with wax, with writing engraved on them. Two wooden tablets represent the scriptures from Judah (the Bible) and Joseph (the Book of Mormon) to 'be one in mine hand' (Ezek. 37:15–19 and fn.). With the two labeled wooden tablets in hand, the prophet was to show his people that the children of Israel will be gathered from among the heathen to become one nation, with one king, never to be 'divided into two kingdoms any more at all' (Ezek. 37:18–22)" (Rasmussen, *Latter-day Saint Commentary on the Old Testament*, 608).

What is the Lord's sanctuary? (37:26–27) Ezekiel prophesied in these verses that a holy sanctuary or temple would be part of Israel's restoration. Shortly after this vision, Ezekiel received a detailed account of what the Jerusalem temple would look like (see Ezekiel 40–48). President Joseph Fielding Smith said: "Ezekiel predicted the building of a temple in Jerusalem which will be used for ordinance work after the gathering of Israel from their long dispersion and when they are cleansed from their transgressions" (*Doctrines of Salvation*, 2:244). ⊕

Ezekiel 38:1–13. The Battle of Gog and Magog Ushers in the Second Coming

Who or what are Gog and Magog? (38:2) "The terms *Gog* and *Magog* are often joined together, as, for example, in the phrase the 'battle of Gog and Magog' (see Revelation 20:8). Thus, many people assume the terms refer to two people by those names. Ezekiel 38:1–2 shows clearly, however, that *Gog* is a name of a person and *Magog* the land from which he comes. Technically, 'Gog *of* Magog' is the correct way to say it. Over the centuries, however, the names have come to mean the combination of nations that will fight against Israel in the last days" (*Old Testament Student Manual: 1 Kings–Malachi*, 284).

How can we prepare for the great spiritual battles ahead? (38:7–13) "All around us, we can see evidence that the battle is already raging today. Although apocalyptic typology often represents entire categories rather than specific individuals or events, there are enough close parallels between this prophecy and others that the timeframe for its fulfillment seems apparent. The key to understanding Ezekiel's vision is to turn to modern revelation, where there is a clearer view of the last days and of the Lord's people in that period. In the time in which we now live, the gathering of the house of Israel and the establishment of Zion have commenced. Satan's forces are engaged in relentless battle against individual Saints and the Church" (Jackson, "What 'Gog' and 'Magog' Represent in Prophecies about the Last Days, after the Millennium").

CHAPTER 38

The battle of Gog, from the land of Magog, against Israel will usher in the Second Coming—The Lord will come amid war and pestilence, and all men will shake at His presence.

1 And the word of the LORD came unto me, saying,

2 Son of man, set thy face against Gog, the land of Magog, the chief prince of Meshech and Tubal, and prophesy against him,

3 And say, Thus saith the Lord GOD; Behold, I *am* against thee, O Gog, the chief prince of Meshech and Tubal:

4 And I will turn thee back, and put hooks into thy jaws, and I will bring thee forth, and all thine army, horses and horsemen, all of them clothed with all sorts *of armour, even* a great company *with* bucklers and shields, all of them handling swords:

5 Persia, Ethiopia, and Libya with them; all of them with shield and helmet:

6 Gomer, and all his bands; the house of Togarmah of the north quarters, and all his bands: *and* many people with thee.

7 Be thou prepared, and prepare for thyself, thou, and all thy company that are assembled unto thee, and be thou a guard unto them.

8 ¶ After many days thou shalt be visited: in the latter years thou shalt come into the land *that is* brought back from the sword, *and is* gathered out of many people, against the mountains of Israel, which have been always waste: but it is brought forth out of the nations, and they shall dwell safely all of them.

9 Thou shalt ascend and come like a storm, thou shalt be like a cloud to cover the land, thou, and all thy bands, and many people with thee.

10 Thus saith the Lord GOD; It shall also come to pass, *that* at the same time shall things come into thy mind, and thou shalt think an evil thought:

11 And thou shalt say, I will go up to the land of unwalled villages; I will go to them that are at rest, that dwell safely, all of them dwelling without walls, and having neither bars nor gates,

12 To take a spoil, and to take a prey; to turn thine hand upon the desolate places *that are now* inhabited, and upon the people *that are* gathered out of the nations, which have gotten cattle and goods, that dwell in the midst of the land.

13 Sheba, and Dedan, and the merchants of Tarshish, with all the young lions thereof, shall say unto thee, Art thou come to take a spoil? hast thou gathered thy company to take a prey? to carry away silver and gold, to take away cattle and goods, to take a great spoil?

Ezekiel 38:14–23. God's Judgment Comes upon Gog and His Followers

14 ¶ Therefore, son of man, prophesy and say unto Gog, Thus saith the Lord GOD; In that day when my people of Israel dwelleth safely, shalt thou not know *it?*

15 And thou shalt come from thy place out of the north parts, thou, and many people with thee, all of them riding upon horses, a great company, and a mighty army:

16 And thou shalt come up against my people of Israel, as a cloud to cover the land; it shall be in the latter days, and I will bring thee against my land, that the heathen may know me, when I shall be sanctified in thee, O Gog, before their eyes.

17 Thus saith the Lord GOD; *Art* thou he of whom I have spoken in old time by my servants the prophets of Israel, which prophesied in those days *many* years that I would bring thee against them?

Why are God's actions against the armies of Gog so catastrophic? (38:18–23) "These verses speak of God defending His nation against Gog and his army with supernatural and earthshaking methods. Unusually strong language concerning the wrath of God is found in these verses. The piling up of intense phrases indicates more than an 'ordinary' future battle. . . . This judgment would rival the magnitude of the judgment Sodom experienced. . . . This terrible battle will reveal God's might to the entire world and His concern for His people (see 39:6)" (*Nelson Study Bible* [NKJV], 1397).

What do we know about the great hailstorm described in this verse? (38:22) "Apparently, this will be one of several hailstorms sent by the Lord to call his children to repentance (D&C 43:25). Isaiah prophesied of hail that would bring the proud and wicked low prior to the time of peace and righteousness (Isaiah 32:15–19). . . . Ezekiel spoke of the destruction of the armies of Gog . . . (Ezekiel 38:22) in the latter-day war against the people of Israel. . . . Further, [the apostle] John saw a time when 'there fell upon men a great hail out of heaven, *every stone* about the weight of a talent' [75.6 pounds; see Bible Dictionary, "Weights and Measures"] (Revelation 16:21). This hailstorm, which will destroy the crops of the earth, as with all of the predicted natural disasters, will come as vengeance upon the wicked" (McConkie and Ostler, *Revelations of the Restoration*, 235–36).

18 And it shall come to pass at the same time
when Gog shall come against the land of
Israel, saith the Lord GOD, *that* my fury shall
come up in my face.

19 For in my jealousy *and* in the fire of my
wrath have I spoken, Surely in that day there
shall be a great shaking in the land of Israel;

20 So that the fishes of the sea, and the fowls
of the heaven, and the beasts of the field,
and all creeping things that creep upon the
earth, and all the men that *are* upon the face
of the earth, shall shake at my presence, and
the mountains shall be thrown down, and the
steep places shall fall, and every wall shall fall
to the ground.

21 And I will call for a sword against him
throughout all my mountains, saith the Lord
GOD: every man's sword shall be against his
brother.

22 And I will plead against him with pestilence and with blood; and I will rain upon
him, and upon his bands, and upon the many
people that *are* with him, an overflowing rain,
and great hailstones, fire, and brimstone.

23 Thus will I magnify myself, and sanctify
myself; and I will be known in the eyes of
many nations, and they shall know that I *am*
the LORD.

Prophecies to Be Fulfilled before the Battle of Gog and Magog (Ezekiel 38:22–23)

"According to the prophets, some important events must take place before the battle actually begins:

"1. The house of Israel will be gathered from among the heathen (the Gentiles) and returned to their own land (see Ezekiel 36:24; 37:21).

"2. The land of Israel will be rebuilt and re-inhabited by the covenant people (see Ezekiel 36:10–12, 33–36).

"3. The land will become highly productive and fruitful, even like the Garden of Eden (see Ezekiel 36:8, 29–30, 34–35).

"4. There will be one nation in the land of Israel again (see Ezekiel 37:22).

"5. Jerusalem will be reestablished as the capital city of the Israelites (see Zechariah 1:16–17; 2:12; 12:6; 3 Nephi 20:46).

"6. Judah will become powerful in politics and warfare (see Isaiah 19:16–17; Zechariah 10:3, 5–6).

"7. A great combination of organizations serving Satan will arise in the last days. This combination has several names: the 'beast . . . out of the sea' (Revelation 13:1), representing the kingdoms of the earth (see JST, Revelation 13:1; 17:8–14; Bruce R. McConkie, *Doctrinal New Testament Commentary*, 3:520); the 'great and abominable church,' 'the church of the devil,' 'the great whore,' and 'the mother of . . . abominations' (Revelation 17:1, 5)" (*Old Testament Student Manual: 1 Kings–Malachi*, 292).

CHAPTER 39

Gog and the land of Magog will be destroyed—For seven years the people in the cities of Israel will burn the weapons of war—For seven months they will bury the dead—Then will come the supper of the great God and the continued gathering of Israel.

8 ¶ Behold, it is come, and it is done, saith the Lord God; this *is* the day whereof I have spoken.

9 And they that dwell in the cities of Israel shall go forth, and shall set on fire and burn the weapons, both the shields and the bucklers, the bows and the arrows, and the handstaves, and the spears, and they shall burn them with fire seven years:

10 So that they shall take no wood out of the field, neither cut down *any* out of the forests; for they shall burn the weapons with fire: and they shall spoil those that spoiled them, and rob those that robbed them, saith the Lord God.

11 ¶ And it shall come to pass in that day, *that* I will give unto Gog a place there of graves in Israel, the valley of the passengers on the east of the sea: and it shall stop the *noses* of the passengers: and there shall they bury Gog and all his multitude: and they shall call *it* The valley of Hamon-gog.

12 And seven months shall the house of Israel be burying of them, that they may cleanse the land.

Summary of Ezekiel 39:1–7

Ezekiel describes the final destruction of the armies of Gog.

Ezekiel 39:8–16. The Dead Are Buried in the Valley of Hamon-gog

Why are the enemies' armor and weapons burned for seven years? (39:9) "The burning of the armour [and weapons] here mentioned has nothing to do with any ancient custom, but was evidently introduced for the purpose of conveying the idea that no remnant should be left of the great conflict to pollute the land; the very weapons of the enemy should be utterly consumed. The *seven years* points to the sacredness and completeness of the number *seven*: It was a great work getting the land thoroughly cleansed from all the implements of heathenism, and the people would not rest till the whole was accomplished. . . . The action, here, therefore, is a sign of the people's zeal for purity" (Fairbairn, *Ezekiel and the Book of His Prophecy*, 419). ⊕

What does the name "Hamon-gog" mean, and where is the valley located? (39:11) "This prophecy is of future events, so it does not necessarily make reference to a known location in Ezekiel's day. Hamon in Hebrew means 'multitude,' so the name Hamon-gog signifies the 'multitude of Gog.' This has reference to the vast numbers buried there. Since the final battle centers around Jerusalem, it is assumed that the valley of Hamon-gog is somewhere nearby— north of Jerusalem and east of the sea" (Chase, *Making Precious Things Plain: Old Testament Study Guide, Part 3*, 318).

How would the burying of such a large group of the dead be accomplished? (39:12–14) "The multitude of carcasses would require more than seven months to bury to cleanse the land. . . . Every person in Israel would be involved. For seven months they would bury the easily observed bodies lying on the ground. After seven months overseers would designate two groups to carry out a 'mopping up' operation (v. 14). One group would search to find any remnant of a body—even a bone—and mark it. These would be collected and taken to the Valley of Hamon Gog for burial by the second group" (*Expositor's Bible Commentary [Abridged]*, 1338).

Ezekiel 39:17–22. "The Supper of the Great God"

Why are the birds and animals invited to feast upon those who have died in this last great battle? (39:17–20) "God will provide the birds of prey and beasts of prey with an abundant meal from this slaughter.... The beasts of prey will make their meal of the corpses before it is possible to bury them, since the burying cannot be effected immediately or all at once.... The picture given of it as a sacrificial meal is based upon Isaiah 34:6 and Jeremiah 46:10. In harmony with this picture the slaughtered foes are

13 Yea, all the people of the land shall bury *them;* and it shall be to them a renown the day that I shall be glorified, saith the Lord GOD.

14 And they shall sever out men of continual employment, passing through the land to bury with the passengers those that remain upon the face of the earth, to cleanse it: after the end of seven months shall they search.

15 And the passengers *that* pass through the land, when *any* seeth a man's bone, then shall he set up a sign by it, till the buriers have buried it in the valley of Hamon-gog.

16 And also the name of the city *shall be* Hamonah. Thus shall they cleanse the land.

17 ¶ And, thou son of man, thus saith the Lord GOD; Speak unto every feathered fowl, and to every beast of the field, Assemble yourselves, and come; gather yourselves on every side to my sacrifice that I do sacrifice for you, *even* a great sacrifice upon the mountains of Israel, that ye may eat flesh, and drink blood.

The Supper of the Great God (Ezekiel 39:17–22)

Concerning what is known as the "Supper of the Great God," Elder Bruce R. McConkie wrote: "After the defeat by the sword of the armies of Gog and Magog, and in the day when the slain of the Lord cover the earth and are as dung upon its face, then the fowls and the beasts shall gorge themselves upon the flesh and blood of the dead. This awful happening, attended by all the stench and stink of the rotting corpses, is set forth in both the Old Testament and the New and in latter-day revelation. It will indeed be something to behold....

"John, in his visions of what was to be in the last days, saw 'an angel standing in the sun' and heard him cry 'to all the fowls that fly in the midst of heaven, Come and gather yourselves together unto the supper of the great God; That ye may eat the flesh of kings, and the flesh of captains, and the flesh of mighty men, and the flesh of horses, and of them that sit on them, and the flesh of all men, both free and bond, both small and great' (Rev. 19:17–18). And our latter-day revelation, speaking of those who have fallen by the plagues and by the sword in Armageddon, says: 'And it shall come to pass that the beasts of the forest and the fowls of the air shall devour them up' (D&C 29:20).

"We have set forth, thus, what the inspired writers say about the blood-soaked scene of gore and corruption that is yet to be. It makes us wonder why it has been revealed in such detail in at least three dispensations. Certainly it will be a literal event in the coming day. But more than this, it surely bears witness of other truths that men should know. It testifies that wickedness shall cover the earth in the last days; that all nations shall take up the sword in the final war of the ages; that men in uncounted numbers will die of plagues and pestilence and by the edge of the sword; and that the dead bodies of all, kings and rulers included, heaped as dung upon the ground, shall, in death, have no more worth than the carcasses of the beasts of the field. Perhaps, above all else, the horror of it all stands as a call to wayward men to repent, to cease their warfare against God, and to seek an inheritance with his people, many of whom will be preserved in that dread day" (*Millennial Messiah*, 489–90).

18 Ye shall eat the flesh of the mighty, and drink the blood of the princes of the earth, of rams, of lambs, and of goats, of bullocks, all of them fatlings of Bashan.

19 And ye shall eat fat till ye be full, and drink blood till ye be drunken, of my sacrifice which I have sacrificed for you.

20 Thus ye shall be filled at my table with horses and chariots, with mighty men, and with all men of war, saith the Lord God.

21 And I will set my glory among the heathen, and all the heathen shall see my judgment that I have executed, and my hand that I have laid upon them.

22 So the house of Israel shall know that I *am* the Lord their God from that day and forward.

CHAPTERS 40–42

A heavenly messenger shows Ezekiel in vision a city where the temple is located—Ezekiel is shown the form and size of the temple and its courts.

Ezekiel sees the inner temple and the Holy of Holies, and he is shown their form and size.

Ezekiel sees in the temple the chambers for the priests.

designated as fattened sacrificial beasts, rams, lambs, he-goats, bullocks; on which [another commentator indicated] that 'these names of animals [signify] different orders of men, chiefs, generals, soldiers'" (Keil and Delitzsch, *Commentary* [on Ezekiel 39:9–20]).

Summary of Ezekiel 39:23–29

After many years of being scattered throughout the earth, the Lord promises His people that He will restore them to their own lands.

Summary of Ezekiel 40–42

Ezekiel is shown a vision of the latter-day temple in Israel. He sees many details of the glorious temple, including the size, its rooms, doors, and courtyards. The design is similar to the temples of both Solomon and Herod.

Ezekiel 43:1–6. Ezekiel Sees God's Glory Fill the Temple

Why does Ezekiel use water to describe the Lord's voice? (43:2) Ezekiel "symbolically describes Jehovah's voice in terms of water. . . . [In vision,] Ezekiel saw the waters flowing from the temple. Clearly the waters that flow from Jehovah's presence symbolize his voice and might. The psalmist writes this beautiful passage: 'The voice of the Lord is upon the waters: the God of glory thundereth: the Lord is upon many waters. The voice of the Lord is powerful; the voice of the Lord is full of majesty' (Ps. 29:3–4)" (Woods, "Waters Which Make Glad the City of God," 286).

In 1836, the Lord manifested Himself to Joseph Smith and Oliver Cowdery in the Kirtland Temple. They described His voice "as the sound of the rushing of great waters" (D&C 110:3).

What vision is Ezekiel referring to in this verse? (43:3) "The high point of the final revelations to Ezekiel is described in this chapter [Ezek. 43] and the next. He saw the return of the Glory of the Lord to the future temple in some of the same imagery he had seen in his call and in the departure of the Spirit of the Lord from the temple (Ezek. 43:1–6; 1:4–28; 3:22–23; 10; 11:23).

"During this vision, the prophet was promised that the Lord will come to dwell in His house on earth forever, but the voice of the Lord reminded him about the inimical acts and attitudes of former Israelite kings, which had caused His Spirit to withdraw before" (Rasmussen, *Latter-day Saint Commentary on the Old Testament*, 611–12).

Ezekiel 43:7–12. The Plans for the Lord's Glorious Temple Are Shown

CHAPTER 43

The glory of God fills the temple—His throne is there, and He promises to dwell in the midst of Israel forever—Ezekiel sees the altar and the ordinances of the altar.

1 Afterward he brought me to the gate, *even*
the gate that looketh toward the east:

2 And, behold, the glory of the God of Israel
came from the way of the east: and his voice
was like a noise of many waters: and the earth
shined with his glory.

3 And *it was* according to the appearance of
the vision which I saw, *even* according to the
vision that I saw when I came to destroy the
city: and the visions *were* like the vision that
I saw by the river Chebar; and I fell upon
my face.

4 And the glory of the LORD came into the
house by the way of the gate whose prospect
is toward the east.

5 So the spirit took me up, and brought me
into the inner court; and, behold, the glory
of the LORD filled the house.

6 And I heard *him* speaking unto me out of
the house; and the man stood by me.

7 ¶ And he said unto me, Son of man, the
place of my throne, and the place of the soles
of my feet, where I will dwell in the midst of
the children of Israel for ever, and my holy
name, shall the house of Israel no more defile, *neither* they, nor their kings, by their

whoredom, nor by the carcases of their kings in their high places.

8 In their setting of their threshold by my thresholds, and their post by my posts, and the wall between me and them, they have even defiled my holy name by their abominations that they have committed: wherefore I have consumed them in mine anger.

9 Now let them put away their whoredom, and the carcases of their kings, far from me, and I will dwell in the midst of them for ever.

10 ¶ Thou son of man, shew the house to the house of Israel, that they may be ashamed of their iniquities: and let them measure the pattern.

11 And if they be ashamed of all that they have done, shew them the form of the house, and the fashion thereof, and the goings out thereof, and the comings in thereof, and all the forms thereof, and all the ordinances thereof, and all the forms thereof, and all the laws thereof: and write *it* in their sight, that they may keep the whole form thereof, and all the ordinances thereof, and do them.

12 This *is* the law of the house; Upon the top of the mountain the whole limit thereof round about *shall be* most holy. Behold, this *is* the law of the house.

Why would the Lord command Ezekiel to show the temple plans to the people? (43:10–11) "In verses 10 and 11, the Lord commands Ezekiel to show Israel the plans for His glorious house. The experience of seeing a potential temple is designed to make Israel realize what they have been missing because of their sins. The hope is that the desire for the temple will cause Israel to change and make themselves into the kind of people who are worthy to have such an edifice. This scenario should also help us realize the value of the temple and enhance our desire to be worthy to attend" (Muhlestein, *Essential Old Testament Companion*, 461).

Summary of Ezekiel 43:13–27

A heavenly guide shows Ezekiel the measurements and specifications of the temple and the altar. He is also taught the ordinances which the future priests would conduct. "Ezekiel was told to communicate these things and teach Israel the modes of worship and the law of the future temple. After being told some specifications about the altar, he was taught the ordinances that the future priests, 'the seed of Zadok,' would conduct" (Rasmussen, *Latter-day Saint Commentary on the Old Testament*, 612).

Summary of Ezekiel 44

Ezekiel's vision continues as the heavenly guide leads him outside the eastern gate, where he observes the glory of the Lord fill the temple. The Lord teaches Ezekiel that holiness should characterize the priests and their work in the temple. They are to teach the people the "difference between the holy and profane, and cause them to discern between the unclean and clean" (v. 23). Those who have not yet received the outward ordinances of the law, and those with an uncircumcised heart, are prohibited from entering or ministering in the temple.

Summary of Ezekiel 45–46

In the future, the promised land will be divided into districts, including a square-mile section around the temple that is to be sacred and set aside for the Lord. Accurate and fair standards of measurement are provided for future sacrifices and offerings. God's people will observe the Sabbath, the Passover, and other feasts as part of their worship at this future temple. The heavenly guide shows Ezekiel the chambers in the outer court of the sanctuary where the priests cook, eat, and change their clothing (see also Ezek. 42:13–14).

Ezekiel 47:1–12. Healing Water Flows from the Temple to the Dead Sea

Why is Ezekiel's vision of the temple important for Latter-day Saints? (47:1) "In the forty-seventh chapter of Ezekiel is a wonderful prophecy that teaches a profound and deeply beautiful lesson on the power and purpose of the temple. It also serves as an excellent illustration of the kind of symbolic teaching found in the House of the Lord. . . .

"As we read [Ezekiel's] words, the Spirit seems to whisper, 'What will literally be true, one day, of the Lord's temple in Jerusalem, is true *now*, spiritually, of all the Lord's temples. From the doors of each one a *healing, life-giving* river flows.'

"Latter-day temples are the source of a powerful, deeply refreshing river. It is a river of peace, revelation, truth, light, and priesthood power. But above all else, it is a river of love" (Wilcox, *House of Glory*, 40, 41).

CHAPTER 44

The glory of the Lord fills the house of the Lord—No strangers may enter the sanctuary—The services of the priests in the temple are explained.

CHAPTERS 45–46

Portions of land will be provided for the sanctuary and the dwellings of the priests—The people are to offer their sacrifices and oblations and keep their feasts.

The ordinances of worship and of sacrifice are explained.

CHAPTER 47

Waters issue from the house of the Lord and heal the Dead Sea—The Lord shows the borders of the land.

1 Afterward he brought me again unto the door of the house; and, behold, waters issued out from under the threshold of the house eastward: for the forefront of the house *stood toward* the east, and the waters came down from under from the right side of the house, at the south *side* of the altar.

2 Then brought he me out of the way of the gate northward, and led me about the way without unto the utter gate by the way that looketh eastward; and, behold, there ran out waters on the right side.

How might the water coming forth from the temple represent Jesus Christ? (47:1–2) When the messenger directed Ezekiel to stand at the east temple door, "water began to flow forth from the temple on its right, or south, side. Whether this water will be literal we cannot say. What is important is the symbolism behind it. The Savior Himself would draw on this imagery. On the great day of the Feast of the Tabernacles, when an enactment of Ezekiel's vision was performed by pouring out water from the temple so that it flowed forth, Christ said that any who thirsted should come to Him and they would then have living water flow from them (see John 7:37–39)" (Muhlestein, *Scripture Study Made Simple*, 468). ⊕

3 And when the man that had the line in his hand went forth eastward, he measured a thousand cubits, and he brought me through the waters; the waters *were* to the ankles.

4 Again he measured a thousand, and brought me through the waters; the waters *were* to the knees. Again he measured a thousand, and brought me through; the waters *were* to the loins.

5 Afterward he measured a thousand; *and it was* a river that I could not pass over: for the waters were risen, waters to swim in, a river that could not be passed over.

6 ¶ And he said unto me, Son of man, hast thou seen *this?* Then he brought me, and caused me to return to the brink of the river.

7 Now when I had returned, behold, at the bank of the river *were* very many trees on the one side and on the other.

8 Then said he unto me, These waters issue out toward the east country, and go down into the desert, and go into the sea: *which being* brought forth into the sea, the waters shall be healed.

9 And it shall come to pass, *that* every thing that liveth, which moveth, whithersoever the rivers shall come, shall live: and there shall be a very great multitude of fish, because these waters shall come thither: for they shall be

How wide and deep was the river? (47:3–5) "One thousand cubits is approximately 1,750 feet. . . . Four times the man uses the measuring line to mark off this distance across the stream, which progressively gets deeper from ankle depth, to knees, to waist, and finally too deep and wide to cross except by swimming" (*NKJV Study Bible* [2018], 1238). ⊕

Which sea will be miraculously healed by the water issuing from the temple? (47:8–10) "The water flows down to the Dead Sea and heals it so that all manner of fish thrive in the sea. Everything thrives around the river and newly healed sea from En-Gedi in the hills west of the Dead Sea to En-Eglaim far to the east. . . .

"The Dead Sea is so saturated with salt that nothing lives in it—not even the kind of shrimp that can survive in the Great Salt Lake. It is the ultimate symbol of the lack of life, and thus its healing is the greatest symbol of God's ability to bring life to us no matter how dead we become" (Muhlestein, *Essential Old Testament Companion*, 464–65).

healed; and every thing shall live whither the
river cometh.

10 And it shall come to pass, *that* the fishers
shall stand upon it from En-gedi even unto
En-eglaim; they shall be a *place* to spread
forth nets; their fish shall be according to
their kinds, as the fish of the great sea, exceeding many.

11 But the miry places thereof and the
marshes thereof shall not be healed; they
shall be given to salt.

12 And by the river upon the bank thereof,
on this side and on that side, shall grow all
trees for meat, whose leaf shall not fade, neither shall the fruit thereof be consumed: it
shall bring forth new fruit according to his
months, because their waters they issued out
of the sanctuary: and the fruit thereof shall be
for meat, and the leaf thereof for medicine.

What do the water and the trees mean in this vision? (47:12) "The waters that flow from the temple have both literal and figurative meaning. The meaning is literal in the physical sense of the waters' renewing and fructifying effects on the land. In the figurative sense they symbolize first the restoration of Israel as a land and a people, eventually including the entire earth. At the same time, they are figurative for the voice, presence, power, and pedagogy [teaching] of Jehovah, which flows down from heaven as revelation to renew and sanctify man. Ezekiel uses the imagery of trees as a symbol of mankind. Just as the waters cause the trees to grow, so hearkening to the voice of Jehovah causes mankind to grow" (Woods, "Waters Which Make Glad the City of God," 282). ✪

Temple and Family History Work Can Bring Healing (Ezekiel 47:1–12)

Reflecting on the blessings of temple service, Elder Dale G. Renlund observed: "A heavenly messenger showed Ezekiel a vision of a temple with water gushing out of it. . . .

"Two characteristics of the water are noteworthy. First, though the small stream had no tributaries, it grew into a mighty river, becoming wider and deeper the farther it flowed. Something similar happens with the blessings that flow from the temple as individuals are sealed as families. Meaningful growth occurs going backward and forward through the generations as sealing ordinances weld families together.

"Second, the river renewed everything that it touched. The blessings of the temple likewise have a stunning capacity to heal. Temple blessings can heal hearts and lives and families. . . .

"God will strengthen, help, and uphold us; and He will sanctify to us our deepest distress. When we gather our family histories and go to the temple on behalf of our ancestors, God fulfills many of these promised blessings simultaneously on both sides of the veil. Similarly, we are blessed when we help others in our wards and stakes do the same. Members who do not live close to a temple also receive these blessings by participating in family history work, collecting the names of their ancestors for temple ordinances to be performed.

"President Russell M. Nelson, however, cautioned: 'We can be inspired all day long about temple and family history experiences others have had. But we must do something to actually experience the joy ourselves.' He continued, 'I invite you to prayerfully consider what kind of sacrifice—preferably a sacrifice of time—you can make [to] do more temple and family history work' [see *Ensign*, Oct. 2017, 39]. As you accept President Nelson's invitation, you will discover, gather, and connect your family. Additionally, blessings will flow to you and your family like the river spoken of by Ezekiel. You will find healing for that which needs healing" ("Family History and Temple Work," 47–49).

CHAPTER 48

The portions of land for the tribes are named—The gates of the city bear the names of the tribes—The name of the city will be The Lord Is There.

Summary of Ezekiel 47:13–23

Sections of land are to be divided among the tribes of Israel. The tribe of Levi is separately given a special land for their residence (Ezek. 45:1–8), and the inheritance of Joseph is divided between Ephraim and Manasseh (the two sons of Joseph who were adopted by Jacob [see Gen. 48:5]). Inheriting the land comes by the covenant made between the Lord and Abraham (Gen. 12:7; 15:7, 18–21; 17:8). Those who are not of Israel, but who had settled in the land and had children there, are to receive an inheritance among the tribes of Israel (see Isa. 56:3–8).

Summary of Ezekiel 48

Additional details are given about the division of the land among the tribes of Israel. The holy city will have twelve gates, each bearing a name of one of the tribes of Israel. Ezekiel concludes his book with a prophecy that Jerusalem will eventually be known by the new name, "The Lord is there" (48:35).

THE BOOK OF DANIEL

Introduction

The Book of Daniel tells the familiar story of Daniel and his three friends as exiles in the court of Babylon around 605 B.C. Daniel was "a prophet of God and a man of great faith. Nothing is known about his parents, although he appears to have been of royal descent (Dan. 1:3). He was taken captive to Babylon, where he received the name Belteshazzar (Dan. 1:6–7)....

"The book has two divisions: chapters 1–6 are stories about Daniel and his three companions; chapters 7–12 are prophetic visions that Daniel saw" (Guide to the Scriptures, "Daniel").

"Although [the Book of Daniel] is placed among the prophetic books in the Christian Old Testament, Daniel is among the Writings in the Hebrew Bible" (Holzapfel, et al., *Jehovah and the World of the Old Testament*, 350).

"Daniel's visions always show God as triumphant (7:11, 26–27; 8:25; 9:27; 11:45; 12:13). The climax of his sovereignty is described in Revelation: 'The kingdom of the world has become the kingdom of our Lord and of his Christ, and he will reign for ever and ever' (Rev 11:15; cf. Da 2:44; 7:27)" (*NIV Study Bible* [1985], 1298).

A study of the book of Daniel is also important as one considers the effect it had on the prophetic mission of Joseph Smith. "Throughout his life, Joseph Smith was exposed to and influenced by the themes and images of the book of Daniel. Wilford Woodruff, a close associate and careful record keeper, reported that one of the scriptures cited by the angel Moroni to the young Joseph Smith in September 1823 was Daniel 2. Toward the end of his life, the [Prophet Joseph] taught, 'I calculate to be one of the instruments in setting up the kingdom of Daniel.' Clearly, the book of Daniel gave focus and meaning to his mission. Just how important it was becomes apparent when we examine more closely the early years of the [Latter-day Saint] movement" (Whittaker, "Book of Daniel in Early Mormon Thought," 159).

In summary, "the book of Daniel teaches its readers the important duty of being true to the God of Israel at all cost and illustrates the blessings of the Lord upon the faithful" (Bible Dictionary, "Daniel, book of").

CHAPTER 1

Daniel and certain Hebrews are trained in the court of Nebuchadnezzar—They eat plain food and drink no wine—God gives them knowledge and wisdom beyond all others.

1 In the third year of the reign of Jehoiakim king of Judah came Nebuchadnezzar king of Babylon unto Jerusalem, and besieged it.

2 And the Lord gave Jehoiakim king of Judah into his hand, with part of the vessels of the house of God: which he carried into the land

Daniel 1:1–7. Daniel and Others Are Trained in the King's Palace

When was Daniel taken captive to Babylon? (1:1–3)

"When the Babylonians conquered Assyria, they moved quickly to control the former holdings of the Assyrian Empire. Nebuchadnezzar took his army on a hasty march through the Fertile Crescent, using swift and powerful military raids.... In 605 or 604 BC, he struck Judah. The Jews quickly yielded. As part of the tribute he demanded, Nebuchadnezzar took many of Judah's young elite with him" (Muhlestein, *Essential Old Testament Companion*, 466).

of Shinar to the house of his god; and he brought the vessels into the treasure house of his god.

3 ¶ And the king spake unto Ashpenaz the master of his eunuchs, that he should bring *certain* of the children of Israel, and of the king's seed, and of the princes;

4 Children in whom *was* no blemish, but well favoured, and skilful in all wisdom, and cunning in knowledge, and understanding science, and such as *had* ability in them to stand in the king's palace, and whom they might teach the learning and the tongue of the Chaldeans.

5 And the king appointed them a daily provision of the king's meat, and of the wine which he drank: so nourishing them three years, that at the end thereof they might stand before the king.

6 Now among these were of the children of Judah, Daniel, Hananiah, Mishael, and Azariah:

7 Unto whom the prince of the eunuchs gave names: for he gave unto Daniel *the name* of Belteshazzar; and to Hananiah, of Shadrach; and to Mishael, of Meshach; and to Azariah, of Abed-nego.

8 ¶ But Daniel purposed in his heart that he would not defile himself with the portion of the king's meat, nor with the wine which he drank: therefore he requested of the prince of the eunuchs that he might not defile himself.

Why were Daniel and other young people chosen by the king? (1:3–4) Nebuchadnezzar "ruled by terror, crushing his enemies by fire and sword, and weakening them with deportations to other parts of his empire. It was in the midst of this battle-torn era that Daniel was born. As a youth, he and certain other Hebrews were taken into the court of Nebuchadnezzar for service. They were chosen because of their wisdom and knowledge and ability to learn. Thus, Daniel was brought into a strange land with strange customs, a strange environment, and a very different religious heritage (see Daniel 1)" (Perry, "In the World," 13).

Why did Daniel and his friends receive new names? (1:6–7) "The fact that Daniel and his friends were given new names signifies their new relationship with a superior power, in this case their Babylonian rulers. Interestingly, we commonly refer to Daniel by his Hebrew name, not his new Babylonian name, Belteshazzar ('protect his life;' e.g., Dan 1:6, 2:26). Based on similar principle, receiving a new name in a religious context of a covenant relationship is illustrated in Genesis 17:1–16; 32:24–30" (Holzapfel, et al., *Jehovah and the World of the Old Testament*, 350). ⊕

Daniel 1:8–16. Daniel and His Friends Refuse to Eat the King's Food

In what way did Daniel not defile himself? (1:8) It appears that Daniel was not only following the Mosaic dietary code when he refused to eat the food provided by the king's servants, but he may have also been exercising caution to avoid giving honor to a pagan deity. "Such meals then became a sort of sacrament through which the king partook of the power of the gods. For Daniel to have eaten the king's food would have been tantamount to idol worship, and an admission that these gods had something to offer" (Draper, "Book of Daniel," 324). ⊕

Who was the "prince of the eunuchs"? (1:9–10) The "prince of the eunuchs" was the king's "chief of his officers" (Daniel 1:3*a*). "In the strict and proper sense they were the persons who had charge of the bed-chambers in palaces and larger houses. . . . [But] some of these rose to be confidential advisers of their royal masters or mistresses" (*Smith's Bible Dictionary*, "Eunuch").

What was unique about Daniel's request? (1:12) "Daniel's strategy was most interesting. He did not challenge the beliefs of the Babylonians. Instead, he volunteered to conduct a test as to which way was best. . . . At the end of the tenth day, Daniel and his friends were found to be healthier and stronger than all the rest. Daniel . . . did not have to adopt a different standard of values when he was 'in the world'" (Perry, "In the World," 14).

Daniel 1:17–21. The Lord Greatly Blesses Daniel and His Friends

How were Daniel and his companions blessed by not eating the king's meat? (1:17) Daniel and his friends were blessed physically with fairer countenances and with knowledge and wisdom for their obedience to God. Daniel was also given the spiritual gift to understand visions and dreams. Similarly, those in our day who remember to keep the Word of Wisdom, "walking in obedience to the commandments, shall receive health in their navel and marrow to their bones; and shall find wisdom and great treasures of knowledge, even hidden treasures; and shall run and not be weary, and shall walk and not faint. And I, the Lord, give unto them a promise, that the destroying angel shall pass by them, as the children of Israel, and not slay them" (D&C 89:18–21).

9 Now God had brought Daniel into favour and tender love with the prince of the eunuchs.

10 And the prince of the eunuchs said unto Daniel, I fear my lord the king, who hath appointed your meat and your drink: for why should he see your faces worse liking than the children which *are* of your sort? then shall ye make *me* endanger my head to the king.

11 Then said Daniel to Melzar, whom the prince of the eunuchs had set over Daniel, Hananiah, Mishael, and Azariah,

12 Prove thy servants, I beseech thee, ten days; and let them give us pulse to eat, and water to drink.

13 Then let our countenances be looked upon before thee, and the countenance of the children that eat of the portion of the king's meat: and as thou seest, deal with thy servants.

14 So he consented to them in this matter, and proved them ten days.

15 And at the end of ten days their countenances appeared fairer and fatter in flesh than all the children which did eat the portion of the king's meat.

16 Thus Melzar took away the portion of their meat, and the wine that they should drink; and gave them pulse.

17 ¶ As for these four children, God gave them knowledge and skill in all learning and wisdom: and Daniel had understanding in all visions and dreams.

18 Now at the end of the days that the king had said he should bring them in, then the prince of the eunuchs brought them in before Nebuchadnezzar.

19 And the king communed with them; and among them all was found none like Daniel, Hananiah, Mishael, and Azariah: therefore stood they before the king.

20 And in all matters of wisdom *and* understanding, that the king inquired of them, he found them ten times better than all the magicians *and* astrologers that *were* in all his realm.

21 And Daniel continued *even* unto the first year of king Cyrus.

CHAPTER 2

Nebuchadnezzar's dream is revealed to Daniel—The king saw a great image, a stone cut from the mountain without hands destroyed the image, and the stone grew and filled the whole earth—The stone is the latter-day kingdom of God.

1 And in the second year of the reign of Nebuchadnezzar Nebuchadnezzar dreamed dreams, wherewith his spirit was troubled, and his sleep brake from him.

2 Then the king commanded to call the magicians, and the astrologers, and the sorcerers, and the Chaldeans, for to shew the king his dreams. So they came and stood before the king.

3 And the king said unto them, I have dreamed a dream, and my spirit was troubled to know the dream.

4 Then spake the Chaldeans to the king in Syriack, O king, live for ever: tell thy servants the dream, and we will shew the interpretation.

5 The king answered and said to the Chaldeans, The thing is gone from me: if ye will not make known unto me the dream, with the interpretation thereof, ye shall be cut in pieces, and your houses shall be made a dunghill.

Daniel 2:1–18. Nebuchadnezzar's Servants Cannot Interpret His Dream

Why was the king so concerned about a dream? (2:1) "In the ancient world, dreams were considered a significant medium of insight for the future, and Babylonian religion especially encouraged the seeking of such portents through dreams and unusual circumstances of everyday life. The success of a king and the welfare of his kingdom were often dependent on the correct interpretation of an unusual dream or some bizarre natural event" (Hill, "Daniel," 60).

Who were these magicians, astrologers, and sorcerers? (2:2) "The 'magician is the translation of the Hebrew word with the root meaning of "stylus" or "pen" and hence can be referred to as a scholar more than a magician in the ordinary sense.' Later in history, among the Persians, they are referred to as the Magi or wise scholars" (Brandt, *Book of Daniel*, 31). "*Sorcerers* cast spells. *Astrologers* were a class of priests who claimed to receive special knowledge through the stars. It's possible that some of these practitioners had demonic powers, but they seem ineffective in the story of Daniel (2:1–12)" (*Quest Study Bible* [1994], 1212).

Why would King Nebuchadnezzar say he forgot his dream? (2:5) "In verse 5 the phrase 'is gone from me' should probably read 'is *certain* with me,' as the Persian word *azda* ('sure') is used. Note in verse 9 that the king makes the point that he knows what he dreamt; therefore if the interpreters can tell him the dream, he will know that *they* know what they are talking about and he will know whether he can have confidence in their interpretation or not!" (Rasmussen, *Introduction to the Old Testament and Its Teachings*, 2:92; see also Dan. 2:5*a*).

6 But if ye shew the dream, and the interpretation thereof, ye shall receive of me gifts and rewards and great honour: therefore shew me the dream, and the interpretation thereof.

7 They answered again and said, Let the king tell his servants the dream, and we will shew the interpretation of it.

8 The king answered and said, I know of certainty that ye would gain the time, because ye see the thing is gone from me.

What was the king accusing his wise men of when using the phrase "till the time be changed"? (2:9)
Another way of saying this is "till with time circumstances will change" (Dan. 2:9*a*). In other words, the king accused his counselors of trying to buy time in hopes that the circumstances would change and the king might forget about his request to interpret his troubling dream.

9 But if ye will not make known unto me the dream, *there is but* one decree for you: for ye have prepared lying and corrupt words to speak before me, till the time be changed: therefore tell me the dream, and I shall know that ye can shew me the interpretation thereof.

10 ¶ The Chaldeans answered before the king, and said, There is not a man upon the earth that can shew the king's matter: therefore *there is* no king, lord, nor ruler, *that* asked such things at any magician, or astrologer, or Chaldean.

11 And *it is* a rare thing that the king requireth, and there is none other that can shew it before the king, except the gods, whose dwelling is not with flesh.

12 For this cause the king was angry and very furious, and commanded to destroy all the wise *men* of Babylon.

13 And the decree went forth that the wise *men* should be slain; and they sought Daniel and his fellows to be slain.

In what way does this account parallel the experience of Joseph in Egypt with Pharaoh? (2:14–16)
"The story echoes earlier biblical traditions. Most widely recognized in this regard are the similarities between this story and the story of Joseph in Egypt, especially Genesis 41. In Daniel as in the Joseph story, we have a foreign ruler whose spirit is troubled by a dream, the failure of professional diviners to assuage the ruler's anxiety, a young Hebrew captive accomplishing what the experts could not, the faithful

14 ¶ Then Daniel answered with counsel and wisdom to Arioch the captain of the king's guard, which was gone forth to slay the wise *men* of Babylon:

15 He answered and said to Arioch the king's captain, Why *is* the decree *so* hasty from the king? Then Arioch made the thing known to Daniel.

16 Then Daniel went in, and desired of the king that he would give him time, and that he would shew the king the interpretation.

17 Then Daniel went to his house, and made the thing known to Hananiah, Mishael, and Azariah, his companions:

18 That they would desire mercies of the God of heaven concerning this secret; that Daniel and his fellows should not perish with the rest of the wise *men* of Babylon.

19 ¶ Then was the secret revealed unto Daniel in a night vision. Then Daniel blessed the God of heaven.

20 Daniel answered and said, Blessed be the name of God for ever and ever: for wisdom and might are his:

21 And he changeth the times and the seasons: he removeth kings, and setteth up kings: he giveth wisdom unto the wise, and knowledge to them that know understanding:

22 He revealeth the deep and secret things: he knoweth what *is* in the darkness, and the light dwelleth with him.

23 I thank thee, and praise thee, O thou God of my fathers, who hast given me wisdom and might, and hast made known unto me now what we desired of thee: for thou hast *now* made known unto us the king's matter.

24 ¶ Therefore Daniel went in unto Arioch, whom the king had ordained to destroy the wise *men* of Babylon: he went and said thus unto him; Destroy not the wise *men* of Babylon: bring me in before the king, and I will shew unto the king the interpretation.

captive attributing his success to God, and the rewarding of the captive and his promotion to a position of enormous influence in the kingdom of his sojourning" (Seow, *Daniel*, 34).

What can we learn from Daniel's actions? (2:17–18) "Daniel was confident that God would answer his prayer. But he also realized that the effectiveness of prayer may be heightened when believers unite in common supplication" (Archer, "Daniel," 43). "Daniel immediately enlists the aid of his three companions (v.17). He exhorts them to 'plead for mercy'. . . . Daniel and his friends know that [Jehovah] is a God of compassion (Ex. 34:6), and they know from the accounts of Joseph's experience in Egypt that God alone reveals the meanings of dreams (Gen. 40:8; 41:16). Thus they have good cause to believe in the power of urgent petition in prayer to God" (Hill, "Daniel," 63–64).

Daniel 2:19–30. Nebuchadnezzar's Dream Is Revealed to Daniel

What qualified Daniel to have the secret revealed to him? (2:19) "Living in harmony with God's will was essential to approaching God in faith. . . . Not only had they not defiled themselves, but they had embraced their covenants. . . . Like Ammon, the son of Mosiah, Daniel saw this crisis as an opportunity and took advantage to act rather than succumb to fear (Alma 17:29). The situation was a matter of life and death, but he had been true and faithful. He could petition the Lord for mercy with trust and confidence that He would provide an answer for the king" (Brandt, *Book of Daniel*, 38, 39).

Why is it important to recognize the source of spiritual blessings and knowledge? (2:28) Daniel confessed God's hand in all things (see D&C 59:21). "Though the king would have given Daniel credit for giving the interpretation of his dream, Daniel made it clear that it was not he, nor any of the wise men or soothsayers, who was able to determine the nature of the dream and its interpretation. Daniel testified that 'there is a God in heaven' (Daniel 2:28), and it was by the power of God that the secret of Nebuchadnezzar's dream was made known. Daniel did not take credit to himself for what the Lord had done for his benefit. To do so would certainly have offended God" (*Old Testament Student Manual: 1 Kings–Malachi*, 298). ⊕

Daniel 2:31–49. Daniel Interprets and Explains Nebuchadnezzar's Dream

25 Then Arioch brought in Daniel before the king in haste, and said thus unto him, I have found a man of the captives of Judah, that will make known unto the king the interpretation.

26 The king answered and said to Daniel, whose name *was* Belteshazzar, Art thou able to make known unto me the dream which I have seen, and the interpretation thereof?

27 Daniel answered in the presence of the king, and said, The secret which the king hath demanded cannot the wise *men,* the astrologers, the magicians, the soothsayers, shew unto the king;

28 But there is a God in heaven that revealeth secrets, and maketh known to the king Nebuchadnezzar what shall be in the latter days. Thy dream, and the visions of thy head upon thy bed, are these;

29 As for thee, O king, thy thoughts came *into thy mind* upon thy bed, what should come to pass hereafter: and he that revealeth secrets maketh known to thee what shall come to pass.

30 But as for me, this secret is not revealed to me for *any* wisdom that I have more than any living, but for *their* sakes that shall make known the interpretation to the king, and that thou mightest know the thoughts of thy heart.

31 ¶ Thou, O king, sawest, and behold a great image. This great image, whose brightness *was* excellent, stood before thee; and the form thereof *was* terrible.

32 This image's head *was* of fine gold, his breast and his arms of silver, his belly and his thighs of brass,

33 His legs of iron, his feet part of iron and part of clay.

34 Thou sawest till that a stone was cut out without hands, which smote the image upon his feet *that were* of iron and clay, and brake them to pieces.

35 Then was the iron, the clay, the brass, the silver, and the gold, broken to pieces together, and became like the chaff of the summer threshingfloors; and the wind carried them away, that no place was found for them: and the stone that smote the image became a great mountain, and filled the whole earth.

36 ¶ This *is* the dream; and we will tell the interpretation thereof before the king.

37 Thou, O king, *art* a king of kings: for the God of heaven hath given thee a kingdom, power, and strength, and glory.

38 And wheresoever the children of men dwell, the beasts of the field and the fowls of the heaven hath he given into thine hand, and hath made thee ruler over them all. Thou *art* this head of gold.

39 And after thee shall arise another kingdom inferior to thee, and another third kingdom of brass, which shall bear rule over all the earth.

40 And the fourth kingdom shall be strong as iron: forasmuch as iron breaketh in pieces and subdueth all *things:* and as iron that breaketh all these, shall it break in pieces and bruise.

41 And whereas thou sawest the feet and toes, part of potters' clay, and part of iron, the kingdom shall be divided; but there shall be in it of the strength of the iron, forasmuch as thou sawest the iron mixed with miry clay.

42 And *as* the toes of the feet *were* part of iron, and part of clay, *so* the kingdom shall be partly strong, and partly broken.

43 And whereas thou sawest iron mixed with miry clay, they shall mingle themselves with the seed of men: but they shall not cleave one to another, even as iron is not mixed with clay.

What does the phrase "cut out without hands" mean? (2:34) "The new kingdom that Daniel envisioned would be 'cut out without hands' (Dan. 2:34), meaning that it would be of *divine* construction, rather than human. This kingdom would subdue the nations of the world and over the course of time would be transformed from a small stone into an immense mountain that would fill the entire earth" (Jackson, "May the Kingdom of God Go Forth," 254–55).

What is the kingdom of God in the last days? (2:44) President Ezra Taft Benson taught: "The Church of Jesus Christ of Latter-day Saints is, as Daniel prophesied, a spiritual kingdom 'cut out of the mountain without hands' (Dan. 2:45), meaning that it was begun through the intervention of God. It is not just another human institution. What other organizations or churches ascribe their founding to the declaration that messengers have come to human beings from the God of heaven with authority and power to restore ordinances and keys lost by apostasy?" ("Marvelous Work and a Wonder," 32). ⊕

44 And in the days of these kings shall the God of heaven set up a kingdom, which shall never be destroyed: and the kingdom shall not be left to other people, *but* it shall break in pieces and consume all these kingdoms, and it shall stand for ever.

Interpretation of Nebuchadnezzar's Dream (Daniel 2:36–45)

Kent P. Jackson explained that "the purpose of the dream was not to show relative strength or value but to outline a succession from one to the next" ("May the Kingdom of God Go Forth," 252).

Jackson outlined each empire or era in that succession. "The Head of Gold: The empire over which Nebuchadnezzar ruled is referred to technically as the Neo-Babylonian empire.... As Daniel explained, this empire was the golden head of the image....

"The Breast and Arms of Silver: The second world power envisioned by Daniel was the Persian empire.... When the city of Babylon was conquered by Cyrus in 539 B.C., the Persian monarch assumed control of the vast territory that had been ruled by Nebuchadnezzar and his successors....

"The Belly and Thighs of Brass: The next great kingdom in Nebuchadnezzar's dream represented the empires of Alexander the Great and his successors.... When Alexander of Macedonia set out in the year 334 B.C. to reconquer the Ionian Greek cities from Persian rule, no one could have imagined either the scope of his future conquests or their lasting impact on the future of the world....

"The Legs of Iron: The kingdom characterized as the image's legs of iron was the Roman empire.... The Romans conquered the territories of the Greeks that had succeeded Alexander the Great....

"The Feet of Iron and Clay:... With the fall of the Roman empire, the world entered into a phase of its history in which one world power would no longer rule over all. Instead, an era began in which numerous regional nations competed for the territories once held by the world powers of the past. Nebuchadnezzar's dream and Daniel's prophetic interpretation are conveyed in the metaphor of the great statue. As with any prophetic metaphor, the imagery is not meant to be interpreted in detail, but in major concepts.... In Daniel's prophetic view of the future, the message is taught clearly that one world power would supersede another until there came a time in which smaller nations would be the pattern of world government" ("May the Kingdom of God Go Forth," 252–54).

KINGDOMS REPRESENTED

Head of fine gold
Babylonian Empire

Breast and arms of silver
Mede and Persian Empires

Belly and thighs of brass
Macedonian Empire

Legs of iron
Roman Empire

Feet and toes of clay
Kingdoms that arose after the fall of the Roman Empire

45 Forasmuch as thou sawest that the stone
was cut out of the mountain without hands,
and that it brake in pieces the iron, the brass,
the clay, the silver, and the gold; the great
God hath made known to the king what shall
come to pass hereafter: and the dream *is* certain, and the interpretation thereof sure.

46 ¶ Then the king Nebuchadnezzar fell
upon his face, and worshipped Daniel, and
commanded that they should offer an oblation and sweet odours unto him.

47 The king answered unto Daniel, and said,
Of a truth *it is,* that your God *is* a God of
gods, and a Lord of kings, and a revealer of
secrets, seeing thou couldest reveal this secret.

In what way is the restoration of the gospel a fulfillment of this prophecy? (2:45) Modern revelation provides the meaning of the "stone" described by Daniel: "The keys of the kingdom of God are committed unto man on the earth, and from thence shall the gospel roll forth unto the ends of the earth, as the stone which is cut out of the mountain without hands shall roll forth, until it has filled the whole earth. Yea, a voice crying—Prepare ye the way of the Lord, prepare ye the supper of the Lamb, make ready for the Bridegroom. . . . Wherefore, may the kingdom of God go forth, that the kingdom of heaven may come, that thou, O God, mayest be glorified in heaven so on earth, that thine enemies may be subdued" (D&C 65:2–3, 6).

Why is God called "God of gods" and also "Lord of kings"? (2:47) "One reason why the Lamb is successful in his battle against his enemies is that he commands the hosts (or armies) of heaven, as the 'Lord of lords, and King of kings.' Not only do both the Father and the Son reign as sovereigns over all the earth and over every earthly ruler of any kind but they also rule over heavenly lords and kings (1:6; 5:10; 15:3; Deut. 10:17; Dan. 2:47; 1 Tim. 6:15)" (Parry and Parry, *Understanding the Book of Revelation*, 230).

The Church of Jesus Christ of Latter-Day Saints Is the "Stone . . . Cut Out of the Mountain without Hands" (Daniel 2:34, 44–45)

"Nebuchadnezzar represented the king of kings, a world power, representing the head of gold.

"Another kingdom would arise and take over world dominion. . . .

"This is a revelation concerning the history of the world, when one world power would supersede another until there would be numerous smaller kingdoms to share the control of the earth.

"And it was in the days of these kings that power would not be given to men, but the God of heaven would set up a kingdom—the kingdom of God upon the earth, which should never be destroyed nor left to other people.

"The Church of Jesus Christ of Latter-day Saints was restored in 1830 after numerous revelations from the divine source; and this is the kingdom, set up by the God of heaven, that would never be destroyed nor superseded, and the stone cut out of the mountain without hands that would become a great mountain and would fill the whole earth. . . .

"We give these truths to you, not in arrogance or worldly pride, but with a deep sincerity and a kindly offer—the gospel without price, the gospel of truth, the gospel of salvation and exaltation.

"I know it is true. I know it is divine. I know it is the little stone that was cut out of the mountain without hands. I know it will fill the earth as prophesied and commanded by the Savior Jesus Christ when in his last moments on earth, he said to his eleven apostles, 'Go ye into all the world and preach the gospel to every creature'—to every nation, kindred, tongue, and people (see Mark 16:15). I know it is true from the birth of Adam to the days of Daniel to the days of Joseph Smith and to this day. I know it is true and divine. We offer it to you without price. We promise to you eternal life if you will follow its precepts strictly" (Kimball, "Stone Cut without Hands," 8–9).

In what way did the king make Daniel "a great man"? (2:48–49) "The empire was divided into provinces, or satrapies, of which Babylon was one. Daniel is exalted to high office in the province, but that vague description finds definition in the next statement that clarifies the nature of his high office: he is made prefect over the wise men. This is more likely ranking within his guild rather than an administrative position in the civil government" (Walton, et al., *IVP Bible Background Commentary*, 734).

48 Then the king made Daniel a great man, and gave him many great gifts, and made him ruler over the whole province of Babylon, and chief of the governors over all the wise *men* of Babylon.

49 Then Daniel requested of the king, and he set Shadrach, Meshach, and Abed-nego, over the affairs of the province of Babylon: but Daniel *sat* in the gate of the king.

CHAPTER 3

Nebuchadnezzar creates a golden image and commands all men to worship it—Shadrach, Meshach, and Abed-nego refuse and are cast into the fiery furnace—They are preserved and come out unharmed.

Summary of Daniel 3:1–7

Nebuchadnezzar sets up an enormous image of gold. When the sounds of various instruments are heard, the people are to kneel and worship the image or be thrown into "a burning fiery furnace" (Daniel 3:6).

Daniel 3:8–18. Shadrach, Meshach, and Abed-nego Refuse to Obey the King's Wicked Command

Why would these Chaldeans accuse Daniel's friends? (3:8) "The accusers are either Babylonian officials generally or members of a special guild of diviners or priestly class of wise men. . . . These 'worship police' have two motives: ethnic or racial distrust (if not hatred) given the references to the 'Jews' (vv. 9, 12), and professional jealousy given the reference to the status of the three Hebrews as rulers over the affairs of the province of Babylon [Dan. 2:49; 3:12]" (Hill, "Daniel," 79).

8 ¶ Wherefore at that time certain Chaldeans came near, and accused the Jews.

9 They spake and said to the king Nebuchadnezzar, O king, live for ever.

10 Thou, O king, hast made a decree, that every man that shall hear the sound of the cornet, flute, harp, sackbut, psaltery, and dulcimer, and all kinds of musick, shall fall down and worship the golden image:

11 And whoso falleth not down and worshippeth, *that* he should be cast into the midst of a burning fiery furnace.

12 There are certain Jews whom thou hast set over the affairs of the province of Babylon, Shadrach, Meshach, and Abed-nego; these men, O king, have not regarded thee: they serve not thy gods, nor worship the golden image which thou hast set up.

13 ¶ Then Nebuchadnezzar in *his* rage and fury commanded to bring Shadrach, Meshach, and Abed-nego. Then they brought these men before the king.

14 Nebuchadnezzar spake and said unto them, *Is it* true, O Shadrach, Meshach, and Abed-nego, do not ye serve my gods, nor worship the golden image which I have set up?

15 Now if ye be ready that at what time ye hear the sound of the cornet, flute, harp, sackbut, psaltery, and dulcimer, and all kinds of musick, ye fall down and worship the image which I have made; *well:* but if ye worship not, ye shall be cast the same hour into the midst of a burning fiery furnace; and who *is* that God that shall deliver you out of my hands?

16 Shadrach, Meshach, and Abed-nego, answered and said to the king, O Nebuchadnezzar, we *are* not careful to answer thee in this matter.

17 If it be *so,* our God whom we serve is able to deliver us from the burning fiery furnace, and he will deliver *us* out of thine hand, O king.

18 But if not, be it known unto thee, O king, that we will not serve thy gods, nor worship the golden image which thou hast set up.

How did Daniel's friends respond to the king's challenge? (3:15–16) "Shadrach, Meshach, and Abed-nego refused to worship the new Babylonian image, knowing full well that the consequence was death (Dan. 3:1–12). . . . [Their] response cast no doubt on God's ability to save; the men responded that if God desired to save them he could. But whether or not he did, the idol was still nothing and they would not worship it. . . .

"The details of the attempted execution magnify the power of God and the helplessness of the king. . . . The furnace was heated seven times hotter than usual and . . . the guards who threw the Jews into the fire died before they could get away from the heat" (Draper, "Book of Daniel," 326, 327).

Why doesn't righteousness provide immunity from tribulation? (3:17–18) "[Daniel's companions] knew that they could trust God—even if things didn't turn out the way they hoped. They knew that faith is more than mental assent, more than an acknowledgment that God lives. Faith is total trust in Him.

"Faith is believing that although we do not understand all things, He does. Faith is knowing that although our power is limited, His is not. Faith in Jesus Christ consists of complete reliance on Him" (Simmons, "But If Not . . . ," 73). ⊕

What does this verse teach us about true devotion to God? (3:18) After retelling the story of Shadrach, Meshach, and Abed-nego, President Howard W. Hunter taught: "The ability to stand by one's principles, to live with integrity and faith according to one's belief—that is what matters, that is the difference between a contribution and a commitment. That devotion to true principle—in our individual lives, in our homes and families, and in all places that we meet and influence other people—that devotion is what God is ultimately requesting of us" ("Standing As Witnesses of God," 61).

Daniel 3:19–30. Shadrach, Meshach, and Abed-nego Are Thrown into a Fiery Furnace and Emerge Unscathed

What could the number seven mean in this instance? (3:19) "The temperature was controlled by the number of bellows forcing air into the fire chamber. Therefore sevenfold intensification was achieved by seven bellows pumping air the same time. But the expression [KJV, 'one seven times more than it was wont to be heated'] may have been figurative for 'as hot as possible' (seven signifies completeness)" (*NIV Study Bible* [1985], 1304).

Who was the fourth man walking in the fire? (3:24–25) "Nebuchadnezzar knew he was looking at a supernatural being, though his *son of the gods* description reflected his belief in many gods. Later the king described the man as an angel (3:28). Some believe the figure was an angel; others feel he was literally the Son of God—Christ making an appearance more than five centuries before his earthly birth" (*Quest Study Bible* [1994], 1216).

What important message can we learn from the three young men in this story? (3:26) "Clearly our individual exit routes from this life vary; so does the timing. There are many who suffer so much more than the rest of us: some go agonizingly; some go quickly; some are healed; some are given more time; some seem to linger. There are variations in our trials but no immunities. Thus, the scriptures cite the fiery

19 ¶ Then was Nebuchadnezzar full of fury, and the form of his visage was changed against Shadrach, Meshach, and Abed-nego: *therefore* he spake, and commanded that they should heat the furnace one seven times more than it was wont to be heated.

20 And he commanded the most mighty men that *were* in his army to bind Shadrach, Meshach, and Abed-nego, *and* to cast *them* into the burning fiery furnace.

21 Then these men were bound in their coats, their hosen, and their hats, and their *other* garments, and were cast into the midst of the burning fiery furnace.

22 Therefore because the king's commandment was urgent, and the furnace exceeding hot, the flame of the fire slew those men that took up Shadrach, Meshach, and Abed-nego.

23 And these three men, Shadrach, Meshach, and Abed-nego, fell down bound into the midst of the burning fiery furnace.

24 Then Nebuchadnezzar the king was astonied, and rose up in haste, *and* spake, and said unto his counsellors, Did not we cast three men bound into the midst of the fire? They answered and said unto the king, True, O king.

25 He answered and said, Lo, I see four men loose, walking in the midst of the fire, and they have no hurt; and the form of the fourth is like the Son of God.

26 ¶ Then Nebuchadnezzar came near to the mouth of the burning fiery furnace, *and* spake, and said, Shadrach, Meshach, and Abed-nego, ye servants of the most high God, come forth, and come *hither*. Then Shadrach, Meshach, and Abed-nego, came forth of the midst of the fire.

27 And the princes, governors, and captains, and the king's counsellors, being gathered together, saw these men, upon whose bodies the fire had no power, nor was an hair of their head singed, neither were their coats changed, nor the smell of fire had passed on them.

28 *Then* Nebuchadnezzar spake, and said, Blessed *be* the God of Shadrach, Meshach, and Abed-nego, who hath sent his angel, and delivered his servants that trusted in him, and have changed the king's word, and yielded their bodies, that they might not serve nor worship any god, except their own God.

29 Therefore I make a decree, That every people, nation, and language, which speak any thing amiss against the God of Shadrach, Meshach, and Abed-nego, shall be cut in pieces, and their houses shall be made a dunghill: because there is no other God that can deliver after this sort.

30 Then the king promoted Shadrach, Meshach, and Abed-nego, in the province of Babylon.

CHAPTER 4

Daniel interprets Nebuchadnezzar's dream of the great tree, describing the king's fall and madness—The king learns that the Most High rules and sets the basest of men over earthly kingdoms.

furnace and fiery trials (see Dan. 3:6–26; 1 Pet. 4:12). Those who emerge successfully from their varied and fiery furnaces have experienced the grace of the Lord, which He says is sufficient (see Ether 12:27)!" (Maxwell, "From Whom All Blessings Flow," 11).

How were Daniel's friends protected in the fiery furnace? (3:27) "It has been suggested that the reason Shadrach, Meshach, and Abed-nego were not harmed in the fire was that God transfigured them (cf. Helaman 5:23; 3 Nephi 28:19–22).

"In the Septuagint (or Greek version) of this narrative, there is an additional lengthy twenty-two verse section (not found in the Hebrew version) in which Abed-nego (aka Azariah) offers a prayer to the Lord. In that additional portion (present today in the Apocrypha and translations like the Latin Vulgate), we learn that Shadrach, Meshach, and Abed-nego 'walked about in the heart of the flames, singing hymns to God and blessing the Lord' [see "Prayer of Azariah" V:1]" (Gaskill, *Miracles of the Old Testament*, 416).

Summary of Daniel 4

Nebuchadnezzar dreams of a great tree whose limbs are cut off and scattered. Daniel reluctantly interprets the dream, warning the king that his empire will be cut off and scattered unless he breaks off his sins "by righteousness" (4:27). Nebuchadnezzar continues in his pride, and is punished with temporary madness until he acknowledges and honors God (4:37).

Summary of Daniel 5

The new king, Belshazzar, son of Nebuchadnezzar, holds a great feast. The revelers mockingly drink from the vessels taken as trophies from the temple at Jerusalem. A mysterious message appears on the wall, and the king is troubled. Daniel interprets the message, announcing that God has numbered the days of Belshazzar's kingdom. Belshazzar has been "weighed in the balances, and . . . found wanting" (5:27). He had not learned from Nebuchadnezzar's example. The king is eventually removed from office because of his pride and arrogance. "Darius the Median [takes] the kingdom" (5:31) and rules in Babylon.

Daniel 6:1–9. King Darius Signs a Law That Forbids Prayer

Who was Darius? (6:1) Darius, "the Mede, king of Babylon after the death of Belshazzar (Dan. 5:31; 6:9, 25–28; 9:1; 11:1). It is impossible to identify him with any of the kings of Babylon known to secular history" (Bible Dictionary, "Darius").

Who were these three presidents and what was Daniel's relationship to them? (6:2–3) "Darius not only appointed 120 satraps [local leaders] for all the provinces and districts of his kingdom, but he also placed the whole body of the satraps under a government consisting of three presidents, who should reckon with the individual satraps. . . . Daniel was one of the triumvirate. . . . In this situation Daniel excelled all the presidents and satraps. . . . On that account the king thought to set him over the whole kingdom, i.e., to make him chief ruler of the kingdom" (Keil and Delitzsch, *Commentary* [on Daniel 6:2–3, 4]).

What was the plan to destroy Daniel? (6:4–7) "As Daniel's talents were recognized by the king, he became a trusted counselor. Many were jealous of the position this outsider had obtained, and they sought to do away with him" (Perry, "In the World," 15). "'We can expect that these men, most of them probably were much younger than Daniel and anxious to get ahead.' Their initial strategy was to 'find occasion against [him]' (Dan. 6:4). They likely searched for discrepancies among the official records with the intent to scrutinize his conduct or expose any evidence to accuse him. . . .

CHAPTER 5

Belshazzar and his revelers drink from the vessels of the temple—A hand writes upon the wall, telling of Belshazzar's downfall—Daniel interprets the words and reproves the king for pride and idolatry—That night Babylon is conquered.

CHAPTER 6

Darius makes Daniel the first of his presidents—Daniel worships the Lord in defiance of a decree of Darius—He is cast into the den of lions—His faith saves him, and Darius decrees that all people are to revere the God of Daniel.

1 It pleased Darius to set over the kingdom an hundred and twenty princes, which should be over the whole kingdom;

2 And over these three presidents; of whom Daniel *was* first: that the princes might give accounts unto them, and the king should have no damage.

3 Then this Daniel was preferred above the presidents and princes, because an excellent spirit *was* in him; and the king thought to set him over the whole realm.

4 ¶ Then the presidents and princes sought to find occasion against Daniel concerning the kingdom; but they could find none occasion nor fault; forasmuch as he *was* faithful, neither was there any error or fault found in him.

5 Then said these men, We shall not find any occasion against this Daniel, except we find *it* against him concerning the law of his God.

6 Then these presidents and princes assembled together to the king, and said thus unto him, King Darius, live for ever.

7 All the presidents of the kingdom, the governors, and the princes, the counsellors, and the captains, have consulted together to establish a royal statute, and to make a firm decree, that whosoever shall ask a petition of any God or man for thirty days, save of thee, O king, he shall be cast into the den of lions.

8 Now, O king, establish the decree, and sign the writing, that it be not changed, according to the law of the Medes and Persians, which altereth not.

9 Wherefore king Darius signed the writing and the decree.

10 ¶ Now when Daniel knew that the writing was signed, he went into his house; and his windows being open in his chamber toward Jerusalem, he kneeled upon his knees three times a day, and prayed, and gave thanks before his God, as he did aforetime.

11 Then these men assembled, and found Daniel praying and making supplication before his God.

"Unable to find culpability in his administrative practices and knowing of Daniel's devotion towards his God they sought occasion to find some peculiarity in his religious observance to use against him" (Brandt, *Book of Daniel*, 143, 144).

How did the presidents and princes manipulate the king? (6:8–9) "Daniel had been circumspect in obeying the laws of the land, but his enemies knew that when the law of the land conflicted with *the law of his God*, Daniel would break the former in favor of the latter. . . .

"Once a royal decree had been issued, it could not be revoked—even by the king himself; it remained in force until its time of expiration. The practice of creating an unchangeable law may follow from the idea that changing a decree was an admission that it had been faulty" (*Nelson Study Bible* [NKJV], 1429).

Daniel 6:10–17. King Darius Is Forced by His Own Law to Place Daniel in a Lion's Den

Why did Daniel face Jerusalem when he prayed? (6:10) "Solomon, in his dedicatory prayer of the temple in Jerusalem, referred to the people's praying 'toward the house that I have built for thy name' (1 Kings 8:44). The Prophet Joseph Smith once counseled the Twelve Apostles to 'make yourselves acquainted with those men who like Daniel pray three times a day toward the House of the Lord.' . . .

"These prophets do not suggest that the direction in which one faces when he prays has some mystical significance, but, rather, that it is an attitude of spiritual 'facing.' To face the temple, which is the temporal representation of the House of God, suggests that one turns his heart to the Lord and the covenants made in the temples" (*Old Testament Student Manual: 1 Kings–Malachi*, 303). ⊕

Despite the king's decree, why did Daniel continue to pray? (6:11) "When Daniel received notice of this new law, he faced a dilemma. Prayer and fellowship with the Lord had safeguarded him from the corrupting influences of Babylonian culture. To preserve his role in government and to save his own life, he would have to compromise his integrity by ceasing to pray to God or by praying privately. But faithful Daniel could not compromise. He would trust the Lord for deliverance. His habit had been to pray regularly toward Jerusalem, the focal point of his hopes and prayers for the progress of the kingdom of God" (*Expositor's Bible Commentary [Abridged]*, 1377).

12 Then they came near, and spake before the king concerning the king's decree; Hast thou not signed a decree, that every man that shall ask *a petition* of any God or man within thirty days, save of thee, O king, shall be cast into the den of lions? The king answered and said, The thing *is* true, according to the law of the Medes and Persians, which altereth not.

13 Then answered they and said before the king, That Daniel, which *is* of the children of the captivity of Judah, regardeth not thee, O king, nor the decree that thou hast signed, but maketh his petition three times a day.

14 Then the king, when he heard *these* words, was sore displeased with himself, and set *his* heart on Daniel to deliver him: and he laboured till the going down of the sun to deliver him.

15 Then these men assembled unto the king, and said unto the king, Know, O king, that the law of the Medes and Persians *is,* That no decree nor statute which the king establisheth may be changed.

16 Then the king commanded, and they brought Daniel, and cast *him* into the den of lions. *Now* the king spake and said unto Daniel, Thy God whom thou servest continually, he will deliver thee.

17 And a stone was brought, and laid upon the mouth of the den; and the king sealed it with his own signet, and with the signet of his lords; that the purpose might not be changed concerning Daniel.

Why is the stone that covered the lion's den sealed with the king's signet? (6:17) "The den of lions is a pit underneath the floor with a small opening capable of being covered with a stone. The stone covering is here laid over the opening, and the king and his nobles place their seals upon it (i.e. make a mark with their rings on some soft substance, probably clay which has been placed around the stone, in order to prevent anyone from tampering with it—since any movement of the stone after this sealing would break this seal and be obvious to the observer). The king is evidently fully conscious of his own failure to rescue Daniel" (Provan, "Daniel," 670–71).

18 ¶ Then the king went to his palace, and passed the night fasting: neither were instruments of musick brought before him: and his sleep went from him.

19 Then the king arose very early in the morning, and went in haste unto the den of lions.

20 And when he came to the den, he cried with a lamentable voice unto Daniel: *and* the king spake and said to Daniel, O Daniel, servant of the living God, is thy God, whom thou servest continually, able to deliver thee from the lions?

21 Then said Daniel unto the king, O king, live for ever.

22 My God hath sent his angel, and hath shut the lions' mouths, that they have not hurt me: forasmuch as before him innocency was found in me; and also before thee, O king, have I done no hurt.

Daniel 6:18–28. Daniel Is Protected from the Lions, and Darius Commands Respect for the God of Israel

What does the king's early visit indicate? (6:19–22) "Darius's devotion to Daniel is further evidenced by his early-morning visit to the lion's den. His faith in God was confirmed when he heard Daniel's voice. Daniel made his reciprocal loyalty clear when he not only declared that he was innocent before God, but that he was also innocent before Darius. He made sure that Darius knew that Daniel was no threat to him" (Muhlestein, *Scripture Study Made Simple*, 480).

Daniel in the Lion's Den (Daniel 6:22)

How can we apply Daniel's experience to our own lives? (6:23) "By way of application, it is worth noting that we have no promise that we will *always* be spared from the hurt our enemies seek to bring upon us. However, *in the end*, we—like Daniel—shall be elevated out of the hands of our enemies, without mar or scar. Similarly, like Daniel's enemies, those who fight against God and His anointed servants shall ultimately be destroyed. Thus, there may be difficult days when we face the lions. However, the end result of the faithful will ever be the same; they shall be raised up and all earthly scars—whether they be physical, emotional, or spiritual—will be removed" (Gaskill, *Miracles of the Old Testament*, 436–37).

Why would the king cast Daniel's accusers, and their families, into the lion's pit? (6:24) "Without any judicial hearing or trial, King Darius, absolute monarch that he was, ordered Daniel's accusers to be hauled before him and then cast *with their families* into the pit they had conspired to have Daniel thrown into. Presumably Darius considered them guilty of devising the decree that could have deprived the king of his most able counselor. Furthermore, they had lied to the king when they had averred that 'all agreed' (v. 7) to recommend this decree, when Daniel (the foremost of the administrators) had not even been consulted.... Perhaps Darius acted as he did to minimize the danger of revenge against the executioner by the family to those who were put to death" (Archer, "Daniel," 82).

Did Darius convert to Judaism? (6:26) The king declared that Daniel's God should be respected. "The implication is not that the Jewish form of worship should supplant the local forms of religion, but that the God of Israel should be treated with the reverence due to a *living God* Whose dominion is everlasting" (Slotki, *Daniel–Ezra–Nehemiah*, 54).

How many kings did Daniel serve after having been captured by the Babylonians? (6:28) "He had served *five* kings: *Nebuchadnezzar, Evil-merodach, Belshazzar, Darius,* and *Cyrus.* Few courtiers [servants of kings] have had so long a reign, served so many masters without flattering any, been more successful in their management of public affairs, been so useful to the states where they were in office, or have been more owned of God, or have left such an example to posterity" (*Adam Clarke's* Commentary [on Daniel 6:28]).

23 Then was the king exceeding glad for him, and commanded that they should take Daniel up out of the den. So Daniel was taken up out of the den, and no manner of hurt was found upon him, because he believed in his God.

24 ¶ And the king commanded, and they brought those men which had accused Daniel, and they cast *them* into the den of lions, them, their children, and their wives; and the lions had the mastery of them, and brake all their bones in pieces or ever they came at the bottom of the den.

25 ¶ Then king Darius wrote unto all people, nations, and languages, that dwell in all the earth; Peace be multiplied unto you.

26 I make a decree, That in every dominion of my kingdom men tremble and fear before the God of Daniel: for he *is* the living God, and steadfast for ever, and his kingdom *that* which shall not be destroyed, and his dominion *shall be even* unto the end.

27 He delivereth and rescueth, and he worketh signs and wonders in heaven and in earth, who hath delivered Daniel from the power of the lions.

28 So this Daniel prospered in the reign of Darius, and in the reign of Cyrus the Persian.

CHAPTER 7

Daniel sees four beasts representing the kingdoms of men—He sees the ancient of days (Adam) to whom the Son of Man (Christ) will come—The kingdom will be given to the Saints forever.

1 In the first year of Belshazzar king of Babylon Daniel had a dream and visions of his head upon his bed: then he wrote the dream, *and* told the sum of the matters.

2 Daniel spake and said, I saw in my vision by night, and, behold, the four winds of the heaven strove upon the great sea.

3 And four great beasts came up from the sea, diverse one from another.

4 The first *was* like a lion, and had eagle's wings: I beheld till the wings thereof were plucked, and it was lifted up from the earth, and made stand upon the feet as a man, and a man's heart was given to it.

5 And behold another beast, a second, like to a bear, and it raised up itself on one side,

Daniel 7:1–8. Daniel Has Visions of Four Beasts

Why must one be careful when interpreting Daniel's vision of beasts? (7:1) "Caution must also be used in the interpretation of figures and symbols like those used in the visions of Ezekiel, Daniel, and the book of Revelation. On this matter Joseph Smith has assured us that 'whenever God gives a vision of an image, or beast, or figure of any kind, He always holds Himself responsible to give a revelation or interpretation of the meaning thereof, otherwise we are not responsible or accountable for our belief in it' [Joseph Smith Papers, "History, 1838–1856, volume D-1 [1 August 1842–1 July 1843]," 1523]" (McConkie, *Gospel Symbolism*, 243).

What did these beasts represent? (7:3) The Prophet Joseph Smith declared, "When God made use of the figure of a beast in visions to the [Old Testament] prophets, he did it to represent those kingdoms who had degenerated and become corrupt—the kingdoms of the world, but he never made use of the figure of a beast nor any of the brute kind to represent his kingdom" (Joseph Smith Papers, "Discourse, 8 April 1843, as Reported by William Clayton–B," 2).

The Vision of the Four Beasts (Daniel 7:3–8)

"Like [Daniel] chapter 2, chapter 7 gives a pictorial representation of history: There are four successive empires, and then the kingdom of God is established....

"The Prophet Joseph Smith taught the following about Daniel's vision of the beasts: ... 'When the prophets speak of seeing beasts in their visions, they mean that they saw the images, they being types to represent certain things' [Joseph Smith Papers, 'History, 1838–1856, volume D-1 (1 August 1842–1 July 1843),' 1523]....

"The first [beast], which was like a lion with eagles' wings, represented the Babylonian kingdom under Nebuchadnezzar. The lion and eagle are both supreme among beasts of their class....

"The second beast ... represented the Median-Persian empire. ... The bear was considered next to the lion as the strongest among animals by the people of the ancient Middle East....

"The third kingdom corresponded to the Greek empire of Alexander the Great. Wings signify power to move and extend influence. Heads signify governing power or the seat of government....

"The fourth beast was not likened to an animal. It was, however, very strong and dreadful and broke into pieces the remains of the former kingdoms. It represented the Roman empire and the forces of evil that were manifest through that empire" (*Old Testament Student Manual: 1 Kings–Malachi*, 304).

and *it had* three ribs in the mouth of it between the teeth of it: and they said thus unto it, Arise, devour much flesh.

6 After this I beheld, and lo another, like a leopard, which had upon the back of it four wings of a fowl; the beast had also four heads; and dominion was given to it.

7 After this I saw in the night visions, and behold a fourth beast, dreadful and terrible, and strong exceedingly; and it had great iron teeth: it devoured and brake in pieces, and stamped the residue with the feet of it: and it *was* diverse from all the beasts that *were* before it; and it had ten horns.

8 I considered the horns, and, behold, there came up among them another little horn, before whom there were three of the first horns plucked up by the roots: and, behold, in this horn *were* eyes like the eyes of man, and a mouth speaking great things.

Daniel 7:9–28. Daniel Has a Vision of the Ancient of Days

Who is the "Ancient of days"? (7:9–10) "Daniel in his seventh chapter speaks of the Ancient of Days; he means the oldest man, our Father Adam, Michael; he will call his children together [thousand thousands] and hold a council with them to prepare them for the coming of the Son of Man. . . . He (Adam) is the father of the human family, and presides over the spirits of all men, and all that have had the keys must stand before him in this grand council" (*Joseph Smith* [manual], 104).

9 ¶ I beheld till the thrones were cast down, and the Ancient of days did sit, whose garment *was* white as snow, and the hair of his head like the pure wool: his throne *was like* the fiery flame, *and* his wheels *as* burning fire.

10 A fiery stream issued and came forth from before him: thousand thousands ministered unto him, and ten thousand times ten thousand stood before him: the judgment was set, and the books were opened.

11 I beheld then because of the voice of the great words which the horn spake: I beheld *even* till the beast was slain, and his body destroyed, and given to the burning flame.

12 As concerning the rest of the beasts, they had their dominion taken away: yet their lives were prolonged for a season and time.

Who is the "one like the Son of Man" in this vision? (7:13–14) "The [New Testament] has made extensive use of Daniel 7 in articulating its vision of the future, when Jesus the Messiah (one of whose titles in the Gospels is 'Son of Man') returns in glory to vanquish

13 I saw in the night visions, and, behold, *one* like the Son of man came with the clouds of heaven, and came to the Ancient of days, and they brought him near before him.

14 And there was given him dominion, and glory, and a kingdom, that all people, nations, and languages, should serve him: his dominion *is* an everlasting dominion, which shall not pass away, and his kingdom *that* which shall not be destroyed.

15 ¶ I Daniel was grieved in my spirit in the midst of *my* body, and the visions of my head troubled me.

16 I came near unto one of them that stood by, and asked him the truth of all this. So he told me, and made me know the interpretation of the things.

17 These great beasts, which are four, *are* four kings, *which* shall arise out of the earth.

18 But the saints of the most High shall take the kingdom, and possess the kingdom for ever, even for ever and ever.

the powers of darkness and to take possession with his church of the kingdom (cf., e.g., Matt 24:30; . . . Rev 1:7, 13–15; . . . 13:1–8)" (Provan, "Daniel," 672). Joseph Smith taught: "The Son of Man stands before [Adam], and there is given him glory and dominion. Adam delivers up his stewardship to Christ, that which was delivered to him as holding the keys of the universe, but retains his standing as head of the human family" (*Joseph Smith* [manual], 104). ⊕

Adam Comes to Visit His People (Daniel 7:9–10)

"Spring Hill is named by the Lord Adam-ondi-Ahman, because, said he, it is the place where Adam shall come to visit his people, or the Ancient of Days shall sit, as spoken of by Daniel the prophet" (D&C 116:1).

"The world has not seen the last of Father Adam. He is coming again; coming as the Ancient of Days, to fulfill the prophecy of Daniel concerning him. And he will come to the very place where, bowed with the weight of his nine centuries . . . he blessed his posterity before the close of his earthly career. In the Valley of Adam-ondi-Ahman, now in Western Missouri, almost within hailing distance of the ancient site of the Garden of Eden, where the New Jerusalem is to rise, will sit the Ancient of Days, counseling his worthy children and preparing them for the second coming of the Son of God" (Whitney, in Conference Report, Apr. 1927, 99).

What caused Daniel concern about the fourth beast? (7:19–22) "Daniel regarded the fourth beast with the greatest curiosity and dread. In particular he wondered about the ten horns and the little horn that emerged and overcame God's holy people. Despite the assurance that the ultimate victory would be the Lord's and that his people would finally prevail, Daniel was deeply concerned about their impending persecution" (*Expositor's Bible Commentary [Abridged]*, 1380). ⊕

What does "time and times and the dividing of time" mean? (7:25) "The number three and one-half is sometimes given in scripture as 'a time and times and the dividing of time' (Daniel 7:25; 12:7)" (Gaskill, *Lost Language of Symbolism*, 117). "It is premature to be dogmatic on specifics. Daniel makes repeated references to time, but they are very oblique. The various time frames that add up to three and one-half seem consistently to symbolize the period when evil will dominate. The number seven is associated with the eventual triumph of the Lord" (Draper, "Book of Daniel," 330).

19 Then I would know the truth of the
fourth beast, which was diverse from all the
others, exceeding dreadful, whose teeth *were*
of iron, and his nails *of* brass; *which* devoured,
brake in pieces, and stamped the residue with
his feet;

20 And of the ten horns that *were* in his head,
and *of* the other which came up, and before
whom three fell; even *of* that horn that had
eyes, and a mouth that spake very great things,
whose look *was* more stout than his fellows.

21 I beheld, and the same horn made war
with the saints, and prevailed against them;

22 Until the Ancient of days came, and judgment was given to the saints of the most
High; and the time came that the saints possessed the kingdom.

23 Thus he said, The fourth beast shall be the
fourth kingdom upon earth, which shall be
diverse from all kingdoms, and shall devour
the whole earth, and shall tread it down, and
break it in pieces.

24 And the ten horns out of this kingdom *are*
ten kings *that* shall arise: and another shall
rise after them; and he shall be diverse from
the first, and he shall subdue three kings.

25 And he shall speak *great* words against the
most High, and shall wear out the saints of
the most High, and think to change times
and laws: and they shall be given into his
hand until a time and times and the dividing
of time.

26 But the judgment shall sit, and they shall
take away his dominion, to consume and to
destroy *it* unto the end.

27 And the kingdom and dominion, and the
greatness of the kingdom under the whole
heaven, shall be given to the people of the
saints of the most High, whose kingdom *is*
an everlasting kingdom, and all dominions
shall serve and obey him.

28 Hitherto *is* the end of the matter. As for me Daniel, my cogitations much troubled me, and my countenance changed in me: but I kept the matter in my heart.

CHAPTER 8

Daniel sees in vision a ram (Media and Persia), a goat (Greece), four other kings, and then, in the last days, a fierce king who will destroy the holy people—This king will be broken when he stands up against the Prince of Princes.

1 In the third year of the reign of king Belshazzar a vision appeared unto me, *even unto* me Daniel, after that which appeared unto me at the first.

2 And I saw in a vision; and it came to pass, when I saw, that I *was* at Shushan *in* the palace, which *is* in the province of Elam; and I saw in a vision, and I was by the river of Ulai.

3 Then I lifted up mine eyes, and saw, and, behold, there stood before the river a ram which had *two* horns: and the *two* horns *were* high; but one *was* higher than the other, and the higher came up last.

4 I saw the ram pushing westward, and northward, and southward; so that no beasts might stand before him, neither *was there any* that could deliver out of his hand; but he did according to his will, and became great.

5 And as I was considering, behold, an he goat came from the west on the face of the whole earth, and touched not the ground: and the goat *had* a notable horn between his eyes.

6 And he came to the ram that had *two* horns, which I had seen standing before the river, and ran unto him in the fury of his power.

Daniel 8:1–14. Daniel's Vision of the Ram and the He-Goat, and the Little Horn

Why was the city Shushan in Elam the setting for Daniel's vision? (8:1–2) "The setting for the dream in Elam was deliberate, as it served to impress upon the prophet's mind from whence the next great empire would arise. The capital city [Shushan] lay before him and eventually became one of three Persian centers (Persepolis and Ecbatana being the other two). It was impressive, flowing with prosperous markets and beautiful Persian styled gardens. Tradition holds that Daniel might have been buried at Susa [Shushan] in a sepulture memorialized today as the Tomb of Daniel" (Brandt, *Book of Daniel*, 214).

What might the ram symbolize? (8:3–4) Later in this chapter (8:20), the angel explains that "the ram which thou sawest having two horns are the kings of Media and Persia" (8:20). Parley P. Pratt adds: "In this vision we have first presented the Medes and Persians, as they were to exist until they were conquered by Alexander the great. Now, it is a fact well known that this empire [Persia] waxed exceedingly great for some time after the death of Daniel, pushing its conquests westward, northward, and southward, so that none could stand before it; until Alexander, the king of Grecia, came from the west, with a small army of chosen men, and attacked the Persians upon the banks of the river" (*Voice of Warning*, 25).

What might the horns of the goat and the "four notable ones" represent? (8:5–8) The divine messenger who instructed Daniel noted that the great horn and the other four horns represented the king of Greece and the four kingdoms which would follow him (see Daniel 8:21–22). "Most commentators interpret the horn of the goat as having reference to Alexander the Great, and the four lesser horns or kingdoms that arose from it are often assigned to Cassander in Macedonia, Lysimachus in Thrace, Seleucus I in Syria, and Ptolemy in Egypt" (Sperry, *Voice of Israel's Prophets*, 265).

7 And I saw him come close unto the ram, and he was moved with choler against him, and smote the ram, and brake his two horns: and there was no power in the ram to stand before him, but he cast him down to the ground, and stamped upon him: and there was none that could deliver the ram out of his hand.

8 Therefore the he goat waxed very great: and when he was strong, the great horn was broken; and for it came up four notable ones toward the four winds of heaven.

Who might the "little horn" typify who halted the daily temple sacrifices in Jerusalem? (8:9–12) "The little horn that desecrated the Lord's sanctuary is identified with Antiochus IV Epiphanes who prohibited Jewish worship from 168 B.C. to 165 B.C. It was at this period of trouble for the Jews that Judas Maccabaeus led them in an uprising against their enemies. A victory resulted in their comparative independence for a long time" (Sperry, *Voice of Israel's Prophets*, 265; see also Daniel 8:23–26). ⊕

9 And out of one of them came forth a little horn, which waxed exceeding great, toward the south, and toward the east, and toward the pleasant *land*.

10 And it waxed great, *even* to the host of heaven; and it cast down *some* of the host and of the stars to the ground, and stamped upon them.

11 Yea, he magnified *himself* even to the prince of the host, and by him the daily *sacrifice* was taken away, and the place of his sanctuary was cast down.

12 And an host was given *him* against the daily *sacrifice* by reason of transgression, and it cast down the truth to the ground; and it practised, and prospered.

13 ¶ Then I heard one saint speaking, and another saint said unto that certain *saint* which spake, How long *shall be* the vision *concerning* the daily *sacrifice*, and the transgression of desolation, to give both the sanctuary and the host to be trodden under foot?

What might the 2,300 days represent? (8:14) "An angel announced that the time of Antiochus's defilement of Israel would only be for *2,300 evenings and mornings*. This is a reference either to the 2,300 full days from Antiochus's appointment of the murderer Menelaus as high priest (171 BC) to the rededication of the temple under Judah Maccabee (164 BC) or to a total of 1,150 morning and 1,150 evening sacrifices

14 And he said unto me, Unto two thousand and three hundred days; then shall the sanctuary be cleansed.

from the defiling of the temple (167 BC) to its rededication (164 BC). In either case, Antiochus's defilement would last only until the temple would be rededicated by Judah Maccabee, an event still celebrated by Jewish people today during the festival of *Chanukah* (English, 'dedication') (cf. Jn 10:22–23)" (Rydelnik, "Daniel," 1301).

Summary of Daniel 8:15–27

The angel Gabriel, who is Noah (see *Joseph Smith* [manual], 104), unfolds the meaning of Daniel's vision. The ram, goat, and horns represent political kingdoms and events which will influence God's covenant people. The kings of Media and Persia will be conquered by Greece. In time, Israel will suffer the consequences of their transgressions at the hands of a wicked ruler, "a king of fierce countenance" who shall persecute "the holy people" (Dan. 8:23–24).

CHAPTER 9

Daniel fasts, confesses, and prays for all Israel—Gabriel reveals the time of the coming of the Messiah, who will make reconciliation for iniquity—The Messiah will be cut off.

1 In the first year of Darius the son of Ahasuerus, of the seed of the Medes, which was made king over the realm of the Chaldeans;

2 In the first year of his reign I Daniel understood by books the number of the years, whereof the word of the LORD came to Jeremiah the prophet, that he would accomplish seventy years in the desolations of Jerusalem.

Daniel 9:1–19. Daniel Confesses His Sins and Prays for His People

Which books did Daniel study to understand the Lord's plan for Judah's captivity? (9:2) "The vision is given in response to the prophet's study of 'the books,' specifically Jeremiah's scriptural prophecies concerning the return of the Jews to the Promised Land. The 'books' included writings of many of the Old Testament prophets and he clearly had copies of the prophecies of his contemporary, Jeremiah. . . . False prophets living at the time scoffed at Jeremiah's prediction; but Daniel, even though he was a youth, remembered his words. Throughout his life, he witnessed their complete realization, and patiently waited until the seventy years were accomplished" (Brandt, *Book of Daniel*, 252, 253).

3 ¶ And I set my face unto the Lord God, to seek by prayer and supplications, with fasting, and sackcloth, and ashes:

Why would Daniel fast as he confessed his sins? (9:3) "The doctrine of fasting is ancient. It has been practiced by biblical heroes from the earliest days. . . . Through Isaiah's writings, the Lord said: 'Is *not* this the fast that I have chosen? to loose the bands of wickedness, to undo the heavy burdens, and to let the oppressed go free?' . . . The Savior Himself declared that certain things go 'not out *but* by prayer and fasting.' . . . So, during times of deep distress . . . the most natural thing for us to do is to call upon our Heavenly Father and His Son—the Master Healer—to show forth Their marvelous power to bless the people of the earth" (Nelson, "Opening the Heavens for Help," 73, 74). See commentary in this volume for Isaiah 58:8–12.

What is the context for Daniel's prayerful pleadings? (9:4–6) Daniel's disturbing visions of the history of the world (chapters 7–8) deeply troubled him (see Daniel 7:15, 28; 8:27). He feared for his people. "Confessing the sins of Israel, Daniel prayed in fasting and humility. He sought mercy and forgiveness for his people, admitting the justice of the punishment. . . . In response, the angel Gabriel was sent with great promises, including the promise of 'the Messiah the Prince,' who was to come at a mysteriously calculated time after the 'commandment to restore and to build Jerusalem' (Dan. 9:25)" (Rasmussen, *Latter-day Saint Commentary on the Old Testament*, 624–25).

What can we learn from reading about the response of God's children to His servants the prophets? (9:6) Joseph Smith taught: "In consequence of rejecting the Gospel of Jesus Christ and the Prophets whom God hath sent, the judgments of God have rested upon people, cities, and nations, in various ages of the world" (*Joseph Smith* [manual], 82, 203). On the other hand, "It is no small thing, my brothers and sisters, to have a prophet of God in our midst. Great and wonderful are the blessings that come into our lives as we listen to the word of the Lord given to us through him. . . . History has shown that there is safety, peace, prosperity, and happiness in responding to prophetic counsel" (Ballard, "His Word Ye Shall Receive," 65).

What is a "confusion of faces"? (9:7–10) This phrase "confusion of faces" is better understood as being shamefaced (see Daniel 9:7*b*). Another Bible version states, "This day we are all covered with shame . . . because of our unfaithfulness to you" (NIV, Daniel 9:7).

4 And I prayed unto the LORD my God, and made my confession, and said, O Lord, the great and dreadful God, keeping the covenant and mercy to them that love him, and to them that keep his commandments;

5 We have sinned, and have committed iniquity, and have done wickedly, and have rebelled, even by departing from thy precepts and from thy judgments:

6 Neither have we hearkened unto thy servants the prophets, which spake in thy name to our kings, our princes, and our fathers, and to all the people of the land.

7 O Lord, righteousness *belongeth* unto thee, but unto us confusion of faces, as at this day; to the men of Judah, and to the inhabitants of Jerusalem, and unto all Israel, *that are* near, and *that are* far off, through all the countries whither thou hast driven them, because of their trespass that they have trespassed against thee.

8 O Lord, to us *belongeth* confusion of face, to our kings, to our princes, and to our fathers, because we have sinned against thee.

9 To the Lord our God *belong* mercies and forgivenesses, though we have rebelled against him;

10 Neither have we obeyed the voice of the LORD our God, to walk in his laws, which he set before us by his servants the prophets.

11 Yea, all Israel have transgressed thy law, even by departing, that they might not obey thy voice; therefore the curse is poured upon us, and the oath that *is* written in the law of Moses the servant of God, because we have sinned against him.

12 And he hath confirmed his words, which he spake against us, and against our judges that judged us, by bringing upon us a great evil: for under the whole heaven hath not been done as hath been done upon Jerusalem.

13 As *it is* written in the law of Moses, all this evil is come upon us: yet made we not our prayer before the LORD our God, that we might turn from our iniquities, and understand thy truth.

14 Therefore hath the LORD watched upon the evil, and brought it upon us: for the LORD our God *is* righteous in all his works which he doeth: for we obeyed not his voice.

15 And now, O Lord our God, that hast brought thy people forth out of the land of Egypt with a mighty hand, and hast gotten thee renown, as at this day; we have sinned, we have done wickedly.

16 ¶ O Lord, according to all thy righteousness, I beseech thee, let thine anger and thy fury be turned away from thy city Jerusalem, thy holy mountain: because for our sins, and for the iniquities of our fathers, Jerusalem and thy people *are become* a reproach to all *that are* about us.

What does "cause thy face to shine upon thy sanctuary" mean? (9:17) This is a plea for the Lord to return His glory to the temple. "The city of Jerusalem had been destroyed by the Babylonians in 586 [B.C.] and was little more than a desolate ruin. Fifty years had come and gone since the temple had been dismantled and razed" (Walton, et al., *IVP Bible Background Commentary*, 744). Daniel now pleaded with the Lord to "look with favor on your desolate sanctuary" (NIV, Dan. 9:17).

Daniel 9:20–27. Daniel's Prayers Are Answered with a Promise to Restore Israel

What can we learn about Daniel from this prayer? (9:20) "In reading [Daniel's prayer] one feels . . . its great warmth, and its earnest pleadings, deep humility, confession of sin and failure touch every spiritually minded believer. . . . Throughout this prayer we read how completely he identified himself with the sins, the failure, the shame and the judgment of the people of God. . . . [Yet] of all the Bible characters Daniel appears as the purest. . . . As far as the record goes he was a perfect man. Of course he too was . . . as we are and as such a sinner. [But] well may we see in him a type of the Lord Jesus Christ who took the sins of His people upon Himself and confessed them as His own" (Gaebelein, *Prophet Daniel*, 123, 125).

Why was Daniel's prayer answered at the time of the evening sacrifice? (9:21–23) The elements of the evening sacrifice point to Jesus Christ and His sacrifice. "The Law of Moses provided for an unblemished yearling lamb to be offered morning and evening along with a meal offering and a drink offering (Num. 28:3–8). The time of the evening oblation was three o'clock in the afternoon (the same time when Christ died on the cross). The ritual of the evening sacrifice was significant. The lamb spoke of Christ's being offered as a spotless burnt offering to God" (Phillips, *Exploring the Book of Daniel*, 161).

17 Now therefore, O our God, hear the
prayer of thy servant, and his supplications,
and cause thy face to shine upon thy sanctuary that is desolate, for the Lord's sake.

18 O my God, incline thine ear, and hear;
open thine eyes, and behold our desolations,
and the city which is called by thy name: for
we do not present our supplications before
thee for our righteousnesses, but for thy great
mercies.

19 O Lord, hear; O Lord, forgive; O Lord,
hearken and do; defer not, for thine own
sake, O my God: for thy city and thy people
are called by thy name.

20 ¶ And whiles I *was* speaking, and praying, and confessing my sin and the sin of my
people Israel, and presenting my supplication
before the Lord my God for the holy mountain of my God;

21 Yea, whiles I *was* speaking in prayer, even
the man Gabriel, whom I had seen in the
vision at the beginning, being caused to fly
swiftly, touched me about the time of the
evening oblation.

22 And he informed *me,* and talked with me,
and said, O Daniel, I am now come forth to
give thee skill and understanding.

23 At the beginning of thy supplications the
commandment came forth, and I am come
to shew *thee;* for thou *art* greatly beloved:
therefore understand the matter, and consider the vision.

24 Seventy weeks are determined upon thy
people and upon thy holy city, to finish the

transgression, and to make an end of sins, and to make reconciliation for iniquity, and to bring in everlasting righteousness, and to seal up the vision and prophecy, and to anoint the most Holy.

25 Know therefore and understand, *that* from the going forth of the commandment to restore and to build Jerusalem unto the Messiah the Prince *shall be* seven weeks, and threescore and two weeks: the street shall be built again, and the wall, even in troublous times.

26 And after threescore and two weeks shall Messiah be cut off, but not for himself: and the people of the prince that shall come shall destroy the city and the sanctuary; and the end thereof *shall be* with a flood, and unto the end of the war desolations are determined.

27 And he shall confirm the covenant with many for one week: and in the midst of the week he shall cause the sacrifice and the oblation to cease, and for the overspreading of abominations he shall make *it* desolate, even until the consummation, and that determined shall be poured upon the desolate.

The Prophecy of the Seventy Weeks (Daniel 9:24–27)

"Seventy literal weeks or 490 days provides no useful framework on which to overlay the prophecy. The period from the days of Daniel to the Messiah and on to the Abomination of Desolation spans over 500 years. Therefore, the meaning cannot be interpreted in its literal English form. It must be viewed within the context of the Hebrew writing in which it was given. The Hebrew translation for Seventy Weeks actually says seventy sevens or seventy sets of sevens and is called a *heptad*.... The interpretation should read 'seventy sets of seven,' but seventy sets of seven what? It cannot be seventy sets of seven days, nor of seven weeks, but to fulfill the tenets of the prophecy, it must appropriately read seventy sets of seven years, or 490 years.... This interpretation satisfies both the prophetic language and fulfills the historical duration" (Brandt, *Book of Daniel*, 268, 269).

"The prophecy of the 'seventy weeks' in chapter nine interests Latter-day Saints because it suggests that the New Testament church would fall into apostasy. The sixty-nine weeks (Dan. 9:24–26) may be symbolic of the period between the Jews' return to Jerusalem (537 B.C.) and the coming of Jesus the Messiah, who would atone ('be cut off') for his people. Verse 27 reports that the Lord would 'confirm the covenant with many for one week.' This seventieth week may typify the decades that Christ's true church endured, led then by living apostles and prophets, ending shortly after A.D. 100, following the ministry of John the Apostle. The prophecy also notes that Jerusalem and its temple would be destroyed 'in the midst of the week' (A.D. 70), mentioning the abomination of desolation and the cessation of temple sacrifice (cf. Mark 13:14)" (Chadwick, "Daniel, Prophecies of," in *Encyclopedia of Mormonism*, 1:356).

Summary of Daniel 10–11

The Lord appears to Daniel in brilliant glory as He has to others (see Ezek. 1:26–28; Rev. 1:13–15; D&C 110:2–3; JS–H 1:17). The Lord announces that He will teach Daniel of the "latter days" (Daniel 10:14). Just as Joseph Smith felt following the First Vision, Daniel's encounter with the Lord leaves Daniel with "no strength" (Dan. 10:8).

"If chapter 10 is indeed concerned with the conquest of Persia by Alexander the Great, as believed by most scholars, then chapter 11 foretells the division of Alexander's empire into two parts—the north headed by Seleucus and the south headed by Ptolemy" (Ludlow, *Companion to Your Study of the Old Testament*, 357).

Daniel 12:1–4. Michael Will Lead God's People to Victory

Who is Michael, the "great prince"? (12:1) "Michael is . . . known in the annals of history as Adam. . . . He successfully led the armies of the Lord in battle against the forces of evil in our pre-earth experience (Rev. 12:7–9) and shall be called upon to perform the same role in the great and last battle with the devil and all who dwell in his demented domain (D&C 88:110–15)" (Brewster, *Doctrine and Covenants Encyclopedia*, 355). "[Dan. 12] is best understood as a prophecy of the end of the wicked world, the deliverance of the righteous with the help of Michael, the resurrection of the just and the unjust" (Rasmussen, *Latter-day Saint Commentary on the Old Testament*, 627). ⊕

Who are the wise that shall shine and "turn many to righteousness"? (12:3) "[This] may be applied to the case of holy and useful men [and women], particularly the faithful ministers of the Gospel, in the day of judgment" (*Adam Clarke's Commentary* [on Daniel 12:3]). Disciples of Jesus Christ have been instructed to "hold up your light that it may shine unto the world. Behold I am the light which ye shall hold up—that which ye have seen me do" (3 Ne. 18:24; see also D&C 86:11; 115:5; 138:30). What can you do to hold up the light of Jesus Christ and help others choose righteousness?

CHAPTERS 10–11

Daniel sees the Lord and others in a glorious vision—He is shown what is to be in the latter days.

Daniel sees the successive kings and their wars, leagues, and conflicts that lead up to the Second Coming of Christ.

CHAPTER 12

In the last days, Michael will deliver Israel from their troubles—Daniel tells of the two resurrections—The wise will know the times and meanings of his visions.

1 And at that time shall Michael stand up, the great prince which standeth for the children of thy people: and there shall be a time of trouble, such as never was since there was a nation *even* to that same time: and at that time thy people shall be delivered, every one that shall be found written in the book.

2 And many of them that sleep in the dust of the earth shall awake, some to everlasting life, and some to shame *and* everlasting contempt.

3 And they that be wise shall shine as the brightness of the firmament; and they that turn many to righteousness as the stars for ever and ever.

4 But thou, O Daniel, shut up the words,
and seal the book, *even* to the time of the
end: many shall run to and fro, and knowledge shall be increased.

Why will knowledge increase in the last days? (12:4) "There has been an explosion of secular knowledge. I believe that God has opened up these treasures of intelligence to enhance His purposes on the earth. . . . Advances in communication and travel during this last century have hastened the pace at which the word of the Lord goes out from Zion. I feel much like Isaiah, who spoke of our time, when 'the earth shall be full of the knowledge of the Lord, as the waters cover the sea.' I believe that this marvelous outpouring of knowledge has heightened our ability to take the Lord's saving message to the world, 'that repentance and remission of sins should be preached in his name among all nations' [Luke 24:47]" (Faust, "This Is Our Day," 18–19).

Summary of Daniel 12:5–13

Daniel sees other wonders in vision and is told they will last "for a time, times, and an half" (12:7). The interpretation of the time periods mentioned in these verses has not been revealed by the Lord as yet. God promises Daniel that he shall rest at the end of his days.

HOSEA

Introduction

"The Hebrew name of the prophet, Hoshea, signifies 'help,' 'deliverance,' and 'salvation,' and is derived from the same root as the names of Joshua and Jesus. By reason of numerous allusions in the prophecy to the Northern Kingdom, it is commonly supposed by commentators that Hosea was a native of that commonwealth. The superscription further informs us that Hosea was a prophet 'in the days of Uzziah, Jotham, Ahaz, and Hezekiah, kings of Judah, and in the days of Jeroboam the son of Joash, king of Israel.' Jeroboam II, the king of Israel, reigned from 788 B.C. until 747 B.C. and Hezekiah, the last-named of the kings of Judah, began to reign in 725 B.C. . . . He was, then, a contemporary of three other great prophets, Isaiah, Amos, and Micah" (Sperry, *Voice of Israel's Prophets*, 274).

"Hosea lived during one of the most prosperous eras of ancient Israel's history. . . . But as his book reveals, his society was deeply marred by depravity and evil. His written record exhibits an extraordinary measure of tenderness and compassion which is combined with a stern resolve against wickedness and, particularly, corruption in high places" (Brown, "Book of Hosea," 61).

The prophet Hosea uses extensive metaphors and symbolism that illustrate God's love for His chosen people. "One of the central messages of the book of Hosea is that Jehovah loves His people even when they are unfaithful to Him, and He will mercifully offer them reconciliation" (*Old Testament Seminary Teacher Material* [2018], 778). "Hosea's fundamental idea is the love of God for His people. In love God redeemed them from Egypt (Hosea 11:1); their history has been but an illustration of His love (11–13); all His chastisements are inflicted in love (2:14; 3); and their restoration shall be due to His love (2:19; 14:4). In contrast with this moral Being, who is Love, Hosea sets Israel, characterized always by want of affection, by treachery and infidelity. Yet he is able to look forward to a final redemption (2:19; 11:12–14:9). The profound thought and pathos of this prophet of the north deeply influenced succeeding writers (see Isa. 40–66; Jer. 2–3; Ezek. 16; 33)" (Bible Dictionary, "Hosea, or Hoshea").

"Portraying God to ancient Israel as a loving, forgiving father, Hosea foreshadowed, more than most Old Testament prophets, the spirit and message of the New Testament, the Book of Mormon, and modern revelation" (Poelman, "God's Love for Us Transcends Our Transgressions," 28).

CHAPTER 1

Hosea and his family are a sign unto Israel—In the day of gathering, the people of Israel will become the sons of the living God.

1 The word of the LORD that came unto Hosea, the son of Beeri, in the days of Uzziah, Jotham, Ahaz, *and* Hezekiah, kings of Judah, and in the days of Jeroboam the son of Joash, king of Israel.

Hosea 1:1–11. God Commands Hosea to Marry Gomer and They Are Blessed with Children

What was the political and religious environment of Hosea's time? (1:1) "The years of Hosea's life were melancholy and tragic. The vials of the wrath of heaven were poured out on his apostate people. . . . The obligations of law had been relaxed, and the claims of religion disregarded; Baal became the rival of Jehovah, and in the dark recesses of the groves were practiced the impure and murderous rites of heathen deities; peace and prosperity fled the land, which was harassed by foreign invasion and domestic broils; might and murder became the twin sentinels of the throne; alliances were formed with other nations, which brought with them seductions to paganism; . . . and but a fraction of its population maintained its spiritual allegiance' [Fallows, *Popular and Critical Bible Encyclopedia and Scriptural Dictionary*, s.v. 'Hosea']" (*Old Testament Student Manual: 1 Kings–Malachi*, 104).

2 The beginning of the word of the LORD by Hosea. And the LORD said to Hosea, Go, take unto thee a wife of whoredoms and children of whoredoms: for the land hath committed great whoredom, *departing* from the LORD.

3 So he went and took Gomer the daughter of Diblaim; which conceived, and bare him a son.

Why would God command a righteous prophet to marry a harlot? (1:2) "'The strange symbolic marriage and family of Hosea parallels the strange covenant relationship of wayward Israel with the LORD. It is the prophet's way of telling of his call from the Lord. Whether the "woman of unfaithfulness" was that way when he took her to wife, or whether she became that way later, no one knows. We do know that Israel was once faithful to God, but became unfaithful later'" (Ludlow, *Companion to Your Study of the Old Testament*, 360).

4 And the LORD said unto him, Call his name Jezreel; for yet a little *while*, and I will avenge the blood of Jezreel upon the house of Jehu, and will cause to cease the kingdom of the house of Israel.

5 And it shall come to pass at that day, that I will break the bow of Israel in the valley of Jezreel.

6 ¶ And she conceived again, and bare a daughter. And *God* said unto him, Call her name Lo-ruhamah: for I will no more have mercy upon the house of Israel; but I will utterly take them away.

What might be the significance of the names of Hosea's children? (1:4–9) "Three children were born into the union of Hosea and Gomer. Each was named by God. The first, a son, was named Jezreel, meaning 'God will disperse,' with the appended prophecy that the nation would be destroyed [Hosea 1:4–5]. The second child was a daughter named Lo-ruhamah, meaning 'not having obtained mercy,' for the Lord said he would have no mercy upon Israel because of their wickedness [Hosea 1:6–7]. And finally, another son was named Lo-ammi, meaning 'not my people' [Hosea 1:9]" (McConkie, *Gospel Symbolism*, 169–70).

Hosea's Marriage to an Unfaithful Wife (Gomer) and Her Eventual Return (Hosea 1–3)

"The stunning sketch of the prophet's marriage consists of three parts: (1) an account in chapter 1 written in the third person, (2) words of the Lord in chapter 2 that draw an analogy between Israel's unfaithful conduct toward him and the infidelity of Hosea's wife, and (3) a second report of Hosea's union in chapter 3 written by the prophet himself, that is, in the first person. Differences among the views of interpreters have focused on how one is properly to understand the connection between the biographical narrative in chapter 1 and the autobiographical sketch in chapter 3. The narrative in chapter 1 reports the Lord's command to Hosea to marry a 'wife of whoredoms' to whom were later born three children, whose names symbolized facets of the Lord's ruptured relationship with his people. The narrative in chapter 3 recounts the divine charge to Hosea that he love an adulteress, purchasing her and then confining her to his home, a virtual house arrest (Hosea 3:1–3)" (Brown, "Book of Hosea," 62).

How was the Lord's promise to miraculously save Judah fulfilled? (1:7) "I will spare [Judah] as a kingdom after Israel has been carried away into captivity by the Assyrians.

"'*And will save them by the Lord their God*'—Remarkably fulfilled in the supernatural defeat of the army of the Assyrians, see 2 Kings 19:35; and so they were saved not by bow, nor by sword, nor by battle, nor by horses, nor by horsemen. The former expression may mean, not in war by horses, i.e., yoked to war chariots, nor by horsemen—nor by cavalry, however efficient such troops might have then been deemed" (*Adam Clarke's Commentary* [on Hosea 1:7]).

How might this promise to become the "sons of the living God" be fulfilled? (1:10) "We believe that through living the gospel of Jesus Christ we can become like the Savior, who is perfect. Considering the attributes of Jesus Christ should quash the pride of the self-satisfied person who thinks he or she has no need to improve. And even the most humble person can take hope in the invitation to become like the Savior. . . .

"Love is the motivating principle by which the Lord leads us along the way towards becoming like Him, *our perfect example*. Our way of life, hour by hour, must be filled with the love of God and love for others" (Eyring, "Our Perfect Example," 70).

What does "great shall be the day of Jezreel" mean? (1:11) This phrase "alludes to the meaning of the word [Jezreel], the seed of God [of the House of Israel]. God who has dispersed—sown, them in different lands, shall gather them together; and that day of God's power shall be great and glorious. It was a wonderful seed time in the Divine justice; it shall then be a wonderful harvest in the Divine mercy. He sowed them among the nations in his wrath; he shall reap them and gather them in his bounty" (*Adam Clarke's Commentary* [on Hosea 1:11]).

Hosea 2:1–13. Hosea Calls Gomer, His Wife, to Repentance

How had Israel "played the harlot" like Gomer did? (2:1–5) Gomer's "return to a life of immorality graphically represents the idolatry and wickedness of Israel. Just as Gomer had been unfaithful to her marriage covenant with Hosea, so had Israel been unfaithful to her covenants with Jehovah. The graphic imagery of physical adultery is used many times in the scriptures to characterize Israel's spiritual idolatry and unfaithfulness. . . .

7 But I will have mercy upon the house of Judah, and will save them by the LORD their God, and will not save them by bow, nor by sword, nor by battle, by horses, nor by horsemen.

8 ¶ Now when she had weaned Lo-ruhamah, she conceived, and bare a son.

9 Then said *God,* Call his name Lo-ammi: for ye *are* not my people, and I will not be your *God.*

10 ¶ Yet the number of the children of Israel shall be as the sand of the sea, which cannot be measured nor numbered; and it shall come to pass, *that* in the place where it was said unto them, Ye *are* not my people, *there* it shall be said unto them, *Ye are* the sons of the living God.

11 Then shall the children of Judah and the children of Israel be gathered together, and appoint themselves one head, and they shall come up out of the land: for great *shall be* the day of Jezreel.

CHAPTER 2

Worshipping false gods brings severe judgments upon Israel—In the last days, Israel will be reconciled to God and become His people.

1 Say ye unto your brethren, Ammi; and to your sisters, Ruhamah.

2 Plead with your mother, plead: for she *is* not my wife, neither *am* I her husband: let her therefore put away her whoredoms out of her sight, and her adulteries from between her breasts;

3 Lest I strip her naked, and set her as in the
day that she was born, and make her as a wilderness, and set her like a dry land, and slay
her with thirst.

4 And I will not have mercy upon her children; for they *be* the children of whoredoms.

5 For their mother hath played the harlot:
she that conceived them hath done shame-
fully: for she said, I will go after my lovers,
that give *me* my bread and my water, my
wool and my flax, mine oil and my drink.

"Hosea was the first Israelite prophet to testify of Jehovah's covenant with Israel by comparing it to marriage, but others who followed amplified the imagery [see, for example, Isa. 54:5–6; Jer. 3:6–8; Ezek. 16:8–9, 14–15]" (Top, "Marriage of Hosea and Gomer," 228, 229).

What Are the Meanings of the Literary Devices in Hosea 2?

"Three prominent features of the book [of Hosea] are reasons for its uniqueness: the use of metaphors (including similes), paronomasia or wordplays, and allusions to prior national history. In terms of frequency of use, the book exceeds all other prophetic books in these three areas. Hosea has the distinction of being the prophetic book most poetic in the employment of metaphor and wordplay, and most historical with respect to allusions to prior national traditions" (Dearman, *Book of Hosea*, 10).

Verse	Metaphor	Meaning
Verse 1	Ammi	"My people"
Verse 1	Ruhamah	"Having obtained mercy," or "those who have obtained mercy"
Verse 2	your mother	The nation Israel
Verse 3	wilderness	The captivity
Verse 5	lovers	The priests, priestesses, and idols of the Canaanite temples or, in the larger sense, any person one loves more than God
Verses 5–9, 13	bread, corn, wool, and jewels	Worldly values and treasures
Verses 9–10	her nakedness and her lewdness	Israel's sin
Verses 11–14	allure her	Jehovah still cares for her and will try to win her back.
Verse 15	Valley of Achor, a rich valley north of Jericho, near Gilgal	The Lord will restore her to great blessings.
Verse 16	*Ishi* (Hebrew for "my husband") and *Baali* (Hebrew for "my master")	Eventually Israel will accept God as her Lord and her true husband.
Verses 19–20	betroth thee unto me forever	The fulness of the new and everlasting covenant restored to Israel in the latter days and the eternal blessings that will result from Israel's faithful marriage to Jehovah
Verse 22	Jezreel (Hebrew for "God shall sow")	The downtrodden and poor Israel. Like the Jezreel Valley, they have great potential and will be resown and made fruitful by the Lord.

(Adapted from the *Old Testament Student Manual: 1 Kings–Malachi*, 106).

How does the unfaithful wife Gomer represent Israel? (2:6–13) "We read of the loss of opportunity to participate in sacred acts of worship (v. 11) and Israel's eventual desire to repent and return to her husband. We read of thorns hedging up the way and of Israel's shame and nakedness being uncovered. . . . These items may relate to some of the images of the Fall in the book of Genesis. . . . Ultimately, Israel had created an environment in which she was destroying herself, and though the Lord had had mercy on her for several hundred years by calling prophets and warning of this destruction, Israel was then Lo-ruhamah ('not obtaining mercy'). . . .

"Hosea 2:14–16 marks a turning point in restoring Israel from her fallen state" (Schade, "Imagery of Hosea's Family and the Restoration of Israel," 241–42).

6 ¶ Therefore, behold, I will hedge up thy
way with thorns, and make a wall, that she
shall not find her paths.

7 And she shall follow after her lovers, but she
shall not overtake them; and she shall seek
them, but shall not find *them:* then shall she
say, I will go and return to my first husband;
for then *was it* better with me than now.

8 For she did not know that I gave her corn,
and wine, and oil, and multiplied her silver
and gold, *which* they prepared for Baal.

9 Therefore will I return, and take away my
corn in the time thereof, and my wine in the
season thereof, and will recover my wool and
my flax *given* to cover her nakedness.

10 And now will I discover her lewdness in
the sight of her lovers, and none shall deliver
her out of mine hand.

11 I will also cause all her mirth to cease, her
feast days, her new moons, and her sabbaths,
and all her solemn feasts.

12 And I will destroy her vines and her fig
trees, whereof she hath said, These *are* my rewards that my lovers have given me: and I
will make them a forest, and the beasts of the
field shall eat them.

13 And I will visit upon her the days of
Baalim, wherein she burned incense to them,
and she decked herself with her earrings and
her jewels, and she went after her lovers, and
forgat me, saith the LORD.

Hosea 2:14–23. Through God's Mercy, Gomer Is Promised Her Former Blessings

14 ¶ Therefore, behold, I will allure her,
and bring her into the wilderness, and speak
comfortably unto her.

15 And I will give her her vineyards from
thence, and the valley of Achor for a door
of hope: and she shall sing there, as in the
days of her youth, and as in the day when she
came up out of the land of Egypt.

16 And it shall be at that day, saith the LORD, *that* thou shalt call me Ishi; and shalt call me no more Baali.

17 For I will take away the names of Baalim out of her mouth, and they shall no more be remembered by their name.

18 And in that day will I make a covenant for them with the beasts of the field, and with the fowls of heaven, and *with* the creeping things of the ground: and I will break the bow and the sword and the battle out of the earth, and will make them to lie down safely.

19 And I will betroth thee unto me for ever; yea, I will betroth thee unto me in righteousness, and in judgment, and in lovingkindness, and in mercies.

20 I will even betroth thee unto me in faithfulness: and thou shalt know the LORD.

21 And it shall come to pass in that day, I will hear, saith the LORD, I will hear the heavens, and they shall hear the earth;

22 And the earth shall hear the corn, and the wine, and the oil; and they shall hear Jezreel.

23 And I will sow her unto me in the earth; and I will have mercy upon her that had not obtained mercy; and I will say to *them which were* not my people, Thou *art* my people; and they shall say, *Thou art* my God.

How does a betrothal and marriage covenant represent the Lord's relationship with Israel? (2:19) "When a man and a woman enter into the sacred covenant of marriage, they make certain promises to each other. . . . Chief among these covenant promises are honesty, unfailing love, and strict faithfulness. Often in the scriptures the covenant which God made with Israel is referred to as a marriage covenant. The same conditions which are at the core of the bond of marriage are also at the core of the bond between Jehovah and Israel—honesty, love, and fidelity. The covenant of marriage and God's covenant with his chosen people are, in fact, very similar. . . . The violation of that covenant of honesty, love, and fidelity is expressed as adultery. . . . The dissolution of that covenant is described as divorce" (Jackson, "Marriage of Hosea and Jehovah's Covenant with Israel," 60).

How is God's character revealed in this account? (2:19–23) President Henry B. Eyring said: "'The book of Hosea . . . uses what seem to me almost poetic images. The symbols in Hosea are a husband, his bride, her betrayal, and a test of marriage covenants almost beyond comprehension. . . . Here are the fierce words of the husband, spoken after his wife has betrayed him in adultery: [Hosea 2:6–7].

"'He goes on (through verse 13) to describe the punishment she deserves, and then comes a remarkable change in the verse that follows [Hosea 2:14–15, 19–23]. . . .

"'This was a story of a marriage covenant bound by love, by steadfast love. What I felt [when I taught this as a seminary teacher], and it has increased over the years, was that the Lord, with whom I am blessed to have made covenants, loves me, and you, and those we teach, with a steadfastness about which I continually marvel and which I want with all my heart to emulate'" ("Covenants and Sacrifice"). ⊕

In what way is the Lord's promise to Hosea being fulfilled in our day? (2:23) "The appeal of the book of Hosea for Latter-day Saints is that we live in a day when the Restoration has begun and when latter-day Israel is under solemn obligation and responsibility to carry forth the work of the Restoration and fulfill the Abrahamic covenant. . . . Indeed we have an opportunity to participate in the events leading up to the millennial reign of Christ and to participate in the fulfillment of Hosea's great prophecies of the Restoration when the Lord will say, 'Thou art my people; and they shall say, Thou art my God' (Hosea 2:23)" (Schade, "Imagery of Hosea's Family and the Restoration of Israel," 243–44).

Hosea 3:1–5. Gomer's Blessings Are Restored and She Is Redeemed and Israel's Future Is Foretold

How is the Lord's mercy reflected in His command for Hosea to forgive and redeem Gomer? (3:1–3) "The Lord commanded Hosea to marry a woman with [a sinful] past. . . . After later abandoning Hosea, Gomer recognized her mistakes and wanted to return; but by then—one must infer—she had become a slave. The Lord directed Hosea to buy her back, a course which he pursued willingly, for he still loved her despite all. The prophet next disciplined Gomer by severely restricting her movements and associations with others before restoring her fully to her former status. On such a view, this sorrowful episode deepened Hosea's appreciation for the Lord's frustration at Israel's infidelity and apostasy" (Brown, "Book of Hosea," 63).

CHAPTER 3

Israel will seek the Lord, return to the Lord, and receive of His goodness in the latter days.

1 Then said the LORD unto me, Go yet, love a woman beloved of *her* friend, yet an adulteress, according to the love of the LORD toward the children of Israel, who look to other gods, and love flagons of wine.

2 So I bought her to me for fifteen *pieces* of silver, and *for* an homer of barley, and an half homer of barley:

3 And I said unto her, Thou shalt abide for me many days; thou shalt not play the harlot, and thou shalt not be for *another* man: so *will* I also *be* for thee.

4 For the children of Israel shall abide many days without a king, and without a prince, and without a sacrifice, and without an image, and without an ephod, and *without* teraphim:

5 Afterward shall the children of Israel return, and seek the LORD their God, and David their king; and shall fear the LORD and his goodness in the latter days.

CHAPTERS 4–5

Israel loses all truth, mercy, and knowledge of God and goes whoring after false gods.

The kingdoms of Judah and Israel will both fall because of their iniquities.

Summary of Hosea 4–5

Hosea brings a controversy (or lawsuit) against covenant-breaking Israel. He accuses them of not practicing truth, not dealing mercifully with others, and not seeking to know God. They transgress several of the Ten Commandments and their sins stain the land and its inhabitants. The corrupt priests preach wickedness and fail to teach God's laws. The pagan rituals promote whoredoms and apostasy among Israel. The wicked leaders trap others in sin as a hunter uses a snare and net to capture animals and birds. The kingdom of Judah shares guilt with Israel. Hosea charges them with seeking political security from neighboring nations rather than relying upon God. The Lord withdraws from Israel until they sincerely repent.

CHAPTER 6

Hosea calls Israel to return and serve the Lord—The mercy and knowledge of God are more important than ritualistic sacrifices.

1 Come, and let us return unto the Lord: for he hath torn, and he will heal us; he hath smitten, and he will bind us up.

2 After two days will he revive us: in the third day he will raise us up, and we shall live in his sight.

Hosea 6:1–3. Hosea Invites Israel to Repent and Return to the Lord

How are we healed by returning to the Lord?

(6:1–2) "As we come unto Jesus Christ by exercising faith in Him, repenting, and making and keeping covenants, our brokenness—whatever its cause—can be healed. This process, which invites the Savior's healing power into our lives, does not just restore us to what we were before but makes us better than we ever were. . . . Through our Savior, Jesus Christ, we can all be mended, made whole, and fulfill our purpose. . . .

What Can We Learn from the Example of Gomer's Repentance? (Hosea 3)

"Gomer, the 'wife of whoredoms,' not only symbolizes wayward Israel who went 'whoring' after other gods (see Deut. 31:16–17; Hosea 9:1) but also represents each of us individually. Just as she was unfaithful to Hosea and to the covenants she had made with him, each of us to some degree has also been remiss. We all have in some manner broken covenants and been unfaithful in our spiritual duties. Hosea, on the other hand, stands as a graphic reminder of the steadfast love that the Savior has for each of us. We cannot help but marvel at the continued compassion and love Hosea demonstrated for his wicked wife. Of course he abhorred her adultery. He could not and did not minimize the severity of her sins or ignore her infidelity, but he loved her still and yearned for her return. . . .

"There are among us those who feel that they have sinned to such an extent that they cannot have any claim upon the mercy of God.

"'While wallowing in deep despair, true repentance is impossible,' wrote Elder Neal A. Maxwell. 'The feeling of futility can render one powerless to further resist the adversary; it can blur the vital difference between understanding the possibility of forgiveness for the sinner, while rejecting the sinful act' ["Hope for the Hopeless," 318]. To these dejected souls, Hosea's marriage account offers the most hopeful and significant message in the scriptures—the central focus of the 'glad tidings' of the gospel: 'And this is the gospel, the glad tidings, which the voice out of the heavens bore record unto us—that he came into the world, even Jesus, to be crucified for the world, and to bear the sins of the world, and to sanctify the world, and to cleanse it from all unrighteousness' (D&C 76:40–41). Not only is Hosea, like Christ, willing to take his adulterous wife back but he actually purchases her back. That is one of the most important symbols in the marriage account, because it represents the atonement of Jesus Christ whereby He, as the apostle Paul testified, 'bought us with a price' (1 Cor. 6:20)" (Top, "Marriage of Hosea and Gomer," 233, 235).

"To heal brokenness by coming unto Him, we need to have faith in Jesus Christ. . . . 'Because He has experienced all our pains, afflictions, and infirmities, He knows how to help us rise above our daily difficulties' [Gospel Topics, 'Faith in Jesus Christ']" (Franco, "Healing Power of Jesus Christ," 61).

How does the Lord heal us? (6:1–2) "When sore trials come upon us, it's time to deepen our faith in God, to work hard, and to serve others. Then He will heal our broken hearts. He will bestow upon us personal peace and comfort. Those great gifts will not be destroyed, even by death. . . . The gift of resurrection is the Lord's consummate act of healing. Thanks to Him, each body will be restored to its proper and perfect frame. Thanks to Him, no condition is hopeless. Thanks to Him, brighter days are ahead, both here and hereafter. Real joy awaits each of us—on the other side of sorrow" (Nelson, "Jesus Christ—the Master Healer," 87–88).

What might the phrase "the latter and former rain unto the earth" mean? (6:3) This verse suggests a conditional promise: "If we follow on to know the Lord . . . [then] he shall come unto us as the rain."

This "is a call to seek the knowledge of Jehovah, whose rising is fixed like the morning dawn and whose blessing is 'as the latter and former rain unto the earth.' To the farmer in ancient Israel, two 'rains' were very critical. The former (or first) rains softened the earth so that he could plow it and plant the seed; the latter (or second) rains gave the crop its growth" (*Old Testament Student Manual: 1 Kings–Malachi*, 108). It may also have reference to the "doctrine of the priesthood [distilling] upon [our souls] as the dews from heaven" (D&C 121:45).

3 Then shall we know, *if* we follow on to
know the LORD: his going forth is prepared
as the morning; and he shall come unto us
as the rain, as the latter *and* former rain unto
the earth.

Hosea 6:4–11. Hosea Declares That Israel and Judah Are Unfaithful

What does God desire more than the outward act of a burnt offering? (6:4–6) "As the morning cloud and the dew rapidly disappear, so the efforts of Israel after real goodness (especially 'kindness') lack endurance. . . . God cared more for goodness and piety—the knowledge and doing of His will—than for formal offerings and sacrifice, and nothing at all for religious observances that were insincere and corrupt. . . . Our Lord twice quotes the first clause in justification of doing good on the sabbath day [Matt. 9:13; 12:7]" (*John Dummelow's Commentary* [on Hosea 6:4, 6]). What can you do to become more sincere and enduring in your personal goodness?

4 ¶ O Ephraim, what shall I do unto thee?
O Judah, what shall I do unto thee? for your
goodness *is* as a morning cloud, and as the
early dew it goeth away.
5 Therefore have I hewed *them* by the prophets; I have slain them by the words of my
mouth: and thy judgments *are as* the light
that goeth forth.

6 For I desired mercy, and not sacrifice; and the knowledge of God more than burnt offerings.

7 But they like men have transgressed the covenant: there have they dealt treacherously against me.

8 Gilead *is* a city of them that work iniquity, *and is* polluted with blood.

9 And as troops of robbers wait for a man, *so* the company of priests murder in the way by consent: for they commit lewdness.

10 I have seen an horrible thing in the house of Israel: there *is* the whoredom of Ephraim, Israel is defiled.

11 Also, O Judah, he hath set an harvest for thee, when I returned the captivity of my people.

CHAPTERS 7–14

Israel is reproved for her many sins—Ephraim is mixed among the people.

Both Israel and Judah have forsaken the Lord—The Lord has written the great things of His law to Ephraim.

The people of Israel are taken into captivity for their sins—Ephraim will be a wanderer among the nations.

Israel has plowed wickedness and reaped iniquity—Hosea calls upon Israel to seek the Lord.

Why does the Lord desire mercy over sacrifice? (6:6–11) "The Lord laments over Israel and Judah's transgressions of the covenant they had made with him [in] this lamentation, one of the more well-known verses [Hosea 6:6]. . . . The Savior quotes it twice during his ministry to refute the self-righteous Pharisees (Matthew 9:13; 12:7). The Lord is more interested in how people relate to each other and come to a knowledge of him than he is in their going through ritual in an attempt to worship him (compare 1 Samuel 15:22–23). This verse also demonstrates that Jehovah, the God of the Old Testament, is a God of mercy as well as justice, something not always understood by readers and teachers of the Old Testament" (Nyman and Nyman, *The Words of the Twelve Prophets*, 31).

What knowledge does God want His children to obtain? (6:6) "Christ came that men might have life abundant and life eternal. . . . And that knowledge, I testify, is the most important treasure one can possess or seek. From Hosea comes the word of the Lord: . . . 'For I desired mercy, and not sacrifice; and the knowledge of God' . . .

"All the prophets taught this truth about God, and their prime purpose was not to argue or try to prove the existence of God but to be his witnesses, to testify that he lives and to make his will known among men, . . . [and the] opportunity for men to know God himself" (Hanks, "Trust in the Lord," 13–14).

Summary of Hosea 7–14

Although Hosea and other prophets plead with Israel to repent, they continue to break their covenants. Their sins result in destruction, scattering, and captivity. The Lord remains bound to Israel with cords of love. He promises that the repentant will be ransomed and delivered from death. Yet in the end, the Lord's mercy reclaims scattered Israel as she repents and returns to the Lord. Northern Israel (Ephraim) is a weak nation compared to Assyria, yet Hosea warns Ephraim to avoid entanglements with powerful nations like Egypt or Assyria.

Israel, as a child, was called out of Egypt in similitude of our Lord, as a child, coming out of Egypt—But Ephraim turns away from the Lord.

The Lord uses prophets, visions, and similitudes to guide His people, but they become rich and will not wait on the Lord—Ephraim provokes Him most bitterly.

Ephraim's sins provoke the Lord—There is no Savior beside the Lord—He ransoms from the grave and redeems from death.

In the last days, Ephraim will repent and return unto the Lord.

JOEL

Introduction

"[Joel was] a prophet of Judah. The date of his prophecy is uncertain; it may have been spoken as early as the reign of Joash, before 850 B.C., or even so late as after [the return of the Jews from Babylonian exile in 538 B.C.]. The occasion of the prophecy was a severe visitation of drought and locusts. He assures the people that on repentance they will again receive the blessings of God. His prophecy of the outpouring of the Spirit (2:28–32) was quoted by Peter on the day of Pentecost (Acts 2:17), and by the angel Moroni to Joseph Smith (JS–H 1:41). There are also traces of Joel in Revelation" (Bible Dictionary, "Joel").

"As is typical of Old Testament prophecies, Joel's prophecies are dualistic: They warn of an immediate and impending destruction (through the conquests of Assyria and Babylonia), but they also refer directly to the last days and the destruction that will again threaten Israel just before the Millennium" (*Old Testament Student Manual: 1 Kings–Malachi*, 83).

The structure of Joel's book can be described as follows: "After the phenomenal series of cataclysms anticipated in chapter 1, great conflicts between armies representing the Lord's people and the adversary are told in chapter 2. . . . Chapter 3 tells of the judgment day to follow the restoration of Judah and Jerusalem, with a gathering of 'all nations' to 'the valley of Jehoshaphat' ('the valley of Jehovah's judgment'). The Lord will plead there for his people. The nations may prepare for war, but it will be to no avail, for they will be already in the final 'valley of decision.' That judgment day will be followed by restoration and renewal of the earth, and the Lord shall dwell in Zion" (Rasmussen, *Latter-day Saint Commentary on the Old Testament*, 639).

"The book of Joel seems to be completely removed from the context of the time and place in which it was written. This absence of contemporary references certainly seems to be deliberate; it is as though Joel wanted us to leave behind all thoughts of the here and now and join him in his visions of the future. And the future is clearly the book's focus. I believe that aside from the names of Joel and his father in Joel 1:1, every word in the book refers to the latter days—from the time of the Prophet Joseph Smith into the Millennium" (Jackson, "Book of Joel," 359–60).

CHAPTER 1

Call a solemn assembly and gather to the house of the Lord, for the day of the Lord is at hand.

Summary of Joel 1

Joel prophesies that Israel's wickedness will bring about awful consequences. He portrays invading armies as locusts and other insects that devour the land and make it desolate. Those who remain will mourn and weep like a young widow who has lost her husband. The priests in the house of the Lord will not be able to offer sacrifices and perform ordinances, which causes a loss of the spiritual companionship of the Lord (v. 16). The religious leaders designate a fast and a solemn assembly and gather Israel to the temple to repent and prepare for the day of the Lord when the Almighty will bring destruction as a judgment upon the wicked. Drought and famine cause all creatures to suffer for lack of food.

Joel 2:1–11. The Day of the Lord Is Coming

What might blowing a trumpet represent? (2:1) "In ancient times a herald would blow a trumpet before making an announcement or introducing the arrival of a king. In the last days, the Lord will have his angels sound a number of trumpets to herald the coming of judgments and other important events. Whether these trumpets will be heard by those on earth or whether they are literal or symbolic is not yet clear" (Parry and Parry, *Understanding the Signs of the Times*, 68).

What is "the day of the Lord"? (2:1) "One of the central themes of the Book of Joel is 'the day of the LORD' (1:15; 2:1, 11, 31; 3:14). This language describes a period of time in which God 'comes down' in a dramatic way to bring wrath and judgment on the wicked and salvation to the righteous. . . .

"Joel reveals that this day is to be heralded by heavenly phenomena (2:30, 31) which will bring sudden darkness and gloom on the earth (2:2). It will be a day of divine destruction (1:15) on the nations that have persecuted Israel (3:12–14). . . . Yet it will also be a time of deliverance and unprecedented blessing for God's people (2:32; 3:16, 18–21; 1 Thess. 5:2–5)" (*NKJV Study Bible* [2018], 1291).

Why will there be darkness and gloominess in the last days? (2:2) "Jesus calls upon us to have a deliberate trust in God's unfolding purposes, not only for all humankind but for us individually. And we are to be of good cheer in the unfolding process.

"We must not underestimate, however, the difficulty of the last days. Joel and Zephaniah both speak of the last days as being 'a day of . . . gloominess' (Joel 2:2; Zeph. 1:15). The coming decades will be times of despair. Why? Because, as Moroni said, despair comes of iniquity (see Moro. 10:22). The more iniquity, the more despair. And unless there is widespread repentance, despair will both deepen and spread—except among those who have gospel gladness" (Maxwell, "Be of Good Cheer," 66–67).

Why do the scriptures refer to the events of the last days as both "great" and "terrible"? (2:2–11) "The 'day of the Lord' will be great because Zion will be a reality, but the events associated with it will also make it terrible, as these verses make clear.

CHAPTER 2

War and desolation will precede the Second Coming—The sun and the moon will be darkened—The Lord will pour out His Spirit upon all flesh—There will be dreams and visions.

1 Blow ye the trumpet in Zion, and sound an alarm in my holy mountain: let all the inhabitants of the land tremble: for the day of the LORD cometh, for *it is* nigh at hand;

2 A day of darkness and of gloominess, a day of clouds and of thick darkness, as the morning spread upon the mountains: a great people and a strong; there hath not been ever the like, neither shall be any more after it, *even* to the years of many generations.

3 A fire devoureth before them; and behind them a flame burneth: the land *is* as the garden of Eden before them, and behind them a desolate wilderness; yea, and nothing shall escape them.

4 The appearance of them *is* as the appearance of horses; and as horsemen, so shall they run.

5 Like the noise of chariots on the tops of mountains shall they leap, like the noise of a flame of fire that devoureth the stubble, as a strong people set in battle array.

6 Before their face the people shall be much pained: all faces shall gather blackness.

7 They shall run like mighty men; they shall climb the wall like men of war; and they shall march every one on his ways, and they shall not break their ranks:

8 Neither shall one thrust another; they shall walk every one in his path: and *when* they fall upon the sword, they shall not be wounded.

9 They shall run to and fro in the city; they shall run upon the wall, they shall climb up upon the houses; they shall enter in at the windows like a thief.

10 The earth shall quake before them; the heavens shall tremble: the sun and the moon shall be dark, and the stars shall withdraw their shining:

11 And the LORD shall utter his voice before his army: for his camp *is* very great: for *he is* strong that executeth his word: for the day of the LORD *is* great and very terrible; and who can abide it?

12 ¶ Therefore also now, saith the LORD, turn ye *even* to me with all your heart, and with fasting, and with weeping, and with mourning:

13 And rend your heart, and not your garments, and turn unto the LORD your God: for he *is* gracious and merciful, slow to anger, and of great kindness, and repenteth him of the evil.

14 Who knoweth *if* he will return and repent, and leave a blessing behind him; *even* a meat offering and a drink offering unto the LORD your God?

15 ¶ Blow the trumpet in Zion, sanctify a fast, call a solemn assembly:

"An event of the latter days known as the battle of Armageddon is described in these verses. . . .

"But the Lord is strong, and He will keep His word. He has promised to rescue the people, and He will (see v. 11; see also Zechariah 14; Revelation 9, 11; Ezekiel 38–39).

"Other events, such as the land being 'as the garden of Eden before them' (v. 3), refer specifically to the latter days. Today the Galilee area and the Jezreel Valley in modern Israel have truly 'blossomed as the rose'" (*Old Testament Student Manual: 1 Kings–Malachi*, 84, 85).

Joel 2:12–17. God Is Merciful to Those Who Serve Him

What does it mean for us to "rend [our] hearts?" (2:13) The Joseph Smith Translation adjusts this passage to read, "And rend your heart, and not your garments, *and repent*, and turn unto the Lord your God: for he is gracious and merciful, slow to anger, and of great kindness, and *he will turn away* the evil *from you*" (Wayment, *Complete Joseph Smith Translation of the Old Testament*, 215).

What does the Joseph Smith Translation say about the Lord needing to repent? (2:14) The Joseph Smith Translation changes verse 14 to read: "*Therefore, repent, and* who knoweth *but* he will return and leave a blessing behind him; *that you may offer* a meat offering and a drink offering unto the Lord your God?" (Joel 2:14*a*).

Who is the bridegroom and who is the bride? (2:16) "A common metaphor for ancient Israel's relationship to Jehovah was as bride to bridegroom in a marriage covenant. Later that same analogy was made in New Testament times, highlighting the relationship of the members of the church to Jesus Christ. . . . The Second Coming of the Lord is likened to the Bridegroom coming to claim His bride, a moment for which all should be prepared, worthy, and dressed properly for the celebration" (Holland, *Witness for His Names*, 27).

16 Gather the people, sanctify the congregation, assemble the elders, gather the children, and those that suck the breasts: let the bridegroom go forth of his chamber, and the bride out of her closet.

17 Let the priests, the ministers of the LORD, weep between the porch and the altar, and let them say, Spare thy people, O LORD, and give not thine heritage to reproach, that the heathen should rule over them: wherefore should they say among the people, Where *is* their God?

Summary of Joel 2:18–27

Joel prophesies of a dramatic reversal of God's judgment upon the house of Israel. Blessings of the covenant will finally come to God's repentant people. In contrast to the famine in the land and the destruction brought about by the invading army described in Joel 1, these verses in Joel 2 promise an abundance of "corn, and wine, and oil" (v. 19) and protection from the "northern army" (v. 20). Israel will recognize that the Lord is in their midst.

Joel 2:28–32. The Lord's Spirit Is Poured Out upon All Flesh

Who will be blessed with the Lord's spirit when this prophecy is fulfilled? (2:28–32) "The message of this passage is fourfold: (1) there will be a rich outpouring of the Spirit of the Lord in the latter days; (2) certain signs will be fulfilled before Christ's Second Coming in the clouds of heaven; (3) His coming will be great for the righteous and terrible for the wicked; and (4) the 'remnant' (v. 32), Israel of the latter days, will be those who are left after the period of tribulation and scattering is over" (*Old Testament Student Manual: 1 Kings–Malachi*, 86).

When has the Lord poured out His spirit upon all flesh? (2:28–29) This prophecy has been fulfilled more than once. On the day of Pentecost in Jerusalem, the Apostle Peter explained that the miraculous manifestations of the Spirit that day were a fulfillment of the prophecy found in Joel 2:28–32 (see Acts 2:14–21). Centuries later, the angel Moroni quoted Joel 2:28–32 when he appeared to Joseph Smith and explained that this prophecy "was not yet fulfilled, but was soon to be" (JS–H 1:41).

28 ¶ And it shall come to pass afterward, *that* I will pour out my spirit upon all flesh; and your sons and your daughters shall prophesy, your old men shall dream dreams, your young men shall see visions:

29 And also upon the servants and upon the handmaids in those days will I pour out my spirit.

In our day, President Gordon B. Hinckley declared: "The era in which we live is the fulness of times. . . . The vision of Joel has been fulfilled wherein the Lord declared: [Joel 2:28–32]" ("Living in the Fulness of Times," 4).

30 And I will shew wonders in the heavens and in the earth, blood, and fire, and pillars of smoke.

31 The sun shall be turned into darkness, and the moon into blood, before the great and the terrible day of the LORD come.

Are these events only symbolic or real? (2:30–31) "This prophecy is found in all of the standard works of the Church, testifying that it is real, that it is important, and that we will witness dramatic things as the earth is being cleansed for the coming of Christ (see Matt. 24:29; 1 Ne. 22:18–19; D&C 45:40–42; JS–M 1:33). Whatever these calamities are, and however they eventually will come to pass, it seems safe to say that they have not happened yet to the fullest degree. We would know it if they had. But for the righteous, this will not be a day of calamity, though it will be both 'great' and 'terrible'" (Jackson, *Lost Tribes and Last Days*, 163–64).

32 And it shall come to pass, *that* whosoever shall call on the name of the LORD shall be delivered: for in mount Zion and in Jerusalem shall be deliverance, as the LORD hath said, and in the remnant whom the LORD shall call.

What does it mean that Zion and Jerusalem will be delivered? (2:32) In revelation, the Lord declared that the city of Zion, the New Jerusalem, would be "a place of safety for the saints" (D&C 45:66–69). "When Joseph Smith translated the Book of Mormon, he learned that America is the land of Zion which was given to Joseph and his children and that on this land the City Zion, or New Jerusalem, is to be built. He also learned that Jerusalem in Palestine is to be rebuilt and become a holy city [3 Nephi 20:22; 21:20–29; Ether 13:1–12]. These two cities, one in the land of Zion and one in Palestine, are to become capitals for the kingdom of God during the millennium" (Smith, *Doctrines of Salvation*, 3:71).

The Spirit of the Lord Has Been Poured Out in the Latter Days

Modern prophets have taught that one fulfillment of the prophecy in Joel 2:28–29 can be found in the way the Spirit of the Lord has prepared the world in the latter days for the events of the Restoration of the gospel. President M. Russell Ballard explained: "The Lord prepared the world for the Restoration of the gospel of Jesus Christ long before the Father and the Son appeared to Joseph Smith in 1820. . . .

"As we look back in history, we will discover that many revolutions swept across the world preparing people for the Lord's Church to be restored in the last days. . . .

"The printing, translation, and literacy revolutions prepared the way for political and technological revolutions that swept across Europe and the Americas between the 17th and 19th centuries. The changing political climate in Europe and America gave people greater freedom to choose their own religious path. Religious freedom was one of many results of the political revolutions that occurred during this period.

"The Lord also began to 'pour out [His] spirit upon all flesh' (see Joel 2:28; Joseph Smith—History 1:41), including on those who were prepared to dream of new transportation and communication technologies that would move His Restoration forward in dramatic ways.

"As the Lord raised up His Prophet, He inspired men and women to invent technologies, such as canals, telegraphs, railroads, and steam engines, so the gospel could go forth to all the world.

"In countless other ways, the Lord prepared the world for the Restoration of His gospel to bless individuals, families, communities, nations, and the world" ("How the Lord Prepared the World for the Restoration," 15, 16, 19).

Joel 3:1–8. All Nations Shall Be at War

Where is the valley of Jehoshaphat? (3:1–2) "This is the name given in modern times to the valley between Jerusalem and the Mount of Olives, and the Kidron flows through it. Here Jehoshaphat overthrew the confederated enemies of Israel (Psalm 83:6–8); and in this valley also God was to overthrow the Tyrians, Zidonians, etc. (Joel 3:4, 19), with an utter overthrow.... Joel speaks of the final conflict, when God would destroy all Jerusalem's enemies, of whom Tyre and Zidon, etc., were types. The 'valley of Jehoshaphat' may therefore be simply regarded as a general term for the theatre of God's final judgments on the enemies of Israel" (*Easton's Bible Dictionary*, "Jehoshaphat, Valley of").

How will the Lord recompense other nations for their harsh treatment of Israel and Judah? (3:4–8) "The Lord promises to settle the score with the enemies who *cast lots* (v. 3) for Judah and treated God's people as mere chattel to be traded off for the pleasures of prostitution and wine. When God judges the nations, the punishment fits the crime. God promises to bring down on the nations what they have done to Israel and Judah (vv. 4–8)" (*Zondervan KJV Commentary*, 1123).

Joel 3:9–21. God's People Will Be Blessed and Protected

CHAPTER 3

All nations will be at war—Multitudes will stand in the valley of decision as the Second Coming draws near—The Lord will dwell in Zion.

1 For, behold, in those days, and in that time, when I shall bring again the captivity of Judah and Jerusalem,

2 I will also gather all nations, and will bring them down into the valley of Jehoshaphat, and will plead with them there for my people and *for* my heritage Israel, whom they have scattered among the nations, and parted my land.

3 And they have cast lots for my people; and have given a boy for an harlot, and sold a girl for wine, that they might drink.

4 Yea, and what have ye to do with me, O Tyre, and Zidon, and all the coasts of Palestine? will ye render me a recompence? and if ye recompense me, swiftly *and* speedily will I return your recompence upon your own head;

5 Because ye have taken my silver and my gold, and have carried into your temples my goodly pleasant things:

6 The children also of Judah and the children of Jerusalem have ye sold unto the Grecians, that ye might remove them far from their border.

7 Behold, I will raise them out of the place whither ye have sold them, and will return your recompence upon your own head:

8 And I will sell your sons and your daughters into the hand of the children of Judah, and they shall sell them to the Sabeans, to a people far off: for the LORD hath spoken *it*.

9 ¶ Proclaim ye this among the Gentiles; Prepare war, wake up the mighty men, let all the men of war draw near; let them come up:

10 Beat your plowshares into swords, and your pruninghooks into spears: let the weak say, I *am* strong.

11 Assemble yourselves, and come, all ye heathen, and gather yourselves together round about: thither cause thy mighty ones to come down, O LORD.

Why are agricultural tools to be turned into weapons? (3:10) "This is quite a different preparatory period than some, even among the elect, have supposed would exist prior to the Second Coming. This coming will not be ushered in by righteousness, but by wickedness. . . . Indeed, the great battle of Armageddon itself will be in progress when the Lord comes. . . . This is said of the last days; it is the opposite of what shall be the millennial day when men shall beat their swords into plowshares and their spears into pruning hooks and shall not learn war anymore at all. . . . [The Lord] will come in the day of war and desolation; then he will judge all men and divide the sheep from the goats" (McConkie, *Millennial Messiah*, 372).

12 Let the heathen be wakened, and come up to the valley of Jehoshaphat: for there will I sit to judge all the heathen round about.

13 Put ye in the sickle, for the harvest is ripe: come, get you down; for the press is full, the fats overflow; for their wickedness *is* great.

How will the Lord judge the heathen nations? (3:12–13) "In Joel's visionary scene, the nations are gathered together for war, but it does not appear that they fight—either against each other or against the Lord's Saints, who are not mentioned. Instead, it is the Lord alone who contends against the world. 'Put ye in the sickle,' Joel wrote, 'for the harvest is ripe.' He invites them to trample down the grapes in the overflowing winepress, 'for their wickedness is great' (Joel 3:13). As was revealed to the Prophet Joseph Smith, when Christ returns he will be 'red in his apparel, and his garments like him that treadeth in the wine-vat' [D&C 133:48, 50–51]" (Jackson, "Book of Joel," 364).

14 Multitudes, multitudes in the valley of decision: for the day of the LORD *is* near in the valley of decision.

15 The sun and the moon shall be darkened, and the stars shall withdraw their shining.

What will happen in the "valley of decision"? (3:14) "The Lord challenges the Gentiles and the heathens (those who worship other gods) to come to the valley of decision, where he will sit to judge the nations (Joel 3:9–14). . . . The decision of who is the true Messiah and God of the nations of all the earth will be rendered. While many multitudes will be gathered, they will be no match for the God of the whole earth" (Nyman and Nyman, *Words of the Twelve Prophets*, 43–44). ⊕

16 The LORD also shall roar out of Zion, and utter his voice from Jerusalem; and the heavens and the earth shall shake: but the LORD *will be* the hope of his people, and the strength of the children of Israel.

17 So shall ye know that I *am* the LORD your God dwelling in Zion, my holy mountain: then shall Jerusalem be holy, and there shall no strangers pass through her any more.

How is the Lord the "hope of His people"? (3:16) "Hope sustains us through despair. Hope teaches that there is reason to rejoice even when all seems dark around us.

"With Jeremiah I proclaim, 'Blessed is the man . . . whose hope the Lord is' [Jer. 17:7].

"With Joel I testify, 'The Lord [is] the hope of his people, and the strength of the children of Israel' [Joel 3:16]. . . .

"This is the quality of hope we must cherish and develop. Such a mature hope comes in and through our Savior Jesus Christ, for 'every man that hath this hope in him purifieth himself, even as [the Savior] is pure' [1 John 3:3]" (Uchtdorf, "Infinite Power of Hope," 24).

What changes will occur after the destruction of the wicked? (3:16–21) After the Lord causes the heavens and the earth to shake, "all shall know that Jehovah is God, 'dwelling in Zion,' and 'then shall Jerusalem be holy,' subject to no more invasions. The earth will be renewed, well-watered, and productive. Former nations shall exist no more, but the righteous who have been cleansed will belong to the kingdom of Zion (Joel 3:17–21)" (Rasmussen, *Latter-day Saint Commentary on the Old Testament*, 642).

What blessings will come to the land of Judah as water flows from the house of the Lord? (3:18) "The future abundance of Jerusalem, described in terms of Edenic lushness (v.18), stands in stark contrast to the conditions of drought and famine in [Joel 1:10]. Flowing from God's presence at the Jerusalem temple, streams of blessing will refresh His people and make their place endlessly fruitful (see Pss. 36:8; 87:7; Ezek. 47:1–12; Rev. 22:1–2)" (*Zondervan KJV Commentary*, 1123).

18 ¶ And it shall come to pass in that day, *that* the mountains shall drop down new wine, and the hills shall flow with milk, and all the rivers of Judah shall flow with waters, and a fountain shall come forth of the house of the LORD, and shall water the valley of Shittim.

19 Egypt shall be a desolation, and Edom shall be a desolate wilderness, for the violence *against* the children of Judah, because they have shed innocent blood in their land.

20 But Judah shall dwell for ever, and Jerusalem from generation to generation.

21 For I will cleanse their blood *that* I have not cleansed: for the LORD dwelleth in Zion.

AMOS

Introduction

The name *Amos* means "burden" (see Bible Dictionary, "Amos"). This seems particularly appropriate for a prophet called to prophesy against a people who were in danger of suffering the judgments of God. Amos "prophesied in the days of Uzziah, king of Judah (died about 740 B.C.), and Jeroboam II, king of Israel (died about 750 B.C.). He was a shepherd (Amos 1:1; 7:14) and a native of Tekoa, 12 miles south of Jerusalem, but his ministry was among those of the northern kingdom of Israel" (Bible Dictionary, "Amos"). "As a wool producer, he probably made trips into the northern towns of Israel and saw the religious and social corruption which he strongly rebuked" (Ludlow, *Unlocking the Old Testament*, 208).

Interestingly, "Amos prophesied during two of the longest-lasting, most competent, most prosperous kings in both the north . . . and the south [which makes him contemporary with Hosea, Jonah, Micah, and Isaiah]. Both kingdoms were prosperous, stable, and expanding at this time. Yet their wickedness meant that great problems were near at hand, and Amos warned them of this" (Muhlestein, *Scripture Study Made Simple*, 501). "Amos spoke out against the empty ritualism of a people who, in time of material prosperity, had lost sight of justice and were indifferent to the plight of the poor and the oppressed" (*Revell Bible Dictionary*, 58).

Amos' message also included "a wholesale condemnation of all the nations surrounding the Dead Sea and the Sea of Galilee, Israel and Judah being threatened the most. Indeed, their punishment would be the greater because they had rejected the greater light. This punishment would stop short of total destruction and in the last days the kingdom would not only be restored but would surpass its ancient glory" (Pearson, *Old Testament*, 65).

"[The] nine chapters [of the book of Amos] are one unit; perhaps they are the speech he delivered 'at Bethel . . . the king's chapel' (Amos 7:10–13). . . . The book of Amos is acclaimed for its religious and humanitarian teachings and also for its literary excellence in Hebrew. . . . Amos wrote as divine inspiration worked in and with his clear and active mind" (Rasmussen, *Latter-day Saint Commentary on the Old Testament*, 642, 643).

CHAPTERS 1–2

Amos shows the Lord's judgments upon Syria, the Philistines, Tyre, Edom, and Ammon.

The Lord will pour out judgments upon Moab, Judah, and Israel for their unrighteousness.

Summary of Amos 1–2

Prophecies and judgments against Israel and the surrounding countries are promised upon its inhabitants if they don't turn to the Lord. The two great commandments of loving God and loving your neighbor are emphasized in these two chapters.

Amos 3:1–8. The Lord Reveals His Secrets to His Prophets

Why does the Lord speak of punishing Israel while describing His closeness with them? (3:1–2) This declaration demonstrates Heavenly Father's foreordained knowledge and love for the house of Israel. Because God had chosen and prepared them for His work throughout their history, Israel was accountable for their actions. A similar principle is taught in Doctrine and Covenants 82:3: "For of him unto whom much is given much is required; and he who sins against the greater light shall receive the greater condemnation" (see also Alma 9:18–24).

How did the Joseph Smith Translation correct this verse and hence our understanding of God? (3:6) The Joseph Smith Translation corrected the phrase "hath not done it" to "hath not *known* it" (Amos 3:6*b*). "Does judgment come by chance? By a series of rhetorical questions, in which the answer is obviously, 'No,' Amos expresses the climactic truth that evil or punishment does not come to a city without God's knowing about it. God reveals it to the prophets. And when God speaks to a prophet, who can help but prophesy? Consequently Amos has no alternative. God has spoken to him. He is under divine compulsion to speak God's word" (Schultz, *Old Testament Speaks* [4th edition], 384).

What is meant by the "secrets" God reveals to His servants? (3:7) "The Hebrew word translated 'secret' in this passage is *sod*, which means 'council,' as well as 'counsel, plan.' Thus the Lord taught Amos that the privilege of a prophet was to take part in the heavenly *council* in order to learn the will and *counsel* of the Lord" (Holzapfel, et al., *Jehovah and the World of the Old Testament*, 262). It is also helpful to know that the Joseph Smith Translation changes the word *but* to *until*. It is comforting to know that God will do nothing until He reveals His secrets to His servants the prophets. ⊕

CHAPTER 3

The Lord reveals His secrets unto His servants the prophets—Because Israel rejects the prophets and follows evil, the nation is overwhelmed by an adversary.

1 Hear this word that the LORD hath spoken against you, O children of Israel, against the whole family which I brought up from the land of Egypt, saying,

2 You only have I known of all the families of the earth: therefore I will punish you for all your iniquities.

3 Can two walk together, except they be agreed?

4 Will a lion roar in the forest, when he hath no prey? will a young lion cry out of his den, if he have taken nothing?

5 Can a bird fall in a snare upon the earth, where no gin *is* for him? shall *one* take up a snare from the earth, and have taken nothing at all?

6 Shall a trumpet be blown in the city, and the people not be afraid? shall there be evil in a city, and the LORD hath not done *it?*

7 Surely the Lord GOD will do nothing, but he revealeth his secret unto his servants the prophets.

8 The lion hath roared, who will not fear? the Lord GOD hath spoken, who can but prophesy?

9 ¶ Publish in the palaces at Ashdod, and
in the palaces in the land of Egypt, and say,
Assemble yourselves upon the mountains of
Samaria, and behold the great tumults in the
midst thereof, and the oppressed in the midst
thereof.

10 For they know not to do right, saith the
LORD, who store up violence and robbery in
their palaces.

11 Therefore thus saith the Lord GOD; An
adversary *there shall be* even round about the
land; and he shall bring down thy strength
from thee, and thy palaces shall be spoiled.

12 Thus saith the LORD; As the shepherd taketh out of the mouth of the lion two legs, or
a piece of an ear; so shall the children of Israel
be taken out that dwell in Samaria in the corner of a bed, and in Damascus *in* a couch.

13 Hear ye, and testify in the house of Jacob,
saith the Lord GOD, the God of hosts,

14 That in the day that I shall visit the transgressions of Israel upon him I will also visit
the altars of Beth-el: and the horns of the altar shall be cut off, and fall to the ground.

15 And I will smite the winter house with
the summer house; and the houses of ivory
shall perish, and the great houses shall have
an end, saith the LORD.

Amos 3:9–15. Israel Rejects the Prophets

What great tumult did Amos prophesy that people would eventually witness "upon the mountains of Samaria" (the capital of the kingdom of Israel)? (3:9–11) "Amos, speaking in the 760s, may have assumed that the Assyrians would ultimately serve as God's instrument to punish Israel, but he does not state this explicitly. In any case, Samaria and the nation of Israel will fall to the Assyrian armies of Sargon II in 722, and much of the population will be deported to other portions of the Assyrian empire" (Walton, et al., *IVP Bible Background Commentary*, 768). ⊕

What do we learn from Amos' use of imagery in this passage? (3:12–14) "Amos used vivid imagery to show that scarcely any would escape and those who did would do so with extreme difficulty. It is like a shepherd who can recover no more of a sheep carried away by a lion than two of its legs or a piece of its ear, just enough to prove that they belonged to his sheep" (*Old Testament Student Manual: 1 Kings–Malachi*, 92). In that day the Lord would no longer protect Israel from her enemies, as symbolized by the cutting off of the horns of the altar.

What were "houses of ivory"? (3:15) "The wicked king Ahab had made an ivory house (1 Kgs. 22:39) which apparently had become a symbol of decadence and wickedness by the days of Amos" (Ludlow, *Companion to Your Study of the Old Testament*, 370–71).

Summary of Amos 4–6

The people of Israel, especially their leaders, were deaf to the prophet Amos' warnings. Not even threats of famine and pestilence moved them to change. Therefore, Amos decries Israel because they oppress the poor. The Lord continually asks them to return unto Him. If they do not repent, they will be overthrown like Sodom and Gomorrah. Israel continues to offer empty rituals such as burnt offerings and meat offerings but they are not accepted by the Lord. Amos warns, "Woe to them that are at ease in Zion" (Amos 6:1).

Summary of Amos 7

Amos receives a series of visions that reveal a prophetic warning to the people of Israel. Here Amos sees destructive grasshoppers (see Amos 7:1–3), a raging fire (see Amos 7:4–6), and a plumb line that measures the land of Israel, which will be laid waste by the Lord (see Amos 7:7–9). The chapter concludes with a confrontation Amos has with the priest of Bethel.

Amos 8:1–3. Amos Sees the End of the Nation of Israel

Why did Amos see a vision of "summer fruit"?

(8:1–3) "An object was shown in this fourth vision (the first three are recorded in Amos 7:1–9), the name of which [reminded] the prophet of the imminence of Israel's fall. Indeed, if the translation were slightly varied to 'a basket of *fall* fruit; . . . the *fall* is come upon my people of Israel,' the original wordplay in Hebrew would be preserved. The prophet foresaw more than the capture and scattering of the ten tribes of northern Israel, for he spoke of lamentation in the temple and 'dead bodies in every place'; evidently, the fall of Judah . . . was included in Amos's general vision of the 'fall' of the people Israel (Amos 8:1–3)" (Rasmussen, *Latter-day Saint Commentary on the Old Testament*, 648–49).

CHAPTERS 4–6

The Lord withholds rain, sends famine and pestilence, and destroys gardens and vineyards as judgments upon His people, yet they do not return unto the Lord.

The people of Israel are exhorted to seek the Lord and do good so that they may live—Their sacrifices to false gods are abhorrent.

Woe to them who are at ease in Zion—Israel will be plagued with desolation.

CHAPTER 7

Amos relates how he was called of God to be a prophet—He prophesies the captivity of Israel.

CHAPTER 8

Amos prophesies the downfall of Israel—There will be a famine of hearing the word of the Lord.

1 Thus hath the Lord GOD shewed unto me: and behold a basket of summer fruit.

2 And he said, Amos, what seest thou? And I said, A basket of summer fruit. Then said the LORD unto me, The end is come upon my people of Israel; I will not again pass by them any more.

3 And the songs of the temple shall be howlings in that day, saith the Lord GOD: *there shall be* many dead bodies in every place; they shall cast *them* forth with silence.

4 ¶ Hear this, O ye that swallow up the needy, even to make the poor of the land to fail,

5 Saying, When will the new moon be gone, that we may sell corn? and the sabbath, that we may set forth wheat, making the ephah small, and the shekel great, and falsifying the balances by deceit?

6 That we may buy the poor for silver, and the needy for a pair of shoes; *yea,* and sell the refuse of the wheat?

7 The LORD hath sworn by the excellency of Jacob, Surely I will never forget any of their works.

8 Shall not the land tremble for this, and every one mourn that dwelleth therein? and it shall rise up wholly as a flood; and it shall be cast out and drowned, as *by* the flood of Egypt.

9 And it shall come to pass in that day, saith the Lord GOD, that I will cause the sun to go down at noon, and I will darken the earth in the clear day:

10 And I will turn your feasts into mourning, and all your songs into lamentation; and I will bring up sackcloth upon all loins, and baldness upon every head; and I will make it as the mourning of an only *son,* and the end thereof as a bitter day.

11 ¶ Behold, the days come, saith the Lord GOD, that I will send a famine in the land, not a famine of bread, nor a thirst for water, but of hearing the words of the LORD:

12 And they shall wander from sea to sea, and from the north even to the east, they shall run to and fro to seek the word of the LORD, and shall not find *it.*

Amos 8:4–10. Amos Gives the Reasons for Israel's Destruction

In what ways can we fail the poor and needy? (8:4–6) "Ancient and modern scriptures are clear in their commands to care for the poor and the needy. . . .

"[President] Nelson has observed that 'when the Lord sent prophets to call Israel back from apostasy, in almost every instance, one of the first charges made was that the poor had been neglected.' ["In the Lord's Own Way," *Ensign*, May 1986, 25]. . . .

"The prophet/king Benjamin declared that we must impart of our substance to the poor, 'such as feeding the hungry, clothing the naked, visiting the sick and administering to their relief' for the sake of 'retaining a remission of [our] sins from day to day, that [we] may walk guiltless before God.' (Mosiah 4:26.)" (Oaks, *Lord's Way*, 102–3).

What actions brought this condemnation from Amos? (8:5) "Man is waiting for the day of sanctity to come to an end so that cheating and exploitation can be resumed. This is a stunning condemnation. We are ready to judge a ritual act on its own merit. Properly performed, its value is undisputed. Yet, the prophet speaks with derision of those who combine ritual with iniquity" (Heschel, *Prophets,* 31). ⊕

What was signified by this prophesied event? (8:9–10) "God's judgment would be a great reversal—of light to darkness and joy to mourning" (*Nelson Study Bible* [NKJV], 1486). Among the superstitious people of the time, "a solar eclipse portends divine punishment and elicits mourning rituals. *Sackcloth* and *baldness* were customary expressions of mourning associated with national disaster (e.g., Isa 22.12)" (*New Oxford Annotated Bible Commentary* [2010], 1295).

Amos 8:11–14. Amos Prophesies of a Famine of the Word of God

For what was Israel so desperately searching? (8:11–12) "Here again one finds a clear case of prophetic dualism. Amos predicted a famine for the word of the Lord, which famine certainly occurred during the period of apostasy in Israel and Judah. The hardness of their hearts reached such a state that from 400 B.C. until the ministry of John the Baptist, which began in A.D. 30, as far as we know there were no prophets in Israel. . . .

"But Amos's prophecy was also fulfilled at a later time. After Christ reestablished his Church on earth, it too eventually fell into apostasy. Again revelation ceased, and there was a great famine for the word of God, this famine lasting for well over a thousand years" (*Old Testament Student Manual: 1 Kings–Malachi*, 94). ⊕

When was Amos' prophecy of a famine of God's words fulfilled? (8:11–12) "The apostasy of the early Christian church after the death of the apostles is sometimes referred to as the Great Apostasy because of its duration (more than a millennium and a half) and its depth. It was foreseen by ancient prophets (Amos 8:11–12; Isaiah 24:5), was universal in scope, and was a time when the powers of God and the doctrines of salvation were either not on earth or existed in an altered form" (Millet, "Apostasy, Great," 46). ⊕

Summary of Amos 9

Amos concludes his book with statements of hope for Israel. He promises them God's mercy if they change their ways and turn to the Lord. Their hope would be fulfilled with the Lord gathering Israel together in the last days.

13 In that day shall the fair virgins and young men faint for thirst.

14 They that swear by the sin of Samaria, and say, Thy god, O Dan, liveth; and, The manner of Beer-sheba liveth; even they shall fall, and never rise up again.

CHAPTER 9

Israel will be sifted among all nations—In the last days, the people of Israel will be gathered again into their own land, and it will become productive.

OBADIAH

Introduction

"Obadiah was a seer who was privileged to see in vision the salvation of Israel and other important events of the latter days" (*Old Testament Student Manual: 1 Kings–Malachi*, 258). "Nothing is known of the prophet for whom the book is named, although Obadiah most likely lived in Judah about the time of Jeremiah, Lehi, and their contemporaries. The Edom against which he prophesied is now known as Petra, the mountainous region southeast of the Dead Sea. . . . *Obadiah*, a Hebrew name, translates as 'servant of [Jehovah]' or 'worshiper of [Jehovah].' Thus *Obadiah* could be an appellation such as *Malachi* ('messenger') or *Theophilus* ('friend of God') instead of a personal name. If *Obadiah* is just an appellation, then almost any righteous servant of God could have been inspired to write this prophecy. This is possible, but it is more likely that a prophet named Obadiah wrote the text" (Gillum, "Obadiah's Vision of Saviors on Mount Zion," 122–23).

"Although there is no direct evidence in the text to accurately date the book, scholars usually date this prophecy to the period immediately after the Babylonian destruction of Jerusalem (586 B.C.) because Edom rejoiced (Lam 4:21) and assisted in Jerusalem's demise (Ps 137:7; Ezek 25:12)" (Holzapfel, et al., *Jehovah and the World of the Old Testament*, 315).

The twenty-one verses in Obadiah can be "divided into three parts. Part one, verses 1–9, contains the prophecy of Obadiah about the judgment and destruction of Edom (see Jer. 49:7–22). Part two, verses 10–14, gives the rationale for judgment against Edom. . . . Part three, verses 15–21, tells of future events when God will impart judgment and salvation to restore Israel" (Black, *400 Questions and Answers about the Old Testament*, 205).

Obadiah's prophecy "had a message for ancient Israel and her prophets. It also inspired Christ's beloved apostle, John [who used similar words and phrases in the book of Revelation]. It can also edify us today as it encourages us to become saviors on Mount Zion lest we want to suffer as did the ancient Edomites" (Ludlow, *Unlocking the Old Testament*, 211).

CHAPTER 1

Obadiah prophesies the downfall of Edom—Saviors will stand upon Mount Zion.

1 The vision of Obadiah. Thus saith the Lord GOD concerning Edom; We have heard a rumour from the LORD, and an ambassador is sent among the heathen, Arise ye, and let us rise up against her in battle.

Obadiah 1:1–9. Obadiah Warns the People of Edom of Their Pride

What is the significance of the vision of Obadiah? (1:1) "*The vision of Obadiah* implies . . . that Obadiah was a seer—seer in the sense that he saw the future with supernatural objectivity. . . . He was what the Hebrews called a *chozeh* or *gazer*. That Obadiah saw the salvation of Israel and other important events in the latter days may be in part responsible for the preservation of his little book" (Sperry, *Voice of Israel's Prophets*, 317).

In what way would Edom be a small and despised nation? (1:2) Clearly, despite her assumed safety, Edom's fortunes were about to change. When the Lord stated: "I have made thee small" (Obad. 1:2), He "does not refer to an accomplished overthrow of Edom, [but] refers to a divine determination already made. . . . *Small* and *despised* refer to the condition in which Edom will be left after the conquest by the nations" (*John Dummelow's Commentary* [on Obadiah 1:2]).

What danger was there for Edom in having too much confidence in their own safety? (1:3–4) "Edom's location was in the Arabah, south of the Dead Sea, with abundant ravines, cliffs, and caves (as at Petra). That terrain had given her a false sense of security. But she was about to be plundered more thoroughly than thieves could do, stripped more bare than harvesters in a vineyard would do, and utterly vanquished" (Rasmussen, *Latter-day Saint Commentary on the Old Testament*, 651–52). As Elder Neal A. Maxwell noted: "As surely as the proud elevate themselves in their own eyes, their neighbors disappear from view. The proud not only fail to look up to God, but the proud look down, if they look at all, on their neighbors" (*Neal A. Maxwell Quote Book*, 266).

What do thieves and grape gatherers searching for hidden things suggest about Edom's future? (1:5–7) "Edom was known for its fine mountain-side vineyards. The destruction of the country is likened to the double despoilings of thieves and gleaners. What the thieves and harvesters leave, the gleaners will take. All that will remain is the rotten and crushed fruit left on the ground. . . . This phrase [KJV, 'hidden things'] occurs only here in the Old Testament. . . . What is indicated by the text is the thoroughness of the plundering of Edom. Secret treasures ['hidden

2 Behold, I have made thee small among the
heathen: thou art greatly despised.

3 ¶ The pride of thine heart hath deceived
thee, thou that dwellest in the clefts of the
rock, whose habitation *is* high; that saith in
his heart, Who shall bring me down to the
ground?
4 Though thou exalt *thyself* as the eagle, and
though thou set thy nest among the stars,
thence will I bring thee down, saith the LORD.

5 If thieves came to thee, if robbers by night,
(how art thou cut off!) would they not have
stolen till they had enough? if the grape-
gatherers came to thee, would they not leave
some grapes?
6 How are *the things* of Esau searched out!
how are his hidden things sought up!

What Do We Know about the Nation of Edom? (Obadiah 1:1)

"The name Edom was given to Esau, the first-born son of Isaac and twin brother of Jacob, when he sold his birthright to the latter for a meal of lentil pottage. The country which the Lord subsequently gave to Esau was hence called 'the country of Edom,' Gen. 32:3, and his descendants were called Edomites. Edom was called *Mount Seir* and Idumea also" (*Smith's Bible Dictionary*, "Edom, Idumea").

"The Edomites were neighbors to Judah and lived in the area south of the Dead Sea. We are told that they were the descendants of Esau, the brother of Jacob (Gen. 36:1; 1 Chron. 1:35–43) and were therefore blood relatives of the Israelites. During the early part of Israel's existence, it appears that there were peaceful relations between the two nations, but with time hostilities developed, especially after David and his army attacked Edom (2 Sam. 8:13–14).

"In Obadiah's revelation, the Edomites were told that they were 'greatly despised' (Obad. 1:2). In their pride they believed that they were secure and that no one would harm them. This false security was about to end. In verse 5 we learn that their destruction would be complete. . . . By the second century B.C. there was no longer an Edomite state" (Matthews, "Book of Obadiah," 265).

7 All the men of thy confederacy have brought
thee *even* to the border: the men that were at
peace with thee have deceived thee, *and* prevailed against thee; *they that eat* thy bread have
laid a wound under thee: *there is* none understanding in him.

8 Shall I not in that day, saith the LORD,
even destroy the wise *men* out of Edom, and
understanding out of the mount of Esau?

9 And thy mighty *men,* O Teman, shall be
dismayed, to the end that every one of the
mount of Esau may be cut off by slaughter.

10 ¶ For *thy* violence against thy brother
Jacob shame shall cover thee, and thou shalt
be cut off for ever.

11 In the day that thou stoodest on the other
side, in the day that the strangers carried away
captive his forces, and foreigners entered into
his gates, and cast lots upon Jerusalem, even
thou *wast* as one of them.

12 But thou shouldest not have looked on
the day of thy brother in the day that he became a stranger; neither shouldest thou have
rejoiced over the children of Judah in the day
of their destruction; neither shouldest thou
have spoken proudly in the day of distress.

13 Thou shouldest not have entered into the
gate of my people in the day of their calamity; yea, thou shouldest not have looked on
their affliction in the day of their calamity,
nor have laid *hands* on their substance in the
day of their calamity;

14 Neither shouldest thou have stood in the
crossway, to cut off those of his that did escape; neither shouldest thou have delivered
up those of his that did remain in the day of
distress.

15 For the day of the LORD *is* near upon all
the heathen: as thou hast done, it shall be
done unto thee: thy reward shall return upon
thine own head.

things'] were known in the ancient world, but this was especially appropriate to Edom, where, because of terrain, whole cities could be kept secret" (Walton, et al., *IVP Bible Background Commentary*, 776).

What was Teman known for? (1:8–9) According to Jeremiah 49:7, the worldly wisdom of the Temanites was well-known among the Israelites. Eliphaz, a Temanite, was the oldest and wisest of the three friends of Job (see *John Dummelow's Commentary* [on Obadiah 1:8, 9]; see also *NIV Study Bible* [1995], 1354).

Obadiah 1:10–16. Because of Her Sins, Edom Will Be Destroyed

Why was Edom condemned for standing "on the other side"? (1:11–15) The Edomites "had betrayed their brothers of the house of Israel and thus would 'be cut off for ever.' Apparently they had assisted the Babylonians in carrying away the captives of Jerusalem and destroying the city. The authors of Psalm 137 and Lamentations both wrote about the involvement of the Edomites in the downfall of Jerusalem (Ps. 137:7; Lam. 4:21–22). Verses 12 through 14 of Obadiah contain the Lord's witness against the Edomites. . . . God's judgment would be decisive. The Edomites would be treated as they treated Judah" (Matthews, "Book of Obadiah," 265–66). ⊕

What was Obadiah referring to by saying that "the day of the Lord is near upon the heathen"? (1:15) "The eternal law of consequences will eventually come upon the Edomites. As they have looted Israel (v. 13) the Israelites will eventually possess the lands of the Edomites" (Ludlow, *Companion to Your Study of the Old Testament*, 373).

What is meant by saying that the Edomites had "drunk upon my holy mountain"? (1:16) "The Edomites had apparently joined the drunken orgies of the Babylonians as they celebrated the destruction of the temple on Mount Zion. Now the Edomites and others that had desecrated God's holy place would have to drink a different beverage—the full cup of God's wrath. In fact, they would drink themselves into oblivion and disappear as a nation—as if they had never existed" (*Quest Study Bible* [2011], 1346).

Obadiah 1:17–21. The House of Israel Will Be Delivered in the Last Days

How does Obadiah contrast the future of both Israel and Edom? (1:17–20) "These verses have both a temporal and a spiritual meaning for Latter-day Saints. If Esau (Edom) represents the worldly wicked, these verses may be seen as referring to that day when Israel will be completely restored and evil eliminated. Mount Zion, a symbol for deliverance and holiness (see v. 17), will be the inheritance of the 'house of Jacob,' whereas the 'house of Esau' will be stubble, fit only to be burned" (*Old Testament Student Manual: 1 Kings–Malachi*, 259).

Who were "the house of Jacob" and "the house of Joseph"? (1:18) Here the "house of Jacob" refers to the southern kingdom of Judah. On the other hand, the northern kingdom of Israel "was frequently called 'Joseph' or 'Ephraim' in the scriptures—[and] was destroyed by the Assyrians. . . . Many of its people who survived the warfare were deported to other parts of the Assyrian empire (see 2 Kgs. 17:1–24), from which their descendants now have lost their identity and have become assimilated into the nations of the world" (Jackson, *Lost Tribes and Last Days*, 117). When the Lord comes again in devouring fire, Esau will be as stubble as all the wicked (see Mal. 4:1), and the houses of Ephraim and Jacob will be gathered once again to their lands (see Jer. 3:14; 16:14–16; see also D&C 133:27–35).

Who are the saviors on Mount Zion? (1:21) Joseph Smith referred to saviors on Mount Zion often. He testified this would be fulfilled in the last days: "But how are they to become saviors on Mount Zion? By building their temples, erecting their baptismal fonts, and going forth and receiving all the ordinances, baptisms, confirmations, washings, anointings, ordinations and sealing powers upon their heads, in behalf of all their progenitors who are dead, and redeem them that they may come forth in the first resurrection and be exalted to thrones of glory with them" (*Joseph Smith* [manual], 473).

16 For as ye have drunk upon my holy mountain, *so* shall all the heathen drink continually, yea, they shall drink, and they shall swallow down, and they shall be as though they had not been.

17 ¶ But upon mount Zion shall be deliverance, and there shall be holiness; and the house of Jacob shall possess their possessions.

18 And the house of Jacob shall be a fire, and the house of Joseph a flame, and the house of Esau for stubble, and they shall kindle in them, and devour them; and there shall not be *any* remaining of the house of Esau; for the LORD hath spoken *it*.

19 And *they of* the south shall possess the mount of Esau; and *they of* the plain the Philistines: and they shall possess the fields of Ephraim, and the fields of Samaria: and Benjamin *shall possess* Gilead.

20 And the captivity of this host of the children of Israel *shall possess* that of the Canaanites, *even* unto Zarephath; and the captivity of Jerusalem, which *is* in Sepharad, shall possess the cities of the south.

21 And saviours shall come up on mount Zion to judge the mount of Esau; and the kingdom shall be the LORD's.

JONAH

Introduction

"The prophet Jonah was an unusual servant of the Lord. Jonah was called on a mission very similar to that of other prophets: he was to cry repentance to a people ripening in iniquity. Unlike other prophets, however, Jonah responded by attempting to flee from his assignment. Had his reason been cowardice, though still wrong, it would have been understandable. The brutality of the Assyrians in the treatment of their enemies was well known. But Jonah's problem does not seem to be cowardice. Rather, it seems to have been resentment against the Lord for giving the hated enemy a chance to repent (see Jonah 4:1–2).

"To someone who has been taught to have Christian love for all men, Jonah's attitude may seem almost unbelievable. But to an Israelite who had been taught that he was of the chosen people and that the Gentiles were corrupt and therefore not acceptable to God, Jonah's attitude was more understandable. Though surprising because we expect a different response from the Lord's prophets, Jonah's response was very human" (*Old Testament Student Manual: 1 Kings–Malachi*, 97).

"It is most probable that this book . . . was not written by the person whose name it bears but about him. This is not to say that Jonah was not a historical figure, but that he did not author the material we now have; that a later author used this well-known story to make a point to people living long after Jonah's day. This probably accounts for the fact that this book is different (containing only one verse of prophecy, the rest being history) than any of the others belonging to the minor prophets" (Pearson, *Old Testament*, 66).

"There are various interpretations of Jonah among modern scholars. Most are content to read this story as a parable or allegory, arguing that the exaggerations in the text seem more like satire than history. . . . Jonah's description of the Ninevites as well as their beasts fasting and repenting in sackcloth and ashes seems to be hyperbole and is not attested to anywhere outside the Bible. Some people, including most Latter-day Saints, continue to believe in the historical interpretation that Jonah was a real prophet who made a journey to Nineveh and preached repentance there" (Holzapfel, et al., *Jehovah and the World of the Old Testament*, 278).

In four short chapters, Jonah teaches "much about the nature of God and man and ultimately has something profound to say about . . . the relationship between a man and his Maker. . . . Because we recognize ourselves in Jonah, we initially smile at his humanness—but by the end we are sobered, as we, like Jonah, are humbled by the grace of God and come to recognize our own hidden duplicities" (Seely, "Book of Jonah," 46).

"The key to the book is to be found in Jonah 3:10–4:11 in the reasons the prophet gives for his flight and unwillingness to preach at Nineveh. The writer is opposing a narrowmindedness that would confine the love of God to a single nation. He shows that Jehovah reigns everywhere, over sea and land; even in the gentile world the minds of men are conscious of sin and prepared to acknowledge that Jehovah is God. The book is a beautiful poem, whether it paints the humanity of the gentile sailors; the mourning of the prophet over the decay of the grass of the field; or the divine tenderness in ministering to the prophet with his imperfect conceptions or in pitying the little children of Nineveh" (Bible Dictionary, "Jonah").

CHAPTER 1

Jonah is sent to call Nineveh to repentance—He flees on a ship, is cast into the sea, and is swallowed by a great fish.

1 Now the word of the LORD came unto Jonah the son of Amittai, saying,

2 Arise, go to Nineveh, that great city, and cry against it; for their wickedness is come up before me.

3 But Jonah rose up to flee unto Tarshish from the presence of the LORD, and went down to Joppa; and he found a ship going to Tarshish: so he paid the fare thereof, and went down into it, to go with them unto Tarshish from the presence of the LORD.

Jonah 1:1–3. Jonah Is Called to Preach in Nineveh and Runs Away

What values and truths are gained by studying the book of Jonah? (1:1) "Many wonder if the story of Jonah is real, especially because of the fantastic element of surviving inside a fish and then getting the city of Nineveh to repent. Other scriptural references to Jonah, including those spoken by the Savior, lend a sense of authenticity (see 2 Kings 14:25; Matt. 12:39–41; 16:4). Furthermore, the Lord has brought about greater miracles than survival inside a fish and the repentance of a large, foreign city. . . . The crucial things are the lessons and messages of the story" (Muhlestein, *Essential Old Testament Companion*, 498).

Where was Nineveh and why was Jonah commanded to preach there? (1:2) "Nineveh was an enormous city in Assyria, which served from time to time as the capital city of the great Assyrian Empire. The ruins of Nineveh are situated beside the River Tigris, just across the river from the modern city of Mosul in Northern Iraq. Excavations . . . have laid bare the splendor of the city that once was. . . . The undoubted grandeur that once typified the physical ambience of Nineveh was no guide, however, to its moral character. The writer describes its character simply as 'wickedness.' . . . But evil of all kinds was a matter of concern to God" (Craigie, "Jonah," in *Twelve Prophets*, 1:215–16). The Lord appointed Jonah to warn wicked Nineveh of its coming destruction.

Why might Jonah have run from God? (1:3) "The Israelite Jonah's attempted flight from the Lord (Jonah 1:3) was motivated by his angry refusal to accept that God in his kindness and mercy would accept Gentiles into his kingdom (4:1, 4, 9). Jonah's view that Gentiles were unworthy of a chance for eternal reward is reflected in the anger of first-hour laborers Jesus taught about in his New Testament parable of the laborers [see Matt. 20:1–16]. . . . All of the worldwide missionary work among Gentile nations, conducted both in the primitive Church and also in these latter days, can be seen as being foreshadowed in Jonah's calling to preach to the foreign people of Nineveh" (Scott, "Book of Jonah," 163).

Where was Tarshish located? (1:3) "The exact location of the Tarshish to which Jonah was fleeing is not known, although some scholars believe it was Tartessus in the southwestern part of what is now

Spain. It is clear from Jonah's account that Tarshish could be reached most easily by sea and it was not in the direction of Nineveh" (Ludlow, *Companion to Your Study of the Old Testament*, 376). The city represented the most distant place known to the Israelites: Jonah tried to escape his calling by traveling as far as he could go in the opposite direction.

4 ¶ But the LORD sent out a great wind into
the sea, and there was a mighty tempest in
the sea, so that the ship was like to be broken.
5 Then the mariners were afraid, and cried
every man unto his god, and cast forth the
wares that *were* in the ship into the sea, to
lighten *it* of them. But Jonah was gone down
into the sides of the ship; and he lay, and was
fast asleep.
6 So the shipmaster came to him, and said
unto him, What meanest thou, O sleeper?
arise, call upon thy God, if so be that God
will think upon us, that we perish not.
7 And they said every one to his fellow,
Come, and let us cast lots, that we may know
for whose cause this evil *is* upon us. So they
cast lots, and the lot fell upon Jonah.
8 Then said they unto him, Tell us, we pray
thee, for whose cause this evil *is* upon us;
What *is* thine occupation? and whence comest
thou? what *is* thy country? and of what people
art thou?

Jonah 1:4–10. A Great Storm Arises on the Sea

How was Jonah humbled by the sailors asking him to pray? (1:6) "In this and succeeding passages there is most delicious irony. Instead of Jonah preaching to the heathen, God is preaching to Jonah by means of a heathen. Imagine one of these despised people calling upon a Hebrew prophet to pray! The watchman on the tower of Zion had fallen asleep at his post. Lots were cast, and it was determined that Jonah was the cause of the trouble to the ship. Jonah's conscience smote him, and he asked to be thrown into the sea; all would be quiet then. Like the Prodigal Son he 'came to himself' at last—least in part. What a fine thing it is when men find their better selves" (Sperry, *Voice of Israel's Prophets*, 330–31).

How did casting lots expose Jonah to the other sailors? (1:7) "In ancient times lots were cast when an impartial decision was desired. . . . The heathens cast lots because, they believed, the gods would guide what happened. In Jonah's case, the Lord seems to have guided the outcome" (*Old Testament Student Manual: 1 Kings–Malachi*, 98).

Why might the sailors have been frightened when Jonah identified himself? (1:9–10) "The label of *Hebrew* identifies him as one of the chosen people—a member of the covenant community of Israel bound to the Lord. . . . His 'fear' of the Lord God who hath made the 'sea and the dry land' ([which] is tantamount to saying 'everything') is a statement of belief—in opposition to the polytheism of his day—in one universal God, who created and thus controls all of creation. The disobedience of a simple Hebrew is enough to bring about this calamity, even in 'international waters.' How could one professing such a belief ever hope to escape from the presence of such an omnipresent Being?" (Seely, "Book of Jonah," 47).

Jonah 1:11–17. Jonah Is Cast into the Sea and Swallowed by a Great Fish

Why did Jonah demand to be cast into the sea? (1:12) "Jonah knew that the only way for the storm to abate was for the sailors to toss him overboard. Jonah was ready to die. . . . His words, *because of me* [KJV, 'for my sake'], are an admission of guilt and show a sense of resignation" (*Nelson Study Bible* [NKJV], 1496).

How is it possible that Jonah was swallowed by a great fish and survived? (1:17) "Are we to reject it as being an impossibility and say that the Lord could not prepare a fish, or whale, to swallow Jonah? . . . Surely the Lord sits in the heavens and laughs at the wisdom of the scoffer, and then on a sudden answers his folly by a repetition of the miracle in dispute, or by the presentation of one still greater. . . .

9 And he said unto them, I *am* an Hebrew; and I fear the LORD, the God of heaven, which hath made the sea and the dry *land.*

10 Then were the men exceedingly afraid, and said unto him, Why hast thou done this? For the men knew that he fled from the presence of the LORD, because he had told them.

11 ¶ Then said they unto him, What shall we do unto thee, that the sea may be calm unto us? for the sea wrought, and was tempestuous.

12 And he said unto them, Take me up, and cast me forth into the sea; so shall the sea be calm unto you: for I know that for my sake this great tempest *is* upon you.

13 Nevertheless the men rowed hard to bring *it* to the land; but they could not: for the sea wrought, and was tempestuous against them.

14 Wherefore they cried unto the LORD, and said, We beseech thee, O LORD, we beseech thee, let us not perish for this man's life, and lay not upon us innocent blood: for thou, O LORD, hast done as it pleased thee.

15 So they took up Jonah, and cast him forth into the sea: and the sea ceased from her raging.

16 Then the men feared the LORD exceedingly, and offered a sacrifice unto the LORD, and made vows.

17 ¶ Now the LORD had prepared a great fish to swallow up Jonah. And Jonah was in the belly of the fish three days and three nights.

CHAPTER 2

Jonah prays to the Lord, and the fish vomits him out on dry ground.

1 Then Jonah prayed unto the LORD his God out of the fish's belly,

2 And said, I cried by reason of mine affliction unto the LORD, and he heard me; out of the belly of hell cried I, *and* thou heardest my voice.

3 For thou hadst cast me into the deep, in the midst of the seas; and the floods compassed me about: all thy billows and thy waves passed over me.

4 Then I said, I am cast out of thy sight; yet I will look again toward thy holy temple.

5 The waters compassed me about, *even* to the soul: the depth closed me round about, the weeds were wrapped about my head.

6 I went down to the bottoms of the mountains; the earth with her bars *was* about me for ever: yet hast thou brought up my life from corruption, O LORD my God.

"I believe . . . the story of Jonah. My chief reason for so believing is not in the fact that it is recorded in the *Bible,* or that the incident has been duplicated in our day, but in the fact that *Jesus Christ, our Lord, believed it* [see Matt. 12:39–40]" (Smith, *Doctrines of Salvation,* 2:314). ⊕

What was notable about the time Jonah spent in the fish's belly? (1:17) "The story of Jonah was referred to by our Lord on two occasions when He was asked for a sign from heaven. In each case He gave 'the sign of the prophet Jonah,' the event in that prophet's life being a foreshadowing of Jesus' own death and resurrection (Matt. 12:39–41; 16:4; Luke 11:29–30)" (Bible Dictionary, "Jonah"). This sign was fulfilled after the death of Jesus Christ, when His body lay in the tomb for three days and nights (see Matt. 27:59–66). ⊕

Jonah 2:1–10. Jonah Prays and Is Delivered from the Belly of the Fish

What do we learn about Jonah through his prayer? (2:2) "Jonah's experience in the belly of the fish taught him to turn back to God. His prayer was one of sincere and meaningful repentance. The language Jonah used is similar to that used by Alma before he received forgiveness (see Alma 36:18). Jonah's promise to pay what 'I have vowed' (Jonah 2:9) is part of what is necessary to repent and be forgiven. These words show a desire and determination toward a new life and are symbolic of a rebirth or baptism (see also Romans 6:1–9)" (Valletta, et al., *Old Testament for Latter-day Saint Families,* 623).

Why does Jonah say, "I will look again toward thy holy temple"? (2:4) "The thought that it is all over with him is met by the confidence of faith that he will still look to the holy temple of the Lord, that is to say, will once more approach the presence of the Lord, to worship before Him in His temple" (Keil and Delitzsch, *Commentary* [on Jonah 2:3–4]). Jonah's words reflect his worshipful desire to return to the Lord and no longer flee from Him.

What did Jonah learn about God through this experience? (2:7–9) "Jonah had begun to envision a broader scope to God's power: He knew God's grace was available to idol worshippers who turned from their idols (v. 8).... Though the Jews had a keen sense of being God's chosen people..., Jonah was beginning to discover that God is the God of all peoples. *Salvation comes from the LORD,* not on the basis of belonging to a particular ethnic background or nationality.

"Jonah found God in the belly of a great fish and again later in a wicked, pagan city—in both cases far from the 'holy land.' Jonah learned that God wanted to make himself known to all people everywhere—even the despised Ninevites" (*Quest Study Bible* [2003], 1326).

Jonah 3:1–10. Jonah Preaches in Nineveh and the People Repent

What does this second call to Jonah teach us about God's merciful nature? (3:1) "Throughout the story of Jonah we can see the very personal manner in which the Lord mercifully relates to His children.... We must not, however, mistake His mercy for a license to endlessly repeat our sins. President James E. Faust... has said: 'Many of us backslide, many stumble, and I believe firmly in the gospel of the second chance. But the gospel of the second chance means that having once been found weak,... thereafter we become steadfast' ['Stand Up and Be Counted,' 71]" (Uceda, "Jonah and the Second Chance," 29). When have you received second chances from the Lord? How have these experiences increased your desire to be obedient to Him?

How large was the city of Nineveh? (3:3) "The size of Nineveh is expressed in terms of the time that it would take Jonah to carry out his assignment. He is not circling the circumference of the walls [a distance of about eight miles] but going to all the public places in the city to make his proclamation. His itinerary would have included many of the dozen gate areas as well as several of the temple areas. There would have been certain times during the day when significant announcements could be made" (Walton, et al., *IVP Bible Background Commentary*, 779).

Why might idol worshippers believe Jonah to be a prophet of the true God? (3:5) "Here it is reported that the Ninevites *believed God* (v. 5), which may mean that the Ninevites genuinely turned to the Lord (see Matt. 12:41). On the other hand, their belief in God

7 When my soul fainted within me I remembered the LORD: and my prayer came in unto thee, into thine holy temple.

8 They that observe lying vanities forsake their own mercy.

9 But I will sacrifice unto thee with the voice of thanksgiving; I will pay *that* that I have vowed. Salvation *is* of the LORD.

10 ¶ And the LORD spake unto the fish, and it vomited out Jonah upon the dry *land.*

CHAPTER 3

Jonah prophesies the downfall of Nineveh—The people repent, and the city is saved.

1 And the word of the LORD came unto Jonah the second time, saying,

2 Arise, go unto Nineveh, that great city, and preach unto it the preaching that I bid thee.

3 So Jonah arose, and went unto Nineveh, according to the word of the LORD. Now Nineveh was an exceeding great city of three days' journey.

4 And Jonah began to enter into the city a day's journey, and he cried, and said, Yet forty days, and Nineveh shall be overthrown.

5 ¶ So the people of Nineveh believed God, and proclaimed a fast, and put on sackcloth, from the greatest of them even to the least of them.

6 For word came unto the king of Nineveh, and he arose from his throne, and he laid his robe from him, and covered *him* with sackcloth, and sat in ashes.

may have gone no deeper than had the sailors' fear of God (see 1:16). It is not likely that the people of Nineveh here experienced a genuine conversion to exclusive faith in the Lord God of Israel, but at least they took the prophet's warning seriously and acted accordingly. . . . The sparing of Nineveh should have taught Israel not only about the wideness of God's mercy but also about the readiness of God to respond with forgiveness to even minimal repentance over sin" (*Zondervan KJV Commentary*, 1148).

7 And he caused *it* to be proclaimed and published through Nineveh by the decree of the king and his nobles, saying, Let neither man nor beast, herd nor flock, taste any thing: let them not feed, nor drink water:

8 But let man and beast be covered with sackcloth, and cry mightily unto God: yea, let them turn every one from his evil way, and from the violence that *is* in their hands.

Why did the Assyrians withhold food from their animals? (3:7) This was a way to demonstrate the depth of the Ninevites' mourning. "Not only men of every rank and age, but the cattle likewise, horses and camels, they used either for their pleasure or business; their oxen, cows, and calves, of their herd; their sheep, goats, lambs, and kids, of their flocks. . . . No food [was] to be put into their mangers or folds: nor were they to be suffered to graze in their pastures, or to be allowed the least quantity of food or drink; this was ordered, to make the mourning the greater. . . . [The animals'] rich trappings were to be taken off, and sackcloth put upon them, for the greater solemnity, of the mourning" (*John Gill's Exposition of the Whole Bible*, [commentary on Jonah 3:7, 8]).

9 Who can tell *if* God will turn and repent, and turn away from his fierce anger, that we perish not?

10 ¶ And God saw their works, that they turned from their evil way; and God repented of the evil, that he had said that he would do unto them; and he did *it* not.

How does the Joseph Smith Translation help us understand the events in Nineveh? (3:9–10) The Joseph Smith Translation of Jonah 3:9–10 clarifies that the people of Nineveh declared, "*We* will repent, and *turn unto God*" (Jonah 3:9*a*) and that "God *turned away* the evil that he had said he would *bring upon them*" (Jonah 3:10*c*). The adjustments made to this passage by the Prophet Joseph Smith remind us that God does not need to repent.

CHAPTER 4

Jonah is displeased with the Lord for His mercy upon the people—The Lord rebukes him.

1 But it displeased Jonah exceedingly, and he was very angry.

2 And he prayed unto the Lord, and said, I pray thee, O Lord, *was* not this my saying, when I was yet in my country? Therefore I fled before unto Tarshish: for I knew that thou *art* a gracious God, and merciful, slow to anger, and of great kindness, and repentest thee of the evil.

Jonah 4:1–3. Jonah Is Angry Because of the Lord's Compassion toward Nineveh

Why did the Lord's kindness to Nineveh anger Jonah? (4:1–2) "Jonah didn't like Assyrians, a not uncommon position held by many of the Northern Kingdom in the time of Jonah, for they were his enemies. . . . While not eager to preach to them in the first place, he found solace in preaching his message only when he could anticipate their ultimate destruction. Though he was eager to proclaim the Lord God of heaven as the Creator of all things and reluctantly admitted that the Lord can control all things on the sea and the earth, he would not allow for a universal application of God's mercy to all of his creatures" (Seely, "Book of Jonah," 49).

Why might Jonah have preferred to die rather than live knowing that Nineveh had repented? (4:3) "In spite of acknowledging that God was merciful and gracious, Jonah was angry and asked that God take his life. Perhaps Jonah was fearful of the people since his prophecy had not been fulfilled [Jonah 3:4], or perhaps he was embarrassed because of this. The latter seems more probable. All the text says is that God questioned Jonah about his anger. Jonah left the city in his anger and went outside the city, where he built a booth to provide some shade and waited to see what would become of the city (Jonah 4:5)" (Nyman and Nyman, *Words of the Twelve Prophets*, 74).

Jonah 4:4–11. God Teaches Jonah Mercy and Forgiveness

What was the meaning of the gourd that grew and then withered? (4:4–11) "The Lord causes a huge gourd to grow and provide shade for Jonah. Then He causes a worm to eat the gourd and fierce heat to come upon Jonah. [God] points out that if Jonah has pity on the gourd, God should have pity on the Ninevites, who are His children and who have repented despite not having a full knowledge of the things of God. . . .

"At least one thing the gourd symbolizes is God's mercy. He provides the gourd to give Jonah comfort, even when Jonah doesn't deserve it. He then compares it to what He is willing to do for Nineveh, especially since its residents have repented" (Muhlestein, *Essential Old Testament Companion*, 500).

3 Therefore now, O LORD, take, I beseech thee, my life from me; for *it is* better for me to die than to live.

4 ¶ Then said the LORD, Doest thou well to be angry?

5 So Jonah went out of the city, and sat on the east side of the city, and there made him a booth, and sat under it in the shadow, till he might see what would become of the city.

6 And the LORD God prepared a gourd, and made *it* to come up over Jonah, that it might be a shadow over his head, to deliver him from his grief. So Jonah was exceeding glad of the gourd.

7 But God prepared a worm when the morning rose the next day, and it smote the gourd that it withered.

8 And it came to pass, when the sun did arise, that God prepared a vehement east wind; and the sun beat upon the head of Jonah, that he fainted, and wished in himself to die, and said, *It is* better for me to die than to live.

9 And God said to Jonah, Doest thou well to be angry for the gourd? And he said, I do well to be angry, *even* unto death.

10 Then said the LORD, Thou hast had pity on the gourd, for the which thou hast not laboured, neither madest it grow; which came up in a night, and perished in a night:

11 And should not I spare Nineveh, that great city, wherein are more than sixscore thousand persons that cannot discern between their right hand and their left hand; and *also* much cattle?

MICAH

Introduction

"The 'word of the Lord . . . came to Micah the Morasthite in the days of Jotham, Ahaz, and Hezekiah, kings of Judah' (Mic. 1:1). . . . [Micah's] prophetic ministry occurred in the kingdom of Judah during the reigns of [these kings], about 750 to 686 B.C., making him a contemporary of the prophets Isaiah, Amos, and Hosea. There is no record of interaction between any of these men. . . . Micah's prophecies focus primarily on the fate of Jerusalem and Judah, but also include a short prophecy directed against Samaria, the capital of the northern kingdom of Israel (Mic. 1:5–6). The twin themes of judgments and hope in a restoration are presented as deriving from Jehovah" (Holzapfel, et al., *Jehovah and the World of the Old Testament*, 283).

"The prophet's name is a short form of *Micayah*, a phrase asking, 'Who is like Jehovah?' Like the names of some of the other prophets and patriarchs, it is appropriate to the life's work of this man, who prophetically demonstrated in many ways that no one indeed is like Him, and everyone should strive to live His ways. No other power is like His power, and no king like this King" (Rasmussen, *Latter-day Saint Commentary on the Old Testament*, 665).

"Little is known about Micah, except for his origin in Moresheth-gath, a settlement in the low hill country of Judah, a region known as the Shephelah [about twenty miles southwest of Jerusalem]. . . . While Micah the person may have disappeared from history, the message of Micah was remembered despite its unpopular laments and foretelling of judgments upon Israel and Judah. When Jeremiah was sentenced to death for prophesying against Jerusalem (Jeremiah 26:11–19), certain elders saved Jeremiah by recalling the prophecy of Micah of Moresheth against Jerusalem and Zion (Micah 3:12)" (Pierce, "Understanding Micah's Lament for Judah," 162–63).

CHAPTERS 1–2

Micah prophesies the downfall of Samaria and Jerusalem.

The destruction of Israel is lamented—The Lord will gather the remnant of Israel.

Summary of Micah 1–2

Micah prophesies of the defeat of Samaria and Jerusalem. The two cities became centers for the wickedness and apostasy of the people. The people of Jerusalem imitate the unrighteous actions of those in Samaria. Micah warns that people are willing to listen to false prophets who encourage them to continue in wickedness but ignore true prophets who counsel them to repent. Although Israel will be taken captive, the Lord will gather them back like sheep to the fold.

Micah 3:1–12. Micah Corrects and Warns False Spiritual Leaders

Who were the heads of Jacob? (3:1) Micah's words were "directed in this instance to the rulers of Judah and Israel. Micah begins this oracle [inspired declaration] with a devastating question: 'Should you not know justice [KJV, "judgment"]?' If any should know the meaning of justice, it is those who have the awesome responsibility of leadership. Here 'justice' is used in the sense of fairness and equity in governmental administration" (McComiskey, "Micah," 7:417).

What is meant by the accusation of eating the flesh of the people? (3:2–3) "Addressing the leaders of Israel, the prophet characterized them as butchers and cannibals in their callous injustice to their own people. It was terribly shocking symbolism, but the prophet wanted them to know that because of their lack of justice in taking advantage of the people, in their own time of need the Lord would 'hide his face from them' [verse 4] and not listen to their pleas" (Rasmussen, *Latter-day Saint Commentary on the Old Testament*, 660).

How would the false prophets experience darkness? (3:6–7) "The end will come for these religious hucksters (v. 6). They sin with the gift of prophecy, so that gift will now be removed from them. There will be no visions and no divination, only darkness. No answers will be forthcoming from God. . . . It will be a time in which false predictions of peace will be discredited by the reality of the captivity. These prophets will 'cover their faces' [KJV, 'cover their lips'], an expression connoting deep mourning" (McComiskey and Longman, "Micah," 8:520).

How have true prophets helped you experience the power of the Lord's Spirit? (3:8) "Prophets speak by the power of the Holy Spirit. . . . They represent the mind and heart of the Lord and are called to represent Him and teach us what we must do to return to live in

CHAPTER 3

Priests who teach for hire and prophets who divine for money bring a curse upon the people.

1 And I said, Hear, I pray you, O heads of
Jacob, and ye princes of the house of Israel; *Is
it* not for you to know judgment?

2 Who hate the good, and love the evil; who
pluck off their skin from off them, and their
flesh from off their bones;

3 Who also eat the flesh of my people, and
flay their skin from off them; and they break
their bones, and chop them in pieces, as for
the pot, and as flesh within the caldron.

4 Then shall they cry unto the LORD, but he
will not hear them: he will even hide his face
from them at that time, as they have behaved
themselves ill in their doings.

5 ¶ Thus saith the LORD concerning the
prophets that make my people err, that bite
with their teeth, and cry, Peace; and he that
putteth not into their mouths, they even prepare war against him.

6 Therefore night *shall be* unto you, that ye
shall not have a vision; and it shall be dark
unto you, that ye shall not divine; and the
sun shall go down over the prophets, and the
day shall be dark over them.

7 Then shall the seers be ashamed, and the
diviners confounded: yea, they shall all cover
their lips; for *there is* no answer of God.

8 ¶ But truly I am full of power by the spirit
of the LORD, and of judgment, and of might,
to declare unto Jacob his transgression, and
to Israel his sin.

9 Hear this, I pray you, ye heads of the house of Jacob, and princes of the house of Israel, that abhor judgment, and pervert all equity.

10 They build up Zion with blood, and Jerusalem with iniquity.

11 The heads thereof judge for reward, and the priests thereof teach for hire, and the prophets thereof divine for money: yet will they lean upon the LORD, and say, *Is* not the LORD among us? none evil can come upon us.

12 Therefore shall Zion for your sake be plowed *as* a field, and Jerusalem shall become heaps, and the mountain of the house as the high places of the forest.

the presence of God and His son, Jesus Christ. We are blessed as we exercise our faith and follow their teachings. By following them, our lives are happier and less complicated, our difficulties and problems are easier to bear, and we create a spiritual armor around us that will protect us from the attacks of the enemy in our day" (Soares, "Prophets Speak by the Power of the Holy Spirit," 99). Consider recording how a prophet's words have drawn you closer to God.

How were the leaders guilty of Micah's accusation? (3:9–11) "It seems that . . . the leaders of Israel—tyrants would be a better name—used professional prophets and seers to cloak their misdeeds . . . [and] cover their actions by flattery and falsehood. The hireling prophet depended upon his rich clients for a living. He could not, therefore, be independent in his thinking and in his judgment. He was high-pressured into siding with the rich, and consequently shut his eyes to the real conditions among the people. Naturally he could not attack the sins of the day that made it possible for his clients to exploit Israel's common people" (Sperry, *Message of the Twelve Prophets*, 116–17).

How have these prophecies about Israel and Jerusalem been fulfilled? (3:12) The Hebrew word *heaps* in this verse means "ruins." Israel was conquered by Assyria during Micah's ministry and the city of Samaria was destroyed (see *Old Testament Student Manual: 1 Kings–Malachi*, 113–14). A century later Jerusalem would be demolished by Babylon. Finally, Roman soldiers would destroy Jerusalem in 70 A.D. The temple mount was laid waste, and the land would literally be plowed by the Roman soldiers. Only a part of the original wall that had surrounded the temple mount would survive (see Horton, "Be Ye Also Ready," 48).

CHAPTER 4

In the last days, the temple will be built, Israel will gather to it, the millennial era will commence, and the Lord will reign in Zion.

Summary of Micah 4

"Micah foretold, as Isaiah had [Isa. 2], the latter-day establishment of the house of the Lord 'in the top of the mountains' with people flowing unto it from many nations to learn the ways and walk in the paths of the God of Israel (Micah 4:1). His word and his law shall go forth from the Zion in the mountains and from Jerusalem. 'Strong nations' (Micah 4:3) will be judged and rebuked, weapon makers will make tools for farming, war will cease, peace will be in each home and nation, and the only government will be that of the Lord" (Rasmussen, *Latter-day Saint Commentary on the Old Testament*, 661).

CHAPTER 5

The Messiah will be born in Bethlehem—In the last days, the remnant of Jacob will triumph gloriously over the Gentiles.

1 Now gather thyself in troops, O daughter of troops: he hath laid siege against us: they shall smite the judge of Israel with a rod upon the cheek.

2 But thou, Beth-lehem Ephratah, *though* thou be little among the thousands of Judah, *yet* out of thee shall he come forth unto me *that is* to be ruler in Israel; whose goings forth *have been* from of old, from everlasting.

3 Therefore will he give them up, until the time *that* she which travaileth hath brought forth: then the remnant of his brethren shall return unto the children of Israel.

4 ¶ And he shall stand and feed in the strength of the LORD, in the majesty of the name of the LORD his God; and they shall abide: for now shall he be great unto the ends of the earth.

5 And this *man* shall be the peace, when the Assyrian shall come into our land: and when he shall tread in our palaces, then shall we raise against him seven shepherds, and eight principal men.

6 And they shall waste the land of Assyria with the sword, and the land of Nimrod in the entrances thereof: thus shall he deliver *us* from the Assyrian, when he cometh into our land, and when he treadeth within our borders.

7 And the remnant of Jacob shall be in the midst of many people as a dew from the LORD, as the showers upon the grass, that tarrieth not for man, nor waiteth for the sons of men.

Micah 5:1–7. The Birthplace of the Messiah Is Revealed

What is noteworthy about the prophecy recorded in these verses? (5:2–4) "Equally definite with the prophecies declaring that the Messiah would be born in the lineage of David are the predictions that fix the place of His birth at Bethlehem, a small town in Judea. There seems to have been no difference of opinion among priests, scribes, or rabbis on the matter, either before or since the great event. Bethlehem, though small and of little importance in trade or commerce, was doubly endeared to the Jewish heart as the birthplace of David and as that of the prospective Messiah" (Talmage, *Jesus the Christ*, 86). ⊕

Who were the shepherds and men who would fight against Assyria? (5:5–6) "The 'seven shepherds' and 'eight leaders' [KJV, 'eight principal men'] are to be understood as an indefinite but substantial number of leaders. The figure stresses the abundance of manpower Israel will enjoy when God accomplishes the work of gathering his people from the godless nations. . . . In most instances the [use of such a] numerical sequence is clearly not to be understood literally but may indicate an indefinite and probably much larger number" (McComiskey and Longman, "Micah," 8:532, 533).

Summary of Micah 5:8–15

In the last days, the house of Israel will triumph over all their foes. In 3 Nephi 20:16–17, Jesus Christ quoted Micah 5:8–9, referring to the desolation and destruction of the wicked at the Second Coming.

CHAPTER 6

In spite of all His goodness to them, the people have not served the Lord in spirit and in truth—They must act righteously, love mercy, and walk humbly before Him.

1 Hear ye now what the LORD saith; Arise,
contend thou before the mountains, and let
the hills hear thy voice.

2 Hear ye, O mountains, the LORD's controversy, and ye strong foundations of the earth:
for the LORD hath a controversy with his
people, and he will plead with Israel.

3 O my people, what have I done unto thee?
and wherein have I wearied thee? testify
against me.

4 For I brought thee up out of the land of
Egypt, and redeemed thee out of the house
of servants; and I sent before thee Moses,
Aaron, and Miriam.

5 O my people, remember now what Balak
king of Moab consulted, and what Balaam
the son of Beor answered him from Shittim
unto Gilgal; that ye may know the righteousness of the LORD.

6 ¶ Wherewith shall I come before the LORD,
and bow myself before the high God? shall I
come before him with burnt offerings, with
calves of a year old?

7 Will the LORD be pleased with thousands
of rams, *or* with ten thousands of rivers of oil?
shall I give my firstborn *for* my transgression,
the fruit of my body *for* the sin of my soul?

8 He hath shewed thee, O man, what *is*
good; and what doth the LORD require of
thee, but to do justly, and to love mercy, and
to walk humbly with thy God?

9 The LORD's voice crieth unto the city, and
the man of wisdom shall see thy name: hear
ye the rod, and who hath appointed it.

Micah 6:1–9. Remember the Lord and Walk in His Ways

Why would the people be invited to bring evidence against God? (6:3) "The Lord and His prophets often imitate language we would normally encounter in other contexts in order to make a point. In this case the Lord indicts Israel as if she was in a court. He calls for witnesses, accuses Israel, offers opportunity for Israel to accuse Him and supplies evidence of His own goodness. Many of the prophets use judicial terminology as [a] way of warning Israel that judgment is coming" (Muhlestein, *Essential Old Testament Companion*, 506).

How do we worship the Lord in righteousness? (6:6–8) Micah perceived that for the Israelites, empty sacrificial rituals had replaced the true worship of God (see Craigie, "Micah," in *Twelve Prophets*, 2:46). "The scriptures advocate a different approach. They suggest that we should be true disciples of Jesus Christ. This entails establishing a powerful feeling of accountability to God and a humble approach to life. . . . I have found a genuine goodness among people of all faiths who are humble and feel accountable to God. Many of them subscribe to the Old Testament prophet Micah, who declared, 'What doth the Lord require of thee, but to do justly, and to love mercy, and to walk humbly with thy God?' [Micah 6:8]" (Cook, "Eternal Everyday," 53).

What can we do to accomplish what the Lord requires? (6:6–8) Elder Dale G. Renlund explained, "To *do justly* means acting honorably with God and with other people. We act honorably with God by walking humbly with Him. We act honorably with others by loving mercy. . . .

"To *do justly* and *walk humbly with God* is to intentionally withdraw our hand from iniquity, walk in His statutes, and remain authentically faithful. A just person turns away from sin and toward God, makes covenants with Him, and keeps those covenants. . . .

"Loving mercy means that we do not just love the mercy God extends to us; we delight that God extends the same mercy to others" ("Do Justly, Love Mercy, and Walk Humbly with God," 109, 111).

When has the Lord shown you His goodness? (6:8) "The consistency of pleas from prophets to reflect on the goodness of God is striking. Our Heavenly Father wants us to recall His and His Beloved Son's goodness, not for Their own gratification but for the influence such remembrance has on us. By considering Their kindness, our perspective and understanding are enlarged. By reflecting on Their compassion, we become more humble, prayerful, and steadfast. . . .

"When we remember the greatness of our Heavenly Father and Jesus Christ and what They have done for us, we will not take Them for granted" (Renlund, "Consider the Goodness and Greatness of God," 41, 43). How has remembering the Lord's greatness and goodness helped you follow Him more faithfully?

Summary of Micah 6:10–16

Micah condemns the wicked practices of Israel's leaders and warns of retribution if the people do not repent.

Micah 7:1–8. The Lord Will Show Israel Compassion and Mercy in the Last Days

What were the expected results of a summer harvest? (7:1) "Summer fruit was rare—[very few] figs or grapes . . . ripened late, after the regular harvest was over. Occasionally, someone walking through the trees or vineyard could find such fruit. Micah uses this image as a picture of his search for any godly people who might yet remain faithful to the Lord" (*Quest Study Bible* [2003], 1337).

CHAPTER 7

Though the people of Israel have rebelled, yet in the last days the Lord will have mercy on them—He will have compassion and pardon their iniquities.

1 Woe is me! for I am as when they have gathered the summer fruits, as the grapegleanings of the vintage: *there is* no cluster to eat: my soul desired the firstripe fruit.

2 The good *man* is perished out of the earth: and *there is* none upright among men: they all lie in wait for blood; they hunt every man his brother with a net.

3 ¶ That they may do evil with both hands earnestly, the prince asketh, and the judge

asketh for a reward; and the great *man,* he uttereth his mischievous desire: so they wrap it
up.

4 The best of them *is* as a brier: the most upright *is sharper* than a thorn hedge: the day
of thy watchmen *and* thy visitation cometh;
now shall be their perplexity.

5 ¶ Trust ye not in a friend, put ye not confidence in a guide: keep the doors of thy
mouth from her that lieth in thy bosom.

6 For the son dishonoureth the father, the
daughter riseth up against her mother, the
daughter in law against her mother in law; a
man's enemies *are* the men of his own house.

Why would Micah counsel the people not to trust others? (7:5–6) "There are, it seems, no honest persons left [among them]. Instead, society is populated by violent and ruthless persons, each one set upon the exploitation of a neighbour. . . . In a sad crescendo of misery, [Micah] notes that you cannot trust a neighbour or a friend, and that even the members of an immediate family no longer live together in mutual trust and respect. Parents, children, relatives—all have been infected by the same plague of evil that has corrupted society as a whole" (Craigie, "Micah," in *Twelve Prophets*, 2:52).

7 Therefore I will look unto the LORD; I will
wait for the God of my salvation: my God
will hear me.

Why is it essential to look to the Lord? (7:7) "We see much that is glorious and reassuring in good human beings, but mortal men have limitations. None of us has ever met a mortal in whom we could comfortably rest our salvation. Only one qualifies for that trust, and he is the Holy One of Israel. His love for us was and is so great that he volunteered for the unspeakable burden of carrying the weight of our sins. He is our Mediator and our Advocate with the Father. The prophet Micah spoke truthfully and faithfully long ago when, in a time of great trouble, he testified: 'I will look unto the Lord; I will wait for the God of my salvation: my God will hear me' (Micah 7:7)" (Hanks, "I Will Look unto the Lord," 13).

8 ¶ Rejoice not against me, O mine enemy:
when I fall, I shall arise; when I sit in darkness, the LORD *shall be* a light unto me.

When have you felt the Lord's light in times of personal darkness? (7:8) "[Jesus Christ] is the source of our power, the Light and Life of the World. Without a strong connection to Him, we begin to spiritually die. Knowing that, Satan tries to exploit the worldly pressures we all face. He works to dim our light, short-circuit the connection, cut off the power supply, leaving us alone in the dark. . . .

"Jesus said, 'I am the light [that] shineth in darkness, and the darkness comprehendeth it not' [D&C 6:21]. That means no matter how hard it tries, the darkness cannot put out that light. Ever. You can trust that His light will be there for you" (Eubank, "Christ: The Light That Shines in Darkness," 73, 75).

Summary of Micah 7:9–15

The Lord will deliver and protect the repentant.

Micah 7:16–20. All Nations Will See and Be Confounded by the Mighty Works of God

What can we learn from Micah's testimony of the Lord? (7:18–20) In Micah's concluding words, "he revels in the prospect of Israel's glorious future and breaks out into a strain of sublime praise and admiration for the divine attributes of loving-kindness, faithfulness, and compassion to be manifested by God in [the] deliverance [of His chosen people]" (Sperry, *Message of the Twelve Prophets*, 127.) It may be here that the meaning of Micah's name becomes a focus of his message: "Who is like Jehovah?"—for greatness, for mercy, or compassion? How might Micah's words be a reminder of who we are to become as a people and as individuals?

16 ¶ The nations shall see and be confounded at all their might: they shall lay *their* hand upon *their* mouth, their ears shall be deaf.

17 They shall lick the dust like a serpent, they shall move out of their holes like worms of the earth: they shall be afraid of the LORD our God, and shall fear because of thee.

18 Who *is* a God like unto thee, that pardoneth iniquity, and passeth by the transgression of the remnant of his heritage? he retaineth not his anger for ever, because he delighteth *in* mercy.

19 He will turn again, he will have compassion upon us; he will subdue our iniquities; and thou wilt cast all their sins into the depths of the sea.

20 Thou wilt perform the truth to Jacob, *and* the mercy to Abraham, which thou hast sworn unto our fathers from the days of old.

NAHUM

Introduction

"The book of Nahum is a short prophecy about the destruction of Assyria. Because Nineveh fell in 612 B.C., Nahum is probably dated between 626 and 612 B.C. Nahum describes God as good—'The LORD is good, a strong hold in the day of trouble; and he knoweth them that trust in him' (Nah 1:7)—and at the same time willing to destroy his enemies. . . . The destruction on Nineveh is described in vivid images" (Holzapfel, et al., *Jehovah and the World of the Old Testament*, 315).

"In Nahum's world Assyria was the embodiment of human evil and terror. Of all the oppressive imperial powers that have stained the pages of human history from the past to the present, Assyria claims a place of pre-eminence among evil nations. . . . Not only were atrocities performed, but they are described with apparent delight and pride. There was indiscriminate killing, . . . soldiers and officers were the willing servants of violence, taking pleasure in the abuse of human life and extolling the very acts which degraded their humanity. . . . Nahum cries out not so much for vengeance as for justice, for the rampant evil of Assyria made a mockery out of all human existence" (Craigie, "Nahum," in *Twelve Prophets*, 2:58, 75).

"Nahum wrote in poetic form, using imagery and symbolism. His tone is markedly hostile toward Nineveh, especially in chapters 2 and 3, which describe the city's destruction and humiliation. [Nahum's] description of the Lord's anger may cause some readers to feel uncomfortable. However, it is important to recognize that underlying the Lord's anger toward Nineveh is a deep sense of concern for the suffering of the many people who had been conquered, slain, enslaved, and terrorized by Assyria (see Nahum 3:19). The Lord's judgments of the wicked are connected to His compassion for their victims.

"The meaning of Nahum's name, 'consoler,' plays an important role in the prophet's message (see Bible Dictionary, 'Nahum'). The unrepentant wicked will receive no comfort (see Nahum 3:7), but the righteous can take comfort from Nahum's message that the Lord cares about them and will one day bring an end to wickedness" (*Old Testament Seminary Teacher Material* [2018], 816–17). The destruction of Assyria can be likened to the destruction of the wicked in the last days.

CHAPTER 1

Nahum speaks of the burning of the earth at the Second Coming and of the mercy and power of the Lord.

1 The burden of Nineveh. The book of the vision of Nahum the Elkoshite.

Nahum 1:1–15. The Lord's Anger against the Wicked of Nineveh

What does the word *burden* mean in this verse? **(1:1)** "It is assumed that the 'burden of Nineveh' is a reference to the hopeless message preached by Nahum. His prophecy regarding the fate of Nineveh does not fit the usual pattern of prophesied gloom followed by a soothing message of hope, because that pattern was reserved for the Israelites, not for their enemies" (Black, *400 Questions and Answers about the Old Testament*, 210–11).

What do we know about Nahum? (1:1) "The prophet's name occurs nowhere else in the Bible except in the genealogy of Joseph, the husband of Mary the mother of Christ (Luke 3:25). It means 'Comforter' or 'Consoler.' The superscription of the Book of Nahum refers to the prophet as the 'Elkoshite' (1:1). This latter designation probably has reference to the place of his birth, rather than to his ancestor's name. It seems to mean that Nahum came from a place called *Elkosh*, in the same sense that Micah the Morashtite came from *Moresheth* (Micah 1:1).... Unfortunately, we do not know the exact location of Elkosh, which is not mentioned elsewhere in the Bible" (Sperry, *Voice of Israel's Prophets*, 352).

How could jealousy be a characteristic of God? (1:2) "*Jealousy* is in its usual sense a sinful trait (Gal. 5:20), but the word can also denote a godly quality (2 Cor. 11:2). In this way God is 'jealous' (the word is related to the word *zealous*) for people's faithfulness. God's jealousy shows his love, not a selfishness or lack of control. This righteous jealousy of God's takes vengeance on those who hurt his children" (*Quest Study Bible* [2003], 1340). "God's jealousy is a claim for exclusive allegiance rooted in His holiness (Josh 24:10) and His role as their Creator and Redeemer (Ps. 95:6, 7; 96:2–5)" (*Nelson Study Bible* [NKJV], 1515).

How might God's power over the elements demonstrate His anger toward wickedness? (1:3–6) "[Jehovah] is portrayed as master of the storm and controller of the winds that can bring both life and destruction.... The majesty of God over the forces of nature is made clear, as is the ability to impose drought on generally fertile areas" (Walton, et al., *IVP Bible Background Commentary*, 788). Demonstrations of God governing the elements in response to wickedness are found in the Old Testament and in the Book of Mormon (examples include 1 Kings 17; Isa. 29; Hel. 11; and 3 Ne. 8).

How can the Lord be a strong refuge for you in times of trouble? (1:7) "As I have seen the storms that affect people's lives, I have concluded that no matter what kind of storm is battering us—regardless

2 God *is* jealous, and the LORD revengeth; the LORD revengeth, and *is* furious; the LORD will take vengeance on his adversaries, and he reserveth *wrath* for his enemies.

3 The LORD *is* slow to anger, and great in power, and will not at all acquit *the wicked:* the LORD *hath* his way in the whirlwind and in the storm, and the clouds *are* the dust of his feet.
4 He rebuketh the sea, and maketh it dry, and drieth up all the rivers: Bashan languisheth, and Carmel, and the flower of Lebanon languisheth.

5 The mountains quake at him, and the hills melt, and the earth is burned at his presence, yea, the world, and all that dwell therein.

6 Who can stand before his indignation? and who can abide in the fierceness of his anger? his fury is poured out like fire, and the rocks are thrown down by him.

7 The LORD *is* good, a strong hold in the day of trouble; and he knoweth them that trust in him.

8 But with an overrunning flood he will
make an utter end of the place thereof, and
darkness shall pursue his enemies.

9 What do ye imagine against the LORD? he
will make an utter end: affliction shall not
rise up the second time.

10 For while *they be* folden together *as* thorns,
and while they are drunken *as* drunkards,
they shall be devoured as stubble fully dry.

11 There is *one* come out of thee, that imagi-
neth evil against the LORD, a wicked counsellor.

12 Thus saith the LORD; Though *they be*
quiet, and likewise many, yet thus shall they
be cut down, when he shall pass through.
Though I have afflicted thee, I will afflict thee
no more.

13 For now will I break his yoke from off
thee, and will burst thy bonds in sunder.

14 And the LORD hath given a commandment concerning thee, *that* no more of thy
name be sown: out of the house of thy gods
will I cut off the graven image and the molten image: I will make thy grave; for thou art
vile.

15 Behold upon the mountains the feet of
him that bringeth good tidings, that publisheth peace! O Judah, keep thy solemn
feasts, perform thy vows: for the wicked shall
no more pass through thee; he is utterly cut
off.

of whether there is a solution to it or whether there is an end in sight—there is only one refuge, and it is the same for all types of storms. This single refuge provided by our Heavenly Father is our Lord Jesus Christ and His Atonement. . . . He has promised that He will make our burdens light if we come unto Him in all that we do" (Giménez, "Finding Refuge from the Storms of Life," 101, 102). Do you trust that Jesus Christ will provide refuge as you come to Him?

Who was the wicked counselor that defied the Lord? (1:10) "Prophesying of Judah's future, Nahum spoke of one very 'wicked counsellor' whose yoke upon Judah, probably a large yearly tribute (see 2 Kings 17:14), was to be broken. Sennacherib, king of Assyria, had invaded Judah with a force of nearly two hundred thousand men. The prophecy foretold that Sennacherib would die shortly, and the house of his gods would become his grave (see Nahum 1:14). While he was worshiping in the temple dedicated to the god Nisrock, Sennacherib's two sons, Adrammelech and Sharazer, murdered their father as Nahum had prophesied (see 2 Kings 19:37)" (*Old Testament Student Manual: 1 Kings–Malachi*, 220).

What is the warning given to Nineveh in this verse? (1:14) "For a long period of time, the Assyrians had spread out from Nineveh to bring into bondage the peoples of the surrounding nations. At their height, their possessions spanned the whole of the Middle East, from the Persian Gulf to the Mediterranean Sea and ultimately to northern reaches of the Red Sea. All of Mesopotamia and the mountainous regions to the east and north were absorbed. The whole of the Levant and the entire kingdom of Egypt were subsumed. That, however, would be the extent of their empire. They and their idolatrous culture would be swept away" (Hyde, *Comprehensive Commentary [Nahum]*, 12). ⊕

Summary of Nahum 2–3

The terrible destruction of Nineveh is prophesied. "These words were addressed to the Assyrians of Nineveh; they were ironically advised to prepare their defenses. It was true that [Israel] had before been emptied out and marred at times, but the time had come for Nineveh to be emptied. . . . The prophet, in satirical phrases told them they could prepare for siege but it would be in vain. . . .

"Although it is a taunt-song, rejoicing over the vanquishing of an inveterate and violent enemy, this prophetic book teaches some religious truths: The Lord is patient, great, and just; he is good, dependable, and helpful; and the time is coming when all wickedness shall cease and He shall reign in peace" (Rasmussen, *Latter-day Saint Commentary on the Old Testament*, 666–67).

CHAPTERS 2–3

Nineveh will be destroyed, which is a symbol of what will be in the latter days.

The miserable downfall of Nineveh is foretold.

HABAKKUK

Introduction

"Habakkuk was a Judahite prophet who lived during the time when Jeremiah, Lehi, Nahum, Zephaniah, and other prophets taught in Jerusalem (see 1 Ne. 1:4). Habakkuk questioned the Lord about the decadence of his people and the power which the wicked seemed to have over the righteous (Hab. 1:1–4). He was also concerned about the ominous Babylonian (also called Chaldean) threat which the people of Judah were experiencing, and he was even more worried about the promised destruction of his country by Babylon. Very little is known about his life and background, although scholars are united in dating his pronouncements around 600 B.C." (Ludlow, "Book of Habakkuk," 187).

"The Book of Habakkuk . . . [is] one single prophecy arranged in two parts. In the *first* part (ch. 1 and 2), under the form of a conversation between God and the prophet, we have first of all an announcement of the judgment which God is about to bring upon the degenerate covenant nation through the medium of the Chaldaeans; and *secondly*, an announcement of the overthrow of the Chaldaean, who has lifted himself up even to the deification of his own power. To this there is appended in ch. 3, as a second part, the prophet's prayer for the fulfilment of the judgment; and an exalted lyric psalm, in which Habakkuk depicts the coming of the Lord in the terrible glory of the Almighty, at whose wrath the universe is terrified, to destroy the wicked and save His people and His anointed, and gives utterance to the feelings which the judgment of God will awaken in the hearts of the righteous" (Keil and Delitzsch, *Commentary* [on Habakkuk Introduction]).

"Habakkuk asked God sincere and bold questions that reflected concern for his people and for the Lord's plans for them. . . .

"Some of Habakkuk's petitions take the form of a grievance, such as 'O Lord, how long shall I cry, and thou wilt not hear!' (Habakkuk 1:2). These reflect the deep emotion and desperation the righteous may feel in times of great suffering (see Psalms 6:3; 13:1; 35:17; 74:10; 79:5; D&C 121:1–6) and can remind us that even in our anguish, we may turn to Heavenly Father and pour out our troubles in honest, heartfelt prayer" (*Old Testament Seminary Teacher Material* [2018], 818).

CHAPTER 1

When Habakkuk learns that the Lord will raise up the Chaldeans to overrun the land of Israel, he is troubled that the wicked can be thus employed.

Summary of Habakkuk 1

Habakkuk is troubled that the wicked do not seem to be punished for their unrighteousness. Habakkuk tells the Lord why he is troubled by the wicked Chaldeans. This is similar to an exchange between the Prophet Joseph Smith and the Lord in D&C 121. In both cases, Habakkuk and the Prophet Joseph Smith express concern that the wicked never seem to be punished.

Summary of Habakkuk 2

In this chapter the Lord responds to Habakkuk's concerns and counsels him to remain faithful and patient, for "the just shall live by his faith" (Hab. 2:4). A series of "woes" are pronounced upon the Chaldeans for their wickedness, and their destruction is assured by the Lord.

CHAPTER 2

The Lord admonishes patience and promises that the just will live by faith—The earth will be filled with knowledge about God—Idols have no power.

Habakkuk 3:1–16. Habakkuk Recognizes the Fairness and Justice of God with All His Children

What are "shigionoth"? (3:1) "The 'shigionoth' are supposed to be stringed instruments. Possibly the prayer was set to music anciently and used in the Temple" (Sperry, *Voice of Israel's Prophets*, 373).

What can we learn from Habakkuk's prayer? (3:2–7) "Habakkuk's prayer, like Job's after the Lord's responses to him, confessed humility and awe and a willingness to abide the Lord's management of things [cf. Job 40:3–5; 42:1–6]. He recalled the Lord's manifestations during the Exodus and on into the conquest of the promised land [Hab. 3:3–16 and fn]" (Rasmussen, *Latter-day Saint Commentary on the Old Testament*,

CHAPTER 3

In his prayer Habakkuk trembles at the majesty of God.

1 A prayer of Habakkuk the prophet upon Shigionoth.

2 O LORD, I have heard thy speech, *and* was afraid: O LORD, revive thy work in the midst of the years, in the midst of the years make known; in wrath remember mercy.

A Tale of Two Prophetic Pleas: Joseph Smith and Habakkuk (Habakkuk 1–3)

"In the book of Habakkuk, the prophet expresses his concern at what seems to be the indifference of a just God to the horrible wickedness rampant in Judah, which was causing those who were righteous to suffer. Habakkuk became even more confused when the Lord informed him that the Chaldeans, who were more wicked than the people of Judah, would administer punishment to the Lord's chosen people. He cried out to the Lord and asked why He would permit the wicked to punish His people (see Hab. 1:1–17). . . .

"In this dispensation, the prophet Joseph Smith, in Liberty Jail, after witnessing the maleficent, murderous, immoral, and inhumane treatment of the Saints, exclaimed, 'O God, where art thou? And where is the pavilion that covereth thy hiding place?

"'How long shall thy hand be stayed, and thine eye, yea thy pure eye, behold from the eternal heavens the wrongs of thy people and of thy servants, and thine ear be penetrated with their cries?

"'Yea, O Lord, how long shall they suffer these wrongs and unlawful oppressions, before thine heart shall be softened toward them, and thy bowels be moved with compassion toward them?' (D&C 121:1–3). . . .

"The wicked do prosper sometimes, but only for a short while; and whatever suffering the righteous may endure is only temporary. In the end, it will be the other way around. The wicked will suffer damnation for their behavior, while the righteous who endure earthly trials well will be blessed with peace here and crowned with exaltation hereafter.

"The Lord has counseled us to recognize that our perceptions are limited and, therefore, we need to have patience and faith in our Heavenly Father as we struggle through our trials and sorrows in this life. As we climb the mountain of mortality, there are times when our vision will be clouded and unclear. It is only when we reach the summit that we can see and know things as they really are. Until then, we must be patient and live by faith.

"The present is a time of probation for all living—righteous and wicked. But eternal joy is the heritage of the righteous" (Thornock, "Do the Wicked Prosper While the Righteous Suffer?" 13, 16).

3 God came from Teman, and the Holy One
from mount Paran. Selah. His glory covered
the heavens, and the earth was full of his
praise.

4 And *his* brightness was as the light; he had
horns *coming* out of his hand: and there *was*
the hiding of his power.

5 Before him went the pestilence, and burning coals went forth at his feet.

6 He stood, and measured the earth: he beheld, and drove asunder the nations; and the
everlasting mountains were scattered, the perpetual hills did bow: his ways *are* everlasting.

7 I saw the tents of Cushan in affliction: *and*
the curtains of the land of Midian did tremble.

8 Was the LORD displeased against the rivers? *was* thine anger against the rivers? *was*
thy wrath against the sea, that thou didst ride
upon thine horses *and* thy chariots of salvation?

9 Thy bow was made quite naked, *according* to the oaths of the tribes, *even thy* word.
Selah. Thou didst cleave the earth with rivers.

670). Habakkuk likely hoped that these recollections would remind the Israelites of God's power for future deliverance.

Why did Habakkuk refer to Teman and Mount Paran? (3:3) "The term [*Teman*] means 'southland' and is a poetic description of the Sinai Desert through which the Israelites traveled after leaving Egypt and where God gave them the law. . . . From there God led them north past *Mount Paran* to the promised land (Dt 33:2)" (*Quest Study Bible* [1994], 1349).

Why is the word "Selah" inserted into these verses? (3:3, 9, 13) "This entire chapter is a prayer of Habakkuk set in poetic form. The word *Selah* is inserted to indicate a break in the reading (chanting) at specified points" (Ludlow, *Companion to Your Study of the Old Testament*, 387). See commentary in this volume for Psalm 24. ⊕

What does it mean that "the bow was made quite naked"? (3:9) "That is, it was drawn out of its case; as the arrows had their quiver, so the bows had their cases. A fine oriental bow and bow-case, with quiver and arrows, are now before me; they show with what propriety Jehovah is represented as taking his bow out of its case, in order to set his arrow upon the cord, to shoot at his enemies. It is not the drawing out, or making bare the arrow, that is mentioned here; but the taking the bow out of its case to prepare to shoot. . . .

"All this was done [according to] the covenant of God, . . . which he made with the tribes, to give them the land of the Canaanites for their inheritance" (*Adam Clarke's Commentary* [on Habakkuk 3:9]).

Habakkuk 3: A Psalm of Praise

"Habakkuk's psalm is a hymn of praise to God for his deliverance of his people in times of oppression. The prophet recounted the redemptive acts of the Exodus as an example of the Lord's power for future deliverance. In the context of his questions and dialogue with the Lord about the problem of suffering, this psalm expresses Habakkuk's trust in God during a time of anxiety. The psalm is easily divided into four segments:

"1. *Introduction* (Hab. 3:1–2). In memorable words, the prophet appealed to the Lord to renew his awesome work of salvation and mercy for his people.

"2. *The divine manifestation (or theophany) in the past* (Hab. 3:3–7). In ancient times, God came out of the southern desert to deliver his people (cf. Deut. 33:2; Judg. 5:4–5).

"3. *The conflict between God and the forces of the earth* (Hab. 3:8–15). God comes to defeat his enemies and the foes of his people, represented by the elements, especially the waters. The purpose of the storm is to subdue the earth, overthrow the enemy, and rescue God's people.

"4. *An affirmation of faith in the Lord* (Hab. 3:16–19). The prophet's fear changed to faith, and he knew he would experience joy despite the adversity he was facing. Verses 17 through 19 are memorable phrases, expressing joy in God's salvation and confidence in his strength" (Ludlow, "Book of Habakkuk," 191–92).

Habakkuk 3:17–19. Habakkuk Learns to Respect and Trust in the Lord

How can one still find joy even when surrounded by wickedness? (3:18–19) "Saints can be happy under every circumstance. . . . When the focus of our lives is on God's plan of salvation . . . and Jesus Christ and His gospel, we can feel joy regardless of what is happening—or not happening—in our lives. Joy comes from and because of Him. He is the source of all joy" (Nelson, "Joy and Spiritual Survival," 82).

How can we learn to trust the Lord like Habakkuk? (3:19) "Like Habakkuk of old, we may in our anguish feel that we could bear anything if we could only understand the divine purpose in what is happening. The ancient prophet learned that the righteous live by faith and that faith is not an easy solution to life's problems. Faith is confidence and trust in the character and purposes of God. . . .

"Our religion is 'not weight, it is wings.' It can carry us through the dark times, the bitter cup. It will be with us in the fiery furnace and the deep pit. . . . It is, in short, not the path to easy disposition of problems, but the comforting assurance of the eternal light, by which we may see, and the eternal warmth, which we may feel" (Hanks, "Trust in the Lord," 14).

10 The mountains saw thee, *and* they trembled: the overflowing of the water passed by:
the deep uttered his voice, *and* lifted up his
hands on high.

11 The sun *and* moon stood still in their habitation: at the light of thine arrows they went,
and at the shining of thy glittering spear.

12 Thou didst march through the land in
indignation, thou didst thresh the heathen in
anger.

13 Thou wentest forth for the salvation of
thy people, *even* for salvation with thine
anointed; thou woundedst the head out of
the house of the wicked, by discovering the
foundation unto the neck. Selah.

14 Thou didst strike through with his staves
the head of his villages: they came out as a
whirlwind to scatter me: their rejoicing *was*
as to devour the poor secretly.

15 Thou didst walk through the sea with
thine horses, *through* the heap of great waters.

16 When I heard, my belly trembled; my
lips quivered at the voice: rottenness entered
into my bones, and I trembled in myself, that
I might rest in the day of trouble: when he
cometh up unto the people, he will invade
them with his troops.

17 ¶ Although the fig tree shall not blossom,
neither *shall* fruit *be* in the vines; the labour
of the olive shall fail, and the fields shall yield
no meat; the flock shall be cut off from the
fold, and *there shall be* no herd in the stalls:

18 Yet I will rejoice in the LORD, I will joy in
the God of my salvation.

19 The LORD God *is* my strength, and he
will make my feet like hinds' *feet,* and he will
make me to walk upon mine high places. To
the chief singer on my stringed instruments.

ZEPHANIAH

Introduction

Zephaniah, whose name means "Jehovah protects or has concealed or has sheltered" (Parry and Parry, "Israelite Names," 54), "was commissioned by God to warn Judah and encourage her to repent. . . . Israel was at a pivotal point between peril and safety. Therefore, Zephaniah's sweeping prose account of God's judgments upon the wicked and the eventual triumph of his kingdom was the message vacillating Judea needed to hear" (*Old Testament Student Manual: 1 Kings–Malachi*, 223).

"Zephaniah . . . prophesied in Jerusalem during Josiah's reign and during the period immediately after his death (640–609 B.C.). . . . [He] ministered at the same time as Jeremiah and added [his] warnings of impending destruction to [Jeremiah's]" (Holzapfel, et al., *Jehovah and the World of the Old Testament*, 315). Apparently, "Zephaniah descended from the royal family of King Hezekiah. . . . [He] lived in Jerusalem and may have been trained by the same teachers who influenced Josiah toward his religious reforms" (Ludlow, *Unlocking the Old Testament*, 224).

This prophetic book's message "contains two main parts. The first is that 'the day of the Lord' is coming with its accompanying judgments. Second, hope can be achieved if the Jews 'turn back to God.' Righteous King Josiah and the Jews obeyed Zephaniah's message, delaying the invasion of Babylon upon the kingdom of Judah" (Valletta, et al., *Old Testament for Latter-day Saint Families*, 633).

"Although Zephaniah does not rank among the best-known books of the Old Testament, its message is one of tremendous importance for latter-day Israel. . . . Impressed by the clarity and the power of his vision of the future, modern seers have used the words of Zephaniah to support and amplify their own teachings concerning the coming day of the Lord. To all who long for that day, the book of Zephaniah is a priceless treasure" (Eames, "Book of Zephaniah," 183).

"Joseph Smith did not make any changes in the text of Zephaniah as he translated the Bible" (Nyman and Nyman, *Words of the Twelve Prophets*, 116).

CHAPTERS 1–2

The destruction of Judah is symbolic of the Second Coming—It is the day of the Lord's sacrifice, a day of wrath and trouble.

Seek righteousness; seek meekness—Judgment will come upon the Philistines, the Moabites, the children of Ammon, the Ethiopians, and the Assyrians.

Summary of Zephaniah 1–2

Zephaniah begins by "speaking of the day of burning that shall attend the Second Coming. . . . Nothing that is evil and wicked shall abide the day; all that falls short of the required standard shall be burned in the fires of fervent heat; it shall be as with man, so with the beast. Nothing that is corruptible shall remain [1:2–3]" (McConkie, *Millennial Messiah*, 541). Chapter 1 also contains the Lord's promised judgments against Judah for their worship of false gods and idols (see vv. 4–5). Judah's spirituality has suffered because of their worldliness (see vv. 6, 8–9). Therefore, Judah would be "devoured by the fire of jealousy" (vv. 10–18).

In Zephaniah 2, the Lord's anger shifts to other nations, such as Philistia, Moab, Ammon, and Egypt, all traditional enemies of Judah. They too shall be destroyed, for "the Lord will be terrible unto them" (v. 11).

Zephaniah 3:1–7. Zephaniah Warns the Wicked in Jerusalem

What led to Jerusalem's eventual downfall? (3:1–4) The prophet Zephaniah clearly understood what precipitated Jerusalem's fall: "she drew not near to her God" (Zeph. 3:2). According to the descriptions in verses 3 and 4, there was wickedness and corruption at the top of the city's social structure. "Shepherds are leaders, those in whose care God has entrusted his children. In ancient Israel and Judah, those leaders included the prophets, the priests, and the kings, individuals charged with the responsibility of providing leadership within their respective spheres. Unfortunately, the Bible shows evidence for all-too-frequent corruption in each of these areas (e.g., Ezek. 22:26–28; Zeph. 3:3–4; Micah 3:11)" (Jackson, *Lost Tribes and Last Days*, 107).

Why is it essential to listen to the Lord's voice in any dispensation? (3:2) Ponder the following from President Russell M. Nelson: "[Our] efforts to *hear Him* need to be ever more intentional. It takes conscious and consistent effort to fill our daily lives with His words, His teachings, His truths.

"We simply cannot rely upon information we bump into on social media. With billions of words online and in a marketing-saturated world constantly infiltrated by noisy, nefarious efforts of the adversary, where *can* we go to hear Him?" ("Hear Him," 89).

How did Zephaniah characterize Jerusalem's leaders? (3:3) Zephaniah compared them to lions and wolves who "devour the flesh in the night, and gnaw the bones and extract the marrow afterwards. They use all violence and predatory oppression, like wild beasts; they shun the light, and turn day into night by their revellings" (*Adam Clarke's Commentary* [on Zephaniah 3:3]). "Like Amos and Micah, the prophet [Zephaniah] sternly denounces the crimes of the ruling classes in Jerusalem, points out their ingratitude to Jehovah, and announces doom that is inevitable" (*John Dummelow's Commentary* [on Zephaniah 3]).

CHAPTER 3

At the Second Coming, all nations will assemble to battle—Men will have a pure language—The Lord will reign in their midst.

1 Woe to her that is filthy and polluted, to the oppressing city!

2 She obeyed not the voice; she received not correction; she trusted not in the LORD; she drew not near to her God.

3 Her princes within her *are* roaring lions; her judges *are* evening wolves; they gnaw not the bones till the morrow.

4 Her prophets *are* light *and* treacherous persons: her priests have polluted the sanctuary, they have done violence to the law.

5 The just LORD *is* in the midst thereof; he will not do iniquity: every morning doth he bring his judgment to light, he faileth not; but the unjust knoweth no shame.

6 I have cut off the nations: their towers are desolate; I made their streets waste, that none passeth by: their cities are destroyed, so that there is no man, that there is none inhabitant.

7 I said, Surely thou wilt fear me, thou wilt receive instruction; so their dwelling should not be cut off, howsoever I punished them: but they rose early, *and* corrupted all their doings.

8 ¶ Therefore wait ye upon me, saith the LORD, until the day that I rise up to the prey: for my determination *is* to gather the nations, that I may assemble the kingdoms, to pour upon them mine indignation, *even* all my fierce anger: for all the earth shall be devoured with the fire of my jealousy.

9 For then will I turn to the people a pure language, that they may all call upon the name of the LORD, to serve him with one consent.

10 From beyond the rivers of Ethiopia my suppliants, *even* the daughter of my dispersed, shall bring mine offering.

11 In that day shalt thou not be ashamed for all thy doings, wherein thou hast transgressed against me: for then I will take away out of the midst of thee them that rejoice in thy pride, and thou shalt no more be haughty because of my holy mountain.

12 I will also leave in the midst of thee an afflicted and poor people, and they shall trust in the name of the LORD.

Why did the Lord destroy the nations surrounding Judah? (3:6–7) "[Verse] 6 seems to revert to the theme of [Jehovah's] judgment of foreign nations, while [verse] 7 expresses his hope that Judah might take warning from this, a hope that was to be disappointed" (Gelston, "Zephaniah," 716).

Zephaniah 3:8–13. The People Are Urged to Wait upon the Lord

When will the Lord gather all nations together for destruction? (3:8) "By way of counsel to his people who shall live in this day of anger and wrath, the Lord says: 'Wait ye upon me, saith the Lord, until the day that I rise up to the prey: for my determination is to gather the nations, that I may assemble the kingdoms'—this, of course, is at Armageddon—'to pour upon them mine indignation, even all my fierce anger: for all the earth shall be devoured with the fire of my jealousy' (Zeph. 3:8)" (McConkie, *Millennial Messiah*, 497–98). ⊕

What is the "pure language" referred to by Zephaniah? (3:9) Many believe that the "pure language" was the Adamic language. "The scriptures state that this language, written and spoken by Adam and his children, was 'pure and undefiled' (Moses 6:5–6)" (Robertson, "Adamic Language," 16).

"However, a second meaning of a 'pure language' is even easier for persons to work on before Christ returns. We can develop a 'purified language' devoid of blasphemies, filthiness, and inappropriate terms. All our words should be clean and worthy of the Lord's ears at any time, whether he is on the earth or not. By purifying our own language today, we will be better prepared for the language of God, Adam, and the Millennium" (Ludlow, *Unlocking the Old Testament*, 225). ⊕

What will the circumstances be like for the children of Israel in the day of the Lord? (3:11–13) "From the farthest reaches of the then-known world, the prophet [Zephaniah] foresaw worshippers of the Lord gathering. None shall be ashamed of their affiliation, and none shall be haughty because of it. The meek of the earth among the 'afflicted and poor people . . . shall trust in the name of the Lord' (Zeph. 3:12; Matt. 5:5). Israel, no longer sinful, will dwell in safety among the peoples. The prophet's final vision was a glorious one, showing the true Zion people rejoicing in the Lord" (Rasmussen, *Latter-day Saint Commentary on the Old Testament*, 675).

13 The remnant of Israel shall not do iniquity, nor speak lies; neither shall a deceitful tongue be found in their mouth: for they shall feed and lie down, and none shall make *them* afraid.

14 ¶ Sing, O daughter of Zion; shout, O Israel; be glad and rejoice with all the heart, O daughter of Jerusalem.

15 The LORD hath taken away thy judgments, he hath cast out thine enemy: the king of Israel, *even* the LORD, *is* in the midst of thee: thou shalt not see evil any more.

Zephaniah 3:14–20. The Lord Rules in the Midst of the Righteous

Who is the "king of Israel" who will reign in the last days? (3:14–15) "The millennial King would be . . . a second King David, restoring the glories of the past to which later generations of Israel looked with longing. 'The Holy One of Israel,' wrote Nephi, will 'reign in dominion, and might, and power, and great glory' (1 Ne. 22:24). His name, Jeremiah foretold, would be 'Jehovah, our Righteousness' (Jer. 23:5–6; 33:16, literal translation). 'The king of Israel, even the Lord,' reported Zephaniah concerning the Millennium, 'is in the midst of thee' (Zeph. 3:15). And to Zechariah God said, 'The Lord shall be king over all the earth . . .' (Zech. 14:9; see also vv. 16–17)" (Jackson, *Lost Tribes and Last Days*, 110).

The Second Coming (Zephaniah 3:14–15)

16 In that day it shall be said to Jerusalem, Fear thou not: *and to* Zion, Let not thine hands be slack.

17 The LORD thy God in the midst of thee *is* mighty; he will save, he will rejoice over thee with joy; he will rest in his love, he will joy over thee with singing.

18 I will gather *them that are* sorrowful for the solemn assembly, *who* are of thee, *to whom* the reproach of it *was* a burden.

19 Behold, at that time I will undo all that afflict thee: and I will save her that halteth, and gather her that was driven out; and I will get them praise and fame in every land where they have been put to shame.

20 At that time will I bring you *again,* even in the time that I gather you: for I will make you a name and a praise among all people of the earth, when I turn back your captivity before your eyes, saith the LORD.

Why was Zephaniah able to conclude his prophecy with a message of hope? (3:16–17) "Zephaniah saw our day and beyond. In it he both suffered and rejoiced. He suffered in spirit because of the desolation and destruction which he saw, but he was able to use this as a warning and threat to his own people. In the redemption and final blessings of Israel he saw a ray of hope to extend to Judah. . . . Not all of Israel are to be destroyed. There will still exist in the centuries to come a righteous remnant with whom God can work and bring to pass His righteous purposes in the earth" (Sperry, *Voice of Israel's Prophets*, 388, 387).

When will the Lord gather the house of Israel? (3:20) "Another subject of great importance in the prophecy of Zephaniah is the gathering and restoration of disgraced and scattered Israel. While Zephaniah hinted that this gathering could commence prior to the great day of the Lord with its attendant devastation (Zeph. 2:1–3), he seemed to assign a major portion of that gathering to the period *after* the Savior's return (Zeph. 3:15–20). The Lord's presence among his gathered Saints will be the cause of much happiness" (Eames, "Book of Zephaniah," 183).

How do Zephaniah's words to the Jews give you hope for the future? (3:20) "The prophet concluded on a note of optimism. The day will come when God's people 'shall not see evil any more' (Zephaniah 3:15). Those who have borne the burden of reproach shall be gathered from afar and become 'a name and a praise' (v. 20) among men" (*Old Testament Student Manual: 1 Kings–Malachi*, 224). When have you felt the blessings of being a member of the house of Israel?

HAGGAI

Introduction

"The book of Haggai is the first of the three post-exile prophets. Haggai was a contemporary of Zechariah. His name means 'my feast(s)' or 'festive.' We are not told anything else about Haggai. Out of Haggai 2:3 many have concluded that he must have seen Solomon's temple before its destruction in 586 B.C. In this case Haggai would have been much older than 70 years when he wrote his book" (*Adam Clarke's Commentary* [on Introduction to Haggai]).

"In the opening verse of Haggai we are given to understand that the prophet uttered the short addresses in the book, and there is little doubt that he did so. But it would seem very probable that these are only brief resumes of what he told his people. A prophet whose enthusiasm is such that he rouses a dilatory [negligent] people to build a temple would not likely be limited to such short statements. Either this is true or else we may conclude that the book contains only the formal revelations of the Lord to Haggai. Upon them the prophet based his exhortations and preaching to the people" (Sperry, *Voice of Israel's Prophets*, 391).

"[Haggai] contains 4 oracles, or prophetic pronouncements, all dating to 520 B.C. 'the second year of Darius the [Persian] king' (Hag 1:1). The first of these (Hag 1:1–15) is an impassioned call to return to rebuilding the Temple, a project commenced years earlier but never completed. Although primarily directed at Zerubbabel the governor and Joshua the high priest (Hag 1:1; Jeshua in Ezra 2: 2), the condemnation was expressed more broadly. Haggai's main message was that the Jews were putting time, energy, and resources into finishing their own homes, but the House of the Lord had not been completed. As long as this situation continued, they could not enjoy the peace and prosperity that would come when the temple was finished. Haggai's stirring words, 'Consider your ways' (Hag 1:5), provoked a positive response. The people 'obeyed the voice of the LORD their God and the words of Haggai the Prophet . . . and they came and did the work in the House of the LORD' (Hag 1:12, 14). The temple was dedicated in 515 B.C.

"The remaining three brief oracles (Hag 2:19; 2:10–19; 2:20–23) focus on how the new Temple would be filled with the glory of the Lord, how the Lord would more fully bless his people with the temple in their midst, and how the Lord would overthrow the nations of the world and establish Zerubbabel (symbolically a future Davidic ruler) as his authorized servant" (Holzapfel, et al., *Jehovah and the World of the Old Testament*, 365).

Haggai 1:1–11. The People Are Rebuked and Asked to Continue Rebuilding the Temple

What attitude did the people have about rebuilding the Lord's house? (1:1–2) "The whole purpose of the gathering of the Jews or of any of the house of Israel at any time is to build a temple unto the Lord so that he may reveal his sacred and saving ordinances to his people [see Joseph Smith Papers, 'History, 1838–1856, volume D-1 (1 August 1842–1 July 1843),' 1572]. Haggai's prophecies illustrate how the Lord works to bring about that purpose. . . .

CHAPTER 1

Haggai exhorts the people to build the temple.

1 In the second year of Darius the king,
in the sixth month, in the first day of the
month, came the word of the LORD by
Haggai the prophet unto Zerubbabel the son
of Shealtiel, governor of Judah, and to Joshua
the son of Josedech, the high priest, saying,

2 Thus speaketh the LORD of hosts, saying, This people say, The time is not come, the time that the LORD's house should be built.

3 Then came the word of the LORD by Haggai the prophet, saying,

4 *Is it* time for you, O ye, to dwell in your ceiled houses, and this house *lie* waste?

5 Now therefore thus saith the LORD of hosts; Consider your ways.

6 Ye have sown much, and bring in little; ye eat, but ye have not enough; ye drink, but ye are not filled with drink; ye clothe you, but there is none warm; and he that earneth wages earneth wages *to put it* into a bag with holes.

7 ¶ Thus saith the LORD of hosts; Consider your ways.

8 Go up to the mountain, and bring wood, and build the house; and I will take pleasure in it, and I will be glorified, saith the LORD.

"Many of the Jews were content in Babylon or did not want to return to Jerusalem. Those Jews who returned found opposition to their rebuilding of the temple from the surrounding inhabitants of the land, the Samaritans (Ezra 4). . . .

"The people in Haggai's day were excusing their inaction by rationalizing that it was not yet time to build the temple (Haggai 1:2)" (Nyman and Nyman, *Words of the Twelve Prophets*, 117, 118).

What is a ceiled house? (1:4) "The term 'paneled' [see Hag. 1:4*a*] can mean 'covered,' 'roofed,' or 'paneled,' but the point in any case is that it represents the finishing touches. Their homes were not in process but were fully appointed while the temple remained a ruin" (Walton, et al., *IVP Bible Background Commentary*, 797).

Why should Saints in all ages "consider [their] ways"? (1:5–7) "Somewhat hidden in the Old Testament book of Haggai is a description of a group of people who . . . got it wrong by not placing Christ at the center of their lives and their service. Haggai paints some thought-provoking word pictures as he reprimands these people for staying in their comfortable houses instead of building the Lord's temple: [quoted Hag. 1:4–7]. . . . Don't you love those descriptions of the futility of prioritizing things of no eternal consequence above the things of God?" (Vinson, "True Disciples of the Savior," 9). What adjustments could you make so that the things of eternal consequence take greater priority in your life? ⊕

What might be the intent of the Lord's rebuke in this verse? (1:6) "Verse 6 outlines what the prophet calls the people to consider deeply. The cadence of this verse *in the Hebrew text* produces a powerful effect beginning with the main verb 'you have planted much' and then followed by staccato bursts of infinitives that are captured by the translation: 'eaten, but there is no satiety; drunk, but there is no quenching; dressed, but there is no warmth'. . . . Through these words, Haggai expects the people to notice that their experience parallels the kinds of curses outlined in the Torah when the covenant relationship between [Jehovah] and his people was strained (see Lev. 26; Deut. 28–30, esp. Deut. 28:38–40)" (Boda, *Haggai, Zechariah*, 90, 91; emphasis added).

What might it mean that the Lord will take pleasure in His temple? (1:8) In the latter days, the Lord called His temple "a house of glory" that includes prayer and fasting, learning and order (D&C 88:119). After the sacrifice of His Saints to build His house, the

Lord accepts His temples and puts His name upon His house—with the promise that He will manifest Himself there, and speak with His people in His own voice (see D&C 110:7–8). Temple work is the foundation of Zion, with her "glory, honor, and endowments" through the "[ordinances] of [His] holy house" (D&C 124:39).

Why would the Lord send a drought upon the land? (1:11) "This then was the divine diagnosis of the people's plight: There was a significant connection between the *hārēb* [v.4] and the *hōreb* [v.11], between the temple's 'ruin' [waste] and the experienced 'drought.' The people considered the adverse circumstances [of the drought] to be a decisive argument against the rebuilding of the temple. The Lord, however, revealed to them that the drought was his punishment for their lack of spiritual fervor and commitment in rebuilding the temple. The postexilic community's priorities were awry: they had not first sought the kingdom of God; rather, they were busy concerning themselves with their own 'kingdoms,' their selfish interests and conveniences" (Verhoef, *Haggai and Malachi*, 78).

Haggai 1:12–15. The People Obey the Lord

What was the effect of Haggai's message? (1:12–14) "The initial response of Zerubbabel, Joshua, and the 'remnant of the people' was twofold: they 'obeyed,' and they 'feared' (v. 12). The Hebrew term [שָׁמַע (*šâma'*)] literally means 'and he heard,' but hearing the word or voice of God meant in Hebrew 'to obey.' If one did in fact 'hear,' one would then 'obey.' . . . They also feared the Lord. The Hebrew term [יָרֵא (*yârê'*)] connotes that they were properly awed before the Lord, who had sent Haggai. They recognized God's awesome power and amazing constancy. . . . In response to the people's fear, the Prophet delivers . . . God's assuring declaration: 'I am with you' (v. 13)" (March, "Book of Haggai," in *New Interpreter's Bible*, 7:719).

Who were Zerubbabel and Joshua? (1:12) Zerubbabel means "*born in Babylon*. . . . Grandson of Jehoiachin, king of Judah, and son of Pedaiah (1 Chr. 3:16–19); in Ezra 3:2 and elsewhere he is called 'son of Shealtiel.' . . . Zerubbabel was also known by the Persian name Sheshbazzar (Ezra 1:8, etc.). When Cyrus

9 Ye looked for much, and, lo, *it came* to little; and when ye brought *it* home, I did blow upon it. Why? saith the LORD of hosts. Because of mine house that *is* waste, and ye run every man unto his own house.

10 Therefore the heaven over you is stayed from dew, and the earth is stayed *from* her fruit.

11 And I called for a drought upon the land, and upon the mountains, and upon the corn, and upon the new wine, and upon the oil, and upon *that* which the ground bringeth forth, and upon men, and upon cattle, and upon all the labour of the hands.

12 ¶ Then Zerubbabel the son of Shealtiel, and Joshua the son of Josedech, the high priest, with all the remnant of the people, obeyed the voice of the LORD their God, and the words of Haggai the prophet, as the LORD their God had sent him, and the people did fear before the LORD.

13 Then spake Haggai the LORD's messenger in the LORD's message unto the people, saying, I *am* with you, saith the LORD.

14 And the LORD stirred up the spirit of Zerubbabel the son of Shealtiel, governor of Judah, and the spirit of Joshua the son of Josedech, the high priest, and the spirit of all the remnant of the people; and they came and did work in the house of the LORD of hosts, their God,

gave permission to the Jews to return to Palestine, Zerubbabel was appointed *pekhah* or governor, as the representative of the Jewish royal house (Ezra 1:8)" (Bible Dictionary, "Zerubbabel").

"Joshua was the high priest in the early postexilic period. His grandfather Seraiah had been executed by Nebuchadnezzar when Jerusalem fell to the Babylonians (2 Kings 25:18–21)" (Walton, et al., *IVP Bible Background Commentary*, 797).

15 In the four and twentieth day of the sixth month, in the second year of Darius the king.

Who was Darius the King? (1:15) "Darius the Great (Darius 1, son of Hystaspes), king of Persia, instigator of the campaign against Greece which resulted in his defeat at Marathon 490 B.C.; reigned 522–486 B.C. He recorded his deeds in the famous trilingual inscription at Behistun rock. . . . Restoring the realm of Cyrus, he continued that ruler's tolerant policy towards the Jewish captives in Babylon, and encouraged them to continue their restoration of the Jerusalem temple. When complaints were lodged against the building . . . Darius searched the well-kept archives of Cyrus, found the original decree role authorizing the work (Ezra 6:1–5) and issued a new edict forbidding hindrance of the Jewish project and ordering a generous contribution to it (Ezra 6:6–12)" (*Harper's Bible Dictionary* [1973], 127).

CHAPTER 2

Haggai speaks about the Messiah—The Desire of All Nations will come—The Lord will give peace in His temple.

Summary of Chapter 2

One month after being exhorted to build the temple, the people are discouraged, but comforted by the word of the Lord (see Hag. 1:1, 2:1). The initial effort to build the temple made it apparent that this temple, built in times of distress and hardship, could not be compared with Solomon's temple. The Lord tells His people to "be strong" (Hag. 2:4), and promises that He would "shake the heavens and . . . the nations" (vv. 6–7), that He will "fill this house with glory" (v. 7), and that "the glory of this house shall be greater than of the former" (v. 9).

Two months later (v. 10), calling to their minds the strictures of purity to be maintained in the temple (vv. 11–13), the Lord counsels them to "consider" (three times in vv. 15–18), before one more stone is laid, the consequences of uncleanness and impurity while building the temple (vv. 16–17). If the people will repent and devote themselves fully to Him, the Lord "from this day will . . . bless [them]" (v. 19) and "overthrow the throne of kingdoms" (v. 22) and esteem Zerubbabel (the governor of Judah) before them (v. 23).

Some have interpreted verse 7 "that the 'desire of all nations shall come' [as] a prophecy of Christ, who will bring a lasting peace to the world. Lasting peace, however, will be brought only after the Lord shakes 'the heavens, and the earth, and the sea, and the dry land . . . and . . . all nations' (vv. 6–7) when He comes in His glory to usher in the Millennium. Then His house will indeed be filled with glory, peace will be established, and the desire of all nations will be completely fulfilled. (The phrase 'desire of nations' is used in the hymn "Come, O Thou King of Kings," *Hymns*, no. 59.)" (*Old Testament Student Manual: 1 Kings–Malachi*, 325–26).

ZECHARIAH

Introduction

Zechariah "was the son of Berechiah, who was the son of Iddo (see Zechariah 1:1). Iddo was a priest who returned to Jerusalem with Zerubbabel, the first Jewish governor of Jerusalem after the Jews' return from the Babylonian exile (see Nehemiah 12:1–7). Zechariah prophesied from the second to the fourth year of the reign of Darius, about 520 to 518 B.C. (see Zechariah 1:1; 7:1)" (*Old Testament Seminary Teacher Material* [2018], 831).

"The times of Zechariah are those . . . mentioned in connection with Haggai. The Jews were under the domination of the Persians, who had permitted them to return and build the Temple. They faltered, however, and became poor and despondent. They lost their initial enthusiasm, and not until Haggai and Zechariah preached to them and revived their spirits did they get the Temple under way. It was under these conditions that Zechariah did his work" (Sperry, *Voice of Israel's Prophets*, 403, 406).

"Zechariah is the largest book among the twelve 'minor' prophets (Hosea through Malachi). . . .

"Zechariah is an important book for Latter-day Saints for three reasons. First, . . . [Zechariah's] prophecies of a scattering and gathering of Israel (especially the Jews) were to be fulfilled in later times. . . .

"A second reason for the significance of his writings is that there are more prophecies about Christ in his book than in any other prophetic book except Isaiah. . . .

"A third reason why Zechariah is important to Latter-day Saints is because of his many other prophecies of the last days" (Ludlow, *Unlocking the Old Testament*, 228, 229).

"The book of Zechariah contains descriptions of visions concerning the rebuilding of Jerusalem and the temple, the gathering of scattered Israel, and the triumph of Israel over its enemies. The book culminates in prophecies of the Savior's mortal ministry and final return in glory. By studying the book of Zechariah, students can learn about the Lord's love for His people and His desire to cleanse and redeem them if they repent and keep their covenants. [Readers] can also learn about events that will occur before and after Jesus Christ's Second Coming and feel the importance of preparing themselves for the Lord's return" (*Old Testament Seminary Teacher Material* [2018], 831).

"The book of Zechariah has two divisions: Zech. 1–8, a series of visions sketching the future of the people of God, and Zech. 9–14, prophecies about the Messiah and events preceding His Second Coming" (Bible Dictionary, "Zechariah").

CHAPTERS 1–10

Zechariah calls upon Judah to repent—He is shown in vision that the cities of Judah and the temple will be rebuilt.

Summary of Zechariah 1–10

"Early in 520 B.C. Zechariah received a series of visions all on the same night. The first three [see Zech. 1:7–17; 1:18–21; 2:1–13] focus on Zion and the glory that the Lord intends to bring to her. The next five [see Zech. 3:1–10; 4:1–14; 5:1–4; 5:5–11; 6:1–15] focus on the work of the Messiah as the Priest-King and the steps he will take to bring about the promised glory. The most important of these steps are the gathering and purging of Israel from sin, the Savior's mediating her cause with God, and finally Christ's presidency over the final confrontation between the forces of good and evil. Satan will be totally overthrown, God's wrath appeased, and his kingdom established on the earth" (Draper, "Book of Zechariah," 352–53).

Judah must learn that going through the rituals of fasting and mourning are not sufficient. They must seek the Lord and demonstrate mercy and justice to their neighbors (chapter 7). With the reversal of past judgments, the Lord promises peace and prosperity for a future Zion (chapter 8). A Messianic prophecy refers to the triumphal entry of Jesus Christ into Jerusalem (Zech. 9:10; Matt. 21:1–5; Mark 11:4–10; Luke 19:28–38; John 12:12–16). God's people are to pray to Him rather than turn to pagan idols. Because of the wickedness of Israel's past leaders, who were to be like shepherds, the Lord will take their place and turn Israel into a prosperous and powerful nation (chapter 10).

In the last days, Judah will gather to Jerusalem—The people will come from the land of the north—The Lord will dwell among them.

Zechariah speaks about the Messiah—The Branch will come—At the Second Coming, iniquity will be removed in one day.

Zerubbabel will lay the foundation of and finish the house of the Lord, the temple of Zerubbabel.

An angel reveals truths to Zechariah by the use of symbolic representations.

Zechariah crowns Joshua, the high priest, in similitude of Christ, the Branch, who will come—Christ will be a priest upon His throne forever.

The Lord reproves hypocrisy in fasts—He calls upon the people to show mercy and compassion and to live godly lives.

Who Is "the Branch" Prophesied of by Zechariah? (Zechariah 3:7–10)

"Through Zechariah the Lord spoke . . . : 'Thus saith the Lord of hosts: . . . I will bring forth my servant the BRANCH. . . . I will remove the iniquity of the land in one day [meaning that the wicked shall be destroyed and the millennial era of peace and righteousness commence]. In that day, saith the Lord of hosts, shall ye call every man his neighbour under the vine and under the fig tree' (Zech. 3:7–10). Of that glorious millennial day the Lord says also: 'Behold the man whose name is The BRANCH; and he shall grow up out of his place, and he shall build the temple of the Lord: Even he shall build the temple of the Lord; and he shall bear the glory, and shall sit and rule upon his throne' (Zech. 6:12–13).

"That the Branch of David is Christ is perfectly clear. We shall . . . see that he is also called David, that he is a new David, an Eternal David, who shall reign forever on the throne of his ancient ancestor. 'It shall come to pass in that day, saith the Lord of hosts,' that is, in the great millennial day of gathering, that 'they shall serve the Lord their God, and David their king, whom I will raise up unto them' (Jer. 30:8–9)" (McConkie, *Promised Messiah*, 193).

In the last days, Jerusalem will be restored, Judah will be gathered, and the Lord will bless His people beyond anything in the past.

Zechariah speaks as the Messiah—The Messiah will come, having salvation, lowly and riding upon an ass—He will free the prisoners from the pit—Judah and Ephraim are instruments of the Lord.

Judah and Joseph will be scattered among the people in far countries—The Lord will hiss for them, gather them, and redeem them.

CHAPTER 11

Zechariah speaks about the Messiah—The Messiah will be betrayed for thirty pieces of silver—They will be cast to the potter in the house of the Lord.

7 And I will feed the flock of slaughter, *even* you, O poor of the flock. And I took unto me two staves; the one I called Beauty, and the other I called Bands; and I fed the flock.

8 Three shepherds also I cut off in one month; and my soul lothed them, and their soul also abhorred me.

9 Then said I, I will not feed you: that that dieth, let it die; and that that is to be cut off, let it be cut off; and let the rest eat every one the flesh of another.

Summary of Zechariah 11:1–6

The Lord God admonishes the leaders charged with watching over the flocks (Israel). He compares the grandeur and might of the cedars of Lebanon and the massive oaks of Bashan to the loftiness and superiority of humanity. Notwithstanding their greatness, they can fall and become spoiled. They will lose their standing when the Lord delivers His people.

Zechariah 11:7–17. The Lord Is Rejected by His People

What is one meaning of Zechariah taking up the two staves? (11:7) "Zechariah obeyed God's commission and took up the duties of shepherding his flock. . . . The *two staffs* [KJV, "staves"] allude to the tools of shepherding, the rod and the staff (cf. Ps. 23:4). The staff or crook was a symbol of leadership in the biblical world. . . . Here the word [Beauty] suggests divine blessing, as in Psalm 90:17. This divine favour may refer generally to [the Lord's] covenants with Israel through Abraham. The term [Bands] has legal connotations and indicates a formal tie between two parties" (Hill, *Haggai, Zechariah, and Malachi*, 231, 232).

What might Zechariah have meant by breaking his staff? (11:10–11) "Unlike the prophet Ezekiel who joined two sticks into one, symbolizing the reunification of the two Hebrew kingdoms (Ezek. 37:15-19), Zechariah dramatized the reversal of [the Lord's] covenant relationship and Israelite unity by breaking the two staffs (vv. 10, 14).... The breaking of the *staff called* [*Beauty*] symbolized the *revoking of the covenant* ('annulling', NEB, NRSV) God had made *with all the nations* (NIV), although there is no explicit reference in the [Old Testament] to a covenant between [Jehovah] and the nations. The prophet may be referring to *a covenant of peace* by which God promised to protect Israel from the nations (cf. Ezek. 34:25, 28)" (Hill, *Haggai, Zechariah, and Malachi*, 233). ⊕

10 ¶ And I took my staff, *even* Beauty, and cut it asunder, that I might break my covenant which I had made with all the people.

11 And it was broken in that day: and so the poor of the flock that waited upon me knew that it *was* the word of the LORD.

What did Zechariah's thirty pieces of silver foretell? (11:12–13) "In chapter 11 Zechariah presented the allegory of the good shepherd who tries to save the sheep but because of opposition cannot do it. Finally, he quits in anger, breaks his two staves, and demands his wages. He is paid the sum of thirty pieces of silver. These he throws down before the potter inside the Lord's house, in testimony before Jehovah of his wrongs and rejection. This allegory reflects the rejection of the true shepherd who was sold for thirty pieces of silver and delivered over to false brethren. This betrayer's ransom later bought a potter's field (Matt. 27:7–10)" (Draper, "Book of Zechariah," 358).

12 And I said unto them, If ye think good, give *me* my price; and if not, forbear. So they weighed for my price thirty *pieces* of silver.

13 And the LORD said unto me, Cast it unto the potter: a goodly price that I was prised at of them. And I took the thirty *pieces* of silver, and cast them to the potter in the house of the LORD.

14 Then I cut asunder mine other staff, *even* Bands, that I might break the brotherhood between Judah and Israel.

15 ¶ And the LORD said unto me, Take unto thee yet the instruments of a foolish shepherd.

What might it mean that God will raise up an unfaithful shepherd? (11:16–17) "Before the great day of gathering when the covenant will be fulfilled again and we will again be God's people, there will first be a long night of scattering. Because Israel continues to follow wicked leaders, they are like a flock led by a foolish shepherd who does not care for them. Just as such a flock will be scattered as they wander and as predators come upon them, so will Israel be driven about by every worldly desire and idea. The leaders of the world will pretend to do us good, but in reality will be scattering and abandoning us which can only lead to our hurt" (Muhlestein, *Scriptures Made Simple*, 517).

16 For, lo, I will raise up a shepherd in the land, *which* shall not visit those that be cut off, neither shall seek the young one, nor heal that that is broken, nor feed that that standeth still: but he shall eat the flesh of the fat, and tear their claws in pieces.

17 Woe to the idol shepherd that leaveth the flock! the sword *shall be* upon his arm, and upon his right eye: his arm shall be clean dried up, and his right eye shall be utterly darkened.

CHAPTER 12

In the final great war, all nations will be engaged at Jerusalem, but the Lord will defend His people—Then the Jews will look upon the Lord, whom they crucified, and there will be great mourning.

1 The burden of the word of the LORD for Israel, saith the LORD, which stretcheth forth the heavens, and layeth the foundation of the earth, and formeth the spirit of man within him.

2 Behold, I will make Jerusalem a cup of trembling unto all the people round about, when they shall be in the siege both against Judah *and* against Jerusalem.

3 ¶ And in that day will I make Jerusalem a burdensome stone for all people: all that burden themselves with it shall be cut in pieces, though all the people of the earth be gathered together against it.

4 In that day, saith the LORD, I will smite every horse with astonishment, and his rider with madness: and I will open mine eyes upon the house of Judah, and will smite every horse of the people with blindness.

5 And the governors of Judah shall say in their heart, The inhabitants of Jerusalem *shall be* my strength in the LORD of hosts their God.

6 ¶ In that day will I make the governors of Judah like an hearth of fire among the wood, and like a torch of fire in a sheaf; and they shall devour all the people round about, on the right hand and on the left: and Jerusalem shall be inhabited again in her own place, *even* in Jerusalem.

7 The LORD also shall save the tents of Judah first, that the glory of the house of David and the glory of the inhabitants of Jerusalem do not magnify *themselves* against Judah.

Zechariah 12:1–8. The Great War Will Center in Israel

When might Jerusalem become a "cup of trembling" upon the nations? (12:2–3) "Many problems have long prevailed in the interpretation of the prophecy recorded in Zechariah 12, but latter-day revelation and events are making the meaning clear. The twentieth century has already seen Jerusalem become 'a cup of trembling' and 'a burdensome stone' for some Middle Eastern nations and for the modern community of nations (Zech. 12:2–3)" (Rasmussen, *Latter-day Saint Commentary on the Old Testament*, 690).

What is the gathering of all people of the earth against Jerusalem? (12:3–7) "All of the people of the earth will be gathered against Jerusalem. The governors, or leaders, of Judah are to devour the people roundabout and the Lord will defend Jerusalem (Zech. 12:1–8). This is another description of the battle of Armageddon (Rev. 16–16)" (Nyman, "Twelve Prophets Testify of Christ," 217). Armageddon is "a Greek transliteration from the Hebrew *Har Megiddon*, or 'Mountain of Megiddo.' . . . Several times the valley of Megiddo was the scene of violent and crucial battles during Old Testament times (Judg. 5:19; 2 Kgs. 9:27; 23:29). A great and final conflict taking place at the Second Coming of the Lord is called the battle of Armageddon. See Zech. 11–14, especially 12:11; Rev. 16:14–21" (Bible Dictionary, "Armageddon"). ⊕

What is the Lord conveying with this imagery? (12:4) "The warring hosts shall be smitten with madness, and a blind rage will overrule all reason. . . .

"How will the battle go, and who will come off victorious? What chance for life will any have, considering the destructive power of the weapons then in the hands of the madmen who command the armies? In answer we are told: 'And it shall come to pass, that in all the land, saith the Lord, two parts therein shall be cut off and die; but the third shall be left therein.'

This is Israel of whom he speaks. These are the armies who are defending Jerusalem and whose cause, in the eternal sense, is just. Two-thirds of them shall die" (McConkie, *Millennial Messiah*, 465).

How will God fulfill His covenant with the inhabitants of Jerusalem and all His people? (12:8) "When the Lord says that he will destroy the nations that come against Jerusalem, He is speaking of fulfilling the promise that God would curse those who curse Abraham's seed and that they would possess the gate of their enemies. This subtly indicates God is fulfilling his covenant" (Muhlestein, *Essential Old Testament Companion*, 517). "When God is with his people, none shall stand against them. While this certainly applies literally to Jerusalem at times, it also applies in a symbolic way to all of God's people. When we are keeping covenants and helping God build his Kingdom, nothing can stand before us. All who are the enemies of our righteous works will eventually fall to God" (Muhlestein, *Scripture Study Made Simple*, 518).

8 In that day shall the LORD defend the inhabitants of Jerusalem; and he that is feeble among them at that day shall be as David; and the house of David *shall be* as God, as the angel of the LORD before them.

Zechariah 12:9–14. There Will Be a Final Great Battle

When will the Jews recognize that Jesus was their anticipated Messiah? (12:9–10) "At the conclusion of the battle [Armageddon], the Lord will appear to his people, the embattled Jews, and they will recognize him as their Messiah, but they 'will look upon me whom they have pierced' (Zech. 12:10). There is a dual of fulfillment of this prophecy. It was quoted by John in his gospel as being fulfilled while Christ was on the cross (John 19:37); however, the same author spoke of his coming in the clouds of heaven 'and every eye shall see him, and they also which pierced him' (Rev. 1:7). The context of Zechariah supports the latter fulfillment" (Nyman, "Twelve Prophets Testify of Christ," 217).

Why will there be great mourning in that day? (12:11–14) "What then? Then they begin to believe, then the Jews are convinced, I mean that portion of them who formerly despised Jesus of Nazareth, and being convinced they begin to mourn . . . and there will be such mourning in Jerusalem as that city never experienced before. What is the matter? What are they mourning about? They have looked upon him whom their fathers pierced, they behold the wounds, they are now convinced that they and their fathers have been in error some eighteen hundred years, and they repent in dust and ashes" (Pratt, in *Journal of Discourses* 15:66).

9 ¶ And it shall come to pass in that day, *that* I will seek to destroy all the nations that come against Jerusalem.

10 And I will pour upon the house of David, and upon the inhabitants of Jerusalem, the spirit of grace and of supplications: and they shall look upon me whom they have pierced, and they shall mourn for him, as one mourneth for *his* only *son,* and shall be in bitterness for him, as one that is in bitterness for *his* firstborn.

11 In that day shall there be a great mourning in Jerusalem, as the mourning of Hadadrimmon in the valley of Megiddon.

12 And the land shall mourn, every family apart; the family of the house of David apart, and their wives apart; the family of the house of Nathan apart, and their wives apart;

13 The family of the house of Levi apart, and their wives apart; the family of Shimei apart, and their wives apart;

14 All the families that remain, every family apart, and their wives apart.

CHAPTER 13

The Jews will gain forgiveness at the Second Coming—They will ask the Lord, What are these wounds in Thine hands?—The remnant, tried and refined, will be His people.

1 In that day there shall be a fountain opened to the house of David and to the inhabitants of Jerusalem for sin and for uncleanness.

2 ¶ And it shall come to pass in that day, saith the LORD of hosts, *that* I will cut off the names of the idols out of the land, and they shall no more be remembered: and also I will cause the prophets and the unclean spirit to pass out of the land.

3 And it shall come to pass, *that* when any shall yet prophesy, then his father and his mother that begat him shall say unto him, Thou shalt not live; for thou speakest lies in the name of the LORD: and his father and his mother that begat him shall thrust him through when he prophesieth.

4 And it shall come to pass in that day, *that* the prophets shall be ashamed every one of his vision, when he hath prophesied; neither shall they wear a rough garment to deceive:

5 But he shall say, I *am* no prophet, I *am* an husbandman; for man taught me to keep cattle from my youth.

Zechariah 13:1–6. The Jews Ask about the Wounds in the Savior's Hands and Feet

What fountain of water will be opened to the house of David? (13:1) Possible meanings to this verse include that "[the Jews at Jerusalem will] look upon him whom their fathers pierced and they mourn for him. . . . But repentance alone would not be sufficient, they must obey the ordinances of the Gospel; hence there will be a fountain opened at that time on purpose for baptism. . . .

"This is the fountain that Zechariah says is open to the inhabitants of Jerusalem and to the house of David for sin and uncleanness. . . . Then the Jews will receive the Gospel and they will be cleansed from all their sins by being baptized in water for their remission" (Pratt, in *Journal of Discourses*, 18:66). ⊕

Why will the false prophets be ashamed? (13:2–5) "To justify the anathema with which the opponents of modern revelation seek to persecute those who believe in the continual flow of God's word to His Church, the following prophecy of Zechariah is quoted: [Zech. 13:2–4]. The day here spoken of appears to be yet future, for the idols and the unclean spirits still have influence; and, moreover, the fact that the prophets here spoken of are false ones is shown by Zechariah's associating them with idols and unclean spirits.

"Such attempts to refute the doctrine of continued revelation as have been made on the authority of the foregoing scriptures are pitiably futile; they carry their own refutation, and leave untouched the truth that belief in current revelation is wholly reasonable and strictly scriptural" (Talmage, *Articles of Faith*, 278).

What might the "rough garment" symbolize? (13:4) See Matthew 3:4. "The people of Jerusalem and of adjacent rural parts went out in great multitudes to hear [John the Baptist]. He disdained the soft garments and flowing robes of comfort, and preached in his rough desert garb, consisting of a garment of camel's hair held in place by a leathern girdle. The coarseness of his attire was regarded as significant. . . . Rough garments had come to be thought of as a distinguishing characteristic of prophets [2 Kgs.1:8]. Nor did this strange preacher eat the food of luxury and ease, but fed on what the desert supplied, locusts and wild honey" (Talmage, *Jesus the Christ*, 114).

How does modern revelation become a second witness and help us understand this prophecy? (13:6) In 1831, the Prophet Joseph Smith recorded a revelation describing the Second Coming of Jesus Christ: "And then shall the Jews look upon me and say: What are these wounds in thine hands and in thy feet? Then shall they know that I am the Lord; for I will say unto them: These wounds are the wounds with which I was wounded in the house of my friends. I am he who was lifted up. I am Jesus that was crucified. I am the Son of God. And then shall they weep because of their iniquities; then shall they lament because they persecuted their king" (D&C 45:51–53). ⊕

Summary of Zechariah 13:7–9

Zechariah prophesies the removal of Israel's shepherds and the scattering of the flock. This will be a time of great testing for Judah but also a time of refining. They will call upon the Lord. He will hear them and make them His people.

Zechariah 14:1–9. The Lord Delivers Jerusalem

What is the significance of gathering "all nations at Jerusalem to battle"? (14:1–3) "We are given to understand that when the armies gather in Palestine will be the time when the Lord shall come in judgment and to make the eventful decision which will confound the enemies of his people and establish them in their ancient land forever" (Smith, *Doctrines of Salvation*, 3:47). President Wilford Woodruff taught: "The Gentiles, in fulfillment of the words of [the] prophets, will go up against Jerusalem to battle and to take a spoil . . . and then, when they have taken one-half of Jerusalem captive and distressed the Jews for the last time on the earth [Zech. 14:2] their Great Deliverer, Shiloh, will come" (in *Journal of Discourses*, 15:277–78).

What happens when Jesus appears on the Mount of Olives? (14:4–5) "And then he shall come in person. The Great God shall appear. 'And his feet shall stand in that day upon the mount of Olives, which is before Jerusalem on the east, and the mount of Olives shall cleave in the midst thereof toward the east and toward the west, and there shall be a very great valley; and half of the mountain shall remove toward the north, and half of it toward the south' [Zech. 14:4].'

6 And *one* shall say unto him, What *are* these wounds in thine hands? Then he shall answer, *Those* with which I was wounded *in* the house of my friends.

CHAPTER 14

At His Second Coming, the Lord will fight for Israel—His feet will stand upon the Mount of Olives—He will be King over all the earth—Plagues will destroy the wicked.

1 Behold, the day of the LORD cometh, and thy spoil shall be divided in the midst of thee.

2 For I will gather all nations against Jerusalem to battle; and the city shall be taken, and the houses rifled, and the women ravished; and half of the city shall go forth into captivity, and the residue of the people shall not be cut off from the city.

3 Then shall the LORD go forth, and fight against those nations, as when he fought in the day of battle.

4 ¶ And his feet shall stand in that day upon the mount of Olives, which *is* before Jerusalem on the east, and the mount of Olives shall cleave in the midst thereof toward the east and toward the west, *and there shall be* a very great valley; and half of the mountain shall remove toward the north, and half of it toward the south.

This shall be part of the upheavals which cause every valley to be exalted and every mountain to be made low. This shall be the immeasurably great earthquake foreseen by John and spoken of by the prophets" (McConkie, *Millennial Messiah*, 468).

5 And ye shall flee *to* the valley of the mountains; for the valley of the mountains shall reach unto Azal: yea, ye shall flee, like as ye fled from before the earthquake in the days of Uzziah king of Judah: and the LORD my God shall come, *and* all the saints with thee.

Who are the saints that will come with the Lord? (14:5) The Apostle Paul in his letter to the Thessalonians explained: "For if we believe that Jesus died and rose again, even so them also which sleep in Jesus will God bring with him" (1 Thess. 4:14). In addition, modern revelation speaks of a trumpet sounding that will announce the resurrection where "the dead which died in me [will] receive a crown of righteousness, and [will] be clothed upon even as I am, to be with me that we may be one" (D&C 29:13; see also D&C 88:97–98).

6 And it shall come to pass in that day, *that* the light shall not be clear, *nor* dark:

7 But it shall be one day which shall be known to the LORD, not day, nor night: but it shall come to pass, *that* at evening time it shall be light.

What is the significance of Zechariah's explanation of "light"? (14:6–7) "All people shall see it together! It shall spread over all the earth as the morning light! 'For as the light of the morning cometh out of the east, and shineth even unto the west, and covereth the whole earth, so shall also the coming of the Son of Man be' (JS–M 1:26). Surely this is that of which Isaiah said: 'And the glory of the Lord shall be revealed, and all flesh shall see it together: for the mouth of the Lord hath spoken it' (Isa. 40:5). Surely this is that of which our revelation speaks: 'Prepare for the revelation which is to come, when the veil of the covering of my

A Modern Prophet Testifies of Ancient Prophecy (Zechariah 14:6–7)

President Joseph Fielding Smith commented on the ancient prophecies regarding the great signs to precede the Second Coming of Christ: "Now I have read these passages of Scripture from these various prophets. Here you will find Isaiah saying the Lord will pour out war upon all the world; Jeremiah saying the same thing and speaking of these terrible things; Daniel saying so; Ezekiel saying so. We find Joel, Zephaniah, Zechariah, all proclaiming that in this last day, the day when the sun shall be darkened and the moon turned to blood and the stars fall from heaven, that the nations of the earth would gather against Jerusalem. All of them speak of it; and when that time comes, the Lord is going to come out of His hiding place. You can see what a terrible condition it is going to be; and the Jews besieged, not only in Jerusalem but, of course, throughout Palestine are in the siege; and when they are about to go under, then the Lord comes. There will be the great earthquake. The earthquake will not be only in Palestine. There will not be merely the separation of the Mount of Olives, to form a valley that the Jews may escape, but the whole earth is going to be shaken. There will be some dreadful things take place, and some great changes are going to take place, and that you will find written in the book of Ezekiel (38:17–23)....

"Now, this is very interesting. You can take your Doctrine and Covenants and turn to Section 45 and read what the Lord says about it, confirming what is written here in the book of Zechariah. During this siege, when the nations are gathered and the Lord comes, there will be a great destruction. The armies will become so confused they will fight among themselves. There will be great slaughter. Then the Lord comes to the Jews. He shows Himself. He calls upon them to come and examine His hands and His feet, and they say, 'What are these wounds?' And He answers them, 'These are the wounds with which I was wounded in the house of my friends. I am Jesus Christ'" (*Signs of the Times*, 144–45).

temple, in my tabernacle, which hideth the earth, shall be taken off, and all flesh shall see me together' (D&C 101:23). Surely this is that day of which Zechariah prophesied" (McConkie, *Millennial Messiah*, 419).

What happens when living water flows from Jerusalem? (14:8) "And a stream will break out from under the threshold of the Temple, says the Prophet, and it will run eastward, and will probably pass directly through the deep valley made by the parting of the Mount of Olives. . . . And this water which breaks out from the threshold of the Temple, will not only run eastward but westward also and there will be a great change in the land there, certain portions rising up, others lowered, rough places made smooth and mountains cast down; and half the waters of this spring which will burst forth, will go towards . . . the Dead Sea and half toward the Mediterranean" (Pratt, in *Journal of Discourses*, 18:66, 67). "[And] the waters of the Dead Sea [shall] be healed [see Ezek. 47:8–9]" (Joseph Smith Papers, "History, 1838–1856, volume D-1 [1 August 1842–1 July 1843]," 1520).

8 And it shall be in that day, *that* living waters shall go out from Jerusalem; half of them toward the former sea, and half of them toward the hinder sea: in summer and in winter shall it be.

What will happen so the Lord will be king over all the earth? (14:9) "All that has been spoken of by the holy Prophets shall be fulfilled . . . until error shall give place to truth, wrong to right; until corruption and tyranny shall give place to justice and equity: instead of man bearing rule and having his own way and . . . 'every tongue confess that Jesus is the Christ' [Philip. 2:10–11]. We are only just commencing in this Work, which will grow, and spread, and increase, and no power on this side of hell shall stop its onward progress; it is onward, onward, onward, until the purposes of God and all he has designed shall be fulfilled and accomplished" (Taylor, in *Journal of Discourses*, 10:132–33).

9 And the LORD shall be king over all the earth: in that day shall there be one LORD, and his name one.

Summary of Zechariah 14:10–19

After the destruction of those who fight against Jerusalem, it will become a land of safety, fully inhabited by God's people. After the war is ended, the nations will be humbled and go to Jerusalem to worship the Lord and keep the appointed annual festivals, especially the feast of tabernacles.

20 ¶ In that day shall there be upon the bells of the horses, HOLINESS UNTO THE LORD; and the pots in the LORD's house shall be like the bowls before the altar.

21 Yea, every pot in Jerusalem and in Judah shall be holiness unto the LORD of hosts: and all they that sacrifice shall come and take of them, and seethe therein: and in that day there shall be no more the Canaanite in the house of the LORD of hosts.

Zechariah 14:20–21. After the Lord Returns, All Will Worship Him

Why will "HOLINESS UNTO THE LORD" be inscribed on all things and the people? (14:20–21) "Our welfare and happiness depends upon our obedience to the laws of God, upon our conduct before him in all our acts. We wish to have inscribed not only in our meetinghouse, but in our hearts and acts, Holiness to the Lord.... Let there be no act of my life, no principle that I embrace, that shall be at variance with these words which were first inscribed by the Almighty.... That is not in name only, but it is to be written on the tablets of our hearts, as with a pen of iron [Jer. 17:1]" (Taylor, in *Journal of Discourses*, 23:177–78).

Holiness to the Lord (Zechariah 14:20)

"Zechariah prophesied that in the day of the Lord's millennial reign, even the bells of the horses would bear the inscription 'Holiness unto the Lord.' In that spirit, the pioneer Saints in these valleys affixed that reminder, 'Holiness to the Lord,' on seemingly common or mundane things as well as those more directly associated with religious practice. It was inscribed on sacrament cups and plates and printed on certificates of ordination of Seventies and on a Relief Society banner. 'Holiness to the Lord' also appeared over the display windows [of] the ZCMI department store. It was found on the head of a hammer and on a drum. 'Holiness to the Lord' was cast on the metal doorknobs of President Brigham Young's home. These references to holiness in seemingly unusual or unexpected places may seem incongruous, but they suggest just how pervasive and constant our focus on holiness needs to be" (Christofferson, "Living Bread Which Came Down from Heaven," 38–39).

MALACHI

Introduction

The Hebrew name *Malachi* means "my messenger" (see Bible Dictionary, "Malachi"). Malachi's message and ministry "marks the close of the prophetic voice in Judah until the fervent cry of John the Baptist four hundred years later. . . . So little is known about this prophet that scholars have credited his work to others, such as Ezra. Through modern revelation, however, it is known that he was a real person with great prophetic power (see D&C 138:46). Apparently his ministry closed around 430 B.C." (Pearson, *Old Testament*, 71–72).

"Malachi spoke to the Jews during a period of religious decline. Seventy years after the spiritual emphasis of Haggai and Zechariah, the people were neglecting their religious duties and criticizing God for their problems. . . . Malachi came to them as a messenger of hope. He promised them immediate blessings if they properly served the Lord and a future glory after the Lord had purged the wicked from the earth in his great and dreadful day" (Ludlow, *Unlocking the Old Testament*, 231).

Malachi's prophecy can be divided into two parts. "The first part (Mal. 1:1–2:9) is addressed to the priesthood, reproving them for their neglect of service to God. The second part (2:10–4:6) is addressed to the people, speaking against marriage outside the covenant, divorces from wives within the covenant, and neglect of tithe paying, and reproving the general spirit of discontent. The faithful are encouraged to remain so, with the assurance that the Lord is mindful of them, and the disobedient shall fail in the day of the Lord's coming. . . . All of Mal. 3 and 4 was quoted by the Savior to the Nephites, as recorded in 3 Ne. 24 and 25" (Bible Dictionary, "Malachi").

Malachi's concluding words "anticipate a forerunner to the Savior; . . . the second advent of the Savior, and the restoration of priesthood power to seal on earth and in heaven blessings in eternal covenants. Indeed, the whole book of Malachi has much relevance for the latter days. Moroni, herald angel of the last dispensation, cited some prophecies by Malachi ['He first quoted part of the third chapter of Malachi; and he quoted also the fourth or last chapter of the same prophecy'] (JS–H 1:36–39), indicating that their fulfillment would come in this dispensation. There are many references to the book of Malachi in the Doctrine and Covenants" (Rasmussen, *Latter-day Saint Commentary on the Old Testament*, 694).

"Malachi's prophecy that Elijah would 'turn the heart of the fathers to the children, and the heart of the children to their fathers' (Malachi 4:6) can be found in all four standard works [see Luke 1:17; 3 Ne. 25:6; D&C 2:2–3; 128:17; JS–H 1:39]. When Elijah appeared to the Prophet Joseph Smith and Oliver Cowdery in the Kirtland Temple, he alluded to this prophecy: 'Behold, the time has fully come, which was spoken of by the mouth of Malachi—testifying that he [Elijah] should be sent, before the great and dreadful day of the Lord come' (D&C 110:14). This prophecy has great significance for Latter-day Saints because it teaches the doctrines of the sealing power, eternal families, and the work we do for the dead in temples (see D&C 138:46–48)" (*Old Testament Seminary Teacher Material* [2018], 843–44).

CHAPTER 1

The Jews despise the Lord by offering polluted bread upon the altar and by sacrificing animals with blemishes—The Lord's name will be great among the Gentiles.

1 The burden of the word of the LORD to Israel by Malachi.

2 I have loved you, saith the LORD. Yet ye say, Wherein hast thou loved us? *Was* not Esau Jacob's brother? saith the LORD: yet I loved Jacob,

3 And I hated Esau, and laid his mountains and his heritage waste for the dragons of the wilderness.

4 Whereas Edom saith, We are impoverished, but we will return and build the desolate places; thus saith the LORD of hosts, They shall build, but I will throw down; and they shall call them, The border of wickedness, and, The people against whom the LORD hath indignation for ever.

5 And your eyes shall see, and ye shall say, The LORD will be magnified from the border of Israel.

Malachi 1:1–5. The Lord Loves the House of Israel

Who is Malachi? (1:1) "Nothing is known about the family background or the life of Malachi, outside the pages of his short book. There is even doubt as to whether 'Malachi' is a proper name. . . . Yet it would be very strange indeed if the Hebrews preserved a prophetic book without giving the name of the author" (Wolf, *Haggai and Malachi*, 58).

Why might the text claim that the Lord loved Jacob but hated Esau? (1:2–4) "The mode of teaching characteristic of Malachi is to pose a question or make an assertion from the Lord and then give his diagnosis and prescription. In this case the Lord, through Malachi, invoked the well-known history—why Israel ('Jacob') had been blessed with many blessings whereas Edom had not. Those were the facts behind the shocking rhetoric, 'I loved Jacob, And I hated Esau,' attributed to the Lord. That treatment was based not upon favoritism for the individual but upon the principle that blessings result from obedience to God's laws. Jacob's blessings were pronounced upon him while he was still unworthy (as is true of many of us), and fulfillment of them came only when he fulfilled the law upon which they were based ([Bible Dictionary], 'Jacob'). Esau and Edom went another way. The Lord does not exalt people who live even on 'the border of wickedness' (Mal. 1:4; [Topical Guide], 'Blessing'; 'Obedience')" (Rasmussen, *Latter-day Saint Commentary on the Old Testament*, 694).

How does Edom's demise show God's love for Israel? (1:4–5) "Judah's cousins, the Edomites (descendants of Esau), were among her most bitter enemies. They had even assisted Judah's other enemies from time to time and had benefited greatly from Judah's fall in 587 B.C., by usurping part of her land. . . . Through Malachi, the Lord stated that this would actually prove their demise; they would never rise to power again. Their empty land would be proof of the Lord's care for Israel and would vouchsafe his right to demand their love and loyalty in return (Mal. 1:2–5)" (Draper, "Book of Malachi," 366–67).

Malachi 1:6–14. Priests of Israel Shall Make a Righteous Offering to the Lord

How were the priests polluting sacred ordinances? (1:7–8) "The altar, or 'table of the Lord,' as Malachi called it [Mal. 1:7], was the place of intercession, peacemaking, expiation [penitence], and sanctification. That which was consumed by its flames had in a figurative sense been consumed by God and was therefore understood to have been accepted by him" (McConkie, *Gospel Symbolism*, 104). "Inasmuch as the sacrifices that they made for the people typified the coming sacrifice and Atonement of the Son of God, the only acceptable sacrifice was that which was spotless. [They] were mocking God by offering sacrifices to the Lord with sick, blind, and lame animals and calling them acceptable. . . . They had no reverence for what they were doing" (*Old Testament Student Manual: 1 Kings–Malachi*, 351).

What error did the priests commit when officiating their offerings? (1:10) "The priests, probably to ingratiate themselves with the people, took the refuse [deformed] beasts, etc., and offered them to God" (*Adam Clarke's Commentary* [on Malachi 1:7]). They did not require of the people what the Lord commanded for their sacrifices and worship. "Trying to please others before pleasing God is inverting the *first and second great commandments* (see Matthew 22:37–39). It is forgetting which way we face. And yet, we have all made that mistake because of the fear of men. . . . Thinking one can please God and at the same time condone the disobedience of men isn't neutrality but duplicity, or being *two-faced* or trying to 'serve two masters' (Matthew 6:24; 3 Nephi 13:24)" (Robbins, "Which Way Do You Face?" 9, 10; emphasis added).

6 ¶ A son honoureth *his* father, and a servant his master: if then I *be* a father, where *is* mine honour? and if I *be* a master, where *is* my fear? saith the LORD of hosts unto you, O priests, that despise my name. And ye say, Wherein have we despised thy name?

7 Ye offer polluted bread upon mine altar; and ye say, Wherein have we polluted thee? In that ye say, The table of the LORD *is* contemptible.

8 And if ye offer the blind for sacrifice, *is it* not evil? and if ye offer the lame and sick, *is it* not evil? offer it now unto thy governor; will he be pleased with thee, or accept thy person? saith the LORD of hosts.

9 And now, I pray you, beseech God that he will be gracious unto us: this hath been by your means: will he regard your persons? saith the LORD of hosts.

10 Who *is there* even among you that would shut the doors *for nought?* neither do ye kindle *fire* on mine altar for nought. I have no pleasure in you, saith the LORD of hosts, neither will I accept an offering at your hand.

11 For from the rising of the sun even unto the going down of the same my name *shall be* great among the Gentiles; and in every place incense *shall be* offered unto my name, and a pure offering: for my name *shall be* great among the heathen, saith the LORD of hosts.

12 ¶ But ye have profaned it, in that ye say, The table of the LORD *is* polluted; and the fruit thereof, *even* his meat, *is* contemptible.

13 Ye said also, Behold, what a weariness *is it!* and ye have snuffed at it, saith the LORD of hosts; and ye brought *that which was* torn, and the lame, and the sick; thus ye brought an offering: should I accept this of your hand? saith the LORD.

14 But cursed *be* the deceiver, which hath in his flock a male, and voweth, and sacrificeth unto the Lord a corrupt thing: for I *am* a great King, saith the Lord of hosts, and my name *is* dreadful among the heathen.

CHAPTER 2

The priests are reproved for not keeping their covenants and not teaching the people—The Jews are condemned for dealing treacherously with one another and with their wives.

CHAPTER 3

The Lord's messenger will prepare the way for the Second Coming—The Lord will sit in judgment—The people of Israel are commanded to pay tithes and offerings—They keep a book of remembrance.

1 Behold, I will send my messenger, and he shall prepare the way before me: and the Lord, whom ye seek, shall suddenly come to his temple, even the messenger of the covenant, whom ye delight in: behold, he shall come, saith the Lord of hosts.

2 But who may abide the day of his coming? and who shall stand when he appeareth? for he *is* like a refiner's fire, and like fullers' soap:

Summary of Malachi 2

The Lord promises punishments to the priests for failing to follow the example of their faithful ancestors, the Levites. Their wickedness causes many people to lose faith in the Lord. Also, "the men of Judah and Levi had turned to foreign women and taken them as wives (Mal. 2:11, 13–15). Many had divorced their Israelite wives in order to accommodate their unrighteous desires. Malachi expressed well the Lord's hatred for this practice and its result: the rejection of all offerings made to him and the forfeiture of the consequent blessings (Mal. 2:12, 16–17)" (Draper, "Book of Malachi," 367).

Malachi 3:1–6. The Lord's Messenger Will Prepare the Way before Him

Who is the messenger in our dispensation sent to prepare the way before the Lord? (3:1) "John the Baptist did this very thing in the meridian of time but it remained for Joseph Smith to perform the glorious work in our day. He is the latter-day messenger who was sent to restore the gospel, which itself prepares a people for the return of the Lord" (McConkie, *New Witness for the Articles of Faith*, 629). Of course, Jesus Christ is the great "messenger of the covenant" who shall come. See commentary in *Book of Mormon Study Guide: Start to Finish, Revised Edition* for 3 Nephi 24:1. ⊕

Why is the Lord described as a refiner's fire? (3:2) A refiner is "a man who separates the precious metals from the dross with which in nature they are usually found mixed. Part of the process consists in the application of great heat, in order to bring the mass into a fluid state, hence the term 'refiner's fire.' Christ is the great Refiner. See Isa. 1:25; 48:10; Zech. 13:9; Mal. 3:2–3" (Bible Dictionary, "Refiner").

How do we respond when hardships come? (3:2) "In real life, we face actual, not imagined, hardships. There is pain—physical, emotional, and spiritual. There are heartbreaks when circumstances are very different from what we had anticipated. . . .

"When difficult things occur in our lives, what is our immediate response? Is it confusion or doubt or spiritual withdrawal? Is it a blow to our faith? Do we blame God or others for our circumstances? Or is our first response to remember who we are—that we are children of a loving God? Is that coupled with an absolute trust that He allows some earthly suffering *because* He knows it will bless us, like a refiner's fire, to become like Him and to gain our eternal inheritance?" (Hallstrom, "I Am a Child of God," 27).

What will the righteous sons of Levi offer up? (3:3) This righteous offering by the sons of Levi seems to encompass at least two elements. First, as Elder John A. Widtsoe notes: "The 'offering in righteousness' [D&C 128:24] is here identified with temple work for the salvation of the dead, which encompasses all the principles of the plan of salvation" (Widtsoe, *Evidences and Reconciliations*, 247). Second, the Lord promised that He will "purge" the Levites so that they will become worthy to function again (Mal. 3:3). When He has done this, He will direct the restoration of sacrifices (see D&C 13). ⊕

Malachi 3:7–12. Israel Will Be Blessed for Paying Tithes and Offerings

Why are we expected to pay tithes like those in Old Testament times? (3:8–9) "When the risen Lord appeared to the faithful on this continent, he taught them the commandments the prophet Malachi had already given to other children of Israel. The Lord commanded that they should record these words [Mal. 3:8–10; 3 Ne. 24:8–10].... Here we see that the law of tithing is not a remote Old Testament practice, but a commandment directly from the Savior to the people of our day. The Lord reaffirmed that law in modern revelation, commanding his people to pay 'one-tenth

3 And he shall sit *as* a refiner and purifier of
silver: and he shall purify the sons of Levi,
and purge them as gold and silver, that they
may offer unto the LORD an offering in righteousness.

4 Then shall the offering of Judah and
Jerusalem be pleasant unto the LORD, as in
the days of old, and as in former years.

5 And I will come near to you to judgment;
and I will be a swift witness against the sorcerers, and against the adulterers, and against
false swearers, and against those that oppress
the hireling in *his* wages, the widow, and the
fatherless, and that turn aside the stranger
from his right, and fear not me, saith the
LORD of hosts.

6 For I *am* the LORD, I change not; therefore
ye sons of Jacob are not consumed.

7 ¶ Even from the days of your fathers ye are
gone away from mine ordinances, and have
not kept *them.* Return unto me, and I will
return unto you, saith the LORD of hosts. But
ye said, Wherein shall we return?

8 ¶ Will a man rob God? Yet ye have robbed
me. But ye say, Wherein have we robbed
thee? In tithes and offerings.

9 Ye *are* cursed with a curse: for ye have
robbed me, *even* this whole nation.

10 Bring ye all the tithes into the storehouse, that there may be meat in mine house, and prove me now herewith, saith the LORD of hosts, if I will not open you the windows of heaven, and pour you out a blessing, that *there shall* not *be room* enough *to receive it.*

11 And I will rebuke the devourer for your sakes, and he shall not destroy the fruits of your ground; neither shall your vine cast her fruit before the time in the field, saith the LORD of hosts.

12 And all nations shall call you blessed: for ye shall be a delightsome land, saith the LORD of hosts.

13 ¶ Your words have been stout against me, saith the LORD. Yet ye say, What have we spoken *so much* against thee?

14 Ye have said, It *is* vain to serve God: and what profit *is it* that we have kept his ordinance, and that we have walked mournfully before the LORD of hosts?

15 And now we call the proud happy; yea, they that work wickedness are set up; yea, *they that* tempt God are even delivered.

16 ¶ Then they that feared the LORD spake often one to another: and the LORD hearkened, and heard *it,* and a book of remembrance was written before him for them that feared the LORD, and that thought upon his name.

of all their interest annually' and declaring that 'this shall be a standing law unto them forever' (D&C 119:4)" (Oaks, "Tithing," 33).

How does the Lord "open [to us] the windows of heaven"? (3:10–12) "The promise following obedience to this principle is that the windows of heaven would be open and blessings would be poured out that we would hardly be able to contain. The opening of the windows of heaven, of course, means revelations from God to him who is willing thus to sacrifice" (Lee, "Way to Eternal Life," 16).

What is a possible meaning of the promise of the Lord to "rebuke the devourer for [our] sakes"? (3:11) President Gordon B. Hinckley said: "The Lord has promised that he will rebuke the devourer for our sakes. Malachi speaks of the fruits of our ground. May not that rebuke of the devourer apply to various of our personal efforts and concerns?"

"There is promised in modern revelation a great blessing of wisdom, of knowledge, even hidden treasures of knowledge. Malachi has told us that ours shall be a delightsome land if we will walk in obedience to this law. . . . What a marvelous condition to be a delightsome people whom others would describe as blessed!" ("Sacred Law of Tithing," 4).

Malachi 3:13–18. A Book of Remembrance Is Written for the Righteous

Why do the wicked often seem happier than the righteous? (3:14–15) "We live in a hedonistic age when many question the importance of the Lord's commandments or simply ignore them. Not infrequently, people who flout divine directives such as the law of chastity, the standard of honesty, and the holiness of the Sabbath seem to prosper and enjoy the good things of life, at times even more so than those who are striving to be obedient. Some begin to wonder if the effort and sacrifices are worth it. . . . The wicked may 'have joy in their works for a season,' but it is always temporary" (Christofferson, "Joy of the Saints," 15–16). ⊕

What is the "book of remembrance" referred to in this verse? (3:16) The Guide to the Scriptures describes this as "a book begun by Adam in which were recorded the works of his descendants; also any similar records kept by prophets and faithful members since that time. Adam and his children kept a book of remembrance, in which they wrote by the spirit of inspiration, and a book of the generations, which contained a genealogy (Moses 6:5, 8). Such records may well have a part in determining our final judgment" (Guide to the Scriptures, "Book of Remembrance").

Who are the Lord's "jewels" and how will they be preserved? (3:17–18) These jewels, or "royal treasure" (Mal. 3:17*b*), are the righteous saints the Lord will find on earth when He comes again. In hopeful imagery, the children of God "shall be as the stones of a crown, lifted up as an ensign" (Zech. 9:16). "At the last day, when wrath is about to be poured out on the earth, the Lord will recollect those whose names he knows and he will spare them from judgment [Mal. 3: 17]. They will be clearly identified as his own people, his special possession. . . . No longer will it be impossible to distinguish between the righteous and the wicked . . . for then all hypocrisy will be stripped away" (Merrill, "Malachi," 861). ⊕

Malachi 4:1–6. The Wicked Will Be Burned at the Second Coming, and the Righteous Will Be Saved

What effect does the burning have on the wicked? (4:1) "Malachi's image is of an altogether more destructive burning. Here, he says that among the proud and wicked there will be absolutely nothing left. Indeed, the burning will not only consume the tree trunks and branches; it will burn the roots out of the ground so that they are gone too. . . . The inference is that the wicked will be totally disconnected and cut off from their ancestors and that they will have no posterity" (Thompson, "Joseph Smith and the Doctrine of Sealing," 10–11). See commentary in *Book of Mormon Study Guide: Start to Finish, Revised Edition* for 3 Nephi 25:1. ⊕

How will the experience of the Lord's coming differ between the righteous and the wicked? (4:2–3) "The great and dreadful day of the Lord! [see Malachi 4:5] . . . Is it a day of sorrow or of joy? Is it our desire to live when that dread hour arrives, or will we plead for a merciful death lest the devastations and suffering be greater than we can bear? . . .

"In truth and in reality, except for faithful members of The Church of Jesus Christ of Latter-day Saints; except for other decent and upright people who are living clean and proper lives in spite of the allurements and enticings of the world; except for those who are living either a celestial or a terrestrial law—except for

17 And they shall be mine, saith the Lord of hosts, in that day when I make up my jewels; and I will spare them, as a man spareth his own son that serveth him.

18 Then shall ye return, and discern between the righteous and the wicked, between him that serveth God and him that serveth him not.

CHAPTER 4

At the Second Coming, the proud and wicked will be burned as stubble—Elijah will return before that great and dreadful day.

1 For, behold, the day cometh, that shall burn as an oven; and all the proud, yea, and all that do wickedly, shall be stubble: and the day that cometh shall burn them up, saith the Lord of hosts, that it shall leave them neither root nor branch.

2 ¶ But unto you that fear my name shall the Sun of righteousness arise with healing in his wings; and ye shall go forth, and grow up as calves of the stall.

3 And ye shall tread down the wicked; for they shall be ashes under the soles of your feet in the day that I shall do *this,* saith the Lord of hosts.

4 ¶ Remember ye the law of Moses my servant, which I commanded unto him in Horeb for all Israel, *with* the statutes and judgments.

5 ¶ Behold, I will send you Elijah the prophet before the coming of the great and dreadful day of the LORD:

6 And he shall turn the heart of the fathers to the children, and the heart of the children to their fathers, lest I come and smite the earth with a curse.

THE END OF THE PROPHETS

these, the Second Coming will be a day of vengeance and of wrath" (McConkie, *Millennial Messiah*, 495–96).

When did Elijah come to fulfill this prophecy? (4:5) "On April 3, 1836, Oliver Cowdery and Joseph Smith saw and received priesthood keys from ancient prophets who held those keys: Moses, Elias, and Elijah. This restoration of keys and authority was so significant the ancient prophet Malachi had prophesied of it (see Malachi 4:5–6). It was necessary that these Old Testament prophets bestow power and authority upon the Church so the kingdom of God could once again be established upon the earth" (Anderson, *Joseph Smith's Kirtland*, 172; see D&C 110:11–16). "When Elijah appeared in the Kirtland Temple April 3, 1836, he acknowledged his appearance was in

Elijah Will Be Sent to Turn the Hearts of Fathers and Children (Malachi 4:4–6)

"The prophet Malachi, in the last book of the Old Testament, prophesied of a time when Elijah the prophet would return to the earth 'before the coming of the great and dreadful day of the Lord . . . [to] turn the heart of the fathers to the children, and the heart of the children to their fathers, lest [He] come and smite the earth with a curse' (Malachi 4:5–6).

"When the angel Moroni appeared to 17-year-old Joseph Smith in 1823, he quoted these same verses from Malachi but rendered them differently [see JS–H 1:38–39]. Four times the angel Moroni repeated Malachi's words to the boy Joseph. . . .

"Only through modern revelation is Elijah's complete role revealed. He was the last prophet to hold the sealing power of the Melchizedek Priesthood before the time of Jesus Christ. With Moses, he appeared to the Savior and Peter, James, and John on the Mount of Transfiguration in the meridian of time (see Matthew 17:1–4; Mark 9:2–5). As a seminal element of the Restoration, Elijah appeared to Joseph Smith and Oliver Cowdery in 1836 in the Kirtland Temple. There, he again restored the keys of the sealing power, this time for sealing families in this dispensation in fulfillment of Malachi's prophecy (see D&C 110:13–16). Because Elijah was sent in this dispensation, the fulness of salvation is available to both the living and the dead.

"Elijah's mission is facilitated by what is sometimes called the spirit of Elijah, which, as President Russell M. Nelson . . . has taught, is 'a manifestation of the Holy Ghost bearing witness of the divine nature of the family' [Nelson, 'New Harvest Time,' 34]" (Cook, "Joy of Family History Work," 30, 31).

It was in the Kirtland Temple that Elijah appeared to Joseph Smith and Oliver Cowdery and committed to them the keys of this dispensation, the keys "to turn the hearts of the fathers to the children, and the children to the fathers" (see D&C 110:13–16).

fulfillment of the prophecy [in Mal. 4:5] 'which was spoken . . . by the mouth of Malachi' (D&C 110:14)" (Ludlow, *Companion to Your Study of the Old Testament*, 404).

What might it mean to "turn" the hearts of the fathers to the children? (4:5-6) Moroni quoted these verses when he first appeared to Joseph. He added that Elijah was acting under and revealing 'priesthood' and he was 'planting in the hearts of the children the promises made to the fathers' so the earth would not be wasted when the Lord returns (Joseph Smith—History 1:36–39). "Now, the word *turn* here should be translated *bind*, or seal. But what is the object of this important mission? or how is it to be fulfilled? The keys are to be delivered, the spirit of Elijah is to come, the Gospel to be established, the Saints of God gathered, Zion built up, and the Saints to come up as saviors on Mount Zion [see Obad. 1:21]" (*Joseph Smith* [manual], 472–73). ⊕

SOURCES

Abernathy, Andrew T. *The Book of Isaiah and God's Kingdom: A Thematic Theological Approach*. 2016.

Abingdon Old Testament Commentaries series. Edited by Patrick D. Miller. 16 vols. 1973–2017.

Ackerman, Susan. "Child Sacrifice: Returning God's Gift." *Bible Review*, Jun. 1993, 20–56.

Adams, L. LaMar. "Isaiah: Disciple and Witness of Christ." In *A Witness of Jesus Christ*, edited by Richard D. Draper, 1–17. Sperry Symposium series. 2013.

———. "Job: The Man and His Message." *Ensign*, Mar. 1982, 72–74.

Alexander, Joseph A. *Commentary on Isaiah*. 1867.

Alexander, Ralph H. "Ezekiel." In *The Expositor's Bible Commentary*, rev. ed, edited by Tremper Longman III and David E. Garland, 7:641–924. 2010.

The Allegory of the Olive Tree: The Olive, the Bible, and Jacob 5. Edited by John W. Welch and Stephen D. Ricks. 1994

Allen, Richard J. *Study Commentary on the Old Testament*. 2013.

Allen, Ronald B. "Numbers." In *The Expositor's Bible Commentary*, edited by Frank E. Gaebelein, 2:655–1008. 1990.

———. "Numbers." In *The Expositor's Bible Commentary*, rev. ed., edited by Tremper Longman III and David E. Garland, 2:23–455. 2012.

Alma, the Testimony of the Word. Edited by Monte S. Nyman and Charles D. Tate, Jr. Vol. 6 of Book of Mormon Symposium series. 1992.

Alter, Robert. *The Art of Biblical Narrative*. 1981.

———. *The Art of Biblical Poetry*, 1985.

———. *The Hebrew Bible: A Translation with Commentary*. 3 vols. 2019.

Amado, Carlos H. "An Eternal Vision." *Ensign*, Nov. 1993, 44–46.

Amerding, Carl E. "Nahum." In *The Expositor's Bible Commentary*, rev. ed., edited by Tremper Longman III and David E. Garland, 8:553–601. 2008.

Amistad, Modesto M., Jr. "Wanted: Modern Nehemiahs." *Ensign*, Dec. 2002, 44–46.

The Anchor Bible series. Edited by William Foxwell Albright and David Noel Freedman. 86 vols. 1956–2008.

Ancient Christian Commentary on Scripture series. Edited by Thomas C. Oden. 29 vols. 2000–2010.

Ancient Israel in Egypt and the Exodus. Ebook. Edited by Margaret Warker, Noah Wiener, and Dorothy Resig. 2012.

Andersen, Neil L. "Come unto Him." *Ensign*, May 2009, 78–80.

———. *The Divine Gift of Forgiveness*. 2019.

———. "Fruit." *Ensign*, Nov. 2019, 116–20.

———. "Power in the Priesthood." *Ensign*, Nov. 2013, 92–95.

———. "The Prophet of God." *Ensign*, May 2018, 24–27.

———. "Prophets and Spiritual Mole Crickets." *Ensign*, Nov. 1999, 16–18.

———. "Repent . . . That I May Heal You." *Ensign*, Nov. 2009, 40–43.

———. "The Spiritual Power of Honesty." *New Era*, Sep. 2019, 2–5.

———. "A Witness of God." *Ensign*, Nov. 2016, 35–38.

———. "Wounded." *Ensign*, Nov. 2018, 83–86.

Anderson, Joseph. "The Road to Happiness." *Ensign*, May 1975, 29–31.

Anderson, Karl Ricks. *Joseph Smith's Kirtland: Eyewitness Accounts.* 1989.

Anderson, Travis T. "Naaman, Baptism, and Cleansing." *Ensign*, Jan. 1994, 28–30.

Andreason, Bruce L. "The Mantle of Elijah." *Ensign*, Aug. 2002, 24–26.

Apocryphal Writings and the Latter-day Saints. Edited by C. Wilford Griggs. 1986.

The Apostle Paul: His Life and His Testimony. Edited by Paul Y. Hoskisson. Sperry Syposium series. 1994.

Archer, Gleason L., Jr. "Daniel." In *The Expositor's Bible Commentary with the New International Version*, edited by Frank E. Gaebelein, 7:1–157. 1985.

Arnold, Bill T. *1 and 2 Samuel.* In The NIV Application Commentary: Old Testament series. Edited by Terry Muck. 2003.

Asay, Carlos E. "The Church Today in the British Isles: An Interview with the Europe Area Presidency." *Ensign*, July 1987, 12–19.

———. "If a Man Die, Shall He Live Again?" *Ensign*, May 1994, 10–12.

———. "The Oath and Covenant of the Priesthood." *Ensign*, Nov. 1985, 43–45.

Ascending the Mountain of the Lord: Temple, Praise, and Worship in the Old Testament. Edited by David R. Seely, Jeffrey R. Chadwick, and Matthew J. Grey. Sperry Symposium series. 2013.

Ashley, Timothy R. *The Book of Numbers.* In The New International Commentary on the Old Testament series. Edited by R. K. Harrison and Robert L. Hubbard, Jr. 1993.

Ashton, Marvin J. "The Measure of Our Hearts." *Ensign*, Nov. 1988, 15–17.

———. "On Being Worthy." *Ensign*, May 1989, 20–23.

———. "Peace—A Triumph of Principles." *Ensign*, Nov. 1985, 69–71.

———. "Rated A." *Ensign*, Nov. 1977, 71–73.

———. "Shake Off the Chains with Which Ye Are Bound." *Ensign*, Nov. 1986, 13–15.

———. "This Is No Harm." *Ensign*, May 1982, 9–11.

———. "What Is a Friend?" *Ensign*, Jan. 1973, 41–43.

Auld, Graeme. "2 Samuel." In *Eerdmans Commentary on the Bible*, edited by James D. G. Dunn and John W. Rogerson, 230–45. 2003.

Austin, Michael. *Re-reading Job: Understanding the Ancient World's Greatest Poem.* 2014.

Baker Commentary on the Old Testament Wisdom and Psalms series. Edited by Tremper Longman III. 7 vols. 2005–2012.

Baker, LeGrand L., and Stephen D. Ricks. *Who Shall Ascend into the Hill of the Lord?: The Psalms in Israel's Temple Worship in the Old Testament and in the Book of Mormon.* 2010.

Baker, William H. "Knowing, Doing, and Being." Brigham Young University devotional, 25 July 2006. Speeches.BYU.edu.

Baldwin, Joyce G. *1 and 2 Samuel.* In Tyndale Old Testament Commentaries series. Edited by D. J. Wiseman. 2008.

Ball, Terry. "Isaiah's Imagery of Plants and Planting." In *Thy People Shall Be My People and Thy God My God*, edited by Paul Y. Hoskisson, 17–35. Sperry Symposium series. 1994.

———, and Nathan Winn. *Making Sense of Isaiah.* 2009.

Ballard, M. Russell. "Beware of False Prophets and False Teachers." *Ensign*, Nov. 1999, 62–64.

———. "God Is at the Helm." *Ensign*, Nov. 2015, 24–27.

———. "His Word Ye Shall Receive." *Ensign*, May 2001, 65–67.

———. "How the Lord Prepared the World for the Restoration." *Ensign*, Jan. 2020, 14–21.

———. "The Law of Sacrifice." Ensign, Oct. 1998, 6–13.

———. "Learning the Lessons of the Past." *Ensign*, May 2009, 31–34.

———. "The Miracle of the Holy Bible." Ensign, May 2007, 80–82.

———. "Precious Gifts from God." *Ensign*, May 2018, 9–11.

Ballard, Melvin J. *Melvin J. Ballard: Crusader for Righteousness.* 1968.

———. "Struggle for the Soul." *New Era*, Mar. 1984, 32–39.

Bangerter, Steven R. "Laying the Foundation of a Great Work." *Ensign*, Nov. 2018, 15–17.

Bangerter, W. Grant. "The Voice of the Lord Is unto All People." *Ensign*, Nov. 1979, 9–12.

Barker, Margaret. "Isaiah." In *Eerdmans Commentary on the Bible*, edited by James D. G. Dunn and John W. Rogerson, 489–542. 2003.

———. "What Did King Josiah Reform?" In *Glimpses of Lehi's Jerusalem*, edited by John W. Welch, David Rolph Seely, and Jo Ann H. Seely, 523–42.

Barney, Kevin L. "Understanding Old Testament Poetry." *Ensign*, June 1990, 50–54.

Bassett, Arthur R. "The King Called David." *Ensign*, Oct. 1973, 62–69.

Bateman, Merrill J. "A Pattern for All." *Ensign*, Nov. 2005, 74–76.

———. "The Power of Hymns." *Ensign*, July 2001, 14–20.

———. "The Power to Heal from Within." *Ensign*, May 1995, 13–14.

———. "Stretching the Cords of the Tent." *Ensign*, May 1994, 65.

Batto, Bernard F. "Red Sea or Reed Sea?" *Biblical Archaeology Review*, Jul/Aug 1984, 57–63.

Beck, David M. "Consecrate." In *Intrepreter's Dictionary of the Bible*, edited by George A. Buttrick, 676–77. 1962.

Bednar, David A. "Clean Hands and a Pure Heart." *Ensign*, Nov. 2007, 80–83.

———. "Honorably Hold a Name and Standing." *Ensign*, May 2009, 97–100.

———. "If Ye Had Known Me." *Ensign*, Nov. 2016, 102–5.

———. "Jesus Christ: The Source of Enduring Joy." *Ensign*, Dec. 2019, 17–21.

———. "Meek and Lowly of Heart." *Ensign*, May 2018, 30–33.

———. "Morning and Evening Prayers." *New Era*, Jan. 2017, 3–4.

———. "On the Lord's Side: Lessons from Zions' Camp. *Ensign*, July 2017, 26–35.

———. "Prepared to Obtain Every Needful Thing." *Ensign*, May 2019, 101–4.

———. "Seek Learning by Faith." *Ensign*, Sep. 2007, 61–68.

———. "The Spirit of Revelation." *Ensign*, May 2011, 87–90.

———. "The Tender Mercies of the Lord." *Ensign*, May 2005, 99–102.

———. "Therefore They Hushed Their Fears." *Ensign*, May 2015, 46–49.

———. "Watchful unto Prayer Continually." *Ensign*, Nov. 2019, 31–35.

———. "We Believe in Being Chaste." *Ensign*, May 2013, 41–44.

———. "Who's on the Lord's Side? Now Is the Time to Show." Brigham Young University–Idaho Education Week devotional, 30 Jul. 2010.

Behold the Lamb of God: An Easter Celebration. Edited by Richard Neitzel Holzapfel, Frank F. Judd Jr., and Thomas A. Wayment. 2008.

Belcher, Richard P. *Finding Favour in the Sight of God: A Theology of Wisdom Literature.* In *New Studies in Biblical Theology*, Book 46. Edited by D. A. Carson. 2018.

Belnap, Daniel L. "'How Excellent Is Thy Lovingkindness': The Gospel Principle of Hesed." In *Gospel of*

Jesus Christ in the Old Testament, edited by D. Kelly Ogden, Jared W. Ludlow, Kerry Muhlestein, Patty Smith, and Thomas R. Valletta, 170–86. Sperry Symposium series. 2009.

———. "'That I May Dwell among Them': Liminality and Ritual in the Tabernacle." In *Ascending the Mountain of the Lord*, edited by David R. Seely, Jeffrey R. Chadwick, and Matthew J. Grey, 12–35. Sperry Symposium series. 2013.

Bennion, Adam S. In Conference Report, Apr. 1955, 109–12.

Bennion, Lowell L. *Best of Lowell L. Bennion: Selected Writings 1928–1988*. Edited by Eugene England. 1988.

Benson, Ezra Taft. "Beware of Pride." *Ensign*, May 1989, 4–7.

———. "The Book of Mormon and the Doctrine and Covenants." *Ensign*, May 1987, 83–85.

———. "Civic Standards for the Faithful Saints." *Ensign*, July 1972, 59–61.

———. In Conference Report, Oct. 1949, 22–29.

———. "Do Not Despair." *Ensign*, Nov. 1974, 65–67.

———. *Ezra Taft Benson*. Teachings of Presidents of the Church series. 2014.

———. "Five Marks of the Divinity of Jesus Christ." *Ensign*, Dec. 2001, 8–15.

———. "Fourteen Fundamentals in Following the Prophet." Brigham Young University devotional, 26 Feb. 1980. In *BYU Speeches of the Year 1981*, 26–30.

———. "Jesus Christ—Gifts and Expectations." *New Era*, May 1975, 16–21.

———. "A Marvelous Work and a Wonder." *Ensign*, May 1980, 32–34.

———. "A Message to Judah from Joseph." *Ensign*, Dec. 1976, 67–72.

———. "Our Obligation and Challenge." Address to regional representatives' seminar, 30 Sep. 1977, 2–3. Cited in David A. Bednar, "On the Lord's Side," *Ensign*, July 2017, 31.

———. "The Power of the Word." *Ensign*, May 1986, 79–82.

———. "Satan's Thrust—Youth." *Ensign*, Dec. 1971, 53–56.

———. *Teachings of Ezra Taft Benson*. Edited by Reed A. Benson. 1988.

———. "To the Mothers in Zion." Fireside address, 22 Feb. 1987. As cited in *Eternal Marriage Student Manual*, 352–57. 2003.

———. "To the 'Youth of the Noble Birthright.'" *Ensign*. May 1986, 43–46.

———. "Watchman, Warn the Wicked." *Ensign*, July 1973, 38–41.

———. "What I Hope You Will Teach Your Children about the Temple." *Ensign*, Aug. 1985, 6–10.

———, Gordon B. Hinckley, and Thomas S. Monson. "First Presidency Statement on the King James Version of the Bible." *Ensign*, Aug. 1992, 80.

Berlin, Adele. "Ruth." *Bible Review*. Aug. 1994, 40–48.

Berrett, LaMar C. *Discovering the World of the Bible*. 1996.

Berrett, William E. *Teachings of the Book of Mormon*. Volume 1. 1962.

The Best of Women's Conference: Selected Talks Selected from 25 Years of BYU Women's Conferences. 2000.

Bewer, Julius A. *The Literature of the Old Testament*. Rev. ed. 1933.

Bible Dictionary. The Church of Jesus Christ of Latter-day Saints. 2013.

Birch, Bruce C. "The First and Second Books of Samuel." In *The New Interpreter's Bible*, edited by Leander E. Keck, 2:947–1383. 1998.

Bird, Randall C. "Moses and the Passover." *Ensign*, Feb. 2002, 31–33.

Biwul, Joel K. *A Theological Examination of Symbolism in Ezekiel with Emphasis on the Shepherd Metaphor*. 2013.

Black, Susan Easton. *400 Questions and Answers about the Old Testament*. 2013.

Blaising, Craig A., and Carmen S. Hardin. *Psalms 1–50.* In Ancient Christian Commentary on Scripture series. Edited by Thomas C. Oden. 2008.

Block, Daniel I. *The Book of Ezekiel, Chapters 1–24.* In The New International Commentary on the Old Testament series. Edited by R. K. Harrison and Robert L. Hubbard, Jr. 1997.

Blumell, Lincoln H. and David M. Whitchurch. "The Coming Forth of the King James Bible." In *The King James Bible and the Restoration*, edited by Kent P. Jackson, 43–60. 2011.

Boda, Mark J. *Haggai, Zechariah.* In The NIV Application Commentary: Old Testament series. Edited by Terry Muck. 2004.

———. "Judges." In *The Expositor's Bible Commentary*, rev. ed., edited by Tremper Longman III and David E. Garland, 2:1044–288. 2012.

Boehm, Bruce J. "Wanderers in the Promised Land." In *Journal of Book of Mormon Studies*, Vol. 3., No. 1 (31 Jan 1994): 187–203.

Book of Mormon Student Manual. 2009.

Bowen, Matthew L. "My People Are Willing: The Mention of Aminadab in the Narrative Context of Helaman 5-6." In Inte*rpreter: A Journal of Latter-day Saint Faith and Scholarship*, 19 (2016): 83–107.

Bowen, Shayne M. "Fasting with Power." *Ensign*, Apr. 2009, 64–67.

Bracke, John M. *Jeremiah 1–29.* In Westminster Bible Companion: Old Testament series. Edited by Patrick D. Miller and David L. Bartlett. 2000.

———. *Jeremiah 30–52 and Lamentations.* In Westminster Bible Companion: Old Testament series. Edited by Patrick D. Miller and David L. Bartlett. 2000.

Bradshaw, Jeffrey M. "Frequently Asked Questions about Science and Genesis." In *Science and Mormonism 1: Cosmos, Earth, and Man*, edited by David H. Bailey, Jeffrey M. Bradshaw, John S. Lewis, Gregory L. Smith, and Michael R. Stark, 193–257. 2016.

———. "The Meaning of the Atonement." *Meridan Magazine* (website). May 30, 2010.

———. "Was Noah Drunk or in a Vision?" *The Interpreter Foundation* (website), KnoWhy #OT106B.

———. "What Are the Most Cited, Recited, and Misunderstood Verses in Deuteronomy?" *The Interpreter Foundation* (website), KnoWhy #OTL17A.

Bragg, Mark A. "Entering the Gate of Heaven." *Ensign*, January 2019, 66–69.

Brandt, Edward J. "Early Families of the Earth." *Ensign*, Mar. 1973, 18.

———. "The Exile and First Return of Judah." *Ensign,* July 1974, 12–13.

———. "The Time of the Divided Kingdoms." *Ensign*, April 1974, 30–31.

———. "What Was the Ark of the Covenant, and Does It Exist in Any Form Today?" *New Era*, May 1973, 49–50.

Brandt, G. Erik. *The Book of Daniel: Writings and Prophecies.* 2018.

Brewster, Hoyt W. *Behold, I Come Quickly.* 1994.

———. *Doctrine and Covenants Encyclopedia*, rev. ed. 2012.

———. *Isaiah Plain and Simple: The Message of Isaiah in the Book of Mormon.* 1995.

Bridges, Ronald, and Luther A. Weigle. *The King James Bible Word Book.* 1994.

Brooke, George J. "Power to the Powerless—A Long-Lost Song of Miriam." *Biblical Archaeology Review*, 20.3 (1994): 62–65.

Brown, Matthew B. *The Gate of Heaven: Insights on the Doctrines and Symbols of the Temple.* 1999.

Brown, Michael L. "Jeremiah." In *The Expositor's Bible Commentary,* rev. ed., edited by Tremper Longman III and David E. Garland, 7:21–572. 2010.

Brown, Raymond. *The Message of Nehemiah.* 1998.

Brown, S. Kent. "Biblical Egypt: Land of Refuge, Land of Bondage." *Ensign*, Sep. 1980, 45–50.

———. "The Book of Hosea." In *1 Kings to Malachi*, edited by Kent P. Jackson, 61–67. Vol. 4 of Studies in Scripture series. 1993.

———. "The Exodus: Seeing It as a Test, a Testimony, and a Type." *Ensign*, Feb. 1990, 54–57.

———. *From Jerusalem to Zarahemla.* 1998.

———. "Trust in the Lord: Exodus and Faith." In *The Old Testament and the Latter-day Saints*, 85–94. Sperry Symposium series. 1986.

———. "Zacharias and Elisabeth, Joseph and Mary." In *The Life and Teachings of Jesus Christ: From Bethlehem through the Sermon on the Mount*, edited by Richard Neitzel Holzapfel and Thomas A. Wayment, 91–120. 2005.

———, and Richard Neitzel Holzapfel. *Between the Testaments: From Malachi to Matthew.* 2002.

———, and Richard Neitzel Holzapfel. "The Lost 500 Years: From Malachi to John the Baptist." *Ensign*, Dec. 2014, 56–60.

———, and Richard Neitzel Holzapfel. *The Lost 500 Years: What Happened between the Old and New Testaments.* 2006.

Browning, Paul K. "Gathering Scattered Israel: Then and Now." *Ensign*, July 1998, 54–61.

Bruce, F. F. *The New International Bible Commentary.* 1986.

Bruckner, James. *Jonah, Nahum, Habakkuk, Zephaniah.* In The NIV Application Commentary: Old Testament series. Edited by Terry Muck. 2004.

Brueggemann, Walter. *Isaiah 1–39.* In Westminster Bible Companion: Old Testament series. Edited by Patrick D. Miller and David L. Bartlett. 1998.

Bunker, Robert L. "Design of the Liahona and the Purpose of the Second Spindle." In *Journal of Book of Mormon Studies*, Vol. 3, No. 2 (31 Jul. 1994): 1–11.

Burgess, Allan K. *New Insights into the Old Testament.* 1993.

Burgess, Henry. *Journal of Sacred Literature and Biblical Record.* 1855.

Burton, F. Howard. "Repentance." *Ensign*, May 1991, 12–14.

Burton, Linda K. "I Was a Stranger." *Ensign*, May 2016, 13–15.

Burton, R. Scott. "The Hymnal of Ancient Israel." In *1 Kings to Malachi*, edited by Kent P. Jackson, 407–25. Vol. 4 of Studies in Scripture series. 1993.

———. "The Nature of God in the Psalms." In *1 Kings to Malachi*, edited by Kent P. Jackson, 426–47. Vol. 4 of Studies in Scripture series. 1993.

———. "Saul and the Institution of Kingship in Israel." In *Genesis to 2 Samuel*, edited by Kent P. Jackson and Robert L. Millet, 281–92. Vol. 3 of Studies in Scripture series. 1985.

Burton, Theodore M. In Conference Report, Oct. 1964, 32–36.

———. In Conference Report, Oct. 1967, 79–82.

———. "The Meaning of Repentance." *Ensign*, Aug. 1988, 6–9.

By Study and Also by Faith: Essays in Honor of Hugh W. Nibley. Edited by John M. Lundquist and Stephen D. Ricks. 2 vols. 1990.

Bytheway, John. *Isaiah for Airheads.* 2006.

Cabal, Ted. *The Apologetics Study Bible.* 2007.

Calabro, David M. "Gestures of Praise: Lifting and Spreading the Hands in Biblical Prayer." In *Ascending the Mountain of the Lord: Temple, Praise, and Worship in the Old Testament*, edited by David R. Seely, Jeffrey R. Chadwick, and Matthew J. Grey, 105–21. Sperry Symposium series. 2013.

Callis, Charles A. In Conference Report, Apr. 1944, 131–34.

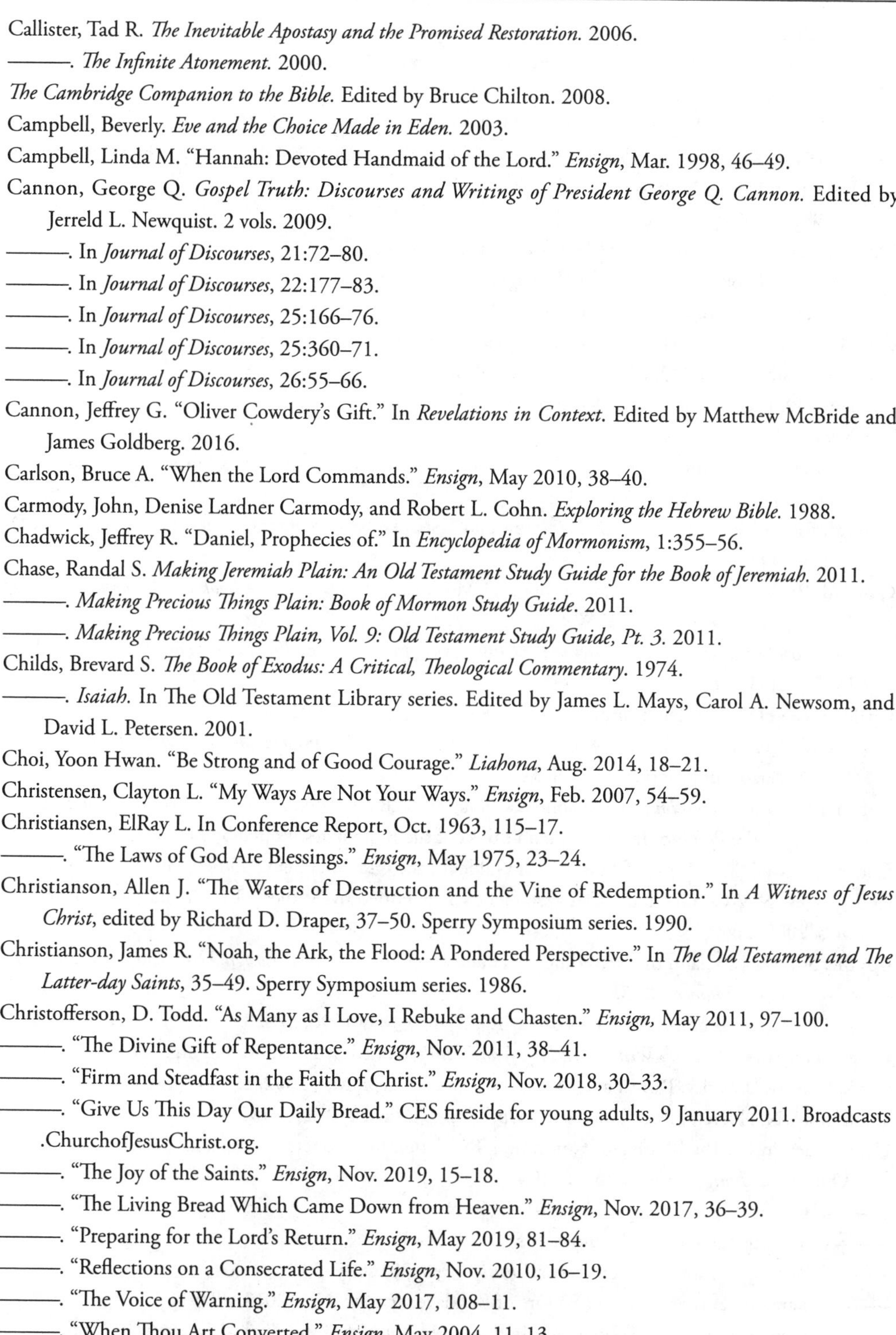

Callister, Tad R. *The Inevitable Apostasy and the Promised Restoration.* 2006.

———. *The Infinite Atonement.* 2000.

The Cambridge Companion to the Bible. Edited by Bruce Chilton. 2008.

Campbell, Beverly. *Eve and the Choice Made in Eden.* 2003.

Campbell, Linda M. "Hannah: Devoted Handmaid of the Lord." *Ensign*, Mar. 1998, 46–49.

Cannon, George Q. *Gospel Truth: Discourses and Writings of President George Q. Cannon.* Edited by Jerreld L. Newquist. 2 vols. 2009.

———. In *Journal of Discourses*, 21:72–80.

———. In *Journal of Discourses*, 22:177–83.

———. In *Journal of Discourses*, 25:166–76.

———. In *Journal of Discourses*, 25:360–71.

———. In *Journal of Discourses*, 26:55–66.

Cannon, Jeffrey G. "Oliver Cowdery's Gift." In *Revelations in Context.* Edited by Matthew McBride and James Goldberg. 2016.

Carlson, Bruce A. "When the Lord Commands." *Ensign*, May 2010, 38–40.

Carmody, John, Denise Lardner Carmody, and Robert L. Cohn. *Exploring the Hebrew Bible.* 1988.

Chadwick, Jeffrey R. "Daniel, Prophecies of." In *Encyclopedia of Mormonism*, 1:355–56.

Chase, Randal S. *Making Jeremiah Plain: An Old Testament Study Guide for the Book of Jeremiah.* 2011.

———. *Making Precious Things Plain: Book of Mormon Study Guide.* 2011.

———. *Making Precious Things Plain, Vol. 9: Old Testament Study Guide, Pt. 3.* 2011.

Childs, Brevard S. *The Book of Exodus: A Critical, Theological Commentary.* 1974.

———. *Isaiah.* In The Old Testament Library series. Edited by James L. Mays, Carol A. Newsom, and David L. Petersen. 2001.

Choi, Yoon Hwan. "Be Strong and of Good Courage." *Liahona*, Aug. 2014, 18–21.

Christensen, Clayton L. "My Ways Are Not Your Ways." *Ensign*, Feb. 2007, 54–59.

Christiansen, ElRay L. In Conference Report, Oct. 1963, 115–17.

———. "The Laws of God Are Blessings." *Ensign*, May 1975, 23–24.

Christianson, Allen J. "The Waters of Destruction and the Vine of Redemption." In *A Witness of Jesus Christ*, edited by Richard D. Draper, 37–50. Sperry Symposium series. 1990.

Christianson, James R. "Noah, the Ark, the Flood: A Pondered Perspective." In *The Old Testament and The Latter-day Saints*, 35–49. Sperry Symposium series. 1986.

Christofferson, D. Todd. "As Many as I Love, I Rebuke and Chasten." *Ensign,* May 2011, 97–100.

———. "The Divine Gift of Repentance." *Ensign*, Nov. 2011, 38–41.

———. "Firm and Steadfast in the Faith of Christ." *Ensign*, Nov. 2018, 30–33.

———. "Give Us This Day Our Daily Bread." CES fireside for young adults, 9 January 2011. Broadcasts .ChurchofJesusChrist.org.

———. "The Joy of the Saints." *Ensign*, Nov. 2019, 15–18.

———. "The Living Bread Which Came Down from Heaven." *Ensign*, Nov. 2017, 36–39.

———. "Preparing for the Lord's Return." *Ensign*, May 2019, 81–84.

———. "Reflections on a Consecrated Life." *Ensign*, Nov. 2010, 16–19.

———. "The Voice of Warning." *Ensign*, May 2017, 108–11.

———. "When Thou Art Converted." *Ensign*, May 2004, 11–13.

———. "Why Marrige, Why Family." *Ensign*, May 2015, 50–53.

Clark, E. Douglas. *The Blessings of Abraham: Becoming a Zion People.* 2005.

———. *Echoes of Eden: Eternal Lessons from Our First Parents.* 2010.

Clark, J. Reuben, Jr. *Behold the Lamb of God.* 1962.

———. In Conference Report, Oct. 1936, 111–15.

———. *Man: God's Greatest Miracle.* Address given at the summer religious course for Seminary and Institute teachers, 21 June 1954. 1975.

———. *Why the King James Version.* 1979.

Clark, James R. *Messages of the First Presidency.* 6 vols. 1965–1975.

Clark, Kim B. "Look unto Jesus Christ." *Ensign,* May 2019, 54–57.

Clarke, Adam. *Adam Clarke's Commentary.* 1832.

Clayton, L. Whitney. "Blessed Are the Pure in Heart." *Ensign,* Nov. 2007, 51–53.

Clayton, Weatherford T. "Our Father's Glorious Plan." *Ensign,* May 2017, 26–29.

Clements, Ronald E. "The Book of Deuteronomy." In *The New Interpreter's Bible,* edited by Leander E. Keck, 2:271–538. 1998.

———. *Jeremiah.* In Interpretation Bible Commentary series. Edited by James Luther Mays, Patrick D. Miller, and Paul J. Achtemeier. 1988.

Clifford, Richard J. *Psalms 1–72.* In Abingdon Old Testament Commentaries series. Edited by Patrick D. Miller. 2002.

Cloward, Robert A. "Isaiah 29 and the Book of Mormon." In *Isaiah in the Book of Mormon.* Edited by Donald W. Parry and John W. Welch, 191–247. 1998.

———. "Lost Scripture." In *Scriptures of the Church: Selections from the Encyclopedia of Mormonism,* edited by Daniel H. Ludlow, 422–23. 1995.

Clyde, Aileen H. "Confidence through Conversion." *Ensign,* Nov. 1992, 88–89.

———. "Old Testament Insights: Women, Wit, Wisdom." In *Women Steadfast in Christ,* edited by Dawn Hall Anderson and Marie Cornwall, 122–23. 1991.

Cohen, Abraham. *The Psalms.* In The Soncino Books of the Bible series. Edited by Abraham Cohen. 1982.

———. *The Twelve Prophets.* In The Soncino Books of the Bible series. Edited by Abraham Cohen. 1969.

Coleman, Gary J. "The Book of Mormon: A Guide for the Old Testament." *Ensign,* Jan. 2002, 45–49.

College Press NIV Commentary: Old Testament series. Edited by Anthony L. Ash and Jack Cottrell. 23 vols. 2000–2009.

Condie, Spencer J. "Claim the Exceeding Great and Precious Promises." *Ensign,* Nov. 2007, 16–18.

———. *In Perfect Balance.* 1993.

———. "Some Scriptural Lessons on Leadership." *Ensign,* May 1990, 27–28.

Congregation: Contemporary Writers Read the Jewish Bible. Edited by David Rosenburg. 1987.

Cook, Gene R. "Charity: Perfect and Everlasting Love." *Ensign,* May 2002, 82–83.

Cook, Mary N. "Never, Never, Never Give Up." *Ensign,* May 2010, 117–19.

Cook, Quentin L. "The Blessing of Continuing Revelation to Prophets and Personal Revelation to Guide Our Lives." *Ensign,* May 2020, 96–100.

———. "Choose Wisely." *Ensign,* Nov. 2014, 46–49.

———. "The Eternal Everyday." *Ensign,* Nov. 2017, 51–54.

———. "The Joy of Family History Work." *Ensign,* Feb. 2016. 28–33.

———. "Lamentations of Jeremiah: Beware of Bondage." *Ensign,* Nov. 2013, 88–91.

———. "Lessons from the Old Testament: In the World But Not of the World." *Ensign,* Feb. 2006, 53–55.

———. "Prepare to Meet God." *Ensign,* May 2018, 114–17.

———. "See Yourself in the Temple." *Ensign*, May 2016. 97–101.

———. "Shipshape and Bristol Fashion: Be Temple Worthy—in Good Times and Bad Times." *Ensign*, Nov. 2015, 39–42.

———. "Valiant in the Testimony of Jesus." *Ensign*, Nov. 2016, 40–43.

Cooper, J. C. *An Illustrated Encyclopaedia of Traditional Symbols*. 1978.

Cordon, Bonnie H. "Trust in the Lord and Lean Not." *Ensign*, May 2017, 6–9.

Cornerstone Biblical Commentary: Old Testament series. Edited by Philip W. Comfort. 12 vols. 2005–2012.

Cornwall, Rebecca J. "The 'Old Dead Book' of Job." *Ensign*, July 1974, 55–59.

"Covenant." In Gospel Topics. The Church of Jesus Christ of Latter-day Saints. 2013.

Covenants, Prophecies, and Hymns of the Old Testament. Edited by Victor L. Ludlow, Dee Darling, Jerome M. Perkins, Patty A. Smith, and Vern D. Sommerfeldt. Sperry Symposium series. 2001.

Cowan, Richard O. *The Church in the Twentieth Century*. 1985.

———. *Temples to Dot the Earth*. 1989.

Craig, Marshall R. "Father Lehi: Prophet and Patriarch." *Ensign*, Sep.1976, 58–63.

Craigie, Peter C. *The Book of Deuteronomy*. In The New International Commentary on the Old Testament series. Edited by R. K. Harrison and Robert L. Hubbard, Jr. 1976.

———. *Ezekiel*. In The Daily Study Bible series. Edited by John C. L. Gibson. 1983.

———. *Twelve Prophets, Volume 1*. In The Daily Study Bible series. Edited by John C. L. Gibson. 1984.

———. *Twelve Prophets, Volume 2*. In The Daily Study Bible series. Edited by John C. L. Gibson. 1985.

Craven, Becky. "Careful versus Casual." *Ensign*, May 2019, 9–11.

Crookston, R. Kent. "The Natural Blessings of the Law." Brigham Young University devotional, 20 March 2001. Speeches.BYU.edu.

Cundall, Arthur E. and Leon Morris. *Judges and Ruth: An Introduction and Commentary*. In Tyndale Old Testament Commentaries series. Edited by Donald J. Wiseman and David Firth. 1968.

Cuthbert, Derek A. "The Spirituality of Service." *Ensign*, May 1990, 12–13.

Dahl, Larry E. "The Abrahamic Test." In *A Witness of Jesus Christ*, edited by Richard D. Draper, 53–67. Sperry Symposium series, 1990.

———, and Donald Q. Cannon. *Encyclopedia of Joseph Smith's Teachings*. 1997.

The Daily Study Bible series. Edited by John C. L. Gibson. 24 vols. 1981–1987.

Dallaire, Helene. "Joshua." In *The Expositor's Bible Commentary*, rev. ed., edited by Tremper Longman III and David E. Garland, 2:817–1042. 2012.

Dalton, Elaine S. "Believe!" *Ensign*, May 2004, 110–12.

———. "Be Not Moved!" *Ensign*, May 2013, 121–24.

———. "Lessons from Ruth and Hannah." *Ensign*, April 2006, 34–37.

———. "Now Is the Time to Arise and Shine!" *Ensign*, May 2012, 123–26.

Damiani, Adhemar. "Serving the Lord." *Ensign*, Nov. 1999, 28–29.

Davidson, Karen Lynn. *Our Latter-day Hymns: The Stories and the Messages*, rev. ed. 2009.

Davies, Dean M. "Come, Listen to a Prophet's Voice." *Ensign*, Nov. 2018, 34–36.

Davis, Garold N. "Book of Mormon Commentary on Isaiah." *Ensign*, Sep. 1998, 54–60.

Dearman, J. Andrew. *The Book of Hosea*. 2010.

———. *Jeremiah, Lamentations*. In The NIV Application Commentary: Old Testament series. Edited by Terry Muck. 2002.

deClaissé-Walford, Nancy, Rolf A. Jacobson, and Beth LaNeel Tanner. *The Book of Psalms*. In The New

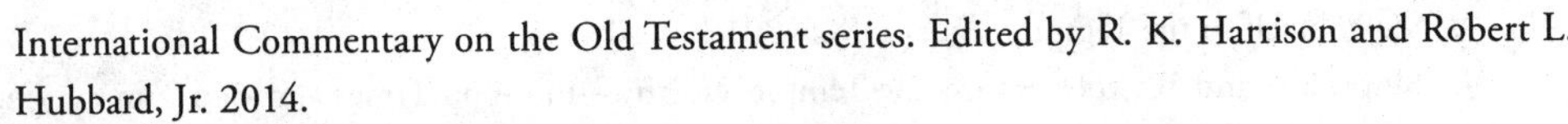

International Commentary on the Old Testament series. Edited by R. K. Harrison and Robert L. Hubbard, Jr. 2014.

de Vaux, Roland. *Ancient Israel: Its Life and Institutions.* 1961.

Dew, Sheri. *God Wants a Powerful People.* 2007.

———. "Our Only Chance." *Ensign,* May 1999, 66–67.

Dibb, Ann M. "Arise and Shine Forth." *Ensign,* May 2012, 117–19.

———. "Be of a Good Courage." *Ensign,* May 2010, 114–16.

———. "I Believe in Being Honest and True." *Ensign,* May 2011, 115–18.

Dickson, John B. "A Brief Introduction to the Church." *Ensign,* May 2000, 82–83.

Dictionary for Theological Interpretation of the Bible. Edited by Kevin J. Vanhoozer. 2005.

Dictionary of Biblical Imagery. Edited by Leland Ryken, James C. Whilhoit, and Tremper Longman III. 1998.

Didier, Charles. "Friend or Foe." *Ensign,* Nov. 1983, 23–24.

Diodore of Tarsus. "Commentary on Psalm 41." In *Psalms 1–50,* edited by Craig A. Blaising and Carmen S. Hardin. 2008.

The Doctrine and Covenants. Edited by Robert L. Millet and Kent P. Jackson. Vol. 1 of Studies in Scripture series. 1984.

Doctrine and Covenants Student Manual (Religion 324–325). 2018.

Doctrines of the Gospel Student Manual (Religion 430–431). 2004.

Donaldson, Lee L. "The Plates of Ether and the Covenant of the Book of Mormon 6." In *Fourth Nephi through Moroni: From Zion to Destruction,* edited by Monte S. Nyman and Charles D. Tate, Jr., 69–80. Vol. 9 of Book of Mormon Symposium series. 1995.

———, V. Dan Rogers, and David Rolph Seely. "Is There Additional Background Information on the Tower of Babel?" *Ensign,* Feb. 1994, 60–62.

Dothan, Trude. "What We Know about the Philistines." *Biblical Archaeology Review* (Jul/Aug 1982): 20–42.

Douglas, Mary. *Leviticus as Literature.* 2009.

Doxey, Joanne Bushman. "Seek the Lord Early." *Friend,* August 2014, 31.

Draper, Richard D. "The Book of Daniel." In *1 Kings to Malachi,* edited by Kent P. Jackson, 320–33. Vol. 4 of Studies in Scripture series. 1993.

———. "The Book of Malachi." In *1 Kings to Malachi,* edited by Kent P. Jackson, 365–72. Vol. 4 of Studies in Scripture series. 1993.

———. "The Book of Zechariah." In *1 Kings to Malachi,* edited by Kent P. Jackson, 351–58. Vol. 4 of Studies in Scripture series. 2003.

———. *Opening the Seven Seals: The Visions of John the Revelator.* 1991.

———. "The Prophets of the Exile: Saviors of a People." In *Voices of Old Testament Prophets,* edited by Dennis Wright, Craig J. Ostler, Dana M. Pike, Dee R. Darling, and Patty A. Smith, 86–109. Sperry Symposium series. 1997.

———, S. Kent Brown, and Michael D. Rhodes. *The Pearl of Great Price: A Verse-by-Verse Commentary.* 2013.

Duguid, Iain M. *Ezekiel.* In The NIV Application Commentary: Old Testament series. Edited by Terry Muck. 1999.

Dummelow, John R. *John Dummelow's Commentary on the Bible.* 1909.

Duncan, Kevin R. "The Healing Ointment of Forgiveness." *Ensign*, May 2016, 33–35.

———. "Our Very Survival." *Ensign*, Nov. 2010, 34–36.

Durham, Louise Gardiner. "Sarah." In *Encyclopedia of Mormonism*, edited by Daniel H. Ludlow, 3:1260. 1992.

Dyer, Alvin R. "Conference: Feast of the Saints." *The Improvement Era*, Dec. 1966, 1151–52.

Eames, Rulon D. "The Book of Zephaniah." In *1 Kings to Malachi*, edited by Kent P. Jackson, 178–83. Vol. 4 of Studies in Scripture series. 1993.

Easterly, Ellis. "A Case of Mistaken Identity." *Bible Review*, Apr. 1997, 41–47.

Easton, Matthew George. *Easton's Bible Dictionary*. 1897.

Eaton, Michael A. *Ecclesiastes*. In Tyndale Old Testament Commentaries series. Edited by Donald J. Wiseman and David Firth. 2009.

Edersheim, Alfred. *Bible History: Old Testament.* 7 vols. 1876–1887. Reprint, 1890.

Edgley, Richard C. "The Condescension of God." *Ensign*, Dec. 2001, 16–21.

The Eerdmans Commentary on the Bible. Edited by James D. G. Dunn and John W. Rogerson. 2003.

The Eerdmans Companion to the Bible. Edited by Gordon D. Fee and Robert L. Hubbard, Jr. 2011.

Eerdmans Dictionary of the Bible. Edited by David Noel Freedman, Allen C. Myers, and Astrid B. Beck. 2000.

Elwell, Walter A., and Philip W. Comfort. *Tyndale Bible Dictionary.* 2001

Encyclopedia of Mormonism. Edited by Daniel H. Ludlow, et al. 4 vols. 1992.

England, Breck. "Let Us Rise Up and Build." *Meridian Magazine*, Nov. 26, 2018.

Enns, Peter. *Exodus.* In The NIV Application Commentary: Old Testament series. Edited by Terry Muck. 2000.

Esplin, Cheryl A. "Filling Our Homes with Light and Truth." *Ensign*, May 2015, 8–10.

Eswing, Zack. *Recovering Eden: The Gospel according to Ecclesiastes.* 2014.

Etz Hayim: Torah and Commentary. Edited by The Rabbinical Assembly: The United Synagogue of Conservative Judaism. 2001.

Eubank, Sharon. "Christ: The Light That Shines in Darkness." *Ensign*, May 2019, 73–76.

Evans, Richard L. In Conference Report, April 1942, 50–51.

The Expositor's Bible Commentary. Edited by Frank E. Gaebelein. 12 vols. 1979–2002.

The Expositor's Bible Commentary: Old Testament. Abridged edition. Edited by Kenneth L. Barker and John R. Kohlenberger III. 1994.

The Expositor's Bible Commentary. Revised edition. Edited by Tremper Longman III and David E. Garland. 13 vols. 2005–2012.

Eyring, Henry B. "The Comforter." *Ensign*, May 2015, 17–21.

———. "Covenants and Sacrifice." Address to religious educators, 15 Aug. 1995, 1–2.

———. "Do Not Delay." *Ensign*, Nov. 1999, 33–35.

———. "Eternal Families." *Ensign*, May 2016, 81–84.

———. "The Family." *Ensign*, Feb. 1998, 10–18.

———. "Fear Not to Do Good." *Ensign*, Nov. 2017, 100–103.

———. "Finding Safety in Counsel." *Ensign*, May 1997, 24–26.

———. "Holiness and the Plan of Happiness." *Ensign*, Nov. 2019, 100–103.

———. "I Love to See the Temple." *Liahona*, May 2021, 28–31.

———. "Man Down!" *Ensign*, May 2009, 63–66.

———. "O Remember, Remember." *Ensign*, Nov. 2007, 66–69.

———. "Our Perfect Example." *Ensign*, Nov. 2009, 70–73.

———. "The Power of Deliverance." Brigham Young University devotional, 15 Jan. 2008. Speeches.BYU .edu.

———. "Prayer." *Ensign*, Nov. 2001, 15–17.

———. "Temples Are a Witness of Our Faith." Groundbreaking and site dedication for the Philadelphia Pennsylvania Temple, September 17, 2011. ChurchofJesusChrist.org.

———. "To Draw Closer to God." *Ensign*, May 1991, 65–67.

———. "Trust in God, Then Go and Do." *Ensign*, Nov. 2010, 70–73.

———. "Watch Over and Strengthen." *Ensign*, May 2000, 66–68.

———. "Watch with Me." *Ensign*, May 2001, 38–40.

Fairbairn, Patrick. *Ezekiel and the Book of His Prophecy.* 1842.

———. *The Visions of Ezekiel.* 1876.

Falk, David A. "Brick by Brick." *Biblical Archaeology Review* (Spring 2020):, 54–57.

"The Family: A Proclamation to the World." *Ensign*, Nov. 1995, 102.

"The Family: A Proclamation to the World." *Ensign*, Nov. 2010, 129.

"The Family: A Proclamation to the World." *Ensign*, May 2017, 145.

Farley, S. Brent. "Job: Parallels with the Savior." *Ensign*, Oct. 1980, 26–27.

———. "Nephi, Isaiah, and the Latter-Day Restoration." In *The Book of Mormon: Second Nephi, The Doctrinal Structure,* edited by Monte S. Nyman and Charles D. Tate, Jr., 227–39. 1989.

Faulconer, James E. *The Old Testament Made Harder: Scripture Study Questions.* 2014.

Faust, Avraham. "Warren's Shaft." *Biblical Archaeology Review* 29.5 (2003): 70, 72–76.

Faust, James E. "Acting for Ourselves and Not Being Acted Upon." *Ensign*, Nov. 1995, 45–47.

———. "Continuing Revelation." *Ensign*, Aug. 1996, 5–7.

———. "A Crown of Thorns, a Crown of Glory." *Ensign*, May 1991, 68–70.

———. "How Near the Angels." *Ensign*, May 1998, 95–97.

———. "Integrity, the Mother of Many Virtues." *Ensign*, May 1982, 47–49.

———. "It Can't Happen to Me." *Ensign*, May 2002, 46–48.

———. "The Lord's Day." *Ensign*, Nov. 1991, 33–35.

———. "Refined in Our Trials." *Ensign*, Feb. 2006, 2–7.

———. "The Refiner's Fire." *Ensign*, May 1979, 53–59.

———. "This Is Our Day." *Ensign*, May 1999, 17–20.

———. "We Seek After These Things." *Ensign*, May 1998, 43-46.

———. "What's in It for Me?" *Ensign*, Nov. 2002, 19–22.

Feasting on the Word: Preaching the Revised Common Lectionary. Edited by David L. Bartlett and Barbara Brown Taylor. 12 vols. 2011.

Featherstone, Vaughn J. *Commitment.* 1982.

Fensham, F. Charles. *The Books of Ezra and Nehemiah.* 1982.

Ferrel, David W. "The Lord Is among Us!" *Ensign*, Feb. 2002, 34–36.

Ferrell, James L. *The Hidden Christ: Beneath the Surface of the Old Testament.* 2009.

Ferris, Paul W., Jr. "Lamentations." In *The Expositor's Bible Commentary*, rev. ed., edited by Tremper Longman III and David E. Garland, 7:573–924. 2010.

1 Kings to Malachi. Edited by Kent P. Jackson. Vol. 4 of Studies in Scripture series. 1993.

First Nephi: The Doctrinal Foundation. Edited by Charles D. Tate and Monte S. Nyman. 1988.

Fisch, S. *Ezekiel.* In The Soncino Books of the Bible series. Edited by A. Cohen. 1966.

Fishelis, Rabbi Avrohom, and Rabbi Shmuel Fishelis. *The Book of Judges: A New English Translation.* In Judaica Books of the Prophets series. Edited by Rabbi A. J. Rosenberg. 1983.

The Five Megilloth. Edited by A. Cohen. 1961.

Fokkelman, Jan P. "Saul and David." *Bible Review,* 5:3:20–32.

For the Strength of Youth. 2011.

Fourth Nephi through Moroni: From Zion to Destruction. Edited by Monte S. Nyman and Charles D. Tate, Jr. Vol. 9 of Book of Mormon Symposium series. 1995.

Fowles, John L. *The Farm Boy Does It Again: Evidences of the Prophetic Calling of Joseph Smith.* 2018.

———. "The Jewish Lectionary and Book of Mormon Prophecy." In *Journal of Book of Mormon Studies.* Vol. 3, No. 2 (31 Jul. 1994): 118–22.

Franco, Cristina B. "The Healing Power of Jesus Christ." *Ensign,* Nov. 2020, 60–62.

Frankel, Ellen, and Betsy Platkin Teutsch. *The Encyclopedia of Jewish Symbols.* 1992.

Frederick, Nicholas J. "Old Wine in New Bottles." In *Prophets and Prophecies of the Old Testament,* edited by Aaron P. Schade, et al., 231–64. Sperry Symposium series. 2017.

Freeman, Emily. *Written on Our Hearts: Invitations from the Old Testament.* 2013.

Freeman, James M. *Handbook of Bible Manners and Customs.* 1874.

Frerichs, W. W. "Hornet." In *The Interpreter's Dictionary of the Bible,* edited by George Arthur Buttrick, et al., 645.

Fretheim, Terence E. "The Book of Genesis." In *The New Interpreter's Bible,* edited by Leander E. Keck, 1:321–674. 1994.

From the Last Supper through the Resurrection: The Savior's Final Hours. Edited by Richard Neitzel Holzapfel and Thomas A. Wayment. Vol. 3 of The Life and Teachings of Jesus Christ series. 2003.

Frymer–Kensky, Tikva. "Deborah 2." In *Women in Scripture: A Dictionary of Named and Unnamed Women in the Hebrew Bible, the Apocryphal/Deuterocanonical Books, and the New Testament,* edited by Carol Meyers, 66–67. 2000.

———. "Jael." In *Women in Scripture: A Dictionary of Named and Unnamed Women in the Hebrew Bible, the Apocryphal/Deuterocanonical Books, and the New Testament,* edited by Carol Meyers, 97–98.

Gaebelein, Arno C. *The Prophet Daniel.* 1911.

Gane, Roy E. *Leviticus, Numbers.* In The NIV Application Commentary: Old Testament series. Edited by Terry Muck. 2004.

Gardner, Ryan S., and David A. Edwards. "How Can I Understand Isaiah?" *New Era,* March 2012, 18–22.

Garner, Brian D. "Ezra Unfolds the Scriptures." *Ensign,* Dec. 2002, 47–49.

Gaskill, Alonzo L. *The Lost Language of Symbolism: An Essential Guide for Recognizing and Interpreting Symbols of the Gospel.* 2003.

———. *Miracles of the Old Testament: A Guide to the Symbolic Messages.* 2017.

Gee, John. "A Different Way of Seeing the Hand of the Lord." *Religious Educator: Perspectives on the Restored Gospel,* vol. 16, no. 2 (2016): 112–27.

Gelston, Anthony. "Zephaniah." In *Eerdmans Commentary on the Bible,* edited by James D. G. Dunn and John W. Rogerson, 715–17. 2003.

Genesis to 2 Samuel. Edited by Kent P. Jackson and Robert L. Millet. Vol. 3 of Studies in Scripture series. 1985.

Gesenius, H.W. F. *Gesenius' Hebrew-Chaldee Lexicon to the Old Testament.* 1979.

Gibson, John C. L. *Genesis, Vol. 2.* In The Daily Study Bible series. Edited by John C. L. Gibson. 1982.

Gilchrist, Donald B. "Wrath of God." In *Encyclopedia of Mormonism*, edited by Daniel H. Ludlow, 4:1598. 1992.

Gill, John. *John Gill's Exposition of the Whole Bible.* 1748–1768.

Gilliland, Steve F. "Forgiveness: Our Challenge and Our Blessing." *Ensign*, Aug. 2004, 44–48.

Gillum, Gary P. "Obadiah's Vision of Saviors on Mount Zion." In *Voices of Old Testament Prophets*, edited by Dennis A. Wright, Craig J. Ostler, Dana M. Pike, Dee R. Darling, and Patty A. Smith, 122–33. Sperry Symposium series. 1997.

Giménez, Ricardo P. "Finding Refuge from the Storms of Life." *Ensign*, May 2020, 101–3.

Ginzberg, Louis. *The Legends of the Jews.* 2 vols. 2003.

Glimpses of Lehi's Jerusalem. Edited by John W. Welch, David Rolph Seely, and Jo Ann H. Seely. 2004.

Goldingay, John A. "Ezekiel." In *Eerdmans Commentary on the Bible,* edited by James D. G. Dunn and John W. Rogerson, 623–64. 2003.

———. *Psalms, Vol. 2: Psalms 42–89.* In Baker Commentary on the Old Testament Wisdom and Psalms series. Edited by Tremper Longman III. 2007.

Goldman, S. *Samuel: Hebrew Text and English Translation with an Introduction and Commentary.* In The Soncino Books of the Bible series. Edited by A. Cohen. 1971.

Gong, Gerrit W. "Good Shepherd, Lamb of God." *Ensign*, May 2019, 97–101.

———. "Hosanna and Hallelujah—The Living Jesus Christ: The Heart of Restoration and Easter." *Ensign*, May 2020, 52–55.

———. "Our Campfire of Faith." *Ensign*, Nov. 2018, 40–43.

The Gospel of Jesus Christ in the Old Testament. Edited by D. Kelly Ogden, Kerry M. Muhlestein, Jared W. Ludlow, Thomas R. Valletta, and Patty A. Smith. Sperry Symposium series. 2009.

Gospel Principles. ChurchofJesusChrist.org. 2011.

Gospel Topics. ChurchofJesusChrist.org.

Gower, Ralph. *The New Manners and Customs of Bible Times.* 1987.

Grahl, Paulo R. "Eli and His Sons." *Ensign*, June 2002, 18–20.

Grant, Jedediah M. In *Journal of Discourses*, 4:70–75.

Grant, Michael. *The History of Ancient Israel.* 1984.

Greenberg, Moshe. *Ezekiel 1–20.* In the Anchor Bible series. Vol. 22. Edited by William Foxwell Albright and David Noel Freedman. 1983.

Greene, Joseph A. "Sodom and Gomorrah." In *The Oxford Guide to People and Places of the Bible,* edited by Bruce M. Metzger and Michael D. Coogan, 294. 2001.

Griggs, C. Wilfred. *Apocryphal Writings and the Latter-day Saints.* 1986.

Grisanti, Michael A. "Deuteronomy." In *The Expositor's Bible Commentary*, rev. ed., edited by Tremper Longman III and David E. Garland, 2:457–814. 2012.

Guide to the Scriptures. ChurchofJesusChrist.org. 2013.

Habershon, Ada R. *Study of the Types.* 1974.

Hafen, Bruce C. *The Broken Heart: Applying the Atonement to Life's Experiences.* 1989.

———, and Marie K. Hafen. *The Contrite Spirit: How the Temple Helps Us Apply Christ's Atonement.* 2015.

Haight, David B. "Temples and Work Therein." *Ensign*, Nov. 1990, 59–61.

Hale, Arta M. "Lessons in Womanhood." *Ensign*, Oct. 1973, 70–75.

Hales, Robert D. "Being a More Christian Christian." *Ensign*, Nov. 2012, 90–92.

———. "Faith through Tribulation Brings Peace and Joy." *Ensign*, May 2003, 15–18.

———. "Hear the Prophet's Voice and Obey." *Ensign*, May 1995, 15–17.

———. "The Holy Scriptures: The Power of God unto Our Salvation." *Ensign*, Nov. 2006, 24–27.
———. "How to Wait on the Lord." *New Era*, June 2015, 48.
———. "Out of Darkness into His Marvelous Light." *Ensign*, May 2002, 69–72.
———. "Tithing: A Test of Faith with Eternal Blessings." *Ensign*, Nov. 2002, 26–29.
———. "Waiting upon the Lord: Thy Will Be Done." *Ensign*, Nov. 2011, 71–73.
Hallen, Cynthia. "Rebekah." *Ensign*, Jan. 2002, 39–41.
Hallstrom, Donald L. "The Heart and a Willing Mind." *Ensign*, Jun. 2011, 30–33.
———. "I Am a Child of God." *Ensign*, May 2016, 26–28.
Halverson, Jared M. "The Rejection and Rehabilitation of Worship in the Old Testament." In *Ascending the Mountain of the Lord: Temple, Praise, and Worship in the Old Testament*, edited by David R. Seely, Jeffrey R. Chadwick, and Matthew J. Grey, 184–201. Sperry Symposium series. 2013.
Hamilton, Victor P. *The Book of Genesis, Chapters 18–50.* In The New International Commentary on the Old Testament series. Edited by R. K. Harrison and Robert L. Hubbard, Jr. 1995.
Hanks, Marion D. In Conference Report, Oct. 1954, 100–102.
———. In Conference Report, Apr. 1967, 123–26.
———. "Forgiveness: The Ultimate Form of Love." *Ensign*, Jan. 1974, 20–22.
———. "Freedom and Responsibility." In *BYU Speeches of the Year 1964*, 5–14.
———. "I Will Look unto the Lord." *Ensign*, Nov. 1986, 11–13.
———. "A Loving, Communicating God." *Ensign*, Nov. 1992, 63–65.
———. "Thou Art You." *The Improvement Era*, Dec. 1964, 1090–91.
———. "Trust in the Lord." *Ensign*, May 1975, 12–14.
Hardison, Amy B. "Theophany on Sinai." In *Ascending the Mountain of the Lord: Temple, Praise, and Worship in the Old Testament*, edited by David R. Seely, Jeffrey R. Chadwick, and Matthew J. Grey, 218–31. Sperry Symposium series. 2013.
Hardy, Ralph W., Jr. "Namaan and Gehazi: A Contrast in Obedience." *Ensign*, Aug. 2002, 27–29.
Harper's Bible Dictionary. Edited by Madeleine S. Miller and J. Land Miller. 1973.
Harper's Bible Dictionary. Edited by Paul J. Achtemeier. 1985.
Harris, James R. "Cain." In *Scriptures of the Church: Selections from the Encyclopedia of Mormonism*, edited by Daniel H. Ludlow, 218–20. 1995.
Hartley, John E. *The Book of Job.* In The New International Commentary on the Old Testament series. Edited by R. K. Harrison and Robert L. Hubbard, Jr. 1988.
Hartley, William G. "The Pioneer Trek: Nauvoo to Winter Quarters." *Ensign*, June 1997, 31–43.
Hawkins, Alan J., David C. Dollahite, and Clifford J. Rhoades. "Turning the Hearts of the Fathers." *BYU Studies* 33, no. 2 (1993): 273–91.
Hedengren, Paul C. "LDS Belief in the Bible." In *Scriptures of the Church: Selections from the Encyclopedia of Mormonism*, edited by Daniel H. Ludlow, 48–49. 1995.
Heltzer, Michael. "The Book of Esther." *Bible Review*, Feb. 1992, 24–29.
Henry, Matthew. *Matthew Henry's Complete Commentary on the Bible.* 1706–1721.
Heschel, Abraham J. *The Prophets.* 1962.
Hess, Richard S. *Joshua: An Introduction and Commentary.* In Tyndale Old Testament Commentaries series. Edited by D. J. Wiseman. 1996.
———. "Leviticus." In *The Expositor's Bible Commentary*, rev. ed., edited by Tremper Longman III and David E. Garland, 1:567–826. 2008

Hill, Andrew E. "Daniel." In *The Expositor's Bible Commentary,* rev. ed., edited by Tremper Longman III and David E. Garland, 8:19–212. 2012.

———. *Haggai, Zechariah, and Malachi.* In Tyndale Old Testament Commentaries series. Edited by David G. Firth and Tremper Longman III. 2012.

Hillam, Harold G. "Future Leaders," *Ensign*, May 2000, 10–11.

Hinckley, Bryant S. *Sermons and Missionary Services of Melvin Joseph Ballard.* 1949.

Hinckley, Gordon B. "The Aaronic Priesthood–a Gift from God." *Ensign*, May 1988, 44–46.

———. "Behold Your Little Ones." *Ensign*, Nov. 1978, 18–20.

———. *Be Thou an Example.* 1981.

———. "Building Your Tabernacle." *Ensign*, Nov. 1992, 51–52.

———. "The Dawning of a Brighter Day." *Ensign*, May 2004, 81–84.

———. "The Empty Tomb Bore Testimony." *Ensign*, May 1988, 65–68.

———. "An Ensign to the Nations, a Light to the World." *Ensign*, Nov. 2003, 82–85.

———. "Everything to Gain—Nothing to Lose." *Ensign*, Nov. 1976, 95–97.

———. "Four Cornerstones of Faith." *Ensign*, Feb. 2004, 3–7.

———. "I Am Clean." *Ensign,* May 2007, 60–62.

———. "If Thou Art Faithful." *Ensign*, Nov. 1984, 89–92.

———. "If Ye Be Willing and Obedient." *Ensign*, Dec. 1971, 123–26.

———. "Living in the Fulness of Times." *Ensign*, Nov. 2001, 4–6.

———. "Of Missions, Temples, and Stewardship." *Ensign,* Nov. 1995, 51–54.

———. "Of You It Is Required to Forgive." *Ensign,* June 1991, 2–5.

———. "Our Solemn Responsibilities." *Ensign*, Nov. 1991, 49–52.

———. "The Sacred Law of Tithing." *Ensign*, Dec. 1989, 2–5.

———. "Stand Strong against the Wiles of the World." *Ensign*, Nov. 1995, 98–102.

———. *The Teachings of Gordon B. Hinckley.* 1997.

———. "This Is the Work of the Master." *Ensign*, May 1995, 69–71.

———. "This Thing Was Not Done in a Corner." *Ensign*, Nov. 1996, 48–51.

———. "The Times in Which We Live." *Ensign*, Nov. 2001, 72–74.

———. "The War We Are Winning." *Ensign*, Nov. 1986, 42–45.

———. "What Are People Asking about Us?" *Ensign*, Nov. 1998, 70–73.

Hinckley, Richard G. "Repentance: A Blessing of Membership." *Ensign*, May 2006, 48–50.

History of The Church of Jesus Christ of Latter-day Saints. Edited by B. H. Roberts. 7 vols. 1932–51.

Hite, Julie M., Steven J. Hite, and R. Tom Melville. *The Old Testament with the Joseph Smith Translation.* 2001.

Hoffmeier, James K. "Out of Egypt." In *Ancient Israel in Egypt and the Exodus*, edited by Margaret Warker, Noah Wiener, and Dorothy Resig, 1–20. 2012.

Holbrook, Brett L. "The Sword of Laban as a Symbol of Divine Authority and Kingship." *Journal of Book of Mormon Studies,* vol. 2, no. 1 (1 Jan. 1993): 39–72.

Holland, Jeffrey R. "Are We Not All Beggars?" *Ensign*, Nov. 2014, 40–42.

———. "As Doves to Our Windows." *Ensign*, May 2000, 75–77.

———. "Behold, the Lamb of God." *Ensign*, Apr. 2019, 44–46.

———. "The Best Is Yet to Be." *Ensign*, Jan. 2010, 23–27.

———. "Cast Not Away Therefore Your Confidence." *Ensign*, Mar. 2000, 7–11.

———. *Christ and the New Covenant: The Messianic Message of the Book of Mormon.* 1997.

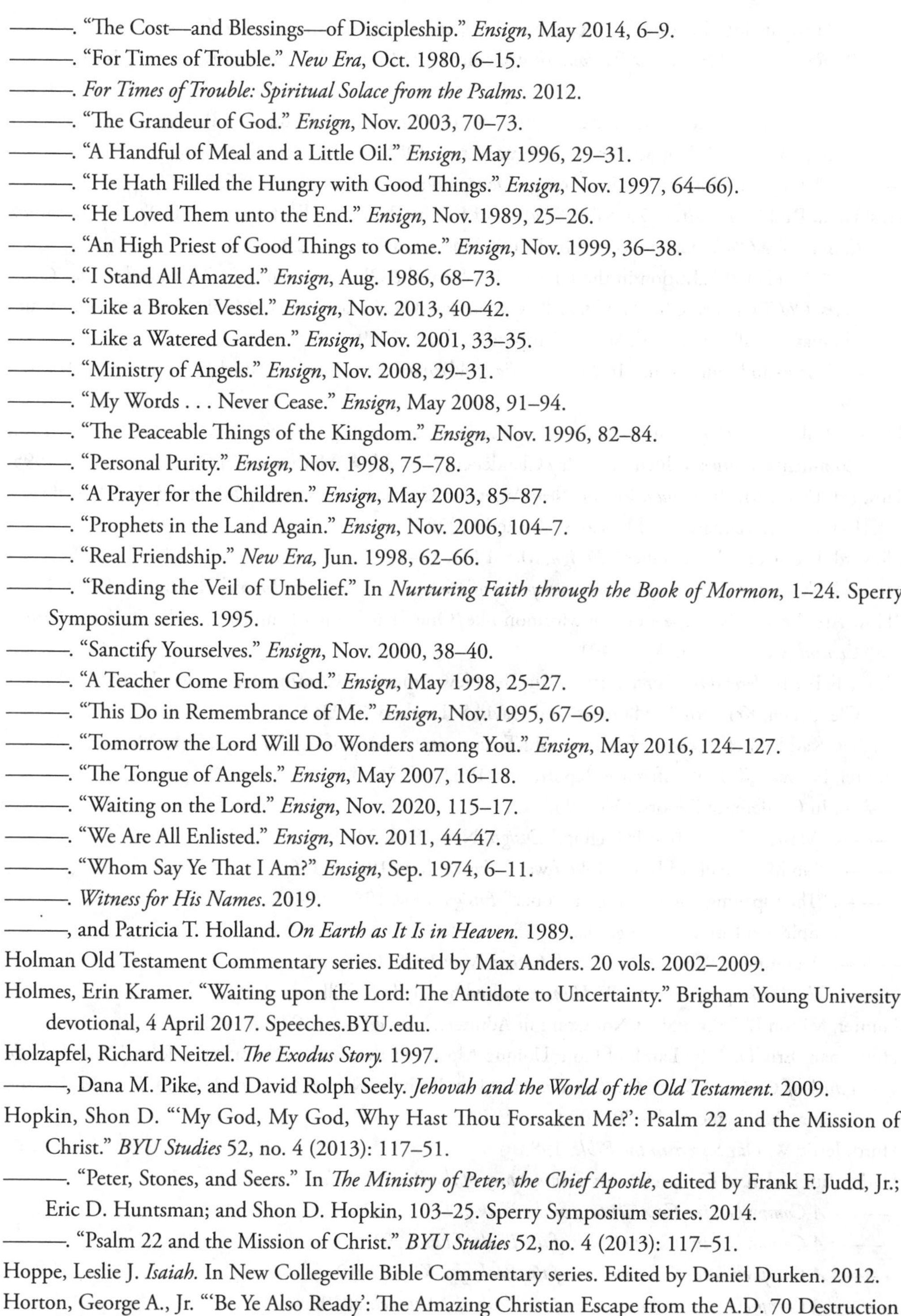

———. "The Cost—and Blessings—of Discipleship." *Ensign*, May 2014, 6–9.

———. "For Times of Trouble." *New Era*, Oct. 1980, 6–15.

———. *For Times of Trouble: Spiritual Solace from the Psalms*. 2012.

———. "The Grandeur of God." *Ensign*, Nov. 2003, 70–73.

———. "A Handful of Meal and a Little Oil." *Ensign*, May 1996, 29–31.

———. "He Hath Filled the Hungry with Good Things." *Ensign*, Nov. 1997, 64–66).

———. "He Loved Them unto the End." *Ensign*, Nov. 1989, 25–26.

———. "An High Priest of Good Things to Come." *Ensign*, Nov. 1999, 36–38.

———. "I Stand All Amazed." *Ensign*, Aug. 1986, 68–73.

———. "Like a Broken Vessel." *Ensign*, Nov. 2013, 40–42.

———. "Like a Watered Garden." *Ensign*, Nov. 2001, 33–35.

———. "Ministry of Angels." *Ensign*, Nov. 2008, 29–31.

———. "My Words . . . Never Cease." *Ensign*, May 2008, 91–94.

———. "The Peaceable Things of the Kingdom." *Ensign*, Nov. 1996, 82–84.

———. "Personal Purity." *Ensign,* Nov. 1998, 75–78.

———. "A Prayer for the Children." *Ensign*, May 2003, 85–87.

———. "Prophets in the Land Again." *Ensign*, Nov. 2006, 104–7.

———. "Real Friendship." *New Era,* Jun. 1998, 62–66.

———. "Rending the Veil of Unbelief." In *Nurturing Faith through the Book of Mormon*, 1–24. Sperry Symposium series. 1995.

———. "Sanctify Yourselves." *Ensign*, Nov. 2000, 38–40.

———. "A Teacher Come From God." *Ensign*, May 1998, 25–27.

———. "This Do in Remembrance of Me." *Ensign*, Nov. 1995, 67–69.

———. "Tomorrow the Lord Will Do Wonders among You." *Ensign*, May 2016, 124–127.

———. "The Tongue of Angels." *Ensign*, May 2007, 16–18.

———. "Waiting on the Lord." *Ensign*, Nov. 2020, 115–17.

———. "We Are All Enlisted." *Ensign*, Nov. 2011, 44–47.

———. "Whom Say Ye That I Am?" *Ensign*, Sep. 1974, 6–11.

———. *Witness for His Names*. 2019.

———, and Patricia T. Holland. *On Earth as It Is in Heaven.* 1989.

Holman Old Testament Commentary series. Edited by Max Anders. 20 vols. 2002–2009.

Holmes, Erin Kramer. "Waiting upon the Lord: The Antidote to Uncertainty." Brigham Young University devotional, 4 April 2017. Speeches.BYU.edu.

Holzapfel, Richard Neitzel. *The Exodus Story.* 1997.

———, Dana M. Pike, and David Rolph Seely. *Jehovah and the World of the Old Testament.* 2009.

Hopkin, Shon D. "'My God, My God, Why Hast Thou Forsaken Me?': Psalm 22 and the Mission of Christ." *BYU Studies* 52, no. 4 (2013): 117–51.

———. "Peter, Stones, and Seers." In *The Ministry of Peter, the Chief Apostle*, edited by Frank F. Judd, Jr.; Eric D. Huntsman; and Shon D. Hopkin, 103–25. Sperry Symposium series. 2014.

———. "Psalm 22 and the Mission of Christ." *BYU Studies* 52, no. 4 (2013): 117–51.

Hoppe, Leslie J. *Isaiah.* In New Collegeville Bible Commentary series. Edited by Daniel Durken. 2012.

Horton, George A., Jr. "'Be Ye Also Ready': The Amazing Christian Escape from the A.D. 70 Destruction of Jerusalem." *Ensign*, June 1989, 48–49.

———. "An Indispensable Foundation." *Ensign*, Mar. 2002, 38–41.

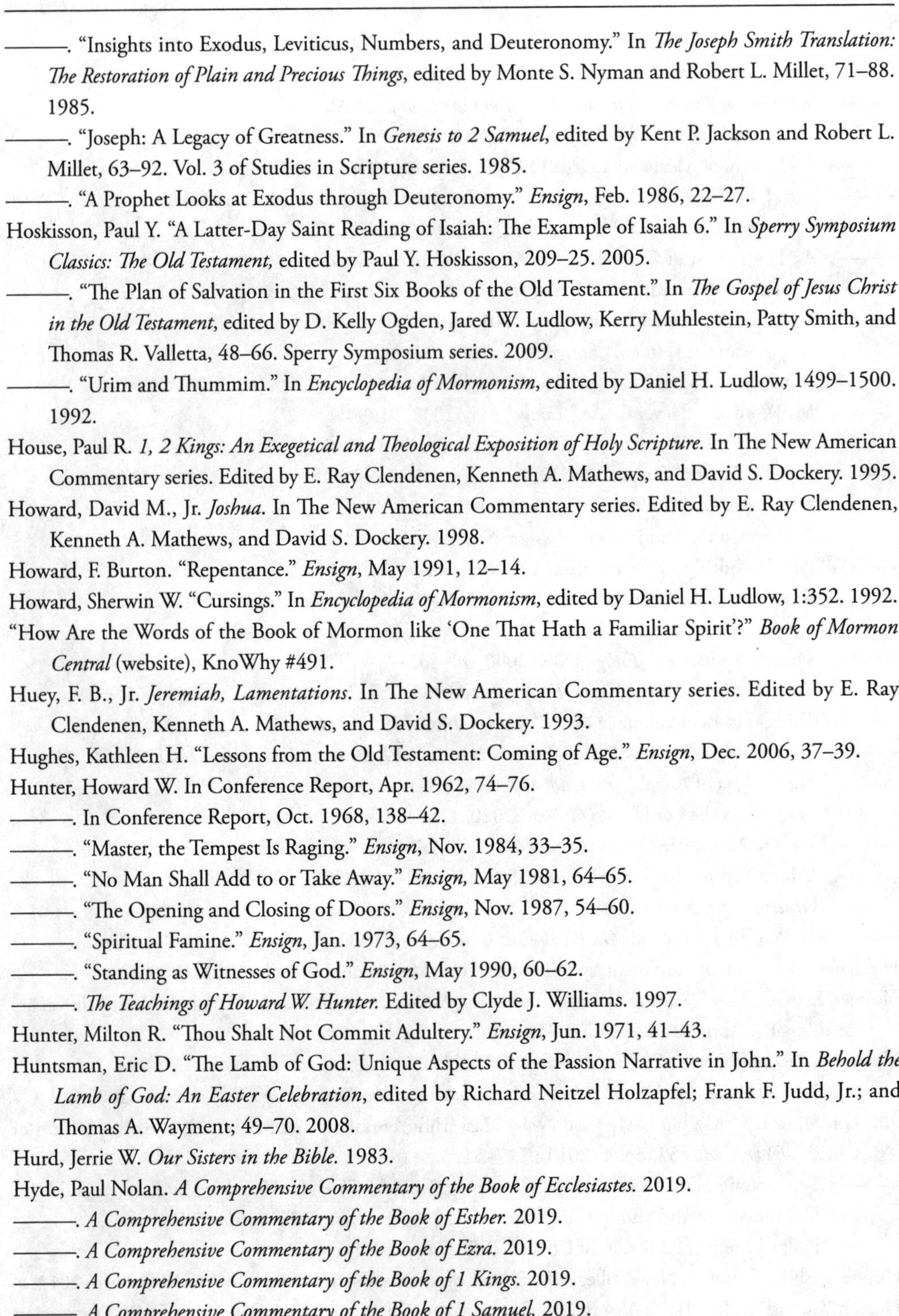

———. "Insights into Exodus, Leviticus, Numbers, and Deuteronomy." In *The Joseph Smith Translation: The Restoration of Plain and Precious Things*, edited by Monte S. Nyman and Robert L. Millet, 71–88. 1985.

———. "Joseph: A Legacy of Greatness." In *Genesis to 2 Samuel*, edited by Kent P. Jackson and Robert L. Millet, 63–92. Vol. 3 of Studies in Scripture series. 1985.

———. "A Prophet Looks at Exodus through Deuteronomy." *Ensign*, Feb. 1986, 22–27.

Hoskisson, Paul Y. "A Latter-Day Saint Reading of Isaiah: The Example of Isaiah 6." In *Sperry Symposium Classics: The Old Testament*, edited by Paul Y. Hoskisson, 209–25. 2005.

———. "The Plan of Salvation in the First Six Books of the Old Testament." In *The Gospel of Jesus Christ in the Old Testament*, edited by D. Kelly Ogden, Jared W. Ludlow, Kerry Muhlestein, Patty Smith, and Thomas R. Valletta, 48–66. Sperry Symposium series. 2009.

———. "Urim and Thummim." In *Encyclopedia of Mormonism*, edited by Daniel H. Ludlow, 1499–1500. 1992.

House, Paul R. *1, 2 Kings: An Exegetical and Theological Exposition of Holy Scripture.* In The New American Commentary series. Edited by E. Ray Clendenen, Kenneth A. Mathews, and David S. Dockery. 1995.

Howard, David M., Jr. *Joshua.* In The New American Commentary series. Edited by E. Ray Clendenen, Kenneth A. Mathews, and David S. Dockery. 1998.

Howard, F. Burton. "Repentance." *Ensign*, May 1991, 12–14.

Howard, Sherwin W. "Cursings." In *Encyclopedia of Mormonism*, edited by Daniel H. Ludlow, 1:352. 1992.

"How Are the Words of the Book of Mormon like 'One That Hath a Familiar Spirit'?" *Book of Mormon Central* (website), KnoWhy #491.

Huey, F. B., Jr. *Jeremiah, Lamentations.* In The New American Commentary series. Edited by E. Ray Clendenen, Kenneth A. Mathews, and David S. Dockery. 1993.

Hughes, Kathleen H. "Lessons from the Old Testament: Coming of Age." *Ensign*, Dec. 2006, 37–39.

Hunter, Howard W. In Conference Report, Apr. 1962, 74–76.

———. In Conference Report, Oct. 1968, 138–42.

———. "Master, the Tempest Is Raging." *Ensign*, Nov. 1984, 33–35.

———. "No Man Shall Add to or Take Away." *Ensign*, May 1981, 64–65.

———. "The Opening and Closing of Doors." *Ensign*, Nov. 1987, 54–60.

———. "Spiritual Famine." *Ensign*, Jan. 1973, 64–65.

———. "Standing as Witnesses of God." *Ensign*, May 1990, 60–62.

———. *The Teachings of Howard W. Hunter.* Edited by Clyde J. Williams. 1997.

Hunter, Milton R. "Thou Shalt Not Commit Adultery." *Ensign*, Jun. 1971, 41–43.

Huntsman, Eric D. "The Lamb of God: Unique Aspects of the Passion Narrative in John." In *Behold the Lamb of God: An Easter Celebration*, edited by Richard Neitzel Holzapfel; Frank F. Judd, Jr.; and Thomas A. Wayment; 49–70. 2008.

Hurd, Jerrie W. *Our Sisters in the Bible.* 1983.

Hyde, Paul Nolan. *A Comprehensive Commentary of the Book of Ecclesiastes.* 2019.

———. *A Comprehensive Commentary of the Book of Esther.* 2019.

———. *A Comprehensive Commentary of the Book of Ezra.* 2019.

———. *A Comprehensive Commentary of the Book of 1 Kings.* 2019.

———. *A Comprehensive Commentary of the Book of 1 Samuel.* 2019.

———. *A Comprehensive Commentary of the Book of Isaiah.* 2019.

———. *A Comprehensive Commentary of the Book of Job.* 2019.

———. *A Comprehensive Commentary of the Book of Joshua.* 2019.
———. *A Comprehensive Commentary of the Book of Judges.* 2019.
———. *A Comprehensive Commentary of the Book of Nahum.* 2019.
———. *A Comprehensive Commentary of the Book of Proverbs.* 2019.
———. *A Comprehensive Commentary of the Book of Psalms.* 2019.
———. *A Comprehensive Commentary of the Book of 2 Kings.* 2019.
———. *A Comprehensive Commentary of the Fifth Book of Moses: Deuteronomy.* 2018.
———. *A Comprehensive Commenatry of the First Book of Moses: Genesis.* 2018.
———. *A Comprehensive Commentary of the Fourth Book of Moses: Numbers.* 2018.
———. *A Comprehensive Commentary of the Second Book of Moses: Exodus.* 2018.
———. *A Comprehensive Commentary of the Third Book of Moses: Leviticus.* 2018.
Hymns of The Church of Jesus Christ of Latter-day Saints. 1985.
"Inspiration Key to Thanksgiving Psalm." *Church News*, Nov. 22, 1975, 12.
The International Bible Commentary. Edited by F. F. Bruce. 1986.
Interpretation Bible Commentary, Old Testament series. Edited by James Luther Mays and Patrick D. Miller. 26 vols. 1985–2012.
The Interpreter's Bible. Edited by George Arthur Buttrick, et al. 12 vols. 1952.
Interpreter's Dictionary of the Bible. Edited by George Arthur Buttrick, et al. 4 vols. 1962.
Isaiah and the Prophets: Inspired Voices from the Old Testament. Edited by Monte S. Nyman. 1984.
Isaiah in the Book of Mormon. Edited by Donald W. Parry and John W. Welch. 1998.
Isbouts, Jean-Pierre. *National Geographic Who's Who in the Bible.* 2013.
Jackson, Kent P. "The Book of Joel." In *1 Kings to Malachi*, edited by Kent P. Jackson, 359–64. Vol. 4 of Studies in Scripture series. 1993.
———. "Genesis and the Early Experiences of Mankind." In *Genesis to 2 Samuel*, edited by Kent P. Jackson and Robert L. Millet, 25–34. Vol. 3 of Studies in Scripture series. 1985.
———. "God's Testament to Ancient Israel." In *Genesis to 2 Samuel*, edited by Kent P. Jackson and Robert L. Millet, 3–12. Vol. 3 of Studies in Scripture series. 1985.
———. "I Will Be Your God." In *1 Kings to Malachi*, edited by Kent P. Jackson, 286–99. Vol. 4 of Studies in Scripture series. 1993.
———. *Joseph Smith's Commentary on the Bible.* 1994.
———, ed. *The King James Bible and the Restoration.* 2011.
———. "The Law of Moses and the Atonement of Christ." In *Genesis to 2 Samuel*, edited by Kent P. Jackson and Robert L. Millet, 153–72. Vol. 3 of Studies in Scripture series. 1985.
———. "The Lord Is There." In *1 Kings to Malachi*, edited by Kent P. Jackson, 300–319. Vol. 4 of Studies in Scripture series. 1993.
———. *Lost Tribes and Last Days: What Modern Revelation Tells Us about the Old Testament.* 2005.
———. "The Marriage of Hosea and Jehovah's Covenant with Israel." In *Isaiah and the Prophets: Inspired Voices from the Old Testament*, edited by Monte S. Nyman, 57–74. 1984.
———. "May the Kingdom of God Go Forth." In *The Doctrine and Covenants*, edited by Robert L. Millet and Kent P. Jackson, 251–57. Vol. 1 of Studies in Scripture series. 1984.
———. *The Restored Gospel and the Book of Genesis.* 2001.
———. "What 'Gog' and 'Magog' Represent in Prophecies about the Last Days, After the Millennium." *LDS Living*, 19 Jul. 2019; adapted from *Lost Tribes and Last Days: What Modern Revelation Tells Us about the Old Testament.*

Jacob, Maude Beeley. *The Message of the Old Testament.* 1942.

Jamieson, Robert, Andrew Robert Fausset, and David Brown. *Jamieson-Fausset-Brown Bible Commentary.* 1871.

Jenkins, Ryan. "Quiet Slumber: Revelation through Dreams." *Religious Educator* 12, no. 1 (2011): 73–89.

Jensen, Jay E. "Remember Also the Promises." *Ensign*, Nov. 1992, 80–81.

Jensen, Marlin K. "Remember and Perish Not." *Ensign*, May 2007, 36–38.

———. "To Walk Humbly with Thy God." *Ensign*, May 2001, 9–11.

The Jewish Study Bible. Edited by Adele Berlin and Marc Zvi Brettler. 2004.

The Jewish Study Bible: Second Edition. Edited by Adele Berlin and Marc Zvi Brettler. 2014.

Johnson, Clark V. "Job's Relevancy in the Twenty-First Century." In *A Witness of Jesus Christ*, edited by Richard D. Draper, 96–111. Sperry Symposium series. 1990.

Johnson, Lane. "Russell M. Nelson: A Study in Obedience," *Ensign*, Aug. 1982, 18–24.

———. "Who and Where Are the Lamanites?" *Ensign*, Dec. 1975, 15–16.

Johnson, Oliver L., Jr. *Isaiah the Prophet: The Imminent Return of Christ: A Bible Commentary Chapters 40–66.* 2015.

Johnson, Paul V. "To Guide Us in These Latter Days." BYU–Hawaii devotional, 18 Feb. 2020. Speeches. BYUH.edu.

Johnson, Peter M. "Power to Overcome the Adversary." *Ensign*, Nov. 2019, 110–12.

Jorgensen, Lynne W. "The Mantle of the Prophet Joseph Passes to Brother Brigham: A Collective Spiritual Witness." In *BYU Studies* 36, no. 4 (1996–97): 125–204.

The Joseph Smith Translation: The Restoration of Plain and Precious Things. Edited by Monte S. Nyman and Robert L. Millet. 1985.

Josephus, Flavius. *Antiquities of the Jews.* In *The Works of Josephus*. Translated by William Whiston. 1875.

———. *The Works of Josephus.* Translated by William Whiston. 1875.

Joshua and Judges. Edited by A. Cohen. 1970.

Journal of Discourses. 26 vols. 1854–86.

The JPS Torah Commentary series. Edited by Nahum M. Sarna. 5 vols. 1989–1996.

Judaica Books of the Prophets series. Edited by Rabbi A. J. Rosenberg, et al. 24 vols. 1976–1992.

Judd, Daniel K. "The Fortunate Fall of Adam and Eve." In *No Weapon Shall Prosper: New Light on Sensitive Issues*, edited by Robert L. Millet. 2011.

Judd, Frank F. Jr. "'Be Ye Therefore Perfect:' The Elusive Quest for Perfection." In *The Sermon on the Mount in Latter-day Scripture*, edited by Gaye Strathearn, Thomas A. Wayment, and Daniel L. Belnap, 123–39. Sperry Symposium series. 2010.

Jukes, Andrew. *The Law of the Offerings.* 1847.

Kaiser, Walter C., Jr. "The Book of Leviticus." In *The New Interpreter's Bible*, edited by Leander E. Keck, 1:985–1191. 1994.

———. "Exodus." In *The Expositor's Bible Commentary*, rev. ed, edited by Tremper Longman III and David E. Garland, 1:333–561. 2008.

Kapp, Ardeth Greene. *Rejoice! His Promises Are Sure.* 1997.

Kasher, Menahem M. *Encyclopedia of Biblical Interpretation.* 8 vols. 1957.

Keener, Craig S. *NKJV Cultural Backgrounds Study Bible.* 2017.

Keetch, Von G. "Blessed and Happy Are Those Who Keep the Commandments of God." *Ensign*, Nov. 2015, 115–117.

Keil, Carl Friedrich, and Franz Delitzsch. *Commentary on the Old Testament.* 1854–1889.

Kidner, Derek. *Genesis: An Introduction and Commentary.* In Tyndale Old Testament Commentaries series. Edited by Donald J. Wiseman and David Firth. 2008.

———. *Psalms 73–150: An Introduction and Commentary.* In Tyndale Old Testament Commentaries series. Edited by Donald J. Wiseman and David Firth. 2009.

Kim, Sung Kuk. *Psalms in the Book of Revelation.* 2013.

Kimball, Heber C. In *Journal of Discourses*, 11:95–97.

Kimball, Spencer W. "The Blessings and Responsibilities of Womanhood." *Ensign*, Mar. 1976, 70–73.

———. In Conference Report, Oct. 1952, 46–51.

———. In Conference Report, Oct. 1954, 50–55.

———. In Conference Report, Apr. 1969, 27–31.

———. "The Example of Abraham." *Ensign*, June 1975, 3–7.

———. *Faith Precedes the Miracle.* 1972.

———. "The Fourth Commandment." In *The Ten Commandments Today*, 54–72.

———. "Give Me This Mountain." *Ensign*, Nov. 1979, 78–79.

———. "Hold Fast to the Iron Rod." *Ensign*, Nov. 1978, 4–6.

———. "The Lord Expects His Saints to Follow the Commandments." *Ensign*, May 1977, 4–7.

———. "Love vs. Lust." *BYU Speeches of the Year: 1965*, 1–30.

———. *The Miracle of Forgiveness.* 1969.

———. "President Kimball Speaks Out on Planning Your Life." *New Era*, Sep. 1981, 46–51.

———. "Revelation: the Word of the Lord to His Prophets." *Ensign*, May 1977, 76–78.

———. *Spencer W. Kimball.* Teachings of Presidents of the Church series. 2011.

———. "The Stone Cut without Hands." *Ensign*, May 1976. 4–9.

———. *The Teachings of Spencer W. Kimball.* Edited by Edward L. Kimball. 1982.

———. "To See the Face of the Lord." Official Report of the San Jose Costa Rica Area Conference Held in San Jose, Costa Rica, 23 and 24 February 1977.

———. "Voices of the Past, of the Present, of the Future." *Ensign*, June 1971, 16–19.

———, et al. *Woman.* 1979.

King, Arthur Henry. *The Abundance of the Heart.* 1986.

The King James Bible and the Restoration. Edited by Kent P. Jackson. 2011.

Kleven, Terence. "Up the Waterspout: How David's General Joab Got Inside Jerusalem." *Biblical Archaeology Review* 20.4 (1994): 34–35.

Knight, George W., and Rayburn W. Ray. *The Illustrated Everyday Bible Companion.* 2005.

Koelliker, Paul E. "Gospel Covenants Bring Promised Blessings." *Ensign*, Nov. 2005, 94–95.

Lalleman, Hetty. *Jeremiah and Lamentations.* In Tyndale Old Testament Commentaries series. Edited by David Firth and Tremper Longman III. 2013.

Lamoreaux, Adam D. "The Work of Ezra and Nehemiah." In *1 Kings to Malachi*, edited by Kent P. Jackson, 373–85. Vol. 4 of Studies in Scripture series. 1993.

Lane, Jennifer Clark. "Hebrew Concepts of Adoption and Redemption in the Writings of Paul." In *The Apostle Paul: His Life and His Testimony*, edited by Paul Y. Hoskisson, 80–95. Sperry Symposium series. 1994.

———. "The Lord Will Redeem His People: Adoptive Covenant and Redemption in the Old Testament." In *Journal of Book of Mormon Studies*, Vol. 2, No. 2 (31 Jul. 1993): 39–62.

———. "Worship: Bowing Down and Serving the Lord." In *Ascending the Mountain of the Lord: Temple,*

Praise, and Worship in the Old Testament, edited by Davie R. Seely, Jeffrey R. Chadwick, and Matthew J. Grey, 122–35. Sperry Symposium series. 2013.

Larson, Knute, and Kathy Dahlen. *Ezra, Nehemiah, Esther.* In Holman Old Testament Commentary series. Edited by Max Anders. 2005.

The Latter-day Saints' Millennial Star. Vol. 4 No. 4 (August 1843): 49–55.

The Latter-day Saints' Millennial Star. 1859.

LDS Beliefs: A Doctrinal Reference. Edited by Robert L. Millet, Camille Fronk Olson, Andrew C. Skinner, and Brent L. Top. 2011.

Lectures on Faith. Delivered to the School of the Prophets in Kirtland, Ohio, 1834–1835. Reprint, 1985.

Legge, David. "The Sovereign's Psalm." Available at https://www.preachtheword.com/sermon/misc0061-sovereignpsalm.shtml.

Lee, Harold B. "Communion with Deity." *The Improvement Era*, Dec. 1966, 1142–44.

———. In Conference Report, Apr. 1943, 131–35.

———. In Conference Report, Oct. 1970, 152–53.

———. *The Teachings of Harold B. Lee.* Edited by Clyde J. Williams. 1996.

———. "Understanding Who We Are Brings Respect." *Ensign*, Jan. 1974, 2–7.

———. "Uphold the Hands of the President." In *Living Prophets for a Living Church*, 165–66. 1973.

———. "The Way to Eternal Life." *Ensign*, Nov. 1971, 9–17.

Lee, Peggy Furniss. "A King for Israel." *Ensign*, June 2002, 21–23.

Leo the Great. "Feast Beyond Compare." In *Psalms 1–50*, edited by Craig A. Blaising and Carmen S. Hardin. 2008.

Levine, Baruch A. *Leviticus.* In The JPS Torah Commentary series. Edited by Nahum M. Sarna. 1989.

Lewis, Barbara A. "Integrity." *Ensign*, Apr. 2018, 50–53.

Lewis, C. S. *Reflections on the Psalms.* 1958.

The Life and Teachings of Jesus Christ: From Bethlehem through the Sermon on the Mount. Edited by Richard Neitzel Holzapfel and Thomas A. Wayment. 2005.

The Lion Encyclopedia of the Bible: Life and Times, Meaning and Message: A Comprehensive Guide. Edited by Pat Alexander, John W. Drane, David Field, and Alan Millard. 1986.

Litchman, Kristen E. "Deborah and the Book of Judges." *Ensign*, Jan. 1990, 32–35.

The Literary Guide to the Bible. Edited by Robert Alter and Frank Kermode. 1987.

Literature of Belief: Sacred Scripture and Religious Experience. Edited by Neal E. Lambert. 1981.

Living Prophets for a Living Church. 1973.

Long, V. Philips. "1 and 2 Samuel." In *Zondervan Illustrated Bible Backgrounds Commentary: Old Testament*, edited by John W. Walton, 2:266–491. 2009.

Longman, Tremper, III. *The Book of Ecclesiastes.* In The New International Commentary on the Old Testament series. Edited by R. K. Harrison and Robert L. Hubbard, Jr. 1997.

———. *How to Read the Psalms.* 1988.

———. *Psalms.* In Tyndale Old Testament Commentaries series. Edited by David Firth and Tremper Longman III. 2014.

The Lord of the Gospels. Edited by Bruce A. Van Orden and Brent L. Top. Sperry Symposium series. 1991.

Ludlow, Daniel H. *A Companion to Your Study of the Book of Mormon.* 1976.

———. *A Companion to Your Study of the Old Testament.* 1981.

———. *Selected Writings of Daniel H. Ludlow.* 2000.

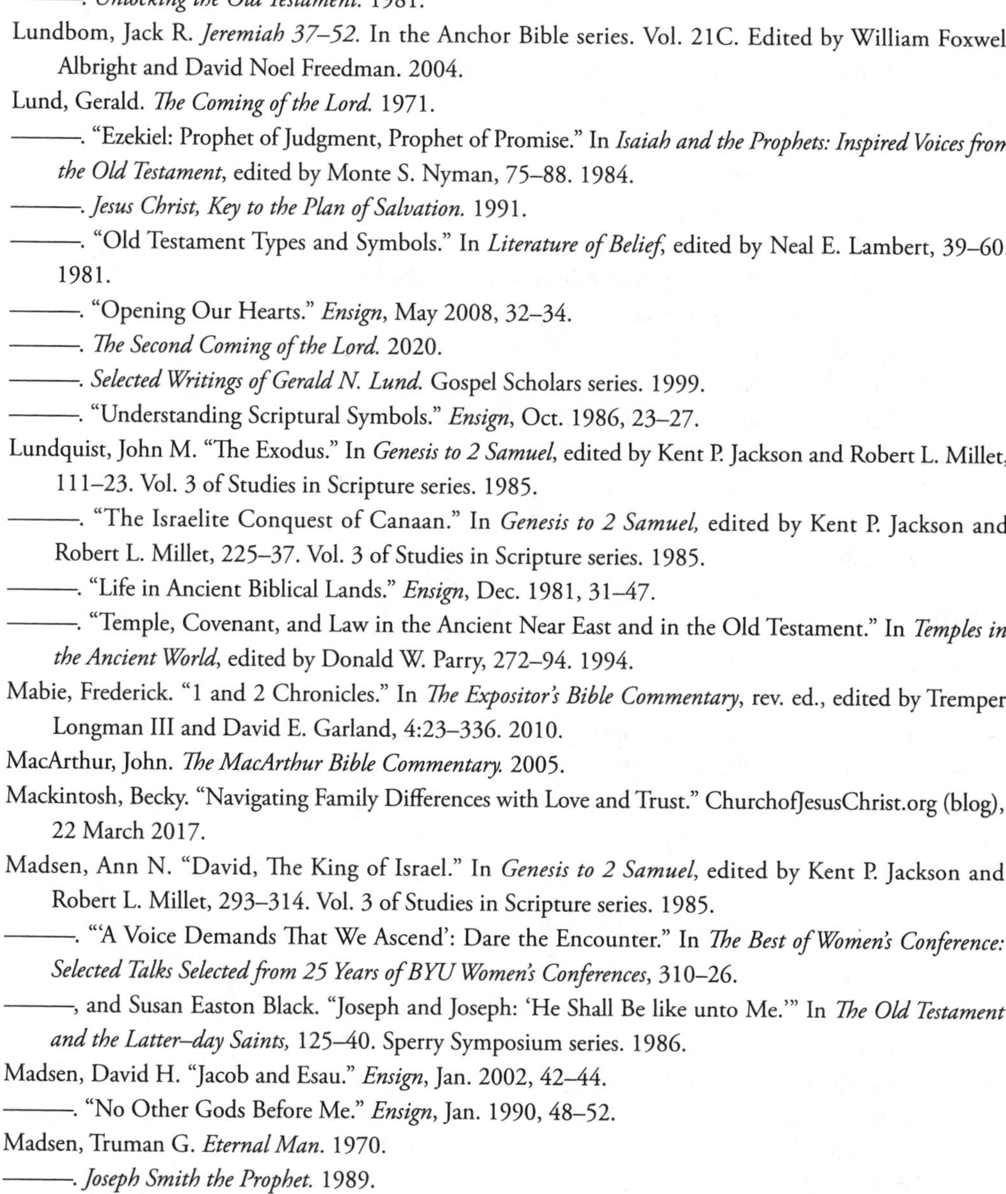

———. “What Laws Governed the Inheritance of Birthright in the Old Testament?” *Ensign*, Sep. 1980, 52–53.

Ludlow, Victor L. “The Book of Habakkuk.” In *1 Kings to Malachi*, edited by Kent P. Jackson, 187–92. Vol. 4 of Studies in Scripture series. 1993.

———. *Isaiah: Prophet, Seer, and Poet.* 1982.

———. *Principles and Practices of the Restored Gospel.* 1992.

———. *Unlocking Isaiah in the Book of Mormon.* 2003.

———. *Unlocking the Old Testament.* 1981.

Lundbom, Jack R. *Jeremiah 37–52.* In the Anchor Bible series. Vol. 21C. Edited by William Foxwell Albright and David Noel Freedman. 2004.

Lund, Gerald. *The Coming of the Lord.* 1971.

———. “Ezekiel: Prophet of Judgment, Prophet of Promise.” In *Isaiah and the Prophets: Inspired Voices from the Old Testament*, edited by Monte S. Nyman, 75–88. 1984.

———. *Jesus Christ, Key to the Plan of Salvation.* 1991.

———. “Old Testament Types and Symbols.” In *Literature of Belief*, edited by Neal E. Lambert, 39–60. 1981.

———. “Opening Our Hearts.” *Ensign*, May 2008, 32–34.

———. *The Second Coming of the Lord.* 2020.

———. *Selected Writings of Gerald N. Lund.* Gospel Scholars series. 1999.

———. “Understanding Scriptural Symbols.” *Ensign*, Oct. 1986, 23–27.

Lundquist, John M. “The Exodus.” In *Genesis to 2 Samuel*, edited by Kent P. Jackson and Robert L. Millet, 111–23. Vol. 3 of Studies in Scripture series. 1985.

———. “The Israelite Conquest of Canaan.” In *Genesis to 2 Samuel*, edited by Kent P. Jackson and Robert L. Millet, 225–37. Vol. 3 of Studies in Scripture series. 1985.

———. “Life in Ancient Biblical Lands.” *Ensign*, Dec. 1981, 31–47.

———. “Temple, Covenant, and Law in the Ancient Near East and in the Old Testament.” In *Temples in the Ancient World*, edited by Donald W. Parry, 272–94. 1994.

Mabie, Frederick. “1 and 2 Chronicles.” In *The Expositor’s Bible Commentary*, rev. ed., edited by Tremper Longman III and David E. Garland, 4:23–336. 2010.

MacArthur, John. *The MacArthur Bible Commentary.* 2005.

Mackintosh, Becky. “Navigating Family Differences with Love and Trust.” ChurchofJesusChrist.org (blog), 22 March 2017.

Madsen, Ann N. “David, The King of Israel.” In *Genesis to 2 Samuel*, edited by Kent P. Jackson and Robert L. Millet, 293–314. Vol. 3 of Studies in Scripture series. 1985.

———. “‘A Voice Demands That We Ascend’: Dare the Encounter.” In *The Best of Women’s Conference: Selected Talks Selected from 25 Years of BYU Women’s Conferences*, 310–26.

———, and Susan Easton Black. “Joseph and Joseph: ‘He Shall Be like unto Me.’” In *The Old Testament and the Latter–day Saints,* 125–40. Sperry Symposium series. 1986.

Madsen, David H. “Jacob and Esau.” *Ensign*, Jan. 2002, 42–44.

———. “No Other Gods Before Me.” *Ensign*, Jan. 1990, 48–52.

Madsen, Truman G. *Eternal Man.* 1970.

———. *Joseph Smith the Prophet.* 1989.

———. “The Joy of the Lord Is Your Strength (Nehemiah 8:10)” Brigham Young University devotional, 21 Nov. 2000. Speeches.BYU.edu.

———. "'Putting on the Names': A Jewish-Christian Legacy." In *By Study and Also by Faith*, edited by John M. Lundquist and Stephen D. Ricks, 1:458–81. 1990.

Malamat, Abraham. "Let My People Go and Go and Go." In *Ancient Israel in Egypt and the Exodus*, edited by Margaret Warker, Noah Wiener, and Dorothy Resig, 21–30. 2012.

March, W. Eugene. "The Book of Haggai." In *The New Interpreter's Bible*, edited by Leander E. Keck, 7:719–21.

Marriott, Neill F. "Abiding in God and Repairing the Breach." *Ensign*, Nov. 2017, 10–12.

Martens, Elmer A. and Larry L Walker. *Isaiah, Jeremiah & Lamentations.* In Cornerstone Biblical Commentary: Old Testament series. 2005.

Matthews, Darrell L. "The Book of Obadiah." In *1 Kings to Malachi*, edited by Kent P. Jackson, 264–66. Vol. 4 of Studies in Scripture series. 1993.

Matthews, Robert J. *Behold the Messiah.* 1994..

———. *A Bible! A Bible!* 1990.

———. "How to Read Isaiah and Enjoy It!" In *Selected Writings of Robert J. Matthews*, 199–210.

———. "Our Heritage from Joseph of Israel." In *Thy People Shall Be My People and Thy God My God*, edited by Paul Y. Hoskisson, 1–16. Sperry Symposium series. 1994.

———. *A Plainer Translation: Joseph Smith's Translation of the Bible, a History and Commentary.* 1985.

———. *Selected Writings of Robert J. Matthews.* Gospel Scholar Series. 1999.

———. "Thou Shalt Not Bear False Witness." *Ensign*, Oct. 1994, 52–57.

Matthews, Victor H. *Manners and Customs in the Bible*, rev. ed. 1991.

Maxwell, Neal A. "Be of Good Cheer." *Ensign*, Nov. 1982, 66–69.

———. "'Behold, the Enemy Is Combined' (D&C 38:12)." *Ensign*, May 1993, 76–79.

———. "Brim with Joy." Brigham Young University devotional, 23 Jan. 1996. Speeches.BYU.edu.

———. "But a Few Days." Address to Church Educational System religious educators, 10 Sep. 1982.

———. "Consecrate Thy Performance." *Ensign*, May 2002, 36–38.

———. *Deposition of a Disciple.* 1976.

———. "Encircled in the Arms of His Love." *Ensign*, Nov. 2002, 16–18.

———. *Even as I Am.* 1982.

———. "For I Will Lead You Along." *Ensign*, May 1988, 7–10.

———. "From Whom All Blessings Flow." *Ensign*, May 1997, 11–12.

———. "God Will Yet Reveal." *Ensign*, Nov. 1986, 52–54, 59.

———. "The Great Plan of the Eternal God." *Ensign*, May 1984, 21–23.

———. "Hope through the Atonement of Jesus Christ." *Ensign*, Nov. 1998, 61–63.

———. "Irony: The Crust on the Bread of Adversity." *Ensign*, May 1989, 62–65.

———. *Men and Women of Christ.* 1991.

———. "Murmur Not." *Ensign*, Nov. 1989, 82–85.

———. *The Neal A. Maxwell Quote Book.* Edited by Cory H. Maxwell. 1997.

———. *Notwithstanding My Weakness.* 1981.

———. *One More Strain of Praise.* 1999.

———. "Our Acceptance of Christ." *Ensign*, June 1984, 69–74.

———. "Overcome . . . Even as I Also Overcame." *Ensign*, May 1987, 70–72.

———. "Patience." *Ensign*, Oct. 1980, 28–31.

———. *Plain and Precious Things.* 1983.

———. "The Precious Promise." *Ensign*, Apr. 2004, 42–47.

———. "Put Off the Natural Man, and Come Off Conqueror." *Ensign*, Nov. 1990, 14–16.
———. "Put Your Shoulder to the Wheel." *Ensign,* May 1998, 37–39.
———. "Repent of [Our] Selfishness." *Ensign*, May 1999, 23–25.
———. "Settle This in Your Hearts." *Ensign*, Nov. 1992, 65–67.
———. "The Seventh Commandment: A Shield." *Ensign*, Nov. 2001, 78–80.
———. "The Stern but Sweet Seventh Commandment." *New Era*, June 1979, 36–38.
———. *That My Family Should Partake.* 1974.
———. *That Ye May Believe.* 1992.
———. *Things as They Really Are.* 1978.
———. "Those Seedling Saints Who Sit before You." Address given to CES religious educators, 19 August 1983.
———. "Yet Thou Art There." *Ensign*, Nov. 1987, 30–33.
Mayfield, James B. "Ishmael, Our Brother." *Ensign*, Jun. 1979, 24–32.
Maynes, Richard J. "The Joy of Living a Christ-Centered Life." *Ensign*, Nov. 2015, 27–30.
Mays, James L. *Psalms: Interpretation: A Bible Commentary for Teaching and Preaching.* 1994.
McCann, J. Clinton, Jr. *Theological Introduction to the Book of Psalms.* 1993.
McCarter, P. Kyle, Jr. *II Samuel.* In the Anchor Bible series. Edited by David Noel Freedman. 1984.
McComiskey, Thomas E. "Micah." In *The Expositor's Bible Commentary*, edited by Tremper Longman III and David E. Garland, vol. 7. 1985.
———, and Tremper Longman III. "Micah." In *The Expositor's Bible Commentary*, rev. ed., edited by Tremper Longman III and David E. Garland, vol. 8. 2008.
McConkie, Bruce R. "Christ and the Creation." *Ensign*, Jun. 1982, 9–15.
———. "Come: Let Israel Build Zion." *Ensign*, May 1977, 115–18.
———. In Conference Report, Apr. 1952, 55–57.
———. In Conference Report, Oct. 1967, 42–44.
———. *Doctrinal New Testament Commentary.* 3 vols. 1965–1973.
———. "Eve and the Fall," in Kimball, et al., *Woman*, 57–68.
———. "How to Worship." *Ensign*, Dec. 1971, 129–31.
———. *The Millennial Messiah: The Second Coming of the Son of Man.* 1982.
———. *The Mortal Messiah: From Bethlehem to Calvary.* 4 vols. 1979–1981.
———. *A New Witness for the Articles of Faith.* 1985.
———. "Our Sisters from the Beginning." *Ensign*, Jan. 1979, 61–63.
———. *The Promised Messiah: The First Coming of Christ.* 1978.
———. "The Promises Made to the Fathers." In *Genesis to 2 Samuel,* edited by Kent P. Jackson and Robert L. Millet, 47–62. Vol. 3 of Studies in Scripture series. 1985.
———. "The Purifying Power of Gethsemane." *Ensign*, May 1985, 9–11.
———. "The Story of a Prophet's Madness." *New Era*, April 1972, 4–7.
———. "Ten Keys to Understanding Isaiah." *Ensign*, Oct. 1973, 78–83.
———. "The Testimony of Jesus." *Ensign*, July 1972, 109–10.
———. "Think on These Things." *Ensign*, Jan. 1974, 45–48.
———. "This Final Glorious Gospel Dispensation." *Ensign*, April 1980, 21–25.
———. "This Generation Shall Have My Word through You." *Ensign*, June 1980, 54–59.
———. "What Think Ye of the Book of Mormon?" *Ensign*, Nov. 1983, 72–74.

McConkie, Carol F. "The Beauty of Holiness." *Ensign*, May 2017, 9–12.

———. "Live according to the Words of the Prophets." *Ensign,* Nov. 2014, 77–79.

McConkie, Joseph Fielding. *Answers: Straightforward Answers to Tough Gospel Questions.* 1998.

———. *Gospel Symbolism.* 1985.

———. *His Name Shall Be Joseph: Ancient Prophecies of the Latter-day Seer.* 1980.

———. "Joseph Smith and the Poetic Writings." In *The Joseph Smith Translation: The Restoration of Plain and Precious Things*, edited by Monte S. Nyman and Robert L. Millet, 103–20.

———. "Joseph Smith as Found in Ancient Manuscripts." In *Isaiah and the Prophets*, edited by Monte S. Nyman, 11–31. 1984.

———. "Premortal Existence, Foreordinations, and Heavenly Councils." In *Apocryphal Writings and the Latter-day Saints*, edited by C. Wilford Griggs, 173–95. 1986.

———. *Prophets and Prophecy.* 1988.

———, and Robert L. Millet. *A Doctrinal Commentary on the Book of Mormon.* Vols. 1–3. 1987–91.

———, Robert L. Millet, and Brent L. Top. *A Doctrinal Commentary on the Book of Mormon.* Vol. 4. 1992.

———, and Craig J. Ostler. *Revelations of the Restoration: A Commentary on the Doctrine and Covenants and Other Modern Revelations.* 2000.

———, and Donald W. Parry. *A Guide to Scriptural Symbols.* 1990.

McConkie, Oscar W. *The Aaronic Priesthood.* 1977.

McKay, David O. In Conference Report, Apr. 1936, 56–61.

McMullin, Keith B. "God Loves and Helps All His Children." *Ensign*, Nov. 2008, 75–78.

———. "Our Path of Duty." *Ensign*, May 2010, 13–15.

Merrill, Byron R. "'Behold, the Lamb of God': The Savior's Use of Animals as Symbols." In *The Lord of the Gospels*, edited by Bruce A. Van Orden and Brent L. Top, 129–47. Sperry Symposium series. 1991.

———. *Elijah: Yesterday, Today, and Tomorrow.* 1997.

———. "Original Sin." In *Encyclopedia of Mormonism*, edited by Daniel H. Ludlow, 3:1052–53. 1992.

Merrill, Eugene H. "Malachi." In *The Expositor's Bible Commentary,* edited by Tremper Longman III and David E. Garland, 8:835–63.

Meservy, Keith H. "Ezekiel, Prophet of Hope." *Ensign*, Sep. 1990, 58¬59.

———. "Ezekiel's Sticks and the Gathering of Israel." *Ensign*, Feb. 1987, 4–11.

———. "God Is with Us." In *1 Kings to Malachi*, edited by Kent P. Jackson, 86–107. Vol. 4 of Studies in Scripture series. 1993.

———. "The Good News of Moses." In *Genesis to 2 Samuel*, edited by Kent P. Jackson and Robert L. Millet, 205–23. Vol. 3 of Studies in Scripture series. 1985.

———. "How Did Proverbs Come to Be—and How Were They Used in Olden Times?" *Ensign*, Oct. 1973, 60.

———. "Jerusalem at the Time of Lehi and Jeremiah." *Ensign*, Jan. 1988, 22–25.

———. "Job: 'Yet Will I Trust in Him.'" In *Sixth Annual Sperry Symposium*, Jan. 28, 1978, 139–59.

———. "Why Did the Lord Permit Israel to War against People in the Land of Promise?" *Ensign*, Oct 1973, 59.

"A Message from the First Presidency." In *Saints*, 1:xv. 2018.

Messages of the First Presidency of The Church of Jesus Christ of Latter-day Saints. Edited by James R. Clark. 6 vols. 1965–71.

Messenger and Advocate. 3 vols. Kirtland, Ohio: October 1834–September 1837. Reprint, 2020.

Meyers, Eric M. and John Rogerson. "Part One. The World of the Hebrew Bible." In *The Cambridge Companion to the Bible,* edited by Bruce Chilton, 39–325.

Mickelsen, Lynn A. "True Friendship and Self-Respect." *Ensign*, June 2006, 30–33.

Midgely, Louis. "The Ways of Remembrance." In *Rediscovering the Book of Mormon*, edited by John L. Sorenson and Melvin J. Thorne, 168–76. 1991.

Milgrom, Jacob. *Numbers.* In The JPS Torah Commentary series. Edited by Nahum M. Sarna. 1990.

Millet, Robert L. *After All We Can Do . . . Grace Works.* 2003.

———. "Apostasy, Great." In *LDS Beliefs: A Doctrinal Reference*, edited by Robert L. Millet, et al., 46–50. 2011.

———. "Cain." In *LDS Beliefs: A Doctrinal Reference,* edited by Robert L. Millet, et al., 87–88.

———. "The Call of Moses and the Deliverance of Israel." In *Genesis to 2 Samuel,* edited by Kent P. Jackson and Robert L. Millet, 93–109. Vol. 3 of Studies in Scripture series. 1985.

———. "Enoch and His City." In *Pearl of Great Price,* edited by Kent P. Jackson and Robert L. Millet, 131–42. Vol. 2 of Studies in Scriptures series. 1985.

———. *An Eye Single to the Glory of God: Reflections on the Cost of Discipleship.* 1991.

———. "Lessons in the Wilderness." In *Genesis to 2 Samuel,* edited by Kent P. Jackson and Robert L. Millet, 173–204. Vol. 3 of Studies in Scripture series. 1985.

———. *Life in Christ: Discovering the Transforming Power of the Savior.* 1990.

———. "Looking Beyond the Mark: Insights from the JST into First-Century Judaism." In *The Joseph Smith Translation: The Restoration of Plain and Precious Things*, edited by Monte S. Nyman and Robert L. Millet, 201–14. 1985.

———. *Men of Covenant: Oaths, Covenants, and Transcendent Promises.* 2015.

———. *Men of Valor: The Powerful Impact of a Righteous Man..* 2007.

———. "Millennium." In *LDS Beliefs: A Doctrinal Reference*, edited by Robert L. Millet, et al., 425–31.

———. *Precept upon Precept: Joseph Smith and the Restoration of Doctrine.* 2016.

———. "Saint." In *LDS Beliefs: A Doctrinal Reference*, edited by Robert L. Millet, et al., 551.

———, and Joseph Fielding McConkie. *The Life Beyond.* 1986.

———, and Joseph Fielding McConkie. *Our Destiny: The Call and Election of the House of Israel.* 1993.

———, Camille Fronk Olson, Andrew C. Skinner, and Brent L. Top. *LDS Beliefs: A Doctrinal Reference.* 2011.

Minert, David R. *Simplified Isaiah for the Latter–day Saints.* 2006.

The Ministry of Peter, the Chief Apostle. Edited by Frank F. Judd, Jr.; Eric D. Huntsman; and Shon D. Hopkin. Sperry Symposium series. 2014.

Monson, Thomas S. "Be an Example and a Light." *Ensign*, Nov. 2015, 86–88.

———. "Be Strong and of a Good Courage." *Ensign*, May 2014, 66–69.

———. "Be Your Best Self." *Ensign*, May 2009, 67–70.

———. "Blessings of the Temple." *Ensign*, Oct. 2010, 12–19.

———. "Blessings of the Temple." *Ensign*, May 2015, 91–93.

———. "The Call of Duty." *Ensign*, Apr. 1986, 37–39.

———. In Conference Report, Oct. 1964, 140–43.

———. "Constant Truths for Changing Times." *Ensign*, May 2005, 19–22.

———. "Dedication Day." *Ensign*, Nov. 2000, 64–66.

———. "Duty Calls." *Ensign*, May 1996, 43–46.

———. "Hopeless Dawn—Joyful Morning." *Ensign*, May 1976, 10–12.

———. "How Firm a Foundation." *Ensign*, Nov. 2006, 62–69.

———. "I Know That My Redeemer Lives!" *Ensign*, May 2007, 22–25.

———. "Meeting Your Goliath." *Ensign*, Jan. 1987, 2–5.

———. "Models to Follow." *Ensign*, Nov. 2002, 60–62, 67.

———. "Obedience Brings Blessings." *Ensign*, May, 2013, 89–92.

———. "The Priesthood in Action." *Ensign*, Nov. 1992, 47–49.

———. "Search and Rescue." *Ensign*, May 1993, 48–51.

———. "The Search for Jesus." *Ensign*, Dec. 1990, 2–5.

———. "Stand in Your Appointed Place." *Ensign*, May 2003, 54–57.

———. *Teachings of Thomas S. Monson.* Compiled by Lynne F. Cannegieter. 2011.

———. "Three Gates to Open." Brigham Young University devotional, 14 Nov. 2006. Speeches.BYU.edu.

———. "We Never Walk Alone." *Ensign*, Nov. 2013, 121–24.

———. "Who Honors God, God Honors." *Ensign*, Nov. 1995, 48–50.

Moody Bible Commentary. Edited by Michael A. Rydelnik and Michael Vanlaningham. 2014.

Moore, Carey A. *Esther.* In the Anchor Bible series. Edited by David Noel Freedman. 1971.

Morales, L. Michael. *Who Shall Ascend the Mountain of the Lord?: A Biblical Theology of the Book of Leviticus.* 2015.

Morgan, Christopher J. "The Sin of Achan." *Ensign*, April 2002, 43–45.

Morton, Ermel J. "I Have A Question." *Ensign*, Aug. 1981, 29.

Motyer, J. Alec. *Isaiah.* In Tyndale Old Testament Commentaries series. Edited by D. J. Wiseman. 1999.

"Move Forward in Faith." *Ensign*, Aug. 2013, 54–57.

Moyle, Henry D. In Conference Report, Apr. 1955, 69–72.

Muhlestein, Kerry. *The Essential Old Testament Companion: Key Insights to Your Gospel Study.* 2013.

———. "Israel's Exodus and Deliverance—Then and Now." *Ensign*, Mar. 2018, 46–51.

———. "Ruth, Redemption, Covenant, and Christ." In *The Gospel of Jesus Christ in the Old Testament*, edited by D. Kelly Ogden, Jared W. Ludlow, and Kerry Muhlestein, 187–206. Sperry Symposium series. 2009.

———. *Scripture Study Made Simple: The Old Testament.* 2017.

———. "Seeking Divine Interaction: Joseph Smith's Varying Searches for the Supernatural." In *No Weapon Shall Prosper: New Light on Sensitive Issues,* edited by Robert L. Millet, 77–91.

Myers, Jacob M. *Ezra–Nehemiah.* In the Anchor Bible series. Edited by David Noel Freedman. 1965.

Nadauld, Margaret D. "Joy of Womanhood." *Ensign*, Nov. 2000, 14–16.

Nelson, Russell M. "The Atonement." *Ensign*, Nov. 1996, 33–36.

———. "Becoming Exemplary Latter-day Saints." *Ensign*, Nov. 2018, 113–14.

———. "Blessed Are the Peacemakers." *Ensign*, Nov. 2002, 39–42.

———. "Celestial Marriage." *Ensign*, Nov. 2008, 92–94.

———. "Children of the Covenant." *Ensign*, May 1995, 32–35.

———. "Closing Remarks." *Ensign*, Nov. 2019, 120–22.

———. "Covenants." *Ensign*, Nov. 2011, 86–90.

———. "The Creation." *Ensign*, May 2000. 84–86.

———. "Decisions for Eternity." *Ensign*, Nov. 2013, 106–9.

———. "Drawing the Power of Jesus Christ into Our Lives." *Ensign*, May 2017, 39–42.

———. "The Exodus Repeated." *Ensign*, July 1999, 6–13.

———. "Face the Future with Faith." *Ensign*, May 2011, 34–36.

———. "The Gathering of Scattered Israel." *Ensign*, Nov. 2006, 79–82.
———. "Go Forward in Faith." *Ensign*, May 2020, 114–16.
———. "Hear Him." *Ensign*, May 2020, 88–92.
———. "Hope of Israel." Supplement to the *New Era* and *Ensign*, Aug. 2018, 8–17.
———. "How Firm Our Foundation." *Ensign*, May 2002, 75–78.
———. "In the Lord's Own Way." *Ensign*, May 1986, 25–28.
———. "Jesus Christ—the Master Healer." *Ensign*, Nov. 2005, 85–88.
———. "Joy and Spiritual Survival." *Ensign*, Nov. 2016, 81–84.
———. "Lessons from Eve." *Ensign*, Nov. 1987, 86–89.
———. "Let God Prevail." *Ensign*, Nov. 2020, 92–95.
———. "Let Your Faith Show." *Ensign*, May 2014, 29–31.
———. "Listen to Learn." *Ensign*, May 1991, 22–26.
———. "Living by Scriptural Guidance." *Ensign*, Nov. 2000, 16–18.
———. "The Love and Laws of God." Brigham Young University devotional, 17 Sep. 2019. Speeches .BYU.edu.
———. "Opening the Heavens for Help." *Ensign*, May 2020, 72–74.
———. "Perfection Pending." *Ensign*, Nov. 1995, 86–88.
———. "Personal Preparation for Temple Blessings." *Ensign*, May 2001, 32–34.
———. "A Plea to My Sisters." *Ensign*, Nov. 2015, 95–98.
———. *The Power within Us.* 1988.
———. "Remnants Gathered, Covenants Fulfilled." In *Voices of Old Testament Prophets*, edited by Dennis Wright, Craig J. Ostler, Dana M. Pike, Dee R. Darling, and Patty A. Smith, 1–21. Sperry Symposium series. 1997.
———. "Revelation for the Church, Revelation for Our Lives." *Ensign*, May 2018, 93–96.
———. "Roots and Branches." *Ensign*, May 2004, 27–29.
———. "The Sabbath Is a Delight." *Ensign*, May 2015, 129–32.
———. "The Savior's Four Gifts of Joy." *New Era*, Dec. 2019, 2–5.
———. "Set In Order Thy House." *Ensign*, Nov. 2001, 69–71.
———. "Stand as True Millennials." *Ensign*, Oct. 2016, 24–31.
———. "Sustaining the Prophets." *Ensign*, Nov. 2014, 74–77.
———. *Teachings of Russell M. Nelson.* 2018.
———. "Thanks Be to God." *Ensign*, May 2012, 77–80.
———. "Thanks for the Covenant." Brigham Young University devotional, 22 Nov. 1988. In *BYU 1988–89 Devotional and Fireside Speeches*, 53–61.
———. "We Are Children of God." *Ensign*, Nov. 1998, 85–87.
———. "We Can Do Better and Be Better." *Ensign*, May 2019, 67–69.
———. "Where Is Wisdom?" *Ensign*, Nov. 1992, 6–8.
———. "Why This Holy Land?" *Ensign*, Dec. 1989, 12–19.
———. "With God Nothing Shall Be Impossible." *Ensign*, May 1988, 33–36.
Nelson's Illustrated Bible Dictionary: New and Enhanced Edition. Edited by Ronald F. Youngblood. 2014.
The Nelson Study Bible [NKJV]. Edited by Earl D. Radmacher. 1997.
Nelson, Wendy Watson. "For Such a Time as This." BYU Women's Conference address, 3 May 2007. WomensConference.ce.BYU.edu.
Neuenschwander, Dennis B. "Ordinances and Covenants." *Ensign*, Aug. 2001, 20–26.

The New American Commentary series. Edited by E. Ray Clendenen, Kenneth A. Mathews, and David S. Dockery. 42 vols. 1991–2015.

The New Bible Commentary: Revised. Edited by D. Guthrie, J. A. Motyer, A. M. Stibbs, and D. J. Wiseman. 1970.

New Collegeville Bible Commentary series. Edited by Daniel Durken. 21 vols. 2007–2015.

The New International Commentary on the Old Testament series. Edited by R. K. Harrison and Robert L. Hubbard, Jr. 26 vols. 1965–2019.

The New Interpreter's Bible. Edited by Leander E. Keck. 12 vols. 1994–1998.

The New Oxford Annotated Bible: New Revised Standard Version. Edited by Bruce M. Metzger and Roland E. Murphy. 1991.

———. Edited by Michael D. Coogan. 2010.

Newsom, Carol A. "The Book of Job: Introduction, Commentary, and Reflection." In *The New Interpreter's Bible*, edited by Leander E. Keck, 4:627–37. 1996.

Nibley, Hugh W. *Abraham in Egypt.* Vol. 4 in The Collected Works of Hugh Nibley series. 1981.

———. *Ancient Documents and the Pearl of Great Price.* 1986.

———. *Approaching Zion.* Vol. 9 in The Collected Works of Hugh Nibley series. Edited by Don E. Norton. 1989.

———. *An Approach to the Book of Abraham.* Vol. 18 in The Collected Works of Hugh Nibley series. 2009.

———. *Brother Brigham Challenges the Saints.* Vol. 13 in The Collected Works of Hugh Nibley series. 1994.

———. The Collected Works of Hugh Nibley series. 19 vols. 1986–2010.

———. *Eloquent Witness: Nibley on Himself, Others, and the Temple.* Vol. 17 of The Collected Works of Hugh Nibley series. 2008.

———. *Enoch the Prophet.* Vol. 2 of The Collected Works of Hugh Nibley series. 1986.

———. *Lehi in the Desert/The World of the Jaredites/There Were Jaredites.* Vol. 5 of The Collected Works of Hugh Nibley series. 1988.

———. *Nibley on the Timely and the Timeless.* 1978.

———. *Old Testament and Related Studies.* Vol. 1 of The Collected Works of Hugh Nibley series. Edited by John W. Welch and Gary P. Gillum. 1986.

———. "On the Sacred and the Symbolic." In *Temples of the Ancient World*, edited by Donald W. Parry, 533–615. 1994.

Nibley, Preston. *Brigham Young: The Man and His Work.* 1960.

The NIV Application Commentary: Old Testament series. Edited by Terry Muck. 23 vols. 1999–2020.

The NIV Study Bible. Edited by Kenneth L. Barker. 1985.

The NIV Study Bible. Edited by Kenneth L. Barker. 1995.

The NIV Study Bible. Edited by Kenneth L. Barker. 1997.

The NIV Study Bible. Edited by Kenneth L. Barker. 2002.

The NIV Study Bible: Fully Revised Edition. Edited by Kenneth L. Barker. 2020.

NKJV Cultural Backgrounds Study Bible. Edited by John H. Walton and Craig S. Keener. 2017.

NKJV Study Bible. Edited by Earl D. Radmacher. 2007.

NKJV Study Bible. Edited by Earl D. Radmacher. 2018.

No Weapon Shall Prosper: New Light on Sensitive Issues. Edited by Robert L. Millet. 2011.

Nyman, Monte S. "The Contribution of the JST to the Old Testament Historical Books." In *The Joseph*

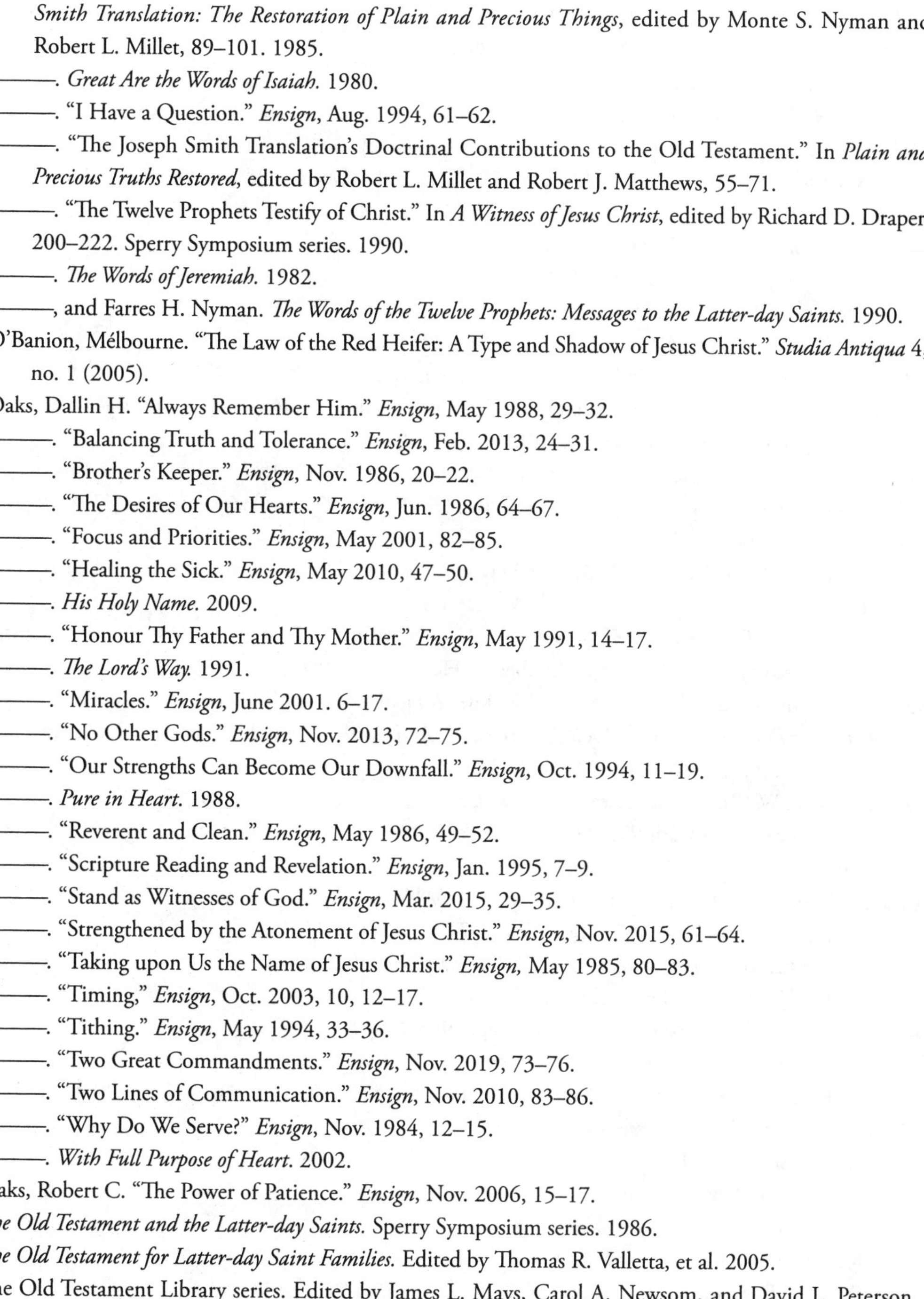

Smith Translation: The Restoration of Plain and Precious Things, edited by Monte S. Nyman and Robert L. Millet, 89–101. 1985.

———. *Great Are the Words of Isaiah.* 1980.

———. "I Have a Question." *Ensign*, Aug. 1994, 61–62.

———. "The Joseph Smith Translation's Doctrinal Contributions to the Old Testament." In *Plain and Precious Truths Restored*, edited by Robert L. Millet and Robert J. Matthews, 55–71.

———. "The Twelve Prophets Testify of Christ." In *A Witness of Jesus Christ*, edited by Richard D. Draper, 200–222. Sperry Symposium series. 1990.

———. *The Words of Jeremiah.* 1982.

———, and Farres H. Nyman. *The Words of the Twelve Prophets: Messages to the Latter-day Saints.* 1990.

O'Banion, Mélbourne. "The Law of the Red Heifer: A Type and Shadow of Jesus Christ." *Studia Antiqua* 4, no. 1 (2005).

Oaks, Dallin H. "Always Remember Him." *Ensign*, May 1988, 29–32.

———. "Balancing Truth and Tolerance." *Ensign*, Feb. 2013, 24–31.

———. "Brother's Keeper." *Ensign*, Nov. 1986, 20–22.

———. "The Desires of Our Hearts." *Ensign*, Jun. 1986, 64–67.

———. "Focus and Priorities." *Ensign*, May 2001, 82–85.

———. "Healing the Sick." *Ensign*, May 2010, 47–50.

———. *His Holy Name.* 2009.

———. "Honour Thy Father and Thy Mother." *Ensign*, May 1991, 14–17.

———. *The Lord's Way.* 1991.

———. "Miracles." *Ensign*, June 2001. 6–17.

———. "No Other Gods." *Ensign*, Nov. 2013, 72–75.

———. "Our Strengths Can Become Our Downfall." *Ensign*, Oct. 1994, 11–19.

———. *Pure in Heart.* 1988.

———. "Reverent and Clean." *Ensign*, May 1986, 49–52.

———. "Scripture Reading and Revelation." *Ensign*, Jan. 1995, 7–9.

———. "Stand as Witnesses of God." *Ensign*, Mar. 2015, 29–35.

———. "Strengthened by the Atonement of Jesus Christ." *Ensign*, Nov. 2015, 61–64.

———. "Taking upon Us the Name of Jesus Christ." *Ensign,* May 1985, 80–83.

———. "Timing," *Ensign*, Oct. 2003, 10, 12–17.

———. "Tithing." *Ensign*, May 1994, 33–36.

———. "Two Great Commandments." *Ensign*, Nov. 2019, 73–76.

———. "Two Lines of Communication." *Ensign*, Nov. 2010, 83–86.

———. "Why Do We Serve?" *Ensign*, Nov. 1984, 12–15.

———. *With Full Purpose of Heart.* 2002.

Oaks, Robert C. "The Power of Patience." *Ensign*, Nov. 2006, 15–17.

The Old Testament and the Latter-day Saints. Sperry Symposium series. 1986.

The Old Testament for Latter-day Saint Families. Edited by Thomas R. Valletta, et al. 2005.

The Old Testament Library series. Edited by James L. Mays, Carol A. Newsom, and David L. Peterson. 49 vols. 1987–2015.

Old Testament Seminary Teacher Manual. 2015.

Old Testament Seminary Teacher Material. 2018.

Old Testament Seminary Teacher Material. Online commentary. 2018. ChurchofJesusChrist.org.

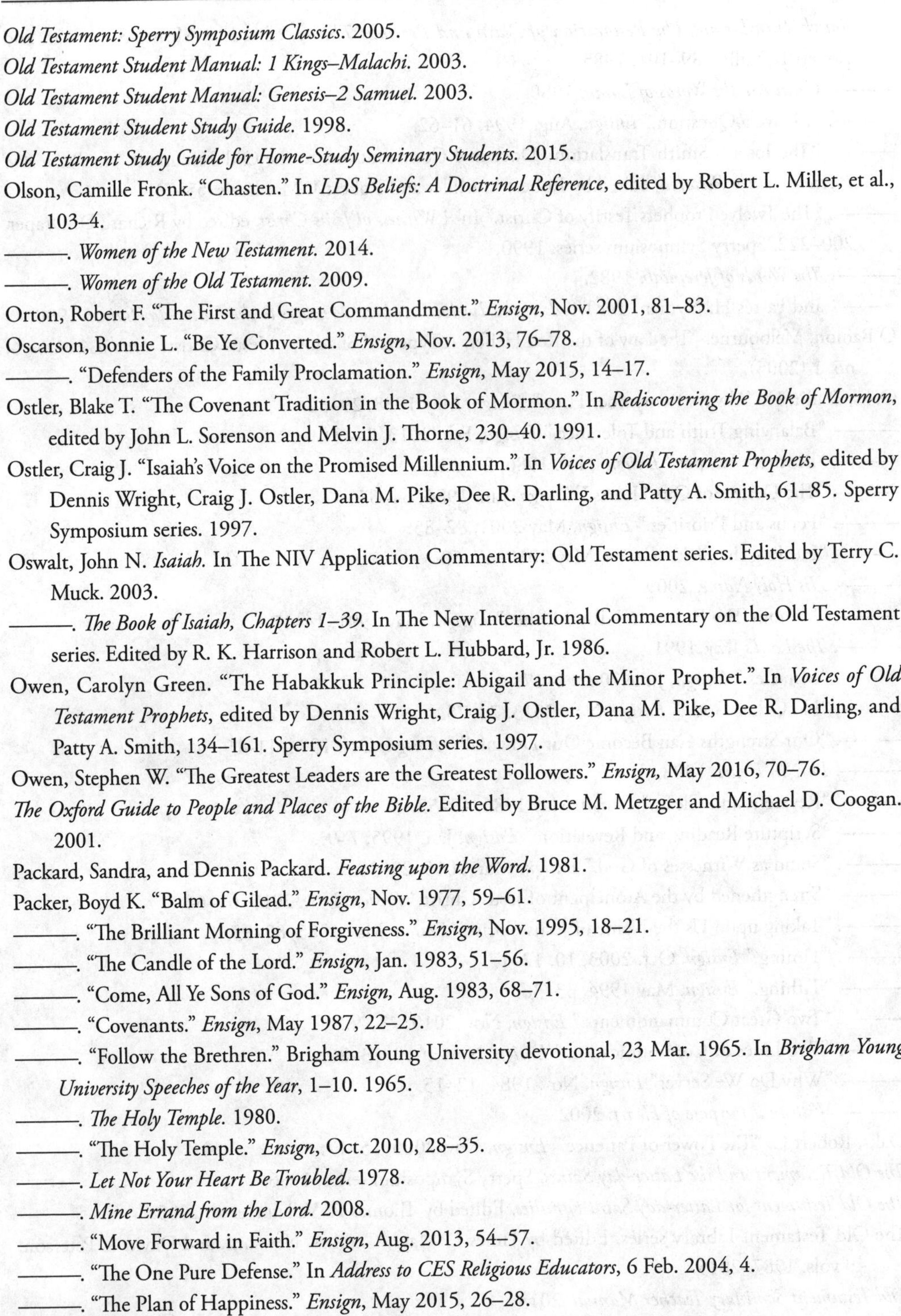

Old Testament: Sperry Symposium Classics. 2005.

Old Testament Student Manual: 1 Kings–Malachi. 2003.

Old Testament Student Manual: Genesis–2 Samuel. 2003.

Old Testament Student Study Guide. 1998.

Old Testament Study Guide for Home-Study Seminary Students. 2015.

Olson, Camille Fronk. "Chasten." In *LDS Beliefs: A Doctrinal Reference*, edited by Robert L. Millet, et al., 103–4.

———. *Women of the New Testament.* 2014.

———. *Women of the Old Testament.* 2009.

Orton, Robert F. "The First and Great Commandment." *Ensign*, Nov. 2001, 81–83.

Oscarson, Bonnie L. "Be Ye Converted." *Ensign*, Nov. 2013, 76–78.

———. "Defenders of the Family Proclamation." *Ensign*, May 2015, 14–17.

Ostler, Blake T. "The Covenant Tradition in the Book of Mormon." In *Rediscovering the Book of Mormon*, edited by John L. Sorenson and Melvin J. Thorne, 230–40. 1991.

Ostler, Craig J. "Isaiah's Voice on the Promised Millennium." In *Voices of Old Testament Prophets,* edited by Dennis Wright, Craig J. Ostler, Dana M. Pike, Dee R. Darling, and Patty A. Smith, 61–85. Sperry Symposium series. 1997.

Oswalt, John N. *Isaiah.* In The NIV Application Commentary: Old Testament series. Edited by Terry C. Muck. 2003.

———. *The Book of Isaiah, Chapters 1–39.* In The New International Commentary on the Old Testament series. Edited by R. K. Harrison and Robert L. Hubbard, Jr. 1986.

Owen, Carolyn Green. "The Habakkuk Principle: Abigail and the Minor Prophet." In *Voices of Old Testament Prophets*, edited by Dennis Wright, Craig J. Ostler, Dana M. Pike, Dee R. Darling, and Patty A. Smith, 134–161. Sperry Symposium series. 1997.

Owen, Stephen W. "The Greatest Leaders are the Greatest Followers." *Ensign,* May 2016, 70–76.

The Oxford Guide to People and Places of the Bible. Edited by Bruce M. Metzger and Michael D. Coogan. 2001.

Packard, Sandra, and Dennis Packard. *Feasting upon the Word.* 1981.

Packer, Boyd K. "Balm of Gilead." *Ensign*, Nov. 1977, 59–61.

———. "The Brilliant Morning of Forgiveness." *Ensign*, Nov. 1995, 18–21.

———. "The Candle of the Lord." *Ensign*, Jan. 1983, 51–56.

———. "Come, All Ye Sons of God." *Ensign,* Aug. 1983, 68–71.

———. "Covenants." *Ensign*, May 1987, 22–25.

———. "Follow the Brethren." Brigham Young University devotional, 23 Mar. 1965. In *Brigham Young University Speeches of the Year*, 1–10. 1965.

———. *The Holy Temple.* 1980.

———. "The Holy Temple." *Ensign*, Oct. 2010, 28–35.

———. *Let Not Your Heart Be Troubled.* 1978.

———. *Mine Errand from the Lord.* 2008.

———. "Move Forward in Faith." *Ensign*, Aug. 2013, 54–57.

———. "The One Pure Defense." In *Address to CES Religious Educators*, 6 Feb. 2004, 4.

———. "The Plan of Happiness." *Ensign*, May 2015, 26–28.

———. "Prayers and Answers." *Ensign*, Nov. 1979, 18–21.

———. "Reverence Invites Revelation." *Ensign*, Nov. 1991, 21–23.

———. "Scriptures." *Ensign*, Nov. 1982, 51–53.
———. "Shield of Faith." *Ensign*, May 1995, 7–9.
———. "To Young Women and Men." *Ensign*, May 1989, 53–60.
———. "The Twelve Apostles." *Ensign*, Nov. 1996, 6–8.
———. "The Word of Wisdom: The Principle and the Promises." *Ensign*, May 1996, 17–20.
———. "Why Stay Morally Clean." *Ensign*, July 1972, 111–13.
Palmer, S. Mark. "The Enduring Influence of Righteous Women." *Ensign*, Oct. 2018, 50–53.
Parker, Jared T. "Cutting Covenants." In *The Gospel of Jesus Christ in the Old Testament*, edited by D. Kelly Ogden, Jared W. Ludlow, Kerry Muhlestein, Patty Smith, and Thomas R. Valletta, 109–28. Sperry Symposium series. 2009.
Parrella, Adilson de Paula. "Essential Truths—Our Need to Act." *Ensign*, Nov. 2017, 115–16.
Parry, Donald W. "The Flood and the Tower of Babel." *Ensign*, Jan. 1998, 35–41.
———. "Garden of Eden: Prototype Sanctuary." In *Temples of the Ancient World*, edited by Donald W. Parry, 126–51.
———. "Ritual Anointing with Olive Oil in Ancient Israelite Religion." In *The Allegory of the Olive Tree: The Olive, the Bible, and Jacob 5*, edited by John W. Welch and Stephen D. Ricks. 1994.
———. "Sinai as Sanctuary and Mountain of God." In *By Study and Also by Faith*, edited by by John M. Lundquist and Stephen D. Ricks, 1:482–500. 1990.
———. *Temples of the Ancient World: Ritual and Symbolism.* 1994.
———, and Jay A. Parry. *Symbols and Shadows: Unlocking a Deeper Understanding of the Atonement.* 2009.
———, and Jay A. Parry. *Understanding Death and the Resurrection.* 2003.
———, and Jay A. Parry. *Understanding the Signs of the Times.* 1999.
———, Jay A. Parry, and Tina M. Peterson. *Understanding Isaiah.* 1998.
———, and Stephen D. Ricks. "The Judges of Israel." In *Genesis to 2 Samuel*, edited by Kent P. Jackson and Robert L. Millet, 239–47. Vol. 3 of Studies in Scripture series. 1985.
Parry, Jay A., and Donald W. Parry. "Israelite Names—Witnesses of Deity." *Ensign*, Dec. 1990, 52–54.
———. *Understanding the Book of Revelation.* 1998.
Patterson, Richard D., and Hermann J. Austel. "1 and 2 Kings." In *The Expositor's Bible Commentary*, rev. ed., edited by Tremper Longman III and David E. Garland, 3:615–954. 2009.
Pearce, Virginia L. "Fear." *Ensign*, Nov. 1992, 90–92.
The Pearl of Great Price. Edited by Robert L. Millet and Kent P. Jackson. Vol. 2 of Studies in Scriptures series. 1985.
Pearson, Glenn L. *The Old Testament: A Mormon Perspective.* 1980.
Penrose, Charles W. In Conference Report, Oct. 1919, 45–60.
———. In *Journal of Discourses*, 21:45–53.
———. In *Journal of Discourses*, 21:220–32.
———. In *Journal of Discourses*, 24:82–99.
———. "The Second Advent." In *Latter-day Saints Millennial Star*, Vol. 21, No. 37 (1859): 581–88.
Perry, L. Tom. "Becoming Goodly Parents." *Ensign*, Nov. 2012, 26–28.
———. "Becoming Men in Whom the Spirit of God Is." *Ensign*, May 2002, 39–41.
———. "Consider Your Ways." *Ensign*, July 1973, 20–21.
———. "Family Traditions." *Ensign*, May 1990, 19–20.
———. "In the World." *Ensign*, May 1988, 13–15.
———. "The Law of the Fast." *Ensign*, May 1986, 31–33.

———. "The Sabbath and the Sacrament." *Ensign*, May 2011, 6–9.

———. "Trust in the Lord." *Ensign*, May 1978, 51–53.

———. "We Believe All That God Has Revealed." *Ensign*, Nov. 2003, 85–88.

Petersen, Mark E. *Abraham, Friend of God.* 1979.

———. "Another Prophet Now Has Come." *Ensign*, Jan. 1973, 116–18.

———. In Conference Report, Apr. 1949, 144–46.

———. In Conference Report, Apr. 1970, 81–82.

———. *Joseph of Egypt.* 1981. .

———. *Joshua, Man of Faith.* 1978.

———. *Moses: Man of Miracles.* 1977.

———. *Noah and the Flood.* 1982.

———. "The Sabbath Day." *Ensign*, May 1975, 47–49.

———. "Salvation Comes through the Church." *Ensign*, July 1973, 108–11.

———. *Three Kings of Israel.* 1980.

Petersen, Morris S. "Earth." In *Encyclopedia of Mormonism*, edited by Daniel Ludlow, et al., 2:431–33.

Peterson, Brian N. *Ezekiel in Context.* 2012.

Pett, Peter. *Peter Pett's Commentary on the Bible.* 2011.

Phillips, Elaine. "Esther." In *The Expositor's Bible Commentary*, rev. ed., edited by Tremper Longman III and David E. Garland, 4:569–674. 2010.

Phillips, John. *Exploring the Book of Daniel.* 2004.

Pierce, George A. "Understanding Micah's Lament for Judah (Micah 1:10–16) through Text, Archaeology, and Geography." In *Prophets and Prophecies of the Old Testament*, edited by Aaron P. Schade, Brian M. Hauglid, and Kerry Muhlestein, 161–84. Sperry Symposium series. 2017.

Pike, Dana M. "'I Will Bless the Lord at All Times': Blessing God in the Old Testament." In *Ascending the Mountain of the Lord*, edited by David R. Seely, et al., 136–55. Sperry Symposium series. 2013.

———. "'How Beautiful upon the Mountains': The Imagery of Isaiah 52:7–10." In *Isaiah in the Book of Mormon*, edited by Donald W. Parry and John W. Welch, 249–91. 1998.

———. "The Proverbs." In *1 Kings to Malachi*, edited by Kent P. Jackson, 448–62. Vol. 4 of Studies in Scripture series. 1993.

Pinegar, Ed J., and Richard J. Allen. *Latter-day Commentary on the Old Testament.* 2001.

———. *Old Testament Who's Who.* Illustrated Edition. 2009.

Pinegar, Rex D. "Decide to Decide." *Ensign*, Nov. 1980, 71–73.

Plain and Precious Truths Restored: The Doctrinal and Historical Significance of the Joseph Smith Translation. Edited by Robert L. Millet and Robert J. Matthews. 1995.

Plastaras, James. *The God of Exodus: The Theology of the Exodus Narratives.* 1966.

"Plural Marriage in Kirtland and Nauvoo." Gospel Essays. ChurchofJesusChrist.org.

Poelman, Ronald E. "God's Love for Us Transcends Our Transgressions." *Ensign*, May 1982, 27–29.

———. "The Gospel and the Church." *Ensign*, Nov. 1984, 64–65.

Polish, Daniel F. *Keeping Faith with the Psalms: Deepen Your Relationship with God Using the Book of Psalms.* 2004.

Porter, Bruce D. "Building the Kingdom." *Ensign*, May 2001, 80–82.

———. *The King of Kings.* 2000.

Prager, Dennis. *The Rational Bible: Exodus.* 2018.

———. *The Rational Bible: Genesis.* 2019.

Pratt, Carl B. "The Lord's Richest Blessings." *Ensign*, May 2011, 101–3.
Pratt, Orson. In *Journal of Discourses*, 12:84–93.
———. In *Journal of Discourses*, 15:53–61.
———. In *Journal of Discourses*, 15:178–91.
———. In *Journal of Discourses*, 16:78–87.
———. In *Journal of Discourses*, 17:289–306.
———. In *Journal of Discourses*, 18:57–69.
———. In *Journal of Discourses*, 19:280–94.
———. In *Journal of Discourses*, 21:272–80.
———. In *Journal of Discourses*, 24:20–32.
———. *Orson Pratt's Works.* 1851.
Pratt, Parley P. *The Voice of Warning.* 1837.
Preparing for an Eternal Marriage: Student Manual. 2003.
Prinsloo, Willem S. "The Psalms." In *Eerdmans Commentary on the Bible*, 364–436. 2003.
Prophets and Prophecies of the Old Testament. Edited by Aaron P. Schade, Brian M. Hauglid, and Kerry Muhlestein. Sperry Symposium series. 2017.
Provan, Iain W. "Daniel." In *Eerdmans Commentary on the Bible*, edited by James D. G. Dunn and John W. Rogerson, 665–75. 2003.
———. *Ecclesiastes, Song of Songs.* In The NIV Application Commentary: Old Testament series. Edited by Terry Muck. 2001
———. *1 & 2 Kings.* In Understanding the Bible Commentary series, edited by Ward W. Gasque, Robert L. Hubbard, Jr., and Robert K. Johnston. 2012.
———. "2 Kings." In *Zondervan Illustrated Bible Backgrounds Commentary*, edited by John H. Walton, 3:108–219. 2009.
Quest Study Bible. 1994.
Quest Study Bible. 2003.
Quest Study Bible. Revised NIV edition. 2005.
Quest Study Bible. 2011.
Ramsay, William M. *The Westminster Guide to the Books of the Bible.* 1994.
Rasband, Ronald A. "Be Not Troubled." *Ensign*, Nov. 2018, 18–21.
———. "Build a Fortress of Spirituality and Protection." *Ensign*, May 2019, 107–9.
———. "Lessons from the Old Testament: Fleeing Temptation." *Ensign*, Mar. 2006, 62–65.
———. "Standing by Our Promises and Covenants." *Ensign*, Nov. 2018, 53–56.
Rasmussen, Ellis T. *An Introduction to the Old Testament and Its Teachings.* 2 vols. 1972.
———. *A Latter-day Saint Commentary on the Old Testament.* 1993.
———. "Old Testament." In *Scriptures of the Church: Selections from the Encyclopedia of Mormonism*, edited by David H. Ludlow, 489–94.
Read, Lenet Hadley. "All Things Testify of Him: Understanding Symbolism in the Scriptures." *Ensign*, Jan. 1981, 4–7.
———. "Elijah and Elisha: Foreshadowing the Latter-day Work." *Ensign*, Mar. 1988, 24–28.
———. "How the Bible Came to Be." *Ensign*, Aug. 1982, 49–55.
———. "The Plates and the Feast of Trumpets." *Journal of Book of Mormon Studies*, Vol. 2, No. 2 (Fall 1993): 110–20.
Rector, Hartman, Jr. "Live above the Law to Be Free." *Ensign*, Jan 1973, 130–31.

Redd, J. Lyman. "Aaron's Consecration: Its Nature, Purpose, and Meaning." In *Thy People Shall Be My People and Thy God My God,* edited by Paul Y. Hoskisson, 118–35. Sperry Symposium series. 1994.
Rediscovering the Book of Mormon. Edited by John L. Sorenson and Melvin J. Thorne. 1991.
Reexploring the Book of Mormon. Edited by John W. Welch. 1992.
Reichert, Victor E. *Job.* In The Soncino Books of the Bible series. Edited by A. Cohen. 1946.
Renlund, Dale G. "Abound with Blessings." *Ensign,* May 2019, 70–73.
———. "Choose You This Day." *Ensign,* Nov. 2018, 104–7.
———. "Consider the Goodness and Greatness of God." *Ensign,* May 2020, 41–44.
———. "Constructing Spiritual Stability." Brigham Young University devotional, 16 Sep. 2014. Speeches .BYU.edu.
———. "Do Justly, Love Mercy, and Walk Humbly with God." *Ensign,* Nov. 2020, 109–12.
———. "Family History and Temple Work: Sealing and Healing." *Ensign,* May 2018, 46–49.
———. "Our Good Shepherd." *Ensign,* May 2017, 29–31.
———. "Preserving the Heart's Mighty Change," *Ensign,* Nov. 2009, 97–99.
———. "Repentance: A Joyful Choice." *Ensign,* Nov. 2016, 121–24.
———. "Unwavering Commitment to Jesus Christ." *Ensign,* May 2019, 22–25.
———. and Ruth Lybbert Renlund. "The Divine Purposes of Sexual Intimacy." *Ensign,* Aug. 2020, 15–19.
———, and Ruth Lybbert Renlund. *The Melchizedek Priesthood.* 2018.
The Revell Bible Dictionary. 1990.
Revised Standard Version of the Bible. 1952.
Reynolds, George, and Janne M. Sjodahl. *Commentary on the Book of Mormon.* 7 vols. 1955–1961.
Reynolds, Noel. "The Israelite Background of Moses Typology in the Book of Mormon." In *BYU Studies,* 44:2 (2005):5–23.
Richards, Franklin D. In *Journal of Discourses,* 4:159–62.
———. In *Journal of Discourses,* 23:311–20.
———. "LDS Hymns—Worshiping with Song." *Ensign,* Nov. 1982, 22–24.
Richards, Lawrence O. *The Bible Reader's Companion.* 1991.
———. *Zondervan Expository Dictionary of Bible Words.* 1991.
Richards, LeGrand. "Be Ye Prepared." *Ensign,* Nov. 1981, 27–29.
———. In Conference Report, Oct. 1956, 22–26.
———. In Conference Report, April 1963, 115–19.
———. In Conference Report, Oct. 1966, 41–44.
———. *Israel! Do You Know?* 1954.
———. *A Marvelous Work and a Wonder.* Revised edition. 1972.
———. "Prophets and Prophecy." *Ensign,* Nov. 1975, 50–52.
———. "The Things of God and Man." *Ensign,* Nov. 1977, 21–24.
———. "Value of the Holy Scriptures." *Ensign,* May 1976, 82–83.
Ricks, Stephen D. "Deuteronomy: A Covenant of Love." *Ensign,* Apr. 1990, 55–59.
———. "The Law of Sacrifice." *Ensign,* June 1998, 24–29.
———. "Ruth." In *Genesis to 2 Samuel,* edited by Kent P. Jackson and Robert L. Millet, 249–57. Vol. 3 of Studies in Scripture series.1985.
———. "A Watchman to the House of Israel." In *1 Kings to Malachi,* edited by Kent P. Jackson, 267–85. Vol. 4 of Studies in Scripture series. 1993.
Ridges, David J. *The Old Testament Made Easier: Part 1, Genesis through Exodus 24.* 2014.

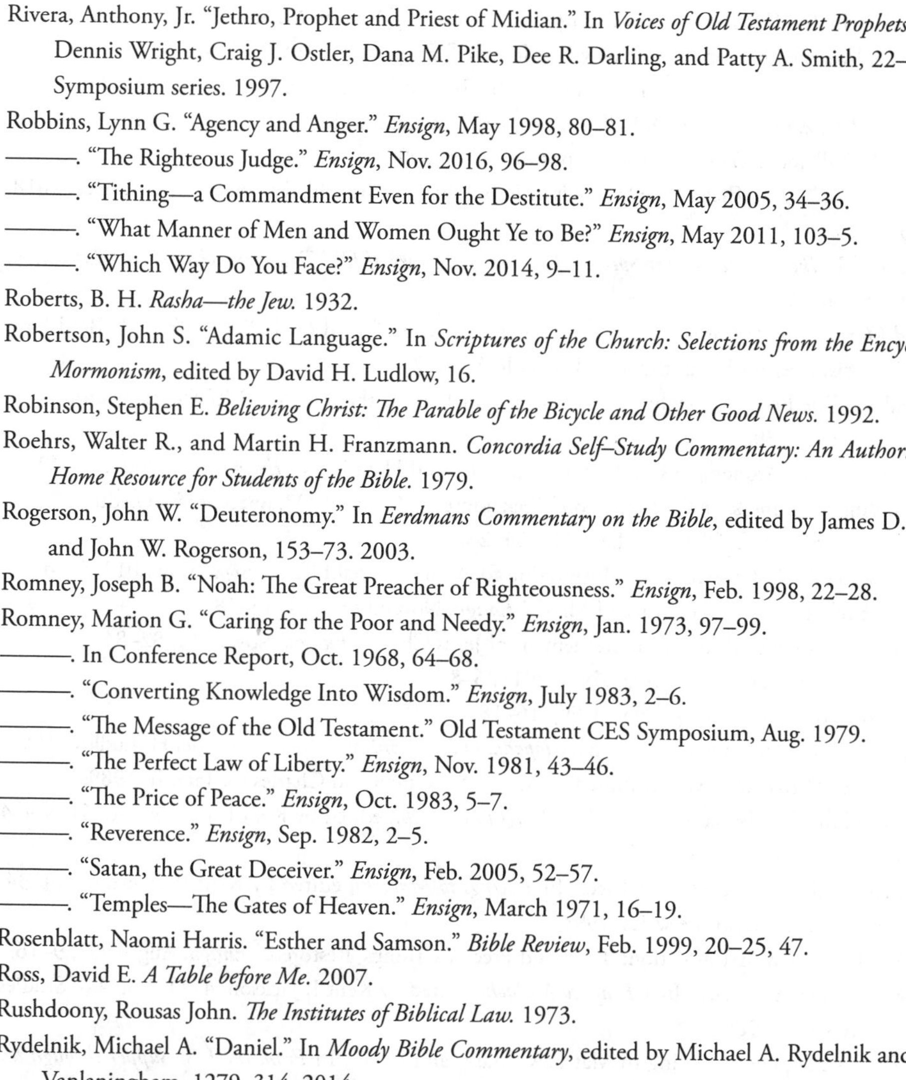

Rivera, Anthony, Jr. "Jethro, Prophet and Priest of Midian." In *Voices of Old Testament Prophets*, edited by Dennis Wright, Craig J. Ostler, Dana M. Pike, Dee R. Darling, and Patty A. Smith, 22–33. Sperry Symposium series. 1997.

Robbins, Lynn G. "Agency and Anger." *Ensign*, May 1998, 80–81.

———. "The Righteous Judge." *Ensign*, Nov. 2016, 96–98.

———. "Tithing—a Commandment Even for the Destitute." *Ensign*, May 2005, 34–36.

———. "What Manner of Men and Women Ought Ye to Be?" *Ensign*, May 2011, 103–5.

———. "Which Way Do You Face?" *Ensign*, Nov. 2014, 9–11.

Roberts, B. H. *Rasha—the Jew.* 1932.

Robertson, John S. "Adamic Language." In *Scriptures of the Church: Selections from the Encyclopedia of Mormonism*, edited by David H. Ludlow, 16.

Robinson, Stephen E. *Believing Christ: The Parable of the Bicycle and Other Good News.* 1992.

Roehrs, Walter R., and Martin H. Franzmann. *Concordia Self-Study Commentary: An Authoritative In-Home Resource for Students of the Bible.* 1979.

Rogerson, John W. "Deuteronomy." In *Eerdmans Commentary on the Bible*, edited by James D. G. Dunn and John W. Rogerson, 153–73. 2003.

Romney, Joseph B. "Noah: The Great Preacher of Righteousness." *Ensign*, Feb. 1998, 22–28.

Romney, Marion G. "Caring for the Poor and Needy." *Ensign*, Jan. 1973, 97–99.

———. In Conference Report, Oct. 1968, 64–68.

———. "Converting Knowledge Into Wisdom." *Ensign*, July 1983, 2–6.

———. "The Message of the Old Testament." Old Testament CES Symposium, Aug. 1979.

———. "The Perfect Law of Liberty." *Ensign*, Nov. 1981, 43–46.

———. "The Price of Peace." *Ensign*, Oct. 1983, 5–7.

———. "Reverence." *Ensign*, Sep. 1982, 2–5.

———. "Satan, the Great Deceiver." *Ensign*, Feb. 2005, 52–57.

———. "Temples—The Gates of Heaven." *Ensign*, March 1971, 16–19.

Rosenblatt, Naomi Harris. "Esther and Samson." *Bible Review*, Feb. 1999, 20–25, 47.

Ross, David E. *A Table before Me.* 2007.

Rushdoony, Rousas John. *The Institutes of Biblical Law.* 1973.

Rydelnik, Michael A. "Daniel." In *Moody Bible Commentary*, edited by Michael A. Rydelnik and Michael Vanlaningham, 1279–314. 2014.

Sabin, Gary B. "Stand Up Inside and Be All In." *Ensign*, May 2017, 52–55.

"Sacred Temple Clothing" (video). ChurchofJesusChrist.org.

Sailhamer, John H. "Genesis." In *The Expositor's Bible Commentary,* rev. ed., edited by Tremper Longman III and David E. Garland, 1:21–331. 2008.

Saints: The Story of the Church of Jesus Christ in the Latter Days. Vol. 1: *The Standard of Truth, 1815–1846.* 2018.

Saints: The Story of the Church of Jesus Christ in the Latter Days. Vol. 2: *No Unhallowed Hand, 1846–1893.* 2020.

"The Salt of the Earth." *Ensign*, Jan. 2014, 66–67.

Sarna, Nahum M. *Exodus.* In The JPS Torah Commentary series. Edited by Nahum M. Sarna. 1991.

———. *Exploring Exodus: The Heritage of Biblical Israel.* 1986.

———. *Exploring Exodus: The Origins of Biblical Israel.* 1996.

———. *Genesis.* In The JPS Torah Commentary series. Edited by Nahum M. Sarna. 1989.

———. "Who Was the Pharaoh 'Who Knew Not Joseph'?" *Ensign*, Dec. 1987, 54–57.

Schade, Aaron. "The Imagery of Hosea's Family and the Restoration of Israel." In *The Gospel of Jesus Christ in the Old Testament*, edited by D. Kelly Ogden, Jared W. Ludlow, Kerry Muhlestein, Patty Smith, and Thomas R. Valletta, 233–49. Sperry Symposium series. 2009.

Schank, Stephen A. "'I Am That I Am': Symbols of Jesus Christ in the Old Testament." *Ensign*, Dec. 2018, 32–35.

Schultz, Samuel J. *The Old Testament Speaks: A Complete Survey of Old Testament History and Literature.* Fourth edition. 1990.

Science and Mormonism 1: Cosmos, Earth, and Man. Edited by David H. Bailey, Jeffrey M. Bradshaw, John S. Lewis, Gregory L. Smith, and Michael R. Stark. 2016.

Scott, David R. "The Book of Jonah: Foreshadowings of Jesus as the Christ." *BYU Studies Quarterly* 53, no. 3 (2014): 161–80.

Scott, Richard G. "The Atonement Can Secure Your Peace and Happiness." *Ensign*, Nov. 2006, 40–42.

———. "Finding Happiness." BYU Education Week address, 19 Aug. 1997. Speeches.BYU.edu.

———. "Finding Joy in Life." *Ensign*, May 1996, 24–26.

———. "How to Obtain Revelation and Inspiration for Your Personal Life." *Ensign*, May 2012, 45–47.

———. "Peace of Conscience and Peace of Mind." *Ensign*, November 2004, 15–18.

———. "Personal Strength through the Atonement of Jesus Christ." *Ensign*, Nov. 2013, 82–84.

———. "The Power of Scripture." *Ensign*, Nov. 2011, 6–8.

———. "Trust in the Lord." *Ensign*, Nov. 1995, 16–18.

Scriptures of the Church: Selections from the Encyclopedia of Mormonism. Edited by Daniel H. Ludlow. 1995.

Second Nephi: The Doctrinal Structure. Edited by Monte S. Nyman and Charles D. Tate, Jr. 1989.

Seely, David Rolph. "The Book of Jonah." In *1 Kings to Malachi*, edited by Kent P. Jackson, 46–51. Vol. 4 of Studies in Scripture series. 1993.

———. "I Am with Thee, to Deliver Thee." In *1 Kings to Malachi,* edited by Kent P. Jackson, 214–34. Vol. 4 of Studies in Scripture series. 1993.

———. "The Joseph Smith Translation: 'Plain and Precious Things' Restored." *Ensign*, Aug. 1997, 9–16.

———. "Kings and Chronicles." In *1 Kings to Malachi*, edited by Kent P. Jackson, 4–11. Vol. 4 of Studies in Scripture series. 1985.

———. "The Last Supper according to Matthew, Mark, and Luke." In *From the Last Supper through the Resurrection*, edited by Richard Neitzel Holzapfel and Thomas A. Wayment, 59–107. 2003.

———. "The Lord Is Our Judge and Our King (Isaiah 18–33)." In *1 Kings to Malachi*, edited by Kent P. Jackson, 108–27. Vol. 4 of Studies in Scripture series. 1993.

———. "The Lord Will Bring Salvation (Isaiah 51–66)." In *1 Kings to Malachi*, edited by Kent P. Jackson, 147–64. Vol. 4 of Studies in Scripture series. 1993.

———. "The Ministry of Jeremiah (Jeremiah 1, 25–29, 32–45, 52)." In *1 Kings to Malachi,* edited by Kent P. Jackson, 193–213. Vol. 4 of Studies in Scripture series. 1993.

———. "A Prophet over the Nations (Jeremiah 21–24, 30–31, 46–51)." In *1 Kings to Malachi*, edited by Kent P. Jackson, 235–52. Vol. 4 of Studies in Scripture series. 1993.

———. "The Restoration as Covenant Renewal." In *Old Testament: Sperry Symposium Classics*, 311–36. 2005.

———. "Samuel: Prophet, Priest, Judge, and Anointer of Kings." In *Genesis to 2 Samuel*, edited by Kent P. Jackson and Robert L. Millet, 271–80. Vol. 3 of Studies in Scripture series. 1985.

———. "The Song of Solomon." In *1 Kings to Malachi*, edited by Kent P. Jackson, 467–70. Vol. 4 of Studies in Scripture series. 1993.

———, and Jo Ann H. Seely, "Lehi and Jeremiah: Prophets, Priests, and Patriarchs." *Journal of Book of Mormon Studies,* 8/2 (1999): 24–35, 85–86.

———, and John W. Welch, "Zenos and the Texts of the Old Testament." In *The Allegory of the Olive Tree: The Olive, the Bible, and Jacob 5*, edited by John W. Welch and Stephen D. Ricks, 322–43. 1994.

Seely, Jo Ann H. "Lamentations." In *1 Kings to Malachi*, edited by Kent P. Jackson, 253–57. Vol. 4 of Studies in Scripture series. 1993.

Segal, Lore. "II Samuel." In *Congregation*, edited by David Rosenburg, 106–25. 1987.

Seow, Choon–Leong. *Daniel.* In Westminster Bible Companion: Old Testament series. Edited by Patrick D. Miller and David L. Bartlett. 2003.

———. *Ecclesiastes.* In the Anchor Bible series. Edited by William Foxwell Albright and David Noel Freedman. 1997.

The Sermon on the Mount in Latter-day Scripture. Edited by Gaye Strathearn, Thomas A. Wayment, and Daniel L. Belnap. 2010. Sperry Symposium series. 2010.

Shannon, Avram R. "'Come Near unto Me': Guarded Space and Its Mediators in the Jerusalem Temple." In *Ascending the Mountain of the Lord: Temple, Praise, and Worship in the Old Testament*, edited by David R. Seely, Jeffrey R. Chadwick, and Matthew J. Grey, 66–84. Sperry Symposium series. 2013.

Shütze, Manfred H. "The Sword of the Lord and of Gideon." *Ensign*, April 2002, 46–49.

Sill, Sterling W. *Wealth of Wisdom.* 1977.

Simmons, Dennis E. "But If Not . . ." *Ensign*, May 2004, 73–75.

Simpson, Robert L. "These Four Things." *Ensign*, May 1976, 57 –59.

Sjodahl, Janne M., and George Reynolds. *Commentary on the Book of Mormon.* 7 vols. 1961.

Sklar, Jay. *Leviticus: An Introduction and Commentary.* In Tyndale Old Testament Commentaries series. Edited by David Firth and Tremper Longman III. 2014.

Skousen, Royal. "Textual Variants in the Isaiah Quotations in the Book of Mormon." In *Isaiah in the Book of Mormon*, edited by Donald W. Parry and John W. Welch, 369–90. 1998.

Slotki, I. W. *Isaiah.* In The Soncino Books of the Bible series. Edited by A. Cohen. 1949.

Slotki, Judah J. *Daniel, Ezra, Nehemiah.* In The Soncino Books of the Bible series. Edited by A. Cohen. 1951.

Smith, Barbara B. "Women for the Latter Day." *Ensign*, Nov. 1979, 107–8.

Smith, Eldred G. "Opposition in Order to Strengthen Us." *Ensign*, Jan. 1974, 62–63.

Smith, Esther Clark. "Psalm." *Ensign*, Apr. 1978, 19.

Smith, Gary V. *Isaiah 1–39.* In The New American Commentary series. Edited by E. Ray Clendenen and Kenneth A. Mathews. 2007.

Smith, George A. In *Journal of Discourses*, 5:66–69.

———. In *Journal of Discourses*, 10:68.

Smith, George Albert. In Conference Report, Oct. 1943, 43–49.

———. In Conference Report, Oct. 1948, 180–90.

———. In Conference Report, Oct. 1949, 4–9.

Smith, Joseph. "Ancient Poetry." In *The Latter-day Saints Millennial Star*, Vol. 4 No. 4 (August 1843): 49–55.

———. "Discourse, 3 October 1841, as reported by *Times and Seasons*," 577. In Joseph Smith Papers.

———. "Discourse, 8 April 1843, as Reported by William Clayton–B," 2. In Joseph Smith Papers.

———. "History, 1838–1856, volume C-1 [2 November 1838–31 July 1842][a]," 904[a]. In Joseph Smith Papers.
———. "History, 1838–1856, volume C-1 [2 November 1838–31 July 1842] [addenda]," 8 [addenda]. In Joseph Smith Papers.
———. "History, 1838–1856, volume D-1 [1 August 1842–1 July 1843] [addenda]," 4 [addenda]. In Joseph Smith Papers.
———. "History, 1838–1856, volume D-1 [1 August 1842–1 July 1843] [addenda]," 6 [addenda]. In Joseph Smith Papers.
———. "History, 1838–1856, volume E-1 [1 July 1843–30 April 1844]," 1727. In Joseph Smith Papers.
———. "History, 1838–1856, volume F-1 [1 May 1844–8 August 1844]," 18. In Joseph Smith Papers.
———. *Joseph Smith*. Teachings of Presidents of the Church series. 2011.
———. The Joseph Smith Papers. JosephSmithPapers.org.
———. "Letter to Noah C. Saxton, 4 January 1833," 14–15. In Joseph Smith Papers.
Smith, Joseph F. *Gospel Doctrine: Selections from the Sermons and Writings of Joseph F. Smith*. 1919.
———. *Joseph F. Smith*. Teachings of Presidents of the Church series. 2011.
———. In *Journal of Discourses*, 11:305–14.
———. In *Journal of Discourses*, 18:89–94.
———. In *Journal of Discourses*, 24:185–94.
———, Anthon H. Lund, and Charles W. Penrose. "Only One God to Worship." In *Messages of the First Presidency*, edited by James R. Clark, 4:269–71.
Smith, Joseph Fielding. *Answers to Gospel Questions*. 5 vols. 1957–1966.
———. *Church History and Modern Revelation*. 4 vols. 1946.
———. In Conference Report, Apr. 1943, 11–16.
———. In Conference Report, Apr. 1956, 58–59.
———. *Doctrines of Salvation , Vols. 1–3: Sermons and Writings of Joseph Fielding Smith*. Revised edition. 1999.
———. *Progress of Man*. 1936.
———. *The Restoration of All Things*. 1945.
———. "The Second Commandment." In *Ten Commandments Today*. 1955.
———. *Signs of the Times*. 1952.
Smith, Robert F., and Benjamin Urrutia. "New Information about Mulek, Son of the King." In *Reexploring the Book of Mormon*, edited by John W. Welch, 142–44. 1992.
Smith, William. *Smith's Bible Dictionary*. 1901.
Snow, Erastus. In *Journal of Discourses*, 5:285–92.
———. In *Journal of Discourses*, 23:181–89.
———. In *Journal of Discourses*, 23:294–302.
Snow, Lorenzo. In *Journal of Discourses*, 12:146–48.
———. In *Journal of Discourses*, 16:272–80.
———. In *Journal of Discourses*, 23:189–95.
Soares, Ulisses. "Confide in God Unwaveringly." *Ensign*, May 2017, 33–35.
———. "Hold to the Rod." Ensign, Mar. 2015, 59–61.
———. "How Can I Understand?" *Ensign*, May 2019, 6–8.
———. "Prophets Speak by the Power of the Holy Ghost." *Ensign*, May 2018, 98–99.
———. "Take Up Our Cross." *Ensign*, Nov. 2019, 113–16.

The Soncino Books of the Bible series. Edited by A. Cohen. 14 vols. 1946–1982.

Sorensen, David E. "Faith Is the Answer." *Ensign*, May 2005, 72–74.

———. "Small Temples—Large Blessings." *Ensign*, Nov. 1998, 64–65.

Speiser, E. A. *Genesis*. In the Anchor Bible series. Edited by David Noel Freedman. 1964.

Sperry Symposium Classics: The Old Testament. Edited by Paul Y. Hoskisson. 2005.

Sperry, Sidney B. "Ancient Temples and their Functions." *Ensign*, Jan 1972, 67–72.

———. *Book of Mormon Compendium.* 1968.

———. *The Message of the Twelve Prophets.* 1941.

———. "A Note on Psalm 8:4–6." *Ensign*, Feb. 1972, 21.

———. *The Spirit of the Old Testament.* 1970.

———. *The Voice of Israel's Prophets.* 1953.

Stephens, Carole M. "If Ye Love Me, Keep My Commandments." *Ensign*, Nov. 2015, 118–20.

Stephenson, Jonathan H. "'I Am He': Jesus' Public Declarations of His Own Identity". In *The Lord of the Gospels*, edited by Bruce A. Van Orden and Brent L. Top, 162–72. Sperry Symposium series. 1990.

Stern, David H. *Complete Jewish Bible.* 2016.

Stevenson, Gary E. "The Safety and Peace of Keeping the Commandments." *Ensign*, Dec. 2012, 62–65.

———. "Shepherding Souls." *Ensign*, Nov. 2018, 110–13.

———. "With All Thy Getting, Get Understanding." *Ensign*, Jan. 2017, 28–33.

Stirling, Mack C. "Job: An LDS Reading." In *Temple Insights*, edited by William J. Hamblin and David Rolph Seely, 99–143. 2014.

Stone, David R. "Zion in the Midst of Babylon." *Ensign,* May 2006, 90–93.

Strathearn, Gaye. "'Holiness to the Lord' and Personal Temple Worship." In *The Gospel of Jesus Christ in the Old Testament*, edited by D. Kelly Ogden, Jared W. Ludlow, Kerry Muhlestein, Patty Smith, and Thomas R. Valletta, 219–32. Sperry Symposium series. 2009.

———. "The Wife/Sister Experience: Pharaoh's Introduction to Jehovah." In *Thy People Shall Be My People and Thy God My God*, edited by Paul Y. Hoskisson, 150–62. Sperry Symposium series. 1994.

Strong, James. *Strong's Exhaustive Concordance of the Bible.* 1890. Reprint, 2009.

Stulman, Louis. *Jeremiah.* In Abingdon Old Testament Commentaries series. Edited by Patrick D. Miller. 2005.

Swainston, Howard D. "Tithing." In *Encyclopedia of Mormonism*, edited by Daniel H. Ludlow, et al., 1480–82.

Swanson, Vern G. "Israel's 'Other Tribes.'" *Ensign*, Jan. 1982, 26–31.

Szink, Terrence L. "The Reign of Solomon." In *1 Kings to Malachi*, edited by Kent P. Jackson, 12–19. Vol. 4 of Studies in Scripture series. 1993.

Talmage, James E. *Articles of Faith: Being a Consideration of the Principal Doctrines of The Church of Jesus Christ of Latter-day Saints.* 1982.

———. *The House of the Lord: A Study of Holy Sanctuaries Ancient and Modern.* 2013.

———. *Jesus the Christ: A Study of the Messiah and His Mission according to Holy Scriptures both Ancient and Modern.* 1973. Reprint, 1981.

Talmon, Shermaryahu. "1 and 2 Chronicles." In *The Literary Guide to the Bible*, edited by Robert Alter and Frank Kermode, 365–72. 1987.

Tanner, J. Paul. "The Literary Structure of the Book of Daniel." *Bibliotheca Sacra*, vol. 160 (2009): 269–82.

Tanner, John S. "The Book of Job." In *1 Kings to Malachi*, edited by Kent P. Jackson, 391–406. Vol. 4 of Studies in Scripture series. 1993.

Tanner, N. Eldon. "Obedience." *Ensign*, Jan. 1974, 92–95.

———. "The Power of Example." *Ensign*, Dec. 1981, 2–4.

Tate, George S. "The Typology of the Exodus Pattern in the Book of Mormon." In *Literature of Belief: Sacred Scripture and Religious Experience,* edited by Neal E. Lambert, 245–62. 1981.

"Tattooing." In Gospel Topics. ChurchofJesusChrist.org.

Taylor, John. *The Gospel Kingdom: Selections from the Writings and Discourses of John Taylor.* 1943.

———. *The Government of God.* 1852.

———. In *Journal of Discourses*, 10:113–20.

———. In *Journal of Discourses*, 20:219–29.

———. In *Journal of Discourses*, 22:312–21.

———. In *Journal of Discourses*, 23:175–80.

———. In *Journal of Discourses*, 26:66–76.

Taylor, John B. *Ezekiel.* In Tyndale Old Testament Commentaries series. Edited by D. J. Wiseman. 1969.

Temple Insights. Edited by William J. Hamblin and David Rolph Seely. 2014.

Temples of the Ancient World: Ritual and Symbolism. Edited by Donald W. Parry. 1994.

The Ten Commandments Today. 1955.

"Then Will I Go unto the Altar of God." *New Era*, Sep. 2015, 8–9.

Theological Wordbook of the Old Testament. Edited by R. Laird Harris, et al. 2 vols. 1980.

Thomas, Carol B. "Integrity." *Ensign*, May 2000, 91–92.

Thompson, J. A. *The Book of Jeremiah.* In The New International Commentary on the Old Testament series. Edited by R. K. Harrison and Robert L. Hubbard, Jr. 1980.

Thompson, Keith A. "Joseph Smith and the Doctrine of Sealing." In *Interpreter: A Journal of Latter-day Saint Faith and Scholarship*, 21(2016): 1–21.

Thornock, A. LaVar. "Do the Wicked Prosper While the Righteous Suffer?" *Ensign*, Oct. 1990, 12–16.

Thy People Shall Be My People and Thy God My God. Edited by Paul Y. Hoskisson. Sperry Symposium series. 1994.

Tice, Richard. "Bekahs, Shekels, and Talents: A Look at Biblical References to Money." *Ensign*, Aug. 1987, 30–34.

Tigay, Jeffery H. *Deuteronomy.* In The JPS Torah Commentary series. Edited by Nahum M. Sarna. 1996.

Tingey, Earl C. *Old Testament Prophecies of Jesus Christ.* 2012.

Top, Brent L. "The Loving Arms of Christ." *Ensign*, April 2012, 51–57.

———. "Man." In *LDS Beliefs: A Doctrinal Reference*, edited by Robert L. Millet, et al., 402–3. 2011.

———. "The Marriage of Hosea and Gomer: A Symbolic Testament of Messianic Love and Mercy." In *A Witness of Jesus Christ*, edited by Richard D. Draper, 223–39. Sperry Symposium series. 1999.

———. "Mercy." In *LDS Beliefs: A Doctrinal Reference*, edited by Robert L. Millet, et al., 422–24. 2011.

———. "New Jerusalem." In *LDS Beliefs: A Doctrinal Reference*, edited by Robert L. Millet, et al., 450–52. 2011.

———. *A Peculiar Treasure: Old Testament Messages for Our Day.* 1997.

———. "Repentance." In *LDS Beliefs: A Doctrinal Reference*, edited by Robert L. Millet, et al., 523–27. 2011.

———. "Sabbath." In *LDS Beliefs: A Doctrinal Reference,* edited by Robert L. Millet, et al., 544–47. 2011.

———. "Thou Shall Not Covet." *Ensign*, Dec. 1994, 22–26.

Topical Guide. ChurchofJesusChrist.org. 2013.

The Torah: A Modern Commentary. Edited by W. Gunther Plaut. 1981.

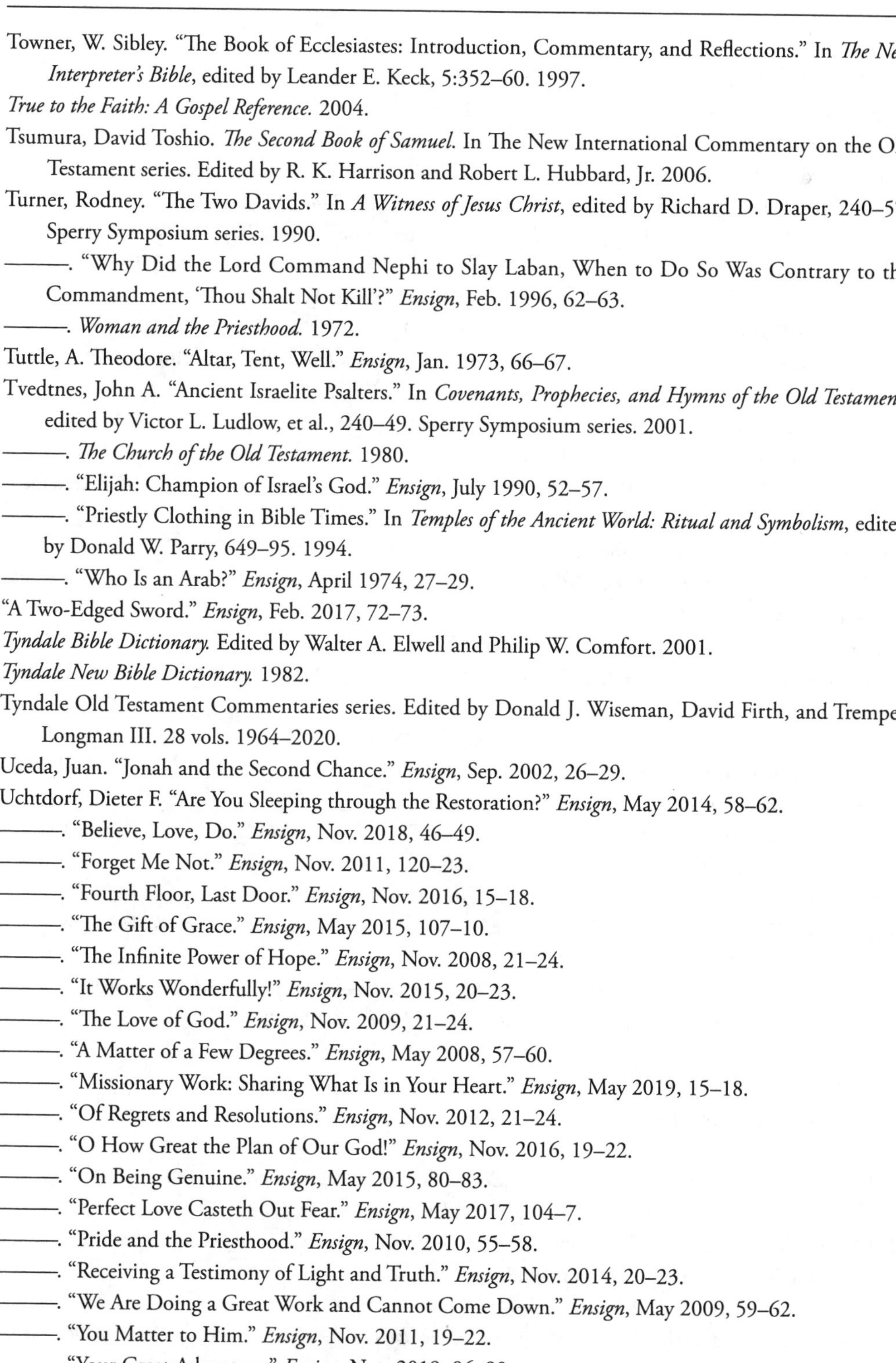

Towner, W. Sibley. "The Book of Ecclesiastes: Introduction, Commentary, and Reflections." In *The New Interpreter's Bible*, edited by Leander E. Keck, 5:352–60. 1997.

True to the Faith: A Gospel Reference. 2004.

Tsumura, David Toshio. *The Second Book of Samuel.* In The New International Commentary on the Old Testament series. Edited by R. K. Harrison and Robert L. Hubbard, Jr. 2006.

Turner, Rodney. "The Two Davids." In *A Witness of Jesus Christ*, edited by Richard D. Draper, 240–57. Sperry Symposium series. 1990.

———. "Why Did the Lord Command Nephi to Slay Laban, When to Do So Was Contrary to the Commandment, 'Thou Shalt Not Kill'?" *Ensign*, Feb. 1996, 62–63.

———. *Woman and the Priesthood.* 1972.

Tuttle, A. Theodore. "Altar, Tent, Well." *Ensign*, Jan. 1973, 66–67.

Tvedtnes, John A. "Ancient Israelite Psalters." In *Covenants, Prophecies, and Hymns of the Old Testament*, edited by Victor L. Ludlow, et al., 240–49. Sperry Symposium series. 2001.

———. *The Church of the Old Testament.* 1980.

———. "Elijah: Champion of Israel's God." *Ensign*, July 1990, 52–57.

———. "Priestly Clothing in Bible Times." In *Temples of the Ancient World: Ritual and Symbolism*, edited by Donald W. Parry, 649–95. 1994.

———. "Who Is an Arab?" *Ensign*, April 1974, 27–29.

"A Two-Edged Sword." *Ensign*, Feb. 2017, 72–73.

Tyndale Bible Dictionary. Edited by Walter A. Elwell and Philip W. Comfort. 2001.

Tyndale New Bible Dictionary. 1982.

Tyndale Old Testament Commentaries series. Edited by Donald J. Wiseman, David Firth, and Tremper Longman III. 28 vols. 1964–2020.

Uceda, Juan. "Jonah and the Second Chance." *Ensign*, Sep. 2002, 26–29.

Uchtdorf, Dieter F. "Are You Sleeping through the Restoration?" *Ensign*, May 2014, 58–62.

———. "Believe, Love, Do." *Ensign*, Nov. 2018, 46–49.

———. "Forget Me Not." *Ensign*, Nov. 2011, 120–23.

———. "Fourth Floor, Last Door." *Ensign*, Nov. 2016, 15–18.

———. "The Gift of Grace." *Ensign*, May 2015, 107–10.

———. "The Infinite Power of Hope." *Ensign*, Nov. 2008, 21–24.

———. "It Works Wonderfully!" *Ensign*, Nov. 2015, 20–23.

———. "The Love of God." *Ensign*, Nov. 2009, 21–24.

———. "A Matter of a Few Degrees." *Ensign*, May 2008, 57–60.

———. "Missionary Work: Sharing What Is in Your Heart." *Ensign*, May 2019, 15–18.

———. "Of Regrets and Resolutions." *Ensign*, Nov. 2012, 21–24.

———. "O How Great the Plan of Our God!" *Ensign*, Nov. 2016, 19–22.

———. "On Being Genuine." *Ensign*, May 2015, 80–83.

———. "Perfect Love Casteth Out Fear." *Ensign*, May 2017, 104–7.

———. "Pride and the Priesthood." *Ensign*, Nov. 2010, 55–58.

———. "Receiving a Testimony of Light and Truth." *Ensign*, Nov. 2014, 20–23.

———. "We Are Doing a Great Work and Cannot Come Down." *Ensign*, May 2009, 59–62.

———. "You Matter to Him." *Ensign*, Nov. 2011, 19–22.

———. "Your Great Adventure." *Ensign*, Nov. 2019, 86–90.

———. "Your Wonderful Journey Home." *Ensign*, May 2013, 125–29.

Understanding the Bible Commentary series. Edited by W. Ward Gasque, Robert L. Hubbard, Jr., and Robert K. Johnston. 36 vols. 2011–2013.

Unger, Merrill F. *The New Unger's Bible Dictionary.* 1988.

———. *The New Unger's Bible Dictionary.* 2005.

Valletta, Thomas R. "The Captain of the Covenant." In *The Book of Mormon: Alma, the Testimony of the Word,* edited by Monte S. Nyman and Charles D. Tate Jr., 223–48. 1992.

———. "The Exodus: Prophetic Type and the Plan of Redemption." In *Thy People Shall Be My People and Thy God My God,* edited by Paul Y. Hoskisson, 178–89. Sperry Symposium series. 1994.

———. "The Length of the Lives of the Ancient Patriarchs." *Ensign,* Feb. 1994, 59–61.

———. "The True Bread of Life." *Ensign,* Mar. 1999, 6–13.

———, et al., eds. *The Book of Mormon Study Guide: From Start to Finish.* Revised edition. 2019.

———, et al., eds. *The Old Testament for Latter-day Saint Families.* 2005.

VanGemeren, Willem A. "Psalms." In *The Expositor's Bible Commentary,* rev. ed., edited by Tremper Longman III and David E. Garland, 5:21–1011. 2008.

Verhoef, Pieter A. *Haggai and Malachi.* In The New International Commentary on the Old Testament series. Edited by R. K. Harrison and Robert L. Hubbard, Jr. 1987.

Viñas, Francisco J. "Listening to the Voice of the Lord." *Ensign,* Nov. 1996, 78–79.

Vine's Complete Expository Dictionary of Old and New Testament Words. Edited by Merrill F. Unger and William White Jr. 1996.

Vinson, Terrance M. "True Disciples of the Savior." *Ensign,* Nov. 2019, 9–11.

Voices of Old Testament Prophets. Edited by Dennis Wright, Craig J. Ostler, Dana M. Pike, Dee R. Darling, and Patty A. Smith. Sperry Symposium series. 1997.

Vorhaus, Renee. "I Have a Question." *Ensign,* September 1980, 64–65.

Voth, Steven. "Jeremiah." In *Zondervan Illustrated Bible Backgrounds Commentary: Old Testament,* edited by John W. Walton, 4:228–371. 2009.

Walker, Gary Lee. "The Fall of the Kingdom of Judah." In *1 Kings – Malachi,* edited by Kent P. Jackson, 165–77. Vol. 4 of Studies in Scripture series. 1993.

Walker, Steven C. "Between Scriptural Lines." *Ensign,* Mar. 1978, 62–63.

Walton, John H. "Genesis." In *Zondervan Illustrated Bible Backgrounds Commentary: Old Testament,* edited by John H. Walton, 1:2–159. 2009

———, and Victor H. Matthews. *The IVP Bible Background Commentary: Genesis—Deuteronomy.* 1997.

———, et al. *The IVP Bible Background Commentary: Old Testament.* 2000.

"Watchmen on the Tower." *Ensign,* Apr. 2016, 28–29.

Wayment, Thomas A. *The Complete Joseph Smith Translation of the Old Testament.* 2012.

———, and Richard N. Holzapfel. *The Life and Teachings of Jesus Christ: From the Last Supper through the Resurrection.* 2003.

Webster, Noah. *An American Dictionary of the English Language.* 1828. Reprint, 1980.

Weis, Ted. "Inclusio and the Gospels." *Living the Biblios* (blog), 6 Mar. 2008.

Welch, John W. "The Calling of a Prophet." In *First Nephi, The Doctrinal Foundation,* edited by Charles D. Tate and Monte S. Nyman, 35–48. 1988.

———. "New Testament Word Studies," *Ensign,* Apr. 1993, 28–30.

———. "The Temple in the Book of Mormon." In *Temples of the Ancient World,* edited by Donald W. Parry, 297–387.

———. "Word Studies from the New Testament." *Ensign,* Jan. 1995, 28–30.

———. Donald W. Parry and Stephen D. Ricks. "This Day." In *Reexploring the Book of Mormon*, edited by John W. Welch, 117–19. 1992.

Welker, Roy A. *Spiritual Values of the Old Testament.* 1952.

Wells, Bruce. "Exodus." In *Zondervan Illustrated Bible Backgrounds Commentary: Old Testament*, edited by John W. Walton, 1:160–283. 2009.

Wells, Daniel H. In *Journal of Discourses*, 5:40–44.

Wenham, Gordon J. *The Book of Leviticus.* In The New International Commentary on the Old Testament series. Edited by R. K. Harrison and Robert L. Hubbard, Jr. 1979.

———. "Genesis." In *Eerdmans Commentary on the Bible*, edited by James D. G. Dunn and John W. Rogerson. 2003.

———. *Genesis 16–50.* In Word Biblical Commentary series. Edited by Bruce M. Metzger, David A. Hubbard, and Glenn W. Barker. 2000.

———. *Numbers: An Introduction and Commentary.* In Tyndale Old Testament Commentaries series. Edited by Donald J. Wiseman. 1981.

Wesley, John. *Wesley's Explanatory Notes.* 1765.

West, Stephen A. "Are You on the Lord's Side?" *New Era*, Sep. 2002, 12–15.

Westminster Bible Companion: Old Testament series. Edited by Patrick D. Miller and David L. Bartlett. 20 vols. 1995–2008.

"What Does the Church Believe about Evolution?" *New Era*, October 2016, 41.

Whiting, Scott D. "Temple Standard." *Ensign*, Nov. 2012, 37–39.

Whitney, Orson F. In Conference Report, Apr. 1927, 96–101.

———. *Gospel Themes.* 1914.

———. *Saturday Night Thoughts.* 1921.

Whittaker, David J. "The Book of Daniel in Early Mormon Thought." In *By Study and Also by Faith.* Edited by John M. Lundquist and Stephen D. Ricks, 1:155–201. 1990.

"Why Does Jacob Quote So Much from the Psalms?" *Book of Mormon Central* (website), KnoWhy #62.

"Why Is the Lord's Hand 'Stretched Out Still'?" *Book of Mormon Central* (website), KnoWhy #49.

"Why Should Readers Pay Close Attention to the Mulekites?" *Book of Mormon Central* (website), KnoWhy #434.

Widtsoe, John A. *Evidences and Reconciliations.* 3 vols. in 1. Reprint, 1976.

———. "The Worth of Souls." In *The Utah Genealogical and Historical Magazine*, Oct. 1934, 187–92.

Wiersbe, Warren W. *The Wiersbe Bible Commentary: Old Testament.* 2007.

Wilcox, S. Michael. "The Abrahamic Covenant." In *A Witness of Jesus Christ*, edited by Richard D. Draper, 271–79. Sperry Symposium series. 1990.

———. "The Abrahamic Covenant." *Ensign*, Jan. 1998, 42–48.

———. *House of Glory: Finding Personal Meaning in the Temple.* 1995.

———. "The 12 Spies." *Ensign*, Mar. 2002, 35–37.

———. *Twice Blessed.* 2016.

———. *Who Shall Be Able to Stand? Finding Personal Meaning in the Book of Revelation.* 2003.

Williams, Clyde J. "Standard Works." In *Encyclopedia of Mormonism*, edited by Daniel H. Ludlow, et al., 3:1415–16. 1992.

Willis, Timothy M. *Jeremiah–Lamentations.* In College Press NIV Commentary: Old Testament series. Edited by Anthony L. Ash and Jack Cottrell. 2002.

Wilson, Garth A. "The Mulekites." *Ensign*, Mar. 1987, 60–64.

Wilson, Gerald H. *Psalms Volume 1.* In The NIV Application Commentary: Old Testament series. Edited by Terry Muck. 2002.

Wilson, Lynne Hilton. "The Holy Spirit: Creating, Anointing, and Empowering." In *The Gospel of Jesus Christ in the Old Testament,* edited by D. Kelly Ogden, Kerry M. Muhlestein, Jared W. Ludlow, Thomas R. Valletta, and Patty A. Smith, 250–81. Sperry Symposium series. 2009.

Winder, Barbara W. "Becoming a Prepared People." *Ensign,* Nov. 1988, 88–90.

Winn, Nathan, and Terry B. Ball. *Making Sense of Isaiah.* 2009.

Wirthlin, Joseph B. *Finding Peace in Our Lives.* 1995.

———. "The Law of the Fast." *Ensign,* May 2001, 73–75.

———. "Living Water to Quench Spiritual Thirst." *Ensign,* May 1995, 18–20.

———. "Never Give Up." *Ensign,* Nov. 1987, 8–10.

———. "One Step after Another." *Ensign,* Nov. 2001, 25–27.

———. "The Straight and Narrow Way." *Ensign,* Nov. 1990, 64–66.

———. "Sunday Will Come." *Ensign,* Nov. 2006, 28–30.

———. "The Virtue of Kindness." *Ensign,* May 2005, 26–28.

Wirthlin, Joseph L. In Conference Report, Oct. 1943, 119–24.

Wiseman, Donald J. *1 and 2 Kings.* In Tyndale Old Testament Commentaries series. Edited by Donald J. Wiseman. 2008.

A Witness of Jesus Christ. Edited by Richard D. Draper. Sperry Symposium series. 1990.

Wolf, Herbert. *Haggai and Malachi.* 1976.

Women in Scripture: A Dictionary of Named and Unnamed Women in the Hebrew Bible, the Apocryphal/ Deuterocanonical Books, and the New Testament. Edited by Carol Meyers. 2000.

Women Steadfast in Christ: Talks Selected from the 1991 Women's Conference Co-sponsored by Brigham Young University and the Relief Society. Edited by Dawn Hall Anderson and Marie Cornwall. 1991.

Wood, Robert S. "Instruments of the Lord's Peace." *Ensign,* May 2006, 93–95.

Woodger, Mary Jane, Kenneth L. Alford, and Craig K. Manscill. *Dreams as Revelation.* 2019.

Woodruff, Wilford. *The Discourses of Wilford Woodruff.* Edited by G. Homer Durham. 1946.

———. In *Journal of Discourses,* 9:221–29.

———. In *Journal of Discourses,* 15:275–83.

———. In *Journal of Discourses,* 16:262–72.

———. In *Journal of Discourses,* 17:188–95.

———. In *Journal of Discourses,* 18:109–22.

Woods, Edward J. *Deuteronomy: An Introduction and Commentary.* In Tyndale Old Testament Commentaries series. Edited by David Firth and Tremper Longman III. 2011.

Woods, Fred E. "Elisha and the Children: The Question of Accepting Prophetic Succession." In *BYU Studies* 32, no. 3 (Summer 1992): 47–58.

———. "The Waters Which Make Glad the City of God: The Water Motif of Ezekiel 47:1–12." In *A Witness of Jesus Christ,* edited by Richard D. Draper, 281–98. Sperry Symposium series. 1989.

Word Biblical Commentary series. Edited by Bruce M. Metzger, David A. Hubbard, and Glenn W. Barker. 61 vols. 2000.

The Words of Joseph Smith: The Contemporary Accounts of the Nauvoo Discourses of the Prophet Joseph. Edited by Andrew F. Ehat and Lyndon W. Cook. 1980.

Workman, H. Ross. "Beware of Murmuring." *Ensign,* Nov. 2001, 85–86.

"Worship through Hymns." *Ensign,* Mar. 2008, 64–67.

Wright, David P. "The Laws and the Sanctuary." In *Genesis to 2 Samuel*, edited by Kent P. Jackson and Robert L. Millet, 143–52. Vol. 3 of Studies in Scripture series. 1985.

———. "Revelations in the Wilderness of Sinai." In *Genesis to 2 Samuel*, edited by Kent P. Jackson and Robert L. Millet, 125–41. Vol. 3 of Studies in Scripture series. 1985.

Wright, Dennis A. "The Prophet's Voice of Authority." In *Voices of Old Testament Prophets*, edited by Dennis Wright, Craig J. Ostler, Dana M. Pike, Dee R. Darling, and Patty A. Smith, 34–45. Sperry Symposium series. 1997.

The Wycliffe Bible Commentary. Edited by Charles F. Pfeiffer and Everett F. Harrison. 1962.

Young, Brigham. *Brigham Young.* Teachings of Presidents of the Church series. 2011.

———. *Discourses of Brigham Young.* Edited by John A. Widtsoe. 1976.

———. In *Journal of Discourses*, 2:248–58.

———. In *Journal of Discourses*, 3:97–105.

———. In *Journal of Discourses*, 6:143–49.

———. In *Journal of Discourses*, 7:331–34.

———. In *Journal of Discourses*, 7:334–38.

———. In *Journal of Discourses*, 8:194–200.

———. In *Journal of Discourses*, 8:205–9.

———. In *Journal of Discourses*, 9:1–6.

Young, Edward J. *The Book of Isaiah.* 1965.

———. *The Book of Isaiah.* 3 vols. 1972.

Young, S. Dilworth. "For Thy Servant Heareth." *Ensign*, Nov. 1974, 90–92.

Youngblood, Ronald F. "1, 2 Samuel." In *The Expositor's Bible Commentary*, rev. ed., edited by Tremper Longman III and David E. Garland, 3:21–614. 2010.

"Your Covenant Path." *New Era*, March 2015, 12–13.

Zohary, Michael. *Plants of the Bible.* 1982.

Zondervan Illustrated Bible Backgrounds Commentary: Old Testament. Edited by John H. Walton. 5 vols. 2009.

Zondervan Illustrated Bible Dictionary. 1987.

Zondervan Illustrated Bible Dictionary. Edited by J. D. Douglas and Merrill C. Tenney; revised by Moisés Silva. 2011

Zondervan King James Version Commentary: Old Testament. Edited by Edward E. Hindson and Daniel R. Mitchell. 2010.

IMAGE CREDITS

Page x Map © Intellectual Reserve, Inc. Used by permission.

Page xii Map © Intellectual Reserve, Inc. Used by permission.

Page 5 Engraving by Cornelius Boel. Public domain.

Page 21 Illustration ca. 1880. Getty Images.

Page 89 Engraving by Gustave Doré. Public domain.

Page 230 Map © Intellectual Reserve, Inc. Used by permission.

Page 260 Photograph © Intellectual Reserve, Inc. Used by permission.

Page 282 Illustration © ArtMari/Shutterstock.com.

Page 284 Illustration © ArtMari/Shutterstock.com.

Page 288 Illustration © ArtMari/Shutterstock.com.

Page 388 Painting by James Tissot. Public domain.

Page 392 Engraving by Gustave Doré. Public domain.

Page 449 Photograph © SourceFlix. Used by permission.

Page 485 Photograph © Intellectual Reserve, Inc. Used by permission.

Page 487 Map © Intellectual Reserve, Inc. Used by permission.

Page 871 Painting by Václav Mánes. Public domain.

Page 885 Painting by James Tissot. Public domain.

Page 1006 Engraving by Gustave Doré. Public domain.

Page 1087 Painting © Robert Barrett. Used by permission.

Page 1182 Photograph © A.Pushkin/Shutterstock.com.

Page 1228 Illustration ca. 1877. Getty Images.

Page 1252 Illustration by Clarence Larkin. Public domain.

Page 1261 Engraving ca. 1873. Getty Images.

Page 1265 Photograph © Norman W. Gardner. Used by permission.

Page 1332 Painting © Robert Barrett. Used by permission.

Page 1357 Photograph courtesy Library of Congress. Public domain.

INDEX